A Brush with Nature

The Gere Collection of Landscape Oil Sketches

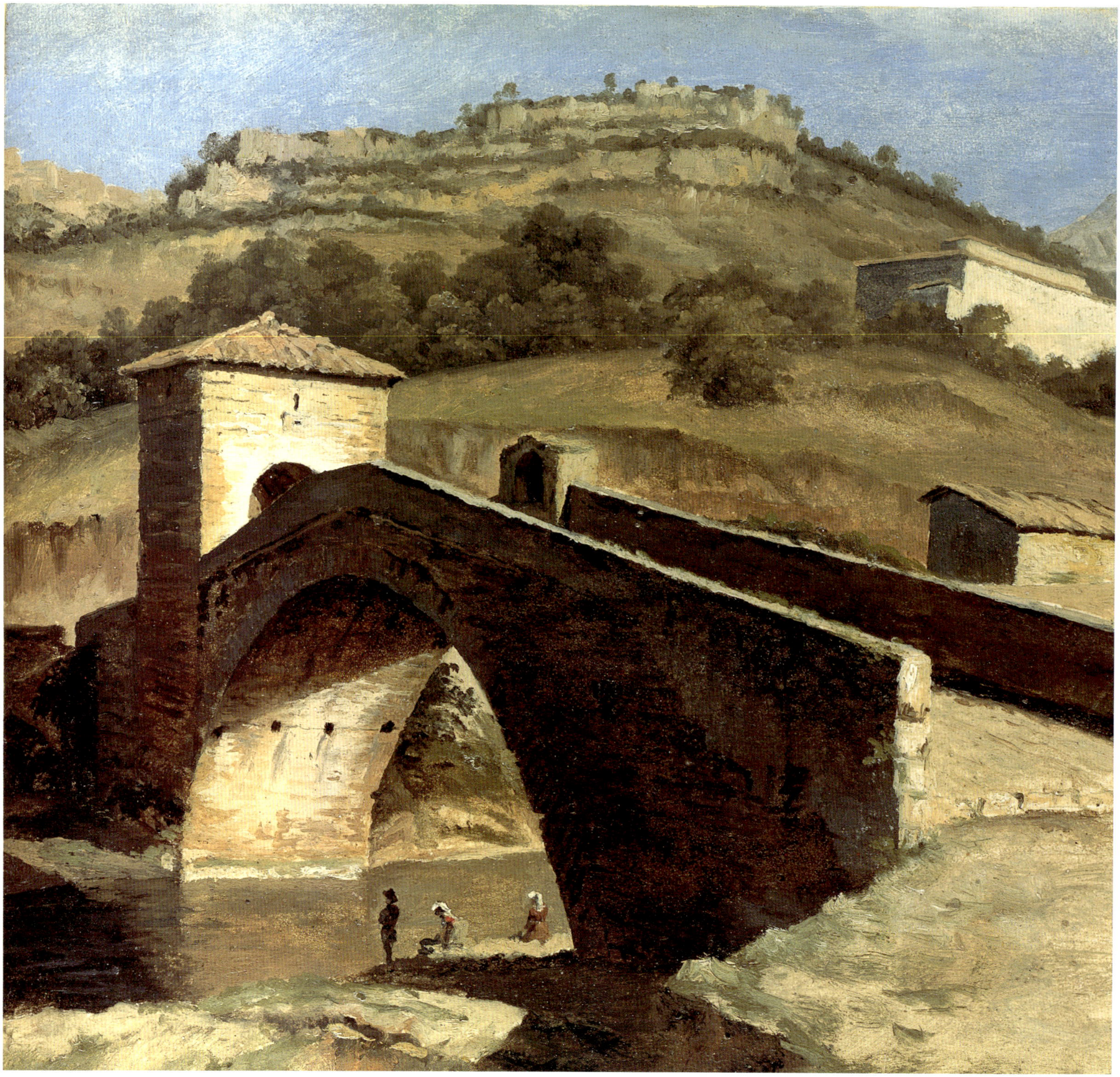

A Brush with Nature

The Gere Collection of Landscape Oil Sketches

CHRISTOPHER RIOPELLE

XAVIER BRAY

with an essay by
CHARLOTTE GERE

National Gallery Publications

Front Jacket: *View of the Cascades at Tivoli* (detail, cat. no. 23) Simon Denis

Back Jacket: *Ruins with Workmen* (detail, cat. no. 33) French School?

Frontispiece: *Bridge at Subiaco* (detail, cat. no. 17) Constantin

Page 6: *Landscape with Trees and Rocks* (detail, cat. no. 11) Camuccini

This book was published to accompany an exhibition at:
The National Gallery, London
23 June – 30 August 1999
Exhibition supported by The Bernard Sunley Charitable Foundation

First published in Great Britain in 1999 by
National Gallery Publications Limited
St Vincent House
30 Orange Street
London WC2H 7HH

ISBN 1 85709 253 8 hardback
525316
ISBN 1 85709 273 2 paperback
525455

British Library Cataloguing in Publication Data.
A catalogue record for this book is available from the British Library.
Library of Congress Catalog Card Number:99-74120

Edited by Caroline Bugler and Celia Jones
Designed by Sarah Davies
Printed and bound in Great Britain by Butler and Tanner, Frome and London

Contents

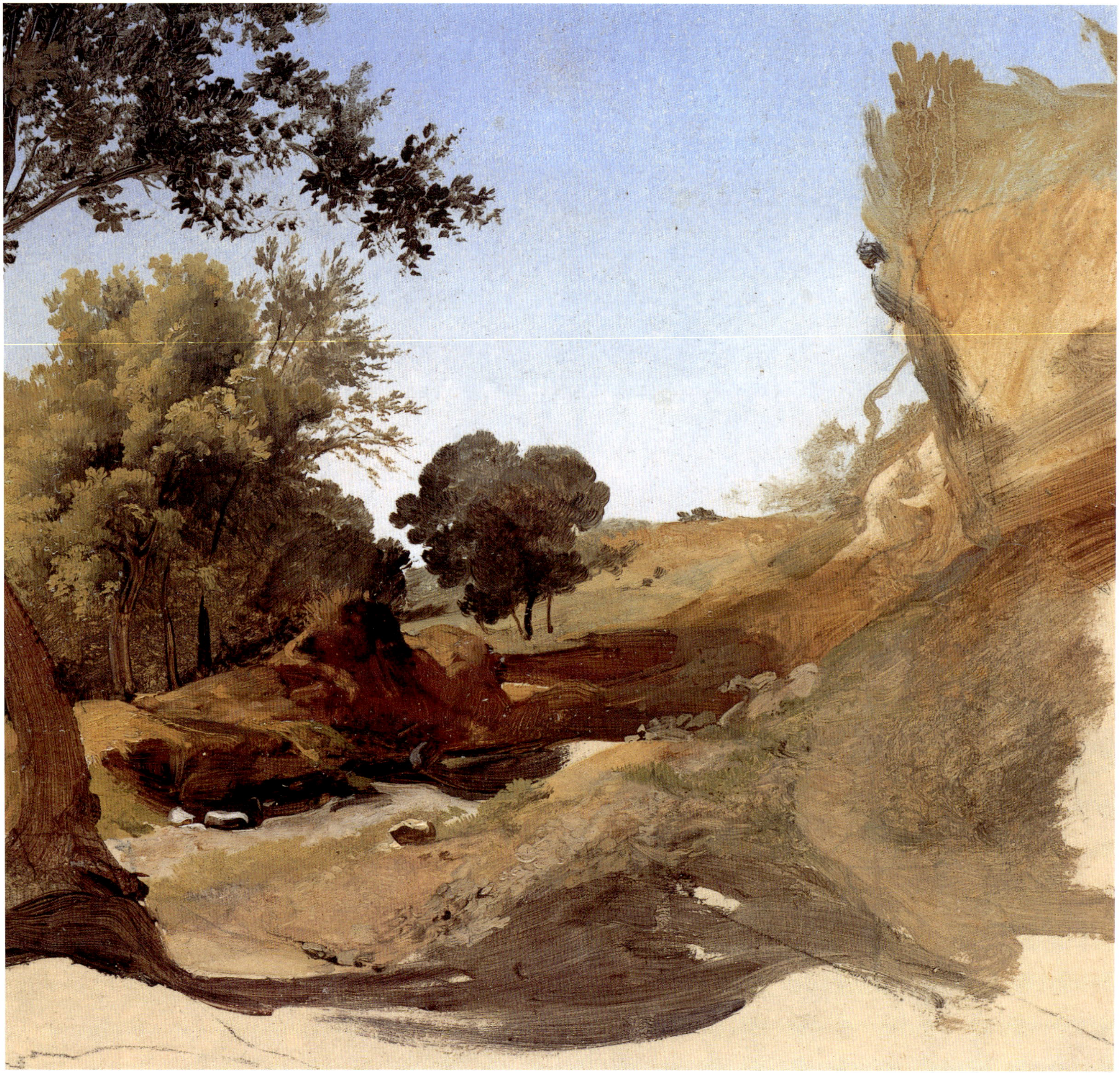

Foreword

This exhibition celebrates a remarkable private collection of a kind of painting that has been passionately admired by a band of enthusiasts for several decades, but which only in recent years has begun to attract wider appreciation. The landscape oil sketch is a small painting, usually on paper or wooden panel, executed out of doors. It is painted quickly – one writer recommended that the artist spend no more than two hours on it – and this speed is essential to capture fleeting effects of light and atmosphere in the landscape. For some two hundred years, from the seventeenth to the nineteenth centuries, artists across Europe painted such sketches not to exhibit them publicly but to test and sharpen their skills of perception and execution.

As you might expect, the practice flourished above all in the Romantic era, and at their best these sketches have a Wordsworthian intensity of response to nature, capturing a beauty entirely visual, that has 'no need of a remoter charm by thought supplied'.

Some decades ago, a few connoisseurs, collectors and curators around the world began to rediscover the freshness and spontaneity of the oil sketch. They also came to enjoy the challenge of identifying the authors of many of these works, which were rarely signed. Foremost among these pioneers were John and Charlotte Gere. Over a period of about forty years, beginning in the 1950s, they assembled a collection of sketches by British, French, German, Scandinavian, Belgian, Spanish and Italian landscape painters. Some of the artists are famous, others hardly known, but the collection as a whole surveys the oil sketch tradition across Europe at a high level of accomplishment. Those fortunate enough to have visited when the paintings hung in the Gere home in London recall the delight of discovering these gems, and the long and lively discussions that ensued, not to mention the renewed delight of rediscovering them on subsequent visits, as new works were added.

The distinguished scholar Peter Galassi has called the Gere collection 'a laboratory for connoisseurship.' That laboratory is now open to the public. John Gere died in 1995, but Charlotte Gere continues to care for and to expand the collection, and she has agreed to exhibit it publicly for the first time at the National Gallery. It will then come here on permanent loan. As long ago as 1918 the National Gallery itself purchased two early nineteenth-century landscape oil sketches, one by Camille Corot, the other by Théodore Rousseau, at the sale in Paris of the Degas collection. They form the core of a small but distinguished group of sketches here that in recent years has grown with the acquisition of works by the Welsh-born Thomas Jones, and the Belgian Simon Denis, both active in Italy at the end of the eighteenth century. Charlotte Gere's generosity in placing on loan to the National Gallery the finest private collection of its kind is a magnificent encouragement to our endeavours, and ensures that the National Gallery is, overnight, one of the world's leading centres for their display and – no less important – study.

We are grateful to The Bernard Sunley Charitable Foundation for its support of this exhibition, as for so many others. Our first debt of gratitude, however, is to Charlotte Gere, who has given us the opportunity to show the collection and who has been unfailing in her encouragement and advice in seeing this exhibition come to fruition.

Neil MacGregor
Director

'Paintings of a unique kind'
Collecting Landscape Oil Sketches

Charlotte Gere

In 1993 Roberta Olson, Professor of Art History at Wheaton College, Massachusetts, asked John Gere about the starting point for his landscape oil sketch collection for a lecture on collectors and collecting she was giving at the Metropolitan Museum in New York. Although he had retired from the Keepership of Prints and Drawings at the British Museum more than ten years earlier, John had been working on two major exhibitions of drawings by Raphael and Michelangelo, both of which were shown in New York, so his name was still known in museum circles there, but that Roberta should assume he would be recognised as a collector by the Metropolitan audience is more surprising. The tiny number of specialist dealers and enthusiasts interested in oil sketches made his – or rather our – collecting a very private project.

Prompted by Roberta, John recalled buying in about 1950 a view of the Crystal Palace at Sydenham (cat. no. 69) by the little-known amateur William White Warren, an indefatigable sketcher with a huge number of surviving works. Warren was discovered by Paul Wallraf, a respected member of a small, tightly knit London circle of connoisseur-collectors, museum men and critics – there were then almost no art historians as such. As a self-proclaimed follower of Constable, Warren was no pioneer and has remained obscure and unappreciated in spite of the fact that his work was – and still is – easy to buy. John eventually owned seven sketches by him and, although he remained attached to them, they were relegated to distant parts of the house as the collection expanded. It was not until the emergence in 1954 of scintillating Neapolitan views by the obscure Welshman Thomas Jones, which had been lost to view since 1803, that the idea of a forgotten but widespread tradition in landscape practice started to take shape for him.

When the Jones oil sketches were auctioned at Christie's their originality was recognised by James Byam Shaw, a director of Colnaghi's in London, who bought nearly all of them. Several museums, including the British Museum, snapped them up for ridiculously small sums – none fetched more than twenty guineas at auction – and John later reproached himself bitterly for missing that opportunity. Jones, a pupil of Richard Wilson, seemed nothing more than an uninspired and largely unsuccessful exponent of romantic mythological landscapes until the discovery of the sketches. In a short article for the *British Museum Quarterly*[1] comparing the print room's Jones of *Buildings in Naples*, with sketches by his French contemporary Pierre-Henri de Valenciennes in the Musée du Louvre, John speculated that 'it may well have been common practice in Rome at that period to make sketches of this kind', and this indeed proved to be the case. He was by then aware that these *al primo* landscape 'snapshots' were 'paintings of a unique kind' that deserved study as a separate entity, and he concluded that the best way to study them was to collect them.

A year or so after the 1954 Jones discovery, John acquired the view of the grotto at Posillipo (cat. no. 43). In 1957, very shortly after I met him, I found a tiny landscape by Jones (cat. no. 44) for five pounds, and, meaning to consult him about whether I should buy it, I told him about it. Without a word, he rose from his desk and with long strides reached the shop long before I could catch up with him, and bought it for himself. He always excused this on the grounds that true collectors have to be ruthless. The point of this anecdote is the speed with which I had been recruited into the band of cognoscenti. I had known John for only a few weeks and we were not yet on Christian name terms, but he had so managed to

1 Gere 1959.

infect me with his ideas of the importance of Jones and his contemporaries that I was able to recognise his hand in a painting no bigger than a postcard from across the width of Museum Street. I think from then on I appeared in a different light to him, possibly even as a future collaborator.

In the 1950s John's energies – and his very limited spare cash – were devoted to Italian sixteenth-century drawings, his own professional field, then available in such abundance that it was possible to buy beautiful things in which the British Museum had no interest for a few pounds. The Pre-Raphaelites were even more of a bargain, with Burne-Jones drawings in great bundles, often costing less than a pound each. However, in 1963 the London dealer John Manning exhibited a group of late eighteenth-century oil sketches and drawings bearing dated inscriptions, identified as Louis Gauffier, and John acquired one of the environs of Rome (see cat. no. 34). It is no coincidence that the oil sketch collection took over when Old Masters and the Victorians had become vastly more expensive. As John explained to Roberta Olson 'they are still cheap enough to collect, because they are often anonymous and on the whole people are reluctant to buy pictures without names attached'.

Knowledge of the open-air sketching tradition in European landscape painting is now so well-established that it is difficult to recall the state of ignorance that existed in the 1950s. Collecting these sketches was a real venture into uncharted waters. There was no established market and it was even difficult to know whether to ask for them as drawings or paintings because of the fact that they were frequently painted on paper. Gradually a list emerged of names to search for, but true sketches appeared only very rarely on the market. As the private working material of the artist, kept in his studio and shown only to pupils and fellow artists, oil sketches were rarely signed and when the contents of a studio were dispersed the sketches, unmounted and often uncared for, gravitated to the local flea market or into job lots at auction. Sketches that reached the mainstream art

Part of the collection as it was hung before the transfer to the National Gallery. Among the oil sketches on show are works by Bidauld, Bertin, Leighton and Wals (photo: Gavin Kingcombe).

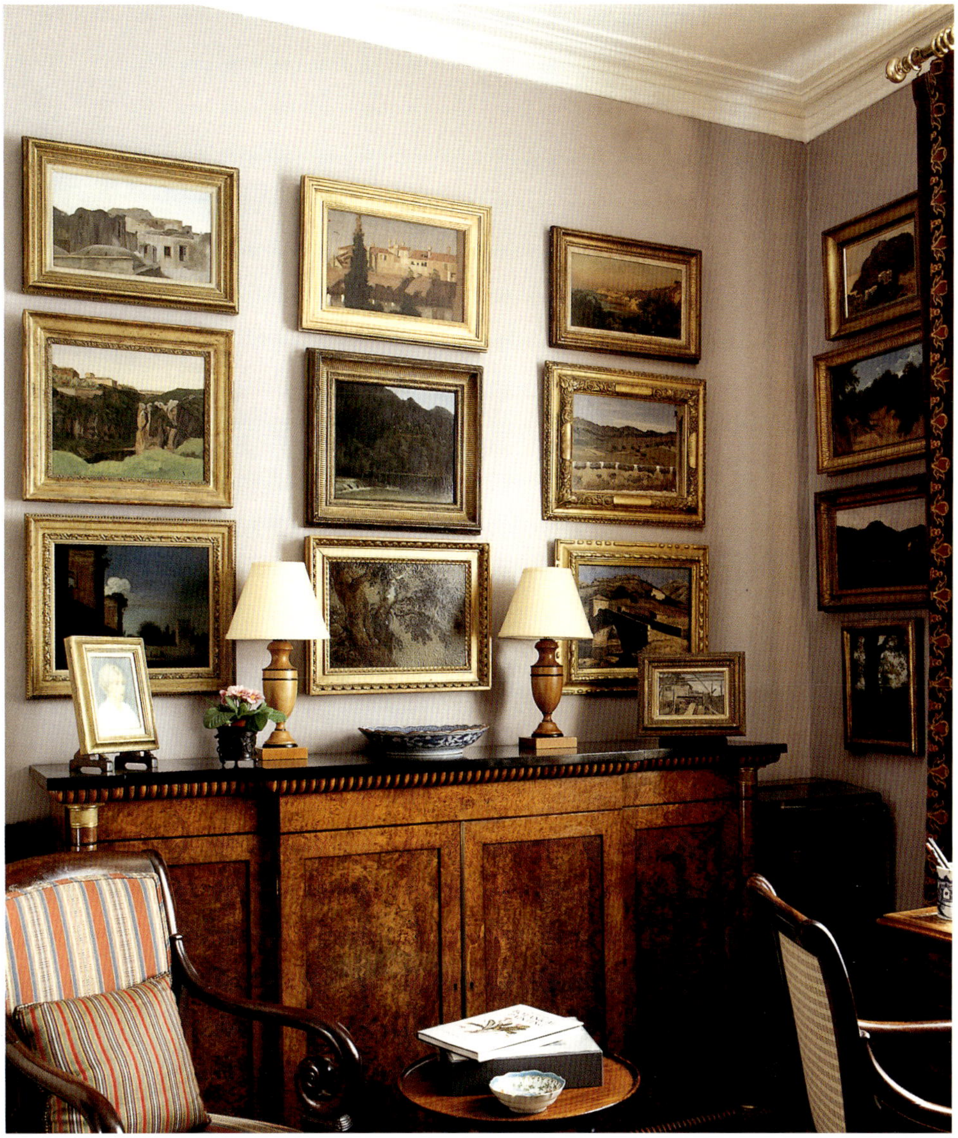

market were likely to turn up anywhere, even in sales of Old Master drawings (the Carl Blechen of Amalfi, cat. no. 3, and the J.-M. Cels sky study (cat. no. 12), are two examples). Even when finds came with names attached to them – usually a matter of indifference to John, who was not at all afraid of anonymity – these often proved to be incorrect. It may constitute something of a record in procrastination that we hesitated for respectively twenty (cat. no. 38) and twenty-one years (cat. no. 2) over the decision to buy two paintings exhibited in 1972 which both carried a patently implausible attribution to Caruelle d'Aligny and are now attributed to François-Marius Granet and Jean-Joseph-Xavier Bidauld respectively. Apart from the

Two oil sketches by Valenciennes and Denis's *View of the Cascades at Tivoli* can be seen as part of the original display (photo: Gavin Kingcombe).

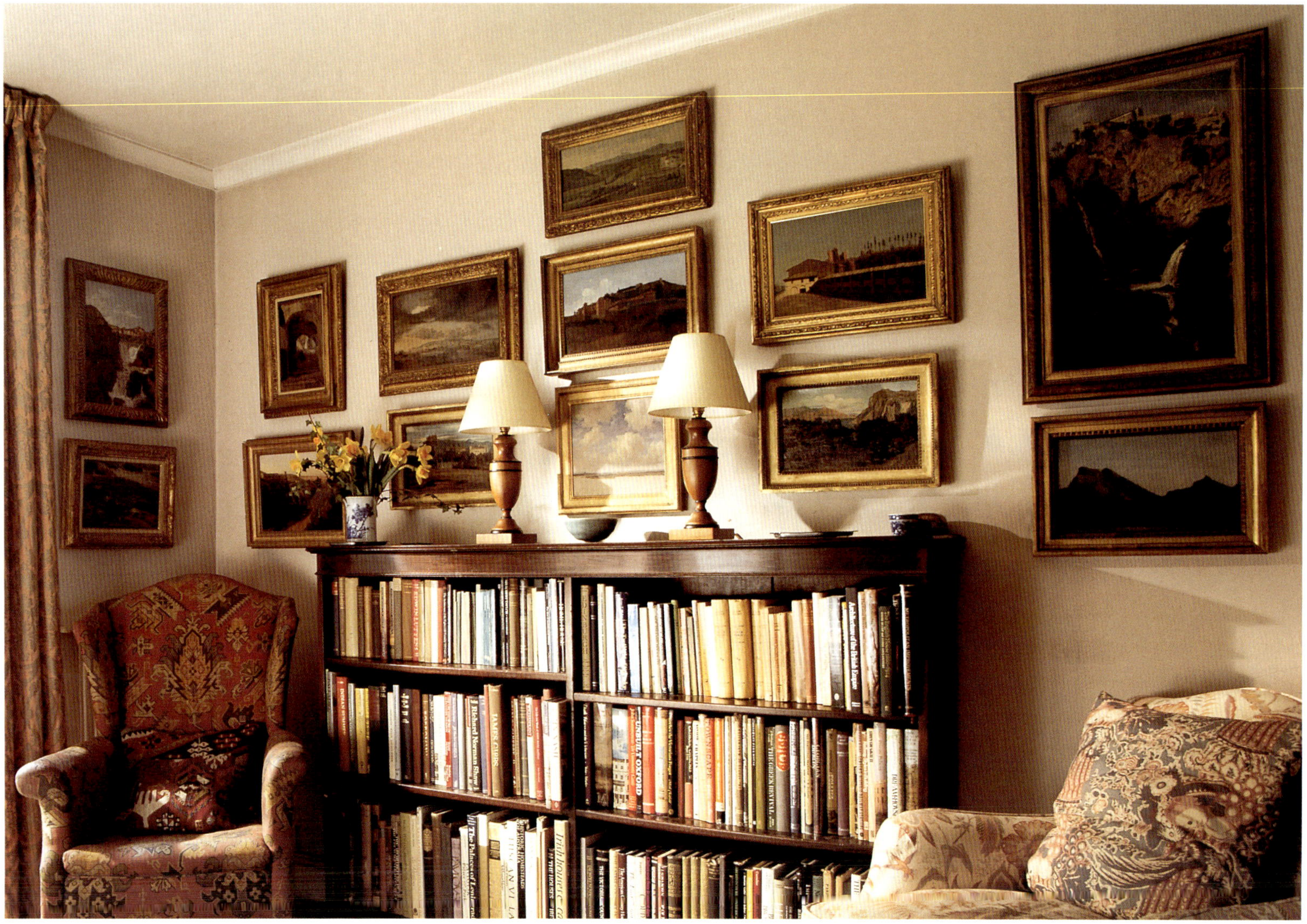

incorrect attribution, John was also dubious about the 'sketch' status of the Granet (cat. no. 38) and this has proved to be justified. However, the information that it provides about Granet's *modus operandi* is worth any slight adjustment in the nebulous concept of the sketch.

The only way to arrive at some idea of the individual personalities of the artists was by comparison of examples, the well-tried method applied to the attribution of Old Master drawings, with which John was intimately familiar. The material, though abundant, is scattered in museums and private collections throughout Europe, rarely catalogued and almost never on show, so ownership of a sufficiently large number of representative examples became a form of scholastic tool as much as an aesthetic experience.

Authorship of individual works was, and still is, very hard to establish owing to the obscurity of most of the artists. Pierre-Henri de Valenciennes, Thomas Jones, Simon Denis, Louis Gauffier, Jean-Joseph-Xavier Bidauld, Edouard Bertin, Achille-Etna Michallon, some of the best-known among them, are hardly household names. In 1971 an exhibition held in London and Cardiff brought Thomas Jones to a wider public, and then in 1977 an exhibition shown at the Cabinet du Dessins at the Louvre and the British Museum, *French Landscape Drawings and Sketches of the Eighteenth Century*, and including oil sketches by Valenciennes and François Desportes, did the same for them. The Valenciennes sketches had been in the Louvre since 1930 and were sometimes shown with the early Roman views by Corot and his master Michallon, in the little cabinet rooms on an upper floor. They were almost unknown in England and proved a revelation to an audience accustomed to regard open-air landscape painting as a nineteenth-century innovation. Some of the Desportes sketches were borrowed from the Manufacture National at Sèvres, where about six hundred had been deposited in 1784 as inspiration for the porcelain painters. The *plein-air* landscapes, which were less useful than the flowers and animals, had been largely forgotten.

Exhibitions at the Louvre dedicated to Valenciennes, Desportes and Michallon (in 1976, 1982 and 1994 respectively), made these artists more familiar, but an enormous quantity of unsuspected material remains in other institutions. Some years ago, when I accompanied John on a courier trip to Frankfurt in connection with a Goya exhibition, I wandered off during the prolonged hand-over negotiations and found myself in a gallery stacked with small, brilliant, unlabelled landscape views. I was hustled out by a warder almost at once, and it seems astonishing to report that we were never able to discover what they were. It was as if I had imagined the whole episode. A wealth of German material emerged in exhibitions devoted to Carl Blechen in Berlin in 1990 and Georg von Dillis in Munich in 1992. In 1990, for some reason which I have now forgotten, we could not get a hotel room in Berlin even for one night, but it seemed crucial to see the Blechen exhibition, and we flew over for the day. On the basis of that visit the long slog of establishing the attribution of the Amalfi view (cat. no. 3) was begun.

For unfathomable reasons the former curator of the Musée Granet would not allow anyone to see the large group of sketches by François-Marius Granet and Jean-Antoine Constantin – the latter had been bought as an act of charity to his family, and discovered much later in parcels labelled to be thrown away – and Professor Lawrence Gowing was forced to make slides surreptitiously, which were then passed round like forbidden books. Since the sketches have

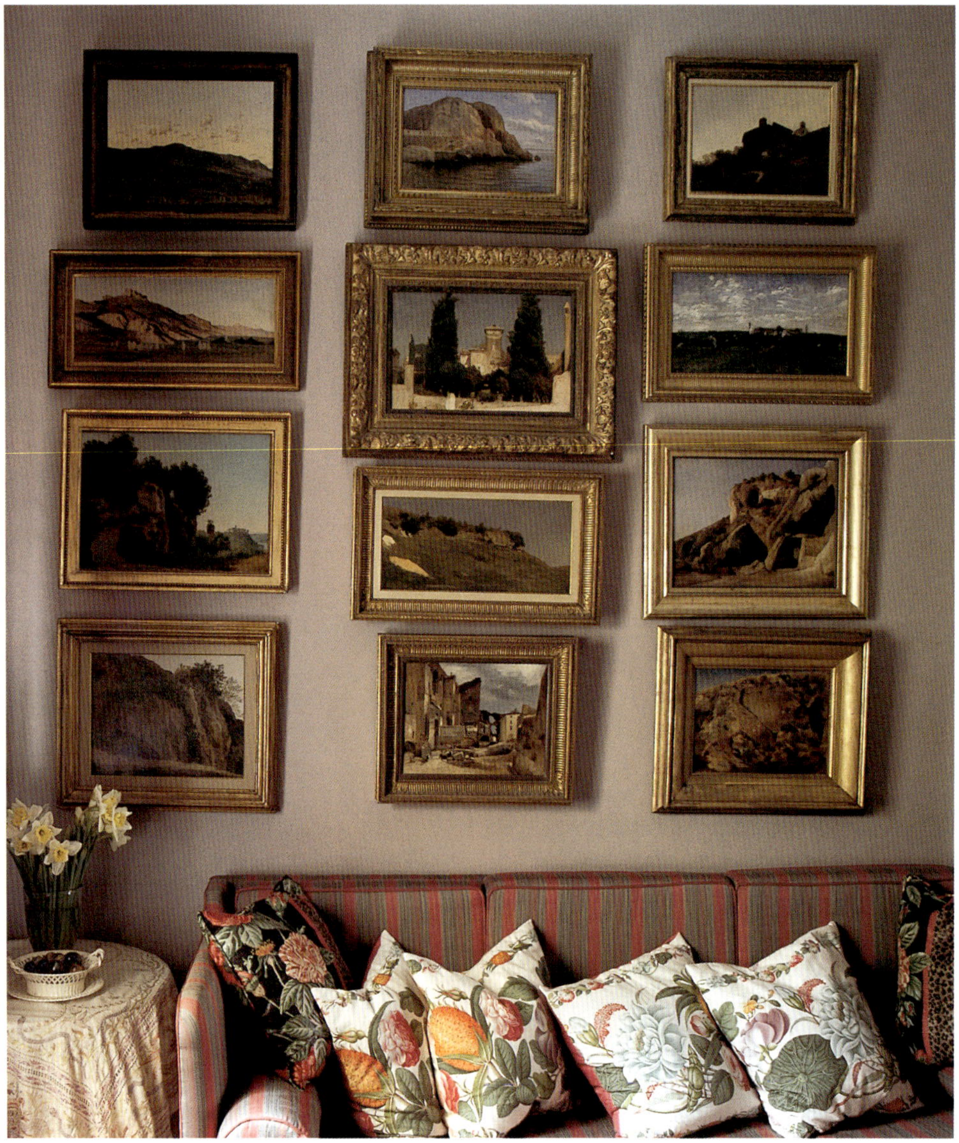

Part of the collection as it was originally hung. Among the works seen here are Lord Leighton's *View of the Villa Malta* and Böcklin's *A Cliff Face* (photo: Gavin Kingcombe).

been made accessible by the present curator, many more have come on the market, and museums have bought them – views of Tivoli by Granet are among the recent acquisitions by the Ashmolean in Oxford and the Metropolitan Museum in New York.

In the 1970s the Paris dealer Jacques Fischer was still finding beautiful sketches in the Marché aux Puces, one of them being the Valenciennes of *Cow-Shed and Houses on the Palatine Hill* (cat. no. 66). John heard about it when it had already found its way into the Galerie du Fleuve from a friend, Colin McMordie, whom he encountered by chance in the street. He was too late to catch it there, and pursued it to London where he bought it from the London oil sketch specialist John Lishawa. This was not a moment for caution and was the first occasion when we were forced to spend real money on the collection.

It seems probable that Jacques also found the sketch of a cliff by Arnold Böcklin (cat. no. 4) in a similar environment. Although he had no ideas about the likely author, or even the date, he thought John would be intrigued by the 'faces' formed by fissures in the rocks, and he must have been surprised – as I was – by John's reaction. Feigning indifference John enquired the price and agreed to buy it immediately. Without staying for the customary lengthy discussion and to make a show – not very convincing on either side – of haggling over the price, he hustled me out. Protesting at this curtailment of one of our principal pleasures in collecting, I asked the reason. 'Quick, quick,' he urged, to get us out of earshot, 'it's by Böcklin.' We had just come from the Musée d'Orsay, and he saw an unmistakable resemblance between the sketch and the background of the large Böcklin there. It was a very daring attribution, and certain to be challenged, but contrary to expectation it has stood the test of rigorous scepticism.

A number of sketches in the collection have a provenance traceable to a descendant of the artist. The three by G.-B. Camuccini (cat. nos. 9–11) came from a large group of forty or more, found by Julien Stock of Sotheby's in the attic of the family villa outside Rome. Two sketches added to the collection since my husband's death, the George Wallis of tree stumps (cat. no. 67) and the sky study by Jean-Michel Cels (cat. no. 12), were found in similar circumstances, as part of bundles of unmounted and scruffy material which had remained with the artist's family.

Specialist dealers are crucial to the small, closely knit group of sketch enthusiasts, but others with a taste for the off-beat, like the late Jeremy Maas, sometimes acquired 'irresistible', but often anonymous and hard to sell, sketches. Maas had the Valenciennes cloud study, *Rome at Sunrise* (cat. no. 65), in 1965, believing it to be by Thomas Jones. He was also an admirer of Frederic, Lord Leighton's landscape sketches. These have remained seriously undervalued – except by such enlightened dealers as the Fine Art Society – in comparison with Leighton's large academic works, in spite of the reaction of critics and public alike to the group included in the Royal Academy's Leighton centenary exhibition in 1996.

Leighton's view of the *Villa Malta* (cat. no. 51) came to us by an odd route. It was owned by Hugh and April Squire, dedicated collectors of Old Master drawings, who thought it was by Corot. They explained away Leighton's label on the reverse as indicating that the painting belonged him, rather than that he was himself the author of it, and their disappointment at receiving convincing proof to the contrary was acute. John enquired delicately if they would consider parting with it, and Hugh indicated that he might sell, asking bluntly what John would give for it. Boldly announcing the largest sum he could possibly think of, viz. £250, John was ecstatic to find himself its owner.

With the pioneering exhibitions of Italian views at Hazlitt, Gooden and Fox in 1978 and 1979 oil sketches became more expensive, but they also became more available. One of the most striking, the torrent of water at Tivoli by Simon Denis (cat. no. 24), came from the 1978 exhibition, which was in the nature of an experiment and prices were still modest. We bought steadily through the next decade, by whatever means we could, a mixture of frugality – John was notoriously reluctant to take taxis however late the hour – and 'trading up' within the collection. The first insurmountable financial crisis arose in 1989 when a painting that John had longed to possess for nearly thirty years, the *Landscape with Figures* (cat. no. 64) attributed to Salvator Rosa, came up for auction. There was nothing for it but to sacrifice a cherished Old Master drawing, but in doing so we unwittingly secured funds that would cover all the purchases of the future. This meant that we could afford the Goffredo Wals (cat. no. 68) and when a group surfaced of Roman views by Gilles Closson, previously known only through the sketches bequeathed to his native city of Liège, we were able to buy three (cat. nos. 13–15).

Sketches are now highly prized and equally highly priced. Jones and Bidauld have long since broken the £50,000 barrier and sketches seem set to reach six figures. Just as we had to stop buying Old Master drawings in the 1960s, we would probably have had to give up this collection as well, but it was an incredibly absorbing enterprise while it lasted.

'Discovering a splendid problem'
Inventing the Landscape Oil Sketch

CHRISTOPHER RIOPELLE

This catalogue tells two stories. The first is the story of the landscape oil sketch. Artists made such free and improvisational sketches out of doors in nature from at least the early seventeenth century. In the mid-eighteenth century, the practice became widespread, especially among the large international community of artists working in Italy. By the turn of the nineteenth century it was a commonplace of artistic training, and for the next fifty years or more almost every landscape painter in Europe, whether travelling in Italy or working at home, honed his or her talent by making these simple, direct oil studies in the open air. The works were rarely intended for public exhibition. They were tests of skill in the observation and transcription of natural phenomena, ways of training the eye and hand to capture fleeting effects of light and atmosphere. Often painted on paper or small wooden panels, the completed sketches were piled in the corner of the studio, sometimes consulted as the artist composed a 'finished' landscape painting, or shown to students, but more often than not, largely ignored once they were completed. When the contents of artists' studios were dispersed following their deaths, such sketches were little valued; the final lot in the 1861 sale of the painter Jules Coignet's effects consisted of '100 different painted studies', otherwise unspecified.[1] The sketches of Jean-Antoine Constantin were almost thrown away before the Director of the Musée Granet in Aix-en-Provence took pity on the artist's impoverished widow and bought them.

In the second half of the nineteenth century the qualities of quickness and spontaneity that characterised the oil sketch came to be admired and adopted by the Impressionist painters, who exhibited their own sketch-like paintings as finished pictures. With this innovation, the rôle of the oil sketch as a painter's private craft – a rehearsal for the 'real' work of painting – diminished. As fewer and fewer artists painted such studies, the reasons why they had once been an important part of artistic training were forgotten.

The second story this catalogue tells – implicitly in the details of provenance and exhibition history in individual entries, and in the acknowledgement of lively disagreements among connoisseurs of the tradition – is that of the slow rediscovery of the landscape oil sketch itself, and the recovery of an understanding of the significant rôle it once played within landscape painting. This process began in the early decades of the twentieth century, and was accomplished by a small group of collectors, connoisseurs, curators and dealers, who became curious about the simple but impressively vivid landscapes they stumbled upon in the reserves of the Louvre, on the walls of provincial museums, at flea markets or in dealers' back rooms. The oil sketches that Camille Corot had painted in Italy early in the nineteenth century had been admired since critics first began to discuss them in the 1850s. They came to the attention of a wider public following the artist's death in 1875.[2] Now the achievements of Corot's teacher Achille-Etna Michallon, and of Michallon's teacher Pierre-Henri de Valenciennes, began to be identified and assessed. Dozens more artists were discovered to have been important and innovative practitioners of the craft. New names like those of Thomas Jones and Simon Denis acquired renown as their sketches came to light. In many cases, these artists are now far more admired for their oil sketches than they ever were for their grander, more artistically self-conscious public works.

It is hard to overestimate how much knowledge had been lost about the oil sketch when connoisseurs and collectors began to detect traces of the tradition

1 Paris 1861.
2 Galassi 1991, p. 3.
3 Galassi in Washington, Brooklyn and St Louis 1996–7, p. 27.
4 For the early history of open-air painting, see Conisbee 1979; and Consibee in Washington, Brooklyn and St Louis 1996–7, pp. 29–47.
5 Cited by Conisbee ibid., p. 32.

and to raise questions about it. The gift of dazzling sketches by Valenciennes and Michallon to the Louvre by the Princesse Louis de Croÿ in 1930 came as a surprise to almost everyone. Who were these artists who, even before Corot, had such freshness of vision? Their works had descended in a single collection from the artists' lifetimes, so at least authorship was not the problem. With many other oil sketches, however, attribution soon emerged as a central issue. The paintings were almost never signed and artists working side by side in front of the same motif, or trained in the same master's studio, frequently painted in a remarkably similar manner. Often, they deliberately attempted to imitate the effects their colleagues were achieving. This was a time-honoured pedagogical practice among painters, and the young Corot, for example, made a deep impact on his contemporaries with his oil sketches. Moreover, painters from all over Europe worked and learned together in Italy, frequently making it difficult to identify a sketch's country of origin. Connoisseurs were repeatedly taken by surprise when evidence revealed that artists who were thought to be minor – flying below the radar scope of critical attention, so to speak – on occasion proved to be among the most innovative and highly original masters of the oil sketch. Students of the oil sketch have necessarily spent much time – and continue to do so – attempting to discriminate one hand from another, and constructing recognisable artistic personalities, just as scholars of early Italian gold-ground painting were doing a century ago.

As the anonymous works in this collection attest – as well as those about which we can only hazard more or less informed opinions – much still remains to be learned about the landscape oil sketch, but the fascination of the task lies in the slow accumulation of answers to what at times have appeared to be intractable problems. By studying the collection as a whole, as well as the individual works, we begin to understand the lineaments of the tradition, its international dimensions, and its evolution from the seventeenth century to the late nineteenth century. In a 1996 tribute to the late John Gere, the oil sketch scholar Peter Galassi said of him that 'he discovered a splendid problem where none had existed before.'[3] This catalogue is a report on the present state of knowledge of that problem, which Gere, and a handful of pioneering colleagues, were among the first to articulate.

It is clear that by the seventeenth century artists were already painting landscapes out of doors.[4] In northern Europe, Peter Paul Rubens was creating small panels with all the freshness and spontaneity of immediate perception, such as his *Landscape after a Storm* of about 1630–5 (fig. 1). At about the same time in Rome, Claude Lorrain was experimenting with a novel way of working. Joachim Sandrart records him first preparing his colours in the countryside, and then later actually beginning to paint there.[5] The left side of his *A View in Rome* of 1632 (fig. 2), may correspond to the view of the church of Santissima Trinità de Monti on the Pincio that he would have seen and painted from the roof of his own house; the right side of the same painting, however, is an imaginary view of ruins. There is fleeting evidence of other artists – Diego Velázquez and Salvator Rosa (see cat. no. 64), for example – also working out of doors. In France, towards the end of the seventeenth century, François Desportes was constantly painting in the open air as he assembled a repertoire of motifs, such as tree trunks, flowers, animals and birds to adapt for use in

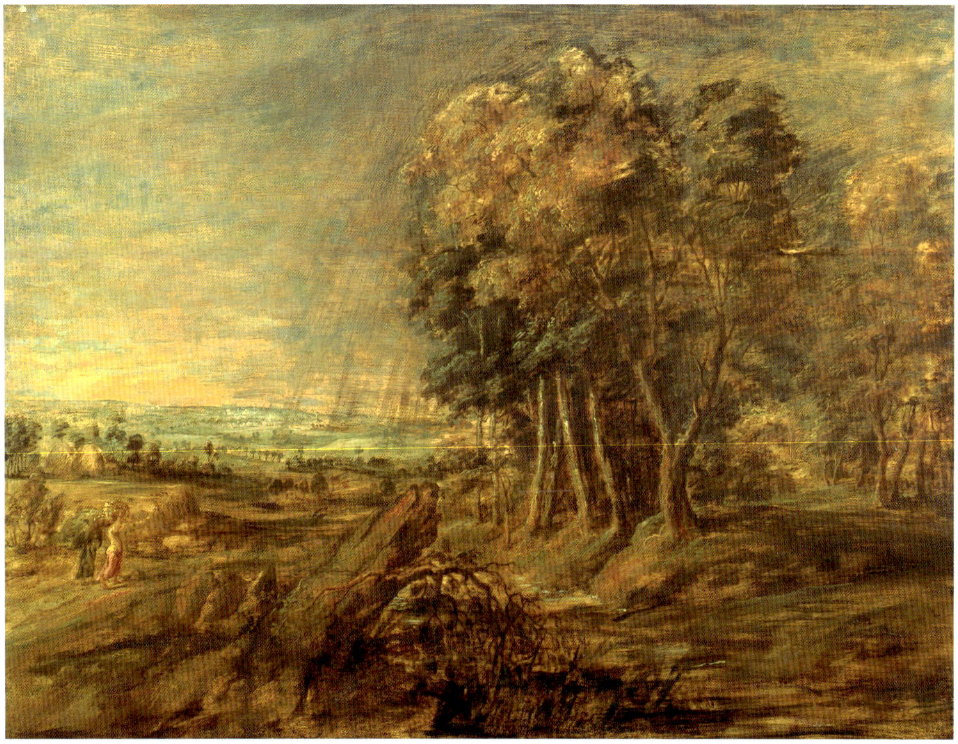

Fig 1 Peter Paul Rubens, *Landscape after a Storm,* 1630–35. Oil on canvas, 49 x 64.6 cm. London, Courtauld Gallery (inv.no.COU. 124.302).

his 'finished' paintings (see cat. no. 26). The custom may have been more popular at an earlier time than we are yet fully aware.

Rome was from the beginning the vital centre of the oil sketch tradition. Artists came to the city from across Europe to study the art of Antiquity and the High Renaissance of Raphael and Michelangelo. They drew the ancient marbles and copied the masterpieces of painting in princely galleries and the vast papal collections. For relaxation they ventured out into the surrounding countryside to draw and paint the picturesque ruins, the waterfalls and temples at Tivoli, and the aqueducts that stepped in stately rhythm across the Campagna,[6] and to study the vivid, ever-changing light effects that swept across the landscape. The practice of painting out of doors spread, particularly during the eighteenth century, probably at the various gathering places the artists frequented, and in the studios where they worked.

A watercolour by Eugène Lacroix of a studio at the French Academy in Rome in the early nineteenth century (fig. 3) shows what an artist might have taken with him on such a painting expedition. Propped up against a wall on the right is a type of portable easel consisting of a box containing paints and sheets of paper or small panels mounted on a pole, that could be pushed into the ground to hold it upright on site. The pair of pistols hanging above are for defence against poisonous snakes or brigands, although the snake slithering across the floor is probably a harmless pet, like the tortoise. The French Academy was the centre of artistic life in Rome for French artists. Originally housed in the Palazzo Mancini on the Corso, in 1802 it moved to the Villa Medici, high on the Pincian Hill, which afforded magnificent views out over the roofs and domes of the city. There, the most promising young artists in France, winners of the prestigious Prix de Rome in painting, sculpture and other art

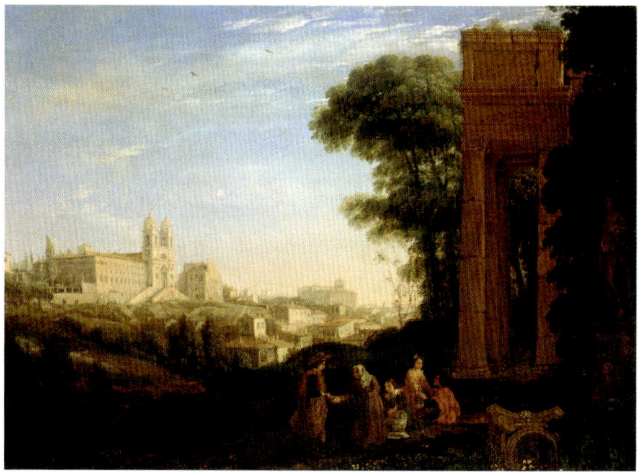

Fig 2 Claude Lorrain, *A View in Rome,* 1632. Oil on canvas, 59.7 x 83.8 cm. London, National Gallery (NG1319).

6 On the sites in and near Rome that were favoured by the painters, see Faunce in ibid., pp. 49–77.

7 See Galassi 1991.

disciplines, were sent for four years of rigorous, carefully supervised study. Within the French academic tradition, only that exposure to Antiquity and the Italian Renaissance prepared an artist to contribute meaningfully to the course of French art. Painters from other countries tended to band together in informal groups according to their nationalities, and there was a lively interchange between these various gatherings.

Other artists flocked to Naples. The Welshman Thomas Jones, a student in London of Richard Wilson, travelled to Italy in 1776, staying in Rome and later Naples until 1783. There he is known to have enjoyed the convivial company of an international group of artists and to have made a living as a minor painter of picturesque Italian scenes. The small, vivid oil sketches he also made there, such as *A Wall in Naples* (fig. 4), were completely unknown until a descendant offered them for sale as recently as 1954. Such uncompromisingly direct transcriptions of the humblest domestic motifs, some made from the rooftop of Jones's house in Naples, astonished viewers when they came to light, and intrigued scholars as they attempted to account for such unprecedented verisimilitude in paintings made decades before the invention of the photographs they seemed so uncannily to resemble.[7] The Belgian Simon Denis's oil sketches have also only fairly recently been rediscovered. The freedom of execution and the sense of drama seen in his *Sunset in the Roman Campagna* (fig. 5), stands in contrast to his more polished, 'correct,' and essentially pedestrian, large-scale landscape paintings. It is a remarkable feature of the oil sketch tradition that, freed from the constraint of painting for the public, working to hone their own perceptions, certain artists intuitively achieved effects of great beauty and freshness.

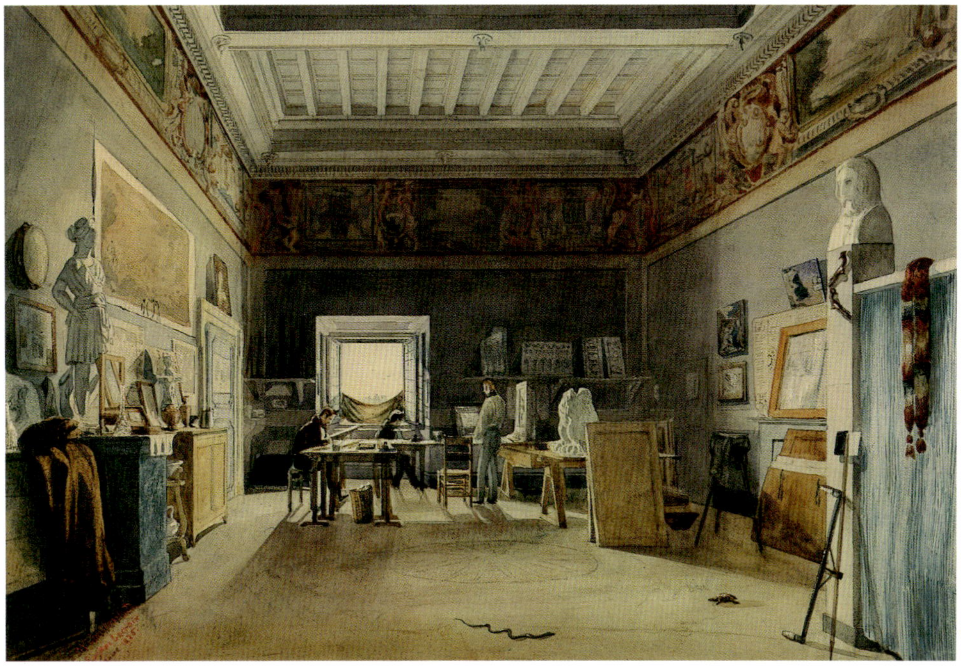

Fig 3 Eugène Lacroix, *Studio in the Villa Medici,* 1835. Watercolour, 22.9 x 32.7 cm. Private Collection.

The advice of a widely respected master of landscape painting, Claude-Joseph Vernet, seems to have influenced many painters to take up the oil sketch. Pierre-Henri de Valenciennes, for one, reported that a day he spent in consultation with Vernet in Paris in 1781 discussing perspective in painting was instrumental for the future direction of his art; he seems to have taken up the oil sketch soon afterwards. Valenciennes took to the craft with gusto and during several years in Rome painted assiduously. His unexpected rooftop views of the city are characterised by a striking and novel disposition of forms and the evocation of rich atmospheric effects with paint that has been laid down with evident speed and aplomb. He thought hard about what he was doing and why, and articulated his thoughts, thus emerging as perhaps the single most influential figure in the early history of the tradition. He later gathered his ideas on perspective

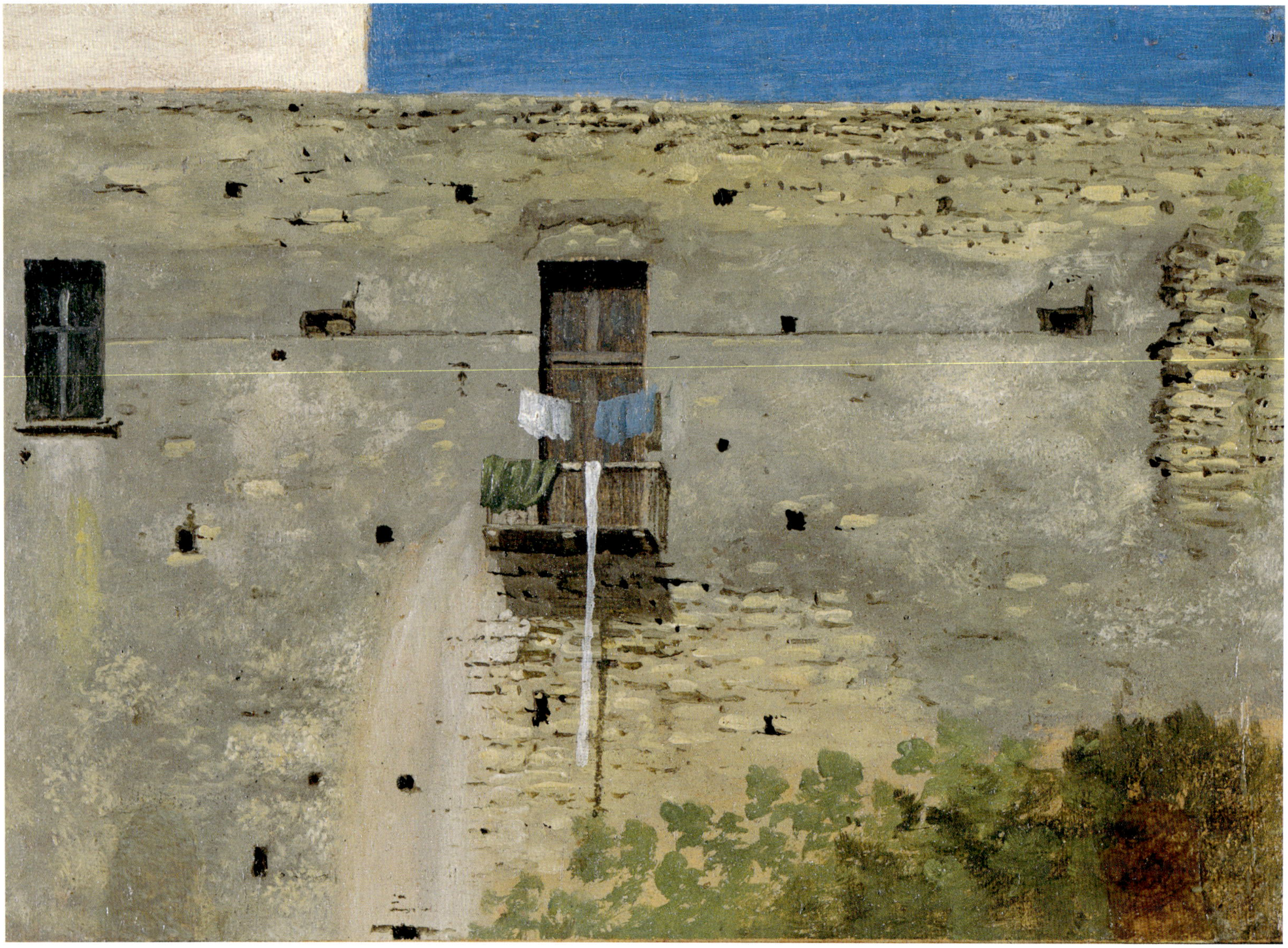

Fig 4 Thomas Jones, *A Wall in Naples,* about 1782. Oil on paper laid on canvas, 11.4 x 16 cm. London, National Gallery (NG6544).

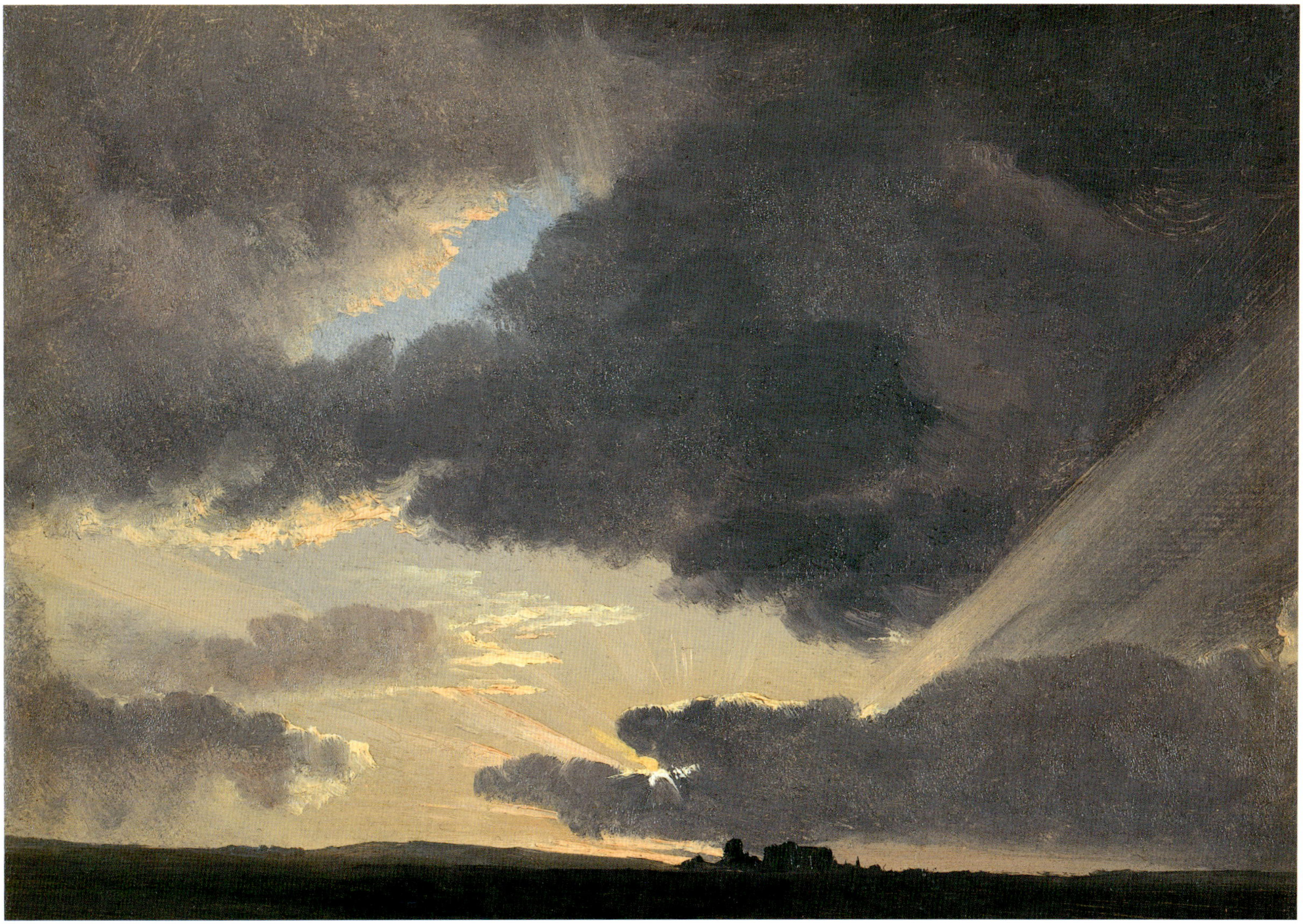

Fig 5 Simon Denis, *Sunset in the Roman Campagna,* between 1786 and about 1803. Oil on paper, 17 x 23 cm. London, National Gallery (NG6562).

and other aspects of art in a publication entitled *Elémens de perspective pratique* that appeared in 1800. The treatise included a chapter on the oil sketch, in which he spelled out the lessons he had learned in Rome and had shared there with fellow painters.

Valenciennes proposed that the artist take only two hours to make a sketch in order to capture specific effects of light. Light conditions changed rapidly, of course, and the artist had to make do with half an hour in the morning or evening. He advised the painter to focus on the middle ground and not to concern himself with the foreground, suggesting that he start his sketch by painting clouds because that would determine the general tone of the image. A work such as *Rome: Houses and a Domed Church* (fig. 6) shows him acting on his own advice. Valenciennes was interested in capturing the subtlest effects and recommended that painters study rushing water so as to understand movement and to differentiate between the shapes and textures of pebbles under water and those on dry land. He urged his students to attend to particularly characterful tree trunks and their aged, weathered barks. Of such minute visual distinctions was the oil sketch made, and artists all over Rome started turning to the very motifs Valenciennes suggested.

Fig 6 Pierre-Henri de Valenciennes, *Rome: Houses and a Domed Church*, about 1783. Oil on cardboard, 18 x 25 cm. Paris, Musée du Louvre (RF3034).

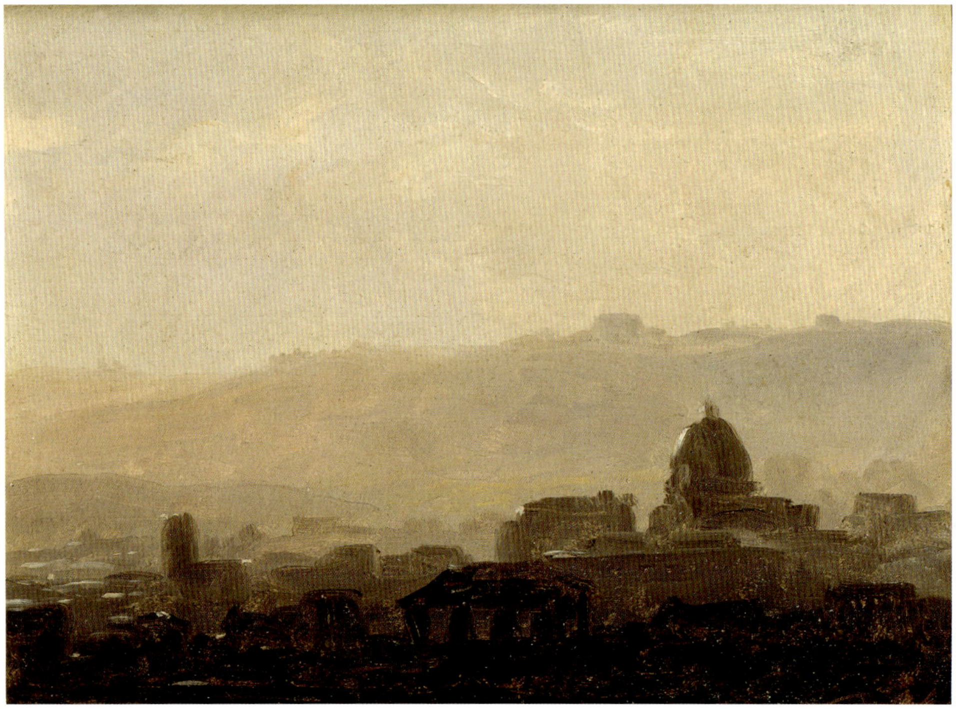

Valenciennes returned to Paris in 1785, where he enjoyed a distinguished career as a painter of carefully composed historical landscapes and as an influential teacher of perspective. The advice that had become the currency of studio talk in Italy now began to make an impact in France, on artists such as his pupils Achille-Etna Michallon and Jean-Victor Bertin. Thanks to the influence of Valenciennes, landscape painting acquired a new importance in France when, in 1817, a Prix de Rome was set up for *paysage historique*, or historical landscape painting. While based on studies from nature, such landscapes were learned, artifical constructs, carefully composed in the studio to achieve noble or picturesque effects and populated with figures from history or mythology. With the institution of that prize, landscape painting assumed the central role in French art that it would occupy for the rest of the nineteenth century. The first winner was the brilliant, but tragically short-lived Michallon. He too travelled to Italy where, like Denis (see cat. nos. 23, 24) and the Briton Philip Reinagle (see cat. no. 61), he followed his master's advice to paint torrents of rushing water, in this case the waterfalls at Tivoli (fig. 7).

The oil sketch was by now a stable part of artistic practice. Six months before Michallon died in 1822, Corot entered his studio, thus establishing a remarkable continuity in the the French landscape tradition

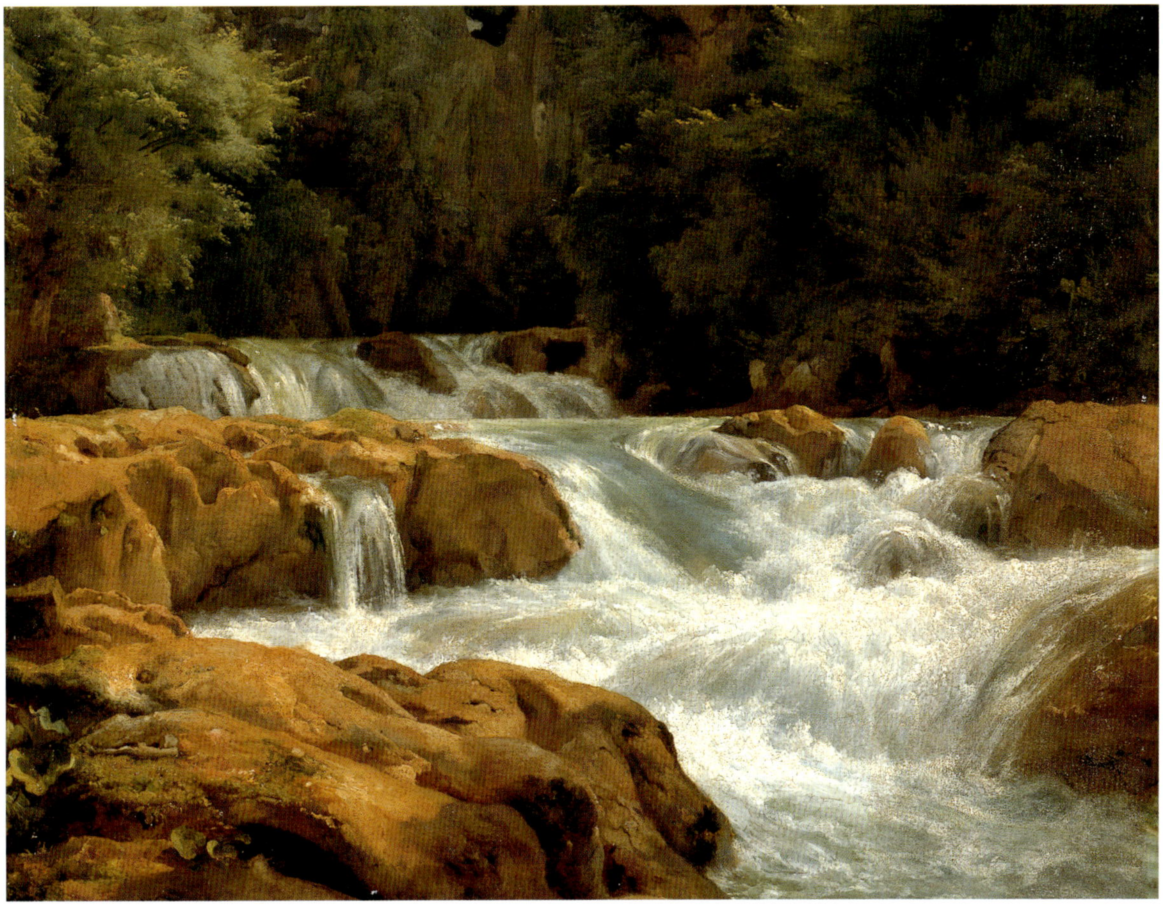

Fig 7 Achille-Etna Michallon, *The Torrent (Tivoli)*, about 1820. Oil on canvas, 48 x 60 cm. Paris, Musée du Louvre (RF2883).

from Vernet to Valenciennes to Michallon and to the man who quickly emerged as the greatest exponent of the art.[8] When Corot arrived in Italy late in 1825 he immediately undertook innovative oil studies of the city and surrounding countryside characterised by structural rigour and a bold handling of paint. He worked side by side with many French artists there and was widely influential in his approach. For Corot, however, young and anxious to establish a name, the distinction observed in the French academic tradition between the oil sketch and the 'finished' exhibition picture remained paramount. In September 1826 he made an oil sketch of the ruined Roman bridge that crossed the Nera river near the town of Narni in the Campagna (fig. 8). A triumph of atmospheric observation and breadth of vision, in which the foreground is left vague, just as Valenciennes had counselled, the sheet has long been widely admired. In 1827, the year of his first submission to the Paris Salon, Corot 'worked up' the Narni sketch in a finished painting (fig. 9). The painting that he showed that year was not merely a larger, more elaborate version of the sketch, however, but an artificial composition that refers to the earlier work almost in passing. Here, Corot

8 On Corot's achievement, see Galassi 1991.

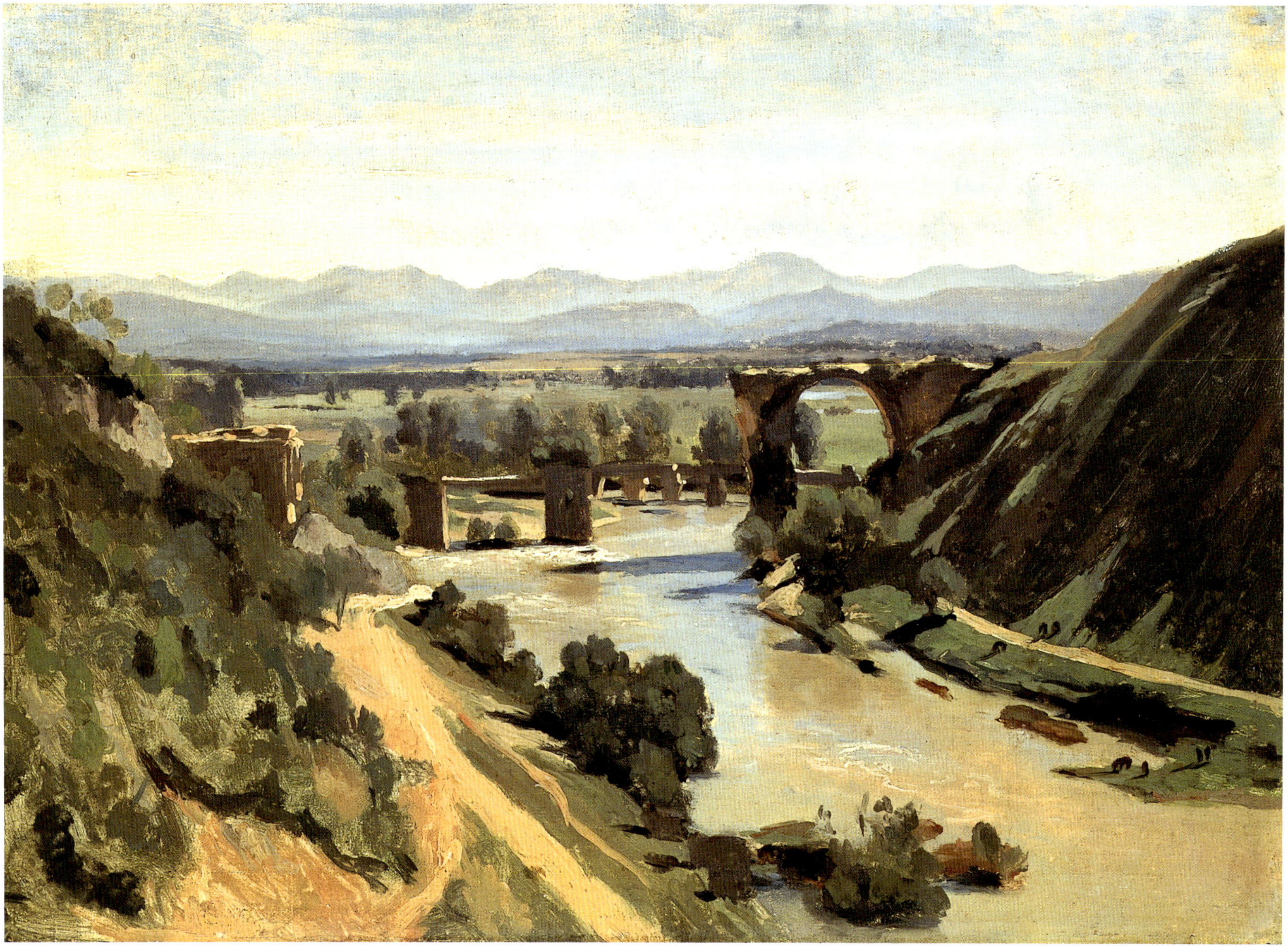

Fig 8 Camille Corot, *The Bridge at Narni,* 1826. Oil on paper laid on canvas, 34 x 48 cm. Paris, Musée du Louvre (RF1613).

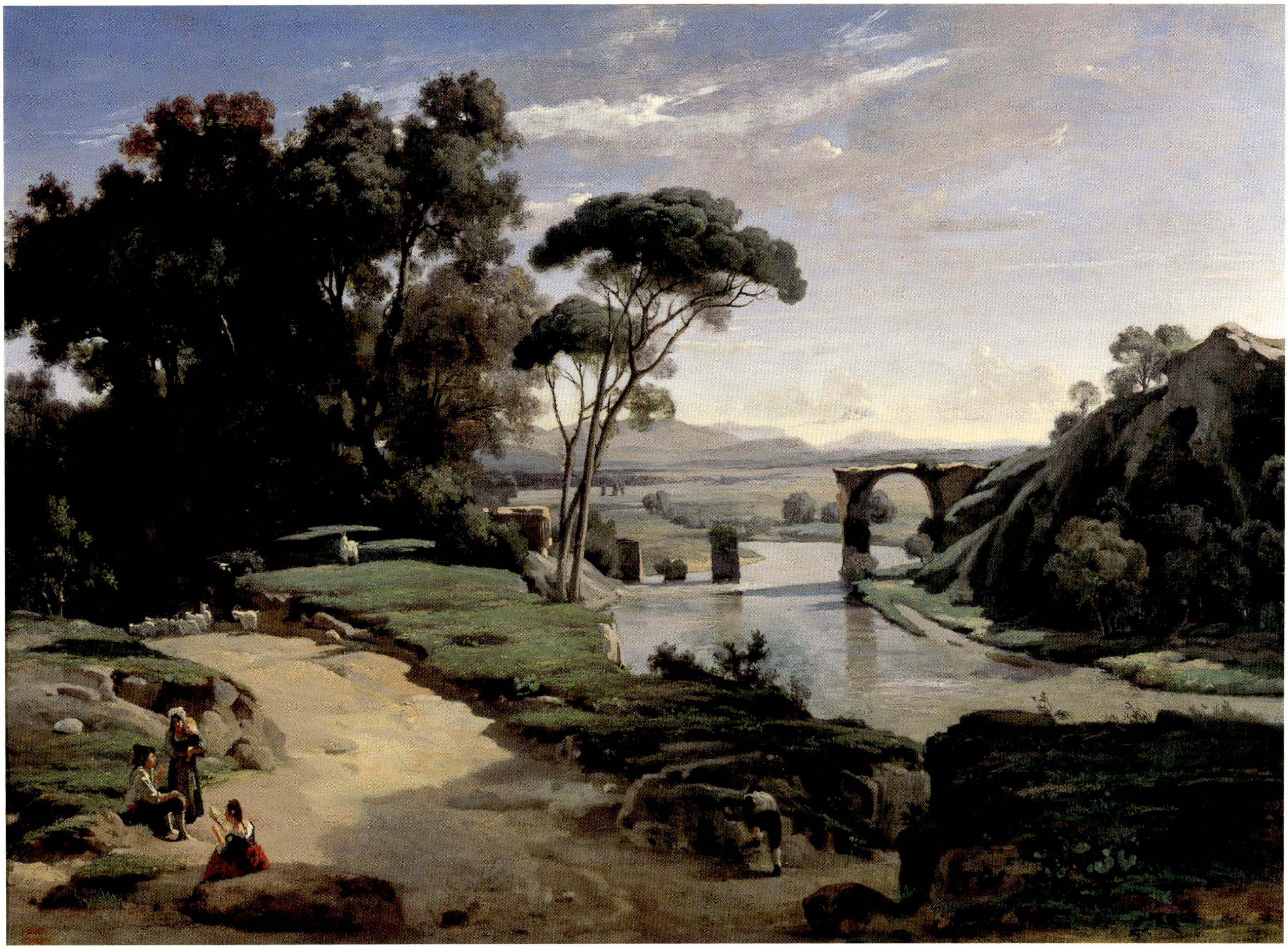

Fig 9 Camille Corot, *The Bridge at Narni,* 1827. Oil on canvas, 68 x 94.6 cm. Ottawa, National Gallery of Canada (purchased 1939).

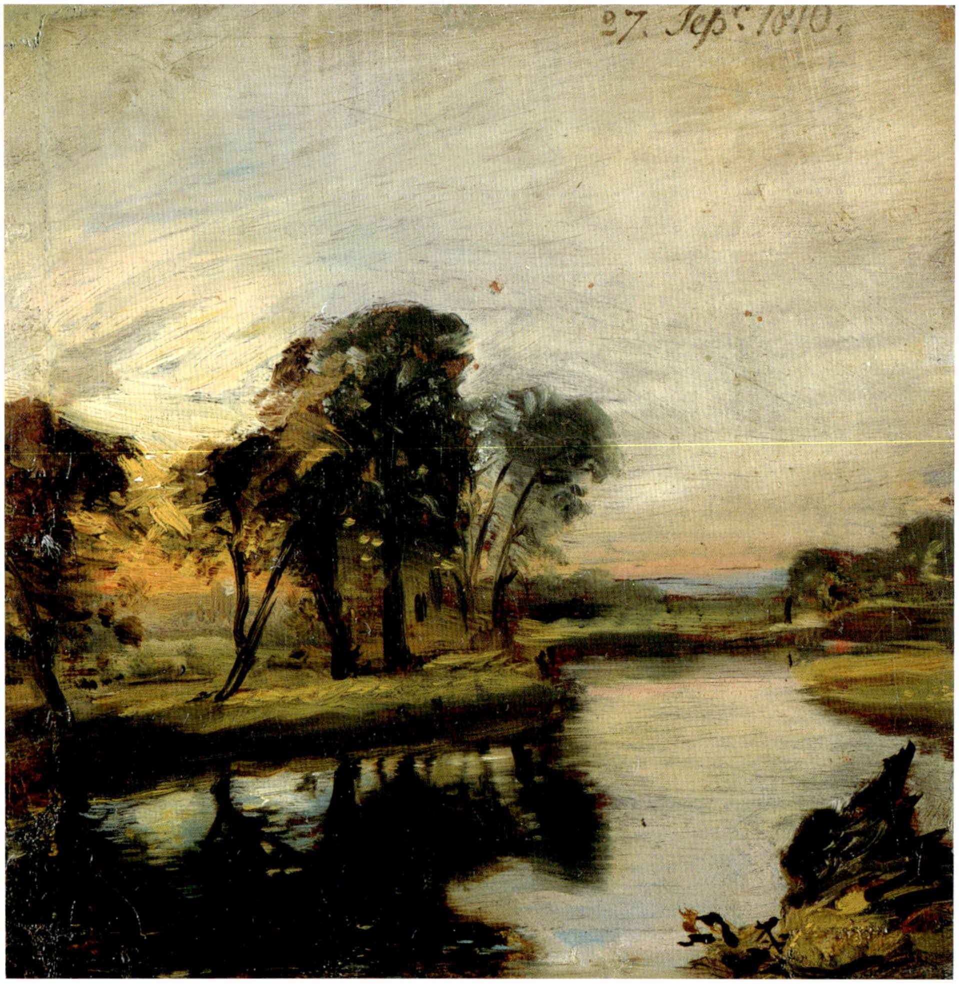

Fig 10 John Constable, *View on the Stour (Afternoon on the River)*, 1810. Oil on canvas, 23.5 x 23.5 cm. Philadelphia, John G. Johnson Collection, Philadelphia Museum of Art (J.857).

brought to bear not merely his skill in observation but his powers of composition, knowledge of landscape tradition, and inventive skills as he added shepherds and their flocks, winding paths and trees. For Corot, the aesthetic worth of the painting lay not in the motif depicted but in his ability to ennoble it. That is the ground on which he staked his claim to artistic success.

The influence of Corot's Italian oil sketches on fellow artists was almost instantaneous. Soon after his arrival in Italy late in 1825 contemporaries were referring to him as 'the master'. Though he visited Italy on two further occasions, Corot's return to France from that first trip, in 1828, can be seen to mark the shift of innovation in landscape oil sketching from Italy to France. A new generation of artists turned its attention to the French landscape when the Barbizon painters went to work in the forest of Fontainebleau.

Across the English Channel another tradition of oil sketching was growing up. Artists such as Thomas Kerrich, seemingly without much exposure to French or Italian practices, spontaneously arrived at novel depictions of the English landscape at an early date, before the turn of the nineteenth century (see cat. no. 45). Although he did not paint oil sketches himself, Richard Wilson awoke a taste in English patrons for Italian landscape, and word of the oil sketch filtered back to England with artists such as Jones and Reinagle. J.M.W. Turner, who travelled widely on the Continent, made sketches. John Constable, who never left England, did so even more assiduously in his jewel-like evocations of a specifically English landscape, such as his spirited *View on the Stour* of 1810 (fig 10). The continuity of that British tradition is represented in the Gere collection by the superb group of oil sketches that Frederic, Lord Leighton, the quintessential Victorian painter, executed at home, in Italy and Spain, in the second half of the century (see cat. nos. 48–55).

Artists in northern Europe were drawn to Italy by an almost mystical yearning for a timeless land. Among the most accomplished was Johan Christian Dahl, Norwegian-born but active in Dresden, who in 1820 found an inherently monumental view when he looked out from the darkness of a grotto near Naples into the brilliant Mediterranean light (fig. 11). Often the Northern painters added an unexpected accent to the oil sketch; when the Swiss painter Arnold Böcklin depicted a cliff side he made it seem alive with human faces and forms (cat. no. 4).

If it took more than two hundred years, from the early seventeenth century to the mid-nineteenth century, for landscape oil sketching to emerge as an artistic practice, and eventually to win a place at the very heart of landscape painting across Europe, the tradition disappeared with remarkable rapidity. This is not to say that people stopped painting oil sketches out of doors; thousands still do so today. But with the innovations of the Impressionists, the oil sketch inevitably lost its status and function. It was no longer a tool for refining perception and painterly skill – a vital adjunct to the painting of 'finished' pictures. The distinction that Corot drew between the sketch and the exhibited painting no longer pertained when the imagery of speed, spontaneity and incompleteness themselves were exploited in the pictures a new generation of artists chose to show.

Claude Monet seemed to announce as much with his *Boat Studio* of 1876 (fig. 12). He shows the artist at work out of doors, capturing the most transient effects of light reflected on water and drifting down through trees. All is ephemeral, floating and unstable, but Monet declines to impose stability. Flux is all and he declares his picture to be complete. In some of the latest works in the Gere collection, by Edgar Degas (cat. no. 22) and Giuseppe de Nittis (cat. no. 25), the Impressionist moment is at hand, but is seen to flow effortlessly out of the oil sketch tradition. In 1888 Paul Gauguin, having passed through his apprenticeship in Impressionist painting, posed a more severe challenge to the oil sketch tradition when he took his friend Paul Sérusier out into nature to paint. When they reached their motif, a lake deep in the forest,

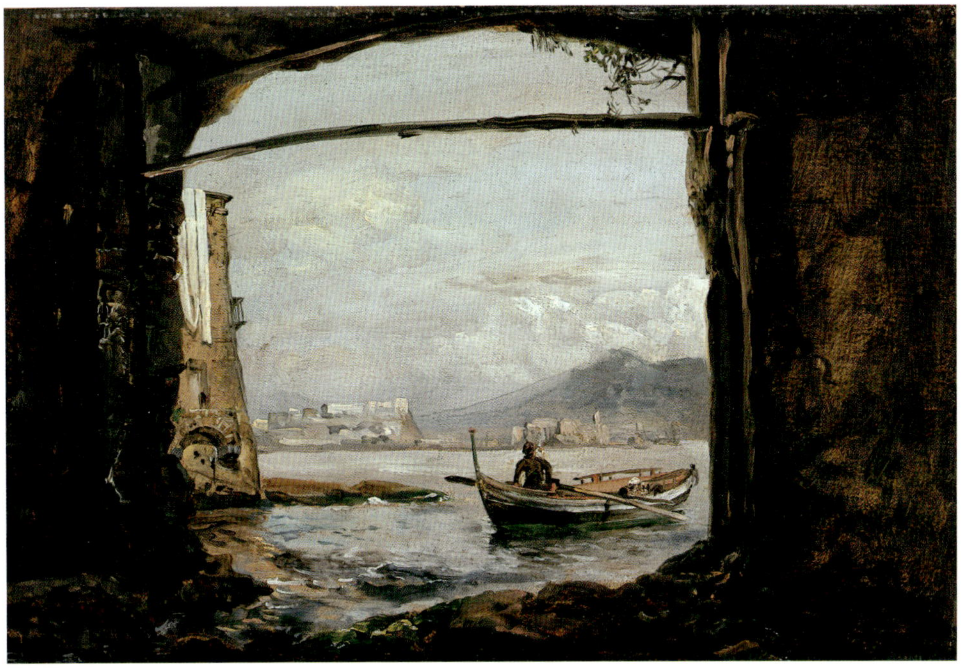

Fig 11 Johan Christian Dahl, *View from a Grotto near Naples*, 1820. Oil on paper laid on canvas, 25.5 x 38.5 cm. Oslo. Nasjonalgalleriet (inv. 426–26).

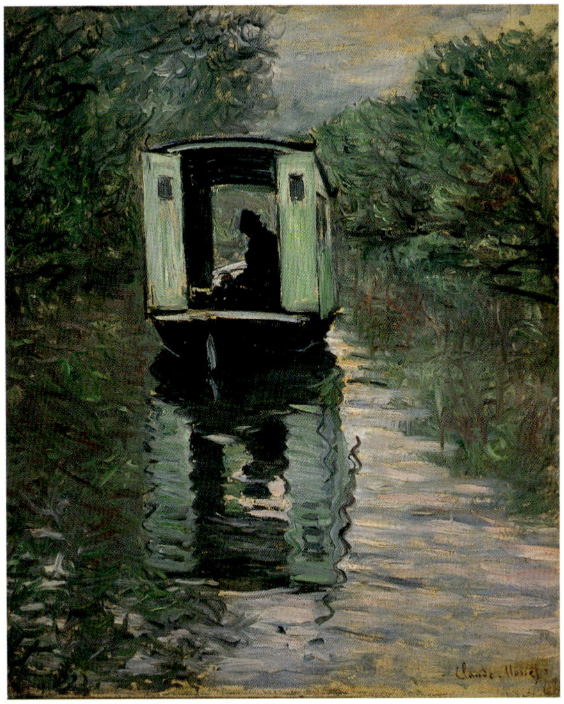

Fig 12 Claude Monet, *The Boat Studio*, 1876. Oil on canvas, 72 x 59.8 cm. Merion, PA, The Barnes Foundation (inv.no.730).

Gauguin told Sérusier to note the colours of the landscape and then, ignoring their true values, to paint each colour as brilliantly, purely and artificially as possible. The resulting tiny painting, *The Talisman* (fig. 13), is symbolic of a wider shift in nineteenth-century art away from naturalism towards stylisation of form, evocation of symbolic resonances and, ultimately, abstraction. This redirection would prove fundamental to Modernism. From that point on, the humble attention to the minute specificities of nature and its changing effects, and the openness to perception that had led to the rise of the landscape oil sketch, no longer stood at the centre of the painter's craft. A great and vital tradition was on the wane. Its rediscovery beginning some two decades later would be the achievement of enthusiastic connoisseurs and collectors like those whose collection is catalogued here.

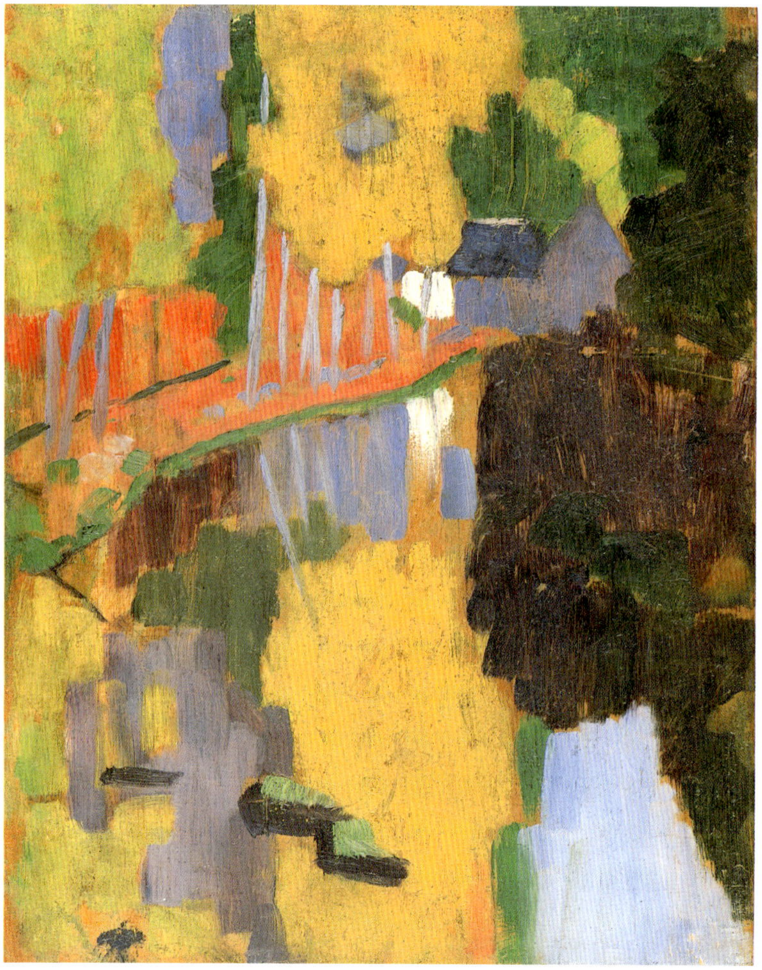

Fig 13 Paul Sérusier, *The Talisman,* 1888. Oil on wood, 27 x 21.5 cm. Paris, Musée d'Orsay (RF1985-13).

The Catalogue

BERTIN, Edouard (1797–1871), attributed to

1. *View of the Gorge at Civita Castellana,* about 1826–7

Oil on paper laid on canvas, 31.0 x 37.0 cm

Technical note

Some underdrawing is visible in the buildings.

Provenance

Bought without an attribution in Paris in the 1970s.

The fortified medieval town of Civita Castellana lies eighty-seven kilometres north of Rome on the Via Flaminia, one of the ancient routes through the Roman Campagna. The area was particularly well known to artists and poets, mainly for the imposing silhouette of Mount Soracte to the southeast. The town itself sits on a narrow plateau above cliffs descending on either side into gorges where the Rivers Vicano and Tréia nourish dense thickets of trees and bushes. In ancient times it was a strategically important Etruscan settlement, whose location made it a natural stronghold against Roman attacks. In the Middle Ages a military fortress was built, which during the Renaissance was converted into an imposing octagonal castle known as La Rocca, following designs by Antonio da Sangallo.[1]

By the eighteenth century, the castle had been converted into a prison, and travellers tended to regard Civita Castellana as a grim place best avoided. None the less, the site attracted many artists. In the 1780s Valenciennes and Jean-Joseph-Xavier Bidauld made trips there, drawing inspiration from the natural rock formations and the varying greens of the foliage. A painting by Bidauld of 1787 shows the gorge at Civita Castellana (fig. 14).[2] In 1815 Petit-Radel, a French guidebook writer, remarked that the town was 'one of the most picturesque' because it was 'built upon a rock in an isolated and very romantic way.'[3]

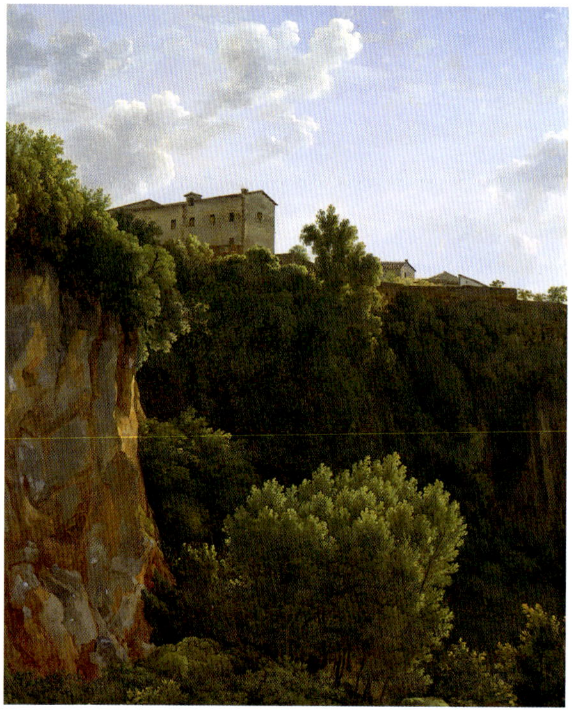

Fig 14 Jean-Joseph-Xavier Bidauld, *Gorge at Civita Castellana,* 1787. Oil on paper mounted on canvas, 50 x 37.5 cm. Stockholm, National Museum.

In the 1820s Bertin was one of several foreign painters to visit the area. Trained initially as a history painter at the Ecole des Beaux-Arts in Paris under Anne-Louis Girodet-Troison, he turned to landscape painting early on in his career. In 1816 he entered Bidauld's studio and two years later he joined the atelier of Louis-Etienne Watelet, a *paysagiste* who had also trained under Valenciennes. After a brief trip to Rome, Bertin returned to Paris in 1823 to pursue his studies under Jean-Victor Bertin (no relation). It was in Jean-Victor Bertin's studio that Edouard Bertin met his future sketching companions, Corot and Caruelle d'Aligny. With them he returned to Rome in 1825, taking up lodgings at the Pensione delle Lepre, sketching in their company in and around Rome, and exchanging ideas on techniques and style.[4] The friendship of the three painters is reflected in the stylistic similarities of their drawings and oil sketches, which often lead to confusion over attributions. This sketch, for example, has in the past been attributed to Caruelle d'Aligny. Even in the 1830s, when the three artists presented paintings at the Salon, art critics such as Etienne-Jean Délécluze commented on the

1 Bertarelli 1934, p. 657.

2 Washington, Brooklyn and St Louis 1996–7, no. 29.

3 Petit-Radel 1815, Vol. I, p. 342. Quoted in Sarah Faunce's essay in Washington, Brooklyn and St Louis 1996–7, p. 75.

4 Washington, Brooklyn and St Louis 1996–7, p. 212.

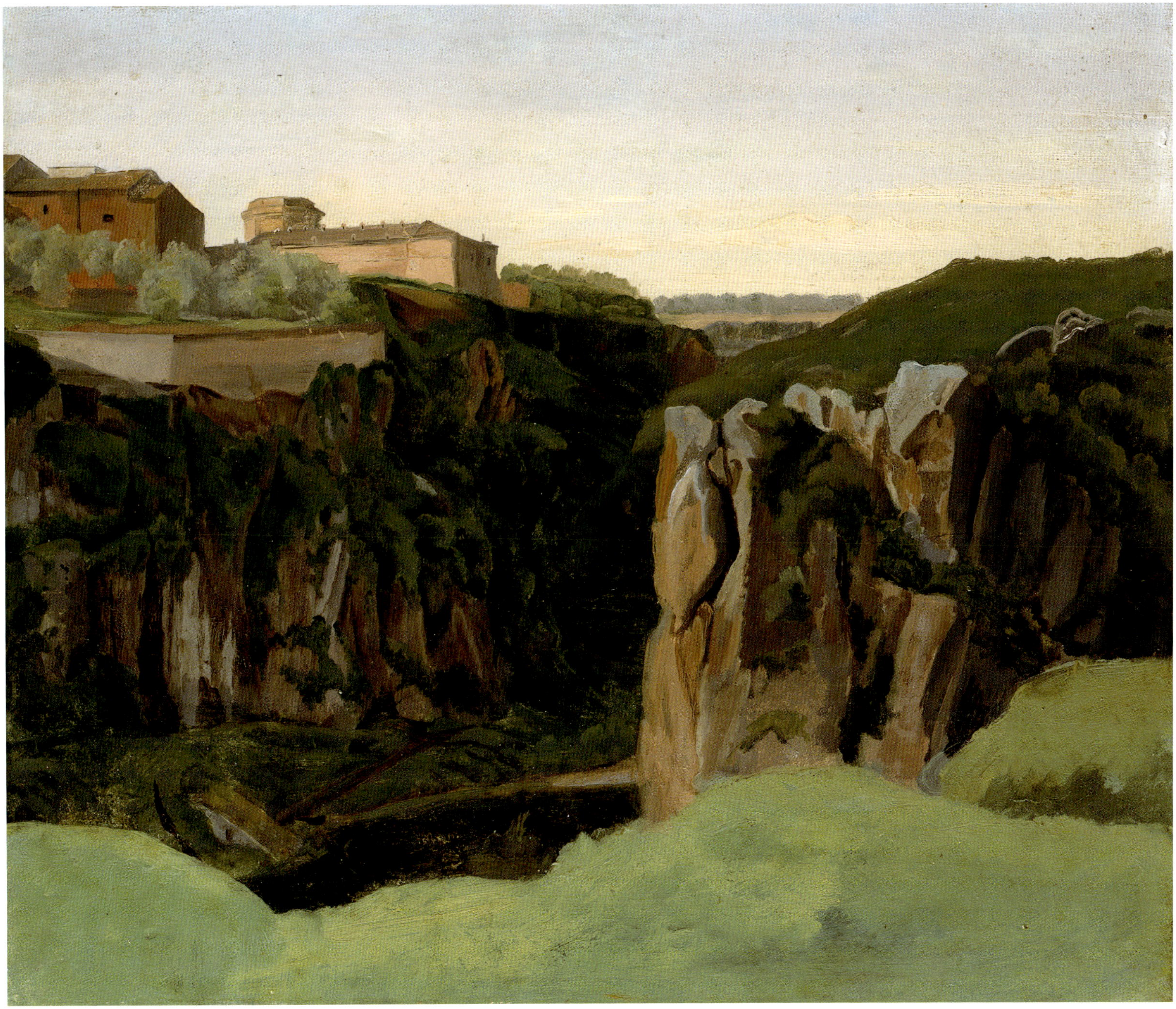

stylistic similarities between their works, claiming that a new school of landscape painting was in the process of emerging.

Bertin spent only two years in Italy, returning to Paris in 1827 to join Ingres as a pupil in his studio. While in Italy, however, he executed numerous drawings, mostly of views of Italian hill towns and famous sites such as Subiaco, Civitella and Ariccia. Many are now in the Musée des Beaux-Arts in Chartres, including thirteen views of Civita Castellana from various viewpoints, one of which has the same viewpoint as the sketch exhibited here (fig. 15).[5]

Using black chalk and graphite, Bertin concentrates on the strong outlines of the buildings and the vertical edges of the cliffs. Characteristic of his style is the manner in which the rocks are drawn, using thicker lines to accentuate their sculptural aspect. This effect is taken up in his oil sketches, particularly in a signed sketch (fig. 16),[6] in which he attempts to emphasise the volume and mass of the cliffs.

Caruelle d'Aligny's drawings of Civita Castellana in the Louvre are similar in execution and taken from viewpoints close to those of Bertin.[7] His classical training led him to structure his compositions clearly,

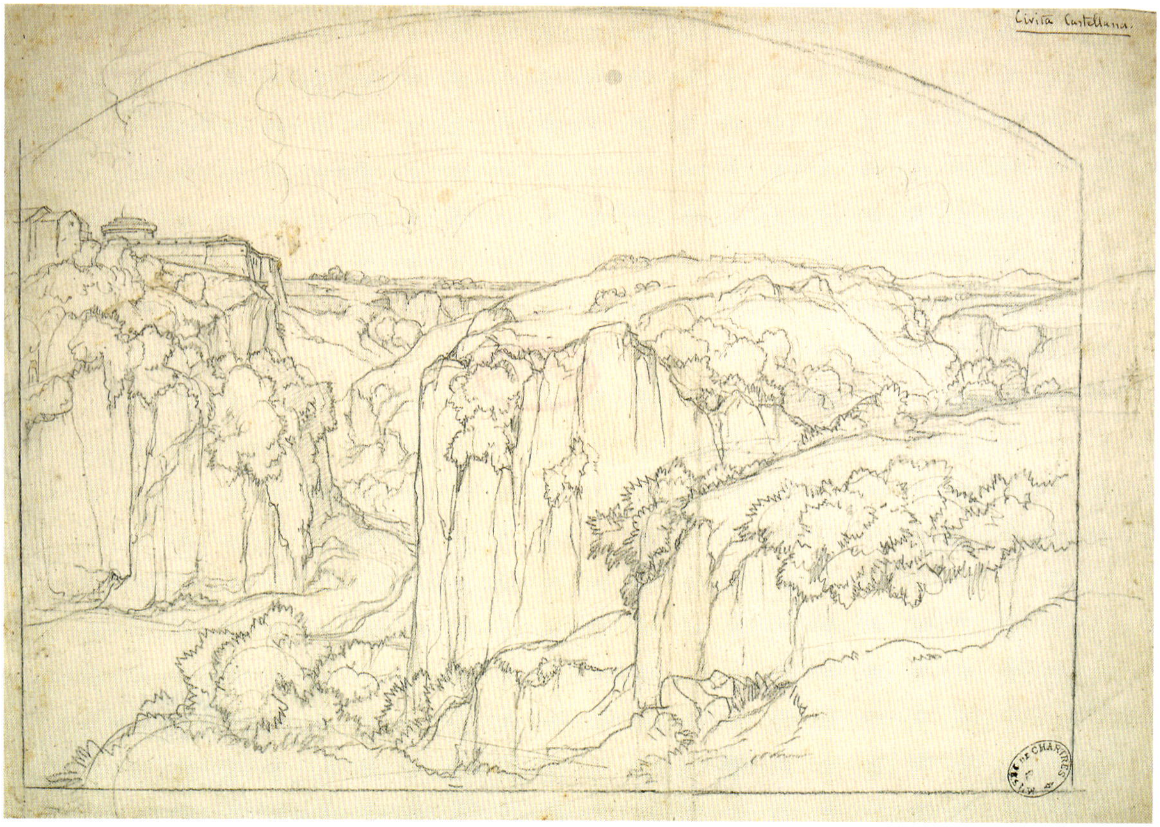

Fig 15 Edouard Bertin, *View of Civita Castellana*, 1826–7. Black chalk, 34.6 x 27.9 cm. Musée de Chartres.

5 Grunchec 1980, p. 141, no. 54, fig. 7.

6 Washington, Brooklyn and St Louis 1996–7, no. 80.

7 Aubrun 1988, pp. 215–6, nos. D. 76 and D. 79.

often using the natural surroundings to balance forms and perspective in a disciplined manner that was to have a strong influence on Corot. Some of d'Aligny's drawings are dated 1826, while Corot is known to have visited Civita Castellana in May 1826 and September 1827. It is quite possible, therefore, that Bertin made this sketch in the company of his two friends.

The sketch reveals a confident drawing style, particularly in the classically shaped buildings which stand out in contrast to the green foliage (some underdrawing is apparent in the octagonal fortress). Its free brushstrokes, reminiscent of Corot's style, convincingly evoke the texture of the natural surroundings and the fall of light on rocks and greenery. *XB*

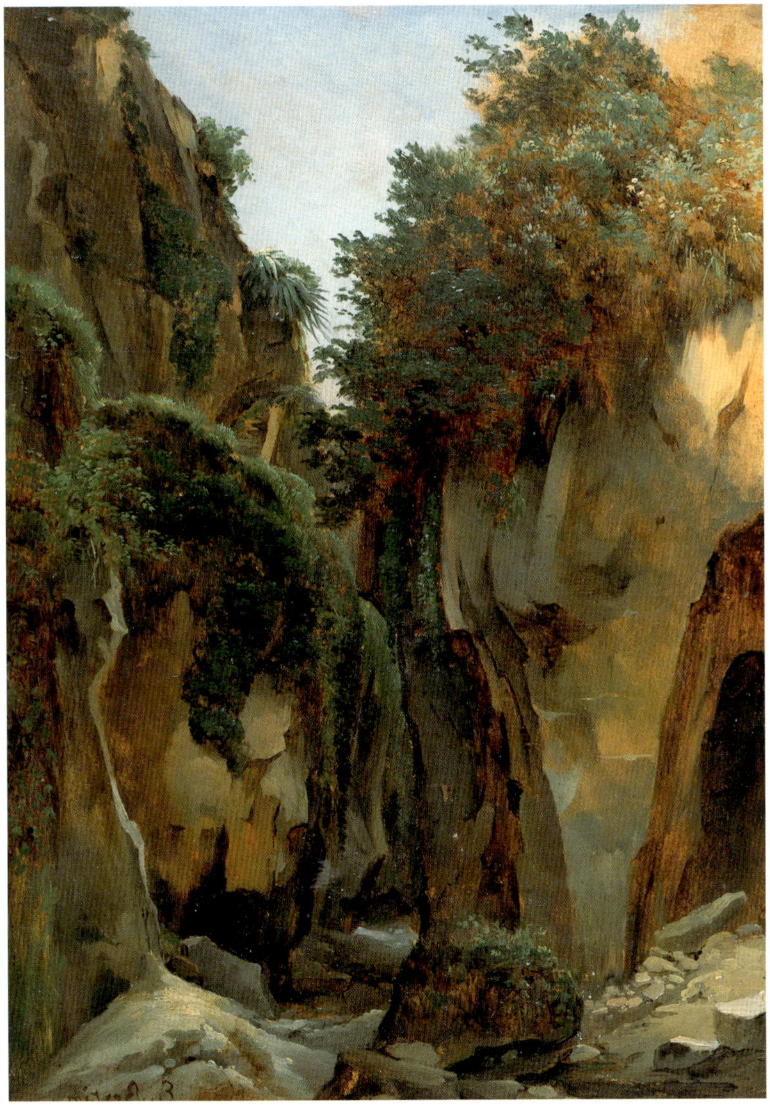

Fig 16 Edouard Bertin, *Ravine at Sorrento,* early 1820s. Oil on paper mounted on cardboard, 40.9 x 29.5 cm. New York, Metropolitan Museum of Art, purchase, Karen B. Cohen Gift, 1986.

BIDAULD, Jean-Joseph-Xavier (1758–1846), attributed to
2. *Buildings by a Weir in a Mountainous Valley,* undated

Oil on paper mounted on board, 30.5 x 35.2 cm

Inscriptions

A series of stickers and annotations on back of board
J3796W
R.B.
From *Julius H. Weitzner* *10 Farm Street*
958 Madison Avenue *London, W.1*
New York 21, N.Y. *England*
Handwritten underneath: *CARVELLE d'ALIGNY*
Handwritten *WEITZNER*
10 Farm Street
London, W.1
W1 England
13
WADSWORTH ATHENEUM
HARTFORD, CONN.
No. T.L. 889
Artist. C.F.T. Aligny
Title: Hilly Landscape
Owner: Julius H. Weitzner
958 Madison Avenue
New York, N.Y.
Handwritten in pencil *M. Shakespeare Soc.*
Roman numerals *LLIX*
Inscribed in red crayon *30*

Provenance

Julius Weitzner, New York; Kurt Popper, New York; Shepherd Gallery, New York, 1972; bought from Shepherd Gallery, New York, in 1992.

Exhibitions

Displayed at Hartford, Wadsworth Atheneum (as Théodore Caruelle d'Aligny); New York 1972, no. 9 (as Caruelle d'Aligny).

Literature

Munich 1991, pl. 31.

When acquired, this subtle depiction of rushing water in a mountainous valley, with what may be mill buildings tucked among the trees, bore the letters *CA* in red paint in the lower left corner. When the picture was cleaned, however, the monogram of the landscape painter Théodore Caruelle d'Aligny (1798–1871) quickly came away. Since then, no strong consensus has emerged on the attribution of the painting, though the architectonic structure of the composition and the minute painterly touch would seem to suggest that this is an earlier, more fully Neoclassical hand than Caruelle d'Aligny's. Heilmann suggested Jean-Victor Bertin, and the name Pierre-Athanase Chauvin (1774–1832) has also been put forward.

For several reasons, Bidauld's name should be added to the equation. Bidauld was drawn to rushing water, repeatedly painting quick-moving mountain streams, as in his *View of a Cascade on the River Isère near Allevard*,[1] and his *Cascade of Water* (Carpentras, Musée Duplessis).[2] Often, as here, steep, densely wooded hills spill down to the water's edge. The hillsides themselves are painted in a gamut of nuanced but saturated green tones, with small, careful, sometimes feathery brushstrokes often seeming to delineate every leaf. Finally, Bidauld seemed to take delight in the eccentric profiles the green hilltops formed against the sky.

Born at Carpentras, Bidauld belonged to the early generation of Neoclassical landscape painters led by Valenciennes and including J.-V. Bertin and Didier Boguet. He was the first landscape painter to enter the Académie des Beaux-Arts, in 1823. Taught by Claude-Joseph Vernet, he painted in Fontainebleau and Switzerland and spent five years in Italy, from 1785 to 1790, working in the Roman Campagna and elsewhere. On returning to Paris, he exhibited historical landscapes at the Salon until his death and was a vocal opponent of naturalism in landscape. Soon forgotten, none the less he was intensely admired by Corot. *CR*

1 Sold Sotheby's, New York, 28 January 1997, lot 350.
2 Carpentras 1978, cat. no. 19; Gutwirth also lists here numerous other water studies by Bidauld.

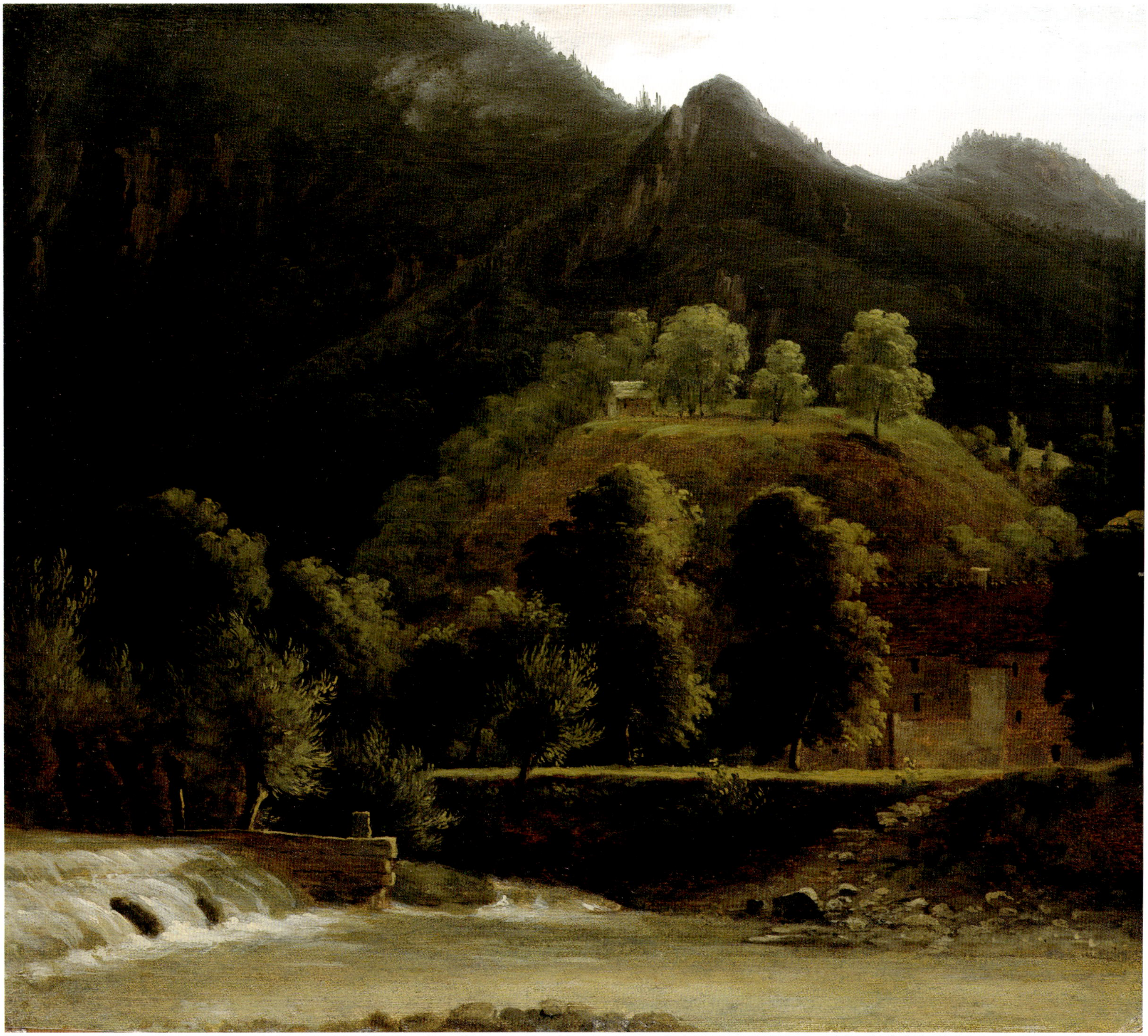

Blechen, Carl (1798–1840)

3. *The Capuchin Convent at Amalfi*, about 1829

Oil on paper, laid on board, 28.5 x 38.7 cm

Inscriptions

Inscribed on back *Sold at Christie's 22/iii/1984*
French (?) School c. 1820

Technical note

Pin marks are found in the four corners of the paper.

Provenance

Bought from Christie's, London, 22 March 1984, lot 19.

Blechen gave up a job in a bank to become an artist in 1820, entering the Academy in Berlin to study landscape. He was influenced by the landscapes of Johan Christian Dahl whom he visited in Dresden in 1823, and was supported by the architect and painter Karl Friedrich Schinkel, both of whom had travelled to and painted in Italy. Late in 1828 Blechen was able to set out for the south in turn. He spent nine months in Italy where, close to the community of German artists in Rome, he painted free and vivid oil sketches in the Campagna, including numerous cloud studies, as Dahl had done. The following summer Blechen travelled to Naples, where he worked assiduously until September when his money ran out, forcing him to return home. Back in Berlin, where he taught at the Academy, he continued to paint, but his studio pictures, which retained much of the freshness and spontaneity of his oil sketches, did not find a ready market. In recent years, however, appreciation for his art has grown, and a major retrospective exhibition was devoted to Blechen in Berlin in 1990.[1]

During the summer of 1829 Blechen painted frequently at Amalfi, down the coast from Naples. It was there that he depicted the Capuchin convent, perched on a great wall of rock, a steep road climbing to it. As was frequently his habit, he brought the vertical mass in the foreground close to the picture plane, suggesting a rapid dive into space beyond. While essentially monochromatic, none the less the rock face is full of animated, pulsing touches. If the compositional structure is similar to other sketches made near Naples in 1829, so too are the palette and brushwork. This sheet was unattributed when it appeared in a drawings sale at Christie's, London, in 1984 and the Munich dealer Matthias Hans was the first to propose an attribution to Blechen.[2] While Helmut Borsch-Supan has not accepted the attribution on the basis of a transparency, in 1993 John Leighton pointed out the close similarity between the oil sketch and Blechen's finished painting of the Capuchin convent in the Oskar Reinhart Foundation, Winterthur.[3] *CR*

1 Berlin 1990.
2 Oral communication.
3 London, Los Angeles and New York 1993, p. 111, fig. 55.

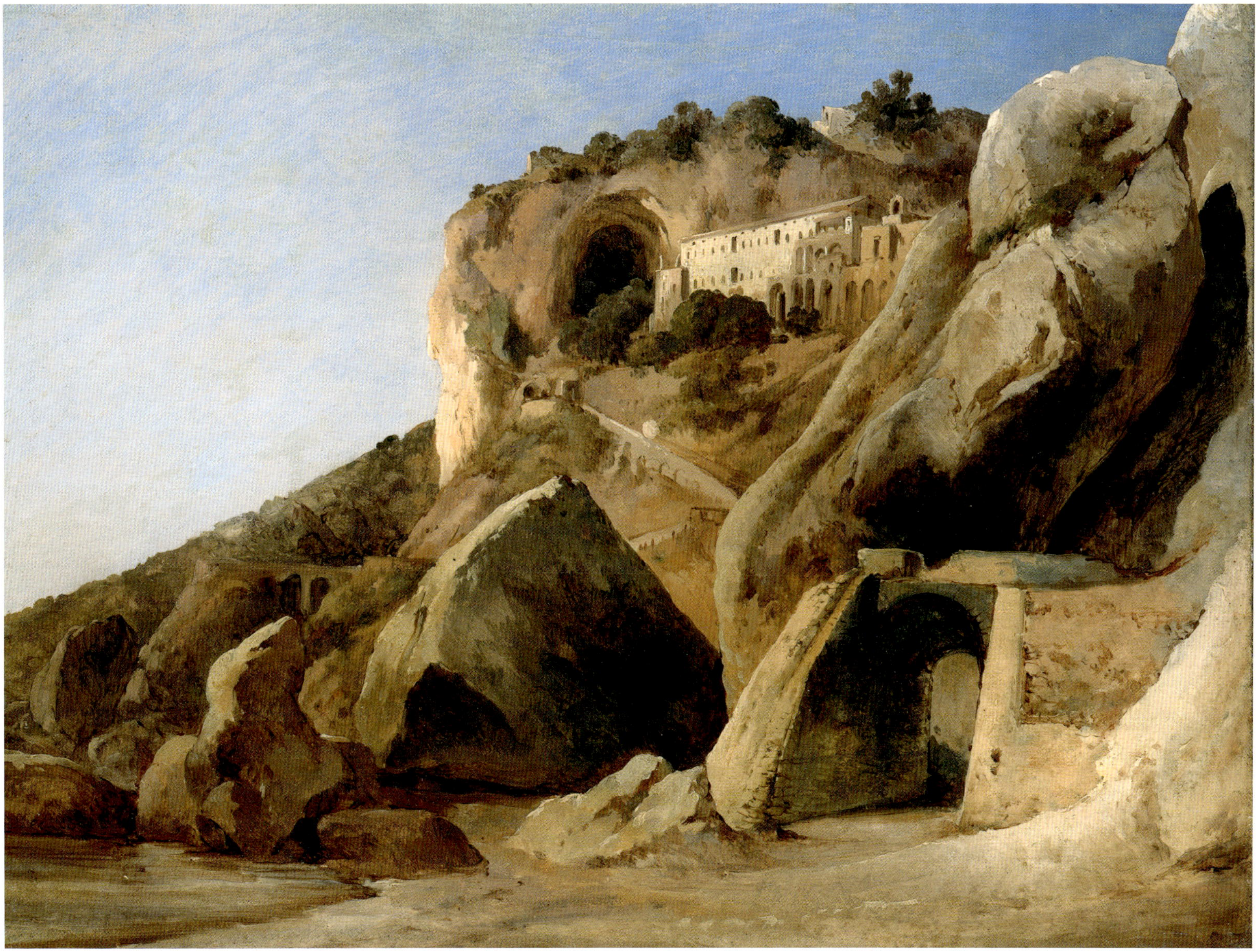

Böcklin, Arnold (1827–1901)

4. *A Cliff Face,* about 1850–55

Oil on paper laid on canvas, 23.1 x 32.0 cm

Inscriptions

Inscribed on stretcher *H 1.5 20.7*

Label inscribed *g.l.*

Provenance

Bought from Fischer et Keiner, Paris, in 1987 (as artist unknown).

The Swiss painter Arnold Böcklin travelled to Italy for the first time in 1850, and remained for seven years, marrying an Italian woman with whom he had fourteen children, and associating with the circle of German artists in Rome known as the *Tugendbund*. He returned to Italy once again in the 1860s for a four-year stay, and moved permanently to Tuscany in 1893, where he died. The Italian landscape, particularly the rocks, cliffs and chasms of its more rugged terrain, often played an important rôle in the large-scale, idealising, mythological paintings for which he is best known. The fauns, satyrs and woodland creatures that inhabit such works are like emanations of the fields and gulleys in which they gambol, and the mossy rocks against which they recline to make music or take their rest. The vertiginous, bare cliffs towering over his *Island of the Dead* (New York, Metropolitan Museum of Art, and four other versions) add to the inchoate sense of dread which pervades that famous composition. Such natural phenomena were often carefully studied by Böcklin in small-scale landscape oil sketches that he made on his Italian travels.

The site of the rock face depicted here is not known, nor can it be directly associated with a finished painting by Böcklin. The attribution of the sketch to him was first proposed by Christoph Heilmann, among others.[1] It shares important characteristics with another oil sketch by Böcklin, his *Study in the Sabine Mountains* (Switzerland, private collection) that Galassi has described as 'an abruptly framed cliff-side study ... horizonless, vivid in its pattern of light and shadow ... not a pastiche but a fresh discovery.'[2] In both works the pitted face of the rock is closely observed, as is the foliage that clings to it here and there. Yet the actual size of the motif depicted is difficult to determine. Details of the cliff face suggest elements of the human face. Noses, eyes and even complete profiles seem about to emerge from the jagged rock, as at upper left. At centre right a dark shadow forms itself into the hawk-nosed profile of an ogre or troll. If Böcklin's finished paintings explore a landscape inhabited by mythological creatures, this sketch suggests that he sought out the animistic dimension to be found in nature itself. *CR*

1 Oral communication.

2 Galassi 1991, p. 222; fig. 283.

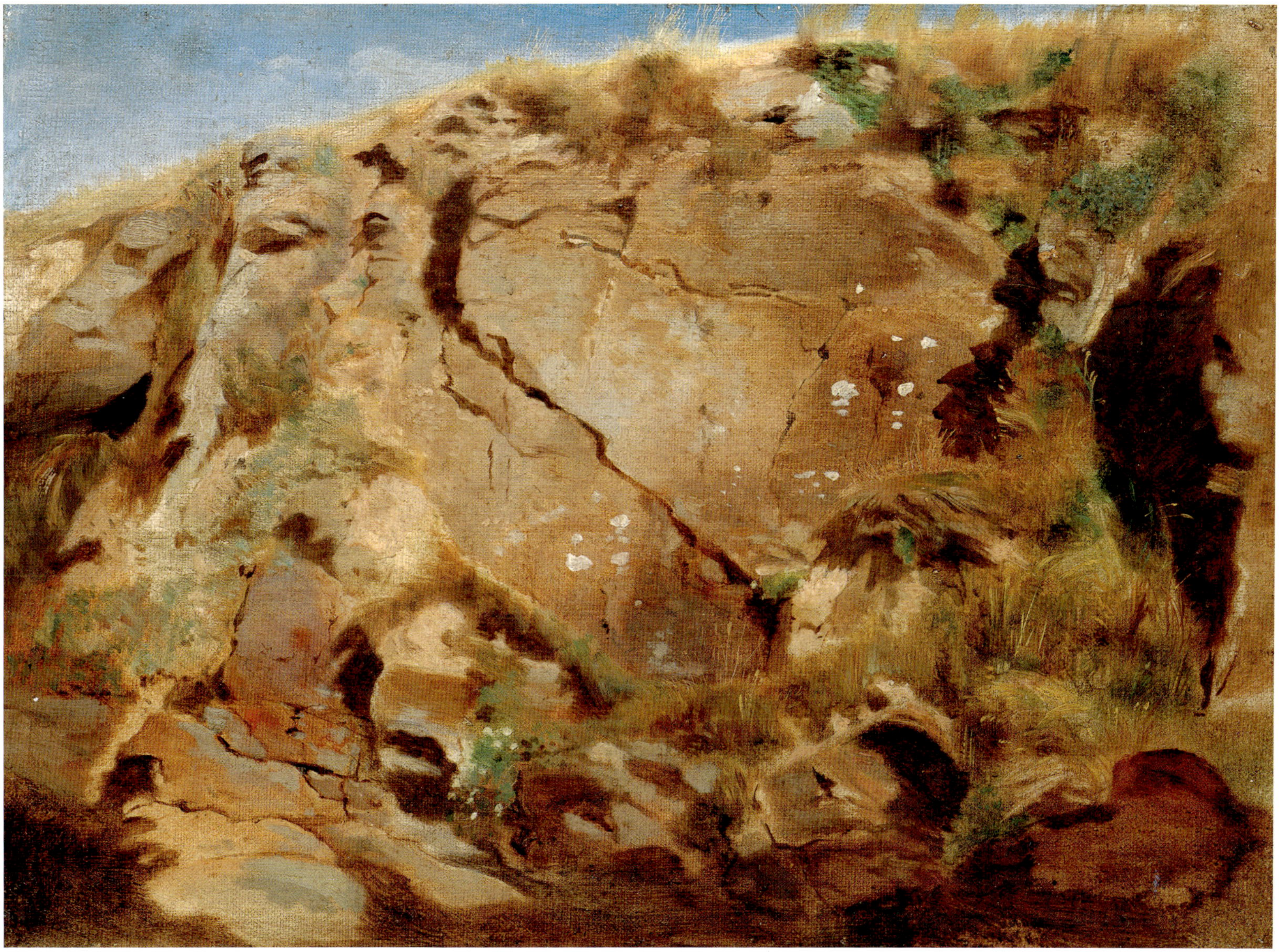

Boldini, Giovanni (1842–1931)

5. *In the Garden*, about 1875

Oil on panel, 23.8 x 19.0 cm

Inscriptions

Signed at lower right *Boldini*

White chalk inscription on reverse *P 2071*

Provenance

Bought from Sotheby's, London, in June 1981.

Best known as a painter of bravura society portraits during the Belle Epoque, the Italian-born Boldini painted landscapes throughout his long career. This was especially true during the several years following his move to Paris in 1871. On his first visit there in 1867 he had met the Impressionist painters, including Degas and Manet, and when he moved there permanently he turned to the cityscapes and scenes of urban life that many of them also painted. Like a number of contemporary artists, Boldini was fascinated by the slightly ramshackle quality of the periphery of Paris. Many of his works depict the area around his home on the Place Pigalle at the foot of Montmartre, as yet only partially built up and retaining a suburban, if raffish, character. His quick, nervous brushstroke proved to be the perfect instrument for capturing the animation and modernity of the quarter, imparting a sense of flux to his paintings.

That same freedom of brushstroke characterises this sprightly depiction of a small garden. As the distant row of rooftops suggests, it may be on the outskirts of Montmartre. The open door of a garden shed in the foreground, the dusty pathway and the tumble-down trellis at centre left, indicate that it is not a particularly well-maintained garden. Perhaps it has been neglected over the winter; the relative bareness of the trees and few flowers suggest that the time of year may be spring, just as the fruit trees come into bud. Boldini depicts the tree trunks and branches with an almost calligraphic verve. The garden has attracted a visitor; with a few deft brushstrokes the artist evokes the presence of a woman, dressed in black and wearing a hat, sitting by a flowerbed and turning her head to examine a bloom. *CR*

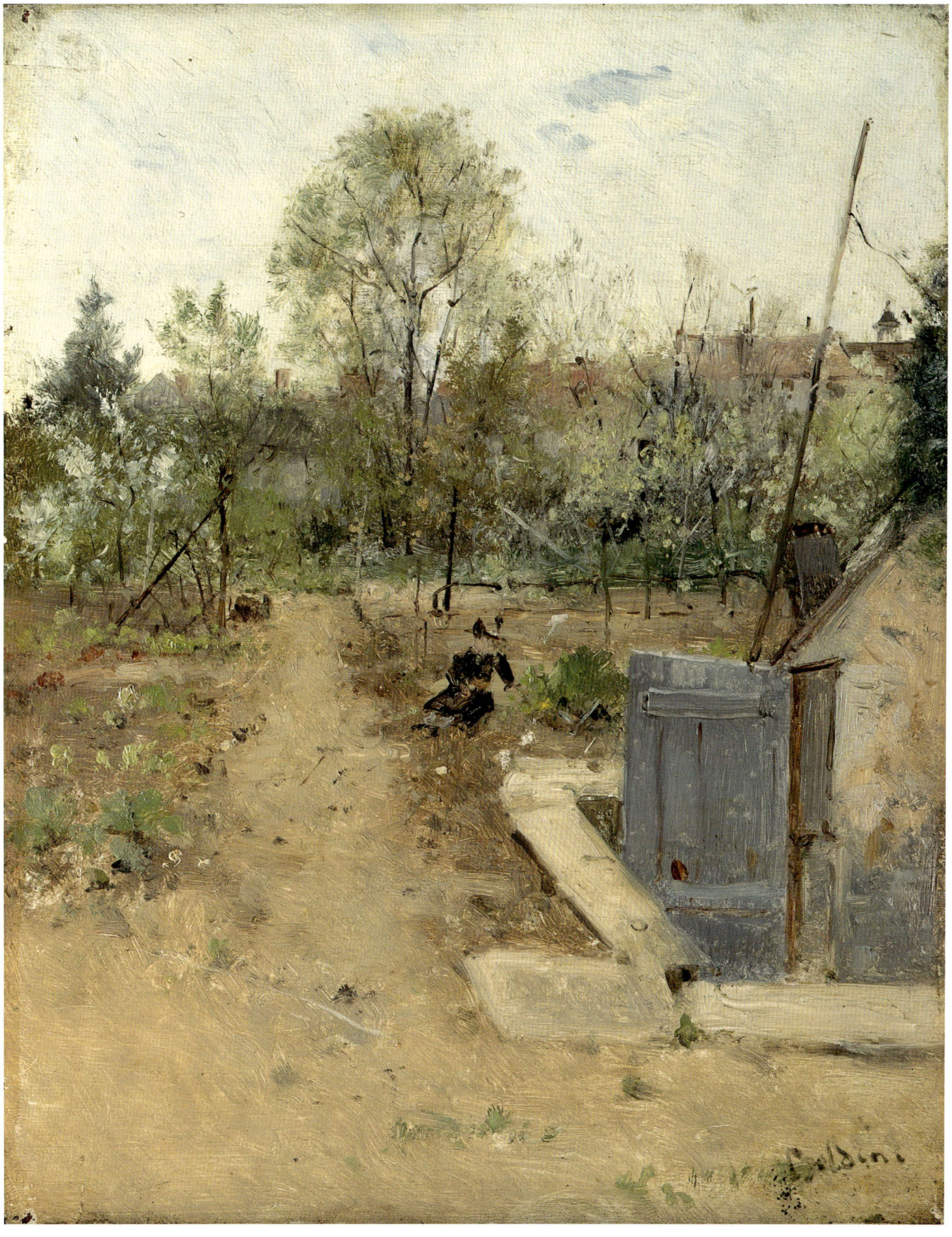

British School

6. *Villa and Town Buildings on a Hill with Roman Remains,* about 1780

Oil on paper laid on wood, 22.3 x 39.5 cm

Technical note

Infra-red photography has revealed under-drawing in the buildings.

Provenance

Paris art market, 1991 (as Hendrik van Lint); bought from John Lishawa, London, in 1992; (as French School, c.1760–80).

Exhibition

Washington, Brooklyn and St Louis 1996–7, no. 6.

The site has not been identified, though it is surely in Italy. The artist has situated himself at the foot of a hill looking up towards an arcuated wall, perhaps ancient Roman in origin, and a red brick town beyond it. The town comprises what appear to be rather modern buildings, including one that is at least five storeys tall. The hill continues to rise and a villa is perched at the top, its cornice lined with free-standing statues. It stands within an enclosed, tree-filled garden where, oddly for Italy, what appears to be the spire of a steeple pokes into the sky. The russet tonality of the landscape, and the crisp architectonic forms, contrast with the blue of the sky and rolling clouds. Such hill-top villas once punctuated the landscape around Naples, but they do so in the Roman Campagna as well, for example at Caprarola.

This beautiful oil sketch, full of vivid colour and detail, and the freshness of an Italian summer's day, is one of the most intriguing 'teasers' of the Gere Collection. Despite close scrutiny by leading scholars in the field, it continues to withold the secret of the artist's name and nationality, and the date of execution. For his part, John Gere suggested that it might be the work of Richard Wilson (1713–1782), or a British artist in his circle, and thus dated it to the middle of the eighteenth century. David Solkin[1] has not supported the attribution to Wilson, however, nor has it found general favour. Other British names suggested have included Francis Towne (?1739/40–1816), Thomas Patch (1725–1782), William Marlow (1740–1813) and Alexander Cozens (1717–1786). The organisers of the exhibition of landscape oil studies *In the Light of Italy*,[2] attempted no attribution; the painting appeared there as the work of an 'Unknown artist around 1780?' In the exhibition catalogue, however, they perceptively placed it immediately following three works by or attributed to the French artist Alexandre-Hyacinthe Dunouy (1757–1841), and immediately before seven works by Wilson's student, the British artist Thomas Jones (1742–1803), thus situating it among the international community of landscape painters active in Italy, and specifically in Naples, during the late years of the eighteenth century. *CR*

1 Oral communication.

2 Washington, Brooklyn and St Louis 1996–7.

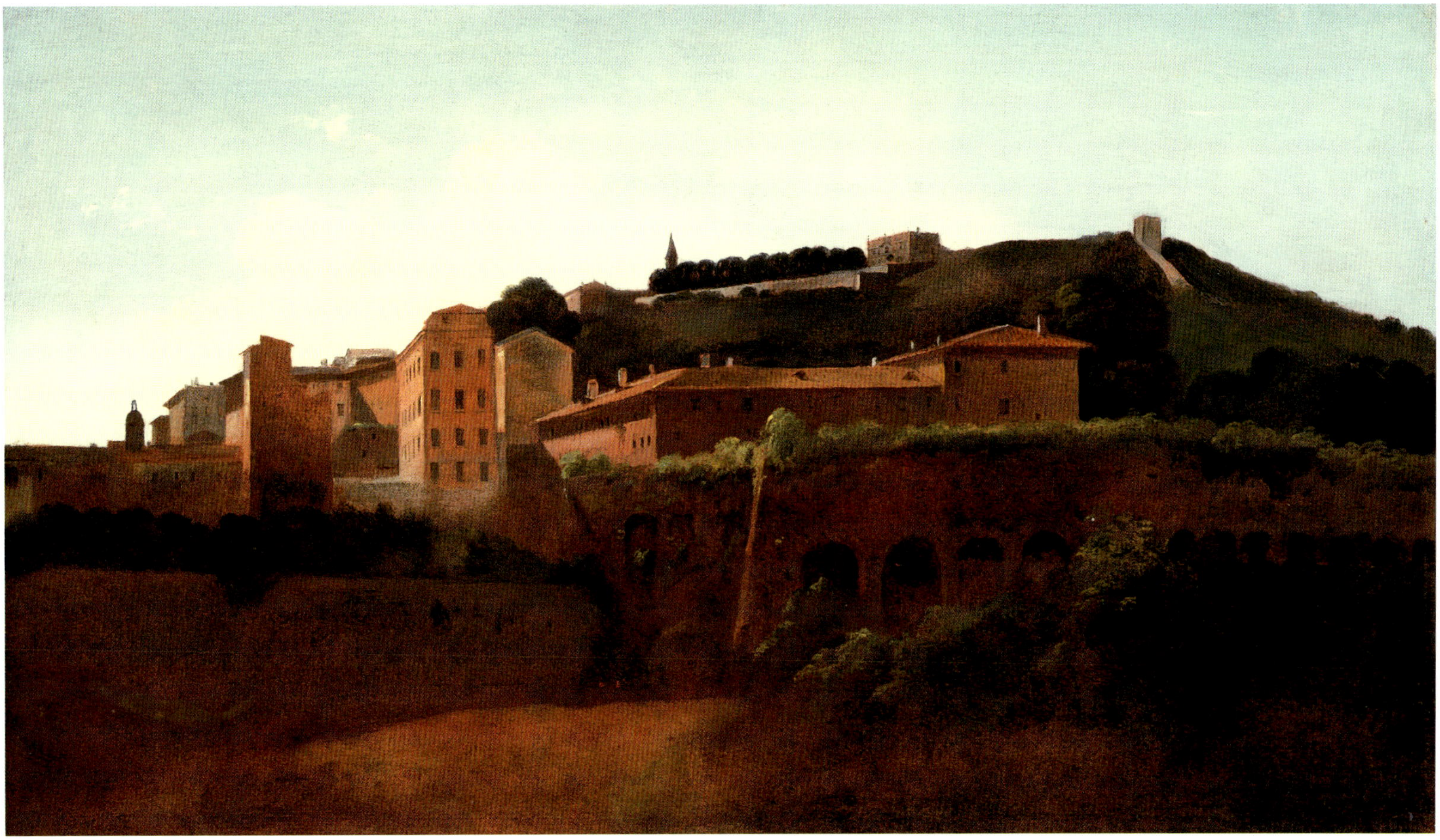

BÜRKEL, Heinrich (1802–1869)

7. *Distant View of Rome with the Baths of Caracalla in the Foreground,* about 1829

Oil on paper, 23.7 x 57.4 cm

Inscriptions

Artist's monogram stamped on the lower left in red *HB*. On the reverse *nachlass Bürkel, (Lught 314c)*; unidentified collector's mark *SG* in a circle

Provenance

Bought from The Drawing Shop, Galerie Osten-Kashey Ltd, New York, in 1971.

Exhibition

New York 1971.

This panoramic view of the Baths of Caracalla (see fig. 17), painted before the ruins were fully excavated, is probably part of a series of oil sketches executed soon after Bürkel's arrival in Rome in 1829 from Munich, where he had been studying. Another oil sketch by him of the Porta di San Giovanni in Rome (Winterthur, Oskar Reinhart Foundation), shows a similar type of view, in which he attempts to record the vista as if using a wide-angle lens.[1] In both sketches the foreground is rapidly sketched in with diluted oils, while the ruins in the middle ground are painted in greater detail, making them appear more sharply in focus. To convey the architectural immensity of the ruins, Bürkel has created a sense of space and distance using light and colour. This is particularly visible in the hazy, violet-purple tones used for the distant view of Rome with its skyline of cupolas, and the bluish tones of the hills in the background.

Although Bürkel stayed in Rome on several occasions, notably in 1829–32, 1837 and 1853–4, he spent most of his working career in Germany, where he was recognised as an important member of the German landscape school. He was made an honorary member of the Dresden and Vienna Academies and of the Munich Academy in 1858. *XB*

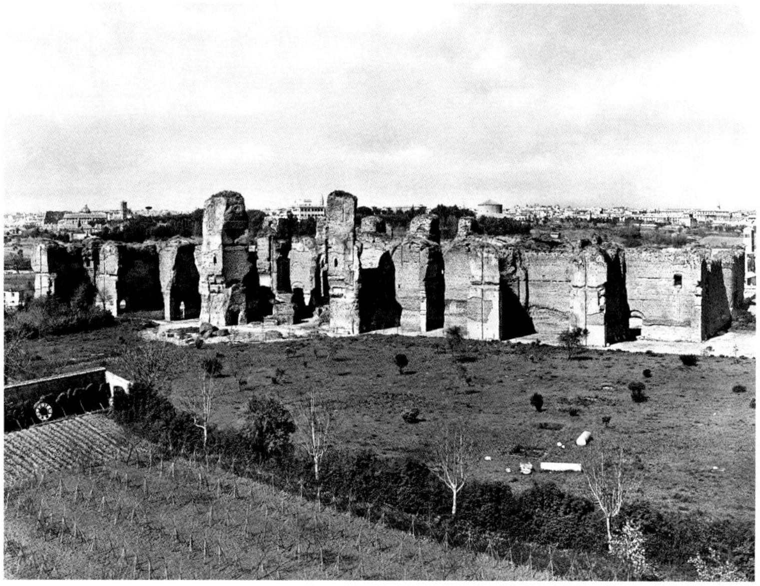

Fig 17 Rome, looking towards the Baths of Caracalla (photo: Alinari).

1 Vignau-Wilberg 1979, cat. no. 16, p. 52, and London, Los Angeles and New York 1993, fig. 52, p. 108. Another sketch of similar format and dimensions was shown as no. 60 in London 1979.

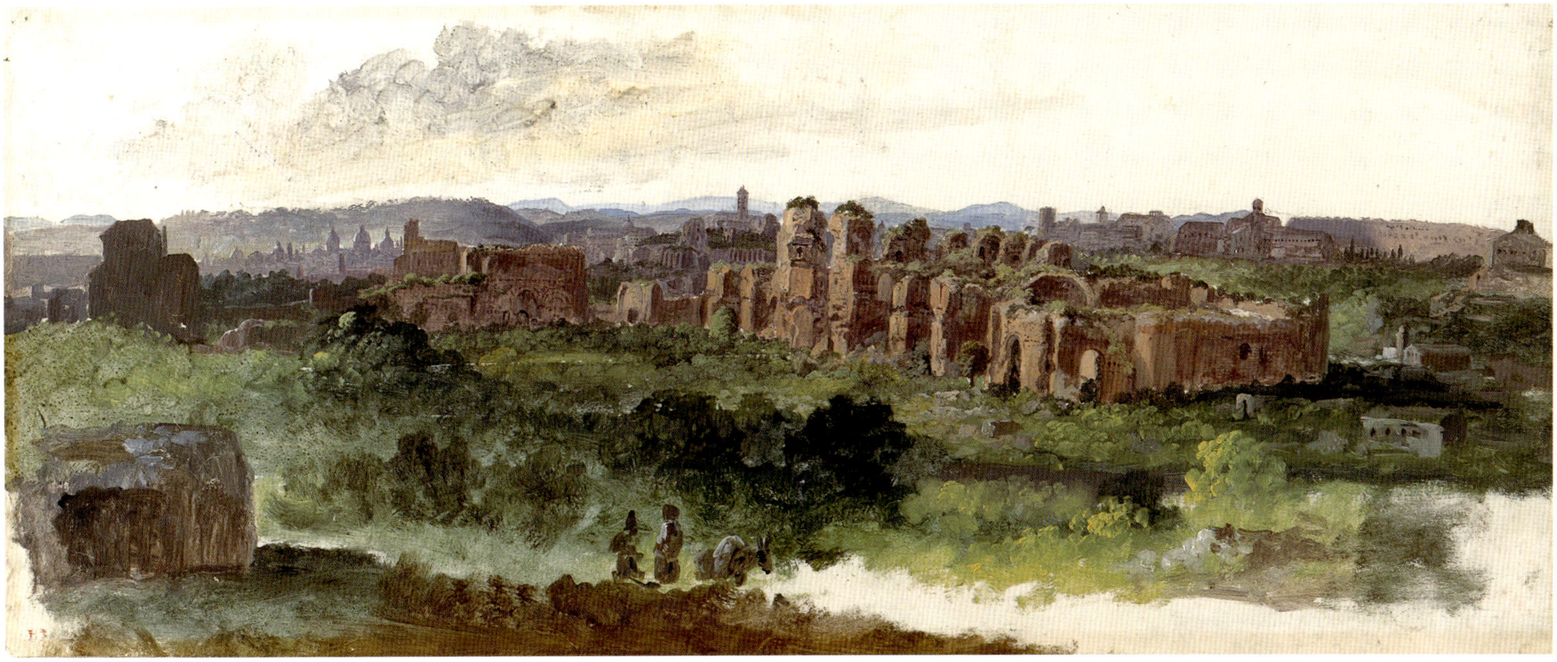

Buttura, Eugène-Ferdinand (1812–1852)
8. *A Road in the Roman Campagna*, around 1840

Oil on paper laid on canvas, 26.5 x 38.5 cm

Inscriptions

Modern labels on reverse *Oil on paper 26.5 x 38.4 cm / 10.5 x 15 1/8 inches and Eugene Buttura (1812–1852). Won Prix de Rome for Landscape 1837 (in Rome 1838–42). This sketch is said by Mark Brady, from whom I bought it in New York in May 1992, to have come from a descendant of the artist*

Provenance

By descent in the artist's family; Paris, Hôtel Drouot, 30 March 1992, lot 3; bought from W. M. Brady & Co. Inc., New York, in 1992.

Buttura studied landscape under both Jean-Victor Bertin (1767–1842) and Jean-Charles-Joseph Rémond (1795–1875). In 1837 he was awarded the Prix de Rome in historical landscape painting for *Apollo, guarding the Flocks of King Admetus, invents the Lyre* (Paris, Ecole Nationale Supérieure des Beaux-Arts). While commentators were less than kind about his skills, generally finding the prize-winning composition stilted and lacking in originality, the anonymous critic of *L'Artiste* noted 'the vigour of [Buttura's] touch.'[1] Travelling to Italy, Buttura remained at the Villa Medici in Rome until 1842, where he made landscape drawings, characterised by his biographer as 'remarkable,'[2] as well as numerous landscape oil sketches and the finished landscape compositions that he submitted to the Salon in Paris. After his return to Paris he continued to exhibit at the Salon until his early death.

The vigorous touch that had attracted critical attention in Paris in 1837 is evident in this oil sketch of a dusty road meandering through the Roman Campagna. The artist probably painted it during his time at the Villa Medici, around 1840. Large touches of paint are laid down confidently to delineate the sides of the sunken road and the greenish shadows that fall across it from the right. Brushy strokes differentiate the foliage of the scrubby trees that line the roadway, while a single curving line of paint establishes the small, dry gulley that runs along its edge. Using a spare gamut of brown and green tones, which contrast with the blue of the sky, Buttura suggests the arid atmosphere of a Roman summer's afternoon. *CR*

1 *L'Artiste*, Vol. 14, 1837, pp. 77–8; Grunchec 1986, p. 334.

2 Gaudissart 1990.

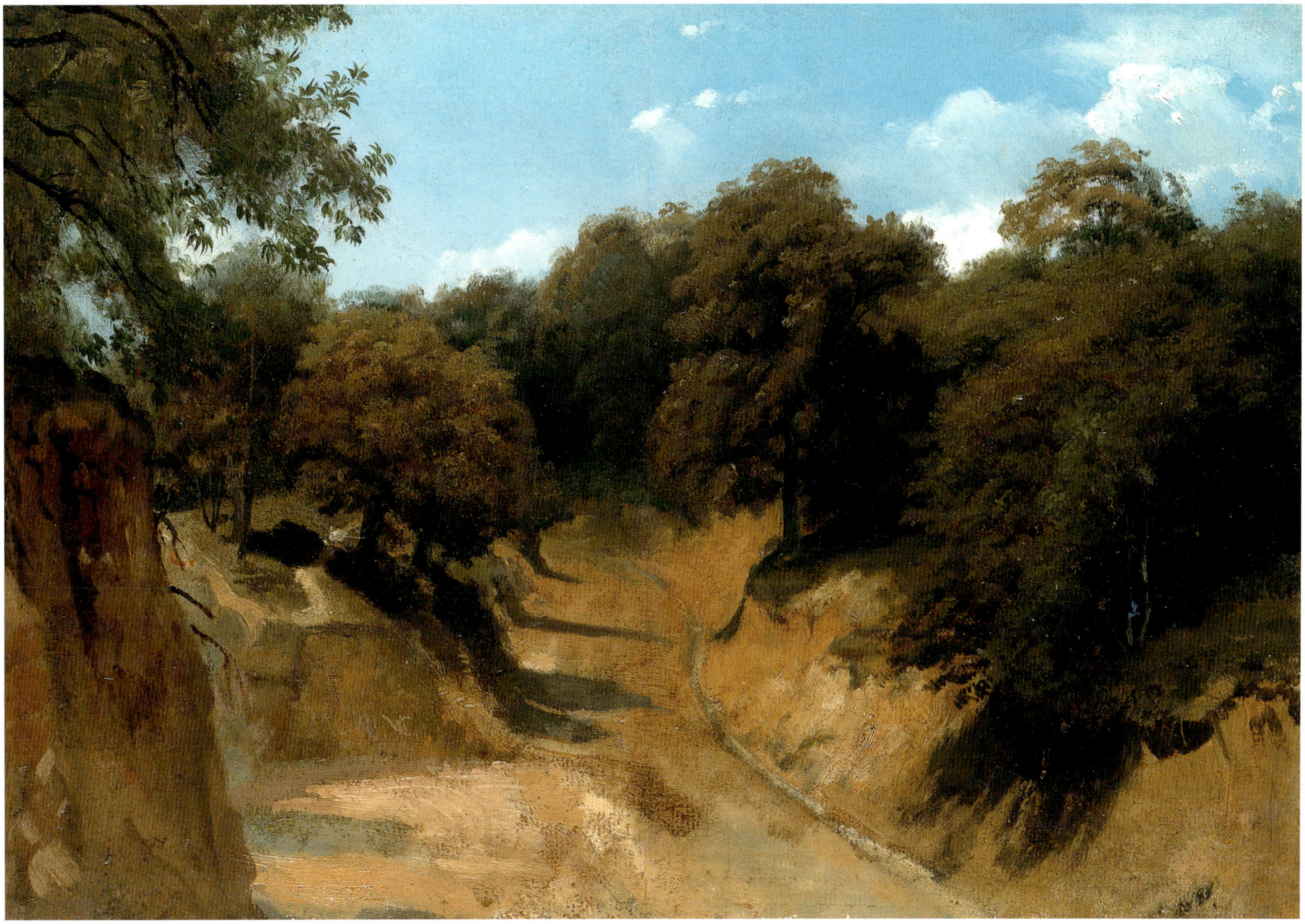

Camuccini, Giovanni-Battista (1819–1902)

9. *Ariccia,* about 1850

Oil on paper laid on a plastic support, 24.2 x 32.8–33.4 cm

Provenance

Camuccini family by descent; bought from the family in 1983.

Giovanni-Battista Camuccini was the son of the Neoclassical portraitist and history painter Vincenzo Camuccini (1771–1844), who was a central figure in the Roman art world of the early nineteenth century, indeed famous throughout Europe. At the time of his father's death, Camuccini inherited responsibility for his studio and there he would have met the young Giovanni Costa (1826–1903) who had recently entered as a student. The latter was a patriot, fought for the unification of Italy, and for several years around 1850 lived in virtual exile in the country near Ariccia in the Roman Campagna (fig. 18). It is interesting to speculate that Camuccini may have painted this study of Ariccia while visiting Costa there, perhaps influenced by his naturalistic approach to landscape.

Camuccini chose an unexpected vantage point from which to sketch the old town. He stood on a hillside covered in scrub looking up a dusty trail to the backs of humble stone buildings. Plaster is peeling, vines climb the walls, grass sprouts from rooftops. At left, the hillside falls away abruptly into forest and thick undergrowth. Camuccini lavishes attention on the textures of the walls and the dry foliage. At upper right, rising above the tumbledown roofs, is the splendid hemispherical dome and belfry, glimmering in the sunlight, of the church of Santa Maria dell'Assunzione, built by Gianlorenzo Bernini in 1662–4 for his patron, Pope Alexander VII. It resembles nothing so much as the rising sun, and the perfection of its Baroque forms stands in contrast to the modest, decayed buildings in the foreground. It is tempting to speculate that the painter was perhaps symbolically contrasting his father's brilliant artistic career during which, like Bernini, he too was a favourite of kings and popes, with his own far humbler artistic aspirations and attainments.

This sketch as well as the two other Camuccinis in the collection (cat. nos. 10 and 11), along with many other works by the artist in oil on paper, were found in a decaying bundle in the family villa at Cantalupo in Sabina several years ago. *CR*

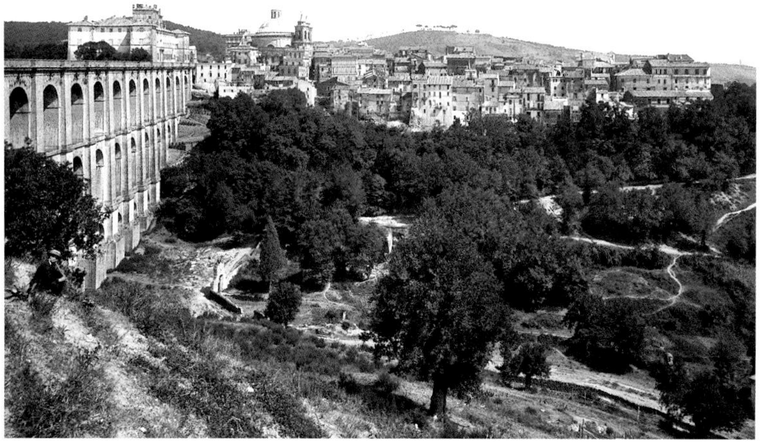

Fig 18 View of Ariccia (photo: Alinari).

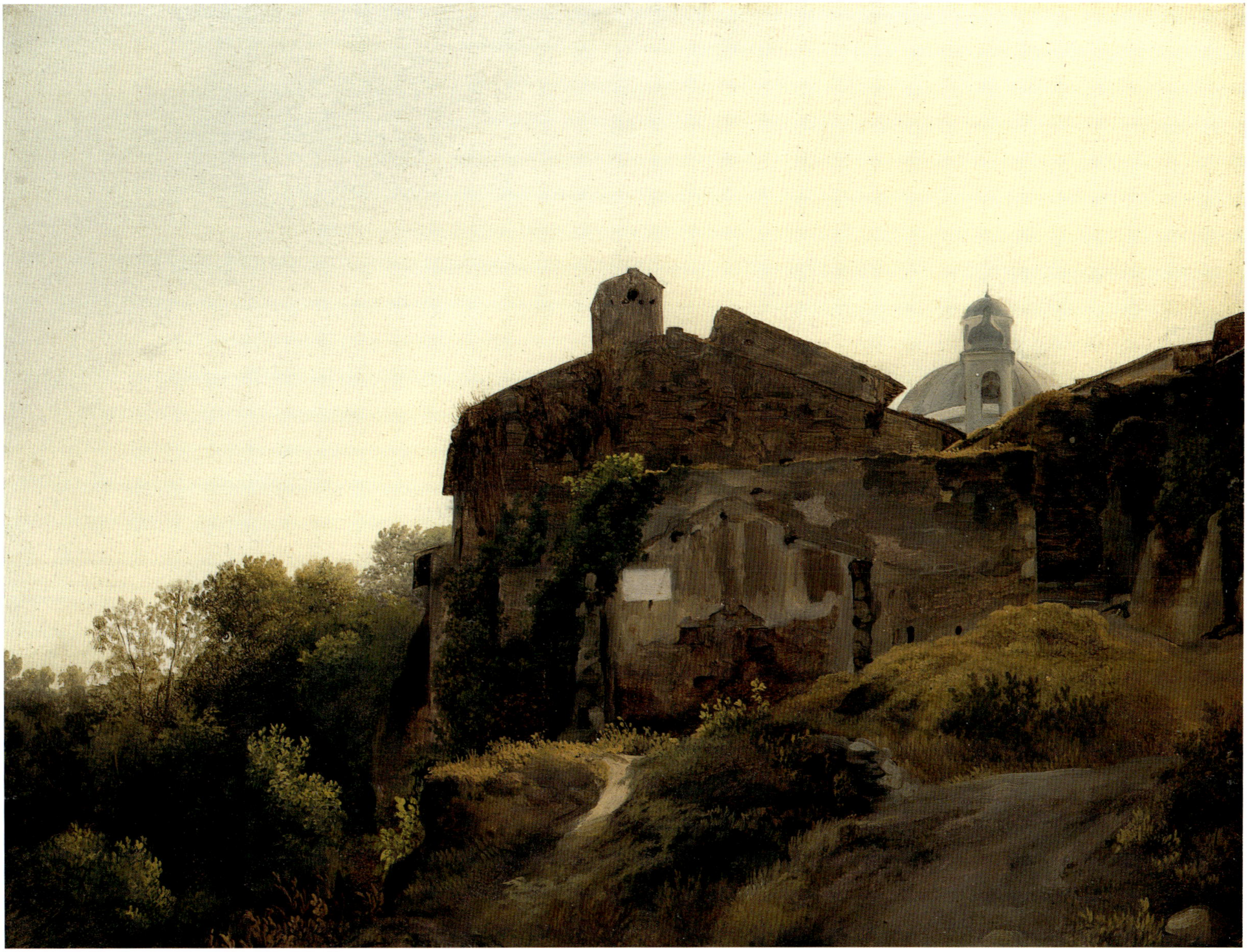

CAMUCCINI, Giovanni-Battista (1819–1902)

10. *A Fallen Tree Trunk,* undated

Oil on paper laid on board, 25.8 x 42.0 cm

Provenance

The Camuccini family by descent; bought from the family in 1983.

Valenciennes recommended that artists make oil studies of trees, focusing on their bark and other characteristic irregularities. Artists such as Wallis (see cat. no. 67) and Michallon (see cat. no. 57) followed this advice early in the century, as did Camuccini when he painted this study, perhaps as much as a half century later. The massive, twisted trunk, moss dappling its curving, broken branches, has fallen somewhere in the countryside. Decay is well advanced as it is slowly, inexorably absorbed back into the earth. A study in death, Camuccini has exploited all the vitality and animation in the form. New life sprouts around it as brilliant sunlight falls. *CR*

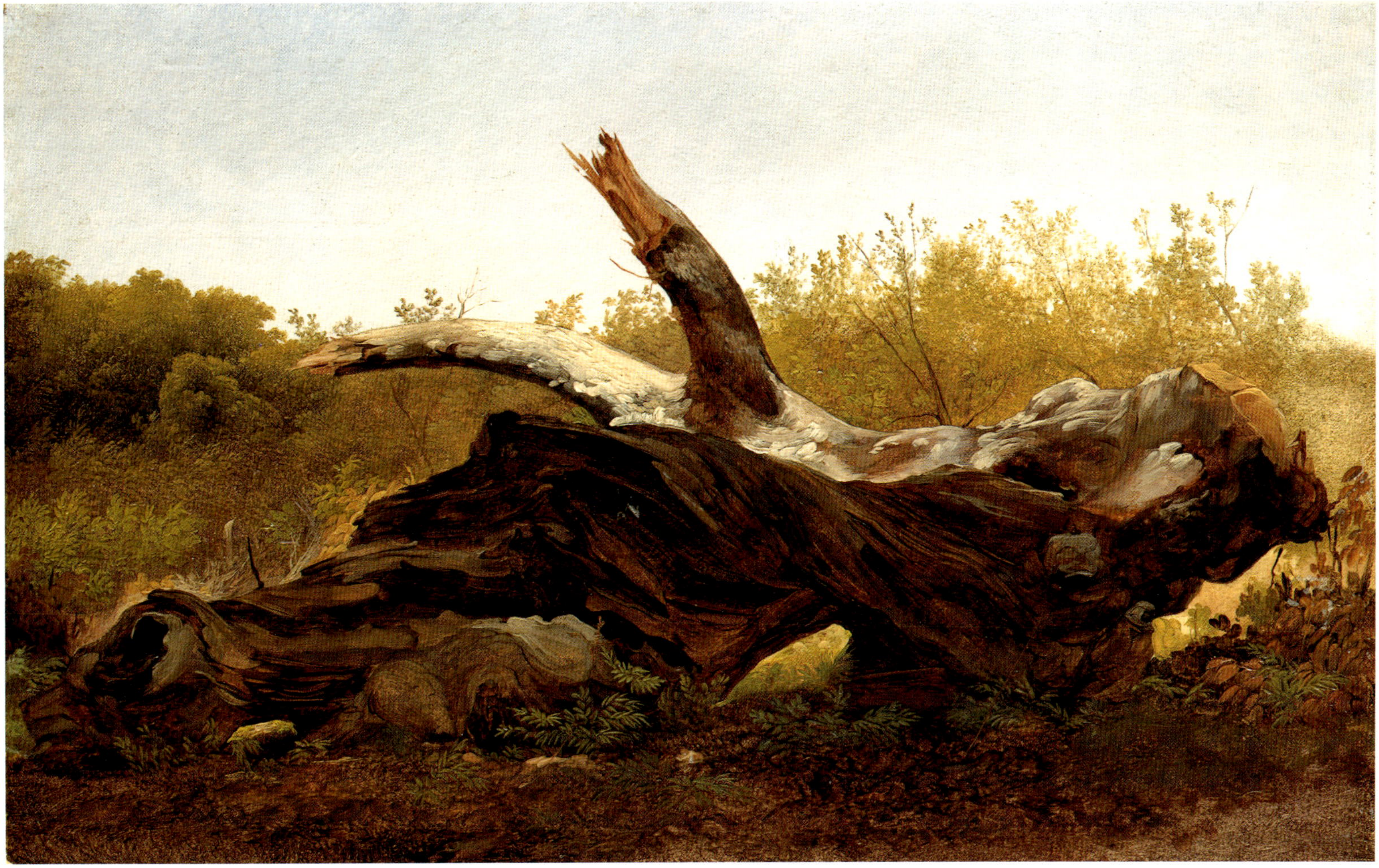

Camuccini, Giovanni-Battista (1819–1902)
11. *Landscape with Trees and Rocks*, undated

Oil and chalk on paper laid on canvas, 27.8 x 37.9 cm

Technical note

Infra-red photography has revealed extensive underdrawing.

Provenance

The Camuccini family by descent; bought from the family in 1983.

When they painted landscapes, students of the oil sketch often sketched in the principal forms of the motif in pencil or chalk before beginning to work with colours. They were also encouraged to focus on the middle distance and quickly capture what they saw there rather than attempt to depict the areas of landscape closest to hand, for which they would need to refocus their gaze. Thus, painters in this collection such as Gilles-François Closson (see cat. no. 13) and Ramsay Richard Reinagle (see cat. no. 62) sometimes left the bottoms of their sketches blank, revealing details of the underdrawing. The son of a well-known artist and certainly aware of such academic strategies, Camuccini adopted these techniques in this free and quickly executed view of a landscape, probably painted in the Roman Campagna.

Camuccini began by making a preliminary drawing, clearly visible in an infra-red photograph of the painting (fig. 19). It shows three thin tree trunks at left, a path moving up the hill from lower right, large rocks at right, and clouds in the sky. Paint was then applied in long, liquid strokes to define two of the tree trunks – the third trunk at far left was not in the end painted – and the play of light and shade on the hillside. Similarly, the path up the hill, originally sketched in chalk, is not delineated in paint nor is there a cloud in the sky. The trees in the background at left are more carefully depicted than other forms in the painting, but the rocks that rise at right are painted thinly and with slapdash freedom. Indeed, the brushstrokes at upper right are applied over the blue of the sky and, as the underdrawing visible there shows, independently of the rock forms previously sketched in chalk. Drawing and painting are different activities, of course, and, like many other artists, Camuccini rethought his treatment of the motif as he moved from one medium to the other. *CR*

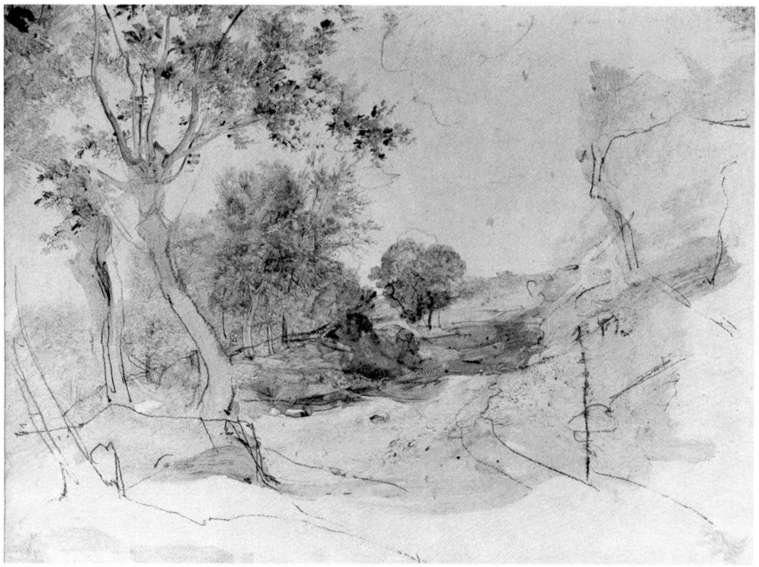

Fig 19 Giovanni-Battista Camuccini, *Landscape with Trees and Rocks*, infra-red photograph.

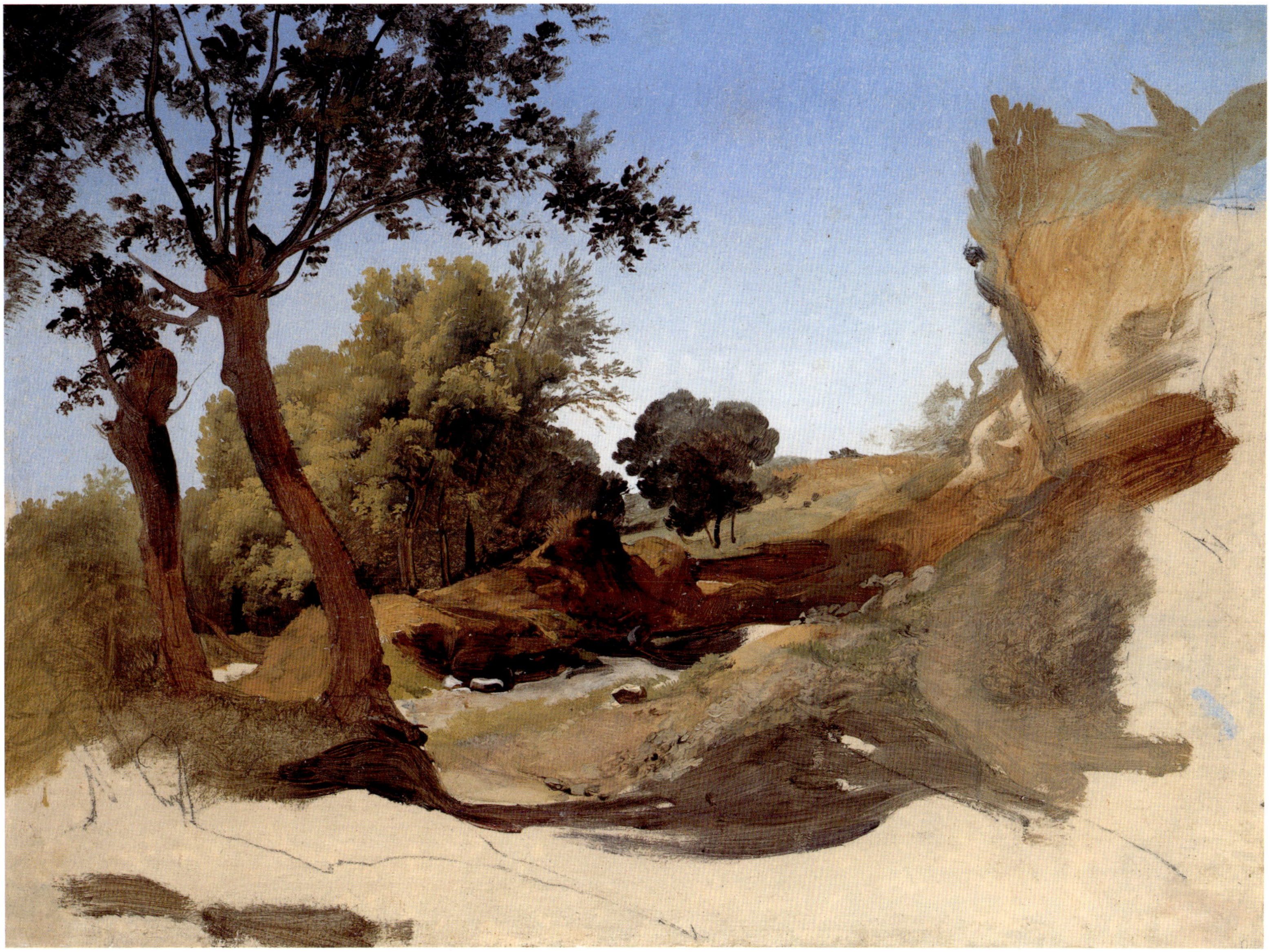

Cels, Jean-Michel (1819–1894)
12. *Sky Study with Birds*, 1842

Oil on paper, 26.6 x 37.3 cm

Inscriptions

Signed and dated on the reverse *JM Cels 1842 Bruxelles*

Inscribed on reverse *V[ernis] cop[al] étendu de térébenthine*

Provenance

Christie's, South Kensington, London, 16 April 1997, lot 310; bought from W. M. Brady & Co., New York, 1997.

A little-known Belgian artist, Jean-Michel Cels was the son of a Neoclassical painter and long-time director of the Académie de Tournai, Cornelis Cels (1778–1859). The elder Cels was his son's first teacher and it was no doubt he who introduced Jean-Michel to the oil sketch, as he had made such studies himself during seven years in Italy early in the century. A number of drawings and oil sketches on paper by the father and son entered the market in 1997, including landscapes and flower studies by Jean-Michel, as well as eight sky studies, of which the present work is one. Several are inscribed with dates, locations and notes on the medium. This sketch was executed at Brussels in 1842, and Cels mixed copal varnish thinned with turpentine with his paint. Unlike some of his other sky studies, in which the artist situated himself in space by including a thin strip of earth at the bottom, this sketch shows only billowing clouds against a blue sky, with two birds wheeling in the breeze.[1]

In painting such oil studies of cloud formations, Cels was building on tradition, for 'skying' – as John Constable called it – played a long and important rôle in the history of the *plein-air* sketch. The Dutch painter Willem van de Velde the Younger is reported to have made such studies in the seventeenth century. In his *Cours de peinture par principes* of 1708, Roger de Piles specifically recommended that artists sketch the changing patterns in the sky at several times of day and in various weather conditions. Valenciennes painted sky studies, and in his *Elémens de perspective pratique* of 1800 advised artists to begin their open-air sketches with the sky, in order to establish a tone. In England, both J. M. W. Turner and John Constable executed numerous cloud studies. Indeed, Constable painted about one hundred of them in a period of concentrated work at Hampstead in 1820–1, dating many of them to the very hour.[2] While speed is of the essence in the landscape oil sketch, it is particularly so with sky studies as cloud formations are constantly altering. *CR*

1 Four others are illustrated in colour in New York 1998, nos. 33–6.

2 For a brief history of cloud painting see Hawes 1969, pp. 344–65.

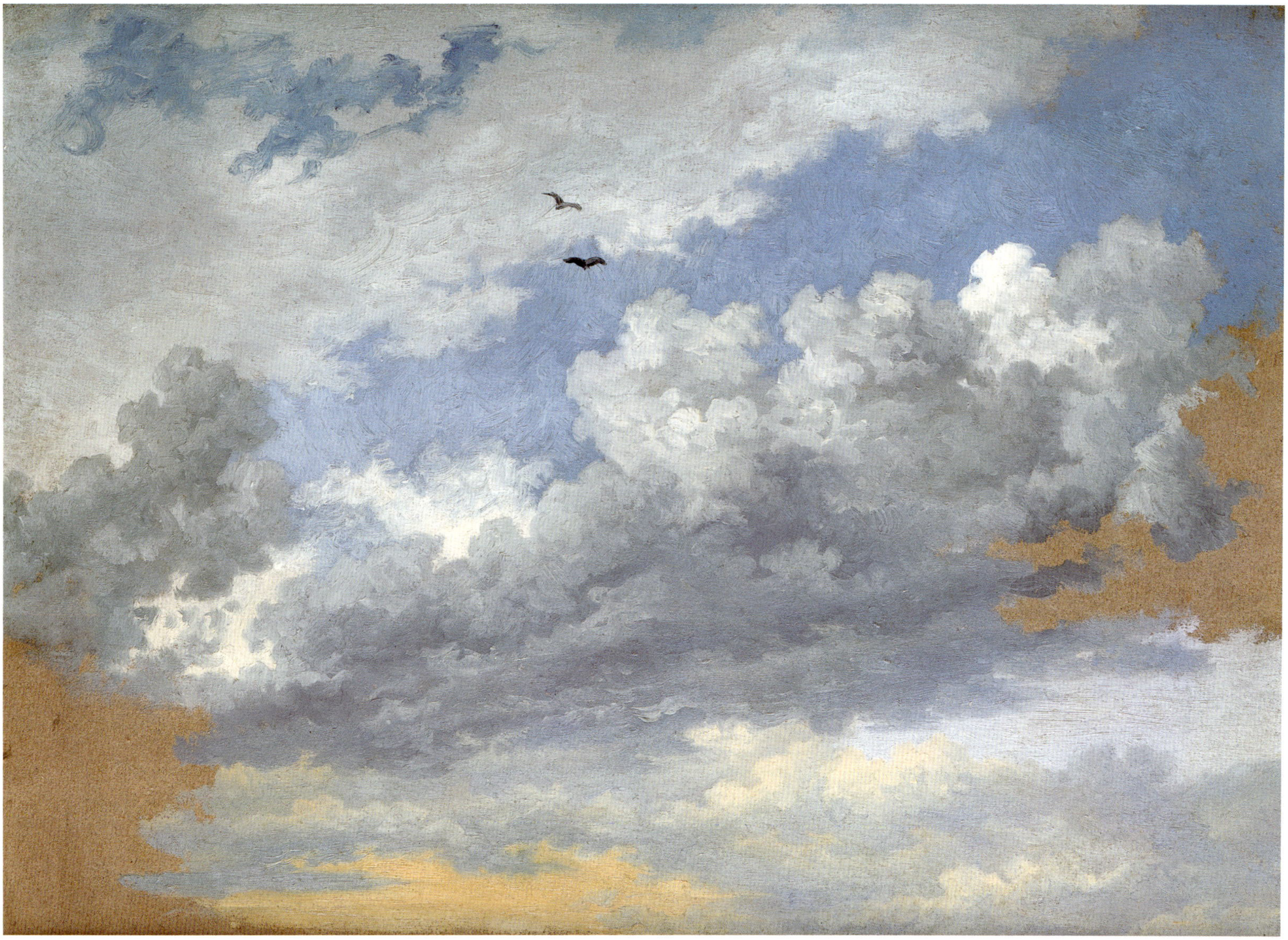

Closson, Gilles-François-Joseph (1798–1842)
13. *The Cascade at Tivoli*, about 1824–9

Oil on paper laid on canvas, 56.2 x 39.6 cm

Provenance

With the Galerie d'Arenberg, Brussels, in 1994; bought from James Mackinnon, London in 1994.

Exhibitions

Brussels 1994, no. 25; Washington, Brooklyn and St Louis 1996–7, no. 109.

Until recently relatively little known, Closson is one the most significant Belgian landscape painters of the nineteenth century.[1] Born in Liège, where he studied with Hennequin in 1813, Closson moved to Paris in 1817 to study under the famous history painter, Baron A.-R. Gros. On his return to Liège, he won a grant from the Darchis Foundation which enabled him to travel to Italy in 1824. There, he gave up history painting in order to dedicate himself fully to landscape, executing a significant number of oil sketches and drawings, most of which are now in the Cabinet des Estampes du Musée des Beaux-Arts in Liège.

In 1829 Closson returned to Liège for good, with the hope of establishing himself as a painter of landscape compositions. On at least three occasions, in 1830, 1833 and 1836, he presented Italian views, mainly of Rome and Tivoli, at the Brussels Salon. Although he failed to obtain the recognition that he desired, mainly because contemporary taste tended more to history paintings and genre scenes, he was eventually made professor at the Liège Academy in 1837, a post which he kept until his death.

The only documents recording his stay in Italy are fifty oil sketches and 300 drawings donated to the Liège Academy by his widow (now in the Musée de Beaux-Arts) and a batch of forty-eight oil sketches first exhibited at the d'Arenberg gallery in Brussels in 1994, three of which are shown here. Like most of his contemporaries, Closson seems to have travelled around Italy randomly recording views of famous sites, mostly in and around Rome, Tivoli and the region of Naples. His paintings are sketches in the real sense of the word, almost all of them left unfinished, revealing his technique and approach to painting out in the open. Before applying oil paints, he made a rapid drawing in graphite as a rough compositional guide. This underdrawing is visible in most of his paintings, suggesting that he kept them in his studio for use when painting larger landscape compositions, probably those he presented for the Salon exhibitions. His sketches on the whole demonstrate an extraordinary ease in capturing the fleeting movement of light, a precision of detail and an admirable feeling for colour and texture.

This sketch was painted from the bottom of the gorge at Tivoli, looking up at the steep rocky cliff and the waterfalls. Rather than including the Temple of Vesta in his sketch, as artists normally did from this viewpoint, Closson chose to concentrate on the dramatic contrast between the texture and colours of the cascading waters and the foliage growing on the cliff rock. To intensify the scene he balanced his composition by positioning in its centre the moment of transition from dark to light, highlighted by the reflection of sunlight on the foam of the cascade. This ability to focus on a specific range of vision reflects his academic training.

This sketch may well have served Closson as a model for a larger, more finished composition. In 1831, when he was trying to re-establish himself on the Belgian art scene, we learn from a letter that he attempted to sell a view of the cascading water at Tivoli to the vice-president of an art society in Ghent.[2] *XB*

1 Brussels 1985–6, pp. 313–15.

2 Ibid., p. 313.

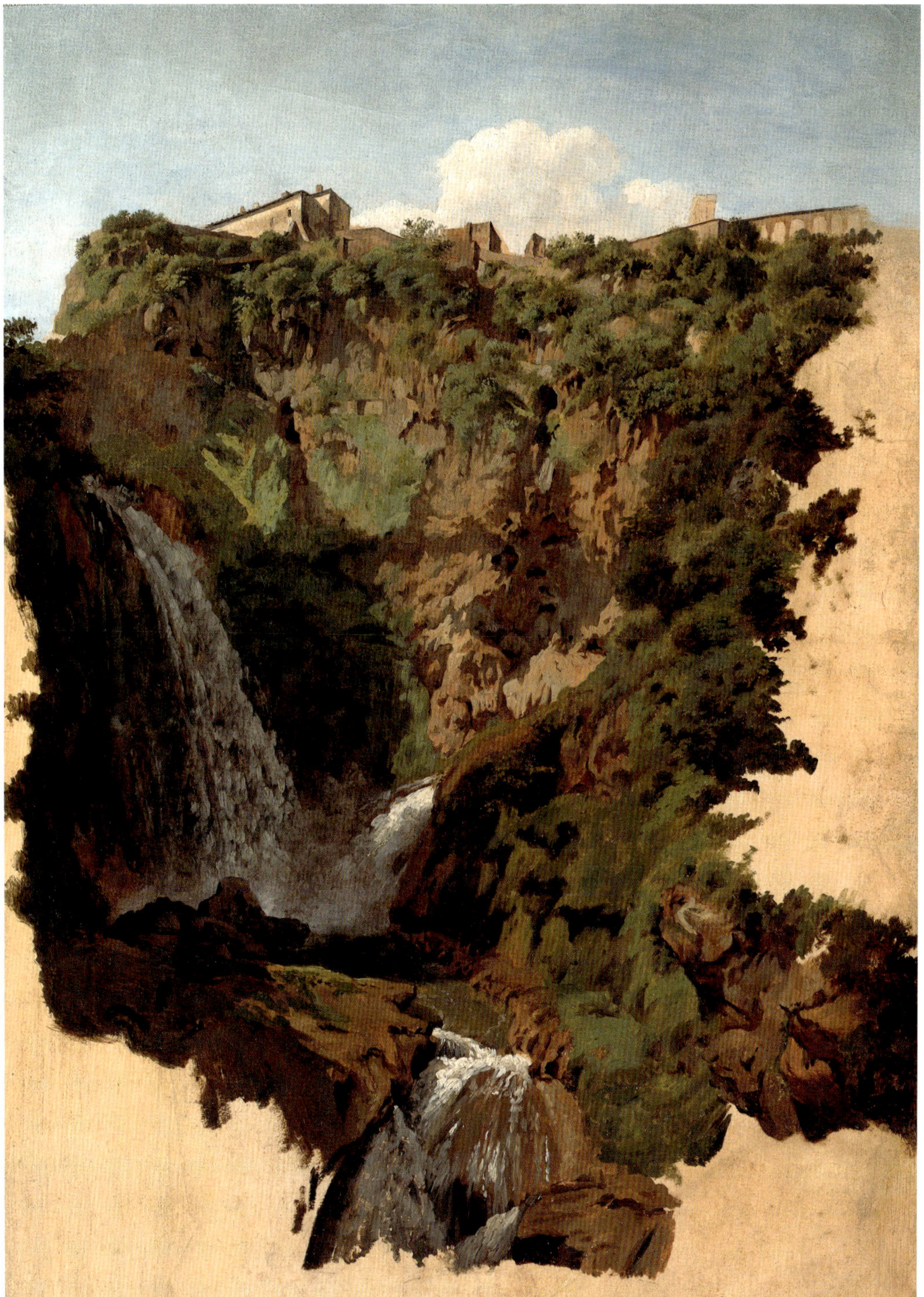

Closson, Gilles-François-Joseph (1798–1842)
14. *Antique Ruins (the Baths of Caracalla?)*, about 1824–9

Oil on paper laid on canvas, 29.5–30.9 x 37.6 cm

Provenance

Galerie d'Arenberg, Brussels; bought from John Lishawa, London, in 1993.

Exhibitions

Brussels 1993, no. 22; Washington, Brooklyn and St Louis 1996–7, cat. no. 108.

As in his oil sketch of the waterfalls at Tivoli (cat. no. 13), Closson has left this sketch unfinished, with the underdrawing still apparent in the lower left-hand corner. The decision to leave it incomplete is characteristic of Closson. On the one hand the unfinished appearance of his sketches suggests spontaneity and a desire to record nature instantly, while on the other hand the compositional advantages offered by the empty spaces suggest a more deliberate method of working. Here, the blank space heightens the solidity of the ruins in the background and the light ground provides an interesting contrast with the walls in shadow on the right.

The ruins in the background have not been identified. The dark red colour of the brickwork and the arches is reminiscent of the ruins in Rome, particularly on the Palatine Hill, and at Hadrian's Villa, near Tivoli. It has been suggested that the arch in the centre, with a slight curve and the shadow of the higher arch on the brick wall above, may be one of the archways in the ruins of the Baths of Caracalla.[1] Located to the southeast of the Palatine Hill, within the walls of Rome, the Baths looked very different in the nineteenth century to how they do today. Before they were fully excavated, the ground level was much higher and the undergrowth much denser, providing an inspirational setting for Closson's painting. *XB*

1 See Washington, Brooklyn and St Louis 1996–7, p. 242.

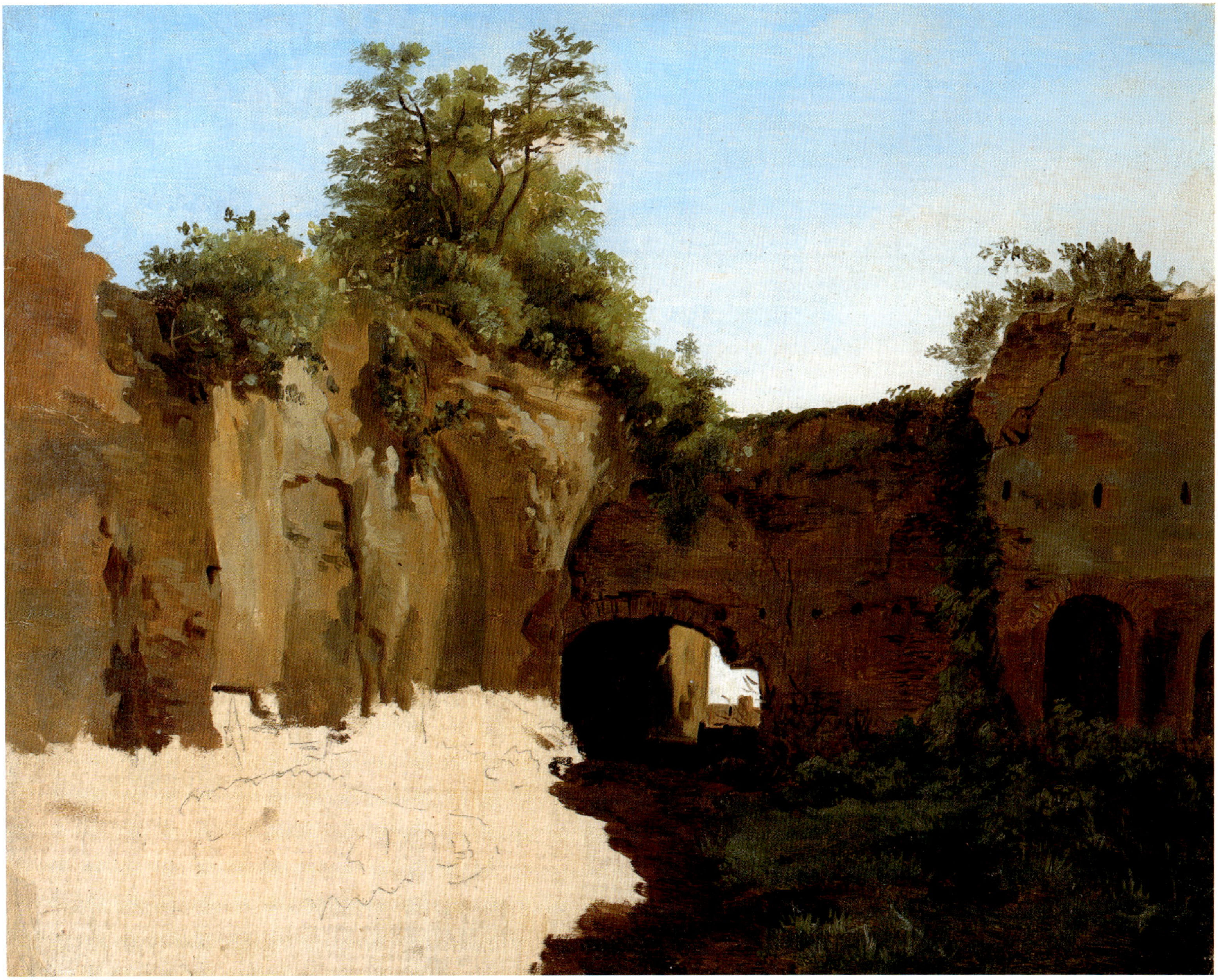

CLOSSON, Gilles-François-Joseph (1798–1842)
15. *Landscape with Cumulus Clouds*, about 1824–9
Oil on canvas, 24.5 x 29.3 cm

Inscriptions
Two stickers with numbers on the stretcher *4* and *35*

Technical note
Infra-red photography has revealed an underdrawing related to a different composition.

Provenance
Galerie d'Arenberg, Brussels, 1994; bought from James Mackinnon, London, in 1994.

The rapidity of execution and the atmospheric rendition of the white cumulus clouds and the landscape stretching to a distant horizon below suggest that Closson was familiar with Valenciennes's advice to painters not to take more than half an hour to record what they saw before them. The range of whites and greys used to give volume to the clouds and the white dabs of paint highlighting the reflection of the sunlight demonstrate the ease and dexterity of Closson's brush. The flat landscape and bulbous clouds recall northern Europe, suggesting that Closson may have made this work on his return to Liège at the end of 1829. However, as it forms part of a group of Italian views, and the Roman Campagna can at times appear to be completely flat, particularly looking westwards from Tivoli towards the coast, we may be justified in assuming that this sketch was executed in Italy.

This assumption is reinforced by the impressive underdrawing revealed by infra-red photography, which shows a completely different type of landscape (fig. 20). Against a background of distant mountains, a hill town in the middle ground is perched on a cliff edge, with a river sweeping down below. In the foreground is a herd of cattle with a herdsman on horseback with another standing in the lower left-hand corner. The drawing has been squared-up, suggesting that Closson intended to transfer the composition, possibly for a finished painting. In 1828 he painted a *View of the Environs of Rome*, exhibited in 1830 at the Salon de l'Emulation in Liège, and it is possible that this drawing is linked to a now lost painting.[1] It was not unusual for landscape paintings presented at Belgian Salons to draw inspiration from Italian scenery, combined with such northern features as well-fed cows and herdsmen, and perhaps Closson was adapting to local taste when composing his picture.[2] *XB*

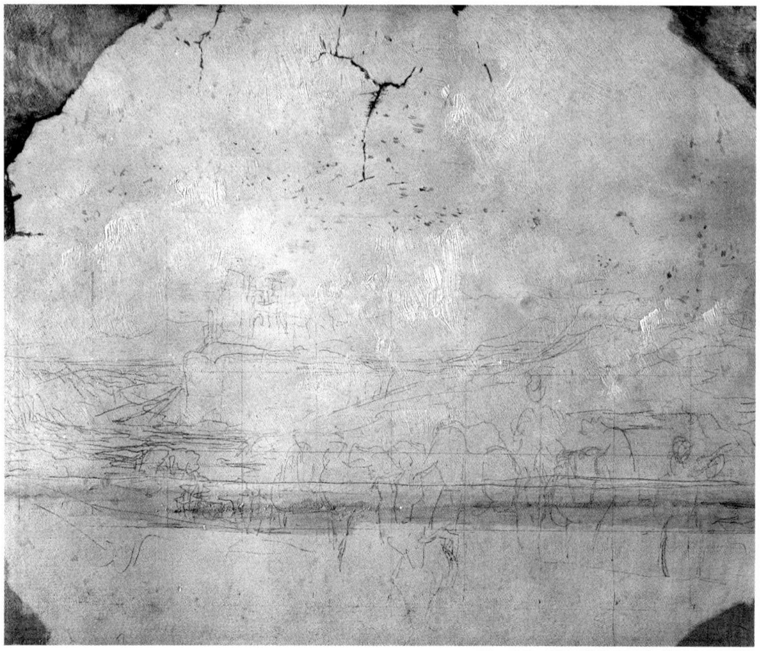

Fig 20 Gilles-François-Joseph Closson, *Landscape with Cumulus Clouds*, infra-red photograph.

1 Brussels 1985–6, p. 313.
2 For comparisons see ibid., pp. 293–5.

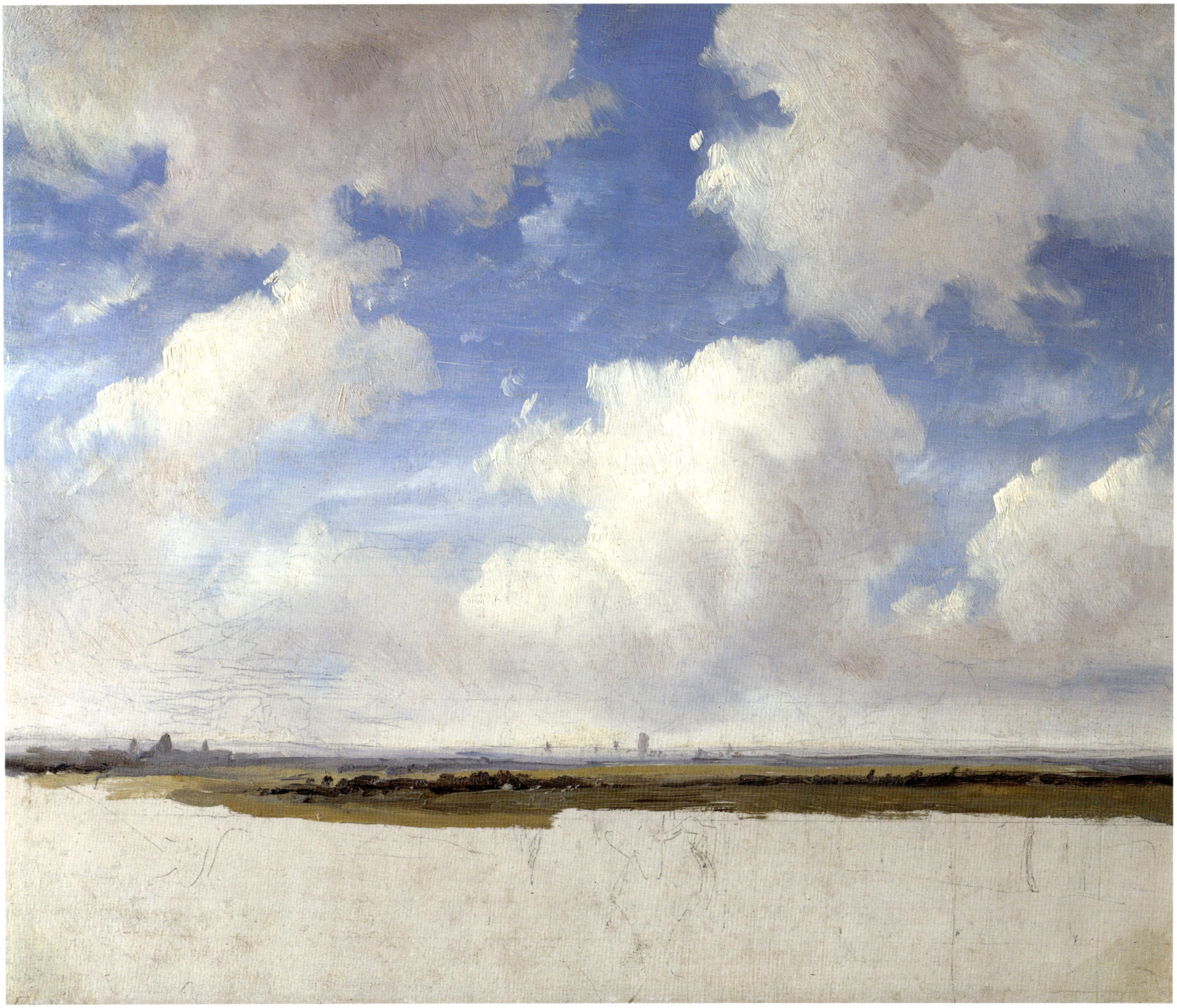

Coignet, Jules-Louis-Philippe (1798–1860), attributed to
16. *River Landscape,* about 1840

Oil on paper laid on canvas, 25.2 x 38.4 cm

Provenance

Said to have been in the Jules Coignet studio sale, Paris, Hôtel Drouot, 8–12 April 1861; bought from James Mackinnon, London, in 1988.

Despite the distinctive profile of the mountain, the site has not been identified. The rustic buildings at right and left suggest that it is Italy, although the lush green of the vegetation may point to France. The artist situated himself on the near side of a river with sheer vertical banks, thus largely eliminating the problem landscape sketchers faced of how to deal with the foreground. He dispatched it here with two broad and largely undifferentiated bands of dark paint representing water and bank and then, as was often recommended, focused his attention on the middle and far distance. While some areas of the landscape are broadly painted, in others the artist has applied numerous small strokes of colour, animating the surface with several shades of green.

An attribution is difficult. Whatever the location, the artist is surely French and the date of execution may be around 1840. By that time a common approach to landscape painting out of doors had developed in France, with numerous painters, many of them forgotten or little-known today, studying under the same masters, adopting their approach and often approximating their touch. According to anecdotal information supplied by James Mackinnon, this painting was in the 1861 studio sale of Jules-Louis-Philippe Coignet. If so, it would probably have been included under lot 307, the final lot in the sale, which is described in the catalogue as containing one hundred diverse painted studies (*100 Etudes peintes diverses*).[1] As the catalogue makes clear, however, the sale also included works by other artists. An influential teacher with numerous students, Coignet may have kept examples of their work in his studio and he may also have had on hand for teaching purposes works by contemporary artists he particularly admired, such as Théodore Caruelle d'Aligny (1798–1871) and André Giroux (1801–1879).

Coignet studied under Jean-Victor Bertin (1767–1842) but was always more interested in naturalistic landscape than in his master's classical compositions. He visited Italy in 1820 and again in 1840, travelling extensively and sketching. He followed the same procedure in France itself, frequently publishing lithographs of the French countryside. While he often showed at the Salon, his greatest impact was as a teacher, and his studio attracted numerous students interested in his naturalistic approach to landscape. It is easy to see this painting as arising from his circle. *CR*

1 Paris 1861.

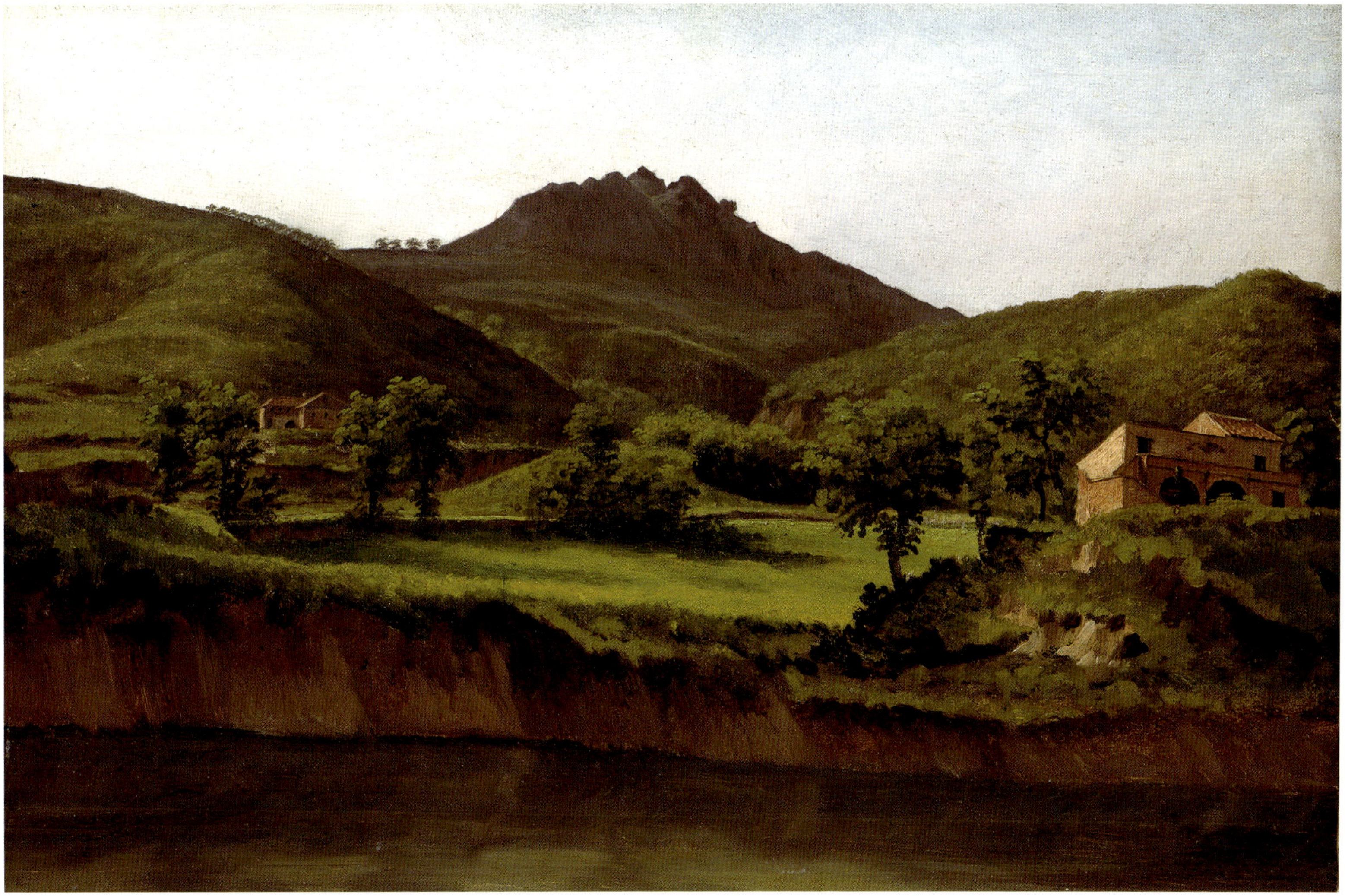

CONSTANTIN, Jean-Antoine (1756–1844), attributed to

17. *Bridge at Subiaco*, about 1777

Oil on paper, 28.7 x 38.4–39.4 cm

Provenance

Said to have been in the Jules Coignet studio sale, Paris, Hôtel Drouot, 8–12 April 1861; bought from James Mackinnon, London, in 1988.

The sketch shows the Bridge of Campo d'Arco which crosses the River Aniene outside Subiaco, a town in the Sabine Hills some seventy kilometres east of Rome. The strong, simple architecture of the old bridge is thrown into relief by the dramatic play of light and shadows across it. Brilliant sunlight even reaches the underside of the bridge, illuminating part of the single stone span as it arches over the river. The façade of the gatehouse is also bathed in light on the opposite bank. Having traversed the bridge, the eye travels up the side of an adjacent hill where rustic buildings are similarly illuminated, and on to grey mountains and cerulean sky above.

The attribution to Constantin is based on the stylistic similarities of the sketch to others by the artist. Working in Italy for some three years beginning in 1777, he painted oil sketches and drew landscapes extensively in Rome and the surrounding countryside. Indeed, he made a more highly detailed wash drawing of this same bridge from a slightly different viewpoint in which he also focused on the play of light and shade across its austere form (Aix-en-Provence, Musée Granet).[1] As with the present oil sketch, many of Constantin's studies took as their motifs works of architecture, either Roman ruins or the more homely medieval structures that dotted the Roman countryside. He often observed them, as here, from acute angles that give rise to unexpected conjunctions of forms and complex spatial configurations.[2] He was drawn to strong architectural forms silhouetted against the sky.[3] Constantin's handling of paint was broad, as here, and he often relied on abrupt divisions between areas of light and shade.

Born in Marseilles, Constantin was a founder of the Provençal school of landscape painting and his work influenced Granet. His talents were recognised early, when local patrons arranged to send him to Rome to study in 1877. He arrived the same year as Valenciennes and the two indefatigable oil sketchers may well have encountered one another there. After three years of hard work, however, Constantin's health gave way and he returned to France. He served as director of the School of Drawing in Aix from 1786 to 1794, after which it was dissolved. Much of the rest of his life was spent in making unremarkable submissions to the Paris Salon, and seeing them duly rewarded. Constantin died in poverty, however, and the oil sketches and some 1,200 drawings now in the Musée Granet were purchased from his widow as an act of charity. They had only just escaped being thrown away. The director of the Musée Granet, Denis Coutagne, has recently questioned the attribution on the basis of a study of a transparency.[4]

As with the *River Landscape* attributed to Coignet (cat. no. 16), this oil sketch is said to have figured in the 1861 Coignet atelier sale which, the sale catalogue makes clear, included works by artists other than Coignet himself.[5] *CR*

1 Marseilles 1986, cat. no. 24.

2 See his *Inside the Colosseum: Chapel and Terrace* (Aix-en-Provence, Musée Granet); Washington, Brooklyn and St Louis 1996–7, cat. no. 27.

3 Compare with the two views in New York 1998, nos. 9 and 10.

4 Oral communication.

5 Paris 1861.

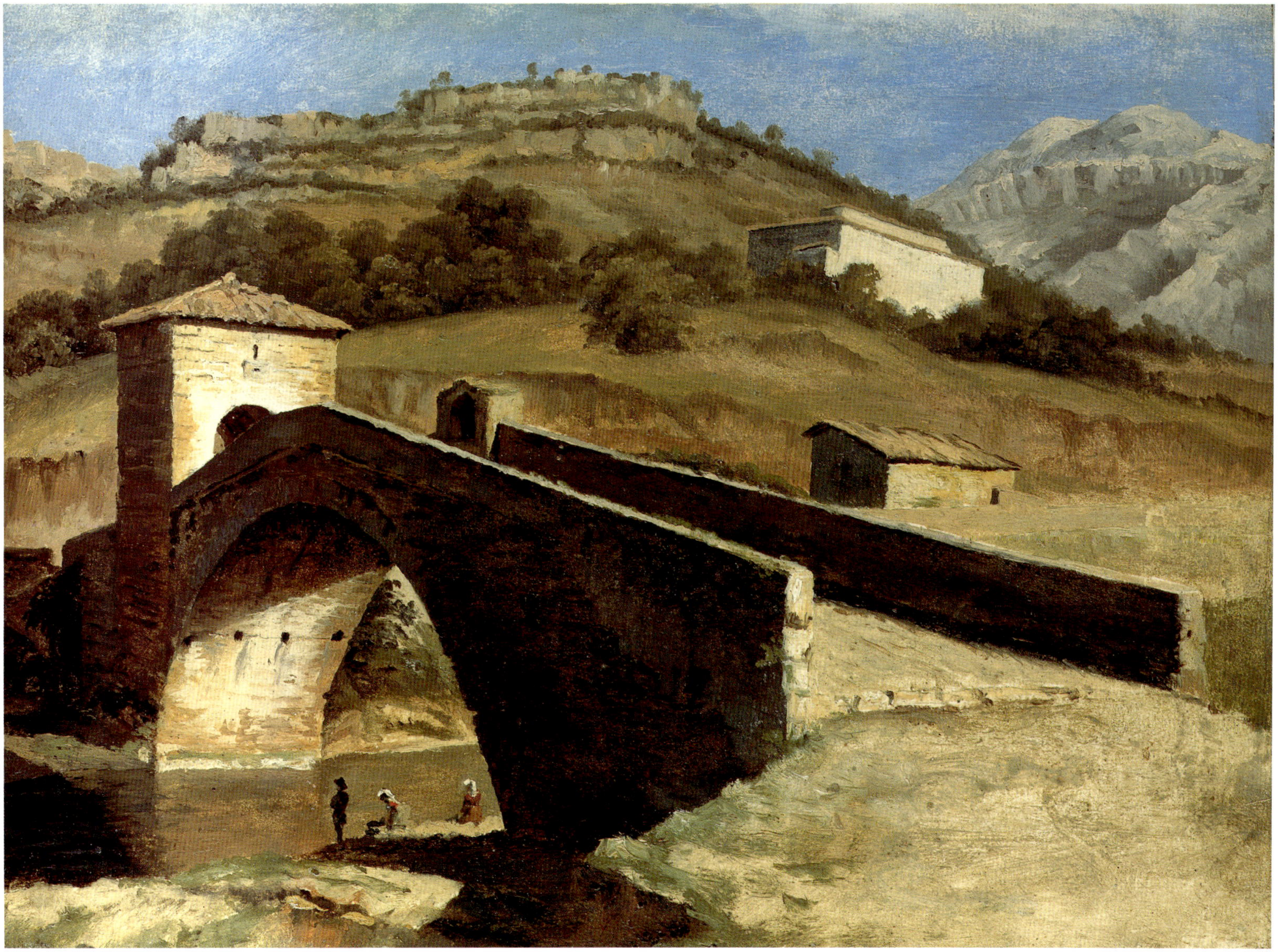

Corot, Jean-Baptiste-Camille (1796–1875), attributed to

18. *Staircase in the Entrance to the Villa of Maecenas at Tivoli*, about 1826

Oil on paper laid on canvas, 29.7 x 21.5 cm

Inscriptions

Lower right *Corot*

On backing paper over the stretcher *J.B.C. Corot S. Agnese fuori le mura* (crossed out) *1826* (?)

In a more recent hand *Granet*

Provenance

Bought from John. Lishawa, London, in 1978 (as Corot).

Together with Valenciennes and Michallon, Corot is a central figure in the French oil sketch tradition. Like those older masters, his most innovative studies were made in Italy, between 1825 and 1828. During those years he travelled widely in the peninsula, painting many of the notable sites that had been attracting landscape artists for generations, including Tivoli. The many sketches he executed are among the most structurally rigorous nineteenth-century studies.[1] Not only are they today among Corot's most admired works, even while he was painting them they were widely influential on the landscape artists with whom he came into contact. Among the artists with whom Corot travelled and painted in Italy were Théodore Caruelle d'Aligny, Edouard Bertin, Léon Cogniet and the German Ernst Fries.

It is easy to see why an artist like Corot, ever on the lookout for challenging motifs, might have been attracted to the spatial complexity and complicated lighting effects on the staircase at the Villa of Maecenas. The old wooden doors at the bottom of the stairs have been pulled open and are depicted obliquely, but five slots in the door at left exactly mirror the five windows through which light pours into the space at the top of the stairs. The perspectival recession into depth up the staircase is also a movement from humid darkness at bottom to dazzling illumination above. The pitted vault over the stairway itself gives way to a higher, brighter space, while the return of the staircase at top creates an almost Cubist architectural interval of contrasting planes. The painting is executed with long, liquid strokes and quick daubs of paint. The horizontal strokes of paint that outline the stairs are freely applied in brown, where the space is in shadow, and white, where the sun has made its way. The figures mounting the stairs are mere squiggles of paint, while the red touches on the costume of the seated peasant woman at bottom provide the highest note of colour.

The attribution of the painting to Corot has not attracted wide support. None the less, it is worth noting that the Corot 'signature' at lower right survived intact when the painting was cleaned. François-Marius Granet has also been proposed. He made his career painting interior spaces, though more often ecclesiastical than ancient Roman ones. Indeed, a drawing by Granet (fig. 21) shows exactly the same site, although the procession of monks bearing tapers that mounts the staircase makes it appear grander and more monumental than it was in reality. If it is by Granet, the painting would date between 1802 and the artist's 1824 return to Paris. Roberta Olson, however, has rejected this attribution.[2] *CR*

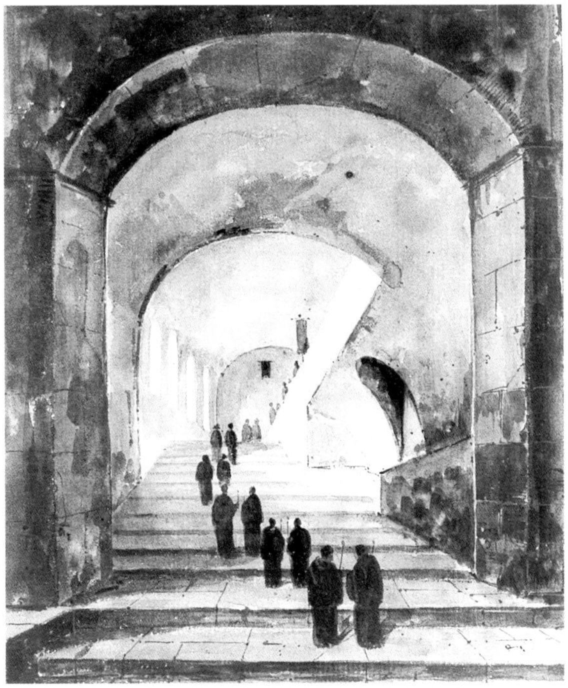

Fig 21 François-Marius Granet, *A Procession*, about 1810. Pen and wash on paper. Private collection.

1 On Corot's achievement in this field, see the seminal study, Galassi 1991.

2 Oral communication.

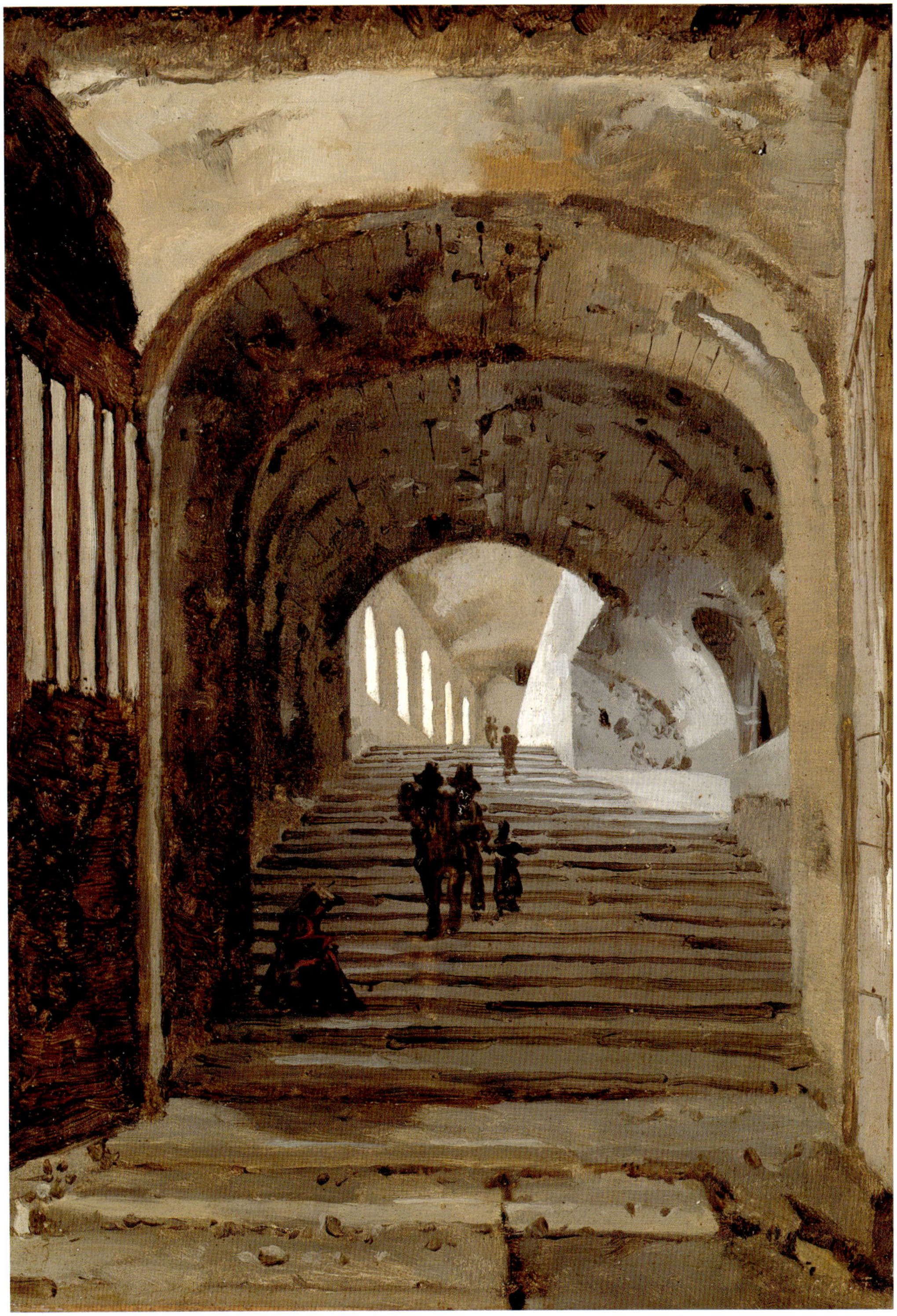

Costa, Giovanni (1826–1903)

19. *Porto d'Anzio*, about 1853

Oil on oak panel, 12.5 x 37.1 cm

Inscription

Stencil on back of panel *BF245*

Provenance

Bought from the Fine Art Society, London, in 1981.

Costa was committed to painting out of doors, rendering the effects of nature but also registering his emotional response to landscape. His luminous, small oil sketches proved influential on such fellow Italian artists as Giovanni-Battista Camuccini and the Macchiaioli painters, as well as such British artists as George Heming Mason and Lord Leighton, both of whom he introduced to oil sketching and who remained lifelong friends. Costa and Mason travelled together on a sketching expedition south of Rome as early as 1853, sleeping in the open air and stopping at Anzio along the coast. The format of Mason's *Porto d'Anzio* (private collection),[1] begun on that trip, is more rectangular than Costa's depiction of the site, his viewpoint more symmetrical, and taken further back from the sea. Costa on the other hand used an emphatically horizontal panel of a kind he favoured, its very format, despite the small scale, imbuing the image with a panoramic sweep. Dense shrubbery gives way to a golden beach against which the white-capped waves break; the purple-tinged coastline disappears to the north; the sky, which occupies more than half of the painting surface, is filled with scudding clouds but opens to streaks of blue at upper right. Like the Macchiaioli painters, Costa used thin paint and allowed the grain of the wooden panel to show through, thus texturing the landscape. No figures are to be seen, but the artist has captured a sense of the timeless rhythms of Mediterranean life. *CR*

1 York, London and Stoke-on-Trent 1989, cat. no. 3, illus.

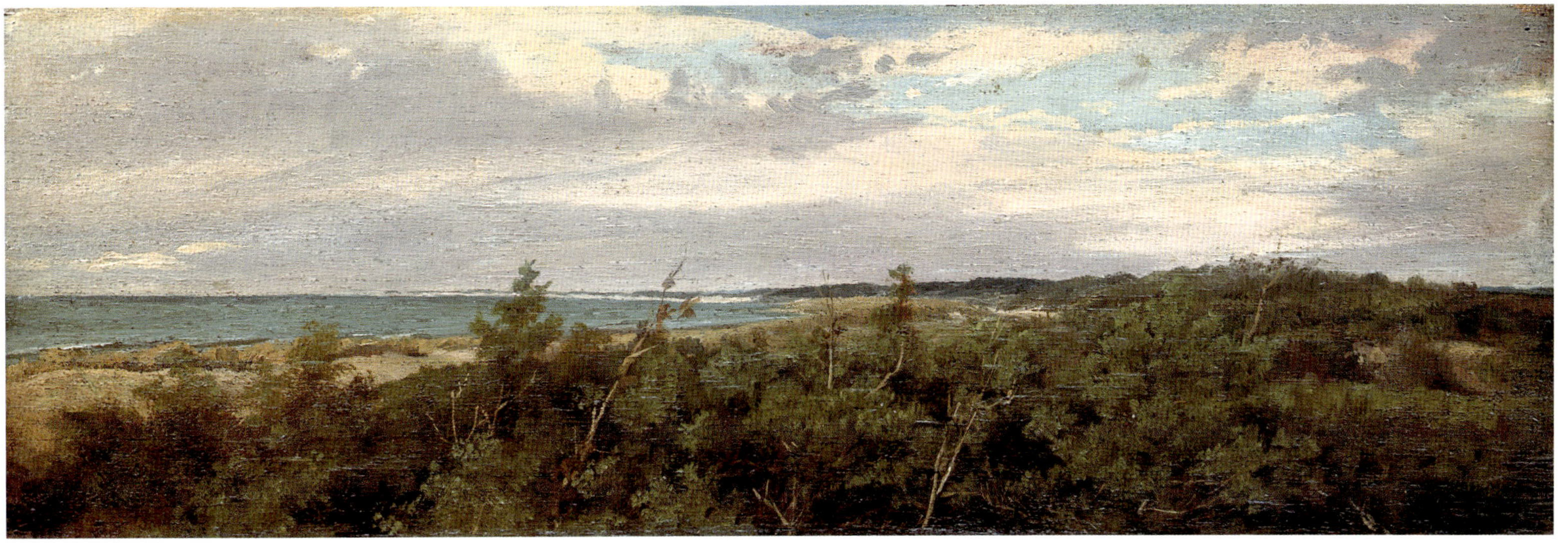

Costa, Giovanni (1826–1903)

20. *After a Shower near Pisa*, undated

Oil on panel, 13.3 x 29.2 cm

Inscriptions

Labels on reverse *No. 31 J 9993*
From ROBERT DUNTHORNE
Print Publisher
The Rembrandt Head
5 Vigo Street London W.
Artist: Giovanni Costa
Subject: After a Shower near Pisa
Oil Painting

After a shower near Pisa by Giovanni Costa
Bt Christie's 18.12.25, no. 72 (?)
In Cole- of Fredk Anthony White
170 Queen's Gate - S.W.

Provenance

Robert Dunthorne, London; Frederick Anthony White, London; Christie's, London, 18 December 1925, lot 72, bought by James Nicoll; bought from Abbott and Holder, London, date not recorded.

Exhibition

London 1976, no. 12.

In the paintings of his later years, Costa moved beyond the broad touch of the Macchiaioli to achieve a more delicate style, full of moist atmospheric effects. This small, subtle painting of damp fields near Pisa, with clouds dancing above a line of trees and hillside, probably dates from late in the nineteenth century. There is an almost Pointillist quality about the countless minute touches of colour that depict the wildflowers in the foreground, although the scale is so small that a shimmering effect is achieved. At the same time, Costa delineates the space with geometric clarity and precision.

The painting has one of the longer provenances in the Gere Collection, and it appears to be entirely English. Through his long years of friendship with George Heming Mason and Frederic, Lord Leighton, Costa enjoyed excellent relations with Britain. In his later years he frequently visited British friends and exhibited at the Royal Academy and the Grosvenor Gallery. Works such as this were particularly admired by British patrons and influenced such British painters as George James Howard, 9th Earl of Carlisle (1843–1911), and Matthew Ridley Corbet (1850–1902). *CR*

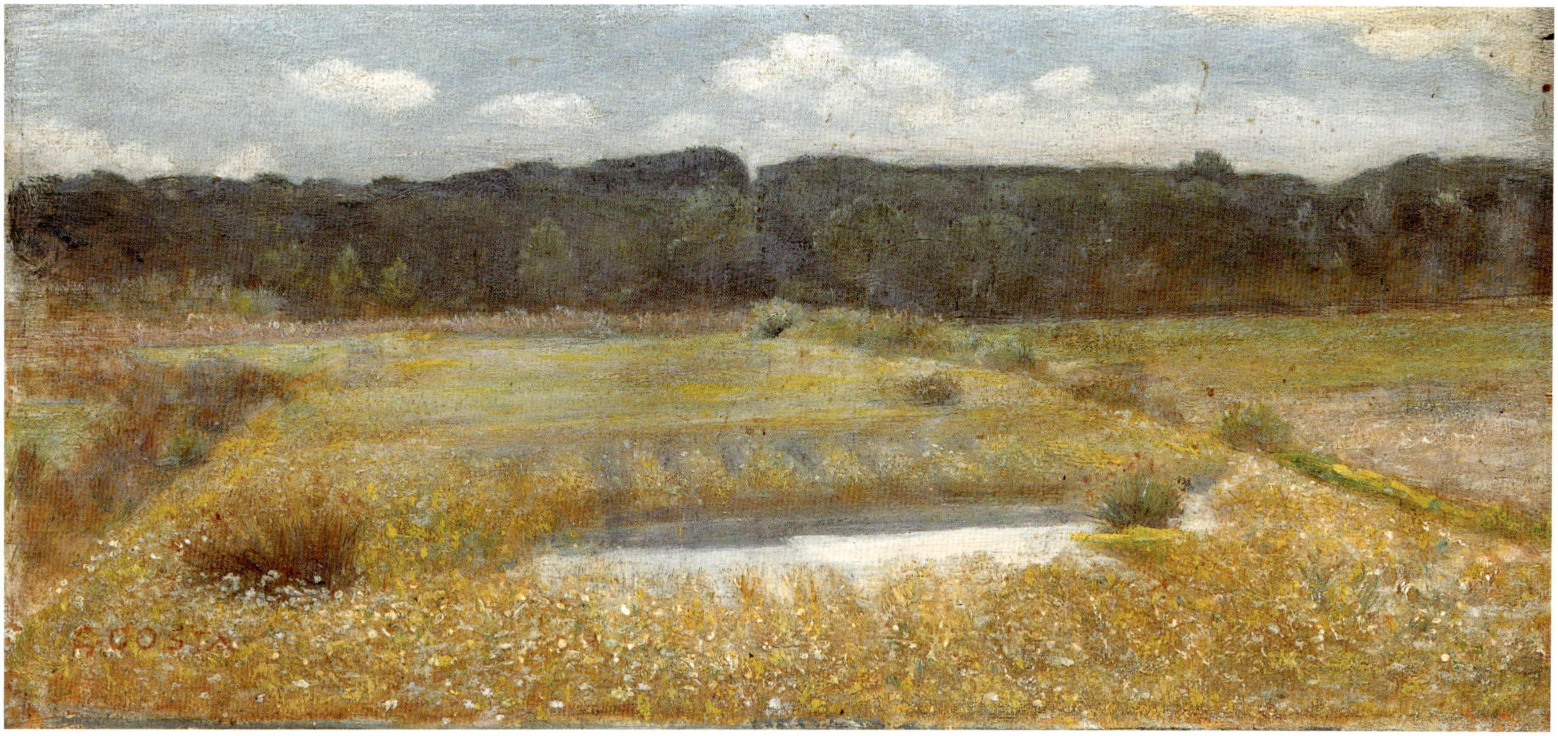
G. COSTA

DANBY, Francis (1793–1861)

21. *A Boat-Builder's Yard*, around 1840

Oil on paper laid on card, 12.2 x 18.5 cm

Inscriptions

In ink at bottom on backing card *Francis Danby. ARA*

Label on reverse *M 639*

Provenance

Bought from the Maas Gallery, London, in 1968.

Exhibitions

Cambridge and London 1980–1, no. 75; New York 1981, no. 194; London 1989, no. 52.

Literature

Adams 1973, no. 46.

Danby was passionate about sailing and the sea. In 1847 he moved to Exmouth in Devon where he worked as a boat-builder while continuing to paint. The following year a critic noted that the artist intended to send a painting to exhibition if 'his amateur boatbuilding does not interfere to prevent its completion on time.'[1] In the 1850s he built his own yacht. This small study of a boat-builder's yard probably dates from somewhat earlier in Danby's career; in the 1989 retrospective exhibition of his works it was assigned to the years around 1840. Danby had recorded his interest in such sites earlier still, when he painted an oil sketch entitled *Boat-building near Dinan* (New Haven, Yale Center for British Art), probably executed in France in the summer of 1838. While that work shows a broad river landscape, including a distant line of hills shrouded in morning mist, the present sheet is a remarkable close-up investigation of a cluttered yard itself. Attention is paid to the implements of the craft – casks, baskets, boards, ropes, levers and pulleys – that to the unknowledgeable appear to be strewn about haphazardly but which to Danby's experienced eye may have seemed the very model of boat-building order and precision. A latticework of thin poles cuts through the space and the heavy wooden boards stacked in the foreground help to establish perspectival recession into depth. Sunlight glints off surfaces, while Danby's quick touches of pale colour capture the humid atmosphere of a waterside site.

Very different from the elegantly composed poetical landscapes and biblical extravaganzas on which his contemporary reputation was based, Danby's oil sketches are direct and immediate records of local sights that caught his eye. This work was included in the 1981 New York exhibition *Before Photography*; it is like a snapshot in its unassuming but unblinkered rendering of a banal workaday motif. But as that exhibition so deftly demonstrated, photography never attained, nor indeed aspired to such informality until decades after pioneering painters of oil sketches, Danby among them, had charted the territory. *CR*

1 Quoted by Francis Greenacre, London 1989, p. 35.

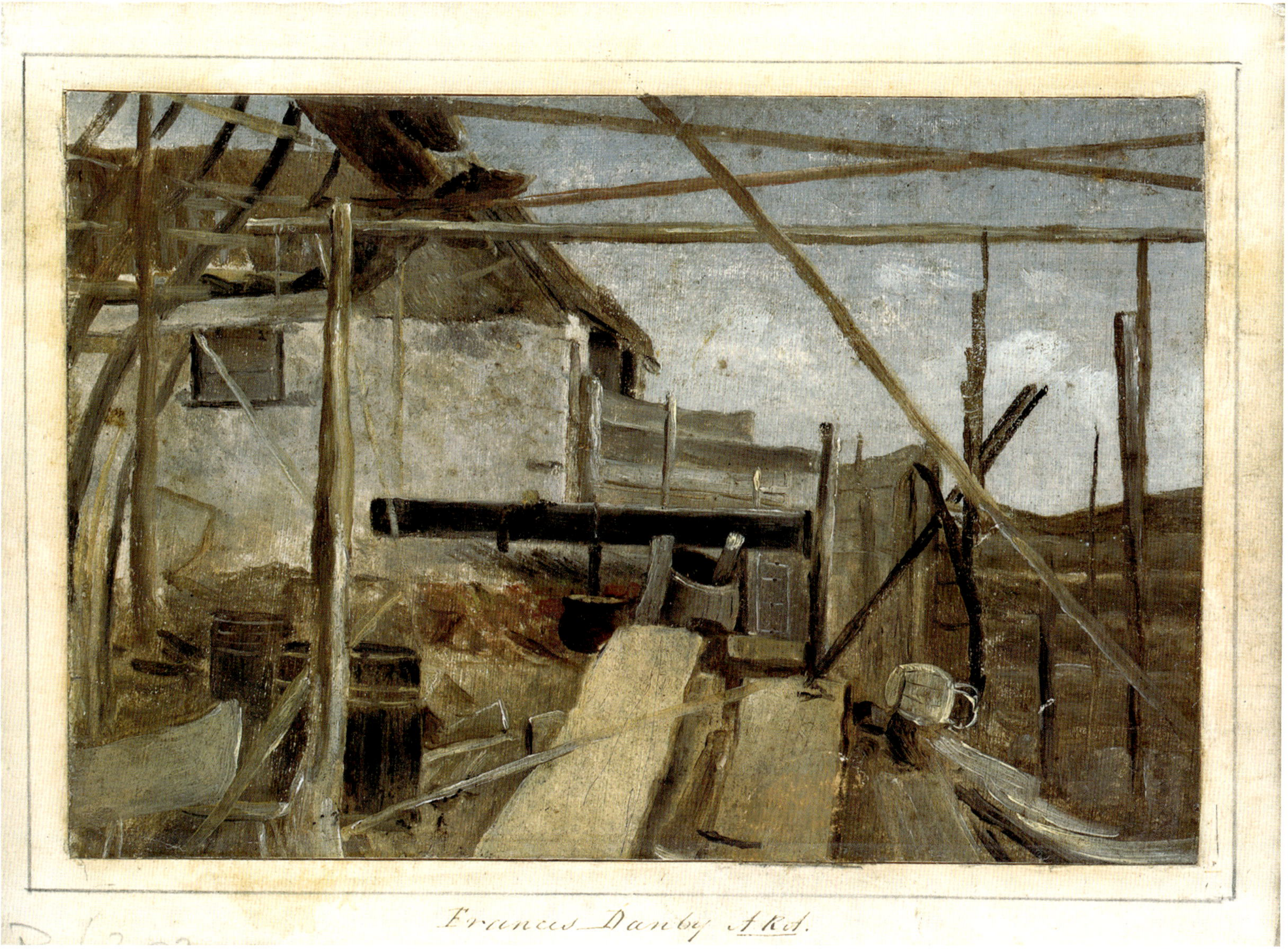
Francis Danby ARA.

Degas, Hilaire-Germain-Edgar (1834–1917)

22. *Promenade beside the Sea*, about 1860

Oil on canvas, 22.4 x 32.4 cm

Inscriptions

Stencils on the stretcher *473; KC*

Provenance

Edmond de Gas, Paris; Gustave Pellet, Paris; Julian Lousada, London; estate of Mrs M. R. Lousada, London; Christie's, London, 8 May 1953, lot 36; Charles Douie, Sussex; thence by descent.

Exhibitions

London 1926; New York and Houston 1994, no. 7; Washington 1998, no. 10.

Literature

Manson 1927, p. 50, pl. 21; Brame and Reff 1984, no. 38; New York and Houston 1994, pp. 61, 64–5, 67, 74, fig. 48; Washington 1998, p. 38.

In this apparently unassuming painting we witness one of the first times the young Degas used a motif of central importance for his art, the horse and rider. At the same time, we see him teaching himself how to combine and adapt preparatory sketches made in nature for a more composed work.

Two riders, one male the other female, both dressed in black and wearing top hats, gallop away from the viewer around the edge of a bay towards a distant row of hills jutting into the sea. The *amazone* is seated side-saddle and a veil billows from her hat. Quick touches of paint between the horses' legs suggest the dust they kick up, while a few white-capped wavelets break on the shore. An overcast sky is evoked by means of long horizontal strokes of grey paint laid over beige across the upper third of the canvas. In his important study of Degas as a painter of landscapes, Richard Kendall was intrigued by the 'explosive entry' of the two riders into the picture, calling this small painting 'one of the most dramatic inventions of Degas' early career.'[1] He brilliantly and concisely situated the canvas in Degas's landscape oeuvre, showing that it is not the swiftly executed *plein-air* sketch that it might at first appear, but a carefully worked up painting, preceded by preparatory studies, that was probably completed some time after Degas had visited the site he depicts.[2]

That site is part of the Bay of Naples. Degas had family in the city, which he first visited in 1856. When he passed through briefly on his return to Paris early in 1860, he made a pencil sketch of the picturesque Castello San Elmo overlooking the bay, with the Castello dell'Ovo further out in the water. In the far distance he showed the distinctive profile of Vesuvius.[3] At about the same time, Degas made an upright drawing in ink and white gouache showing the two riders and traces of the same landscape, the sky filled with billowing clouds.[4] A low barrier to the right of the riders on that sheet establishes that they are following a path slightly elevated above the seashore, a detail that is left ambiguous in the painting. As he spent only a short time in Naples in 1860, it is probable that Degas executed this painting, in which he combined his two studies in different media, after he returned to France.

As Kendall noted, the landscape, with its distinctive architectural and natural features, is muted and generalised in the painting, and Vesuvius is suppressed. As he also recognised, the artist inserted the figure of the *amazone* and her horse into a quite different pictorial context in *On the Racecourse* (Basel, Offentliche Kunstsammlung), a painting set in Normandy which he probably executed the following year.[5] This borrowing was a strategy that Degas refined and adapted throughout his life. *CR*

1 New York and Houston 1994, p. 63.

2 For Kendall's analysis, on which this discussion is based, ibid., pp. 61–5.

3 The pencil sketch is Degas Notebook 19, pp. 6 and 7 (Paris, Bibliothèque Nationale); ibid., fig. 49.

4 That sketch is Degas Notebook 18, p. 55 (Paris, Bibliothèque Nationale); ibid., fig. 51.

5 The painting is ibid., fig. 52.

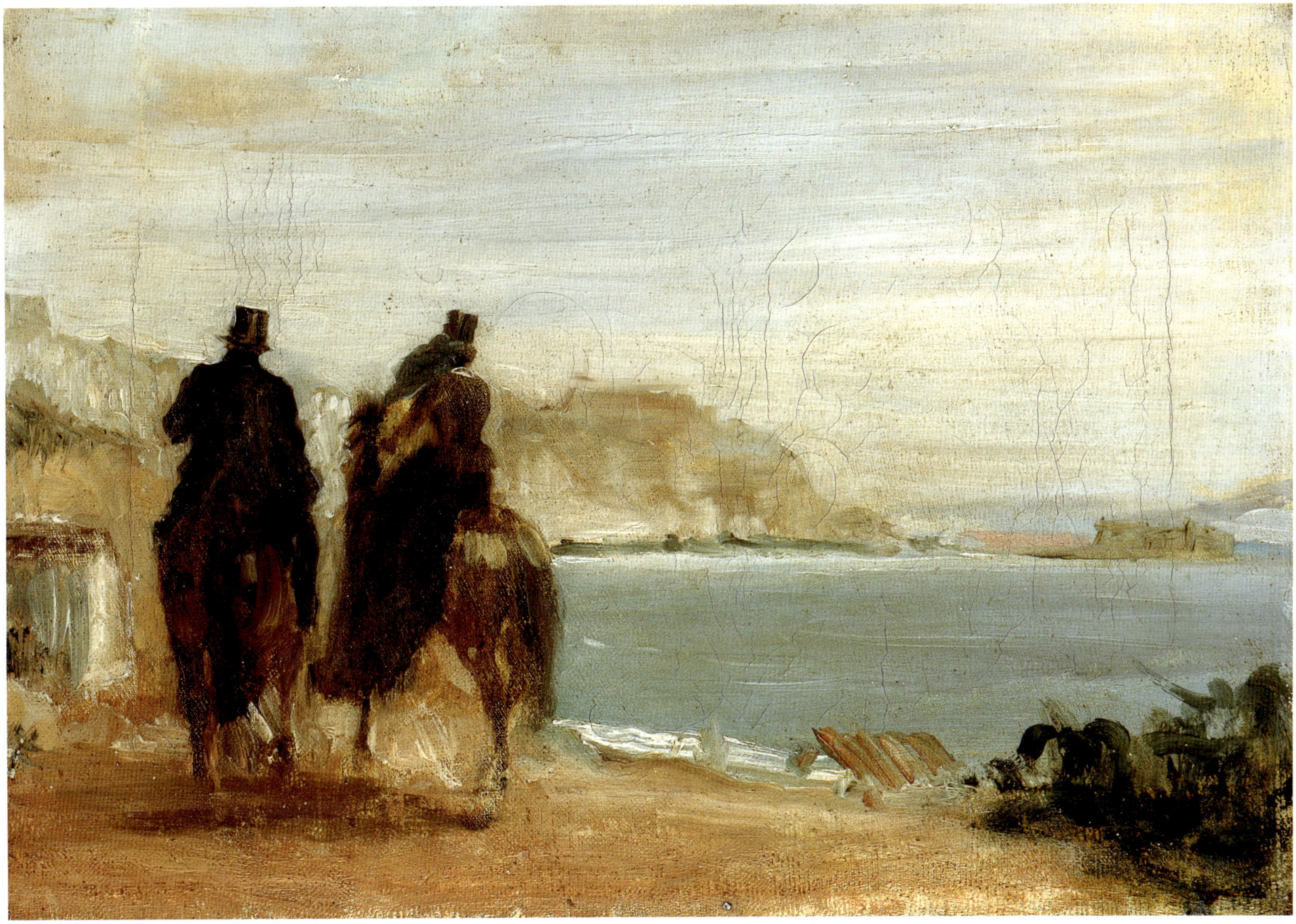

Denis, Simon (1755–1812)
23. *View of the Cascades at Tivoli*, about 1789–93
Oil on paper laid on linen, 38.6 x 25.8 cm

Technical note
Underdrawing is visible in many areas, particularly in the buildings and the rocks below.

Provenance
In the collection of Dr John Maxon, Chicago; bought from Mia Weiner, New York, in 1992 (as a French or Scandinavian artist).

Simon Denis was born in Antwerp and trained there with the landscape and animal painter H. J. Antonissen (1737–1794), before moving to Paris in 1775 to work under the genre painter and picture dealer Jean-Baptiste Lebrun (1769–1801). Thanks to Lebrun, Denis was able to make his first visit to Italy in 1786. His talent as a landscape painter was quickly recognised in Rome, where his ability to paint interesting light effects and his convincing observation of detail won him membership of the Academy of St Luke in 1803. After marrying a Roman woman he decided to stay in Italy. He travelled between Rome and Naples, where he finally settled on being appointed court painter to Joseph Bonaparte in 1806, a position he held until his death in 1812. In addition to academic landscapes reminiscent of Claude Lorrain's classical canvases, Denis painted wonderfully free and vibrant *plein-air* oil sketches, becoming one of the most expressive landscape artists of the late eighteenth century. His ability to render glowing colour and capture elusive light effects as they occur can be seen in his sketch *Sunset in the Roman Campagna* in the National Gallery, London (fig. 5).

The town of Tivoli, or Tibur as it was known in Latin, lies thirty-two kilometres northeast of Rome, along the ancient Tiburtine road. A country retreat in

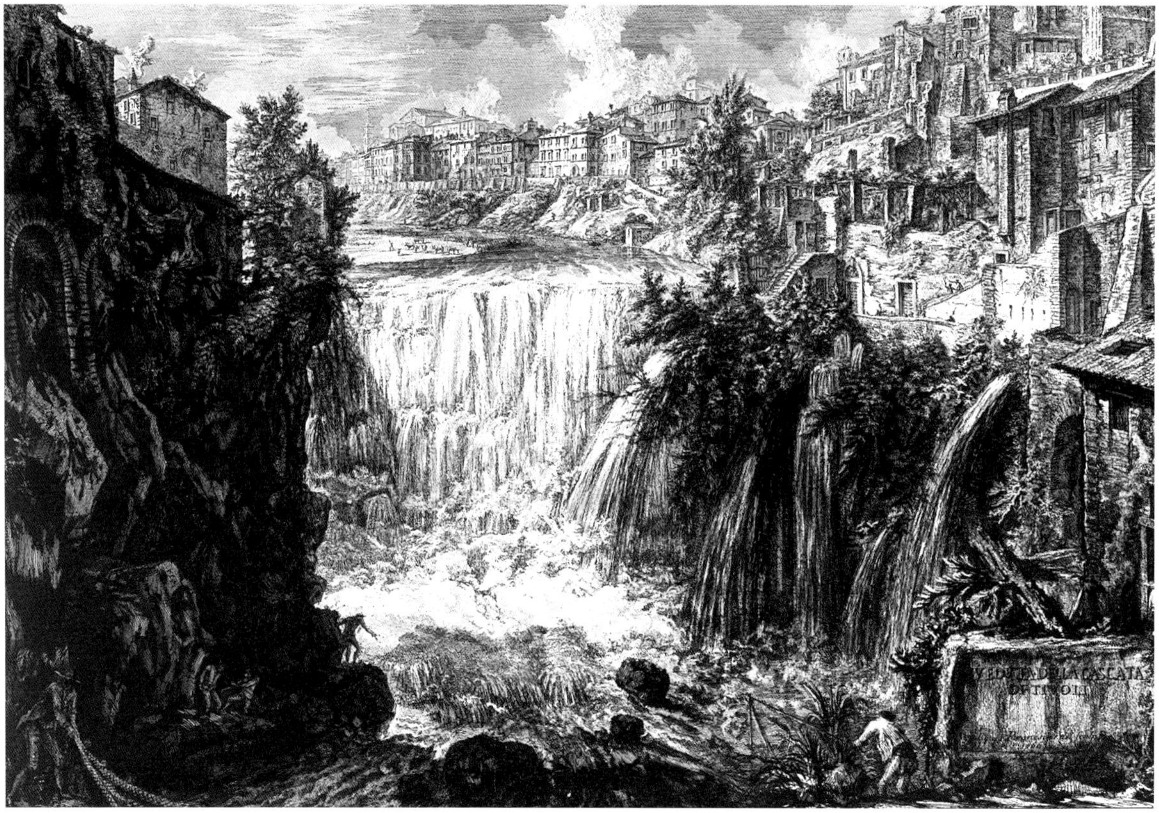

Fig 22 Giovanni Battista Piranesi, *The Cascades at Tivoli*, 1776. Etching, 47 x 70 cm. London, British Museum.

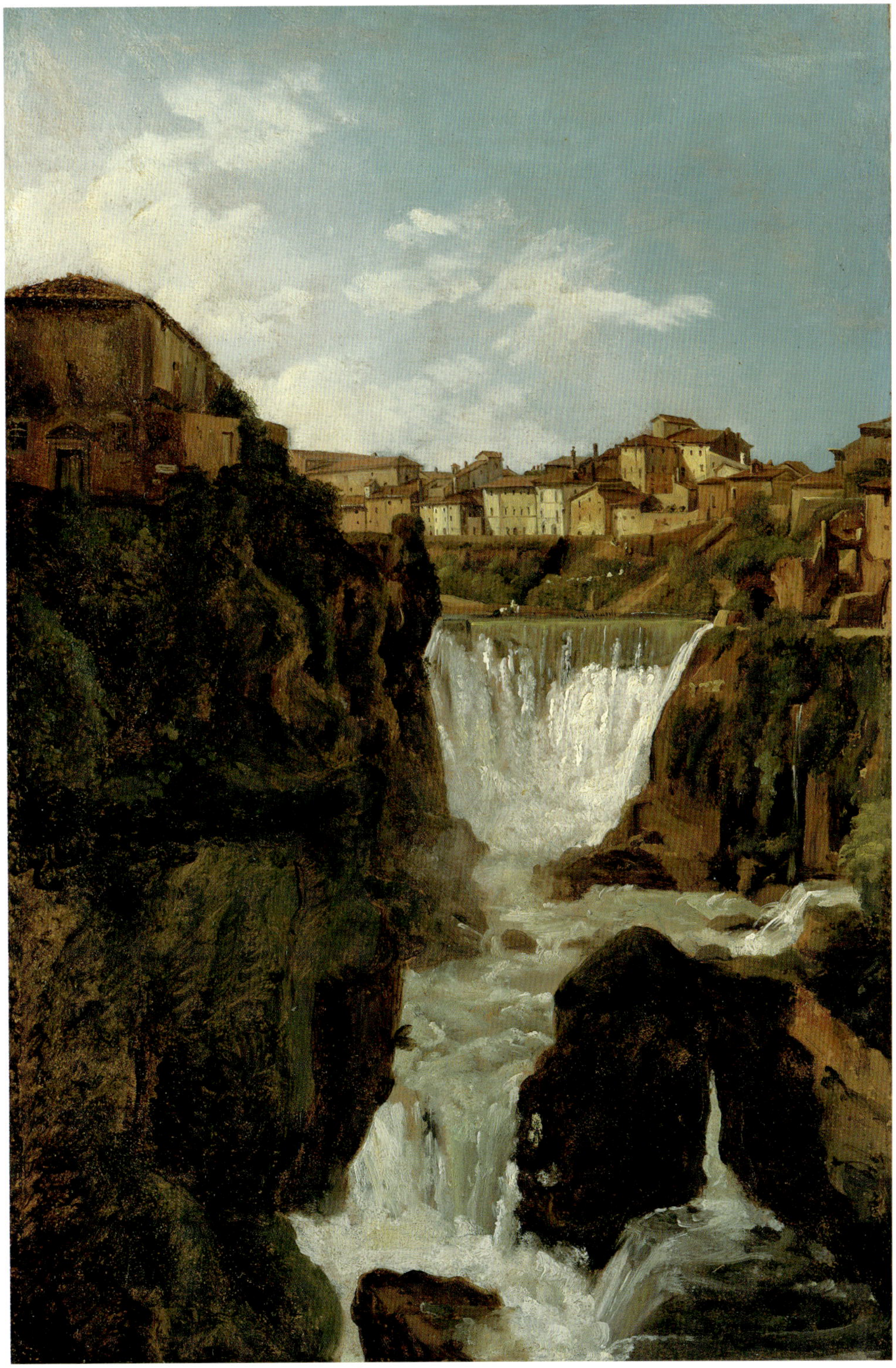

classical times for those escaping the summer heat and the political intrigues of Rome, it has been associated with poets and painters since antiquity. Maecenas, the patron of Horace and Virgil, built his villa there, commissioning poems from his *protégés* extolling the beauty of Tivoli. Later, painters were to evoke the natural beauty of the site with their brushes, particularly in the seventeenth century, when Claude Lorrain and Gaspard Dughet included views of Tivoli in their ideal landscape compositions. By the eighteenth and nineteenth centuries it was practically obligatory for artists visiting Italy to include Tivoli on their itinerary.

The main attractions at Tivoli were the cascades and watercourses just outside the town. Known as the Grande Cascata and the Cascatelle, these impressive waterfalls were formed by the waters of the Aniene river as it plunged down high cliffs into the valley below before joining the Tiber. In the sixteenth century, under Pope Sixtus V, a wall was built to steer the waters more directly towards the precipice, but aside from that intervention the falls were entirely natural and of stunning beauty. Artists depicted them from all angles, choosing different positions in order to convey their gushing and rumbling waters whose spray, illuminated by the sunlight, created extraordinary visual effects ranging from rainbows to colours of fire.

As the guidebook writer Vasi remarks, artists were especially captivated by the 'agreeable and enchanting contrasts' of the light as it fell on the whiteness of the cascading waters plunging down onto the gigantic rocks at the base of the falls.[1] Panoramic views could be obtained from the belvedere on the Via delle Cascatelle, where one could look across the Grande Cascata over to the immense vaulted arches of the structure known as the Villa Maecenas, which was in fact the foundations of an ancient temple complex. In the distance lay the flat Campagna, stretching out to the southwest where the dome of St Peter's was just visible in the distance.

This view is almost certainly taken from the Ponte San Rocco looking across the gushing waters towards the town of Tivoli in the distance. An English traveller known as Eustace noted that 'the first fall may be seen from the windows of the inn or from the temple; but it appears to the greatest advantage from the bridge thrown over the narrow channel a little below it. From this bridge you may also look down into the shattered rock, and observe far beneath the writhings and agitation of the stream struggling through its rocky prison.'[2] This was a particularly popular view and often treated by artists, particularly Piranesi who

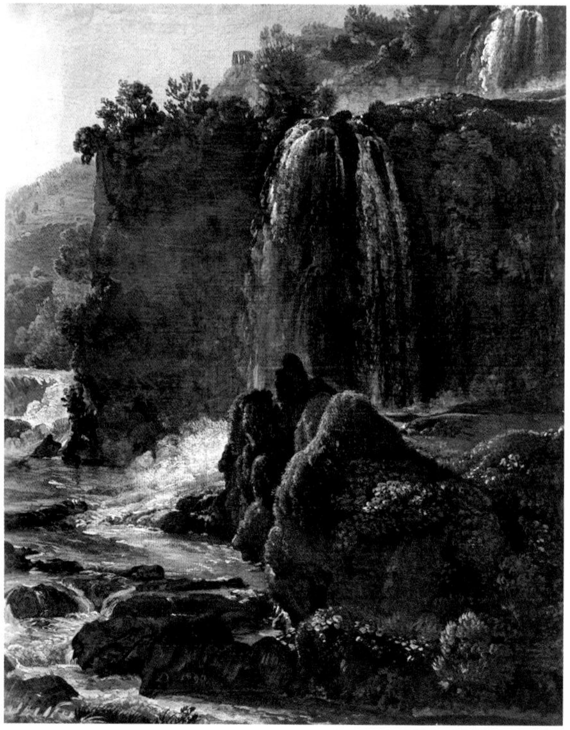

Fig 23 Simon Denis, *Cascatelle at Tivoli*, 1793. Oil on canvas, 47 x 39 cm. Antwerp, Koninklijk Museum voor Schone Kunsten.

1 Vasi 1797, Vol. 1, p. 622.
2 Quoted in Rome 1992, p. 230.
3 Vigée-Lebrun 1869, Vol. 1, p. 179. A sketch by Denis in a German private collection shows Vigée-Lebrun drawing under a tree near the falls with her daughter.
4 The sketch is monogrammed and dated 'D. 1793', with an inscription on the back *Cascatelles a Tivoly il y avoit peu d'eau. Si. Denis.* See Antwerp 1874, p. 114.
5 Brussels 1985–6, p. 299.

interpreted it in one of his etchings (fig. 22). It offered the opportunity to contrast the cubic and symmetrical shapes of the buildings with the white foam of the waters and dark greens of the vegetation. To emphasise the tranquillity in the top half of the composition, the painter here has left the sky open and has included two washerwomen rinsing their laundry in the river just before it turns into a violent torrent.

The attribution to Simon Denis, tentatively suggested in the past, is confirmed here on the basis of stylistic comparisons with other oil sketches he executed while visiting the falls at Tivoli. Denis is known to have visited Tivoli on two occasions. He was there in 1789, with the celebrated French portrait painter Elisabeth Vigée-Lebrun and her daughter, and François Ménageot, director of the French Academy at Rome.[3] A signed and dated oil sketch on paper of the Cascatelle confirms that he returned to Tivoli in 1793 for another sketching session (fig. 23).[4] At that time, Denis was probably getting together a series of sketches which he could use for a panoramic view of Tivoli, commissioned along with seven other landscapes of the Roman Campagna by Friederich von Reventlow to decorate his castle in Schleswig-Holstein.[5] The Antwerp sketch shows a similar treatment to the present sketch in its loose depiction of rocks and greenery, letting the light-brown ground appear below. For the falling water, Denis has applied pure white dabs of paint, a characteristic of his technique apparent in other sketches, particularly in the *Falls at Terni* (fig. 24). The extensive underdrawing is visible to the naked eye – Denis seems to have sketched out the composition beforehand, and then filled it out in colour, a practice that was to prove influential for later painters. *XB*

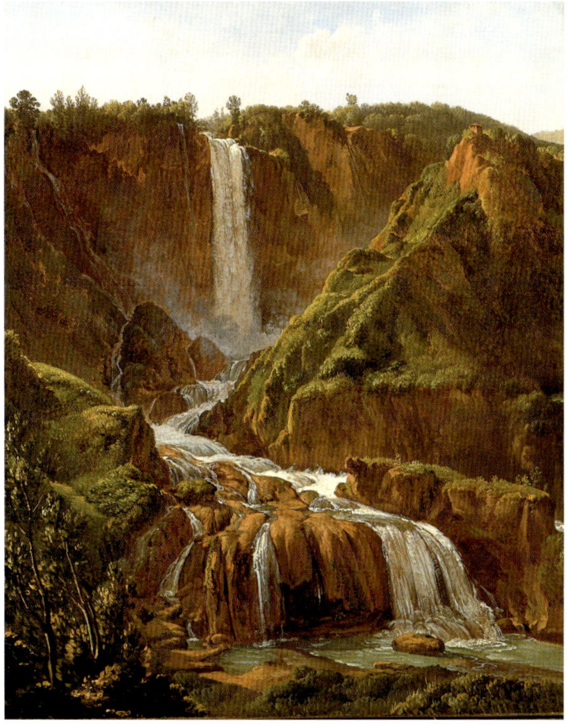

Fig 24 Simon Denis, *The Falls at Terni*, 1790s. Oil on canvas, 74 x 60 cm. James Mackinnon Collection.

Denis, Simon (1755–1812)
24. *A Torrent at Tivoli*, about 1789–93
Oil on paper laid on a plastic support, 21.2 x 37.8 cm

Inscriptions
Signed and inscribed in ink on the reverse
à Tivoly, Sn Denis
In pencil on the top right-hand corner
Dame Sam Sebastian.

Provenance
Bought from Hazlitt, Gooden and Fox, London, in 1978.

Exhibitions
London 1978, no. 2; Cambridge and London 1980–1, no. 34; Washington, Brooklyn and St Louis 1996–7, no. 35.

Literature
Brussels 1985–6, p. 298; Galassi 1991, pl. 115; Munich 1991, pl. 26.

In addition to making studies of sky and clouds and recording the changing effects of light on landscape, part of the *plein-air* artist's training included the painting of specific details from close up, such as dead tree trunks, leaves and running water. Close-up views of water rushing over rocks had become an essential part of such artists' repertoire by the late eighteenth century, and Denis seems to have excelled in this. Such sketches may have been done with the intention of using them for larger paintings or for reference purposes in the studio, but they seem also to have been painted as studies for their own sake. They enabled the artist to demonstrate his dexterity in reproducing in paint the effects of foaming water gushing over rocks, its translucency and the shadows beneath the surface. Valenciennes, whom Denis may have met in Rome in the late 1780s, recommended in his treatise on landscape painting, that in order for the artist 'to place truth in every portion of his works' he should 'make several studies of transparent water through which one sees small stones' and take into account the varying shapes of the stones caused by the friction of the running water.[1] By making such sketches, artists were able to develop their concentration and ability to record nature in full movement. To the twentieth-century eye, their simplicity in theme and execution often verges on abstraction, making them appear very direct and almost modern.

As the inscription indicates, Denis painted this sketch while visiting the falls at Tivoli, probably in the early 1790s when he also painted the *View of the Cascades at Tivoli* (cat. no. 23). He seems to have produced a series of such sketches, concentrating on running and falling water, as indicated in another sketch, inscribed '*au pied des cascatelles a Tivoli*' (fig. 25). It is quite probable that Denis used these as guides or for reference when painting larger compositions, particularly the series for Friedrich von Reventlow's castle in Schleswig-Holstein (see cat. no. 23). *XB*

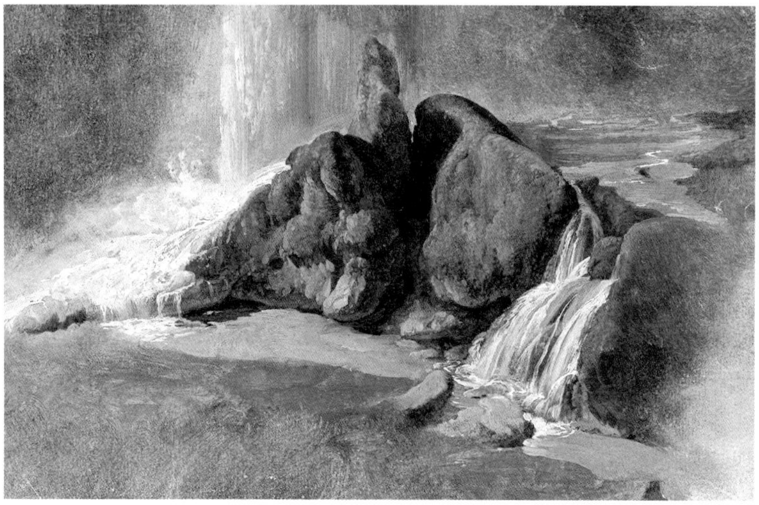

Fig 25 Simon Denis, *At the Foot of the Cascatelle at Tivoli*, Oil on paper, 21 x 33.3 cm. Karlsruhe, Staatliche Kunsthalle (inv. no. 2857).

1 Valenciennes 1800, 1973, p. 412.

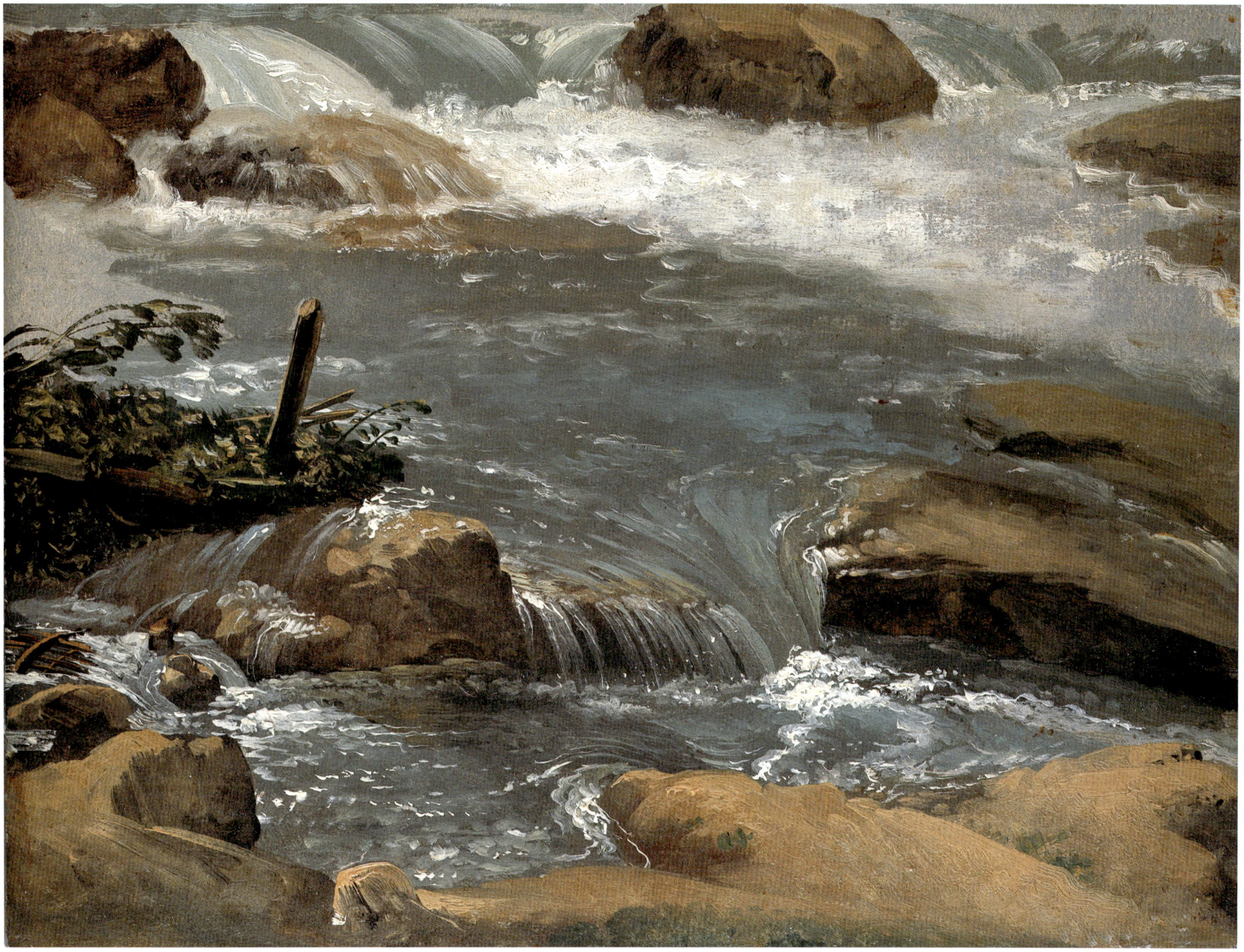

De Nittis, Giuseppe (1846–1884)
25. *Winter Landscape*, about 1880
Oil on panel, 21.4 x 26.8 cm

Provenance
Bought from Fischer et Keiner, Paris, date not recorded.

Under a leaden sky a solitary female figure makes her way across a snow-covered garden plot. Perhaps she is gathering twigs or branches, or returning from market via a wooden gate at the bottom of the garden, summarily indicated at lower right. The plot has only recently been planted, as is suggested by the row of four thin, bare trees at right, smaller than the trees in adjacent plots and more vulnerable to the snow and cold. A low trellis, meant to support climbing plants, pokes out of the snow and runs across the plot in a line parallel to the stone wall at left. The garden appears to be walled on three sides, but is open on the fourth to a tall suburban villa. Like the garden, the house too is new; its box-like proportions, red-brick construction decorated with stone quoining, and mansard roof are all typical of French domestic architecture of the late nineteenth century. A road runs in front of the house and passes beneath another new construction, a railway bridge at left. The setting would seem to be a distant suburb of Paris, only recently and rather haphazardly built-up and still relatively empty. Thanks to the railway, however, such sites were newly accessible to the capital. The foreground is unpainted and the artist's vantage point is high; perhaps he looked down on the scene from the upper window of a neighbouring house.

When this oil sketch was acquired it carried no attribution. It can be associated, however, with the work of the Italian-born painter Giuseppe de Nittis. Trained in Naples and close to the Macchiaioli painters in his native country, De Nittis settled in Paris in 1868 where he befriended many of the Impressionist artists. He exhibited five paintings in the First Impressionist Exhibition of 1874, and was influenced by the work of his closest friend among the group, Edgar Degas. Like the Italian and French contemporaries with whom he allied himself, De Nittis was committed to a naturalistic art that explored the changing play of light. He often painted out of doors on small wooden panels, as here, covering them quickly with thin layers of colour deftly evoking atmospheric effects. He frequently painted snow scenes, almost monochromatic works in tones of white and grey, animated with a few touches of colour. Such images often show solitary figures in snow-swept streets or parks. Like such contemporaries as Jean Béraud and Norbert Goeneutte, he specialised in depictions of the newly constructed areas of Paris and its suburbs. More than them, however, De Nittis experimented with audacious compositions in which strong diagonals cut into the pictorial space, as with the stone wall here. Influenced by Japanese prints, he often left large open areas in his pictures, arranging buildings around the perimeter.[1]
CR

1 For a recent study of the artist, see Milan and Bari 1990.

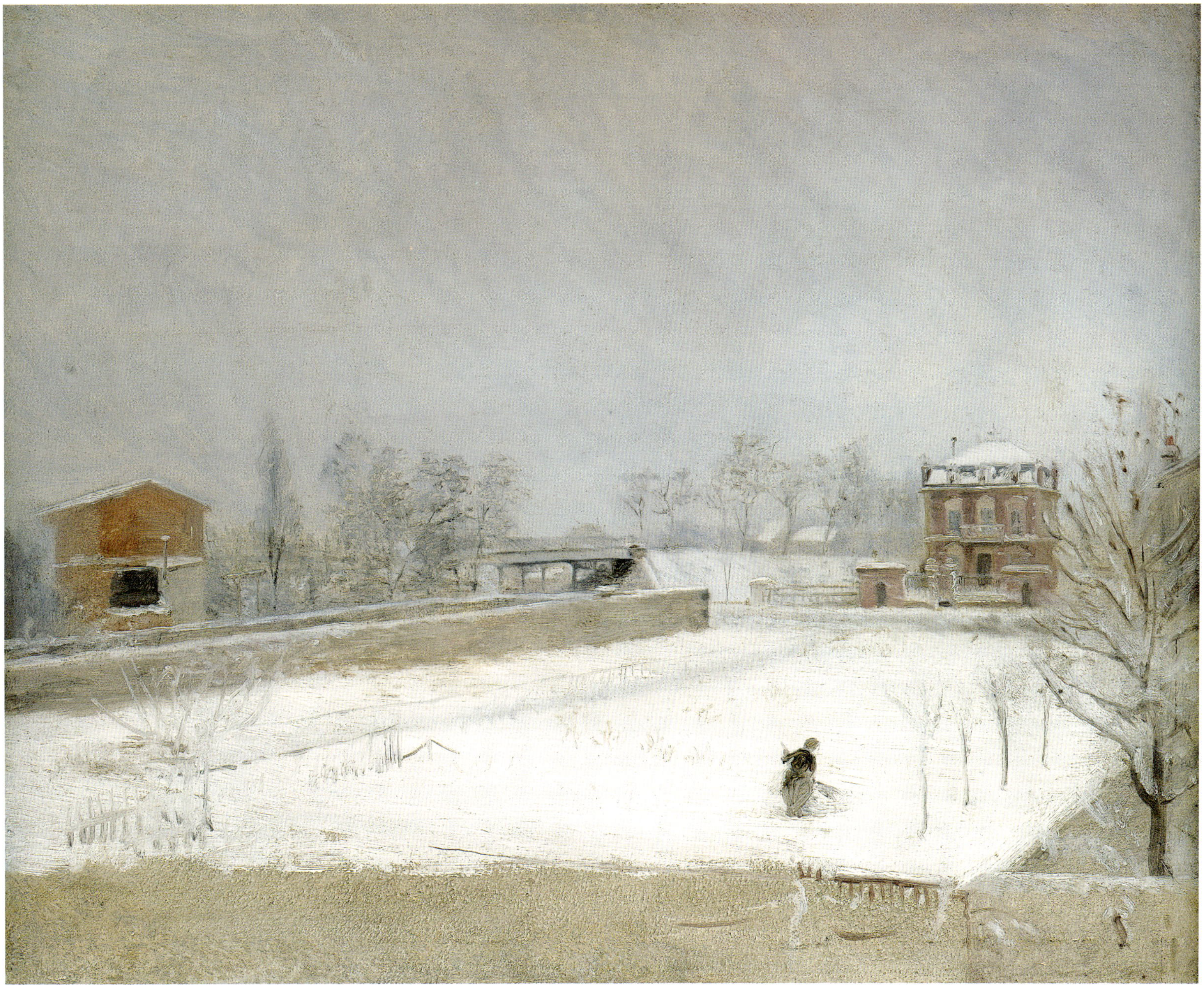

Desportes, François (1661–1743), attributed to

26. *Study of Two Trees*, about 1700

Oil on paper laid on cardboard, 27.1 x 39.2–40.2 cm

Inscriptions

Sticker on reverse *O 11*. Inscription from an old print stuck onto the frame *MUS INTEREA CELERI NOS L London, W. IUDIMUS HORA III Austriaco Magno Hecturiae Duci Joannes Volpato, et Raphael Morghen D.D.D.*

Provenance

Bought from James Mackinnon, London, in 1993 (as French School, eighteenth-century).

The attribution of this beautiful, fresh study of two intertwining tree trunks has proven to be one of the most elusive of any work in the Gere Collection. There is not even a strong consensus on its country of origin, much less on the century in which it was painted. When acquired the sheet was ascribed to a French artist working in the first half of the eighteenth century. Names such as Jean-Baptiste Oudry (1686–1755), Nicolas de Largillière (1656–1746) and Jean-François de Troy (1679–1752) have been proposed. François Bourne, on the other hand, has suggested that the use of brilliant highlights on the sheet would indicate an earlier date, and possibly an artist with a living memory of Peter Paul Rubens (1577–1640).[1] He proposed the name of the Flemish painter of landscape and woodland scenes, Jacques Fouquier (1590–1659). Alastair Laing has also seen it as a Flemish work of the seventeenth century and has suggested the name of Pieter Boel (1622–1674).[2]

The present author offers the tentative suggestion that the work is by a French artist, perhaps François Desportes or someone in his large studio, where skill in rendering such naturalistic motifs was highly valued. Such studies were incorporated into the backgrounds of Desportes's hunting landscapes and the 'portraits' of royal hunting dogs that he executed between 1702 and 1714. An inventory of the contents of Desportes's studio, drawn up in 1784 by his nephew Nicolas Desportes, includes mention of '49 sheets (studies of tree trunks and plants)'.[3] Like Desportes, one of the great innovators in the history of the oil sketch, the author of the present sheet was particularly drawn to twisting, characterful tree trunks.[4] The first public exhibition of the study may help to resolve the issue, or it may bring even more names into play. *CR*

1 Oral communication.

2 Oral communication.

3 Cited in Paris 1982–3, p. 59.

4 Compare the sketch with works by Desportes illustrated in ibid, cat. nos. 59, 64, 67.

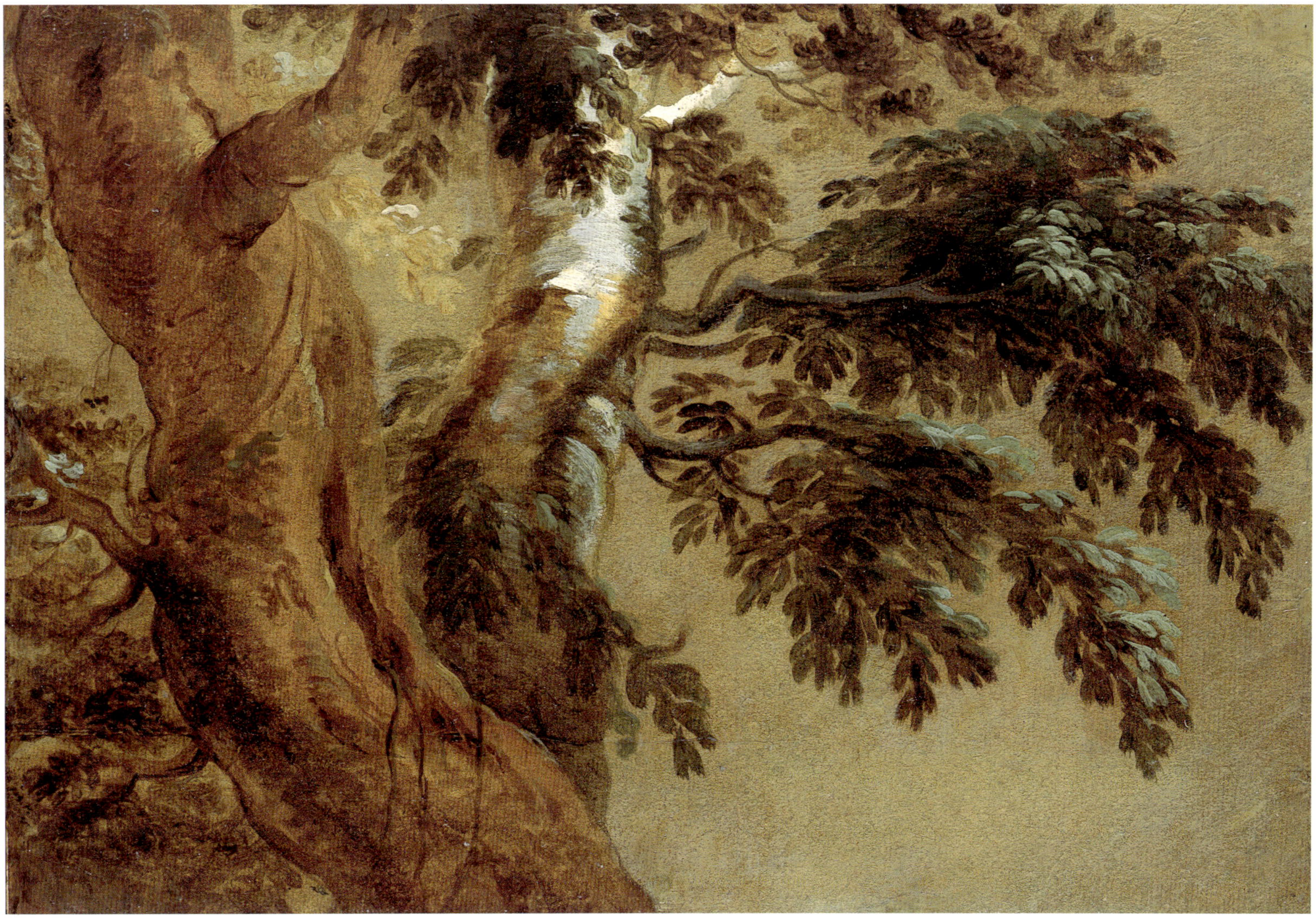

Dunouy, Alexandre-Hyacinthe (1757–1841)

27. *Panoramic View of the Bay of Naples*, about 1783–9 or 1810–15

Oil on paper laid on canvas, 29.2 x 45.2 cm

Technical note

Some pentimenti are apparent in the lighthouse and in one of the buildings at the bottom right of the composition. Infra-red photography reveals underdrawing in some of the buildings, particularly those above the castle on the right. Indications that the sketch was originally squared-up are apparent at the bottom of the composition, where paint was not applied. The view is painted on two sheets of paper of a printed form stuck together: *Gardes Françoise, Magazin Générale de l'Habillement – Année 1783 – Mois de Janvier – Recette en Deniers – Dépense en Deniers*. It appears to be a listing of military equipment or dress for the French army.

Provenance

Sold at Christie's, London, 20 June 1979, lot. 253 (as Jean-Joseph-Xavier Bidauld); bought from John Lishawa, London, in 1980.

Exhibitions

Washington, Brooklyn and St Louis 1996–7, no. 5.

The view shown in this wonderfully atmospheric sketch is probably from a rooftop just below the Spanish quarter in Naples. This kind of view, with its concentration on the varying volumes of the architecture massed against each other and dramatic lighting effects, bears many affinities with the oil studies that Thomas Jones was painting in the early 1780s while in Naples. The painter here is looking southeast across the Bay of Naples, towards the hills of the Sorrento peninsula. Great care has been taken in the structure of the composition, which contains all the elements that interest a *plein-air* sketcher. The green foliage in the foreground, possibly surrounding a cloister, contrasts with the almost cubic architecture of the houses and roof terraces.

Emerging from these, prominent buildings break the skyline and give additional structure to the composition. The fifteenth-century castle built by Alfonso V of Aragon, known as the Castel Nuovo, is strategically placed on the right, with its northeastern façade bathed in the morning light, counterbalancing the dark tones of the steeple and dome of the church of San Diego. The eighteenth-century lighthouse, now destroyed, appears at left of centre, balanced by the golden-tiled dome on the right, possibly that of the no-longer extant church of Santa Maria dei Poveri. Visible to the naked eye are pentimenti where the painter, dissatisfied with the original position of the lighthouse, moved it slightly to the left. The masts of the ships in the harbour, just apparent against the blue of the sea, lead the eye out towards the volcanic hills of Sorrento. The painter seems to have taken particular delight in depicting the contrast between the urban and the natural scenery through subtle lighting effects and the use of suggestive shapes in the architecture and the rolling hills.

Before the paper was laid onto the canvas it was observed that the sketch was painted on two sheets of paper stuck together, on one of which is printed a list of military equipment for the French army. At the top of this list is the date January 1783, providing a possible *terminus post quem* for the dating of this sketch. We might therefore presume that it was painted in the mid-1780s by a French hand. Soon after the sketch was acquired, Pierre Lamicq proposed Alexandre-Hyacinthe Dunouy (1757–1841) as a possible candidate.[1] This attribution was subsequently endorsed by Philip Conisbee and John Lishawa, who compared the sketch with other similar views of Naples and Italian hill towns made by Dunouy while he was in Italy in the 1780s. The manner in which the buildings, the windows and the wall textures are painted bears a strong resemblance to Dunouy's *Palazzo Reale and the Harbour, Naples* (New York, private collection). However, apart from a signed and dated painting of a *View of Sora* (1789; private collection), there is no proof he was in Naples in the 1780s.[2] It is therefore possible that Dunouy painted this sketch at a later date, between

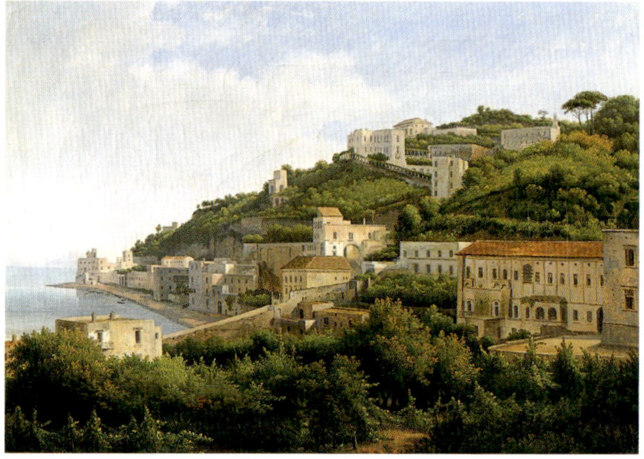

Fig 26 Alexandre-Hyacinthe Dunouy, *View of the Coast of Posillipo*, 1810–15. Oil on paper mounted on canvas, 33.3 x 46.7 cm. Private collection (Courtesy Didier Aaron, Inc.).

1 Dunouy's near contemporary, Jean-Joseph-Xavier Bidauld, also painting similar views in Italy between 1785 and 1790, was suggested by John Whiteley (oral communication).

2 Edinburgh 1986, p. 29: *View of Sora* is signed and dated by Dunouy in Rome, 1789. Sora is near Naples.

3 Sotheby's New York, 28 January 1999, lot. 338.

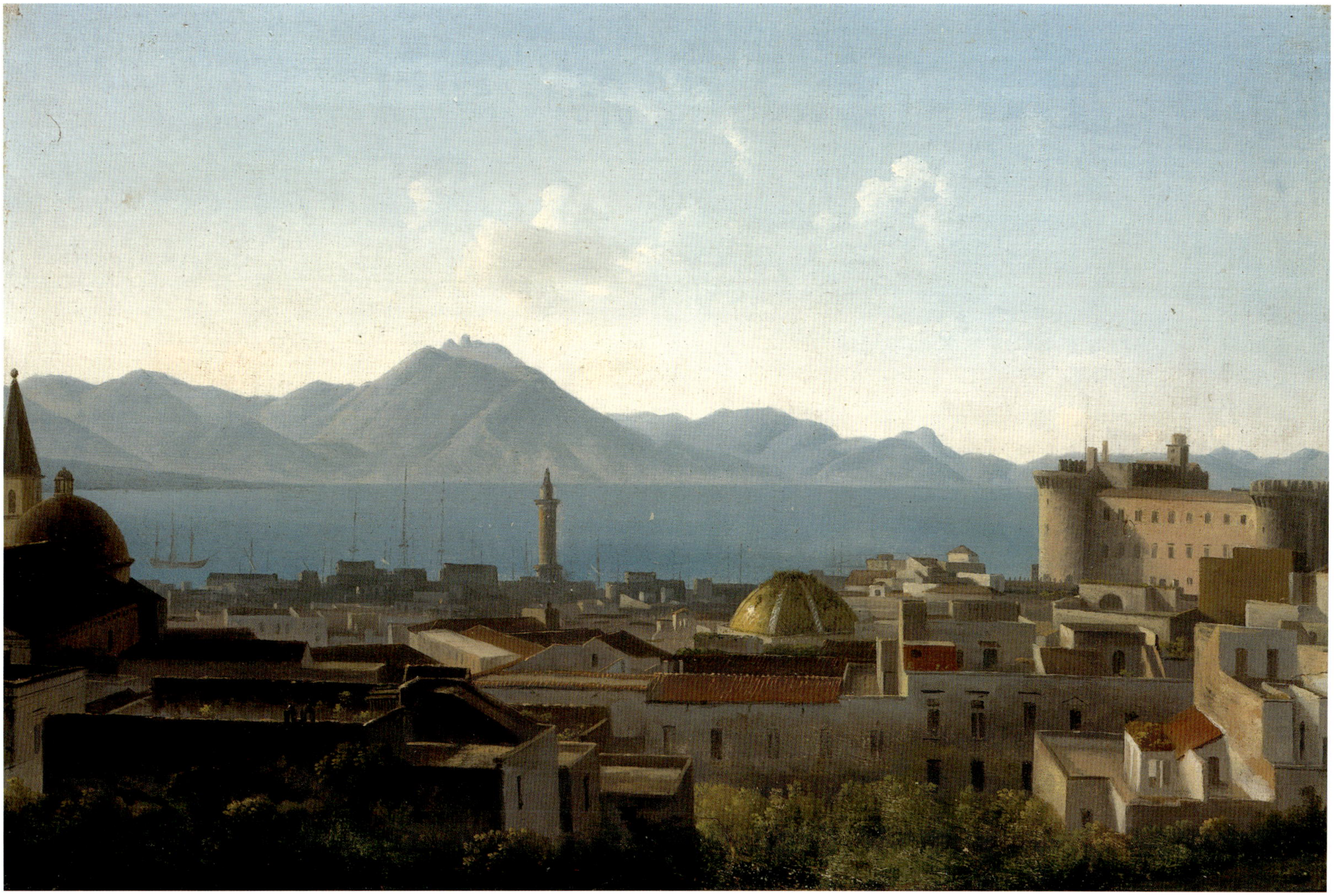

1810 and 1815, when he was definitely in Naples working for Caroline Murat. Two sketches datable to that period have strong affinities with the present sketch. One of these, a *View of the Coast of Posillipo* (fig. 26),[3] is similar in execution, particularly in the architecture and manner in which the windows are painted. The other, a *View of Vesuvius* (private collection) recalls the bluish haze of the mountains in the background. *XB*

FEARNLEY, Thomas (1802–1842)

28. *Coast Scene, possibly Capri,* about 1834

Oil on paper mounted on board, 22.2 x 34.9 cm

Inscriptions

Modern inscriptions on back of board

15116

75

Inscribed in pencil on the former mount in a nineteenth-century hand *T Fearnley*

Provenance

Bought from Abbott and Holder, London, date not recorded.

Exhibitions

Manchester and Cambridge 1993.

The grandson of a Yorkshireman, Fearnley was born in Norway and had his early artistic training there and in Denmark. He met his fellow Norwegian, the landscape painter and master of the oil sketch, Johan Christian Dahl (1788–1857), in 1826 and was much influenced by the eighteen months he spent working with him in Dresden during 1829 and 1830. Like Dahl, Fearnley alternated between oil sketches and larger, composed landscapes meant for exhibition. Dahl urged him to specialise in Norwegian scenes, but Fearnley was a peripatetic and convivial man, and not overly fond of the Norwegian climate. He travelled and sketched widely in Europe, including Italy, where he spent three years beginning in 1832. In a letter of 1836 to Dahl that must have shaken the earnest older master's confidence in Fearnley's commitment to working from nature, he indicated that he would be quite content to paint Norwegian scenes but remain in the Italian sunshine.[1] At the age of thirty-nine Fearnley contracted typhus and died.

During his years in Italy, Fearnley worked in Rome, where he was friendly with the German artists, and travelled to the south to sketch. The great rocky outcrop here recalls landscape features on the southern Italian coast. The organisers of the 1993 exhibition *Nature's Way* very tentatively proposed that it might represent a coastal scene on Capri, showing it in conjunction with two oil sketches of rocky coast inscribed *Capri* and dated September 1833.[2] It has also been suggested that the site is on the mainland near Naples, but the actual location still remains to be identified.

In a letter to Dahl Fearnley cited a series of Italian nature studies he had painted which he described as 'finished.'[3] The adjective could as well be applied here, as the surface of the paper is entirely covered in paint, and delicate strokes of colour have been carefully added to depict the water lapping the shore. Fearnley is at pains to depict the change in water colour from blue to brown as the wavelets approach the shore and begin to reflect the rock face. A thin mauve line and a few boats at the distant horizon are all that distinguish the blue of the water from that of the sky. The rock itself is more broadly handled in tones of brown and gold. While finished for an oil sketch, many of Fearnley's nature studies share this same quality. There is, however, nothing composed about this sketch. The artist delights in the abrupt bluntness of the rock, rounded by time and, as a deep line of shadow suggests, almost cleft in two. *CR*

1 Quoted in Manchester and Cambridge 1993, p.52, cat. no. 28.

2 Ibid., nos. 27, 28.

3 Ibid., p. 27, cat. no. 27.

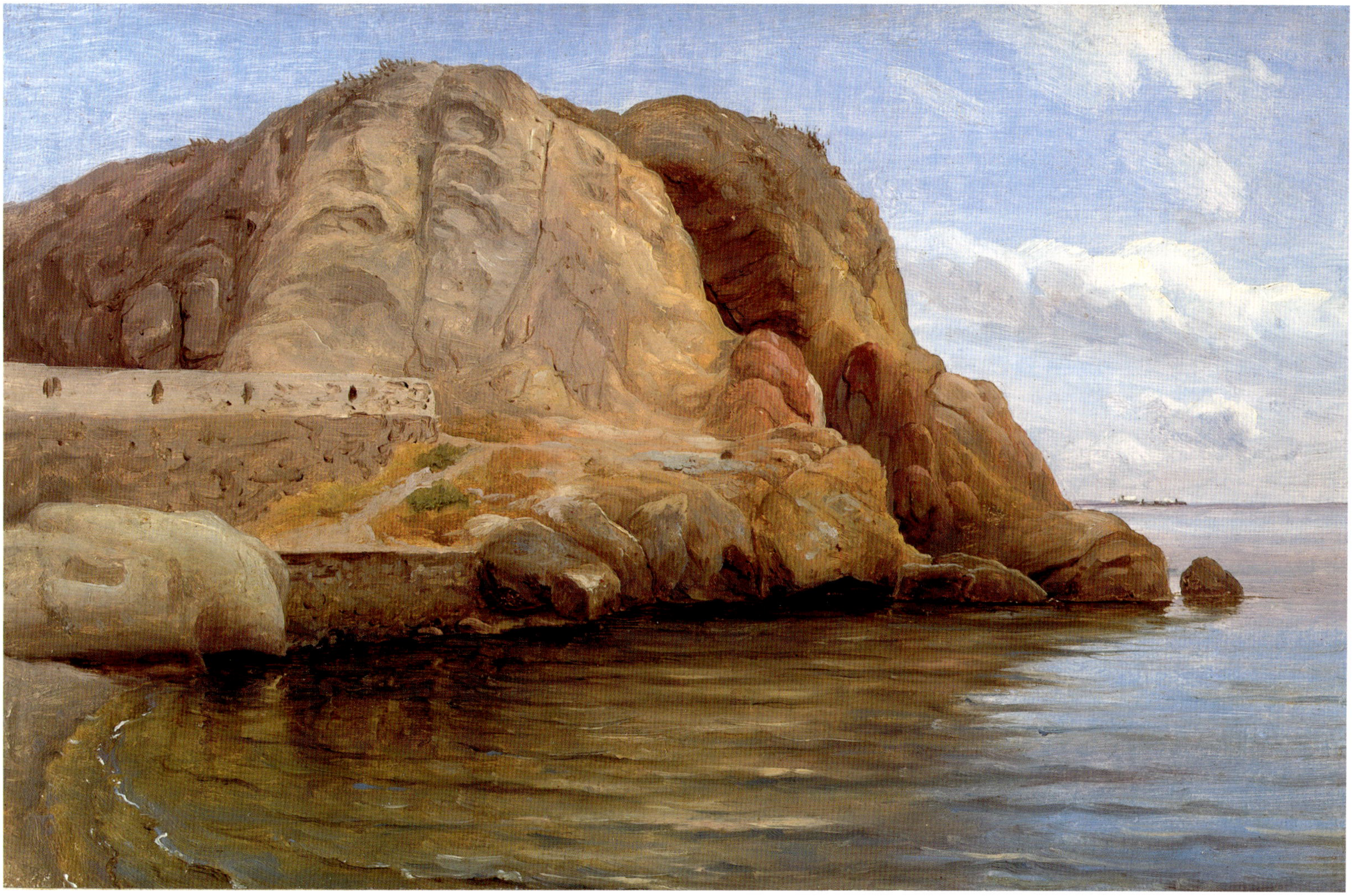

Fleury, Léon (1804–1858)

29. *View in the Villa Borghese: The Casino del Muro Torto and the Aqueduct of the Acqua Felice,* about 1827–30 Oil on paper laid on canvas, 15.5 x 26.0 cm

Inscriptions

Various inscriptions and labels on the back of the stretcher read: *Vente Cals*; label *7014*; *(Leon Fleury)*; *F.A.L. Fleury 1804–1858, Vue 15 x 25*; label *45/18*

Technical note

Infra-red photography (fig. 27) has revealed extensive underdrawing for a different composition, particularly in the area of the sky.

Provenance

Possibly sold at the Vente Cals on 16–17 February, 1881; bought from the Hazlitt Gallery, London, in 1970.

Exhibitions

Cambridge and London 1980–1, no. 92.

Literature

Galassi 1991, p. 109, pl. 127.

The attribution to Fleury is based on the inscriptions on the back of the stretcher. From these we can presume that the landscape painter, Adolphe-Félix Cals (1810–1880), acquired this oil sketch at the sale of Fleury's atelier in 1859. The sketch was then sold when Cals's collection was auctioned in 1881.

Léon Fleury trained under Hersent and the landscape painter Jean-Victor Bertin (a student of Valenciennes) before leaving for Italy in 1827 to join Corot and Caruelle d'Aligny. He worked closely with Corot, accompanying him on sketching expeditions to the Apennines. Their technique and style were so similar that their oil sketches were often confused by contemporaries. Corot is on record as remarking that 'we do not know whether Fleury or I painted this sketch.'[1] Fleury stayed on in Italy, making occasional trips to Naples, until his return to Paris in 1830. There he exhibited at the Salon of 1831 a group of seven small oils painted in Italy, which were well received. Bought by King Louis-Philippe, they are now in the Château de Compiègne. Fleury subsequently enjoyed a successful career as a landscape painter specialising in views of the forest of Fontainbleau.

This picture is one of his quickly executed oil sketches, or *pochades*. It was probably painted between 1827 and 1830 while he was in Rome. The view shows part of the Villa Borghese, with the Casino del Muro Torto, or orangery, on the right and part of the Acqua Felice aqueduct on the left. The motif, which combined ancient ruins and effulgent, leafy nature,

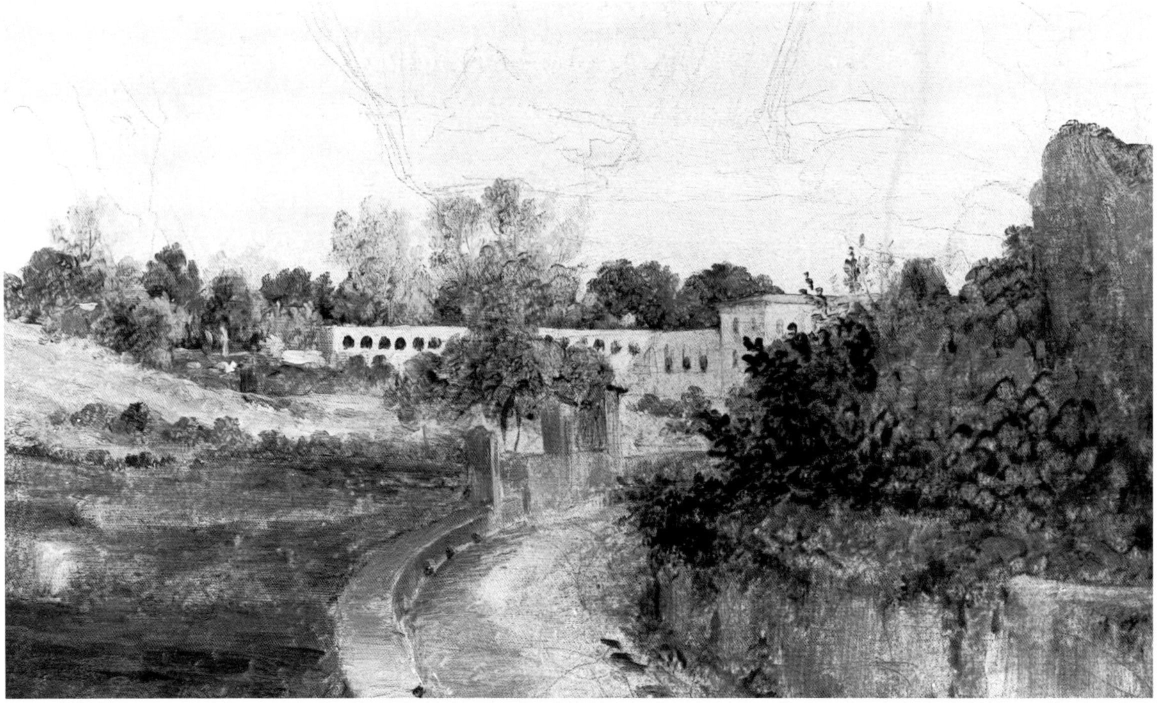

Fig 27 Léon Fleury, *View in the VIlla Borghese: The Casino del Muro Torto and the Aqueduct of the Acqua Felice*, infra-red photograph.

1 'Nous ne savons plus qui de Fleury ou moi a fait cette étude.' Quoted in Harambourg 1985, p. 147.

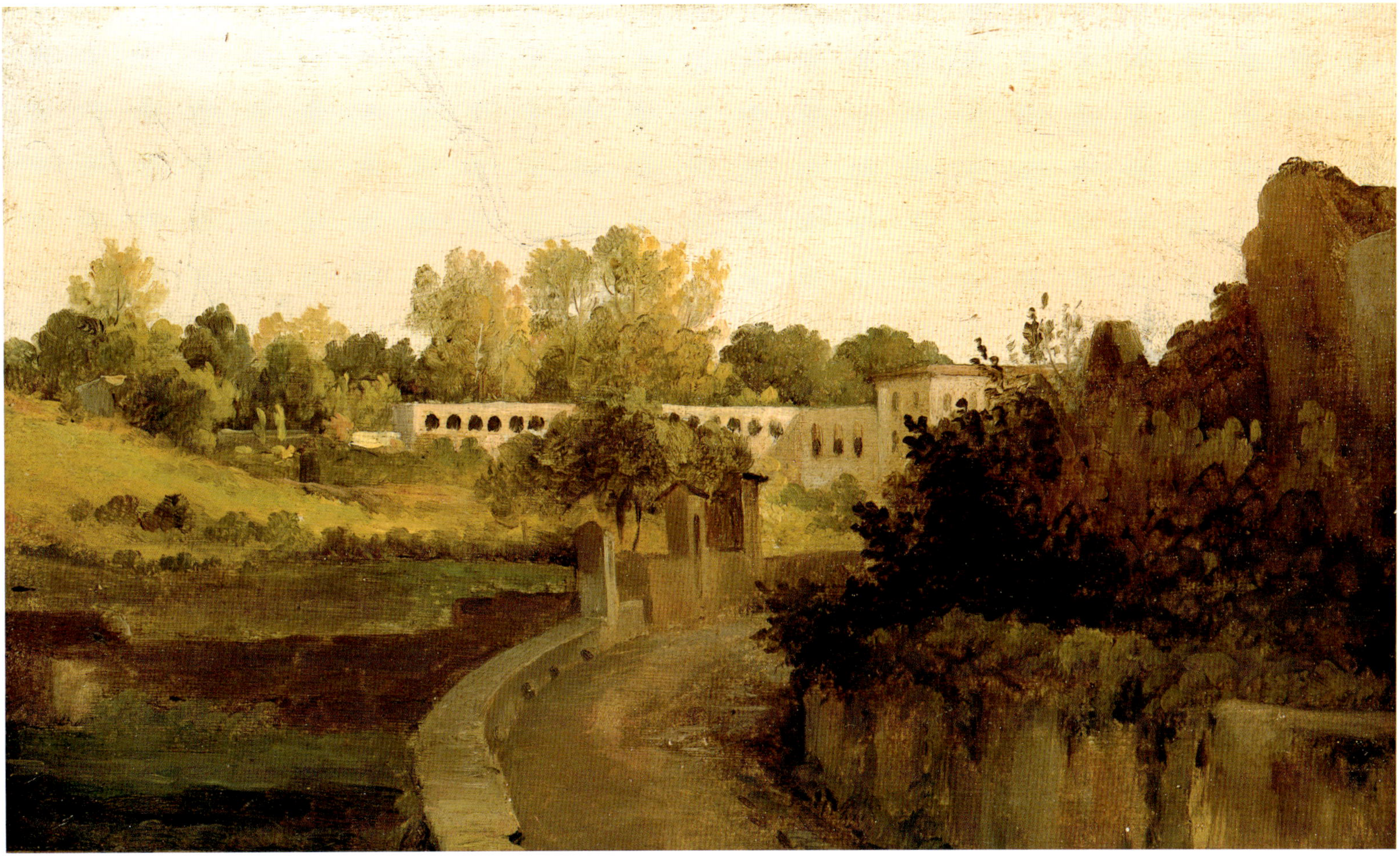

had proved popular with painters in Rome since the time of Valenciennes. Although Fleury seems to have recorded the view in a spontaneous manner, using quick brushstrokes for the foliage and the architecture, his viewpoint has been carefully chosen in order to create a balanced composition. He has positioned the path in the middle of the foreground, leaving our eye to follow its graceful curve upwards, around the rocks and into the background. The picture is divided by a strong diagonal moving from the bottom left to the top right, separating the dark shadow of the foreground from the beautifully sunlit background. *XB*

French School

30. *The Temple of the Sibyl at Tivoli seen from the Gorge*, undated

Oil on paper laid on canvas, 28.7 x 18.7 cm

Inscriptions

Inscribed on the original stretcher in ink *Hubert Robert – Tivoli*; in another hand *Temple de Vesta ? Tivoli*. Chalk inscription on the stretcher *G60666*

Provenance

Bought from John Lishawa, London, in 1997 (as Louis Gauffier).

Exhibition

London 1988, no. 16 (as Louis Gauffier).

Literature

Galassi 1991, p. 110, pl. 128 (as Bidauld ?).

Situated on the edge of the cliff dominating the valley below Tivoli is the famous antique Temple of Vesta, commonly but wrongly known as the Temple of the Tiburtine Sibyl (fig. 28). This small circular building, dating from the last years of the Roman republic, was originally composed of eighteen fluted Corinthian columns, of which ten only remain, supporting an entablature with a frieze of bucrania (ox-skulls), garlands and rosettes. Converted into a church known as Santa Maria della Rotonda in the Middle Ages, it was admired from the seventeenth century onwards as a fine example of antique architecture. Nearby stands the original Temple of the Sibyl, visible in this picture on the right. Consisting of a rectangular temple with a tetrastyle Ionic façade, this temple was also converted into a church, known until 1884 as San Giorgio.

The legend of the Tiburtine Sibyl is a combination of local legends and a tale taken from Ovid's *Metamorphoses*. The Sibyl is believed to have been Ino, sister of Semele, who was Jupiter's lover and the mother of Bacchus. Jupiter's jealous wife, Juno, having succeeding in eliminating Semele, was anxious also to remove Ino. After various adventures and terrible misfortunes, Ino was washed up on the shores of the Tiber and made a prophetess by Hercules and the prophetess Carmenta. The temple at Tivoli was built in her honour. Tradition has it that her effigy was found at the bottom of the cliff and taken to the Capitol in Rome.

The dating of this sketch is problematic. Most scholars have rejected the attribution to Hubert Robert, whose name appears inscribed on the back of the stretcher. John Lishawa, having exhibited it as Louis Gauffier, now proposes Claude-Joseph Vernet (1714–1789) as a possible candidate.[1] Vernet did sketch outdoors and encouraged his contemporaries to do likewise, drawing and painting from nature. We know for certain that he painted oil sketches, as the sale of his estate after his death in 1789 included '33 Tableaux & Etudes, peints d'après nature, tant à Rome qu'à Naples . . .'[2] Stylistically, the sketch here is similar to the backgrounds of the landscapes he executed in Italy in the 1740s and compares particularly well with two small views of Rome of the *Castel Sant'Angelo* and the *Ponte Rotto*, both in the Louvre. Philip Conisbee[3] and other scholars, however, have suggested a later date, preferring to associate the style and manner of execution with sketches by Bidauld and Gauffier executed in the late 1780s.[4] Nevertheless, the attribution remains an open question. *XB*

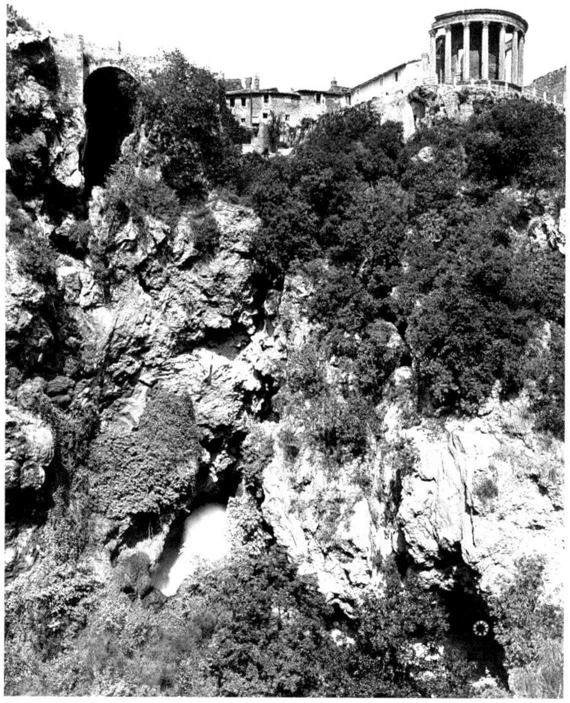

Fig 28 The Temple of Vesta at Tivoli (photo: Alinari).

1 Another possible oil sketch by Vernet was exhibited in Washington, Brooklyn and St Louis 1996–7, no. 2, p. 113.

2 Ibid.

3 Oral communication.

4 The attribution to Bidauld suggested by Galassi was based on similarities with the view of the *Gorge at Civita Castellana* (Stockholm Nationalmuseum). Although the Gauffier attribution was rejected by Jean-François Mejanes who was writing a catalogue raisonné on the artist, the sketch was thought to have strong affinities with an oil sketch on paper by Gauffier of a *View of the Monastery of Santa Scholastica at Subiaco*, in the Musée des Beaux-Arts in Lille (see London 1993).

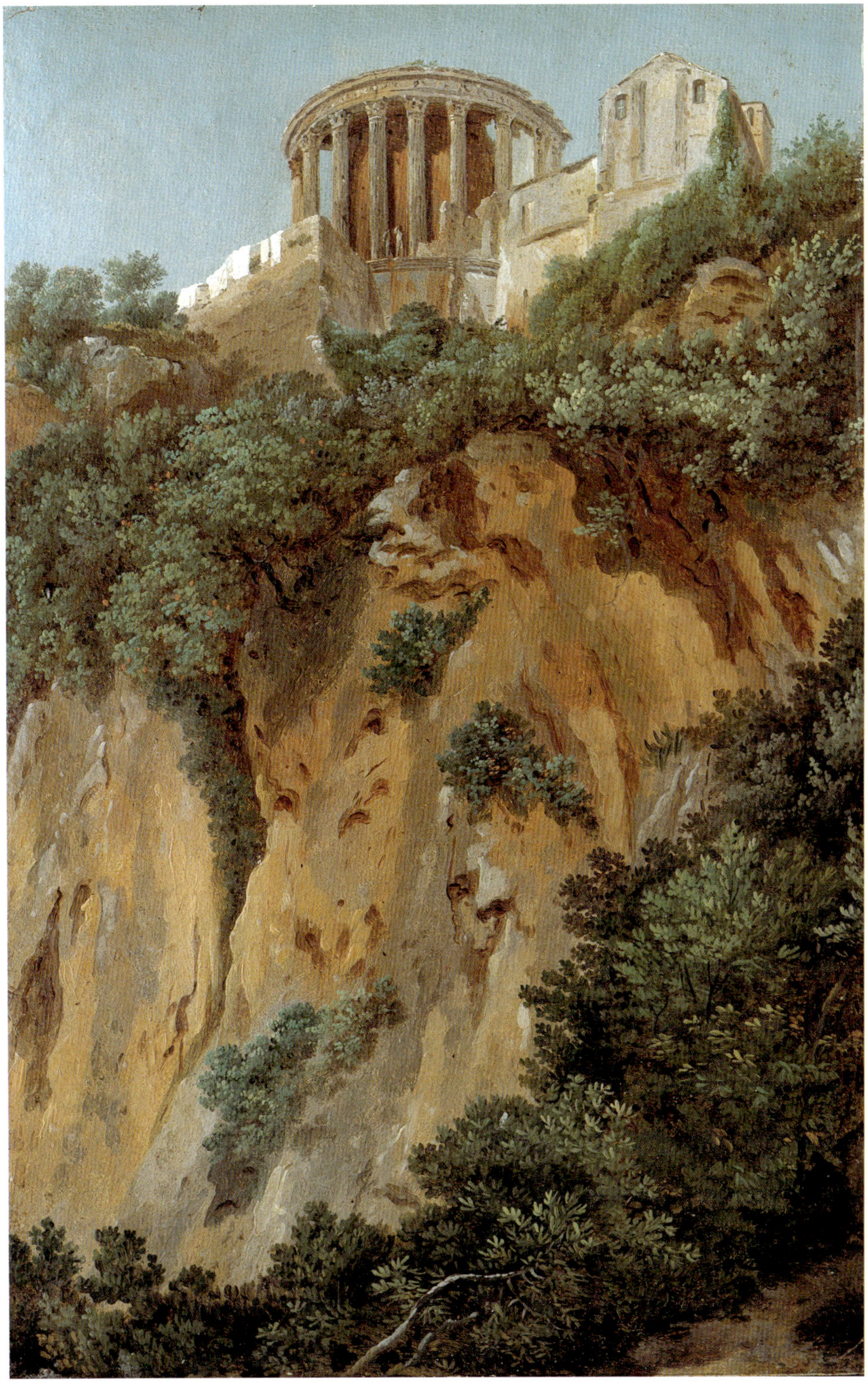

French School

31. *Panoramic Landscape with a Farmhouse*, 1780s–1820s

Oil on canvas, 17.7 x 40.4 cm

Provenance

Bought from William Drummond, Covent Garden Gallery, London, in 1980.

This sketch was probably painted in the Roman Campagna. The mountains in the distance are similar to those found to the north of Rome on the way to Civita Castellana, and there appears to be an Italian farmhouse on the right. However, the exact location of the site, which at one point was considered to be either in France or in Spain, remains to be resolved.

Various attributions have been proposed. Some have considered it an early example of a French *plein-air* oil sketch from the early eighteenth century, mainly because of its resemblance in style and handling to oil sketches by François Desportes (1661–1743), most of which are now in the Musée National de la Céramique, in Sèvres.[1] Desportes is known to have gone out into the countryside around Paris and along the River Seine, armed with a makeshift easel, to sketch freely with diluted oils. However, he is not documented as having been to Italy, and since most of his sketches are on paper it is unlikely that this painting is by him. In addition, a close comparison between Desportes's work and this sketch shows differences in execution and conception. Other suggestions have included the French painter Michel-Ange Houasse (1680–1730), who travelled to Spain, where he worked as court painter to the Bourbon king, Philip V, in 1715. There he executed a series of landscape paintings around Madrid, including some of royal palaces.[2] However, these bear little stylistic resemblance to this painting and the landscape here does not look like the countryside around Madrid.

Although it is difficult to date this sketch, it is likely that it was actually painted at a much later date, between the 1780s and 1820s.[3] The author was almost certainly familiar with Valenciennes's treatise and teaching techniques, and had probably seen his oil sketches, executed while he was in Italy in the late 1770s. The manner in which the house is rapidly sketched in, and the treatment of the foliage, applied with thick brushstrokes, is reminiscent of Valenciennes's *View of the Pyramid of Cestia* (Paris, Musée du Louvre). However, the present sketch does not have the strength or freedom of execution found in Valenciennes's oil sketches, making it difficult to attribute it definitively. *XB*

1 Paris 1982–3, pp. 58–63.

2 Madrid 1981–2, no. 33.

3 Philip Conisbee has supported this opinion.

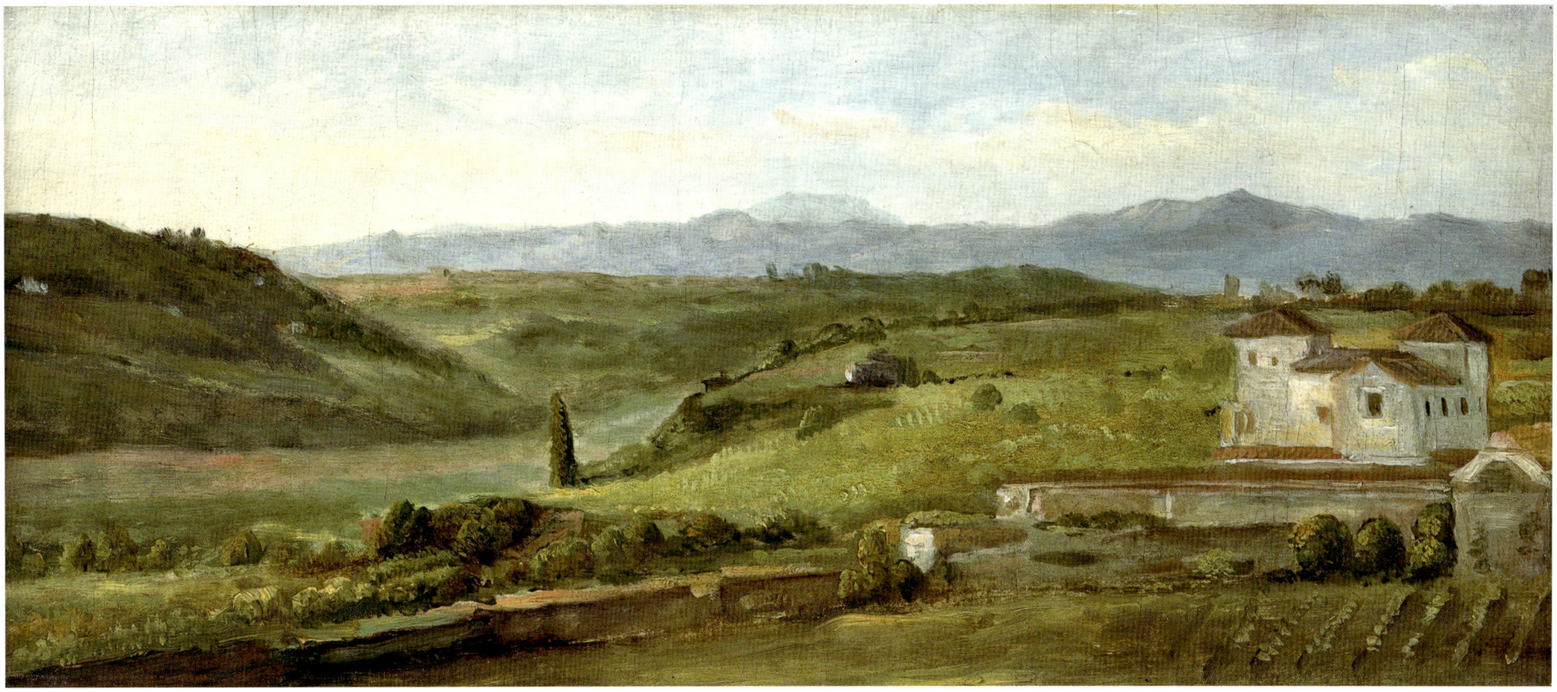

French School(?)

32. *View looking into the Val de Villé in the Vosges, France,* 1830s

Oil on paper on canvas, 27.9 x 38.5 cm

Inscription

Inscribed on the original stretcher *Entrée du Val de Villé a S...(illegible) & 8 ? 9m. 8bre.*

Provenance

Bought from John Lishawa, London, in 1977.

Until recently, the view shown in this sketch was unknown. Thanks to the combined evidence of an inscription on the stretcher and a photograph in a guide book, it can now be identified as Val de Villé, a valley in the Bas-Rhin region of Alsace in France. Named after the small town of Villé, thirty-two kilometres south of Strasbourg and five kilometres to the west of the town of Sélesta, the valley is in the Vosges mountain range that runs parallel to the River Rhine. By coincidence, a photograph in the *Blue Guide to France* (1984 edition) shows the same view, taken from roughly the same position as the present sketch (fig. 29).[1] The photograph is captioned 'Landscape near Turkheim,' a town south of Villé, but the exact site is not specified. The rest of the inscription on the stretcher, *'8 ? 9m. 8bre,'* probably refers to the date and to the time of day at which the sketch was painted, in the month of October (8 standing for Latin *octo*). This area of the Vosges is famous for its fortified crag-top castles, built to defend France from threatening German armies, and its fruity white wines. In the foreground are rows of vines, rapidly sketched in translucent black oil paint with a warm beige ground apparent beneath. In the middle distance are slate-roofed houses, with smoke curling upwards from their chimneys. More vines are visible on the mountain slopes to the left, which cut across the composition. Behind, the dark shadows of mountains contrast strongly with the morning sky above. On a crag-top in the middle are the ruins of a castle, most probably the fifteenth-century castle of Haut-Koenigsbourg, built at an altitude of 755 metres. Sacked and burnt by the Swedish army in 1633, its ruins were purchased from the town of Sélesta early this century by the German Emperor Wilhelm II and fully restored. The most evocative part of the sketch is the early morning light, rendered with even layers of buttery whites and beige colours, on top of which the artist has painted passing clouds with quick flicks of his brush.

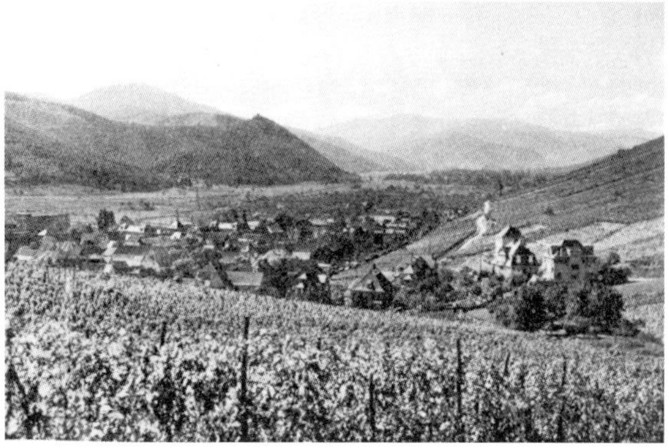

Fig 29 View looking into the Val de Villé in the Vosges (*Blue Guide to France*, 1984).

This sketch has in the past been attributed to the French landscape painter François-Marius Granet (1775–1849) on account of technical and stylistic similarities to other mountain landscapes by him. However, since the location of the site is here confirmed and knowing that Granet never made a trip to Alsace, we can safely reject that attribution.[2] James Mackinnon[3] has suggested Louis-Auguste Lapito (1803–1874) as a possible candidate. Lapito is known to have travelled extensively through Germany, Switzerland and regions of France, so it is quite possible that he visited Alsace. A *View of the Alps* by Lapito in a private collection shows a similar use of the brush and thinly applied translucent black paint in the foreground.[4] Nevertheless the attribution remains an open question. *XB*

1 We are very grateful to Simon Bainbridge for pointing out the photograph to us.

2 Denis Coutagne at the Musée Granet in Aix-en-Provence has also rejected the attribution.

3 Oral communication.

4 London 1998, cat. no. 20, p. 49.

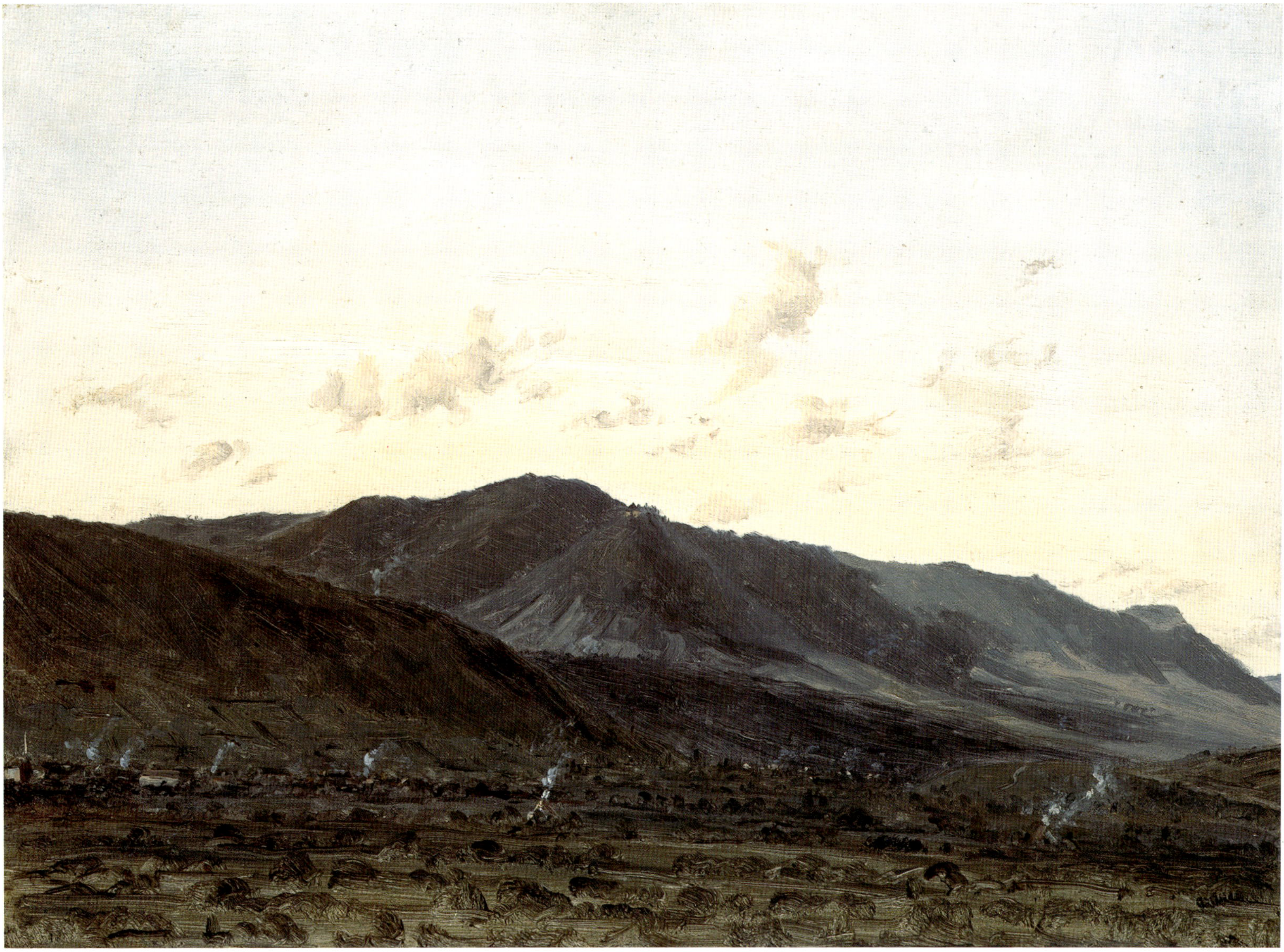

French School(?)

33. *Ruins with Workmen*, about 1850s

Oil on paper laid on canvas, 24.7 x 32.7cm

Inscription

A blind-embossed stamp on the other side of the paper, in the upper right-hand corner, reads: *C WISE* with traces of the word *Limited* underneath.

Technical note

Some underdrawing executed in graphite is apparent in most of the composition.

Provenance

Sold at Sotheby's, 24 June 1981, lot. 117 (with an attribution to Caruelle d'Aligny and a suggested date of 1825); bought from Brandt Dayton, New York, in 1986.

Exhibition

New York 1983, no. 2.

Both the author and the location of this remarkable oil sketch have yet to be identified. In it, the artist records spontaneously an almost nondescript ruin in a state of flux. From what we can gather, contemporary houses have been pulled down in order to reveal classical ruins behind and beneath them. The impressive arched door and the buttresses supporting the wall on the left tower over the figures below, who busy themselves with the Herculean task of clearing up the ruins. As the underdrawing indicates, the artist quickly sketched in the structure of the composition before applying his oil paints, with which he masterfully captures the play of light on the texture of the brickwork and plastered walls.

The range of attributions and sites tentatively put forward in the past is so extensive that it is probably more useful to concentrate on the physical aspects of the sketch before making any further suggestions. Close examination of the paper reveals that the sketch was executed on lightweight writing paper, made in England probably in the first half of the nineteenth century.[1] Such paper, however, was readily available on the Continent and could have been used by an artist of any nationality. A clue to the date of the paper's manufacture is provided by the blind-embossed stamp on the reverse of the upper right-hand corner, which reads *C. WISE Limited*. Such stamps were commonly used by stationers and paper merchants, and sometimes by the papermakers themselves, in order to identify their product. No stationer of that name has yet been identified, but a certain Charles Wise and other members of that family were active papermakers between 1810 to 1832 in the Maidstone area of Kent.[2] The word *Limited* below *C. WISE*, however, suggests a later date, as limited liability only became available for companies after 1854.[3] It is more likely therefore that C. Wise was a stationer or merchant and perhaps a descendant of the Wise family.[4] In any case, the evidence points towards a later date for the sketch's execution, most probably in the 1850s.

It is believed by some that this sketch was painted in Rome. Apart from the fragment of a fluted column visible in the middle of the composition, the blocks of volcanic stone, often used by the Romans for large construction projects, and the brickwork of the left-hand wall; recall antique Roman architecture. Several ruins in Rome, such as the Theatre of Marcellus, were used by local citizens as a skeleton on which to erect modern buildings in the manner indicated in this sketch. The arches through which the sky is visible at the back are also reminiscent of classical ruins and Roman aqueducts, notably the walls and arches of the former Palace of Domitian on the south side of the Palatine near the Circus Maximus (fig. 30). It is therefore possible that the sketch was painted on top of the Palatine, within the walls, looking out through the arches. Rich Roman families such as the Mattei and the Spada had built their country villas in this area. In 1830 a Scot named Charles Mills acquired a plot of land on what used to be Domus Augustana and built a neo-Gothic villa there, completed by 1850. It is visible in the top left-hand corner of the photograph.

However, since the Roman Empire extended its influence across Europe, it is also possible that the ruins are somewhere in France or Spain. The arches in the background are not unlike those of the amphitheatres found in cities in the south of France, such as Nîmes or Arles. Between 1826 and 1830 the Arles amphitheatre was being restored and 212 houses that had been built within the ruins were demolished.[5] A further possibility is that the ruins are actually the

1 We are grateful to Peter Bower for his help on the identification of the paper.

2 John, Edward, Charles and Stacey Wise worked several mills, sometimes alone or in partnership with members of the family and other papermakers such as John Hayes, Christopher Patch and Charles Brenchley. See London 1990b pp. 72–9.

3 Bryer, R. 'The Mercantile Laws Commission of 1854 and the political economy of Limited Liability', *Economic History Review*, l, 1, 1997, pp. 37–56.

4 To confuse the matter further, another C. Wise is listed in Thieme-Becker. An English engraver, mainly of portraits in stipple, he is known to have left England in 1850 for the United States to work as a publisher in Boston, New York and Philadelphia. It is possible that he was at one point a paper supplier.

5 Rouquette and Sintès 1989, p.64.

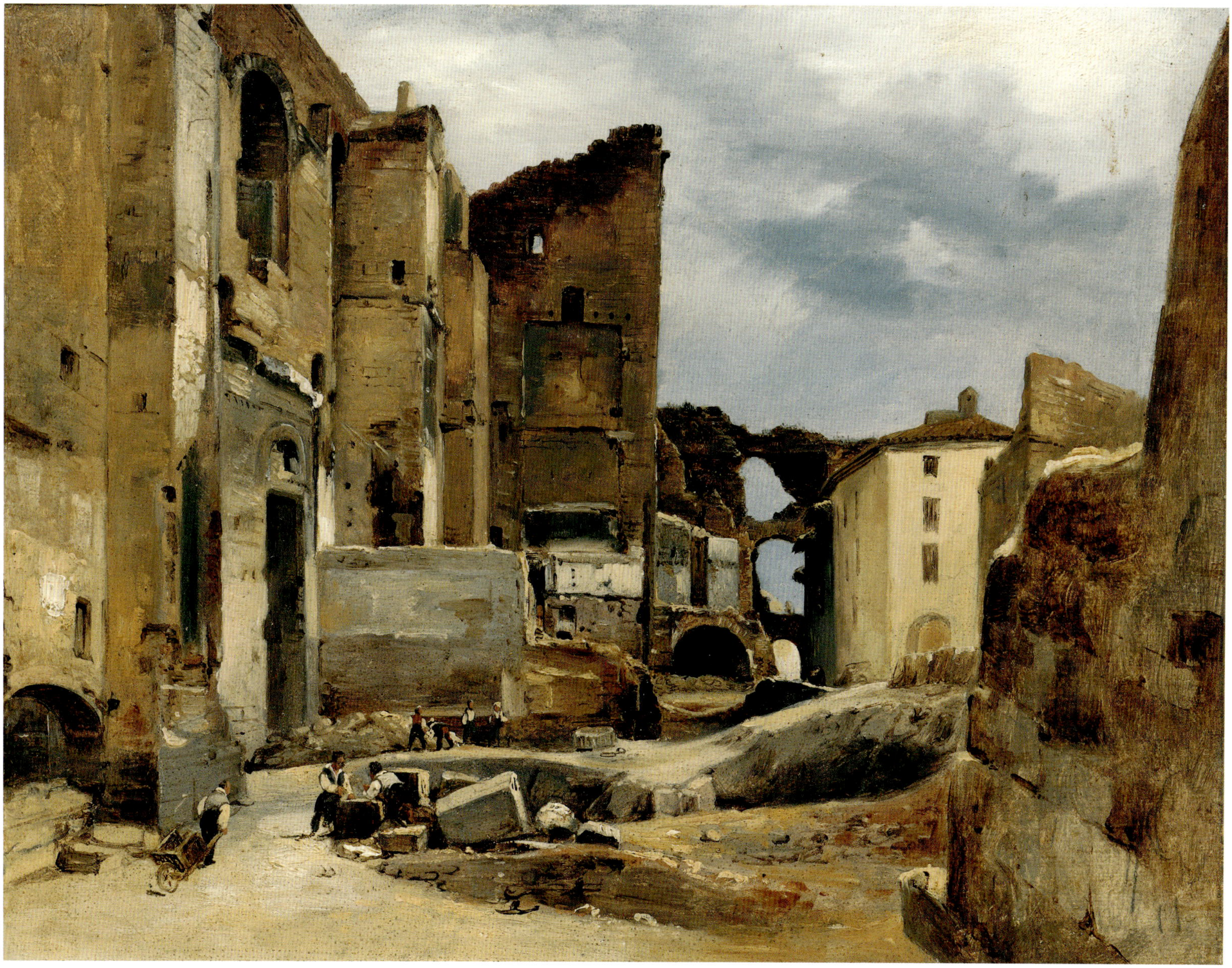

remains of a collapsed church. The alcove or niche on the left resembles a tomb with possibly a sepulchral monument or *gisant* inside.

With the location unidentified, it is hard to make any sensible attribution. The cool tones of the palette have reminded some of a northern hand, particularly Danish painters such as Martinus Rorbye (1803–1848). Others have been more inclined to see a French hand, proposing names such as Jules Coignet (1798–1860) and Charles Rémond (1795–1875). The best candidate so far, however, is the French painter Adrien Dauzats (1804–1868).[6] Dauzats travelled extensively throughout Europe and North Africa. With Baron Taylor, he visited and painted a series of views in most of the regions and towns of France, compiling an illustrated book known as *Voyages pittoresques et romantiques dans l'ancienne France*. The great majority of his paintings and sketches show architectural sites, either interiors of churches and mosques or the exteriors of cathedrals usually dwarfing figures below, such as the *Exterior of the Abbey of St Denis* (Sceaux, Musée d'Ile de France).[7] A more telling comparison, however, is

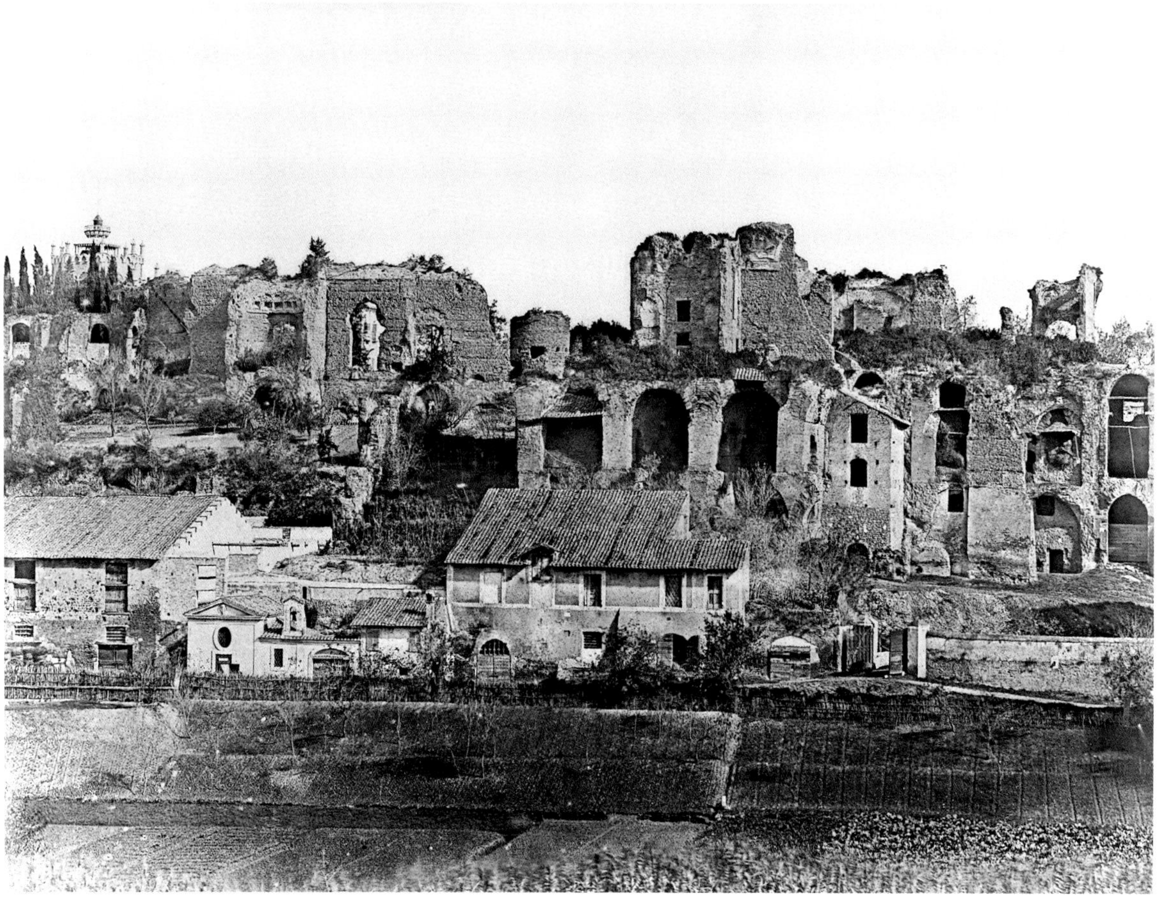

Fig 30 The Circus Maximus in Rome (photo: Alinari).

6 Patrick Noone and James Mackinnon support the possibility of this attribution.

7 Plessier 1990, cat. no. 11, p. 44.

8 Ibid., cat. no. 39, p. 74.

his 1844 painting *The Porte de Mars at Reims,* which shows workmen restoring an ancient Roman triumphal arch (fig. 31).[8] The treatment of the cracks in the masonry, the texture of the stones and the study of light are all compatible with elements in this sketch. *XB*

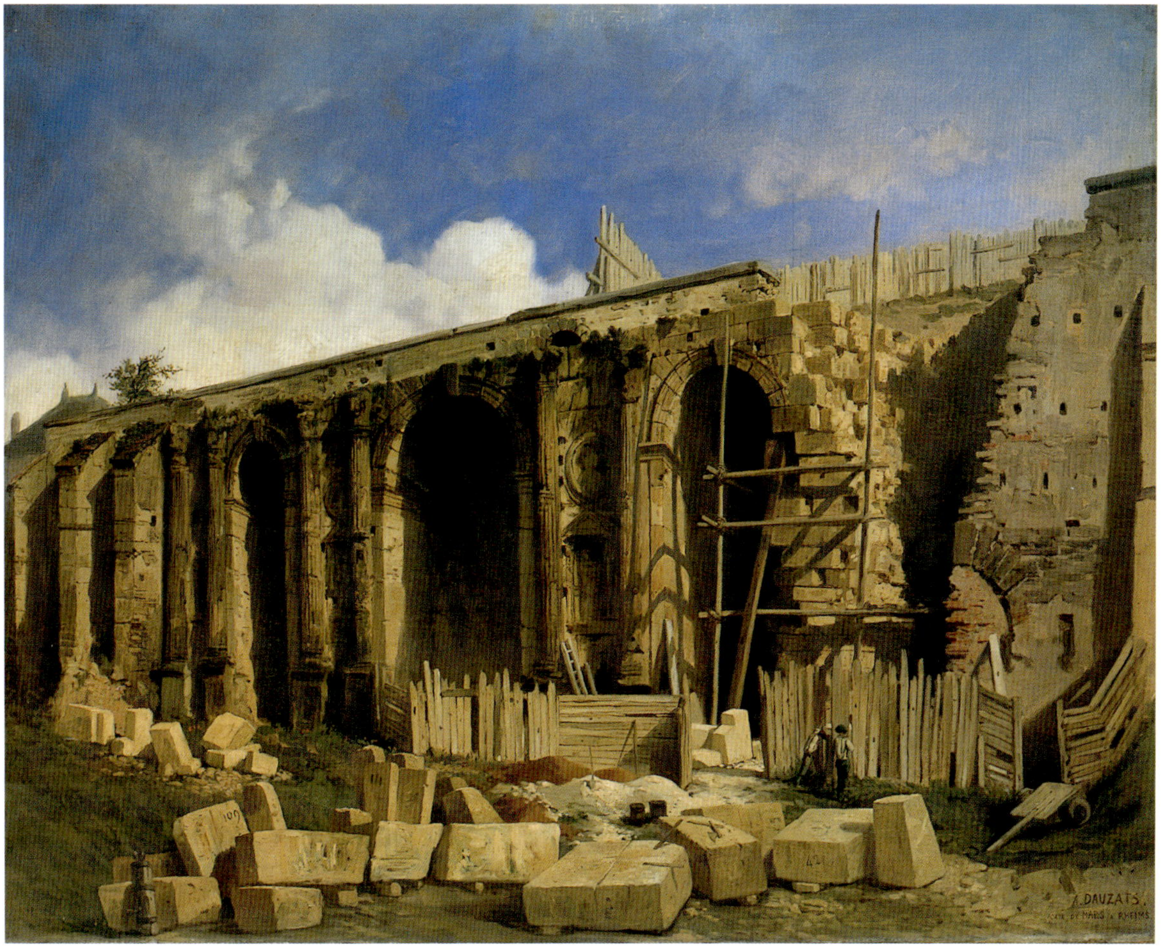

Fig 31 Adrien Dauzats, *The Porte de Mars at Reims*, 1844. Oil on canvas, 73 x 92 cm. Narbonne, Palais des Archevêques.

Gauffier, Louis (1762–1801), attributed to
34. *Cliff at Vicovaro*, 1787
Oil on paper laid on board, 27.3 x 34.9 cm

Inscription
Sticker on reverse of preserved fragment inscribed in ink, bottom right-hand corner *Vicovaro 1787*

Technical note
The right edge of the sheet was irreparably damaged by damp and a strip measuring 5.2 cm wide and bearing the inscription *Vicovaro 1787* was trimmed off at the time the painting was sold in 1963. The fragment is preserved in the Gere archives, The National Gallery, London.

Provenance
Bought from the Manning Gallery, London, in 1963.

Vicovaro is near Tivoli in the Roman Campagna, some forty kilometres east of Rome. This characterful and carefully observed view of a cliff there alternates between broad strokes of paint to indicate the planes of stone and careful touches to delineate the leaves and branches that cling to the rock face. The foreground has been lightly touched in.

The sketch is one of a group of paintings and drawings of Italian and Swiss views that appeared on the London art market in 1963. Dates inscribed in ink on various sheets in the group indicate that they were made between 1786 and 1790. From the group, two views of Caprarola, dated 1789, were acquired in 1963 by the British Museum. The attribution of this sketch to Gauffier rests primarily on the resemblance of the handwriting to that found in a sketchbook of Italian views inscribed on the inside cover of the sketchbook: *Gauffier à l'Académie de France à Rome*.[1] Anna Ottani Cavina notes, however, that the sketchbook contains inscriptions in two hands.[2] The first, on the inside cover, is indeed Gauffier's own, seemingly made at the time of his arrival in Rome in 1784. The second, more elegant hand is later in date and not by the artist. It is this hand, not Gauffier's, that appears on the preserved fragment trimmed from the present sketch, and also on other works in the group that emerged in 1963. One of these works is inscribed *Geneve* and dated 1790. Ottani Cavina is not aware that Gauffier made a Swiss visit; as she notes, however, by 1790 Gauffier was no longer a pensioner of the French Academy in Rome and his travels would not necessarily have been documented.[3] Thus, while the sheet cannot be ascribed securely to Gauffier, it is necessarily by an artist working within his orbit. The handling of paint in leaves and rock seems to resemble closely that on another sheet, showing a vine-covered arched passageway, that is also given to Gauffier.[4]

Gauffier, a student of the history painter Hugues Taraval, won the Prix de Rome in 1784 and quickly travelled to Italy where, with the exception of a brief return to Paris in the year of French Revolution, 1789,[5] he seems to have spent the rest of his short life. There he showed a propensity for painting landscapes out of doors. As life became difficult at the French Academy with the political upheavals of the Revolution, Gauffier removed himself to Florence where he made a living painting portraits of French military officers and itinerant international figures, often with landscape backgrounds. He also painted large-scale landscapes such as the vertiginous views at Vallombrosa now in the Musée Fabre, Montpellier, and at the Philadelphia Museum of Art. He died in Florence in 1801. *CR*

1 Marmottan 1926, pp. 281 ff. On the album, now with Wildenstein & Co. Inc., New York, see Ottani Cavina 1994.
2 Letter dated 24 April 1998 (Gere archives, The National Gallery, London).
3 Letter dated 20 July 1990 (Gere archives, The National Gallery, London).
4 Location unknown; photograph in the Gere archives, The National Gallery, London.
5 It was then that he would have painted the famous *Presumed View of the Luxembourg Gardens* (Paris, Musée du Louvre), long ascribed to Jacques-Louis David, but more recently attributed to Gauffier; see Ottani Cavina 1992, pp. 27–33.

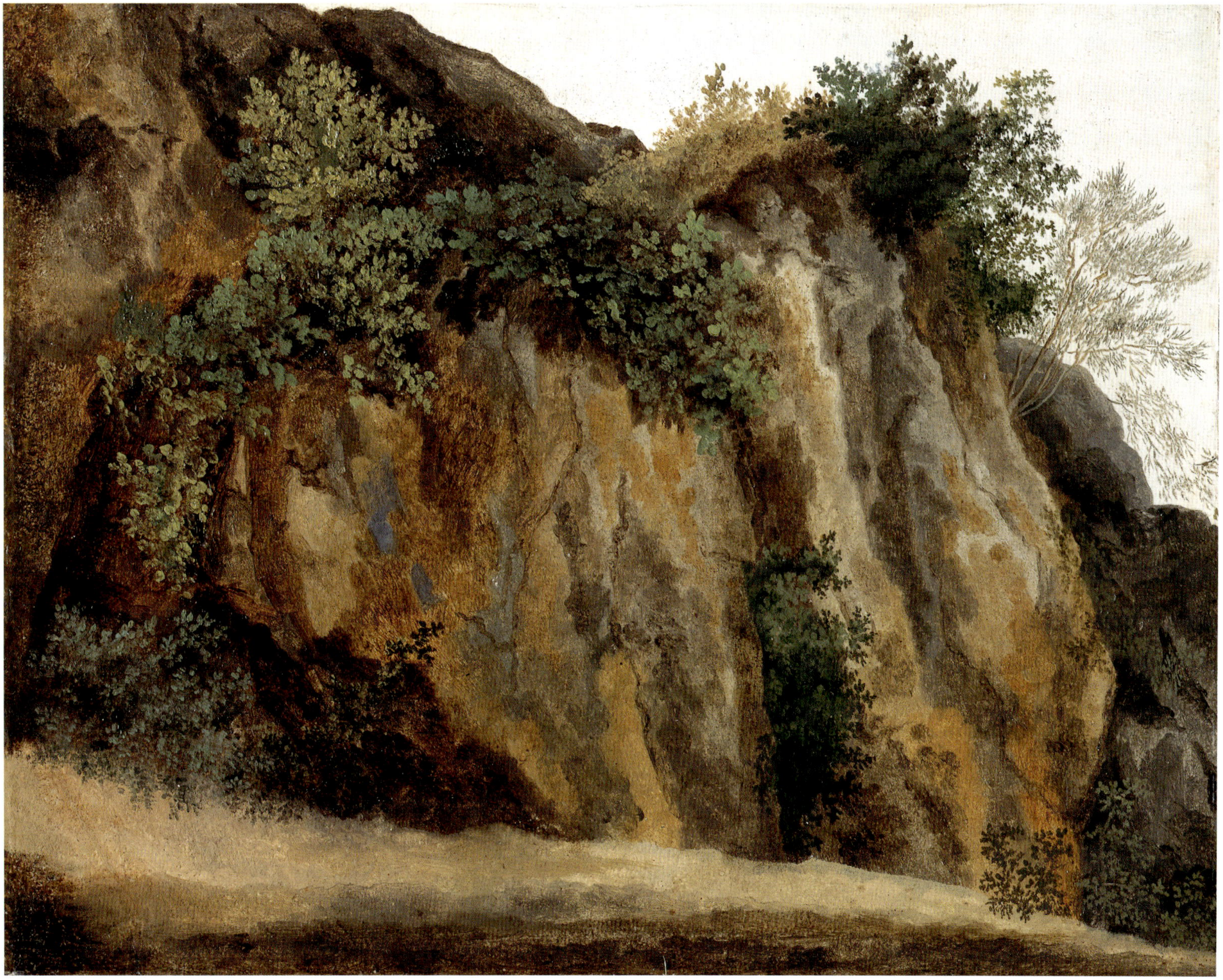

GERMAN SCHOOL

35. *A Rustic House by the Sea*, 1843

Pencil and oil on paper laid on canvas, 21.0 x 28.5 cm

Inscription

At bottom *4 Jan 1843 auf dem Fels?..gegenuber...II Blätter einseln zu...?* (on the rock?...Opposite...II loose sheets...?)

Technical note

An infra-red photograph reveals extensive underdrawing.

Provenance

Bought from P. & D. Colnaghi Ltd, London, in 1970.

When the Hamburg painter Friedrich Nerly (1807–1878) arrived in Rome in 1828, as many as 130 German artists were already living there.[1] Many of them were practising their skills by making landscape oil sketches, and it is often difficult to distinguish one hand from another. The experience of Italy was important for generations of German painters, and there would still have been large numbers of them in the city fifteen years later when this sketch, whose inscription remains for the most part frustratingly illegible, was painted by a German artist in the New Year of 1843.[2] The publication and first public exhibition of the work may help to lead to an identification of its author. One name that deserves serious consideration is that of Franz Catel (1778–1856), who showed a lively interest in the traditional architecture of Italy.

The rustic and asymmetrical stone house that the artist has chosen as a motif is set high on a rocky hill overlooking a distant domed church and campanile at right, perhaps a monastic complex, and the blue sea beyond. A cross hanging on the closed door at right, and the two cloaked figures sketched in pencil huddled in front of it, may suggest that this is an

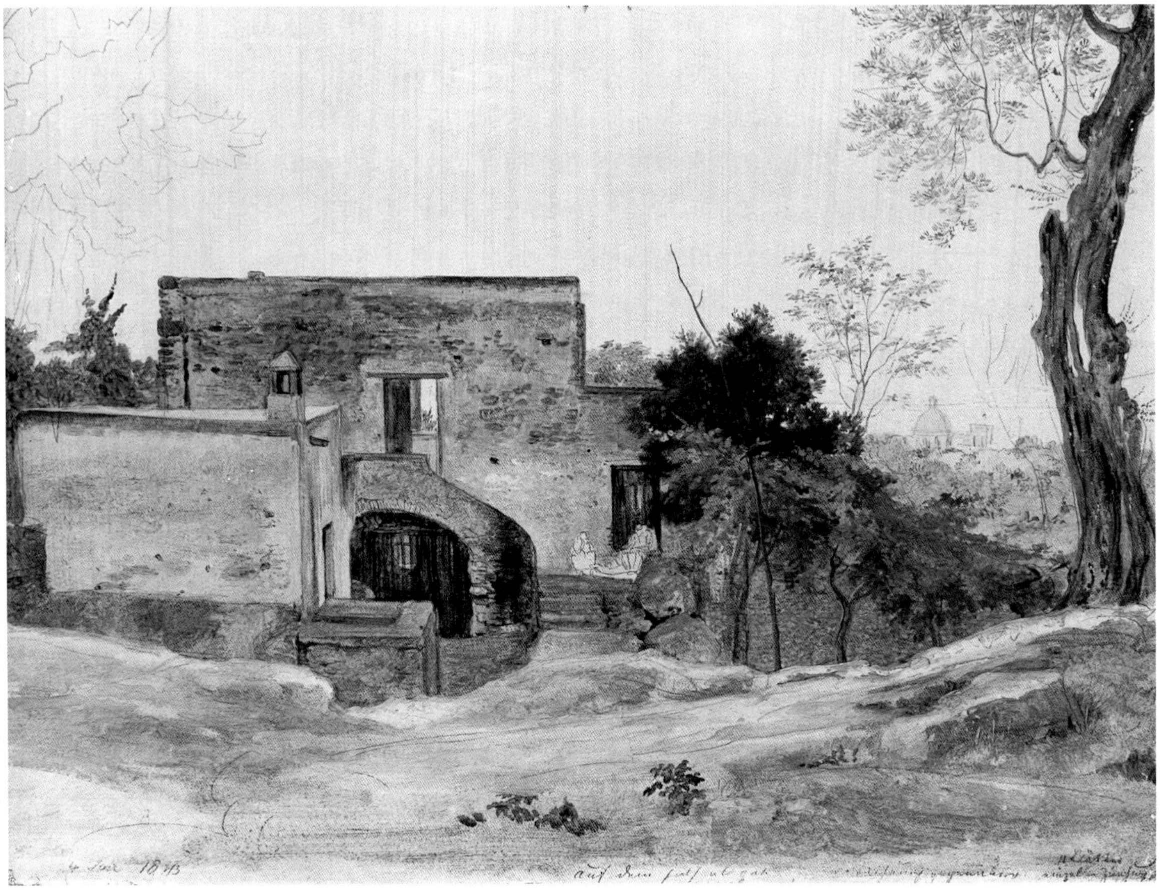

Fig 32 German School, *A Rustic House by the Sea*, infra-red photograph.

1 Washington, Brooklyn and St Louis 1996–7, p. 256.

2 While it has been suggested that the date inscribed on the sheet at lower left should be read as 1813, the infra-red photograph reproduced here makes it clear that the date is indeed 1843.

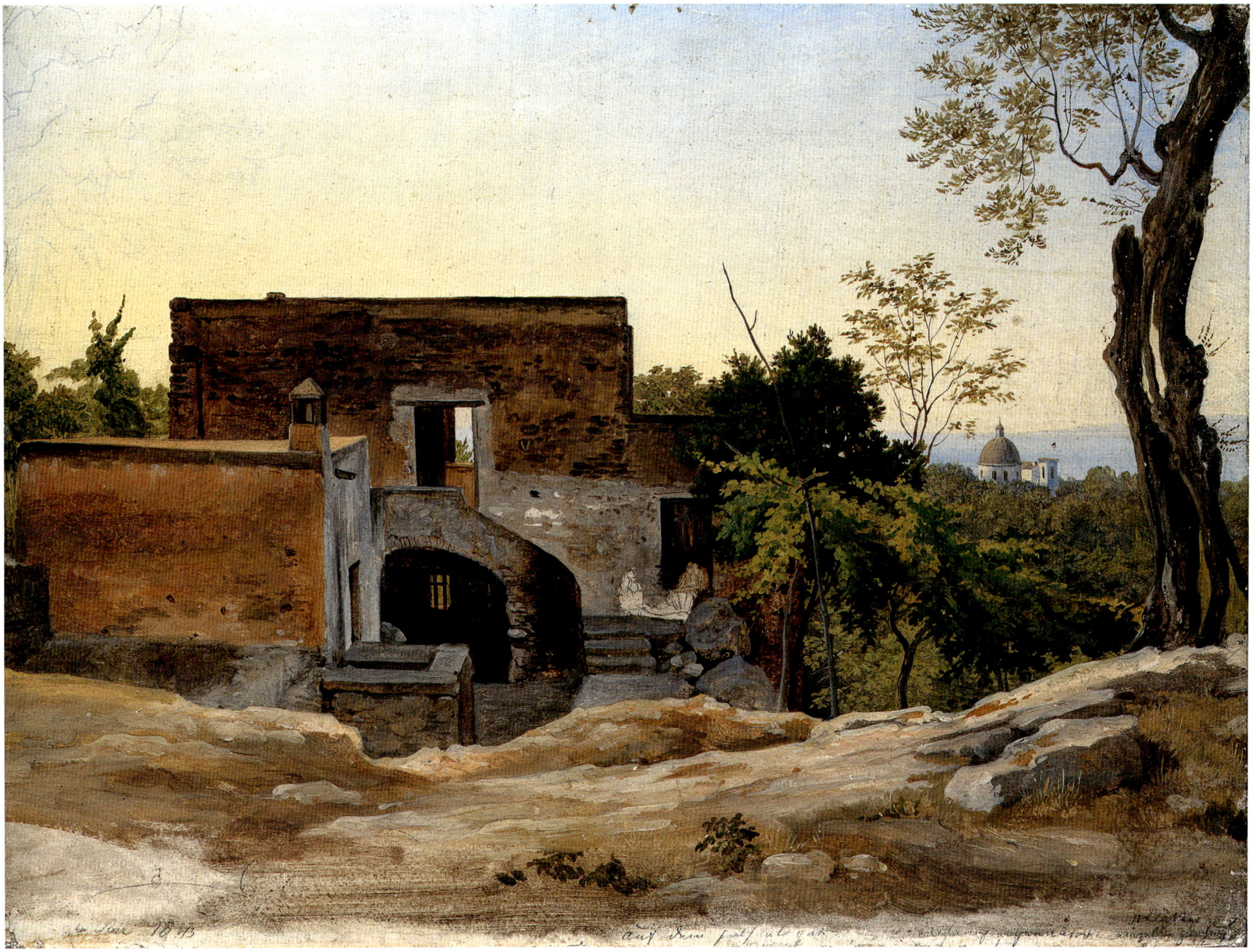

almshouse, or some sort of charitable shelter, perhaps for pilgrims making their way to Rome. As an infrared photograph (fig. 32) reveals, the artist first sketched in the composition in pencil, indicating extensive foliage at upper left that was never painted. The gnarled tree at right, included in the pencil sketch, was painted only after the sea had been brushed in – blue can be seen through a fissure in the trunk – while a second, slim tree, included in the pencil sketch, was not in the end included in the painted study. *CR*

Giroux, André (1801–1879)
36. *Ruins on the Palatine,* before 1830
Oil on paper laid on canvas, 21.8 x 31.0 cm

Inscriptions

Inscribed on stretcher *VII – 11773; A/228.6*

Provenance

Said to have been included in the Vente Giroux, Paris, 1970; bought from the Hazlitt Gallery, London, probably in 1970.

Exhibitions

Washington, Brooklyn and St Louis 1996–7, no. 105.

Literature

Galassi 1991, p. 104, pl. 121.

By the time André Giroux won the Prix de Rome for historical landscape painting in 1825, he had already been exhibiting his composed, classicising landscapes at the Salon for several years. In Rome, where he remained until 1830, he befriended the young and innovative French landscape painters living in the city, including Corot, Caruelle d'Aligny, Edouard Bertin and Léon Fleury. He frequently painted and sketched out of doors with them, both within Rome and further afield in the Campagna, and works by members of this group of artists often resemble each other. Giroux sent many of his oil sketches back to Paris, where one such series of Italian studies won him a first-class medal at the Salon of 1831. In later years he regularly exhibited French and Swiss views, and idealised 'souvenirs' of his Italian sojourn.

The contents of Giroux's studio were dispersed in a Paris auction as recently as 1970. Although this small, vivid sketch on paper does not bear a stamp, it is said to have been included in the sale, and the attribution to him is uncontested. The sketch shows ancient Roman ruins on the southeast corner of the Palatine Hill.[1] It is not evident from the picture where the artist stood to paint, as no ground plane is shown. Rather, a wall of piers and enclosed arches, marked by dark windows and passageways, rises up abruptly in front of the viewer. The crisp geometry of the architecture has been softened and muted by age and by invading trees and shrubs that cling to fissures in the stone and take root. They blur the edges of the ancient buildings, making them seem to blend into nature. The sunlight flickering on the leaves bathes the whole in a warm, atmospheric glow. *CR*

1 The specific site is identified in Washington, Brooklyn and St Louis 1996–7, cat. no. 105.

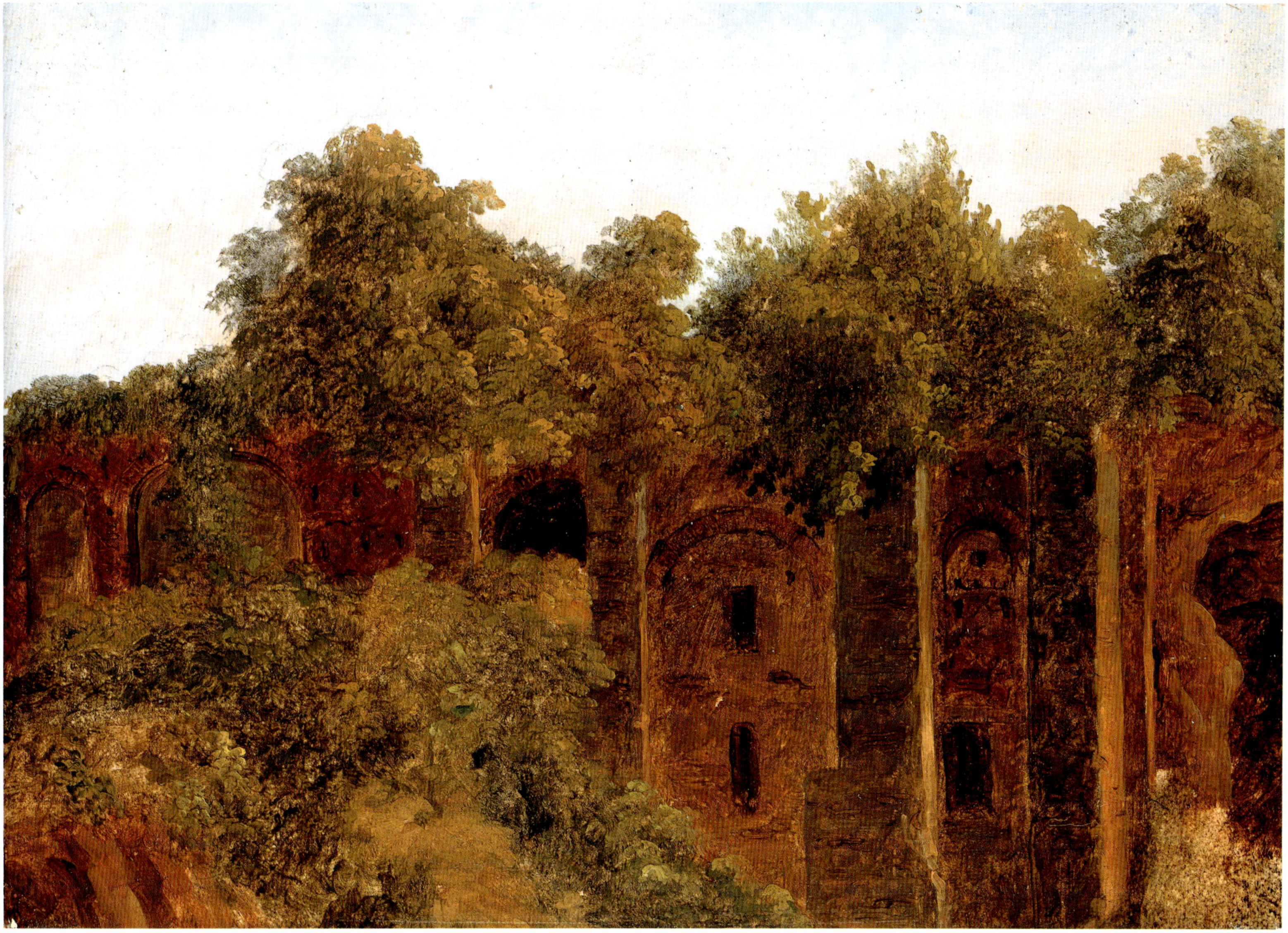

GOURLIER, Paul-Dominique (1813–1869)

37. *Acqua Acetosa,* 1837

Oil on canvas, 22.7 x 60.7 cm

Inscriptions

Signed and dated in red at lower right

Rome 1837 PG

Labels on stretcher *7040; 7/22*

Provenance

Bought from the Hazlitt Gallery, London, in 1970.

A student of Corot, Gourlier showed landscapes at the Paris Salon, many of them Italian scenes, from 1841 until 1869. He seems to have travelled to Italy frequently; this 1837 sketch showing a vista in the Roman Campagna must date from one of his first trips. It depicts the site of a mineral spring known as the Acqua Acetosa, below the Nazons rocks, seen at left, and near the River Tiber, visible in the distance. Corot himself had made oil sketches at the site in the 1820s.[1] This painting most closely resembles another Corot, entitled by Robaut *Torre di Quinto – Les Rochers de Nazons (Campagne de Rome)*,[2] but apparently showing the same site. Like Corot, when he came to paint the Acqua Acetosa, Gourlier chose an emphatically horizontal canvas. Despite the small scale of the painting, the conception is panoramic. Long, liquid brushstrokes outline the swelling land, and trace the trails that run across it. Thick slabs of dark paint establish the rock face. The distant mountains and long low clouds that meander across the sky almost merge with one another. *CR*

1 Robaut and Moreau-Nélaton 1905, nos. 76, 95, 147.

2 Ibid., no. 167.

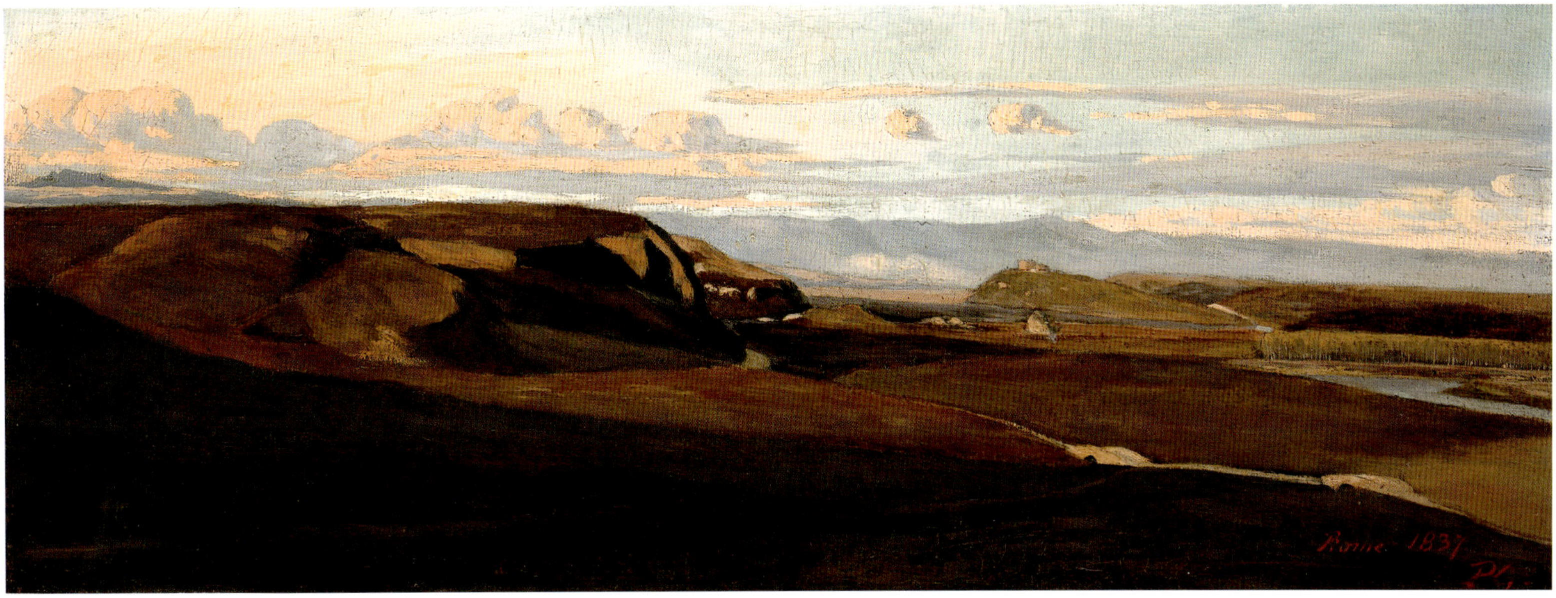
Rome. 1837

GRANET, François-Marius (1775–1849), attributed to

38. *View of the Falls at Tivoli,* about 1808–10

Oil on paper laid on canvas, 27.6 x 36.6 cm

Provenance

With the Shepherd Gallery, New York, in 1972; bought from the Shepherd Gallery in 1992 (as Robert-Leopold Leprince).

Exhibition

New York 1972 (as Caruelle d'Aligny).

François-Marius Granet, to whom this painting is attributed, was one of the most gifted and expressive landscape painters of the first half of the nineteenth century.[1] Born in Aix-en-Provence, he studied in the 1790s with Jean-Antoine Constantin and Jacques-Louis David, before travelling briefly to Rome in 1802. He was so enchanted with what he found there that soon after his return to France he set off once again for Italy, and ended up by spending a further twenty-one years there as a member of a community of French artists including Ingres, Fabre, Chauvin and Boguet. Granet finally returned to France in 1824 to become a curator at the Louvre and later director of the Museum of French History at Versailles, a post he kept until the Revolution of 1848. Before his death in 1849, he bequeathed the contents of his studio, consisting of approximately 1,800 paintings, drawings and watercolours, to the local museum in Aix-en-Provence, now the Musée Granet.

Granet's Italian oil studies show a fascination with the irregular forms and textures of antique Roman ruins and houses. He was particularly interested in the varying effects of light, which he interpreted either by using highly diluted oils or by smudging the paint surface. In contrast, when painting foliage and flowers, he often used a very fine brush, applying delicate touches for the leaves and light impastos for the petals.

Like his predecessor Valenciennes, Granet enjoyed painting from unconventional viewpoints, at times disregarding topographical accuracy. This picture, for example, is a complete reinterpretation of a view he had already drawn from the esplanade near the Temple of Vesta at Tivoli, looking across to the other side of the River Aniene (fig. 33).[2] Rather than moving buildings around and rearranging them according to his own aesthetic imperatives, as in two oil sketches now in the Musée Granet,[3] Granet completely reversed the composition of the houses but kept the riverbank and the waterfall on the correct side. When comparing the drawing and the oil sketch, if one takes as a reference point the waterfall and the small pedimented shrine at the edge of the torrent on the left-hand side of the riverbank, the differences become clear. However, when the block of houses in the oil sketch is

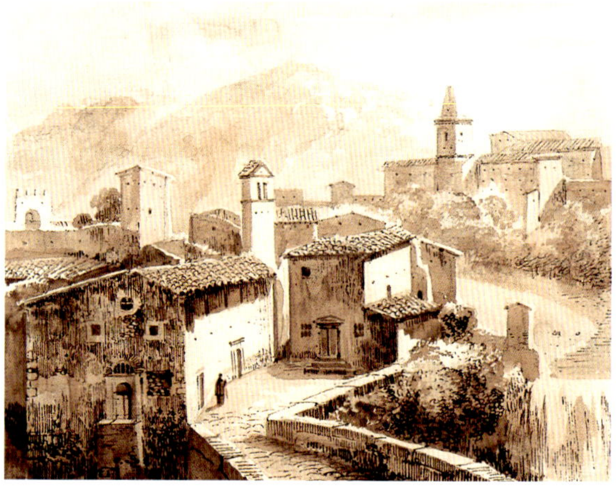

Fig 33 François-Marius Granet, *View from the Temple of Vesta,* c.1805–8. Pen and wash on paper, 13 x 10.2 cm. Aix-en-Provence, Musée Granet.

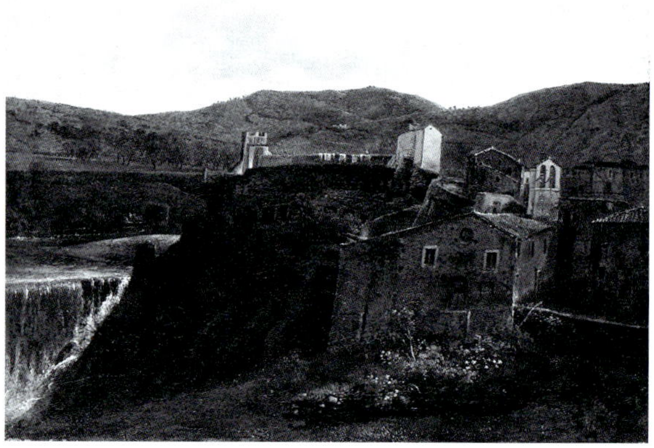

Fig 34 Reversed view of François-Marius Granet, *View of the Falls at Tivoli.*

1 The attribution to Granet is tentatively suggested here for the first time, and has been supported on stylistic grounds by Denis Coutagne, Director of the Musée Granet.

2 The drawing is on p.22 of an album known as *Souvenirs de Rome 1805–1808,* put together by Granet for his friend Simon, which is now in the Musée Granet.

3 Néto-Daguerre and Coutagne 1992, p.256. figs. 295 and 296.

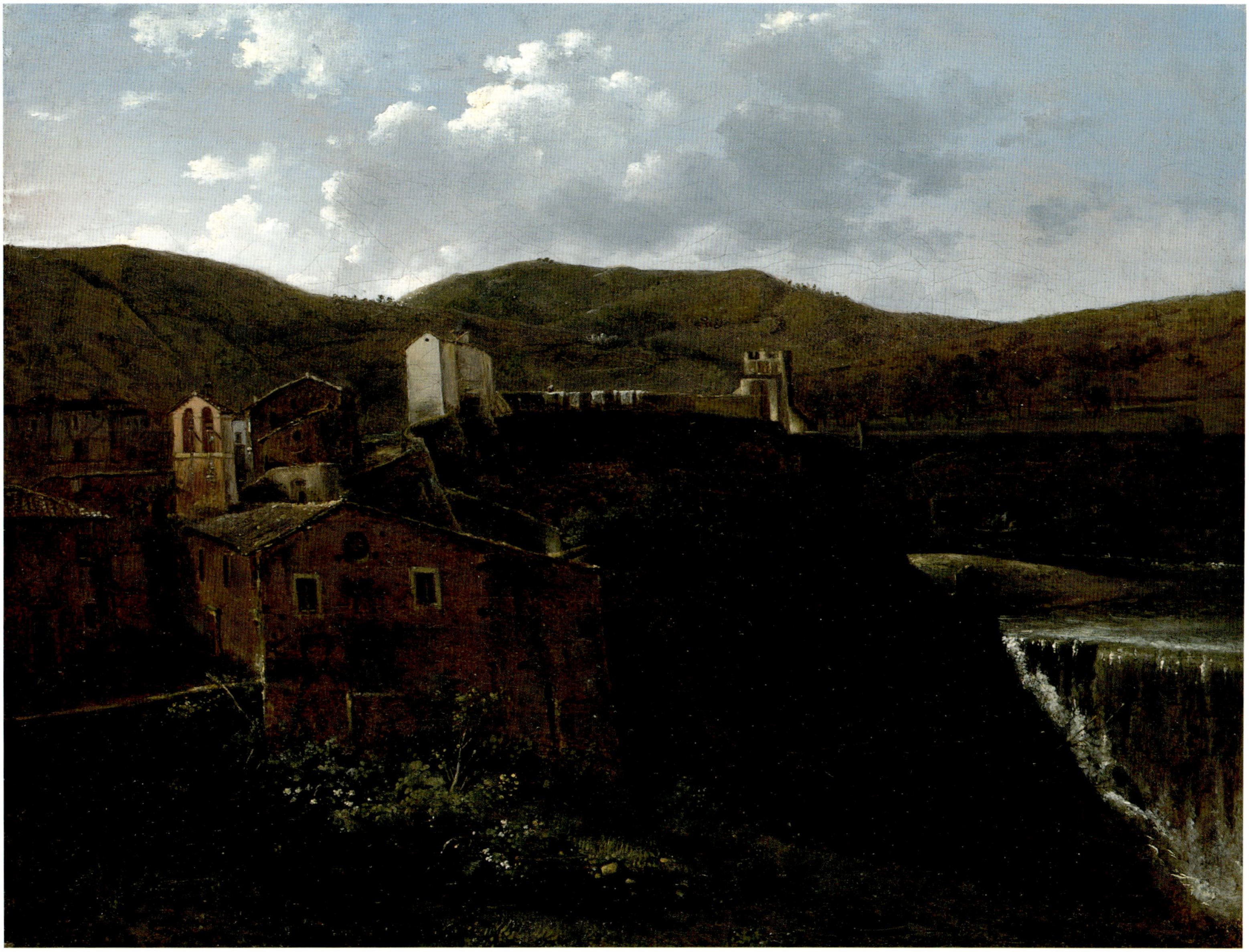

reversed, the two representations match almost exactly (fig. 34). The bell tower of the chapel of the Madonna del Ponte, the house on the right and the bridge with drying laundry, suddenly make sense in relation to the drawing when the composition is switched round. In creating his composition, Granet has painted an extension to the house on the right and replaced the gorge with flowers and greenery, suggesting that the picture was not painted directly from nature but most probably in the studio, either from memory or from a counter-proof of an earlier composition, with a view to selling it as a finished composition. *XB*

Guillaumet, Gustave (1840–1887)

39. *Mountains in North Africa, with a Bedouin Camp*, about 1862–87

Oil on paper laid on canvas, 19.0 x 46.0 cm

Inscriptions

Three stamps on stretcher and back of canvas *ATELIER GUILLAUMET*

Provenance

Bought from Fischer et Keiner, Paris, date not recorded

A student at the Ecole des Beaux-Arts in Paris, while he was *en route* to Rome in 1862, Guillaumet suddenly changed his mind at Marseilles and sailed for North Africa instead. Over the years he returned to Algeria and Morocco again and again, and made a successful, if brief, career as a painter of Orientalist subjects that were enthusiastically received in Paris. Indeed, he is said to have been considered the Orientalist Millet, combining naturalism and exoticism in equal measure in his paintings. Guillaumet was particularly drawn to lower Algeria, and the lives of the nomadic peoples he found in the desert there. The Musée d'Orsay in Paris has some large-scale paintings of these subjects, including *The Desert (The Sahara)* of 1867 and *The 'Seguia', Biskra* of 1884.

As Guillaumet visited North Africa ten times in fifteen years, it is all but impossible to date this oil sketch precisely. It depicts a range of rugged hills rising from a valley floor, with white-robed Bedouins moving across the foreground, away from their dark tents at right. The emphatically horizontal format recalls that used by such contemporary landscape artists as Giovanni Costa and Frederic, Lord Leighton. The loose, broad strokes and thick impasto, both indicative of quick application, are very different from the enamel-like surfaces of the artist's more highly finished compositions. This suggests that for Guillaumet, as for the majority of his contemporaries, the oil sketch was a different category of painting from the exhibitable picture. By the third quarter of the nineteenth century, however – in the wake of Realism and Naturalism, and with the advent of Impressionism – artists had become increasingly conscious of the appeal of spontaneity, and of the seemingly improvisatory oil sketch. *CR*

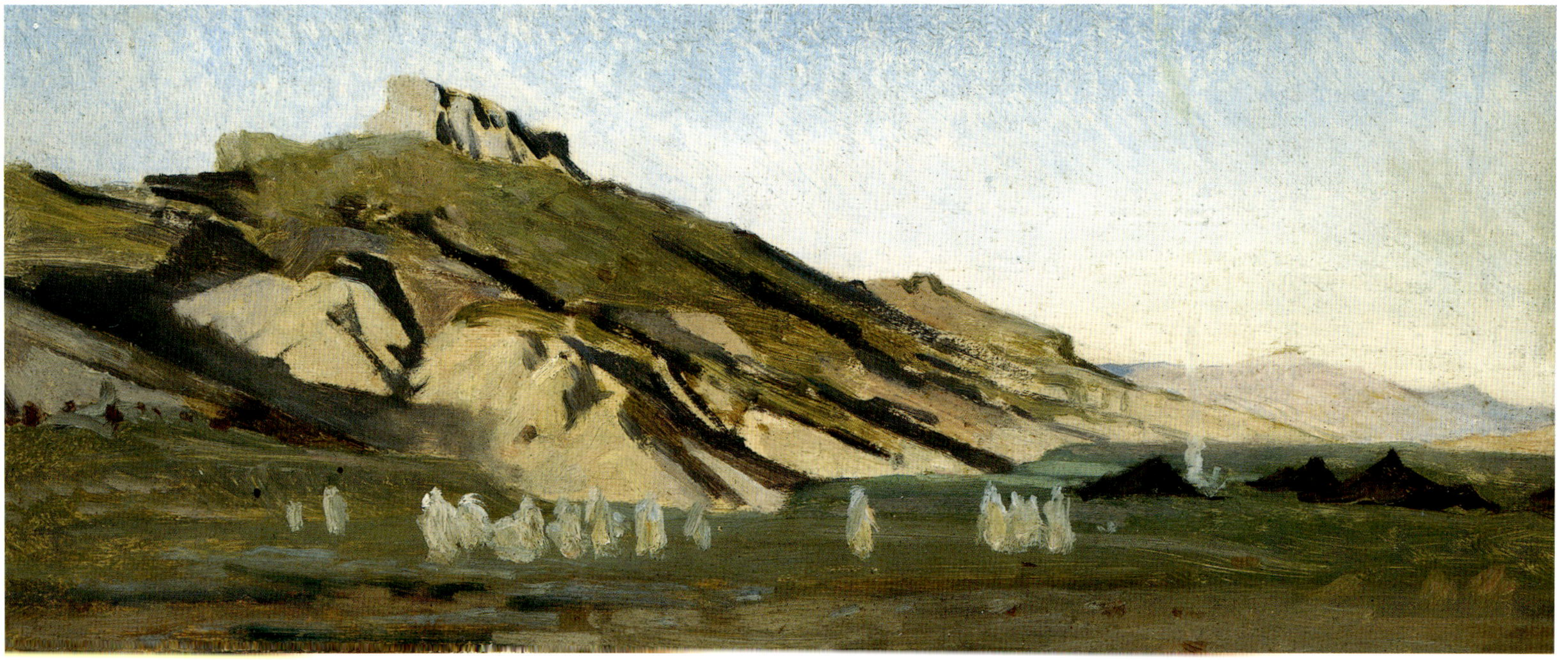

Haes, Carlos de (1826–1898), attributed to

40. *View of Madrid,* about 1855–65

Oil on paper laid on canvas, 25.2 x 45.2 cm

Provenance

Bought from Fischer et Keiner, Paris, before 1986 (as Alexander Cals).

Literature

Gowing 1986.

The view of Madrid seen here has changed little since the early nineteenth century, apart from the addition of a few modern office buildings and high-rise apartment blocks. It is taken from one of the highest points of the Casa de Campo, an area dotted with small oak trees and shrubs that was formerly a royal hunting ground and is now a municipal park to the west of the Royal Palace. With a few quick strokes of white paint, the painter has accurately depicted the royal palace in the middle of the composition, along with church spires and the dome of San Francisco el Grande on the far right. Completed in 1744 under Philip V, Spain's first Bourbon king, the royal palace was a replacement for the Moorish palace known as the Alcázar, which had burnt down in 1734. The impressive edifice was designed by the Italians Juvarra and Sacchetti, and decorated with frescoes by Anton Rafael Mengs and Giambattista Tiepolo.

This sketch was once attributed to Francisco de Goya, on the grounds that it was similar in conception to his oil sketch of the *Meadow of San Isidro* (Madrid, Prado Museum), the background of which contains a beautifully observed view of Madrid. However, pigment analysis undertaken at the National Gallery in 1993 has determined a later date for the picture. Notably, this analysis revealed the presence of viridian in the greens of the foliage, a pigment that first came into use in 1838 and did not become widely available until after 1859.[1]

The sketch bears similarities to the work of the Spanish landscape painter, Carlos de Haes (1826–1898), as well as to the work of members of his entourage. Born in Brussels, Haes spent his youth in Malaga, southern Spain, before returning to Belgium in 1850 to study with the landscape painter Joseph Quineaux (1822–1895), who encouraged his students to paint in the open air. After travelling through France, Germany and the Netherlands, acquainting himself with contemporary Realist trends, Haes returned to Madrid in 1855. Two years later he presented a landscape *View of the Royal Palace from the Casa de Campo*[2] for which he was offered the fourth chair for landscape painting at the Royal Academy of San Fernando. Still hanging at the Academy, that view is from a different angle to the sketch exhibited here. It focuses on the reflection of the trees on the pond in the foreground, with the Royal Palace appearing in the background. Its general atmosphere reflects a knowledge of the Barbizon School of landscape painting, also apparent in the present sketch, particularly in the effects of light and use of intense greens.

When rivals asked Haes how he had achieved such truth to nature, he responded that they should sketch in the open air before painting in the studio.[3] Possibly the sketch exhibited here is one of those he executed in preparation for his academic piece. Made Academician of Merit in 1861, Haes became an influential figure at the Academy. He travelled around Spain during the 1870s, producing *plein-air* studies before painting full-scale works in larger format. One of the first landscape painters to encourage this practice in Spain, he particularly influenced his student Aureliano Berruete (1845–1912), who was to become one of the leading Spanish Impressionists.[4] *XB*

1 See correspondence between David Bomford at the National Gallery and John Gere, dated 6 October 1993, in the Gere archive (now at the National Gallery).

2 Royal Academy of San Fernando, no. inv. 762, 69 x 100 cm.

3 Quoted in González de Amezúa del Pino 1998, p. 96.

4 The present sketch had been attributed to Berruete. However, although he worked closely with de Haes and accompanied him on several sketching expeditions, Berruete's style is closer to the French Impressionists than that of his master.

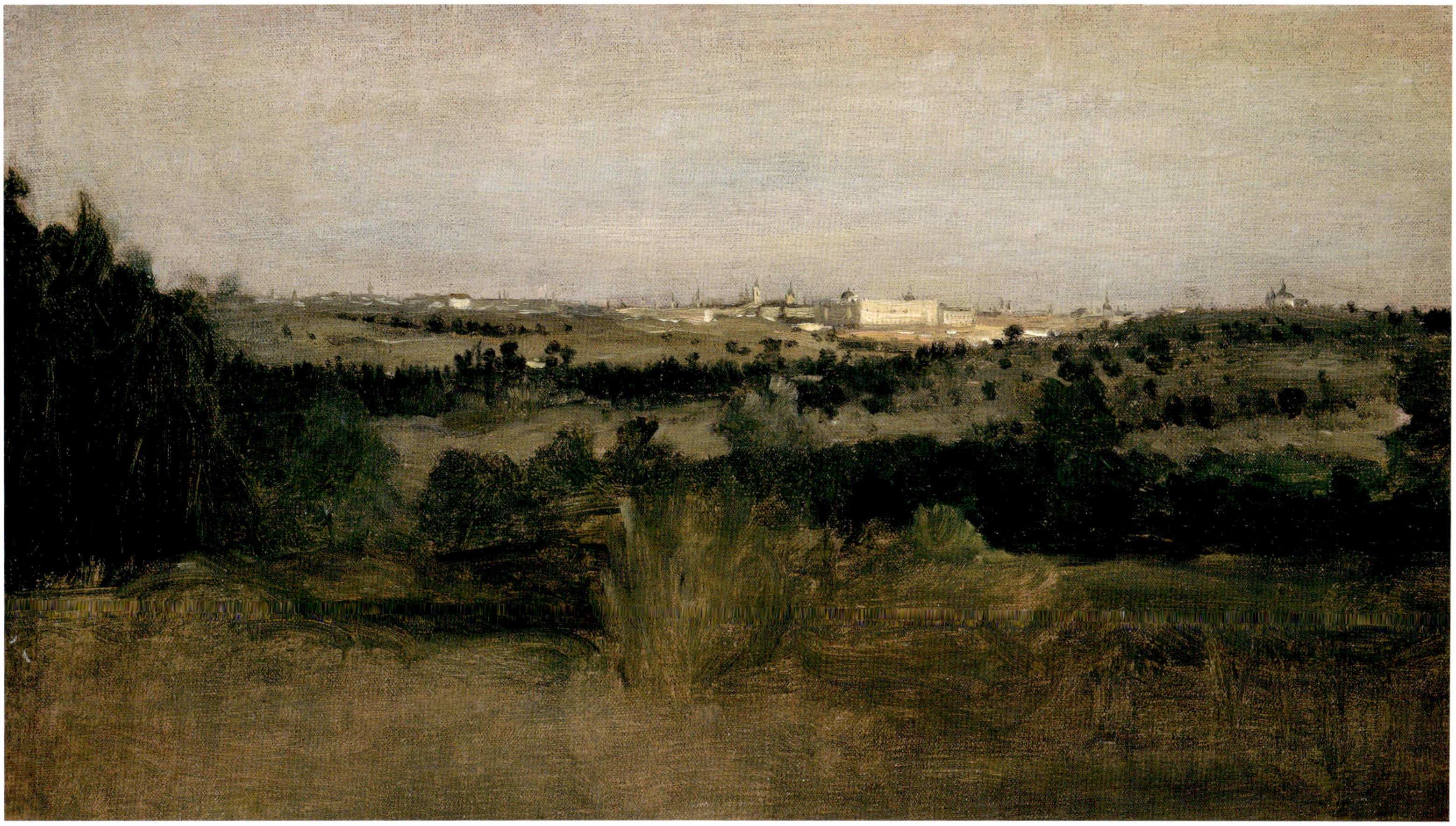

Heinrich, Johann August (1794–1822), attributed to

41. *Landscape with Figures bathing*, about 1820

Oil on paper laid on canvas, 28.5 x 31.2 cm

Inscription

In pencil on original stretcher *Landschaft Spitzweg*

Provenance

Bought from Rupert Cavendish, London, in 1990 (as Heinrich).

A wall of sandy rock overgrown with shrubbery, tall grasses, tendrils and angular roots, rises steeply from a pond or slow-moving stream. The textures of the rocks and the play of light on the leaves are both captured with painterly economy, as is the dense luxuriance of the undergrowth. At top, shrubs are silhouetted against a cloudy sky. At bottom, three female bathers clad in white shifts ease themselves into the water. These women, however, immediately call into question the status of the work. Like the *banditti* figures added to the not dissimilar sketch of a rocky ridge attributed here to Salvator Rosa (cat. no. 64), they serve to turn a landscape oil study into a finished composition. Moreover, the diminutive scale of the figures is disproportionate to the natural motif itself, which can only have measured a metre or so in height. With the women, we are forced to read the rocks and shrubbery as at least six metres high, and certain grasses as being far taller than a human being. For artists in the early nineteenth century the landscape oil sketch was rarely an end in itself but could serve as one stage in the evolution of a composition. Here we see an artist taking the next step in that process, adding generalised figures redolent of a timeless arcadia to a highly specific landscape motif which had been sketched out of doors.

An old inscription on the stretcher identifies it as the work of Carl Spitzweg (1808–1885). While that attribution can be discounted, it is clear that the painting is by a German artist active in the early nineteenth century. Heinrich's name was proposed when the painting was on the market. The sheet bears comparison with Heinrich's detailed and meticulous pencil sketches of rocks and trees deep in the forest, such as his drawing *In the Rabenauer Grund* of about 1820 (Berlin, Alte Nationalgalerie).[1] Heinrich studied in Dresden and Vienna where he knew members of the Nazarene Brotherhood. In 1819 he met both Johan Christian Dahl (1788–1857), a master of the oil sketch, and Caspar David Friedrich (1774–1840). The next year he was listed among Friedrich's students. Often in frail health, Heinrich died of pulmonary disease in 1822, while travelling to Italy for the first time. Helmut Borsch-Supan has not accepted the attribution, however, which remains open to discussion. *CR*

1 New York 1988, cat. no. 95, illus. p. 235.

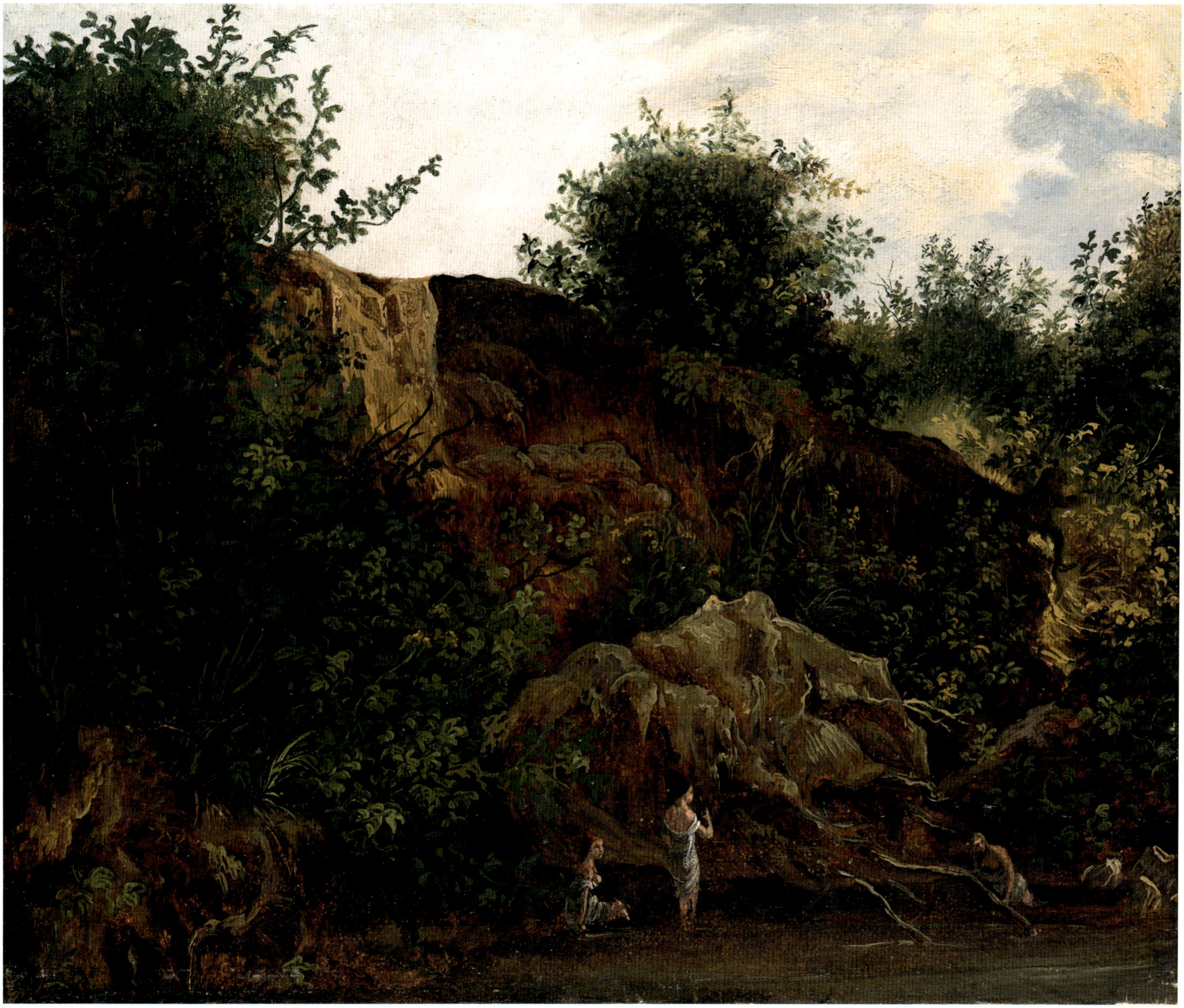

Joinville, Antoine-Victor-Edmond-Madeleine (1801–1849)

42. *A Distant View of Tivoli*, 1824

Oil on canvas, 25.7 x 39.7 cm

Inscriptions

Inscribed on the lower right in red *Tivoli 1824*; in a different hand in white *Joinville*

Provenance

Bought from John Lishawa, London, in 1977.

This is one of the few oil sketches by Joinville to be signed and dated, possibly suggesting that the painter was thinking of selling it. The view is taken from the opposite side of the valley to the Temple of Vesta, to the right of the Grande Cascata (large waterfalls), looking towards the Villa Maecenas and the Roman Campagna in the distance (see fig. 35).

Joinville, who trained in 1818 at the Ecole des Beaux-Arts in Paris under Hersent, was a member of the second generation of classical landscape painters working in Italy which included Edouard Bertin, Caruelle d'Aligny, Desgoffe and Corot. This sketch documents his visit to Italy in 1824. Two years later he exhibited for the first time at the Lebrun gallery a finished painting of *Campo-Vaccino in Rome* (Chartres, Musée des Beaux-Arts). He seems to have stayed on in Italy, as he produced several paintings of views of Genoa, Venice, Rome and Naples between 1831 and 1848, travelling on at least one occasion to north Africa during this period.

The smudgy application of paint, particularly in the trees and rocks, shows some affinity with Corot's oil sketches executed around that date. *XB*

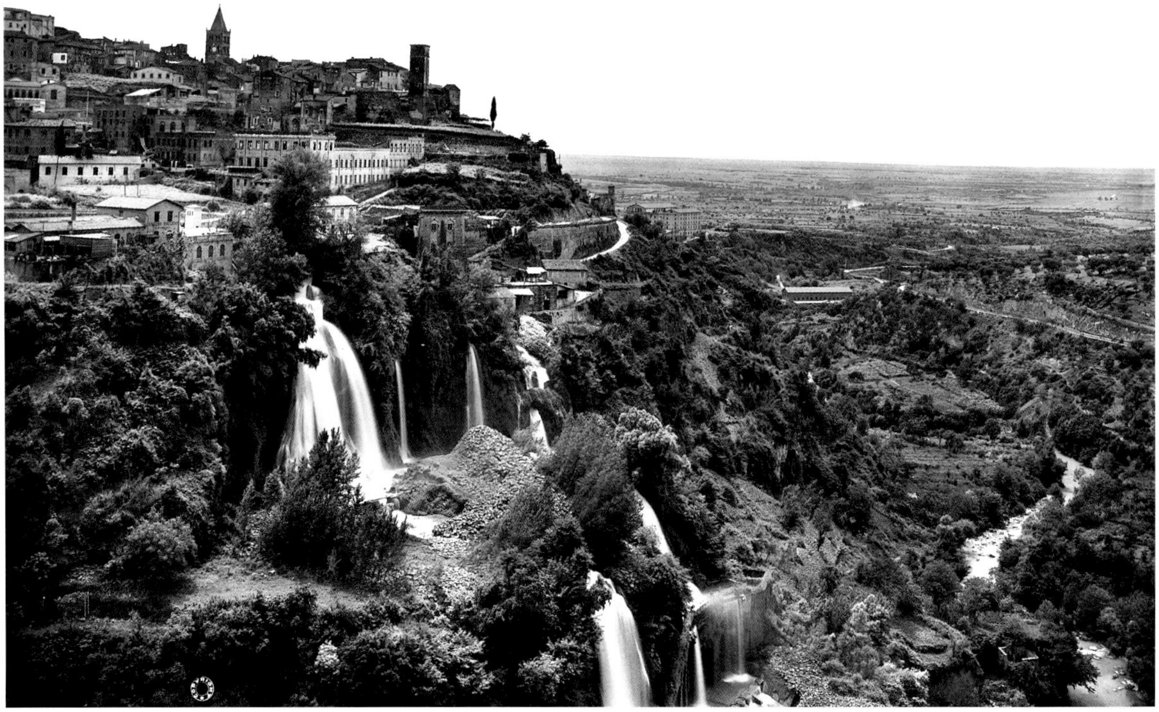

Fig 35 The falls at Tivoli (photo: Alinari).

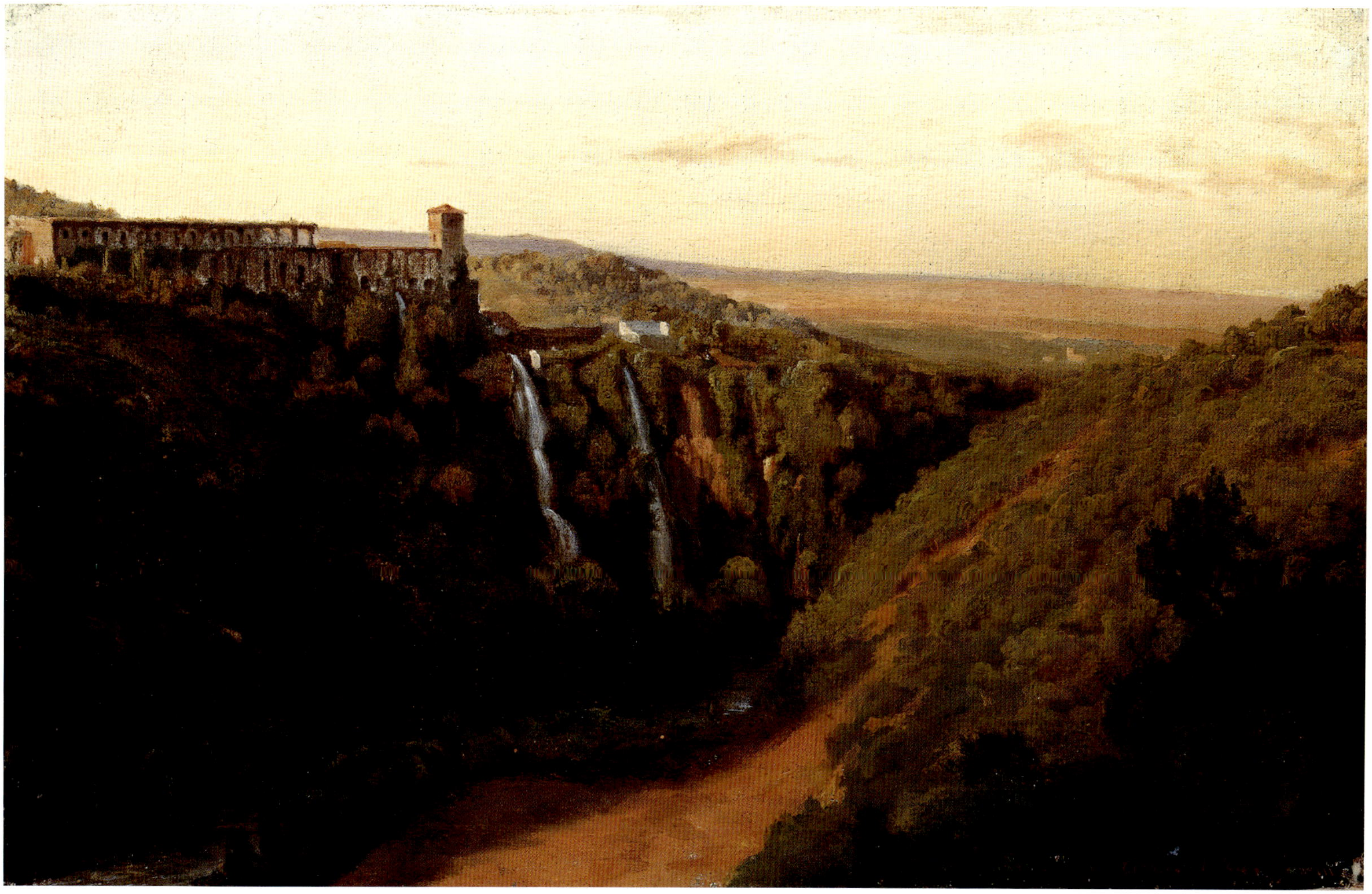

Jones, Thomas (1742–1803)

43. *The Grotto of Posillipo,* 1782

Oil on paper laid on board, 20.3 x 27.3 cm

Inscriptions

Signed and dated on reverse of the paper, now laid down, *TJ Naples August 1782*
Inscribed on reverse of board in brown watercolour *The Grotto at Posillippo/ Thomas Jones*

Provenance

Bought from Colnaghi, London, in 1956.

Exhibitions

Naples 1962, no. 55; London 1970, no. 71; Washington, Brooklyn and St Louis 1996–7, no. 12.

Literature

Gowing 1985, p. 47, p. 53; Galassi 1991, pp. 34–5, pl. 36.

Born in Radnorshire, Wales, Jones studied painting in London between 1763 and 1765 under the most advanced British landscape painter of the day, his fellow Welshman Richard Wilson. He may have learned the rudiments of painting oil sketches out of doors from Wilson. On more than one occasion in the early 1770s, Jones reported that he was making such oil studies on paper. The young painter travelled to Italy in 1776 where he met numerous artists from across Europe. He continued to paint oil sketches as well as larger, more highly finished and generalised views of Rome and Naples and the surrounding countryside. The latter found a ready market among international tourists seeking souvenirs of their Italian visit, though Jones's artistic production was small. Returning to Wales from Italy in 1783, the painter succeeded to his wealthy father's estate at Pencerrig and ended his days as a figure of standing in the local community, though largely forgotten as an artist.

Jones's small-scale Italian oil sketches on paper, many of them, as here, carefully inscribed with a date, were never intended for public view but for later studio reference. He found his motifs in the famous ruins of Antiquity and the natural wonders that had long attracted artists to Italy. Unusually, he also found subjects for his brush in unprepossessing sights such as the old stone walls and shuttered windows he viewed from his studio rooftop. One example is the National Gallery's *A Wall in Naples* of about 1782 (fig. 4). These intimate works became known only when a descendant of the artist sent a group of them for auction as late as 1954. They were quickly recognised as among the most audacious oil sketches of their time, remarkable for their immediacy and close observation. Today, they are considered key documents in the history of the *plein-air* oil sketch.

Jones visited Naples between September 1778 and January the following year, and then settled there from May 1780 to August 1783. The city was far larger than Rome, boasted a lively international artistic community and, with figures like Sir William Hamilton in residence, was a magnet for British visitors who were potential patrons. This sketch was made in 1782 during Jones's second, longer residence in the city. It depicts the grotto at Posillipo, a tunnel cut by the ancient Romans to link Naples with Pozzuoli, further west along the coast. The tall, thin tunnel, depicted by numerous artists besides Jones, was a marvel of ancient engineering, and the tomb of Virgil was to be found there, a site no cultivated tourist could miss.

Nature and the man-made fuse in this austere image. Omitting foreground detail – though there is evidence of sketching on the sheet, at left – Jones set out to capture the distinctions between brilliant sunlight and shadow falling on the rock face at right and the impenetrable darkness of the vertical entrance to the tunnel at centre. Virgil's tomb itself is summarily indicated to the right of the main entrance. Above, green foliage echoes the rounded form of the white cloud in a brilliant sky. Jones also made a more detailed watercolour drawing of the grotto from a different angle (now in a private collection). *CR*

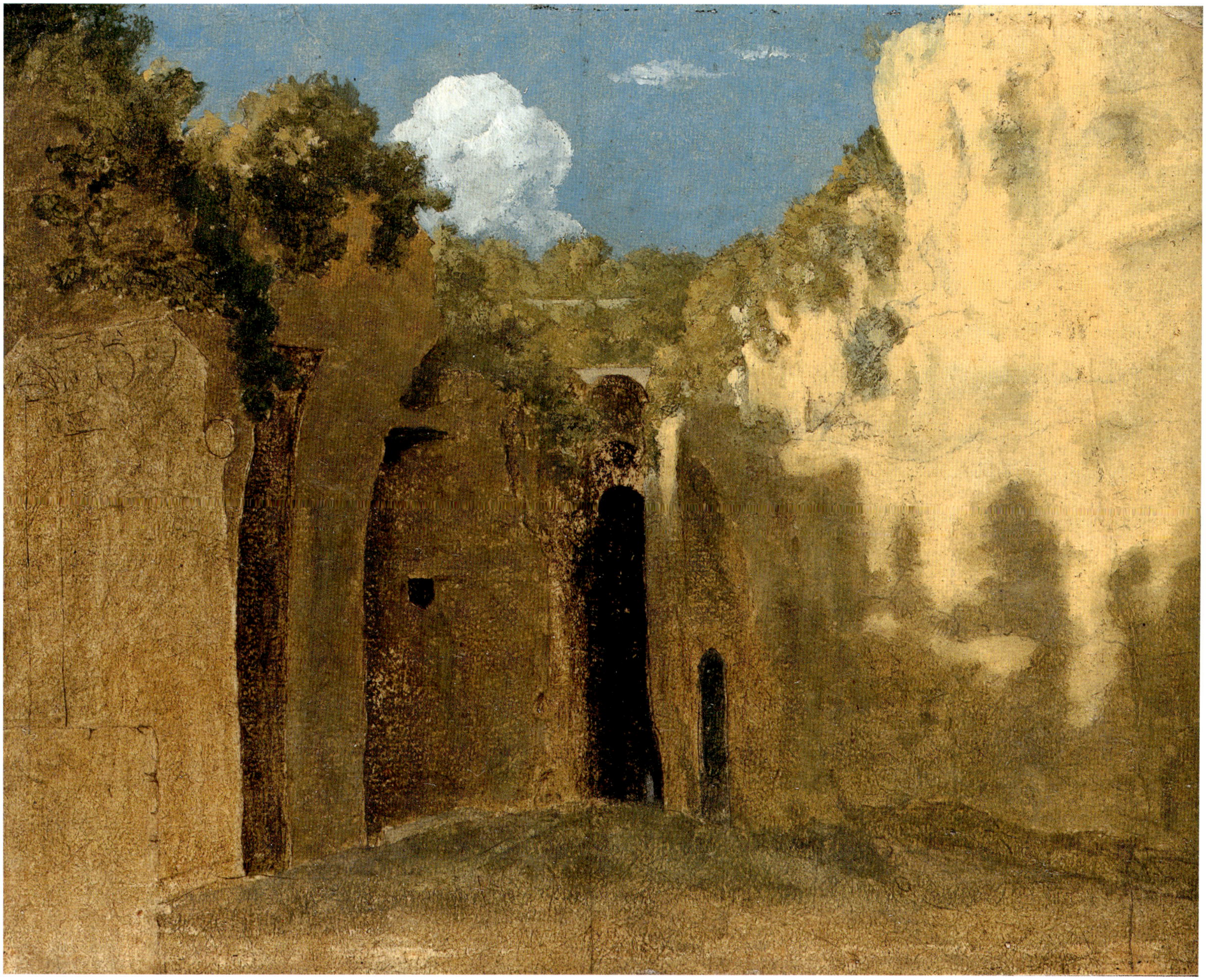

JONES, Thomas (1742–1803)

44. *Landscape with a Distant View of the Sea (Wales or Italy)*, undated

Oil on paper mounted on board, 14.7 x 22.1 cm

Inscriptions

Printed label on reverse of board

Thomas Jones (1742–1803)

First exhibition of the artist's recently discovered oil sketches of Wales, Rome and Naples.

Marble Hill House

Twickenham

1 June – 16 August

Provenance

Bought from Meatyard, London, in 1957.

Exhibition

London 1970, no. 18.

Literature

Gowing 1985, pp. 29–30, pl. 20.

The generalised features of this broad, sweeping landscape do not allow for a precise identification of the site. Gowing argued that the landscape was Welsh and that the painting was made before Jones departed for Italy in 1776. In his *Memoirs*, Jones himself reported making oil studies in his native Wales on three occasions in the 1770s.[1] The rounded forms of the landscape, the crisp division of the fields and the directness with which the motif is captured compare with Jones's known Welsh oil sketches, such as his *View at Pencerrig* of 1772 (private collection).[2] However, it also somewhat resembles a watercolour view that Jones made in the environs of Rome, at Larici.[3] The depiction of the fields also resembles the hillside in Jones's *View from Ponte Loreto, an Antique Bridge near Nettuno*.[4] The farm buildings in the middle ground could be Italian as well as Welsh. *CR*

1 Cited in Washington, Brooklyn and St Louis 1996–7, p. 118.

2 Illustrated Gere 1970, p. 469.

3 Auctioned at Phillips, London, 3 November 1986, lot. 20.

4 Auctioned at Christie's, London, 10 June 1999, lot 14.

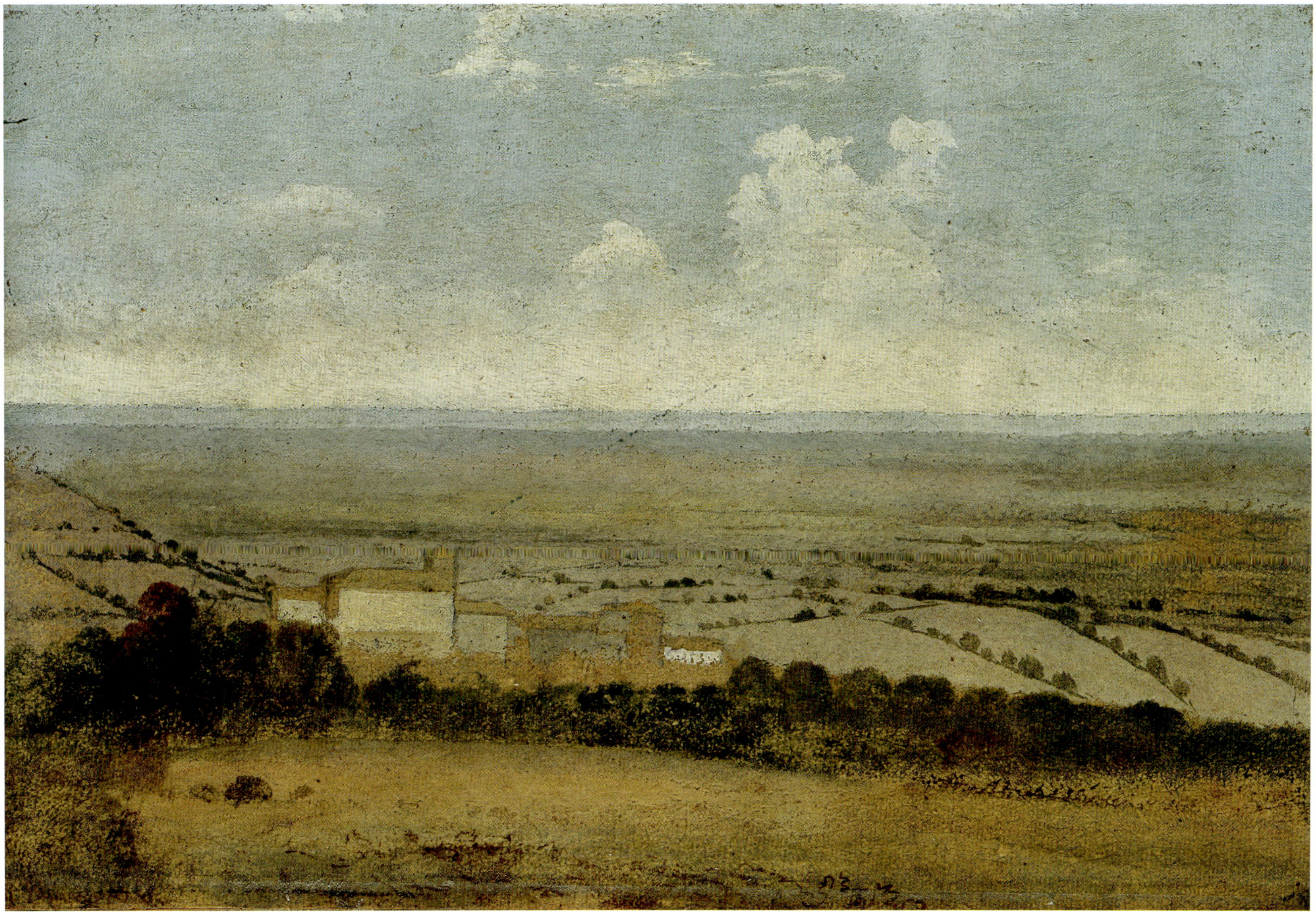

KERRICH, Thomas (1748–1828)

45. *Distant View of Lowestoft from the South,* perhaps 1794

Oil on panel, 16.5 x 34.9 cm

Inscription

Inscribed on the reverse *Lowestoft By T. Kerrich*

Provenance

Sotheby's, London, 28 October 1987, lot 320; bought from David Routledge, Suffolk, in 1989.

Kerrich had a distinguished career as an antiquarian, fellow of Magdalene College, Cambridge, and librarian of the University of Cambridge. During continental travels in the 1770s he was awarded a silver medal in Antwerp for a drawing, and it is as a draughtsman rather than a painter that he is best known. He bequeathed to the British Museum forty-eight volumes of his sketches of ancient costumes, and prints were made after several of his portrait drawings of Cambridge worthies. His important study of the prints of Martin van Heemskerck (1498–1574) was published in 1829.

This oil study is painted on a thick oak panel, not unlike a floorboard. It depicts a broad, calm bay along the Suffolk coast dotted with sailing ships. White-tipped waves lap a sandy beach. At lower left, above the beach, the artist includes the grassy outcrop on which he must have stood as he worked, and a trail leads along the knoll back towards what the inscription on the reverse of the panel identifies as the town of Lowestoft. A group of Kerrich's landscape drawings in a private collection[1] includes a sheet signed and dated 'Lowestoft, 1794', thus establishing a possible date for this work as well. Another sheet in the same collection is inscribed 'Pakefield', a village on the Suffolk coast immediately south of Lowestoft. Pakefield may be the vantage point from which this sketch is painted; the view remains almost unchanged to this day. On a third sheet, of 1802, a later hand has added: 'I have a small oil painting on panel'. The annotation could imply that, when confronted by a motif, Kerrich made both drawn and painted sketches out of doors, or conversely that his landscape paintings were based on his earlier drawings. Although Kerrich's other landscape paintings have not been identified, the simplicity and directness of this image suggest a precocious and original approach to landscape. The work of a trained artist, but not essentially a painter, it is at the same time remarkably unfettered by a reliance on conventional landscape formulae. *CR*

1 Known from photographs in the Witt Library, Courtauld Institute.

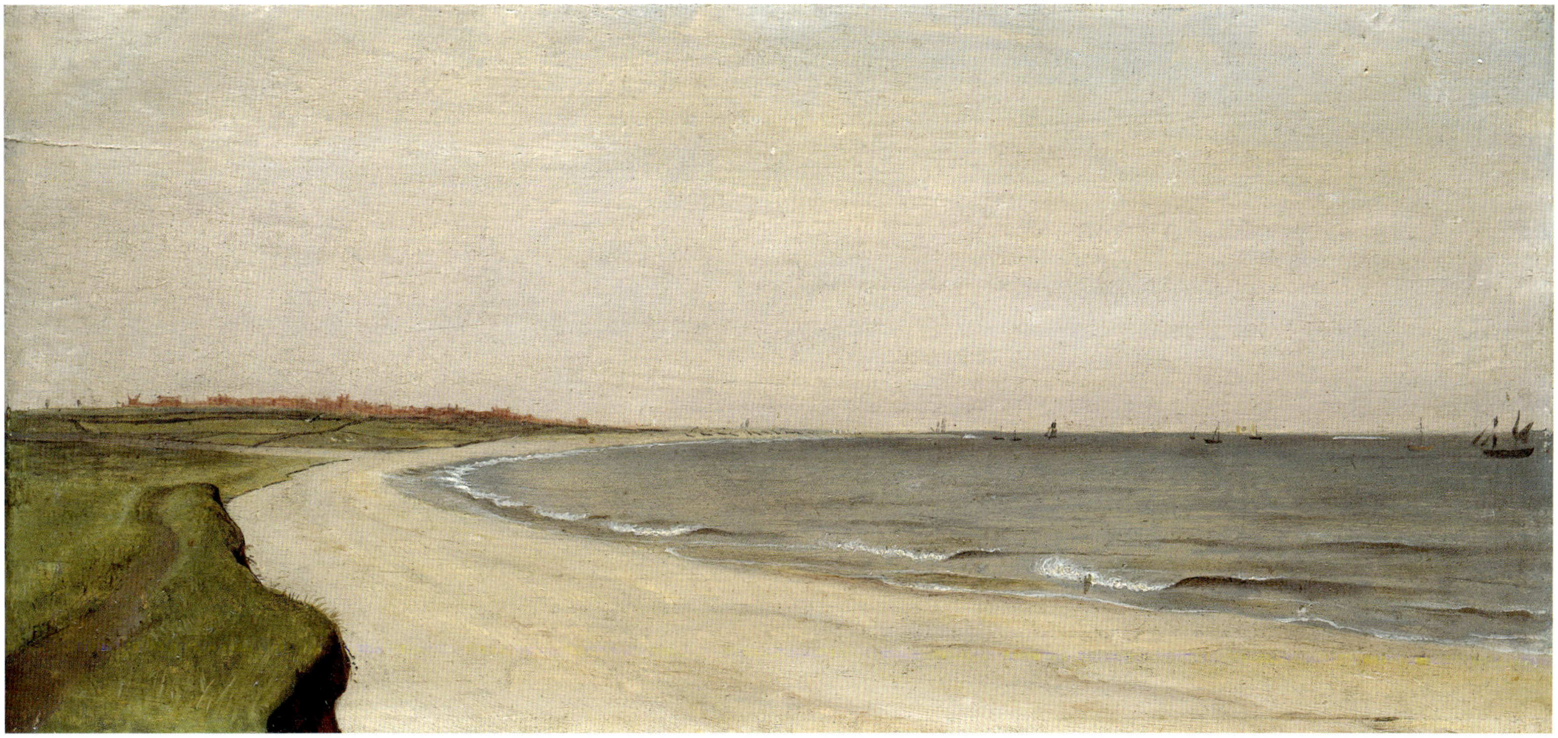

Knip, Josephus Augustus (1777–1847), attributed to
46. *Green Mountains,* around 1810
Oil on paper laid on canvas, 20.0 x 37.0 cm

Inscriptions

In chalk on back of canvas *289 426 Wol*
Stencil on stretcher *DS 300*
Label on stretcher *Christie's South Kensington 8 February 1984, lot 201 (Follower of Thomas Jones)*
Label on stretcher *289426*

Provenance

Bought at Christie's South Kensington, London, on 8 February 1984, lot 201 (as Follower of Thomas Jones).

The location of these tall mountains, with their distinctive peaks silhouetted against a blue sky, has not been identified. It is clear, however, that we are not meant to read them as rising abruptly from a flat, bare plain. Rather, the artist seems to have followed the advice, articulated by Valenciennes and often given to painters making oil sketches in the early nineteenth century, to concentrate attention on a motif in the middle distance while leaving the foreground empty. The pale green strip in the foreground here is either a thinly applied underpaint or a wash added when the sketch was finished in order to establish tonal unity on the sheet. The attribution to Knip, first advanced by John Gere, is based on the resemblance of this sketch to other depictions of green Italian mountains by the artist, especially in the use of a mottled brushstroke and broken blue pigment in the sky. Most striking is its resemblance to Knip's *Lake Albano with Palazzolo* and *A View in the Campagna*, both in the Hamburger Kunsthalle.[1]

Knip is the best-known member of a dynasty of Dutch painters active from the late eighteenth century to about 1900. He worked in Paris for several years in the early nineteenth century. The large, composed Neoclassical landscapes on which he built his reputation derive, however, from motifs that appear in wash drawings and oil sketches executed in Italy between 1809 and 1813, which Knip consulted throughout his later career. That career was cut short in the late 1820s when the artist lost the sight of one eye. Total blindness followed in 1832, as it had for Knip's father thirty-seven years earlier. *CR*

1 The former painting is illustrated in colour in Washington, Brooklyn and St Louis 1996–7, cat. no. 52; both are illustrated in Howoldt and Baer 1993, p. 102.

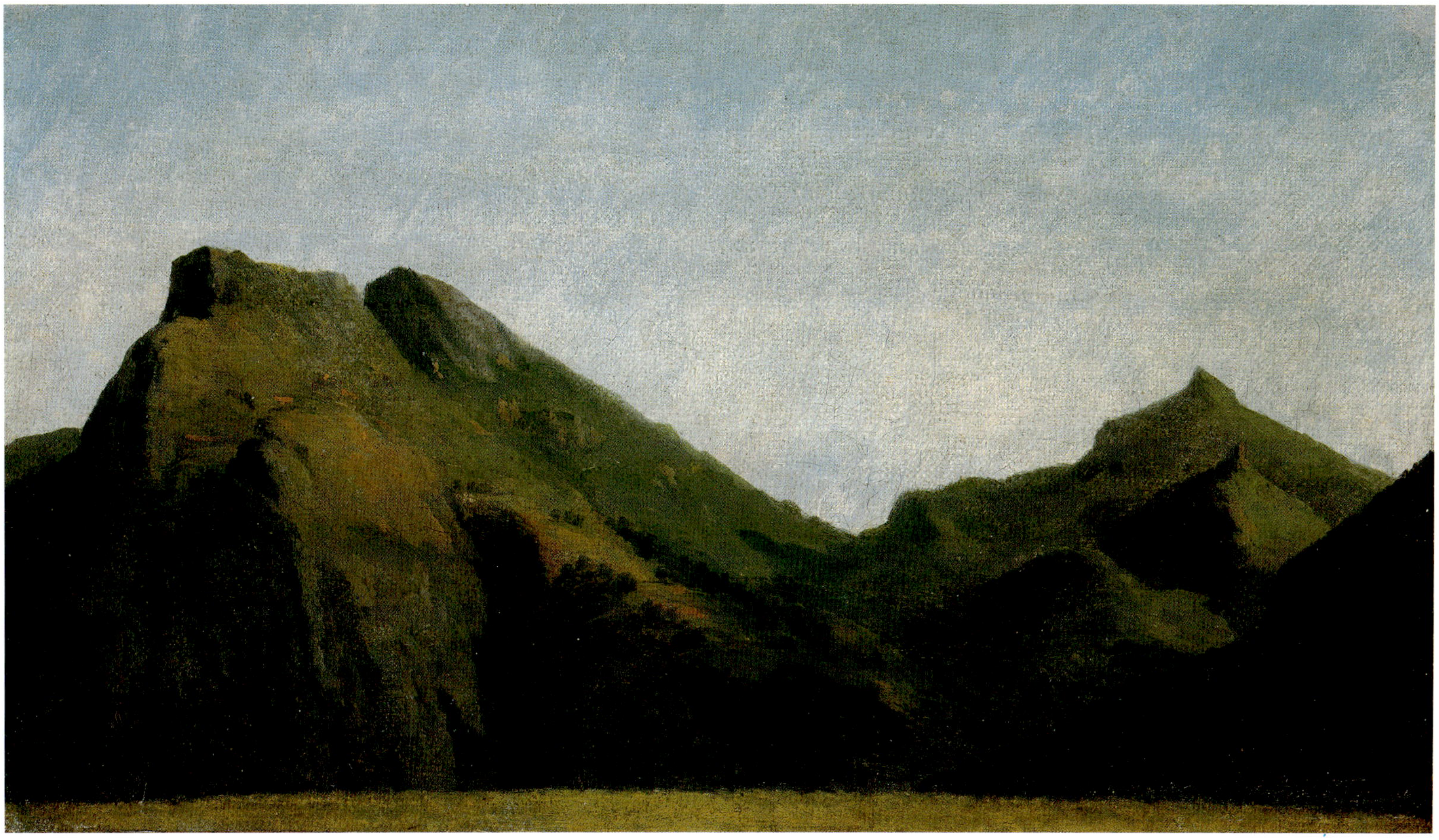

KØLLE, Claus Anton (1827–1872)

47. *A Courtyard in Rome*, 1860s

Oil on canvas, 27.8 x 24.1 cm

Inscriptions

On label on stretcher *J erst Flave I Rom, males af Kolle UDSALC, St. Kjöbmargerade 15, 1 KJÖBENHAVN*

Ink inscription on stretcher *1.43; 14 48 50*

Provenance

Bought from the Bury Street Gallery, London, in 1990.

A Danish painter of portraits, landscapes and theatrical decorations, Kølle visited Rome in 1860–1 and again in 1867. This view into a Roman courtyard was perhaps made from the first- or second-storey window of an inn. The artist looked down on the metal dome of a conservatory seen through the branches of a fir tree. A leafy orange tree is heavy with fruit, which provides the brightest notes of colour in the painting. The oranges echo in miniature the rounded dome below. It must have been springtime as the largest tree, whose branches dance across the upper half of the canvas, has only begun to come into leaf. At top, windows on the other side of the courtyard are open to the breeze, while the tiled roof of a shorter building stands at right angles to them. Sunlight casts irregular shadows at right. Kølle must have enjoyed the complicated grouping of solid and changing forms that he spied through his window. His vision is made even more ambiguous by the fact that neither the floor of the courtyard nor the sky are shown. We are aware only of a tightly contained space, bursting with new life. *CR*

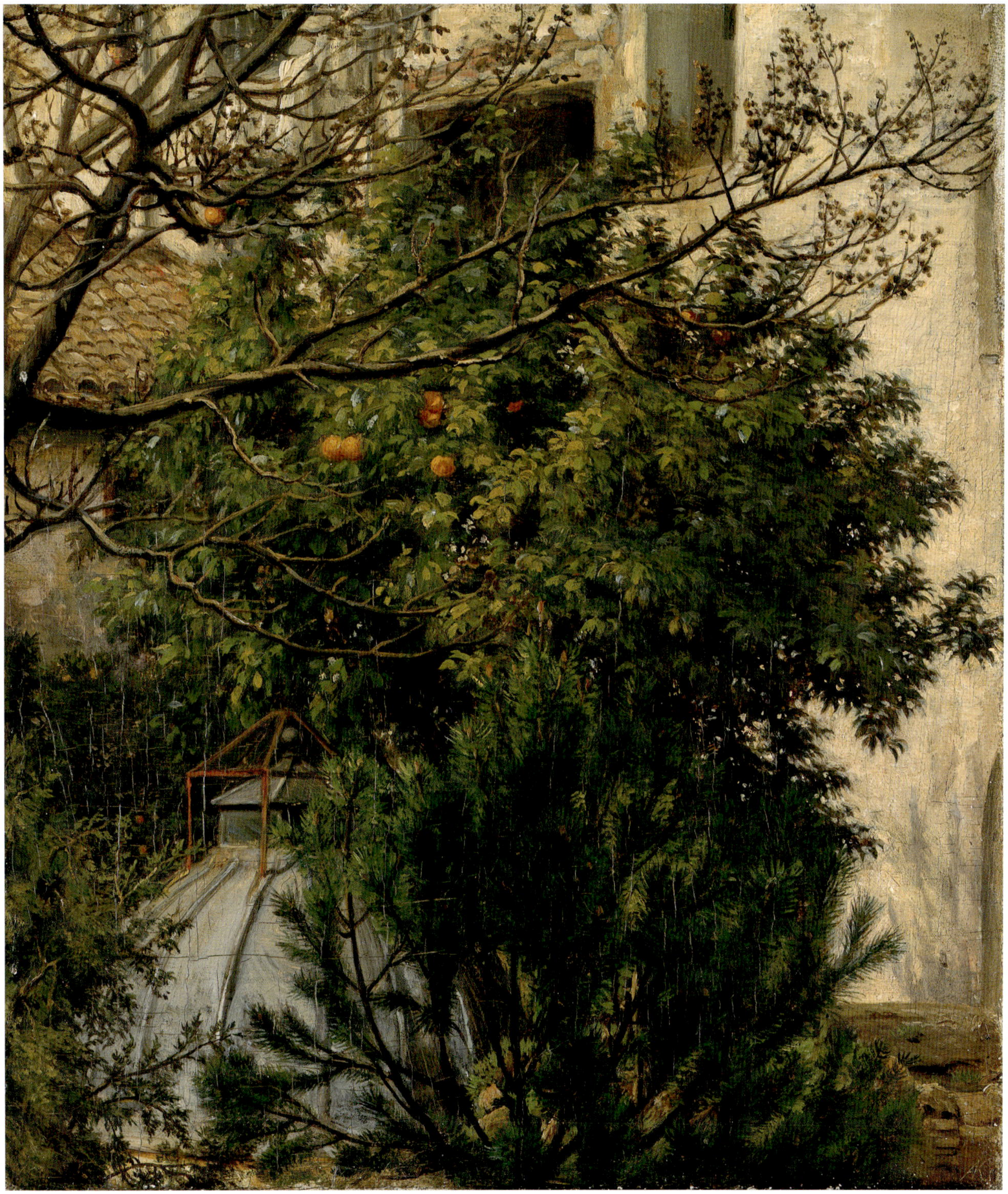

Leighton of Stretton, Frederic, Baron (1830–1896)

48. *Archway on the Palatine,* undated

Oil on canvas, 29.0 x 19.0 cm

Inscriptions

Inscribed on bottom edge of canvas *11 x 7*

Stencil on stretcher *82*

Label on reverse, from posthumous studio sale of 1896 *Lord Leighton, P.R.A.*

Inscribed in pencil *35 N Ashely Rd. ... Mr. Oult*

Inscribed on label in ink *KING GUSTAV IV ADOLF SOFIRO CASTLE*

Provenance

The artist's studio sale, Christie's, London, 11 and 13 July 1896, unidentified lot; King Gustav IV Adolf of Sweden; bought from Sotheby's Belgravia, 29 July 1975, lot 31.

As the President of the Royal Academy for eighteen years from 1878, Lord Leighton was at the centre of the Victorian art world. Showered with honours, a month before he died he became the only British artist ever elevated to the peerage. His monumental, precisely detailed canvases on Italian Renaissance and ancient mythological themes were admired in his day, although not widely influential after the beginning of the twentieth century. A resurgence of interest in Leighton's work in recent years culminated in 1996 in a highly popular retrospective exhibition at the Royal Academy itself.

Less well known than Leighton's large-scale figure paintings, and a particular pleasure of that exhibition, were the vivid landscape oil sketches that the artist made during much of his career, but only occasionally exhibited. From youth Leighton was an indefatigable traveller. He especially loved Italy, but also journeyed to Greece and the Greek Islands, Asia Minor, Spain and North Africa, making oil sketches as he went. He was friendly with the landscape painters Giovanni Costa and George Heming Mason, whom he first met in Rome in 1853, and with whom he often worked. Like them, he attempted to capture the play of brilliant Mediterranean light on the distinctive landscapes and indigenous architecture of the areas through which he passed. As Christopher Newall has shown, Leighton's interest in the oil sketch was also strongly influenced by the example of Corot, several of whose paintings he came to own, including his brilliantly improvisatory *Four Times of Day* (Loyd Collection, on loan to the National Gallery, London).[1]

Leighton lived in Rome from 1852 to 1855. Newall suggests, however, that the artist's earliest surviving oil sketches date from his visit to Capri in 1859.[2] Thus he probably painted this view of ancient ruins on the Palatine Hill during a subsequent visit to the Eternal City, perhaps during the 1860s. The eye is drawn into the pictorial space through the tall Roman archway to the blue sky beyond, and at the same time up the wall face, a subtly modulated passage of earth tones, to the foliage that has invaded the scene and another patch of blue sky above. As photographs taken at the time of Leighton's death show, the artist filled his studio with his oil sketches (figs. 36, 37). Mounted in simple gold frames, they hung in rows around the walls, amid casts of ancient and Renaissance sculpture, and a wealth of exotic bric-à-brac. Those sketches were dispersed at a posthumous auction in July 1896. This painting can be seen in one of the studio views (fig. 36), and on the back it bears a label from the studio sale, but its lot number has not been identified. The subject of antique ruins must have appealed to a former owner of the sketch, King Gustav IV Adolf of Sweden, who was himself an archaeologist. *CR*

1 London 1996 p. 45.

2 Ibid.

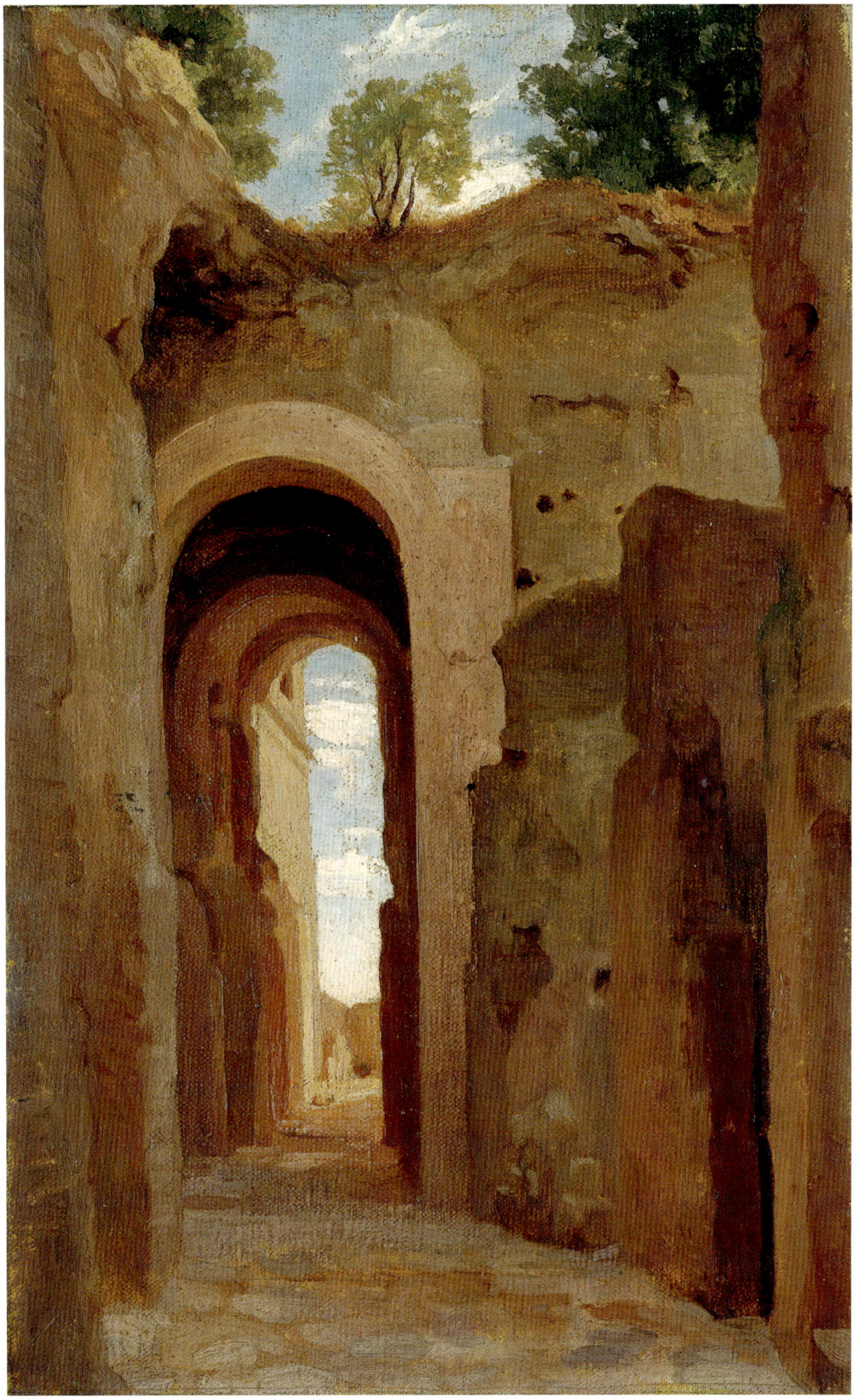

Leighton of Stretton, Frederic, Baron (1830–1896)

49. *View in Capri,* perhaps 1859

Oil on canvas, 21.2 x 29.3 cm

Inscriptions

Inscribed on bottom turned-over edge

11 x 7 3/4 inches

Stencil on stretcher *S (8?) 20p (1?)*

Provenance

Probably included in the artist's studio sale, Christie's, London, 11 and 13 July 1896, unidentified lot; bought from the Fine Art Society, London, in 1981.

The painting can be seen in one of the series of photographs of Leighton's studio taken after his death in 1896, which show walls lined with the artist's framed landscape oil sketches (fig. 36). Those sketches were sold at auction in July the same year, and this work was probably included in that studio sale, although its lot number has not been identified.

Leighton spent five weeks on the island of Capri in the early summer of 1859, and his first securely dated oil sketches were made during the sojourn. Like those of his friend Giovanni Costa, the majority of Leighton's 'pure' landscape sketches, as opposed to those in which the built environment dominates, are resolutely horizontal in disposition. Here, however, he tries his hand at a particularly complicated spatial configuration of houses, hills and sea. Standing high on a rugged hillside, the artist looks down onto the roofs of a small group of simple peasant houses. With their light colour, distinctive shallow domes and chimneys, they stand in stark contrast to the landscape they inhabit. Leighton then raises his eyes to follow a meandering trail up and across a steep crest of hills. Skittering trails of paint lead the way across this harsh, timeless terrain. The distant summit which the eye finally reaches is almost exactly at the vertical mid-point of the painting. At left, the cliffs fall away vertiginously to the sea.

The site is redolent of ancient Mediterranean civilisation – one can imagine a trireme, seeking shelter for the night, pulling into the cove at lower left – though the artist does not seem to have used the motif in any of his later mythological scenes. Indeed, Newall quite correctly draws a distinction between Leighton's essentially private landscape sketches, made to capture fleeting effects in nature, and the landscapes he composed so carefully in his studio for the backgrounds of his large figure paintings.[1] *CR*

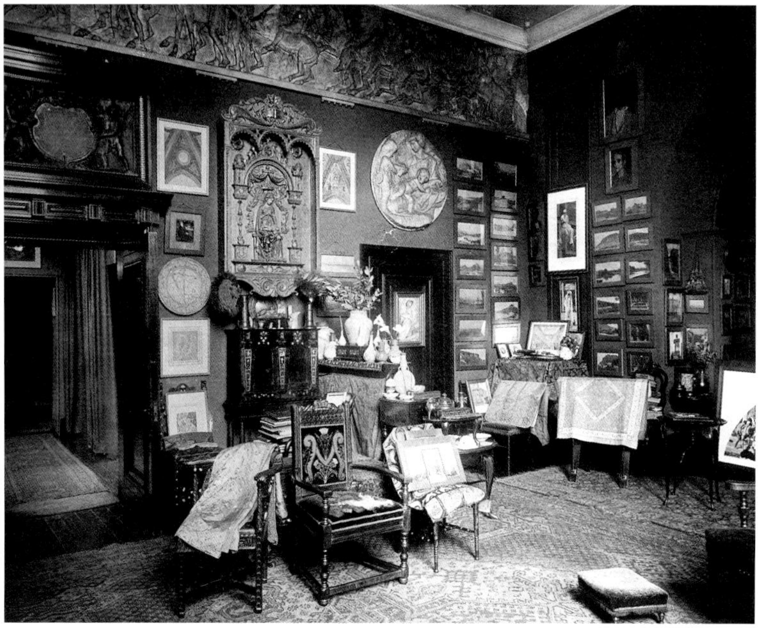

Fig 36 Frederic, Lord Leighton's studio in 1896.

1 London 1996, p. 52.

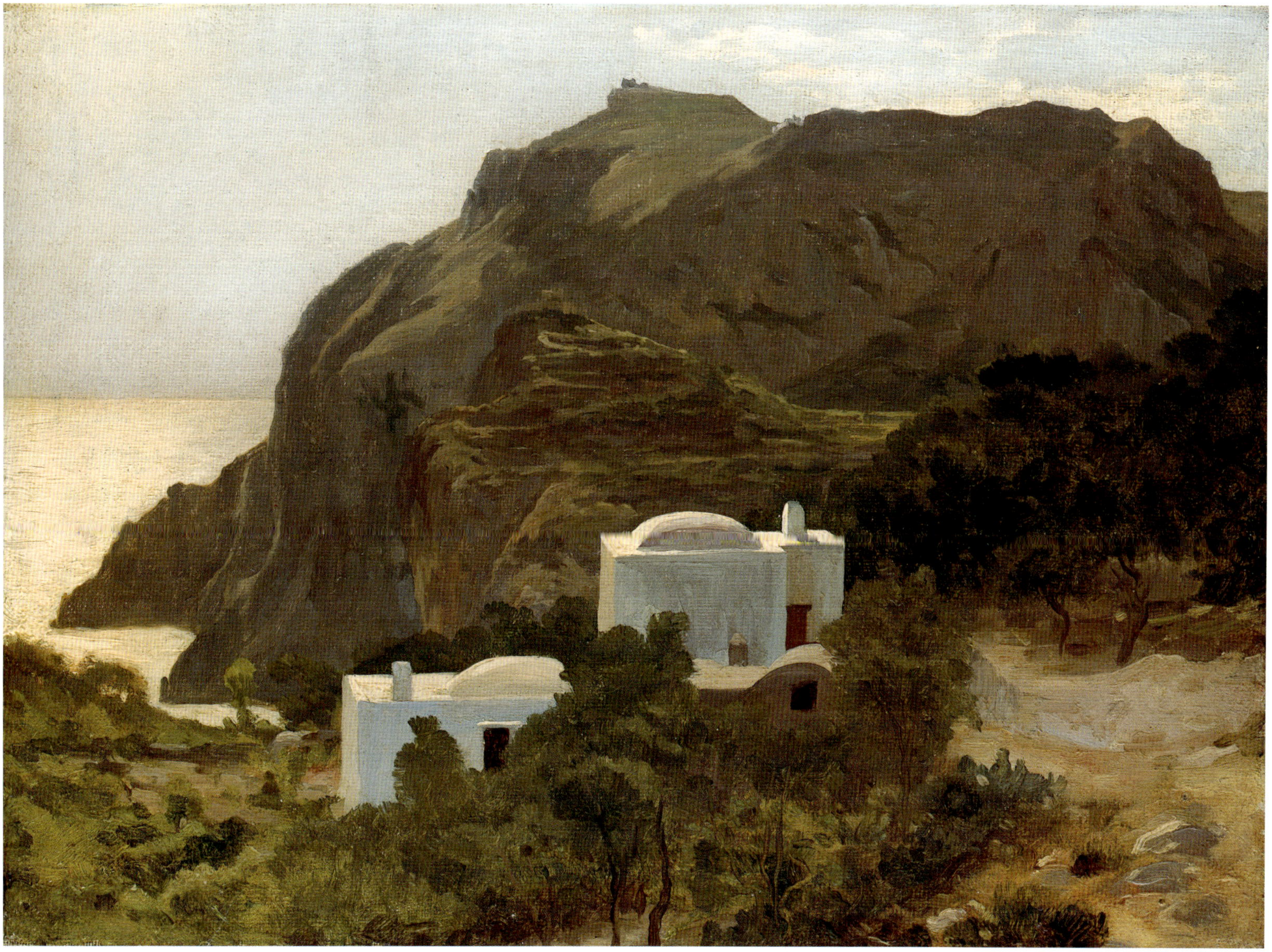

Leighton of Stretton, Frederic, Baron (1830–1896), attributed to
50. *Houses in Capri,* perhaps 1859

Oil on canvas, 22.3 x 38.5 cm

Inscription

Inscribed on brown edging paper *Matera (Poulu)*

Provenance

Bought from Fischer & Keiner, Paris, date not recorded.

This painting was unattributed when acquired but the attribution to Leighton is generally accepted, notably by Peyton Skipwith of the Fine Art Society. It compares well with the oil sketches made on Capri, where the artist delighted in depicting the jumble of white-washed houses, narrow, angular streets and rugged hills towering over buildings in the centre of the island. He practised painting at different times of day, in order to capture changing light effects. Many of his Capri views are characterised by a limited range of colours, as here, but subtle discrimination of tones. At the same time, this picture is less fully resolved than other Capri sketches, especially at lower right.

There is some possibility that the site depicted is not Capri, but elsewhere. An inscription on the edging paper reads: *Matera (Poulu)*, although whether there is any relation between that inscription and the painting itself is not clear. The inland town of Matera is a provincial capital in southern Italy. It is not known if Leighton visited the town but he did travel in southern Italy in the spring and summer of 1859, reaching Paestum before crossing to Capri. *Poulu* would appear to be a French word, the precise significance of which is unknown. *CR*

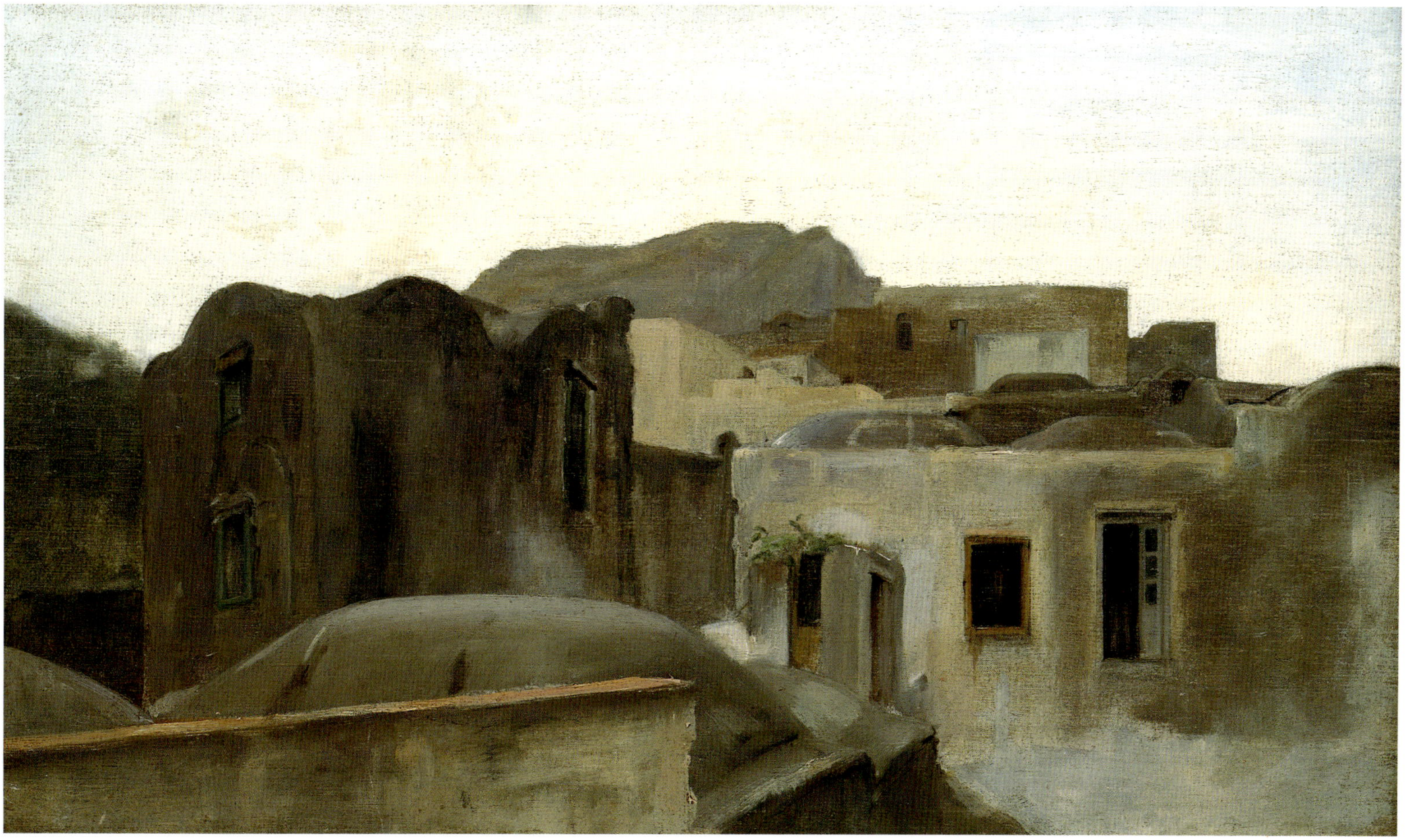

Leighton of Stretton, Frederic, Baron (1830–1896)
51. *The Villa Malta, Rome,* 1860s
Oil on canvas, 27.2 x 41.5 cm

Inscriptions
Inscribed on reverse *16 ⅛ x 10 ⅛*
Inscribed on stretcher *S20p*
Label on stretcher *Villa Malta*
Label on frame *RA exhibition 1996 cat. no. 51*

Provenance
The artist's studio sale,Christie's, London, 11–16 July 1896, lot 54; bought by Valentine Cameron Prinsep for £52.10s; bought from Hugh Squire, date not recorded.

Exhibitions
According to 1896 Leighton sale catalogue, exhibited in Dublin and York; London 1897, no. 104; London 1976, no. 35; London 1996, no. 51.

Literature
Rhys 1898, p. 92; Ormond 1975, p.133, no. 504; Washington, Brooklyn and St Louis 1996–7, p. 25, fig. 1.

The painting is visible in a photograph of Leighton's studio taken after his death (fig. 37), and it figured in the 1896 sale of the contents of Leighton's studio. The collector Hugh Squire had convinced himself that it was by Corot, one of the most influential and imitated artists of the nineteenth century and in his disappointment at discovering that it was 'merely' by Leighton, agreed to sell it to John and Charlotte Gere.

As Newall points out, however, the connection with Corot is vital to an understanding of the painting.[1] In the late 1850s Leighton had come to appreciate deeply the work of the French painter, and particularly the free, spontaneous, but structurally rigorous, oil sketches that he had made in Italy a few decades earlier. Leighton sought to approach the immediacy of perception that characterised the finest works of the French master, as well as his architectonic structuring. This view of the Villa Malta contrasts the tall cypresses and the foliage in the middle ground with the tall tower of the villa at the centre of the canvas and the rich and simple forms of the villa's architecture. Johan Christian Dahl painted the same motif, more crisply, with its tall, asymmetrical tower on the Pincio where Leighton often stayed when he was in Rome, in his *A View from the Villa Malta*, 1820 (Oslo, Nasjonalgalleriet). Newall believes the work was painted after 1859, when Leighton painted his first securely dated group of oil sketches on Capri, and when he was particularly under the influence of Corot. *CR*

Fig 37 Frederic, Lord Leighton's studio in 1896.

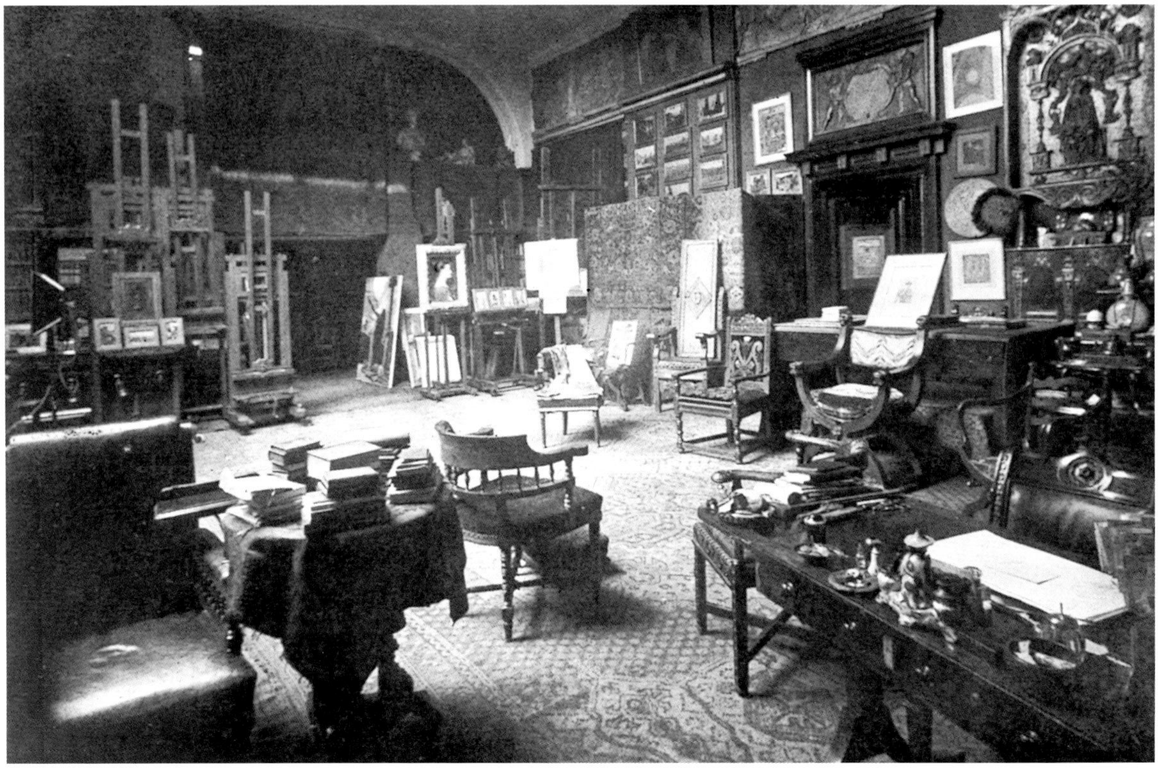

1 London 1996, cat. no. 51.

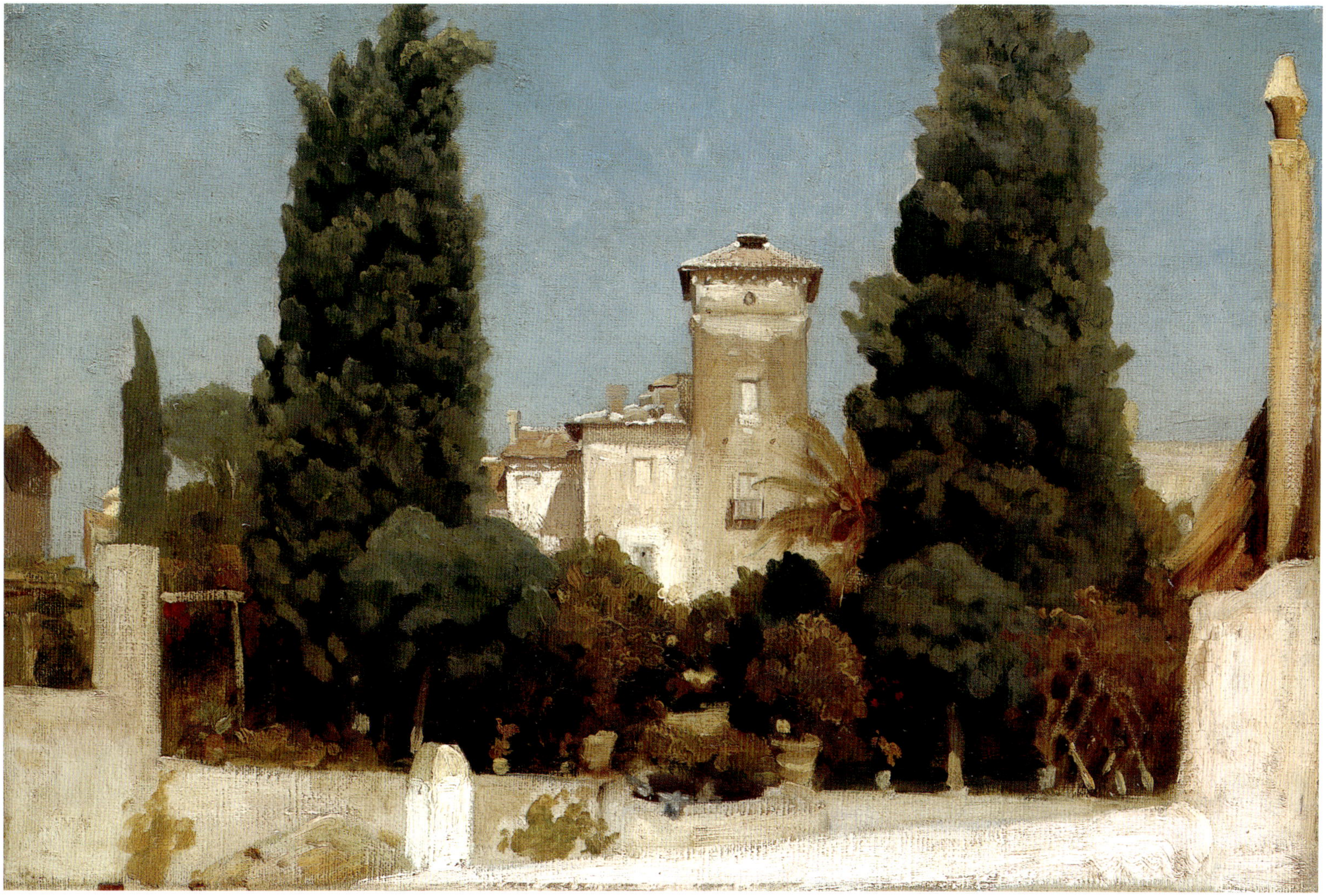

Leighton of Stretton, Frederic, Baron (1830–1896)

52. *An Outcrop in the Campagna,* perhaps 1866

Oil on canvas, 20.2 x 43.5 cm

Inscription

Stencilled on reverse *820 p and 9 5 (?)*

Provenance

The artist's studio sale, Christie's, London, 11 and 10 July 1896, lot unidentified; Christopher Gibbs (?); Sotheby's, London, 12 November 1992, lot 113; bought from The Fine Art Society, London, in 1992.

This simple image of a rocky outcrop silhouetted against a cerulean sky is a recent rediscovery. It reappeared in a 1992 London sale, together with a more panoramic view of *Monte Sacro, in the Roman Campagna, showing the Ponte Nomentano.*[1] The painting can be seen in a photograph of Leighton's studio taken after his death in 1896 (fig. 36) but before the landscape oil sketches he displayed there were sold at auction in July that year. Probably included in that sale, the lot number of the present sketch is unidentified.

In the autumn of 1866 Leighton, Giovanni Costa and William Blake Richmond undertook a painting expedition in the Roman Campagna when, Newall has suggested, the *Monte Sacro* sketch might well have been painted.[2] This sketch may also date from that expedition. It employs the horizontal format that Costa and Leighton often preferred for oil sketches, and achieves a compelling level of directness in the transcription of natural phenomena and the play of light that is characteristic of Leighton's finest Italian oil sketches. The emphatic daub of pure white pigment at the left is an unexpected animating touch. *CR*

1 They were Sotheby's, London, 12 November 1992, lots 112 and 113 respectively.

2 London 1996, cat. no. 52.

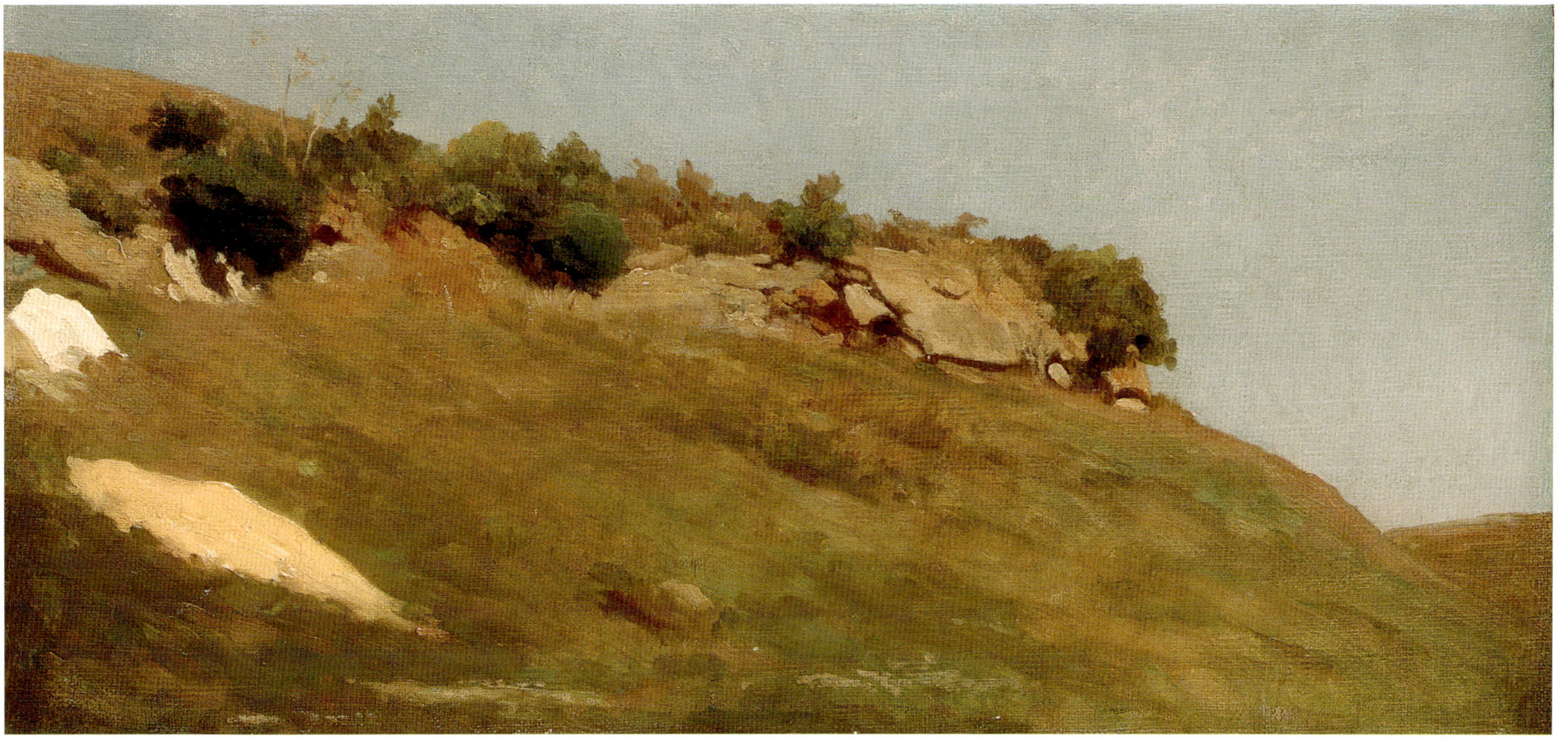

LEIGHTON OF STRETTON, Frederic, Baron (1830–1896)

53. *A View in Spain*, 1866

Oil on canvas, 27.3 x 39.7 cm

Inscription

Stencilled on the stretcher *7 AT 820p*

Provenance

The artist's studio sale, Christie's, London, 11 and 13 July 1896, possibly lot 56; Wickham Flower; bought from The Fine Art Society, London, date not recorded.

Exhibition

Perhaps London 1897, no. 174.

Literature

Ormond 1975, no. 518.

Leighton went to Spain for the first time in 1866, travelling extensively and making oil sketches as he went. This study can be seen in a photograph of the artist's studio (fig. 36), and was almost certainly included in his posthumous auction of July 1896, although its lot number has never been known. Now that Newall has identified an oil sketch from the Spanish trip acquired by the Tate Gallery in 1924 with lot 14 in the 1896 sale,[1] rather than with lot 56, *A View in Spain*, with which it was traditionally associated, it is possible that the present work is the one sold under that title.

The sketch shows an old stone wall dividing a farmyard from green fields, sparsely dotted with trees. Rugged hills, perhaps part of the Serranía de Ronda range, rise in the distance. Leighton used several shades of green, olive and brown to differentiate the various aspects of the landscape. Darker green is worked into the hillside in vivid touches. The wall, worn and rounded with age, is as irregular as the hills themselves; Leighton finds here an equivalence between natural and man-made forms. Daubs of white animate the very bottom of the canvas. On the right, the wall and doorway of the farmhouse provide a stong vertical accent and establish where Leighton stood in order to make his sketch, perhaps in the shade of an overhanging eave. He used a similar device, a window frame at right, to show where he positioned himself to sketch his *Houses in Venice* (cat. no. 54). *CR*

1 London 1996, cat. no. 36.

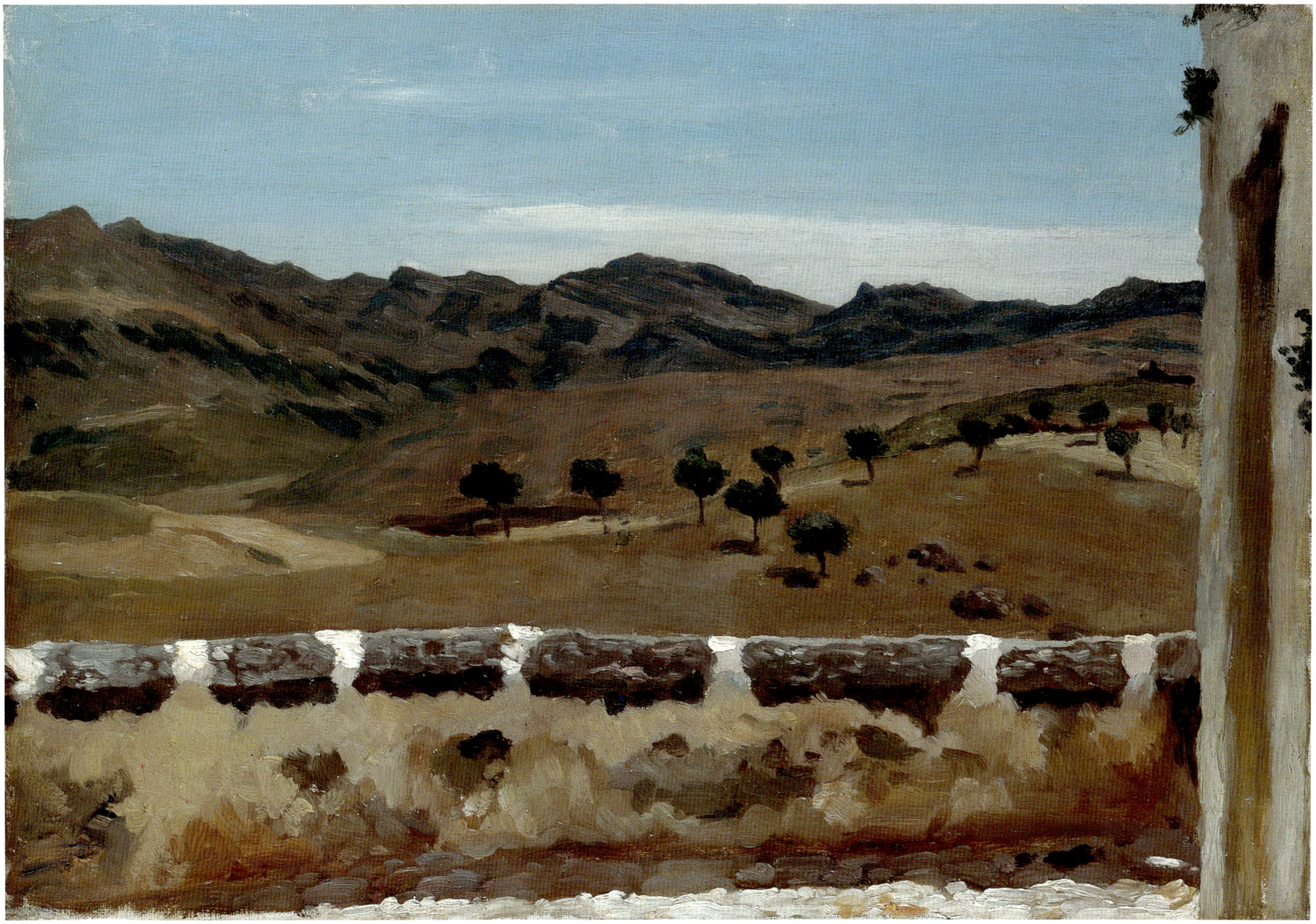

LEIGHTON OF STRETTON, Frederic, Baron (1830–1896)

54. *Houses in Venice,* perhaps 1867

Oil on canvas, 25.0 x 39.5 cm

Newall characterises this as 'one of the most extraordinary and original' of Leighton's oil sketches.[1] The view is probably from a hotel window in Venice, as the vertical band of paint at far right suggests a window frame. It looks out over red-tiled roofs, stuccoed walls and chimney pots, in an unidentified quarter of the city. At left a tall, thin cypress, its very tip caught in the sunlight as it breaks above the roof line, rises from a courtyard. Long shadows fall across the roof running across the middle ground of the painting, while brilliant touches of light, perhaps reflected from the water of a canal far below, dance across the wall. In its play of flat and angled planes, this is an almost proto-Cubist composition, but redolent of the specific atmosphere of a waning Venetian afternoon. Newall suggests that it might have been painted during a stop in Venice on Leighton's return from Asia Minor in 1867.[2] *CR*

Inscriptions

On back of plyboard: *8* or *S 0p*

Label *Lord Leighton, P.R.A. SN. 7563*

On back of wood panel protecting plywood support

Royal Academy winter Exhibition, 1897

Belonged to T.W. Bacon Esq.

4 Lyndhurst road, Hampstead

From Robert Dunthorne

Print Publisher

The Rembrandt Head

5 Vigo Street, London W

Oil sketch from the Leighton Collection

The Fine Art Society Ltd.

148 New Bond Street, London, W1Y 0JT

No. 5841

March 1974

Exhibited: RA, Winter 1897

Provenance: T.W. Bacon, R. Thesiger

Provenance

The artist's studio sale, Christie's, London, 11 and 13 July 1896, lot 2 (*A Study of Houses in Venice*); bought by Robert Dunthorne for £31.10s; 1897, T. W. Bacon; Roderick Thesiger; Mrs Robert Frank, 1973; bought from the Fine Art Society, London, in 1973.

Exhibitions

According to 1896 Leighton sales catalogue, exhibited in Dublin; London 1897, no. 150; London 1930, no. 34; London 1976, no. 36; Cambridge and London 1980–1, no. 102; London 1996, no. 97.

Literature

Rhys 1898, p. 91; Ormond 1975, no. 529, pl. 150; Newall 1990, p. 64, pl. 41.

1 London 1996, cat. no. 97.

2 Ibid.

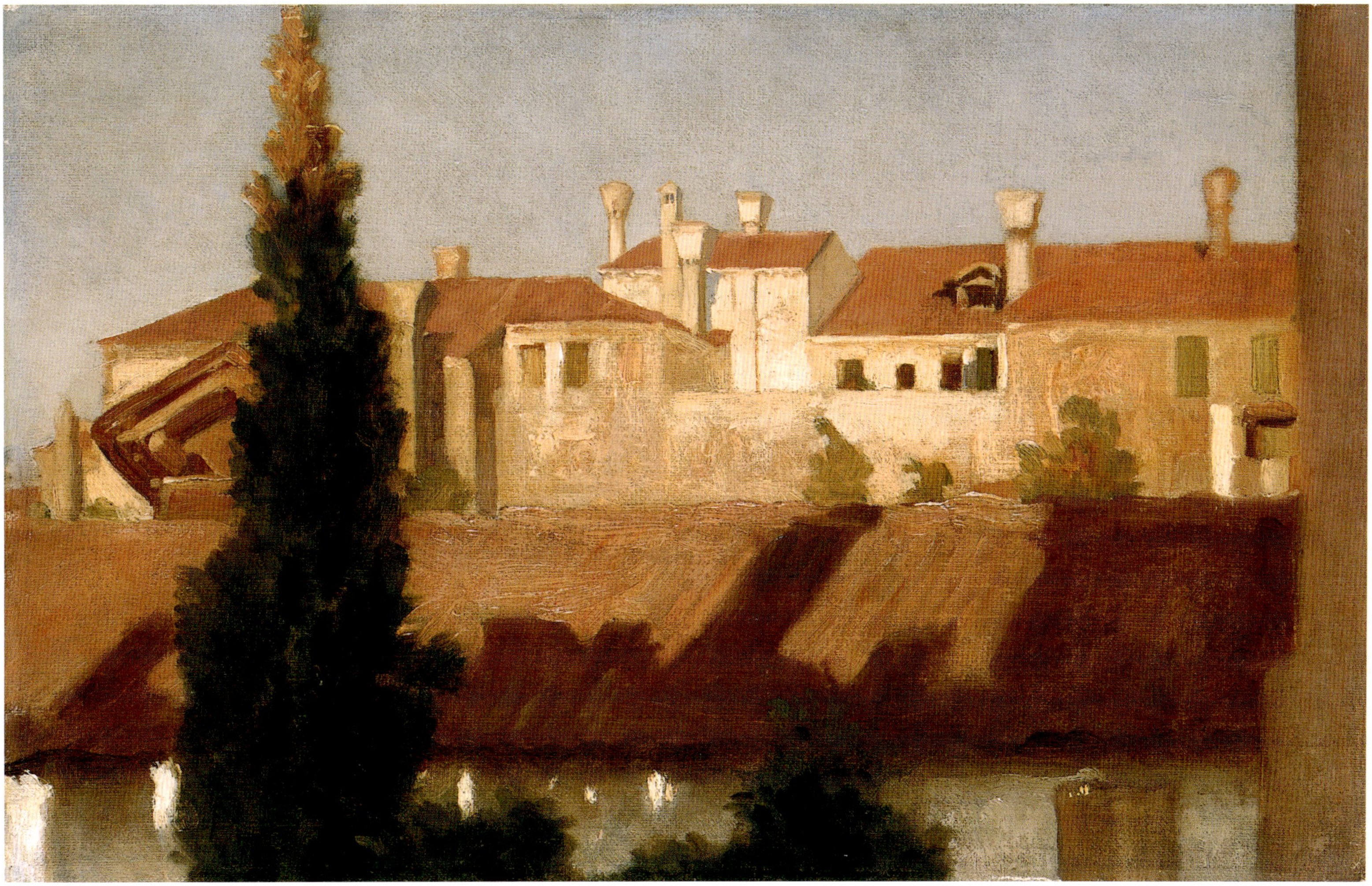

LEIGHTON OF STRETTON, Frederic, Baron (1830–1896)

55. *Coastal Landscape,* around 1880

Oil on canvas laid on board, 21.5 x 39.3 cm

Provenance

Sir Malcolm Bullock, Bt.; Christie's, London, 17 March 1967, lot 64; bought from the Fine Art Society, London, in 1968.

Literature

Ormond 1975, no. 536.

It is not certain when or where Leighton painted this rugged coastal landscape. It may perhaps be the coast of Cornwall which the artist frequently visited, attracted by its dramatic rock formations. He was also drawn to such natural phenomena in Ireland and Scotland. The broad stokes of the brush, and the dynamic silhouetting of forms against the sky somewhat resemble the vivid treatment of the motif in a very different kind of oil sketch, the portrait of a single, massive rock at Kynance Cove in Cornwall, painted in 1884 (private collection).[1] In structure, the study owes a debt to the works of Leighton's mentor in oil sketching, Giovanni Costa. As with Costa's *Porto d'Anzio* (cat. no. 19), the artist has chosen a horizontal format, viewing the shoreline from behind a screen of shrubbery. The sandy beach and coastline cliffs diminish toward the horizon at left. The muted red of the roof on a hut or shelter at right is the highest note of colour in the painting. *CR*

1 London 1996, cat. no. 92.

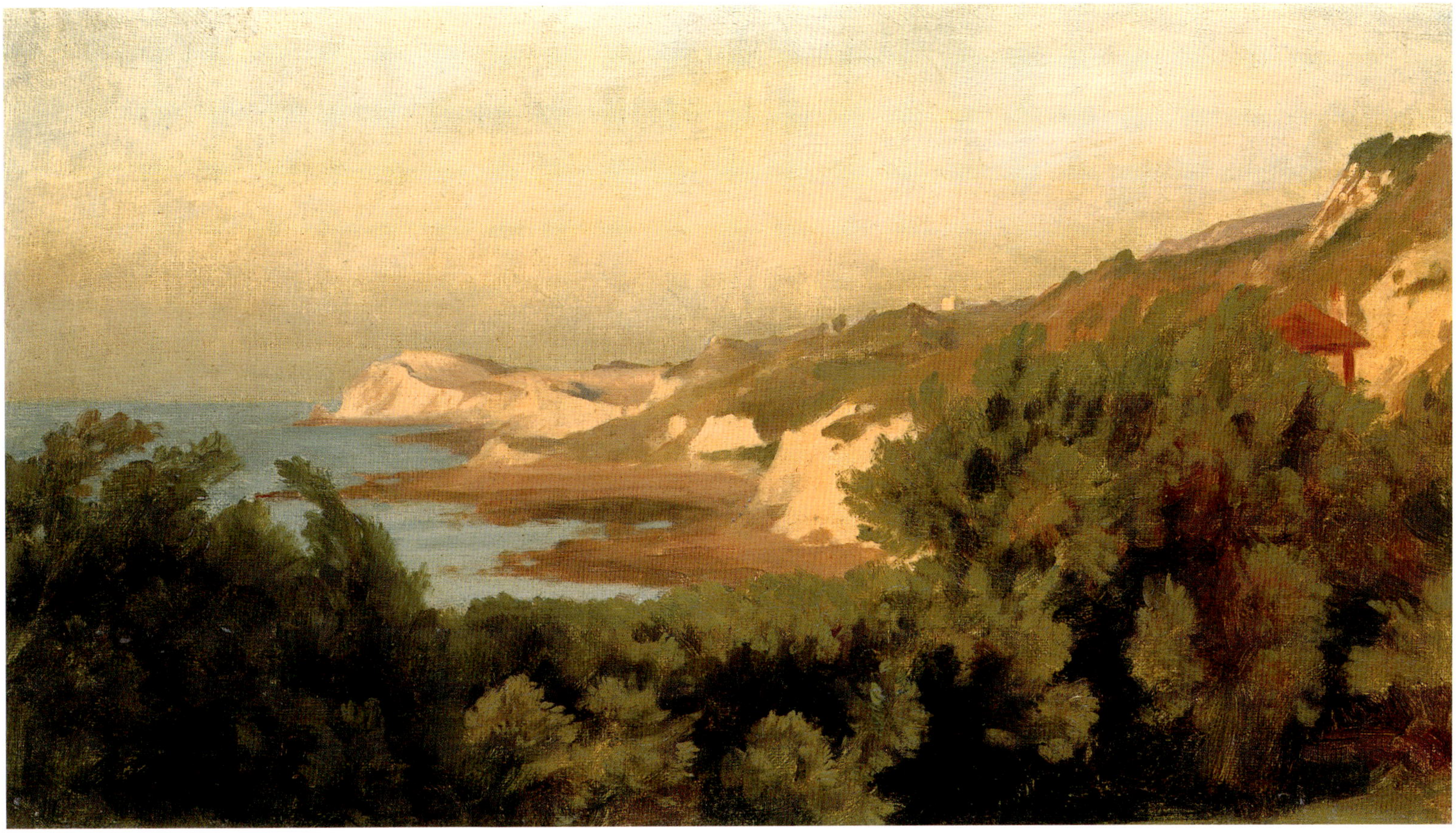

MASON, George Heming (1818–1872)
56. *The Villa Borghese*, about 1852–3

Oil on paper mounted on board, 13.5 x 36.1 cm

Inscription

Inscribed on the original gold mount *George Heming Mason, The Park of the Villa Borghese*. On the back under adhesive tape *George Mason ARA*.

Provenance

1976, Fine Art Society, London; bought from Virginia Surtees in 1976.

Exhibitions

London 1976, no. 48; Cambridge and London 1980–1.

Until the First World War George Heming Mason was considered one of England's leading landscape painters. Sir John Everett Millais described him as the 'biggest genius of the present day' and his landscapes, particularly those painted in England on his return from the Continent in 1858, were admired for their poetic evocation of the mystery and beauty of the English countryside.

Born at Fenton Park in Staffordshire, Mason studied as a surgeon in Birmingham between 1839 and 1843 while at the same time taking lessons in painting from the portraitist James John Hill. In autumn 1844 he left suddenly with his brother for Italy, against his father's wishes, settling in Rome in 1845. When his father's pottery firm went bankrupt in 1848, Mason's allowance was suspended and he found himself in penury. Amid the turmoil of the 1848 revolt of Garibaldi's Red Shirts against the papacy, he narrowly evaded execution after being accused of espionage by the papal authorities. To make ends meet, he found himself obliged to paint souvenir views of the landscape around Rome. In 1850 he went on expeditions into the Roman Campagna and in 1852, while staying at the Pension Martorelli at L'Ariccia, he was introduced to the Italian landscape painter Giovanni Costa. Eight years younger than Mason, Costa was already an established artist and was to have a great influence on the English painter. For the next five years the two worked closely together, going on 'twenty days sketching' expeditions.[1] Like other contemporary artists, such as the German Nazarenes and the Roman Puristi, Costa believed that the painter should work directly from nature with a clear and uncluttered style, hailing the oil sketch as the basis for all subsequent ideas in painting, inspired 'by the love for eternal truth.'[2]

Mason adjusted his style to that of Costa, absorbing his ideas, and together with other foreign painters such as George Howard, Frederic, Lord Leighton, Sir William Blake Richmond and Arnold Böcklin, they founded a new school of landscape painting. Years later, in 1884, this group came to be known as the Etruscans, after Costa, the 'Etruscan'. In 1853 Mason met Leighton, who was to make a permanent impression on him and support him in later years when he was depressed and once again in dire financial straits. Leighton's Italian sketchbook would have opened Mason's eyes to the merits of a sound technical training, and there is no doubt that he was dazzled by Leighton's knowledge, social accomplishments and technical mastery. Likewise, Leighton is known to have admired Mason's work, prophesying that one day his rare talent would be appreciated.

This sketch was painted in the gardens of the Villa Borghese, a popular site for landscape artists within Rome, due mainly to its picturesque broken ground, hillocks, buildings and clumps of trees. Probably executed between 1852 and 1853, it follows closely Costa's oil sketch technique. Apparent at the bottom of the canvas is the mid-toned grey ground, on which Mason has applied loose but confident brushstrokes to depict the foliage of the trees and the shadows on the walls below. *XB*

1 Agresti 1904, p. 68.
2 Costa 1927, p. 120.

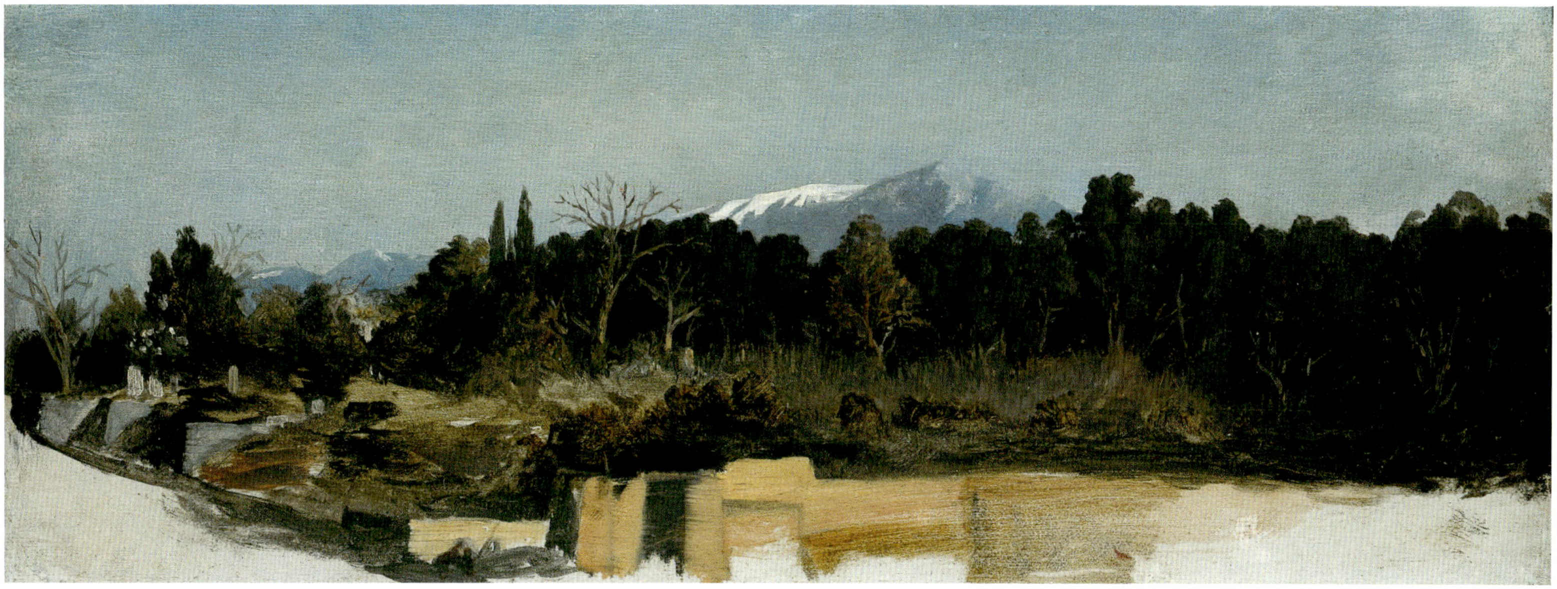

MICHALLON, Achille-Etna (1796–1822)
57. *A Torrent in a Rocky Gorge*, undated

Oil on paper laid on canvas, 38.4 x 30.6 cm

Inscriptions

Label on reverse: *64/51*

Label on frame:

Arts Council of Great Britain

105 Piccadilly London W1

Exhib. Paintings from Nature

Cat. No. 78

artist. Michallon

title: Torrent

Owner. Private collection

Provenance

Bought from John Lishawa, London, in 1978.

Exhibitions

Cambridge and London 1980–1, no. 78; Edinburgh 1986, no. 21; London 1988, no. 35.

Michallon played a pivotal rôle in the history of the landscape oil sketch in France as the student of Valenciennes and the teacher of Corot, the two most brilliant exponents of the art. He had a talent for friendship as well, and was a companion of such landscape painters as Dunouy, Jean-Victor Bertin, Granet and Coignet – the last a particular friend – as well as members of the international community of artists he met in Rome. Michallon's talent was recognised and encouraged from an early date, and in 1817 he was the first winner of the Prix de Rome for historical landscape painting. He set off for Italy where he arrived early in 1818 and remained until 1821, travelling as far south as Sicily. In Italy, Michallon painted both oil sketches and larger, more finished landscapes. In some instances motifs sketched in oil were adapted for his composed landscapes. Back in Paris early in 1822, Michallon opened his atelier to students, including Corot and Léon Fleury. In September, however, a sudden illness carried him away, ending the brief career of perhaps the most promising landscape painter of his generation.

An important group of drawings and paintings by Michallon, including twenty-six oil sketches, entered the Louvre in 1930. They had been acquired by the family of the artist's friend, Comte Pierre-Charles de l'Espine, at the studio sale following Michallon's death, and stand as the core works against which new attributions to the artist must be tested. The attribution of the present work to Michallon is not universally accepted. Lesage did not include it in her recent, cautious catalogue raisonné of the artist.[1] She comments there on the thorny problems raised by Michallon attributions. It is often very difficult, she remarks, to distinguish his hand from that of several talented contemporaries. Moreover, his oil sketches were passed around among friends and copied early on, notably by Coignet. Michallon was a prolific artist – although he was only twenty-five when he died, the inventory made upon his death listed no fewer than 410 works. Even though much is surely lost, more oil sketches wait to be recognised.

Like many of his contemporaries, Michallon frequently painted foaming water rushing over rocks, as well as rocky grottoes and crags, both in France and Italy.[2] This sketch has been compared with the artist's horizontally disposed *View of a Grotto at Royat (The Grotto of the Washerwomen in the Auvergne)* (Paris, Musée du Louvre, RF 2892), sharing with it a broad handling of colours in the rock face laid down in rectangular patches, and quick touches of white paint to capture the swift-moving water. The *View of a Grotto* was executed in France around 1814, or certainly before the end of 1817 when the artist incorporated the motif in a composed landscape signed and dated that year.[3] The present sketch can also be compared with Michallon's *Waves at the Foot of Rocks* (Paris, Musée du Louvre, RF 2869), especially in the greater agitation of the water and the subtle gamut of green and blue tones the artist uses in the water. That sketch was probably painted in Italy, perhaps at Tivoli, between 1818 and 1821.[4] Lishawa originally acquired this sketch as part of a group of works, some of which bore Michallon's signature, which may suggest an origin in the artist's studio. *CR*

1 Lesage 1997, pp.101–42.

2 In Michallon's *Inventaire après décès*, nos. 239–46 are described together as *Fabriques, rochers lointains et torrents*.

3 *Landscape with Ruins and a Man frightened by a Snake* (Barnard Castle, The Bowes Museum), Paris 1994, cat. no. 20, illus.

4 Paris 1994, cat. no. 50, colour illus. p. 73.

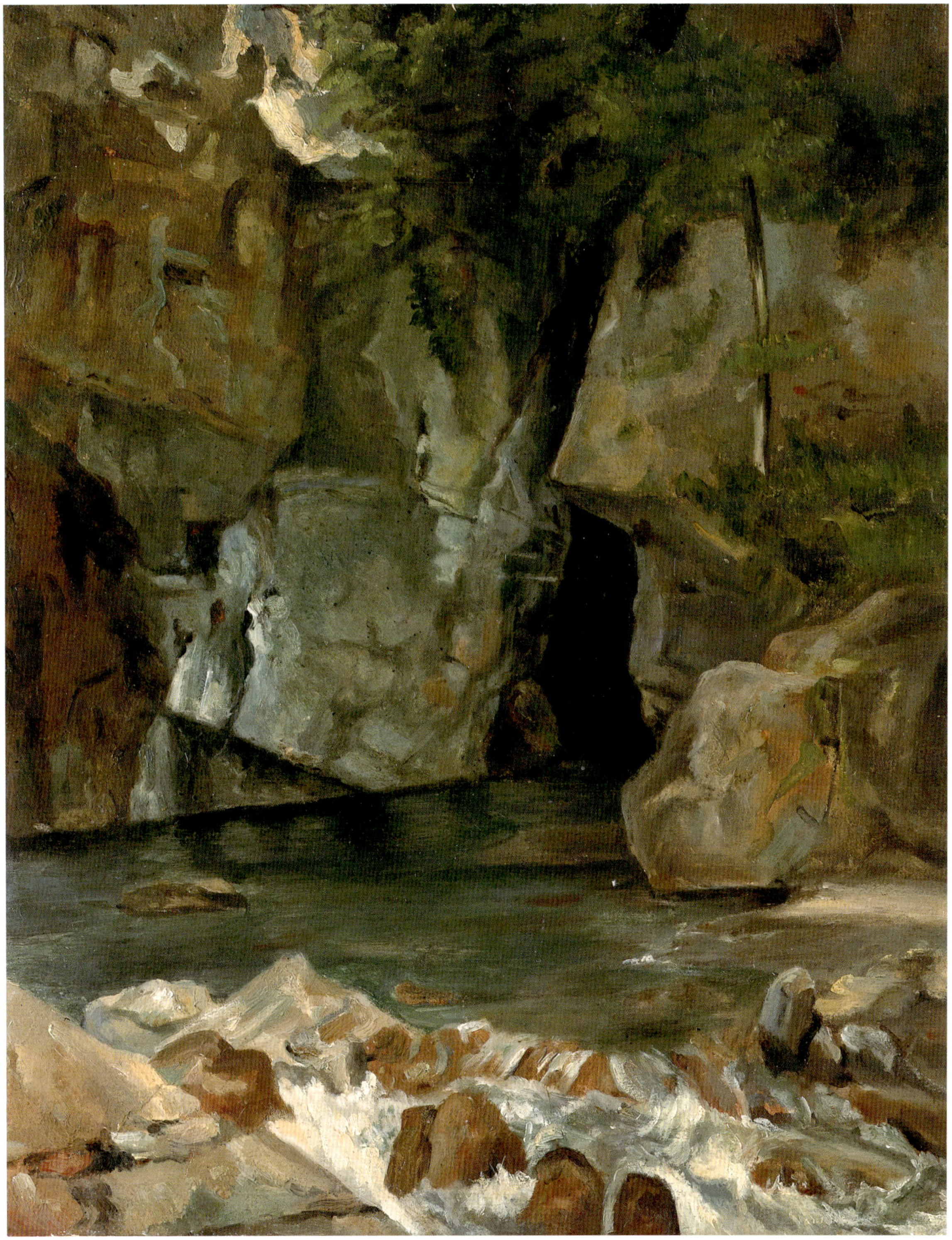

MICHALLON, Achille-Etna (1796–1822)
58. *A Tree*, about 1817

Oil on paper, 30.5 x 24.0 cm

Inscription

Inscribed at lower left in red *TOT* [?]

Technical note

There is some underdrawing in some tree branches, particularly at upper left. On the recto of the sheet is a drawing of a farmhouse.

Provenance

Bought from James Mackinnon, London, in 1990.

In his *Elémens de perspective pratique* of 1800, Michallon's teacher Valenciennes advised his students to make oil studies of beautiful trees, either isolated or *en masse*. He urged them to pay particular attention to the bark of trees, the mosses attached to them, roots, branches and all the irregularities that establish their individual characters.[1] He also recommended that his students study the seventeenth-century Dutch landscape masters in the Louvre, and in about 1816 Michallon painted a study of a tree trunk based on a detail of a painting by Jacob van Ruisdael (Puy-en-Velay, Musée Crozatier).[2] Such studies may also lie behind a highly finished painting such as his *The Oak and the Reed* (1816; Cambridge, Fitzwilliam Museum), a subject taken from La Fontaine's *Fables*. Homely, aged tree trunks, their forms shaped by time and the elements, offered infinite variety to the artist's observing eye, and trees played a central rôle in Michallon's oil studies as well as his composed landscapes.

Here, an ancient, shattered tree trunk still towers over the younger growth. The bark is composed of countless quick touches of colour that suggest its rough texture while its branches twist and curl dramatically. The oil sketch is neither signed nor inscribed with Michallon's name; perhaps the reason Lesage did not include it in her catalogue. However, she has compared it to a signed tree study by the artist in a French private collection.[3] In a later communication she went on to suggest that the latter *Tree* was painted around 1815–16.[4] The sketch can also be compared to several other paintings attributed to Michallon in which trees figure prominently.[5]

The reverse of the sheet has a, probably unfinished, painting of a farmhouse set against a row of trees with a cloud-filled sky above (fig. 38). The buildings seem to be French, which would further suggest that the sketches were made before Michallon left for Italy in 1817. *CR*

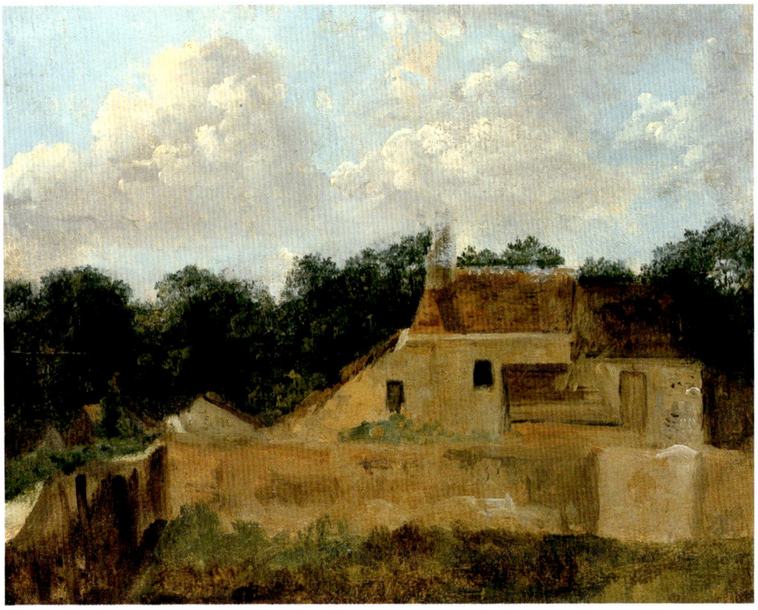

Fig 38 Achille-Etna Michallon, verso of *A Tree*.

1 Valenciennes 1800, 1973, p. 409.
2 Lesage 1997, cat. no. 16.
3 Letter to John and Charlotte Gere, dated 12 March 1993, in the Gere archive at the National Gallery. The painting to which she compares the study is Lesage 1997, cat. no. 15, illus.
4 Letter to John Gere, dated 31 March 1993, in the Gere archive at the National Gallery.
5 See London 1988, nos. 37, 38. *Vue du château de Meudon, Vue du château de Vincennes, Vue du château de Versailles*, reproduced in New York 1982, but not exhibited.

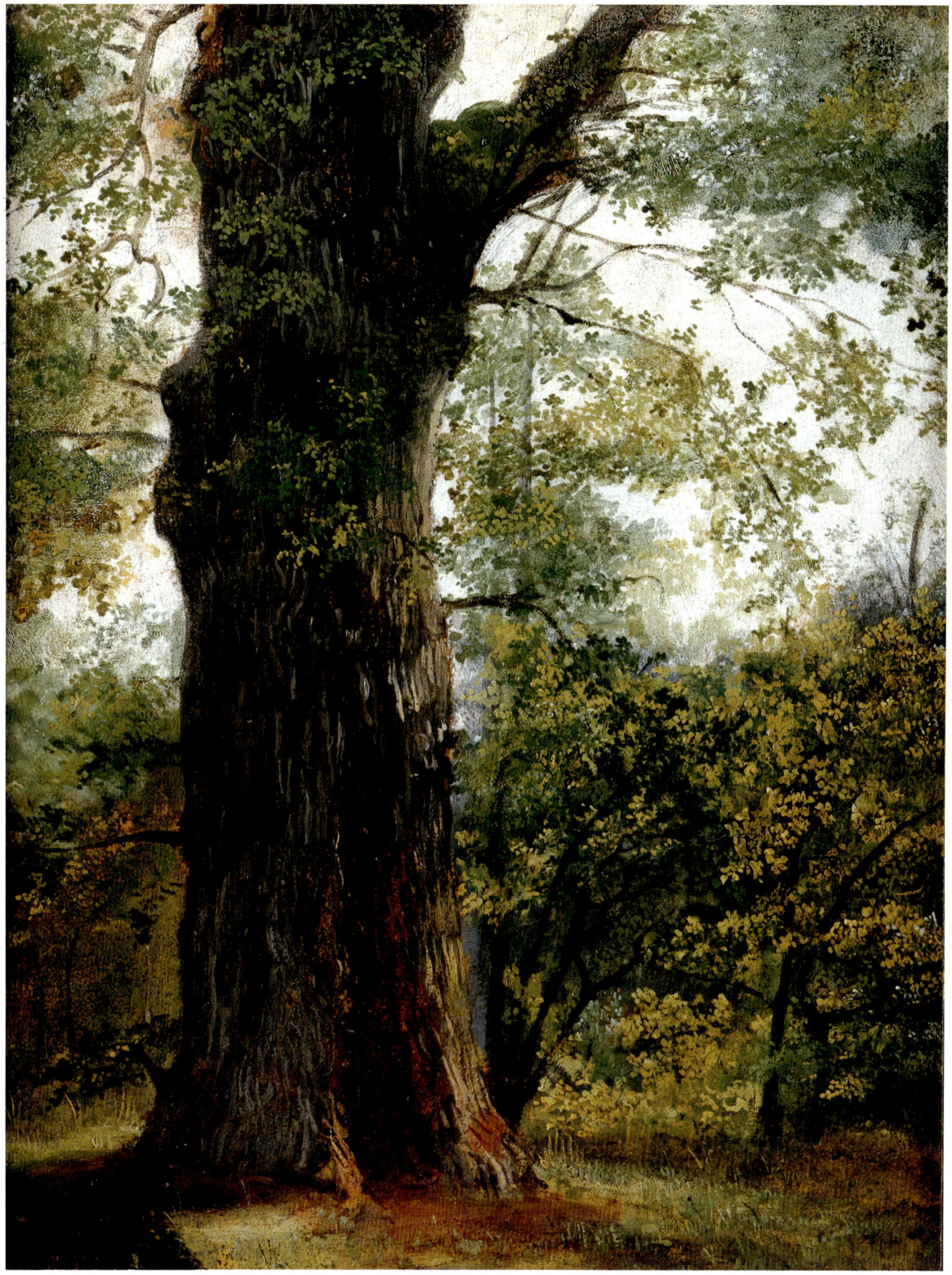

Pitloo, Anton Sminck van (1791–1837)
59. *View of the Aventine Hill from the Palatine*, about 1811–15

Oil on paper laid on canvas, 31.8 x 44.3 cm

Inscriptions

In ink on the reverse *Farnese Gardens on the Palatine looking towards St. Alexis on the Aventine. 7.*

Under the stretcher is another inscription in pencil *On Palatine, Tiber, Hs of Malta.*

Stencil marks on the frame *HZ 701.*

Provenance

One of two paintings in this exhibition thought to have come from a collection in the north of England, where they had been called school of Posillipo and attributed to Pitloo; bought from Hazlitt, Gooden and Fox, London, in 1989 (as French school, c.1825).

Although Sminck van Pitloo was of Dutch origin, he spent most of his life outside the Netherlands. He studied in Paris between 1808 and 1810 under Jean-Joseph-Xavier Bidauld and Jean-Victor Bertin and then left for Italy, where he was to spend the rest of his life. On his arrival in Rome in 1811 he was quickly accepted as a member of the Dutch and Flemish community of landscape painters, which included such artists as Abraham Teerlink (1776–1857) and Martin Verstappen (1773–1852). Pitloo's success was rapid, thanks to commissions from a number of foreign patrons. In 1815 he moved to Naples where, apart from short trips to Switzerland and Sicily, he spent the remainder of his career. Today he is best remembered as the master of two Italian painters, Giacinto Gigante (1806–1876) and Achille Vianelli (1803–1894), with whom in the 1820s he founded a school of landscape painting known as the school of Posillipo, named after the bay north of Naples.[1]

This view of a scene on the Palatine Hill in Rome looking across the Circus Maximus towards the church of Saint Alexis on the Aventine Hill, was most probably painted before Pitloo's departure for Naples in 1815. His classical training shows in the structure of his composition, in which the mass of the ruined wall on the right contrasts with the almost empty space on the left, where the Tiber appears in the lower corner. Linking the two halves together, the path leads our eye from the lower left-hand corner round into the ruins covered in foliage. *XB*

1 See Rome 1985.

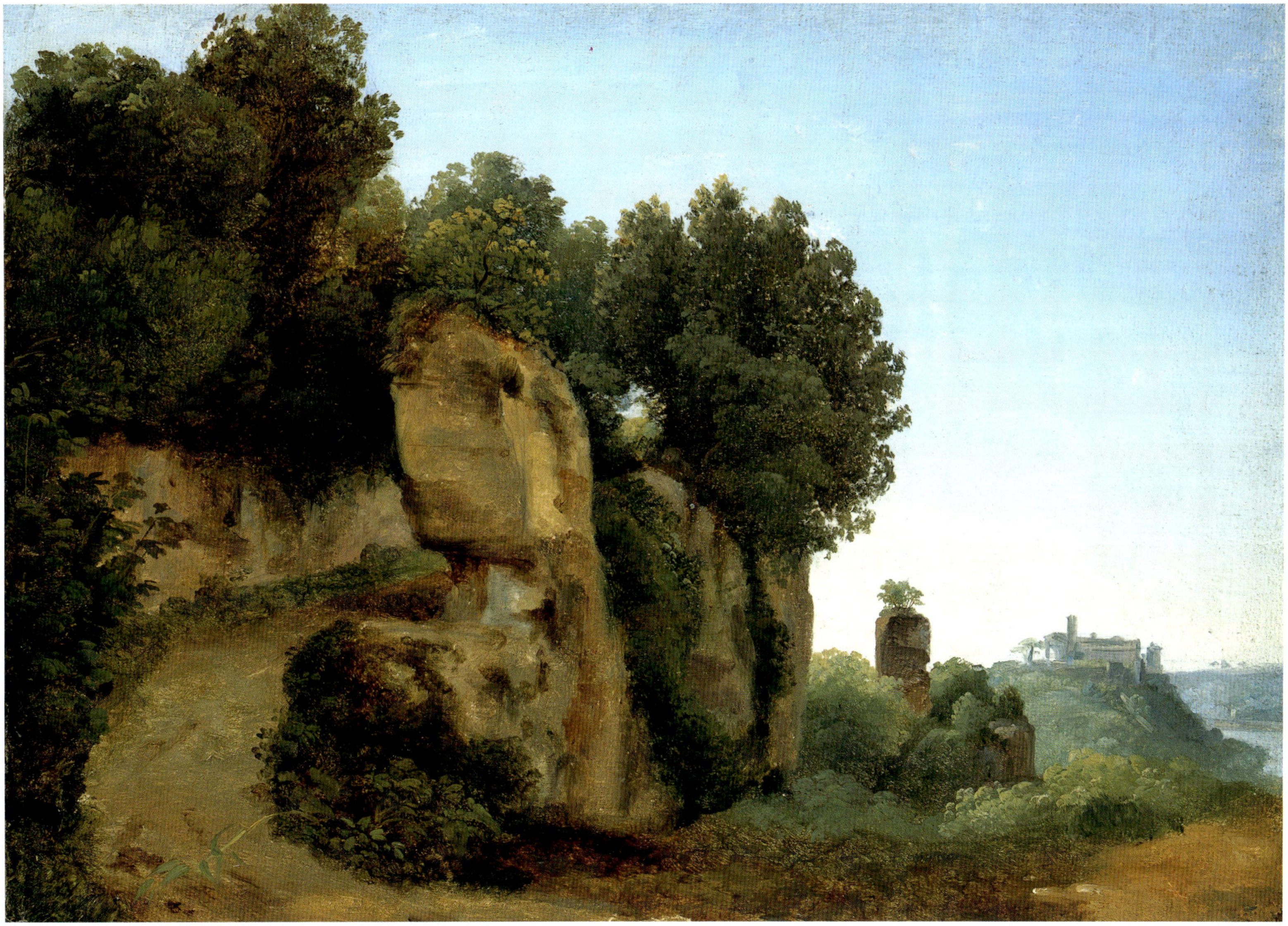

Pitloo, Anton Sminck van (1791–1837)
60. *Vines at Báia,* about 1820–30

Oil on paper laid on canvas, 40.5 x 29.3 cm

Inscriptions

In ink, in an early nineteenth-century hand, on a label stuck on the reverse of the canvas *Study of Trees nr. Naples at Baiae*
Below in ink *2* and in pencil *41*

Provenance

One of two paintings in this collection thought to have been owned previously by a collector in the north of England, where they had been called School of Posillipo and attributed to Pitloo; bought from Hazlitt, Gooden and Fox, London, in 1981 (as French school, c.1825).

As the inscription on the reverse indicates, this sketch was painted at the fishing town of Báia, on the Mediterranean coast five kilometres north of Naples. Famous for its thermal springs, this site was often visited by tourists and artists attracted by the antique Terme Báiane, an impressive complex dating from the first and fourth centuries. In this painting, Pitloo shows more interest in the vines growing in what seems to be an orchard than he does in the antique ruins. With a very oily palette typical of his later technique, he explores the range of greens offered by the light shining through the leaves. *XB*

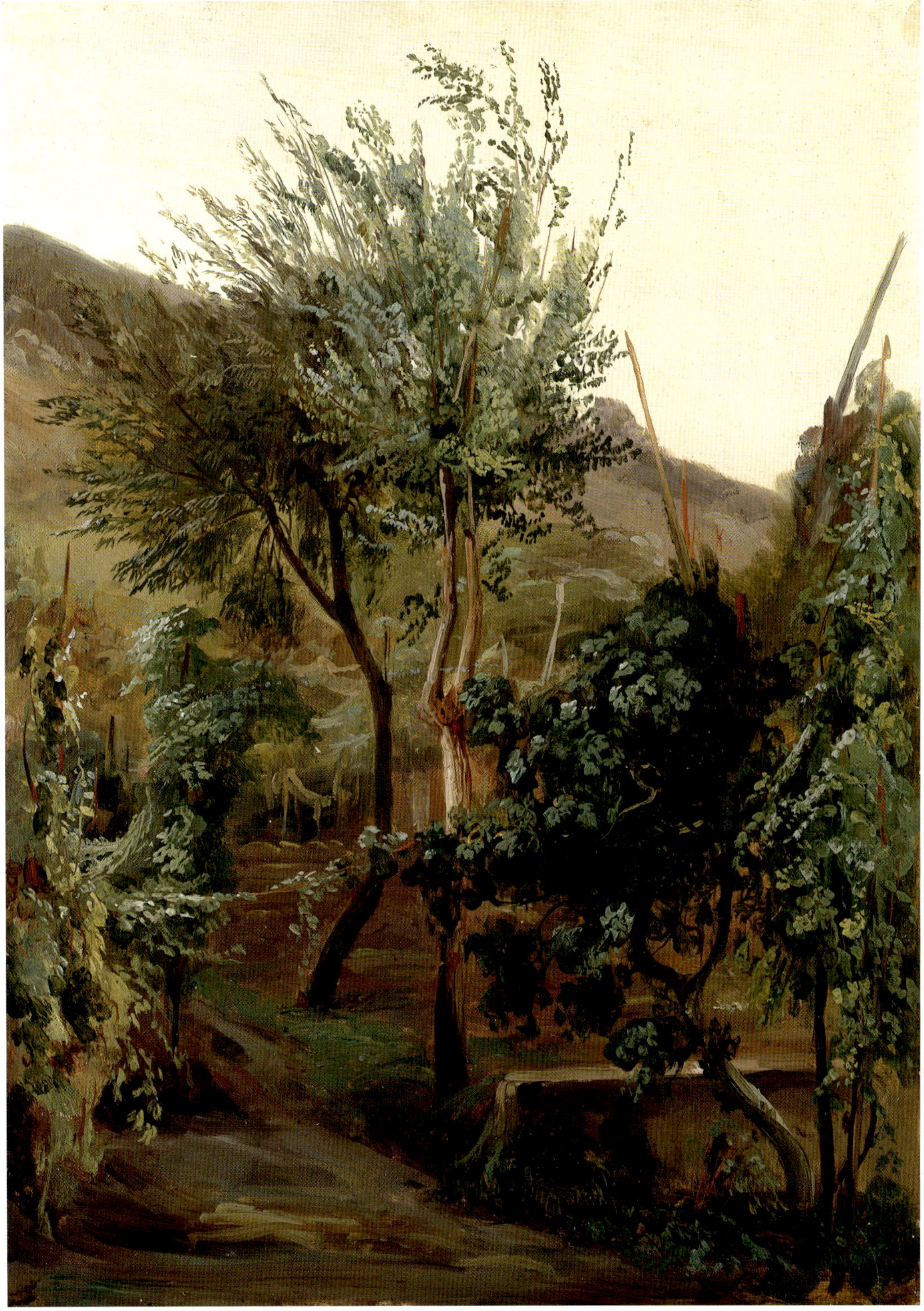

Reinagle, Philip (1749–1833)

61. *A Trout Stream*, about 1810

Oil on paper laid on canvas, 23.0 x 28.6 cm

Inscriptions

On the reverse *A trout Stream Philip Reinagle. R..a.*
From his Daughter- O.G. Reinagle.
To J.H. Smith
Caradoc Lodge
Church Stretton
Stencils on stretcher *JG51* and *28* repeated
Chalk inscription *ENG*

Provenance

From the artist to his daughter, O. G. Reinagle; J. H. Smith, Church Stretton, Shropshire; bought from Hazlitt, Gooden and Fox, London, in 1989.

The scion of a family of painters, illustrators and printmakers, Philip Reinagle, RA, trained under Allan Ramsay as a portraitist. Later, he specialised in landscape and often copied the works of such seventeenth-century Dutch masters as Meindert Hobbema (1638–1709) and Jacob van Ruisdael (1628/9?–1682). Reinagle travelled to Italy in the 1790s where he met Simon Denis. In Rome in 1796 Frederick Hervey, 4th Earl of Bristol – the eccentric Earl Bishop of Derry – proposed commissioning pendant paintings from the two artists, although the subject is not known.

The inscription by the artist's daughter on the reverse of this sketch, identifying the site as a trout stream, suggests that she thought the work was painted after Reinagle's return to Britain from the Continent, probably early in the new century. None the less, the painting can be compared profitably with Simon Denis's *A Torrent at Tivoli* (cat. no. 24). Both show swift-moving, relatively shallow streams, with water dancing over rocks and breaking into curling white rivulets of foam. Denis, who was six years younger than Reinagle but more experienced in painting sketches out of doors, may have told him of the advice of Valenciennes, who had left Rome in 1784. Valenciennes specifically recommended the practice of painting such streams, maintaining that it sharpened the artist's eye to the visual effects of movement. He included the recommendation in his *Elémens de perspective pratique* of 1800, but that publication codified practices that had emerged among the international community of artists in Rome in the preceding decades. Like Thomas Jones when he returned from Italy over a decade earlier, in 1783, Reinagle was one of the handful of artists who gradually brought news back to Britain of the novel continental approach to landscape painting. *CR*

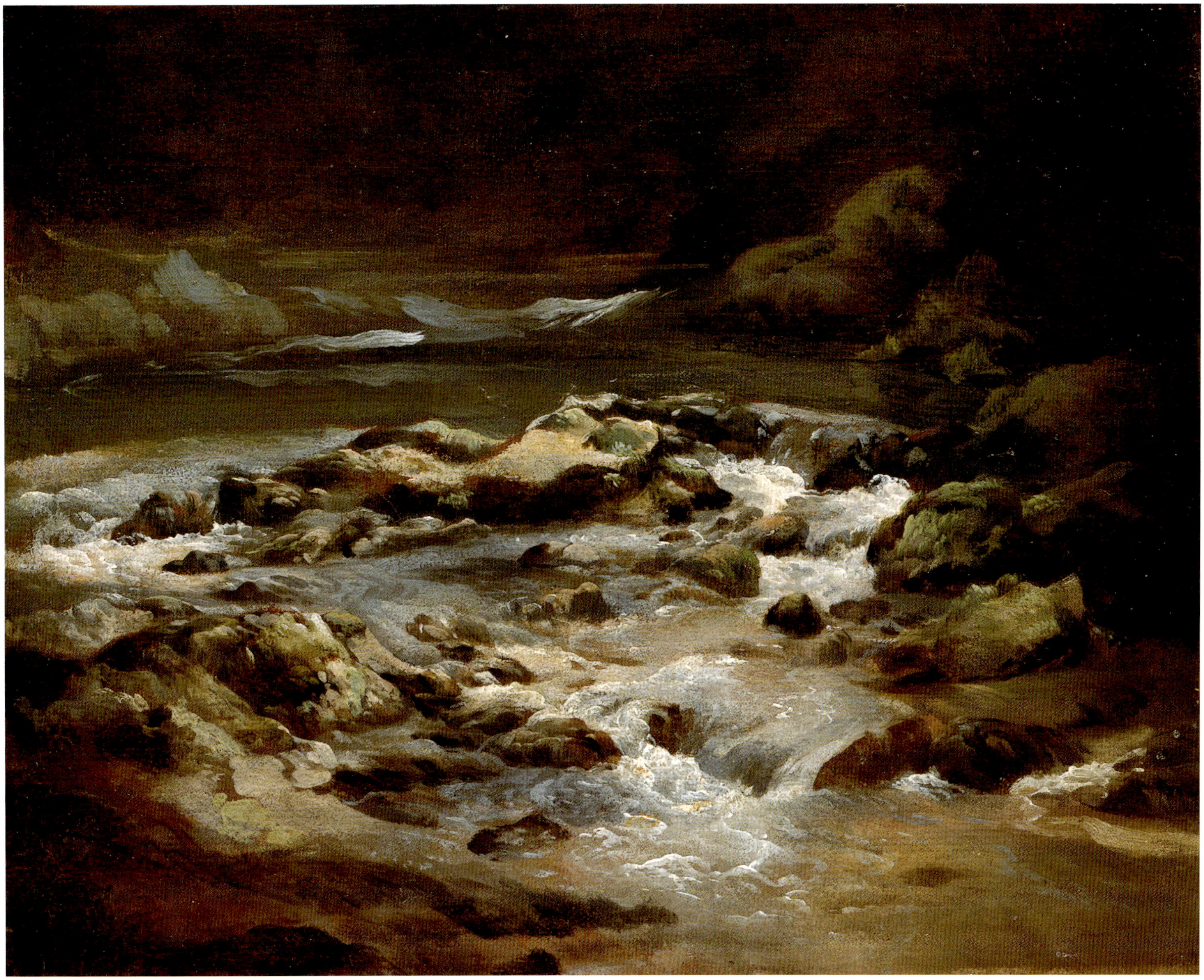

Reinagle, Ramsay Richard (1775–1862)

62. *Rome: Part of the Aurelian Wall (the Muro Torto) with the Villa Ludovisi beyond, about 1796* Oil on paper laid on canvas, 33.0 x 43.5 cm

Inscription

Inscribed in pencil *walls of Rome, Villa Ludovisi, Villa Borghese*

Provenance

Private collection, Yorkshire; Hazlitt Gallery, London, 1962–3; Marcello Sestieri, Rome; bought from Hazlitt, Gooden and Fox, London, in 1978.

Exhibition

London 1979, no. 26 (as Sir Charles Eastlake).

This is one of eight Roman landscape sketches said to have come from a Yorkshire collection in the 1960s. The view is towards the southeast from the northern end of the Pincian Hill. Beyond the grounds of the Villa Borghese is a section of the Aurelian Wall and the umbrella pines of the Villa Ludovisi. The artist focuses on the middle distance, inscribing the spared foreground with indications of the location. At the time of the 1979 exhibition, *The Lure of Rome*, Wheelock Whitney attributed the group to Sir Charles Eastlake (1793–1865) who spent some fourteen years in Italy from 1815, and made numerous landscape oil sketches. While the attribution is plausible, as Duncan Bull has said of another sketch from the same group of eight, now in the Yale Center for British Art, New Haven, 'sketches of this type are often extremely similar, varying little even in artists of different nationalities.'[1]

This sketch and another rather different one in the collection, from the same Yorkshire source (cat. no. 63), are both characterised by an insistent horizontality that is reminiscent of panorama painting. This has led to them being attributed to the panorama painter Ramsay Richard Reinagle, and the suggestion that the sketch may be a preparatory study for one of Reinagle's panoramas, such as the view of Rome seen from the Capitol that he exhibited in London in 1803.

The precociously gifted son of Philip Reinagle (see cat. no. 61), named after his father's master, Allan Ramsay, Reinagle first showed at the Royal Academy at the age of thirteen, in 1788. After studies in Holland he visited Italy, arriving there in 1796 and travelling as far south as Naples. He later reported painting two panoramas in Rome, one from the Capitoline Hill, the other from the Villa Ludovisi. Back in London, he worked on panorama paintings for the impresario Robert Barker, who exhibited them in Leicester Square, and then formed a partnership with Barker's son, Thomas Edward Barker. Beginning in 1803, the two young men erected an exhibition building in the Strand and showed a series of ten panoramas, including views of Naples, Florence and Paris. The first of these was the view of Rome as seen from the Capitoline Hill. The exhibition was visited by Reinagle's friend, John Constable, who reported: 'He views nature minutely and *cunningly*, but with no greatness or breadth.'[2] Reinagle boasted of his skill in imitating the styles of the Old Masters, worked as a picture restorer and dabbled in art dealing. In old age he was forced to resign from the Royal Academy when he passed off the work of a young painter as his own.
CR

1 New Haven and London 1981, cat. no. 80, p. 56.
2 Quoted in Smart 1975.

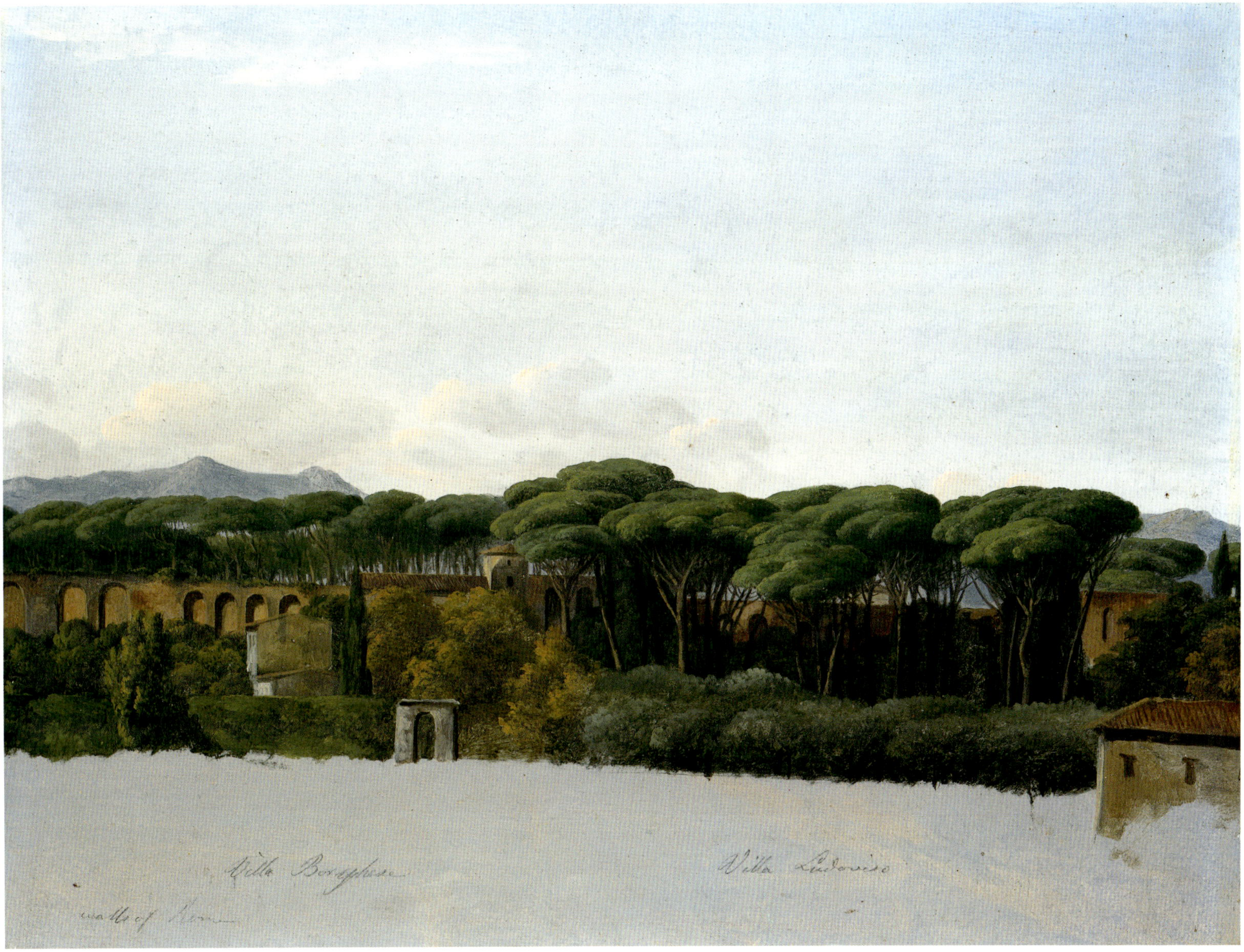
Villa Borghese
Villa Ludovisi
walls of Rome

Reinagle, Ramsay Richard (1775–1862)

63. *Mountainous Landscape with Ruins and Buildings*, 1796

Oil on paper laid on canvas, 13.0 x 33.4 cm

Inscription

Inscribed in the middle distance at the right *Green* and *Grey*

Technical note

An infra-red photograph reveals under-drawing and colour notations, in English.

Provenance

Private collection, Yorkshire; Hazlitt Gallery, London, 1962–3; Marcello Sestieri, Rome; bought from Hazlitt, Gooden and Fox, London, 1978.

Exhibition

London 1979 (as Charles Eastlake).

This view across the Roman Campagna to distant hills came from the same group of eight oil sketches as *Rome: Part of the Aurelian Wall (the Muro Torto) with the Villa Ludovisi beyond* (cat. no. 62), found in a Yorkshire private collection in the early 1960s. The colour annotations in English at the right appear to be in the same hand as the annotations on that sketch. Another painting from the group, *The Church of Santa Saba and the Pyramid of Caius Cestius* is now in the British Art Center, Yale University, New Haven, where it is tentatively attributed to Charles Eastlake (1793–1865).[1]

As with catalogue number 62, the emphatic horizontality of the sketch may associate it with panorama painting, and Reinagle has been proposed as the artist. A painter of panoramas, he exhibited a view of Rome as seen from the Capitol in London in 1803. It may have included distant views of the countryside surrounding the Eternal City, and the characteristics of this sketch suggest that it could have been made as a study for such a detail. Unlike the crisply delineated *Rome: Part of the Aurelian Wall (the Muro Torto) with the Villa Ludovisi beyond*, however, which shows an area not far distant from the centre of Rome, the colours here are muted, the forms not sharply distinguished from one another, and the paint applied thinly, almost like watercolour. The space seems compressed, with the farm buildings and ruins in the middle distance forming a single horizontal line, as objects appear to when seen from a great distance. The artist may have been taking into account the convention of aerial perspective whereby the most distant areas depicted in a painting are shown as more subdued and tonally unified than near ones. As he sketched he may well have contemplated the rôle that such a detail would play, and what visual weight it would carry in a vast panorama. *CR*

1 See New Haven and London 1981, cat. no. 80; and Cormack 1985, p. 90.

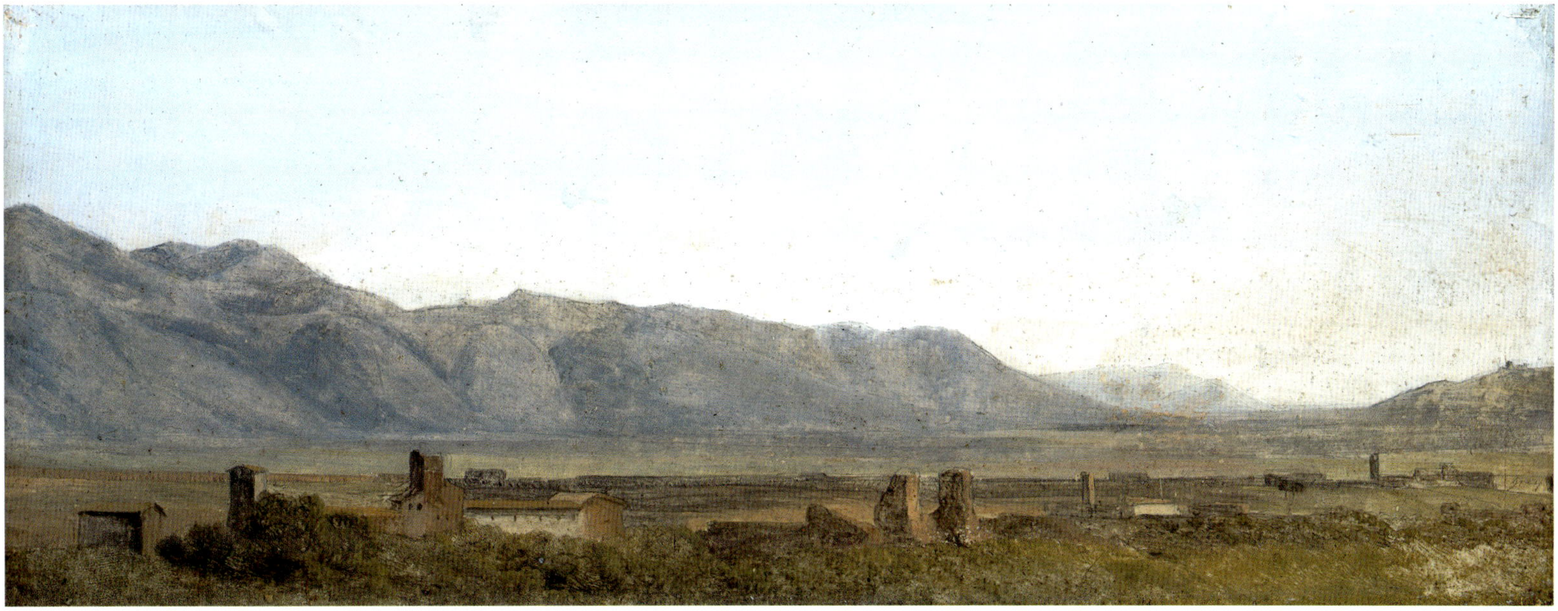

Rosa, Salvator (1615–1673), attributed to
64. *Wooded Bank with Figures,* probably 1660s
Oil on paper laid on board, 28.1 x 41.7 cm

Inscriptions
Inscribed on the reverse in an old hand *Salvatore Rosa Napoletano Nato nel 1615 Morto del* [sic] *1673*. Also on the reverse are Italian customs stamps dated 15 December 1959.

Technical note
The paper was primed with a light-brown ground, which is particularly apparent in some areas of the sky. The bluest parts of the sky at the edge, upper left, consist of smalt and lead white. The retouchings along the edges contain viridian, only available after 1839. A sample taken from the mid-grey-green foliage on the left revealed green earth (*terra verde*), white and a yellow-brown earth pigment. The browner foliage consists largely of translucent golden-brown earth pigments.

Provenance
Bought by Malcolm Waddingham from a stranger on a train to Bologna in 1959; sold at Sotheby's London, 5 July 1989, lot 13 (as Salvator Rosa); bought from Hazlitt, Gooden and Fox, London, in 1990 (as Salvator Rosa).

Exhibitions
London 1973, no. 3; Cambridge and London 1980–1, no. 2; London 1990a, no. 10.

Literature
Conisbee 1979, p. 419, pl. 23; Kitson 1990 no. 13, p. 26; Washington, Brooklyn and St Louis 1996–7, fig. 10.

Salvator Rosa is known to have been active as a landscape painter before leaving Naples for the last time in 1635. His first biographer, Passeri, tells us how 'after having primed some sheets of paper and put them in a folder he would go out into the countryside around Naples and whenever he saw a view that pleased him, whether a landscape or a marine view, he would sit down wherever seemed most appropriate and record it from nature with oil paints.'[1] This anecdote confirms that Rosa was one of the first artists known to have painted *en plein air*. Other painters, such as Claude, who settled in Rome in 1627, also made a practice of going out into the Roman countryside to sketch. The German writer and painter, Sandrart, tells us that he and Claude often went on sketching trips to such nearby towns as Tivoli and Subiaco, where they 'began to paint entirely from nature with colours on prepared paper and cloths, the mountains, grottoes, valleys and deserted places...'[2]

The preference for working on paper seems to have been purely practical. Prepared sheets of paper were easy to transport. Paper soaked up the oil in the paints quickly, making it easier for the pigment to dry and giving the artist time to complete his sketch in a single session. Sandrart seems to have found this technique particularly satisfying, as he emphasises that it was in his opinion the 'best manner to impress the truth precisely on the mind: because body and soul are, as it were, brought together in it.'[3]

Unfortunately, no other coloured sketches on paper by Rosa seem to have survived, and we have no idea of what they looked like. However, this picture does seem to illustrate the working methods described by Passeri. Throughout his career, Rosa produced numerous landscapes, either for private patrons or for himself. Unlike Claude, who aimed for idealised landscapes capturing the atmosphere of an imagined Golden Age, Rosa was more interested in the impressive power of nature. In a letter to his friend Giovanni Battista Ricciardi, Rosa expressed his appreciation of the 'wild beauty' he found in the Apennine mountain scenery.[4] The majority of his landscapes evoke the grandeur of nature and its power over man. To emphasise this Rosa often included small figures, such as bandits and hermits in attitudes of conversation or prayer. This proto-Romantic approach was to have a strong influence on later painters, particularly nineteenth-century artists such as Sir George Hayter who produced similar landscapes.[5]

The dating of this picture is problematic. None of Rosa's pre-1635 landscapes have come to light and it is unlikely that this sketch dates from that period. The composition, with the three figures in the foreground and rocks looming above, is comparable to that of the small landscapes executed by Rosa later in his career, notably in the 1660s. Examples such as the *Landscape with Saint Anthony Abbot and Saint Paul the Hermit* and *Desolate Landscape with Two Figures* (Denis Mahon collection) with similar backdrops both come to mind. Other parallels, particularly the interpretation of the rocks, are apparent in a *Rocky Landscape with Two Figures* in the Galleria Nazionale d'Arte Antica, in Rome.[6] Rosa's drawings for the *condotti* figures, also datable to the later part of his career, can be compared with those in the sketch exhibited here.[7]

On close inspection, the sketch seems to have been painted on two occasions. The fissures and cracks in the rocks and foliage above are loosely painted in an almost impressionistic manner. Details such as the bamboo leaves, grass and flowers, however, seem to have been added at a later date. This is particularly obvious on the right of the composition, where painted

1 Passeri 1934, p. 386.
2 Röthlisberger 1961, Vol. I, p. 51.
3 Ibid.
4 Quoted in London 1997, p. 146.
5 Sir George Hayter (1792–1871) was in Italy between

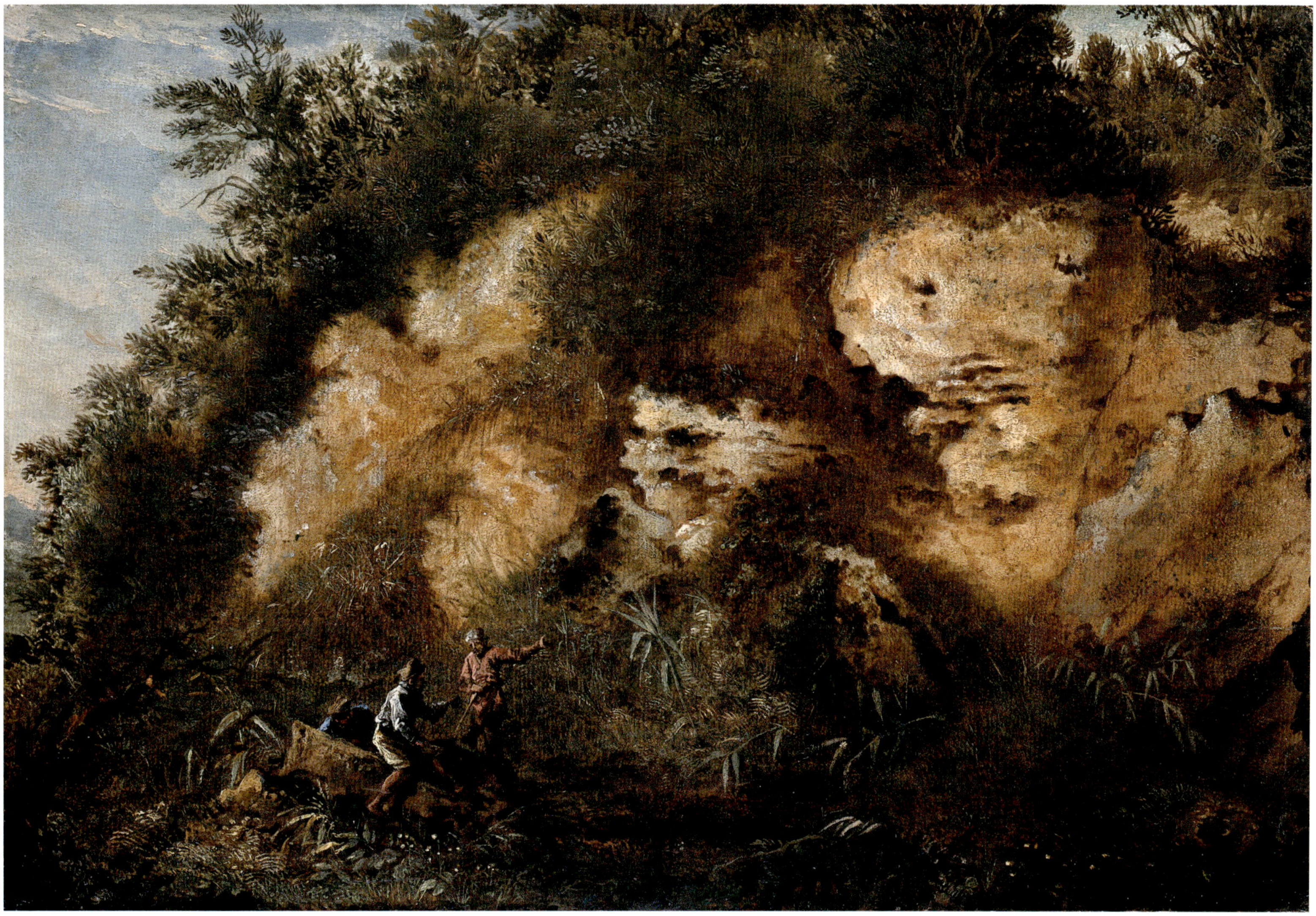

foliage has been added, as if to extend the volume of the original foliage. It is quite possible that Salvator Rosa added these details in the studio, but it is also possible that they were painted later by someone who wanted to transform a loose sketch into a painting.[8]
XB

1816 and 1816. An interesting comparison between this painting and a work by Hayter is offered by his *Banditti at the Mouth of a Cave* (RBF61) dated 1817, in the Brinsley Ford collection. See Ford Collection 1998, Vol. I, fig. 111, and Vol. I, p. 157.

6 London 1997, cat. nos. 68 and 69, pp.146–7. For the painting in Galleria Nazionale see Salerno 1963, cat. no. 79, p. 133.

7 Mahoney 1977, Vol. II, nos. 8.3 and 10.6.

8 Several Rosa scholars have questioned the attribution to Rosa. Although Michael Kitson catalogued this painting as by Rosa in 1973, in 1990 he expressed doubts about the painting being a seventeenth-century oil sketch and also questioned the attribution to Rosa (Kitson 1990, no. 13, p. 26). Helen Langdon and Jonathan Scott, have also doubted the authorship of this painting (oral communication).

VALENCIENNES, Pierre-Henri de (1750–1819)

65. *Rome at Sunrise, from the Janiculum*, about 1780

Oil on paper laid on board, 23.3 x 41.3–42.4 cm

Inscriptions

On the reverse, label in typescript *Thomas Jones, 1742–1803* (crossed out). Added in red ink *Pierre-Henri de Valenciennes, 1750–1806.*
J.S. Maas & Co. Ltd. Dealers in fine art 15a Clifford Street, New Bond Street W1: Telephone REGent 2302
Inscribed in ink *P4103*
Label *K.707.*
Inscribed *Griffin V.25/1065D.*
T.WX

Provenance

Bought from the Maas Gallery, London, in 1965 (as Thomas Jones).

Valenciennes is a central figure in the development of the landscape oil sketch, indeed in the history of landscape painting in the late eighteenth and nineteenth centuries, important both as a theoretician and a practitioner. Born in Toulouse, and trained at the academy there, he first travelled to Italy in 1769 and again in 1777, when he remained for some eight years. Influenced by Claude-Joseph Vernet, whom he met on a brief visit to Paris in 1781, Valenciennes studied perspective and devoted himself to painting landscape studies out of doors. He most often chose humble motifs in and around Rome and his small oil paintings on paper captured changing light and atmospheric effects with remarkable economy.

Valenciennes taught at the Ecole des Beaux-Arts in Paris from 1812, where he encouraged his students, including Achille-Etna Michallon and Jean-Victor Bertin, to paint such informal studies, arguing that the direct experience of nature obtained through sketching in oils was the prerequisite for painting more ambitious, composed landscapes. Indeed, Valenciennes was committed to raising the status of landscape painting to that of history painting, arguing in his *Elémens de perspective pratique* of 1800, which included a treatise on landscape painting, that idealised landscapes should be imbued with mythological or literary meanings. Due to his influence a prize for *paysage historique*, or historical landscape, was instituted in 1816. Valenciennes was largely forgotten after his death and it was only with the gift to the Louvre of 124 landscape oil studies in 1930 that a reappraisal of his work began, and the major rôle he played in landscape painting came to be recognised.

To paint this scene, the artist took up a position looking eastwards from a point at the southern end of the Janiculum Hill in Rome. In the distance at the far left is the church of San Giovanni in Laterano, seen from the rear. The recently completed monumental marble statues of Apostles crowning its attic are indicated by tiny vertical paint strokes. The large white building in the foreground is the Ospedale di San Michele, which stood on the west bank of the Tiber. The tall campanile beyond it is the church of Sant' Alessio on the Aventine Hill, and in the distance, their highest reaches lost in the clouds, are the Alban Hills.[1] The buildings of eighteenth-century Rome take up only the bottom third of the painting, however, while the upper two thirds are given over to a scudding dance of black, grey and white clouds at dawn, hurrying across a blue sky that breaks through in an irregular band of brightness at the centre of the sheet and again at upper left.

Originally attributed to Thomas Jones, John Gere re-attributed this sketch to Valenciennes and identified it with the sky studies the artist made in Rome following his meeting with Claude-Joseph Vernet in Paris in 1781, which had important consequences for his art. Valenciennes credited Vernet with teaching him in a single lesson the importance of sky and clouds in landscape. In his treatise on landscape painting Valenciennes himself later advised the student to 'begin his study with the sky, which gives tonality for the background.'[2] Light effects can change rapidly, however, especially at the beginning and end of the day. Indeed, Valenciennes cautioned that if an artist wished to capture light effects at dawn or dusk, he had only a half hour to do so.[3] These clouds seem to be moving particularly swiftly and it is possible that the painting was not made out of doors but was based on a rapid pencil sketch with colour annotations, of a kind that Valenciennes is known to have made and used.[4] On the other hand, Valenciennes was

1 John Gere identified the artist's viewpoint and the buildings depicted.
2 Valenciennes 1800, 1973, p. 338.
3 '... *toute étude d'après Nature doit être fait rigoureusement dans l'intervalle de deux heures au plus; et si c'est un effet du soleil levant ou couchant, il n'y faut pas mettre plus d'une demi-heure.*' Ibid., p. 338.
4 See Lacambre 1976, p. 4, illus.
5 See *Rocca di Papa in the Mist* and *Rocca di Papa under Clouds* (both Paris, Musée du Louvre), Washington, Brooklyn and St Louis 1996–7, cat. nos. 21, 22, illus.

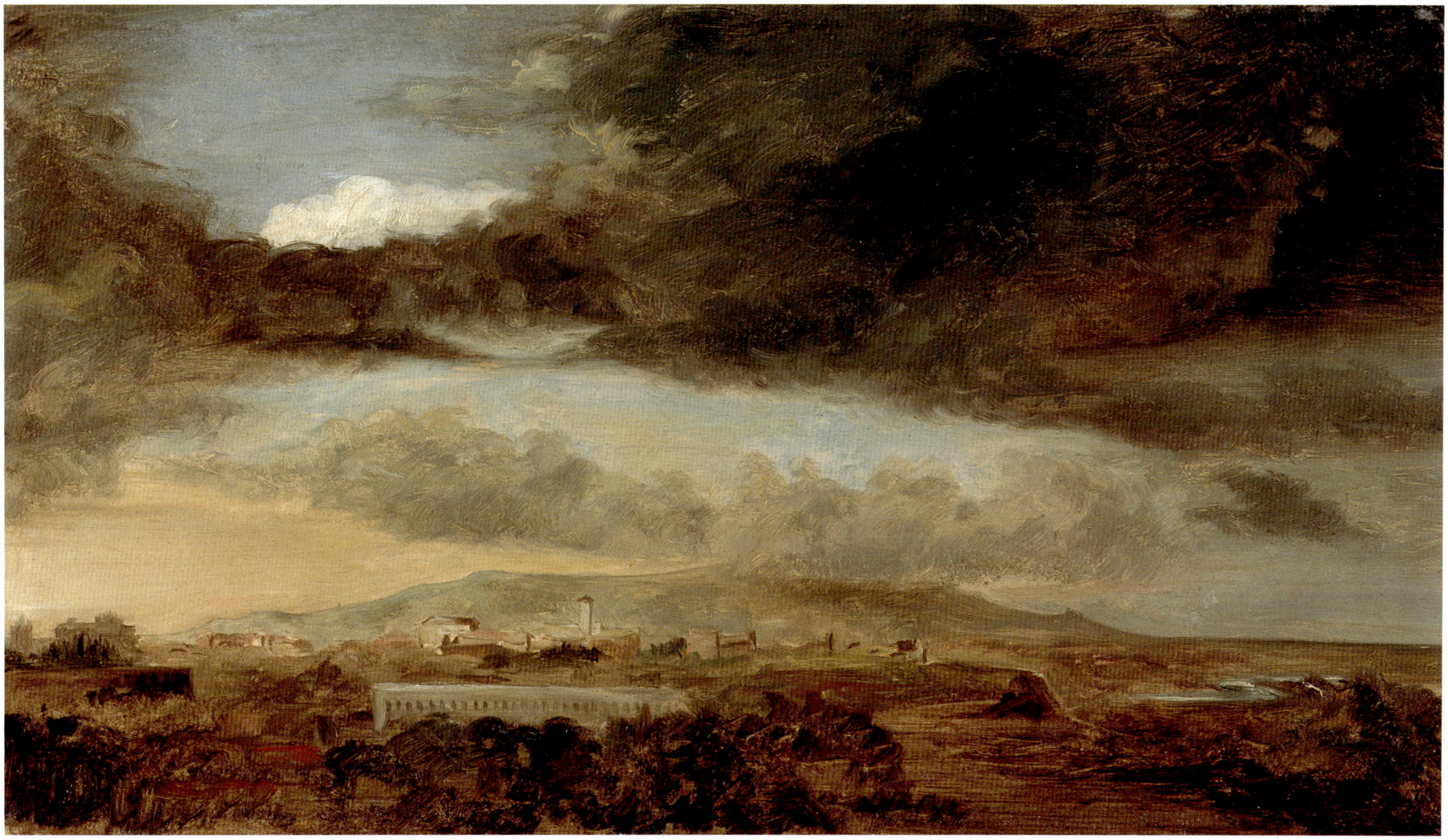

exceptionally dextrous with the paint brush, able to capture evanescent atmospheric effects, cloud and mist, with a few, deft touches of colour.[5] The attribution of this sheet to Valenciennes has not been universally accepted. *CR*

VALENCIENNES, Pierre-Henri de (1750–1819)
66. *Cow-Shed and Houses on the Palatine Hill*, about 1870

Oil on paper laid on canvas, 23.1 x 37.8 cm

Provenance

Galerie du Fleuve, Paris, 1976; bought from John Lishawa, London, in 1977.

Exhibitions

Cambridge and London 1980–1, no. 31; Edinburgh 1986, no. 17; London 1988, no. 6, Washington, Brooklyn and St Louis 1996–7, no. 17.

Here, Valenciennes depicts modern houses and a long, open shed on the Palatine Hill in Rome. They stand in front of a grander, ancient Roman arcade erected in the second century by Septimus Severus. Brilliant sunlight falls from upper right onto the façade of the house and dapples the roof of the shed. Valenciennes captures the complicated play of bands of lighter and darker shadows under the eaves of the shed and on the ground in the forecourt. The tops of tall, thin trees beat a staccato rhythm against the cloudless sky at right. Some twenty years earlier Hendrik van Lint had incorporated the same motif in a view of the western flank of the Palatine as seen from the Aventine Hill.[1]

Valencienne's painting corresponds closely to a pen-and-wash drawing, inscribed '*à la villa neron*' (at Nero's villa), in one of his Louvre sketchbooks (fig. 39). The drawing includes the outline of billowing clouds and, at left, the distant dome of St Peter's, both omitted in the painting. This is not the only case in Valenciennes's work of a drawing and painting treating the same motif. A painting, *Ruins in the Grounds of the Villa Farnese* (Paris, Musée du Louvre), corresponds to a sketchbook drawing inscribed '*aux thermes de neron*' (at the baths of Nero) (Musée du Louvre, RF 12976, fol. 26, Paris).[2] Observing the similarity of the latter painting and drawing, Conisbee suggested that 'a drawing rather than the *immediate* inspiration of nature' may have been the source for the painting.[3] The same suggestion, that the painting was made after the drawing rather than out of doors in front of the motif, might be made here too. Even if that is the case, it is clear here that the oil sketch and wash drawing impart very different kinds of information. Whereas the draughtsman delineates roofs with parallel hatching lines, the painter uses small touches of bright colour in a proto-pointillist manner to suggest the flickering play of light. Similarly, the forecourt in the drawing is two-toned, while the same area of the painting contain a subtle medley of tones. Valenciennes exploited the distinctive properties of the media, pen and wash accentuating architectonic structure, and oil paint accentuating strong distinctions between light and shadow. *CR*

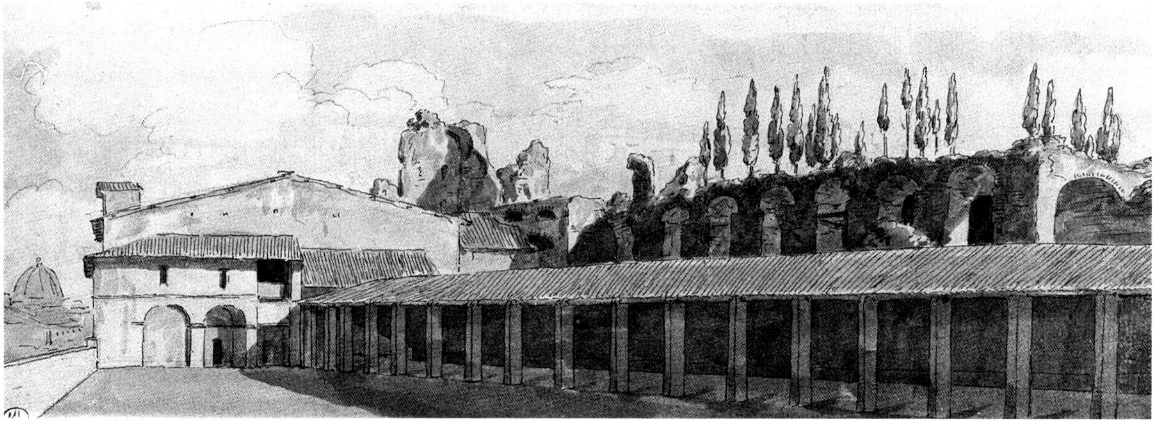

Fig 39 Pierre-Henri de Valenciennes, *At Nero's Villa*, about 1870. Pen and wash on paper, 19.4 x 27.1 cm. Paris, Musée du Louvre (R.F-12976, fol. 23).

1 Sotheby's, London, 8 July 1987, lot. 66.

2 Both are illustrated in Conisbee 1979, p. 337, figs. 95, 97.

3 Conisbee 1979, p. 336.

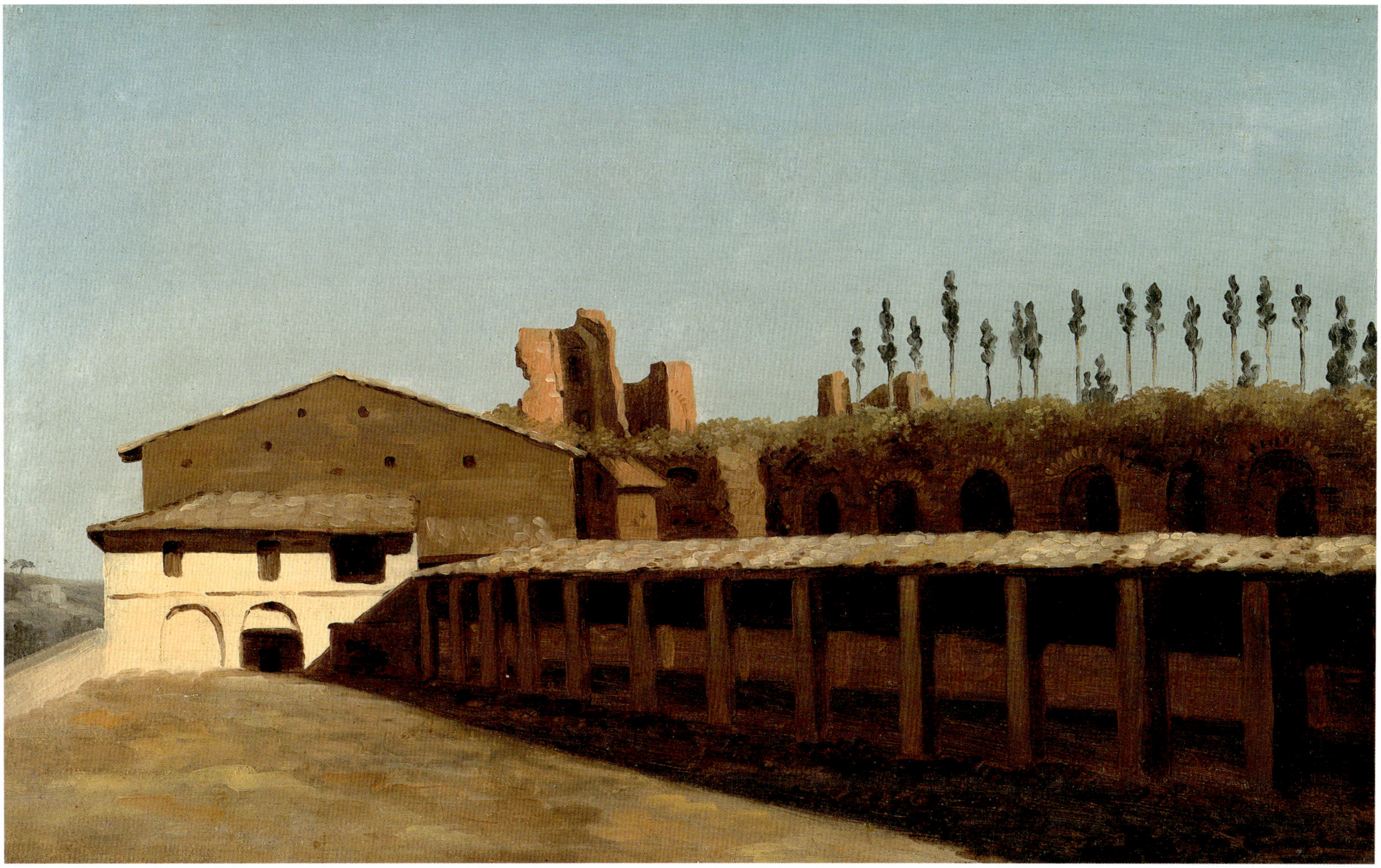

Wallis, George Augustus (1761–1847)

67. *Rocks, Tree-Trunks and Branches,* about 1800

Oil on paper, 46.2 x 44.3 cm

Provenance

Bought from James Mackinnon, London, in 1996.

Literature

New York 1996.

Born at Merton in England in 1788, Wallis travelled to Italy with the financial support of Lord Warwick. After passing through Rome he settled in Naples, painting the surrounding countryside and travelling to Sicily as well. In 1794 Wallis returned to Rome where he met the international community of artists there. His large, highly finished historical landscapes on Christian and mythological themes led to him being made a member of the Rome Academy in 1806. Wallis also operated as an art dealer in Italy and later, between 1807 and 1810, in Spain, most often working for British clients. He was instrumental in bringing Velázquez's *The Toilet of Venus* (*'The Rokeby Venus'*) to Britain, where it is now part of the National Gallery's Collection. In 1812 he settled in Heidelberg where he taught Karl Rottman and Ernest Fries. In 1817 the artist returned to Italy where he taught at the Academy in Florence and executed frescoes and portraits. He died in Florence in 1847.

Wherever he went, Wallis made oil sketches in nature. These paintings were unknown until 1996, when eight of them were exhibited as works by his French contemporary, Valenciennes.[1] In the same year, Mackinnon exhibited a number of Wallis's oil sketches and drawings, including another version of this bleak yet powerful depiction of rocks and branches.[2] It was probably painted during Wallis's sojourn in Italy between 1788 and 1806. Such works are characterised by a stark monumentality of form. With a broad but subtle touch, the artist deftly records the texture of moss on rocks and bark. Forms are silhouetted against a sky through which a few clouds scud. Wallis often chose such simple motifs, also recording the rocky outcrops, forest paths, ancient ruins overgrown with greenery and, as here, the accidental conjunctions of nature. Often he positioned himself very close to the motif. While his broad hand is distinctive, Wallis is still relatively unknown among the oil sketch artists working in Italy around 1800, and the attribution of works to him will remain the subject of lively discussion for some time to come.[3] *CR*

1 Spoleto 1996.
2 New York 1996.
3 See most recently Paris 1998.

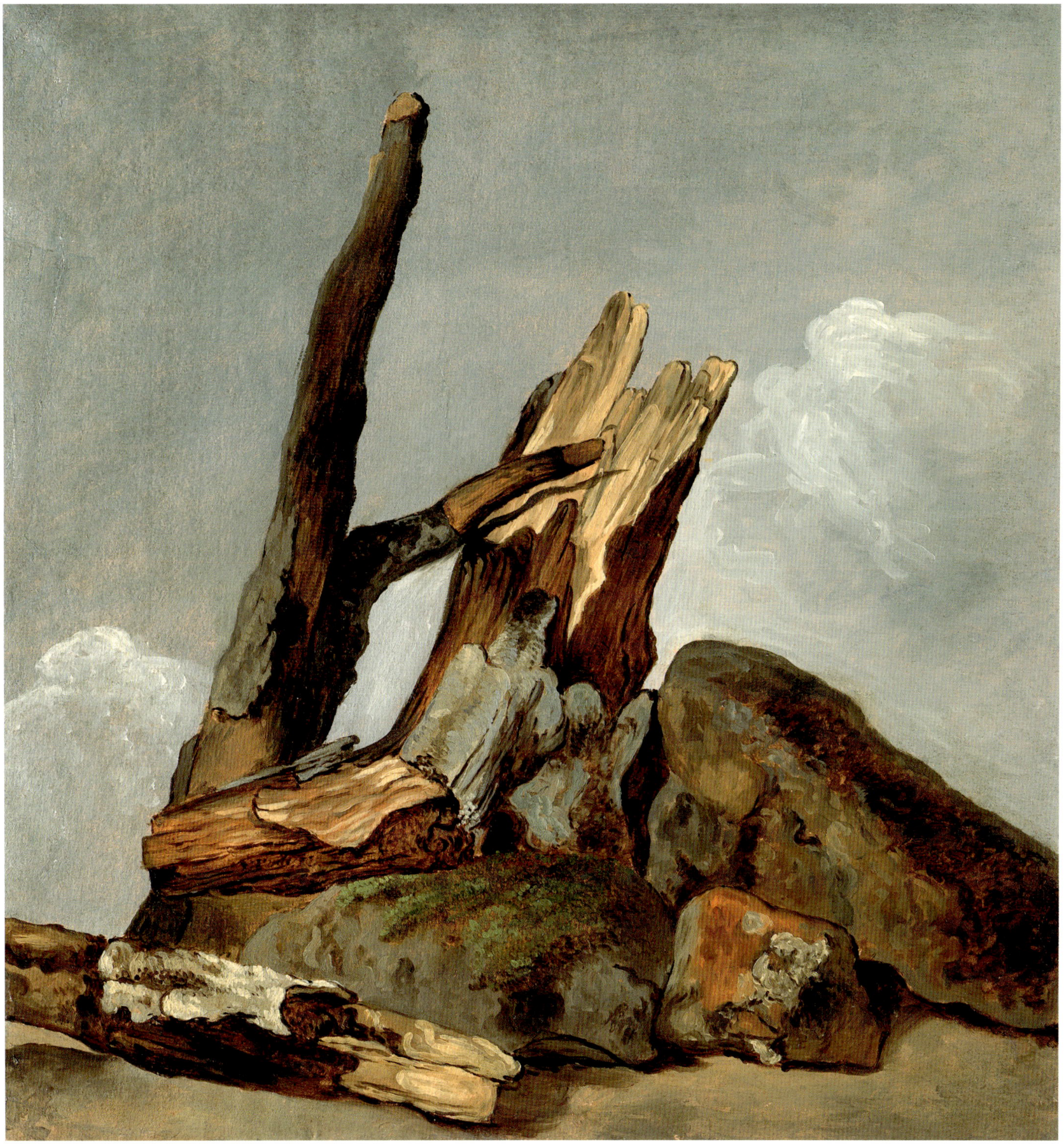

Wals, Goffredo (around 1590/95–late 1630s)
68. *The Walls of Rome,* about 1616–1630s

Oil on canvas, 30.2 x 38.0 cm

Provenance

Hazlitt Gallery, London, in 1970 (as Agostino Tassi); purchased by Eugene Victor Thaw, New York; bought from Hazlitt, Gooden and Fox, London (as Goffredo Wals), date not recorded.

Exhibition

London 1990b, no. 5.

Literature

Salerno 1974, p. 49 (as Bartolomeus Breenbergh); Salerno 1977–8, p. 187, cat. no. 37.15 (as Wals with a suggestion that the figures are by Napoletano); Repp 1983, cat. no. 17 (incorrectly described as being on copper).

Biographical details on Goffredo Wals are scarce. He was born in Cologne, worked as a landscape painter in Naples, Rome and Genoa, and died in an earthquake in Calabria. We know that a certain 'Goffredo fiammingo' worked with the landscape painter Agostino Tassi in Rome between 1616 and 1618, and this may well have been Wals. According to one of his biographers, Baldinucci, Wals then moved to Naples where he was 'much lauded' as a painter of 'landscapes, distant views, and perspectives.'[1] While in Naples during the 1620s he is thought to have taught Claude the art of painting landscapes. However, few of his works have survived and his artistic career remains obscure.

The basis for most attributions to Wals is a monogrammed circular engraving of a landscape with a river.[2] He also seems to have produced several small circular paintings on copper, composed as if viewed through a telescope, with delicate brush-strokes influenced by the work of Adam Elsheimer and Filippo Napoletano. Soprani, another biographer who probably knew Wals personally, remarked that his paintings 'brought such delight to the eye that in looking at the painted view the real one was quite forgotten.'[3]

Wals's landscapes are usually composed of simple, naturalistic motifs, such as farm buildings on riverbanks, quiet country roads or overgrown ruins in the Roman Campagna. Unlike the small paintings on copper, this painting has a rectangular format and canvas support. However, it shares with them an atmosphere of peace and purity, underscored by the strong shadows cast by the towers that it depicts in an open space. Although the exact site has not been identified and is probably imaginary, it is certainly based on *plein-air* observation. The walls may be inspired by the Aurelian walls near the Porta di San Paolo in Rome, of which Wals made a pen and brown wash drawing (fig. 40). The architectural motif of the towers with arched windows and vegetation growing on top also appears in one of his copper paintings, *Landscape with Architecture*, formerly in the De Boer Gallery.[4] *XB*

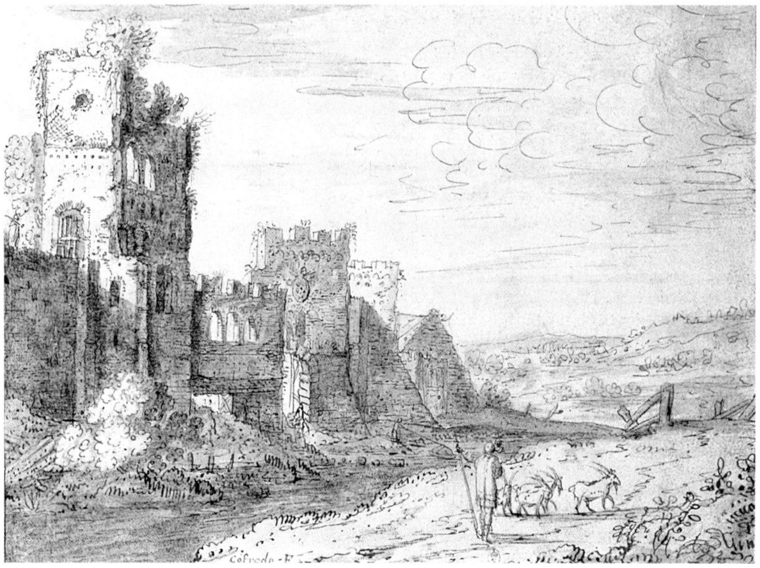

Fig 40 Goffredo Wals, *Porta di San Paolo, Rome.* Pen, brown and blue wash, 16.7 x 22.5 cm. Paris, Musée du Louvre.

1 See the life of Claude in Baldinucci 1845–7, Vol. 4, p. 357.

2 Harris 1978, pp. 399–403.

3 Quoted in Salerno 1977–8, Vol. I, p.186.

4 Röthlisberger 1979, p. 18, ill. 26.

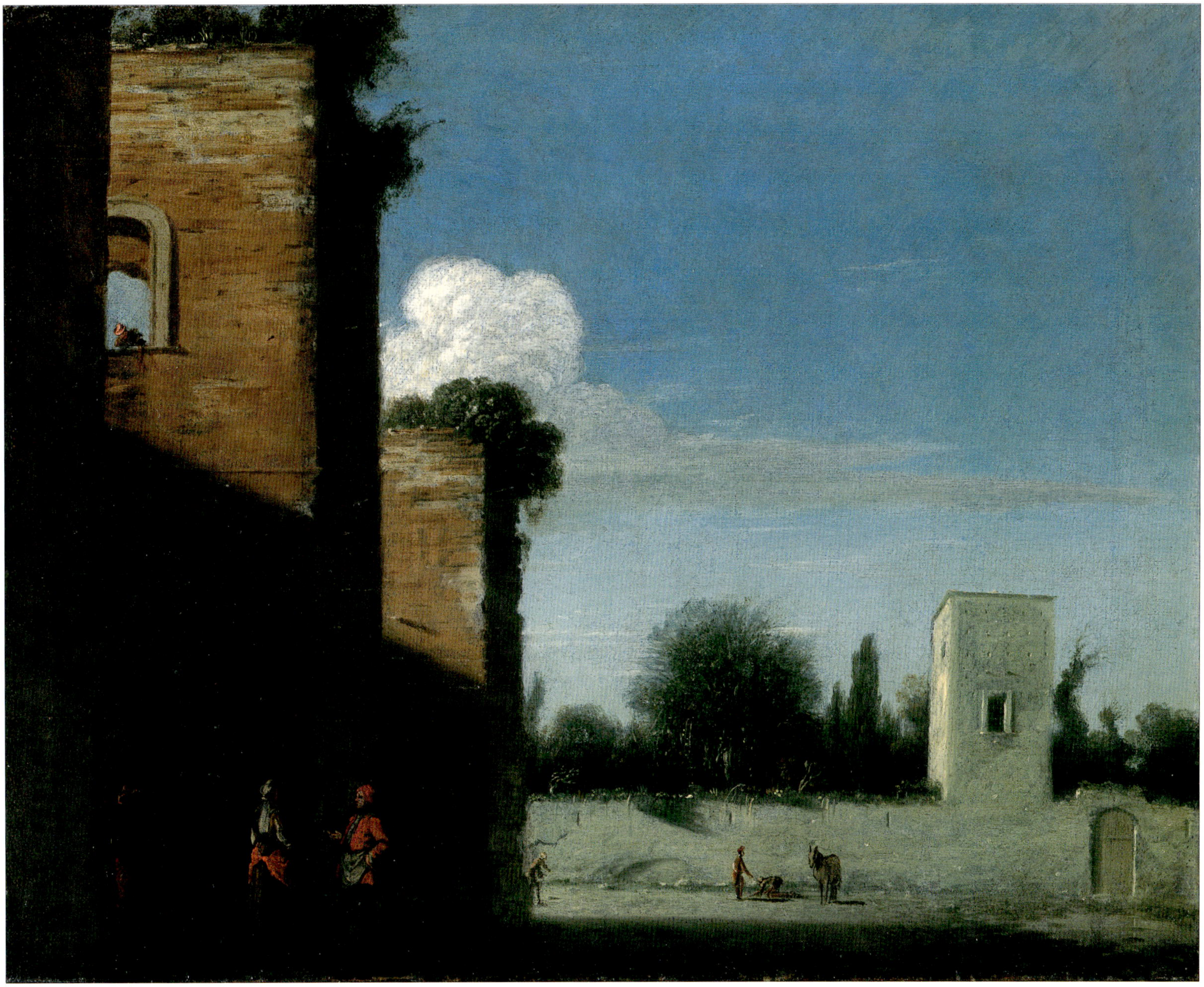

WARREN, William White (1832–*c.* 1912)

69. *The Crystal Palace from Penge*, perhaps 1870s

Oil on canvas laid down on cardboard, 22.3 x 41.6 cm

Inscriptions

On reverse of cardboard backing *William*
(rest erased)
The Crystal Palace from Upper Norwood
c. 1870
From Baer Feb 1954 J.A.G.
F.O.
Mr. Gere
[illegible]
MUA 1555 Px 110
CARVED OAK FRAME

Provenance

Bought from Jack Baer in 1954.

This lively, unassuming sketch by the British painter of landscapes and coastal scenes, William White Warren, plays a special rôle in the Gere Collection as the first landscape oil sketch that John Gere purchased in the collection that he and Charlotte Gere were to form over the next forty years. In its quickness, Gere recognised the spontaneity and immediacy of perception that he sought out and admired in the oil sketch tradition.

The painting shows the Crystal Palace, the monumental glass pavilion designed by Sir Joseph Paxton (1803–1865) and originally erected in Hyde Park to house the Great Exhibition of 1851. Following the exhibition, the structure, which covered eighteen acres, was dismantled and erected for a second time, to a slightly different plan, at Sydenham in south London, opening in 1854. Warren shows the Crystal Palace shimmering in the sun, like a heat mirage, at its new site, surrounded by what remained largely open countryside. The building attracted other painters as well, including Charles-François Daubigny (1817–1878), who painted it in 1866, and Camille Pissarro (1830–1903), who painted it in 1871. It was destroyed by fire in 1936. *CR*

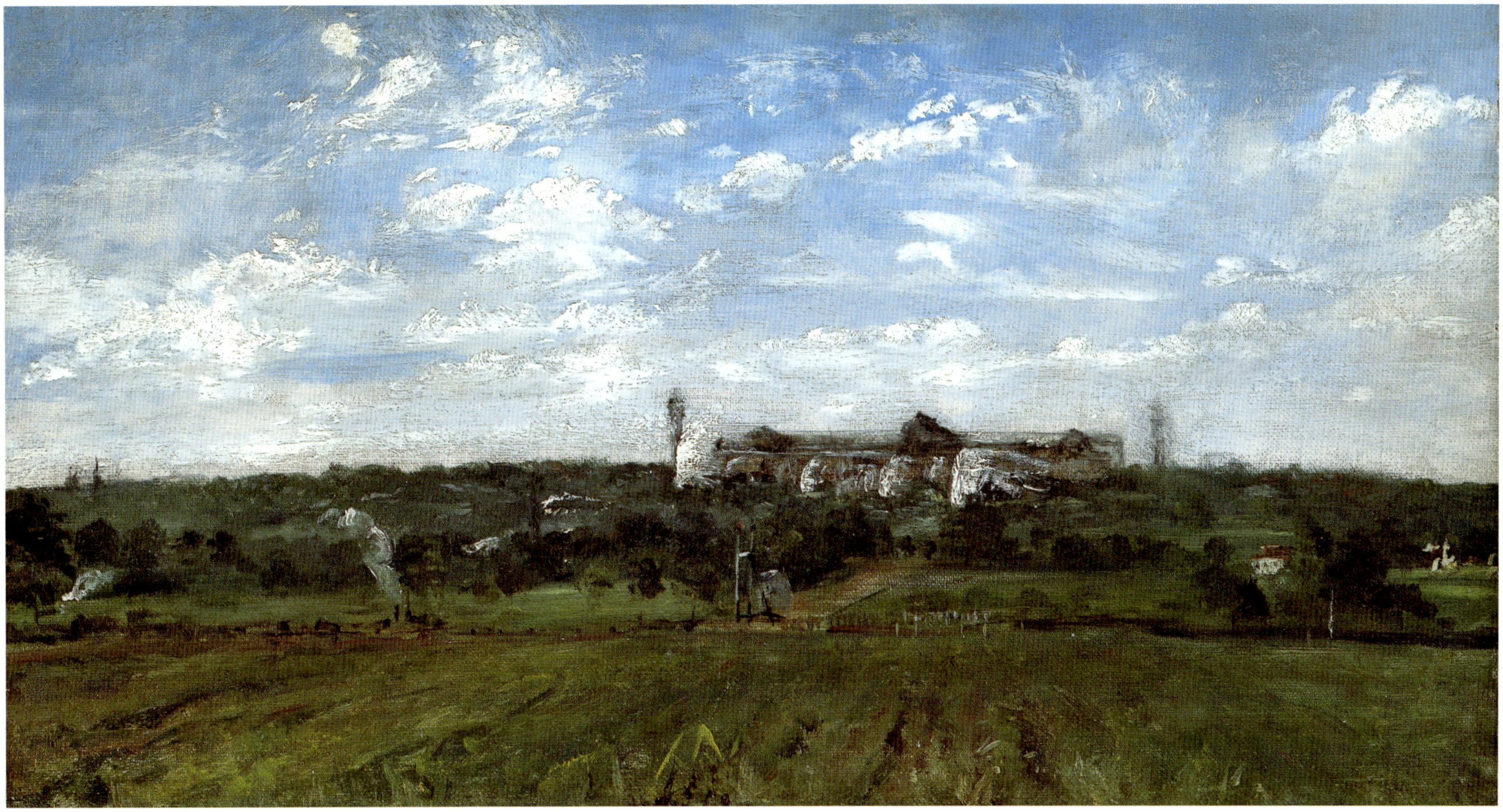

Bibliography

Adams 1973 Eric Adams, *Francis Danby: Varieties of Poetic Landscape*, New Haven and London, 1973.

Agresti 1904 O. R. Agresti, *Giovanni Costa, his life, work and times*, London, 1904.

Antwerp 1874 *Catalogue du Musée d'Anvers*, Antwerp, 1874.

Aubrun 1988 Marie-Madeleine Aubrun, *Théodore Caruelle d'Aligny, 1798–1871*, Paris, 1988.

Baldinucci 1845–7 F. Baldinucci, *Notizie dei professori del disegno da Cimabue in quà*, F. Ranalli ed., 5 vols., Florence, 1845–7.

Berlin 1990 *Carl Blechen, Zwischen Romantik und Realismus*, exh. cat., Berlin, Nationalgalerie, 1990.

Bertarelli 1934 L.V. Bertarelli, *Guida d'Italia del Touring Club Italiano: Roma e dintorni*, Milan, 1934.

Brame and Reff 1984 Philippe Brame and Theodore Reff, *Degas et son oeuvre: a supplement*, New York and London, 1984.

Brussels 1985–6 *Autour du Néo-Classicisme en Belgique, 1770–1830*, exh. cat., Brussels, Musée des Beaux-Arts d'Ixelles, 1985–6.

Brussels 1993 *Tableaux de Maîtres anciens du XVIe au XIXe siècle*, exh. cat., Brussels, Galerie d'Arenberg, 1993.

Brussels 1994 *Souvenirs d'Italie (1825–1829) de Gilles-François-Joseph Closson (Liège 1796–1842)*, exh. cat., Brussels, Galerie d'Arenberg, 1994.

Cambridge and London 1980–1 *Painting from Nature*, exh. cat., Cambridge, Fitzwilliam Museum, and London, Royal Academy of Arts, 1980–1.

Carpentras 1978 Suzanne Gutwirth, *Jean-Joseph-Xavier Bidauld (1758–1846), peintures et dessins*, exh. cat., Carpentras, Musée Duplessis, 1978.

Coignet 1848 Jules-Louis-Philippe Coignet, *Cours complet de paysage*, Paris, 1848.

Conisbee 1979 Philip Conisbee, 'Pre-Romantic *Plein-Air* painting', *Art History*, Vol. II, 1979, pp. 413–28.

Cormack 1985 Malcolm Cormack, *A Concise Catalogue of Paintings in the Yale Center for British Art*, New Haven, 1985.

Costa 1927 Giovanni Costa, *Quel che vidi e quel che intesi*, Milan, 1927.

Cottbus 1990 *Carl Blechen, Bilder aus Italien*, exh. cat., Cottbus, Bezirksmuseum, 1990.

Edinburgh 1986 Michael Clarke, *French Impressionism and its Origins: Lighting up the Landscape*, exh. cat., Edinburgh, National Gallery of Scotland, 1986.

Ford Collection 1998 Luke Herrmann, 'Sir Brinsley Ford Collection', *The Walpole Society*, Vol. 60, 1998.

Galassi 1991 Peter Galassi, *Corot in Italy: Open-Air Painting and the Classical Landscape Tradition*, New Haven and London, 1991.

Gaudissart 1990 Patricia Gaudissart, 'La Vie et l'oeuvre d'Eugène Buttura (1812–1852), peintre paysagiste'. Unpublished Mémoire du Maîtrise for the Département d'Histoire de l'art de l'Université de Clermont II, 1990.

Gere 1959 John Gere 'An oil sketch by Thomas Jones', *British Museum Quarterly*, Vol. XXI, no. 4, 1959, pp. 93–4.

Gere 1970 John Gere, 'Thomas Jones: An eighteenth-century Conundrum', *Apollo*, Vol. XCI, no. 100, June 1970, pp. 469–70.

González de Amezúa del Pino 1998 Mercedes González de Amezúa del Pino, *La Real Academia de Bellas Artes de San Fernando y su Museo*, Madrid, Fundación Airtel Movil, 1998.

Gowing 1985 Lawrence Gowing, *The Originality of Thomas Jones*, (Walter Neurath Memorial lecture) London, 1985.

Gowing 1986 Lawrence Gowing, 'Goya's "Black" Paintings', *Burlington Magazine*, Vol. CXXVIII, no. 1000, July 1986, pp. 506–8.

Grunchec 1980 Philippe Grunchec, 'Edouard Bertin (1797–1871): Sa participation au Prix de Rome et des dessins au musée de Chartres', *La Revue du Louvre et des Musées de France*, 30, 1980, pp. 147–152.

Grunchec 1986 Philippe Grunchec, *Les Concours des Prix de Rome 1797–1863, vol. II, Pièces d'archives et d'oeuvres documentées*, Paris, 1986.

Harambourg 1985 Lydia Harambourg, *Dictionnaire des peintres paysagistes français au XIXe siècle*, Neuchâtel, 1985.

Harris 1978 Anne Sutherland Harris, 'A Drawing by Goffredo Wals,' *Master Drawings*, Vol. XVI, no. 4, 1978, pp. 399–403.

Hawes 1969 L. Hawes, "Constable's Sky Studies", *Journal of the Warburg and Courtauld Institutes*, 32, 1969, pp. 349–66.

Howoldt and Baer 1993 Jenns Eric Howoldt and Andreas Baer, *Die Gemälde des 19. Jahrhunderts in der Hamburger Kunsthalle*, Hamburg, 1993.

Kitson 1990 Michael Kitson, 'The Seventeenth Century: Claude to Francisque Millet', in *Claude to Corot: The Development of Landscape Painting in France*, exh. cat., New York, Colnaghi, 1990.

Lacambre 1976 Geneviève Lacambre, 'L'Art de peindre les paysages', in *Les Paysages de Pierre-Henri de Valenciennes, 1750–1819*, exh. cat., Paris, Musée du Louvre, 1976.

Lesage 1997 Blandine Lesage, 'Achille-Etna Michallon (1796–1822). Catalogue de l'oeuvre peint', *Gazette des Beaux-Arts*, Vol. CXXX, August 1997, pp. 101–41.

London 1896 *The Studio Sale of Frederic, Lord Leighton, P.R.A.*, Christie's, London, 11–16 July 1896.

London 1897 *Winter Exhibition*, exh. cat., London, Royal Academy, 1897.

London 1926 *Opening Exhibition of the Modern Foreign Gallery*, exh. cat., London, Tate Gallery, 1926.

London 1930 *Centenary Exhibition*, exh. cat., London, Leighton House, 1930.

London 1970 *Thomas Jones*, exh. cat., London, Marble Hill House, Twickenham, 1970.

London 1973 *Salvator Rosa*, exh. cat., London, Hayward Gallery, 1973.

London 1976 *The Etruscan School*, exh. cat., Fine Art Society, London, 1976.

London 1978 *From Revolution to Second Republic*, exh. cat., London, Hazlitt, Gooden and Fox, 1978.

London 1979 *The Lure of Rome*, exh. cat., London, Hazlitt, Gooden and Fox, 1979.

London 1988 *The Art of Landscape*, exh. cat., Crawley and Asquith with John Lishawa, London, 1988.

London 1989 Francis Greenacre, *Francis Danby, 1793–1861*, exh. cat., London, Tate Gallery, 1989.

London 1990a *Italy and the Italianate*, exh. cat., London, Hazlitt, Gooden and Fox, 1990.

London 1990b Peter Bower, *Turner's Paper: A Study of the Manufacture, Selection and Use of his Drawing Papers, 1787–1820*, exh. cat., London, Tate Gallery, 1990.

London 1993 *Tradition and Revolution in French Art*, exh. cat., London, National Gallery, 1993.

London 1996 *Frederic, Lord Leighton*, exh. cat., London, Royal Academy, 1996.

London 1997 G. Finaldi and M. Kitson, *Discovering the Baroque: The Denis Mahon Collection*, exh. cat., London, National Gallery, 1997.

London, Los Angeles and New York 1993 *Caspar David Friedrich to Ferdinand Hodler: A Romantic Tradition*, exh. cat., London, National Gallery, Los Angeles County Museum of Art and New York, Metropolitan Museum of Art, 1993.

Madrid 1981–2 *Miguel-Ange Houasse. Pintor de la Corte de Felipe V*, exh. cat., Madrid, Museo Municipal, 1981–2.

Mahoney 1977 Michael Mahoney, *The Drawings of Salvator Rosa*, New York, 1977.

Manchester and Cambridge 1993 *Nature's Way: Romantic Landscapes from Norway*, exh. cat., Manchester, Whitworth Art Gallery, University of Manchester, and Cambridge, Fitzwilliam Museum, 1993.

Manson 1927 J. B. Manson, *The Life and Work of Edgar Degas*, London, 1927.

Marmottan 1926 Paul Marmottan, 'Le peintre Louis Gauffier', *Gazette des Beaux-Arts*, Vol. XIII, 1926.

Marseilles 1986 *Jean-Antoine Constantin*, exh. cat., Marseilles, Musée des Beaux-Arts, 1986.

Milan and Bari 1990 Raffaele Monti et al., *Giuseppe De Nittis: Dipinti 1864–1884*, exh. cat., Milan, Palazzo della Permanente, and Bari, Pinacoteca Provinciale, 1990.

Minorco 1998 *Minorco Collection: Paintings and Drawings from the 18th and 19th Centuries*, London, 1998.

Munich 1991 Christoph H. Heilmann, *Johann Georg von Dillis, 1759–1841: Landschaft und Menschenbild*, exh. cat., Munich, Neue Pinakothek, 1991.

Naples 1962 *Il Paesaggio Napoletano nella Pittura Straniera*, exh. cat., Naples, Palazzo Reale, 1962.

Néto-Daguerre and Coutagne 1992 Isabelle Néto-Daguerre and Denis Coutagne, *Granet: Peintre de Rome*, Aix-en-Provence, 1992.

Newall 1990 Christopher Newall, *The Art of Lord Leighton*, Oxford, 1990.

New Haven 1981 Duncan Bull, *Classic Ground: British Artists and the Landscape of Italy, 1740–1830*, New Haven, 1981.

New York 1971 *Autumn Exhibition*, exh. cat., New York, Shepherd Gallery, 1971.

New York 1972 *The Forest of Fontainebleau: French landscapes 1800 to 1870*, exh. cat., New York, Shepherd Gallery, 1972.

New York 1981 *Before Photography*, exh. cat., New York, Museum of Modern Art, 1981.

New York 1982 *Consulat, Empire, Restauration: Art in early nineteenth-century France*, exh. cat., New York, Wildenstein, 1982.

New York 1983 *Early French and other Nineteenth-Century Landscape Paintings and Drawings*, exh. cat., New York, Brandt Dayton, 1983.

New York 1988 *The Romantic Spirit: German Drawings, 1750–1850, from the Nationalgalerie (Staatliche Museen, Berlin) and the Kupferstich-Kabinett (Staatliche Kunstsammlungen, Dresden)*, New York, Pierpont Morgan Library, 1988.

New York 1996 James Mackinnon, *Aspects of Landscape 1760–1880*, exh. cat., New York, Mark Brady Gallery, 1998.

New York 1998 James Mackinnon, *Paintings and Sketches, 1780–1870*, exh. cat., New York, Mark Brady Gallery, 1998.

New York 1999 Simon Dickinson, *Oil Sketches by Auguste-Jean-Baptiste Vinchon and other French Arists*, exh. cat., New York, Newhouse Galleries Inc., 1999.

New York and Houston 1994 Richard Kendall, *Degas Landscapes*, exh. cat., New York, Metropolitan Museum of Art, and Houston, Museum of Fine Arts, 1994.

Ormond 1975 Richard and Leonée Ormond, *Lord Leighton*, New Haven and London, 1975.

Ottani Cavina 1992 Anna Ottani Cavina, 'Louis Gauffier and the question of J.-L. David's "Vue présumée du jardin du Luxembourg"' *Burlington Magazine*, Vol. CXXXIV, no. 1066, January 1992, pp. 27–33.

Ottani Cavina 1994 Anna Ottani Cavina, *I paesaggi della ragione*, Turin, 1994.

Paris 1861 *Catalogue des tableaux et études peintes, pastels, aquarelles, sépias, dessins et croquis laissés par M. Jules Coignet et des tableaux et dessins par divers maitres ... provenant de son cabinet*, Paris, Hôtel Drouot, 8-12 April 1861.

Paris 1982–3 *L'Atelier de Desportes: Dessins et esquisses conservés par la Manufacture nationale de Sèvres, Paris*, exh. cat., Paris, Musée du Louvre, 1982–3.

Paris 1994 Vincent Pomarède, *Achille-Etna Michallon*, exh. cat., Paris, Musée du Louvre, 1994.

Paris 1998 *George Augustus Wallis (1761–1847)*, exh. cat., preface by John Lishawa, Paris, Galerie Eric Coatalem, 1998.

Passeri 1934 G. B. Passeri, *Vite dei Pittori*, ed. J. Hess, Leipzig, 1934.

Plessier 1990 Ghislaine Plessier, *Adrien Dauzats ou la tentation de l'Orient*, Bordeaux, 1990.

Portoghesi 1968 Paolo Portoghesi, *Un'altra citta*, Rome, 1968.

Repp 1983 A. Repp, *Goffredo Wals, Zur Landscaftsmalerei zwischen Adam Elsheimer und Claude Lorrain*, Cologne, 1983.

Rhys 1898 Ernest Rhys, *Frederic Lord Leighton: Late President of the Royal Academy of Arts: an Illustrated Record of his Life and Work*, London, 1898.

Robaut and Moreau-Nélaton 1905 Alfred Robaut and Etienne Moreau-Nélaton, *L'Oeuvre de Corot. Catalogue raisonné et illustré*, 5 vols., Paris 1905.

Rome 1985 Elena di Majo, *Anton Sminck Van Pitloo (1796–1837): Un paesaggista Olandese a Napoli. Ventisette Opere Ritrovate*, exh. cat., Rome, Galleria Carlo Virgilio, 1985.

Rome 1992 Tony Cubberley and Luke Herrmann, *Twilight of the Grand Tour, A catalogue of the drawings by James Hakewill in the British School at Rome Library*, exh. cat., Rome, British School, 1992.

Röthlisberger 1961 Marcel Röthlisberger, *Claude Lorrain: The Paintings*, 2 vols., New Haven and London, 1961.

Röthlisberger 1979 Marcel Röthlisberger, 'Additional Works by Goffredo Wals and Claude Lorrain,' *Burlington Magazine*, Vol. CXXI, no. 910, January 1979, pp. 20–8.

Rouquette and Sintès 1989 J. M Rouquette and C. Sintès, *Arles Antique*, Paris, 1989.

Salerno 1963 L. Salerno, *Salvator Rosa*, Milan, 1963.

Salerno 1974 L. Salerno, 'Precisiazione su Filippo Napoletano e I suoi "Affini"', *Arte Illustrata*, no. 37, 1974.

Salerno 1977–8 L. Salerno, *Pittori di paessaggio del seicento a Roma*, vol. I, Rome, 1977–8.

Smart 1975 Alastair Smart, 'Ramsay Richard Reinagle', *Antique Collector*, March 1975, pp.18–19.

Spoleto 1996 Bruno Mantura and Geneviève Lacambre, *Pierre-Henri de Valenciennes, 1750–1819*, exh. cat., Spoleto, Palazzo Racani Arroni, 1996.

Valenciennes 1800 P. -H. de Valenciennes, *Elémens de perspective pratique, à l'usage des artistes, suivis de réflexions et conseils à un élève sur la peinture, et particulièrement sur le genre de paysage*, Paris, 1800. Reprinted Geneva 1973.

Vasi 1797 Giuseppe Agostini Vasi, *Itineraire instructif de Rome: ou description générale des monumens antiques et modernes et des ouvrages les plus remarkables de peinture, de sculpture et d'architecture de cette célébre ville et de ses environs*, Rome, 1797.

Vigée-Lebrun 1869 Marie-Louise-Elisabeth Vigée-Lebrun, *Souvenirs de Mme Vigée-Lebrun*, Claudine Herrmann, ed., Paris, 1869.

Vignau-Wilberg 1979 Peter Vignau-Wilberg, *Stiftung Oskar Reinhart, Sammlungskatalog vol. 2. Deutsche und oesterreichische Maler des 19 Jahrhunderts*, Zurich, 1979.

Washington, 1998 Jean Sutherland Boggs, *Degas at the Races*, exh. cat. Washington, National Gallery of Art, 1998.

Washington, Brooklyn and St Louis 1996–7 *In the Light of Italy: Corot and early open-air painting*, exh. cat., Washington, National Gallery of Art,Brooklyn Museum and Saint Louis Art Museum, 1996–7.

York, London and Stoke-on-Trent 1989 *Painters of the Italian Landscape 1850–1900*, exh. cat., York City Art Gallery, London, Leighton House, Stoke-on-Trent Museum and Art Gallery, 1989.

Authors' Acknowledgements

The authors' overriding debt is to Charlotte Gere. Not only did she give us the exciting and challenging opportunity of writing the catalogue of the collection that she and the late John Gere formed, but she generously placed at our complete disposal her knowledge of individual paintings, and of the landscape oil sketch tradition. The invaluable starting point for every entry in this publication has been the exhaustive notes that Charlotte Gere compiled on each painting. Now in the Gere archive at the National Gallery, these include information on provenance, exhibition history and publication but, perhaps more importantly, they record John and Charlotte Gere's evolving opinions on the authorship and dating of individual works. They also document the enthusiasm for the oil sketch that they have shared over the years with fellow connoisseurs, collectors, curators and dealers who have offered their own thoughts and ideas on the attribution and dating of specific works. Thus we are in the unique position here of acknowledging the assistance of almost everyone in Britain, Europe and America who, over the last forty-five years, has concerned himself or herself with the landscape oil sketch, as they all shared their perceptions with John and Charlotte Gere. In many cases there is a wide divergence of opinion, and we hope that the catalogue reflects this. Knowledge of the oil sketch continues to grow but, as Charlotte Gere reminded us at every step in our work, there are still many answers we do not have.

In October 1998 a small group of scholars and connoisseurs of the landscape oil sketch accepted our invitation to study the Gere collection over a period of a day and a half in the conservation studios of the National Gallery. There, with the paintings in front of us, we discussed each work in turn, every participant generously sharing their knowledge, experience and insights. These lively and thought-provoking conversations helped to clarify many issues for us, and were of crucial importance in shaping our later investigations. We thank Sir Jack Baer, Anna Ottani Cavina, Michael Clarke, Adrian Eeles, Sarah Faunce, Jacques Fischer, Susan Galassi, Christoph Heilmann, Catherine Johnston, Alastair Laing, John Leighton, James Mackinnon, William Vaughan, John Whiteley and Wheelock Whitney.

Others not able to join us in our meetings also generously offered their advice and encouragement when they passed through London or when we importuned them further afield, including Sylvia Ballantyne, Peter Bower, Mark Brady, Duncan Bull, Denis Coekelberghs, Philip Conisbee, Denis Coutagne, Stephen Duffy, Peter Gailes, Peter Galassi, John House, Helen Langdon, John Lishawa, Jane Munro, Peter Nahum, Lord Poltimore, Vincent Pomarède, Régine Rémon, Kate de Rothschild, Martin Royalton-Kisch, Jonathan Scott, David Scrase, David Solkin, Gary Tinterow and Dacia de Viejo.

We are grateful to all the staff and colleagues at the National Gallery and at National Gallery Publications who have made the exhibition and the catalogue possible.

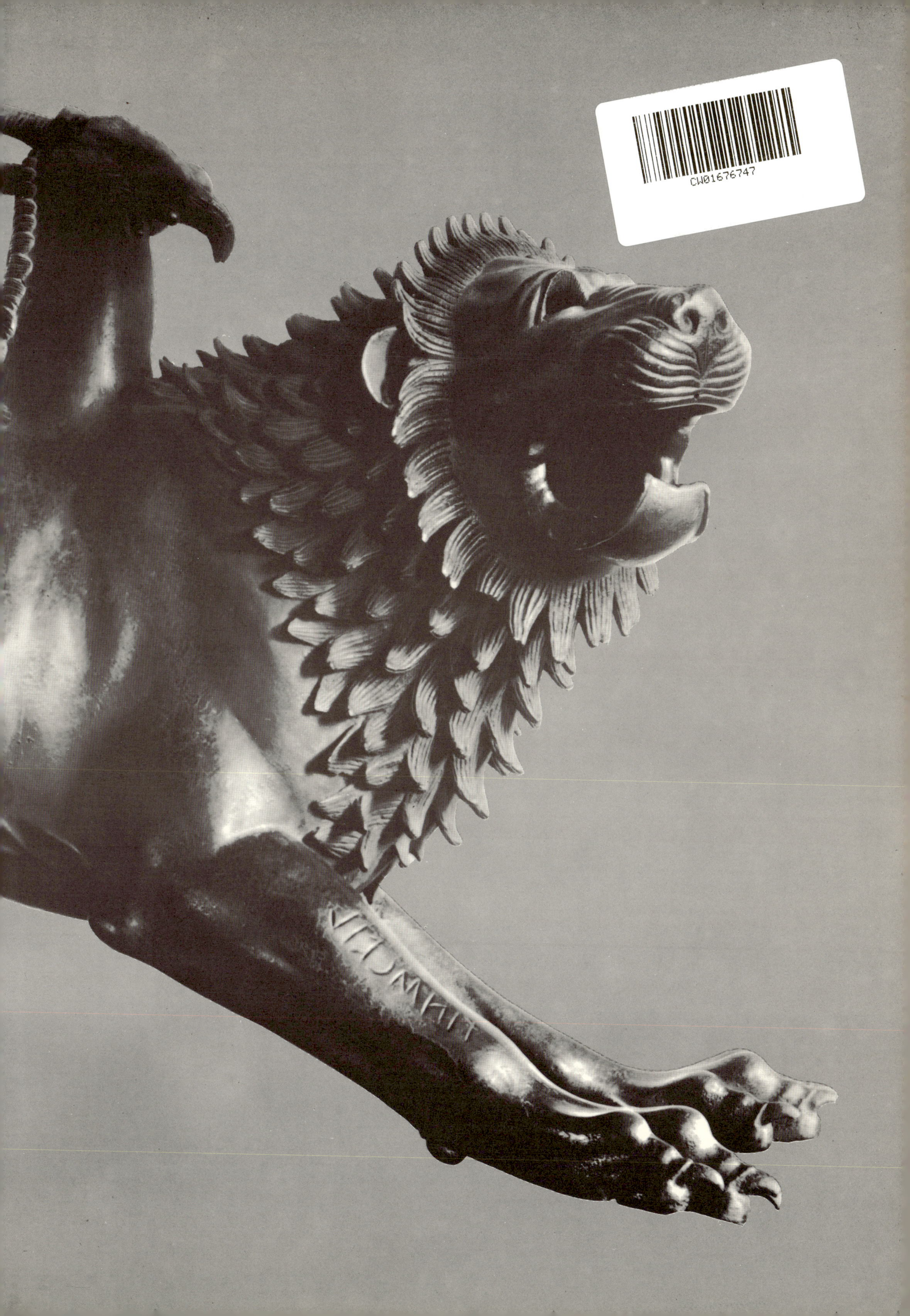

New Larousse Encyclopedia of Mythology

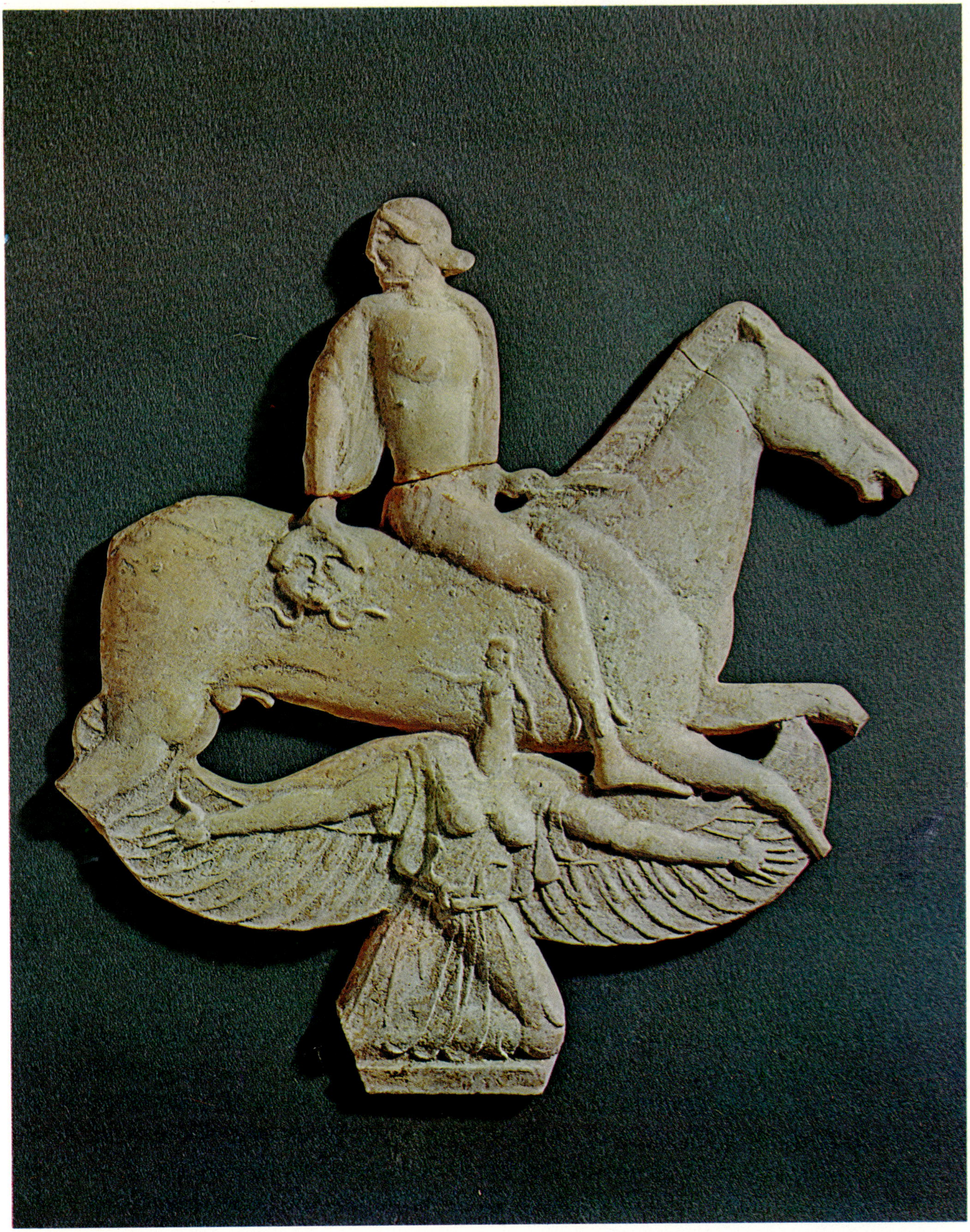

Perseus and Medusa. With Athene's assistance, the hero has just slain the Gorgon Medusa with a bronze *harpe*, or curved sword, given him by by Hermes and now, seated on the back of Pegasus who has just sprung from her bleeding neck and holding her still-dripping decapitated head in his right hand, he turns to watch her two sisters who are pursuing him in fury. Beneath him kneels the headless body of the Gorgon with her arms and golden wings outstretched. From her neck emerges Chrysaor, the father of the monster Geryon. Perseus later presented Medusa's head to Athene who placed it on her shield. Relief from Melos. British Museum.

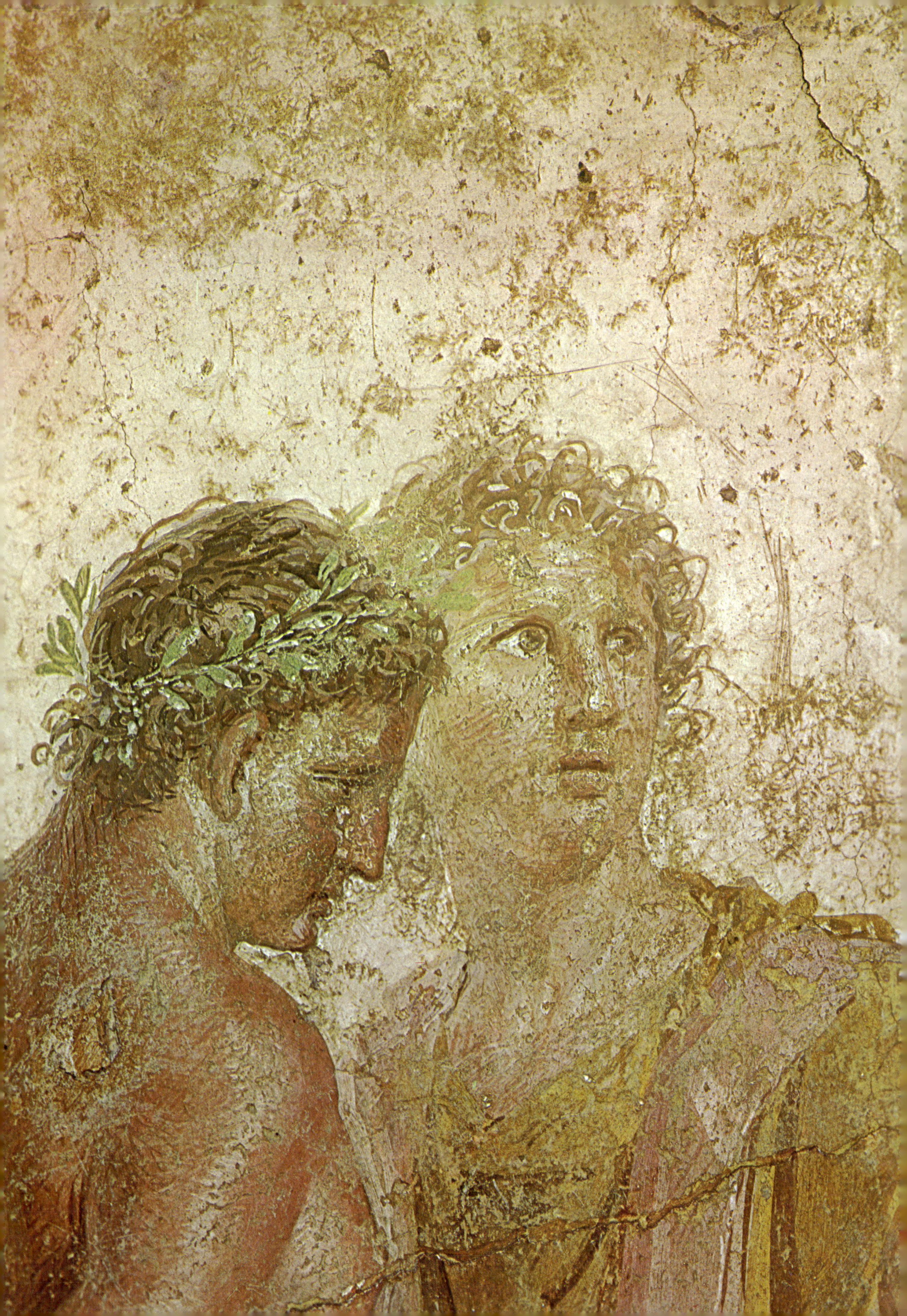

New Larousse Encyclopedia of Mythology

Introduction by
Robert Graves

Book Club Associates
London

Other titles in this series:
Larousse Encyclopedia of Animal Life
Larousse Encyclopedia of Astronomy
Larousse Encyclopedia of Prehistoric and Ancient Art
Larousse Encyclopedia of Byzantine and Medieval Art
Larousse Encyclopedia of Renaissance and Baroque Art
Larousse Encyclopedia of Modern Art
Larousse Encyclopedia of the Earth
Larousse Encyclopedia of Ancient and Medieval History
Larousse Encyclopedia of Modern History
Larousse Encyclopedia of World Geography
Larousse Encyclopedia of Music
Larousse Encyclopedia of Archaeology
Larousse World Mythology
Larousse Science of Life

This edition published 1973 by
Book Club Associates
by arrangement with
The Hamlyn Publishing Group Limited
London New York Sydney Toronto

First published in 1959

New edition 1968
Ninth Impression 1974

New Larousse Encyclopedia of Mythology
Translated by Richard Aldington and Delano Ames
and revised by a panel of editorial advisers from the
Larousse Mythologie Générale edited by Felix Guirand
and first published in France by
Augé, Gillon, Hollier-Larousse, Moreau et Cie,
the Librairie Larousse, Paris

Printed in Hong Kong by Toppan for
THE HAMLYN PUBLISHING GROUP LIMITED
LONDON NEW YORK SYDNEY TORONTO
Hamlyn House, The Centre, Feltham, Middlesex, England

ISBN 0 600 02420 2

INTRODUCTION

By Robert Graves

Mythology is the study of whatever religious or heroic legends are so foreign to a student's experience that he cannot believe them to be true. Hence the English adjective 'mythical', meaning 'incredible'; and hence the omission from standard European mythologies, such as this, of all Biblical narratives even when closely paralleled by myths from Persia, Babylonia, Egypt and Greece; and of all hagiological legends. Otherwise, the New Larousse Encyclopedia of Mythology offers a comprehensive and compact *Who's Who* or *Who Was Who* of the better known gods, goddesses, heroes, monsters, demons, angels and saints from all over the world, including certain Moslem ones. It does not discuss philosophic theory or religious experience, and treats each cult with the same impersonal courtesy.

Myth has two main functions. The first is to answer the sort of awkward questions that children ask, such as: 'Who made the world? How will it end? Who was the first man? Where do souls go after death?' The answers, necessarily graphic and positive, confer enormous power on the various deities credited with the creation and care of souls – and incidentally on their priesthoods.

The second function of myth is to justify an existing social system and account for traditional rites and customs. The Erechtheid clan of Athens, who used a snake as an amulet, preserved myths of their descent from King Erichthonius, a man-serpent, son of the Smith-god Hephaestus and foster-son of the Goddess Athene. The Ioxids of Caria explained their veneration for rushes and wild asparagus by a story of their ancestress Perigune, whom Theseus the Erechtheid courted in a thicket of these plants; thus incidentally claiming cousinship with the Attic royal house. The real reason may have been that wild asparagus stalks and rushes were woven into sacred baskets, and therefore taboo.

Myths of origin and eventual extinction vary according to the climate. In the cold North, the first human beings were said to have sprung from the licking of frozen stones by a divine cow named Audumla; and the Northern afterworld was a bare, misty, featureless plain where ghosts wandered hungry and shivering. According to a myth from the kinder climate of Greece, a Titan named Prometheus, kneading mud on a flowery riverbank, made human statuettes which Athene – who was once the Libyan Moon-goddess Neith – brought to life, and Greek ghosts went to a sunless, flowerless underground cavern. These afterworlds were destined for serfs or commoners; deserving nobles could count on warm, celestial mead-halls in the North, and Elysian Fields in Greece.

Primitive peoples remodel old myths to conform with changes produced by revolutions, or invasions and, as a rule, politely disguise their violence: thus a treacherous usurper will figure as a lost heir to the throne who killed a destructive dragon or other monster and, after marrying the king's daughter, duly succeeded him. Even myths of origin get altered or discarded. Prometheus' creation of men from clay superseded the hatching of all nature from a world-egg laid by the ancient Mediterranean Dove-goddess Eurynome – a myth common also in Polynesia, where the Goddess is called Tangaroa.

A typical case-history of how myths develop as culture spreads: – Among the Akan of Ghana, the original social system was a number of queendoms, each containing three or more clans and ruled by a Queen-mother with her council of elder women; descent being reckoned in the female line, and each clan having its own animal deity. The Akan believed that the world was born from the all-powerful Moon-goddess Ngame, who gave human beings souls, as soon as born, by shooting lunar rays into them. At some time or other, perhaps in the early Middle Ages, patriarchal nomads from the Sudan forced the Akans to accept a male Creator, a Sky-god named Odomankoma; but failed to destroy Ngame's dispensation. A compromise myth was agreed upon: Odomankoma created the world with hammer and chisel from inert matter, after which Ngame brought it to life. These Sudanese invaders also worshipped the seven planetary powers ruling the week – a system originating in Babylonia. (It had spread to Northern Europe, by-passing Greece and Rome; which is why the names of pagan deities – Tuisto, Woden, Thor and Frigg – are still attached to Tuesday, Wednesday, Thursday and Friday.) This extra cult provided the Akan with seven new deities, and the compromise myth made both them and the clan-gods bisexual. Towards the end of the fourteenth century A.D., a social revolution deposed Odomankoma in favour of a Universal Sun-god, and altered the myth accordingly. While Odomankoma ruled, a queendom was still a queendom, the king acting merely as a consort and male representative of the sovereign Queen-mother, and being styled 'Son of the Moon': a yearly dying, yearly resurrected, fertility godling. But the gradual welding of small queendoms into city-states, and of city-states into a rich and populous nation, encouraged the High King – the king of the dominant city-state – to borrow a foreign custom. He styled himself 'Son of the Sun', as well as 'Son of the Moon', and claimed limitless authority. The Sun which, according to the myth, had hitherto been re-born every morning from Ngame, was now worshipped as an eternal god altogether independent of the Moon's life-giving function. New myths appeared when the Akan accepted the patriarchal principle, which Sun-worship brought in; they began tracing succession through the father, and mothers ceased to be the spiritual heads of households.

This case-history throws light on the complex Egyptian corpus of myth. Egypt, it seems, developed from small matriarchal Moon-queendoms to Pharaonic patriarchal Sun-monarchy. Grotesque animal deities of leading clans in the Delta became city-gods, and the cities were federated under the sovereignty of a High King (once a 'Son of the Moon'), who claimed to be the Son of Ra the Sun-god. Opposition by independent-minded city-rulers to the Pharaoh's autocratic sway appears in the undated myth of how Ra grew so old and feeble that he could not even control his spittle; the Moon-goddess Isis plotted against him and Ra retaliated by casting his baleful eye on mankind – they perished in their thousands. Ra nevertheless decided to quit the ungrateful land of Egypt; whereupon Hathor, a loyal Cow-goddess, flew him up to the vault of Heaven. The myth doubtless records a compromise that consigned the High King's absolutist pretensions, supported by his wife, to the vague realm of philosophic theory. He kept the throne, but once more became, for all practical purposes, an incarnation of Osiris, consort of the Moon-goddess Isis – a yearly dying, yearly resurrected fertility godling.

Indian myth is highly complex, and swings from gross physical abandon to rigorous asceticism and fantastic visions of the spirit world. Yet it has much in common with European myth, since Aryan invasions in the second millennium B.C. changed the religious system of both continents. The invaders were nomad herdsmen, and the peoples on whom they imposed themselves as a military aristocracy were peasants. Hesiod, an early Greek poet, preserves a myth of pre-Aryan 'Silver Age' heroes: 'divinely created eaters of bread, utterly subject to their mothers however long they lived, who never sacrificed to the gods, but at least did not make war against one another.' Hesiod put the case well: in primitive agricultural communities, recourse to war is rare, and goddess-worship the rule. Herdsmen, on the contrary, tend to make fighting a profession and, perhaps because bulls dominate their herds, as rams do flocks, worship a male Sky-god, typified by a bull or a ram. He sends down rain for the pastures, and they take omens from the entrails of the victims sacrificed to him.

When an invading Aryan chieftain, a tribal rain-maker, married the Moon-priestess and Queen of a conquered people, a new myth inevitably celebrated the marriage of the Sky-god and the Moon. But since the Moon-goddess was everywhere worshipped as a triad, in honour of the Moon's three phases – waxing, full, and waning – the god split up into a complementary triad. This accounts for three-bodied Geryon, the first king of Spain; three-headed Cernunnos, the Gallic god; the Irish triad, Brian, Iuchar, and Iucharba, who married the three queenly owners of Ireland; and the invading Greek brothers Zeus, Poseidon, and Hades who, despite great opposition, married the pre-Greek Moon-goddess in her three aspects, respectively as Queen of Heaven, Queen of the Sea, and Queen of the Underworld.

The Queen-mother's decline in religious power, and the goddesses' continual struggle to preserve their royal prerogatives, appears in the Homeric myth of how Zeus ill-treated and bullied Hera, and how she continually plotted against him. Zeus remained a Thunder-god, because Greek national sentiment forbad his becoming a Sun-god in Oriental style. But his Irish counterpart, a thunder-god named The Dagda, grew senile at last and surrendered the throne to his son Bodb the Red, a war-god – in Ireland, the magic of rain-making was not so important as in Greece.

One constant rule of mythology is that whatever happens among the gods above reflects events on earth. Thus a father-god named 'The Ancient One of the Jade' (Yu-ti) ruled the pre-revolutionary Chinese Heaven: like Prometheus, he had created human beings from clay. His wife was the Queen-mother, and their court an exact replica of the old Imperial Court at Pekin, with precisely the same functionaries: ministers, soldiers, and a numerous family of the god's sisters, daughters and nephews. The two annual sacrifices paid by the Emperor to the August One of the Jade – at the winter solstice when the days first lengthen and at the spring equinox when they become longer than the nights – show him to have once been a solar god. And the theological value given to the number 72, suggests that the cult started as a compromise between Moon-goddess worship and Sun-god worship: 72 means three-times-three, the Moon's mystical number, multiplied by two-times-two-times-two, the Sun's mystical number, and occurs in solar-lunar divine unions throughout Europe, Asia and Africa. Chinese conservatism, by the way, kept these gods dressed in ancient court-dress, making no concessions to the new fashions which the invading dynasty from Manchuria had introduced.

In West Africa, whenever the Queen-mother, or King, appointed a new functionary at Court, the same thing happened in Heaven, by royal decree. Presumably this was also the case in China; and if we apply the principle to Greek myth, it seems reasonably certain that the account of Tirynthian Heracles' marriage to Hera's daughter Hebe, and his appointment as Celestial Porter to Zeus, commemorates the appointment of a Tirynthian prince as vizier at the court of the Mycenaean High King, after marriage to a daughter of his Queen, the High Priestess of Argos. Probably the appointment of Ganymede, son of an early Trojan king, as cup-bearer to Zeus, had much the same significance: Zeus, in this context, would be more likely the Hittite king resident at Hattusas.

Myth, then, is a dramatic shorthand record of such matters as invasions, migrations, dynastic changes, admission of foreign cults, and social reforms. When bread was first introduced into Greece – where only beans, poppy-seeds, acorns and asphodel-roots had hitherto been known – the myth of Demeter and Triptolemus sanctified its use; the same event in Wales produced a myth of 'The Old White One', a Sow-goddess who went around the country with gifts of grain, bees, and her own young; for agriculture, pig-breeding and bee-keeping were taught to the aborigines by the same wave of neolithic invaders. Other myths sanctified the invention of wine.

A proper study of myth demands a great store of abstruse geographical, historical and anthropological knowledge; also familiarity with the properties of plants and trees, and the habits of wild birds and beasts. Thus a Central American stone-sculpture, a Toad-god sitting beneath a mushroom, means little to mythologists who have not considered the world-wide association of toads with toxic mushrooms or heard of a Mexican Mushroom-god, patron of an oracular cult; for the toxic agent is a drug, similar to that secreted in the sweat-glands of frightened toads, which provides magnificent hallucinations of a heavenly kingdom.

Myths are fascinating and easily misread. Readers may smile at the picture of Queen Maya and her pre-natal dream of the Buddha descending upon her disguised as a charming white baby elephant – he looks as though he would crush her to pulp – when 'at once all nature rejoiced, trees burst into bloom, and musical instruments played of their own accord'. In

English-speaking countries, 'white elephant' denotes something not only useless and unwanted, but expensive to maintain; and the picture could be misread there as indicating the Queen's grave embarrassment at the prospect of bearing a child. In India, however, the elephant symbolises royalty – the supreme God Indra rides one – and white elephants (which are not albinos, but animals suffering from a vitiliginous skin-disease) are sacred to the Sun, as white horses were for the ancient Greeks, and white oxen for the British druids. The elephant, moreover, symbolises intelligence, and Indian writers traditionally acknowledge the Elephant-god Ganesa as their patron; he is supposed to have dictated the *Mahabharata*.

Again, in English, a scallop-shell is associated either with cookery or with medieval pilgrims returning from a visit to the Holy Sepulchre; but Aphrodite the Greek Love-goddess employed a scallop-shell for her voyages across the sea, because its two parts were so tightly hinged together as to provide a symbol of passionate sexual love – the hinge of the scallop being a principal ingredient in ancient love-philtres. The lotus flower sacred to Buddha and Osiris has five petals, which symbolise the four limbs and the head; the five senses; the five digits; and, like the pyramid, the four points of the compass and the zenith. Other esoteric meanings abound: for myths are seldom simple, and never irresponsible.

CONTENTS

COLOUR PLATES

PREHISTORIC MYTHOLOGY

THE RELIGION OF THE FIRST MEN

Mythology, which will be examined in the following chapters by specific regions and epochs, implies a belief in supernatural forces, that is to say in beings who are both different from and superior to living men in that they exercise, either directly or through the intermediary of natural phenomena, a benign or harmful influence. It is the function of ritual practices or ceremonies to encourage the former influence and prevent or neutralise the latter.

As an introduction to the study of the varied forms and the often poetic embellishments which these beliefs assumed among different peoples throughout the ages, it is appropriate to inquire into their origins: when in the life of mankind did such beliefs first appear?

Supernatural beings, the objects of these beliefs, can be divided into two categories which, though in principle distinct, overlap in a number of cases. On the one hand there are the dead, ancestors or *manes*, who have been known to their contemporaries in the form and condition of normal men. On the other hand there are the divinities, strictly speaking, who never existed as ordinary mortals.

Our information about the religious beliefs of peoples known to history can be derived from written documents; about primitive peoples who still exist we have the oral reports of travellers and ethnologists. But for prehistoric ages both of these sources of information are entirely lacking, and we never find ourselves in the actual presence of prehistoric religious beliefs. The only materials we possess are either physical traces of what appear to be vestiges of ritual practices or else pictorial representations of such practices from which can be inferred – with the aid of ethnological parallels – a belief in the existence of the supernatural beings to whom they were addressed. One cannot, therefore, insist too strongly on the hypothetical character of conclusions based on such material.

We shall confine ourselves to the study of those people we call Palaeolithic because of their industry in chipped, not polished, stone, and who lived during the Pleistocene geological epoch. We shall retrace our way cautiously through the course of time and, ignoring facts which are too ambiguous, try to discover what may reasonably be conjectured about their religious beliefs.

Mythology in the strict sense of the word. It is not impossible that the Magdalenians – the least ancient of Palaeolithic peoples – had a mythology in the strict sense of the word: that is to say, that they attributed to certain supernatural beings not only a specific form but specific acts. This at least is an acceptable interpretation of wall-drawings discovered in the cavern of the Trois-Frères in the Ariège department of southern France. There are three of them, and two at least seem to form an intentional group. Objectively the one on the right depicts a personage whose upright posture, legs and rump belong to a man. He has a horse's tail, a bison's head and the front legs of an animal, with one hoof distinctly cloven. He is perhaps dancing, and is certainly playing some kind of bowed musical instrument. He is preceded by an animal which turns its

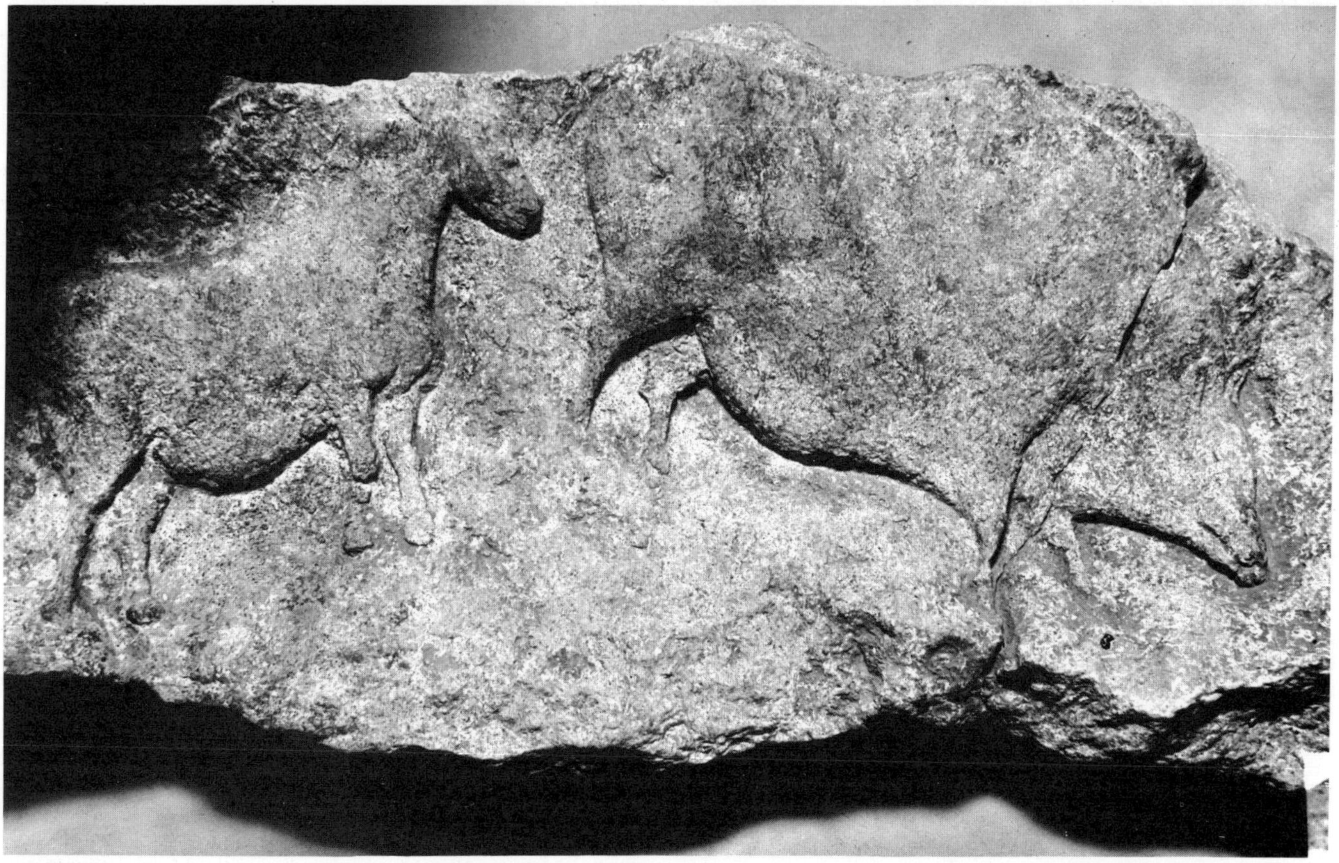

Part of the Relief Frieze of Le Roc, Charente (according to Dr. Henri Martin). Effigies of female animals connected with fertility magic.

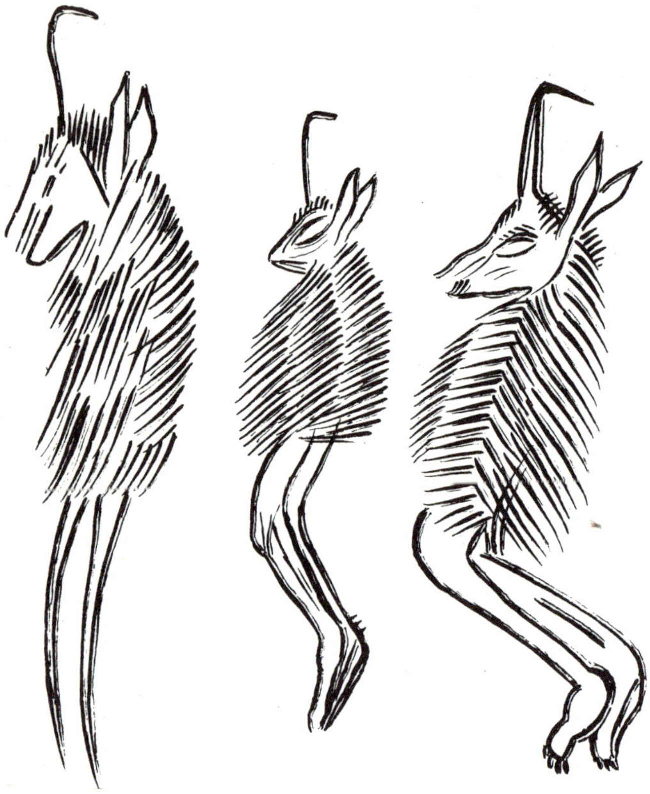

Engraved shaft from the Mège Shelter at Teyjat, Dordogne (according to H. Breuil). Men disguised as chamois. Hunting magic.

head towards him. To be sure, the human figure may be a magician in disguise who is charming the animal in front of him; but it would seem difficult to disguise the arms of an actual man with imitation hooved forelegs. Moreover, neither of the two animals who precede him is altogether real. The one nearest to him, a female whose sex is carefully accentuated, has the hind-quarters of the deer tribe and the forequarters of a bison. The forelegs of the reindeer in front terminate in the hooves of anything but a reindeer. We may thus suppose that this group of figures, of which not one entirely corresponds to reality, was intended to represent a mythological scene – a sort of Palaeolithic Orpheus charming equally mythical animals by means of his music and dancing.

The Magicians. But this interpretation of the Trois-Frères group is by no means the only one possible. Actually, the combination in the same animal of characteristics belonging to different species is found again elsewhere, not only in other drawings from the same cave. In the Trois-Frères cavern there are two bears, one with a wolf's head, the other with a bison's tail. A Solutrean bas-relief at Roc in the Charente shows a swine with a bull's back.

Such figures, as we shall see, are connected with the magic of hunting and fertility and represent not mythological but real animals who are partially deformed in order to avert the hostility which might be aroused in them were their exact resemblance drawn. In addition, personages who combine human and animal characteristics occur elsewhere in Magdalenian art, both in wall-paintings and household possessions. Some of them also seem to be dancing and – according to ethnological parallels – may quite probably represent magicians in disguise. Such are, to cite only the least debatable specimens, another figure carved and painted on a wall of the same Trois-Frères cave – a man with a bearded head, bull's ears, stag's antlers and a horse's tail – and the three personages with chamois heads carved on a staff found in the Mège shelter at Teyjat in the Dordogne. Though all these figures may equally be interpreted as either divinities or magicians, it would seem that the figure cut on one side of a limestone pebble from La Madeleine, in which human features are represented under a covering mask, must be that of a magician. On the other face of the same stone there is a feminine figure whose animal head is not so certainly a mask. If we assume that she also is a magician we reach the interesting conclusion that at least in the Lower Magdalenian period magic functions were not an exclusively masculine prerogative.

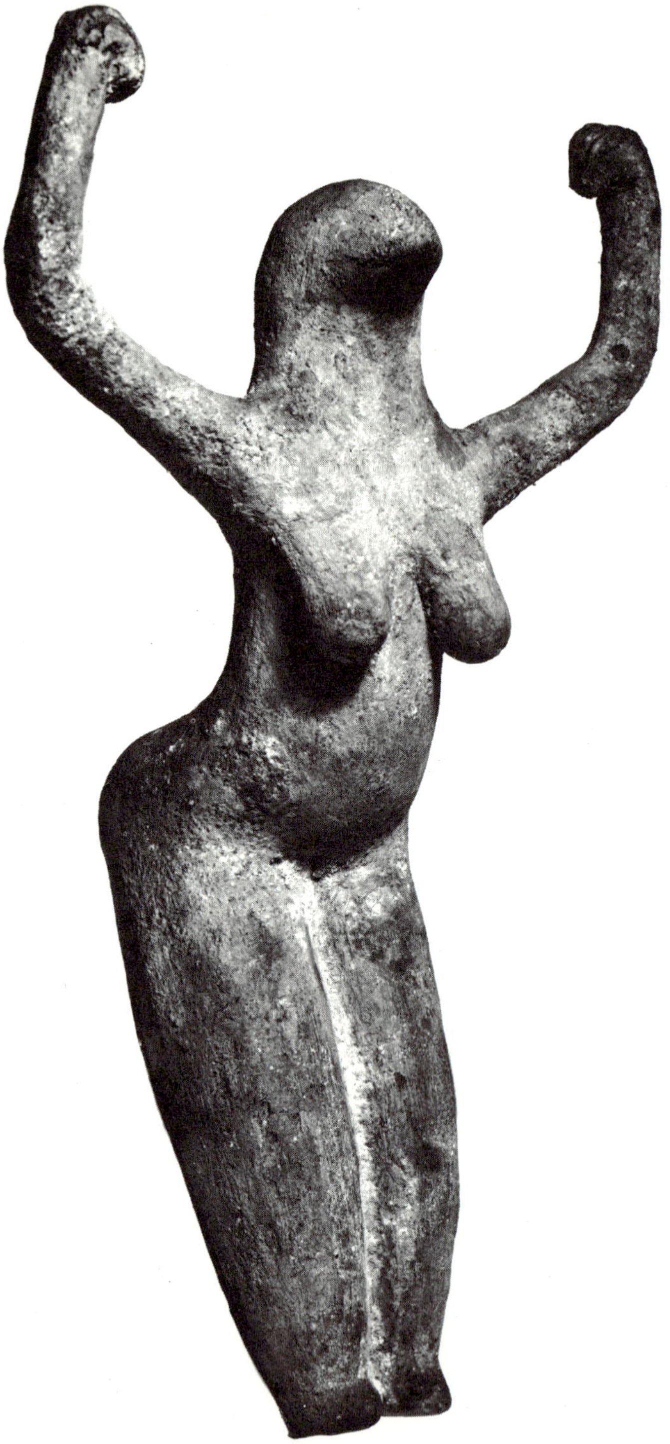

Egyptian terracotta figurine. Fashioned from Nile mud, these female figures were probably fertility goddesses or served as simple representations in magic rites. Prehistoric period.

Whether any of the figures mentioned above actually represented a hybrid deity or not, it is easy to see how the use of magic disguise contributed to the belief in such deities. The power of the magician was attributed to his disguise. It played the role of establishing a mystic communion, a fusion of essence, between him and the animals on which he proposed to act. Magic power and the magician's appearance were naturally associated. His aspect, simultaneously animal and human, naturally led to the conception of gods under the same hybrid form. The god possessed similar powers, and the magician, at least in the exercise of his functions, was in some way the god's incarnation. In any case, whether these figures represented divinities or magicians, they bear witness to the existence of religious beliefs. There can be no doubt that during the Magdalenian period many caverns, either wholly or at least in their lower depths, were sanctuaries.

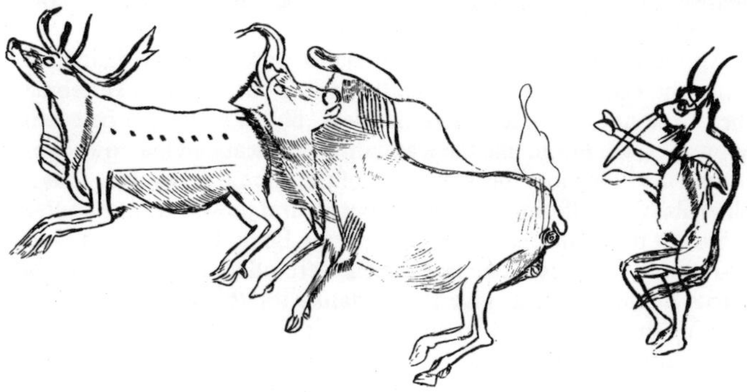

Wall Engraving in the Trois-Frères, Ariège (according to H. Begouen and H. Breuil). Mythical scene or representation of some form of hunting magic.

Hunting Magic. Food in Palaeolithic times depended primarily on hunting, and the essential role of magic was to assure its success. Mimetic magic with animal disguises must have contributed. But Magdalenian man certainly had recourse to sympathetic or homoeopathic magic, which relies on the theory that an operation performed on an image of a real being will produce the same effect on the being itself. Many of the drawings and clay figures of the cave of Montespan in the Haute-Garonne seem to have been made in order to be slashed or pierced with holes with the object of wounding real animals. Particularly remarkable is a statue of a bear cub, modelled in the round and placed on a stand, which seems to have been destined for this purpose. The statue never had a head. There is a cavity in the neck which seems to have been produced by a wooden peg supporting some object – and the skull of a bear cub was found on the ground between the statue's two front paws. This suggests that the headless statue, which is riddled with more than thirty holes, was completed by the head of an actual animal. There are other indications that it was perhaps covered with an animal's hide which also played a part in the magic ceremony.

Also sculptured in the round at Isturitz in the Basses-Pyrénées is a feline creature, perforated in a manner which does not seem to suggest that the holes were made in order to hang up the figure. They must therefore represent wounds; and there are also arrows or harpoons scratched on the figure's thighs and spine. Another sculpture in the same grotto was even more obviously intended for sympathetic magic. This is a bison in sandstone. On its flank there is a deep vertical incision, at the side of which an arrow is cut. It is even possible that the original fracturing of the head and feet was the result of intentional mutilation which completed the magic ceremony.

From these examples, in which the magic operation consists of actually wounding the animal's image, ancient man passed gradually to merely portraying the wounds or even simply evoking them by drawing the weapons which were supposed to inflict them. This can be seen, among many other examples, in a wall-drawing of a bear at Trois-Frères. Its body is depicted as having been stoned. It bristles with arrows, and from the muzzle flow copious streams of blood.

In these figures, and in others which seem to represent animals being hunted not with weapons but with snares, it is almost certain that the portrayal of a wished-for event was intended to bring about the event itself.

Two drawings on limestone of animals pierced with arrows, a rhinoceros and a stag, found at La Colombière in the Ain, must antedate the Magdalenian and correspond chronologically to the Solutrean period in a region to which this civilisation did not penetrate.

Fertility Magic. Since hunting of necessity required the existence of game it is natural that Palaeolithic man, in order that game should be plentiful, also practised fertility magic. In this case sympathetic magic could not, as with hunting magic, consist of performing in animal images the operations which would produce the desired result on the animals themselves. Fertility could only be caused artificially in effigy. We can therefore consider the representation of certain animal couples, and certain females, as examples of fertility magic. Such animal couples are the clay-modelled bisons of Tuc d'Audoubert, the reindeer sculptured in ivory of Bruniquel and the bull following a cow at Teyjat. To these may be added a wall-drawing of bison at Altamira. A female fertility figure is the drawing on a flagstone at La Madeleine of a doe accompanied by her fawn. All these specimens are of the Magdalenian period. But the older Solutrean frieze at Roc presents several bas-reliefs of female forms: the sow with cow's back already mentioned and some mares, one of which seems to be accompanied by the rough outline of a male.

It is possible, though disputable, that certain figures of wounded men – for example a drawing in the shelter at Saltadora – were intended to bewitch an enemy, and thus correspond to a war magic similar to hunting magic. We consider it even more doubtful that representations of amorous scenes between human beings or the figurines of women with exaggerated bellies were intended to cause fertility among women. There is the Magdalenian 'Woman with a Reindeer' of Laugerie-Basse and the luxuriant females who are particularly abundant in, though not exclusive to, the Aurignacian period. But their role, we believe, was purely erotic. There is, however, a curious drawing on a blade of bone at Isturitz in which a woman, followed by a man, bears on her thigh a harpoon similar to those which in the picture on the opposite side of the blade have wounded a bison. This we are tempted to interpret as a love charm.

To sum up, there seem to be no indications of hunting magic or fertility magic during Aurignacian times. They only appear with the Solutrean and continue into the Magdalenian period, reaching their apogee in its first phase.

Pre-Mousterian Offerings. Different religious practices are encountered in pre-Mousterian central Europe, a period which goes back to the last ice age. The most characteristic remains come from Drachenloch, above Vattis in the valley of the Tamina (canton of Saint-Gall, Switzerland), which is the highest known Palaeolithic cavern, over 7,500 feet above sea level. In two of the chambers there are low stone walls nearly three feet high, which were certainly made by the hand of man. They run along the cave wall, leaving between it and them a space about fifteen inches wide. This space is filled with the bones of cave bears. These bones are chiefly skulls and are usually accompanied by the two first cervical vertebrae. There are also leg bones belonging, with rare exceptions, to different individual bears. At the entrance and in the forepart of one of these chambers similar bone-heaps were accumulated in half a dozen rectangular stone chests, covered by large slabs which form lids. In the far end of the same chamber three skulls were gathered together in an empty space between fallen blocks. Another skull had been carefully placed beneath a huge stone which was wedged in a manner to protect it

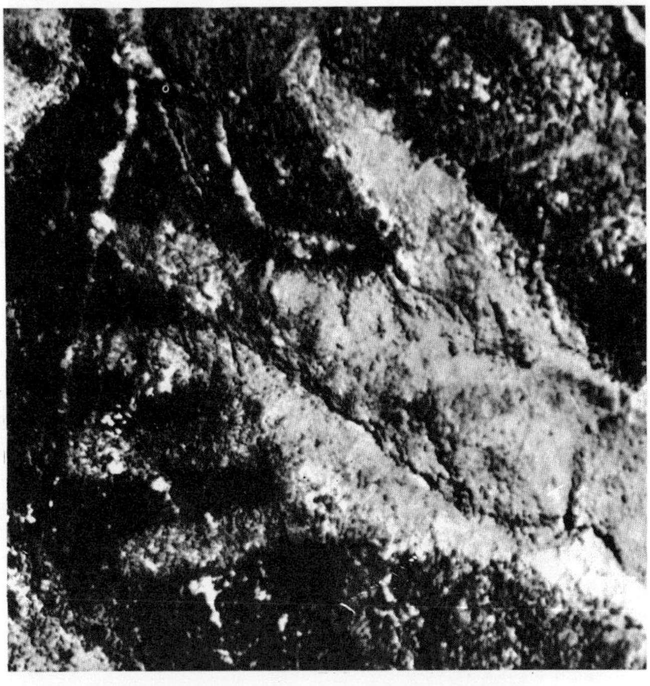

Negative hand print in red ochre. A very early example of man expressing man, leading later to more complicated examples and to sympathetic magic. Grotte de Gargas (Hautes-Pyrénées).

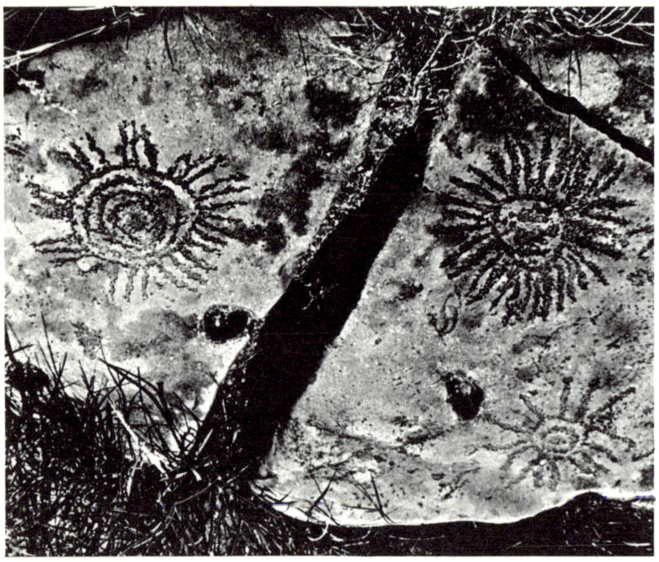

Designs resembling symbolic suns which from their frequency in the later engraving period would appear to point to the existence of sun worship in this area. Cave in the Matopo Hills, Rhodesia.

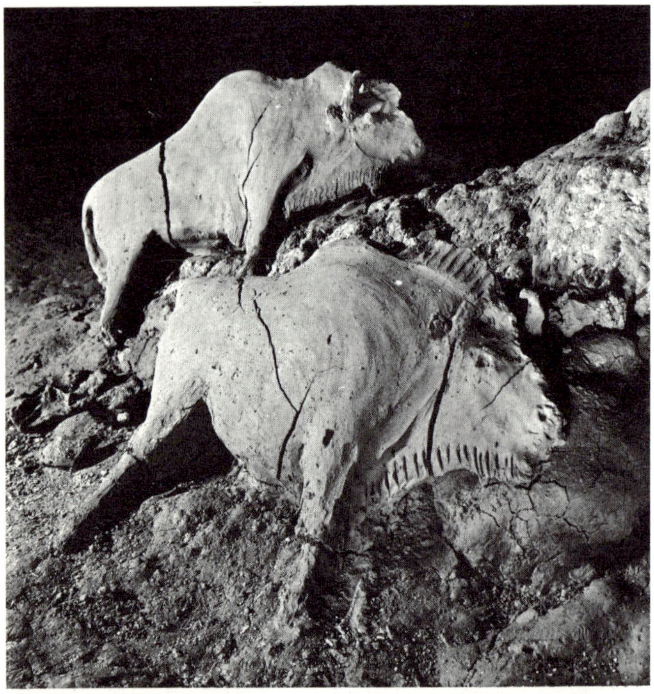

Male bison about to mount a female. Representations of animals coupling are believed to have been made as part of fertility rites. Clay figures of the Magdalenian period. Le Tuc d'Audoubert (Ariège).

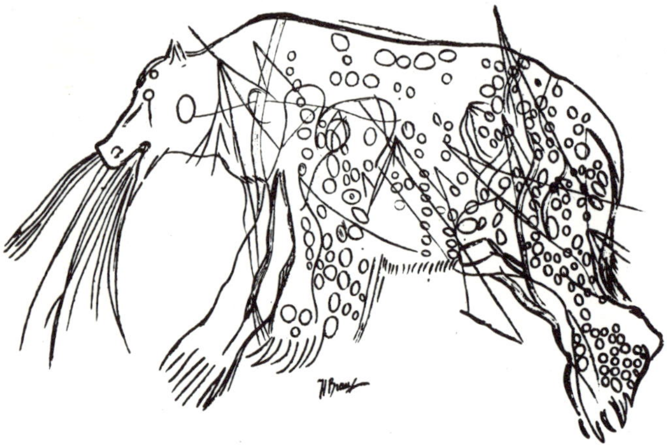

Wall Engraving from the Trois-Frères (according to H. Begouen and H. Breuil). Bear stoned and pierced with arrows, vomiting blood. Sympathetic magic.

against the pressure of the earth. It was encircled by a sort of stone crown adapted to the shape of the head.

All these collections of bears' remains were certainly deliberate. Since the skulls were generally attached to the first two vertebrae, they were not deposited there fleshless, but in a state to be eaten. Moreover, the brain, like the legs with their meat and marrowbones, represented the most succulent part of the animal. They were thus in all probability offerings to some supernatural power. It is, of course, arbitrary to see in this power a Supreme Being like our own God, and more likely these choice morsels were offered to conciliate the spirits of the game, to give them thanks for the success of a past hunting expedition and to solicit the continuance of their favour in the future. In any case we have here what may be the oldest known example of practices addressed to supernatural powers.

THE CULT OF THE DEAD

The dead, too, were considered to be supernatural powers. Corpses were the object of practices which give evidence not only of deference but also, in the broad sense of the word, of a cult. The skeletons which have been found in artificially dug trenches or surrounded and covered by durable materials, like stones or bone fragments, were incontestably buried with funerary intention.

Many of them, moreover, were buried with funerary furnishings such as the jewels and ornaments which have been found on or near them. Doubtless these were objects which they had owned during their lifetimes. But even if they had not been presented with these ornaments on burial, at least the survivors had not, in spite of their considerable value, taken them away as they could have done. The fact that they belonged to the dead rendered them in some way taboo. And then other objects found with the bodies could only have been placed there by the survivors, and constitute genuine funerary furnishings, destined for the use of the dead man in after-life: utensils, works of art, food.

In many cases red ochre (clay coloured with haematite or iron peroxide) was sprinkled over the corpse's grave and has left traces of its colour on the skeleton and surrounding objects. Because of its colour certain primitive peoples of to-day, in particular the Australian aborigines, liken red ochre to blood (even we call it haematite) and for this reason consider it a symbol of life and strength. It is reasonable to suppose that the ochre spread over the tombs and bodies of Palaeolithic man was intended, like the deposits of food, to strengthen the dead one during his journey to the after-world and his sojourn in his new abode.

Among numerous examples of these various funeral practices we shall call attention only to those that are particularly characteristic, and establish at which periods such practices were in force.

The Magdalenian skeleton of Hoteaux in the Ain, covered with red ochre, was found in a small trench. Behind the head a large stone had been placed. Beside it were chipped flint instruments and a chieftain's staff in reindeer horn on which was engraved a stag. The skeleton of Sordes in the Landes had several slabs placed on its skull and had been covered with red ochre. Beside it were found about forty bears' and three lions' canine teeth, almost all carefully pierced. Some twenty of them were carved with seals, fish and arrows. In view of their position they must have constituted a necklace and a belt. The perforated shellfish which formed the adornment of 'the crushed man' of Laugerie-Basse belonged to two species which are native to the Mediterranean. Having come from such a distance they must have been especially valuable.

Under the right hand of the skeleton of Solutré there were numerous flints chipped in the shape of laurel leaves and also a pierced scallop shell. Found with it were two crude statuettes of reindeer in stone.

The skeleton of Klause in Bavaria was enclosed between boulders fallen from the ceiling. They had been arranged to make a place for the body. It was completely surrounded by a mass of red powder. Above and beneath the head was a great heap of fragments of mammoths' tusks.

For the Aurignacian period a number of consonant facts have been established in the caverns of Grimaldi, near Menton. In the grotto '*des Enfants*' the two negroid skeletons lie in a trench about thirty inches deep. The head of the old woman was found in a tightly closed chest formed by two lateral blocks of stone, covered over by

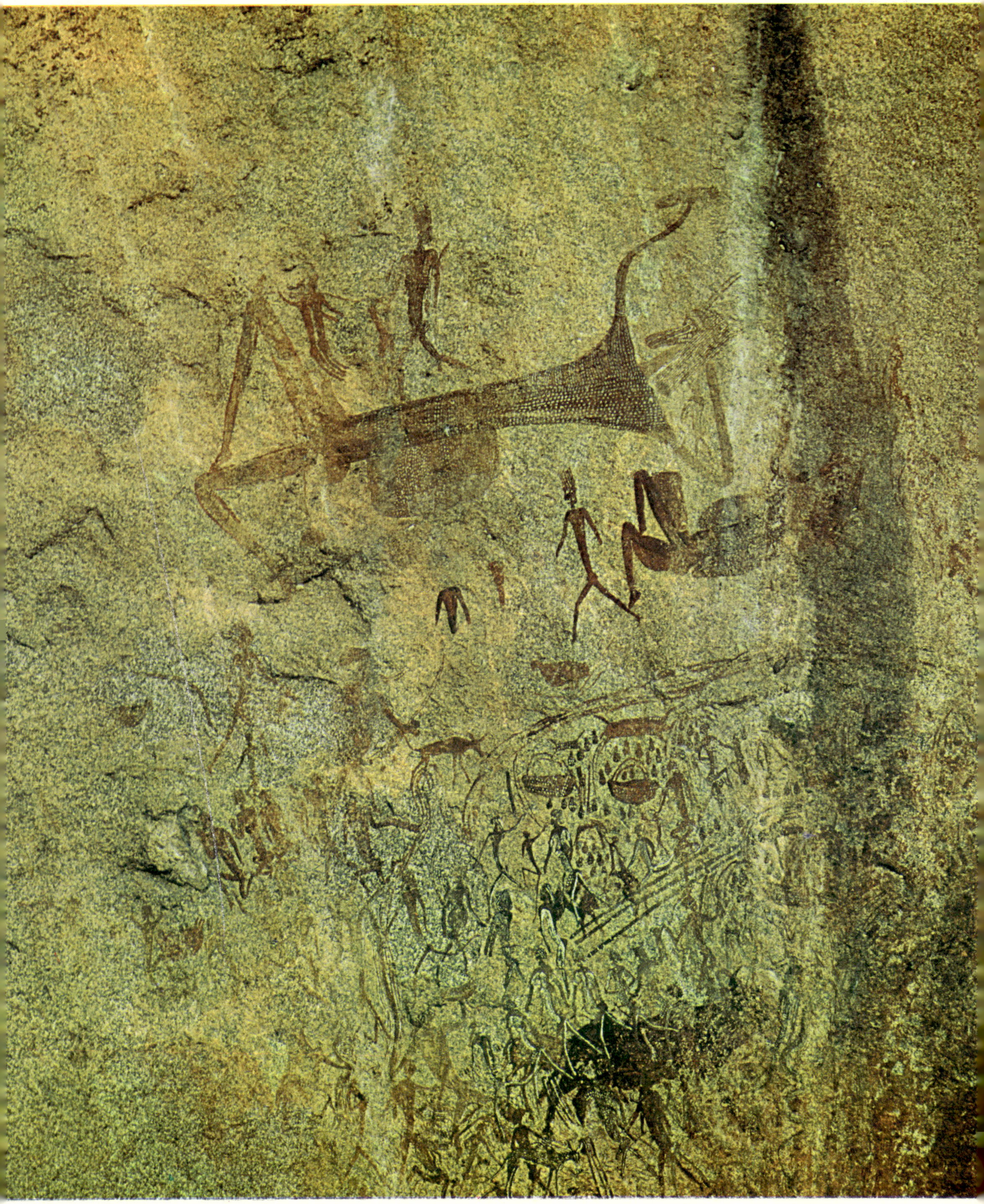

Funeral scene. The large reclining figure in the upper half is a masked and bandaged body, probably of a chief or someone of rank, wearing an antelope mask and ready for burial. The figure below with raised knees is possibly a wife mourning him, but she could also be prepared for burial with him – in effect to follow him into the next world. The curved lines in the lower part may represent a river, a frequent symbol among primitive peoples for the barrier to be crossed before reaching the next world. Numerous other figures are shown, and offerings of food. Rock painting believed to be about 5,000 years old at 'Diana's Vow' Farm near Rusape, Rhodesia.

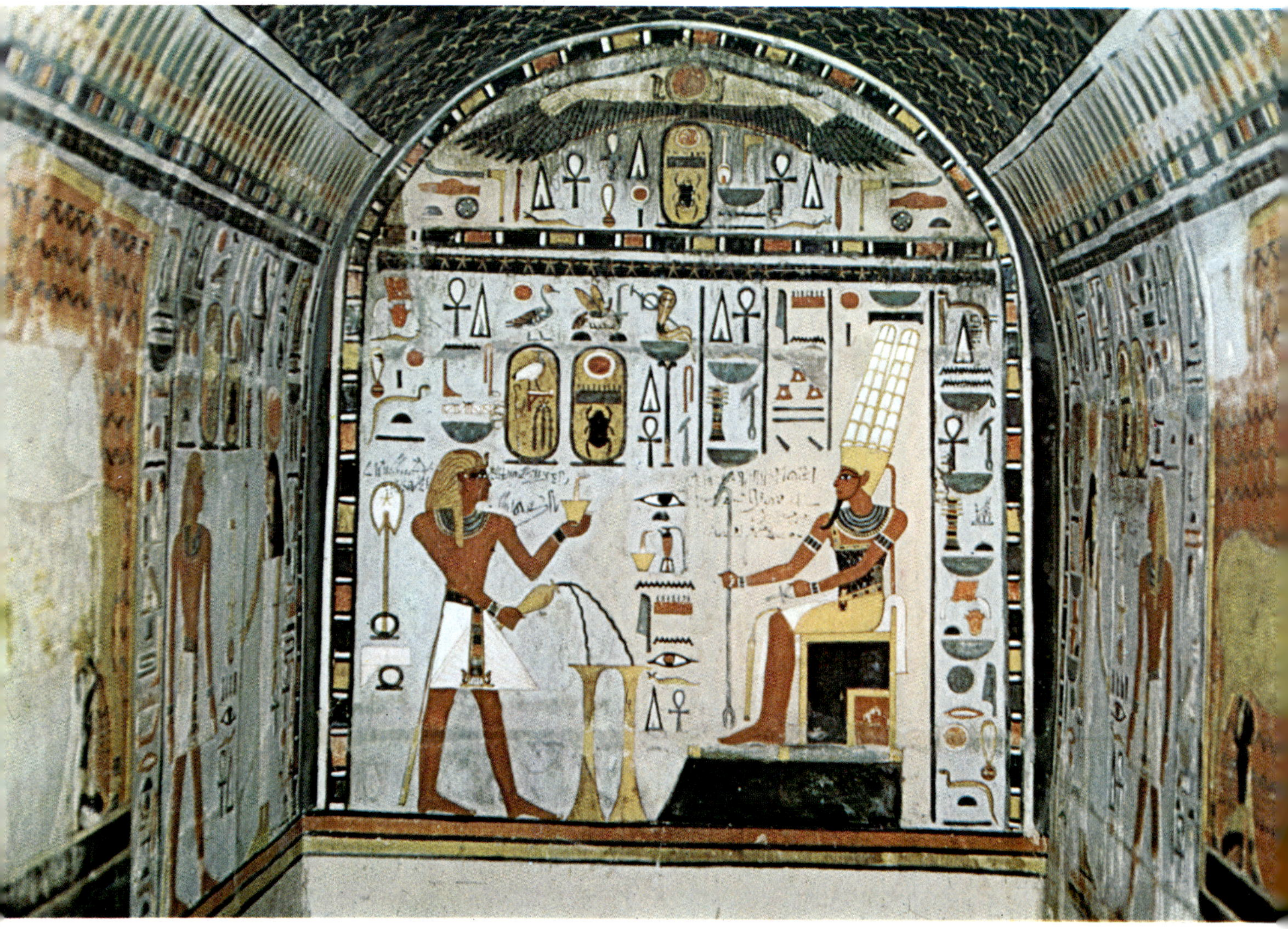

Thutmoses III pours a libation to the god Amon-Ra. The pharaoh stands before the seated god pouring a double libation with his right hand and holding burning incense in his left. The god is portrayed seated on a throne wearing his head-dress of a crown surmounted by two tall plumes and holding a sceptre and the *ankh,* or symbol of life. Originally a god of Thebes, Amon was raised by the conquests of Thutmoses III to the position of supreme god of the known world. Tomb of Thutmoses III from Deir el-Bahri. Eighteenth dynasty, 1580 to 1350 B.C.

a horizontal slab. The young man was wearing a sort of crown made of four rows of pierced nassas. The same shellfish provided the two bracelets on the old woman's left arm. This tomb contained red powder in the rubble, around the head and on parts of the young man's skeleton. The two children, to whom the cave owes its name, were wearing a kind of apron made of thousands of perforated nassas. In the same cave a female skeleton was covered over with animal bones, the jawbones of a wild boar and some chips of flint. Under its head there was a white stone bearing traces of red colouring. It was literally lying in a bed of trochus shells. Not being pierced, these shells could not have been for adornment, but had been put near the body for food.

At La Barma Grande the three bodies stretched side by side were placed in an obviously man-made trench and had a bed of red earth. They wore adornments composed of shells, teeth, fish vertebrae and artificial pendants in bone and ivory. Particularly remarkable is the young man's necklace, which was held in its original position by a coating of clay and, in the symmetry and rhythm of its arrangement, bears witness to a sense of artistry. These skeletons were accompanied by very beautiful flint instruments, and the woman's head reposed on the femur of an ox.

The corpse of Paviland in Wales was powdered with iron oxide which stained the earth and burial objects, and in some places formed a coating on the bones. Although probably male, it has for this reason been christened 'The Red Lady'. Beside it was found the entire head of a mammoth complete with tusks. Near the thighs were found two handfuls of small shells drenched in red, and near the chest some fifty fragments of round ivory rings.

At Predmosti in Moravia twenty human skeletons were gathered under a veritable lid of stones. A child's skeleton wore a necklace of fourteen pendants. Beside the skeleton of Brno there were more than six hundred fragments of fossilised shells, strung together to form conical tubes. Some were still inserted in each other and together they must have made a kind of breastplate for the body. Near it were also found large perforated stone disks, small disks decorated with incisions, three solid disks made of mammoth's or rhinoceros's ribs, some rhinoceros ribs, and finally an ivory statuette of a human being. The skeleton and some of the objects in the tomb were partially stained red.

The skeleton of La Chapelle-aux-Saints belongs to the Mousterian period. It lay in a trench a little less than five feet long, about three feet wide and a foot deep. The head lay against a corner of the trench, propped by stones and covered over with broad slabs of bone. At La Ferrassie the two children at least were laid in artificial trenches. The man's skeleton was covered by rubble and protected by chips of bone. The skeleton of Moustier had its skull placed on a sort of pillow formed by a heap of flint fragments carefully adapted to the shape of the head. The nose seems to have been especially protected by two chips of flint. The bodies of both La Chapelle-aux-Saints and Moustier were provided with funerary furnishings, instruments and joints of game.

The use of red ochre has not been observed in the Mousterian period, but burial rites are as apparent then as in later Magdalenian times. What, then, was their intention? Since they were performed for people whose earthly life was finished they imply a belief that the dead continue after death to lead some kind of existence. This posthumous life appears to have been conceived as similar to life on earth, with the same needs and the same means of satisfying them. This explains the ornaments left with the dead, the implements, the food (quarters of venison and piles of shellfish) and the red ochre.

In thus providing for the posthumous needs of the dead, the survivors seem, however, to have acted less from disinterested affection than from self-interest. Their care seems to have been to encourage the deceased's favourable disposition towards themselves, to soften his possible hostility or to put him physically in a position where he could do no harm. Generally speaking, primitive people believe that death, like sickness, is the result of a magic operation. Deaths to which we assign natural causes are attributed by them to an evil spell, the author of which, whether unconscious or malevolent, they attempt to discover by various means.

This being so, it can be understood that the dead were thought to harbour vengeance against their presumed murderers and, in consequence of the idea of collective responsibility, against all those who survived them. At the very least they would entertain sentiments

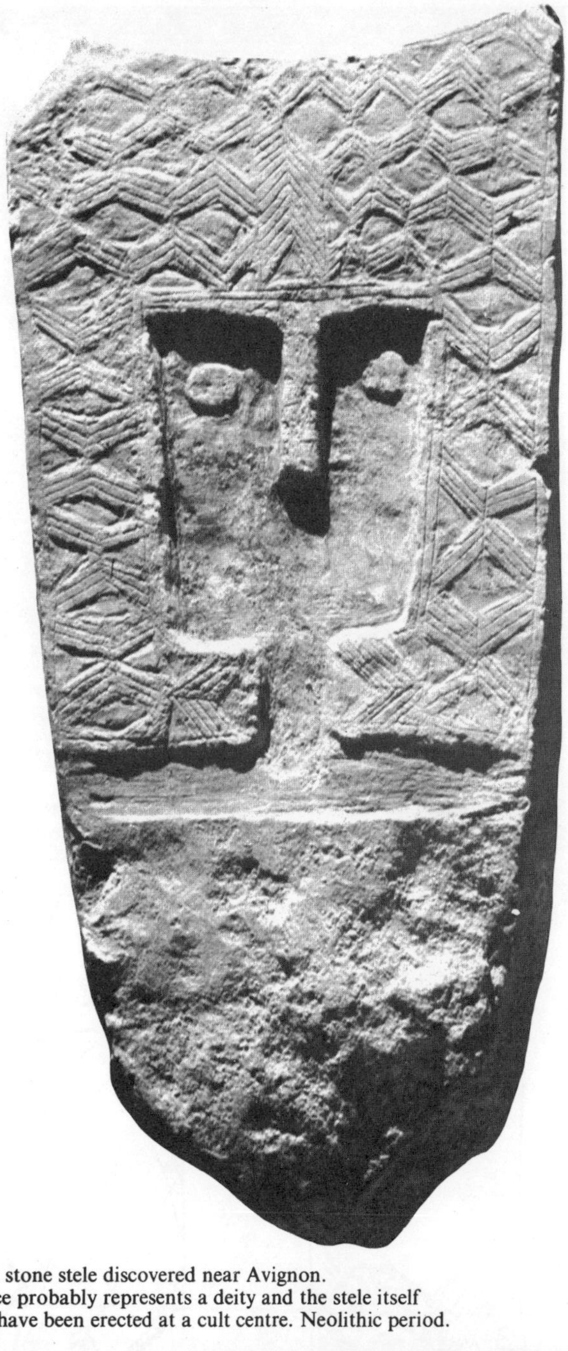

Carved stone stele discovered near Avignon.
The face probably represents a deity and the stele itself would have been erected at a cult centre. Neolithic period.

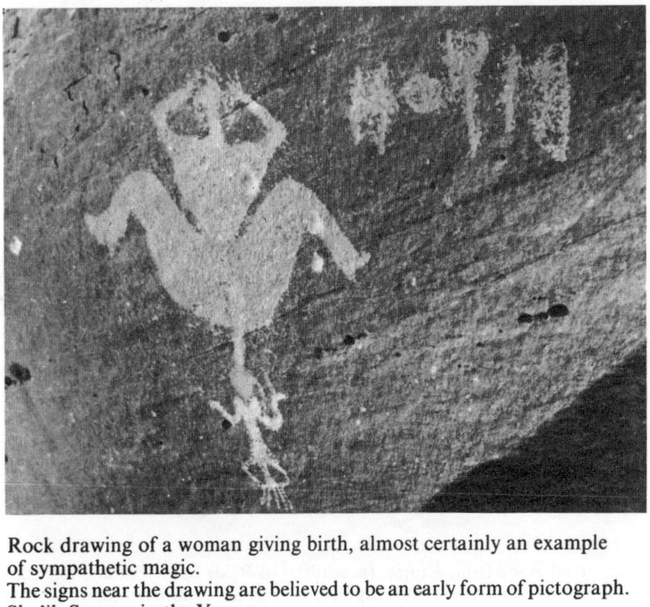

Rock drawing of a woman giving birth, almost certainly an example of sympathetic magic.
The signs near the drawing are believed to be an early form of pictograph. Sha'ib Samma in the Yemen.

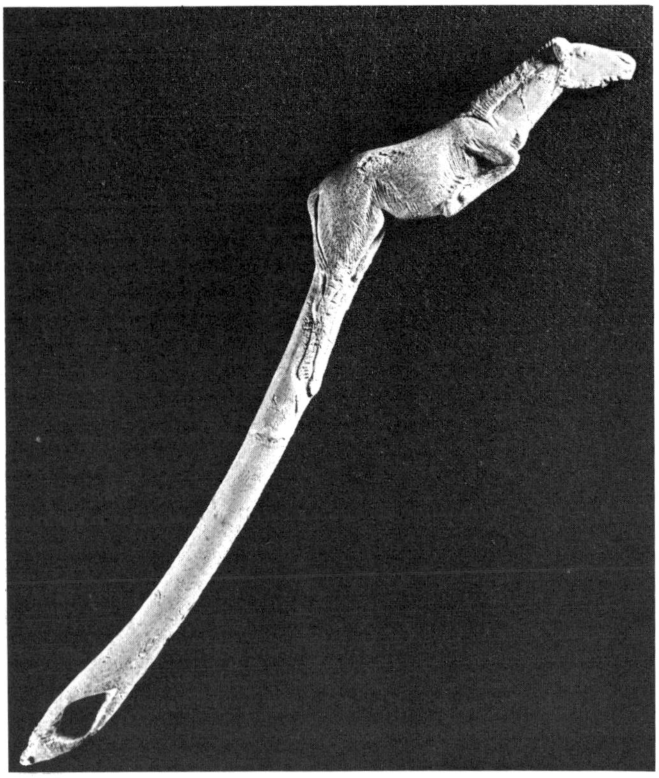

Spear thrower in carved bone. The spear shaft fitted into the hole to provide additional leverage. The figure of the horse suggests that wild horses were hunted for food. Palaeolithic period.

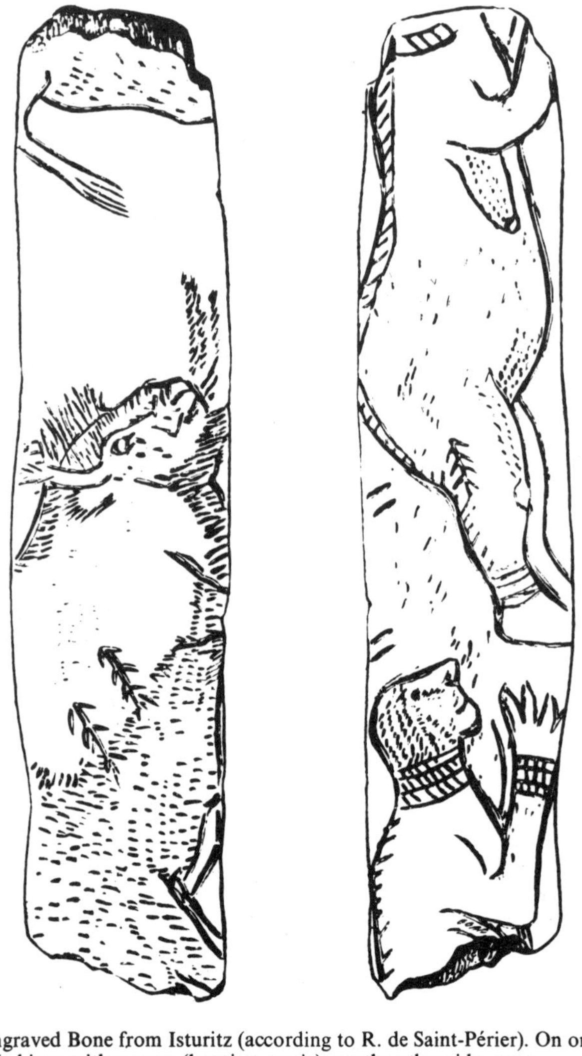

Engraved Bone from Isturitz (according to R. de Saint-Périer). On one side bison with arrows (hunting magic); on the other side, man following a woman with an arrow in her thigh (possibly love charm.)

of envy towards those who still enjoyed the earthly life of which they themselves had been deprived. It seems, then, that the basic attitude towards the dead was one of fear, and that burial rites were originally measures of protection against the deceased. Thus Palaeolithic trenches and tombs may have been intended less to shelter the dead than to imprison them. The statuette of Brno, very probably masculine and buried with a masculine corpse, could have played the role of a 'double', meant to keep the dead one in his tomb and prevent him from 'returning' to torment the living. This would account for the statuette's being made with neither legs nor right arm.

Particularly remarkable is the trussed-up position in which many of these bodies were found. A typical example from the Magdalenian period is the old man of Chancelade in the Dordogne, covered with red ochre, with arms and legs folded and the vertical column bent to such a degree that the skeleton only occupies a space little more than two feet long and sixteen inches wide. In the grotto '*des Enfants*', which is Aurignacian, the negroid young man's legs were completely drawn up to his thighs. The old woman's thighs were raised as far as possible so that her knees reached the level of her shoulders. The legs were sharply folded under the thighs and the feet nearly touched the pelvis. The forearms were bent upwards so that the left hand was just beneath the shoulder-blade. In the Mousterian period the woman of La Ferrassie had her legs doubled up; the bent right forearm rested along the thigh, the hand on a knee. This arm and the legs formed a letter 'N', the knee reaching a distance of only six inches from the shoulder. The legs of the skeleton of La Chapelle-aux-Saints were folded and raised so that the kneecaps were more or less on a level with the chest.

This contracted condition which has been observed in so many skeletons from the Mousterian until the Magdalenian period could, of course, only have been imposed on the body by those who buried it. In addition, it means that the body must have been tied up at the moment of death: for *rigor mortis* would later have prevented its being forced into such a position. It seems, then, that among Palaeolithic as among other primitive peoples who share similar burial customs, the doubled-up posture of the body was only a result of the trussing-up and binding – this being the essential operation, intended to prevent the dead from coming back to torment the living. This also explains the diversity of positions in which Palaeolithic bodies are found: provided that they were securely bound and could not leave their graves, the actual position of the body was of secondary importance and could be left to individual initiative.

Although fear of the dead seems to have been the dominant sentiment it does not follow that in some cases at least there was not also a belief that the dead could be helpful and beneficent, especially when funeral rites devised to assure their maximum well-being in the after-life had been performed. This seems to account for certain practices which differed from burial in the strict sense, in that they tended not to set the dead apart from the living but, on the contrary, to preserve their remains and keep them, as it were, to hand. Such, notably, was the practice of stripping the flesh from the body before burial. This was done by various means, especially by natural putrefaction in a provisional grave. The object was to conserve the skeleton or its bones, which were sometimes worn by the survivors as amulets. The practice seems to have existed from Palaeolithic times. A Lower Magdalenian example is found in the grotto of Le Placard in the Charente. An entire skull of a woman, complete with lower jawbone, was placed on a rock and surrounded by a hundred and seventy shells of different sorts, some pierced, some not. Skulls in the same cave, belonging to Lower Magdalenian and Upper Solutrean periods, show clear traces of deliberate flesh-stripping and have undoubtedly been cut and altered. In the Aurignacian cave of Le Cavillon at Grimaldi three such bones were found: the broken radius of a child and two bones from a man's foot, coloured a vivid red. Scattered nearby was a set of pierced and unpierced shells. A tomb at Predmosti contained only a few bone-remains which had been scraped; the head was missing but must once have been there, for two teeth still remained. A Mousterian skeleton, found in a trench at La Ferrassie, had its skull, deprived of face and jawbone, placed nearly four feet away from the body. At Le Pech de l'Aze the skull of a five or six years old child was surrounded by deliberately broken animal bones, by teeth and by a quantity of implements. Finally, we must take into

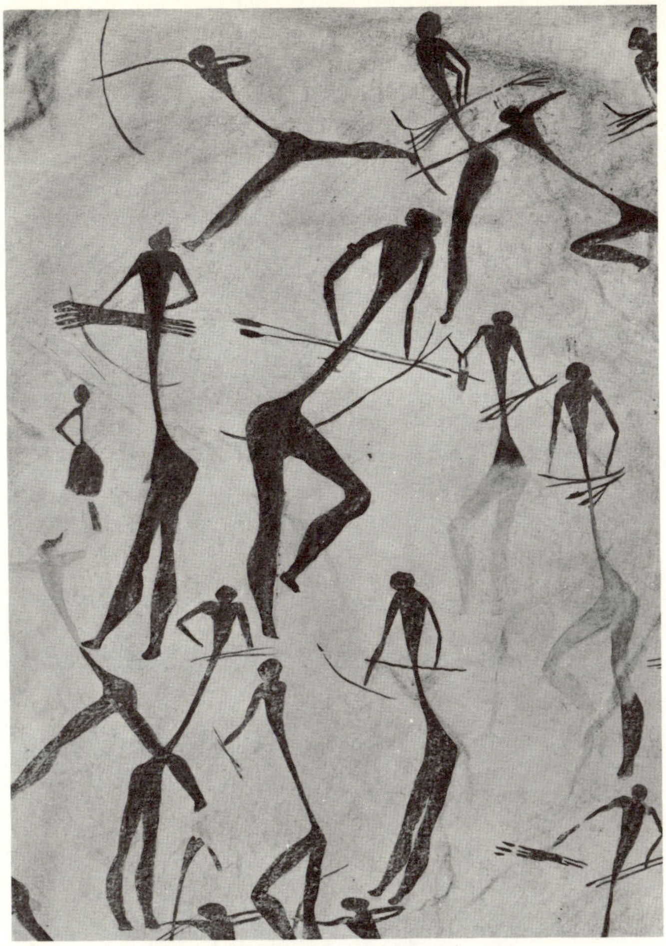

Stone age men armed with bows and arrows preparing for battle or the hunt. In the world of primitive magic success in either was sought by formal representations such as these. From a cave painting at Teruel.

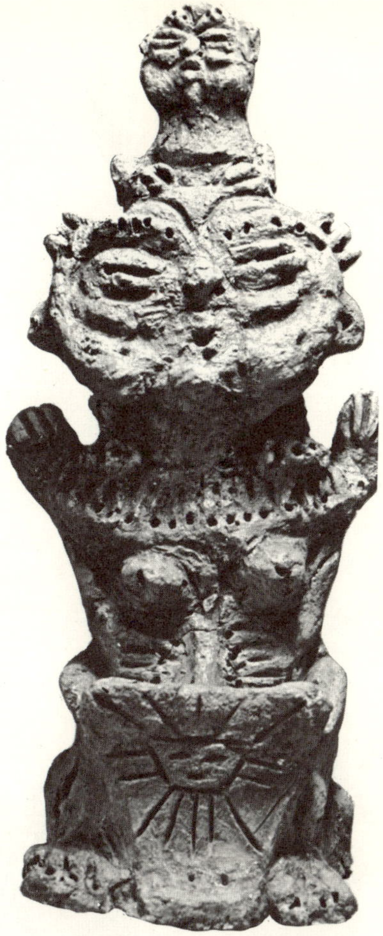

Pottery figure discovered in Lake Maracaibo, Venezuela. Of unknown date, it probably represents a primitive mother goddess. The sun sign on the base would seem to anticipate the later sun cultures.

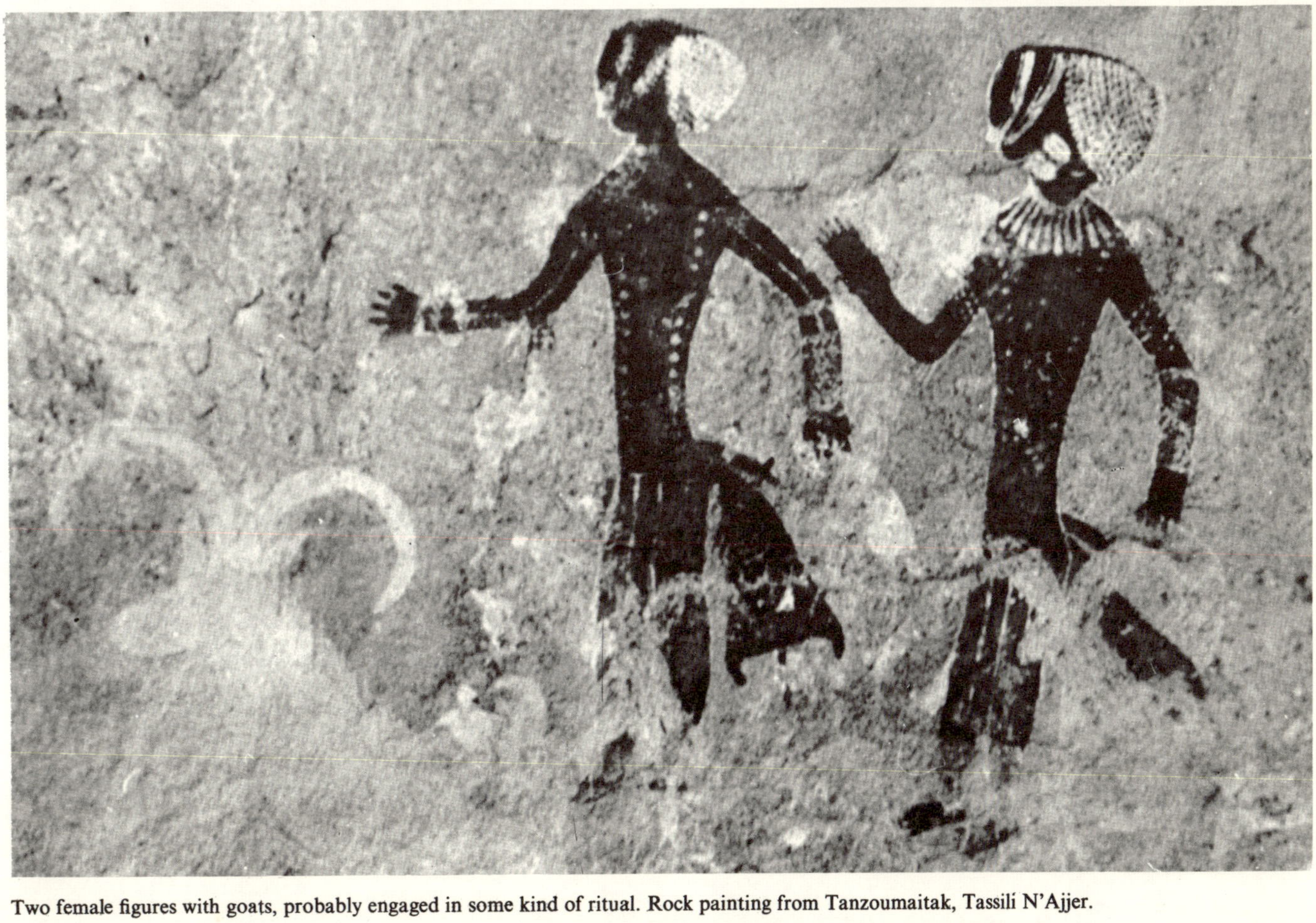

Two female figures with goats, probably engaged in some kind of ritual. Rock painting from Tanzoumaitak, Tassili N'Ajjer.

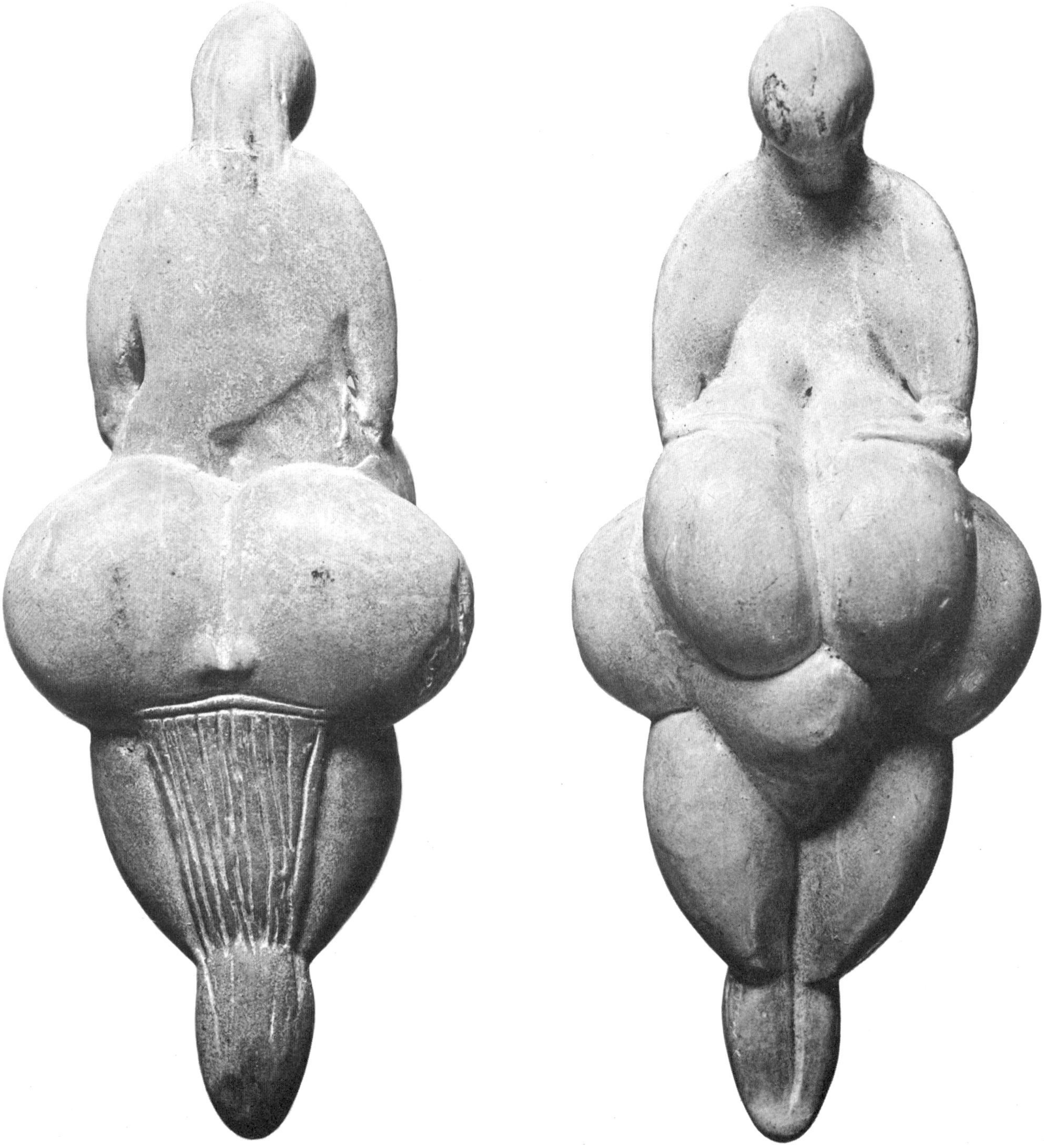

Ivory Statuette from the Cave of Les Rideaux at Lespugne, Hte. Garonne (according to R. de Saint-Périer). Connected with fertility magic.

account many finds of isolated human bones from all periods, generally skulls or jawbones.

Sinanthropus. The deposits of Fu-Ku-Tien near Peking permit us to go back to the earliest Pleistocene times. They have yielded – together with abundant vestiges of fire, and work in bone and stone – the remains of a dozen human beings, halfway between Pithecanthropus man of Java and Neanderthal man of Mousterian Europe. For the moment these remains are confined to skull and lower jaw, without traces of cervical vertebrae, while the animals on which these men fed are represented by bones from all parts of the body. There can thus be no question of cannibalism or of the heads being cut from corpses immediately after death. To all appearances these skulls must have been preserved after the bodies had been stripped of flesh.

Hence from the remotest times when, on the evidence of the skull which is all we have of his body, man was still closely related to the ape, it would seem that there are proofs of his industry and that, at least in the form of a cult of the dead, he revealed traces of religion.

EGYPTIAN MYTHOLOGY

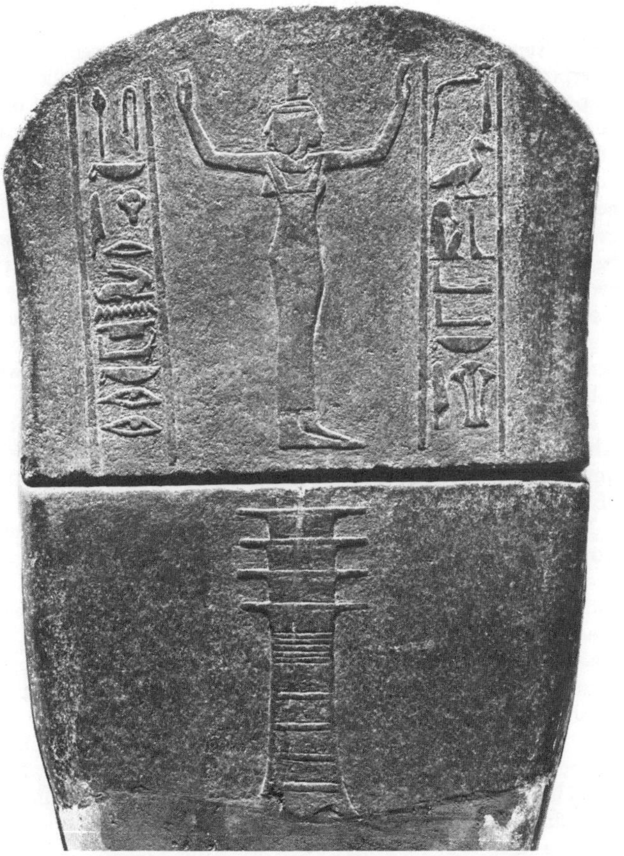

Isis, the sorrowing wife and eternal mother. Protectress of the dead, the goddess stands mourning with upraised arms at the foot of a sarcophagus. She bears a throne upon her head, the ideogram of her name. Below is the *djed* symbol of stability, which also represents her husband Osiris. Stone relief.

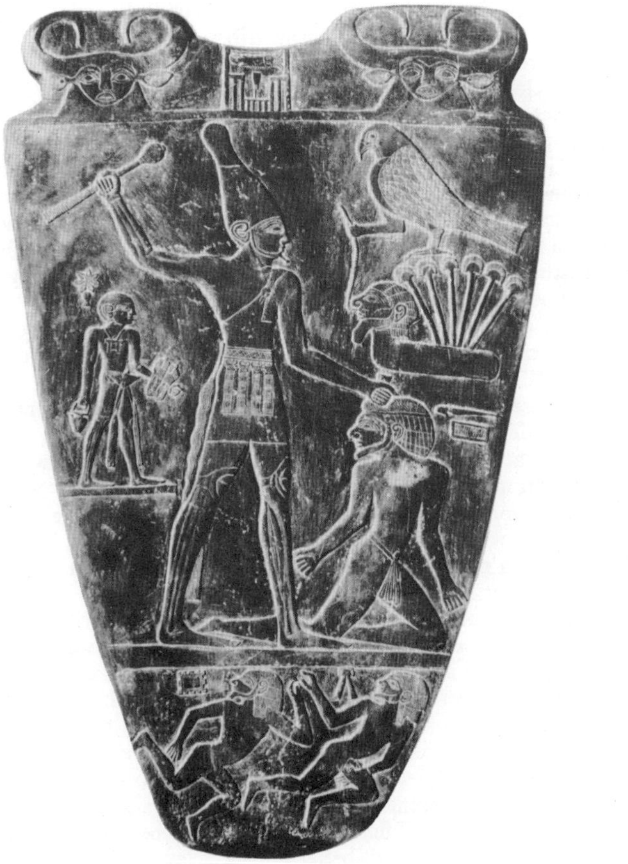

Horus, in the form of a falcon with a human arm, delivers six thousand captives to King Narmer, who is brandishing his mace over the defeated chief. First Dynasty, about 3200. Cairo.

INTRODUCTION

No one who strolls through the Egyptian galleries of a museum can fail to be struck by the multitude of divinities who attract attention on all sides. Colossal statues in sandstone, granite and basalt, minute statuettes in glazed composition, bronze, even in gold, portray gods and goddesses frozen in hierarchical attitudes, seated or standing. Sometimes these male or female figures have heads with human features. More often they are surmounted by the muzzle of an animal or the beak of a bird. The same divinities, receiving adoration and offerings or performing ritual gestures for the benefit of their worshippers, can be seen again on the bas-reliefs of massive sarcophagi or sculptured on funerary stelae and stone blocks stripped from temple walls. They recur on mummy cases and in the pictures which illuminate the papyri of the Book of the Dead.

In view of such a multiplicity of divine images it may seem strange to suggest that the religion of Ancient Egypt is very imperfectly known to us. Such, however, is the case; though we know the names of all these gods and goddesses and the temples in which they were worshipped, we understand little of their nature and seldom know even the legends concerning them.

It is true that the innumerable religious texts which have survived often allude to mythological occurrences. The full stories themselves, however, are almost never set down; for they were known to every early Egyptian and handed down from generation to generation by word of mouth alone.

Only the myth of Osiris – one of the greatest gods in the Egyptian pantheon – has been transmitted in detail to us by Plutarch. Plutarch, though Greek and writing of times already long past, was evidently well informed; for in ancient texts we find frequent references to the events he relates, notably in those texts which the old kings of the sixth dynasty had engraved inside their pyramids – twenty-five centuries before him.

It seems that the earliest representations of Egyptian deities appeared about the middle of the fourth millennium, long before the first hieroglyphs. In those days the inhabitants of the Nile valley lived in tribes. Each tribe had its own god, who was incarnated in the form either of an animal, of a bird or of a simple fetish. There is a fragment of a palette for grinding malachite in the Louvre on which we see men of one of these early tribes setting forth to hunt. They are bearded, unlike the clean-shaven men of later historical epochs, and they wear only a belted loin-cloth. At the back of the belt is attached the bushy tail of an animal. At their head marches their chief. In one hand he brandishes a club. In the other he grasps the staff of a standard or totem pole which bears a kind of perch for a falcon. On other objects of the same class the hawk is replaced by an ibis, a jackal, a scorpion, or perhaps by a thunderbolt, a bucranium, or two crossed arrows on a shield. These are the gods of the tribe who led their followers into battle and, when necessary, fought for them. Often, indeed, one of the divine animal's paws is a human hand which grasps a weapon to slaughter the enemy or an implement to attack his fortress.

These animal deities, however, gradually gave way to gods in human form, and at the end of his anthropomorphic evolution nothing of the primitive animal is left except the head surmounting the body of a man or woman. Sometimes the head, too, has become human and all that remains are vestigial ears or horns.

From the second dynasty on, the divine types seem to have become definitely fixed and to remain unchanged until the end of paganism. Like the hunters of the ancient tribes seen on the palette in the Louvre, the gods of the historical epoch are shown dressed in short loin-cloths ornamented by animals' tails. The goddesses, like great ladies, wear a narrow robe, held at the shoulders by shoulder-straps and falling nearly to their ankles.

Gods and goddesses alike often retain the head of the animal from which they were derived. They wear heavy wigs, thanks to which the transition between the snout of an animal or the beak of a bird and their human bodies takes place so smoothly that our aesthetic sense is scarcely violated and these hybrid beings seem almost real.

At other times the head is human, and in this case the shaven chin of the god is adorned by an artificial plaited beard, which recalls the bearded faces of the first Egyptians.

These divinities are distinguished and immediately identified by their different head-dresses and by various attributes inherited from the original fetish or from the primitive animal which surmounts their heads. Sometimes too their names are written in hieroglyphic signs. Like the ancient tribal chieftains, the gods carry sceptres with one end forked and the other decorated by, say, the head of a greyhound. Goddesses bear in their hand a simple stalk of papyrus.

By the time that the animals and fetishes of the prehistoric epoch had become divinities in human form the nomad warriors whom they once led into battle had long since settled down to till the soil. Their gods were installed in the towns they built, and were thus transformed from tribal into local deities. Every town, village and district had its god who bore the title: 'Lord of the City'. There he resided and yielded priority of rank to no one. Conceived in the image of a man, but of a man infinitely strong and powerful, he possessed a vital fluid – the 'sa' – which he could renew at will by having another god, better provided, lay hands on him. But he could not defend himself for ever against old age, and sometimes he even died. He delighted in revealing himself to men, and he would become incarnate in the temple statue, in a fetish, or in a chosen animal which the initiated could recognise by certain signs.

At first the god lived alone, jealous of his authority. But the Egyptian could not conceive of life without a family and soon he married off his god or goddess and gave him or her a son, thus forming a divine triad or trinity in which the father, moreover, was not always the chief, contenting himself on occasion with the role of prince consort, while the principal deity of the locality remained the goddess. This occurred at Dendera, where the sovereign was the goddess Hathor.

The god resided in the temple, which was his palace, with his family and sometimes with other gods whom he permitted to surround him. Only Pharaoh, the king, whom he called his 'son' had the right to appear in his presence. But as the king naturally could not officiate everywhere at once he delegated high priests to each sanctuary to perform in his place the ceremonies of the cult, while numerous priests and priestesses composed the domestic staff of the god and administered his sometimes immense domains. On certain dates the 'Lord of the City' brought joy to his people by deigning to show himself to them in all his glory. Abandoning the deep shadows of the *naos* (the inner sanctuary of the temple) where only Pharaoh's representative had the privilege of worshipping him daily, he would emerge majestically and be borne through the streets in his golden barque on the shoulders of his priests.

In addition to such local gods, some of whom imposed their authority over several provinces at a time and even throughout the entire land, the Egyptians worshipped, though generally without cult, the great divinities of nature: the Sky, the Earth, the Sun, the Moon and the mighty river which, in the words of Herodotus, created Egypt – the Nile.

In the Egyptian language the word 'sky' is feminine. Thus the Egyptians made the sky a goddess, Nut or Hathor, whom they represented either as a cow standing with her four feet planted on earth, or as a woman whose long, curved body touches the earth only with the tips of her toes and fingers. It was the starry belly of the goddess which men saw shining in the night above them. Sometimes also they imagined the sky as the head of a divine falcon whose eyes, which he opened and closed alternately, were the sun and the moon.

The earth, on the contrary, is masculine. Thus it was a man lying prone, from whose back sprouted all the world's vegetation. They called him Geb, the earth-god.

The sun had many names and gave rise to extremely varied interpretations. In his aspect of solar disk the sun was called Aten. Depending upon whether he rose, or climbed to the zenith, or set, he was given the names Khepri, Ra or Atum. He was also called Horus and it was under this name, joined with that of Ra, that he later reigned over all Egypt as Ra-Harakhte. It was claimed that he was reborn every morning of the celestial cow like a sucking calf, or like a little child of the sky-goddess. He was also said to be a falcon with speckled wings flying through space, or the right eye only of the great divine bird. Another conception of him was that of an egg laid daily by the celestial goose, or more frequently a gigantic scarab rolling before him the incandescent globe of the sun as, on earth, the sacred scarab rolls the ball of dung in which it has deposited its eggs.

The moon, too, was called by different names: Aah, Thoth, Khons. Sometimes he was the son of Nut, the sky-goddess. Sometimes he was a dog-headed ape, or an ibis; at others, the left eye of the great celestial hawk whose right eye was the sun.

Not content with explaining the phenomena of the external world, the priests of the principal sanctuaries busied themselves in constructing cosmological systems to demonstrate how the gods had successively appeared and how all that exists had been created. We have a fair knowledge of four of these systems which were taught in the four great religious centres of Hermopolis, Heliopolis, Memphis and Busiris. In each of these sanctuaries the priests attributed the work of creation to the great local god.

In his own temple Thoth, Ra, Ptah and Osiris was each proclaimed to have created the world, but each in his own way. Sometimes it was taught that the gods had issued from the mouth of the Demiurge and that all had been created by his voice. Sometimes it was alleged that they were born when the creator spat or performed an even cruder act. Again it was said that men had been engendered by his sweat or by a flood of tears gushing from his eyes. Another explanation was that men, together with the entire animal world, had emerged from the sun-dried mud of the Nile. It was also taught that the Demiurge had modelled them from the earth and fashioned them on a potter's wheel.

Like all people in antiquity the Egyptians explained everything by the intervention of a god, and for them there was nothing which was not capable of containing supernatural power. Consequently the number of gods worshipped in the Nile valley was considerable, and a list found in the tomb of Thuthmosis III enumerates no fewer than seven hundred and forty. Of most of them we know only the names and it would serve no useful purpose to mention them here.

We shall limit ourselves in this study to those deities who enjoyed a genuine cult or who occupied a real place in Egyptian mythology, beginning with the study of the gods and goddesses associated with the Ennead (or company of gods) of Heliopolis; that is to say, with the cosmological system taught by the priests of Heliopolis. We shall then review the great protective divinities of the Pharaohs and the kingdom, enumerating them in chronological order when in the course of the royal dynasties they appear particularly important.

Afterwards we shall come to river gods and desert gods not included in the above categories; then to the various divinities who concerned themselves with men's birth or death; and finally to deified humans among whom will be found the living Pharaoh who was himself a veritable god.

We shall conclude with a study of the sacred animals which,

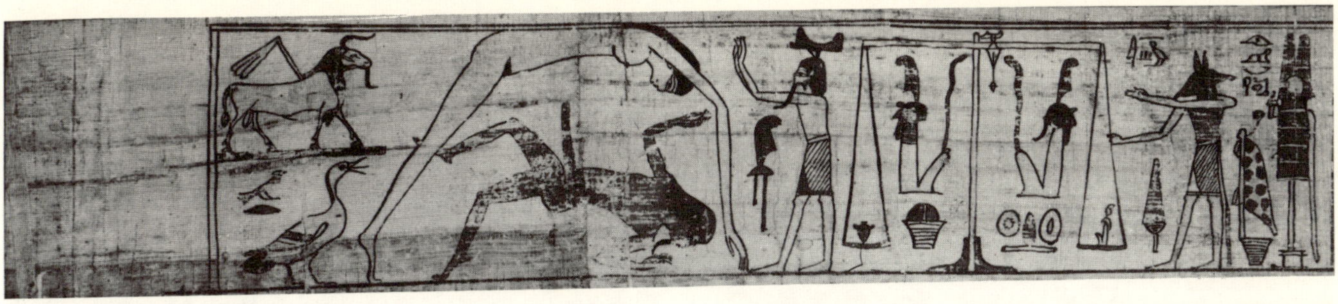

Geb, the earth god, tries to reach his wife and twin sister, the goddess Nut, after being separated from her on the orders of Ra. With her body arched over the world, which she touches only with her toes and finger-tips, she forms the vault of the sky. Papyrus of Tameniu, twenty-first dynasty, 1102 to 952 B.C.

towards the end of paganism, were without doubt the most popular divinities in Egypt. We append a list of quadrupeds, birds and even insects from whom the gods and goddesses borrowed either the features or the attributes.

THE ENNEAD OF HELIOPOLIS AND THE FAMILY OF OSIRIS

Nun (or **Nu**) is Chaos, the primordial ocean in which before the creation lay the germs of all things and all beings. The texts call him the 'father of the gods', but he remains a purely intellectual concept and had neither temples nor worshippers. He is sometimes found represented as a personage plunged up to his waist in water, holding up his arms to support the gods who have issued from him.

Atum (or **Tum**), whose name seems to come from a root which signified 'not to be' and 'to be complete', was originally a local god of Heliopolis where his sacred animal was the bull Merwer (Greek Mneuis). From very early times his priests identified him with Ra, the great sun god. They taught that inside Nun, before the creation, there had lived a 'spirit, still formless, who bore within him the sum of all existence'. He was called Atum, and he manifested himself one day under the name of Atum-Ra and drew from himself gods, men and all living things.

Later, Atum was personified as the setting sun and the sun before its rising. His cult spread rather widely through Egypt, conjointly with that of Ra.

Atum was ordinarily considered to be the ancestor of the human race. He is always represented with a man's head, wearing the double crown of the Pharaohs – the 'pschent'. Originally unmarried, Atum was supposed to have fathered the first divine couple without the aid of a wife. Only later was he given a spouse, indeed two – since at Memphis he was united sometimes with Iusaas and sometimes with Nebhet Hotep, who bore him the twin gods Shu and Tefnut.

Ra (or **Re** or **Phra**), which probably signifies 'creator', is the name of the sun, sovereign lord of the sky. He had his principal sanctuary at Heliopolis. The priests of this city affirmed that it was here Ra first manifested himself in the stone object in the form of an obelisk called benben, piously preserved in the temple named for this reason Het Benben – the 'palace of the obelisk'.

Formerly, according to the priests of Heliopolis, the sun-god reposed, under the name of Atum, in the bosom of Nun, the primordial ocean. There, in order that his lustre should run no risk of being extinguished, he took care to keep his eyes shut. He enclosed himself in the bud of a lotus until the day when, weary of his own impersonality, he rose by an effort of will from the abyss and appeared in glittering splendour under the name of Ra. He then bore Shu and Tefnut who, in their turn, gave birth to Geb and Nut, from whom issued Osiris and Isis, Set and Nephthys. These are the eight great gods who with their chief Ra – or more exactly Ra Atum, since Ra and Atum were identified with each other – form the divine company or Ennead of Heliopolis.

Ra drew from himself and without recourse to woman the first divine couple. It is not until much later that he was given as his spouse Rat – which is only his own name feminised – or Iusaas, Eus-os, Uert-Hekeu, 'the great of magic'. As for men and all other living creatures, it was said that they came from Ra's tears – perhaps a play on words as 'tears' and 'men' sound the same in Egyptian.

At the same time Ra had created a 'first' universe, different from the present world, which he governed from the 'Prince's Palace' in Heliopolis where he normally resided. The Books of the Pyramids minutely describe for us his royal existence and how, after his morning bath and breakfast, he would get into his boat and, in the company of his scribe, Weneg, inspect the twelve provinces of his kingdom, spending an hour in each.

As long as Ra remained young and vigorous he reigned peacefully over gods and men; but the years brought with them their ravages and the texts depict him as an old man with trembling mouth from which saliva ceaselessly dribbles. We shall see later how Isis took advantage of the god's senility, made him reveal his secret name and thus acquired sovereign power.

Even men perceived Ra's decrepitude and plotted against him. These projects finally reached Ra's ears. Justly enraged, he summoned his council and, having consulted the gods one by one on the measures which should be taken, he decided to hurl his divine Eye against his rebellious subjects. Farther on we shall tell how the divine Eye (taking the form of the goddess Hathor) rushed upon the guilty and massacred them without pity until Ra, appeased, managed to put an end to the bloodshed; for his goodness would not permit him to allow the entire human race to be exterminated.

The ingratitude of men had, however, inspired in him a distaste for the world and a desire to withdraw himself beyond reach. So on the orders of Nun, the goddess Nut changed herself into a cow and took Ra on her back. She raised him high into the vault of heaven and at the same time, as we shall later relate, the present world was created.

From the moment that the sun-god left earth for heaven his life was immutably regulated. During the twelve daylight hours he rode in his boat from east to west across his kingdom. He took great care to avoid the attack of his eternal enemy Apep, the great serpent who lived in the depths of the celestial Nile and sometimes – for instance during total eclipses – succeeded in swallowing the solar barque. But Apep was always at last vanquished by Ra's defenders and cast back into the abyss.

During the twelve hours of darkness the perils which Ra faced were even greater. But again they were overcome and at night he passed from cavern to cavern, receiving the acclamations of the inhabitants of the underworld who waited with impatience for the light he bore and after his departure fell back into the agony of darkness.

Ra, it was also taught, was born each morning in the guise of a child who grew until midday and afterwards fell into decline, to die that night an old man.

We see him represented in many fashions: as a royal child resting on the lotus from which he sprang at his birth; as a man, seated or walking, whose head is surmounted by the solar disk around which is wreathed the Uraeus, the terrible sacred asp who spits flame and destroys the god's enemies; as a man with a ram's head, Efu Ra, in whom the dead sun is embodied during his nocturnal transit.

Often also we find a personage with the head of a falcon, surmounted by a disk with the Uraeus. This is Ra-Harakhte, the great solar god of Heliopolis, sovereign lord of Egypt. The forms and names of Ra are innumerable and the Litanies of the Sun, engraved at the entrance of the royal tombs, list no fewer than seventy-five.

Universally recognised as the creator and ruler of the world, Ra, with whom all the other gods were finally identified, became from the time of the Old Kingdom the divinity particularly revered

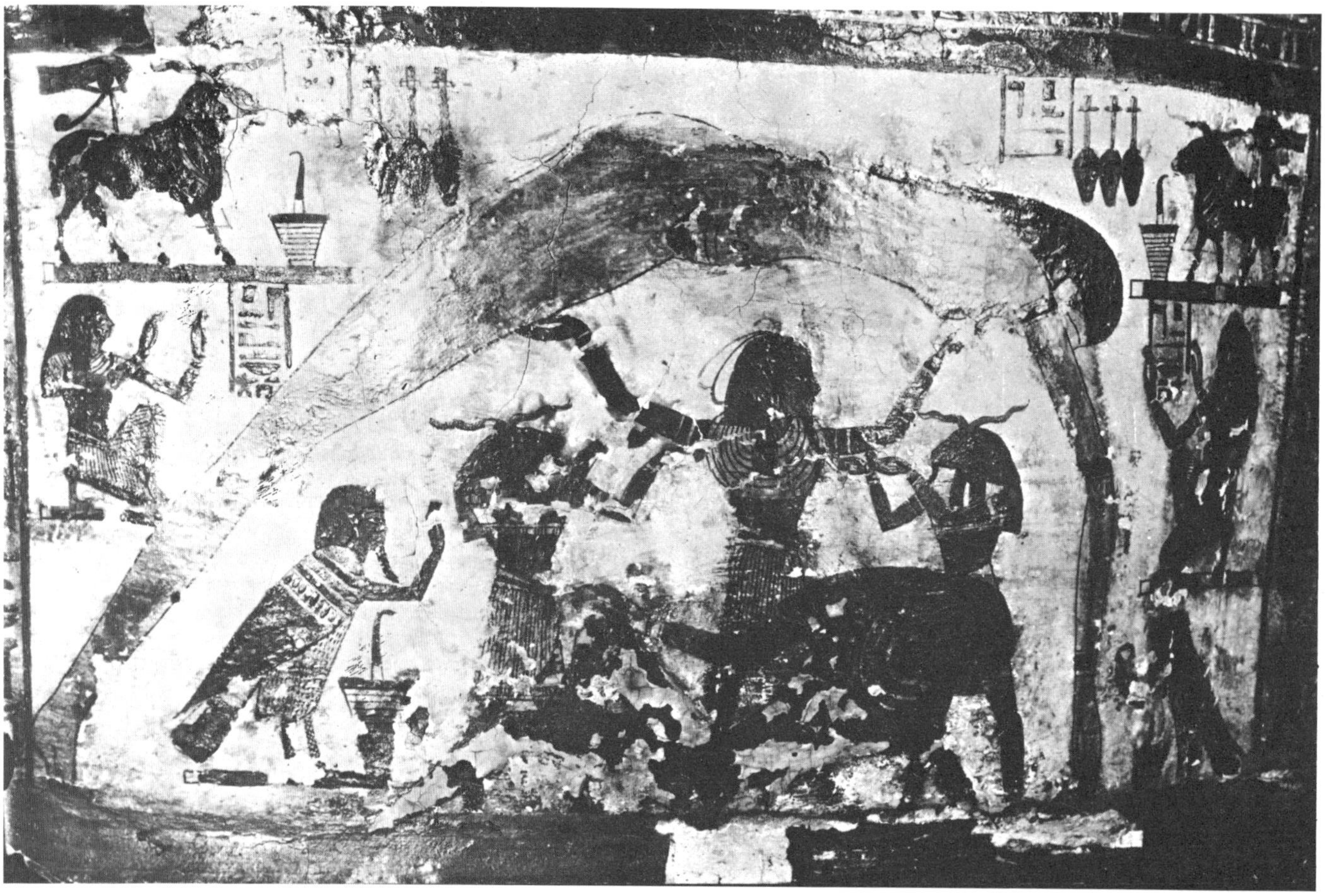

The creation of the universe. Shu, the god of the atmosphere, holds aloft the body of Nut, the sky goddess, whom he has just separated from her husband Geb. The latter lies at his feet resting on one elbow with his knees raised and forming with the angles of his body the hilly surface of the earth. Painted coffin of Butehamon.

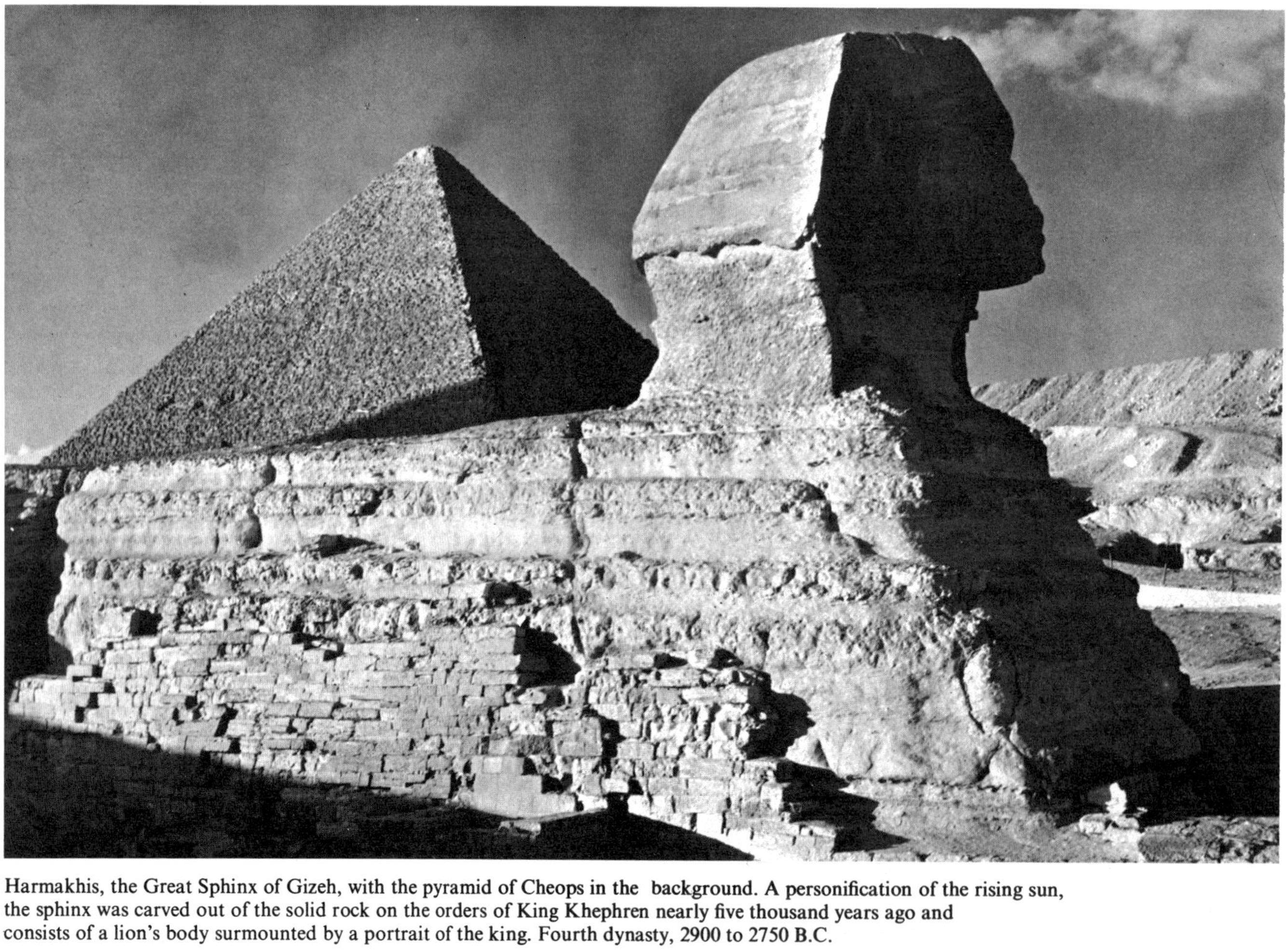

Harmakhis, the Great Sphinx of Gizeh, with the pyramid of Cheops in the background. A personification of the rising sun, the sphinx was carved out of the solid rock on the orders of King Khephren nearly five thousand years ago and consists of a lion's body surmounted by a portrait of the king. Fourth dynasty, 2900 to 2750 B.C.

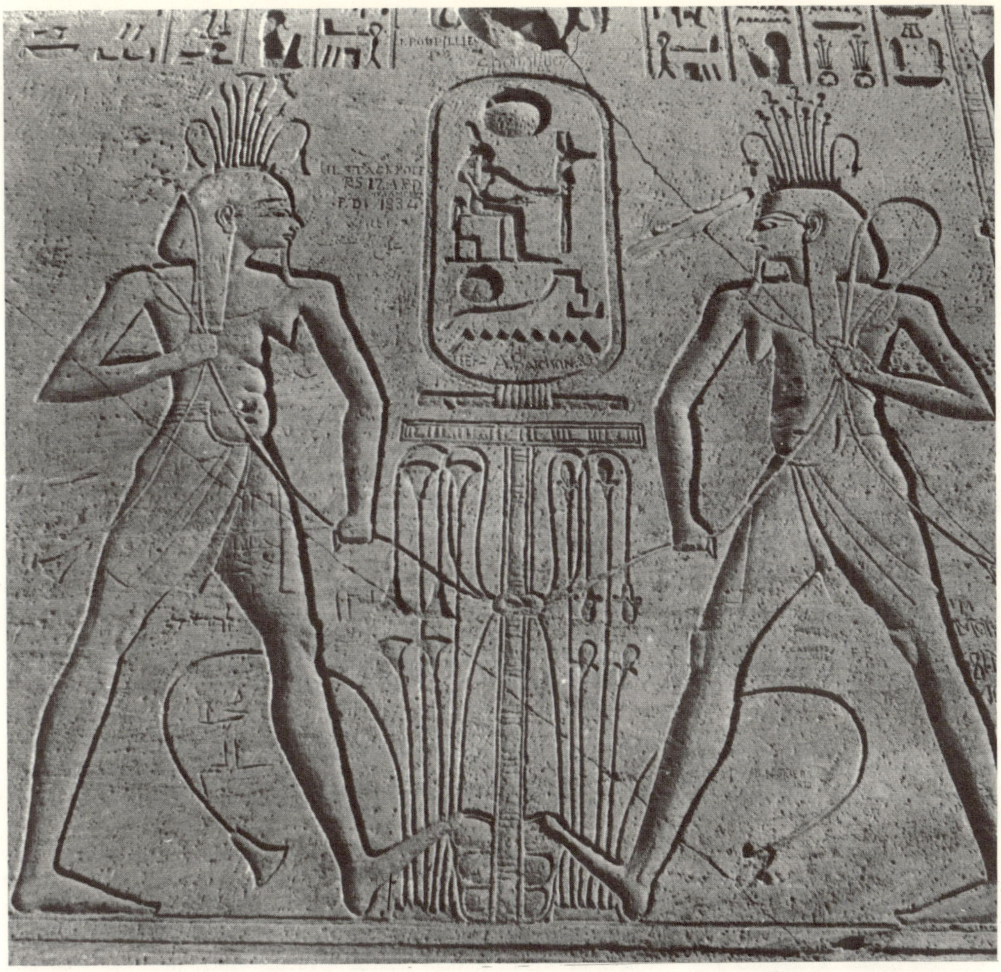

The two gods of the Nile binding the ties of lotus and papyrus to symbolise the union of Upper and Lower Egypt – the symbolic gesture of *sam-taui*. The god on the left represents Upper Egypt and wears a crown of lotus plants, that on the right, Lower Egypt, with a crown of papyrus. Bas-relief from a pedestal beneath the colossal statues of Rameses II in front of the great temple at Abu Simbel. Nineteenth dynasty, 1375 to 1202 B.C.

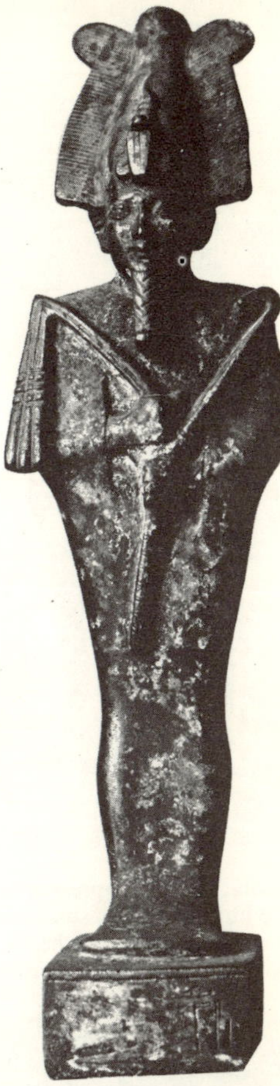

A statue of Osiris showing him swathed in mummy wrappings, wearing the *atef* crown and *uraeus*. His arms are free and he carries the crook and flail, supreme symbols of power. To those who passed the final ordeal of judgment he gave the blessing of eternal happiness.

by the Pharaohs, who called themselves 'sons of Ra'. One story tells us how the sun-god came to Reddedet, the high priest's wife, in the guise of her husband and how from this union were born the three first kings of the fifth dynasty. Each time that a Pharaoh was conceived Ra was said to return to earth to espouse the queen.

Of the celebrated sanctuary of Heliopolis, where the god was worshipped in the form of a gigantic obelisk – a petrified sun's ray – and where he used to take the form of the bull Merwer, or, at times, the bird Bennu, there remain to-day only shapeless ruins and an obelisk, the oldest in Egypt, erected during the twelfth dynasty by the king, Senusert I.

Khepri (or **Khepera**) signifies at the same time 'scarab' and 'he who becomes'. For the Heliopolitans he represented the rising sun which, like the scarab, emerges from its own substance and is reborn of itself. Khepri was the god of the transformations which life, for ever renewing itself, manifests. He is represented as a scarab-faced man or as a man whose head is surmounted by this insect. Sometimes he appears simply as a scarab.

Shu, who with Tefnut his twin sister comprised the first couple of the Ennead, was created by Ra without recourse to woman. His name derives from a verb which means 'to raise' and can be translated as 'he who holds up'. He is the Atlas of Egyptian mythology and supports the sky. It was told of him how, on the orders of Ra, he slipped between the two children, Geb the earth-god and Nut, goddess of the sky, who had until then been closely united. He threw them violently apart and elevated Nut high into the air, where he maintained her with his upraised arms.

Shu is also the god of air: emptiness deified. But like the other great divinities of nature he enjoyed no especial cult.

He is always represented in human form. On his head he normally wears, as a distinctive sign, an ostrich feather which is an ideogram of his name.

Shu succeeded Ra as king on earth. But like his father he experienced the vicissitudes of power; for the children of Apep plotted against him and attacked him in his palace of At Nub. He vanquished them, but disease riddled him so that even his faithful followers revolted. Weary of reigning, Shu abdicated in favour of his son Geb and took refuge in the skies after a terrifying tempest which lasted nine days.

Tefnut seems to have been a theological conception rather than a real person. At Heliopolis she was said to be Shu's twin sister and wife, but she appears to have been paired in earlier times with a certain god Tefen of whom we know nothing but the name.

Goddess of the dew and the rain, it seems, she also had a solar character. She was worshipped in the form of a lioness or of a woman with the head of a lioness, and the Greeks sometimes identified her with Artemis. She is depicted in the texts as a pale copy of Shu, whom she helps to support the sky and with whom each morning she receives the new-born sun as it breaks free from the eastern mountains.

Anhur (the Greek rendering is *Onouris*) seems to signify 'he who leads what has gone away' but has also been translated as 'sky-bearer'. God of Sebennytus and This, it is believed that he symbolised the creative power of the sun. He was very soon identified with Shu and invoked under the name Anhur-Shu. He is assumed to be a warlike personification of Ra, and was identified by the Greeks as Ares, the god of battle.

He is represented with the traits of a warrior wearing a head-dress adorned with four tall straight plumes. He is covered by a long embroidered robe and often brandishes a lance. Sometimes

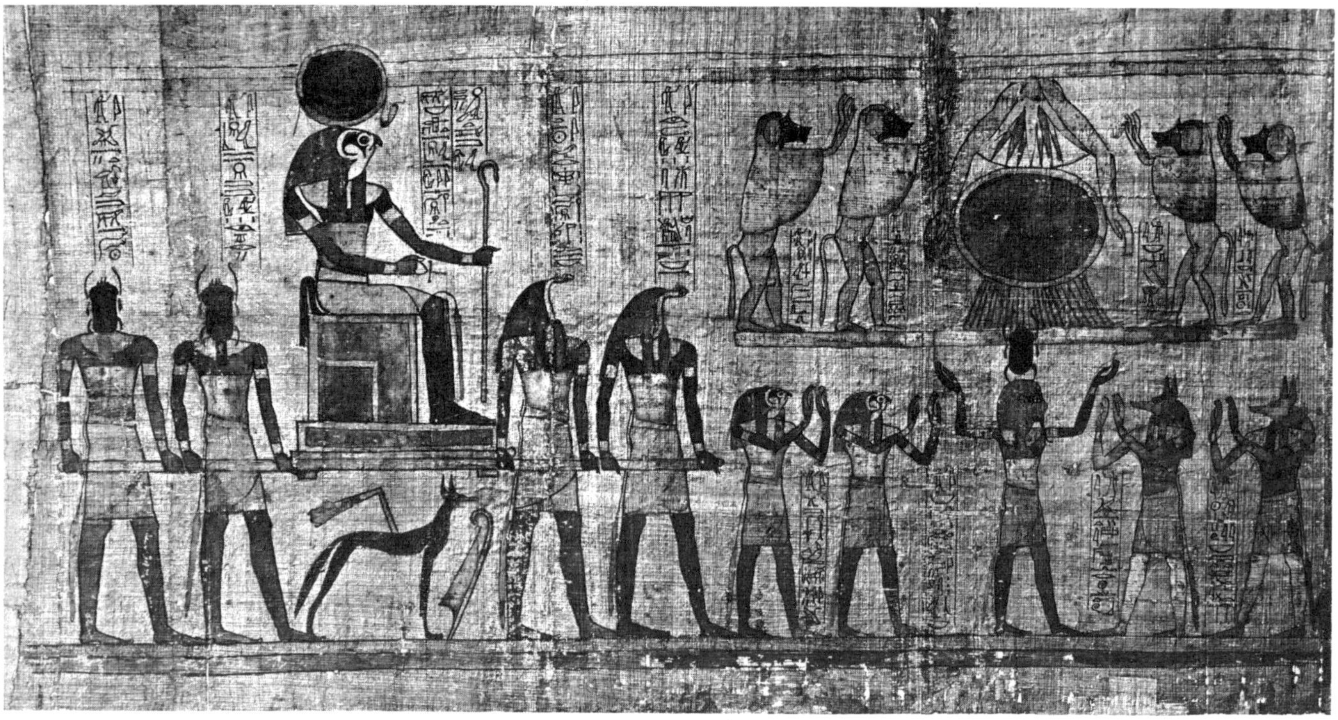

Symbolic Tableau representing the course of the Sun. Two jackal-headed gods and two falcon-headed gods worship the god Khepri, whose human head is surmounted by a scarab. Above, four dog-headed apes greet the birth of the sun. To the left four lesser divinities, with serpent and scarab heads, triumphantly bear Ra-Harakhte across his kingdom. New Kingdom, 1580 to 1090. Papyrus in the Bibliothèque Nationale.

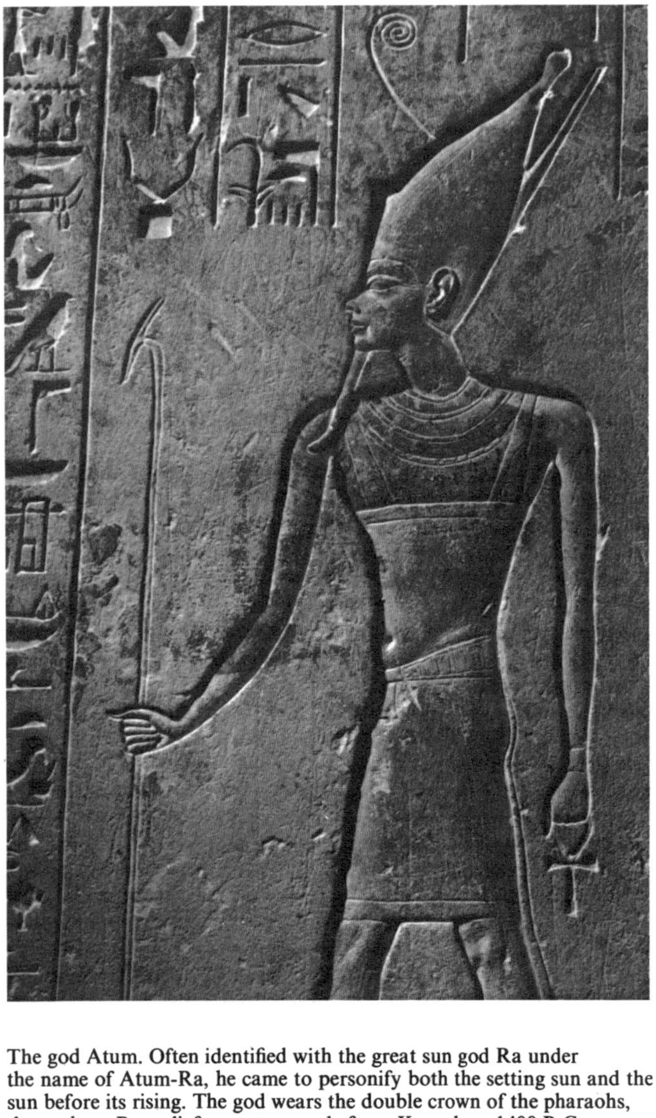

The god Atum. Often identified with the great sun god Ra under the name of Atum-Ra, he came to personify both the setting sun and the sun before its rising. The god wears the double crown of the pharaohs, the *pschent*. Bas-relief on a stone stele from Karnak, *c*. 1400 B.C.

he holds the cord by which he leads the sun. Legend recounts how an Eye of Ra which had fled from Egypt was brought back from Nubia by Anhur, and how this divine Eye became enraged upon seeing that another Eye had taken its place. Ra then set it on his forehead where it became the Uraeus which protected the god against his enemies.

Anhur was very popular under the New Empire and was called 'the Saviour' and 'the Good Warrior'. He was fervently invoked against enemies and against noxious animals, whom he hunted without respite from his chariot. His popularity was of long duration; Herodotus speaks of the great festivals he saw celebrated at Papremis and of the innumerable cudgel blows which priests and the faithful enthusiastically exchanged in honour of their god.

As a wife Anhur was given Mehit, who seems to be a mere double of Tefnut, the sister-wife of Shu. She was worshipped at This, and is pictured as a lion-headed goddess.

Geb (or **Seb, Keb**) constituted with Nut the second pair in the Ennead. Plutarch identifies him with Cronus. In reality he was the earth-god, the physical foundation of the world; but in classical times he scarcely had anything resembling a cult.

We have already seen how Geb had been separated by Shu from Nut, his sister-spouse. Since that time he had remained inconsolable and his lamentations could be heard night and day.

Geb is often represented lying under the feet of Shu, against whom he had vainly struggled to defend his wife. Raised on one elbow, with one knee bent, he thus symbolises the mountains and the undulations of the earth's crust. His body is sometimes covered with verdure.

Geb is nearly always depicted as a man without especial attributes, but on occasion his head is surmounted by a goose, which is an ideogram of his name. Certain legends, moreover, describe him as a gander – the 'Great Cackler' – whose female has laid the egg of the sun. Others make him a vigorous bull who has fertilised the celestial cow.

Most frequently, however, Geb was reputed to be the father – and Nut the mother – of the Osirian gods, and for this reason was known as the 'father of the gods'.

He was the third divine Pharaoh and succeeded Shu to the throne. His reign also was disturbed. One text tells us how Geb caused the golden box in which Ra's Uraeus was kept to be opened in his presence. Ra had deposited the box, together with his cane and a lock of his hair, in a fortress on the eastern frontier of his empire

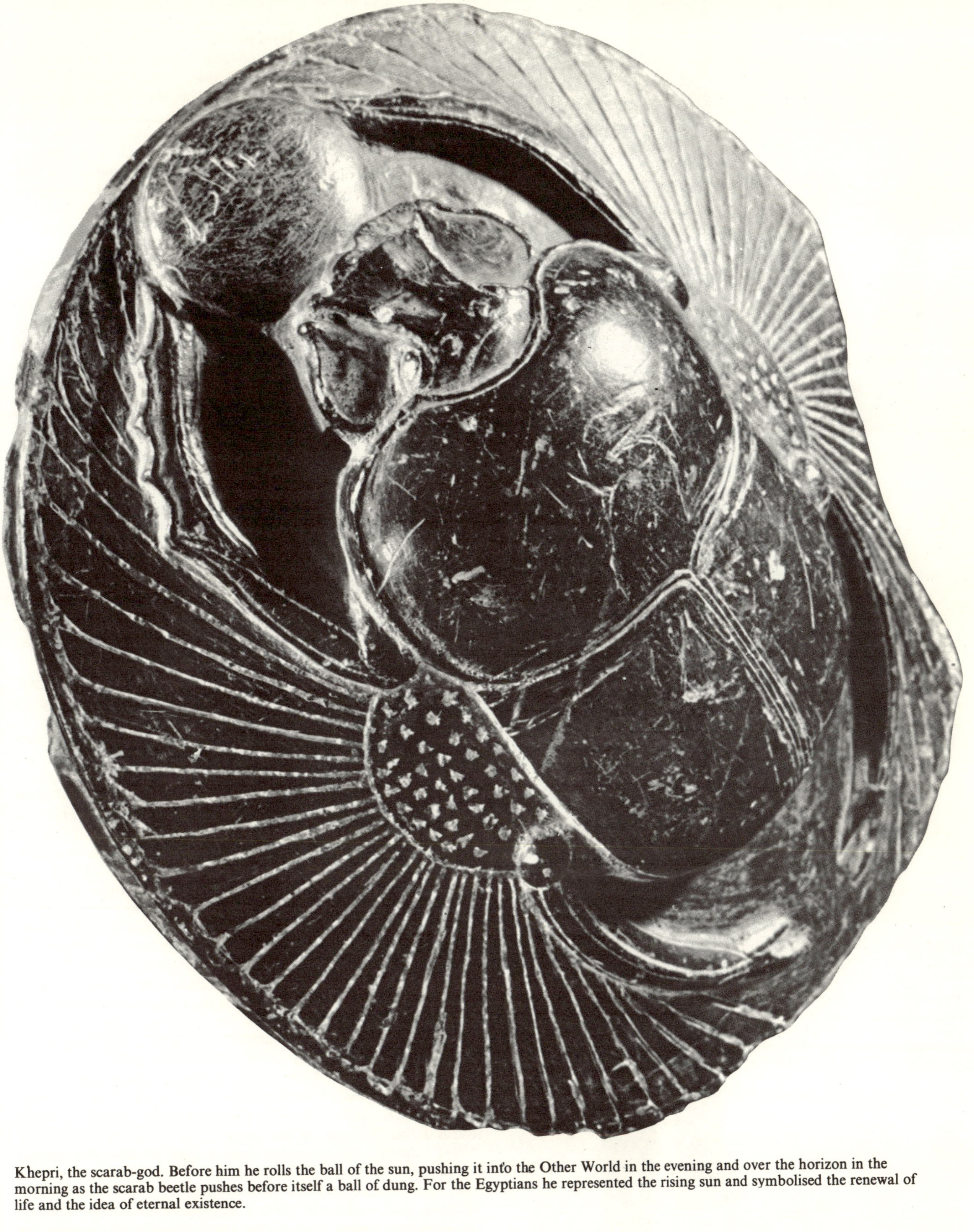

Khepri, the scarab-god. Before him he rolls the ball of the sun, pushing it into the Other World in the evening and over the horizon in the morning as the scarab beetle pushes before itself a ball of dung. For the Egyptians he represented the rising sun and symbolised the renewal of life and the idea of eternal existence.

as a potent and dangerous talisman. When opened, the breath of the divine asp within killed all of Geb's companions then and there, and gravely burned Geb himself. Only the lock of Ra's hair, applied to the wound, could heal Geb. So great, indeed, was the virtue of this divine lock of hair that years later when it was plunged for purification into the lake of At Nub it immediately turned into a crocodile. When he was restored to health Geb administered his kingdom wisely and drew up a careful report on the condition of every province and town in Egypt.

Then he handed over his sovereignty to his eldest son, Osiris, and ascended to the heavens where at times he took the place of Thoth as Ra's herald and arbiter of the gods.

Nut, whom the Greeks sometimes identified with Rhea, was goddess of the sky, but it is debatable if in historical times she was the object of a genuine cult. She was Geb's twin sister and, it was said, married him secretly and against the will of Ra. Angered, Ra had the couple brutally separated by Shu and afterwards decreed that Nut could

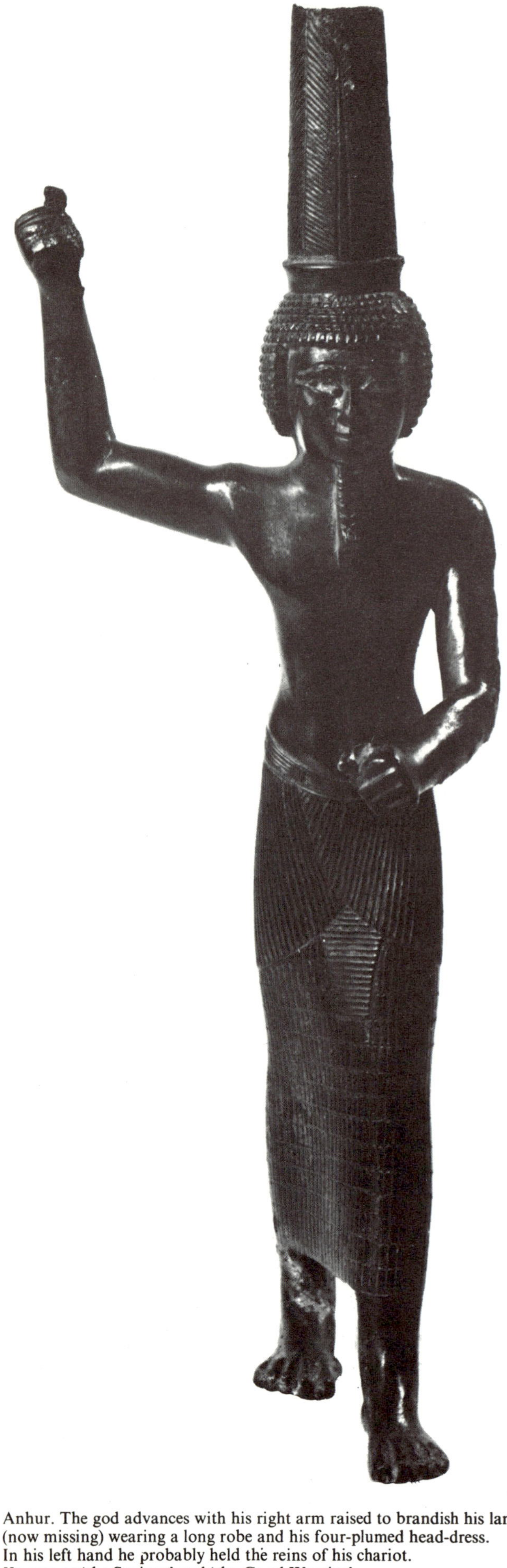

Anhur. The god advances with his right arm raised to brandish his lance (now missing) wearing a long robe and his four-plumed head-dress. In his left hand he probably held the reins of his chariot. Known as 'the Saviour' and 'the Good Warrior', Anhur was invoked against enemies and noxious animals. Bronze statuette of the twenty-sixth dynasty, 672 to 525 B.C.

not bear a child in any given month of any year. Thoth, Plutarch tells us, happily had pity on her. Playing draughts with the Moon, he won in the course of several games a seventy-second part of the Moon's light with which he composed five new days. As these five intercalated days did not belong to the official Egyptian calendar of three hundred and sixty days, Nut was thus able to give birth successively to five children: Osiris, Haroeris (Horus), Set, Isis and Nephthys.

The sky-goddess is often represented as a woman with elongated body, touching the earth with toes and fingertips, while her star-spangled belly is held aloft by Shu and forms the arch of the heavens. She also sometimes appears as a cow; for this is the form she assumed when, on the orders of Nun, she bore Ra on her back to the sky after Ra, as already related, decided to abandon his rebellious subjects. The dutiful cow rose obediently to her feet, rose higher and higher until she became dizzy and it was necessary to appoint a god to each of her four legs – which became the four pillars of the sky – in order to steady them. Shu, meanwhile, supported her belly, which became the firmament and to which Ra attached the stars and the constellations to light our earth. Though she was often qualified by the title 'Daughter of Ra', Nut was also the mother of the sun, which, as we have already had occasion to see, was reborn in various fashions each morning from her womb.

When she is pictured as a woman Nut often wears a rounded vase on her head, this being an ideogram of her name. She is protectress of the dead and we frequently see her holding the deceased close in her arms. On the inner lid of sarcophagi her starry body stretches above the mummy, watching maternally over him.

Osiris, which is the Greek rendering of the Egyptian Ousir, was identified by the Greeks with several of their own gods, but principally with Dionysus and Hades. At first Osiris was a nature god and embodied the spirit of vegetation which dies with the harvest to be reborn when the grain sprouts. Afterwards he was worshipped throughout Egypt as god of the dead, and in this capacity reached first rank in the Egyptian pantheon.

Hieroglyphic texts contain numerous allusions to the life and deeds of Osiris during his sojourn on earth; but it is above all thanks to Plutarch that we know his legend so well.

The first son of Geb and Nut, he was born in Thebes in Upper Egypt. At his birth a loud, mysterious voice proclaimed the coming of the 'Universal Lord', which gave rise to shouts of gladness, soon followed by tears and lamentations when it was learned what misfortunes awaited him. Ra rejoiced at the news of his birth in spite of the curse he had pronounced against Nut; and, having Osiris brought into his presence, he recognised his great-grandson as heir to his throne.

Osiris was handsome of countenance, dark-skinned and taller than all other men. When Geb, his father, retired to the heavens, Osiris succeeded him as king of Egypt and took Isis, his sister, as queen. The first care of the new sovereign was to abolish cannibalism and to teach his still half-savage subjects the art of fashioning agricultural implements. He taught them how to produce grain and grapes for man's nourishment in the form of bread, wine and beer. The cult of the gods did not yet exist. Osiris instituted it. He built the first temples and sculptured the first divine images. He laid down the rules governing religious practice and even invented the two kinds of flute which should accompany ceremonial song.

After this he built towns and gave his people just laws, thus meriting the name Onnophris – 'the Good One' – by which, as the fourth divine Pharaoh, he was known.

Not satisfied with having civilised Egypt, he wished to spread the benefits of his rule throughout the whole world. He left the regency to Isis and set forth on the conquest of Asia, accompanied by Thoth, his grand vizier, and his lieutenants Anubis and Upuaut. Osiris was the enemy of all violence and it was by gentleness alone that he subjected country after country, winning and disarming their inhabitants by songs and the playing of various musical instruments. He returned to Egypt only after he had travelled the whole earth and spread civilisation everywhere.

On his return Osiris found his kingdom in perfect order; for Isis had governed wisely in his absence. But it was not long before he became the victim of a plot organised by his brother Set, who was jealous of his power. Farther on we shall relate in detail (see *Isis* and *Set*) how on the 17th Athyr, in the twenty-eighth year of his

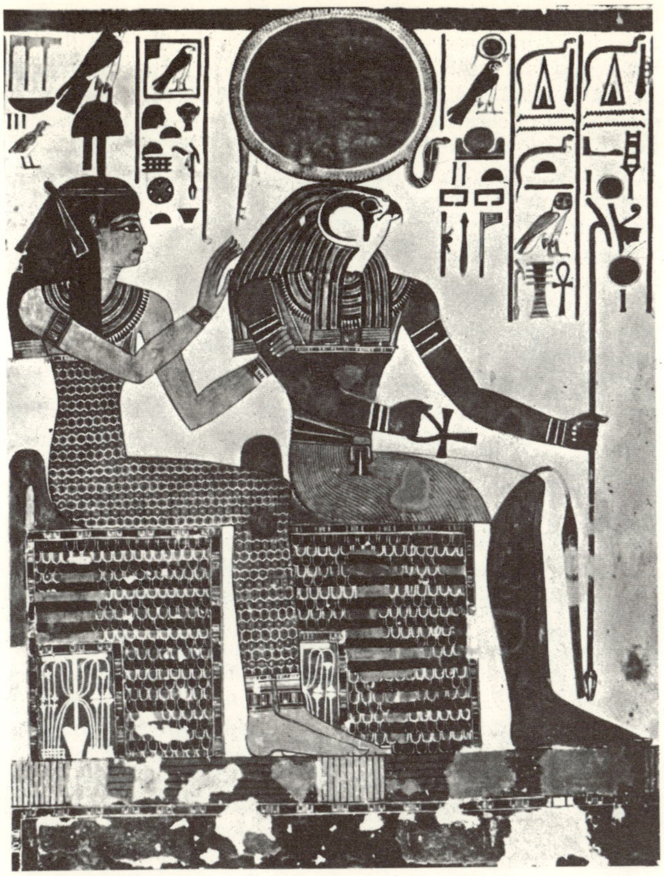

Ra-Harakhte and Ament, goddess of the West. The god is falcon-headed and wears the solar disk encircled by a serpent on his head while the goddess wears her emblem, the hawk.
Originally the goddess of a Libyan province to the west of Egypt, Ament became the goddess of the underworld when 'west' came to signify the land of the dead. Fresco from the tomb of Nefertari. Nineteenth dynasty, 1375 to 1202 B.C.

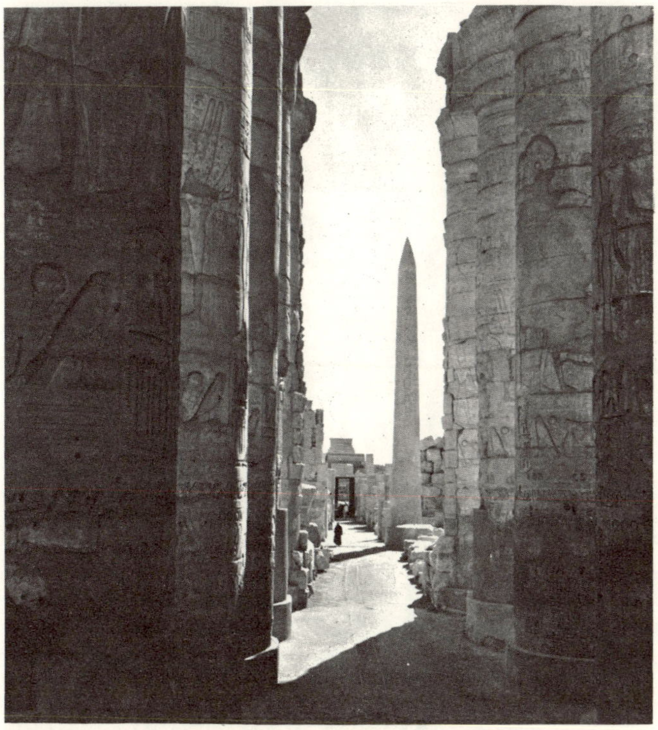

Colossal carved columns in the temple of Amon at Karnak in Thebes. Probably the largest religious building of all time, the temple was nearly a quarter of a mile long and the work of extension, rebuilding and decoration went on for a period of nearly two thousand years. A hundred men could stand on each of the capitals of the columns in the nave of its great hall.

reign, Osiris 'the Good One' fell under the blows of the conspirators and how his faithful wife found his body and bore it back to Egypt. For the moment it suffices to say that Isis, thanks to her powers of sorcery and the aid of Thoth, Anubis, and Horus, succeeded in restoring her husband's dead body to life. Osiris soon answered Set's accusations and vindicated himself before the tribunal of gods, presided over by Geb.

Resurrected and from thenceforward secure from the threat of death, Osiris could have regained his throne and continued to reign over the living. But he preferred to depart from this earth and retire to the 'Elysian Fields' where he warmly welcomed the souls of the just and reigned over the dead.

Such is the legend of Osiris. What we can guess of his actual origin suggests that he was a fetish of a conquering clan which first installed its god at Busiris in Lower Egypt. There he took the place of the preceding Lord of the City, Andjeti, whose form he borrowed. Perhaps he borrowed his name also, since later in Abydos in Upper Egypt he became identified with Khenti Amenti, the wolf-god, and became the great god of the dead, sometimes known as Osiris Khenti Amenti, 'Lord of the Westerners' – that is, the dead, who dwell in the west where the sun sets.

Here we can only indicate briefly the many cosmic interpretations which the myth of Osiris has been given.

As a vegetation spirit that dies and is ceaselessly reborn, Osiris represents the corn, the vine and trees. He is also the Nile which rises and falls each year; the light of the sun which vanishes in the shadows every evening to reappear more brilliantly at dawn. The struggle between the two brothers is the war between the desert and the fertile earth, between the drying wind and vegetation, aridity and fecundity, darkness and light.

It was as god of the dead that Osiris enjoyed his greatest popularity; for he gave his devotees the hope of an eternally happy life in another world ruled over by a just and good king.

He was worshipped throughout Egypt in company with Isis, his wife, and with Horus, his posthumous son, who formed with him a trinity. But he was particularly venerated at Abydos where priests showed his tomb to the innumerable pilgrims who visited it. Happy were the favoured ones who were buried in the shadows of the august sanctuary or who at least had a stela erected nearby in their name to assure the benevolence of Osiris in after-life!

Osiris is represented sometimes standing, sometimes seated on his throne, as a man tightly swathed in white mummy wrappings. His greenish face is surmounted by the high white mitre flanked by two ostrich feathers which is called 'Atef', the crown of Upper Egypt. Around his neck he wears a kind of cravat. His two hands, freed from the winding sheet, are folded across his breast and hold the whip and the sceptre in the form of a crook, emblems of supreme power.

The names and appellations of Osiris were countless. There are about a hundred in the litanies of the Book of the Dead.

Like many other gods he delighted in incarnations. He appeared not only in the form of various animals – the bull Onuphis, the sacred ram of Mendes, the bird Bennu – but also in the 'Djed', a simple fetish which seems to have been his primitive form in the days when he led his prehistoric followers into battle. The 'Djed' was originally the trunk of a fir or some other conifer; but in classical times it was a kind of pillar with four capitals, which certain texts alleged to be the god's vertebral column, preserved in the famous sanctuary of Busiris.

Space is lacking to describe the festivals which marked critical dates in the Osiris legend. They were publicly celebrated, and in the course of the Mysteries then presented priests and priestesses would mime the passion and resurrection of the god.

Isis (a Greek rendering of **Aset, Eset**) was identified by the Greeks with Demeter, Hera, Selene and even – because of a late confusion between Isis and Hathor – with Aphrodite. In later days the popularity of Isis became such that she finally absorbed the qualities of all the other goddesses; but originally she seems to have been a modest divinity of the Delta, the protective deity of Perehbet, north of Busiris, where she always retained a renowned temple.

Very soon she was given as wife to Osiris, the god of the neighbouring town. She bore him a son, Horus, who formed the third member of the trinity. Her popularity grew rapidly with that of her husband and son. This is her legend as Plutarch tells it to us:

The first daughter of Geb and Nut was born in the swamps of the

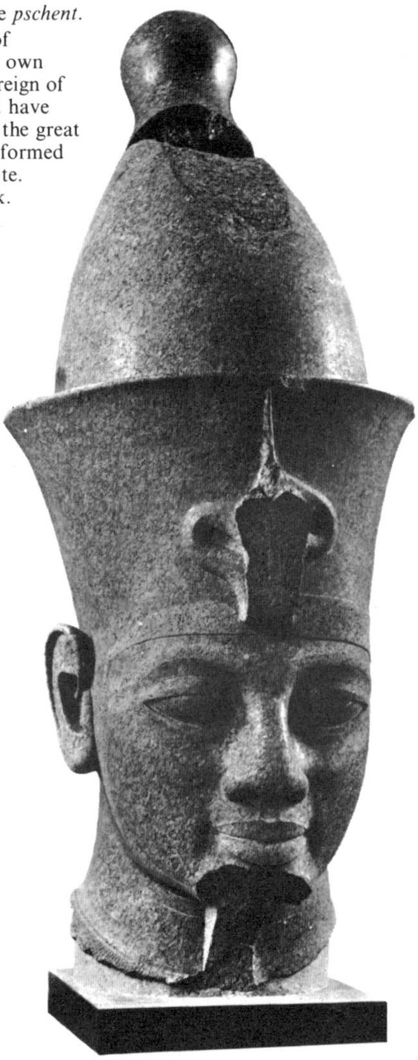

Tuthmoses III. wearing the *pschent*. The Pharaohs were fond of depicting the gods in their own likenesses and during the reign of Tuthmoses III they would have resembled this portrait of the great Pharaoh which originally formed part of a statue. Red granite. *c.* 1550 B.C. From Karnak.

Delta on the fourth intercalary day. Osiris, her eldest brother, chose her as his consort and she mounted to the throne with him. She helped him in his great work of civilising Egypt by teaching women to grind corn, spin flax and weave cloth. She also taught men the art of curing disease and, by instituting marriage, accustomed them to domestic life.

When her husband departed on his pacific conquest of the world she remained in Egypt as regent. She governed wisely while awaiting his return.

She was overwhelmed with grief at the news that Osiris had been assassinated by their brother, the violent Set. She cut off her hair, tore her robes and at once set forth in search of the coffer in which the good Osiris had been enclosed and which the conspirators had cast into the Nile.

This coffer had been carried out to sea by the waters of the Nile and borne across the waves to the Phoenician coast where it came to rest at the base of a tamarisk tree. The tree grew with such astonishing rapidity that the chest was entirely enclosed within its trunk.

Now Malcandre, the king of Byblos, gave orders that the tamarisk should be cut down in order to serve as a prop for the roof of his palace. When this was done the marvellous tree gave off so exquisite a scent that its reputation reached the ears of Isis, who immediately understood its significance. Without delay she went to Phoenicia. There the queen, Astarte, confided to her the care of her newly born son. Isis adopted the baby and would have conferred immortality upon it had its mother not broken the charm by her cries of terror upon seeing the goddess bathe the baby in purificatory flames. In order to reassure her, Isis revealed her true name and the reason for her presence. Then, having been presented with the trunk of the miraculous tree, she drew forth the coffer of her husband, bathed it in tears, and bore it back in haste to Egypt where, to deceive Set, she hid it in the swamps of Buto. Set, however, regained possession of his brother's body by chance and in order to annihilate it for ever cut it into fourteen pieces which he scattered far and wide.

Isis, undiscouraged, searched for the precious fragments and found them all except the phallus which had been greedily devoured by a Nile crab, the Oxyrhynchid, forever accursed for this crime.

The goddess reconstituted the body of Osiris, cunningly joining the fragments together. She then performed, for the first time in

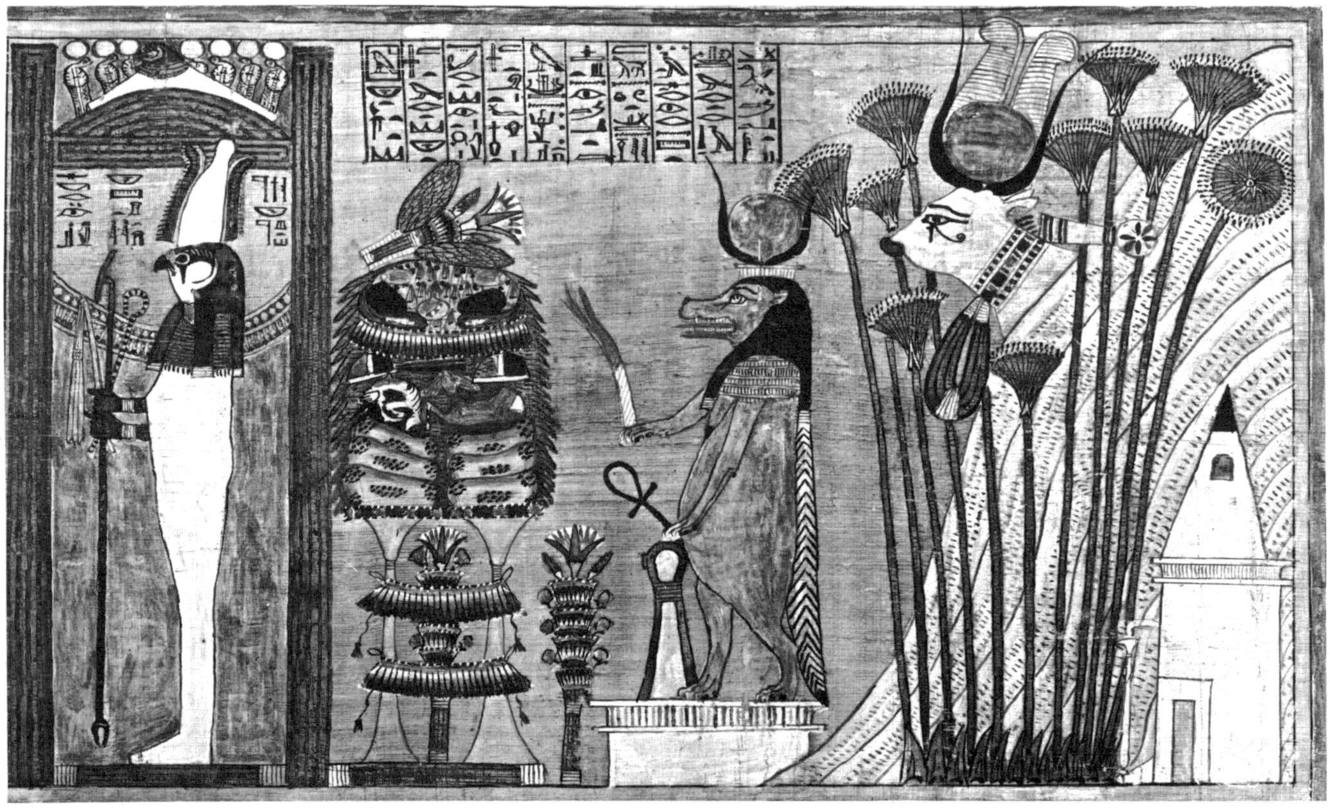

Seker, Taueret and Hathor – scene from the Papyrus of Ani. On the right, the goddess Hathor, in the form of a cow, emerges from the Libyan mountain to protect the tomb of Ani. Before her stands the hippopotamus goddess, Taueret, while on the left Seker, the hawk-headed god of the dead of the Memphis necropolis, stands guard. Painting on papyrus. Nineteenth dynasty, 1375 to 1202 B.C.

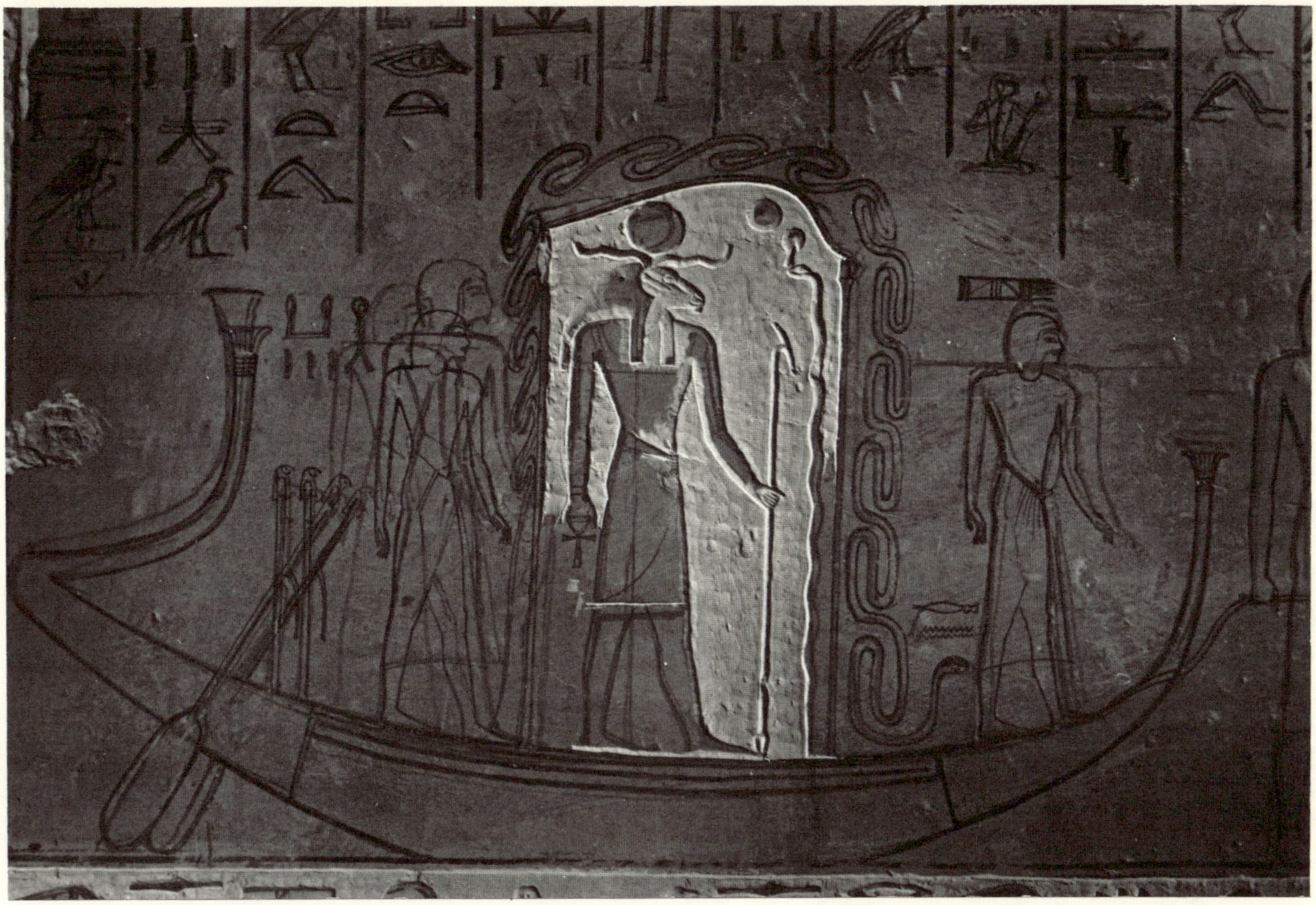

Efu Ra. The dead sun, portrayed as a man with a ram's head surmounted by the solar disk, is drawn in the Evening Boat through the Realm of Night. Around his cabin the serpent Mehen throws its coils to protect him from the terrible serpent Apep who sought to destroy him every night. Sketch and bas-relief on the wall of a tomb in the Valley of the Kings, Thebes.

history, the rites of embalmment which restored the murdered god to eternal life. In this she was assisted by her sister Nephthys, her nephew Anubis, Osiris' grand vizier Thoth and by Horus, the posthumous son whom she had conceived by union with her husband's corpse, miraculously re-animated by her charms.

Afterwards she retired to the swamps of Buto to escape the wrath of Set and to bring up her son Horus until the day when he should be of an age to avenge his father. Thanks to her magic powers Horus was able to overcome every danger which threatened him.

Isis, indeed, was a potent magician and even the gods were not immune from her sorcery. It was told how, when she was still only a simple woman in the service of Ra, she persuaded the great god to confide to her his secret name. She had taken advantage of the fact that the sun-god was now an old man with shaking head and dribbling mouth. With earth moistened with his divine spittle she fashioned a venomous snake which bit Ra cruelly. Ra was incapable of curing himself of a wound whose origin he did not understand, and had recourse to the spells of Isis. But Isis refused to conjure away the poison until Ra, overcome with pain and hiding himself from the other gods, consented to reveal his true name, which he caused to pass directly from his own bosom into that of Isis.

Isis, in the Osirian myth, represents the rich plains of Egypt, made fruitful by the annual inundation of the Nile which is Osiris, who is separated from her by Set, the arid desert.

Her cult continued to grow in importance until it ultimately absorbed that of nearly all other goddesses. It even crossed the frontiers of Egypt; seamen and merchants in the Graeco-Roman era carried her worship as far as the banks of the Rhine – Isis, star of the sea, and patron divinity of travellers.

In the Nile valley she kept her worshippers until well into Christian times. It was not until the middle of the sixth century, in the reign of Justinian, that the temple of Philae – her chief sanctuary in the extreme south of the country – was closed to her cult and turned into a church.

Great festivals were celebrated in spring and autumn in honour of Isis. The splendours of the processions which then took place have been described to us by Apuleius, who was an initiate in the mysteries of Isis. Thanks to him we can raise a corner of the veil which conceals the secret ceremonies of initiation.

Isis is normally represented as a woman who bears on her head a throne, the ideogram of her name. Occasionally, but later, her head-dress is a disk, set between cow's horns, occasionally flanked with two feathers. Finally we sometimes find her represented with a cow's head set on a human body. These horns and the cow's head merely prove that Isis was by then identified with Hathor; but Plutarch, though he says he does not believe it, gives us another explanation. Isis, he tells us, wished to intervene on behalf of Set who, though her husband's murderer, was also her own brother. She tried to cheat her son Horus of his just vengeance; but Horus turned in rage against his mother and cut off her head. Thoth then transformed it by enchantment and gave her the head of a cow.

This cow is, on the other hand, the animal sacred to Isis who also possessed, as fetishes, the magic knot 'Tat', called 'The Knot of Isis', and the Sistrum, the emblem of Hathor.

Sculpture and painting often represent her beside Osiris, whom she helps or protects – as she does the dead – with her winged arms. She may be seen mourning at the foot of sarcophagi or watching over canopic jars. She also frequently appears in the role of mother, suckling the infant Horus or joining him in his struggles with Set.

Set (Seth, Sutekh), whom the Greeks called Typhon, was the name of Osiris' evil brother who finally became the incarnation of the spirit of evil, in eternal opposition to the spirit of good.

The son of Geb and Nut, he was, Plutarch tells us, prematurely born on the third intercalary day. He tore himself violently from his mother's womb. He was rough and wild, his skin was white and his hair was red – an abomination to the Egyptians, who compared it to the pelt of an ass.

Set was jealous of Osiris, his elder brother, and secretly aspired to the throne. In order to seize it he availed himself of the great festivals which were celebrated at Memphis on the occasion of Osiris' victorious return to his kingdom. Having first assured

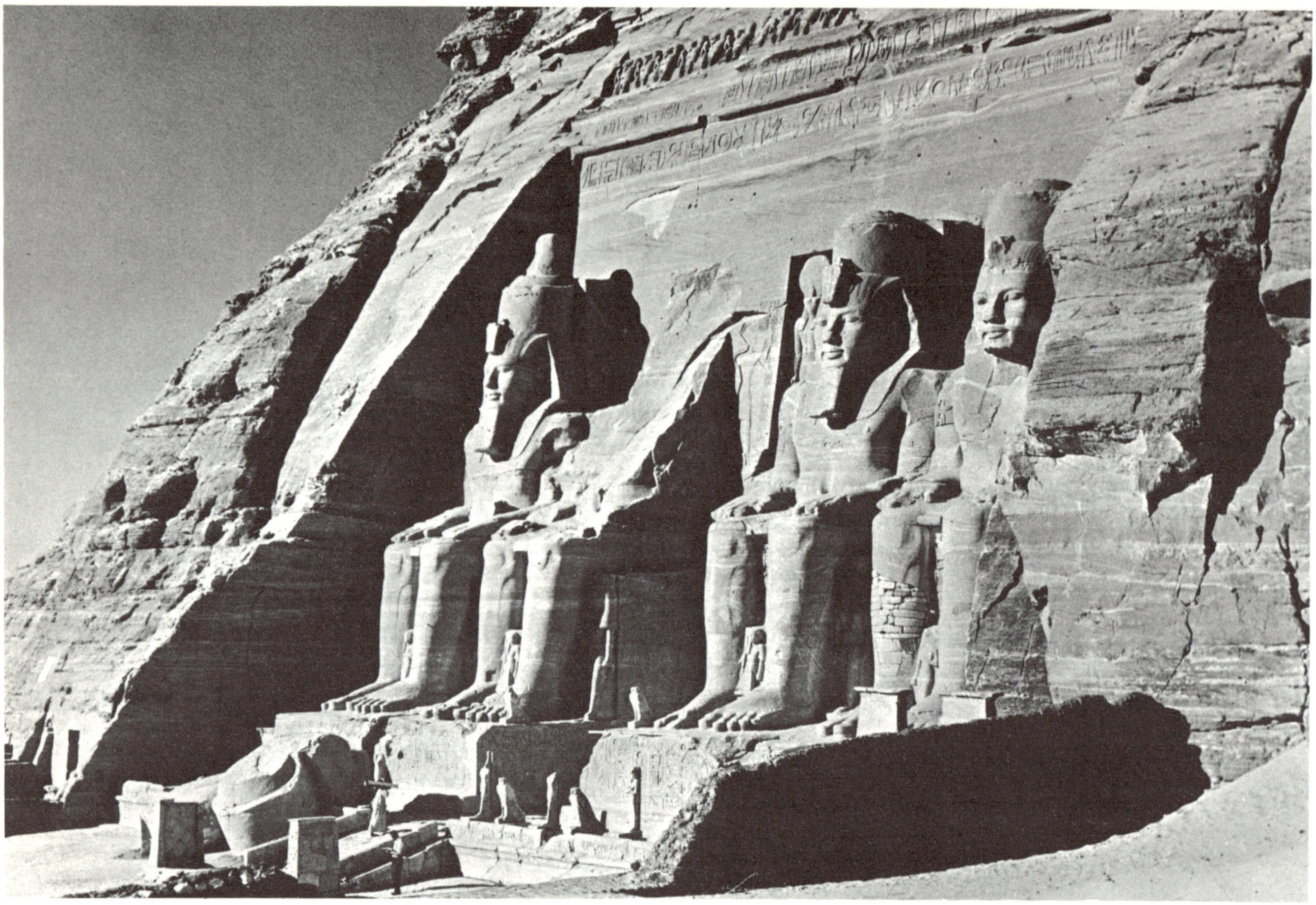

The facade of the great temple at Abu Simbel in Egyptian Nubia. Flanking the entrance are four colossal seated statues over sixty feet high of the Pharaoh Rameses III wearing the double crown of Upper and Lower Egypt while above it stands the falcon-headed figure of the sun god. Smaller figures represent wife, princes and gods. Nineteenth dynasty, 1375 to 1202 B.C.

himself of the presence of seventy-two accomplices he invited his brother to a banquet during the course of which he gave orders that a marvellously fashioned coffer should be brought in. This chest, he explained jokingly, would belong to whomsoever fitted it exactly. Osiris, falling in with the pleasantry, lay down in the coffer without suspicion. The conspirators at once rushed forward, closed the lid and nailed it solidly down. They threw it into the Nile, whence it was carried to the sea and across to Byblos. We have already seen how Isis brought it back to Egypt and how Set, hunting by moonlight in the swamps of the Delta, found it again by chance, and how, when he had recognised his brother's corpse, he cut it up into fourteen pieces which he scattered far and wide. This time the usurper felt that the possession of the realm was assured, and it worried him little that his wife Nephthys had left him. Nephthys, indeed, had joined the party of Osiris as most of the other gods had done, escaping from the cruelties of the tyrant by taking refuge in the bodies of various animals. Meanwhile Horus, son of Isis, was growing to maturity in the shelter of the Delta swamps, and we shall see how he avenged the murder of Osiris, his father, and reclaimed his heritage from Set.

As we have already said, Set, in Osirian myth, figures as the eternal adversary, a personification of the arid desert, of drought and darkness in opposition to the fertile earth, life-bringing water and light. All that is creation and blessing comes from Osiris; all that is destruction and perversity arises from Set.

In primitive times, however, the evil character of Set was not so accentuated. The old pyramid texts make him not the brother of Osiris, but the brother of Horus the Elder, and speak of terrible struggles between them which were terminated by the judgment of the gods, who proclaimed Horus the victor and banished Set to the desert.

It was only later, when the Osirian myth had grown and when the two Horuses had become confused, that Set was made the uncle of Horus and the eternal enemy of Osiris.

Originally Set seems to have been the Lord of Upper Egypt who was overthrown by the worshippers of the falcon god. The legendary struggles between the brother gods may thus reflect historical events.

The bas-reliefs of the Old and the Middle Kingdoms show Set and Horus together leading prisoners to the king, or else together at the base of the royal throne binding the plants of Upper and Lower Egypt around the emblem which expresses the idea of union – thus making the symbolic gesture of '*sam-taui*', the union of the two countries.

Under the domination of the Hyksos, the new rulers identified Set with their own great warrior god Sutekh and had a temple built for him in Avaris, their capital. Under the New Empire Rameses II, whose father was named Seti, the 'Setian', did not hesitate to proclaim himself the 'Beloved of Set'. The worshippers of Osiris, however, were indignant that a cult should be devoted to the murderer of the 'Good One', and Seti caused the cursed image to be effaced from the engraved tablets on the walls of his tomb and proclaimed himself no longer the 'Setian' but the 'Osirian'.

It is only towards the middle of the tenth century, under the kings of the twenty-second dynasty, that the assassin of Osiris really began to undergo the punishment for his crime. His statues were broken and on the bas-reliefs his features were smashed with hammers. Anyone who wrote his name was forced to erase it. Finally he was driven from the Egyptian pantheon and made a god of the unclean. Set, the ancient Lord of Upper Egypt, ended up by becoming a kind of devil, enemy of all the gods.

Asses, antelopes and other desert animals were supposed to belong to Set, and also the hippopotamus, the boar, the crocodile and the scorpion, in whose bodies the god of evil and his partisans had sought refuge from the blows of the conquering Horus. Legend says that Set, in the guise of a black pig, had once wounded Horus in the eye. In this form each month he attacked and devoured the moon where, some said, the soul of Osiris had taken refuge.

Set is represented as having the features of a fantastic beast with a thin, curved snout, straight, square-cut ears and a stiff forked tail. This creature cannot with certainty be identified and is commonly called the 'Typhonian animal'. Sometimes Set is depicted as a man with the head of this strange quadruped.

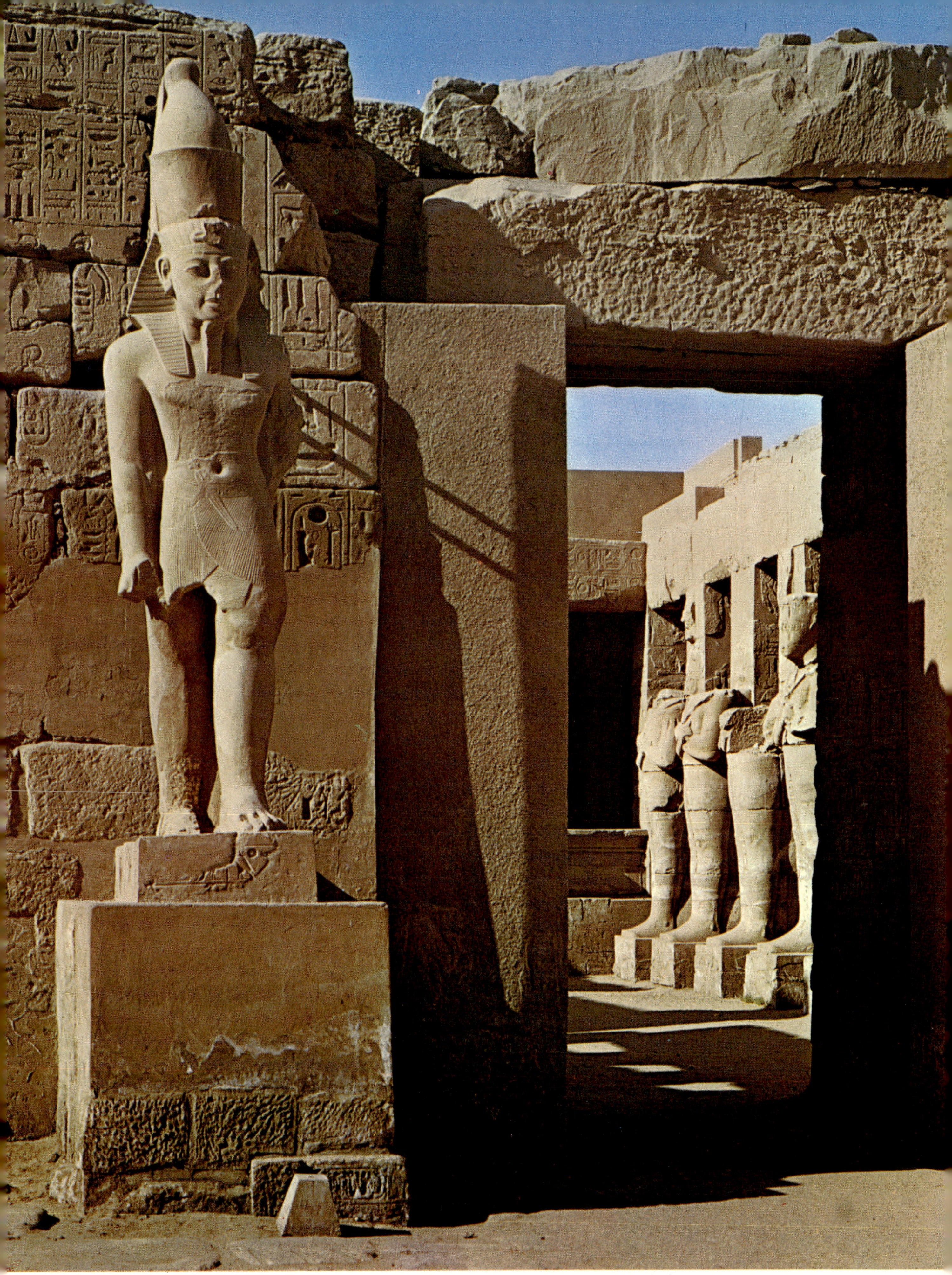

The temple of Rameses III at Karnak. The pharaoh wears the double crown of Upper and Lower Egypt, the *pschent*. The statues in the inner court, though much damaged by time, show clearly the familiar Osiris posture with their arms folded across their breasts, holding the flail and the sceptre in the shape of a crook, the emblems of supreme power. Twentieth dynasty, 1202 to 1102 B.C.

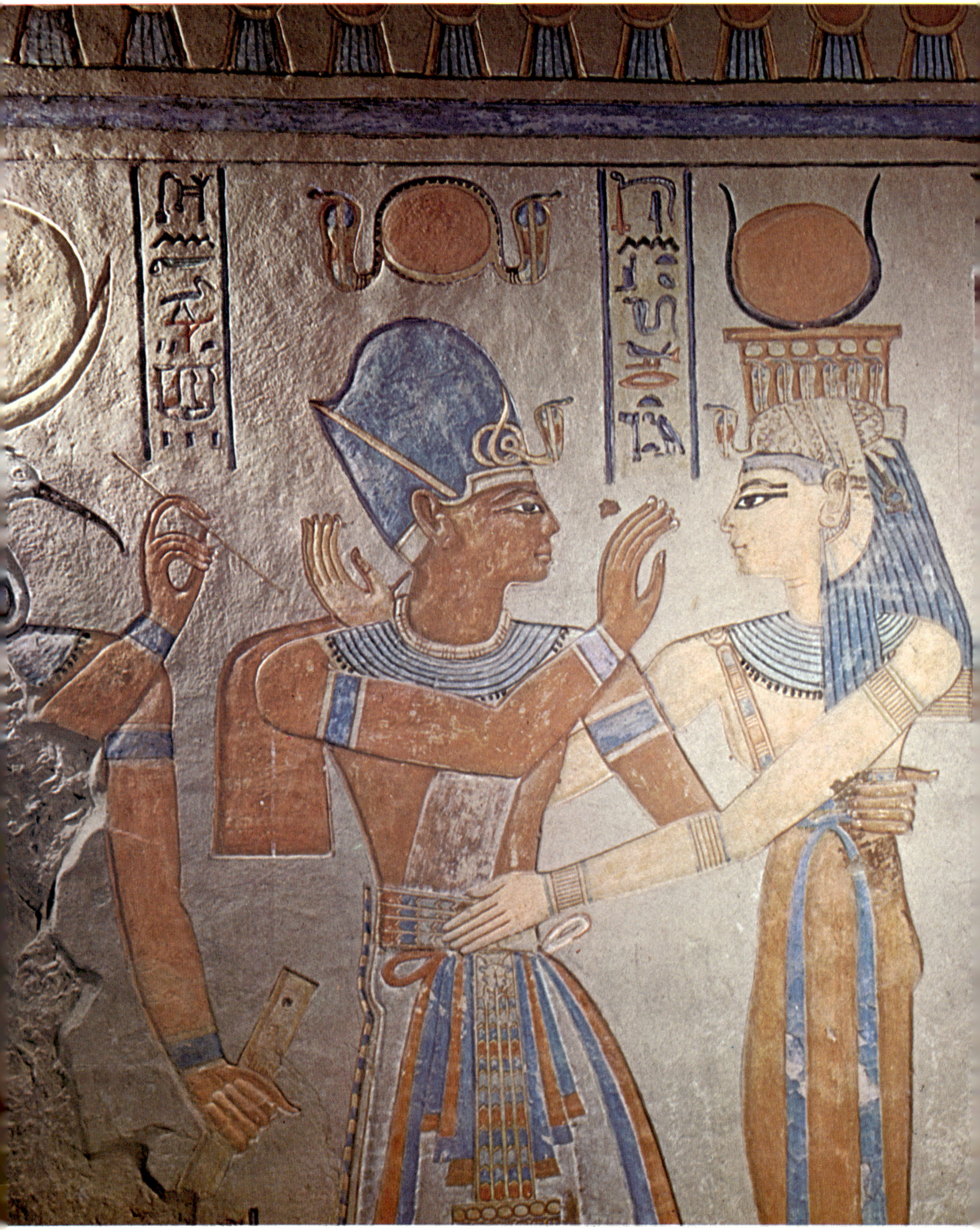

The goddess Isis embraces Prince Amun-kher-khopsh. The protectress of the dead, the goddess wears a disk set between cow's horns on her headdress, having become identified with Hathor, the cow-goddess, by this date. The prince, who was the son of the Pharaoh Rameses III, wears the blue *khepresh,* or war helmet. Behind him stands the ibis-headed god Thoth holding a read pen in his upraised right hand and with a writing palette in his left to record the prince's deeds. Painting from the tomb of Prince Amun-kher-khopsh, Twentieth dynasty, 1202 to 1102 B.C.

Nephthys is the Greek rendering of Nebthet and is called by Plutarch Aphrodite and Nike.

She is pictured as a woman wearing on her head the two hieroglyphs with which her name, which signifies 'Mistress of the Palace', was written: i.e., a basket (*neb*) placed on the sign for a palace (*het*). In origin a goddess of the dead, Nephthys in the Osirian legend becomes the second daughter of Geb and Nut. Set, her second brother, took her for his wife, but she remained barren. She wanted a child by her eldest brother Osiris and with this object she made him drunk and drew him into her arms without his being aware of it. The fruit of this adultery was Anubis.

Nephthys, according to this legend, seems to represent the desert's edge, ordinarily arid but sometimes fruitful when the Nile floods are especially high. When Set committed fratricide his wife abandoned him in horror and, joining the party of Osiris' defenders, she helped her sister Isis to embalm the corpse of the murdered god, alternating with her in the funereal lamentations. A papyrus still preserves for us the text of these lamentations.

Just as Nephthys and Isis had protected the mummy of their brother so the 'twins', as they are often called, also watched over the bodies of the dead who, by virtue of funeral rites, had become 'Osirises'. On coffin-lids and the walls of sarcophagi we often see them represented, standing or kneeling, stretching forth their long, winged arms in a gesture of protection.

Horus is the Latin rendering of the Greek Horos and the Egyptian Hor. He was a solar god constantly identified with Apollo and represented by a falcon or a falconheaded god.

Under the name Hor – which in Egyptian sounds like a word meaning 'sky' – the Egyptians referred to the falcon which they saw soaring high above their heads, and many thought of the sky as a divine falcon whose two eyes were the sun and the moon. The worshippers of this bird must have been numerous and powerful; for it was carried as a totem on prehistoric standards and from the earliest times was considered the pre-eminent divine being. The hieroglyph which represents the idea of 'god' was a falcon on its perch.

Wherever the followers of the falcon settled, Horus was worshipped, but in the course of time and in the different sanctuaries which were dedicated to him his role and attributes varied. Thus we find in the Egyptian pantheon some twenty Horuses, among whom it is important to distinguish Horus the Elder, 'Haroeris', and other falcons of a solar character such as Hor Behdetite, Horus of Edfu, from Horus, son of Isis, of the Osirian legend – i.e., 'Harsiesis', the infant avenger of his father.

Haroeris is the Greek rendering of Har Wer, which signifies Horus the Great, Horus the Elder.

He was worshipped at Latopolis under the name Horkhenti Irti, 'Horus who rules the two eyes', and at Pharboethos under the name Hor Merti, 'Horus of the two eyes'. He is the god of the sky itself and his two eyes are the sun and the moon, whose birth, according to Herodotus, was celebrated on the last day of Epiphi, when these two astral bodies are in conjunction.

In the pyramid texts Haroeris is the son of Ra and brother of Set, and the eternal struggle between darkness and light is symbolised by the endless battles in which Set tears out the eyes of Horus while Horus emasculates his implacable enemy. We shall presently see how the tribunal of the gods gave judgment in favour of Horus, who from the end of the second dynasty was considered to be the divine ancestor of the Pharaohs in whose records he is given the title Hor Nubti: 'Horus the Vanquisher of Set'.

Behdety, 'He of Behdet' (or Hor Behdetite) is another name of the great celestial Horus. He was worshipped at Behdet, a district of ancient Edfu. The Greeks called it Apollinopolis Magna and recognised Apollo as Lord of the sanctuary.

Behdety is usually represented in the form of a winged solar disk; his followers liked to sculpture his image above temple gates. He often appears in battle scenes hovering above the Pharaoh like a great falcon with outspread wings which clutches in its claws the mystic fly-whisk and the ring, symbolic of eternity.

The bas-reliefs in the temple at Edfu portray him as a falcon-headed god leading into battle against Set the armies of Ra-Harakhte, the great god of whom we have already spoken

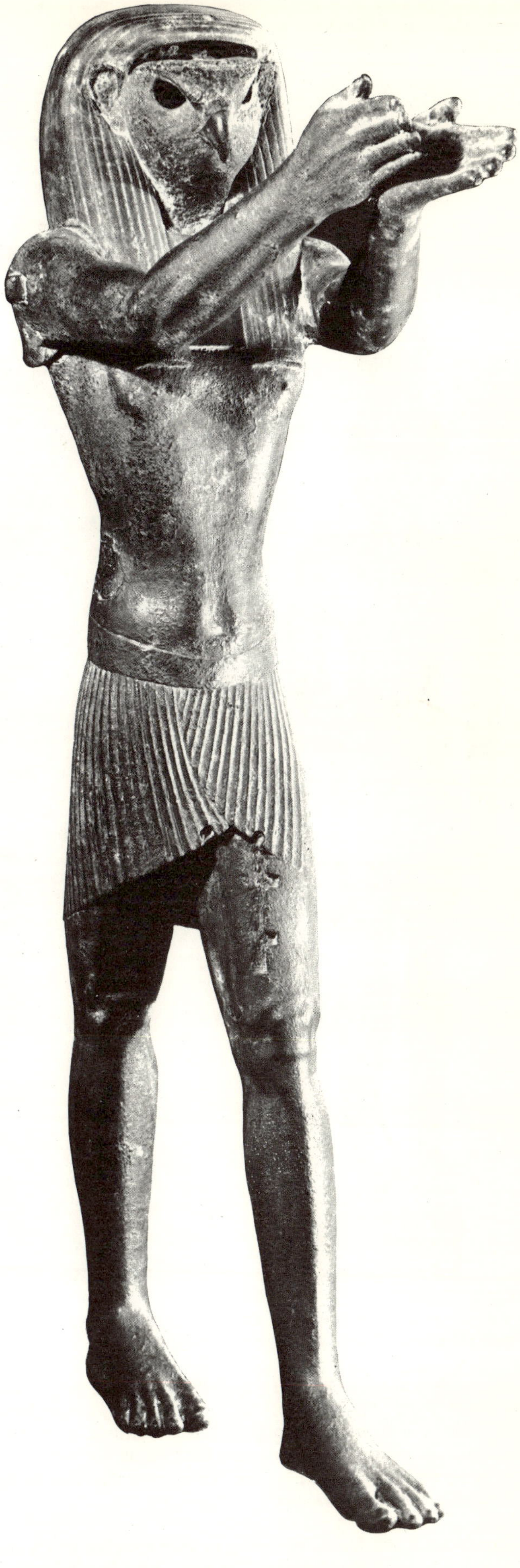

Horus. The falcon-headed solar god of Memphis makes a purificatory gesture towards a Pharaoh – possibly Amenhotep II. His gesture, formerly completed by the god Set, in company with whom he performed the coronation and purification of the Pharaoh, would at this period have been completed by the god Thoth. Statue of the nineteenth dynasty, 1587 to 1375 B.C.

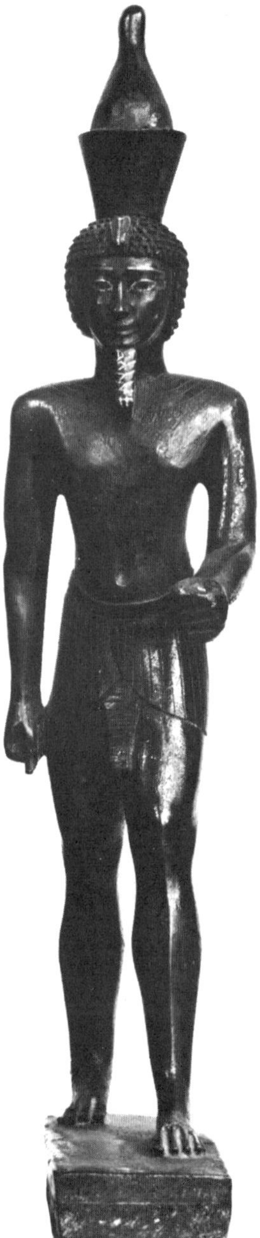

Haroeris. The great sky-god Horus the Elder or Horus the Great is portrayed with the head of a man instead of that of a falcon probably by confusion with the younger Horus, the son of Isis and Osiris. and wears the double crown upon his head. Statue in bronze.

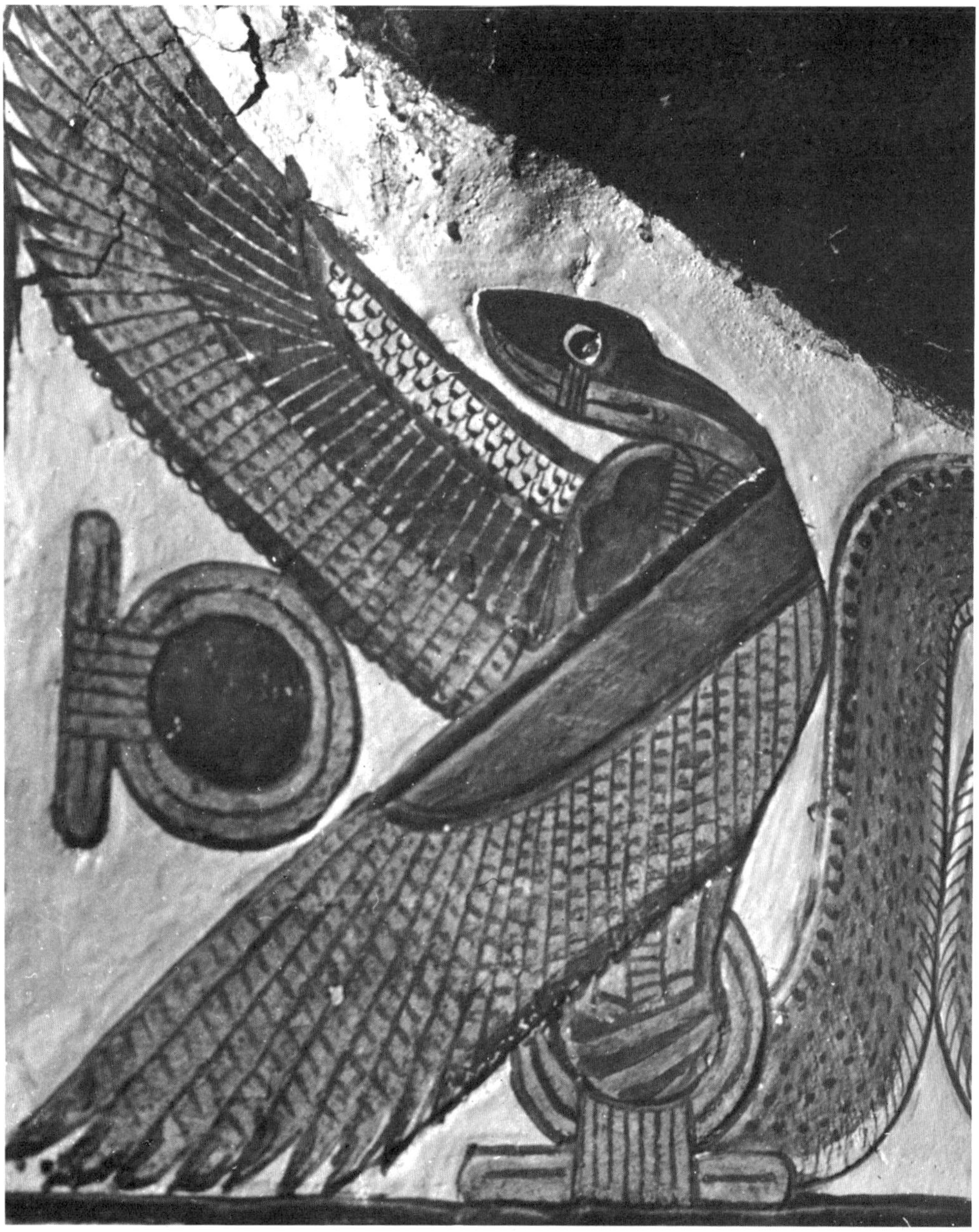

Snake-goddess. This tomb painting from the Valley of the Kings probably represents Mertseger, the snake goddess of the Theban necropolis, who protected the desert tombs. Another goddess also portrayed as a winged cobra was Buto, the protector of the Pharaoh. New Kingdom period, 1738 to 1102 B.C. Thebes.

(see *Ra*) who embodied in a single deity the union of Ra and a special form of Horus worshipped at Heliopolis.

Harakhtes is the Greek rendering of Harakhte and means 'Horus of the Horizon'. He represents the sun on its daily course between the eastern and western horizon. Early confused with Ra, he successively usurped all of Ra's roles until Ra, in his turn, assumed all of Horus' epithets and became pre-eminent throughout Egypt under the name Ra-Harakhte.

Harmakhis is the Greek rendering of Hor-m-akhet which means 'Horus who is on the Horizon'. The name has often been wrongly employed in the form of Ra Harmakhis for Ra-Harakhte. It is the proper name of the huge sphinx sixty feet high and more than a hundred and eighty feet long sculptured nearly five thousand years ago in the image of King Khephren in a rock near the pyramid which it guards. He is a personification of the rising sun and a symbol (for the comfort of Khephren) of resurrection.

Raised on the edge of the desert, even its colossal size did not in ancient days protect it against the invading sands. A stela tells us how it appeared in a dream to the future Thuthmosis IV. Thuthmosis was at the time a simple royal prince and not heir to the throne. While hunting he fell asleep in the shadow of the sphinx and dreamed that it spoke to him, ordering him to remove the covering sand and promising in return to heap favours upon him. 'Oh my son Thuthmosis,' it cried, 'it is I, thy father, Harmakhis-Khepri-Atum. The throne will be thine... so that thou shalt do what my heart desires...'

Harsiesis is the Greek rendering of Hor-sa-iset, i.e. 'Horus, the son of Isis'. We have already seen how Isis was reputed to have conceived Horus without husband or lover and how the popularity of mother and son continued to increase, together with that of Osiris himself. This popularity became such that Harsiesis – originally a minor falcon-god from the neighbourhood of Buto who was called Horus the Younger in order to distinguish him from the great sky-god Horus the Elder – ended up by eclipsing all the other Horuses whose roles and attributes he successively took over.

The Osirian legend recounts the posthumous birth of the child which Isis obtained from Osiris by magical means, re-animating the corpse of the murdered god. It relates how she gave premature birth to Horus on the floating island of Chemmis, not far from Buto. In early youth he was frequently called 'the infant Horus' – Harpakhrad – or Harpokrates.

Harpokrates is represented as a baby, nude or adorned only with jewellery. His head is shaved, except for the sidelock of youth which falls over his temple. Often he is seated on his mother's lap while she offers him her breast. He sucks his thumb like a baby, a gesture which was misinterpreted by the Greeks, who took it for a symbol of discretion, and won the young god fame as the divinity of silence.

For fear of the machinations of Set, Horus was brought up in seclusion. He was extremely weak at birth and escaped from the numerous dangers which menaced him only by his mother's power of sorcery. He was bitten by savage beasts, stung by scorpions, burnt, attacked by pains in the entrails. The memory of these sufferings is preserved for us in the magic formulas which were employed by sorcerers to cure patients similarly afflicted.

The child Horus grew, and Osiris appeared frequently to him and instructed him in the use of arms so that he should soon be able to make war on Set, reclaim his inheritance and avenge his father. This glorious action earned for Horus the epithet Harendotes, which is the Greek for Har-end-yotef, 'Horus, protector of his father'.

The campaigns of the young god against the murderer of Osiris are sculptured on the walls of the temple at Edfu whose great god Behdety was, in this later epoch, identified with Horus, while Set was confused with Apep, the eternal enemy of the sun. In a long series of bas-reliefs we see him, under the name Hartomes, 'Horus the Lancer', piercing his adversaries with his lance while his followers cut Set's followers – who vainly attempt to seek refuge in the bodies of crocodiles, hippopotami, antelopes and so on – into pieces.

The war dragged on, and in order to terminate it a tribunal of the gods summoned the two adversaries before it. Set pleaded that his nephew was a bastard, only the alleged son of Osiris; but Horus victoriously established the legitimacy of his birth. The gods, after condemning the usurper, restored Horus' heritage and declared him ruler of the two Egypts, by which he then earned the two further titles: Harsomtus or Heru Sam Taui ('Horus who unites the two countries') and Har-pa-neb-taui ('Horus, Lord of the two lands').

He now everywhere re-established the authority of Osiris and the solar cycle. He erected temples in which he was represented in the various forms he had assumed during the wars against his irreconcilable enemies, the followers of Set. He then reigned peacefully over Egypt, of which he always remained the national god, ancestor of the Pharaohs, who each took the title of 'the Living Horus'.

With his father Osiris and his mother Isis, Horus was worshipped throughout Egypt. He figures in the triads or trinities of numerous sanctuaries, either as chief, as prince consort, or as divine infant. Thus at Edfu and at Ombos he is the great god with Hathor as his companion; while Hathor is the uncontested mistress at Dendera, and Horus, in his role of the sovereign's husband, only a privileged guest.

Until the beginning of the New Kingdom, temple figures represent Horus acting in consort with Set to crown and purify the king. They show the king into the sanctuary or perform the symbolic gesture of *'sam-taui'*. But later Thoth everywhere replaces Set. Elsewhere we see Horus fighting Set and his partisans, mourning Osiris and performing for him the burial duties. Finally in the next world Horus ushers the deceased into the presence of 'the Good One' and often presides over the weighing of his soul.

Hathor (Athyr) is the name of the great Egyptian deity whom the Greeks identified with Aphrodite.

A sky-goddess, she was originally described as the daughter of Ra and the wife of Horus. She was, however, sometimes called the mother of Horus; for her name can also signify 'the dwelling of Horus' and it was explained that within her the sun-god resided, being enclosed each evening in her breast, to be born again each morning.

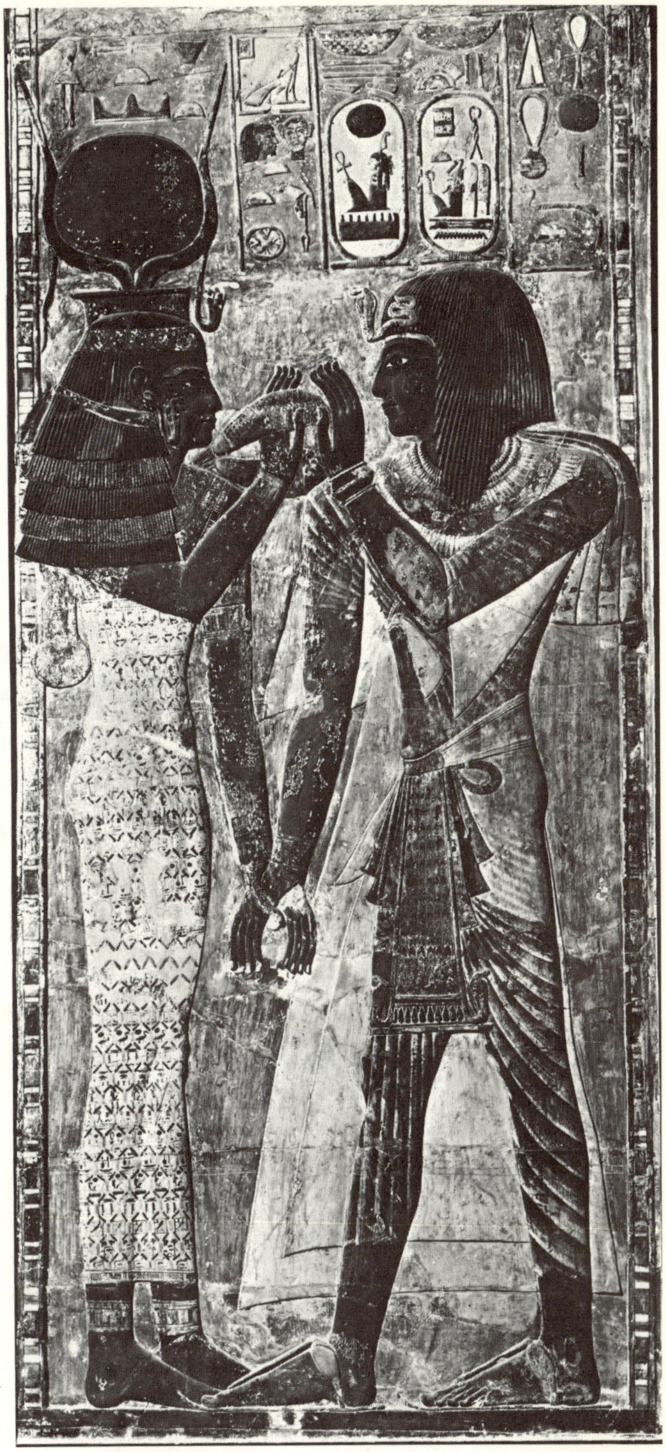

Hathor and the Pharaoh Seti I. The goddess, wearing an embroidered robe and a horned head-dress with the solar disk and the *uraeus* embraces the Pharaoh and presents him with the 'Menat' collar, thus transmitting to him her protective fluid.
Painted bas-relief. Nineteenth dynasty, 1350 to 1202.

The texts also say that she was the great celestial cow who created the world and all that it contains, including the sun.

She is in consequence represented as a cow – her sacred animal – or as a cow-headed goddess. Still more often she is given a human head adorned either with horns or simply cow's ears and heavy tresses framing her face.

Hathor also had a fetish in which she liked to embody herself: the sistrum, a musical instrument which drove away evil spirits. It was in a spirit of piety that the architect of Dendera conceived the columns of Hathor's temple as so many colossal sistrums.

Hathor was the protectress of women and was supposed to preside at their toilet. She enjoyed immense popularity as the goddess of joy and love. She was proclaimed mistress of merriment and sovereign of the dance, mistress of music and sovereign of song, of leaping and jumping and the weaving of garlands. Her temple was

Selket. One of the four goddesses who protected the dead, Selket, wearing her sacred animal, the scorpion, on her head, spreads her winged arms around the sarcophagus of the young Pharaoh Tut-ankh-Amon. The other three goddesses were similarly carved in high relief at each of the other corners of the sarcophagus. Yellow quartzite. Eighteenth dynasty, 1587 to 1375 B.C.

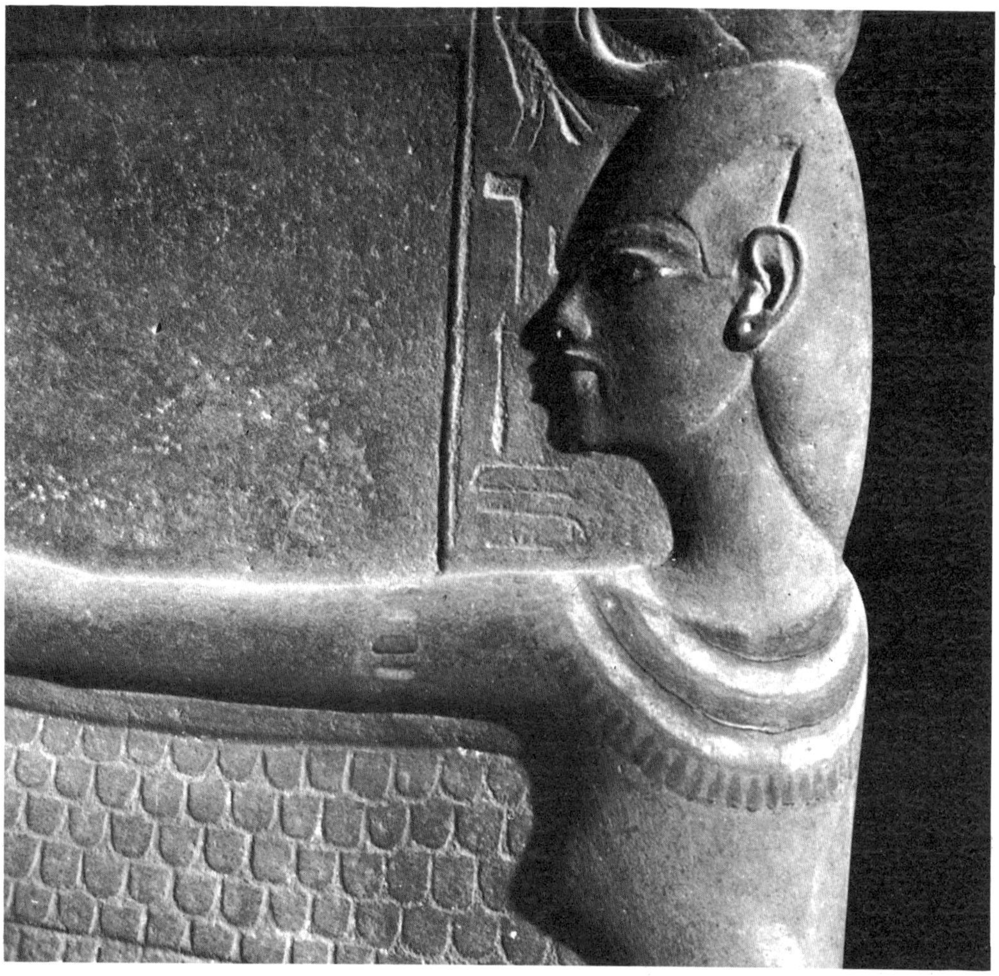

Sebek, the crocodile god. In this bas-relief on the small south-western outer wall of the court of the temple of Kom Ombo where his triad was worshipped, Sebek is portrayed as a seated man with a crocodile's head though he could also be represented as the animal itself. At one time a patron of the Pharaohs, he was later reviled in some areas as an enemy of Osiris.

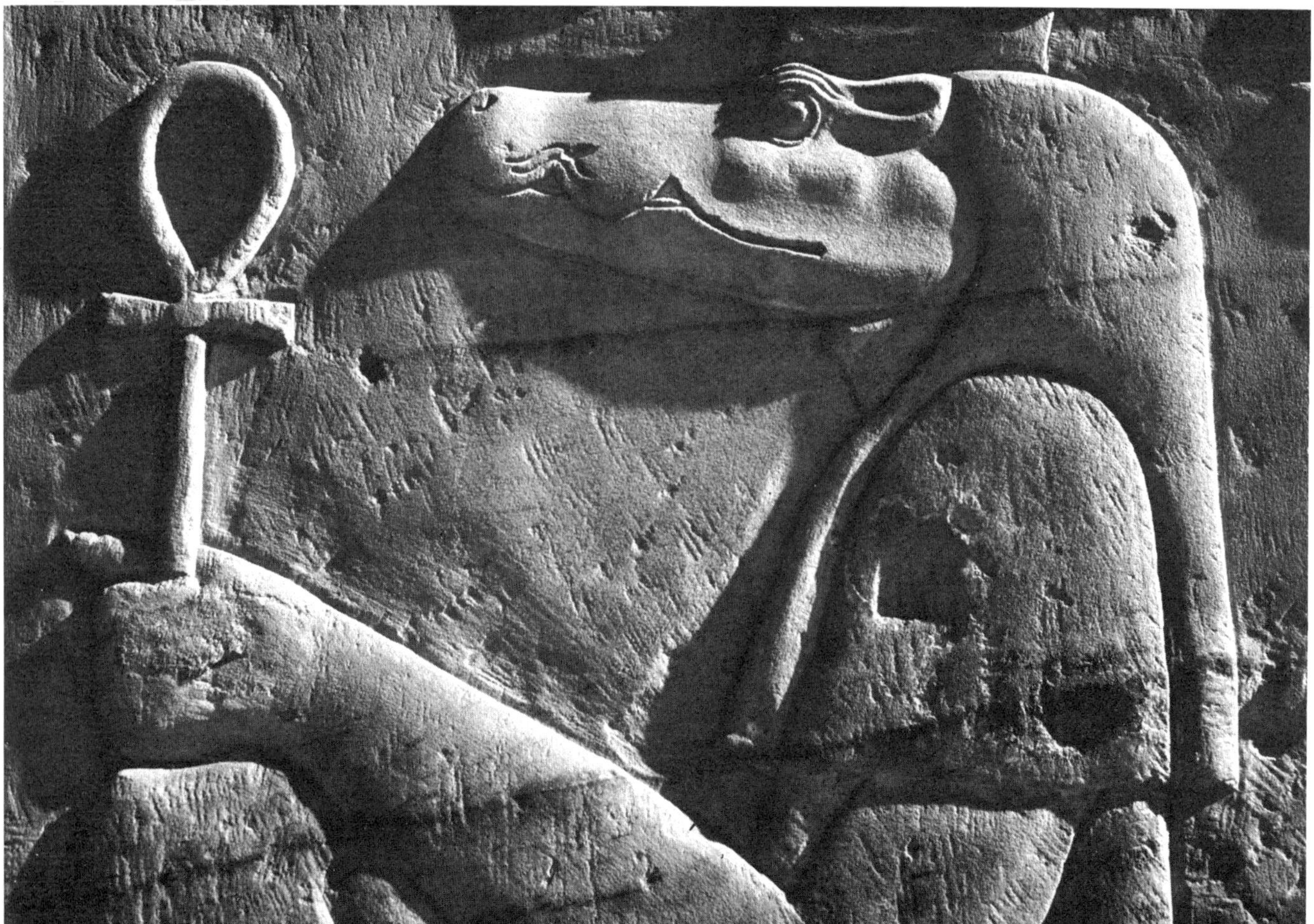

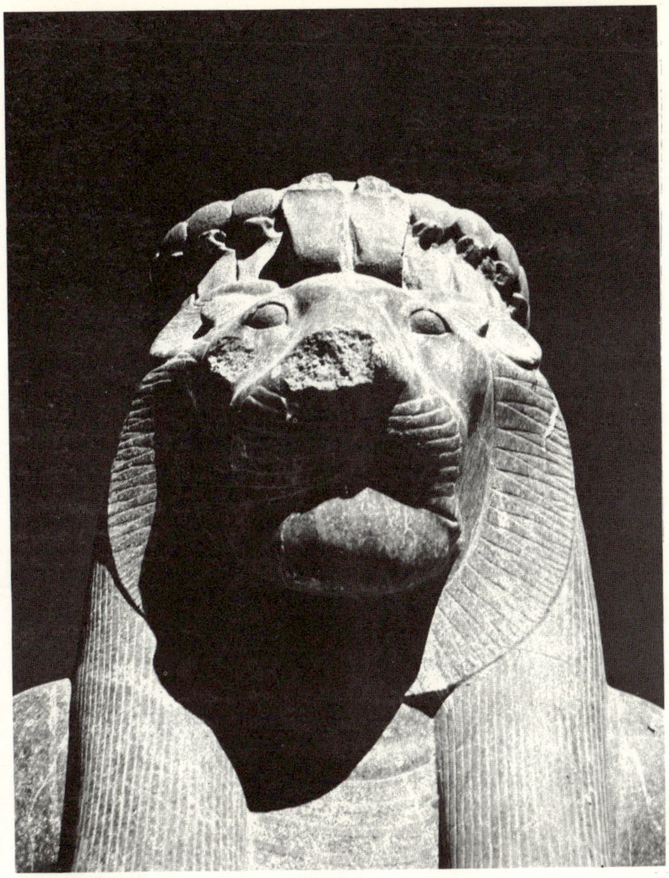

Sekhmet, the terrible lioness-headed goddess of war and battle. The goddess of vengeance, who at one time attempted to exterminate the human race and who punished the damned in the Underworld, she was also a fire goddess and symbolised the devouring fire of the sun. Head of a statue in the third court of the temple of Mont at Karnak. Eighteenth dynasty, *c.* 1400 B.C.

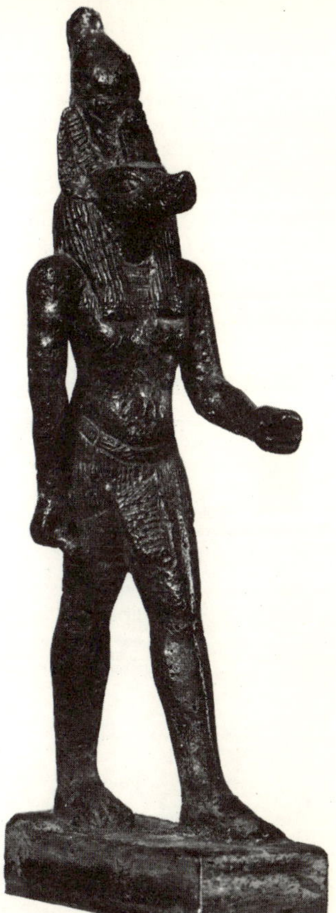

Anubis, 'Lord of the Land' (i.e. the cemetery). The jackal-headed god advances wearing the double crown of Upper and Lower Egypt. Originally the fourth son of Ra, he was later admitted into the family of Osiris, and from being the god of death of the Pharaoh only, became the god of death for all. Bronze statuette.

the 'home of intoxication and a place of enjoyment'.

Hathor nourished the living with her milk. We see her giving her breast to the king whom she holds in her arms or on her knees and, again, in the form of a cow, suckling the Pharaoh.

Although she was well disposed towards those who were alive she cherished the dead even more tenderly. Under the name 'Queen of the West' she was the protectress of the Theban necropolis. Vignettes in the Book of the Dead show the good cow half-emerged from the Libyan Mountain – the westernmost limit of human habitation – to welcome the dead on their arrival in the other world. Those who understood how to beseech her aid by means of the prescribed formulas she would carry in safety on her back to the after world.

She was also called 'the Lady of the Sycamore', for she would sometimes hide in the foliage of this tree on the edge of the desert and appear to the dead with the bread and water of welcome. It was she, they believed, who held the long ladder by which the deserving could climb to heaven. More and more the goddess specialised in her role of funerary deity until in the last epoch a dead person was no longer called 'an Osiris' but 'a Hathor'.

Her principal sanctuary was at Dendera where she was worshipped in company with her husband, Horus of Edfu, who here ceded first place to her, and with their son Ihi (Ahi), 'the Sistrum Player', who is represented as an infant jingling the sistrum at her side. Great festivals were celebrated in this temple, above all on New Year's Day, which was the anniversary of her birth. Before dawn the priestesses would bring Hathor's image out on to the terrace to expose it to the rays of the rising sun. The rejoicing which followed was a pretext for a veritable carnival, and the day ended in song and intoxication.

Hathor was also worshipped at Edfu with Horus, Lord of the temple, and their son Harsomtus, as well as at Ombos, where she took part in both trinities at the same time.

Even beyond Egypt, on the coast of Somaliland, she was called 'Mistress of the land of Punt', from which perhaps she had come in very ancient times. In the Sinai peninsula she was known as 'Mistress of the land of Mefket'; and in Phoenicia, where part of the Osirian legend had early taken root, as 'the Lady of Byblos'.

Anubis, the Greek rendering of Anpu, was identified with Hermes, Conductor of Souls. It was Anubis who opened for the dead the roads of the other world. He is represented as a black jackal with a bushy tail, or as a blackish-skinned man with the head of a jackal or the head of a dog, an animal sacred to Anubis. For this reason the Greeks called the chief city of his cult Cynopolis.

From the earliest dynasties Anubis presided over embalmments. Funeral prayers, in which he was always to occupy a preponderant position, were in those days almost exclusively addressed to him.

In the pyramid texts Anubis is the 'fourth son of Ra' and his daughter is Kebehut, the goddess of freshness. But later he was admitted into the family of Osiris and it was said that Nephthys, left childless by her husband Set, bore him adulterously to Osiris.

Abandoned by his mother at birth, he was, it is related, found by his aunt, Isis. Isis, feeling no rancour at the thoughtless infidelity of her husband, undertook to bring up the baby. When he had grown to man's estate Anubis accompanied Osiris on his conquest of the world, and when 'the Good One' was murdered he helped Isis and Nephthys to bury him.

It was on this occasion that Anubis invented funeral rites and bound up the mummy of Osiris to preserve him from contact with the air and subsequent corruption. He was known, therefore, as 'Lord of the Mummy Wrappings'. From then on he presided over funerals and it is in this role that we often see him, first proceeding with the mummy's embalming and later receiving it at the door of the tomb. Anubis also makes sure that offerings brought by the deceased's heirs actually reach him.

Afterwards we see Anubis take the dead by the hand and, in his capacity of Osiris' usher, introduce him into the presence of the sovereign judges before whom he then weighs the soul of the dead.

This role of god of the dead won Anubis a universal cult and his admission into the circle of Osiris kept his worship alive until the latest epoch when, because of his identification with Hermes, Conductor of Souls, he was given the name Hermanubis. In the great procession in honour of Isis which Apuleius describes, it is the dog-headed god, bearing in his hands the caduceus and the palms, who marches at the head of the divine images.

Upuaut (or **Ophois Wepwawet**) is a wolf-headed or jackal-headed god who should not be confused with Anubis. Upuaut signifies 'he who opens the way'. In prehistoric representations we see the wolf-god, borne high upon his standard, guiding the warriors of his tribe into enemy territory. Similarly, during his principal

Anubis preparing a mummy. The god bends forward to adjust the mask of the bandaged mummy which lies on a lion-headed couch. Anubis was believed to have invented funeral rites and the art of embalming when he bound up the body of Osiris to preserve it from corruption. Painting from the first tomb of Sennedjem at Deir el Medinah in the necropolis of Thebes. Twentieth dynasty, 1202 to 1102 B.C.

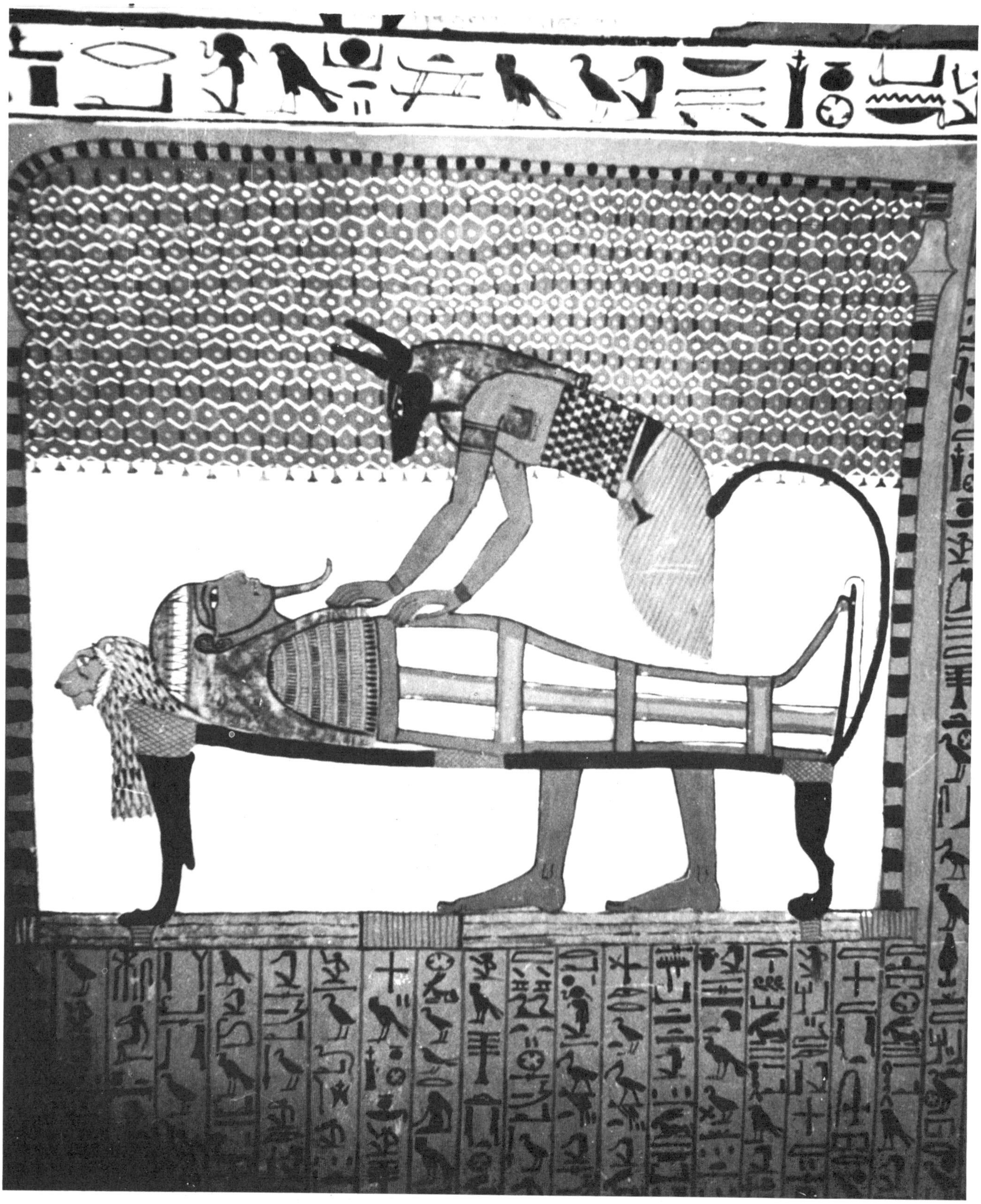

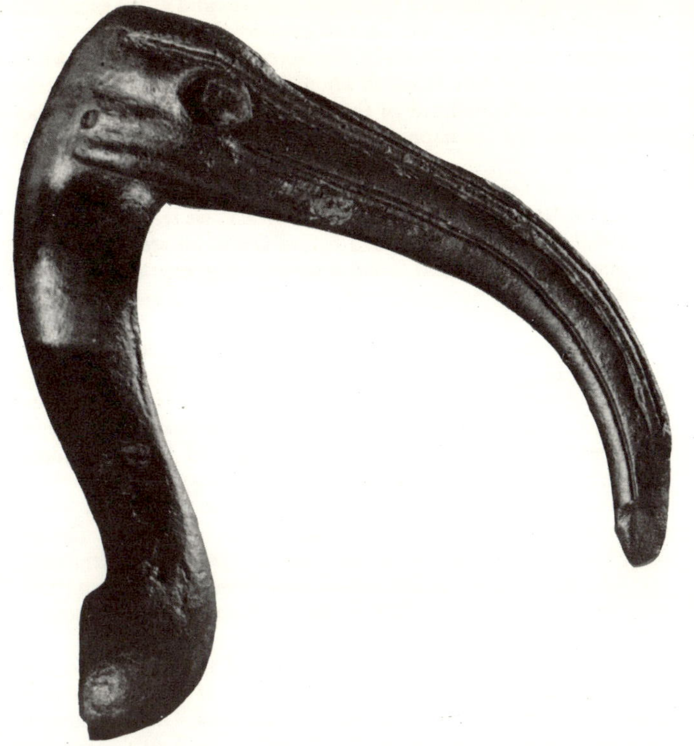

Head of Thoth. Represented generally as an ibis or an ibis-headed man, Thoth was worshipped at Hermopolis as the divine ibis who created the world. The god of learning, the inventor of hieroglyphs and the scribe of the gods, he was also portrayed as a dog-headed baboon, probably as the result of a fusion in early times with another deity. Bronze.

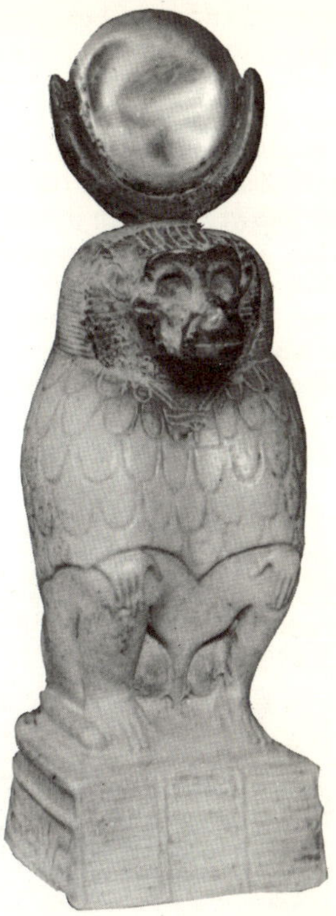

Thoth as a baboon. The god is seated and wears a crescent moon upon his head. Worshipped as a lunar deity throughout Egypt, he was believed to take the place of Ra in the sky while the latter made his journey through the Underworld during the hours of night, and was responsible for regulating the months and seasons.

procession, Upuaut, carried on his shield, leads the cortège at the festivals of Osiris. Sometimes he is also shown piloting the sun's boat during its nocturnal voyage and, if necessary, towing it along the edge of the southern and northern sky.

A former warrior-god, he was also worshipped as god of the dead; and notably at Abydos, before Osiris deposed him, he was worshipped as Lord of the Necropolis under the name Khenti Amenti 'he who rules the West'.

Upuaut was feudal god of Siut, the Greek Lycopolis, and a later addition to the Osirian legend. He was an ally of Osiris and, with Anubis, one of his chief officers during the conquest of the world. As such, they both sometimes appear in later times dressed as soldiers.

Thoth is the form which the name Djehuti or Zehuti had taken in Graeco-Roman times. He was identified by the Greeks with Hermes, Messenger of the Gods, and was worshipped throughout Egypt as a moon-god, patron of science and literature, wisdom and inventions, the spokesman of the gods and their keeper of the records.

Djehuti seems merely to mean 'he of Djehut', the name of the old province in Lower Egypt whose capital, Hermopolis Parva, must have been the cradle of Thoth's cult before he had established his principal sanctuary at Hermopolis Magna in Upper Egypt.

Thoth is ordinarily represented with the head of an ibis, often surmounted by a crescent moon, or simply as an ibis. He liked to appear as a bird of this sort, but also at times as a dog-headed ape, which makes us suspect that the god of historical ages may have been derived from a fusion, in very remote times, of two lunar divinities, one figured as a bird, the other as an ape.

According to the theologians of Hermopolis, Thoth was the true universal Demiurge, the divine ibis who had hatched the world-egg at Hermopolis Magna. They taught that he had accomplished the work of creation by the sound of his voice alone. When he first awoke in the primordial 'Nun' he opened his lips, and from the sound that issued forth four gods materialised and then four goddesses. For this reason the future Hermopolis was called Khnum, 'City of the Eight'. Without real personality these eight gods perpetuated the creation of the world by the word; and the texts tell us that they sang hymns morning and evening to assure the continuity of the sun's course.

In the Books of the Pyramids, Thoth is sometimes the oldest son of Ra, sometimes the child of Geb and Nut, the brother of Isis, Set and Nephthys. Normally, however, he does not belong to the Osirian family and is only the vizier of Osiris and his kingdom's sacred scribe.

He remained faithful to his murdered master and contributed powerfully to his resurrection, thanks to the trueness of his voice which increased the force of his magic incantations, and to the thoroughness of the way in which he purified the dismembered body of Osiris. Afterwards he helped Isis to defend the child Horus against the perils which beset him. We are told how on the orders of the gods he drove out the poison from the child's body when he had been stung by a scorpion. Later we see him intervene in the merciless struggle between Horus and Set, curing the former's tumour and the latter's emasculation by spitting on their wounds. Finally, when the two irreconcilable enemies were summoned to appear before the tribunal of the gods sitting in Hermopolis, Thoth earned the title 'He who judges the two companions'. He decided between the two adversaries and condemned Set to return his nephew's heritage.

As he had been the vizier of Osiris, so afterwards was he that of Horus. When Horus resigned earthly power Thoth succeeded him to the throne. During three thousand two hundred and twenty-six years Thoth remained the very model of a peaceful ruler.

Endowed with complete knowledge and wisdom, it was Thoth who invented all the arts and sciences: arithmetic, surveying, geometry, astronomy, soothsaying, magic, medicine, surgery, music with wind instruments and strings, drawing and, above all, writing, without which humanity would have run the risk of forgetting his doctrines and of losing the benefit of his discoveries.

As inventor of hieroglyphs, he was named 'Lord of Holy Words'. As first of the magicians he was often called 'The Elder'. His disciples boasted that they had access to the crypt where he had locked up his books of magic, and they undertook to decipher and learn 'these formulas which commanded all the forces of nature and subdued the very gods themselves'. It is to this infinite power which his followers attributed to him that he owes the name Thoth – three times very, very great – which the Greeks translated as Hermes Trismegistus.

After his long reign on earth Thoth ascended to the skies where he undertook various employments.

First of all he was the moon-god, or at least the god in charge of guarding the moon; for this astral body had its own individuality and name: Aah-te-Huti. We have already recounted the legend (see *Nut*) which tells how Thoth played draughts with the moon and won a seventy-second part of its light from which he created the five intercalary days. Elsewhere we are told that the moon is the left eye of Horus, watched over by either an ibis or a dog-headed ape. On the other hand a passage in the Book of the Dead tells us that Ra ordered Thoth to take his own place in the sky whilst he himself 'lighted the blessed in the underworld'. The moon then appeared and in its boat began its nocturnal voyages, each month exposed to the attack of monsters who slowly devoured it but who, happily, were constrained by the moon's faithful champions to disgorge it.

In his quality of lunar divinity Thoth measured the time, which he divided into months (to the first of which he gave his own name) and into years, which in turn were divided into three seasons.

He was the divine regulative force and charged with all calculations and annotations. At Edfu we see him before the temple trinity presenting the register in which is recorded all that concerns the geographical division of the country, its dimensions and resources. At Deir el Bahri we see him proceeding scrupulously with an inventory of treasures brought to the gods of Egypt by a naval expedition on its return from the land of Punt.

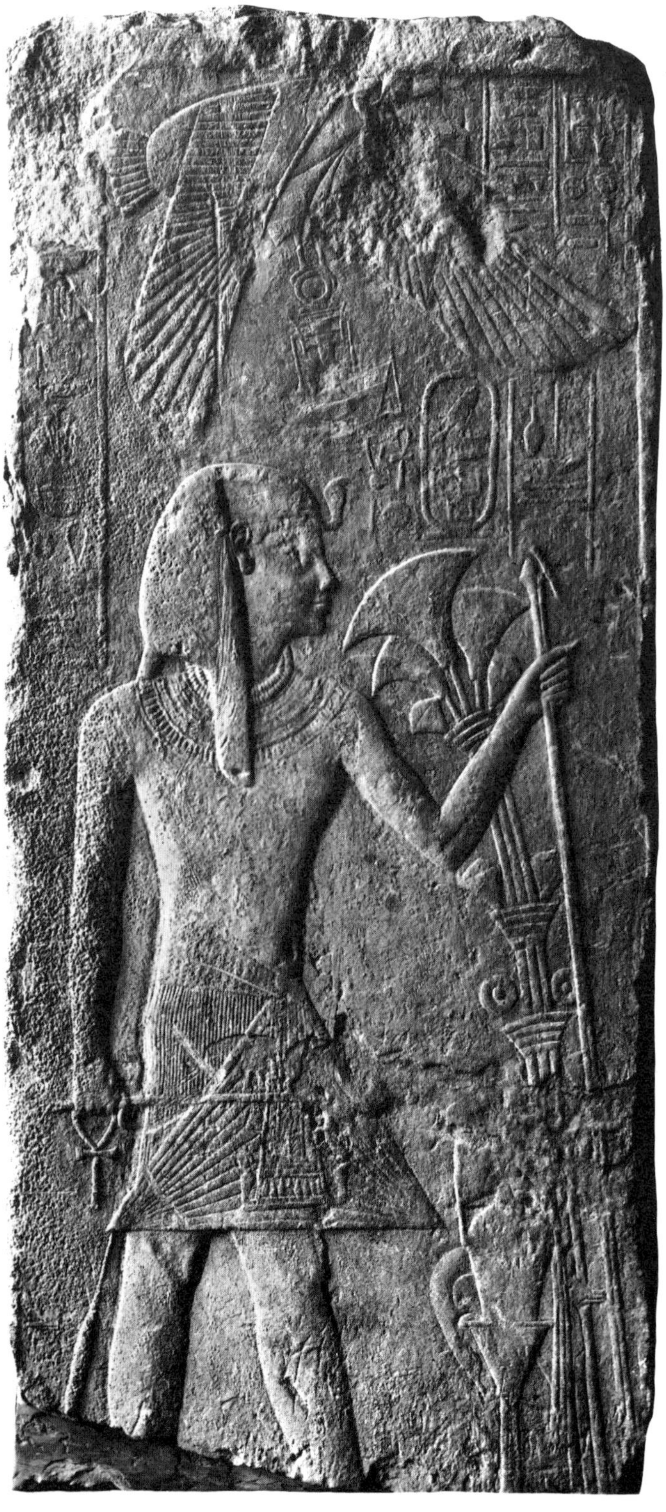

Nekhebet, the goddess, in the form of a vulture with outstretched wings, hovers protectively over the Pharaoh Mem-kau-Heru, of the Fifth Dynasty. Louvre.

Thoth was the keeper of the divine archives and at the same time the patron of history. He carefully noted the succession of the sovereigns and, on the leaves of the sacred tree at Heliopolis, wrote the name of the future Pharaoh whom the queen had just conceived after union with the Lord of the Heavens. On a long palm shoot he also inscribed the happy years of reign which Ra had accorded to the king.

He was the herald of the gods and also often served as their clerk and scribe. 'Ra has spoken, Thoth has written', we read. And during the awful judgment of the dead before Osiris we see Thoth, who has weighed the heart and found it not wanting, proclaim in a loud voice the verdict 'not guilty' which he has just registered on his tablets.

He was invested with the confidence of the gods and chosen by them as arbiter. We have already seen him awarding judgment to Horus and condemning Set. Also, at least from the time of the New Empire, he everywhere replaces Set in coronation scenes, in scenes in which libations are offered to the king, and in the symbolic ceremony of '*sam-taui*'.

The texts often couple him with Maat, the goddess of Truth and Justice; but in no temple do we find them together. On the other hand two spouses of his were known, Seshat and Nehmauit, 'she who uproots evil'. In Heliopolis they form with him two triads with, in the first instance, Hornub as divine son, and in the second Nefer Hor.

Plutarch tells us that the chief festival of the ibis-headed god was celebrated on the nineteenth of the month of Thoth, a few days after the full moon at the beginning of the year. His friends were then approached with the words, 'Sweet is the Truth', and they were presented with many gifts of sweetmeats, honey, figs and other dainties.

Seshat (or **Sesheta**) was Thoth's principal spouse. In reality she is, in her quality of goddess of writing and history, merely his double. At first she was portrayed with the features of a woman wearing on her head a star inscribed in a reversed crescent, surmounted by two long straight plumes, an ideogram of her name which signifies 'the secretary'. Later, due probably to a misunderstanding on the part of sculptors, the crescent was replaced by two long, turned-down horns, from which the goddess derived the title Safekh-Aubi, i.e. 'she who wears (or, perhaps, raises) the two horns'.

She was a stellar divinity who served to measure time; to her – as to Thoth – was ascribed the invention of letters. She was called 'mistress of the house of books'.

She was also called 'mistress of the house of architects' and was represented as the foundress of temples, helping the king to determine the axis of a new sanctuary by the aid of the stars, and marking out the four angles of the edifice with stakes.

As goddess of history and record-keeper for the gods, we see her, alone or in the company of her husband, writing the names of the sovereigns on the leaves of the sacred tree at Heliopolis, or registering on a long palm-leaf the years of reign accorded to the Pharaoh and, on this occasion, drafting the minutes of jubilee celebrations.

As mistress of the scribes she writes on a tablet the balance due to the king from captured enemy booty. When the great sovereign of the eighteenth dynasty, Queen Hatshepsut, sends an expedition to the land of Punt it is Seshat who, on the expedition's return to Thebes, makes the inventory of the treasures brought back. 'Thoth made a note of the quantity', we are told, 'and Seshat verified the figures.'

PROTECTIVE DIVINITIES OF THE PHARAOHS AND THE KINGDOM

In the course of this study we have already met several gods who enjoyed the especial favour of the kings who considered them to be their divine ancestors. Such were Set, formerly Lord of Upper Egypt, but later expelled from the Egyptian pantheon; Horus, of whom every Pharaoh boasted that he was the living incarnation; and Ra, whose son each Pharaoh from the fifth dynasty onwards, proclaimed himself to be. We shall now review, in the chronological order in which their dynastic importance appears most marked, certain other divinities.

Nekhebet, who was identified by the Greeks as Eileithyia, protectress of childbirth, was from the earliest times the protective goddess of Upper Egypt. The centre of her cult was at El Kab, the former Nekheb, which the Greeks called Eileithyiaspolis, capital of the oldest kingdom in the South.

In war and offertory scenes she often appears hovering over the Pharaoh's head in the form of a vulture, holding in her claws the fly-whisk and the seal.

She is also sometimes portrayed as a divinity with the bald head of a vulture, or as a woman wearing the white crown of Upper Egypt either on her head or on a headdress shaped like a vulture.

As a mother goddess Nekhebet suckled the royal children; often we see her suckling the Pharaoh himself.

Buto, a transcription of Per Uadjit, 'the dwelling of Uadjit', was the name which the Greeks gave to the Delta town and also to the goddess who was worshipped there. She was the ancient protectress of Lower Egypt.

The Osirian legend recounts that Buto, sovereign of the Delta, allied herself with Isis and helped protect her infant child. She gathered up the baby Horus from the floating island of Chemmis, for which reason she was afterwards identified with Latona, the mother of Apollo.

Buto was a snake-goddess, frequently represented in the form of a cobra, sometimes winged and sometimes crowned. She also often has the features of a woman wearing, either directly on her head or on a head-dress in the form of a vulture, the red crown of the North, of which she was the official protectress as Nekhebet was of the white crown of the South.

The vulture-goddess and the cobra-goddess, known conjointly as Nebti – 'the two mistresses' – appear side by side on royal documents. Sometimes they embellish the Pharaoh's forehead in order to protect him against his enemies, though normally only the Uraeus appears.

Mont (Menthu) was the Theban god of war whom the Greeks, because of his solar character, identified with Apollo. He appears at the beginning of the Middle Kingdom when he was particularly venerated by the kings of the eleventh dynasty, many of whom took the name Menthu-hetep, 'Mont is satisfied'.

He is usually represented as a personage whose falcon head is surmounted by the solar disk and two tall straight plumes. At a later period he also appears as a man with a bull's head embellished with the same attributes. The bull was actually the animal sacred to him. The bull in which he preferred to become incarnate was the celebrated Buchis which was piously tended at Hermonthis, the sun's residence in Upper Egypt. Hermonthis was the former capital of this region and Mont, the sun-god, was for many long centuries its lord and master before he was demoted to second rank by his former vassal, Amon of Thebes, who became king of the gods.

Having ousted Mont, Amon, whose wife was barren, wished to adopt him as divine son in the Theban Triad; but the former sovereign of the entire region could not long be happy in such a subordinate position. Mont therefore chose to dwell apart at Hermonthis, of which he remained the uncontested master, and at Medamud, in the suburbs of Thebes, where numerous votaries came to worship him in company with his wife Rat-taui.

A solar god of warlike character, Mont was represented as the god of war under the New Kingdom. He brandished the *khepesh,* which was a kind of very curved scimitar, and cut off the heads of the Pharaoh's enemies. We see him offering the Pharaoh his invincible weapon and leading his vanquished enemies in chains. Temple bas-reliefs also often show Mont, as sun-god of the South, with Atum, sun-god of the North, escorting the king into the sanctuary.

Amon (Amun, Ammon) is the name of the great Egyptian deity who was often given the title 'king of the gods'. For this reason the Greeks identified him with Zeus. He was almost unknown in the time of the Old Kingdom. His name – which seems to be derived from a root meaning 'hidden' – only appears four times in the Heliopolitan texts of the pyramids. Perhaps he originally belonged to the cosmological system of Hermopolis which we have already discussed, and was one of those 'eight gods' who emerged from the mouth of Thoth. Thebes, which afterwards was to erect such gigantic temples in his honour, was at that time only a village in the fourth nome (or province) of Upper Egypt, the capital of which was Hermonthis, city of Mont, who was then Lord of all that region.

It was with the first king of the twelfth dynasty, whose name, Amenemhat, signifies 'Amon leads', that Thebes and its god began to take on an importance which was to become considerable under the great conquerors of the eighteenth dynasty – called Thuthmosis and Amenhotep and proudly proclaiming themselves to be 'sons of Amon'.

Amon by this time had dispossessed Mont and become the great divinity of the whole country of which Thebes – which was called Nut Amon, the 'city of Amon', or simply Nut, 'the city' – was henceforth the capital.

Amon normally appears with bronzed human features wearing as a head-dress a kind of crown which supports two straight tall parallel plumes. Sometimes he is seated majestically on a throne. Sometimes he stands with a whip raised above his head, in the ithyphallic pose of the god Min.

He is also at times represented with the head of a ram with curled horns, and at Karnak an animal of this sort was religiously tended, a living incarnation of the god. They also kept a goose which was Amon's other sacred animal.

The phallic Amon represented the forces of generation and reproduction. He was often called 'his mother's husband' and was supposed to initiate and then maintain the continuity of creative life. He was the god of fertility, and we see the king, in his presence, sowing grain and cutting the first sheaf.

He was the patron of the most powerful Pharaohs; he acknowledged them as his sons and gave them victory over their enemies. It was, then, quite natural that the god of Thebes should become pre-eminently the national god. The faithful proclaimed him 'king of the gods' under the name Amon-Ra; for when the theologians had obligingly identified him with Ra, the old sun-god, Amon assumed Ra's position as universal Demiurge and chief of the great Ennead. Pictured in the royal tombs we see Amon-Ra enthroned in the sun's boat and, during the twelve hours of night, illuminating the underworld.

Ra, however, had never abdicated his ancient authority, and under the name of Ra-Harakhte he always enjoyed his own distinct cult. Indeed, under the reign of Amenhotep III, there was a reaction in Ra's favour, no doubt encouraged by the priests of Heliopolis who were jealous of Amon's immense fortune and the omnipotence which this parvenu among the gods claimed. The texts and bas-reliefs on the walls of the temple of Luxor glorify the divine birth of Amenhotep as a result of Amon's love for the queen-mother, wife of Thuthmosis IV. But on the death of Amenhotep the cult of Ra-Harakhte gained new importance. Under the already venerable name 'Aten of the Day' – i.e. 'The solar disk whence issues the light of day', his visible form and true name – Ra-Harakhte, it would seem, engaged in a struggle against his rival Amon which was so successful that Amon was momentarily humbled. In the fourth year of his reign Amenhotep's son and successor proclaimed a great religious reform and decreed that only the religion of Aten was official.

Full of zeal for his new god, the reforming Pharaoh began by changing his name Amenhotep ('Amon is satisfied') to Akhenaton ('The glory of Aten'). He hastened to abandon Thebes for a new capital city, Akhetaten – the present-day Tell-el-Amarna – which he had built in Middle Egypt to the glory of the solar disk.

There were no statues of Aten. Bas-reliefs and paintings always represent him in the form of a great red disk from which fan out long rays tipped with hands which have seized offerings laid on altars, or which present to the king, the queen and their daughters the hieroglyphs of life and strength. The Pharaoh was his only priest, and his cult was celebrated in a temple resembling the ancient solar temples of the Old Kingdom and called, like the celebrated sanctuary of Ra at Heliopolis, Het Benben, 'the Palace of the Obelisk'. There, at the extremity of a vast courtyard, rose the obelisk of the sun. The ceremony consisted of an oblation of fruits and cakes and the recitation of hymns of great beauty, which were composed by the king himself, in honour of his god. In them the sun was glorified, as in olden days, as creator of mankind and benefactor of the world, but without those allusions to early mythological legends of which the ancient hymns to Ra had been full. The hymns could thus be sung and understood not only by the inhabitants of the Nile

Pillars decorated with stylised lotus and papyrus plants in the temple of Amon at Karnak, one of two great sanctuaries dedicated to the sovereign god of Thebes. Amon was worshipped here in company with Mut, his wife, and their son Khons.

Amon. The god is portrayed in human form wearing his characteristic plumed head-dress and seated on a throne. Between his knees he holds a headless figure of Tut-ankh-Amon whom he places under his protection. Having suffered a temporary eclipse under Akhenaton, the god had been restored to his position of supremacy by the young Pharaoh, probably under pressure from the priests. Statue from Thebes. Eighteenth dynasty, 1587 to 1375 B.C.

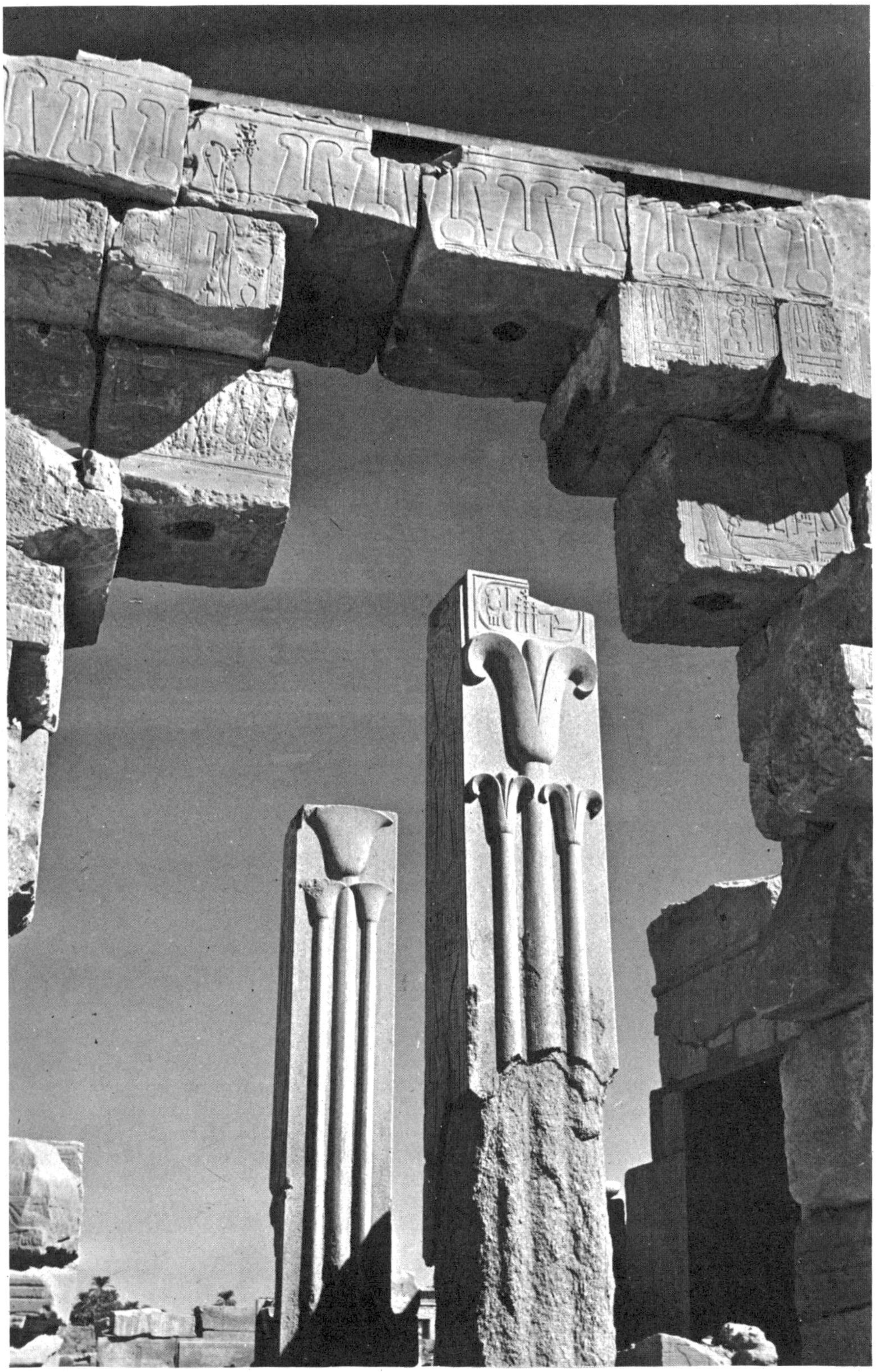

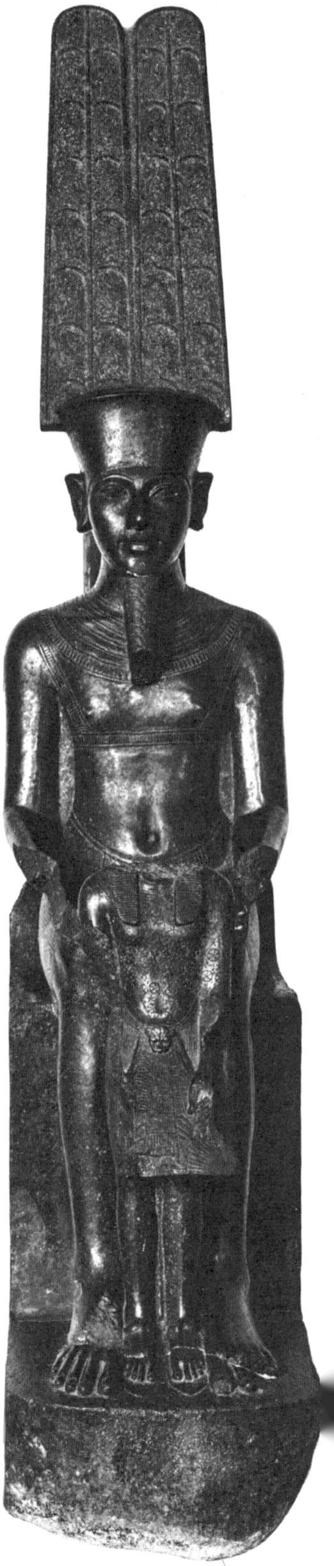

Amon. The king of the gods is represented seated on his throne and with the head of a ram. Originally represented as a goose or a ram when still a local deity of Thebes, he retains here, in addition to the ram's head, two goose feathers which he wears upon his head. His curved horns were adopted by Alexander the Great after he was recognized as the Son of Amon in 332 B.C. Statuette of the twenty-sixth dynasty, 672 to 525 B.C.

Akhenaton and Nefertiti, followed by one of their daughters, present offerings to their god Aten, who is represented by a solar disk the rays of which terminate in hands. Stela of the Eighteenth Dynasty, 1580 to 1350. Cairo.

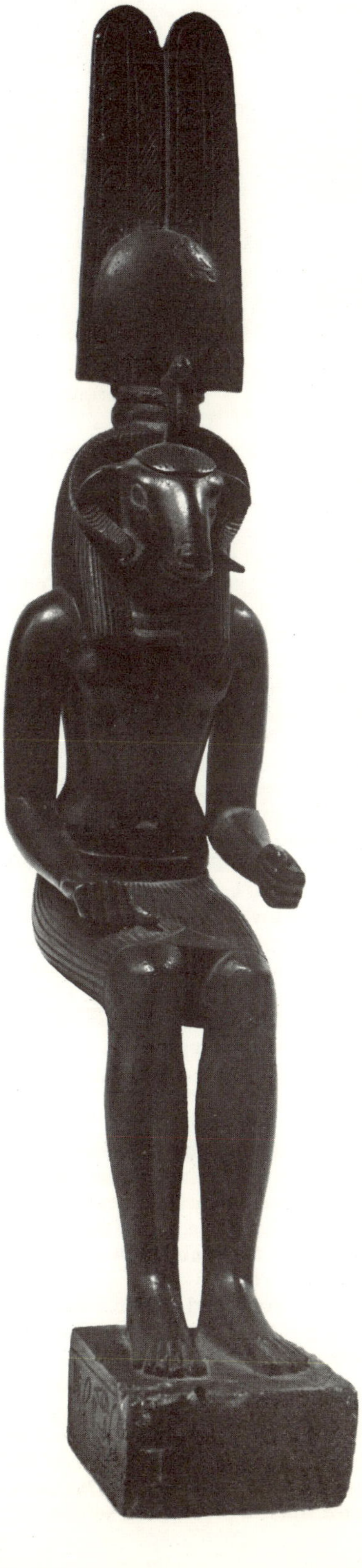

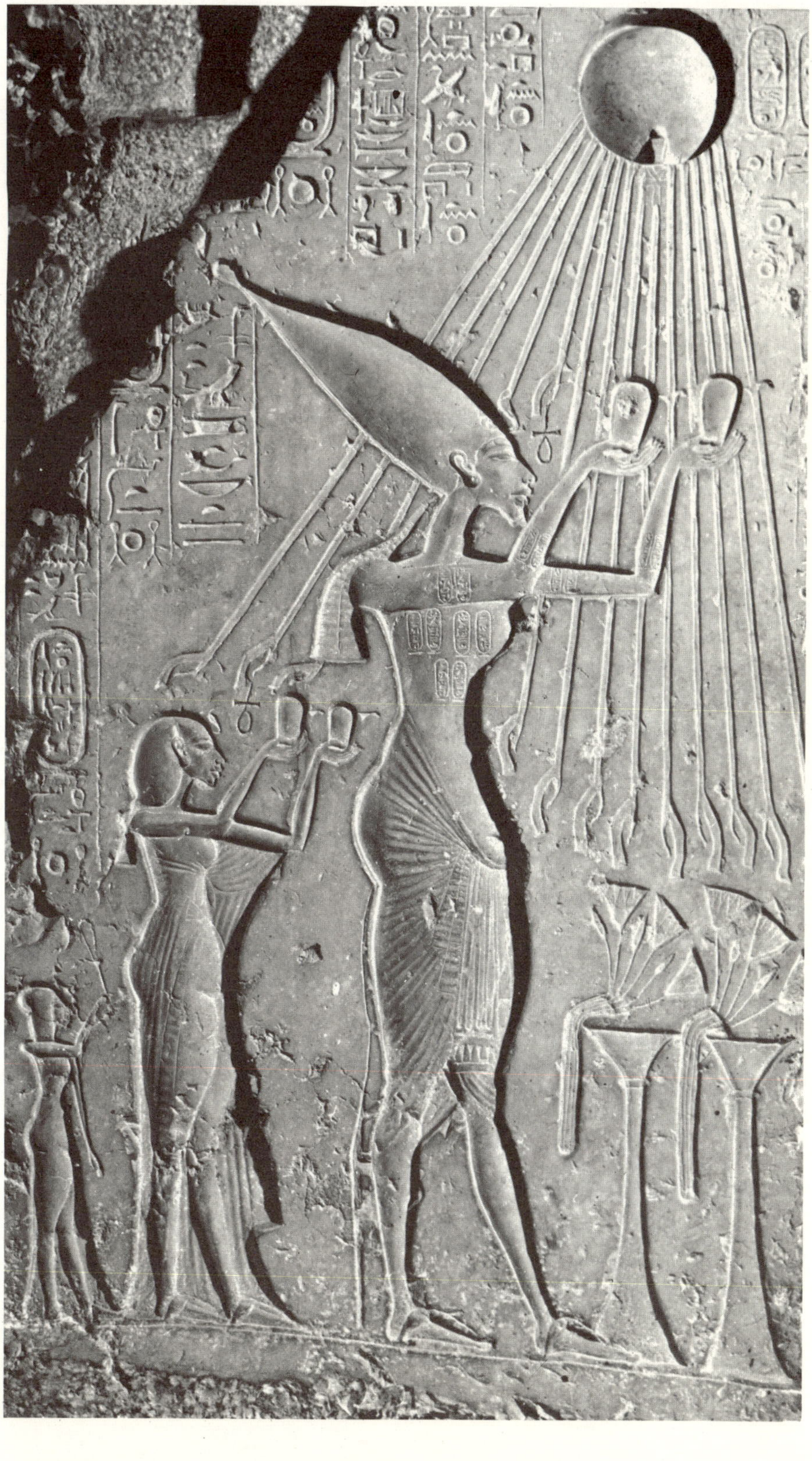

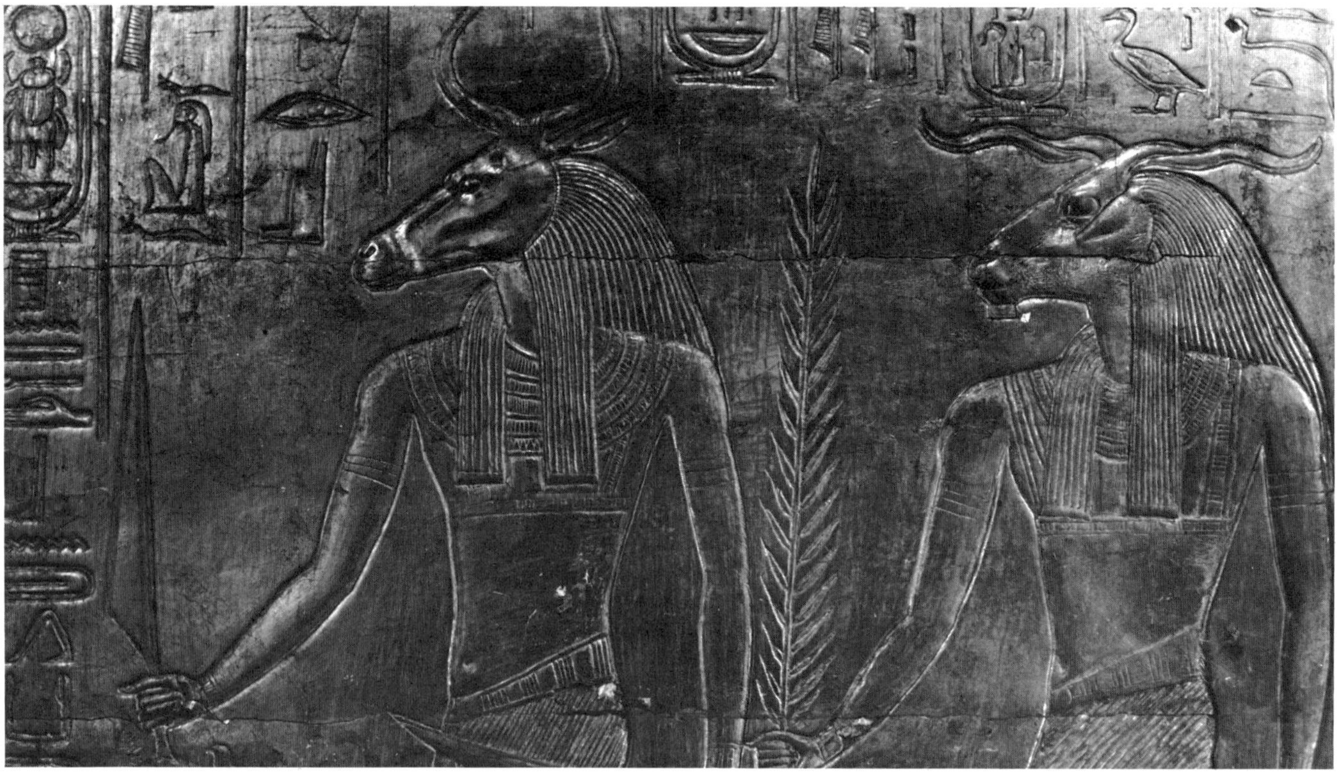

Gods of the Underworld. Two zoomorphic gods, one bullheaded, the other ram-headed, holding knives and a bough, stand guard over the third gate of the Underworld. Detail from the second shrine of Tut-ankh-Amon. Relief incised into gold foil on a thin layer of gesso. Eighteenth dynasty, 1587 to 1375 B.C.

Valley but also by foreigners. All men, they proclaimed, were equally the children of Aten. In this modified attempt at monotheism we may suspect plans for an Empire-wide religion, especially if it is remembered that at this time Egyptian domination extended as far as Asia, where the Syrians worshipped Adonis and the Jews worshipped Adonai.

As long as the king lived there was no official god in Egypt but Aten. The other gods were proscribed and bitter war declared against them, especially against Amon and his trinity. Their temples were despoiled and their riches given to the solar disk. Their statues were broken and the bas-reliefs on which they appeared were mutilated, while Amon's name was harried from the most inaccessible places. It was chiselled off and removed from all the royal tablets, even from those of Amenhotep III, the Pharaoh's own father.

The new religion, it is true, was ephemeral, and on the death of the reformer, or very shortly afterwards, his own son denied his father's name and restored the cult of Amon. He changed his heretical name Tut-ankh-Aten ('Living image of Aten') into the orthodox Tut-ankh-Amon ('Living image of Amon'). Wherever it was found, the old name was replaced by the new. But there were oversights, and on the magnificent throne of the young Pharaoh, recently removed from his celebrated tomb, we can still read the two names almost side by side – a silent witness to the prince's heresy and to its abjuration.

Restored to all his former splendour by Horemheb and the kings of the nineteenth dynasty who heaped his temples with gifts, Amon, from thenceforth definitely incorporated with Ra, saw his fortune grow to such a point that it reached three-quarters of that of all the other gods combined. An inventory of his wealth made under Rameses III tells us that he possessed, among other riches, 81,322 slaves and 421,362 head of cattle. His high priests, the first prophets of Amon, were chosen from among the most powerful lords. They soon became hereditary and, after playing the role of royal comptrollers to the weak sovereigns of the twentieth dynasty, finally seized the crown itself. Herihor, the priest, succeeded the last of the Rameses to the throne. During the troubles that ensued Thebes ceased to be the royal seat and political capital of Egypt. It remained from then on the exclusive property of Amon and became a kind of theocratic state where the god wielded power, either directly through his oracles or by the mediation, no longer as in the past of his chief prophet, but of his earthly spouse. This was normally the king's daughter, 'the god's wife', 'the god's adorer'. She was paid the highest honour, ruled the town and administered the immense domains of the god, her husband.

Sovereign of Thebes, Amon extended his power beyond the frontiers of Egypt into Ethiopia where, through his oracles at Napata and Meroe, he himself chose the kings. He deposed them and ordered their death, thus exercising a tyrannical domination which only ended in the third century B.C. when Ergamenes threw off the priests' yoke and had them put to death.

Amon's power over the desert tribes of Libya was equally great and until the latest epoch pilgrims crowded in great numbers to that venerable oasis-temple of Amon – or of Jupiter Ammon – where the celebrated oracle had, in 332 B.C., saluted Alexander the Great and called him 'Son of Amon'.

Amon's most magnificent sanctuaries were, however, at Thebes on the right bank of the Nile, at Luxor and at Karnak, whose ruins to-day still fill us with admiration, and where he was worshipped in company with Mut, his wife, and their son Khons. On the bas-reliefs which cover the walls and columns we see the king of the gods on his throne, where he receives the perpetual adoration of the Pharaoh, whom at times he embraces and whom he infuses with the magic fluid 'sa'. Elsewhere he gives the breath of life to him and grants him long years of reign. He hands him the *khepesh* of battle and, trampling the vanquished underfoot, delivers over enemy towns. Finally Amon is shown holding on his knees the queen with whom he will unite in order to produce the next Pharaoh, his son.

Mut, being Amon-Ra's wife, was identified by the Greeks with Hera. She is a vague and ill-defined deity whose name signified 'Mother'. She is represented as a woman wearing a head-dress in the form of a vulture, an ideogram of her name. Again she wears a heavy wig surmounted by the *pschent* – the double crown to which, as wife of the king of the gods, she had a right.

She grew in stature along with her spouse and when he, under the name Amon-Ra, had become the great god of the heavens she also became a solar deity. She was sometimes identified with Bast, whose cat-form she assumed; and with Sekhmet, from whom she borrowed the head of a lioness.

A text tells us that as a sky-goddess she remained – in the form of a cow – behind Amon when he emerged from the waves and broke from the egg at Hermopolis. 'He mounted on her back, seized her horns, and dismounted where it pleased him so to do.'

When she had long been childless Mut first adopted Mont, then Khons. It is with Khons as child that she entered the celebrated Theban triad of which Amon was the chief.

Khons (Khensu), whose name means 'the Navigator' or 'He who crosses the sky in a boat', seems originally to have been a moon-god, little known beyond the region of Thebes. It is a puzzle why the Greeks sometimes identified him with Hercules.

Khons is ordinarily represented in the form of a personage swathed like Ptah, whose composite sceptre he holds before him. His head is completely shaven except for one temple which is adorned by the heavy tress of a royal child. He wears a skullcap surmounted by a disk in a crescent moon. At first rather obscure, Khons rose to the ranks of the great gods when he was adopted by Amon and Mut and replaced Mont as their son in the Theban triad. It is only under the New Kingdom, however, that he seems to have begun to enjoy great popularity as an exorcist and healer. The possessed and the sick from all over Egypt and even from abroad had recourse to him. In the case of those from abroad Khons delegated his powers to a statue in which he incarnated a double of himself, commanding it to go forth and cure his suppliants. Thus we see the great Khons Neferhotep of Karnak, whose aid the Syrian prince of Bakhtan had implored on behalf of his daughter, delegate a second Khons in Syria who was named 'He who executes the designs and who expels the rebels'. Space is lacking to recount in detail how the divine substitute accomplished his mission and drove from the princess's body the demon which had tormented her; how at the end of three years and nine months he appeared in a dream to her father in the form of a golden falcon who flew swiftly towards Egypt; and how the grateful prince then hastened to take back the divine statue with the greatest ceremony together with costly gifts which were deposited in the temple of Karnak at the feet of the great Khons Neferhotep.

Khons was much venerated at Thebes and also worshipped at Ombos where he formed the third person in the triad of Sebek under the name Khons Hor, who was represented as a man with a falcon's head surmounted with a disk in a crescent moon.

In conclusion it may be remarked that one of the months of the year was named Pakhons, which means 'the month of Khons'.

Sebek (in Greek, Suchos) is the name of a crocodile divinity who figured among the patrons of the kings of the thirteenth dynasty, many of whom were called Sebekhotep, 'Sebek is satisfied'.

The god was represented either as a man with the head of a crocodile or simply as a crocodile. In a lake attached to his chief sanctuary an actual crocodile was kept. It was called Petesuchos, 'He who belongs to Suchos' (or to Sebek), and it was said that the god was incarnate therein.

We know little of the origins of Sebek. A pyramid text calls him the son of Neith. But, as Maspero has pointed out, it is easy to conceive that the presence nearby of a swamp or a rock-encumbered rapid could have suggested to the inhabitiants of the Fayyum of Ombos that the crocodile was the supreme god who must be appeased by sacrifice and prayers. To his worshippers no doubt Sebek was none other than the Demiurge who, on the day of creation, issued from the dark waters where until then he had reposed, in order to arrange the world – as the crocodile emerges from the river to deposit her eggs on the bank. Possibly because the name Sebek sounds in Egyptian a little like Geb he was sometimes given Geb's titles.

Sebek was especially venerated in the Fayyum. The whole province was under his protection and his principal sanctuary was in the former Shedet, the Crocodilopolis of the Greeks. We shall have occasion to speak further of this when we study the animals sacred to the Egyptians.

Sebek was the object of a cult in Upper Egypt also. One can still see to-day at Kom Ombo – the former Ombos – ruins of the temple where Sebek's triad was worshipped, as was a second triad of which Horus was the chief. Perhaps here Sebek really replaced the former Lord, Set the Ombite, whom the pious worshippers of Horus would not tolerate. What is certain is that Sebek often shared Set's evil reputation. He was reproached with having aided the murderer of Osiris when Set, to escape punishment for his crime, took refuge in the body of a crocodile. That was why these animals, worshipped in certain provinces, were hunted down and destroyed in others.

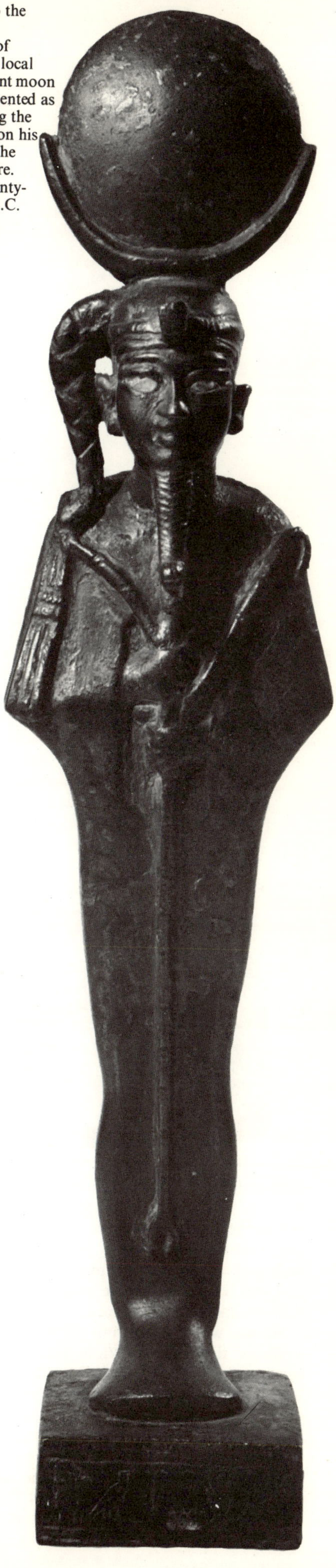

Khons. A later addition to the Theban triad in which he replaced Mont as the son of Amon and Mut, Khons, a local moon god, wears the crescent moon upon his head and is represented as a youthful mummy wearing the tress of the royal children on his right temple and carrying the crook and flail and a sceptre. Bronze statuette of the twenty-sixth dynasty, 672 to 525 B.C.

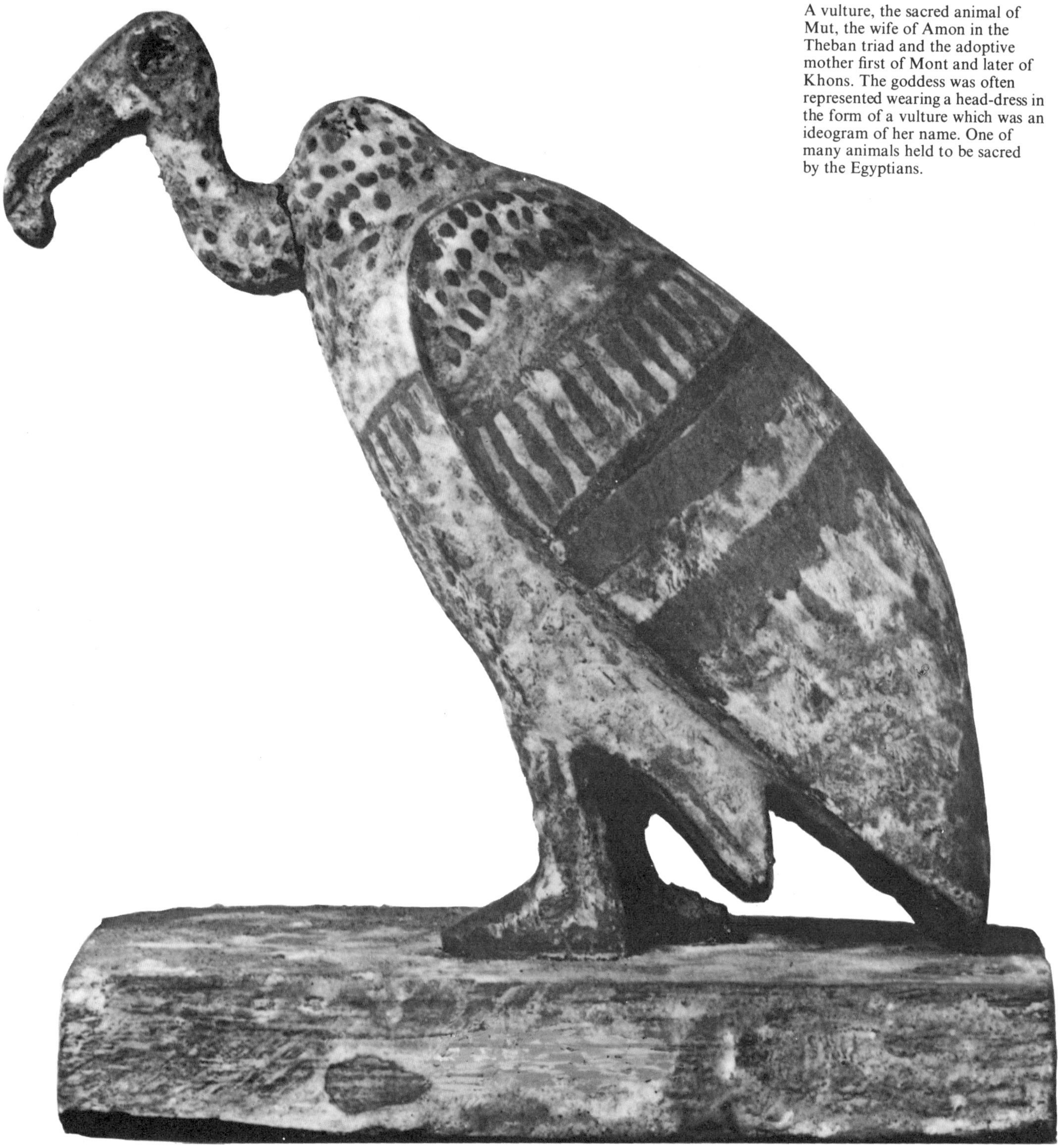

A vulture, the sacred animal of Mut, the wife of Amon in the Theban triad and the adoptive mother first of Mont and later of Khons. The goddess was often represented wearing a head-dress in the form of a vulture which was an ideogram of her name. One of many animals held to be sacred by the Egyptians.

Ptah of Memphis, in his aspect ot protector of artisans and artists, was identified by the Greeks with Hephaestus. He is normally represented as a mummified figure, often raised on a pedestal inside the *naos* of a temple, his skull enclosed in a tight head-band and his body swathed in mummy-wrappings. Only his hands are free and hold a composite sceptre uniting the emblems of life, of stability and of omnipotence.

He was worshipped from the earliest times at Memphis where, south of the ancient 'White Wall' of Menes, he possessed the celebrated temple of Ptah-Beyond-the-Walls. Ptah must always have been of first importance as sovereign god of the old capital of the North, the city where the Pharaohs were crowned. But little is known of his role before the advent of the nineteenth dynasty, whose great kings, Seti I and Rameses II, held him in particular devotion, while one soveregin of the same dynasty even bore the name Siptah, which signified 'Son of Ptah'.

It was, however, after the extinction of the last of the Rameses, when the political role of the Delta had become predominant, that the god of Memphis attained his full glory. Of all the gods of Egypt he was then third in importance and wealth, yielding only to Amon and Ra; and not even to them in the estimation of his own priest, who proudly proclaimed him to be the Universal Demiurge who had with his own hands fashioned the world.

Ptah was the patron of artisans and artists and the inventor of the arts. He was at the same time designer, smelter of metal and builder. His high priest at Memphis bore a title analogous to the 'Master Builder' of our medieval cathedrals. It was he who during the construction of a temple directed architects and masons.

To-day there remain only shapeless ruins of the celebrated temple of Memphis where priests showed Herodotus the ex-votos commemorating the great miracles performed by Ptah. Among others was the occasion on which he had saved Pelusium from Sennacherib's attacking Assyrians by raising an army of rats, who forced the assailants to retreat by gnawing their bowstrings, quivers, and the leather thongs of their shields.

In this temple Ptah was worshipped in company with his consort

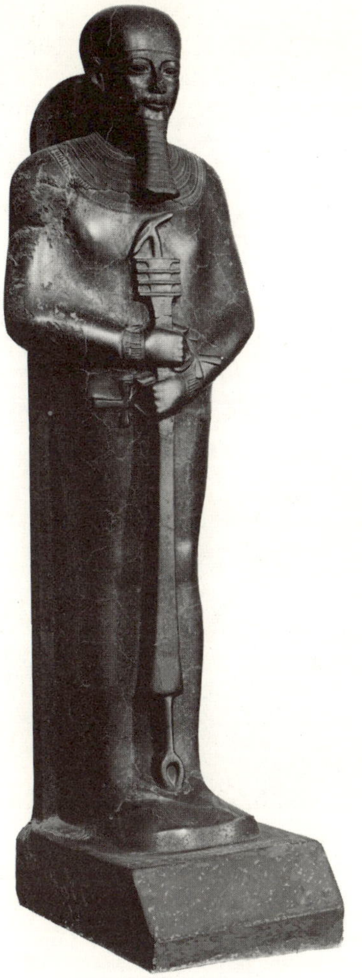

Ptah. The sovereign god of Memphis, the old capital of the north, Ptah was proclaimed the creator of the world by his priests and was the object of the particular devotion of a number of the Pharaohs. He was normally represented as a mummified figure holding a composite sceptre uniting the emblems of life, stability and omnipotence. Bronze statue.

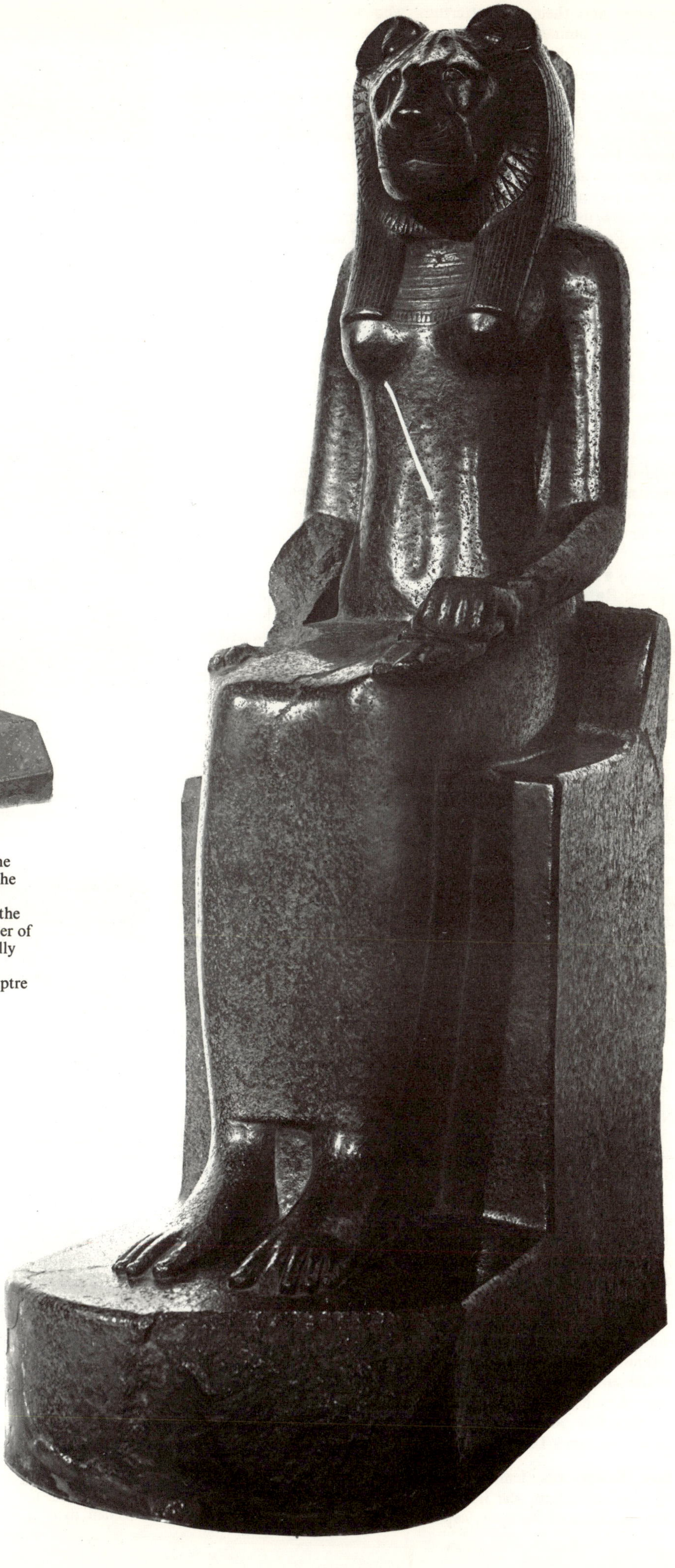

Sekhmet. 'The Beloved of Ptah' is represented as a woman with the head of a lioness seated on a throne. Originally a divinity of Latopolis to the north of Memphis, she joined the Memphis triad as the wife of Ptah to whom she bore a son, Nefertum, later replaced by the deified human, Imhotep. Black granite statue of the eighteenth dynasty from Karnak *c.* 1500 B.C.

Sekhmet and their son Nefertum, who was later succeeded by Imhotep, a human hero deified. Near the sanctuary was piously tended the celebrated bull Apis, a living incarnation of the god. We shall speak of Apis in the final section of this study.

Although Ptah was apt to be called 'fair of face' he is sometimes depicted as a deformed dwarf with twisted legs, hands on hips and a huge head, shaved except for the childish lock. Thus represented, Ptah plays the role of protector against noxious animals and against all kinds of evils. He was early identified with the very ancient and obscure earth-god Tenen and also with Seker, of whom we shall write briefly below. He was frequently invoked under the names Ptah Tenen, Ptah Seker and even Ptah Seker Osiris.

Seker (the Greek rendering is Sucharis) was doubtless a vegetation god before he became the god of the dead in the Memphis necropolis. There, in the form of a greenish hawk-headed mummy, he was worshipped in a sanctuary called Ro Stau ('the doors of the corridors') which communicated directly with the underworld. He was early identified with Osiris and brought to Osiris all his own local worshippers. It was under the name Seker Osiris that the god of the dead was usually worshipped in Memphis. In the end the great funerary divinity became Ptah Seker Osiris.

Sekhmet (rendered in Greek as Sakhmis) is the name of the terrible goddess of war and battle who is usually represented as a lioness or a woman with the head of a lioness.

Her name, which means 'the Powerful', is simply a title of Hathor which was given to Hathor on the occasion when in the form of a lioness she hurled herself on the men who had rebelled against Ra. As we have already seen she attacked them with such fury that the sun-god, fearing the extermination of the human race, begged her to arrest the carnage. 'By thy life', she answered him, 'when I slay men my heart rejoices', and she refused to spare her victims. For this reason she was later given the name Sekhmet and represented in the form of a savage lioness. In order to save what remained of the human race Ra had recourse to a stratagem. He spread across the bloody battlefield seven thousand jugs containing a magic potion composed of beer and pomegranate juice. Sekhmet, who was thirsty, mistook this red liquid for human blood and drank it so avidly that she became too drunk to continue the slaughter. The human race was saved; but to appease the goddess, Ra decreed that 'on that day there should be brewed in her honour as many jugs of the philtre as there were priestesses of the sun'. This was henceforth done annually on the feast day of Hathor. The great massacre had taken place on the twelfth day of the first month of winter; thus the calendar of lucky and unlucky days carefully notes: 'Hostile, hostile, hostile is the 12th Tybi. Avoid seeing a mouse on this day; for it is the day when Ra gave the order to Sekhmet.'

The goddess was called 'the beloved of Ptah'; for, though originally a divinity of Latopolis, she joined the Memphis Triad as Ptah's wife, bearing him a son, Nefertum.

Attached to her cult were bone-setters who, with her intercession, cured fractures.

Nefertum, which the Greeks rendered as Iphtimis, is the name of the original divine son of the Memphis Triad. The Greeks identified him with Prometheus, perhaps because his father was said to be Ptah Hephaestus, the discoverer of fire.

He is habitually represented as a man armed with the curved sabre called the *khepesh.* His head is surmounted by an open lotus flower from which springs a horned stalk, and he often appears standing on a crouched lion. Sometimes he has the head of this lion, which he doubtless owes to his mother, the lion-goddess Sekhmet.

His name, which signifies 'Atum the Younger', clearly indicates that he was at first an incarnation of Atum of Heliopolis, a rejuvenated Atum who at dawn sprang from the divine lotus, asylum of the sun during the night. A native of Lower Egypt, he was considered as the son of Ptah, and his mother became that god's spouse. He therefore occupied – before Imhotep – the third place in the oldest Memphis Triad.

Bast (Bastet) was identified by the Greeks with Artemis, probably by confusion with the lioness-headed goddess Tefnut. She was local goddess of Bubastis, capital of the eighteenth nome or pro-

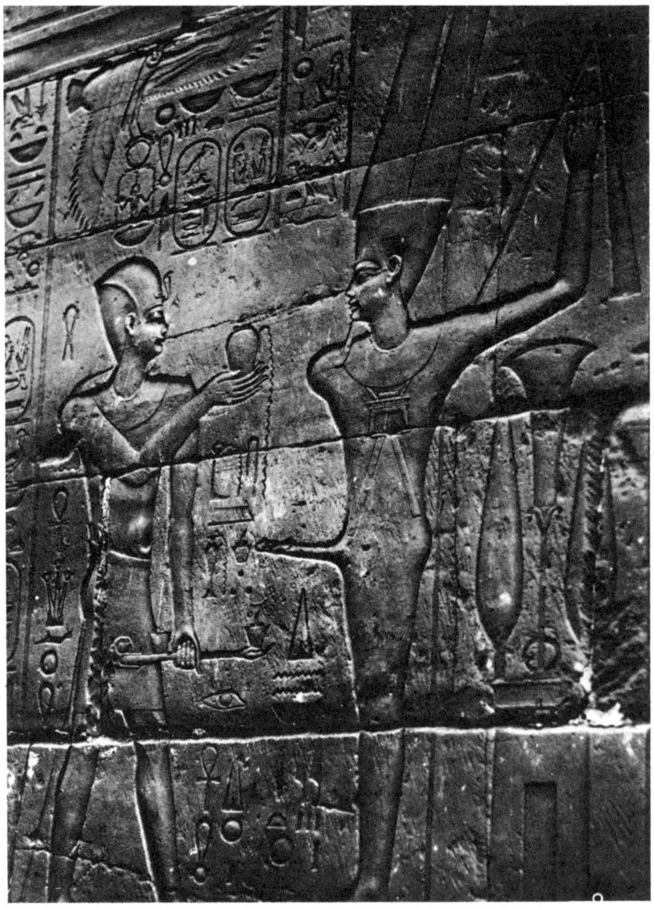

Min receiving a libation. The ithyphallic fertility god stands with his flail raised behind his head and wearing a plumed head-dress which was probably borrowed from Amon.
The Pharaoh pours him a libation with his right hand and holds burning incense in his left. The local god of Coptos,
Min was chiefly worshipped in the classical period as the protector of travellers. Bas-relief, Luxor.

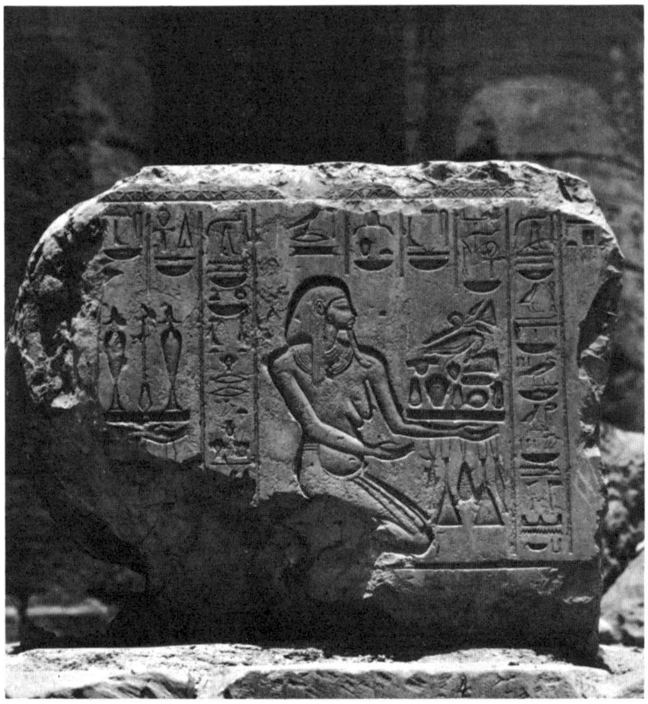

Hapi, the god of the Nile. The kneeling god wears the narrow belt of the Nile fishermen and boatmen and holds in his hands the riches provided by the fertilising waters. Invoked to procure the flooding of the river, Hapi was not connected with any theological system.
Bas-relief in the temple of Medinet Habu.
Twentieth dynasty, 1202 to 1102 B.C.

vince of Lower Egypt. Bubastis is a transcription of Per Bast, i.e. 'The House of Bast'. She became the great national divinity when, about 950 B.C., with Sheshonk and the Libyan Pharaohs of the twenty-second dynasty, Bubastis became the capital of the kingdom.

Though in origin a lioness-goddess, personifying the fertilising warmth of the sun, her sacred animal later became the cat, and she is represented as a cat-headed woman holding in her right hand either a sistrum or an aegis, composed of a semi-circular breastplate surmounted with the head of a lioness. In her left hand she carries a basket.

She was related to the sun-god whom some called her father and others her brother-spouse; and she became – like Sekhmet, with whom she is frequently confused in spite of their very dissimilar characters – the wife of Ptah of Memphis and with him formed a a triad in which Nefertum was the third person.

Although, as patron of the kings of Bubastis, Bast had already become one of the great divinities of Egypt, it was in the fourth century B.C. that she achieved her greatest popularity. She existed also in secondary forms as Pekhet, the cat or lion-headed goddess of Speos Artemidos, to the east of Beni Hasan.

Like Hathor she was a goddess of pleasure and loved music and the dance. She would beat time with the sistrum, often decorated with the figure of a cat, which she grasped in her hand. In her benevolence she also protected men against contagious disease and evil spirits.

Great and joyful festivals were periodically celebrated in her temple at Bubastis. Herodotus tells us that it was one of the most elegant in Egypt and recounts how the devout came in hundreds of thousands from all over the country for the huge annual fair. The journey took place by barges to the sound of flutes and castanets. Buffoonery and jokes were bandied between the pilgrims and the women on the banks of the river who watched the barges as they passed, and everything was a pretext for pleasantry and masquerade. On the appointed day a splendid procession wound through the town and festivities followed during which, it seems, more wine was drunk than during all the rest of the year.

To please the cat-goddess her devotees consecrated statues of this animal in great numbers, and in the shadow of her sanctuaries it was a pious custom to bury the carefully mummified bodies of cats who during their lifetime had been venerated as animals sacred to Bast. (See *Sacred Animals.*)

Neith (Neit), whom the Greeks identified with their Pallas Athene, is the name of a Delta divinity. She was protectress of Sais, which became capital of Egypt towards the middle of the seventh century B.C. when Psammetichus I, founder of the twenty-sixth dynasty, mounted the throne, thus assuring the wealth and importance of his local goddess.

She was, in fact, an extremely ancient divinity; for her fetish – two crossed arrows on an animal skin – was carried on the standard of a prehistoric clan, and two queens of the first dynasty derived their names from hers.

Her epithet Tehenut, 'the Libyan', suggests that she probably originated in the west. She always remained important in Sais after having been, in very early times perhaps, considered to be the national divinity of Lower Egypt whose red crown she habitually wears. The crown was called 'Net', which sounds like her own name.

In the beginning she was worshipped in the form of a fetish composed of two crossed arrows on a shield or the mottled skin of an animal. Later she was represented with the features of a woman wearing the crown of the North and holding in her hand a bow and arrows. Still later her attribute became a weaver's shuttle, an ideogram of her name, which she sometimes wears on her head as a distinguishing emblem.

Neith, indeed, appears in a double role: as a warrior-goddess and as a woman skilled in the domestic arts. This is why she was identified with Athene, who also played this double role.

When, with the advent of the Sais dynasty, her preponderance was established, she played a part in many cosmogonic myths. She was made a sky-goddess like Nut and Hathor, and she was proclaimed to be mother of the gods in general and of Ra in particular 'whom she bore before childbirth existed'.

She was the great weaver who wove the world with her shuttle as a woman weaves cloth. Under the name Mehueret she was the Celestial Cow who gave birth to the sky when nothing existed.

She was introduced into the Osirian cult and confounded with Isis; she became protectress of the dead and we sometimes see her offering them the bread and water on their arrival in the other world.

Just as Isis and Nephthys are frequently found together in pictures and texts, so Neith often appears with Selket, either as guardian of the mummy and viscera of the dead, or as protectress of marriage.

To-day nothing remains of her celebrated temple at Sais where, Plutarch tells us, could be read the following inscription: 'I am all that has been, that is, and that will be. No mortal has yet been able to lift the veil which covers me.'

To this sanctuary was annexed a school of medicine, 'The House of Life', directed by the priests. Later, under the Persians, Darius' Egyptian doctor boasted that he had re-organised this medical school under royal protection.

DIVINITIES OF RIVER AND DESERT

Khnum (Khnemu), which was rendered in Greek as Khnoumis, was a god of the region of the Cataracts. He is portrayed as a ram-headed man with long wavy horns, unlike the curved horns of the ram-headed Amon.

He was a god of fecundity and creation and was originally worshipped under the form of a ram or a he-goat. Like all gods of this sort he doubtless, according to Maspero, symbolised the Nile which comes from the heavens to fertilise the earth and make it fruitful. His chief sanctuary was near the Cataracts, not far from the spot where the earliest Egyptians placed the source of their great river, on that Isle of Elephantine of which Khnum was proclaimed sovereign lord.

From his temple, where he received offerings in company with his two wives, Sati and Anukis – who were, as far as we know, childless – Khnum watched over the sources of the Nile.

Khnum means 'the Moulder' and it was taught that he had formerly fashioned the world-egg on his potter's wheel. At Philae, moreover, he was called 'the Potter who shaped men and modelled the gods'. We see him moulding the limbs of Osiris; for it was he, they said, who 'shaped all flesh – the procreator who engendered gods and men'.

In this quality he presided over the formation of children in their mothers' wombs. Temple bas-reliefs show him fashioning the body of the young Pharaoh on his sculptor's turntable. At Armant this young Pharaoh is none other than the son of Julius Caesar and Cleopatra, here identified with the divine child Harsomtos.

The celebrity of Khnum soon crossed the nearby frontier and penetrated Nubia, whose god Doudoun was also a ram, or a ram-headed god. This facilitated the identification of the two gods and attracted new and numerous worshippers to the Isle of Elephantine.

Harsaphes, the Greek rendering of Hershef ('He who is on his lake'), was the name of another ram-headed god identified by the Greeks with Hercules. His principal sanctuary was at Heracleopolis Magna in the Fayyum. Probably a Nile god, like all ram-headed gods according to Maspero, Harsaphes was from the earliest times the object of great veneration; for already under the first dynasty we see King Ousaphais consecrating a *naos* to him.

Sati (Satet) was one of Khnum's two wives and as such a guardian goddess of the Cataracts. According to Maspero her name signifies 'She who runs like an arrow'. She is the Archer who lets fly the river's current with the force and rapidity of an arrow. She is represented as a woman wearing the white crown of the South, flanked by two long horns. Like Neith she often holds arrows and a bow in her hands. She was worshipped in the extreme south of Egypt, where her favourite abode was on the island of Seheil. She gave her name to the first *nome* of Upper Egypt which was called Ṭa Setet, the 'Land of Sati'. Its capital was Abu, 'City of the Elephant', the Elephantine of the Greeks, where Sati took her place in the temple of Khnum in company with Anuket.

Anuket (Anquet), the Greek for which was Anukis, was Khnum's second wife. She is represented as a woman wearing a tall plumed crown. Her name seems to mean 'the Clasper' – she who clasps the river bank and presses the Nile between the rocks of Philae and Syene. She was worshipped at Elephantine with Khnum and Sati as a regional goddess of the Cataracts. She liked to reside on the island of Seheil, which was consecrated to her.

Min, whom the Greeks identified with Pan, was a very ancient god whose totem, a thunderbolt apparently, appeared at the top of old prehistoric standards. Wearing a crown surmounted by two tall straight plumes which seem to have been borrowed from Amon, Min is always represented standing with a flail raised in his right hand behind his head and always with phallus erect.

This latter trait seems to indicate that Min was originally considered by his priests to be the creator of the world. He is often identified with Horus; and we may wonder if his name was not in earlier days simply a special name for the sun-god.

Be this as it may, Min was in the classical epoch chiefly worshipped as god of the roads and protector of travellers in the desert. The principal centre of his cult was Coptos, 'the town of caravaneers', a point of departure for commercial expeditions. Their leaders, before risking themselves in the deserts, never failed to invoke the great local god Min, god of the Eastern desert and 'Lord of Foreign Lands'.

He was worshipped also as a god of fertility and vegetation and protector of crops. On temple walls we see scenes from the ceremonies which were celebrated in his honour as harvest-god during the king's enthronement. We see the Pharaoh offering him the first sheaf which he has just cut and we see the homage which is rendered to the white bull, sacred to Min.

As well as in Coptos he was worshipped in Akhmin, the former Chemmis, known as Panopolis to the Greeks, who identified Min with Pan. There in his honour gymnastic games were celebrated, and it is perhaps for this reason that the Greek historian Herodotus praised the inhabitants of Panopolis for being the only Egyptians who liked Greek customs.

Hapi was the name of the deified Nile. He is given the figure of a man, vigorous but fat, with breasts developed like those of a woman, though less firm and hanging heavily on his chest. He is dressed like the boatmen and fishermen, with a narrow belt which sustains his massive belly. On his head he wears a crown made of aquatic plants – of lotus if he is the Nile of Upper Egypt, of papyrus if he represents the river in Lower Egypt.

Hapi, in fact, played the two parts of Southern Nile and Northern Nile. There were two corresponding goddesses who personified the river banks and they are sometimes seen standing with outstretched arms, as though begging for the water which will render them fertile.

The Egyptians thought of the Nile as flowing from Nun, the primordial ocean which waters the visible as well as the invisible world. It was also said that Hapi resided near the First Cataract, on the Isle of Bigeh, in a cavern where he poured water to heaven and earth from his urns. Towards the middle of June the Nile would rise and the devotees of Osiris affirmed that the inundation – on the height of which depended the year's prosperity – was caused by Isis weeping for her husband, treacherously slain by his wicked brother Set. The suitable height of the inundation was, in Graeco-Roman times, fixed at sixteen cubits – as the sixteen infants which decorate the famous statue of the Nile in the Vatican indicate. In order that the river should attain this height the Egyptians in June would make offerings to Hapi, imploring him with fervour and singing hymns, often of great poetic quality.

Apart from this, Hapi scarcely played a part in religion as such, and he was not connected with any theological system.

In temples he occupied a secondary role, and appears as a servant offering his river products to the great gods. On the foundations of buildings we often find long processions of alternate gods and goddesses who resemble Hapi and are known as 'Niles'. They represent the sub-divisions of the two Egypts bringing, in tribute to the Lord of the sanctuary, the products of all the provinces.

DIVINITIES OF BIRTH AND DEATH

Taueret (Apet, Opet) 'the Great' was a popular goddess of childbirth and symbolised maternity and suckling.

She is represented as a female hippopotamus with pendant mammae, standing upright on her back legs and holding the hieroglyphic sign of protection, 'sa', a plait of rolled papyrus. She was especially worshipped in Thebes where, under the New Kingdom, she enjoyed great popularity among people of the middle class, who often gave her name to their children and decorated their houses with her images.

As well as her role of protectress Taueret sometimes fulfilled that of an avenging deity: then she would appear as a goddess with the body of a hippopotamus but the head of a lioness who brandished a dagger in a menacing manner.

Heket was a frog-goddess or a frog-headed goddess who, it seems, symbolised the embryonic state when the dead grain decomposed and began to germinate.

A primitive goddess, it was taught at Abydos that she came with Shu from the mouth of Ra himself and that she and Shu were the ancestors of the gods. She was, they also said, one of the midwives who assisted every morning at the birth of the sun. In this aspect she figures, like Nekhebet and others whom we shall mention, among the patrons of childbirth.

Meskhent is sometimes represented as a woman wearing on her head two long palm shoots, curved at their extremities. She was a goddess of childbirth and personified the two bricks on which, at the moment of delivery, Egyptian mothers crouched. Sometimes we see Meskhent in the form of one of these bricks, terminated by a human head.

She appeared beside the expectant mother at the precise moment the baby was born; and she was said to go from house to house bringing relief to women in labour. Often, too, she played the role of fairy godmother and pronounced sentence on the newly born and predicted its future.

The old story in which the birth of the three first kings of the fifth dynasty is described permits us to determine the roles which these various divinities played during childbirth. When, we read, Reddedet approached the term of her confinement, Ra, the true father of the child she bore in her womb, ordered Isis, Nephthys, Heket and Meskhent to go to her bedside. The four goddesses, disguised as dancers and accompanied by Khnum who carried their luggage, set forth. When the moment had come Isis placed herself in front of Reddedet, Nephthys, behind her, while Heket helped her. Isis received the child. The goddesses then washed it and placed it on a bed of bricks. Finally Meskhent approached the newborn baby and said: 'It is a king who will rule over all the land.' Khnum then put health and strength into its body.

The Hathors were kinds of fairy godmothers who sometimes appeared at the birth of the young Egyptian to prophesy his destiny, much as we have seen Meskhent do. There were seven or even nine of them and we see them, in the form of young women, at the confinement of Ahmes at Deir el Bahri, of Mutemuia at Luxor and of Cleopatra at Armant. Their predictions were sometimes favourable, sometimes not; but no one escaped the fate they foretold.

Shaï was 'Destiny', and was sometimes made a goddess: Shaït. He was born at the same moment as the individual, grew up with him and shadowed him until his death. Shaï's decrees were inescapable. After death, when the soul was weighed in the presence of Osiris, Shaï could be seen in the form of a god without special attributes attending the trial in order – Maspero says – 'to render exact account before the infernal jury of the deceased's virtues and crimes, or in order to prepare him for the conditions of a new life'.

Renenet was the goddess who presided over the baby's suckling. She nourished him herself and also gave him his name – and, in consequence, his personality and fortune. At his death we see her with Shaï when his soul is weighed and judged. She is variously represented: as a woman without attributes, as a snake-headed woman, as a woman with the head of a lioness, or as a uraeus, dressed and with two long plumes on her head. As a nursing goddess she symbolised nourishment in general and sometimes appears as a harvest goddess with the title, 'Lady of the Double Granary'. She gives her name to the month of Pharmuti, 'the month of Renenet', which was, in later epochs, the eighth month of the Egyptian calendar.

Renpet was the goddess of the year, the goddess of springtide and of youth. As a deity of time's duration she was called 'Mistress

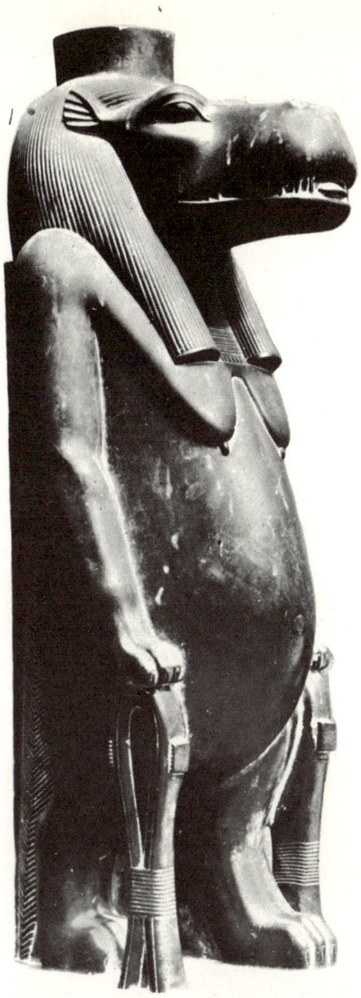

The Hippopotamus goddess Taueret, supported by two plaits of rolled papyrus which form the hieroglyphic sign 'sa'.
Statuette of the twenty-sixth Dynasty, 663 to 525. Cairo.

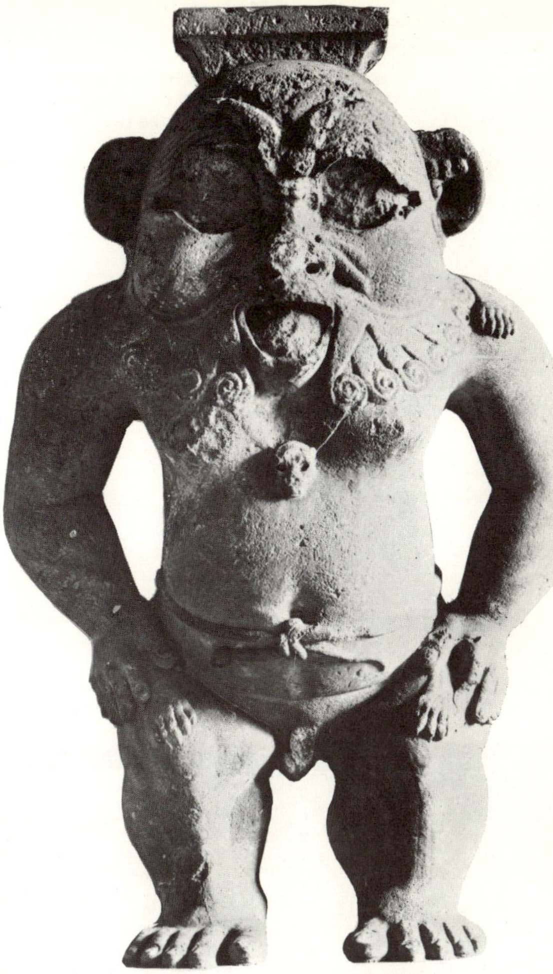

Bes. A foreign god who was introduced into Egypt, Bes is represented as a hideous bearded dwarf dressed in a leopard skin and wearing an ostrich-feather head-dress. One of the most popular gods in Egypt, he was both a protector and the guardian of sheep.
Statue of the twenty-sixth dynasty.

of Eternity'. She is represented as wearing above her head a long palm-shoot, curved at the end – an ideogram of her name.

Bes often appeared at birth, but chiefly he was a marriage-god and presided over the toilet of women.

Bes was a popular god who perhaps originated in the land of Punt of which he was sometimes called the Lord. He appears in the form of a robust dwarf of bestial aspect. His head is big, his eyes huge, his cheeks prominent. His chin is hairy and an enormous tongue hangs from his wide-open mouth. For head-dress he has a bunch of ostrich feathers; he wears a leopard skin whose tail falls behind him and is visible between his bandy legs. In bas-reliefs and paintings he is frequently represented full-face, contrary to the old Egyptian usage of drawing only in profile. He is normally immobile, hands on hips; though occasionally he skips cheerfully but clumsily and plays the harp or tambourine or, again, brandishes a broad dagger with a terrible and menacing air.

At once jovial and belligerent, fond of dancing and fighting, Bes was the buffoon of the gods. They delighted in his grotesque figure and contortions, just as the Memphite Pharaohs of the Old Kingdom enjoyed the antics of their pygmies.

At first Bes was relegated to the lowest rank among the host of genii venerated by the common people, but his popularity grew; and under the New Kingdom the middle classes liked to place his statue in their houses and name their children after him.

From this epoch we often see Bes represented in the *mammisi* of temples – that is to say, in the birth houses where divine accouchements took place. He thus presided over childbearing and at Deir el Bahri he appears with Taüeret and other tutelary genii beside the queen's bed as a protector of expectant mothers.

He also presided over the toilet and adornment of women, who were fond of having his image carved on the handles of their mirrors, rouge boxes and scent bottles. Bed-heads are also frequently found ornamented with various representations of Bes; for he was the guardian of sleep who chased away evil spirits and sent the sleeper sweet dreams.

He was moreover an excellent protector not only against evil spirits but against dangerous beasts: lions, snakes, scorpions, crocodiles. Against their bite or sting the whole family could be preserved by taking care to place in the house a little stela or pillar, covered with magic formulas, on which was sculpted Bes' menacing mask above a figure of the infant Horus, standing on two crocodiles.

At the end of paganism Bes was even supposed to be the protector of the dead, and for this reason became as popular as Osiris.

After the triumph of Christianity Bes did not immediately vanish from the memory of man; for we are told of a wicked demon named Bes whom the holy Moses had to exorcise because he was terrorising the neighbourhood. To this day, it would seem, the monumental southern gate of Karnak serves as a dwelling-place for a knock-kneed dwarf whose gross head is embellished with a formidable beard. Woe to the stranger who, coming across him in the dusk of evening, laughs at his grotesque figure! For the monster will leap at his throat and strangle him. He is the Bes of Ancient Egypt who, after long centuries, is not yet resigned to abandoning altogether the scenes which once witnessed his greatness.

Selket (Selquet) is the name of the old scorpion-goddess who was depicted as a woman wearing on her head a scorpion, the animal sacred to her. She was also at times a scorpion with a woman's head.

According to certain texts she was a daughter of Ra. She often played the role of guardian of conjugal union. At Deir el Bahri she appears with Neith supporting the hieroglyph of the sky, above which Amon is united with the queen-mother. The two goddesses protect the couple from all annoyance.

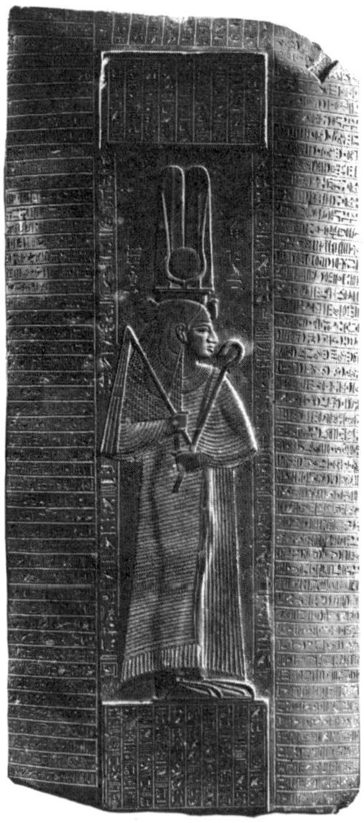

Meskhent, the goddess of childbirth. The goddess wears her palm-shoot head-dress and an elaborate wig and carries the crook and flail. The personification of the two bricks on which Egyptian women crouched to give birth, she brought relief to women in labour and foretold the future of the child.
Relief carving on stone.

Selket played an especial part in the ceremony of embalming. She protected the entrails and, as we shall later explain, guarded the canopic vase which contained the intestines.

As we have already noticed, Selket is often found in company with Neith, as Isis is with Nephthys. Like the other three goddesses, Selket protected the dead, and like them we see her extending winged arms across the inner walls of sarcophagi.

The four sons of Horus, who were members of the Third Ennead, were supposed to have been born to Isis; but it was also said that Sebek, on Ra's orders, caught them in a net and took them from the water in a lotus flower. It is on a lotus flower that they stand before the throne of Osiris during the judgment of the dead.

They were appointed by their father, Horus, to guard the four cardinal points. He also charged them to watch over the heart and entrails of Osiris and to preserve Osiris from hunger and thirst.

From then on they became the official protectors of viscera. Since the time of the Old Kingdom it had been usual to remove the viscera from the corpse, to separate them and preserve them in cases or jugs called – wrongly – 'canopic' jars. Each of these was confided to the care not only of one of the four genii but also of a goddess.

Thus the human-headed Imsety watched with Isis over the vase containing the liver. The dog-headed Hapi guarded the lungs with Nephthys. The jackal-headed Duamutef with Neith protected the stomach. And the hawk-headed Qebhsnuf with Selket had charge of the intestines.

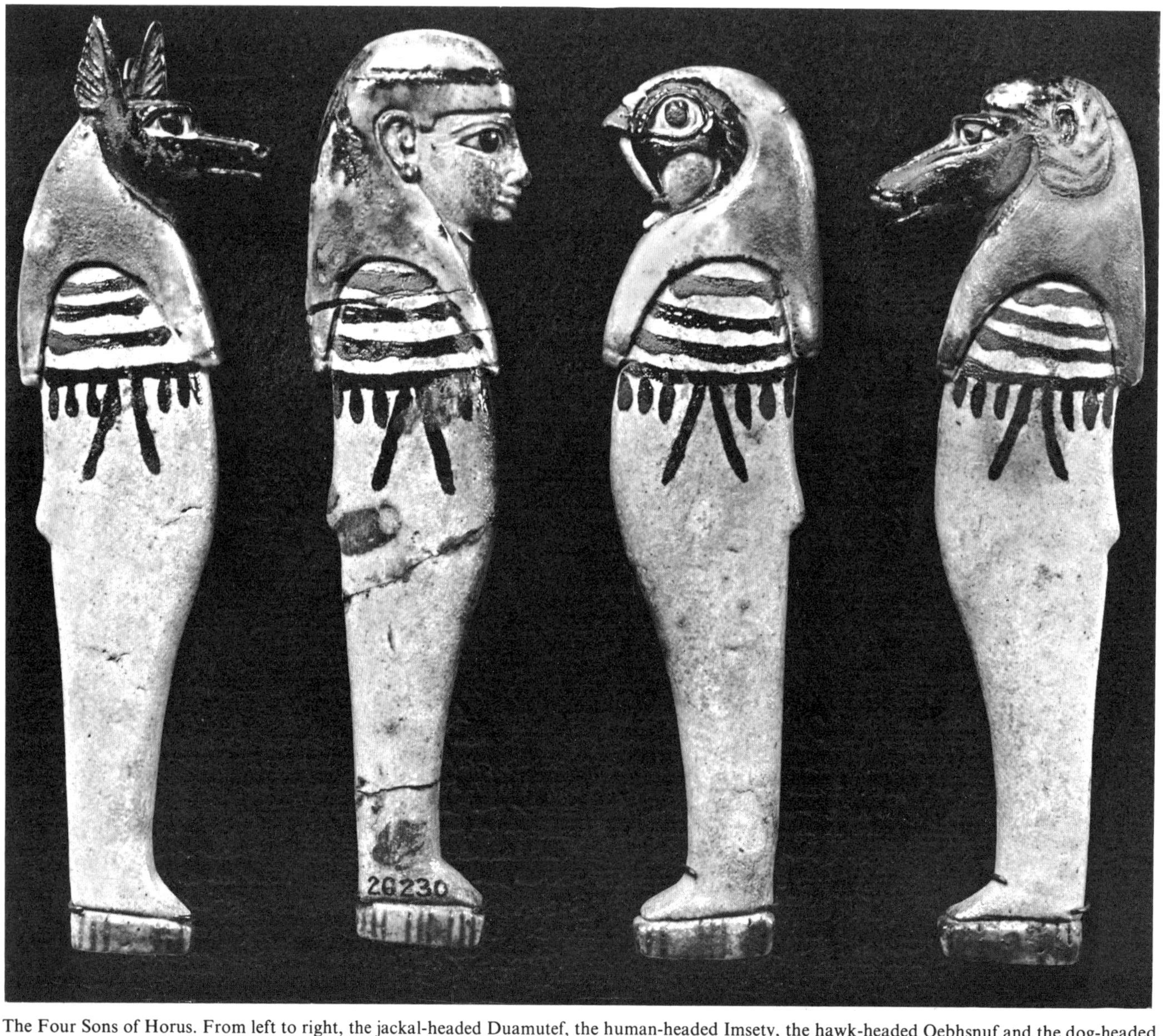

The Four Sons of Horus. From left to right, the jackal-headed Duamutef, the human-headed Imsety, the hawk-headed Qebhsnuf and the dog-headed Hapi. As protectors of the viscera their heads appeared on the lids of the so-called 'canopic' jars, Duamutef guarding the stomach, Imsety the liver, Qebhsnuf the intestines and Hapi the lungs.

Ament, whose name is a simple epithet meaning 'the Westerner', is represented as a goddess wearing an ostrich feather on her head or sometimes an ostrich plume and a hawk.

This feather, the normal ornament of Libyans, who wore it fixed in their hair, was also the sign for the word 'Western' and was naturally suitable to Ament, who was originally the goddess of the Libyan province to the west of Lower Egypt.

Later 'the West' came to mean the Land of the Dead, and the goddess of the West became the goddess of the dwelling-place of the dead.

At the gates of the World, at the entrance of the desert, one often sees the dead being welcomed by a goddess who half-emerges from the foliage of the tree she has chosen to live in to offer him bread and water. If he drinks and eats he becomes the 'friend of the gods' and follows after them, and can never return. The deity who thus welcomes the dead is often Ament, though she may frequently be Nut, Hathor, Neith or Maat, who take their turn in replacing the goddess of the West.

Mertseger (Merseger), whose name signifies 'the Friend of Silence' or 'the Beloved of Him who makes Silence' (i.e. Osiris), was the name of a snake-goddess of the Theban necropolis. More accurately she pertained to one part of the funerary mountain at Thebes – the peak, shaped like a pyramid, which dominated the mountain chain and earned Mertseger the epithet Ta-dehnet, 'the peak'.

She is represented as a human-headed snake or even as a snake with three heads: namely, a human head surmounted by a disk flanked by two feathers between two others: a snake's head similarly embellished and a vulture's head. Although Mertseger was benevolent she could also punish. We have the confession of Neferabu, a modest employee at the necropolis, who admitted having sinned and been justly stricken with illness. Afterwards he proclaims that he has been cured by 'the Peak of the West', having first repented and ardently besought her forgiveness.

The Judges of the Dead and the Weighing of the Soul. When, thanks to the talismans placed on his mummy and especially to the passwords written on the indispensable Book of the Dead with which he was furnished, the deceased had safely crossed the terrifying stretch of country between the land of the living and the kingdom of the dead, he was immediately ushered into the presence of his sovereign judge, either by Anubis or by Horus. After he had kissed the threshold he penetrated into the 'Hall of Double Justice'. This was an immense room at the end of which sat Osiris under a *naos,* guarded by a frieze of coiled uraeus: Osiris, 'the Good One', redeemer and judge who awaited his 'son who came from earth'. In the centre was erected a vast scale beside which stood Maat, goddess of truth and justice, ready to weigh the heart of the deceased. Meanwhile Amemait, 'the Devourer' – a hybrid monster, part lion, part hippopotamus, part crocodile – crouched nearby, waiting to devour the hearts of the guilty. All around the hall, to the right and to the left of Osiris, sat forty-two personages. Dressed in their winding-sheets, each held a sharp-edged sword in his hand. Some had human heads, others the heads of animals. They were the forty-two judges, each corresponding to a province of Egypt; and each was charged with the duty of examining some special aspect of the deceased's conscience.

The deceased himself began the proceedings and without hesitation recited what has been called 'the negative confession'. He addressed each of his judges in turn and called him by name to prove that he knew him and had nothing to fear. For, he affirmed, he had committed no sin and was truly pure.

Then followed the weighing of his soul, or psychostasia. In one of the pans of the balance Anubis or Horus placed Maat herself, or else her ideogram, the feather, symbol of truth. In the other he placed the heart of the deceased. Thoth then verified the weight, wrote the result on his tablets and announced it to Osiris. If the two pans of the balance were in perfect equilibrium Osiris rendered favourable judgment. 'Let the deceased depart victorious. Let him go wherever he wishes to mingle freely with the gods and the spirits of the dead.'

The deceased, thus justified, would lead from then on a life of eternal happiness in the kingdom of Osiris. It is true that it would be his duty to cultivate the god's domains and keep dykes and canals in good repair. But magic permitted him to avoid all disagreeable labour. For at burial he would have been furnished with *Shabtis (Ushabtis)* or 'Answerers' – those little statuettes in stone or glazed composition which have been found in tombs by the hundreds and which, when the dead man was called upon to perform some task, would hasten to take his place and do the job for him.

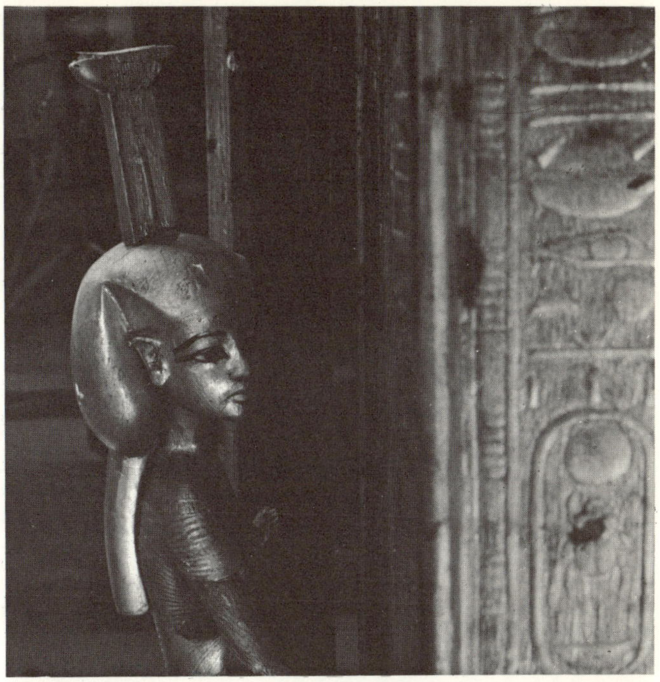

Nephthys. One of the four tutelary goddesses who protected the dead, Nephthys wears her ideogram on her head – a basket surmounting the sign for a palace. With Hapi she was responsible for the lungs of the corpse and here she guards the canopic shrine containing the viscera of Tut-ankh-Amon. Carved wood overlaid with gold upon gesso. Eighteenth dynasty, 1587 to 1375 B.C.

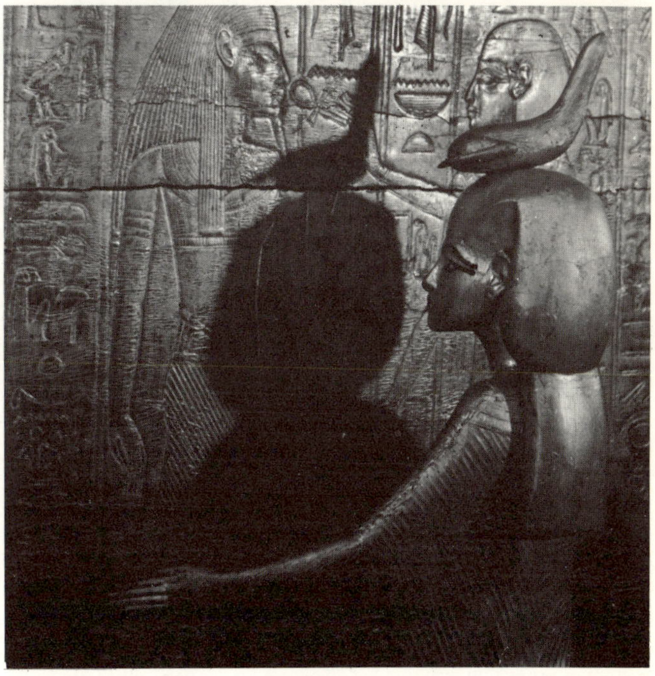

Selket guarding the canopic shrine of Tut-ankh-Amon.
The scorpion goddess wears the *khaet* head-dress surmounted by her ideogram and extends her arms in a gesture of protection.
The fourth of the tutelary goddesses, she was responsible for the intestines of the dead person in company with Qebhsnuf. Carved wood overlaid with gold upon gesso. Eighteenth dynasty, 1587 to 1375 B.C.

Maat is depicted as a woman standing or sitting on her heels. On her head she wears the ostrich feather which is an ideogram of her name – truth or justice. She was the goddess of law, truth and justice. The texts describe her as the cherished daughter and

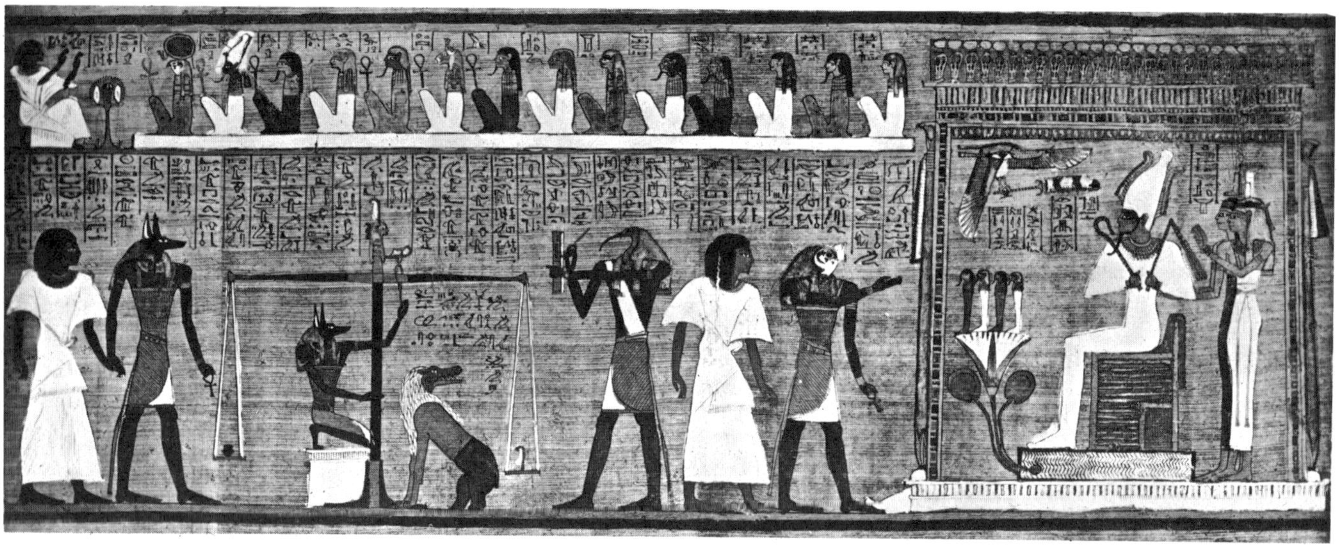

Judgment scene from the Book of the Dead. The dead man, dressed in white, is led into the judgment hall by Anubis who then weighs his heart while the monster Amemait and the ibis-headed Thoth look on. Horus then conducts him into the presence of Osiris who is seated on a throne set upon water from which springs a lotus bearing the Four Sons of Horus. Behind him stand Isis and Nephthys. Above, the dead man is shown addressing the forty-two personages. Painting on papyrus, *c.* 1450. B.C.

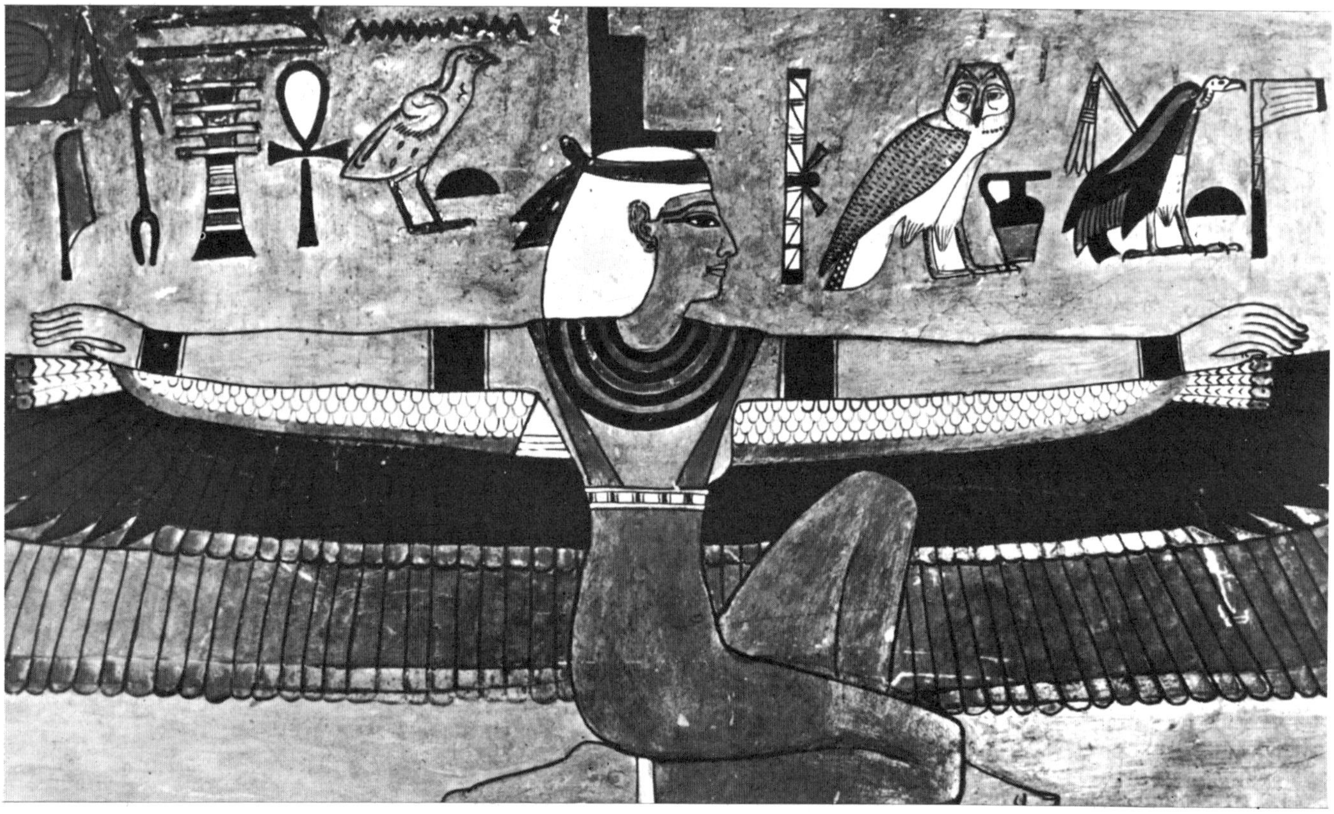

The goddess Isis. The wife of Osiris and the chief of the four goddesses who protected the dead, Isis kneels with her winged arms outstretched in a gesture of protection, wearing her ideogram on her head. With her wings she was believed to have transmitted the breath of life to the dead Osiris. Wall painting from the tomb of Seti I. Nineteenth dynasty, 1375 to 1202 B.C. Thebes.

confidante of Ra, and also the wife of Thoth, the judge of the gods who was also called 'the Master of Maat'.

She formed part of the retinue of Osiris, and the chamber in which the god held his tribunal was named the 'Hall of Double Justice', for Maat was often doubled into two absolutely identical goddesses who stood one in each extremity of the vast hall. As we have just seen, Maat also took her place in one pan of the balance opposite the heart of the dead in order to test its truthfulness.

In reality Maat was a pure abstraction, deified. The gods, it was taught, loved to nourish themselves on truth and justice. Thus, in the ritual of the cult, it was the offering of Maat which genuinely pleased them; and in the temples we see the king, at the culminating point of divine office, presenting to the god of the sanctuary a tiny image of Maat – an offering which was more agreeable to him than all the others he had received, no matter how rich they were.

Neheh (Heh), 'Eternity', is another deified abstraction. The god of eternity is represented as a man squatting on the ground in the Egyptian manner and wearing on his head a reed, curved at the end. We often see him thus, carved on furniture and other homely objects, holding in his hands the sign for millions of years and various emblems of happiness and longevity.

MEN DEIFIED AND THE PHARAOH GOD

Imhotep, in Greek Imuthes, signifies 'He who comes in peace'. Imhotep was by far the most celebrated among those ancient sages who were admired by their contemporaries during their lifetime and after their death finally worshipped as equals of the gods.

Imhotep lived at the court of the ancient King Zoser of the third

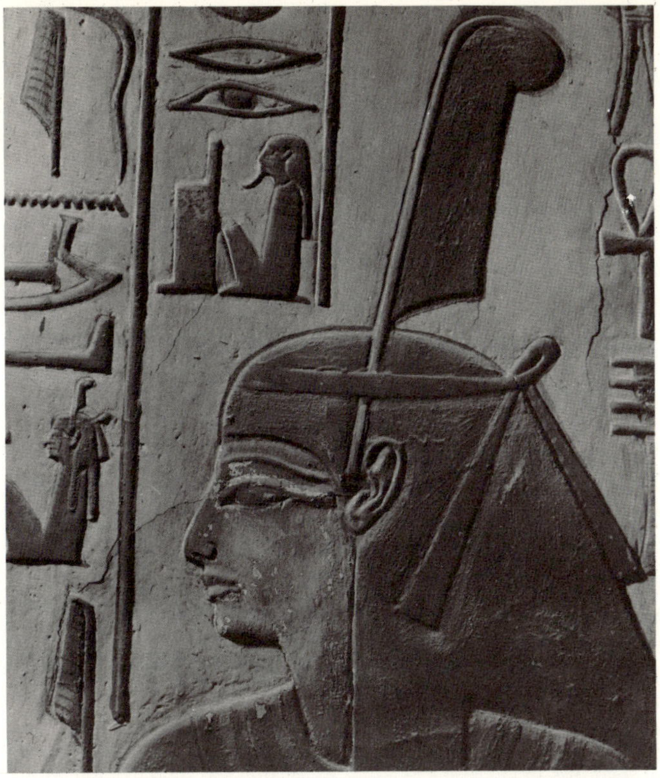

Maat. The goddess of truth and justice, Maat wears an ostrich feather on her head-dress, the ideogram of her name.
The goddess played an important part in the judgment of the dead, either herself or her feather being placed in the scales opposite the heart of the dead person in order to test its truthfulness. Painted relief from the tomb of Nefertari. Nineteenth dynasty, 1375 to 1202 B.C.

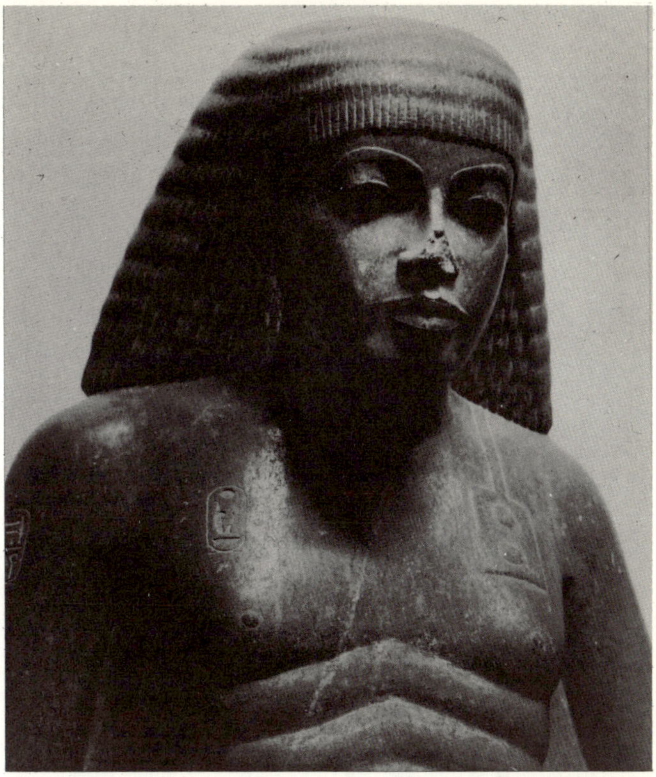

Amenhotep, son of Hapu, the architect and vizier of Amenhotep III, the father of Akhenaton. Like Imhotep before him, Amenhotep was revered as a sage during his lifetime and was finally deified.
He is portrayed as a scribe seated cross-legged with a papyrus unrolled on his knees. Life-size statue in black granite.
Eighteenth dynasty, 1587 to 1375 B.C. Karnak.

dynasty. He was Zoser's greatest architect and Zoser was the constructor of the oldest of the pyramids. During his reign, as recent discoveries have revealed, the stone column seems to have been employed for the first time in the history of architecture.

By the time of the New Kingdom Imhotep was already very famous. He was reputed to have written the 'Book of Temple Foundations', and under the Pharaohs of Sais his popularity increased from year to year. Some time later, during the Persian domination, it was claimed that Imhotep was born not of human parents but of Ptah himself. He was introduced into the Triad of Memphis with the title 'Son of Ptah', thus displacing Nefertum.

He is represented with shaven head like a priest, without the divine beard, crown or sceptre and dressed simply as a man. He is generally seated or crouching, and seems to be attentively reading from a roll of papyrus laid across his knees.

He was patron of scribes and the protector of all who, like himself, were occupied with the sciences and occult arts. He became the patron of doctors. Then – for ordinary people who celebrated his miraculous cures – he became the god or, more accurately, the demi-god of medicine. He was thus identified by the Greeks with Asclepius. Towards the end of paganism Imhotep seems even to have relegated his father Ptah to second rank, and to have become the most venerated god in Memphis.

Amenhotep, son of Hapu, whom the Greeks called Amenophis, was a minister of Amenhotep III and lived in Thebes in the fifteenth century B.C.

'A sage and an initiate of the holy book,' we are told, 'Amenhotep had contemplated the beauties of Thoth.' No man of his time better understood the mysterious science of the rites. He was remembered by the Thebans for the superb edifices he had had built. Among these, one of the most imposing was the funeral temple of the king, his master, of which to-day there remain only the two statues that embellished the façade. They are gigantic statues and one of them was renowned throughout antiquity under the name of the Colossus of Memnon. Throughout the centuries the renown of Amenhotep continued to grow. In the Saite epoch he was considered to be a man 'who, because of his wisdom, had participated in the divine nature'. Magic books were attributed to him and miraculous stories told about him.

In the temple of Karnak there were statues of Amenhotep, son of Hapu, to which divine honours were paid; but he never became a real god like Imhotep, son of Ptah. He was, however, venerated in company with the great divinities in the little Ptolemaic temple of Deir el Medineh.

The old sage is generally portrayed as a scribe, crouching and holding on his knees a roll of papyrus.

Pharaoh must also be named among the gods of Egypt; for the king's divinity formed part of the earliest dogmas. To his subjects, moreover, he was the Sun-god, reigning on earth. He wore the Sun-god's uraeus which spat forth flame and annihilated his enemies. All the terms which were used in speaking of him, of his palace and of his acts could apply equally to the sun. It was taught that he actually perpetuated the solar line; for, whenever there was a change of king, the god Ra married the queen, who then bore a son who, in his turn, mounted the throne of the living.

In temples, and particularly those of Nubia, many ancient kings and the living king himself were often worshipped in company with the great gods. Thus we sometimes see pictures of the reigning Pharaoh worshipping his own image.

Among the countless sacred animals which, especially in later times, were worshipped in the Nile Valley we shall here give details of only the most celebrated, those who were worshipped under their own names in the temples.

THE SACRED ANIMALS

Apis is a Greek rendering of Hapi. As the 'Bull Apis' he is to-day the best known of the sacred animals. Very popular and honoured throughout Egypt, he was tended and worshipped at Memphis, where he was called 'the Renewal of Ptah's life'. He was Ptah's sacred animal and believed to be his reincarnation. Ptah in the form of a celestial fire, it was taught, inseminated a virgin heifer

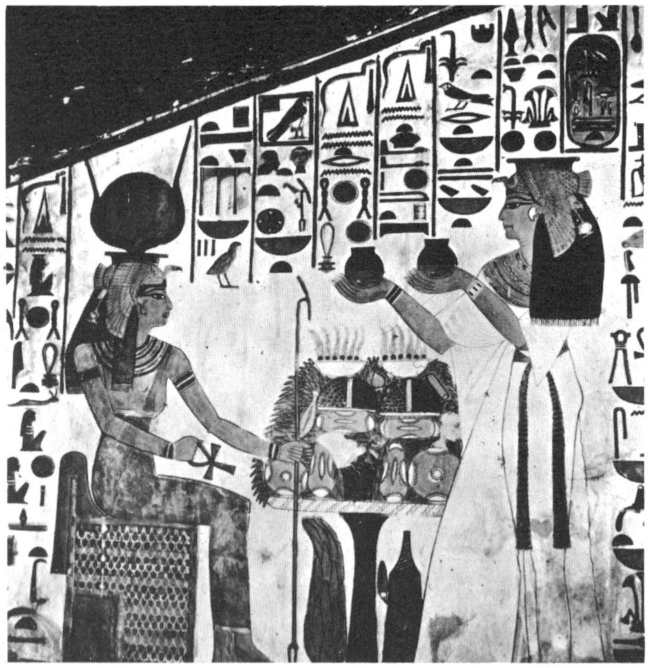

The goddess Hathor receiving an offering.
The goddess is represented seated on a throne wearing a horned head-dress and holding a sceptre and the *ankh*. Before her stands Queen Nefertari, the wife of Rameses II, who presents her with two vases. The protectress of women, Hathor, as 'Queen of the West', was also protectress of the Theban necropolis. Wall-painting from the tomb of Queen Nefertari. Nineteenth dynasty, 1375 to 1202 B.C.

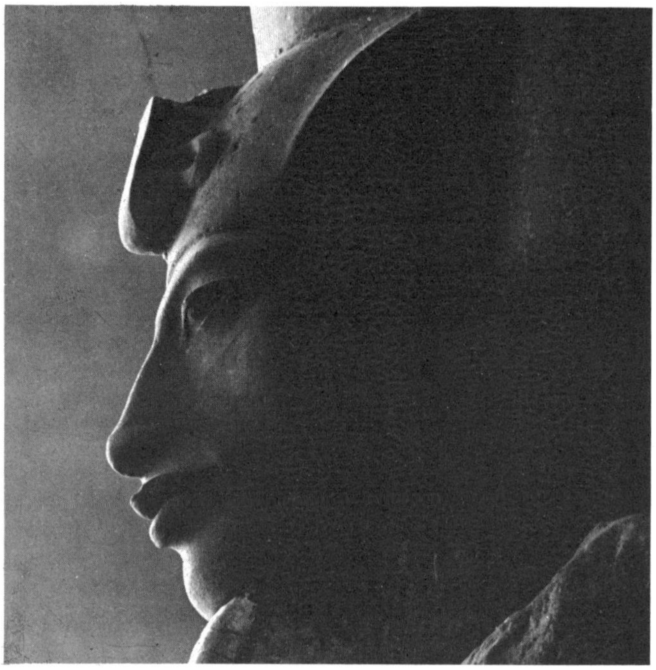

Akhenaton, the heretical Pharaoh. Head from an Osirian pillar-statue portraying the king at the beginning of his reign from the temple of Ra-Harakhte to the east of Karnak. It was the Aten.
or solar disk of the Rising Sun that Akhenaton was soon to adopt as the sole god of his new religion. Eighteenth dynasty, 1587 to 1375 B.C.

and from her was himself born again in the form of a black bull which the priests could recognise by certain mystic marks. On his forehead there had to be a white triangle, on his back the figure of a vulture with outstretched wings, on his right flank a crescent moon, on his tongue the image of a scarab and, finally, the hairs of his tail must be double.

As long as he lived Apis was daintily fed in the temple which the kings had had built for him in Memphis opposite the temple of Ptah. Every day at a fixed hour he was let loose in the courtyard attached to his temple, and the spectacle of his frolics attracted crowds of the devout. It also drew the merely curious; for a visit to the sacred animals was a great attraction for the tourists who were so numerous in Egypt during the Graeco-Roman era.

Each of his movements was interpreted as foretelling the future; and when Germanicus died it was remembered that the bull, shortly before this, had refused to eat the delicacies which Germanicus had offered him.

Normally Apis was allowed to die of old age. Ammianus Marcellinus, however, tells us that if he lived beyond a certain age he was drowned in a fountain. During the Persian tyranny the sacred bull was twice assassinated, by Cambyses and by Ochus. Space is lacking to describe how the Egyptians mourned the death of Apis, and their transports of joy at the announcement that his successor had been found. We should also have liked to describe the vast subterranean chambers discovered in 1850 at Saqqarah where the mummified bodies of the sacred bulls were, after splendid funeral services, buried in immense monolithic sarcophagi of sandstone or pink granite.

Above these underground galleries arose a great temple of which to-day nothing remains. In Latin it was called the Serapeum. Here the funeral cult of the dead bull was celebrated. He had become, like all the dead, an 'Osiris' and was worshipped under the name Osiris Apis. This in Greek was Osorapis, which caused him quickly to be confused with the foreign god Serapis, who was worshipped according to a purely Greek ritual in the great Serapeum at Alexandria. A god of the underworld, Serapis was confused at Memphis with Osorapis and was worshipped with Osorapis in his funerary temple. Due to this confusion the temple was thenceforth called Serapeum.

Other Sacred Bulls. To be brief we shall only enumerate the three other important bulls of Egypt.

Mneuis is the Greek rendering of Merwer, the Bull of Meroe also called Menuis. He was the bull sacred to Ra Atum at Heliopolis. It seems that he was of a light colour, although Plutarch speaks of his black hide.

Buchis, the Greek for Bukhe, was the bull sacred to Menthu at Hermonthis. According to Macrobius, the hair of his hide, which changed colour every hour, grew in the opposite direction from that of an ordinary animal. The great vaults where the mummies of Buchis were buried were discovered near Armant by Robert Mond, who in 1927 had already found the tombs of the cows which bore these sacred bulls.

Onuphis, the Greek rendering of Aa Nefer, 'the very good', was the bull in which the soul of Osiris was said to be incarnated, as Ra Atum re-appeared in Mneuis and Mont was re-embodied in Buchis.

Petesuchos is the Greek rendering of an Egyptian word meaning 'he who belongs to Suchos' (or Sebek). He was the sacred crocodile in which was incarnated the soul of Sebek, the great god of the Fayyum who had his chief sanctuary in Crocodilopolis, the capital of the province, which was called Arsinoe from the time of the second Ptolemy.

At Crocodilopolis, in a lake dug out near the great temple, Petesuchos was venerated. He was an old crocodile who wore golden rings in his ears. His devotees riveted bracelets to his forelegs. Other crocodiles, also sacred, composed his family and were fed nearby.

In the Graeco-Roman era the crocodiles of Arsinoe were a great attraction for tourists. Strabo tells us how in the reign of Augustus he paid a visit to Petesuchos. 'He is fed,' Strabo writes, 'with the bread, meat and wine which strangers always bring when they come to see him. Our friend and host, who was one of the notabilities of the place and who took us everywhere, came to the lake with us, having saved from our luncheon a cake, a piece of the roast and a small flagon of honey. We met the crocodile on the shore of the lake. Priests approached him and while one of them held open his jaws another put in the cake and the meat and poured in the honey-wine. After that the animal dived into the lake and swam towards the opposite shore. Another visitor arrived, also bringing his offering. The priests ran round the lake with the food he had brought and fed it to the crocodile in the same manner.'

For many centuries no one has worshipped Petesuchos, but in

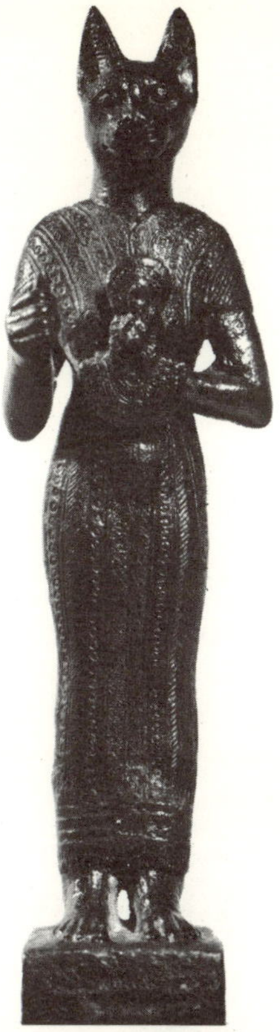

Bast. The cat-headed goddess of Bubastis wears a long embroidered robe and in her left hand holds the 'aegis of Bast' – a semi-circular breastplate surmounted by the head of a lion. Originally a lioness-goddess, she was frequently confused with Sekhmet and as a goddess of pleasure became one of the most popular Egyptian deities. Bronze statuette.

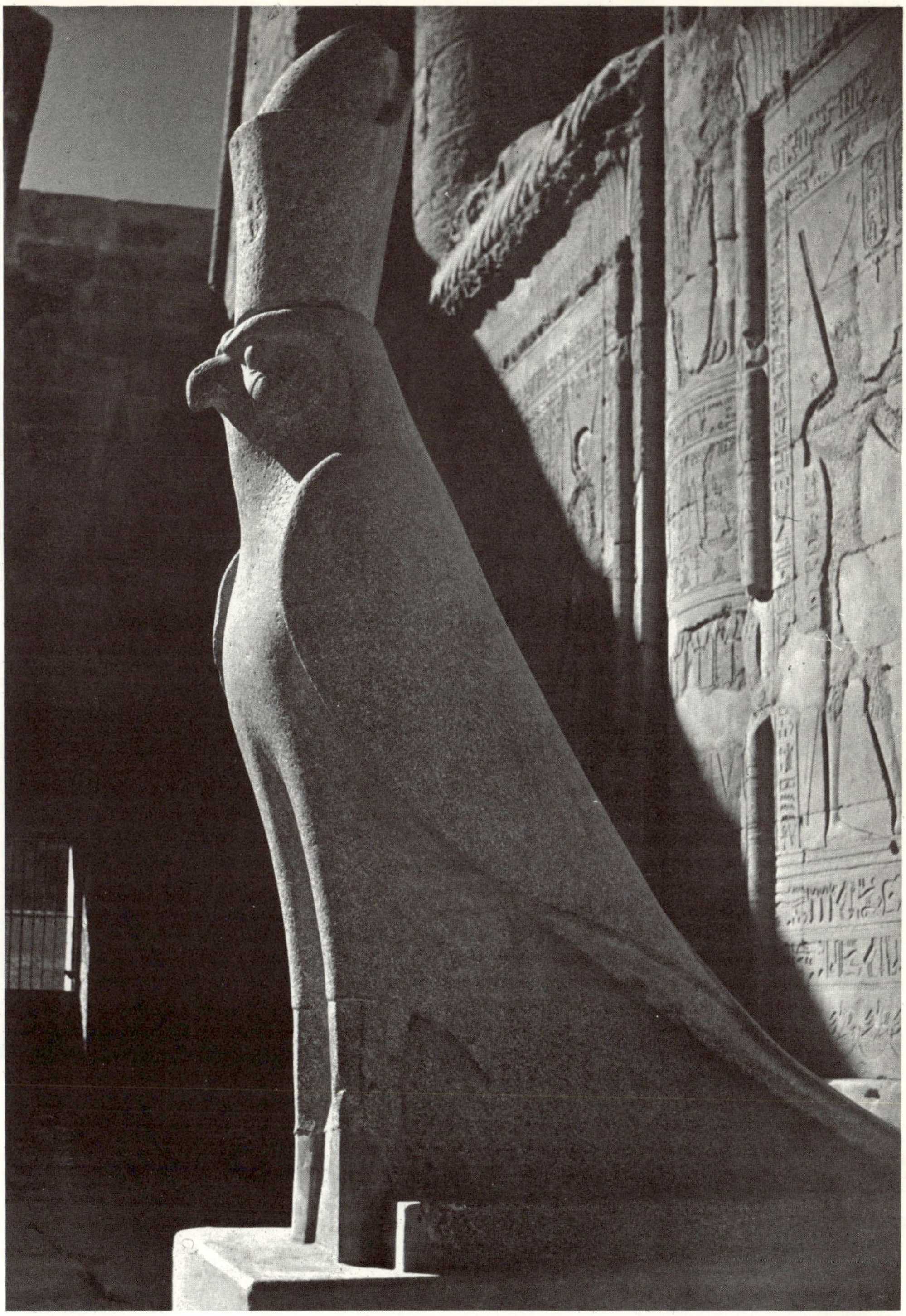

Horus. The great sky-god is portrayed as a falcon in this statue in the court of the temple of Edfu in Upper Egypt – one of the great temples dedicated especially to his worship. Closely connected with the Pharaoh, he wears the double crown of Upper and Lower Egypt. The falcon was considered the pre-eminent divine being from the earliest times and was the ideogram of 'god'. Twenty-sixth dynasty, 672 to 525 B.C.

the centre of Africa those who dwell on the southern shores of Lake Victoria-Nyanza today still venerate Lutembi, an old crocodile who for generations has come to the shore each morning and evening at the call of the fishermen to receive from their hands the fish they offer him.

Like Petesuchos of old, the crocodile Lutembi has become a profitable source of revenue for his votaries. For, since many people come to see him out of curiosity, the natives demand a fee for calling him to the shore and make the visitor pay well for the fish they give him.

Sacred Rams were also very popular in Egypt. Chief among them was Ba Neb Djedet, 'the soul of the lord of Djedet', a name which in popular speech was contracted into Banaded and in Greek rendered as Mendes. In him was incarnated the soul of Osiris, and the story which Herodotus brought back about the ram – which he wrongly calls 'the He-goat of Mendes' – confirms the veneration in which this sacred animal was held. Thoth himself, said his priests, had formerly decreed that the kings should come with offerings to the 'living ram'. Otherwise infinite misfortune would spread among men. When Banaded died there was general mourning; on the other hand immense rejoicing greeted the announcement that a new ram had been discovered, and great festivals were held in order to celebrate the enthronement of this king of Egyptian animals.

The Bird Bennu must also be mentioned among the sacred animals; for, though he was purely legendary, the ancients did not doubt his reality. Worshipped at Heliopolis as the soul of Osiris, he was also connected with the cult of Ra and was perhaps even a secondary form of Ra. He is identified, though not with certainty, with the Phoenix who, according to Herodotus' Heliopolitan guides, resembled the eagle in shape and size, while Bennu was more like a lapwing or a heron. The Phoenix, it was said, appeared in Egypt only once every five hundred years. When the Phoenix was born in the depths of Arabia he flew swiftly to the temple of Heliopolis with the body of his father which, coated with myrrh, he there piously buried.

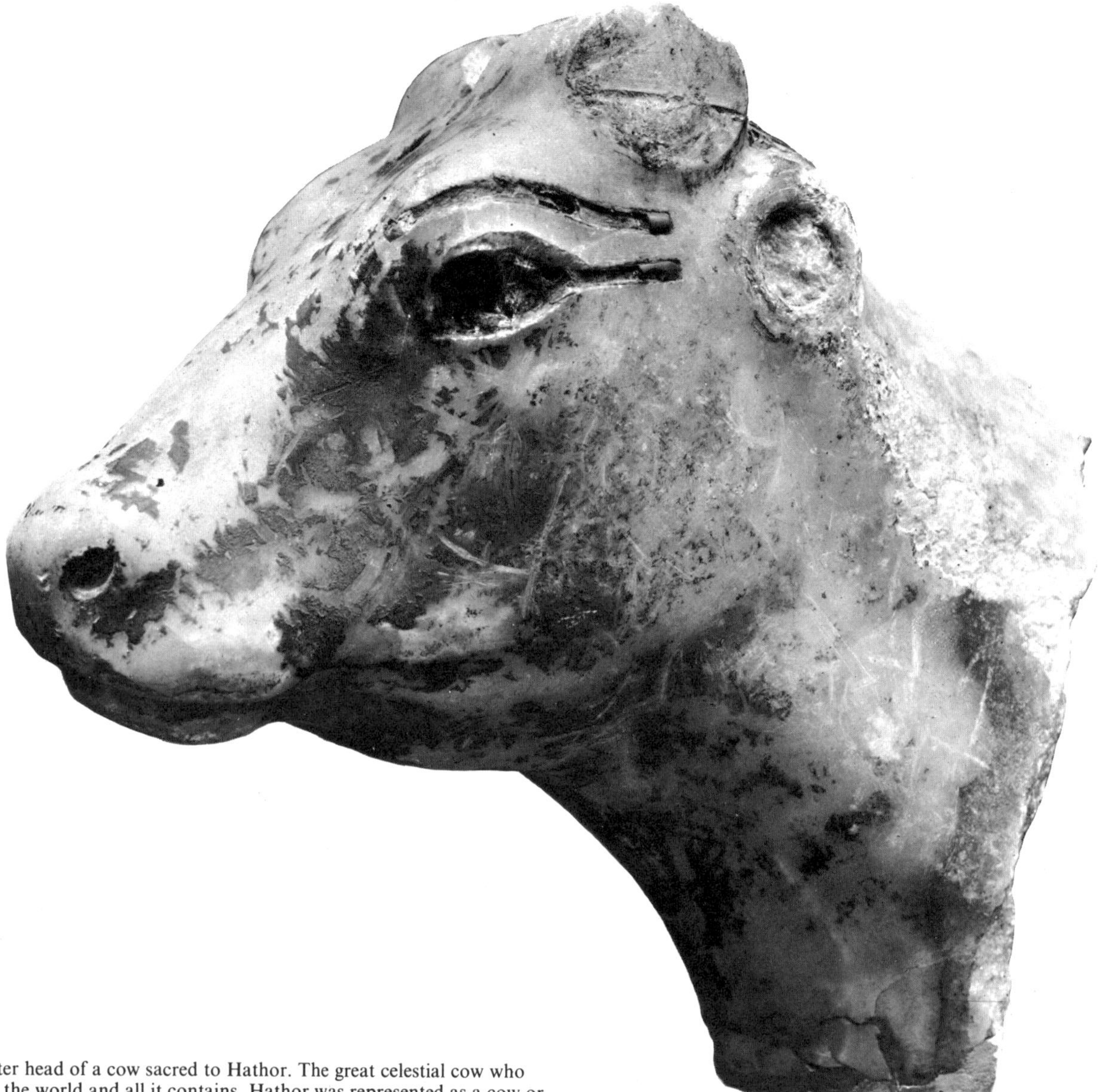

Alabaster head of a cow sacred to Hathor. The great celestial cow who created the world and all it contains, Hathor was represented as a cow or as a cow-headed woman or, more often, simply wearing cow's horns upon her head. Special reverence was paid to the sacred cows at the temple of Deir el Bahri where the goddess had a chapel. Eighteenth dynasty, 1587 to 1375 B.C.

CONCLUSION

Much more remains to be said on the subject of the sacred animals. In most sanctuaries the god or goddess of the locality was supposed to be incarnate in the animal kept: a cat in the temple of Bast, a falcon or an ibis in the temple of Horus or Thoth. In addition, popular superstition in later times so grew that every individual of the species of animal in whose body the provincial god was incarnate was regarded as sacred by the inhabitants of that province. It was forbidden to eat them, and to kill one was a heinous crime. Since, however, different nomes venerated different animals it could happen that a certain species which was the object of a cult in one province was mercilessly hunted in the neighbouring province. This sometimes gave rise to fratricidal wars such as that which, in the first century of the Christian era, broke out between the Cynopolitans and the Oxyrhynchites. The latter had killed and eaten dogs to avenge themselves on the former for having eaten an oxyrhynchid, a kind of spider crab. Plutarch writes:

'In our days, the Cynopolitans having eaten a crab, the Oxyrhynchites took dogs and sacrificed them and ate their flesh like that of immolated victims. Thus arose a bloody war between the two peoples which the Romans put an end to after severely punishing both.'

Certain animals – cats, hawks, ibis – were venerated all over Egypt and to kill them was punishable by death. 'When one of these animals is concerned,' writes Diodorus, 'he who kills one, be it accidentally or maliciously, is put to death. The populace flings itself on him and cruelly maltreats him, usually before he can be tried and judged. Superstition towards these sacred animals is deeply rooted in the Egyptian's soul, and devotion to their cult is passionate. In the days when Ptolemy Auletes was not yet allied to the Romans and the people of Egypt still hastened to welcome all visitors from Italy and, for fear of the consequences, carefully avoided any occasion for complaint or rupture, a Roman killed a cat. The populace crowded to the house of the Roman who had committed this "murder"; and neither the efforts of magistrates sent by the king to protect him nor the universal fear inspired by the might of Rome could avail to save the man's life, though what he had done was admitted to be accidental. This is not an incident which I report from hearsay, but something I saw myself during my sojourn in Egypt.'

Cats, indeed, were so venerated that when a building caught fire the Egyptians, Herodotus tells us, would neglect the fire in order to rescue these animals whose death to them seemed more painful than any other loss they might sustain. When one of the sacred animals died it was considered an act of great merit to provide for its funeral; and in certain cases, such as the bull Apis, the king himself made it his duty to take charge of the obsequies.

Pity for dead animals reached an almost unbelievable degree. To give an idea of this it may be mentioned that crocodile cemeteries have been discovered where the reptiles were carefully mummified and buried with their newly born and even with their eggs.

The goddess Hathor protecting the Pharaoh Psammetichus. The goddess is represented as a cow, her sacred animal, with the solar disk and the uraeus between her horns. A protector and nourisher of the living, Hathor came increasingly to be regarded as the protector of the dead. Copy of a statue of the twenty-sixth dynasty, 572 to 525 B.C.

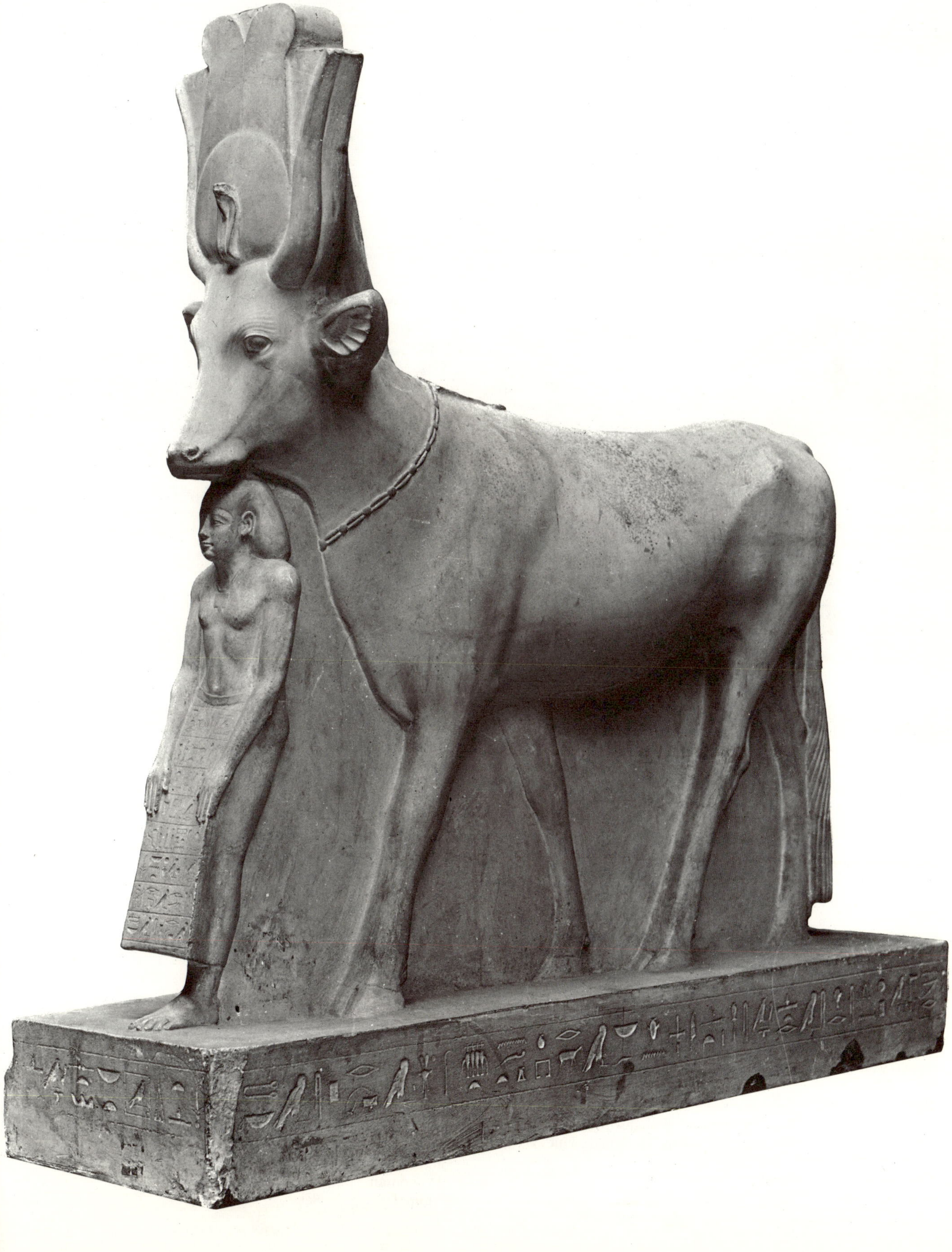

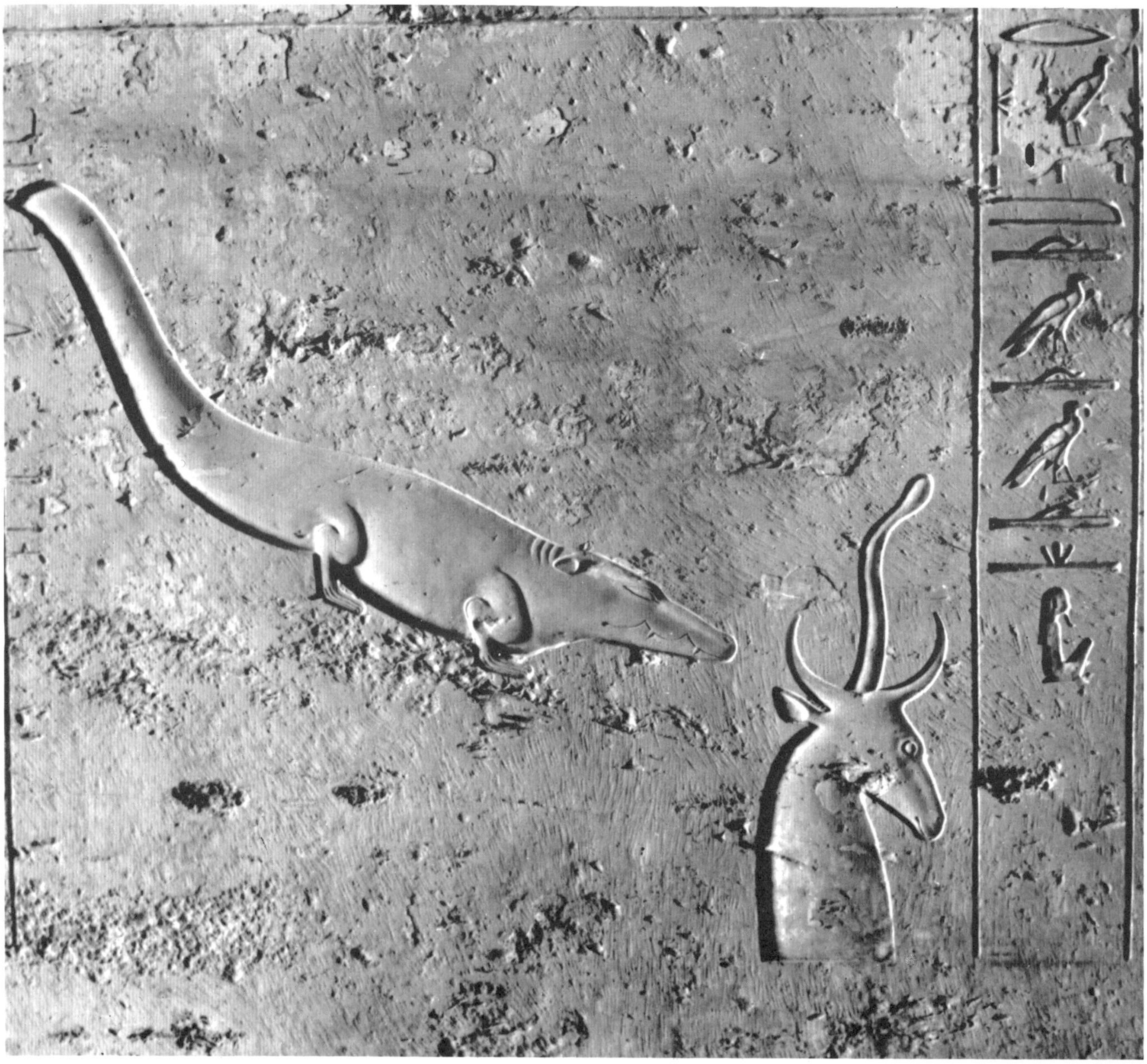

Petesuchos, the sacred crocodile. 'He who belongs to Suchos (or Sebek)'. Petesuchos was venerated in a lake dug out near Sebek's great temple at Crocodilopolis, it being believed that the god's soul was incarnate in him. Worshipped in some provinces, crocodiles were hunted down in others. Bas-relief in the tomb of Seti Meremptah in the Valley of the Kings. Nineteenth dynasty, 1375 to 1202 B.C. Thebes.

Animals, birds, fish, reptiles of all kinds that were venerated by the ancient inhabitants of the Nile valley were interred by the hundreds of thousands. An example of the abundance of these corpses can be found at Beni Hasan, where the cats' cemetery has been commercially exploited for the extraction of artificial fertiliser.

Herodotus did not exaggerate when he wrote that the Egyptians were the most religious of men.

A LIST OF ANIMALS WHOSE HEADS APPEAR ON EGYPTIAN DIVINITIES

The following is a table, in alphabetical order, of those animals whose heads were borne by certain gods. Only the gods mentioned in this study are listed. We have omitted the countless genii and lesser divinities who on tomb decorations and in illustrations of funerary papyri were also represented with animal heads.

Bull:	Osorapis. See also Apis, Mont.
Cat:	Bast. (Sometimes, perhaps, Mut.)
Cow:	Hathor, Isis when identified with Hathor. See also Nut.
Crocodile:	Sebek.
Dog-faced ape:	Hapi, Thoth at times.
Donkey:	Set (in later times).
Falcon:	Ra-Harakhte, Horus, Mont, Khons Hor, Qebhsnuf.
Frog:	Heket.
Hippopotamus:	Taueret.
Ibis:	Thoth.
Jackal:	Anubis, Duamutef.
Lion:	Nefertum, sometimes.
Lioness:	Sekhmet, Tefnut (sometimes Mut and Renenet).
Ram with curved horns:	Amon.
Ram with wavy horns:	Khnum, Hershef or Harsaphes.
Scarab:	Khepri.
Scorpion:	Selket.
Serpent:	Buto. See also Mertseger and Renenet.
Uraeus:	See Serpent.
Vulture:	Nekhebet.
Wolf:	Upuaut, Khenti Amenti.
Indeterminate animal called the Typhonian Animal:	Set.

ASSYRO-BABYLONIAN MYTHOLOGY

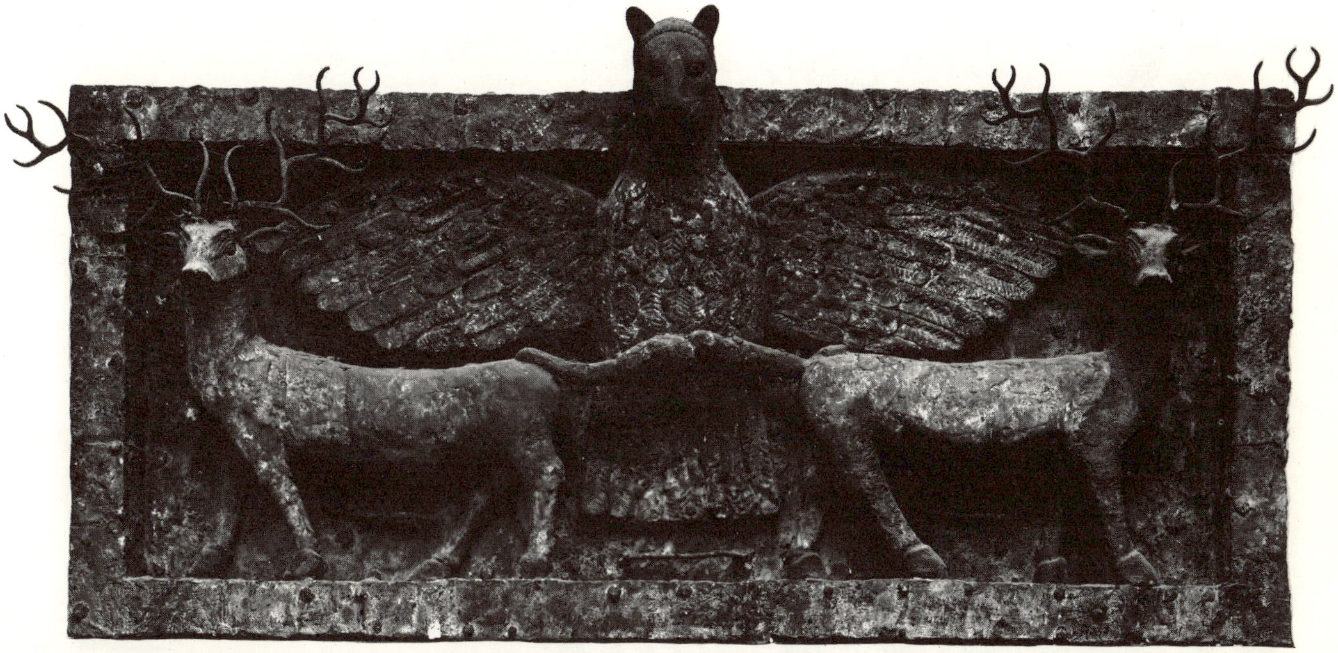

Large copper panel from the temple of Ninkhursag at Tell-el Obeid, near Ur, showing the divine, lion-headed eagle, Imdugud, with two stags. The personification of the benevolent rainstorm after drought, his outstretched wings were believed to shroud the heavens with clouds. Originally erected over the doorway of the temple, this relief shows the balanced arrangement of figures which was one of the great creations of Sumerian art. *c.* third millennium B.C.

INTRODUCTION

From the beginning of the third millennium B.C., a flourishing civilisation existed on the lower banks of the Tigris and the Euphrates, due to two neighbouring peoples: the Akkadians and the Sumerians. The land of Sumer was situated around the upper end of the Persian Gulf, which in those days probably extended much further inland than it does to-day, although this belief has recently been challenged. The towns of Eridu to the south and Nippur to the north marked its extreme limits: other towns were Lagash, Umma, Erech, Larsa and Ur. The Sumerians had probably come from central Asia or the Siberian steppes. The land of Akkad, which lay immediately to the north of Sumer, was peopled by Semites who had probably come from northern Syria. The site of the city, Agade, from which it took its name, has not yet been identified. Its other principal towns were – from south to north – Borsippa, Babylon, Kish, Kutha and Sippar.

The question of which of these two peoples was the older has been disputed, as has the part attributable to each in the development of civilisation. As to the respective contributions of the two races to religion which is all that concerns us here, it is probably most accurate to regard Assyro-Babylonian religion as not primarily a Semitic religion but as one resulting from the semitisation of an originally Sumerian or, to employ a more general term, Asian basis.

However that may be, there was indubitably a reciprocal penetration between the religions of Sumer and Akkad. Each city doubtless venerated its own divinities, but each also welcomed those of neighbouring cities. Conquerors, moreover, would impose their own gods on regions subdued. In time, these new gods would become identified with the indigenous gods and, if not actually assimilated, form affiliations and relationships with them. It is this intermixture of the Akkadian and Sumerian pantheons, completed by the contributions of later epochs, which constitutes Assyro-Babylonian mythology.

THE CREATION

The myth of the Creation is given to us in a series of seven tablets which in the main come, like most of the other religious texts which we shall make use of, from the library of Ashurbanipal in Nineveh. Tablets date from the seventh century B.C., whilst there are some pieces from Ashur going back to 1000 B.C. The work as we have it must be based on much older original texts.

Water is the primordial element. From the fusion of sweet water (Apsu) and salt water (Tiamat) arose all beings, beginning with the gods.

The *Apsu,* which is here personified, was a kind of abyss filled with water which encircled the earth. The earth itself was a round plateau. This plateau was bounded by mountains on which rested the vault of heaven, and it floated on the waters of the Apsu. From the Apsu came the springs which broke through the surface of the earth. The Apsu may be compared to the River Oceanus of the Greeks, which Homer also called the father of all things.

Tiamat was a personification of the sea and represented the feminine element which gave birth to the world. In the continuation of the story she represents the blind forces of primitive chaos against which the intelligent and organising gods struggle.

Lakhmu and *Lakhamu* were the first two to be born. They are rather vague gods, and seem to be a pair of monstrous serpents. They gave birth to *Anshar*, the male principle, and to *Kishar*, the female principle, who represented respectively, so some think, the celestial and the terrestrial worlds. In the same way the Greek

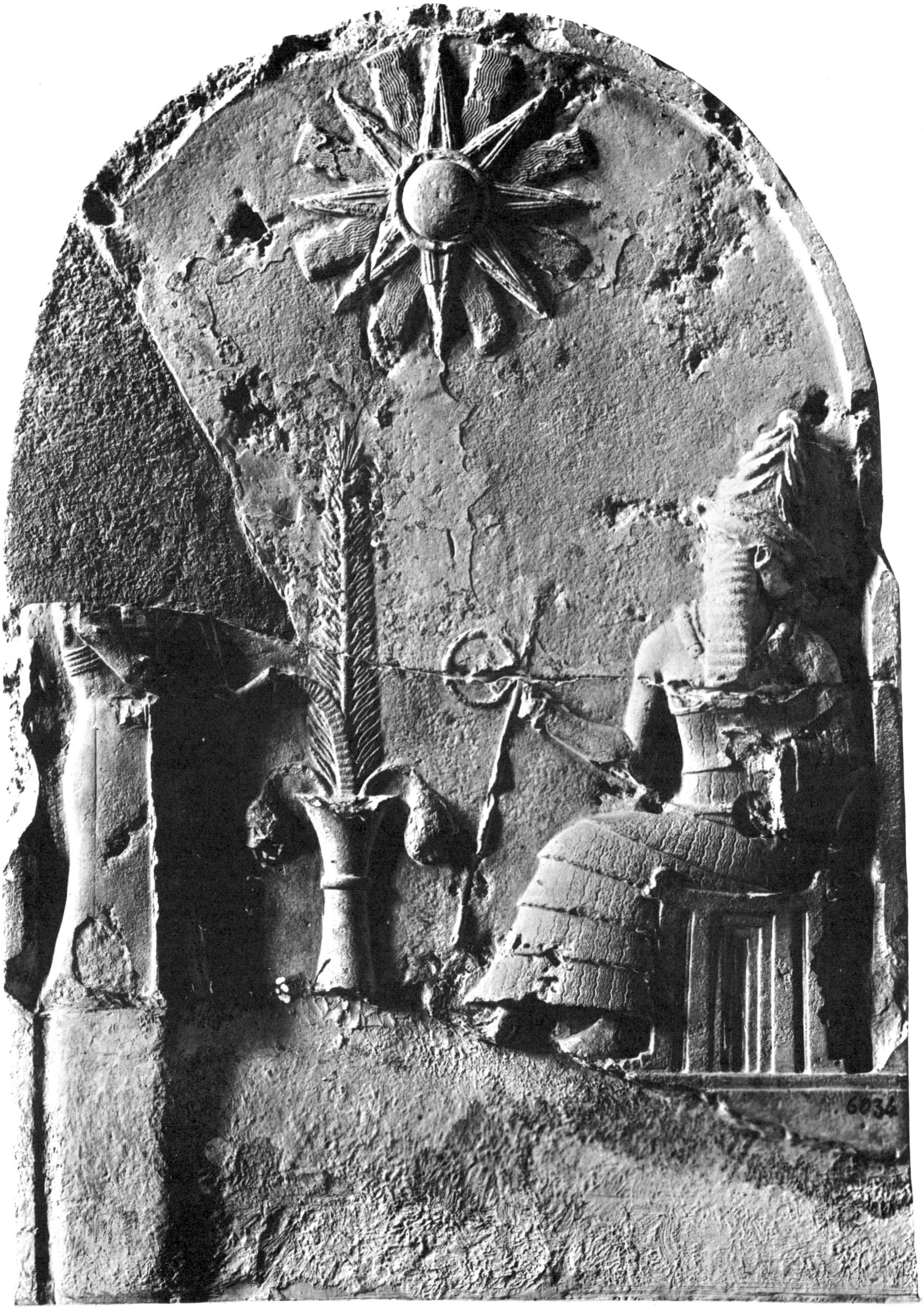

Scene of worship. A devotee waters the sacred plant before a seated divinity, doubtless the god Shamash. Archaic stela. Louvre.

Figure of a bison. Possibly a votive offering, the tuft under its chin and the long, shaggy hair on its head and body are elaborately chased. Sumerian work. *c.* 2500 B.C. From Van (Eastern Turkey).

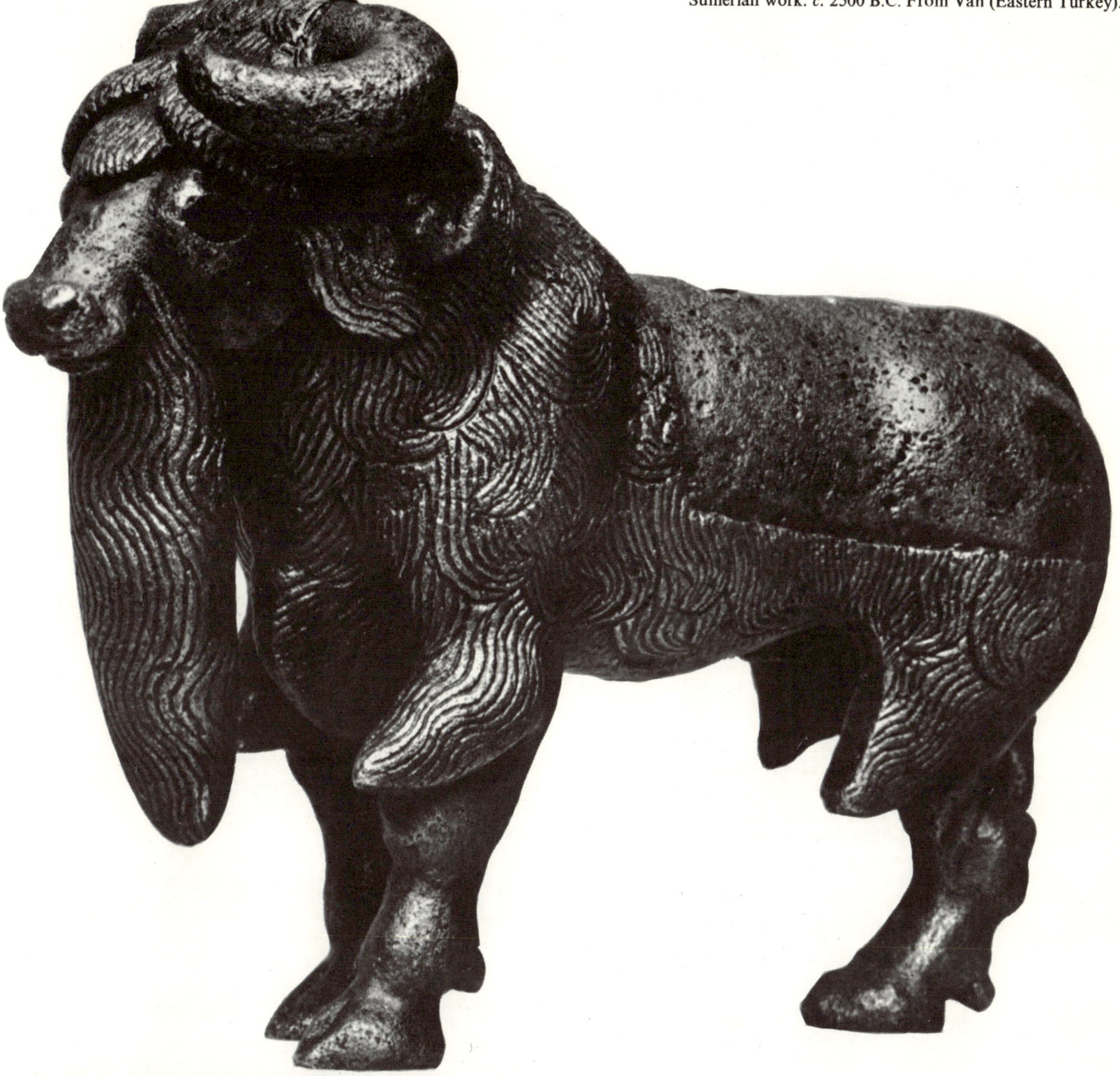

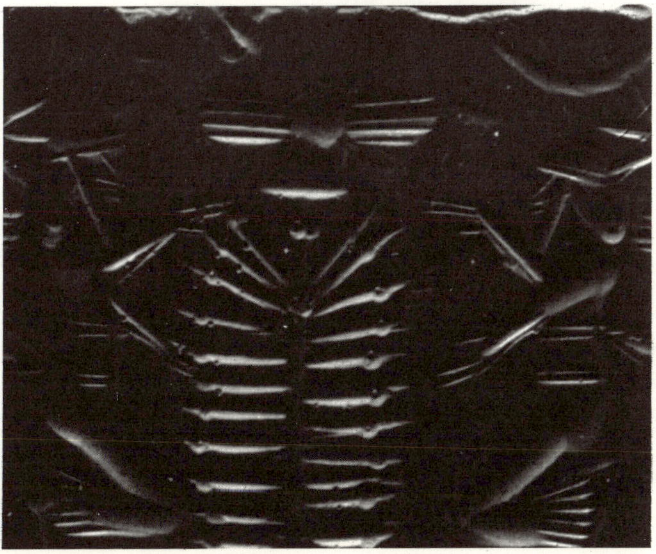

Sacred tree with two worshippers. Above the tree hovers the winged disk, emblem of Asshur. Assyrian cylinder. Louvre.

gods were born of the union of Uranus, the sky, and Gaea, the earth. But while in Greek mythology Gaea played an important role Kishar does not appear again in the story.

In the *Epic of the Creation* it will be noticed that the principal role is played by *Marduk*; it is he who triumphs over Tiamat and organises the universe. This is explained by the Babylonian origin of the poem, for Marduk was, as we shall later see, the great god of Babylon.

Now this is how the people of Sumer and Akkad explained the origin of the world.

In the beginning when 'the sky above had not been named and the earth below was nameless' there existed only Apsu, the primordial ocean, and Tiamat, the tumultuous sea. From their mingled waters came forth first *Mummu* (the tumult of the waves) then a pair of monstrous serpents, *Lakhmu* and *Lakhamu*, who in their turn gave birth to *Anshar*, the celestial world, and to *Kishar*, the terrestrial world. To Anshar and Kishar were born the great gods: Anu, the powerful; Ea, of vast intellect; and the other divinities. These latter were the *Igigi* who peopled the sky, and the *Anunnakę* who were scattered over the earth and through the underworld.

Soon the new gods with their turbulence disturbed the repose of old Apsu who complained to Tiamat: 'During the day I have no rest and at night I cannot sleep.' The two ancestors argued about

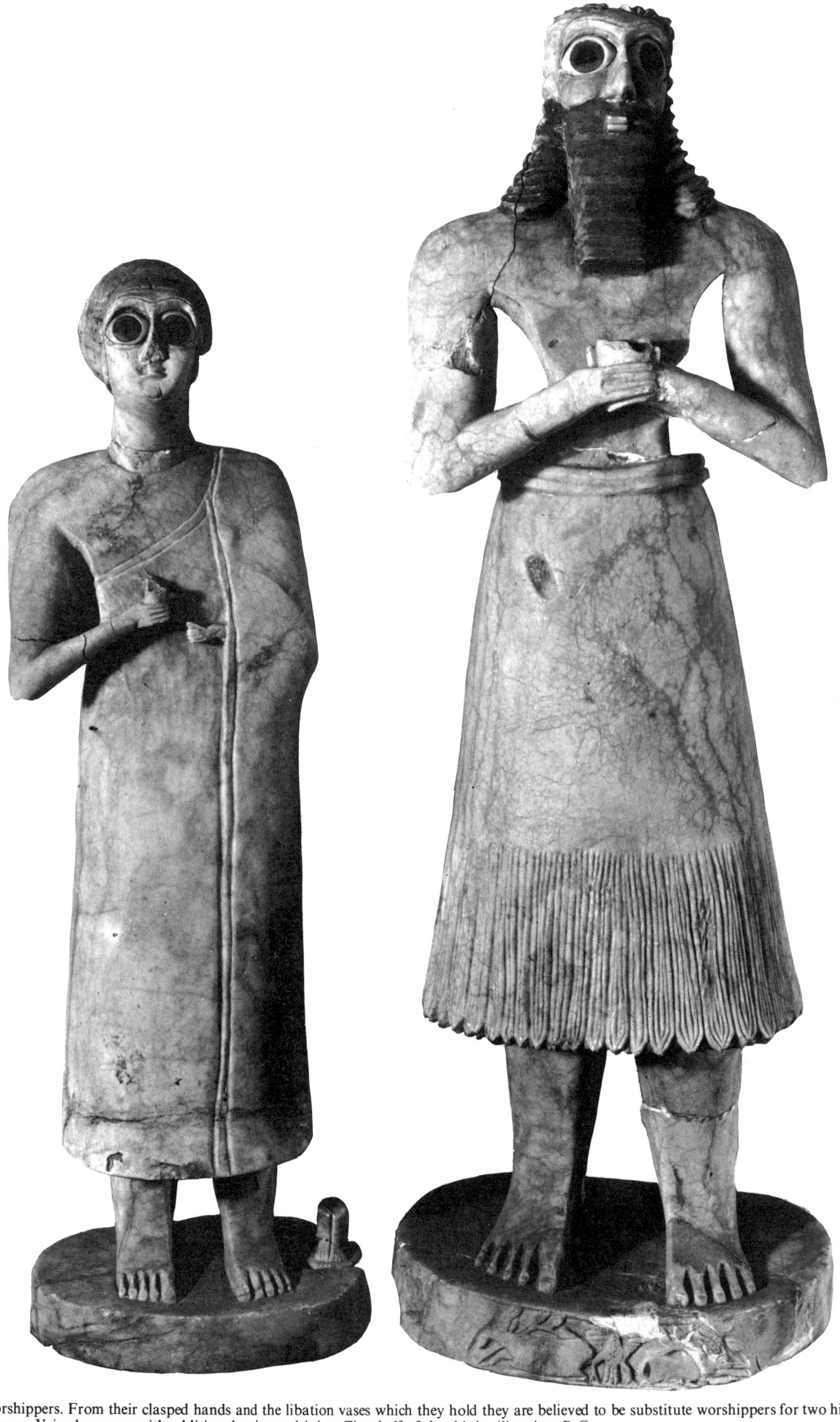

Two worshippers. From their clasped hands and the libation vases which they hold they are believed to be substitute worshippers for two high-ranking personnages. Veined gypsum with additional paint and inlay. First half of the third millennium B.C.

A priest, or possibly a hero, approaching an altar. In his outstretched hands he holds a lotus plant. Ivory panel from Fort Shalasar, Assyria.

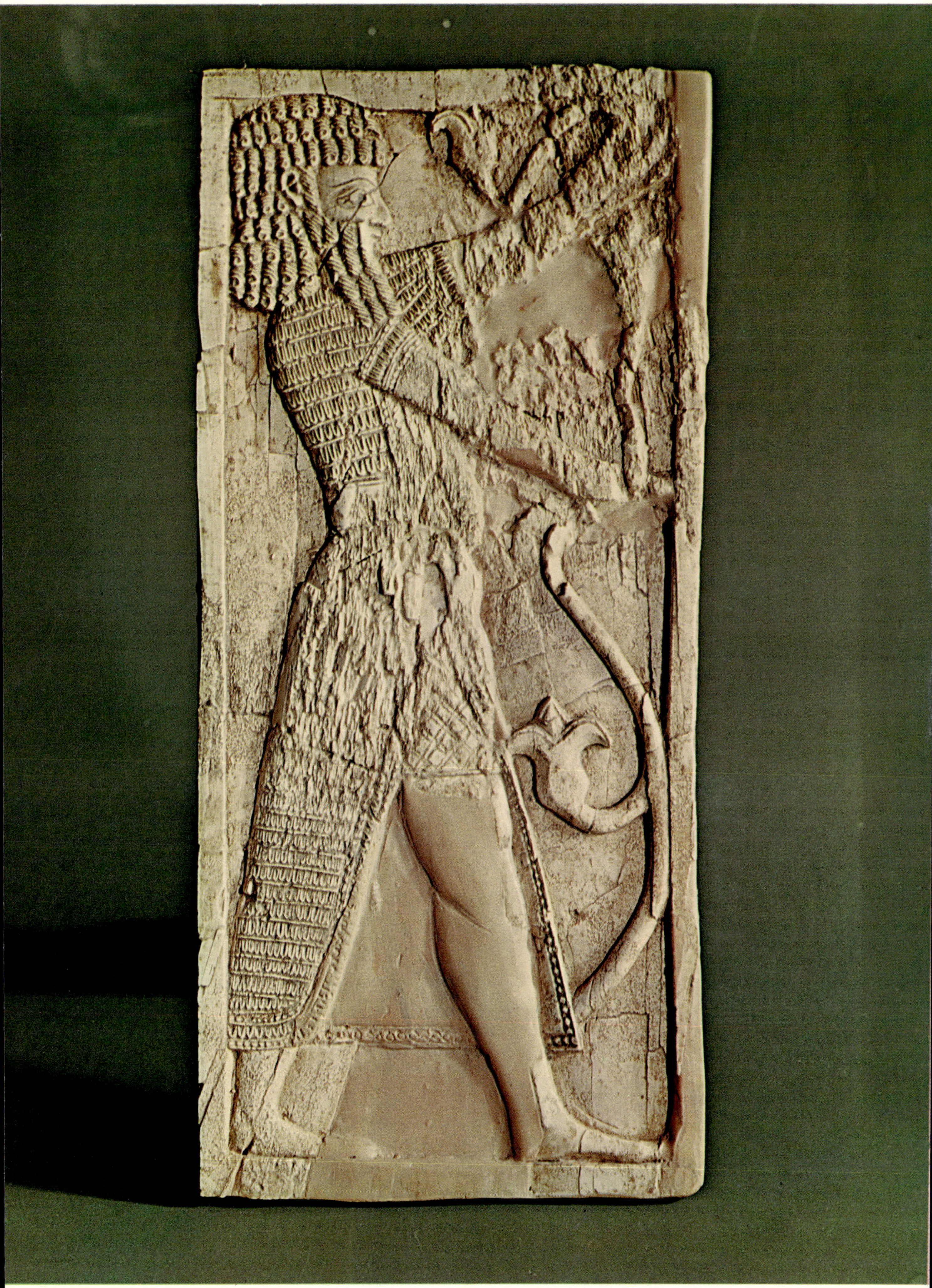

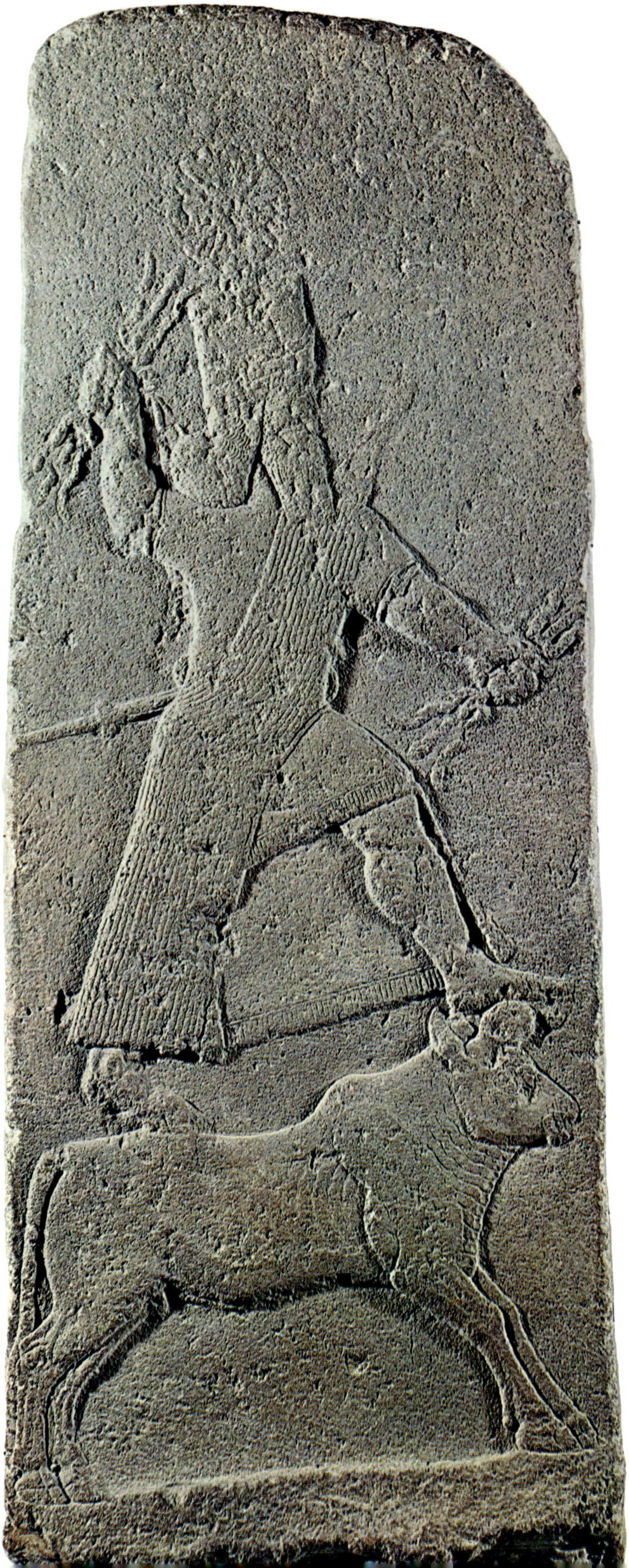

Adad, the Babylonian god of tempests. He could be both beneficent and terrifying – while he was feared in the fury of the storm he was also worshipped as the bringer of the life-giving rain. On this stele from Arslan-Tash he is seen riding on a bull, his emblem, and carrying thunderbolts in his hands. *c.* Eighth century, B.C.

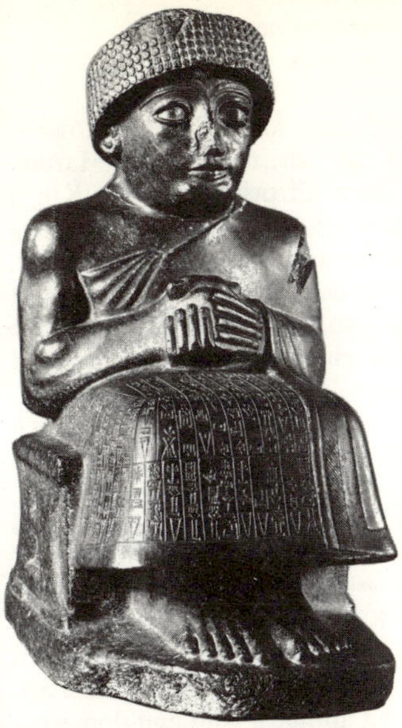

Small seated statue of Gudea, the *patesi*, or governor, of the Sumerian city-state of Lagash. Like most rulers of his time, Gudea was also a priest. Here he is portrayed in the presence of his god wearing a turban-like head-dress and with his hands clasped before him in prayer. The original Sumerian beliefs contributed much to the myths and religion of Assyria and Babylonia. Alabaster. End of the third millennium B.C.

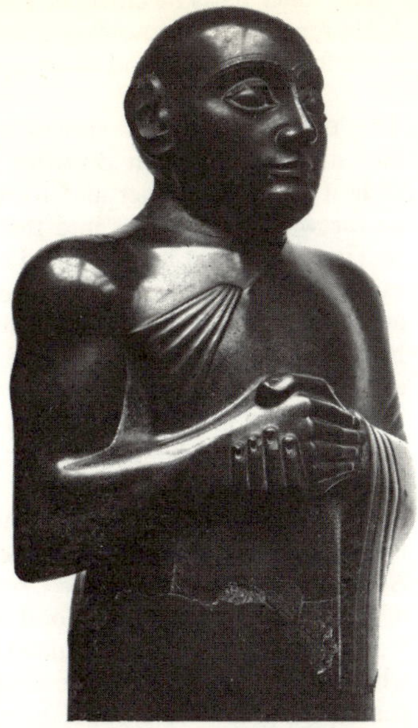

Votive figure of Gudea of Lagash. The *patesi* stands bare-headed wearing a simple robe which leaves his right shoulder bare and with his hands again clasped in the ritual attitude of prayer. As the result of a dream Gudea built a temple to Ningirsu at Lagash and this statue may well have come from this. Black basalt. End of the third millennium B.C.

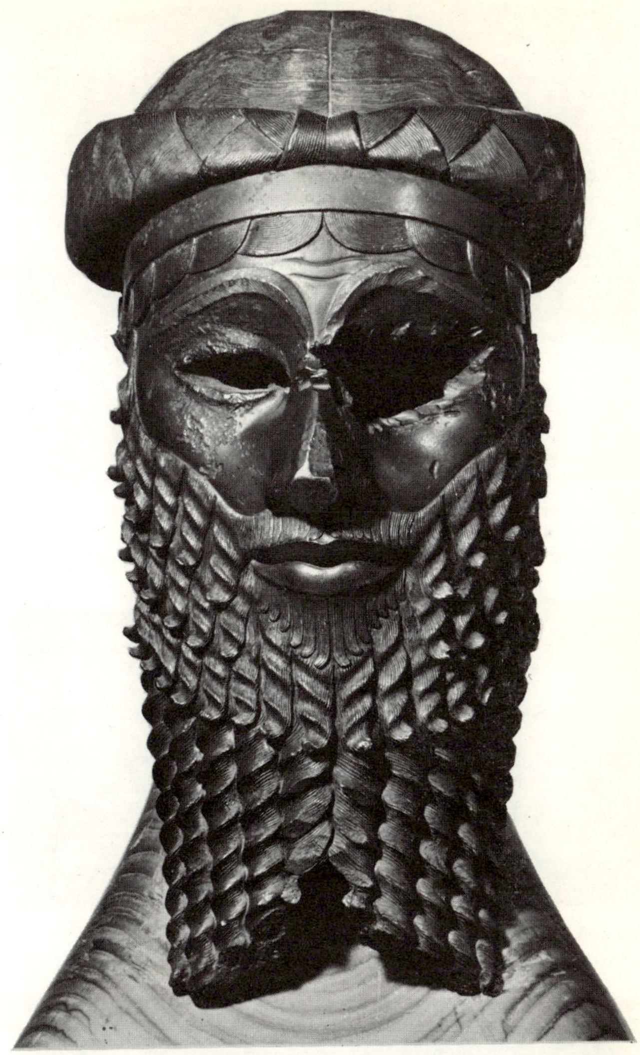

Life-size bronze head of an Akkadian priest or king from Nineveh. The functions of priest and king were often combined during this period so that this head could well represent a man who was both. The hair, beard and eyebrows are elaborately worked while the eyes were probably made of precious stones. *c.* 2200 B.C.

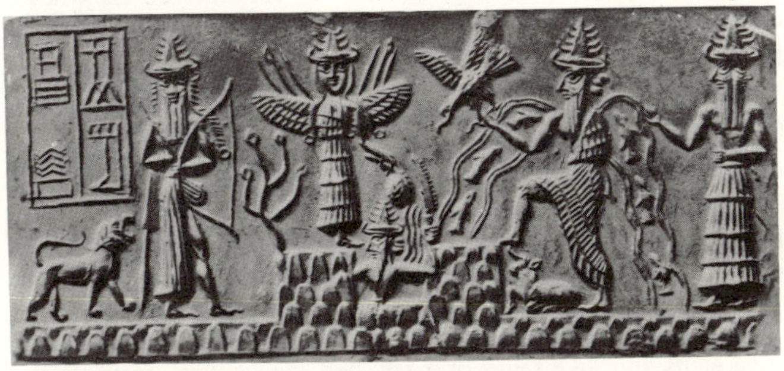

The liberation of the sun god. In the centre Shamash, the sun god, rises from the Mountain of the East before a winged goddess wearing the *kaunakes*. A god with a bow and arrow stands on the left while on the right a water or river god ascends the mountain before a two-faced god. Impression from a Sumerian cylinder seal. *c.* 2250 B.C.

the annihilation of their descendants. 'Why should we destroy all that we have made?' asked Tiamat. 'Even though their way is troublesome!' But Ea, who perceived all things, learnt of Apsu's design and by his magic incantations was able to seize Apsu and Mummu. Tiamat, enraged, gathered around her a certain number of the gods and gave birth to enormous serpents 'with sharp teeth, merciless in slaughter', to terrible dragons with glittering scales, to tempest-monsters, savage dogs, to scorpion-men, furious hurricanes, fish-men and rams. To command this troop she chose *Kingu*, to whom she gave sovereignty over all the gods, pinning on his breast the tablets of fate.

Meanwhile Ea, who knew of Tiamat's plans, went to his father Anshar. 'Tiamat, our mother,' he said, 'has conceived a hatred against us. She is gathering an army together, she storms with fury.' Listening to his son, Anshar was moved. He 'struck his thigh, he bit his lip, his stomach knew no more rest'. At first he sent Anu against Tiamat, but Anu lacked the heart to confront the goddess. Ea was no more courageous. Then Ea summoned Bêl-Marduk, 'the son who makes his heart swell', and bade him to do battle with Tiamat, promising him the victory. Marduk accepted, but first insisted that the assembled gods should confer on him supreme authority. Anshar consented and at once sent his messenger Gaga to Lakhmu and Lakhamu, as well as to the other Igigi. All hastened to the Upshukina and, having kissed each other, sat down to a banquet. After they had eaten bread and drunk wine they prepared a princely dwelling for Marduk, the king. They acknowledged his rule over all the world and accorded him the sceptre, the throne and the *palu,* giving him the unrivalled weapon which repelled all enemies, 'Go', they said to him, 'and slay Tiamat. May the winds carry her blood to secret places!'

Thus invested Marduk took in his right hand a bow, fixed the string, hung a quiver at his side, set lightning before him and made a net in which to entangle Tiamat. He loosed the winds which he posted beside him; then, taking his chief weapon, the hurricane, he mounted his chariot – a terrifying tempest – which was drawn by four swift and violent steeds, fearful in battle. Thus 'arrayed in terror' he went forth to challenge Tiamat to battle.

They rose up, Tiamat and Marduk the Wise, among the gods. The *Epic of the Creation* (Tablet IV, vs. 93-104. Dhorme's translation), tells us:

> They marched to war, they drew near to give battle.
> The Lord spread out his net and caught her in it.
> The evil wind which followed him, he loosed it in her face.
> She opened her mouth, Tiamat, to swallow him.
> He drove in the evil wind so that she could not close her lips.
> The terrible winds filled her belly. Her heart was seized,
> She held her mouth wide open.
> He let fly an arrow, it pierced her belly.

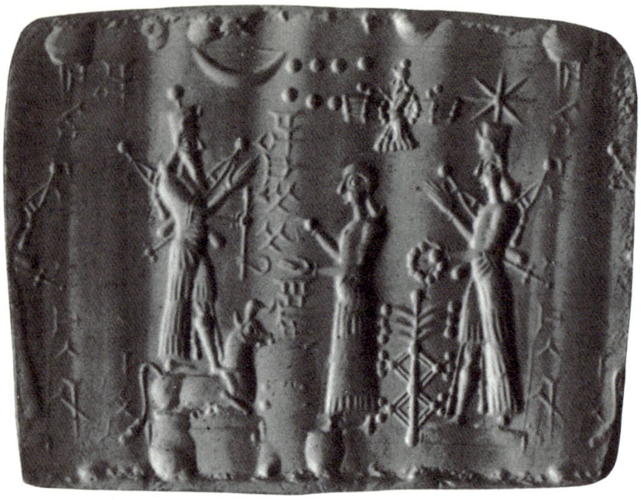

Worshipper between two divinities: the god with the axe, the goddess with the crown. Perhaps Marduk and Ishtar. Above, the emblem of Asshur. Assyrian cylinder. Bibliothèque Nationale.

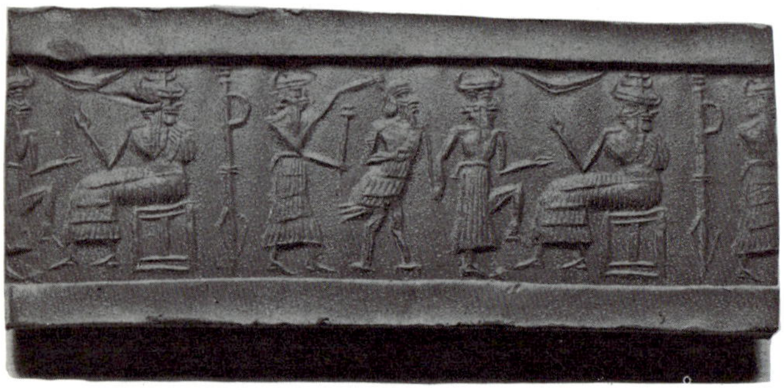

The god with two heads leads to Anu (?) the tempest-bird Zu. Assyrian cylinder. Louvre.

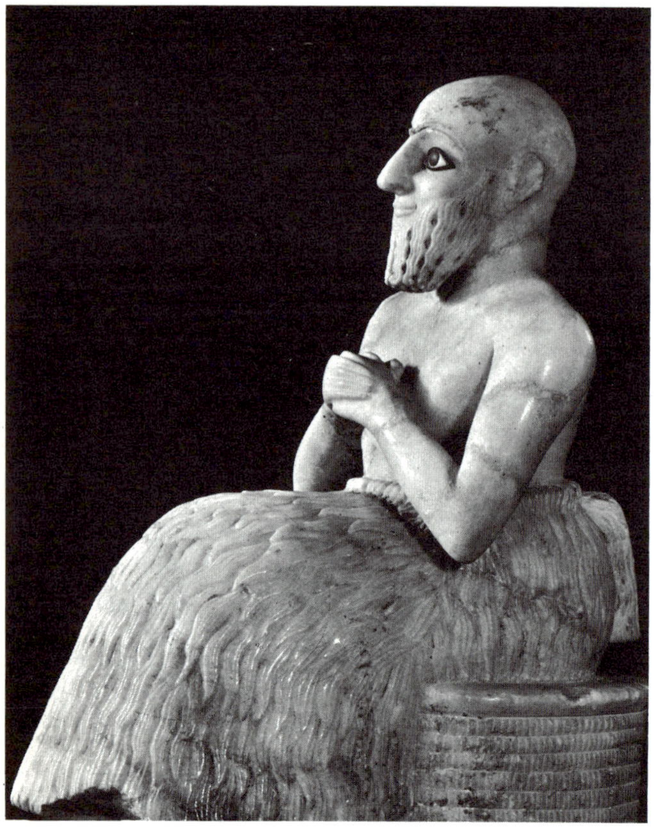

Ebih-il worshipping the goddess Ishtar. One of the most popular deities in the pantheon, the goddess had numerous devotees. This seated statue portrays one of them – the steward Ebih-il – who is shown with his hands clasped before him in prayer, ritually clad in an elaborate skirt. It was dedicated by him to the goddess and comes from her temple at Mari in Sumeria. Alabaster. *c.* 2500 B.C.

Her inner parts he clove, he split her heart.
He rendered her powerless and destroyed her life.
He felled her body and stood upright on it.

The death of Tiamat spread confusion among her followers. Her auxiliaries fled in disorder to save their lives, but Marduk caught them in his net and took them all prisoner. With Kingu he threw them in chains into the infernal regions. Then, returning to Tiamat, he split her skull and cut the arteries of her blood. And, as he contemplated the monstrous corpse, he 'conceived works of art'. He clove the body 'like a fish into its two parts'. From one half he fashioned the vault of the heavens, from the other the solid earth. That done, he organised the world. He constructed a dwelling-place for the great gods in the sky and installed the stars which were their image; he fixed the length of the year and regulated the course of the heavenly bodies.

Thus the earth was formed. Then 'in order that the gods should live in a world to rejoice their hearts' Marduk created humanity. According to the *Epic of the Creation* Marduk moulded the body of the first man using the blood of Kingu. A neo-Babylonian text from Eridu says that he was aided in his work by the goddess Aruru who 'produced with him the seed of mankind'. Finally there appeared the great rivers, vegetation and animals, wild and domestic. The work of creation had been achieved.

THE WORLD OF THE GODS

The essential privilege of the gods was immortality. But they had the same needs and passions as mortals.

They were subject to fear. During the deluge the gods were disquieted to see the waters rise. They climbed to the sky of Anu and there:

The gods crouched like dogs; on the wall they cowered.

The gods were also greedy. When they forgathered they never failed to feast and drink themselves into a state of boisterous intoxication. The *Epic of the Creation* says:

They grow drunk with drinking, their bodies are joyful,
They shout aloud, their hearts exult.

They were equally fond of sacrifices. When Uta Napishtim was saved from the Deluge and, in gratitude, placed offerings on the summit of the mountain, 'the gods smelled the good odour, the gods swarmed like flies above him who offered them sacrifice'.

Like men the gods had wives and families. They were celestial sovereigns and, like kings of earth, had their courts, servants and soldiers. They inhabited palaces situated either in regions above the sky, on the great Mountain of the East, or in the subterranean depths of the underworld. Although each had his own sphere of influence they would sometimes gather together to debate common problems. They would then assemble in a hall called the Upshukina. In particular they would congregate there at the beginning of each year, on the feast of Zagmuk, in order to determine men's destiny. The gods thus formed a thoroughly organised and hierarchical society.

The divine hierarchy was not immediately established and was often modified. The great primordial principle of fertility and fecundity, at first worshipped by the Sumerians, was quickly dispersed into a crowd of divinities who had no precise connection with each other. Later, under the influence of national pride, the gods acquired rank, the dignity of which corresponded to the importance in the country as a whole of the city in which they were particularly venerated. Finally the official theologians of Babylon fixed the hierarchy of the gods more or less definitely, dividing them into triads. The two principal triads were those of the great gods Anu, Enlil and Ea, and of the astral gods Sin, Shamash and Ishtar.

THE GREAT GODS

When the victory of Marduk over Tiamat had re-established peace and order in the world of the gods each divinity received his own particular sphere of influence. The universe was divided into three regions each of which became the domain of a god. Anu's share was the sky. The earth was given to Enlil. Ea became the ruler of the waters. Together they constituted the triad of the Great Gods.

Anu. Anu was the son of Anshar and Kishar. His name signified 'sky' and he reigned over the heavens. There he resided in the uppermost region which was called the 'sky of Anu'. He was god in the highest sense, the supreme god. All the other deities honoured him as their 'father', that is to say, their chief. They came to him for refuge when danger threatened them, during the Deluge for example. It was to him they came when they had complaints to lodge. Thus the goddess Ishtar, harshly repelled by the hero Gilgamesh, goes to find Anu, her father. 'Oh my father,' she said to him, 'Gilgamesh has cursed me,' and she requested him to make 'a celestial bull' to send against Gilgamesh. In the same way Anu summoned all cases of importance before his tribunal. When Adapa broke the wings of the South Wind Anu ordered him to appear before him. He combined power and justice, all the marks of sovereignty. Before the raised throne on which he sat were placed the insignia of royalty: 'the sceptre, the diadem, the crown and the staff of command.' On monuments Anu was represented by a tiara placed on a throne. He had, moreover, an army at his command: the stars which he had created to destroy the wicked were called 'the soldiers of Anu'.

Anu never left the heavenly regions, never came down to earth. When he abandoned his majestic immobility it was to walk in that portion of the sky which was exclusively reserved for him, the name of which was 'Anu's Way'.

In spite of his uncontested supremacy he was not, however, exempt from weaknesses. We have seen, that, for example, when he was sent to do battle against Tiamat he was unable to face the monster and left the glory of victory to Marduk.

Aided by his companion, the goddess Antu, he presided from above over the fates of the universe and hardly occupied himself with human affairs. Thus, although he never ceased to be universally venerated, other gods finally supplanted him and took over certain of his prerogatives. But the great god's prestige remained such that the power of these usurper gods was never firmly established until they, too, assumed the name Anu.

Enlil (Bel). Enlil was much more involved in the events which took place on earth. In the land of Sumer, and particularly at Nippur, Enlil, Lord of the Air, had been worshipped from early times. Enlil was the god of the hurricane and his weapon was the amaru, that is, the deluge. Like the Greek Zeus he symbolised the forces of nature and again like Zeus he was soon considered to be the master of men's fates.

When the people of Babylon took over the gods of Sumer, far from overlooking Enlil they made him the second element in their supreme triad. They virtually assimilated Enlil to their god Marduk, to whom they applied the name Bel, which means 'Lord'. Bel then became Lord of the World and his rule extended throughout the earth. He was called 'King of the Land' or 'Lord of all Regions'.

Enlil, like Anu, had a reserved promenade in the heavens – 'Enlil's Way' – but he normally resided on the Great Mountain of the East.

Like Anu, Enlil (Bel) held the insignia of royalty which he dispensed to the person of his choice. Earthly kings, then, were only the representatives or vicars of Enlil (or Bel). In order to raise them above other men it was enough that the god should pronounce their name, for the word of Bel was all-powerful.

> The word of Enlil is a breath of wind, the eye sees it not.
> His word is a deluge which advances and has no rival.
> His word above the slumbering skies makes the earth to slumber.
> His word when it comes in humility destroys the country.
> His word when it comes in majesty overwhelms houses and brings weeping to the land.
> At his word the heavens on high are stilled.

For men, then, Enlil is the dispenser of good and evil. It was he who in an angry mood sent down the deluge to annihilate the human race.

In the most ancient period Enlil was associated with the goddess Ninkhursag, 'Lady of the Great Mountain', though to the systematising theologians his consort was Ninlil. When Bel took over

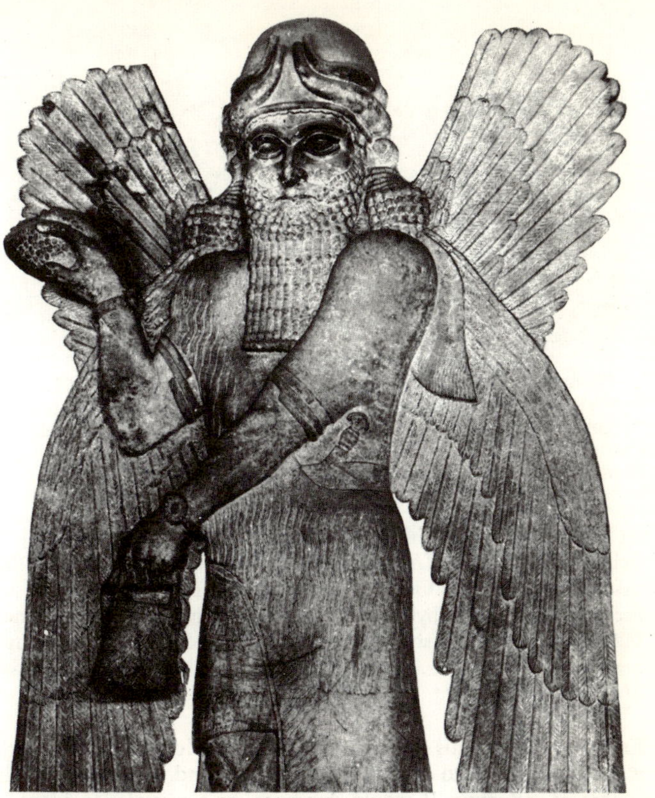

Benevolent winged genie from one of the gates of the palace of Sargon II at Khorsabad. Dressed in a long fringed robe and the horned head-dress of divinity, he holds a lustral vase and pine-cone sprinkler with which to purify those entering the palace after they have passed the guardian bulls at the entrance. His function may also have been to drive away evil spirits and demons.
Relief carving of the eighth century B.C.

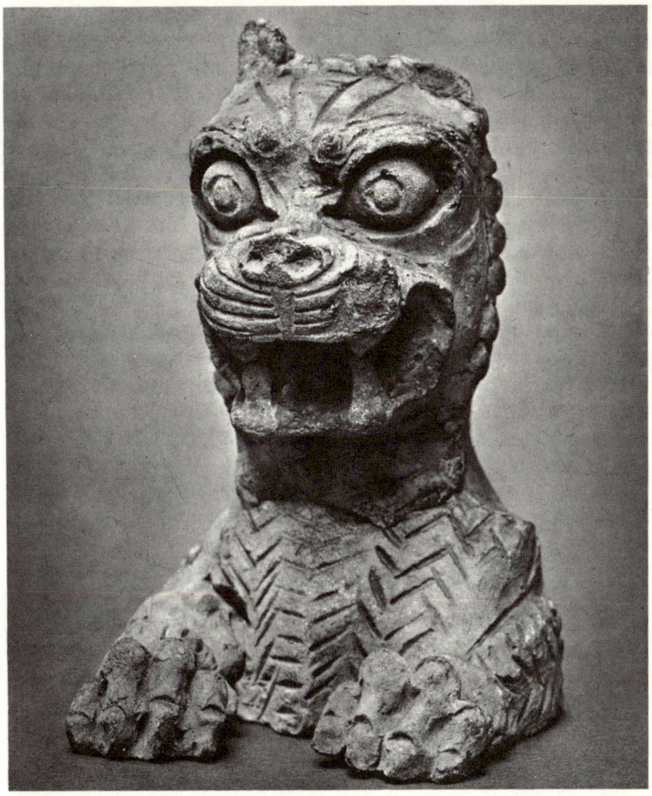

Lion-headed Babylonian monster. This creature probably represents one of the seven evil genii who were believed to have been born in the Mountain of the West and lived in holes in the ground or among ruins, spreading discord and disease among men and decimating their flocks. Genii, both good and evil, were believed to play a major role in men's daily lives by the Babylonians. Terra-cotta. Seventh to sixth centuries B.C.

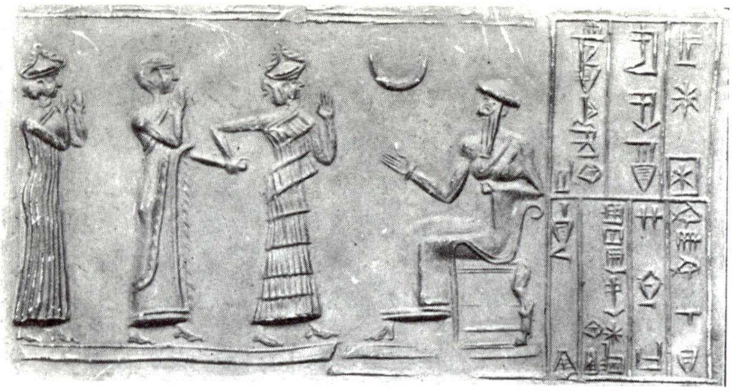

Ur-Nammu deified as the god Sin. On the right, the great king of Ur is shown seated on a throne extending his hand in greeting to Khashkhamer, the governor of Ishkun Sin, who is led into his presence by two goddesses wearing conical horned head-dresses with their hands raised in intercession. In the centre is a crescent moon.
Impression from a Sumerian cylinder seal. 2500 B.C.

the attributes of Enlil, his consort could correspondingly be called Belit, that is to say, 'The Lady'. Although she sometimes bore the title 'Mother of the Gods', Ninkhursag or Belit enjoyed no supremacy over the Babylonian Olympus. On the contrary, with her sacred milk she nourished those whom Bel had chosen to be kings among men. Thus, thanks to her, earthly sovereigns could boast of divine origin.

Ea. The name of this divinity, which means 'House of the Water', is alone sufficient to indicate his character and the nature of his sphere of influence. It would, however, be a mistake to identify him with the Poseidon of the Greeks. Ea was not a marine deity. His proper domain was the Apsu – in other words that stretch of fresh water which surrounded the earth and on which at the same time the earth floated. The springs which gushed from the earth, the great rivers which watered the Chaldean plain came from the Apsu. We have seen how, during the creation, the fertilising waters of the Apsu encountered the salty and tumultuous waves of the sea. In the same way the Greeks distinguished between the River Oceanus and the 'sterile sea'. While the waters of the Apsu spread abundance and happiness over the earth they were also the source of all knowledge and wisdom.

In the land of Sumer, Ea bore the name of *Enki*, 'Lord of the Earth'. As god of the Apsu he was also god of supreme wisdom. He presided over magic incantations and the gods themselves willingly consulted him. Sometimes he was also called 'Lord of the sacred Eye', *Ninigiku*, that is to say 'he whom nothing escapes'. When necessary his vigilant wisdom corrected the errors of the gods themselves. When Bel decided to drown the race of man by flood it was Ea who warned Uta-Napishtim and prevented the destruction of mankind.

God of knowledge, Ea, jointly with Shamash, spoke oracularly and he was invoked in incantations. But he also presided over men's work. Carpenters, stone-cutters, goldsmiths venerated him as their patron. It is even possible, on one interpretation of a very damaged text, that Ea was sometimes regarded as the creator of man, whom he had fashioned with clay.

The earthly residence of Ea was the holy city of Eridu which, situated in the extreme south of the land of Sumer on the Persian Gulf, had been the first city to be raised from the waters. Here Ea had his dwelling, the *Ezuab*, or the 'House of the Apsu'. Nearby rose a wondrous tree, a black *Kishkanu*, the foliage of which shone like a lapis-lazuli and cast a thick shade like that of a forest.

Ea is represented as a goat with a fish's tail. He is also seen in human form with waves springing from his shoulders or from a vase held in his hands.

Ea's companion, whose physiognomy is rather vague, bears the name of Ninki, 'Lady of the Earth', or else Damkina, or again Damgalnunna, 'The Great Spouse of the Lord'.

Such was the triad of the great gods, and such it remained until the day when Babylon became mistress of all the land of Sumer and Akkad. Then, naturally, she placed her own national god, Marduk, at the head of the pantheon.

Marduk. Marduk was the oldest son of Ea. He came from the Apsu and originally personified the fertilising action of the waters; it was he who made plants grow and grain ripen. He thus had above all the character of an agricultural deity, as his attribute the *marru*, which is simply a spade, testifies. His fortunes grew with the greatness of Babylon, the city of his choice, and finally he occupied the first place among the gods. He had, moreover, attained this position by right of conquest. It will be remembered how, after the failure of Anu and Ea – the *Epic of the Creation* does not mention Bel in this connection – Marduk dared to face the monstrous Tiamat. And it will also be remembered how before he joined battle he insisted that the assembly of the gods should invest him with supreme authority and the privilege of determining fates. All this was accorded to him. After his victory the gods showed their gratitude by awarding him fifty titles, each of which corresponded to a divine attribute. In this way the fullness of divinity was united in Marduk. He was not only 'he who created grain and plants and made green things to grow' but also:

> The light of the father who begot him,
> He who renews the gods,
> The Lord of pure incantation, making the dead to live,
> He who knows the hearts of the gods,
> Guardian of justice and law,
> The creator of all things,
> Among lords, the first,
> The Lord of Kings,
> The shepherd of the gods.

Bel conferred upon him his own title of 'Lord of the Land' and Ea, overjoyed at his son's victory, cried:

> Let him, like me, be called Ea;
> The commands that I command let him pronounce them!

Thus Marduk absorbed all the other gods and took over all their various functions and prerogatives. It was he who organised the universe, assigned dwelling-places to the gods, and fixed the course of the heavenly bodies. It was he who created man from the blood of Kingu; he was the 'Lord of Life', the great healer and took the place of his father, Ea, in magic incantations. From Enlil he obtained the governorship of the four quarters of the earth. Henceforward he was the supreme commander of the Anunnaki and each year he himself determined men's fates in the Duku, i.e. 'the pure abode', during the feast of *zagmuk*. Even Anu, the supreme god, felt the effects of Marduk's growing glory. Marduk took from him the *Anutu* – that is, his own dignity – and his word became 'like the word of Anu'.

It was the privilege of the supreme gods to ordain the destiny of men. The possession of the Tablets of Fate was the token of omnipotence. Now, one day, the storm-bird Zu stole the famous tablets. Anu offered the divine kingship to the one who recovered them. When approached, Adad and Shara each in turn declined. Though the text then becomes fragmentary, another composition makes it probable that it was Marduk who succeeded in overcoming the thief Zu and recovering the stolen tablets.

Marduk proved his indomitable courage on another occasion. Evil genii were provoked by the god Sin, whose watchfulness pursued nocturnal malefactors. They wove a plot against him and with the complicity of Shamash, Ishtar and Adad they succeeded in eclipsing his light. As in the days of Tiamat, Anu and Ea were seized with terror. But Marduk gave battle to the rebels, put them to flight and gave back Sin his brilliance. The poet was right when he said:

> When he is angered no god can resist his wrath,
> Before the sharp blade of his sword the gods flee.
> Terrible master, without rival among the great gods!
> In the tempest his weapons flash,
> In his flames steep mountains are overthrown.

Marduk was generally represented armed with a kind of scimitar felling a winged dragon, a souvenir of his victory over Tiamat. In this way he could be seen in the *Esagil*, his famous temple in Babylon, where he was enthroned beside his spouse Zarpanit.

Each year on a fixed date the god's statue was carried solemnly through the immense crowd out of the Esagil and out of the city to a place in the country called the *Akitu* which was a sort of temple. Here it remained for several days. The ritual of this ceremony, which has been restored for us by Thureau-Dangin, comprised prayers chanted by the priests, magic ceremonies, purifications and sacrifices: the king himself came to receive investiture from Bel-Marduk. These festivals lasted no less than ten days. It seems that during them a mystery play was given in which were represented the death of the god, his resurrection and finally his marriage with the goddess.

Similar ceremonies, arranged in the same way, took place annually at Uruk in honour of Anu and Ishtar, and at Ur in honour of Nannar.

Asshur. But the day came when the might of Babylon faded before that of Nineveh. The national god of the Assyrians, Asshur, then took the first place. In order to make this substitution easier Asshur was identified with the ancient Babylonian god Anshar. Thus Asshur became 'king of all the gods, self-created, father of the gods, maker of the sky of Anu and of the underworld, author of mankind, who lives in the bright heavens, Lord of the gods, he who ordained men's fate...'

Asshur was above all a warrior-god who shared the bellicose instincts of his people. He accompanied their armies into battle, fought at their side, directed the soldiers' blows and rendered their arms victorious. Thus he received the first fruits of the booty and the vanquished became his subjects. Nor did he disdain to appear to his followers in order to stimulate their courage and strengthen their confidence. Such was that king of Lydia to whom he showed himself and said: 'Kiss the feet of the king of Asshur, Ashurbanipal, and in his name thou shalt surely triumph over thine enemies.'

Asshur is generally represented in the form of a winged disk, or mounted on a bull, or floating through the air. These are warrior representations. But he was not merely a warlike god. In his quality of supreme divinity he was also the great god of fertility. He is then represented surrounded by branches and his attribute is a female goat.

Asshur's principal consort was the goddess Ninlil.

THE SIDEREAL DIVINITIES

Sin. The moon-god occupied the chief place in the astral triad. Its other two members, Shamash the sun and Ishtar the planet Venus, were his children. Thus it was, in effect, from the night that light had emerged.

In his physical aspect Sin – who was venerated at Ur under the name of Nannar – was an old man with a long beard the colour of lapis-lazuli. He normally wore a turban. Every evening he got into his barque – which to mortals appeared in the form of a brilliant crescent moon – and navigated the vast spaces of the nocturnal sky. Some people, however, believed that the luminous crescent was Sin's weapon. But one day the crescent gave way to a disk which stood out in the sky like a gleaming crown. There could be no doubt that this was the god's own crown; and then Sin was called 'Lord of the Diadem'. These successive and regular transformations lent Sin a certain mystery. For this reason he was considered to be 'He whose deep heart no god can penetrate'.

Because he illuminated the night Sin was an enemy of evil-doers whose criminal enterprises were favoured by darkness. We have already seen how wicked spirits plotted against him. They had won to their cause even the god's children Shamash and Ishtar as well as Adad, the god of thunder. Their combined efforts succeeded in eclipsing Sin, and only Marduk's intervention re-established order.

Sin had other functions. It was he who measured time; for so Marduk had decided on the day of the creation.

At the month's beginning to shine on earth
Thou shalt show two horns to mark six days.
On the seventh day divide the crown in two;
On the fourteenth day, turn thy full face.

Sin was also full of wisdom. At the end of every month the gods came to consult him and he made decisions for them.

His wife was *Ningal,* 'the great Lady'. He was the father not only of Shamash and Ishtar but also of a son *Nusku,* the god of fire.

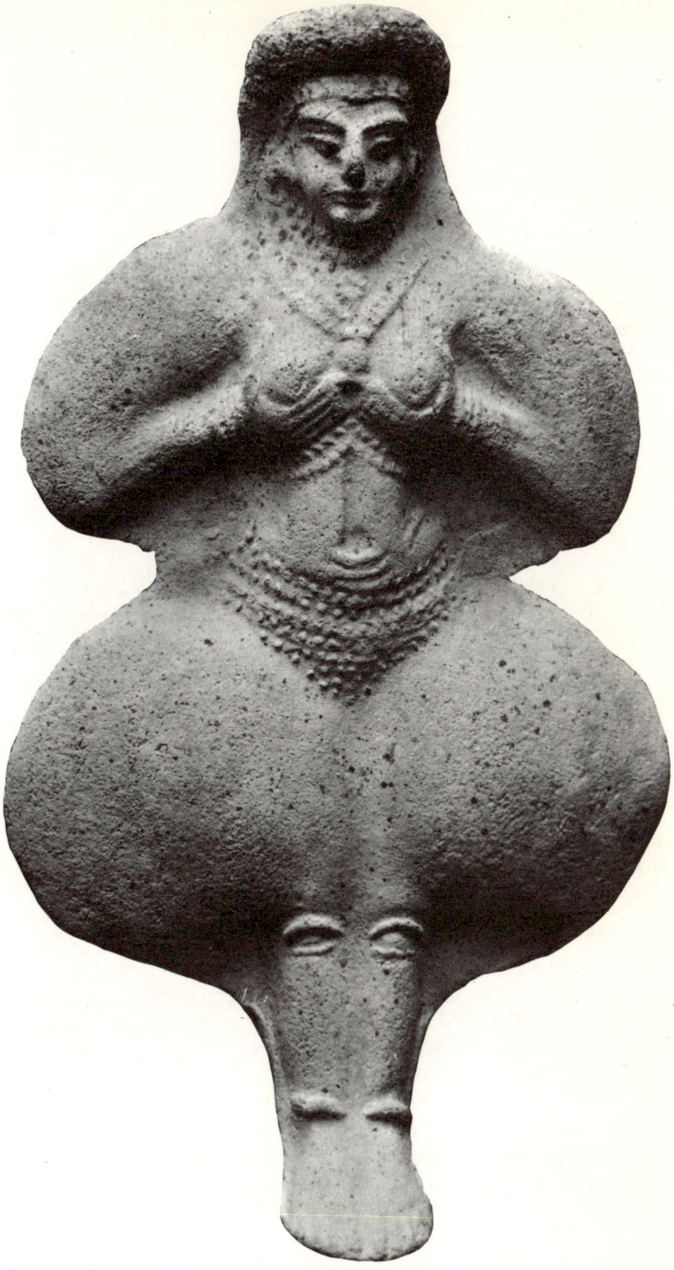

The Goddess Ishtar. Terracotta. Sumerian period. Louvre.

Shamash. Every morning the scorpion-men who inhabit the Mountain of the East and defend its approaches, open in the mountain's flank a great folding door. From it will spring, on his daily journey, Shamash, the sun-god. The god appears. Luminous rays seem to issue from his shoulders. In his hand he grasps an object which resembles the blade of a saw: is it a weapon or more simply the key to the Eastern Gate? With alert footstep he climbs the mountain and joins Bunene, his coachman, who is harnessing the chariot in which the god will take his place. In a dazzle of light Shamash begins slowly to mount the sky. When evening falls Shamash guides his chariot towards the great Mountain of the West. A gate opens and he penetrates the depths of the earth. The sun has disappeared. During the night Shamash pursues his subterranean course so that before dawn he shall have regained the Mountain of the East.

Vigour and courage were the distinctive qualities of this god who triumphed over the night and put the winter to flight. But above all he was the god of justice. His bursting light which chased away the shadows where crime throve made him the terror of the evil-doer: he 'breaks the horn of him who meditates evil'. How could one escape him? Not only did he see everything, but his rays were a vast net which caught all who committed iniquities. Thus he bore the title of 'Judge of the Heavens and the Earth', 'Sublime Judge of the Anunnaki', 'Lord of Judgment'. His temple in Babylon was called the 'House of the Judge of the World'. In his role of judge the god was represented seated on a throne, holding

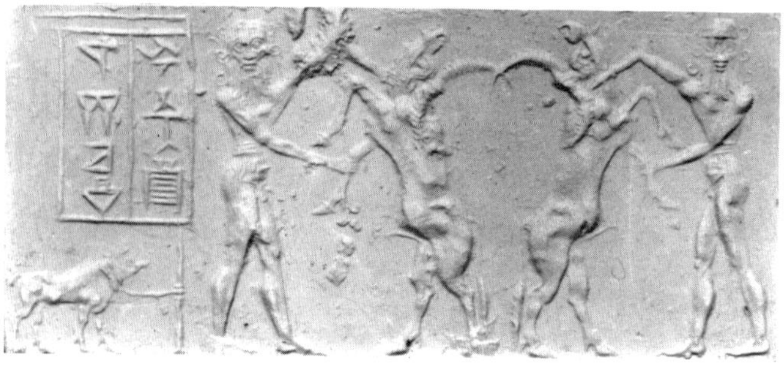

Gilgamesh in conflict. The great Sumerian hero is probably shown here wrestling with the celestial bull which was sent against him by the goddess Ishtar after he had repulsed her advances, the duplication of the figures being for the purposes of symmetry and balance – a common device in Sumerian art. Impression from a mother of emerald Akkadian cylinder seal. *c.* 2340 to 2180 B.C.

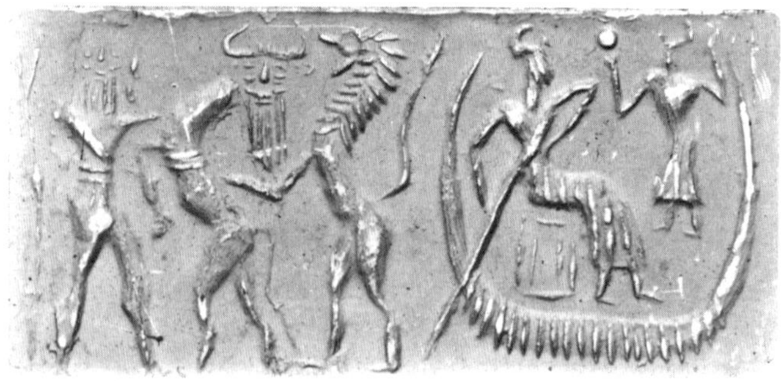

Two scenes from the story of Gilgamesh. On the left Gilgamesh and his friend the half man – half bull, Enkidu, are shown in conflict with a lion, an animal which they loved to hunt together, while on the right the hero is probably shown crossing the waters of Death in the boat of Urshanabi in search of his dead companion. Impression from an Akkadian cylinder seal. 2340 to 2180 B.C.

in his right hand the sceptre and the ring.

Shamash had another role. Like the later Greek Apollo, who was also a sun-god, Shamash was the god of divination. Through the intermediary of a soothsayer, the *baru,* he revealed to men the secrets of the future. After he had offered sacrifice to Shamash the soothsayer would observe the various shapes assumed by oil poured on the water in the sacred tub, or examine the liver of the sacrificial victim, or decipher what the gods had decreed from the position of the stars, the movements of the planets, the appearance of meteorites. It was especially at Sippar, where the sun-god was particularly honoured, that the art of divination flourished.

There Shamash with his wife, *Aya,* was venerated. To the divine couple two gods of abstract character were born: *Kittu* who was justice, and *Misharu* who was law.

Ishtar. According to some, Ishtar was the daughter of Anu; according to others, of Sin. She called herself 'goddess of the morn and goddess of the evening'. One of the most prominent figures in the Assyro-Babylonian pantheon, Ishtar was the divine personification of the planet Venus. While the Assyro-Babylonians made Ishtar a goddess, the Arabs made her a god under the name *Athtar.*

The same complexity occurs in her functions, depending on whether she was considered to be the daughter of Sin or of Anu. In the former case she was a war-goddess, in the latter the goddess of love.

The warrior Ishtar was the daughter of Sin and the sister of Shamash. She was the 'Lady of Battles, valiant among goddesses'. She retained this character in the forms in which she was worshipped by the Assyrians. Like Asshur she went on expeditions, took part in battles 'covered with combat and arrayed in terror'. She is represented standing on a chariot drawn by seven lions, with a bow in her hands. She was particularly worshipped at Nineveh and Arbela (Erbil). She was the sister of Ereshkigal, queen of the underworld, and she helped greatly to people the infernal regions; for she was the 'Star of Lamentation' who 'made brothers who were on good terms quarrel among themselves, and friends forget friendship'.

On the other hand at Erech, Ishtar, daughter of Anu, was above all the goddess of love and voluptuousness, not indeed that her character manifested much more tenderness. On every occasion the goddess was irritable, violent and incapable of tolerating the least obstacle to her wishes. 'If you do not create the celestial bull,' she said to her father Anu, 'I shall break (something) open...the dead will become more numerous than the living.' Finding that the gates of the underworld did not open quickly enough for her she threatened the porter:

> If you open not the gate that I may pass,
> I shall burst it in and smash the lock,
> I shall destroy the threshold and break the doorposts,
> I shall make the dead to rise and they will outnumber the living!

It was, however, she who roused amorous desire in all creatures. As soon as she withdrew her influence:

> The bull refuses to cover the cow, the ass no longer approaches the she-ass,
> In the street the man no longer approaches the maid-servant.

Sacred prostitution formed part of her cult and when she descended to earth she was accompanied by 'courtesans, harlots and strumpets'. Her holy city Erech was called the 'town of the sacred courtesans'. Ishtar herself, moreover, was the 'courtesan of the gods' and she was the first to experience the desires which she inspired. Her lovers were legion and she chose them from all walks of life. But woe to him whom Ishtar had honoured! The fickle goddess treated her passing lovers cruelly, and the unhappy wretches usually paid dearly for the favours heaped on them. Animals, enslaved by love, lost their native vigour: they fell into traps laid by men or were domesticated by them. 'Thou hast loved the lion, mighty in strength', says the hero Gilgamesh to Ishtar, 'and thou hast dug for him seven and seven pits! Thou hast loved the steed, proud in battle, and destined him for the halter, the goad and the whip.'

Even for the gods Ishtar's love was fatal. In her youth the goddess had loved Tammuz, god of the harvest, and – if we are to believe Gilgamesh – this love caused the death of Tammuz. Ishtar was overcome with grief and burst into lamentations over her dead lover. In such a way, later, Aphrodite was to bewail the death of Adonis.

In order to find Tammuz again and snatch him from his sad abode, Ishtar conceived the audacious plan of descending into the underworld, 'to journey towards that land without return, towards that house from which he who enters does not come out again'. She had the gates opened and penetrated the seven precincts, at each gate stripping off one by one a piece of adornment or dress: the great crown from her head, pendants from her ears, the necklace from her throat, the jewels from her breast, her girdle adorned with birthstones, the bracelets from her hands and from her feet; and finally the garment which covered her nakedness. She arrived in the presence of Ereshkigal, queen of the infernal regions. But Ereshkigal called Namtaru, her messenger, and ordered him to lock up Ishtar in the palace and to let loose against her the sixty maladies. Thus Ishtar was a prisoner, and on earth there was desolation and in the heavens great sorrow. Shamash and Sin, her father, carried their grief to Ea. Ea, in order to deliver Ishtar, thereupon created the effeminate Asushu-Namir and sent him to the land of no return, instructed with magic words to restrain the will of Ereshkigal. In vain the queen of the infernal regions strove to resist. In vain did she attempt 'to enchant Asushu-Namir with a great enchantment'. Ea's spell was mightier than her own, and Ereshkigal had to set Ishtar free. Ishtar was sprinkled with the water of life and, conducted by Namtaru, again passed through the seven gates, recovering at each the adornment she had abandoned.

In spite of the violence of her character Ishtar's heart was not a stranger to kindness. Mortals often experienced her benefactions. Many a king owed his elevation to the throne to Ishtar's love and the story of Sargon, King of Agade, related by himself, is significant.

'My mother was a priestess. I did not know my father. The priestess, my mother, conceived me and gave birth to me in hiding. She placed me in a basket made of reeds and closed the lid with pitch. She put the basket in the river which was not high. The river carried me away and brought me to Akki who was a man responsible for libations. Akki looked upon me with kindness and drew

Colossal human-headed winged bull from the palace of Sargon II at Khorsabad. This awe-inspiring figure represents a benevolent genie and was one of a pair which together guarded an entrance to the palace. It wears the horned head-dress of divinity and is provided with five legs as it was intended to be seen from both the front and the side. Eighth century B.C.

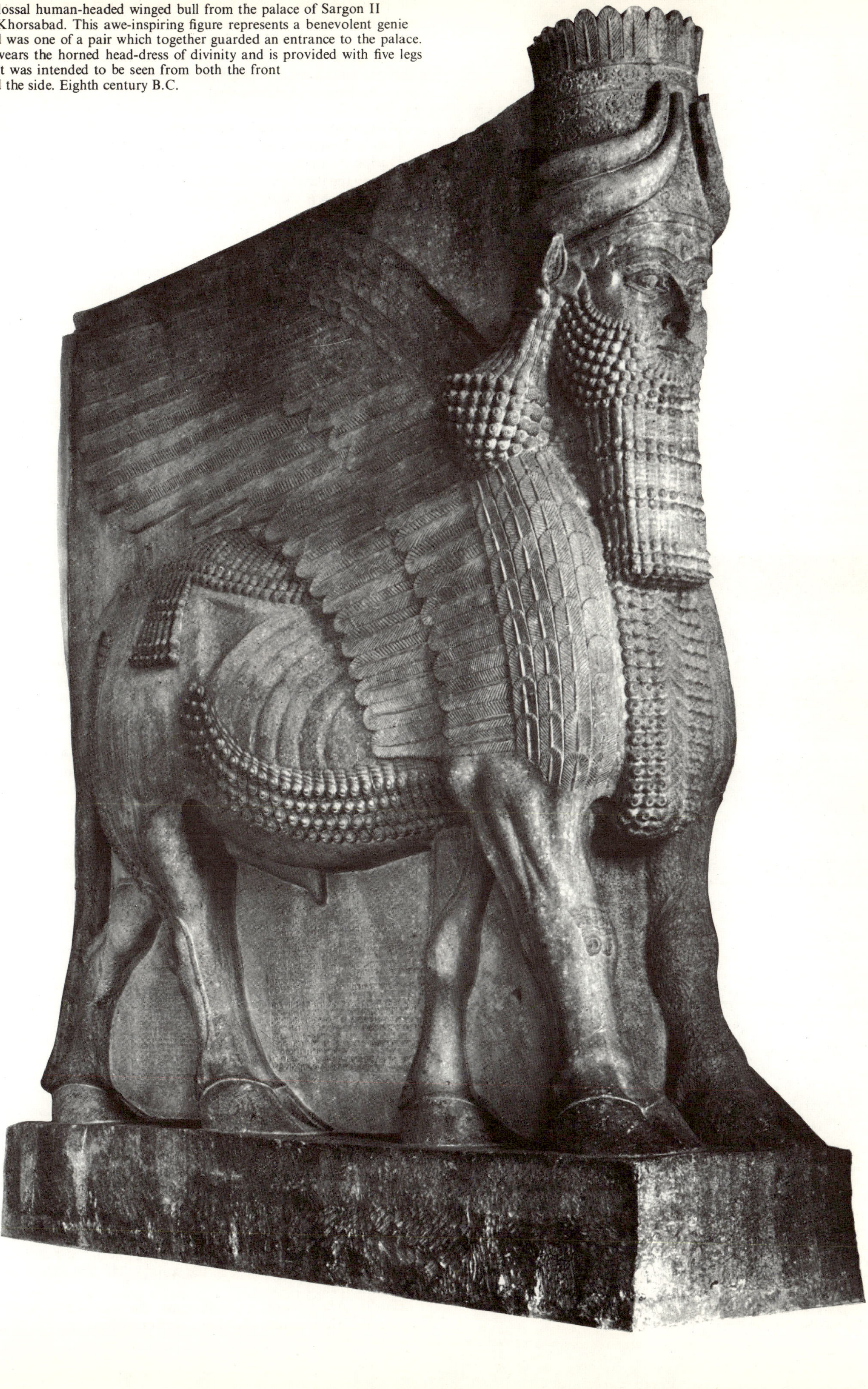

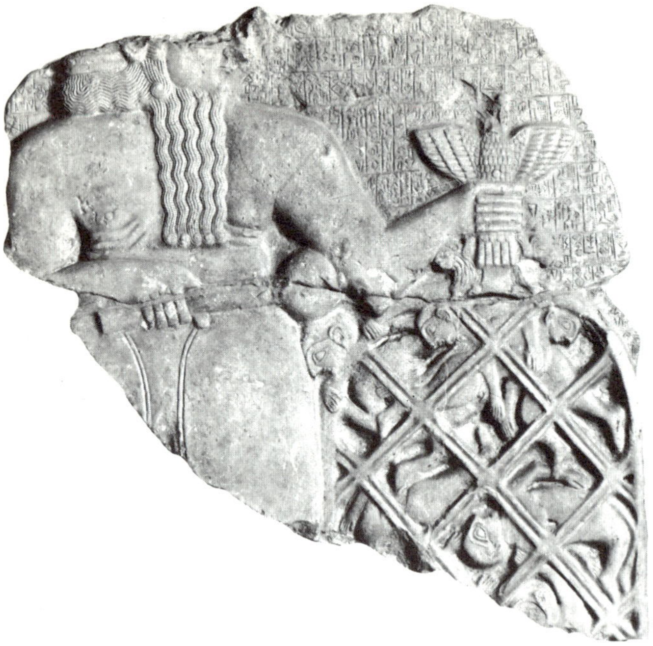

Ningirsu, god of Lagash, clasping in one hand the eagle with outstretched wings, his emblem, and in the other a club, with which he seems to threaten the captives taken in his net. Fragment of the Vulture Stela. Sumerian archaic art. Beginning of the third millennium. Louvre.

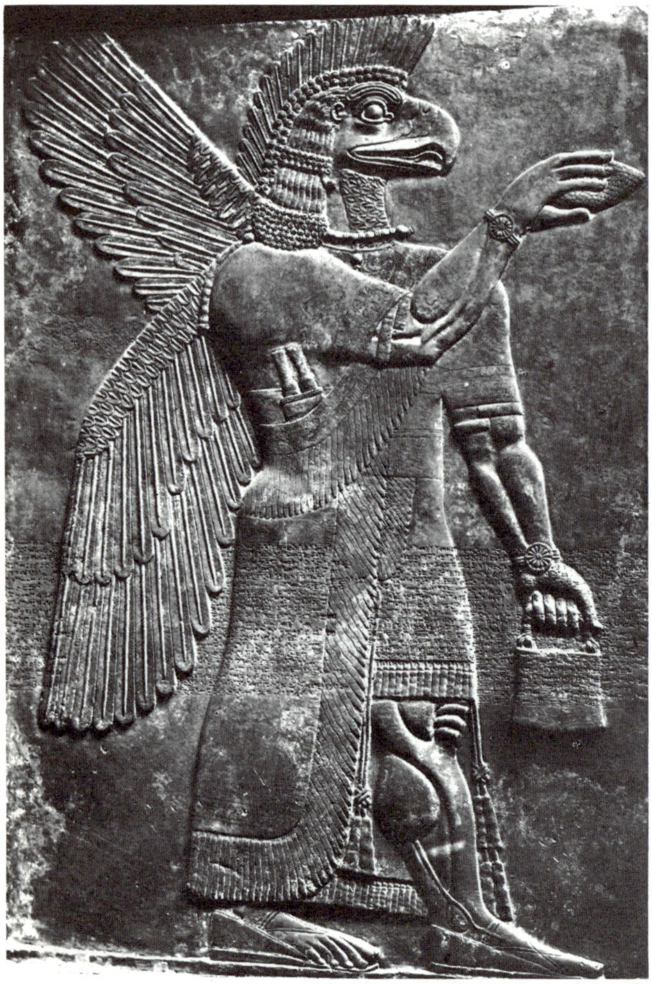

Eagle-headed winged genie carrying a vessel of lustral water and a pine-cone sprinkler – one of the benevolent genie who accompanied men in their daily lives and protected them from disease and evil forces. His long fringed robe is held at the waist by a belt into which a dagger is thrust and he wears thonged sandals on his feet.
Assyrian bas-relief in marble. 885 B.C.

me from the river. He adopted me as his child and brought me up. He made me his gardener. It was while I was his gardener that the goddess Ishtar loved me. Then I became king.' (Dhorme's translation.)

Those whom she cherished Ishtar treated with maternal tenderness. Addressing Ashurbanipal she says:

> My face covers thy face like a mother over the fruit of her womb,
> I will place thee like a graven jewel between my breasts,
> During the night will I give thee covering.
> During the day I shall clothe thee,
> Fear not, oh my little one, whom I have raised.

Sovereign of the world by virtue of love's omnipotence, Ishtar was the most popular goddess in Assyria and Babylonia. Under the name Astarte she was one of the great goddesses of Phoenicia and bequeathed more than one of her traits to the Greek Aphrodite.

Ninurta. Ishtar completes the great triad of the astral deities. In Sumer and Akkad, however, another god continued to be honoured who was of much the same character and who has been identified with the constellation Orion. His name, according to place, was variously Ningirsu or Ninurta.

Ningirsu, who was worshipped at Lagash, was the son of Enlil. Ninurta was similarly a part of the Enlil cycle. Ningirsu, patron of a part of the city of Lagash, was not only concerned with irrigation, as 'the god of fields and canals, who brings fertility', but was also a war-god and this is the aspect which Ninurta retained, a hunter and warrior. He was called the 'champion of the celestial gods'. He was the 'strong one who destroys the wicked and the enemy'. His weapon and attribute was a kind of club flanked by two S-shaped snakes.

The warlike disposition of Ninurta caused a fearful coalition to rise against him, in which the whole of nature joined. The very stones took part in the struggle. Some ranged themselves on the side of Ninurta while others went to swell the ranks of his enemies. When Ninurta emerged victorious he did not forget his humble allies. He blessed the stones which had remained faithful to him and cursed the others. And that is why certain stones such as the amethyst and lapis-lazuli shine with such glittering brilliance, are valued by man and are reserved for noble usage while others are trodden under foot in disdain.

Ningirsu's wife was the goddess Bau, daughter of Anu, she who breathed into men the breath of life. Every year, on New Year's Day, the solemn nuptials of Ningirsu and Bau were celebrated. The goddess was ushered into the bridal chamber in the midst of a cortège of worshippers who bore wedding gifts. To this divine couple were born septuplet virgins. At other places and times Bau's role was assumed by others, such as Nin-Karrak or Gula.

GODS OF THE STORM AND WINDS

We have already seen that the god of Nippur, Enlil, was the god of the hurricane, 'Lord of the winds'. But when he became Lord or *ba'al* of the earth, Enlil slowly lost this primitive character.

Adad. From the beginning of the second millennium the mastery of the storm was conferred on a special divinity: Adad. Adad is usually represented standing on a bull and grasping thunderbolts in each hand; he is the god of lightning and the tempest. It is he who lets loose the storm, makes the thunder growl and bends the trees under the fury of the winds. Enveloped in black clouds he roars with his mighty voice. While Bêl decreed the deluge Adad executed his will, and the tumult rose to the very heavens.

But Adad's aspect was not always so terrifying. Adad, the tempest-god, was also the god who brought the beneficent wind and with it the welcome rains. He was the god of the inundation which fertilises, he who each year caused the river to rise and cover the earth with nourishing slime. Hence, when Bêl wished to send a series of plagues to chastise men he first addressed Adad: 'From on high Adad hoarded the rains. Below, the flood-waters were stubborn and no longer rose in the springs. The abundance of the fields diminished.'

Finally, Adad shared with Shamash the privilege of revealing the future. He was also the 'Lord of Foresight'.

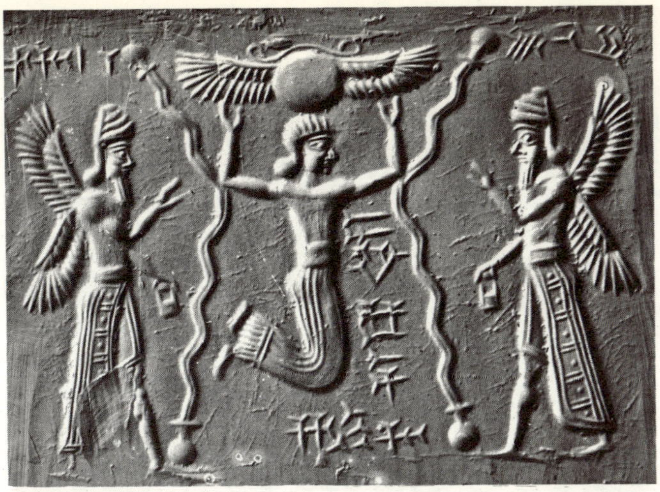

Mythological scene. Two winged deities wearing horned head-dresses and bearing vessels of lustral water stand on either side of a floating female figure wearing a tiara. Above her she supports a winged disk, the emblem of the god Asshur, while from two vases in the heavens two streams of water pour into two similar vases on the earth. Impression from a late Assyrian chalcedony cylinder seal. 990 to 600 B.C.

In his various functions Adad was associated with his companion, the goddess Shala.

FIRE GODS

May Gibil devour you! May Gibil catch you!
May Gibil kill you! May Gibil consume you!

Such was the imprecation pronounced by the wizard, the Ashipu, as he consigned to the flames the clay image of a sorcerer whose malignant charm he wished to break, or – infallible method of destroying spells – as he burned a peeled onion and a crushed date.

Gibil, the divinity thus invoked, was the god of fire and was called the son of Anu.

Another fire-god was Nusku whose attribute was a lamp shaped like a wooden clog. More especially he represented the sacred fire which consumed burnt offerings and carried their delectable fragrance up to the gods. Thus he was called 'Bêl's sublime messenger'. He was invoked during sacrifices:

Without thee, a banquet cannot be prepared in the temple,
Without thee, the great gods cannot breathe the incense.

Gibil and Nusku helped – and sometimes took the place of – Sin and Shamash in dispensing justice.

O mighty Nusku, warrior-god! He burns the wicked,
He orders and decrees, he is attentive to the smallest fault;
Equitable judge, he sees into the hearts of men,
He makes justice and law to shine forth.
O Gibil, the powerful, the roaring tempest,
Thou governor of gods and kings,
Thou sittest in judgment on the unjust judge.

WATER GODS

Enki (or **Ea**), god of the Apsu, was the principal divinity of the liquid elements. But he had a daughter, the goddess Nanshe who shared his functions. She was the goddess of springs and canals. Like her father she was particularly honoured in Eridu, the holy city, which was situated at the mouth of the Apsu. She was also worshipped at Lagash and each year, on a canal near the city, there was a procession of boats to escort the sacred barge in which the goddess rode. Nanshe's emblem was a vase in which a fish swam.

Finally, the rivers too were deified. They were invoked not only as the creators of all things but also as instruments of the gods' justice.

It is thou, O river, who judges man's judgment,
O great river, O river sublime, O river of the sanctuaries.

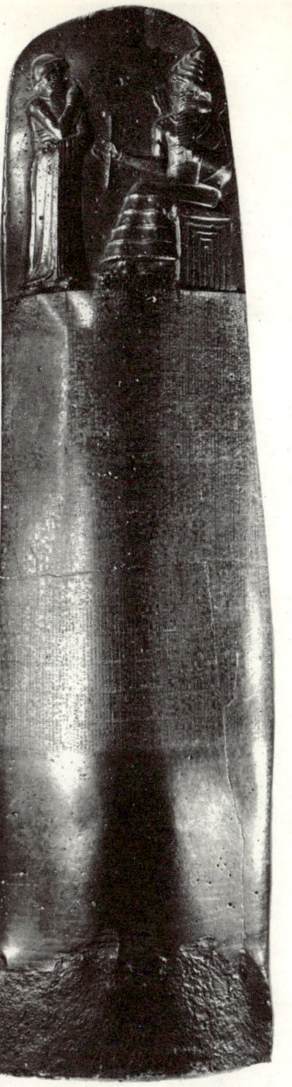

The god Shamash dictates his laws to Hammurabi. Top of the Stela of Hammurabi. About 2000 B.C. Louvre.

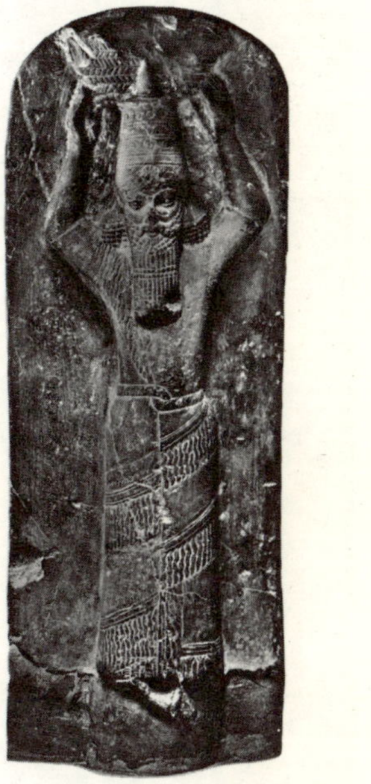

Ashur-bani-pal building a temple to a god. On his head the great Assyrian emperor bears the brick basket which marked the founder of a temple. The first great private collector of books known to history, it was in his library at Nineveh that were discovered the tablets containing the text of the story of Gilgamesh. Stone stele from Babylon. Seventh century B.C.

EARTH GODS

From remotest times the Earth-mother was worshipped under the names of Ga-Tum-Dug at Lagash, of Bau and Innini at Der and at Kish, or of Gula and of Ninkhursag.

All these divinities represented, like the Gaea of the Greeks, the great creative principle.

Later the specialised role of these earth divinities became more marked.

Over the harvest presided Nisaba, goddess of the grain, the Babylonian Ceres. She was the sister of Nanshe.

The vine had its own goddess: Geshtin.

But the chief vegetation god was Tammuz, who was probably originally a tree god.

Tammuz, or Dumuzi, to use a more original form of the name, was the son of Ningishzida, 'Lord of the wood of life', whose own father was Ninazu, 'Lord of Soothsaying by means of water'. He was loved by Ishtar but, for a mysterious and doubtless involuntary reason, this love caused his death. Like the ear of corn which the reaper's scythe cuts off in the glory of its yellow ripeness, Tammuz, the harvest-god, was ravished by death in the fullness of youth, and forced to descend into the underworld. Heartbroken by the death of her lover Ishtar bewailed her sorrow in bitter lamentations which she poured forth from the midst of a choir of weeping men and women. This tradition was perpetuated among the people and each year when the earth, sweltering under the summer sun, had lost its harvest mantle, the death of Tammuz was bewailed in funeral chants. Similarly at Byblos the 'passion' of Adonis was commemorated by public mourning.

Ishtar descended into the infernal regions to dispute with her sister Ereshkigal possession of the 'lover of her youth'. Tammuz returned to the abode of the gods and remained thenceforth at the gate of Anu where with his father Ningishzida he stood guardian.

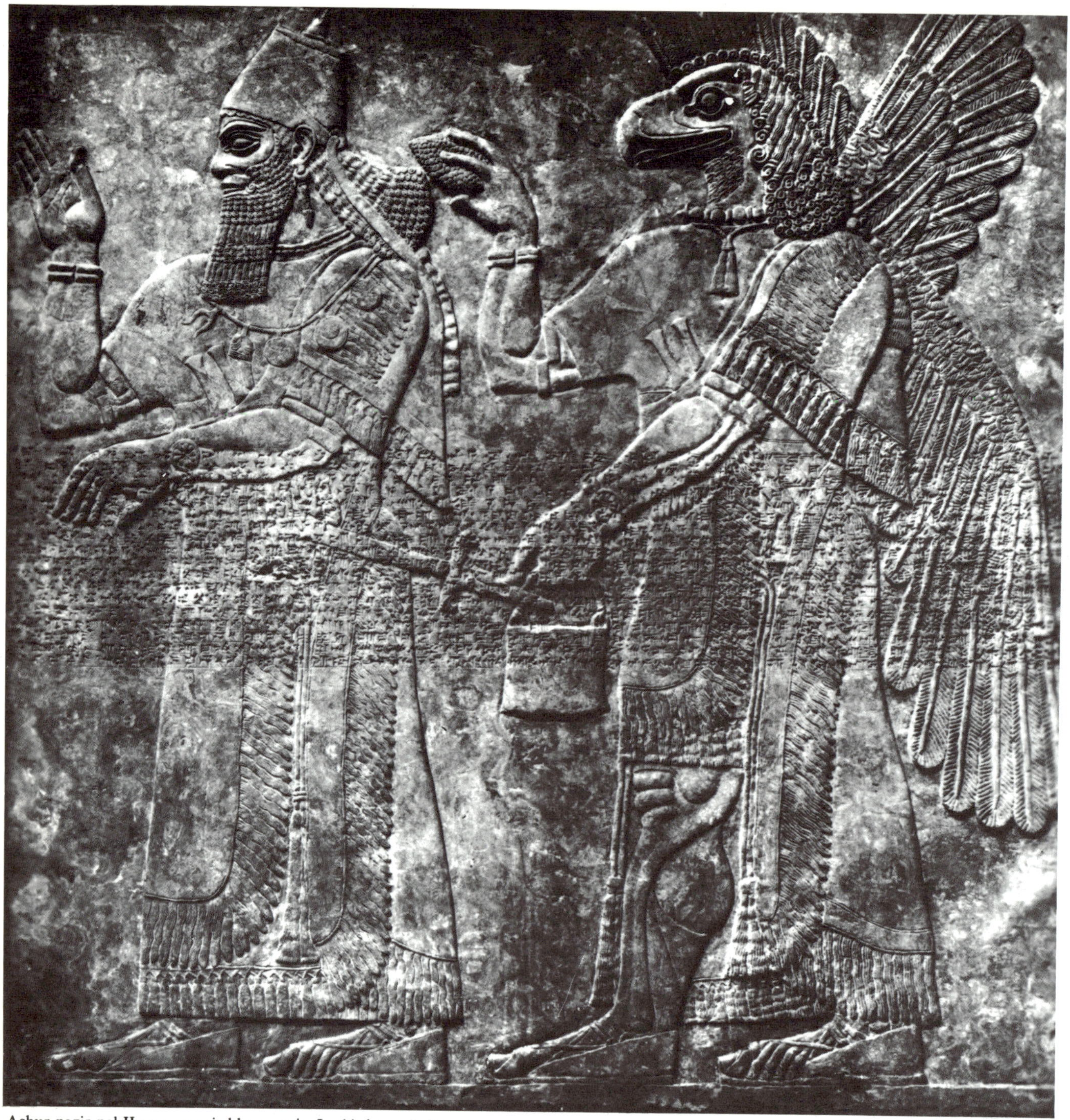

Ashur-nazir-pal II accompanied by a genie. In this bas-relief the Assyrian emperor is shown followed by a winged, eagle-headed divinity who carries a lustral vase and a pine-cone sprinkler with which he makes a purificatory gesture over the king. Stone bas-relief, 883 to 859 B.C.

GODS CONCERNED WITH THE LIFE OF MAN

The Origin of Humanity: The Deluge. Whether man was moulded by Marduk with his own blood, whether he was born of the union of Marduk and the goddess Aruru, or whether – as they told at Eridu – he had been fashioned by the goddess Mami from clay mixed with the blood of a god whom Ea had slain, one point is clear: namely, that humanity was the work of divine hands – men were children of the gods.

Nevertheless the gods one day resolved to destroy the human race. The motive for this remains unexplained. Assembled in the town of Shuruppak, which is situated on the banks of the Euphrates, the great gods Anu, Enlil, Ninurta and Ennugi decided to drown the earth with a deluge. But Ea, who was also present, took pity on mankind. He confided the secret of the project to a reedhut. As Ea intended, the secret was overheard by an inhabitant of Shuruppak named Uta-Napishtim:

> Man of Shuruppak, son of Ubar-Tutu,
> Destroy thy house, build a vessel,
> Leave thy riches, seek thy life,
> Store in thy vessel the seeds of all of life.

Uta-Napishtim listened to Ea's advice and set to work without delay. He built a great ship a hundred and twenty cubits high. He loaded it with all he possessed in gold and silver. He took his family aboard and herded in his cattle, together with the animals and birds of the land. Meanwhile the hour appointed by Shamash had arrived. That evening the Lord of Shadows caused the rain to fall, a rain of filth. Uta-Napishtim hastened to board his vessel and make fast the door.

> When dawn broke
> A cloud black as night rose from heaven's foundation.
> Within it Adad bellowed!
> Shullat and Khanish march at the head,
> Nergal tears away the mast.
> He comes, Ninurta, he spurs the attack,

The Anunnaki are bearing torches,
Their brilliance lights up the land,
Adad's tumult reaches the skies,
All that is bright is changed into darkness.

The terror which spread through the universe reached the gods themselves. Seized with fear they sought refuge in the sky of Anu. They crouched like dogs on the ramparts and their burning lips quivered with fright. Ishtar 'cried out like a woman in labour'. She repented having supported, perhaps even provoked, the decision of the gods. She had not contemplated a chastisement so dreadful.

May that day become as mud,
That day when I spoke evil to the assembled gods,
For I spoke evil to the assembled gods,
In order that my people might perish, I commanded the battle.
I give birth to my people!
Like the spawn of fish they fill the sea!

But nothing could stop the scourge. 'Six days and six nights the winds were abroad and the deluge descended.' At last, on the dawn of the seventh day the evil wind grew peaceful, the sea became calm; the voices of men were stilled, 'and all mankind was changed into mud'.

At this spectacle Uta-Napishtim could not hold back his tears. Meanwhile his ship had come to rest on the summit of Mount Nisir, the only land which had emerged from the waves. Uta-Napishtim let loose a dove and then a swallow, but they came back to the ship, having found nowhere to alight. A raven, in his turn released, did not come back at all. Then Uta-Napishtim came out from his boat. He poured a libation and placed a burnt offering on the summit of the mountain. With joy the gods smelled the good odour of sacrifice. Only Enlil was enraged to see that some mortals had escaped the disaster. But Ea managed to appease him by carefully chosen words. In token of reconciliation Enlil took Uta-Napishtim and his wife by the hand. He touched them on the face and said:

Formerly Uta-Napishtim was a human being,
Now Uta-Napishtim and his wife will be like unto us, gods.

And he fixed their abode 'far away, at the mouth of the rivers', in an inviolable retreat.

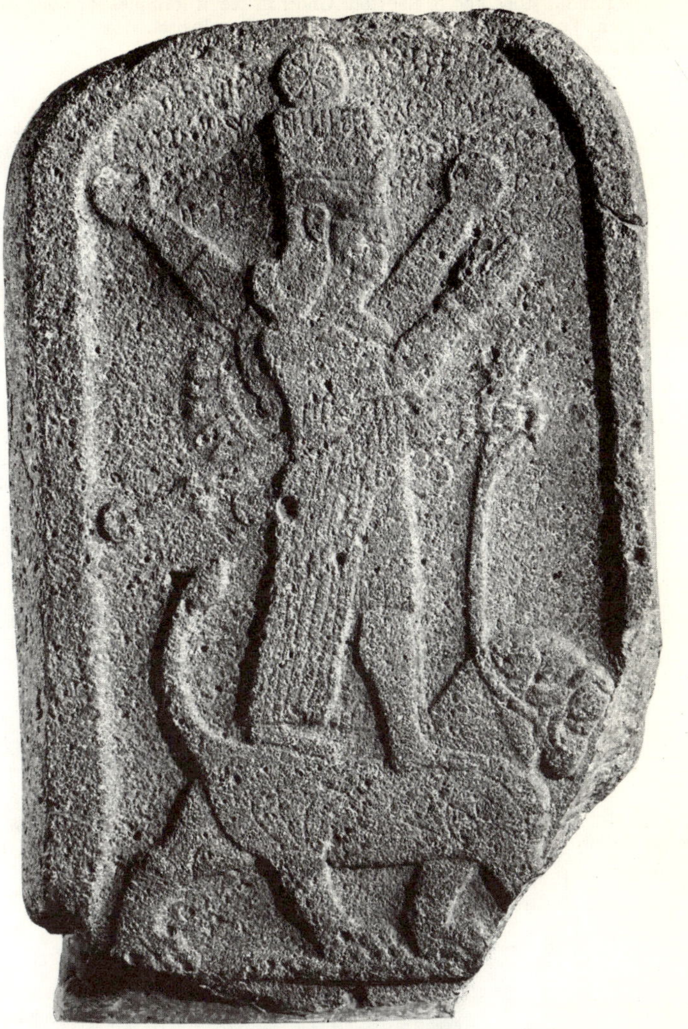

The goddess Ishtar riding on a lion. 'The goddess of the morn and the goddess of the evening', Ishtar was the personification of the planet Venus and was both a goddess of love and of war. Here she is depicted in her role of warrior goddess as 'Lady of Battles', armed and riding on her sacred animal, the lion. On her headdress she wears a star. Bas-relief on a stone stele from Tell Ahmar. Eighth century B.C.

Gods and Men. Numerous divinities presided over the various phases of human life. When a mother felt the first pains of labour Mami was invoked, she who had created the new race of men. BELIT-ILI, 'the Lady of the Gods', who then took the name NINTUD, or 'The Lady of Childbirth', also watched over the birth of the newly born whose destiny was determined, from the moment of his arrival in the world, by the goddess MAMMITU.

The entire course of human life was, moreover, regulated by the sovereign will of the gods, whose chief attribute was deciding the fates of men. We have already seen how highly the gods valued this privilege which fell successively to Anu, Enlil, Ea and Marduk. Although it was the supreme god who made the final decision, all could discuss it. At the beginning of every year, while on earth the festival of the Zagmuk was being celebrated, the gods assembled in the Upshukina, the Sanctuary of Fates. The king of the gods in the later Babylonian period, Bêl-Marduk, took his place on the throne. The other gods knelt with fear and respect before him. Removing from his bosom the Tablet of Fates, Bêl-Marduk confided it to his son Nabu, who wrote down on it what the gods had decided. Thus the fate of the country was fixed for the coming year.

These decisions naturally remained secret. Men could, however, receive warnings from the gods, either in dreams or by apparitions. Dreams were sent to men by the god ZAQAR, the messenger of Sin. If they were too obscure one consulted the goddess NANSHE, 'the interpreter of dreams'. Apparitions were less frequent and only occurred to people of importance. Thus it was that Gudea, who reigned at Lagash, undertook the construction of the temple of Ningirsu in that city on the formal order of the god who had appeared to him while he was asleep. 'In the midst of my dreaming, a man as tall as the sky, as big as the earth, who as to his head was a god, as to his arms was the divine bird Imdugud, as to his feet was the hurricane, to the right and left of whom crouched a lion, has ordered me to construct his house...'

Happiness and unhappiness came from the gods. It was they who sent disease, having for this purpose recourse to IRRA, an aspect of NERGAL, king of the underworld, and NAMTAR, a plague demon. Men's health, on the other hand, depended especially on the goddess NIN-KARRAK and on the goddess GULA. Both were thought to be daughters of Anu. Gula could at will inflict illness or restore health. She was called 'the Great Doctoress' and her symbol was a dog.

Morality was also under the control of a deity. We have seen that Shamash and Nusku were the gods of justice. The same role was shared by KADI, the goddess of Der who had at first symbolised the creative earth. Kadi's attribute was a snake with, sometimes, a human bust.

Intellectual activity was placed under the protection of NABU whose principal sanctuary was at Borsippa, near Babylon. Nabu was the son of Marduk. The prestige of his father was reflected on to him and in the end he took over some of the paternal power. We have already seen how on the day when destinies were determined it was Nabu who engraved the gods' decisions on the sacred tablets. But his role was not confined to that of a simple scribe: he could, at will, increase or diminish the number of days allotted to each mortal being, and from this he derived his importance. Nabu had been chosen as secretary of the assembled gods because he – and his wife TASHMETUM – had invented writing. For this reason he also presided over *belles-lettres*. His attribute – like that of his father Marduk – was the serpent-headed dragon, and additionally the chisel and engraving tablet.

Various other divinities presided over men's arts and crafts. We have seen that Ea was the patron of carpenters and goldsmiths. The latter also appealed to the god GUHKIN-BANDA, if we can

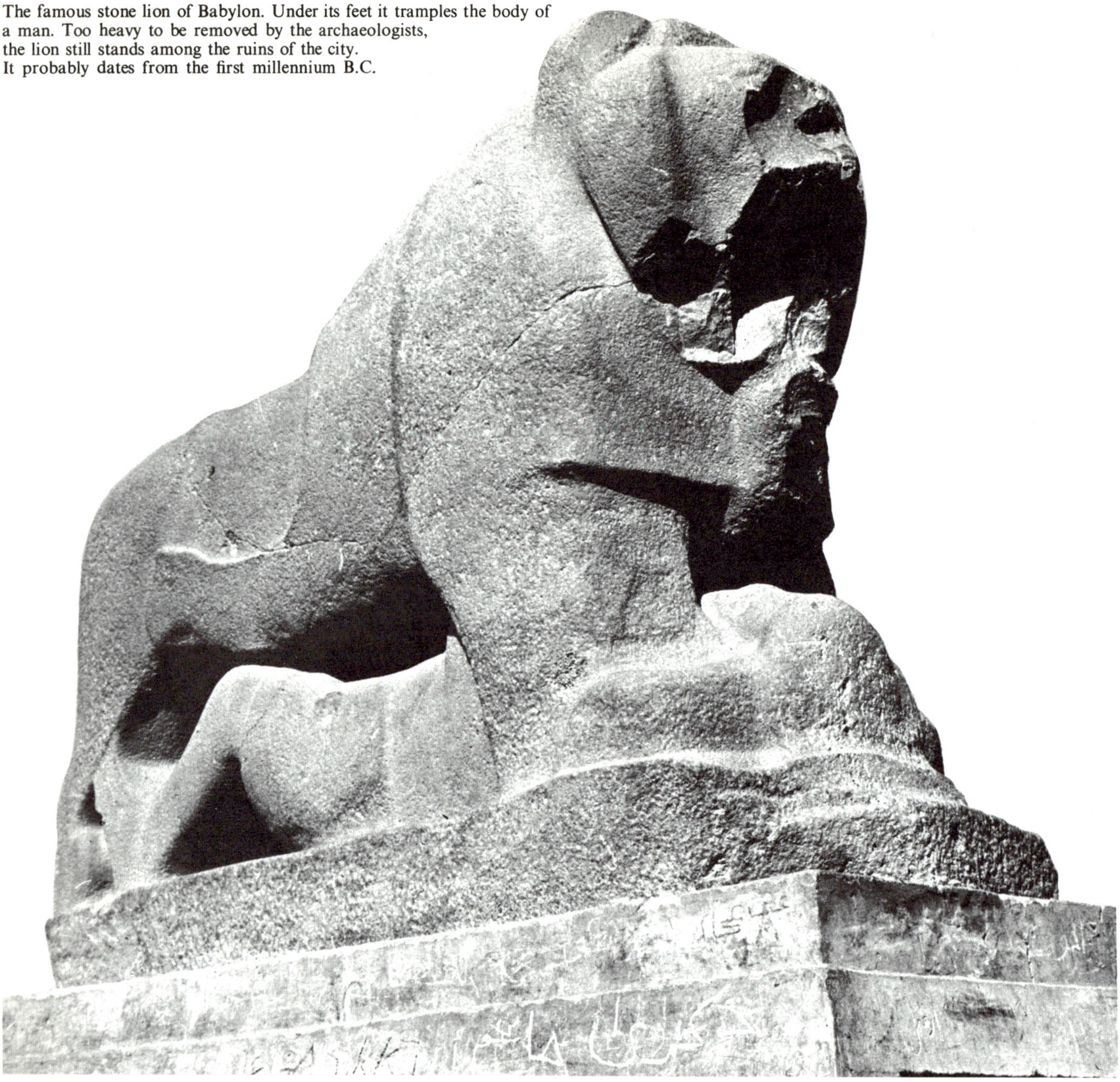

The famous stone lion of Babylon. Under its feet it tramples the body of a man. Too heavy to be removed by the archaeologists, the lion still stands among the ruins of the city. It probably dates from the first millennium B.C.

believe Ashurbanipal's statement: 'With the help of the god Guhkin-Banda I have made as an offering an artistic platter in bright gold.'

THE UNDERWORLD AND ITS DIVINITIES

Under the earth, beyond the abyss of the Apsu, lay the infernal dwelling-place to which men descended after death. It was the 'Land of no return', 'the house from which he who enters does not come out'. What hope was there to escape from this kingdom defended by seven-fold walls? To enter it a man had successively to penetrate seven gates, abandoning at each a part of his apparel. When the last gate had closed behind him he found himself naked and imprisoned for ever in the 'dwelling-place of the shadows'. The audacious Ishtar who had imprudently ventured into the land of no return was unable to escape, goddess though she was, and remained there a prisoner. To free her nothing less than the aid of Ea and the power of his magic incantations had been required. Sometimes the gods gave an especially privileged inhabitant of the underworld permission to come up for a moment into the light. Thus Enkidu, the companion of the hero Gilgamesh, was authorised to go and tell his friend what took place in the kingdom of the shadows. It was a sad picture. In these regions of eternal darkness the souls of the dead – *edimmu* – 'clad, like birds, in a garment of wings' are all jumbled together:

In the house of dust
Live lord and priest,
Live the wizard and the prophet...
Live those whom the great gods
Have anointed in the abyss.
Dusk is their nourishment
And their food is mud.

Only certain *edimmu*, especially favoured, had the right to a bed and fresh water.

As well as the souls of the dead the underworld also contained the 'captive gods' – Kingu and his accomplices who in the great civil war among the gods had taken the side of Tiamat and been vanquished by Marduk.

Over all this subterranean world reigned the goddess Ereshkigal, 'Princess of the great earth'. Originally she was sole sovereign. But one day the god NERGAL, 'Lord of the great dwelling' – who under another form bore the name Meshlamthea – invaded the infernal regions. With him were fourteen demons whom he posted at the different gates. To obtain peace Ereshkigal consented to take Nergal for her husband. 'Thou shalt be my husband', she said to him, 'and I shall be thy wife. I shall make thee ruler over the vast kingdom and place in thy hand the tablet of wisdom.' And so Nergal, who until then had been god of destruction and war, became the overlord of the dead. His symbol was a sword or a lion's head. To administer his commands he had Namtaru, god of the plague, 'who crouches by Nergal'. Among other infernal deities we meet BELILI, the sister of Tammuz, and the scribe BELIT-SERI.

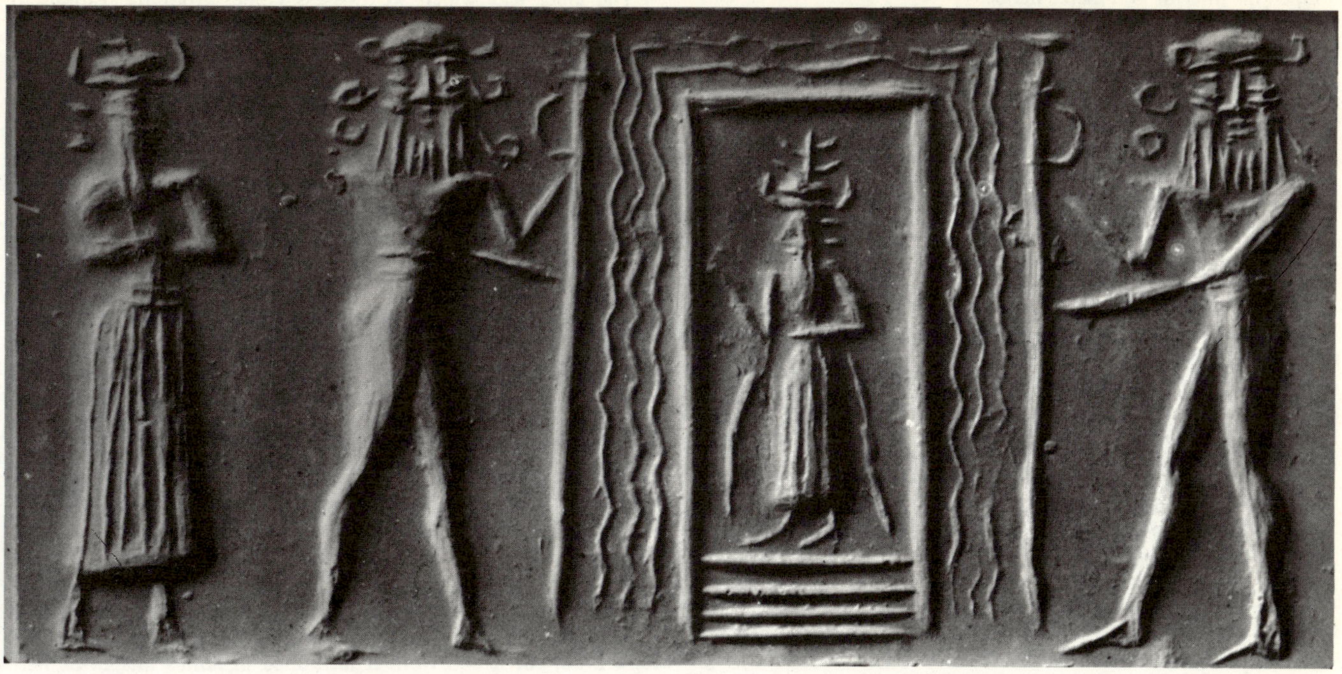

Gilgamesh with two gods. In the centre, twin figures of the hero holding a gate-post stand on either side of a water-god with two streams of water flowing from his waist who stands in a shrine surrounded by water. This is possibly a representation of the water-god Ea in his dwelling, the House of the Apsu. On the left, a minor deity approaches in an attitude of worship. Impression from an Akkadian cylinder seal. 2340 to 2180 B.C.

THE GENII

Inferior to the gods but nevertheless participating in their nature and sharing certain prerogatives with them were the genii, the *utukku*. They were divided into two groups, the good and the evil. Even more than the gods they played a major role in the daily life of man.

The good genii, who were called *shedu* or *lamassu*, acted as guardian spirits. They defended the individual against evil powers, carried his homage to the gods and drew down on him divine favour. They could be seen standing before the gates of temples in the form of winged bulls with human heads. But their duty was not only to stand guard over sacred enclosures. Invisible but omnipresent they remained at a man's side, following him in the streets and into battle; for, as it was said, 'he who has no god when he walks in the street wears a headache like a garment'.

This was because men were constantly exposed to malignant forces, represented by the evil *utukku*. These were, firstly, the *edimmu* – the souls of the dead – who had not received burial or whose funeral rites had been neglected: they avenged themselves by tormenting the living. They could, to be sure, be appeased by the offer of a funeral repast, the *Kispu*, or by a libation of water. But there were other, more redoubtable *utukku* to be reckoned with. These evil genii issued from the lower world, the *arallu*, or emanated from the bile of Ea, and overwhelmed men with disease, inspired them to criminal acts, spread disunion among families, decimated the flocks. They were rightly compared with 'the storm which breaks loose with fury in the skies', or the 'rising wind which casts darkness over the bright day'. There was no way of appeasing them, 'for they heeded neither prayer nor supplication'. We have seen how they had no respect even for the gods and how they dared to attack Sin whose benevolent light they attempted to eclipse. Who precisely were these malevolent spirits? It is not known, only that 'they do not take wives and beget no children'. Seven of them were particularly dangerous. 'They were born in the Mountain of the West, they dwell in holes in the ground, they live among the ruin of the earth.' When they appeared to mortals it was in the form of terrifying creatures, as for example an apparition with a human body, the head of a lion bristling with horns, and feet armed with powerful claws. They could not be driven away except by incantations. The victim had recourse to the exorcist – the *ashipu* – who in Ea's name pronounced the liberating formula:

> Evil *alu*, turn thy breast and depart!
> O, inhabitant of the ruins, get thee to thy ruins;
> For the great Lord Ea has sent me:
> He has made his incantation fitting for my mouth,
> He has given into my hand the cauldron for the Seven, according to the holy ordinances.

THE HEROES

Tradition retained the memory of legendary persons who had been in direct contact with the gods and whose adventures were of a mythical character. The most famous of these – omitting Uta-Napishtim, the hero of the deluge – were Etana, Adapa and above all Gilgamesh. If we wish to attribute a moral significance to these myths we can interpret them as men's efforts to rise above their wretched surroundings, conquer the heavens and achieve immortality.

Etana. In the days before there was a king on earth, when the 'sceptre, the diadem, the crown and the staff of office were placed before Anu in the heavens' the great Anunnaki, who determined men's fate, held counsel on the subject of the earth. The gods, especially Ishtar and Enlil, set about finding a king for men and, it seemed, chose Etana. All went well, until Etana complained that he had no heir. He addressed Shamash and said:

> O my Lord, by your order let it come forth:
> Grant me the herb of birth.
> Tell me which is the herb of birth.
> Set aside my shame, set for me a name.

Shamash, to whom Etana's libations and offerings of wild sheep had been agreeable, answered him: 'Take to the road and reach the mountain.'

Now this mountain had recently been the scene of a drama enacted by an eagle and a serpent. The two creatures lived side by side with their progeny. One day the eagle conceived the criminal design of eating the serpent's little ones. He accomplished the heinous crime in spite of the wise remonstrance of one of his little ones, 'young, but very intelligent', who put into him the fear of Shamash's wrath:

> The net, the spell of Shamash would fall upon thee and seize thee.
> He who trespasses on what is Shamash's, Shamash will punish him with his own hand.

And the serpent, in fact, brought his plaint before the god of justice, who said to him:

> Take to the road and reach the mountain.
> I will keep thee a buffalo.

Open his interior and pierce his belly!
Make thy habitation in his belly.
Birds of all kinds will descend from the sky.
The eagle will descend with them.
He will seize on the flesh.
When he comes inside the beast thou shalt clutch him by the wing:
Cut off his wings, his pinions, his claws,
Tear him and throw him into a ditch;
Let him die there from hunger and thirst!

And so it was done. Deceived by the serpent's stratagem, the eagle fell into his power and was condemned to perish slowly in the ditch.

When Etana had come to the mountain he found the eagle in his prison and, as Shamash had counselled him to do, he asked for the herb which would give him a son. The eagle promised to procure it for him as soon as he had regained his strength. For eight months Etana brought food until the eagle was at last able to fly again. He offered to carry Etana up to the very sky of Anu.

On my bosom place thy back,
In the feathers of my wings place thy hands,
Place thy flanks on my flanks,
And I shall carry thee to Anu's sky.

Either from curiosity, or ambition to seize the insignia of power, or, more probably, in the hope of obtaining the wondrous herb, Etana accepted; and the two companions soared into the air. At the end of three double-hours the sea below looked to Etana no more than 'a small ditch in a garden'. The travellers reached the sky of Anu without incident and prostrated themselves before the gods. But the eagle wished to fly further until he reached Ishtar. For two double-hours more they rose and Etana marvelled to see the earth turn into a garden while the vast sea was like a basket. But at the third double-hour he was seized by vertigo. In vain he cried to the eagle: 'My friend, I can climb no higher into the sky! Stop!' The fall was appalling. The eagle spun downwards with Etana and the two imprudent ones crashed to the ground.

Adapa. In the holy city of Eridu, Adapa had been created by Ea to reign among men. The god had given him great wisdom and extreme prudence; only immortality, reserved for the gods, had been denied him. Every day Adapa issued from the enclosure of Eridu, approached the bright harbour and, boarding his boat, sailed out on to the broad sea to fish. One day while he was fishing the South Wind rose, upset his boat and sent Adapa to the home of fishes. In a fury Adapa broke the wings of the South Wind, and for seven days the wind blew no more. Anu grew uneasy and, learning of the affair, summoned Adapa into his presence with the intention of offering him the food of death.

But Ea, who watched over his protégé, taught him how to conciliate the gods who kept vigil at Anu's threshold, at the same time warning him to accept from Anu neither food nor drink. Adapa then put on a robe of mourning and, conducted by Ilabrat, Anu's messenger, arrived at the gates of heaven. There he met the two guardians, Tammuz and Ningishzida, who, seeing him, asked: 'Man, for whom dost thou wear a robe of mourning?' Adapa answered as Ea had instructed him to do: 'On earth two gods have perished and therefore do I wear mourning.' 'And who are these gods?' they asked, and Adapa replied: 'Tammuz and Ningishzida.' Delighted with this mark of respect Tammuz and Ningishzida ushered Adapa into Anu's presence and interceded on his behalf. The great god was appeased and, wishing in his turn to honour the magnanimous Adapa he offered him the Food of Life. But Adapa remembered Ea's warning and refused either to eat or drink. This was how he lost the chance to become immortal.

Was he the victim of bad luck, or was it not that Ea, whom nothing escaped, had foreseen Anu's offer and had not willed that Adapa – and with him humanity – should acquire that immortality which he had judged it best to deny him?

Gilgamesh. Of all the Assyro-Babylonian heroes the most famous is certainly Gilgamesh whose figure and exploits have been immortalised in a vast poem, the masterpiece of Babylonian literature, and entitled, according to how it is interpreted, either as 'He who discovered the source' or 'He who saw all'.

The chief text which we possess comes from the Library of Ashurbanipal of Nineveh and dates from the seventh century B.C. It comprises twelve cantos of about three hundred verses each. The poem, however, is much more ancient, for a Babylonian fragment of it has been preserved which goes back to the beginning of the second millennium.

The hero of the poem – Gilgamesh – does not seem to have been purely imaginary. It is generally agreed that he was a king of the land of Sumer who reigned in the third millennium over the city of Uruk or Erech in probable succession to the king Dumuzi. Among the chiefs of these small Sumerian towns Gilgamesh doubtless distinguished himself for his courage and the success of his enterprises. As happened in similar cases a legend grew up about him and he became the central figure in a series of marvellous adventures which form the material of the poem of which the following is a résumé:

Over the ancient walled city of Erech, where Anu had his earthly dwelling, 'Eanna the holy', there once reigned a wise but despotic prince whose name was Gilgamesh. 'His two-thirds was a god, his other third a man.' He spread consternation among local families, taking daughters from their fathers, maidens from heroes, wives from their husbands. The inhabitants of Erech complained to the gods. The gods, too, were moved and spoke to Aruru the Great: 'Thou hast created Gilgamesh. Now create another man in his image so that they shall fight each other and leave Erech in peace.' Aruru took mud, cut it and from it fashioned in Anu's image the hero Enkidu – who was also called Eabani. His body was covered with hair; on his head his hair was like a woman's, 'growing like the harvest'. He grew up in the desert among the wild beasts.

With gazelles he ate the grass,
With the cattle he quenched his thirst,
With the flocks his heart rejoiced to drink.

In order to defend his friends, the beasts, he filled in the trenches dug by hunters, removed the nets they had spread and, as his strength equalled an army of Anu, no one dared to venture into the desert. It was decided to seize him. But how? Gilgamesh suggested an expedient:

Go, my hunter, and take with thee a harlot. While he accompanies his flock to the drinking trough, she – let her remove her robe. Let him take his pleasure of her. He will see her and approach her.

Thus it was done. Posted near the drinking trough the hunter and the harlot, after waiting for two days, saw Enkidu and his familiar flock arrive. The girl exposed her bosom and drew off her robe. Enkidu was overcome with passion and lay with her. When he had his fill of pleasure he returned to his flock, but upon seeing him the gazelles fled. 'The desert cattle shunned him.' Deprived of his innocence Enkidu was no longer worthy to live in familiarity with animals. In vain he tried to rejoin them. His knees betrayed him, his body was as though paralysed. He returned and sat sadly at the harlot's feet and she completed his enslavement by flattering words.

Thou art beautiful, Enkidu, thou art like a god.
Why dost thou roam the desert with wild flocks?
Come! I shall lead thee to Erech within the walls,
Where Gilgamesh is perfect in strength
And, like a wild ox, has established himself over the people.

And without resistance Enkidu let himself be conducted to Erech.

Meanwhile Gilgamesh, in his palace, was disturbed by a dream: in his sleep he had seen a man of prodigious strength with whom he had vainly attempted to struggle. He went to find his mother Ninsun who 'knew all knowledge' and confided to her his uneasiness.

My mother, I have seen a dream in the night:
Whilst there were stars in the heavens,
Someone swooped down upon me like an army of Anu;
I bore him and he was stronger than I,
His anger I repulsed violently, but I could not shake him off...
I overlaid him like a woman.
I laid him at thy feet:
Thou madest him measure himself with me.

Ninsun, who knew all knowledge, reassured her son. The dream signified that Enkidu, who surpassed Gilgamesh in strength, would

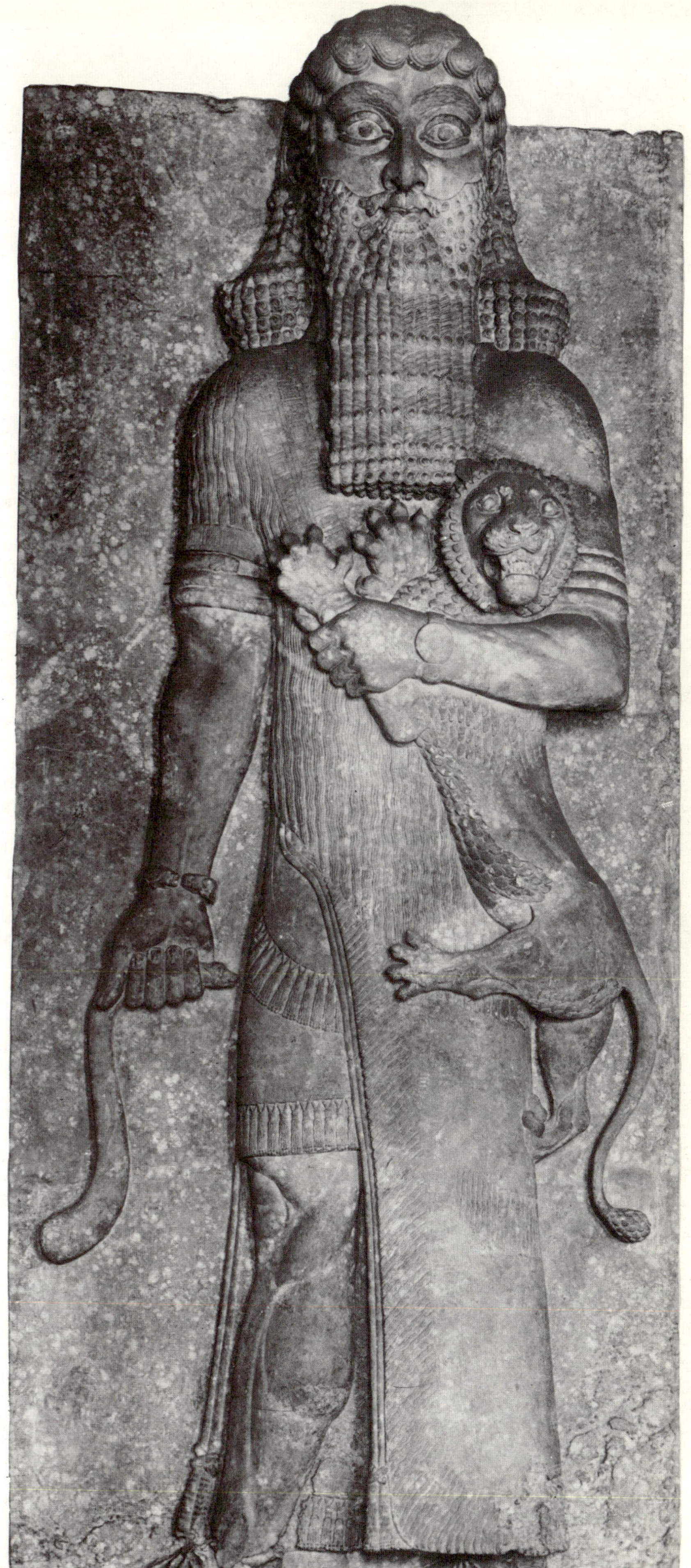

The hero Gilgamesh holding a lion that he has captured. Bas-relief from Khorsabad. Eighth century B.C. Louvre.

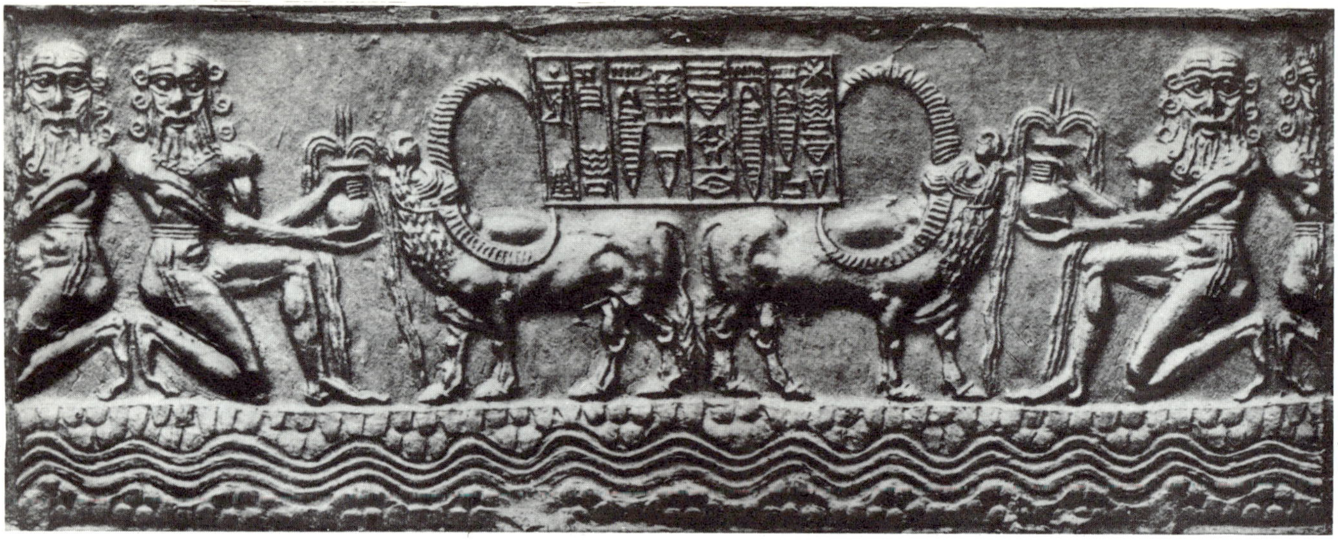

Gilgamesh watering a bull from a gushing vase. Cylinder seal. Clercq Collection.

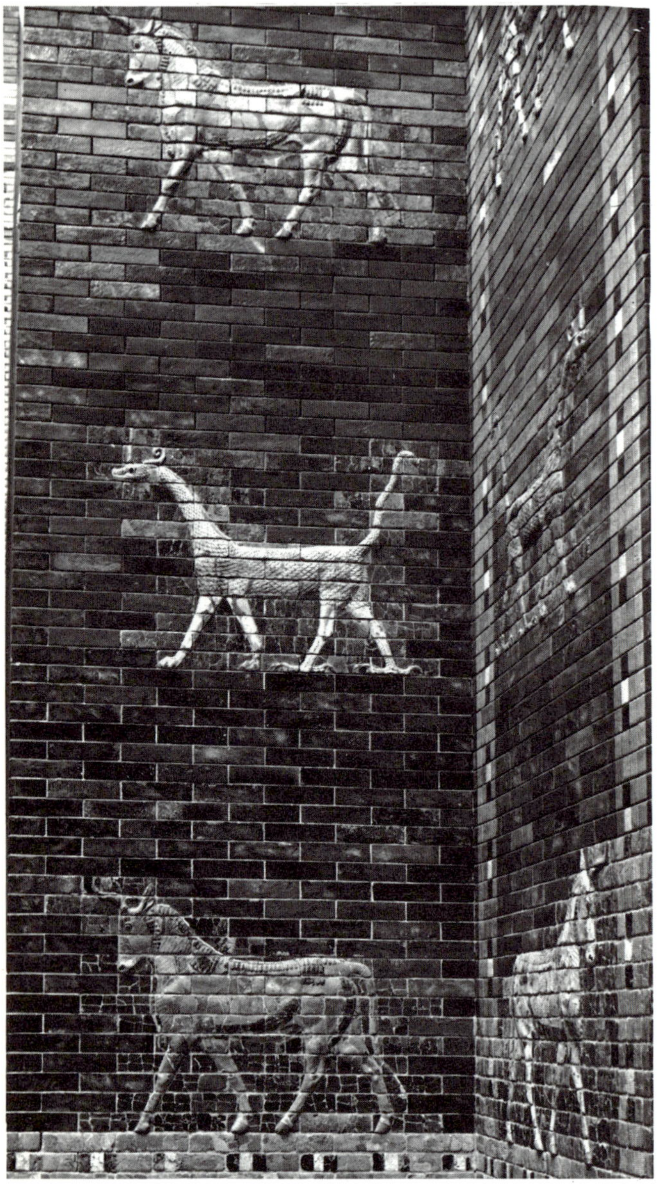

Detail of the Ishtar Gate of Babylon. Dedicated to the goddess whose name it bears, this great double gate spanned the processional way linking the temple of Marduk with the palace of Nebuchadnezzar. It is decorated with bulls and dragons, the animals sacred to Adad and Marduk, in brown, white and yellow on a blue ground. Reconstruction in the Berlin Museum from the original glazed bricks. Between 604 and 561 B.C.

become his friend. And indeed when Enkidu presented himself at the palace, after a fierce wrestling bout, Gilgamesh welcomed him with friendliness and the two sat down side by side like brothers.

Enkidu became Gilgamesh's inseparable companion and led a royal existence. He was dressed in a magnificent robe, he slept in a well-made bed and sat in peace at Gilgamesh's left hand. The kings of the earth kissed his feet and the people of Erech acclaimed him with their voices. One night, however, Enkidu had a bad dream: a mysterious being with sombre visage and the claws of an eagle carried him above the clouds and cast him into the house of shadows where Nergal dwelt, 'the house from which he who enters does not come out'.

When day broke Enkidu recounted his dream to Gilgamesh and described the vision he had brought back from the nether world. Gilgamesh filled a pot of jet with honey, filled a pot of lapis-lazuli with butter and offered them as gifts to Shamash. The god advised Gilgamesh to go and fight Khumbaba the Strong, king of the Cedar Mountain.

As soon as she heard of the project Ninsun, the mother of Gilgamesh, dressed in her sacred ornaments and went up to the terrace of the palace. There she offered incense to Shamash and addressed him with a mother's tears.

'Why,' she asked, 'hast thou given my child a heart which does not sleep? And now thou hast touched him and he is going away by far-off paths towards Khumbaba. He faces a combat which he understands not; he undertakes a campaign which he does not understand.'

In vain the inhabitants of Erech attempted to restrain Gilgamesh by pointing out the perils of the enterprise. Khumbaba was a terrifying monster, and it required a march of twenty thousand hours to reach his retreat. In vain Enkidu himself showed his distaste for the expedition. Gilgamesh stubbornly insisted on carrying out his plan. He closed his ears to the advice of his elders, overcame Enkidu's hesitations and the two friends set out.

The itinerary of Gilgamesh and Enkidu has been widely discussed. For long it was believed that the Mountain of the Cedars was in Elam, in the neighbourhood of Susa in south-west Persia. But Virolleaud, on the strength of new fragments of the poem recently deciphered, has demonstrated that the mysterious Mountain of the Cedars was probably the Amanus, the mountain which separates Syria on the north-west from Asia Minor. So Gilgamesh's expedition, stripped of its legendary trimmings, simply commemorates the first expeditions of the inhabitants of Babylonia, who, lacking wood and stone in their own land, ascended the Euphrates valley in search of these materials which they finally found on the rocky and wooded slopes of the Amanus.

But to return to our heroes. After a long journey they arrived at the green mountain, mantled with its forest of cedar, which was the domain of Khumbaba. Enlil had placed Khumbaba there to keep the cedars intact. His voice was a tempest, his mouth was the mouth of the gods, his breath was a wind. 'Whoever cuts down his cedars is stricken with infirmity.' Enkidu again wished to dissuade Gilgamesh 'My friend,' he said, 'let us not go into the forest. My hands are weak and my ribs are paralysed.' But Gilgamesh led him on.

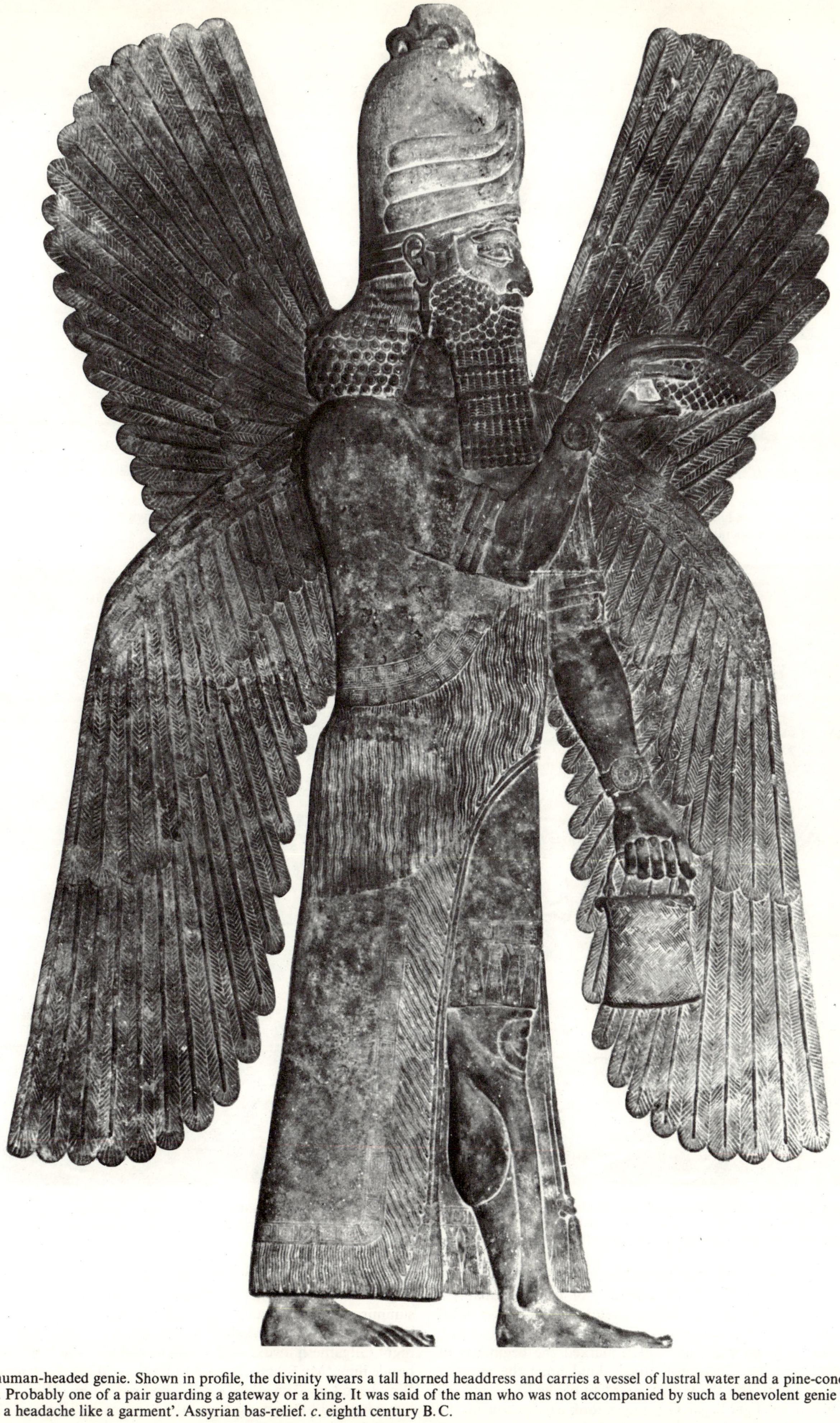

Winged human-headed genie. Shown in profile, the divinity wears a tall horned headdress and carries a vessel of lustral water and a pine-cone sprinkler. Probably one of a pair guarding a gateway or a king. It was said of the man who was not accompanied by such a benevolent genie that he 'wears a headache like a garment'. Assyrian bas-relief. *c.* eighth century B.C.

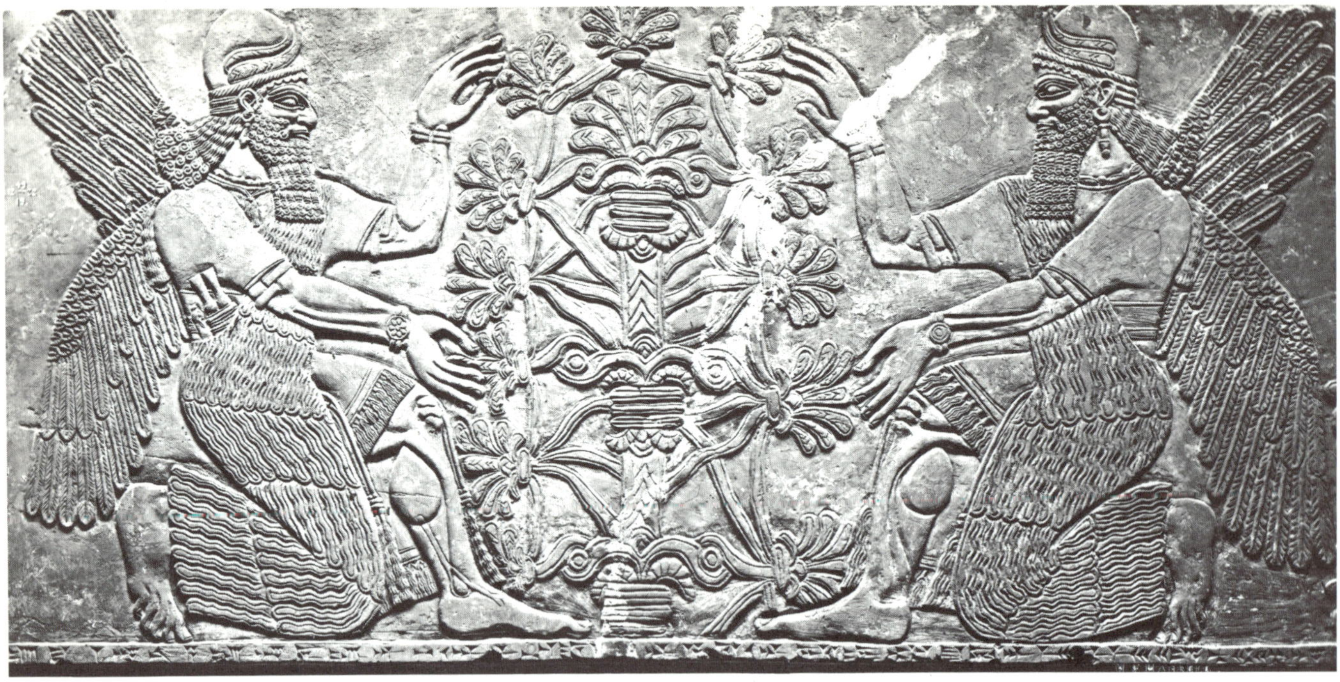

Two winged deities with a sacred tree. The two bearded figures wearing horned headdresses kneeling on either side of a stylised tree, towards which they stretch out protective hands, probably represent Enlil, or Bel, the god of the earth, or perhaps his twin guardian figures. Sacred trees, or trees of life, were particularly associated with the worship of Enlil. Bas-relief from Nimrud. *c.* 900 B.C.

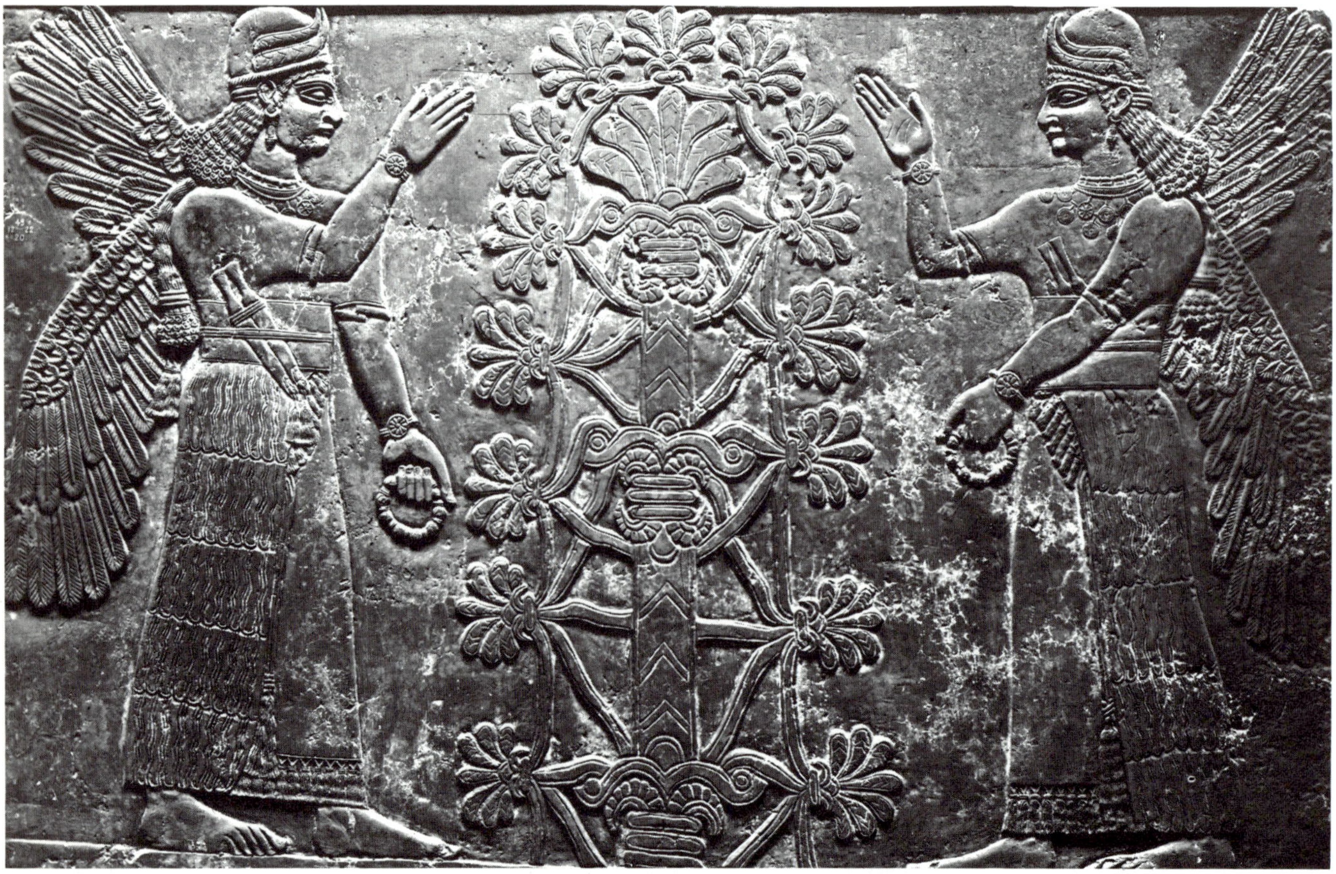

Two winged female deities with a sacred tree. Holding a ring in one hand and extending the other towards a sacred tree, these two figures probably represent Ninlil, or Beltis, the consort of Enlil, or Bel, or her twin guardian figures. Ninlil, or Beltis, was a fertility goddess and, in this case, the stylised growing tree may represent her. Bas-relief from the north-west palace of Nimrud. *c.* 900 B.C.

The forest, covered with majestic and sweet-smelling cedars, was the dwelling of the gods and the sanctuary of Irnini, probably a form of Ishtar. Before the two heroes stretched its shadows, filled with delights and well-traced paths. The two friends took a path and soon came to an enclosure which marked the beginning of Khumbaba's domain. Gilgamesh called aloud upon the monster and challenged him. But the savage guardian of the forest refused to reply. Before the fight began Gilgamesh took care to consult the omens. He made an offering to the dead, chanted the funeral dirge, dug a trench into which he threw seed-corn and, climbing to the summit of the mountain, invoked Shamash: 'O Lord,' he said, 'send a dream for Enkidu.' And suddenly in the middle of the night Gilgamesh awoke and spoke to Enkidu who knelt, watching beside him. 'My friend,' he said to Enkidu, 'didst thou not call me? Why have I awakened? Has not a god passed by? Why is my flesh overwhelmed? Dreaming I saw the heavens cry out and the earth

Part of the great stele of Ur-Nammu, king of Ur. Above, on the left, the king pours a libation to the goddess Ningal while, on the right, he offers a similar libation to her consort Nannar – the moon-god Sin. The builder of the great ziggurat at Ur, Ur-Nammu is shown below with mason's tools on his shoulder following a god. Relief carving on stone. Second millennium B.C.

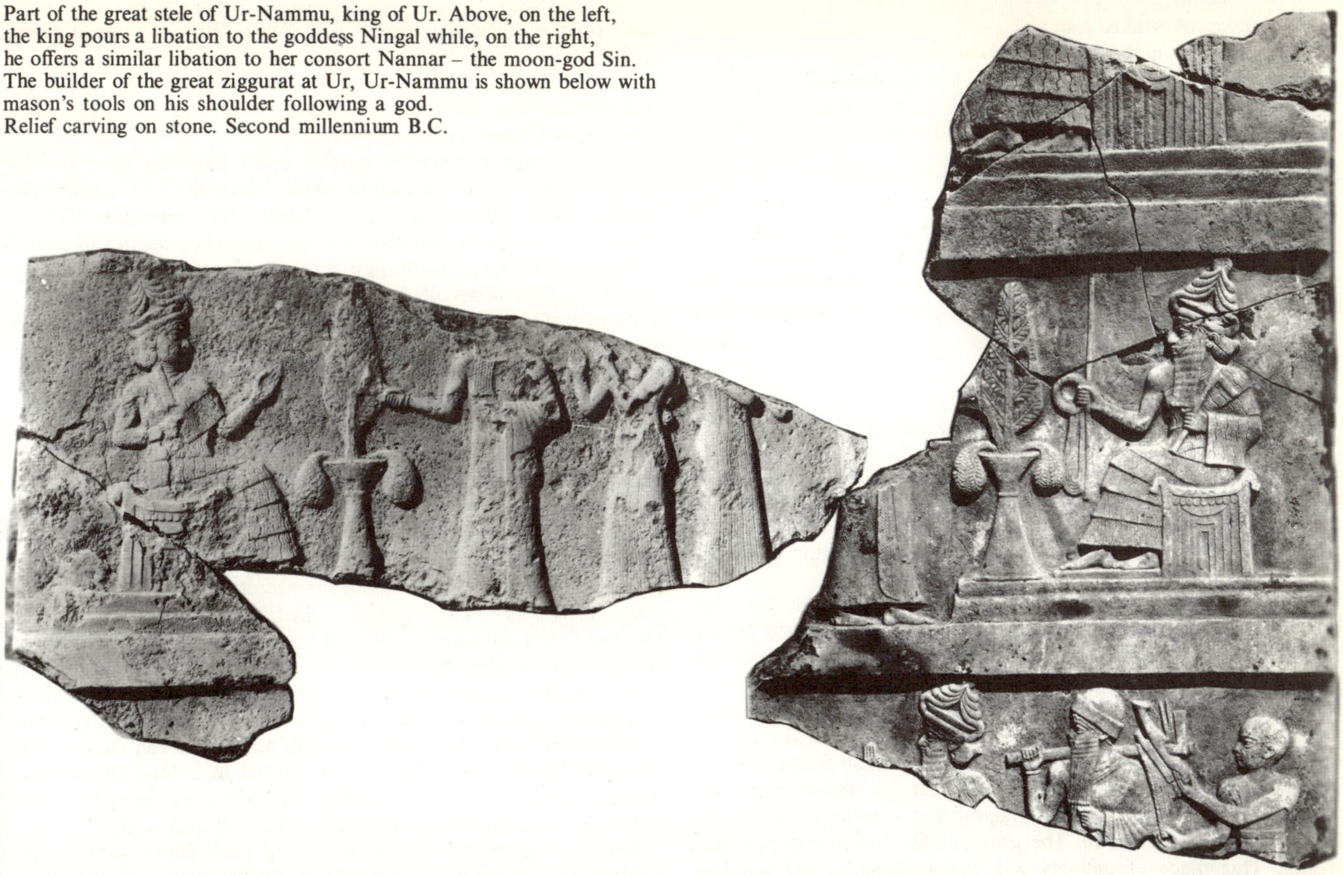

roar. In the darkness lightning flashed, fire burst forth; death fell like rain. Then the fire was extinguished...' Enkidu presumably interpreted the dream as an omen of victory, though the next part of the text is lost. He invoked the aid of the gods and went into battle. The gods let loose the elements against Khumbaba who confessed himself vanquished and was slain by Gilgamesh.

After his triumph Gilgamesh purified himself of his battle-stains, rearranged his hair and put on clean raiment. He fastened his robe and resumed his crown. The goddess Ishtar saw the hero and, struck by his beauty, spoke to him:

Come, Gilgamesh, be my lover!
Be my husband and I shall be thy wife!
I shall harness thee a chariot of lapis-lazuli and gold.
Come into our dwelling, in the perfume of the cedars.
When thou comest in our dwelling
They who sit on thrones will kiss thy feet,
Kings will prostrate themselves before thee, Lords and Princes...

But Gilgamesh roughly repelled the goddess. He well knew how inconstant she was and what wretched fate she reserved for her lovers when they had ceased to please her.

Come, I will reveal thy harlotry!
For Tammuz, lover of thy youth,
Year after year thou hast mourned.
The bird, the 'little gardener', the speckled one,
Thou hast loved him:
And struck him and broken his wing!
Thou hast loved the lion, mighty in strength:
And thou hast dug for him seven and seven pits.
Thou hast loved the steed, proud in battle,
And destined him for the halter, the goad and the whip.
Thou hast loved the shepherd:
To thee each day he sacrificed his kids;
Thou hast struck him and changed him into a leopard...
Me, too, wilt thou now love – and like them transform.

On hearing these harsh words Ishtar smouldered with rage. She rose to the skies, approached Anu, her father, and said: 'Gilgamesh has cursed me! Gilgamesh has recounted my shame...To chastise his impudence create a celestial bull to send against him!' Anu granted his daughter's request. He sent against Gilgamesh a furious bull who was about to overthrow the hero when Enkidu rushed to his assistance, seized the beast by its tail and tore it to pieces. Then, seeing Ishtar on the walls of Erech, weeping in the midst of her sacred courtesans, he skinned off the right flank of the celestial bull and flung it derisively into the goddess's face, saying: 'And thou too, let me but catch thee – I shall do as much to thee.'

Gilgamesh removed the bull's vast horns, which could hold much oil, and reserved them for the ritual of anointing required by the cult of Lugal-banda for whom he had an especial veneration. After which the two friends, having washed their hands in the Euphrates, returned to Erech amidst the acclamations of the people who cried:

Gilgamesh is dazzling among men!
Gilgamesh is mighty among men!

Having accomplished their marvellous exploits our heroes rested. But the cruel Ishtar meditated her revenge. Enkidu was stricken with illness and for twelve days struggled against it. Thus was fulfilled the funereal dream which had disturbed him at the beginning of the poem. At dawn on the thirteenth day Enkidu expired in the arms of his friend. Gilgamesh bewailed him:

Enkidu, my friend, my little brother, who chased the tiger of the desert;
Together have we gone everywhere and climbed mountains:
What sleep has seized thee now?
Darkness has come over thee and thou hearest me not!

He felt his heart and his heart no longer beat. Suddenly seized with panic before the corpse Gilgamesh rushed from his palace and fled through the countryside. Those whom he met said to him:

Why is thy strength devoured? Why is thy face lowered?
Thy heart is in a sorry state; thy features are cast down.
And there is sorrow in thy bowels;
Sadness and mourning burn thy visage.

And Gilgamesh answered them:

Why should I not flee through the land?
Enkidu, my friend, my little brother, who chased the panther of the desert,
My friend who with me killed lions,
My friend who faced with me all difficulties,

His fate has overtaken him.
Six days and six nights have I wept over him.
Then was I afraid of death and I fled through the land.
My friend whom I loved has become like unto mud.
And I, must I too, lie down like him and never rise again?

So it was the fear of death which made Gilgamesh flee.

But where could he discover the secret of how to escape this inevitable fate? Finally he thought of going to consult Uta-Napishtim, that fortunate man who, having survived the deluge, had received from the gods the gift of immortality. To reach him the road was long and dangerous. To Gilgamesh that mattered not: he would face all perils.

If I meet lions and am afraid,
I shall raise my head and call upon Sin;
To Ishtar, courtesan of the gods, my prayers shall rise.

First he reached Mount Mashu. It was here that every evening the sun sought repose. The gates of the mountain were guarded by scorpion-men whose heads touched the terrace of the gods and whose breasts reached the netherworld. 'Their dazzling brilliance overthrew mountains.'

Seeing them Gilgamesh felt his face grow dark with fear and horror. Nevertheless he recovered his courage and bowed before them. A scorpion-man, who had recognised in Gilgamesh the flesh of the gods, obligingly indicated the route, and the hero strode forward into the depths of the mountain. For eleven double-hours he marched through impenetrable darkness. Finally, at the twelfth double-hour, the light again shone, and Gilgamesh found himself in a wonderful garden which lay beside the sea. Before him rose the tree of the gods whose fruits, magnificent to behold, were borne on branches of lapis-lazuli. The ground was strewn with precious stones. This place of delights was the dwelling of the goddess Siduri Sabitu (that is, the inn-keeper) 'who lives at the edge of the sea'. At the sight of the hero, dressed in the skin of a wild animal, Siduri took fright and locked herself in her house. But Gilgamesh threatened to break the bolt and smash in the door. The goddess then consented to listen to him. When he had told her the object of his journey she first pointed out that it was useless.

O Gilgamesh, why dost thou run in all directions?
The life thou seekest thou shalt never find.
When the gods created man
They gave him Death.
Life they kept in their own hands.

Let Gilgamesh, then, be satisfied with earthly joys.

Fill thy belly,
Night and day rejoice,
Make every day a festival!
Put on lavish raiment,
Let thy head be washed! Wash thee with water,
Consider the child who grasps thy hand,
Let thy wife rejoice on thy bosom!

Moreover, to what perils would he not expose himself if he persisted in his design:

O Gilgamesh! There has never been a way,
And no one since the days of old has passed the sea.
The way is hard and the road is rough,
And deep are the waters of Death which close the entrance.
Where, then, Gilgamesh, shalt thou pass over the sea?
When thou reachest the waters of Death, what shalt thou do?

Being, however, unable to overcome the hero's stubbornness Siduri advised him to seek Urshanabi, Uta-Napishtim's boatman, who alone could guide him on this difficult voyage.

Urshanabi bade Gilgamesh cut in the forest a hundred and twenty poles each sixty cubits long. After that he invited him on board his boat. They reached the waters of Death which surrounded the paradise of Uta-Napishtim and defended its approaches. Woe to him who touched these waters! But thanks to Urshanabi's foresight Gilgamesh avoided their deadly contact. He threw away each pole after having used it only once. With the one hundred and twentieth pole the crossing was accomplished.

Gilgamesh found Uta-Napishtim and explained his desire for immortality. But 'he who had found everlasting life' urged upon him death's inescapable necessity.

'Do we make a house to last for ever? Does the river rise for ever? No one knows the face of death. Mammitu who created fate decides, with the Anunnaki, the fates. They determine life and death and they never make known the days when death will come!'

If, after the deluge, he himself had become immortal the privilege was due to the benevolence of a god. And to prove to Gilgamesh the force of destiny he proposed an experiment. Since sleep is the image of death let Gilgamesh not go to bed for six days and seven nights. Alas! Gilgamesh had scarcely sat down before he was asleep! Uta-Napishtim said with contempt to his wife:

Behold the strong man who desired everlasting life!
Sleep, like a hurricane, breaks over him.

So Gilgamesh returned home and retained his mortal state. Before he departed, however, Uta-Napishtim at his wife's request revealed to Gilgamesh a wondrous secret: at the bottom of the ocean there was a prickly plant – 'like the bramble its thorn pricks the hand, but its name is "the-old-man-becomes-young" and he who eats of it regains his youth.' Gilgamesh at once attached heavy stones to his feet, plunged into the ocean, gathered the plant which pricked his hand and, removing the stones, rose again and regained Urshanabi's boat. His journey would not have been useless. But alas! during his return journey he bathed in a fountain of fresh water; when a snake, attracted by the odour of the plant, stole the magic branch. Then Gilgamesh sat down and wept.

Doubly disappointed, Gilgamesh regained Erech with its enclosure. Still haunted by the fear of death he evoked the shade of Enkidu, to learn from him the 'law of the world'; but Enkidu could only describe to his friend the mournful condition of those who are everlastingly imprisoned in the sombre kingdom of Nergal. And it is upon this disheartening vision that the adventures of Gilgamesh close.

THE GODS OF ELAM

In the mountainous country east of Babylonia lay the land of Elam – which was once, in the fourth millennium B.C., the scene of a flourishing civilisation whose chief centre was the city of Susa.

This civilisation was closely related to that of the land of Sumer and their religions had much in common. Unless they had a common origin – which some have suggested – their similarity of religious belief can be simply explained by their propinquity.

The chief divinity of the Elamites was IN-SHUSHINAK, 'He of Susa' who was not only, as his name seems to indicate, Susa's local god, but was also considered the 'Sovereign of the Gods', 'Master of heaven and earth', 'Maker of the Universe'. These are the same titles which in Babylon were given to supreme gods. IN-SHUSHINAK is a personal name rather than an indication of origin.

It is not easy to identify In-Shushinak exactly, but it is generally agreed that he corresponded to Ninurta, 'the champion of the celestial gods', or even Adad, god of lightning and the tempest. We must not forget that these two divinities had, as well as their terrible aspect, a more beneficent function: they were gods of the welcome rain and fruitful flood and, hence, gods of fertility. In-Shushinak must without doubt have also shared this double nature.

Among the other divinities who peopled the Elamite pantheon and who, since we know scarcely more than their names, can only be enumerated are: KIRIRISHA, the sovereign goddess whose spouse was the god KHUMBAM who is identified with the Babylonian Marduk; LAGAMAL, described as the son of Ea; NAH-HUNTE, the sun who, like Shamash, was at the same time god of light and of justice; TESHUB, god of the tempest, who was, moreover, worshipped throughout Western Asia; NARUTI, whom we only know from an offering presented to the deity by the *ishakku* of Susa.

These national deities were later joined by the gods and goddesses of Sumer and Akkad who may have been imported into Elam when it fell under the hegemony of the rulers of Agade, Ur and Lagash; or else may have been introduced when the Elamites extended their domination over Babylonia.

PHOENICIAN MYTHOLOGY

INTRODUCTION

The Phoenicians were a part of the Canaanite world which was formed at the dawn of history by Semitic immigration into the territories between the Mediterranean and the Syrian desert. The mythology of the Phoenicians is thus largely derived from a background common to a more widely extended ethnic group. We know much less about it than about the mythology of the Egyptians or the Assyro-Babylonians. In the last few decades, however, such progress has been made, thanks to excavations at Byblos and Ras Shamrah, that our sources of information have been much enlarged.

At the moment our sources consist of four groups of texts.

The most ancient go back to the times of the Old Kingdom in Egypt, that is to say to the beginning of the third millennium B.C. They were discovered by Pierre Montet in central Phoenicia, in the ruins of Gubla, the Byblos of the Greeks, to-day Jebeil, a little village of the Lebanon Republic, north of Beirut. They are of especial value when studied in conjunction with Egyptian texts of various periods and the illustrations on contemporary monuments.

The second group of Phoenician mythological texts comes from Schaeffer and Chenet's excavation in the ruins of Ugarit, a town which was a little to the north of the Phoenicia of classical authors, a place which to-day is called Ras Shamrah. They are very valuable documents, written in the first half of the fourteenth century B.C., discovered in 1929 and the years following, transcribed and translated by Virolleaud in the review *Syria* and the subject of a brilliant commentary by R. Dussaud in the *Revue de l'histoire des religions*.

The third group consists of certain inscriptions and illustrations on monuments, of the literary works of Philo of Byblos, of Damascius, Mochus, the Bible and of Assyrian and Egyptian texts.

One cannot overlook the mythology peculiar to Carthage, Phoenicia's principal colony. Carthaginian documents thus form the fourth and last of these groups which we shall now consider in turn.

BYBLOS, AT THE BEGINNING OF THE THIRD MILLENNIUM

In the days of the first Egyptian dynasties Byblos was a small town on a hill beside the sea. It did a lively trade in the wood of the neighbourhood. The Egyptians came to Byblos in search of the timber they required for the construction of sea-going ships, the masts decorated with streamers which rose before their temples, the hewn planks they used in making furniture and coffins. From Byblos they also brought back the resin which was so important in embalming. Many documents bear witness to these economic relations, which were non-existent between Egypt and any other towns on the Phoenician coast. The result was an exchange of myths between Egypt and Byblos.

The chief deity of Byblos was a goddess. She was probably already known under the title of Ba'alat, that is 'the Lady (of Byblos)'. On a cylinder seal, engraved at Byblos itself for a prince whose name has not come down to us, she is represented seated, dressed in a tight robe with shoulder straps, wearing her hair in the Egyptian manner, her head surmounted by a disk between two horns. Thus she resembles the goddess Hathor, who was venerated on the banks of the Nile.

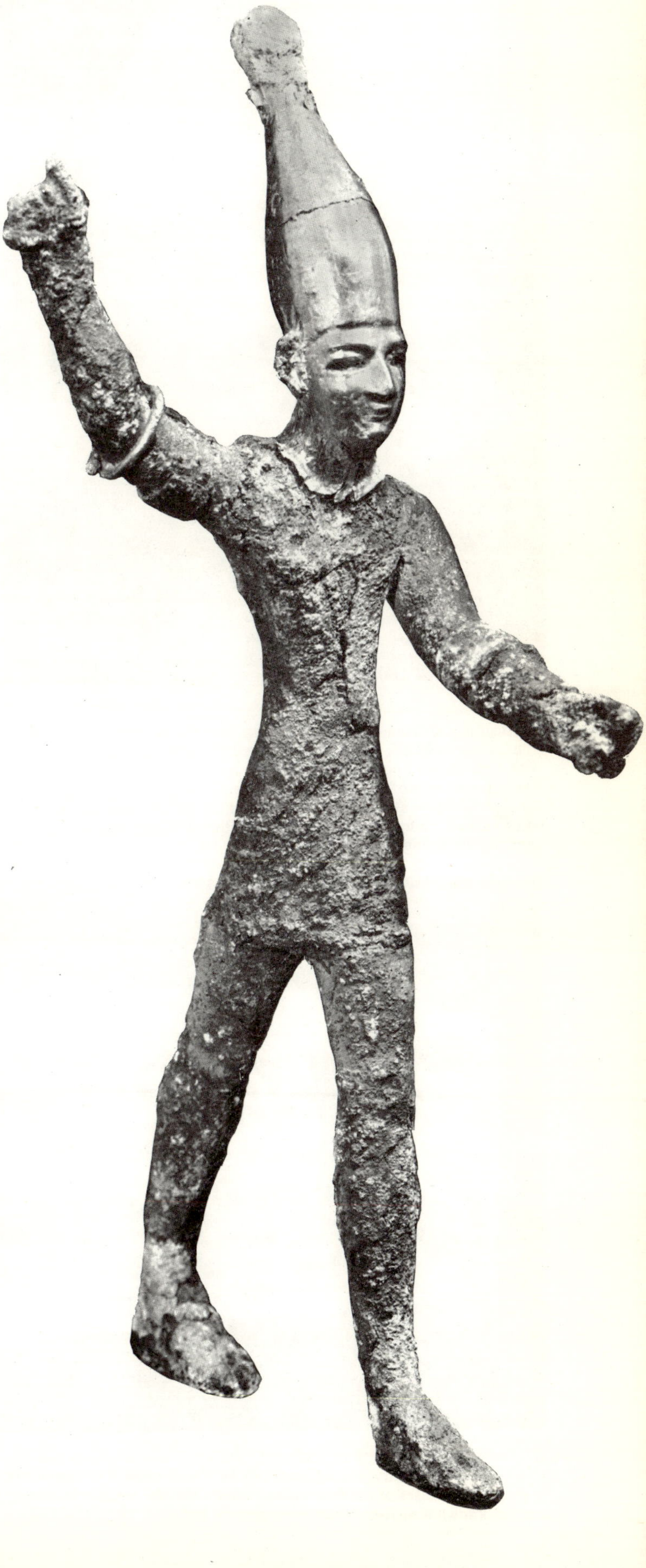

Statuette of Ba'al from Ras Shamrah. Ba'al, or 'Lord', was a title conferred on a number of gods by the Phoenicians. At Ras Shamrah it was given to Hadad, the god of the tempest, portrayed here as a young warrior with his left arm outstretched to wield his lightning spear. In his right hand he would have held a club. Copper inlaid and overlaid with gold and silver. Fourteenth century B.C. Louvre.

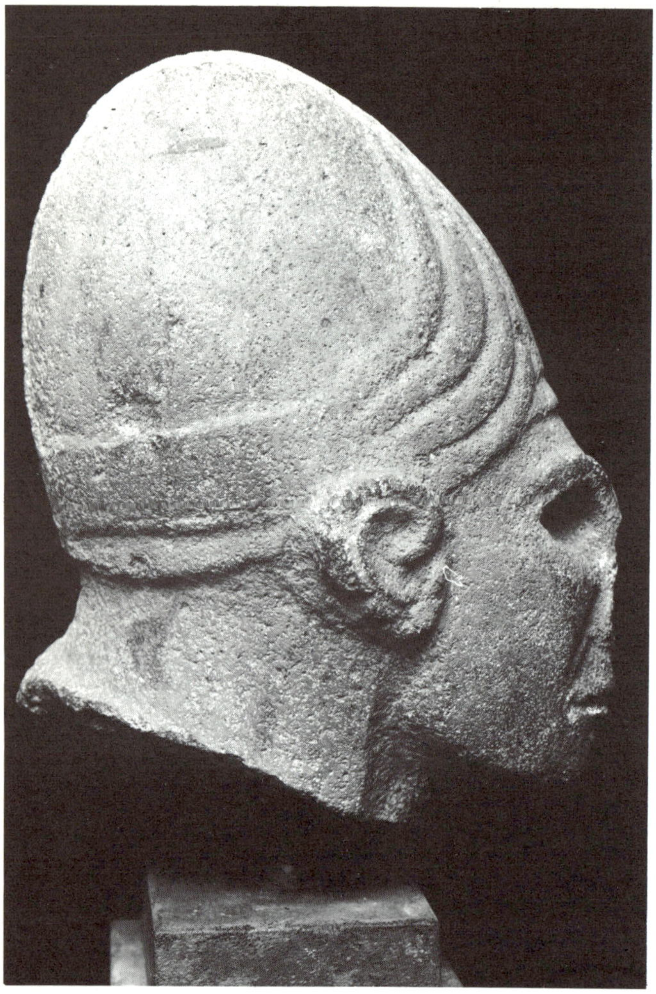

Head of a god from Djabboul in Syria. Possibly a representation of El, 'the Father of Men', the god is portrayed wearing a helmet adorned with four superimposed rows of bull's horns – the emblems of divinity. The supreme god of the Semitic pantheon, El was worshipped throughout Syria alongside the local gods, or 'Ba'als', one of his titles, indeed, being 'the Bull' – an appellation which probably signified his strength.

An Egyptian bas-relief, discovered by Renan and preserved in the Louvre, portrays her welcoming and embracing a Pharaoh. From one of the horns above her face is suspended a uraeus which poises its head against that of the uraeus ornamenting the brow of the king.

Another bas-relief in the museum of Beirut has two symmetrical scenes in each of which a king of some dynasty between the fifth and the eleventh – probably one of the Pepis – kneels and presents two vases to a divinity. In one scene it is the Lady of Byblos; in the other a lion-headed god, who, like the goddess, is designated by the epithet: 'Beloved of Hathor'.

From the time of the twelfth dynasty, relations between Egypt and Byblos became such that the Lady of Byblos was finally equated with Hathor. Henceforth she seems eager to copy the Egyptian manner of attitude and costume. For example, the stela of Yehawmelek, during the Achaemenian Empire, shows the Lady of Byblos wearing the head-dress of the goddess Hathor of Ptolemaic times – a vulture skin surmounted by a mortier.

According to the cylinder seal already mentioned there existed in Byblos a great god who was assimilated to the Egyptian sun-god Ra. He was distinguished by two epithets which were not used in Egypt: he was called 'Ra, of Foreign Lands' and 'Ra, who is on Pharaoh's Lake'.

His son was the god of Byblos, to whom the cylinder gives the Egyptian name of Ruti, that is to say, 'He who resembles a Lion'. It is he whom we have already seen on the bas-relief with symmetrical scenes, depicted with a human body and a lion's head.

The cylinder seal gives us the name of a fourth divinity: Hay-Tau of Nega, of whom the prince calls himself the well-loved.

Nega is mentioned several times in Egyptian texts. It was either the territory between northern Lebanon and the sea, which later formed the district of Byblos, or else merely the region of Nahr Ibrahim, five miles to the south of Jebeil, which became the centre of the cult of Adonis. It was a wooded region where grew various species of conifers, junipers and a tree with red wood called the *mer*. The god of Nega, Hay-Tau, a prototype of Adonis, was the spirit of forest vegetation. At some period he became metamorphosed into a tree.

The Egyptians adopted Hay-Tau and identified him with their Osiris, according to the legend recounted by Plutarch which has been referred to in the section on Egyptian mythology. The resin of the conifers was the tears of Osiris; and, if the coffins of Egyptian priests were by preference made of resinous wood, that was because the priests had become 'Osirises'. The pyramid texts mention the god Hay-Tau of Nega three times, with whom the Pharaoh is

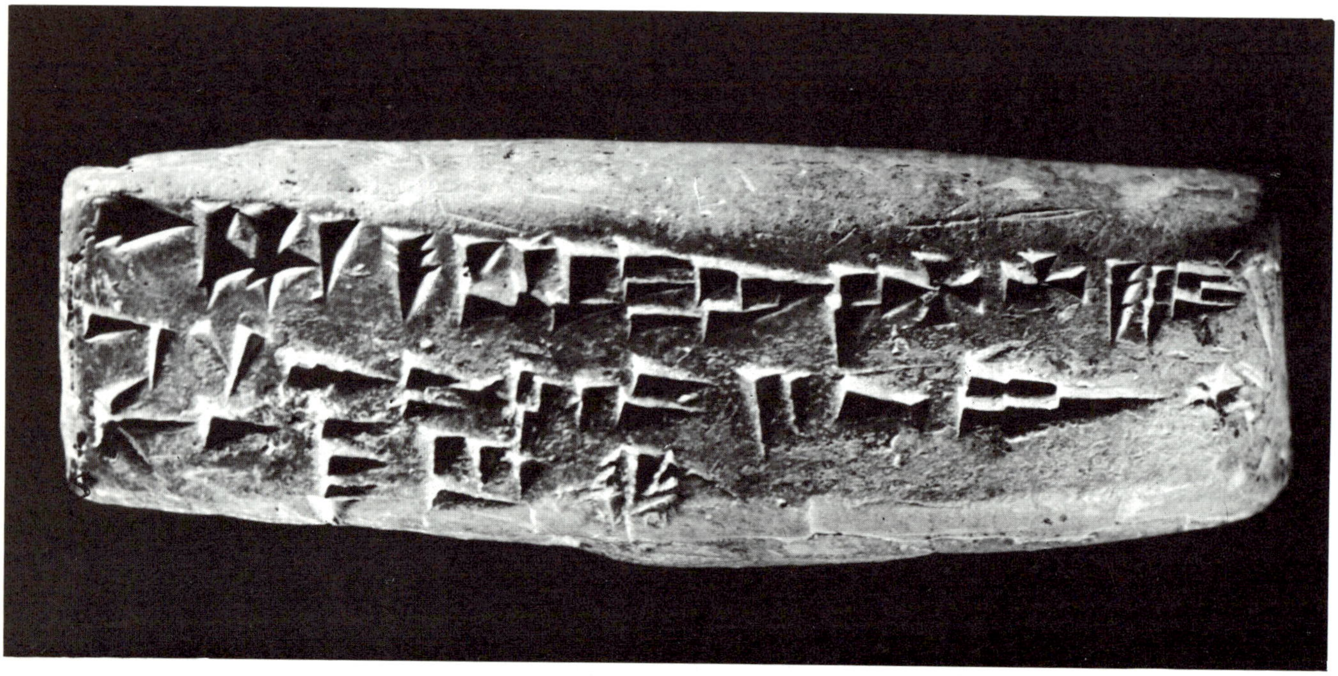

Clay tablet inscribed with the different signs of the alphabetic cuneiform script in which the mythological texts of Ras Shamrah were set down. Discovered in a library in the former city of Ugarit (now Ras Shamrah), the texts recount the stories concerning El, Ba'al and Asherat and the other gods and goddesses of the Phoenician religion and the legends involving mortals such as Keret and Danel. The tablet is the earliest known alphabet. Fourteenth century B.C.

identified in his tomb. It is requested, moreover, that the dead king shall not be treated like Osiris who is changed into a tree in Nega.

An Egyptian document long before Plutarch, the Story of the Two Brothers, shows another form of Hay-Tau's introduction into Egyptian mythology. The Egyptian hero is called Ba-Tau. His brother had wished to kill him. He therefore fled to the Valley of the Pine, very likely the Valley of Nahr Ibrahim, and placed his heart on the topmost branch of the pine. Egyptian soldiers came to carry off his wife. She had the tree cut down and immediately Ba-Tau died. He came to life again four years later when his brother found the heart. He transformed himself into a bull and returned to Egypt, carrying his brother on his back. The identification of Ba-Tau with Hay-Tau was for the Egyptians especially clear because the god of Nega, in the hieroglyphic texts, was associated with a bull. We shall see that in Phoenician mythology, as the Ras Shamrah texts present it, the bull is frequently associated with gods.

THE LEGENDS OF RAS SHAMRAH

The cuneiform tablets of Ras Shamrah reveal in the fourteenth century B.C. mythological material of a tradition which was already ancient and which, moreover, was to continue, though not without modifications, until the end of paganism, since echoes of it are found in the works of Philo of Byblos.

The basis of this mythology was the cult of the elements and of natural phenomena. In it, all the divinities have clearly been transformed into human shape and are arranged in a strict hierarchy.

At the head of the pantheon stood El, the great god who from remote times was honoured among all the western Semites. He governed the entire land of Canaan. He made the rivers flow into the abyss of the ocean and thus assured the fertility of the earth. As 'father of years', for he regulated their course, and as 'the king', El dwelt in a pavilion near the shore where rivers flow into the sea. He was honoured under various titles. The most important of these seems to have been 'Bull' or 'Bull-El'; not that he was identified with an animal, though in certain cases he was thus represented. But the idea of power and strength was symbolised among the Canaanites by the bull, which was also the symbol or animal-attribute of other divinities.

After El the greatest god was Ba'al. He was often El's enemy. He was less ancient than El in Phoenician mythology. Ba'al did not appear before the arrival of the Phoenicians on the Mediterranean coast when they emigrated from the Negeb, south of Palestine, where they had previously lived. Ba'al, in the Ras Shamrah texts, is the same god as Ba'al Tsaphon, a name which can be translated 'Lord of the North'. He is the same god as Ba'al Lebanon, 'Lord of Lebanon', later venerated in all the places of cult in the Lebanon Mountains, in the attitude popularised by the images of the Heliopolitan Jupiter.

But, as in all the other cases where a Canaanite divinity was called Ba'al, the name was never a proper name. It was an appellation that hid the god's true name, which was known only to the initiated. Like the name of the god of Israel it could, apparently, be pronounced only in exceptional cases which were laid down by tradition. Ba'al, in the Ras Shamrah texts, is Hadad, god of the atmosphere, of clouds and the tempest. His voice sounded in the clouds, he wielded the thunderbolt, he dispensed rain.

This god did not, like El, exist before the birth of the gods. He had a mother, the goddess Asherat-of-the-Sea. His consort also is Asherat, but it is impossible to say whether she is the same goddess or one of her hypostases. In Ugarit, the ancient city whose ruins to-day bear the name Ras Shamrah, she was many times represented on the stelae erected in his temple.

After 1350 B.C. we see him on a stela with the general traits of the god Sutekh – a type created by the Egyptians to represent foreign gods. This stela indicates the influence of the Pharaoh in Phoenicia, an influence of which we were already aware thanks to the famous diplomatic correspondence called the 'Letters of el Amarna'.

Elsewhere, under the influence of the Hittites who disputed the control of Upper Syria with the Egyptians, the same god, wearing a pointed helmet adorned with the symbolic horns which the Sumerians reserved for the head-dress of their gods, thrusts his spear into the earth and the shaft of his spear appears to simulate the lightning's zigzag.

A famous cylinder seal in the Boston Museum, though not

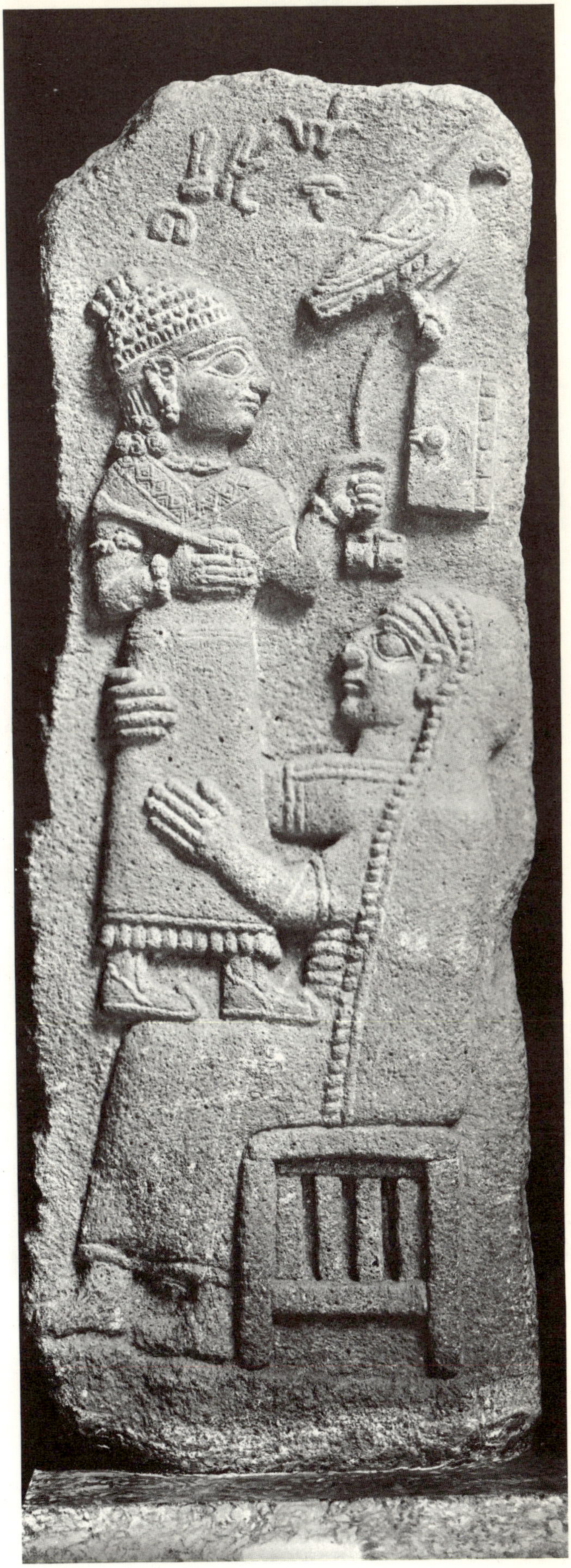

Funeral stele from Marash in Anatolia. The scribe Tarhunpiyas is portrayed standing on the knees of a seated woman, probably a mother goddess, who clasps the lower part of his body in her arms. He holds – or is connected to – the figure of a falcon.

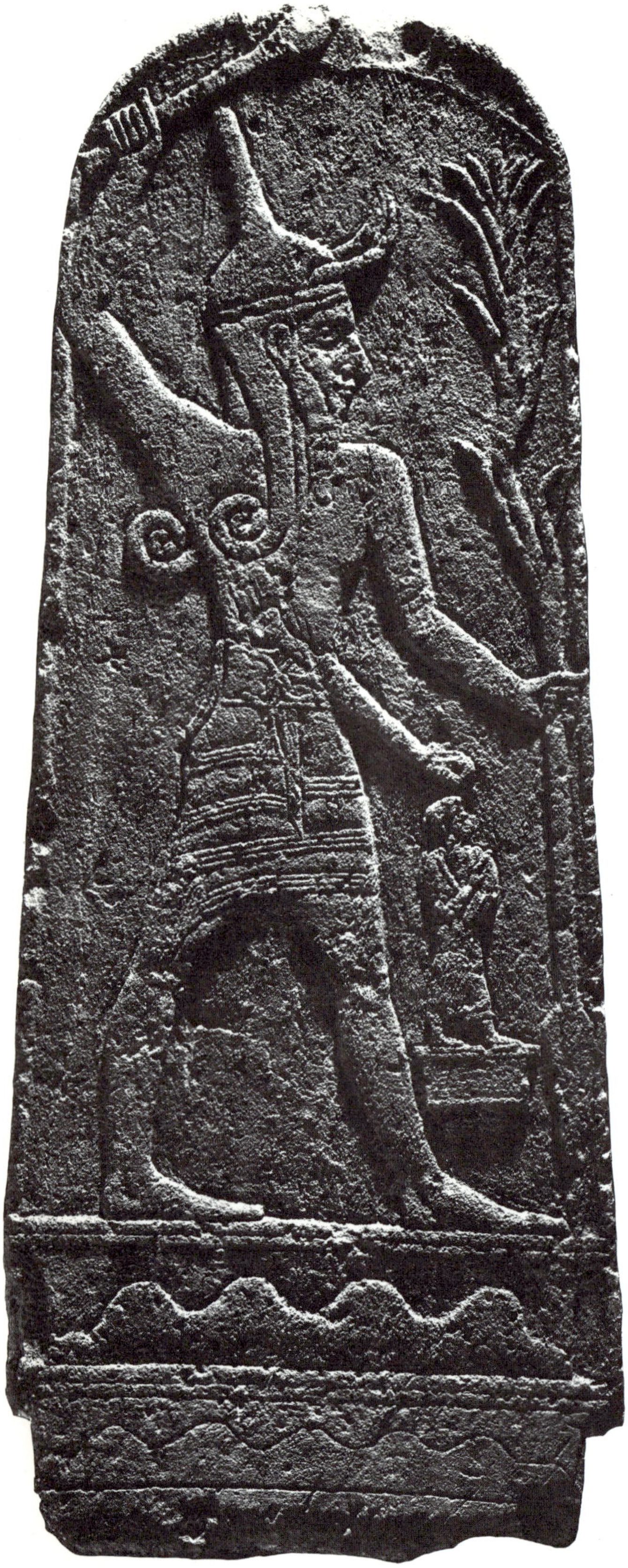

The Ba'al Tsaphon. Stela from Ras Shamrah. Fourteenth century B.C. Louvre.

actually of Phoenician origin, represents Ba'al Hadad. Not only has he overthrown a man with his lance, but behind him there is a representation of his animal attribute, the bull. This representation was traditional among the western Semites. At the beginning of the second millennium in the Semitic colonies of Asia Minor, Hadad, armed with a thunderbolt and standing on a bull, faces a god who holds a spear with its point lowered towards a man stretched at his feet.

Mot, one of the sons of El, was the spirit of the harvest. He ruled the countryside when the ground lay dry beneath the burning sun, when the corn had reached maturity. The plains on which it never rains were the domains of Mot, the divine son. He was the god El's favourite son.

At the time of the harvest Mot was sacrificed by the goddess Anat, but he did not remain dead for long. Almost immediately he was reborn and his reign seemed scarcely to have been interrupted. But he was to be vanquished in a combat with the son of Ba'al at the beginning of the rainy season and abandoned by El his father, who himself had determined that such should be the unfortunate Mot's fate.

Aleyin, Mot's opponent, was the son of Ba'al. As with Mot, his relationship and dependence upon his father was close. Indeed it seems that he was merely another concept of Ba'al with the special function of maintaining the water supply. Most of the rivers in Phoenicia had divine names which were connected with the cycle of Aleyin. Aleyin, the spirit of springs, fostered vegetation which relied upon the season of the rains. He was called the 'Ba'al of the Earth', 'the House of Water'. Perhaps it was he who was honoured later with those monuments called 'Memnonia' erected at the mouths of most rivers in Phoenicia, temples where mourning rites were celebrated.

Aleyin, 'he who rode the clouds', was accompanied by seven companions and a troop of eight wild boars.

The goddess Asherat-of-the-Sea was called 'Mother of the Gods' and was said to have seventy children. She was also 'Creator of the Gods', and In Wisdom the Mistress of the Gods'. She was El's counsellor and the mother of Ba'al. Asherat, consort of Ba'al, may be merely a hypostasis of Ashtart. There was also an Asherat of Tyre.

Ashtart (in Greek Astarte) and Elat, whose names occur together in a list of sacrifices, are only rarely mentioned in the Ras Shamrah texts.

Ashtart of the Sky of Ba al was the most beautiful of heavenly bodies, the planet Venus.

Elat is the feminine form of the name El. There was a goddess Elat of the Sidonians.

The virgin Anat was the daughter of Ba'al and the sister of Aleyin. She was above all a divinity of bellicose temperament. We see her proceeding to the ritual murder of the god Môt. Later she finds herself obliged to ask her father's aid to put an end to the life of the harvest-god. The role which El had assigned to her was that of perpetuating the life of the gods – not in giving them life but in procuring for them the means of preserving it, especially by being responsible for constant sacrifices.

The Hyksos introduced her into Egypt. At Avaris she was honoured as the consort of a god sometimes called Ba'al, sometimes Sutekh. Her cult continued to flourish after the expulsion of the Hyksos.

As a daughter of the rain-god and sister of the water-god, Anat also played a part in fostering vegetation. She sprinkled the earth with dew; for the dew, like the rain, is the 'fat of the earth'.

At Ugarit great care was taken to ensure that the dead were supplied with water. Wells, cisterns covered with a flagstone pierced with a hole, gutters and jars sunk into the ground, provided reservoirs of water not only for those buried in the cemetery but also for those who had perished far from home. For the latter, funeral rites were piously performed and gifts deposited in the tombs which they would never occupy; for their souls could return to the land of their fathers to receive offerings and sacrifices.

Qadesh, the 'Holy', whose animal-attribute was the lion in Egyptian documents, was only an epithet of the goddess Anat. By this name she was the consort of the god Amurru, god of the 'West', who in Egyptian texts was given the name Reshef. They appeared together in the sacrifice of the ass at harvest time.

Offerings and Sacrifices. To nourish the gods, who like mortals were obliged to eat, one offered them bread and wine on a golden table.

Come, give them drink. Put bread upon the table, bread. And pour wine into the cups. In the golden goblet the blood of trees.

They were also offered a great variety of sacrifices, many of which are mentioned in the Bible. There were, for instance, expiatory sacrifices. When Anat reproaches Mot for the death of her brother Aleyin, Mot answers her:

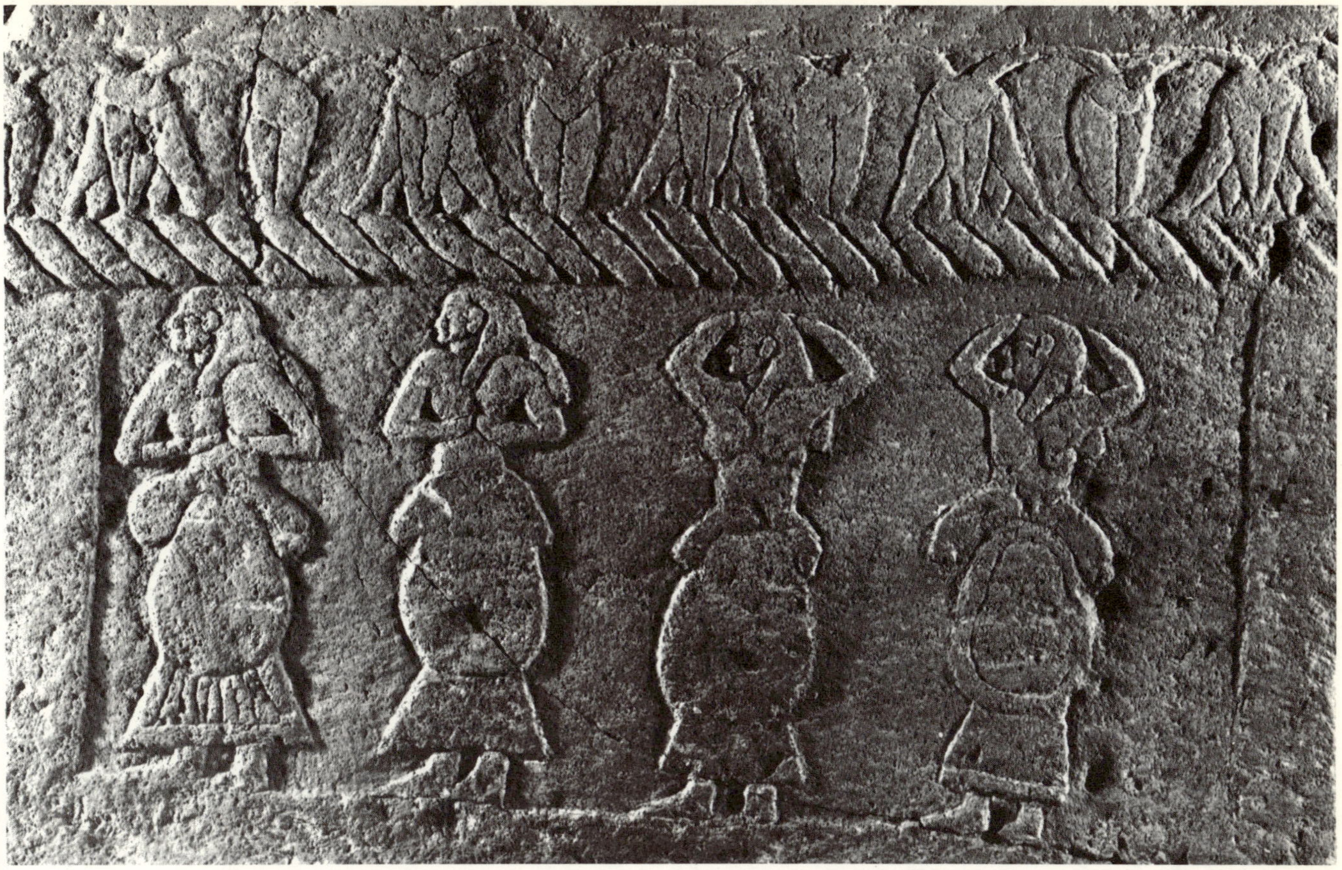

End panel of the sarcophagus of king Ahiram of Byblos. Four mourning women with their upper garments loosed and their breasts bare are shown performing a ritual dance. In addition, the first two lacerate their breasts—a mourning rite known from the Ba'al myth of Ras Shamrah – while the other two tear their hair or pour dust upon it. Though Ahiram reigned in the early tenth century B.C., the sarcophagus in which he was interred probably dates from three centuries earlier. Limestone.

I am Aleyin, son of Ba'al. Make ready, then, the sacrifice. I am the lamb which is made ready with pure wheat to be sacrificed in expiation.

Animals offered in sacrifice were the ox, the sheep, the ram, the calf, the lamb. No female animal is mentioned, at least in the ceremonies which accompanied the consecration of a temple.

A special sacrifice at the season of the harvest, to reawaken the spirit of the vine which the ass, nibbling the leaves, might have eaten, shows Qadesh and Amurru – in other words, Anat and Aleyin – intervening. Asherat-of-the-Sea gives them the following order:

Tie up the ass, bind the stallion. Make ready the vine-shoots with silvery leaves – of vivid green. Remove the she-asses from the vine.

Qadesh and Amurru obey. They tie up the ass, bind the stallion. They make ready the vine with silvery leaves, of vivid green. They remove the she-asses from the vine.

Qadesh and Amurru cross their hands. Asherat installs the ass on the high place. The stallion on the ... of the high place.

Qadesh seizes them, Amurru embraces them – when the morning star appears before the sanctuary of the virgin Anat. Then the sailor protects the sailor of Tsapuna.

The struggle between Aleyin and Mot. One of the poems of Ras Shamrah presents the two vegetation-gods and tells of their struggle which recurs every year.

The part of this poem which has been preserved begins at the moment when Aleyin, son of Ba'al, has just died. Asherat, his grandmother, and Ba'al, his father, are deeply distressed.

Latpon, one of the sons of the god El, goes to find his father in the tent he inhabits where 'the rivers meet the sea', to ask that the dead god be given a successor. El addresses Asherat-of-the-Sea and begs her to designate one of her sons.

Here part of the text is missing. Later the goddess Anat demands that Mot give her back her brother. She sets her dogs on the murderer's flocks, seizes him and puts him to death.

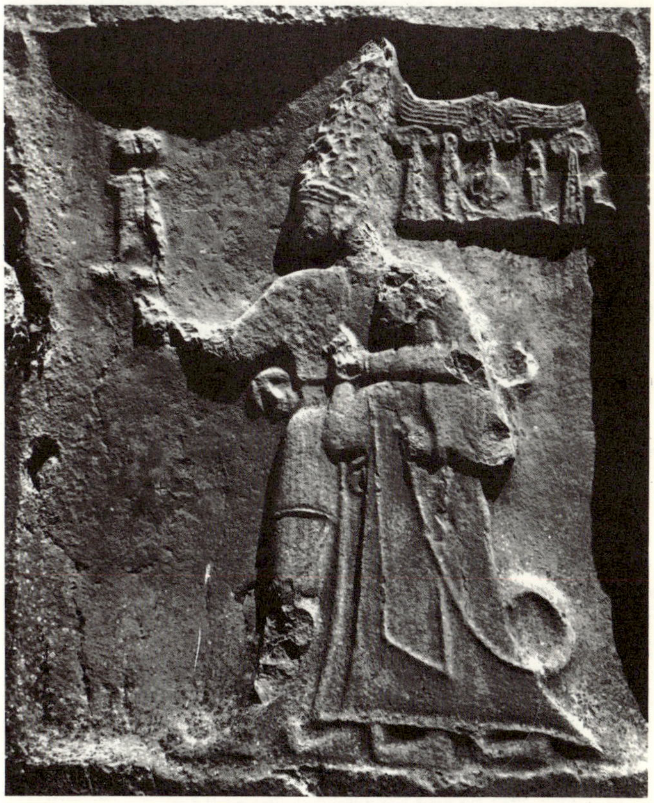

Sharrupa protecting king Tuthaliya IV. The god is shown over life-size to emphasize his divine character and wears a tall, multi-horned head-dress and a short kilt together with a sword. He embraces the king with his left arm – a gesture denoting honour and protection. To the right and left, above, are divine ideograms. Relief in the rock shrine of Yazilikaya near Hattusa, the former capital of the Hittite Empire.

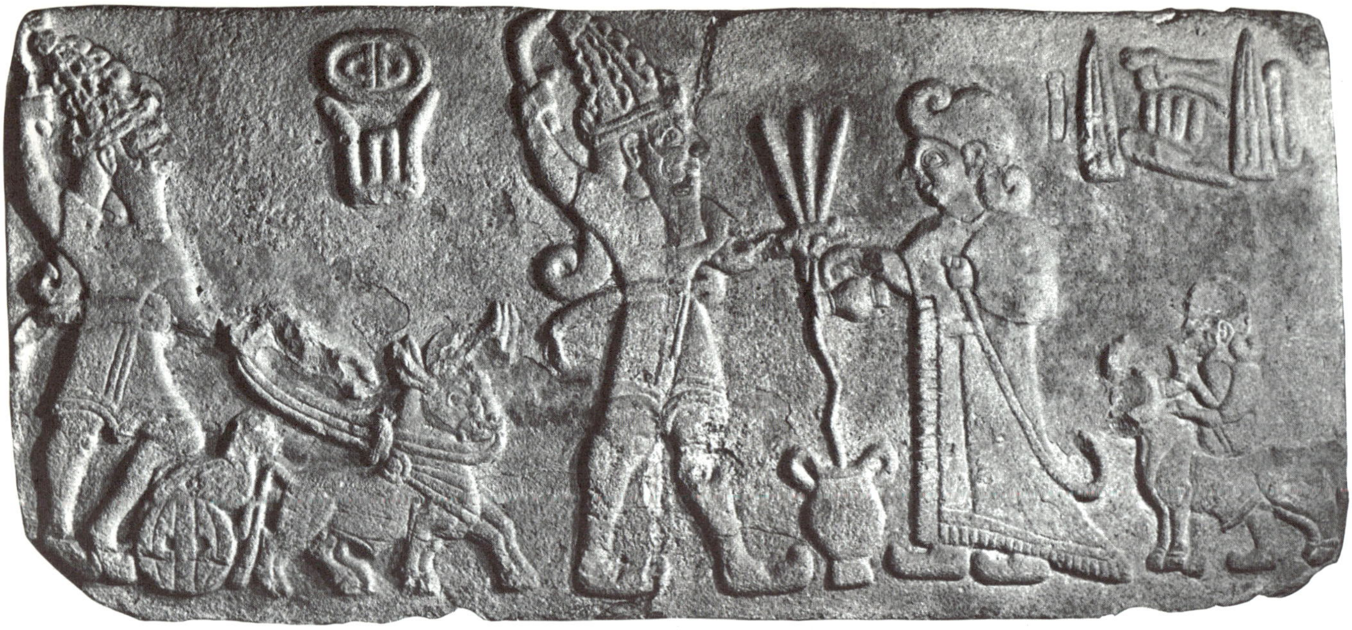

King Sulumeli and the weather-god. The bearded weather-god appears twice on this Hittite relief from Malatya. On the left he is seen riding in a chariot drawn by two bulls while in the centre he receives a libation from the king. Dressed in a horned head-dress and short tunic, he holds a thunderbolt in his left hand and brandishes a boomerang in his right. The king holds the royal staff. Tenth century B.C.

She seizes Mot, the son divine. With her sickle she cleaves him. With her flail she beats him. With fire she grills him. With her mill she grinds him. In the fields she scatters him. To consume his leaven, so that he no longer withholds his share (of the crop).

When Mot, the divine son, has perished, then Aleyin, son of Ba'al, is alive. The rains fall in abundance, rivers overflow, floods threaten. El orders Anat to inquire into the situation. Anat addresses the goddess Sapas, one of El's daughters, who is called the 'Torch of the Gods'. Sapas departs in search of Aleyin.

Finally Ba'al intervenes when, at the end of seven years, Mot threatens Aleyin with the seven chastisements of which he himself has been a victim. Aleyin takes up the challenge and the goddess Sapas announces Mot's downfall.

'Listen well, Mot, O son of the Gods! Behold, thou shalt do battle with Aleyin, son of Ba'al. Behold, thy father, Shor-El, will not listen to thee! May he tear away the gates of thy dwelling-place! May he overthrow the throne of thy royalty! May he break the sceptre of thy sovereignty!'

Mot, vanquished, descends into the underworld. Aleyin is re-established in his own, and his triumph is the subject of another poem.

The death of Ba'al and the death of Aleyin. Ba'al was hunting in the desert, probably the desert of Qadesh, when he suddenly found himself face to face with strange creatures, as big as wild bulls. El had created them to bar Ba'al's way, and Amat Asherat, whom El had banished to the desert, had brought them into the world.

The battle was merciless and at first Ba'al had the advantage. Finally, however, he succumbed and fell like a bull.

Anat soon arrived to undertake the burial of him whom the legend here calls her son. She dug a grave, transformed part of the desert into a garden and, after announcing the death of the god, descended with him into the tomb, accompanied by the sun-goddess who remained there until she became surfeited with the tears which she drank as though they were wine.

Aleyin also died. Anat bore him on her shoulders as far as the Mountain of the North. There she offered perfume to the deities of the underworld, then six sacrificial bulls, rams, stags, ibex and asses, in order that Aleyin should have enough to eat during his six months in the underworld. Finally she sent an announcement to El saying that he and his wife Asherat could rejoice since Ba'al and Aleyin were dead.

El and his wife rejoiced, but as Aleyin fulfilled an indispensable role they set about seeking someone to replace him.

Then Anat appeared again and accused the god Mot of responsibility for her brother's death.

The temple of Ba'al. Another poem of ancient origin which describes the construction of the Temple of Ba'al is purely mythical in substance and contains no mortals.

Though Ba'al was the owner of all space it was better that he, like other divinities, should possess a dwelling less vast as a place of prayer.

Ba'al has not a temple like a god; neither a sacred enclosure like a son of Asherat.

Before beginning the construction, the authorisation of El had to be obtained, without which all work would be in vain. To make sure of El's benevolence he was presented with a golden throne and a golden table covered with offerings. It was the work of Hiyon, the divine craftsman, who with his bellows and tongs 'melted silver, plated gold' and fashioned images of bulls in precious metals to decorate the future sanctuary.

Asherat-of-the-Sea undertook to present the request to El. Then to Latpon – the god who shared with her the gift of wisdom – she gave orders to begin work.

Latpon El Dped answered: 'I shall labour, I, the magician of Asherat. I shall work, I who perceive. Behold, Amat Asherat fashions the bricks. A house shall be constructed for Ba'al, for he is a god; and a holy enclosure, for he is a son of Asherat.'

Later the goddess urges Latpon to rest.

And the Lady Asherat-of-the-Sea, of all the gods Mistress in Wisdom, said: 'Rest from thy toil, for thou art of great age. Rest, because of thy lungs... And delight also in his rain.'

Ba'al himself took part in the work. With the lightning – 'his earthly saw' – he felled cedars for the roof of his dwelling. A message sent to Ba'al's son, Aleyin, shows that the erection of the holiest part of the edifice was reserved for him.

'Build a chapel of gold and silver. It will be the chapel of the pure. I shall watch over them.'

Ba'al was finally installed, and Anat offered to him the sacrifice of a bull. Then two brothers, Kusor and Hasisu, appeared and proposed to install windows in the temple.

And Kusor-and-Hasisu said: 'Listen, Aleyin, son of Ba'al, mark our words, O Rider of the Clouds. Behold, I shall put a sky-light in the sanctuaries, a window in the middle of the temples.'

But this did not suit Aleyin who retorted:

'Thou shalt place no sky-light in the sanctuaries, nor window in the middle of the temples.'

The argument was not settled; they had to appeal to a higher divinity, Ba'al, or perhaps even to the supreme god, El. Then Aleyin proposed a compromise.

'I myself shall place them, Kušor, the mariner, Kusor, son of the law (?), he shall open the window in sanctuaries, the sky-light in the middle of temples. And Ba'al shall open a fissure in the clouds – above the (face) of Kusor-and-Hasisu.'

Thenceforth the waters above would no longer spill from the heavens entirely by hazard and a deluge need be feared no more. Ba'al would let the rain fall only when Kusor opened the windows of the temple. Kusor became the regulator of the seasons, as Philo teaches us. Kusor also possessed the art of incantation and soothsaying. He was the inventor of mechanical devices and of the fishing boat.

The Epic of Keret. In the texts of Ras Shamrah Phoenician mythology is not exclusively occupied with gods. There are also legends in which mortals appear, together with gods and with god-like heroes who have commerce with the daughters of men.

Keret was a son of the supreme god, El, and the soldier of the goddess Sapas. He was also king of Sidon. El, his father, ordered him to resist an invasion conducted by Etrah or Terah, a moon-god.

Allied with the enemy were the people of Zabulon – a tribe which was later to form part of the people of Isra... and occupy the country between Carmel and the Lake of Galilee. Also with the enemy were the Koserites, who are mentioned in the lists of enemy towns inscribed on Egyptian vases at the end of the eleventh dynasty.

Far from hastening to obey El's orders, Keret shut himself up in his chamber and burst into tears. But in dreaming he regained his confidence: he dreamed that he would be the father of a son. This decided him to execute the orders he had received, but before he departed on the campaign he ascended a migdol, sat on the parapet of the tower and there, raising a hand to the sky, offered in sacrifice wine in a silver cup, honey in a golden vase, and the blood of a bird and of a lamb.

He then returned to the town and made arrangements for six months' food supplies for the population. But Terah had already occupied five towns and was attempting to cut the territory of the Phoenicians in two. The battle took place in the Negeb to the south of Palestine. The vanquished were obliged to emigrate: some did so in a body, others in small groups. Keret does not seem to have emerged victorious from the struggle. When he returned to Sidon he bought a wife and paid for her in gold and silver. By this wife he had a son, beautiful as Ashtart and gracious as Anat. This son was a prodigy: he had scarcely been born before he cried out: 'I hate the enemy!' He demanded justice for the widow, protection for the orphan and assistance against the plunderer.

Danel is another mythological hero. He was versed in the art of divination and his daughter knew all the secrets of astrology. His memory was preserved and, it seems, it is to Danel that the prophet Ezekiel compares the king of Tyre when he says to him: 'Thou art wiser than Daniel, no secrets are hidden from thee.' (XXVIII. 3.)

Poem of the birth of the gracious and fair gods. This myth, like the Epic of Keret, reminded the Phoenicians in mythological form of their land of origin, the Negeb, from where, via what was later called the Philistine coast, they reached, towards the beginning of the third millennium, Tyre, Sidon, Gubla and Arvad. In the fourteenth century B.C. they had not yet been driven by the Philistines from the coast near Egypt and they continued to use the trade routes of the Negeb.

This poem, in its essential features, has survived in a sort of mnemonic for the use of reciters during a religious ceremony which seems to have accompanied sacrifices made towards the end of winter.

Mot-and-Shur is then very tired. Dussaud, following Jeremiah II. 21, sees Mot as the spirit of the withering vine when it has the aspect of dead wood, in this hyphenated form of the god's name.

Mot-and-Shur sits down, holding in his hand a sceptre of sterility, holding in his hand a sceptre of unfruitfulness.

This is the moment in the vineyard when the vine is pruned, the shoots are tied and the terraces made ready. Among the sacrifices for the occasion was that of cooking a kid in the milk of its mother, a Canaanite custom which Mosaic law condemned and formally forbade.

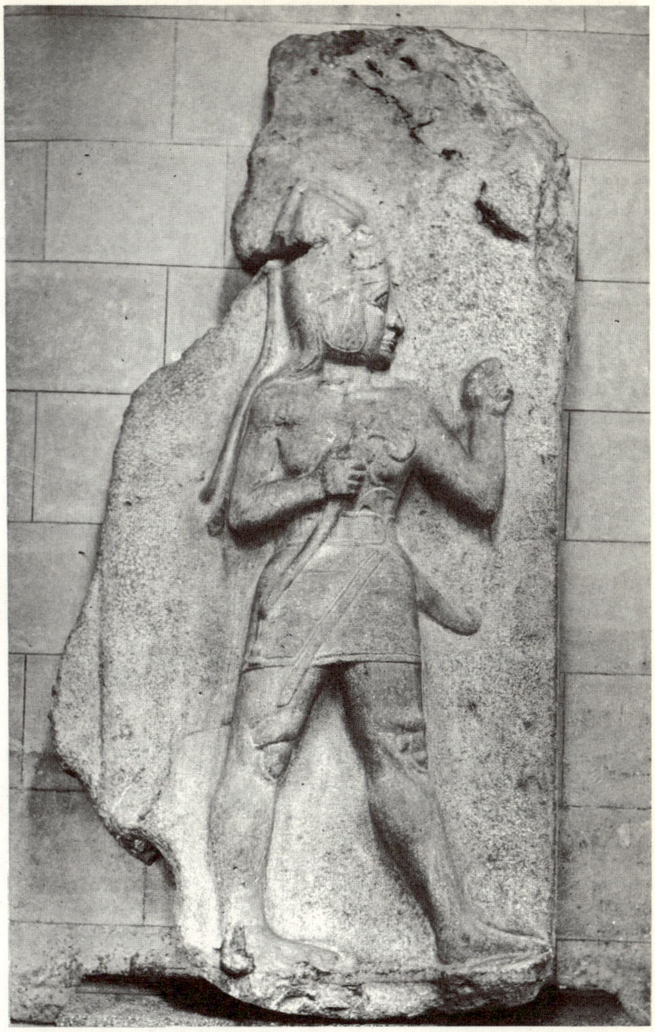

Hittite war god. The vigorous young god strides forward grasping an axe in his right hand with a curved sword thrust into his belt.
On his head he wears a pointed helmet with cheek and neck flaps, its plume falling to his elbow. His short kilt is fastened by a sash which falls to his knee. His feet are bare.
Relief from the inside of the King's Gate at Hattusa.
Fourteenth century B.C. Ankara Museum.

To this fertility rite, a rite of procreation was added in which El, the supreme god, took direct part in order to create the gods 'gracious and fair'.

El, the sun-god, advanced along the shore, on the banks of the abyss. The celebrants called upon Mot lamenting. Then they called upon the 'Mother' – probably Asherat-of-the-Sea. El plunged into the waves.

The hands of El reach out like the sea. And the hands of El reach out like the waves. El stretches his hand like the sea. El stretches his hand like the waves.

With this the god obtained two objects which he put in his house. El placed the wave in the sky, and when it fell again as rain upon the earth it bent Mot's sceptre and his hands began nervously to tremble.

When El had made his wives fruitful, they accused themselves of Mot's misfortunes.

O Mot, Mot, it is we who made thy sceptre to bend, we who caused thy hand to tremble.

The narrative then says:

El leaned over their lips; then he raised his voice and said: 'Behold, their lips are sweet as a bunch of grapes.'

The continuation concerns the ritual of divine marriage. After having recounted that,

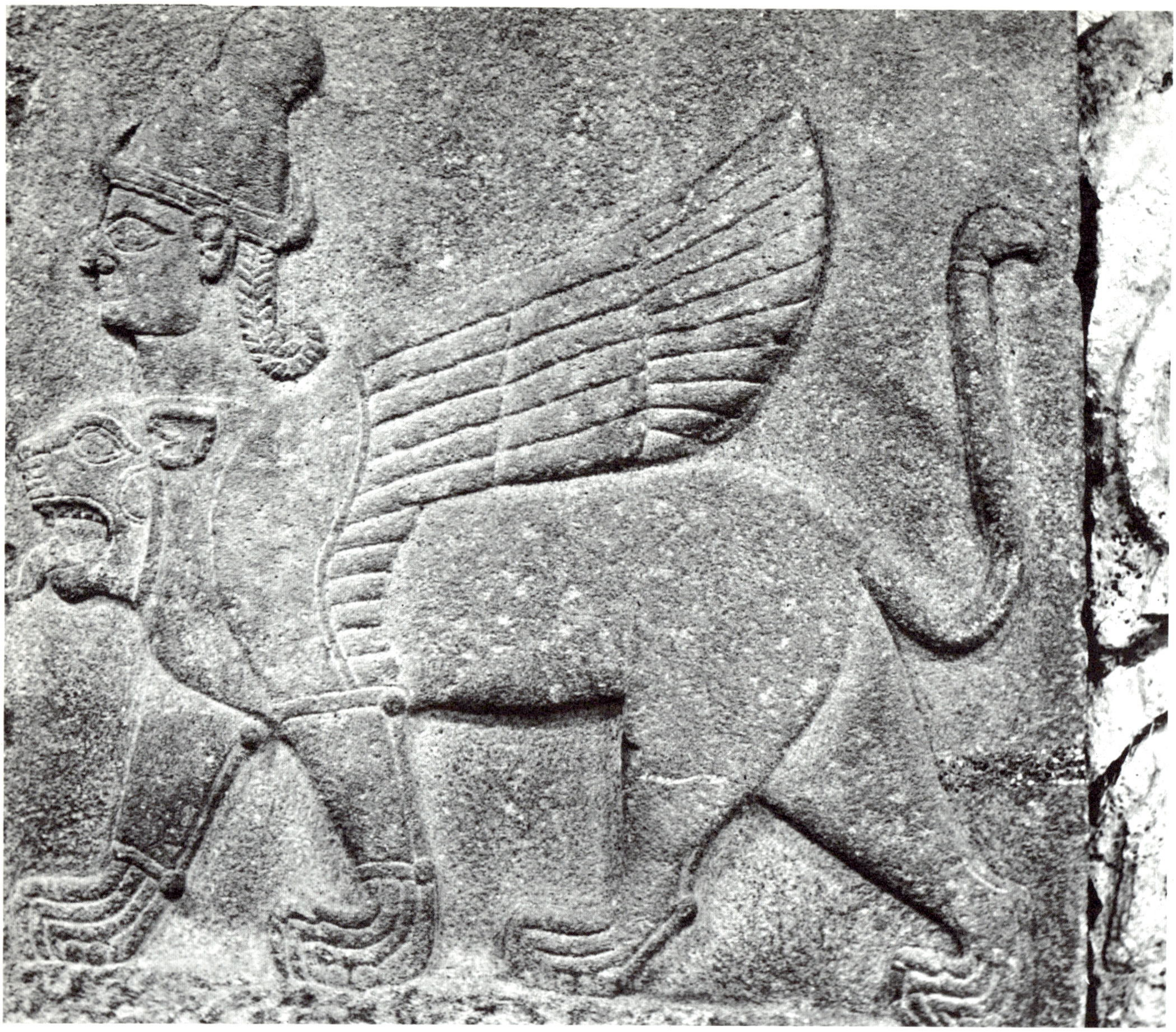

Mythical animal. This two-headed winged animal with the head and body of a lion surmounted by a second, human head wearing a tall head-dress is probably derived from the sphinxes of Egypt which were taken over by the Hittites and put to a similar use as protective images. The shape of the head-dress on the human head is reminiscent of the white crown of Upper Egypt. Bas-relief, 1050 to 850 B.C. Ankara Museum.

In the kiss and the conception, in the embrace...She...and she bore Sahar and Salem ('the Dawn' and 'the Evening'),

the principal actor says:

Send to El this message: 'My wife, O El, has given birth.'

El asks:

'To whom has she given birth?'

And the answer is:

'Sahar and Salem are born to me.'

Then follows the birth, under the same conditions, of five gracious gods, and finally of Sib'ani ('the seventh') whose father is called Etrah, perhaps the same personage as the moon-god Terah who is mentioned in the poem of Keret.

The myth thus takes on an historical interest. It takes us to the south of Palestine, to the Negeb, a region which was in Palaeolithic times, as recent research has shown, already populated. It shows the Phoenicians building one of the towns which would be among the most important in the land of the Philistines, and contracting an alliance with the desert Bedouins in order to ensure safe passage towards the Aelanitic gulf. The mother of Sib'ani lived in the desert for seven years, in order to purify herself, and at the end of the seven years she returned and asked for food and drink.

Set down in its present form in the thirteenth or fourteenth century B.C., this poem was already evidence of a distant past. A fortunate discovery made in 1932 at Byblos gives us further evidence: the carved scabbard of a gold dagger corroborates pictorially what is known by the texts of journeys to Ophir. The episodes depicted take place before a king, mounted on a mule. One, in the desert, shows an attack from behind on a lion who is busy seizing a gazelle. In the land of monkeys we see a servant leading a dog-faced baboon. Finally, since to reach this far-off region it was necessary to cross the sea, the goldsmith has suggested the idea of this journey by carving a fish.

PHOENICIAN GODS OF THE FIRST MILLENNIUM B.C.

In the first millennium B.C. every town in Phoenicia honoured its Ba'al – that is, its 'Lord', its 'Master', who was the proprietor of the soil and supreme ruler of its inhabitants. Instead of a Ba'al the deity honoured could be a Ba'alat, a 'Lady'. In certain regions there also existed Ba'alim: the Ba'al Tsaphon, 'Lord of the North' whom we have met in the myths of Ras Shamrah; the Ba'al Shamim, 'Lord of the Skies' of the Bible; the Ba'al Lebanon, 'Lord of Lebanon'.

The real name of the divinity is almost never known. As in Israel, one avoided pronouncing it, though perhaps for different reasons. In Phoenicia the object was to prevent strangers from discovering it lest, in their turn, they invoked the god, drew his benevolence upon themselves and succeeded by diverting his interest in turning him from his own people.

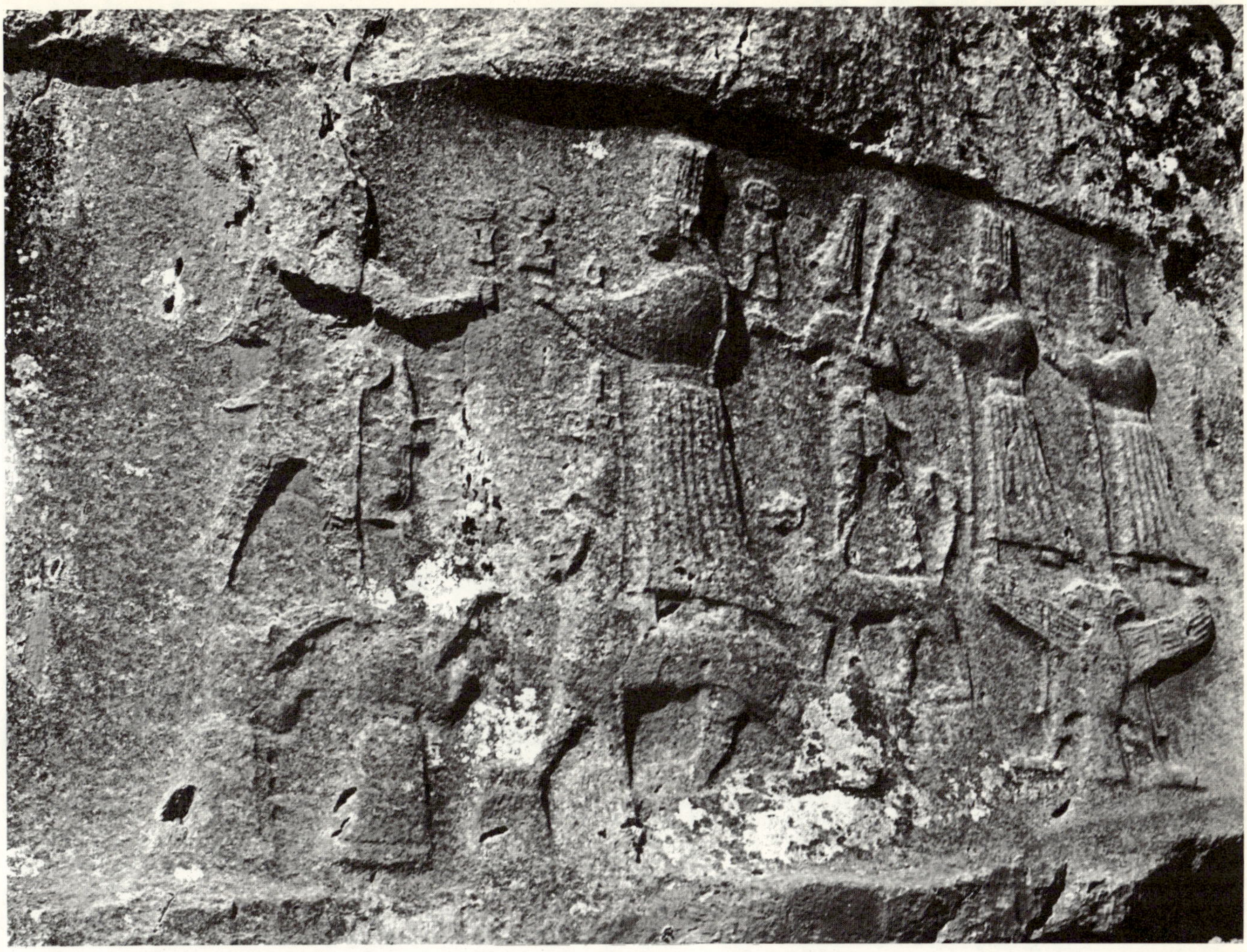

The meeting of the gods. In the centre the divine couple greet one another, the Weather-god of heaven, on the left, standing on the backs of two mountain gods while Hepat, the sun-goddess of Arinna, rides on her sacred animal, the lion. Behind her is their son, Surruma, also standing on a lion, followed by two goddesses above their emblem, a two-headed eagle. On the far left is the weather-god of Hattusa. Relief from the rock shrine of Yazilikaya. Thirteenth century B.C.

From the earliest times Gubla had had a Ba'alat as its chief divinity. She was identified with the Egyptian Hathor and for the Greeks she was a form of Astarte.

Berytus also worshipped a 'Lady', a nymph whom the god Adonis wooed, but a marine Ba'al was more fortunate than he.

The Ba'al of Tyre was a solar god in origin. Later, like the other divinities of Phoenician ports, he added to his primitive characteristics the characteristics of a marine deity. He was known under the title of Melkart, 'God of the City'. The Greeks identified him with Heracles.

Sidon venerated Eshmun, who became a god of health and was equated by the Greeks with Asclepius. The same town also worshipped an Ashtart in honour of whom King Solomon built a sanctuary in Jerusalem. Kings and queens were priests and priestesses of this lascivious goddess, whose cult was practised in grottoes in the place which is to-day called Maghdusheh.

Of the Phoenician divinities of this epoch we know only the adventures of one, to whom the Greeks gave the name Adonis. Details of the story were collected in the fifth century B.C. by the poet Panyasis.

The Myth of Adonis. Adonis is the direct successor of Hay-Tau of Nega and he replaced the two vegetation gods Aleyin and Mot of the Ugarit poems.

Born of a tree into which his mother had transformed herself, Adonis was of an extraordinary beauty. At his birth Aphrodite put him a coffer which she confided to the goddess of the underworld, Persephone. When later she came to reclaim the coffer she found that Persephone had already opened it, beheld the great beauty of the child and refused to give him up. The dispute between the two goddesses was brought before Zeus, who decided that Adonis should spend half the year on earth and half in the underworld.

According to other legends, Aphrodite fell deeply in love with the young god. She feared that a tragic fate would befall him and tried to discourage his passion for the chase. Adonis persisted in hunting and was killed by a wild boar or by a bear.

Adonis was an agricultural divinity and a vegetation spirit who, like Aleyin, was manifest in the seed of corn. His name, Adonis, is only known in Greek texts. It is a Hellenised form of the Semitic word *adoni*, 'my Lord, my master', which was ceaselessly repeated by Phoenician women in their lamentations during the god's festivals. In the Bible Ezekiel calls him Tammuz, the name of the Mesopotamian vegetation and corn-god. His actual Phoenician character was revealed only in the sixth century of our era by Damascius: Adonis is Eshmun.

The cult of Adonis was common to all Phoenicia, but it was in the territory of Byblos that it was celebrated with the greatest pomp.

Halfway between Byblos and Baalbek, near the source of the Nahr Ibrahim which the Greeks called the River Adonis, was the village of Aphaca, to-day called Afka. There, on a site which modern travellers all praise for its extraordinary charm, rose a sanctuary to Ashtart which was destroyed by the Emperor Constantine.

From the terrace of the sanctuary one sees the impressive circle of tall cliffs and the river, springing from a grotto, as it splashes tumultuously from cascade to cascade between verdant and wooded banks until at last it plunges into the depths of the gorge where the god perished.

At Ghineh one of the monuments erected in honour of Adonis still exists. Sculptured in the rock, the god grasps a spear in his hand and is on the watch for the animal which is about to attack him. The goddess, meanwhile, sits in an attitude of deep affliction.

It was believed that every year Adonis returned to such places,

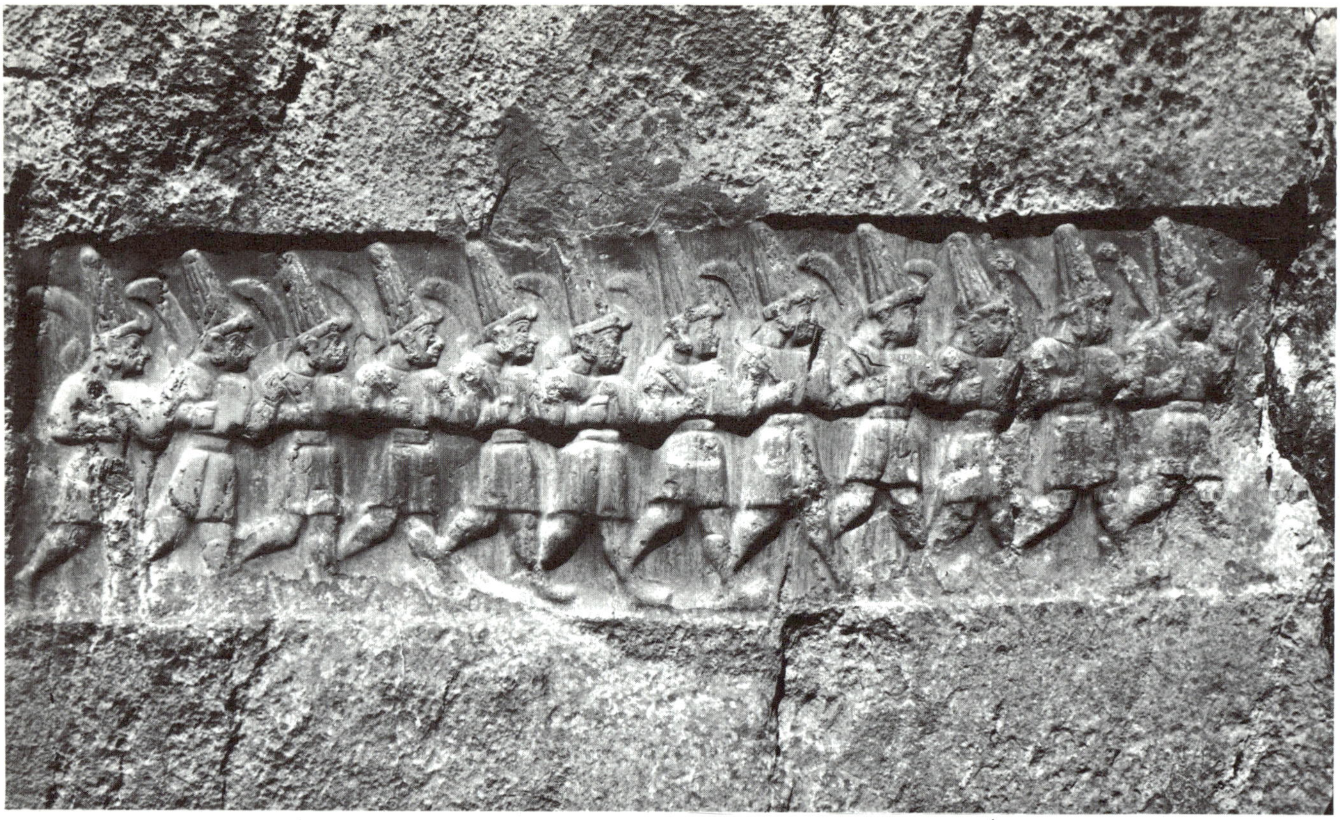

Procession of gods. Twelve running warrior gods bearing curved swords are shown on this Hittite relief at Yazilikaya near Hattusa. They are identically dressed in tall, ribbed head-dresses and short belted tunics and on their feet wear the shoes with upturned toes characteristic of a mountain people. The Hittites had a large and varied pantheon of a 'thousand gods and goddesses'. The names of these particular gods and the part they played in their religion, however, is not yet known.

there to be mortally wounded. The waters then would change to blood: a phenomenon due to the particles of red haematite which become detached from the rocks during certain natural conditions such as the season of high waters.

Festivals of Adonis. The *Adonia*, as the Greeks called the annual festivals which commemorated the death of Adonis, were the most beautiful of Phoenician festivals and were celebrated immediately after the harvest. Saglio described them in outline as follows:

'It seems that nothing was lacking which normally took place at funerals: neither the oiling and toilet of the dead, nor the exhibition of the body, funeral offerings and communal repasts. Images of Adonis in wax and terracotta were placed before the entrance or on the terraces of houses. Women crowded round them or carried them through the town, wailing and beating their breasts with every sign of the deepest grief. They danced and chanted dirges to the strident sound of short flutes – called *giggros* or *giggras* – which the Phoenicians use for their funeral ceremonies.' This picture must be completed by Theocritus's description of the festival celebrated with oriental pomp at Alexandria in the palace of Arsinoe, wife of Ptolemy Philadelphus. Under an arbour of greenery in which cupids flutter, the beautiful adolescent Adonis lies on a silver bed, covered with rich purple tissue. Venus is beside him. Around him are arranged vases full of perfumes, fruits, honey, cakes, and finally silver baskets containing what were called 'gardens of Adonis'. It was the custom to sow in vessels, normally not so valuable as the vases found in Arsinoe's palace, but in earthenware pots, in bottoms of cups, sherds, sometimes in baskets, all kinds of plants which germinate and grow rapidly, such as fennel, barley, wheat, and especially lettuce, which played a part in the legend of Adonis. (It was said that Venus had laid the body of her lover on a bed of lettuce.) These plants grew in a few days under the influence of the June sun, but, having no roots, faded and withered immediately. They were thus a symbol of the ephemeral existence of Adonis. These little artificial gardens were displayed with images of the god during the pomp and ceremony of the *Adonia*; afterwards they were thrown into the sea or into fountains.

Lucian mentions a joyful rite which was added to the ancient lamentations to celebrate the resurrection and ascension of Adonis.

The Works of Philo. Towards the end of the first century of our era, Philo undertook to demonstrate that Greek mythology was based on Phoenician mythology, which itself can be explained by the history of the first generation of human beings. Philo's authority was a rather mysterious Phoenician writer named Sanchuniathon. Among the fragments of Philo's works which have survived we can distinguish a cosmogony, a primitive history and the history of the Uranus group.

The *Cosmogony* of Philo is a combination of traditional elements over which 'troubled and windy air or a breath of wind and dark chaos' presides as ruling principle. Thus it was for many centuries; then, 'the breathing air became enamoured of its own principles and made a mingling and this union was called Desire. This was the principle of creation of all things, but the breath knew not its own creation and from embracing itself produced Mot. Some say that this was slime and others a rotting of aquatic composition. From it came all the germs of all created things and it was the origin of everything.'

This conception of spontaneous creation was accompanied by the idea of a cosmic egg, borrowed from Egypt. Then, by means of evolution, beings were differentiated and those beings who were to have intelligence finally became conscious of themselves.

Greek authors mention other Phoenician cosmogonies. One of these, attributed to the philosopher Eudemus, has in the beginning Time – then Desire and Darkness. 'From the union of these two first principles were born Aer (air) and Aura (breath). Aer represented pure intelligence and Aura the first living creature proceeding therefrom by movement. This couple then produced the cosmic Egg, in conformity with the intelligible spirit.'

According to Damascius, in the sixth century A.D., the first principle of the Phoenicians was 'cosmic Time which contained all things within it'. For Mochus, in the second century A.D., there was in the beginning a double principle: Aether and Air. Then came the Wind and afterwards the two winds Lips and Notos; later Oulomos (the Ages) and still later Chousor, the Opener, and the Egg.

'The air was illuminated', Philo continues, 'due to the flaming of the earth and sea; and winds were formed and clouds. And there was a vast downpouring of waters and floods from the sky. And when, after the sun's heat, all things were separated and left their appointed place to meet in the air and there collide, thunder and lightning resulted. At the sound of the thunder the intelligent animals awoke and took fright at the noise and wandered over the earth and in the sea, as males and females.'

Philo's *Primitive History* is an account of the progress of civilisation and religion.

The first generations deified the products of the earth, considered them to be gods and worshipped them, 'for from the earth they drew their substance, they and those who followed them and all those who had been before them; and they made libations and ritual aspersions'. When a plant died there was lamentation, and also at the birth or death of an animal.

Progress was attributed to Aeon, who discovered edible fruits. From the race of Aeon and Protogonos, both sons of Kolpia and his wife Baau, issued Genos and Genea, who were the first inhabitants of Phoenicia. 'There was a drought and they lifted their hands to the sun in the sky. For they considered the sun to be a god and the sole lord of the sky. They named him Beelsamin, which to the Phoenicians means "Lord of the Sky", or to the Greeks "Zeus".'

The invention of fire was due to mortal offspring of the same race named Light, Fire and Flame. 'They found fire by rubbing sticks of wood together and taught others to do likewise.'

This important step in civilisation was followed by the appearance of giants. Their names – Cassios, Lebanon, Antilebanon and Brathy – were given to the mountains over which they ruled. It seems that these giants must be considered the inventors of burning incense; for all these mountains were renowned for their fragrant woods.

In the meanwhile men's morals had become so licentious that 'children took the name of their mothers; for women in these days would give themselves to the firstcomer'. One of these children of an unknown father was Hapsouranios, who was said to live in Tyre. He was the inventor of huts built of rushes and papyrus. His brother Ousoos was the first to make garments from animal skins. 'The rains came and with them violent winds so that the trees which grew at Tyre brushed together and caught fire, and the forest was consumed. Ousoos took a tree, stripped it of its branches and was the first who dared to venture out to sea. He consecrated two stelae, one to Fire and one to Wind, and worshipped them and sprinkled them with libations of the blood of beasts which he had killed in the chase.'

Hypsouranios and Ousoos were deified after death. Their stelae were worshipped: every year festivals were held in their honour.

Two of their descendants invented hunting and fishing. Later two brothers invented iron and the manner of working it. 'One of them, Kusor, practised the arts of magic formulas, incantation and divination...he invented the fish-hook and bait, the fishing-line and fishing-boat, and he was the first man who learned to navigate.' This Kusor, whom we have already met in the myth of the temple of Ba'al at Ugarit, was identified by Philo and by Herodotus with the Greek god Hephaestus.

He, whom the people of Byblos called the greatest of gods, discovered how to 'add to houses courtyards, porches and cellars' and thus to turn them into luxurious dwellings. The same period saw the beginning of hunting with hounds. A little later pastoral life developed: Amynos and Magos taught the people how to live in villages and tend flocks.

Then came the discovery of salt by Misor and Sydyk. A descendant of Misor's, Taautos, whom the Egyptians called Thoth, invented the first written characters. The Cabeiri, descendants of Sydyk, perfected navigation.

Finally 'others discovered the use of herbs and simples and a remedy for the bite of poisonous animals'.

In this primitive history the actors follow one another and the various inventions are made, so to speak, without particular sequence or connection. Philo's *History of the Uranides* has a more logical sequence. In it Philo treats the gods as ordinary mortals who take part in a series of adventures from which result the creation of royalty, the foundation of the first town, the invention of the plough and the cultivation of wheat, the institution of votive sacrifices and of human sacrifices, the construction of temples, the transition from free love to polygamy and finally monogamy.

Uranus, the Sky, had a sister Ge (or Gaea), the Earth. Their father Hypsistos (Elioun, the All Highest) 'having ended his life in a struggle against ferocious beasts, was deified, and his children offered sacrifices and libations to him'.

When Uranus had succeeded to his father's authority, he took his sister Ge in marriage and they had four children. Uranus had numerous other children by other wives. Ge was distressed by his infidelity and tormented with jealousy, so that they finally separated. When, however, the fancy took him, Uranus would approach his wife with violence and many times he attempted to destroy the children she had borne him. Ge defended herself as best she could. When Cronus (El), one of her sons, had become a man he declared war upon his father in order to avenge his mother. Hermes Trismegistus, secretary and adviser to Cronus, harangued his master's allies with magic words and the struggle ended in the overthrow of Uranus, whose authority passed to Cronus. During the battle Uranus' favourite concubine, who was pregnant to him, fell into the hands of Cronus, who gave her as a wife to Dagon. Uranus' son whom she bore received the name Demarus. He was to become the father of Melkart, the god of Tyre.

Cronus surrounded his house with a wall and founded Byblos, the first city. Fearing the schemes of his brother Atlas, he buried him, on the advice of Hermes, in the depths of the earth. He killed his own son, against whom he harboured suspicions, and cut off the head of his own daughter 'so that all the gods stood stupefied before the decrees of Cronus'.

In those days the descendants of the Cabeiri had perfected ships. They disembarked on the coast near Mount Cassios and there consecrated a temple.

Uranus had long since fled, but he still planned to avenge himself on his son. He sent three of his daughters – Ashtart, Rhea and Dione – to kill Cronus by treachery. Cronus seduced them and made them his wives 'although they were sisters'. Uranus did not admit defeat. He sent against his son Hour and Destiny together with other allies. These, too, Cronus seduced and kept at his side.

By Ashtart, Cronus had seven daughters and two sons, Pothos and Eros. Rhea presented him with seven children, the youngest of whom was recognised as a god from the moment of his birth.

Sydyk married one of Ashtart's daughters, who bore Asclepius. Demarus begat Melkart, identified with Heracles, and to Pontus was born Poseidon and Sidon. She was endowed with a wondrous voice and invented the chanting of hymns. In these days Dagon made the first plough and began the cultivation of grain.

Because of Uranus the war continued. Pontus, the father of Sidon, put Demarus to flight. Demarus was the first to make a vow to offer sacrifice to the gods if they helped him to escape from the critical situation in which he found himself. In the thirty-second year of his reign Cronus caught his father in an ambush and cut off his sexual organs. The spirit of Uranus was dispersed: the blood of his severed genitals flowed in the water of springs and rivers.

In the following period we meet the divinities of the Phoenician towns. Cronus – that is to say the Phoenicians themselves – undertakes long voyages.

Cronus decided that Ashtart, Demarus and Adod should rule over the country. 'Ashtart placed on her head a bull's head as a royal insignia. While travelling the world she found an aerolith which she brought back to Tyre to consecrate on the holy island.

'...Cronus also made a tour of the world. He made his daughter Athene sovereign of Attica. There was famine and plague and Cronus offered his own son in sacrifice to his father Uranus. He circumcised himself and forced his allies to do likewise. Shortly afterwards he deified another child whom Rhea had borne him and who had died. He was named Moûth, and the Phoenicians called him Death and Pluto.

'Cronus gave the city of Byblos to the goddess Baltis, who is Dione. He gave Berytus to Poseidon and to the Cabeiri, who were either hunters or fishermen, and deified the remains of Pontus there. Previously the god Taaut (the Egyptian Thoth), who had taken on the outward appearance of Cronus, Dagon and all the other gods combined, had drawn the sacred characters of writing.

'Taaut also designed the insignia of royalty for Cronus: four eyes, two in front and two behind, two opened and two closed; on his shoulders four wings, two spread in flight, two hanging limp. The eyes were a symbol to show that Cronus slept while he watched and watched while he slept. The wings on his shoulders meant that he flew while at rest and rested in flight. The other gods each had two wings on their shoulders to indicate that they flew with Cronus. The god El also had two wings on his head, one for pure intelligence, the other for feeling.

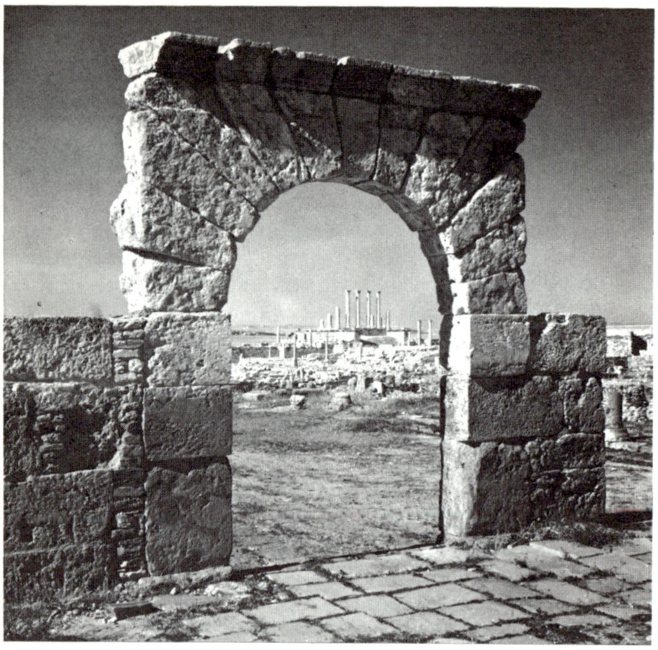

The entrance to the temple of Ba'al at Thuburbo Majus near Carthage. Ba'al-Hammon, the Phoenician sky – and fertility-god, was the chief god of Carthage, Phoenicia's principal colony, and it was doubtless to the same Ba'al that the temple in the Roman city of Thuburbo Majus was dedicated – the Romans confusing the god with the African god Jupiter Ammon.
The god was normally associated with the great goddess of Carthage, Tanit.

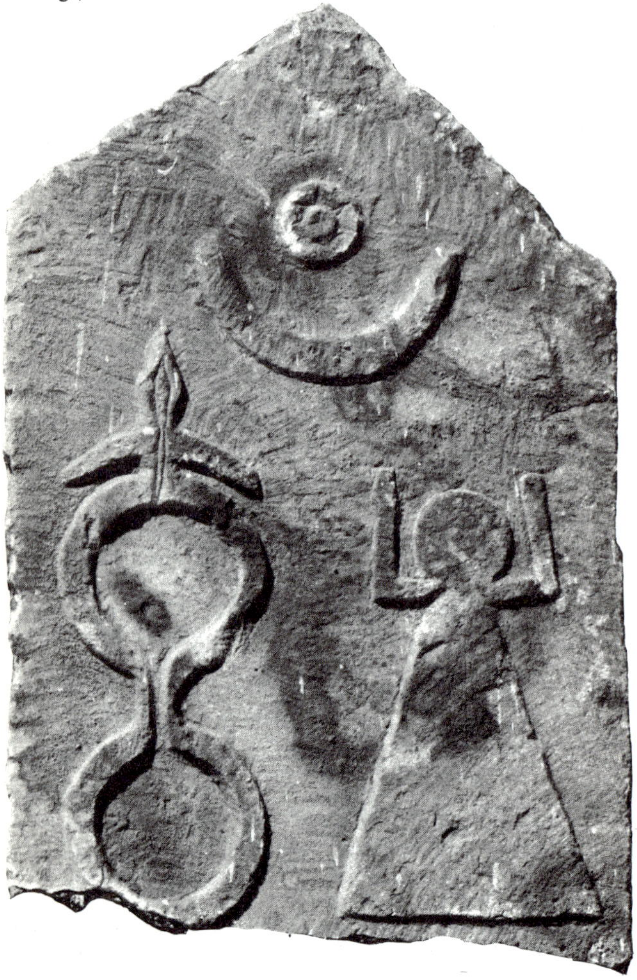

Ashtar was known by various names, including Astarte, Ishtar (to the Babylonians), Ashtoreth (to the Hebrews), and when the great city of Carthage was founded she became known as Tanit. The Phoenicians adopted her as the protective deity of the city which was to become their greatest glory. She is symbolically represented in this stele found at Dougga in Tunis – not far from the site of ancient Carthage.

'Cronus, having arrived in the land of the South, gave all Egypt to the god Taaut to be his kingdom.'

THE GODS OF CARTHAGE

In the trading posts and colonies which the Phoenicians founded on the coasts of Africa and on the islands of the Mediterranean the gods were those of Phoenicia.

At Carthage, their chief foundation, Ba'al-Hammon was worshipped. He was a dignified old man with a beard, and his head was embellished with ram's horns. He sat on a high-backed throne and rested his hands on the heads of two rams which formed the arms of the seat. Ba'al-Hammon was a sky-god and a god of fertility; the Romans confused him with the African god Jupiter Ammon.

Carthage also honoured, with Eshmun and Adonis, the god Bes, who was a frightening dwarf with bow-legs and prominent belly. Bes was also known in Egypt and western Asia, where images of him were widely spread.

The great goddess of Carthage, normally associated with Ba'al-Hammon in inscriptions, was called Tanit. She was described as the 'face of Ba'al'. On numerous little stelae, designed to commemorate sacrifices, Tanit is represented by a symbol the meaning of which has not yet been determined. Some think it is a degenerated human figure in outline, others a primitive representation of an altar. This 'symbol of Tanit', of which one example is known in Phoenicia, is in the form of a truncated cone surmounted by a disk. Sometimes between the disk and the truncated cone is inscribed a horizontal line the two ends of which turn up at right angles.

Another symbol, equally common on Carthaginian stelae, is the open hand – a gesture of propitiation.

THE HITTITE GODS

The mythology of the Hittites has not yet been studied in all its details, but in the chaos of the pantheon where the 'thousand gods and goddesses' dwell, one can distinguish groups of extremely varied origin: ancient indigenous gods worshipped before the advent of the Indo-European Hittites, Irbitiga, Kalhisapi, Teteshapi and Wasezzel; Luwian divinities such as Santa, Tarhunza and Wandu; Hurrian divinities like Teshup and Hepat; gods of Babylon and Assyria, who are less easy to recognise because their names can also represent Hittite names in consequence of the system of allography (or name substitution) adopted by the Hittites.

Thus the Sumerian name Ishkur, adopted as an ideogram in Akkad for the god Hadad, and the number X, a name of the same god, were utilised by the Hittites for the still unknown name of their god who presided over tempests and beneficial rainfall, as Ishkur and Adad did, as Teshub did in Hurrian lands, or Hadad did in Canaan.

At the head of the Hittite pantheon can be distinguished the divine couple, symbolising vital forces, which is common to all Asian peoples. In the thirteenth century B.C. this couple can be seen leading a long procession of other gods on the rocks at Yazilikaya, a mile and a half from the ruins of Hattusa, the capital of the empire.

We shall mention only two of the Hittite myths: that of the Great Serpent and that of Telepinu.

The Great Serpent had dared to attack the weather-god. The god demanded that he be brought to justice. Inar, a god who had come southward with the Indo-European Hittites, prepared a great feast and invited the serpent with his family to eat and drink. The serpent and his children, having drunk to satiety, were unable to go back into their hole, and were exterminated.

Telepinu had vanished and all life withdrew from the earth. Fire was extinguished, the gods died of hunger in their sanctuaries, animals perished in their stables, the trees lost their leaves and the fields their verdure. The Sun gave a festival. His divine guests could not eat their fill nor could they quench their thirst. The weather-god explained the situation to them: his son, Telepinu, was angry and had gone no one knew where, taking all his goods with him. All the gods, great and small, set about searching for the fugitive. Twice the eagle vainly explored the entire land. Then, on the orders of the Lady of the gods, the bee flew off with instructions that if she found Telepinu she should 'sting him in the hands and feet to make him reappear'.

Telepinu returned, and at once life resumed its normal course.

GREEK MYTHOLOGY

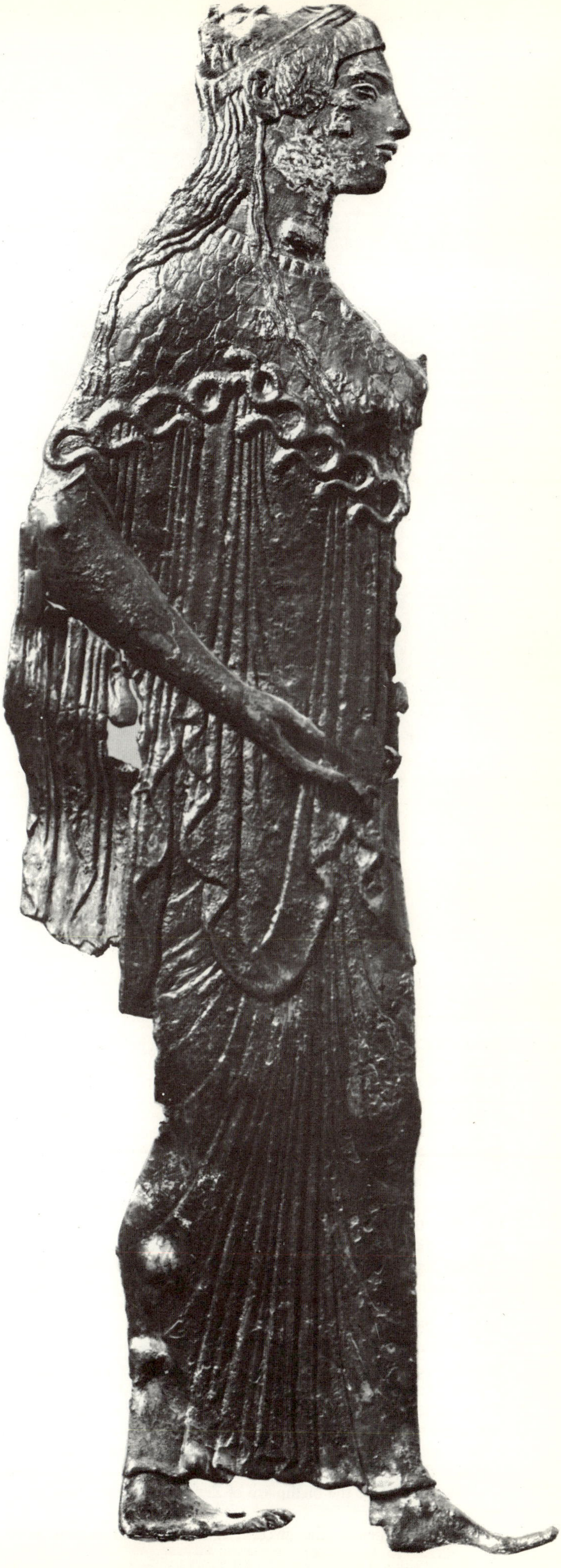

It is now known that well before the peoples whom we know as the Greeks had emerged from primitive barbarism there existed in the basin of the Aegean Sea a Mediterranean civilisation which had its centre in Crete. Aegean civilisation, which had already made tentative beginnings in the third millennium, reached its apogee towards the sixteenth century B.C. when it spread to continental Greece, starting in Argolis (Mycenae). It was destroyed in the twelfth century by the Dorian invasions.

In Aegean civilisation, religion naturally had its place. But the only silent documents which archaeology has yet furnished are insufficient to allow an exact estimate of its character and elements. As with all peoples the first form Aegean religion took was fetishism– the worship of sacred stones, the cult of pillars, the cult of weapons (particularly the double-axe), the cult of trees and animals.

Later, when an anthropomorphic conception of divinity had arisen, the Cretan pantheon was formed and myths were created. We find survivals of such myths in a great many Greek legends; for instance, the birth of Zeus in Crete, Europa and the bull, Cretans brought by Apollo to Delphi to be priests of his cult, the Minotaur, etc. When they moved to continental Greece, however, the Aegean divinities took on a Hellenic aspect beneath which their original physiognomy disappeared. Thus what we know about the Aegean pantheon is reduced to very little.

THE AEGEAN PANTHEON

The Great Goddess. The chief deity of the Aegeans was – like that of many Asiatic cults – feminine. She was the *Great Goddess,* the *Universal Mother,* in whom were united all the attributes and functions of divinity. Above all she symbolised fertility, and her influence extended over plants and animals as well as humans. All the universe was her domain. As celestial goddess she regulated the course of the heavenly bodies and controlled the alternating seasons. On earth she caused the products of the soil to flourish, gave men riches, protected them in battle and at sea guided them on their adventurous voyages. She killed or tamed fierce beasts; and finally she also reigned over the underworld: mistress of life, she was also sovereign of death.

The Great Goddess is represented, depending on the epoch, either crouching or standing. Sometimes she is nude, sometimes dressed like a Cretan woman. In the latter case she wears a flounced skirt and her bosom is either entirely bare or covered with a corsage which leaves her breasts exposed. Her head-dress varies: the hair may be free, knotted with a simple fillet; it may be covered either by a sort of turban decorated with flowers or aigrettes, or by a conical tiara in the Oriental manner, or, again, by a very tall tiara in the shape of a topless cone.

Although the type is always the same and only the attributes and details of dress vary, it is questionable if a single divinity is concerned or if, on the contrary, these various representations do not depict distinct goddesses, each having her own character. The procreative goddess with broad hips who presses her raised arms to heavy breasts – could she be the same as the virgin warrior who advances, escorted by a lion, striking the ground with her spear? Could the vegetation-goddess whom we see sitting under the sacred

The Protectress of Athens. Perhaps the most characteristically Greek of all the Olympians, Athene is also the most positively identified as having developed from an archaic local cult. The daughter of Zeus, according to the Greeks, she sprang fully armed from his brow. Warrior goddess, patroness of the arts, and the personification of intelligence, she was a deity much revered and respected. Her formidable character is well caught in this striking bronze statue of the fifth century B.C.

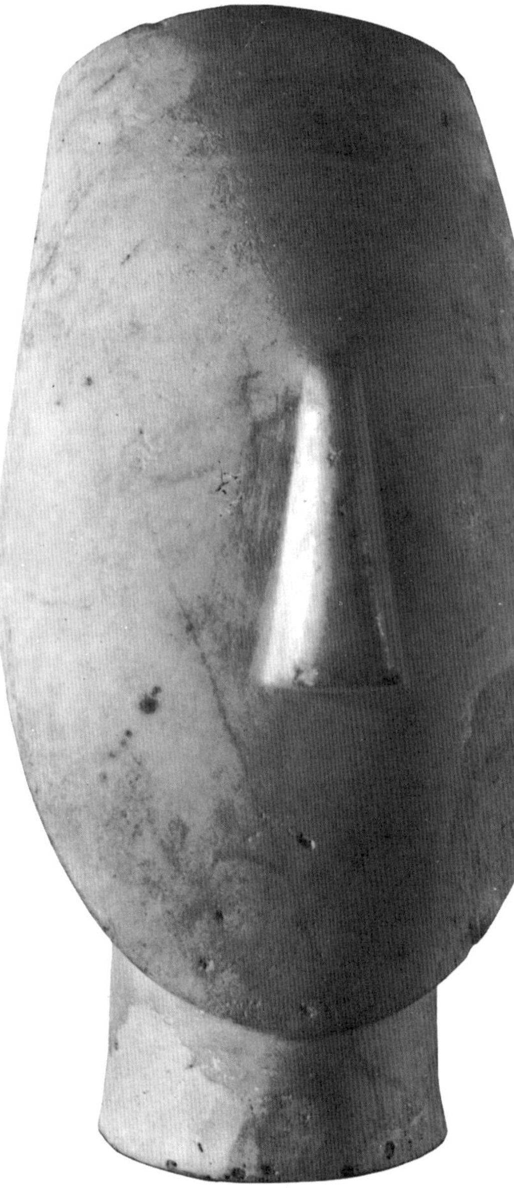

Head of a Cycladic idol. This simple head depicts a deity of the early Mediterranean civilisation which grew up in the islands of the Aegean in the third millennium B.C. The Cyclades, the islands round Delos, were once, according to ancient tradition, inhabited by the Carians (a people of Asia Minor) who were later driven out by Minos, King of Crete. Though some four thousand years old, this head bears a striking resemblance to some modern sculpture.
Third millennium B.C.

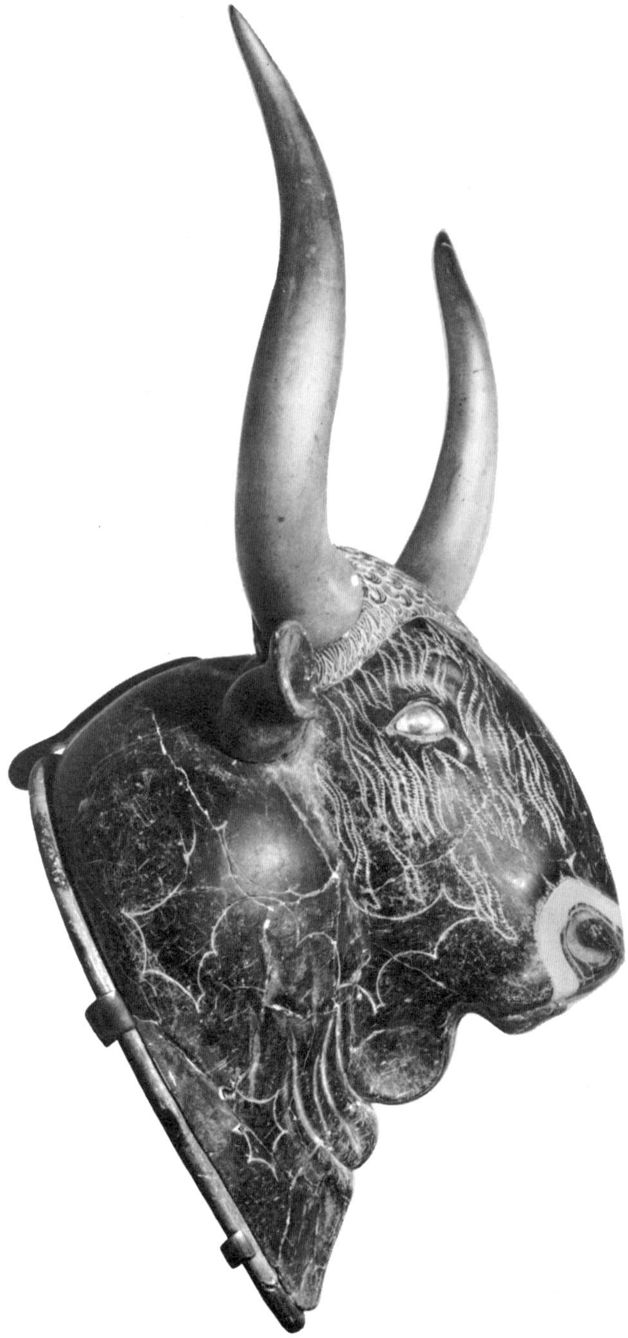

Cretan rhyton, or ritual vase, in the shape of a bull's head.
The bull played an important part in Cretan mythology being the emblem of the Great God who was associated with the Great Goddess in the religion of the Aegean. Survivals of these Cretan legends are found in the legends of Greece. Black steatite with inlay of tridacna shell and rock crystal, and horns of gilded wood. From Cnossos, *c.* 1500 B.C.

tree, receiving from her priestesses the first fruits and flowers, be the same as the sea-goddess who is carried across the waves in a boat, or the earth-goddess around whom serpents intertwine?

What was the name of the mother-goddess of the Aegeans? Here again in the absence of documentation we are left to conjecture. It seems that she was worshipped in Crete under the vocable *Rhea*. At least this was the name later associated with the ancient Cretan divinity in the cult of Zeus. Zeus was made her son, a tradition revived, as we shall see, by Hesiod in his *Theogony*.

Two other names of Cretan goddesses have been preserved: *Dictynna* and *Britomartis*. In their legends the Greeks applied the two names to the same divinity.

Dictynna, whom the Greeks called the 'goddess of the nets', was perhaps the goddess of Mount Dicte, a mountain in Crete which was later said to be the birthplace of Zeus. She would, then, be the mother-goddess.

Britomartis means 'the sweet virgin', a denomination which could not very well be applied to the Great Mother of the universe.

According to the Greek legend, Britomartis was a young virgin huntress who pursued wild beasts in the forests of Crete. She was said to be the daughter of Zeus. Minos saw her and was captivated by her beauty. He offered her his love, but was refused. He then attempted violence but Britomartis fled and, after a race which lasted no less than nine months, in order finally to escape Minos she flung herself off a high rock into the sea. She fell into the nets of a fisherman and for that reason received the name Dictynna. Artemis, in reward for her chastity, raised her to the rank of the immortals and thenceforth she appeared during the night to navigators. The Greeks made the assimilation even closer and called Dictynna-Britomartis the Cretan Artemis.

The God. With the Great Goddess the Aegeans associated a god. It would seem that this god, at least originally, was, in imitation of the cults of Western Asia, subordinate to the goddess; but though we are informed of the relationship between Tammuz and Ishtar, between Attis and Cybele, and between Adonis and Astarte, no indication has yet come to light with regard to the relationship between the Aegean god and goddess.

A celestial divinity, like the goddess with whom he was associated, the Aegean god bore the epithet *Asterius* (the 'starry'). He is found again under the name Asterion, king of Crete, who married Europa after her adventure with Zeus. Afterwards he was assimilated with Zeus himself, whose legend was thus enriched with the older Cretan contributions.

The peculiarity of the Cretan god was the mingling of animal and human features which composed his nature. The bull, as in many Asiatic religions, had been adopted since the earliest ages as the Aegean symbol of strength and creative energy. It later became the emblem of the Great God, and as such played an important part in Cretan legends. It even became incorporated in the divine nature: Minotaur is analogous to the bull-god of the Elamites and to the Enki of the Sumerians, who was also 'the savage bull of the sky and the earth'.

The bull-god was not the only aspect under which the Cretan god appeared. Besides the *Minotaur* there was also *Minos*. Therefore the god was also conceived in human form, and it was thus that he sometimes appeared to his worshippers in all his terrifying majesty.

But whether we are concerned with Minos or the Minotaur we know them only through the modifications they underwent when Hellenised. We shall therefore only mention them here in passing and reserve a later occasion to discuss them at greater length, when we meet them again in the heroic legends of classical Greece.

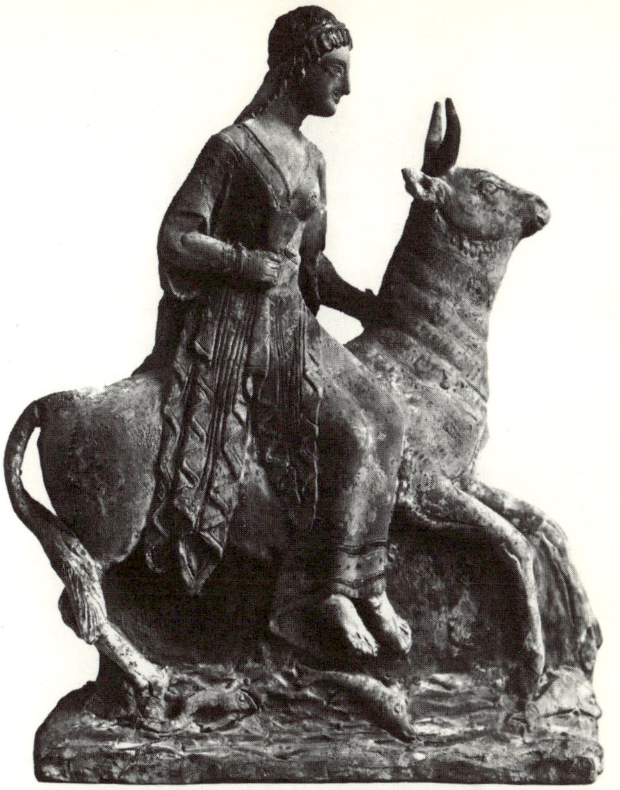

The abduction of Europa – one of the legends originating in Crete which were later incorporated into the mythology of Greece. The daughter of Phoenix, or Agenor, the king of Phoenicia, she is seated on the back of a bull – in reality Zeus in disguise – who plunges into the waves to carry her off to Crete. She later gave birth there to Minos, Rhad-amanthys and Sarpedon. Terracotta from Tanagra in the archaic style.

THE MYTHOLOGY OF CLASSICAL GREECE

INTRODUCTION

Greek Theogonies. The Greek pantheon was established as early as the Homeric epoch. The many divinities of which it was composed generally appear in the *Iliad* and the *Odyssey* with their characteristic physiognomy, their traditional attributes and their own time-honoured legends. But the poet tells us nothing of their origin or their past. At the most he mentions that Zeus is the son of Cronus and says incidentally that Ocean and his spouse Tethys were the creators of gods and living beings.

It was only later that the Greeks felt the need to provide their gods with a genealogy and a history. Hesiod's poem, the *Theogony*, written in about the eighth century B.C., is the oldest Greek attempt at mythological classification. While recounting the origin of the gods, recalling their chief adventures and establishing their relationships, he also claims to explain the formation of the universe. The poem is thus as much a cosmogony as a theogony. A reflection of popular beliefs, the *Theogony* of Hesiod had, in Greece, a kind of official recognition.

From the sixth century B.C., however, until the beginning of the Christian era other theogonies were elaborated under the influence of Orphic doctrines; and these theogonies departed widely from the traditions of Hesiod. But the Orphic theogonies, known only to the initiated, were never popular. In addition they were too intermingled with foreign contributions, notably Asiatic, to be specifically Greek in character. We shall therefore merely give a summary of their principal features, having first given Hesiod's version of the origins of the world.

THE FORMATION OF THE WORLD AND THE BIRTH OF THE GODS

Chaos and Gaea. In the beginning, Hesiod says, there was Chaos, vast and dark. Then appeared Gaea, the deep-breasted earth, and finally Eros, 'the love which softens hearts', whose fructifying influence would thenceforth preside over the formation of beings and things.

From Chaos were born Erebus and Night who, uniting, gave birth in their turn to Ether and Hemera, the day.

On her part Gaea first bore Uranus, the sky crowned with stars, 'whom she made her equal in grandeur, so that he entirely covered her.' Then she created the high mountains and Pontus, 'the sterile sea', with its harmonious waves.

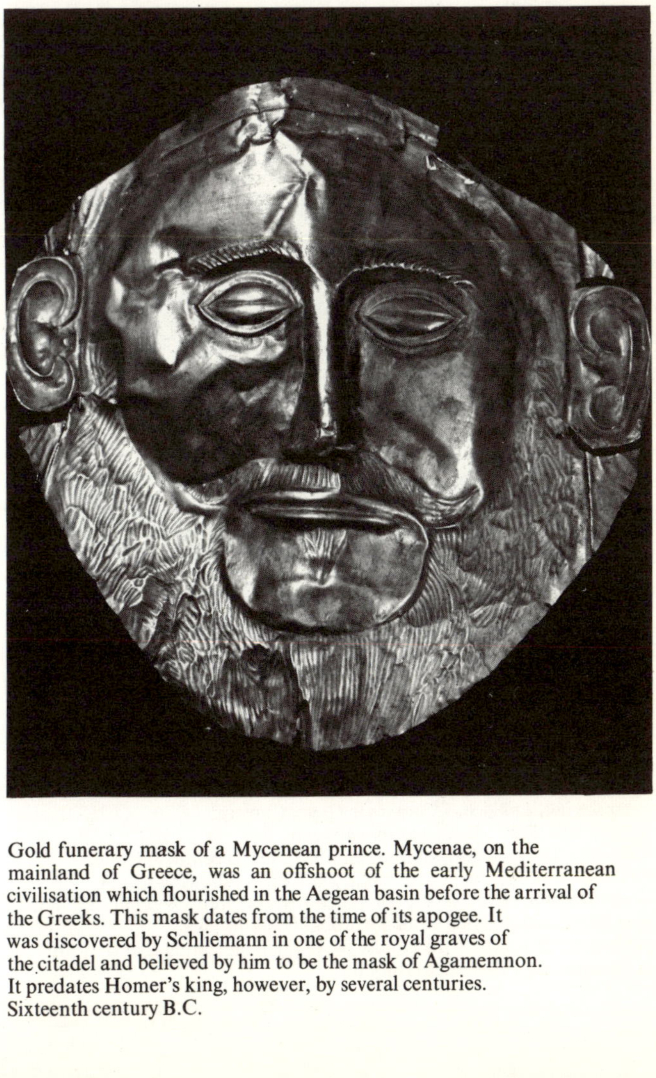

Gold funerary mask of a Mycenean prince. Mycenae, on the mainland of Greece, was an offshoot of the early Mediterranean civilisation which flourished in the Aegean basin before the arrival of the Greeks. This mask dates from the time of its apogee. It was discovered by Schliemann in one of the royal graves of the citadel and believed by him to be the mask of Agamemnon. It predates Homer's king, however, by several centuries. Sixteenth century B.C.

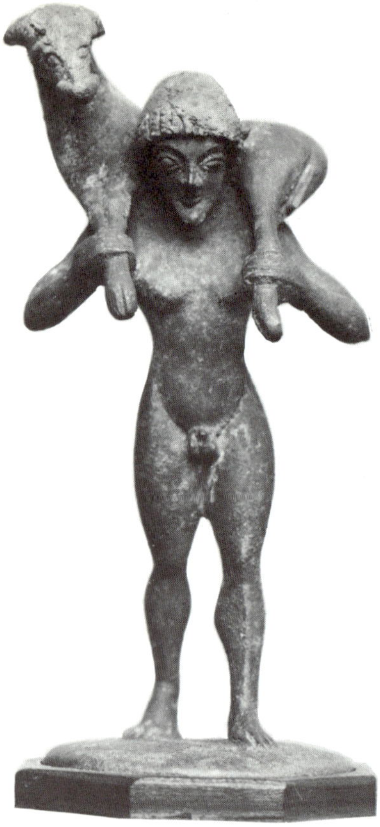

Hermes Kriophoros, the Ram-bearer. Probably a very ancient divinity of the Pelasgians (the pre-Hellenic Aegean inhabitants of Greece), Hermes is shown in this archaic statuette carrying out his original functions as protector of flocks and herds. After the Dorian invasion he lost much of his prestige, his functions being taken over by Apollo Nomius, while he himself became the son of Zeus and the messenger of the gods. *c.* sixth century B.C.

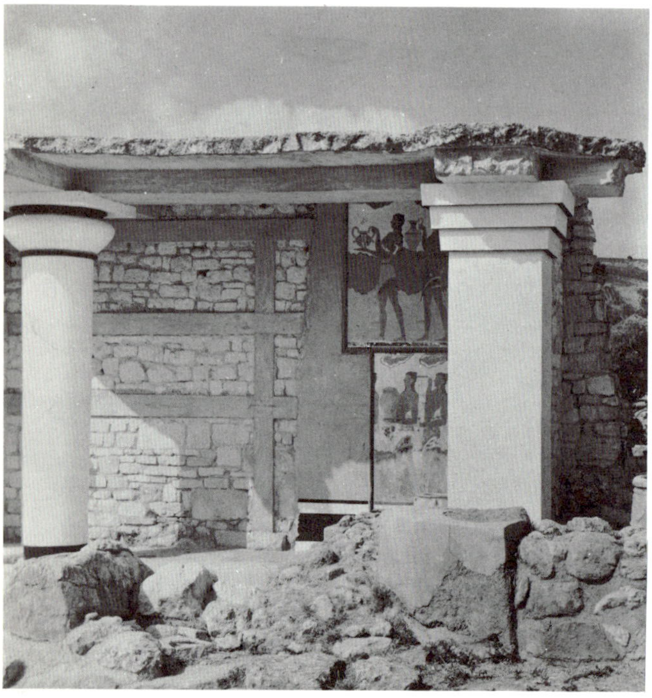

Frescoes in the palace at Cnossos in Crete. Cnossos, in the north of the island, was the capital of the pre-Hellenic Aegean civilisation which had its centre in Crete. Its palace was decorated with numerous frescoes showing scenes from daily life. Here two superimposed rows of youths wearing ceremonial loin-cloths and carrying vases are probably taking part in some religious rite – the clouds above them indicating that they are in the open air. Fifteenth century B.C.

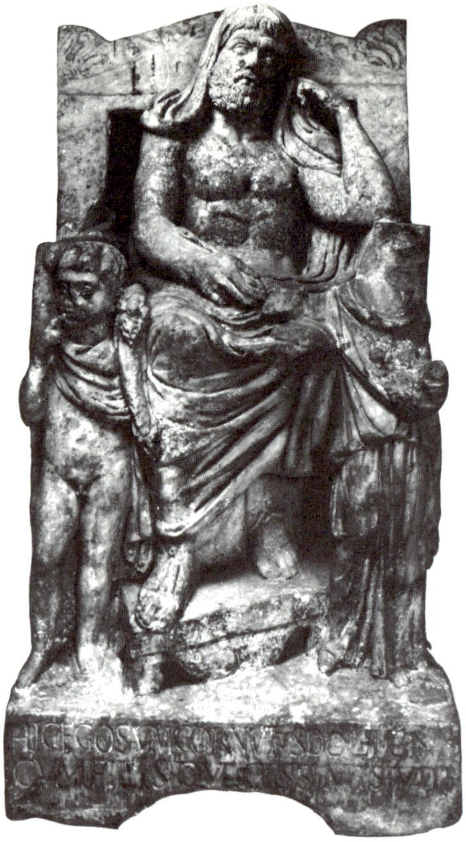

Cronus seated on his throne. The youngest son of Uranus, the starlit sky, and Gaea, the earth, Cronus castrated his father at the instigation of his mother and became the head of a new dynasty. By his sister Rhea he was the father of Hades, Poseidon, Zeus, Hestia, Demeter and Hera. The later Greeks read Cronus as Chronos and thought of him as Time. Roman statue.

Uranus and Gaea: The Uranus group. The universe had been formed. It remained to be peopled. Gaea united with her son Uranus and produced the first race – the Titans. There were twelve of them, six male and six female: Oceanus, Coeus, Hyperion, Crius, Iapetus, Cronus; Theia, Rhea, Mnemosyne, Phoebe, Tethys and Themis.

Uranus and Gaea then gave birth to the Cyclopes: Brontes, Steropes and Arges, 'who resembled the other gods but had only one eye in the middle of their forehead'. Finally they bore three monsters: Cottus, Briareus and Gyges. 'From their shoulders sprang a hundred invincible arms and above these powerful limbs rose fifty heads attached to their backs'. For this reason they were called the Hecatoncheires or the Centimanes.

Uranus could only regard his offspring with horror, and as soon as they were born he shut them up in the depths of the earth. Gaea at first mourned, but afterwards grew angry and meditated terrible vengeance against her husband. From her bosom she drew forth gleaming steel, fashioned a sharp sickle or *harpe* and explained to her children the plan she had made. All of them hesitated, struck with horror. Only the astute Cronus, her last-born, volunteered to support his mother. When evening fell Uranus, accompanied by Night, came as usual to rejoin his wife. While he unsuspectingly slept, Cronus, who with his mother's aid lay in hiding, armed himself with the sickle, mutilated his father atrociously and cast the bleeding genitals into the sea. From the terrible wound black blood dropped and the drops, seeping into the earth, gave birth to the redoubtable Furies, to monstrous giants and to the ash-tree nymphs, the Meliae. As for the debris which floated on the surface of the waves, it broke into a white foam from which was born a young goddess, Aphrodite, 'who was first carried towards the divine Cythera and thence as far as Cyprus surrounded with waves'.

The Character of the First Gods. Such are the first divine figures and the first drama they underwent. Some of the actors are, it is true, rather vague and ill-defined.

The Chaos of Hesiod, the name of which comes from a Greek root meaning 'to gape', simply designates open space. Only later,

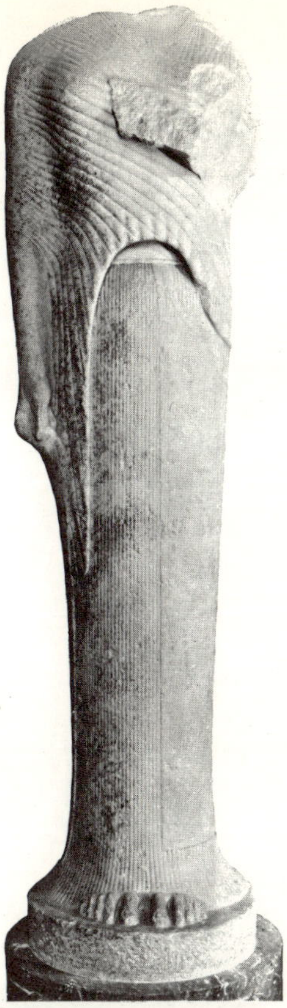

Statue of the goddess Hera. The wife of Zeus and, as such, the chief feminine deity of Olympus, Hera presided over all phases of feminine existence and was above all the goddess of marriage and maternity. Her chief sanctuary was at Samos, where she was believed to have been born, and it was here that this over-lifesize statue was discovered. It was dedicated to the goddess by Cheramyes and was originally painted. Marble. *c.* 560 B.C.

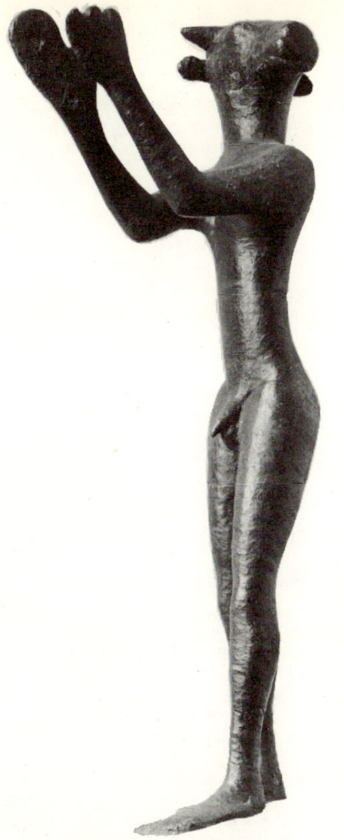

The Minotaur. The Cretan bull-god appeared in Greek mythology as the offspring of Pasiphaë, the wife of Minos, King of Crete, and a bull. Half human and half bull, it is depicted in this archaic statuette as a man with a bull's head and upraised arms. the Minotaur fed exclusively on human flesh and lived in a palace called the Labyrinth. It was finally killed by Theseus. Bronze. *c.* eighth century B.C.

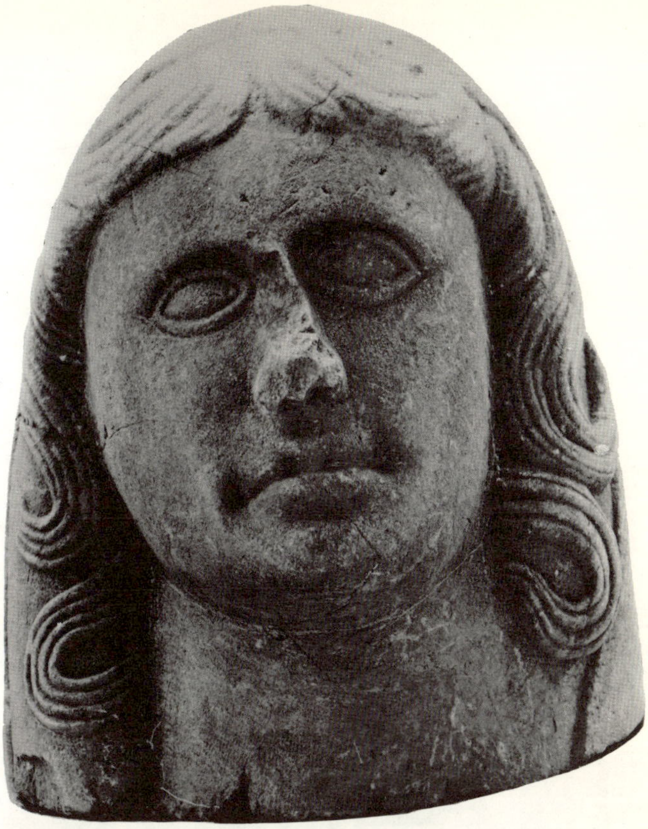

Head of Gaea. Probably the great deity of the early Greeks, Gaea represented the earth and was worshipped as the universal mother who had created the universe and borne both the first race of gods and the first humans. She was later superseded by other divinities but continued to preside over marriages and oaths and be honoured as a prophetess. She had a number of sanctuaries.

because of a false derivation from a word meaning 'to pour', was Chaos considered to mean the confused and unorganised mass of the elements scattered through space. Chaos is moreover a pure cosmic principle devoid of god-like characteristics.

The same may be said of Hesiod's Eros, who has nothing in common with the Eros whom we shall meet in later legends. Here Eros has only a metaphysical significance: he represents the force of attraction which causes beings to come together.

Uranus, son and husband of Gaea, is the starlit sky. It may be pointed out that he received no cult in Greece. This conception of the sky and the earth, considered as two primordial divinities, is common to all Indo-European peoples. In the Rig-Veda the sky and the earth were already called 'the immortal couple' and the 'two grandparents of the world'.

Gaea. The only divinity with well-defined features is Gaea, the earth. According to Hesiod it seems likely that Gaea, from whom all things issued, had been the great deity of the primitive Greeks. Like the Aegeans and like the peoples of Asia, the Greeks must doubtless have originally worshipped the Earth in whom they beheld the mother-goddess. This is again confirmed by the Homeric hymn in which the poet says: 'I shall sing of Gaea, universal mother, firmly founded, the oldest of divinities.'

Gaea, 'the deep-breasted', whose soil nourishes all that exists, and by whose benevolence men are blessed with fair children and all the pleasant fruits of earth, was thus at one time the supreme goddess whose majesty was acknowledged not only by men but by the gods themselves. Later, when the victorious dynasty of the Olympians was established, Gaea's prestige was not lessened. It was still she whom the gods invoked when they made oaths: 'I swear by Gaea and the vast sky above her,' Hera proclaims when, in the *Iliad*, she answers Zeus' accusations.

Gaea the omnipotent not only created the universe and bore the first race of the gods, but also gave birth to the human race. Thus in the myth of Erichthonius she draws him forth from her own bosom and offers him to Athene: he was the first inhabitant of Attica.

The power of Gaea was also manifest in her gift of foretelling the future. The Oracle of Delphi, before it passed into Apollo's hands, had originally belonged to Gaea.

Later, as other divinities rose in the estimation of men, the role of Gaea gradually became less important. Her cult, however, always continued in Greece. She presided over marriages and was honoured as pre-eminent among prophetesses. At Patras the sick came to consult her. She was particularly venerated at Aegae, at Delphi and at Olympia. She had sanctuaries at Dodona, Tegea, Sparta and at Athens, near the Areopagus. She was offered first fruits and grain; but when she was invoked as the guardian of the sanctity of oaths a black ewe was immolated in her honour. She was commonly represented in the form of a gigantic woman.

The Titans. The Titans, who formed the first divine race, had for the most part no very clearly defined personality. The etymology of their name which Hesiod gives (from a word meaning 'to stretch out', because they had stretched out their hand against their father) is fanciful. Their name probably derives from a Cretan word which meant 'king'.

In Greece the Titans were honoured as the ancestors of men. To them was attributed the invention of the arts and of magic.

Cyclopes and Hecatoncheires. In Hesiod the Cyclopes were storm genii, as their names indicate: Brontes, thunder; Steropes, lightning; Arges, thunderbolt.

As for the Hecatoncheires or Centimanes – the 'hundred-handed' – their names are sufficient to characterise them. They, too, were three in number: Cottus, the Furious; Briareus, the Vigorous; Gyges, the Big-limbed.

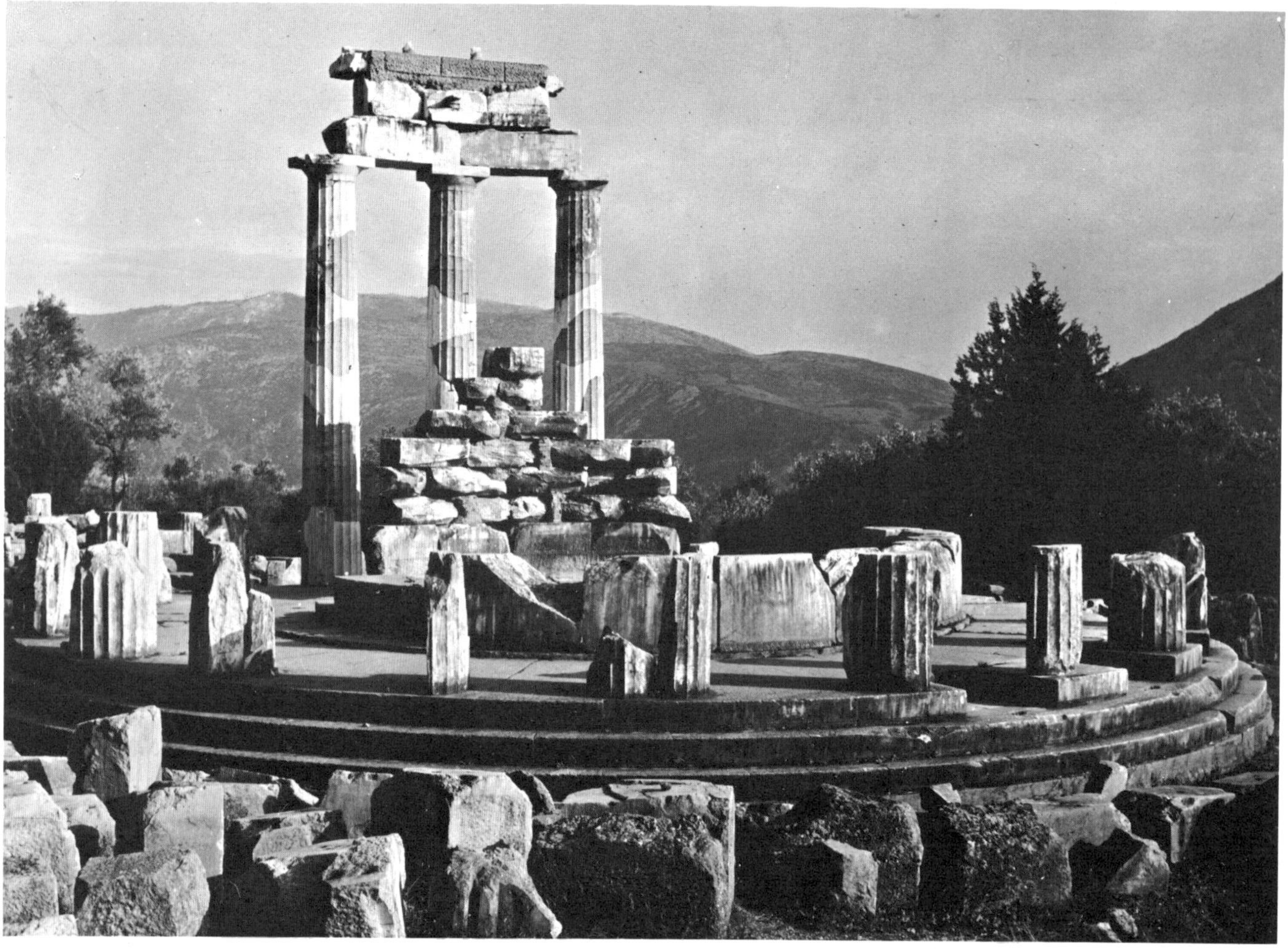

The Tholos at Delphi. Situated on the lower slopes of Mount Parnassus, Delphi was the most ancient and sacred sanctuary in Greece. Its famous oracle was presided over by Apollo and drew worshippers from far and near. The Tholos is one a number of buildings standing in a precinct dedicated to Athene – the only deity apart from Apollo to have her own temple at Delphi. Pentelic marble. Beginning of the fourth century B.C.

Titans, Cyclopes and Hecatoncheires symbolised the tumultuous forces of nature.

Orphic Cosmogonies. To the above primitive and popular cosmogony followers of Orphism opposed other explanations of the origin of things. They claimed as their authority the apocryphal writings attributed to Orpheus which seem actually to have been written by a priest named Onomacritus. The philosophic and scientific pre-occupations which all these systems reflect, the subtleties in which they delight, and the many abstractions which they employ, remove them from the realm of the primitive. They are metaphysical systems rather than mythology.

Taken as a whole this is roughly what they come to: the first principle was Cronus, or Time, from which came Chaos, which symbolised the infinite, and Ether, which symbolised the finite.

Chaos was surrounded by Night, which formed the enveloping cover under which, by the creative action of the Ether, cosmic matter was slowly organised. This finally assumed the shape of an egg of which Night formed the shell.

In the centre of this gigantic egg, whose upper section formed the vault of the sky and whose lower section was the earth, was born the first being, Phanes – the Light. It was Phanes who, by union with Night, created Heaven and Earth. It was he also who engendered Zeus.

We shall not dwell longer on this brief summary of Orphic doctrine; for we shall meet it again when we come to the god Dionysus, who became the supreme god of Orphism. Meanwhile Hesiod continues to recount the fate of the second divine dynasty.

CRONUS: THE BIRTH OF ZEUS: THE COMING OF THE OLYMPIANS

The Reign of Cronus. When Uranus was reduced to impotence, Cronus liberated his brothers, the Titans – with the exception of the Cyclopes and the Hecatoncheires – and became chief of the new dynasty.

Under his reign the work of creation continued. Night gave birth to Doom (Moros), to black Ker (Moera) and to Death; then to Sleep and his retinue of Dreams. She then bore bantering Gaiety (Momus) and wailing Misery (Oizus), and the Hesperides who guarded the golden apples beyond the Ocean. Then came the Fates: Clotho, Lachesis and Atropos, who when a mortal was born apportioned his share of good and evil. Night also bore Nemesis, fearful to mortals, Fraud, Incontinence, Old Age and Eris (Strife) who in turn gave birth to Sorrow, Forgetfulness and Hunger, to Disease, Combat, Murder, Battles, Massacres, Quarrels, Lies and Equivocations, to Injustice and Oaths.

Pontus, the sea, united with Gaea, the earth, to produce Nereus the Truthful, Thaumas the Monstrous, Phorcys the Intrepid and pretty-cheeked Ceto and Eurybia with the heart of steel.

To Nereus and Doris, daughter of the Ocean, were born fifty daughters, the Nereids. To Thaumas and Electra were born Iris, the rainbow, and the Harpies with their fair tresses. By Phorcys Ceto bore the Graeae (the Old Ones) who came into the world with white hair, and the Gorgons who lived beyond the Ocean in the land of the Hesperides.

The Titans also begot children either with their sisters or with nymphs.

Oceanus and Tethys had three thousand sons, the Rivers, and three thousand daughters, the Water Nymphs, plus Metis (Wisdom), Tyche (Fortune), and Styx (the Infernal River). To Hyperion and Theia were born Helios (the Sun), Selene (the Moon) and Eos (the Dawn). Coeus and Phoebe engendered Leto and Asteria. By Eurybia Crius had: Astraeus, Pallas and Perses. By the Oceanid Clymene or, according to others, by Asia, Iapetus fathered Atlas, Menoetius, Epimetheus and Prometheus. Finally Cronus married his sister Rhea, who gave him three daughters: Hestia, Demeter and Hera; and three sons: Hades, Poseidon and Zeus.

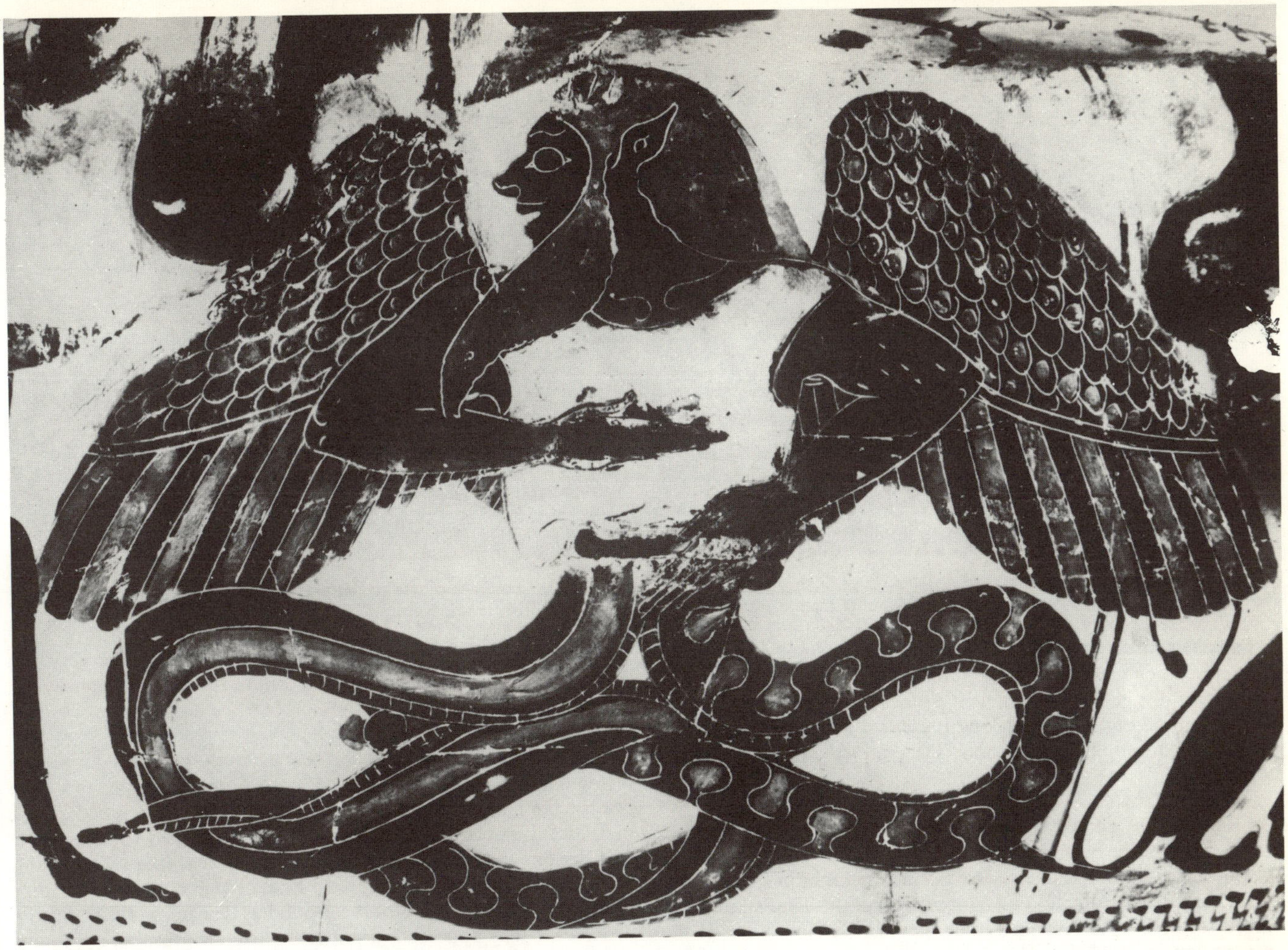

Typhon. In her fury that Zeus had given birth to Athene alone and unaided, Hera prayed that she too might bear a child unaided and produced the monster Typhon. Her son is confused with another Typhoeus, or Typhon, the son of Gaea and Tartarus, the lower half of whose body was composed of coiled serpents and whose wings blotted out the sun. Detail from a red-figured vase.

But whether it was that he feared, as it seems an oracle had predicted, that he would be supplanted by one of his children, or whether he had agreed with his older brothers, the Titans, to leave no posterity, Cronus swallowed each of his children as it was born.

The Birth and Childhood of Zeus. Rhea, his wife, was overwhelmed with boundless grief. She asked herself in despair if she were condemned to see all her progeny thus disappear. When the time approached for her to give birth to Zeus she beseeched her own parents, Uranus and Gaea, to help her save this child. On their advice she went to Crete and there, in a deep cavern under the thick forests of Mount Aegeum, she brought forth her son. Gaea took the new-born baby and undertook to bring it up. Meanwhile Rhea wrapped up an enormous stone in swaddling clothes and presented it to the unsuspecting Cronus, who swallowed it at once.

Meanwhile Gaea had carried her grandson to Mount Ida (others say to Mount Dicte) and given him for safe keeping into the hands of the nymphs Adrasteia and Ida, daughters of Melisseus, king of Crete. The two nymphs surrounded the young god with care and attention. They put him in a golden cradle and to amuse him Adrasteia presented him with a ball composed of hoops of gold. So that Cronus should not hear the baby crying the Curetes executed around the cradle warlike dances, beating their bronze shields with their swords.

Who exactly were these Curetes? In primitive times there had been a tribe of this name settled in Aetolia. On the other hand the Greeks gave them the epithet *Gegeneis* (children of the earth) or *Imbrogeneis* (children of the rain), so they may have been earth-spirits. Herodotus, however, calls them Phoenicians, followers of Cadmus, who had settled in Crete. Others say they came from Phrygia. Probably the Curetes were Cretan priests devoted to the orgiastic cult of the great goddess Rhea. They were distinguished by their half-warrior, half-sacredotal character. To increase their prestige the first among them were deified and thus became the sacred Curetes, the protectors of Zeus. They had temples, in Messina notably, and – which tends to confirm their earth-spirit origin – they were invoked in making oaths. The Curetes appear many times in the mythological history of Greece; on Hera's orders they spirited away at birth the young Epaphus, son of Zeus and Io, and were in consequence put to death by Zeus.

Thus sheltered from his father's cruelty the young Zeus grew up in the forests of Ida. For a wet-nurse he was given the goat Amaltheia. She was a wondrous animal whose aspect terrified even the immortals. In gratitude Zeus later placed her among the constellations and from her hide, which no arrow could pierce, he made the redoubtable aegis. To the nymphs he gave one of her horns, conferring upon it the marvellous property of refilling itself inexhaustibly with whatever food or drink was wished for; this was the horn of plenty (cornucopia). According to certain authors Amaltheia was the wife of Melisseus and suckled the young god with her milk. Others make her a nymph who simply watched over the child Zeus, claiming that the god was fed on ambrosia and nectar brought to him by doves and an eagle. And if Adrasteia and Ida are called daughters of Melisseus (from the Greek *melissa,* a bee) was this not because the bees of Ida brought their scented honey to the divine child?

The oracle which had predicted to Cronus that he would one day be overthrown by one of his sons had not lied. As soon as Zeus had reached manhood he planned to punish his father. Apollodorus tells us that he summoned to his aid Metis, daughter of Oceanus. Metis gave Cronus a draught that made him vomit up the stone and with it the gods, his own children, whom he had swallowed. Vanquished by the might of Zeus, Cronus was driven from the sky and cast to the very depths of the universe and there enchained in the region which stretches beneath the earth and the fruitless sea. This at least is what Homer says; according to others Cronus was sent to the ends of the earth to dwell in bliss, or plunged into mysterious slumber in distant Thule.

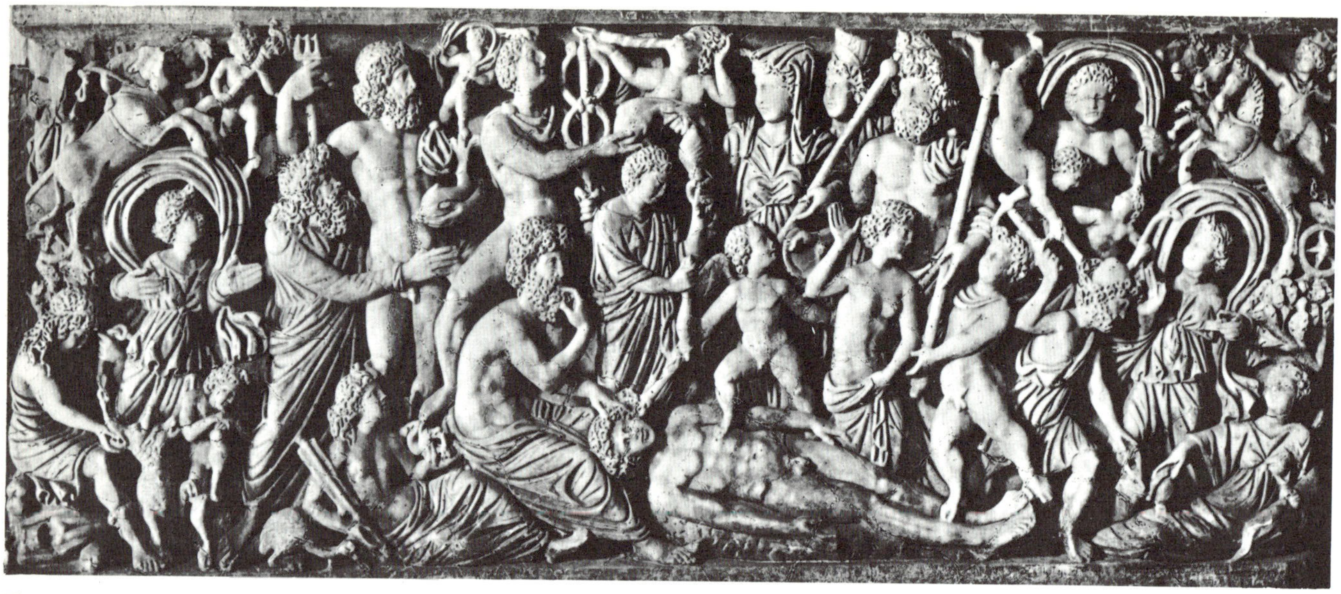

The creation of Man. In the presence of the gods of Olympus (Poseidon, Hermes, Hera, Zeus, Apollo) Prometheus prepares to animate the body of the first man whom he has just fashioned. Bas-relief from a sarcophagus in the National Museum, Naples.

To bear witness to his victory Zeus placed the stone Cronus had disgorged in divine Pytho, at the foot of Parnassus, 'to be one day in the eyes of mortals a monument to these wonders'.

This famous stone was for long preserved at Delphi within the walls of the tomb of Neoptolemus. The era of the Olympians now began.

The Revolt of the Titans. The Titans, with the exception of Oceanus, were jealous of the new gods and wished to reconquer the kingdom of which they had been dispossessed. Then the terrible struggle began. From their stronghold on Mount Othrys the Titans launched furious attacks upon Olympus. For ten years the outcome of the war remained doubtful. Zeus descended into Tartarus where, guarded by the monster Campe, the Hecatoncheires and the Cyclopes were kept prisoners. He set them free and made them his allies. The Cyclopes gave him the thunderbolt and the Hecatoncheires put their invincible arms at his service. Seizing in their enormous arms great boulders, they crushed the Titans. 'Sea and earth resounded with the horrifying clamour and the shaken firmament groaned aloud.' Zeus, too, was unable to curb his warlike rage and joined in the fray. From the heights of Olympus, Hesiod tells us, from the heights of the heavens he hurled thunder and lightning. With unwearying hand he flung bolt after bolt, and the air was rent with sound and fury. The fertile earth shuddered and burned; vast forests flamed and all things melted and boiled: the River Ocean, the immense sea and the entire earth. Around the infernal Titans arose stifling mists and blazing air; their bold glances were blinded by flashes of lightning. The fire even reached Chaos, and from what the eye could behold and the ear distinguish one would have said that sky and earth were confounded, the earth shaken on its very foundations, the sky crashing down from its heights. Such was the mighty uproar of this battle among the gods!

In spite of their pride and courage the Titans were finally defeated and, bound with chains, cast into the abysmal depths of the earth – as far below its surface as is the earth itself from the sky. 'It is there among impenetrable shadows and foul vapours, at the very end of the world, that the Titans, by the will of the king of the heavens, are buried.'

The War of the Giants. Zeus had scarcely put down this dangerous revolt when he was forced to undergo a new struggle, this time against the Giants. The Giants had sprung from the blood of the mutilated Uranus and were not only distinguished for their size. For these monstrous sons of the Earth had legs like serpents and their feet were formed of reptiles' heads. At the instant that they emerged from the entrails of the ground at Phlegra, in the peninsula of Pallene, they appeared in glittering armour grasping enormous spears. Porphyrion and Alcyoneus were their leaders. They at once attacked Olympus, whose mass dominated the plain of Phlegra on the west. Islands, rivers, mountains, all gave way before them. 'While one,' says Claudian, 'with vigorous arm shook Mount Oeta of Thessaly in the air, another balanced the summits of Mount Pangaea in his powerful hand. One armed himself with the ice of Mount Athos, another seized Ossa and lifted it, while still another tore up Rhodope. . . From everywhere the horrible din echoed.' To reach the heights of Olympus the giants piled the surrounding mountains one upon another, Ossa on Pelion. But grouped around Zeus the gods – with the exception of Demeter who took no part in the struggle – stood their ground before the assailants. Apollo struck down Ephialtes. Clytius fell under the blows of Hecate or Hephaestus. The impetuous Ares pierced Pelorus and Mimas with his sword. Poseidon pursued Polybutes across the sea, flung the island of Nisyros on top of him and buried him.

The gods alone, however, could not triumph, for the oracle had declared that the sons of Gaea would succumb only to the blows of a mortal. This mortal was Hercules (Gk. Heracles), with whom Dionysus was sometimes associated. While Dionysus struck down Rhaetos (or Eurytus), Hercules attacked Alcyoneus. At first the giant resisted his blows. Hercules was astonished, but Athene revealed to him that Alcyoneus was invulnerable as long as he stood

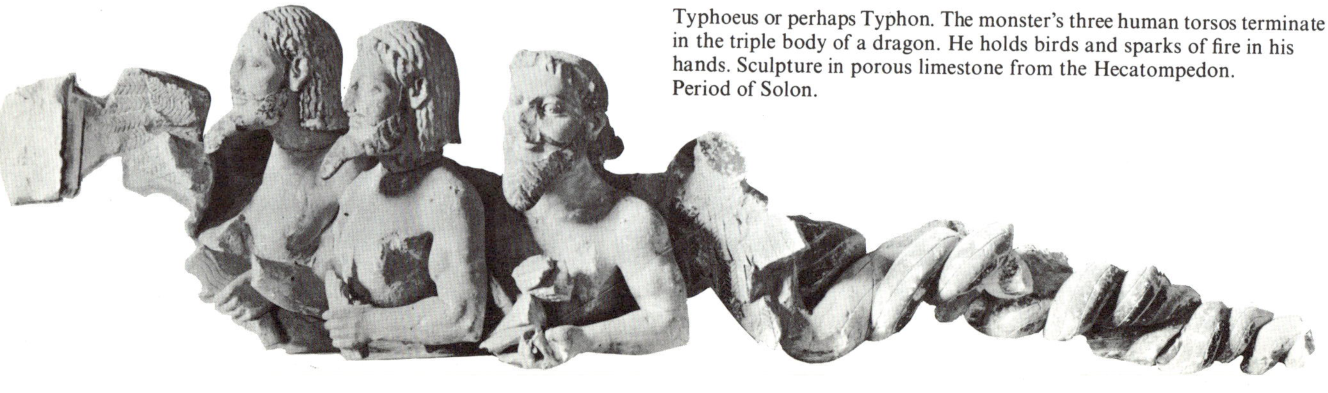

Typhoeus or perhaps Typhon. The monster's three human torsos terminate in the triple body of a dragon. He holds birds and sparks of fire in his hands. Sculpture in porous limestone from the Hecatompedon. Period of Solon.

on the soil which had given him birth. The hero then seized the giant in his arms and carried him away from the territory of Pallene and at once slew him. Porphyrion wished to avenge his brother, but Zeus inspired in him a sudden passion for Hera. While the giant pursued Hera, Hercules pierced him with a deadly arrow. From that moment the defeat of the giants was assured. In vain Pallas and Enceladus attempted to struggle against Athene; one after the other they were overcome. With the skin of Pallas Athene fashioned the aegis. As for Enceladus, she buried him under the island of Sicily. And even today when the giant turns over, the entire island quakes.

Typhoeus. Gaea, however, could not resign herself to the defeat of her children. Against Zeus she raised up a final monster, Typhoeus, whom she had borne to Tartarus. He was a terrifying creature whose hands worked ceaselessly and whose feet were never still. From his shoulders sprang a hundred horrible dragons' heads, each with a darting black tongue and eyes which spurted searing flame. From his thighs emerged innumerable vipers; his body was covered with feathers; thick bristles sprouted from his head and cheeks. He was taller than the tallest mountain. At sight of Typhoeus the gods were seized with fear and fled as far as Egypt. Only Zeus stood firm before the monster; but entwined in the myriad coils of the serpents he fell into the hands of Typhoeus who cut the tendons of his hands and feet and imprisoned him in his den in Cilicia. Rescued by Hermes, Zeus renewed the struggle. With his thunderbolts he overwhelmed Typhoeus, who fled to Sicily, where under Etna the god crushed him.

Thus in the first ages of the world, when the elements were not yet mastered and matter was still rebellious, there occurred terrifying cataclysms which threatened to overthrow everything. The ground writhed and trembled, the mountains crumbled or split apart to belch forth enormous boulders and molten stone, rivers broke from their courses, the seas rose and engulfed the earth. But the divine wisdom, regulator of the universe, finally imposed its will over all these disorderly elements. The earth became firm, the volcanoes subsided, the now well-behaved rivers again irrigated the plains and the tumultuous sea no longer tossed its waves beyond the sands of its shores. Harmony was born anew and man, reassured, gave thanks to the god whose might had triumphed over the forces of evil.

The defeat of Typhoeus assured the final and lasting supremacy of Zeus. From then on no serious adversary dared to measure his strength with this god who had vanquished all the powers of evil. His reign, established by triple victory, would never be seriously disturbed; and among the Olympians Zeus maintained his rank of uncontested master of gods and men.

THE ORIGINS OF HUMANITY

Prometheus. The Titan Iapetus was the father of four sons. Their mother, according to Hesiod, was the Oceanid Clymene; according to Aeschylus, she was Themis. Two of these sons, Menoetius and Atlas, were punished by Zeus, doubtless for having taken part in the revolt of the Titans. Menoetius was plunged into darkest Erebus, in punishment for 'his wickedness and boundless audacity'. As for Atlas, he was condemned to stand for ever, before the Hesperides on the edge of the world, and to bear upon his shoulders the vault of the heavens. The other two – Prometheus (who foresees) and Epimetheus (who reflects after the event) – had a different fate and played an important role in the legendary history of the origins of humanity.

In view of the unchallengeable might of the Olympians, Prometheus' only weapon was cunning. During the revolt of the Titans he had kept a prudent neutrality and had even made overtures to Zeus when it seemed likely that the war would be won by him. Thus Prometheus had been admitted into Olympus and the circle of the Immortals. But he entertained a silent grudge against the destroyers of his race and revenged himself by favouring mortals to the detriment of the gods.

He had, perhaps, other reasons for his interest in the human race; for a tradition – rather late, it is true – said that Prometheus was the creator of mankind. It was he who with earth and water – some said with his own tears – had fashioned the body of the first man into which Athene breathed soul and life. In Phocis the author Pausanias saw bits of hardened clay which had the odour of human skin and which were plainly the residue of the slime employed by Prometheus.

But it seems that this creation took place only after the earlier race of man had been destroyed in the deluge. Current opinion actually attributed to mankind an older and nobler origin. 'Men and gods,' says Pindar, 'we are of the same family; we owe the breath of life to the same mother.'

The Four Ages of Man. The first men, who were contemporaries of Cronus, enjoyed complete happiness. It was the Golden Age. Hesiod says: 'They lived like gods, free from worry and fatigue; old age did not afflict them; they rejoiced in continual festivity.' Their lot did not include immortality, but at least 'they died as though overcome by sweet slumber. All the blessings of the world were theirs: the fruitful earth gave forth its treasures unbidden. At their death, men of the Golden Age became benevolent genii, 'protectors and tutelary guardians of the living'.

After the Golden Age came the Silver Age, during which lived a race of feeble and inept men who obeyed their mothers all their lives (i.e. it was a matriarchal age). They were also agriculturalists, Hesiod says.

The men of the Bronze Age were robust as ash trees and delighted only in oaths and warlike exploits. 'Their pitiless hearts were as hard as steel; their might was untameable, their arms invincible.' They ended by mutually cutting each other's throats. From this generation, however, dated the discovery of the first metals and the first attempts at civilisation.

After the Bronze Age Hesiod places the Heroic Age, peopled by the valiant warriors who fought before Thebes and under the walls of Troy. But the more widespread opinion was that after the Bronze Age came the Iron Age – the contemporary age, a period of misery and crime 'when men respect neither their vows, nor justice, nor virtue'.

Thus they explained the progressive degeneration of mankind.

The Theft of Fire: Pandora. As long as Cronus had reigned, gods and men had lived on terms of mutual understanding. Hesiod says: 'In those days meals were taken in common; men and the immortal gods sat down together.' Everything changed with the coming of the Olympians. Over men Zeus asserted his divine supremacy. A meeting of gods and men was held at Sicyon to determine which portion of victims offered in sacrifice was owed to the gods. Prometheus, who was in charge of the partition, laid out an enormous ox which he had cut up in his own way. He arranged the flesh, the entrails and the most succulent morsels in the skin and placed them on one side; on the other side he perfidiously laid the fleshless bones which he had covered with a rich layer of fat. Zeus, who was invited to take first choice, chose the bones; but when he had removed the white, gleaming fat and discovered nothing but the animal's bones he fell into a rage. In his anger he withheld fire from the unfortunate race who lived on earth. But the astute Prometheus went to the island of Lemnos, where Hephaestus kept his forges. There he stole a brand of the holy fire which he enclosed in a hollow stalk and carried back to men. Another version of the story claims that he lighted his torch at the wheel of the sun.

Outraged by the theft, Zeus sent a fresh calamity to men. He ordered Hephaestus to fashion clay and water into a body, to give it vital force and human voice, and to make therefrom a virgin whose dazzling beauty would equal that of the immortal goddesses. All the divinities heaped their especial gifts on this new creature, who received the name of Pandora. Hermes, however, put perfidy into Pandora's heart and lies into her mouth. After which Zeus sent her as a gift to Epimetheus. Although his brother Prometheus had warned him against accepting any gift from the ruler of Olympus, the imprudent Epimetheus was enchanted by Pandora's beauty, welcomed her, and made a place for her among men. Unhappy imprudence! For Pandora brought in her arms a great vase – which is incorrectly called 'Pandora's Box'. She raised its lid, and the terrible afflictions with which the vase had been filled escaped and spread over the earth. Hope alone did not fly away. Thus, with the arrival of the first woman, misery made its appearance on earth.

The Deluge: Deucalion and Pyrrha. Zeus' rage, however, was not appeased. In his anger he resolved to annihilate the human race

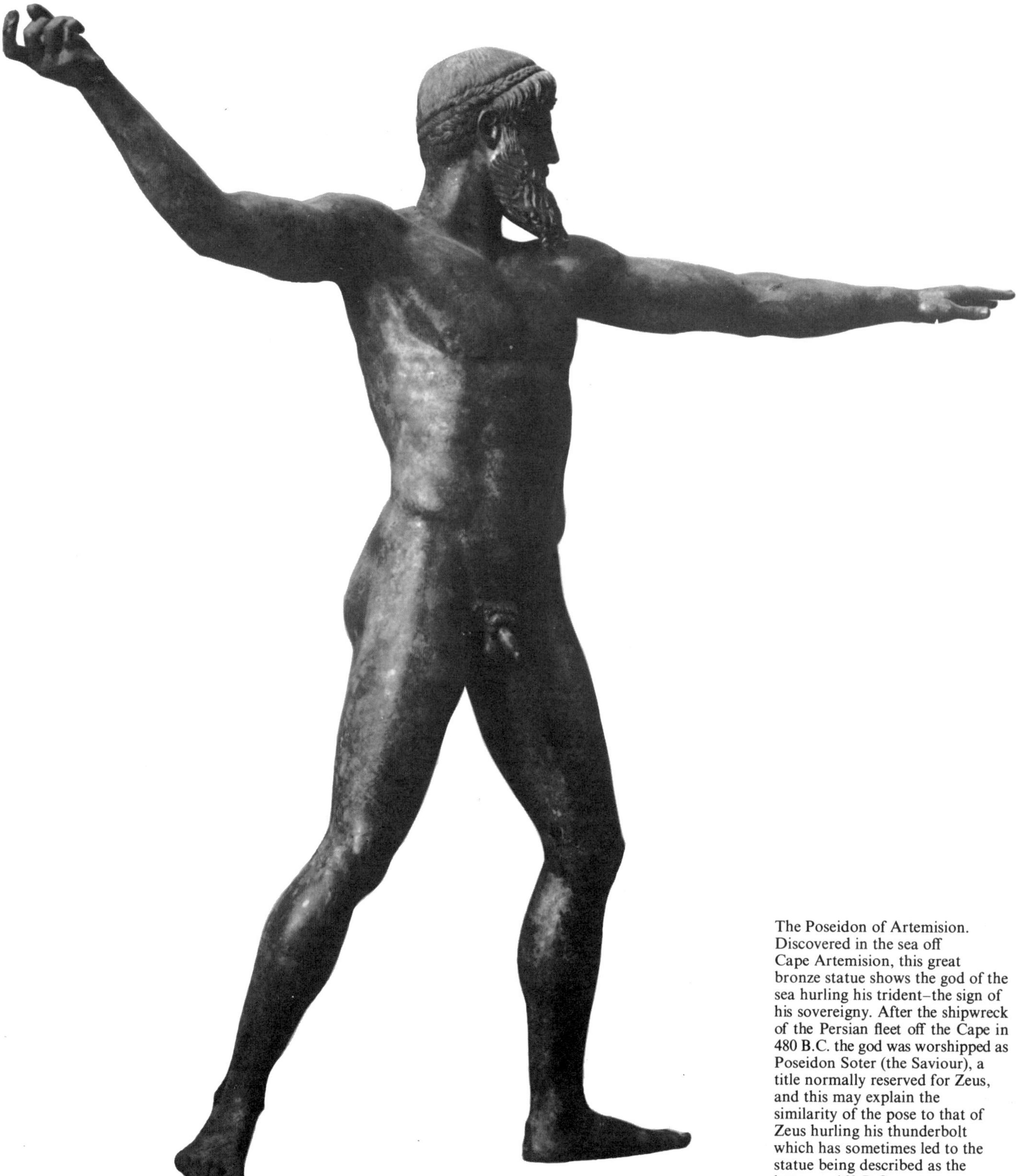

The Poseidon of Artemision. Discovered in the sea off Cape Artemision, this great bronze statue shows the god of the sea hurling his trident–the sign of his sovereigny. After the shipwreck of the Persian fleet off the Cape in 480 B.C. the god was worshipped as Poseidon Soter (the Saviour), a title normally reserved for Zeus, and this may explain the similarity of the pose to that of Zeus hurling his thunderbolt which has sometimes led to the statue being described as the latter. *c.* 460 B.C.

by burying it beneath the waves of a deluge. But once again Prometheus was on guard. He warned his son Deucalion who, with his wife Pyrrha, daughter of Epimetheus and Pandora, then reigned in Thessaly. On the advice of his father, Deucalion constructed an ark and with his wife went aboard. For nine days and nine nights they floated on the waters. On the tenth day the downpour ceased and the two survivors disembarked on the crest of Mount Othrys or Mount Parnassus. Deucalion offered up sacrifice to Zeus Phyxius (protector of fugitives) and the god, touched by his piety, promised to grant him his first wish. Deucalion asked Zeus to renew the human race.

Another legend says that Deucalion and Pyrrha, having gone to Delphi, addressed their prayers to Themis. 'Veil your heads,' replied the goddess, 'remove the girdles of your robes and cast behind you the bones of your first ancestor.' Stricken at first with astonishment, Deucalion and Pyrrha at last solved the mystery of this ambiguous command. They veiled their heads and walked across the plain, throwing over their shoulders stones torn from the earth – for were they not descendants of Gaea, the earth, and were not the rocks her very bones? The stones which Deucalion threw were changed into men, those that Pyrrha cast were transformed into women.

The human race was renewed and Zeus recovered from his anger. Deucalion was regarded as the father of the Hellenes, the first king and founder of towns and temples. It was he, they said, who built the temple of Olympian Zeus at Athens, and nearby the temple his tomb was pointed out. In Cynos, however, they also boasted of having the tomb of Deucalion and his wife Pyrrha.

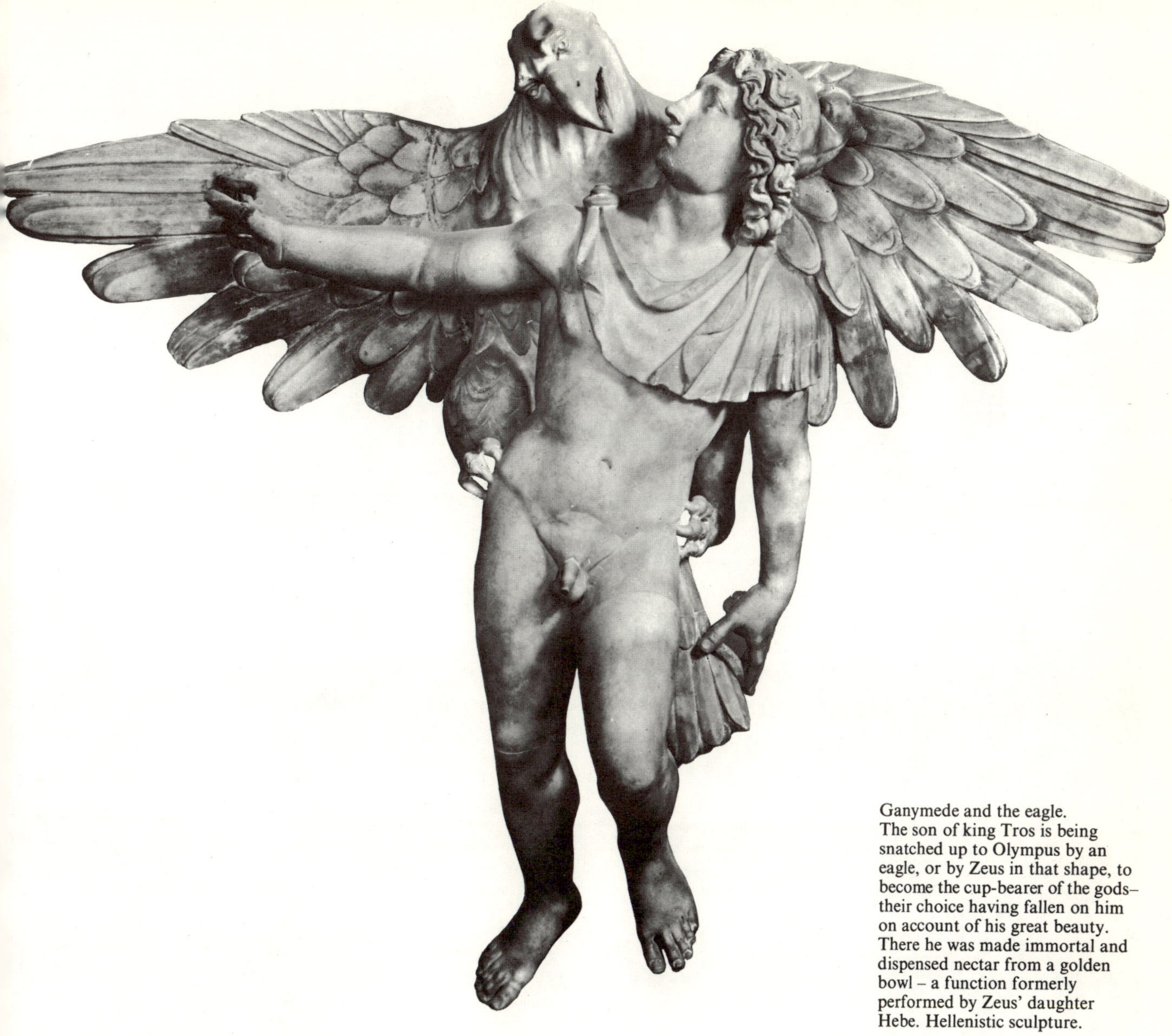

Ganymede and the eagle.
The son of king Tros is being snatched up to Olympus by an eagle, or by Zeus in that shape, to become the cup-bearer of the gods– their choice having fallen on him on account of his great beauty. There he was made immortal and dispensed nectar from a golden bowl – a function formerly performed by Zeus' daughter Hebe. Hellenistic sculpture.

The Torture of Prometheus. Although peace had been concluded between Zeus and mankind, Prometheus had to pay cruelly for his trickery and thefts. At the command of Zeus, Hephaestus, assisted by Kratos and Bia, seized and bound Prometheus with indestructible chains to one of the crests of Mount Caucasus. There, 'an eagle with outstretched wings, sent by Zeus, fed upon his immortal liver; as much as the winged monster devoured during the day, that much grew again during the night'. In spite of the torture the Titan persisted in his attitude of revolt. Disdaining complaints and humiliating prayers he never ceased to defy the lord of Olympus and to express his hatred in violent outbursts. For was he not in possession of a secret which dangerously concerned the future of Zeus himself?

Finally after thirty years of suffering – others say thirty thousand years – he was with Zeus' permission rescued by the divine Hercules, who slew the eagle and broke the prisoner's chains. Prometheus then revealed to Zeus his famous secret and warned him that if he continued to pay court to Thetis, daughter of Nereus, he would run the risk of seeing a son born who would dethrone him. Not wishing to chance the same misadventure that had befallen his father and his grandfather, Zeus abandoned his amorous enterprise and allowed Thetis to marry a mortal, Peleus.

Prometheus, however, could not acquire divine immortality unless some immortal consented to exchange destinies with him. Now the centaur Chiron, whom Hercules had struck with a poisoned arrow, was in despair lest his wound never healed. To put an end to his suffering Chiron begged to be allowed to descend into Hades in the place of Prometheus. Zeus consented, and from then on the son of Iapetus took his permanent place on Olympus. And the Athenians, who saw in Prometheus the benefactor of mankind and the father of all the arts and sciences, raised an altar to him in the gardens of the Academy.

OLYMPUS

Mount Olympus. On the confines of Thessaly and Macedonia, along the shores of the Aegean Sea from which it is separated only by a narrow littoral, rises the chain of Olympus. While on the north the mountain group descends to the plain by a series of gentle hills, the south face – that which the Greeks saw – falls precipitously and the mountain offers the aspect of a rocky cliff. Above a sort of monster plateau, itself steeply flanked which serves as a base, Mount Olympus soars in one sweep up to more than nine thousand feet. Down its sheer slopes, covered with dark woods, tumble numerous torrents which dig deep furrows, rather like the folds of a garment. Thus the poets called it 'Olympus of the innumerable folds'. The line of the mountain peaks is rounded into a kind of amphitheatre and the upper tiers of rock, formed by the heaping up of huge boulders round which cling shreds of cloud, look like gigantic seats arranged there for the use of supernatural beings.

The mariner who sailed into the gulf of Therme (today the gulf of Salonica) would feel himself filled with religious awe when he perceived against the hard blue line of sky the lofty profile of Mount Olympus. Everything concurred to reveal to him the fearful majesty of the gods. In the first place he had no doubt that Olympus was the highest mountain in the world. Then he would remember that the

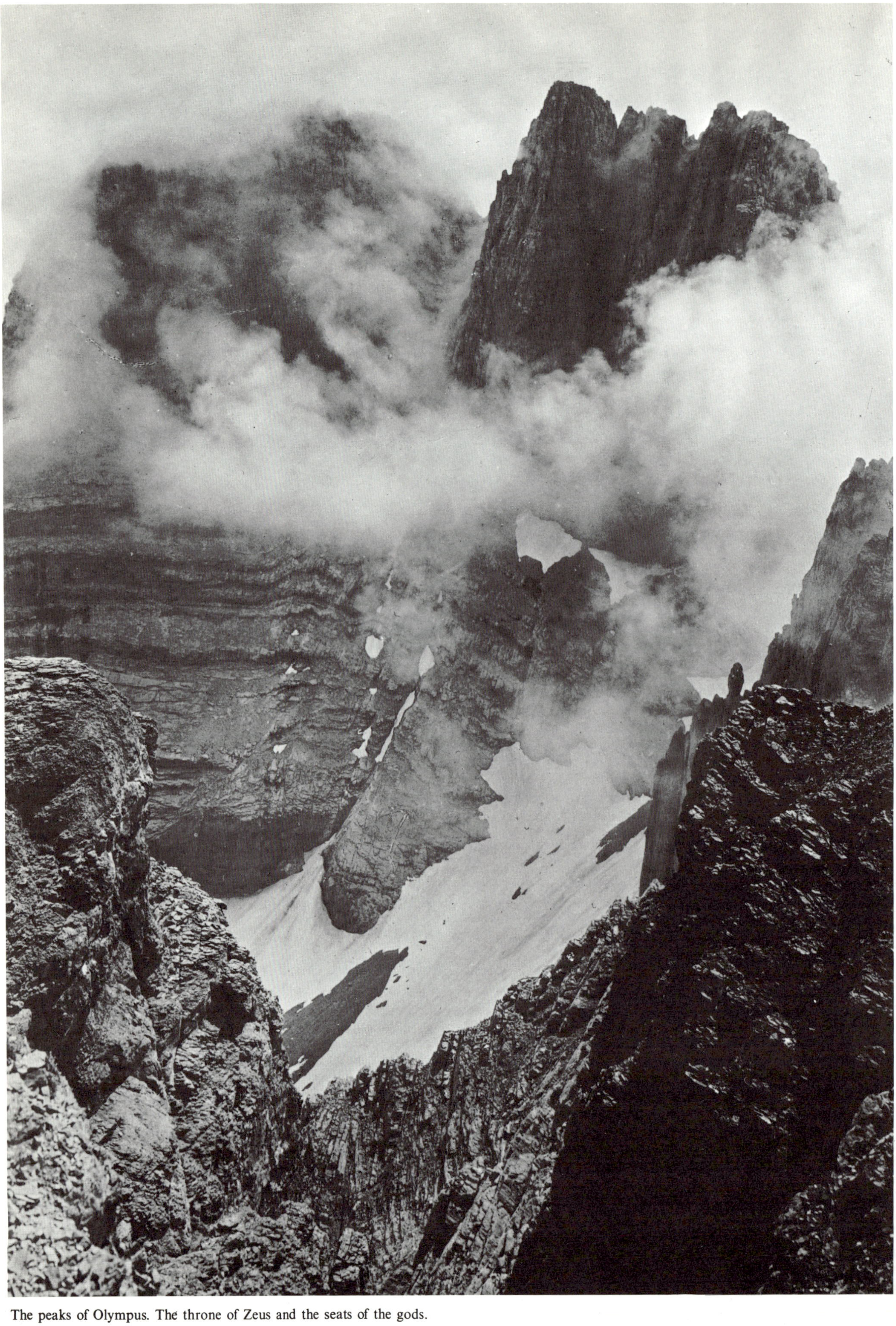

The peaks of Olympus. The throne of Zeus and the seats of the gods.

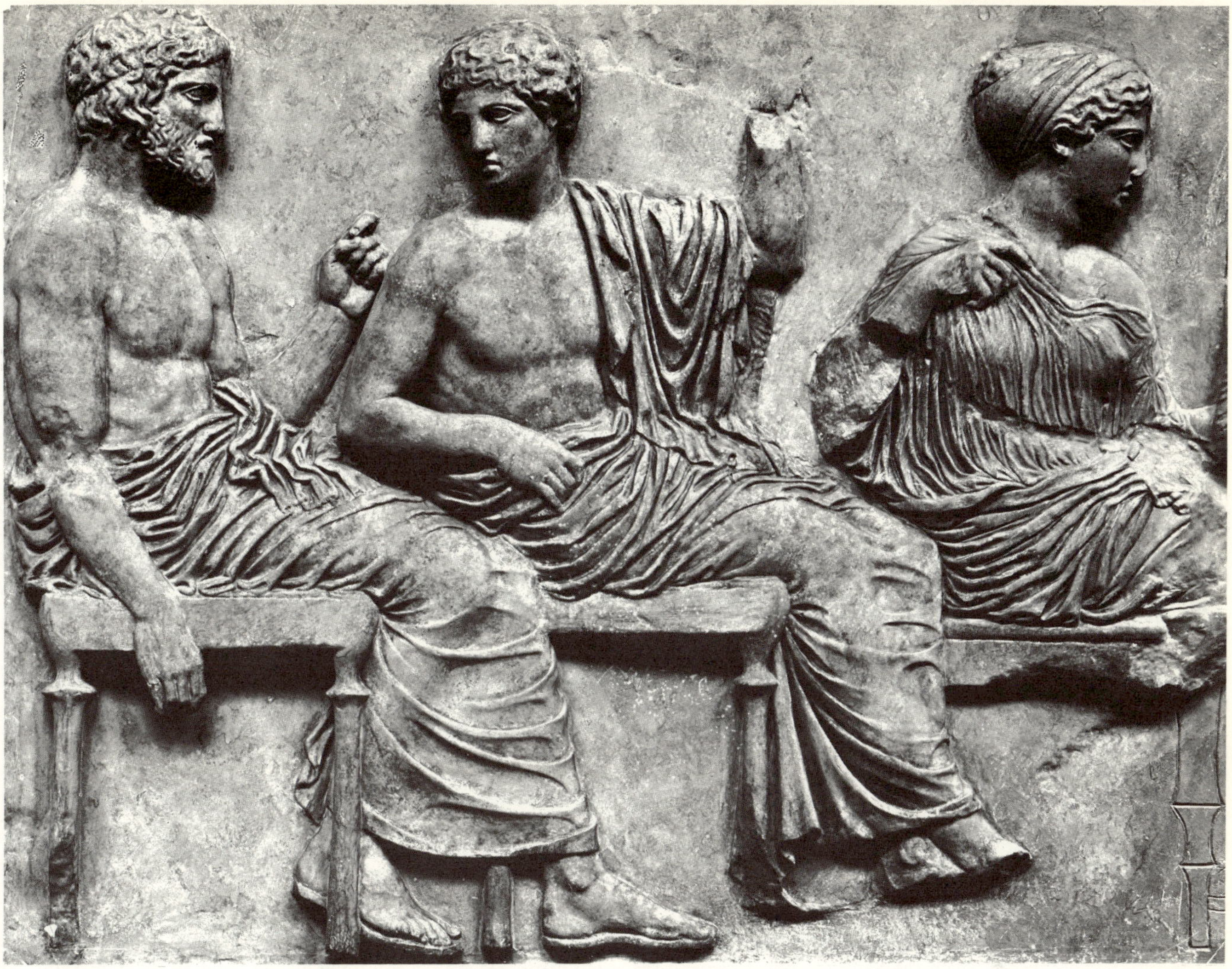

The gods on Olympus. Poseidon, Apollo, Artemis. Frieze from the Parthenon, Pentelic marble. Acropolis Museum, Athens.

narrow Vale of Tempe, which separates Olympus from Ossa and cradles under its willows and plane-trees the peaceful stream of Peneus, had been hollowed out by Zeus during his struggle with the Titans. Finally he would scarcely dare raise his eyes towards the summits; for he knew that up there, behind the veil of clouds which hid them from mortal regard, dwelt the almighty gods. Bending over his oars he would repeat the words of old Homer who, speaking of Olympus, had said: 'Never is it swept by the winds nor touched by snow; a purer air surrounds it, a white clarity envelops it and the gods there taste of a happiness which lasts as long as their eternal lives.'

Actually when the sons of Cronus drew lots for the partition of the empire of the world, Zeus received as his share the sublime regions of the Ether, Poseidon the tumultuous sea, and Hades the sombre depths of the earth. But it was agreed that Olympus should be held in common by all the gods and that there they should make their dwelling-place.

The Gods on Olympus. Assembled on Olympus, the gods formed a society with its own laws and hierarchy. First came the twelve great gods and goddesses: Zeus, Poseidon, Hephaestus, Hermes, Ares and Apollo; Hera, Athene, Artemis, Hestia, Aphrodite and Demeter. Beside them were ranged other divinities, some of whom did not relinquish pride of place to the great twelve. Such were Helios, Selene, Leto, Dione, Dionysus, Themis and Eos. Then, of a lower rank, forming as it were the courtiers of the Olympians and sworn to their service, came: the Horae, the Moerae, Nemesis, the Graces, the Muses, Iris, Hebe, Ganymede. It must be pointed out that Hades, although a brother of Zeus, did not frequent Olympus and, with the goddesses Persephone and Hecate, remained in his subterranean empire.

Over this society Zeus reigned as sovereign ruler. If at times the gods were tempted by rebellious impulses they were quickly reduced to obedience. In Homer we see how Zeus speaks to them: 'Let no god, let no goddess attempt to curb my will . . . or I shall seize him and cast him into darkest Tartarus. Then will he recognise how much mightier am I than all the gods! Come, then, try it, O gods! And you will discover with whom you have to deal. Hang from the heavens a golden chain and attach yourselves all, gods and goddesses, to it, and no matter how hard you strive, you will not drag Zeus in his supreme wisdom from the sky down to earth. But when, afterwards, I begin to pull I shall draw you, you and the earth and the sea together, I shall draw you up and roll the chain around the summit of Olympus and you will all remain there suspended in the air.' Without quite carrying out this threat Zeus nevertheless inflicted severe penalties on gods who had displeased him. For instance he would make them serve as slaves to mortals; such was the fate of Poseidon and Apollo. Therefore the gods did not resist him and even the irascible Hera counselled prudence. 'Foolish that we are to lose our tempers with Zeus . . . He sits apart and neither worries nor is disturbed; for he boasts of being incontestably superior to the immortal gods in might and power. So resign yourselves.'

Above the gods, however, and above Zeus himself hovered a supreme power to whom all were subject: Moros, or Destiny. Son of the Night, Moros, invisible and dark like his mother, prepared his decrees in the shadows and extended his inescapable dominion over all. Zeus himself could not set aside his decisions and had to submit to them like the humblest mortal. He had, moreover, no desire to set aside the decisions of Destiny; for, being himself Supreme Wisdom, he was not unaware that in upsetting the destined course of events he would introduce confusion into the universe it was his mission to govern. Thus, even when it was a matter of saving the life of his own son Sarpedon, the hour of whose death the Fates had marked down, Zeus preferred to bow his head and let what was ordained be fulfilled.

The days of the gods passed in merrymaking and laughter. Sometimes, when they intervened in the affairs of men whose quarrels they enthusiastically adopted, the gods would disagree. But these passing storms did not affect the normal serenity of Olympus.

Seated around their golden tables the gods dined on celestial nectar and ambrosia, and savoured the rising fragrance of fatted cattle which mortals burned in their honour on their altars below. Even when Zeus called them together in counsel on the topmost peak of Olympus where he resided, the fair Hebe would move among them pouring nectar, and the golden cups would pass from hand to hand.

While they drank, Apollo would delight them with the harmony of his lyre and the Muses would sing in turn in their sweet voices.

Finally, 'when the brilliant torch of the sun had disappeared the gods would take their leave and return to the dwelling Hephaestus had built with wondrous cunning for each of them, there to rest and repose'.

If the gods' daily life resembled that of men it was because, at least in appearance, their natures were not dissimilar. Their bodies were like mortal bodies, but superior in stature, strength and beauty. Ares' body, stretched on the ground, covered a length of seven plethra – well over two hundred yards – and when Hera from the heights of Olympus swore by the Styx, she could touch the earth with one hand and with the other reach the seas.

In the case of the gods, however, blood was replaced by a more fluid substance, the ichor, which rendered the body imperishable and incorruptible. This did not prevent the gods from being vulnerable to weapons used by men. But their wounds, no matter how painful, always healed and their bodies retained eternal youth.

Another privilege which the gods enjoyed was the power of metamorphosis, to change themselves if they wished into animals or even to take on the aspect of inanimate objects.

Like mortals the gods were subject to human passions. They were accessible to love, hate, anger, even to envy. They cruelly punished all who aroused their enmity, but showered favours on those who revered and honoured them with gifts.

ZEUS

The very name Zeus, in which the Sanskrit root *dyaus* and the Latin *dies* (the day) are found, evokes the idea of the luminous sky. Originally, then, Zeus was the god of the sky and of atmospheric phenomena. He was lord of the winds, of the clouds, of rain both destructive and beneficial, of the thunder. He resided in the ether, the upper part of the air, and on mountain tops. He was literally the All-high. Hence he was worshipped in elevated spots such as Mount Lycaeus in Arcadia, Mount Apesas in Argolis, Parnassus and Hymettus in Attica, Helicon in Boeotia, Pelion in Thessaly, Olympus in Macedonia, Pangaea in Thrace, Ida in Crete and so forth.

His Attributes. Later Zeus took on a moral personality and became the supreme god who united in himself all the attributes of divinity. He was omnipotent, he saw everything and knew everything. Thus he was the fountainhead of all divination, whether he spoke oracularly in person as on Olympus and at Dodona, or whether he had recourse as at Delphi to the intermediary of Apollo, his prophet. A wise sovereign, he ordained all according to the law of Fate with which his own will was merged. To mortals he dispensed good and evil; he was, moreover, kind and compassionate. Though he chastised the wicked he was capable of pity. He averted threatening dangers (*Alexikakos*); he protected the weak, the indigent, the fugitive and, in general, all suppliants (*Milichios*). His solicitude also extended to the family as god of the hearth (*Ephestios*), of marriage (*Gamelios*), of friendship (*Philios*), and of the peoples' assemblies (*Agoraios*). Finally he was the protector-god of all Greece – Panhellenic Zeus.

His Cult. The most famous sanctuary of Zeus was that of Dodona, in Epirus. It was also the oldest, dating back to the Pelasgians. People came there from all parts of Greece to consult the oracle of a sacred oak whose rustling and murmurs were regarded as the words of Zeus himself. On the origin of this oracle Herodotus, who claims to have heard it from the lips of the priestesses of Dodona, says: 'Two black doves flew from Thebes in Egypt, one to Libya and the other to Dodona. The latter, alighting in an oak tree, began to speak in a human voice and to say that an oracle of Zeus should be founded in this place. The people of Dodona believed that they had received an order coming from the gods, and on the dove's advice founded the oracle.' The interpretation of the oracles of Dodona was entrusted to a college of priests, the Selli, a name which was undoubtedly none other than that of the former inhabitants of the country. These priests practised asceticism, slept on the ground and never washed their feet. To the Selli were later added three priestesses, called the Peleiades. They were more especially attached to the service of the goddess Dione, who was venerated at Dodona at the side of Zeus, here taking over the role of Hera. Dione was a Pelasgian divinity and, according to Hesiod, the daughter of Oceanus and Tethys. She was said to be mother of Aphrodite.

Among Zeus' other sanctuaries must be mentioned that of Mount Lycaeus in Arcadia on the summit of which was a mound of earth, fronted by two columns with engraved eagles. Here, it was said, human sacrifice was once practised. The root from which the word Lycaeus was formed (it means 'light') reveals that Zeus was here originally a solar deity.

Finally there was the celebrated temple of Olympus with its famous statue of the god sculptured by Phidias. It rose on a richly ornamented pedestal which was about ten yards high and seven yards wide. The statue itself was more than thirteen yards in height. Seated on a throne of bronze, gold, ivory and ebony, the god held in his right hand a crowned Victory while his left hand rested on a sceptre surmounted by an eagle. He was dressed in a golden mantle strewn with flowers. On his brow there was an olive wreath and his countenance, framed by a long beard, wore an expression of serene majesty.

Representations. The Olympian Zeus of Phidias represented the ideal which inspired subsequent artists. The god was normally depicted as a man in the fullness of maturity, of robust body, grave countenance and with broad forehead jutting out above deeply set eyes. His face is framed by thick waving hair and a finely curled beard. Except in primitive images he is rarely nude. He usually wears a long mantle which leaves his chest and right arm free. His attributes are the sceptre in his left hand, in his right hand the thunderbolt and at his feet the eagle. Often on his brow he wears a crown of oak-leaves.

The Marriages of Zeus. Before marrying Hera and associating her officially with his sovereignty, Zeus, among whose many functions that of procreation was pre-eminent, had contracted numerous unions.

His first wife was Metis (Wisdom) who, says Hesiod, 'knew more things than all the gods and men put together'. But Gaea and Uranus warned Zeus that if he had children by Metis they would be more powerful than he, and dethrone him. So, when Metis was about to give birth to Athene, Zeus, in order to forestall the danger, swallowed the mother and with her the unborn baby. By avoiding the risk of an embarrassing posterity in this manner he also now embodied supreme Wisdom – a double benefit.

Next he married Themis, daughter of Uranus and Gaea. Themis was the Law which regulates both physical and moral order. It is not surprising, then, that her children should be: the Horae or Seasons; Eunomia (Wise Legislation); Dike (Justice); Eirene (Peace), and finally the Fates or Moerae who were also said to be the daughters of Night. Even when she was replaced by Hera, Themis continued to remain near Zeus as an adviser, and she was always revered on Olympus.

Another Titaness, Mnemosyne, was the wife of Zeus. The god stayed nine nights with her, and when her time had come Mnemosyne gave birth to nine daughters, who were the Muses.

Zeus was also enamoured of Demeter, but the goddess repulsed his advances. He changed himself into a bull and violated her, and from this union was born Kore, also called Persephone.

The Oceanid Eurynome was also among Zeus' wives and was the mother of the three Graces or Charites.

Zeus and Hera. And then Zeus married Hera. Actually their relationship was already long established. In the days when Cronus

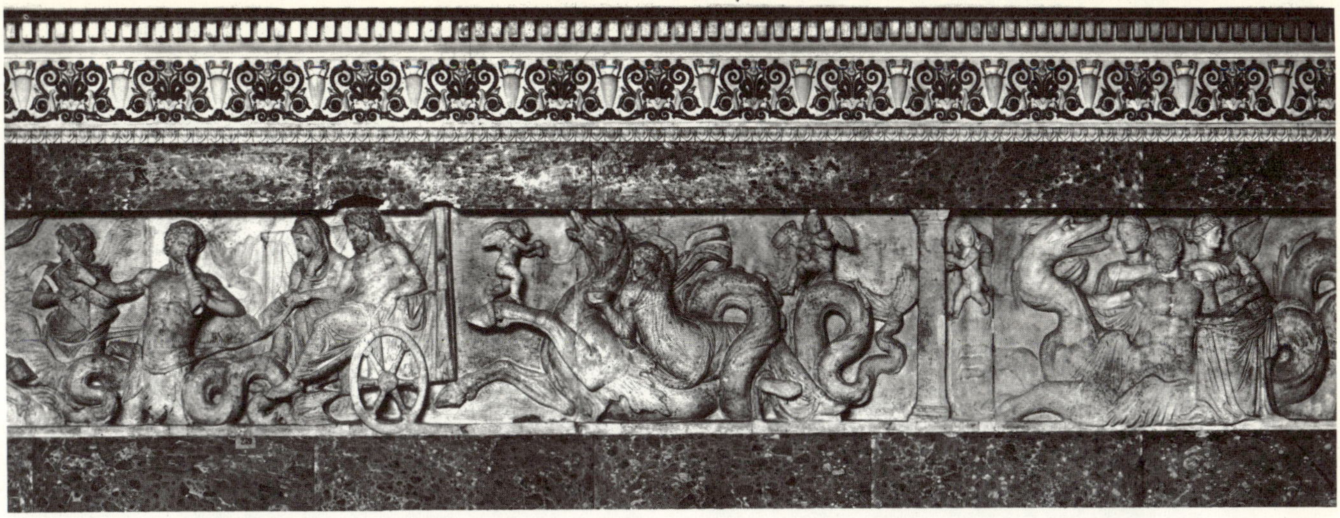

The marriage of Poseidon and Amphitrite. Poseidon and Amphitrite are seated in a carriage drawn by two Tritons one of whom plays a conch-shell and the other a lyre. Behind them follow a procession of Tritons and Nereids. The daughter of Oceanus or Nereus, Amphitrite at first fled from Poseidon but was later brought back by a dolphin to become his wife. Frieze from an altar in the temple of Neptune at Rome.

still reigned, the young goddess grew up in the island of Euboea under the care of her nurse Macris. Zeus came to her one day and bore her to Mount Cithaeron on the confines of Attica and Boeotia, where he lay with her. Another legend places the first encounter between Zeus and Hera in the region of the Hesperides, while at Cnossus in Crete, near the river Theris, they also pointed out the exact spot where the marriage of the divine couple was consummated. Pausanias relates the adventure differently. In order not to awaken his sister's suspicions Zeus came to her in the form of a cuckoo. It was winter and the bird seemed to be frozen with the cold. Touched by pity, the young goddess warmed the cuckoo by holding it against her breast. Zeus then reassumed his natural form and attempted to take advantage of the situation. Hera resisted at first and gave way only after Zeus had promised to marry her. The marriage, solemnly celebrated on Olympus, did not, however, put an end to Zeus' amorous enterprises. Braving Hera's jealousy and ignoring the misfortunes which this jealousy could bring upon its victims, Zeus continued enthusiastically to pursue goddesses and mortal women.

Zeus and the Titanesses. Zeus was not always successful. Thus, on the advice of Prometheus, he freely renounced Thetis for fear of begetting by her a son who would dethrone him. Nor could he overcome the resistance of the nymph Asteria, daughter of Coeus and Phoebe, who in order to escape him changed herself into a quail and threw herself into the sea where she became a floating island called, at first, Ortygia, and later Delos.

Leto was less shy than her sister Asteria and surrendered to Zeus' seductions. In this way she earned Hera's enmity and, as we shall later see, it was only after many misadventures that she was finally able to bring into the world her two children: Apollo and Artemis.

Maia, daughter of Atlas and Pleione, was more adroit and succeeded in evading Hera's jealous eye. She lived in Arcadia on Mount Cyllene. 'Escaping from the crowd of happy immortals,' says the Homeric hymn, 'Maia of the fair tresses lived in the depths of a dark cavern. It was here that the son of Cronus lay all night with the nymph whilst sweet sleep held alabaster-limbed Hera, sleep who thus deceives immortals and feeble men alike.' Maia gave birth to Hermes.

It was said that another daughter of Atlas, Electra, bore Zeus Harmonia – whom Hesiod, however, calls the daughter of Ares and Aphrodite – and Dardanus. Finally a third daughter of Atlas, Taygete, was pursued by Zeus. According to some accounts she was protected by Artemis, who turned her into a hind and only later restored her to her original form. In gratitude Taygete consecrated to the goddess a hind whose horns she had gilded and which we shall meet again during the labours of Hercules. According to other accounts Taygete submitted to Zeus and gave birth to Lacedaemon.

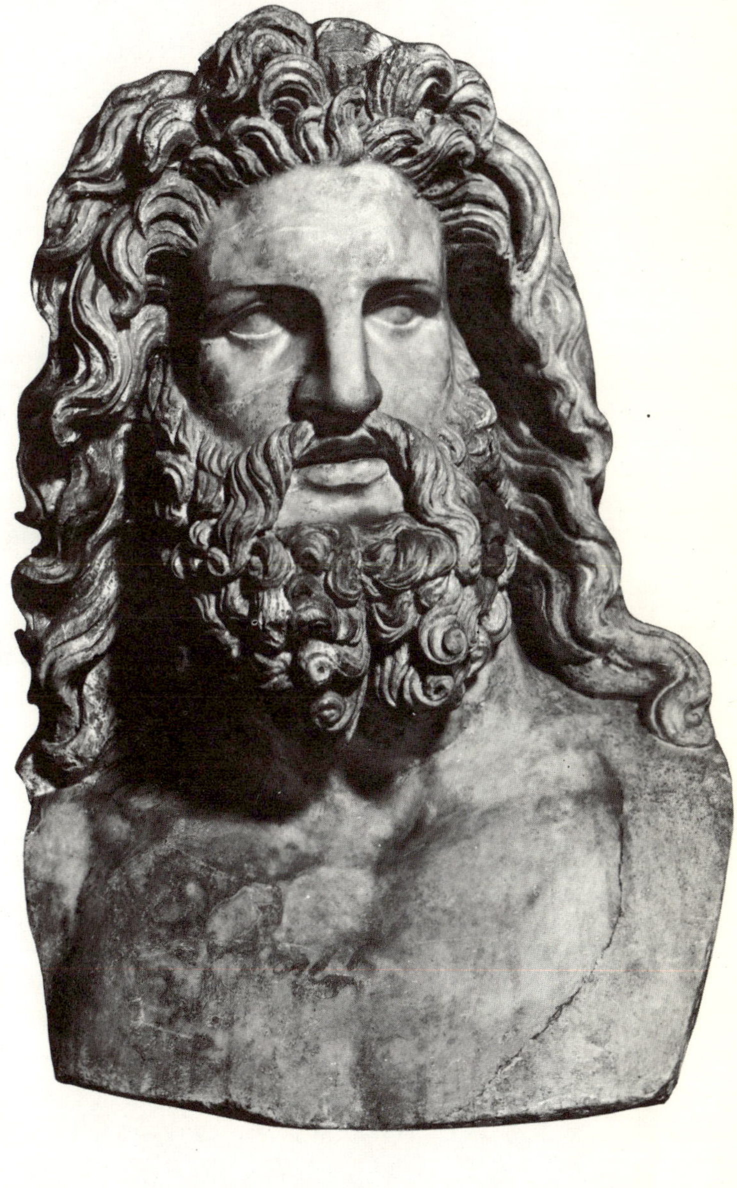

Zeus, 'The Father of gods and men'. He was the supreme god of the Greeks, the protector of laws and morals and the dispenser of good and evil. After defeating his father Cronus, he reigned supreme over the gods of Olympus and was the father of Athene, Artemis, Apollo, Ares and Dionysus and of innumerable other children by nymphs and mortals. His most famous sanctuary was at Dodona.
Greek sculpture, fourth century, B.C.

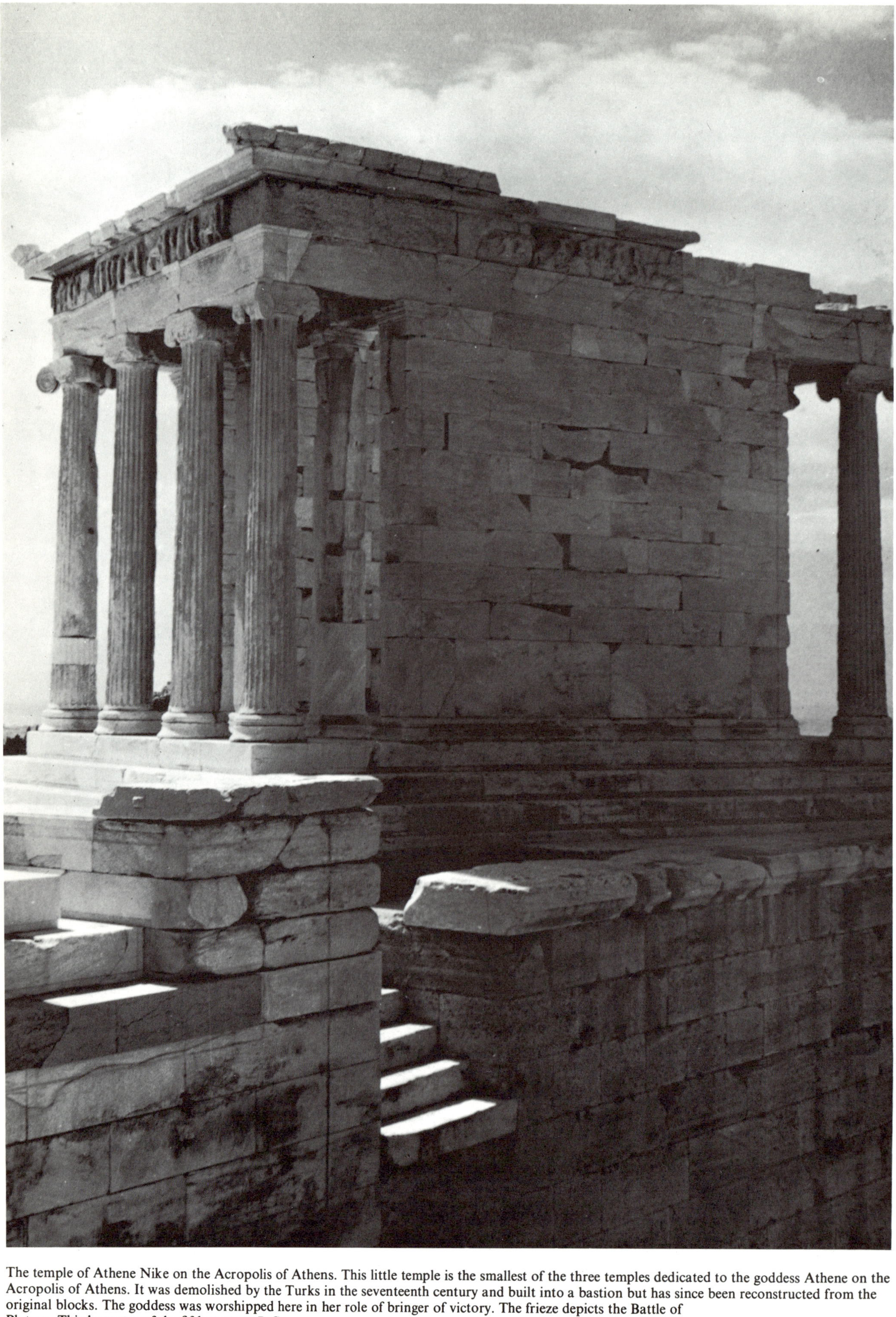

The temple of Athene Nike on the Acropolis of Athens. This little temple is the smallest of the three temples dedicated to the goddess Athene on the Acropolis of Athens. It was demolished by the Turks in the seventeenth century and built into a bastion but has since been reconstructed from the original blocks. The goddess was worshipped here in her role of bringer of victory. The frieze depicts the Battle of Plataea. Third quarter of the fifth century B.C.

Zeus and the Nymphs. Among the nymphs loved by Zeus must also be mentioned Aegina and Antiope, the daughters of the river-god Asopus. The former had been carried off by Zeus who, assuming the shape of an eagle or a flame, had borne her to the island of Oenone or Oenopia, where she gave birth to Aeacus. Asopus set out in search of them. From Sisyphus he discovered the name of his daughter's ravisher and the place where she had hidden herself. He was on the point of finding her when Zeus struck him with a thunderbolt and forced him to return to his river-bed. Others relate how Asopus surprised the two lovers: to protect Aegina from the paternal fury Zeus changed her into an island and himself into a rock.

As for Antiope – who, according to Pausanias, was not the daughter of Asopus but of Nycteus – Zeus approached her in the form of a satyr and surprised her when she was asleep. To hide her shame Antiope fled to Sicyon, where she married the king, Epopeus. Her father Nycteus killed himself with despair, but before he died he charged his brother Lycus to avenge his honour. Lycus seized Sicyon, put Epopeus to death and brought Antiope back, a prisoner. At Eleuthere Antiope gave birth to twins, Amphion and Zethus, whom she exposed on Mount Cithaeron and who later figured among the chief heroes of Theban legend.

The nymph Callisto was a daughter of Lycaon. She was a companion of Artemis and had made a vow of chastity. But Zeus was captivated by her extraordinary beauty. One day while the nymph was reposing in the woods Zeus presented himself to her in the form of Artemis. The young virgin welcomed him unsuspectingly, and when she realised her mistake it was already too late. She tried to hide her shame, but Artemis discovered what had occurred when one day she saw Callisto bathing with her companions. In order to shield the nymph from the rage of the goddess, Zeus changed Callisto into a bear. But Artemis pierced her with her arrows and she died giving birth to a son, Arcas, who was the ancestor of the Arcadians. As for Callisto, she was transformed into a constellation and became the Great Bear.

A similar adventure overtook Mera, daughter of Praetus. Mera too was a follower of Artemis and was also killed by the goddess for having given herself to Zeus. Before dying she gave birth to Locri, ancestor of the Locrians.

Zeus and Mortal Women. The first mortal woman whom Zeus loved was Niobe, daughter of Phoroneus and the nymph Laodice. She gave birth to Argos, founder of the city of that name. The same Phoroneus, son of Inachus, had a sister named Io who, in the former Heraeum, between Mycenae and Tiryns, exercised the functions of priestess of Hera. Zeus fell in love with her. In order to lie with her he took the form of a cloud. In spite of this stratagem Hera's suspicions were aroused. Zeus pleaded innocence and, in order to put his wife off the scent, changed his mistress into a white heifer. Hera pretended to be deceived and asked him for the heifer as a gift. Once it was in her possession she placed the animal under the care of Argus Panoptes – 'who sees all'. This Argus, son of Arestor, was a giant of redoubtable strength: he had once killed a bull which was ravaging Arcadia, and slain Echidna, daughter of Tartarus and Gaea. In addition he had one hundred eyes, of which fifty remained open while the other fifty closed in sleep. Zeus, however, ordered the cunning Hermes to set Io free. Hermes succeeded in charming the giant to sleep with the sound of his flute, and cut off

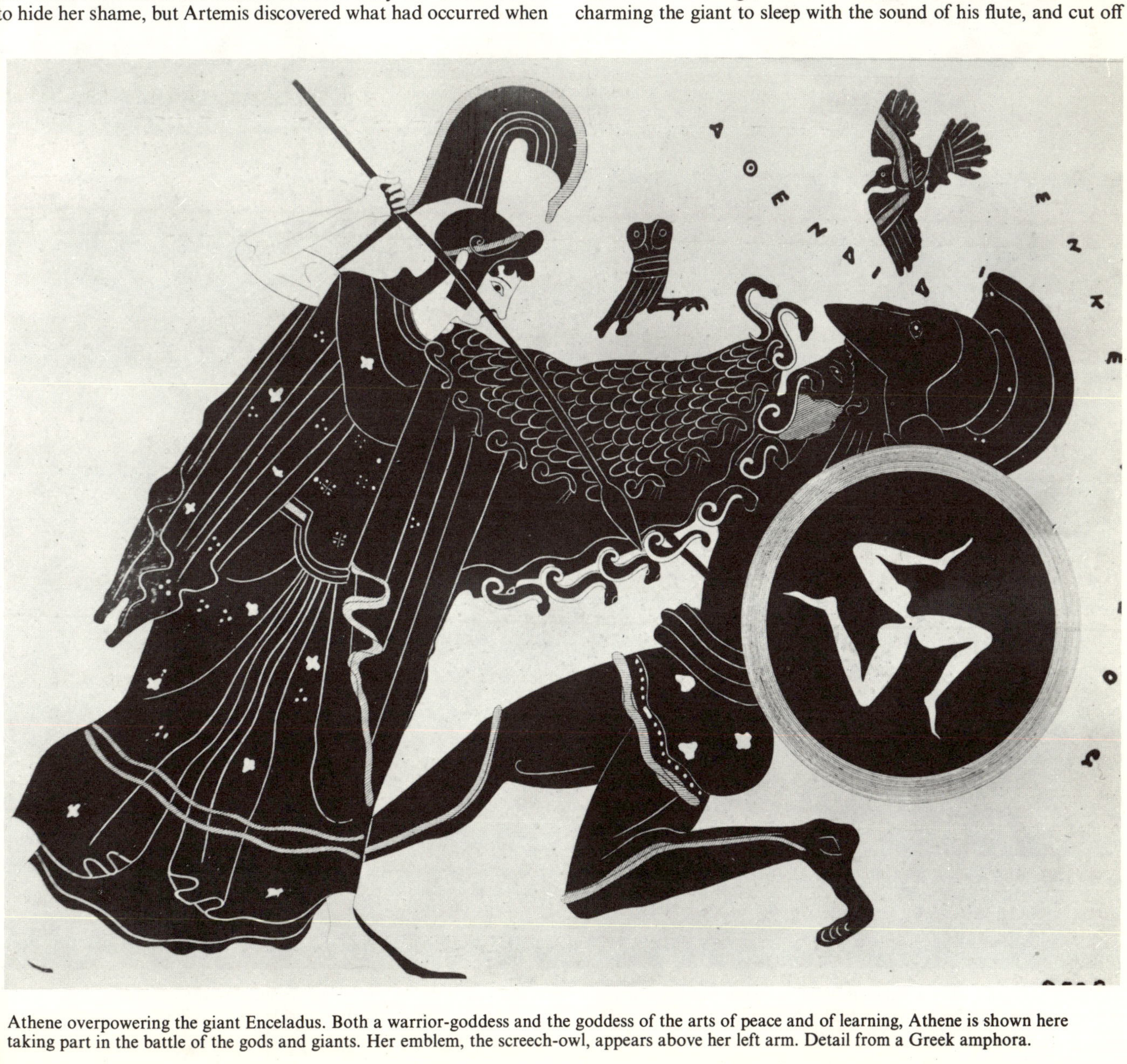

Athene overpowering the giant Enceladus. Both a warrior-goddess and the goddess of the arts of peace and of learning, Athene is shown here taking part in the battle of the gods and giants. Her emblem, the screech-owl, appears above her left arm. Detail from a Greek amphora.

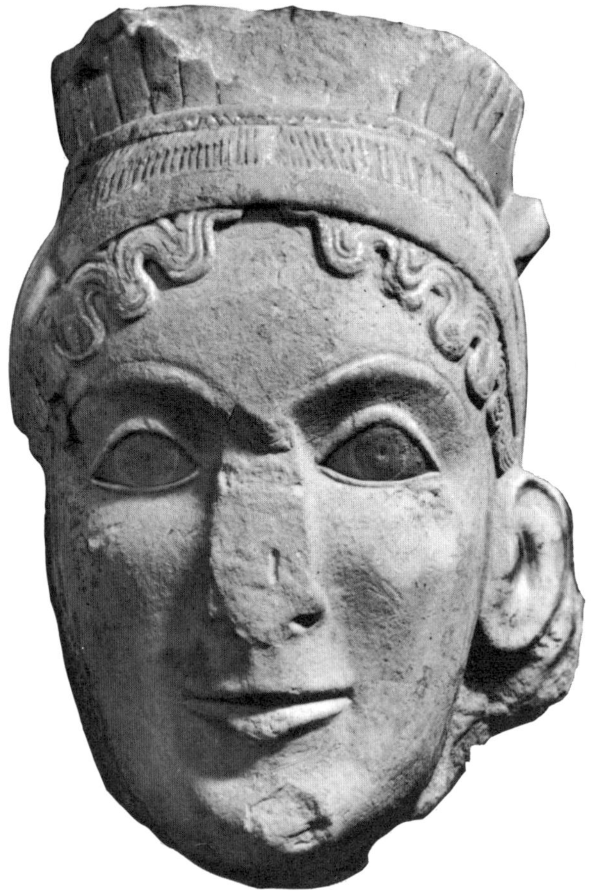

Head of Hera. This head is all that remains of a colossal cult group from the goddess's temple at Olympia which showed her seated on her throne with her husband Zeus standing armed beside her. Her hair is held by a narrow hairband while she wears a crown of leaves and blossoms on her head. The statue was originally painted, the goddess's hair being reddish-yellow and her hairband dark red. Grey limestone. *c.* 600 B.C.

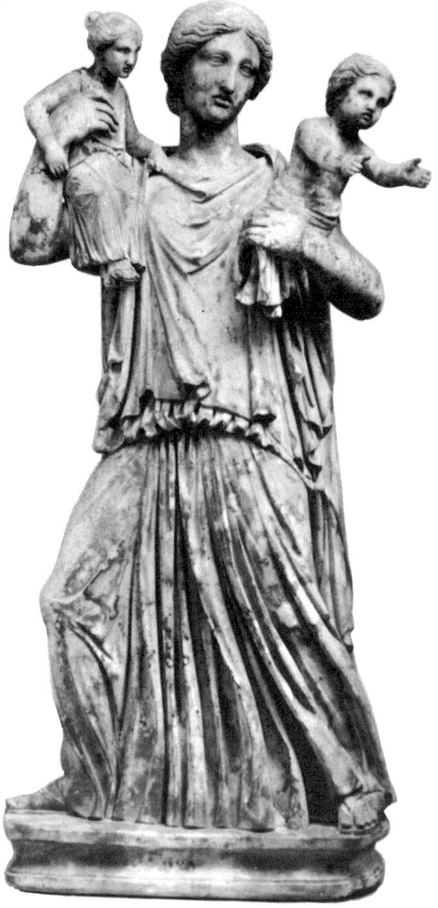

Leto with Apollo and Artemis. According to ancient tradition, Leto was the wife of Zeus before he married Hera. The daughter of the Titans Coeus and Phoebe, she bore him the twins Apollo and Artemis, the latter preceding her brother into the world by a day. It was only later that Leto was made a mistress of Zeus and a victim of Hera's jealousy. Her wistful expression betrays her sufferings.

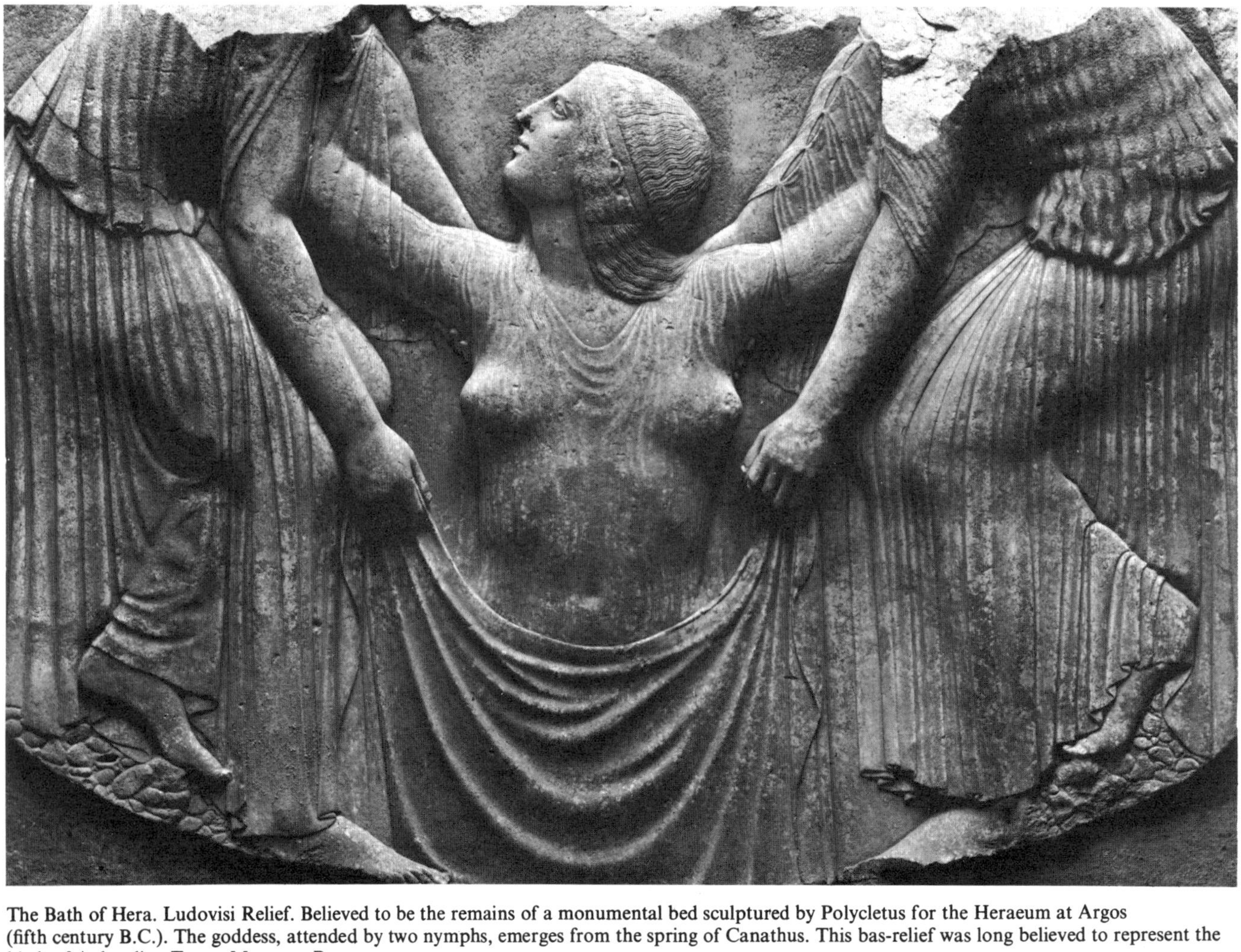

The Bath of Hera. Ludovisi Relief. Believed to be the remains of a monumental bed sculptured by Polycletus for the Heraeum at Argos (fifth century B.C.). The goddess, attended by two nymphs, emerges from the spring of Canathus. This bas-relief was long believed to represent the birth of Aphrodite. Terme Museum, Rome.

Interior of the temple of Hera at Paestum. Founded by Doric speaking colonists *c.* 600 B.C., Paestum (or Posidonia) in southern Italy possesses some of the most imposing ruins of the Hellenistic world. Of its three Greek temples the second temple of Hera (illustrated below) is not only the finest but is also the best-preserved Greek temple outside Attica. Built in the fifth century B.C. in the Doric style, it was for long believed to be a temple of Poseidon.

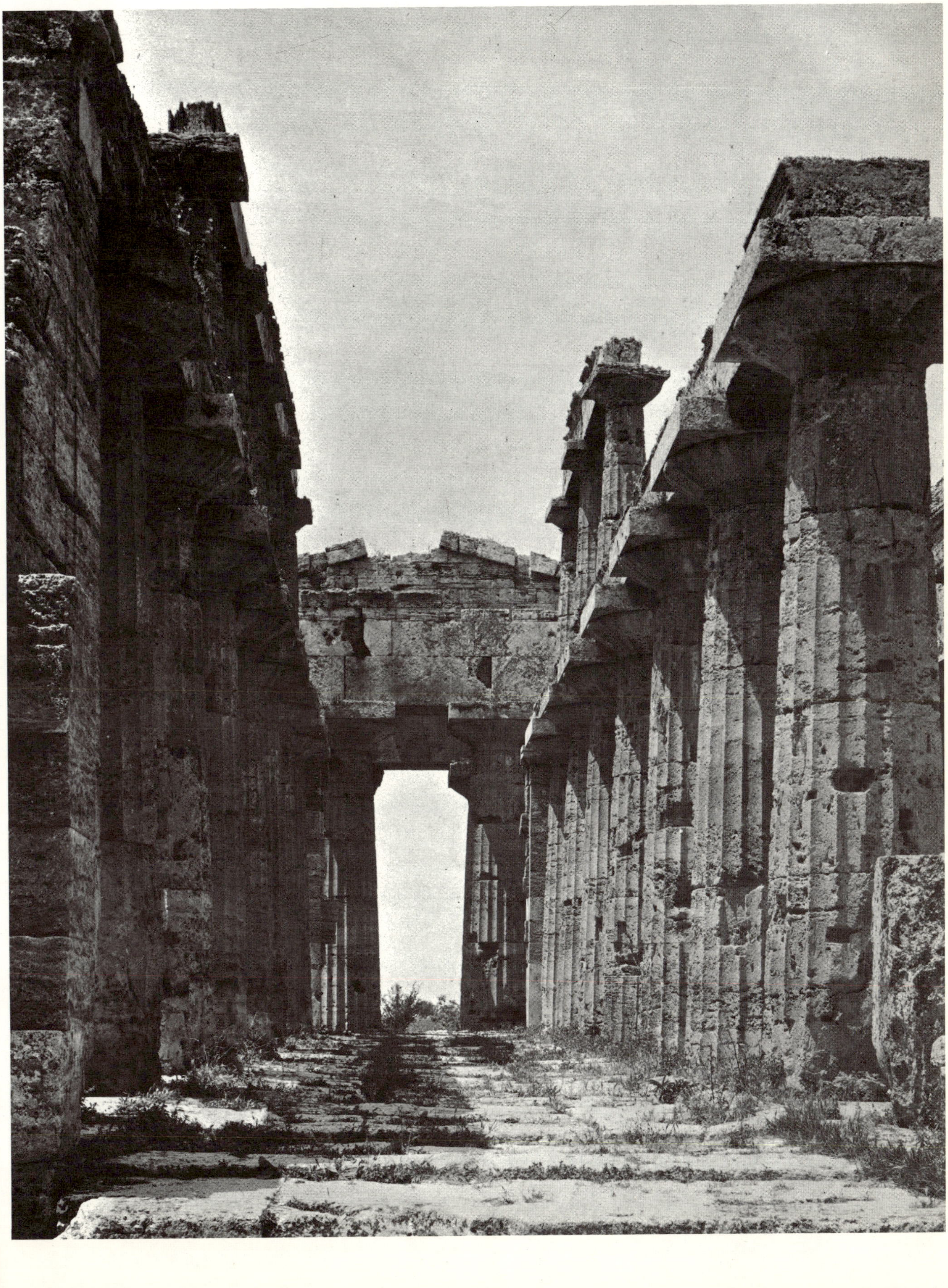

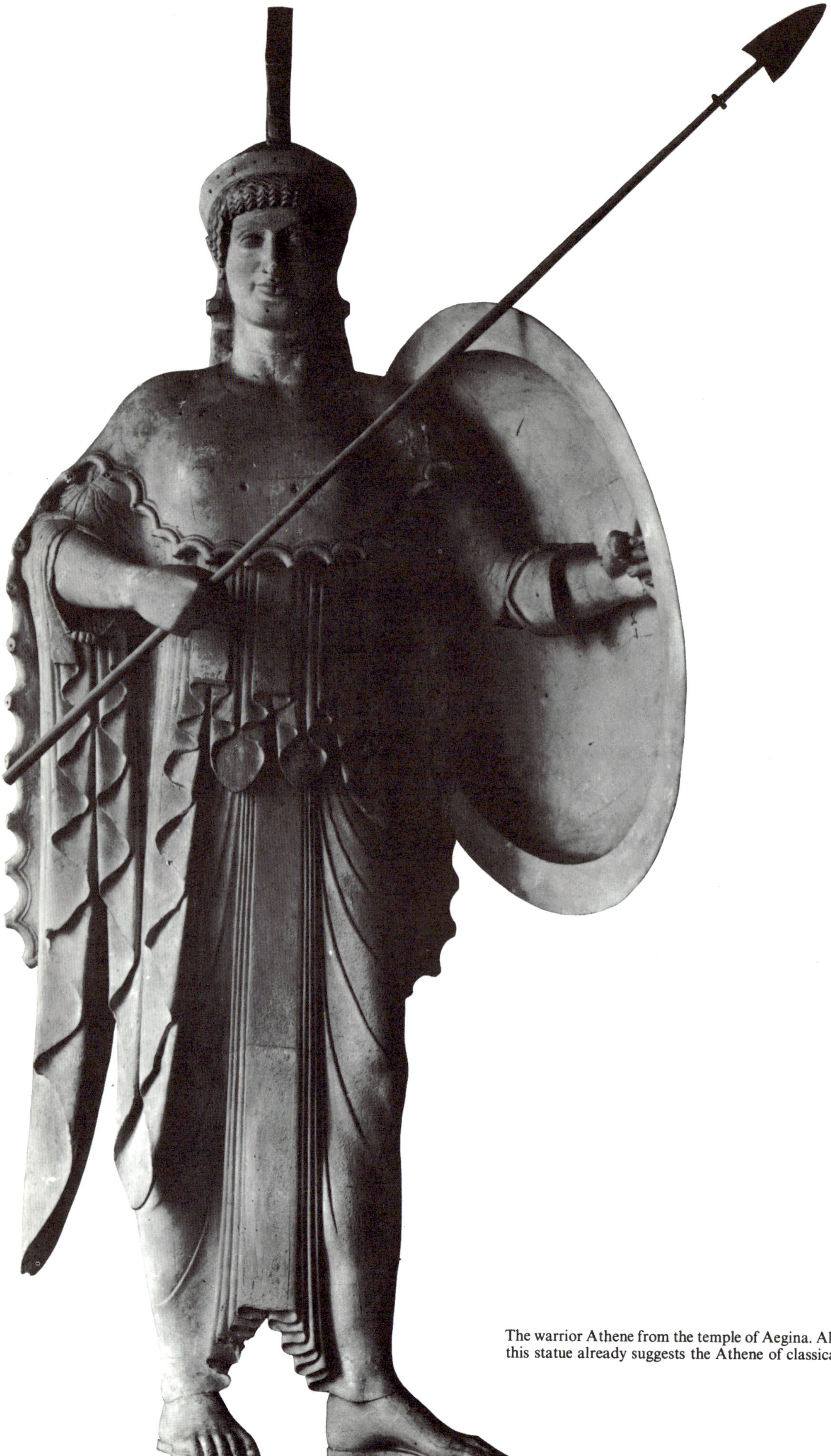

The warrior Athene from the temple of Aegina. Although archaic this statue already suggests the Athene of classical art. Munich Museum.

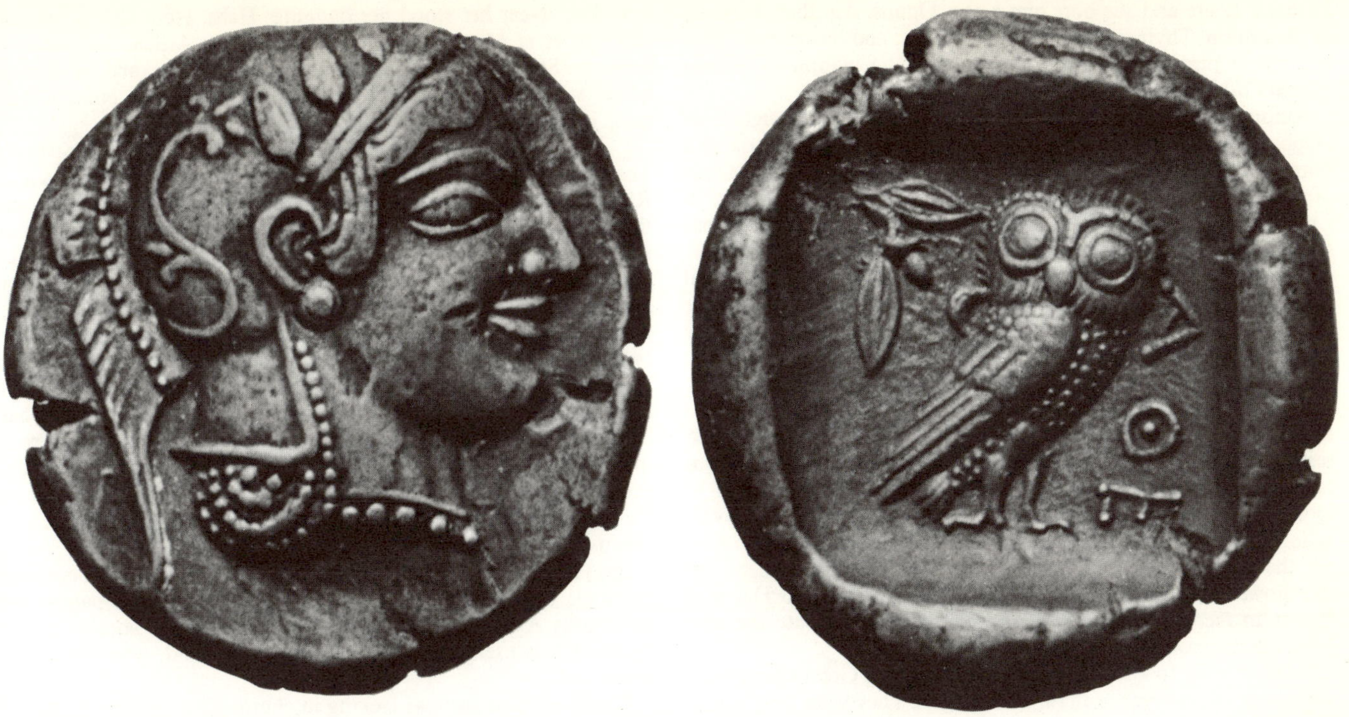

Archaic Head of Athene, helmeted. On the reverse side, the owl. A four drachma piece. Athens. Fifth century B.C.

his head. To honour Argus, who had served her, Hera distributed his eyes over the tail of her favourite bird, the peacock, whose plumage was thenceforth so brilliant. As for the unfor unate heifer, Hera sent a gad-fly to torture her. Driven mad by the stinging insect, Io fled across the world. She swam the Thracian Bosphorus, crossed the Ionian Sea which took her name and, having ranged Asia Minor, finally reached Egypt where, by a simple touch of the hand, Zeus restored her to her human form. She then bore a son, Epaphus – child of 'the touch'. But Hera was not disarmed. She ordered the Curetes to abduct the child. They obeyed and for this reason were slain by Zeus. Io at last found her child in Syria and returned to Egypt where she married the king, Telegonus. In later days Io became confused with the Egyptian goddess Isis and her son Epaphus with Apis.

At Argos reigned Acrisius who had but one daughter, Danae. An oracle had told Acrisius that one day his daughter would bring into the world a son by whose hands he would perish. Acrisius thereupon had a chamber of bronze built underground – or some say a tower – and in it locked Danae with her nurse. But Zeus, who had been attracted by the girl's charms, found a way to enter the chamber in the form of a shower of gold and frequently visited Danae. The result was the birth of a son, Perseus. Acrisius was terrified when he learned of this miraculous birth, and shut up both mother and child in a chest which he cast into the sea. Tossed by the waves, the chest was finally carried to the island of Seriphus where a fisherman, one Dictys, brother of King Polydectes, caught it in his nets. Danae and Perseus were thus saved. We shall see, when we come to Perseus, how this romantic adventure continued.

More terrible still was Hera's jealousy of and the vengeance she took on another of Zeus' loves, Semele, daughter of Cadmus. When she learned of the relationship between her husband and this mortal girl Hera came to her rival in disguise and suggested that Semele ask her lover to appear before her in all the brilliance of his majesty. Zeus tried in vain to dissuade Semele from making such an unreasonable demand. Semele insisted. The god gave in, and visited her in his chariot of glory, surrounded by lightning and thunder. The sight of the great god in all his dazzling splendour was too much for mortal eyes and Semele perished, consumed by celestial flames. Zeus gathered up the child she bore in her womb and enclosed it in his own thigh until the day set for its birth: it was to be Dionysus.

The rape of Europa had less tragic consequences. Daughter of Phoenix or of Agenor, King of Phoenicia, and of Telephassa, the young Europa was playing one day at the water's edge, gathering flowers with her companions. Her attention was caught by the sight of a bull with glistening hide who browsed peacefully among her father's herd. His air, gentle and at the same time majestic, struck her. She did not suspect that this bull was none other than the master of the gods, Zeus himself, who had assumed this shape in order to deceive the girl of whom he had become enamoured. Trustingly Europa approached and caressed the animal, who very gallantly knelt before her. She climbed playfully on to his mighty back, and began to wreathe flowers around his powerful horns. Suddenly the bull reared to his feet, at a bound sprang into the waves, and carried the weeping virgin across the vast sea. They finally reached the southern coast of Crete, at Gortyna. In the days of Theophrastus the plane tree under which Zeus made the young Phoenician his mistress was still pointed out. Because it had witnessed and sheltered the divine union this tree received the privilege of retaining its foliage in all seasons. Europa gave birth to Minos, Rhadamanthys and Sarpedon. All three were adopted by the King of Crete, Asterius, who subsequently became Europa's husband.

Although it was within his province to guard the sanctity of marriage, Zeus on occasion did not hesitate to pay court to married women. Thus he fell in love with Leda, the wife of Tyndareus. One evening when the young woman was bathing in a pool she saw floating majestically towards her a swan of dazzling whiteness. It was Zeus. The same night Leda also lay with her own husband; afterwards she bore Pollux and Helen, children of Zeus; and Castor and Clytemnestra, children of Tyndareus.

In order to seduce Alcmene, Zeus employed another stratagem. He wished, Hesiod says, 'to produce a son who would one day be a powerful protector for gods and men alike', and he had set his heart on the wife of the Theban chief, Amphitryon. But as he knew she was virtuous and incorruptible he took advantage of Amphitryon's absence to assume Amphitryon's own appearance. Alcmene welcomed Zeus in this disguise exactly as though he were her actual husband. When the real Amphitryon returned a few hours later he was surprised by his wife's lack of enthusiasm while she, in her turn, was astonished that he had so quickly forgotten the marks of tenderness she had so recently bestowed upon him. The mystery was finally cleared up by the soothsayer Teiresias. From the double union twins were born: Hercules, son of Zeus; and Iphicles, son of Amphitryon.

Such were the more memorable of Zeus' love affairs. But many more were attributed to him and his progeny was enormous.

By him the Oceanid Pluto had Tantalus. The Danaid Anaxithea and Hesione had, respectively, Olenus, founder of Olenus in Achaia, and Orchomenus, king of the city of the same name in Boeotia. Orchomenus' own daughter, Elara, was also loved by Zeus who, to protect her from Hera's jealousy, hid her under the earth, where she gave birth to the giant Tityus. Zeus also loved Neaera, who bore Aegle. He carried off Protogenia, daughter of Deucalion, from her husband Locre and she bore him a son, Opuns. Another daughter of Deucalion, Thyia, was also loved by Zeus; and he changed himself into a pigeon in order to seduce a young nymph of Achaia named Phthia.

Among the other mistresses of Zeus were Thalia, daughter of Hephaestus, who became the mother of the Palici; Thymbris who bore a son, Pan; Dia, wife of Ixion, whom Zeus seduced in the shape of a horse and who became the mother of Pirithous; finally, in Crete, Carme, who gave birth to Britomartis; and Cassiopeia, whose son Atymnius was honoured at Gortyna with Europa.

One could prolong the list, which was enriched by the regional pride of various provinces of Greece or even small towns, eager to give themselves a divine ancestor. We have seen, in fact, how a number of Zeus' offspring became the ancestors of a tribe or the founders of cities. But some of these unions of the god can be explained in other ways. Some are solar myths: for instance the union of Zeus, god of the luminous ether, with Leto and Leda, who seem to have been deities of the night. Others are merely allegorical accounts of historical facts: the Phoenician Europa brought to Crete by a bull could represent the contribution of Asiatic civilisation to that of Crete, symbolised by the bull-god. Finally others are the romanticised expression of great natural phenomena: in the shower of gold which penetrates to the subterranean Danae it is easy to recognise the rays of the sun which germinate the seed buried in the ground.

In attributing to Zeus all these adventures, the Greeks then were not guilty of irreverence towards their god. They were only translating the emotions they felt in face of nature's great mysteries into gracious and poetic form. Or else, more naively, they were creating for themselves a noble ancestry.

HERA

The name Hera was once believed to be connected with the Latin root *herus* (master) and with an old Greek word which meant 'earth'. Today, however, it is agreed that Hera is related to the Sanskrit *svar* (the Sky). Hera was then originally queen of the sky, the celestial virgin (hence her epithet Parthenia), and at first quite independent of Zeus. Their marriage was arranged afterwards, in order to explain the fusion of two cults which had at first been distinct. Some authorities even see in the hostility of Hera towards her husband a vestige of the resistance which the worshippers of Hera opposed to the rival cult of Zeus. Others interpret the noisy quarrels of the divine couple as a mythological translation of storms or the 'struggle of the meteors and atmospheric disturbances in revolt against the sky'.

Her Functions. Hera, however, soon lost her cosmic character and retained only her moral attributes. She was thought of as Woman deified. She presided over all phases of feminine existence. Thus Temenus, son of Pelasgus, consecrated at Stymphalus three temples to her: the first to the child-goddess, the second to the wife-goddess, the third to the widow-goddess. But primarily she was the goddess of marriage (*Gamelia*) and maternity. She represented the idealised type of wife.

Representations. Hera was depicted as a young woman, fully developed, of a chaste and rather severe beauty. Her forehead is normally crowned with a diadem or with a high crown of cylindrical shape, the *polos*. She wears a long tunic or *chiton* and is enveloped in a veil which adds to her bearing of nobility, reserved and full of modesty. Her attributes are a sceptre surmounted by a cuckoo (in allusion to the circumstances of her nuptials) and a pomegranate, symbol of conjugal love and fruitfulness. The bird sacred to her is the peacock, whose spangled plumage recalls the stars in the vault of heaven – and testifies to the service of hundred-eyed Argus.

Her Cult. Like Zeus, Hera was venerated on the summits of mountains. In Greece the chief centre of her cult was Argos. Here she had five or six temples, the oldest of which had been built by Phoroneus. It was the Heraeum at Argos which housed the famous statue of Hera in gold and ivory by Polycletus. The goddess was represented seated on a throne, her brow crowned by a diadem on which were depicted the Horae and the Graces. In her left hand she held a pomegranate and in her right a sceptre surmounted by a cuckoo. Near her stood her daughter Hebe. Hera also possessed sanctuaries at Mycenae, Olympus, Sparta, in Attica, Boeotia and Euboea. She was particularly venerated in Crete and at Samos where stood the greatest of her temples, which was built, it was said, by the Argonauts.

The Legend of Hera. Hera was the oldest daughter of Cronus and Rhea, born, according to the Samians, on the isle of Samos, on the banks of the river Imbrasos near a waterwillow which could still be seen in the days of Pausanias. She had been brought up, according to some, by Macris or by the daughters of the river Asterion; according to others, by the Horae or Seasons. Her childhood was spent on the isle of Euboea and we have seen how her brother Zeus found her there and made her his wife. From then on Hera was associated with Zeus' sovereignty and became the chief feminine deity of Olympus. She sat on a golden throne beside her husband, and when she entered the assembly of the gods all rose in homage to her. On Olympus her marriage to Zeus had been the occasion of great rejoicing. All the Immortals had taken part in the procession and the Fates themselves had chanted the hymeneal chorus.

But Hera's happiness was not unclouded. She had given Zeus four children: the gracious Hebe, Ilithyia, mother of birth-pangs, the impetuous Ares, and the skilful Hephaestus. Her fidelity to her husband was exemplary. He, on the other hand, was constantly unfaithful.

It was not that she was lacking in charm. She took great care of her beauty. Every year she went to bathe in the spring Canathus at Nauplia and in these marvellous waters each time renewed her virginity. The 'white-armed goddess' was irresistible when she anointed her lovely body with an oil whose sweetness was such that it filled the whole earth and sky with its fragrance. When she had arranged her divine tresses, when she had pinned to her breast with golden clasps the robe Athene had woven for her with such art, put on her ear-rings, exquisitely worked and set with precious clusters of three drops, and draped from her head a glorious veil white as the sun, Zeus himself, seeing her thus arrayed, cried: 'Never has love for goddess or mortal woman so flooded my senses and filled my heart!'

Hera would never have lacked suitors had she wished them. Ixion, King of the Lapithae, when invited to dine with the gods, had only to turn his eyes towards her to be inflamed with irresistible desire. In the madness of his passion he even embraced a cloud which Zeus had shaped to resemble Hera. Ixion was chastised for his insolence: he was bound to a fiery wheel which whirled him perpetually through the sky.

Hera, proud of her own virtue, did not endure the continual faithlessness of her husband without protest. Shortly after her marriage she left Olympus in vexation and returned to the isle of Euboea. In order to bring her back again Zeus employed a pleasant stratagem. He had a veiled statue carried around in a chariot and let it be everywhere known that this was the new fiancée of the master of the gods. In a transport of jealousy and wounded pride Hera arrested the chariot, lacerated the robes of her supposed rival and, discovering the trick her husband had played on her, returned somewhat crestfallen to Olympus.

The renewed infidelities of Zeus incited her to avenge herself physically on his person. One day, assisted by Poseidon, Apollo and Athene, she succeeded in binding him with thongs. It would have been the end of Zeus' power had not Thetis summoned to his rescue the hundred-armed giant whom the gods called Briareus and men called Aegaeon. 'Proud of his glory, he sat beside the son of Cronus; and the gods were struck with terror and did not enchain Zeus.'

Hera considered it equally outrageous that Zeus alone and unaided had given birth to Athene. In her rage she invoked the earth and the vast heavens and the Titans imprisoned in Tartarus, and implored their favour so that she, too, might bear unaided a child 'who should be in no way inferior in strength to Zeus'. Her wishes were granted and when her time came she gave birth 'not to a son who resembled gods or men, but to the frightful, the terrible Typhon, scourge of mankind'. This monster is confused with Typhoeus, son of Gaea and Tartarus, against whom Zeus had had so hard a struggle.

Hera was roughly punished for these vain attempts to revolt. One day Zeus beat and bruised her, and when Hephaestus tried to defend his mother Zeus seized his too-zealous son by one foot and flung him from the heights of Olympus. On another occasion Zeus attached an anvil to each of Hera's ankles, bound her hands with bracelets of unbreakable gold and suspended her from the sky, surrounded by clouds.

Though Hera was forced to submit she could at least vent her fury on her rivals. She caused Semele's death, for a long time persecuted Io, and tried to prevent the confinement of Leto and of Alcmene. She was equally remorseless towards the children of her rivals and towards their families. Hercules was her victim, and Ino, Semele's sister, was cruelly punished for having cared for the infant Dionysus.

The vindictive temper of the goddess was not only displayed when her conjugal honour was at stake. Because Antigone, daughter of Laomedon, had boasted of having hair more beautiful than Hera's, Hera turned her locks into serpents. Because they had treated a wooden statue of the goddess with contempt the daughters of Proetus, Lysippe and Iphianassa, were stricken with leprosy and madness. They went raging half-nude through the Peloponnese and were only cured by the costly intervention of the seer Melampus. Melampus demanded as the price of his services a third of Proetus' kingdom. Proetus at first refused; but his daughters' madness became worse. He went again to Melampus, who raised his price and insisted on a second third of the kingdom for his brother Bias. Proetus consented, and from Hera Melampus obtained the two girls' restoration to health. Another tradition, to be sure, attributes the madness of Proetus' daughters to the anger of Dionysus.

Finally Hera never forgave the Trojan Paris for having preferred Aphrodite on the occasion of the famous beauty contest on Mount Ida, and her rancour was only satisfied when the entire Trojan race had been annihilated.

ATHENE

Of the many derivations proposed for the name of Athene (or Athena) none is really satisfactory. The Sanskrit *vadh* (to strike) and *adh* (hill) have been suggested, as well as the Greek for 'flower' and 'nurse'! The poetic epithet *Pallas* frequently joined to the name Athene comes either from the Greek 'to strike' or more probably from the Greek 'girl'.

Her Character and Functions. Although certain scholars have seen in Athene a personification of moisture, analogous to the Hindu Sarasvati, it seems more probable that she was in origin a storm- and lightning-goddess. Hence her normal attribute, the aegis – which in primitive times signified the stormy night – and her epithet as a goddess 'of the brilliant eyes'. She would thus be analogous to the Vedic goddess Vach. But Athene very quickly lost this meteorological character.

Her functions were many: she was venerated among the great divinities in her quality of warrior-goddess, as goddess of the arts of peace and as goddess of prudent intelligence.

To Athene the warrior – her oldest manifestation – belong the epithets *Promachos* ('who fights in the foremost ranks') and *Alalcomeneis* ('who repulses the enemy'). She was the protectress of towns and the guardian of acropolises.

The pacific Athene protected various industries. She was pre-eminently the *Ergane,* or working woman, and was the patron of architects and sculptors, as well as of spinners and weavers. She also protected horses (*Hippia*) and oxen (*Boarmia*). The olive tree owed to her its fruit. Her wisdom, which earned her the epithet *Pronoia* (the Foreseeing), made her the counsellor-goddess (*Boulaia*) and the goddess of the Assembly (*Agoraia*). Athene's emblem was the owl.

Her Cult. Though she was honoured throughout Greece Athene was the object of an especial cult in Athens. On the Acropolis she had, besides the Parthenon, two other temples: the temple of Athene Nike and the Erechtheum.

The chief festivals of the cult of Athene were: the *Arrephoria,* in the course of which two little girls of noble family, from seven to eleven years old, descended from the Acropolis to deposit in an underground chamber near the sanctuary of Aphrodite mysterious objects which they carried in a basket; the *Scirophoria,* when priests and priestesses walked in solemn procession under a vast parasol (*sciron*); and finally the *Panathenaea* which dated from the days of Theseus and consisted of a solemn procession to the Acropolis in which was carried to the goddess a *peplos* made by the most skilled workmen in Athens. Taking part were not only priests and magistrates but also girls carrying baskets, old men bearing olive branches and young men on horseback. During the Panathenaea were held races, gymnastic games, regattas and contests of music, singing and dancing.

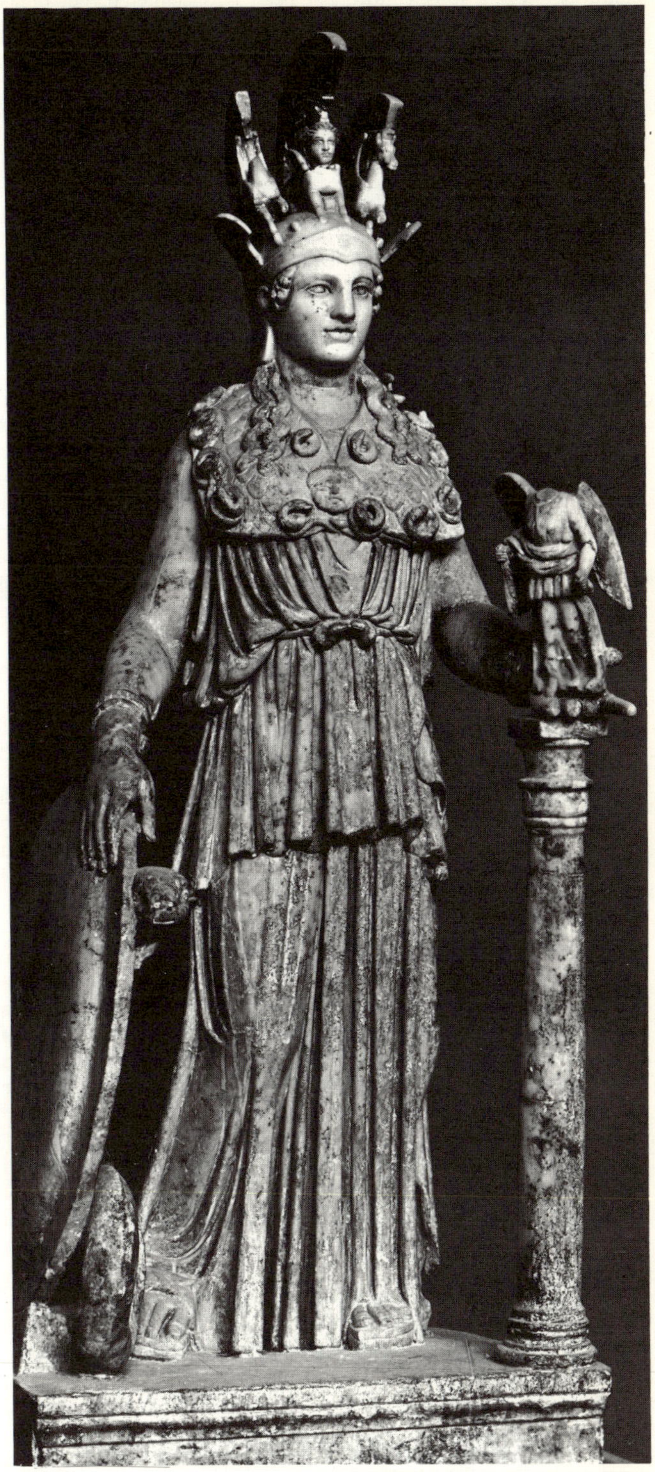

Athene Parthenos. This statue reproduces, with a slight variation in posture, the celebrated Athene of Phidias. Athens Museum.

Representations. The oldest representations of Athene were the *palladia.* Originally the palladia were stones which were said to have fallen from the sky and to which protective power was attributed. Later these stones were replaced by statues in wood (*xoana*) which had the same celestial origin. In them the goddess was depicted with her body sheathed in tight draperies, and in her hands she held a shield and spear. The most celebrated statue of the warrior Athene was that of the Parthenon, the work of Phidias. The goddess, standing, wore a long chiton; her head was helmeted, her breast covered with the aegis, her right hand rested against a spear and in her left hand she held a winged victory.

The Birth of Athene. When Zeus swallowed his wife Metis she had been about to give birth to a child. Shortly afterwards Zeus was tortured by an intolerable headache. To cure him Hephaestus – some said Prometheus – split open his skull with a bronze axe and from the gaping wound, shouting a triumphant cry of victory, sprang Athene – 'fully armed and brandishing a sharp javelin'. At the sight all the Immortals were struck with astonishment and filled with awe. 'Great Olympus was profoundly shaken by the dash and impetuosity of the bright-eyed goddess. The earth echoed with a terrible sound, the sea trembled and its dark waves rose...'

In Crete they said that the goddess had been hidden in a cloud and that it was by striking this cloud with his head that Zeus had caused Athene to emerge. The event was supposed to have taken place near Cnossus beside a stream, the Triton: whence the epithet Tritogeneia (born of Triton) often given to Athene. It was also explained by making her the daughter of Poseidon and of Lake Tritonis. Finally some said that Athene's father was the giant Pallas whom she had killed because he wished to ravish her. But these various relationships were dubious and it was generally agreed that Athene was the daughter of Zeus, engendered by the god himself.

This birth, in which she had played no part, infuriated Hera who, in reprisal, gave unassisted birth to the monster Typhon.

Athene was Zeus' favourite child. His preference for her was marked and his indulgence towards her so extreme that it aroused the jealousy of the other gods.

'Thou hast fathered,' says Ares to Zeus, 'a rash and foolish daughter who delights only in guilty acts. All the other gods who live on Olympus obey thee and each of us submits to thy will. But she, thou never curbest neither by word nor deed; she does as she pleases.'

Athene, the Warrior Goddess. The manner in which Athene made her first appearance revealed her warlike proclivities. And, indeed, she delighted above all in battle. We have seen her taking part in the war against the giants, killing Pallas and hurling her chariot against Enceladus whom she finally crushed under the island of Sicily. We find her again, equally belligerent and ardent, in the battles which raged beneath the ramparts of Troy. Not satisfied with stimulating the ardour of the Greeks – whom she favoured – she entered the skirmish herself. She put on her head a helmet of gold with jutting crest 'vast enough to cover the foot-soldiers of a hundred towns'. Over her shoulder she slung the aegis which she had fashioned, according to some, from the skin of the giant Pallas or which – as was more generally held – was made from the hide of the goat Amaltheia. Zeus had used it for the first time during the war with the Titans and afterwards presented it to his daughter. It was a sort of cuirass or breastplate, fringed and bordered with snakes and bearing in the centre the horrifying head of the Gorgon. Thus armed, Athene mounted on to the chariot of Diomedes, seized the whip and reins herself, and flung the horses against Ares, whom she stretched on the ground with a blow of her spear.

The memory of Athene's warlike prowess was perpetuated in Libya in annual festivals during which girls, divided into two camps, would stage a furious battle with sticks and stones.

Athene, Protectress of Heroes. Herself a warrior, Athene protected the brave and valorous. When Hercules, a victim of Hera's hostility, undertook his arduous labours Athene stood at his side to help and comfort him. It was she who gave him the brazen cymbals whose sound frightened the birds of Lake Stymphalus. It was she who escorted him when he brought Cerberus from the underworld. Finally it was she who, after his death, welcomed him on the threshold of Olympus. And so, when Hercules won the golden apples of the Hesperides, he offered them in homage to this tutelary goddess.

In the same way Athene also guided Perseus on his expedition against the Gorgons. As the hero dared not look into the terrifying face of the Medusa she guided his arm so that he could strike the monster. In gratitude Perseus afterwards gave Athene the Gorgon's head which she placed on her shield. Athene's part in the adventures of Perseus was so active that certain traditions say that she herself killed the Medusa by striking her during her sleep. This theory gave rise to several legends; for instance, that the battle between Athene and the Gorgon was the result of a beauty contest; and that the goddess gathered up the blood of her victim and made a gift of it either to Asclepius or to Erichthonius – blood which had issued from the left vein brought death, blood from the right vein restored life.

Athene was also kindly disposed towards Bellerophon: she appeared to him in a dream and gave him a golden bridle, thanks to which he was able to tame the horse Pegasus.

Finally she protected Odysseus successfully against all the perils which assailed him on his return from Troy, and in the guise of the sage Mentor she guided young Telemachus during his efforts to find his father again.

Athene's Chastity. On all these occasions when Athene came to the aid of heroes it was because they were worthy of her esteem, not because of any amorous attraction. Athene was a striking exception to Olympian society because of her absolute chastity. In spite of calumny and insinuations about supposed relations with Helios, Hephaestus and even Hercules, her heart remained insensitive to the pangs of love and she defended her virginity fiercely. Woe to anyone who wounded her modesty!

One day when she was bathing with the nymph Chariclo, Teiresias by chance beheld her. He was guilty of no more than involuntary indiscretion. Athene, nevertheless, punished him by depriving him of his sight. In spite of her companion's plea for pity she refused to revoke her decision, but to soften the harshness of the punishment she conferred upon the unhappy Teiresias the gift of foretelling the future.

Hephaestus became enamoured of Athene. One day when the goddess came to see him about making a suit of armour for her he attempted to violate her. Athene fled, pursued by the limping god. He caught up with her, but she defended herself so effectively that Hephaestus was unable to accomplish his criminal design and, instead, scattered his seed on the earth, which shortly afterwards gave birth to a son, Erichthonius. The child was found by Athene, who brought him up unknown to the other gods. She enclosed the infant in a basket which she confided to the daughters of Cecrops, forbidding them to open it. One of the sisters, Pandrosos, obeyed; the other two, Herse and Aglauros, could not control their curiosity. But the moment they opened the basket they fled in terror; for around the infant a serpent was coiled. They were stricken with madness by Athene, and flung themselves off the top of the Acropolis. Erichthonius grew to maturity and became king of Athens, where he established the solemn cult of Athene.

The Quarrel between Athene and Poseidon. Previously the goddess had already shown particular benevolence to the land of Athens. In the days of King Cecrops a dispute had arisen between her and Poseidon for the possession of Attica. To affirm his rights Poseidon struck the rock of the Acropolis with his trident and a salt water spring gushed forth. According to another tradition it was a horse which appeared under Poseidon's trident. Athene, in her turn, caused an olive tree to sprout on the Acropolis, a tree which could be seen in the time of Pericles, still alive in spite of having been burned by the Persians during the invasion of Xerxes. Asked to settle the dispute the gods, on the evidence of Cecrops, pronounced in favour of Athene.

The Gifts of Athene. Athene was as benevolent in peace as she was redoubtable in war, and rendered valuable service to mankind. She taught the people of Cyrene the art of taming horses. She showed Erichthonius how to harness the first war chariots. She was present while Jason's companions were building the ship *Argo*. Her skill was revealed in the humblest handicrafts: she invented the potter's wheel and made the first vases. But above all she excelled in woman's work. The art of weaving cloth and embellishing it with wonderful embroidery had no secrets from her. The Immortals relied on her skill and it was she who embroidered Hera's veil. She was jealous of her accomplishments and allowed no one to surpass her.

In Lydia there lived a girl named Arachne who was renowned for her skill in handling needle and spindle. One day she dared to challenge the goddess to compete with her. Athene arrived in the guise of an old woman and asked Arachne to withdraw her impious challenge. Arachne refused. Athene reassumed her divine form and accepted the challenge. Arachne at once drew threads across her loom and with cunning hand guided the shuttle through the taut netting. As a subject, she had chosen to weave the loves of the gods. When she had finished she submitted her work to Athene for examination. The goddess tried in vain to discover any imperfection in it. Furious at her failure and unwilling to admit defeat, Athene changed Arachne into a spider and condemned her eternally to spin, and to draw from her own body the thread with which to weave her web.

Although Athene's activities were chiefly concerned with useful work she was not averse to artistic creation. Certain traditions originating in Boeotia attributed to her the invention of the flute. They said that the goddess had thought of blowing into a stag's horn, pierced with holes, in order to imitate the plaintive whistling sound made by the Gorgon when Perseus cut its throat. But in Athens it was said that Athene had not persevered with her musical efforts because the Olympians had laughed at her when she blew out her cheeks and pursed her lips. So she had contemptuously tossed the flute aside and pronounced a curse against any person who picked it up. The satyr Marsyas, who dared to take possession of the instrument, was cruelly punished for his imprudence.

Athene also at times filled the role of goddess of health: everyone knew how the architect Mnesicles who, while working on the construction of the Propylaea, had fallen and was in danger of death, had been miraculously healed by Athene who was called for this reason Hygieia.

Athene extended her protection not only to individuals but also to entire cities. She was symbolised by the *Palladia* or statues of herself which had, it was claimed, fallen from heaven. The possession of a palladium was a pledge of security. Athens guarded one jealously in the Erechtheum. When Danaus fled from Egypt he was careful not to forget his palladium which he carried to Lindus in the isle of Rhodes. The most celebrated palladium was that of Troy which Zeus had presented to King Dardanus. According to others it had been made by Athene herself: heartbroken at having accidentally killed young Pallas, her playmate and the the daughter of Tritonis, her foster-father, Athene carved from a tree trunk a statue reproducing the features of Pallas which she left with Zeus. Later Electra, whom Zeus seduced, took refuge behind this palladium. Zeus tossed it away and it fell on the land of Ilium, where Ilus had a temple built for it. When the Greeks laid siege to Troy they realised that they would never be victorious so long as the city retained its palladium. Diomedes and Odysseus therefore decided to steal the precious idol, and its theft spread discouragement among the Trojans. It was said, to be sure, that Dardanus had taken the precaution of exposing to the faithful only a copy of the palladium, and had carefully concealed the original in the adytum – or innermost sanctuary – of the temple. Thus it was the replica that the Greeks had stolen. As for the genuine palladium, it was taken after the fall of Troy to Italy by Aeneas. But it did not remain there. After many vicissitudes it was brought back to Amphissa in Locris, where it could be seen and venerated by all.

APOLLO

The etymology of the word Apollo is uncertain. A connection has been suggested between the name and an old Greek verb which means 'to repel or set aside', and also an ancient form of a verb meaning 'to destroy'. (In the latter case Apollo would be the 'destroyer', as he appears to be in the *Iliad*.) A relationship between Apollo and the English word apple which would make of him a primitive apple-tree god is equally unsatisfactory.

Origin, Character and Functions. The same uncertainty surrounds Apollo's origin. Some authorities believe that he came from Asia and was either a Hittite god, a Hellenic double of the Arab god Hobal, or a god of Lycia. Others, because of his close relations with the Hyperboreans, think that he was a Nordic divinity, brought by the Greeks from the North in the course of their migrations. It is difficult to decide between these two opposing schools of thought because, though both advance plausible arguments, neither can actually prove its case.

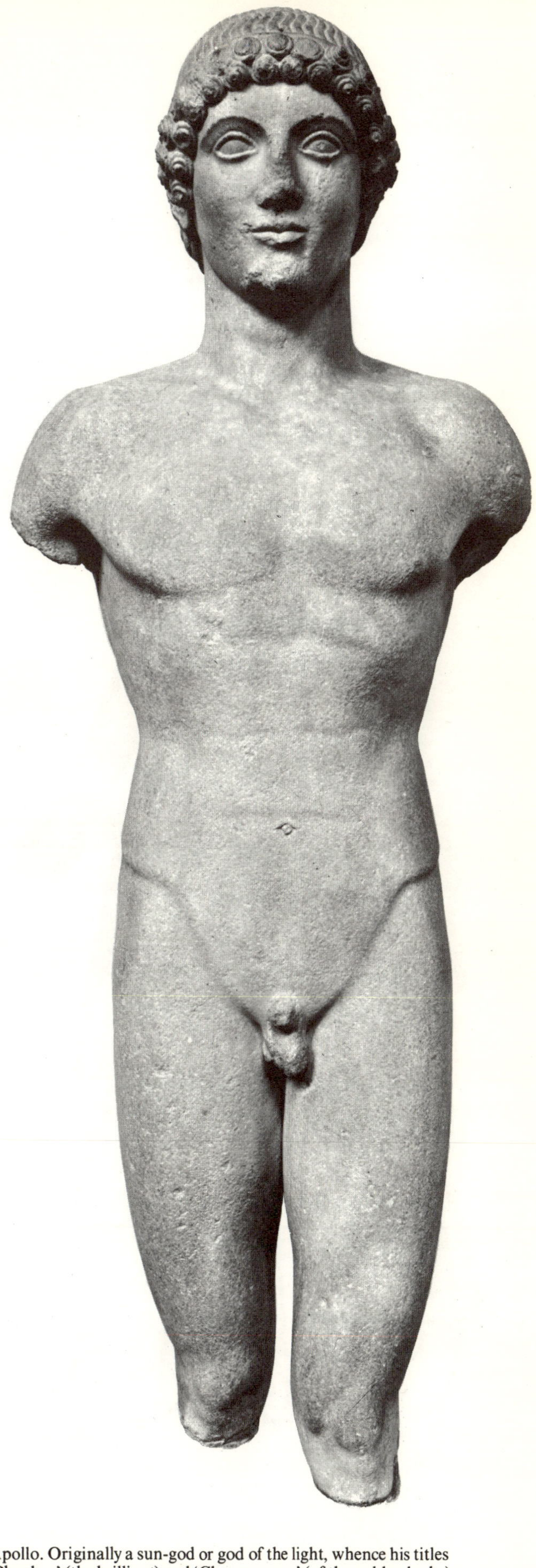

Apollo. Originally a sun-god or god of the light, whence his titles 'Phoebus' (the brilliant) and 'Chrysocomes' (of the golden locks), Apollo was also a pastoral and musician-god and a god of prophecy. His oracle at Delphi, where he had his chief shrine, was famous. He was the son of Zeus and Leto and the twin brother of Artemis. Statue in Parian marble from the island of Lemnos, *c.* 480 B.C.

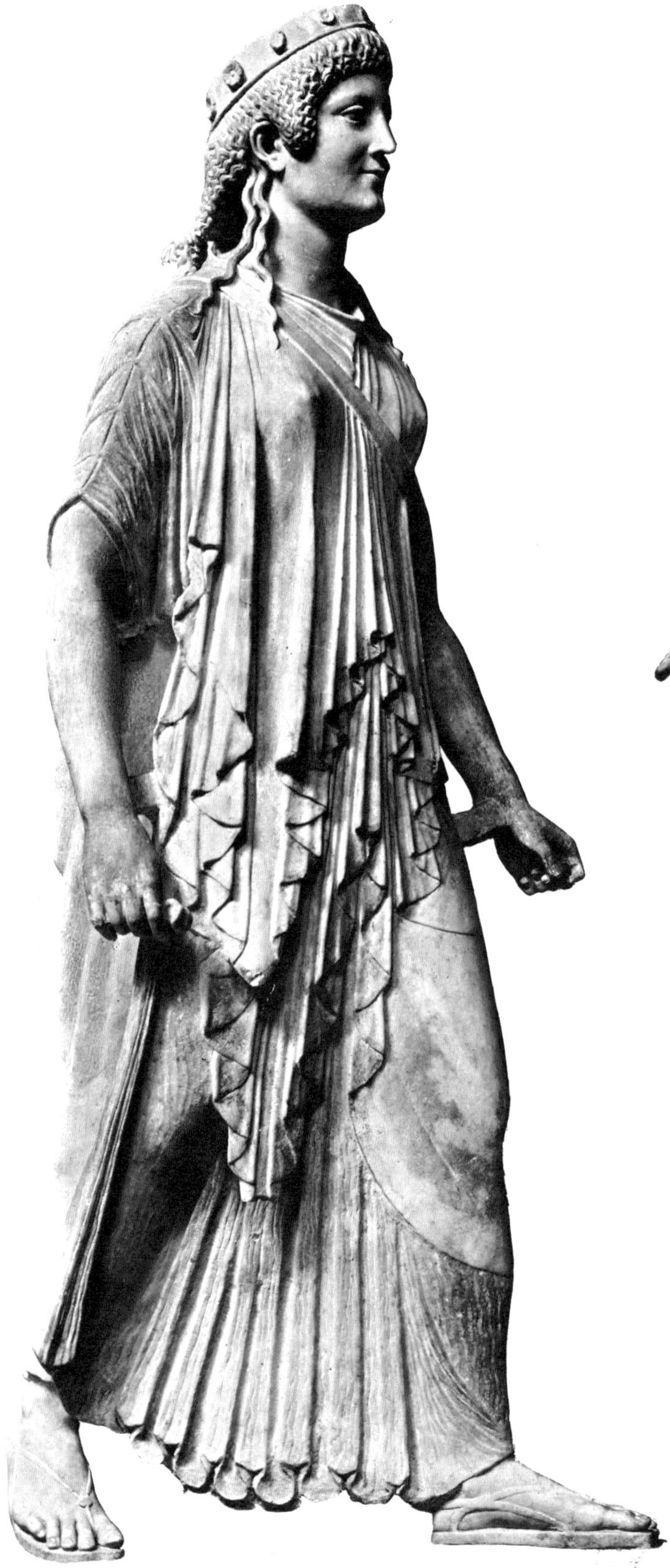

Artemis, the virgin-huntress. The goddess of the chase and of forests, Artemis loved the pleasures of the hunt in the woods and glades of Arcadia accompanied by her band of nymphs. Like her twin brother Apollo she could dispense sudden death with her arrows but though implacable towards those who aroused her anger she could be benevolent towards those who honoured her. Greek statue from Pompeii.

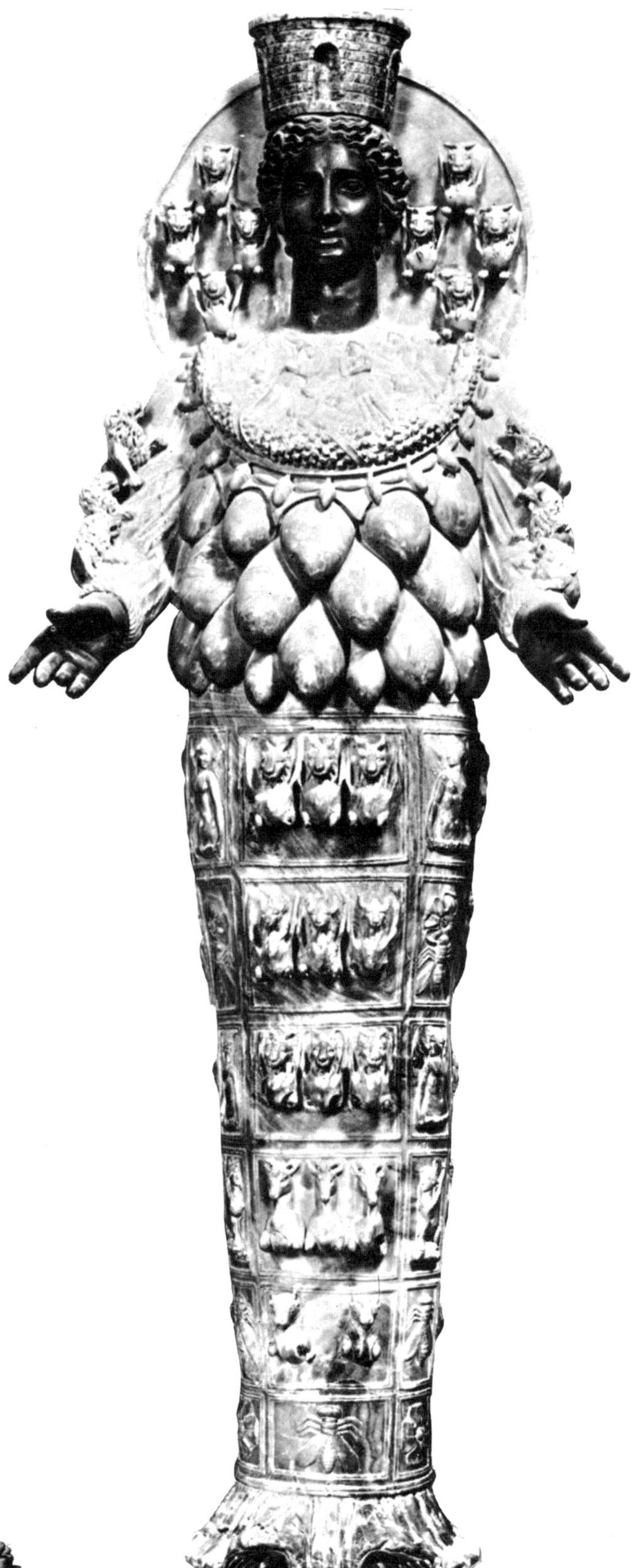

The Ephesian Artemis, a fertility goddess of Asia Minor. Sometimes confused with the virgin goddess of the Greeks, she was in fact an Ionian deity of completely different character.

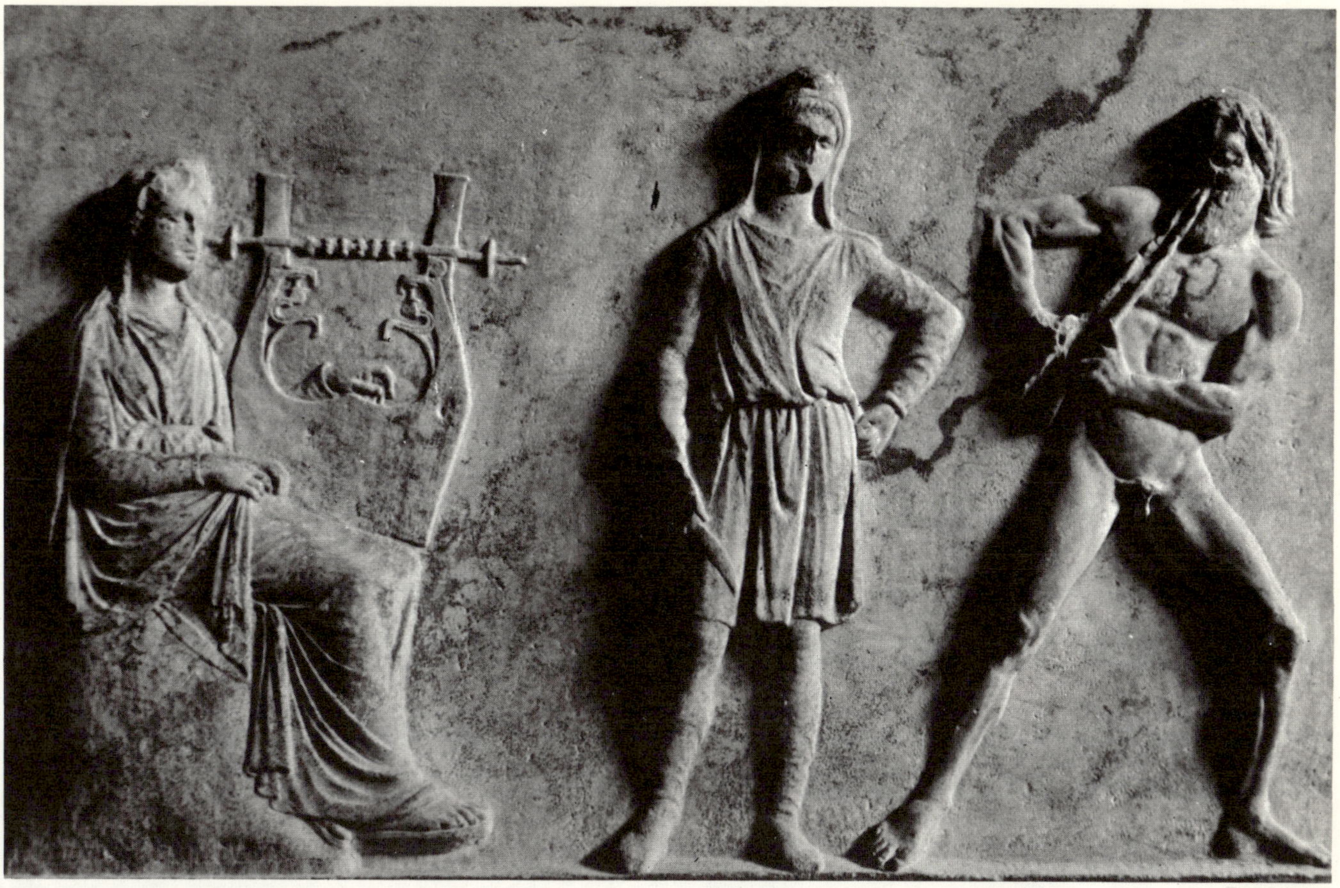

Apollo and Marsyas. Emboldened by the praise that he had received for his playing, the satyr Marsyas had challenged Apollo to a musical contest, the winner to inflict whatever punishment he wished on the loser. Apollo is seated on the left listening to the satyr who is playing on the flute. Marsyas was defeated and flayed with the knife held by the servant in the centre. Bas-relief from the pedestal of the statue of the goddess Leto by Praxiteles. *c.* 366 B.C.

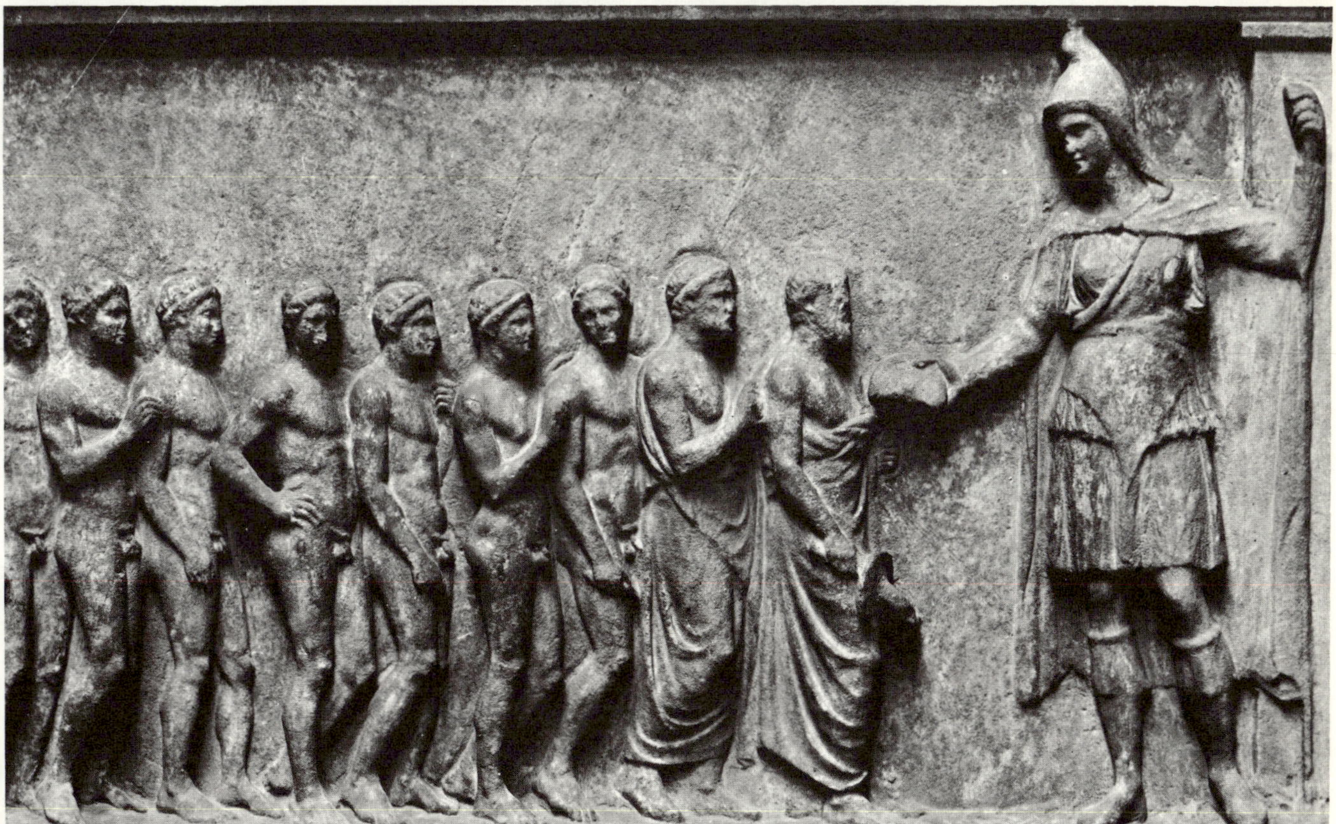

Artemis Bendis. Dressed in her saffron hunting tunic and buskins and with a hooded cape fastened over her shoulders, the goddess receives a torch which had been passed from horseman to horseman in the annual race held in her honour at the Piraeus. In addition to her role as goddess of the chase, Artemis was also a moon-goddess and she has here taken over a rite belonging to another moon-goddess, the Thracian Bendis. Relief sculpture, fourth century B.C.

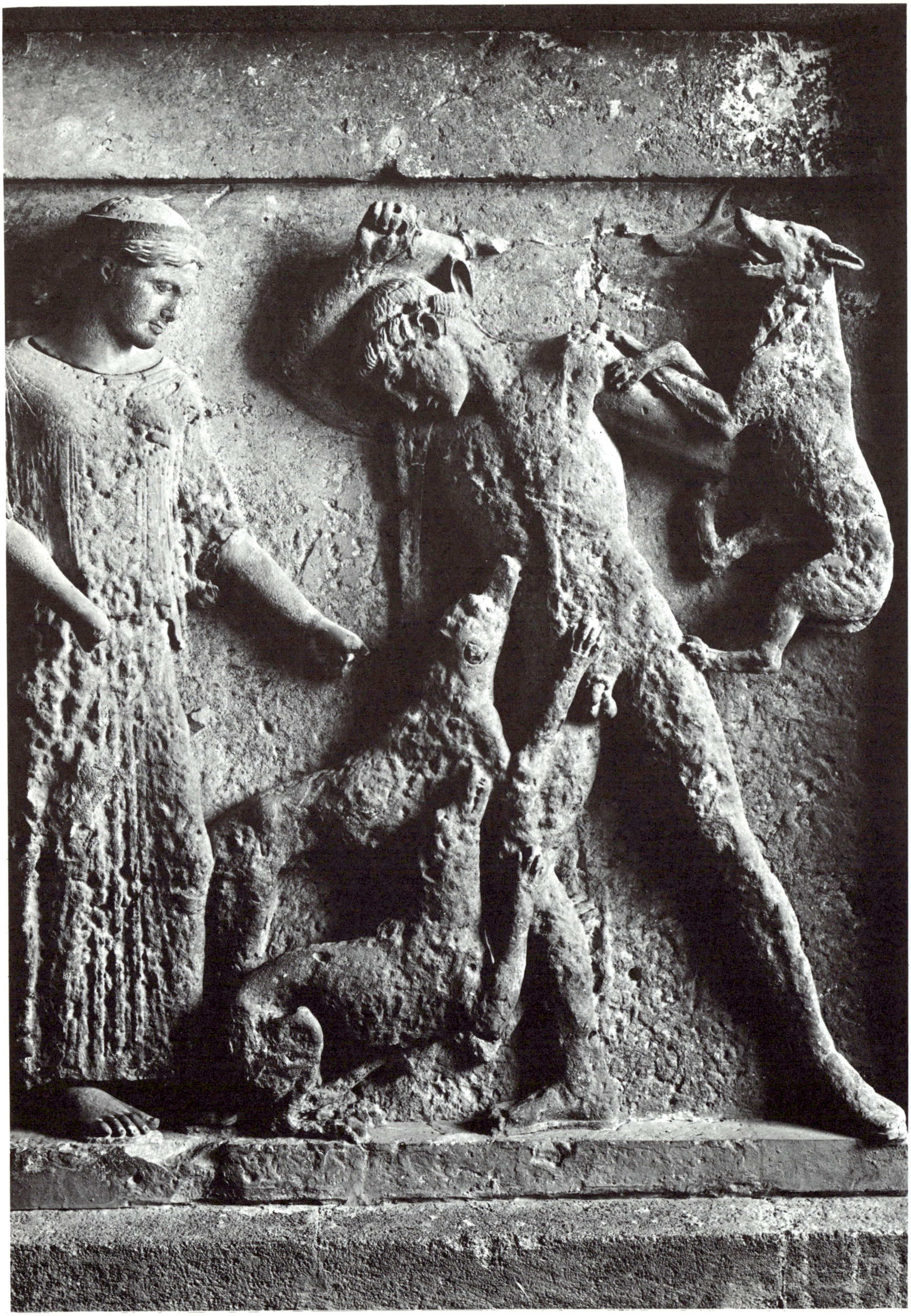

Artemis causes Actaeon to be devoured by his hounds. Metope from Temple E, Selinus. National Museum, Palermo.

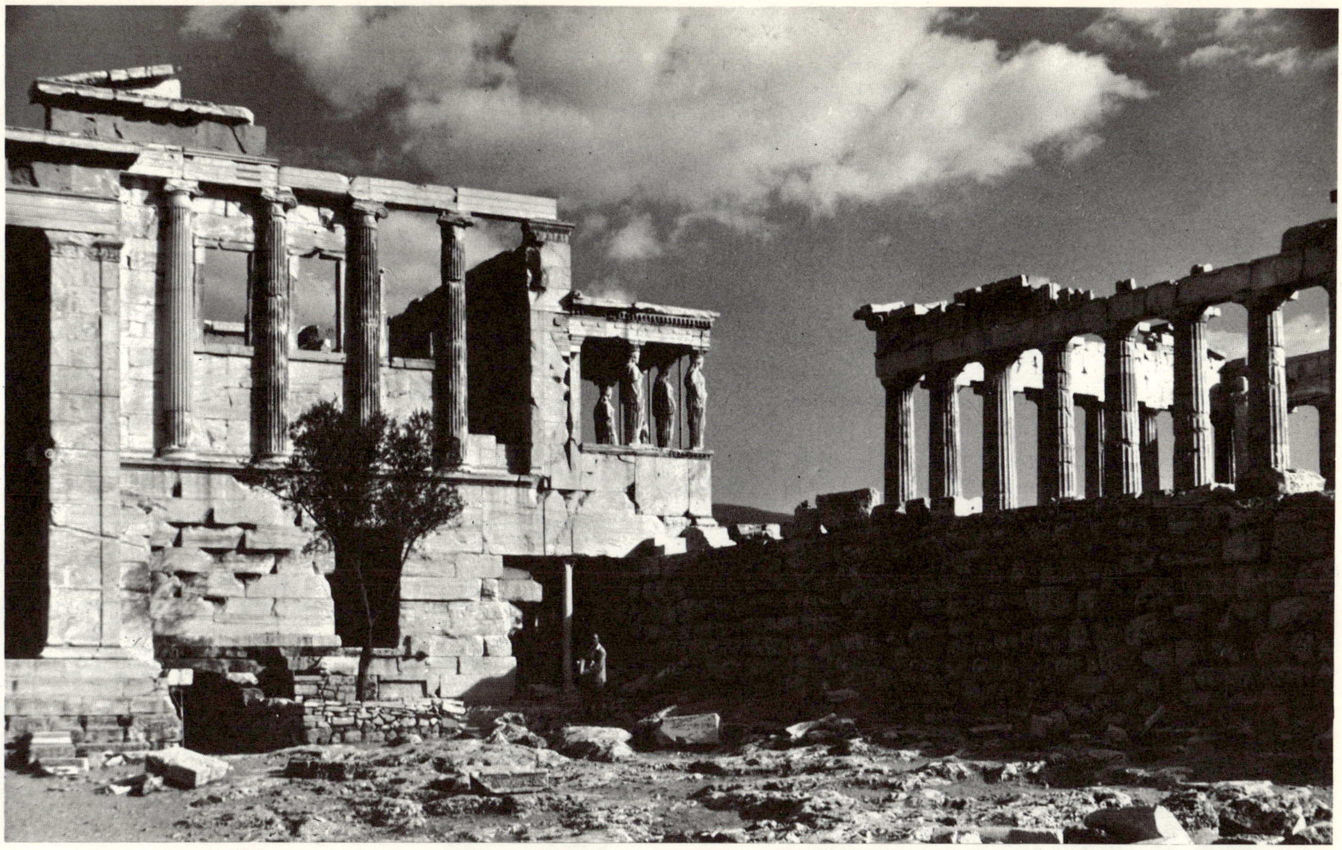

The Erechtheum and the Parthenon from the west. Both these temples were dedicated to the goddess Athene – the Parthenon to Athene Parthenos and the Erechtheum to Athene Polias. The Parthenon, the masterpiece of the Doric style, was commenced in 447 B.C., dedicated in 438 B.C. and completed in 432 B.C. The Erectheum was built some decades later in the Ionic style on the most sacred spot on the Acropolis. In the precinct before it grew Athene's olive tree.

The difficulty is that the legend of Apollo and his functions reveal divergences which are sometimes even contradictory. How is it, for example, that this pre-eminently Greek god was, in the *Iliad*, the ally of the Trojans – that is to say, the Asiatics? And if he was in fact of Asiatic origin, how can we explain his retreat in the Vale of Tempe and among the Hyperboreans? In this it is tempting to see a return of the god to the land of his origin.

As to his functions, they are so multiple and complex that it is often hard to connect one with another.

Apollo was first of all a god of the light, a sun-god–without, however, being the sun itself, which was represented by a special divinity, Helios. From this arose his epithets: Phoebus, the 'brilliant'; Xanthus, the 'fair'; Chrysocomes, 'of the golden locks'; as such he delighted in 'high places, the frowning peaks of high mountains, wave-lapped, beetling promontories'. This god of the light was the son of Latona or Leto – probably a double of the Asiatic Lada – who was undoubtedly a divinity of the night.

As a solar god Apollo made the fruits of the earth to ripen, and at Delos and Delphi the first crops were therefore consecrated to him. In addition he protected the crops by destroying the mice which infested the fields (*Apollo Smintheus*) and drove off the locusts which devastated the harvest (*Apollo Parnopius*).

Because the sun is murderous with its rays which strike like darts, and at the same time beneficent because of its prophylactic powers, Apollo was thought of as an archer-god who shot his arrows from afar (*Hecatebolos*) as the god of sudden death; but also as a healer-god who drove away illness (*Alexikakos*). In this latter function he had apparently supplanted a primitive deity Paeon (the healer) whose name is closely related to the divinity whom Homer calls the physician of the gods, Paeëon.

Apollo was also the god of divination and prophecy. Without speaking of the many early oracles he possessed in Asia Minor, at Thymbra, Clarus, Grynia, Didymus, all over Greece he had sanctuaries where men came to consult him and where he pronounced judgment through the intermediary of priestesses, the Sibyls. Famous were those of Tegyra, near Orchomenus, and of Thebes in Boeotia, over which presided Teiresias' own daughter, Manto. At Thebes in the days of Pausanias the stone from which the priestess delivered her oracles could still be seen. It was called the Seat of Manto. Manto was afterwards led to Delphi, where she devoted herself to the cult of Apollo. The god, it was said, sent her to Asia Minor to found the oracle of Clarus.

But of all the sanctuaries of Apollo the most celebrated was that of Delphi, situated in a deep cavern from which emanated prophetic vapours. The priestess, or Pythia, sat on a tripod placed on the threshold of the cavern. Soon, under the god's influence, she would fall into a trance and, possessed by prophetic delirium, begin to pour forth broken phrases and obscure words which were then interpreted by the priest and members of the sacred counsel of Delphi.

This role of prophecy conferred on a sun-god is surprising in view of the fact that in Greece divination was reserved for underworld divinities. It is a fact, however, that Apollo ousted them all little by little. We must then assume that he already possessed this function when he came to Greece; and we cannot fail to notice his resemblance in this respect to the Assyro-Babylonian sun-god Shamash, who also had the gift of prophecy – an argument in favour of Apollo's being of Asiatic origin.

But there are other aspects of the sun-god which are not easy to relate to the above.

For Apollo was also a shepherd-god (*Nomius*) whose mission it was to protect the flocks. We shall see later that flocks are often associated with Apollo. His epithet, Lycian – unless it simply signifies that he was of Lycian origin – can clearly be derived from the root *lux*, light, and would then be a qualifying epithet for a solar-deity. But 'Lycian' is also related to the Greek word meaning wolf. Apollo could then have primitively been a wolf-god (as Reinach conjectured) or else a god who killed wolves (*Lukoktonos*) – both equally applicable to a rural divinity. Apollo Nomius may be linked with Apollo Carneios (the ram-god of the Dorians) who was also a pastoral divinity.

Apollo is a musician-god as well, the god of song and the lyre. This is how Homer shows him when he described the gods listening to 'the sound of the gracious lyre which Apollo held'.

He is also a builder and a colonising-god who, as Callimachus

Hermes resting. Greek bronze. National Museum, Naples.

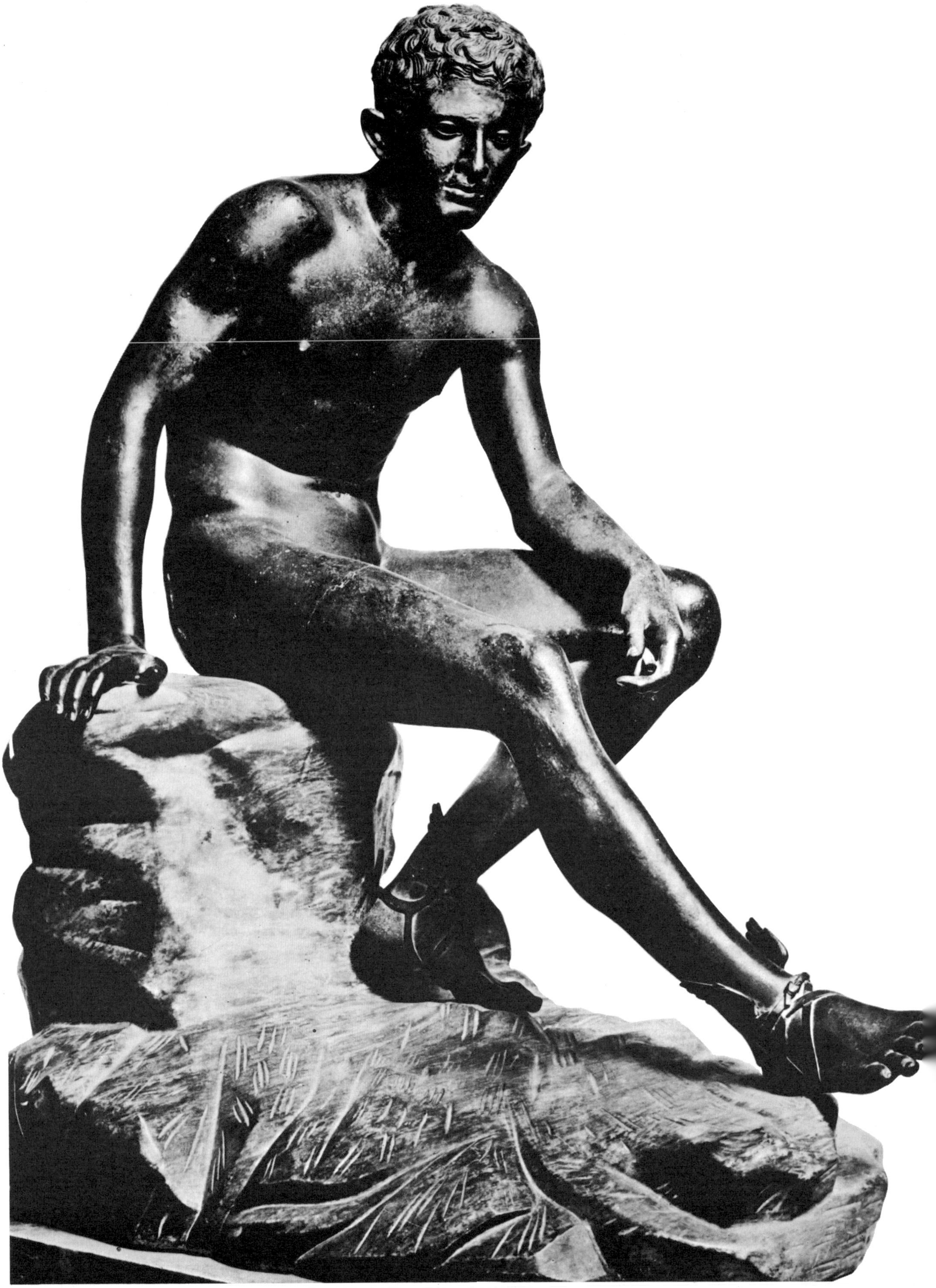

Hermes Psychopompus leads Eurydice to Orpheus. Attic bas-relief. Villa Albani, Rome.

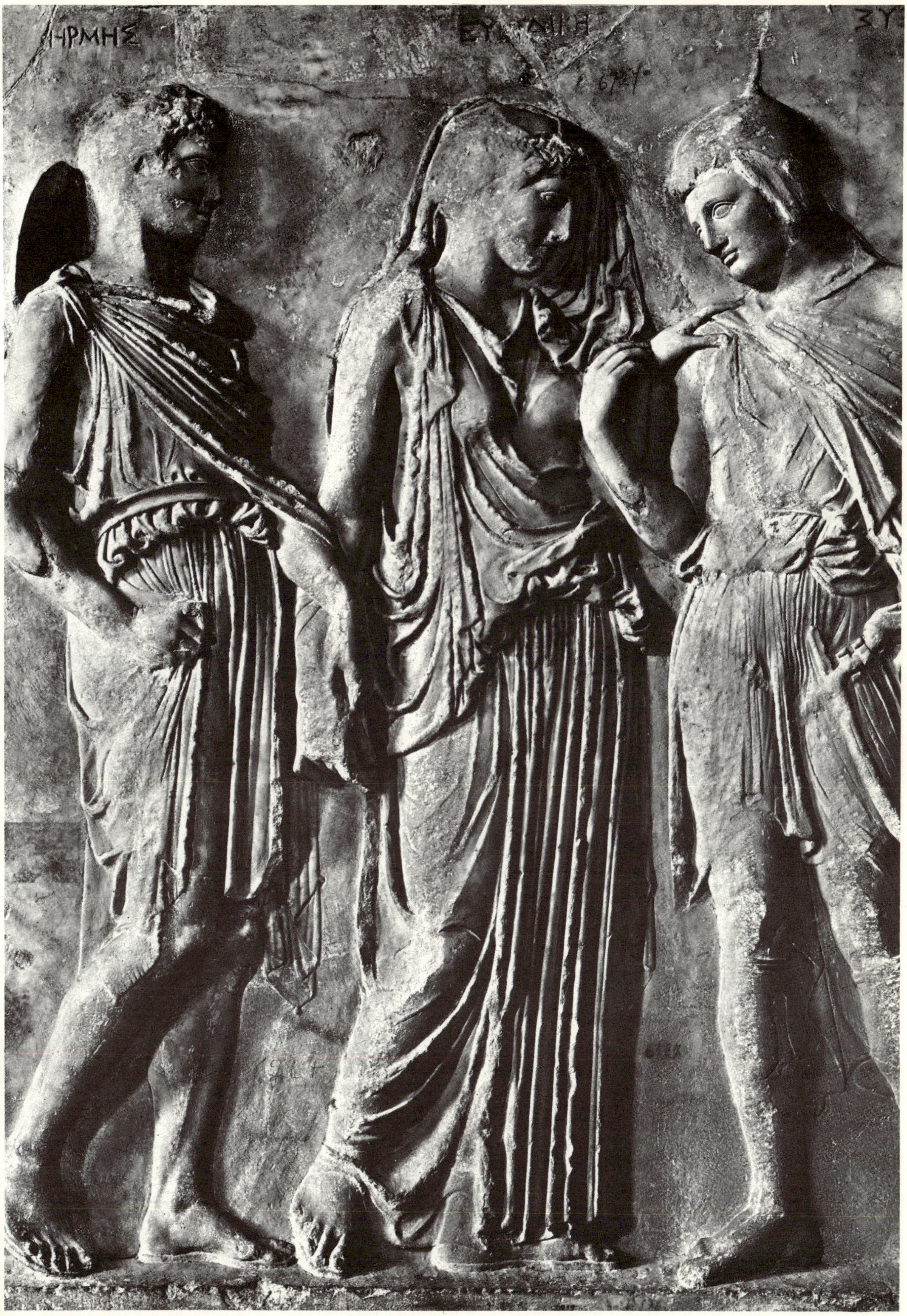

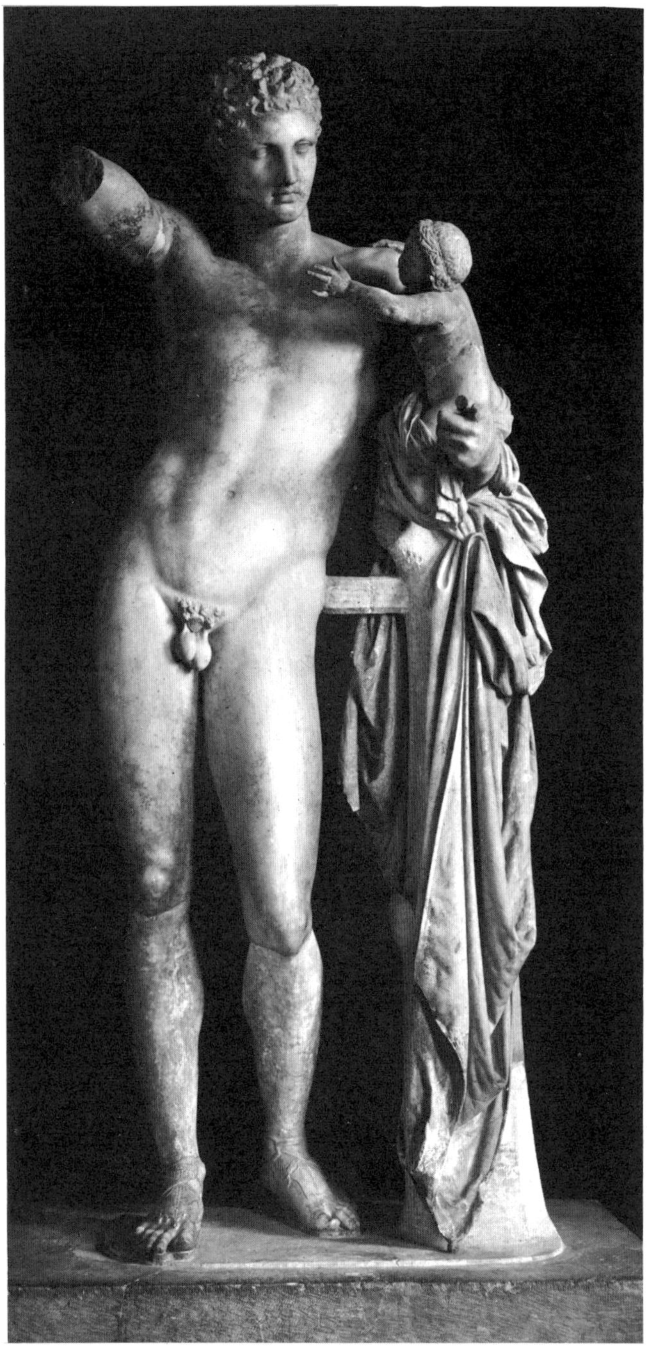

Hermes and the infant Dionysus. The messenger of the gods rests on his journey to the nymphs of Nysa to whose care he is to entrust his little half-brother Dionysus on the orders of Zeus. In his right hand he held a bunch of grapes with which to amuse the child. Originally thought to be Praxiteles' original of *c.* 330 B.C., the statue, which was found in the temple of Hera at Olympia is now believed to be a later copy. Parian marble.

says, 'delights in the constructions of towns of which he himself lays the foundations'.

So many varying functions lead one to suspect that in Apollo there were many personalities, and the problem of his origin would be clarified by considering him to be a solar-god from Asia who was merged with a pastoral-god, the chief god of the Dorians, who came from the north of Greece.

Representations. In spite of his multiple character Apollo always appears as a single type in the representations which were made of him. He was depicted as a young man of idealised beauty, with a vigorous body, a broad chest and slim hips. His beardless face with its delicate features is surmounted by a high forehead and thick, long hair which sometimes falls freely behind him, sometimes is knotted on top or at the nape of his neck so that only a few curls fall to his shoulders. He is generally nude or wears only a chlamys thrown over his shoulder. Sometimes, particularly when he is represented as a musician, he wears a long tunic with loose folds.

His attributes are the bow, the quiver, the shepherd's crook, the lyre. The animals which are sacred to him are the swan, the vulture, the crow, the cock, the hawk, the cicada, the wolf and the serpent. His favourite plants are the laurel, the palm, the olive and the tamarisk.

The Birth of Apollo. According to the oldest traditions Apollo's mother, Leto, daughter of Coeus and Phoebe, was the wife of Zeus before Zeus was married to Hera. This is how she appears in the *Iliad* where, like her son – and doubtless because of her Asiatic origin – she protects the Trojans. Hesiod also depicts her in the same role and represents her as enveloped in a veil of sombre hue, a garment natural to a goddess of the night. Only later was Leto made a mistress of Zeus and a victim of Hera's jealousy; and it is chiefly the history of her misfortunes which enriches her legend.

When Leto was pregnant with the twins Zeus had given her she wandered the earth in search of a place to give birth to them. But she was pursued by Hera's jealous fury and ranged Attica, Euboea, Thrace and the islands of the Aegean sea, begging in vain of each of these countries to receive her. All feared the anger of Hera and all 'were seized with dread and terror' and none dared receive her. But Leto at last found shelter. It will be remembered that Leto's sister, Asteria, had been changed into a quail because she had resisted the ardours of Zeus, then into the floating isle of Ortygia. On the promise that Apollo would erect a splendid temple on its stony and barren soil, the isle of Ortygia consented to receive Leto. Hera, however, had sworn that her rival would only give birth in a place where the sun's rays never penetrated. In order that this vow should not be broken Poseidon raised the waves like a dome over the isle of Ortygia which, at the same time, he anchored to the depths of the sea with four pillars. After the birth of Apollo, Ortygia changed its name to Delos – 'the Brilliant'.

No longer able to prevent the birth she loathed, Hera attempted at least to delay it. While all the other Immortals hastened to Delos to be with Leto, Hera kept Ilithyia, the goddess of childbirth, behind. During nine days and nine nights Leto was the victim of atrocious suffering. Finally Iris was dispatched to Olympus and succeeded in fetching Ilithyia. Then, says a Homeric hymn to Apollo, 'Leto clasped a palm-tree in her arms, pressed the soft ground with her knees, and the earth beneath her smiled and the child leapt into the light. All the goddesses cried out with joy. Then, O Phoebus, the goddesses washed thee in sweet water, limpid and pure, and they gave thee for swaddling clothes a white veil of tissue, light and fresh, which they tied with a golden girdle'.

Leto, at the same time, gave birth to a daughter, Artemis.

Due to the similarity of names the birth of Apollo is sometimes placed in the sacred grove of Ortygia, in the neighbourhood of Ephesus.

Leto's tribulations did not end with the birth of Apollo. For fear of Hera she left Delos in haste and went to Asia Minor, to the land which later became Lycia. There one day she paused at the edge of a pool. She wished to quench her thirst but was prevented from doing so by rude shepherds who stirred the water to make it muddy. Leto punished them by turning them into frogs.

The Childhood of Apollo: The Serpent Python. Unlike other children Apollo was not nourished on his mother's milk. Themis put nectar and sweet ambrosia to his lips. Immediately the new-born baby threw off his swaddling clothes and was endowed with manly vigour, which he proved without delay in doing battle with the serpent Python.

This monster was a female dragon which the earth had given birth to and which had acted as nurse to Typhon. Hera, who was resolved to exterminate her rival, sent Python against Leto at the moment of Apollo's birth. But thanks to Poseidon, who had hidden Leto's retreat among the waves, Leto was saved and the serpent Python returned to its lair on the wooded slopes of Parnassus. Now, four days after his birth, Apollo set forth in search of a place to establish his sanctuary. Armed with the arrows which Hephaestus had forged for him, he descended from the heights of Olympus, crossed Pieria, Euboea, Boeotia, and arrived in the valley of Crissa. On the treacherous advice of the nymph Telphousa, who reigned over this region and wished to retain her position, Apollo wandered into the savage gorge of Parnassus which was the serpent Python's lair. The serpent saw the god and sprang at him. But Apollo let fly an arrow. 'Torn with cruel pain the monster lies shuddering: he rolls in the sand. He plunges into the forest and twists on the ground, now here, now there, until the moment when, with poisonous breath, he exhales his life in a torrent of blood.' Apollo contemptuously pushed his victim aside with one foot and said: 'Now rot where you lie.' And in memory of the occasion the spot where this dramatic encounter took place was called by the name *Pytho* – from the Greek 'to rot'. It was later changed to Delphi. As for Telphousa, the god punished her treachery by smothering her under a rock.

In order to purify himself from the stains he had got when killing the serpent, Apollo exiled himself to Thessaly, in the Vale of Tempe. When his period of expiation was concluded he returned to Delphi, his head crowned with sacred laurel, and escorted by a procession of priests, chanting hymns of triumph.

The memory of these events was perpetuated at Delphi by the festival of the *Septeria* (or Veneration) which was celebrated every nine years. An adolescent youth, chosen from among the nobility, represented Apollo. Accompanied by other young folk he would go and set on fire a wooden hut which symbolised the dragon's lair. At the close of the Septeria the same youths would make a pilgrimage to the Vale of Tempe, practise expiatory rites and return to Delphi carrying sacred laurel.

The Foundation of Delphi. Delphi was in fact Apollo's chosen land. Soon after his victory over the serpent Python he built an altar in harsh Pytho, in the midst of a sacred grove. The place was deserted and Apollo was wondering where he would find priests for his new cult when he perceived in the distance on the dark sea a ship manned by some Cretans. Immediately assuming the form of a dolphin, he sped after the ship and leapt on to the deck, to the great terror of the sailors, who were even more terrified when their ship suddenly ceased to obey the oars and, deviating from its course, rounded the Peloponnese, entered the Gulf of Corinth and ran aground on the shores of Crissa. Apollo then reassumed his his divine appearance and told the Cretans his will. 'From now on none of you will again return to your pleasant city. You will see your rich dwellings and your cherished wives no more; but you will guard my temple. You will know the designs of the immortal gods and, by their will, you will be perpetually honoured. You will have in abundance all that the illustrious tribes of men bring to me. And since you first beheld me on the dark sea in the shape of a dolphin, you shall invoke me by the name of the Delphinian.' Such was the origin of Delphi. The same episode explains the role of Apollo as god of navigation and marine expeditions, particularly colonisation.

But Apollo did not always remain at Delphi. Every year at the end of autumn he went away, beyond the Rhipaei mountains where the impetuous Boreas reigned, towards the mysterious land of the Hyperboreans. There, under a sky eternally bright, lived a happy and virtuous race of men devoted to the cult of Apollo. Leto herself, they said, was a native of this blessed land, which she had left in the guise of a she-wolf to come to Delos. With the return of the good weather Apollo would come to Delphi again in a chariot drawn by white swans or monstrous griffins. Some placed this annual exile of the god in Lycia.

The Exploits of Apollo. Apollo, the celestial archer whose arrows were long-ranged and infallible, was distinguished for many exploits. He fought against the Aloadae, Ephialtes and Otus. These two giants, sons of Aloeus or Poseidon, aspired to the hands of Hera and Artemis, and repeating the audacious attempt of the Titans to scale Olympus, piled Pelion on Ossa to achieve their daring objective. They would have succeeded had not Apollo struck them down with his arrows. It is true that another tradition attributes the death of the Aloadae to Artemis. Apollo, in the same way, slew the giant Tityus who had dared to assail the honour of Leto, his mother.

The god was no less ruthless towards mortals. In Phocis there was a man of extraordinary strength named Phorbas, chief of the Phlegyians. He would lie in wait beside the road which led to the temple of Delphi and force the passing pilgrims to fight with him. Having vanquished them he would then put them painfully to death. Apollo, disguised as an athlete, appeared one day and felled Phorbas with a mighty blow of the fist. Apollo even measured his strength against Hercules. Hercules had come to Delphi, but, not obtaining from the Pythia the oracle he hoped for, he seized the sacred tripod and carried it away. Apollo hastened after him, overtook him and prepared to fight it out. It required the intervention of Zeus himself to put an end to the combat. Zeus obliged Hercules to restore the tripod and reconciled the two adversaries. Apollo, indeed, tolerated no insult to his person or his cult. The archer Eurytus, who had dared to challenge him, perished for his presumption; and because Agamemnon at Troy had gravely offended his priest Chryses, Apollo for nine days let fly his exterminating arrows against the Greek army, sending innumerable warriors to the kingdom of Hades.

Among the Olympians Apollo enjoyed especial consideration. When he entered, the assembly of the gods all rose in sign of respect. Leto, his mother, would relieve him of bow and quiver, which she would hang from a golden nail. Zeus would welcome his son and give him nectar in a golden cup. The Immortals would then resume their places. Leto was proud to have borne this illustrious son who wielded the redoubtable bow.

Only the cunning Hermes dared to play tricks on his half-brother; we shall see later how he stole Apollo's heifers.

Apollo's Servitude. In spite of the marked favour which the master of the gods showed him, Apollo twice aroused the wrath of Zeus. The first time was when Apollo took part in the plot which Hera formed against her husband and which failed thanks to Thetis. In fury Zeus condemned Apollo, together with Poseidon, to go to Troy, there to enter the service of King Laomedon for a year. While Poseidon worked on the construction of the Trojan ramparts, Apollo pastured the royal oxen on the slopes and in the wooded gorges of Mount Ida. When the year had run its course Laomedon refused to pay the two gods the wages which had been agreed upon and even threatened to cut off their ears. In revenge Apollo spread plague through the country and Poseidon summoned a a monster from the sea which killed men in the fields.

The second time Apollo incurred his father's anger was when, in order to avenge the murder of his son, Asclepius, whom Zeus had struck with a thunderbolt, Apollo killed the Cyclopes who had made the thunderbolt. Zeus punished him by sending him to serve Admetus, king of Pherae. Apollo tended his mares and ewes. He showed devotion to his mortal master, helped him to get married and even saved his life. These two episodes demonstrate the pastoral character of Apollo Nomius.
was the most important of musician-gods. Attracted by the divine music, the fallow deer and hinds would come to frisk, and even the savage beasts of the forest joined in. Did Apollo invent the lyre? According to some he did; though it seems more likely that he received the instrument from Hermes.

Apollo would have it that no instrument could compare in beauty with the lyre or the cithara. One day while strolling on Mount Tmolus he was challenged to a musical contest by the satyr Marsyas,

While he watched his flocks Apollo would play his lyre, for he who had acquired a remarkable virtuosity on the flute which Athene had once cast aside. A jury was constituted among whom sat the Muses and Midas, king of Phrygia. When the tournament was finished Apollo was declared the victor. Only Midas voted for Marsyas. The god punished Midas by bestowing upon him a pair of ass's ears. As for his unfortunate rival, he attached him to a tree trunk, flayed him alive and suspended his body at the entrance of a cavern which could be seen in the neighbourhood of Celaenae in Phrygia. According to other traditions the contest took place between Apollo and Pan.

The Loves of Apollo. It would seem that a god endowed with all the charms of youth, strength and grace would find few to resist him. Indeed the amorous adventures of Apollo were numerous; but several of them were singularly unfortunate – his mistresses were unwilling and the dénouements were tragic.

To be sure, he was loved by the Oceanid Melia, whom he made mother of Ismenius, by Corycia who gave him a son Lycoreus, and by Acacallis, mother of Phylacides and Philandros; but he tried in vain to seduce Daphne. This nymph, daughter of the river Peneius, was as chaste as she was beautiful. When she refused to submit to Apollo he attempted to ravish her; but she fled. He overtook her and she already felt the eager arms of the god around her when she called upon the venerable Gaea to aid her. Immediately the earth gaped open. Daphne disappeared, and in her place a laurel tree sprang from the ground. Apollo made it the plant sacred to him.

The nymph Cyrene, who was said to be the daughter of King Hypseus, was a huntress. Apollo saw her one day on the wooded slopes of Mount Pelion, wrestling with a lion. Charmed by her beauty and courage, he carried her away in a golden chariot to Libya, where she gave birth to Aristaeus.

Nor did all mortal women submit to Apollo's desires. There was Castalia, a girl of Delphi, who, in order to escape the god's pursuit, threw herself into the fountain which afterwards took her name.

Acacallis – who must not be confused with the nymph of the same name – and Chione were loved simultaneously by Hermes and Apollo. Chione, daughter of Daedalion, had Autolycus by Hermes and Philammon by Apollo. Very proud of the beauty of her sons she had the imprudence to scoff at the barrenness of Artemis, who in punishment pierced her with arrows. Acacallis, also called Deione, was the daughter of Minos. Her father had sent her to Libya, where she knew Apollo. She had two sons by him, Amphithemis or Garamas and Miletus. When Miletus was born his mother, for fear of Minos, had him carried into a forest where, thanks to Apollo's protection, the wolves took care of the newly born babe who grew up among them. Shepherds discovered him and removed him from this savage existence. Later Miletus aroused the suspicions of Minos and fled to Asia Minor, where he founded the town of Miletus. Less fortunate was Linus, Apollo's son by Psamathe, daughter of Crotopus, King of Argos. Linus had been exposed by his mother, who wished to conceal his birth, and he was devoured by dogs. At the news Psamathe was overcome with grief and betrayed herself. Her father had her put to death. Apollo immediately struck the city of Argos with a terrible plague which only ceased when Crotopus was exiled. This Linus, who died in infancy, is not the musician hero whom Apollo had by Urania.

The adventure of Apollo and Coronis had a tragic sequence. Coronis, daughter of Phlegyas, King of the Lapiths, had yielded to Apollo and conceived a son. When she was on the point of becoming a mother she married the Arcadian Ischys. A crow, that Apollo had left with Coronis to watch over her, came at once to tell Apollo of the girl's infidelity. In his rage Apollo cursed the crow, whose plumage suddenly turned black, and put Coronis and Ischys to death. According to others he let Artemis avenge him. The two bodies were placed on the funeral pyre and the body of Coronis was already half consumed when Apollo arrived and tore from the flames the child who was about to be born. The child became the god of medicine, Asclepius. When Phlegyas learned who was responsible for the tragedy he marched on Delphi and burnt the temple of Apollo. But he perished under the blows of the god and was thrown into Tartarus, where he was cruelly tortured for his sacrilege.

One day while gathering flowers on the slopes of the Acropolis, Creusa, daughter of Erechtheus and Praxithea, was surprised by Apollo. She lay with him in a neighbouring cavern. Here she later gave birth to a son, Ion. Apollo sent Hermes to fetch the child and bring him to Delphi, where he entered the service of the temple. Meanwhile Creusa had married Xuthus, but their union remained childless. The couple came to Delphi, where the oracle proclaimed that the first being whom they beheld would be their son. As they emerged from the temple the first person they encountered was the young Ion. Xuthus adopted him. Creusa, jealous, attempted to poison Ion, and Ion himself tried to kill Creusa. The Pythia herself cleared up the misunderstanding and revealed to Creusa and Ion that they were mother and son. Athene also told Xuthus the truth, and from Apollo Xuthus received the promise that he would become the father of two sons, Dorus and Achaeus who, with Ion, were the ancestors of the Greek race.

By Thyria Apollo had a son Cycnus, a youth of rare beauty who was attached by a tender affection to his companion of the chase, Phylius. When Phylius abandoned him, Cycnus in despair threw himself into Lake Canopus. Thyria, his mother, threw herself in after him; and Apollo changed them both into swans.

By a certain Cyrene, sometimes also called Asteria, Apollo had another son, Idmon, whom he endowed with the gift of foreseeing the future. When he was invited to take part in the expedition of the Argonauts, Idmon foresaw that he would die in the course of the voyage. He went, nevertheless, and was in fact killed by the bite of a snake.

Evadne bore Apollo Iamus, a celebrated soothsayer and chief of the family of the Iamidae at Olympia.

Divination naturally plays an important role in the legends of Apollo. Thus, when Apollo fell in love with Cassandra, daughter of King Priam, he conferred upon her the gift of foretelling the future on her promising to yield herself to him. But Cassandra refused to fulfil her part of the bargain. Apollo then begged a single kiss. In this way he breathed into her mouth and, though he left her with the power of foretelling the future, he took from her the power of persuasion so that from then onwards no one would believe what Cassandra predicted.

Several youths were also loved by Apollo. Such was Cyparissus, whom the god changed into a cypress because the young man was heartbroken at having carelessly killed a favourite stag. Such also was Hyacinthus, son of Amyclas, King of Laconia. Now Hyacinthus was loved not only by Apollo but also by Boreas and Zephyrus. One day when Hyacinthus and Apollo were throwing the discus, Boreas and Zephyrus jealously directed the discus which Apollo had just thrown so that it struck Hyacinthus on the head and immediately killed him. From the blood which gushed from the wound sprang the flower which bears his name, the hyacinth. In memory of this sad event they celebrated annually in Laconia the festival of the *Hyacinthia*, which began with funeral offerings and lamentations and ended with songs of joy in honour of the young hero who had become immortal.

THE RETINUE OF APOLLO

The Muses. In his aspect of god of music, Apollo's habitual companions were the Muses. Thus he was called *Apollo Musagetes*.

Originally the Muses, like the Nymphs, seem to have been deities of springs. Afterwards they became goddesses of memory, and then of poetic inspiration.

This number varied. The first Muses worshipped on Mount Helicon were three in number: Melete, Mneme and Aoide. There were also three at Sicyon, as well as at Delphi, where their names – Nete, Mese and Hypate – personified the three strings of the lyre. There were seven Muses in Lesbos and in Sicily, eight for the Pythagoreans and in primitive Athens. It was finally agreed that there were nine Muses: Clio, Euterpe, Thalia, Melpomene, Terpsichore, Erato, Polyhymnia, Urania and Calliope.

Functions. The Muses were for long merged in an indissoluble choir which presided over music and poetry in general. It was only later that a special province was assigned to each.

Clio thus became the Muse of History. Her attributes were the heroic trumpet and the clepsydra.

Euterpe presided over flute-playing and her attribute was the flute.

Thalia, who was at first considered a bucolic Muse, became the Muse of Comedy. In her hands she carried the shepherd's staff and the comic mask.

Melpomene was the Muse of Tragedy. Her attributes were the tragic mask and also the club of Hercules.

Terpsichore, whose attribute was the cithara, was the Muse of Lyric Poetry and of the Dance.

Erato was the Muse of Love Poetry.

Polyhymnia, after having been the Muse of heroic hymns, became the Muse of Mimic Art. She was represented in an attitude of meditation with a finger on her mouth.

Urania was the Muse of Astronomy and her attributes were the celestial globe and a compass.

Calliope, who was first in rank among her sisters, was considered in turn to be the Muse of Epic Poetry and Eloquence. Her attributes were the stylus and tablets.

Places of Cult and Representations. The cult of the Muses originated in Thrace, or more precisely in Pieria, as their oldest sanctuary testifies. It was established at Libethrum on the eastern slopes of Olympus, whence it spread to Boeotia where, around Helicon, the centres of the cult were the towns of Ascra and Thespiae. At Thespiae festivals in honour of the Muses were celebrated every five years and included poetic contests. In the rest of Greece the cult

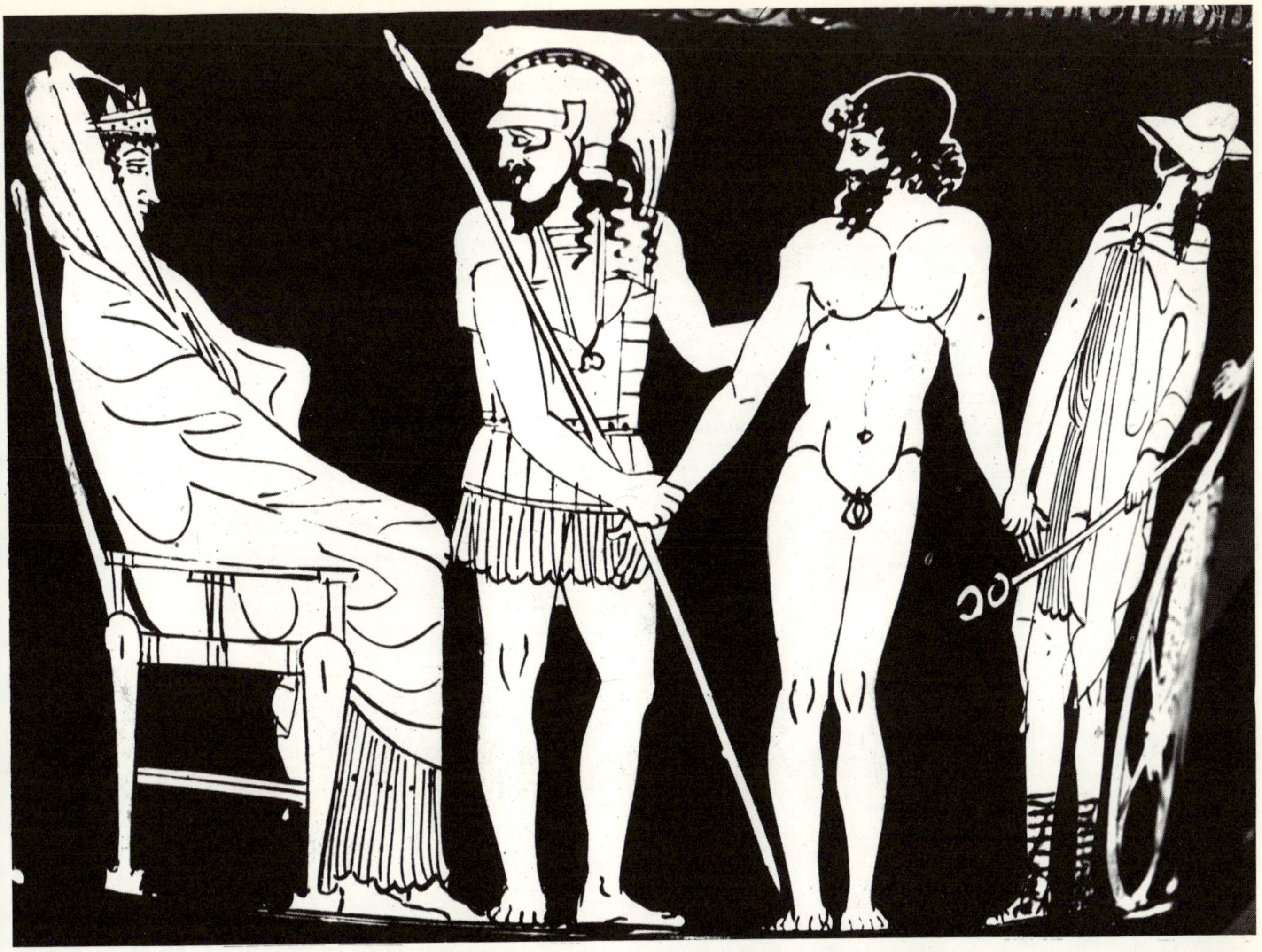

The punishment of Ixion. Invited to Olympus by Zeus, Ixion, the king of the Lapithae, had cast eyes upon Hera and was deceived by Zeus into embracing a cloud made in her image. Here he stands before her, grasped by Ares and Hermes, awaiting his punishment. Zeus condemned him to be scourged by Hermes and he was then bound to a fiery wheel which rolled him ceaselessly through the sky. Detail from a red-figured vase.

of the Muses was no less fervent. In Athens a hill near the Acropolis was consecrated to them and they were worshipped on the banks of the Ilissus. At Delphi they were venerated with Apollo. The Muses also had sanctuaries at Sparta, Troezen, Sicyon, Olympus, in the islands and in several towns in Magna Graecia.

Their former character of spring nymphs explains why numerous fountains were sacred to the Muses.

Offerings to the Muses consisted of grains of wheat kneaded with honey. Libations were poured to them of water, milk and honey.

The Muses are represented as young women with faces smiling, grave or thoughtful, according to their function. They are dressed in long floating robes, covered by a mantle. Urania and Clio are normally depicted sitting. They are otherwise distinguished by their individual attributes.

The Legend of the Muses. As to the origin of the Muses traditions vary. According to Mimnermus and Alcman they were born of Uranus and Gaea; they were also said to be daughters of Pierus and Antiope or else the nymph Pimplea, of Zeus and the Arcadian nymph Neda, of Apollo and so forth. Hesiod's opinion was, however, generally accepted, and he called them the daughters of Zeus and the Titaness Mnemosyne (or Memory).

It was told how after the defeat of the Titans the gods had asked Zeus to create divinities who were capable of celebrating the victory of the Olympians. The master of the gods then went to Pieria, where he shared Mnemosyne's couch for nine consecutive nights. When her time had come Mnemosyne gave birth to nine daughters who formed the choir of the Muses.

Although the Muses often frequented Olympus, where they added gaiety to the feasts of the Immortals with their singing, they preferred to dwell on Helicon, a high mountain in Boeotia whose wooded slopes were covered with fragrant plants which had the property of depriving snakes of their venom. Here numerous springs caused an agreeable freshness: the most celebrated were Aganippe and Hippocrene, which gushed forth under the hoof of Pegasus. Both had the virtue of conferring poetic inspiration on those who drank their waters. On the tender greensward which bordered these fountains the Muses 'with tireless feet would trace the graceful figures of a dance, full of charm, while they displayed the harmony of their brilliant voices', and when they were tired they would restore the freshness of their complexions in the azure waters of Hippocrene. When night came they would abandon the summits of Helicon and, wrapped in a thick cloud, draw near the habitations of men, who could then hear the melodious sound of their voices.

The Muses also liked to visit Parnassus in Phocis where they shared the company of Apollo. From the flank of this mountain came forth a spring, the fountain Castalia, which was sacred to them and whose waters also gave poetic inspiration. This fountain which, they said, communicated with the Cephisus – which also had its source on Parnassus – was regarded as a mouth of the River Styx. The waters of Castalia were used in purification rites in the temple at Delphi, and they were given to the Pythia to drink. The Muses, indeed, were closely connected with the cult of Apollo and as well as being patrons of poetry were guardians of the oracle of Delphi. They themselves, moreover, had the gift of prophecy: 'they said that which is, what will be, and what has been'. It was they who taught Aristaeus the art of divination.

But their legend is chiefly concerned with them as goddesses of song. Hesiod shows us the Muses on Olympus charming the great soul of Zeus. 'Their tireless voices flow from their mouths in sweet accents, and this bewitching harmony as it spreads afar brings smiles to their father's palace, their father who wields the thunderbolt.'

Like all goddesses the Muses were easily offended and harshly punished anyone who dared compete with them.

When the Thracian Bard Thamyris boasted that he surpassed

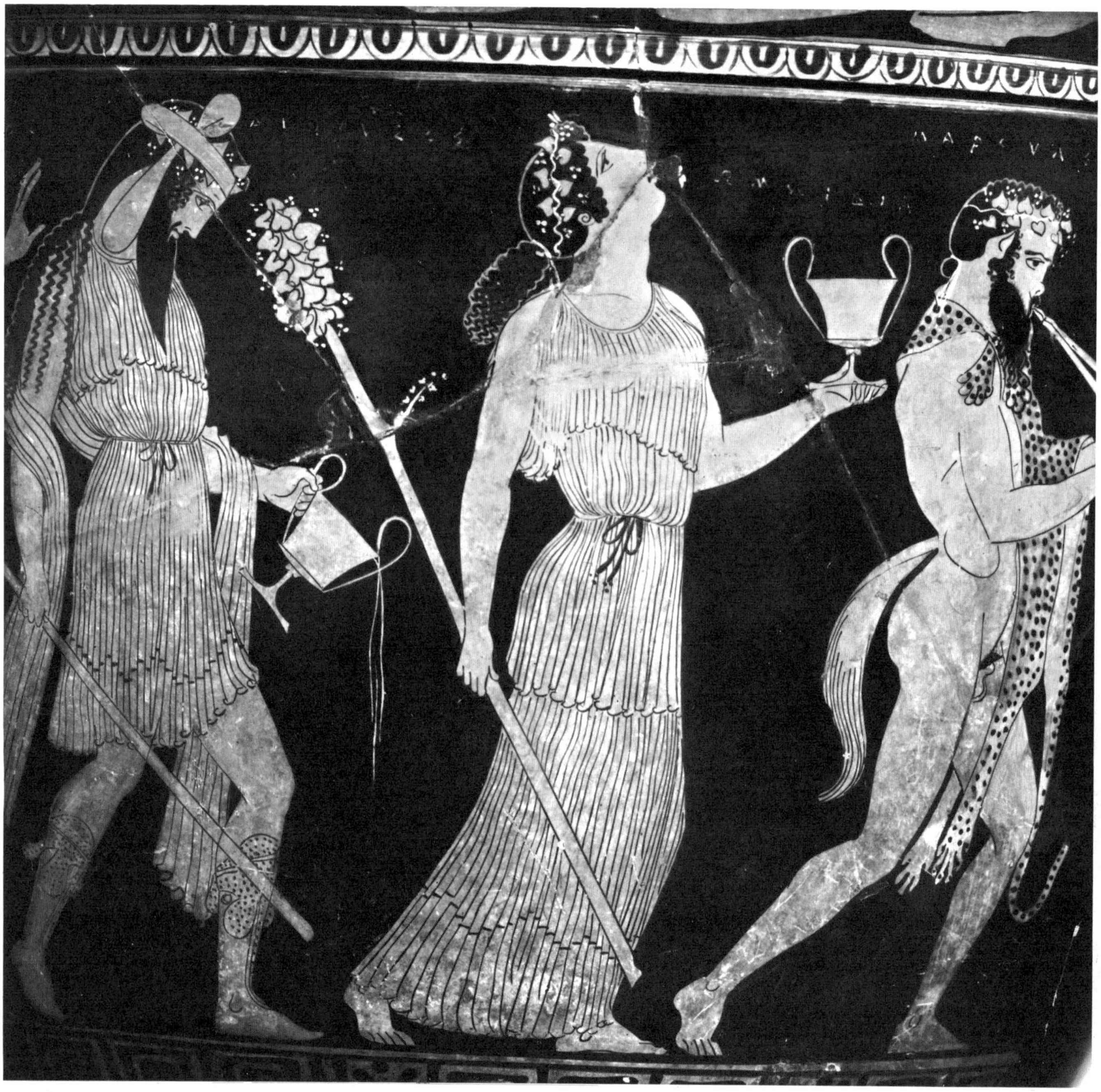

Hephaestus returns to Olympus. Detail from an Attic crater. Louvre.

even the Muses, they struck him blind and dumb.

Pierus, King of Emathia in Macedonia, had nine daughters, the Pierides, who dared to challenge the Muses for the prize of poetry. They were changed into magpies by Apollo and the Muses took over their name.

Finally, the Sirens paid dearly for their presumption. Having issued a challenge to the Muses they were vanquished in spite of the irresistible sweetness of their voices, and in consequence were deprived of their wings.

Originally the Muses were represented as virgins of the strictest chastity. They had taken shelter one day with Pyreneos, King of Daulis in Phocis, when the king attempted to violate them. The Muses then took their wings and flew away. Pyreneos tried to follow them, but he fell from the top of his palace and was killed.

Later numerous love-affairs were attributed to the Muses.

Calliope was not only loved by Apollo, by whom she had two sons, Hymenaeus and Ialemus; she also married Oeagrus, to whom she bore Orpheus, the celebrated singer of Thrace.

Melpomene lay with the river-god Achelous and became the mother of the Sirens.

Euterpe – others say it was Calliope or Terpsichore – had by Strymon, the river-god of Thrace, a son Rhesus who was slain during the Trojan war by Odysseus and Diomedes; for an oracle had said that if the horses of Rhesus drank the waters of the Xanthus Troy would become impregnable.

Clio, having reproached Aphrodite for her passion for Adonis, was punished by Aphrodite, who roused in her heart an irresistible love for Pierus, King of Macedonia. By him Clio had Hyacinthus, whose unfortunate history we have already read.

Thalia gave birth to the Corybantes after lying with Apollo.

By Amphimarus, the musician, Urania had Linus, who was also said to be the son of Apollo and Calliope or Terpsichore. To Linus was attributed the invention of melody and rhythm. It was told how he challenged Apollo to a song contest and how Apollo killed him. Linus had a statue on Helicon where he was honoured as an equal of the Muses. Thebes claimed to possess his tomb.

Finally, Thamyris was supposed to be the son of Erato, and Triptolemus the son of Polyhymnia.

ARTEMIS

The etymology of the name Artemis is obscure and gives us no precise indication of her character. The laws of phonetic derivation are against connecting the name with the world for 'bear', and 'quail' has been suggested in memory of her birth in the isle of Ortygia. The adjective meaning 'safe and sound' has also been proposed, which would make Artemis 'she who heals sickness'. But none of the etymologies take into consideration the goddess's complex character in which, it would seem, different divinities are merged, as in the case of Apollo.

Character and Functions. The primitive Artemis, probably a replica of *Apollo Nomius*, was an agricultural deity, worshipped especially in Arcadia. She was the goddess of the chase and of forests (*Agrotera*). Her symbol was a she-bear, which suggests that she was originally confused with Callisto, who was later made her companion. One is tempted to connect the Arcadian Artemis with Artio, the Celtic goddess of Berne, whose symbol was also a she-bear.

From the beginning Artemis was associated with Apollo and could not fail to participate in his nature: thus she is also a divinity of the light (Phoebe), though of the moon's light. Similarly, her lunar character gradually became less marked, as the appearance of a special moon-goddess, Selene, testifies. In her aspect of light-goddess she has the same functions as Apollo. Like him armed with bow and quiver, she bore the epithet *Apollousa*, the destructress; or *Iocheaira*, who liked to let fly with arrows, strike down mortals with her fearful darts, and assail their flocks with deadly disease. Like Apollo she was the deity of sudden death, though it was usually women whom she struck. She was, however, equally benevolent and brought prosperity to those who honoured her.

In her capacity of moon-goddess Artemis presided over childbirth, jointly with Ilithyia.

Finally Artemis was likened to other divinities who had no connection with her, such as the moon-goddess of Tauris, as a result of confusion caused by the epithet *Tauropolos* which Artemis had in certain towns like Samos, Amphipolis and Icarus. She was also compared to the Cretan goddess Britomartis, and to Hecate, a Thracian divinity who was at the same time a moon-goddess and a goddess of the underworld. There is even less connection between the Greek Artemis and the Artemis or Diana of Ephesus, a personification of fecundity, one of the forms of the Great Mother-goddess of the Orient.

Artemis, particularly venerated in Arcadia, was worshipped throughout Greece, notably in the Peloponnese, at Sparta, at Caryae in Laconia, at Athens, Aegina, Olympia and Delos, where the laurel was consecrated to her and where Hyperborean girls brought their offerings to her. She was revered, too, in Crete, Asia Minor and Magna Graecia.

Representations. Although the lunar character of Artemis is sometimes recalled on coins by a torch held in her hand, or by the moon and the stars which surround her head, sculptors have chiefly emphasised her rural aspect. She appears to us as a young virgin, slim and supple, with narrow hips and regular features. Her beauty is a little severe, with her hair drawn back or partly gathered in a knot on her head. She wears a short tunic which does not fall below her knees: this is, in fact, the Dorian chiton which has been turned up and the folds retained by a girdle. Her feet are shod with the cothurnus or laced buskin. She is usually accompanied by a hind or a dog.

Very different is the appearance of the crowned Artemis of Ephesus, whose body is tightly sheathed in a robe covered with animal heads which leaves her bosom with its multiple breasts exposed: a striking image of a fertility-goddess who has nothing to do with the Greek Artemis.

The Legend of Artemis. Artemis was occasionally presented as the daughter of Zeus and Demeter or Persephone; or else of Dionysus and Isis. But according to the tradition general among the Greeks she was the daughter of Leto, and Apollo's twin sister.

She was born, they said, on the sixth day of the month of Thargelion – a day before her brother – on the isle of Ortygia which only took the name Delos after the birth of Apollo. She shared the vicissitudes which marked the childhood of her brother, accompanying him on his expedition against the serpent Python and during his exile in Thessaly. Then she chose Arcadia for her favourite place of abode. In this savage and mountainous region, where torrents tumbled down the woody slopes and plunged through narrow gorges, Artemis, accompanied by sixty young Oceanids and twenty nymphs appointed to the care of her pack of swift hounds gave herself to the pleasures of the chase. As soon as she was born she had, in fact, gone to find her father Zeus and, embracing his knees, begged from him, not ornaments or jewellery, but a short tunic, hunting boots, a bow and a quiver full of arrows.

As skilled as her brother, 'on the shady mountainside, on the wind-lashed mountain tops, she bends her bow of sparkling gold and lets fly her deadly arrows'.

When she had tired of tracking wild beasts or pursuing the light-footed roebuck she would pause beside the clear waters of a fountain and bathe with her companions until the freshness of the waters had assuaged her fatigue.

In this rude, out-door existence there was no place for love. To the virgin huntress even the legitimate joys of marriage were repugnant, and she made of chastity a strict law which she imposed on her companions. Woe to the nymphs who had joined Artemis' band and then so far forgot their duty as to taste of forbidden pleasures! Even were she a victim of some god's trickery she was nonetheless cruelly chastised. The unfortunate Callisto, who had been approached by Zeus in the guise of the goddess herself and seduced, fell beneath Artemis' arrows when her disgrace became known.

Woe, also, to the imprudent man who gave way to his curiosity! Actaeon, son of Aristaeus and Autonoë, was himself a passionate huntsman. One day with his hounds he was chasing a stag when he came to the valley of Gargaphia, near the fountain Parthenius, where at that moment Artemis and her companions happened to be bathing. Ravished by the beauty of the goddess, Actaeon paused to contemplate her. He was observed. Enraged that a mortal should have seen her in her nakedness, Artemis changed Actaeon into a stag and set his own pack on him. The hounds tore Actaeon to pieces and devoured him.

But on one occasion, it would seem, Artemis' own heart was stirred by the hunter Orion. Perhaps she might even have married him had not Apollo intervened. One day when Orion, a strong swimmer, was bathing in the sea, he had swum far from shore and had nearly vanished on the horizon when Apollo challenged his sister to hit the scarcely perceptible point which, far out to sea, moved on the surface of the waves. Artemis, not realising that the distant object was Orion, accepted the challenge, bent her bow and shot an arrow. It pierced the temple of him she loved. Did Apollo wish to safeguard his sister's honour, or was he motivated by secret jealousy? Certain traditions do, indeed, claim that he had ravished Artemis on his own altar at Delos. But we prefer to believe in the intact purity of the goddess.

Elsewhere it was told that Orion perished for having dared to touch the goddess one day when they were hunting together in the island of Chios. Artemis summoned a deadly scorpion from the earth which stung Orion on the heel.

This version agrees better with what we know of the dark and vindictive character of Artemis. When Apollo punished Tityus for the outrage done to Leto, his mother, Artemis seconded him. To her also the death of the Aloadae was sometimes attributed: the two giants having attempted to violate her, Artemis turned herself into a white doe and got between them in such a way that, trying to strike the beast with their javelins, they ran each other through instead.

We have seen how Artemis killed Chione whom her brother loved, because Chione was vain of her children's beauty. Niobe was punished still more harshly. Daughter of Tantalus, Niobe had six sons and six daughters by her husband Amphion. In her maternal pride she dared to disparage Leto, who had brought only two children into the world. To punish this insolence Apollo and Artemis struck down all twelve of Niobe's children with their arrows and Niobe, heartbroken, at last persuaded Zeus to change her into a rock.

The slightest negligence towards Artemis was apt to be punished. Admetus, who had omitted to offer sacrifice to the goddess on his marriage, had when he entered the bridal chamber the disagreeable surprise of finding it full of snakes. Oeneus, who reigned at Calydon in Aetolia, forgot to consecrate the first fruits of his crop to Artemis: his territory was ravaged by a prodigious boar and, in the course of the adventures which accompanied and followed the capture of the monster, his whole family perished.

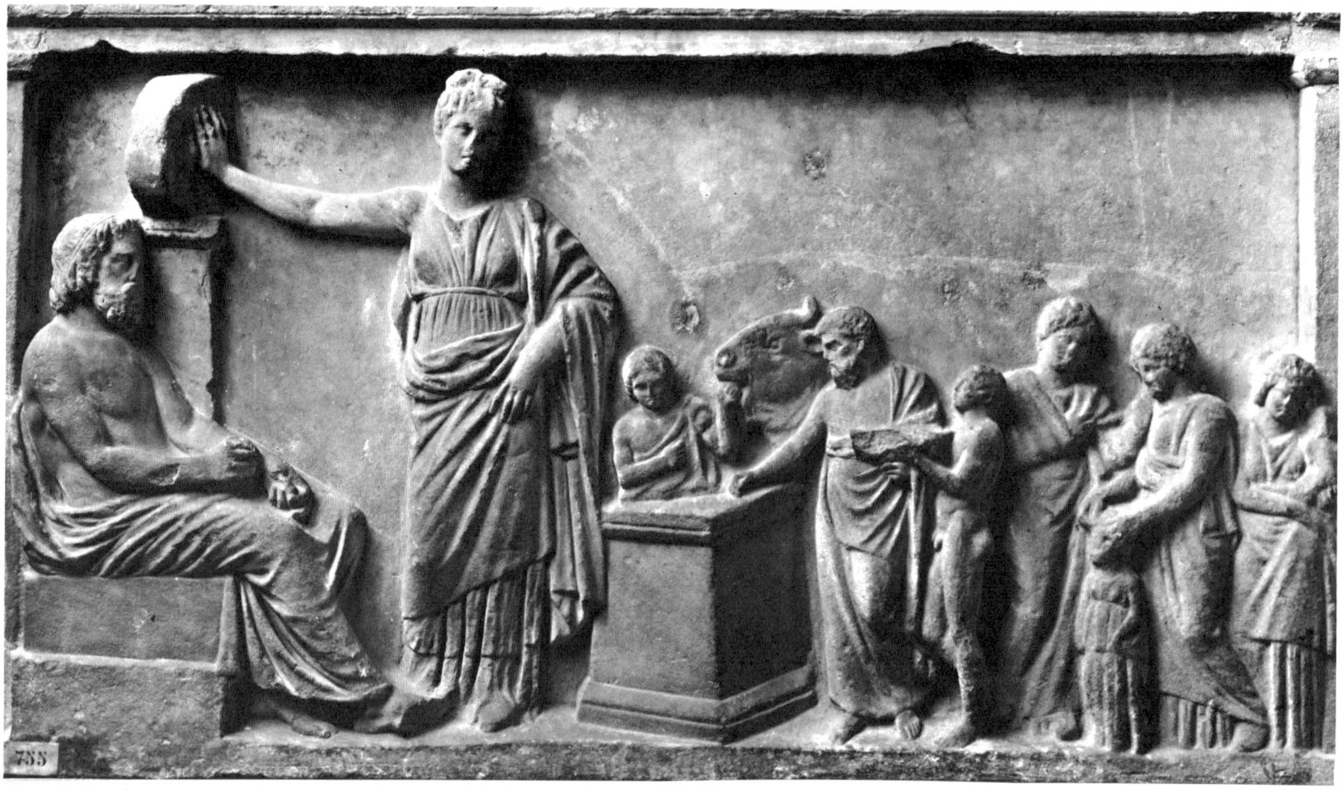

Votive relief to Asclepius and Hygieia. The god of health is seated on the left with his daughter Hygieia standing before him. On the right a family lead a sacrificial bull to the altar. Patients would spend the night on the skin of the sacrificed animal in one of the god's sanctuaries after observing special purificatory rites of a religious and medical nature. Cures were marked by ex-votos such as this.

It was also for offending the goddess, either by killing a stag in a wood that was sacred to her or by boasting that he was a more skilled hunter than she, that Agamemnon was wind-bound in the port of Aulis, together with the Greek fleet. He could obtain the return of favourable winds only by immolating to Artemis his own daughter, Iphigenia. But the goddess took pity on the innocent victim and snatched Iphigenia away at the moment of sacrifice, bearing her to Tauris where she was made a priestess of Artemis' cult.

In the Tauric Chersonese there existed, in fact, a local divinity who was later identified with the Hellenic Artemis and who was honoured by blood sacrifices. All strangers who were shipwrecked on the coasts of Tauris were sacrificed to her. Iphigenia presided over the sacrifices. One day her brother Orestes approached these inhospitable shores. He was condemned to death, but he revealed himself to his sister and together they fled, carrying with them the statue of the goddess, which was deposited in the town of Brauron in Attica and later transferred to a sanctuary on the Acropolis in Athens. It was venerated under the name of *Artemis Brauronia*, the bear being sacred to her. It was told a tame bear which wandered freely through the villages of Attica one day lacerated a girl with its claws. It was killed by the girl's brothers. Artemis in anger at once sent a deadly plague to Athens. The oracle, when consulted, replied that the scourge would cease only if the inhabitants consecrated their daughters to Artemis. And so, every five years, a procession of little girls from five to ten years old, dressed in saffron-coloured robes, would wend its way solemnly to the temple of Artemis.

The town of Limnaion in Laconia also gloried in the possession of the true Taurian Artemis. The statue had been found standing upright in the middle of a thicket – for this reason it was called Artemis Orthia (the upright) – and the discovery had been accompanied among the inhabitants of Limnaion and the neighbouring villages by an outbreak of madness, murders and epidemics. They succeeded in appeasing the bloodthirsty goddess by human sacrifices, later replaced by the flagellation of youths in front of the statue of Artemis. The statue was carried by the priestess, and it became heavier whenever the zeal of those performing the flagellation slackened.

We should be wrong, however, to consider the daughter of Leto only under this rough and barbarous aspect. Though she loved to roam the mountains and the valleys, she also permitted herself more gentle amusements. She was the sister of Apollo, god of the cithara, and she too was a musician-goddess: song and dancing were pleasing to *Artemis Hymnia*. 'When the chase has rejoiced her heart she unbends her bow and enters the vast dwelling-place of her brother in the rich land of Delphi and joins the lovely choir of the Muses and the Graces. There she hangs up her bow and arrows and, dressed in gracious style, leads and directs the choir.'

Artemis of Ephesus and the Amazons. We have said above that by a rather strange confusion the name of Artemis had been given to a fertility-goddess particularly venerated at Ephesus. The origin of this cult was said to go back to the Amazons, a mythical people of female warriors who had come from the region of the Caucasus to settle in Cappadocia on the banks of the Thermodon. There the Amazons founded a state whose capital was Themiscyra and which was ruled over by a queen. Men were not admitted. Once a year the Amazons would go to their neighbours the Gargarensians to form temporary unions. Of the children which resulted therefrom they would keep only the girls who, from infancy, were trained for the chase and for war. The ancient Greeks derived their name from *mazos*, 'breast', and '*a*', 'no', and explained that they removed their right breast in order to draw the bow more easily. But, apart from the fact that no trace of such mutilation is ever seen in representations of the Amazons, the peculiar aspect of Artemis of Ephesus, their great goddess, suggests that the prefix '*a*' has, on the contrary, an augmentative value.

To the Amazons was attributed the foundation of many towns: Smyrna, Ephesus, Cyme, Myrina and Paphos. From Cappadocia they reached the islands, landed at Lesbos and Samothrace, and had even penetrated Boeotia and Attica. The motive for this invasion of Attica was to avenge the abduction or the abandonment – one does not know exactly which – of Antiope by Theseus. Antiope was the sister of the Amazon queen, Hippolyta. In Athens they used to show the tombs of the Amazons who had perished in the course of the war, and every year the Athenians offered sacrifices to the *manes* of their enemies. The Amazons also fought in Lycia against Bellerophon, and against Hercules, who slew Hippolyta, their queen. During the Trojan war they came to the aid of Troy and saw their young queen, Penthesileia, fall beneath the blows of Achilles. It was also told how they sent an expedition against the isle of Leuce in the Black Sea, where they were put to flight by the shade

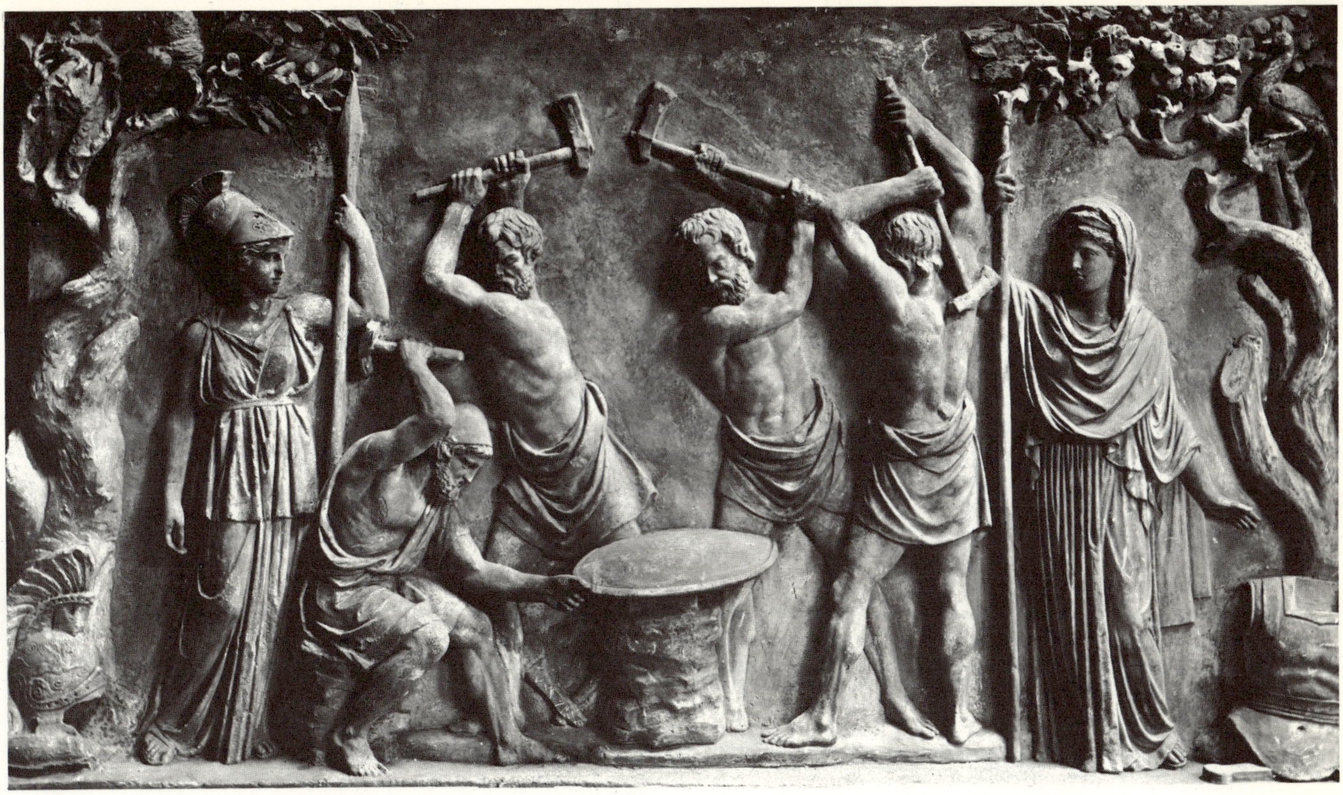

Hephaestus and the Cyclopes forging the shield of Achilles. Antique bas-relief. Rome. To the left, Athene, to the right, Hera.

of Achilles, whose sanctuary they were about to sack. By their warlike habits and their horror of men the Amazons offer some resemblance to the Greek Artemis, which is doubtless the reason why their great goddess was given the same name.

HERMES

As in the case of the other Greek gods, many etymologies have been proposed for the name Hermes. Some suggest a connection with the Vedic Sarameya, derived from Sarama, god of the storm or of the dawn; others relate Hermes to a Greek word which conveys the idea of movement; still others – thinking of the early representations of the god – suggest the word for 'stone' or 'rock', and also the verb which means 'to protect'.

Character and Functions. Certain details of Hermes' legend suggest that he was either a god of the twilight or of the wind. Such are his birth, his theft of Apollo's heifers – analogous to the cows of the Vedic Indra, which personified the clouds – the myth of his slaying Argus, later thought to explain the epithet *Argephontes*, a probable deformation of *Argeiphantes*, 'he makes the sky clear'. It is, however, more probable that Hermes was a very ancient Pelasgian divinity, of Thracian origin, who was particularly honoured by the shepherds of Arcadia and whose mission was to watch over their flocks and protect their huts. From this doubtless arose the Greek habit of placing at the doors of houses a more or less crude image of this god. The Dorian invasion lessened the prestige of Hermes. Apollo Nomius took his place, and the primitive Hermes of the shepherds and of animal fertility took on another character.

Hermes was above all thought of as the god of travellers, whom he guided on their perilous ways. His images were placed where country roads branched and at crossroads in towns. It is without doubt a natural extension of this role that Hermes was also charged with conducting the souls of the dead to the underworld. Unless, indeed, this *Hermes Psychopompus* (conductor of souls), who is sometimes differentiated from the celestial Hermes, was not a substitute for some older subterranean divinity, a kind of *Zeus Plutos*.

Since in primitive times voyages were scarcely undertaken except for commerical purposes, Hermes was consequently the god of commerce, the god of profit – lawful and unlawful – and the god of games of chance. And, since buying and selling require much discussion. and the art of the trader is to overcome the buyer's hesitation by subtle and persuasive words, Hermes became the god of eloquence, the god *Logios*.

To these various functions Hermes added that of being the messenger of Zeus. This is how he appears in Homer, where he is qualified with the epithet *Diactoros* (the messenger). He comes to earth ceaselessly with orders from the king of the gods and undertakes the most delicate missions. In Hesiod, Hermes is the god who brings to men's hearts the impressions and sentiments which Zeus has inspired.

This indefatigable runner could scarcely fail to be honoured by athletes. Thus he had the epithet *Agonios*, 'who presides over contests', especially in Boeotia. His statue stood at the entrance to the stadium at Olympia, and to him was attributed the invention of pugilism and racing.

Representations. The classic aspect of Hermes is that of an athlete-god. In primitive times he had been represented as a mature man with a thick, long beard, his hair bound with a fillet and falling in curls to his shoulders. Afterwards he became the idealised type of the *ephebe* or young gymnast, with lithe and graceful body. His hair is short and crisp, his features fine; he carries his head slightly inclined as though listening with friendly interest. His nervous and supple body is largely exposed by the chlamys tossed over his shoulder or wound round his left arm. He often wears a round, winged hat – a *petasus* – and on his feet there are winged sandals. In his hand he holds a winged staff around which serpents are entwined; this is the *caduceus*.

The Theft of Apollo's Heifers. Hermes, son of Zeus and Maia, was born in the depths of a cave on Mount Cyllene in Arcadia. On the very day of his birth Hermes displayed his mischievous humour by stealing the cattle which had been confided to the care of Apollo. Sneaking furtively from his cradle, the infant god climbed the mountains of Pieria, where he found the divine herd. From it he separated fifty lowing heifers which he drove before him under cover of the night to the banks of the Alpheus. He made them walk backwards so that their hoofmarks should not betray the direction they had taken. He himself had cautiously put enormous sandals of tamarisk and myrtle twigs on his delicate feet. Before shutting up the heifers in a cavern he picked out two of the fattest and, having ingeniously produced fire by rubbing twigs of laurel together, he roasted them, dividing the flesh into twelve equal portions in honour of the twelve great gods. After which he regained the heights of

Cyllene, re-entered his cave through the keyhole, 'like vapour or a breath of autumn', and crawled into his cradle again. On the following day Apollo noticed the disappearance of his heifers. He grasped – by divination – what had occurred and went at once to Cyllene, where Hermes stubbornly denied all knowledge of the theft. Apollo seized the infant in his arms and carried him to the tribunal of Zeus on Olympus. The master of the gods could not but laugh at the cunning of his new-born child but, as he also cherished Apollo, he instructed Hermes to return the heifers. 'The two handsome sons of Zeus then hastened to sandy Pylus, near the ford of the Alpheus, and they reached the fields and the tall stable where the objects of the theft had been shut in at nightfall.'

The Invention of the Lyre. Reconciliation between the two gods was completed by the gift Hermes made to Apollo of a musical instrument he had ingeniously devised. When he had set out on his nocturnal adventure, Hermes found a tortoise in his path. He picked it up and, with a bright chisel, emptied the shell. Around it he stretched oxhide with the aid of reeds and arranged over a bridge seven strings made from sheep gut which then gave out harmonious sounds. It was the first lyre.

When Apollo, still annoyed by the theft of his heifers continued bitterly to reproach him, Hermes struck the strings of the instrument he had just fashioned. Apollo was charmed by the sound and his anger died – 'while the delightful sound of the divine music penetrated his senses, a sweet desire took possession of him'. Hermes guessed that Apollo coveted the lyre and spontaneously gave it to him. In exchange Apollo gave Hermes a bright whip or a golden wand – a prototype of the caduceus – and entrusted him with the care of the celestial herd. From then on Apollo became the god of music and Hermes the protector of flocks and herds. The friendship of the two gods was never broken. On many occasions Hermes was of service to Apollo and, in particular, took charge at their birth of several of Apollo's children.

The Good Offices of Hermes. In spite of his malicious pranks Hermes won the sympathy of all the gods. Even the vindictive Hera forgot her jealousy where Hermes was concerned. Alone among the illegitimate children of Zeus, the son of Maia found favour with her and the august goddess even consented to suckle him.

Hermes was always willing to be helpful, and his ingenuity made him a valuable ally. During the war against the giants he put on the helmet of Hades – which made him invisible – and killed the giant Hippolytus. We have already seen how he freed Zeus, when Zeus was a prisoner of Typhoeus. He restored Zeus' strength by replacing the nerves which the giant had cut. During Zeus' amorous adventures, Hermes' aid was invaluable: he put the giant Argus to sleep with the sound of his flute and then, in order to free Io, killed him. When Dionysus was born it was Hermes who carried the child to Orchomenus and delivered him into the hands of Ino, Semele's sister. Zeus moreover made him his messenger. In order rapidly to cross the celestial spaces Hermes wore winged sandals which bore him 'over the watery sea or over the vast earth like a breath of wind'. To aid his flight he sometimes added wings to his hat.

When Ares fell into the hands of the Aloadae and was kept captive for thirteen months without anyone's knowing the place of his captivity, it was Hermes who finally discovered his prison and set him free. Again it was Hermes who, with the help of Iris, found in the abode of Tantalus the golden dog Pandareus had stolen from Zeus.

Hermes' protection was also extended to heroes: when Perseus faltered he restored his courage, and he accompanied Hercules during his descent to the underworld.

Hermes was a benefactor of mankind, and protected their flocks, guided them on their voyages, presided over their business affairs and inspired in them melodious speech and eloquence. Often he also took a direct part in their affairs. He plunged the Greeks into deep slumber with the aid of his magic wand 'with which he made drowsy the eyes of mortals or, if he so desired, roused them from sleep'. In doing this he made it possible for Priam to bring the body of his son Hector back into the walls of Troy. He gave Odysseus a magic plant which made him immune to the enchantments of Circe. We even see him one day, when the Euboeans were preparing to attack the city of Tanagra, put himself at the head of the youths of that city in order to repel the invaders.

Hermes, as we have seen, was also concerned with the underworld; for it was he who conducted the souls of the dead to their final dwelling-place. For this reason he was called *Psychopompus*.

Homer shows us the souls of Penelope's suitors slain by Odysseus as they fly after Hermes, rustling like bats, until they reach the 'fields of asphodel where dwell the phantoms of those who are no longer'. Hermes could also lead back the souls of the dead into the world of light. When Tantalus cut his own son into pieces and served them as a feast for the gods, Hermes, on the instructions of Zeus, re-assembled the pieces and restored the young man to life. Hermes also accompanied Orpheus on his search for Eurydice.

The Sons of Hermes. Hermes, like the other gods, had many amorous adventures. Among the goddesses he was, it appears, the lover of Persephone, Hecate and Aphrodite. Among nymphs, whom he pursued in the shady depths of forests, his conquests were wider. By them he had a numerous progeny among whom it is sufficient to mention: Saon, son of the nymph Phene, who colonised Samothrace; Polydorus, son of the Thessalian nymph Polymele; Daphnis, the beautiful and unhappy shepherd of Sicily, who was born in the neighbourhood of Etna; and above all Pan, the rustic god of Arcadia. While tending the flocks of Dryops on the slopes of Mount Cyllene, Hermes saw Dryops' daughter and loved her. She brought into the world a son who was covered with hair and had the horns and feet of a goat. In horror she abandoned him, but Hermes picked him up, wrapped him in the skin of a hare and then carried him to Olympus where the gods delighted in the spectacle. According to another tradition, Pan was the son of a mortal, Penelope, whom Hermes came to in the guise of a he-goat.

Among the mortals whom Hermes loved were Acacallis, daughter of Minos, whom he made mother of Cydon, founder of the Cretan town of Cydonia, and Chione, who also bore him a son, Autolycus. Autolycus received from his father the gift of rendering what he touched invisible. In this way he was able to commit numerous thefts until one day Sisyphus, whose oxen he had stolen, caught him. Another son of Hermes was Myrtilus, who was killed by Pelops: the god avenged himself on the murderer's descendants.

ARES

Should we, with Max Muller, connect the name Ares – like Mars – with the Sanskrit root *mar*, from which derive the Vedic *maruts*, storm-divinities? Or with the Greek root which means 'carry away, destroy'? Both hypotheses are equally ingenious and equally uncertain.

Character and Representations. Ares originated in Thrace. He was always thought of by the Greeks with more terror than sympathy, and his role was strictly limited. He was simply the god of war, of blind, brutal courage, of bloody rage and carnage. Hypotheses which would make him primitively a fertility-god or a solar deity seem to be unfounded.

Actually we know little more about this god than what the poets tell us. He was, however, honoured throughout Greece and his cult was particularly developed in Thrace and Scythia. He had a temple in Athens. Olympia honoured him under the name Ares-Hippios, and Sparta under that of Ares-Enyalius (the warlike). A spring was consecrated to him near Thebes, beneath the temple of Apollo.

In Greek sculpture Ares was not represented by any especially fixed type. We scarcely know him except from vase paintings. At first he was depicted as a bearded warrior wearing a helmet with a tall crest and dressed in heavy armour. Later he appears as a young man, almost nude, who has retained little of his warlike attributes except the spear and helmet.

The Rages of Ares. 'Of all the gods who live on Olympus', says Zeus in the *Iliad* to Ares, 'thou art the most odious to me; for thou enjoyest nothing but strife, war and battles. Thou hast the obstinate and unmanageable disposition of thy mother Hera, whom I can scarcely control with my words.'

In expressing these unfriendly sentiments to his son, the master of the gods exactly defines the character of Ares, 'a furious god, by nature wicked and fickle', who in the immortal society of Olympus found, it seems, very little sympathy.

As god of war it was natural that he enjoyed fighting. Mounted

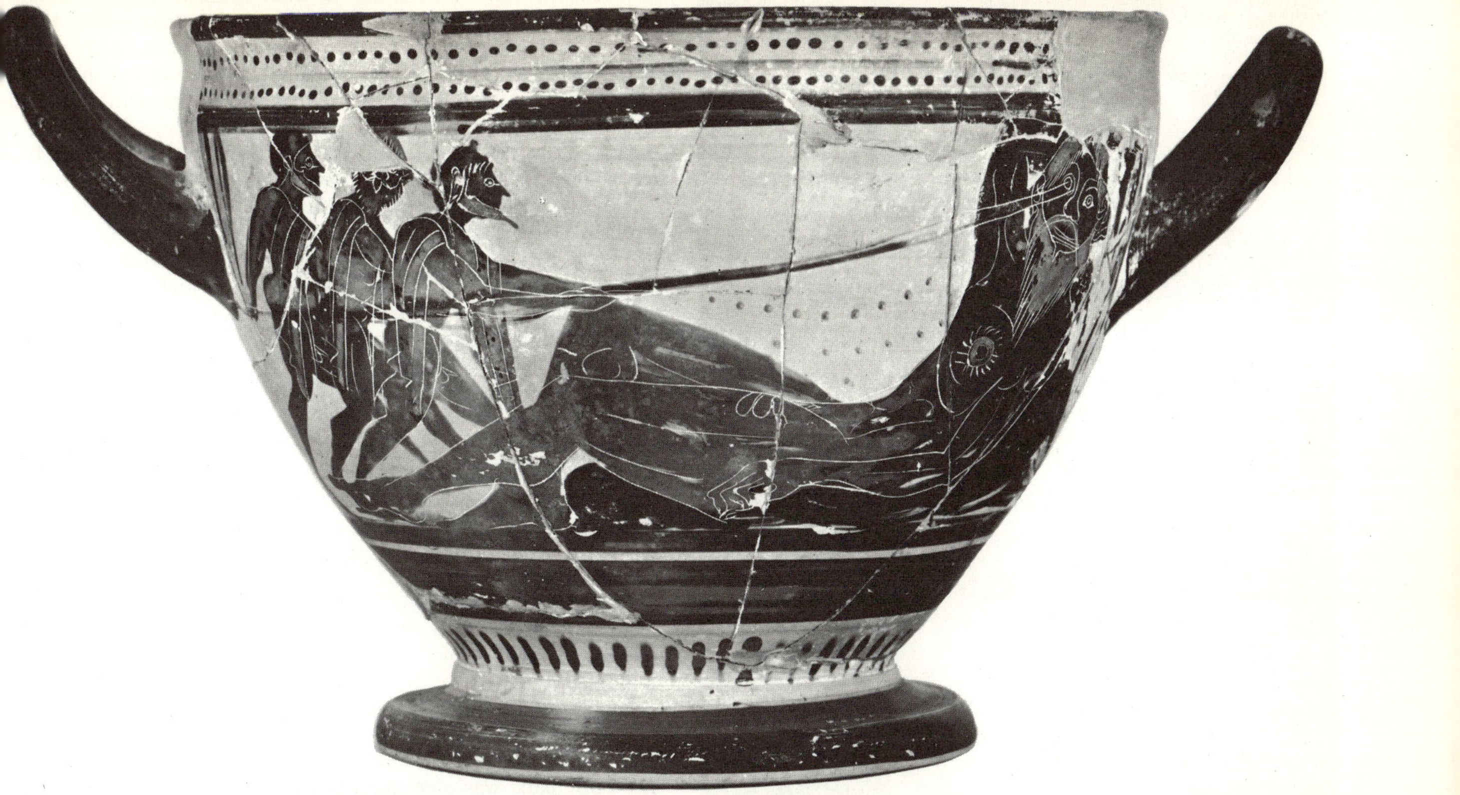

The blinding of Polyphemus. Odysseus and two of his companions drive a sharpened stake into the eye of the sleeping Cyclops who had been keeping them prisoner on their return journey from Troy in order to devour them. Though the Cyclopes traditionally only had one eye in the middle of their foreheads, the artist has depicted Polyphemus as having two in the normal manner. Black-figured Boeotian skyphos, second quarter of the sixth century B.C.

on a chariot drawn by swift horses with golden brow-bands, clad in bronze armour and grasping in his hands an enormous spear, Ares ranged the battlefield, striking deadly blows on all sides. His two squires, Deimos (Fear) and Phobos (Fright) – sometimes said to be his sons – accompanied him, together with Eris (Strife), 'insatiable in her fury', Enyo, 'destroyer of cities', and the Keres, sombre divinities, eager to drink the black blood of the dying.

Though none disputed his warlike ardour, Ares was disliked not only for his perpetual thirst for blood and slaughter which made him the 'scourge of mortals', but for his brutality and blind violence. It was in this, especially, that he differed from Athene who, as a warrior-goddess, represented cool and intelligent courage. Ares and Athene were thus constantly opposed. Many times they encountered each other on the plains of Ilium where they fought on opposite sides. The very sight of Athene set Ares in a rage. 'Why, then, shameless fly, dost thine insatiable audacity enflame the war between the gods? What ardour carries thee away? I think that to-day thou shalt pay for all thou hast done to me!' With these words he struck the terrible aegis which even the thunderbolt of Zeus could not break. Athene, drawing back, took up a stone which was lying on the plain: a black stone, rugged and enormous, which men of past ages had put there to serve as a boundary stone for the field. She hurled it at the neck of the impetuous Ares. His knees gave way and when he fell his body covered seven acres. Dust soiled his hair and about him his armour jangled. Pallas Athene smiled and, glorying in her exploit, addressed to him winged words: 'Vain fool! Hast thou not yet learned how superior my strength is to thine?'

Indeed the impetuous Ares, contrary to what one might expect, rarely emerged victorious from combat. Nor was it only the immortal gods who got the better of him. Otus and Ephialtes, the two Aloadae, succeeded in binding and keeping him captive for thirteen months. When he challenged Hercules, who had just killed his son Cycnus, Ares was wounded by the hero and forced to return groaning to Olympus. According to others, Zeus, who did not wish to see his two sons quarrel, put an end to the fight by dropping a thunderbolt between the two combatants.

The Loves of Ares. He was scarcely more happy in his love affairs. Impressed by the glamour of the handsome warrior whom she doubtless compared with Hephaestus, her ill-favoured husband, Aphrodite fell in love with Ares. The sentiment was quickly reciprocated. Ares took unscrupulous advantage of Hephaestus' absence to dishonour the marital couch; but Helios, who had observed the two lovers, reported the business to the smith-god. Although a deceived husband is usually an object of ridicule, Hephaestus was able to parry the laughter by an ingenious artifice. Secretly he forged a net so fine that it could not be seen, but so strong that it could not be broken. He arranged this net above the couch where the lovers normally frolicked, and pretended to leave for Lemnos.

'As soon as Ares saw the industrious Hephaestus depart he directed his steps towards the dwelling-place of the illustrious god, burning with love for Cytheraea of the fair crown. She was seated. He took her hand and said, "Come, my dear, let us lie on the couch of Hephaestus, for thy good man has gone to Lemnos, the land of the barbarous-tongued Sintians."' Thus he spoke, and his words were pleasing to the goddess. Soon they fell asleep and the invisible net of the ingenious Hephaestus spread over them. Then the limping god, who had retraced his steps, cried out in a terrible voice to all the gods:

'"Zeus and ye Immortals! Come in haste and see this intolerable thing, worthy of your laughter. Because I am lame Aphrodite despises me. She loves the fatal Ares because he is agile and handsome. See them both, asleep on my couch. Soon they will no longer care to sleep; for these cords will keep them bound together until Zeus returns the gifts I made him in order to obtain this impudent wench who cannot restrain her lust!"'

Then the gods gathered together in the palace of bronze and from their throats rose roars of uncontrollable laughter which threw Ares and Aphrodite into a state of extreme confusion. Hephaestus at last consented to free the two guilty ones when Ares promised to pay him the price of the adultery. The guilty wife fled to Paphos in the island of Cyprus and the seducer retired into the mountains of Thrace. From the union of Ares and Aphrodite a daughter was born, Harmonia, who later became the wife of Cadmus, King of Thebes.

Whether Ares had other misadventures of this nature is unknown, but he had little luck with his children.

By the nymph Aglauros Ares had a daughter, Alcippe. One day

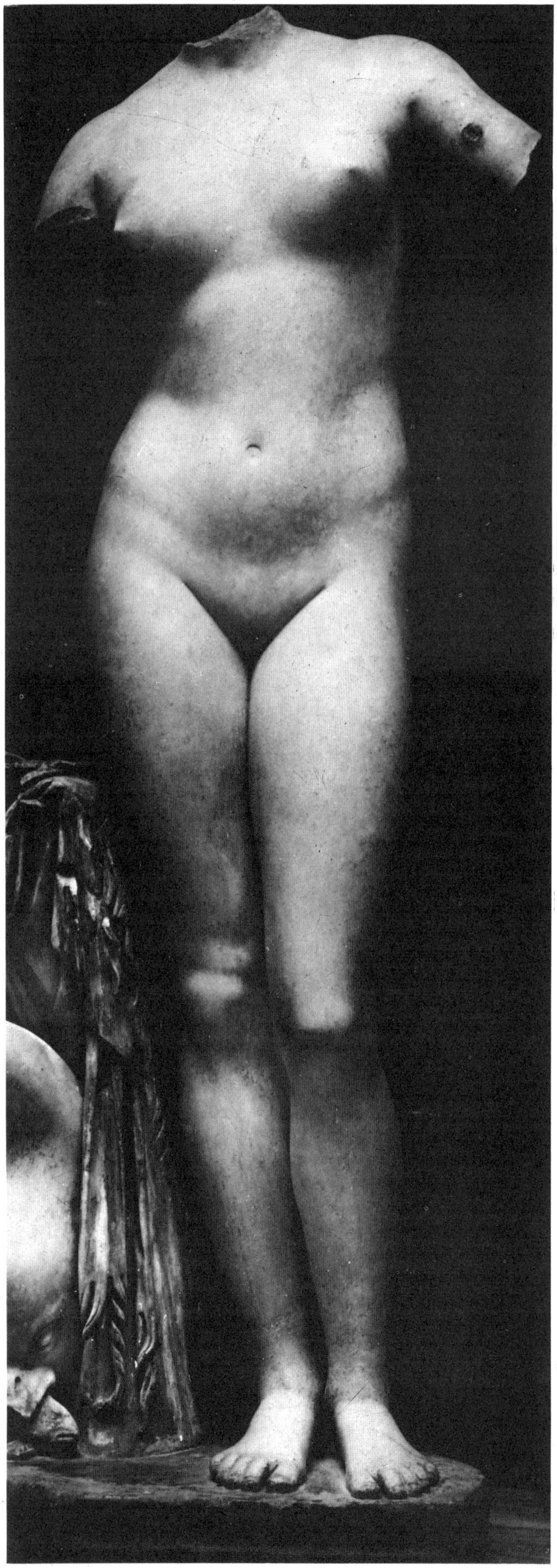

Aphrodite of Cyrene. Inspired by Hesiod's account of the goddess' birth, this statue from Cyrene in Libya shows Aphrodite, 'the foam-born', freshly risen from the sea in the act of wringing out her hair.
A dolphin frolics by her feet. The goddess of love was worshipped throughout the Greek world, her cult reaching as far West as Italy and Sicily. Early Hellenistic original, or possibly a Roman copy.

Halirrhothius, son of Poseidon, ravished her and Ares killed him. For this murder Poseidon summoned him before the tribunal of the twelve great gods, which met on a hill situated in front of the Acropolis in Athens. Ares was acquitted. In memory of this event the hill received the name of the Areopagus, and afterwards criminal cases continued to be judged there.

Among the other children of Ares who came to unhappy ends it is sufficient to mention: Phlegyas, son of Chryse, who was killed by Apollo; Diomedes, King of the Bistones of Thrace, who was put to death by Hercules; Cycnus, son of Pelopeia or of Pyrene, who was also killed by Hercules: cruel and belligerent like his father, Cycnus used to attack travellers in the region of Tempe and use their bones for building a temple to his father. He challenged Hercules, who struck him down and, into the bargain, wounded Ares himself, who had tried to defend his son. Some genealogies say that the unhappy Meleager, son of Oeneus and Althaea, was also the son of Ares.

Having seduced Harpina, daughter of the river-god Asopus, Ares had by her a son, Oenomaus, who reigned near Olympia, and himself had a daughter, Hippodameia. Since an oracle had predicted that he would be killed by his son-in-law, Oenomaus, in order to get rid of her suitors, announced that he would give his daughter only to the man who beat him in a chariot race. He was certain he would always win, because Ares his father had made him a gift of winged steeds. Pelops, however, carried away the prize, thanks to a treacherous ruse of Hippodameia herself, and Oenomaus found death in defeat.

Finally, among mortal women who were loved by Ares, there was Aerope, daughter of Cepheus, who died in giving birth to a son, Aeropus. However, thanks to the intervention of Ares, the new-born babe was able miraculously to suckle at the breast of his deceased mother.

HEPHAESTUS

Origin, Function and Representations. Whether we see in the name Hephaestus the Greek form of the Sanskrit *Yavishtha* (the very young), an epithet of Agni, the Vedic god of fire, or whether we derive it from the Greek words for 'hearth' and 'to kindle', there is no doubt that Hephaestus was, from remotest times, the personification of terrestrial fire, of which volcanoes were the most terrifying manifestation.

Thus the cult of Hephaestus, who was perhaps an Asiatic divinity, a native of Lycia, first arose on the volcanic island of Lemnos. From there it was brought to Attica and, with the colonisations, introduced into Sicily.

It is possible that in primitive times Hephaestus personified celestial fire and that he had thus been a thunder-god; his limping gait would then symbolise the zigzag of the lightning. If fire is of celestial origin then there is no reason why Hephaestus should not have such a character.

The fire which he represents is not, however, the destroying element, but rather the beneficent element which permits men to work metal and foster civilisation. Thus Hephaestus appears as the divine blacksmith, the artisan-god, the demiurge who has created admirable works and taught men the mechanical arts.

That is why Hephaestus – who was at first depicted as a beardless young man – was afterwards traditionally represented as a robust smith, with bearded face, powerful neck and hairy chest. His short and sleeveless chiton leaves his right shoulder bare; on his head he wears a conical bonnet and in his hands he grasps a hammer and tongs.

The Birth of Hephaestus. Although Hesiod's genealogy claims that Hephaestus was, like Typhon, born by Hera alone, it was generally admitted that he was the son of Hera and Zeus. At most one was sometimes given to understand that he was conceived before the official marriage of the two deities and that Hera had invented this legend of a miraculous birth in order to conceal her shame.

In contrast with the other Immortals, who were distinguished by beauty and the symmetry of their bodies, Hephaestus was ill-made and lame in both legs. His feet were twisted. His stumbling gait and dislocated hip aroused the 'unquenchable laughter of the Immortals' when he walked among them.

His Misadventures. Contrary to what was often said Hephaestus' infirmity was not the result of an accident. He was lame from birth. Homer, in fact, recounts that Hera, ashamed of the ugliness of her son, tried to hide him from the Immortals 'because he was lame'. She threw him from the heights of Olympus into the sea, where he was taken in by Thetis, daughter of Nereus, and Eurynome, daughter of the old Ocean. For nine years he remained concealed in their deep grotto, 'forging a thousand ingenious objects for the two nymphs', and at the same time preparing a cunning revenge. One day Hera received a gift from her son, a golden throne artistically wrought. She sat on it with delight, but when she tried to rise again she was suddenly gripped by invisible bands. The Immortals tried in vain to extricate her from the throne. Only Hephaestus was capable of releasing her, but he refused to leave the depths of the Ocean. Ares tried to drag him up by force, but was put to flight by Hephaestus who threw burning brands at him. Dionysus was more successful: he made Hephaestus drunk and, while he was drunk, perched him astride a mule and thus brought him back to Olympus. But they still had to meet his demands: Hephaestus refused to set Hera free unless they gave him the loveliest of the goddesses, Aphrodite – though some say Athene – for a bride. According to another tradition the reason why Hephaestus bound up Hera was to make her tell him the secret of his birth.

From then on there was peace between Hera and her son. Indeed, forgetting his former rancour, Hephaestus at the peril of his life attempted to defend his mother when she was beaten by Zeus. Irritated by his son, Zeus seized him by one foot and flung him from the courts of heaven. All day long he tumbled through space and, at sunset, fell more dead than alive on to the island of Lemnos, where the Sintians gathered him up.

The Blacksmith of Olympus. Under this graceless exterior, however, lurked a subtle and inventive spirit. Hephaestus excelled in the art of working metals. On Olympus he built palaces for the gods. For himself he constructed a 'sparkling dwelling of glittering and incorruptible bronze'. In it he had his workshop. There he could be seen beside the flaming furnaces, bathed in sweat, bustling about his bellows, poking the fires under twenty crucibles at a time, or hammering out the molten metal on an enormous anvil. When some god came to visit him, the gigantic blacksmith would pause to sponge his face, his hands, his powerful neck and hairy chest. He would put on a tunic and, leaning against a heavy staff, reach his gleaming throne. In order to steady his unsure footsteps – for his frail legs supported his massive body with difficulty – he had even fashioned two golden statues which resembled living girls. They had been endowed with movement and hastened to his side to aid him as he walked.

The Earthly Dwellings of Hephaestus. Homer placed the workshop of Hephaestus on Olympus. But the fire-god also haunted the earth, where he maintained various underground places of residence. He had done his apprenticeship as a blacksmith in the isle of Naxos and it was said that he unsuccessfully disputed the possession of the island with Dionysus. If so, understanding between the two gods was quickly re-established, and they always remained on excellent terms. Often the Sileni and the Satyrs helped Hephaestus in his work. To initiate him in the art of the forge Hera, it was said, had confided Hephaestus to the dwarf Cedalion, whose identity is rather mysterious. Some call him the son, others the father of Hephaestus. All that is known is that he always remained attached to the fire-god and followed him to Lemnos when Hephaestus set up an establishment there.

Hephaestus, indeed, had never forgotten the welcome the Sintians had given him on the occasion of his fall from Olympus and, in gratitude, settled in this volcanic island. His presence there was attested by the flaming vapours which escaped from Mount Moschylus to the accompanying sound of dull rumbling. This was the sound of the divine blacksmith's hammers from the workshop he had set up in the bowels of the mountain. Beside him worked the faithful Cedalion from whom he was never separated, except on the occasion when he lent him as a guide to the blind giant Orion who wished to be conducted to the West in order to recover his eyesight. Hephaestus was also helped by the Cabeiri, who were probably his sons. One tradition says Prometheus came to Lemnos to steal the divine fire which he then gave to mankind.

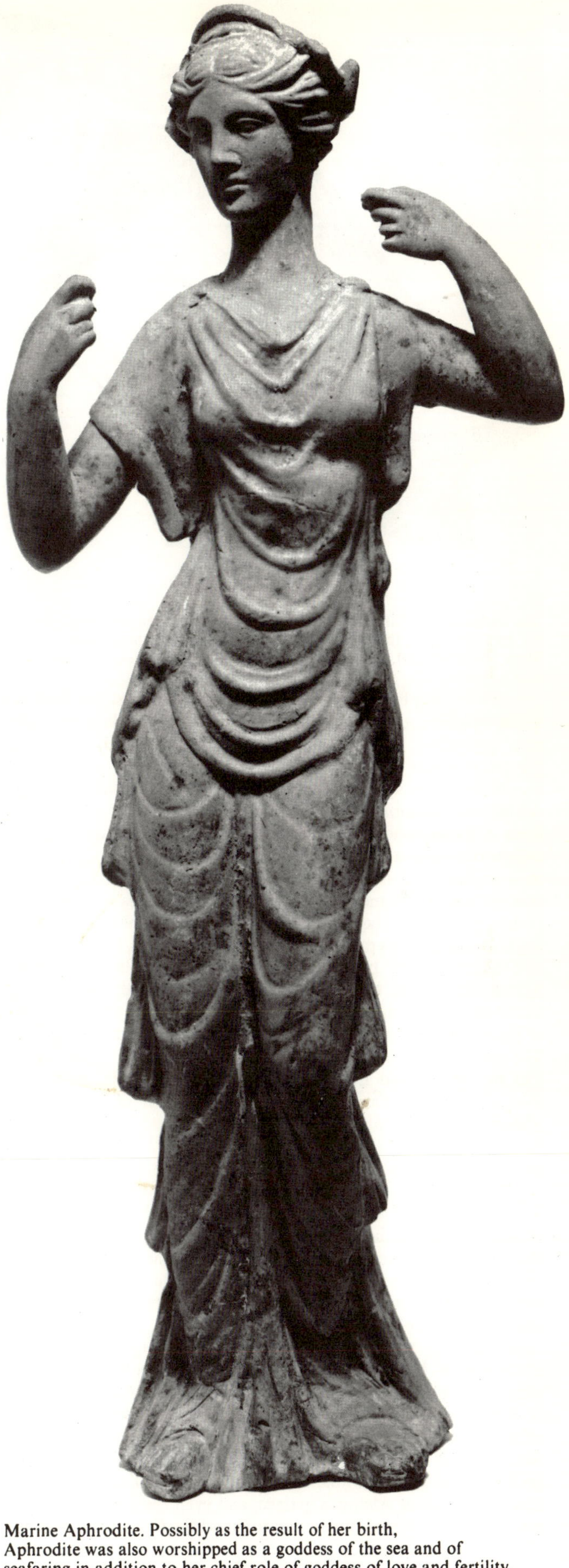

Marine Aphrodite. Possibly as the result of her birth, Aphrodite was also worshipped as a goddess of the sea and of seafaring in addition to her chief role of goddess of love and fertility. As Aphrodite Euploia she gave prosperous voyages and as Aphrodite Galenaia, fair weather, her shrine as a marine goddess being at Hermione. Of her numerous other sanctuaries the most famous were at Paphos, Cythera and Corinth. Late first century B.C.

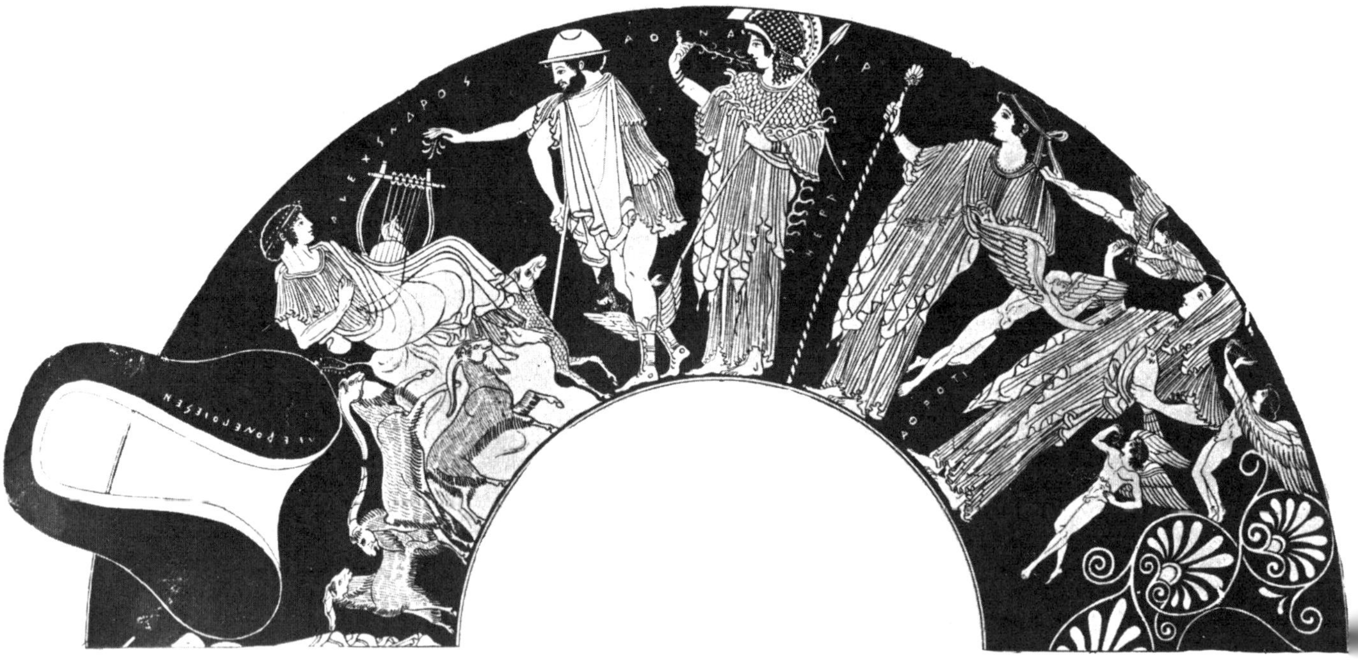

The Judgment of Paris. Hermes leads the three contending goddesses into the presence of Paris who is seated on the left guarding his father's flocks and playing the lyre. Behind the messenger of the gods in his winged sandals comes Athene, armed with her helmet and spear, followed by Hera, with her staff, and Aphrodite, who is accompanied by Erotes and carries a dove. Detail from a red-figured kylix by Herron.

Later on Hephaestus emigrated to Sicily. At first we find him in the volcanic archipelago of the Lipari Islands. He it doubtless was, mysterious and obliging blacksmith, who at night wrought the metal which was left in the evening on the edge of a crevasse and found there again next morning wondrously worked. Subterranean ramifications connected the Lipari Islands with Mount Etna in Sicily, where Hephaestus finally settled. He dislodged an indigenous demon called Adranus. In Etna Hephaestus also acted as a gaoler to Typhoeus who, it will be remembered, had been crushed under this mountain by Zeus. Earthquakes and eruptions of lava were due to the convulsions of this monster when he attempted to break from his prison. But he could not escape, for Hephaestus had placed on his head heavy anvils on which he energetically hammered bronze and iron. When sailors skirted the coasts of Sicily and saw long streamers of smoke escaping from the crest of Etna they had no doubt that it was Hephaestus lighting his forge. The god was helped in his task by the Palici, twins whom he had had by the Oceanid Etna (though others say that the Palici were sons of Zeus and the nymph Aethalia, daughter of Hephaestus). The giant Cyclopes also assisted him.

His Works. The activity of Hephaestus was prodigious and only equalled by his skill. He was ceaselessly employed on some work of great delicacy. As well as the palaces on Olympus with their bronze trimmings, he fashioned Zeus' golden throne, sceptre and thunderbolts, the fearful aegis, the winged chariot of Helios, the arrows of Apollo and Artemis, Demeter's sickle, Hercules' cuirass, the arms of Peleus, the armour of Achilles, the necklace which Harmonia, wife of Cadmus, wore for her nuptials, Ariadne's diadem, Agamemnon's sceptre, the hypogeum or underground chamber of Oenopion. Nor should one forget the golden goblet which Zeus offered to Aphrodite, a vase given by Dionysus to Ariadne, the *harpe* of Perseus and Adonis' hunting equipment. To Hephaestus were also attributed such works of wonder as the tripods with golden wheels which rolled of their own accord into the assembly of the gods, the bronze bulls whose nostrils spurted forth flame, the golden and silver dogs of Alcinous' palace, and even the giant Talos 'that man of bronze' whose duty it was to guard the Cretan tree and prevent its being approached.

Nothing was impossible to him. When Zeus, in order to punish men, decided to create the first woman, Pandora, it was to Hephaestus that he turned. He ordered Hephaestus to mould the body of a woman with water and clay, to give it life and a human voice, and to form from it a virgin of ravishing beauty. To perfect his work Hephaestus encircled Pandora's brow with a golden crown which he himself had engraved.

On many other occasions Hephaestus gave assistance to Zeus. He split his skull with an axe in order that Athene might spring out. On his orders he bound Prometheus to the Caucasus. Doubtless he remembered the harsh lesson his father had given him when he had dared to cross Zeus' will. For this reason Hephaestus would pacify the other gods on Olympus, and especially Hera, when they were angry with Zeus. To all he preached submission: 'Have patience, O my mother, and, in spite of thy sorrow, be resigned so that I shall not see thee struck before my eyes. No matter how distressing this would be I could not come to thine aid; for it is hard to oppose the master of Olympus.' And all these quarrels spoiled the joy of living. 'The finest feast is without pleasure when discord triumphs.'

His Loves. Hephaestus was addicted to all pleasures. In spite of his ugliness he became the husband of Aphrodite. The position was not without its compensations, nor without its risks: his wife was continually unfaithful to him, especially with Ares. We have already seen with what spirit Hephaestus avenged himself by imprisoning the two lovers in a net and exposing them thus to the laughter of the Olympians. This misadventure did not prevent Hephaestus himself from aspiring to the love of the wise Athene. But the goddess successfully resisted him and he tried in vain to ravish her in the plain of Marathon. Certain legends say that Hephaestus' passion for Athene dated from the very moment of her birth. Before he struck Zeus with the axe which would liberate Athene from his head, Hephaestus had demanded the hand of the virgin who was about to appear. Zeus, they said, consented; but Athene herself refused to keep her father's promise. Must one see in these pursuits and evasions a symbol of the rivalry between these two working-gods, or an antagonism between celestial fire (Athene) and terrestrial fire (Hephaestus)? It is more probable that their histories are mingled simply because both were patrons of men's work and hence frequently associated.

Hephaestus was also said to have married the beautiful Charis and Aglaia, one of the Graces. By Cabeiro, daughter of Proteus, he was the father of the Cabeiri. The Oceanid Etna bore him twins, the Palici, the Dioscuri of Sicily; though another tradition says that they were sons of Zeus and the nymph Aethalia, daughter of Hephaestus. To escape Hera's vengeance Aethalia begged the earth to conceal her until the day of her delivery. Her prayers were granted and when her time came the two children sprang from the earth, whence their name: 'They who return to the light'. Two small lakes at the foot of Etna, always full of boiling sulphur water, marked the place where they had appeared. Their temple was there, and there they delivered oracles.

Among the other sons of Hephaestus may be mentioned Ardalus, Palaemon, Pylius – who cared for Philoctetes in Lemnos – and Periphetes who, like his father, was lame – which did not, however, prevent him from attacking travellers on the outskirts of Epidaurus and slaying them with his brazen club. He was killed by Theseus.

The Companions of Hephaestus. We have seen that Hephaestus was aided in his work by a certain number of subterranean divinities or fire genii. The best known were the Cyclopes, who assisted him at the forges under Etna. The first Cyclopes who appear in Greek mythology were the three sons of Uranus and Gaea: Arges, Steropes and Brontes. It may be remembered how after their father had cast them into Tartarus they were delivered by Zeus, whom they helped in his struggle against the Titans. Apart from thunder, the thunderbolt and the lightning which they gave Zeus, they presented Hades with a bronze helmet and Poseidon with a trident. They were put to death by Apollo, who took his vengeance on them for the death of his son Asclepius.

These earlier Cyclopes had nothing in common with the Cyclopes whom Homer introduces us to in the *Odyssey.* The latter were men of gigantic stature and repellent ugliness with their single eye in the middle of their forehead, who inhabited the south-west coast of Sicily. Given to a pastoral existence, they were gross and ill-mannered, living in isolated caverns, slaughtering and devouring any strangers who approached their shores. The best known among them was Polyphemus, who took Odysseus and his companions prisoner. In order to escape, the Greek hero made Polyphemus drunk and put out his single eye by means of a sharpened, burning stake; Odysseus and his companions then escaped from the cavern by tying themselves under the bellies of rams. Before this misfortune Polyphemus had fallen in love with the Nereid Galatea. He paid court to her by sending her a daily present of a bear or an elephant. To this inelegant suitor Galatea preferred the shepherd Acis, son of the nymph Symoethis. Jealous of this rival Polyphemus crushed him beneath a rock, and Acis was changed by the gods into a river.

When tradition made Mount Etna the abode of Hephaestus he was given the Cyclopes as companions. They borrowed their features from the Cyclopes of Hesiod and Homer. They were, says Callimachus, 'enormous giants, as big as mountains, and their single eye, under a bushy eyebrow, glittered menacingly. Some made the vast bellows roar, others, laboriously raising one by one their heavy hammers, struck great blows at the molten bronze and iron they drew from the furnace.' Their number was not stated. Among the names which were given to them we find those of Brontes, Steropes, Acamas and Pyracmon.

At Lemnos the Cyclopes were replaced by the Cabeiri, divinities whose origin and nature have remained rather mysterious especially since they occur in various regions with quite distinct characters. The Cabeiri of Lemnos, said to be the sons of Hephaestus, were benevolent genii, underground smiths evidently associated with the volcanic nature of the island's structure. At Samothrace the Cabeiri were a kind of inferior god, sworn to the service of the great gods of the island; tradition made them the sons of Zeus and Calliope. At Thebes in Boeotia the Cabeiri appear to have been associated with the cult of Demeter and Kore, since their temple was situated near a grove sacred to these two goddesses. In Thessaly they spoke of a Cabeire who was put to death by his two brothers and buried at the foot of Olympus. Finally we find Cabeiri at Pergamus in Phoenicia, and Herodotus believed he recognised them in Egypt. From all this it would seem that the Cabeiri, whose name has been compared with the Phoenician *qabirim,* 'the powerful', were in primitive times underground spirits, originating in Phrygia, who in the volcanic islands naturally took on the character of fire genii. They were reputed to be the first metal-workers.

The Greeks, however, recognised other metallurgical genii who, without being directly concerned with the cult of Hephaestus, must be mentioned here.

In the forests of Phrygian Ida there lived cunning magicians called the Dactyls. Originally there were three of them: Celmis, Damnameneus and the powerful Acmon, 'who in the caves of the mountains was the first to practise the art of Hephaestus, and

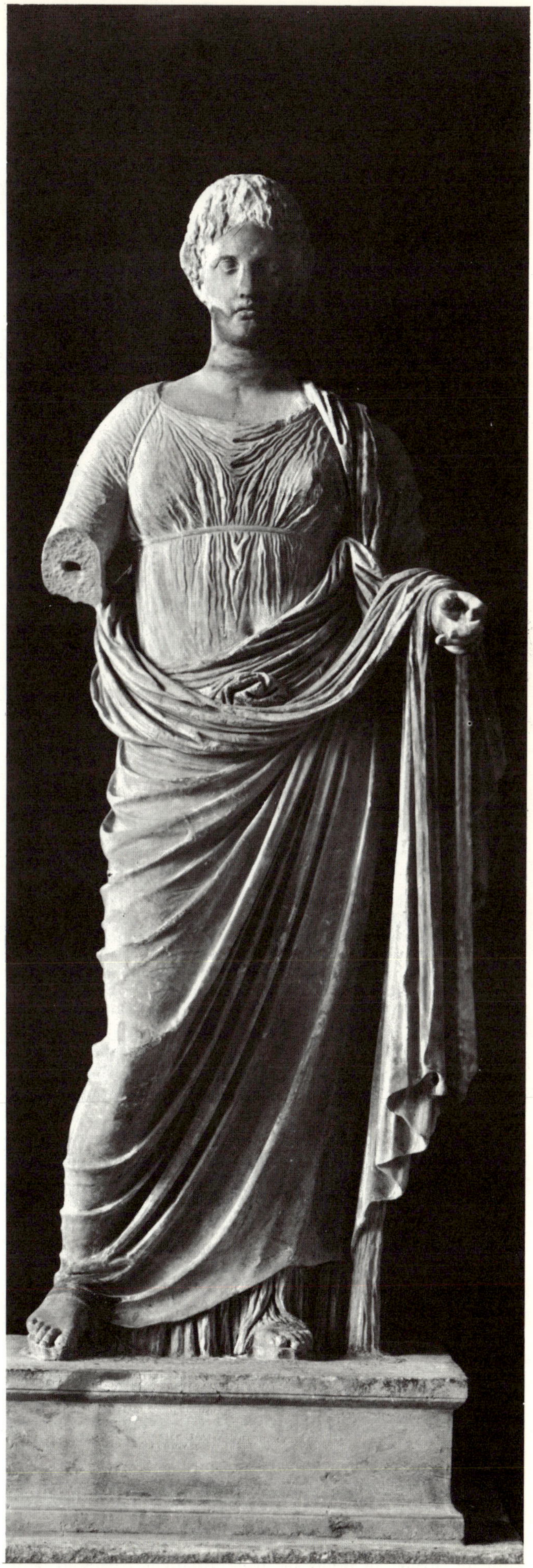

The Themis of Rhamnus. National Museum, Athens.

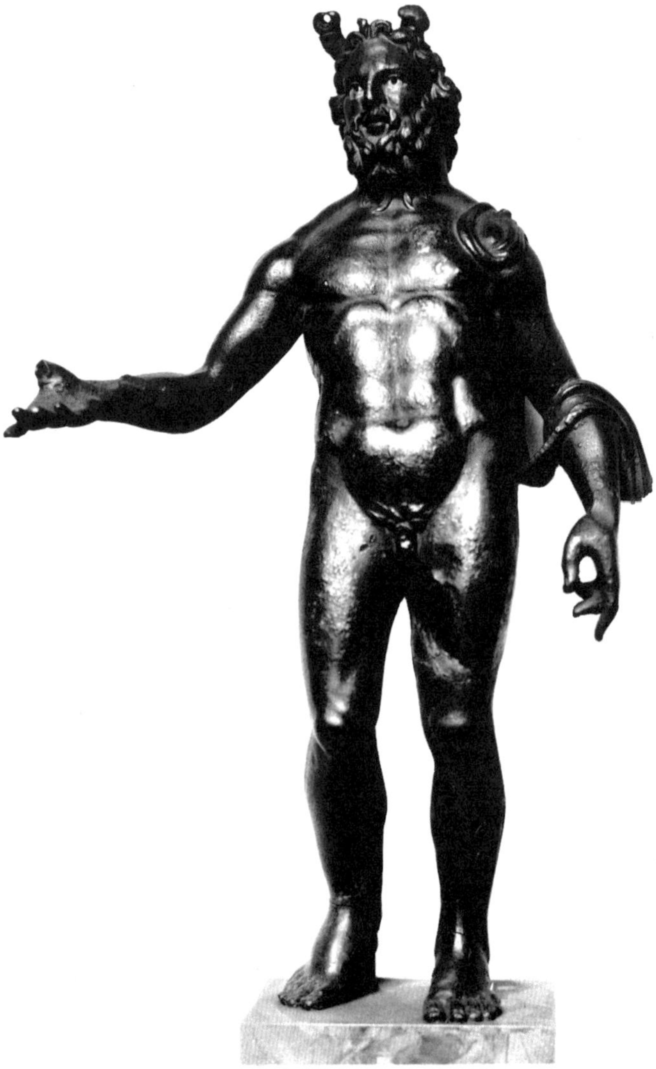

Oceanus. The father of the three thousand Oceanids and the three thousand rivers, Oceanus is portrayed as a vigorous middle-aged man with marine animals in his hair in this antique bronze. Originally conceived as one of the great elemental forces which had helped form the world, Oceanus was believed to encircle the entire universe with his waters from which rose the sun and the stars. His importance diminished in the later stages of Greek culture.

who knew how to work blue iron, casting it into the burning furnace'. Later their number increased. From Phrygia they went to Crete where they taught the inhabitants the use of iron and how to work metals. To them was also attributed the discovery of arithmetic and the letters of the alphabet.

Genii who also played a civilising role but afterwards assumed a malignant character were the Telchines, said to be the sons of Poseidon and Thalassa, though another tradition makes them Poseidon's guardians. The centre of their cult was the Isle of Rhodes, whence they spread to Crete and Boeotia. They were great metalworkers, as the names of three of them suggest: Chryson, Argyron and Chalcon. They forged the first statues of the gods, and among their works were the sickle of Cronus and the trident of Poseidon. But they were feared for their enchantments. They could cast the evil eye and, by sprinkling the ground with the waters of the Styx mixed with sulphur, they blighted the harvest and killed the flocks.

APHRODITE

Origin and Character. Though the primitive Greeks certainly had a goddess of love it would seem she was not Aphrodite. We must not be misled by the legend which arose later to justify an etymology based on a sort of pun which connects her name with the Greek word for 'foam'. In reality the name Aphrodite seems to be of oriental origin, probably Phoenician, like the goddess herself – sister of the Assyro-Babylonian Ishtar and the Syro-Phoenician Astarte. From Phoenicia the cult of Aphrodite passed to Cythera, a Phoenician trading-post, and to Cyprus (whence the epithets Cytheraean and Cyprian which the goddess has in Homer); then it spread throughout Greece and even reached Sicily.

In origin Aphrodite was – like the great Asiatic goddesses – obviously a fertility goddess whose domain embraced all nature, vegetable and animal as well as human. Afterwards she became the goddess of love in its noblest aspect as well as in its most degraded.

Aphrodite Urania, or the celestial Aphrodite, was the goddess of pure and ideal love. Aphrodite Genetrix or Nymphia favoured and protected marriage: unmarried girls and widows prayed to her in order to obtain husbands. Aphrodite Pandemos (common) or Aphrodite Porne (courtesan) was the goddess of lust and venal love, the patroness of prostitutes. Under the influence of her legend Aphrodite later became a marine deity (Pelagia, Pontia).

Cult and Representations. The chief centres of the cult of Aphrodite were Paphos in Cyprus and Cythera in Crete. Among her most famous sanctuaries were the temple of Cnidus in Caria and the temple on the Isle of Cos. Aphrodite Pandemos was venerated at Thebes, where a statue of the goddess could be seen, made, they said, of the battering-rams of the ships which had brought Cadmus to Greece. In Athens there was a temple of Aphrodite Hetaera, in which the goddess was represented sitting on a he-goat. She was venerated at Abydos, at Ephesus and above all at Corinth, where the prostitutes of the town were her veritable priestesses. Aphrodite Genetrix was worshipped at Sparta and at Naupactus. Aphrodite Urania had temples at Sicyon, Argos and Athens. Finally the marine Aphrodite Pelagia was especially honoured at Hermione. In Thessaly they venerated an Aphrodite Anosia (the impious) in memory of the murder of the courtesan Lais by the wives of the region. In Sicily Aphrodite had a celebrated temple on Mount Eryx.

The representations of Aphrodite vary according to the character in which she was envisaged.

At Sicyon they venerated an ivory-adorned statue in which the goddess was crowned by a *polos*. Nobility and modesty characterised this statue, which evidently depicted Aphrodite Urania or Genetrix.

The note of sensuality is emphasised in the later effigies of Aphrodite. Indeed, the models whom the sculptors employed were often courtesans like Cratina, Phryne or Cambyse, the mistress of Alexander. Such were the nude Aphrodites of Praxiteles which, it is said, shocked the piety of the inhabitants of Cos. The Aphrodite which was honoured at Cnidos was particularly voluptuous.

Hesiod's myth of the birth of Aphrodite inspired the various types of Aphrodite *anadyomene* – i.e., rising from the waters – like the celebrated Aphrodite (or Venus) de Medici, and the Aphrodites at the bath so popular in statuary.

A type rather different from the preceding is Aphrodite the Warrior, represented armed and wearing a helmet. She was particularly venerated at Sparta. She is an echo of the warrior Ishtar of Babylonia.

The Birth of Aphrodite. Homer describes Aphrodite as the daughter of Zeus and Dione – a rather vague divinity who was said to be the daughter of Oceanus and Tethys and of whom we know only that she was closely associated with the cult of Zeus at Dodona. Even her name, which is merely the feminine form of Zeus, suggests her lack of defined personality. Popular imagination could scacely be satisfied with so poor a legend, and the Homeric tradition was thus supplanted by another, richer in popular appeal.

When, at the instigation of his mother, Gaea, the audacious Cronus had castrated his father, Uranus, he cast the severed genitals into the sea. They floated on the surface of the waters, producing a white foam from which rose Aphrodite. Carried on the moist breath of Zephyrus, the West Wind, across the tumultuous sea, the goddess was borne along the coast of Cythera and finally landed on the shores of Cyprus. She was greeted by the Horae, who dressed her richly, adorned her with precious jewels and conducted her to the assembly of the Immortals. Beside her walked Love and Himeros, tender Desire. When they saw her the gods were struck with admiration for such beauty and each, says the poet, 'wished in his heart to take her as a wife and lead her to his abode'.

It was natural that they should be moved; for Aphrodite was the essence of feminine beauty. From her gleaming fair hair to her silvery feet everything about her was pure charm and harmony. To be sure Hera and Athene were also very lovely, but the haughty beauty of Hera imposed respect and the severe beauty of Athene arrested desire. Aphrodite exuded an aura of seduction. To the perfection of her figure and the purity of her features she added the grace which attracted and conquered. 'On her sweet face she always wore an amiable smile.'

The Judgment of Paris. One can imagine that the other goddesses did not accept the presence on Olympus of this redoubtable rival without resentment. They were determined to dispute the prize of beauty with her. Now, to the nuptials of Thetis and Peleus all the Immortals had been invited except Eris, or Discord. Infuriated by the omission, Eris tossed into the hall where the guests were gathered a golden apple with this inscription: *For the fairest.* Hera, Athene and Aphrodite all three claimed it. To settle the affair Zeus ordered them to submit the argument to the judgment of a mortal. Choice fell upon one Paris, son of King Priam of Troy. Hermes then conducted the three goddesses to Phrygia where Paris was tending his father's flocks on the slopes of Mount Ida. Paris was acutely embarrassed and tried to refuse, but he had to submit to the will of Zeus, expressed by Hermes. One by one the three goddesses appeared before him and attempted to influence his decision by reinforcing the power of their charms with alluring promises. 'If you award the prize to me,' said Hera, 'I shall make you lord over all Asia.' Athene promised to see that the young shepherd was always victorious in battle. Aphrodite, who could offer neither sceptres nor victories, merely loosened the clasps by which her tunic was fastened and unknotted her girdle; then she promised to give Paris the most beautiful of mortal women. The verdict was then delivered, and the shepherd of Mount Ida awarded the coveted apple to Aphrodite. In this way Paris won possession of Helen, wife of Menelaus; but neither Hera nor Athene forgave him the wound to their pride, and avenged themselves cruelly by delivering his country, his family and his people to devastation and making sure that he, too, fell beneath the blows of the Greeks.

But from that time Aphrodite's supremacy remained uncontested. Even Hera, when she wished to recapture her husband's wayward love, did not hesitate to run to her former rival to borrow the magic girdle which was endowed with the power of enslaving the hearts of gods and men alike. It was a girdle wondrously worked and cunningly embroidered. It contained every seduction, Homer tells us – love and desire and sweet dalliance – which enthrals the heart of even the wisest.

Goddess of love, Aphrodite was mistress of seductive conversation, 'gracious laughter, sweet deceits, the charms and delights of love.' This was her empire, though, like the other gods, she sometimes espoused the quarrels of mankind. On such occasions she too threw herself into the fray and we see her defending the Trojans and taking part in the battles which raged beneath the walls of Ilium with, it may be added, little success. One day when she had come to the aid of her son Aeneas and was shielding him from the Greek arrows with a fold of her sparkling veil, Diomedes recognised her. Well aware that she was a divinity without courage, he attacked her, and with the point of his spear lightly wounded her delicate hand. Aphrodite retired hastily to Olympus, regarded mockingly by Athene who said: 'Doubtless the Cyprian has been persuading some Greek woman to fight for her dearly beloved Trojans, and while she was caressing the woman a golden clasp has scratched her delicate hand!' Aphrodite complained bitterly to the father of the gods. Zeus smiled and said to her: 'You, my child, were not meant to concern yourself with matters of war. Go, attend to the sweet tasks of love.'

The Loves of Aphrodite. Aphrodite's beauty had stirred all the gods; but it was Hephaestus, the ugliest and most graceless among them, who obtained her for a wife. Such an ill-matched union could not be happy, and even on Olympus Aphrodite found those to console her, among others Ares, with whom she was surprised by her husband, and Hermes who, it seemed, was more adroit. Aphrodite, moreover, took a wicked delight in rousing the passionate desires of the Immortals and launching them on amorous adventures. With the exception of Athene, Artemis and Hestia, all came under her influence. The master of the gods himself yielded to her power. 'She distracts the mind of Zeus, deceives his prudent soul, and sends him chasing after mortal women.'

To avenge himself 'Zeus, in his turn, inspired in Aphrodite the sweet desire to lie with a mortal man'. And so the goddess was seized by an irresistible passion for the Trojan Anchises, whose beauty rivalled that of the gods. One day when Anchises was pasturing his flocks on Mount Ida Aphrodite came to join him. First she had visited her sanctuary at Paphos where the Graces had anointed her body with fragrant and incorruptible oil and adorned her in her most precious jewels. 'Her veil was more dazzling than flame, she wore bracelets and ear-rings, round her throat there were golden necklaces, her delicate bosom shone like the moon.' While she climbed the slopes of Mount Ida shaggy wolves, bristling lions and agile panthers frisked around her; 'at this spectacle she rejoiced and instilled love in their hearts'.

When she came to Anchises she explained that she was the daughter of Otreus, King of Phrygia, and confessed her desire to become his spouse. Without further ado Anchises conducted Aphrodite to his well-prepared couch, covered with the skins of bears and lions. And there 'a mortal man, by the will of the gods and destiny, slept with an immortal goddess without knowing who she was'.

Upon awaking Aphrodite appeared before Anchises in all her divine splendour. The shepherd beheld her in terror, fearing the premature old age with which a man who has lain with an immortal goddess is stricken. But Aphrodite reassured him and promised him a son who would be like a god. She asked of him only that he should never reveal the name of the child's mother. The child was later the pious Aeneas.

Anchises was not the only mortal loved by Aphrodite. The Phoenicians who frequented the isles of the Aegean and the ports of the Peloponnese had brought with them the tale of the love of their own goddess Astarte for Adonis. The Greeks naturally retold it of Aphrodite, and the story of Aphrodite and Adonis was one of the episodes most often treated by poets and artists.

Among Aphrodite's favourites must be mentioned Phaethon, son of Eos and Cephalus, who was carried off as a child by the goddess and became 'the nocturnal guardian of her sacred temples'. There was also Cinyras, sometimes described as the father of Myrrha – and consequently of Adonis. He was usually regarded as the founder of the cult of Aphrodite in the island of Cyprus over which he reigned.

In this same island of Cyprus, in Amathus, there lived a sculptor named Pygmalion. Passionately devoted to his art, Pygmalion was only happy in the silent world of statues which his chisel had created. His misanthropy was attributed to the disgust he felt at the conduct of the Propoetides. These were girls in Amathus who rashly denied the divinity of Aphrodite. To punish them Aphrodite inspired in them such immodesty that, losing all sense of shame, they would prostitute themselves to all comers. In the end they were turned into rocks. Thus Pygmalion shunned the society of women, but nonetheless fervently venerated Aphrodite. Now it came about that he made an ivory statue of a woman of such extraordinary beauty that he fell in love with it. Alas! the cold image did not respond to his transports of love. Aphrodite took pity on this singular lover. One day while pressing the inert statue in his arms Pygmalion felt the ivory suddenly moving; his kisses were returned. The statue was miraculously alive.

This prodigy is only an example of the sovereign power of Aphrodite over all creation. Throughout all nature she spread her life-bringing joy: at her appearance, Lucretius says, 'the heavens are assuaged and pour forth torrents of light; the waves of the sea smile on her'. Aphrodite, however, was also the terrifying divinity who filled women's hearts with the frenzy of passion. Unhappy were they whom Aphrodite chose for her victims; such would betray their own fathers like Medea or Ariadne. They would abandon their homes, like Helen, to follow a stranger. They would be overcome, like Myrrha or Phaedra, with incestuous desires, or, like Pasiphaë, be torn by monstrous and bestial passions.

The same Aphrodite nevertheless protected legitimate unions and figured among the divinities who presided over the sanctity of marriage. Spartan mothers offered a sacrifice to her when their daughters were married. It was she who cared for the daughters of Pandareus, Merope and Cleothera, after the death of their parents, fed them on milk and honey and delectable wine and, when they had grown up, asked the almighty Zeus that their nuptials should be blessed. Had it depended on Aphrodite alone, Merope and Cleothera would have become happy and respected wives; but the two unfortunate young women, at the moment of their marriage, were carried off by the Harpies and made into followers of the odious Furies.

Hermaphroditus. Among Aphrodite's children were Harmonia, a daughter, whom she bore to Ares and who married Cadmus, and a son, Hermaphroditus, whose father was Hermes.

To conceal his birth Aphrodite immediately confided Hermaphroditus to the nymphs of Mount Ida who brought him up in the forests. At the age of fifteen he was a wild and savage youth whose chief pleasure was to hunt in the wooded mountains. One day in Caria he arrived at the banks of a limpid lake whose freshness tempted him to bathe. The nymph Salmacis who ruled the lake saw him and was enamoured of his beauty. She told him so, and in vain the shy youth attempted to repulse her. Salmacis threw her arms around him and covered him with kisses. He continued to resist and the nymph cried out: 'Cruel youth! You struggle in vain. O ye gods! Grant that nothing may ever separate him from me, or me from him!' Immediately their two bodies were united and became as one. 'In their double form they are neither man nor woman; they seem to have no sex yet to be of both sexes.'

In consequence of this event the waters of the lake received the property of causing those who bathed therein to lose their virility. This was in accomplishment of the final wish that Hermaphroditus had pronounced just before Salmacis drew him down into the depths of the water.

Some have interpreted this strange fable as a survival of the cult of the Bearded Aphrodite of Cyprus.

THE RETINUE OF APHRODITE

Eros. Among Aphrodite's normal companions the most important was Eros. Unknown in Homeric times, he appears in Hesiod's *Theogony* as the son of Erebus and the Night. His role was to co-ordinate the elements which constitute the universe. It is he who 'brings harmony to chaos', and permits life to develop. This primitive deity, a semi-abstract personification of cosmic force, has little resemblance to the traditional Eros whose physiognomy was only developed in later times.

About his origin there is little agreement. Some say his mother was the goddess Ilithyia; others say he was born to Iris and Zephyrus. Sometimes he is supposed to have been born before Aphrodite, whom he and the Horae welcomed on the shores of Cyprus. Sometimes – and this was the most widespread tradition – he was considered to be the son of Aphrodite. As to his father, the ancients hesitated between Ares, Hermes and Zeus.

Eros was the youngest of the gods; he was a winged child, gracious though rebellious, whose pranks and caprices caused much suffering among men and gods. He was armed with a bow and arrows whose prick stirred the fires of passion in all hearts. In his malice he respected not even his own mother, and Aphrodite sometimes had to punish him by taking away his wings and quiver. Normally, however, he was her zealous servant. He helped with her toilet and accompanied her abroad. While the goddess lingered in the arms of Ares, Eros amused himself by handling the war-god's heavy weapons and trying on his helmet with its gleaming plume. In much the same way we see him later playing with the weapons of Hercules.

This cruel and charming young god who delighted in torturing men and who, according to Anacreon, repaid hospitality offered to him by an artfully released dart, was himself sometimes a victim of the passions he inspired in others. This is illustrated by the charming tale of Psyche, although the story is of late invention and more philosophical than mythological.

Eros and Psyche. Psyche (in Greek the word means 'soul') was a princess of such remarkable beauty that Aphrodite herself was jealous of her. She instructed her son Eros to punish the audacious mortal. Shortly afterwards an oracle commanded Psyche's father, under threat of terrifying calamities, to conduct his daughter to the summit of a mountain where she would become the prey of a monster. Trembling but resigned, Psyche was awaiting on a solitary rock the fulfilment of the oracle, when suddenly she felt herself gently lifted in the arms of Zephyrus, who carried her to a magnificent palace. When night fell Psyche was on the verge of sleep when a mysterious being joined her in the darkness, explaining that he was the husband for whom she was destined. She could not see his features, but his voice was soft and his conversation full of tenderness. Before the return of dawn the strange visitor disappeared, first making Psyche swear never to attempt to see his face. In spite of the oddness of the adventure, Psyche was not discontented with her new life; in the palace nothing she could desire was lacking except the constant presence of her delightful husband, who only came to visit her during the dark hours of night. Her happiness could have continued in this way had not her sisters – who were devoured by envy – sown the seeds of suspicion in her heart. 'If your husband,' they said, 'is afraid to let you see his face it is because he must really be some hideous monster.' They nagged her so much that one night Psyche, in spite of her promise, rose from the couch she shared with her husband, stealthily lighted a lamp and held it above the mysterious face. Instead of a fearful monster she beheld the most charming person in the world – Eros himself. At the foot of the couch lay his bow and arrows. In her delight Psyche, in order to study her husband's features more closely, held the lamp nearer. A drop of scalding oil fell on the god's bare shoulder. He awakened at once, reproached Psyche for her lack of faith and immediately vanished.

The palace vanished at the same time, and poor Psyche found herself on the lonely rock again in the midst of terrifying solitude. At first she considered suicide and threw herself into a nearby river; but the waters bore her gently to the opposite bank. From then on she was pursued by Aphrodite's anger and submitted to a series of terrible ordeals. She succeeded, however, in overcoming them one by one, thanks to mysterious assistance. She even had to descend into the underworld. Finally, touched by the repentance of his unhappy spouse, whom he had never ceased to love and protect, Eros went to Zeus and implored permission for Psyche to rejoin him. Zeus consented and conferred immortality on Psyche. Aphrodite forgot her rancour, and the wedding of the two lovers was celebrated on Olympus with great rejoicing.

At the side of Eros other divinities were often seen, of which the chief were Himeros and Pothos, both personifications of amorous desire.

The Graces. Aphrodite's retinue was usually completed by the Graces. Though sometimes said to be the daughters of Helios and Aegle, the Graces were more generally considered to have been born to the Oceanid Eurynome and fathered by Zeus. They were smiling divinities whose presence spread joy not only throughout the external world but also in the hearts of men. 'With you,' Pindar says to them, 'all becomes sweetness and charm.' Their number and their names often varied. According to epochs and regions they were called: Charis and Pasithea (by Homer); in Sparta, Cleia and Phaenna; Hegemone and Auxo in Athens. But the most widely accepted tradition fixed their number as three and their names as Aglaia, Euphrosyne and Thalia. They were Aphrodite's companions and attended to her toilet. The goddess made use of their services when she wished to adorn herself in all her seductions.

With the return of Spring the Graces delighted in mingling with the nymphs, forming with them groups of dancers who tripped the ground with nimble step. This was because these divinities – in whom some have seen a personification of the sun's rays, but who were originally nature-goddesses – also presided over the budding of plant-life and the ripening of fruits. Aglaia was 'the brilliant'. Thalia was 'she who brought flowers'. The joy which results from the sun's blessings is revealed in Euphrosyne's name: 'she who rejoices the heart'. In origin as well as function the Graces were closely connected with Apollo: hence they often form part of his retinue.

They were also considered to be the goddesses of gratitude. Thus their mother was sometimes said to be Lethe (oblivion) because gratitude is quickly forgotten.

The most celebrated sanctuary of the Graces was at Orchomenus in Boeotia, where they were worshipped in the form of aeroliths or meteorites. They also had two sanctuaries in Athens.

The Graces were at first clad in long chitons and wore crowns. However, from the end of the fourth century B.C. they were represented as three nude young women holding one another by the shoulder.

POSEIDON

Character and Function. Although Poseidon's dominion was the sea, he held his own appointed position among the great gods on Olympus.

Far from being a Libyan importation, as Herodotus claims, he was actually a very ancient Pelasgian deity, older even than Zeus. His province, later confined to the waters, was in primitive times much wider.

The etymology which the ancients gave his name, connecting it with 'drink' and 'river', is doubtful. The name Poseidon seems rather to derive from the root meaning 'to be master' which is found again in the Latin *potens*.

It is not impossible that this primitive Poseidon, this sovereign 'master', had once been a celestial god, as his attribute, the trident – probably a symbol for the thunderbolt – seems to indicate. Though supplanted by Zeus, Poseidon continued to exercise his empire over the entire earth, as is proved by those struggles he had with other divinities who contested with him the supremacy of various parts of Greece, and also by the titles Homer gives him, such as *Enosichthon* – 'earth-shaker'. Poseidon was, indeed, the god of earthquakes. Even when his sphere was more narrowly confined to the sea Poseidon retained his character of a great god: he remained the equal of the celestial Zeus, the Zeus Elalios (marine), whose power extended over the whole physical universe.

As a personification of the watery element Poseidon was always considered a god of fecundity and vegetation.

Cult and Representations. Poseidon was a national god of the Ionians of the Peloponnese, who brought him with them when they emigrated from Asia, and was particularly worshipped in this part of Greece. At Sparta he was even called *Genethlios*, the creator. But his cult was spread throughout Greece, especially in maritime towns. In Corinth, Rhodes and Taenarus he actually succeeded in supplanting the local divinity.

Animals which were sacred to him were the horse, symbol of gushing springs, and the bull, emblem either of his power to fertilise or of his impetuosity. In the course of certain festivals dedicated to Poseidon and called Taureia, black bulls were thrown into the waves.

In the same way horse races were celebrated in honour of Poseidon. This custom originated in Thessaly where the god, they said, had created the horse with a blow of his trident.

In the art of classical antiquity Poseidon very much resembles Zeus: he has a similar majesty when he is depicted standing, his chest bare, grasping his trident. But normally his features are less serene and, with his thick beard and disorderly hair, reveal a careworn expression.

The Legend of Poseidon. Poseidon was a son of Cronus and Rhea. He shared the fate of his brothers and sisters, and at birth was swallowed by his father. He was disgorged with the others when Zeus, on the advice of Metis, gave Cronus the draught which made him vomit up his children. According to another tradition Rhea managed to shelter Poseidon from his father's voracity by giving Cronus a young foal to swallow, meanwhile hiding her son in the midst of a flock of lambs near Mantinea. Poseidon was then confided to a nurse named Arne and grew up without his father's knowledge. It was also said that Rhea gave Poseidon to Capheira, a daughter of Oceanus who, with the aid of the Telchines, brought him up in Rhodes.

When Zeus fought the Titans and the Giants, Poseidon fought at his side and killed the giant Polybutes by hurling at him a fragment of cliff torn from the island of Cos, which later became the islet of Nisyros. After their common victory the paternal heritage was, as we remember, divided into three parts: Zeus took the vast heavens, Hades the murky underworld, and Poseidon obtained the immense sea.

Although he was the equal of Zeus by birth and dignity Poseidon was nevertheless subject to his brother's sovereign power. The sea-god complained and grumbled at times. Once he went so far as to conspire with Hera and Athene to dethrone Zeus. Zeus was the stronger and Poseidon was forced to pay for his attempted revolt by spending a year in the service of the haughty Laomedon, for whom he constructed the walls of Troy.

Poseidon's empire, however, was not unworthy of his ambitions. He was master not only of the sea but of the lakes and rivers. In a sense even the earth belonged to him, since it was sustained by his waters and he could shake it at will. Indeed, during the war with the Giants he split mountains with his trident and rolled them into the sea to make the first islands. And it was he who, in the days when Thessaly was merely a huge lake, had cleared the road for the River Peneius by splitting the mass of Mount Ossa in two.

Poseidon's thirst for possession was so keen that he often found himself in conflict with the other gods.

We have already mentioned the dispute he had with Athene for the possession of Attica, a dispute which ended to Athene's advantage. Out of spite Poseidon flooded Attica. Nor could he win Troezen from the same goddess; Zeus awarded it to them in common.

Poseidon was no more fortunate with Hera, with whom he contested the dominion of Argolis. The decision was submitted to the judgment of the river-god Inachus, assisted by the rivers Asterion and Cephissus. It was unfavourable to Poseidon, who avenged himself by drying up the three rivers and with them Argolis.

There was also a contest between Poseidon and Helios over the isthmus of Corinth. Briareus, chosen to arbitrate, awarded the Corinthian Acropolis to Helios and left the rest of the isthmus to Poseidon. This was the origin of the cult in which Poseidon was honoured in the isthmus of Corinth; during his festivals the celebrated Isthmian Games were held.

Finally Poseidon unsuccessfully disputed Aegina with Zeus, and Naxos with Dionysus. He had to cede the territory of Delphi, which until then he had held in common with Gaea, to Apollo, receiving in exchange the island of Calauria.

On the other hand no one ever disputed Poseidon's rule over the sea. He established his abode in the depths of the Aegean Sea where 'there had been built for him a magnificent palace, glittering with gold, which would endure for ever'. When he left the palace he would harness to his chariot swift steeds with golden manes and shod with bronze. Clad in golden armour he would seize a cunningly wrought whip in his hand and hurl his chariot across the watery plain. Around him would frolic sea monsters, come up from the abysmal depths to render homage to their sovereign. The joyful sea would open before him as his chariot flew lightly across waves which did not even so much as wet the bronze axle. More often, however, the appearance of Poseidon was accompanied by wild tempests, a manifestation of the god's furious rage.

Amphitrite. Poseidon's wife was Amphitrite who was in origin the feminine personification of the sea. She was a daughter of Oceanus or of Nereus. Poseidon picked her out one day when she was dancing with her sisters on the isle of Naxos. When he asked for her hand in marriage Amphitrite at first refused and fled to Atlas. Poseidon sent a dolphin to look for her. The dolphin discovered where she had taken refuge and brought her back to his master; as a reward Poseidon placed him among the constellations.

From then on Amphitrite shared Poseidon's kingdom. We see her at her husband's side on the divine chariot drawn by tritons blowing conch-shells. In her hand she sometimes holds the trident, insignia of Poseidon's sovereignty.

From the union of Poseidon and Amphitrite were born a son, Triton, and two daughters: Rhode, who gave her name to the island of Rhodes and was the mother of the Heliades; and Benthesicyme, who settled in Ethiopia.

Amphitrite was an accommodating wife and patiently put up with her husband's frequent infidelity. Only once did she show jealousy: this was with regard to Scylla, who was originally a nymph of rare beauty. Enraged by the love Poseidon showed her, Amphitrite threw magic herbs in the pool where Scylla used to bathe, and the nymph was changed into a frightful monster. Her metamorphosis is sometimes attributed to Circe.

The Loves of Poseidon. Of Poseidon's innumerable mistresses we shall mention only the principal ones.

Among the goddesses there was Gaea, whom he made mother of the fearful giant Antaeus. There was Demeter, who changed herself into a mare in order to escape him. But Poseidon took the form of a stallion and from their union was born – apart from a daughter whose name remains mysterious (perhaps it was Despoena) – the wild horse, Arion, whose right feet were

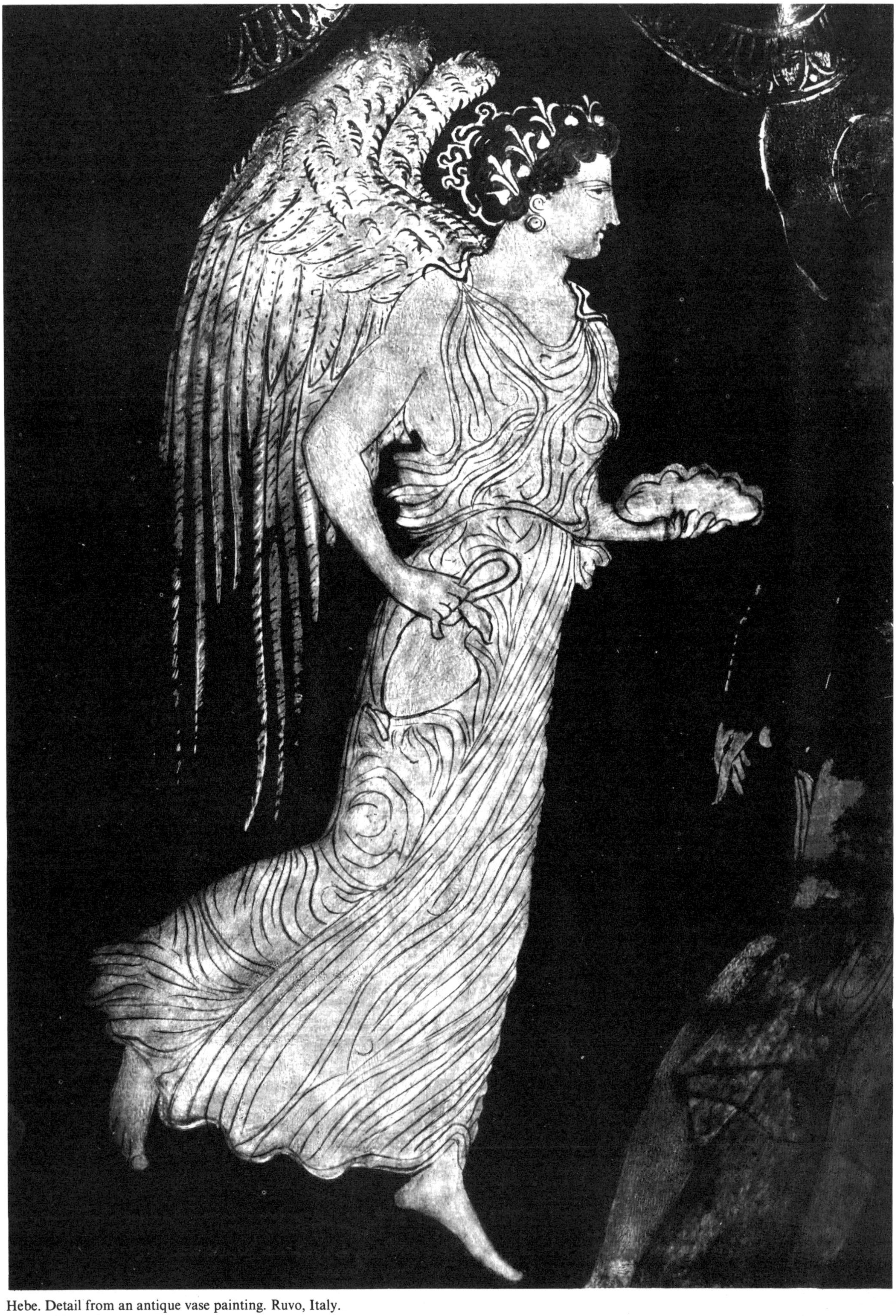

Hebe. Detail from an antique vase painting. Ruvo, Italy.

those of a man and who was endowed with the power of speech.

It was also in the shape of a horse – though others say a bird – that Poseidon succeeded in seducing Medusa, in the very temple of Athene. Infuriated by this profanation, Athene turned Medusa's hair into snakes. When Perseus decapitated Medusa, the blood which escaped from the wound gave birth to Chrysaor and the horse Pegasus.

By Alcyone, one of the Pleiades, Poseidon had a daughter, Aethusa, who was loved by Apollo, and two sons: Hyperenor and Hyrieus. The latter reigned in Boeotia and by the blessing of the gods became father of the giant Orion, of whom we shall speak later.

By the harpy Celaeno, Poseidon had two sons: Lycus, who reigned over the Fortunate Isles, and Eurypylus, who distinguished himself at the siege of Troy and took part in the expedition of the Argonauts.

Another Eurypylus, who reigned over the isle of Cos and was killed by Hercules, and the Argonaut Ancaeus were born to Poseidon and Astypalaea, sister of Europa.

Chione, daughter of Boreas, was seduced by Poseidon and had a son, Eumolpus. To hide her shame she threw the child into the sea; but Poseidon saved it and carried it to Ethiopia where he confided it to his daughter Benthesicyme, who later became Eumolpus' mother-in-law.

Aethra was the daughter of Pittheus, King of Troezen. Athene ordered her in a dream to go to the isle of Sphaeria and there on the tomb of Sphaerus to offer a sacrifice. Aethra was surprised in the temple by Poseidon and ravished. She afterwards married Aegeus and became the mother of Theseus.

Because of her great beauty Theophane, daughter of Bisaltes, was besieged by suitors. To protect her from their attentions Poseidon, who loved her himself, carried her to the isle of Crinissa (Crumissa). The suitors followed her. Poseidon then turned her into a ewe, the inhabitants of the island into sheep, and himself into a ram. Theophane gave birth to the famous ram with the golden fleece.

Alope, daughter of Cercyon, had a son by Poseidon. She exposed him, after having covered him with a rich robe. The infant was suckled by a mare and found by herdsmen who carried him to Cercyon. Cercyon at once recognised the rich robe and discovered his daughter's disgrace. He condemned her to perpetual imprisonment and once more exposed the infant. But the faithful mare again came to suckle him. For this reason he was named Hippothous. Later, when Cercyon was slain by Theseus, Hippothous mounted the throne of his grandfather.

For having plundered a grove sacred to Demeter, Erysichthon, King of Thessaly, was afflicted with insatiable hunger. To appease it he was obliged to sell everything he possessed. At the end of his resources he finally put his own daughter Mestra up for sale. Now Poseidon loved Mestra and granted her the gift of metamorphosis, so that each time she was able to escape her purchasers. This stratagem allowed Erysichthon to sell his daughter over and over again, until at last the ruse was discovered and he had no alternative but to devour himself.

During the drought in Argolis which was the result of Poseidon's fury with Inachus, Danaus sent his daughters in search of water. One of them, Amymone, carelessly wounded a sleeping satyr who then leapt at her. Others say that Amymone was surprised by the satyr while she herself was asleep. In either case Poseidon arrived, put the satyr to flight and rescued Amymone, whose favours he then enjoyed. In gratitude the god struck a rock with his trident and the springs of Lerna gushed forth. By this union Amymone had a son, Nauplius, who later founded Nauplia and was swallowed by the waves for having blasphemed the gods. The origin of the fountain of Pirene, near Corinth, was also connected with a legend of Poseidon. By the nymph Pirene, daughter of Achelous or Asopus, the god had two sons who perished miserably. Pirene was inconsolable and could not stop weeping; it was her tears which gave birth to the celebrated fountain.

The nymph Tyro, daughter of Salmoneus and Acidice, had conceived a passion for the river Enipeus. Poseidon, who loved her, despaired of moving her heart. One day when Tyro was strolling along the banks of the Enipeus Poseidon assumed the appearance of the river-god and approached her. The nymph was deceived by this disguise and yielded. She bore two sons, Pelias and Neleus, whom she exposed. They were found by shepherds and brought up among herds of horses. Meanwhile Tyro had married Cretheus, King of Iolcus, and was ill-treated by Sidero, her mother-in-law. When Pelias and Neleus returned to their mother they killed the wicked Sidero.

The Posterity of Poseidon. Among Poseidon's numerous offspring we shall limit ourselves to mentioning a few names:

Euphemus, son of Europa, who received from his father the power of walking on the waters and who was the second pilot during the expedition of the Argonauts.

Halirrhothius, son of the nymph Euryte, who was put to death by Ares for having ravished his daughter Alcippe. This murder gave rise to a quarrel between Ares and Poseidon, to settle which the tribunal of the Areopagus was instituted at Athens.

Evadne, daughter of Pitane, who at her birth was confided to Aepytus, King of Phoesane in Arcadia, and who afterwards bore a son to Apollo, Iamus.

The Molionids, twin sons of Molione, who were born of a silver egg and who so resembled each other that later tradition said they had but a single body with two heads, four arms and four legs. It was they who commanded the troops of Augias against Hercules who, moreover, killed them.

Cycnus, son of Calyce or Harpale, who was exposed on the seashore at birth and taken in by fishermen. Later, he became king of Colonae in the Troad, and by his first wife, Procleia, had two children, Tenes and Hemithea. His second wife, Phylonome, conceived a passion for her stepson Tenes but, unable to seduce him, slandered him to his father. Cycnus had Tenes and his sister Hemithea locked up in a chest and set them adrift on the sea. But the two young people were saved by Poseidon, and Tenes, landing at Tenedos, became its king. When Cycnus learned the truth he killed Phylonome and went to join his son. Both fought in the Trojan ranks against the Greeks and perished by the hand of Achilles. Since Cycnus was invulnerable, Achilles strangled him with the strap which secured his helmet; but when he attempted to despoil him of his arms the body of Cycnus changed into a swan.

Finally we mention a certain number of monstrous and malignant beings who were also among Poseidon's progeny.

Amycus, born of the nymph Melia, reigned in Bithynia. He was of prodigious strength and challenged all strangers who approached his kingdom to a fatal boxing match. When the Argonauts arrived in Bithynia he at once defied them, but Pollux accepted the challenge and killed him.

The Aloadae were children of Poseidon by Iphimedeia, wife of Aloeus. They were twin brothers, Ephialtes and Otus, who each year grew so fast that at the age of nine they were nearly twenty yards high. We have seen how they attempted to scale Olympus, kept Ares captive for thirteen months and finally perished either beneath Apollo's blows or through a stratagem of Artemis'. They were thrown into Tartarus for their crimes and there bound, back to back, to a column by means of a chain made of interlaced serpents. To them were attributed the foundation of Ascra and the institution of the cult of the Muses on Mount Helicon.

Cercyon, son of a daughter of Amphictyon, lived in Eleusis. He forced all travellers to wrestle with him and he killed the vanquished. Only Theseus succeeded in beating him, and put him to death. Cercyon was the father of Alope, who was herself loved by Poseidon.

Another son of Poseidon's was also killed by Theseus. This was the brigand Sinis, who lived in the Isthmus of Corinth. He submitted all passers-by to an odious torture: he tied them to the tops of two pine-trees which he had bent down. When the trees were released the victims were torn asunder. Theseus made him suffer the same torture.

No less cruel was the King of Egypt, Busiris, son of Poseidon and Anippe. When drought devastated his kingdom Busiris consulted a soothsayer of Cyprus, who declared that the scourge would cease only if each year he immolated a stranger. Busiris began by immolating the soothsayer and continued this bloody practice until the day when Hercules arrived in Egypt and was chosen as a victim. They were about to cut his throat when Hercules burst from the chains which bound him and killed Busiris and his attendants. From that day human sacrifice was no longer practised in Egypt.

To this list of monsters may be added the Cyclops Polyphemus, son of Poseidon and the nymph Thoösa.

In this monstrous progeny attributed to Poseidon may perhaps be seen a survival of the impression of terror felt by primitive men at the rages of the stormy sea. Similarly it was said that Poseidon often summoned up fearful monsters against his enemies. He sent such a monster to ravage the Troad to revenge himself on Laomedon; another, at the prayers of the Nereids, desolated Ethiopia in order to punish the pride of Cassiopeia, mother of Andromeda. He sent a wild bull to devastate the plain of Marathon and a dragon which caused the death of the son of Theseus, Hippolytus.

HESTIA

Character and Functions. The Greek word 'hestia' means the hearth, the place in the house where the fire was maintained. The difficulty which primitive man experienced in procuring fire easily explains why he tended it with care and also venerated it. Moreover it was around the hearth that the family gathered. When one of its members departed to found a new family he took with him a parcel of fire from his parents' hearth, which thus symbolised the continuity of the family. When families began to form groups in towns, each town had its communal hearth where the public fire was maintained. Finally the fire of the *hestia* was used in sacrifices. For these various reasons the *hestia*, like the Vedic Agni, very early took on a sacred character. This character was afterwards personified in a deity who took the actual name of the object she symbolised.

Hestia, then, was, like Hephaestus, a fire-divinity. But while Hephaestus represented the fiery element in its celestial and subterranean manifestations, Hestia symbolised the household fire – fire, as it were, domesticated. Hence the homely and social character of this goddess, whose province was to protect not only the house and the family but also the city. Later Hestia, by analogy, represented the fire in the centre of the earth and the earth itself; but this conception was less mythological than philosophical.

Hestia was venerated in all Greek towns; she had her altar in every prytaneum – or Public Hearth. The Hestia of Delphi was the object of an especial cult, because Delphi was believed to occupy the centre of the universe and its hearth was therefore the common hearth of all Greece. Temples of Hestia were characterised by their circular form.

Representations of Hestia are rare. Glaucus of Argos sculptured one for Olympia. There was also a very celebrated one in Paros. The goddess was depicted sometimes seated, sometimes standing, but always in an attitude of immobility.

Hestia did not spring, like the other divinities, from popular imagination, and legends about her are few.

According to Hesiod – for Homer, before him, did not know of the goddess Hestia – she was the first child born to Cronus and Rhea. Thus she was the oldest of the Olympians and always maintained her precedence. Men understood this well and when they offered sacrifices consecrated the first morsels of the victims to Hestia and in festivals poured her the first and last libations. On Olympus Hestia's dignity was unquestioned and her rights as the eldest were recognised. She seems to have taken little advantage of this and played a minor role in Olympian drama. 'In the dwelling of the gods,' says Plato, 'Hestia alone maintains repose.' We only know of her that both Poseidon and Apollo sought her hand in marriage. She would have neither one nor the other. In order to put an end to their attentions she placed herself under Zeus' protection and made a solemn vow, touching the head of the master of the gods, to remain a virgin for ever. Zeus accepted her vow and 'instead of marriage offered her a handsome recompense: seated in the midst of the celestial dwelling-place she receives the richest part of sacrifices, and among men she is of all the deities the most venerated'.

Hestia thus shared with Athene and Artemis the prerogative of chastity. She was one of those over whom Aphrodite never succeeded in exercising her power.

THE LESSER GODS OF OLYMPUS

Olympian society was made in the image of human society and beneath the great gods there were lesser gods who held various positions.

Themis. Of these Themis may be said to be the most important. She was the daughter of Uranus and Gaea and belonged to the race of Titans which the Olympians had supplanted. Far from sharing the disgrace of her brothers, however, Themis never ceased to be honoured on Olympus. Indeed, at the beginning of his reign Zeus had chosen her for his wife. The Moerae, they said, had brought her to Zeus from the far-off regions where Uranus dwelt. Later, when Hera became the wife of Zeus, Themis remained at his side to offer counsel and service. It seems that Hera took no offence at this; when Hera arrived in the assembly of the gods it was from the hand of Themis that she received the cup of nectar.

Themis' mission on Olympus was not only to maintain order but also to regulate the ceremonial; she invited the gods to forgather and prepared their feasts.

She was moreover helpful and obliging. It was she, they said, who had received the infant Zeus from Rhea when Rhea wished to shelter him from the voracity of his father, Cronus. Later she presided over the laborious birth of Apollo and Artemis. It was also said that she made Apollo a present of the oracle at Delphi which she had inherited from her mother, Gaea.

On earth her province was also extensive; above all she was the goddess of justice. She protected the just – whence her epithet *Soteira* – the protectress – and punished the guilty. In her name and according to her advice judges gave their verdicts. Themis was also goddess of wisdom and was called *Euboulos*, the good counsellor; under this title she presided over public assemblies. Finally, since she was the interpreter of the gods' will, she had the gift of delivering oracles. It was she who, after the deluge, suggested to Deucalion the means of re-peopling the earth. We have just seen that she once owned the oracle of Delphi.

From her union with Zeus Themis had several children: the Horae, and the Moerae or Fates. The Hesperides were also sometimes said to be her daughters.

The cult of Themis was spread throughout Greece; a temple was consecrated to her in the citadel of Athens. She also had sanctuaries at Troezen, Tanagra, Olympia and at Thebes, where she was worshipped with Zeus Agoraios.

She is represented as a woman of grave countenance and austere features. Her attribute is a pair of scales.

Iris. Pontus and Gaea had had, among other children, a son Thaumas who united with Electra, daughter of Oceanus and Tethys. From this union were born the Harpies and Iris. On Olympus Iris, who to the ancients personified the rainbow, was the messenger of the gods. She was assigned in particular to the service of Zeus. When Zeus had an order to give another Immortal, Iris delivered it. If he wished to make his will known to men, Iris flew lightly down to earth where she either borrowed mortal shape or appeared in her divine form. In her divine form she wore a long, full tunic, her hair encircled by a bandeau, and in her hand held the caduceus. She could be recognised by the golden wings attached to her shoulders. Occasionally, like Hermes, she wore winged sandals. Sometimes she cleaved the air as swiftly as the wind, at others glided down the rainbow which bridged sky and earth. She sped through the waters with equal ease. When Zeus sent her in search of the marine-goddess Thetis, Homer tells us how she dived into the dark waves between Samos and the cliffs of Imbros, making the gulf itself groan aloud. Even the underworld opened before Iris when, at the command of Zeus, she went to refill her golden cup with the waters of the Styx by which the Immortals bound themselves with fearful oaths.

Iris was devoted to Zeus but even more so to Hera. She not only delivered Hera's messages but also effected her vengeance, such as the time when she went to Sicily and, in the guise of Beroe, set fire to Aeneas' fleet. Iris also fulfilled the role of Hera's faithful servant. She prepared Hera's bath, helped her with her toilet, and night and day stood at the foot of her mistress's throne, never falling asleep or even loosening her girdle or sandals.

She also waited on the other gods. When they returned to Olympus in their chariots she would unharness steeds and give them nectar and ambrosia. When Aphrodite was wounded by Diomedes, Iris 'took the overwhelmed goddess and led her away from the battle', helped her to mount the chariot of Ares, and took the reins and whip into her own hands.

Even mortals experienced her good nature. When she heard Achilles bitterly complain that the flames of the pyre were slow in consuming the body of Patroclus she immediately went to find the Winds – who had just foregathered in the dwelling of the violent

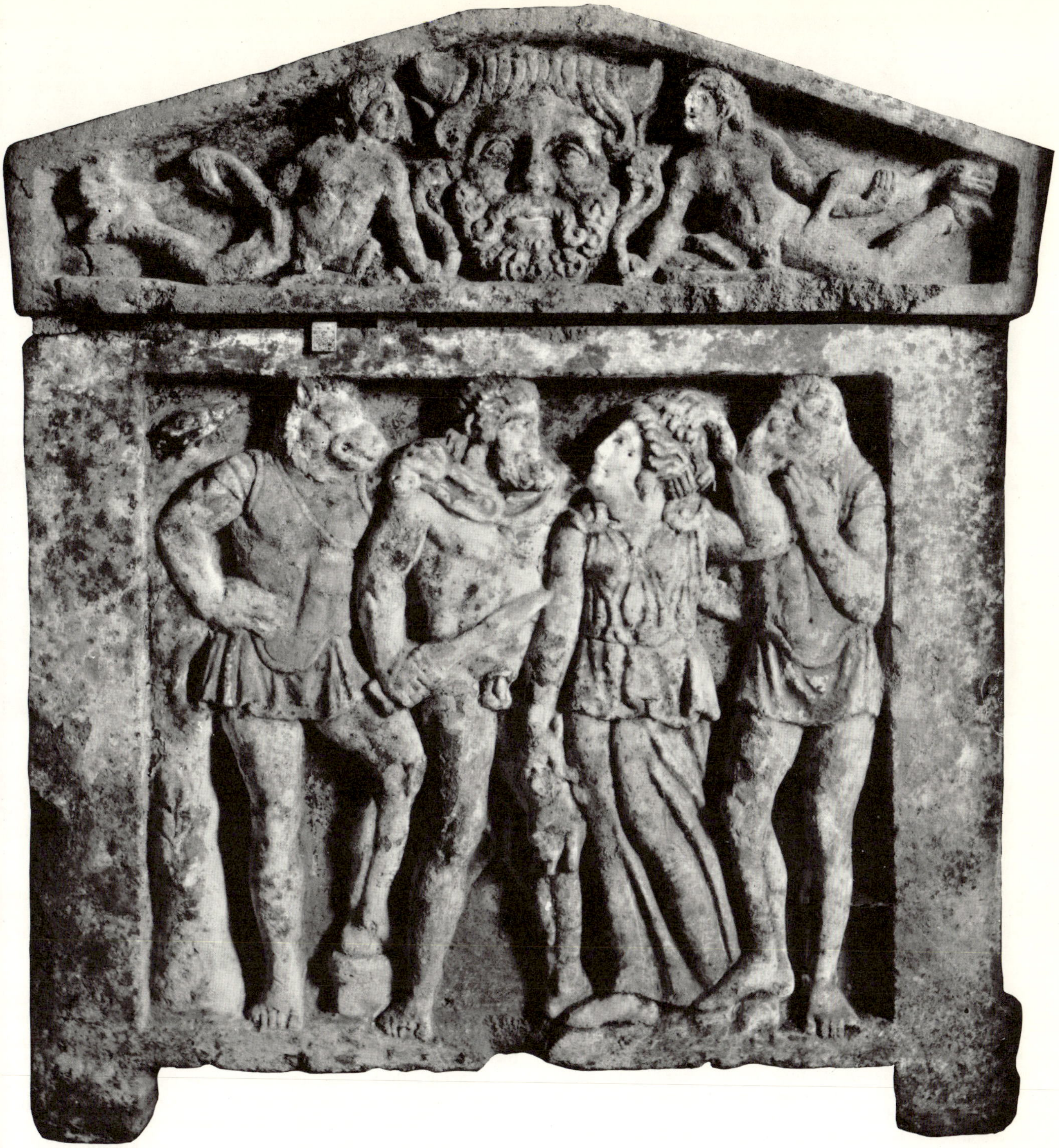

Odysseus forces Circe to restore his companions to human form. Polychrome funerary urn. Fourth century B.C. Orvieto Museum.

Zephyrus for a solemn feast – and begged Boreas and Zephyrus to come and fan the funeral pyre.

Some said that this same Zephyrus was the husband of Iris and claimed that Eros was the fruit of their union.

On earth Iris was particularly honoured at Delos, where she was offered dried figs and cakes of wheat and honey.

Hebe. Hebe was worshipped by the Greeks as the goddess of youth. She had an altar in the Cynosarges at Athens. At Phlius a grove of cypresses which possessed the right of asylum was sacred to her. She also had a sanctuary at Sicyon.

She was the daughter of Zeus and Hera. She had the gift of eternal youth and represented the deified type of young maiden who in the primitive family was devoted to domestic occupations. Thus on Olympus she performed many duties.

She assisted her brother Ares to dress, bathed him and clad him in magnificent robes. When her mother Hera wished to go forth from Olympus, Hebe prepared the chariot, 'rapidly fixing the curved wheels to the iron axle, tying to the end of the shaft a handsome golden yoke to which she attached reins of gold'. But her chief duty was to hand around nectar and ambrosia to the gods during their feasts. She would move among them, bearing the ewer with the divine draught with which she would fill their goblets. It was claimed that as a result of a fall in which Hebe exposed herself to the eyes of all in a rather indecent posture, she lost her job and was replaced by Ganymede.

When Hercules, having at last appeased Hera's wrath, was admitted on his death to Olympus with the rank of a god, he was given the gracious Hebe for a wife. They had two children, Alexiares and Anicetus.

Ganymede. In primitive times Ganymede seems to have been conceived as the deity responsible for sprinkling the earth with heaven's rain. He is compared with the Vedic *Soma* who, like him, was ravished by Indra – and changed into a sparrow-hawk. Ancient astronomers identified him with Aquarius, the Water-carrier.

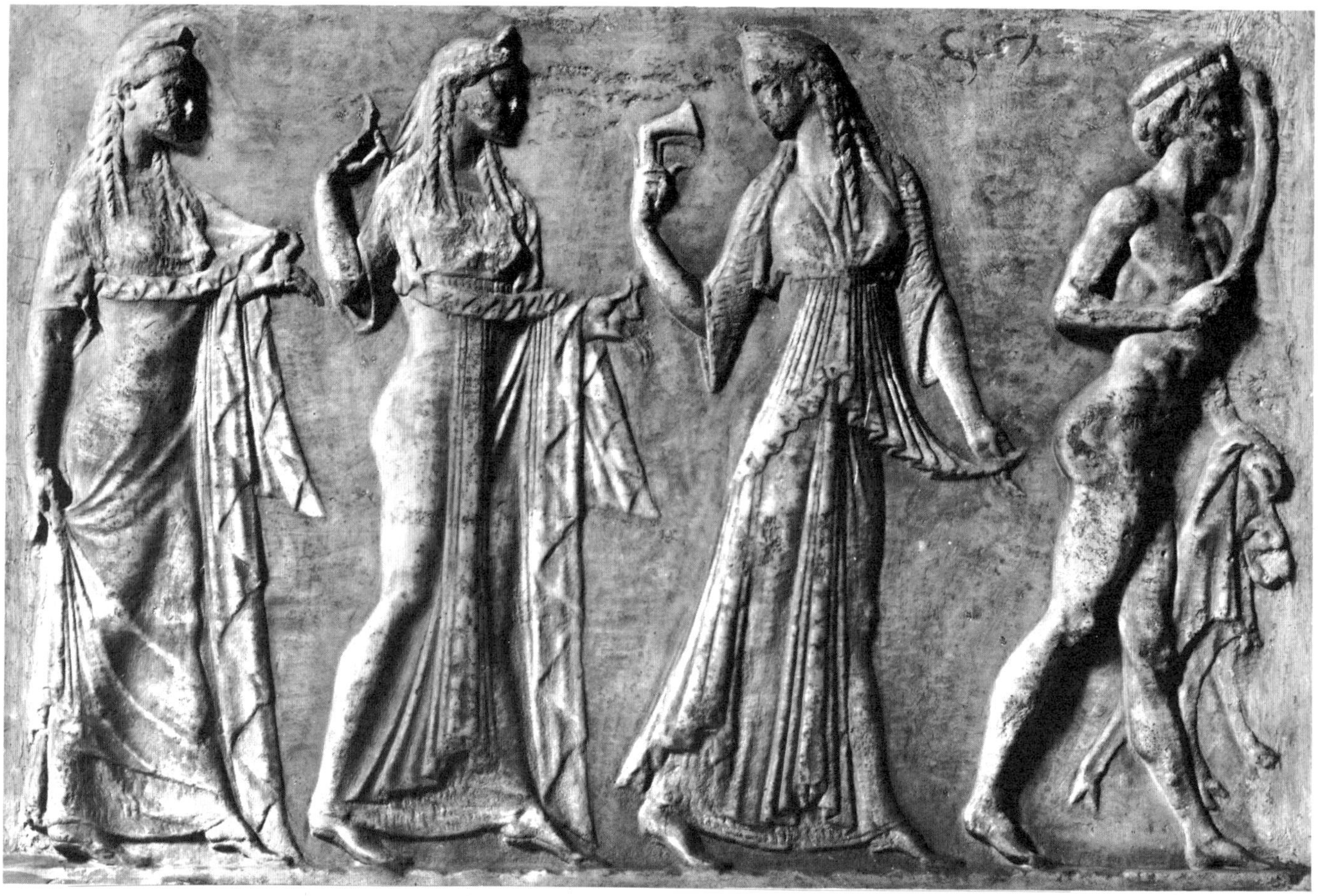

The Horae and the god Pan. Votive bas-relief. Capitol Museum, Rome.

Ganymede was venerated at Sicyon and at Phlius conjointly with Hebe.

He is depicted as an adolescent in a Phrygian cap and a mantle thrown back over his shoulders, either seated beside Zeus or carried through the air by an eagle.

In spite of the honorary position he occupied on Olympus, Ganymede was not of divine birth, being the son of Tros, King of Phrygia, and of Callirrhoe. At least this was the general opinion, although some said his father was Laomedon, Ilus, Assaracus or even Erichthonius. He was distinguished among mortals for his extraordinary beauty. Zeus was charmed and, wishing to make him his favourite, had him swept up by an eagle from the plains of the Troad and brought to Olympus. It was also said that Zeus himself took the form of an eagle in order to carry off the fair adolescent. The abduction of Ganymede took place, according to various versions, in either Mysia, Harpagia, on Phrygian Ida or on the promontory of Dardanus.

To recompense Tros for the loss of his son Zeus presented him with magnificent steeds, 'swift as the storm'.

On Olympus Ganymede became the cup-bearer of the gods and rejoiced the eye of all by his beauty.

The Horae. The Greek word from which the Horae derive their name signifies a period of time which can be applied equally to the year, the seasons, and the hours of the day. These different meanings influenced the successive conceptions of the Horae.

First the Horae were divinities of a meteorological character whose function was limited to showering the earth with life-giving rain. They encouraged the blossoming and ripening of fruits and therefore symbolised spring and summer. Afterwards they presided over the order of nature and the succession of the seasons, with whom in the end they were confused.

The number of the Horae varied. The Athenians venerated two: Thallo, who brought the flowers; and Carpo, who brought the fruits. Hesiod counted three Horae: Eunomia, Dike and Irene. Then their number became four and, according to the classification of Hyginus, as many as ten or eleven.

Their sphere of influence soon became moral as well as physical. Guardians of the order of nature, they also watched over the moral order: Eunomia saw that the laws were observed; Dike attended to justice, Irene to peace. According to Hesiod's expression 'they mellowed the behaviour of men'. Finally they were regarded as the protectors of youth.

The Horae were honoured at Athens, Argos, Olympia and particularly at Corinth.

They are depicted as young maidens, holding in their hands the products of the various seasons: a branch in flower, an ear of corn, a vine stock.

Even before their number was determined and their names decided, the Horae had their appointed occupations on Olympus. In particular it was their duty to guard the gates of heaven, which they opened or closed to the passage of the Immortals by removing or replacing a thick cloud. This is how they appear in the Homeric poems, where we can also see them harnessing Hera's chariot with the celestial steeds which they fed with ambrosia.

Later their character became definite: it was known that their number was three, that their names were Eunomia, Dike and Irene, and that they were the daughters of Zeus and Themis. They were charming maidens with lovely hair, golden diadems and a light footstep. On Olympus they loved to dance in company with the Graces, and thus formed part of the retinue of Aphrodite, whom they adorned with their own hands.

When Zeus to man's perdition sent Pandora down to earth the Horae enhanced her attractions by embellishing her hair with floral garlands.

On many occasions they demonstrated their tenderness towards childhood and youth. It was they who nurtured Hera. It was they again who swaddled Hermes at his birth and wove garlands to shelter him. They received Dionysus when he emerged from the thigh of Zeus. Thallo, the Athenian Hora, was venerated by youthful athletes in the temple of Agraulos.

The adventures which were related of them sometimes appear to arise from confusion with other divinities. For example, it was told that the Hora of springtime had been loved by Zephyrus, to whom she bore a son, Carpos; but the tale seems to apply rather to Chloris, the Flora of the Latins. In the same way Pausanias makes

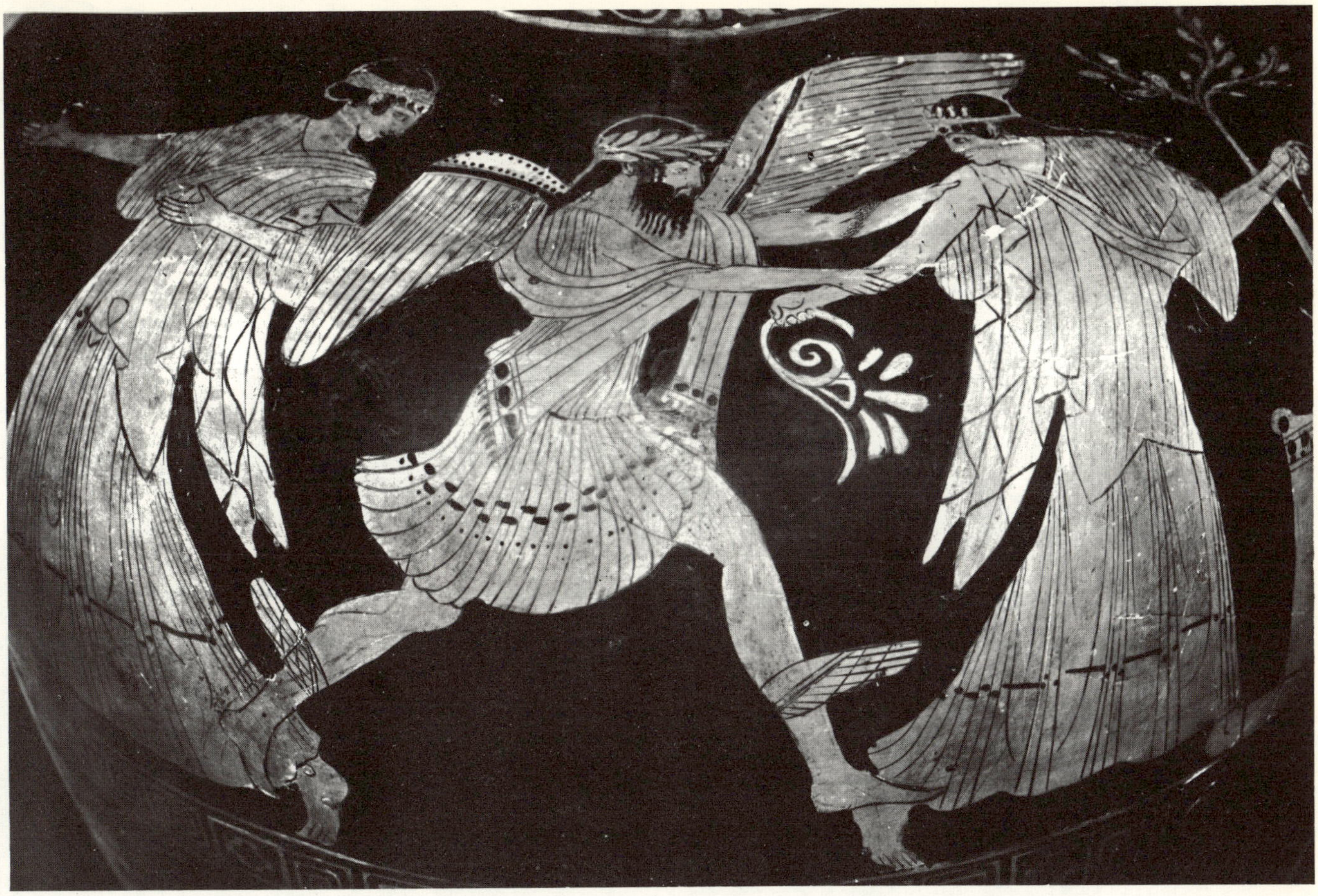

Boreas abducting Oreithyia. Detail of an Attic hydria. Fifth century B.C. Vatican Museum, Rome.

Irene the mother of Plutus because in Athens there was a statue of Irene with Plutus in her arms; nothing, however, authorises such a relationship. Of Carpo, one of the two Athenian Horae, it was said that she fell in love with young Camillus, son of the river-god Maeander, and that in despair she drowned herself in the waters of the river, whereupon Zeus changed her into fruit.

SIDEREAL AND METEOROLOGICAL GODS

By his sister Theia (or by Euryphaessa) the Titan Hyperion, son of Uranus and Gaea, had three children: Helios, the sun; Selene, the moon; and Eos, the dawn.

HELIOS

Although the Greeks considered Apollo to be the god of solar light, the sun itself was personified by a special divinity, Helios. In Greece the cult of Helios was very ancient and was practised throughout the land, at Elis, at Apollonia, on the Acropolis of Corinth, at Argos, at Troezen, on Cape Taenarum, at Athens, in Thrace and finally, and especially, in the island of Rhodes which was sacred to him. In Rhodes could be seen the colossal statue of Helios, the renowned work of the sculptor Chares. It was about thirty yards high, and ships in full sail could pass between the god's legs.

It was related that Helios was drowned in the ocean by his uncles, the Titans, and then raised to the sky, where he became the luminous sun.

Every morning Helios emerged in the east from a swamp formed by the river-ocean in the far-off land of the Ethiopians. To his golden chariot, which Hephaestus had fashioned, the Horae harnessed the winged horses. They were of dazzling white, their nostrils breathed forth flame and their names were Lampon, Phaethon, Chronos, Aethon, Astrope, Bronte, Pyroeis, Eous and Phlegon. The god then took the reins and climbed the vault of heaven. 'Drawn in his swift chariot, he sheds light on gods and men alike; the formidable flash of his eyes pierces his golden helmet; sparkling rays glint from his breast; his brilliant helmet gives forth a dazzling splendour; his body is draped in shining gauze whipped by the wind.'

At midday Helios reached the highest point of his course and began to descend towards the West, arriving at the end of the day in the land of the Hesperides, where he seemed to plunge into the Ocean. In reality, there he found a barque or a golden cup, made by Hephaestus, in which his mother, wife and children were awaiting him. He would sail all night and in the morning regain his point of departure.

The abode of Helios was also said to be on the isle of Aeaea where his children Aeëtes and Circe lived. Again it was said that his horses rested on the islands of the Blessed, at the western extremity of the earth, where they browsed on a magic herb.

Helios possessed other domains on earth. When the gods had divided up the world Helios was absent and was forgotten. He complained about this to Zeus and obtained an island which was just beginning to emerge from the waves. He called it Rhodes after the nymph Rhode, whom he loved.

A dispute arose one day between Helios and Poseidon for the possession of the Isthmus of Corinth. The giant Briareus, who was chosen to arbitrate, awarded the Isthmus to Poseidon but gave Acrocorinth to Helios, who later relinquished it to Aphrodite.

As well as his horses, Helios owned on the isle of Thrinacia seven herds of oxen and seven flocks of ewes with beautiful fleece, each herd and flock being of fifty head. This number always remained constant, like the three hundred and fifty days and three hundred and fifty nights of the primitive year. Two daughters of the god, Phaetusa and Lampetia, guarded these animals. When Odysseus and his companions landed on the isle of Thrinacia the men, in spite of their chief's warning, laid hands on the sacred cattle. 'Chasing before them the handsome broadbrowed heifers which grazed not far from the azure-prowed vessel, they cut their throats, then cut up the flesh in morsels which they fixed to their skewers.' When Helios was told by Lampetia what had occurred he complained to the gods and threatened to shut himself up in the kingdom of Hades and shed his light on the dead. Zeus calmed him by promising to strike these foolish mortals with a thunderbolt.

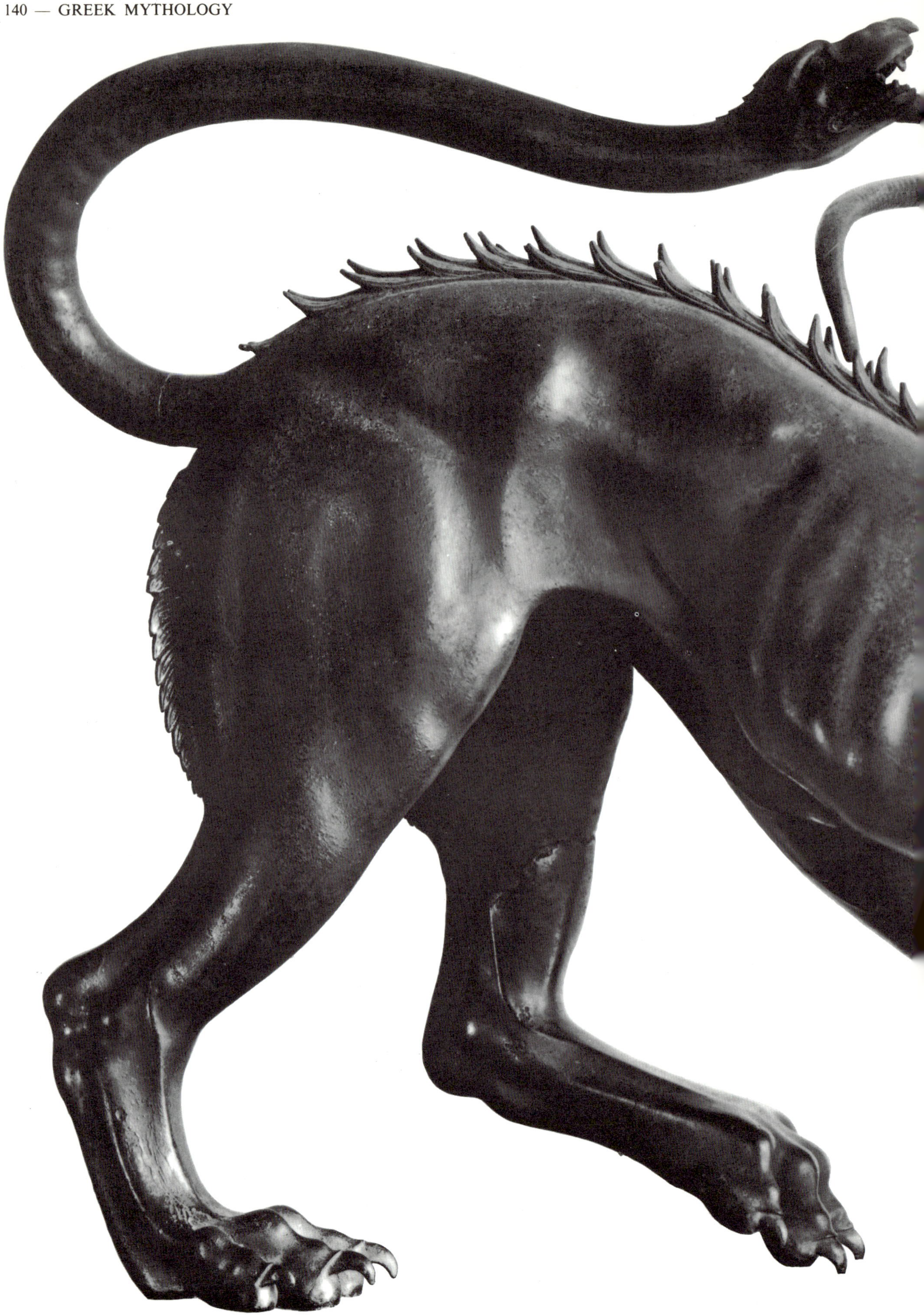

The Chimaera. Etruscan Bronze. Archaeological Museum, Florence.

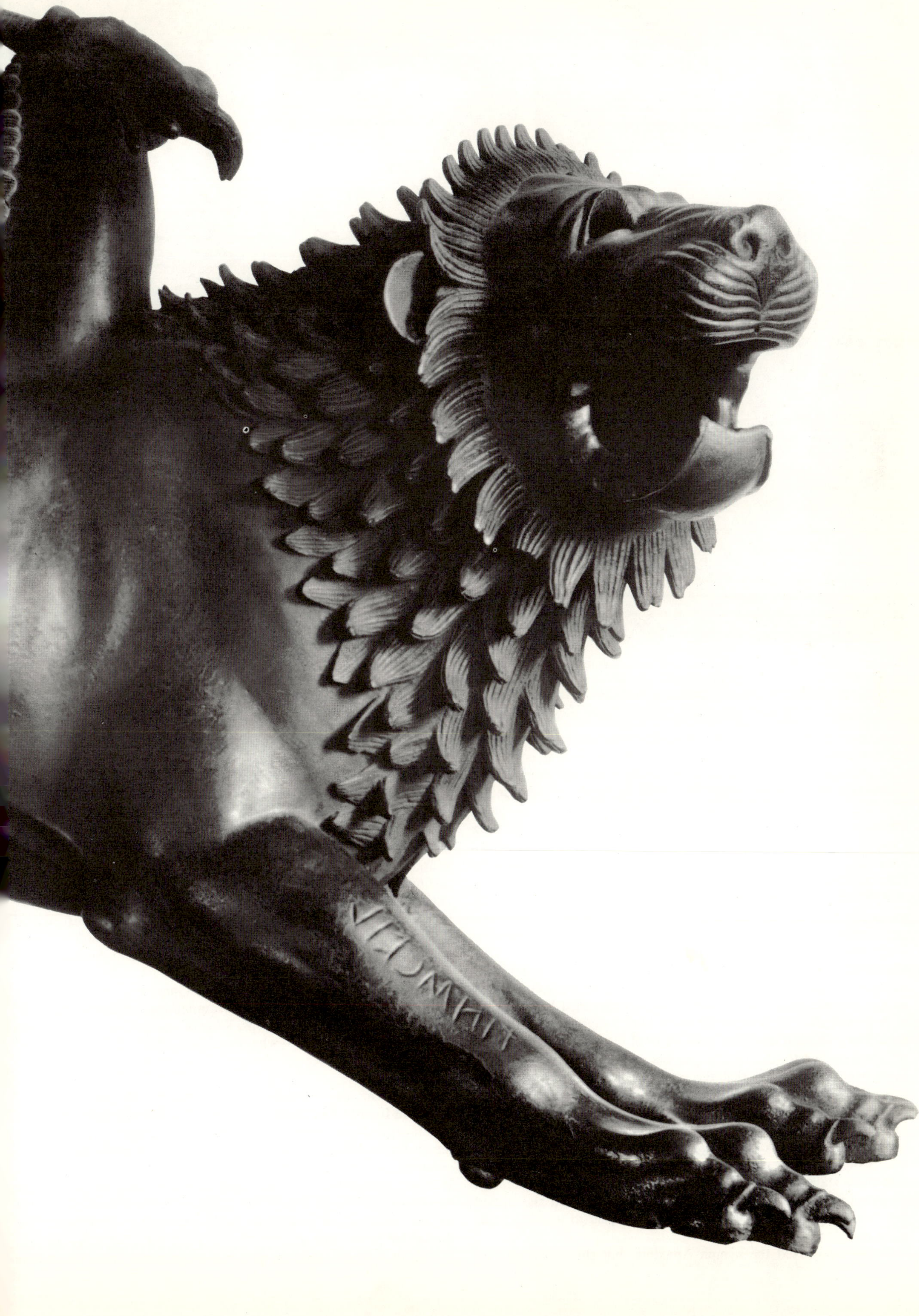

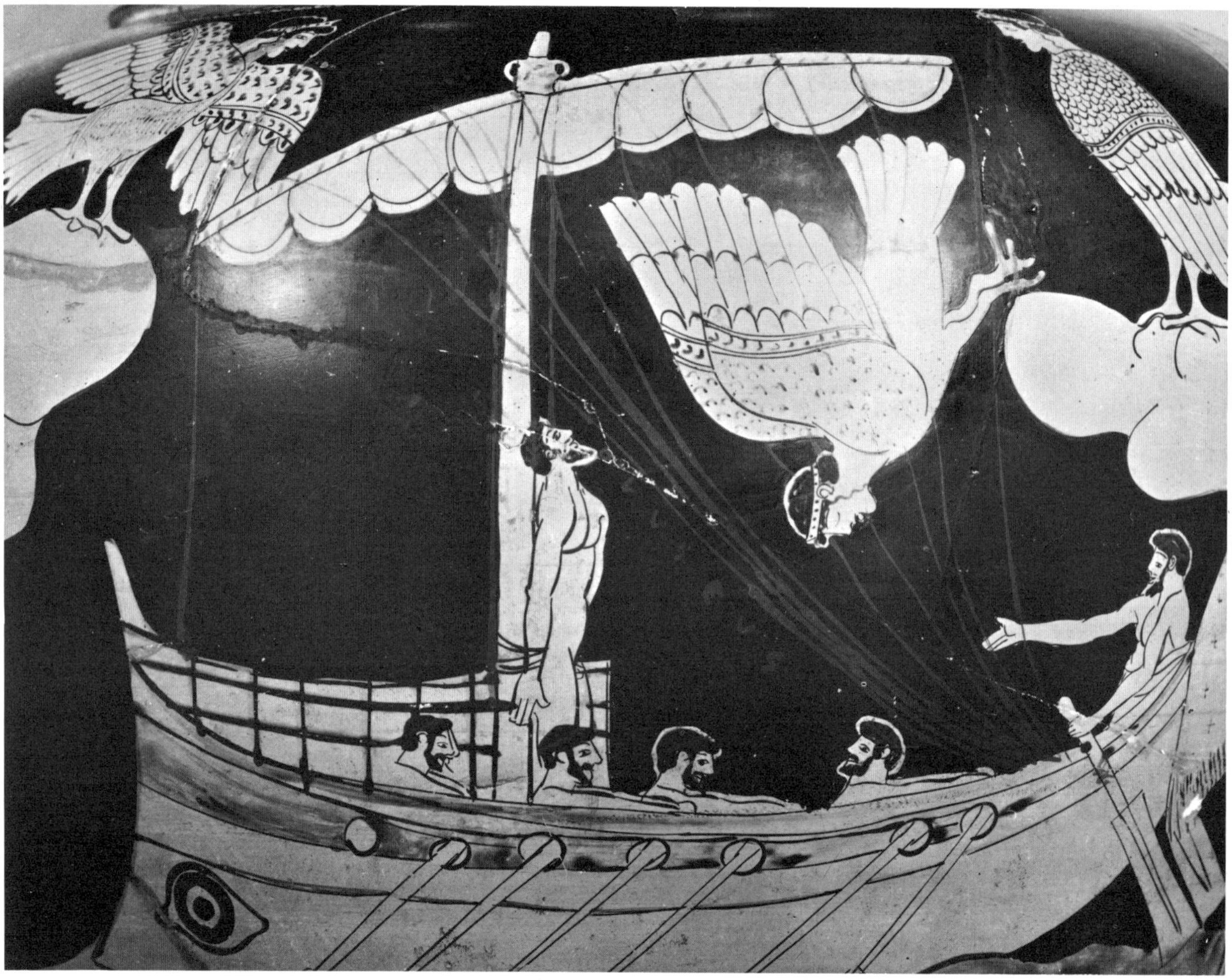

Odysseus and the Sirens. Perched on rock or fluttering overhead, the three sirens seek to lure Odysseus and his companions to their deaths with their melodious voices. Forewarned by Circe, Odysseus has had himself securely bound to the mast of his ship while his companions row on, their ears stopped with bees-wax, unable to hear the sirens' song. Detail from a Greek red-figured stamnos from Vulci. Early fifth century B.C.

As god of light Helios saw everything and knew everything. Of him it could be said what Pindar said of Apollo: 'He is the god who plumbs all hearts, the infallible, whom neither mortals nor immortals can deceive either by action or in their most secret thoughts.' Similarly the Assyro-Babylonian sun-god Shamash was also the god who discovered the crimes of the wicked. Nothing escaped Helios. It was he who informed Demeter of the rape of her daughter. It was he who revealed Aphrodite's unfaithfulness to Hephaestus.

Aphrodite avenged herself by inspiring in Helios a burning passion for Leucothea, daughter of Orchamos, King of Babylon, and Eurynome. Having assumed the appearance of the venerable Eurynome, Helios was about to approach the young maiden, who received him without suspicion. But Clytie, Leucothea's sister, who had herself enjoyed the favours of the god, was jealous of Leucothea's happiness. She informed Orchamos, who condemned his daughter to be buried alive. Helios came in haste, but his rays could not 'bring back living warmth into the frozen limbs of his mistress'. Incapable of restoring her to life, he changed her into an incense shrub. As for Clytie, she realised that the god was now indifferent to her love and, according to Ovid, died of despair. 'Exposed to the weather's inclemency, night and day she slept naked on the ground; for nine days without food or water she could quench her thirst only with the dew and her own tears. . . Her body at last took root in the soil; a mortal pallor spread over her and her limbs changed into a colourless stalk; her head became a flower bright as the violet, and in spite of the root which held her fast to the ground she turned her face towards Helios whom she never ceased to worship.' She is the heliotrope.

Helios also loved the nymph Anaxibia, but she fled from him and took refuge in the temple of Artemis Orthia and disappeared. Helios was unable to find her and rose up into the sky; the place took the name of Anatolius, which means ascension.

Helios had numerous wives as well: the Oceanid Perse, by whom he had two sons, Aeëtes and Perses, and two daughters, Circe and Pasiphaë; Neaera, who bore him Phaetusa and Lampetia, the guardians of his flocks; the nymph Rhode, by whom he had seven sons, the Heliads, and one daughter, Electryone. The Heliads were distinguished for their intelligence and to them was attributed the perfecting of naval architecture as well as the division of the day into hours. One of them, Tenagis, was outstandingly learned and finally aroused the jealousy of his brothers, who murdered him. After the murder they dispersed among the islands in the neighbourhood of Rhodes.

Among the wives of Helios were also Gaea, who gave him a son, Achelous; Iphinoë (or Iphiboë) or Naupiadame, mother of Augeias; finally Clymene, wife of Merops, King of the Ethiopians, by whom he had seven daughters – who were also called the Heliads – and one son, Phaethon.

Phaethon. One day Phaethon had a dispute with Epahus, son of Zeus and Io, who had thrown doubts on his divine origin. Phaethon was mortified and went to his mother to complain. In order to reassure him, she advised him to go to Helios himself and ask for confirmation of his divine birth. Phaethon obeyed and begged Helios to accord him a favour which would prove to all eyes that he was indeed the son of Helios. The god gave his promise and swore it by the Styx, which made the oath irrevocable. Phaethon then demanded permission to drive the sun's chariot for one day. In vain Helios tried to dissuade the presumptuous youth from this insane project. Phaethon insisted and Helios was bound by his oath; he had, therefore, to confide the sun's impetuous steeds to Phaethon. The horses, no longer restrained by the firm hand of their usual driver, rushed wildly through space, carrying the unhappy Phaethon, who had lost all control over them, on their mad career. The chariot came too near the earth; the rivers dried up and the soil began to burn. The universe would have been destroyed by flame had not Zeus struck the rash youth with a thunderbolt and sent him tumbling into the waters of the Eridanus. Phaethon was buried by the nymphs. His sisters, the Heliads, came to weep beside his tomb and were changed into poplar trees. Their tears became the amber which was gathered in abundance on the banks of the Eridanus.

Circe. A daughter of Helios was equally celebrated in the mythological annals of Greece: Circe. Because she lived in the west of the isle of Aeaea some have tried to see in Circe a moon-goddess. But more probably she was a goddess of love – of degrading love – comparable to the Babylonian Ishtar who was so roughly treated by Gilgamesh.

Circe was above all known for her evil spells and enchantments. Married to the king of the Sarmatians, she poisoned her husband and went to live in the isle of Aeaea where she built herself a magnificent palace. She cast a spell over all who landed on the island and, by means of magic potions, turned them into animals. Thus she changed Odysseus' companions into swine. Odysseus alone escaped their fate, thanks to a herb, *moly*, which Hermes had given him. Better still, he forced the sorceress to restore his companions to their human form. Nevertheless he spent a year with Circe, forgetting his wife and his country. Circe, it was said, was slain by Telemachus, who had married her daughter, Cassiphone.

SELENE

Selene, who was also called Mene, was the sister of Helios, and with her golden crown illuminated the shadowy night. Every evening, beginning her journey when her brother had finished his, the divine Selene of the broad wings, 'after bathing her lovely body in the Ocean, clad herself in splendid robes and rose in the sky on her chariot drawn by shining steeds'. Sometimes we also see her mounted on a horse, a mule or even a bull.

Although she was generally considered to be the daughter of Hyperion and Theia (or Euryphaessa) her father was sometimes said to be Helios or even Zeus.

Her beauty attracted the love of Zeus, who made her mother of three daughters: Pandia, 'remarkable for her beauty among the Immortals'; Erse, the dew; and Nemea. It was claimed that the Nemean Lion was also born to Zeus and Selene, and that it fell from the moon on to the earth.

Selene was loved by Pan, who took the shape of a white ram and drew her into the depths of a wood in Arcadia.

Selene and Endymion. The best-known legend of Selene was that of her love for Endymion. The story was told differently in Elis and in Caria. According to the Elians, Endymion was a king of Elis whose tomb was still shown at Olympia and to whom Selene bore fifty daughters. According to the Carian tradition Endymion was a young prince who, hunting on Mount Latmus one day, lay down to rest in a cool grotto where he fell asleep. Selene saw him and, captivated by his beauty, stole a kiss while he slept. Endymion asked Zeus to grant him immortality and eternal youth; Zeus consented on condition that he remained eternally asleep.

Another tradition explains this eternal sleep as a punishment inflicted by Zeus on Endymion who, on his admission to Olympus, had been rash enough to aspire to Hera's love.

Be this as it may, Selene came faithfully night after night silently to contemplate her sleeping lover. Thus the rays of the amorous moon come to caress the sleep of mortals.

EOS

The third child of the Titans, Hyperion and Theia, was Eos (Aurora), the rosy-fingered dawn with the snowy eyelids. It was she who brought the first glimmer of day to men. Every morning at dawn she slipped from the couch of her husband, Tithonus, and emerging from the ocean rose into the sky. Sometimes she appeared as a winged goddess tilting an urn from which fell the morning dew. Sometimes she was mounted on the horse Pegasus and bore in her hands a torch. Most often saffron-robed Eos rode on a purple chariot drawn by two horses.

It was only later that Eos was distinguished from Hemera, goddess of the day; originally she was represented as accompanying her brother Helios during his whole journey.

Eos at first united with the Titan Astraeus, to whom she bore the winds, Boreas, Zephyrus, Eurus, Notus and various astral bodies.

Eos was young and lovely and made to awaken desire. She was loved by Ares, which earned her the enmity of Aphrodite. To avenge herself, Aphrodite inspired Eos with love for numerous mortals.

She conceived a passion for the giant Orion, whom she carried off and kept with her, to the great annoyance of the gods. Artemis finally killed him by accident in the isle of Ortygia.

Eos and Tithonus. Then Aphrodite filled the heart of Eos with love for Tithonus, one of Laomedon's sons. Wishing to be bound to her new husband for eternity, Eos begged Zeus to confer immortality on him; but, alas, she had forgotten to ask at the same time for perpetual youth! As the years passed the young and handsome lover of former days became an old man with wrinkled brow. In vain Eos fed him on the celestial ambrosia which rendered the flesh incorruptible; old age gave way to decrepitude. The goddess then shut Tithonus up in a chamber where the impotent old man remained in solitude until the day when the gods took pity and changed him into a cicada.

Eos and Cephalus. Meanwhile the inconstant Eos sought consolation among other mortals. There was Cleitus, grandson of the soothsayer Melampus, for whom she obtained the favour of being admitted into Olympus. There was Cephalus, son of Hermes, or of Deion, King of Phocis, whose fate was more tragic. Cephalus had just married Procris, whom he dearly loved, when Eos saw him hunting on Mount Hymettus and carried him off to Syria. Far from responding to the goddess's love, Cephalus thought only of his beloved Procris. Not unnaturally irritated, Eos filled him with doubts about his wife's fidelity and advised him to test her. Cephalus then approached Procris in disguise and, offering her rich jewels, tried to seduce her. Procris repelled him at first, but finally the temptation was too strong for her. Cephalus revealed his identity and drove her away. The unhappy Procris retired to Euboea and put herself under the protection of Artemis. Artemis – or some say it was Minos – gave her a dog who never lost the scent and a javelin which never missed its mark, and sent her back in disguise to Cephalus. This time Cephalus, offered the dog and the javelin, was himself tempted and, in fact, made the same mistake his wife had previously made. The couple then became reconciled. But Procris still feared that her husband might be unfaithful to her and followed him when he went hunting, spying on him without his suspecting it. One day when Procris was hidden in a thicket Cephalus heard a rustling sound. Thinking it was some wild beast, he threw the javelin which never missed its mark. Procris was slain and Cephalus was summoned before the Areopagus, which banished him from Athens. He went to Thebes, where he visited Amphitryon, and then retired to an island which was named Cephallenia after him. According to another version of the story Cephalus was inconsolable at the death of Procris and threw himself from the promontory of Leucas into the sea.

The Offspring of Eos. By her marriage with Tithonus, Eos had two sons: Memnon and Emathion. Emathion reigned over Arabia and was killed by Hercules. Memnon was King of Ethiopia and went to Troy with an army of Ethiopians and Susians to assist Priam. He was 'the most handsome warrior who appeared before Troy'. Having killed Antilochus, son of Nestor, he was himself killed by Achilles. Eos obtained immortality for him; nevertheless she never ceased to weep each morning for her dearly beloved son, and it was her tears which formed the dew. It seems likely that this hero represents some former Asiatic divinity. Memnon, indeed, was reputed to have founded Susa – where his tomb was – and to have built the walls of Babylon. He was also venerated in Egypt: the colossal statue at Thebes was called the statue of Memnon.

Among the other sons of Eos must be mentioned Phaethon, son of Tithonus (or of Cephalus) who was carried off by Aphrodite to be the guardian of her temple. He is thus connected with the planet Venus, of which two other sons of Eos, Phosphorus and Hesperus, represent the planet's double aspect of morning star and evening star.

Phosphorus was the son of Astraeus; with a torch in his hand he could be seen in the guise of a winged spirit flying through the air before his mother's chariot.

Hesperus, 'the most splendid star which shines in the firmament', was sometimes said to be the son of Atlas. Hesperus' own children were: Daedalion, who in despair at the death of his daughter Chione threw himself from the heights of Parnassus and was changed by Apollo into a sparrow-hawk; and Ceyx, who married Alcyone. Ceyx and Alcyone were both turned into birds for having dared to compare themselves to Zeus and Hera. Another version is that when Ceyx perished in a shipwreck Alcyone threw herself in despair into the sea and Thetis changed the couple into halcyons or kingfishers.

The Hesperides. Hesperus was also said to be father of the Hesperides; though others said they were daughters of Night and Erebus, or of Phorcys and Ceto, or of Zeus and Themis. The Hesperides were three or four in number: Aegle, Erytheis, Hespera, Hestia or Arethusa. Their abode was beyond the river-ocean, at the extreme western limits of the world, where they personified the clouds gilded by the setting sun. They lived in a wondrous garden and guarded the golden apples which grew there. Since, however, the Greeks had two identical words for 'apple' and for 'flock of sheep', it has been wondered if the Hesperides were not rather guardians of the celestial flocks which in Indo-European mythology symbolised clouds.

ORION: THE PLEIADES: THE HYADES

The constellations of Orion, the Pleiades and the Hyades, occupied a particular place in Greek mythology.

Orion. Orion was a giant of Boeotia famous for his beauty. He was variously described as the son of Mother Earth, of Poseidon and Euryale, and of Hyrieus, King of Hyria in Boeotia. One day when Zeus, Hermes and Poseidon were travelling together on earth they were handsomely received by Hyrieus. In gratitude for his hospitality they promised to grant whatever he asked for. Hyrieus asked for a son. The three gods then took the hide of a heifer, urinated on it and buried it. Nine months later Orion emerged from the ground. This singular mode of procreation seems to arise from a play on words, Orion and urine being similar also in Greek. Orion was of such gigantic stature that he could walk on the bottom of the sea without wetting his head. He was endowed with prodigious strength and was a passionate hunter. He followed his favourite sport accompanied by his dog Sirius. He had married Side who, because she boasted that she was more beautiful than Hera, was cast by that goddess into Tartarus. Afterwards Orion fell in love with Merope, daughter of Oenopion, ruler of Chios. He rid the island of all its savage beasts in vain: he was rejected by Oenopion. Orion therefore took Merope by violence. Her father then implored the aid of Dionysus, who plunged Orion into deep slumber; while Orion slept, Oenopion put out his eyes. The giant, however, discovered from an oracle that he could regain his sight if he travelled towards the sun. He went to Lemnos, where Hephaestus gave him his son Cedalion for a guide. When his sight was restored Orion sailed on to Crete, where he went hunting with Artemis. We have seen that he was carried off by Eos. The end of Orion was attributed to Artemis, though there are various versions of how it occurred. Some said she struck him down on the isle of Ortygia after Eos had carried him off, others that she shot him by accident at Apollo's instigation, or that she caused his death by a scorpion's sting after he had attempted to ravish her, or, again, because he boasted of having destroyed all the wild beasts in Crete. Asclepius attempted to resuscitate Orion, but Zeus struck him with a thunderbolt. Orion descended into the realm of Hades, where his shade with a brazen club continued to hunt the wild beasts. But according to the more popular tradition Orion was transported to the sky where, in golden armour and sword in hand, he shines on winter nights. His brilliance, however, fades when the constellation Scorpio appears.

Pleiades and Hyades. The Pleiades were daughters of Atlas and Pleione or Aethra. There were seven of them: Maia, Taygete, Electra, Alcyone, Celoeno, Sterope and Merope. The first three were loved by Zeus. Poseidon obtained the favours of Alcyone and Celoeno. Ares was Sterope's lover. Only Merope had to be content with the love of a mere mortal, Sisyphus – hence she shines less brightly in the sky than her sisters. They had all been changed into stars. They were being pursued across the mountains of Boeotia by the hunter Orion. They were about to fall into his clutches when they cried to Zeus for help. He turned them into doves, then placed them in the sky. It was also related that the Pleiades, inconsolable at the death of their sisters, the Hyades, killed themselves in despair and were then changed by Zeus into stars. They appeared in the sky in the middle of May and thus announced the return of the good weather.

The appearance of the Hyades on the contrary was the signal for the rainy season. Their very name meant the Rainy Ones. They were also daughters of Atlas and Aethra or Pleione. Their number varies among different authors from two to seven. Nor are their names fixed. The ones most frequently listed are: Ambrosia, Eudora and Coronis. It was related that they had brought up Zeus in Dodona, and later Dionysus in Nysa. In recognition of these services they were placed among the heavenly bodies, where they formed a group of stars in the constellation Taurus. Their metamorphosis was also explained as a recompense for the unhappiness they suffered at the death of their brother Hyas, who was killed while hunting by a serpent or a wild boar.

GODS OF THE WINDS

The empire of the winds was shared between the four sons of Eos, the dawn, and Astraeus, the starry sky. They were called: Boreas, the North Wind; Zephyrus, the West Wind; Eurus, the East Wind; and Notus, the South Wind.

Boreas dwelt in the mountains of Thrace. It was there that Iris came in search of him to fan the funeral pyre of Patroclus. It was said that Boreas carried off Oreithyia, daughter of Erechtheus, from the banks of the Ilissus, and by her had several children, notably Chione, who was loved by Poseidon; Cleopatra, who married Phineus; and the twins Zetes and Calais, also called the Boreades, who took part in the expedition of the Argonauts, fought victoriously against the Harpies, and were slain by the arrows of Hercules in the island of Zenos. They were changed into favourable winds which blew from the north-east and were given the name *Prodromes,* forerunners, because they came shortly before the rise of the Dog Star.

Boreas assumed the form of a stallion to mate with the mares of Erichthonius, and from this union were born twelve young mares so light of step that 'they ran across fields of standing corn without bruising an ear of grain and over the crests of the sea without wetting their feet'.

In memory of the abduction of Oreithyia the Athenians raised a temple to Boreas on the banks of the Ilissus. They especially venerated Boreas because he had dispersed the fleet of the invader Xerxes. Boreas was represented as a winged man of mature age with hair floating in the wind. On the chest of Cypselus, however, he is depicted as having serpents for legs.

The normal companion of Boreas was Zephyrus who was not, originally, the soft and beneficial wind at whose breath the spring flowers open. Like his brother he was a savage and baleful wind who took pleasure in brewing storms and tossing the waves of the sea. With Boreas he lived in the caves of mountainous Thrace. From his union with the Harpy Podarge were born the two horses Xanthus and Balius, who drew the chariot of Achilles.

Later Zephyrus' violent disposition softened. He became a sweet-scented wind which gently fanned the blessed regions of Elysium. For a wife he was given the gracious Chloris by whom he had a son, Carpus – or fruit.

The Athenians consecrated an altar to Zephyrus on the road to Eleusis.

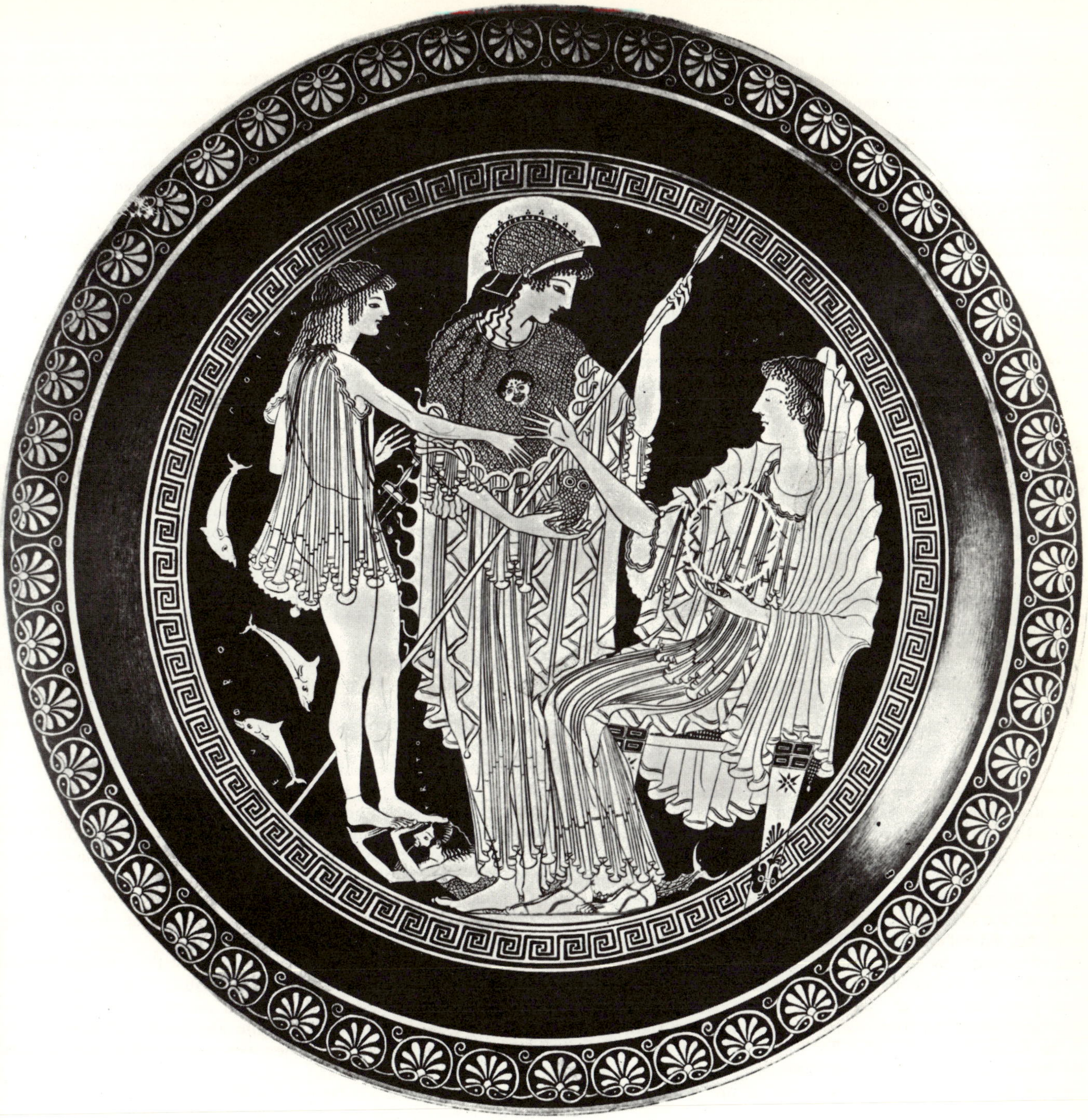

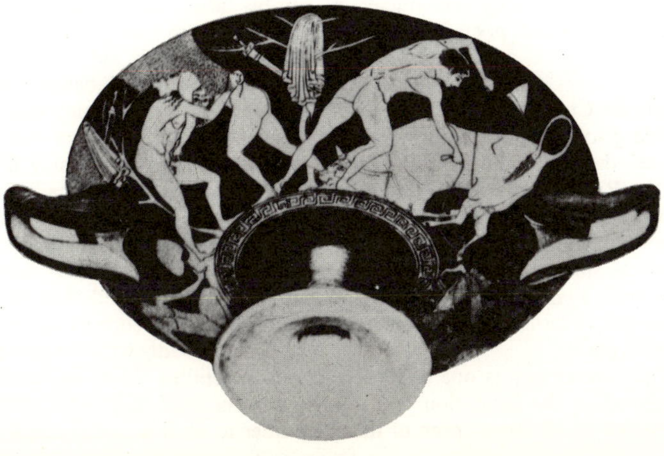

Theseus receiving a jewelled crown from Amphitrite, the goddess of the sea. Challenged by Minos to prove his claim to be the son of Poseidon by retrieving a golden ring thrown into the sea, the Attic hero has plunged into its depths, escorted by a school of dolphin, and now stands before the goddess. Detail from the bottom of a Greek cup decorated with scenes showing the exploits of Theseus.

As for Notus and Eurus, their individualities were never clearly defined.

Aeolus. Another tradition, which has its source in the *Odyssey*, places the abode of the winds in the Aeolian Islands, where they were kept under the guardianship of Aeolus. Aeolus was the son of Poseidon and Arne, and a brother of Boeotus. After an adventurous youth he settled in the Lipari Islands and married Gyane, the daughter of King Liparus. Because of his piety and justice Aeolus became a friend of the gods. It was said that he invented ships' sails. Zeus appointed him guardian of the winds which he could, at will, excite or soothe. When Odysseus landed on his island Aeolus welcomed him hospitably and on his departure gave him a wine-skin in which were tied up those winds which would impede his voyage. Overcome by curiosity the companions of Odysseus untied the wine-skin and let the deadly contrary winds escape.

At first Aeolus was simply the guardian of the winds, but later he became their father and, in Roman mythology, the god of wind. He resided, they said, on the isle of Lipara, where he kept the winds chained up in deep caverns.

The Chimaera and the Harpies. In opposition to these regular winds there were various monsters who personified the storm winds who, 'pouncing suddenly on the darkened waves, unleashed the raging tempests to destroy men'. Their father was Typhon, son of Typhoeus, spirit of the hurricane, and their mother was Echidna, the upper part of whose body was that of a young nymph but whose lower part was that of a horrifying serpent covered with scales. Among these monsters it will be sufficient to mention the Chimaera and the Harpies.

The Chimaera had the head of a lion, the body of a goat and the tail of a dragon. She vomited forth horrible flames. It is agreed that she was a personification of the storm-cloud.

The Harpies – who were also said to be daughters of Thaumas and Electra – were tempest-goddesses, 'the ravagers'. Homer only names one of them, Podarge. Hesiod mentions two, Aello and Ocypete, winged creatures as swift as birds and the winds. Later the Harpy type became definite: they were monsters with the face of an old hag, the ears of a bear, and the body of a bird with long hooked claws. It was their habit to snatch and devour food from tables, or else to soil the table, spreading filth and stench and causing famine. Thus when the soothsayer Phineus was condemned by Zeus to eternal old age and everlasting hunger, the Harpies came to steal the food which was laid before him, soiling with their excrement what they did not carry away. They were attacked by the Argonauts and particularly by the Boreades Zetes and Calais, who pursued them through the air and vanquished them. They granted them their lives, however, at the request of Iris. According to other traditions one of the Harpies drowned herself in the Tigris, a river in the Peloponnese; the other fled to the Echinade Islands where she turned round and fell to the shore. Thus the islands took the name of the Strophades, from the Greek 'to turn'.

GODS OF THE WATERS

Pontus. The oldest divinity of the waters was Pontus, whom Gaea produced from herself at the beginning of time. Pontus is no more than the personified sea. He was without physiognomy or character, and all that remained of him was his name, which poets later used to designate the sea.

Oceanus. The primitive Greeks, like the Chaldeans, imagined an immense river which formed a liquid girdle around the universe. It lay beyond the sea and embraced the sea without, however, mingling with its waters. It was the River Ocean, or Oceanus, who, having himself neither source nor outlet, gave birth to 'all the rivers, the entire sea, to all waters which gushed from the earth, to all deep wells'. From him arose all the stars – with the exception of the Great Bear – only to plunge back again. On the shores of Oceanus were the fabulous lands of the virtuous Ethiopians, the fog-bound Cimmerians, the minute Pygmies.

Son of Uranus and Gaea, the Titan Oceanus was one of those elemental forces which had contributed to the formation of the world. In him Homer salutes the essence of all things, even of the gods, and regards him as a divinity whose power was inferior to none but Zeus'.

Oceanus married his sister Tethys and by her had the three thousand Oceanids and the three thousand rivers. According to one tradition Oceanus and Tethys cared for the infant Hera, whom they sheltered in their palace in the west of the world.

The Olympians, however, finally established their empire over the waters, as over the rest of the universe, and the watery element was inherited by Poseidon, who from then on became the uncontested lord of the sea and the rivers, while the aged Oceanus was confined to his distant place of retirement.

DIVINITIES OF THE SEA

The importance assumed by Poseidon in Greek religious belief caused the other and more ancient marine deities to play secondary roles, and their cult retained no more than a popular character.

Nereus. Nereus was the son of Pontus and Gaea. He was born in the first ages of the world, and the accumulation of centuries had made of him a venerable greybeard. He was, indeed, called 'The Old Man of the Sea'. He was kindly and helpful, 'having known only thoughts of justice and kindness'. He only left the dwelling he occupied with his wife Doris in the depths of the Aegaean Sea in order to come to the assistance of sailors and give them useful advice. Like other marine deities, however, he only spoke when he had to. Hercules resorted to force in order to learn from him how to reach the land of the Hesperides. Nereus also possessed the gift of prophecy; Paris one day beheld him emerging from the waves and heard from his mouth the announcement of the coming destruction of Troy.

Of the marriage of Nereus and Doris were born fifty daughters, the Nereids, fair virgins with golden hair who lived with their father in his submarine abode, but who might sometimes be seen when the sea was calm frolicking with the Tritons on the crest of the waves.

Of most of the Nereids we know only the names; some of them, however, played a part in the legends of Greece.

Arethusa was seen one day by the hunter Alpheius, who immediately fell in love with her. He pursued her, and to escape him Arethusa took refuge on the isle of Ortygia, where she was changed into a spring. Alpheius, who remained in the neighbourhood of Olympia, was himself changed into a river and his waters, crossing the sea without mingling with it, then joined the waters of the spring Arethusa on the isle of Ortygia.

Galatea, another Nereid, was courted by the Cyclops Polyphemus, but she preferred a young herdsman of Sicily, named Acis. Polyphemus surprised the two lovers one day while they were conversing in the hollow of a grotto and crushed Acis under an enormous boulder. Galatea, however, succeeded in having Acis changed into a river.

Psamathe had a son by Aeacus, Phocus, who reigned over the island of Aegina and who was assassinated by Peleus and Telamon. To avenge the murder of her son Psamathe sent a monstrous wolf who devastated Peleus' flocks.

The most celebrated of the Nereids was Thetis. For her beauty she was sought in marriage by both Zeus and Poseidon. But Themis declared that Thetis would give birth to a son more powerful than his father, and both gods prudently renounced their project. Zeus decided to marry Thetis to a mortal, and chose Peleus, King of Thessaly. Thetis did not accept this alliance which she, being immortal, considered beneath her dignity, without protest. She attempted to escape from Peleus by taking on various shapes: she changed herself into a fish and then into an animal, into a fluid wave, then into burning flame. Thanks to the advice of the centaur Chiron, Peleus finally succeeded in seizing her and their marriage was celebrated with great pomp in the presence of the gods, who showered handsome gifts on the couple. To Thetis and Peleus was born a son, Achilles. Some said that Achilles was their seventh child and that Thetis had thrown the first six into the fire to destroy such evidence of an unworthy union. This story agrees rather badly with the tenderness which Thetis always showed towards Achilles. When she learned the fatal destiny which awaited her son she tried to prevent it by rendering Achilles invulnerable. In order to do this, she exposed him every night to the flames and dressed his wounds with ambrosia. But Peleus caught her unawares one night and, terrified, snatched the child away. According to a more accredited version, as soon as Achilles was born Thetis plunged him into the Styx, thus making his body invulnerable, all except the heel by which she held him.

Thetis plays a part in many legends. It will be recalled that she came to the assistance of Zeus when he was nearly overcome by Hera, Apollo, Poseidon and Athene: she brought the giant Briareus to defend Zeus. Thetis and her sister Eurynome sheltered Hephaestus after his fall from Olympus. She also sheltered Dionysus when he fled before Lycurgus.

She was honoured in various parts of Greece, in Thessaly, in Messenia and at Sparta.

Proteus. Proteus was another 'Old Man of the Sea'. He was the son of Oceanus and Tethys, and his duty was to guard Poseidon's herd of seals. At noon each day he would emerge from the waves and come ashore to rest in the shelter of a rock. Around him slept the tight-packed herd of seals, sons of the fair Halosydne. It was the propitious moment to obtain from wise Proteus a revelation of what fate held in store; for he saw into the future and he spoke the truth. But, since he never spoke oracularly unless forced to do so, it was first necessary to catch hold of him – no simple matter, for Proteus could change shape at will and in order to escape from whoever held him would in succession turn himself into a lion, a dragon, a panther, into water, fire, a tree... The important thing was not to be intimidated by these metamorphoses, for then Proteus would admit himself vanquished and talk. In this manner Menelaus, following the advice of Idothea, Proteus' own daughter, learned from him how to return to his own country. Proteus was represented with the features of an old man, and he lived on the isle of Pharos on the Egyptian coast.

This localisation no doubt resulted from a confusion with a fabled King of Egypt who was also named Proteus. It was said that this king welcomed Paris and Helen when they fled from Sparta, but that he kept Helen with him in order to return her to her legitimate husband. It was also said that he went from Egypt to Thrace, where he married. Later, angered by the cruelty of his two sons, Tmolus and Telegonus, he decided to return to Egypt, and Poseidon hollowed out for him under the sea a road which led him back to Pharos.

Phorcys. The character of Phorcys is more vague. Homer calls him 'the old man who rules the waves'. He says that his daughter was the nymph Thoosa who by Poseidon had the monstrous Polyphemus. According to Hesiod, Phorcys was the son of Pontus and Gaea. He married his sister Ceto and fathered the Graeae, the Gorgons, the dragon Ladon and, perhaps, the Hesperides. It was also said that Scylla was born of his love for Hecate. To judge by his wild progeny Phorcys must in the eyes of the Greeks have personified the perfidious and evil sea. His very name seems to indicate the whitish foam which crowns the crest of the waves.

Glaucus. The name Glaucus evokes a picture of the dark greenish-blue which the sea assumes when the winds begin to rise. There were various legends about Glaucus. One related that he was a humble fisherman from Anthedon. One day when he returned from fishing he set down his fish among some herbs which grew beside the shore. He saw them immediately leap up and fling themselves back into the sea. He tasted the herbs himself and was changed into a Triton. He jumped into the sea and was admitted among the marine deities as one of their own number. Another legend recounts that while pursuing a hare Glaucus saw the creature swallow a blade of this herb and at once recover its agility. In curiosity Glaucus also tasted the mysterious herb and thus acquired immortality. He took to the sea either in obedience to a secret impulse sent by Zeus, or because he was vexed at being unable to make his fellow men acknowledge his immortality.

Glaucus normally dwelt in Delos. Apollo conferred on him the gift of prophecy which he transmitted to his daughter, the sibyl Deiphobe. Once a year Glaucus left his abode in Delos and made a tour of the islands of the Aegaean Sea. He would appear to sailors, with his thin body covered with seaweed and seashells, and predict sinister occurrences.

He was a lugubrious divinity and even his love affairs were unhappy. Except for Syme, whose love he won and whom he carried to a small island near Rhodes, all to whom he paid court repulsed him. He discovered Ariadne on the isle of Naxos and attempted to console her, but Dionysus arrived, bound him up with vine-shoots, and consoled Ariadne himself. It was also said that Glaucus turned Scylla into a monster out of resentment though, it is true, Scylla's metamorphosis was also attributed to the jealousy of Amphitrite.

Sometimes confused with Glaucus was another personage of human origin who was raised to the rank of a marine divinity: Melicertes Palaemon.

Melicertes was the son of Athamas and Semele's sister Ino who had incurred the wrath of Hera for having fed and sheltered young Dionysus after his mother's death. Hera, in vengeance, unbalanced Athamas' mind and Athamas slew one of his own sons, Learchus. To save the other son, Melicertes, from his father's madness, Ino seized the child and jumped with it into the sea. She was welcomed by the Nereids and became, under the name Leucothea, a divinity who protected mariners. As for Melicertes, his body was carried by a dolphin to the coast of Corinth. Sisyphus found it and erected a tomb for Melicertes on the shore. Under the name Palaemon, Melicertes was from then on venerated as a god. On the instructions of the Nereids the Isthmian games were instituted in his honour. He is usually represented as a child carried by dolphins.

Triton. Around the chariot of Amphitrite, who was escorted by the gracious Nereids, frisked strange creatures, half-men, half-fish, whose bodies were covered with scales, whose teeth were sharp and whose fingers were armed with claws. Their breast and belly were supplied with fins, and instead of legs they had the forked tail of a marine monster. This lascivious troop played among the waves, noisily blowing on conch shells. They were the Tritons. Some of their number, who were furnished with a pair of horse's legs as well, were known as Centaur-Tritons.

Although they lived in the sea the Tritons sometimes ventured on to land. At Tanagra, people remembered a Triton who had desolated the country and ravished the women. To capture him they placed a vase filled with wine on the beach. The Triton drank it, and during his drunken slumber a fisherman cut off his head. They placed a statue of a headless Triton in the temple of Dionysus at Tanagra to commemorate the event.

These marine genii took their name from a primitive god, son of Poseidon and Amphitrite, whose name was Triton. He also was half-man, half-fish, and lived with his father in the depths of the sea, although his favourite place of abode was near the coast of Libya. It even seems that in origin Triton was a purely Libyan divinity, unless the Minyaen colonists had brought with them to Africa the former god of the river Triton which flowed into Lake Copais in Boeotia.

As Poseidon's son, Triton shared some of his father's powers: like him he could raise or quieten the waves. He could be seen riding the waves on his chariot drawn by steeds whose hooves were the claws of crayfish.

On two occasions he did Zeus a good turn. During the war with the Giants, Triton contributed to the victory of the Olympians by frightening the giants with the terrible sounds he made with his conch. Later, it was Triton whom Zeus made responsible for seeing that the waters withdrew after the deluge.

Benevolent and obliging, Triton saved the Argonauts when a tempest drove their ship on to the Libyan coast. He helped them, and his advice enabled them to continue their voyage.

Triton shared the gift of prophecy with the other marine gods, Nereus and Proteus, of whom he was originally, perhaps, only a local form. It seems, however, that he more especially personified the roar of the sea or its wild movement, as his attribute, the conch, tends to indicate.

Sea Monsters: The Sirens. The name Siren derives from a Greek root meaning 'to bind or attach' and clearly alludes to the role the Sirens played in mythology. One is inclined, however, to consider them as divinities who symbolised the souls of the dead. They would thus be funerary genii, avid for blood and hostile to the living. With their bird's body and woman's head, they recall the human-headed Egyptian hawk who also incarnated the souls of the dead. The Sirens were invoked at the moment of death, and their

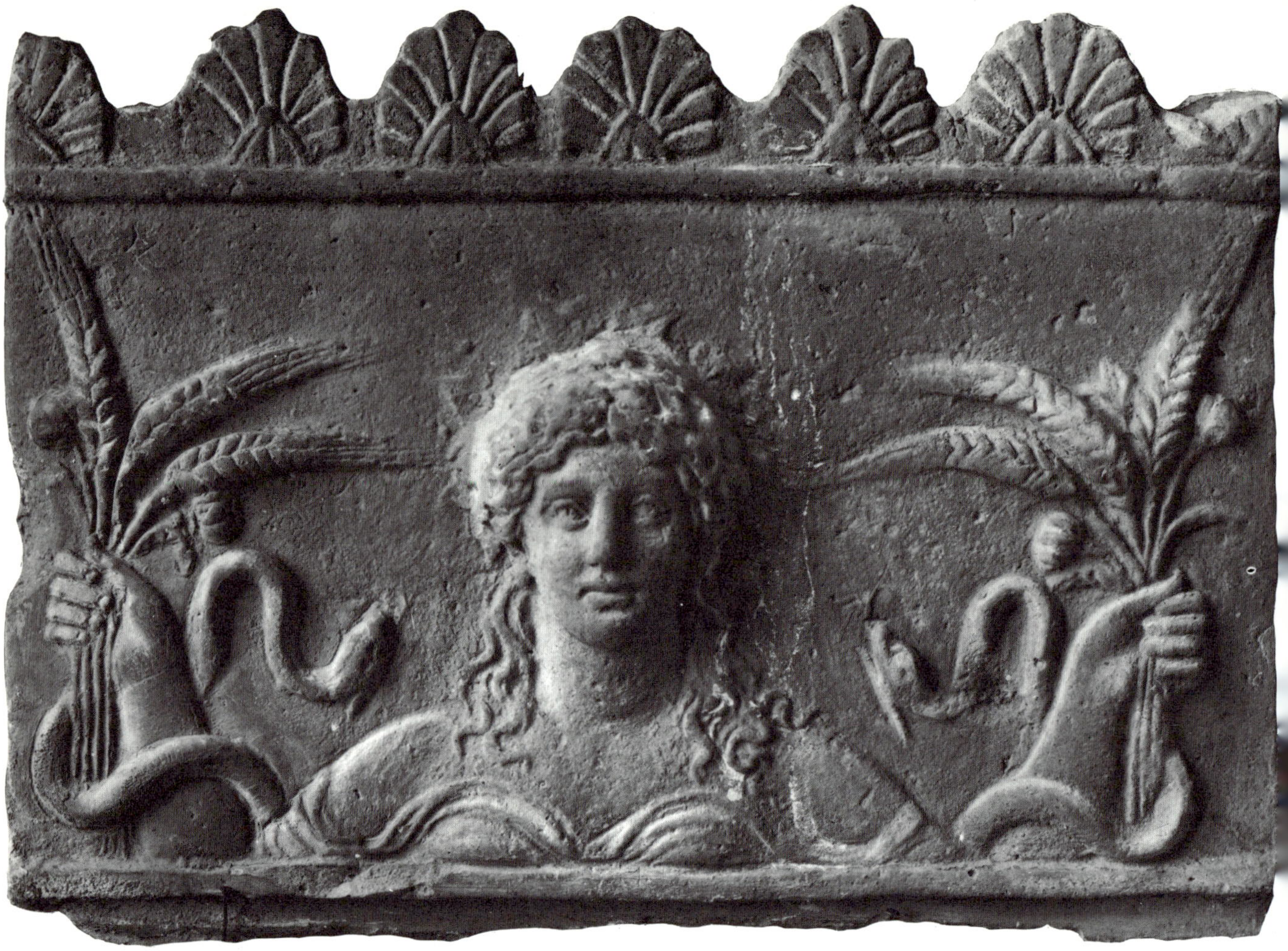

Head of Demeter with her attributes: sheaves of corn, poppies and snakes. Terra-cotta. Terme Museum, Rome.

images are frequently found on tombs. Legend, however, has retained nothing of this conception of them, and depicts the Sirens only as malevolent monsters of the sea.

At first they were represented with the head and bust of a woman and the body of a bird, and only later depicted as women whose bodies terminated in fish tails. Their attribute was a musical instrument – a lyre or a double flute. They had a temple at Sorrento.

When Odysseus was about to leave Circe and take to his swift ships again, she warned him of the dangers of the voyage and in particular said:

'First thou shalt arrive where the enchanter Sirens dwell, they who seduce men. The imprudent man who draws near them never returns, for the Sirens, lying in the flower-strewn fields, will charm him with sweet song; but around them the bodies of their victims lie in heaps.'

And so it was that Odysseus came in sight of a rocky islet where he perceived the bizarre creatures, half-women, half-birds, who, seeing his ship, began to sing. They were the Sirens and what they sang was:

'Draw near, illustrious Odysseus, glory of the Achaeans, stop thy ship and come to us. None has yet passed by this isle without having listened to the enchantment of our voices and heard us sing of the mighty deeds done by the Greeks beneath the walls of Troy. For we know all that happens on the fruitful earth.'

The sweetness of their voices was such that Odysseus could not have resisted their invitation had he not followed Circe's advice and taken the precaution of having himself lashed to the mast of his ship. As for his companions, he had cautiously stopped up their ears with wax.

Thus they escaped the fearful danger. But the human bones scattered over the green fields of the Siren Island bore mute witness to the imprudence of former sailors and to the ferocity of these insidious-voiced creatures.

They had not always been like this. In primitive times the Sirens, who were daughters of the river Achelous, had been river deities. In number they were – depending on different authors – two, three, four or even eight. They had names which emphasised the charm of their voices: Aglaophonos or Aglaophone (of the brilliant voice); Thelxepeia (of the words which enchant); Peisinoë (the persuasive); Molpe (song).

There were various explanations of their strange shape. According to some they were with Persephone when she was ravished by Hades, and it was at their request that Zeus gave them wings so that they could fly in pursuit of the ravisher. According to others they owed their birds' bodies to the wrath of Aphrodite who punished them in this way for having been rebellious to love.

The Sirens were excessively proud of their voices and their musical talent and had, it was said, dared one day to challenge the Muses. But the Muses vanquished them and pulled out their wing feathers. They then abandoned the springs and dales and went to hide their shame among the jagged rocks along the coasts of Southern Italy. Their abodes were Cape Pelorus, Capri, the isle of Anthemusa, and the Siren Isles. There from the shores they attracted sailors by their songs and devoured the unhappy wretches who had been unable to resist their seduction.

In the end, however, they found their master. When the ship of the Argonauts sailed past their island they tried as usual to exert their power. But only Butes, son of Zelion, jumped overboard to join the treacherous goddesses. The others were prevented by Orpheus who was with them. He tuned his lyre and began to sing; and his persuasive voice overcame the allure of the Sirens.

Vanquished, the Sirens from that moment lost all power to do harm and were changed into rocks. One of them, Parthenope, threw herself into the sea in vexation. Her body was tossed on to the shore by the waves, and a tomb was erected for her on the very spot where later the city of Naples rose.

Charybdis and Scylla. This same Sicilian sea where the Sirens dwelt also harboured two other redoubtable monsters, Charybdis and Scylla.

Of Charybdis we know little more than what Homer tells us. 'Divine Charybdis with a terrible roar swallows the waves of the bitter sea and three times each day she throws them up again.' She lived under a rock crowned by a green fig tree. She was called the daughter of Poseidon and the Earth and it was because she had stolen the oxen of Hercules that Zeus struck her with a thunderbolt and changed her into a whirlpool whose vortex swallowed up ships.

The legend of Scylla was more extensive. She was the daughter of Phorcys and Crataeis, or of Typhon and Echidna, or of Poseidon. According to others, her mother was Lamia, that queen of Libya who was loved by Zeus and saw her children perish as a result of Hera's jealousy. In her misery she went out of her mind and devoured babies whom she tore from their mothers' arms. Scylla was at first a nymph of rare beauty. Whether it was because she repelled the advances of Glaucus and Glaucus punished her for disdain, or whether, on the contrary, she had given herself to Poseidon and thus excited Amphitrite's jealousy, Scylla was changed by Circe into a monster. While she was bathing in a pool into which Circe had thrown certain magic herbs, six necks suddenly sprang from her shoulders, necks of monstrous length, surmounted by six frightful heads, each supplied with a triple row of teeth. She lurked in a dark cavern hollowed in the middle of a reef from which emerged only her heads, which snapped up passing dolphins, the dogs of the sea, and those of 'the enormous monsters nurtured by the noisy Amphitrite whom she was able to seize'. When a ship passed within her reach each of her heads would carry off a man from the bench of rowers, and no vessel could boast of escaping Scylla without loss.

When Hercules brought Geryon's herd through the straits of Sicily, Scylla seized and devoured one of the oxen. Hercules killed her, but she was resuscitated by her father Phorcys, and mariners passing the straits of Sicily continued to dread the twin perils of Charybdis and Scylla.

FRESH-WATER DIVINITIES

The Rivers. There were three thousand rivers according to Hesiod, sons of Oceanus and Tethys, who partook of the divine nature of their parents and were worshipped by mortals.

Young folk consecrated their hair to them; rams were immolated to them and into their waters were cast living horses and bulls.

The rivers were represented as vigorous men with long beards; their strength was symbolised by the pair of horns which adorned their brow.

The most celebrated and venerated of rivers was the Achelous, which was also the largest watercourse in Greece. Achelous fought against Hercules for the hand of Deianeira. Vanquished, he changed himself into a serpent, then into a wild bull, Hercules, however, overthrew him and tore off one of his horns, with which the nymphs made the Horn of Plenty. Achelous, ashamed of his defeat, threw himself into the river which thenceforth bore his name. Achelous was revered throughout Greece and even in Sicily – six rivers were named after him – and he was invoked when taking oaths. It was for having omitted to do him honour during a sacrifice that the daughters of the soothsayer Echinus were changed into islands and became the Echinades.

Almost as famous was the Asopus, a name also found in Thessaly and the Peloponnese. Asopus was a river-god of Boeotia. By his wife Merope he had two sons, Pelasgus and Ismenius, and twelve daughters, among them Sinope, who was carried off by Apollo; Corcyra and Salamis, who were loved by Poseidon; and Aegina, who was ravished by Zeus. Asopus went in search of Aegina and learned from Sisyphus – in exchange for a spring which he made gush forth on Acrocorinth – the name of his daughter's ravisher. He attempted to obtain justice, but Zeus struck him with a thunderbolt and forced him to return to his river bed.

Inachus, river-god of Argolis, also had one of his daughters, Io, seduced by Zeus. During the dispute between Hera and Poseidon for possession of Argolis, Inachus was chosen to arbitrate. He pronounced in favour of Hera, and Poseidon, in annoyance, dried up his waters.

Cephissus was a river-god of Phocis and Boeotia. He only appears in mythology as the father of Narcissus, whom he had by the Oceanid Liriope. There was a sanctuary consecrated to him at Argos.

Among the other river-gods may be mentioned: Peneius in Thessaly; in Arcadia, Ladon, who was the father of Syrinx and Daphne; in the Peloponnese, Alpheius, who, they said, fell in love with Artemis. To elude him Artemis took refuge in Elis and when she reached Letrini made herself unrecognisable by daubing herself with mud. It was also related that Alpheius was a hunter who fell in love with the nymph Arethusa and pursued her to the isle of Ortygia, where she changed into a spring. Alpheius, in his turn, was changed into a river, but he still obstinately pursued Arethusa. He crossed the sea without mingling with its waters and in Ortygia rejoined her whom he loved. When bulls were sacrificed in Olympia, past which the Alpheius flowed, it appeared that the waters of the fountain of Arethusa were also tinted with blood. The Eurotas in Laconia had, it was said, been a king of that country, and son of Taygete. Among his daughters was Sparta, who was married to Lacedaemon. He was responsible for draining the marshes which covered Laconia, and his name was given to the canal he dug to carry away the waters. Others said he threw himself into the river which bears his name in despair at having lost a battle.

In Phrygia the two principal river-gods were the Scamander (or Xanthus) and the Maeander. It was Hercules, seized by thirst, who had scooped out the earth and caused the Scamander to gush forth. Scamander took part in the Trojan war and Homer describes his battle with Achilles. He caught up the hero in his nets and it required the intervention of Hephaestus to appease the river-god. As for the Maeander, it owed its name to Maeander, King of Pessinonte, who in the course of a war made a vow that if he were victorious he would immolate the first person who came to congratulate him. The first person to do so was his son. Maeander fulfilled his vow, but threw himself in despair into the river which took his name.

Water Nymphs. Just as every river had its own divine personality, so every stream, brook, spring and pool harboured in its waters a divinity who was known as a nymph.

Water nymphs were classified according to their place of abode. Potamids were nymphs of rivers and streams; Naiads were nymphs of brooks; Crenae or Pegae were nymphs of springs; Limnads were nymphs of stagnant waters.

Although in the divine hierarchy they occupied an inferior rank, they were occasionally admitted to Olympus, and mortals honoured them with a religious cult.

Their functions were many. They had the gift of prophecy and could deliver oracles. They were benevolent deities and cured the sick; they watched over flowers, fields and flocks.

Sometimes they lived in the depths of the waters, sometimes in grottoes near the springs over which they presided. There they would busy themselves weaving and spinning. Sometimes they would mingle with the retinue of certain divinities.

In spite of their divine character they were not immortal. According to Plutarch the average life span of a nymph did not exceed nine thousand six hundred and twenty years. But it was their privilege always to remain young and beautiful, for their nourishment was ambrosia.

Although they were generally benevolent, they could become dangerous to those mortals whom they distinguished with their favours. Like the Rusalki of the Slavs, they sometimes dragged such mortals down into the depths of the waters. This, as we have seen, was the fate of Hermaphroditus, victim of the nymph Salmacis. A similar fate overtook young Hylas, the handsome companion of Hercules. When the ship of the Argonauts reached the coasts of the Troad, Hylas, who was a member of the expedition, was sent to shore by his companions in search of water. As it happened he discovered a fountain, but the nymphs of the place were so charmed by his beauty that they carried him to the depths of their watery abode, and in spite of the cries of Hercules which made the shores reverberate with the name Hylas, the young man was never seen again.

Among the nymphs whose name is known to legend may be mentioned Aganippe, nymph of the spring of that name which flowed at the approaches of Mount Helicon and whose waters inspired those who drank of them; Cassotis and Castalia, nymphs of prophetic springs on Parnassus; Hago, who presided over a fountain on Mount Lycaeus. During periods of drought the priest of Lycaean Zeus would touch the surface of the fountain with an oak branch. At once a mist would arise which would thicken into a cloud and soon pour forth the wished-for rain. There were also Pirene whose tears at the death of her son formed a fountain which could be seen near Corinth; Cyane, a Sicilian nymph who accompanied Persephone when she was carried off by Hades: heartbroken, she turned herself into a fountain. According to another tradition this fountain sprang from the hole Hades made when he plunged into the earth. Every year the people of Syracuse would come there and throw in a bull. Argyra, nymph of a fountain in Arcadia, loved the shepherd Selemnos. When she deserted him Selemnos was so broken-hearted that Aphrodite took pity on him and changed him into a river, granting him oblivion to cure the sickness of his heart. Thus whoever bathed in the river Selemnos found oblivion from the sorrows of love.

Calypso was the daughter of Atlas and Tethys and reigned, according to ancient tradition, over the isle of Ortygia in the Ionian Sea. When Odysseus was thrown by a tempest on her shores she welcomed him hospitably and kept him with her for seven years. To retain him forever she offered him immortality, but Zeus ordered her to release him. As her name – derived from a root which means 'to hide' – indicates, Calypso personified the depths of the waters.

DIVINITIES OF THE EARTH

GAEA, RHEA AND CYBELE

A personification of the earth, Gaea was, as we have already seen, the primitive goddess of the Greeks. Though her cult persisted throughout the ages her individuality became submerged in that of other similar divinities. The Pelasgian Gaea was early supplanted by Rhea whose origin was probably Cretan and who was herself only the earth deified. Her very name seems to derive from an archaic word meaning earth.

The legend of Rhea was formed by more or less repeating that of Gaea. The couple Rhea-Cronus correspond exactly to the couple Gaea-Uranus. Both goddesses have the same maternal anxieties and both husbands come to the same unhappy end. In the same way that the primitive Greeks made Gaea the Great Mother and and author of all beings, so the supremacy of Rhea was affirmed by the fact that she was made mother of the great ruling gods of Olympus.

In spite of her foreign origin Rhea soon took on a physiognomy which was plainly Greek. Several regions of Greece claimed the honour of having been the theatre of the divine episodes of her legend. For instance, it was near Chaeronea, on the cliff of Petrachus, that Rhea presented the stone to Cronus; the same scene was also localised at Methydium in Arcadia. Thebans pointed out the place where Rhea brought Zeus into the world, while the Arcadians said he was born on Mount Lycaeus. The god had grown up either in Olympia of Elis, or on Mount Ithome in Messenia. Finally Rhea was supposed to reside on Mount Thaumasium in Arcadia.

The Hellenic character of Rhea was, however, altered by the influence of the great Phrygian goddess Cybele whose cult was early introduced into Greece; but in the end the two goddesses were merged.

Etymologically Cybele was the goddess of caverns. She personified the earth in its primitive and savage state and was worshipped on the tops of mountains: on Ida in Phrygia, on Berecyntus, Sipyle, Dindymus. She exercised dominion over wild beasts who habitually formed part of her retinue.

Greek representations of Cybele retained an Asiatic character. The goddess with her turreted crown – the normal attribute of Asian mother-goddesses – is seated on a throne flanked by two lions, or else is placed in a chariot drawn by the same animals. Sometimes she holds a whip decorated with knuckle-bones. This attribute, emblem of power, was the instrument with which the *Galli*, priests of Cybele, flagellated themselves.

The Galli were an odd fraternity who celebrated the cult of their goddess with convulsive dances to the sound of flutes, drums and cymbals, while clashing their shields with their swords. In their orgiastic fury they would sometimes voluntarily mutilate themselves. They were known in Greece under the name of the Corybantes and were the issue, it was said, of a certain Corybas, son of Cybele. Later they were identified with the Cretan Curetes.

With the great Phrygian goddess a god of lesser rank was associated: Attis, whose role in respect to Cybele was analogous to that of Tammuz to the Babylonian Ishtar, or Adonis to the Phoenician Astarte. Like them he was a vegetation god; the Phrygians honoured him under the name *Papas,* the father.

As the cult of Cybele spread through Greece the figure of Attis became modified. He was presented as a young and handsome shepherd from Celaenae with whom Cybele fell in love. She chose him as her priest and imposed upon him a vow of chastity. When Attis broke his vow and espoused the daughter of the river Sangarius, Cybele struck him with frenzied delirium in the course of which he mutilated himself. When he recovered from his madness he was on the point of killing himself when Cybele changed him into a fir-tree. According to another tradition – obviously inspired by the myth of Adonis – Attis perished a victim of the jealousy of Zeus who sent a wild boar against him. The tomb of Attis was at Pessinus, and each year at the beginning of spring his festival was celebrated for five days. The first was a day of mourning when in the midst of lamentation a sacred fir wound with woollen bands was carried through the streets. On the second day the Galli worked themselves into a fever to the sound of savage music. The third day was marked by bloody mutilations. On the fourth day joyful dancing commemorated the resurrection of Attis. Finally the fifth day was devoted to rest.

Cybele became united with the King of Phrygia, Gordius, who had devised the famous Gordian knot. By him she had a son, Midas, who succeeded to his father's throne. He was a wise and pious king who established the cult of the Great Zeus of Ida and instituted the mysteries of Cybele. His kindness to Silenus who, on the banks of the Sangarius one day was drunk and had been tied up by peasants, earned Midas the gratitude of Dionysus. The god asked him to make a wish and Midas asked that everything he touched should be turned into gold. He soon regretted this indiscretion, for even the food he ate immediately turned into gold. Dionysus took pity on him and sent him to purify himself in the river Pactolus, which thenceforth flowed with gold dust.

Midas was less fortunate with Apollo. Asked to arbitrate between Apollo and Marsyas as to which played the lyre or the flute better, Midas voted against Apollo who, as a reward, gave him a pair of ass's ears. Midas was able to hide these ears under his Phrygian cap and his disgrace was known only to his barber. The secret weighed heavily on the poor barber who dug a hole in the ground and confided it to the earth. Now reeds grew in this spot and whenever the wind stirred among them they could be heard to repeat: 'King Midas has ass's ears.' In despair Midas killed himself by drinking, they say, the blood of a bull.

DEMETER

Character and Functions. Gaea and her substitutes, Rhea and Cybele, personified the earth as such, while Demeter represented the fertile and cultivated soil. Of the two elements which compose her name – an alteration or a more ancient form of a word meaning 'earth mother' – the maternal part finally assumed the greater importance among the Greeks.

Without doubt the primitive character of Demeter was preserved in certain regions of Greece, notably in Arcadia where the goddess was represented with a horse's head, surrounded by serpents and ferocious beasts, bearing in one hand a dolphin and in the other a dove. But elsewhere, and particularly in Attica, Demeter appeared above all as a goddess of the fruits and riches of the fields. She was especially the corn-goddess. She presided over the harvest and all the agricultural labours which attend it.

Goddess of the earth, Demeter's sphere of influence also reached the underworld; though her character of underworld divinity soon devolved on a special goddess – Persephone – who was made the daughter of Demeter.

Demeter always remained in contact with mortals whom she heaped with the benefits of civilisation. Thus she was called *Thesmophoros* 'who gives laws', though this title may have been given to her in her capacity of goddess of marriage.

Cult and Representations. Demeter was worshipped in Attica, Arcadia and Argolis, at Delos, in Crete, in Asia Minor and in

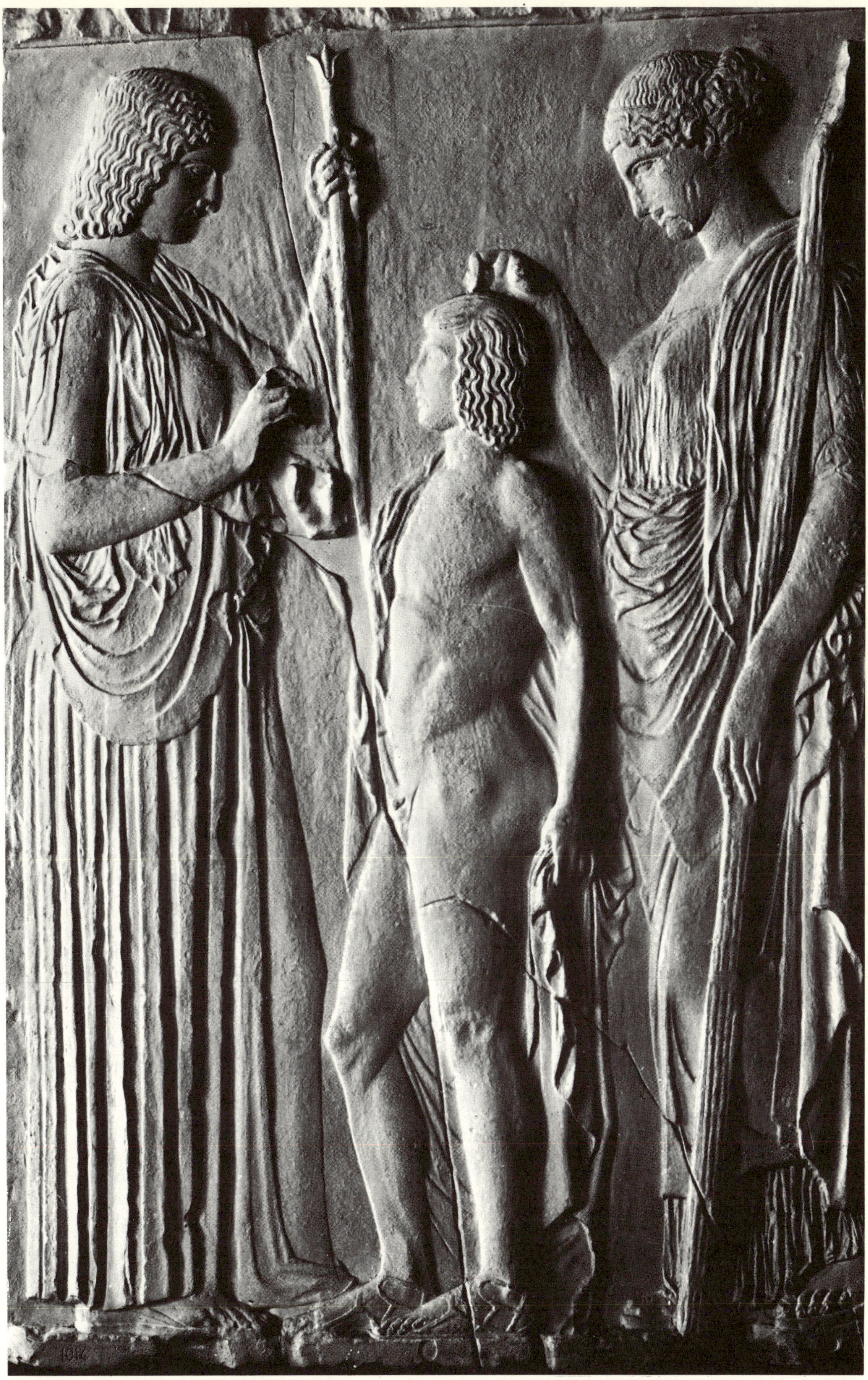

Eleusinian divinities. Tripotolemus between Demeter and Kore. Bas-relief of the fifth century B.C. National Museum, Athens.

Sicily. Her cult remained mysterious and was accompanied by orgies. Her temples, called *Megara*, were often found in forests.

It is above all Demeter's maternal aspect that art has accentuated in the various portrayals of the goddess. She appears sometimes seated, sometimes walking, dressed in a long robe and often wearing a veil which covers the back of her head. Sometimes she is crowned with ears of corn or a ribbon, and holds in her hand either a sceptre, ears of corn, or a torch.

Demeter's Suitors. Demeter was a daughter of Cronus and Rhea and thus belonged to the group of the great Olympians. She was of a severe beauty, a beauty scarcely relieved by her hair, which was as fair as ripened grain.

Poseidon coveted her, but Demeter refused herself to him. To escape him she fled to Arcadia where, assuming the shape of a mare, she mingled with the herds of King Oncus. Poseidon, however, succeeded in finding her, changed himself into a stallion and made her the mother of the horse Arion who was endowed with the gift of speech and had the right feet of a man. By Poseidon Demeter also had a daughter whose name has remained concealed and who was known only as the mistress – Despoena. She was particularly honoured in Thessaly.

Demeter was infuriated at the outrage to which Poseidon had submitted her and left Olympus. She took on the aspect of a Fury – thus in Arcadia she was entitled Erinnys – and hid her shame in a cavern. In order to bring her back to Olympus Zeus himself had to intervene. She resumed her place among the Immortals after purifying herself in the waters of the Ladon.

Demeter was also coveted by Zeus whom she resisted in a similar fashion. Zeus, however, deceived her by turning himself into a bull and made her mother of Kore.

But the heart of Demeter was not always untouched by sentiment. It was said that she loved Iasion, 'lay with him in a thrice-ploughed field' and had by him a son, Plutus. According to some Zeus was jealous of Iasion and struck him with a thunderbolt; according to others, he lived for a long time with Demeter and introduced her cult into Sicily.

Demeter and Kore. Demeter, however, was chiefly celebrated for her maternal tribulations. She loved her daughter Kore tenderly. One day Kore was gathering flowers in the fields of Nysa with her companions when she suddenly noticed a narcissus of striking beauty. She ran to pick it, but as she bent down to do so the earth gaped open and Hades appeared. He seized her and dragged her with him down into the depths of the earth. According to another tradition, the abduction of Kore took place on the heights near the town of Enna in Sicily. And in the neighbourhood of Syracuse they showed the place where Hades plunged back into the earth, hollowing out a vast cavity in the process, since filled by waters from the spring of Cyane. Colonus in Attica, Hermione in Argolis, Pheneus in Arcadia and even Crete, likewise claimed for their territory the honour of this divine abduction.

Demeter meanwhile had heard her child's despairing cry for help. 'Then,' says the poet of the Homeric hymn, 'bitter sorrow seized her heart...Over her shoulders she threw a sombre veil and flew like a bird over land and sea, seeking here, seeking there...For nine days the venerable goddess ranged the world, bearing flaming torches in her hands. At last on Hecate's advice, she went to consult the divine Helios who revealed to her the name of her daughter's ravisher. 'No other god is guilty,' he said to her, 'but Zeus himself, who awarded thy daughter to his brother Hades so that he might call her his flowering bride.' This revelation overwhelmed Demeter. In rage and despair she withdrew from Olympus and in the guise of an old woman sought refuge among the cities of men. For long she wandered aimlessly. One day she arrived in Eleusis and sat down to rest near the palace of the wise Celeus, who reigned in that country. The king's daughters saw her and questioned her kindly. Demeter told them that she had been carried off by Cretan pirates who had brought her to these parts where she was a stranger. She was, she added, in search of refuge and would be glad to work as a servant or nurse.

Now it happened that Metaneira, the wife of Celeus, had just been delivered of a son, Demophoön. Metaneira, therefore, welcomed the goddess under her roof; but when Demeter crossed the threshold her head brushed the rafters and from her emanated a divine radiance. Metaneira was filled with respect and offered her her own seat. But Demeter remained standing and silent, her eyes fixed on the ground, refusing food and drink; for longing for her flower-girdled daughter consumed her. Finally young Iambe who, though she was the daughter of Pan and Echo, served as a slave in Celeus' palace – and to whom was attributed the invention of iambic verse – succeeded in cheering up Demeter with her buffoonery. She persuaded Demeter to drink a little *kykeon,* a beverage made of water, flour and mint.

Later legend substituted Baubo for Iambe. Baubo was upset when Demeter refused the drink she offered her and made an obscene gesture at which the goddess, in spite of herself, laughed.

Demeter was put in charge of bringing up the infant Demophoön. She gave him nothing to eat, but instead breathed softly on him, anointed him with ambrosia and at night hid him in the fire, like a burning coal, in order to destroy all that was mortal in him. Thus, to the amazement of his parents, the child grew like a god. Intrigued by this prodigy Metaneira spied on the nurse and caught her just as she was placing the little boy in the middle of the flames. Metaneira screamed with terror. Incensed, the goddess withdrew Demophoön from the fire and put him on the ground. 'Had it not been for your imprudence,' she said to his mother, 'I should have put this child forever beyond the reach of old age and death; but now it is no longer possible for me to shelter him from death.' Then she appeared before the wife of Celeus in her divine form. She revealed her name and ordered that a temple be erected for her in Eleusis where the initiated should celebrate her mysteries. Then she went forth from the palace.

Before departing, however, she wished to show her gratitude to her hosts; she gave Triptolemus, Celeus' oldest son, the first grain of corn, and taught him the art of harnessing oxen to the plough and how to sow the soil with grain from which would spring fair harvests. She gave him as well a winged chariot harnessed with dragons, and bade him travel the world spreading the benefits of agriculture among all men. Thus Triptolemus ranged all Greece, taught Arcas, King of Arcadia, how to make bread, and in Arcadia founded many towns. He also visited Thrace, Sicily and Scythia where King Lyncus tried to murder him while he was asleep and was changed by Demeter into a lynx. He visited Mysia where the King of the Getae, Carnabon, tried in vain to harm him, and finally returned to Eleusis. There Celeus plotted to have him slain, but was prevented by Demeter. Celeus was then forced to resign the throne to Triptolemus.

It should be pointed out that originally no bond of relationship united Celeus and Triptolemus who in the Homeric hymn is merely described as one of the kings who were guardians of justice. Very much later Triptolemus was identified with Demophoön and attributed with the marvellous adventure in infancy of which Demophoön was originally the hero.

Demeter's stay at Eleusis was the chief episode in the course of her wanderings on earth, but she also stayed with Pelasgus in Argos. She visited Phytalus to whom she gave the olive tree. She was received in Attica by Misme whose son Ascalabos made Demeter the butt of his jokes and was punished by being turned into a lizard.

Still inconsolable at the loss of her daughter, Demeter retired to her temple at Eleusis. There 'she prepared for mankind a cruel terrible year: the earth refused to give forth any crop. Then would the entire human race have perished of cruel, biting hunger if Zeus had not been concerned.' He hastened to send his messenger Iris to Demeter, but without success. Then all the gods came one by one to supplicate the implacable goddess. She stated flatly that she would not permit the earth to bear fruit unless she saw her daughter again. There was no solution except to give in. Zeus commanded Hermes to descend into the kingdom of Hades and obtain Hades' promise to return young Kore – who since her arrival in the underworld had taken the name Persephone – to her mother. Hades complied with the will of Zeus, but before sending his wife up to earth tempted her to eat a few pomegranate seeds. Now this fruit was a symbol of marriage and the effect of eating it was to render the union of man and wife indissoluble.

When Kore returned to the world of light her mother hastened to her and embraced her with transports of joy. 'My daughter,' she cried, 'surely thou hast eaten nothing during your imprisonment in the dark regions of Hades! For if thou hast not eaten thou shalt

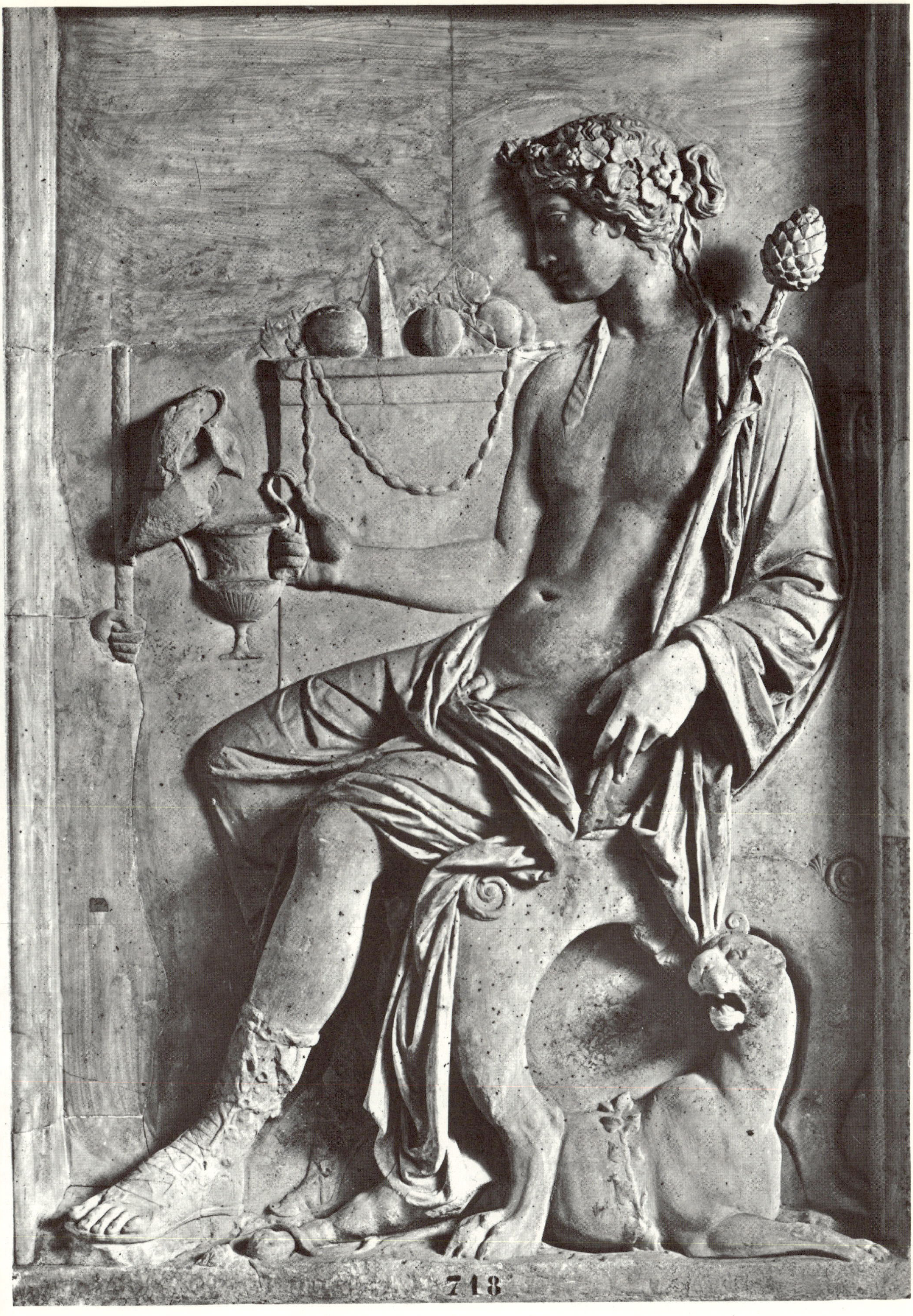

Dionysus, holding in one hand the thyrsus and in the other a cantharus. The god is portrayed as an ephebe. Bas-relief from Herculaneum. National Museum, Naples.

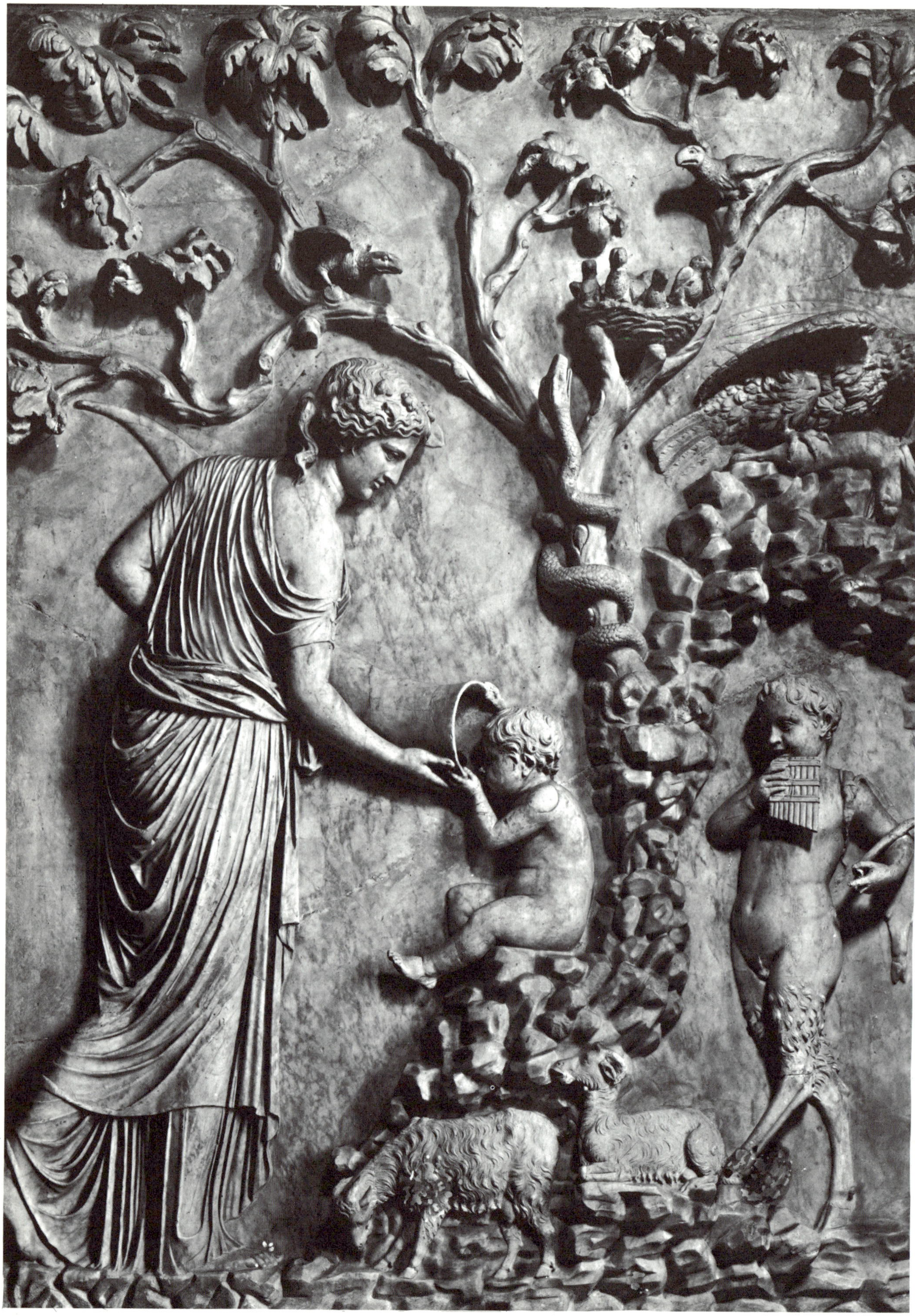

The Nymph Leucothea (Ino) gives the infant Dionysus a drink from the Horn of Plenty. Antique bas-relief. Lateran Museum, Rome.

live with me on Olympus. But if thou hast, then must thou return to the depths of the earth!' Kore admitted that she had tasted of the fatal pomegranate. It seemed that Demeter was again to lose her daughter.

As a compromise Zeus decided that Persephone should live with her husband for one-third of the year and pass the other two-thirds with her mother. The august Rhea herself brought this proposal to Demeter who agreed to it. She set aside her anger and bade the soil again be fertile. The vast earth was soon covered with leaves and flowers. Before she returned to Olympus, Demeter taught the kings of the earth her divine science and initiated them into her sacred mysteries.

And thus they explained why each year when the cold season arrived the earth took on an aspect of sadness and mourning: no more verdure, nor flowers in the fields, nor leaves on the trees. Hidden in the bowels of the ground the seeds slept their winter sleep. It was the moment when Persephone went to join her husband among the deep shadows. But when sweet-scented spring came the earth put on its mantle of a thousand flowers to greet the return of Kore, who rose in radiance, 'a wondrous sight for gods and men'.

The Eleusinian Mysteries. This double event – the disappearance and return of Kore – was the occasion of great festivals in Greece. In the *Thesmophoria* which were celebrated in Attica in the month of October, the departure of Kore for the sombre dwelling was commemorated. According to Herodotus the origin of these festivals went back to the daughters of Danaus who imported them from Egypt. They were exclusively reserved for married women and lasted three days.

The return of Kore was celebrated in the *Lesser Eleusinia*, which took place in the month of February.

As for the *Greater Eleusinia*, which took place every five years in September, it seems that they had no direct connection with the story of Kore. It was a solemn festival – the greatest festival of Greece – in honour of Demeter, and its principal object was the celebration of the mysteries of the goddess. The scene of the Greater Eleusinia was Athens and Eleusis.

On the first day the *ephebi* (youths) of Athens would go to Eleusis to fetch the sacred objects (*hiera*) kept in the temple of Demeter, and bring them back with great pomp to Athens where they were placed in the Eleusinion, at the foot of the Acropolis. The following day the faithful (*mystae*) who were judged to be worthy of participating in the mysteries would assemble in Athens at the call of the hierophant. Afterwards they would go to purify themselves in the sea, taking with them pigs which were bathed and then sacrificed. Finally the solemn procession towards Eleusis took place and the *hiera* were returned with the same ceremonial as before. At the head of the procession was carried the statue of Iacchus, a mystic name for Dionysus who was early associated with the cult of Demeter.

In Eleusis the actual mysteries themselves were then celebrated. Only the initiated could participate and they were forbidden to divulge what occurred. Initiation comprised two stages; the second, the *epoptae*, could only be undertaken after a year's probation.

As far as one can conjecture, the *mystae*, after drinking the *kykeon* and eating the sacred cakes, entered the *Telesterion*, where they attended a liturgical drama concerning the abduction of Kore. The *epoptae* – or those belonging to the highest grade – attended another liturgical drama the subject of which was the union of Demeter and Zeus, and of which the priestess of Demeter and the hierophant were the protagonists.

It is not easy to understand the exact meaning of these mysteries. They were, however, probably more than a simple commemoration of the legend of Demeter and must also have had to do with the problem of future life, the revelation of which the initiated awaited from the goddess.

DIONYSUS

Character and Functions. Dionysus is etymologically the 'Zeus of Nysa' and seems, by several similarities of legend and function, to be the Greek form of the Vedic god *Soma*. The cradle of his cult was Thrace. It was brought to Boeotia by Thracian tribes, who established themselves in that country, and was afterwards introduced to the island of Naxos by Boeotian colonists. The cult of Dionysus spread throughout the islands, whence it returned to continental Greece, first to Attica, then later to the Peloponnese.

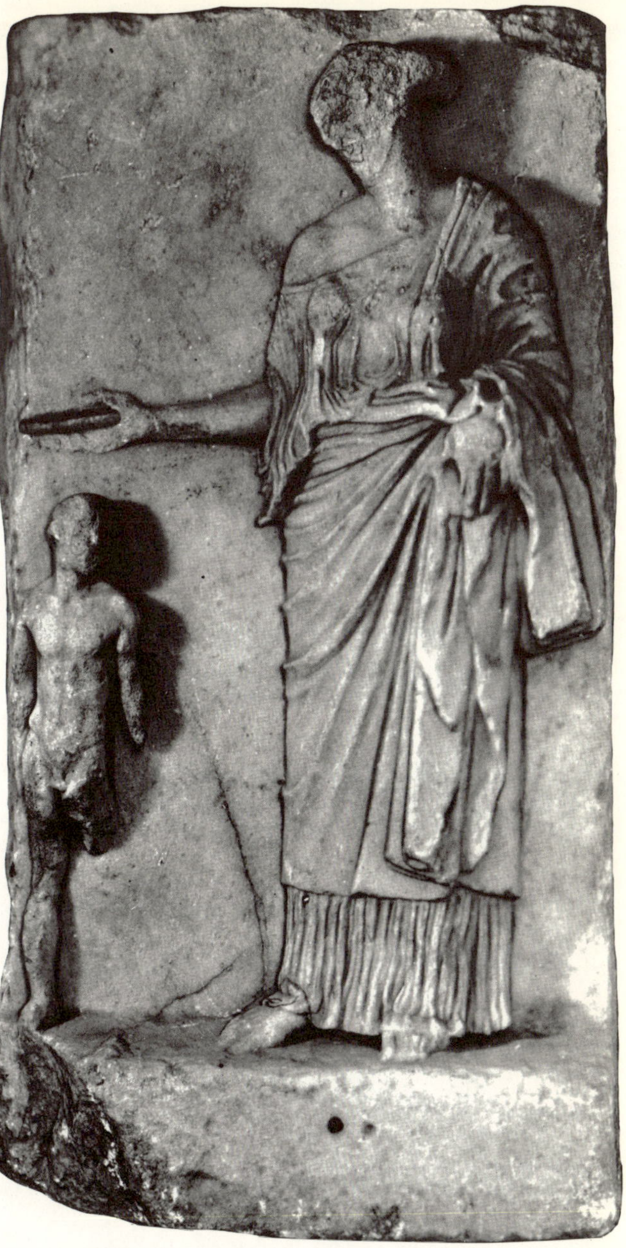

Votive relief from Eleusis showing Persephone pouring water on an initiate. It was from Eleusis, according to the priests of Demeter, that the goddess' daughter Persephone, or Kore, was abducted by Hades and carried off to the Underworld and it was here that Demeter had her great sanctuary where mother and daughter were worshipped conjointly and where their Mysteries were celebrated. Only the initiated were allowed to take part in these.

The figure of the primitive Dionysus is complicated by traits borrowed from other and foreign gods, notably the Cretan god Zagreus, the Phrygian god Sabazius, and the Lydian god Bassareus. Thus his sphere of influence widened as his character became enriched with fresh contributions. In origin Dionysus was simply the god of wine; afterwards he became god of vegetation and warm moisture; then he appeared as the god of pleasures and the god of civilisation; and finally, according to Orphic conceptions, as a kind of supreme god.

Cult and Representations. Dionysus was honoured throughout Greece; but the character of the festivals which were dedicated to him varied with regions and epochs.

One of the most ancient festivals was that of the *Agrionia*, first celebrated in Boeotia, especially at Orchomenus: the Bacchantes immolated a young boy. Human sacrifice was also practised at Chios and at Lesbos; it was later replaced by flagellation. In Attica, they celebrated rural *Dionysia*: in December the *Lenaea*, festival of the wine press, when the god was offered the new wine; at the

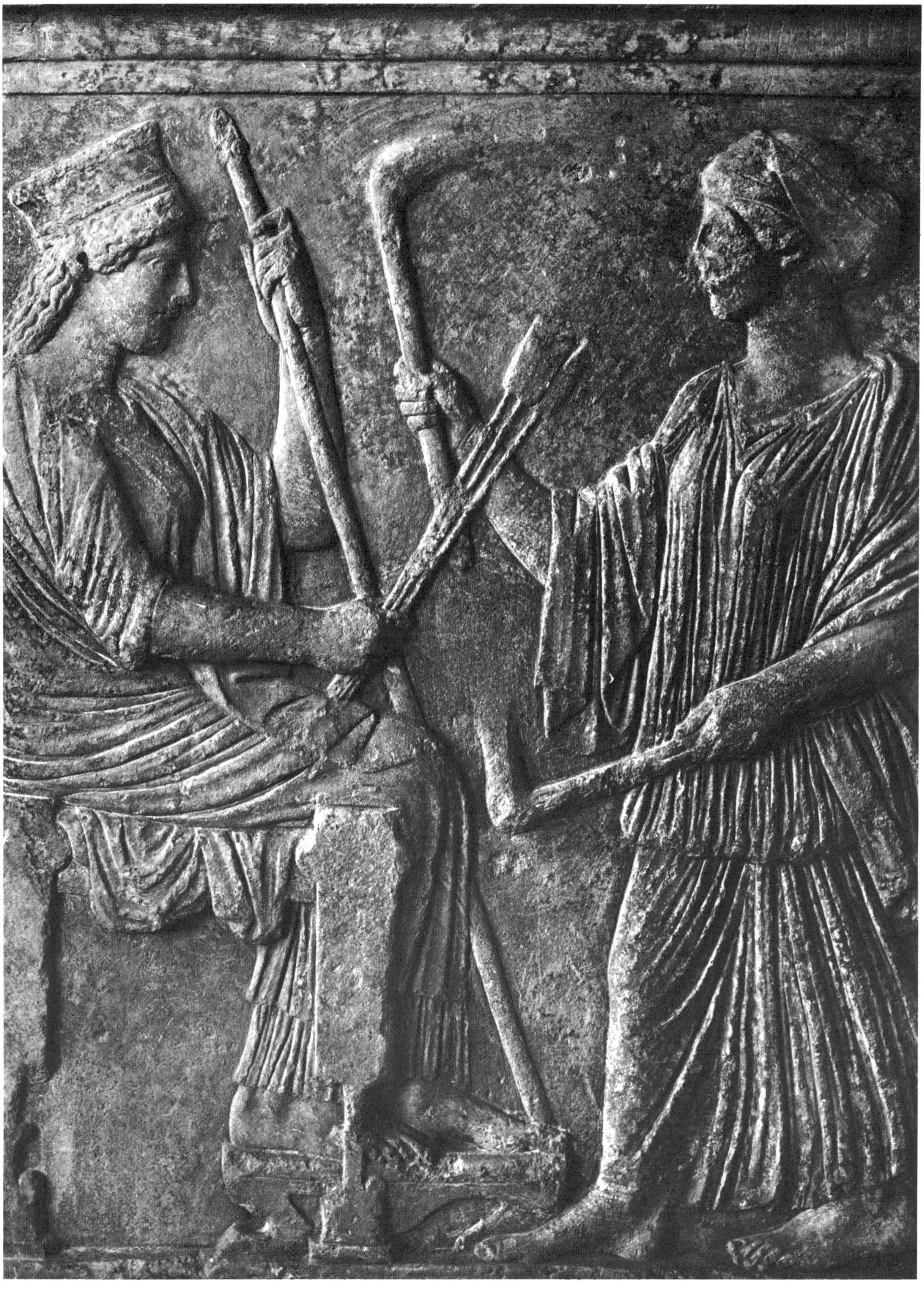

Demeter and Persephone. This votive relief from Eleusis shows Persephone's return to her mother in the springtime after her winter's sojourn in the Underworld. The corn goddess is seated on the left grasping her staff in one hand and with her attribute – three ears of corn – in the other while her daughter stands before her holding two flaming torches. It seems probable that Persephone was originally merely another aspect of Demeter. Fifth century B.C.

end of February the *Anthesteria,* floral festivals which lasted three days, during which wine of the last vintage was tasted. In the sanctuary of Lenoeon there was a procession followed by a sacrifice offered by the wife of the archon-king, and finally boiled seed was offered to Dionysus and Hermes. The most brilliant festivals were the *Greater Dionysia,* or urban Dionysia, at the beginning of March. It was during these festivals that dramatic representations were given. In addition to those dignified ceremonies all Greece celebrated festivals of orgiastic character as well, such as those which took place on the slopes of Mount Cithaeron.

The appearance of Dionysus altered at the same time as his legend. He was first depicted as a bearded man, of mature age, with brow generally crowned with ivy. Later he appears as a beardless youth of rather effeminate aspect. Sometimes the delicate nudity of his adolescent body is half-covered by the *nebris,* a skin of a panther or fawn; sometimes he wears a long robe such as women wore. His head with its long curly hair is crowned with vine leaves and bunches of grapes. In one hand he holds the *thyrsus,* and in the other, grapes or a wine cup.

The Birth and Childhood of Dionysus. When the earth has been made fertile by life-giving rains it must, in order that its products may reach maturity, endure the bite of the sun which burns and dries it up. Only then do its fruits develop and the golden grapes appear on the knotty vine. This seems to be the meaning of the myth of Semele who was normally considered to be the mother of Dionysus.

Semele, daughter of Cadmus, King of Thebes, was seen by Zeus and yielded to him. Zeus would come to her father's palace to visit her. One day, at the suggestion of the treacherous Hera who had assumed the guise of her nurse, Semele begged Zeus to show himself to her in his Olympian majesty. She was unable to endure the dazzling brilliance of her divine lover and was consumed by the flames which emanated from Zeus' person. The child she carried in her womb would also have perished had not a thick shoot of ivy suddenly wound around the columns of the palace and made a green screen between the unborn babe and the celestial fire. Zeus gathered up the infant and, as it was not yet ready to be born, enclosed it in his own thigh. When the time was come he drew it forth again, with the aid of Ilithyia, and it is to this double birth that Dionysus owed the title *Dithyrambos.*

Zeus confided his son to Ino, sister of Semele, who lived at Orchomenus with her husband Athamas.

Such was the commonest version of the story. It was also related that Cadmus, learning of the guilty liaison of his daughter Semele, had her shut up in a chest and thrown into the sea. The chest was carried by the waves as far as the shores of Prasiae in the Peloponnese; when it was opened Semele was dead, but the child was still alive. He was cared for by Ino.

Hera's jealous vengeance was unappeased and she struck Ino and Athamas with madness. Zeus succeeded in saving his child for the second time by changing him into a kid whom he ordered Hermes to deliver into the hands of the nymphs of Nysa.

Where was Nysa? Was it a mountain in Thrace? One seeks its precise situation in vain; for every region where the cult of Dionysus was established boasted of having a Nysa.

Dionysus, then, passed his childhood on this fabled mountain, cared for by the nymphs whose zeal was later recompensed; for they were changed into a constellation under the name of the Hyades. The Muses also contributed to the education of Dionysus, as did the Satyrs, the Sileni and the Maenads. In Euboea, according to tradition, Dionysus was confided by Hermes to Macris, the

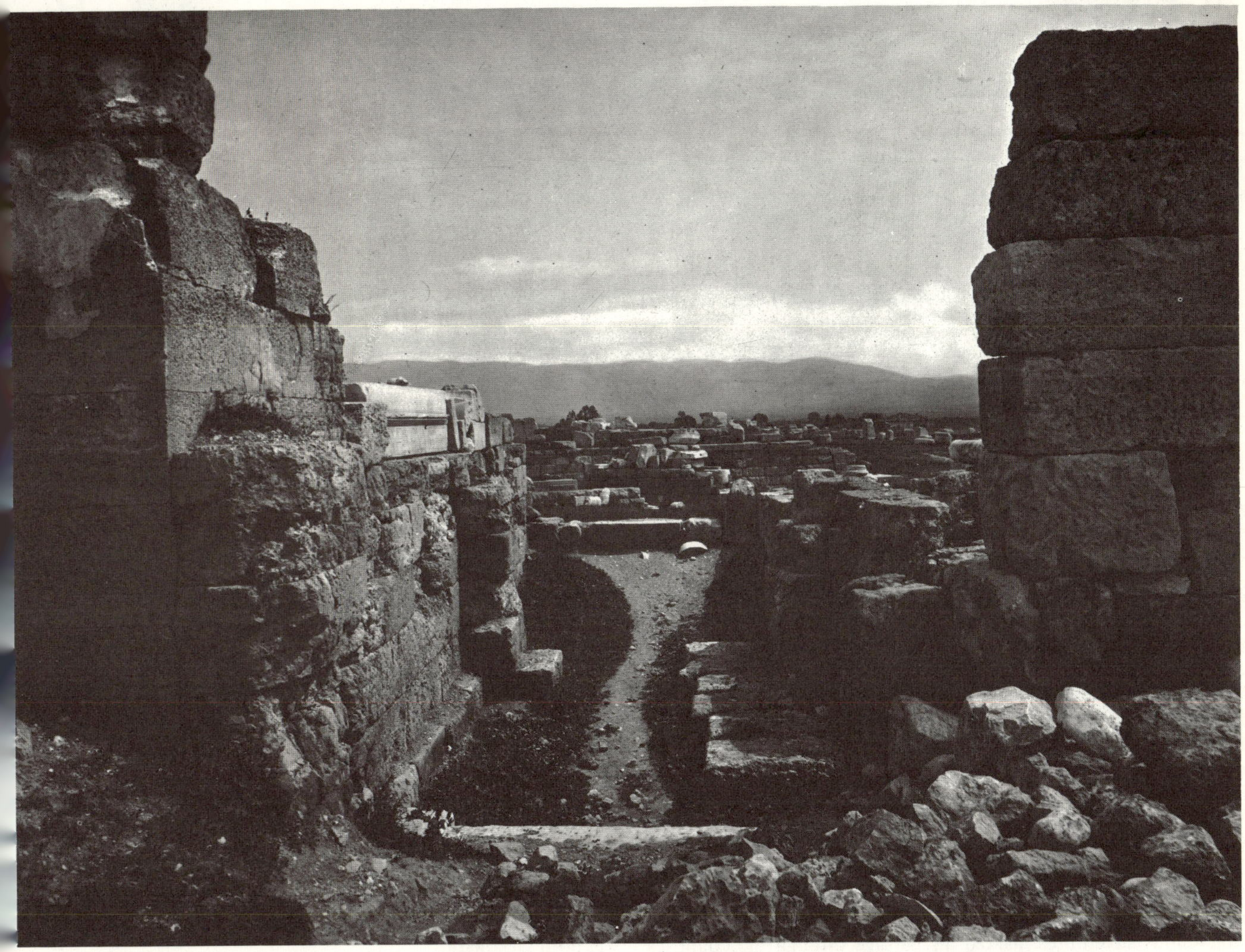

The wall surrounding the sacred precinct at Eleusis. Some fourteen miles west of Athens, Eleusis was the home of the most holy rites of the Greek religion until the end of the pagan period. Its sacred precinct was filled with altars and inscriptions while within it stood the great hypostyle hall called the Telesterion in which the mysteries of Demeter and Persephone were celebrated. The sacred buildings were destroyed by Alaric in A.D. 396.

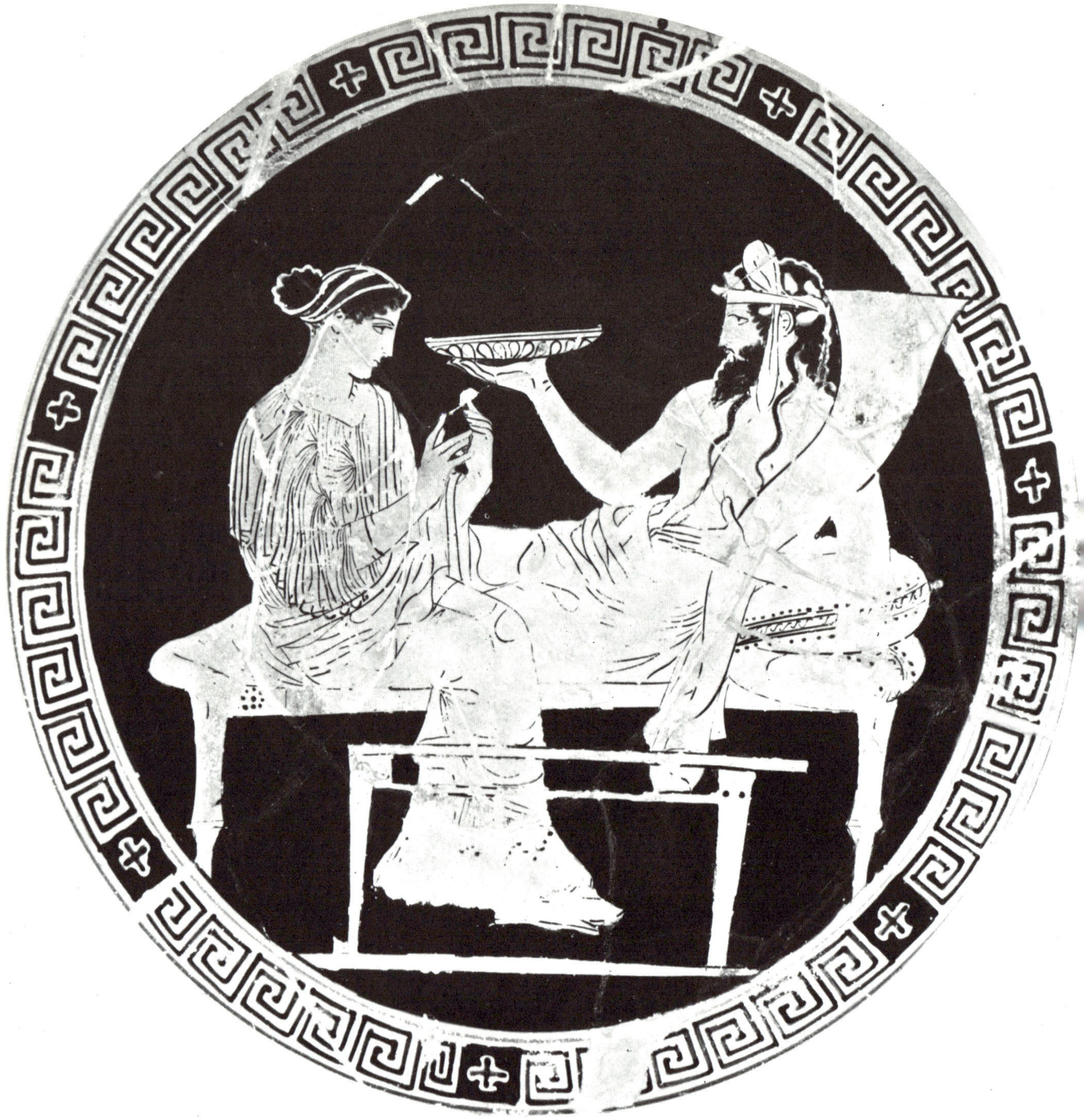

Persephone and Hades. Condemned by Zeus to spend a third of each year in the Underworld with her husband Hades after eating the fatal pomegranate seeds, the symbol of marriage, Persephone is shown here seated at the foot of her husband's couch while he reclines upon it clasping a cornucopia or horn of plenty. Feared as the god of the Underworld, Hades was more widely venerated as Pluto, the god of riches.

daughter of Aristaeus, who then nourished him with honey.

With his head crowned by ivy and laurel the young god wandered the mountains and forests with the nymphs, making the glades echo with his joyful shouts. In the meanwhile old Silenus taught his young mind the meaning of virtue and inspired him with the love of glory. When he had grown up Dionysus discovered the fruit of the vine and the art of making wine from it. Doubtless he drank of the wine without moderation at first, for they said Hera had stricken him with madness. But the disease was short-lived. To cure himself Dionysus went to Dodona to consult the oracle. On the way he came to a marsh which he crossed by mounting an ass. To reward the animal he bestowed on it the gift of speech. When he was cured Dionysus undertook long journeys across the world in order to spread the inestimable gift of wine among mortals. Marvellous adventures marked his passage through the countries he visited.

The Travels of Dionysus. Coming from the mountains of Thrace he crossed Boeotia and entered Attica. In Attica he was welcomed by the king, Icarius, to whom he presented a vine-stock. Icarius had the imprudence to give his shepherds wine to drink; as they grew intoxicated they thought they were being poisoned and slew him. The daughter of Icarius, Erigone, set out to look for her father and, thanks to her dog Maera, at last discovered his tomb. In despair she hanged herself from a nearby tree. In punishment for this death Dionysus struck the women of Attica with raving madness. Icarius was carried to the heavens with his daughter and her faithful dog. They were changed into constellations and became the Waggoner, Virgo and the Lesser Dog Star.

In Aetolia Dionysus was received by Oeneus, King of Calydon, and fell in love with Althaea, his host's wife. Oeneus pretended not to notice and the god rewarded his discretion by giving him a vine-stock. From the fleeting union of Dionysus and Althaea was born Deianeira.

In Laconia Dionysus was the guest of King Dion who had three daughters. Dionysus fell in love with the youngest, Carya. Her two older sisters threatened to expose the affair by warning their father. Dionysus struck them with madness, then changed them into rocks. As for Carya, it was her fate to be turned into a walnut tree.

After continental Greece Dionysus visited the islands of the Archipelago. It was in the course of this voyage that the god, walking one day by the seashore, was abducted by Tyrrhenian pirates and carried aboard their ship. They took him for the son of a king and expected a rich ransom. They tried to tie him up with heavy cords, but in vain. The knots loosened of their own accord and the bonds fell to the deck. The pilot, terrified, had a presentiment that their captive was divine and attempted to make his companions release him. The pirates refused. Then occurred a series of prodigies. Around the dark ship flowed wine, fragrant and delicious. A vine attached its branches to the sail, while around the mast ivy wound its dark green leaves. The god himself became a lion of fearful aspect. In horror the sailors leapt into the sea and were immediately changed into dolphins. Only the pilot was spared by Dionysus.

On the isle of Naxos Dionysus one day perceived a young woman lying asleep on the shore. It was the daughter of Minos, Ariadne, whom Theseus had brought with him from Crete and just abandoned. When she awoke Ariadne realised that Theseus had left her and gave way to uncontrollable tears. The arrival of Dionysus consoled her and shortly afterwards they were solemnly married. The gods came to the wedding and showered gifts on the couple. Dionysus and Ariadne had three sons: Oenopion, Euanthes and Staphylus. The Homeric tradition has a different version of the Ariadne episode. Ariadne was supposed to have been killed by Artemis and it was only after her death that Dionysus married her. In Naxos they showed the tomb of Ariadne and in her honour two festivals were celebrated: one mournful, bewailing her death; the other joyful, commemorating her marriage to Dionysus.

The travels and adventures of Dionysus were not limited to the Greek world. Accompanied by his retinue of Satyrs and Maenads he went to Phrygia, where Cybele initiated him into her mysteries. At Ephesus in Cappadocia he repulsed the Amazons. In Syria he fought against Damascus who destroyed the vines which the god had planted and was punished by being skinned alive. Then he went into the Lebanon to pay a visit to Aphrodite and Adonis whose daughter, Beroë, he loved. After having reigned for some time over Caucasian Iberia, Dionysus continued his journey towards the East, crossing the Tigris on a tiger sent by Zeus, joined the two banks of the Euphrates by a cable made of vine-shoots and ivy-tendrils, and reached India where he spread civilisation. We also find him in Egypt where he was received by King Proteus; and in Libya where he helped Ammon to reconquer his throne from which he had been deposed by Cronus and the Titans.

After these glorious expeditions Dionysus returned to Greece. He was no longer the rather rustic god recently come down from the mountains of Boeotia. His contact with Asia had made him soft and effeminate: he now appeared in the guise of a graceful adolescent, dressed in a long robe in the Lydian fashion. His cult became complicated by orgiastic rites borrowed from Phrygia. Thus he was received in Greece with distrust, sometimes even with hostility.

When he returned to Thrace, notably, the king of that country, Lycurgus, declared against him. Dionysus was obliged to flee and seek refuge with Thetis, in the depths of the sea. Meanwhile, Lycurgus imprisoned the Bacchantes who followed the god, and Dionysus struck the country with sterility, depriving Lycurgus of his reason. In his madness Lycurgus killed his own son, Dryas, whom he mistook for a vine-stock. The desolation of Thrace did not cease until the oracle ordered that Lycurgus be conducted to Mount Pangaeum where he was trampled to death under the hooves of wild horses.

Dionysus was no better received by Pentheus, King of Thebes, who threw the god into prison. Dionysus escaped without trouble and struck Agave, the mother of Pentheus, as well as the other women of Thebes, with madness. They were transformed into Maenads and rushed to Mount Cithaeron where they held Dionysian orgies. Pentheus had the imprudence to follow them and was torn to pieces by his own mother. This terrible drama forms the subject of Euripides' *Bacchae*.

A similar tragedy overtook the inhabitants of Argos who had also refused to recognise the divinity of Dionysus: the women, driven out of their minds, tore up and devoured their own children.

Among the chastisements which Dionysus inflicted, one of the most famous concerned the daughters of Minyas, King of Orchomenus. They were three sisters: Alcithoë, Leucippe and Arsippe.

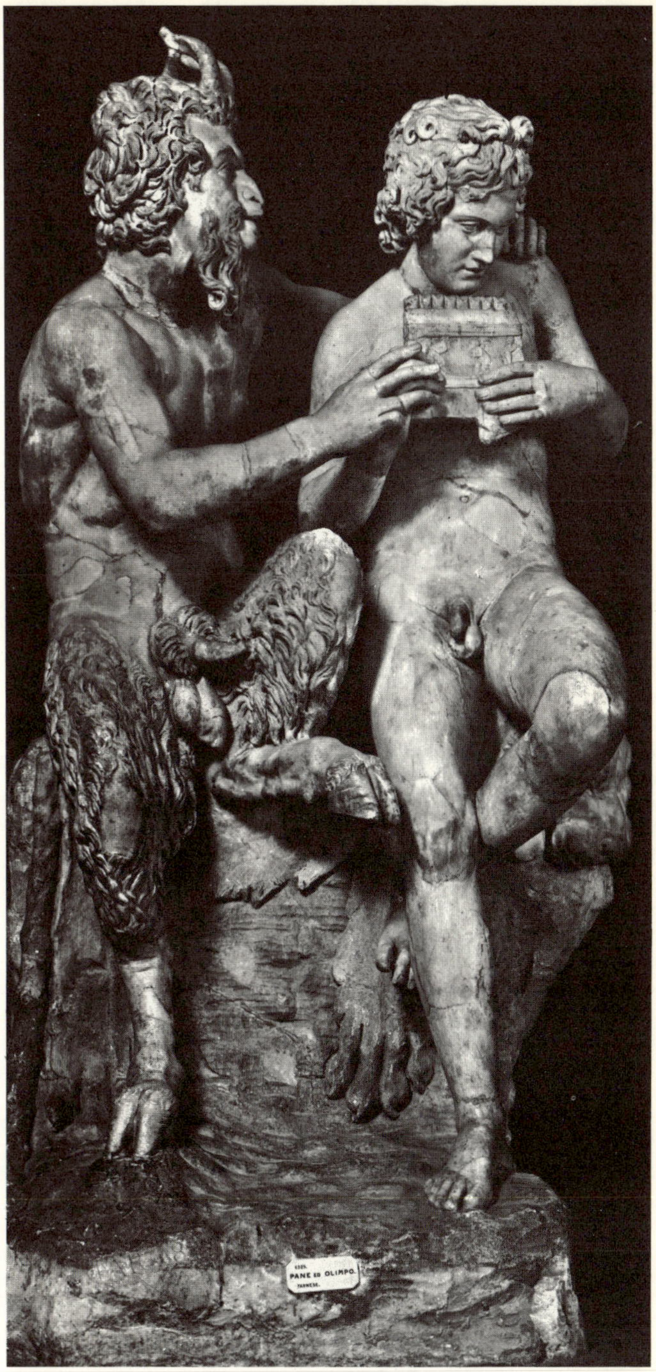

Pan Teaching Olympus to play the syrinx. National Museum, Naples.

Since they refused to take part in the festivals of Dionysus, he visited them in the guise of a young maiden and tried to persuade them by gentleness. Being unsuccessful, he turned himself successively into a bull, a lion and a panther. Terrified by these prodigies, the daughters of Minyas lost their reason and one of them, Leucippe, tore her son Hippasus to pieces with her own hands. Finally they underwent metamorphosis: the first became a mouse, the second a screech-owl, the third an owl.

Thenceforth no one any longer dreamed of denying the divinity of Dionysus or of rejecting his cult.

The god crowned his exploits by descending into the infernal regions in search of his mother, Semele. He renamed her Thyone and brought her with him to Olympus among the Immortals. At Troezen, in the temple of Artemis Soteira, they showed the exact place where Dionysus had returned from his subterranean expedition. According to the tradition of Argos the route to the underworld had been shown to the god by a citizen of Argos, one Polymnus, and Dionysus had come up again via the sea of Alcyon.

On Olympus Dionysus took part in the struggle against the Giants; the braying of the ass on which he rode terrified the Giants and Dionysus killed Eurytus or Rhatos with his *thyrsus*.

Foreign Divinities Assimilated by Dionysus. The exuberance of the legends of Dionysus is explained not only by his great popularity but also because the personality of Dionysus absorbed, as we have already said, that of several foreign gods, notably the Phrygian Sabazius, the Lydian Bassareus and the Cretan Zagreus.

Sabazius, who was venerated as the supreme god in the Thracian Hellespont, was a solar-divinity of Phrygian origin. Traditions concerning him were very diverse. Sometimes he was the son of Cronus, sometimes of Cybele whose companion he became. His wife was either the moon-goddess Bendis or Cotys (or Cottyto), an earth-goddess analogous to the Phrygian Cybele. Sabazius was represented with horns and his emblem was the serpent. The *Sabazia* were celebrated in his honour – nocturnal festivals of orgiastic character.

When Sabazius was later assimilated by Dionysus their legends became amalgamated. Some said that Sabazius had kept Dionysus enclosed in his thigh before confiding him to the nymph Hippa; others claimed on the contrary that Sabazius was the son of Dionysus. It was in consequence of such confusions that Dionysus was finally supposed to have come from the Thracian Hellespont.

Sometimes the Bacchantes were called *Bassarids* and Dionysus himself had the epithet *Bassareus,* in which case he was represented wearing a long robe in the Oriental fashion. The lexicographer Hesychius considered this to be a reference to the fox-skins which the Bacchantes wore; but it would rather seem to be an allusion to an Oriental divinity absorbed by Dionysus. Indeed, in Lydia a god similar to the Phrygian Sabazius was venerated. The place of his cult was Mount Tmolus where, according to Orphic-Thracian legend, Sabazius delivered the infant Dionysus to Hippa. Tmolus actually became one of the favourite haunts of Dionysus. What was the name of the Lydian god? It has been conjectured that his name was Bassareus. He was doubtless a conquering god and to him may be attributed the origin of Dionysus' distant conquests. Bassareus could also explain the visit of Dionysus to Aphrodite and Adonis, and perhaps also the legend of Ampelus, a youth of rare beauty whom Dionysus cherished with particular affection. One day when he was attempting to master a wild bull Ampelus was tossed and killed by the animal. Dionysus was heartbroken and obtained the gods' permission to change Ampelus into a vine.

The identification of Dionysus with the Cretan god, Zagreus, who was very probably in origin the equivalent of the Hellenic Zeus, introduced – under the influence of Orphic mysticism – a new element into the legend of the god, that of the Passion of Dionysus.

This is what they said of Dionysus-Zagreus:

He was the son of Zeus and Demeter – or of Kore. The other gods were jealous of him and resolved to slay him. He was torn into pieces by the Titans who threw the remains of his body into a cauldron. Pallas Athene, however, was able to rescue the god's heart. She took it at once to Zeus who struck the Titans with thunderbolts and, with the still beating heart, created Dionysus. As for Zagreus, whose remains had been buried at the foot of Parnassus, he became an underworld divinity who in Hades welcomed the souls of the dead and helped with their purification.

On these sufferings and resurrection the adepts of Orphism conferred a mystic sense, and the character of Dionysus underwent profound modification. He was no longer the rustic god of wine and jollity, formerly come down the mountains of Thrace; he was no longer even the god of orgiastic delirium, come from the Orient. Henceforth Dionysus – in Plutarch's words – 'the god who is destroyed, who disappears, who relinquishes life and then is born again', became the symbol of everlasting life.

Thus it is not surprising to see Dionysus associated with Demeter and Kore in the Eleusinian mysteries. For he, too, represented one of the great life-bringing forces of the world.

THE RETINUE OF DIONYSUS: RURAL DIVINITIES

From early times in Greece the vintage festivals were occasions for joyful processions in which priests and the faithful, men and women, of the cult of Dionysus took part. These devotees were called Bacchants and Bacchantes or Maenads. It was the habit to provide the god with a cortège or *thiasus* composed of secondary divinities more or less closely bound up with his cult: Satyrs, Sileni, Pans, Priapi, Centaurs, Nymphs.

Satyrs and Sileni. The Satyrs represented the elementary spirits of the forests and the mountains. They were a kind of wood-genii whose sudden appearance would terrify shepherds and travellers. There was something about them of both monkey and he-goat with their low forehead, their snub nose, their pointed ears, their hairy body ending in a goat's tail, their cloven hooves. Such at least was their primitive aspect; later traces of the beast which at first do-

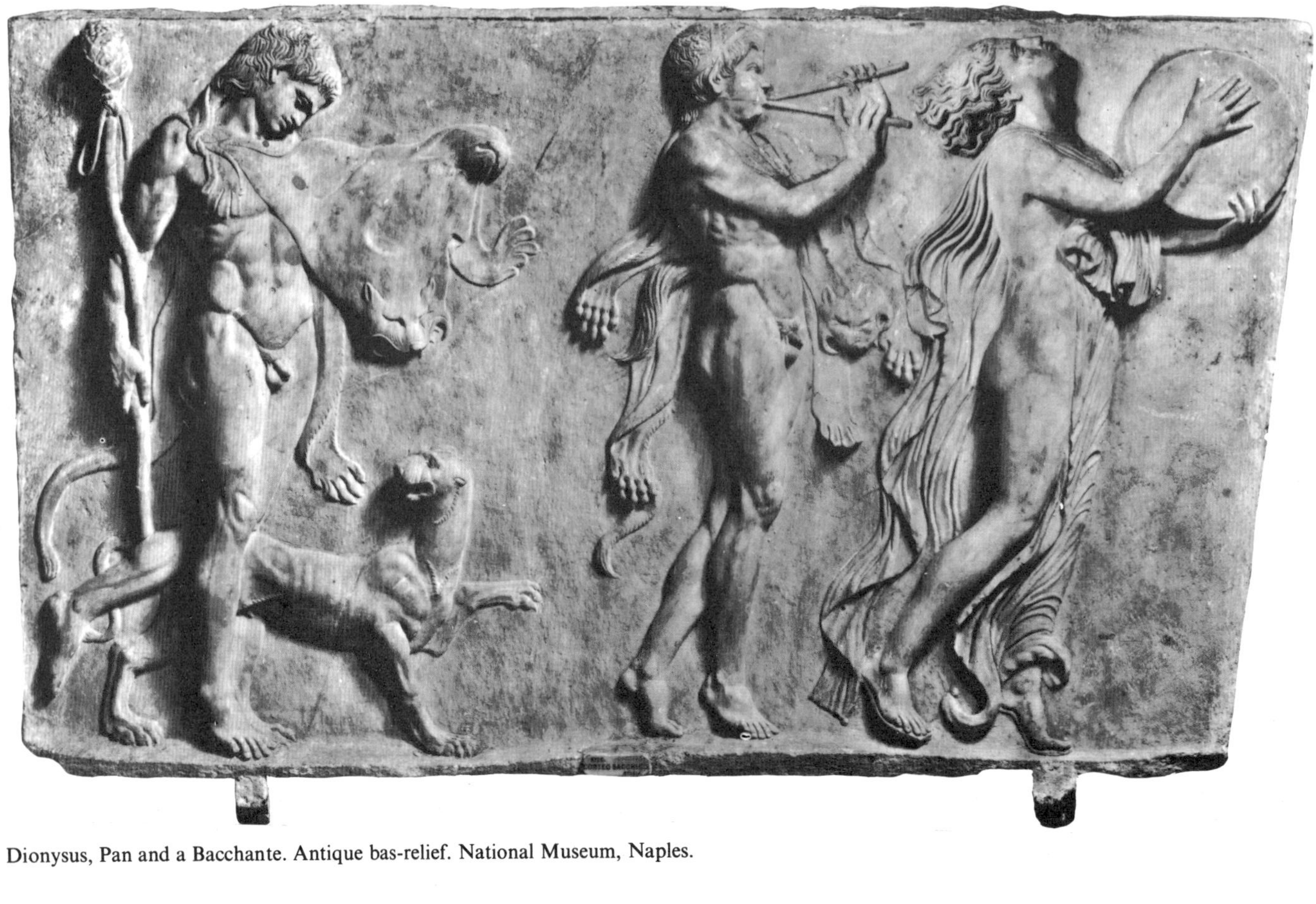

Dionysus, Pan and a Bacchante. Antique bas-relief. National Museum, Naples.

minated survived only in their pointed ears and the small horns on their brow, while their features took on an expression of youth and gentleness. Their character also altered. According to Hesiod the Satyrs were originally a lazy and useless race who loved only pleasure and good cheer. Sensual and lascivious, they delighted in chasing the nymphs through the forests. Later, although they preserved their malicious nature, they acquired more grace and specialised in the pleasures of music and the dance. They were thought to be brothers of the nymphs and the Curetes. Another tradition relates that they were originally men, sons of Hermes and Iphthima, but that Hera turned them into monkeys to punish them for neglecting to keep watch on Dionysus. They were, however, faithful companions of the god and played the principal role in his orgiastic festivals.

One of the most picturesque figures in the retinue of Dionysus was Silenus, a fat old man, bald, snub-nosed, always drunk, who followed the god sometimes supported by Satyrs, sometimes swaying precariously on an ass. Nevertheless this cheerful drunkard was full of wisdom. He had been the tutor of Dionysus and had helped to form his character. His knowledge was immense, he knew both the past and the future, and could reveal the destiny of anyone who succeeded in tying him up during the heavy slumber which followed his drinking-bouts. Plato felt no irreverence in comparing his master Socrates with Silenus. Silenus was, it appears, the son of Hermes and the Earth. Others say that he was born of the blood of Uranus after Cronus had mutilated him. Pindar says his wife was Nais.

In reality the name Silenus is a generic term which applies to a category of rural divinities, rather similar to the Satyrs and often confused with them. The Sileni were native not to Greece, but to Phrygia, and personified the genii of springs and rivers. Their name seems to mean 'water which bubbles as it flows' and their fluvial character is evident from certain peculiarities of their bodies: unlike the Satyrs who derive chiefly from the he-goat, the Sileni derive rather from the horse – a water symbol – whose tail, hooves, and even ears they possess. Marsyas, who is generally made a Satyr, was in reality a Silenus and, at the same time, a river-god of Phrygia. That was why the Phrygian Midas – whose legend is closely connected with that of the Sileni – voted for Marsyas in the famous music contest with Apollo.

Pan, Aristaeus, Priapus. Another divinity later incorporated in the retinue of Dionysus, and often confused with the Satyrs because of his physical resemblance to them, was the god Pan, whose cult was for long localised in Arcadia. Hence he was made the son of Hermes, the great Arcadian god. His mother was either the daughter of King Dryops, whose flocks Hermes had tended, or Penelope, whom he had approached in the form of a he-goat. Pan himself came into the world with the legs, horns and beard of a goat.

Various etymologies have been proposed for the name Pan. The Homeric hymn connects it with the adjective which means 'all' under the pretext that the sight of Pan on Olympus amused *all* the Immortals. The same etymology was invoked by the mythologists of the school of Alexandria who considered Pan to be the symbol of the Universe. Max Muller found a connection between Pan and the Sanskrit *pavana*, the wind, and believed that Pan was the personification of the light breeze. In our opinion, however, it seems more likely that the name comes from the root which means 'to eat' which gave the Latins the verb *pascere*, 'to graze or pasture'. Pan, indeed, was above all a shepherd-god, of woods and pastures, protector of shepherds and flocks. He lived on the slopes of Mount Maenalus or Mount Lycaeus, in grottoes where the Arcadian shepherds came to worship him. He made their goats and ewes prolific – whence his aspect of a phallic divinity – and caused wild beasts to be killed by hunters; when the hunt was unsuccessful they would whip his image by way of reprisal. Pan himself delighted in roving the forests, frisking with the nymphs whom he sometimes terrified with his appearance. One day he was chasing the nymph Syrinx and had nearly caught her when she cried aloud to her father, the river-god Ladon, to change her into a reed. Her prayer was granted. Pan consoled himself for his disappointment by cutting some reeds with which he made a flute of a new sort, giving it the name Syrinx, or Pan-pipes. He was more successful with the nymph Pitys who preferred him to Boreas. Boreas, the bitter North Wind, was enraged and flung himself on Pitys, throwing her against a rock where her limbs were crushed. In pity Gaea transformed her into a pine. It was told that Pan succeeded in seducing the moon-goddess Selene; he disguised himself in the fleece of a dazzling white ewe and drew her into the forest with him, or he himself assumed the shape of a white ram.

For long he was confined to the mountains of Arcadia where he amused himself by giving the lonely traveller sudden frights, called for this reason panics. He penetrated into Attica only at the time of the Persian wars. Shortly before the battle of Marathon he appeared to the ambassadors whom the Athenians had sent to Sparta and promised to put the Persians to flight if the Athenians consented to worship him in Athens. In gratitude they erected a sanctuary for him on the Acropolis and from there the cult of Pan spread throughout Greece.

We have said that Pan finally symbolised the universal god, the Great All. In this connection Plutarch recounts how in the reign of Tiberius a mariner sailing near the Echinades Islands heard a mysterious voice call out to him three times, saying: 'when you reach Palodes proclaim that the great god Pan is dead.' This was at the exact time that Christianity was born in Judea. The coincidence has always seemed strange; but Reinach has demonstrated that the sailor simply heard the ritual lamentations in honour of Adonis.

Every region in Greece had its own Pan. That of Thessaly was called Aristaeus. Without doubt this Aristaeus was a great primitive deity of this land, for his name means 'the very good', which was also the epithet of Zeus in Arcadia. Moreover Pindar says that 'Aristaeus was carried after his birth by Hermes to Gaea and the Horae who fed him on nectar and ambrosia, and transformed him into Zeus, the immortal god, and into Apollo, the pure, the guardian of flocks and the chase and pasturage.' According to legend Aristaeus was the son of Uranus and Gaea or of Apollo and Cyrene. He was brought up by the Centaur Chiron and instructed in the arts of medicine and soothsaying. He was considered as the protector of flocks and agriculture, particularly of the vine and olive. It was he who taught men bee-keeping.

His civilising influence was felt throughout Greece. In Boeotia he married the daughter of Cadmus, Autonoë, by whom he had a son, Actaeon. During his stay in Thrace he fell in love with Eurydice, the wife of Orpheus. It was in fleeing from Aristaeus that she was mortally bitten by a serpent. The end of Aristaeus was mysterious; he vanished from the earth on Mount Haemus.

The Pan of Mysia, in Asia Minor, was Priapus. He was particularly venerated at Lampsacus. His orgin is rather vague. His mother was said to be Aphrodite or Chione and his father Dionysus, Adonis, Hermes or Pan.

It was told that Hera, jealous of Aphrodite, caused him to be born with the extraordinary deformity to which he owes his name. His mother abandoned him and he was taken in by shepherds. Priapus presided over the fecundity of fields and flocks, over the raising of bees, the culture of the vine and over fishing. He protected orchards and gardens where his phallic image was placed. He was evidently introduced into the retinue of Dionysus by way of Asia.

The Centaurs. In addition to the Satyrs and the Sileni another kind of monstrous creature formed part of the cortège of Dionysus: the Centaurs. Their torso and head were those of a man; the rest of their body belonged to a horse. They had not always been like this: the first representations of Centaurs show them as giants with hairy bodies; then they were depicted as men with the hind-quarters of a horse. Their definitive appearance goes no farther back than the period of Phidias.

Natives of Thessaly, the Centaurs were descendants of Ixion, son of Ares. Ixion was engaged to marry Dia, daughter of Eioneus. There was a dispute between Ixion and his future father-in-law and Ixion threw him into a burning ditch. This crime earned universal reprobation and Ixion was forced to seek refuge with Zeus who offered him hospitality. But Ixion had the audacity to covet Zeus' own wife, Hera. In order to test how far his impudence would go, Zeus formed a cloud into the likeness of Hera and gave it to Ixion. From this strange union was born a monster, Centaurus, who, himself uniting with the mares of Pelion, fathered the race of the Centaurs.

Some have interpreted all this as a Hellenic equivalent of the Vedic Gandharvas. But it is more likely that the Centaurs – whose name etymologically signifies 'those who round up bulls' – were a primitive population of cowmen, living in Thessaly, who, like American cowboys, rounded up their cattle on horseback. Their behaviour was rude and barbarous, whence the savagery which was always attributed to the Centaurs – gross creatures, cruel, and given to lechery and drunkenness.

Some of their number were, however, famed for their wisdom. Such was Pholus who entertained Hercules. Such, especially, was Chiron who was educated by Artemis and Apollo themselves, and who in his turn was the teacher of many heroes. He perished in consequence of a wound made by Hercules with a poisoned arrow. The wound was incurable and Chiron exchanged his immortality for the mortality of Prometheus. Zeus placed him among the stars where he became part of the constellation Sagittarius.

The chief episode in the legend of the Centaurs was their battle with the Lapiths on the occasion of the nuptials of Peirithous. The Lapiths were also a fabulous people from Thessaly. Their king, Peirithous, was marrying Hippodameia and had invited the Centaur Eurytion to the festivities. Excited by the wine Eurytion attempted to abduct the bride, but was prevented from doing so by Theseus. Eurytion returned to the attack with a troop of Centaurs armed with slabs of stone and the trunks of pine trees. A general battle took place from which the Lapiths at last emerged victorious, thanks to the courage of Theseus and Peirithous. The Centaurs were driven to the frontiers of Epirus and took refuge on the slopes of Mount Pindus.

The Nymphs. Among these graceless and brutal divinities the nymphs were conspicuous for the charm of their youth and beauty. The nymphs of Dionysus' retinue were in all points similar to their sisters who peopled the rivers and springs. Like the nymphs also found in the retinue of Artemis and Apollo they were tutelary deities of the forests and mountains. Their names varied according to their place of abode. The Oreads were nymphs of the mountains and the grottoes. The Napaeae, the Auloniads, the Hylaeorae and the Alsaeids haunted the woods and valleys. Only the Dryads, forest nymphs responsible for trees, never mingled with divine processions. Crowned with oak-leaves, sometimes armed with an axe to punish outrages against the trees which they guarded, they would dance around the oaks which were sacred to them. Certain of their number, the Hamadryads, were still more closely united with trees of which, it was said, they formed an integral part.

Among the nymphs who followed Hera there was an Oread named Echo who, every time that Zeus paid court to some nymph, would distract Hera's attention with her chattering and singing. When Hera discovered this she deprived Echo of the gift of speech, condemning her to repeat only the last syllable of words spoken in her presence. Now shortly afterwards Echo fell in love with a young Thespian named Narcissus. Unable to declare her love she was spurned by him and went to hide her grief in solitary caverns. She died of a broken heart, her bones turned into stone, and all that was left of her was the echo of her vioce. Her unhappy end was also attributed to the wrath of Pan who was unable to win her love and had her torn to pieces by shepherds. Gaea received her mortal remains but even in death she retained her voice.

As for Narcissus, the gods punished him for having spurned Echo by making him fall in love with his own image. The soothsayer Teiresias had predicted that Narcissus would live only until the moment he saw himself. One day when he was leaning over the limpid waters of a fountain Narcissus caught sight of his own reflection in the water. He conceived so lively a passion for this phantom that nothing could tear him away from it, and he died there

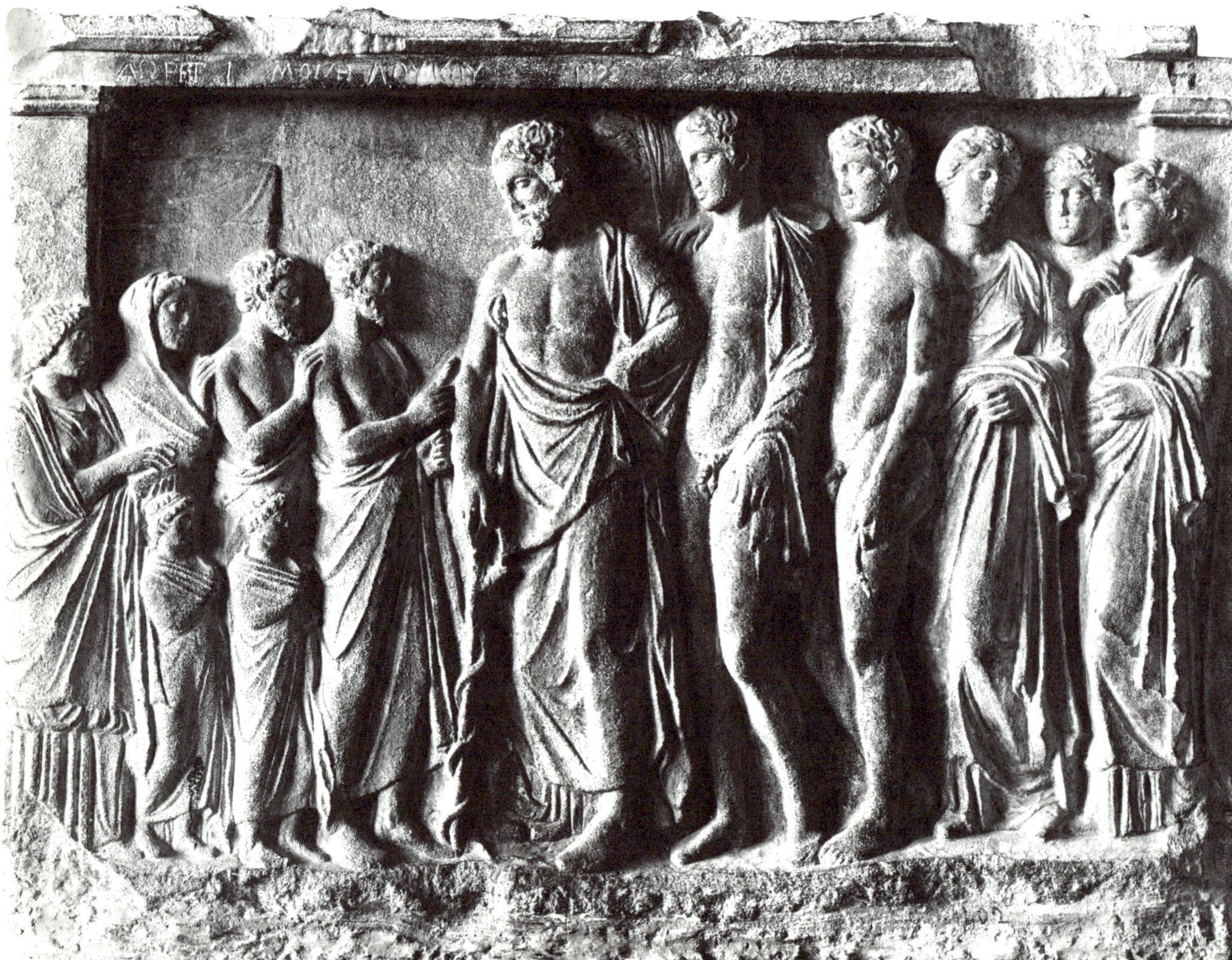

Votive relief to Asclepius. The faithful come to beseech the god's aid. With him are his wife Epione, his sons Machaon and Podaleirius, and his daughters Hygieia, Aegle and Panacea. National Museum, Athens.

of languor. He was changed into the flower which bears his name and which grows at the edge of springs.

Another victim of the nymphs was the handsome Sicilian herdsman Daphnis. Daphnis was the son of Hermes and a nymph. He was abandoned by his mother and taken in by shepherds whose daily life he shared at the foot of Etna. He was loved by a nymph, Echenais, Xenaea or Lyce, who made him swear eternal fidelity to her under pain of going blind. Intoxicated by the princess Chimaera, Daphnis broke his vow and at once lost his sight. He tried to console himself with poetry and music; he was called the inventor of pastoral poetry. He killed himself one day by falling from the top of a cliff.

THE LIFE OF MAN

Zeus, sovereign lord of mortals, did not rule directly over their fate. He delegated this task to secondary divinities who accompanied men throughout their physical and moral life.

DIVINITIES OF BIRTH AND HEALTH

Ilithyia. In primitive times there were two Ilithyias, daughters of Hera, who presided over birth and brought to women in labour both pain – the keen arrows of the Ilithyias – and deliverance. No child could be born unless they were present, no mother could find relief without them. Thus, when Apollo was born, the jealous Hera detained Ilithyia on Olympus for nine days and nine nights when she had been on the point of going to the aid of Leto. Hera repeated this manoeuvre when Alcmene was about to give birth to Hercules.

The two Ilithyias finally merged into a single person, the goddess of childbirth. She was, in fact, a very ancient divinity believed to have originated in Crete. She is most often depicted kneeling, a position which was believed to aid delivery, and carrying a torch, symbol of light, while with her other hand she makes a gesture of encouragement.

Certain goddesses known to be particularly concerned with women were sometimes given the epithet Ilithyia: Hera at Argos, for instance, and Artemis at Delos. It may even be asked if Ilithyia is not simply a double of Hera's.

Asclepius. We have seen, in discussing Apollo, the tragic circumstances of the birth of Asclepius, son of Apollo and Coronis. Apollo snatched him from the burning pyre on which his mother's body had just been consumed and carried him to Mount Pelion where he was confided to the care of the Centaur Chiron. Chiron taught him to hunt and instructed him in the science of medicine. The medical career of Asclepius then began. With his miraculous cures he soon earned immense renown. He even succeeded in restoring the dead to life, thanks either to the Gorgon's blood which Athene had given him or to the properties of a plant which a serpent had told him about. Hades felt that he was being wronged. He went to Zeus to complain, and Zeus agreed that mortals must follow their destiny. Thus Asclepius was guilty of thwarting the order of nature and Zeus struck him dead with a thunderbolt.

Apollo avenged the death of his son by exterminating the Cyclopes who had forged the thunderbolt. Apollo was banished from Olympus for a considerable time as a result of this massacre.

At Epidaurus another tradition of the birth of Asclepius was current. They said that Coronis gave birth to her son Asclepius while her father, Phlegyas, was on an expedition to the Peloponnese. She exposed the new-born child on Mount Titthion where a goat fed it and a dog guarded it. One day Aresthanas, a shepherd, discovered it and was struck by the supernatural light which played over the child.

Be that as it may, the god of health was always considered to be the offspring of light or fire. To the sick he restored the warmth they had lost. Hence he was the object of great veneration in Greece. He was surrounded by auxiliary divinities: to begin with, Epione, his wife, who bore the two Asclepiads, Podaleirius and Machaon. Both took part, at the head of the Thessalians of Tricca, in the Trojan war. They were as skilled in medicine as their father. Machaon, especially, cured Menelaus of an arrow wound. He also cured Philoctetes. He himself was killed before Troy and Nestor brought his body back to Greece. Podaleirius survived the expedition and on his return was cast by a tempest on to the shores of Caria where he settled.

Asclepius also had daughters: Iaso, Panacea, Aegle and, above all, Hygieia, who was closely associated with the cult of her father as goddess of health. Finally we must mention the guardian spirit of convalescence, Telesphorus, who was represented wearing a hooded cape, the costume of those who had just recovered from illness.

Asclepius was sometimes represented as a serpent, but more frequently as a man of middle age with an expression of benevolence, and his cult was at the same time a religion and a system of therapeutics. His sanctuaries, such as those at Tricca, Epidaurus, Cos and Pergamus, were built outside the towns on particularly healthy sites. The priests in charge of them at first held a monopoly of medical knowledge which was handed down from father to son. It was only later that they admitted outsiders as neophytes.

In the *Asclepeia* special rites were observed. After much purificatory preparation, baths, fasting, sacrifices, the patient was permitted to spend the night in the temple of Asclepius where he slept either on the skin of the sacrificed animal or on a couch placed near the statue of the god. This was the period of incubation. During the night Asclepius would appear to the patient in a dream and give him advice. In the morning the priests would interpret the dream and explain the god's precepts. Patients would thank Asclepius by tossing gold into the sacred fountain and by hanging ex-votos on the walls of the temple.

DIVINITIES CONCERNED WITH MORALITY

The Moerae or Fates. The Moerae, whom the Romans called the Parcae, were for Homer the individual and inescapable destiny which followed every mortal being. Only in Hesiod's *Theogony* are they treated as goddesses. They were three in number, daughters of Night, and they were called: Clotho, Lachesis and Atropos. Clotho, the spinner, personified the thread of life. Lachesis was chance, the element of luck that a man had the right to expect. Atropos was inescapable fate, against which there was no appeal. The whole of man's life was shadowed by the Moerae. They arrived at his birth with Ilithyia. When he was married the three Moerae had to be invoked so that the union should be happy. And when the end approached the Moerae hastened to cut the thread of his life. Hesiod placed them with the Keres, thus giving them the role of divinities of violent death.

The Moerae were submitted to the authority of Zeus who commanded them to see that the natural order of things was respected They sat in the assemblies of the gods and possessed the gift of prophecy.

Nemesis. Like the Fates, Nemesis had at first been a moral idea, that of the inexorable equilibrium of the human condition. Man could displease the gods in two manners, either by offending the moral law – in which case he incurred their wrath – or by attaining too much happiness or riches – in which case he excited their jealousy. In either of these cases the imprudent mortal was pursued by Nemesis, or the divine anger. If he had offended only by an excess of good fortune he might hope to propitiate the goddess by sacrificing a part of his happiness.

Polycrates, tyrant of Samos, was terrified of the unheard-of luck which followed him, and wished to forestall the jealousy of the gods by throwing into the sea a priceless ring of which he was especially fond. But when the ring was returned to him by a fisherman who had found it in the belly of a fish, Polycrates realised that Nemesis had refused to accept his sacrifice and that unhappiness was in store for him. And, indeed, it overtook him shortly afterwards.

Nemesis later became a goddess with more definitely defined personality, and various genealogies were ascribed to her. According to some she was the daughter of Oceanus. According to others she was born of Night and Erebus, in which case she was a deadly power. But when Dike was made her mother she became an equitable divinity. She was, however, always responsible for seeing that order was maintained. One of her titles was Adrasteia – the Inevitable. She is sometimes depicted with a finger to her lips – suggesting that silence is advisable in order not to attract the divine anger. The principal sanctuary of Nemesis was at Rhamnus, a small town in Attica. There was a statue of the goddess there

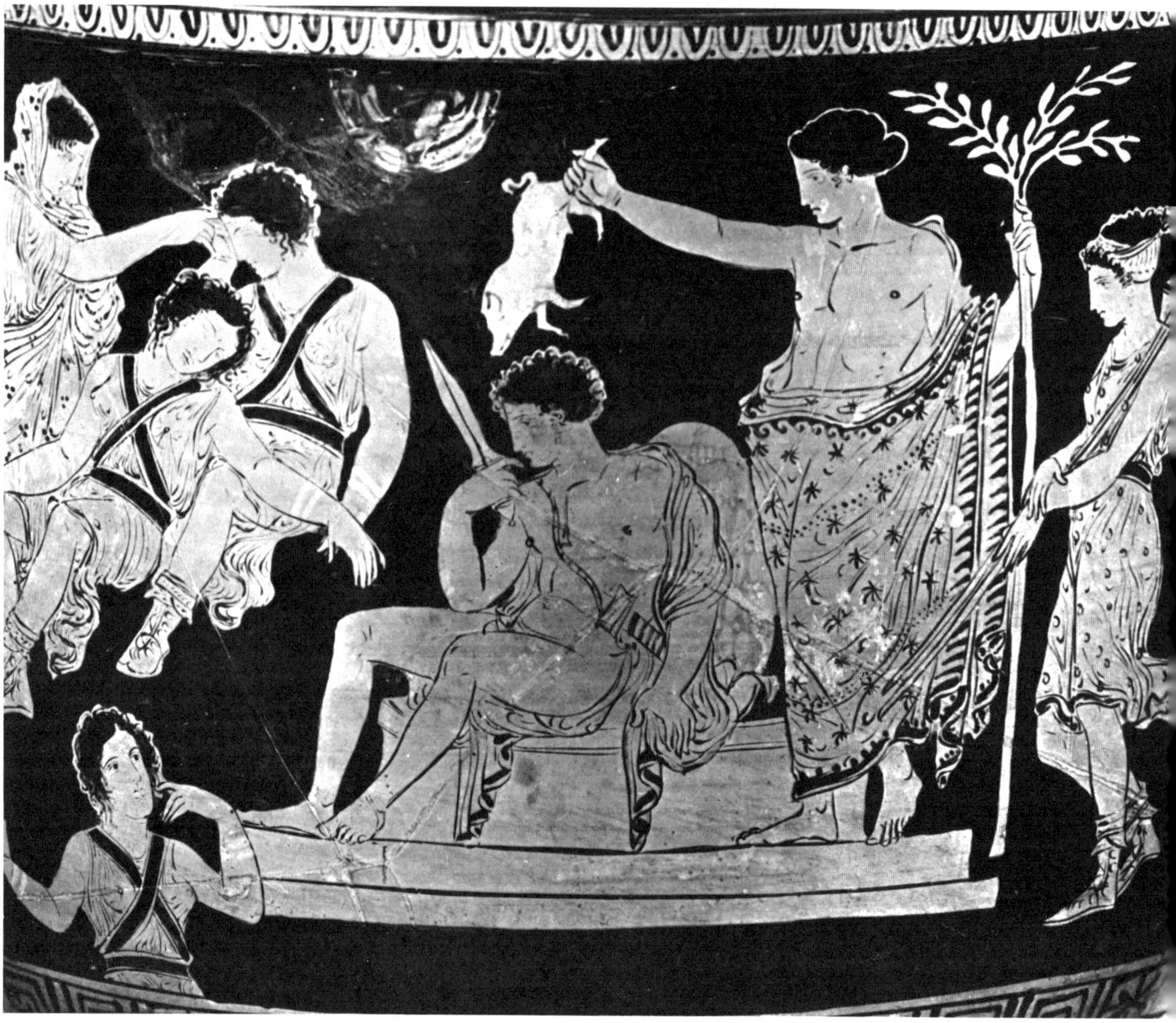

The Eumenides. Greek crater. The Eumenides sleep while Apollo purifies Orestes with a young pig. Louvre.

which Phidias carved from the marble which the Persians, rashly counting on victory in advance, had brought with them before the battle of Marathon, expecting to erect a trophy with it.

Tyche, Ate, Litae. To complete the list of divinities whose functions were moral, there is Tyche, goddess of fortune. Hesiod calls her the daughter of Oceanus and Tethys. She was represented variously by various cities, each having its own Tyche. Adorned with the mural crown, she wears the attributes of abundance.

Ate, daughter of Eris or of Zeus, was on the other hand a malevolent divinity who prompted men to irresponsible acts. She led both men and gods into error and aberration. It was she who, when Hercules was born, suggested to Zeus the imprudent vow which caused the hero such subsequent misery. Hence the master of the gods punished the wicked goddess by banishing her permanently from Olympus and 'from the heights of heaven flung her into the midst of man's affairs'.

In order to repair the damage done by the treacherous Ate, Zeus sent the Litae after her. The Litae were Prayers and also daughters of Zeus. Wrinkled and lame, they limped after their sister Ate, trying to mitigate the evils she caused. Whoever welcomed the Litae with respect was showered with blessings.

THE UNDERWORLD

In Greek mythology the Infernal Regions were the mournful abode where, separated from their bodies, the souls of those who had finished their earthly existence took refuge. There were two successive conceptions of where the afterworld was situated. 'The Afterworld,' says Circe to Odysseus, 'lies at the extremity of the earth, beyond the vast Ocean.' The earth was thought of as a flat surface limited by an immense encircling river Ocean. One must cross this river in order to reach the desolate and uncultivated shore of the infernal regions. There few things grew, the soil was barren and no living being could survive, for the sun's rays could not penetrate so far. Black poplars were found there and willows which never bore fruit. The ground supported asphodel, a funerary plant of ruins and cemeteries.

This was the tradition of the epic poems. It was altered with the progress of geography when navigators discovered that very far to the west – where the infernal regions were supposed to be – there existed lands which were in fact inhabited. Popular belief then placed the kingdom of Shadows elsewhere: from then on it was situated in the centre of the earth. It continued to remain a place of shadows and mystery, of Erebus. Its approaches were no longer the Ocean. The Underworld communicated with the earth by direct channels. These were caverns whose depths were unplumbed, like that of Acherusia in Epirus, or Heraclea Pontica. Near Cape Taenarum there was one of these entrance gates and also at Colonus in a place dedicated to the Eumenides.

In the same way certain rivers whose course was partly underground were thought to lead to the infernal regions. Such was the Acheron in Thesprotia into which flowed the Cocytus. It must be remarked, moreover, that the names of these rivers were given to them because they were believed to flow into the underworld. Acheron derives from the word which means 'affliction'. It was the river of sadness and Cocytus was the river of lamentation.

Though the ancients carefully described the exterior appearance and approaches of the underworld, they were vaguer about its interior. On this aspect of the Infernal Regions we have little information. According to what we have, the actual Underworld was preceded by a vestibule called the Grove of Persephone. Here the black poplars and sterile willows were again found. It had to be crossed before reaching the gate of the Kingdom of Hades. At the gate was posted Cerberus, the monstrous watch-dog with fifty heads and a voice of bronze. He was born of the love of the giant Typhoeus for Echidna. Cerberus was variously represented. Sometimes he had only three heads, sometimes he bristled with serpents and his mouth dribbled black venom. He was always to be feared. When entering the underworld, to be sure, the terrible beast would appear prepossessing, wagging its tail and ears. But never again could one come out. Cerberus, however, could be appeased by tossing to him cakes of flour and honey. Hermes could calm him down with his caduceus and Orpheus charmed him with his lyre. Only Hercules dared measure his strength with Cerberus and, vanquishing him, carried him for a moment up to earth. Cerberus infected certain herbs with his venom which were afterwards gathered by magicians and used in the preparation of baleful philtres.

Within the Underworld flowed subterranean rivers: Acheron with its affluent the Cocytus swelled by the Phlegethon, Lethe and, finally, the Styx. Acheron was the son of Gaea. He had quenched the thirst of the Titans during their war with Zeus and been thrown into the Underworld where he was changed into a a river. To cross Acheron it was necessary to apply to old Charon, the official ferryman of the Underworld. He was a hard old man, difficult to deal with. Unless before embarking the shade of the deceased newcomer presented Charon with his obolus, he would mercilessly drive away an intruder so ignorant of local usage. The shade was then condemned to wander the deserted shore and never find refuge. The Greeks therefore carefully put an obolus into the mouths of the dead.

The Styx surrounded the Underworld with its nine loops. The Styx was personified as a nymph, daughter of Oceanus and Tethys. She was loved, it was said, by the Titan Pallas and by him had Zelos (Jealousy); Nike (Victory); Kratos (Force); and Bia (Violence). As a reward for the help she rendered the Olympians during the revolt of the Titans it was decided that the Immortals should swear by her name, and such vows were irrevocable.

Those who drank of the waters of Lethe forgot the past. Lethe flowed, according to some, at the extremity of the Elysian fields; according to others at the edge of Tartarus. The Elysian fields and Tartarus were the two great regions of the Underworld.

THE SOVEREIGN OF THE UNDERWORLD

It seems that the name of the ruler of the Underworld derives from the privative prefix 'a' and the verb 'to see', evoking an idea of mystery. He was the Invisible. He was also called Pluto, from the word for 'riches'. It was he who received buried treasure: he was then considered the god of agricultural wealth. From the centre of earth he exerted his influence on cultivation and crops.

Hades – he was also called Aidoneus – was the son of Rhea and the ferocious Cronus who devoured him as he devoured his brothers and sisters. Fortunately he was delivered by his brother Zeus, from whom he received as his share of the inheritance the Kingdom of the Underworld.

Over this domain Hades ruled as absolute master. He seemed happy there and was only seen to leave his Kingdom on two occasions: once to abduct Persephone and the other time to go in search of Paean in order to be cured of a wound inflicted by Hercules who struck his shoulder with a sharp-pointed arrow. On the other hand, if an impulse to emerge from the Underworld seized him, no one could see him; for his helmet made him invisible.

Hades was not a particularly inconstant husband. Persephone had only twice to complain of his infidelity. First he became interested in Minthe, a nymph of the Cocytus. Persephone – or perhaps it was Demeter – pursued the unfortunate nymph and trod her ferociously underfoot. Hades transformed her into a plant which first grew in Triphylia; it was mint which was afterwards sacred to Hades.

Hades also brought a daughter of Oceanus to his kingdom, one Leuce, who died a natural death and became a white poplar, the tree of the Elysian Fields. When Hercules came up from the Underworld he was crowned with its foliage.

Hades was very little venerated, though as Pluto he received much more homage. This was because Hades was essentially a god of terror, mystery and the inexorable. Pluto, on the contrary, was regarded as a benevolent deity and his cult was sometimes associated with that of Demeter.

To pray to him – Homer says – one struck the ground with bare hands or with rods. One sacrificed to him a black ewe or a black ram. Plants sacred to the god of the Underworld were the cypress and the narcissus.

Persephone. The name of the wife of Hades occurs in several forms: Persephone, Persephoneia, Phersephone, Persephassa, Phersephatta. It is difficult to discover the etymology of all these variations. It is believed that the last half of the word Persephone comes from a word meaning 'to show' and evokes an idea of light. Whether the first half derives from a word meaning 'to destroy' – in which case Persephone would be 'she who destroys the light' – or from an adverbial root signifying 'dazzling brilliance' as in the name Perseus, it is difficult to decide.

The problem is complicated by the fact that Persephone is not a purely infernal divinity. Before marrying Hades she lived on earth with her mother Demeter who had conceived her by Zeus. Her name had then been Kore.

It is probable that originally mother and daughter were merged in one and the same divinity. Demeter, as we have seen, had in her province not only the surface of the earth, but also its interior. Subsequently the personality of Demeter split and her subterranean function devolved on a distinct goddess who was, however, an offspring of the primitive goddess. This is the meaning of the Kore-Persephone myth.

The dramatic circumstances of Kore's abduction will be recalled: how Hades surprised her while she was gathering flowers in a field, carried her away in his chariot and plunged with her into the depths of the earth; how Demeter, unable to regain full possession of her daughter, accepted the gods' proposal that Persephone should pass at least part of the year with her.

Persephone's legend is limited to this single episode, though the initiates of Orphism tried to enrich it by making the goddess the mother of Dionysus-Zagreus. Confined, like Hades, to her shadowy empire, Persephone was exempt from the passions which swayed other divinities. At most she was said to have felt a certain tenderness for the beautiful Adonis.

As goddess of the Underworld Persephone's attributes were the bat, the narcissus and the pomegranate. She was honoured in Arcadia under the names Persephone Soteira and Despoena. She was also venerated at Sardes and in Sicily. But usually her cult was joined to Demeter's and the rites of both were almost always similar.

Hecate. Hecate is best treated as a divinity of the Underworld, though she was in origin a moon-goddess. She was a native of ancient Thrace and in some ways she resembled Artemis with whom she was sometimes merged. Her name seems to be the feminine form of a title of Apollo's – the far-darter. Thus Hesiod makes her the daughter of the Titan Perses and the Titaness Asteria, both symbols of shining light. Hecate's lunar character always remained: she and Helios together witnessed the abduction of Kore by Hades.

Hecate was powerful both in the sky and on earth: she gave men riches, victory and wisdom; she watched over the prosperity of flocks and presided over navigation. During the war with the Giants she was the ally of Zeus; thus she continued to be honoured on Olympus.

A later tradition says that Hecate was the daughter of Zeus and Hera. It was said that she incurred her mother's wrath by stealing her rouge to give to Europa. She fled to the earth and hid in the house of a woman who had just been brought to bed with a child, contact with whom rendered Hecate impure. To remove the stain the Cabeiri plunged her into the Acheron, and that was how Hecate became a divinity of the Underworld. In the infernal regions Hecate's authority was considerable: she was called Prytania of the dead or the Invincible Queen. She presided over purifications and expiations. She was the goddess of enchantments and magic

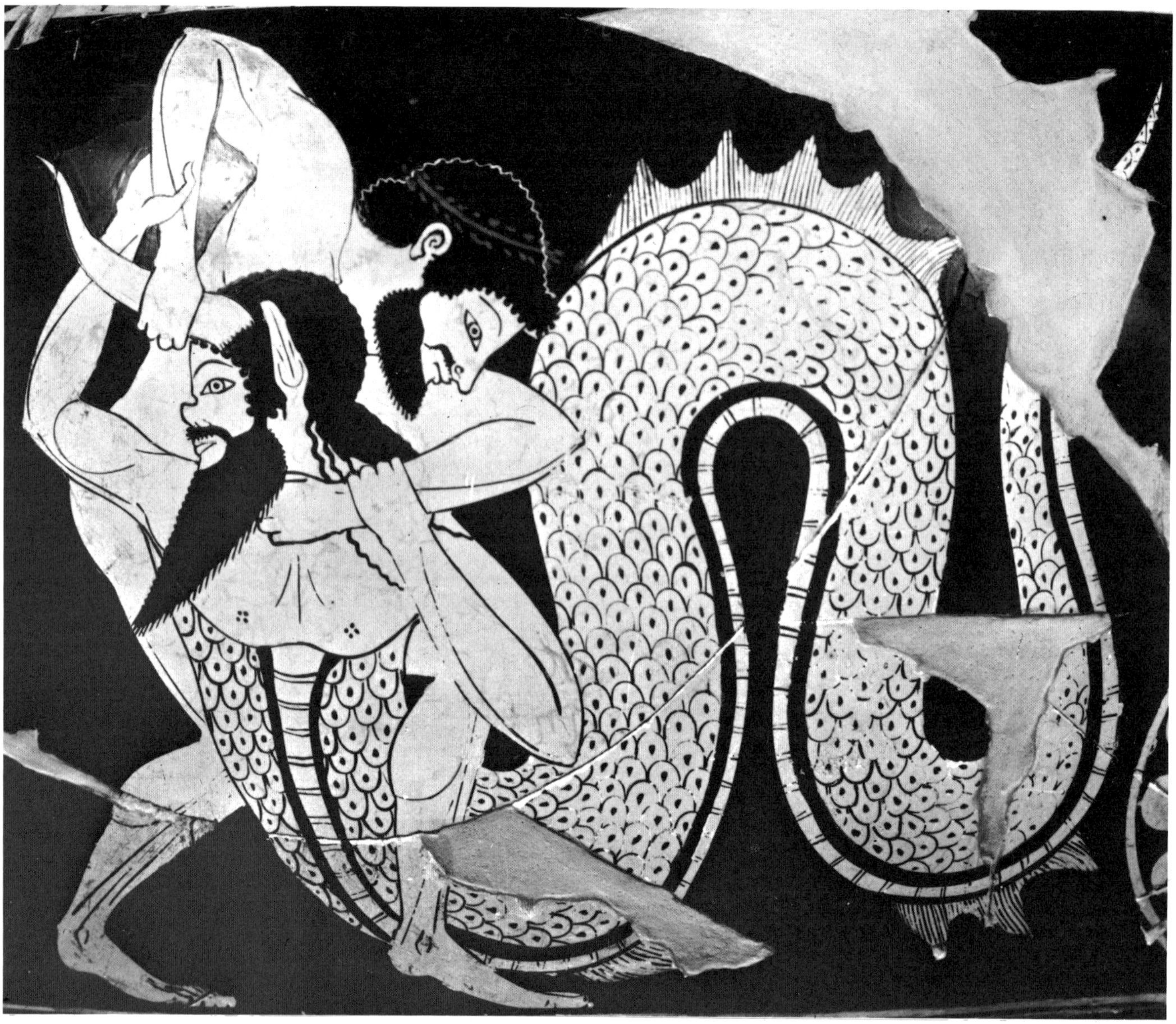

Hercules wrestling with Achelous. The river-god has turned himself into a speckled serpent in an attempt to overcome his rival for the hand of the lovely Deianeira but he was finally overcome by the hero who snapped off one of his horns. Rivers were worshipped by the Greeks who believed them to be the divine offspring of Oceanus and Tethys. The Achelous was the largest watercourse in Greece. Detail from a Greek red-figured vase.

charms as well. She sent demons to the earth who tormented men. She herself would appear at night accompanied by her retinue of infernal dogs. The places that she haunted most frequently were crossroads, or near tombs or the scenes of crimes. Thus at crossroads her image could be found, either columns or statues of the goddess with three faces – they were called triple Hecates – and, on the eve of the full moon, offerings would be left before these images to propitiate the redoubtable goddess.

THE AUXILIARIES OF HADES

Thanatos and Hypnos. Thanatos – Death – naturally supplied Hades with his subjects. He was the son of Night. Euripides shows him dressed in a black robe holding in his hand the fatal sword, as he walks among men. But normally Death did not appear in this sinister aspect; Thanatos was more usually represented as a winged spirit. He then completely resembled his brother Hypnos – Sleep – who lived with him in the Underworld. Hypnos put men to sleep by touching them with his magic wand or by fanning them with his dark wings. He had power also over the gods and Homer tells us how at Hera's request he took the form of a night bird and sent Zeus to sleep on Mount Ida. The son of Hypnos was Morpheus, god of dreams.

The Keres. The Keres executed the will of the Moerae or Fates and were no doubt originally confused with them. When the implacable deities had fixed the fatal hour, it was the Keres who appeared. They would then seize the unhappy mortal, deliver the decisive blow, and carry him down to the land of shadows. In the midst of battle especially they could be seen to hover, with a sparkling eye, grimacing mouth, and sharp teeth whose whiteness contrasted with the sombre hue of their visage. They wore red robes and cried out dismally as they finished off the wounded. They would dig in their sharp claws, then greedily drink the streaming blood. Not without reason were they called the dogs of Hades.

The Erinnyes. The Erinnyes were also sometimes called the 'dogs of Hades'. They, too, were infernal deities whose special mission was to punish parricides and those who had violated their oaths. Their genealogy was rather vague: according to Hesiod they were born to Gaea fertilised by the blood of Uranus. Aeschylus calls them 'the children of Eternal Night' and Sophocles 'Daughters of the Earth and the Shadow'. It seems that they were first venerated in Arcadia where a Demeter Erinnyes, from whom they were perhaps derived, was worshipped. Their number for long remained undetermined, but was later fixed at three when they were given the individual names of Tisiphone, Megara and Alecto.

When a crime was committed in a family – above all when a son's hands were stained with the blood of his parents – the black goddesses would immediately appear, their hair bristling with serpents, armed with torches and whips. They would sit at the threshold of the guilty one's house and it was in vain to attempt escape. Even in the Underworld they pursued their vengeance and tormented the guilty in Tartarus.

The cult of the Erinnyes was spread throughout all Greece, above all in Athens where they had a temple near the Areopagus. Here they were honoured under the name of the Eumenides – the Benevolent Ones – in memory of the mildness they had shown towards Orestes, who, after the murder of his mother, had come to seek refuge in Athens.

Life in the Underworld. Souls of the dead, when they had left the earth, only retained a pale reflection of their former personality. Physically they were diaphanous and insubstantial. Morally they were also shadows: their courage and intelligence had disappeared. Only a few privileged persons lived in the Underworld as they had lived on earth, following the same occupations. Orion continued to hunt, Minos judged souls, Hercules was always ready to overthrow some monster or other.

In brief the Underworld, in this primitive conception of it, was a sort of dismal house of retirement. Only the outstandingly guilty suffered eternal torture.

Little by little, however, the Underworld came to be thought of, not as a limbo, but as a place of justice where each received exactly what he deserved.

Souls on their arrival appeared before a tribunal composed of Hades and his three assessors: Aeacus, Minos and Rhadamanthys.

The latter two were sons of Zeus and Europa and had reigned, Minos over Crete and Rhadamanthys over the Cyclades. Aeacus was the son of Zeus and Aegina and during his life had been distinguished for his piety and love of justice. The gods themselves had chosen him as an arbiter. After his death he was appointed in the Underworld especially to judge Europeans, while Rhadamanthys tried Asiatics. It was Aeacus who held the keys of the Underworld.

After they had been examined and judgment pronounced, the souls of the dead were either cast into Tartarus or conducted to the Elysian Fields or to the Islands of the Blessed.

Tartarus with its gates of bronze was the sombre gaol of those who had committed crimes against the gods. It was surrounded by a triple wall and bathed by the waters of the Phlegethon. The avenue which led to Tartarus was closed by a diamond gate. Here the most notorious prisoners were the Titans and the giant Tityus on whom two vultures fed because he had attempted to violate Leto. Tantalus could also be seen, eternally tortured by hunger and thirst; Sisyphus, who without respite rolled his rock up a steep cliff; Ixion, bound to his flaming wheel spinning in the air; and the Danaids, condemned eternally to fill a bottomless barrel.

In Elysium, on the contrary, snow and rain and tempests were unknown. Soft breezes forever refreshed this abode of happiness which was at first reserved for the children of the gods, but later opened to the favourites of the Olympians and the souls of the just.

THE HEROES

The Greeks' Idea of the Hero. The Greek Hero was not always a supernatural being related to the gods. Homer made him a man of strength and courage or one who was especially venerated for his wisdom, like Laertes, Aegyptus and Demodocus. The hero could also be simply a prince of an illustrious family like Odysseus and Menelaus, for example. It is only incidentally that the heroes of Homer's poems are related to gods.

Hesiod on the other hand generalised the idea of the superman and recounted his origin. According to him, heroes were the offspring of the fourth generation of mythical men, that is to say the generation which took part in the battles of Troy and Thebes. At that epoch, indeed, gods and mortals often mingled.

Cult of the Heroes. The cult which the Greeks rendered to their heroes closely resembled the devotion with which they honoured their own ancestors. The hero, they believed, was in fact their most illustrious ancestor. Heroes and ancestors alike were offered sacrifice at the end of the day: the sacrificial victim was turned towards the West and at the foot of the altar a trench was dug to receive the victim's head. But the chief role of the hero was to act as intermediary between men and the gods. While men after death became insubstantial shadows, heroes retained their original

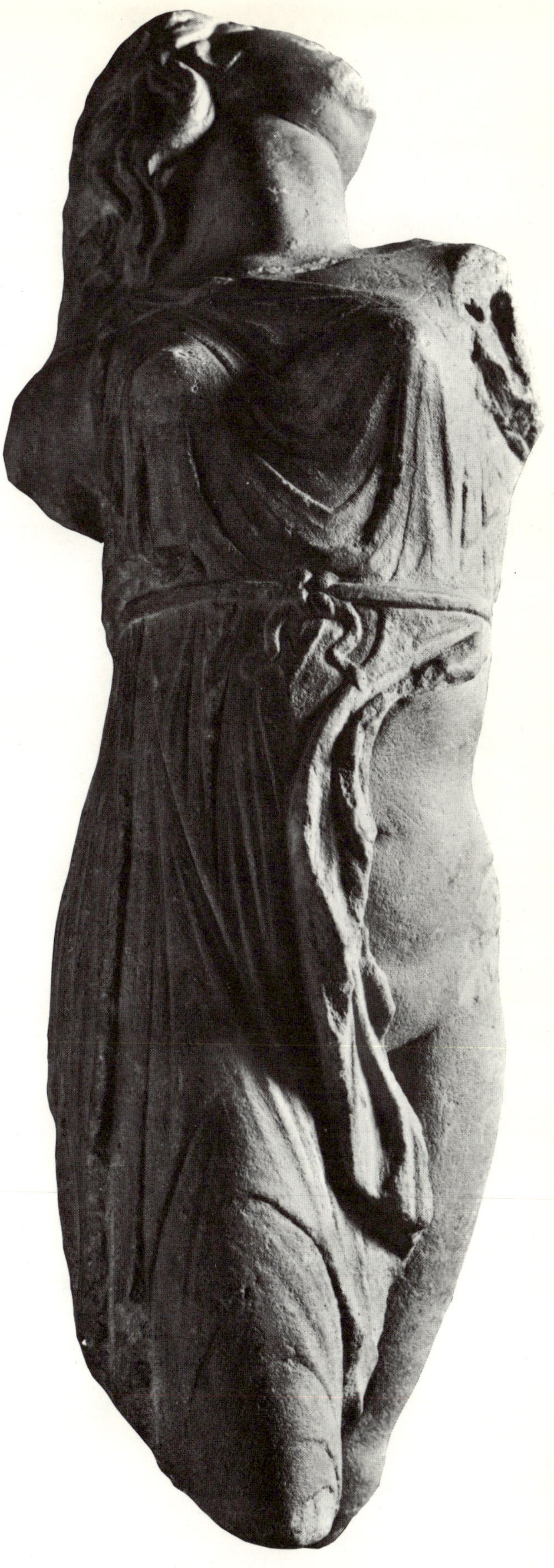

Dancing Maenad. With her head thrown back in ecstasy, one of Dionysus' female retinue follows in the wake of the god. Modelled in an idealised fashion upon the god's frenzied Thracian worshippers, the Maenads accompanied Dionysus on his travels crowned with wreaths of ivy, oak or fir and draped in the skins of animals. Under a more peaceful aspect they gathered grapes and prepared wine. Statue ascribed to the fourth century B.C. sculptor, Scopas.

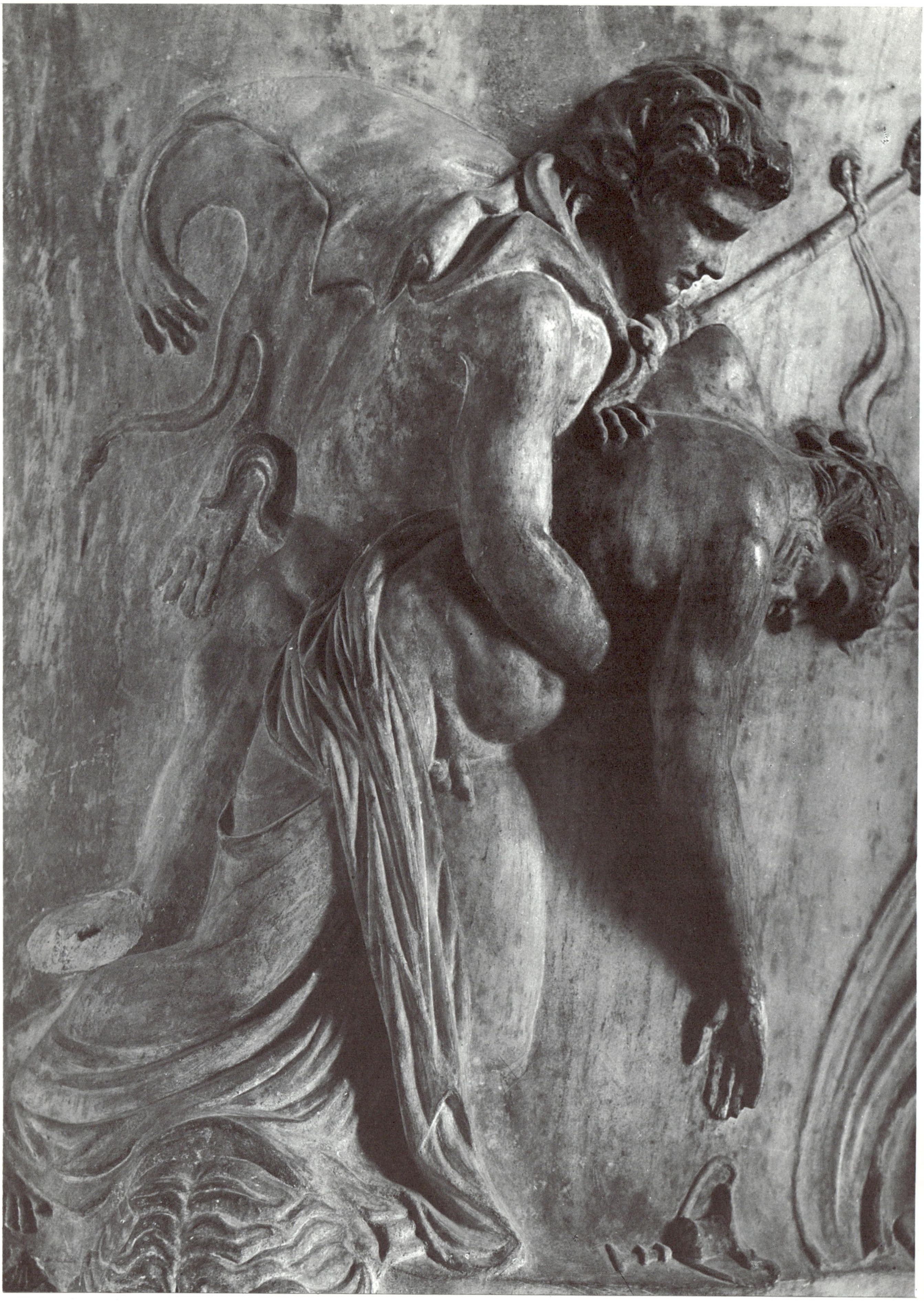

Silenus supported by a young satyr. One of the most picturesque figures in the retinue of Dionysus, Silenus was always depicted as a drunken, fat old man. In spite of his unprepossessing appearance he was nevertheless possessed of great wisdom and had formerly been the god's tutor. He is assisted by a young satyr wearing a panther skin, or *nebris*, and carrying the *thyrsus*. Detail from the Borghese vase.

qualities and could intercede for mortals. In brief, the heroes, who were originally idealised men, became demi-gods and in the hierarchy occupied a position midway between men and the Olympians.

HERCULES

We are not very certain about the etymology of the word Heracles (the Latinised form being Hercules, which is used here throughout). Various hypotheses have been suggested to explain the name. The ancients claimed that Heracles was thus named because he owed his glory to Hera. The name has also been translated as 'glory of the air'. But no one of the theories advanced is more convincing than the others.

The Functions of Hercules. Hercules was thought of as the personification of physical strength. In his aspect of athlete-hero the foundation of the Olympic Games was ascribed to him. Pindar says that he arranged all the rules and details. But the chief function of Hercules was to play the part of a protector. When men were in danger Heracles *Alexikakos* was their chief resort. In consequence he even had medical powers: he was invoked in case of epidemics, while certain medicinal springs at Himera and Thermopylae were sacred to him. Finally, sometimes as Heracles Musagetes he played the cithara. To sum up, he presided over all aspects of Hellenic education and, after being the god of physical prowess, he was the god who sang of victory and accompanied himself on the lyre. More than any other he was the friend and counsellor of men.

Representation and Cult. The glorious hero, the invincible athlete, is depicted as a man of mature strength, endowed with muscular power, whose head is rather small in relation to his body. Generally Hercules stands, leaning on his heavy club. In his statues and busts we observe a rather sad and severe expression, as though Hercules, the eternal conqueror, never knew repose. His appearance suggests that he is waiting for yet another superhuman task to fulfil.

Hercules was venerated like other heros and with the same rites, but his cult was much more general. All Greece honoured him. His exploits, indeed, took place all over the Hellenic world. Thebes and Argos were the centres from which his legend spread.

The Birth of Hercules. His Childhood and First Exploits. Hercules descended from Perseus, whose son Alcaeus (the Strong) was the father of Amphitryon, the supposed father of Hercules. On the other hand, Electryon (the Brilliant), another son of Perseus, was the father of Alcmene (woman of might). Hercules, then, was born under the sign of strength and light; and, into the bargain, his paternity was divine. Zeus, wishing to have a son who should be a powerful protector of both mortals and Immortals, descended one night to the city of Thebes where he assumed the appearance of Amphitryon and lay with Amphitryon's wife, Alcmene. Shortly afterwards Amphitryon himself returned from a victorious expedition and took his wife in his arms. From the two successive unions Alcmene conceived twins: Hercules and Iphicles.

Their birth was not without difficulties. On the day Hercules should have been born Zeus swore a solemn and irrevocable oath before the Olympians that the descendant of Perseus who was about to be born should one day rule Greece. At these words Hera, doubly jealous, hurried to Argos where she caused the wife of one Sthenelus – himself a son of Perseus – to be brought prematurely to bed. She gave birth to Eurystheus. Hastening to Thebes, Hera simultaneously retarded the birth of Hercules. Thus Eurystheus came into the title of ruler of Greece and Zeus, bound by his solemn oath, was obliged to recognise him. And that was why Hercules all his life found the hardest tasks imposed on him by the rival whom Hera had set up against him. Nor was her vengeance yet satisfied. One night while all in the palace of Amphitryon were asleep, two serpents attacked the infant Hercules. While Iphicles screamed pitifully, Hercules firmly grasped the two monsters, one in each hand, and wrung their necks. To encourage such promise Hercules was then handed over to illustrious tutors. Rhadamanthys taught him wisdom and virtue while Linus taught him music. Linus was killed by the young hero in a fit of temper. Amphitryon then confided his divine offspring to some shepherds who lived in the mountains. There Hercules gave himself over to physical exercise and developed his strength. At the age of eighteen he killed

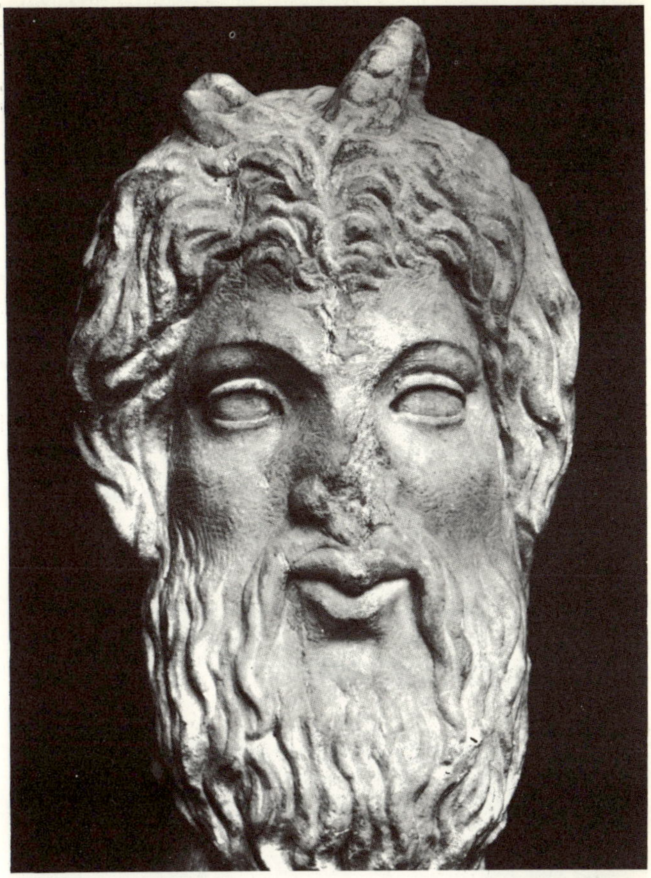

Head of Pan. An Arcadian shepherd-god who protected flocks and herds and made them prolific, Pan loved to roam the woods and mountains of Arcadia joining in the revels of the nymphs and playing on the pipes. He was later incorporated into the retinue of Dionysus. Half man and half goat, he was portrayed with a man's body but with the legs, ears, horns and beard of a goat.
Athenian sculpture in Pentelic marble, *c.* 400 B.C.

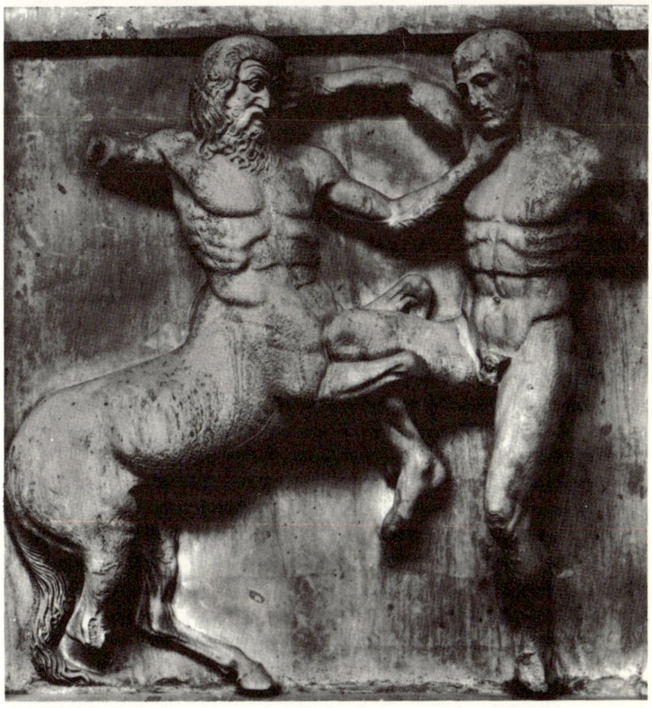

Centaur fighting a Lapith. The Centaurs, half man and half horse, also formed part of the retinue of Dionysus and were probably originally inspired by the horse-breeders of Thessaly. Though barbarous and sensual for the most part, some of them were famed for their wisdom. Here a Centaur struggles with a Lapith at the wedding feast of King Peirithous. It was this series of reliefs by Phidias and his assistants that fixed their appearance definitively. Metope from the Parthenon.
Pentelic marble, *c.* 445 B.C.

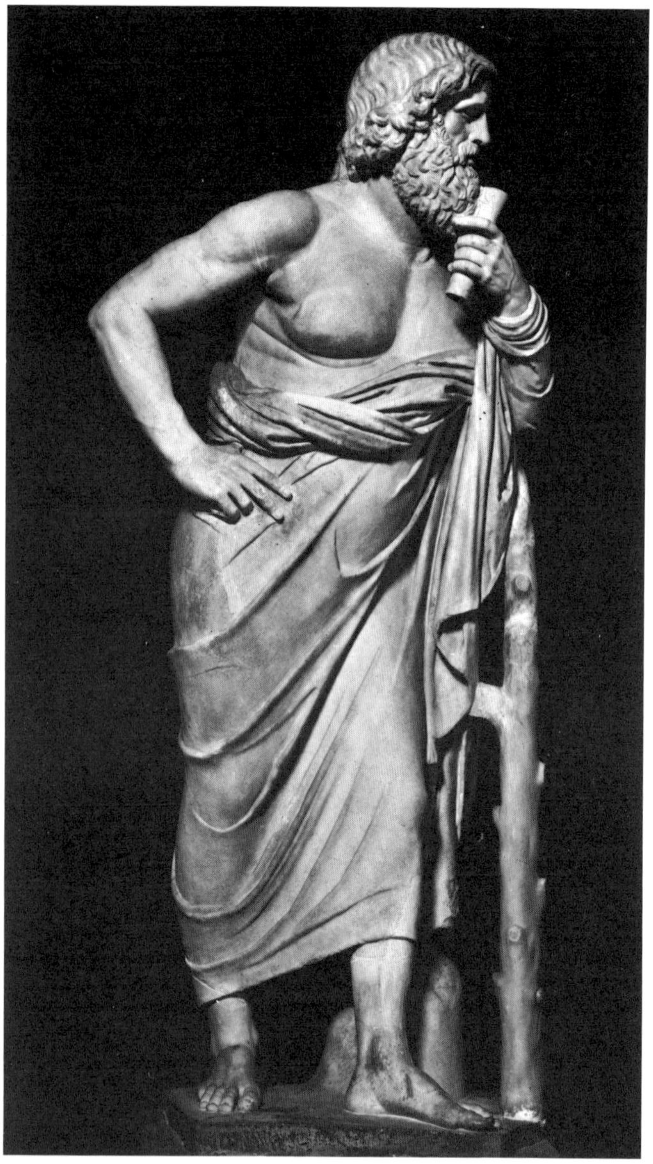

Asclepius. The god of health and healing leans on a tree-trunk lost in meditation grasping a scroll representing medical learning. The son of Apollo, he had learned the science of medicine from the Centaur Chiron but was later killed by Zeus for raising the dead. His image was set among the stars. Greatly venerated throughout Greece, he had numerous shrines, his priests holding a monopoly of medical knowledge.

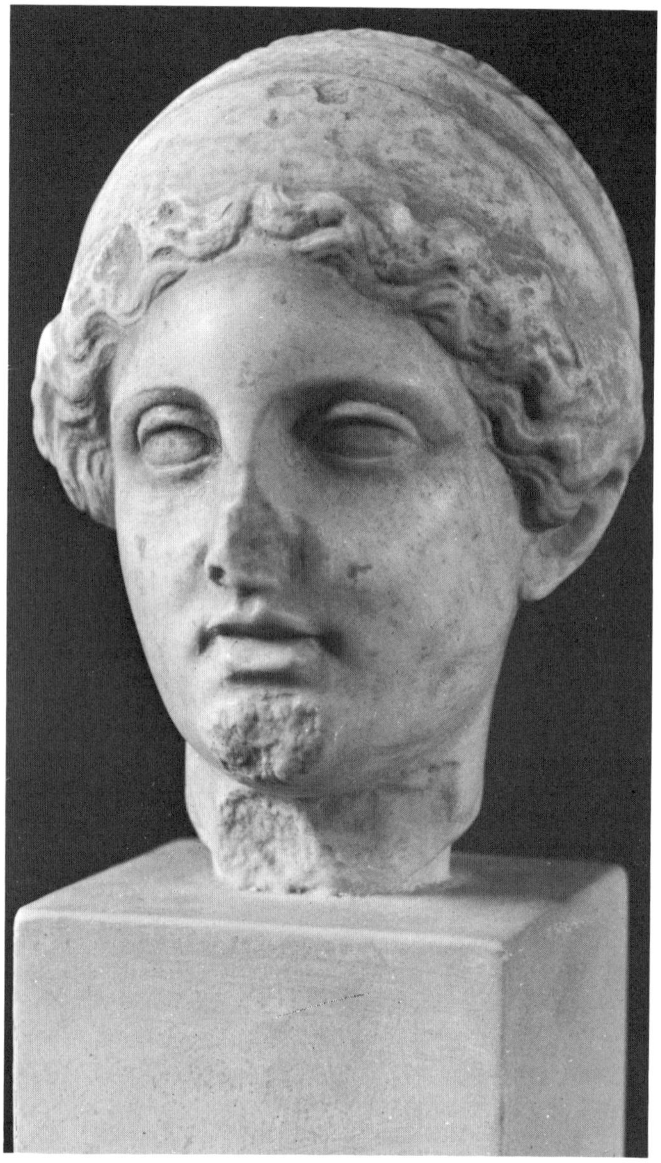

Head of Hygeia. The daughter of Asclepius, Hygeia was closely associated with her father's cult as the goddess of health and was frequently portrayed with him. The most important of his attendants, her mother, brothers and sisters also being auxiliary divinities of the god, she had a cult at Titane which was almost as honoured as his. Her name follows immediately after his and before that of her sister Panacea in the Hippocratic oath.

a ferocious lion which came to devour Amphitryon's herds. The hero, while waiting for the beast, hid in the house of King Thespius and, legend recounts, he made use of the occasion to lie in a single night with his host's fifty daughters.

Hercules shortly afterwards defended his native city against Orchomenus. He met the herald of Orchomenus, who had come to Thebes to collect the tribute, and cut off his nose and ears, thus starting the war. Amphitryon, fighting beside his two sons, was killed. But Hercules, aided by Athene, defeated Erginus, King of Orchomenus. Creon became king of that country and gave his daughter Megara to Hercules as a wife. Their marriage was unhappy. Hera sent Lyssa, the Fury of madness, to Hercules. The hero was seized with the deadly malady, mistook his own children for those of Eurystheus, and massacred them and their mother. After this grim crime Hercules had to flee the country. He went to Argolis where he spent twelve years under the orders of Eurystheus who imposed upon him the most arduous labours. For thus the oracle of Delphi had commanded when Hercules, wishing to remove the stain of his crime, consulted her.

THE TWELVE LABOURS

The Nemean Lion. The first monster that Hercules had to exterminate was the Nemean Lion, the skin of which Eurystheus ordered him to bring back. Hercules attempted in vain to pierce the beast with his arrows, then he engaged it hand to hand and finally strangled it in his powerful grip. But he kept the skin and from it made a garment which rendered him invulnerable. He then returned to Tiryns with his trophy.

The Lernaean Hydra. This hydra, born of Typhon and Echidna, was an enormous serpent with nine heads. Its den was a marsh near Lerna in the Peloponnese. It would issue forth to ravage the herds and crops; its breath moreover was so poisonous that whoever felt it fell dead.

Accompanied by Iolaus, son of Iphicles, Hercules arrived at Lerna, found the monster near the spring of Amymone and forced it to emerge from the marshes by means of flaming arrows. Then he tried to overwhelm it by means of his mighty club. But in vain; for every time he struck off one of the hydra's nine heads two grew in its place. Then Iolaus set the neighbouring forest on fire and with the help of red-hot brands burnt the serpent's heads. Hercules cut off the final head and buried it. Then he soaked his arrows in the hydra's blood which made them poisonous and deadly.

The Wild Boar of Erymanthus. This savage beast came down from Mount Erymanthus, on the borders of Arcadia and Achaia, and

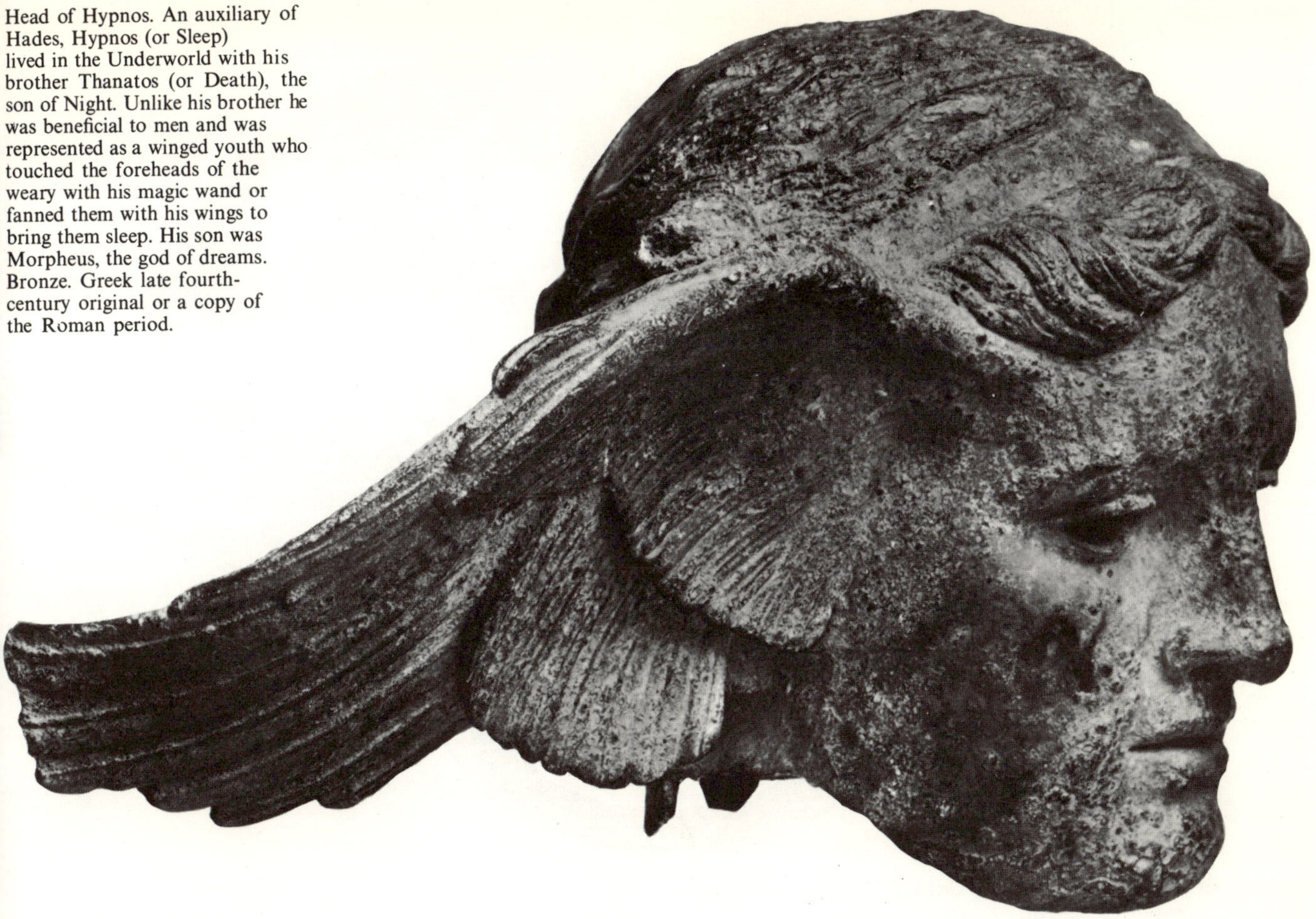

Head of Hypnos. An auxiliary of Hades, Hypnos (or Sleep) lived in the Underworld with his brother Thanatos (or Death), the son of Night. Unlike his brother he was beneficial to men and was represented as a winged youth who touched the foreheads of the weary with his magic wand or fanned them with his wings to bring them sleep. His son was Morpheus, the god of dreams. Bronze. Greek late fourth-century original or a copy of the Roman period.

devastated the territory of Psophis. Hercules succeeded in capturing it and carried it to Tiryns. Eurystheus was so terrified at the sight of the monster that he ran away and hid himself in a bronze jar.

On his way to Mount Erymanthus Hercules had received the hospitality of the Centaur Pholus, who in his honour broached a barrel of delicious wine which had been a present from Dionysus. The other Centaurs were attracted by the bouquet of the wine and came running to the house of Pholus, armed with stones and uprooted fir trees, to demand their share of the wine. Hercules drove them off with his arrows. The Centaurs were decimated, and took refuge near Cape Malea.

The Stymphalian Birds. The marshes of Stymphalus in Arcadia were peopled by monstrous birds whose wings, beaks and claws were of iron. They fed on human flesh and were so numerous that when they took wing the light of the sun was blotted out. Hercules frightened them with brazen cymbals and slew them with arrows.

The Ceryneian Hind. Eurystheus then ordered Hercules to bring him back the hind of Mount Ceryneia alive. Her hooves were of bronze and her horns of gold. Hercules chased her for an entire year before he at last caught her on the banks of the Ladon.

The Stables of Augeias. Augeias, King of Elis, owned innumerable herds of cattle among which were twelve white bulls sacred to Helios. One of them whose name was Phaethon was privileged to shine like a star. Unhappily these magnificent animals lived in foul stables, heaped high with manure of many years' accumulation. Hercules undertook to clean them out in one day on condition that the king gave him a tenth part of the herd. In order to do this he breached the walls of the building and, altering the course of the rivers Alpheus and Peneius, made them rush though the cow-sheds. When the job was done Augeias, under the pretext that Hercules was merely executing the orders of Eurystheus, refused to fulfil his part of the bargain. Later the hero was to punish this dishonesty.

The Cretan Bull. Poseidon had given Minos a bull, believing that Minos would offer it in sacrifice to him. As the king did nothing of the sort, Poseidon drove the animal mad. The country was terrorised and Minos appealed to Hercules who at the time happened to be in Crete. The hero managed to capture the animal which he carried on his back across the sea to Argolis.

The Mares of Diomedes. Diomedes, son of Ares and king of the Bistones, owned mares which he fed on human flesh. Hercules, accompanied by a few volunteers, approached Thrace and captured these terrible mares, having first killed their guardians. The alert was given, the Bistones rushed upon him and the battle began. Hercules at last vanquished his assailants and Diomedes was given to his own mares to eat.

The rescue of Alcestis is usually said to have taken place at this same time. Admetus, King of Pherae, had obtained from the Fates, through the intermediary of Apollo, an assurance that he would not die if someone consented to die in his stead. When the fatal moment arrived his wife, Alcestis, took his place. They were about to bury the unhappy woman when Hercules passed by and engaged in dreadful struggle with Thanatos – Death himself. Hercules succeeded in wrenching Alcestis from death's grasp and returned her to her husband.

The Girdle of Hippolyte. Hippolyte, whom some call Melanippe, was the Queen of the Amazons in Cappadocia. As a mark of her sovereignty she possessed a magnificent girdle given to her by Ares. Admete, daughter of Eurystheus, greatly coveted this marvellous adornment, and Hercules was therefore given orders to go and fetch it. Accompanied by several celebrated heroes – Theseus, Telamon, Peleus – he embarked. His first port of call was Paros where he fought with the sons of Minos. Next he reached Mariandyne in Mysia where he helped King Lycus to conquer the Bebryces. In gratitude Lycus built the town of Heracles Pontica.

When at last he reached the country of the Amazons Hercules at first encountered no obstacle: Hippolyte agreed to give him the girdle. But Hera was enraged and, disguising herself as an Amazon, spread abroad the story that Hercules planned to abduct the queen. The Amazons seized their weapons. Hercules, believing they had betrayed him, slaughtered the Amazons, together with their queen. He took the girdle and then proceeded towards Troy.

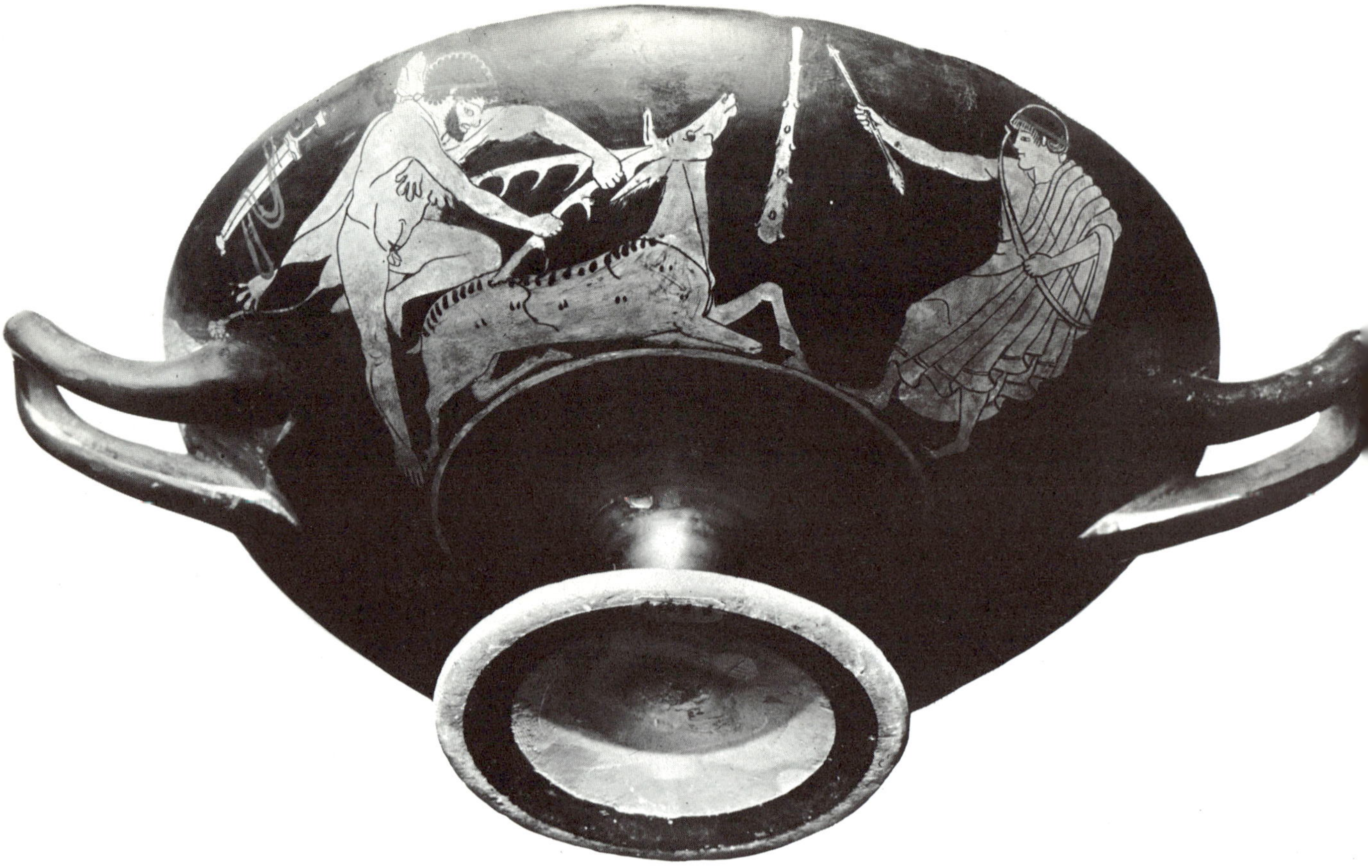

The Hind with the Brazen Hooves. The Cretan bull. Greek cup. Louvre.

The Cattle of Geryon. Geryon was a triple-bodied monster who reigned over the western coast of Iberia or, according to others, over the Epirus. He owned a herd of red oxen which were guarded by the herdsman Eurytion and the dog Orthrus. Hercules, on the orders of Eurystheus, took possession of the oxen after killing Eurytion, Orthrus and finally Geryon. On his return journey he had various adventures. He slew the sons of Poseidon who attempted to steal the oxen, and he had to go to Eryx, king of the Elymans, in Sicily, to recapture an ox which had escaped and been put in the stables of Eryx. Eryx refused to return the beast unless Hercules beat him in a series of boxing and wrestling bouts. Hercules finally overthrew and killed him. In the hills of Thrace Hera sent a gadfly which drove the animals mad; they dispersed through the mountains and Hercules had great trouble in herding them together again. When he had done so he brought the cattle to Eurystheus who sacrificed them to Hera.

It was in the course of this expedition that Hercules penetrated Gaul where he abolished human sacrifice. He fought the Ligurians with the aid of stones which Zeus caused to rain down from the sky and which covered the plain of the Crau. The river Strymon refused to let him cross and he filled up its bed with stones.

The Golden Apples of the Hesperides. Eurystheus next commanded Hercules to bring to him the golden apples which the Hesperides, daughters of Atlas and Hesperus, guarded in their fabulous garden at the western extremities of the world. Hercules first travelled towards the north where, on the banks of the Eridanus, the nymphs of the river advised him to consult Nereus about the route. Hercules succeeded in capturing the prophetic god who told him how to reach the garden of the Hesperides. Crossing Libya Hercules measured his strength with Antaeus, a monstrous bandit who forced all travellers to wrestle with him. Antaeus was the son of Gaea, Mother Earth, and had the power of regaining his strength by touching the earth with his feet. Hercules in the end choked him to death by holding him high in the air in his arms. Hercules was next attacked while asleep by the Pygmies. He sewed them up in his lion skin. Then he arrived in Egypt where Busiris, the king, sacrificed a foreigner every year in order to put an end to a terrible famine. Hercules was chosen as victim, put in chains and conducted to the temple. But he threw off his chains suddenly and slew Busiris and his son Amphidamas (Iphidamas). He then resumed his journey. He crossed Ethiopia where he killed Emathion, son of Tithonus, and replaced him by Memnon. He crossed the sea in a golden barque which the Sun had given him. In the Caucasus he slew with his arrows the eagle which gnawed the liver of Prometheus and finally reached the garden of the Hesperides. He killed the dragon Ladon which guarded the entrance, seized the apples and delivered them to Eurystheus. Eurystheus made him a gift of them and Hercules in his turn presented them to Athene who returned them to the Hesperides.

It was also related that Hercules was aided by Atlas on this enterprise. He persuaded Atlas to pick the apples while he, Hercules, meanwhile supported the world on his shoulders. When Atlas returned with the apples he was reluctant to reassume his traditional burden and would have refused to do so had not Hercules outwitted him.

Hercules' Journey to the Underworld. In despair of ever getting the better of Hercules, Eurystheus, as a final labour, commanded him to fetch Cerberus, guardian of the infernal gates. Hercules first had himself initiated into the infernal mysteries at Eleusis and then, guided by Hermes, he took the subterranean passage which descended at Cape Taenarum. Everything fled before him except Meleager and the Gorgon. Farther on Theseus and Peirithous, who had imprudently ventured into the Underworld, implored his assistance. Hercules saved Theseus, but was prevented from rescuing Peirithous by a sudden earthquake. He relieved Ascalaphus of the boulder which was crushing him, overthrew Menoetes, or Menoetius, the herdsman of Hades, wounded Hades himself and finally obtained the permission of Hades to carry off Cerberus, provided that he could conquer the monster without other weapons than his bare hands. Hercules leapt on Cerberus and at last mastered him by strangulation. Then he dragged the brute by the scruff of its neck back to earth, showed him to Eurystheus, and sent him back to Hades again.

Other Exploits of Hercules. When he was at last freed from servitude Hercules, far from resting on his laurels, set forth on new adventures.

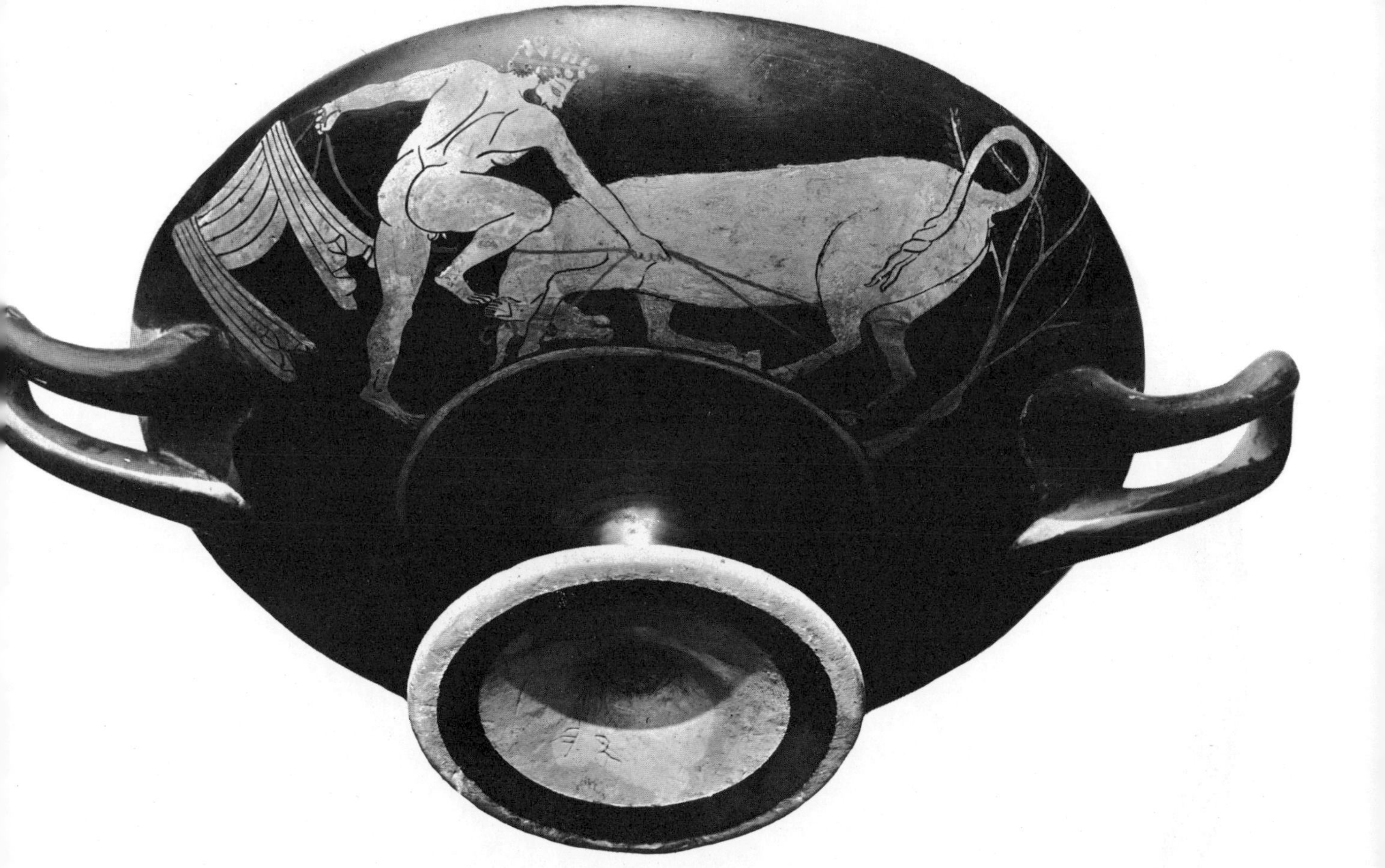

When King Eurytus promised the hand of his daughter Iole to him who vanquished him in an archery contest, Hercules arrived and triumphed. The king refused to keep his word. Shortly afterwards the king's son, Iphitus, asked Hercules to help him search for some stolen horses, and Hercules, distraught with fury, killed him. For this crime Hercules went to Delphi to be purified. The Pythia refused to answer him and Hercules made off with her tripod. A bitter quarrel with Apollo ensued in which Zeus himself had to intervene. At last the oracle condemned Hercules to a year's slavery, and obliged him to hand over his year's wages to Eurytus. It was Omphale, Queen of Lydia, who bought the hero when he was offered for sale as a nameless slave, for three talents. In spite of the tradition which showed Hercules during this period softened by pleasures and dressed in a long oriental robe while he spun wool at the feet of his mistress, he did not remain inactive. He captured the Cercopes, evil and malicious demons who were, perhaps, only a horde of brigands camped near Ephesus. He killed the king of Aulis, Syleus, who forced strangers to work in his vineyards and then cut their throats. He rid the banks of the Sagaris of a gigantic serpent which was ravaging the countryside, and finally threw the cruel Lityerses into the Maeander. Lityerses had been in the habit of forcing strangers to help with his harvest and then of cutting off their heads with a scythe. Omphale was overcome with admiration and restored the hero's freedom.

Hercules then offered to rescue Hesione, daughter of Laomedon, King of Ilium. This unfortunate princess had been chained to a rock, as an expiatory victim against an epidemic. A dragon had come to devour her. Hercules prevented the tragedy, but Laomedon refused to give him the reward which had been agreed upon. The hero returned to Ilium with six ships, besieged the town, took it by assault, killed Laomedon and his sons, and gave Hesione in marriage to his friend Telamon. On his return journey he was thrown onto the shores of the island of Cos by a storm raised by Hera. The inhabitants received him badly and he avenged himself by sacking the island and slaying its king, Eurypylus. Next, he took part at Phlegra in the battle between the gods and the giants.

Hercules had not forgotten the dishonesty of Augeias in the matter of the Augeian Stables. He marched against him and devastated his domain. He had on this occasion to fight the Molionids, sons of Poseidon. It was said that they had been hatched from a silver egg and had but one body with two heads, four arms and four legs.

While he was laying siege to Pylus Hercules did battle with Periclymenus who had the power of metamorphosis. When Periclymenus turned himself into an eagle Hercules destroyed him with a blow of his club.

Hercules also restored Tyndareus to his throne after he had been deprived of it by Hippocoon and his sons. Passing through Tegea in Arcadia Hercules seduced Auge, daughter of Aleus and a priestess of Athene. She bore him a son Telephus, whom she hid in the temple of the goddess. Athene, angered by this profanation, sent a plague to the country. Aleus discovered his daughter's shame and drove her away. She took refuge with King Teuthras in Mysia and exposed her child on Mount Parthenius. When Telephus grew to manhood he went in search of his mother. He found her in Mysia and, not recognising her, was on the point of marrying her when Hercules intervened and prevented the incest.

The last adventure of Hercules took place in Aetolia and in the land of Trachis. He obtained the hand of Deianeira, daughter of Oeneus, king of the Aetolians, after having triumphed over another suitor, the river-god Achelous. But shortly afterwards the accidental murder of young Eunomus, who served at his father-in-law's table, obliged Hercules to fly from the country, together with his wife. When he arrived at the river Evenus Hercules gave Deianeira to the Centaur Nessus to carry across to the opposite bank. But halfway across Nessus attempted to violate Deianeira. Hercules saw this and at once struck him with an arrow. As Nessus died he gave his blood to Deianeira, telling her that it would preserve the love and fidelity of her husband.

Unfortunately Hercules then conceived the fateful idea of going back to punish Eurytus. He slew Eurytus, together with his sons, and brought away Iole whom he had never ceased to love. On his return he stopped at Cenaeum in Euboea to offer a sacrifice to Zeus. Before doing so he sent his companion Lichas to Deianeira in Trachis to fetch a white tunic. Deianeira was worried at the thought that Iole was with her husband and, remembering the words of Nessus, soaked the tunic in the Centaur's blood before sending it to Hercules, hoping thus to regain his love. Scarcely had Hercules put

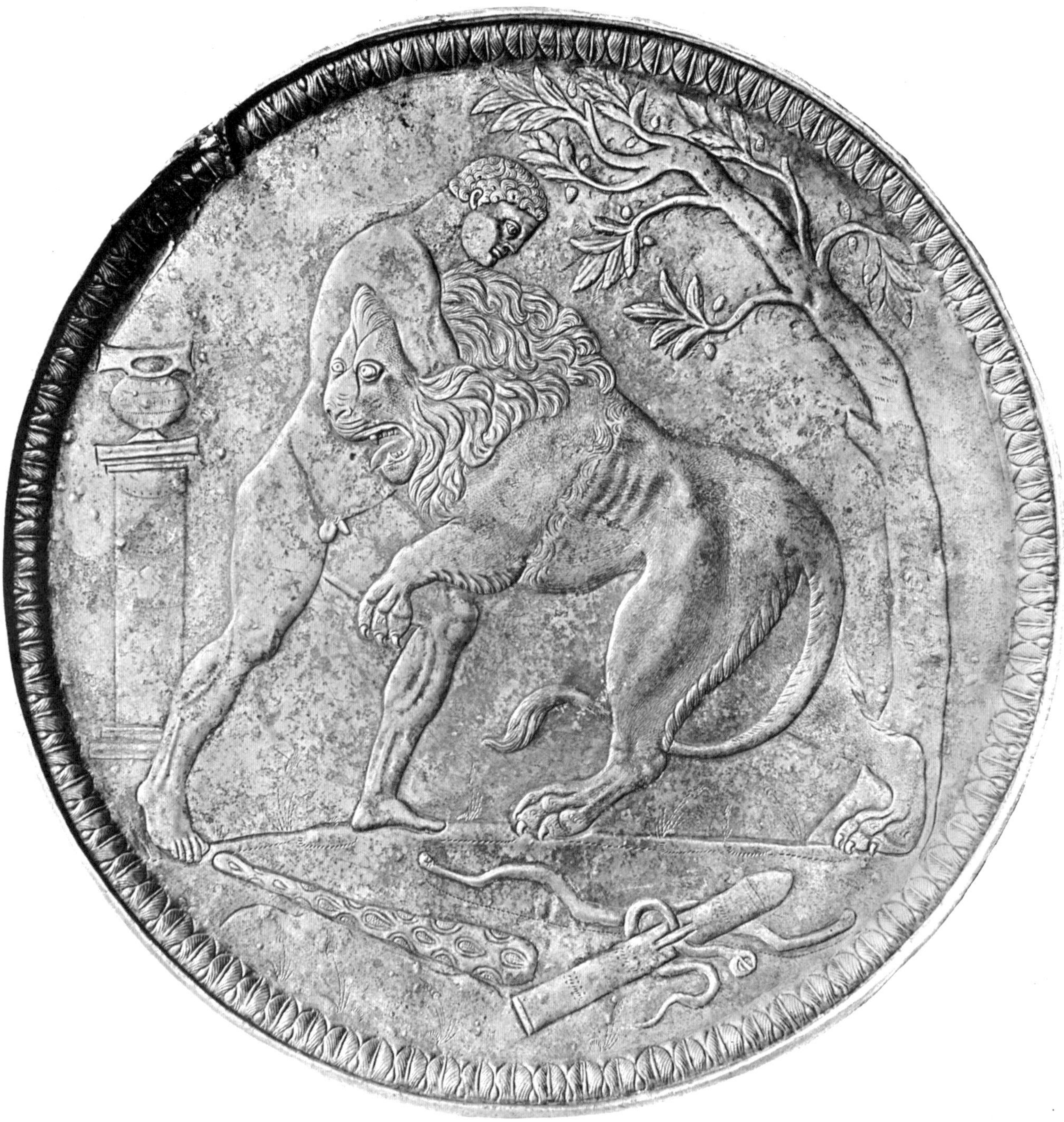

Hercules strangling the Nemean Lion. Silver platter. Bibliothèque Nationale, Paris.

on the tunic when he felt himself devoured by inner fire. Maddened with pain, he seized Lichas by the feet and flung him into the sea; then, tearing up pine-trees by their roots he made himself a funeral pyre, mounted it and ordered his companions to set it alight. All refused. Finally Poeas, father of Philoctetes, lighted the pines and Hercules rewarded him by giving him his bow and arrows.

The flames crackled and rose around the hero. At the moment they reached his body a cloud descended from the skies and in an apotheosis of thunder and lightning the son of Zeus disappeared from the eyes of men. He was admitted to Olympus where he was reconciled with Hera. He was married to her daughter Hebe and from then on lived the blissful and magnificent life of the Immortals.

The Progeny of Hercules. Legend ascribes nearly eighty sons to Hercules; their fortunes varied. Certain of them, more especially designated the Heraclids, distinguished themselves by conquering the Peloponnese.

After their father's death the sons of Hercules, fearing Eurystheus' persecution, left Mycenae and for a long time searched for refuge in vain. Finally Demophon, son of Theseus, received them in Athens. This was sufficient pretext for war between Eurystheus and the inhabitants of Attica. Iolaus, a former companion of Hercules, killed Eurystheus. The Heraclids then thought they could return to the Peloponnese. Their return was premature and caused an outbreak of the plague, and again they had to exile themselves.

Afterwards they attempted five consecutive invasions. Only the last one was successful. Its leaders were Temenus, Cresphontes and Aristodemus, great-grandsons of the hero. Allied with them were Dymas and Pamphylus, sons of the king of the Dorians. They chose the sea route and embarked at Naupactus to sail through the straits of Corinth. Before they left they had the misfortune to kill a prophet of Apollo. In anger the god destroyed their fleet and struck the expedition with famine. When the oracle of Delphi was consulted, it told the allies that they required a guide with three eyes. In the end they discovered a one-eyed man, Oxylus, who rode towards them on a horse and thus, with his mount, fulfilled the conditions of the oracle. Oxylus became leader of the expedition.

Tisamenus, son of Orestes, who reigned in Argos, perished in battle against the Heraclids and their Dorian allies, who then divided his country among themselves. Oxylus received Elis, Temenus was given Argos, the sons of Aristodemus obtained Sparta and Cresphontes took Messenia.

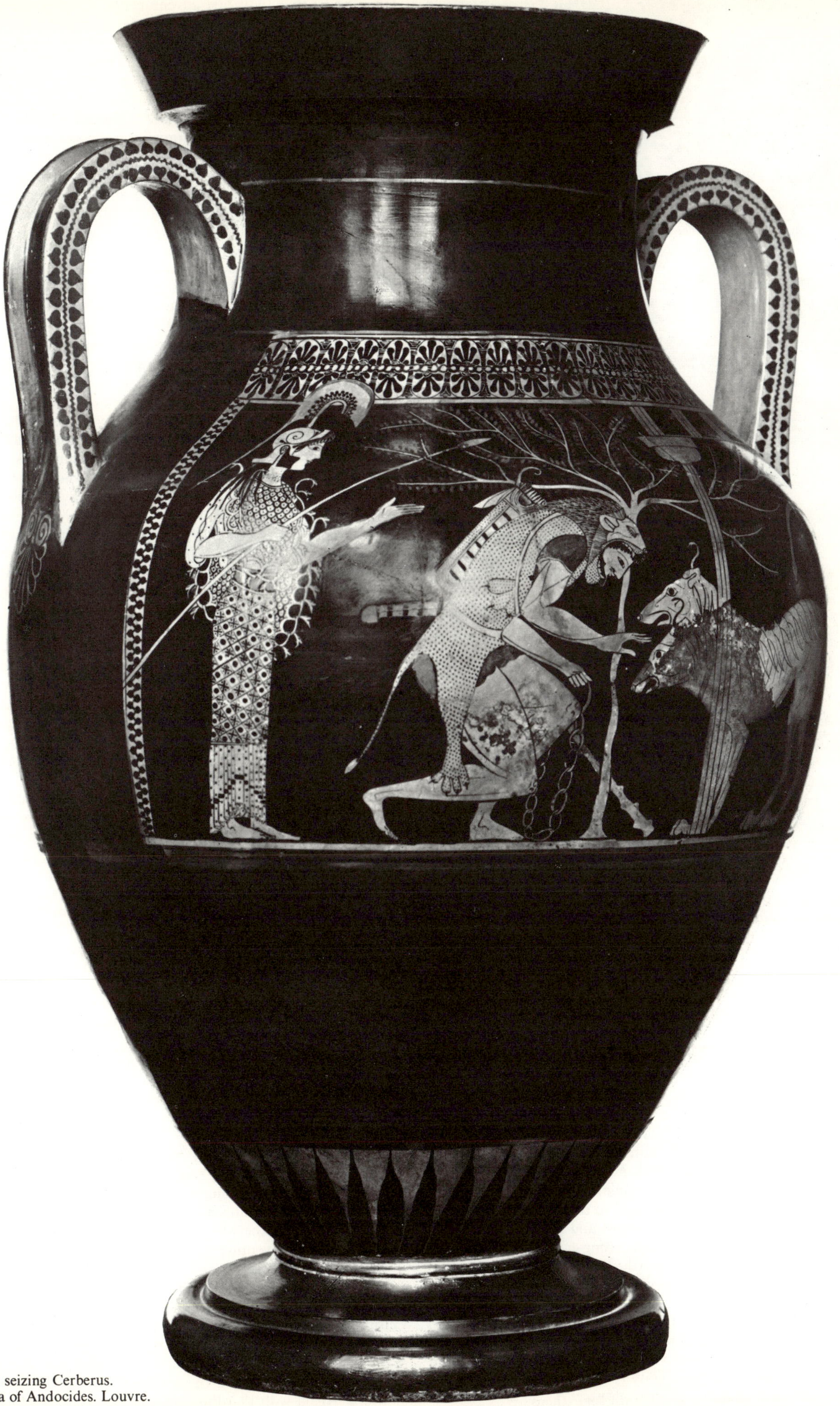

Hercules seizing Cerberus.
Amphora of Andocides. Louvre.

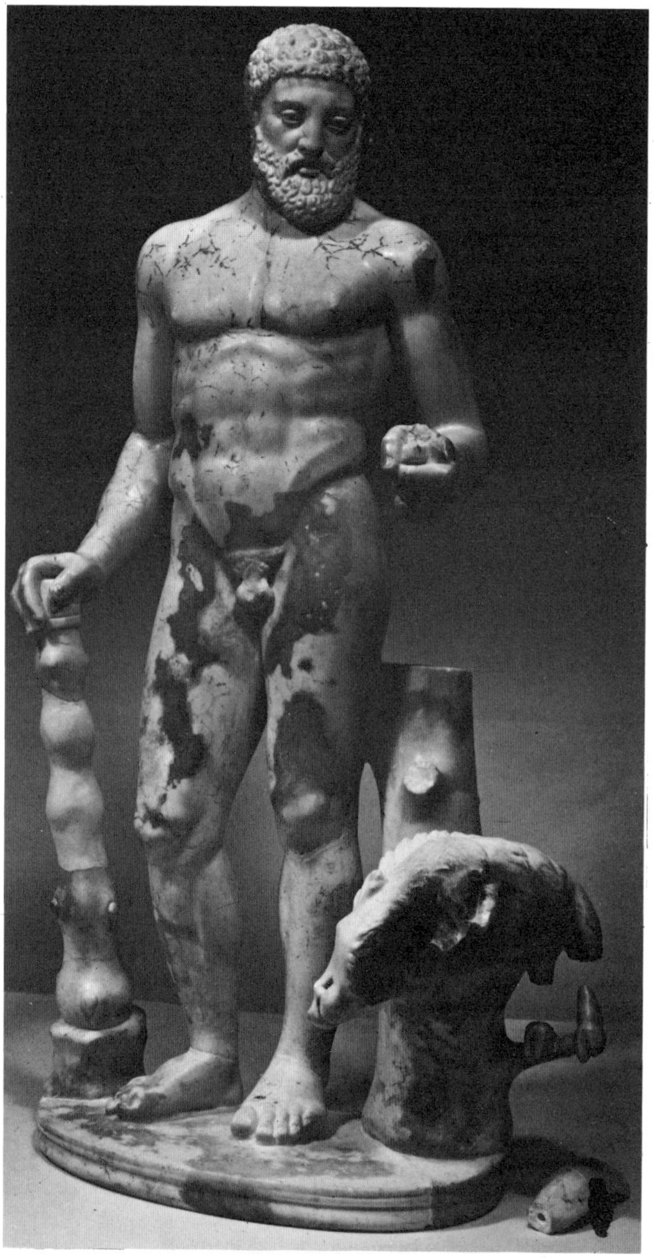

Hercules. The most popular of the Greek heroes, Hercules was worshipped throughout the whole of Greece. The personification of physical strength and the protector and counsellor of men, he was the son of Zeus and Alcmene who was herself descended from another hero – Perseus.
This statuette depicts him leaning on his club with a boar – possibly that of Erymanthus – caught in the branches of a tree beside him. Marble. Roman copy of a fifth-century Greek original.

THESEUS AND THE HEROES OF ATTICA

The Birth and Youth of Theseus. Theseus, like Hercules, was a great destroyer of monsters; and like Hercules he perished tragically. His birth was also analogous to the Theban hero's. His mother was Aethra, daughter of Pittheus, King of Troezen. She was loved at the same time by Aegeus, King of Athens, and by Poseidon. Theseus, who was conceived by this double union, thus had two fathers, a mortal and a god. Aegeus was obliged to return to Athens before the child was born and he hid his sword and his sandals under a heavy rock. When Theseus had grown strong enough to lift the rock and find these, he was to come to Athens and rejoin his father. So Theseus spent his childhood with his mother. When he was sixteen years old Aethra revealed the secret of his birth and showed him the famous rock of his father. Theseus had already shown bravery. As a child he had attacked, thinking it was alive, the body of the Nemean Lion which Hercules, visiting Pittheus, had placed on a table. Theseus now lifted the mighty rock, took possession of his father's sword and sandals and set forth for Athens.

His First Exploits. His first adventures occurred on his journey to Athens. Near Epidaurus, he killed a dangerous bandit, Periphetes, son of Hephaestus, and took from him his terrible club. In the forests of the Isthmus he inflicted on Sinis, son of Poseidon, the same torture which Sinis imposed on others; namely, tearing them asunder by tying them to sprung pine-trees. He killed the wild sow of Crommyon, called Phaea. On the slopes of Megaris he dashed Sciron against a boulder. Sciron had forced travellers to wash his feet and when they stooped to do so he would kick them over the cliff into the sea where they were devoured by a monstrous turtle. At Eleusis he vanquished Cercyon the Arcadian and, a little farther on, put an end to the criminal career of the giant Polypemon, known as Procrustes, who forced his victims to lie on a bed too short for them and then cut off whatever overlapped. Alternatively he would stretch them if the bed proved too long. Theseus made him undergo the same treatment. When he had purified himself after all these killings on the banks of the Cephissus, Theseus at last reached Athens.

He had donned a white robe and carefully arranged his beautiful fair hair. Hence, the workmen building the temple of Apollo Delphinios mocked at his innocent air and foppish appearance. Without deigning to reply Theseus picked up a heavy ox-cart and tossed it clean over the temple. Then he arrived at his father's palace. Aegeus had meanwhile married Medea who was instinctively jealous of the unknown newcomer and during the ensuing feast attempted to poison him. When Theseus drew his sword, his father recognised it and him. Aegeus then drove Medea and her children away and shared his throne with his son. From then on Theseus fought to strengthen his father's authority. First he exterminated the Pallantids who were nephews of Aegeus and had schemed to overthrow their uncle. Then he went in search of a wild bull which was devastating Attica. He succeeded in capturing the beast near Marathon, brought it back to Athens and sacrificed it to Apollo Delphinios.

Theseus and the Minotaur. In the midst of all this arrived ambassadors from Crete who for the third time had come to collect the annual tribute – seven virgins and seven young men – which had been imposed on Athens since the murder of Androgeus. These unfortunate young people were, when they arrived in Crete, thrown as food to a monster called the Minotaur. Theseus embarked with the victims with the intention of destroying the monster. He told his father that if he were victorious the ship when it returned would carry a white sail; if he were vanquished the black sail would be retained. When he arrived in Crete Theseus said that he was the son of Poseidon. Minos, to test this boast, tossed a golden ring into the sea and requested the hero to bring it back to him. Theseus dived in and returned not only with the ring but with a crown which Amphitrite had given him. Ariadne, the daughter of Minos, fell in love with Theseus and furnished him with a ball of string by means of which he could guide himself through the Labyrinth in which the Minotaur was kept and, after killing him, return. When Theseus had slain the beast he left Crete and took Ariadne and her sister Phaedra with him; but he abandoned Ariadne on the isle of Naxos. We have already seen how she was consoled by Dionysus.

In the joy of victory Theseus forgot to change the black sail which his ship was carrying. Aegeus saw it from the shore and, believing that his son was dead, threw himself into the sea. The ship which had been used on this expedition was piously preserved by the Athenians and carefully kept in a state of repair. It was named the Paralia and every year took gifts from Attica to Delos.

The Last Exploits of Theseus. At the death of his father Theseus became King of Attica and endowed his people with wise institutions. He united them in a single group, built a communal prytaneum in Athens, divided the citizens into three classes, erected temples and instituted the Panathenaea. At the same time he continued his wandering life of adventure.

He accompanied Hercules on his expedition against the Amazons, took part in hunting the wild boar of Calydon and sailed with the Argonauts. He was usually accompanied by his faithful friend Peirithous who at first had been his enemy. With Peirithous he also attacked the Amazons and abducted one of them, Antiope – which was the motive for an Amazonian invasion of Attica. Antiope bore him a son, Hippolytus, but he repudiated her and instead married Phaedra. Again with Peirithous he went to Sparta and carried off

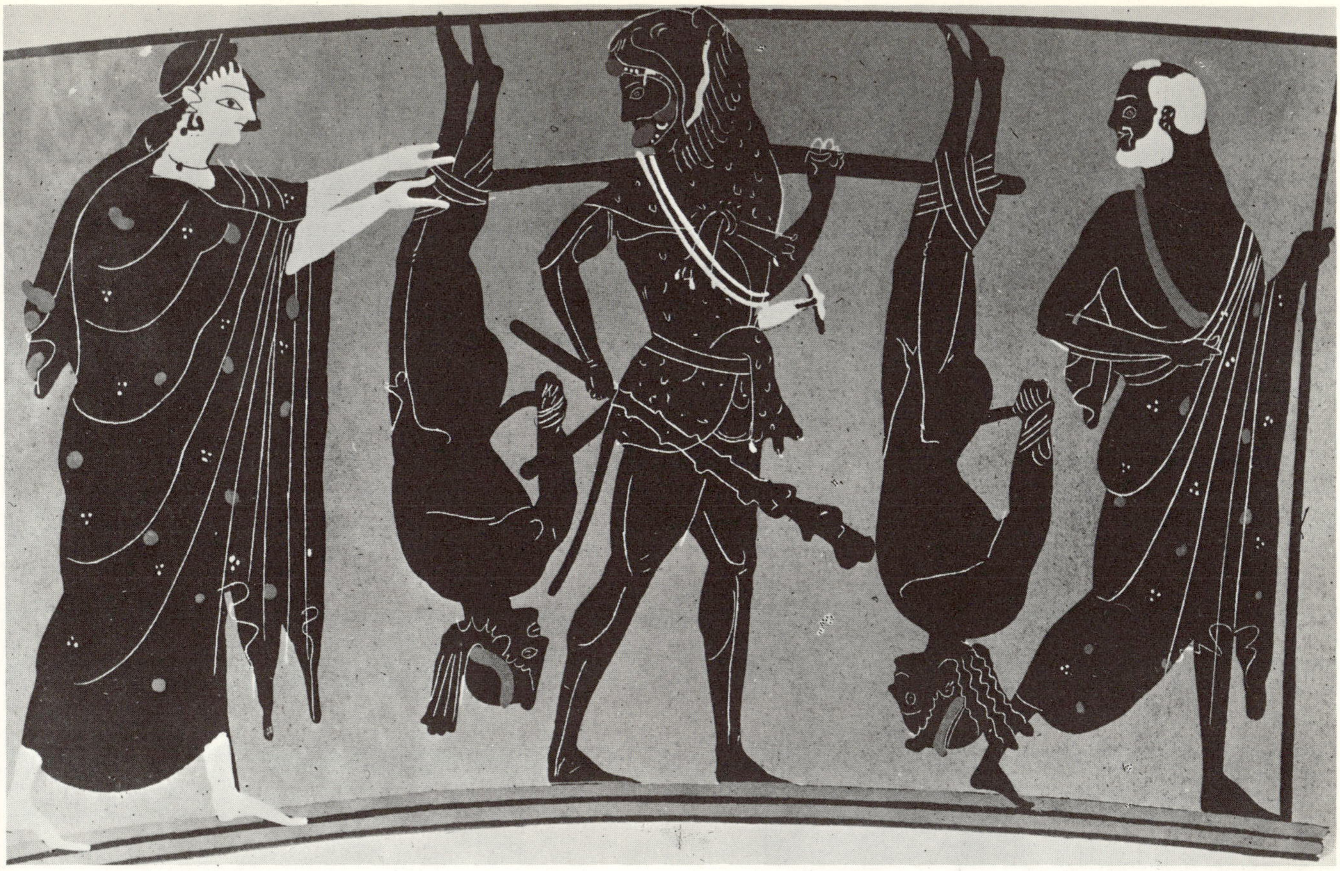

Hercules carrying the Cercopes. While spending a year as the slave of Omphale, queen of Lydia, as his punishment for carrying off the Pythia's tripod from Delphi, Hercules did not entirely relinquish his heroic character and succeeded in capturing the two Ephesian Cercopes who travelled the world working mischief and who had constantly plagued him. Here he carries off the two brothers dressed in the invulnerable pelt of the Nemean lion.

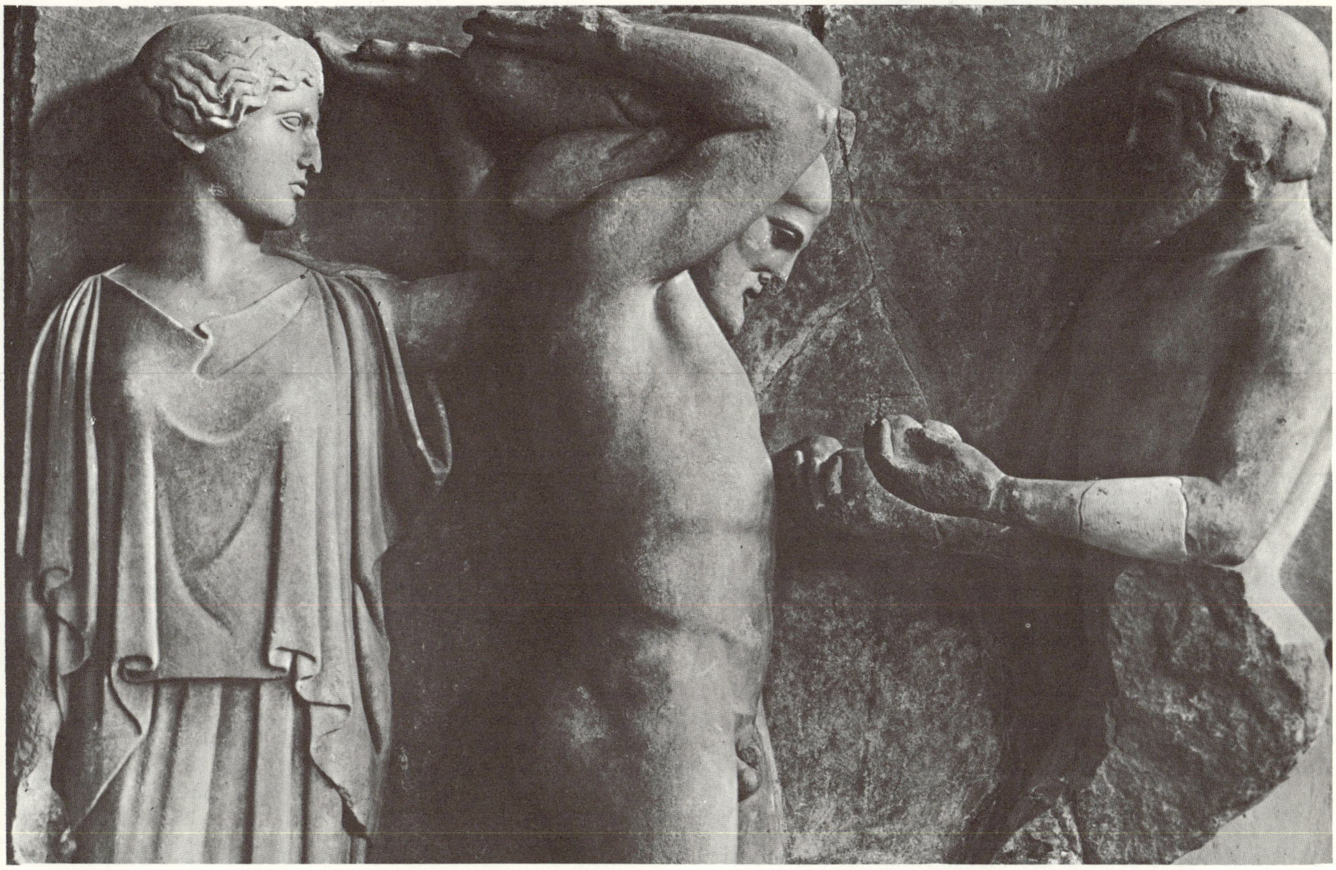

Atlas bringing Hercules the apples of the Hesperides. As the eleventh of his twelve labours Hercules had been ordered to bring back the golden apples guarded by Atlas' daughters, the Hesperides. In the second version of the story Atlas himself fetched the apples while the hero supported the world on his shoulders in his place. In this relief he is assisted in this task by Athene. Metope from the temple of Zeus at Olympia. Parian marble, *c.* 450 B.C.

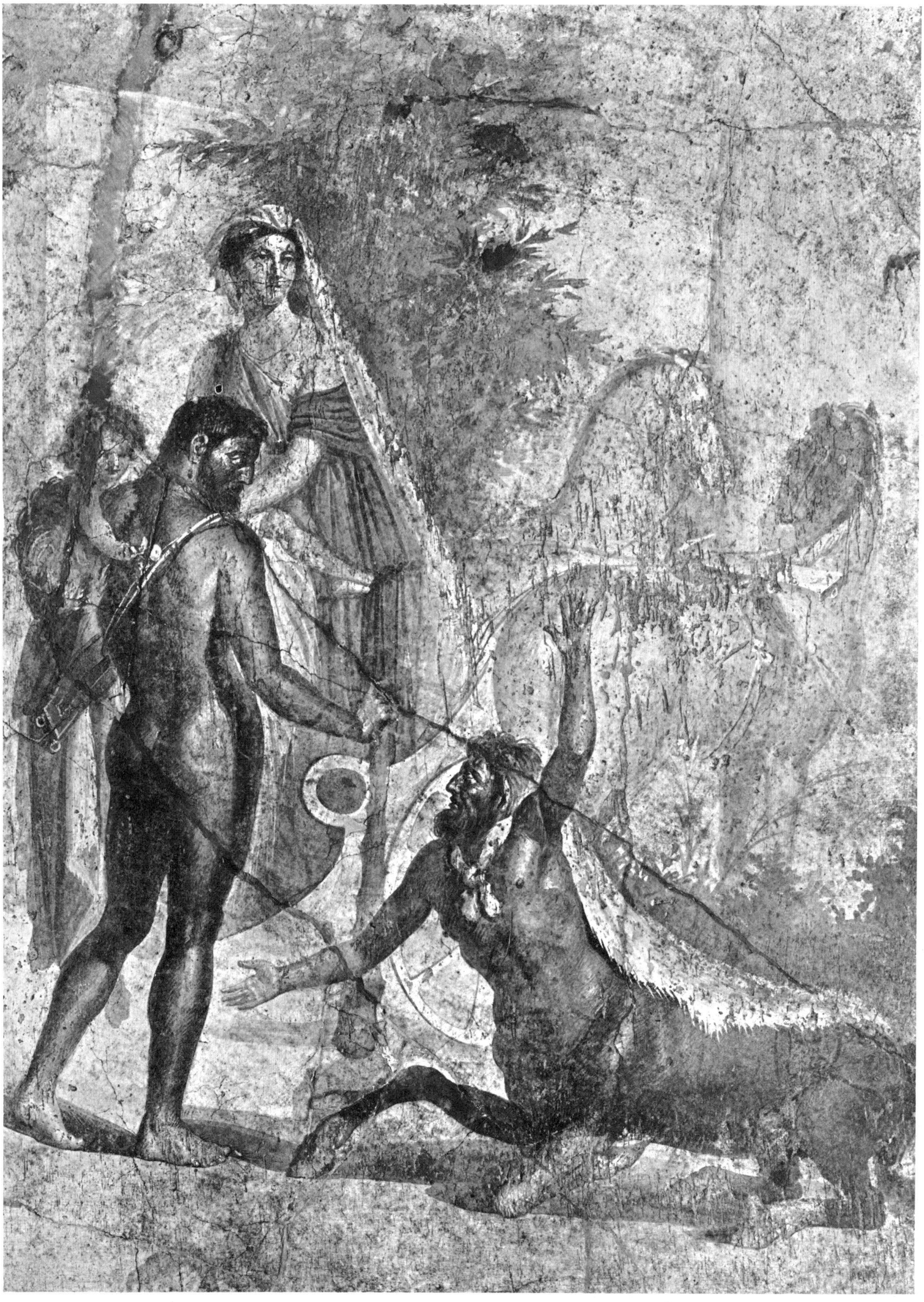

Hercules and Nessus at the river Evenus. Obliged to flee from Aetolia with his wife and son, Hercules had been held up by the river Evenus which was in flood. Here, with his son on his back, he asks the Centaur Nessus to carry Deianeira across to the other bank. The Centaur attempted to carry her off and Hercules killed him with a poisoned arrow. Wall-painting from Pompeii.

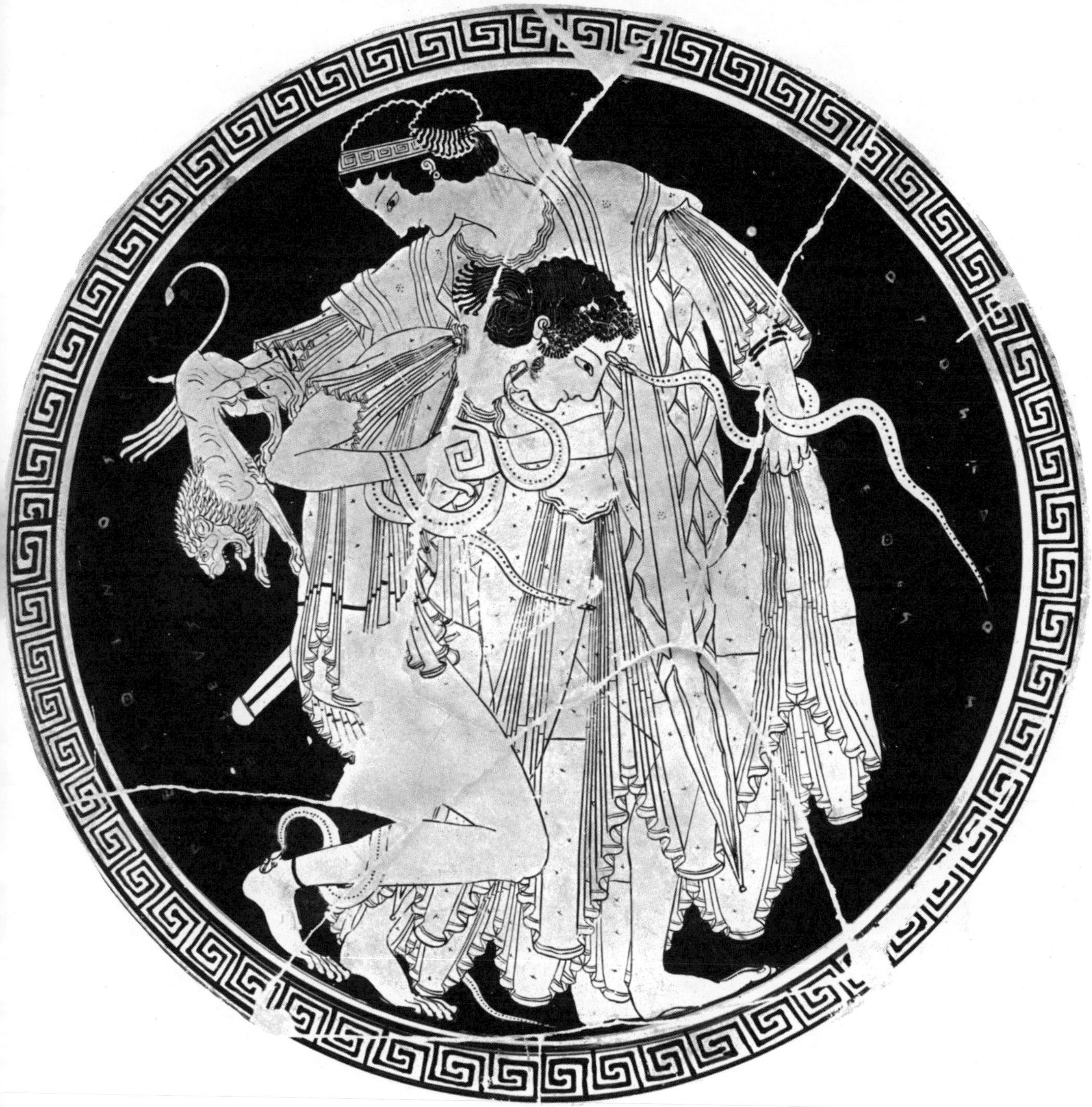

Peleus wrestling with Thetis. Humiliated at being ordered to marry a mortal, the Nereid Thetis attempted to escape from her future husband by turning herself successively into fire, water, a lion and a serpent. With Chiron's advice the Thessalian hero succeeded in overcoming her resistance and they were finally married. Their son was Achilles. Bottom of a Greek cup by the painter Peithinos. Late sixth century B.C.

young Helen. The two friends drew lots for her and she fell to Theseus. To console himself Peirithous decided to abduct Persephone, and the two heroes set forth for the Underworld. They succeeded in getting in, but they could not get out again and it required Hercules to rescue Theseus. When he returned to Athens the king found his house in an uproar. The Dioscuri, as Helen's brothers were called, had come to take their sister back; and Phaedra had conceived an incestuous passion for her son-in-law Hippolytus, who, being consecrated to Artemis, had made a vow of chastity and refused her. In chagrin Phaedra told Theseus that his son had made an attempt on her honour, and Theseus, too credulous, banished Hippolytus and called down Poseidon's wrath on the youth. The god summoned up a marine monster who terrified Hippolytus' chariot horses, and Hippolytus was crushed to death. At Troezen his tomb could be seen near the tomb of Phaedra. In the temple which was consecrated to him maidens, on the vigil of their wedding, would hang up a lock of their hair.

Sorely stricken by these tragedies, Theseus left Athens and retired to Scyros, to the palace of King Lycomedes. But Lycomedes was jealous of his guest's great fame and treacherously threw him into the sea. The remains of Theseus were interred at Scyros and later found by Cimon who brought them back to Athens and placed them in the sacred enclosure of the Theseum.

OTHER HEROES OF ATTICA

Cecrops. Cecrops, who was called Autochthonus or 'born of the earth', was regarded as the founder of Athens. It was during his reign that the dispute between Athene and Poseidon for the possession of Attica took place.

Erichthonius. Erichthonius was the son of Hephaestus who had engendered him by Gaea, the Earth, after being repulsed by Athene. In spite of this, Athene took charge of the infant, enclosed him in a chest which she confided to Pandrosos, the eldest daughter of Cecrops, forbidding her to open it. But the sisters of Pandrosos could not control their curiosity. When they saw that the newly born child was entwined by a serpent they were seized with terror.

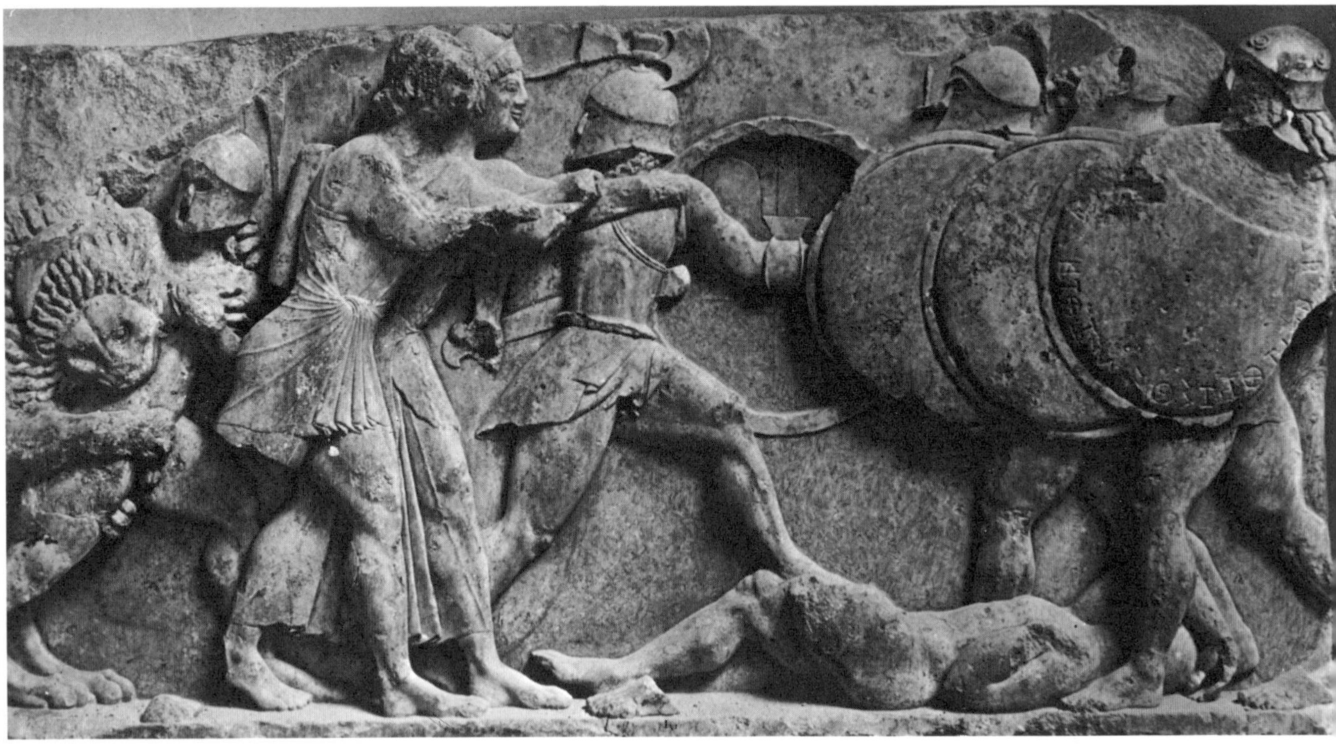

The battle between the gods and giants. The gods are advancing from left to right against the attacking giants in this archaic relief from Delphi. On the left one of the lions drawing Cybele's chariot seizes a giant while Apollo and Artemis advance before him shooting arrows behind a fleeing giant. On the right three more giants advance over the body of a fallen comrade. Detail from the north frieze of the Siphnian treasury at Delphi. Parian marble, *c.* 525 B.C.

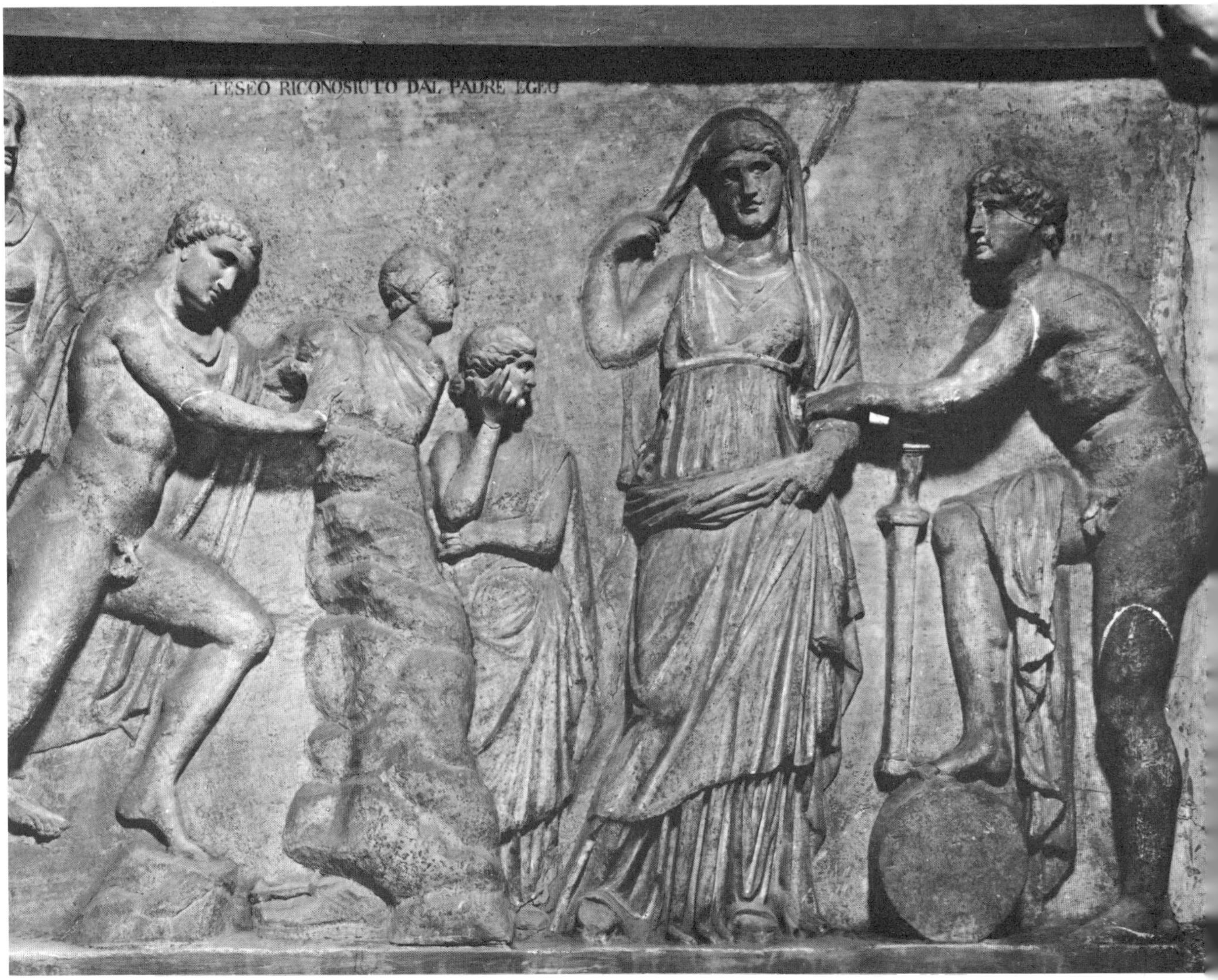

Theseus is recognised by his father. Bas-relief. Villa Albani, Rome.

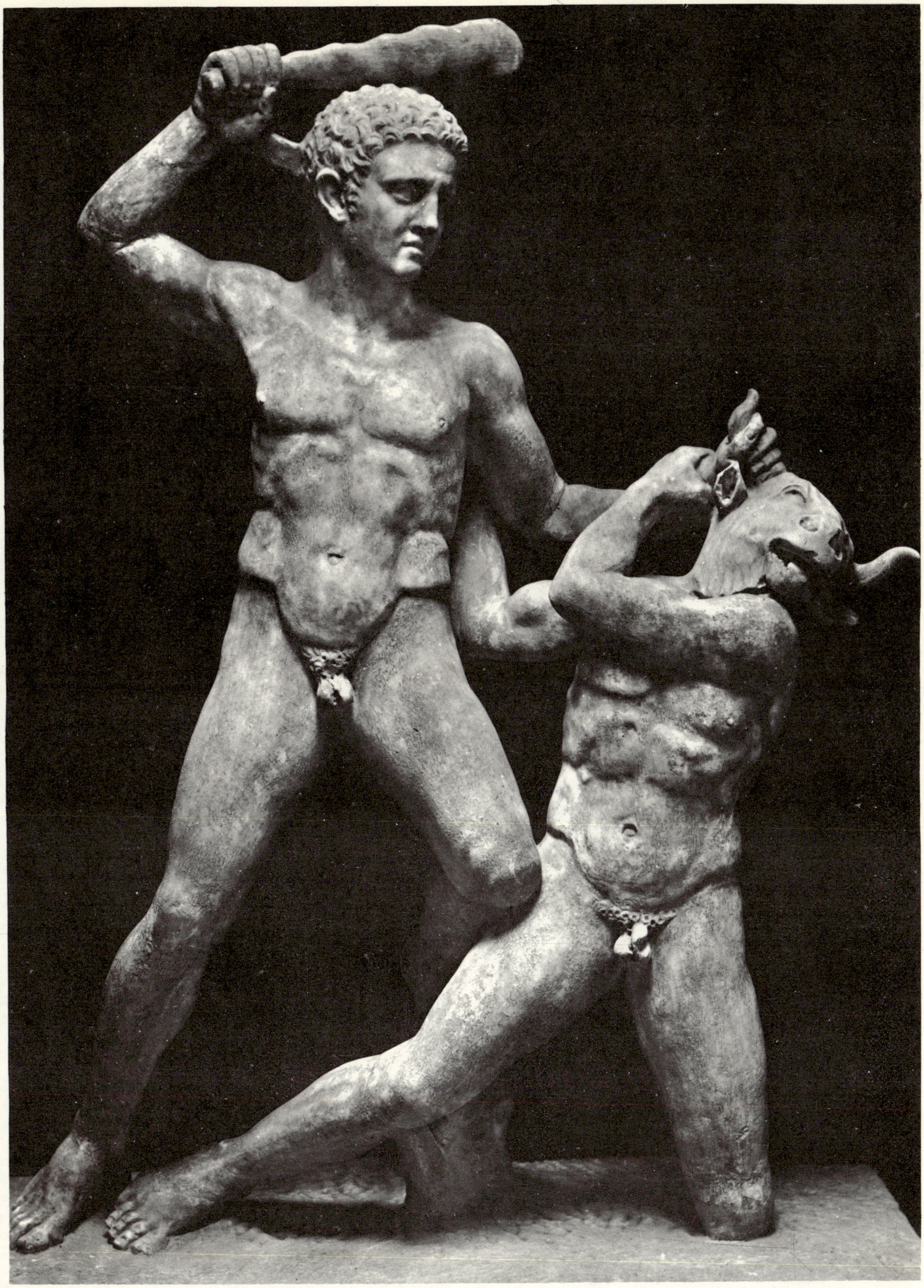

Theseus killing the Minotaur. When Minos sent to Athens for the third time for his annual tribute of seven youths and seven maidens to be fed to the Minotaur, Theseus offered himself as one of the victims and sailed with them to Crete. With the assistance of Ariadne, the daughter of Minos, he succeeded in finding the monster within the labyrinth and slew him with his club.

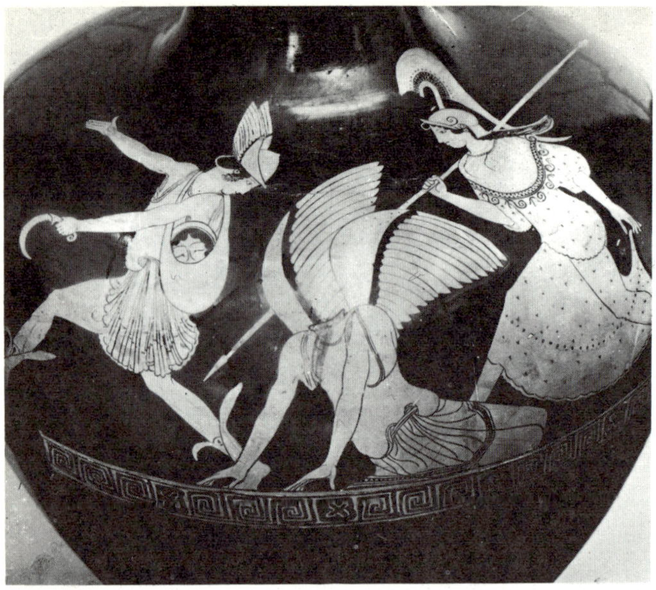

Persus fleeing after slaying the Gorgon, Medusa.
The hero of Argolis makes off towards the left, his head turned to look at the decapitated body of the Gorgon which sinks to the ground behind him. In his left hand he carries the *harpe* with which he has just killed her while in a wallet round his neck he bears her severed head. The goddess Athene follows behind him. Greek red-figured vase.

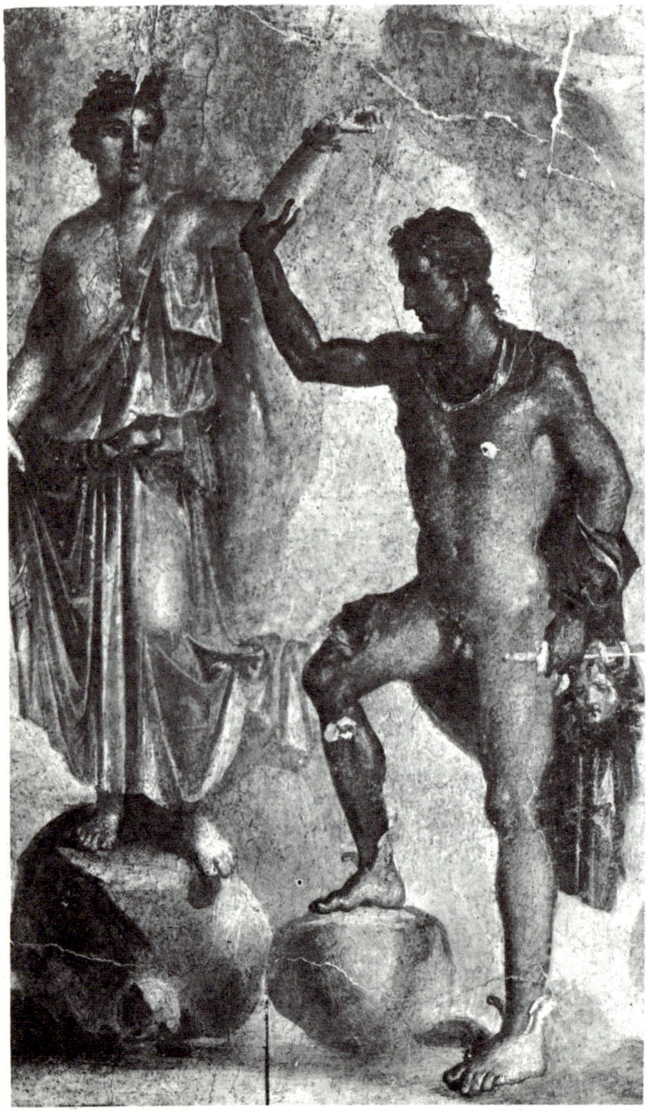

Perseus rescuing Andromeda.
Mural painting from Pompeii in the National Museum, Naples.

In their wild flight they fell from the top of the Acropolis and were killed.

Erichthonius was King of Athens; he introduced the worship of Athene and the use of silver. He made war on Eumolpus and the Eleusinians. This Eumolpus, son of Poseidon, had come from Thrace to Eleusis and there instituted the mysteries of Demeter. It was told how Eumolpus was slain by Erichthonius and how, in expiation of the murder, Poseidon demanded the death of one of the King of Athens' daughters. There were four of them and they decided to die together. As for Erichthonius, Zeus struck him dead with a thunderbolt.

Descendants of Erichthonius. One of his daughters, Oreithyia, was seen one day by Boreas while she was playing on the shore; he carried her off and married her. Another daughter, Creusa, was loved by Apollo and by him had a son, Ion, whose adventure has been related in the chapter on Apollo.

Pandion, son of Erichthonius, succeeded him to the throne of Athens. He had three daughters: Procris, Philomela and Procne. All three had tragic fates. Procris was married to Cephalus and we have already seen how the jealousy of Eos brought unhappiness to the couple.

Philomela and Procne. When Pandion made war on Labdacus, King of Thebes, he was assisted by Tereus, King of Thrace, to whom he had given his daughter, Procne, in marriage. Procne bore Tereus a son, Itys. But when Tereus laid eyes on Philomela, his sister-in-law, he fell in love with her, violated her and, for fear that she would reveal the crime, cut out her tongue. Nevertheless the wretched Philomela was able to tell her sister what had occurred by embroidering the shocking story on a peplos. Procne, out of her mind with rage, killed Itys and served him to Tereus for dinner. Then she and Philomela fled while the tyrant Tereus pursued them with drawn sword. A benevolent deity intervened and turned Tereus into a hoopoe, Procne into a swallow and Philomela into a nightingale. As for Itys, he was resuscitated and changed into a goldfinch.

BELLEROPHON AND THE HEROES OF CORINTH

Sisyphus. If Bellerophon was Corinth's most valiant hero, his grandfather, Sisyphus, was its most cunning. Sisyphus was the son of Aeolus and founded Ephyra, the ancient name of Corinth. As far back as Homeric times he was reputed to be the craftiest of men. Sometimes he was even alleged to be the father of Odysseus, so great was their resemblance in this respect. It was Sisyphus who told the river-god Asopus that his daughter Aegina had been abducted by Zeus. Zeus in fury sent Thanatos for him, but the cunning Sisyphus succeeded in trapping the god of death and it required Ares to set him free. This time Sisyphus had to submit to his destiny. But before dying he advised his wife not to pay him funeral honours. He had scarcely arrived in the Underworld when he went to Hades to complain of his wife's negligence and to ask for permission to go back to earth for a moment in order to punish her. Permission was granted and Sisyphus, back on earth again, refused to return to the Underworld. Hermes had to deal personally with this recalcitrant shade. Sisyphus was punished for his bad faith by being condemned eternally to roll up the slope of a mountain an enormous boulder which, each time it nearly reached the summit, rolled down again.

Bellerophon. Sisyphus had a son, Glaucus, who offended Aphrodite and, in the course of funeral games, was trampled and killed by his horses, whom the goddess had driven mad. Afterwards the ghost of Glaucus continued to frighten horses. The son of Glaucus, Hipponous, was more celebrated under the name of Bellerophon, which was given to him after he had murdered a Corinthian named Bellerus. In expiation of the murder Bellerophon went to the palace of Proetus, King of Tiryns. The King's wife, Stheneboea, at once fell in love with the young hero. Bellerophon scorned her and she told her husband that he had attempted to seduce her. Proetus did not dare to kill a man who was his guest and, instead, sent him to his father-in-law, Iobates, with a sealed message containing his death sentence. Iobates imposed various tasks on Bellerophon, trusting that in the attempt to accomplish them he would perish. First, he ordered Bellerophon to fight the Chimaera. Now Bellerophon had a marvellous winged horse called Pegasus, born of the Gorgon's

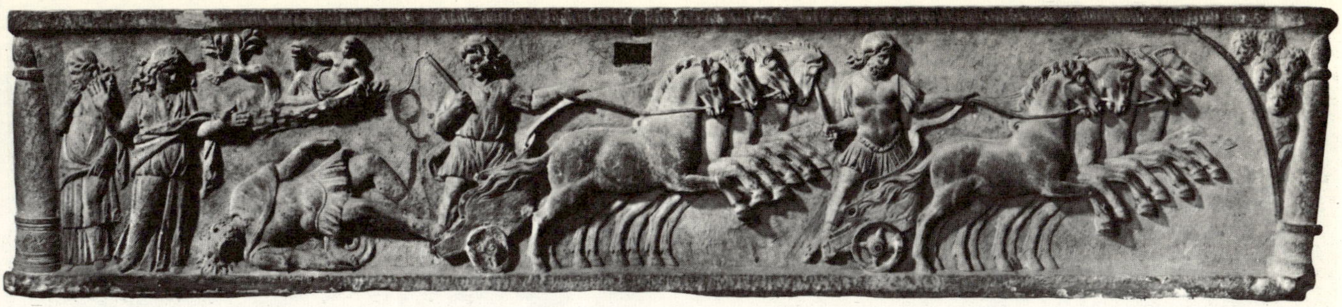

Chariot race between Pelops and Oenomaus. Bas-relief on a sarcophagus in the Vatican Museum, Rome.

blood, which he had succeeded in taming thanks to a golden bridle that Athene gave him. Mounted on Pegasus, Bellerophon flew over the Chimaera and stuffed the monster's jaws with lead. The lead melted in the flames which the Chimaera vomited forth and killed it.

Bellerophon next triumphed over the savage tribes of the Solymia and the Amazons. On his return he successfully overcame an ambuscade which Iobates had laid for him. Iobates was so filled with admiration that he gave the hero his daughter in marriage. The end of Bellerophon's life, however, was tragic. His two children, Laodameia and Isandrus, were slain, the first by Artemis, the second by Ares. According to Pindar Bellerophon himself attempted to reach Olympus on his flying steed, but was flung to earth by Zeus and lamed by his fall. Odious to all the Immortals, Homer says, Bellerophon wandered the earth, his heart consumed with misery, alone, fleeing the haunts of men.

PERSEUS AND THE HEROES OF ARGOLIS

When Io, daughter of the river-god Inachus, arrived in Egypt after all her tribulations she brought a son into the world, Epaphus. The great-grandsons of Epaphus were Aegyptus and Danaus. Both married, and Aegyptus had fifty sons while Danaus had fifty daughters. A quarrel broke out between the two brothers and on Athene's advice Danaus embarked with his fifty daughters and sailed towards Greece. He landed on the Peloponnesian coast and was received at Argos by Gelanor, the King, whose crown he shortly afterwards seized.

Some time later the sons of Aegyptus came to find their uncle, Danaus, and as a token of reconciliation asked him for the hand of his daughters. Danaus consented, but his rancour still seethed. On their wedding day he gave each of his daughters a dagger and ordered her to kill her husband during the night. All obeyed with the exception of Hypermnestra, who fled with her husband Lynceus. We have seen how the Danaids were condemned to everlasting torture in the infernal regions.

The grandsons of Hypermnestra, Proetus and Acrisius, were also brother enemies. Proetus was finally driven from Argos by his brother and retired to Lycia where he married the daughter of Iobates, Stheneboea. Then he laid claim to his share of Argolis and seized Tiryns where he settled, after having made peace with his brother Acrisius.

Acrisius, who grieved at having no heir, learned from the oracle at Delphi that his daughter Danaë would have a son who would kill his grandfather, namely himself. In vain he shut Danaë up in a subterranean chamber. We have already seen how Zeus, in the guise of a shower of gold, reached Danaë and made her the mother of a son, Perseus. Again, in vain, Acrisius put mother and son into a chest which he cast into the sea: they were washed ashore at Seriphos and taken in by Polydectes, king of that country. Some years later Polydectes fell in love with Danaë, but was embarrassed by the presence of Perseus who had become a robust young warrior. He therefore pretended that he wished to marry Hippodameia and asked his vassals to bring wedding gifts. Each did his best and Perseus, anxious to distinguish himself, promised to bring back the Gorgon's head. Polydectes was relieved to think he had seen the last of him.

Perseus then left Seriphos and reached the abode of the Graeae, frightening old shrews who among them had but one tooth and one eye which all three used in turn. Perseus stole their single tooth and only eye, and in this way persuaded them to tell him where the Gorgons lived. From them he also stole a magic wallet and a dark helmet which rendered its wearer invisible.

Thus equipped Perseus reached the westernmost extremities of the earth where, says Aeschylus, 'dwell monsters abhorred by mortals, with locks of serpents, whom none look upon without perishing'. They were the three sisters Stheno, Euryale and Medusa, daughters of Phorcys and Ceto. Instead of teeth they had the tusks of wild boars, their hands were of bronze, golden wings were fixed to their shoulders, and whoever dared to look them in the face was instantly turned to stone. Only one of them was mortal, Medusa. It was therefore she whom Perseus attacked. Armed with a bronze

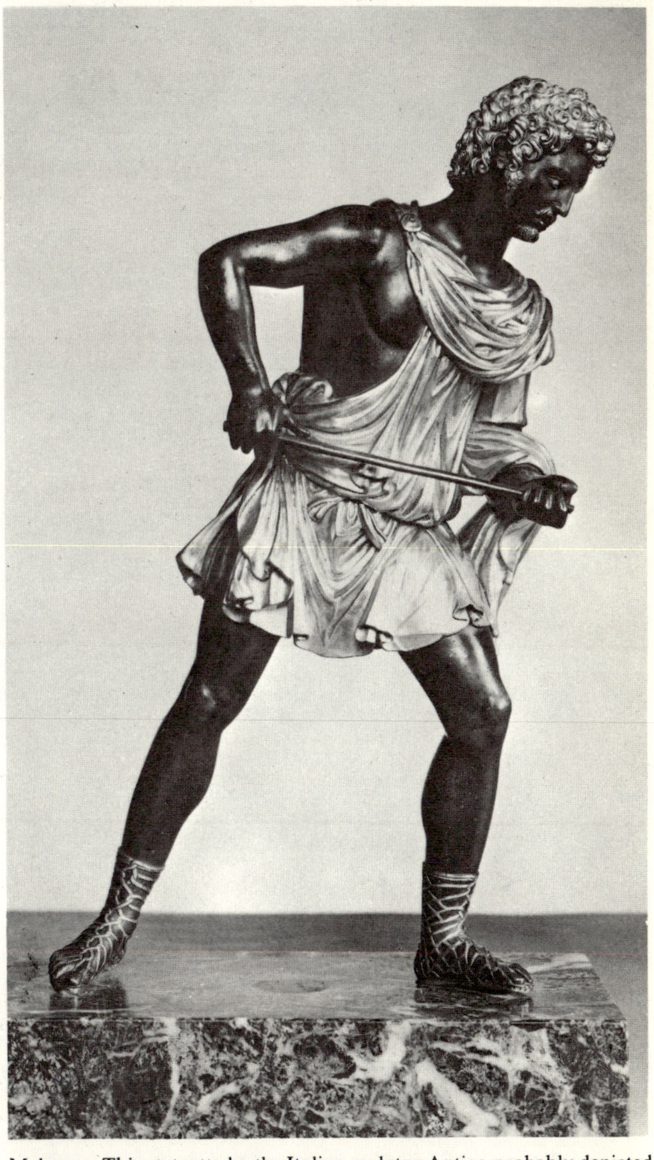

Meleager. This statuette by the Italian sculptor Antico probably depicted the Aetolian hero dispatching the Calydonian boar.
Unfortunately, in an ensuing quarrel over its pelt, Meleager killed his two uncles and some say that to revenge their deaths his mother then destroyed the brand which preserved his life. Others say that she merely cursed him and that he was finally killed in battle by Apollo.
Bronze, parcel gilt.
Late fifteenth or early sixteenth century.

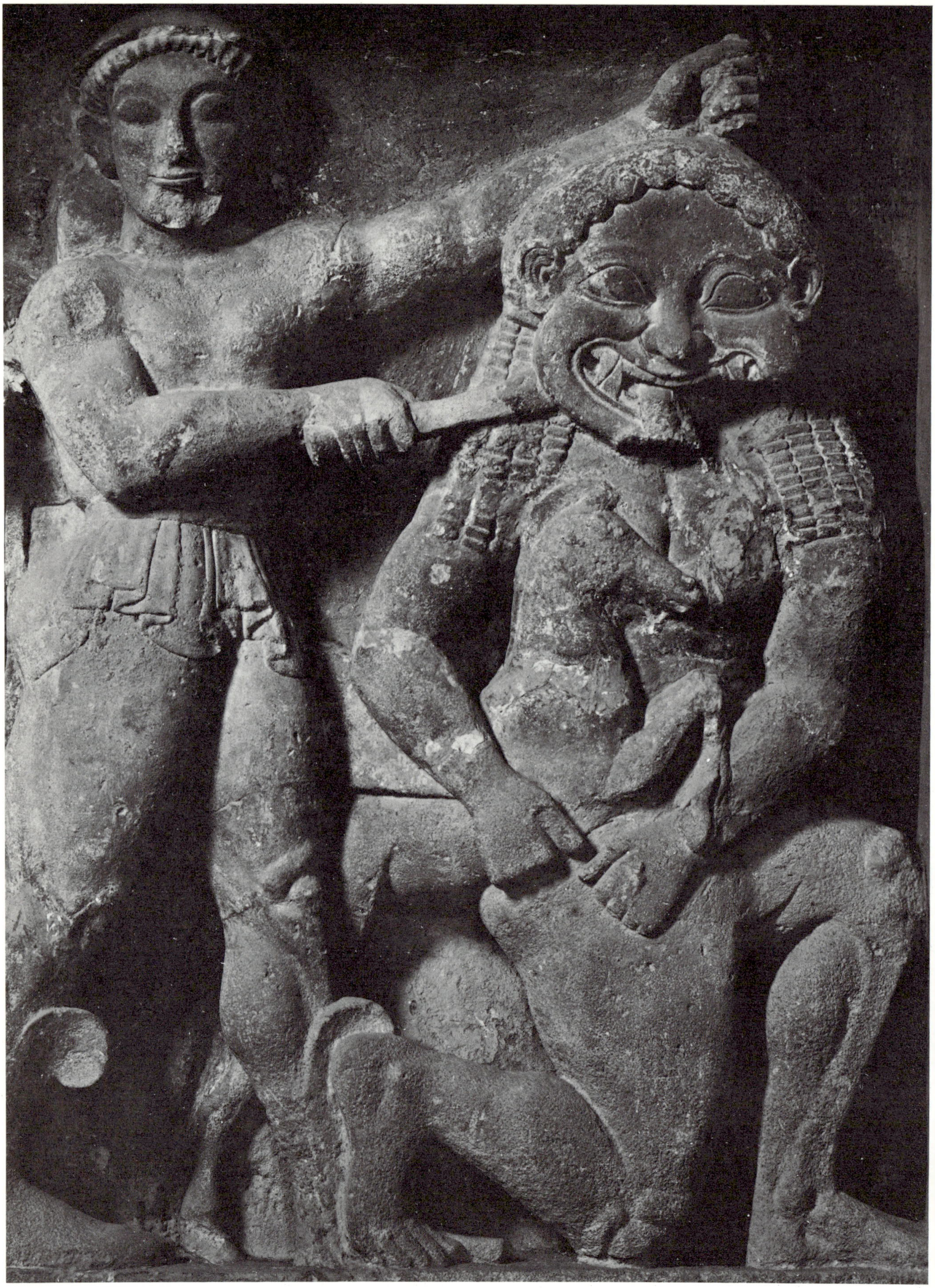

Perseus killing the Gorgon. Metope from Selinus. Palermo Museum.

Facing: Pegasus followed by a Centaur. Born of the Gorgon's blood, the winged horse Pegasus was later tamed by Bellerophon with the help of Athene and finally ascended to Olympus where he carried Zeus' thunderbolts. A favourite of poets and painters, it was he who had stamped out the spring Hippocrene on Mount Helicon for the Muses. The Centaur is shown as a man with only the hindquarters of a horse in this early portrayal.

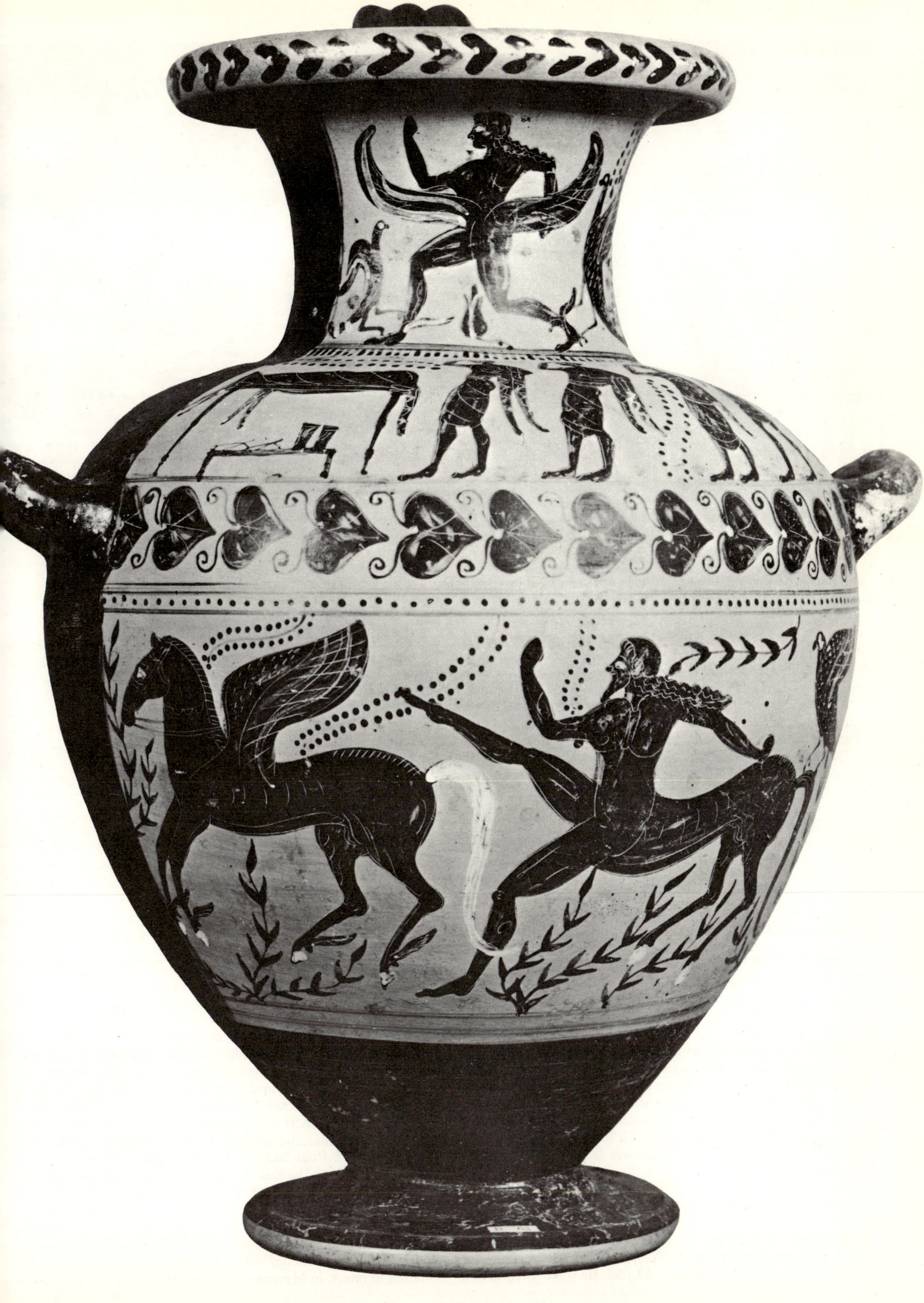

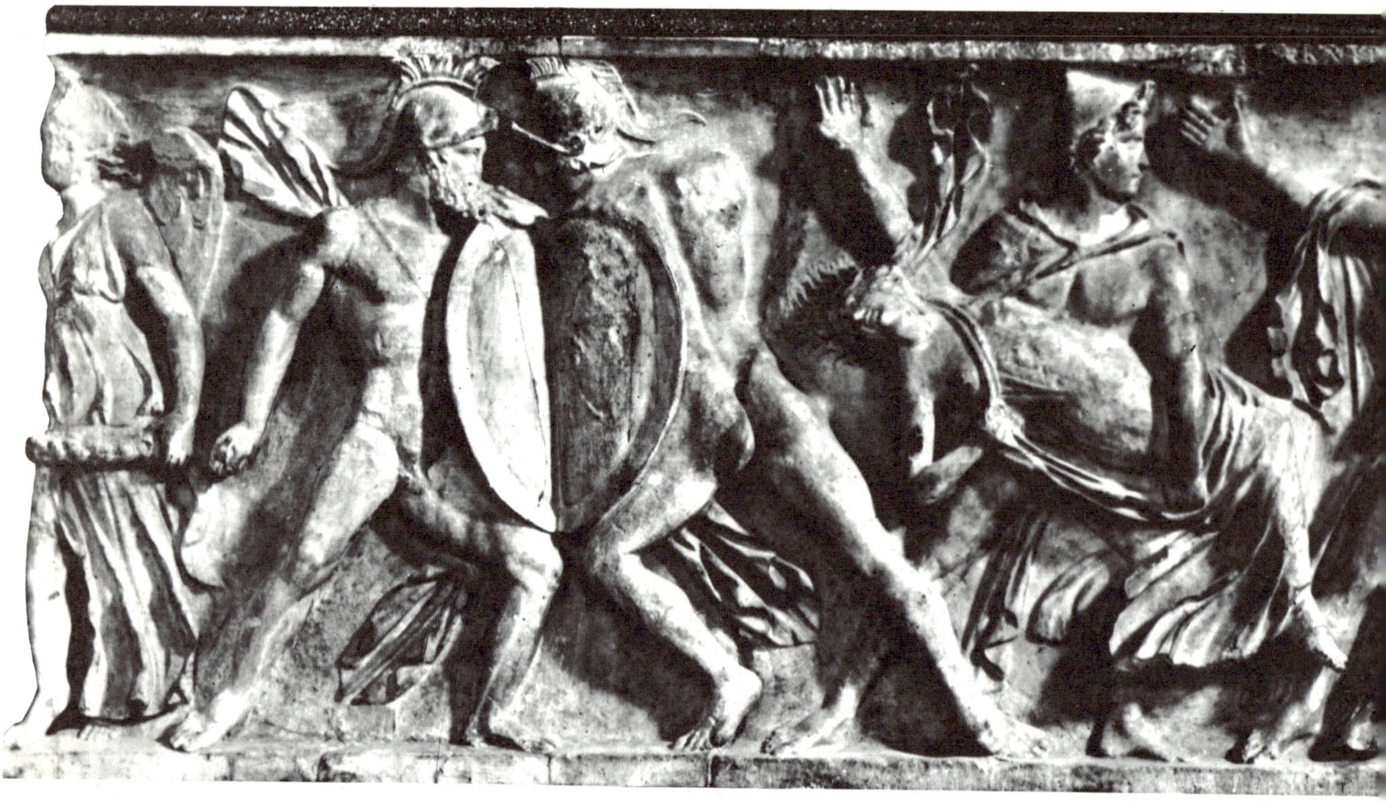

The Dioscuri carry off the daughters of Leucippus. Bas-relief on a sarcophagus in the Uffizi Gallery, Florence.

harpe which Hermes had given him, he averted his eyes and, letting Athene guide his arm, he struck. Or, some say, he fixed his eyes on her reflection in the polished surface of his shield. Then he cut off Medusa's head with one stroke of the sickle, and from her bleeding neck sprang Pegasus and Chrysaor, father of the infamous Geryon. Perseus put the terrible head into his wallet and fled on Pegasus' back while the other two Gorgons pursued him in vain.

Perseus reached Ethiopia to find the country in a state of desolation. Cassiopeia, wife of the king, Cepheus, had offended the Nereids by proclaiming that she was more beautiful than they. In this quarrel Poseidon had taken the part of the Ocean nymphs and sent a marine monster to devour men and beasts. When the oracle of Ammon was consulted he answered that only Andromeda, daughter of King Cepheus, could save the country by offering herself as a victim to the monster. When Perseus arrived on the scene he found the unhappy Andromeda chained to a rock, awaiting death. He fell in love with her at first sight. The sequel may be guessed: he killed the monster, freed Andromeda and married her. He took her back with him to Seriphos, where he found that his mother was being persecuted by Polydectes. He put an end to this and to Polydectes by holding up the head of Medusa. Polydectes saw it and was turned to stone then and there.

Perseus returned the magic wallet and dark helmet to Hermes and presented Athene with the head of the Gorgon which she placed on her shield. Then, with his mother and his wife, he set forth for Argos. Acrisius, remembering what the oracle had said long ago, fled at the approach of his daughter's son. But fate ordained that one day while Perseus was throwing the discus during funeral games Acrisius was present and the discus struck and killed him. Perseus did not wish to succeed to his grandfather's throne and instead reigned only over Tiryns and Mycenae. He founded the family of the Perseids of which one day Hercules was to be such a glorious representative.

OTHER HEROES OF ARGOLIS.

The Pelopids. Although the race of Pelopids took their name from Pelops, they owed their origin to Pelops' father, Tantalus.

Tantalus was king of Phrygia or of Lydia. He was invited to dine with the gods on Olympus and he stole their nectar and ambrosia. He returned their invitation, and when they sat at his table he served to them, in order to test their divinity, the body of his own son, Pelops. The guests immediately realised this; Demeter alone, more absent-minded or else more hungry than the others, ate flesh from the shoulder. Zeus ordered that the child's remains should be thrown into a magic cauldron and Clotho restored Pelops to life. Only one of his shoulders was missing and had to be replaced in ivory.

For these crimes Tantalus was cast into the infernal regions. He stood waist-deep in the middle of a lake in Tartarus surrounded by trees laden with delicious fruit. Thirst and hunger which he could never satisfy tortured him; for when he reached out his hand the fruit evaded him, when he leaned down to drink the water receded.

When he was grown up Pelops left Phrygia and went to Pisa in Elis where he competed for the hand of Hippodameia. Her father, Oenomaus, had promised to give his daughter to the first suitor who vanquished him in a chariot race. Fifteen suitors had already been defeated and killed. Pelops bribed Myrtilus, Oenomaus' charioteer, to loosen one of his master's chariot wheels, and thus he won the race and the hand of Hippodameia. Afterwards he killed Myrtilus in order to get rid of an embarrassing accomplice. But the father of Myrtilus was Hermes, and Hermes avenged the death of his son by laying a curse on Pelops and all his house.

By Hippodameia Pelops had several children, among them Atreus and Thyestes. By another wife he had a son Chrysippus, whom he particularly loved. At Hippodameia's instigation Atreus and Thyestes murdered Chrysippus and for this crime were forced to go into exile. They reached Mycenae. At the death of Eurystheus, King of Mycenae, Atreus succeeded to the throne. His brother Thyestes was jealous and seduced the wife of Atreus, Aerope, and in addition stole from him a ram with a golden fleece which had been a present from Hermes. He was driven from Mycenae but left Pleisthenes to avenge him. Now Pleisthenes was Atreus' son, who had been brought up by Thyestes as his own son. Pleisthenes was on the point of striking down Atreus, but Atreus killed him instead, realising too late that it was his son. To avenge himself Atreus pretended to be reconciled with Thyestes and invited him and his children to return to Mycenae. In the course of a feast he served to

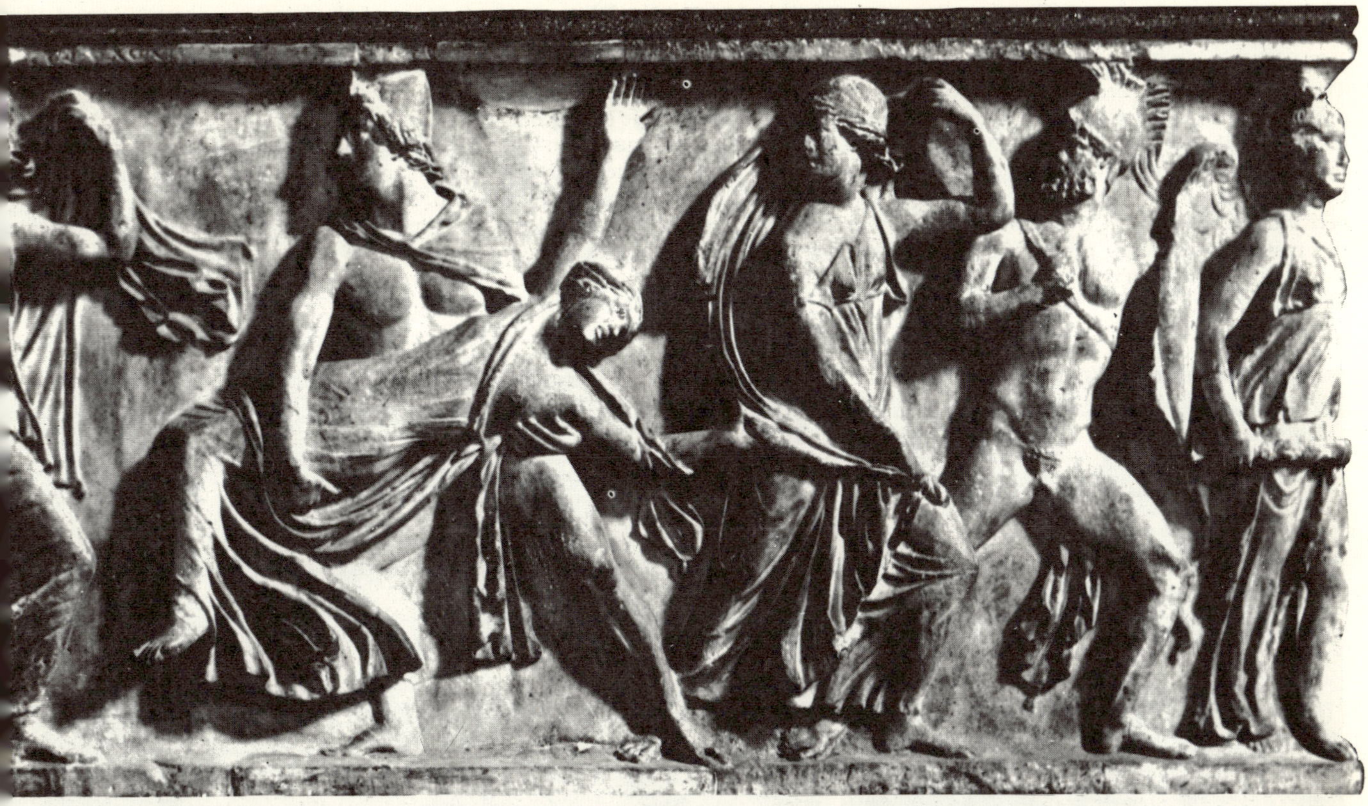

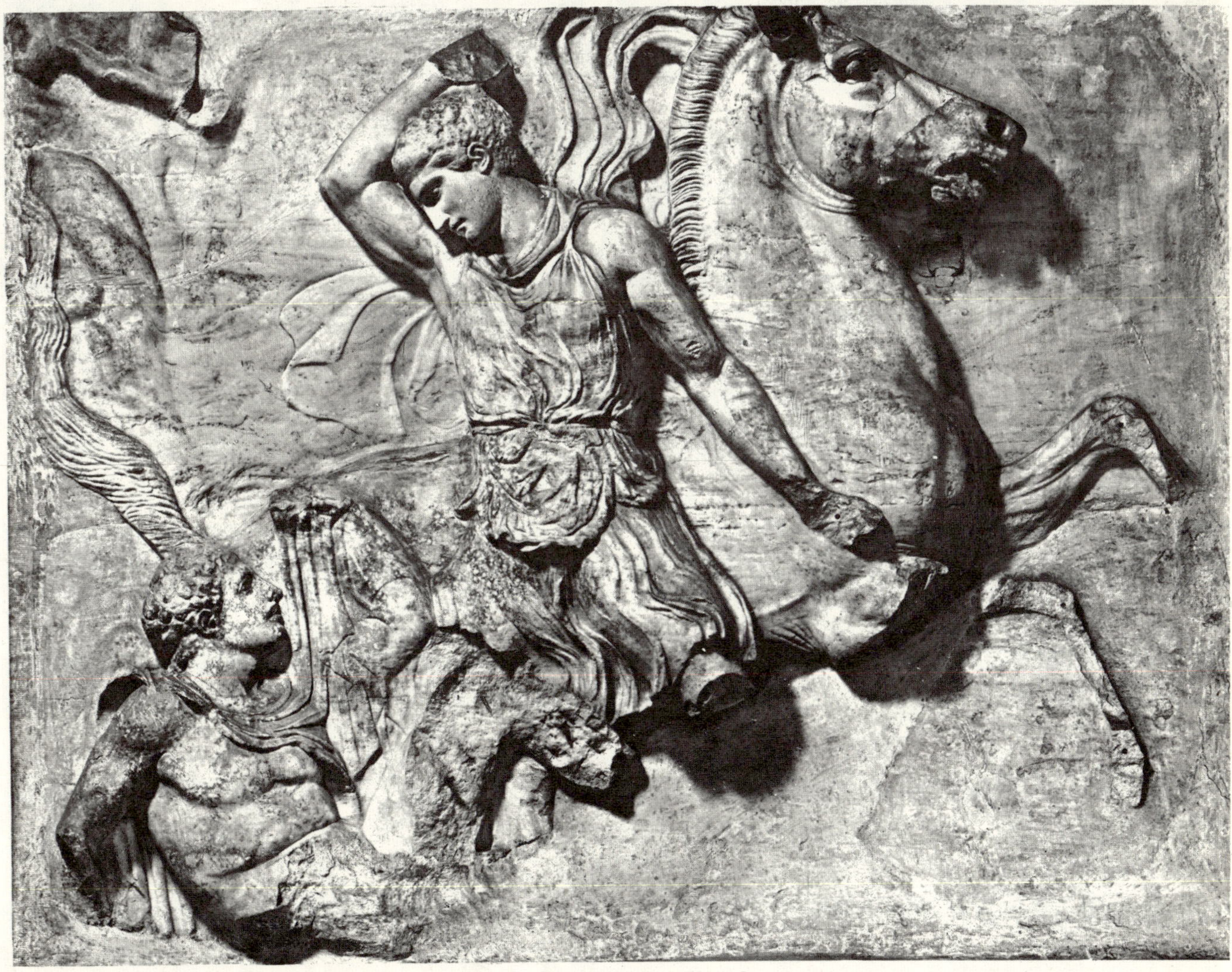

Pollux killing Lynceus. Antique bas-relief. School of Phidias. Villa Albani, Rome.

Thyestes the bodies of two of his sons. The sun, it was said, hid in order not to cast light on such a crime. Later Atreus was killed by Aegisthus, another son of Thyestes, whom Atreus had brought up with his own children, Agamemnon and Menelaus.

The series of these revolting crimes did not stop at this point. Thyestes who had succeeded his brother to the throne of Argos was driven from it by his nephews Agamemnon and Menelaus. On his return from the Trojan War, Agamemnon, in his turn, was murdered by Aegisthus who was living in adultery with Agamemnon's wife, Clytemnestra. Eight years later Aegisthus and Clytemnestra perished by the hand of Clytemnestra's son, Orestes, who expiated this matricide by a long period of suffering. Then only were the Furies satisfied and an end put to the atrocities which had stained the family of Atreus with blood.

THE DIOSCURI AND THE HEROES OF LACONIA

The Dioscuri. The founder of the Laconian dynasties was Lelex who, by his union with a Naiad, had a son Eurotas, whose daughter Sparta married Lacedaemon. Lacedaemon reigned over Sparta and gave his name to that city. The most famous of his descendants were Hippocoön, who was killed by Hercules: Icarius, to whom Dionysus taught the secret of wine-making and who was killed by drunken shepherds; and finally Tyndareus, husband of Leda and father of Helen, of Clytemnestra, and of the Dioscuri: Castor and Pollux.

It was said that Zeus had played a certain part in this paternity since, in the guise of a swan, he had visited Leda. Leda had been brought to bed with two eggs from one of which issued Pollux and Helen, regarded as the children of Zeus, and from the other Castor

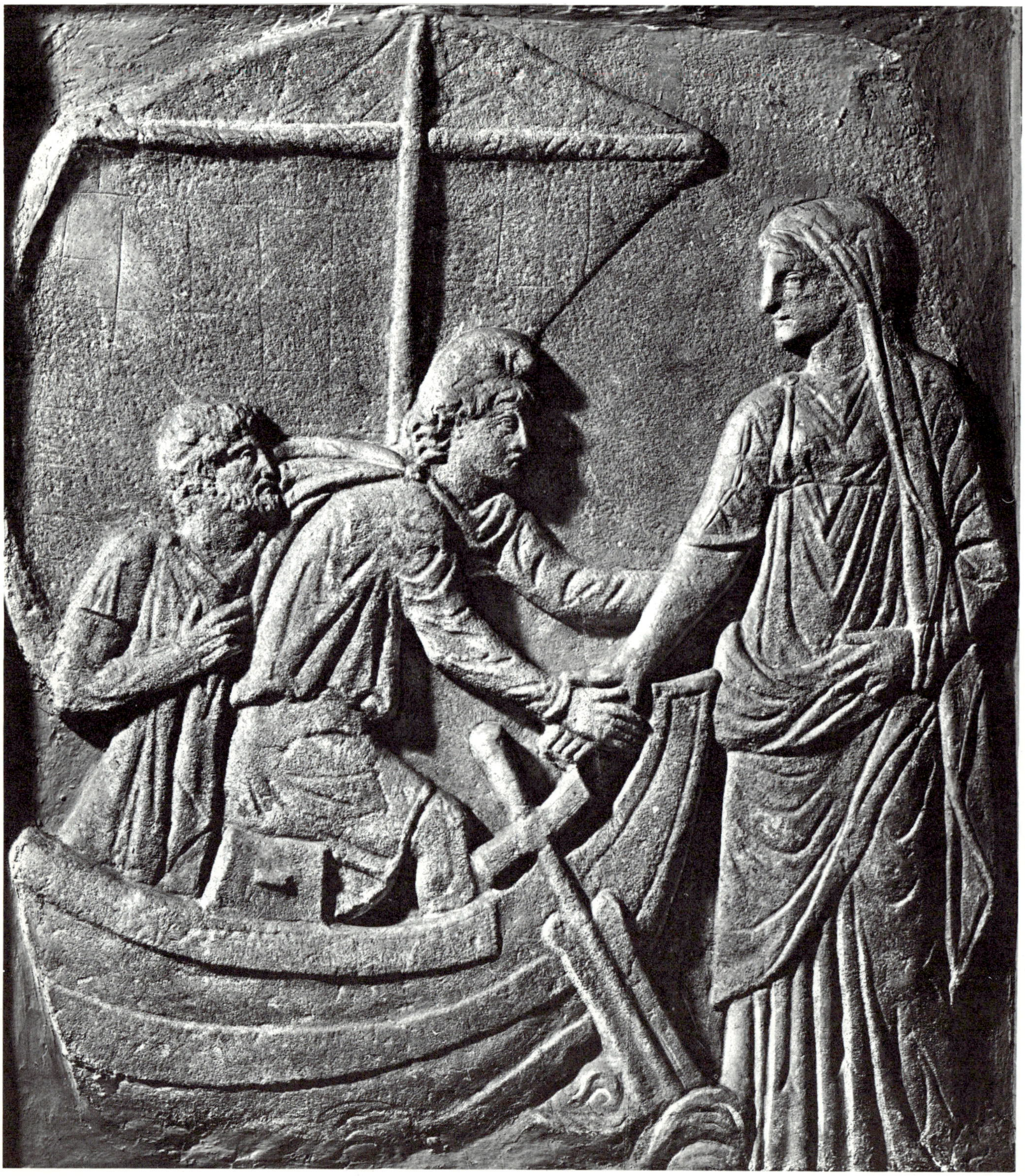

The Abduction of Helen. Greek bas-relief in the Lateran Museum, Rome.

and Clytemnestra, who were reputed to be the children of Tyndareus.

In spite of their different paternity Castor and Pollux were both qualified as Dioscuri, which meant young sons of Zeus. They always lived on terms of close friendship.

The semi-divine character of the Dioscuri has been explained by A. H. Krappe as the superstition which surrounds the birth of twins among most primitive peoples. The phenomenon, being not common, was interpreted either as ill-omened – hence the persecutions often inflicted on twins and their mother – or as fortunate. In either event the anomaly was justified by assuming that one at least of the children was of divine origin; this was the case with Hercules and Iphicles, and also with Castor and Pollux.

Among the exploits of the Dioscuri may be mentioned their expedition against Athens to rescue their sister Helen from Theseus who had abducted her. They also joined Jason on the Argonauts' expedition, and Zeus showed his benevolence towards them during a storm which assailed the ship *Argo* in the sea of Colchis. While Orpheus called upon the gods, two flames descended from the sky and hovered over the heads of the Dioscuri. It was the origin of Saint Elmo's Fire which still today announces to sailors the end of a storm.

Afterwards Castor and Pollux carried off the two daughters of Leudippus and married them. This was the occasion of their quarrel with the Aphareids, Idas and Lynceus, who were also paying court to the young women. This rivalry must have been unfortunate for the Dioscuri although no one knows exactly how it turned out. According to Pindar the Dioscuri went on an expedition with the Aphareids and cheated them out of their share of the booty. Ac-

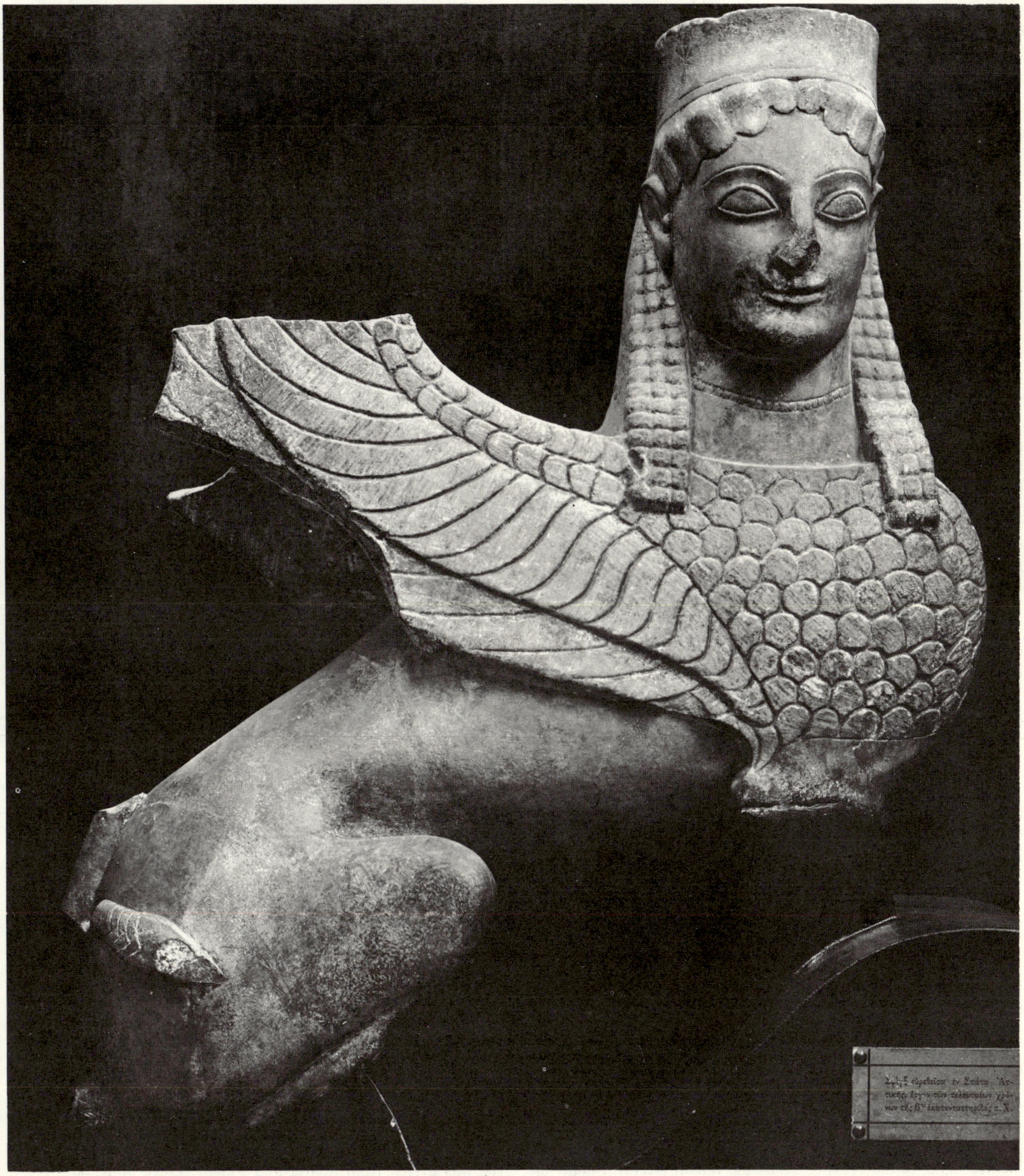

The Sphinx. Archaic statue found at Sparta. National Museum, Athens.

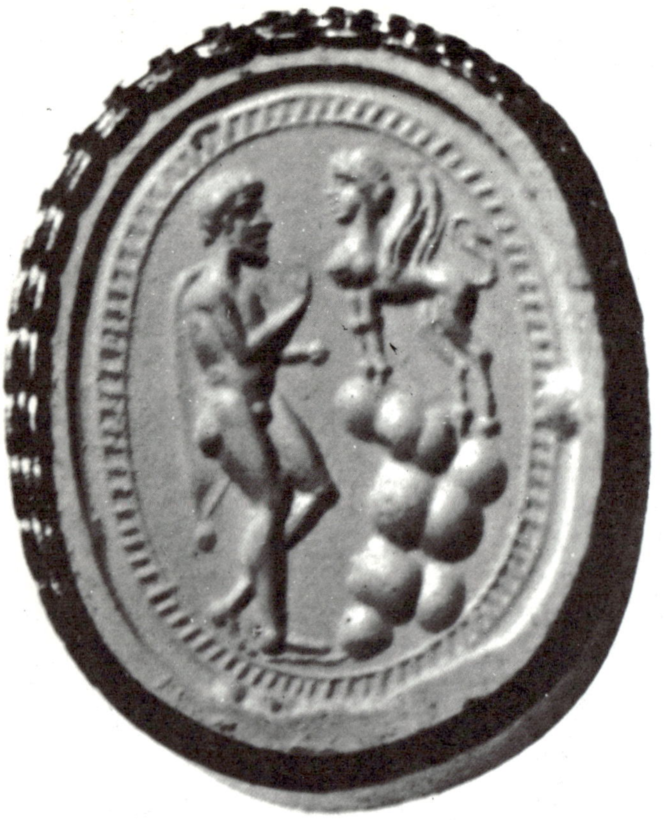

Oedipus and the Sphinx. 'What is the animal that has four feet in the morning, two at midday and three in the evening?' Perched on Mount Phicium near Thebes the Sphinx has just put her riddle to Oedipus who is in the process of answering her. A monster, part woman, part lion and part bird, she was accustomed to devour all those who could not solve it. Oedipus succeeded, however, and she threw herself to her death. Etruscan seal.

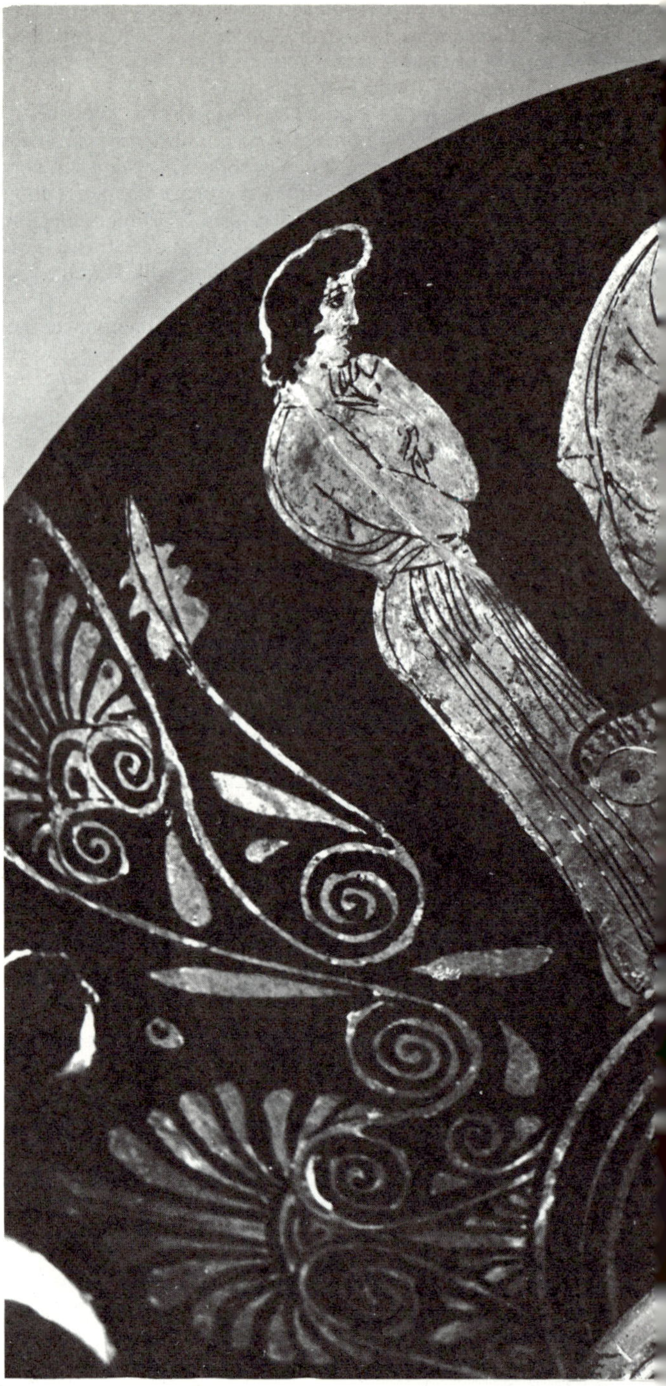

The death of Pelias. One of his daughters leads the old man from his seat while another waits by a cauldron with a sword in her hand. On the left Medea looks on. In order to effect her revenge Medea had told Pelias' daughters that she could rejuvinate their father if they first cut him up and boiled him in a cauldron. Two of them obeyed her and thus killed their father. Detail from a Greek red-figured vase, *c.* 420 B.C.

cording to other authors the four young men had a dispute over the division of a herd of oxen. Idas quartered an ox and ruled that half the spoil should go to the man who ate his share first, the other half going to the man who finished second. So saying he swallowed his own quarter and his brother's quarter and drove off the whole herd.

The Dioscuri then led an expedition against the Aphareids and in the course of the battle Pollux killed Lynceus while Castor was mortally wounded by Idas. Pollux wept over the body of his brother; for being himself immortal he could not follow him to the kingdom of Hades. Zeus was touched by this fraternal devotion and authorised Pollux to share with his brother the privilege of immortality: thus the Dioscuri continued to live each on alternate days. Another tradition says that Zeus placed them among the stars, in the constellation Gemini, The Twins.

Venerated at first in Achaia, the Dioscuri were afterwards honoured throughout Greece as the tutelary divinities of sailors and as protectors of hospitality. Sometimes they can be seen, dressed in white robes and purple mantles, starred bonnets on their heads, arriving in cities to test what sort of welcome the inhabitants will give to strangers.

Helen. Their sister Helen was celebrated for her beauty. When she had scarcely reached the age of ten Theseus carried her off, but the Dioscuri brought her home again. She was besieged by suitors. Her father Tyndareus made each of them swear that he would in case of need come to the aid of the lucky man who became Helen's husband. He then chose Menelaus. For three years the couple lived happily together. Then Paris, son of the Trojan King Priam, visited the court of Menelaus, fell in love with Helen and carried her off. This was the cause of the Trojan War. All the princes of Greece, faithful to their oaths, took arms under the command of Agamemnon to avenge the outrage done to Menelaus. For ten years the struggle raged before the walls of Troy. Neither the craft of Odysseus, the bravery of Diomedes, nor the dash of Achilles could conquer the resistance of the Trojans, led by the valiant Hector. Finally the Greek warriors were able to enter the city by hiding in the hollow flanks of a huge wooden horse which the Trojans themselves dragged into the city. Troy was taken and set on fire. Old Priam was slain and the rest of his family immolated or carried away as slaves. Menelaus regained his wife and was reconciled with her. To be sure it was said that the real Helen had always remained in Egypt where her husband later found her, and that Paris had brought only the phantom of Helen back with him to Troy. However, it seems obvious that this account was invented simply to save the self-esteem of the unfortunate Menelaus.

The end of Helen was variously reported. After her husband's death she was admitted among the stars with the Dioscuri. Or else she was united to Achilles in the Islands of the Blessed. Or, again, she was driven from Sparta and sought refuge in Rhodes where she was hanged from a tree on the orders of the queen, Polyxo.

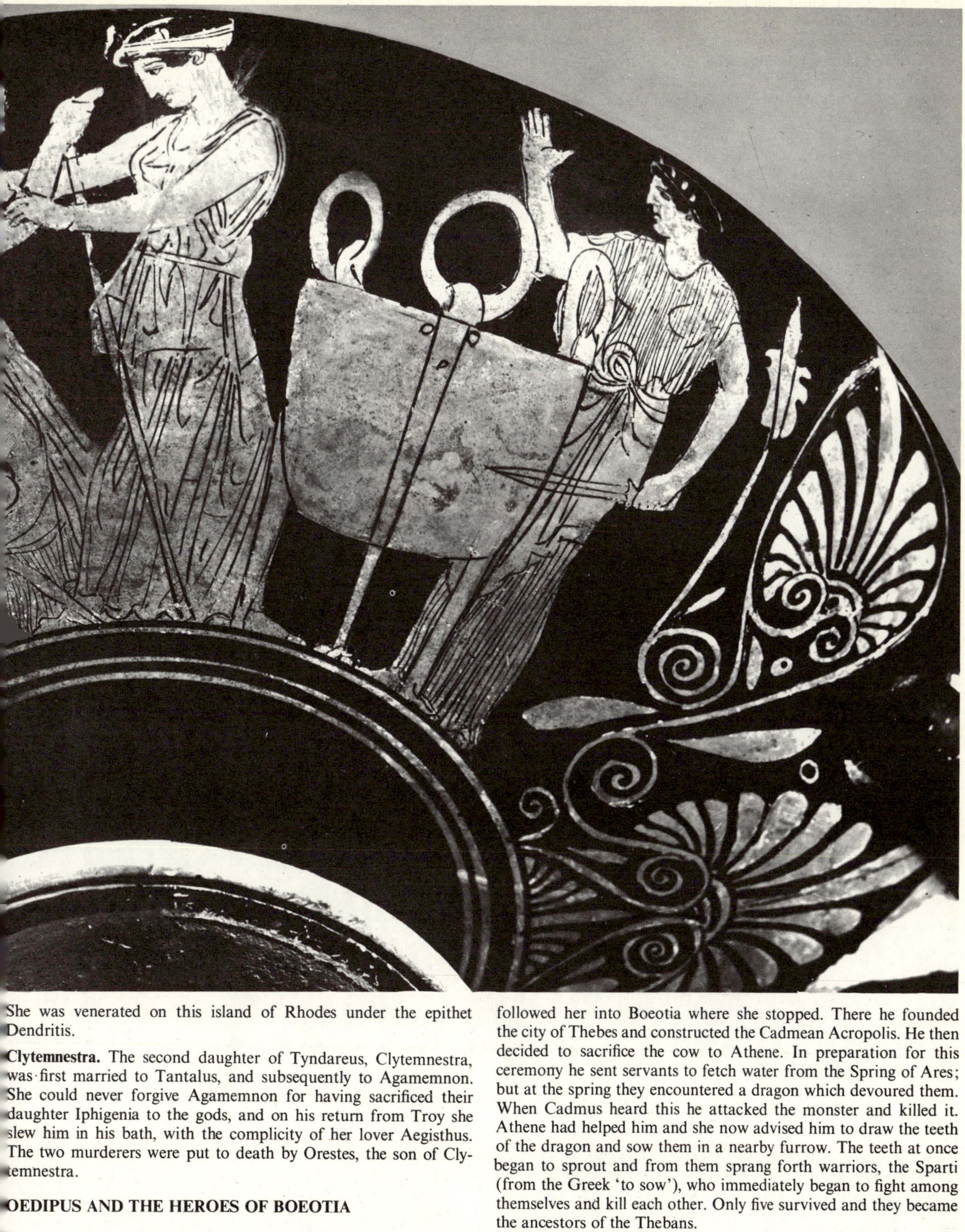

She was venerated on this island of Rhodes under the epithet Dendritis.

Clytemnestra. The second daughter of Tyndareus, Clytemnestra, was first married to Tantalus, and subsequently to Agamemnon. She could never forgive Agamemnon for having sacrificed their daughter Iphigenia to the gods, and on his return from Troy she slew him in his bath, with the complicity of her lover Aegisthus. The two murderers were put to death by Orestes, the son of Clytemnestra.

OEDIPUS AND THE HEROES OF BOEOTIA

Cadmus. The principal heroes of Thebes belonged to the family of the Labdacids whose founder was Cadmus. He was the son of Agenor and Telephassa. Phoenix and Cilix were his brothers and Europa his sister. When Europa was carried off by Zeus, the three brothers set out to find her. Cilix and Phoenix soon tired of the search and settled down in the countries which were to be known as Cilicia and Phoenicia. Cadmus was more persistent and consulted the oracle of Delphi who advised him to abandon his search and when he came across a cow to let her guide him, and where she stopped, there to build a city. In Phocis Cadmus found the fateful animal and followed her into Boeotia where she stopped. There he founded the city of Thebes and constructed the Cadmean Acropolis. He then decided to sacrifice the cow to Athene. In preparation for this ceremony he sent servants to fetch water from the Spring of Ares; but at the spring they encountered a dragon which devoured them. When Cadmus heard this he attacked the monster and killed it. Athene had helped him and she now advised him to draw the teeth of the dragon and sow them in a nearby furrow. The teeth at once began to sprout and from them sprang forth warriors, the Sparti (from the Greek 'to sow'), who immediately began to fight among themselves and kill each other. Only five survived and they became the ancestors of the Thebans.

Meanwhile in order to expiate the murder of the dragon who was a son of Ares, Cadmus had to spend a few years serving as a slave. After this Athene recompensed him by awarding him the crown of Thebes, while Zeus granted him the hand of the shining Virgin Harmonia, daughter of Ares and Aphrodite, or perhaps, of Zeus and Electra.

The couple lived happily together. Their children were Semele, mother of Dionysus; Ino, mother of Melicertes; Autonoë, mother of Actaeon; Agave, mother of Pentheus; and Polydorus, father of Labdacus who was the ancestor of the Labdacids. Towards the end of their lives Cadmus and Harmonia went to reign over Illyria, then were changed into dragons and transported to the Islands of the Blessed.

In Greece Cadmus was considered to be a divine legislator and the promoter of Boeotian civilisation: to him were ascribed the discovery of casting metal and the invention or importation of the alphabet.

Amphion and Zethus. Amphion and Zethus were twins, and the legends concerning them belong to the earliest days of Theban royalty. They were sons of Zeus and Antiope. Persecuted by her father, Antiope sought refuge with Epopeus at Sicyon. Epopeus married her, but her brother, Lycus, marched on Sicyon, killed Epopeus and brought Antiope back a captive. On the return journey, in a wayside thicket, Antiope brought her twins into the world. They were exposed on Mount Cithaeron and taken in by shepherds. Antiope was long held prisoner, but one day her chains fell from her of their own accord. She fled and rejoined her sons, Amphion and Zethus, who then attacked Thebes where Lycus now reigned. They killed Lycus and also his wife, Dirce, who was tied to the horns of a wild bull. The two brothers then fortified the city. Zethus carried stones while Amphion, with the magic sounds of his lyre, caused the stones to move of their own will and gently slide into the desired position in the walls.

Afterwards Zethus married Thebe and Amphion married Niobe who bore him twelve children. Niobe was proud of her twelve children and unfortunately dared to scoff at Leto, who had only had two. Apollo and Artemis punished this insult to their mother by shooting down all of Niobe's children. The unhappy mother, prostrate with grief, was changed by Zeus into a rock on the deserted summits of Mount Sipylus.

Oedipus. Laius, son of Labdacus, king of Thebes, had married Jocasta. Having been warned by an oracle that his son would one day kill him Laius carried the child to which Jocasta had just given birth to Mount Cithaeron. He pierced the infant's feet with a nail and tied them together solidly, hoping thus to be rid of him. But a shepherd found the child and took him to Polybus, King of Corinth, who adopted him and named him Oedipus because of his wounded foot. When Oedipus had grown up he learned his destiny from an oracle who told him that he would kill his father and marry his mother. Oedipus believed that he could escape this fate by exiling

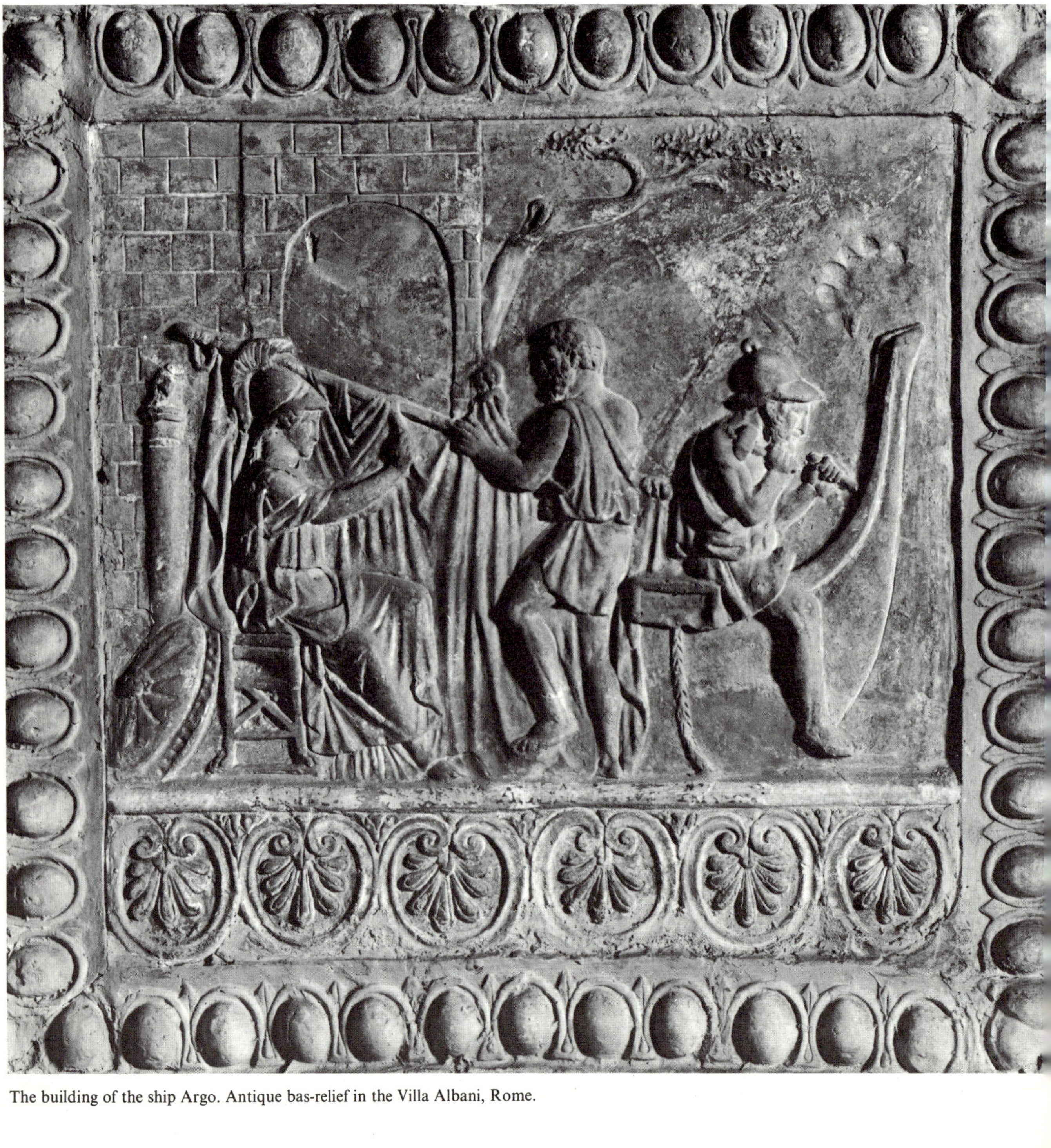

The building of the ship Argo. Antique bas-relief in the Villa Albani, Rome.

himself for ever from Corinth, never again seeing Polybus and his wife whom he assumed to be his true parents. This scruple was his own undoing. He went to Boeotia and on the road quarrelled with an unknown man whom he struck with his staff and killed. The victim was, indeed, Laius, his own father. Oedipus continued on his journey without suspecting that the first half of the oracle's prediction had been fulfilled. He arrived in Thebes where he learned that the region was being devastated by a fabulous monster with the face and bust of a woman, the body of a lion and the wings of a bird. Guarding the road to Thebes the Sphinx – as the monster was called – would stop all travellers and propose enigmas to them; those who were unable to solve her riddles she would devour. Creon, who had governed Thebes since the recent death of Laius, promised the crown and the hand of Jocasta to the man who delivered the city from this scourge. Oedipus resolved to attempt the feat. He was successful. The Sphinx asked him: 'Which is the animal that has four feet in the morning, two at midday and three in the evening?' He answered: 'Man, who in infancy crawls on all fours, who walks upright on two feet in maturity, and in his old age supports himself with a stick.' The Sphinx was vanquished and threw herself into the sea.

And thus, still without realising it, Oedipus became the husband of his mother, Jocasta. From their union two sons were born, Eteocles and Polyneices, and two daughters, Antigone and Ismene. Oedipus, in spite of the double crime he had innocently committed, was honoured as a sovereign devoted to his people's welfare, and appeared to prosper. But the Erinnyes were waiting. A terrible epidemic ravaged the land, decimating the population, and at the same time an incredible drought brought with it famine. When consulted, the oracle of Delphi replied that these scourges would not cease until the Thebans had driven the still unknown murderer of Laius out of the country. Oedipus, after having offered ritual maledictions against the assassin, undertook to find out who he was. His inquiries finally led to the discovery that the guilty man was none other than himself, and that Jocasta whom he had married was his mother. Jocasta in shame and grief hanged herself and Oedipus put out his own eyes. Then he went into exile, accompanied by his faithful daughter Antigone. He took refuge in the town of Colonus in Attica and, at last purified of his abominable crimes, disappeared mysteriously from the earth.

As for his sons, victims of the paternal curse, they perished by each other's hand. They had agreed to reign for alternate years. But when the time came Eteocles refused to hand over the crown. Polyneices gathered together an army of Argives and laid siege to Thebes. It was during this siege that the two brothers slew each other in the course of single combat. The senate of Thebes decreed that the body of Polyneices should be left unburied, but Antigone nevertheless rendered her dead brother funeral honours. For this she was condemned to be buried alive. Her sister Ismene shared her fate. And thus the unhappy family came to an end.

MELEAGER AND THE HEROES OF AETOLIA

The ancestor of the Aetolians was Aetolus, son of Endymion. Because of an accidental murder Aetolus was forced to leave the land of his father and he established himself in the region of Greece which afterwards took his name. Among his descendants was Oeneus, to whom Dionysus made a gift of the first vinestock. Oeneus had by two different wives two sons, Meleager and Tydeus.

Meleager. Meleager's mother was Althaea, the first wife of Oeneus. When he was seven days old the Fates appeared to his mother. Clotho predicted for the child great generosity; Lachesis, extraordinary strength; Atropos declared that he would live only so long as a certain brand which was burning on the hearth continued to exist. Althaea hastened to rescue the brand, extinguished it and put it in a place of safety. Meanwhile Meleager became, as the Fates had foretold, a hero full of valour. His father Oeneus once forgot to offer to Artemis the first fruits of his harvest and the angry goddess sent a monstrous wild boar to ravage Aetolia. To hunt the monster Meleager invited all the most celebrated heroes of Greece, among them a young Arcadian woman named Atalanta. The hunt was cruel and hard. Many were killed by the wild boar. Atalanta was the first to wound it with an arrow in the back and Meleager finished it off with his spear. A dispute arose among the huntsmen over the monster's remains which Meleager had presented to Atalanta. Meleager's uncles attempted to take it away from her and Meleager killed them. When she learned how her brothers had been slain by her too quick-tempered son, Althaea, it was said, threw the fatal brand into the fire and Meleager immediately died. Another tradition says that Althaea merely dedicated her son to the Furies.

According to this latter version, war meanwhile broke out between the Aetolians and the Curetes over whom Meleager's uncles had reigned. The hero fought valiantly at first, but when he learned that his mother had cursed him he shut himself up in his house. The Curetes thus gained the advantage and broke into the town, setting fire to the houses. Stubbornly Meleager ignored the entreaties of relations and friends and refused to fight. He gave in at last to the prayers of his wife, Cleopatra, and resuming his place at the head of his troops put the enemy to flight. During the battle he was killed, they said, by Apollo.

Atalanta. Atalanta, the unconscious cause of Meleager's troubles, was the daughter of the Arcadian Iasus. Iasus had wanted a son and he exposed his infant daughter on Mount Parthenius where she was suckled by a bear and taken in by hunters whose rough life she shared. When she had grown up Atalanta continued to live in rural solitude, taking pleasure only in the chase and despising the thought of marriage. She slew the Centaurs, Rhaecus and Hylaeus, who had tried to ravish her. She took an illustrious part in Meleager's boar hunt, and vanquished Peleus in wrestling at the funeral games held in honour of Pelias. Her father Iasus finally recognised her and decided to have her married. She declared that she would only marry the man who could beat her in a foot race. More than one suitor had competed and been killed by Atalanta when a certain Melanion thought of a trick. While he ran he dropped one by one three golden apples which Aphrodite had given him. Atalanta paused to pick them up. She was thus beaten and married Melanion. The couple were later turned into lions for having profaned a temple of Zeus.

Tydeus and Diomedes. Meleager's half-brother, Tydeus, killed his cousins who had plotted against his father. He had to leave Aetolia and went to Argos where he married the daughter of King Adrastus. He took part in the expedition of the seven chieftains against Thebes and distinguished himself by various exploits, notably by killing fifty Thebans who had laid an ambush for him. He fell, however, under the blows of the Theban Melanippus. Though grievously wounded Athene brought him an elixir which would have cured and made him immortal. She was about to offer it to him when the soothsayer Amphiaraus who was a personal enemy of Tydeus, presented him with the head of Melanippus. In a transport of rage Tydeus split open his recent enemy's skull and devoured his brain. Outraged by such savagery, Athene left him to his fate and Tydeus died shortly afterwards.

His son Diomedes avenged him by sacking Thebes with the Epigoni. The same Diomedes was renowned for his exploits before Troy: he wounded Aphrodite and even Ares. With Odysseus he seized the Palladium on which the safety of Troy depended. After the war his return to Greece was marked with adventures. He was tossed by a storm on to the coast of Lycia and very nearly immolated to Ares by King Lycus, but was saved by the king's daughter, Callirrhoë, who loved him and when he departed killed herself in despair. When he returned to Argos he learned that his wife was unfaithful to him. He left Argos, which he later reconquered. He finished his valorous career in Italy with King Daunus whose daughter he married.

PELEUS, THE ARGONAUTS AND THE HEROES OF THESSALY

Peleus. Although Peleus was one of the most famous heroes of Thessaly he was not a native of that country. He was the son of Aeacus who reigned over the island of Aegina. Peleus with his brother Telamon fled from Aegina after they killed their half-brother Phocus. Telemon established himself in Salamis where he inherited the crown of Cychreus, the king. Peleus first went to Phthia where he visited Eurytion. Unwilling to present himself without an escort, he prayed to Zeus who changed certain ants into men who were henceforth called *Myrmidons*. Eurytion welcomed him warmly and gave him a third of his estates, together with the

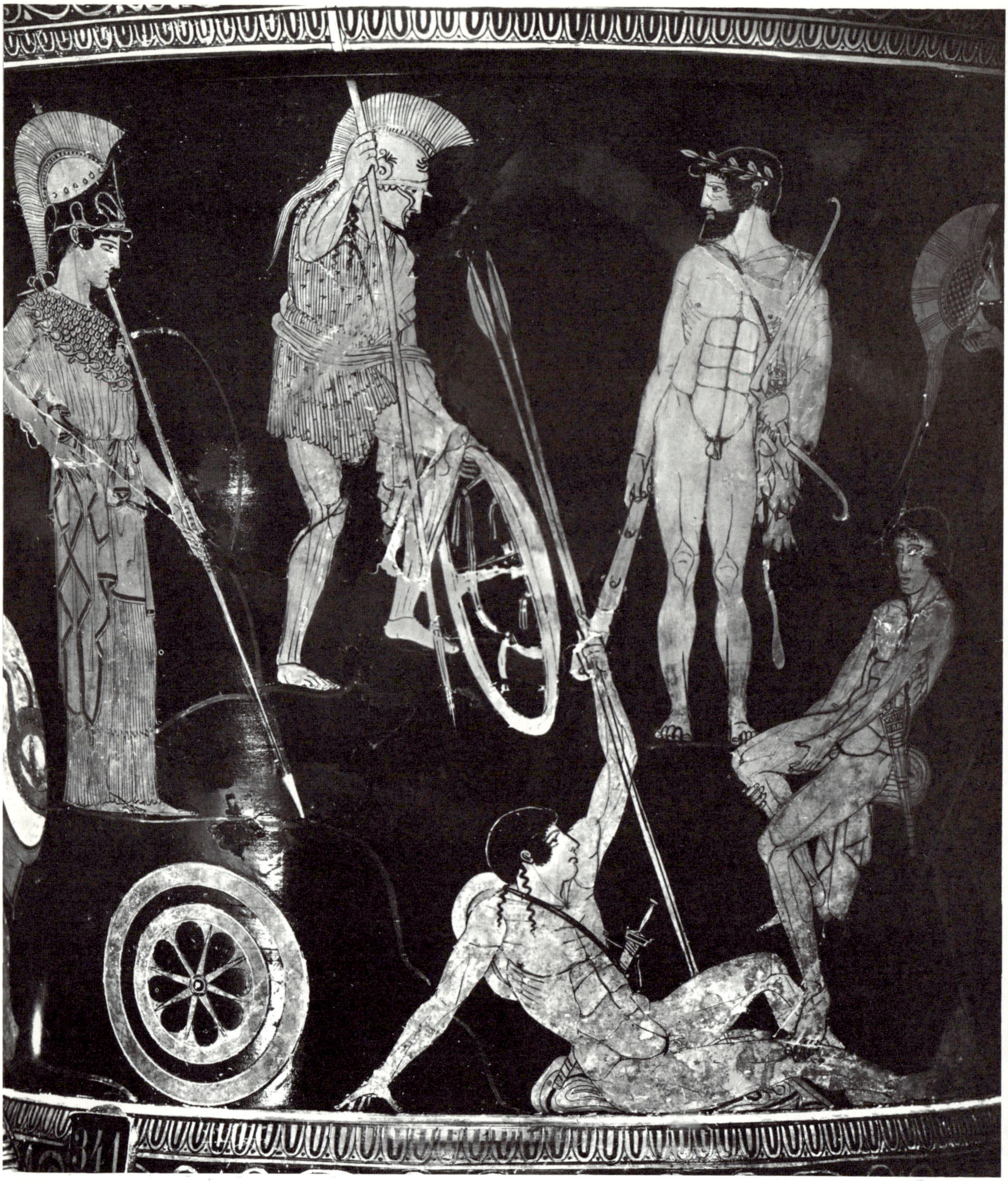

The Argonauts gather under the protection of Athene. Detail of a crater from Orvieto. Louvre.

hand of his daughter Antigone. Unfortunately Peleus and Eurytion took part in Meleager's boar hunt during which Peleus accidentally killed his father-in-law. He then took refuge in Iolcus with Acastus who purified him. The wife of Acastus conceived an amorous passion for Peleus, but was repulsed by him. She avenged herself by falsely telling Antigone that Peleus had been unfaithful to her. Antigone hanged herself in grief. She also told her husband the same story. The laws of hospitality forbade Acastus to kill Peleus; instead he took his guest hunting on Mount Pelion, hoping to see him killed. But Peleus vanquished the wildest and most dangerous beasts, thanks to a fabulous dagger which had been made by Hephaestus. While Peleus was asleep Acastus stole this dagger and hid it, thinking in this way to leave him without defence against the ferocious Centaurs who peopled the mountain. The project nearly succeeded, but by luck Peleus was saved by the Centaur Chiron who returned his dagger. Peleus used it to punish Acastus and his treacherous wife, and himself became king of the land.

Shortly afterwards Peleus married the Nereid Thetis, not without resistance on the part of the bride who, once courted by Poseidon and Zeus himself, considered marriage to a mortal to be an insult to her dignity. Thanks to the advice of Chiron Peleus overcame the efforts of Thetis to elude him and the marriage was sumptuously celebrated in the crests of Mount Pelion. From their union Achilles was born. We have already seen how Thetis attempted to bestow immortality on her son. The achievement of this work was interrupted by Peleus, and Thetis in vexation rejoined her sisters, the Nereids.

Young Achilles was confided to the Centaur Chiron who fed him on the marrowbones of bears and the entrails of lions.

Achilles. Thus Achilles grew in years and strength. He was nine when the seer Calchas predicted that he alone would conquer Troy. Thetis, who knew that in Troy he would meet his death, tried to avoid the peril by hiding him, disguised as a girl, in the palace of Lycomedes, King of Skyros. But the Greeks, helped by Odysseus, discovered the so-called 'maiden' by an ingenious trick. Odysseus one day came to Lycomedes' palace with gifts for the king's daughters. Among them he slipped a shield and a spear. Then he and his companions gave battle cries and sounded the trumpets. Achilles thinking they were being attacked, rushed for the weapons. The Greeks then took him with them; for he could not escape his destiny. We know what valour he displayed beneath the walls of Ilium; in single combat he killed the valiant Hector. But he himself perished before Troy was taken, pierced in his vulnerable heel by an arrow, shot either by Apollo or by Paris.

But to return to Peleus: while his son grew up his own adventurous life continued. He took part in the voyage of the Argonauts. He

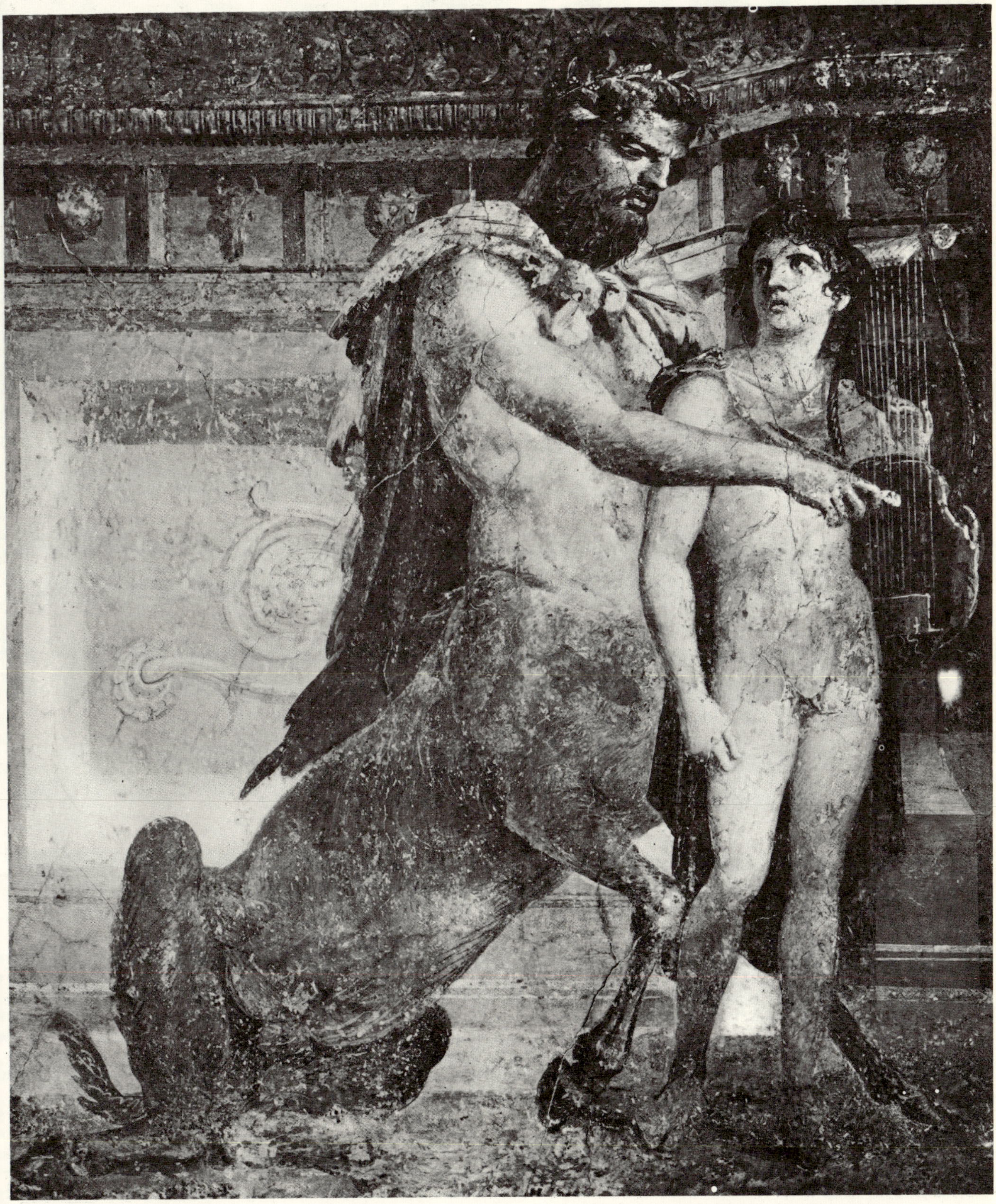

The Centaur Chiron instructing the young Achilles. When Thetis deserted her husband Peleus, their son, Achilles, was entrusted to the care of the wise old Centaur Chiron on Mount Pelion who fed him on the entrails of lions and the marrowbones of bears to give him courage and instructed him in the arts of riding, hunting, pipe-playing and healing. Here he teaches him to play on the lyre. Wall-painting from the basilica of Herculaneum.

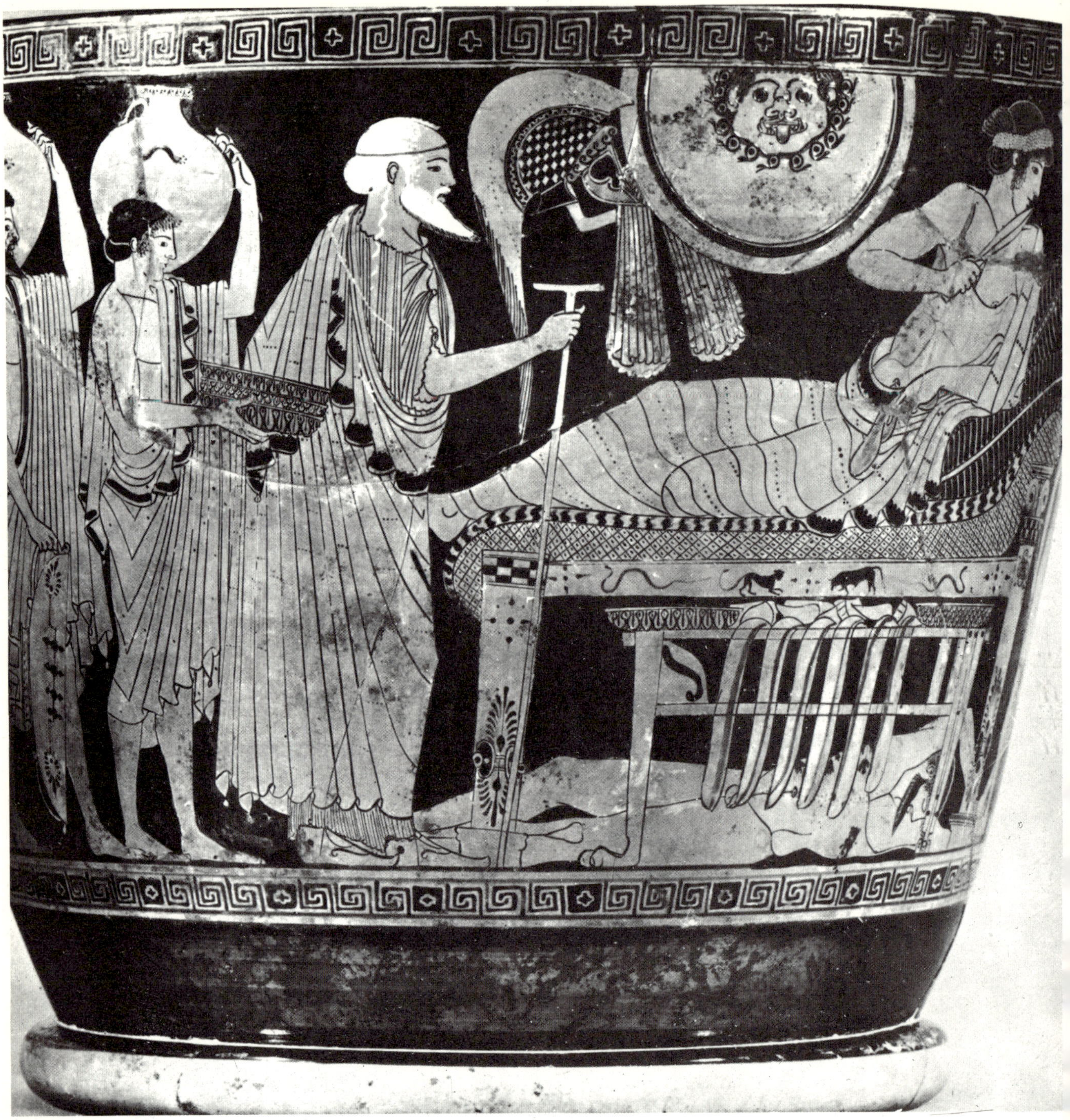

Priam pleading with Achilles for the body of his son Hector. Achilles reclines on his couch with his head averted while the aged Priam addresses him. Above him hangs the armour forged for him by Hephaestus while beneath his couch lies the mangled body of the Trojan hero. Though Achilles had refused Hector's dying plea that his body might be ransomed for burial he finally yielded to Priam's entreaties and accepted Hector's weight in gold. Greek vase painting.

fought with the Lapiths against the Centaurs. He seconded Hercules during his own expedition against Ilium. He outlived his son and had a listless old age. The circumstances of his death are unknown.

Jason and the Argonauts. The expedition of the Argonauts was celebrated in the annals not only of Thessaly but of all Greece. Its object was the conquest of the Golden Fleece, the origin of which was this: Phrixus and Helle, the two children of the Boeotian King Athamas, were hated by their step-mother Ino. Their very lives were threatened and they fled, mounted on a fabulous ram which was a gift of Hermes. This ram was endowed with reason and speech; had a fleece of gold and could move through the air as well as it could over the earth. In the course of their flight Helle fell into the sea and gave her name to the Hellespont. Phrixus was luckier and reached Colchis on the Black Sea. There he sacrificed the ram to Zeus, and offered its fleece to the king of the country, Aeëtes, who hung it from a tree and set a dragon who never slept to guard it.

Meanwhile at Iolcus in Thessaly reigned Pelias who had wrenched the throne from his brother, Aeson. Aeson's son, Jason, had been confided to the care of the Centaur Chiron. When he reached man's estate Jason went to his uncle and demanded his share of the kingdom. Pelias was sorely disturbed, for an oracle had once told him to 'beware of the man who wears but one sandal', and Jason had appeared before him with only one foot shod. He therefore told his nephew that he would willingly comply with his demand on condition that Jason first brought him back the Golden Fleece.

With the help of Hera or Athene Jason immediately built a ship with fifty oars, the *Argo*, in which he had set a bough of the prophetic oak of Zeus at Dodona. He gathered together the most famous heroes, among whom were Amphion, the Dioscuri, Hercules, Orpheus, Peleus, Theseus and Meleager. Then the hardy adventurers set forth in search of the fabled Golden Fleece. Their voyage was full of incident: they were forced to struggle against the elements as well as against men. Finally they reached the mouth

The young Apollo. Bronze statue of the fifth century B.C

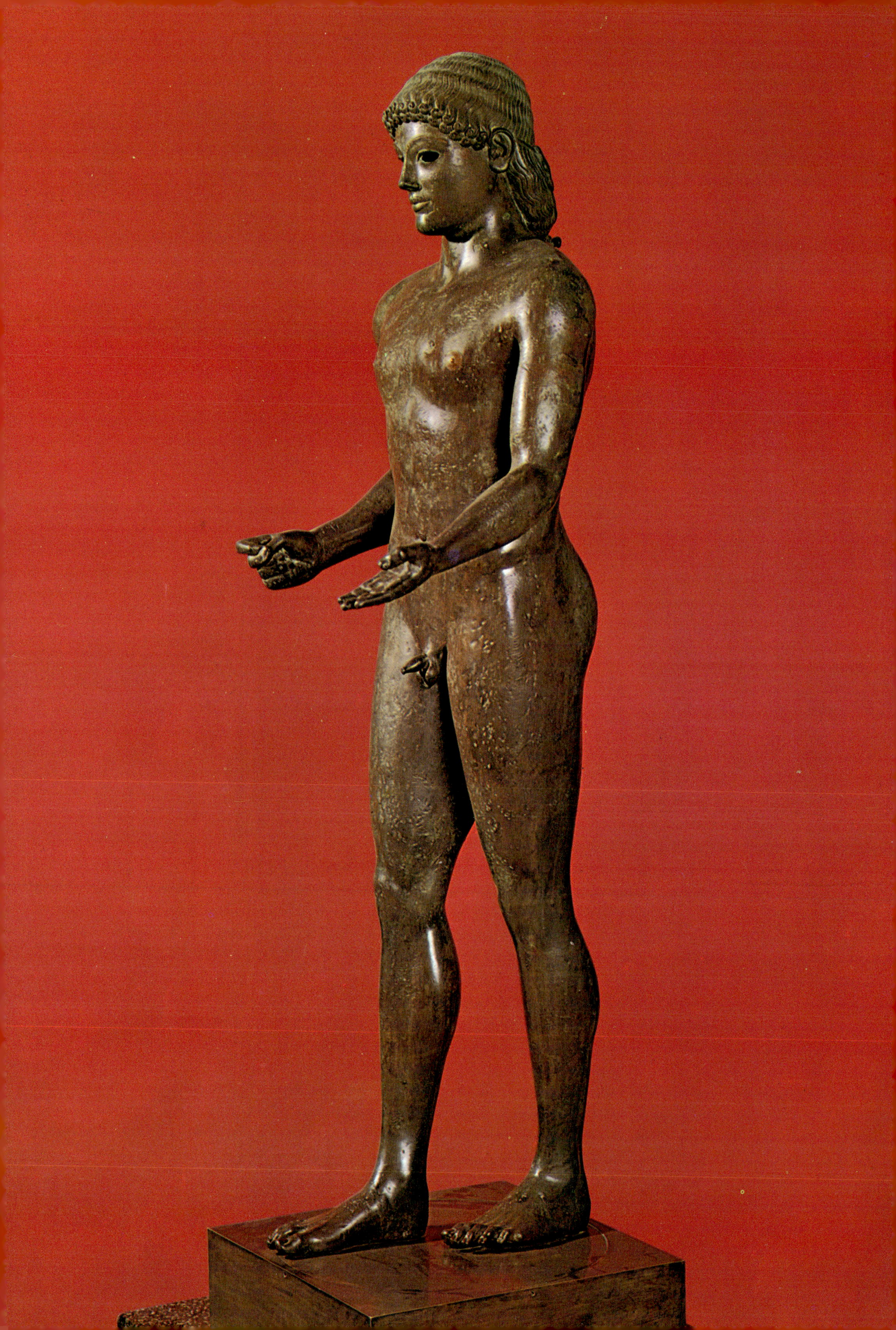

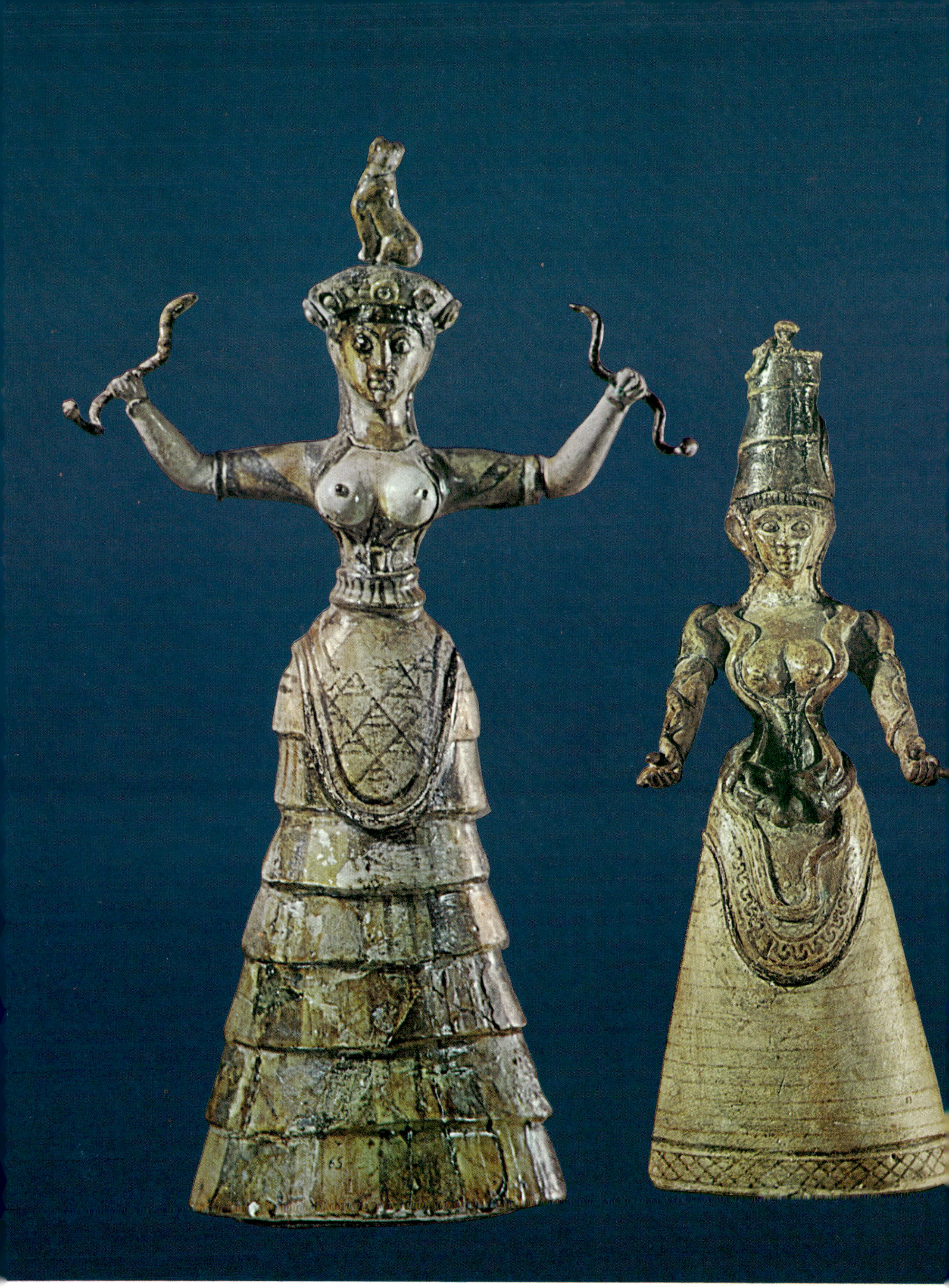

Two figures from the palace of Knossos, now in the Heraklion Museum. They probably represent priestesses of the great earth-mother and fertility goddess of the eastern Mediterranean. The serpents which they carry are age-old symbols of fertility *c.* 1600 B.C.

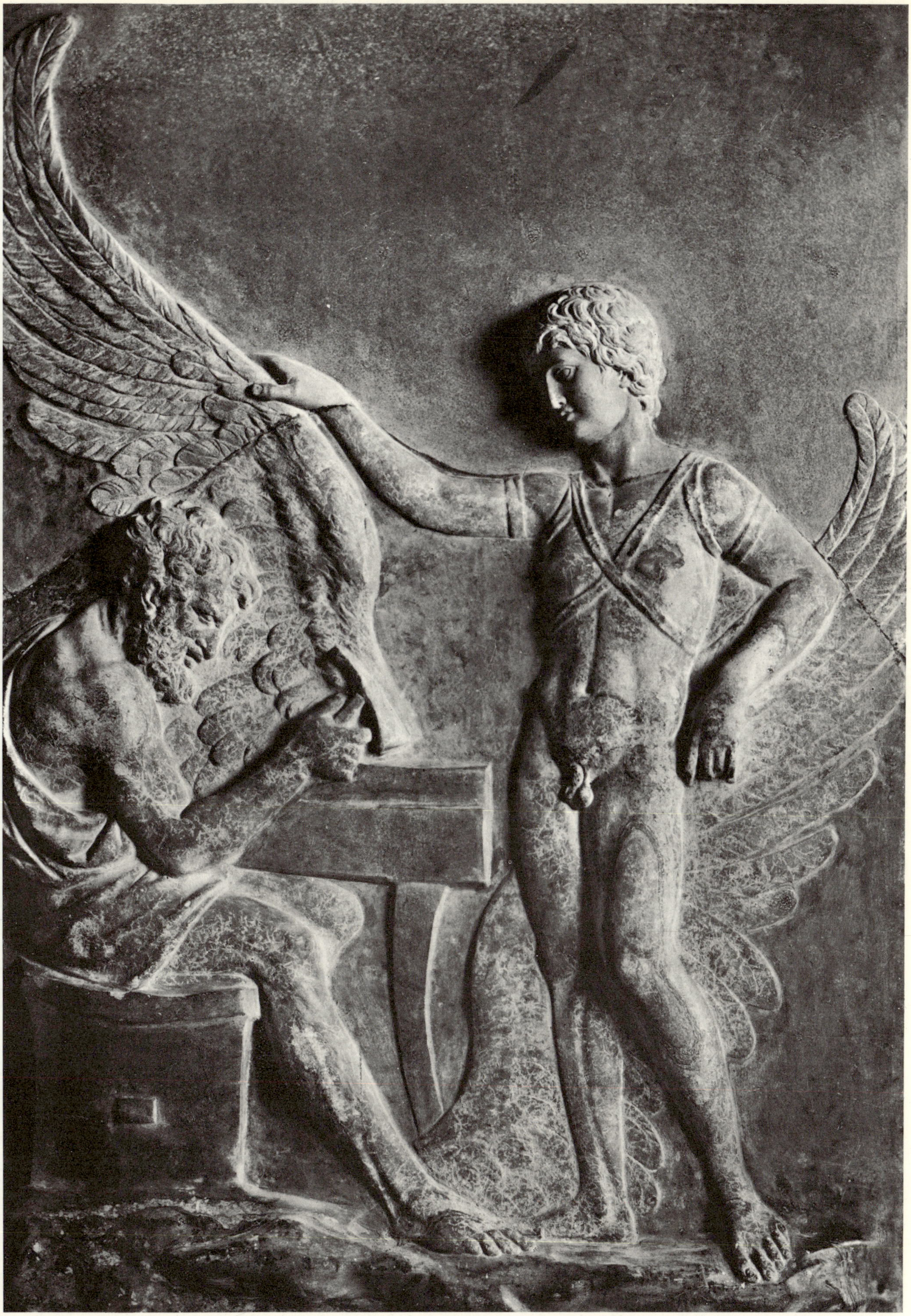

Daedalus and Icarus. Antique bas-relief. Villa Albani, Rome.

of the Phasis and rowing up the river came to the kingdom of Aeetes. Aeetes consented to give up the Golden Fleece, but imposed his own conditions. Jason had first to harness a plough with two wild bulls whose hooves were of bronze and whose breath was of flame. With them he must plough a field and plant it with dragons' teeth. Luckily for Jason the daughter of Aeetes, Medea, fell in love with him and, as she was a skilled magician, showed him how to overcome these fearful conditions. Then Aeetes refused to keep his word; Medea again helped Jason to vanquish the dragon who guarded the Golden Fleece and to seize the precious trophy. Both left the country in haste, pursued by Aeëtes. In order to delay her father's pursuit Medea did not hesitate to scatter the route with the dismembered body of her own brother whose throat she had cut. After a long and perilous voyage which took them across the Danube, the Ocean, the Libyan deserts, the Red Sea and the Mediterranean, the Argonauts finally returned to Iolcus. During Jason's absence Pelias had put Aeson to death. Others say that Aeson was still alive and was even rejuvenated by one of Medea's magic philtres. In any case, Jason avenged himself on his uncle. Medea persuaded the daughters of Pelias that she could with her charms rejuvenate their father, but that first they must cut him up into pieces and cook him. They carried out these instructions and Medea left matters as they were. After this atrocious murder Medea and Jason withdrew to Corinth. There they lived happily for ten years, whereupon Jason fell in love with Creusa (or Glauce), daughter of King Creon, and abandoned Medea. Medea avenged herself by sending a wedding present to the new bride: a magnificent robe which consumed her with inextinguishable fire. Medea then cut the throats of the children she had had by Jason and fled to Athens where she married Aegeus. She had to leave Athens when she tried to poison Theseus and went to her father at Colchis.

As for Jason, some say that he grew weary of life and killed himself. Others say that while resting in the shade of the ship *Argo,* the poop fell on him and accidentally crushed him to death.

ORPHEUS AND THE HEROES OF THRACE

Orpheus, the great hero of Thrace, was very different in character from the other Greek heroes. He was not distinguished for his warlike exploits. He was in origin perhaps a Thracian king, and he owed his fame above all to his amazing musical talent. Son of Apollo, he sang and played the lyre with such art that the savage beasts came running to listen and even trees would follow him. His talent performed miracles during the voyage of the Argonauts. The ship *Argo,* high on the beach, descended to the sea of its own accord at the sound of his singing. His songs arrested the Symplegades, those terrible moving rocks which threatened to crush the ship, and sent them down to the bottom of the sea. He lulled the dragon, guardian of the Golden Fleece, to sleep by singing, and thus facilitated the Argonauts' escape.

Such was the power of his voice and the harmony of his lyre that even the infernal deities submitted to them. He had married the nymph Eurydice whom he passionately loved. One day when Eurydice was fleeing from Aristaeus she was mortally bitten by a snake hidden in the grass. Orpheus was heartbroken at the death of his wife and resolved to descend into the Underworld to reclaim her. He was able to charm Hades and Persephone who gave him permission to take Eurydice back to earth on the sole condition that he should not turn to look at her during the journey. The couple had almost reached the gates of Hades when Orpheus impatiently and imprudently turned to look at his wife. At once she was whisked back into the sombre abode of the dead and vanished, this time for ever.

Orpheus was inconsolable and, some said, killed himself. But the more widely held opinion was that he was torn in pieces by Thracian women who were infuriated at this single-minded love for his wife. His head and his lyre were flung into the River Hebrus and carried as far as Lesbos. The head of the divine singer was caught in a fissure of rock where for long it delivered oracles. In the days of Lucian his lyre could still be seen in a temple at Lesbos and it was sacrilege to lay hands on it. One day Neanthus, son of the Tyrant of Lesbos, tried to play the wondrous lyre and was devoured by dogs who had been attracted by the sound. They also said that the head of Orpheus was found by a shepherd on the banks of the Melas, and in the town of Libethra in Macedonia they pointed out his tomb.

Other Thracian Poets. Thrace took pride in other famous poets and musicians, such as Philammon, also said to be a son of Apollo, and to whom was attributed the institution of choral dance in the temple of Delphi.

Philammon's son, Thamyris, an equally celebrated musician, once dared to challenge the Muses. For his presumption they deprived him of his voice and, into the bargain, blinded him.

To Thrace also belonged Eumolpus, son of Poseidon and Chione who was a daughter of Boreas. Eumolpus was thrown into the sea by his mother who wished to conceal her shame. He was found by Boreas who carried him to Ethiopia. From there Eumolpus went to the court of Tegyrius, King of Thrace. He was killed by Erechtheus when he was fighting with the Eleusinians against Athens. Some say that Eumolpus instituted the Eleusinian mysteries in honour of Demeter who had taught him how to cultivate the vine and trees. He also taught Hercules to sing and play the lyre.

MINOS AND THE HEROES OF CRETE

The ancient legends of Crete were early imported into Greece and were, as we have seen, a basis of Hellenic mythology, taking on new aspects as they became adapted to continental traditions. They centred for the most part around the figure of the fabulous King Minos. It seems, however, that more personages than Minos were concerned, and we should distinguish at least two Minoses of which one was the grandson of the other. But makers of myths are never worried about chronology or verisimilitude and wove all their legends around the single figure of Minos.

Minos then – with Rhadamanthys and Sarpedon – was a son of Zeus and Europa. Europa after her arrival in Crete married the king of the island, Asterius, who adopted her children. Minos succeeded Asterius to the throne of Crete. He distinguished himself by the wisdom of his laws and his sense of justice which, after his death, earned him promotion to the dignity of judge of the Underworld.

Minos had married Pasiphae. She had already given him several children when Poseidon, angered by Minos, inspired her with a monstrous passion for a bull. From this union was born the Minotaur, a monster half-human, half-bull.

The Athenians had killed the son of Minos, Androgeus, and in consequence Minos laid siege to Athens. Previously he had besieged Megara and vanquished the king Nisus, thanks to the treason of Scylla, Nisus' daughter. Scylla was in love with Minos and had therefore cut a golden lock of hair – on which the safety of the city depended – from her father's head. Minos took advantage of this treacherous act, but punished its author. He had the infatuated Scylla drowned in the Saronic Sea, where she was changed into a lark. Before Athens, however, Minos was less successful. The siege dragged on. Minos implored the aid of Zeus who visited Athens with a plague. To rid themselves of this plague the Athenians consented to send Minos an annual tribute of seven youths and seven maidens who were to be fed to the Minotaur. We have already seen how Theseus freed his city from this wretched servitude.

The Minotaur, who fed exclusively on human flesh, had been enclosed by Minos in an amazing palace from which no one could find an exit: the Labyrinth. The Labyrinth had been constructed by Daedalus, an Athenian distinguished for his ingenuity and cunning. To Daedalus was ascribed the invention of the axe and the saw. It was he, they said, who first fixed arms and legs to the *xoana,* the shapeless primitive statues of the gods. He killed his nephew who was a rival craftsman and sought asylum with Minos. Daedalus helped Ariadne when she gave Theseus the precious ball of thread which enabled the hero to find his way out of the Labyrinth. For this act of treachery Minos had Daedalus and his son Icarus locked up in the Labyrinth for a while. They flew to freedom by means of an ingenious pair of wings which Daedalus devised. In the course of their flight Icarus was imprudent enough to approach too near the sun. The wax by which his wings were attached melted and he plummeted into the sea which henceforth took his name, the Icarian Sea. Daedalus landed in Cumae, and from there went to Sicily where he gained the favour of King Cocalus. Thus when Minos pursuing Daedalus landed on the island, Cocalus refused to hand over his guest. Indeed, he smothered Minos in a bath. Such was the end of this famous monarch whose tomb was, nevertheless, shown in Crete.

ROMAN MYTHOLOGY

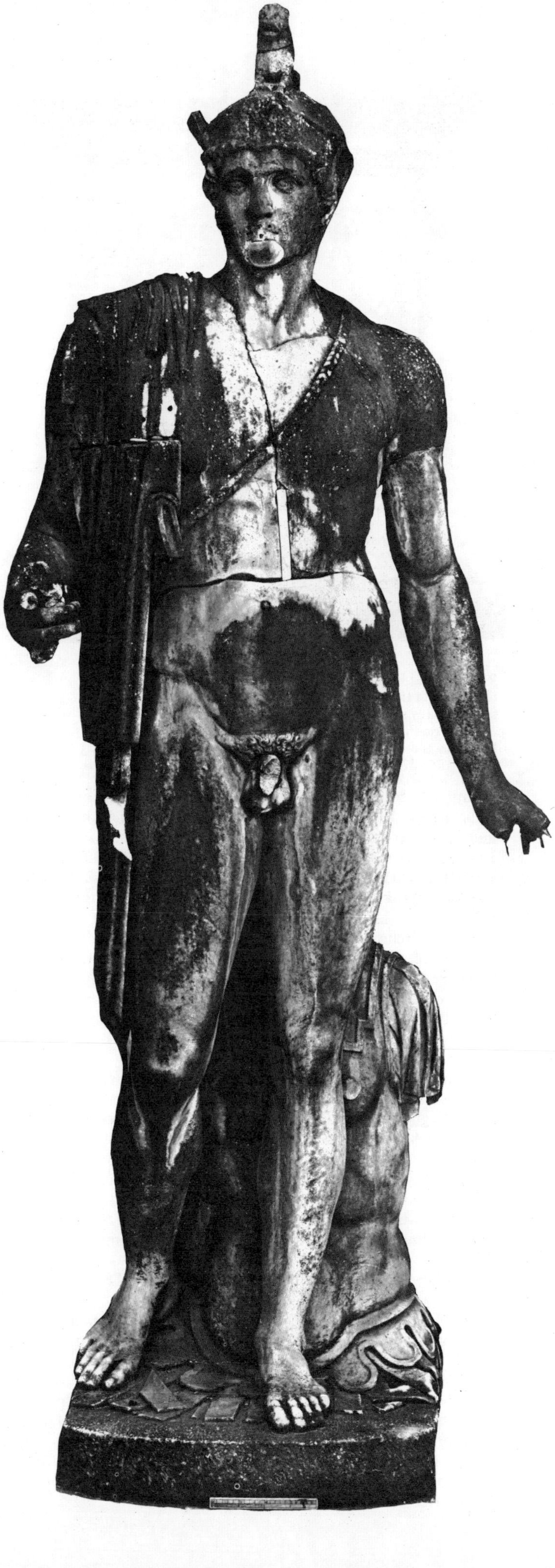

INTRODUCTION

The term Roman Mythology requires some explanation, even justification. The religious system whose centre is placed for convenience in Rome was not in fact purely Roman; the elements which composed it were numerous and varied. It was not monolithic, but a mosaic in which can be recognised contributions which were Etruscan, Alban, Sabine, Greek, Syrian, Persian, Egyptian. Obviously there were Roman elements too; but not to such a degree that they dominated the system and gave it a specifically national character.

Roman mythology seems poor when compared with the poetic and spiritual richness of Greek and Oriental mythologies. The Romans were a practical people with little imagination and they sought to form a religion which corresponded to their needs. It was important to them to feel sheltered from the perils which threatened the group or the individual; but they experienced no mystic necessity to love and worship the superhuman powers to whom they had recourse. Their gods were protectors for whose services they paid; and in case of failure their wages were withheld. *Do ut des:* I give to thee so that thou givest to me; such was the cynical profession of faith that one might inscribe above the entrance of the Roman Pantheon.

We use the term Roman pantheon inaccurately, for there was no genuinely Roman pantheon. The term was a Greek importation of the third century B.C. Was there not, then, a hierarchy of divinities worshipped in Rome? There was. But it was not at all like that great assembly of splendid personages, all possessing their individual traits and each easily recognised, which composed the Greek pantheon. It was something more abstract and utilitarian: a register, an actual catalogue (*Indigitamenta*) in which those who were interested could find the names of protective powers with special functions attributed to them and the rites which must be performed in order to purchase their favours.

In the course of time, when the fortunes of war had given the Romans empire over the ancient world, this utilitarian spirit which they had shown in constructing their own religious system led them without effort to build on their own soil the temples of the peoples they had defeated. These foreign gods whom they installed in the family circle, as it were, were new protectors who joined those who already stood guard over the Roman family and city. Rome, capital of the Empire, accepted within its walls gods who were formerly enemies but henceforth formed part of Roman political organisation.

ITALIC GODS

There were a certain number of purely Italic gods. It must not, however, be forgotten that foreign influences, and above all Greek influence, were felt from very early times. To give a few dates: the traditional foundation of Rome was 753 B.C. Now during the course of that century Greek colonies were established in Sicily and in southern Italy which was, indeed, called Magna Graecia. The Dorians founded Syracuse in 734 and Tarentum in 707. The Achaeans founded Sybaris in 721, Metapontum and Croton. The Euboeans installed themselves on both sides of the Straits of Messina, at Rhegium (Reggio) in Italy and at Messina in Sicily.

Mars, the most Roman of the gods, second in importance only to Jupiter himself. Originally an agricultural deity his character changed with that of the Roman people and he became instead the god of war of a conquering and warring nation, his agricultural functions devolving on to lesser gods. Mars had numerous temples both in Italy and throughout the empire, his chief festivals being in the spring. Roman marble.

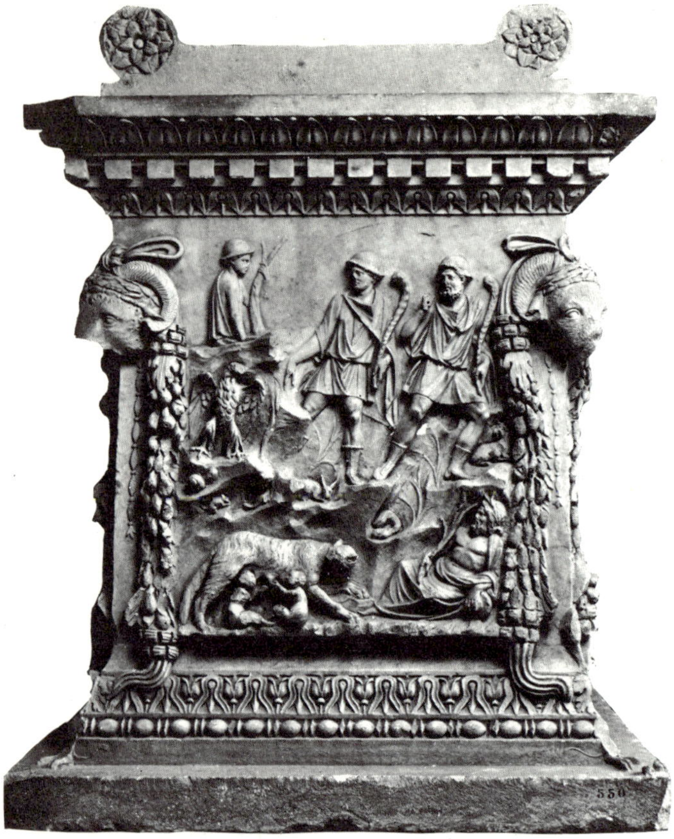

Romulus and Remus discovered by the shepherds.
Deposited at the foot of the Palatine by the flooded river Tiber, the twin baby sons of Mars and Rhea Silvia are shown being suckled by the she-wolf on this bas-relief from Ostia. On the right is the Tiber. Romulus and Remus later returned to the Palatine to found the city of Rome – according to tradition in 753 B.C. Roman altar discovered at Ostia.

Relations obviously sprang up between these Greeks and the Italic tribes. In particular, Etruscan towns like Tarquinii, Vulci and Caere were in regular touch with the Hellenic colonies. Now the Etruscans were closely involved in the history of primitive Rome, which they perhaps conquered. In any case, during the sixth century tradition speaks of the Etruscan kings of Rome: Tarquinius the Elder – who was of Greek origin – Servius Tullius and Tarquinius Superbus. Hence it is evident that the Romans, through the intermediary of the Etruscans, were very early exposed to Hellenic influence, which explains why in these notes devoted to the Italic gods we shall encounter certain details already observed in Greek mythology. This early hellenisation of the Roman pantheon foreshadows the more complete assimilation which took place in the course of the third and second centuries B.C.

We have seen that the Romans considered their gods as protectors. There were thus two chief classes of Italic gods: those whose function it was to guard the State, and those who watched over the family – the family being considered as an integral cell of the State.

We shall study first the gods of the State; but this does not imply that in the eyes of the Romans these were in any way more important than the gods of the family. Indeed the cult rendered by the *Paterfamilias* – who acted as an actual priest – to his lares, his penates and his manes was just as important as the cult of Janus or Jupiter.

GODS OF THE STATE: PRINCIPAL DIVINITIES

Janus. Janus is unique in that he was an essentially Italic god or, more precisely, Roman. He appears in no other mythology.

The origin of his name is uncertain. Cicero tried to find it in the verb *ire*. Others preferred the root *div* (*dividere*), and assumed that the first form of the name was *Divanus*. A third hypothesis suggests a form *Jana*, sometimes employed for Diana, of which the root *dius* or *dium* evokes the idea of the luminous sky.

This last etymology agrees with the established fact that Janus was in origin a solar deity. But his functions were wide and important and derived one from another.

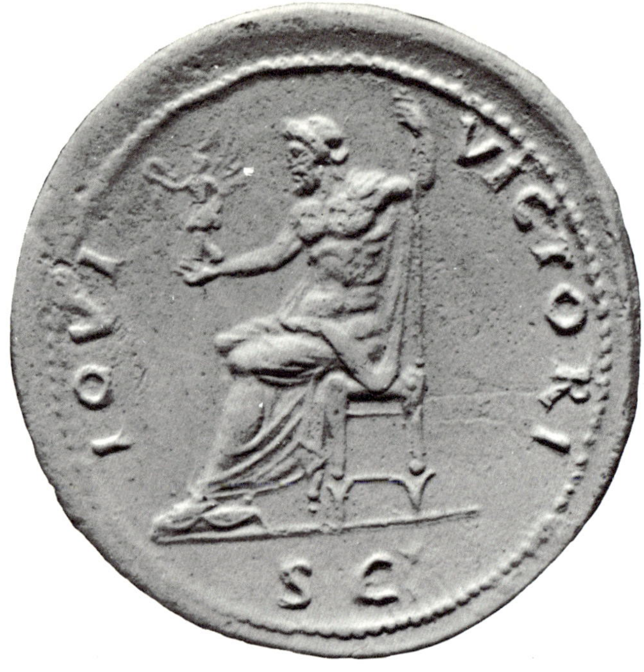

Bearded Janus. Roman Coin. Bibliothèque Nationale, Paris.

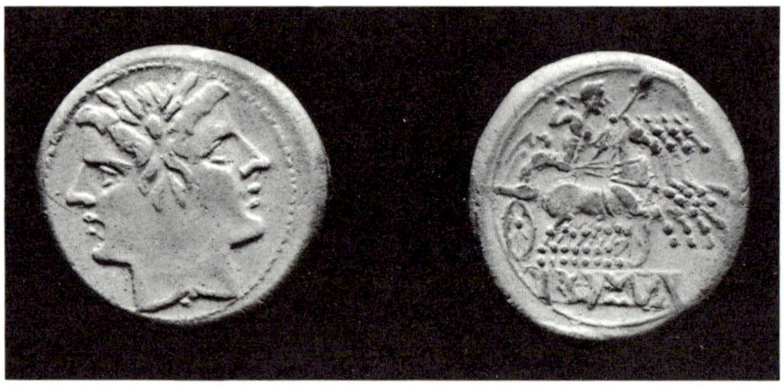

Beardless Janus. On the reverse, Jupiter mounted on a quadriga. Roman Coin. Bibliothèque Nationale, Paris.

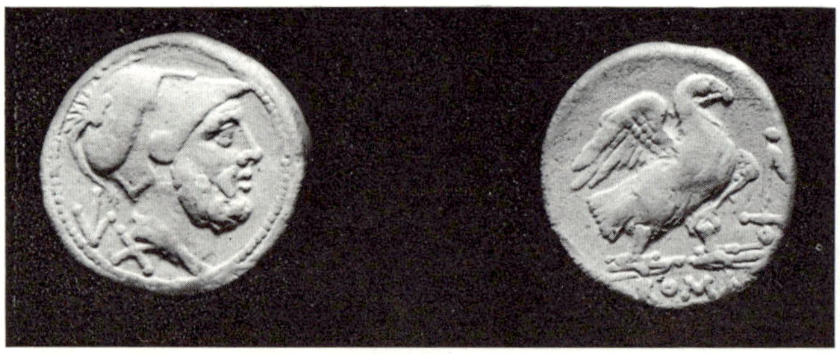

Mars bearded and helmeted. Roman Coin. Bibliothèque, Nationale, Paris.

Janus was first the god of all doorways: of public gates (*jani*) through which roads passed, and of private doors. His insignia were thus the key which opens and closes the door, and the stick (*virga*) which porters employed to drive away those who had no right to cross the threshold. His two faces (*Janus bifrons*) allowed him to observe both the exterior and interior of the house, and the entrance and exit of public buildings.

Being god of the gates he was naturally the god of departure and return and, by extension, the god of all means of communication. Under the name Portunus he was the god of harbours; and since travel can be either by land or sea, he was supposed to have invented navigation.

Janus was also the god of 'beginnings'. As a solar god he presided over daybreak (*Matutinus Pater*). He was soon considered as the promoter of all initiative and, in a general way, he was placed at the head of all human enterprises. For this reason the Romans ascribed to him an essential role in the creation of the world. He was the god of gods, *Janus Pater*. Ovid relates that Janus was called *Chaos* at the time when air, fire, water and earth were all a formless

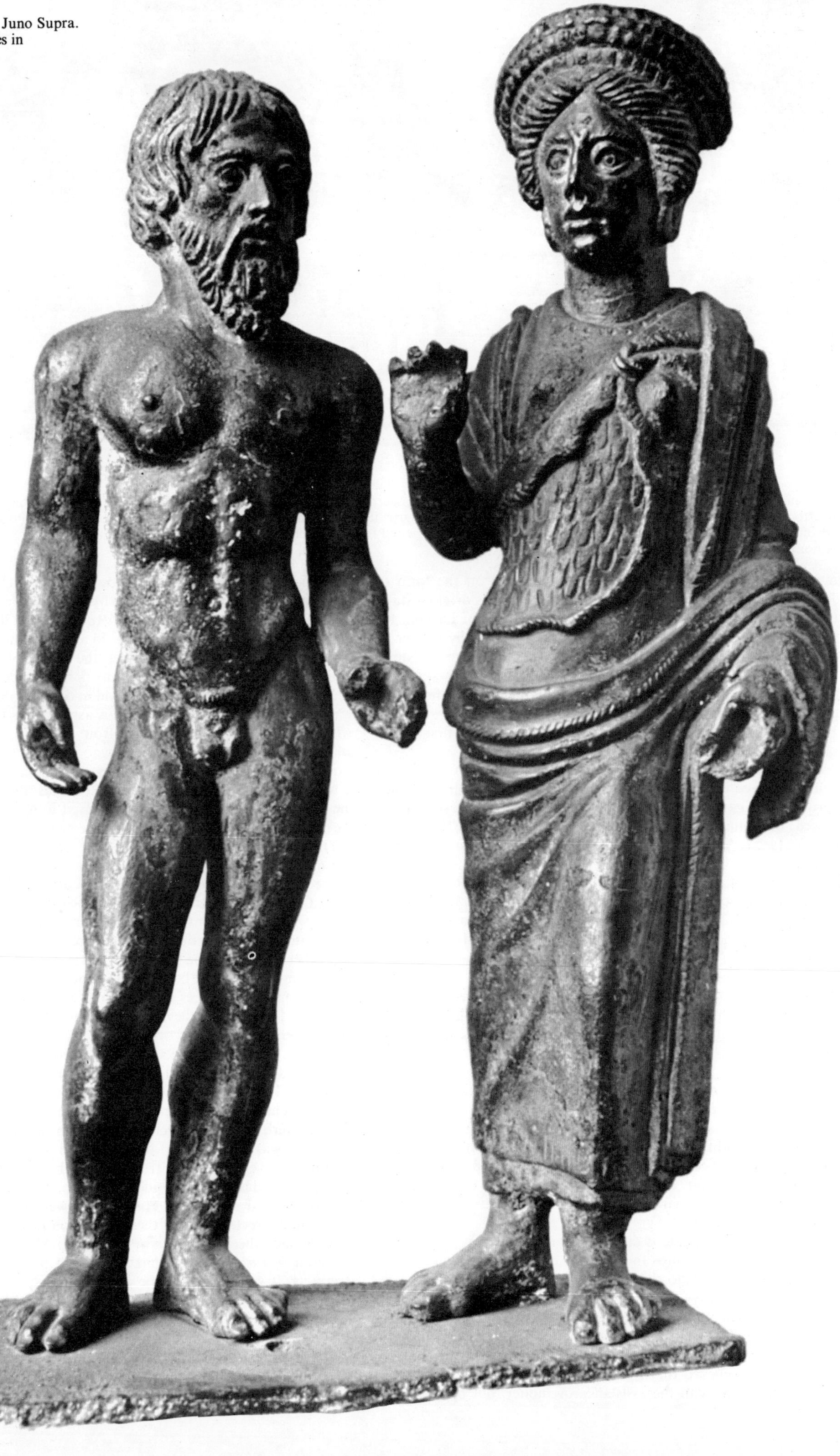

Jupiter Tinia and Juno Supra. Etruscan statuettes in bronze. Louvre.

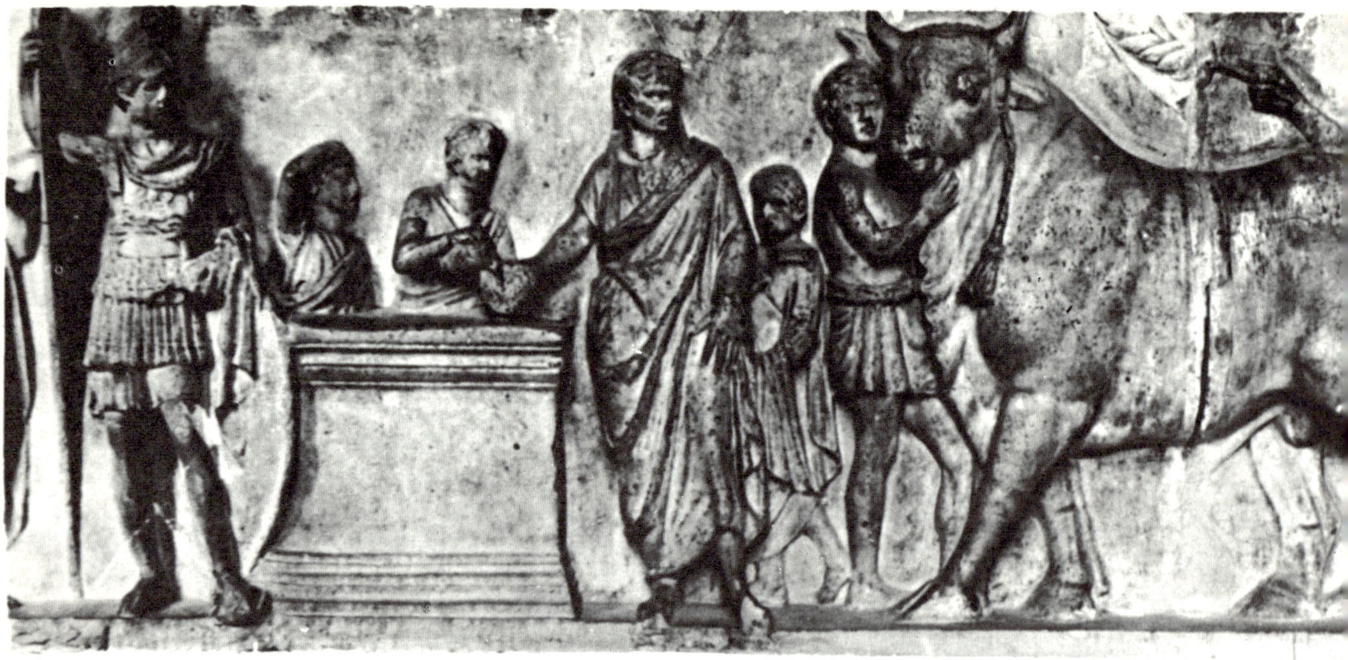

A Roman sacrifice. This relief probably depicts the *suovetaurilia*, a sacrifice consisting of a bull, a ram and a pig (the most valuable items of Roman livestock) which was offered to Mars in his original capacity as an agricultural deity during the spring festival of the *Ambarvilia*. Prior to becoming a war-god Mars had been responsible for protecting crops and fields and for increasing the fertility of animals. A horse was sacrificed to him each October.

mass. When the elements separated, Chaos took on the form of Janus: his two faces represented the confusion of his original state. Other legends made Janus a king of the golden age of Latium. He was said to have welcomed Saturn driven from the sky by Jupiter.

The cult of Janus was established either by Romulus or by Numa and always remained popular among the Romans. Janus appeared at the head of religious ceremonies and, in his quality of father of the gods, was the first on the Romans' list, coming even before Jupiter. He was honoured on the first day of every month and the first month of the year (*Januarius*) bore his name.

In the Forum he had a temple whose gates were open in times of war and closed in times of peace. The reason for this custom is not certain. The gates of the temple of Janus were, however, rarely closed: once under Numa, three times under Augustus, then under Nero, Marcus Aurelius, Commodus, Gordius III, and in the fourth century.

It was told of this temple how, during an attack on Rome by the Sabine Tatius, a Roman woman was bribed by jewels to show the enemy the path to the citadel. But Janus – whose function it was to open a channel for fountains – caused a jet of boiling water to gush forth which stopped Tatius short. On the spot where the water spurted the temple of Janus was erected.

We possess no statue or bust of Janus, but on coins his effigies are numerous. He is normally represented with a double face, or as an older man with a beard. The crown of laurel does not appear on all his images.

Mars. Mars is without doubt the most Roman of the gods. His cult was more important than that of Jupiter. This was due to the fact that Mars was very intimately concerned with Roman history, first because tradition made him the father of Romulus, then because of his functions as an agricultural god, and finally because he was the god of war. He thus corresponded to the two successive conditions of the Roman citizen, who was himself first a farmer and then a conqueror.

The origin of his name is disputed. Some connect it with a root *mar* or *mas* which signified the generative force. Others give to the root *mar* the sense of 'to shine', which would imply that Mars was at first a solar divinity.

The most ancient forms of his name are *Maurs* and *Mavors* which were contracted into the usual form Mars. Other forms – *Marspiter* and *Maspiter* – were created by the addition of the word *pater*.

The Latins believed that Mars was the son of Juno. Juno gave birth to him, not with the assistance of Jupiter, but by means of a mystic union with a fabulous flower. Mars was the husband of the vestal Rhea Silvia. He took her by surprise while she was sound asleep, and he became the father of Romulus and Remus.

His functions were at first rustic. In ancient times he was the god of vegetation and fertility. Under the name of *Silvanus* – who afterwards became a distinct divinity – he presided over the prosperity of cattle. He lived in forests and in the mountains. In a general way he protected agriculture; in this aspect he is found associated with *Robigus* who preserved corn from the blight (*robigo*). Several animals were sacred to him: the woodpecker, the horse and the wolf whose image frequently appears in the sanctuaries of the god; it was a she-wolf who had suckled Romulus and Remus. Among the plants and trees which were dedicated to him were the fig-tree, the oak, the dog-wood, the laurel and the bean.

These details, together with the fact that Mars was the god of Spring, when his most important festivals were celebrated, demonstrate that Mars was essentially an agricultural god. He was called Mars *Gradivus*, from *grandiri*, 'to become big, to grow'.

His warrior functions only came afterwards, but in the end they supplanted his former duties which were then transferred to Ceres and Liber. Mars became the god of battle. Honour was paid to him in his temple at Rome before setting out on military expeditions. Before combat sacrifices were offered to him, and after victory he received his share of the booty. Moreover he sometimes appeared on the field of battle, escorted by Bellona and Vacuna, warrior-goddesses, by Pavor and Pallor, who inspired terror in the enemy ranks, and by Honos and Virtus, who instilled in the Romans honour and courage. Mars still preserved his former title of *Gradivus*, but it had changed in meaning and by corruption was now connected with the verb *gradi* 'to march'. Mars was now a foot-soldier. After victory he was accompanied by Vitula and Victoria.

Mars was venerated in Etruria, in Umbria, among the Sabines who associated him with the goddess Nerio, in Samnium and among the Oscans and in Latium. His temples were very numerous and the Romans erected more of them in the conquered territories.

At Rome where he was worshipped as Mars and as Quirinus he had a *sacrarium* on the Palatine Hill in the *Roma Quadrata* of Romulus. It was there that the god's sacred spears were kept and the twelve shields, *Ancilia*, which were objects of his cult. Wishing to bestow upon King Numa a token of his benevolence Mars – or according to Ovid, Jupiter – caused a shield to fall from the sky, to which the fate of Rome was thenceforth attached. In order to avoid all risk of theft or destruction, Numa had eleven identical shields constructed and placed them under the guardianship of

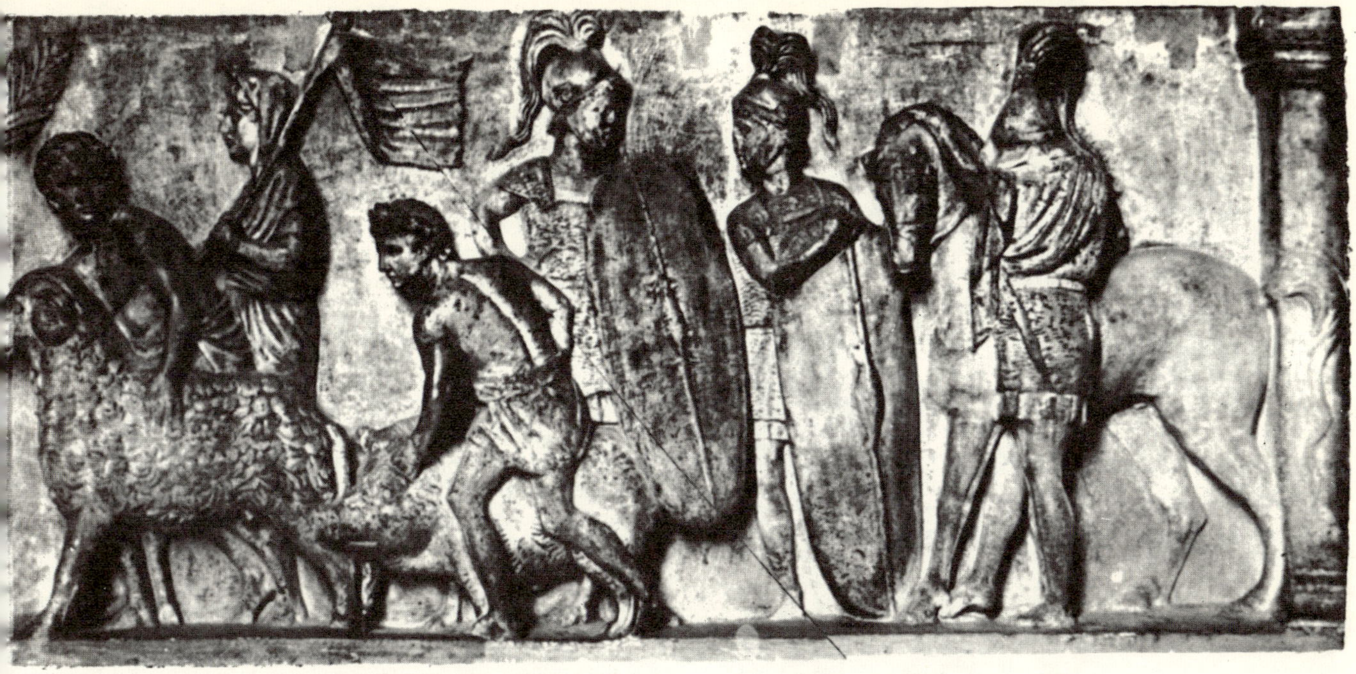

a special college of priests, called the Salii. Primitively the rites of the Salii were intended to protect the growth of plants.

Mars appeared as a purely agricultural god in the festivals of the *Ambarvalia* which were celebrated in Rome on the twenty-ninth of May. They were purification festivals. During them Mars was offered the *suovetaurilia*, in the course of which a pig, a ram and a bull were led around before being immolated to the god.

Mars also figures in the chanting of the *Arvales*, a college of priests who were responsible for the cult of Dea Dia, a rural goddess, closely related to Ceres.

Representations of Mars almost all derive from Greek art. The most Roman image of him is probably a bearded Mars, with cuirass and helmet, reproduced from a statue of Mars Ultor in the temple constructed by Augustus. As for the numerous figures of Mars engraved on medals, they are in the Greek style and copy the Ares type.

Bellona, his companion – sister, wife or daughter – had a celebrated temple in Rome near the gate of Carmenta. There the senate gave audience to ambassadors. In front of the temple rose the 'war column' which the fetialis struck with his lance when war was declared. The priests of Bellona were chosen from among the gladiators.

Jupiter. In the name Jupiter can be found the root *di, div,* which corresponds to the idea of brilliance, the celestial light.

The function of the Etruscan Jupiter, who was called *Tinia,* was to warn men and, on occasion, to punish them. For this purpose he possessed three thunderbolts. He could hurl the first whenever he felt like it, as a warning; but to hurl the second, which was also premonitory, he had to obtain the permission of twelve gods, *consentes* or *complices*. The third thunderbolt was the one which punished. It could only be released with the consent of superior or hidden gods – *dii superiores, involuti*. This primitive Jupiter can be compared with Summanus, another Etruscan thunder-god who presided over the night sky.

The Latin Jupiter was first of all the god of light – sun and moon – and of celestial phenomena: wind, rain, thunder, tempest and lightning. His role was thus important to the agricultural population. Several epithets correspond to his diverse duties: Jupiter Lucetius was the god of light; Jupiter Elicius (*elicere*, to elicit, to draw forth) caused the rain to fall; Jupiter Liber was the god of creative force; Jupiter Dapalis presided over sowing; Jupiter Terminus watched over the boundary stones of fields.

Jupiter rapidly lost his rural functions and became the great protector of the city and the State. He was a warrior-god (Jupiter Stator, Feretrius, Victor). He symbolised the great virtues of justice, good faith and honour; he protected youth. In short he was the great tutelary power of the Empire: Jupiter Optimus Maximus. Solemn titles were reserved for him: Conservator orbis, Conservator Augustorum, Propugnator, etc. A more prosaic title, Pistor – 'baker' – recalled that Jupiter once advised the Romans, who were besieged in the Capitol by the Gauls, to throw bread over the walls in order to show the enemy that they were in no fear of starvation.

Jupiter was worshipped throughout Italy. On the Quirinal he had a very ancient temple, the Capitolium vetus, where he formed a triad with Juno and Minerva. This temple was built on the Capitoline Hill under the Tarquins and the three gods there formed the Capitoline Triad. There Jupiter bore the name Optimus Maximus.

It was under the aegis of the Capitoline Jupiter that the senators assembled to declare war. Generals appeared before him prior to setting out to war and after victory returned to offer him a crown of gold and part of the booty.

The *ludi romani,* annual games, were celebrated in the circus in his honour. Their foundation was attributed to the Elder Tarquin. They consisted of athletic contests, especially chariot races.

As well as the ludi romani there were the *ludi plebeii* which consisted of foot races and theatrical entertainments.

Images of Jupiter are practically all derived from Greek art. The Volscian Jupiter is, however, curious in that it is beardless and the god is depicted as a young man.

Juno. Sister and consort of Jupiter, Juno was a very great Italic goddess. In the remotest epochs she was found among the Sabines, the Oscans, the Latins, the Umbrians and the Etruscans.

Her oldest titles, Lucetia and Lucina, correspond to her chief functions.

Juno Lucetia was the feminine principle of the celestial light, of which Jupiter was the masculine principle. Like Jupiter she was also a moon-goddess; in this latter aspect she was coupled with Diana.

Goddess of light, she was by derivation the goddess of childbirth, for the new-born baby is brought into the light. The goddess was then Juno Lucina.

In this aspect she occupied an important part in the ceremonies of marriage and afterwards. She had many titles: Juno Pronuba watched over the arrangement of marriages; Juno Domiduca conducted the bride to the house of her husband and saw that she crossed the threshold; Juno Nuxia coated the doorposts with perfume; Cinxia unknotted the bride's girdle. Later Juno Lucina protected the pregnant wife, strengthened the bones of the infant (Juno Ossipago) and assured the mother's supply of milk (Juno Rumina). Juno Sospita received fervent invocations at the time of labour and delivered the baby.

As a goddess of childbirth she was naturally invoked by wives who were barren. It was Juno Lucina who rescued the Sabine women from the scourge of sterility with which they had been stricken after their abduction.

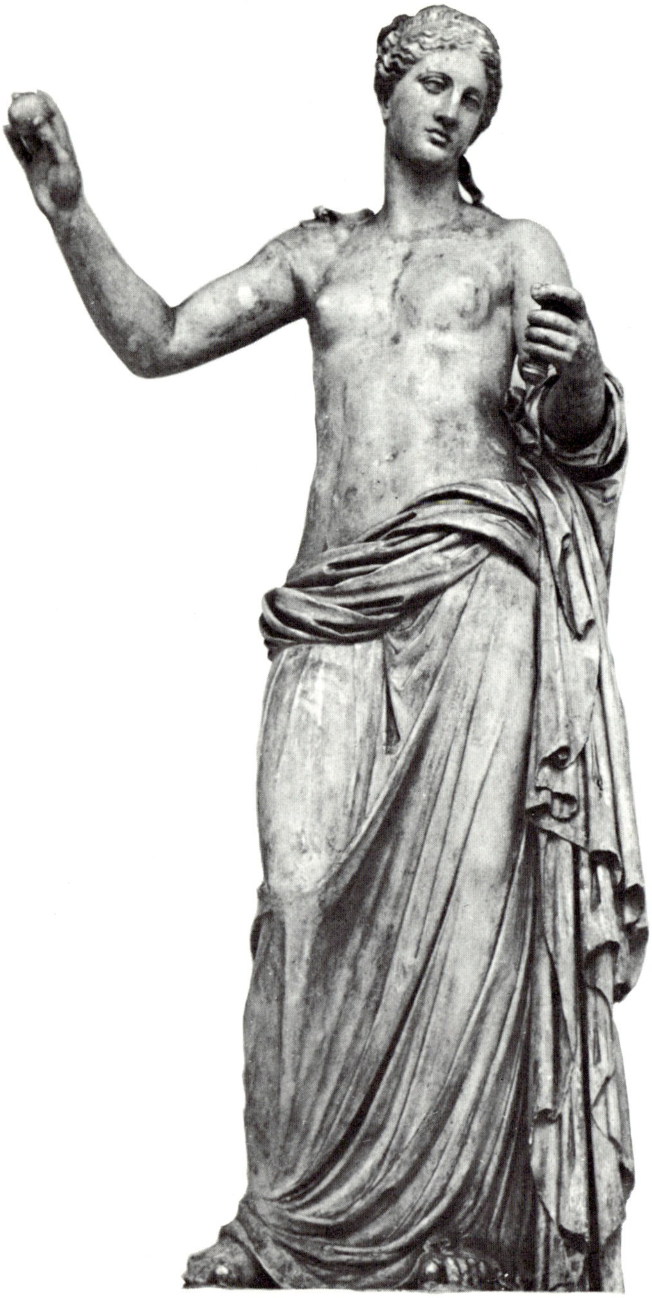

The Venus of Arles. The Roman goddess of love is shown holding an apple and admiring herself in a mirror in this antique sculpture restored by Pradier in the nineteenth century. Originally an Italian goddess of horticulture who brought beauty and fruitfulness to gardens, Venus later became identified with the Greek goddess Aphrodite and extended her influence to human beings as well.
Probably a copy of a Praxitelean work of *c.* 360 to 350 B.C.

To sum up, Juno Lucina was the goddess and symbol of the Roman matron – a logical consequence of her own title of spouse of Jupiter, the supreme god.

Her role of goddess of childbirth was not confined to the protection of the Roman wife. Under the name Populonia, Juno also watched over the multiplication of the race. Under the name Martialis, mother of Mars, she was the goddess of birth and finally of fertility – Caprotina. This is what they said of the origin of this epithet: taking advantage of Rome's weakness after the invasion of the Gauls, the neighbouring tribes marched against the city under the leadership of Posthumius Livius. They threatened to destroy Rome unless all the women and girls were turned over to them. Some female slaves offered to go to the camp of Posthumius, disguised as free women. The stratagem was successful. But that night, when the enemy was asleep, they unfurled from the top of a wild fig-tree (*caprificus*) a signal to the Romans who hastened to come and slaughter the aggressors. The slaves were set free and rewarded by the State; and their act of heroism was commemorated every year on the seventh of July, known as the Nonae Caprotinae.

Juno Moneta, after having been the adviser of those about to be married, became the adviser of the Roman people. When the Gauls attempted to scale the walls of the citadel of the Capitol it was Juno's sacred animals, the geese, who warned (Latin *monere,* to warn) the defenders of the peril. Later this epithet Moneta changed its meaning, due to the installation near the temple of Juno of the mint where *money* was coined.

Juno Sospita, protectress of confinements, became in a broader sense she who was always willing to help, the liberator. She had two temples at Rome. At Lanuvium, Juno Sospita had a temple which was guarded by a serpent. Every year a maiden would offer cakes to the serpent. If it accepted, this was a sign that the girl was a virgin. Its refusal was an evil omen and a year of sterility was to be feared.

A temple to Juno Lucina was built on the Esquiline in 735 B.C. only a few years after the foundation of Rome. In the temple of the Capitoline Triad, built by the Tarquins, Juno's title was Regina. There she held the golden sceptre, the Patera and the thunderbolt. She then played the role of august consort of Jupiter and protectress of the Roman people. Her cult was spread throughout the Empire.

The festivals of Juno Lucina, the *Matronalia,* were celebrated by Roman matrons at the Kalends of March. After a ceremony in the sacred grove of the Palatine it became a family festival. The mistress of the house was its central figure; she received a present from her husband and served her slaves at the table.

Juno Regina is almost always represented standing; her attributes are the sceptre, the patera, the veil and the peacock.

Juno Sospita is armed with spear and shield.

Juno Lucina carries a child in her arms; there are two more at her feet. She is also represented with a child in her arms and in her hand a flower which recalls the circumstances in which she conceived the god Mars.

Vesta. Vesta is the most beautiful of Roman divinities, bright and pure like the flame which is her symbol. Her name derives – like the name Hestia – from a Sanskrit root, *vas,* which expresses the idea of 'shining'.

The Latins had made Vesta a goddess who personified the earth and fire. The Romans kept only the second of these personifications. Nor was Vesta the goddess of fire in its broadest sense, but only of fire required for domestic use or in religious ceremonial.

In the beginning Vesta was associated with Janus Pater and Tellus Mater, and was the protectress of sown fields. She was also a symbol of idealised maternity – although she was a virgin – because fire nourishes.

As a goddess of fire she received both a private and a public cult.

Every hearth had its Vesta. With Jupiter Dapalis she presided over the preparation of meals; she was offered the first food and drink. With the Lares and the Penates she held a pre-eminent position in the house.

At Rome the centre of her cult, which was said to have been originated by Romulus, was in the Regia. It lasted almost all the year, being interrupted only during the months of January and November. The chief festivals of Vesta were the Vestalia which were celebrated on the seventh of June. On that day her sanctuary (which normally no one except her priestesses, the Vestal Virgins, entered) was accessible to mothers of families who brought plates of food. The Vestals officiated. The ceremonies were simple and unsanguinary. The objects of the cult were essentially the hearth fire and pure water drawn into a clay vase, handmade, and narrow at the base so that it could not stand on the ground.

The Vestals, who played a role of first importance in Roman liturgy, enjoyed exceptional prestige. When Numa first instituted them they were two in number; Servius increased them to six. They were chosen by lot from patrician families and entered the college between the ages of six to ten. They remained there for thirty years. During the first ten years they received instruction in their duties which they exercised for the following ten years. Then, in their turn, they taught the younger Vestals.

They took vows of absolute chastity. Those who broke their vows were punished by death. Originally they were whipped to death, but the Elder Tarquin modified this torture: they were then whipped and walled-up alive in a tomb which was sealed after a few provisions had been deposited in it. Vestals accused of impurity sometimes managed to clear their reputation. It was told how Tuccia proved her virginity by bringing back water from the Tiber in the sacred sieve. The accomplice of the guilty Vestal was whipped to death in the Forum Boarium. During the course of eleven centuries only twenty Vestals broke their vow and suffered punishment.

If a Vestal let the sacred fire go out she was whipped by order of Pontifex Maximus.

When the Vestals had finished the thirty years of their engagement they could marry. They rarely took advantage of this right, however, preferring to maintain the privileges of their position. Whenever they appeared in public they were preceded by a lictor, and if a man condemned to death chanced to meet a Vestal he was immediately reprieved.

Statues of Vesta are not numerous. Her image is found on coins, mostly imitations of Greek art. She is always veiled.

Vulcan. Vulcan was one of the oldest of Latin gods, ante-dating even Jupiter. Under the name Volcanus, he was the first Jupiter of Rome whose foundation he protected. In his aspect of Jupiter he formed a couple with Juno. He was also associated with Maia, an incarnation of the Earth Mother, and with Vesta, considered as goddess of the earth. He was not allied with Venus who in those remote times still played a small part in Roman mythology. Volcanus was the father of Cacus, whose legend will be recounted later. To him was also attributed the paternity of Servius Tullius, king of Rome.

A maiden in the neighbourhood of Praeneste was seated one day near the fire when a spark fell on her; some months afterwards she gave birth to a son. She exposed him in the forest where some girls found him beside a lighted fire. For this reason he was regarded as a son of Vulcan and because of the smallness of his eyes they named him Coeculus. When he grew up he founded the town of Praeneste, celebrating the occasion with public games. As some of those present cast doubts on his paternity he invoked his father Vulcan and the crowd was immediately surrounded by flames.

Vulcan was the god of the thunderbolt and of the sun, then the god of fires whose ravages he could arrest, and finally became the god who was associated with the attribute of life-giving warmth.

He was invoked as the divinity of the hearth and, as he was united with Maia, mother of springs, he was considered the first god of the Tiber. He even possessed warlike functions and may have preceded Mars as god of battles. In the early history of Rome, then, Volcanus was a more important personage than the later Vulcan.

The *Volcanalia* were celebrated on the twenty-third of August. On the twenty-seventh of August Vulcan was fêted in the *Volturnalia* in his role of god of the Tiber, Volturnus being one of this river's religious names. The seventeenth of August was the festival of the *Portunalia,* also consecrated to the Tiber. It is probable that in ancient times human sacrifices were offered to Vulcan. His altar in the Forum was the Volcanal.

The Romans always represented him as bearded, sometimes with a slight facial deformity which doubtless recalled his infirmity. Near him stand the hammer, tongs and anvil, attributes which came from Greece. He wears a bonnet (*pileus*) and a short tunic which leaves his right arm and shoulder free.

Saturn. Saturn was a very ancient agricultural divinity of Latin and Roman origin; he was of the same rank as Janus and Jupiter. His name may be connected with *satur* (stuffed, gorged) or with *sator* (a sower); in either case he is synonymous with abundance.

Saturn was a working god and a vine-grower (*vitisator*). Under the name Stercutius he saw to the manuring of fields. He was associated with Ops, who was a personification of the earth's riches. Saturn was supposed to have been king of Italy during the golden age. Driven from the sky by Jupiter he hid himself (*latuit*) in the country since called Latium, and indeed beneath the Capitol at Rome itself. His reign brought prosperity and abundance.

The *Saturnalia,* celebrated on the seventeenth of December, originally consisted of a series of rural festivals, *sementivae feriae, consualia larentalia, paganalia.* The Saturnalia assumed their real importance in 217 B.C., a time when the defeat at Lake Trasimene, a prelude to the disaster of Cannae, caused a religious revival among the Romans.

The Saturnalia lasted seven days, from the seventeenth to the

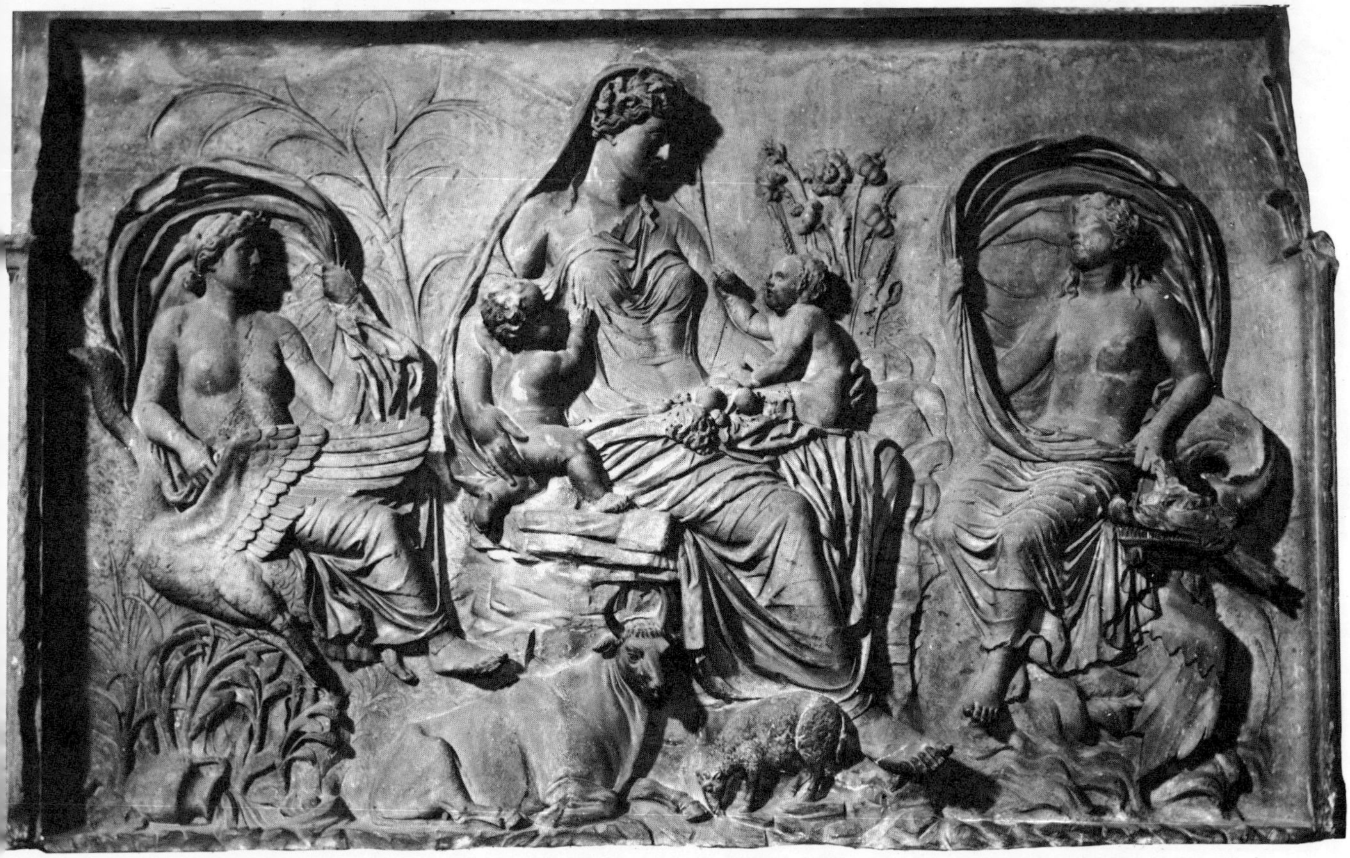

Tellus Mater with Air and Water. An earth-goddess and goddess of fecundity, Tellus Mater protected the fruitfulness of the soil and watched over marriage and the procreation of children. Here she is portrayed holding two children while fruit, flowers, plants and corn fill her lap and grow beside her. On her right is Air seated on the back of a swan while on her left Water is shown with a marine monster. Bas-relief from the Ara Pacis, or Altar of Peace, erected on the Campus Martius between 13 B.C. and 9 B.C.

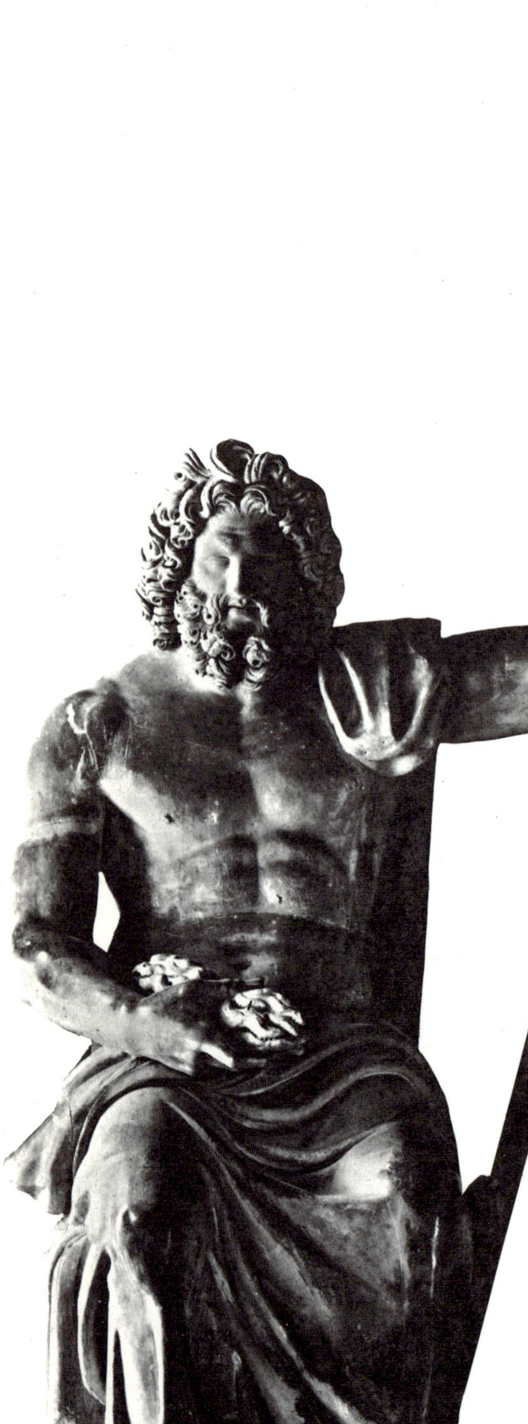

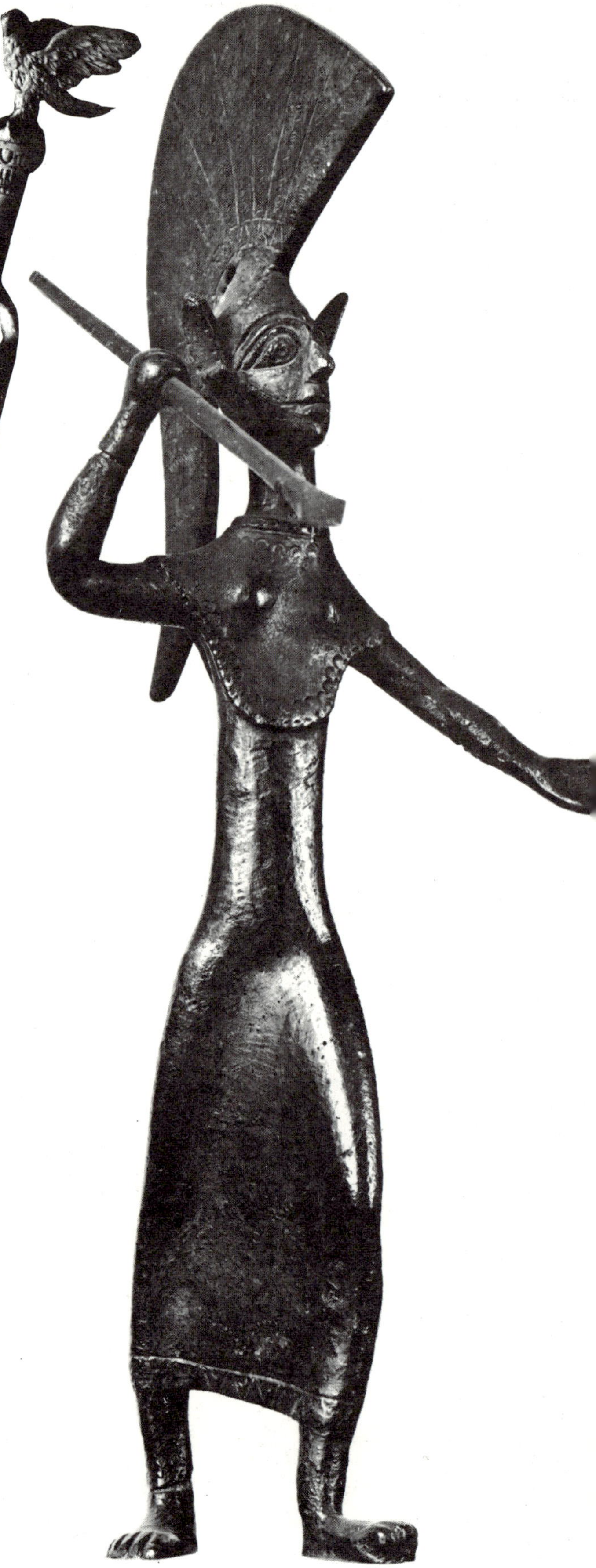

Jupiter. The supreme god of the Roman pantheon, he was the great protector of the city and the state and the guardian of public morality being concerned with oaths, treaties and leagues. Originally an Italian sky-god he was later closely identified with the Greek Zeus, his cult being introduced to Rome by the Etruscan kings shortly before their fall.
With Juno and Minerva he formed the Capitoline triad.

Minerva. This Etruscan figure of the goddess shows her wearing a helmet and breastplate like the Greek goddess Athene, with her right arm raised to hurl her spear. One of the twelve great figures of the Roman pantheon, Minerva first appeared in Etruria and was possibly a goddess of the thunderbolt. She was merged with Athene very early however and was consequently the least Roman of the divinities of the Capitoline triad. Bronze of the sixth century B.C.

twenty-third of December. It was a period of unrestrained festivity. After the religious ceremony there was an immense feast: people even took the precaution of bathing in the morning in order to remain all day at table. Encumbering togas were removed and they ate at ease in tunics. In memory of the golden age the masters served the slaves who, during the festivals, could say and do what they liked. There was a general suspension of public activity. Law courts did not sit, schools were closed, commercial and military operations were suspended.

In the temple of Saturn near the Capitol the State treasury was kept, as well as the standards of the legions which were not on campaign. The god's effigy was bound with woollen strips which prevented him from leaving Roman territory. His bands were untied during the Saturnalia.

In a painting from Pompeii Saturn is standing, his chest half bare, a sickle in his hand. On coins he carries a sickle or ears of corn.

Minerva. The name Minerva is connected with the root *manas* or *mens*. She first appeared in Etruria under the names of *Menrva, Menrfa, Meneruva, Menarva,* and was perhaps a goddess of the thunderbolt. It seems that this Etruscan Minerva very early merged with the Greek Athene. Minerva is hence the least Italic of the divinities with whom she formed the triad Jupiter-Juno-Minerva.

The Roman Minerva was especially the protectress of commerce and industry and of schools. It was only later that she assumed the character of a warrior-goddess.

According to Roman tradition the cult of Minerva originated in Falerii. When in 241 B.C. the Romans took this town they carried Minerva off, built her a temple at the foot of Mount Coelius and gave her the name Minerva *Capta*. There was, however, a temple already consecrated to Minerva in Rome on the Aventine. In any case her cult was not ancient in Latium or among the Sabines.

Minerva was honoured, in association with Mars, in the *Quinquatrus* which lasted five days during the Spring equinoxes.

Minerva was venerated throughout the Empire. Particularly homage was paid to her by corporations of artisans, flute-players, doctors and so forth.

There was no purely Roman figure of Minerva. The Etruscans had represented her with wings, holding a screech-owl in her hand. It will be remembered that this bird was sacred to Athene.

Mercury. The name Mercury is connected with the root *merx* (merchandise) and *mercari* (to deal, trade). He is not very ancient for he does not appear in the *Indigitamenta*. The early Romans, being above all countrymen, had no need for a god of commerce.

The Roman Mercury appeared only about the fifth century B.C. and was exclusively the god of merchants. For long he was known only in this capacity, so that Plautus, in his prologue to *Amphitryon*, reminds his audience that Mercury presided over messages and commerce. Like certain other minor divinities – Pecunia, Aesculanus, Argentinus – he watched over tradesmen's profits.

Mercury had a temple on the Aventine. Among animals the cock was especially sacred to him.

To portray him Roman artists generally drew upon representations of Hermes. They gave Mercury a beardless face and, for attributes, the caduceus and the winged petasus, with a purse in his hand.

AGRICULTURAL DIVINITIES

Faunus. Legend made Faunus the son of Picus and the grandson of Saturn. He was thought to have been one of the first kings of Latium. He gave laws to the still barbarous tribes and invented the shawm or rustic pipe. He deified his father Picus and his mother Canente who on the death of her husband wasted away with grief until there was nothing left of her. Faunus was one of the first Roman rustic divinities and, above all, a fertility god. He also possessed the gift of prophecy and caused voices to be heard in the countryside. But to obtain oracular information from him he had first to be bound, as King Numa succeeded in doing. Under the name Lupercus he had a temple on the Palatine, the Lupercal – the name of the grotto where the she-wolf suckled the twins, Romulus and Remus. The *Lupercalia* were celebrated on the fifteenth of February and were among the most important festivals on the Roman calendar. Their function was purificatory. Goats

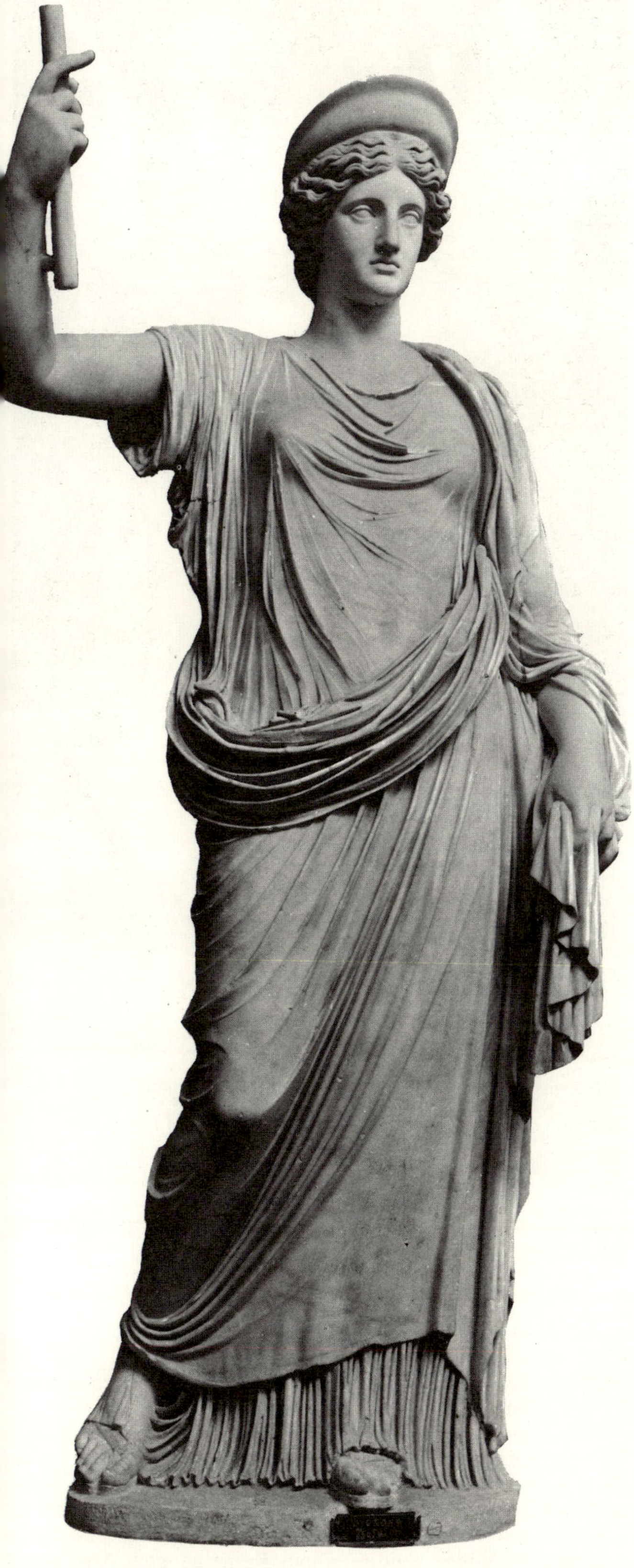

Juno. The consort of Jupiter, she was a very important Italian goddess who already had a temple on the Esquiline as early as 735 B.C. Like Hera, with whom she was identified, Juno was the protectress of women and marriage but unlike the Greek goddess she also developed wider functions and as Juno Regina of the Capitoline triad became the protectress of the State. This statue probably shows her in this role.

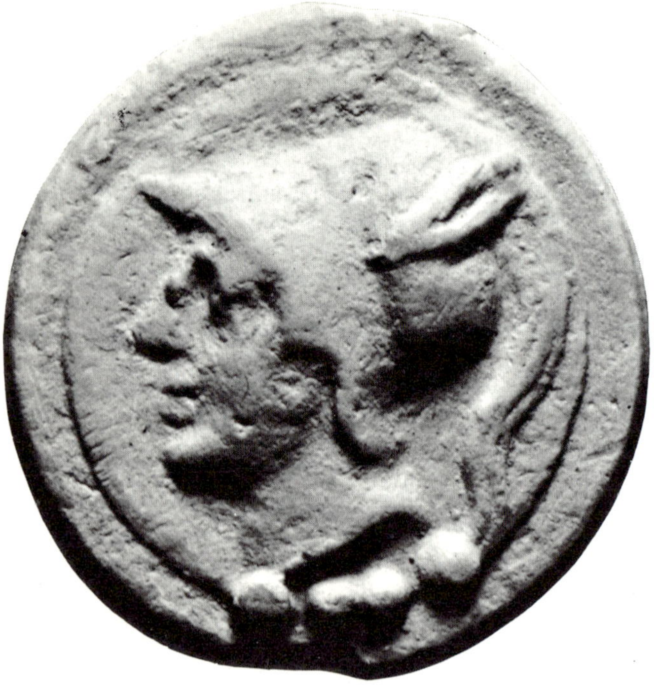

Minerva, portrayed as the goddess Roma. Roman Coin. Bibliothèque Nationale, Paris.

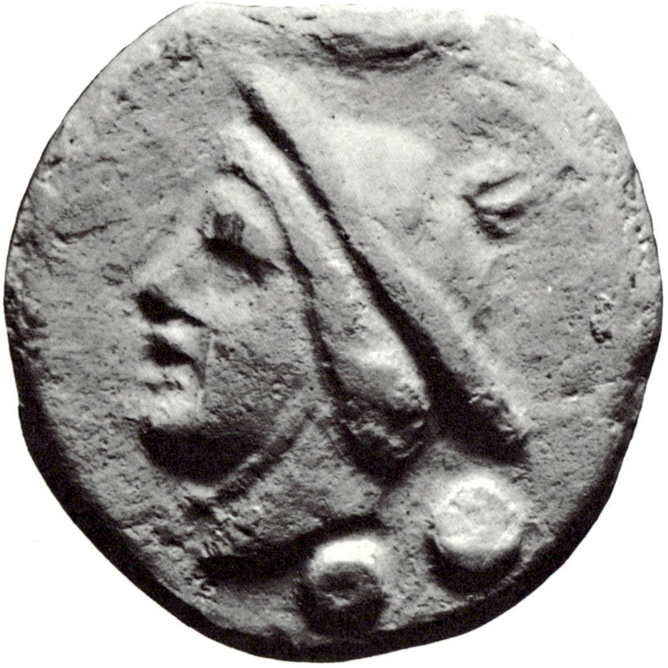

Mercury. Effigy on a Roman Coin. Bibliothèque Nationale, Paris.

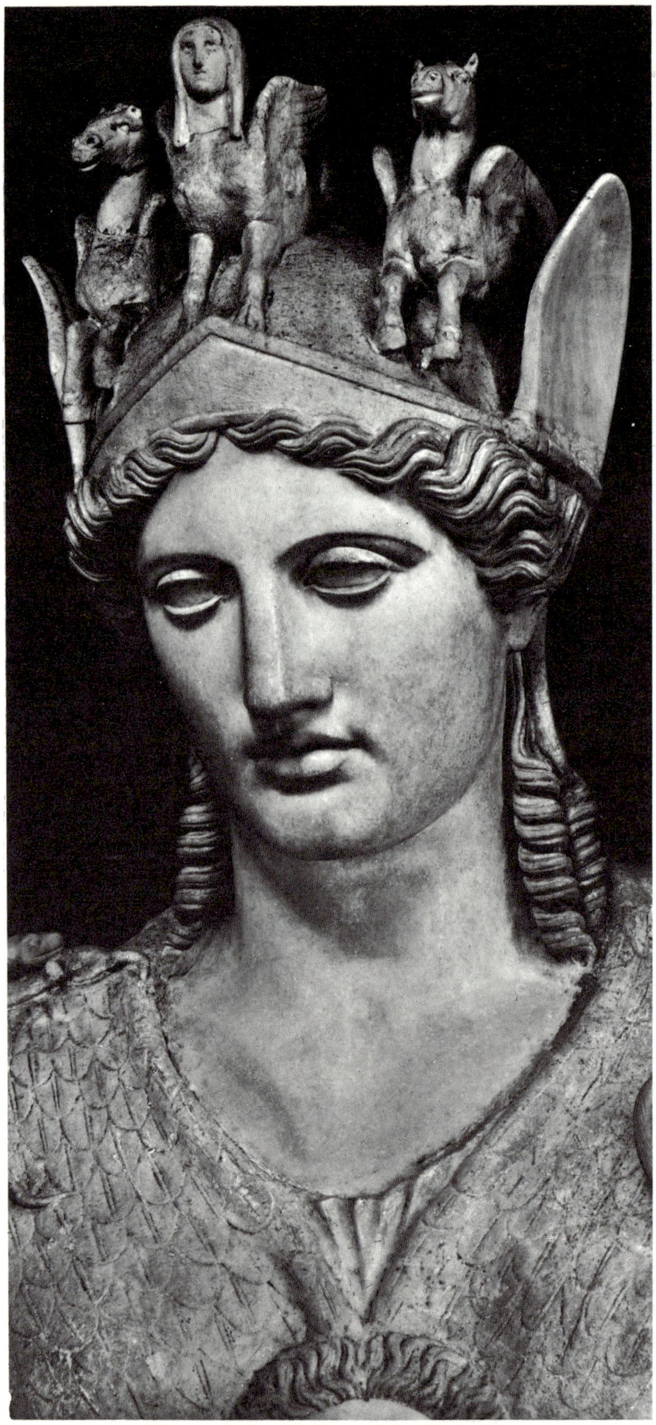

Head of Minerva. To the Romans Minerva was above all the goddess of handicrafts, learning and the arts and as such was particularly venerated by the guilds of artisans, artists and professional men.
She later assumed Athene's other role as a warrior-goddess and was worshipped in association with Mars in the *Quinquatrus* – a festival which finally came to be considered her own.
Statue after the Athene Parthenos of Phidias.

and he-goats were sacrificed, and perhaps dogs. After the animals were immolated two youths were led to the altar. The priests touched their brows with the bloody knife and wiped them with a wad of wool soaked in milk, after which the youths would burst out laughing. The priests of the college of the Luperci, half naked, draped only in the skins of the sacrificed goats, would then perform a ceremony during which women who wanted to become pregnant would hold out their hands and turn their backs to be struck with a whip of goat's hide. Ovid gives a rather amusing explanation of the nudity of the Luperci. One day Faunus surprised Hercules and Omphale asleep in a grotto. Faunus wished to take advantage of the sleeping young woman, but the lovers had playfully exchanged garments. In the darkness Faunus did not notice this and, deceived by the softness of the robe Hercules was wearing, approached him instead of Omphale. He was, as can be imagined, rudely repulsed. To avoid such misadventures in the future, Faunus insisted that his priests should be naked when they celebrated his festivals. The Lupercalia were only suppressed in 494 A.D. by Pope Gelasius who replaced them by a festival in honour of the ritual Purification of the Virgin.

With Faunus, god of fertility, was associated Fauna, who was his wife or daughter. Fauna was invoked under the name of *Bona Dea:* women celebrated her cult at the beginning of December with a mysterious festival which was forbidden to men and degenerated into an orgy. Also associated with Faunus was Ops, a very ancient Sabine goddess whom Rome adopted. Ops was a personification of creative force and agricultural fertility. She was venerated in the *Opalia* on the nineteenth of December and invoked by sitting down and touching the earth with the hand. Fauna, or Bona Dea, was also closely related to Maia who symbolised the earth's Spring fertility and was honoured in May. Another goddess of Latium, Marica, was loved by Faunus who, according to

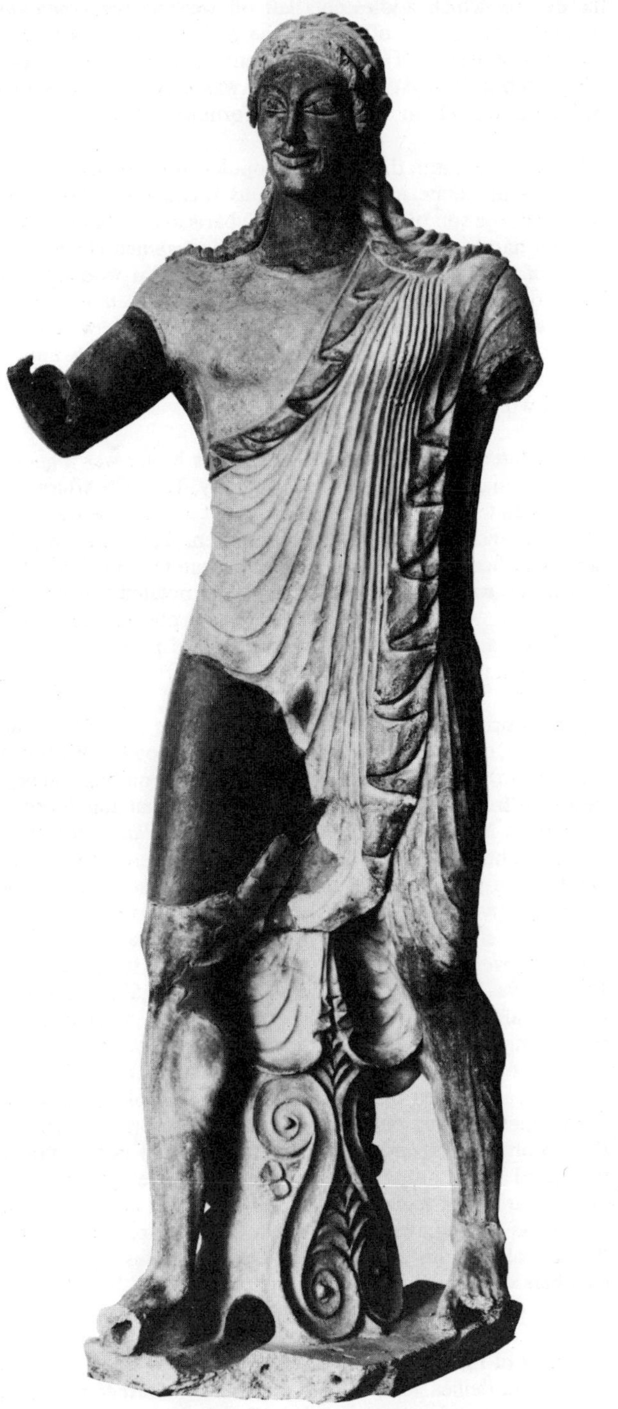

The Apollo of Veii. Apollo was introduced into Italy at a very early date and his cult was first established in Rome in the fifth century B.C. following an outbreak of plague. During the Republican period he was chiefly worshipped as a god of healing and prophecy but under Augustus he became one of the chief gods of Rome and as Apollo Palatinus was in some ways the equal of Jupiter Optimus Maximus. Etruscan terracotta, late sixth century B.C.

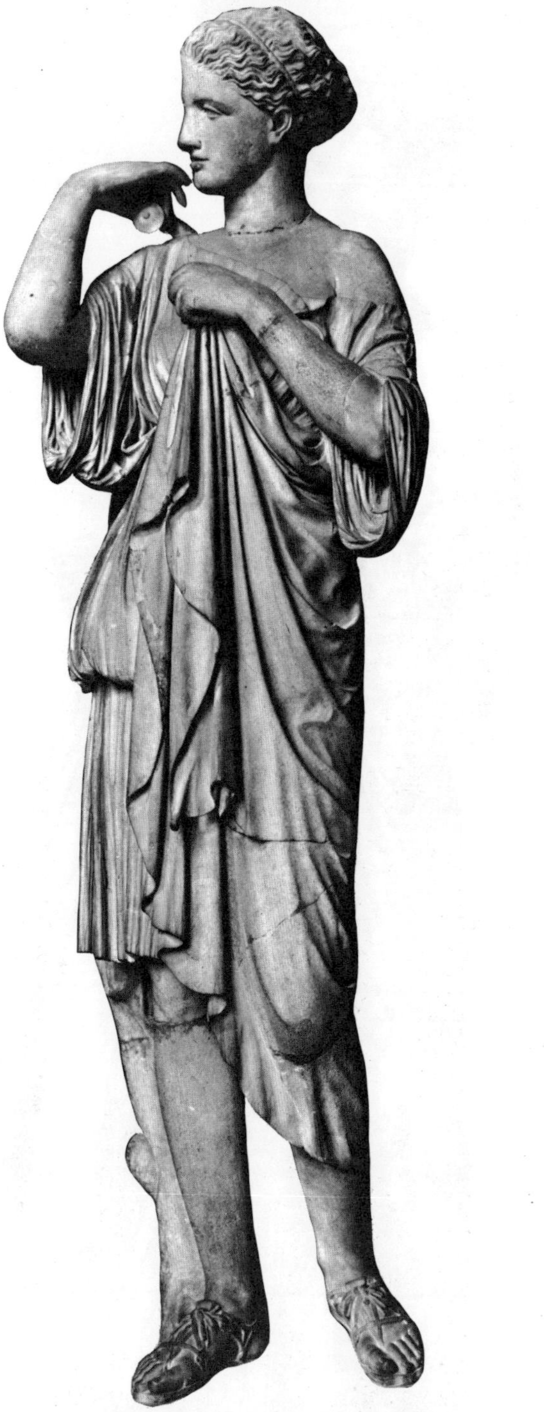

The Diana of Gabii. An Italian goddess of mountains and woods and of women and childbirth, Diana was anciently identified with the Greek goddess Artemis who possessed a similar character and functions. Her cult was widespread, her most famous shrine being at Nemi while at Rome she was worshipped in a temple on the Aventine traditionally founded in the sixth century B.C. This life-size Roman marble statue possibly reproduces Praxiteles' Artemis Brauronia of 346 B.C.

Virgil's interpretation, made her the mother of the king, Latinus.

Consus. Consus was one of the most ancient gods of Rome. He presided over sowing. His festivals, the *Consualia,* consisted of two distinct ceremonies. In the first, which took place on the twenty-first of August after the harvest, Consus was associated with Ops. There were chariot races and horse races, entertainments, dancing and a curious race on oxhides rubbed with oil. The second ceremony of the Consualia took place on the fifteenth of December after the sowing. Chariot races with mules were held in the circus. Consus had an altar near the Circus Maximus. During the year this altar was covered with earth to evoke the idea of sowing. It was only swept for the Consualia. It was during the festivals of Consus that the Romans abducted the Sabine women.

Pales. Pales was at first a masculine divinity attached to the person of Jupiter. Afterwards Pales took on feminine form and became the protectress of flocks, giving vigour to the males and fecundity to the females. Her festivals, the *Palilia,* were celebrated on the twenty-first of April, the date of the foundation of Rome. On the eve of the festival a purification ceremony took place in houses and stables in which a sacred mixture made by the Vestals was employed. Then the livestock and stables were sprinkled with lustral water. Pales gave her name to the hill where Roma Quadrata rose, the Palatine.

Liber Pater. This Italic god's first function was to preside over the fertility of the fields. He was also a god of fecundity. He was honoured on the seventeenth of March in the *Liberalia.* This was

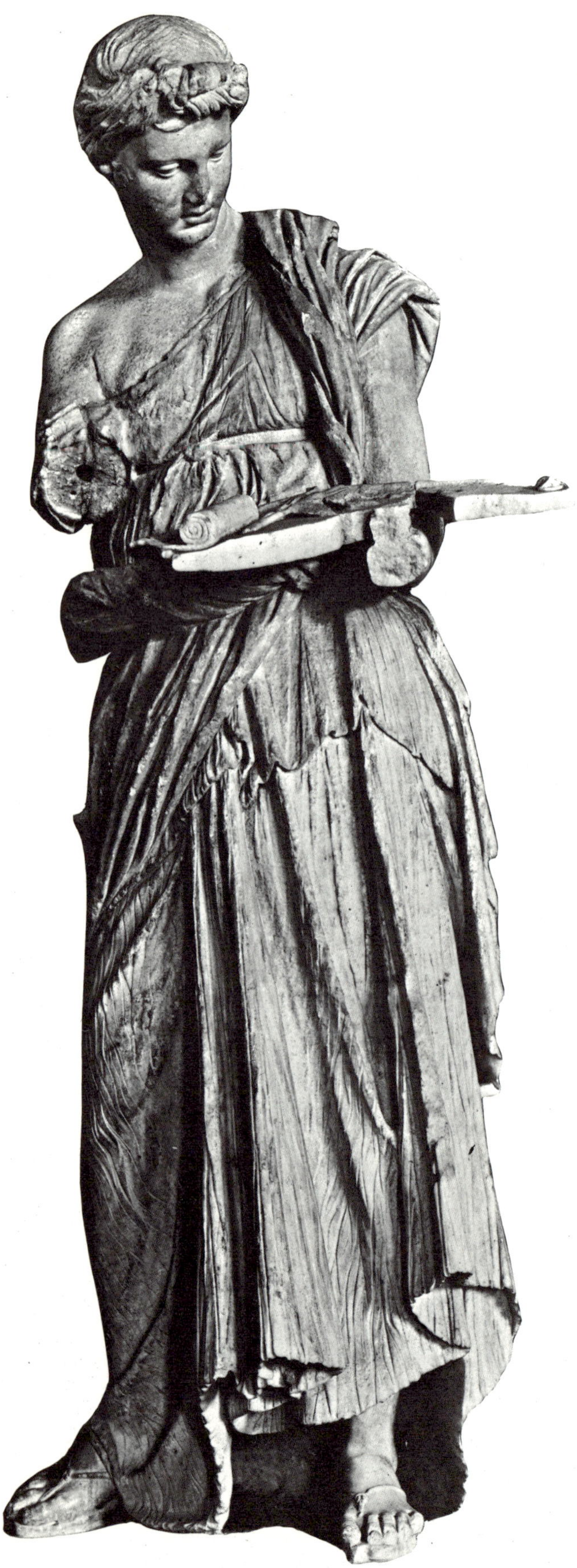

The Antium Girl. This life-size statue from Antium depicts a young temple servant or priestess performing a religious rite.
On her arm she balances a circular salver on which were originally arranged a rolled-up strip of woollen cloth, a laurel twig and a vessel, of which only one foot remains. She wears a linen chiton and a woollen cloak. Probably a Roman copy of a Hellenistic bronze of the mid third century B.C. Parian marble.

the day on which adolescents left off wearing the *praetexta* and assumed the apparel of a man (the *toga virilis*). Liber Pater did not become the god of vine-growers until after he had been confused with Iacchus Dionysus. His consort was Libera, an ancient Italic goddess about whom there is little information.

Silvanus. This Latin divinity was popular in Rome from very early days. As his name indicates Silvanus was a forest god. He was, they said, the son of a shepherd of Sybaris and a she-goat or else a maiden named Valeria Tusculanaria. He watched chiefly over the work of clearing land and making pastures in wooded country. His province extended to all arboriculture, as well as to guarding herds and to the tilling of the soil. Domestic cattle were sacrificed to him. He was often confused with Faunus or with Pan whose physical aspect he had. Silvanus was particularly feared by children and by women in labour.

Tellus Mater. In the remotest times Tellus Mater was a goddess of fecundity in company with a male divinity, Telluno. Afterwards she was associated with Jupiter. In her role of mother she watched over marriage and the procreation of children. The bride would offer her a sacrifice when she entered her husband's house. She had her part in the *porca praecidanea,* the sow immolated to Ceres 'before the harvest'. As an agricultural deity she protected the fruitfulness of the soil and all the states which the seed passes through when it is sown in the soil.

Flora. In primitive central Italy Flora was the goddess of budding springtime, of cereals, fruit trees, the vine and flowers. With Robigus (or Robigo) she prevented wheat-rust. With Pomona she watched over fruit trees. She had a temple on the Quirinal and another near the Circus Maximus. Her festivals, the *Floralia,* lasted from the twenty-eighth of April to the third of May and were rather licentious. On the twenty-third of May there was another festival in her honour, a rose festival. The Sabines and the Latins venerated another goddess, Feronia, who shared some of Flora's functions and watched over spring flowers and vegetation. It is possible that Feronia was originally an underworld divinity. She was associated with Soranus, a Sabine divinity who became a solar god after first having been a god of the underworld. In the course of a sacrifice which mountaineers were offering on Mount Soracte wolves appeared and seized the offerings; they then took refuge in a cave from which escaped pestilential vapours. The oracle declared that these wolves were under the protection of the god Soranus and instructed the mountaineers to live by rapine, like the wolves. Whence arose the name *Hirpi Sorani* which was given to them. The name was perpetuated in a Roman family, especially devoted to the cult of Soranus and Feronia. During the festivals of Feronia members of this family, the Hirpini, would walk bare-footed over glowing coals without burning themselves.

Divinities of the Waters. All stretches of water, all springs and all rivers were deified. The nymph Juturna – or rather Diuturna – a native of Latium, was the goddess of still waters and of rivers over which Jupiter gave her empire in reward for her love. She was venerated in the *Juturnalia* on the eleventh of January by the college of the *Fontani* who were artisans assigned to aqueducts and fountains.

Neptunus was perhaps originally a water-god or a protector against drought. During the *Neptunalia* on the twenty-third of July they would build huts of branches for shelter against the sun.

As for the Nymphs, they were in a general way water divinities. Usually they were associated with some superior deity like Jupiter, Diana or Ceres. Their cult originated in Latium. Their springs were found near the Capena gate. The most famous was the fountain of the nymph Egeria whom Numa, the king, would come to consult during the night. According to Ovid she married Numa and after his death retired to the woods in the valley of Aricia where Diana changed her into a fountain. She is reputed to have foretold the fate of new-born babies.

Among the other nymphs may be mentioned the Camenae who were prophetic nymphs. One of them, Antevorta, knew the past; another, Postvorta, the future. The most important of the Camenae was Carmenta who first dwelt in Arcadia where she had a son by Mercury, Evander. When Evander left his native land and came to Italy, where he founded the town of Pallantium, Carmenta came with him. She changed the fifteen Greek letters brought by Evander into Roman letters; she had the gift of prophecy and lived until she was a hundred and ten. After her death she received divine honours.

Ceres and Diana. In their aspect of Italic divinities Ceres and Diana offer no particular interest. Ceres, who came from Campania, had a temple in Rome; but her rites, like the temple itself, were Greek. Diana retained only briefly her primitive character as a goddess of light, mountains and woods. She was rapidly hellenised. Among other sanctuaries Diana had a temple on the shores of Lake Nemi whose priest was traditionally an escaped slave. In order to obtain this office he had first to kill his predecessor in single combat. From then on he, too, was a target for any assassin who might wish to supplant him.

Venus. Venus, too, in early days occupied a very modest position in the Roman pantheon. With Feronia and Flora she symbolised spring and fruitfulness. She had her place in the *Floralia* (twenty-eighth of April to the third of May) and in the *Vinalia rustica* on the ninth of August.

Vertumnus. It is not known whether Vertumnus was Etruscan or Latin. In any case the origin of his name is clearly Latin: *vertere*, 'to change'. He was a god of fruit trees like Ceres and Pomona. Pomona was courted by all the rural gods, but she yielded only to Vertumnus. In order to seduce her he was forced to assume several different guises, appearing before her as a labourer, a vinegrower and a harvester. In the end he overcame her suspicions by assuming the aspect of an old woman. Vertumnus was also associated with Silvanus, and he was venerated with the god of the Tiber, the course of which he was supposed to have altered. Tradition shows him revolving in the assembly of gods, where he was constantly changing shape.

GODS OF THE UNDERWORLD.

It was above all from primitive Etruria that the Romans borrowed their conception of the infernal regions and its inhabitants. In the Etruscan underworld the naive and terrifying visions common to all primitive religions mingle with the abstract conceptions of more developed systems. Both were submitted to Greek influence while they retained their national characteristics. In the infernal regions Eita or Ade (Hades) with his consort Persipnei (Persephone) reigned. The chief infernal figures were Charun (Charon) and Tuchulcha, a female demon with ferocious eyes, the ears of an ass, a beak in place of a mouth, two serpents twined around her head and a third around her arm. At the moment of death the soul was seized by two groups of genii. The first were malevolent and were led by Charun who carried a mallet or a torch. The second group were benevolent and were led by Vanth. Their dispute symbolised the struggle between good and evil. The deceased travelled to the afterworld either in a chariot, on horseback, or on foot. He is sometimes depicted with two genii, one leading him by the hand and the other following him; sometimes accompanied by a winged divinity who carries in his right hand a scroll on which is inscribed the dead man's record. Another subterranean divinity, Tages, taught the Etruscans haruspicy – that is to say the rules for foretelling the future by the examination of entrails and by the observation of lightning. Tages in the guise of a child suddenly rose from a furrow before a certain labourer, Tarchon, and revealed to him certain magic formulas which were afterwards gathered together in books.

The Romans had no great Underworld divinities. Those of whom we shall speak have a confused personality which only developed under Hellenic influence. In the primitive epoch the real infernal gods were the Manes.

Dis Pater. His name signified that he was the richest of all the gods – *dis* is a contraction of *ditis*, 'rich' – and indeed the number of his subjects continued ceaselessly to increase. In much the same way the Greeks called the god of the dead Pluto, *ploutos* being 'riches'. Dis Pater was never popular; his altars were rare. The Romans being superstitious did not care to worship a personification of death; or perhaps they reserved their homage for the Manes.

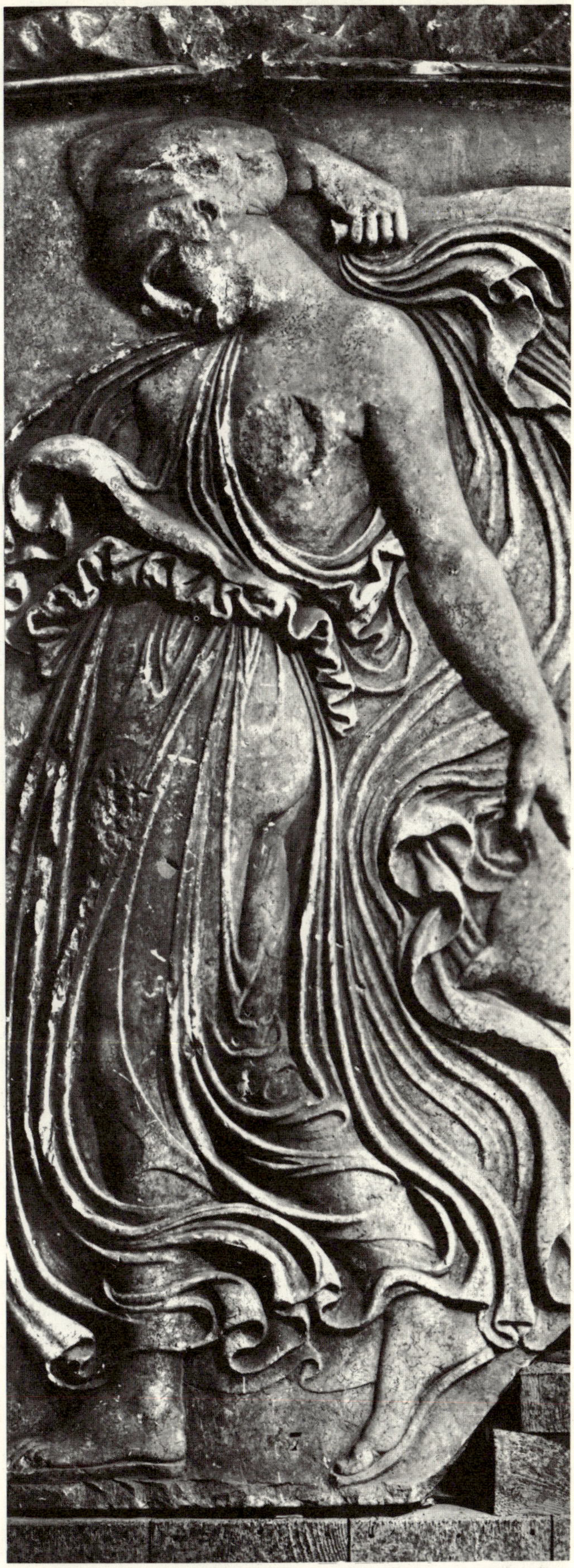

Maenad. The worship of Dionysus was introduced into Rome from lower Italy, its popularity being attested by numerous artistic representations. Here one of the god's female followers brandishes the knife with which she has just cut off the head of a wild animal which she will devour raw in the *omophagia*. Women, as successors of the Maenads, had a special place in the worship of Dionysus. Antique bas-relief.

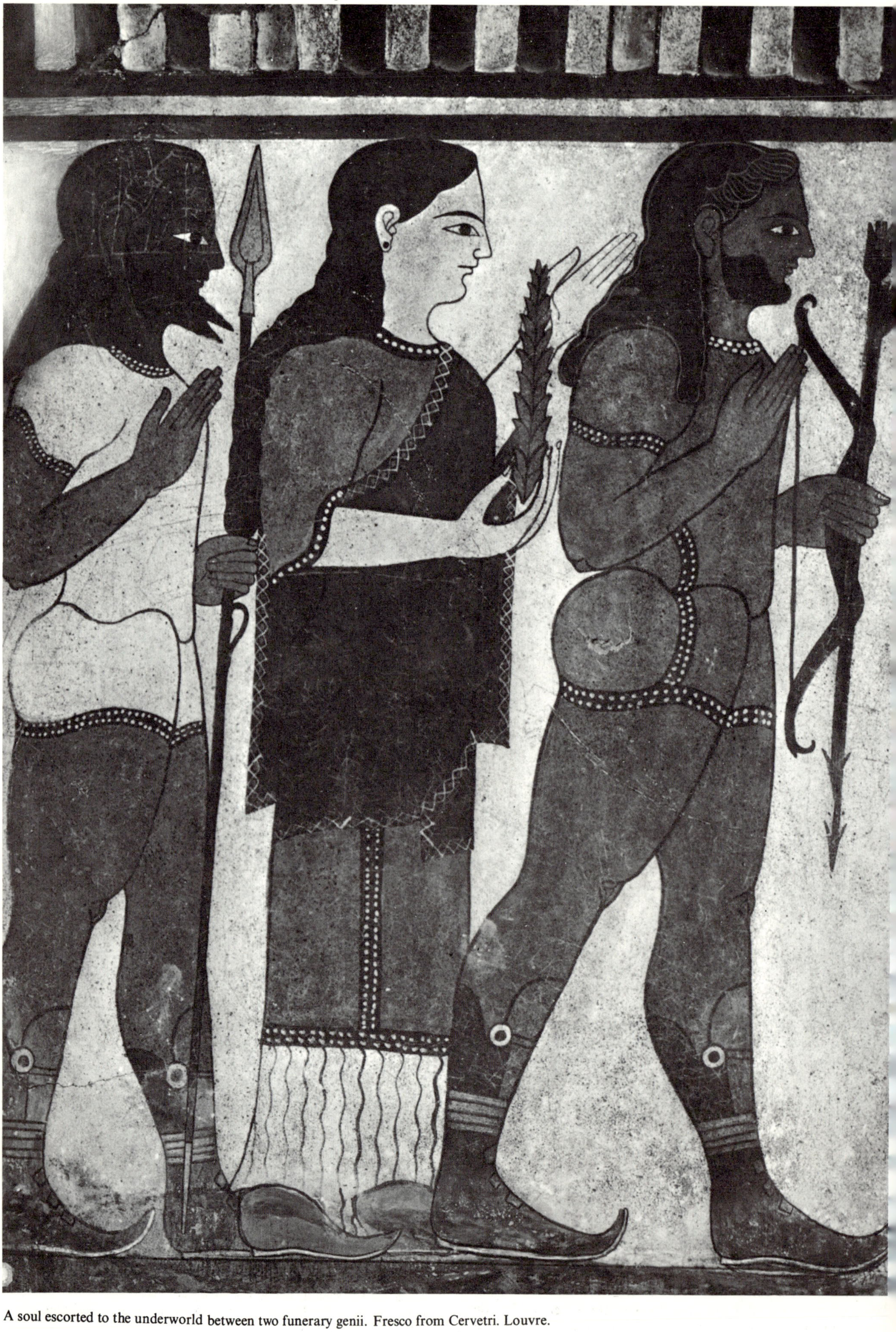

A soul escorted to the underworld between two funerary genii. Fresco from Cervetri. Louvre.

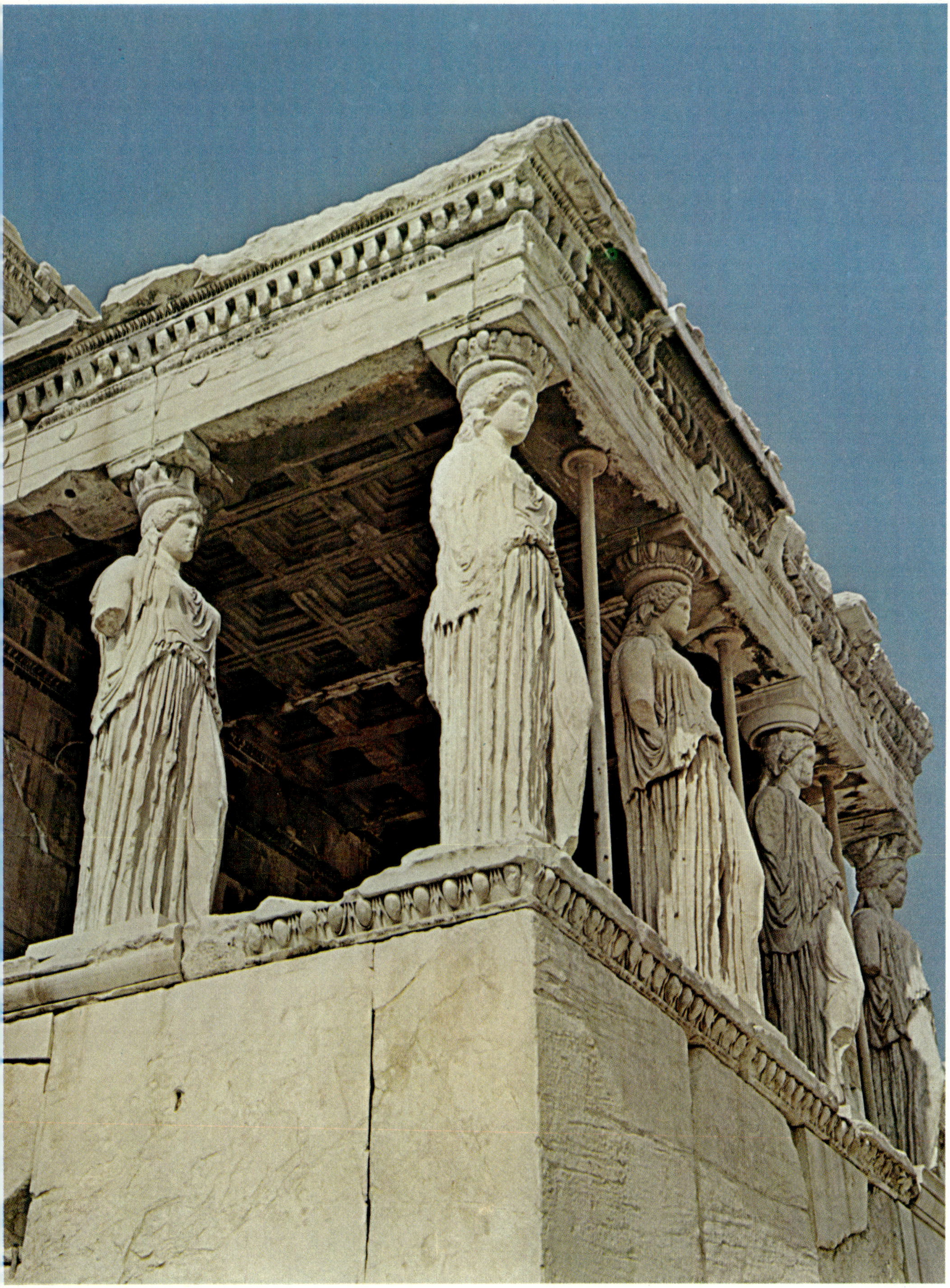

The Acropolis of Athens from the south west. Occupied from the earliest times, the sacred hill with its temples towers some five hundred feet above the modern city which stretches away to the north. Set on fire and laid waste by the Persians in 480 B.C., its present buildings date from the restoration of Pericles. On the left, where the ground rises less precipitously, is the entrance with the little temple of Athene Nike while in the centre of the hill stand the Erechtheum and the great temple of the Parthenon dedicated to the worship of Athene Parthenos, or 'Athene the Virgin', the protectress of the city.

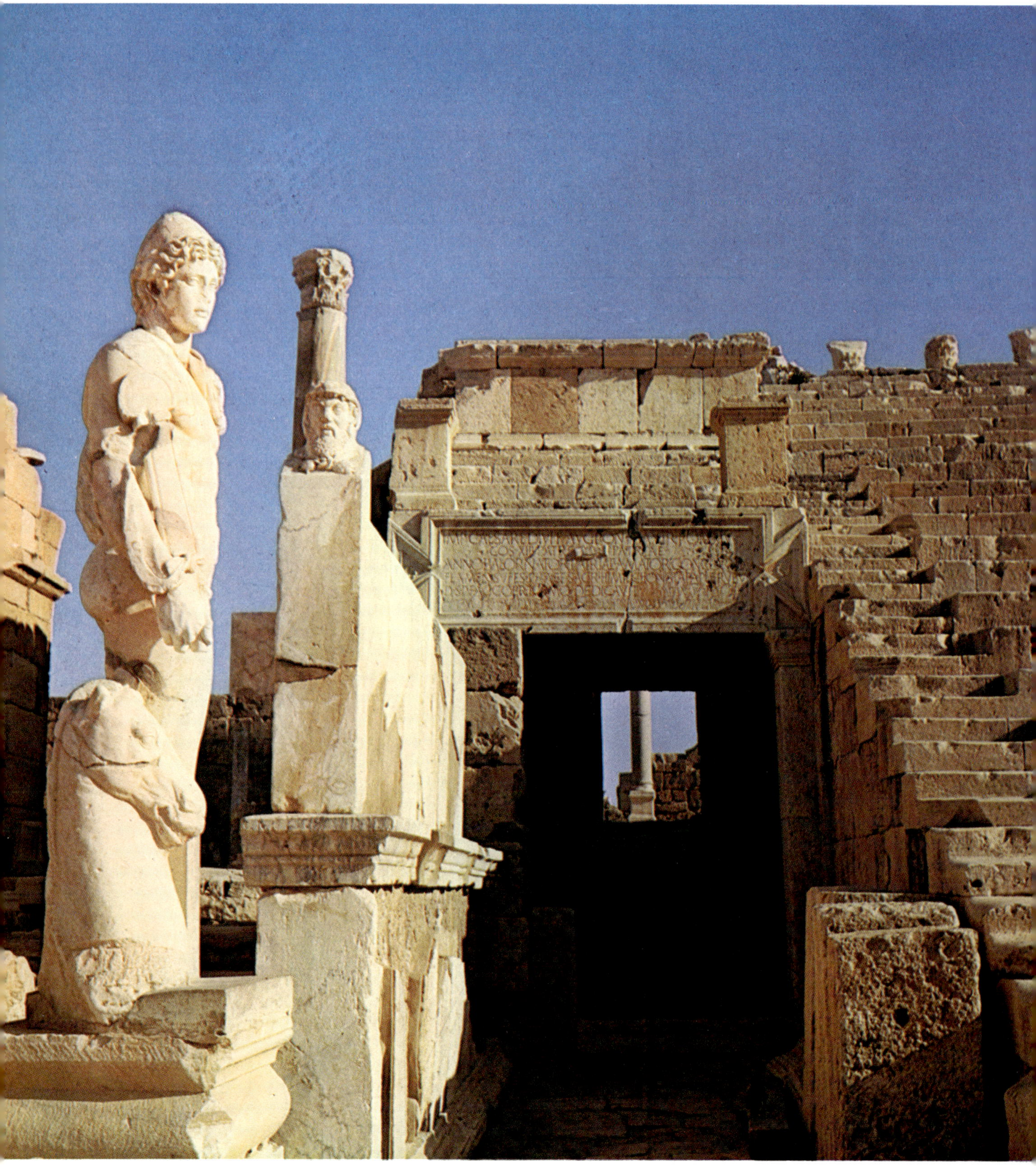

One of the Dioscuri, seen in the Roman theatre at Leptis Magna. Castor and Pollux were hatched from eggs like Helen and Clytemnestra – a sequel to the coupling of Leda with a swan, who proved to be Jupiter (Zeus) in one of his many guises. The Romans embraced the cult of the Dioscuri at an early date; it was probably adapted from an Etruscan source but this did not prevent the Romans from claiming that the twins in fact fought on their side at the Battle of Lake Regillus. Statues of Castor and Pollux stood at either side of the orchestra in the Leptis Magna theatre and were recently restored to the position they occupied in the first century A.D.

Orcus. Orcus represented Death. His name was also applied to the Underworld. He carried off the living by force and conducted them to the infernal regions. He was sometimes confused with Pluto.

Februus. Februus was probably the Etruscan god who corresponded to Dis Pater. It seems that the month of February was sacred to him; it was the month of the dead. In Etruria they also invoked a certain Mancus who must have been another Dis Pater.

Libitina. Libitina was an ancient Roman divinity, originally perhaps an agricultural divinity, who became the goddess of funerals and was identified by some with Proserpina. Whenever anyone died a piece of money had to be brought to her temple. Undertakers were called *libitinarii.*

Mania, Lara. These two divinities were probably one and the same person who was considered to be the mother of the Lares and the Manes. Lara was a nymph who talked so much that Jupiter cut out her tongue. For this reason she was called *Muta* or *Tacita.* Mania took part in the festivals of the *Compitalia* and the *Feralia*; she became a kind of ogress who frightened small children. *Maniae* were grotesque figurines which represented the dead; woollen dolls which were hung on doors in honour of the Lares were also called maniae.

Lemures, Larvae. These were the ghosts of the dead whose activities were mischievous. They returned to earth to torment the living. The *Lemuria* on the ninth, eleventh and thirteenth of May were instituted by Romulus in expiation of the murder of his brother; for Remus had appeared after his death to the shepherd Faustulus and to Acca Larentia to demand reparation. Romulus then created the *Remuria* which by corruption of the first letter became the *Lemuria.*

On this occasion every father of a family went through an extraordinary ritual: he arose, bare-footed, at midnight, he snapped his fingers to drive away the shades and washed his hands three times. He filled his mouth with black beans, then tossed them behind him, saying: 'I throw away these beans and with them I redeem myself and mine.' He repeated this invocation nine times. Meanwhile the funerary spirits picked up the beans. The father then again purified his hands, struck a brazen instrument and repeated nine times: 'Paternal manes, go.' After this he could safely look behind him.

The Manes. They were called *Di Parentes* or *Manes.* The latter term derived from an archaic adjective *manus* – 'good' – which was the opposite of *immanis.* Thus the Manes were, properly speaking, the 'Good Ones'. They were the object of a public and a private cult. Whenever a town was founded a round hole would first be dug. In the bottom of it a stone, *lapis manalis,* which represented a gate to the Underworld, would then be embedded. On the twenty-fourth of August, the fifth of October and the eighth of November this stone would be removed to permit the Manes to pass through. The object of the cult rendered to them was to appease their anger. Originally they were offered blood sacrifices, and it is probable that the first gladiatorial combats were instituted in their honour. Their festivals, the *Parentalia* and the *Feralia,* were celebrated in February. From the thirteenth to the twenty-sixth business ceased and temples were closed. Tombs were decorated with violets, roses, lilies and myrtle and on them was deposited food of various kinds.

Like the Greeks the Latins placed the Infernal Regions in the centre of the earth. It could be reached by various openings – caves, lakes, marshes. One of the most celebrated of these was Lake Avernus in Campania, a grim and deserted spot in the neighbourhood of Pozzuoli. The hills which surrounded it were formerly covered with woods sacred to Hecate (*luci averni*) and pitted with cavities through which, according to Cicero, one called forth the souls of the dead. Near Avernus the cave called the Cave of the Cumaean Sibyl can still be seen.

GODS OF THE CITY

Fortuna. Called Fors, then Fors Fortuna, she represented fate with all its unknown factors. Her name derives from *fero.* She was from remotest antiquity venerated in many Italian provinces, but her most important cult was celebrated at Praeneste in Latium where a certain Numerius Suffustus, digging in a cliff, discovered some tablets in oak inscribed with mysterious formulas, by means of which oracles could be delivered.

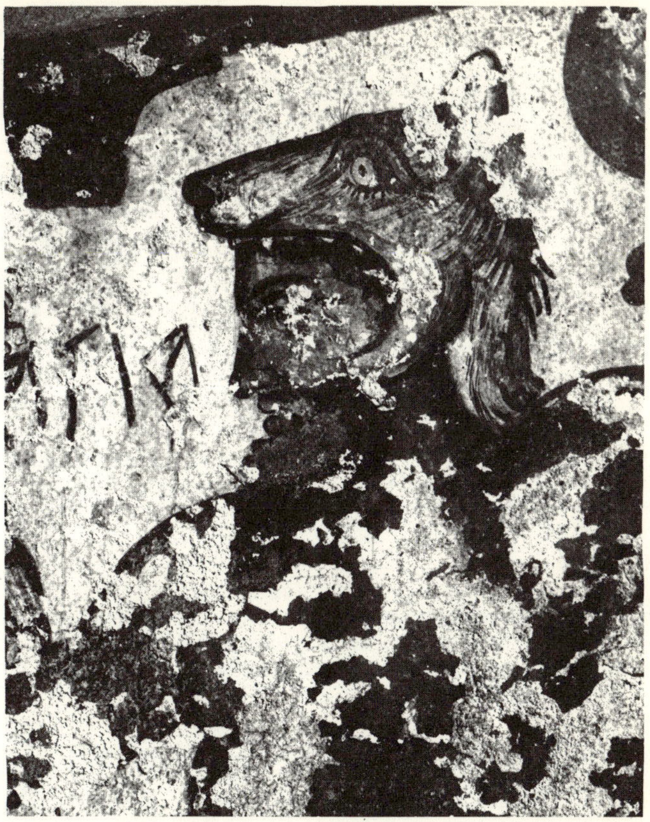

Underworld scene. Fresco from the tomb of Orcus. Tarquinii. Ade (or Hades) seated on his throne with his wife Persipnei (Persephone) beside him addresses the triple-headed Geryon who stands before him.

At Praeneste Fortuna was called Primigenia – firstborn (of Jupiter) – and, with an inconsequence which is not rare in the history of ancient myths, she was considered to be Jupiter's nurse and daughter at the same time.

Fortuna Primigenia was introduced to Rome in 204 B.C. during the second Punic war. However, the Romans already had a Fortuna who, they said, had favoured the astonishing political career of Servius Tullius, the slave who became king. One legend makes Servius Tullius the son of Fortuna; another said he was her lover. The goddess, in order to visit him, would slip during the night through the skylight. The *Porta Fenestella* in Rome recalled this memory.

Fortuna was honoured under many names. In Rome she was Fortuna *publica populi romani.* Fortuna *Muliebris* – protectress of matrons *univirae* namely, only once married – persuaded Coriolanus to raise the siege of Rome at the prayers of his mother and the Roman wives. A golden statuette of Fortuna had always to remain in the sleeping quarters of Roman Emperors. Citizens who were distinguished by outstanding good or bad luck had a Fortuna. When overtaken at sea by a storm Caesar said to the terrified pilot: 'What do you fear? You carry Caesar and his Fortuna.'

The countless representations of Fortuna show her chief attributes to be the wheel, the sphere, a ship's rudder and prow, and a cornucopia. The goddess is sometimes seated, sometimes standing. Occasionally she has wings.

Genius. The Genius was the anonymous deity who protected all groups of people and the places of their group activities. The number of genii was unlimited. The most important genius was, naturally, the *Genius publicus populi romani* who appeared on coins, sometimes with the features of the reigning emperor. After this Genius came the genii of districts, of *curia* and *decuria*; then those of towns, tribes and colonies. Every corporation had its Genius, as well as every house, gate, street and so on. The Roman emperors subsequently instituted the public cult of their own personal Genii for the entire duration of their term of office.

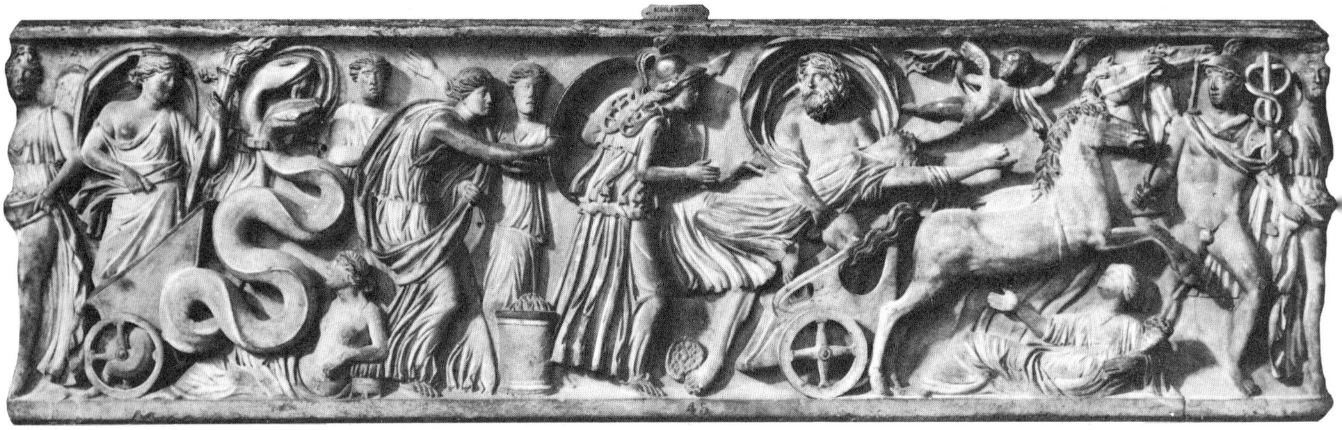

The rape of Proserpina. The Romans had no great Underworld divinities of their own and instead borrowed those of the Etruscans which had themselves been subjected to Greek influence. Hence they believed that the Underworld was ruled by Hades (or Pluto) and his wife Persephone, whose name was corrupted in Latin into Proserpina. This antique sarcophagus depicts her abduction by Hades while Minerva and Hecate follow in pursuit.

Lares and Penates. The public cult of the Lares was later than their private cult. Their role in the city was, however, identical to that which they played in the family.

Among the Latins, Sabines and Etruscans the public Lares – or *Compitales* – were originally placed where two fields joined, and as they were found at the intersections of roads there were two Lares for the same *compitum* – or crossroads. This distinguished the public Lares from the family Lar which was always single.

From the country they came into the towns. The *Lares compitales* became national divinities. When Decius Mus undertook to save the Roman army he first invoked the Lares (and the Manes) as well as Janus, Jupiter and Mars. The public Lares kept Hannibal away from the walls of Rome. In the end they represented the city's and even the Empire's illustrious dead. Alexander Severus venerated the Lares of Orpheus, of Abraham, of Apollonius of Tyana and of Jesus Christ.

In the epoch of the kings the Penates already enjoyed a public cult. They were called *Penates populi romani* and they were venerated in the *Regia* where the sacred fire burned and the *penus* of Vesta stood. There were two of them and they carried spears. The objects of their cult – which continued until the end of paganism – were guarded by the Vestals and by the pontiffs.

Tiberinus. The god of the Tiber naturally received a particular cult at Rome. To prevent him from overflowing the Vestals would on the fifteenth of May throw from the Sublicius bridge twenty-four wicker manikins, without doubt images of former human sacrifices. On the seventeenth of June the *Ludi piscatorii* – the festival of fishermen and divers – took place, and on the seventeenth of August, the *Tiberinalia.* The Tiber was so venerated that in the first century the Senate rejected a project for altering its course. Rhea Silvia, mother of the twins, was thrown into the Tiber and became its spouse.

Angerona. Very little is known about the goddess Angerona who was depicted holding a finger to her bound and sealed mouth. She may have been the goddess of Silence or, as some claim, the hidden name of Rome, which it was forbidden to pronounce.

Terminus. Social life received the protection of several divinities such as Terminus. He played a very important role, for he watched over property, which was a holy thing, and presided over the fixing of boundaries and frontiers. Actually Terminus was at first only a title of Jupiter's; but a legend gave him his own personality: it was told how Terminus – and Juventas – refused to make way for Jupiter when Jupiter came to install himself on the Capitol. At first the god was represented by a plain block of stone. Later he was depicted as a column surmounted by a human head.

Fides: Deus Fidius: Semo Sancus. These three divinities were responsible for the sincerity of public and private transactions. Fides, who was of Sabine origin, personified good faith, especially in verbal contracts: *Aedes Fidei Populi Romani.* Deus Fidius, also of Sabine origin, was the guardian of hospitality. Semo Sancus, a Latin god, was the god of oaths. Thus honest people found themselves protected. The rest were not, however, without patrons. Laverna and Summanus accepted the prayers of thieves and impostors.

Bonus Eventus. Success in enterprises was the responsibility of Bonus Eventus; he was at first a rural god in charge of the harvest. Then his province spread to all kinds of initiative. He had a temple in Rome and a statue on the Capitol.

Victoria. This Latin goddess was probably the same as the Sabine Vacuna. After having been the protectress of fields and woods she became responsible for the Romans' success in arms. They considered her as one of their most ancient divinities. With her they honoured Vica Pota and Vitula or Vitellia who presided over victory celebrations.

After victory came *Pax* (Peace), but her cult was neither ancient nor widespread. She had a temple in Rome only after A.D. 75 *Concordia* symbolised the union of citizens. A temple was erected to her in 367 at the time when the plebeians won political equality. *Felicitas* personified happy events. *Laetitia* and *Annona* were connected with incidents particularly desirable for the city of Rome: namely, the arrival of corn.

DEIFIED HEROES AND ALLEGORIES.

Hercules (Greek, Heracles). In primitive times the functions of Hercules – whom some people merged with Semo Sancus, Deus Fidius and Silvanus – were rural. He assured the fruitfulness of the countryside, watched over families and guarded their heritage. Certain authorities see in him the particular Genius of man as Juno was of women.

He was linked with the history of Rome's very site. When he carried off the cattle of Geryon, the triple-bodied monster who reigned over the western coast of Iberia, Hercules made a stop between the Aventine and the Palatine hills under the hospitable roof of Evander. During the night the brigand Cacus – half man, half satyr, the son of Vulcan – stole some of his heifers. To hide the theft Cacus dragged the animals by the tail to his den on the Aventine. The following morning the stolen heifers bellowed in answer to the bulls which Hercules was preparing to drive on. Guided by the sound, Hercules removed the boulder which concealed the den of Cacus and after a terrible struggle slew the bandit in spite of the flames which he belched forth. The scene of this battle was later called the Forum Boarium.

Romulus and Remus. Romulus and Remus were sons of Mars. Mars had surprised the Vestal, Rhea Silvia, daughter of Numitor, King of Alba, while she was asleep and lain with her. The resulting twins were placed in a winnowing basket and set afloat on the Tiber. The river overflowed and deposited the basket before the grotto Lupercal, under the fig-tree Ruminal. There a she-wolf came to suckle the infants who were sheltered and brought up by the shepherd Faustulus and his wife Acca Larentia.

When the twin brothers decided to found a new city they first carefully studied the flight of birds. In that section of the sky which the Augur's wand had apportioned to Romulus he saw twelve vultures. In Remus' section only six could be seen. Romulus proceeded, with a plough harnessed to a white cow and a white bull, to draw a furrow which should mark the boundary of the new city's walls. Remus jumped over this shallow furrow in derision and his brother killed him. It is possible that this rivalry between the two brothers was a symbol of the rivalry between the two districts of ancient Rome – the Cermalus (or the Aventine) and the Palatine.

In order to people his town, which was more or less in the shape of a square – the Roma Quadrata – Romulus founded a place of asylum beyond the ramparts. The neighbours refused to marry such outlaws and Romulus took advantage of the rustic festival called the Consualia to abduct the daughters of the Sabine tribe whom he had invited to the ceremonies. The mysterious death of Romulus and his disappearance during a storm are the invention of the poet Ennius. Afterwards Romulus was identified with Quirinus and worshipped under that name.

Acca Larentia, wife of the shepherd Faustulus and the foster-mother of Romulus, had another legend according to which she was a notorious courtesan in the days of Romulus and Ancus. Hercules played dice with the guardian of her temple. He won and in consequence ordered her to unite with a certain rich Tuscan named Tarrutius who left her a large fortune. Acca Larentia left it to the Roman people who in her honour instituted the *Larentalia*.

Castor and Pollux. At the battle of Lake Regillus in 496 B.C. during the war with Latium, the Roman dictator Aulus Posthumius made a vow to erect a temple to Castor and Pollux who were honoured at Tusculum, a town which was an enemy of Rome's. A few seconds later Castor and Pollux were seen at the head of the Roman cavalry leading it to victory. That same evening the inhabitants of Rome saw two young men, dressed in purple chlamydes, watering their white horses at the fountain of Juturna in the Forum. They were Castor and Pollux who had come to announce the victory and, incidentally, to become part of the religion of Rome. They were of Greek origin and had arrived via Etruria where they were called Kastur and Pultuke by the Etruscans; but they rapidly became altogether Roman. A magnificent temple was erected to them in the Forum. They accompanied the Roman army on its campaigns and during battles appeared in the midst of the cavalry. They also protected sailors and travellers at sea. At Ostia they calmed a storm which was preventing ships loaded with corn from entering port. In their quality of marine gods they naturally presided over commerce. In the second century A.D. they were incorporated in funeral rituals and their popularity was so great that even Christians did not deny that they were symbols of life and death.

Aeneas. Although he afterwards became the national hero of Rome, Aeneas was of foreign origin. He was the son of Anchises and Aphrodite, son-in-law of Priam and chief of the Dardanians. In the *Iliad* he figures among the allies of Troy and appears as a warrior both intrepid and full of wisdom. There are various traditions about him. According to one he valiantly defended the citadel of Ilium; according to another he delivered the town to the Greeks and succeeded Priam. But the most accredited story is that which – according to Stesichorus, Timaeus and Lycophron – relates how Aeneas left Troy after its fall with his warriors and the remaining Trojans in search of a new fatherland. After vain attempts to establish himself in Thrace, in Crete and in Sicily, he finally reached the banks of the Tiber. There he helped the king of the Aborigines, Latinus, in his struggle with the Rutuli. He married the daughter of Latinus, Lavinia, and built a town which was called Lavinium. Later he succeeded Latinus and after a four years' reign perished rather mysteriously in a battle with the Rutuli. Long before Virgil made him the hero of the *Aeneid* Aeneas was venerated by the Romans – under the name *Jupiter indiges* – as the founder of their race. Many of the great Roman families, notably that of the Julii, boasted that they descended from him.

Connected with the cult of Aeneas was that of Anna Perenna, sister of Dido, who had sought asylum with Aeneas and, persecuted by Lavinia's jealousy, drowned herself in the river Numicus. When the plebeians took refuge on the Mons Sacer, Anna Perenna, in the guise of an old woman, brought them food to eat and for this reason was honoured with a temple in Rome.

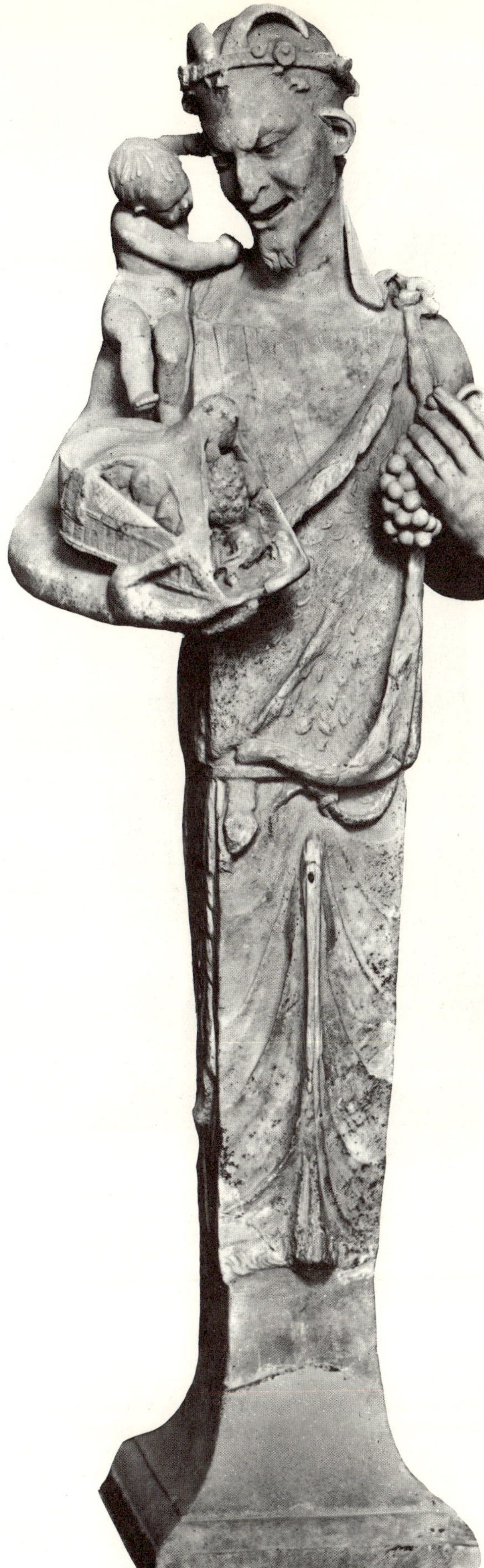

Herm of a faun with a baby boy on his shoulder.
One of a class of Latin rural deities with horns, pointed ears, beards and tails, fauns were derived from the Italian god Faunus who brought fruitfulness to fields and animals and was later identified with Pan. Here one plays with a baby boy, dressed in a goatskin and holding a basket of fruit and a bunch of grapes.

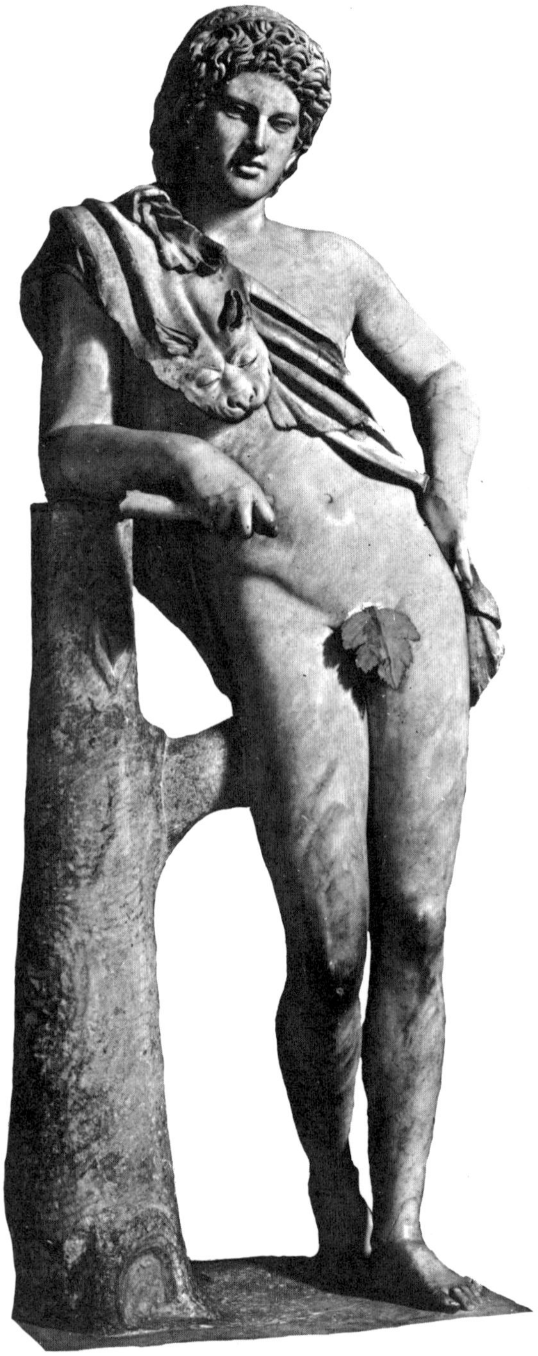

A satyr. Dressed in a panther-skin and holding a flute in his right hand, this youthful companion of Dionysus retains the pointed ears of an earlier, more animal, appearance. The worship of Dionysus (or Bacchus as he was known to the Romans) was banned by the Senate in 186 B.C. but later became a respectable mystery religion and enjoyed immense popularity in the first and second centuries A.D.

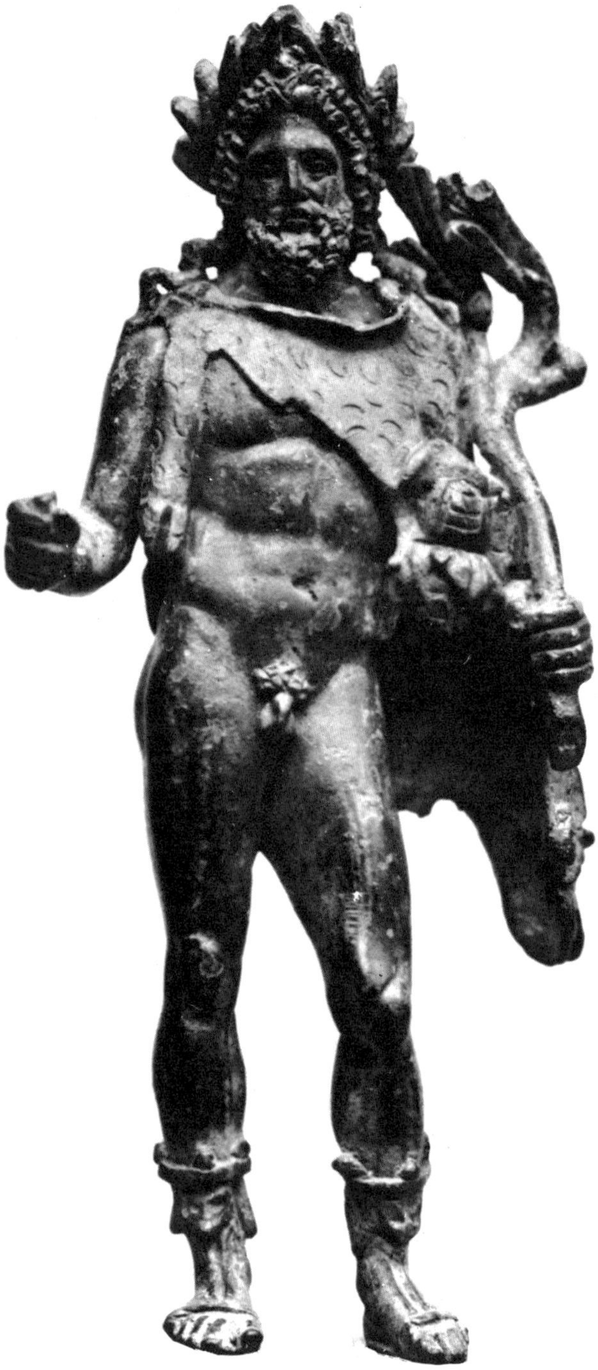

Silvanus. A deity of woodland and uncultivated land, Silvanus also watched over the cleared fields and protected herds. He was worshipped by farmers as guardian of pasture-land, boundaries and homesteads and was one of the few Roman rural deities to retain the same character to the end. Here he carries a tree in his left hand and the shaft of a pruning hook in his right – the symbols of his dual nature.

The Emperors. The deification of sovereigns was not a Roman invention: in eastern countries kings had for a long time been the objects of religious worship. In Rome it was the Senate that awarded the honour of apotheosis. An immense pyre was erected on top of which an image of the new god was placed. From the midst of the flames an eagle would carry the soul of the emperor to his celestial abode.

Even before the Empire Julius Caesar had, after his death, achieved apotheosis. Augustus was the first emperor to be deified. Then Claudius, then still others and finally even empresses. These honours were the logical consequence of those which they received during their lifetime. Even before death raised them to the rank of divinities people spoke of their *numen* and of their *aeternitas*. Some of the emperors were aware of the irony of these excessive homages. When Vespasian was dying he announced that he felt himself becoming a god. Referring to his brother, Geta, whom he caused to be put to death by centurions, the emperor Caracalla declared that Geta would be a god provided he was not living. The triumph of Christianity did not immediately put an end to the custom of deification.

Allegories. The Romans deified numerous virtues and devoted cults to them. *Aequitas,* scale in one hand and in the other a rod which corresponded to a unit of measurement, was equity. *Pudicitia* watched over the chastity of matrons and only accepted homage from wives who were *univirae*. The *Aeternitas* and *Clementia* of the emperors were venerated and the *Fecunditas* of empresses. The latter were created in order to celebrate the birth of a daughter to Poppaea, the wife of the emperor Nero. Veneration was also paid to *Spes* (Hope), *Libertas*, *Virtus* (Courage), *Pietas* (Piety), etc. These cults are merely a random selection mentioned to give some idea of the incalculable number which then existed.

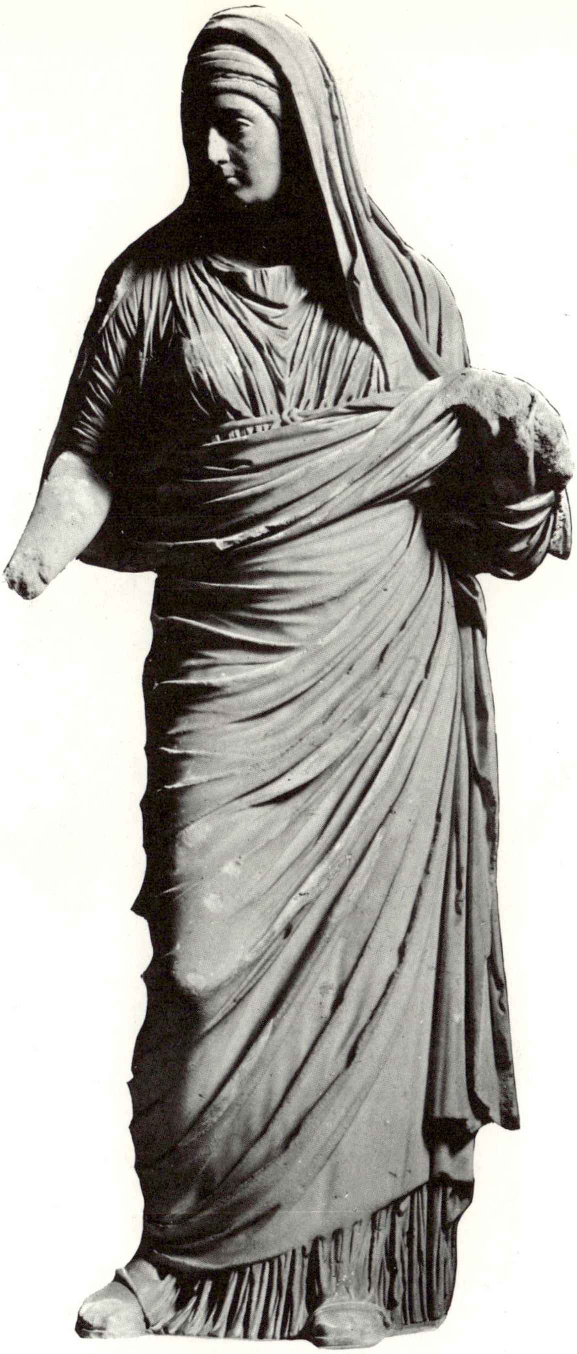

A Vestal Virgin. Originally two in number, then four and finally six, the Vestal Virgins were the priestesses of Vesta, the Roman goddess of the hearth, whose cult occupied a position of the first importance in the Roman religion. Admitted between the ages of six and ten, the Vestals served for thirty years, their chief duty being to keep alight the godesses' sacred fire.

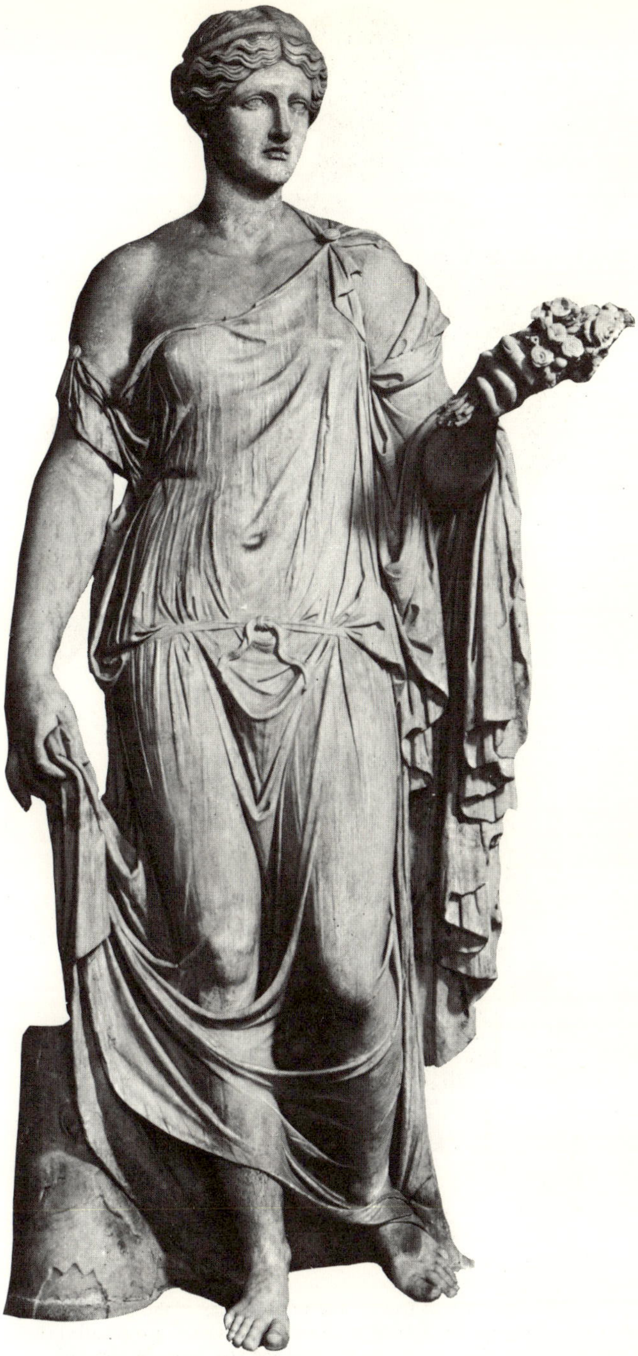

The Farnese Flora. The goddess of spring and flowering or blossoming plants, Flora was an Italian goddess whose cult was in existence at Rome at an early date. A temple was dedicated to her in 238 B.C. on the advice of the Sibylline Books and her festivals, the *Floralia*, were celebrated annually. She was later identified with the Greek goddess Chloris. May-blossom was associated with her worship.

GODS OF THE FAMILY

Genius. The Genius was by definition the creative force which engendered the individual; it watched over his development and remained with him until the hour of his destruction. It presided over his marriage and over the nuptial bed, for this reason being entitled *genialis*. It appeared at the birth of the being whose function it was to protect. It formed the infant's personality. The power of the child's Genius depended on luck. If it was a boy its tutelary spirit was a Genius; if a girl it would be a Juno.

The Genius and the Juno did not accomplish their protective mission unassisted. They had many auxiliaries. *Nundina* presided over the infant's purification. *Vaticanus* made it utter its first cry. *Educa* and *Potina* taught it to eat and drink. *Cuba* kept it quiet in its cradle. *Ossipago* and *Carna* saw to the development of its bones and flesh. *Abeona* and *Adeona* taught it to walk. *Sentinus* saw to the awakening of the infant's intellectual faculties, and such like.

In a word, the Genius fostered the growth and all the intellectual and moral faculties of the individual of whom it was a kind of abstract double. The cult rendered to the Genius was very simple: on the day of birth it was offered wine and flowers, after which there was dancing. The Genius was first represented as a serpent. Later the Genius of the head of the family was depicted as a man in a toga. He was installed between the Penates and the Lar. With him sometimes appeared the Juno of the wife.

The Penates. Their name derives from *penus*, the larder or room where food was stored. Their first function was to see to the preservation of food and drink. Indeed, they were closely bound to the life of the family and shared its joys and sorrows. Their role was so important that they received the epithet of *dii* or *divi* which was not accorded, in fact, to either the Genius or to the Lar.

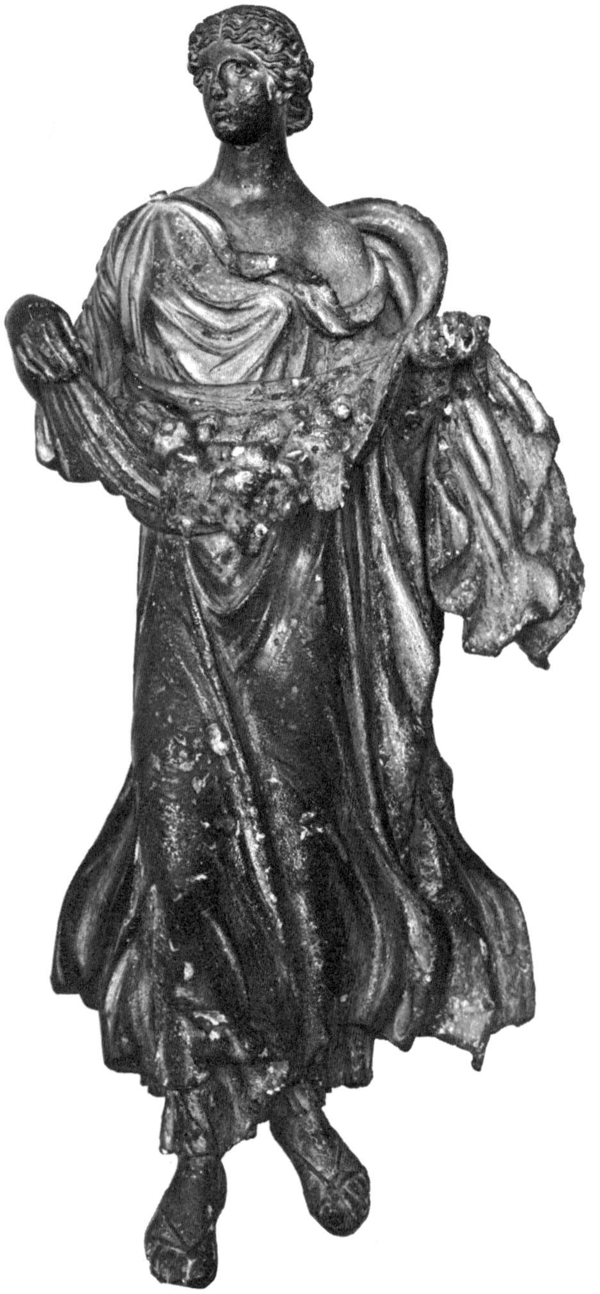

Pomona. The goddess of fruits – and in particular of those which grow on trees – Pomona had a priest at Rome and a sacred grove called the Pomonal near Ostia. According to Ovid she was loved by the god Vertumnus who adopted various disguises in order to win her but the story is a late one. Her festivals, if any, are not known.
Roman statuette of the first century B.C., found near Padua.

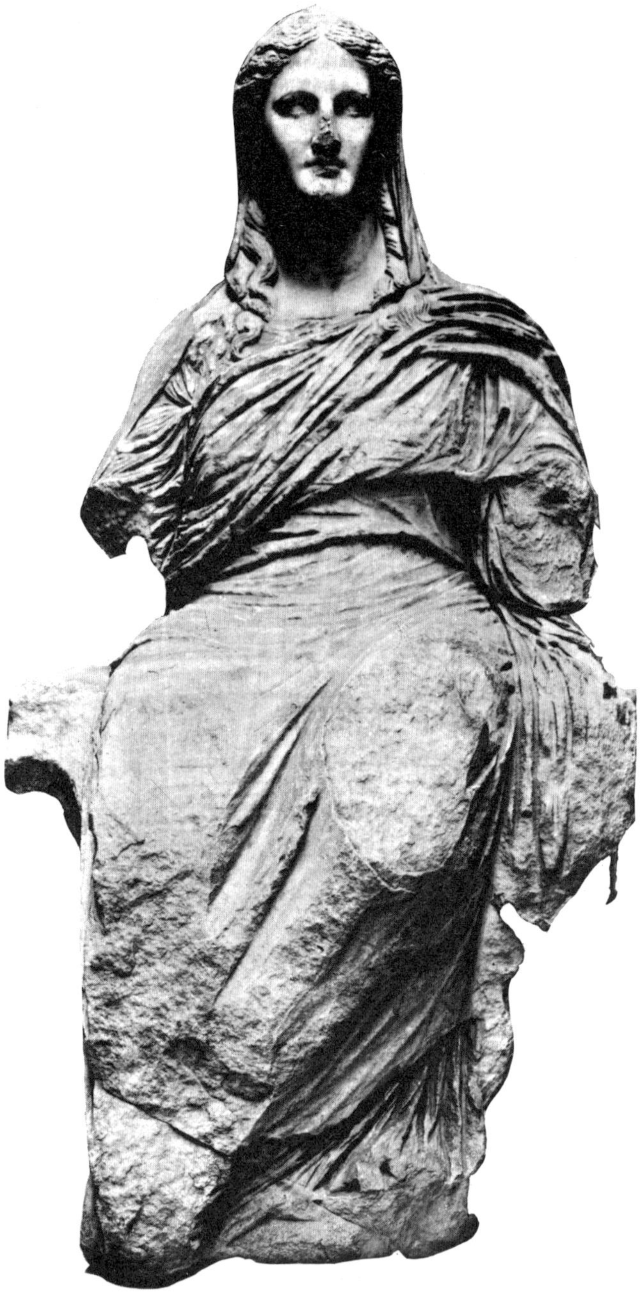

Ceres. An ancient Italian corn-goddess, Ceres was identified with the Greek goddess Demeter at an early date and as a result of this association became one of the twelve great deities of the Roman pantheon. Her most famous cult was on the Aventine where a temple was built to her, in conjunction with Liber and Libitina, in 493 B.C. Her festival, the *Cerialia*, was celebrated on 19th April.

The Penates were always two in number. Their altar was the hearth which they shared with Vesta. Their images were placed before that of the Genius, at the back of the atrium. At every meal they were put between the plates and offered the first helping of food.

These simple practices dated back to the remotest times. In later days they were observed only in rural districts. To the Penates were often added gods who exercised a particular protection over the particular family: Mercury appeared among the Penates of a merchant, Vesta in the house of a baker, Vulcan in the house of a blacksmith. When the family moved the Penates moved with it. In the same way, when the family became extinct they disappeared.

The Lar. The term Lar was Etruscan and signified chief or prince. The Lares found among the Latins, the Sabines and the Etruscans belong to the most ancient Italic mythology.

First they were protectors of agriculture, associated with Consus and the agricultural Mars. They played the role of guardians – *custodes agri*. Their image was crudely sculptured from a tree-stump and was usually situated at the approaches of the farmhouse.

Their functions and their cult did not greatly differ from those of the Penates. Actually they were frequently confused. Their altar was also the hearth and they received similar homage. On festive occasions they were decorated with garlands and offered incense, fruit and libations of wine.

Unlike the Penates there was only one family Lar. He symbolised the house. The phrase: *ad larem suum reverti* meant to come home. He was invoked on all important occasions of family life: departures, marriages, funerals. The bride when she crossed the threshold of her new house offered the Lar a sacrifice and gave him a coin. After funerals two rams were immolated to him in order to purify the house. The family Lar was habitually represented in a juvenile aspect with curly hair, a short tunic and in a dancing posture. Above his head he raises the rhyton from which wine flows into a patera.

Numerous divinities were concerned with family life. We have already mentioned some of the ones who watched over the child's birth and first footsteps. In discussing the epithets of Juno we have alluded to certain divinities who presided over various aspects of marriage. In addition to all these there were *Orbona,* the goddess

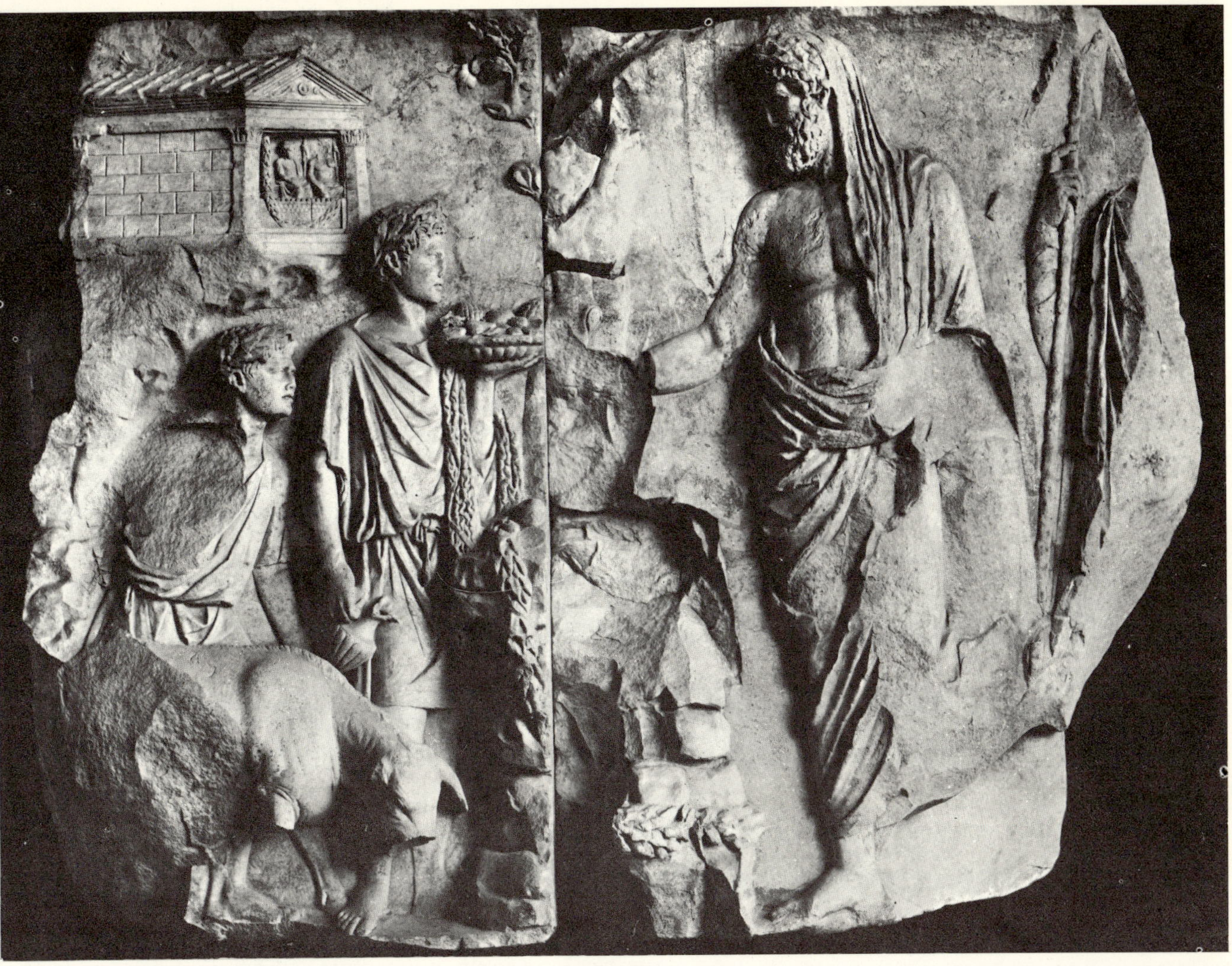

Aeneas (?) offering a sacrifice to the Penates, whose altar we see in the background. Bas-relief from the altar of Peace. Terme Museum, Rome.

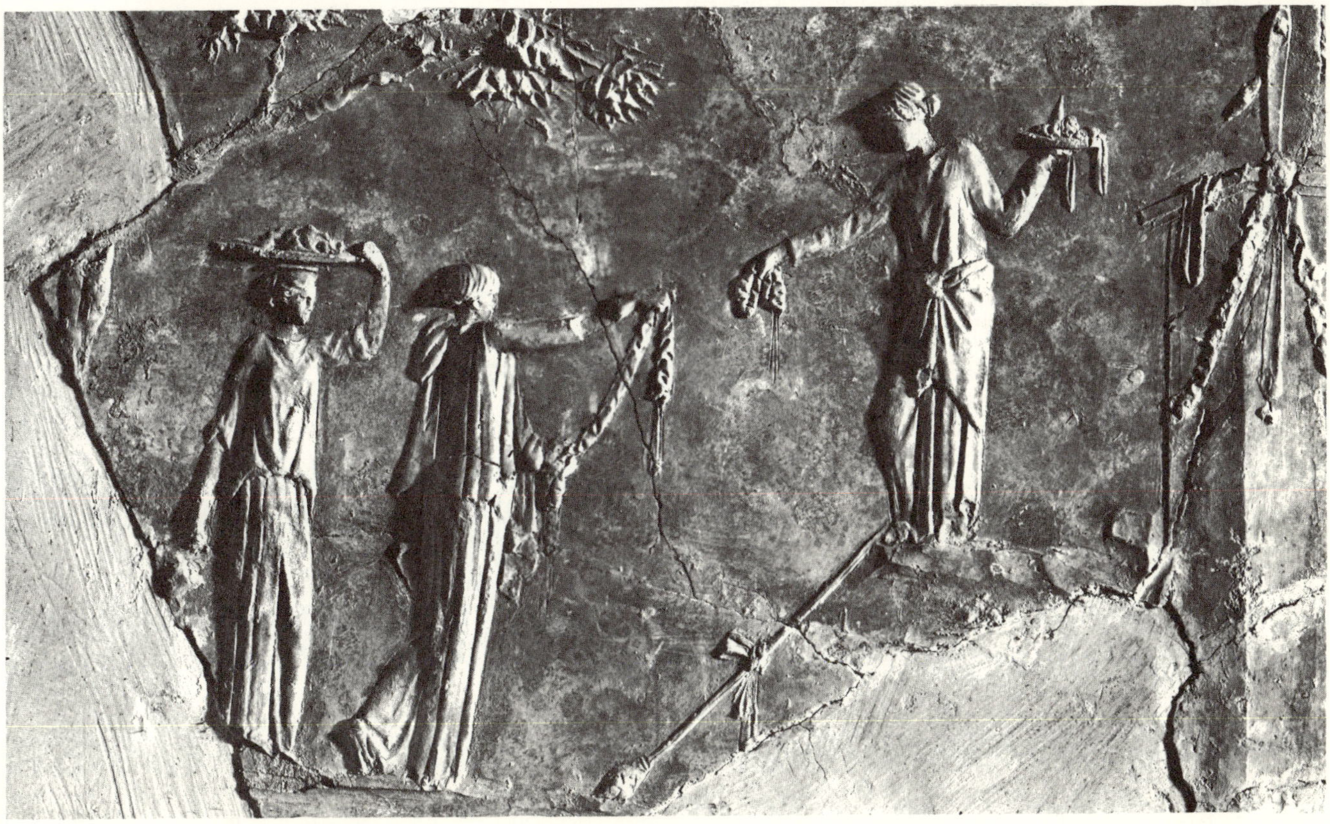

Offering to Isis. Stucco from the so-called House of the Priestess of Isis, in the National Museum, Rome.

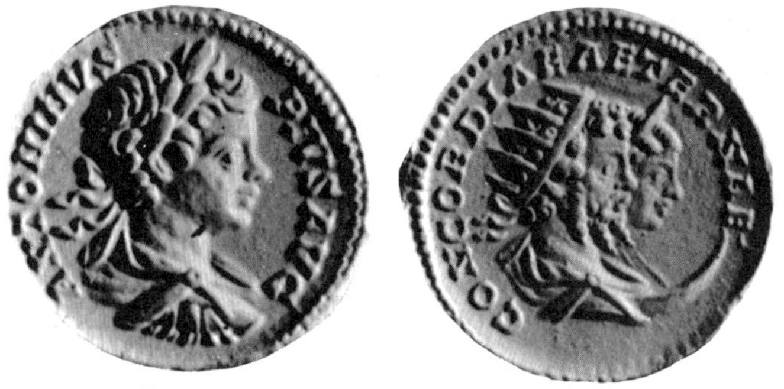

Aureus of Antoninus Pius. In addition to their main gods the Romans later came to deify their Emperor also in imitation of Eastern custom where kings had long been the object of religious worship. Emperors were regarded as gods during their lifetime while some also achieved apotheosis after their deaths. There was a shrine to Antoninus and his Empress Faustina in the Forum.

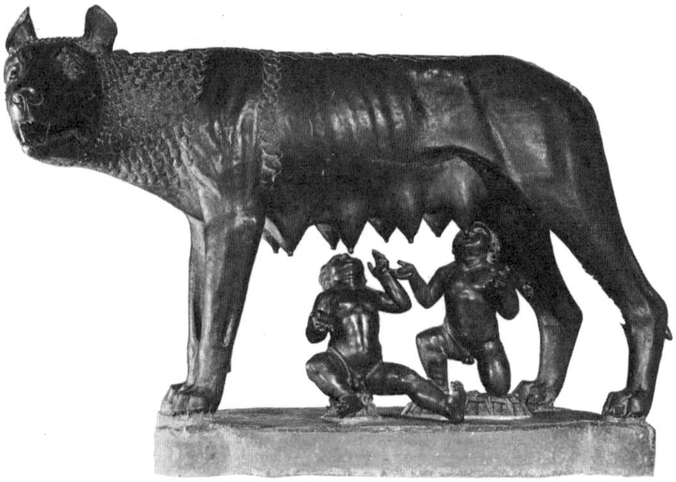

The wolf suckling Romulus and Remus. Bronze. The wolf is fifth century B.C. The children are later additions. Capitoline Museum.

who protected orphans: *Viriplaca,* who soothed quarrels between husband and wife; *Deverra, Intercidona, Pilumnus* were divinities of the broom, the axe and the mortar, whose intervention at the moment of childbirth drove away rustic evil spirits. In the conjugal chamber there was even a bed made for Pilumnus and his twin brother *Picumnus* who were both responsible for looking after the new-born baby. The list of such divinities could still be extended.

THE GREEK CONTRIBUTION

In the third century B.C. the poet Ennius enumerated the twelve great gods of the Graeco-Roman pantheon: Juno, Vesta, Minerva, Ceres, Diana, Venus, Mars, Mercurius, Jove, Neptunus, Volcanus, Apollo.

Janus and Saturn, purely Italic divinities, officially lost their pre-eminence although they continued to receive an important cult. The other great gods found their functions augmented by those they possessed under other names in the Greek pantheon. At the same time they changed their nature, ceased to be abstractions and took on human shape. Certain secondary divinities were promoted to the first rank: Ceres, Diana and Venus acquired their full stature by joining forces with Demeter, Artemis and Aphrodite. Neptune, a rather slight personage with ill-defined duties, inherited the maritime empire of Poseidon. Liber Pater, a modest Italian peasant, was attached to the fortunes of Iacchus-Dionysus.

Apollo sprang in all his novelty into the midst of the Roman gods and won for himself a position of great eminence. It was, indeed, Apollo who opened the road for his Greek compatriots. In the fifth century the Sibyl of Cumae, a priestess of Apollo, offered to sell King Tarquin nine books of prophecy. Twice the king refused, finding the price too high. Each time the priestess tossed three books into the fire and doubled the price of those remaining. Tarquin finally bought the last three which were preserved in the temple of the Capitol and called the Sibylline Books. They contained instructions for gaining the favours of foreign gods, Greek and Oriental. This was how Apollo made his entrance into Rome, following an epidemic in 431. For the same reason an appeal was made in 293 to the god of Epidaurus, who was the serpent-god Aesculapius.

In succession all the great gods of Greece were introduced into Roman religion, some reinforcing already established deities, others bringing with them entirely new cults. At the same time the Hellenic ritual and manner of praying appeared, including the rites of *lectisternia* and *supplicationes.* To celebrate a lectisternium beds were set up for pairs of deities; their effigies were laid on the beds and before them a meal was set. The first lectisternium was celebrated in 399 B.C. The supplications consisted of public processions which began at the temple of Apollo and visited different sanctuaries in the city.

The hellenisation of Roman mythology began at an early date and continued steadily and rapidly. It was complete between the third and the second centuries. Livy attributed this retreat of old Roman tradition before foreign influence to the political and moral crisis which attended the Punic wars.

THE ORIENTAL CONTRIBUTION. Divinities from the Orient were introduced into Italy with all their functions and all their rites. They retained their personalities unaltered. They underwent not an adaptation, but simply a physical transfer.

Asia Minor. The great goddess of Phrygia, Cybele, first penetrated Italy with her spouse Attis under the name of *Magna Mater deum Idaea.* In 205 B.C. the Romans, terrified by a shower of stones, consulted the Sibylline Books. These promised that Hannibal, who was still established in Bruttium, would be driven from Italy by the presence of the Great Mother of Ida. The Senate sent ambassadors to King Attalus from whom they received the black meteoric stone which was supposed to be the throne of the goddess. This sacred object was received at Ostia by Scipio Nasica, 'the best citizen of Rome', and carried by matrons to the Palatine and placed in the temple of Victory (April, 204). In 202 Hannibal was defeated at Zama by Scipio Africanus. A temple was then built for Cybele on the summit of the Palatine and games were instituted in her honour. The cult of Cybele assumed its full importance at the beginning of the Empire.

Another divinity from Asia Minor was Ma, a personification of fruitfulness. Ma was introduced into Rome by the dictator Sulla in about 85 B.C.

Egypt. The cult of Isis and of Serapis penetrated Italy by way of Sicily and the south of the Peninsula. It was at first practised by slaves and freed men during the second century. The Senate tried in vain to arrest its progress, but was unable to prevent its spreading

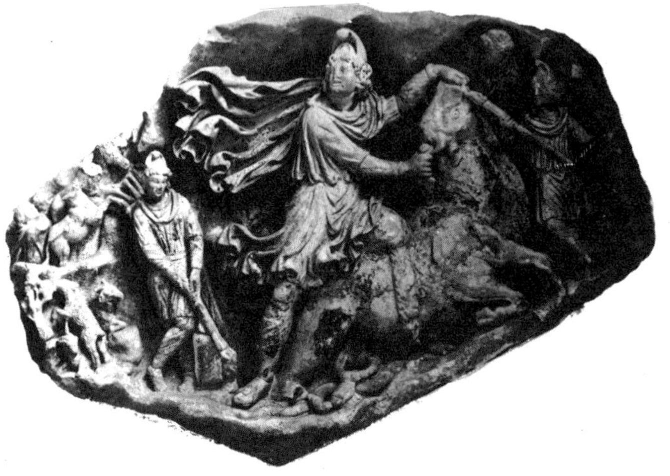

Deity of the Mithraic cult. In passing west into Europe from Persia the worship of Mithras absorbed many foreign elements including a strong strain of astrology. This winged, lion-headed deity covered with the signs of the zodiac and enclosed in the coils of a serpent has been identified by some as Aion, or Time, the god of the astrologers, believed by many to be the Creator himself.
Marble statue of the second and third centuries A.D.

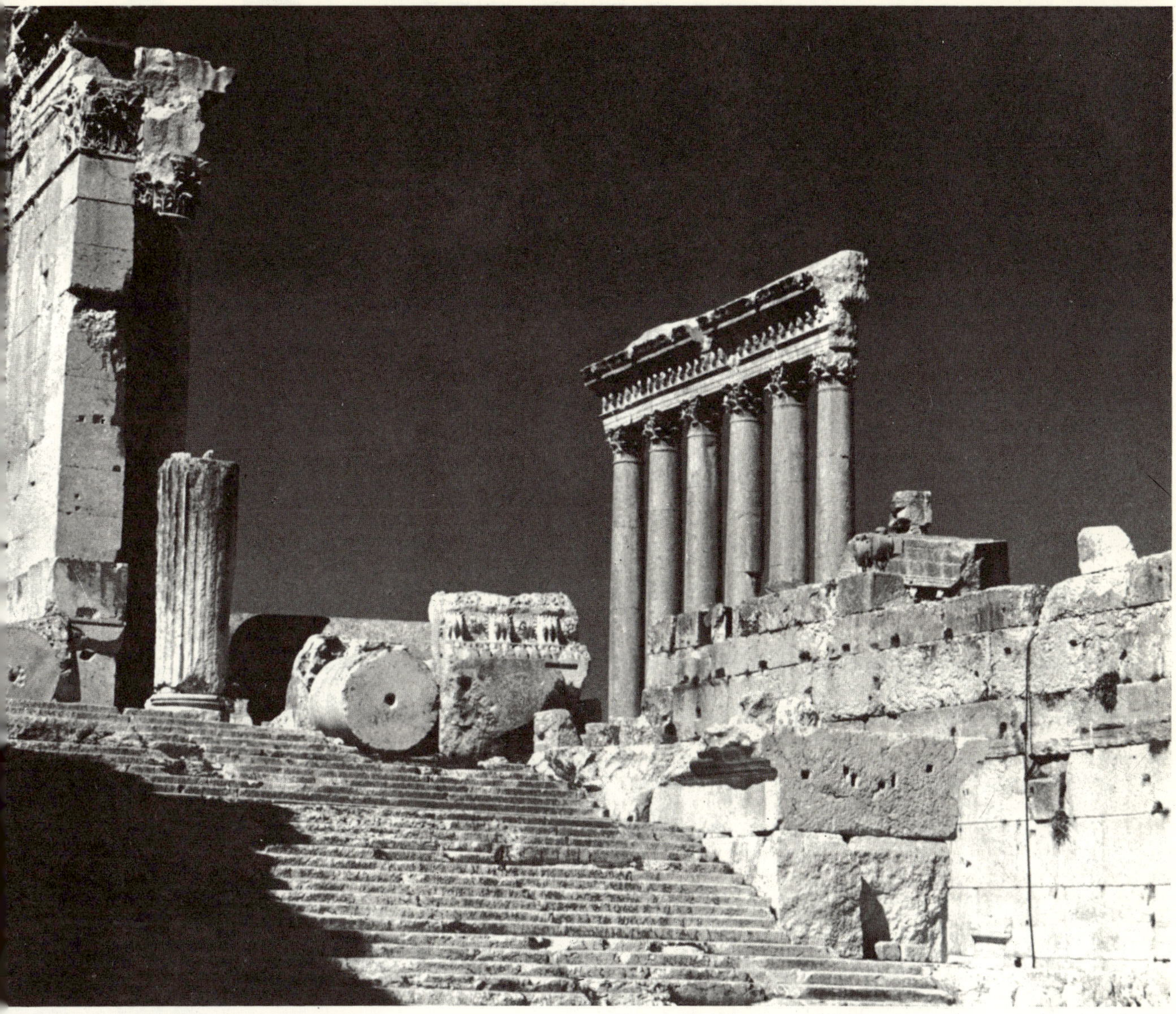

View of the temples of Jupiter and Bacchus at Baalbek in Syria. Originally the cult centre of a local Baal, the god was identified with Jupiter after the city became a Roman colony and was worshipped under the title of Jupiter Heliopolitanus in the great temple dedicated to him on the right. On the left is the smaller temple of Bacchus – one of the best preserved Roman temples in existence. First to third centuries A.D.

to the centre and north of Italy. Caligula installed it solemnly in Rome and in the Field of Mars erected a temple of Isis Campestris. Caracalla built another one on the Quirinal.

The Egyptian gods who never lost their character remained for long popular in Rome. Their greatest popularity dated from the third century. At the end of the fourth century there were still processions in honour of Isis.

Syria. *Atargatis*, known under the name of *Dea Syria*, first entered Latin territory as far back as the second century B.C. She was at first worshipped by slaves.

A consequence of Rome's various annexations was the introduction and assimilation of various foreign cults. The numerous Syrian Baals and the goddess Baltic were brought to Rome by Syrian recruits, excellent troops which the Emperors incorporated into the Roman army.

Their cults were established by the first century and reached the apogee of their importance in the third. The Emperor Heliogabalus attempted to have the Baal of Ephesus recognised as the principal god of the Empire.

Persia. The cult of Mithras was the last to appear in Rome, during the course of the first century B.C. It became very important and persisted until the end of paganism. It was practised by the functionaries and by the Emperors themselves. Commodus had himself initiated into its mysteries. In 307 Diocletian consecrated at Carnuntum on the Danube a temple to Mithras, 'Protector of the Empire'.

We have come far from the humble and rustic divinities whom in primitive days the peasants of Latium worshipped. Most of them were forced to give way before the more brilliant gods, or else, in order not to disappear completely, to combine with them. Those who, thanks to the persistent devotion of country folk still survived, had a faded air and appeared like poor relations in the sumptuous pantheon which Rome, mistress of the world, erected as a measure of her glory.

CELTIC MYTHOLOGY

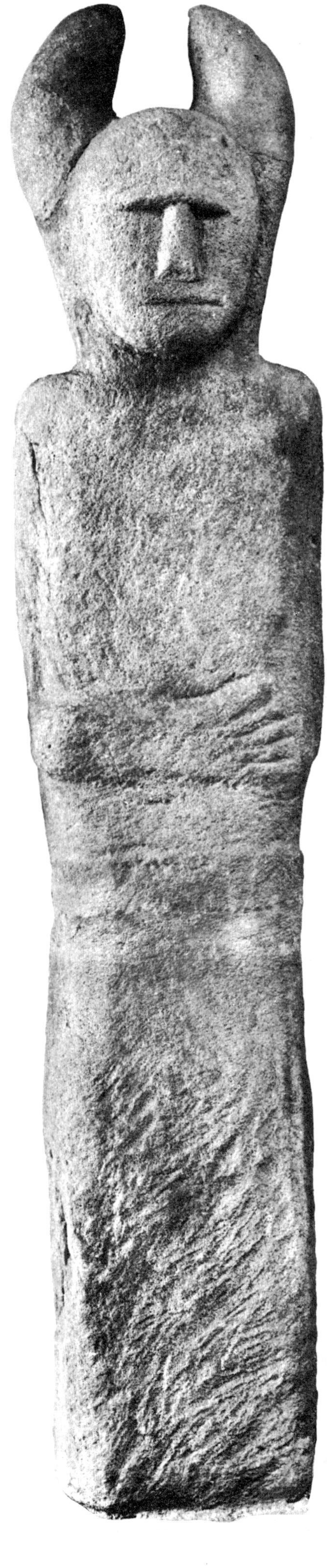

INTRODUCTION

The mythology of the Celts which has been preserved in written form since the early Middle Ages contains evidence of their beliefs in pre-Christian times. During the period of Rome's expansion into north-west Europe references to Celtic beliefs were made in the writings of classical authors. Similarly, in those parts of the Empire which had been predominantly Celtic in the time of their independence native deities continued to be worshipped alongside the gods of the Roman pantheon. A considerable body of evidence exists in the form of inscriptions to Celtic deities in France, southern Britain and, to a lesser extent, in Spain and other parts of the Roman Empire in which Celtic influence had existed. It might be assumed that it would be possible to correlate closely the literary and epigraphic evidence of the pre-Roman and Roman period with the myths themselves but, with few exceptions, this is not possible. This apparent dichotomy, however, may be resolved after an examination of both the mythology proper and the evidence, literary and archaeological. From a study of any of the main sources alone it would be possible to be misled as to the nature of Celtic Mythology. By considering evidence other than the purely mythological the chance of error is minimised, although complete certainty of interpretation is not possible in the study of any mythology remote in time.

THE CELTIC TRADITION

The Celtic tradition is preserved in a large number of texts both of prose and of poetry, the earliest of which in its present form dates to the eighth century A.D., although most belong to the centuries following. Most important and valuable are those from Ireland, for example the Books of Leinster, of the Dun Cow, of Ballymote, and the Yellow Book of Lecan. Of less value in the present context, although important in its own right, is the literature of the Welsh tradition, for example the Mabinogion preserved in the White Book of Rhydderch and the Red Book of Hergest dating from the fourteenth century A.D. It may be seen that their compilation dates to the Christian period but much of their contents, Irish and Welsh alike, dates from internal evidence to a much earlier period. In using this Celtic literature as a source for mythology it has always to be remembered that even the earliest extant texts date to the Christian period and that in all probability they were written by monks. For this reason one must expect Christian accretions and the possibility that certain important evidence may have been suppressed so as to conform with the Christian ethic. Any such suppressions have, of course, been irretrievably lost and could never be reconstructed. In the Irish literature the native gods are hardly, if at all, disguised and are therefore immediately recognisable. The Welsh literature tends to disguise deities as kings or knights, or even clerics, but they are, nevertheless, of some value when used in conjunction with Irish evidence.

THE MYTHOLOGICAL CYCLE IN IRELAND

Modern scholars have classified much of the mythology of the Celts into Cycles. The Mythological Cycle is important in that it gives something of the early history of Ireland in the form of myths or, as has been said with some justification, it treats some of the native myths as history, even fixing definite dates to what must

Two-faced statue from Holzgerlingen, Württemberg, Western Germany.

A relief of the Romano-Celtic Mars from Custom Shrubs, Gloucestershire. Mars was worshipped throughout the Roman Empire in a number of roles, but in Celtic Britain he figures chiefly as a warrior god.

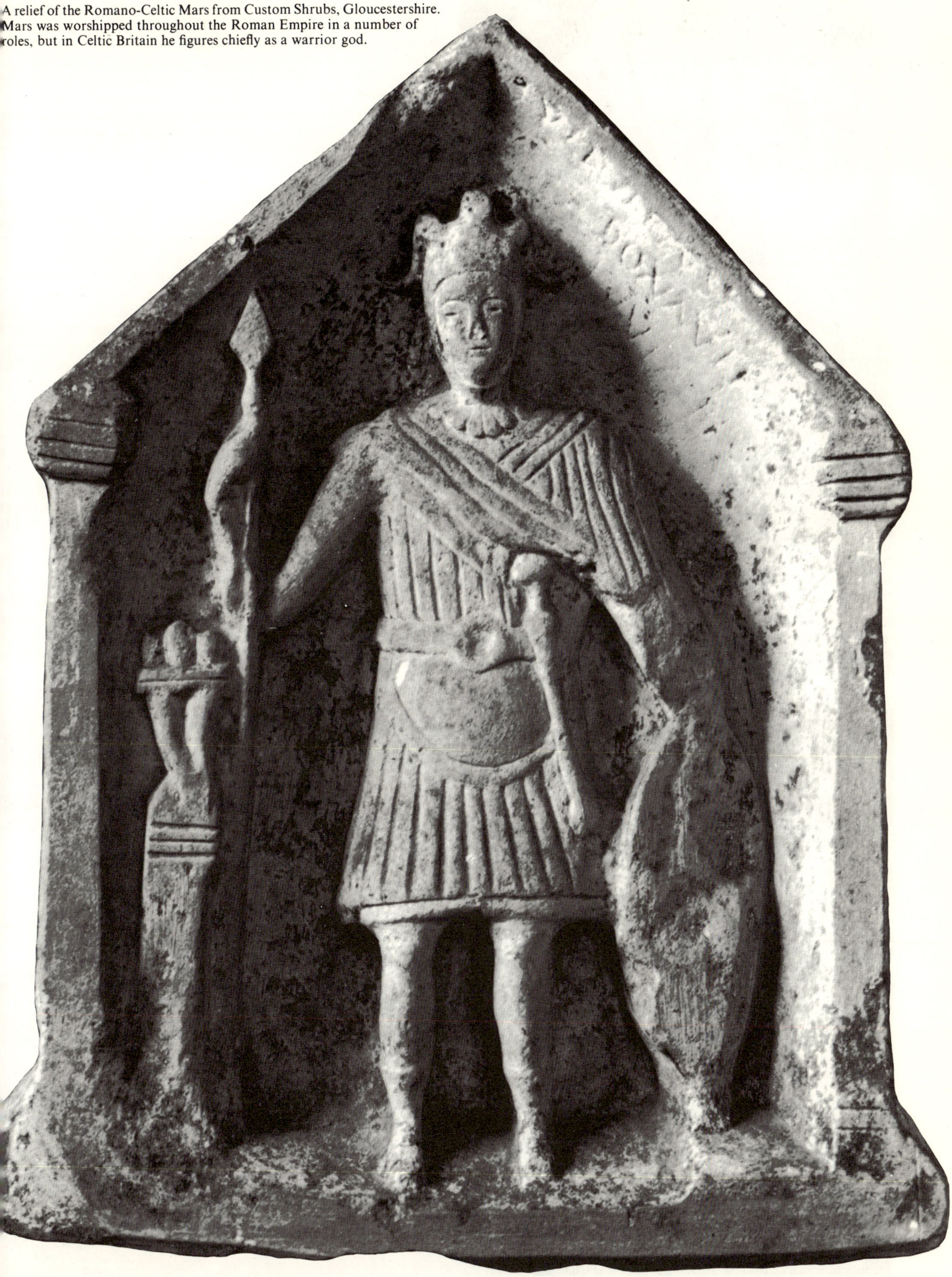

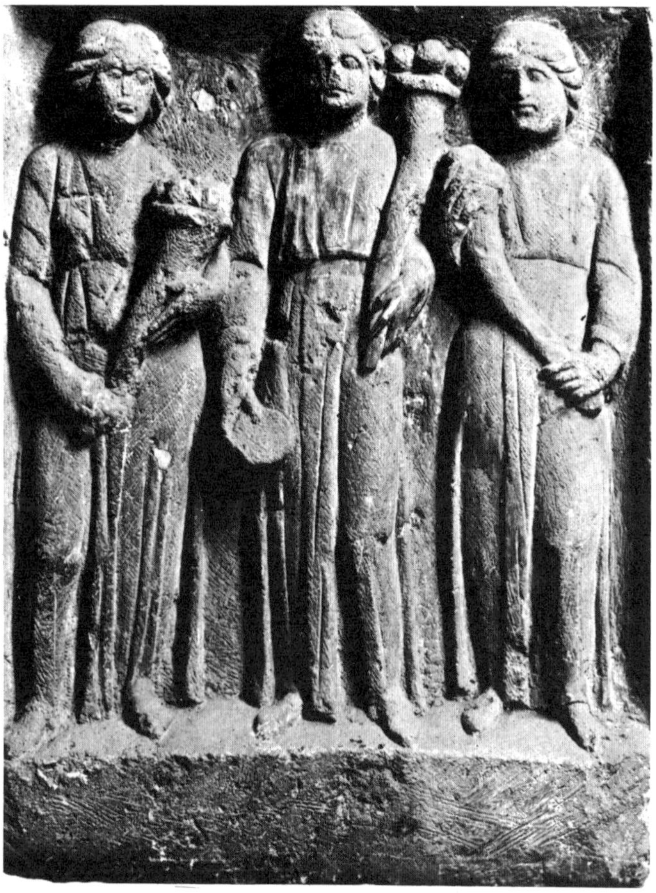

Three mother goddesses. Celtic goddesses often enjoyed a wider distribution than the male gods and appear to date from an earlier period. Particularly popular was the triad of mother or fertility goddesses, here shown with horns of plenty, who were worshipped under various epithets throughout most of Britain and Gaul. Their cult seems to have been chiefly confined to the humbler classes. It is unusual for all three goddesses to be shown standing. Relief sculpture.

surely have been mythical events. The *Lebor Gabála*, the 'Book of Conquests', tells of successive invaders of Ireland, an account slightly modified by suitable obeisances to orthodox Christianity but retaining much of the flavour of pre-Christian times. The first race which inhabited Ireland perished in the biblical Flood. It was followed two-hundred and sixty-eight years later, on the first of May, by a group of twenty-four males and twenty-four females led by Partholón. At that time there were in Ireland only one treeless and grassless plain, three lakes and nine rivers, but during Partholón's time four plains were cleared and seven new lakes were formed. Before his time there had been no tilling of the soil. After three centuries the population had grown to five thousand but on the tercentenary of Partholón's landing his people were wiped out by an epidemic, gathering together to die on the original plain in Ireland. Although there were no survivors the knowledge brought and augmented by Partholón's people did not perish, the knowledge and working of gold, the first brewing of beer, the first cauldron and the introduction of domesticated cattle. To this period are also attributed some of the less tangible assets of civilisation, law giving and ritual practices. As did their successors, so did the people of Partholón fight against and defeat the Fomorians. These latter were a race of demons, generally monstrous and hideous, who fought against Partholón with supernatural powers.

After an interval of thirty years the people of Nemed came into Ireland and in their time the face of the countryside was again changed by the clearance of twelve new plains and the formation of four new lakes. Decimated by the same epidemic which had annihilated Partholón they were unable to defend themselves adequately against the Fomorians and became their vassals. Part of their tribute was the delivery on the first of November of two-thirds of the children born to them each year, two-thirds of their corn and their milk. After a battle with the Fomorians in which Conann and many Fomorian followers were killed, the remnants of the people of Nemed fled from the country.

Next followed on the first of August the Fir Bolg together with the Fir Gaileoin and Fir Domnann. The similarity of these names to those of the Belgae, the Dumnonii and Gauls, has suggested

The god Cernunnos. He holds in one hand a torc (collar) and in the other a ram-headed serpent; he is surrounded by various animals. Silver plaque from the Gundestrup bowl. Belzeaux Zodaique.

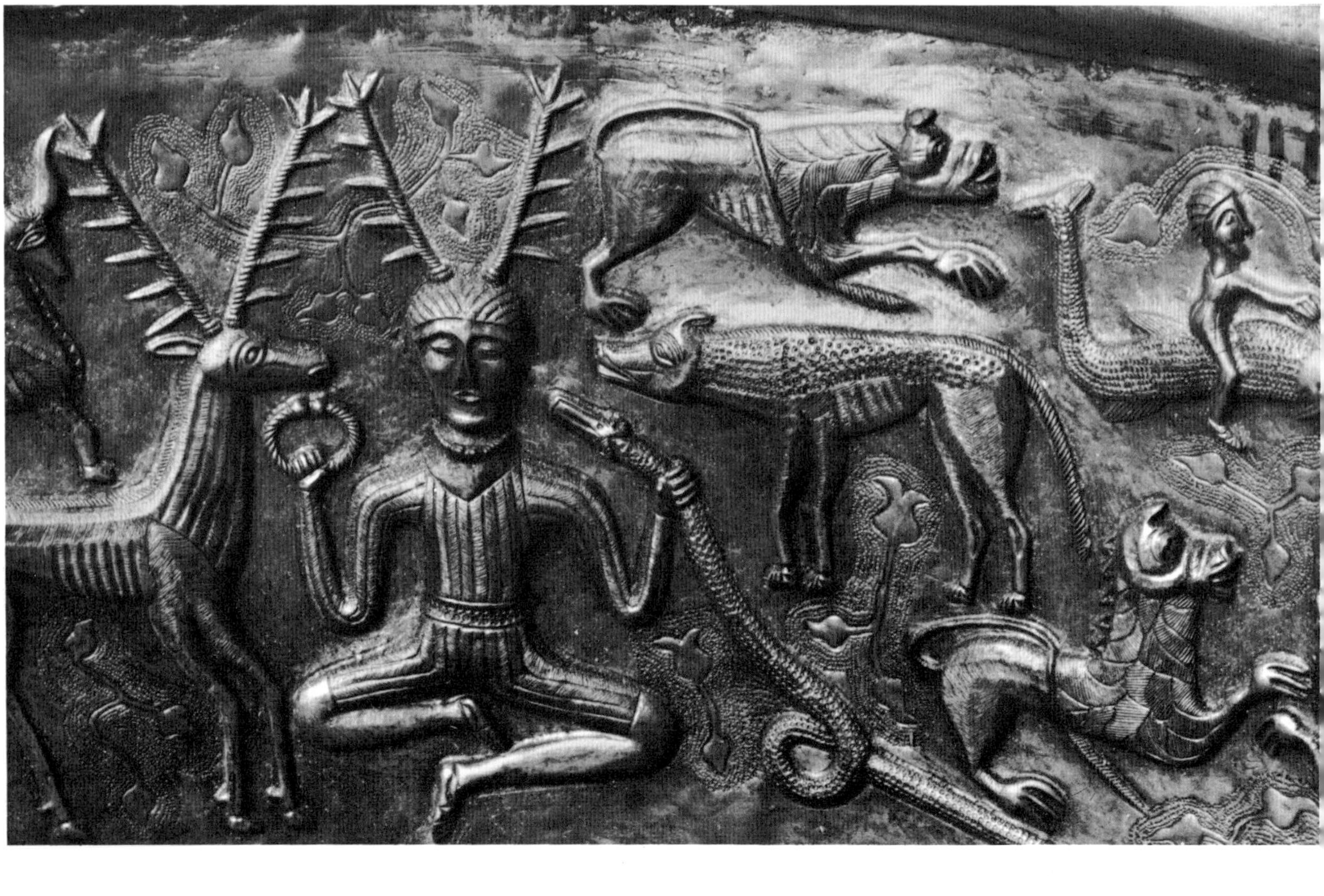

hat this 'invasion' refers to the arrival of certain tribes of the proto-ıistoric period. Whether or not these are to be in any way connected vith the Celtic people is uncertain, but their mythical contribution o the cumulative wealth of the country lies in the warlike sphere of their armament and the aristocratic notion of monarchy. Their ule did not remain undisputed for long although they were not ıttacked by the Fomorians, but they were soon dispossessed by the *Tuatha Dé Danann*, the People of the Goddess Danu.

The *Tuatha Dé Danann* landed on the first of May and after some ınsuccessful negotiations with the Fir Bolg battle was joined at *Mag Tuireadh*. The *Tuatha* were victorious and allowed the conquered to retain the Province of Connacht while they took possesion of the remainder of the island, building their capital at Tara. Still unconquered the Fomorians disputed the ownership of the and of Ireland but the *Tuatha*, perhaps recognising the strength of their ancient powers, attempted an alliance. During the battle of *Mag Tuireadh* Nuada, king of the *Tuatha*, had lost his right hand ınd, as a king had to be without physical blemish, he was obliged o abdicate. In his place Bres, the son of a Fomorian father and a nother from the *Tuatha Dé Danann*, was elected and the alliance urther strengthered by dynastic marriages including that of Bres to Brigit, the daughter of the Dagda, one of the chieftains of the *Tuatha*. Despite these precautions the alliance was ıneasy, aggravated by the lack in Bres of the generosity demanded of a king of the *Tuatha* and his imposition of excessive taxes. Eventually Bres in his turn lost his eligibility for the kingship ıaving been satirised so successfully by Cairbre, the principal bard of the *Tuatha*, that boils appeared on his face. His enforced abdication resulted in formal war between the *Tuatha* and the Fomorians, a war fought after seven years of preparation with he help of magical weapons. The Fomorians were defeated at he second battle of *Mag Tuireadh*, or Moytura the Northern,

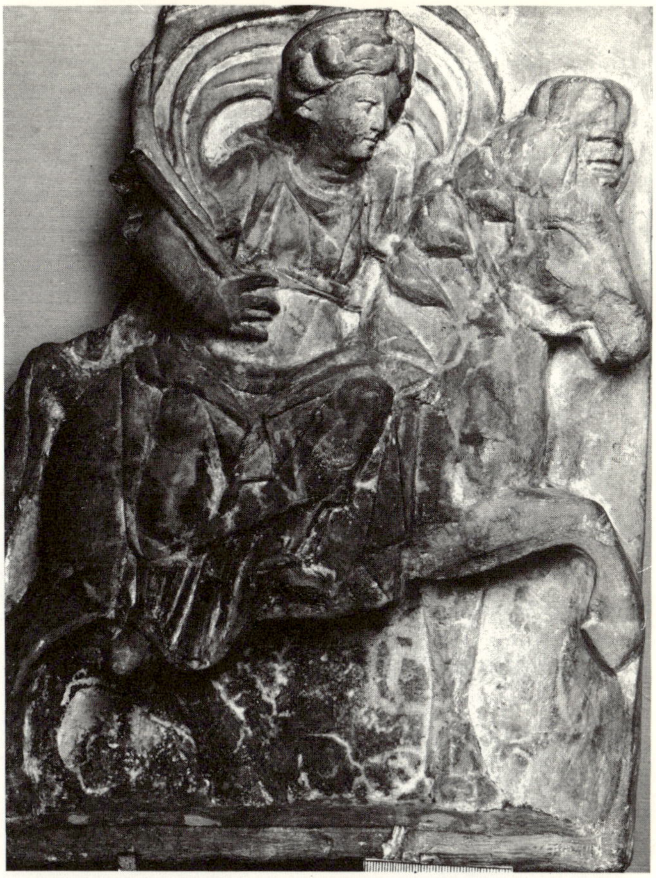

Epona. The goddess is shown seated side-saddle on her horse, wearing a long robe, a cloak and a diadem and carrying a stable key. One of the few Celtic goddesses to enjoy a widespread cult, Epona was taken over by the cavalry units of the Roman army as a protective goddess of horses and her cult spread with them throughout Europe. Her effigy was placed in stables. Gallo-Roman bas-relief from Gannat in central France.

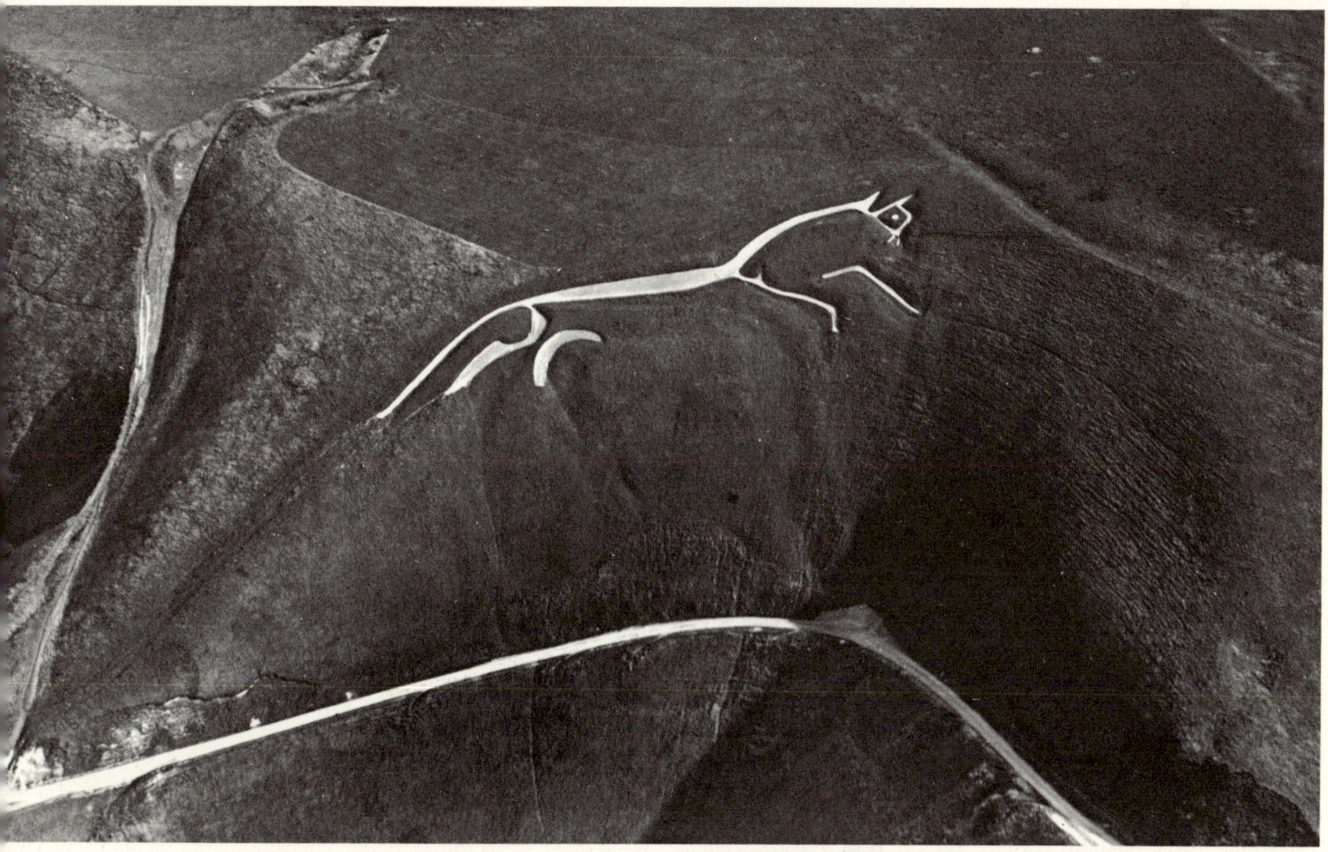

The White Horse at Uffington in Berkshire. Perhaps the most dramatic representation of the horse in Celtic times, this gigantic figure over 370 feet long was probably cut into the chalk of the hillside close to an Iron Age fort in the first century B.C. The horse was one of a number of animals held sacred by the Celts and was particularly associated with the horse-goddess Epona. Here it may possibly represent her in zoomorphic form. The figure has the beaked head typical of Celtic portrayals of this animal.

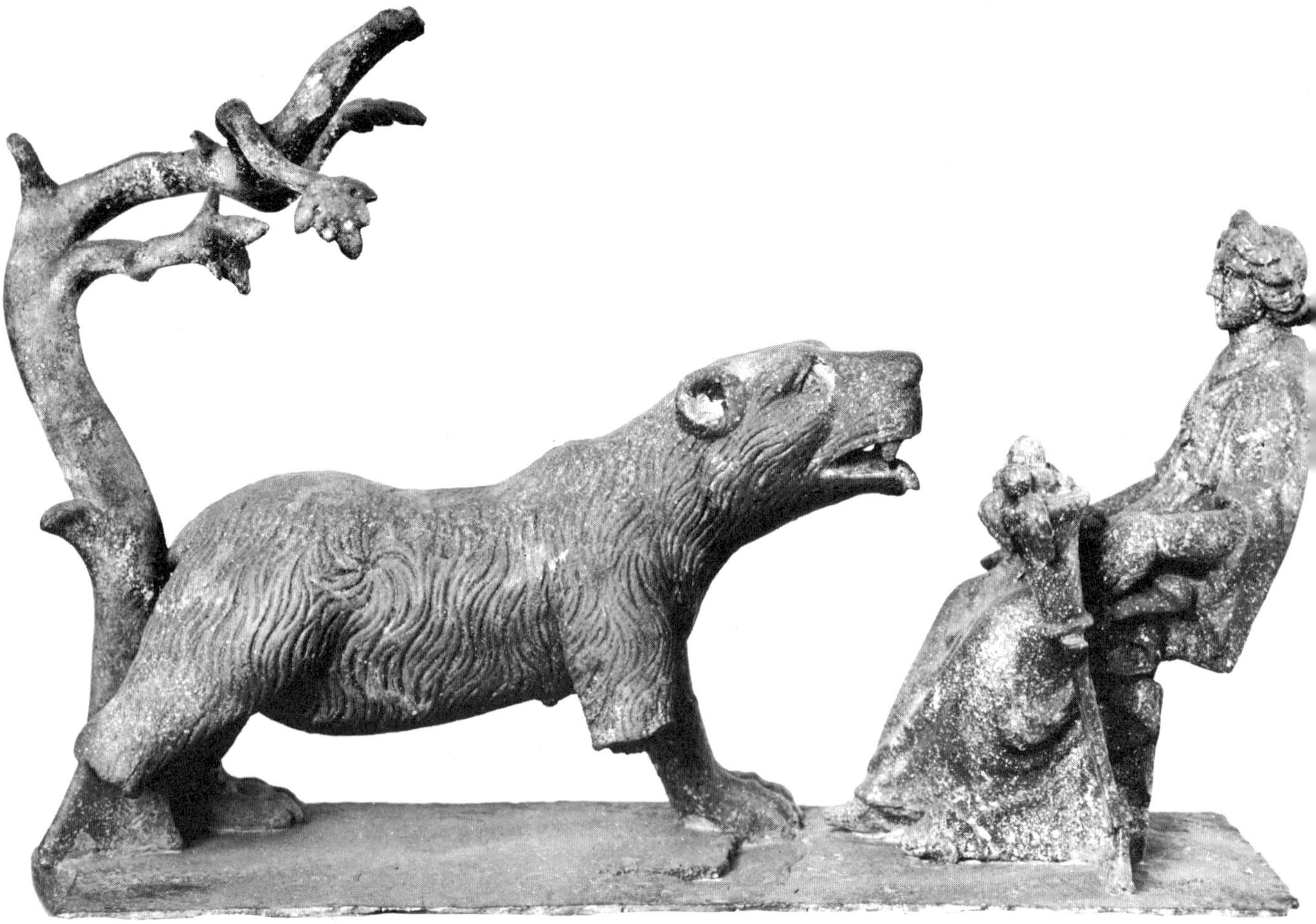

The goddess Artio worshipped by the Helvetii in the neighbourhood of Bern.

used to distinguish it from the earlier battle of the same name.

The *Tuatha* themselves, however, were destined in turn to be dispossessed by the last race to take possession of Ireland, the Sons of Mil, the Milesians. The latter's arrival on May the first and the subsequent battle for supremacy of the island was attended by formal and ritual observances, similar to those noticed in the conflict between the *Tuatha* and the Fomorians. Similarly, magical powers were used by both sides but in two successive battles the *Tuatha* were defeated and, according to popular tradition, made terms with their conquerors. The *Lebor Gabála* states that they were expelled from the island but this is in contradiction to the remainder of Irish tradition. The *Tuatha* became the gods of the Celts and the majority retired to the *síde*, the prehistoric burial mounds of the country.

This, then, is the mythological history of Ireland and a somewhat similar history may be found in the Welsh literature for the island of Britain although this is far less clearly defined than that of the neighbouring island. It is obvious that this sequence of invasions cannot be accepted as an entirely factual account of the arrival of successive peoples into Ireland. The reference to the Fir Bolg, however, may suggest that the later invasions refer to the arrival of peoples who are historically attested. The arrival of the Sons of Mil may have been added in Christian times to provide the ruling families with a genealogy respectable in the eyes of the Church. It would have been inappropriate for them to have claimed descent from the superhuman *Tuatha Dé Danann*. There seems little doubt that the Tuatha were the gods of the Celts in pre-Christian Ireland and the myth of their dispossession refers to the eventual conversion of the human Milesians to Christianity. Of the other invasions it may be suggested that these refer to the struggles of successive colonists to give their cult-practices pre-eminence over those of the previous inhabitants. It would be unwise to attempt a correlation of such events with known prehistoric migrations, but the internal evidence of some of the myths suggests that they may refer to a period as early as the Bronze Age. The complete annihilation of Partholón and his followers may refer to the complete eclipse of one cult by its successor, whereas the attempts at a *modus vivendi* discernible in the relations between the Fir Bolg and the *Tuatha* suggest a form of compromise. Within the *Tuatha* itself the functio of the Dagda and Lug appear to overlap to considerable exten and this may refer to some such compromise. The Fomorians whos presence underlies so much of the mythological history are be interpreted as a reference to some of the ritual practices of ver early inhabitants who had not accepted either the culture or th cults of newcomers. Material evidence of such people exists in th archaeological record in Ireland.

THE DEITIES OF CELTIC MYTHOLOGY

Outstanding in the invasion myths are superhuman figures wh are thinly disguised deities. Of the invasions prior to that of th *Tuatha Dé Danann* it is not possible to be certain of much more tha the names of their leaders. Partholón may symbolise the who group of his people, all of whom may have possessed superhuma attributes. Among their several functions appears to have been, a one would expect at any early date, some concern with the fertilit of the soil, the role of a vegetation god. Among the Fir Bolg the king Eochaid mac Eire appears to represent some form of benevolen father-figure. In his time the country witnessed an extended perio of happiness and wealth, probably as a result of his marriage wit Tailtiu who was evidently an earth goddess.

IRISH GODS

It is among the *Tuatha Dé Danann*, however, that the gods o Celtic Mythology may be recognised. As a group they watched ove the whole of human activity but as individuals some had the special functions. The most important deities were skilled in man spheres and attempts made by scholars to equate them with th specialised gods of other pantheons have been unsuccessful. For most were the Dagda and Lug.

The Dagda. By his epithet, *Eochaid Ollathair*, 'father of all', an *Ruad Ro-fhessa*, 'lord of perfect knowledge', the Dagda may b recognised as one of the omnicompetent deities of the Celts. He father of all, neither in the sense that he was the progenitor of all the gods nor that he was given special honours, but that he was omnicompetent, a true father-figure. In appearance he was pictured as gross and ugly, pot-bellied and coarse, and wearing the short tunic and hood of the peasant with rawhide sandals. Among his attributes was a club so large that it would have needed eight men to carry it and was therefore mounted on wheels. When dragged along the ground it left a furrow like a frontier dyke. Under the club the bones of his people's enemies were like hailstones under horses' hooves. With one end he could kill nine men at a time and with the other restore them to life. He was therefore lord of life and death. His other great possession was his cauldron which could never be emptied and from which no one ever went away unsatisfied. This symbolises his role of nourisher of his people, perhaps that of a fertility god, and this interpretation is strengthened by the myths of his union with the Morrigan by the River Unius in Connacht on the first of November and with the Boann, the goddess of the River Boyne, also on the first of November. During the time of the domination of the *Tuatha* by the Fomorians the Dagda was able to display his skill as a builder in constructing fortresses. It was at this time, too, that he appears to have undergone a ritual ordeal on the first of November when he was obliged to eat a gargantuan meal of porridge, which was produced from out of a huge hole in the ground. After this feast he had intercourse with one of the daughters of the Fomorians.

The whole episode is redolent of the ritual acts imposed on the chiefs of primitive tribes at specific times of the year in order to increase the fertility of the land and the well-being of the people. Although gross in essence it was a necessary ritual act and the myth may be referring to the actual ordeals imposed on Celtic chieftains at the most important feast of the year. If the Dagda is to be regarded as a personification of the ideal leader of a people this interpretation is quite apposite. Certainly the practice of ritual offerings in pits in the ground is well known in European prehistory.

Not all the attributes of the Dagda were so fundamentally gross. As a harpist he was able to call into existence the seasons of the Celtic year, again, perhaps, indicative of his guardianship of the fertility of the earth.

Lug. Similar in function to the Dagda was Lug, known as *Lámfhada*, 'of the long arm', and *Samildánach*, 'many skilled'. The myth of his arrival to join the *Tuatha* under Nuada underlies his omnicompetence. When asked by the guard at the gate of the royal palace of Tara to state his craft he replied that he was a carpenter. On being told that the *Tuatha* already had a carpenter Lug retorted that he was a smith, and learning further that there was also a smith went on to state that he was also a warrior, a harper, a poet, a historian, hero, sorcerer and so forth. All these posts were filled but Lug demanded that Nuada should be asked whether or not he had in his court any single person who was master of all these skills. There was not and Lug was admitted to membership of the *Tuatha De Danann*.

Despite this overlap of function with the Dagda, Lug in his person and in his attributes was in complete contrast. In place of the crude club Lug was armed with spear and sling, weapons more highly specialised and which were capable of accurate aim beyond the immediate reach of a man's arm. With his sling Lug killed Balor, the champion of the Fomorians at the battle of *Mag Tuireadh* (Moytura the Northern) by hurling a slingstone into his one enormous eye. This was the final defeat of the Fomorians and Lug was cast as the hero of the *Tuatha*.

It has been suggested that this myth tells of the replacement of one form of solar worship, as represented by the single eye of Balor, by the radiant Lug. If Lug was a solar deity, which has been doubted, it was but one of his functions and his appearance as a young and handsome man with his superior weapons is more in keeping with the Celtic ideal of an all-efficient deity. He appears to have replaced the Dagda but without any of the violence attendant on the dispossession of the gods of earlier people. Perhaps the Celts prior to their arrival in Ireland had retained one of the older deities of their continental homeland, or even adopted some older deity *en route* and granted him admission to the ranks of the *Tuatha*, for the grossness of the Dagda is not in keeping with the more refined arts of the remainder of the *Tuatha*. There is nothing to suggest that their number had always been limited as the arrival of Lug shows.

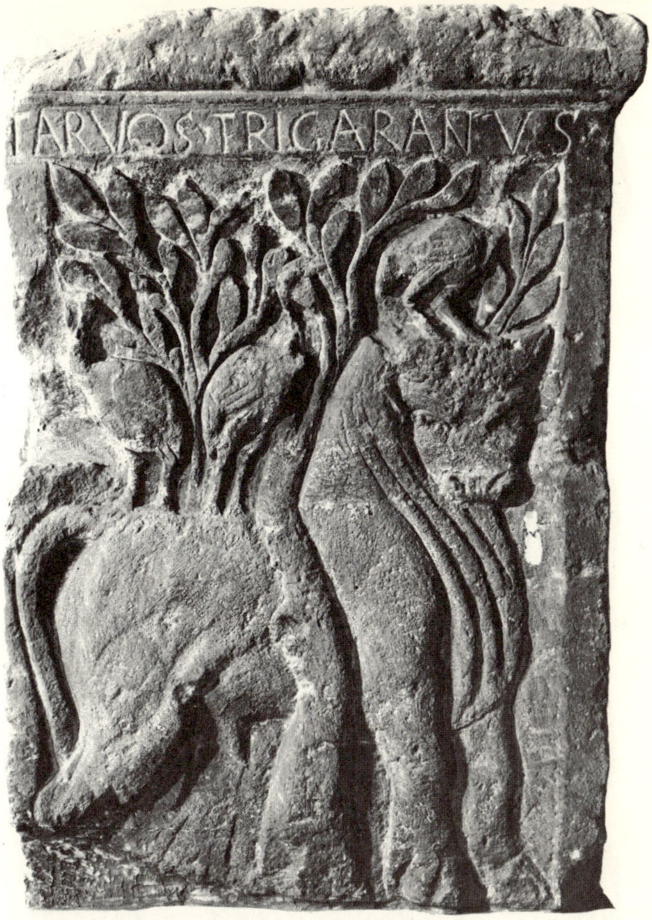

Tarvos Trigaranus or the Bull with Three Cranes.
Altar from Paris in the Cluny Museum.

Other Gods. The remaining male deities of the *Tuatha* are less easily understood. The functions of some of them appear to have duplicated those of Dagda and Lug whereas others were clearly the gods of specialised skills. Nuada, the king of the *Tuatha*, had attributes which place him in a category similar to that of the Dagda and Lug, a type of chieftain-god. He is a shadowy figure, known as Nuada Argatlam, Nuada of the Silver Hand, after the first battle of Moytura in which he lost a hand subsequently replaced by one of silver by Dian Cécht, the leech of the *Tuatha*. In his keeping was one of the treasures of the *Tuatha*, the sword of Nuada which, when unsheathed, was so powerful that no enemy could escape it. He was killed in the second battle of Moytura after which the territory allotted to them by the victors, the Milesians, was apportioned by the Dagda. The other leading figures among the *Tuatha Dé Danann* were deities with somewhat more particular functions, Ogma the champion, Gobniu the smith and brewer of beer, and Dian Cécht the leech. These, together with the Dagda, Lug and Nuada, did not comprise the whole of the people of the Goddess Danu, but the Celts visualised their gods living in a society similar to their own, aristocratic and warlike, in which they were served by their inferiors, craftsman and peasant. The gods referred to in this section were the chieftain-gods and it is important to understand that the ideal of the Celts was not to be found in the simple agrarian deities of earlier times but it was appropriate to the advanced and more secure economy of the Celtic Iron Age. This interpretation is supported by the available archaeological evidence. The chieftain-gods of the *Tuatha* were expected through the agency of the supernatural powers which they possessed and with the aid of their four magical treasures, the cauldron of the Dagda, the spear of Lug, the sword of Nuada and the Stone of Fál which cried out aloud when stepped on by the lawful king of Ireland, to secure the general well-being of their people and increase their prosperity.

The position of the *Tuatha Dé Danann* has been emphasised not because they were the sole deities of the Celts even in Ireland, but because from the literature it is possible to make some attempt at a reconstruction of their meaning as deities. There also existed other gods, sometimes more localised deities such as the chieftain-gods Midir of Bri Leith Bodb of Síd ar Femen, or minor deities, frequently

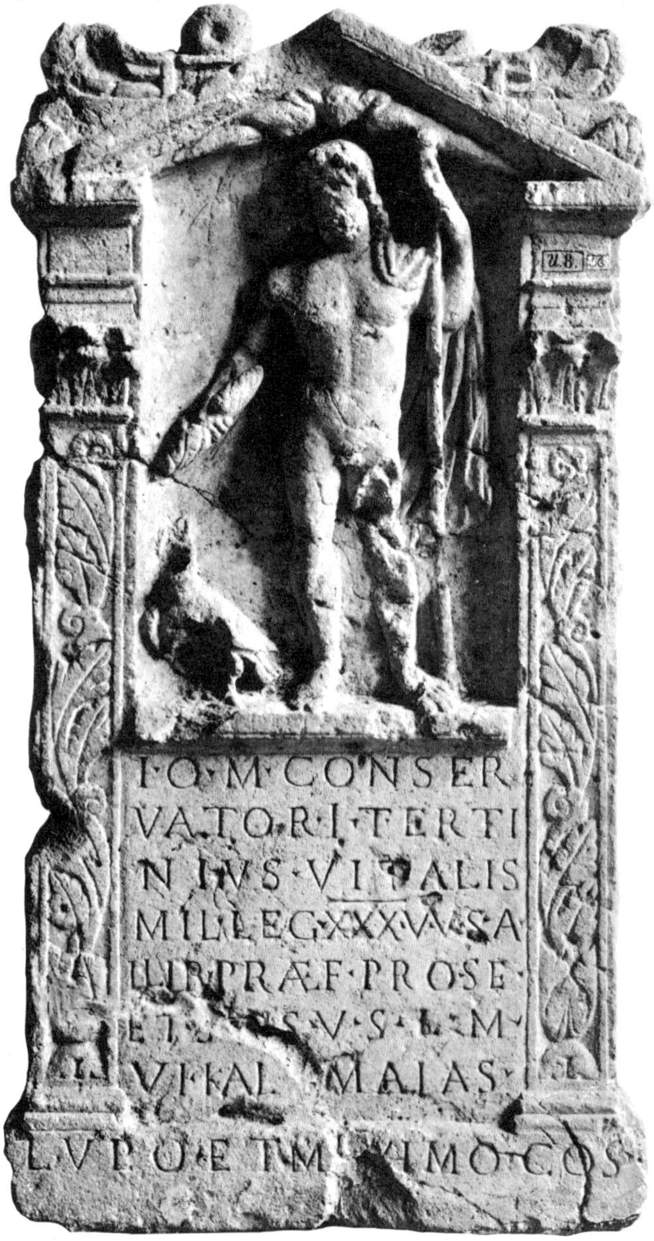

Jupiter with a goose. Like a number of other Roman gods, Jupiter became identified with various aspects of omnicompetent Celtic gods and was worshipped among the Celtic peoples, but he lost the supreme position he occupied in the Roman pantheon and was worshipped chiefly as a sky-god and god of storms.
On this bas-relief found at Xanten in western Germany he is shown in company with a goose – a bird sacred to the Celts, which appears to have been especially associated in their mythology with gods of a martial character.

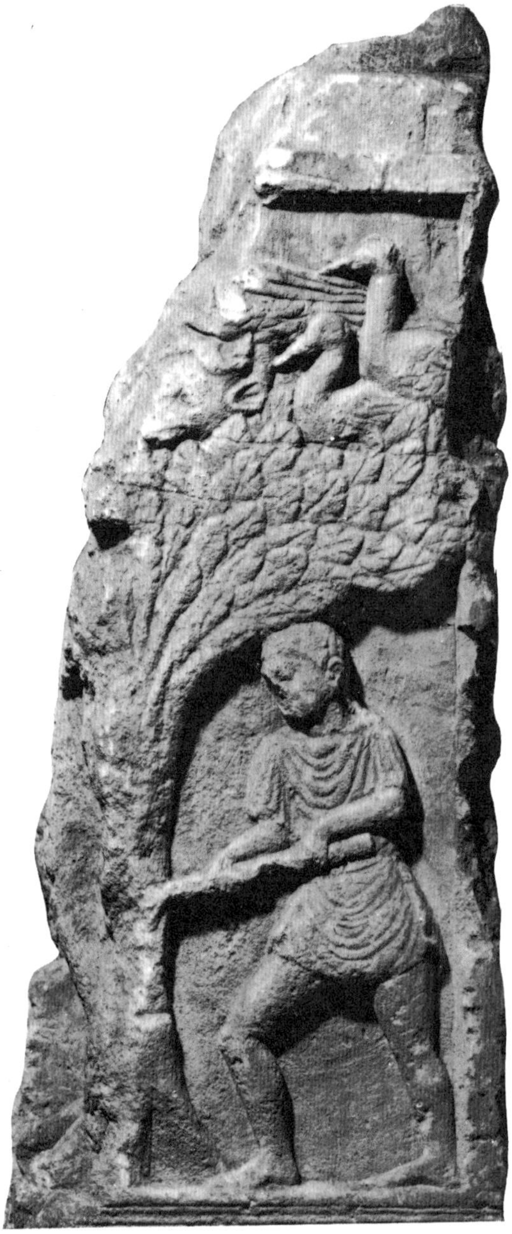

Esus cutting down a willow-tree. The god is shown in his usual role as a wood-cutter and is engaged in chopping down a willow-tree in the branches of which can be seen a bull's head and three egrets. The particular legend associated with this scene is not known but marsh birds often appear in Celtic iconography in connection with solar deities, in their role as gods of healing, and occasionally as war-gods. Bas-relief.
First century A.D.

the offspring of the major chieftain-gods, such as Angus Og, the son of the Dagda and Boanna. The heroes of the Celts such as Cú Chulainn and Finn, although of divine ancestry, are in a different category and are discussed separately. Finally, the sea-gods of the Celts in Ireland although, in the case of Manannán mac Lir, included among the chieftain-gods of the *Tuatha* should be considered apart from their terrestrial counterparts. Manannán was lord of the sea beyond and under which lay *Tír na nOc*, the Celtic otherworld. One of the most colourful of the *Tuatha* in his invulnerable mail, a helmet which shone like the sun and armed with his sword which never failed to kill, he sailed in his boat which needed neither sail nor oars but went wherever he willed it. His pigs were important for the well-being of the *Tuatha*. Killed and eaten daily, they returned to life the following day and provided the *Tuatha* with some of their supernatural food. Manannán in fact appears to have been a fertility deity, sharing at least some of the functions of the mother-goddess, but, as in the case of the preceding sea-gods whom he supplanted, it is extremely difficult to fit him into any exact classification.

IRISH GODDESSES

The gods of the Celts emerge from mythology as little occupied specifically with the fertility of the earth. In this they differed from, and perhaps complemented, the functions of the goddesses who, in their turn, appear to have retained the concept of the Mother-Goddess which had evolved in much earlier times and which persisted through and beyond the Celtic period. Whereas the Celtic gods were specifically Celtic in that they could have existed only in the climate engendered by the warrior-aristocratic society of their period, the goddesses were restatements of an age-old theme.

Danu: Anu and Brigit. The gods of the Celts in Ireland are frequently called the People of the Goddess Danu, but this does not mean that she actually gave birth to all of them. The Dagda, for example, was sometimes referred to as her father. The only direct descendants of Danu who appear in mythology are Brian, Iuchar and Iucharba, probably an example of the triple concept of one deity which is common in Celtic iconography. With Danu was confused Anu or Ana after whom were called the hills, the Paps of Anu in Co. Kerry.

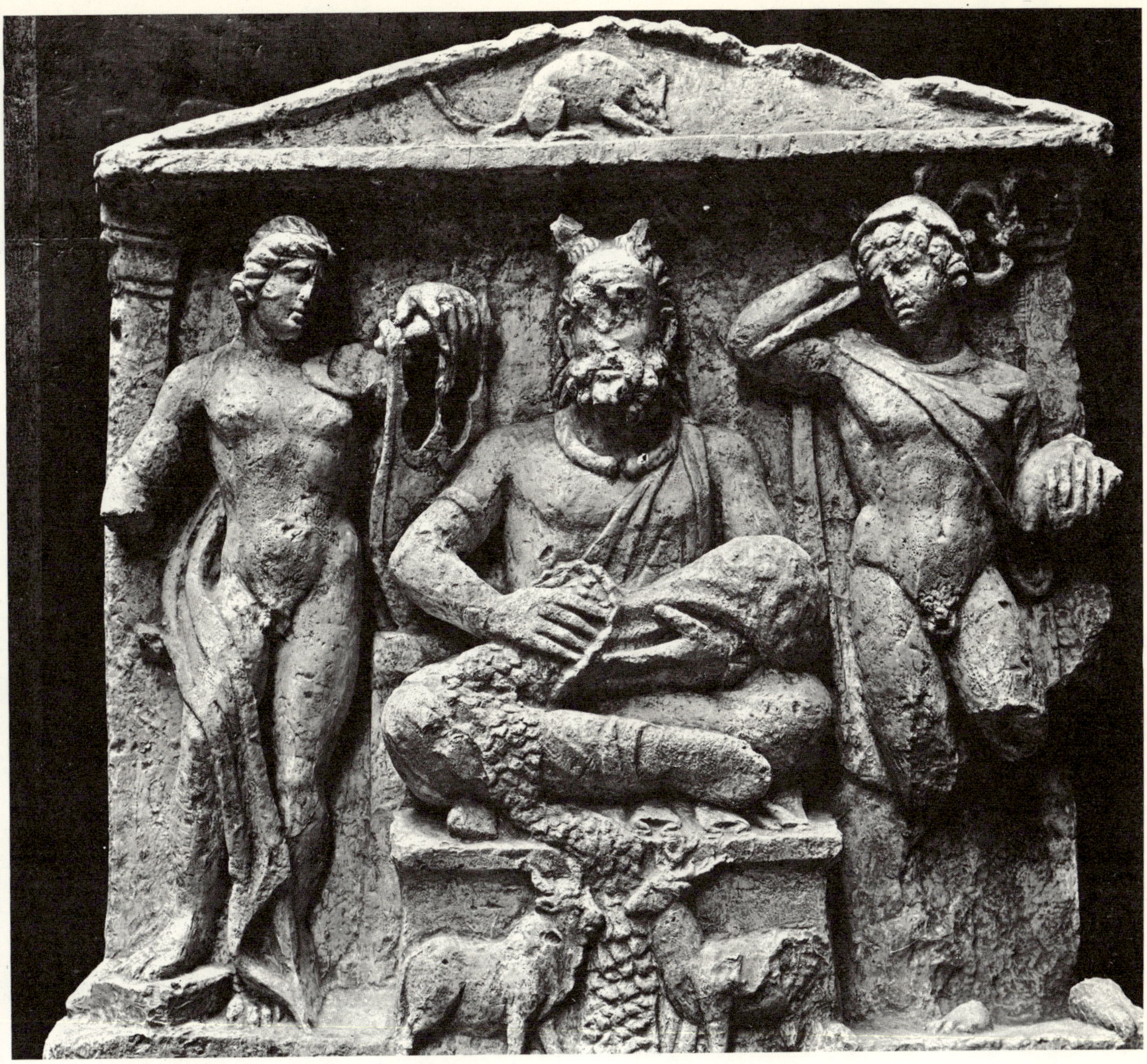

Cernunnos with Apollo and Mercury. Celtic gods often continued to be worshipped alongside the gods of the Roman pantheon even when the countries themselves had been absorbed into the Roman Empire. Here Cernunnos is shown pouring out coins or grain before a bull and a stag with Apollo on his right and Mercury on his left. The Roman gods are clearly inferior to him in Celtic belief. Gallo-Roman stele found at Rheims.

Similarly confused was Brigit who again was frequently regarded as a triple goddess. Her worship appears to have been more widespread than that of either Danu or Anu and she survives in Christianity as Saint Brigid (or Bride). It seems probable that all these deities are different concepts of the same mother-goddess figure. All were goddesses of plenty and should find their place in the concept of fertility-cults. Brigit, however, had additional functions as a tutelary deity of learning, culture and skills.

Macha. Macha, the eponymous deity of the capital of Ulster, Emain Macha, was a more complex deity. The mythology suggests that she was perhaps a survival of a mother-goddess worshipped in parts of Ireland prior to the arrival of the Celts. Her earlier functions are obscure but appear to have been appropriate to those of a fertility goddess. She was, for example, the wife of Nemed, a leader in one of the earlier invasion myths. In the Ulster Cycle she was the wife of Crunnchu, a peasant farmer, and this close association with the soil is in contrast with the more exalted role of the male deities. Against her will and although pregnant she was forced to race against the horses of Conchobor at Emain Macha. She was successful but died giving birth to twins. In dying she put a curse on the warriors of Ulster which subjected them for nine generations to the pangs of childbirth for five days and four nights in the hour of their greatest need. It has been thought that this myth refers to some collective ritual practised at one of the feasts of Ulster in honour of Macha, the mother-goddess, and in times of national distress. Macha is here again a fertility deity, concerned not only with the fertility of the earth but also man's fertility.

In another myth Macha appears as a warrior-queen in her own right, forcing the sons of her enemies to build the fortifications of her capital, Emain Macha. Here she had acquired a more warlike role which is paralleled in the myths of other goddesses. It might be expected that tutelary deities, male or female, would have been expected to fight for their devotees and, as in Celtic society in the pre-Christian period it was not unusual for women to fight in battle, there is no need to feel that the Celts were being unethical in casting their goddesses in warlike roles. The historic queens, Boudicca and Cartimandua, are evidence of this and the mythical queen, Medb of Connacht, is in the same tradition. Macha was sometimes associated with the Morrigan and the Badb to form a triad of warrior goddesses who presided over battle. As such they did not fight with mortal weapons but used their supernatural powers, for example the Morrigan in fighting against Cú Chulainn. They frequently resorted to shape-shifting and it is evident that many Celtic goddesses undertook personal transformations at different times.

The other female deities that are discernible in Celtic mythology are variations on the theme of the Mother-Goddess who not only

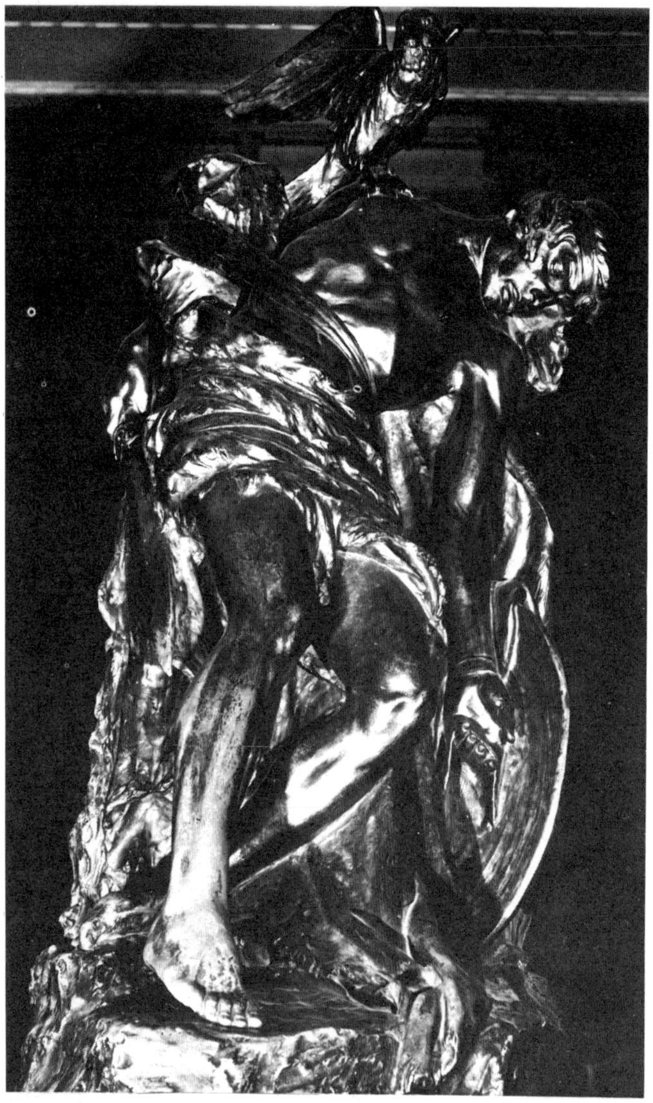

The death of Cu Chulainn. Lured to the Plain of Muirthemne by Queen Medb and tricked into violating his *geasa*, or taboos, the great Ulster hero has thus been deprived of his supernatural powers and now, fatally wounded, has had himself bound to a pillar-stone by his belt so that he may defy his enemies to the end and die on his feet. Bronze statue.

saw to the fertility of the earth, animals and men, but who would have aided with supernatural powers their devotees in their distress. There were many local deities fulfilling much the same functions as those more fully documented in the literature, and some had local festivals dedicated in their honour similar in intent, if not in size, to that of Tailtiu. That Tailtiu had been the daughter of one of the Fir Bolg but subsequently married the *Tuatha Dé Danann* is another instance of the continuity of the mother-goddess figure.

BRITISH DEITIES

Due to the nature of Welsh mythology and the stronger influences of Christianity imposed on it before the production of the earliest extant manuscripts it is more difficult to reconstruct the main features of the gods and goddesses of Britain. In the Four Branches of the Mabinogi it is possible to trace a mythological history of Britain, similar to that of Ireland in that there is the dispossession of gods by those of newcomers. It is, however, by no means as complete as the Irish Mythological Cycle but this lacuna may be filled by reference to other parts of the Welsh literature.

The Children of Don. Some of the Irish deities reappear in Wales in the native tradition but this may have been the result of Irish immigration into Britain in the late Roman period. Parallel to the *Tuatha Dé Danann*, although by no means identical in every respect, are the Children of Don. Among them was Govannan, the smith and brewer, who was the British equivalent of Gobniu. Ludd or Nudd was the analogue of Nuada, both being credited in

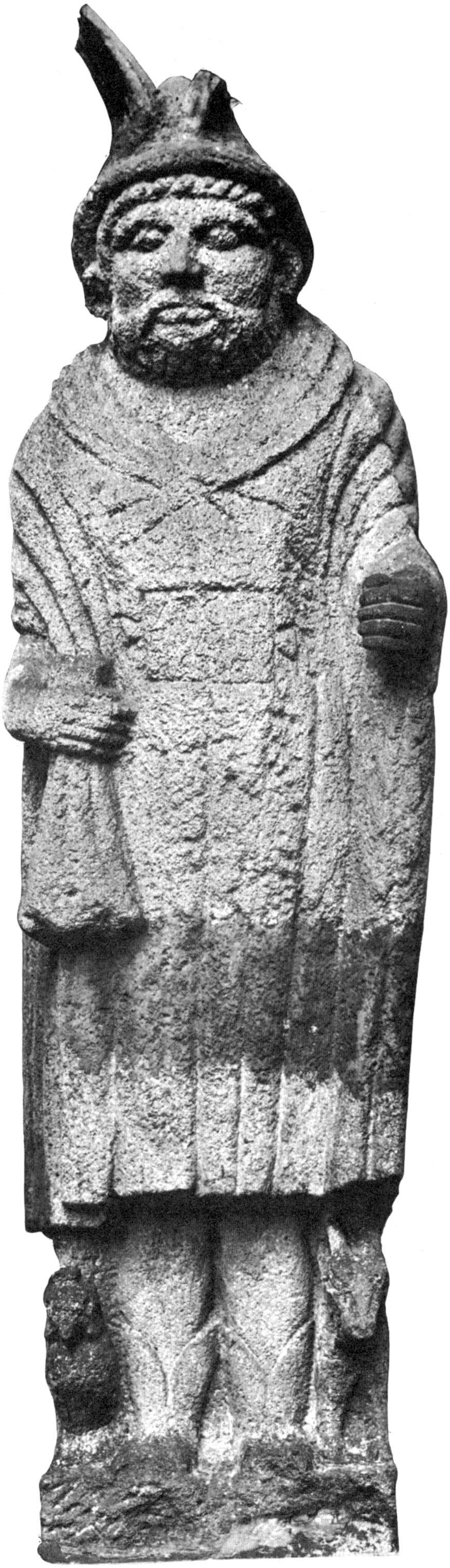

Another aspect of the Gallic Mercury, bearded and in travelling costume.

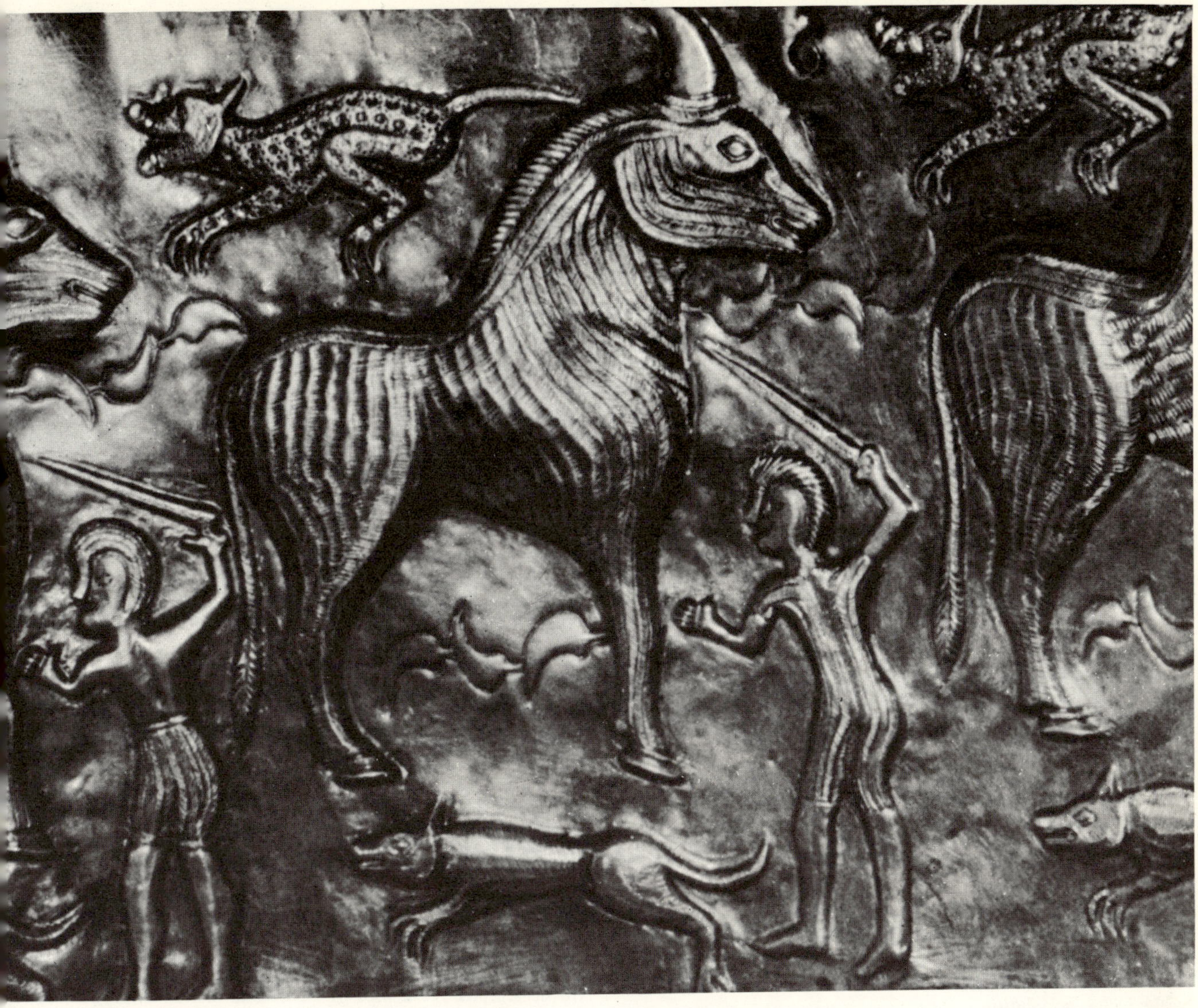

Scene from the interior of the Gundestrup bowl. Here three figures accompanied by dogs are about to plunge their swords into the necks of three bulls. Though the scene suggests a hunt, the formal repetition would suggest a ritual significance. Relief in silverplated copper probably of the second century A.D.

their respective myths with silver hands, Llaw Ereint, 'silver hand', being the epithet of Ludd, and both having been rulers.

Perhaps the greatest of the Children of Don was Gwydion who was more of an omnipotent god such as the Dagda and Lug. He was skilled in the arts of war and peace and underwent trials at the hands of hostile powers, much in the way that the Dagda suffered ordeals when subject to the Fomorians. In this case, as with the Dagda, this myth probably represents a ritual ordeal imposed on the Celtic chieftains. He possessed magical powers and was skilled in poetry and eloquence. Despite his strongly defined attributes in the literature his worship was apparently restricted to north-west of Wales.

Among the Children of Don was Arianrod, a goddess, after whom the Corona Borealis was sometimes named. She was the mother of Llew, again a somewhat indistinct figure who has been compared not very satisfactorily with the Irish Lug. Llew was known as *Llew Llaw Gyffes*, 'Llew of the strong hand', perhaps similar in intent to the *Lámfhada* of Lug. Like Lug he had a spear and a sling after which the rainbow was called. He appears to have been another manifestation of the chieftain-god idea. It is interesting to note that many of the Children of Don gave their names to constellations, such as Cassiopeia – Llys Don ('the Court of Don'), the Milky Way – Cær Gwydion, Corona Borealis – Cær Arianrod. However, this does not imply they were neccessarily part of a sky myth.

The Children of Llyr. As in Irish literature Manannán was more renowned than his father, Lir, so in the Welsh is Manawyddan more clearly defined than was his father, Llyr. The attributes of Manawyddan ab Llyr were less clearly defined than his counterpart, and sometimes even contradictory, but he appears to have been a god of fertility and craftsmanship. The myth of his fortress in Gower, built from human bones, may hide some reference to sacrifice.

His brother Bran the Blessed, *Bendegeit Bran*, is more clearly defined. Of enormous size and commensurate strength he possessed those supernatural powers attributed to their deities by the Celts in Ireland. He had a cauldron which would restore to life the dead but without the power of speech. This cauldron had originally come from Ireland and was returned there as a gift to Matholwch, king of Ireland. Bran was later forced to fight Matholwch and in the episode of this war his superhuman powers were emphasised. He waded across the Irish Sea, his body like a mountain, his two eyes lakes on either side of a ridge which was his nose. When he laid himself down across a river a whole army could march across his back. In addition he was a skilled harpist and poet. At the final battle with Matholwch Bran was wounded in the foot with a poisoned arrow. Realising he was dying he ordered his head to be cut off and be taken to the White Hill in London facing the continent as a protection against invaders. Thus Bran appears as yet another omnipotent god who watched over his people, fighting for them, and ultimately sacrificing himself for them.

It has been suggested that the Children of Llyr were deities of the underworld as opposed to the Children of Don who were sky deities. This is disputable, but the two groups appear to have represented successive groups of gods worshipped in Britain. As in the case of the *Tuatha Dé Danann* and the Fomorians in Ireland there was intermarriage suggesting some form of rapprochement between contending groups. British archaeological evidence shows that in the highland zone where most of the myths were preserved the remains of earlier cultures lingered and prospered long after the newer cultures had become dominant in the lowland zone. It would not be surprising if remnants of pre-Celtic beliefs had become incorporated into the purely Celtic tradition. The interpretation of the Welsh tradition is complicated by many factors including the Irish influences which must have been strong in parts of Wales in the sub-Roman period, the possibility of still later Scandinavian influences, and the late date of the extant British literary sources. The Christian Church appears to have been less generous to its pagan forerunners in Britain and the Celtic gods in Welsh mythology were much more mutilated than their Irish counterparts.

Other British Deities. Deities who did not strictly belong to either the Children of Don or of Llyr included a counterpart in Welsh myth of the Irish Morrigan, a goddess appearing in battle in changing horrid guises. Pwyll appears in the first branch of the Mabinogi to have become the lord of the underworld in a myth which tells of how he changed places for a year and a day with Arawn, prince of Annwn, the British Hades. Henceforth he was known as *Pwyll Pen Annwn,* Head of Annwn. He married Rhiannon who was an earlier fertility-goddess and they produced Pryderi, a later lord of the underworld and around whose exploits the myths enshrined in the four branches of the Mabinogi were woven. The large number of supernatural beings who appear in Welsh mythology remain indistinct but the central theme which recurs frequently is that of strife, all of which should point to a struggle between beliefs in conflicting deities, but centred mainly on that between the Children of Llyr and the Children of Don and their various allies.

Arthur. Some considerable difficulty impedes a completely satisfactory interpretation of Arthur. As the legends surrounding him took shape in the literature of the Middle Ages writers borrowed material from different sources and confused what they did not understand in an attempt to produce a coherent narrative. There seems little reason to doubt that a historic Arthur existed in the person of Ambrosius Aurelianus who lived in the turbulent century following the collapse of Roman rule in Britain. He appears to have been a Romanised Briton who successfully commanded a mobile force of cavalry against Saxon invaders. It is not improbable that the accounts of his exploits would have been cherished and magnified by the Celtic population.

Behind the historic Arthur was a mythical person who has been variously interpreted as a god, Artor, the ploughman, and a bear god, neither of whom are entirely convincing. By the time the Welsh myths were written down the mythical Arthur had become as indistinct as the majority of other Welsh deities. In the story of Culhwch and Olwen Arthur appears most strongly in his mythological aspect, surrounded by other mythical persons. He appears to have been yet another chieftain-god with his consort, Gwenhwyfar, perhaps originally a fertility goddess. To the early relatively simple conception of Arthur had been attracted myths belonging to other deities and the exaggerated exploits of the historic Arthur. Despite the strong influence of Christianity in the later versions it is possible to detect the Celtic myth in which the Grail is the thinly disguised cauldron of plenty and the opponents of Arthur and his Knights are the last echoes of various long-displaced deities.

THE CELTIC HERO-FIGURE

Distinct from the full-scale gods who were divine were the heroes of the Celts who, although basically human, possessed superhuman powers which they used for the benefit of their people. Foremost in the extant literature is the life and death of Cú Chulainn whose exploits figure so largely and in great detail in the Ulster Cycle. Cú Chulainn is the epitome of the Celtic hero who was the defender of his tribe, a mortal endowed with superhuman faculties which he exercised solely for the good of his people. From his birth to his early death the epics centred on Cú Chulainn are probably representative of similar stories woven around the heroes of lesser tribes and which have been lost. In the story of Culhwch and Olwen some of Culhwch's exploits resemble Cú Chulainn's and the former suggests the existence of similar hero-figures among the British Celts.

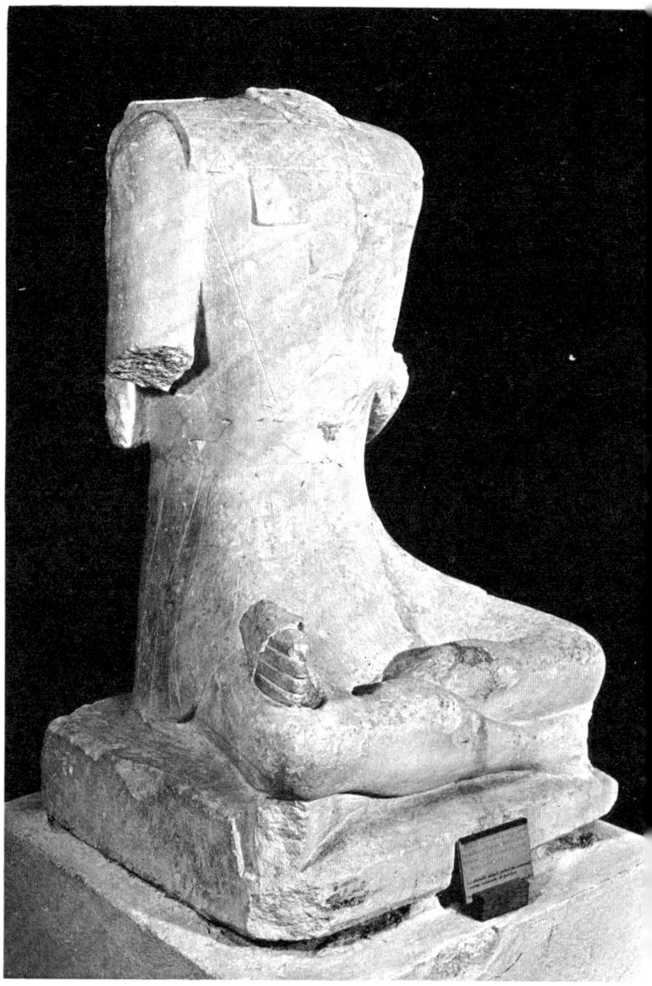

Seated figure from the entrance to the sanctuary of La Roquepertuse. The figure, which is dressed in a tunic and a kind of scapular which was originally decorated with incised and painted ornament, represents a Gallic chieftain with the attributes of a hero or god. The seated, crosslegged pose is one used by the Celts to indicate divinity and is frequently met with gods of an indigenous character *c.* 400 B.C.

In the story of Cú Chulainn's birth there is an element of mystery and doubt. In one version it appears that he was the son of at least one divine being, Lug, and in another version that he was born three times, a further instance of Celtic triplication. His original name was Sétanta and this is connected with the British tribe, the Setanti, whose tribal hero he may originally have been. His name, Cú Chulainn, 'the Hound of Culann', was given him at the age of seven after he had been forced to kill the watch-dog of Culann, the smith. In recompense Cú Chulainn undertook to guard the kingdom of Ulster and thus became the champion of his people. In his childhood he is pictured as bearing typically human attributes and was brought up in circumstances appropriate to those of the son of any high-born Celt. Following custom he was sent away to foster-parents, although his education from Sencha, Fergus and Cathbad who taught him wisdom, warfare and magic, in addition to the more normal fosterage given by Amairgin the poet, was to fit him for his special role in society. He later received further tuition from the sorceress, Scáthach, who taught him much of the art of magic. This over-emphasis of human attributes and needs was typical of all things surrounding the person of the hero but essential humanity was never obscured. Similarly, Cú Chulainn came to full manhood at an earlier age than his contemporaries and won his position by force. Violence to gain his objective is typical of the hero. Cú Chulainn's entry into the court of Conchobor was violent and his disturbance of the king's chessboard was as ill-mannered as the Welsh hero Culhwch's entry on horseback into Arthur's court. Later on he was similarly required to win his bride by force after undergoing violent and dangerous ordeals in foreign lands.

After undergoing his ritual ordeals, one of which was to fight the hound of Culann, Cú Chulainn received his warrior's armour, again by a form of trickery. Now he was a full warrior but before e could become the full protector of his people he had to prove imself in further exploits. Once completed he was able to take his lace at courts as the full champion of his people, fully equipped nd skilled in the arts of war and culture. He was the exaggerated deal of Celtic nobility, proud, brave and skilled in magic and the rts. The Celtic warrior was no uncouth soldier but was able to onverse on equal terms with poets and druids.

In his normal state Cú Chulainn is pictured as a young man vith well-defined physical attributes. He had seven pupils in each ye, seven fingers on each hand and seven toes on each foot. His heeks were multi-coloured, yellow, blue, green and red. His long lark hair was of three tints, dark close to the roots, red in the niddle and lighter in colour towards the tips, suggestive of the ractice of the Celts of smearing their hair with a thick wash of ime. Rich and gorgeous jewellery adorned him, a hundred strings f jewels on his head, a hundred golden breast ornaments. Far lifferent was Cú Chulainn in his battle-frenzy when his body was eized by contortions. He turned round in his skin so that his feet nd knees were to the rear and his calves and buttocks to the front. lis long hair stood on end and on the tip of each hair was a spot f blood or a spark of fire. From his open mouth spurted fire and rom the top of his head a jet of black blood rose mast high. One ye receded far back into his skull while the other protruded onto is cheek. Finally, on his forehead appeared the 'hero's moon', a trange inexplicable sign. When in this state Cú Chulainn's fury vas uncontrollable and he needed to be plunged into three vats of old water before he could be pacified.

Thus endowed he was well-nigh invincible in battle and was able o defend Ulster single-handed against the four provinces of Ireland luring the time when the men of Ulster were laid prostrate with he curse of Macha. This is the great central action in the story of Cú Chulainn, the Cattle Raid of Cualnge, which in itself is full of ignificance. Although invincible he was not invulnerable and his ody was sorely wounded on a number of occasions. To the Celts heir hero had to suffer as a mortal else he would have been lessened in their eyes. Similarly, he had to die without descendants yet die unconquered, and this was brought about by supernatural means against which he was powerless.

During his life-time Cú Chulainn had made enemies who, if he spared them, plotted for revenge. Among them was Queen Medb who had intitiated the Cattle Raid of Cualnge in her attempt to steal the brown bull of Cualnge. She had trained sorcerers from childhood as part of her plan to bring about Cú Chulainn's downfall. Again Ulster was invaded by the four provinces and again Cú Chulainn hastened to its defence. This time he realised that he was fighting against supernatural powers which had been carefully organised against him. In Irish mythology there is the frequent occurrence of the *geis* which was a ritual injunction to avoid certain actions in some circumstances and to perform others in the appropriate circumstances. Cú Chulainn was burdened with several *geasa* and in his last battle, the 'Great Carnage of Mag Muirthemne', he realised that he had been 'overtaken' by his *geasa*.

Before the actual battle Cú Chulainn was thus overtaken by his *geasa*. Three of the sorceresses of Medb were roasting a dog at a hearth as he passed. It was one of his *geasa* not to pass a hearth without tasting the food being prepared but it was also another *geis* for him to eat dog. By taking the dog's shoulder offered to him his powers were diminished. Another series of demands were made on him by a poet who threatened to satirise him if he refused. This succeeded in disarming and mortally wounding him. Washing himself in a lake he killed an otter which came to drink the blood-stained water. He realised that his end was near as it had been foretold that his first and last exploits would be the killing of a dog – the first was the Hound of Culann and the last a water-dog, the otter. In his death agony he bound himself to a pillar-stone and defied his enemies until the end. And so he died with his honour unimpaired.

All the features which distinguish the Celtic hero are discernible in the Cú Chulainn story and all tribal heroes must have followed this pattern to a greater or lesser extent. Cú Chulainn, however,

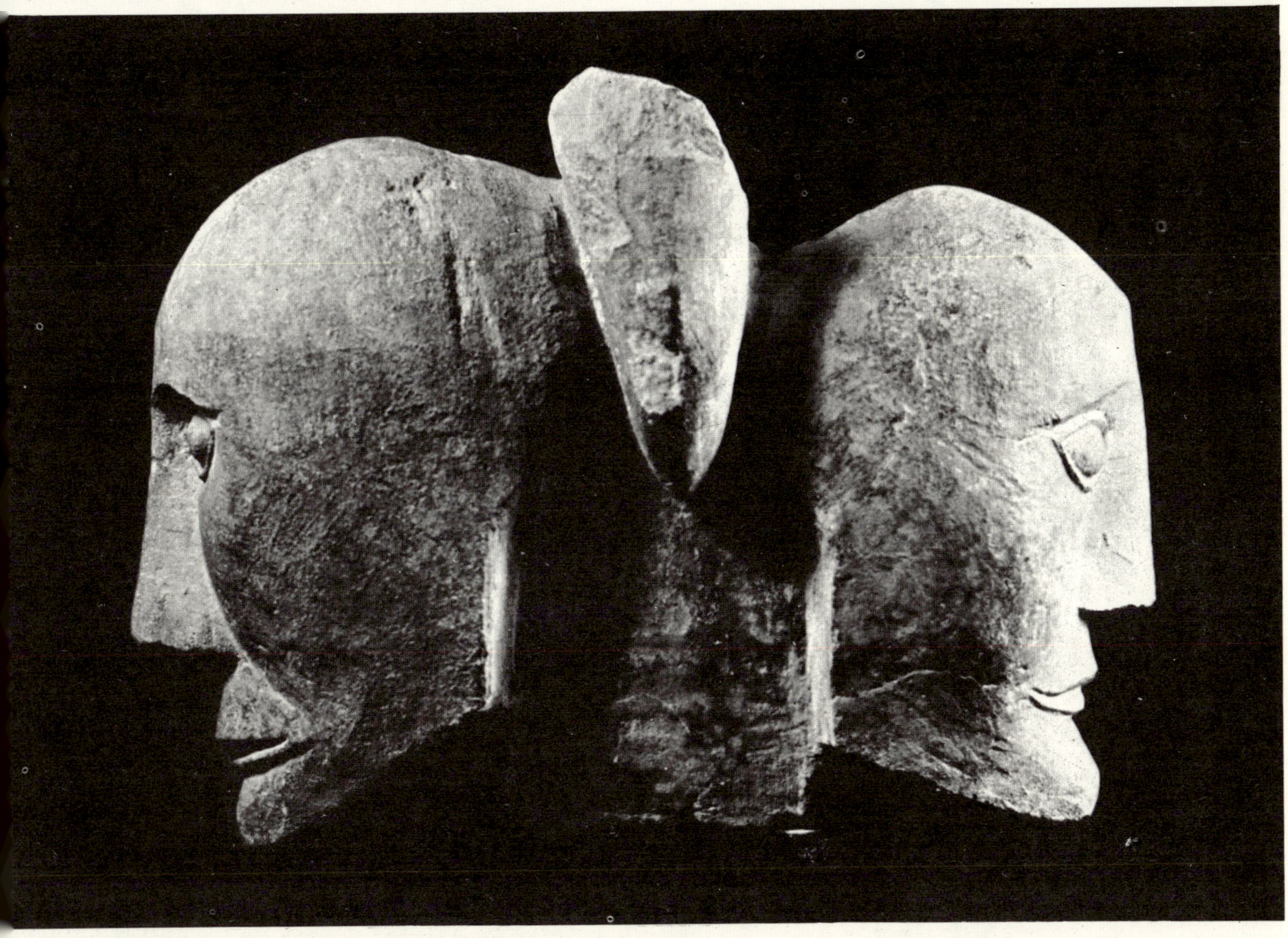

Janiform head from La Roquepertuse. This double head from the early Celtic sanctuary at La Roquepertuse in the south of France was formerly believed to be a bicephalic representation of Mercury but it is now thought that it may represent the heads of defeated enemies.

was a hero within the tribe, fighting for his people. Beyond the minutely ordered social life of the tribe existed another hero-figure best typified by Finn. Finn shared the more important of the personal qualities of Cú Chulainn but he and his peers were conceived of as extra-tribal heroes. The exact meaning of the myths centred on the *fiana*, the bands of young warriors in the Ossianic Cycle, has brought forth a number of interpretations. The background of this cycle differs in externals from that of the Ulster Cycle in that it clearly relates to a later period. It would be a mistake to regard the *fiana* as groups of deities, for Finn and his band were not gods but heroes, mortal yet endowed with superhuman attributes. They were frequently in close contact with the otherworld.

The *fiana* of mythology, such as that of Finn mac Cumal and his band, apparently had purely human prototypes in Celtic society. They were groups of young warriors who, for a variety of reasons, were unable to fit comfortably within the precisely defined pattern of tribal life. As such they were free of the normal obligations due to their respective tribes. A great part of their activities was devoted to hunting and mercenary warfare. They were, in fact, a form of mobile army whose allegiance could be granted temporarily to any ruler who had immediate need of their services. In this way they have sometimes been conceived of as defenders of Ireland against Norse attacks, but this is clearly a later interpolation. The human *fiana* may very well have taken part in the historically attested Irish raids on Roman Britain.

As the hero of the tribe was basically human but was a magnifie ideal so were the mythological *fiana* bands of human warrio whose exploits were similarly magnified. Many of their huntin and fighting expeditions were set in magical environments. Fre quently they ventured into the Celtic otherworld, into the *síd* c one of the gods and across the sea to the Isles of the Blessed. The fought on the side of the gods, particularly as allies of the *Tuath Dé Danann*, against their enemies. Their genealogy often include ancestors among the gods, Finn, for example, having ancestor among both the *Tuatha Dé Danann* and the Fir Bolg. In their per sons they possessed the attributes expected of the tribal hero bravery and loyalty, skill in fighting and the more cultured arts particularly poetry. Ossian, the son of Finn, after whom the Ossiani Cycle is named, was perhaps the greatest poet of them all.

The hero, therefore, was human. He had superhuman power but not enough to prevent his being wounded in his encounter with enemies. Being mortal the hero had to die although, as i the case of Finn who lived to be two hundred and thirty, his life span was sometimes superhuman. In sum, the hero was the mag nified ideal of the Celtic warrior aristocracy.

THE CELTIC OTHERWORLD

After their defeat the *Tuatha Dé Danann* in popular traditio left the land of Ireland. Some of the survivors went undergroun

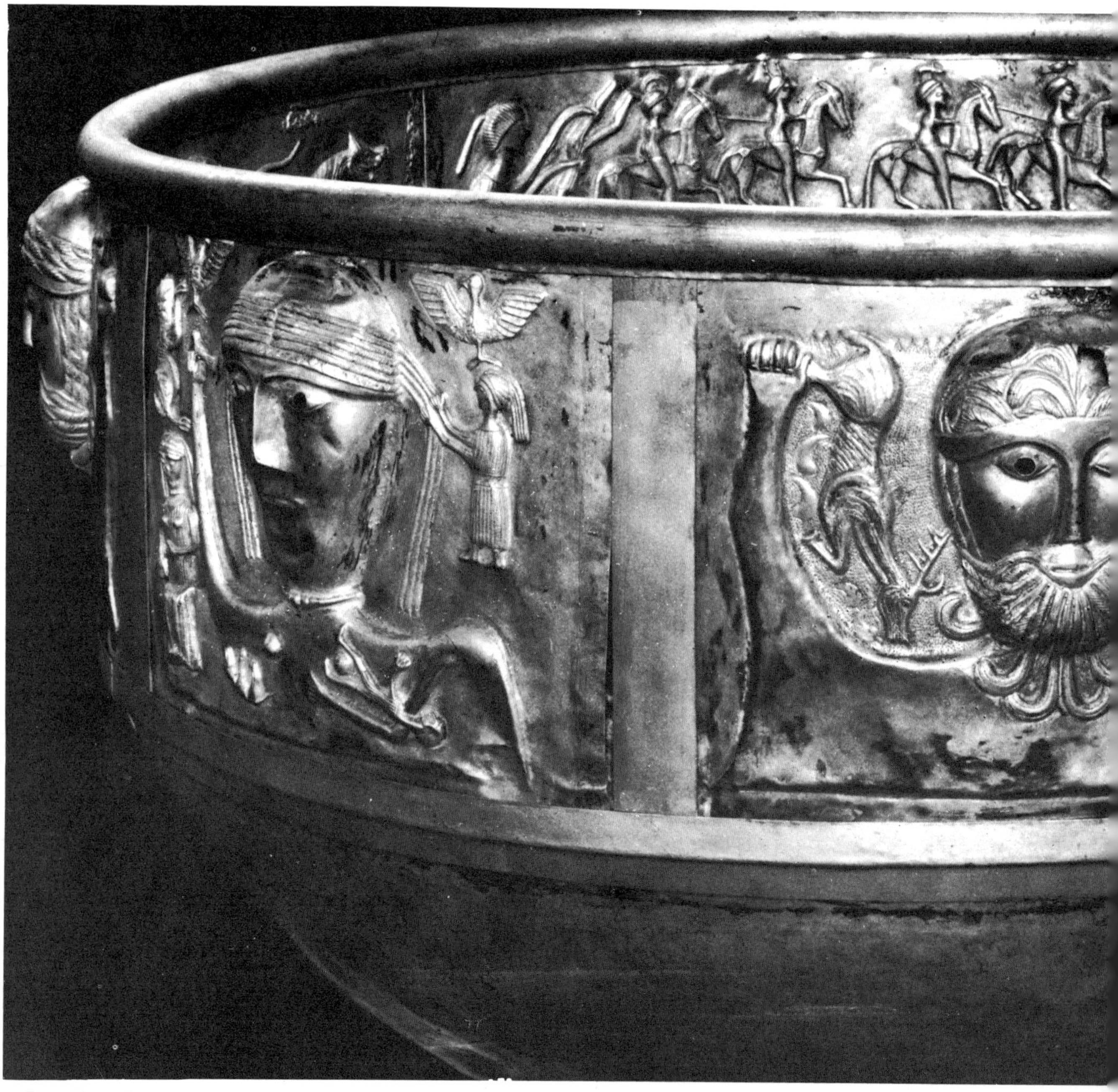

to take possession of the *síde*, natural mounds and tumuli of prehistoric Ireland. Within a *síd* a whole supernatural world could be encompassed. Other gods went under the sea where lay *Tír fo Thuinn*, 'The Land under the Waves'. Others voyaged westwards over the sea to *Tír na nOc*, the 'Land of Youth', or *Mag Mell*, the 'Field of Happiness', imaginary islands towards the setting sun.

However it was conceived, the otherworld of the Celts was a place of supreme happiness. All the yearning of the Celtic soul for a Golden Age seems to have inspired the poets in their descriptions of *Tír na nOc*, or the *síde*. Time ceased to have terrestrial meaning, a minute in a *síd* might be the equivalent of several mortal years, a period of days in a *síd* might be only as long as a minute in the human world. As soon as one of Bran's companions, in returning to look at their homeland after a sojourn in the otherworld, set foot on land he turned to ashes. To them it seemed that they had been away for only a year, yet it had really been centuries.

In the otherworld the Celtic vision of mortal perfection is idealised. The land was rich in food and the delights of nature. No unpleasantness existed, neither in nature nor in man. Music, feasting, love-making and, proper to the ideal of a warrior-aristocracy, even fighting were unlimited and devoid of any sense of satiety. All were immortal and if wounds and death resulted from battle, on the following day the wounds were healed and the dead restored to life. And so it continued into eternity.

This was a land of magic, ruled over by the dispossessed gods and inhabited by supernatural beings. In the myths, however, man is sometimes pictured as entering this world either on the invitation of a god or goddess or by force. In particular, the Celtic heroes were invited to help perhaps the ruler of a *síd* against an enemy in return for the love of a divine woman. Again, there are stories of men forcing their way into the *síde* to steal the treasures of the gods for the benefit of man. There several such stories woven around the theft of a magic cauldron of plenty or of magic cattle. As in many Celtic myths the ideal is magnified and this is clearly the significance of the idealised picture of the Celtic otherworld.

In contrast with the delights of *Tír na nOc*, there was also an otherworld in which fear rather than bliss was predominant. The domain of giants, such as that of Ysbaddaden in the tale of Culhwch and Olwen, or the kingdom of Scathach surrounded by phantoms and horrors in the Cú Chulainn epic may be cited. It is difficult to reconcile these two apparently contradictory concepts of the otherworld but a simple explanation is possible. If a Celtic hero was pictured as proving his valour against supernatural forces the myth would tend to exaggerate the horror in his difficulties. If he was invited into the world of the *Tuatha Dé Danann* as a guest or as an ally the supernatural delights of that world would also be emphasised. Clearly a hero could not have proved his valour in a land of plenty peopled by divine and gracious beings, but he could have done so in a land of demons.

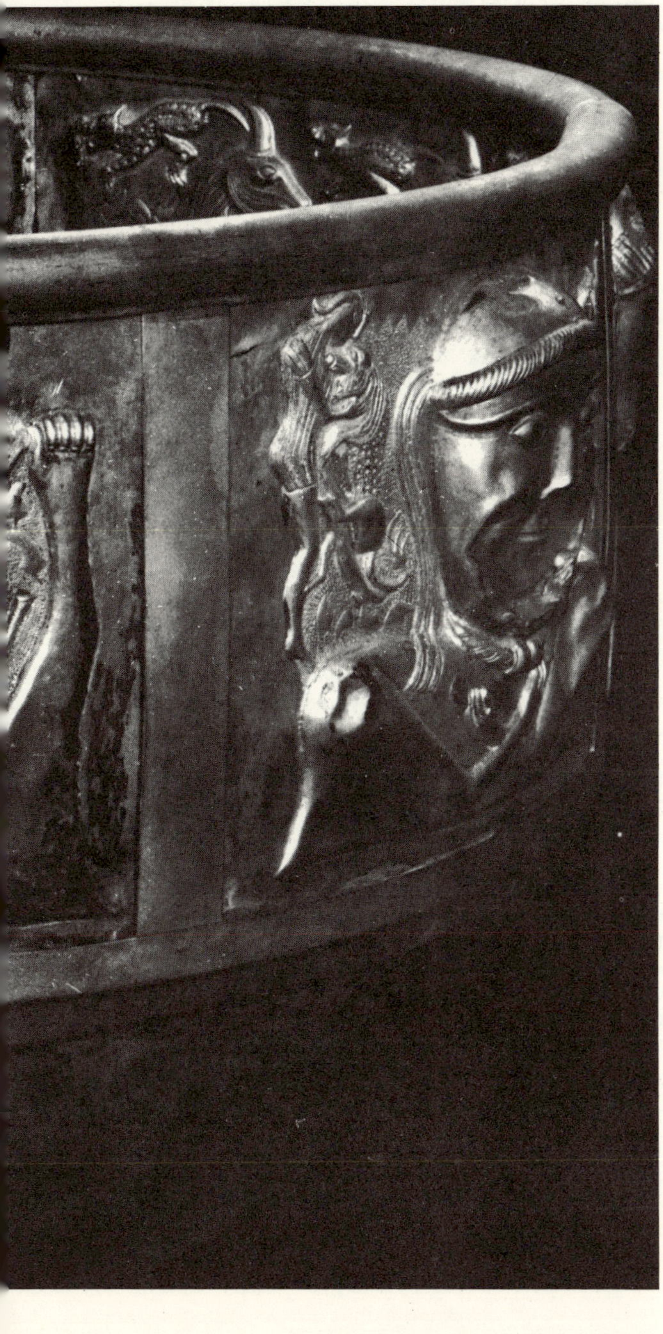

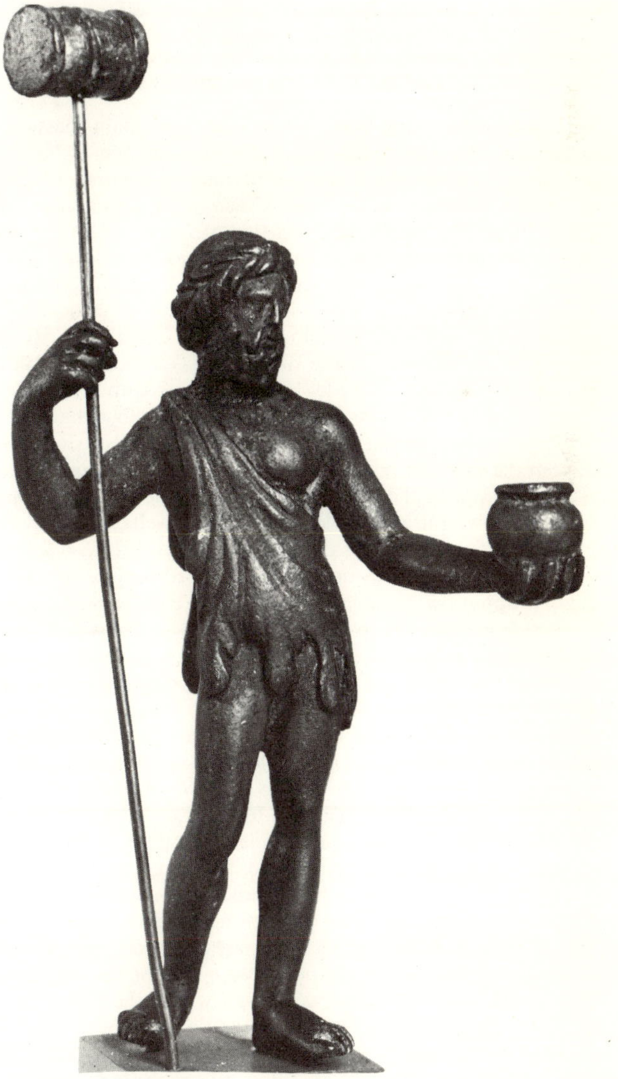

Dis Pater or Sucellus with his attributes: the mallet and the drinking cup.

The silver bowl found in a bog at Gundestrup in Denmark. The plates are decorated in relief with figures of deities, including Cernunnos, and with scenes of ritual activity. National Museum of Denmark, Copenhagen.

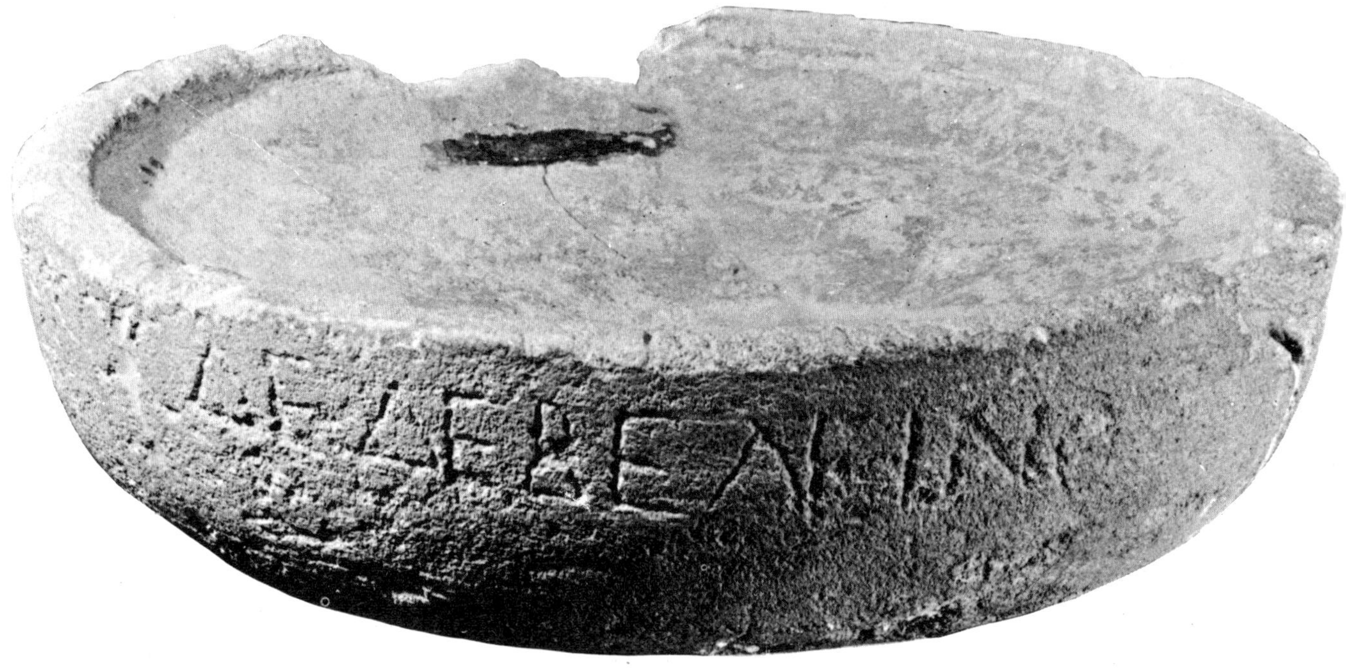

Offering table to Belenus. Belenus (or Belinus as he was called in the British Isles) was one of the most ancient and widespread Celtic gods associated with pastoralism, his cult being practised throughout Northern Italy, Gaul and the British Isles. Some thirty-one dedications bear witness to his popularity – an unusually large number for one god. The feast of Beltain on the first day of May during which cattle were driven between fires for their ritual protection was possibly dedicated to him. Stone.

The Feasts of the Celtic Year. There were four main feasts in the Celtic year. The year began on what is now the first of November with the feast of *Samain*. Three months later on the first of February was *Imbolc* followed by the feast of *Beltine* or *Cétshamain* on the first of May. The fourth feast was that of *Lugnasad* on the first of August. Of these four *Samain* and *Beltine* were the more important and in the myths many important events took place on those days.

The beginning of the Celtic New Year was a particularly important event and the mythological cycle contains in its many references to *Samain* evidence of ritual acts which took place at this time. On the eve of the feast, time appeared to belong neither to the old year nor to the new. There was a feeling that this lack of distinction in time was matched by a similar indistinct boundary between the world of man and that of his gods. Although man had taken possession of the land after their defeat the *Tuatha Dé Danann* were still powerful and could affect man's welfare. Whereas the mythical heroes of the Celts could venture bravely into *side* to meet their gods either as allies or enemies, the ordinary people felt less sanguine about the possibility that on the eve of *Samain* the people of the *side* left their domain and wandered in the world of man. Furthermore the beginning of the year was a solemn event, coming as it did at the beginning of winter, to a people whose agricultural economy was still liable to failure.

The origins of the feast may remount in time to the pre-Celtic period. In the Mythological Cycle the people of Nemed were forced to render to the Fomorians on this day two-thirds of their milk, their corn and children. Allowing for exaggeration this seems to refer to a distant memory of a considerable offering of agricultural produce and perhaps of human sacrifice too. Similarly, there is an echo in the *Dindshenchas*, the mythological geography of Ireland, of human sacrifices to *Crom Cruaich* and hideous and terrifying ritual at *Samain* in Celtic times. There are references, too, to ordeals by fire and water, which are probably myths of human sacrifice. Entering the darkness and insecurity of winter the Celts, in common with other primitive peoples, felt at this time of the year their insecurity in the face of the supernatural. The stories of attacks by hostile supernatural powers and of sacrifices are indicative of this insecurity and the need for propitiation.

There is less fear in those myths of *Samain* centred on the union of male deities with a mother-goddess figure. Such is the myth of the Dagda's union with the Morrigan by the River Unius and with Boann, the goddess of the River Boyne. Possibly at this feast, too, there were rites performed to ensure the fertility of the land during the coming year.

The feast of *Beltine*, possibly dedicated to the god Belenus, was a happier festival. On the first of May both the races of Partholón and the *Tuatha Dé Danann* landed in Ireland. On this day fires were lit and the cattle were driven between them for ritual protection. The people danced, probably in a sunwise direction and carried burning torches around the fields, a form of sympathetic magic to aid the sun in his all-important role in an agricultural economy. At this time of renewed hope and delight at the end of the winter there were also fertility rites, possibly in honour of the Mother-Goddess.

The feasts of *Imbolc* and *Lugnasad* are less easy to interpret. *Imbolc*, on the first of February, has been connected with the lactation of ewes, and, although the sheep appears to have had little significance in Celtic mythology, its place in the economy of the Celts is well attested. It would have been appropriate to celebrate a feast at a point half-way though the Celtic winter. In later times this became the feast of Saint Brigid, a Christianised retention of a Celtic goddess of fertility, Brigit. *Lugnasad*, on the first of August, appears to have been connected with the god Lug, but it was also in some way connected with fertility as shown by the association of mother-goddesses, such as Macha, in the celebrations held on this day.

That the feasts of *Samain* and *Beltine* were of considerable antiquity is suggested by the strongly pastoral basis of the Celtic economy. Although the sun appears to have been invoked at *Beltine* the Celtic year had no solar orientation. There is nothing here of the solstice or equinox and one is reminded of Caesar's comment that the Celts measured time by nights instead of days. The feast of *Lugnasad* with its more agrarian bias should, on this supposition, be later in its inception. Its association with Lug, who, in turn, appears to have been introduced at a later date than, for example, the Dagda, supports this hypothesis. It is possible that Lugnasad replaced an earlier feast, possibly more simply a fertility festival. Although crop-raising figures little in the myths of a predominantly pastoral society, it has to be remembered that primitive corn-growing had been practised in Ireland as early as the Neolithic period. Perhaps the ordinary peasant farmer was disregarded in the cult-practices which were primarily devoted to the well-being of a warrior aristocracy.

THE GREEK AND ROMAN VIEW OF CELTIC RELIGION

Celtic Mythology contains invaluable evidence as to the beliefs of the Celts in the pre-Christian period. At its greatest extent Celtic influence covered much of Western Europe and penetrated as far as Asia Minor, but the mythology is strictly relevant only to the

Celts of the British Isles. There was an undoubted basis of common belief shared by all Celtic peoples, and to obtain any evidence as to the beliefs of the continental Celts it is necessary to consider both the opinions of Greek and Roman writers and the archaeological record. The evidence of the classical writers is particularly valuable because, although fragmentary, it is a contemporary record. Set against this, however, was their inability to view beliefs of other peoples against anything but a classical background. They constantly sought parallels within the framework of their own religious experience. Allowing for this their evidence is valuable, if at times apparently in conflict with that derived from mythology.

Caesar spent ten years in Gaul at a time when that part of Europe was being brought fully into the Empire. Before his time Greek and Roman influences had been entering the country and the attitudes of the Celts, particularly among the aristocracy, may well have been modified as much by classical belief as by the material imports. Caesar's evidence is, nevertheless, of considerable value. He said that the whole people were devoted to their beliefs and stated that Mercury was worshipped more than any of their other gods. This is supported by the archaeological evidence from Roman Gaul whence over four hundred inscriptions and more than three hundred statues survive. After Mercury, Apollo, Mars, Jupiter and Minerva were worshipped and the Celts held beliefs similar to those of other people; Apollo was a healing god, Minerva a goddess of craftsmanship, Jupiter a heavenly ruler and Mars a war-god. Mercury emerges as a chieftain-type god, the inventor of all the arts, the presiding deity of commerce and guardian of travellers. Caesar also referred to Celtic belief in descent from Dis Pater.

It would be easy to dismiss Caesar's evidence as inaccurate, but remembering his long stay in Gaul and the accuracy of so much of his *Gallic War* it is obvious that his opinions are not so obviously incorrect. In the first place he did not concern himself with the native name for Celtic deities but equated them as closely as possible with his own gods. It is unlikely that Mercury and the other Roman gods were worshipped by name in pre-Roman Gaul and Britain and it would appear that reference was being made to Celtic deities. It is unnecessary to attempt a complete identification of Roman with Celtic gods. Irish mythology shows that the male gods were regarded as omnicompetent, father-figures, warriors and poets. It would have been easy for a Roman to have interpreted any of these individual functions in terms of a single god of his own pantheon. It is possible that different tribes would have emphasised some particular attribute of their tribal gods at different times according to their ritual needs. Caesar could have equally misinterpreted the function of the Celtic goddess, although it is inexplicable how he could have completely overlooked the cult centred on Celtic fertility-goddesses whose existence is so well attested in epigraphy. Perhaps Caesar was drawing his evidence from those tribes who had received the greatest classical influence. What might have been true in the time of the Celts in southern Gaul in the first century B.C. would not necessarily have been applicable to the insular Celts.

Lucan in his *Pharsalia* refers to three deities, Teutates, Esus and Taranis to whom sacrifice respectively was offered by drowning, hanging and burning. Attempts have been made to equate these deities with Mercury, Mars, Jupiter and Dis Pater. It has also been suggested that in pre-Roman Gaul the Celts worshipped a single omnicompetent god who, after contact with classical influences, was conceived of as a number of specialised deities. This appears to oversimplify the problem. In Roman Gaul, Spain and Britain the equations between Celtic and Roman gods was not always consistent. A Celtic Cocidius might be equated with both Mars and Silvanus at the same Roman fort and does not suggest the existence of specialised Celtic divinities. In discussing the Celtic gods in the insular mythology it has been shown that, with few exceptions, Celtic gods were omnicompetent deities with little of the specialist in their make-up. It is probable also that with a few specific exceptions such as Lug, worship of individual deities was confined to restricted areas, probably coterminous with some tribal or other area. Archaeological evidence shows that Esus was worshipped in north-eastern Gaul and although similar evidence for the worship of the Gallo-Roman Teutates and Taranis is not great it is more widespread. Undue prominence has sometimes

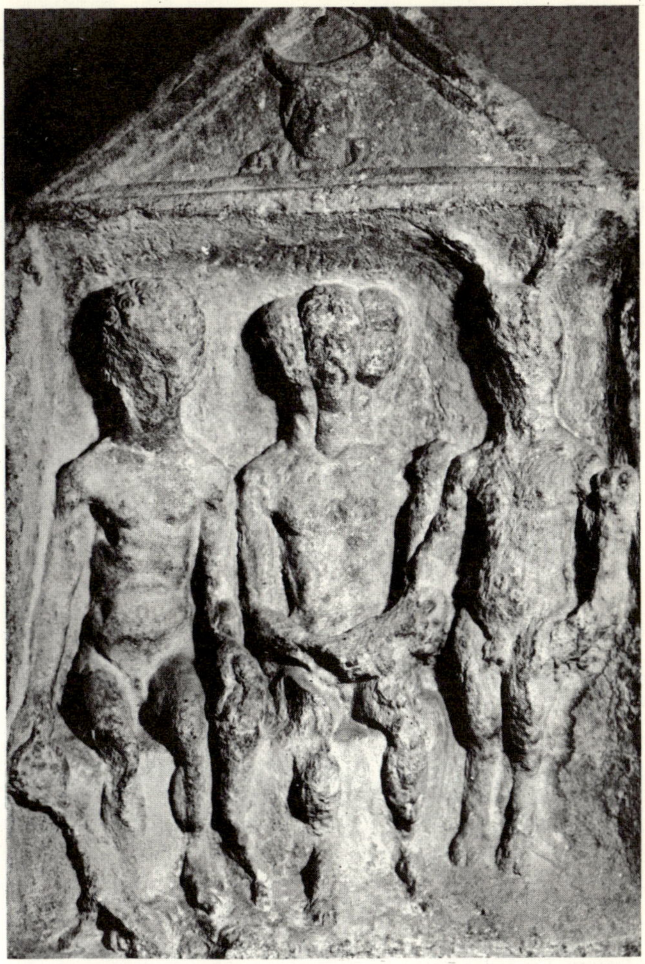

Gallic Triad. In the centre, the triple-headed Cernunnos. Beaune Museum.

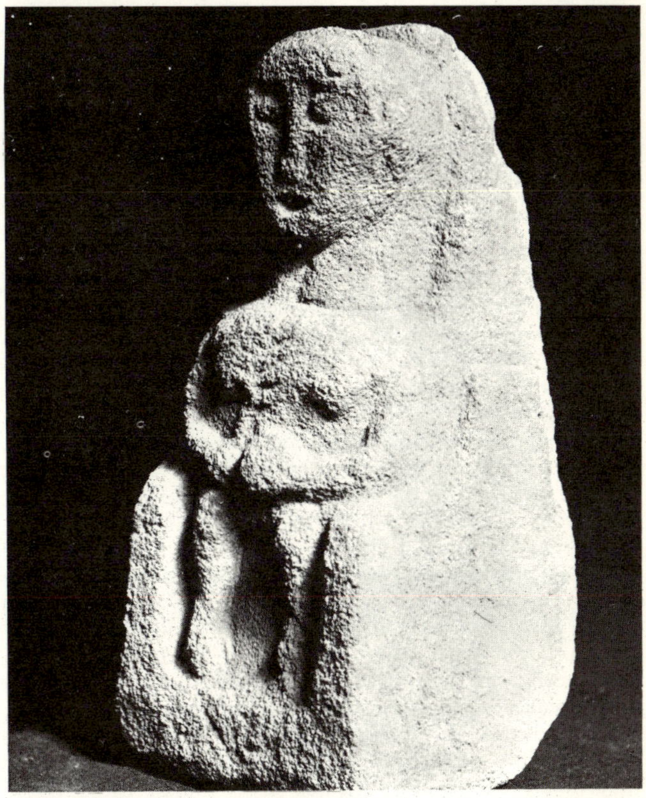

Seated goddess. This crude figure of a mother goddess was discovered during excavations on the site of the Romano-British town of Venta Siluram (or Caerwent) in Monmouthshire and appears to be of native workmanship. The goddess is portrayed seated, naked, on a high-backed chair or throne holding a stem of foliage, or possibly wheat, upright between her breasts in her right hand and a spherical object, probably fruit, in her left. Sandstone.

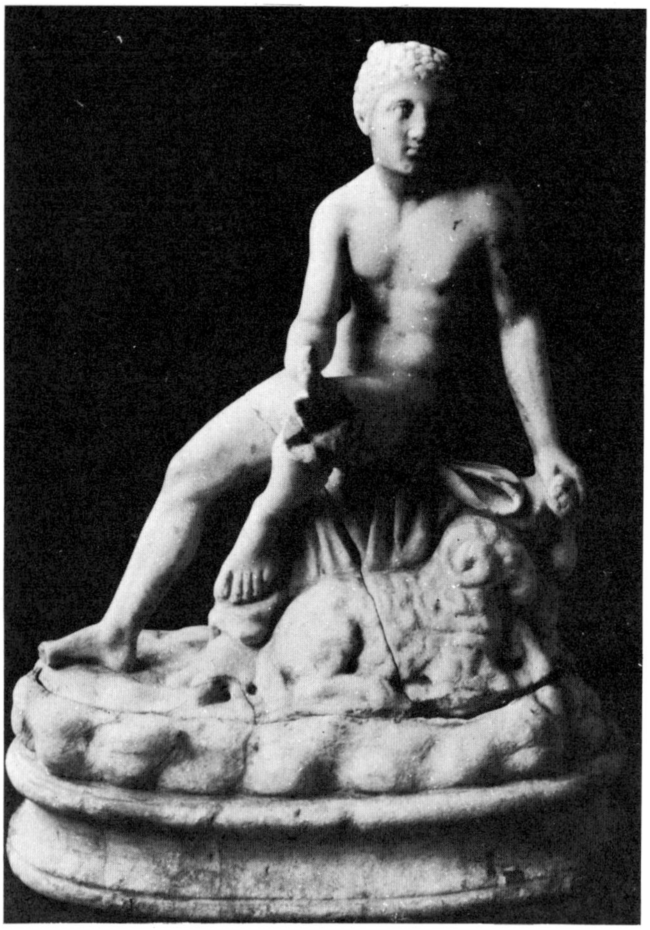

Mercury. The god is seated naked on a rock with a ram lying on the ground beside him. The most popular of all the Roman gods to be adopted by the Celts, Mercury was worshipped by them in preference even to Jupiter, Mars, Apollo and Minerva, his role being that of a chieftain-type god, the inventor of all the arts, the presiding deity of commerce and the guardian of travellers.

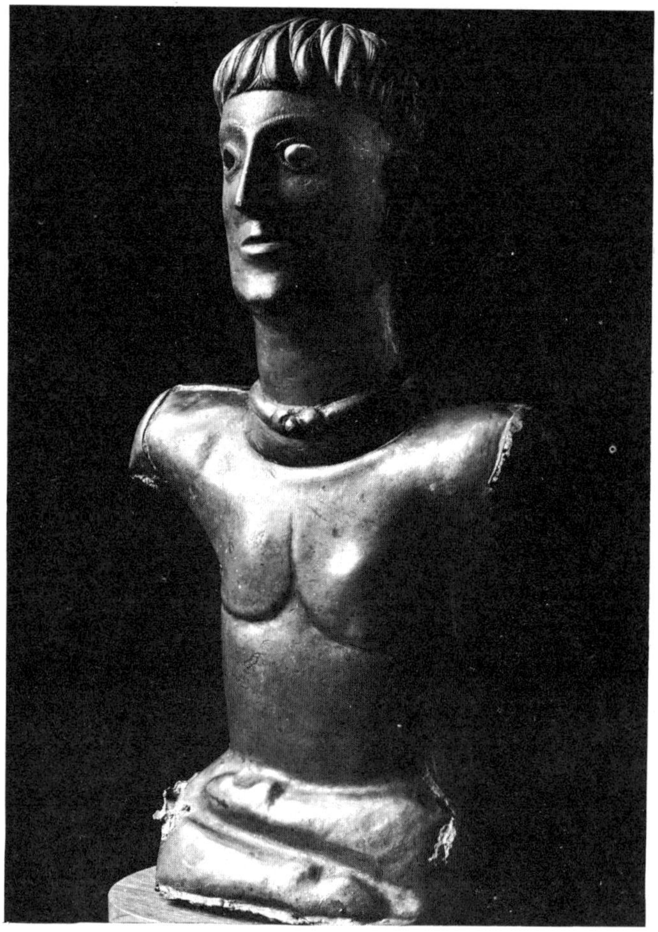

Seated god. Found at Bouray near Paris this iron and cast bronze figurine shows a god seated in the cross-legged position associated with Celtic deities and wearing a torc round his neck, the symbol of divinity. It was originally made in two parts and is of Gaulish workmanship. The eyes, only one of which remains, were of inlaid enamel. It is not known which particular deity it represents. *c.* first century A.D.

been given to Lucan's reference and it is now obvious that the triad, Esus, Taranis, and Teutates were either manifestations of a tribal deity or simply a local triad. The name Taranis means 'thunder' and Teutates is cognate with *Tuatha,* 'people', epithets which might have applied to almost any tribal god. In another passage Lucan describes the Gaulish Ogmios from whom may have been derived Ogma, the champion of Irish mythology.

The setting for worship is sometimes referred to in Greek and Roman writers. During the Roman period worship was formally organised in properly constructed temples and although there is evidence to suggest that some form of built 'temple' may have been used in the period of Celtic independence the main ritual activity of the Celts was conducted in the open air, in woodland clearings or by lakes, rivers, streams and springs. A writer in the fourth century B.C. refers to the existence in Britain of a magnificent circular temple dedicated to Apollo. It is difficult to understand this reference. Perhaps Stonehenge or Avebury is intended but the original use of these sites dates to the Early Bronze Age, at least one thousand years earlier, and the allusion to the sky-god is obscure. The barbarism of certain Celtic rites is brought out in their writings by Caesar, Tacitus, Lucan and others. Caesar states that human sacrifices were made by burning, the victims placed in huge images, and other writers frequently refer to blood-stained altars and the like. Allowing for literary licence there seems to be no doubt that the Celts practised human sacrifice, perhaps not as a frequent part of their ceremonial, but certainly in times of trouble and possibly, in the earlier period at least, at certain annual ritual gatherings. This helps in the interpretation of various myths involving death by fire or burning. Similarly, there are many references to the offering of human heads to the gods, and both the archaeological and mythological evidence provide comparable evidence. The head of Bran and Cú Chulainn's juggling with human heads may be cited. More frequent were the animal sacrifices, some of which were substitutes for earlier human sacrifices.

It is from Latin writers, particularly from Caesar, that most of present-day knowledge of Druids is derived. The Druids were the holy men of the Celts. In them was vested the responsibility for the ritual welfare of their people. As the dividing line between ritual and secular was finely drawn and sometimes indefinably drawn, the Druids held considerable power in most spheres of Celtic life. In addition to their priestly duties they were also judges and teachers. As judges they were able to enforce their decisions by excommunication of the guilty and the resultant deprivation of tribal protection. As teachers their influence was strong among the aristocracy whom they educated.

Powerful in their organisation, their secular influence was immense but in the present context reference to their ritual functions is more apt. All ceremonial observances were naturally under their control. In them, too, rested the ritual lore of the Celts. This was not written down but had to be learned by rote during the long training of the Druid. In Ireland, at least, it appears that regular colleges of Druids existed. They were so well organised and the training given extensive enough to include non-ritual accomplishments that it was possible in the early days of Christianity for their conversion to Christian monastic establishments. In them the traditional love of learning continued and aided the preservation of Celtic Mythology which was ultimately committed to writing.

In the discussion of the mythology of the insular Celts an attempt has been made to indicate the nature of belief in the deities worshipped. Some amplification of the full nature of Celtic belief may be obtained from a study of Greek and Latin writers. According to Caesar the Druids taught that their souls did not die but passed at death into other bodies. Their belief in personal immortality was so strong that the Celts had no fear of death in battle. But this

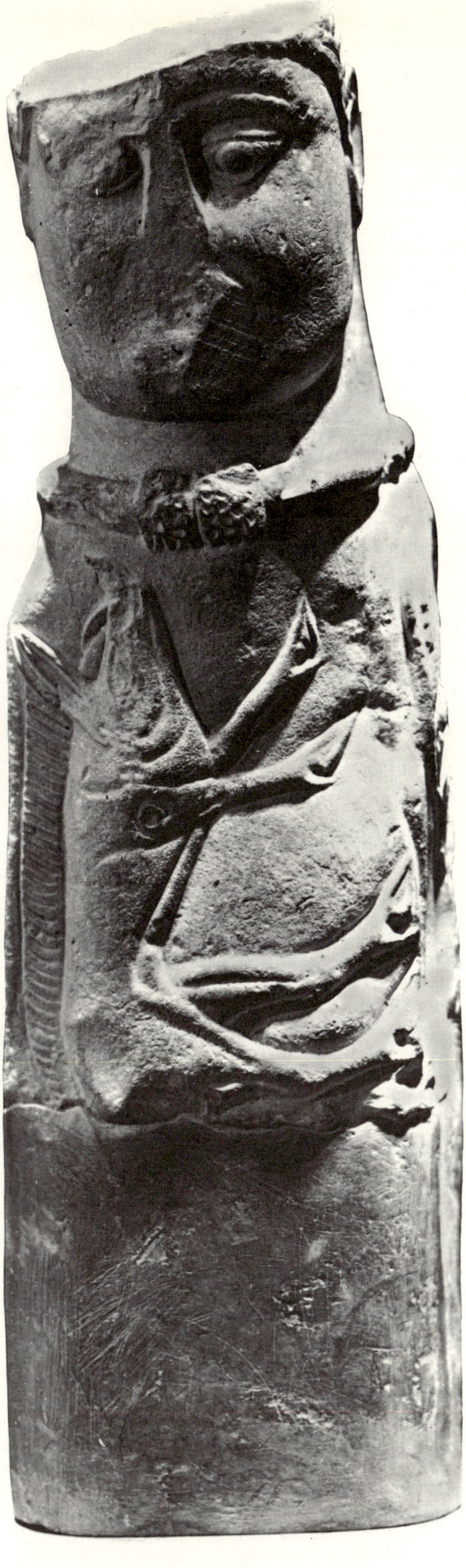

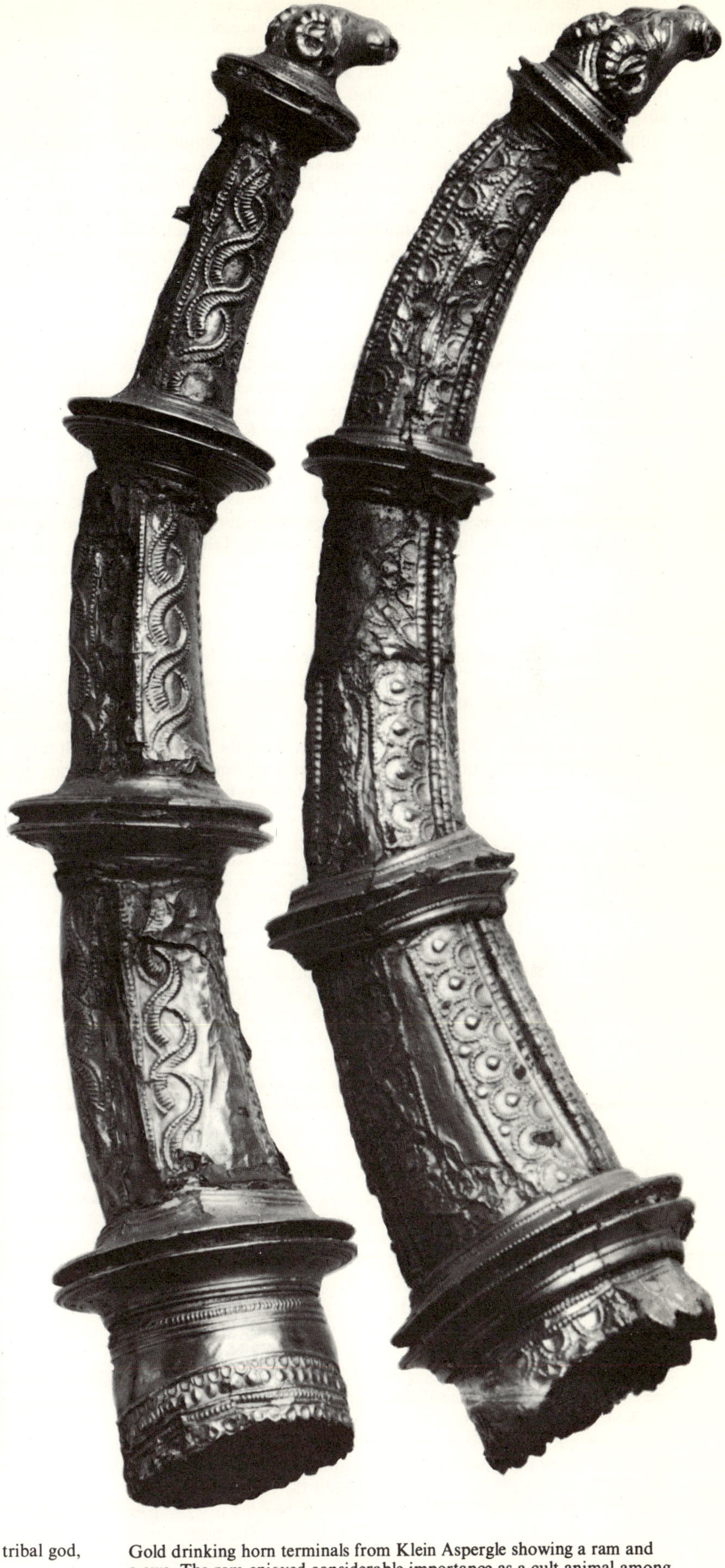

Stone figure from Euffigneix in France. Probably a local or tribal god, this figure, which pre-dates the Roman conquest of Gaul, wears a torc and has a large boar carved on its chest.
The boar was the principal cult animal of the Celts during this period and was believed to be closely associated with the otherworld.
Its flesh was prized for ritual feasts for the living and was buried with the dead for their feasts beyond the grave.

Gold drinking horn terminals from Klein Aspergle showing a ram and a ewe. The ram enjoyed considerable importance as a cult animal among the Celts and was frequently associated with the horned god Cernunnos, its composite form of a ram-headed serpent in particular being a regular attribute of the god. It is also found accompanying the Gaulish god equated with Mars and the Gallic Mercury.
Its connections with fertility rites are age old.

Druidical teaching of the after-life led some classical writers to connect it with the Pythagorean doctrine of metempsychosis, Diodorus Siculus writing, 'the Pythagorean doctrine prevails among them, teaching that the souls of men are immortal and live again for a fixed number of years inhabited in another body'. The imputation of such a sophisticated concept to the Celts is one which cannot stand careful study. It is likely that the Romans could easily have confused true metempsychosis with Druidic teaching. Lucan recognised the profound differences of belief between Romans and Celts, but neither he nor any other ancient writer mentioned the basis of metempsychosis common to Pythagoreanism and other beliefs, the expiation of sin in other bodies after death until complete perfection is attained. Indeed there seems to be no evidence for a Celtic belief in retributive justice in the next world, no Hell, only an indeterminate land of the blessed. These remarks by Diodorus Siculus and others cannot be completely rejected and, although imperfectly understood today, some belief, no matter how vaguely it resembled true metempsychosis, may have been held. Some such similar belief may be hidden in the myths which tell of shape-shifting, such as those centred on *Badb Catha*, the Raven of Battle.

Finally, there are frequent allusions to the Celts' use of representations of their deities. It is shown below that very few Celtic anthropomorphic representations are known prior to the assimilation of classical influences. Caesar speaks of images to Mercury and other writers mention crude figures, generally of wood. References of this type date to as early as the third century B.C.

THE EVIDENCE OF ARCHAEOLOGY

In this section an attempt is made to interpret the archaeological evidence derived from Celtic Europe in prehistoric and Roman times in terms of Celtic mythology.

Pre-Roman Evidence. Although in pre-Roman times the Celts, with the exception of those subject to strong classical influences, appear to have worshipped in sacred places as opposed to formal buildings there are a number of sites dating from the Celtic Iron Age both on the continent and in the British Isles. In Britain a wooden-built 'temple', similar in plan to the later stone-built Romano-Celtic temples was discovered at Heathrow in Middlesex and is believed to date from the third century B.C. Under the Romano-Celtic temple at Frilford in Berkshire a small Iron Age shrine appears to have had affinities with earlier British Bronze Age ritual sites and cannot, on present evidence, be accepted as typical of Celtic practice. Continental sites have also revealed wooden-built structures, such as the first century B.C. circular roofed building at St. Margarethen-am-Silberberg. An open-air ritual site surrounded by an earthwork in the Kobener Wald contained at the centre a very tall wooden post set at the centre of a raised area. This site, known as the Goloring, appears to date from the sixth century B.C. and would have served as a ritual centre in which a large congregation could have been accommodated with room for such activities as ritual games and the like. It has been suggested that some of the sites at Tara and elsewhere in Ireland may have resembled the Goloring in function as well as in physical appearance. In this connection the reference to a circular temple in Britain to Apollo by a writer of the fourth century B.C. is apposite.

Zoomorphic Representation. In the art of the Celts in pre-Roman times there is frequent reference to animal motives and much of this can only have been ritual in intent. Among the animals which are well represented in the metal-work of Iron Age Britain is the boar, as for example on the Witham shield, the boar's head from Banffshire and the helmet crests and numerous small votive boars. On the continent large stone sculptures of boars are known from Iberia and generally associated with hill-forts of the Celtic period. The bull figures in similar environments and the fine sacrificial bull on the base plate of the Gundestrup bowl may be cited as examples of the use of this animal in Celtic inconography. The importance of the bull in the predominantly pastoral economy of pre-Roman times is immediately obvious and the participation of cattle in the ceremonies of *Beltine*, at the election of a king at Tara and in their sacrifice at *Bron Trograin*, the August festival, links the archaeological with the mythological evidence. More obviously ritual are the three-horned bulls such as that from Maiden Castle, Dorset, and the *Tarvos Trigaranus* of Roman Gaul, paralleled by the three-horned Gaulish boar.

The White Horse at Uffington in Berkshire, cut into the chalk of the hillside and probably dating to the Iron Age, is perhaps the most dramatic representation of the horse in Celtic times. This animal is closely connected with the cult of Epona, a horse-goddess, shown in some Gaulish statuary as seated on a horse. In time there may have been some confusion between the goddess and her horse and the deity equated with the animal. Inscriptions in the Roman period show that the cult of Epona was widespread and stretched from Spain to Eastern Europe and Northern Italy to Britain. A similar goddess may be identified in some aspects of Irish goddesses such as Macha of Ulster and Medb of Connacht and Rhiannon of the Welsh tradition. In Ulster there is evidence of a symbolic union of a new king with a mare representing the fertility of earth. The horse-goddess emerges as another manifestation of the mother-goddess, a protectress of the dead no less than the living as is suggested by the embossed horses on the Aylesford funerary bucket in the archaeological record and in the three red horsemen from the kingdom of Donn, lord of the dead in Irish Mythology.

Anthropomorphic Representation. It has been sometimes suggested that the Celts were incapable of satisfactory anthropomorphic representation and this has been held to account for the apparent lack of human figures in pre-Roman iconography. The literary evidence tells of images, such as Caesar's reference to the many images of Mercury. The transitional period between the Late Bronze Age and the Iron Age in the British Isles and Northern Europe has revealed a number of cult-figures, some quite small but others more than life-size. That wooden figures were perhaps frequently used in Celtic times is possible as the literary evidence suggests and as is shown sparingly in the archaeological evidence. The pre-Roman sculptures of Gaul and Ireland, the coin evidence and a limited corpus of bronzes, proves that the Celts were able to portray the human – or divine – figure. Any apparent paucity of such representation in pre-Roman times might possibly be attributed to a reluctance to portray any deity in the same way that gods were rarely mentioned by name in swearing oaths.

Much of the sculpture from Gaul was influenced by foreign traditions, Greek and Etruscan. In the Rhineland anthropomorphic figures are pictured on pillars and wearing 'leaf-crowns', similar in some respects to the head-dress on the head of the Aylesford bucket. Cruder figurines are also known such as the stone figure from Stackach, Württemberg, and a small clay figurine from Co. Antrim. Iberia and Ireland have both produced small bronze figurines wearing crescentic head-dresses. The three-faced head of stone from Corleck, Co. Cavan, has parallels in Roman Gaul and is another example of the Celtic devotion to its triads.

It is difficult to equate the majority of the anthropomorphic figures of the pre-Roman period with individual deities. The hillside figure of a naked man wielding a club at Cerne Abbas in Dorset may represent a deity, perhaps the Dagda himself. An important exception is Cernunnos, the horned god, who is pictured with other deities on the Gundestrup bowl. Squatting in a pose known from south Gaulish sculpture, he is pictured holding a torc in his right hand and grasps a ram-headed serpent in his left. He wears breeches and a tunic and a torc around his neck. His horns are identical to those of a deer standing close by him. Perhaps the ritual significance here is connected in some way with the cycle of fertility symbolised by the shedding of antlers. Whatever the significance of this deity his cult was widespread in time, from a fourth-century B.C. rock-engraving in Northern Italy to Romano-Celtic sculptures such as the serpent-legged Cernunnos in Cirencester Museum and elsewhere. In Ireland this horned god appears carved on a sandstone block at Tara.

The other deities pictured on the Gundestrup bowl include the god with the wheel who may perhaps be equated with Taranis. In Roman times his cult was wide-spread in Gaul and appeared in Britain. Also represented on the bowl are scenes in which sacrifices are being made and ritual processions are taking place. There is a contrast to be drawn between the large, torc-wearing busts of the deities and the smaller human figures and animals, some of which can be interpreted as sacrificial. The whole bowl, although Celtic, was found in Jutland and had been dismantled

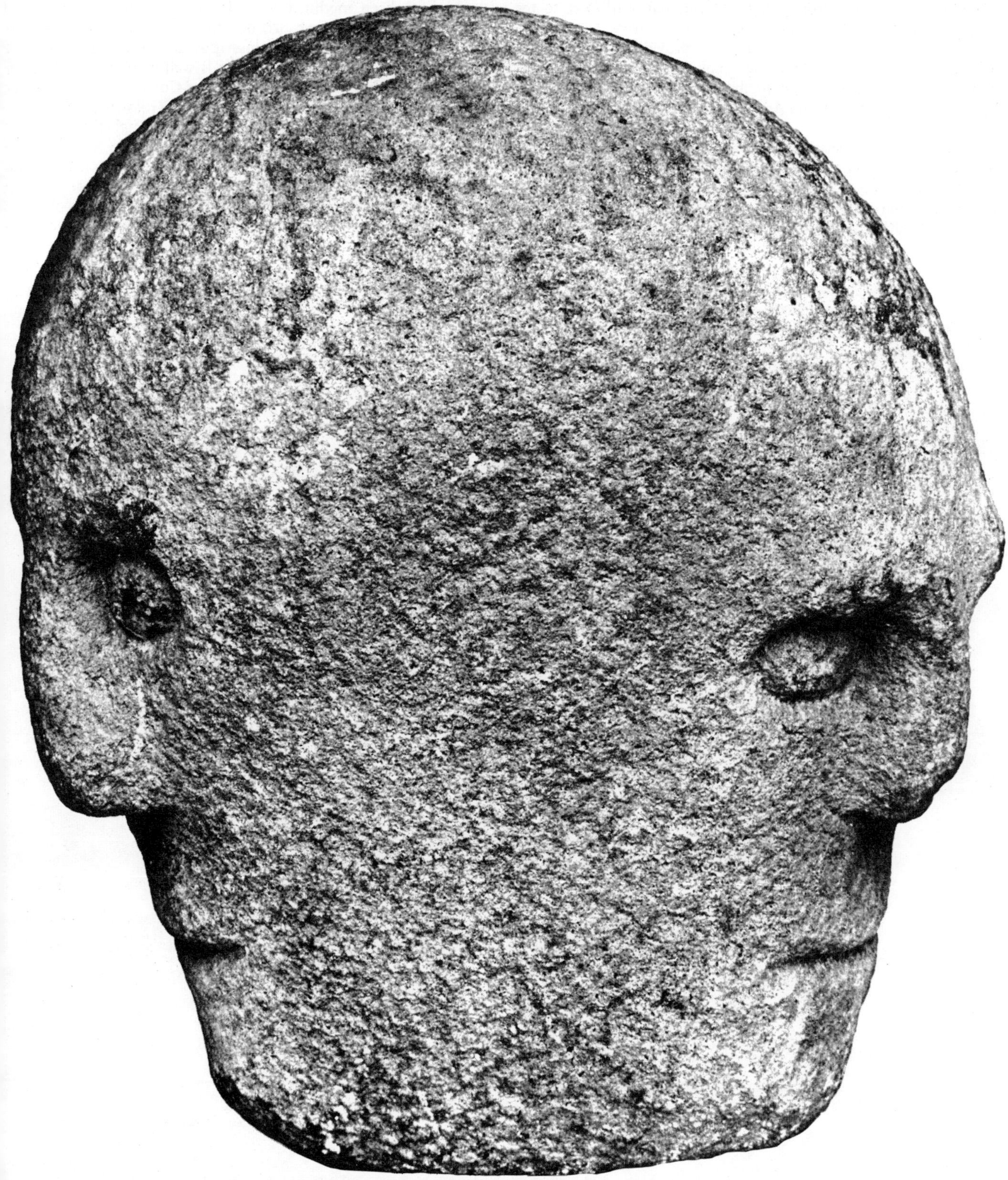

Three-faced stone head from Corleck, Co. Cavan. National Museum of Ireland.

and deposited in a bog as an offering, and presumably was itself an important cult-object.

Other Artifacts. In addition to human and animal sacrifice the Celts are known to have made other offerings to their deities. Throughout the area of Celtic influence in Europe there is ample evidence of the deposition in streams, rivers and lakes of valuable objects. The Gundestrup bowl has been mentioned as a single offering but at Llyn Cerrig Bach in Anglesey deposits of valuable metal objects were made over a period of time. The close connection of the Druids with Mona is significant. It is known from contemporary sources that the Celts on the continent dedicated to their gods the spoils of war and evidence similar to that of Llyn Cerrig Bach is known from La Tène and elsewhere.

The torc appears on the Gundestrup cauldron and on several Romano-Celtic sculptures as well as being mentioned in Irish mythology. There exist many splendid torcs of bronze and gold, including the beautiful examples from Broighter, Co. Derry and Snettisham, Norfolk. They appear to have been some form of amulet, perhaps serving a purpose similar to that of the votive wheels of Britain and Gaul.

Objects accompanying burials are proof that the Celts believed in some form of personal immortality. Grave furniture was provided according to the status of the deceased and varied between the elaborate chariot burials of the Marne and Yorkshire to the simple peasant burials with their frugal joints of pork. In between, the members of an intermediate class were provided with the armament and finery appropriate to their rank. The strong Celtic belief in a future life as shown in contemporary literature is supported by the ample evidence of Iron Age burial rites.

Romano-Celtic Evidence. Archaeological evidence dating from the period of Roman occupation of Celtic areas must be used sparingly to amplify that of mythology and pre-Roman archaeology. It is immediately obvious that Roman influence would have been strong and, although the basic beliefs of the Celts in their deities may not have changed significantly, there is no doubt that they would have been modified to a degree commensurate with the degree of Romanisation absorbed. This can be seen in the proliferation of Romano-Celtic altars, inscriptions and sculptures and of Romano-Celtic temples. The change is well epitomised in the replacement by the Gallo-Roman 'Jupiter-Column' of the simpler wooden ritual posts which once stood at the Goloring.

The epigraphic evidence is valuable even though the bulk of it might appear to be negative. It is seldom possible to equate the dedications with the figures of mythology. An exception is Mabon who is the Maponus of dedications and classical reference. Among the large numbers of inscriptions there is a high proportion of single dedications and of very small groups of dedications restricted to one place. Many of the inscriptions and altars must have been

The dolmen at Bruniquel in southern France. Grave mounds and burial sites were in a sense regarded as sanctuaries by the Celts, who had a great veneration for the dead, and served as a focal point for ritual and for religious games. The burial places of earlier inhabitants were brought into their mythology; they were believed to be entrances to the otherworld and the dwelling places of the departed and to the retreats of dispossessed gods.

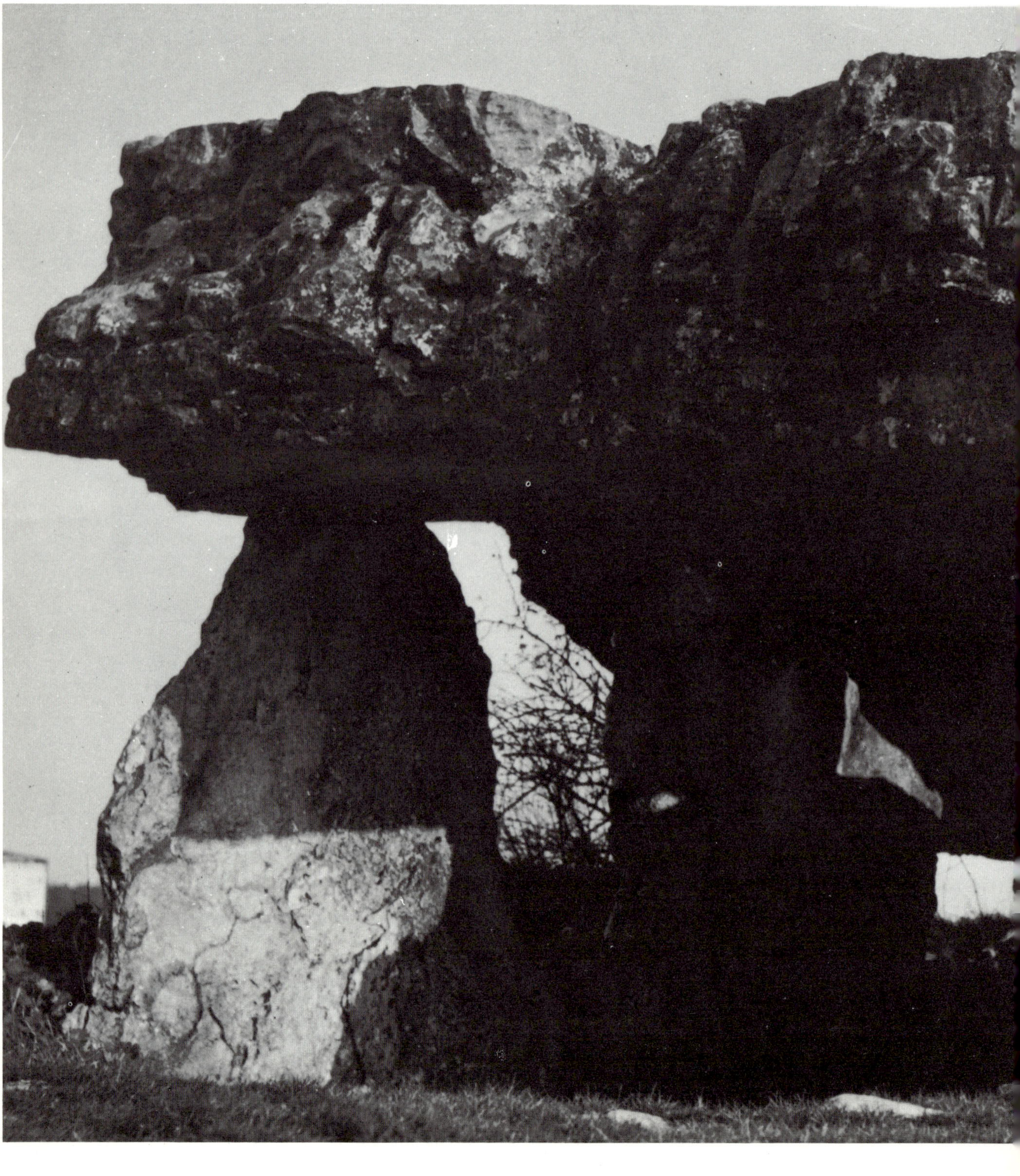

edicated to very minor deities, *genii loci,* rather than to full-scale ibal gods or mother-goddesses. The dedications to Coventina in orthern Britain, spirit of a sacred well, and to similar presiding eities of streams, rivers, mountains and other natural features in ritain and the continent do not so much offer proof of a pre-Roman eification of such natural features as the adoption in Roman times the Roman trappings of a popular cult. It is not necessary to sume that such popular cults were so highly organised before e adoption of such elaborate aids to devotion, although the basic ements of reverence must have existed hitherto in a vaguer form. n the other hand the distribution of Romano-Celtic inscriptions ithin a limited area, such as those to Belatucadrus or Cocidius Northern Britain, is suggestive of the cult of a tribal god. In an ea of military occupation, however, the existence of troops from her parts of the Empire complicates to a degree not so evident the more civilised provinces the interpretation of the epigraphic idence. On the whole a study of the inscriptions supports the

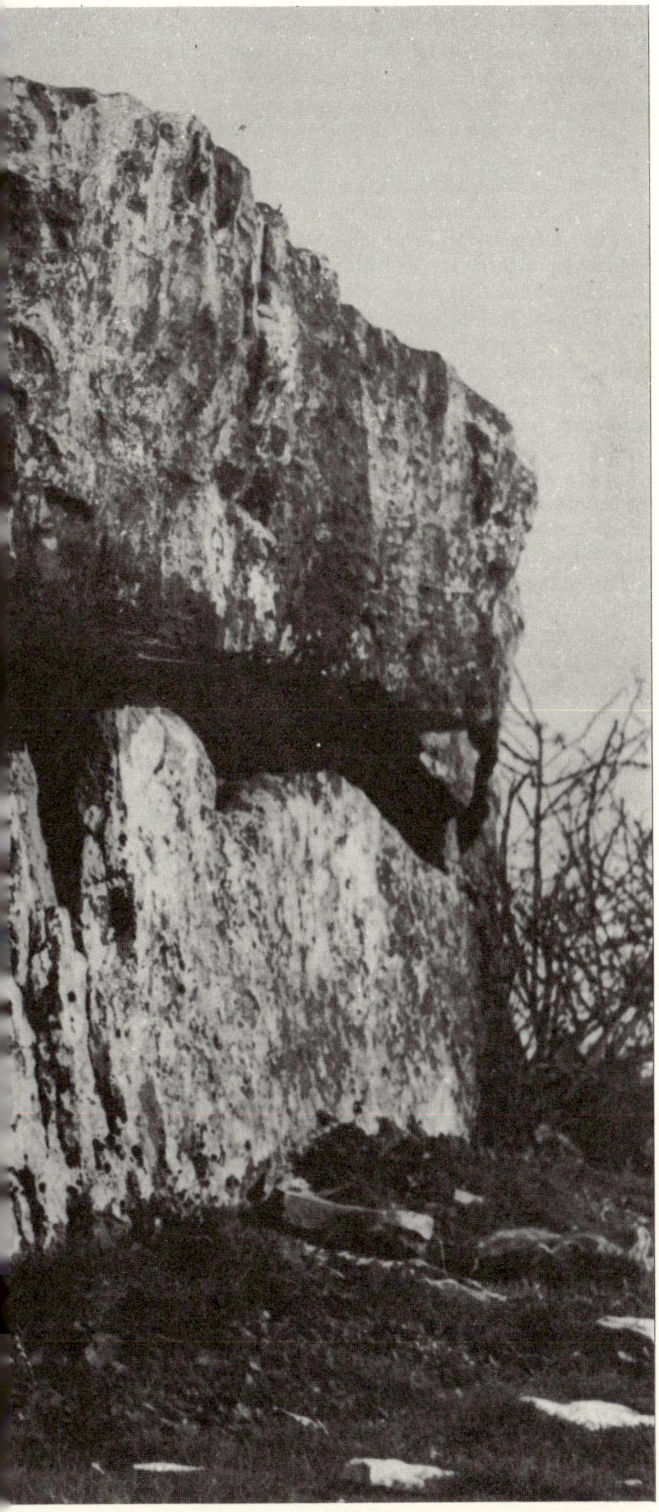

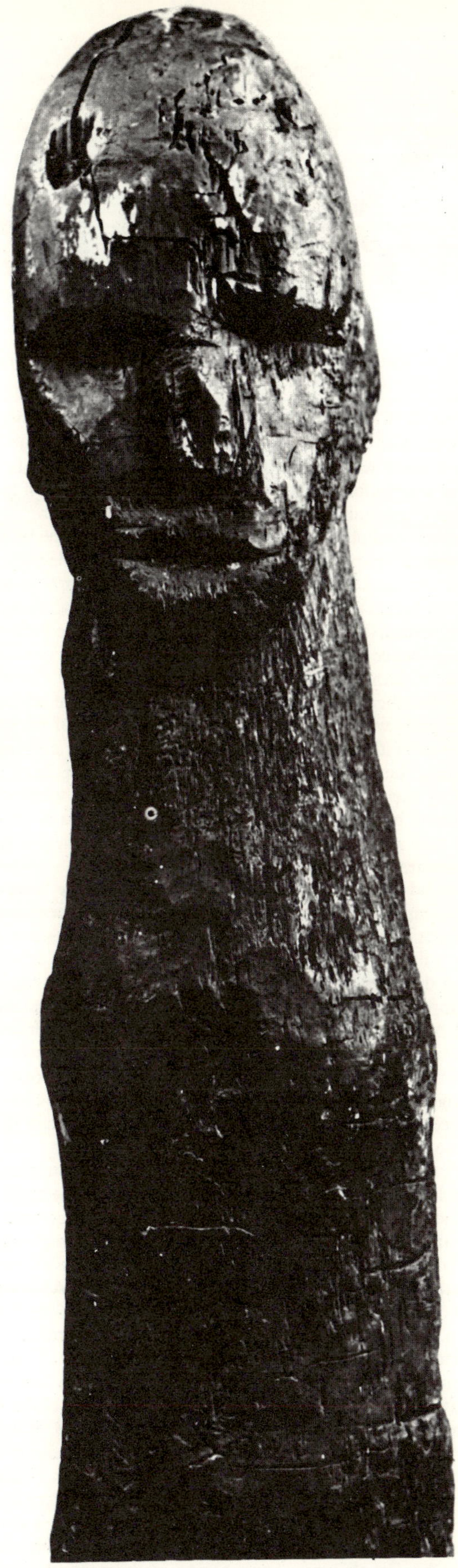

Head of a wooden male idol from Ralagham in Co. Cavan, Ireland. Trees were of the first importance in Celtic mythology and definite links were established from the earliest times between certain gods and certain trees. The evidence furnished by classical authors, and to a lesser extent by archaeology, shows that the Celts frequently worshipped wooden idols. The selection of the wood for this kind of anthropomorphic idol was made with great care.

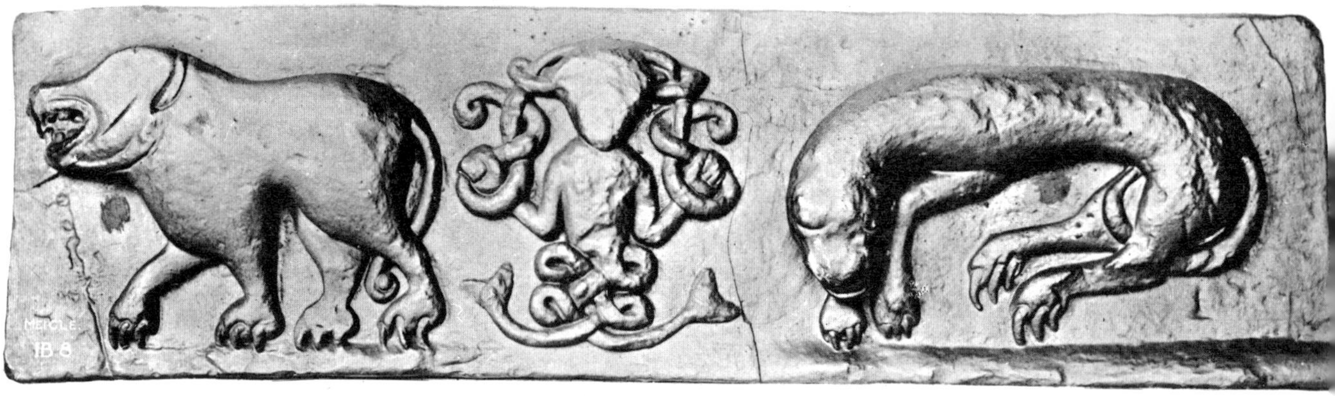

The god Cernunnos between two animals. The god is depicted with a bull's head and a man's torso; his legs are serpents and end in fishtails. Stone from Meigle. Edinburgh Museum.

belief that the Celts worshipped their local tribal gods. Local goddesses were also worshipped but it has been shown that Epona enjoyed a more widespread devotion. More apparent is the large corpus of inscriptions dedicated to the Matres, the triad of fertility-goddesses whose cult embraced most of Gaul and Britain.

A further complication in the interpretation of the Romano-Celtic evidence is apparent when the inscriptions include dedications to Celtic linked with Roman gods. This *interpretatio romana* is seldom consistent as a single Celtic god appears to have been identified with several Roman, even in the same place. The bulk of epigraphic evidence is to be found in the Romanised parts of the Celtic areas, either in civilised Gaul and Spain or in the military areas of Northern Britain and the Rhineland where dedications to Celtic gods were made by soldiers, the majority of whom were not natives of the region in which they served. In making their dedications they may well have misunderstood the local deities whom they wished to honour. The Celts of Gaul, too, were obviously influenced by Roman cult-practices as may be seen in the sculptures of their gods who, although bearing Celtic names, frequently assume the trappings of a Mercury or a Mars.

The rapid spread and use of the Romano-Celtic temple was another symptom of Romanisation applied to the ceremonial of native cults. It is not known whether or not this was a result of Roman policy for, although native cults were allowed to continue provided that they were not in conflict with Roman law, the Druids were suppressed in Britain as being a potential political menace. Instead of being permitted to practise their ritual observances in secret woodland groves the Celts may well have been encouraged to build a Romano-Celtic temple in a town or the open countryside. This, together with the novelty of Roman trappings, could have accounted for their spread. Although substantially built of stone and decorated in the Roman manner these temples, with their central *cella,* either square, circular or polygonal in plan, with surrounding portico, were not based on the classical temple. They sometimes attracted to themselves the classical additions of a theatre and baths. At Lydney in Gloucestershire the temple-complex dedicated to Nodens included a temple of basilica plan, together with baths, an inn and a long building in which sick devotees slept in the hope of a nocturnal visit by the god. Dating to the first century A.D. it exhibits the interesting amalgam of classical and Celtic ideas, more particularly as it was probably the zeal of Irish immigrants into the region which made it possible. Nodens himself may be equated with Nuada of Irish mythology and Nudd of the Welsh. The archaeological evidence from this last phase of Roman influence in Britain is particularly valuable for, in addition to the strong possibility of an identification of Nodens with Nuada and Nudd, there is ample evidence that the devotees of Nodens accepted him as an omnicompetent god. He was a healing god, a protector of fishermen on the River Severn and was associated with a fertility deity. In his temple was a triple shrine, perhaps another instance of the triplication of a deity.

CONCLUSION. There is little doubt that Celtic mythology, particularly that of Ireland, tells of the gods of the Celts. The myths themselves speak of Celtic belief in their deities and, although it is impossible to be certain how strong was Christian belief at the time they were written down, it is possible that a good proportion of this mythology is directly derived from the sacred lore of the Druids. In no way do either the references to Celtic belief by Greek and Roman writers or the archaeological evidence conflict with modern interpretations of the mythology. Provided that too rigid a rapprochement is avoided all three sources may be made to provide material for the study of the beliefs of the Celts. All the evidence points to the existence of comparatively localised cults and it is rare to find deities worshipped over wide areas. The cult of Lug is exceptional. Place and tribal names hint at his cult in Spain, Switzerland and Gaul as well as in Ireland. The restricted distribution of Romano-Celtic inscriptions and the existence of eponymous tribal deities suggest local tribal interpretations of chieftain-gods and mother-goddesses, although the latter frequently enjoyed a wider distribution than those of male gods. The mythology itself cannot be taken as evidence that there was a widespread belief in specific gods. This is not to say that similar gods were not worshipped under different names among different tribal groups.

The strongly marked aristocratic nature of Celtic society in the days of independence suggests that the mythology relates to the gods of the aristocracy and it is not certain either how far the ordinary peasant shared in these beliefs, or how far he was allowed to participate in ritual observances. The sorceress, Mongfhinn, to whom 'the women and common people addressed their prayers' is the only figure in mythology who appears to have been definitely worshipped by the ordinary people. The large number of single inscriptions from Romano-Celtic times may refer to similar popular cults centred on very localised *genii loci* who were frequently associated with a more primitive worship of minor natural features. Among the common people, too, there were many of pre-Celtic descent to whom the cult-practices of earlier times may have proved adequate. To such people the aristocratic gods of the *Tuatha De Danann* may have been too unapproachable, even if access had been allowed them. It seems likely that the secret lore of the Druids would have been denied to such people. Even the Celtic aristocracy seems to have been impressed by the burial places of earlier inhabitants, so much so that they were brought into their myths. To the peasantry in close contact with the soil such relics of earlier cults, in which their ancestors perhaps participated, may have seemed more potent than the gods of their newly arrived overlords.

As part of the earliest European literature after Greek and Latin, Celtic mythology has a value over and above that of a source for ancient beliefs. In it is a rich store of priceless evidence for the way of life of the Celtic aristocracy, their hopes and fears. It is an important part of the record of a people who have made no small contribution to the European heritage, in no way diminished by its lack of general recognition.

TEUTONIC MYTHOLOGY

INTRODUCTION

Three or four centuries before the Christian era the Teutons were established in the south of the Scandinavian peninsula, in the islands of the Baltic sea and on the great flat plain of north Germany between the Rhine and the Vistula. They formed a fairly populous group of tribes who were not politically united and indeed frequently fought each other, but they nevertheless spoke the same language, had a certain community of culture, and very probably shared the same religious beliefs. Some of these beliefs were inherited from their Indo-European ancestors; for the language and cultural structure of the Teutons was derived, some thousand years earlier, from the great Indo-European complex, and their distant kinship with the Latins, Celts, Greeks, Slavs and certain other peoples may explain the similarity of some of their general conceptions, and even of certain of their legends, with those of Greece, Rome and the Orient. The Teutons, however, had lived so long separated from other Indo-European peoples that in the end they had devised an original religion.

Lacking monumental illustrations and written documents, we shall never know the exact nature of this religion in the days when it was still more or less the same for all the German peoples. We only know it in the relatively developed form it had taken towards the beginning of the Christian era, and in the course of the ensuing centuries among the branches of the ancient Teutonic nation.

In the historical epoch the Teutons were divided into three great groups: those of the East, or Goths, who, at first establishing themselves between the Oder and the Vistula, left this region towards the end of the second century A.D. and emigrated in great numbers towards the Black Sea; then the Teutons of the North, who occupied the Scandinavian countries; and finally the West Germans, ancestors of the present Germans and the Anglo-Saxons, who were at first confined to North Germany and little by little spread towards the Rhine and the Danube where they were soon to clash with the Romans. Meanwhile certain of their tribes prepared to cross the sea and establish themselves in Britain. This dispersion of the Germanic peoples was not without influence on their culture and, consequently, on their religious conceptions.

On their contact with Byzantine civilisation great numbers of the Goths were in the fourth century converted to Christianity. The only examples of their language which have survived are translations of the Bible and commentaries on sacred texts. The rare ancient historians who speak of the Goths tell us practically nothing of their pagan traditions. We must therefore abstain from speaking of the religion of the Eastern Germans. Teutonic mythology is known to us only through the literary products of the North and West Germans, as well as through certain works in Latin or Greek. Now at the period when historians of classical antiquity and authors who wrote in German, Anglo-Saxon or Norse began to note the religious traditions of the various Germanic tribes their mythology was very far from everywhere presenting the same features. The cult of certain divinities was very developed on one shore of the Baltic while it was neglected or even unknown on the opposite shore. The same gods did not enjoy equal prestige among neighbouring tribes. Also, Christian influences were already beginning to be felt.

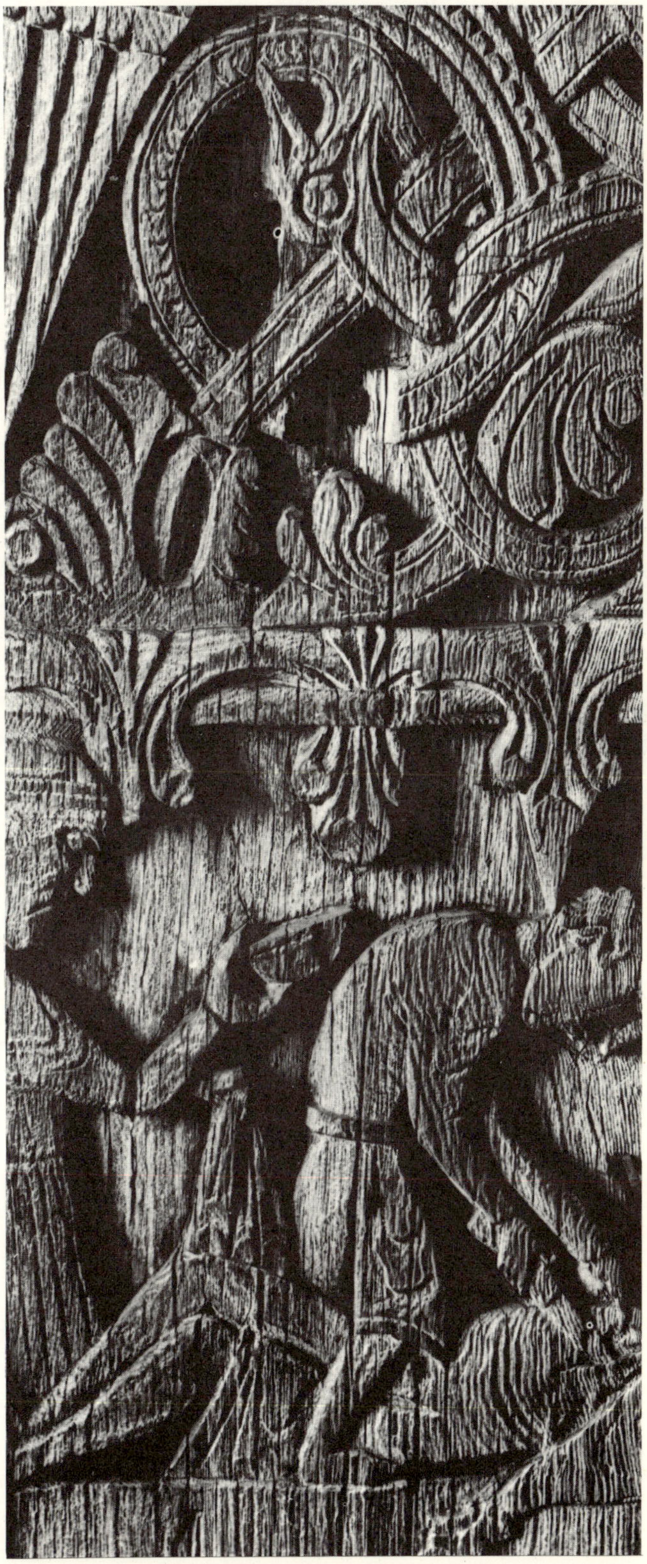

The death of Hogni. This wood-carving from Austad stave church in Norway is an example of a scene from an old pagan saga finding its way into a Christian church. Here the heart of Hogni is cut from his breast while a servant stands by to receive it in a bowl.

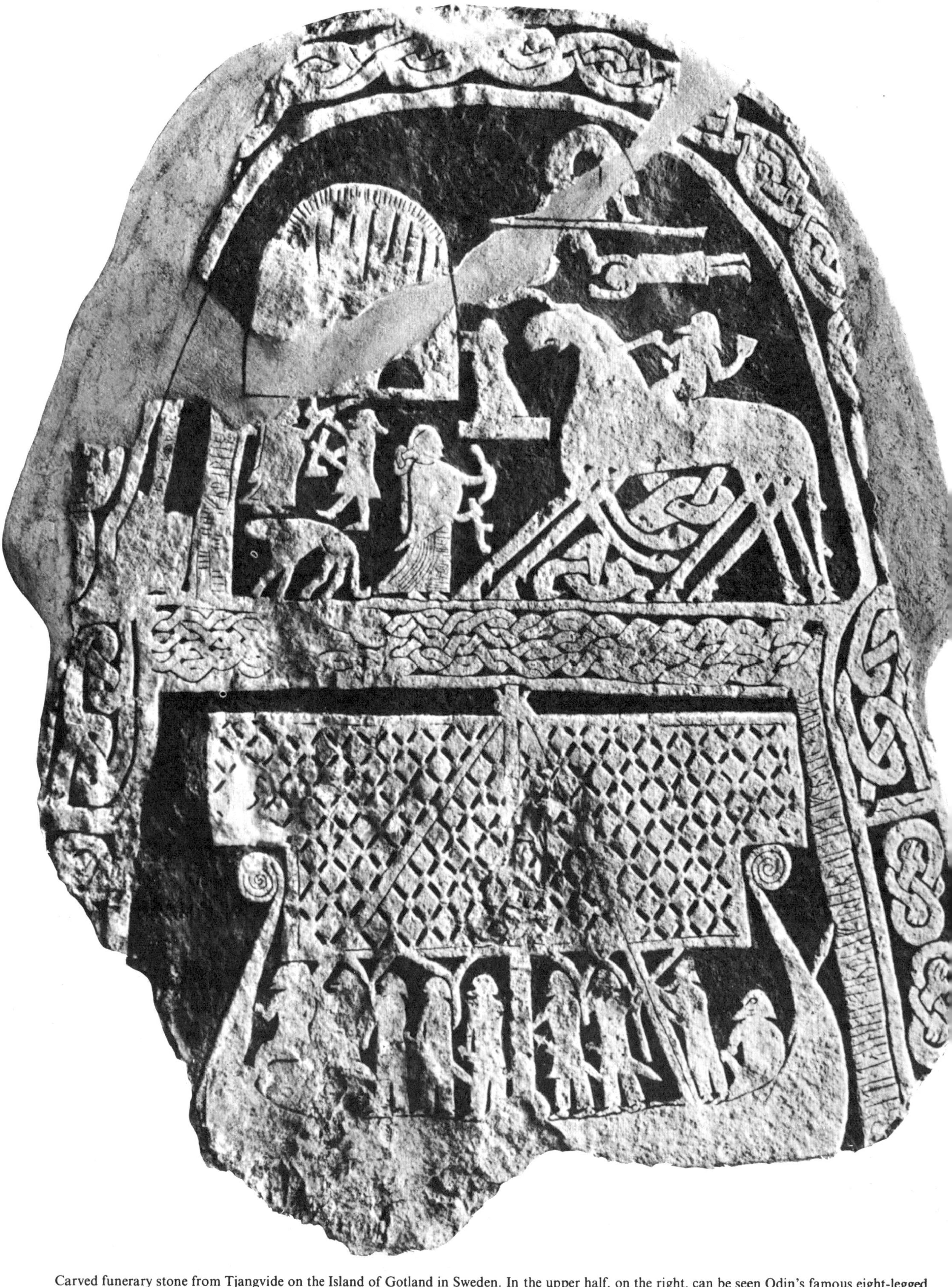

Carved funerary stone from Tjangvide on the Island of Gotland in Sweden. In the upper half, on the right, can be seen Odin's famous eight-legged horse, Sleipnir. The figure on his back may represent Odin himself or alternatively the dead man, in whose honour the stone was erected, being carried by Sleipnir to Valhalla where he is welcomed by a woman holding out a drinking horn. Below is a ship in full sail – possibly representing the ship of the dead. Eleventh century A.D.

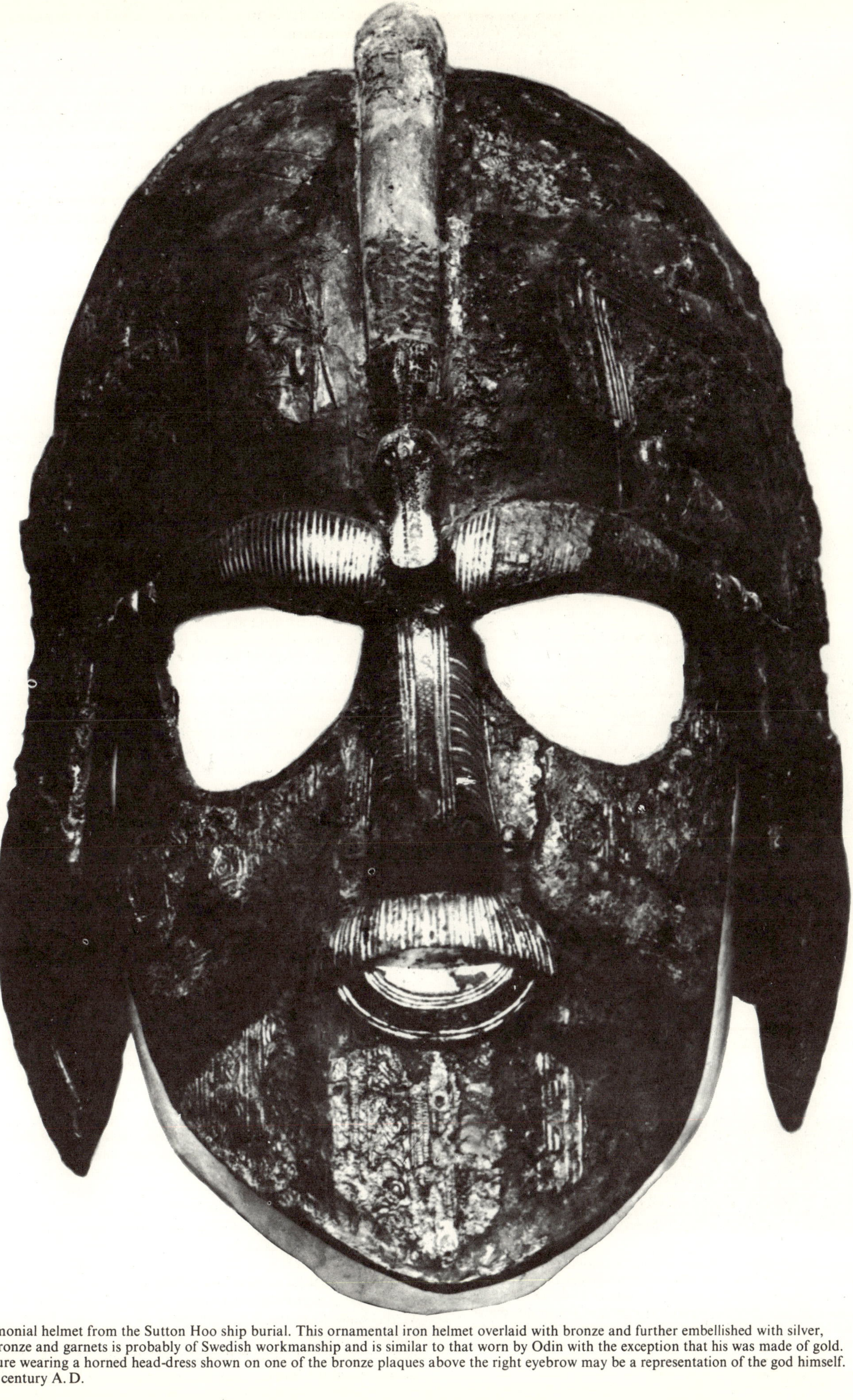

Ceremonial helmet from the Sutton Hoo ship burial. This ornamental iron helmet overlaid with bronze and further embellished with silver, gilt bronze and garnets is probably of Swedish workmanship and is similar to that worn by Odin with the exception that his was made of gold. A figure wearing a horned head-dress shown on one of the bronze plaques above the right eyebrow may be a representation of the god himself. Sixth century A. D.

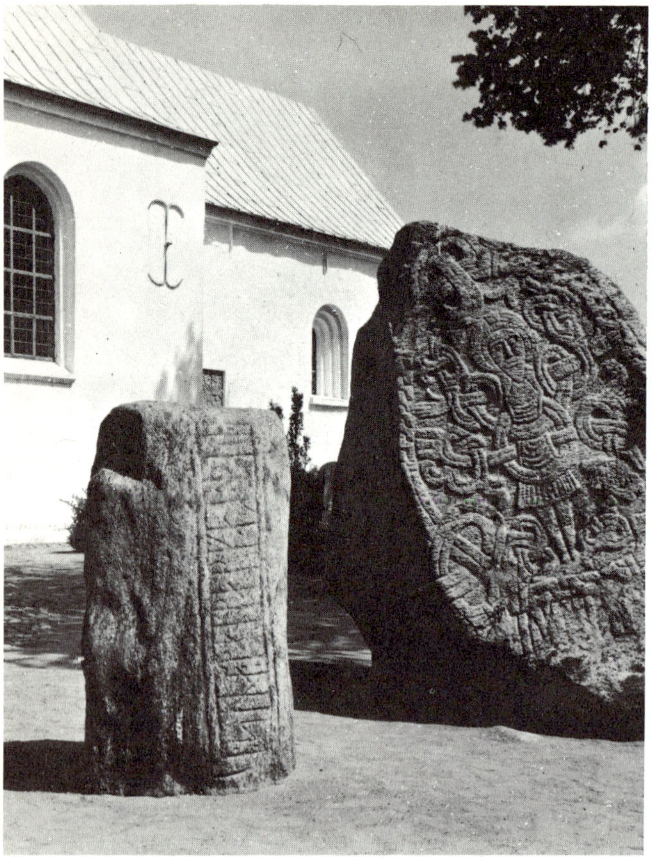

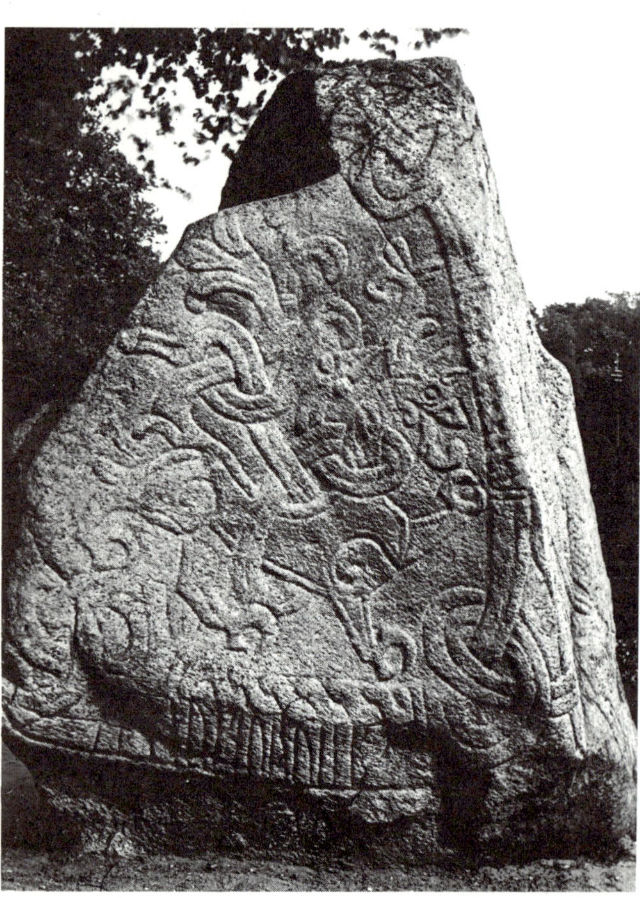

The Jelling Stone. Pagan elements survived alongside the new beliefs in Scandinavia long after the official establishment of Christianity. On the Jelling Stone, which marks the conversion of the Danish king to Christianity in A.D. 965 the outstretched arms of Christ are shown entwined with the complicated interlace designs commonly found on the runic stones of the old pagan religion while the inscription itself is in runes. An ornamental lion decorates another face of the stone. *c.* A.D. 980.

The Anglo-Saxons of Britain were converted to Christianity from the commencement of the seventh century. Anglo-Saxon missionaries soon began the evangelisation of Germany. Charlemagne completed by force the work which they had undertaken peaceably. The Scandinavian countries in their turn adopted the new faith between the ninth and the eleventh centuries. With the exception of certain Greek and Latin historians and a few Scandinavian poets the writers from whom we derive our information about German mythology were themselves Christians. They are apt to give a Christian tone to the old pagan myths. They lived, moreover, at quite different epochs and the traditions they collected at a remove of several centuries do not often agree very satisfactorily.

For the Germanic tribes of the West, the ancestors of the Germans and the Anglo-Saxons, documentary sources of information are sparse. Latin historians like Caesar and Tacitus had at their disposal only second-hand information and they attempted to explain Teutonic religion in terms of Roman religion. For instance, Donar the thunder-god, became for them *Jupiter tonans*. Woden received the name Mercury and Tiw was called Mars. The missionaries, monks and clerks who, from the eighth century, pursued their work of conversion and were at the same time the first to write the German language could, had they wished to, have given us a complete picture of German mythology in the early centuries. But their chief concern was to save souls. Hence they scarcely alluded to pagan myths except to condemn them. We should know practically nothing of the old German beliefs if 'popular' tales and epics had not preserved much that pertains to secondary divinities, demons, giants and spirits of all sorts.

The Scandinavians alone had the heart to save and perpetuate the memory of ancient beliefs. Their poets and scholars, even when they belonged to the Christian church, piously noted down the legends of the pagan gods. The old collection of anonymous poems known as the *Eddas* – one section of which dates from before the introduction of Christianity into Scandinavia – the songs of the skalds, the sages, the manuals of poetry, the works of history and erudition which medieval Iceland, Norway, Denmark and Sweden have left us, bring to life with much vigour and colour the ancient gods of the Teutonic pantheon and their cohorts of innumerable secondary divinities. It is almost entirely through the literature of Scandinavia that we know the legends of the great gods like Woden-Odin and Donar-Thor. It is, then, these legends especially which will be quoted in the following sections. But it does not therefore follow that these gods were exclusively Scandinavian. On the contrary they were, under various names, revered by the majority of the Teutons. Almost without exception the legends which were told among the ancestors of the Germans and the Anglo-Saxons have not been handed down to us. Hence in any account of Teutonic mythology the Scandinavian traditions must of necessity form a major part.

THE BIRTH OF THE WORLD, OF THE GODS, AND OF MEN

At the dawn of time, say the old bards and poets of Iceland, there was neither sand nor icy waves. The earth did not exist, nor the sky which to-day covers it. Nowhere did grass grow. Only a yawning abyss stretched through space. But, long before the sea was created, Niflheim, a world of clouds and shadows, formed in the regions to the North of the abyss. In the midst of Niflheim surged the fountain Hvergelmir, from which spread the glacial waters of twelve rivers. To the South lay the land of fire, Muspellsheim. From there poured rivers whose waters contained a bitter poison which little by little set and became solid. On contact with the ice coming from the North this first deposit became covered with thick coatings of hoar-frost which partly filled up the abyss. But warm air blowing from the South began to make the ice melt; and from the tepid drops which thus formed was born a giant in human form, Ymir – the first of all living beings.

Ymir was the father of all the giants. Once while he was asleep it happened that he became completely bathed in sweat: under his left arm were then born a man and a woman, both giants like him. At the same time the ice, continuing to melt gave forth a cow, Audumla, the wet-nurse of the giants. Ymir quenched his thirst at her udders from which flowed four streams of milk. The cow herself licked the blocks of ice and was nourished by the salt which

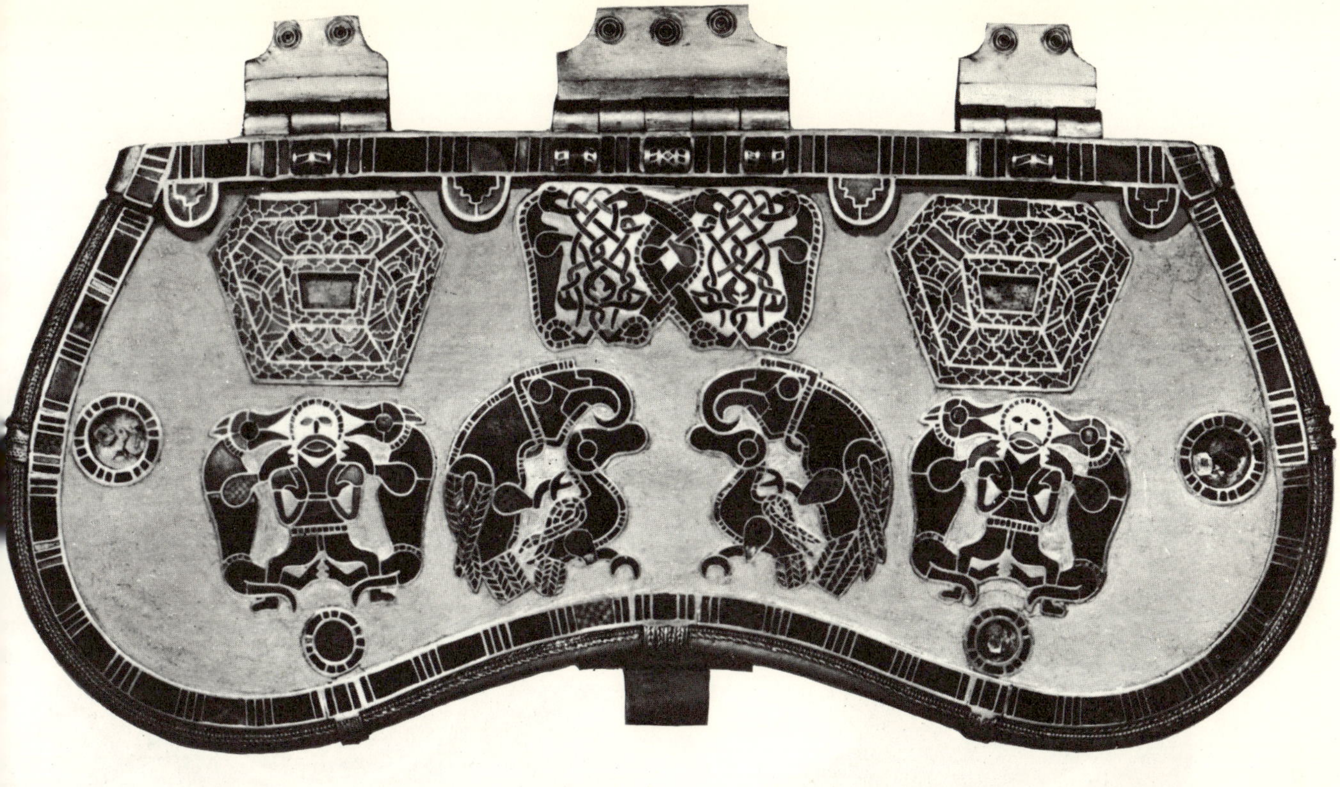

Jewelled purse lid from the Sutton Hoo ship burial. Some eight inches long, this richly decorated purse lid is set with seven ornamental gold plaques and four circular studs inlaid with garnets and coloured glass. The two outside plaques at the bottom show the figure of a man between two rampant beasts and it seems likely that the artist was probably thinking here of the myth of Odin being swallowed by the wolf Fenrir. Seventh century A.D.

they contained. Now, in thus licking the ice which melted under her warm tongue, she brought to light first the hair, then the head, and finally the entire body of a living being whose name was Buri. Buri had a son Bor, who married one of the giant's daughters, Bestla. With her he fathered the three gods Odin, Vili and Ve.

These three sons of the Giants' race at once began a struggle against the Giants which ceased only with their annihilation. At first they killed the aged Ymir. So much blood flowed from his body that the yawning abyss was filled with it, and in it all the Giants were drowned with the sole exception of Bergelmir who had launched a small boat on the stormy waves and with his wife succeeded in escaping. It was from this couple that the new race of giants issued.

Meanwhile the sons of Bor raised the inert body of Ymir from the sea and with it formed the earth which was given the name Midgard, or the 'middle abode', for it was situated halfway between Niflheim and Muspellsheim. The flesh of Ymir became the land and his blood the resounding sea. From his bones the gods made mountains and from his hair the trees. Then they took his skull and placing it on four raised pillars they made it into the vault of the heavens. In the vault they placed the haphazard sparks which escaped from the kingdom of fire, Muspellsheim. Thus they created the sun, the moon and the countless stars. The gods regulated their course and determined the succession of days and nights, as well as the duration of the year. The sun, travelling across the southern sky, threw its light and warmth over the vast stretches of the earth. And soon there appeared the first blades of green grass.

Other gods, during this time, had come to join the sons of Bor. Where they came from and whether they too were sons of giants the old Scandinavian authors do not say. In association with Odin these new gods worked to build their celestial dwelling-place. In this vast abode which was called Asgard, 'the abode of the Aesir', each of them had his own mansion. The North Germans thought that these divine palaces were exactly like the great farms of their petty nobility: the chief part was a large room, the hall, where one received visitors and gave banquets.

Between their place of residence and that of mankind the gods built a vast bridge to which they gave the name Bifröst, which was the rainbow.

Then they assembled and deliberated on the manner in which the earth might best be peopled. In the rotting corpse of the giant Ymir whom Odin and his brothers had killed grubs were beginning to form. From these grubs the gods made dwarfs to whom they gave human form and whom they endowed with reason. Because the dwarfs were born of the flesh of Ymir, the gods decided that they should continue to live in what had formerly been this flesh and since become earth and stone. For this reason the dwarfs led a subterranean existence. There were no women among them and hence they had no children. But, as and when they disappeared, two princes whom the gods had given them replaced them by other dwarfs, moulded from their natal earth. Thus the race of dwarfs endlessly continued.

As for men, they sprang directly from the vegetable world. Such at least was the general tradition among the North Teutons. Three gods, Odin, Hoenir and Lodur, one day were travelling together on the still deserted earth. On the way they came across two trees with inert and lifeless trunks. The gods resolved to make mortals of them. Odin gave them breath, Hoenir a soul and reasoning faculties. Lodur gave them warmth and the fresh colours of life. The man was called Ask ('Ash') and his wife was Embla ('Vine'?). From them proceeded the entire race of man.

Tacitus in his *Germania* attributes to the West Germans – the ancestors of the Germans of to-day – a different tradition. The first man, according to these tribes, was called Mannus, and his father was a god or a giant, born of the earth, whose name was Tuisto. Mannus had three sons each of whom later fathered one of the three principal groups of the German tribes. This relationship was perhaps invented by some kind of primitive philosopher; for the names Tuisto and Mannus are probably not without significance. The first seems to mean 'the two-sexed being', and the second apparently means Man as a creature endowed with thought and will.

In the imagination of the North Teutons the earth on which man lived had the shape of a vast circumference, surrounded everywhere by water. In the circular ocean which thus bordered the inhabited world, and was itself only limited by the primitive abyss, there lived an immense reptile, the Serpent of Midgard, whose countless coils encircled the earth.

Beneath Midgard there was a third world, which was not without similarities to the infernal regions imagined by the Greeks and other peoples in antiquity. It was the abode of the dead and the Scandinavians gave it the name of Niflheim ('Mist-world') or Niflhel. This underworld was represented as a sombre, damp and

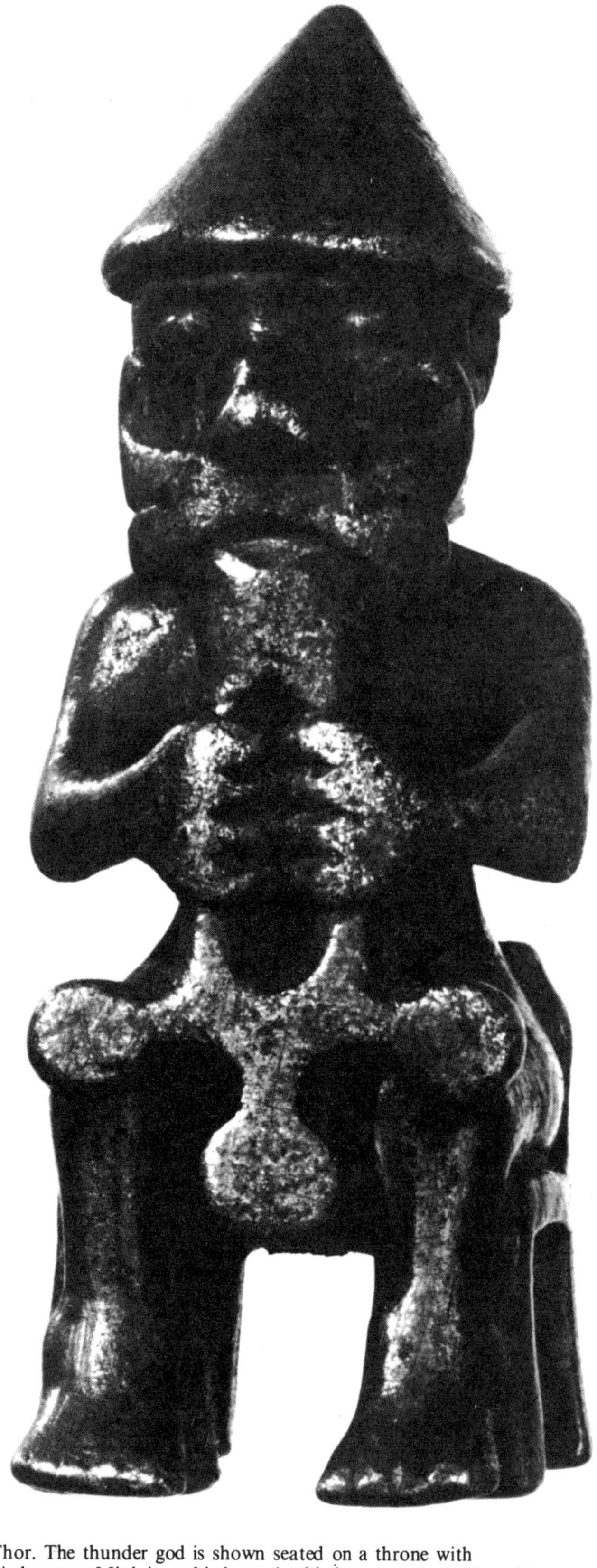

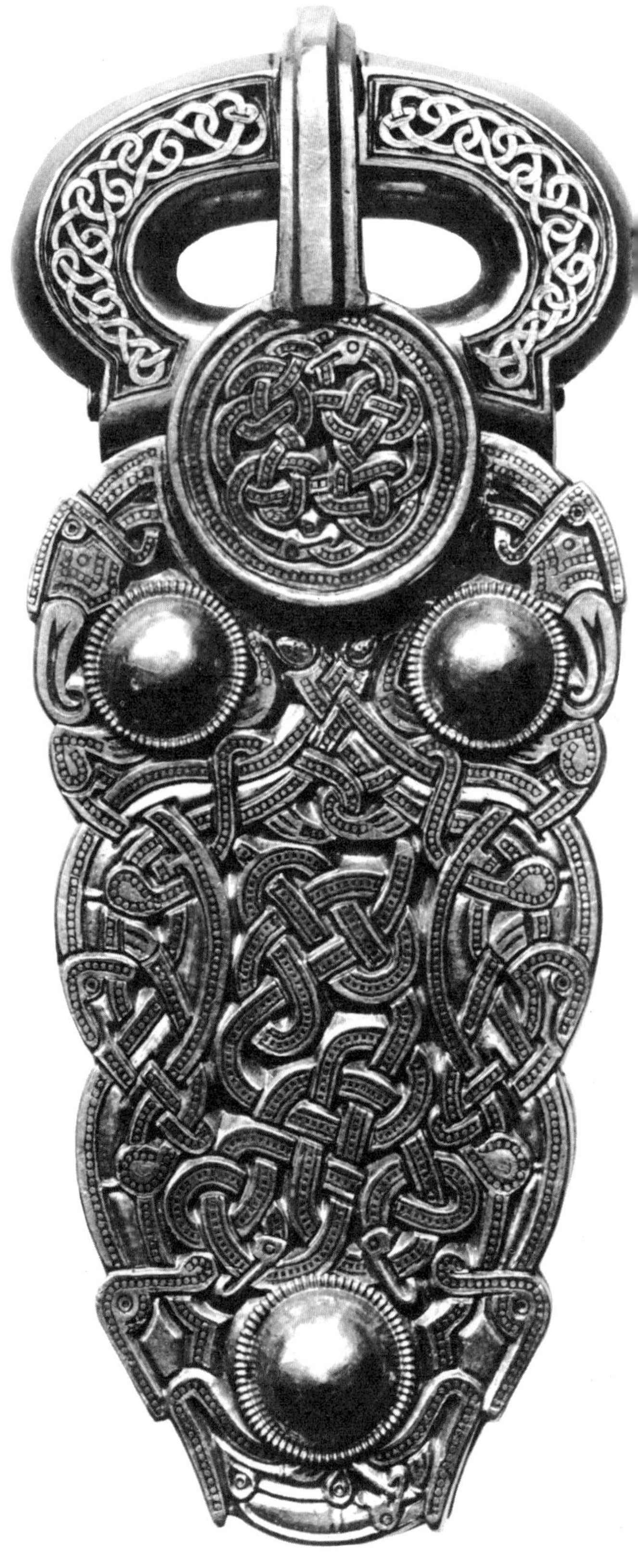

Thor. The thunder god is shown seated on a throne with his hammer Mjolnir on his knees in this bronze statuette found in northern Iceland. One of the most popular of the Teutonic gods, Thor finally came to occupy a position superior even to that of Odin himself in certain northern countries – particularly in Norway and above all in its colony, Iceland. His cult survived until the advent of Christianity. *c.* A.D. 950 – 1000.

The great gold buckle from the Sutton Hoo ship burial. One of nineteen pieces of gold jewellery found in the grave, this great belt-buckle of solid gold is five inches long and weighs over fourteen ounces. Its surface is almost entirely covered with the interlaced bodies of snakes and other animals. Though the buckle bears a striking resemblance in the style of its ornament to articles found in Swedish graves it is of English workmanship. Seventh century A.D.

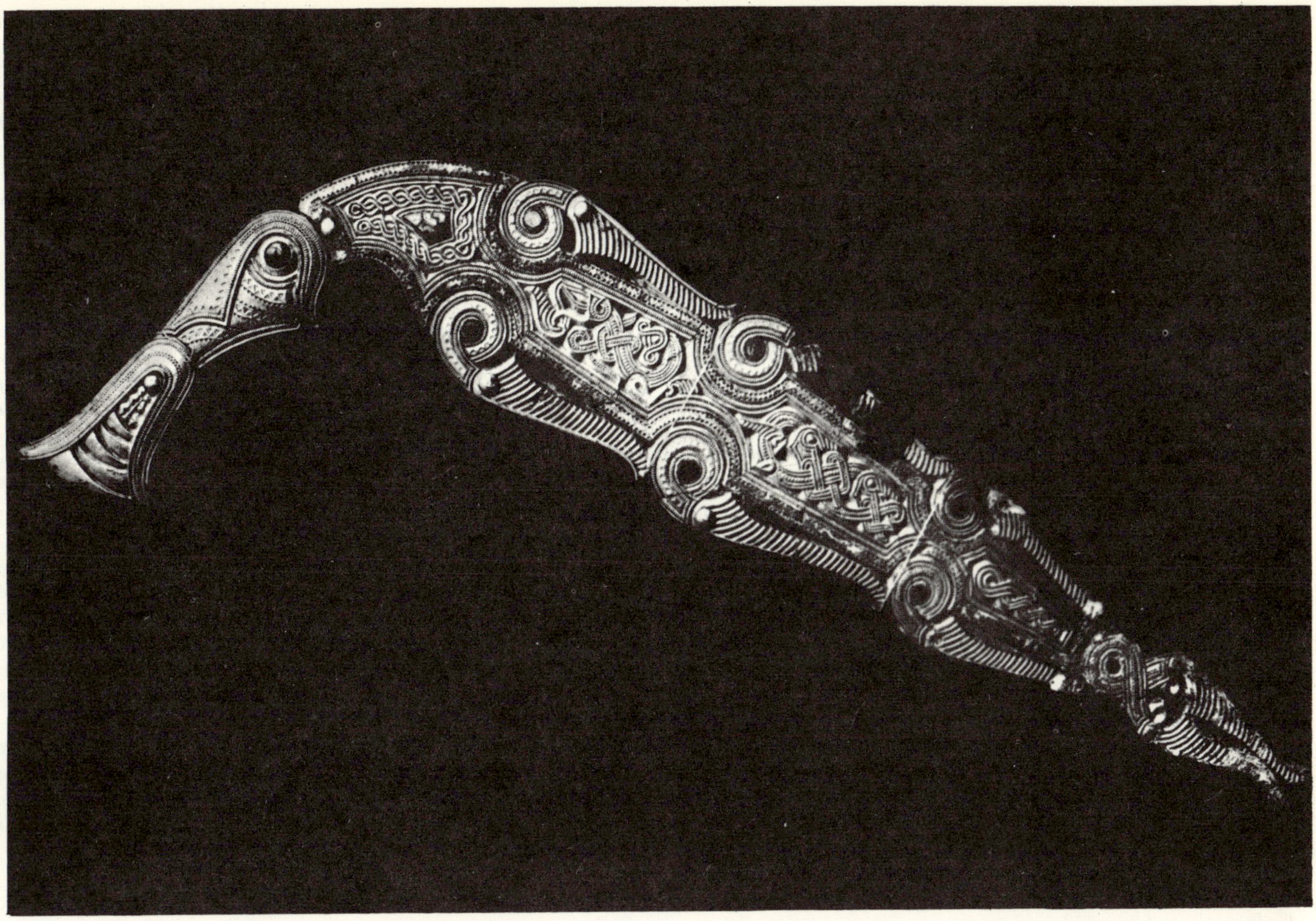

Dragon ornament from the Sutton Hoo ship burial. This ferocious animal with its wickedly curved fangs and four pairs of wings or legs comes from the front of a large, circular wooden shield. Its body is decorated with interlaced ornament and the entire animal is eleven inches long. The dragon was repaired in antiquity before the shield was buried, its last pair of wings, or legs, being made of plaster covered with gold leaf. Gilt bronze. Seventh century A.D.

glacial place. In it lived giants and dwarfs whom the poets sometimes described as being covered with snow and hoar-frost. This subterranean kingdom was the domain of the goddess Hel. Its entrance was guarded by a monstrous dog named Garm who saw that no living person penetrated into the world of the dead.

This division of the universe into three super-imposed worlds does not correspond to the very oldest north Teutonic conceptions. We have already seen that their poets, explaining the origin of the world, placed Niflheim to the north of the immense abyss from which the world was soon to emerge. It is not impossible that in remote times the Teutons had conceived the universe merely as a kind of vast plane: in the centre stretched the earth and beyond the ocean and the original abyss lay vague countries inhabited by giants. Doubtless it was only later, and perhaps under the influence of Greek or Oriental cosmogonies, that they began to represent the world of the gods, the world of men and the world of the dead as situated one on top of the other.

Thus there is some uncertainty and even contradiction in the tales which have come down to us. There is still another tradition which ill-accords with those just given, but which is nevertheless familiar to all Norse poets: namely, the tradition that depicts the entire world as a tree of prodigious dimensions. This tree whose foliage was always green was the ash tree Yggdrasil. One of its roots reached down into the depths of the subterranean kingdom and its mighty boughs rose to the heights of the sky. In the poetic language of the skalds Yggdrasil signified the 'Steed of the Redoubtable' (Odin) and the gigantic tree received its name because, they said, Odin's charger was in the habit of browsing in its foliage. Near the root which plunged into Niflhel, the underworld, gushed forth the fountain Hvergelmir, the bubbling source of the primitive rivers. Beside the second root, which penetrated the land of giants, covered with frost and ice, flowed the fountain of Mimir, in which all wisdom dwelt and from which Odin himself desired to drink even though the price demanded for a few draughts was the loss of an eye. Finally under the third root of Yggdrasil – which according to one tradition was in the very heavens – was the fountain of the wisest of the Norns, Urd. Every day the Norns drew water from the well with which they sprinkled the ash tree so that it should not wither and rot away.

In the highest branches of the tree was perched a golden cock which surveyed the horizon and warned the gods whenever their ancient enemies, the Giants, prepared to attack them. Under the ash tree the horn of the god Heimdall was hidden. One day this trumpet would sound to announce the final battle of the Aesir against all those who wished to cause their downfall. Near the vigorous trunk of the tree there was a consecrated space, a place of peace where the gods met daily to render justice. In its branches the goat Heidrun browsed; she gave Odin's warriors the milk with which they were nourished.

Malevolent demons continually schemed to destroy the ash Yggdrasil. A cunning monster, the serpent Nidhögg, lurked under the third root and gnawed at it ceaselessly. Four stags wandered among its foliage and nibbled off all the young buds. Thanks however to the care and attention of the Norns the tree continued to put forth green shoots and rear its indestructible trunk in the centre of the earth.

The Germans also, it seems, believed that the universe was supported by a gigantic tree. Doubtless the architecture of their own dwellings suggested this idea: it was their habit to support the framework of their houses by a huge tree trunk. Some German tribes set up pillars made of a single tree-trunk on hilltops. These apparently represented the tree of the universe and such monuments were called *Irmensul,* which means 'giant column'. In 772 during an expedition against the Saxons, Charlemagne, in what is now Westphalia, had one of these pillars, which was an object of great veneration, destroyed.

This world was not eternal. In the end it would perish, and in its ruin the gods themselves would be involved. A day would come when the Giants and the demons of evil who lived in remote or subterranean regions of the universe would attempt to overthrow the order established and maintained by the gods. Nor would their uprising be in vain; it would be the Twilight of the Gods and the collapse of the universe. But before relating the death of the gods we must describe what they had been, what their functions were, their powers and their personality.

THE GREAT TEUTONIC GODS

The Teutonic pantheon never contained a strictly defined number of divinities. The number varied, growing or diminishing according to tribes and epochs. Certain divinities who for a time were powerful gradually in the course of centuries lost the prestige they had once enjoyed. Others, on the contrary, grew in power and dignity. For the Germanic gods were never thought of as more than men of superior essence; and like men they were mortal and subject to the vicissitudes of fortune.

Three of them seem to have been the object of a cult which extended throughout the lands inhabited by the Teutons. These were Woden, whom the Northern Teutons called Odin; Donar, whose Scandinavian name was Thor; and Tiw – or as the Southern Germans said, Ziu – and who in Scandinavia was named Tyr. These three gods and a few others who will be discussed later belonged to the race of the Aesir. Besides the Aesir the Teutons – or at least the Scandinavians – considered that there was a second race of gods, the Vanir. The most important and best known of the Vanir was Frey. Between the Aesir and the Vanir a terrible struggle once took place which ended in a compromise; and Frey became, like Odin and Thor, an inhabitant of Asgard. When the great rising of the Giants took place the Aesir and the Vanir went into battle side by side, and side by side succumbed. Conceived by a warlike people, the Teutonic gods were nearly all distinguished for their warlike virtues. Even the goddesses, though few in number, reveal themselves on the occasion to be fearful in battle.

The basic structure of the Teutonic pantheon is a concept shared by all the Indo-European peoples, who are to be distinguished from all other cultural groups by a certain close correspondence between their social and religious structure. A comparison between the religions of the most conservative of the Indo-European groups, notably the Germans, Romans and Indo-Aryans, reveals a tripartition of their society, reflected in a tripartition of their religion. This history of the Indian caste system reveals three original groupings: a royal and priestly caste, a warrior caste, and a caste of agricultural workers. To these correspond three types of gods: those connected with the government of the world, both in its regular and its mysterious aspect; those connected with force and physical strength, largely but not entirely warlike; those connected with fecundity and all related concepts, such as peace, health, pleasure, and the well-being of the 'plebs'. Early religious writers had seen the correspondence between this triple division and the division of the universe into heaven, atmosphere and earth. In India, we have the grouping of Mitra and Varuna for the first function, Indra for the second, and the Asvin twins for the third; at Rome, there is the ancient trinity of the *flamines maiores,* Jupiter, Mars and Quirinus. Among the Germanic peoples, the Indo-European inheritance is represented by Woden and Tiw in the first position, Donar in the second, and the Vanir in the third. The representation of the first function by two divinities is a feature which the Teutons share with the Indian peoples, and which derives from the double aspect of the sovereignty as conceived by primitive peoples; firstly, there is the ruler who is the priest king, who works by the incalculable and terrifying means of magic, and secondly, the king who reflects the order of the world and of society, the constitutional monarch, as it were, who incarnates Law. The Indian Varuna and the Germanic Woden represent the first type, Mitra and Tiw the other. Similarly, the representation of the third function, that of fecundity, has, by the very nature of the concept, a tendency to split up into plurality, and among the various Indo-European peoples may be expressed, not only by a single divinity, but by twins, by a pair of gods reinforced by a goddess or by any other large grouping. It is, therefore, only with special reservations that we can refer to Indo-European gods as 'sky-gods' or 'storm-gods' or the like. To take one simple example: the name of the Indian god Varuna has been identified etymologically with that of the Graeco-Roman god Uranus (Greek, Ouranos), also a common noun for 'heaven'. This does not mean that Varuna's – or Uranus' – original function was the personification of the sky; for the name comes from some conception like 'master of the bond', a reference to the magical activities of the terrible master of the world whose powers are likened to those of a bond which renders his opponents powerless rather than to those resulting from physical force.

Woden-Odin. Woden is supposed to be the principal god of the Teutonic peoples and has been regarded as such for centuries, especially among the ancestors of the Germans. At the time when Tacitus described the customs of the Germans, that is to say towards the beginning of the second century A.D., the cult of Woden prevailed over all others. When in the fifth century the Angles and the Saxons invaded Great Britain they invoked Woden before setting out; and Woden was regarded by them as the ancestor of their kings. The fourth day of the week still bears his name, Wednesday, which is a direct transposition of the Latin *Mercurii dies,* which in French became *Mercredi.*

For some time, scholars have regarded Woden as a 'jumped-up' god; originally a minor demon, he has managed to oust the more

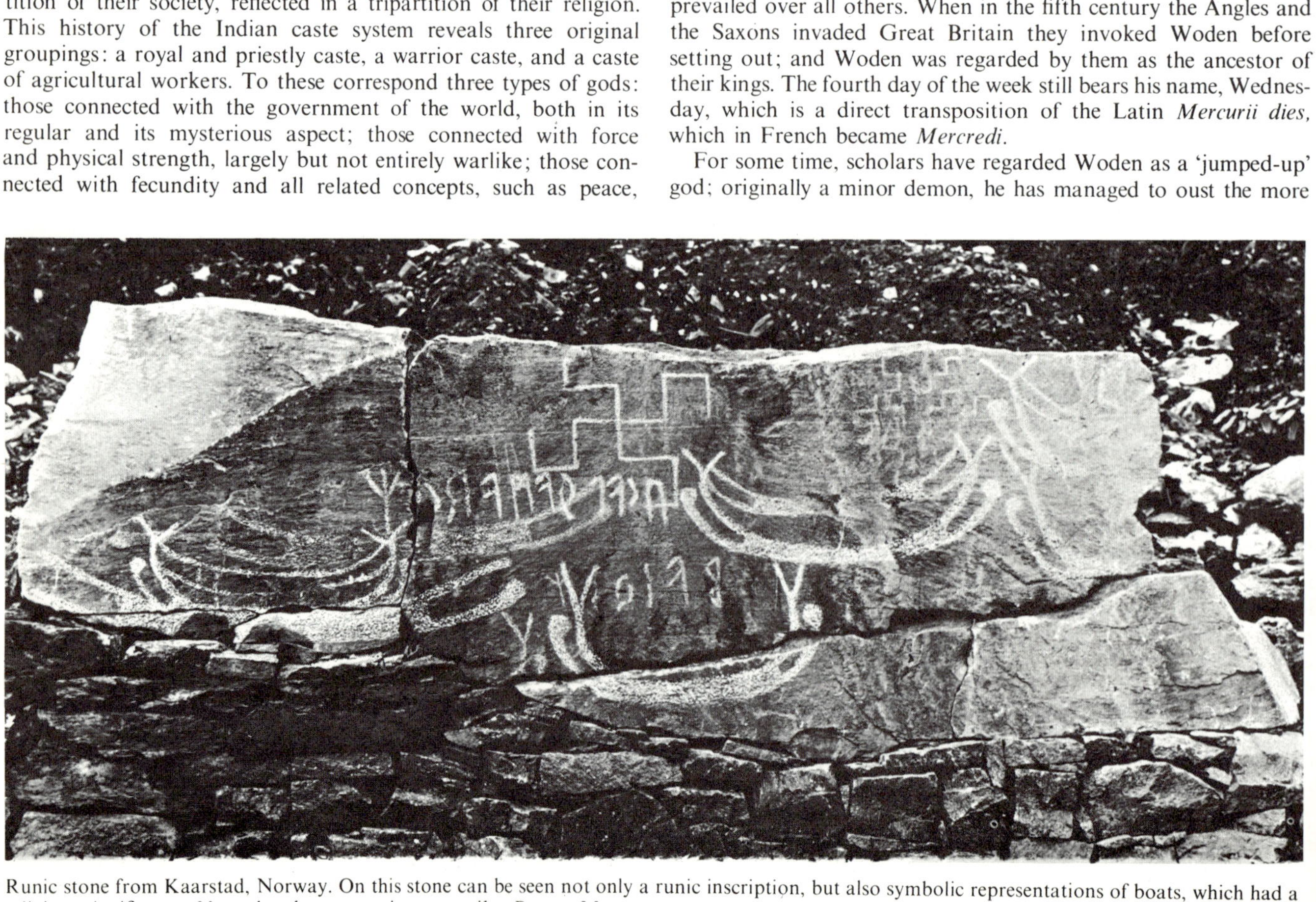

Runic stone from Kaarstad, Norway. On this stone can be seen not only a runic inscription, but also symbolic representations of boats, which had a religious significance. Note also the very curious swastika. Bergen Museum.

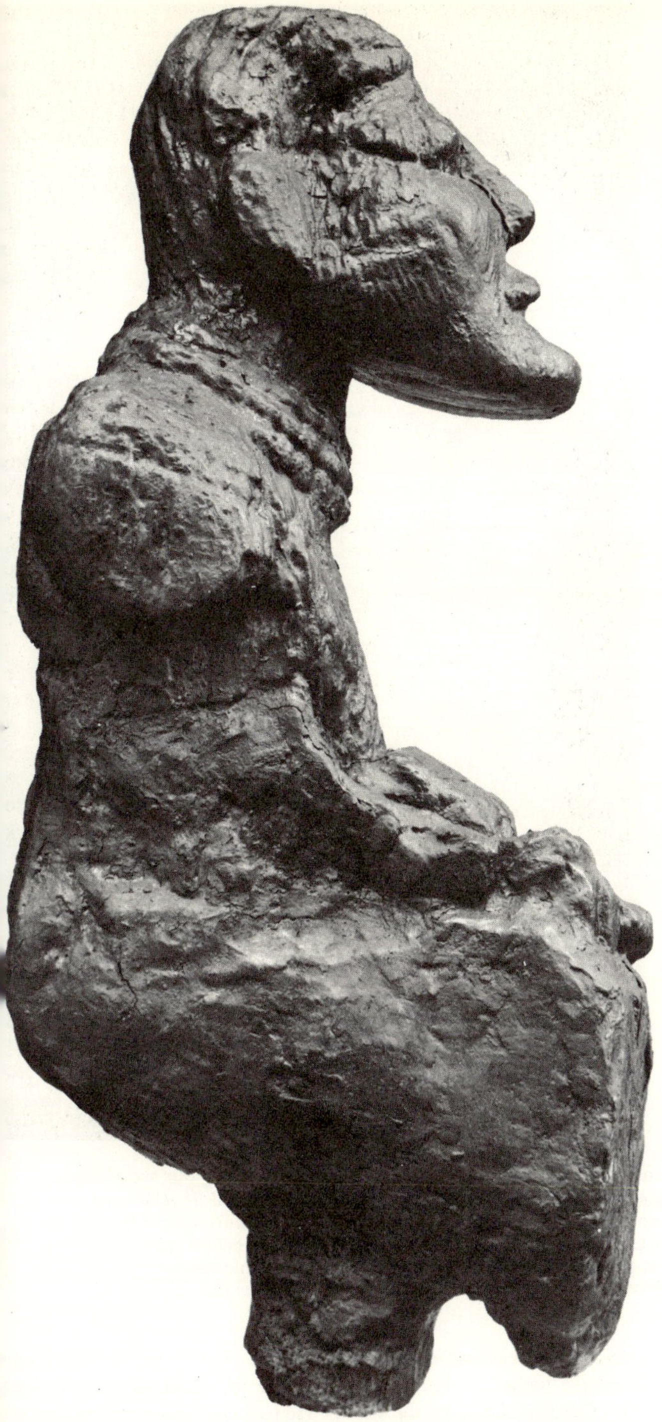

Figurine of a god. This early wooden figurine from Rude Eskildstrup in Zealand shows a seated god wearing a triple neck-ring and is seventeen inches high. Though Teutonic mythology has been preserved in poems and legends, the Christian missionaries were only too successful in destroying temples and idols and it is only by a lucky chance that this figure was found in a Danish bog. From its dress it would appear to date from about the time of the birth of Christ.

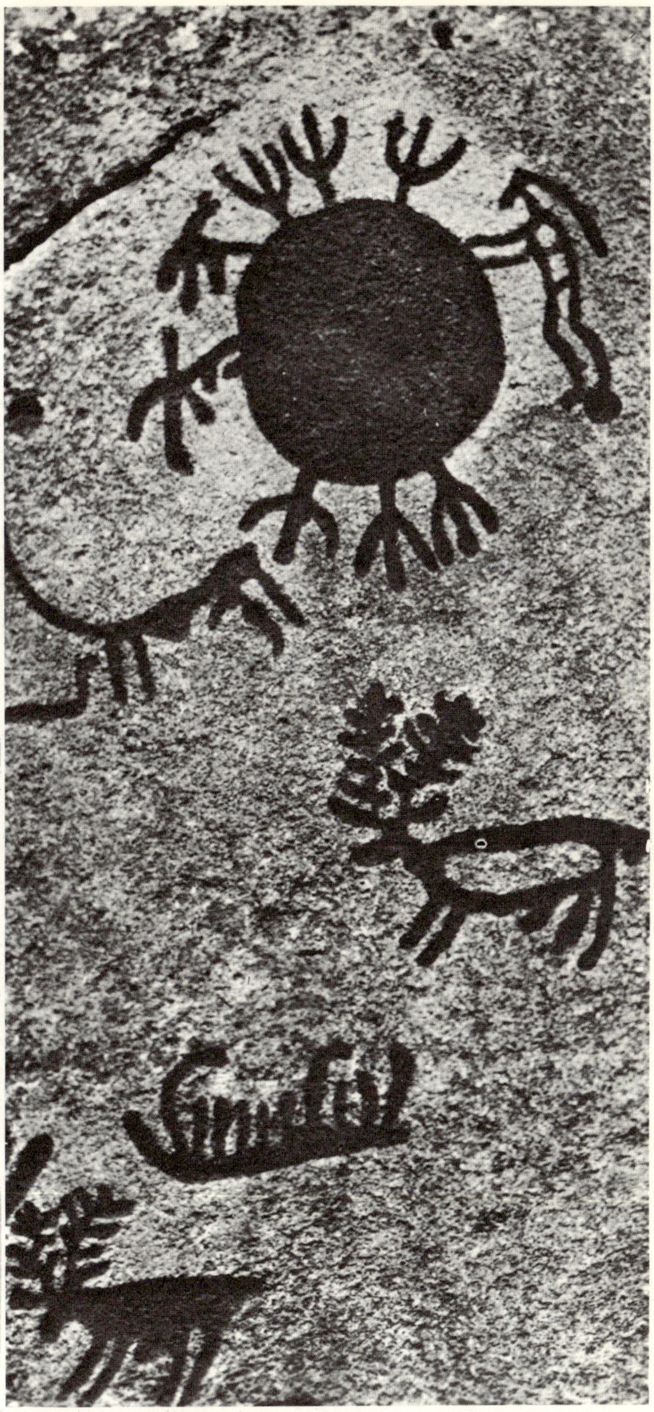

Scandinavian rock engraving at Aspeberget in Sweden. The circular design at the top may be a sun symbol while below are shown deer – the hunters' quarry – and boats, the Scandinavians of this period portraying the objects most familiar to them. The boats may possibly represent those which were believed to carry the dead on their last voyage and the carving may therefore be commemorative in character. *c.* eleventh century B.C.

important divinities such as Donar, 'storm-god' or Tiw, 'sky-god'. Recent researches have shown that this is not the case, that Woden is a prolongation of an Indo-European type. The old theory ran as follows: In all Germanic lands the belief was widespread that on certain stormy nights the tumultuous gallop of a mysterious troop of riders could be heard in the sky. They were believed to be the phantoms of dead warriors. This was the 'furious army' or the 'savage hunt'. This raging army had a leader whose name was derived from the very word which in all Germanic languages expresses frenzy and fury (in modern German *wüten*, 'to rage); his name was Wode. The name was transformed as the divinity assumed more definite character in the imagination of believers; among the ancestors of the Germans it became Woden or Wotan, among the ancestors of the Scandinavians Odin. In the beginning this god of nocturnal storms was represented as a horseman who, in a flowing mantle, a wide-brimmed hat and mounted on a horse, sometimes black, sometimes white, would range the sky in pursuit of fantastic game. But as he rose in dignity he ceased to be a divinity of the night. He became the god who granted heroism and victory and who, from on high, decided man's fate. Furthermore he was regarded as the god of spiritual life which is doubtless why the Latins compared him to Mercury. There is no evidence to suggest that leading the wild hunt was Woden's original function; on the other hand, these activities concord well with Woden's position as the magician-god of the Other World. There is no evidence, either, to suggest that the name *Wode* precedes *Woden*; both may be synchronous, *Woden* signifying 'master of the *Wode*, or fury', the fury which is the sign of the unchaining of all the brute forces of

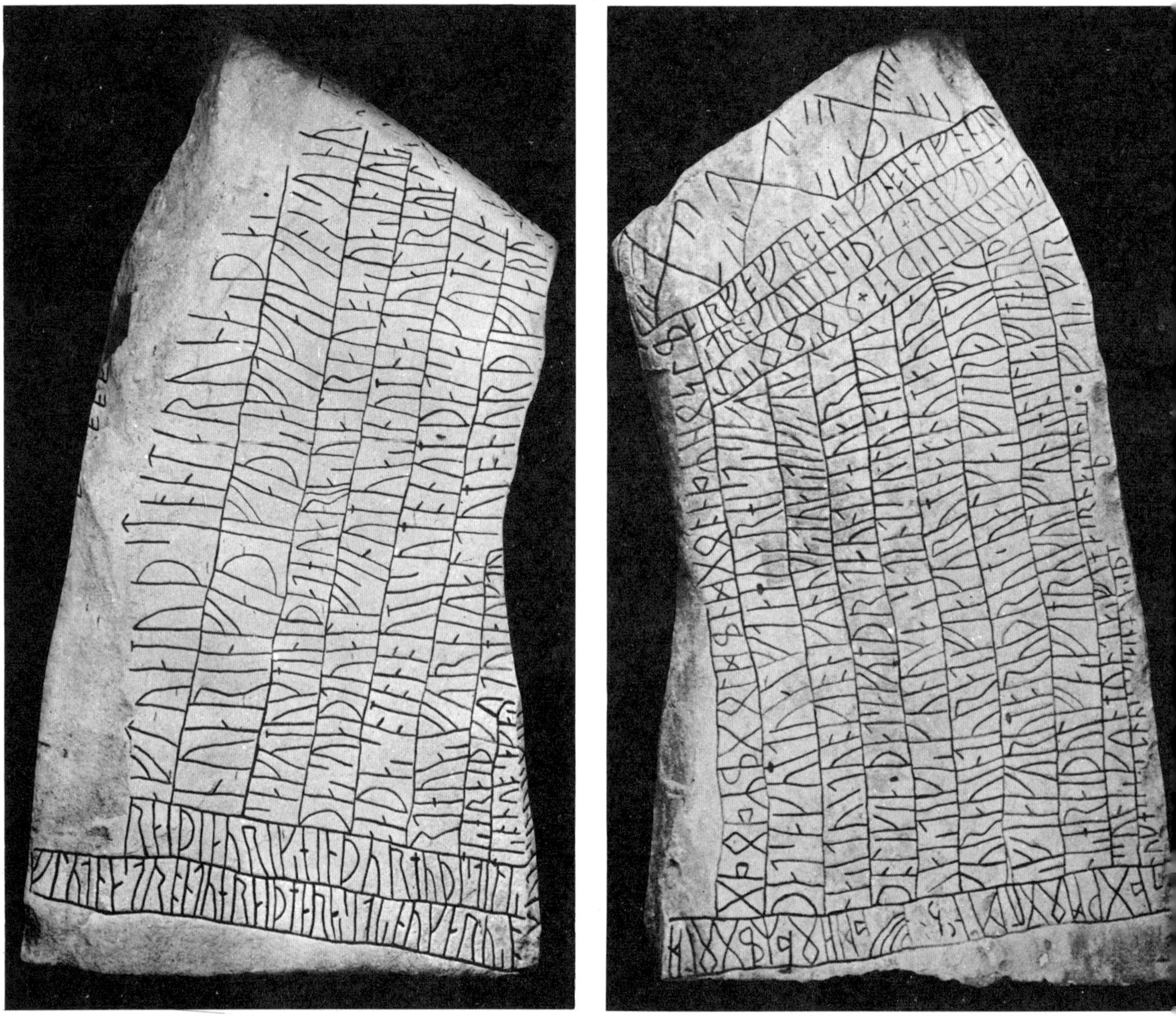

Runic stone from Rok, Sweden . From left to right: *The front face.* Runic inscriptions of the pagan period always have a religious significance. Runes were attributed magic powers. The inscription illustrated is the longest and most important of all those yet discovered. It celebrates in solemn words – occasionally breaking into verse – the merits of a young warrior who died prematurely in battle. It dates from the first half of the ninth century. The stone is about eight feet high and in its broadest part about five feet wide. *The back.* The three branched crosses with crotchets seen at the top are ciphers. *The right side and top.* The signs engraved on the upper surface are cryptographic characters. *The left side.* The nineteen signs engraved in the form of 's' and separated by a vertical line which can be seen in the lower half of this side of the stone represent, in cipher, the name of the god Thor.

the world, as distinct from its organised forces. Like Varuna, Woden rules principally by magic and notably takes an interest in the wider universe, not only in the world of living men, but also in the 'Other World'. Germanic mythology, and this is but a reflection of social conditions, has been noticeably militarised, and if Woden seems to take an undue interest in battle and warriors it is because the old 'royal' caste was more interested in war than anything else. But his shamanic origin is more than once stressed: in spite of his patronage of battles, he does not fight in them, but intervenes magically, making use of his *herfjöturr*, his army-fetter, a paralysing panic. The fury over which he presides, like other magician-gods, has been turned towards war; consequently he has in a certain way become the god of war, but only by being the sovereign god and the master of the most powerful weapon, magic.

The ancient Germans certainly provided this god – who for them surpassed all others – with legends. But for lack of literary works in their language, none of these legends is known to us. We only know – thanks to an old magic formula which has come down to us – that they appealed to Woden to cure cases of sprains and dislocations. We also know that warriors invoked him in battle and prayed to him to give them victory. But only in Scandinavian countries have legends about his person and adventures survived.

In the North Woden was called Odin. He was the god of war and of intelligence. He was handsome. He spoke with such ease and eloquence that all he said seemed true to those who hear him. He liked to express himself in verse, cadenced according t the rules laid down by the skalds. He had the power to change him self instantly into whatever shape he wished; he would in tur become a fish or a bull, a bird, a snake or a monster. When he ad vanced in battle his very approach would suddenly strike his enemie deaf, blind and impotent.

It was Odin who ordained the laws which ruled human society It was on his command that dead warriors were burned with a that belonged to them on funeral pyres. For by thus taking wit him all his worldly possessions the dead warrior would find then again when he reached Valhalla.

Odin was armed with a shining breastplate and a golden helme In his hand he grasped the spear Gungnir which had been forge by the dwarfs and which nothing could deflect from its mark. Hi horse, Sleipnir, was the best and swiftest of all stallions. It ha eight hooves and no obstacle existed which it could not overcome

One day Odin was riding in the land of the Giants. One of th inhabitants of the country, a certain Hrungnir, admired this horse man in the golden helmet who cleaved the air and waters so effort lessly, and began to praise the qualities of his steed. 'But,' he adde 'I myself have a stallion which is even stronger and swifter.' Odi challenged him. Both raced across the vast plain. Hrungnir dug hi spurs into his horse, but in vain. In his wild race whenever he reache

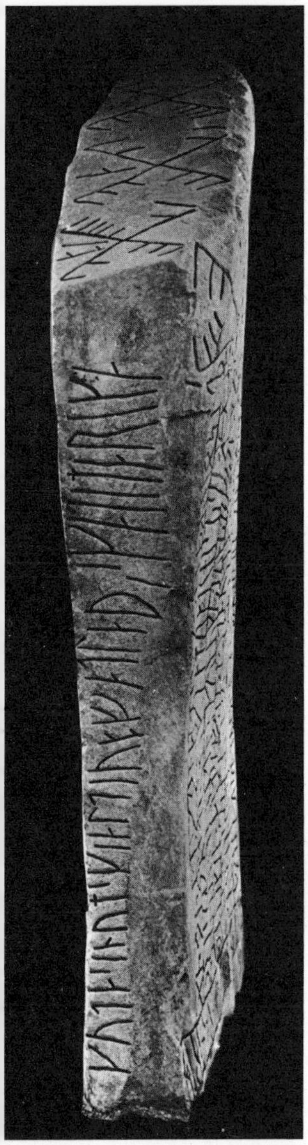

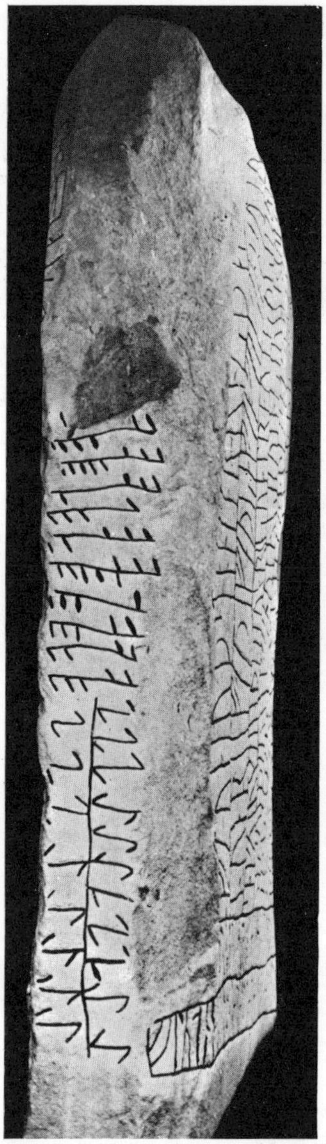

the crest of a hill he saw Odin in front of him flying on Sleipnir towards the next crest. On another occasion Odin wished to rescue one of his protégés, Hadding, from the pitiless enemies who were chasing him. He took up Hadding, wrapped him in the folds of a broad cloak and placed him on the saddle before him. Then he took him home. Now while the horse galloped the astonished young man became curious and glanced out through a hole in the cloak. Stupefied, he saw Sleipnir's hooves pound the waves of the sea as though the road had been paved with stone.

Odin held court in a vast hall glittering with gold which was called Valhalla. Here he summoned to his presence the heroes whom it pleased him to distinguish among those warriors who had fallen on the field of battle. The framework of the huge chamber was formed by spears. The roof was covered not by tiles but by gleaming shields. Breastplates lay on the benches. In the evening this immense hall was lighted by the flash of swords which reflected the huge fires burning in the midst of the festive tables. There were five hundred and forty doors, each wide enough to admit eight hundred soldiers abreast.

In this palace dead heroes passed their time in warlike games and feasts. Odin presided at their libations. On his shoulders perched two crows who whispered in his ear all that they had heard said and all that they had seen with their eyes. Their names were Hugin and Munin (that is, 'thought' and 'memory'). Every morning Odin sent them far and wide; they ranged all the inhabited world, questioned the living and the dead, and returned before breakfast to bring to their master news of the great world.

With Odin in Valhalla lived supernatural women called Valkyries. They acted as both guardians and servants. They brought to Odin's guests beer and mead and attended to the plates and drinking vessels needed during feasts. But their role was not only domestic; they had more martial duties. When there was a battle on earth Odin sent them to mingle with the combatants; it was their task to determine which warriors should fall, and they awarded victory to the side or to the chieftain who gained their favour. They rushed ceaselessly through space on their fiery chargers. Their appearance even was that of warriors; they wore breastplates, helmets and shields and brandished in their hands spears of gleaming steel. They were invisible except to those heroes who were fated to die. To him whom they had chosen to become a companion of Odin they would appear suddenly and make his imminent fate known. Then they would return to Valhalla and announce to Odin the impending arrival of those warriors who were about to join the countless band of his followers.

Odin often mingled in the affairs of men, though he rarely appeared to them in the splendour of his divinity. More often he assumed the disguise of a simple traveller. Among men he had his favourites and to them he always awarded victory. His favour, however, was inconstant and sometimes it happened that he himself would cause the death of a hero whom he had long protected. But even this could be a form of benevolence since such a dead warrior was immediately admitted to the joys of Valhalla.

There was one family to which Odin had been especially prodigal of his favours; the Volsungs. It was said that the founder of this family, one Sigi, was one of his sons. Thanks to the protection of his omnipotent father Sigi had been able to escape all dangers and to conquer a kingdom. He had a son, Rerir. Rerir himself for long remained without posterity. He addressed urgent prayers to Odin who heard him and sent his wife an apple. Rerir's wife ate the apple, and in due course gave birth to Volsung, who became a mighty warrior. Volsung's son was Sigmund. Now one evening when Sigmund and other warriors were seated around the great fires in a vast hall, whose centre was supported by a huge tree-trunk, an unknown man entered. He was tall, already old, and blind in one eye. His head was covered with a broad-brimmed hat, his body was wrapped in a wide cloak. In his hand he carried a naked sword which he thrust up to the hilt into the tree-trunk. The sword, he declared, should belong to him who proved strong enough to draw it out again. Then he vanished.

Every man present attempted to wrench the sword from the tree-trunk. Only the last to try succeeded. This was Sigmund himself, who from then on won many a victory with the aid of the divine sword. But the day came when Sigmund grew old. He was struggling with an adversary when suddenly he saw before him a one-eyed man, wearing a broad-brimmed hat and wrapped in a wide cloak. The unknown man did not speak. He simply pointed with his lance in Sigmund's direction. Sigmund's sword broke in two pieces on the wooden shaft of the lance. The unknown man was Odin himself who had decided that his favourite should die, and thus disarmed him after having furnished him with the weapon of his former triumphs. Sigmund fell dying beneath his opponent's blows. When Hjördis, his wife, heard, she hastened to the battlefield to tend his wounds and, if possible, to save his life. But Sigmund refused all assistance: Odin desired his death and he insisted on submitting to the god's will. He made only one dying wish: he asked that the two fragments of his broken sword be kept so that one day they should be welded together again. The reforged sword was, in the hands of Sigmund's son, to accomplish further glorious exploits. This son was Sigurd – the legendary Siegfried of German tradition, the hero whom Wagner's operas have made celebrated.

Odin was the hero of many an amorous adventure. Although he was the husband of the most revered of the goddesses, Frigg – in German, Frija – he was no more faithful to her than she was to him. We often find him seeking the favours of mortal women, of female giants, or of supernatural beings.

He was not only a warlike and an amorous god, but also a god of wisdom and poetry. Many poems recount the wise counsels he offered men and the rules of conduct which he taught them. He was helpful and benevolent. He knew the magic formulas which cured illness, those which rendered the weapons of the enemy powerless, those which would break a prisoner's chains, rouse or calm the waves, make the dead speak, or gain women's love. He was naturally the lord of the runes, since runes – those characters carved on stones or wood – always had a magic meaning and power.

Odin had not been born with this science. He had acquired it little by little, by questioning everybody he met in the wide world,

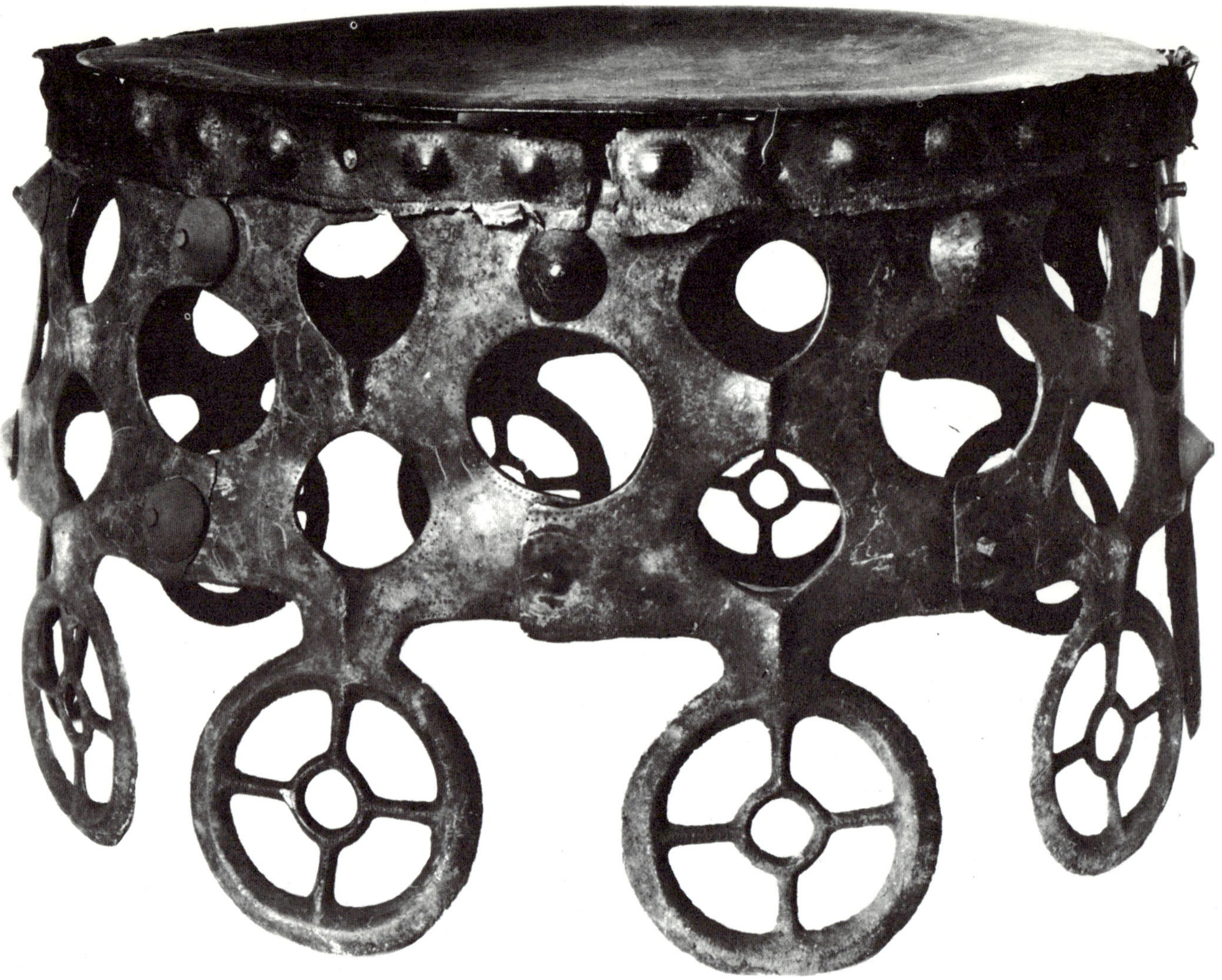

Bronze altar found at Balkaakra, near Ystad, Sweden. This curious work in bronze seems to represent the sun. It is circular in shape and stands on ten round supports which probably represent wheels. It is impossible to say with certainty when it was made; but it belongs to a period well before the introduction of Christianity. How it was used in pagan ritual is also unknown.

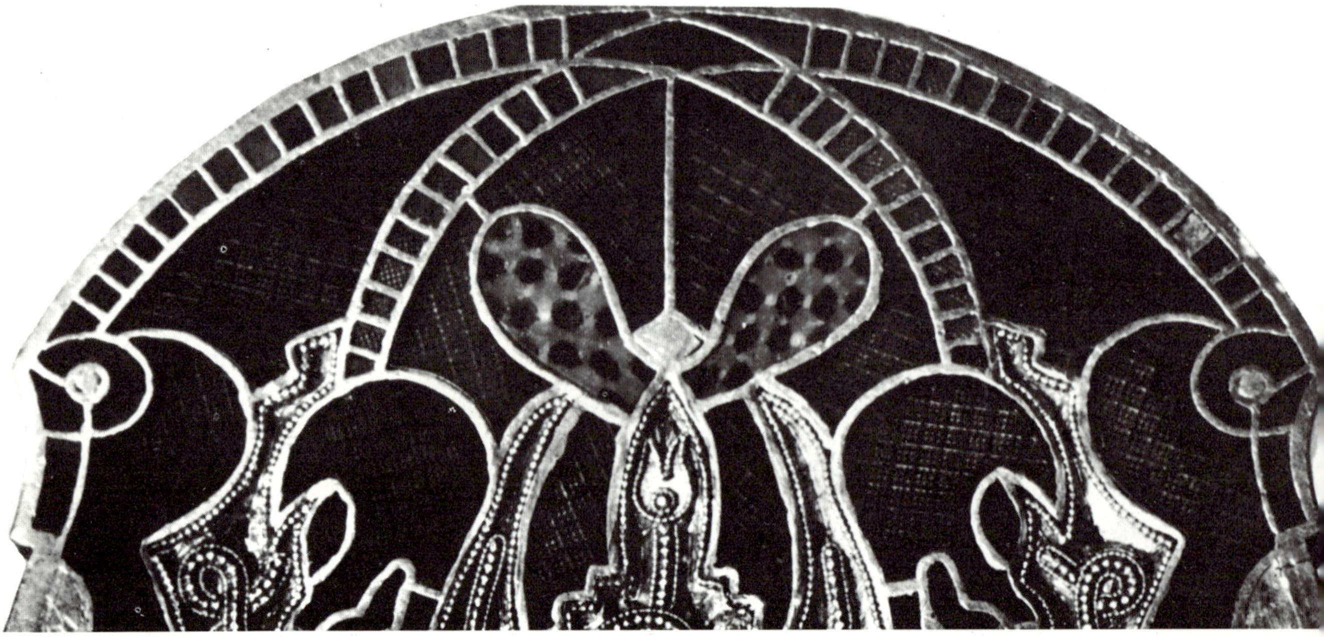

Detail of a gold clasp from the Sutton Hoo ship burial showing two interlaced boars. The hindquarters of the boars are on the outside, their heads crossing in the centre. The boar was a symbol of fertility and was associated with Frey who had a boar with gold bristles to draw his chariot. It was also commonly used as a protective emblem on helmets. Gold with garnets, enamel and filigree work. Seventh century A. D.

giants, elves, water-sprites and wood-sprites. The wisest counsellor whom he consulted was his maternal uncle Mimir whose fountain was situated near one of the roots of the ash tree Yggdrasil. Mimir – 'he who thinks' – was a water demon known and revered by all the Teutons. In the fountain which bore his name all wisdom and knowledge were hidden. Odin, with his thirst to know everything, desired to drink from this fountain, but Mimir only permitted him to do so after he had handed over an eye as a pledge. Mimir perished during the war between the Aesir and the Vanir. But Odin embalmed his head and pronounced magic formulas over it so that it retained the power to answer him and tell him of things which were hidden from others.

If Odin was the god of poetry this was because he had had the skill and cunning to steal the 'mead of the poets', the hydromel, from the giants who had it. This hydromel was of divine origin. When, after their prolonged struggle, the Aesir and the Vanir finally concluded peace they met and spat in turn into the same vase. From their mingled saliva they formed a man, Kvasir, who surpassed all other men in wisdom. But two dwarfs secretly killed Kvasir and mixed his blood with honey. They kept this mixture in two pitchers and in the cauldron Odrerir. This was how the famous hydromel was made. It, too, received the name of Odrerir. Whoever drank of it became both a poet and a sage.

Now, as it happened, the same two dwarfs killed the father of the giant Suttung, and Suttung avenged himself by forcing them to give to him the precious draught. He hid it in a huge underground chamber closed by heavy rocks and set his daughter Gunnlöd to guard it. Odin resolved to get hold of the hydromel by stratagem. Having won the friendship of Suttung's brother, the giant Baugi, whom he had served for a time in the capacity of valet, Odin persuaded him to pierce a hole through the rocks which concealed Suttung's underground dwelling. He then changed himself into a snake and glided through the hole and into the great hall. There he reassumed his divine form and introduced himself to Suttung and Gunnlöd under a false name. His conversation was so skilful and persuasive that he succeeded in winning the father's confidence and the daughter's love. He passed three nights at Gunnlöd's side and the enamoured giantess each night let him drink a few mouthfuls of hydromel. In three goes Odin emptied the two pitchers and the cauldron Odrerir. Then he changed himself into an eagle and flew swiftly away. Suttung also changed himself into an eagle and attempted to catch him in flight, but perished in the attempt. When Odin regained Asgard he spat out the hydromel he had swallowed into large vases, and thus it was that he got possession of the magic beverage which, later, he dispensed to the poets whom it pleased him to favour. A few drops which he had let escape during his flight fell to earth; with this inferior residue bad poets had to content themselves.

One of the most extraordinary episodes in the life of Odin is the one which concerns his voluntary self-sacrifice and resurrection. 'For nine nights,' he says in an old poem, 'wounded by my own spear, consecrated to Odin, myself consecrated to myself, I remained hanging from the tree shaken by the wind, from the mighty tree whose roots men know not.' The tree was the ash Yggdrasil. By wounding and hanging himself from the branches of the world tree Odin was accomplishing a magic rite, the purpose of which was his own rejuvenation. For the gods themselves, like men, were doomed to decrepitude. During the nine days and nine nights that this voluntary sacrifice lasted Odin waited in vain for someone to bring him food and drink. But, attentively observing what lay beneath him, he perceived some runes. With an effort which made him groan aloud with pain he managed to lift the runes, and was immediately set free by their magic power. He dropped to the ground and discovered that he was filled with new vigour and youth. Mimir gave him a few sips of hydromel and again Odin became wise in word and fruitful in deed. Thus was his resurrection accomplished.

This myth of Odin's voluntary self-sacrifice has sometimes been compared to the death of Christ on the Cross. Since legends about Germanic gods were, generally speaking, formed during the course of the first centuries of our era one cannot automatically rule out the possibility of Christian influence. This influence, however, was slight and the myth of Odin's resurrection appears in strictly pagan form. Later we shall see, moreover, that Odin was never considered to be an immortal god. The time would come when he was to perish

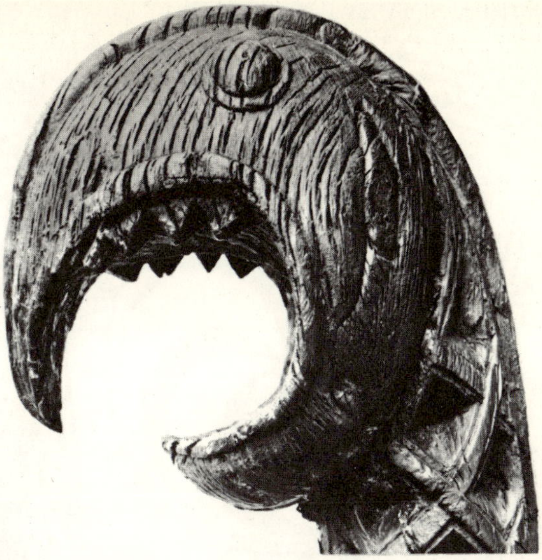

Head of the wooden stem-post from a Viking ship found in the River Scheldt near Termonde in Belgium. Ships had a religious significance in the north from very early times and were particularly associated with Frey and the gods of the Vanir. From the bronze age onwards they were employed in different forms in funeral ceremonies and by about A.D. 600 the dead were being buried or burned inside them. Two famous ship-burials were those of Oseberg and Sutton Hoo. *c.* eighth century A.D.

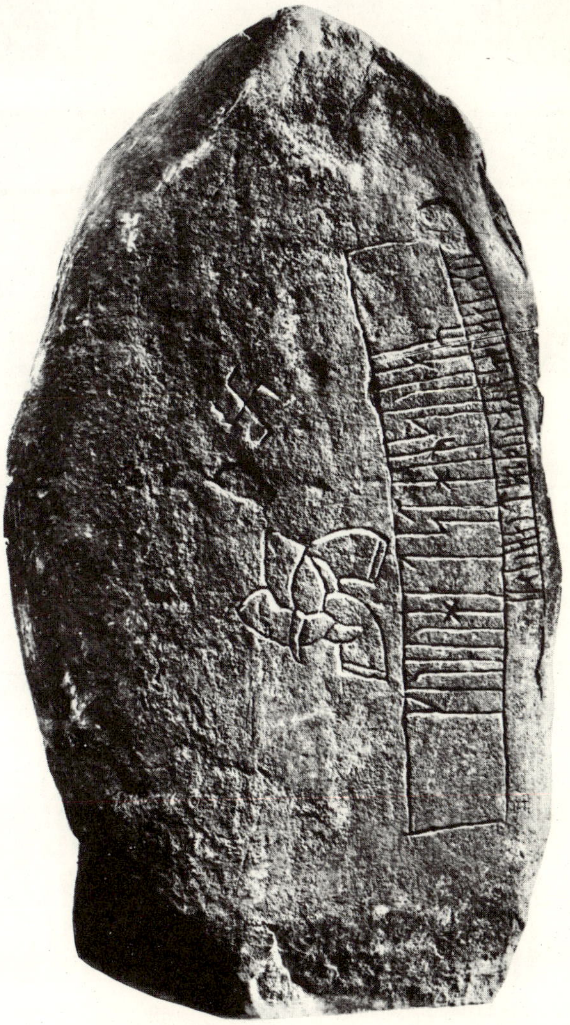

Runic stone from Snoldelev, Denmark. This stone bears, in addition to an inscription concerning the dead man whom it must commemorate, a swastika and a figure which represents three interlocked drinking horns. According to the great Danish scholar Axel Olrik, the swastika is the sign of Thor and the three horns are the sign of Odin. National Museum, Copenhagen.

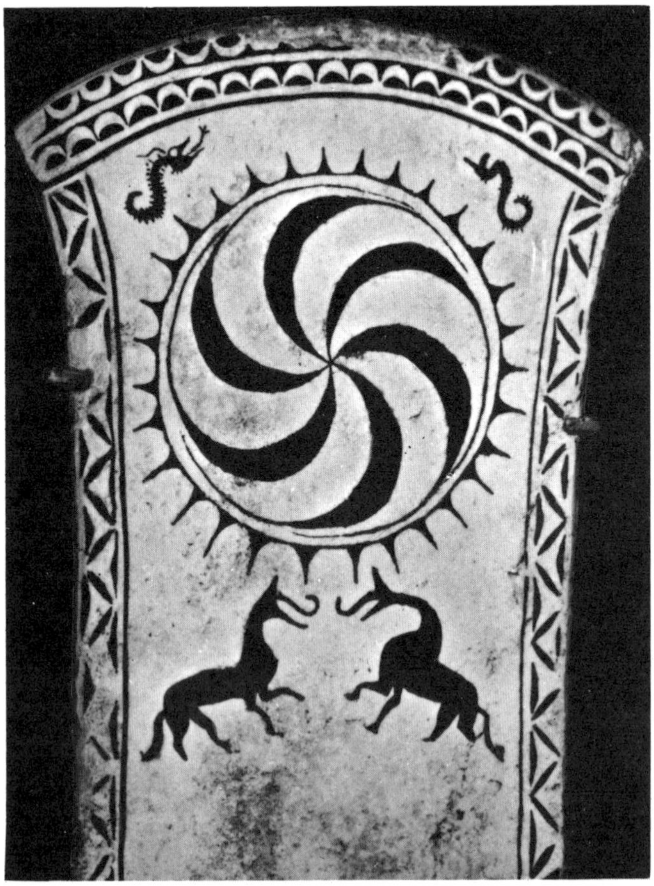

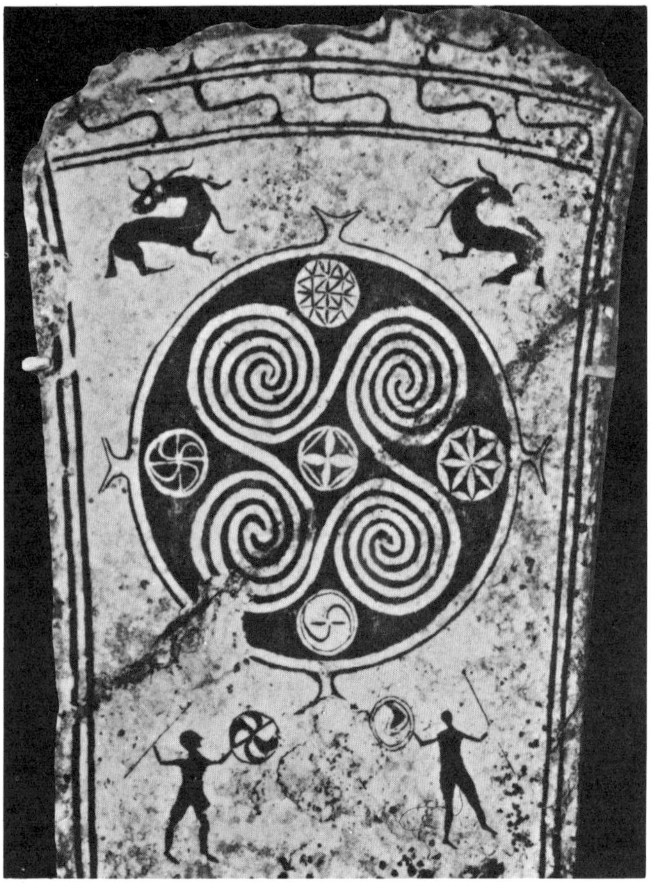

Picture stones from the island of Gotland in Sweden.
Picture stones were first employed in Gotland at the beginning of the Later Iron Age under continental influence and were used as monuments to the dead. These two date from the first period and show horses, fabulous animals and armed men surrounding two circular decorative motifs which are thought to be sun symbols. About 250 of these stones survive either whole or in fragments. Painted limestone, fifth century A.D.

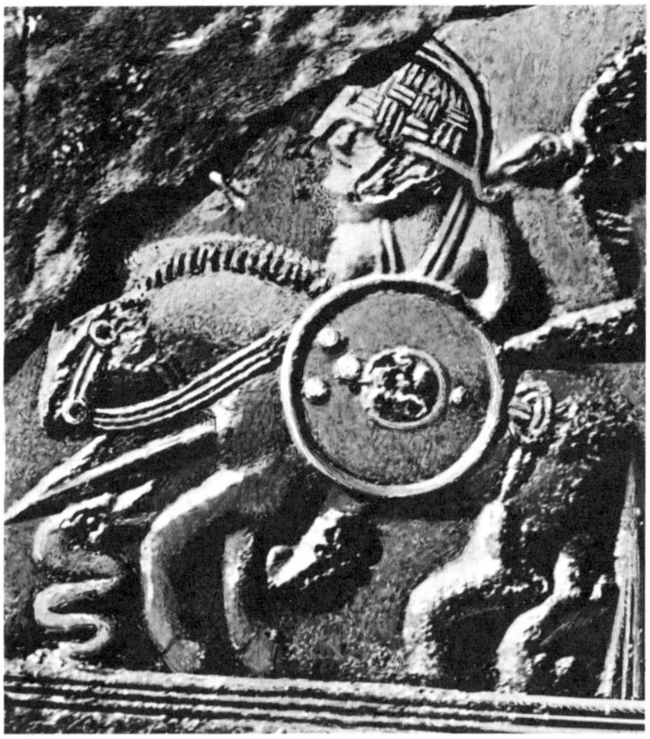

Plaque from a helmet found in a grave at Vendel, Sweden.
It is very probable that the personage here represented is the god Odin. He is accompanied by his two familiar crows and holds the lance Gungnir in his hand. One should, however, point out that this horse Sleipnir has not the eight hooves which legend later attributes to it.

and disappear for ever. This myth of Odin's self-sacrifice has very strict parallels in certain shamanic practices from Central Asia, where initiations have as their usual scenario apparent forms of death, including fasting, cataleptic immobility or feigned executions.

Donar-Thor. The god of thunder, whose name in old German was Donar, had been revered by all the Teutonic tribes. Some of them even considered him as the first and most powerful of all the gods, and Roman authors often identified him with Jupiter. Moreover, in imitation of the Romans who dedicated one of the days of the week to Jupiter – Thursday, *Jovis dies*, 'jeudi' in French – the Germans in all the lands where they became established have named Thursday after Donar (or Thor, which is only another form of the same name). Thus the Germans still say *Donnerstag* and the English *Thursday*.

We know, however, very little of the characteristics and attributes which the Germans of the first centuries ascribed to this god. The very limited information which is furnished by the historians of antiquity, the clerks of the Middle Ages, and by certain Latin inscriptions carved on votive monuments by German soldiers in the service of Rome, scarcely permit us more than a glimpse of the rites of the cult rendered to Donar. His appearance, adventures and functions remain obscure. He was a much feared divinity. When the thunder rolled people believed they heard the wheels of Donar's chariot on the vault of heaven. When the thunderbolt struck they said the god had cast his fiery weapon from on high. This weapon was represented, it would seem, as a missile axe, or perhaps simply as a stone hammer made to be thrown at an enemy's head. It was a form of defence and attack which the Teutons had used from remote times, and in Northern lands this hammer was regarded as Thor's habitual attribute.

Donar was not only the god of thunder. He was to a certain extent the god of war, since – according to Tacitus – the Germans invoked him and chanted his glory when marching into battle.

In Germany, it seems, Donar did not enjoy a prestige equal to that of Woden. But in certain Northern countries, and particularly in Norway, Thor – the German Donar – finally prevailed over all the other gods. In temples it was to Thor that the most richly ornamented altars were consecrated. Temples were even erected to his exclusive cult and many Norwegian peasants gave their children the name Thor in order to place them under his protection.

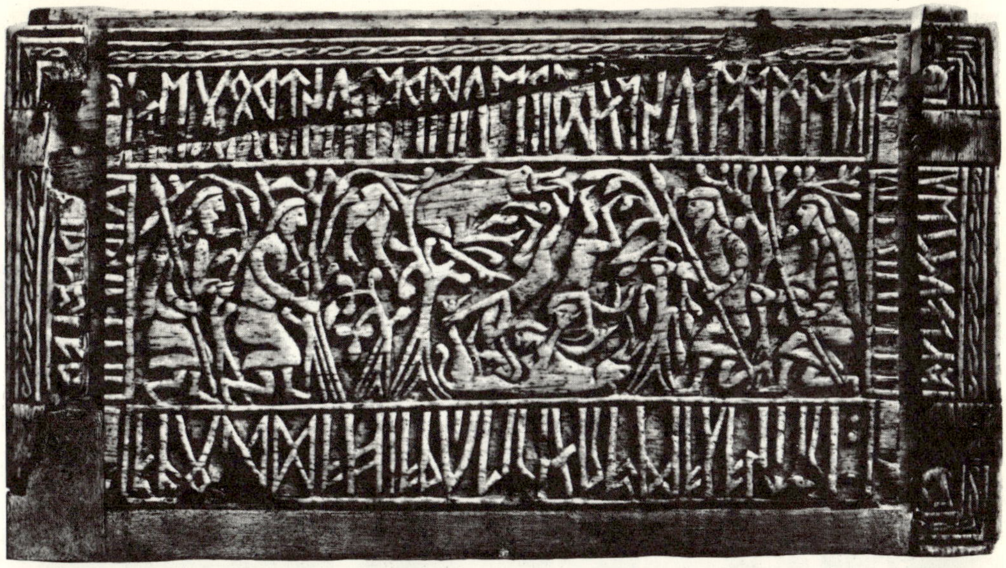

anel from the Franks' Casket. his small whalebone ivory asket not quite nine inches long nd just over four inches high is of lorthumbrian workmanship and decorated with scenes from a niversal history. This panel om the left side of the casket ıows a scene from Roman ıythology with, in the centre, omulus and Remus being ıckled by the she-wolf, the gures being surrounded by ınic inscriptions.

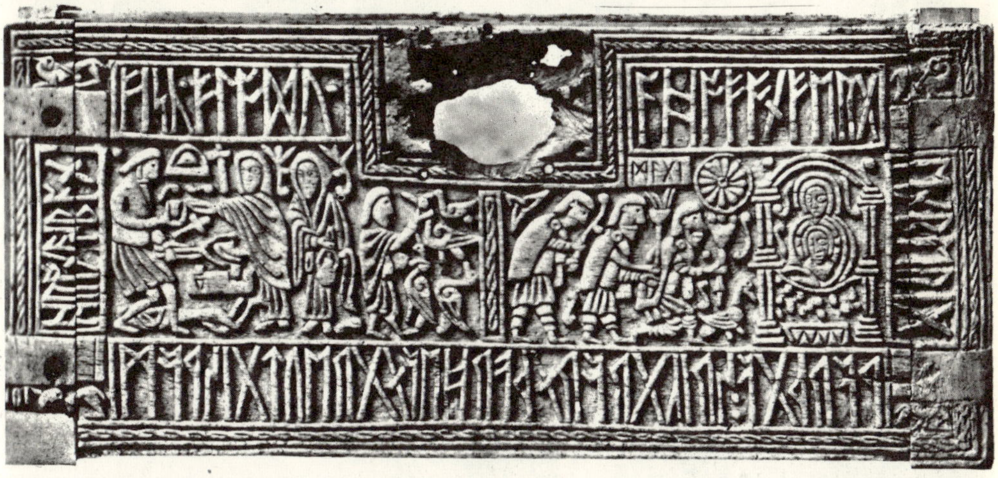

'he panel forming the front of he Franks' Casket shows a cene from pagan mythology on he left and one from the Bible on he right, the whole surrounded by runic inscription. On the left Vayland the Smith receives odvild and her servant after illing her brothers while on the ight is depicted the Adoration of ne Magi. The juxtaposition f Teutonic, classical and Christian motifs is particularly nteresting. *c.* A.D. 700.

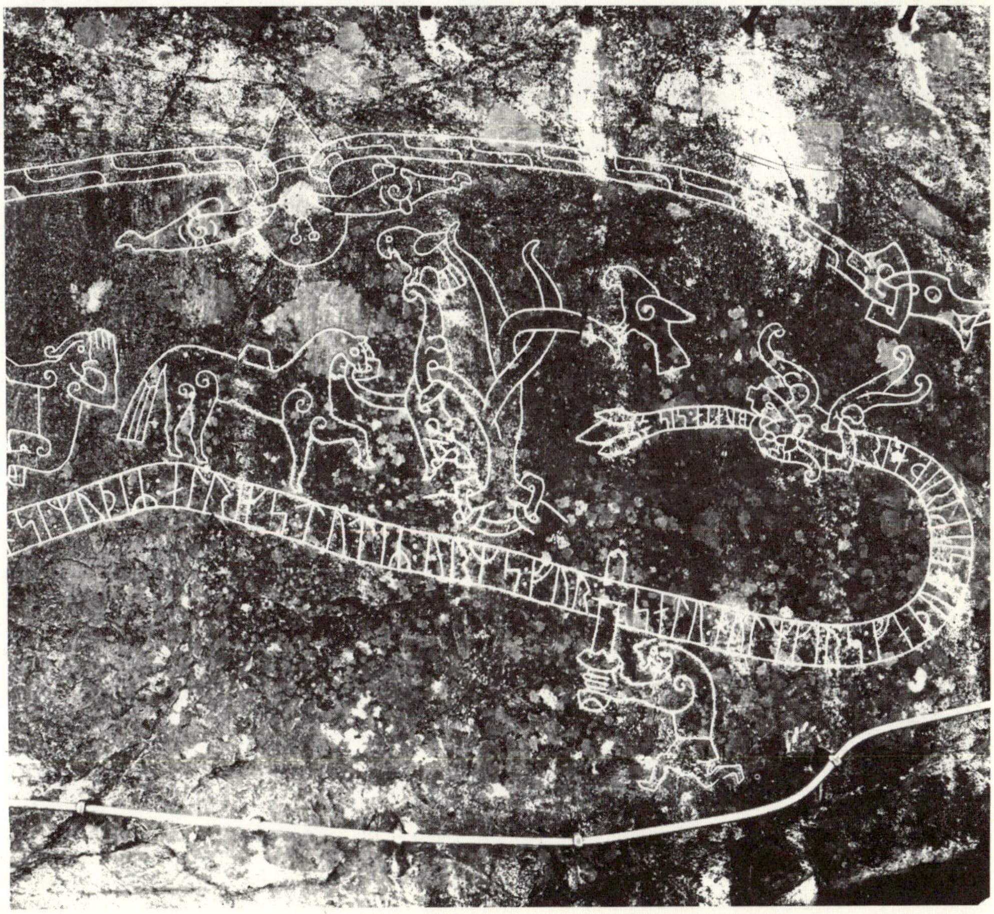

gurd and Fafnir. Design engraved n a rock in Uppland, Sweden. n the right Sigurd drives his word through the monster afnir, represented by a long and, with a runic inscription, in e form of a serpent. In the entre can be distinguished a tree which Sigurd's horse Grani is ed, and in which are perched the vo birds who have come to arn Sigurd against the navish designs of Regin. The ersonage to the left of the orse is Sigurd again. He is oasting Fafnir's heart over a re and is raising one of his left ngers to his mouth, for he urned the finger when he touched ne heart to see if it was roperly cooked. Thus, nintentionally, he has asted the monster's blood, and rom now on he will understand the anguage of the birds.

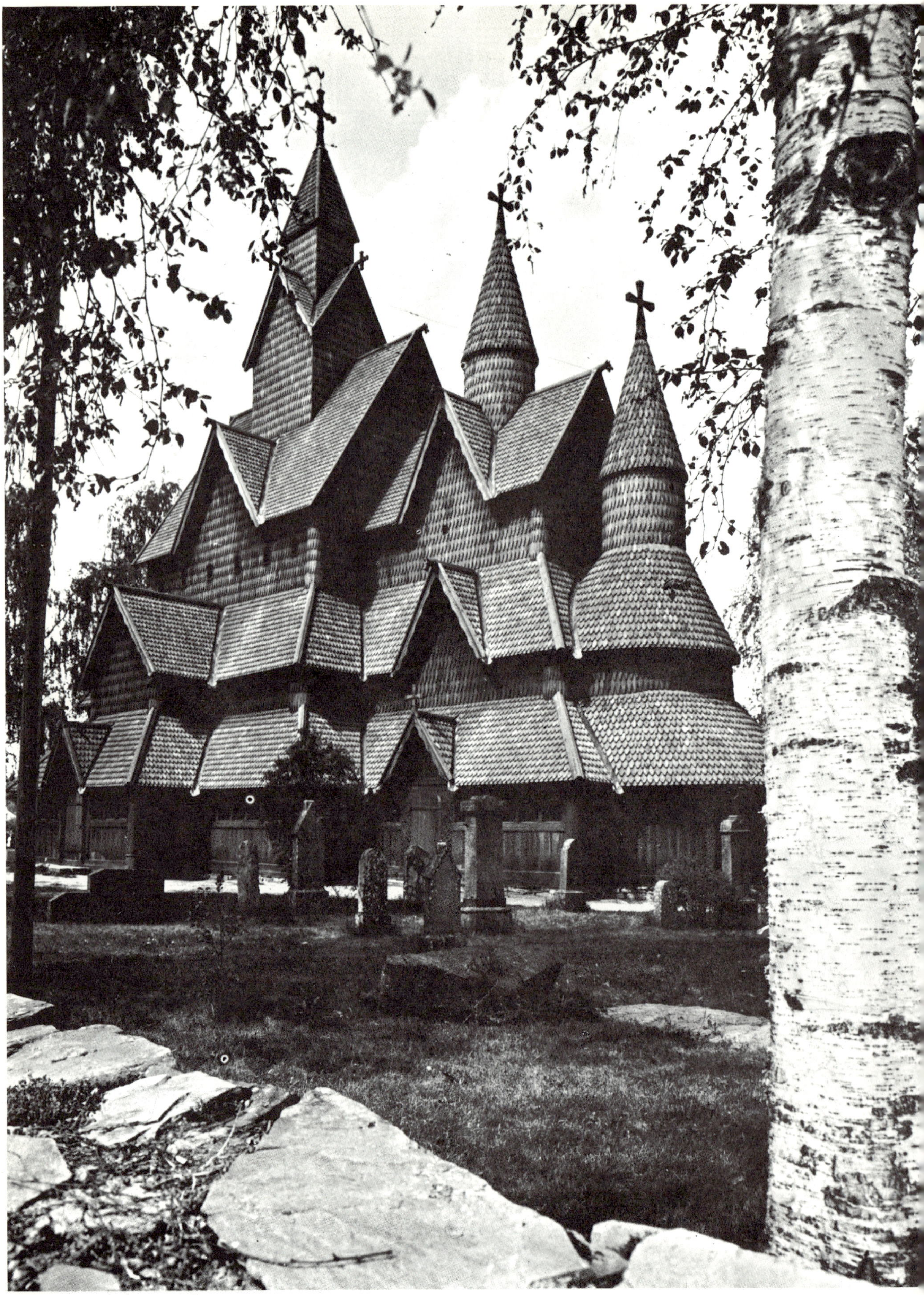

Heddal stave church in Norway. Paganism held out much longer in the Scandinavian countries than in England and Germany and it was not until the tenth and eleventh centuries that the Norwegian people were finally converted to Christianity. Though idols were destroyed, temples burne and heathen worshippers either driven out or put to death, it is thought that the form of pagan temples has been preserved in the so-called stave churches of which that at Heddal is an example.

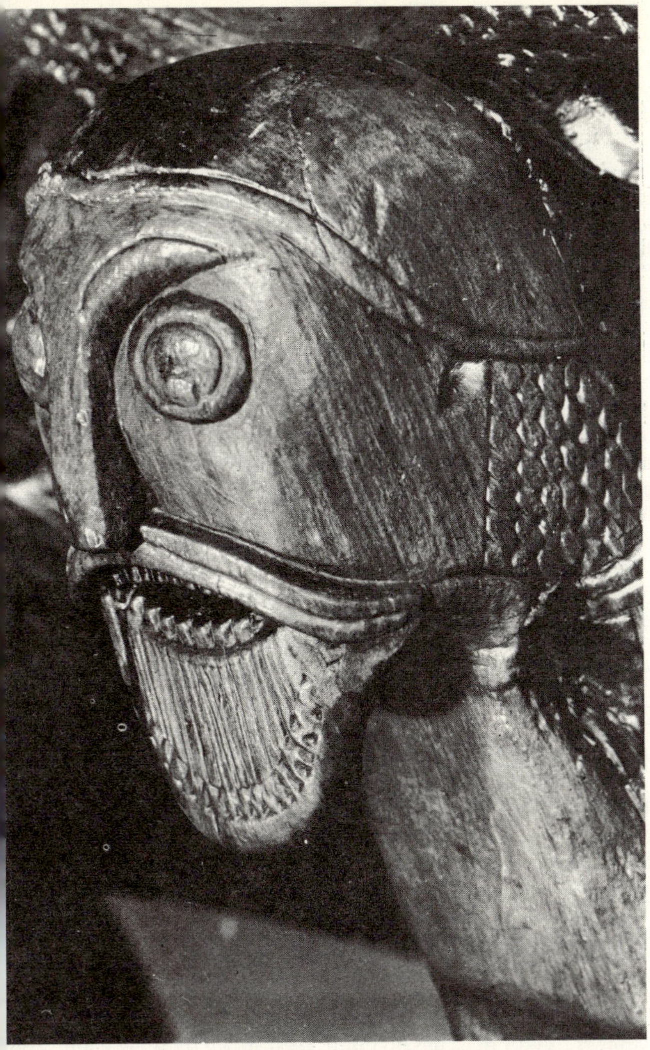

Left Man's head detail from the Oseberg chariot. Chariots were often associated with the gods in Teutonic mythology – the most famous probably being those of Thor and Frey. Tacitus describes a ceremonial progress made in a chariot by the goddess Nerthus and it is possible that the Oseberg chariot may have been used in some such ceremony, the occupant of the grave having been suggested by some to have been a priestess of the Vanir.
Ninth century A.D.

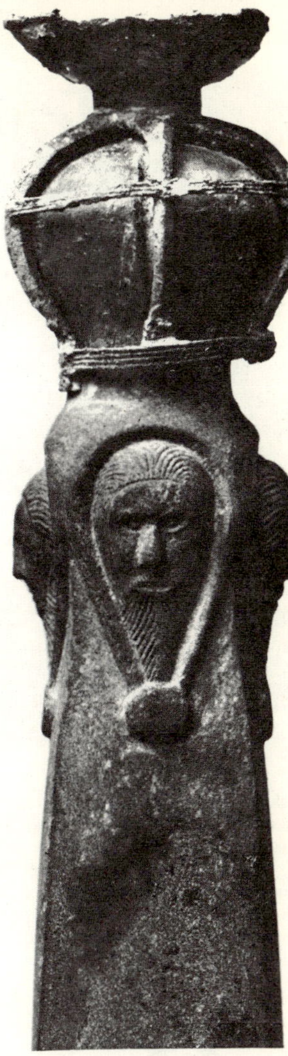

Right Ceremonial whetstone from the Sutton Hoo ship burial. This great, four-sided whetstone, twenty-two inches long and over six in height, is far too elaborate to have served for such a purpose and was probably used as a sceptre. Four human masks carved in low relief decorate the two ends which taper towards a red-painted terminal knob surmounted by a bronze saucer only one of which survives. The burial appears to have been the cenotaph of an East Anglian king. Seventh century A.D.

This distinction is understandable if we take into account the two kinds of societies. Germany, especially at the times of the migrations, still reflected a primitive society of the religious-monarchic type; Scandinavia of the Eddic and saga time, in particular Norway and to an even greater extent its colony Iceland, shows the resistance of a great number of chieftains against the establishment of a unified monarchy of the 'Odinic' type. While kingly society looked to Woden as its principal god, a society composed of independent warriors, relying more on physical force than on cunning or birth, looked to Donar.

Norse poets have drawn Thor very vividly. In him they saw the very apotheosis of the warrior, rude, simple and noble, always ready to face combat and danger, a tireless adversary of giants and demons, a hero without fear, who disdained repose. In one of the poems of the *Edda* he confronts Odin, and the poet not without humour shows Thor's gaucherie and, in spite of the nobility of his character, something of his brutality.

In the course of his travels across the world Thor one day reached the shore of a sea inlet which he could not cross. He hailed the ferryman on the opposite bank. Now this ferryman, who had disguised himself and taken the name Harbard, or 'Grey Beard', was none other than Odin himself. 'Take me to the other side,' Thor shouted to him, 'and I'll give you a share of the good things in my sack, my oatmeal porridge and my herrings.' 'Peasant!' replied Odin. 'You are only a penniless vagabond, a barefooted beggar, a brigand and a horse-thief. My ferry is not made for the likes of you.' Thor then explained who he was and enumerated some of his mighty deeds. 'It was I,' he said, 'who killed Hrungnir, the giant with a head like a rock. And what, pray, were you up to at that time?' 'Me?' the false Harbard answered mockingly, 'I, for five years running, helped a king to fight his enemies and I took advantage of the occasion to win the love and favours of his daughter. Isn't that an exploit quite as glorious as yours?' 'I have also vanquished women,' said Thor, 'and I have exterminated malevolent giants. A thing very necessary to do, for otherwise the race of giants would increase too fast,' 'Quite,' said Odin, 'but you also once hid yourself in terror in the glove of the giant Skrymir!' Odin was alluding to an adventure (which will be related shortly) in which Thor had cut a rather ridiculous figure. Less skilled than the ferryman in finding words and in marshalling his arguments, Thor decided not to defend his reputation; instead he continued to recount the victories he had gained against the giants of the East. 'And I, too,' Odin interrupted banteringly, 'I have been in these Eastern parts. There I met a beautiful maiden, clad in white linen and adorned with golden jewels. She responded to my caresses and yielded to me.' In vain Thor attempted to boast of past triumphs; Odin continued to mock him and, refusing to take him in the ferry, sent him away. On this occasion Thor appeared awkward and oafish. This poem reflects a distinctly Odinic attitude, and defines clearly, though with satirical exaggeration, the distinction between the two divine functions. 'Odin has the nobles who fall in battle, while Thor has the race of peasants.'

He was none the less the favourite god of many tribes. He was the fearless and invincible warrior of imposing stature whose protection one hoped to obtain. His face was adorned with a long red beard. His powerful voice rose above the tumult of battle and filled the enemy with terror. Following his example, the Teutons would go into battle hoping to frighten their opponents with shouts and protracted bellows. Thor's normal weapon was the stone hammer already mentioned, which the Latins compared with the club of Hercules.

In origin this hammer was doubtless a meteorite which, they imagined, had fallen with a thunderbolt during a storm. Afterwards a legend sprang up and it was said that this hammer was the work of a dwarf, skilled in iron work. Never did this dreaded weapon – which was thrown – miss its mark. Afterwards it would return of its own accord to Thor's hand and, when necessary, become so small that he could easily hide it under his garments. It had a name,

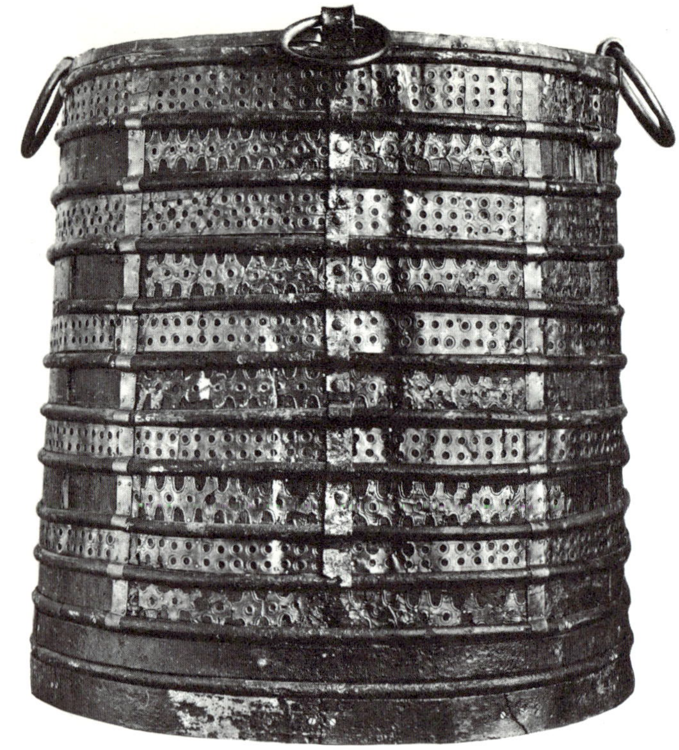

Bucket from the Oseberg ship burial. The Teutons believed in the existence of a subterranean land for the dead, who were consequently provided with the objects they would need in another life. This richly-decorated bucket formed part of the funerary equipment of Norwegian lady of the Viking period and was one of a large collection of personal possessions buried with her. Wood with brass rim, bands and handles. Ninth century A.D.

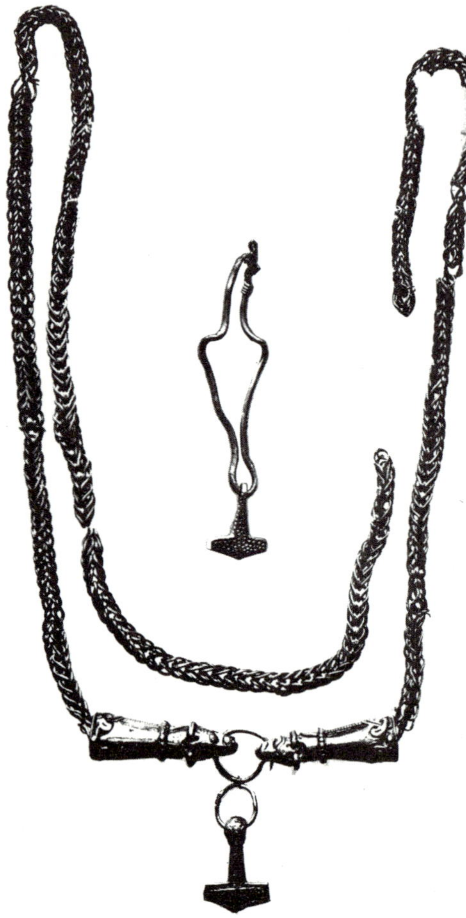

Thor's hammer in the form of pendants. This jewellery is in silver. Magic power was certainly attributed to it. National Museum, Copenhagen.

Mjolnir, which meant 'The Destroyer'. A magic object, the hammer Mjolnir not only served to fight the enemy but also to give solemn consecration to public or private treaties, and more especially to marriage contracts. Hence Thor was for long considered in Norway as the patron of nuptials and the protector of married couples.

In addition to this miraculous hammer Thor possessed two other talismans. One was a girdle which doubled the strength of his limbs as soon as he belted it around his waist; and the other a pair of iron gloves which he needed in order to grasp and hold the shaft of his hammer.

Like the other gods Thor had his own dwelling in Asgard; it was called the palace of Bilskirnir and was situated in the region named Thrudvang, 'the field of Strength'. Bilskirnir had no fewer than five hundred and forty rooms; it was the largest palace anyone had ever heard of. When he left it Thor loved to roam the world in a vehicle drawn by two he-goats. This singular means of transport on occasion took him as far as the kingdom of the dead. If, in the course of his travels, Thor was overtaken by hunger he would kill and cook the goats. The following day he had merely to place his sacred hammer on the hide of the dead beasts for them to leap to their feet again, alive and ready for the road.

A certain tradition makes Thor Odin's son. But this story was only believed in those regions where Odin was regarded as the supreme lord of all the gods. His mother, they said, was the goddess Jörd, that is to say 'the Earth'. Thor had a wife, Sif, who was the personification of conjugal fidelity. He was the father of several children who were, like himself, distinguished for prodigious bodily strength. His two sons Magni (Strength) and Modi (Anger) would one day inherit his hammer and in a new-made world replace him.

As the idealised image of the Germanic warrior Thor was an immensely popular god and the hero of numerous legends. The old bards usually took pleasure in telling how he got the better of evil giants. It sometimes happened that Thor, who was a little lacking in finesse, would let himself be hoodwinked by demons more subtle than himself; but as soon as it came to blows there was no one capable of withstanding him.

One morning Thor woke up to find that his hammer was missing. Worried and not knowing what to do, he went to ask the advice of Loki, whose wits were sharp and who was full of wile. 'The precious hammer,' said Loki, 'has no doubt been stolen by some giant.' And he offered to go himself in search of the talisman. From the goddess Freyja he borrowed the magic robe of feathers which enabled its wearer to fly through the air, and swiftly he reached the abode of the giants. There he soon ran into the giant Thrym, questioned him and discovered that he was the thief. The hammer had been hidden underground at a depth of eight fathoms. Thrym consented to return it only if he were given the goddess Freyja as a wife. When this reply was brought back the Aesir were thrown into a state of consternation. They assembled and deliberated but could find no way of avoiding Thrym's demand. Then they resigned themselves to asking Freyja to accept the proposed bargain. But Freyja refused in indignation. Her fury was so great that the veins in her neck swelled until they burst her golden necklace which rolled to the ground. Embarrassed, the Aesir then resolved on a stratagem. They would dress up Thor himself in women's clothes, cover him with a bridal veil and adorn his neck with Freyja's necklace.

At first hesitating, Thor finally agreed to the scheme. Dressed as a woman he went to the land of Thrym. Loki, disguised as a servant, accompanied him. The two Aesir were given a magnificent welcome in the giant's palace, and Thrym immediately gave orders for the wedding banquet to be prepared. The alleged bride ate with an appetite which astonished one and all. 'She' devoured everything which had been reserved for the women of the palace, namely: one entire ox, eight large salmon and numerous side-dishes. In addition 'she' drank three barrels of mead. The giant marvelled at such voracity. The wily Loki was quick to offer an explanation. For eight days running, he said, Freyja had refused all food and drink, so eager had she been to come to the land of the giants.

Thrym was reassured and more smitten with love than ever. Lecherously he eyed his fiancée and raised her veil to snatch a kiss. But when he saw the goddess's ruddy face and the lightning which flashed from her eyes he leapt away as though he had been stung. Loki again reassured him. For the last eight nights, he explained, Freyja had been unable to sleep, so excited was she, and so feverish with longing to depart for the land of the giants. That was why her eyes flashed fire. Thrym by now was impatient to make his union with Freyja legal and to give it ritual consecration. He therefore sent for the hammer Mjölnir and ordered that it be placed, according to the custom, on the bride's knees. Thor's heart laughed in his bosom. His hand closed firmly on the weapon. Then throwing off his veil he brandished Mjölnir joyfully, struck down Thrym and all Thrym's band of giants. Then contentedly he returned to the other Aesir.

Thor loved to fight not only giants but also monsters. In youth he had resolved to slay the great serpent of Midgard whose innumerable coils caused such violent tempests in the ocean which surrounded the earth. He travelled to distant lands where one day he asked shelter from a giant named Hymir. The next morning Hymir was preparing to go fishing when Thor begged to come along and help. The giant was contemptuous of the suggestion: what possible aid could be expected from a man so young and puny? Thor was annoyed by these insulting words and with difficulty restrained himself from letting Hymir feel the weight of his hammer then and there. But he put off his vengeance for later. 'What sort of bait?' he asked the giant, 'ought one to take along?' 'If you don't know,' Hymir answered rudely, 'it's none of my business to tell you.' Calmly Thor grabbed hold of one of the giant's bulls, wrenched off its head and tossed it into the boat. Then he took the oars and began to row. Hymir who at first had regarded him sarcastically was soon forced to admit that his guest was a first-class seaman. Some time later they reached the spot where it was the giant's habit to fish. He had never, he said, dared row out any farther, and he ordered Thor to ship the oars. But Thor ignored him and continued to row towards the region where he supposed the great serpent of Midgard to be.

Then he prepared his tackle, fixed the bull's head to his hook and cast it into the sea. The serpent immediately plunged for the bait and swallowed it greedily. It had scarcely felt the prick of the hook before it began to thrash about wildly. It tugged on the line with such violence that Thor's two fists were dragged and banged against the gunwales. Thor stiffened and propped his knees against the inner boards of the boat. The boards gave way and he suddenly found himself standing on the bottom of the sea. Thanks to this firm foothold he succeeded in lifting the serpent and half-hoisting it into the boat. One cannot, says the old Icelandic bard, imagine a spectacle more terrifying than Thor fixing the monster with eyes which flashed like lightning while, from the bottom of the boat, the monster stared back at him, spitting venom. Hymir was seized with fright. Taking advantage of a moment when Thor reached out for his hammer he approached, knife in hand, and cut the line. The serpent wriggled free and fell back into the water. In haste Thor threw his hammer, but he was too late: the monster had already vanished into the depths of the sea.

A long time was to elapse before the two adversaries again found themselves face to face. Only at the moment of the great struggle between the gods and the coalition of all their enemies did the serpent of Midgard finally perish beneath Thor's blows. As for the giant whose cowardice had permitted the serpent to escape, Thor struck him so roughly on the head that the blow sent him rolling into the ocean waves where he was drowned. Then Thor peacefully regained the shore by walking across the bottom of the sea.

It happened only once that Thor believed himself vanquished by a giant. But this was merely an illusion; an adroit magician had succeeded in hoodwinking him. One day, accompanied by Loki and two young peasants, Thor crossed the sea and landed in the country of the giants. The four travellers soon arrived in a forest so vast that even after marching all day they had not reached the end of it. When evening fell they looked for shelter and were delighted to see in the midst of the forest a large empty house. True, it was a rather odd construction and they noted with astonishment that the front door was as wide as the house itself. But they were travel-weary and did not pause to examine it further. They entered, made themselves comfortable and fell asleep.

At midnight there was a sudden and violent earthquake. The floor pitched like a ship tossed by the waves. Our travellers woke with a start, fled from the house and took refuge in a small adjoining shed. Thor took up a position before the door, hammer in hand, prepared to repel all enemies. All night long they heard dull sounds and rumblings in the surrounding darkness. No one, however, made an appearance.

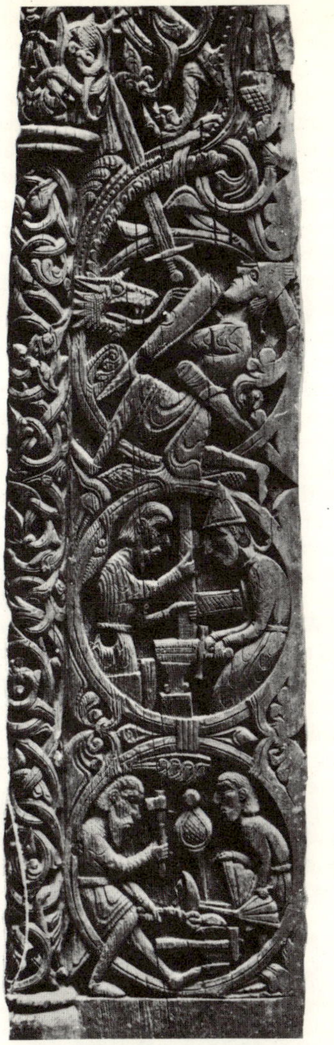

Scenes from the life of Sigurd. The old pagan mythology was of remarkable vitality and scenes from the story of the Volsungs are even found carved on the door-jambs of the twelfth-century church of Hylestad in Norway. In the bottom circle Regin is shown forging a sword for Sigurd who then puts it to the test in the scene above. In the circle at the top he kills the dragon Fafnir.

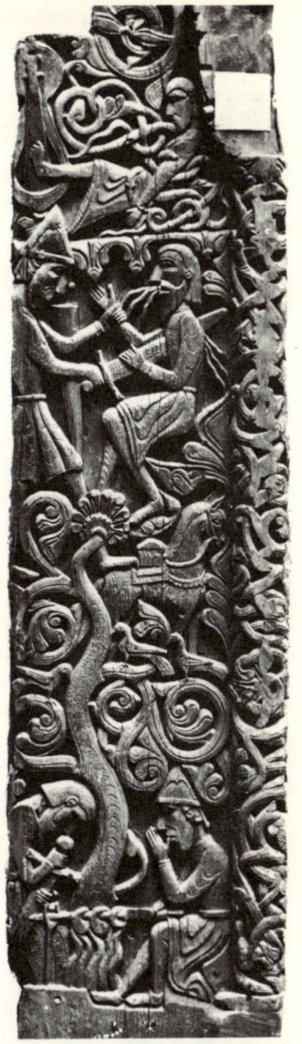

Further scenes from the life of Sigurd at Hylestad church. Below Sigurd and Regin roast the dragon's heart. By tasting its blood Sigurd is enabled to understand the language of the birds who warn him against Regin and he kills him, above. At the top Gunnar is shown in the snake pit with his hands tied behind him. He is playing the harp with his feet in order to charm the snakes.

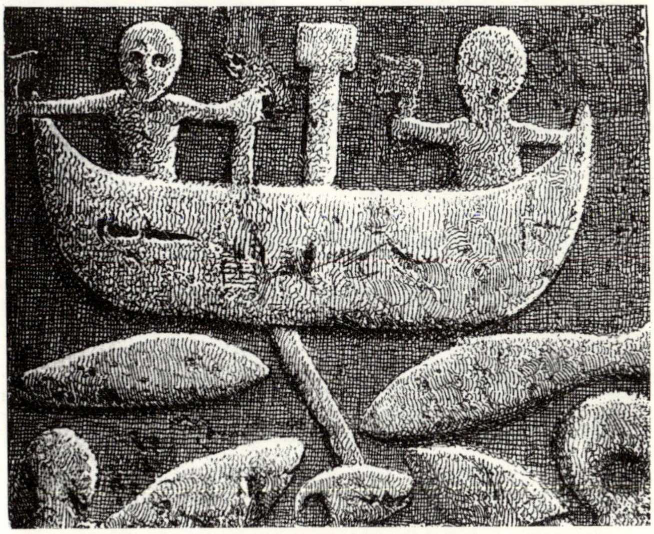

Thor fishing for the serpent of Midgard. Thor is seated on the left. In his right hand he holds his hammer and in his left the line, which he has baited with a bull's head.
Detail from one of the bas-reliefs on the Gosforth Cross, Cumberland.

At dawn Thor ventured out into the forest. Soon he came upon a man of vast stature stretched on the ground and snoring loudly. He now understood the origin of the nocturnal rumblings. In anger he was on the point of striking the noisy sleeper with his hammer when the fellow woke up. He jumped to his feet and introduced himself. He was a giant and his name was Skrymir. 'As for you,' said Skrymir to the silent god, 'there's no need to ask your name. You are Thor, the As. But tell me, where have you dragged my glove?' Stupefied, Thor then realised that he and his three companions had spent the night in the giant's glove which they had mistaken for a house. The small shed in which they had afterwards taken refuge was the thumb of the glove.

Skrymir joined Thor's little group and even politely offered to carry the sack in which they kept their food on his own back. All day the five companions continued the journey together and when night came they halted beneath an oak. Skrymir, saying he was exhausted, stretched out on the ground and immediately fell asleep.

Meanwhile Thor, Loki and the two young peasants, who were dying of hunger, began to loosen the knots of the sack which contained the food they had brought; but discovered that they could not. The giant had tightened the knots in such a fashion that all efforts to untie them failed. Thor was seized with rage. He grasped his hammer and brought it down smartly on Skrymir's head. The giant half woke up. 'It seemed to me', he yawned, 'that a leaf fluttered down on my head.' Then he dropped off to sleep again.

Some hours later Thor, whose irritation had only increased, again struck the giant. This time he put such strength behind the blow that the head of the hammer sank deep into the giant's skull. 'It felt,' murmured the giant, waking up, 'almost as though an acorn dropped on my head.' And he closed his eyes again.

By daybreak Thor was unable to control himself and he landed Skrymir such a blow on the temple that the hammer disappeared up to the shaft. The giant sat up and rubbed his cheek. 'Birds,' he said, 'probably perched up there in the tree. Some of their droppings seem to have fallen on me.' Then, turning towards Thor, he inquired 'Are you awake? It's time to be off. You're not far from Utgard where you're going. There you'll find fellows much stronger than I. And buckling up his sack he disappeared into the forest.

Thor, Loki and their two companions continued the journey alone and towards midday arrived in front of a great fortified castle. Its walls were so high that the travellers had to throw back their heads to see the battlements. The entrance was barred by a heavy grille. In vain the gods attempted to open it. In the end they had to slide through the bars. They then walked forward and entered a huge hall where numerous giants were assembled. King Utgardaloki, lord of the castle, scarcely bothered to return their salute. He shrugged contemptuously and ironically inquired if it could be true that the puny weakling he beheld was the celebrated god Thor. He added that no one was authorised to enter the castle without first proving by some noble deed that he was worthy to approach those who lived there. It would thus be necessary that each of the newcomers measure his prowess, in the art he best understood, with one of the giants here present.

Loki first stepped forward. He boasted of his prowess in eating, much and quickly. The king gave him the giant Logi for an opponent. The two contestants were served with vast quarters of meat on plates as big as vats. In a brief space of time Loki had eaten all his meat, leaving behind nothing but the bones. But his adversary had, in the meantime, gulped down both meat and bones, and the plate as well.

Then came the turn of the young peasant Thjalfi. He claimed to be able to outrun any man or any giant. For an opponent he was given Hugi. Thjalfi ran as quickly as lightning itself, but in vain: Hugi left him far behind.

At last it was Thor's turn to show his skill. No one, he declared with complete assurance, could drink as much or as quickly as he. Utgardaloki then sent for the horn which the warriors of his establishment were accustomed to empty in one, or at the most, two

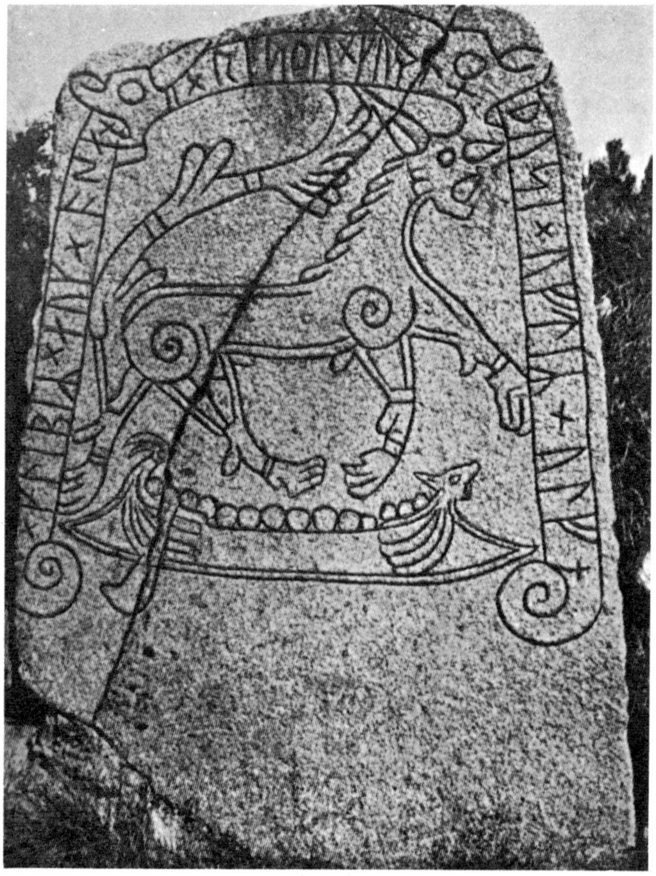

Fenrir. The most terrible of Loki's offspring, Fenrir fathered the brood of wolves whose coming heralded the waning of the power of the gods. Here he strides across the sky above the ship of the North as he accompanies Loki and the other giants against the assembled gods at *ragna rok*. In the final titanic battle between the gods and giants he swallowed Odin but was himself slain by Odin's son, Vidar. Detail from engraved stone at Skaane.

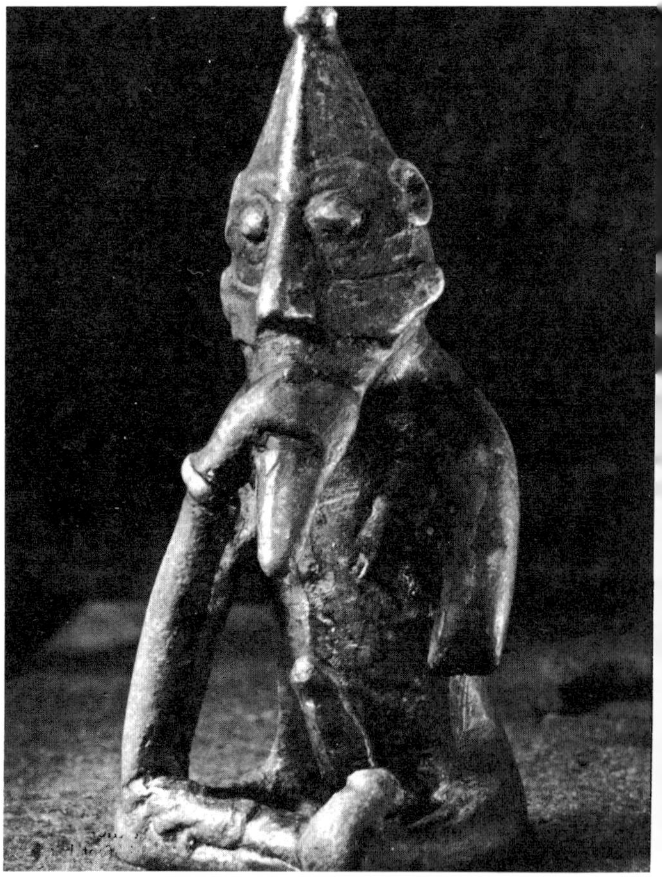

Frey. The best known and most important of a second race of gods worshipped by the Scandinavians, the Vanir, Frey was a god of plenty and fertility. Unlike the gods of the Aesir who were essentially of a warlike character, the gods of the Vanir were pacific and benevolent and concerned themselves with the fruitfulness of plants, animals and men.
Frey was particularly popular in Sweden and was worshipped in the great temple at Uppsala. Statuette from Sodermanland, Sweden.

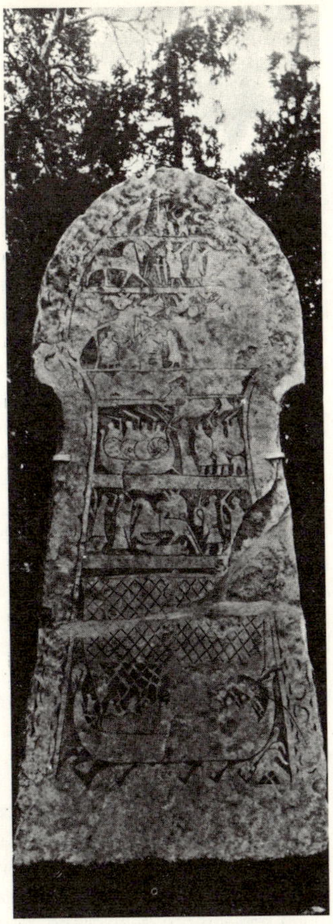

Funerary stone with decorative designs. Hammars, island of Gotland. The war scenes engraved on this stone doubtless recall the mighty deeds of a vanished hero. At the same time, however, their object was to assure that the deceased was nobly received in the Kingdom of the dead.

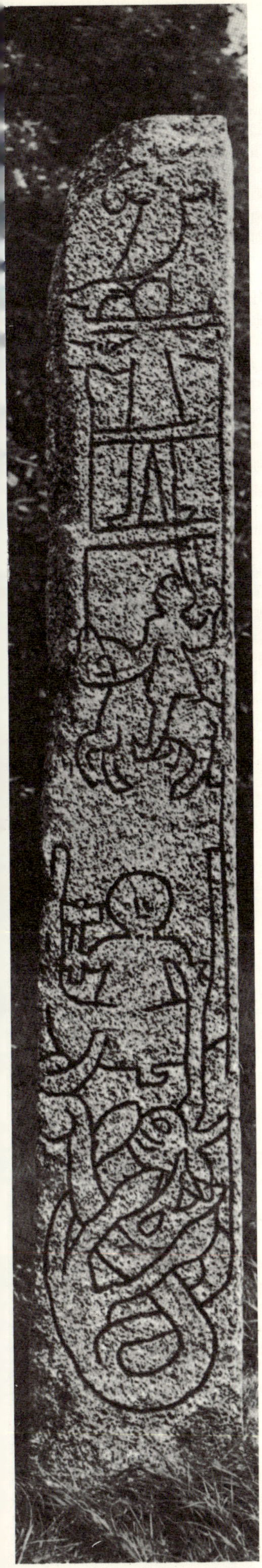

Thor and the Serpent of Midgard. Thor is standing in Hymir's boat holding his hammer in his right hand and the line baited with the bull's head with which he has caught the serpent in his left. His feet have gone through the bottom of the boat in the course of the struggle. On this occasion the serpent escaped but in the final battle Thor succeeded in killing him only to die immediately afterwards. Runic stone from Uppland in Sweden.

draughts. Thor seized the drinking horn and once, twice, thrice took long, deep draughts. But, when he put it down again, the level of the liquid was scarcely lower than when he had begun.

Thor was covered with confusion and, in order to regain the company's esteem, willingly accepted a second test of his valour. They invited him to lift a certain cat from the ground where he was sitting. Thor bent down and seized the animal. With all his might he struggled to lift it, but the cat was immovable. At most one of its paws rose an inch or two from the ground. 'Would you,' Utgardaloki then suggested, 'care to wrestle with Elli, my nurse? She is only a poor old woman.' Thor accepted the challenge, but the more he struggled the more unshakable his adversary appeared to become. In the end it was Thor himself who fell on one knee.

Bitterly humiliated, the Aesir next morning prepared to take their departure. But before they left their host, Utgardaloki, suddenly decided to explain what had actually occurred the day before.

'Never,' he told Thor, 'would I have dared admit you to my castle had I known that your strength was so terrifying. It was I myself whom you met in the forest. I called myself Skrymir. The blows of your hammer would infallibly have killed me had I not protected my head with solid mountains.' And he showed Thor the chain of mountains nearby and pointed out the deep valleys which Thor's hammer had dug.

Then he explained why the gods had been vanquished in the tests he had proposed. If Loki had been unable to equal his opponent, it was because that opponent had been fire itself – for such is the meaning of the word Logi. If Thjalfi had been outrun by Hugi, it was because Hugi was none other than 'thought'. Finally Thor had been unable to empty the drinking-horn because the end of the horn was plunged into the inexhaustible sea. Thor had, however, actually succeeded in slightly lowering the sea-level and had thus produced the first ocean tides. The beast whom he thought was a cat, was in reality the serpent of Midgard whose coils surrounded the earth itself and when he lifted its paw earthquakes had shaken the world. As for the old woman with whom Thor had wrestled in vain, she was Elli, old age itself, which no one could ever conquer.

When he learned how he had been made a fool of Thor seized up his hammer to kill Utgardaloki, but the enchanter had already vanished and with him the castle. Around him Thor saw only the great deserted plain and the grass which grew there.

Thus, even though Thor sometimes appeared rather simple and even a little slow-witted, he never failed to win the Teutons' admiration for the might of his arm and his physical courage. He is found again in many a legend; for in the end he took part in the career of practically every other god.

Tiw-Tyr. This god, in spite of many scholars who have claimed him as the original great god of the Germanic peoples, belongs to the same stratum as Donar and Woden. The South Germans gave him the name Ziu, the North Germans Tiuz. The Scandinavians called him Tyr, the Anglo-Saxons Tiw. It is generally admitted that all these Germanic appellations correspond to the Sanskrit *dyaus*, the Greek *Zeus* and the Latin *Deus*. If this is the case, then the Germanic names for the god must derive from a common Indo-European name which began by simply signifying 'divinity'. Later the name in many countries designated the sky god. Originally Tiw had been a god corresponding to the Indian Mitra, who was patron of the legal side of government, but with the gradual militarisation of Germanic society, he had gradually been restricted to the field of rules governing battle, at which time the Romans identified him with their Mars, and the Latin *Martis dies* (French *Mardi*) by transposition became the day of Tiw, or Tuesday; and finally he was relegated to a position of very minor importance. In German the same god had a second name which was *Things*, and from which the German Tuesday, *Dienstag*, is derived.

Perhaps it is Tiw who is alluded to in a curious Latin inscription on a Roman altar discovered at Housesteads in Northumberland, near to Hadrian's Wall. This altar dates from the third century and was erected by German soldiers serving with the Roman legions. It bears this Latin inscription: '*Deo Marti Thincso et duabus Alaisiagis Bede et Fimmiline et numini Augusti Germani cives Tuihanti v. s. l. m. (votum solverunt libenter merito).*' That is: To the god Mars Thincsus and to the two goddesses Alaisiages Beda and Fimmilina and to the majesty of the divine Augustus the German citizens of Twenthe address this merited homage. (The province of Twenthe was north of the Rhine on the present frontiers of Holland and Germany.)

The epithet *Thincsus* shows that Tiw was seen as a Mars, who presided over the *thing*, the assembly where discussions of the community are regulated according to law. It has been pointed out that Tiw's spear is less a weapon than a sign of juridical power.

The two goddesses Beda and Fimmilina are quite unknown. The interpretation of their names and also of the term Alaisiages which applies to them both presents the greatest difficulties. But it is agreed that they were probably Teutonic goddesses.

Since Donar very early pushed Tiw into the background, Tiw occupies a very small place in German legend. Traditions about him are scarcely more abundant in the North. The name Tyr, however, occurs fairly often in Norse poetry. The skalds attempted to bring Tyr into the great family of Teutonic divinities. Some made him son of the giant Hymir, others said that he was the son of Odin. He was supposed to be extremely brave and enterprising. It was often he who awarded victory to one of the sides engaged in combat. Thus it was prudent to invoke him when going into battle.

In one legend the poets give him the leading role, a tale which bears witness to the energy of his character. An oracle had warned the gods that the giant wolf Fenrir was one of their most dangerous enemies whom it would be wise to reduce to a state in which it could do no harm. They decided not to kill it – for that would be to soil consecrated ground – but instead to chain it up. Twice they had chains forged, but the wolf Fenrir had only to stretch himself in order to break them. Then they begged the dwarfs to fashion a chain which nothing could break.

Soon the dwarfs brought them a wonderous chain composed of six ingredients: the miaul of a cat, the beard of a woman, the roots of a mountain, the tendons of a bear, the breath of a fish and the spittle of a bird. This chain was supple and soft as a silk ribbon and yet of a solidity which passed every test. The gods, now confident that they could bind Fenrir, threw him a challenge. Each of them, they said, had tried to break the chain and none had succeeded. They proposed that the wolf should have a try in order to show his strength.

But Fenrir was full of suspicion, fearing a trap. He did not wish to appear a coward, however, and consented to make the attempt, but on one condition: one of the gods must, he insisted, place a hand in his jaws. In case of trickery the hand would be bitten off. The Aesir exchanged glances. Knowing full well the trickery which had been planned, none was prepared to sacrifice a hand.

Tyr then calmly extended his right hand and placed it between the wolf's jaws. The other gods bound Fenrir who then attempted to break the chain. But the more he struggled the tighter the bonds became. When they saw that his efforts were vain the gods began to laugh. Only Tyre refrained from laughter; for he knew what was coming. And indeed the wolf, understanding that he had been outwitted, bit off the god's right hand at the wrist. Thenceforth Tyr was one-handed. It is significant that Tiw's most important appearance in mythology is in a matter of legal contract. With Woden, he forms a couple which is found elsewhere among the Indo-European peoples, the one-handed and the one-eyed, the man of law and the man of magical fury.

Loki. Loki is not one of the oldest gods in the Germanic pantheon, but in Scandinavian legend his name appears as often, if not more often, than those of Odin or Thor. It seems certain that he was at first regarded as a benevolent divinity; but little by little they preferred to represent Loki as a kind of superior demon, almost always occupied with making mischief. Among the gods he was a sort of *enfant terrible*. He shared their lives and on many occasions zealously served them, and yet he almost never ceased working to undermine their power. It was he in the end who brought about their downfall. Thus we should know something about him as a prelude to an account of the 'Twilight of the Gods'. He was, however, a creation of Scandinavian imagination only. He belonged in no way to the communal tradition of the whole Germanic peoples. It is above all the skalds of the ninth and tenth centuries whose poems have preserved the story of his adventures.

Loki was first conceived as a fire demon. His name is related to a Germanic root which signifies 'flame'. His father was Farbauti, 'who by striking gave birth to fire'. His mother was Laufey, 'the wooded isle', who furnished material for lighting the fire. Popular locutions still current in Scandinavian countries frequently associate his name with phenomena in which fire plays a part. In Norway, for example, when a fire is heard crackling on the hearth they say that Loki is thrashing his children.

This former demon slowly grew in dignity. In the legends in which he plays a part he always appears as one of the Aesir. At the beginning of time Loki and Odin exchanged vows of friendship which, consecrated by ritual practices honoured among the Germans, made the two gods 'blood brothers'. Loki was handsome, attractive and very attentive to the goddesses who rarely resisted him. There was something of the diabolic about him; and as the legends concerning him are of rather late invention it is not impossible that he was attributed with certain traits borrowed from the medieval Christian conception of the Devil.

We have already seen how Loki helped Thor to recapture the hammer which the giant Thrym had stolen. Loki was not always so helpful. When his own interests were at stake he did not hesitate to betray this same Thor. One day he borrowed from the goddess Freyja her falcon-plumed robe, put it on and flew through the air. Soon he reached the house of the giant Geirröd and landed on the roof. The giant perceived this singular bird, caught it and put it into a cage. For three months Loki thus remained a prisoner. Geirröd, not content with depriving him of his liberty, also refused to feed him. At the end of the three months Geirröd had the captive bird brought before him, and only then did Loki decide to explain who he was. He begged the giant to release him.

Geirröd consented to do so only on condition that Loki undertook to deliver to him the most powerful and redoubtable of all the Aesir: Thor himself. He also insisted that Thor should be turned over to him without the attributes which rendered him invincible; that is, without his hammer, his iron gloves and the girdle which lent him supernatural strength. Loki accepted all these conditions and seemed to find it quite natural to betray one of the Aesir in order to get himself out of a scrape. He was then set at liberty and returned to Asgard where by means of specious arguments and illusory promises he persuaded Thor to depart for Geirröd's abode, leaving behind his girdle, gloves and hammer. Thor would have been irretrievably lost had he not on the road met the giantess Grid who was devoted to him and who had borne him a child, the As Vidar. Grid put him on his guard against the wily Geirröd and lent him her own gloves, girdle and magic wand. Thanks to these talismans Thor succeeded in avoiding Geirröd's cunningly laid traps and, indeed, in killing the giant and all his followers. But it was not Loki's fault that Thor did not fall into the power of one of the enemies of the gods.

On another occasion it was a goddess whom Loki was ready to sacrifice. He was wandering the earth one day with Odin and Hoenir. The three gods were famished and they had stopped to roast an ox. But an eagle, perched in a tree above them, cast a spell which prevented the meat from cooking – unless the gods promised to accept him as their table-mate. After the gods had acceded to this demand, the eagle claimed the best cuts of the roast. Annoyed by this Loki grabbed a rod and struck the intruder. The eagle flew away, carrying with it the rod which remained fixed to its body, together with Loki himself who was unable to let go. Dragged across the ground, bruised and bleeding, Loki begged for mercy.

Now the eagle was a giant named Thjazi. Delighted to have captured a god, Thjazi immediately imposed conditions. Loki should recover his liberty only if he swore a solemn oath to deliver to Thjazi the goddess Idun and the apples she possessed, miraculous apples which had the power of preserving youth. Idun was one of the inhabitants of Asgard and it was thanks to her magic apples that the gods never grew old. Ignoring the harm he would cause the Aesir, Loki at once agreed to Thjazi's demands. He lured Idun into the forest on the pretext of showing apples to her that were even more beautiful than those she normally offered to the gods. Thjazi, arriving as arranged, seized the goddess and dragged her off to his abode.

The Aesir were not long in noticing the absence of Idun. Deprived of the apples to which they owed their imperishable vigour they began to grow old. They turned on Loki with such threats that he had no alternative but to promise to bring Idun back again. He assumed the form of a hawk and flew towards the kingdom of the giants. He found Idun, changed her into a nut and carried her back towards Asgard. But Thjazi at once realised what had occurred and,

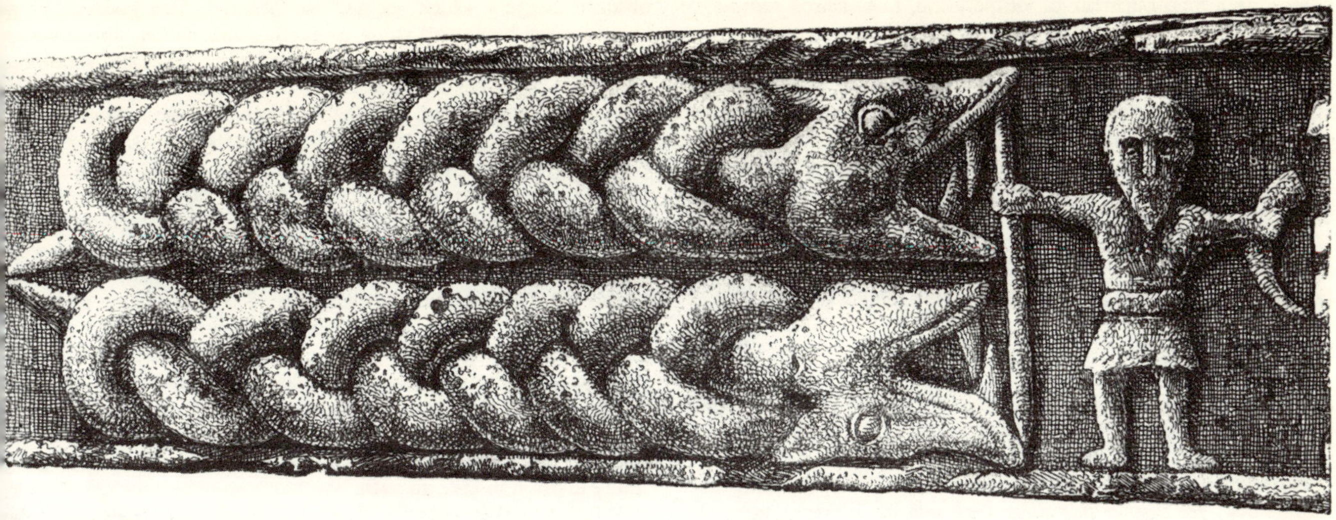

Heimdall, holding in his left hand the horn with which he wakens the gods. Detail from the Gosforth Cross.

changing himself into an eagle, sped through the air after Loki. He might have overtaken him had the gods not hastily built a huge bonfire in which the eagle, as it reached Asgard, burned its wings, fell and was consumed.

Thor's wife, Sif, also suffered from Loki's malice. One day he craftily cut off her lovely tresses. When Thor discovered this he seized Loki in his powerful grip and began industriously to break his bones. Loki cried for mercy and swore an oath that he would persuade the dwarfs to fashion for Sif tresses of pure gold which would grow of their own accord like natural hair. Thor calmed down and Loki visited the forges of the dwarfs, sons of Ivaldir. They promised to make not only the golden tresses but a ship, *Skidbladnir*, which as soon as its sails were hoisted would speed straight towards the desired destination, and also a spear, Gungnir, which would never stop in flight. The two latter talismans were intended for Odin.

Next the imprudent Loki bet a dwarf named Brökk that his brother Sindri, in spite of the great reputation of his skill, would not be able to make such marvels as those which the sons of Ivaldir made. Brökk and Sindri at once set to work. Fearing that they might win the bet – in which his own head was at stake – Loki assumed the form of a gadfly and began to sting and harass them in order to distract them from their work and thus prevent them from finishing it. The two brothers nevertheless succeeded in fashioning the ring Draupnir, which had the virtue of making its owner constantly richer; the golden boar which later belonged to the god Frey, and Thor's famous hammer.

The Aesir were chosen to arbitrate. They declared that Thor's hammer surpassed anything that any dwarf had yet made and that such a treasure would for ever be Asgard's chief protection. The dwarfs Brökk and Sindri had thus won the wager – and Loki's head therefore belonged to them. Loki at first tried to arrange a compromise. Brökk refused it. 'I am yours, then,' said Loki, 'take me.' But as the dwarf was about to seize him Loki vanished. Loki, as it happened, was the owner of shoes which could, at will, immediately carry him beyond the earth and the sea.

The dwarf then went to Thor and complained. Thor lost no time in recapturing the fugitive and handing him over to Brökk. Brökk assured of his rights, announced his intention of cutting Loki's head off. But Loki's resources were not yet exhausted and he began to discuss the matter with vivacity. It was, he admitted, quite true that Brökk had a right to his head, but in the wager nothing had been said about his neck. The dwarf must not, then, remove the slightest part of his neck. Brökk, whose mind was less fertile in such quibbles, did not know what to reply to this fine point. In his embarrassment he resolved at the very least to sew the deceiver's lips together so that he could no longer take advantage of people. He pierced Loki's lips with an awl, and threading stout cord through the holes, knotted it firmly. The precaution was in vain. Loki succeeded in tearing the cord away and thus lightly escaped from a dangerous adventure.

In the end Loki's treachery and love of intrigue got him into trouble with all the other gods. A curious scene in one of the poems of the *Eddas* shows him insulting all the gods of Asgard one after another. A giant, Aegir, lord of the seas, had invited all the gods and all the goddesses to a great feast. Only Thor, who was then travelling in Eastern lands, was absent. A good time was had by all and Aegir's guests were enjoying the simple pleasures of the banquet when suddenly Loki forced open the door of the hall.

Loki had not been invited to the feast, for there was no one against whom he had not played some shabby trick. At the sight of him everyone fell silent. But this frigid welcome did not alter Loki's plans. He began modestly, almost with humility. He was, he explained, only a thirsty traveller. Surely the gods would not refuse him the cup which was given, unasked for, to all passers-by, even strangers. No one answered him. He continued, with affected moderation: let them at least offer him a chair, according to the laws of hospitality; or else let them at least say in so many words that they refused to welcome him.

The gods discussed the matter among themselves and, wishing to respect custom, were inclined to make a place for him among them. Only Bragi, the god of poetry, whose duty it was to welcome the newly arrived, insisted on refusing Loki the seat which he desired. Loki, without yet abandoning his courteous manners, turned towards Odin and reminded him how in the old days they had sworn to be blood brothers. Odin was touched by the memory and ordered Vidar to give up his seat to Loki. A cup was brought and filled according to usage.

Loki began by drinking the health of all the gods present. He added, however, that his good wishes did not extend to Bragi. Bragi, wh , wished to restore peace, apologised for the wounding words he had spoken. He did even more: he offered a horse, a sword and some rings as a mark of reconciliation. But Loki, far from accepting the apology, assumed a haughty tone. Bragi, he said, was a coward; he fled from combat and, while the others exposed themselves to danger, lolled shamelessly on the benches. Bragi, indignant, was about to reply, but his wife Idun begged him not to answer such calculated calumnies.

The contempt which Idun's words betrayed merely fanned Loki's anger. He then attacked all the gods in the hall. In pitiless detail he reminded each of them of the most scandalous episodes in his past life. Nor did he spare the goddesses. There was not one whom he did not accuse of being unfaithful to her husband; he boasted that he himself had enjoyed the favours of many of them. And he named them. With savage delight he confessed to the gods the crimes of which he was voluntarily guilty against each of them. In vain Aegir's guests attempted to return insult for insult. Not one of them could stand up to Loki. Even Odin, who was always praised for his presence of mind and eloquent tongue, was disconcerted by the flood of mockery and abuse which flowed from Loki's lips. Sif approached him and held out a cup of mead, begging him to put an end to the dispute. Loki's response was a further string of insults. He boasted that he had held her in his arms, happy and consenting, she, the wife of the great Thor.

But scarcely had the name of the storm-god been pronounced when in the distance a long rumbling was heard in the mountains. It was Thor who rode in his chariot in the midst of the sounding tempest. He entered the hall, majestic and terrible, commanding silence. In a final outbreak of vituperation, Loki risked reminding the most powerful of all the gods of the humiliating role he had once played in the castle of the enchanter Utgardaloki. Thor brandished his hammer and looked as though he were about to smash in the insulter's skull. Loki was for the first time intimidated: he retreated, but before he left the hall he issued a final threat. Never again, he said to the giant Aegir, would he be able to give a feast like tonight's; for very soon his palace and all that he possessed would be destroyed by flame.

In these words the vindictive Loki announced not only the fate of Aegir's palace, but the burning of the entire world. We shall see later what grim events followed Loki's menacing words.

Heimdall. Among the great Aesir must be counted Heimdall. But of this god who certainly held an important place in Germanic mythology almost nothing is known. He is familiar to us only through the allusions which the poets make to his person, role and power.

He was a god of light. His name probably signifies 'he who casts bright rays'. He may in particular represent the morning light, the dawn of day. He may also personify the rainbow.

In the Indo-European perspective, he occupies a particularly important position, corresponding to that of the Indian Vayu and the Roman Janus. He is the god who presides over the ambiguous beginnings of things, over the *prima* as distinct from the *summa*. Like the guardian Janus, he is guardian of the gods, installed on the threshold of the world of the gods, born in the most ancient times and ancestor of gods and men, considered in their social classes. In the divine assembly, it is he who speaks first, and eschatologically it is he who opens the final phase of the world at the Twilight of the Gods.

The Scandinavians, who are the only Teutons by whom he is mentioned, depict him as tall and handsome. His teeth are of pure gold. He was armed with a sword and mounted on a charger with a glittering mane. He was normally to be found near the great bridge Bifröst (the rainbow) which led from the dwelling-place of men to that of the gods. He was the guardian of this road, the divine sentinel, who warned the Aesir of the approach of their enemies. He required less sleep than a bird. He could see at night as easily as during the day. He could hear the grass growing on earth and the wool on the backs of sheep. He owned a trumpet the sound of which could be heard throughout the world.

He was the sworn enemy of Loki. Loki had only contemptuous laughter for the monotonous sentinel-duty which Heimdall performed, and for the long periods during which he was obliged to remain at the gates of Asgard. Since the beginning of time, as Loki ironically remarked, Heimdall had had to sit, getting his back wet, at his post. But this modest and noble god was able, on occasion, to chastise the diabolical Loki. One day Loki happened to steal the goddess Freyja's necklace. He went to hide it under a reef situated in the far-off Western sea. But Heimdall in the guise of a seal also slipped under this reef and after a fierce struggle with Loki – who had also turned himself into a seal – succeeded in taking possession of the necklace and restoring it to Freyja.

In the final struggle in which the gods fought for their very existence it was, as we shall later see, Heimdall who struck Loki the fatal blow. But he, too, fell beneath his adversary's blows.

Balder. Balder, like Heimdall, was a god of the light. He was the son of Odin and the goddess Frigg. He was so beautiful that he shed radiance around him. None of the Aesir was his equal in wisdom. It was enough to see or hear him to love him. He was the favourite of the gods.

Balder was not only revered in Scandinavia. He was equally popular in Germany. One celebrated magic formula in old German shows him riding with the god Woden. While trotting, his horse sprains a foot, but with a few words filled with esoteric virtue Woden cures it. It is only, however, in the Northern lands that legends of Balder have been preserved. These legends are mainly connected with the history of his death, which was brought about by Loki's malice.

Balder's life had for long been filled with harmony and happiness. But a time came when he was troubled by dreams and presentiments of evil. He explained his disquietude to the other Aesir. Since they were all immensely fond of him they made an effort to forestall the obscure dangers which seemed to threaten. The goddess Frigg begged every being and thing on earth – fire, metal, water, stones and minerals, plants and trees, illnesses, beasts, birds and venomous creatures – to swear an oath never to harm Balder. All undertook this solemn engagement. Balder from then on was invulnerable and the Aesir, as a game, submitted him to various tests. They placed him in the midst of their assembly and shot arrows at him, threw stones or struck him with their weapons. But no projectile, no blow caused him the slightest damage. He remained unwounded and unhurt, to the hilarious mirth of the company.

Loki watched the spectacle and in secret his heart was full of loathing. He assumed the appearance of an old woman and went to see Frigg in her palace. Feigning ignorance, he asked why the gods were so amused. She told him what she had done and how everything on earth had promised to spare Balder. 'Everything? Really everything?' said Loki. 'Have you forgotten nothing?' 'I only overlooked one small plant,' said Frigg. 'It grows to the west of Valhalla and is called Misteltein (mistletoe). It seemed too young to ask it to take an oath.'

Without further inquiries Loki left Frigg and, reassuming his normal shape, hastened to gather the mistletoe from the place indicated. Then he returned to the great field where the gods continued to hurl inoffensive objects at Balder. He turned to one of them, Höd, who held back from the sport because he was blind. 'Why are you not taking part in the game?' Loki asked. 'Why do you not throw something at Balder?' 'It is because I cannot see,' Höd said. 'Besides, I have no weapon.' 'In that case,' said Loki, 'try this wand. Throw it. I will direct you.' Höd took the branch of mistletoe and flung it towards Balder. It pierced him and Balder fell dead. The Aesir, aghast, wept bitterly at the loss of their fair companion. Willingly would they have punished Loki's crime then and there, but the place where they were assembled was consecrated to peace. There it was forbidden to spill blood and no one dared infringe the law.

When they had recovered from their first shock of grief they began to deliberate. Frigg asked if there was not among them one who was prepared to descend into the kingdom of Hel (that is, the kingdom of the dead) to rescue Balder. To him who dared, no matter who he was, she promised her favours in advance. One of Odin's sons, Hermod, at once leapt astride Sleipnir, his father's famous charger, and set forth.

Meanwhile the gods bore the body of Balder to the sea and built the funeral pyre on the boat which had once belonged to him. On it they placed the dead god. Thor, raising his hammer solemnly in the air, gave the pyre its ritual consecration, and then it was set on fire. Balder's horse, fully accoutred, was led to the pyre and the flame consumed him at the same time that it consumed the body of his master. Almost all the gods attended the funeral and even many giants were present, come from their lands of ice and mountains.

While Balder was paid this final tribute Hermod continued his journey through deep and shadowy valleys. For nine days he never left the saddle. He finally reached the river Gjöll at the edge of the underworld. It was crossed by a bridge covered with gold. From the guard he learned that Balder had travelled this way last night with five hundred men. Hermod pursued his way and at last reached the barred gates of the Kingdom of Hel.

There for an instant he dismounted, tightened his saddle-girth, then remounting dug spurs into his steed which leapt the gates at a bound, without even brushing them with its hooves. He penetrated Hel's palace and in the great hall, occupying the seat of honour, he saw the object of his search, his brother Balder. As it was already late he let the night pass before approaching Hel. But early the next morning he explained to the goddess of the infernal regions why the Aesir had sent him here. He beseeched her to allow Balder to return with him to Asgard. Hel was not without pity. If, she said, it was truly the desire of every being and thing in the world that Balder should return to Asgard, then she would willingly set him free. If, on the other hand, there was a single being in the universe who refused to weep for Balder, then she would be obliged to keep him with her.

Hermod returned with this reply to the Aesir. The Aesir then sent forth messengers throughout the world, begging everyone and everything to display his or its grief. At the gods' request the entire world, men and beasts, earth and stones, wood and metal, began to weep for Balder. But when the messengers, delighted with the

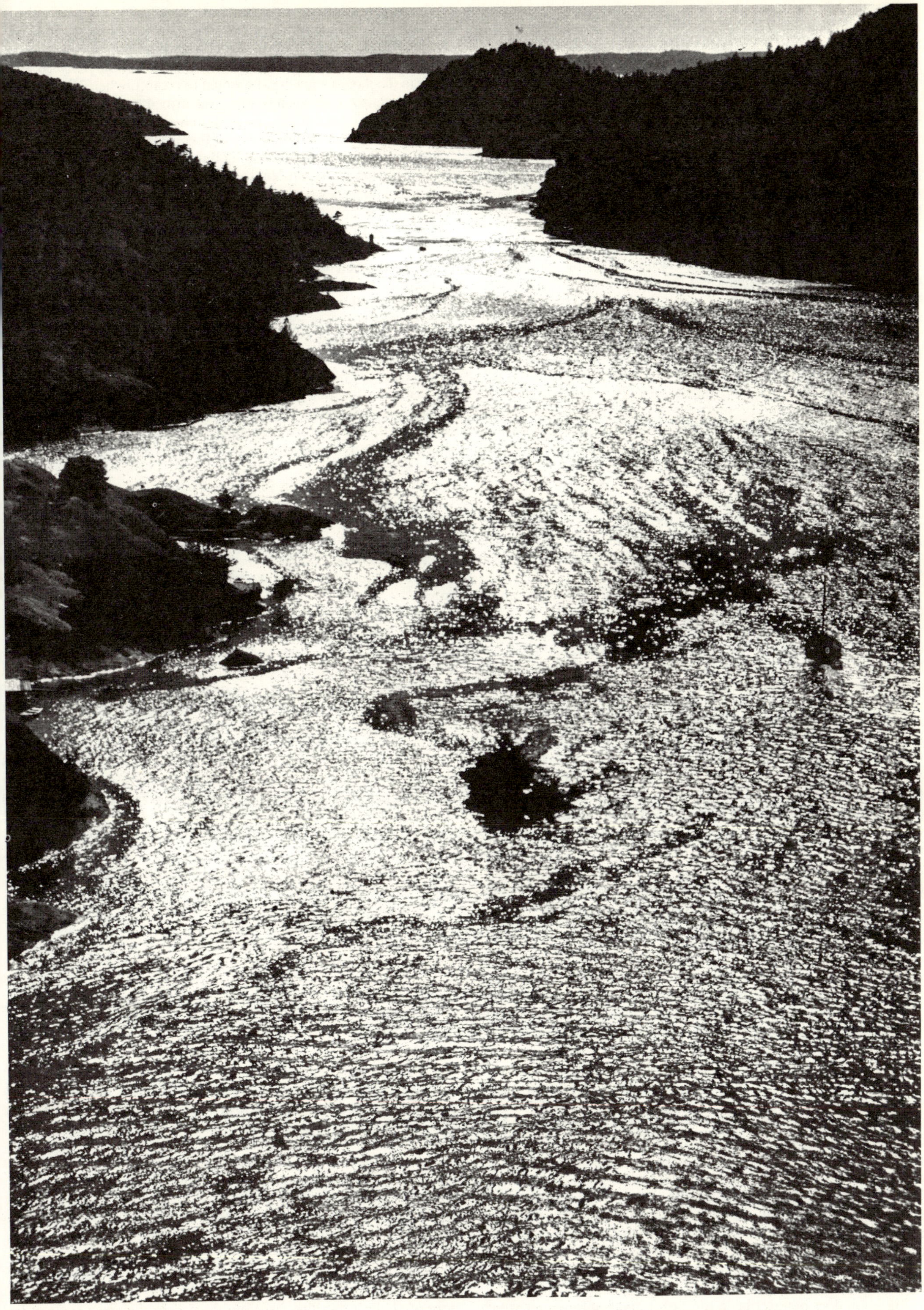

Typical Viking country. The climate and conditions of life have not changed much in rural Scandinavia since the days of the Vikings and it is from such inhospitable shores as these that they sailed in their longships a thousand years ago. The great saga literature of medieval Iceland preserves the spirit of this heroic age while the old pagan religion was kept alive by them long after the rest of Europe had been converted to Christianity.

success of their mission, were returning to Asgard they perceived in a mountain cavern a certain giantess named Thökk who, in spite of their supplications, refused to shed a single tear. 'Neither during his life nor after his death,' she said, 'has Balder rendered me the slightest service. Let Hel keep what is hers.'

Now this elderly giantess was Loki himself who, thus disguised, had found a means of making sure that Balder never returned.

The Vanir: Njörd and Frey. The Aesir were not the only Teutonic gods. In Scandinavia, and especially in Sweden, they also believed in the existence of another race of gods, the *Vanir*. While the Aesir were above all regarded as warrior gods, the Vanir were pacific and benevolent. They provided the fields and pastures and forests with sunlight and life-giving rain. Plants, animals and men themselves multiplied under their guardianship. It was in Spring and Summer that men enjoyed the abundance of their gifts. From them came the harvests, game, and all kinds of riches in general. The Vanir were also the protectors of commerce and navigation.

One Nordic tradition reports that war broke out one day between the belligerent Aesir and the peace-loving Vanir. For some time, scholars imagined that this is a symbolic and poetic account of a conflict which took place in the Scandinavian area between the worshippers of Odin and those of Frey, based on the assumption that the cult of Odin was not introduced into Northern lands until that of Frey was already widespread. But recent investigation has shown that this is not the case, and the war of the Aesir and the Vanir is the continuation of an Indo-European myth represented in India by the struggle of the Nasatya to enter divine society, and at Rome in the mythical history of the war of the Romans and the Sabines. The Vanir have, in fact, no existence apart from those who were sent to Asgard in order to complete the divine society in its triple function of sovereignty, force and fecundity.

However this may be, the following is what the Scandinavian poets and scholars told:

One day the Vanir sent to the Aesir – on a mission which is not explained – a goddess by the name of Gullveig. This goddess was highly skilled in all the practices of sorcery and by her art had acquired much gold. When, alone, she reached the Aesir they were, it is supposed, tempted by her riches. They seized her and submitted her to savage torture. The Vanir demanded satisfaction. They insisted that either a large sum in money should be paid in reparation, or else that their rank should be recognised as equal to that of the Aesir so that they henceforward would receive an equal right to the sacrifices made by the faithful. After taking counsel the Aesir decided to settle the question by fighting. But in the long and cruel war which followed they were very often defeated by their adversaries. They therefore came to an understanding and resigned themselves to treating the Vanir as their equals. On both sides hostages were exchanged. The Aesir turned over the robust Hoenir and the wise Mimir. The Vanir sent their former enemies the mighty Njörd and his son Frey who, from then on, lived in Asgard and were often confused with the Aesir.

The relationship between the three Vanir, Njörd, Frey and Freyja, is a complex one. Tacitus mentions a female deity Nerthus who personified the maternal earth, but says nothing about a male consort. In historical times, the Scandinavian Njörd is a male divinity accompanied by a son and a daughter. Three theories have been put forward to account for the difference in sex between Nerthus and Njörd: the first, which is the stranger but the more widely accepted is that a change in grammatical gender in nouns brought about the change in sex in the divinity; the second, which follows on from the first, is that this grammatical change was aided by the fact that Nerthus was, in fact, a bisexual deity; the third suggests a mistake on the part of Tacitus, who assumed that the major fertility deity of the Teutons would be an earth mother, as in Mediterranean lands. However this may be, the whole of the representation of the fertility function among the Scandinavians has been rearranged; it should be noted that Frey and Freyja are not properly speaking names, but epithets meaning Lord and Lady, and could perhaps have displaced some earlier proper names like Nerthus-Njörd.

Tradition does not ascribe to this father and son functions which are noticeably different. Both are dispensers of wealth, the guarantors of oaths and the protectors of navigation.

Njörd's favourite place of residence was at Noatun, on the shores of the sea. He almost always remained there whereas his wife, Skadi, preferred the mountains. Skadi was the daughter of the giant Thjazi. We have already seen how Thjazi with Loki's complicity, succeeded in getting possession of the goddess Idun and how he perished as an eagle in the flames when he attempted to recapture her. His daughter Skadi undertook to avenge him and armed herself to attack the Aesir. But the gods did not care to fight with a woman and in reparation offered her the choice of one of themselves for a husband. They all stood behind a curtain, leaving only their bare feet visible. Skadi studied the god's feet at length, trying to guess by their shape and instep to whom they belonged. She was burning with desire to obtain Balder for a husband: he was the noblest, most handsome and desirable of all the Aesir. Finally she made her choice: the god she pointed out was so well made that surely he could be none other than Balder. But it was Njörd.

Faithful to the arrangement she had made with the gods Skadi married him. But she wanted to continue living where her ancestors had dwelt, which was among the high rocky uplands. After passing several days with her in these rude surroundings Njörd returned to a more smiling land, explaining: 'The song of the swan seems sweeter to me than the howling of wolves.' To this Skadi replied: 'Here at the seashore the sharp cry of the birds disturbs my sleep. Every morning I am wakened by gulls.' And she returned to the mountains of her birth. She was an indefatigable huntress who on her snow-shoes constantly roved the icy slopes and who always came home laden with game.

Frey was the son of this ill-assorted couple. He was the only Van who in some regions achieved a popularity equal to that of the Aesir, Odin and Thor. In Sweden especially, at Uppsala, his cult was practised. The largest and most splendid of all his temples was erected there. Animals were sacrificed to him and sometimes human beings. His festivals were marked by great rejoicing, dances and games.

Like Odin and Thor he possessed valued servants and wonder-working talismans. He had a horse which crossed mountains and torrents in spate like wind and did not draw back even when faced with flame. He owned a sword which flashed through the air of its own accord: unhappily he gave away this sword and he had sore need of it during the great struggle between the gods and their enemies the giants and demons. If Thor had two he-goats to draw his chariot, Frey had a golden boar, armed with redoubtable tusks. This boar had been forged by the dwarfs Brökk and Sindri. It sped through the air or across the earth more quickly than a galloping horse. As soon as it appeared the night would be illuminated. Other dwarfs built for Frey the ship *Skidbladnir* which no other boat was capable of following at sea. As soon as its sails were hoisted it made straight for the desired port of destination. This ship was large enough to take all the Aesir, together with their weapons and equipment. On the other hand, when it was not in use at sea Frey could easily fold it up and carry it in one of his pockets.

Frey's wife, like his mother, belonged to the race of giants. He was drawn to her by irresistible love. One day while sitting on Odin's throne he amused himself by contemplating from on high that which was taking place on earth. In the kingdom of the giants he suddenly observed a maiden of incomparable beauty coming out of her father's house. She was Gerda, daughter of the giant Gymir. The gleam of her white arms filled the sky and the broad sea with light. Frey's heart was at once inflamed with vehement love; never had man felt such violent passion for a girl. But profound melancholy began to weigh on Frey's soul; for he knew not how to win his beloved. When his parents, old Njörd and the beautiful Skadi, saw the change that had come over him they hastened to send Skirnir to him. Skirnir was both friend and servant, and they asked him to discover the secret of Frey's unhappiness.

Skirnir did not take long to find out what the trouble was, and he offered to go to the young maiden on his friend's behalf and ask for her hand. He only begged of Frey to lend him the famous sword which moved through the air of its own accord and the horse which was not frightened of the red flames stirred up by the enchanters. Through the sombre night, past rocks shining in the mountain torrents, Skirnir rode until he reached the land of the giants. At the door of Gymir's dwelling ferocious dogs were chained. On a nearby hill a herdsman sat and kept watch on the roads. Great flames surrounded the giant's palace with their fiery tongues. But Skirnir did not let himself be frightened. He passed the foaming jowls of

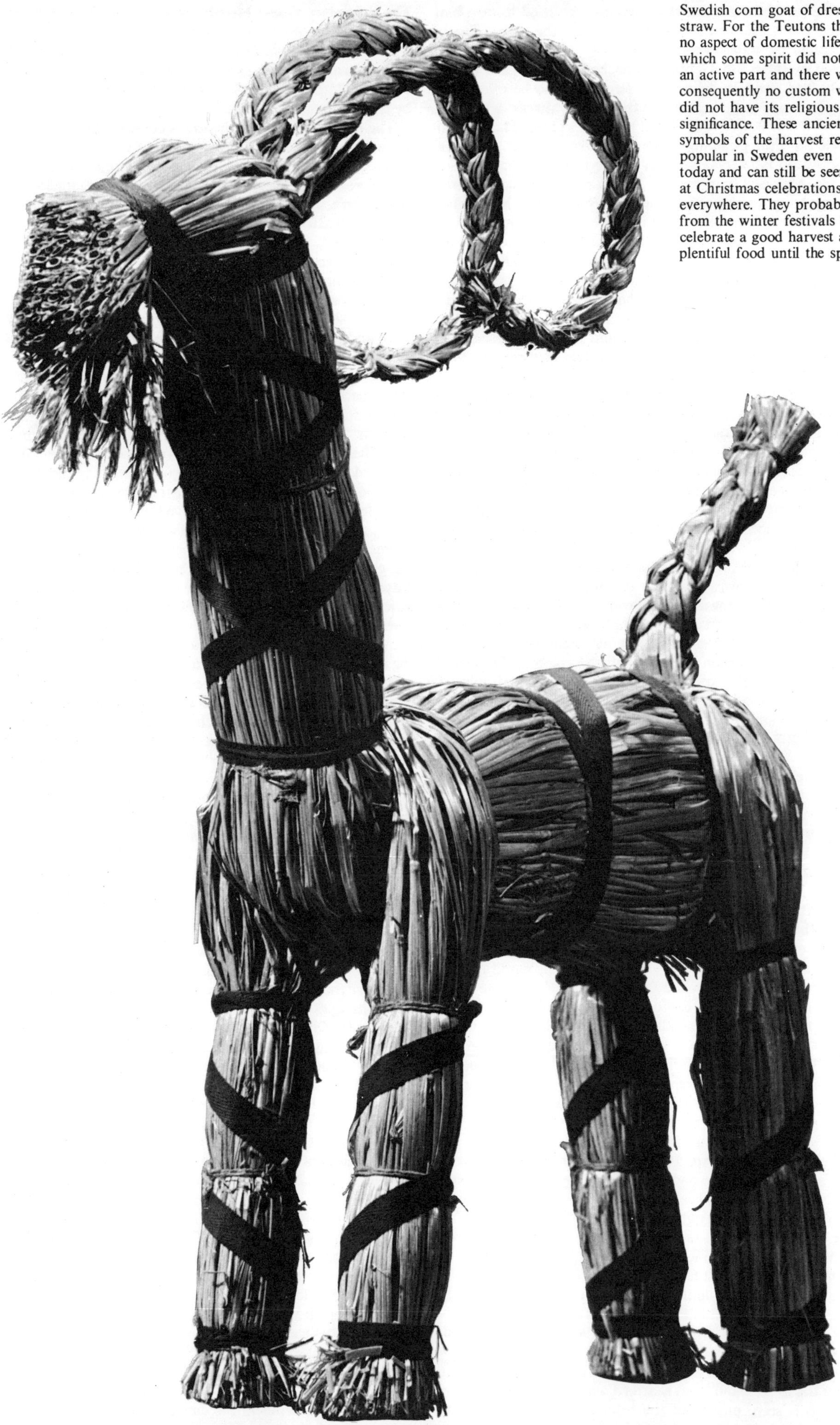

Swedish corn goat of dressed straw. For the Teutons there was no aspect of domestic life in which some spirit did not take an active part and there was consequently no custom which did not have its religious significance. These ancient symbols of the harvest remain popular in Sweden even today and can still be seen at Christmas celebrations everywhere. They probably come from the winter festivals to celebrate a good harvest and plentiful food until the spring.

the dogs, he ignored the shout of the guard who tried to stop him. He spurred his horse which bounded through the magic flames, and penetrated the palace walls.

Attracted by the noise, Gerda approached. Skirnir gave her the message he had come to deliver. At the same time he offered her eleven apples made of pure gold and the ring Draupnir, which had belonged to Odin. But Gerda refused to listen to him. Then Skirnir brandished the thin gleaming blade of his sword and looked as though he would kill Gerda and her father too. The threat was in vain; Gerda remained unimpressed. Despairing of success, Skirnir had recourse to spells and conjurations; he had found, he told her, a magic wand in the forest. He threatened to carve the most terrifying runes on it unless she accepted the gifts in token of agreement to the proposed marriage. He would bring it about, by means of these runes, that she should lead a solitary existence, far from men, at the opposite end of the world where in the icy depths she would dry up like a thistle.

This time Gerda was indeed terrified and no longer resisted. In sign of conciliation she offered Skirnir the cup of welcome, filled with mead. Skirnir pressed her to make a rendezvous with Frey then and there, for Frey was consumed with impatience. This Gerda refused to do, but she promised to meet the god, after nine nights had elapsed, in a sacred grove which she named.

Frey meanwhile waited in agony for news. When Skirnir brought him Gerda's reply his heart was again filled with joy. Only the delay imposed by her caused him pain. 'A night is long, but how much longer are two nights! How can I be patient for three nights! A month has often seemed shorter to me than half a night of this waiting.'

This love story, retold in a beautiful Norse poem of the beginning of the tenth century, was doubtless completed by other legends which have not come down to us. Probably Frey was only able finally to win Gerda after a desperate fight with the giants. In the course of the battle he must have lost his precious sword. For, when the great war between the gods and the giants – the prelude to the end of the world – began, Frey was to find himself without the weapon which rendered him invincible and succumbed to the blows of his adversary.

The great Germanic gods are known to us above all through the prose tales of the *Eddas* and through the Eddic poems. These documents are relatively late, being roughly of the tenth to the thirteenth centuries. But by a lucky chance excavations in Denmark and Sweden have yielded objects on which many of these gods are represented with the features given to them by certain Teutons of the first centuries of our era. In the seventeenth century at Gallehus in the island of Seeland a golden horn was found on which could be distinguished personages and animals in curious attitudes. A hundred years later in the same place a second golden horn was discovered which was, perhaps, the work of the same artist, or at least was closely related to it in style. These two horns were of the fifth century approximately. They were not properly cared for and were stolen by thieves who melted them down. We therefore know them only through eighteenth-century drawings made of them. The figures depicted have long seemed enigmatic and have been interpreted in various ways. The most satisfactory explanation has been given by the eminent Danish scholar Axel Olrik and is here relied on.

The personage who can be seen in the middle of the upper band of the shorter of the two horns is the god Odin. He holds a spear in his right hand and in his left a circle and a staff, which is perhaps a sceptre. He wears a helmet surmounted by two horns. The stag and the two wolves on his left are animals which are often associated with Odin's adventures. The god on the extreme right of this band and who, like Odin, wears a head-dress with two horns, holds in his left hand a sceptre and in his right a sickle: he is Frey, god of fertility. Thor, the third of the great Germanic gods, is represented on the second band as a personage with three heads. In his right hand he holds an axe and in his left a rope attached to a goat. The other figures represent lesser divinities, who are impossible to identify. The two warriors on the left of the upper band seem to be twin gods: they may be the same as the two warriors, similarly dressed and armed, which are represented on one of the very ancient bronze plaques found on Swedish territory, in the Isle of Öland. A personage, on the lower band, who is armed with two daggers may be the god who is seen, on one of the bronze plaques from Öland, occupied in a struggle with two savage beasts.

The Secondary Gods: Hoenir, Bragi, Vidar, Vali, Ull. Around the great Aesir revolved gods whose roles were much more limited, and whose cult was doubtless far from being practised by all the Germanic peoples. These gods, moreover, only appear in Scandinavian legends. Nothing leads us to believe that they were known or revered by the Germans of the South.

The name Hoenir has already occurred in more than one legend. He was one of the usual companions of Odin and Loki during their journeys across the world. In the dawn of time Hoenir played a part in the creation of men, since it was he who breathed a soul into the first couple. But it was not normally his qualities of spirit which distinguished him. He was strong and handsome, in warfare he was intrepid, but his intelligence was considered rather limited. When the Aesir delivered him as a hostage to the Vanir – after the great war between the two races of gods – they were careful to give him the wise Mimir for a companion.

Generally Hoenir occupies a minor role in the legends of which Odin and Loki are the principal actors. The following tale is another example of this.

One day a giant forced a peasant to play a game of draughts with him; the loser was to lose his own life as well. It was the peasant who won. To save his head the giant immediately proposed a bargain: he undertook in a single night to build for the peasant a magnificent house, filled with provisions of all kinds. At this price he should recover his liberty. The following day the peasant did, in fact, find himself the owner of a truly seigniorial estate and with his wife and children happily moved in.

His new life of opulence, however, did not last. The giant found means of making him play another game of draughts, and this time the giant won. Now, according to the agreement between the two players, the peasant would have to turn over his son to the giant, at least unless he could somehow manage to conceal him from the eyes of his subtle enemy. But by what sorcery could he hoodwink the giant? In his distress the peasant first appealed to the king of the Aesir, Odin. During the night Odin caused a field of barley to spring up and he changed the child into a single grain of barley concealed in one of the ripened ears. But the giant scythed the entire field and in order to find the child struck each ear of barley with his sharp sword. The grain he was looking for, however, slipped from his hand and Odin was able to return the child to its parents. But he confessed his inability to do more.

The peasant then appealed to Hoenir. He hastened with the child to the edge of the sea. At that moment seven swans happened to swim past; two of them came ashore. Hoenir at once commanded the child to become one of the feathers which grew on the head of one of the swans. But the giant suddenly appeared, seized the bird and wrung its neck. He did not, however, notice that the feather he was looking for had floated away. Hoenir, restoring the child to its natural form, was able to return him to his parents safe and sound.

The peasant finally called on Loki to help him. Loki turned the boy into one of the eggs contained in the roe of a turbot. The giant fished for the turbot and succeeded in catching it. Then he began to count its eggs one by one; the one he sought, however, slipped between his fingers. The boy reassumed his normal form and fled across the sand of the beach. The giant clumsily pursued him and stupidly blundered into the trap which Loki had prepared. There he died and the child was saved.

Here, too, Hoenir plays only a secondary role – which is his normal fate. Other gods appear in the legends even less frequently than he. Such is the case with Bragi, god of poetry, who was in fact a late creation of Scandinavian imagination. In the ninth century there lived a skald of great renown; his name was Bragi Boddason and he was the inventor of a celebrated type of strophe. It seems probable that after his death he was deified and made one of the Aesir. Until then Odin himself was attributed with the honour of having taught men the art of song and learned rhyme. During the final two centuries of paganism it was Bragi who became the master of the skalds. He was distinguished for wisdom and the noble ease of his speech. It was said that runes were engraved on his tongue – which is a poetic manner of saying that his skill in composing poems was unrivalled.

He married the goddess Idun. The poets imagined him as an old man with a long beard. He was Odin's skald. In Valhalla it was his duty to offer newcomers the cup of welcome and to receive them with words of courtesy. During feasts he would relate fascinating stories to Odin's guests, tales of times long past, the origin of the bardic art, or the adventures of the gods in love and war.

There were two divine personages to whom the poets tried to give a certain significance, but who nevertheless remain somewhat vague: Vidar and Vali.

Vidar was a son of Odin's. He was called the 'Silent As' because he rarely spoke in the assembly of the gods. He was even called a little slow-witted. He was one of those heroes whose great simplicity or even stupidity does not prevent them from succeeding where more subtle heroes fail. The greatest exploit in his life was, as we shall see later, when he surpassed Odin himself in courage and killed the wolf Fenrir. He was, indeed, to survive the merciless war between the gods and the giants, and to be one of the gods of a regenerated world.

Vali, like Vidar, was a god of secondary importance. He is scarcely known except for the part he played in the struggle which preceded the 'Twilight of the Gods'. He too was a son of Odin's. He was scarcely one day old when he undertook to avenge Balder's death on Höd. The wish to kill and with his own hands to place the murderer of the favourite of the gods on the funeral pyre was so ardent in his heart that he did not even pause to wash his hands or comb his hair. The day of his birth was also that of his most valiant exploit.

Neither Vali nor Vidar are very ancient gods. They were invented in order to serve the greater gods as avengers or replacements. They were not genuinely popular, but simply creations of the poets. It is not certain that they were objects of an actual cult.

Ull, on the other hand, was long worshipped in some parts of Scandinavia. It even seems that in the eyes of some of the faithful he was counted among the most important gods of the North. But he must, at an early period, have been put in the background by younger divinities. Without doubt he was already half forgotten in the days of the skalds, and in their poems he occupies a very minor position.

He was, they said, the son of Sif – Thor's wife – and consequently Thor's stepson. His name meant the 'Magnificent'. Ull was a handsome huntsman, skilled in crossing vast frozen stretches on snowshoes and winging game with his arrows. There was so much nobility and majesty about him that the Aesir, it was said, once chose him for a while to replace Odin. Odin had been accused of employing unworthy methods in overcoming the resistance of a maiden he coveted and had been banished from the skies by the other gods. In his absence it was Ull, with the consent of all, who took over the command of the Aesir. But at the end of ten years Odin reappeared and drove Ull away. Ull took refuge in Sweden where he acquired the reputation of a powerful enchanter. He owned a bone on which he had engraved magic formulas which were so powerful that he could use it as a ship to cross the seas.

The Goddesses. Scandinavian bards, story-tellers and learned men have spoken less of the goddesses than of the gods. This is perhaps because Teutonic literature was made more for men than for women. It was above all at the end of banquets, when warriors reposed after battle or distant campaigns, that the bards recited their poems filled with mythological allusions. The wives of the gods remain practically always in the background. The number of goddesses seems to have been great enough, but of many of them we know scarcely more than the name. Their cult, moreover, was rarely practised by the majority of the Germanic peoples. Only one seems to have been revered by all the tribes: she who in old German was called Frija, in Anglo-Saxon Frig, and in old Norse Frigg.

Indeed the very name Frija is only a former adjective, raised little by little to the dignity of a proper name. It meant the 'well-beloved', or 'spouse'. This meaning was undoubtedly known to the Romans since they identified Frija with Venus. And the Roman interpretation was accepted without difficulty by the Germans themselves who translated the name *Veneris dies* (Friday, in French *Vendredi*) by Frija's day (in modern German: *Freitag*). But we know nothing of the character or role which the ancestors of the Germans ascribed to this goddess. It is extremely probable that she was regarded as Woden's wife. But we have no genuinely German legend about her.

On the contrary the Scandinavians show Frija-Frigg taking part in various adventures. The wife of Odin, she shared his wisdom and foresight. It would seem that she did not always agree in all matters with her husband. Sometimes she protected warriors whom Odin tried to harm; and in the resulting quarrels it was not always she who got the worst of it. Her stratagems often succeeded in defeating Odin's will.

She protected men's marriage and made them fruitful. But she personally did not always remain faithful to her own marriage vows, and from time to time, through coquetry or self-interest, she bestowed her favours on various gods, not to mention personages of inferior rank.

Frigg is often confused with Freyja whose origin is, however, different, in spite of the similarity of their names. Originally Freyja did not belong to the race of the Aesir but to that of their rivals, the Vanir. She was the sister of the god Frey and certain Norwegian and Icelandic writers have taken great care to distinguish her from Frigg. But in many cases she was completely confused with Frigg and like her is described as Odin's wife. In the sky she had a rich dwelling, called Folkvang. There she received deceased heroes and assigned them seats in her great banqueting hall. For every time she accompanied Odin to a field of battle she had the right to bring back to her palace half the warriors who had fallen, weapon in hand. She was, in fact, the first of the Valkyries and their supreme commander. Sometimes it even happened that in Valhalla she would pour out the beer and the mead for Odin's warriors, like an ordinary Valkyrie.

Like Frigg, Freyja loved ornaments and jewellery. Not far from her palace, in a grotto which served as their workshop, lived four dwarfs, celebrated for their skill in working metal. One day when she was visiting them she noticed on their table a marvellous golden necklace which they were on the point of finishing. She was seized with an irresistible desire to possess it and offered the dwarfs gold, silver and other precious objects. But the dwarfs, lords of all metals buried in the earth, merely laughed at her offer. To obtain the trinket, they said, she must pay a quite different price: in brief, she must pass one night with each of them. The goddess did not hesitate and did as the dwarfs desired. The necklace then belonged to her.

But the treacherous Loki lost no time in reporting to Odin what had occurred. Odin ordered him to steal the necklace so ill-acquired. Loki then proceeded towards Freyja's bed-chamber, but the door was locked. He turned himself into a fly and buzzed around for some time seeking a crack through which he could slip. Finally in the roof he perceived a hole, the size of the eye of a needle. By this hole he entered the bed-chamber. Freyja, wearing the necklace, was asleep, but she was lying in such a position that it was impossible to reach the clasp. Loki changed himself from a fly into a flea and bit the goddess on the cheek. Freyja stirred in her sleep and turned over so that Loki was finally able to steal the necklace. He then unlatched the door and walked calmly away. When she woke up Freyja discovered the theft and easily guessed who had committed it. She went to Odin and demanded that he return her property. Odin reproached her bitterly for the manner in which she had obtained it and only consented to give her back the necklace on strict conditions.

To obtain his pardon Odin insisted that Freyja should provoke a war between two kings, each of whom commanded twenty kings less powerful than himself. At nightfall all the heroes who had fallen in the battle must be resuscitated in order to renew the struggle on the following day. At this point of the Norse narrative is inserted a passage evidently of Christian inspiration which can only be considered an interpolation. This war should not end until a Christian came in his turn to fight and vanquish all these pagans. Then only should the dead earn repose. Freyja gave her promise to arrange this and regained possession of her necklace.

Freyja was so lovely that often the giants tried to obtain her favours freely or by force. We have already seen how the giant Thrym demanded her from Loki as the price of returning Thor's hammer. The following story was also told: a giant promised to build the gods a magnificent palace in the course of a single winter. The only condition he imposed was that they give him Freyja for a wife and, into the bargain, present him with the sun and the moon. The gods agreed. He would have finished the palace just in time had not Loki intervened. Loki turned himself into a mare and in this guise lured away the stallion on which the giant relied for the transport of his building materials. Freyja was thus narrowly saved from the humiliating fate which awaited her.

It is sometimes difficult to tell the Germanic goddesses apart.

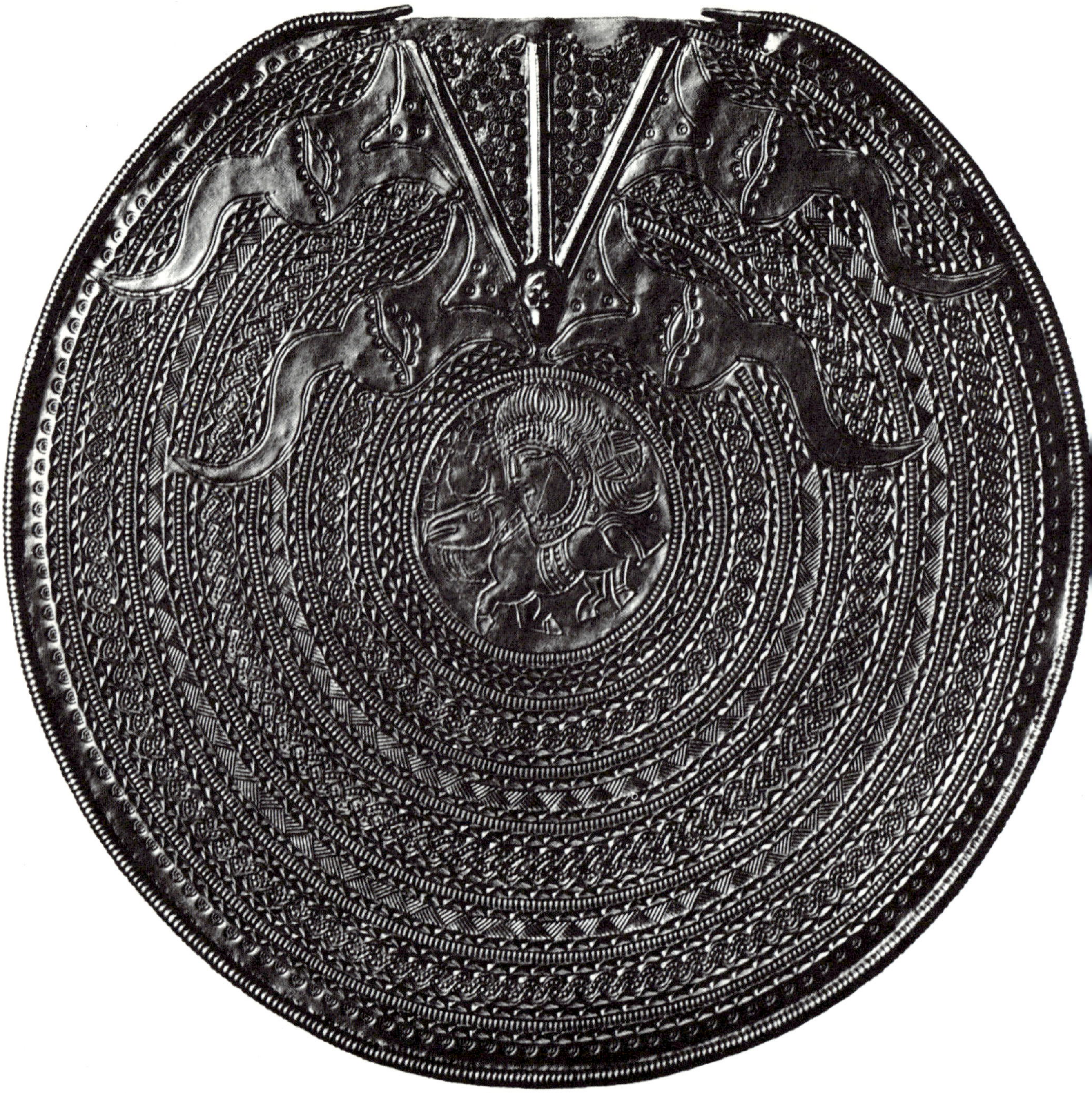

Golden bracteate found in Scania, Sweden. Bracteates are medals made of thin sheets of gold with, on one side, in relief, ornaments, religious symbols, and various scenes or human figures inspired by Roman art. The bracteate was a kind of amulet which was worn around the neck, hanging on a small chain or a cord.

Freyja, who is often confused with Frigg, is also frequently identified with Gefjon, 'the Giver'. Gefjon was a fertility goddess who was particularly honoured in the island of Seeland. A legend explains the origin of the cult which she enjoyed on this island. In olden days there reigned over the land which to-day is called Sweden a king named Gylfi. An unknown woman who wandered about the country gave the king such pleasure by magic arts of which she knew the secrets that he offered to give her as much land as she could mark out in the space of a day and a night with a plough drawn by four bullocks. Now this unknown woman was the goddess Gefjon and she had learned her magic from the Vanir. The four bullocks with which she harnessed the plough were in reality her four sons whom she had by a giant who lived far off in the icy regions of the North. Drawn by these giant bullocks the ploughshare dug so deeply into the ground that it tore away the entire crust of the earth. The bullocks dragged the immense amount of earth thus detached from its native habitat as far as the sea, where, filling in the sea-bottom, it became the island of Seeland. In the place where Gefjon's bullocks had torn away the soil there remained a vast stretch of water, to-day known in Sweden as Lake Mälar.

The Scandinavian poets often cite the names of the wives of th great gods, but they rarely make them the chief characters in thei poems. They have already been mentioned in the preceding page and here it will be sufficient to recall their names. These are – apar from Freyja – Sif, the wife of Thor; Idun, the wife of Bragi; Skad the wife of Njörd; Gerda, the wife of Frey.

The ancestors of the Germans revered, in addition to Frija, th goddess Nerthus of whom Tacitus gives a few details in Chapte XL of his *Germania*. She was perhaps the personified Earth or fertility goddess. Her festival was celebrated in the spring. On a island in the Ocean a grove was sacred to her: here was preserve her chariot which only the priest could approach. By mysteriou signs the priest could recognise the moment when the goddess wa present in her sanctuary. Oxen were then hitched to her chario and, with solemn ritual, the invisible goddess was carried aroun the whole island. When Nerthus was in this way present in th midst of her people all swords remained in their scabbards an no one dared to break the peace. It continued thus until the momen when the priest, advised that the goddess no longer cared to sojour among men, reconducted her to her sanctuary. The chariot, th eils which adorned it and the goddess herself were then plunged nto sea water to purify them. Immediately afterwards the slaves vho had taken part in the ceremony of purification were drowned; or no living person, the priest excepted, must be able to boast that e had penetrated the mysteries of the sanctuary.

Now Nerthus, who among the Germans was of the feminine ex, became among the Scandinavians a masculine divinity; namely, Njörd, of whom we have already spoken. It is possible that the leity who preceded both Nerthus and Njörd was considered among he primitive Germanic tribes as possessing both sexes. This ancient livinity, whom we can only glimpse, probably personified fecundity.

As well as the goddesses who inhabited the luminous regions of he sky, there was the goddess of the underworld. Like the Greeks nd the Romans the Germanic peoples believed in the existence of a subterranean world where the souls of the dead dwelt after eparation from their bodies. They called it by a word which corresponds to the modern German *Hölle* and to which they early gave the sense of the 'infernal regions'. The Teutons, however, at east before their conversion to Christianity, did not consider this nderworld to be a place of punishment; it was simply the residence of those who had ceased to live.

We do not know whether the Germans personified the underworld in the form of a god or goddess. But we do know that the Scandinavians accomplished the personification. Their word *Hel*, which at first merely meant the place where the dead went, finally became the name of a goddess who was considered to be the overeign of the underworld.

Legends about the goddess Hel are few. They date from a time vhen the Northern countries were already converted and bear the vident imprint of Christianity. As Lucifer, for the Christians, was nseparable from Hell and Loki was often identified with Lucifer, t was said that Hel was the daughter of Loki. The tendency was to make her the companion of fearful monsters. She was said to have been brought up in the land of the giants with the wolf Fenrir and he great serpent of Midgard. She was even made the sister of these evil demons. It was told that in her subterranean kingdom she offered asylum to the monster Nidhögg who night and day gnawed at the roots of the ash tree Yggdrasil. She was not supposed to be, however, a divinity of perverse or malevolent character. It was Odin himself who had assigned her to Niflheim; he gave her power over nine different worlds so that she could fix in each the place of her abode. About her appearance there was something strange and even terrifying. Her head hung forward. Half of her face was ike that of a human being, but the other half was totally blank. In he depths of Niflheim she possessed a vast palace where she received, each according to his rank, the heroes and even the gods vho descended into her kingdom. There life was not very different rom that led in the great houses of the Scandinavian chieftains. It vas a sort of underground replica of Odin's celestial palace, Valhalla. When the god Balder, after being killed by Höd, appeared before the goddess of the underworld the great reception hall was esplendent with gold, and servants hastened to put cups of bright mead on the tables for Balder and his retinue.

Hel herself had scarcely any other role except to preside at these eceptions. She was much more the creation of erudite poets than he object of a genuine popular cult. She never took part in the ives of the other gods and, queen of the shadows, remained herself a vague and shadowy figure.

THE TWILIGHT OF THE GODS: THE END OF THE WORLD AND ITS REBIRTH

The Teutons did not believe that the world would endure for ever nor even that the gods were immortal. Like men the gods had ceaselessly to struggle against enemies who were full of envy and deceit. To maintain their pre-éminence over these demons they had incessantly to remain on the alert. We have already seen how one of them, Heimdall, was appointed to stand guard night and day before the bridge, Bifröst, which gave access to Asgard. But in spite of the precautions taken and in spite of their warlike virtues the Aesir were to finish by succumbing to their enemies. And the world which they had sustained and protected was to crumble in ruins with them.

To this grandiose catastrophe – which is recounted with power and brevity in the Völuspa, one of the best poems in the *Eddas* – the name Götterdämmerung or the 'Twilight of the Gods' has been given. This name, which Wagner's opera has made universally familiar, in point of fact arises from a misunderstanding and even a contradiction. The Icelandic term employed by the oldest bards was *ragna rök*, which simply means 'the fatal destiny, the end of the gods'. But from the twelfth or thirteenth century Norse writers substituted for this expression the words *ragna rökkr* which roughly amounted to the same thing and doubtless had in their opinion the advantage of containing a more striking metaphor: *rökkr* meaning, in effect, 'obscurity, shadows, twilight'. From then on the phrase 'twilight of the gods' became habitual.

In the dawn of time the gods in their palaces in Asgard had led a peaceful and industrious life. They had taken pleasure in building temples, erecting altars, working in gold and forging tools with hammer and anvil, or in playing draughts together. Had they only been able to dominate their passions this golden age of peace would never have come to an end. But the gods brought down the blows of destiny on their own heads. That day in Valhalla when they tortured Gullveig, the envoy from the Vanir, in order to extract her gold, they committed a crime from which the first wars resulted. Later they broke their word to a giant who had reconstructed their celestial dwelling. As the price of his labour they had promised him the goddess Freyja, the sun and the moon. But when the time came to pay they permitted Loki to deceive the giant by a dishonest trick. From that moment all the oaths, all treaties concluded in the world began to lose their force and validity. A new era opened, characterised by perjury, violence and warfare. Men, giants and gods were swayed by hatred and anger. The Valkyries ranged the world continually, flying from one battle to another. Evil dreams began to trouble the sleep of the Aesir. Odin uneasily watched the sinister portents accumulate. He understood that the supreme struggle was being prepared. Calmly and resolutely he made ready to face it.

It was the murder of Balder which marked the beginning of the great ordeal. Before his body the Aesir swore an oath to avenge him bitterly. They were not unaware that it was Loki who had armed and guided the hand of the blind murderer. They seized him at once and put him in irons. This ignominious treatment only served further to envenom the wicked god. He broke his chains and joined the Aesir's irreconcilable enemies, the demons and the giants, and with them fought against his former companions.

Meanwhile the baleful omens redoubled. In a distant forest in the East an aged giantess brought into the world a whole brood of young wolves whose father was Fenrir. One of these monsters chased the sun to take possession of it. The chase was for long in vain, but each season the wolf grew in strength, and at last he reached the sun. Its bright rays were one by one extinguished. It took on a blood red hue, then entirely disappeared. For the space of several years the world was enveloped in hideous winter. Snowstorms descended from all points of the horizon. War broke out all over the earth. Brother slew brother, children no longer respected the ties of blood. It was a time when men were no better than wolves, eager to destroy each other. Soon the world was going to sink into the abyss of nothingness.

Everywhere people armed themselves and spied on the enemy. At the frontier of the kingdom of the giants a watchman, Eggther, a redoubtable warrior and a fine harpist, sat on an eminence and kept watch on the kingdoms of men and gods alike. Near the river which bordered the underworld, Garm, the terrible dog, howled furiously, calling all who were confined to his guardianship to battle. In the South, where the land of the fire giants began, Surt, the lord of those countries, had already raised his flaming sword.

On the edge of the sky Heimdall, watchman of the gods, was posted. No one in the world had an eye more piercing or an ear more acute than Heimdall, and yet he allowed his sword to be stolen by Loki and only began to sound his horn when the giants were already on the march. The wolf Fenrir, whom the gods had so carefully chained up, broke his bonds and escaped. As he shook them from him he made the whole earth tremble. The aged ash tree Yggdrasil was shaken from its roots to its topmost branches. Mountains crumbled or split from top to bottom, and the dwarfs who had their subterranean dwellings in them sought desperately and in vain for entrances so long familiar but now disappeared.

From the West, in a ship manned by a phantom crew, approached the giant Hrym. He held himself proudly erect, ready for battle;

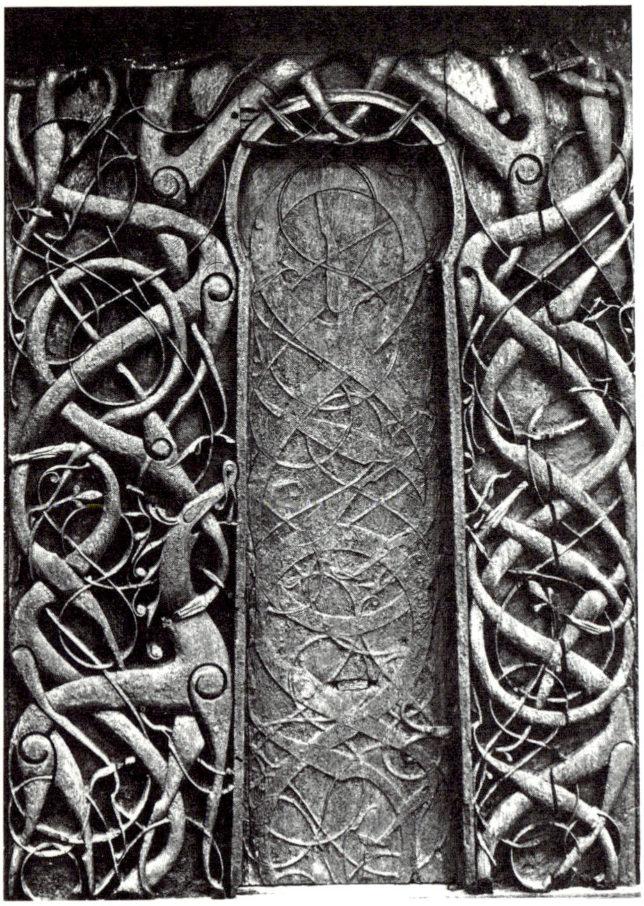

Deer eating the leaves of the world tree, Yggdrasil.
According to Scandinavian mythology, the fabric of the universe was maintained by a gigantic ash tree which remained always green, thanks to the care of the Norns, although four deer browsed ceaselessly on its foliage. It was from the wood of this tree that would emerge the ancestors of a future race of men after the death of the old gods.
Wood-carving from Urnes stave church.

in his left hand he raised his shield, in his right he grasped the tiller. His ship rode forward on the giant waves which the serpent Midgard stirred up as it swam. In its unbridled rage the monster thrashed the waters with its enormous tail and advanced at a furious pace.

Another ship came from the North. Its sails bellied in the wind and it carried the inhabitants of the underworld: Loki sat at the helm. The wolf Fenrir accompanied him. Fire spurted from the beast's eyes and nostrils; from his gaping jaws dripped blood. His upper jaw touched the heavens and his lower jaw brushed the earth.

From the South appeared Surt, followed by innumerable fire giants. Lightning flashed from his sword and all around him flames sprang from the cracking earth. As he drew near rocks crumbled away and men collapsed lifeless. The vault of the heavens was shaken by the tumult of this army in march and, scorched by the breathing furnace beneath, suddenly cracked in two. And when the sons of the fire giants drove their steeds across the rainbow bridge stretched between earth and Asgard, it burst into flames and caved in.

Following the ancient Germanic custom the opposing armies had by agreement fixed the field for their encounter. This was the field of Vigrid, which stretched before Valhalla and was a square which measured a thousand leagues on each side. Here gods and giants, together with warriors whose numbers were countless, pitilessly butchered each other.

Odin wore a golden helmet, plumed with vast eagles' wings. In his hand he grasped the good spear Gungnir. Like a hurricane he flew in the forefront of his warriors who swarmed endlessly from the gates of Valhalla. Around him, like a winged host, flew the Valkyries on their dazzling chargers. Odin caught sight of the wolf Fenrir and, sword raised, fell upon him. But the monster's gaping jowls were so vast that they swallowed up the father of the gods then and there. Thus Odin perished, the first casualty of this titanic battle. At the sight Frigg, his wife, was on the point of fainting with grief. But vengeance was near. Vidar, the son of Odin, advanced fearlessly towards Fenrir. He placed one foot on the monster's lower jaw and kept it thus fixed to the ground. His shoe was made of indestructible leather which the wolf's sharp teeth could not penetrate. Vidar's right hand raised the beast's upper jaw towards the sky and into the yawning gullet he thrust his sword – so deep that it pierced Fenrir's very heart.

Meanwhile Frey, the dazzling Van, and Surt, chief of the fire giants, found themselves face to face. Frey would have made short work of his adversary if he had still possessed the wondrous sword which the dwarfs had forged for him. But he had lost it while seeking the hand of his wife Gerda. Now this weapon which none could resist was in the hands of the giant Surt – and it was the god who succumbed.

Thor saw before him the monster which once long before he had attempted to kill: the great serpent of Midgard. Since that day when the god had almost torn him from the water the serpent had kept itself hidden in the bottom of the sea. To-day it had emerged for the first time and it crawled towards the thunder-god, spitting out so much venom that sea and air alike were poisoned. With his terrible hammer Thor crushed the monster's skull and it fell back, dying. But Thor himself had breathed in so much poison that his strength failed. He tried to stagger away; but at the ninth step he fell to the ground, dead.

Loki in the old days had already found in Heimdall an adversary to be feared; Heimdall had once forced him to restore the necklace he had maliciously stolen from Freyja. Hatred had filled Loki's heart ever since. He now sought out Heimdall, found him and killed him; but lost his own life in doing so.

Only one of the great Aesir was still alive: Tyr. With vast strides Tyr ranged the battlefield, hoping to find and slay the wolf Fenrir who had once bitten off his right hand. He was too late, for Vidar had already killed Fenrir. Suddenly, however, Tyr heard a fearful howling; it was Garm, the dog of the infernal regions. Tyr flung himself on the creature and with his left hand sank his sword deep into its heart. But he himself was so badly mauled that in his turn he, too, died.

All the great gods were dead. And now that Thor, protector of mankind, had disappeared, men were abandoned. They were driven from their hearths and the human race was swept from the surface of the earth. The earth itself was beginning to lose its shape. Already the stars were coming adrift from the sky and falling into the gaping void. They were like swallows, weary from too long a voyage, who drop and sink into the waves. The giant Surt set the entire earth on fire; the universe was no longer more than an immense furnace. Flames spurted from fissures in the rocks; everywhere there was the hissing of steam. All living things, all plant life were blotted out. Only the naked soil remained, but like the sky itself the earth was no more than cracks and crevasses.

And now all the rivers, all the seas rose and overflowed. From every side waves lashed against waves. They swelled and boiled and slowly covered all things. The earth sank beneath the sea, and the vast field of battle where the lords of the universe had faced each other was no longer visible.

All was finished.

And now all was about to begin again. From the wreckage of the ancient world a new world was born. Slowly the earth emerged from the waves. Mountains rose anew and from them sprang cataracts of singing waters. Above the torrent the eagle again began to hover, ready to swoop suddenly down on the fish which played in the waters. As of old the fields became covered with verdure. Ears of corn grew where no human hand had scattered seed. A new sun – the son of that which a wolf had once devoured – shone serenely in the sky.

And a new generation of gods appeared. On the field of peace where formerly the Aesir had assembled the new gods gathered in their turn. Who were these new gods? Had they no connection with the gods of olden days? None at all. They had already been in existence, but having never shared the passions, or quarrels, of the former gods, having committed neither perjury nor crime, they had not perished. To them it was reserved to renew the world.

There was even one resurrection: Balder, the fairest and most beloved of the gods of former days, was reborn; and, accompanied by his brother, Höd, he occupied the great festival hall where Odin had once sat. Odin himself would never return, but two of his sons

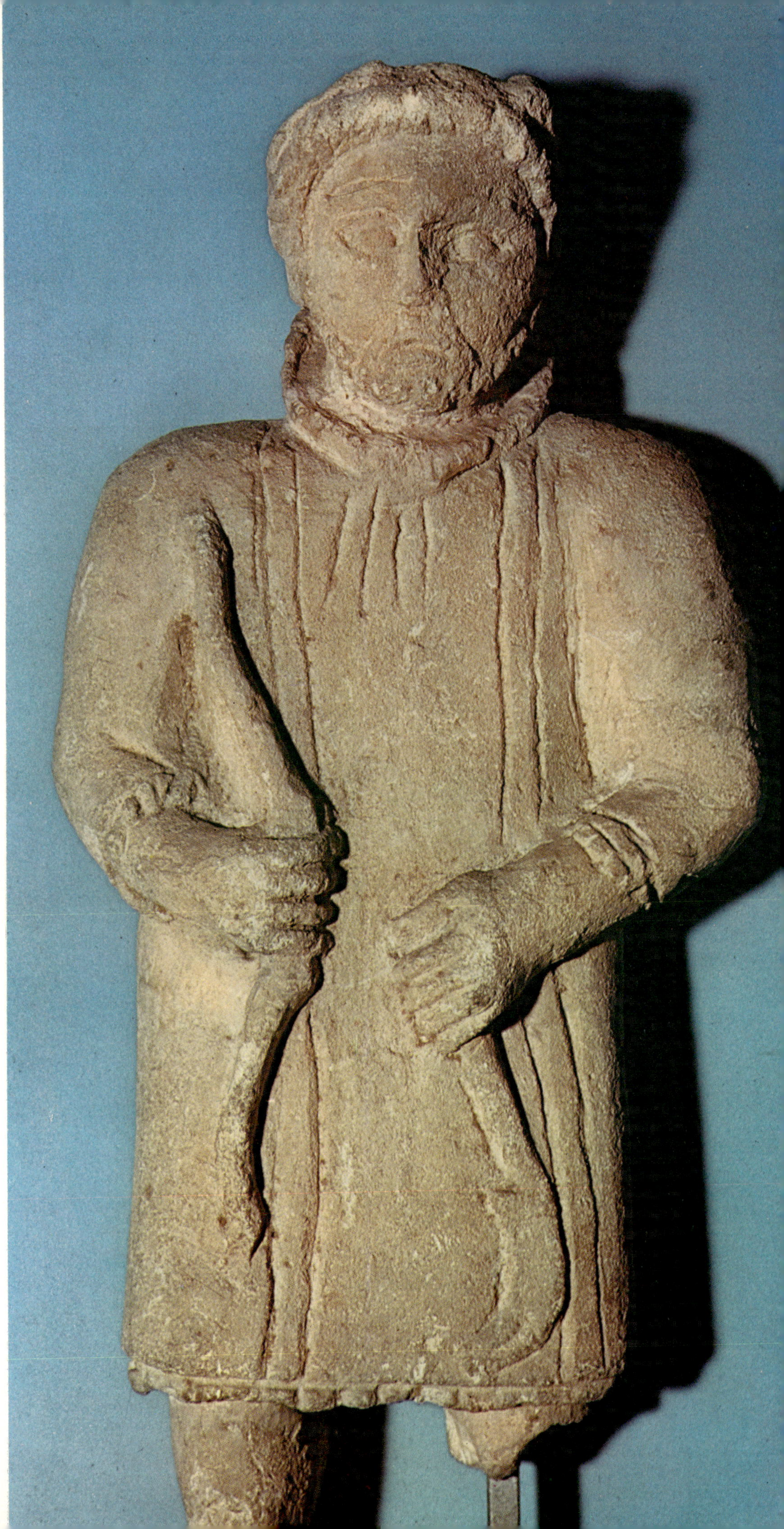

A Celtic deity carrying a bow and a sickle. He is possibly an aspect of Esus the woodcutter god – the region where the image was found was the hilly, wooded country to the north of the Loire. The bow suggests a local attribution, a hunters' patron or deity was likely to have been honoured in a forest area.

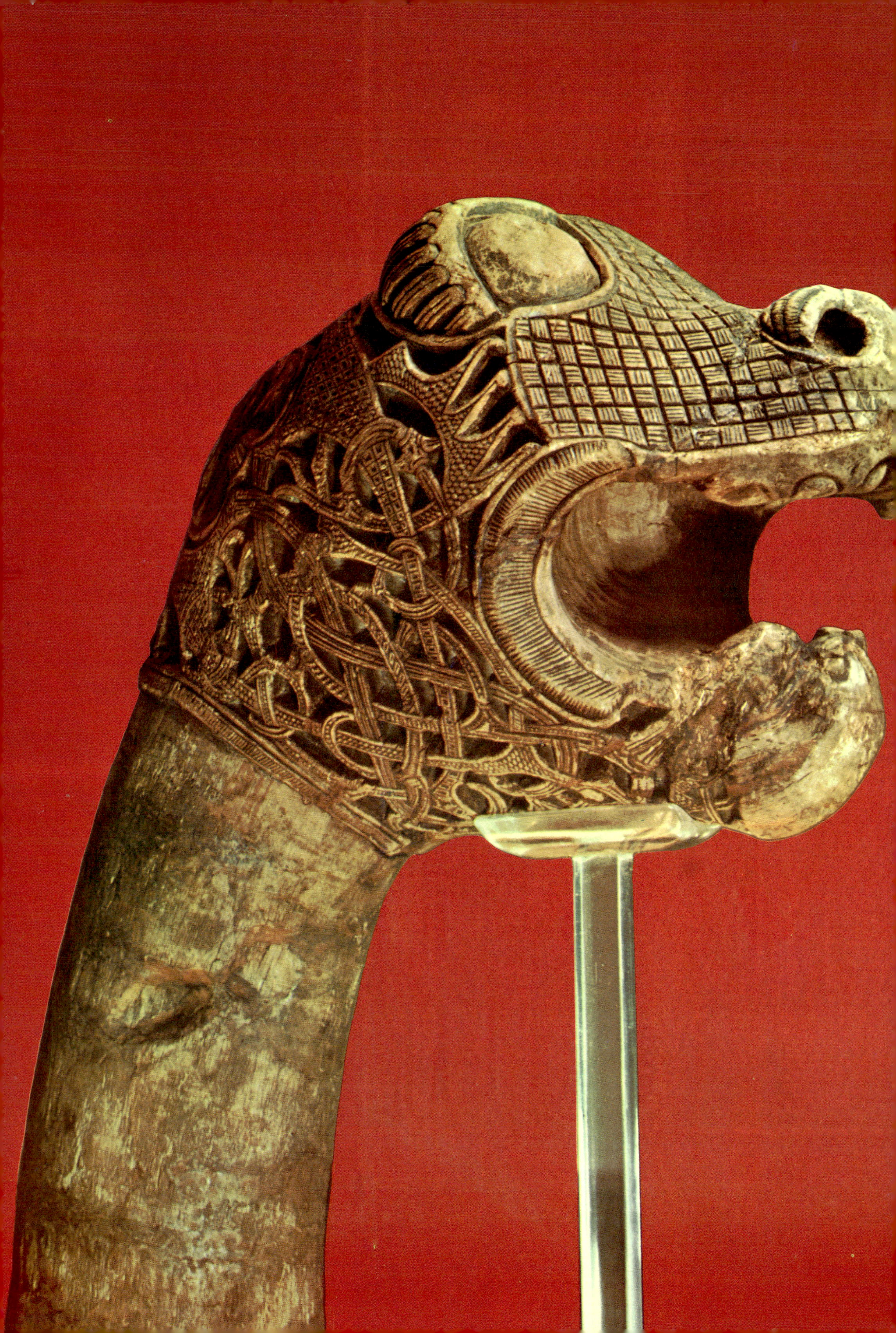

Vidar and Vali, and two of his brothers' sons, Vili and Ve, now lived in the sky. Hoenir, who was Odin's faithful companion, survived. Hoenir now studied the runes engraved on magic wands and, thus penetrating the secrets of the future, was able to tell the new race what happiness awaited them. Two sons of Thor, Magni and Modi, completed the new Teutonic pantheon.

Men also reappeared. For all of them had not perished in the great catastrophe. Enclosed in the wood itself of the ash tree Yggdrasil – which the devouring flames of the universal conflagration had been unable to consume – the ancestors of a future race of men had escaped death. In the asylum they had found, their only nourishment had been the morning dew.

SPIRITS, DEMONS, ELVES AND GIANTS

In the belief of the Teutons the earth was peopled by countless creatures of superhuman nature. Here we shall enumerate only the principal categories of these mysterious beings.

Spirits. Everywhere in Germanic lands the souls of the dead were held in fear and reverence. It was believed that they were able to exercise magic powers. Hence the Teutons sometimes buried their dead under the actual threshold of the house. They thought that the soul of the deceased always remained near its place of burial and could act as a protective spirit to the house of the survivors. They believed that souls on occasion even assumed bodily form and appeared either as they had been during their lifetime or in the guise of an animal. Sometimes it happened, they said, that these souls made the living expiate an ancient crime. For instance everyone knew the legend of the wicked bishop Hatto who, in punishment for his misdeeds, was pursued by an army of mice. He took refuge in a tower built on an islet in the middle of the Rhine, but the mice swam across the river and devoured the bishop alive. These mice were the souls of the poor folk whom the bishop had had burned to death.

In certain lands they believed, on the contrary, that the souls of the dead gathered together in places far removed from human habitation. This was how the idea of the 'Savage Hunt' originated. Thousands of phantoms – who were the souls of the dead – on aerial mounts would in a wild chase follow their leader, the demon Wode, a degenerate form of the god Woden. It was their furious ride which could sometimes be perceived among storm clouds.

In Scandinavia the souls of dead warriors were generally assigned to Valhalla or to the other palaces of the gods. In Germany it was sometimes thought that the abode of souls was in the West, towards the place where the sun sank into the sea. Certain German tribes even specifically named Great Britain as the final refuge of the dead. The historian Procopius recounts that on the coast facing Great Britain there were many villages whose inhabitants, though submitted to Frankish authority, paid no tribute because it had always been their painful duty to carry the souls of the dead across the Channel. Towards midnight an invisible being would knock on their doors and summon them to work. They would rise at once and, as though moved by some strange compulsion, go down to the shore. There they would find mysterious ships waiting, ready to sail. The ships belonged to no one in the village and appeared to be empty. As soon as they embarked and grasped the oars, however, they would realise that the boats were so heavily laden that they sank into the water nearly to the gunwales. It took them only an hour to reach the opposite shore whereas in an ordinary boat the crossing required a day and a night. Scarcely would they touch the far shore when the boat would suddenly seem to empty and ride high in the water. Neither during the voyage nor at the moment of unloading could the sailors see whom they had ferried, but they would hear a voice distinctly proclaim the name, condition and place of origin of each new arrival.

Even the souls of the living were supposed to be able to leave the body and lead a semi-independent existence. The distinction which the Germans made between soul and body did not altogether correspond to the Christian conception of these two elements in human nature. While, for Christians, the soul was entirely immaterial and impalpable, the second 'ego' which the Germans believed all men to possess could exercise bodily functions, speak, move, act, even appear in the form of a human being or of an animal.

The Scandinavians called this half-material 'ego', the *fylgja*, which means roughly 'the follower, the second'. The following story was told of the Frankish king Gontran, son of Clotaire. One day when he returned from hunting he was overwhelmed with fatigue. He sat down under a tree and, propping his head on the knees of a faithful servant who was with him, closed his eyes and fell asleep. Suddenly the servant saw a little creature emerge from the king's mouth. It resembled a snake and crawled until it reached a neighbouring stream where it stopped, as though embarrassed by this unexpected obstacle. The servant drew his sword from its scabbard and laid it across the water; and on this improvised bridge the mysterious creature crossed the stream. It then reached a mountain nearby and disappeared into a hole in the ground. At the end of a few hours it reappeared, again crossed the stream by means of the naked sword and re-entered the king's mouth. Gontran at once woke up and said to his companion: 'I have had a strange dream which I should like to tell you. Before me stretched a great river which I crossed on an iron bridge. I soon reached a cavern situated under a high mountain. In this cavern I beheld a prodigious treasure in gold and silver coins, collected there by our forefathers.' The servant then related to the king what had occurred during his sleep and both were astonished by a dream which so resembled reality. Excavations were made in the mountain, where an immense treasure was discovered which had lain there for many long years.

Although the *fylgja* could leave the body it nevertheless shared the body's fate. Any damage sustained by one of these parts of the individual was immediately felt by the other. If one were killed the other also died. This belief persisted even after the end of paganism. In the Middle Ages they would tell how witches could, without their bodies leaving the house, wander abroad in the guise of an animal; but if someone happened to wound or kill this animal the witch would be found in her house bleeding or dead.

Belief in the existence in every man of a spirit capable of leaving the body to take on a non-human shape gave rise among the Teutons, as among many other peoples, to the conviction that certain men could at will change themselves into animals. All Teutons have believed in the existence of the werewolf; that is of a man who has the power to turn himself into a wolf, in order either to attack other men or to ravish their flocks. It was also admitted that in certain cases the metamorphosis was involuntary and resulted from a spell cast by an enemy skilled in the practice of sorcery.

A Norse story relates that Sigmund and Sinfjöth, wandering through a forest, once found two men in a cabin sound asleep. Above them hung the hides of two wolves. The two unknown men had formerly been turned into wolves by the malevolence of a sorcerer; but he had granted them permission to leave their wolfskins every ten days and for a period of twenty-four hours to resume their human form. It was during one of these periods that they were sleeping in the cabin. Sigmund and Sinfjöth decided to slip into the empty skins, but the moment they did so they found it impossible to take them off again. It was now they who were victims of the enchantment. They at once began to howl like wolves. They sprang on the sleeping men and even bit each other. When they went home they waited for the tenth day. The wolfskins then automatically fell from their shoulders and the two warriors reassumed their normal appearance. They hastened to burn the skins and the spell was broken.

Little by little the Teutons came to consider the *fylgja* as an independent being, as a demon that had no connection with any specific individual. Ultimately it was supposed to be able to incarnate the soul of ancestors or even the soul of a religion. In appearance it was an armed woman, a sort of goddess riding through the air. Though originally protective spirits, the *fylgjur* (plural of *fylgja*) began, with the introduction of Christianity, to be feared as noxious demons. In a saga about some of the chieftains who converted Scandinavia it was told how a certain Thidrandi, an Icelander by birth, one clear night heard a knock on the door of his house. Although he had been warned never in such a case to go out he had the imprudence to cross the threshold, sword in hand, ready to face the enemies whom he expected to find outside. He saw nine women dressed in black, mounted on dark steeds, naked swords in their hands, riding towards him from the North. Turning, he beheld in the South nine other women on white steeds and dressed in white also bearing down on him. In haste he tried to regain his house, but it was too late. The women in black had fallen upon him and mortally wounded him. They found him next day

The Head of an elaborately carved post from the ship burial at Oseberg in Norway. The people of northern Europe and Scandinavia believed that malignant spirits inhabited the forests; these fearsome images have been found at burial sites and are believed to have been placed there for the protection of the dead.

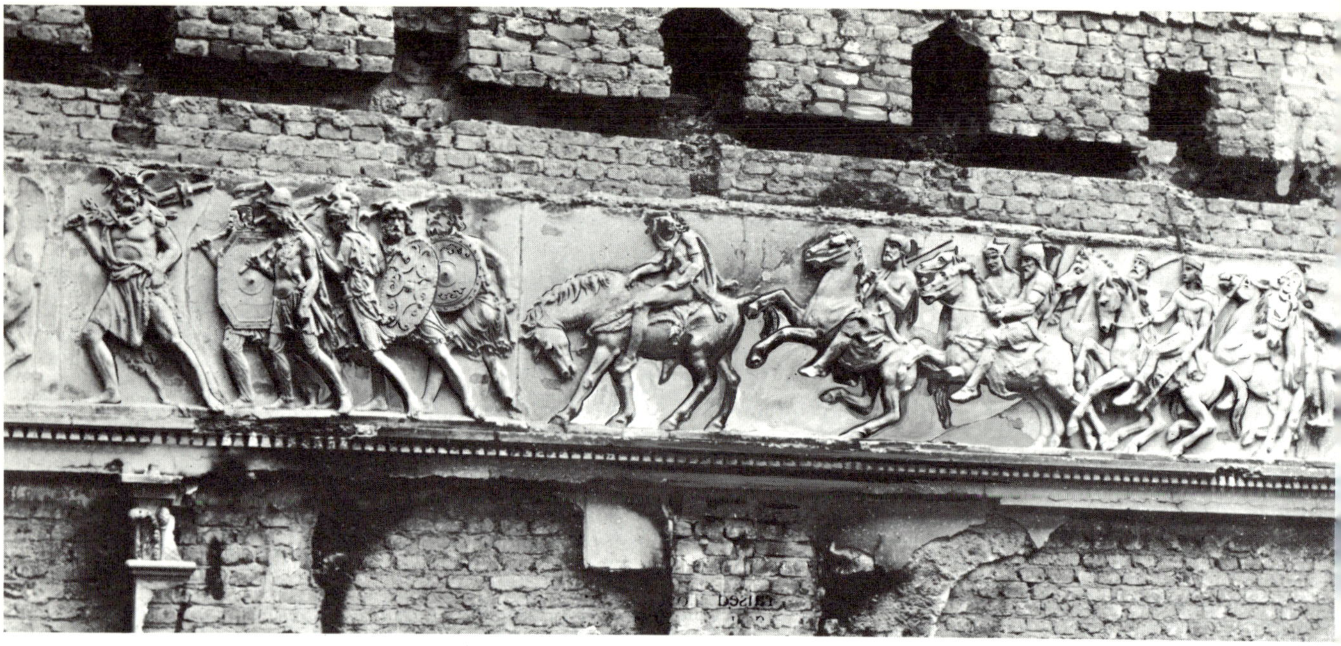

The end of the gods. Frieze in imitation of Greek art, by the Danish sculptor H. E. Freund. Attacked by the giants and other enemies, the gods assemble their warriors in Valhalla and set forth for the field where the decisive battle will be fought.

lying on the ground. He had only time enough to relate what had happened and then he died. His contemporaries explained this strange occurrence in the following way: the women were all protective spirits, *fylgjur* of the race. The black *fylgjur* were those who had remained faithful to paganism. The white were those who were already inclined to accept Christianity. But before being converted the pagan *fylgjur* had demanded a last sacrifice and the unfortunate Thidrandi had been the victim.

NORNS AND VALKYRIES

Other spirits frequently intervened in the life of men and could alter their destiny. They were often women known for their great wisdom. In Scandinavia these female spirits, mistresses of fate, were called Norns. This was the name under which they were universally known; for it was not only the Scandinavians but all the Germanic peoples who believed in their existence. They were thought of as spinners who held the threads of destiny in their hands. They were learned in the old customs, the ancient precepts of right and wrong, and could judge the fate each man merited. They even pronounced the fate of the gods, for the Aesir could no more escape their destiny than could men.

It is possible that at one time they believed in only one dispenser of fate. The word which designated fate (*wurd* in Low German, *wyrd* in Anglo-Saxon, *urdr* in Old Norse) was little by little transformed into a proper name, which was that of a kind of goddess who was both just and inexorable. But this first Norn was soon provided with sisters. It was eventually considered that some of them exerted themselves in the cause of man's happiness while others did everything in their malignant power to render him disservice. It is without doubt from these ancient deities of destiny that the fairies were derived, the fairies which in story appeared at the child's cradle to offer him magic gifts or, on the contrary, to utter maledictions which would shadow him the whole of his life.

The Scandinavian legend of Nornagest relates that at the hero's birth women endowed with the gift of prophecy appeared at his cradle. Beside the baby two candles were burning. The first two women bestowed on the newly born child virtues of all kinds and announced that he would be the happiest man of all his race. But the third woman rose up in fury, because the people crowding around the cradle had elbowed her and even pushed her to the floor. She decided to punish the infant for this affront to her dignity and cried out: 'I foretell that he will cease to live on the day that candle beside him ceases to burn!' Immediately the oldest of the three women seized the candle, extinguished it and warned the mother never to light it again until her son's last day had arrived. That was why the child was baptised Nornagest, 'the guest, the protected of the Norns'.

In Scandinavian countries the Norns became – though it is difficult to say exactly when – three in number. The first among them was the aged Urd (that is to say, Destiny). There was a fountain which bore her name near one of the roots of the ash tree Yggdrasil. It was here that the three Norns could usually be found. Every day they sprinkled the giant tree with water from the fountain so that it should not wither. Urd's two companions were in some documents called Verdandi and Skuld, names which medieval Icelandic scholars interpreted as signifying the Present and the Future; from which it followed that Urd was the Norn of the Past. But this interpretation was only the late invention of the erudite. Even the fact that the Norns were reduced to three in number betrays a classical influence: they wished to have three Norns just as there had been three Fates.

The Valkyries were also dispensers of destiny. But their power extended to only one class of men, namely warriors. It was they who, on the field of battle, gave victory to one or the other side, decided which heroes must perish, and chose which among them should be admitted to Valhalla to drink beer and mead at Odin's feasts. They themselves took part in the fighting. Belief in these warrior goddesses was common to all Germanic people. But the name by which they were designated varied among different tribes. The Germans in general called them *idisi*. The name which has become customary is the Norse *valkyrja* (in Anglo-Saxon *waelcyrie*). Its meaning is clear: the Valkyrie is 'she who chooses warriors destined to die in battle'.

The poets normally described the Valkyries as helmeted goddesses, grasping spears crowned with flame, and mounted on flying steeds from whose manes the dew falls in the valleys or hail descends on the forests. But they were also sometimes depicted as maidens in swans' plumage who could fly through the air. Every swan-maiden was not necessarily a Valkyrie; but a Valkyrie always had the power to turn herself into a swan-maiden. These strange and gracious creatures delighted in haunting the lakes and pools of lonely forests. They could, when it pleased them to do so, cast their plumage aside and appear in human form. But if a man succeeded in stealing their plumage they could never escape from him and were forced to obey his will.

The great medieval German epic, the *Nibelungenlied,* gives us a characteristic example. The fierce Hagen, seeking for a place to cross the Danube, suddenly heard a slight plash of water in a nearby pool. He crept silently through the shaded woods to the water's edge and there he saw two maidens who had slipped out of their swans' plumage and were bathing in the limpid water. He immediately seized their plumage and refused to restore it until he had learned from their lips what fate the future held for the army of the Burgundians who were marching towards the land of the Huns.

It was because she had allowed herself to be surprised by a man that the Valkyrie Brynhild – heroine of Wagner's musical drama – incurred the wrath of Odin. One day she and eight of her sisters were flying far from Valhalla. They landed on earth and removed their plumage. King Agnar approached, seized the discarded apparel and hid it under an oak. From then on the nine Valkyries were in his power. He demanded that Brynhild should help him in the war which he was waging against his old adversary Hjalmgunnar, and that she should make sure that Hjalmgunnar perished. She had no alternative but to agree. Now Hjalmgunnar was Odin's protégé and Odin had decided to give him the victory. Angered at having his will thwarted Odin pricked Brynhild with a magic thorn which had the quality of plunging all whom it touched into profound slumber. Then he enclosed her in a dwelling encircled by a wall of flame. Thenceforward Brynhild would return no more to Valhalla; she had ceased to be a Valkyrie; she was stripped of her divine privileges and condemned to lead a terrestrial life. The only man who could marry her would be the fearless hero who dared ride his horse through the flames which separated her from the world. This hero was to be Sigurd – the German Siegfried.

Valkyries and swan-maidens could become the mistresses and wives of men. In Iceland they told the touching history of Helgi who was united by an ardent and faithful love to the Valkyrie Kara. She would accompany him to war, dressed in her swan's plumage; flying above the battlefield she would sing a song of such charm and sweetness that the enemy would lose all ambition to defend himself. One day while she was hovering above Helgi he raised his sword to strike his adversary, but instead struck Kara in flight and fatally wounded her. It was the end of Helgi's happiness.

Elves and Dwarfs. In the world of nature there was not a spot which was not inhabited by some spirit. Some of these sprites were small, or at least no larger than men. They may be called by the general term of elves. The others, who played an important part in mythology, were giants.

To-day the word 'elf' in all Germanic languages – and consequently in other languages which have borrowed the word – has a more restricted meaning than it formerly had. It once served to designate all spirits or demons associated with nature, who were supposed to inhabit the waters, the woods or the mountains. Elves were sometimes helpful, but at other times they were full of malice. In English poetry of the Middle Ages they were above all celebrated as aerial and luminous beings, full of benevolence and kindness, and that is how they are normally thought of to-day. But the ancient Teutons felt a certain fear of them.

Ordinarily the elves were thought of as beings handsomer and better made than men, although smaller. They were organised in societies in the manner of men with kings whom they faithfully served. They loved games and dancing. Often they passed the entire night tirelessly dancing, interrupted only by the crowing of the first cock; for they feared the sunlight and avoided the eyes of men. If, while they danced by moonlight, a man chanced to pass the clearing where they frolicked he would be unable to tear his eyes from the faces of the young female elves. He would be bewitched by their beauty. If he allowed himself to take part in their dance he was lost: either he would never be seen again, or only his body would be found. Usually their dancing was without witnesses, but in the morning traces of their feet could be discovered in the moist grass. They were wise and subtle creatures to whom the future was known.

Dwarfs may be considered as a special class of elves. They too were of small stature, lived in secret places, usually underground, and were endowed with supernatural intelligence and foresight. They were, however, very far from being beautiful. They were almost always deformed; they were hunchbacked or twisted, they had big heads, pale faces and long beards.

Although they were rather wild and shy they would sometimes come into men's dwellings. One night a troop of dwarfs gathered in the great hall of Eilenburg castle in Saxony to celebrate a wedding. The noise wakened the Count, lord of the castle, who rose and entered the hall. Immediately a dwarf herald stepped forward and invited him, in the most courteous terms, to take part in the festivities. The Count willingly accepted the invitation. When morning came the little folk vanished, but not without first warmly thanking the Count for his hospitality, as politeness required.

Miners, they said, frequently met dwarfs in the galleries they dug in the flanks of mountains. It was said that these dwarfs were themselves often dressed as miners and wore leather aprons, carried lanterns, picks and hammers. More ingenious and learned than men they only frequented places where useful and precious metals abounded; hence to come across them forehadowed the discovery of rich booty. They were considered to be the rightful owners of buried treasure. One of these treasures is celebrated in German epic poetry: the treasure which belonged to the king Nibelung, of which the dwarf Alberich was the guardian. Siegfried, the hero of the *Nibelungenlied,* appropriated it after he had vanquished the dwarf Alberich and demanded an oath of fidelity from him. And it was to gain possession of the fabulous treasure for his master King Gunther that Hagen later treacherously slew the noble Siegfried.

This form of the famous legend of the Nibelungen is, however, peculiar to the German epic. In Norse poetry the matter occurred in another fashion. There, too, it concerned a hidden treasure, but the treasure belonged to a dwarf, one Andvari, who had the power to change himself into a fish and live in the water. One day Loki succeeded in capturing him with the aid of a magic net and only consented to set him free in exchange for the treasure. The dwarf was forced to agree and turned over all the gold he possessed to his enemy. He attempted, meanwhile, to conceal in the hollow of his hand a certain magic ring which had the property of creating further treasure and making it accumulate indefinitely. But Loki saw him and, deaf to the dwarf's piteous appeals, made him hand over the ring. Andvari thereupon laid a solemn curse upon the gold and the ring which had been extorted from him: they should cause the death of all who successively possessed them. Andvari's prophecy was fulfilled. Later the giant Fafnir, who had gained possession of the treasure by murdering his own father, changed himself into a dragon to guard it; but he fell beneath the blows of Sigurd, who himself perished not long afterwards.

Proprietors of the gold and precious stones buried in the ground, the dwarfs were cunning goldsmiths and incomparable blacksmiths. The weapons of the gods and the jewellery of the goddesses were their work. To them Odin owed his spear Gungnir whose flight nothing could arrest, and the ring Draupnir which, like the ring of Andvari, had the power of indefinitely augmenting the riches of its possessor. It was from the dwarfs that Thor acquired his hammer, Frey his golden boar and magic boat, Sif her golden locks and Freyja her beautiful necklace.

Others, not dwarfs in the strict sense of the word, were elves of a particular sort who peopled springs and rivers. In the eyes of the German peoples water-sprites usually took on human appearance. The best known of these were called 'nixies'. Though commonly supposed to be feminine the early German Nix, the undine, the water-sprite, could be masculine and was also called *Wassermann*, waterman. The water-sprites were apt to appear to men, though frequently to men's undoing. The nixie women were supposed to be dazzlingly beautiful. They loved to sit in the sun on the river bank and comb their long golden hair. They sometimes fell in love with handsome young men whom they dragged down to the bottom of the water and who were never seen again. Some who had seen them, or heard their melodious songs, lost their wits. They were, by and large, cruel spirits who delighted in doing harm to men.

There were, on the other hand, others who installed themselves in people's houses and became familiar spirits. They were then called 'kobolds'. They were in appearance not unlike men; of aged aspect, their faces were all wrinkles, and they wore pointed hoods on their heads. Normally they frequented the barns and stables and cellars; and they liked to make themselves useful about the house. They would go and fetch water, chop wood, feed the cattle, currycomb the horses, remove the manure. A kobold brought good luck to the house which sheltered him. He demanded very little for the services he rendered: a little milk and what was left over from the dinner table. But the servant must take good care not to forget his share. Otherwise the little creature could be vindictive and see that she scalded her fingers in the hot water, broke a pot or upset the dishes. When such mishaps occurred she would hear in a corner the malicious chuckle of the kobold.

Finally, the fields and forests were inhabited by innumerable spirits. The appearance of those who dwelt among the trees – 'men and women of the woods' – recalled the environment in which they lived: their bodies were hairy and seemed to be covered with moss; their faces were as wrinkled and gnarled as the bark of the trees. Hunters and woodcutters sometimes saw them in thickets. They were as a rule not unhelpful. They knew the secret virtues of herbs which they made use of in stopping outbreaks of disease. They were, however, sometimes accused of assuming the form of insects, moths and worms, in order to spread illness among men.

The spirits of the fields were generally believed to have animal forms. The ruffling of a field of ripe wheat by the wind was attributed to the passage of an invisible animal, the 'corn-wolf' or the 'rye-dog'. The grain itself was sometimes thought of as the body of this invisible spirit, just as the tree was the body of the tree-sprite. During the harvest the corn-wolf would, they said, try to escape from the harvesters. He would take refuge in that part of the field where the grain still stood; but they would take him prisoner with the final sheaf. When that happened they would make the gesture of killing him with scythe or flail, or – in other parts of the country – take him respectfully home in the sheaf knotted like a scarecrow and piled on top of the other sheaves.

Giants. In many ways the power and the role ascribed to the giants resembled those exercised by various kinds of elves or dwarfs. Often the only difference between them was their size. Like the dwarfs the giants were sometimes hostile, sometimes benevolent. On the whole, however, they inspired fear; and the surly, not to say evil character which the Teutons were apt to attribute to them was explained by their origin. They were, indeed, simply the personification of great natural phenomena, such as hurricanes, winter, volcanic eruptions, earthquakes and so on.

We have already seen that of all living creatures the giants were supposed to be the first to appear on the earth. They ante-dated even the gods. They retained in their appearance and vast bodies something of the rudeness and brutality of those days when the earth first emerged from the icy void. The names by which they were known varied with the country. One name has been adopted in other languages: the Scandinavian *troll.*

Like the dwarfs they were scattered throughout nature. It was thought that they could be glimpsed in the black clouds driven before the storm winds. They were accused of causing hail to fall on the harvest. It was believed that their voices could be heard when thunder rolled through the valley or echoed in the mountains. It was said, when clouds whipped by the wind sped by, that such and such a giant was chasing a pretty girl whom he hoped to seize by force. In this respect the giant resembled Woden.

These giants, so close to the gods, did not hesitate to defy them. We remember the audacity with which Thrym stole Thor's hammer. Another giant, Geirröd, having succeeded in luring Thor to his castle, challenged the god to a singular sort of duel, hoping to reduce him to his mercy. From one of the gigantic fires which burned in the middle of the great hall Geirröd drew forth a lump of incandescent iron by means of vast tongs. The two adversaries were to hurl it at each other in turn. The giant began. Without flinching or dodging the blow Thor caught the molten mass in flight in his iron gloves. The giant, who had expected to kill Thor outright, now only thought of his own skin. With a bound he hid behind an iron column. But Thor flung the glowing missile with such force that the entire edifice was shaken. The monstrous object first pierced the iron column, then the giant's body and the castle wall before plunging into the ground. The symbolism is obvious: demon and god in turn hurled the thunderbolt at each other; but despite his power the giant cannot overthrow the thunder-god.

Other giants lived in the mountains. In Germany the *Nibelungenlied* preserved the memory of twelve giants who lived in the midst of wild mountains and took their orders from the kings Nigelung and Schilbung. The grumbling which can sometimes be heard in the depths of gorges, the crumbling of cliffs and the sudden overflowing of torrents were produced by angered giants.

Finally in the sea there were giants, just as there were nixies in the rivers. Scandinavian legend made a special place for the giant Aegir, lord of the sea. His rank was not quite that of a god but his relations with the Aesir were friendly. He was readily welcomed to their feasts and in his turn received them in his marine palace. He had no need for fire to illuminate his great hall; the gold which adorned it spread a brilliant light. The Teutons doubtless imagined that treasures swallowed up by the sea during shipwrecks were piled high in Aegir's palace.

Aegir had a wife whose name was Ran, that is, 'the ravisher'. She owned a vast net in which she tried to capture and draw to her side every man who ventured on the sea. It was she who stirred up the waves and caused them to lash violently together in the hope of imperilling ships. The terror which she inspired was so great that in the end she rose in popular imagination from the rank of a simple demon to that of a veritable goddess. Moreover she welcomed the drowned magnificently in her great hall and served them with the delicate flesh of fish. Nine daughters were born of her marriage to Aegir. The names which the skalds gave them show that they were merely personifications of the waves. They were temptresses who reached out seductive arms to young men and, if they responded, dragged them to the bottom of the sea.

The wise Mimir, who so often appears in Scandinavian legends and whom Odin willingly consulted, was himself a water giant. But his domain was limited to springs, to pools and inland lakes; it did not extend to the sea. Mimir moreover lived in such close communion with the gods that he was often considered one of them.

The belief in dwarfs, giants and demons of all kinds persisted in Germanic lands for many centuries after the introduction of Christianity, as is witnessed by certain twelfth and thirteenth century epics, tales and countless popular locutions. Some superstitions have persisted even to our days. There was a period – roughly between the ninth and thirteenth centuries – when pagan legends were sometimes amalgamated with Christian legends. It was told, for instance, that Olaf Tryggvason, one of the most energetic converters of Norway, forced a troll – in other words a giant – to build a church. This legend belongs to a well-known type of story in which the role of the hoaxed demon is often played by the devil: the giant – or the devil – offers to erect a building in a given time. He demands, as the price of his labour, either the sacrifice of a human being or else the possession of his soul. At the last minute the endangered man's partner always finds a way of outwitting the demon: the edifice remains while the demon retires in vexation.

There were also cases cited of demons who desired to be accepted into the bosom of the Church. Two children were playing one day on the banks of a river which flowed past their father's house. A water-sprite suddenly rose to the surface of the river and, taking his harp, began to play in wondrous fashion. One of the children interrupted him. 'What good does it do you to play like that?' the child asked. 'You will never attain eternal salvation.' At these words the water-sprite began to weep bitterly; then, tossing his harp away, he plunged back into the waters. When the two children returned to the house they told their father, who was a pastor, what had taken place. He censured them harshly for having filled an inoffensive being with such despair, and sent them back to the river-bank with orders to promise the 'man of the waters' the remission of his sins and his eternal salvation. When they reached the bank the two children saw the water-sprite sitting on the surface of the water. He was still weeping. They said to him: 'Water-sprite, do not grieve like that. Our father says that for you, too, the Saviour came to earth.' Immediately the water-sprite dried his tears, took up his harp again and again broke into sweet melody.

The mingling of Christian and pagan elements, which is not rare, can be easily explained: more than one Germanic tribe had accepted Christianity without thereby rejecting traditional beliefs. Among the Vikings who in the ninth century settled in Great Britain and Ireland there were many who spontaneously adopted the religion of the country they had colonised, but felt no obligation to stop believing in their own Germanic gods. They simply super-imposed one religion on the other, and were, perhaps, not enthusiastically attached to either. More or less the same thing happened with the first colonists in Iceland. In Norway, pious and energetic chieftains had, towards the year One Thousand, forced the whole population to adopt Christianity. But more than one petty prince only accepted the situation for political reasons. Actually it took paganism many centuries to die out, nor can one even say that it is totally dead to-day. The great gods have doubtless been without devotees for many years. The same is not, however, true of the familiar demons by whom the people still have a tendency to believe themselves surrounded. There are spirits in country districts who have not lost all credit, spirits to whom the peasants, either by invoking their aid, attempting to allay their anger, or by associating their name with the practice of witchcraft, still render, without realising it, a certain sort of cult.

SLAVONIC MYTHOLOGY

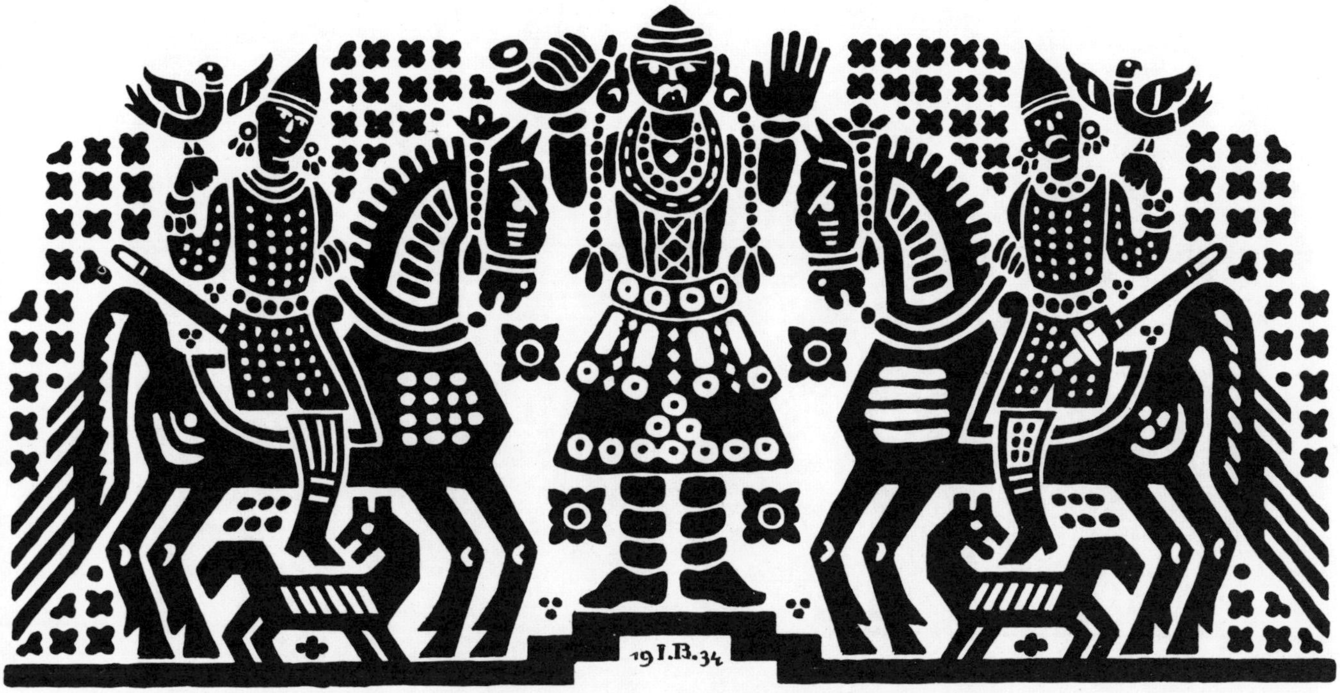

Pre-Slavonic ornamental motif, inspired by Russian embroidery and representing a stylised god flanked by two horsemen equipped for hawking.

INTRODUCTION

We have very few precise data on the Slavonic world in the days of paganism. A few scraps of information provided by Roman historians and Greek 'chroniclers', some vague observations on the part of Arab geographers, and, above all, the frequently erroneous details appearing in the chronicles of Orthodox monks: these are all the material documents which we have available to reconstruct the history of the pagan Slavs and of their religious beliefs.

As, however, the material and spiritual evolution of the Slavs was much later and slower than that of the Latin and Germanic peoples of Western Europe we sometimes find in the more recent history of the Slavonic races vestiges and memories of bygone periods, a fact which allows us to utilise the present in order to reconstruct the past.

The mythological background can still be discovered in folklore – in legends, tales, songs, proverbs and, above all, in exorcisms. For in certain Slavonic countries exorcism of pagan origin is still currently practised.

It was only in the sixth century A.D. that the Slavonic world began to emerge distinctly from the varied and mobile ethnographic mass which peopled the Balkans, Central and Eastern Europe. Very probably it was from the Carpathians that the Slavonic tribes dispersed in various directions to form the three great groups which still exist, namely the Southern Slavs, the Western Slavs and those of the East.

The countries which the Slavs penetrated and colonised were almost everywhere characterised by immense spaces covered with forests and cut up by marshes, lakes and rivers. They lived by fishing and hunting, tended cattle in forest clearings and natural meadows, and planted a little corn in the ground they cleared. The forest provided wood for the construction of their crude houses.

Living in small groups of families, they would feel isolated and defenceless before the powerful forces of nature, before the mystery of day and night, the change of the seasons, the storms and tempests, the flooding rivers, and the irregular succession of good and bad crops.

To rid themselves of perpetual fear before the mysterious manifestations of nature the ancient Slavs needed to find explanations. This imperious necessity to explain natural phenomena found expression in their mythology which constituted their cosmogony and all their science in general.

The ancient Slav was physically incapable of fighting the forces of nature and could only aspire to moderating the evil for which they were responsible. It was therefore necessary for him to find out whom to address himself to. Compelled to submit himself to the domination of these mysterious forces of nature, he submitted them, too, to the domination of other powers which were personified by the numerous divinities with whom he peopled the clouds and the earth, the forests and the rivers, his own field of corn, the stable where his cattle slept, and the house which sheltered his family.

Thus little by little a mythology common to all the Slavonic tribes was formed, an extremely rustic mythology, but perfectly adapted to the general conditions of primitive life. It was only in the outposts of the Slavonic world – where they encountered other peoples – that more complex beliefs were created and a less rustic mythology developed. Only at Kiev and on the littoral of the Baltic Sea (in the island of Rugen) do we find among the Slavs traces of a more or less fixed hierarchy of superior divinities, with a few crude idols, priests and rites.

In general, however, Slavonic mythology found no material expression definite enough to present its divinities in precise form. It remained vague and amorphous like the landscape of most of the countries inhabited by the Slavonic race.

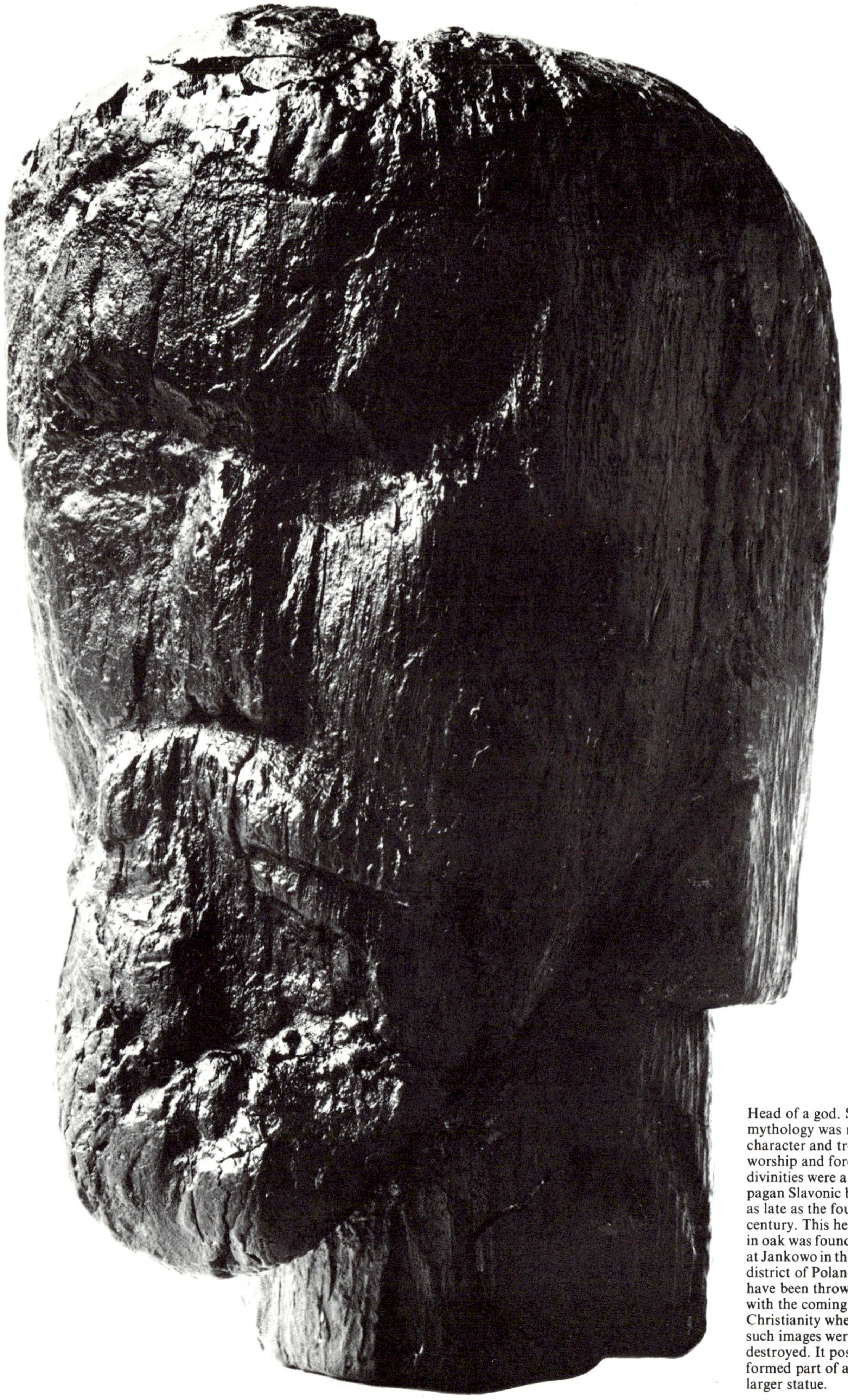

Head of a god. Slav mythology was rustic in character and tree worship and forest divinities were a feature of pagan Slavonic belief until as late as the fourteenth century. This head carved in oak was found in a lake at Jankowo in the Mogilno district of Poland. It may have been thrown there with the coming of Christianity when many such images were destroyed. It possibly formed part of a larger statue.

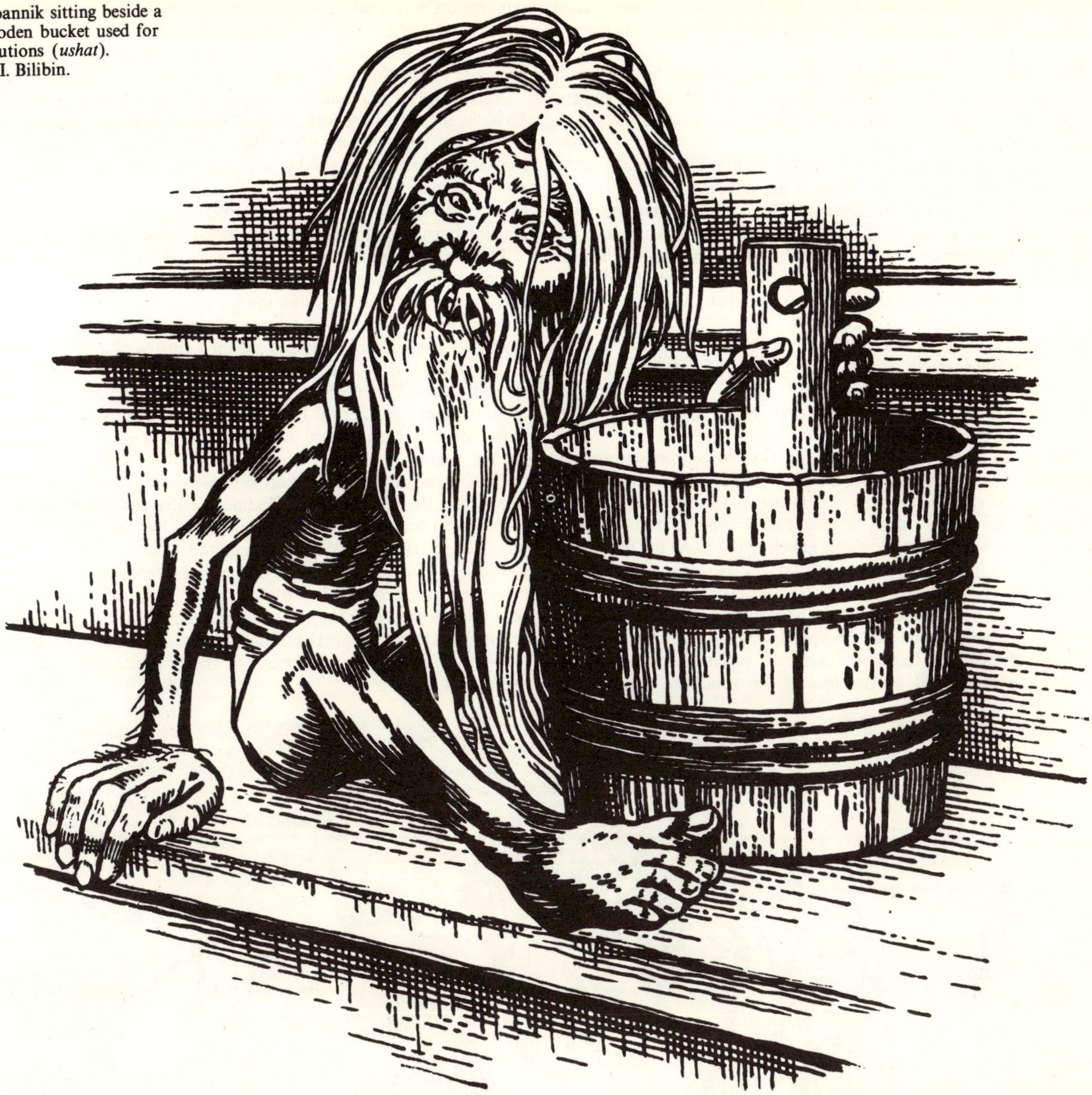

A bannik sitting beside a wooden bucket used for ablutions (*ushat*). By I. Bilibin.

THE BIRTH OF THE GODS:

Byelobog and Chernobog. (The White God and the Black God.) At the basis of Slavonic mythology we find a primitive dualism which had its source in the opposition between light, the creative force, and darkness, the destructive force. This elemental opposition gave birth to two divine images which are found among the peoples of the Western branch of the Slavonic world: Byelobog and Chernobog.

The composition of their names reveals their character. Byelobog is made up of the adjective 'byely' which means 'white', and the noun 'bog' which means 'god'. The adjective 'cherny' on the other hand means 'black'. Thus there is a white god, god of light and day, and a black god, god of the shadows and of night: a god of good and a god of evil, opposed one to the other.

The *volkhvy*, half priests, half sorcerers, of the pagan Slavs would say, according to certain written testimony: 'There are two gods, one above and the other below.'

The Ukrainians still say: 'May the black god exterminate you!'

In White Russia they believed in the existence of *Byelun* (derived from 'byely' – 'white'). In popular legends this divinity appeared as an old man with a white beard, dressed in white. He only showed himself during the daytime. His actions were always benevolent: he saved from harm those who had lost their way and helped unfortunate peasants with their work in the fields.

The simple opposition of Byelobog and Chernobog being insufficient to explain the great variety of natural phenomena, other visions began to take shape against the black-white background of primitive mythology.

THE WORSHIP OF NATURE: RUSTIC GODS: THE SKY AND ITS CHILDREN

When the pagan Slav addressed his prayer to the sky and said: 'Sky, thou seest me! Sky, thou hearest me!' he was not using a metaphorical expression. He thought of the sky as a god, as a supreme being.

Later, when anthropomorphic elements had penetrated the primitive religion of the pagan Slavs, they personified the sky as the god Svarog. The root of this name (*svar* means bright, clear) is related to the Sanskrit.

The sky (Svarog) gave birth to two children: the Sun, called Dazhbog, and Fire, which was called Svarogich, meaning 'son of Svarog'.

John Malala, a Byzantine chronicler, sums up the mythological cosmogony of the pagan Slavs in these terms:

'After Svarog reigned his son, named Sun who was also called Dazhbog... The Sun is the king and son of Svarog; he is named Dazhbog, for he was a mighty lord.'

The other son of Svarog, Fire (or *ogon* which can be compared to the Sanskrit *agni*) is mentioned in the work of a very ancient author called 'Unknown Admirer of Christ' who said of the pagan Slavs:

'They also address prayers to Fire, calling him Svarogich.'

Svarog (the Sky) is thus the father of all other gods.

According to an old Slavonic myth Svarog, after reigning over the universe, transmitted his creative sovereign power to his children.

In many Slavonic countries rural folk still retain a mystic respect for fire, which has always had a sacred character. The old forbade the young to swear or shout at the moment when the fire was being lighted in the house.

Legends and folk stories still retain poetic traces of the ancient myths when they speak of the 'Fire Serpent', a winged monster who breathed flames from his mouth.

The Russian savant Afanasiev says of Svarog's other son, Dazhbog, the sun:

'Svarog, as a personification of the sky, sometimes lighted by the sun's rays, sometimes covered with clouds and brilliant with lightning, was considered to be the father of the Sun and of Fire. In the shadows of the clouds he would kindle the lightning's flame and thus he appeared as the creator of celestial fire. As for terrestrial fire, it was a divine gift brought to earth in the form of lightning. Hence it will be understood why the Slav worshipped Fire as a son of Svarog. Afterwards, splitting the clouds with flashing arrows, Svarog would cause the sun to appear, or, in the metaphorical language of antiquity, he would light the torch of the sun which had been extinguished by demons of the shadows. This poetic conception was also applied to the morning sun emerging from the veils of night. With the sunrise and the renewal of its flame the idea of its rebirth was connected. Svarog was thus a divinity who gave life to the Sun and birth to Dazhbog.'

According to Slavonic myths and legends the Sun lived in the East, in a land of eternal summer and abundance. There he had his golden palace from which he emerged every morning in his luminous chariot, drawn by white horses who breathed fire, to cross the celestial vault.

In a popular Polish tale the sun rode in a two-wheeled diamond chariot harnessed to twelve white horses with golden manes.

In another legend the sun lived in a golden palace in the East. He made his journey in a car drawn by three horses, one silver, one golden and the third diamond.

Among the Serbs the Sun was a young and handsome king. He lived in a kingdom of light and sat on a throne of gold and purple. At his side stood two beautiful virgins, Aurora of the Morning and Aurora of the Evening, seven judges (the planets) and seven 'messengers' who flew across the universe in the guise of 'stars with tails' (comets). Also present was the Sun's 'bald uncle, old Myesyats' (or the moon).

In Russian folklore the Sun possessed twelve kingdoms – the twelve months or signs of the Zodiac. He lived in the solar disk and his children on the stars. They were served by the 'solar daughters' who bathed them, looked after them and sang to them.

The daily movement of the Sun across the celestial sphere was represented in certain Slavonic myths as a change in his age: the Sun was born every morning, appeared as a handsome child, reached maturity towards midday and died in the evening as an old man. The annual movement of the Sun was explained in an analogous fashion.

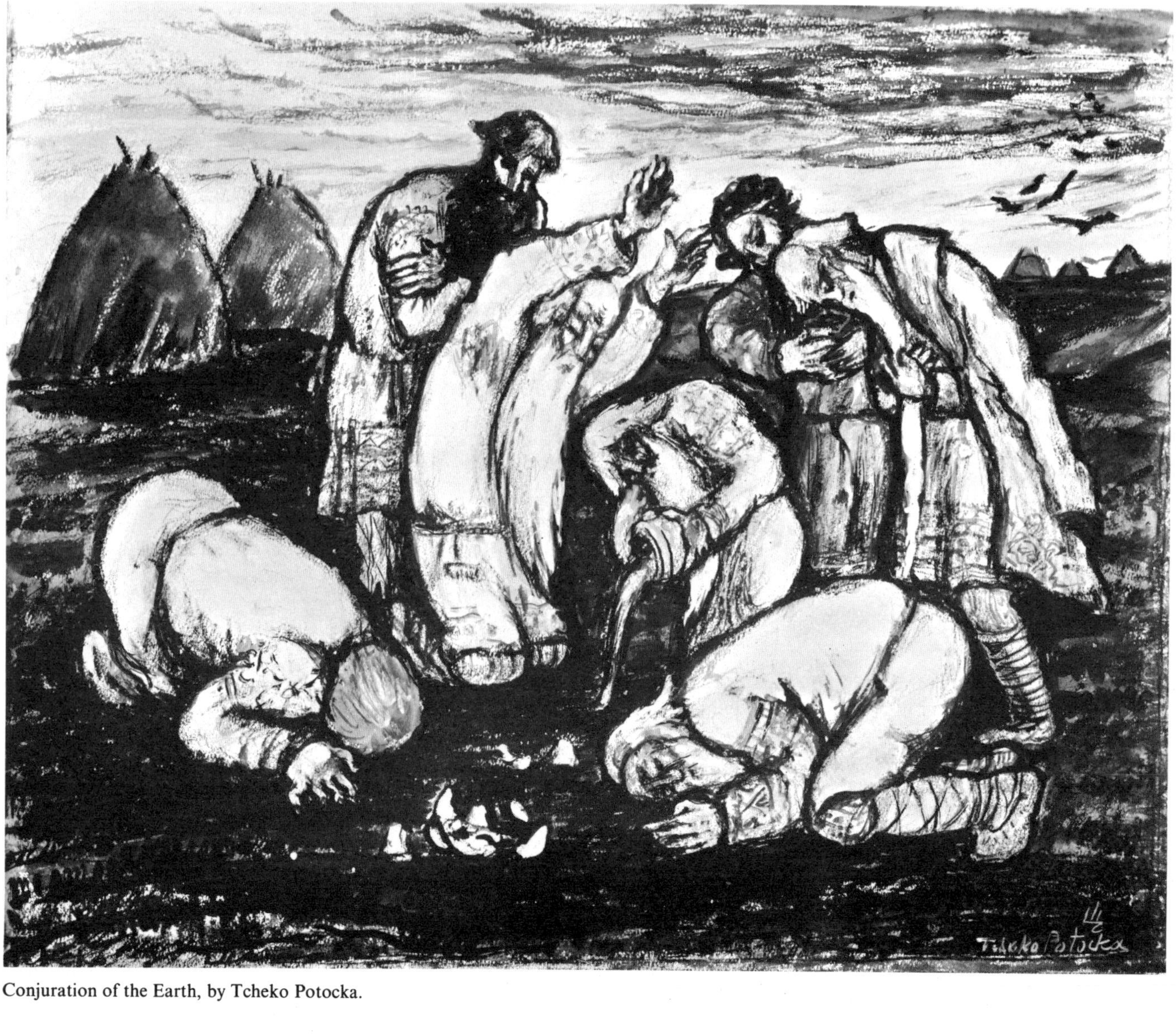

Conjuration of the Earth, by Tcheko Potocka.

Certain Slavonic myths and legends give an anthropomorphic interpretation to the relationship between the Sun and the Moon. Though the name of the Moon – Myesyats – is masculine many legends represent Myesyats as a young beauty whom the Sun marries at the beginning of summer, abandons in winter, and returns to in spring.

The divine couple of the Sun and the Moon gave birth to the stars. When the pair were in a bad mood and not getting on well together an earthquake would result.

In other myths Myesyats is, on the contrary, the husband, and the Sun is his wife. A Ukrainian song speaks of the heavenly vault, 'the great palace whose lord is bright Myesyats with his wife the bright Sun and their children the bright Stars.'

Even to-day certain Slavonic exorcisms are addressed to 'pretty little moon' and beseech her to cure illness etc. The hero of a Ukrainian song-legend speaks to 'little Sun: God, help me, man!'

The Sun-god Dazhbog, great divinity of day and the light of day, conqueror of the shadows, of cold and of misery became synonymous with happiness. Men's destiny depended on him. He was just. He punished the wicked and rewarded the virtuous.

The Slav of Galicia still says, when he wishes ill to a person: 'May the Sun make you perish!' And the Croatian peasant says: 'May the Sun avenge me on you!'

We have referred above to a legend according to which the two 'solar daughters', the Auroras, stood at the Sun's side. The dawn – in Slavonic Zorya or Zarya – was also believed to be a divinity. Aurora of the Morning (Zorya Utrennyaya – *utro* meaning 'morning') opened the gates of the celestial palace when the Sun set forth on his daily journey across the heavens. Aurora of the Evening (Zorya Vechernyaya – *vecher* meaning 'evening') closed them again when the Sun came home.

A myth of a later period attributes a special mission to the Zorya. 'There are in the sky,' it says, 'three little sisters, three little Zorya: she of the Evening, she of Midnight, and she of Morning. Their duty is to guard a dog which is tied by an iron chain to the constellation of the Little Bear. When the chain breaks it will be the end of the world.'

The three little Zorya are thus the great protectresses of the entire universe.

In some myths the two sister Auroras (Zorya) are accompanied by two sister Stars, the morning star Zvezda Dennitsa and the evening star Vechernyaya Zvezda. They share the work of the Zorya and tend the Sun's white horses.

One of them, Dennitsa, in some legends replaces the Sun as wife of Myesyats (the male Moon). In a Serbian song-legend Myesyats reproaches Dennitsa: 'Where hast thou been, star Dennitsa, where hast thou been? Where hast thou wasted thy days? Where hast thou wasted thy days, three bright days?'

In an old Russian exorcism Dennitsa appears as a divinity almost equal to the greatest of the gods. 'In the morning let us arise and pray to God and Dennitsa,' says this exorcism.

In another exorcism the Evening Star is addressed: 'My mother, Vechernyaya Zvezda, to Thee I complain of twelve daughters, twelve wicked girls.' i.e. fevers.

Pagan Slavs also believed in the god or the gods of the winds. A trace of this belief survives in a curious exorcism: 'On the sea, the ocean, on the isle of Buyan, live three brothers, the Winds: one is of the North, the second of the East, the third of the West. Blow, ye Winds, blow unbearable sadness to . . . (such and such a girl) so that she cannot live a single day, a single hour without thinking of me!'

The West Wind, soft and caressing, was named Dogoda.

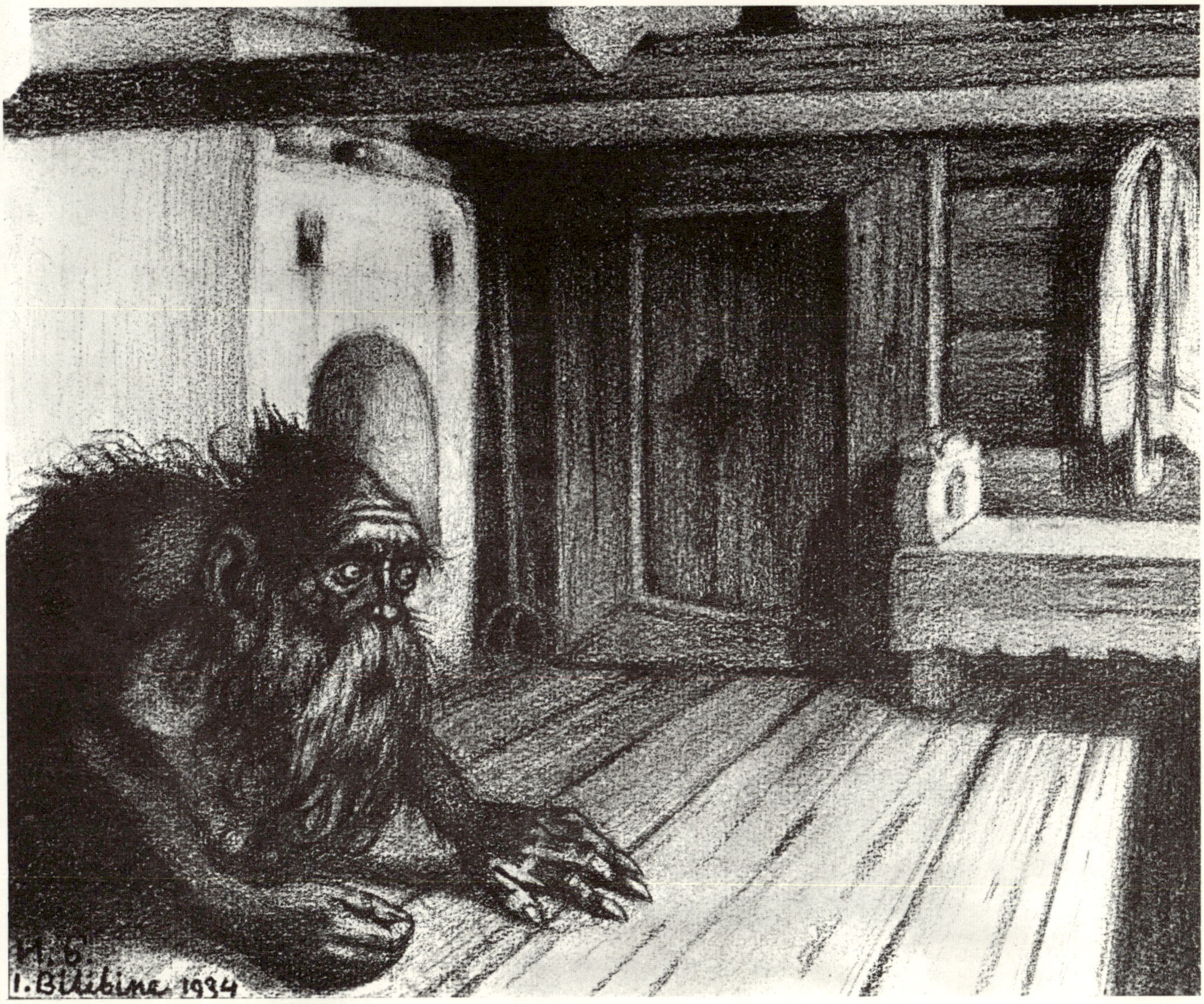

Domovoi, familiar genie of the house. By I. Bilibin.

Little Slav god. An ancient bronze found in a tomb in Poltava. Museum of the University of Kiev.

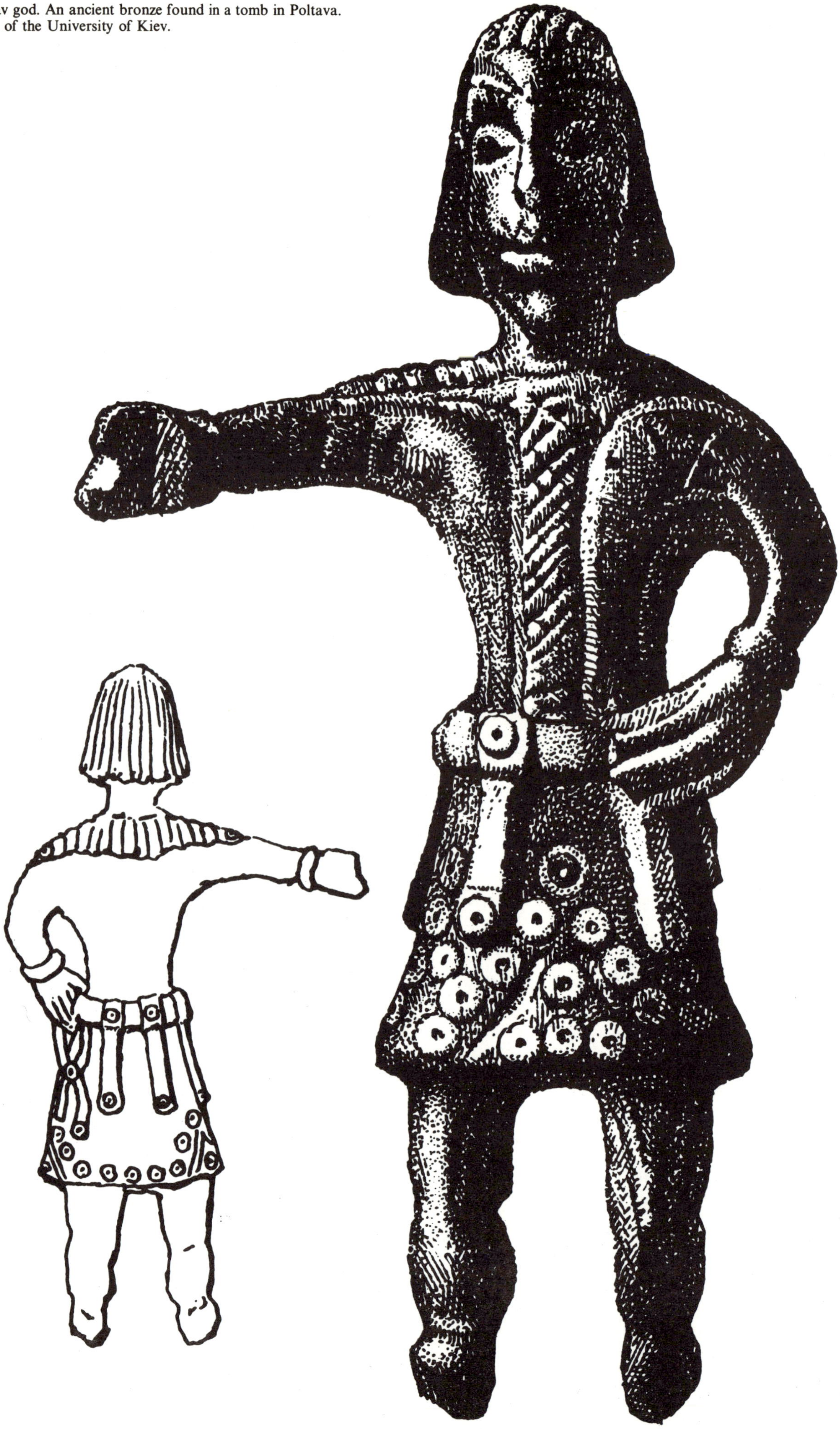

In certain legends there were as many as seven Winds.

Among several Slavonic tribes we find the worship of a god of the Winds named Stribog. They also spoke of a Wind-god named Varpulis who formed part of the retinue of the god Perun and caused the noise of the storm. Erisvorsh was the god of the holy tempest. But the sound of these last names suggests a Lithuanian or Teutonic origin.

MATI-SYRA-ZEMLYA

The pagan Slavs worshipped the Earth as a special divinity, but we have little information about either her appearance or her cult. We only know that among the Russians she was called Mati-Syra-Zemlya which means 'Moist Mother Earth'.

Mythological and ritual memories of belief in the Moist-Mother-Earth can be found in various customs and practices of the Slav peasants.

In certain regions in the month of August the peasants arrive in the fields at dawn with jars filled with hemp oil. Turning towards the east they say: 'Moist Mother Earth, subdue every evil and unclean being so that he may not cast a spell on us nor do us any harm.' While they pronounce this prayer they pour the oil on the ground. Then they turn towards the west and say: 'Moist Mother Earth, engulf the unclean power in thy boiling pits, in thy burning fires.' Turning to the south they pronounce these words: 'Moist Mother Earth, calm the Winds coming from the South and all bad weather. Calm the moving sands and whirlwinds.' And finally turning towards the north they say: 'Moist Mother Earth, calm the North Winds and the clouds, subdue the snowstorms and the cold.' After each invocation oil is poured out and finally the jar which contained it is thrown to the ground.

The Earth was a supreme being, sentient and just. She could predict the future if one knew how to understand her mysterious language. In certain parts of Russia the peasant would dig in the earth with a stock or simply with his fingers, apply his ear to the hole and listen to what the Earth said. If he heard a sound which reminded him of the sound made by a well-filled sleigh gliding over the snow his crop would be good. If, on the contrary, the sound was that of an empty sleigh his crop would be bad.

The Earth was just and one must not deceive her. For centuries Slav peasants settled legal disputes relating to landed property by calling on the Earth as a witness. If someone swore an oath while placing a clod of earth on his head the oath was considered binding and incontestable.

Traces of the ancient worship of the Earth could still be found in Russia on the eve of the first world war in an odd rite to which the peasants had recourse when they wished to preserve their village against an epidemic of plague or cholera. At midnight the old women would perambulate the village, secretly summoning the other women so that the men knew nothing about it. They would choose nine virgins and three widows who would be led out of the village. There they would all undress down to their shifts. The virgins would let down their hair, the widows would cover their heads with white shawls. They would then hitch one of the widows to a plough which was driven by another widow. The nine virgins would seize scythes while the other women grasped various objects of terrifying appearance including the skulls of animals. The procession would then march around the village, howling and shrieking, while they ploughed a furrow to permit the powerful spirits of the Earth to emerge, and so to annihilate the germs of evil. Any man who had the bad luck to meet the procession was felled without mercy.

LITTLE RUSTIC DIVINITIES

Christianity attacked pagan Slavonic mythology before it had completely bloomed. It was nipped, as it were, in the bud.

With the victory of Christianity the great divinities vanished. But the *dii minores*, the little divinities, were able to escape the massacre. The Slavs, though Christians, preserved many pagan beliefs well into the twentieth century and peopled their material and spiritual world with a countless crowd of little gods and goddesses, of spirits good and evil.

Domovoi. The Domovoi – derived from the word *dom* meaning 'house' – was the divinity or spirit of the house. From superstition the Slav peasant avoided calling him by his official name: some designated him by the word 'grandfather' or 'master of the house' while others spoke of 'him' or 'himself'.

The outward aspect of the Domovoi was vague. Usually he was a being in human shape, but hairy; he was covered with silky fur even to the palms of his hands which, otherwise, resembled a man's. Sometimes he had horns and a tail. On occasion he had the aspect of a domestic animal or even of an ordinary bundle of hay.

It was difficult, not to say dangerous, for a person actually to see the Domovoi. His voice, however, was often heard and his groans and stifled sobs; his speech, while ordinarily soft and caressing, could also be abrupt or gloomy.

This is how they explained the origin of the Domovoi and certain other little divinities: when the supreme god created heaven and earth one party of the spirits who surrounded him revolted. He drove these rebellious spirits from the sky and cast them to earth. Some fell onto the roofs of people's houses or into their yards. Unlike others who fell into the water or forests and remained wicked, these, through their association with men, became benevolent.

The Domovoi would become so much at home in the house where he lived that he would be reluctant to leave it. When a Russian peasant built a new *izba*, his wife, before moving in, would cut a slice of bread and put it under the stove in order to attract the Domovoi to the new house. The Domovoi loved to live near the stove or under the threshold of the front door. As for his wife, called Domania or Domovikha, she preferred to live in the cellar.

The Domovoi forewarned the inhabitants of the house of the troubles which threatened them. Before the death of someone in the family he wept. He would pull the wife's hair to warn her that her husband was going to beat her.

The Domovoi appeared among the Slavs only after the family group became distinct from the tribal group. Previously there had been a spirit of the tribe itself, called Rod or Chur, terms which are impossible to translate but which signified ancestor or forefather.

OTHER DOMESTIC SPIRITS

In the neighbourhood of the Domovoi there were other spirits who may be considered as his near relations.

Such were, for example, the Dvorovoi (from the word *dvor* or yard) who was the spirit of the yard; the Bannik (from the word *banya* or bath) who was the spirit of the baths and who lived in the little outhouse situated beside the izba, where the peasants took their baths; the Ovinnik (from the word *ovin* or barn) who was the spirit of the barn.

A little farther removed from human company than the Domovoi, they were less friendly than he, without, however, being as fierce as the forest and water spirits.

The Dvorovoi particularly detested all animals with white fur, such as white cats, dogs or horses. Only white chickens had no fear of the Dvorovoi because they were protected by a special divinity, the god of the chickens who was represented by a round stone with a hole in it which is sometimes found in the fields.

To appease a Dvorovoi one could put a little sheep's wool in the stable, some small glittering objects and a slice of bread. When making this offering one had to say: 'Tsar Dvorovoi, master, friendly little neighbour, I offer thee this gift in sign of gratitude. Be kind to the cattle, look after them and feed them well.' If the Dvorovoi behaved too badly one could punish him by sticking a pitchfork into the wooden fence around the yard, or by beating the demon with a whip in which must be woven a thread drawn from a winding-sheet. The Dvorovoi also dreaded the dead body of a magpie hung up in the yard.

Sometimes the Dvorovoi would fall in love with a woman. One of them conceived a passion for a girl and lived with her for several years. He plaited her hair and forbade her to unplait it. When she was thirty-five years old she decided to marry a man and on the even of her wedding she combed out her hair. Next morning she was found dead; she had been strangled in her bed by the Dvorovoi.

The Bannik lived in the washhouse. He would permit three groups of bathers to enter, but the fourth turn was his. He would invite devils and forest-spirits to visit him. If he were disturbed

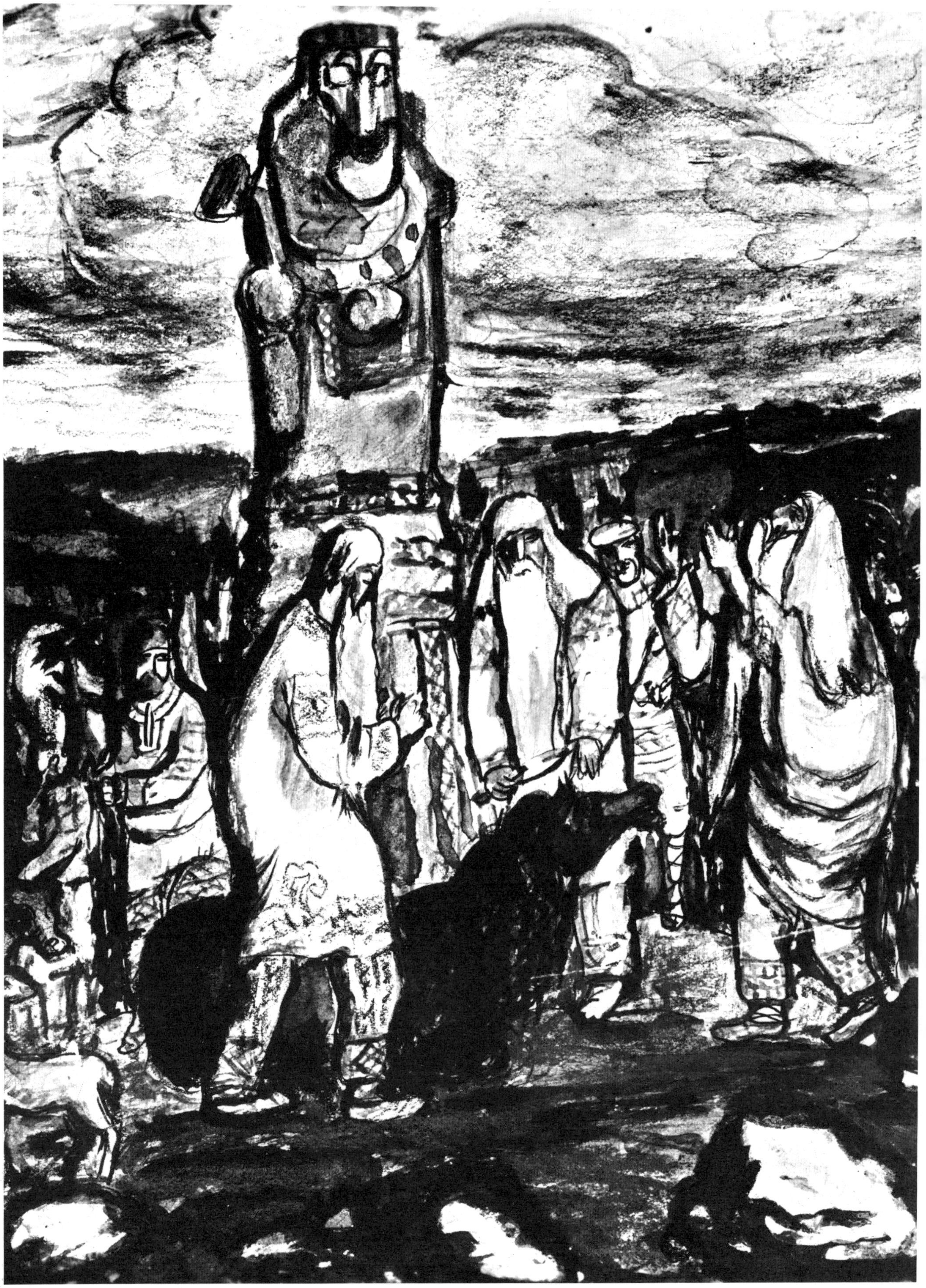

Sacrifice of a horse to Volos. Like the great majority of Slavonic gods, Volos, the god of the beasts, was of rustic origin and character. He later became associated with the war-god Pyerun but with the advent of Christianity he returned to his rural haunts and regained his former role as a protector of flocks. His function and attributes were finally transferred to Saint Vlas or Blaise. Painting by Tcheko Potocka

Kikimora, domestic divinity. Drawing by I. Bilibin.

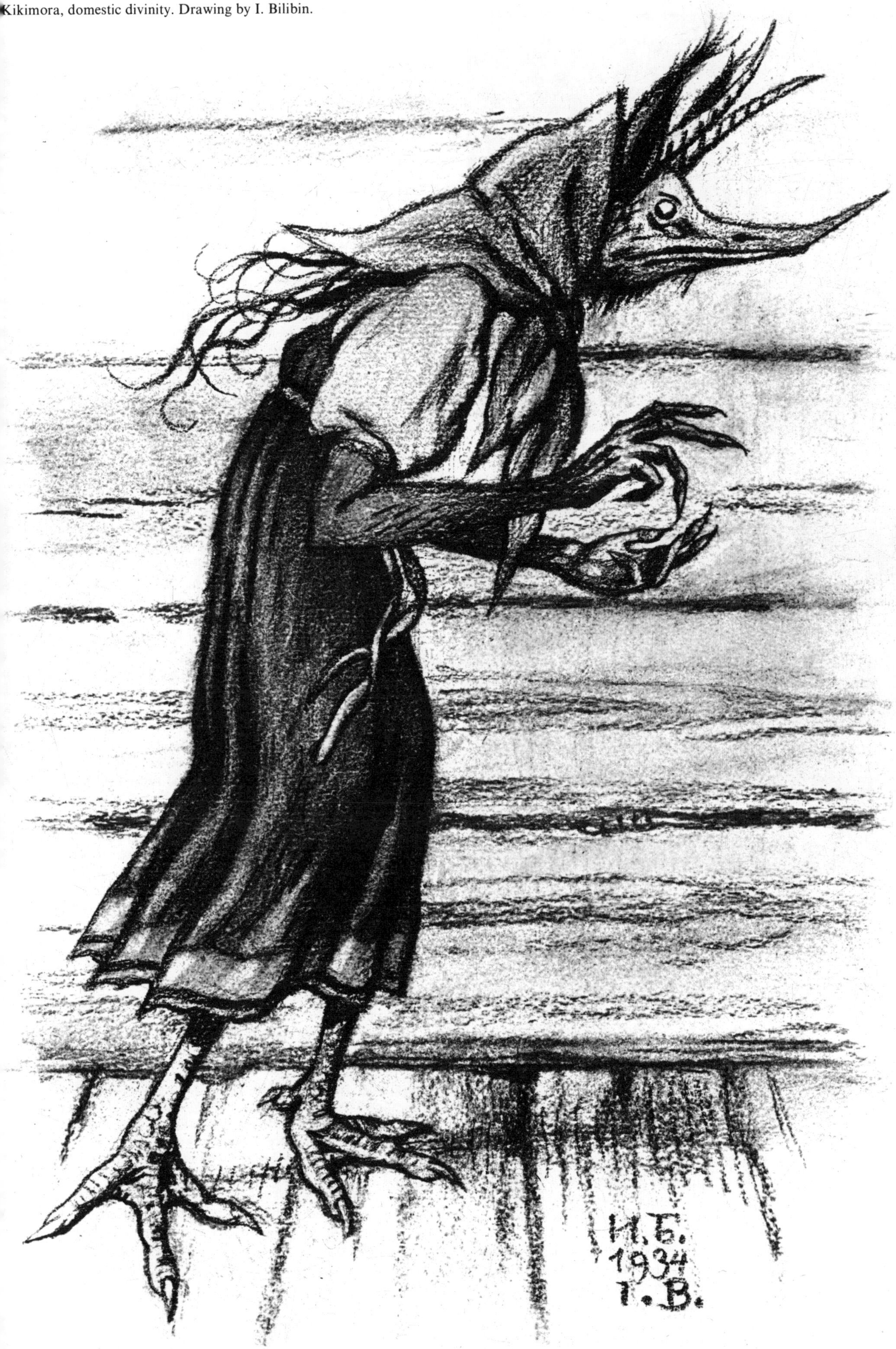

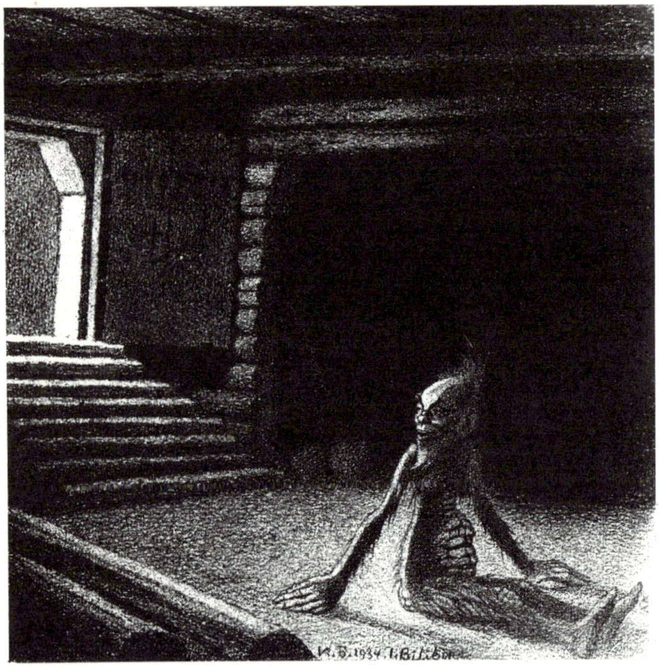

Ovinnik, divinity of the barns. By I. Bilibin.

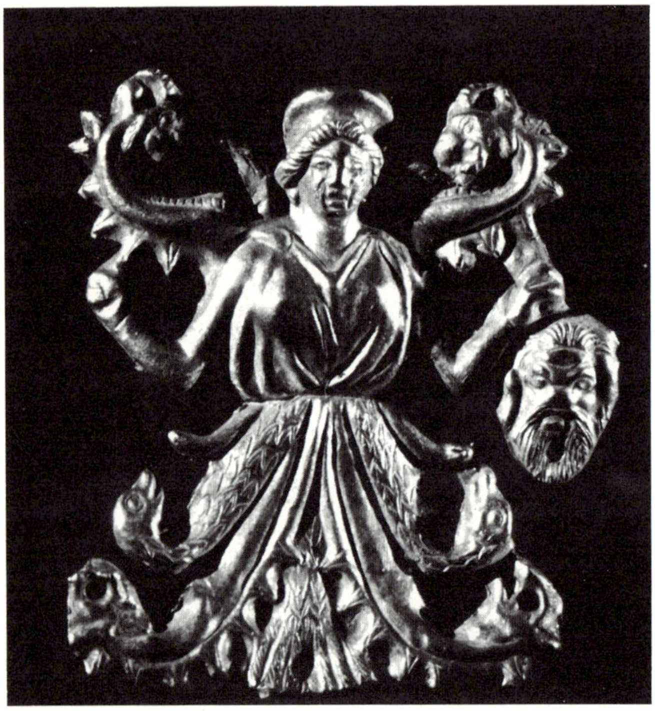

Figure of a goddess. This embossed gold plaque from Scythia showing a winged goddess wearing a calathos may represent the divine huntress of the Scythians – a deity familiar to their Slavonic neighbours under various names. Young and beautiful and accompanied by a pack of hounds, she galloped through the forests of the Elbe and the Carpathians and was almost certainly an aspect of the goddess known to the Greeks as Artemis.

while he himself was washing he would pour boiling water over the intruder and sometimes even strangle him. When leaving the bath it was necessary to leave a little water behind for the Bannik.

The Bannik could be interrogated about the future. To do this you put your naked back through the half-open door of the wash-house and waited patiently. If the Bannik struck you with his claws it was a bad omen; if he caressed your back tenderly with the soft palm of his hand then the future was rosy.

The Ovinnik (spirit of the barns) lived habitually in a corner of the barn. He generally had the aspect of a large dishevelled black cat. He could bark like a dog and laugh his head off. His eyes shone like burning coals. He was so ill-behaved that he was capable of setting the barn on fire.

Only one domestic spirit was feminine. This was Kikimora who, in some regions, passed for the Domovoi's wife. The numerous myths, tales and legends about the Kikimora give no precise picture of her. Sometimes her sole duty was to look after the poultry; sometimes she took part in all household tasks, though only if the mistress of the house was herself diligent and hardworking. If she was lazy, the Kikimora gave her much trouble and tickled the children during the night. The only way to make friends with the Kikimora again was to go into the forest, gather ferns and prepare a fern-tea with which all the pots and pans in the kitchen must then be washed.

The belief, still living, in all these domestic spirits is no more than a survival of the cult which the primitive Slavs rendered to divinities who protected their homes.

We shall limit ourselves to listing in addition: Peseias and Krukis who protected the domestic animals (Krukis was also the patron of blacksmiths); Ratainitsa who watched over the stables; Pri-girstitis whose hearing was so acute that he distinguished the faintest murmurs and loathed shouting; Giwoitis who could be recognised in the shape of a lizard and who was given milk to drink. Among feminine divinities there were: Matergabia who directed the house-keeping and to whom one offered the first piece of bread from the kneading trough; Dugnai who prevented the dough from spoiling; Krimba, a goddess of the house who was worshipped principally in Bohemia. These names again sound Lithuanian, Scandinavian and Germanic.

LESHY

The lands which the ancient Slavs colonised and peopled were densely wooded. The colonisers had to cut their way across enormous forests, filled with dangers and the unexpected. It was natural that they should have run into the Leshy. Leshy, whose name is derived from the word *les*, the forest, was the spirit of the forest.

Popular legends ascribed a human aspect to Leshy, but his cheeks were of a bluish hue because his blood was blue. His green eyes often popped out of their sockets, his eyebrows were tufted and he wore a long green beard. His hair was like a priest's. Sometimes popular imagination dressed him in a special costume: he wore a red sash and his left shoe on his right foot. He also buttoned his 'kaftan' the wrong way round. The Leshy threw no shadow. Even his stature was unstable; when he walked in the depths of the forest his head reached the tops of the tallest trees. When he walked on the forest's edge, through small bushes and grass, he turned into a tiny dwarf and could hide himself under a leaf.

He avoided trespassing on his neighbour's land, but he jealously guarded his own kingdom. When a solitary traveller crossed the forest, or a peasant came to gather mushrooms or berries, or a hunter ventured too deep into the woods, then the Leshy would not fail to lead him astray, to make him blunder in every direction through the undergrowth, only to bring him back to the same spot again.

He was, however, good-natured and almost always ended by releasing his victim, especially if the victim knew how to escape his spells. In order to do this, the wanderer must sit down under a tree-trunk, remove his clothes and put them on again backwards. Nor must he forget to put his left shoe on his right foot.

The Leshy was not mortal although, according to certain legends he was the offspring of a demon and a mortal woman.

On the other hand 'Leshies' had at the beginning of every October to disappear or temporarily die – until the following spring. In spring they were wild and particularly dangerous. Full of anger and anguish – no doubt at the thought of their next disappearance – they would range the forest, whistling and shouting, imitating the strident laughter of over-excited women, sobbing in a human voice and crying out like birds of prey and savage beasts.

Some legends say that the Leshy had family instincts and give him a wife, the Leshachikha, and children, the Leshonki. They lived in the depths of the woods and committed their misdeeds in common.

POLEVIK

If every forest was inhabited by a Leshy every field was ruled by a Polevoi or Polevik. *Pole* meant 'field'.

The outward appearance of the Polevik varied according to region. Sometimes he was simply someone 'dressed in white'. Sometimes the Polevik had a body as black as earth and two eyes of different colours. Instead of hair, long green grass grew on his head. At times he would appear in the guise of a deformed dwarf who spoke a human language.

The Polevik liked to amuse himself in the same fashion as the Leshy by misguiding belated travellers. It could happen that he would strangle a drunkard who had gone to sleep in his field instead of working in it. When this occurred the Polevik was often helped by his children who would run along the furrows, catching birds, which they would give to their parents to eat.

To earn the good will of the Polevik one could make him an offering by placing in a ditch two eggs and an elderly cockerel who could no longer crow. But this must be done so that no one was present at the sacrifice.

In the north of Russia the Polevik was sometimes replaced by the Poludnitsa (*Poluden* or *polden* means noon.) She was a beautiful girl, tall in stature and dressed entirely in white. In summer, at harvest time, she would walk in the fields and if she found a man or a woman working at midday she would seize him by the hair and pull it mercilessly. She would lure little children into the fields of corn and lose them.

Other rustic divinities did not survive the victory of Christianity. We shall limit ourselves to mentioning only a few of them.

Among the Poles the prosperity of the fields was the business of the gods Datan, Tawals, Lawkapatim, who especially presided over tilling the soil, and of the goddess Marzanna who fostered the growth of fruit. Modeina and Siliniets were gods of the forest. Cattle were placed under the protection of Walgino. Kurwaichin was especially responsible for lambs and Kremara for pigs. He was offered beer, poured into the fireplace. Priparchis weaned sucking pigs from their mother.

Among other Slavs, divinities like Kricco were honoured. He protected the fruits of the field. Kirnis saw that the cherries ripened successfully. Mokosh was the god of small domestic animals and had an altar at Kiev. Zosim was the tutelary god of bees. Zuttibur was god of the forest. Sicksa was a forest sprite, a teasing, mischievous genie who could assume any form.

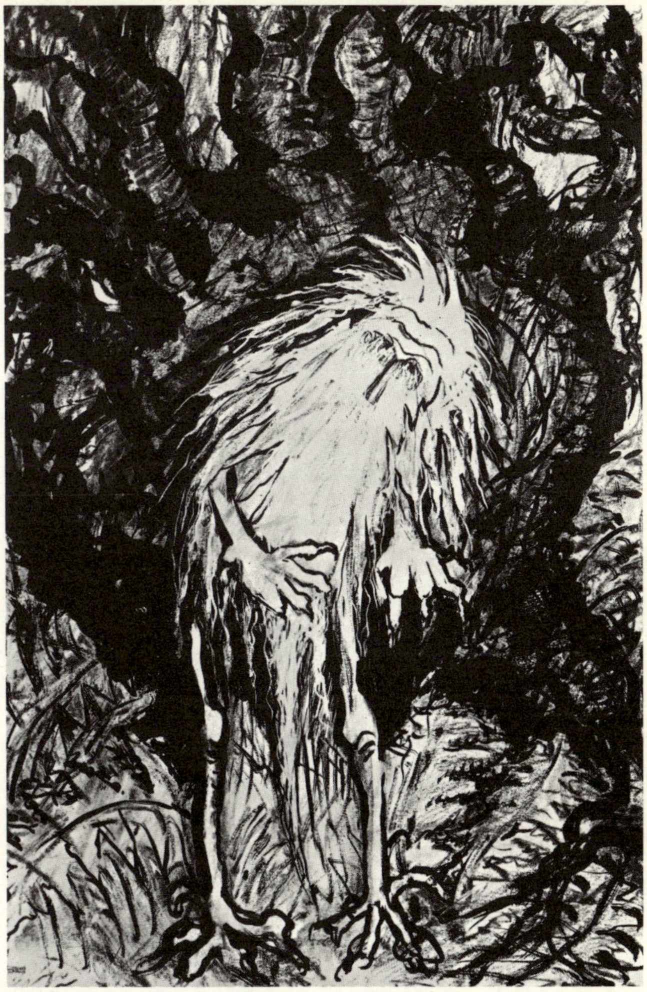

Leshy, forest divinity. Drawing by Tcheko Potocka.

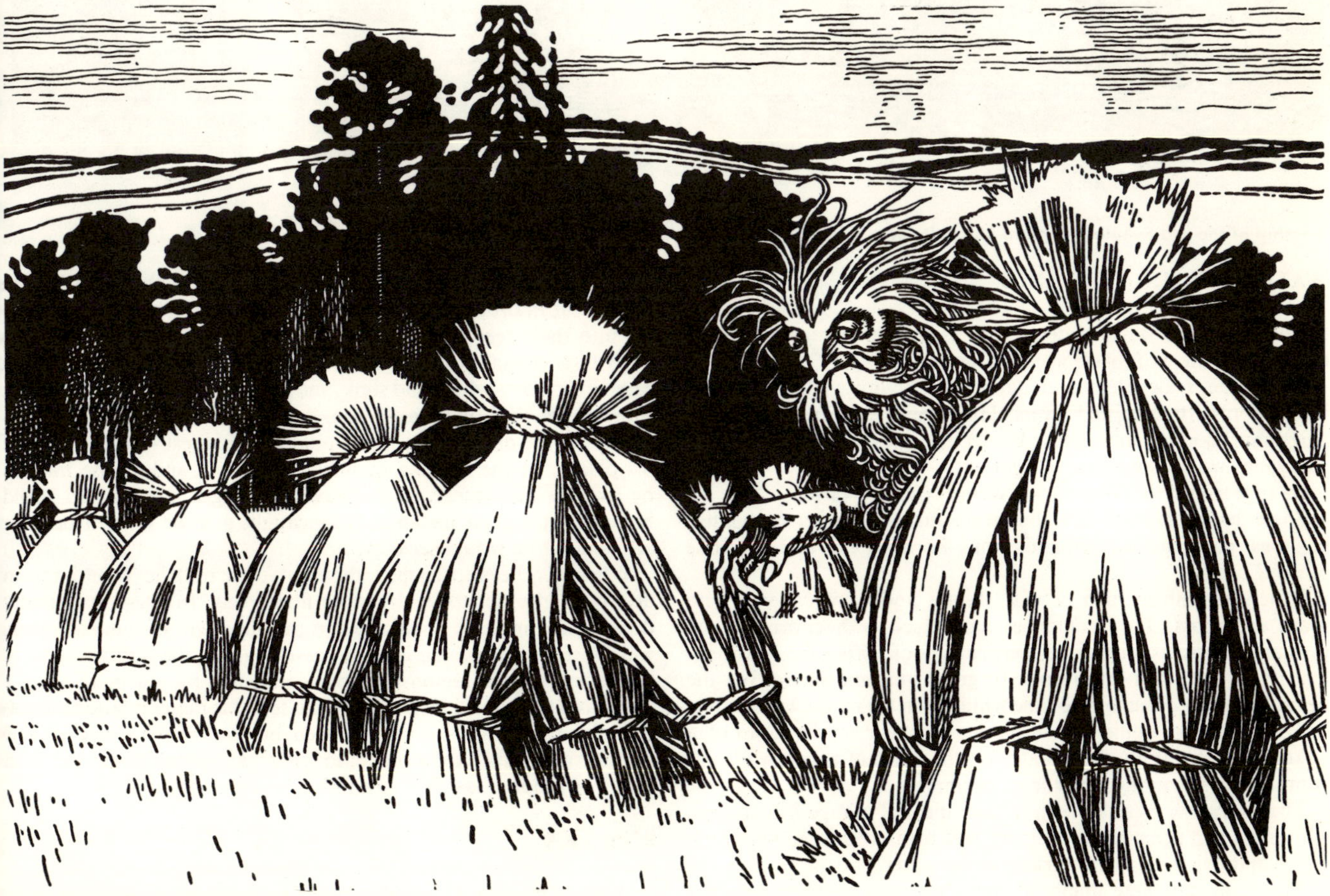

Polevik, field divinity. By I. Bilibin.

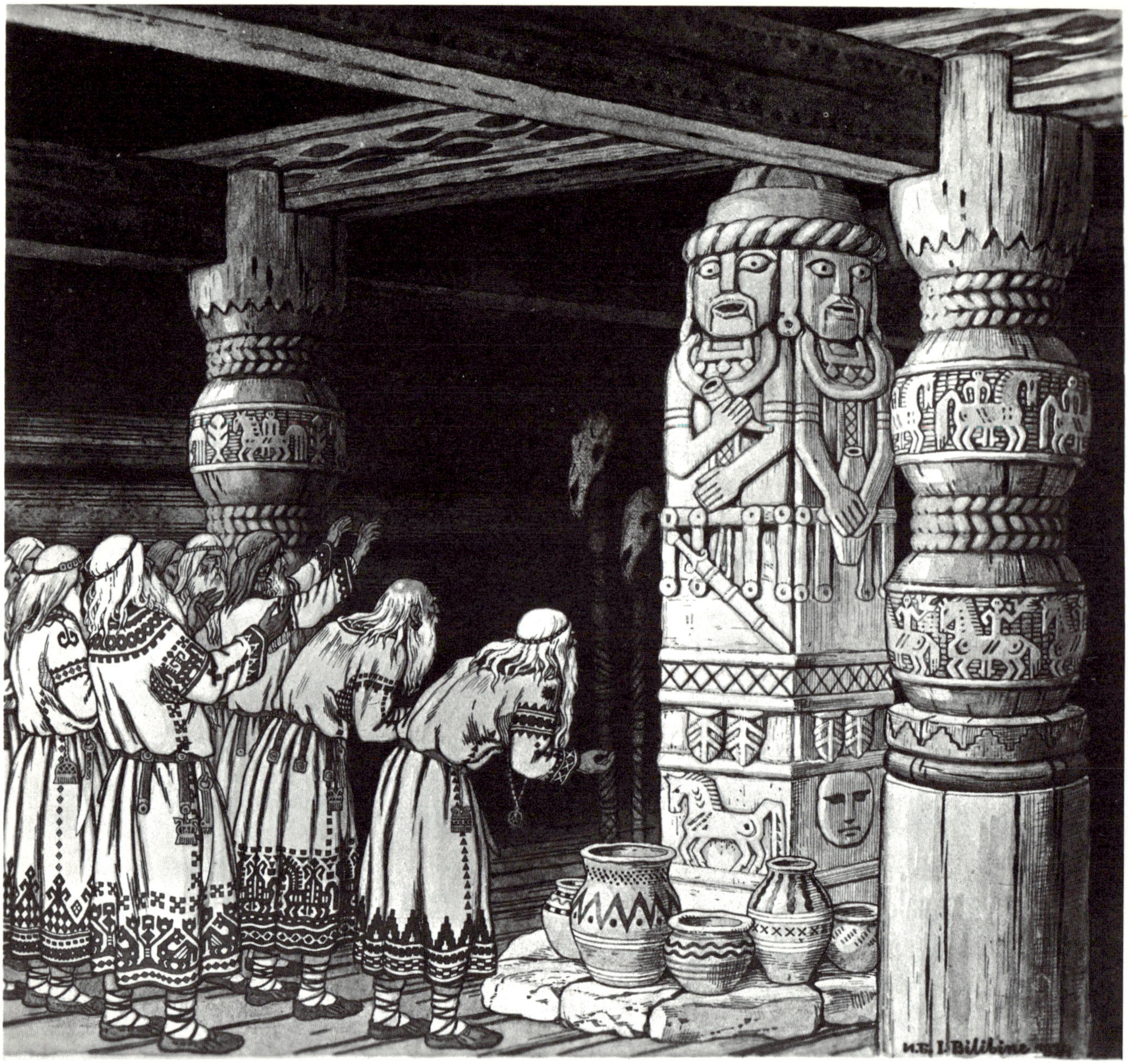

Worship of the god Svantovit among the Baltic Slavs. By I. Bilibin.

WATER SPIRITS: VODYANOI

The Vodyanoi was a water sprite, as his name suggests; for it comes from the word *voda* which means water.

He was a malevolent and dangerous divinity who inhabited lakes, pools, streams and rivers. His favourite haunt was in the neighbourhood of mill-dams. Under the great mill-wheel many Vodyanoi would sometimes forgather.

In appearance the Vodyany-ye were extremely varied.

Some had a human face, but were furnished with outlandish big toes, paws instead of hands, long horns, a tail and eyes like burning coals.

Others resembled men of vast stature and were covered with grass and moss. They could be quite black with enormous red eyes and a nose as long as a fisherman's boot. Often the Vodyanoi had the aspect of an old man with green hair and beard, but the beard changed colour and became white when the moon was waning.

The Vodyanoi could also sometimes appear in the guise of a naked woman sitting in the water on the roots of a tree while she combed the streaming water from her hair.

The Vodyanoi was also seen in the aspect of a huge fish covered with moss and again as an ordinary tree-trunk furnished with little wings and flying along the surface of the water.

The Vodyanoi were immortal, but they grew younger or older with the phases of the moon.

The Vodyanoi did not like human beings and lay in wait for the imprudent in order to drag them into the water. The drowned who fell into their deep and watery kingdom became their slaves. They lived in a crystal palace, ornamented with gold and silver which came from boats which had sunk, and lighted by a magic stone which shone more brightly than the sun.

During the day a Vodyanoi would take his rest in the depths of his palace. In the evening he would come out and amuse himself by striking the water with his paws, making a noise which could be heard at a great distance. If he caught men or women bathing after sunset he would seize them.

Whenever he approached the dam of a mill he would try to destroy it in order to let the water flow freely. In Russia not many decades ago millers, hoping to win the good will of the Vodyanoi, went so far as to push a belated passer-by into the millrace.

In a lake in the region of Olonets in north Russia there lived a Vodyanoi who had a large family. To feed his many relations he required the corpses of animals and men, but the folk who lived around the lake were much too prudent to fetch water from it or bathe in it. The Vodyanoi at last fled to another lake by way of a river.

RUSALKA

When a maiden drowned – either by accident or on purpose – she became a Rusalka. This belief was common to all Slavonic

Ahura Mazda, the god of the Achaemenid kings of Persia, carved in relief at Persepolis. The winged disk was his symbol and the usual method of representing him, but the sculptors of Persepolis sometimes represented him as a bearded figure, looking rather like the reigning monarch.

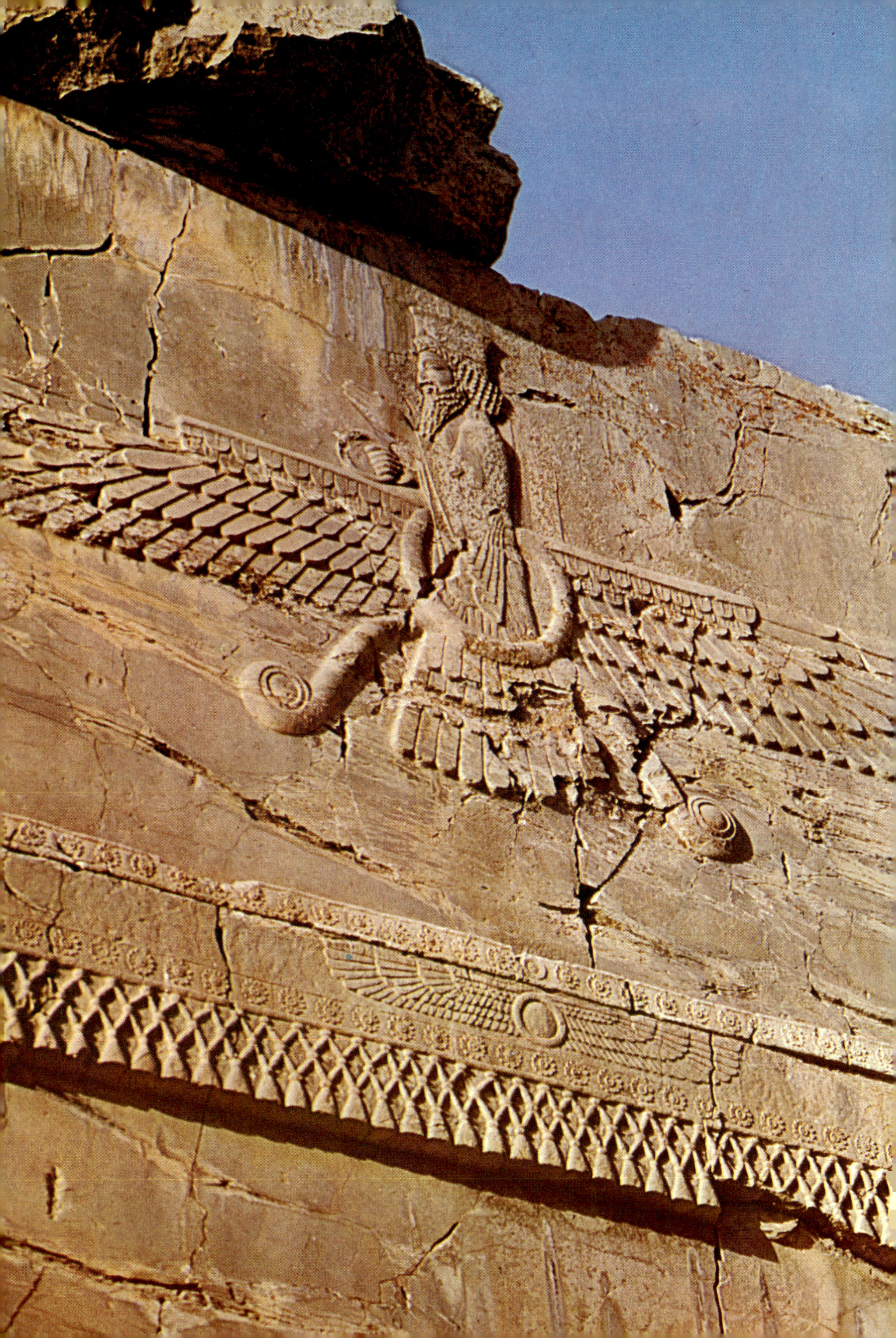

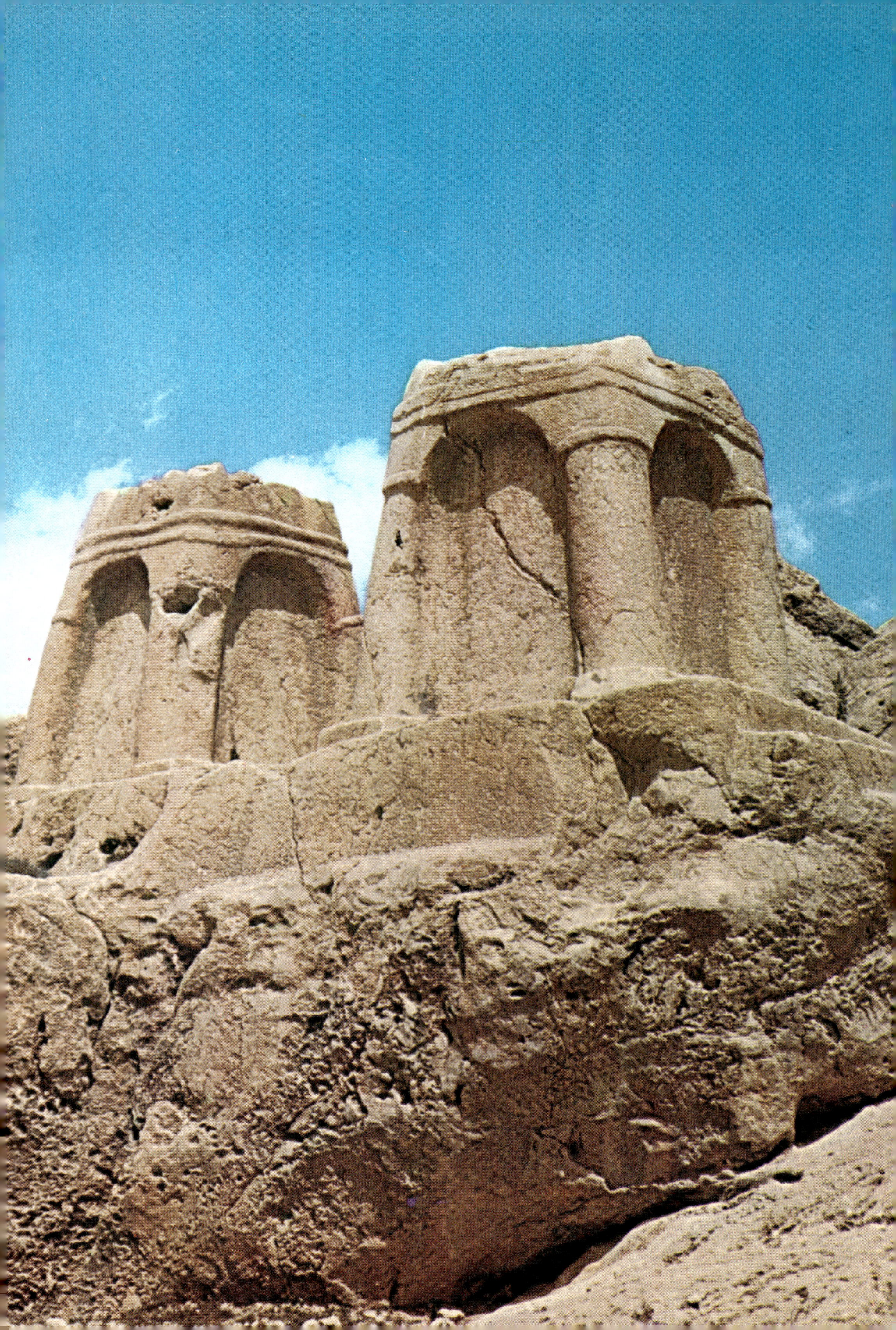

peoples. But the image of this water-divinity was not everywhere the same. One could say that she varied according to climate and the colour of the sky and the waters.

Among the Slavs of the 'blue' Danube the Rusalka – who in this case was called Vila – was a gracious being who retained some of her maidenly charm. Among the northern Russians the gracious, gay and charming Rusalki (plural of Rusalka) of the Danube and the Dnieper were transformed into wicked girls, of unattractive appearance, with uncombed and dishevelled hair. The facial pallor of the southern Rusalka resembled moonlight. Her northern sisters were wan and cadaverous, like the bodies of the drowned, and their eyes shone with an evil green fire. The Rusalki of the south often appeared in light robes of mist; those of the north were always crudely naked. The Rusalki of the Danube and the Dnieper sang delicious songs which were unknown to their sisters of the northern lakes and rivers. The southern Rusalki bewitched the passers-by with their beauty and their sweet voices. Those of the north thought only of brutally seizing the imprudent man or woman who late at night chanced to walk along the water's edge, to push him in and drown him. Death in the arms of a Rusalka from the land of sunshine and blue sky was almost agreeable, a kind of euthanasia. The Rusalki of the northern lands, on the contrary, submitted their victims to cruel and refined tortures.

Slavonic legends attribute to the Rusalki a double existence, aquatic and silvan. Until the beginning of summer – until, in fact, 'Rusalki Week' – they lived in the water. During Rusalki Week they emerged from the water and went into the forest. They would choose a weeping willow or a birch with long slim branches which leaned over the river and climb up into it. At night in the moonlight they would swing in the branches, call out to each other, slip down from the trees and dance in the clearings. The southern Slavs believed that where the Rusalki trod when dancing, there the grass grew thicker and the wheat more abundant.

But their behaviour could also be harmful. When they frolicked in the water they would climb onto the millwheel and stop it, they would break millstones, damage dikes and tear fishermen's nets. They could also send storms and torrential rains down on the fields, steal linen and thread from sleeping women. Luckily there was a sure method for thwarting the wickedness of the Rusalki: one need only hold in one's hand a leaf of absinth, 'the accursed herb'.

Myths concerning the Rusalki reflect the general beliefs of the Slavs on the subject of death and the dead. Green trees, according to these beliefs, were the abode of the dead. When the sun had not yet 'entered the road of summer' the Rusalki, souls of the dead, could remain in the dark and chilly waters. But when these waters were warmed by the rays of the life-giving sun the Rusalki could no longer stay there. And they returned to the trees, the abode of the dead.

CITY GODS AND WAR GODS

We have already seen that on the edges of the Slavonic world where the Slavs came in contact with other peoples, such as the Germans and the Scandinavians, their mythology lost its primitive and rustic character, found fresh inspiration and took on new and less naïve forms.

Certain Russian scholars are even inclined to distinguish two mythologies – and almost two religions – among the pagan Slavs: the one that we have just described, which was common to the great masses composed of peasants, hunters, and fishermen and a second which was the mythology of the upper classes, of town dwellers and those who lived in fortified castles.

In any case it is certain that the Slavs of the Baltic coast and those of Kiev had a more highly developed mythology than that which was based on the mere worship of elemental forces and the phenomena of nature.

The Baltic Slavs – those of the Isle of Rügen, the mouth of the Elbe, etc. – worshipped a divinity named Svantovit. Some of the old chroniclers – Helmgolf, Saxo Grammaticus, etc. – have left us almost contemporary descriptions of Svantovit. In addition a statue of Svantcvit was discovered in 1857 in Galicia on the banks of the river Zbruch. It was a crude and simplified copy of the statue which once occupied his principal temple at Arcona.

The statue of Svantovit at Arcona, placed in a richly ornamented temple, was of great size. It had four heads facing in four directions.

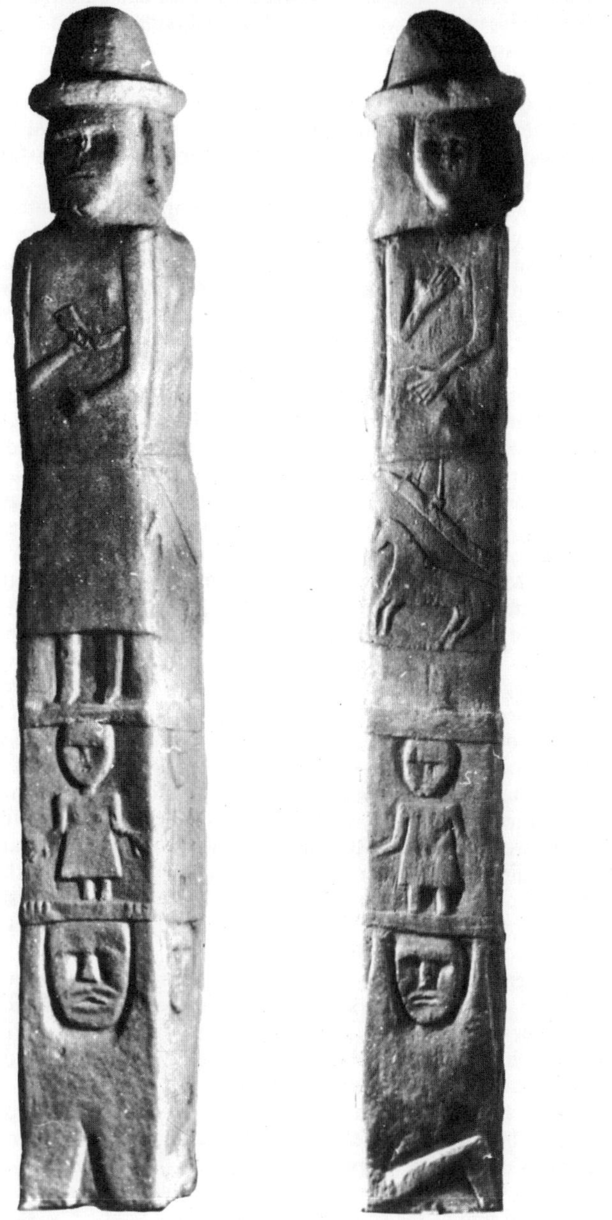

Statue, which is believed to be of Svantovit, found near Husjiatyn, Galicia. The square column is over eight feet in girth. The four sides are each surmounted by a personage arbitrarily identified as the god Svantovit.

Svantovit held in his right hand a bull's horn filled with wine. Beside him hung an enormous sword, a saddle and bridle. In the temple there was a white horse.

Each year the high priest would solemnly examine the contents of the bull's horn which Svantovit held in his hand; if much wine remained in it, that was a good omen – the year would be fruitful and happy. But if the quantity of wine in the horn had considerably diminished a year of famine and trouble must be expected.

The white horse of Svantovit, maintained at the expense of the temple and venerated like its divine master, also served to reveal the future. The priests would fix in the ground several rows of spears and drive the horse of Svantovit through them. If it made the course smoothly without catching any of the spears with its hooves the future promised well.

A flag – a war banner – was kept in the temple. The priests would show it to Svantovit's worshippers before they went to war. Besides the priests, an armed detachment of three hundred men was assigned to the temple of Svantovit.

As well as Svantovit, the old chroniclers mention, among the peoples of the western branch of the Slavonic world, certain other divinities whose attributes were warlike: Rugievit, who was armed with eight swords, seven hanging from his girdle and the eighth in his right hand: Yarovit, who had a great golden shield which was venerated as a holy object. He also had his own banners, and the faithful would carry them and the shield when they went into battle.

The fire altars at Naqsh-i-Rustem. Both the Persians and the related Aryan people who moved east into India were familiar with the cult of fire and certain gods were invested with this particular attribute. Sassanian period, third to seventh centuries A.D.

Then there was Radigast, who grasped in his hand a double-edged axe. On his chest he wore a bull's head and on his curly head a swan with outstretched wings. He was a sure counsellor, god of strength and honour.

It is difficult to say if these gods were identical with Svantovit or if they were distinct and individual divinities. All at least had traits in common from which arose their character of gods of warfare and the city.

According to the testimony of an old chronicler, Svantovit was considered to be the 'god of gods' and beside him all others were no more than demi-gods. Like Svarog he was the father of the sun and of fire. At the same time – as can be seen by his emblem, the bull's horn filled with wine – he was the god of plenty. Above all, however, he was a warrior and in war he always had his share of the booty.

At the opposite end of the Slavonic world we find a divinity analogous to Svantovit, namely the god Pyerun. The origin of this name goes back to remotest Aryan times. Among the Hindus the god Indra was surnamed Parjanya, a word which has the same root as Pyerun. The word Pyerun is known in many Slavonic languages: Pyerun in Russian, Piorun in Polish, Perun in Czech, Peron in Slovak. Among the Lithuanians we often find the name Perkaunas. In the Mater Verborum (1202) the name Pyerun is translated by the name Jupiter.

In the popular language of Poland we discover not only the semantic origin of the name Pyerun but also an explanation of his mythological character. For in Polish *piorun* means 'thunder'.

Neither history nor tradition has preserved anything exact on the subject of Pyerun's divine image. We only know that there was in Kiev until the end of the tenth century a wooden idol of Pyerun. He was incontestably the god of war. For not only was the thunderbolt considered by the pagan Slavs to be the most redoubtable divine weapon but old Russian chronicles explicitly state that there was a direct connection between war and Pyerun. When the first princes of Kiev brought a war with the Greeks to a conclusion by an honourable peace their troops pledged their word by their weapons and invoked the name of Pyerun.

We read in an old chronicle that Olga, one of the first sovereigns of Kiev, 'led her warriors into batlle; and according to the Russian law they swore by their arms and invoked Pyerun. Igor, prince of Kiev, climbed the hill where the image of Pyerun stood and there placed his arms, his shield and his god...'

In Procopius, the sixth century Greek historian, we find a curious detail about Slavonic religion; it probably refers to Pyerun and permits us to place his position among the other gods.

'He is the god who wields the thunderbolt and they, the Slavs, recognise him as the sole lord of the universe.'

This warlike mythology in which foreign elements were mingled – for we must not forget that the 'principality' of Kiev had been founded by Varyags, or Scandinavian warriors – was not without its influence on the rustic mythology from which originally it profoundly differed.

As an example of this influence the god Volos or Vyelyes may be cited. Volos, 'god of cattle', who was of rustic origin and character, was afterwards associated with Pyerun's warlike exploits. The monk Nestor, author of the celebrated *Chronicle*, relates how the warriors of the Princess Olga 'swore by their arms and invoked their god Pyerun and Volos, god of the beasts'. In a treaty concluded between the Greeks and Prince Svyatoslav, the prince and his fighting men declared: 'Let us be bound by our oath before the god in whom we believe – Pyerun – and before Volos, god of the beasts.'

Another no less curious example is the transformation undergone by the image of the Zorya (Aurora) whom we have already mentioned. As long as she remained beside the Sun, god of light, she was only a simple guardian of the gates of his golden palace. But when she was found with Pyerun, god of war, the gentle Zorya assumed the aspect of a well-armed virgin warrior, patroness of warriors whom she protected with her long veil. When asking for her protection one repeated an exorcism which was still used in the nineteenth century:

'Unsheath, O Virgin, the sacred sword of thy father, take up the breastplate of thy ancestors, thy doughty helmet, bring out thy black horse. Fly to the open field. In the open field there is a mighty host with numberless weapons. Cover me, O Virgin, with thy veil and protect me against the power of the enemy, against blunderbuss and arrow, against all adversaries and all arms, against weapon of wood, of bone, of iron, of steel, of copper.'

In the same way the winds – 'grandchildren of Stribog, god of winds' – took on a warlike character and 'from the direction of the sea let arrows fly'.

The Slavs of certain countries such as Lusatia, Bohemia and Poland – in other words the Slavs who were in contact with Teutonic races – did not confine themselves to peopling their forests with Leshye and Rusalki. They created a goddess of the hunt. Young and fair, mounted on a swift steed and accompanied by a pack of hounds, she galloped through the forests of the Elbe and the Carpathians, weapon in hand. Even her name – Diiwica among the Serbians of Lusatia, Devana among the Czechs, Dziewona among the Poles – connects her with Diana.

It may be pointed out that although Svantovit had a temple and priests at Arcona the Slavs of other lands knew neither temples nor a priestly caste. At Kiev the idol of Pyerun was erected on a hill under the open sky, and the functions of the priest were performed by the *Kniaz*, or prince, military chieftain of the 'city'. And it sufficed that the prince changed his religion for all his officials and soldiers and all the ruling class of the city, to feel obliged to imitate his example. When in 988 Prince Vladimir of Kiev decided to become converted to Byzantine Orthodoxy he ordered all his soldiers to be baptised. Pyerun's idol was torn down and thrown into the Dnieper and history has retained not so much as a hint of any kind of effort on the part of Pyerun's worshippers to defend their god. This can have only one explanation: the divinity and his cult formed no part of popular belief, but only that of the dominant military group. When this group renounced its faith there was no one left to defend it.

In the rare cases when the rural population retained a vague memory of the warrior and city dweller's mythology it was touched up to suit peasant taste. The White Russians left Pyerun his weapon the bow, but instead of a war chariot they gave him a simple millstone on which he roamed the sky.

As for Volos, 'god of the beasts', when he left Kiev, now under triumphant Christian occupation, he returned to his rural habitat, stripped of his military functions and attributes. And even when Christianity invaded the Slavonic countryside Volos was able to retain the sympathy of the peasantry. In the nineteenth century Russian peasants still kept the custom of 'curling Volos' hair'. During the harvest they would leave one sheaf of corn in the field and 'curl' its ears – undoubtedly the survival of a pagan sacrifice.

Little by little, deprived of his warlike accessories, Volos again became a simple shepherd, who watched faithfully over the flocks. And if Pyerun himself was remembered by the Slavs long after the days of the Principality of Kiev he was venerated as a divine and mighty labourer tracing furrows in a copper sky with his miraculous plough.

GODS OF JOY

In addition to the divinities already described, Slavonic mythology offers a pair of extremely interesting and picturesque gods who might be called gods of joy. Their names were Yarilo and Kupala.

The origin of the name Yarilo, transcribed as Erilo, may – it has been suggested – be found in the Greek Eros. If this explanation were plausible it would considerably simplify mythological research; for Yarilo was a god of carnal love. But Yarilo probably derives from the adjective *yary*, which means 'ardent, passionate, uncontrolled'. On the other hand the word *yarovoi* is used in speaking of corn sown in springtime as against *ozimoi* which signifies that which is sown in the autumn.

Thus in the name Yarilo we find linked the idea of spring regeneration and that of sexual passion.

The cult of Yarilo was so widespread and deeply rooted among certain Slavonic peoples that even as late as the eighteenth century the orthodox bishop of Voronezh had to take very strict measures against the people of his diocese who were given to it. From his sermons we learn that the pagan Slavs venerated an ancient idol, Yarilo; and in his honour they organised festivities and 'satanic games' which went on for days.

Popular legends from White Russia have preserved a curious description of the outward appearance of the god Yarilo. He was

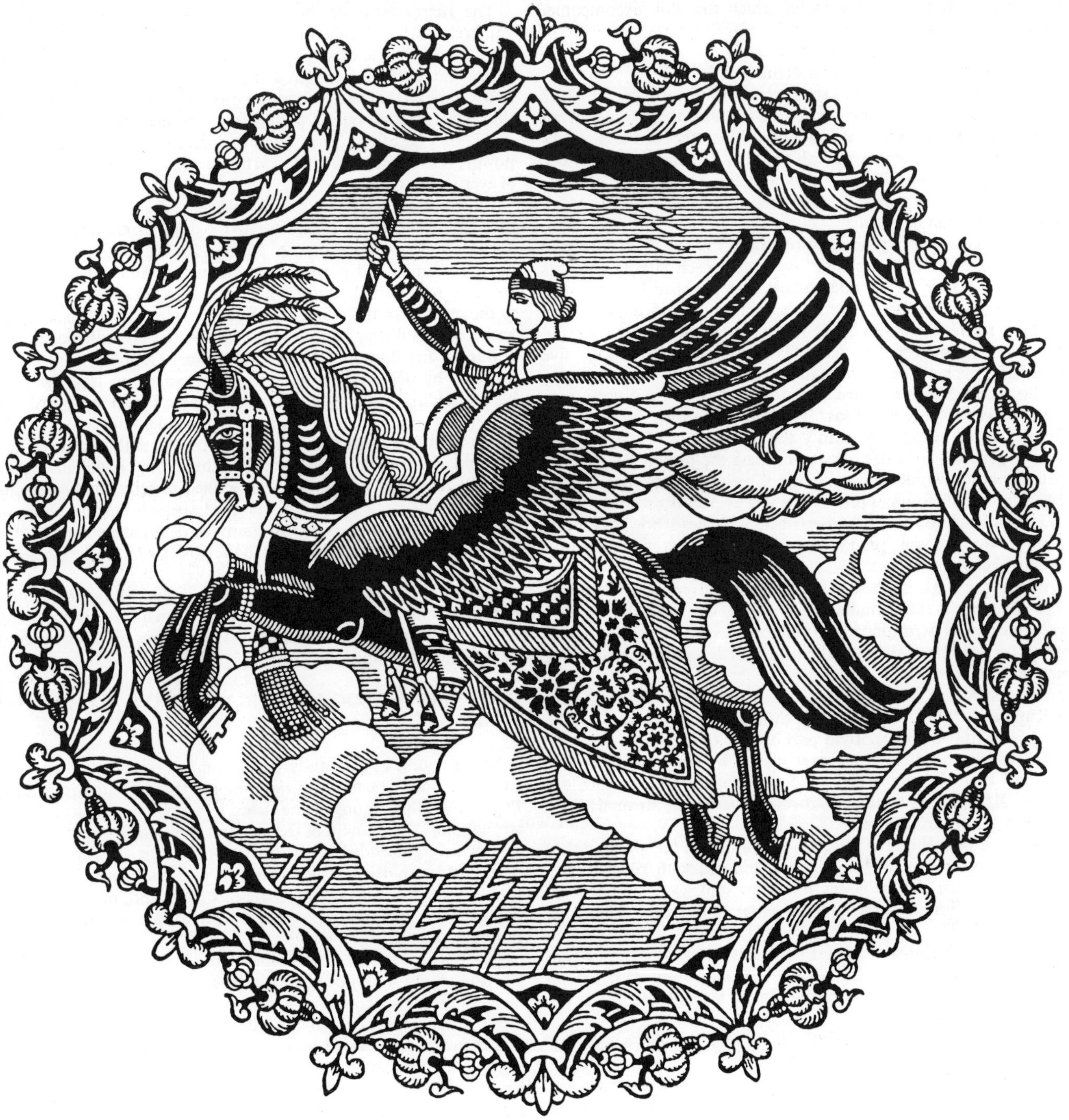

Ilya-Muromyets on his flying horse. Though the old pagan religion was finally vanquished by Christianity in the Slav countries vestiges are still found of it in the celebrated *byliny*, the epic and heroic poems of the Russian people. Among the most popular of these are the series devoted to Ilya-Muromyets, the 'peasant's son', who though a good Christian is portrayed with a number of features which appear to be derived from the old pagan god Pyerun. By I. Bilibin.

young and fair. He rode a white horse and was dressed in a white cloak. On his head he wore a crown of wild flowers. In his left hand he held a bunch of wheat ears. His feet were bare.

Two elements entered into the pagan rites consecrated to Yarilo, and also into the popular festivals which were in Christian times celebrated in his honour. As a god of springtime and fecundity he was honoured in certain Slavonic countries in spring, during the days of the first sowing. In White Russia in the nineteenth century the village maidens would get together and elect the most beautiful of their number who would be dressed in the white garments of Yarilo, crowned with flowers and mounted on a white horse. Around her gathered a *khorovod* (a curious Slavonic derivative of the antique Greek 'chorus'). This was a long circle of dancing girls crowned with freshly gathered flowers. The festival was celebrated on the newly sown fields in the presence of the old men and women of the village. The *khorovod* would chant a song which glorified the blessings of the god.

'Where he sets his foot,
The corn grows in mountains;
Wherever he glances,
The grain flourishes.'

In summer they celebrated the 'funeral' rites of Yarilo. This solemnity was very widespread among Slavs of the east and west alike and for centuries resisted all assaults by Christian preachers – above all in Russia.

During these festivals the men, women and girls would gather together to eat, drink and dance. At sunset a straw idol of Yarilo would be brought to the place where the festival was being held. It was the image of the dead god. The women, intoxicated with drink and dancing, would approach the idol and sob: 'He's dead, he's dead!' The men would come running and seize the idol. Shaking it they would cry: 'Yes, the women do not lie. They know him well, they know that he is sweeter than honey.' Lamentations and prayers would continue, after which the idol, accompanied by the women, would be carried to his place of burial. They would then all begin to eat, drink and dance again.

Like Yarilo Kupala was also a divinity of joy.

The name Kupala has the same root as the verb *kupati* which means to bathe. This is explained by the fact that during the festivals of Kupala, which were celebrated in June, they bathed in the rivers and washed themselves with the 'dew of Kupala', dew which was gathered during the night of the festival. The worship of water and the belief in its mystic powers were one of the elements which composed the cult of Kupala.

This belief was very general among pagan Slavs. Their folk tales often speak of 'dead water' and 'live water', each of which had its miraculous power. When a legendary hero perished by the sword of his enemy and his body lay stretched on the ground, cut to pieces, the fairy sprinkled it with 'dead water' which allowed the severed members to come together again. Then she sprinkled it with 'live water' and the hero was resuscitated.

The ancient Slavs venerated sacred springs, near which were often found places of prayer and sacrifice. Some countries retained until the end of the nineteenth century the odd custom of 'begging the water's pardon'. In order to cure sickness the person begging the water's pardon would throw a piece of bread into the water, greet the water and three times pronounce this ancient exorcism:

'I come to thee, little water-mother, with head bowed and repentant. Forgive me, pardon me – and ye, too, ancestors and forefathers of the water.'

We may remark in passing that the great rivers which watered Slavonic lands – the Danube, the Dnieper, the Don, the Volga – were glorified, personified and almost deified in the Russian *byliny* (or epic poems) under the aspect of legendary heroes, half men, half gods.

The veneration of water was closely connected with the cult of Kupala: bathing, ablutions, and throwing floral crowns into the water, constituted an important part of the ritual.

No less important was the part played by the worship of fire. The holy fires of the holy night of Kupala possessed a purificatory virtue. Kupala's worshippers formed *khorovods* around these fires and jumped over them.

After the official end of paganism we still find the straw idol of Kupala, dressed in a woman's gown, adorned with ribbons, women's necklaces, etc. In places the straw idol was supplied with wooden arms from which hung floral garlands and various feminine ornaments.

At sunset the idol was carried in procession to the river where it was drowned, or else to the holy fire where it was burned. Among the pagan Serbs the idol was not drowned, but only bathed in the water.

An essential element in the cult of Kupala was the worship of trees, herbs and flowers.

During the festival the idol was placed under a tree which had been cut and fixed in the ground. Among the Baltic Slavs the sacred tree was the birch. Women, harnessed to a wagon, would go in procession into the forest and choose a birch which would be transported solemnly to the festive place. The tree was stripped of all but the upper branches which formed a kind of crown around the top. With equal solemnity it was then fixed into the ground and hung with garlands of flowers. All these operations were performed exclusively by women. Men must not touch the sacred tree.

Before this sacred tree sacrifices were made and a cock's throat was cut.

But the more picturesque and mysterious side of the cult of Kupala was undoubtedly the search made for sacred and magic herbs and flowers.

At dawn on the morning of the festival one had to find the plakune-trava, that is 'the tear-weed' (purple loose-strife). Its root had the power to tame impure demons. The sorcerer who possessed it had only to recite this exorcism:

'Tear-weed, tear-weed, thou hast wept much and for a long time, but thou hast gained little. May thy tears not flow in the open field, and thy sobs not sound over the blue sea. Frighten wicked demons, demi-demons and old witches. If they do not submit to thee then drown them in thy tears. If they flee from thy glance engulf them in precipices and pits. May my speech be firm and strong for centuries and centuries!'

The *razryv-trava* or 'herb which breaks' (saxifrage) must be gathered during the daytime. It possessed the virtue of breaking iron, gold, silver and copper into tiny crumbs, simply by its touch. When the scythe encountered this herb it broke. In this case one had to take all that had been mown down and throw it into the water: that which floated on the surface was 'the herb that breaks'.

Another herb, which was 'nameless', had an even more mysterious power; the man who carried it on his person could read the thoughts of every other man.

But the chief sacred herb of Kupala was the fern: for, according to popular belief, it only flowered – and produced, moreover, a single flower – once a year, during Kupala's night. This flower possessed unlimited power. It dominated demons. It knew where treasure was buried. It gave one access to everything, to riches, to the most beautiful women. Before him who had the luck to have gathered this flower kings and potentates bowed their heads.

But the 'fire-flower' of the fern, the flower of Kupala, was jealously guarded by demons. To gather it one had to go into the forest before midnight, the hour when the magic flower appeared. The flower bud would climb up the length of the plant like a living thing; it ripened and, exactly at midnight, it exploded with a bang, forming a bloom of fire so luminous and bright that the eye could not support its brilliance. The brave man who wished to seize the flower must trace a magic circle around it. He must keep within this circle and not look at the monsters, whose guise the demons assumed in order to terrify him, nor must he reply to the voices which addressed him. If he did he was lost.

During Kupala's night trees had the power to leave the ground, to move about and speak among themselves in a mysterious tongue. Only the fortunate possessor of the fire-flower of Kupala could understand their language.

PAGAN MYTHOLOGY AMONG THE SLAVS IN CHRISTIAN TIMES

In the course of our study we have many times noted powerful survivals and pagan memories among the Christianised Slavs. Pagan mythology though vanquished by Christianity in its principal stronghold – the domain of the city and war gods – was deeply and very widely embedded in the hearts of the vast rural population. A sort of symbiosis, a co-existence of paganism and Christianity, took place, especially among Orthodox Slavs and, more especially, in Russia where the country clergy itself was not unwilling to tolerate this religious symbiosis, the 'double-belief'.

A rich source for the study of these curious pagan survivals among Christian Slavs is supplied by the celebrated *byliny* (plural of *bylina*, derived from the word *byl*, which means 'that which has been'), the epic and heroic poems of the Russian people.

The *byliny* are divided into two cycles: one concerned with the *bogatyri* or 'elder valiant champions', and the other with the younger heroes. The first cycle is the older in origin and is full of mythological elements.

The poem about the bogatyr Svyatogor describes him as being so strong that he supported his own strength 'like a heavy burden'. In his pride he declared that if he could find the place where all the weight of the earth was concentrated he would lift up the earth itself. On the steppe he found a small bag. He touched it with his staff; it did not budge. He touched it with his finger; it did not move. Without getting off his horse he seized the bag in his hand; he could not lift it.

'Many years have I travelled the world (he says)
But never yet have I met with a miracle like this.
A little bag
Which will not stir or move or be lifted.'

Svyatogor descended from his good steed. He seized the bag in both hands and raised it as high as his knees. But he himself had sunk knee-deep into the earth! It was not tears which rolled down his face, but blood. He was unable to raise himself from the hole into which he had sunk. And such was the end of Svyatogor.

The mysterious and divine power of the Moist-Mother-Earth is well depicted in this poem. In another we meet a miraculous labourer, the bogatyr Mikula, whose 'little wooden plough' was so heavy that a whole troop of bogatyri could not lift it, whereas

Mikula lifted it with one hand. Mikula's little horse was swifter than the finest chargers, because 'Mikula was loved by the Moist-Mother-Earth'.

The poem of the bogatyr Volkh or Volga depicts him as a mythical being, able to turn himself into a bright falcon, a grey wolf, a white bull with golden horns and into a tiny ant. This *bylina* is remarkable for the name of its hero: Volkh is certainly a deformation of the word Volkhv which among pagan Slavs signified 'priest" and 'sorcerer'.

All these figures are obviously mythical in character, but pagan mythology is mingled with Christian ingredients.

'Svyatogor', the bylina concludes, 'had indeed found the weight of the earth, but God punished him for his pride'.

Mikula, the miraculous labourer, himself says 'that he needs God's aid to till the soil and accomplish his peasant's work'.

And even Volkh, who has all the traits of a werewolf and can 'make sorcery', employs his mysterious gifts to defend Kiev, the orthodox city, against the perfidious 'Indian Tsar' who wishes to 'send up the churches of God in smoke'.

This mixture of pagan and Christian elements is no less striking in the poems about the younger *bogatyri*. Among these the most popular was Ilya-Muromyets, the 'peasant's son'. The numerous byliny which are devoted to him portray him with features which give him a resemblance to the god of lightning, Pyerun.

Ilya-Muromyets' horse did not run over the earth, but flew through the air, 'above the motionless forest and a little below the clouds scudding across the sky'. The arrow which Ilya-Muromyets shot from his miraculous bow resembled that which flew from the divine bow of Pyerun: it brought down church cupolas and split robust oaks into thin slivers.

The origin of Ilya's strength was mythical. He was sickly when born and for thirty-three years 'he remained sitting' unable to rise. One day two passing vagabond minstrels gave him a 'honey draught' to drink, and in him he felt the upsurge of mighty strength.

But the bogatyr was a good Christian. His exploits of prowess were only accomplished after he had been blessed by his elderly parents. He defended the faith of Christ against the infidels. And when the time came for him to die he built a cathedral at Kiev. After this final act Ilya died and turned to stone and his body 'has remained intact until now'.

In the poem of the bogatyr Potok-Mikhailo-Ivanovich we find vestiges of pagan funeral rites. According to certain evidence the wife of a pagan Slav would voluntarily follow her husband to death. The poem relates that when the bogatyr Potok-Mikhailo-Ivanovich was married he and his bride took an oath that whichever survived the other should voluntarily commit suicide. Now Potok's young wife died a year and a half after the wedding. Potok had a grave dug, 'deep and big', summoned 'priests with their deacons' and, having buried his wife, descended himself into the tomb, fully armed and on horseback. 'Overhead had been built a ceiling in oak and yellow sand; room had been left only for a rope which was attached to the cathedral bell.' Above, a wooden cross was placed. The bogatyr Potok remained in the tomb with his brave steed from noon to midnight and, 'to give himself courage he lighted wax candles'. At midnight all the monster reptiles gathered round him and then came the great Serpent who burned with a flame of fire. With his 'sharp sabre' Potok killed the Serpent, cut off his head and 'with this Serpent's head he anointed the body of his wife' – who immediately came to life again. Then Potok pulled the rope and set the cathedral bell ringing. They were freed, he and his wife. The priests sprinkled them with holy water 'and ordered them to live as formerly'. Potok lived to a great age but died before his wife who 'was buried alive with him in the dank earth'.

In other poems dealing with the younger bogatyri we find personifications – under the aspect of legendary heroes – of the great Slavonic rivers, the Danube, Dnieper and Don.

The epics we have mentioned speak of the bogatyri of Kiev. Those which concern the heroes of Novgorod also contain many pagan and mythological elements mingled with Christian ideas. Such are the byliny about the bogatyr Sadko, the Rich Merchant. Sadko, with his ships, was sailing the blue sea.

Suddenly his ship stopped in the middle of the sea and refused to advance. Sadko remembered that he had sailed the blue sea for twelve years, but never paid tribute to the Tsar of the Sea. He filled a great cup with pure silver, another with red gold and a third with

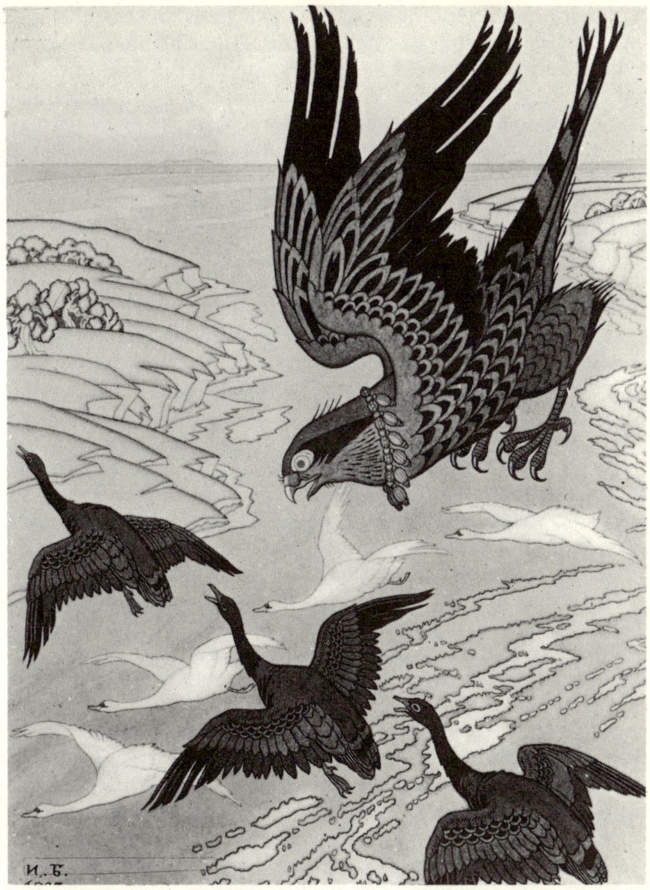

The bogatyr Volga had the power of assuming diverse forms. Here he takes on that of a hawk. By I. Bilibin.

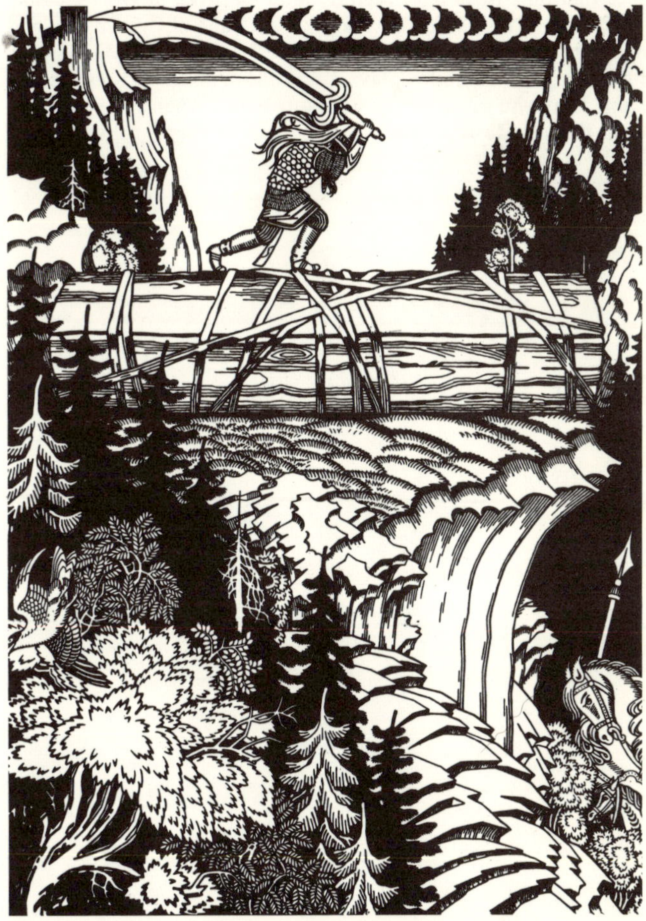

The bogatyr Ilya-Muromyets vainly attempts to break the coffin in which his companion, the bogatyr Svyatogor, has imprudently shut himself. By I. Bilibin.

rare pearls. He placed the cups on a small plank and cast the plank into the blue sea. But the small plank did not sink and floated like a duck. Sadko interpreted this as meaning that the Tsar of the Sea did not want money, but that he demanded the head of a man. They drew lots and it was Sadko who had to descend to the sea lord's abode. With him he took an icon of Saint Nicholas and his *gusli* – a stringed musical instrument. Then he climbed out of his ship and on to the small plank. There he fell asleep to wake up again in a white stone palace. He played his *gusli* before the Tsar of the Sea and the Tsar began to dance. He danced so furiously that he caused a tempest and innocent sailors perished on the sea. In order to stop the dancing – and the attendant hurricane – Sadko broke the strings of his *gusli*.

After his fortunate and miraculous return to land Sadko sailed a further twelve years on the river Volga. When he wished to return to Novgorod he cut a huge slice of bread, put salt on it and put it on the waves of the Volga. To thank him for his kindness the Volga spoke to him in human language and asked him to go and give his regards to his brother, the Lake of Ilmen. In recompense the Lake told Sadko to cast into its waters three great nets which were at once filled with fish. When the fish were taken to Sadko's warehouses they were miraculously transformed into silver.

The end of the heroes was also mystical. It is recounted in a bylina entitled: *Why there are no more bogatyri in Holy Russia.*

After a successful battle, one of the bogatyri had in his pride the imprudence to say: 'If we were to face an army from "over yonder" we would beat it, too!' Immediately two unknown warriors appeared and challenged the bogatyri to combat. A bogatyr struck them with his sword and sliced each of them in two. But instead of two unknown opponents there were now four! When attacked, the four became eight, all very much alive. Then sixteen and so on, without end. 'For three days, three hours and three brief minutes' the bogatyri fought against the army from 'over yonder' whose numbers kept doubling. The mighty bogatyri were seized with fear. They fled to the stony mountains and took refuge in dark caves. And there every one of them was turned to stone. 'And since that time there have been no more bogatyri in Holy Russia.'

We have already said that many of the traits of Pyerun, the god of lightning, were handed down to the bogatyr Ilya-Muromyets. But among the Orthodox Slavs it was above all the prophet Elijah (Saint Ilya) who inherited Pyerun's attributes. When a Slav peasant hears thunder he says that it is the Prophet Elijah rolling across the sky in his fiery chariot.

As for Volos, god of the beasts, he has transferred his functions and attributes to Saint Vlas (or Vlassy: Blaise). The day of Saint Vlas, the eleventh of March, 'the cow begins to rewarm her flanks in the sunshine. A prayer is addressed to Saint Vlas which strangely resembles an ancient exorcism: 'Saint Vlas, give us good luck, so that our heifers shall be sleek and our oxen fat.'

In Russia, during outbreaks of disease among cattle, an icon of Saint Vlas was carried – without the priest's assistance – to the sick animal. A ewe, a sheep, a horse and a cow would be tied together by the tail and pushed into a ravine and there stoned to death – in memory, says Maximov, of pagan rites. During this sacrifice they would chant: 'We kill thee with stones, we bury thee in the ground, O death of cows, we push thee into the depths. Thou shalt not come again to our village.' Finally they would cover the bodies of the sacrificed animals with straw and wood and burn them completely.

It is interesting to note that churches dedicated to Saint Vlas are always situated on the edge of former pasture lands.

Many pagan customs have become an integral part of the religious ceremonial of Christian Slavs. For example, after an interment the friends of the deceased are invited to a funeral repast in the cemetery itself during which they eat and drink copiously. It is a vestige of the former *trizna,* a feast dedicated to the spirit of the dead man, which was customary among pagan Slavs.

In Easter week, in many Slavonic countries, orthodox families go to the cemetery to eat and drink on the graves of their kinsmen and forefathers. What remains of the drink is poured over the grave.

Often pagan superstitions penetrate even the church itself. For example, the exorcism recited by the fortunate possessor of the 'tear-weed', picked on Kupala's Day, had to be recited inside a church before the icons.

Similar examples are countless. It is characteristic that the date of the festival of Kupala, preserved with the majority of its pagan details, was after the introduction of Christianity altered to the twenty-first of June, the summer solstice, not far from the feast of Saint John the Baptist. Now John, in many Slavonic languages, is Ivan; and, quite naturally, the festival of the pagan god Kupala became in many Slav countries that of Ivan-Kupala. This extraordinary association of the mythical name of a pagan divinity with that of a great Christian saint is a perfect example of the naïve and simple manner in which paganism survived into Christian times, and of how the two religions managed to co-exist among the masses of the Slavonic world.

FINNO-UGRIC MYTHOLOGY

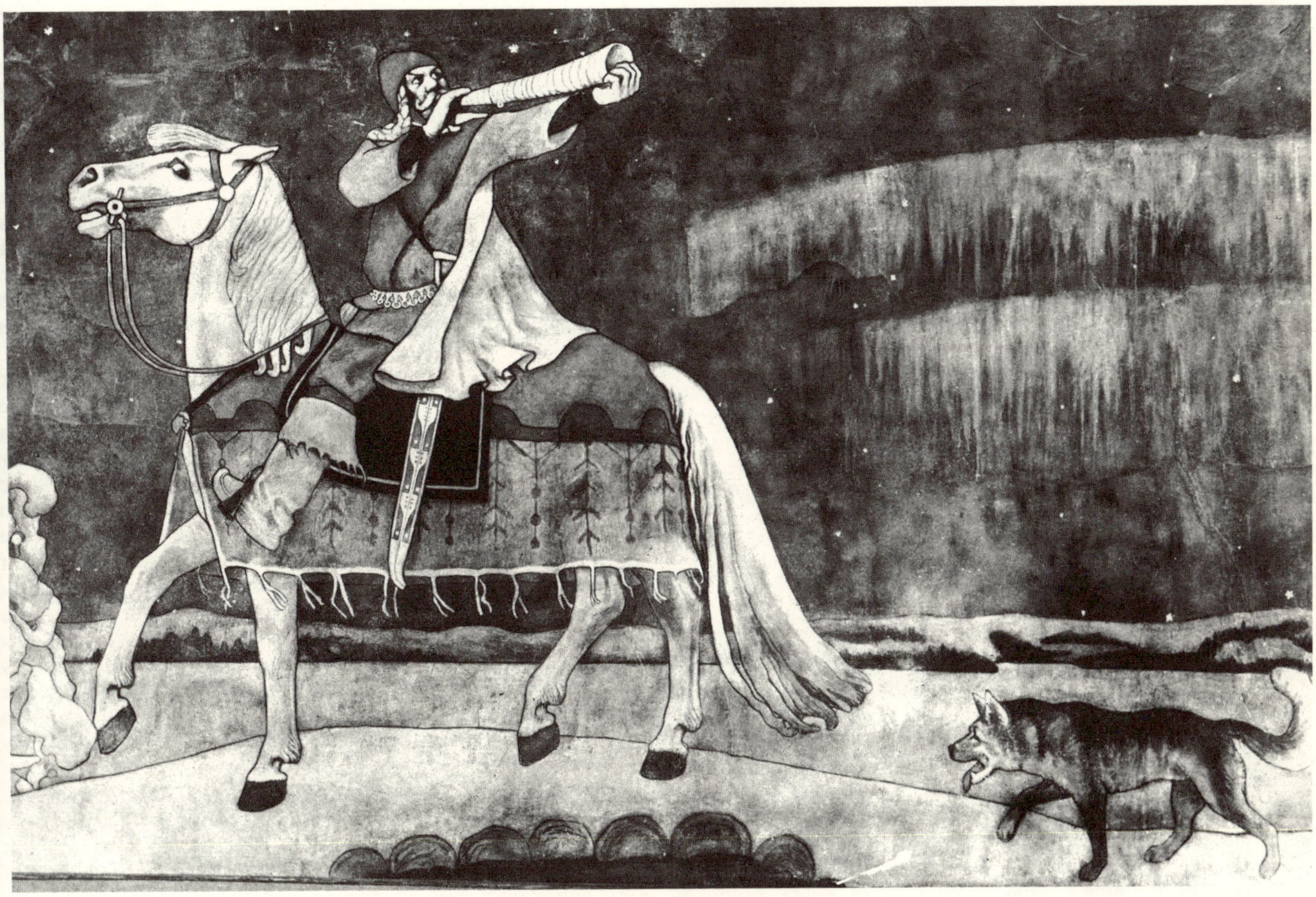

Kullervo. One of the great figures of the *Kalevala*, Kullervo was a wicked and gloomy individual who put his great strength to evil uses and employed magic to avenge himself on a mistress who had incurred his wrath. It is from the *Kalevala*, the Finnish national epic, that we obtain much of our knowledge of the mythology and ancient religious beliefs of the Finno-Ugric peoples. From a painting by A. Gallen-Kallela.

INTRODUCTION

The Finno-Ugric race comprises a considerable number of tribes and peoples who speak different dialects descended from the same parent language. They live not in compact masses but in isolated groups, surrounded on all sides by powerful neighbours of other races.

They can be divided into four principal groups: the Ugrian, to whom belong the Voguls and the Ostyaks, established in Western Siberia, and the Magyars who came from the same region; the Permian group which includes the Zyrians, the Votyaks and the Permyaks who live in the provinces of Vyatka and Perm in Russia; the Cheremis-Mordvin with the Cheremis on the left bank of the upper Volga and the Mordvins on the middle Volga; and finally the Western group, represented by the Finns, the Karelians, the Esthonians and the Livonians on the one hand, and the Lapps on the other.

Scattered and separated from each other the Finno-Ugric peoples have been subjected to various influences: Iranian, Slav, Scandinavian. Their religious evolution has also been extremely varied: the Magyars became one of the chief ramparts of Catholicism; the Finns of Finland and the Esthonians a bulwark of the Lutheran church. The Finno-Ugrians of Russia were largely converted to Orthodoxy with a minority who embraced Islam – though both long kept survivals of their ancient pagan beliefs, survivals which were particularly strong among the Finno-Ugrians of Asia.

With the aid of such survivals and by comparing them with the important evidence furnished by the great mythic epic of the Finnish West – the *Kalevala* – one can draw a reasonably complete picture of the mythology and ancient religious beliefs of the Finno-Ugric peoples.

THE KALEVALA

In about 1828 the Finnish scholar Lönnrot conceived the idea of gathering together the popular songs of ancient Finland. He then began to travel the country, visiting the humblest villages where he collected a considerable quantity of songs or *runot* (runes) which had been handed down by generation after generation of peasants. By patient comparison and arrangement he combined all these songs into a heroic epic which he entitled the *Kalevala*.

When the poem appeared in 1835 it contained about twelve thousand verses. By successive additions it continued to grow and in the definitive edition of 1849 there were twenty-two thousand eight hundred verses.

The subject of the epic is the struggle between Kalevala – which

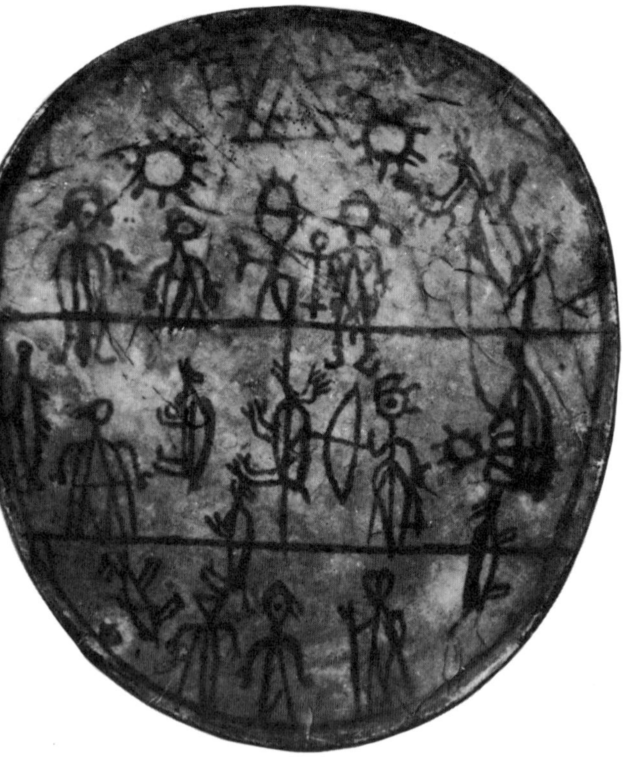

Figures on the skin of a Lapp drum from northern Sweden. Shamanism and magic formed the basis of the primitive Finno-Ugric religion, Lapland in particular being celebrated for its magicians. A sacred drum such as this would have formed an essential part of a shaman's equipment and in the sixteenth and seventeenth centuries the Laplanders' *quodbas*, or 'magic drums', were consequently sought out by the Swedish authorities and confiscated. This example dates from *c.* 1800.

according to the usually authorised interpretation signifies the 'Fatherland of Heroes' – and Pohja or Pohjola, the 'back country' – Northern Finland or Lapland.

The chief hero of the *Kalevala* is Vainamoinen, son of the Virgin of the Air. The beginning of the poem describes his miraculous birth. He clears the ground and sows it. He triumphs over Joukahainen the Laplander, whose sister Aino he plans to marry. But Aino throws herself into the sea and Vainamoinen, having escaped Joukahainen's ambushes, goes to search for a bride among the daughters of Pohja. Louhi, protectress of Pohja, promises him the hand of her own daughter if he can forge the *sampo* – a mysterious talisman which cannot be precisely identified – for her. Vainamoinen confides this task to the smith Ilmarinen; but the daughter of Louhi prefers the smith to the hero and the wedding of the young couple is celebrated with great splendour.

Now a new character appears, Lemminkainen. He is a cheerful youth, a great seducer of girls, quarrelsome and turbulent. He too has come to the land of Pohja in search of a wife. He has even perished in the course of the voyage and all his mother's skill in magic was needed to recall him to life. Furious at not having been invited to the wedding of Louhi's daughter, Lemminkainen undertakes an expedition against Pohja. He kills the great chief of the family, but has to flee from the wrath of the people of Pohja who burn his house and devastate his fields. In vain does he attempt a new expedition. Louhi's magic power triumphs over his courage.

Meanwhile Ilmarinen is stricken with grief at the loss of his wife, devoured by the bears of Kullervo, the spirit of evil. He returns to Pohja to ask for Louhi's second daughter in marriage. When he does not obtain the mother's consent he carries off the girl. But she takes advantage of a time when he is asleep to give herself to another man. Her husband then changes her into a seagull.

When Ilmarinen returns to Kalevala he tells Vainamoinen about the prosperity which the *sampo* has brought to the land of Pohja. The two heroes thereupon make plans to go and seize the precious talisman. Lemminkainen joins them. On the way their ship runs into an enormous pike from whose bones Vainamoinen fashions a wondrous *kantele,* a sort of five-stringed dulcimer. After having lulled his adversaries to sleep with the sounds of this instrument Vainamoinen takes possession of the *sampo*; but an untimely song sung by Lemminkainen awakens the people of Pohja. Louhi rouses a horrifying tempest in the course of which the *kantele* is carried away by the waves and the *sampo* is broken. Vainamoinen is able to rescue only its scattered fragments. This, however, is sufficient to assure the prosperity of the land of Kalevala. Louhi is enraged and unleashes a series of scourges against Kalevala. She goes as far as to shut up the sun and the moon in a cavern; but in the end Vainamoinen triumphs. Then, deciding that his mission has been completed, he embarks alone in a ship he has built and, carried by the waves, he disappears forever on the boundless sea.

From this tissue of legends which embrace, at times rather obscurely, the traditions and aspirations of the Finnish race, one thing at least stands out clearly: the richness and originality of the mythological element. Hence it is only necessary to turn the pages of the *Kalevala* in order to reconstruct the Finnish pantheon, together with the beliefs and practices connected with it.

MAGIC AND SHAMANISM

Beauvoir, in his study of magic among the Finns, wrote: 'All people who have been able to get to know the Finns have regarded them as masters in the occult sciences and, leaving national pride aside, have proclaimed their superiority. Norwegian kings in the Middle Ages forbade people to give credence to Finnish beliefs and prohibited voyages to Finnmark in order to consult magicians.'

Magic, indeed, was the basis of the primitive religion of the Finno-Ugric peoples.

In the sixteenth and seventeenth centuries the Swedish authorities searched for and confiscated the Laplander's 'magic drums' – or *quodbas* – to the sound of which Lappish sorcerers chanted their sacred exorcisms. Among the Finno-Ugrians of Siberia magic drums were still used at the end of the nineteenth century and even at the beginning of the twentieth by the priest-conjurers known as *Shamans.* Shamanism is distinguished from other religions by the power that man or rather certain men particularly endowed, the Shamans, exercise over nature or over the divine or demonic beings who represent and govern nature. Among Finnish peoples magic made its influence felt throughout all aspects of material and intellectual life. If the magic drum which is still found among the Ostyaks of Siberia has under Christian influence fallen into disuse among the Finns of Finland, their popular poetry remains thoroughly impregnated with the spirit of Shamanistic magic. The *Kalevala* is thus in the first place a magic poem which not only abounds in scenes of magic, in conjurations and incantations, but offers a complete repertory of spells by which the Finns claimed to exert power over men, animals, inanimate beings and, in general, over all the forces of nature.

This power, of course, was not conferred upon everyone, but remained the privilege of certain beings especially favoured or gifted.

Magic in the Kalevala. The great future pre-ordained for the imperturbable Vainamoinen was foreboded by the amazing circumstances of his birth. 'He passed thirty summers and as many winters in his mother's womb; he reflected, he meditated how to live, how to exist in this sombre hiding-place. . . . And he cried out: "Break my bonds, O Moon! Sun, deliver me! And thou, radiant Great Bear, teach the hero how to pass through these unknown gates!" But the Moon did not break his bonds, nor did the Sun deliver him. Then Vainamoinen grew bored with his existence. He knocked loudly at the fortress gate with the finger which has no name (namely the ring-finger). He forced the wall of bone with his left big toe and he dragged himself by the fingernails across the threshold and on his knees issued from the vestibule.'

As for the debonair Lemminkainen his mother had bathed him, when he was a little baby, three times in the course of one summer night, and nine times one night in autumn, so that he should become a scholar and a magician in every way, a singer in the house and in the world a man of ability.

When Lemminkainen tried to slay the swan of Tuoni, the infernal river, and perished for his temerity because he had not learned the magic words which gave protection against the bite of serpents; and when his body was torn to pieces by the son of Tuoni and scattered in the waters of the black river, Lemminkainen's mother with

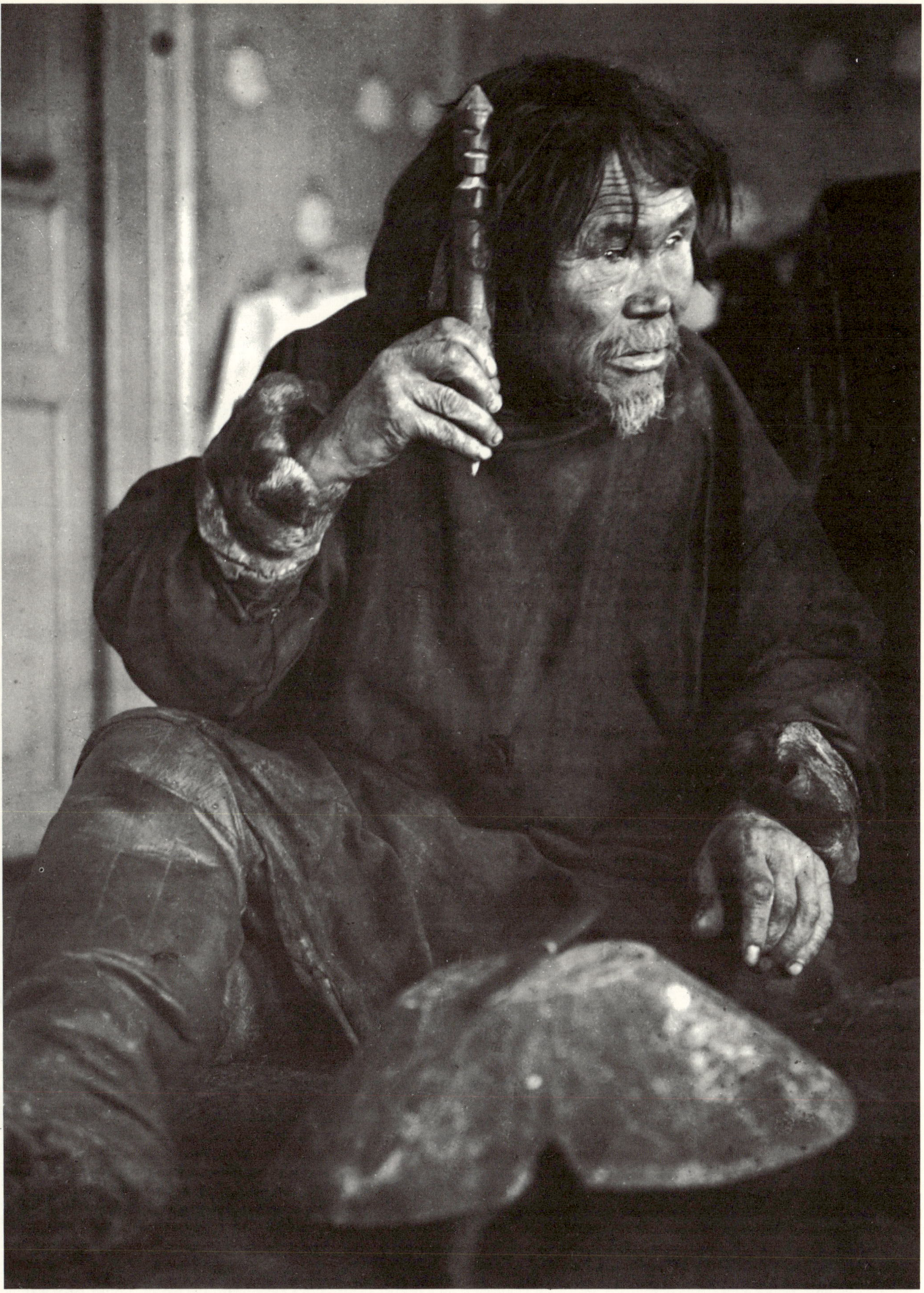

A Samoyed soothsayer from Siberia. The Samoyeds are one of a number of scattered groups which together form the Finno-Ugric race and were among the first to separate from the parent stem at about the beginning of the fourth millennium B.C. Survivals of ancient,pagan beliefs are particularly strong among the Finno-Ugrians of the east and magic drums were still being used by Siberian shamans as late as the present century.

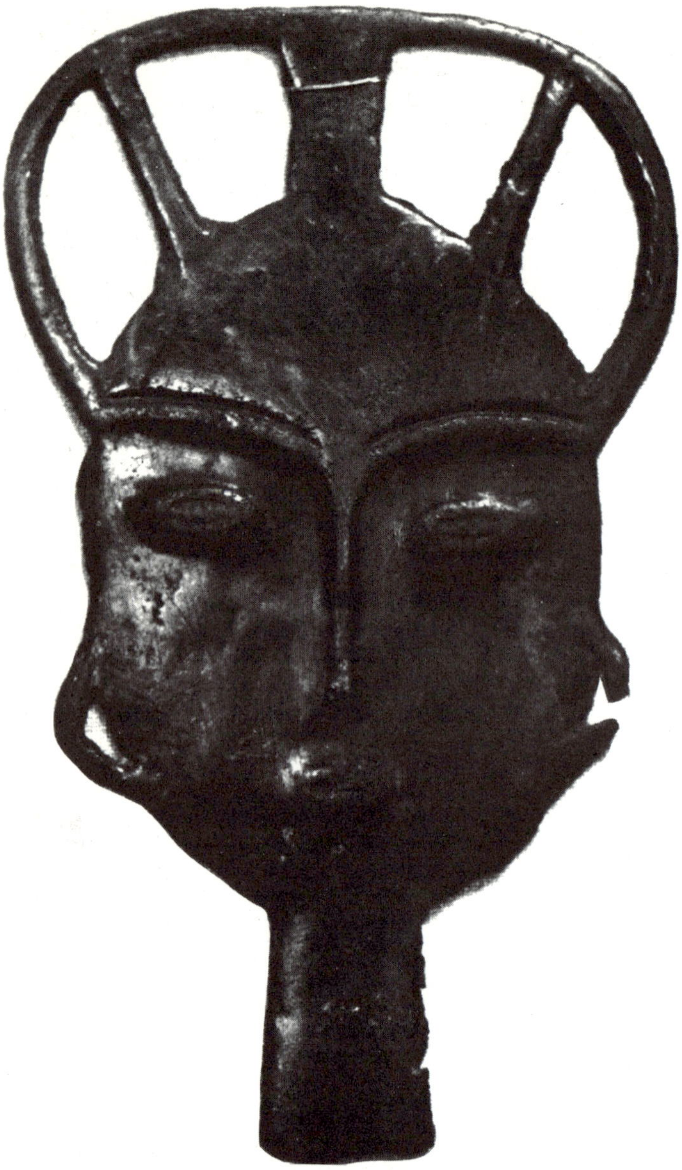

A shaman-ancestor. This cast bronze representation of a shaman-ancestor was found in the valley of the River Ili in 1905.
Unlike most religions which believe rather in the existence of superior and all-powerful gods, the Finno-Ugric pantheon was vague and confused, and certain privileged human beings, known as shamans, were credited with supernatural powers which enabled them to overcome the divine or demoniac spirits which resided in all things.
Irkutsk Museum, Siberia.

her magic arts succeeded in restoring him to life. She fished out the pathetic shreds, 'fitted flesh to flesh, bone to bone, joints to joints, and veins to veins', then she invoked the aid of the goddess of veins, Suonetar, and with her assistance gave her son life once more. But he was unable to speak. The mother magician then called upon Mehilainen, the bee, asking him to go and search beyond the ninth heaven for a wondrous balm which Jumala himself used. When she received the balm she applied it to the exhausted hero's wounds. He awoke from his dreams, he rose and he said: 'I've slept for a long time.'

It was less with the strength of their arms than with the power of their incantations that the heroes fought each other.

When the rash Joukahainen, 'the thin son of Lapland', came to challenge Vainamoinen he called all his knowledge to his assistance. Vainamoinen listened to him impassively and then sang in his turn. And 'behold, the swamps roared and the earth trembled and the copper mountains swayed and the thick boulders were shattered... He overwhelmed young Joukahainen with his spells, he changed his sleigh into a withered shrub, his pearl-handled whip into a seaside reed, his horse with its starred forehead into a rock of the cataracts...Then he hoaxed young Joukahainen himself; he threw him waist-deep into a swamp, into a meadow as deep as his loins, into a patch of briars up to his ears...' To escape from this tigh corner Joukahainen had to promise his conqueror the hand o his sister Aino. Later on he attempted to avenge himself by letting fly an arrow at Vainamoinen; but he only hit Vainamoinen's horse and the hero, thrown into the sea, was pulled out again by an eagle

It was above all the land of the North, Lapland, which wa celebrated for its magic singers and enchanters. We learn from the *Kalevala* that when the light-hearted Lemminkainen went to the house of Louhi he saw that it was full of *tjetajat* (wizards), powerfu magicians, learned soothsayers, skilled sorcerers. All were singing Lappish *runot* (runes) and shouting out the songs of Hiisi – the goo of evil. The cheerful Lemminkainen entered the house and 'began to shout his own savage runes and to display his own great powers of wizardry. Fire spurted from his leather tunic, flame shot from his eyes. He laughed at the proud men, he dispersed them on al sides, into waste lands, fields where nothing grew, swamps where there were no fish. He laughed at the warriors with their swords the heroes with their weapons. He laughed at the old, laughed at the young...'

Like men, animals too were submitted to the power of the magicians. When she sent her cattle to pasture, the wife of Ilmarinen the smith, did not forget to invoke all the divine powers in order to assure the protection of the herd. She also conjured the bear whom she flattered with soft words. 'O handsome Otso, man of the woods, with feet running with honey, let us make a pact, a peace treaty for our lifetime. Swear to me not to attack my crooked-legged givers of wool.' In the same episode the shepherd Kullervo, wishing to avenge himself on his mistress for her cruelty, changes the cows into bears and wolves, and the wicked wife of Ilmarinen is devoured by her own cattle.

Magic powers also affected the elements. To triumph over Lemminkainen the Lady of Pohjola, Louhi, unleashed the Cold. 'O Cold, my gentle son, go where I bid thee. See that the audacious one's ship is held fast in the ice.' And the Cold set about submitting the sea to its power: on the first night he attacked the gulfs and lakes; on the following night he displayed terrible violence: the ice rose by an ell. He also thought of seizing the great hero and freezing him; but Lemminkainen quickly got the better of him, for he knew efficacious words, he understood the 'origins' of the Cold.

It is, in fact, rather curious that one of the chief magic formulas in the *Kalevala* consists of retracing the origin of the things over which one wishes to have a hold. It is only thus that one can subjugate them.

Vainamoinen one day accidentally wounded himself in the knee with his axe. He went to consult an old man who was a celebrated healer. But the healer could do nothing until he was told the origin of the Iron, which he did not know.

The magic element influenced all work, even the most pedestrian. Every time that a man, in work, had to deal with matter he must, in order to deal with it successfully, know the formula. When Vainamoinen was building his ship 'he would sing a song, a powerful song, to each part that he constructed. But when it was time to join planks together three words suddenly failed him.' From that moment it was impossible to finish the ship. Vainamoinen then set about searching for the magic words. He even descended into the underworld to find them, and finally, on the advice of a shepherd, he visited the giant Antero Vipunen. He found him 'lying under the earth with his songs, stretched out on the ground with his magic words. The poplar was growing from his shoulders, the birch from his temples, the alder from his cheeks, the willow from his beard, the fir from his forehead, the wild pine between his teeth.' After having felled all these trees Vainamoinen plunged his iron-clad staff into the giant's throat. The giant then opened his mouth and between his jaws swallowed up the hero and his sword. But 'Vainamoinen turned himself into a blacksmith. From his shirt he made a forge, from his shirt-sleeves and his fur-lined coat he made bellows, from his knee an anvil, from his elbow a hammer. And he began to strike mighty blows in the belly of the prodigious giant.' To Vipunen's imprecations Vainamoinen retorted: 'I shall sink my anvil farther into the flesh of your heart, I shall install my forge in a deeper place until I have heard the words, until I have learned from you the magic words.' Vipunen had to give in. 'He opened the coffer full of words, the coffer full of songs, in order to sing the efficacious words, the profound words of the origin...' Vainamoinen, having thus torn the magic chants from their cavern,

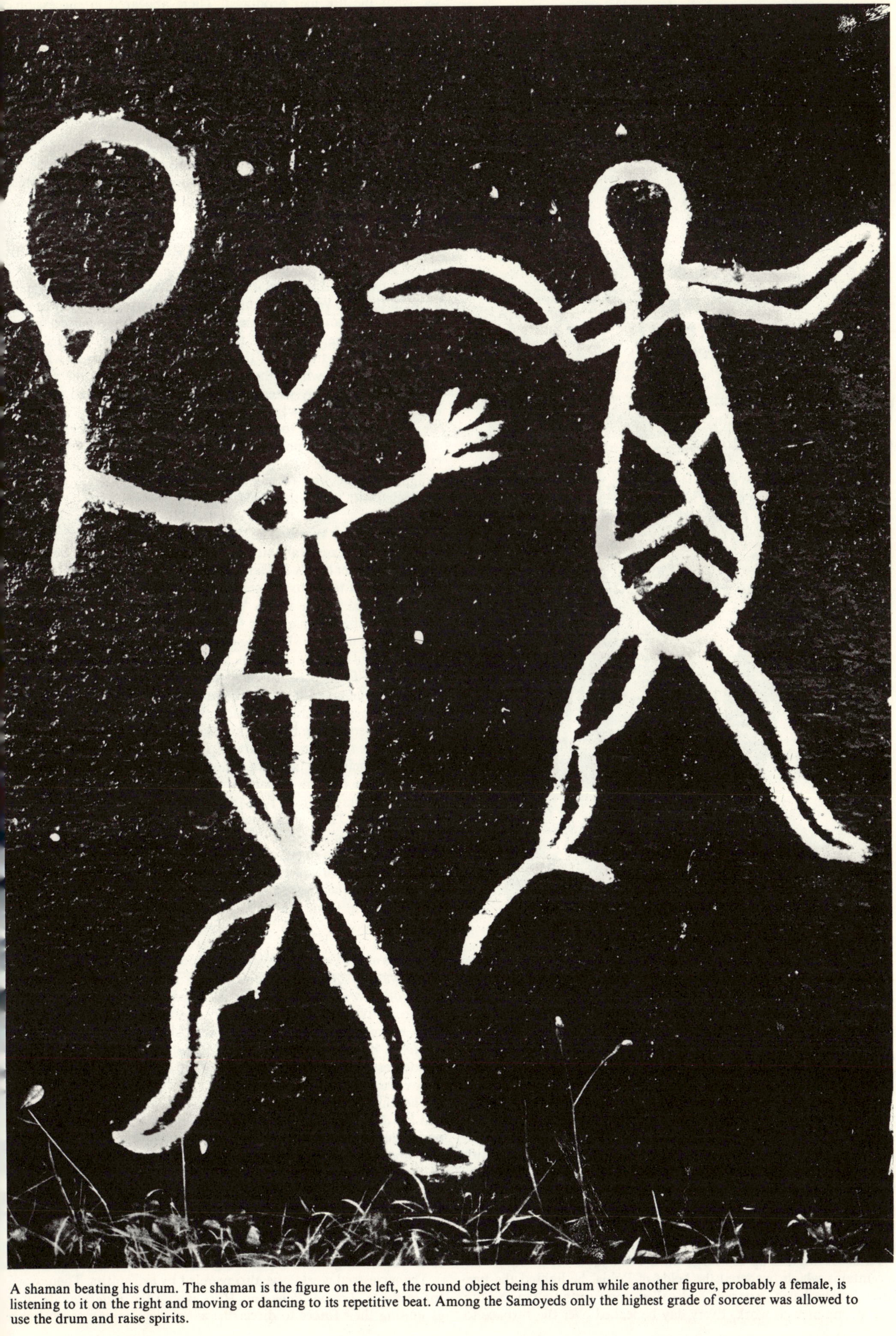

A shaman beating his drum. The shaman is the figure on the left, the round object being his drum while another figure, probably a female, is listening to it on the right and moving or dancing to its repetitive beat. Among the Samoyeds only the highest grade of sorcerer was allowed to use the drum and raise spirits.

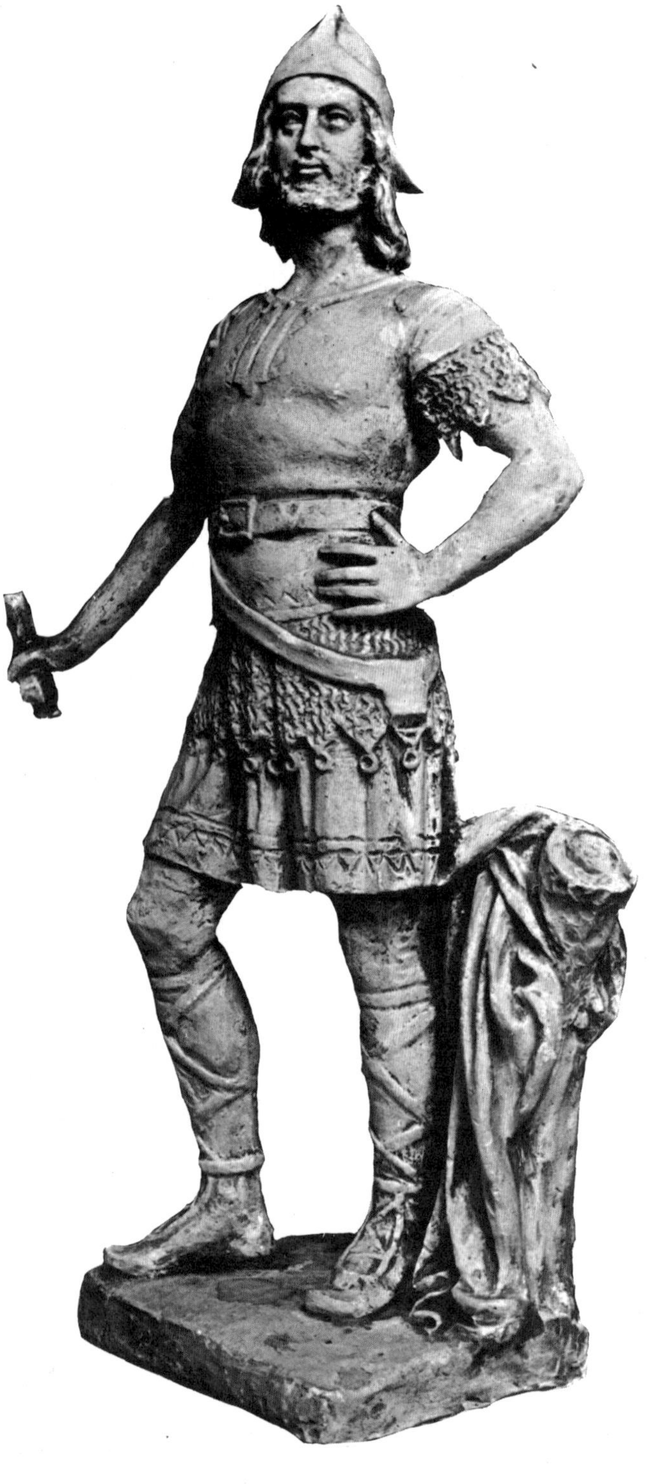

Lemminkainen. One of the heroes of the Kalevala, Lemminkainen was a cheerful, reckless person. When a baby, his mother had ritually bathed him so that he might become a scholar and a magician and he was subsequently able to overcome his enemies by magic and incantations though he was also physically brave. It is possible that he was the same person as the water god Ahti. Plaster statuette by C.A. Sjostrand.

returned to his ship which by the power of words alone was finished without the aid of an axe.

It was also magic which was the basis of the work of the smith Ilmarinen, the unceasing beater of iron. Nothing is more characteristic than the fashioning of the mysterious *sampo* which Ilmarinen undertook to forge 'with the point of a swan's feathers, the milk of a sterile cow, a small grain of barley and the fine wool of a fecund ewe'.

After having set up his forge on a thick block of stone in the mountains which bordered the fields of Pohja, he lighted the fire, threw in the basic materials and called upon serfs to fan the fire and strong men to work. Every day he leaned over the furnace to see what the fire had produced. There appeared in succession a golden bow, a red ship, a heifer with golden horns, a plough with a golden ploughshare and a silver handle. But the smith broke all these objects. Finally, as he leaned again over the furnace, he saw that the *sampo* had been created.

THE GODS OF THE KALEVALA

Confining ourselves to the *Kalevala* alone we find Finno-Ugric mythology rich in its number of divinities. The Swedish scholar Castren listed them in his *Nordiska Resor* ('Nordic Travels') which has been utilised in what follows.

The Celestial Gods. At the head of the Finno-Ugric pantheon stands Jumala, the supreme god, the creator. He is a semi-abstract entity whose sacred tree was the oak. His name is related to a word which signifies twilight, dusk, and it is probable that Jumala was originally a god of the sky. Without completely disappearing Jumala was later replaced by another supreme god, Ukko, whose personality is a little less vague. Ukko was the 'ancient father who reigns in the heavens'. He was the god of the sky and the air. It was he who supported the world, who gathered the clouds and made the rain fall. He was invoked only when all the other gods had been called on in vain. Ukko's wife was Akka, who was also called Rauni from the Finnish word for the mountain ash which was sacred to her.

The other celestial powers were *Paiva*, the Sun; *Kuu*, the Moon; *Otava*, the Great Bear; and above all *Ilma*, divinity of the air, whose daughter *Luonnotar*, Vainamoinen's own mother, was closely connected with the myth of creation.

The Birth of the World. The *Kalevala* recounts how Luonnotar – whose name means Daughter of Nature – grew weary of her sterile virginity and her lonely existence in the midst of the celestial regions, and let herself fall into the sea and float on the white crests of the waves. Tossed by the waves 'the breath of the wind caressed her bosom and the sea made her fertile'. For seven centuries she thus floated without being able to find a resting place. She was lamenting this fact when an eagle – or a duck – appeared. He too was searching the vast sea for a place to build his nest. Perceiving Luonnotar's knee which emerged from the water he built his nest on it and deposited his eggs which he sat on for three days. 'Then the daughter of Ilma felt scorching heat on her skin; she bent her knee violently and the eggs rolled into the abyss. They were not, however, lost in the slime: their remains were changed into beautiful and excellent things. From the lower part of the eggs was formed the earth, mother of all creatures. From their upper part the sublime heavens were formed. Their yolks became the yellow radiant sun, their whites the gleaming moon. Their spotted fragments were the stars, and their black fragments the clouds in the air.' Finally Luonnotar completed the work of creation by causing promontories to spring up, flattening the shores and digging out gulfs. 'Already islands were emerging from the waves; pillars of air rose on their base. The earth, born of a word, displayed its solid mass...'

Divinities of the Earth and Waters. Among the divinities of the earth, which was personified by the *Mother of Mannu*, may be mentioned the *Mother of Metsola*, who personified the forest; *Pellervoinen*, the protective god of fields, lord of trees and plants; *Tapio*, 'of the dark beard, the fir bonnet and moss cloak', who with his wife *Mielikki*, his son *Nyyrikki* and his daughter *Tuulikki*, represented the deities of the woods, invoked by the ancient Finns in order to assure the abundance of game.

The chief water-god was *Ahto* or *Ahti*. With his wife *Vellamo* and his daughters he lived 'at the far end of the cloudy headland, under the deep waves, in the midst of the black slime, in the heart of a thick cliff.' It may be remarked that Lemminkainen bore the epithet Ahti, which suggests that the god and the hero were but one and the same person. Ahti was surrounded by the genii of the waters, generally harmful, such as *Vetehinen*, who was perhaps derived from the Slavonic Vodyanoi, and *Tursas*, a genie of monstrous aspect who, in the *Kalevala*, rises from the bottom of the sea to set fire to the grass cut by the virgins of the billows.

The terrestrial world was also peopled by evil spirits. There were, for instance, *Lempo*, *Paha* and *Hiisi*, whom the *Kalevala* describes as uniting their forces to direct the axe which Vainamoinen holds

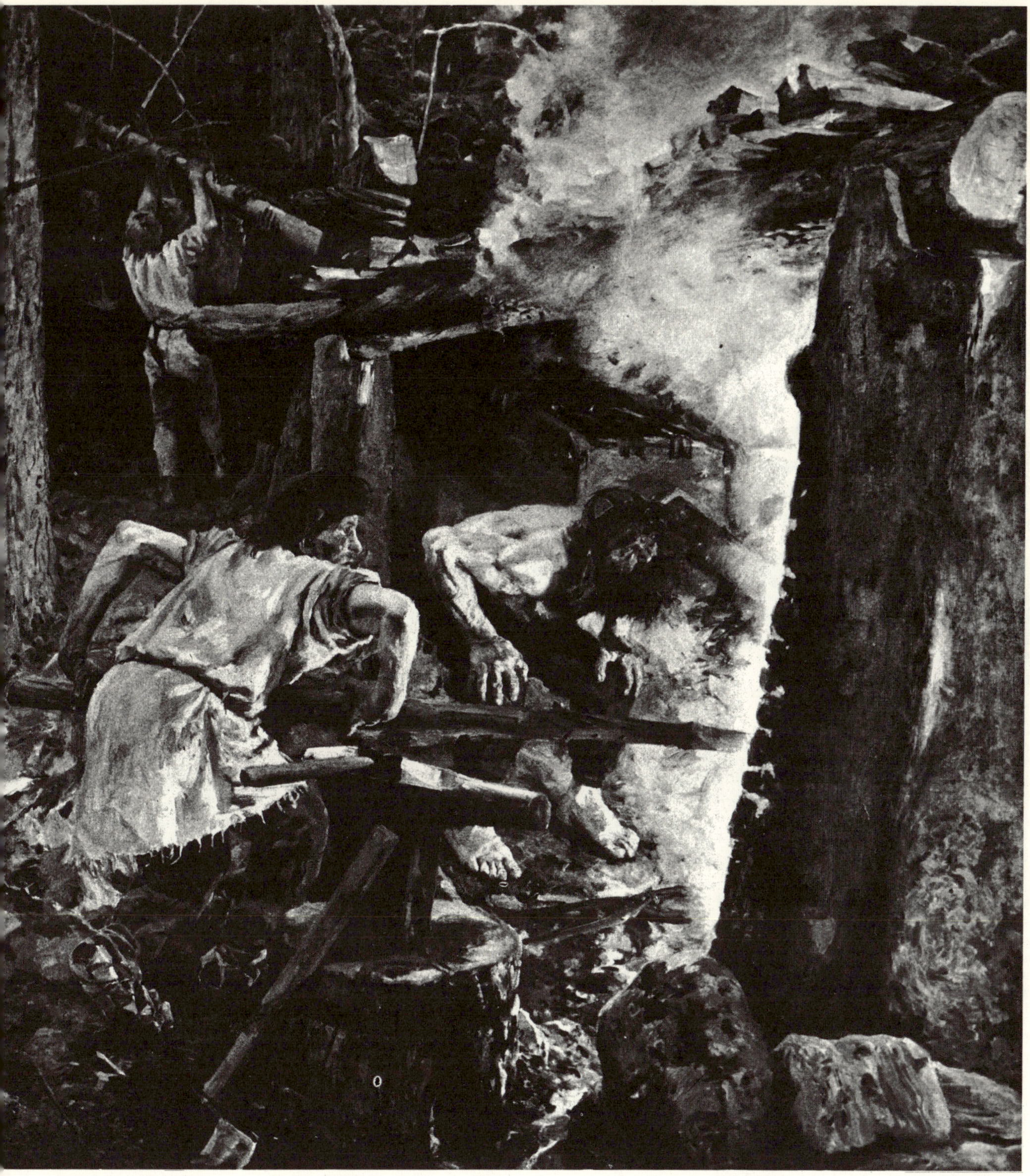

he forging of the Sampo, by A. Gallen-Kallela. Ateneum, Helsinki.

gainst his own knee. 'Hiisi made the handle shake, Lempo turned e cutting edge towards him, Paha misdirected the blow. The axe en split the hero's knee. Lempo plunged it into his flesh, Hiisi ushed it through his veins and the blood began to flow.'

he Underworld of the Kalevala. The idea of the afterworld as a place punishment is not found in Finno-Ugric mythology. In the *alevala* the infernal region, or rather the kingdom of the dead, as the appearance of a land darker than other lands, though in the sun shines and forests grow. The entrance to *Tuonela,* the land Tuoni, or to *Manala,* the land of Mana – names of the Finnish nderworld – was protected by a river with black billows. It required long march to reach it: a week through thickets, another week rough woods, and a third week through deep forests. Woe to those who attempted to penetrate this accursed territory! 'Many enter Manala, but very few come out again.' Lemminkainen, to satisfy the demands of Louhi, ventured as far as the banks of the black river in order to shoot with his arrow the beautiful bird of Tuoni, the long-necked swan. But he was thrown into the depths of the river and his body, torn to pieces by the bloodstained son of Tuoni, was dispersed in the funereal waves of Manala.

Only Vainamoinen escaped unscathed from this perilous expedition. He had come to the land of Tuonela in the hope of finding there the magic words which he needed in order to finish the building of his ship. When he arrived at the river's edge he perceived Tuoni's daughters. They were short of stature and stunted of body and they were busy washing their old rags in the low waters of the Manala. By insisting, he succeeded in being taken to the other bank of the

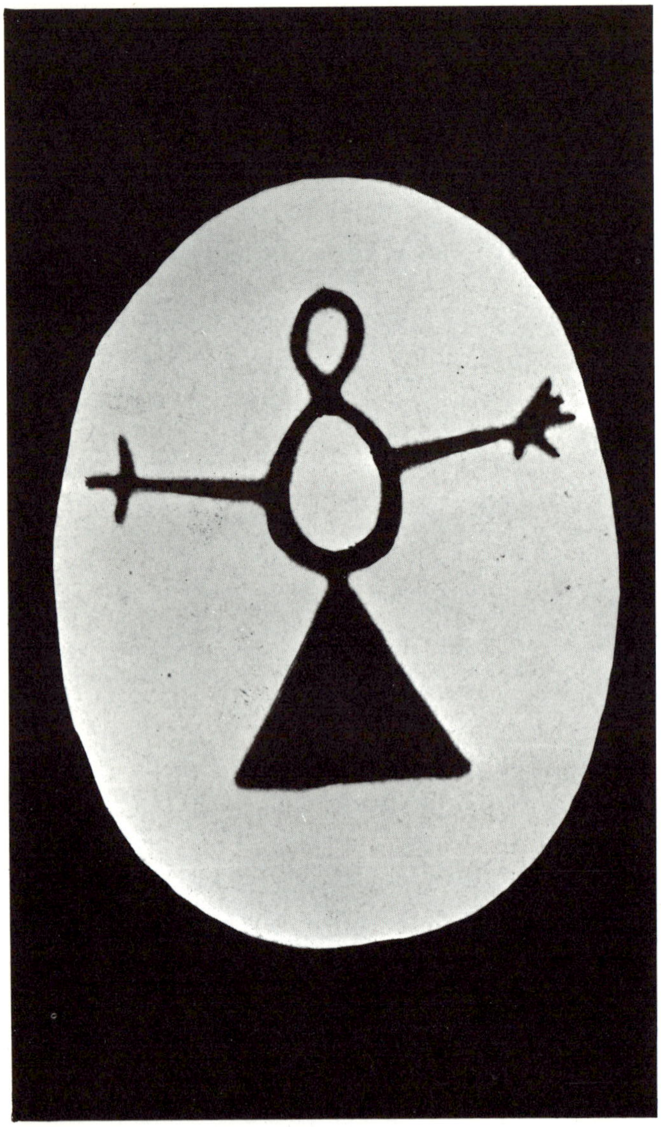

Mader-Atcha. According to a myth preserved by the Lapps, Mader-Atcha with his wife Mader-Akka formed the divine couple who together created men – Mader-Atcha being responsible for the soul and his wife for the body. As Ukko, the sky – or thunder-god, he was the supreme deity of the Finno-Ugric pantheon and was invoked when all the other gods had been called upon in vain. Design from a Lapp shaman's drum.

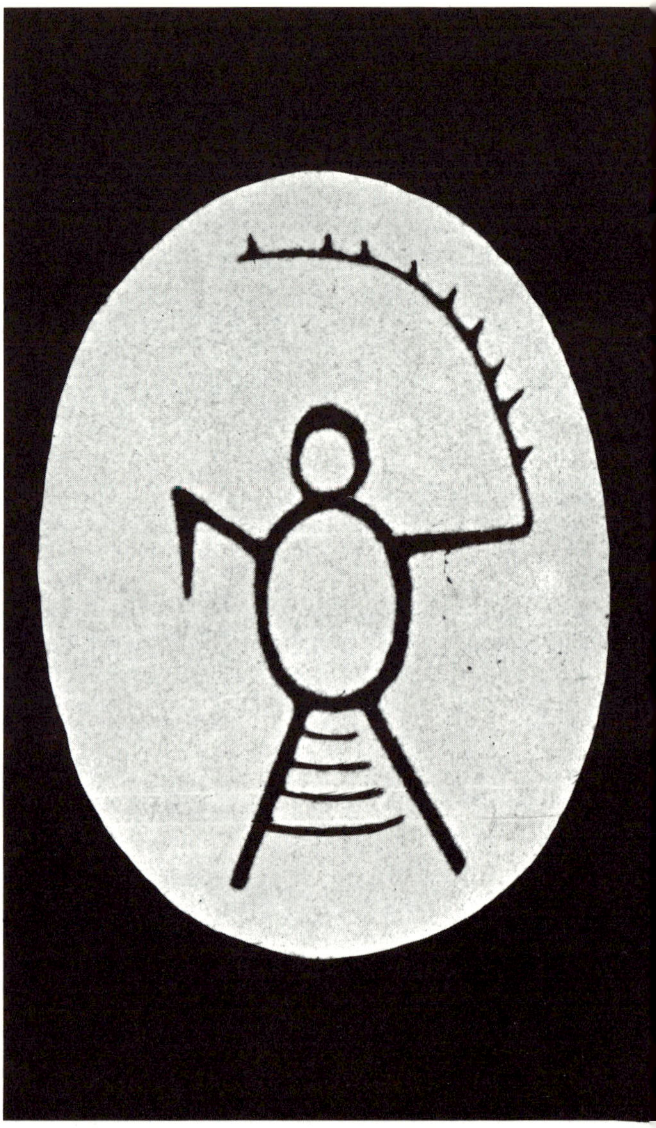

Mader-Akka. One of the few Finno-Ugric deities to possess any individuality was Mader-Akka, the wife of the high god Ukko and the female half of the divine couple. She was also known as Rauni. Mader-Akka saw to the success of the harvest and the fecundity of women and was always depicted as a triangle or a sextant. It is unusual for her to appear on a drum. Lapp drum design.

river, to the isle of Manala, the land of the dead. There he was received by Tuonetar, the queen of Tuonela, who politely offered him beer in a pot swarming with frogs and worms, but informed him that he would never leave the place. And, while Vainamoinen slept, Tuoni's crooked-fingered son threw across the river a net with iron mesh a thousand fathoms long in order to detain the hero for the rest of his life. But Vainamoinen, suddenly changing his form, dived into the water and 'glided like a steel serpent, like a viper, across the billows of Tuonela, and through the net of Tuoni'.

Over the land of Tuonela reigned *Tuoni* and his wife *Tuonetar*. Their daughters were divinities of suffering: notably *Kipu-Tytto*, goddess of illness, and *Loviatar*, 'the most despicable of Tuoni's daughters, source of all evil, origin of a thousand scourges. Her face was black and her skin was a horrible sight.' By her union with the Wind she gave birth to nine monsters: Pleurisy, Colic, Gout, Phthisis, Ulcers, Scabies, Canker, Plague and 'a fatal spirit, a creature eaten up with envy' who was not given a name. Among the goddesses of pain and disease there was also *Kivutar* and *Vammatar*. As for Death, she was personified by *Kalma* who reigned over the graves. It should be pointed out that in Finnish the word *kalma* means 'the odour of a corpse'. On the threshold of the abode of Kalma stood the monster *Surma*, personification of fatal destiny or of violent death, who was ever ready to seize in his murderous teeth and swallow in his vast gullet the imprudent man who came within reach of his fangs.

Mythological Value of the Kalevala. Such was the world of the gods as the *Kalevala* reveals it. It is as well to remember, however, that the poem is a collection of popular songs, no doubt primitive in their inspiration, but collected at a late date, so that some of them show signs of foreign influence. The *Kalevala* must not, then, be regarded as an exact reflection of the basic beliefs of the Finno-Ugric race. And even if it were, the pantheon as depicted in the *Kalevala* in no way resembles the Olympus of the Greeks. It is therefore excessively rash to make comparisons such as, for example that attempted by George Kahlbaum who assimilated Ilmarinen 'the eternal hammerer of iron' with Hephaestus, and the *sampo* with Pandora's Box. Actually the divinities of the *Kalevala* are only vaguely sketched and even the relationships between them are impossible to establish. Castren himself was obliged to recognise that 'the religious doctrine of the Finns was half-way between the direct worship of nature and a kind of religion which to phenomena and to natural objects attributes spirits or divinities who inhabit these phenomena and these objects and animate them'. This is a truer description of Finno-Ugric mythology.

FINNO-UGRIC ANIMISM

Shamanism, which as we have seen is the basis of primitive Finno-Ugric religion, is scarcely compatible with the idea of gods who are essentially superior to humanity, because the Shaman is

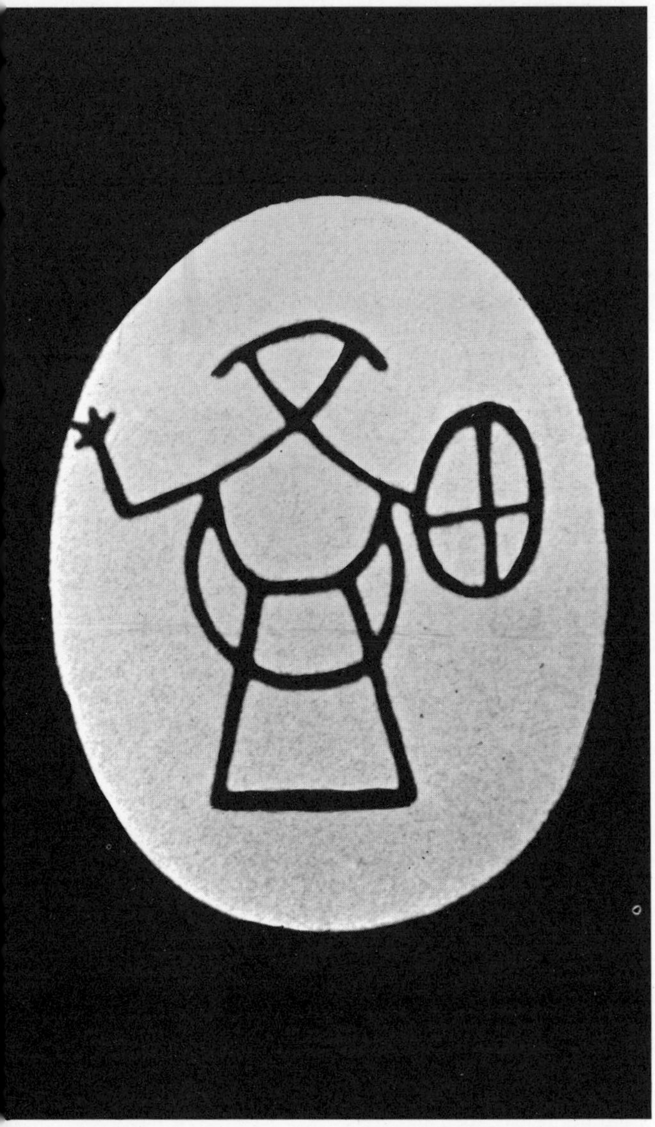

A shaman with his drum. The Finno-Ugric peoples believed that shamans were able to communicate with spirits both good and evil and that they had the power to overcome the spells of the former and transmit the wishes of the latter. In order to enter into such communication the shaman would beat with a spoon-shaped stick upon a sacred drum covered with cabalistic signs until a trance was induced. Lapp drum design.

capable of subduing everything with the magic of his spells. Shamanism presupposes an elemental force in all objects which can be dominated by a greater force, namely that of the magician. Hence the animistic character of Finno-Ugric religion.

The Soul of Things. For the Finno-Ugrians every being, every object, was endowed with a soul which the Finns called *haltija*, the Votyaks *urt*, the Cheremis *ort*. Thus among the Votyaks *d'u-urt* is the soul of the corn, *busi-urt* the soul of the cornfield; and among the Cheremis *pu-ort* is the soul of the tree.

The soul is, however, indissolubly linked to the body with which it forms an indivisible whole. Having no independent existence it dies with the body. That is why the Ingrians went to weep over the grave of the deceased and placed offerings there during a period roughly equivalent to the time of the body's decomposition. Afterwards the grave was no longer visited for, they said, 'there is no longer anything left of the soul'.

For the Voguls the heart and the lungs were the seat of the soul. Thus their warriors would eat the heart and lungs of the vanquished in order to absorb their vital force, that is, their soul. Other tribes attributed a particular importance to the skeleton, the framework of the soul as well as of the body. The Lapps, for example, would avoid breaking and destroying the skeleton of a sacrificed animal, believing that the gods used it again for making a new animal.

The belief that the soul lasts as long as the skeleton exists is also clear from the ceremonies of the 'Bear's festival' of which the *Kalevala* gives us a curious description. After the bear had been hunted and killed its flesh was eaten; then its bones were put in a tomb with skis, a knife and other objects. The slain animal was treated as a friend and asked to tell the other bears about all the honours men had paid to it. The account in the *Kalevala* is merely a lyrical paraphrase of this custom which was practised among the pagan Finns.

Just as all animals possessed a soul, so did all plants, the earth and the waters. When the Lapps of Kola cut down trees in the forest they never omitted, before felling the tree, to 'kill' it with a special blow of the axe. Otherwise the tree would not burn properly on the fire. When the Finns drew water from a well they would pour back two drops so that the 'well should not be killed'.

Hence man was surrounded by a multitude of living beings against whom he must ceaselessly be on guard and whose goodwill he sought to win by prayers and offerings. Thus in the mountainous regions of the Altai in Siberia the natives, who have remained Shamanists, would attach bags made of birch bark to birch-trees and fill them with gifts intended for the good spirits. Not long ago they still sacrificed horses and hung up their skulls and hides on poles: an obvious survival of a very ancient custom, since in the *Kalevala* Vainamoinen does the same thing with the remains of a bear which he carries to the summit of a mountain and suspends from the top of a sacred tree.

The Divine Multitude. This infinity of spirits or genii who peopled the universe presents a rudimentary form of divinity. It was, as it were, an anarchical polydemonism. Absolute individualism reigned in this mythological world. There was no systematic organisation and no genealogical order. All the gods and genii were independent of each other in their respective spheres of influence.

The genii or gods who animated various beings, living or inert, were too closely allied to them to have a distinct individuality.

This explains the indeterminate character of the gods in the *Kalevala*: we glimpse scarcely more than a vague attempt at anthropomorphism in the differentiation of sex between the divinities. Among the Votyaks there are two terms, *murt* ('man') and *mumi* ('mother'), which designate the god and the goddess. Hence *korka-murt* is the 'man of the house' or the spirit of the hearth; *obin-murt* is the rain man, *vu-murt* the water man. *Shundimumi* is the 'mother of the sun'; *gudiri-mumi* the 'mother of the thunder', *muzem-mumi* the earth-mother, and so forth.

It is not easy to keep our bearings in this almost anonymous divine multitude. Only a few personalities emerge with a slightly more marked individuality, such as the goddess *Maan-Eno*. This name was given by the Esthonians to the wife of Ukko, the god of thunder. She saw to the success of the harvest and the fecundity of women. Then there was *Rot*, the god of the Underworld in Lappish mythology. But usually we meet only genii whose names merely recall their functions.

Water Spirits. Such, among others, were the very numerous water spirits. To *Vu-murt*, the Votyaks' water-man, corresponds the *Vizi-ember* of the Magyars. He was a water genie who lived in lakes and rivers and was apt to demand human victims. When these were slow in forthcoming those who lived beside the river would hear his mysterious voice crying: 'The time is come and no one has yet arrived.' After that someone was certain to drown. In addition to a water-man, Magyar mythology had its water-mother – *Viz-anya* – and the 'maiden of the water' – *Vizi-leany*. The appearance of these spirits always foretold misfortune. With these harmful genii may be classed the *Kul'* of the Ostyaks who haunted big lakes and deep waters; the *Va-kul'* of the Zyrians who was represented as a man or a woman with long hair; the *Yanki-murt* and the *Vu-vozo* of the Votyaks. When a Votyak drank water in a strange village he would conjure away the possible malevolence of the vu-vozo with this prayer: 'Do not attack me. Attack, rather, a Russian woman or a Cheremis!'

On the other hand the water sheltered benevolent spirits as well, such as the tonx of the Voguls who brought men luck when hunting or fishing, and cured illness; the *as-iga* or 'old man of the Ob', venerated by those Ostyaks who live beside the great Siberian river; the *Vu-nuna*, 'the water-uncle', who defended the Votyaks against the wicked yanki-murt; and the *Vu-kutis*, 'the aquatic aggressor', who, the same tribe believed, fought disease.

The Finno-Ugrians also had sacred rivers and lakes. Among the Voguls these were the *jelpin-ja* and the *jelpin-tur*; among the Lapps, the *passe-jokka* and the *passe-javrre*, inhabited by the *tchatse-olmai* or water-men; among the Finns, the *pyhajoki* and the *pyhajarvi*. Waterfalls and torrents also had their divinities.

The Finns of Finland had a large number of aquatic divinities among whom the most widespread was *Nakki*, genie of the Water. The population of the West and South of Finland still believes that in lakes there are places which are bottomless. Such places are entrances to the kingdom of the water-god who lives in a superb castle filled with riches.

Nakki emerged from his abode and came to visit the earth at sunrise and sunset. He could assume all kinds of shapes. When bathing one had to cry out before diving in: 'Nakki, come out of the water! I'm the one who's in the water!' For protection against Nakki it was useful to toss a coin into the water and recite this exorcism: 'May I be as light as a leaf and Nakki as heavy as iron.'

We could similarly enumerate the spirits of the forests and the trees. All of this, however, belongs to the study of folklore rather than to mythology.

The Myths. Myths in the strict sense of the word are rather rare. The *Kalevala* has preserved a few, such as the myth of the origin of the serpent, that of the origin of iron and of the origin of fire. Fire came from a spark which Ukko made when he struck his flaming sword against his fingernail. He confided the spark to one of the virgins of the air. But she negligently let it escape from her fingers and the spark 'rolled through the clouds, through the nine vaults and the six lids of the air'. Finally it fell into a lake where it was snapped up by a blue trout who was gulped down by a red salmon who in his turn was swallowed by a grey pike. Vainamoinen, aided by Ilmarinen, succeeded in catching this grey pike. He freed the spark which, after causing numerous fires, was captured by the hero under the stump of a birch and shut in a copper jar.

The Lapps preserve a myth concerning the creation of man by a divine couple: *Mader-Atcha* and *Mader-Akka*. The former created the soul, his wife created the body. If the child to be born was to be a boy Mader-Atcha sent it to his daughter *Uks-Akka*; if a girl, he sent it to another daughter, *Sar-Akka*. The product of this celestial creation was then placed in the womb of its earthly mother.

The Sejda of the Lapps. The same Lapps distinguished a 'wooden god' who in the form of a birch trunk represented the god of thunder and a 'stone god' who had the aspect of either an animal or a man. Traditions concerning these two divinities are, however, extremely vague. More concrete is the existence of certain sacred stones called *sejda*, which the pagan Finns put in various places and which can still be seen in Finland, Karelia and above all in Lapland where they are especially numerous. The sejda – called *saivo* or *saite* by the Lapps of Sweden – served also as talismans. Castren relates that a Lappish sorcerer named Lompsalo owned a sejda thanks to which he caught large quantities of fish. On the opposite bank another sorcerer was in despair at catching nothing. One night when Lompsalo was asleep he stole his sejda and the fish came swimming into his nets. But Lompsalo procured a new and more powerful sejda and all the fish swam back again until the rival sorcerer destroyed his sejda.

CONCLUSION

We see in the above example the usefulness and importance of magic talismans in Finno-Ugric belief. It was thanks to these talismans that a man could control the countless haltija scattered through the universe. It was by the secret magic of sorcerers, by the sacred chants of the eternal bards that he succeeded in penetrating the great mystery of nature and in communicating with the forces hidden in the deep 'origins' of things. That was why as soon as the imperturbable old Vainamoinen began to sing to the accompaniment of his *kantele* all the animals drew near to listen with delight to his joyful tunes. The austere old man of Tapiola, all the forest folk, the queen of the woods herself hastened to enjoy the beautiful harmony. The eagle deserted his eyrie and the wild duck the deep waves; the lovely virgins of the air also lent an attentive ear to the voice of the great hero. Kuutar, the resplendent daughter of the moon, Paivatar, the glorious daughter of the sun, dropped shuttle and spindle. Ahto, king of the blue waves with his mossy beard, rose from his humid kingdom and reclined on a bed of water-lilies. The virgins of the water's edge, adorned with reeds, forgot to smooth their luxuriant hair, while the sovereign of the billows, the old lady whose bosom was enveloped in willows, emerged from the depths of the sea to hear the wondrous melody of the *kantele*...

And thus the lovely Finnish poem brings before our eyes the picture of a mystic and sacred festival in which are united the forces of nature, beasts, men and gods.

MYTHOLOGY OF ANCIENT PERSIA

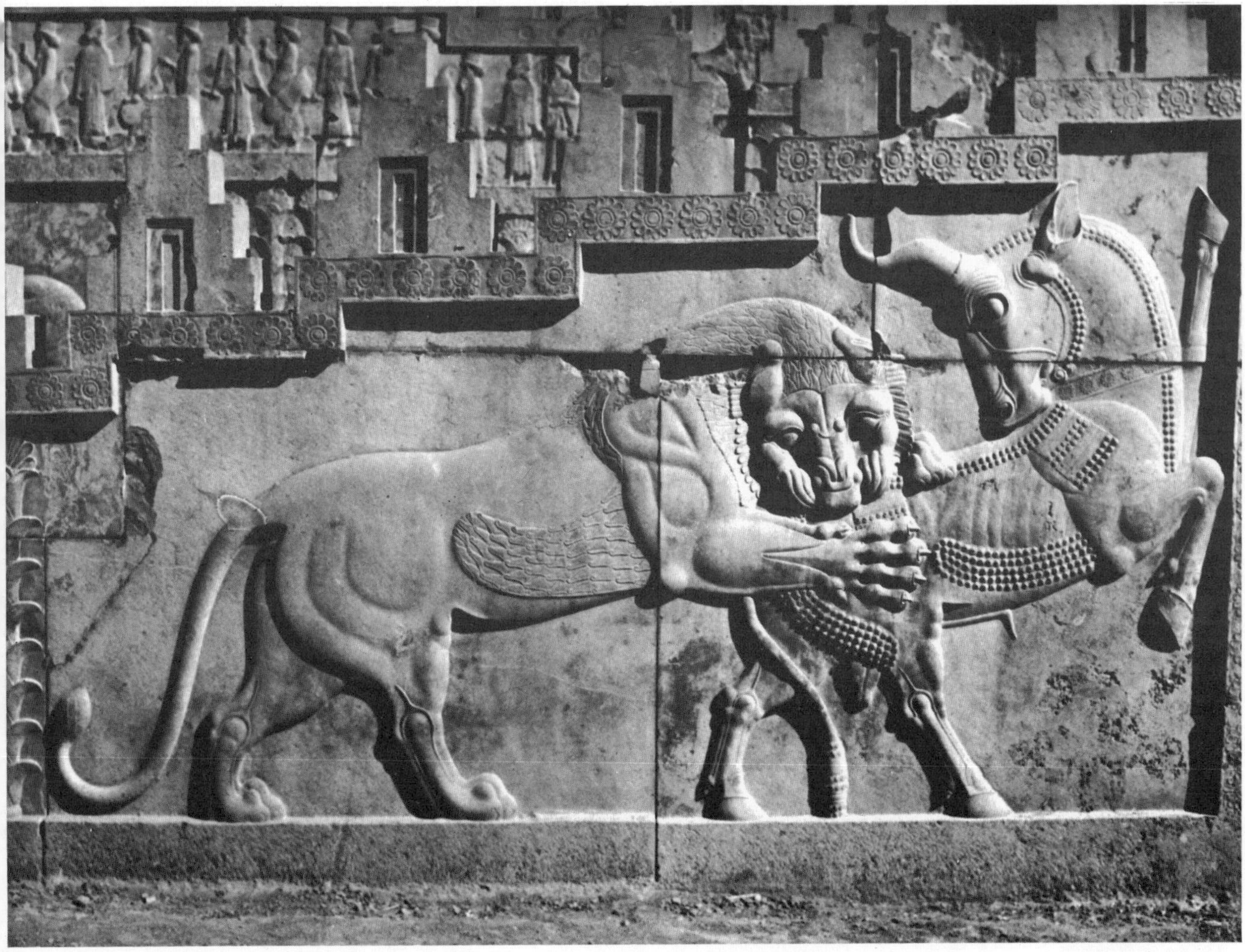

A lion attacking a bull. Darius's great palace at Persepolis, started shortly after 518 B.C., was intended as a shrine for the New Year festival and most of its decoration is consequently associated with this event. This bas-relief from one of the stairways, one of a number, shows a lion, the symbol of royalty, attacking a rearing bull, the animal of sacrifice. The relief may symbolise the new year overcoming the old.

RELIGION OF THE ZEND-AVESTA

THE HISTORICAL AND RELIGIOUS SETTING

The Iranians are an offshoot of that branch of the Indo-European race which is known as Aryan ('noble'). Iran, or Eran, is the land of the Aryans, who without doubt came from Southern Russia, passed into Asia either by way of the Caucasus or the Dardanelles, and gained the plateau of 'Iran'. Their language, which is very similar to the Vedic of India, is a variety of the same tongue which is inferred to be the parent language of Slavonic, Teutonic, Celtic, Greek and Latin.

Among the Indo-European peoples the Aryan tribes were those which established themselves farthest in the East of Eurasia, either in Iran, in the valleys of the Indus, or, to the North of Pamir, in what is now known as Chinese Turkestan.

We find no mention of the future 'Iranians' previous to the ninth century B.C. The first allusion to the Parsua or Persians, who were then in the mountains of Kurdistan, and to the Madai or Medes, already established on the plain, occurs in 837 B.C. in connection with an expedition of the Assyrian king Shalmaneser III. About a hundred years afterwards the Medes invaded the plateau which we call Persia (or Iran), driving back or assimilating populations of whom there is no written record; and Deioces (708—655) established a Median Empire. One of his successors, Cyaxares, became strong enough to ally himself with the Babylonians against the Assyrians, destroyed Nineveh (606) and annexed Assyria. In the following century it was another Iranian people, the Persians, who gained pre-eminence in Western Asia when their king, Cyrus, in 538 seized Babylon. Henceforth the Iranians took the historical place of the Assyro-Babylonians although the Persian Achaemenian Empire represented in Iran a return to Aryanism – an Aryanism purer than that of the Medes.

Iranian Religions. The complexity of the religion of classical Persia is due not only to the fact that it arose from a mingling of Assyro-Babylonian and Aryan beliefs, but also to the great change it underwent during three successive dynasties: the Achaemenian (558—330 B.C.), the Parthian (250 B.C.—191 A.D.) and the Sassanian (224—729 A.D.).

Now, leaving on one side inscriptions (the most valuable being that of Darius at Bisutun) and the documentary evidence of neighbouring civilisations, Iranian cults and myths are known to us only through the *Zend-Avesta* which, though many of its themes are rooted in prehistoric Aryanism, was written at a very late date, during the Sassanian period.

The Cult of Fire. Before being considered in Iran as a symbol of the supreme god, fire must have been the object of a direct cult, in which more or less all the Indo-Europeans participated. The Mazdaians were called 'ateshperest' or fire-worshippers. Several Parthian princes bore the title of 'fratakara' – fire-maker. In the traditionalist organisation of the Magi during the Sassanian period the 'herbedh' – fire-chiefs – occupied an eminent position. Two fire altars, possibly very archaic, survive at Naqsh-i-Rustem and 'fire places' (atesh-gah) – the prytaneum of the Greeks – are preserved in many localities. The various Iranian religions maintained this basic and primitive cult, with the result that light and purity have enjoyed incomparable prestige in all that bears the mark of Iranianism. In the ritual of Brahmanism all that concerns the use of fire obviously arises from this same Aryan belief.

The myth of Atar – Fire, the fire of the sky as well as that which resides in wood – is only an expression of this cult. It is true that Atar is represented as the son of Ahura Mazda, but the student will suspect that the son must be older than the 'father'. He is much more than the element Fire. Personified he brings men comfort, grants them the wherewithal to live, wisdom, virility, noble offspring and a paradise reserved for the virtuous. He accompanies the sun's chariot. He defends the world against the enterprises of the Evil One. One crime only is in his eyes unforgivable: to burn or cook dead flesh. This is the supreme insult to the Life Principle.

The Rite of the Haoma and Immortality. From the same Aryan root springs the rite of ambrosia, the beverage of immortality – the *haoma* of the *Zend-Avesta* which is equivalent to the Vedic *soma*. Though the plant differs – due to the difference of habitat – it is in both cases a sacred herb, pressed through a strainer and producing a liquor which when fermented was believed to heighten spirituality. The incantations pronounced during the haoma ritual drove away evil genii and prepared the way for the reign of the good. (*Yasna*, X, I.)

Haoma was made a mythical personage, 'correct in faith and the adversary of death'. He proclaimed what mortal humanity owed to him: 'Vivanhvat was the first mortal in the corporeal world who prepared me. The fate which was imparted to him and the grace which he was awarded were to have for a son Yima the Splendid, the good shepherd, the most glorious of those who were born, the sole mortal possessor of the solar eye; and, because of his power, to render men and beasts non-mortal, water and plants exempt from drying up, so that man could consume food preserved from all evil spells. In the kingdom of the potentate Yima there was neither cold nor heat, old age nor death, nor envy which is the work of devs (demons).' (*Yasna,* IX, 4 & 5).

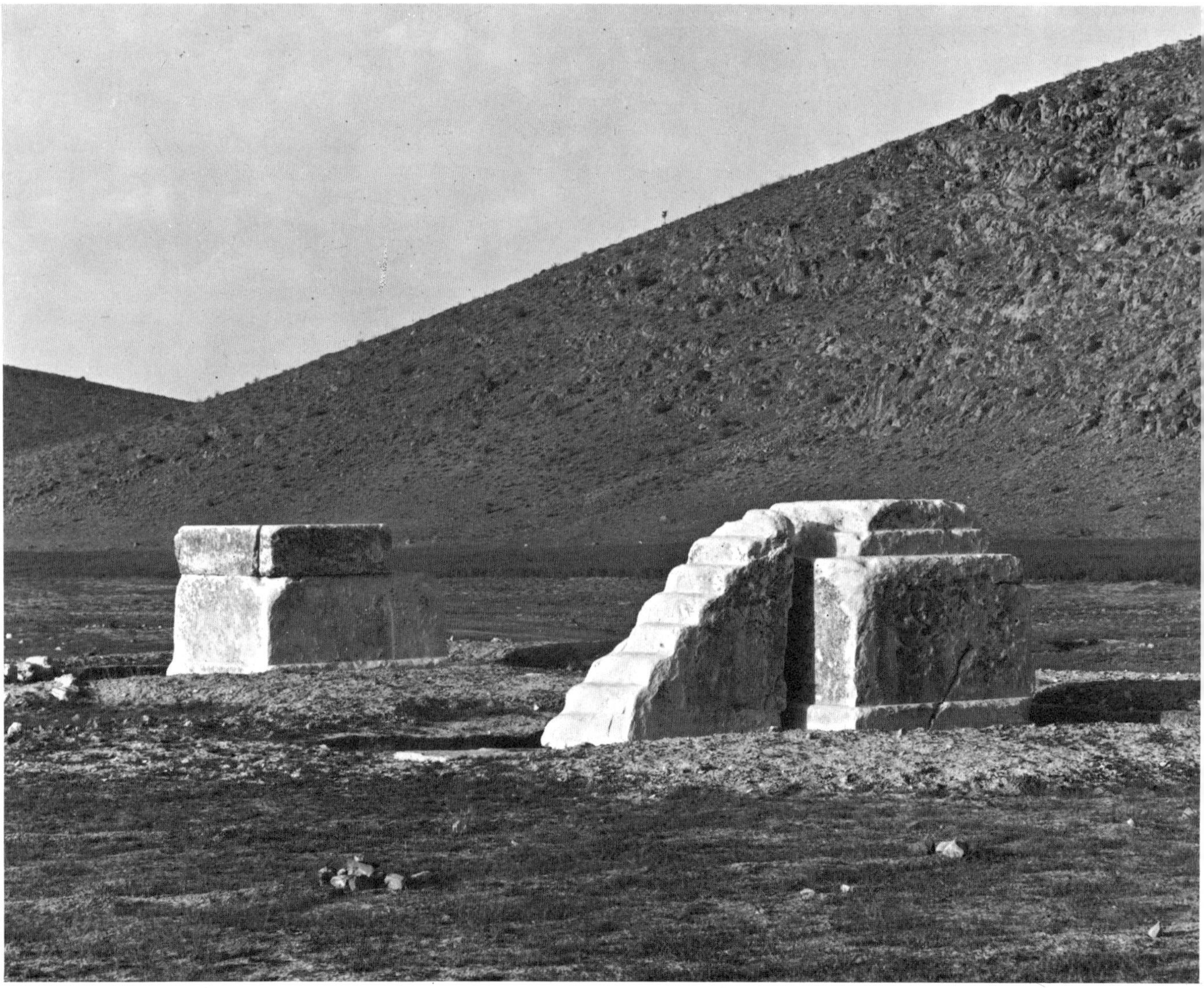

Achaemenian fire altars. Fire appears to have been the object of a direct cult among almost all the Indo-European peoples in early times and was retained in the Mazdaian cult as a visible symbol of the purity and brilliance of the supreme god. Its importance in the Mazdaian cult was such that the Mazdaians were called fire-worshippers by their neighbours. These altars still stand in a sanctuary near Cyrus's capital of Pasargadae. Sixth century B.C.

rchaic Gods. One of the Indo-European migrations has left traces ı Northern Mesopotamia, as is proved by a cuneiform inscription ı Cappadocia. In the text of a treaty the people of Mitanni, a ingdom of the Upper Euphrates, come to an agreement with the Iittites and, fourteen hundred years before Christ, call upon the ods to witness it. The list of these gods is entirely Indian though ɔme of them are also Iranian: Mitra and Varuna, Indra and the Iasatyas. Indra, so important in the mythology of India, is in ·an only a rather featureless demon; but Mitra, although under ɔmewhat different aspects, plays an important part in both civiliıtions. Associated with the goddess of the waters, Anahita, Mithra ppears in the inscriptions of Artaxerxes Mnemon and Ochus. ıt first a god of contracts and friendship, he became the protector f truth and the enemy of falsehood.

In the pre-Zoroastrian period Mithra, often associated with the ıpreme Ahura, was a god of the first magnitude. His military valour ·as without rival. He possessed not only strength but at the same me knowledge; for in essence he was Light. As such he led the ɔlar chariot across the sky. From him victory could be expected as ɹell as wisdom, though his anger with cheating or felony was ıerciless. Beasts were sacrificed to him and he was offered libations f haoma which humans could partake of only provided that scrupuɔus ritual and penitence were observed.

Under the influence of Chaldean astrology the heavenly bodies ɹere the objects of particular veneration: Hvare-Khshaeta, the ıazzling Sun with his chariot and swift steeds; Mah, the Moon; ʌnahita, identified with the planet Venus; Tishtriya, the Dog Star.

Apo, the Water (the Vedic *apas*), recalls the Apsu of Mesopotamia. ·ight, both solar and lunar, was deeply revered.

Above these gods – who afterwards appeared as minor divinities – a chief god was to rise, under three influences which in this respect converged. These were namely, that of the Magi, the Persian kings and Zoroaster.

The Magi. The Magi appear to have been a priestly corporation which originated in a certain Median tribe. They were given to the practice of a special ritual which expressed the ancient Aryan cult. The famous revolt against Cambyses of the Magus Gaumata, the double of his brother Bardiya, leads one to suspect that these priests, in their hostile attitude towards the Persian hegemony, retained an ancient fidelity to the ideals of the Medes.

This corporation for long kept in touch with communities in the mountainous region of the Azerbaijan where the practices of the primitive Aryans persisted in their purest form.

It is, however, a misuse of terms when Greek authors, through ignorance or prejudice, call the Magi the Iranian clergy. They were, indeed, invested with religious functions, but they had no monopoly of them. The Magi must have been no more than a sect until, under the Sassanians, they became an official priesthood which organised Mazdaism. No doubt they had first been fire-priests rather than zealots of Mazda.

Mazda, the God of Persian Royalty. Mazda eclipsed all other divinities only because he was the god of the Achaemenian kings. His mythological triumph was simply a symbol of the pre-eminence achieved in the Iranian world, with its many tribes, by a certain Persian family. The god of gods, master of the heavens and creator of all creatures, was a reflection of the king of kings, master and

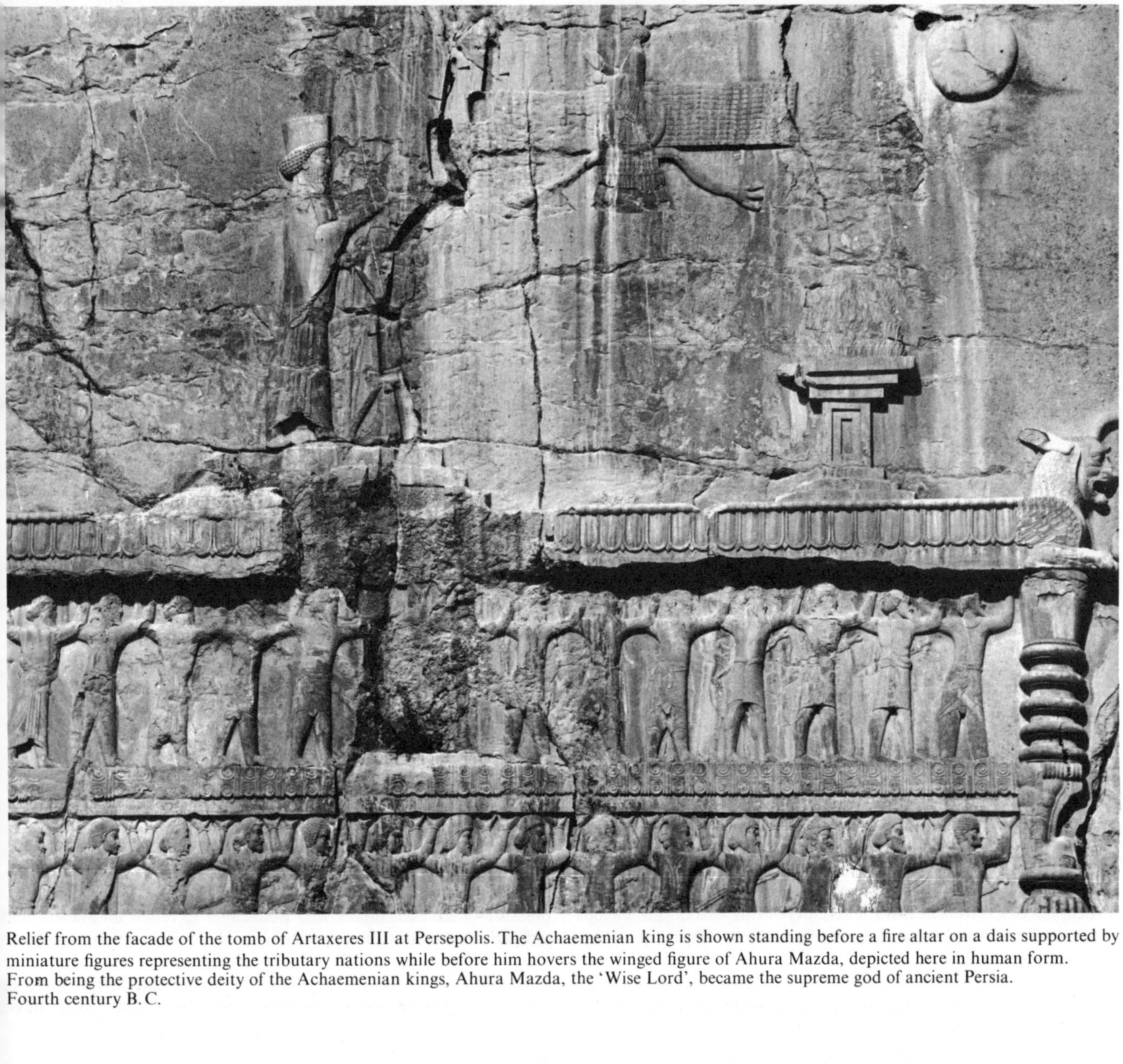

Relief from the facade of the tomb of Artaxeres III at Persepolis. The Achaemenian king is shown standing before a fire altar on a dais supported by miniature figures representing the tributary nations while before him hovers the winged figure of Ahura Mazda, depicted here in human form. From being the protective deity of the Achaemenian kings, Ahura Mazda, the 'Wise Lord', became the supreme god of ancient Persia. Fourth century B.C.

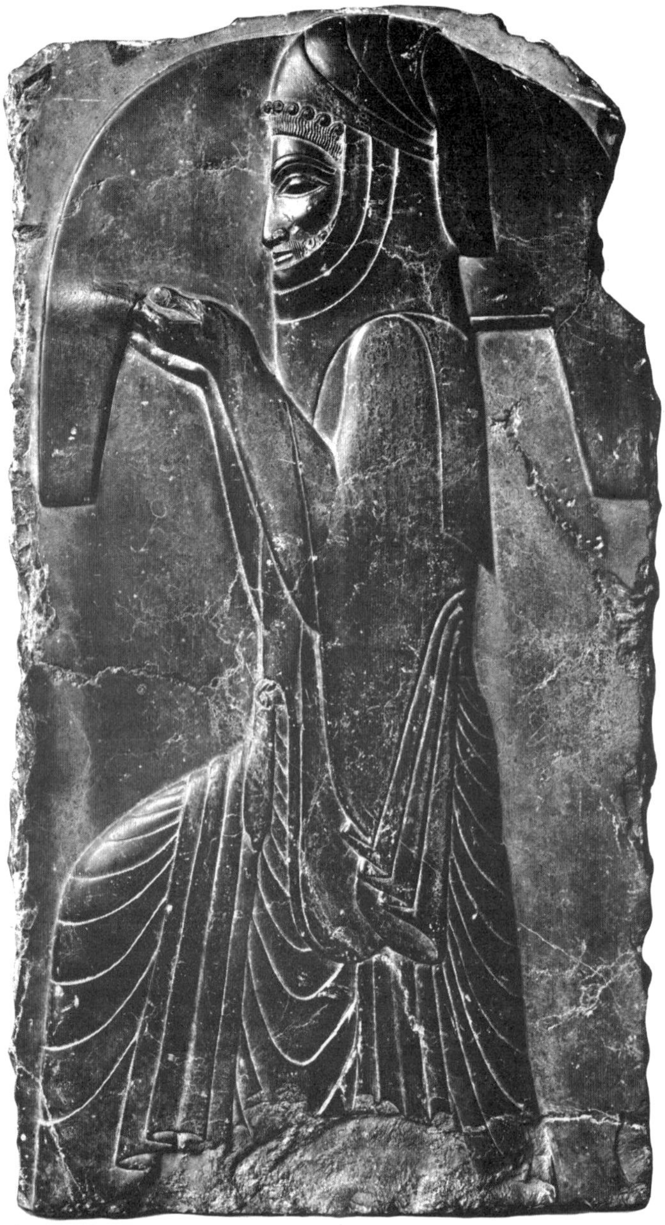

Tribute bearer carrying a chest. Having little art of their own the Iranians adopted that of other peoples – the most popular form employed being that of relief sculpture which was borrowed from the Assyrians. This bas-relief comes from a stairway at Persepolis and shows one of a long line of tribute bearers taking part in the procession for the New Year festival. The figures were originally painted. Achaemenian period, sixth to fourth centuries B.C.

ruler of all peoples. The etymology of Mazda is disputed. It seems to be related to the Sanskrit *medha*, 'wisdom'. But this explanation has, by some authorities, been abandoned for an alleged connection with *mada*, 'intoxication', and *mastim*, 'illumination'; and the god would then be the dispenser of 'transcendent powers'. Other scholars compare the Iranian term Ahura Mazda with Assara Mazaas, god of Ashurbanipal (668–626 B.C.), creator and chief among the gods. They also point out a connection between *ahura* (Iranian), *asura* (Indian) and *Asshur* (Assyrian). Thus, at least, it is certain that the god of the Achaemenians had existed before them and had already enjoyed the respect of an Assyrian sovereign. As early as 715, in the inscriptions of Sargon, the expression 'mazdaka' twice appears in names of Medes.

The sculptors of Persepolis represented the protective divinity of Darius as a man with a venerable beard in the Assyrian style. His body is plumed with symmetrical and majestic wings and a vertical tail of a bird. The hieratic serenity of this lord of the heavens hovers in the atmosphere and bears witness to his impressive royal qualities.

Ahura Mazda, to whom these bas-reliefs give human features, belongs, however, to metaphysics rather than to myth: to picture him in human shape was simply an artifice of sculpture. This kin of nature who created all things surpassed humanity in every way The *Asha* – the universal law – was born of him, as Descartes eternal verities are born of the divine spirit. This god had no huma weaknesses and he operated in his capacity of a spirit. The celestia personages who composed his retinue – a species of archangel – wer abstractions made concrete. It is a stiff and hieratic pantheon, a different from the pantheon we find in the Vedas, as the mosaic of Ravenna are from the reliefs of Angkor.

The Reform of Zoroaster. Zoroaster, in a certain sense, reconcile the religion of the Magi with that of the kings. But this recon ciliation did not become official or orthodox until about eigh centuries after the time of Zoroaster himself who, according t Parsee tradition, lived between 660 and 583, when the *Zend-Avest* was written down in its present form.

Zoroaster's biography consists of marvel after marvel. He wa born amidst universal rejoicing and at his birth he neither wep nor cried but laughed. The hostility, however, of the kavis and th karpans – heretical priests and idolaters – was to surround hi with a network of deceit. In the drama the Turanian karpan Duras robo played the part of a Herod. When the future prophet wishe to marry he submitted to his parents' choice, but like a good Irania devotee of frankness and light he insisted on seeing his fiancée' face before the marriage.

His religious vocation was in many ways similar to that of Buddha At the age of twenty he left the paternal roof in search of the ma who 'was most in love with rectitude and most given to feedin the poor'. To feed animals and the wretched, to tend the fire wit wood, to pour the juice of haoma in the water – such, accordin to him, were the works of piety. He remained in silence for seve years in the depths of a cavern decorated with an image of th world, on a mountain which recalls Sinai. At the age of thirty h received from each of the archangels various revelations whic gave him a hold over the various elements of the cosmos. The firs revelation came to him from Vohu-mano, the Spirit of Wisdom who conferred on him ecstasy in the presence of Ahura Mazd on the banks of the Daiti (Azerbaijan). At once he began to wande and to preach, travelling as far as Ghazni on the borders of Afghanistan and the Eastern fringe of Iran. Other revelations, obtained i other specified regions, initiated him into the manner of treatin domestic animals, fire, metals, the earth, water and plants.

The prophet henceforth knew what he had to know. Angr Mainyu came from the North in order to tempt him, so that h might abstain from killing the demons, his creatures. He offere him an earthly kingdom but, armed with exorcisms, Zoroaste avoided the temptation. 'With the sacred mortar, the sacred cup the word of Mazda, my own weapon, I shall vanquish thee.'

In the course of the twelfth year of the restored faith the con version of Vishtaspa, king of Balkh, took place. Conversion extended as far as the Hindus and the Greeks. The science of th prophet apart from its ritual aspect, included physics, a knowledg of the stars and of precious stones. With herbs he cured a blind man But in these last years the propagation of the faith was no longe pacific: against the infidel Turk, enemy of Vishtaspa, a holy wa raged in which the valour of Insfendiar shone with splendour. Her the *Shah Nameh* adds a note of heroism to the ritualism of th *Zend-Avesta*, and Zoroaster was believed to have been killed i his seventy-seventh year by an odious Turanian.

The mortal aim of Zoroaster consisted essentially of striving after perfection by thought, word and deed. After death the sou was weighed in a balance and judged according to its deeds.

Vicissitudes of Mazdaism. Mazdaism, the religion of Mazda, eclipse all other Iranian cults. But it varied greatly in form. The traditiona 'Iranian Dualism' popularised by books on the history of religion is far from corresponding to the reality of the beliefs which were held between the days of Cyrus and the Moslem conquest.

Though preached by Zoroaster as one aspect of his system, this dualism only became implanted much later under the politica pressure of the Sassanians who were eager to renew an ancient and indigenous tradition in opposition to Hellenistic influences. Unti then it had been merely the opinion of one sect.

The Mazda of the Achaemenians was the god of the 'king o kings'. The Mazda of the Sassanians was the god of a priesthood

Votive bronze pin from Luristan. Before the future Iranians migrated south into Persia from southern Russia in about 1,000 B.C., an indigenous population, probably also of Indo-European stock, inhabited the deep valleys of the Zagros ranges.
These Luristan craftsmen are celebrated above all for their small bronzes many hundreds of which have been recovered from their graves during the present century. The frequent use of animal motifs has been seen by some as evidence of shamanistic practices.

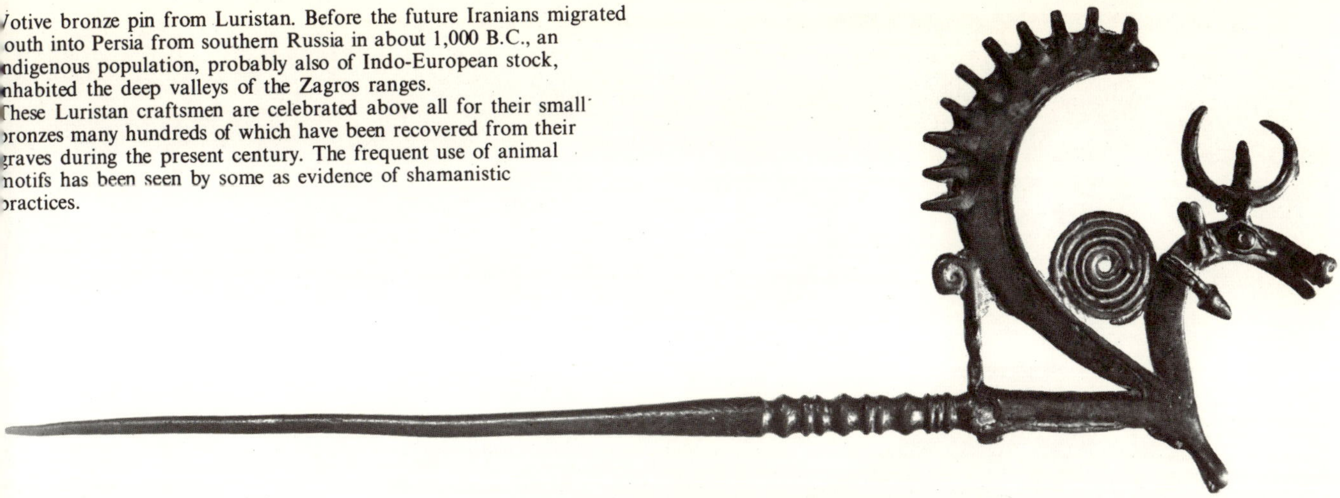

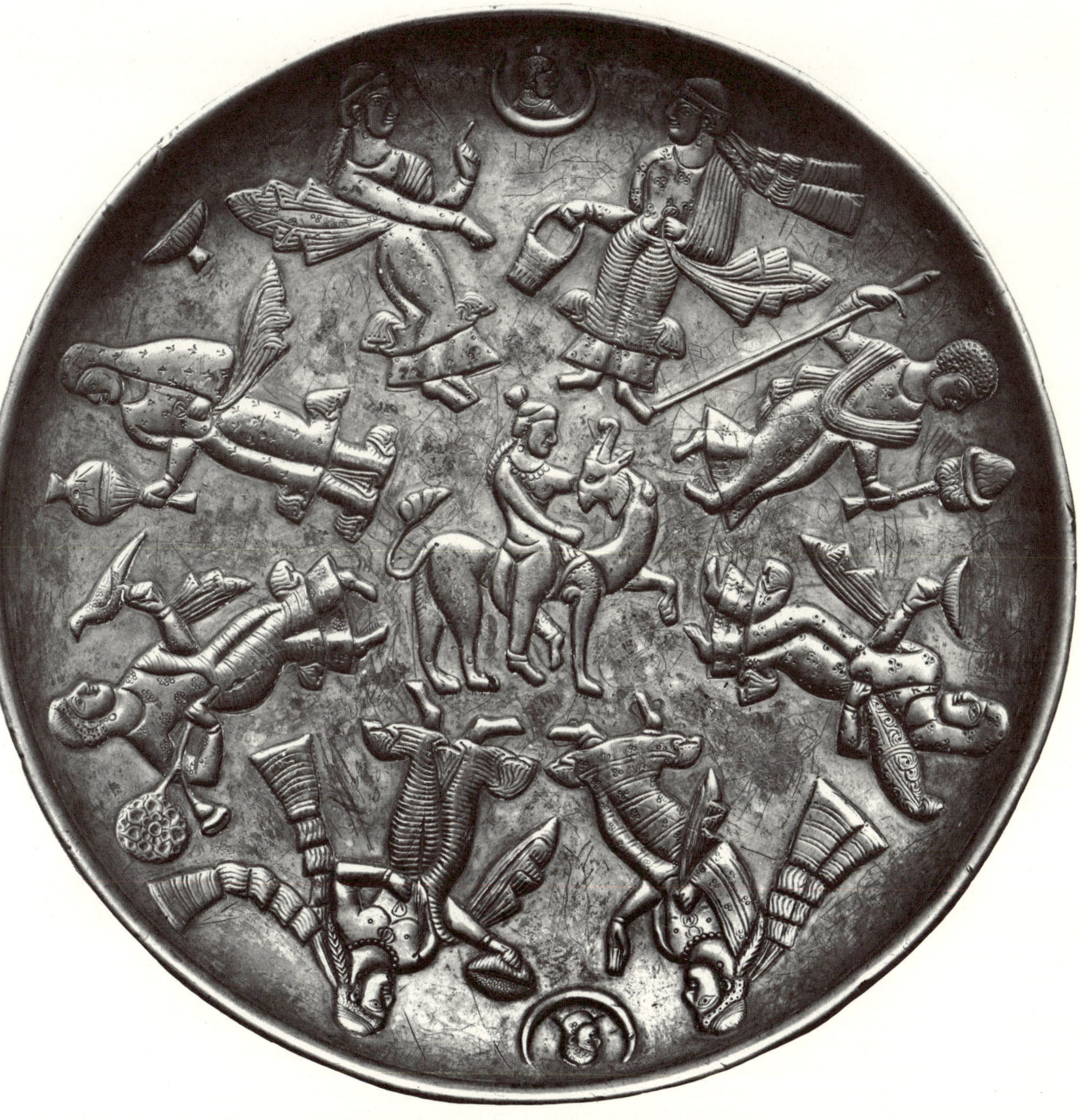

Sassanian silver dish with the goddess Anahita in the centre. The goddess of waters, fecundity and procreation, Anahita was widely worshipped in Achaemenian times and was associated with Mithras in the inscriptions of Ataxerxes, Mnemon and Ochos. Under the Hellenistic name of Anaitis she later acquired considerable popularity throughout Asia Minor and the Occident and her reappearance in Sassanian times may have been the result of foreign influence. She was sometimes identified with the planet Venus.

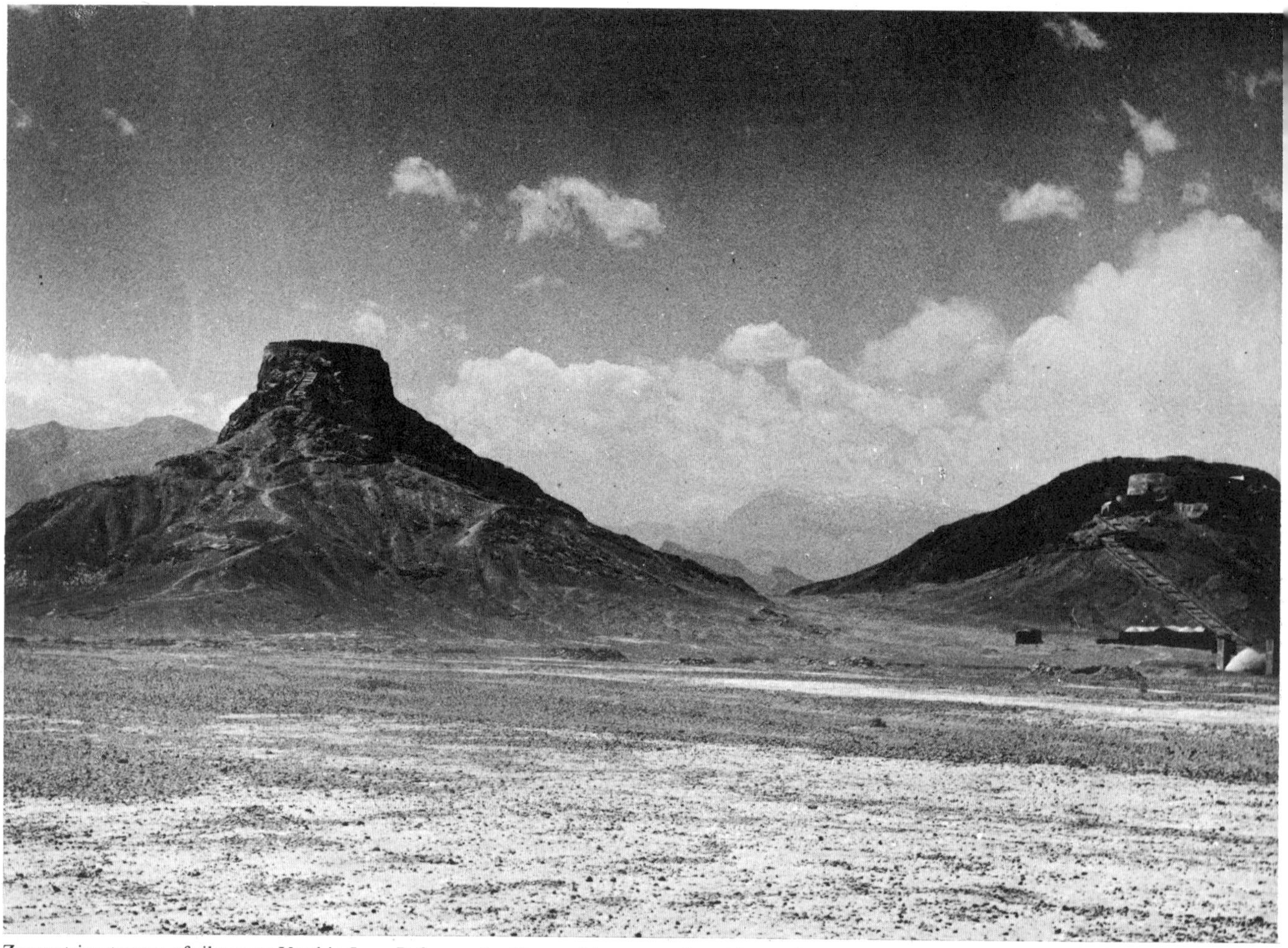

Zoroastrian towers of silence at Yezd in Iran. Before embarking on his career of teaching and conversion, Zoroaster, the reformer of the Persian religion, is said to have spent seven years in silence in a cavern on a mountain. Believed to have lived some time between 660 and 583 B.C., Zoroaster retained the old gods of the Persian people in his new religion but placed the emphasis on the struggle between the forces of Good and Evil

claiming kinship with the ancient Magi. But between these two forms of Mazdaism – the Achaemenian and the Sassanian – there was the age of the Parthians during which other religions monopolised the Iranian conscience.

Religion under the Arsacids. The balance-sheet of these religions is extremely confused and obscure. First must be reckoned the beliefs of the Parthians (Pahlavas, whence the name of the language Pahlavi) who were Iranians originally from Scythia and to whom belonged the founder of the dynasty, Arsaces. They practised ancestor-worship. Afterwards there was Buddhism, which was widespread in Bactria. Then there were various cults influenced by abstract philosophy which revealed a mixture of Greek, Gnostic and Iranian elements. The most famous of these was Mithraism which penetrated not only Western Asia but, carried by the Roman armies, very nearly conquered Europe which it reached in the first century before Christ.

Mithraism. The origin of Mithraism goes back to the Mitra of the Aryans, though it underwent many transformations. Herodotus mentions a sky-goddess Mitra and in Persian *mihr* meant 'Sun'. This is a long way from the old god of contracts, common to India and Iran; however the duality Mithra-Ahura of the *Zend-Avesta* corresponds to the duality Mitra-Varuna of the Vedas. According to one authority the Mithra of Mithraism was a divinity who formed a link between the Ahura Mazda and the Angra Mainyu of Zoroaster; for it is time, marked by the revolutions of the sun, which regulates the alternation of light and darkness.

Hellenistic sculpture has popularised the scene of the immolation of a bull by Mithra, wearing a Phrygian cap, in one of those grottoes where the initiates gathered. In it the god accomplished a fecundity rite, as is witnessed by the vegetation of all kinds which luxuriates around the wound through which the victim's blood escapes.

Far though this Mithraism may have been from the Mazdaism of Zoroaster, it maintained in common with it its two essential ideas: an ardent zeal for moral purity obtained and preserved by a belligerent attitude, that of a 'soldier' of the faith (whence the prestige of this cult among the Roman legions) and a veneration of light; for the sole principle which is 'unconquered' – in other words absolute – is the Sun (*sol invictus*).

Manichaeism. A similar inspiration, but nearer to Zoroastrianism, was found in the sect of Mani, in which the religion of Christ met a dangerous rival – to such an extent, indeed, that Manichaeism was denounced as a Christian heresy. Mani undertook his apostolate in the beginning of the Sassanian era, at the accession of Sapor I to the throne in 242 A.D. A native of Babylonia, Mani combined with Mazdaian dualism the Gnostic tradition borrowed from the Christians of John the Baptist, the Mandaeans of the Lower Euphrates. He propagated the Gospels and the Epistles of Saint Paul and proclaimed himself to be the ultimate spokesman of Christ. He founded a Church in which the Christian hierarchy was closely copied. According to his teaching, asceticism, more or less strict according to the degree of initiation, was necessary in order that the conflict of the universal dualism should, in the individual, end in the final victory of the luminous principle.

Exploration in the neighbourhood of Turfan and the discovery of a medieval library in the grottoes of Tunhwang have brought Manichaean texts to light. Knowledge of the sect is also accessible through the refutations of its detractors, Christian, Mazdean and Moslem. A proof of its immense influence is found in the profound traces it left in France and Spain, in Africa and even in China. No doctrine carried the Iranian spirit farther afield.

A legendary history recounted how the science of salvation had been revealed in various epochs by the Christ, Son of the First Man, who had taken on the guise of flesh in order to denounce its wickedness. It taught how the dualist faith, the only true faith, preached in India by the Buddha, in Persia by Zoroaster, in Palestine by Christ,

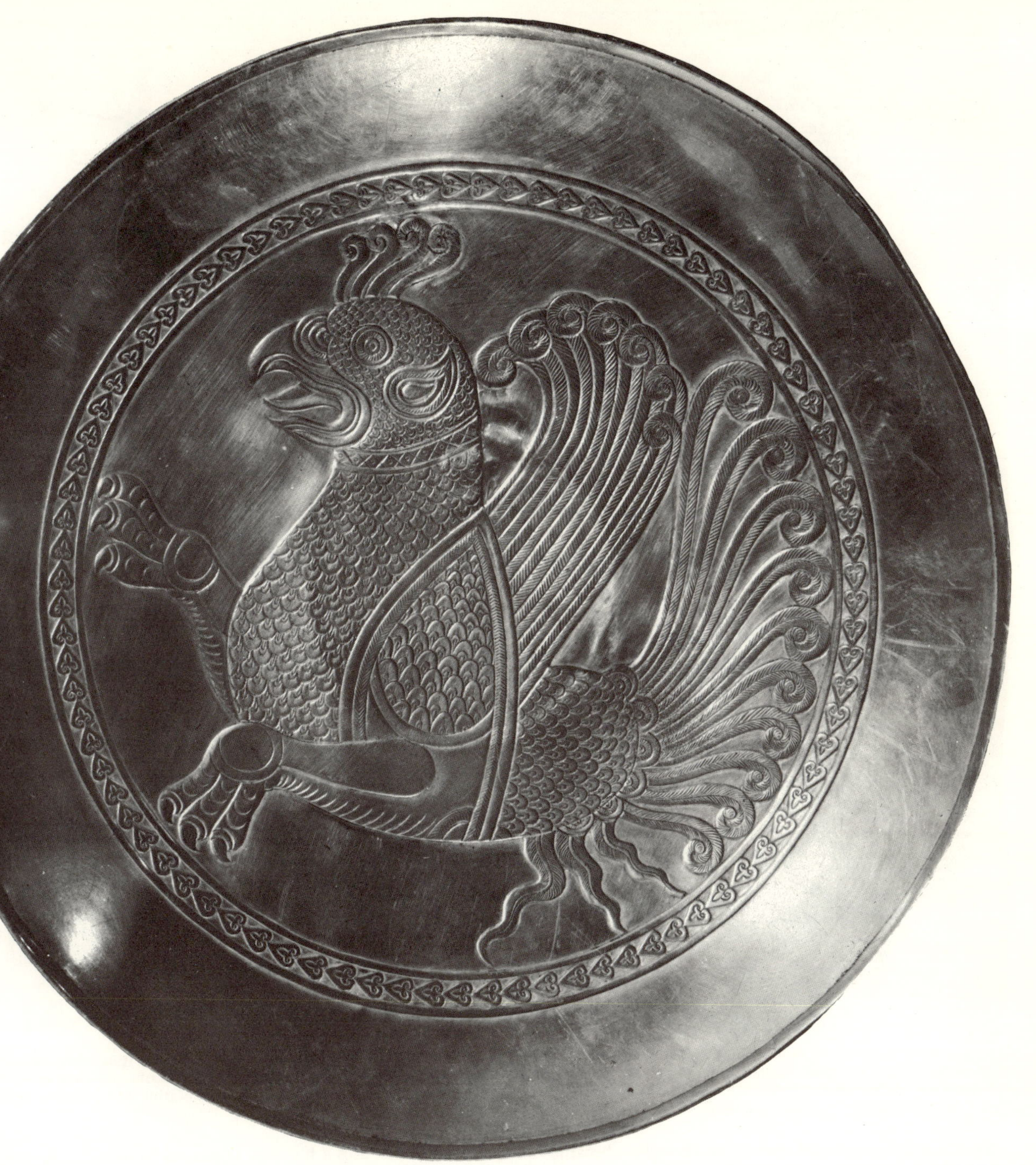

Gold dish decorated with a simurgh. According to Iranian legend, the simurgh, a fabulous bird generally depicted as a composite creature made up of elements borrowed from the peacock, the lion, the griffin and the dog, was a bird of good omen. In the *Shah-Nameh* Simurgh was the noble vulture who rescued Zal, the infant son of Sam, and reared him as his own on Mount Elburz. Persian. Sixth to seventh centuries A. D.

had at last been proclaimed in its full purity in Babylonia and from there throughout the entire universe by Mani and his apostles.

Apart from the revelations he received when he was twelve and twenty-four years old, the life of Mani with its forty years of apostleship gave rise to few legends. One of them is related in a fragment from Turfan. Mihirshah, the brother of Sapor, was hostile to Mani. 'In the Paradise you celebrate,' he demanded, 'can there be a garden as beautiful as mine?' The apostle of the light answered by revealing his luminous Paradise to Mihirshah's eyes and at the sight the Prince remained for three hours in ecstasy.

Prophetic and apocalyptic books proclaimed what would be the fate of the Elect who faithfully followed the holy precepts, of the Hearers who only half followed them, and of the Sinners who continued to violate them. They foretold that the Elect, once rid of their fleshly bonds, would take the road for heaven and return to their fatherland. The Hearers would remain on earth and their souls would enter other bodies. Finally the Sinners, slaves to matter, would follow it into inferno. On the day, such books added, when every spirit who was to be liberated had regained its first abode (Paradise) the world would be left to itself and abandoned by the Ornament of Splendour which sustained it in the North and by Atlas who in the South bore it on his shoulders. Then the stars would fall, the mountains would crumble and all the material elements would gather in the dark abysses of inferno, there to burn as though in an immense furnace. They would at once be covered over by a stone as vast as the earth itself and to the stone would be attached the souls of sinners. Thenceforth Good and Evil, returned to their first estate, would remain separated by an impassable barrier.

DIVINE FIGURES AND LEGENDS

The following exposition, which is dogmatic and not historical, will briefly describe the final stages of Iranian mythological evolution under the Sassanians.

The Antagonism between Ormazd and Ahriman. The omniscient Lord, Ahura Mazda, by a fusion of his two names, became Ormazd.

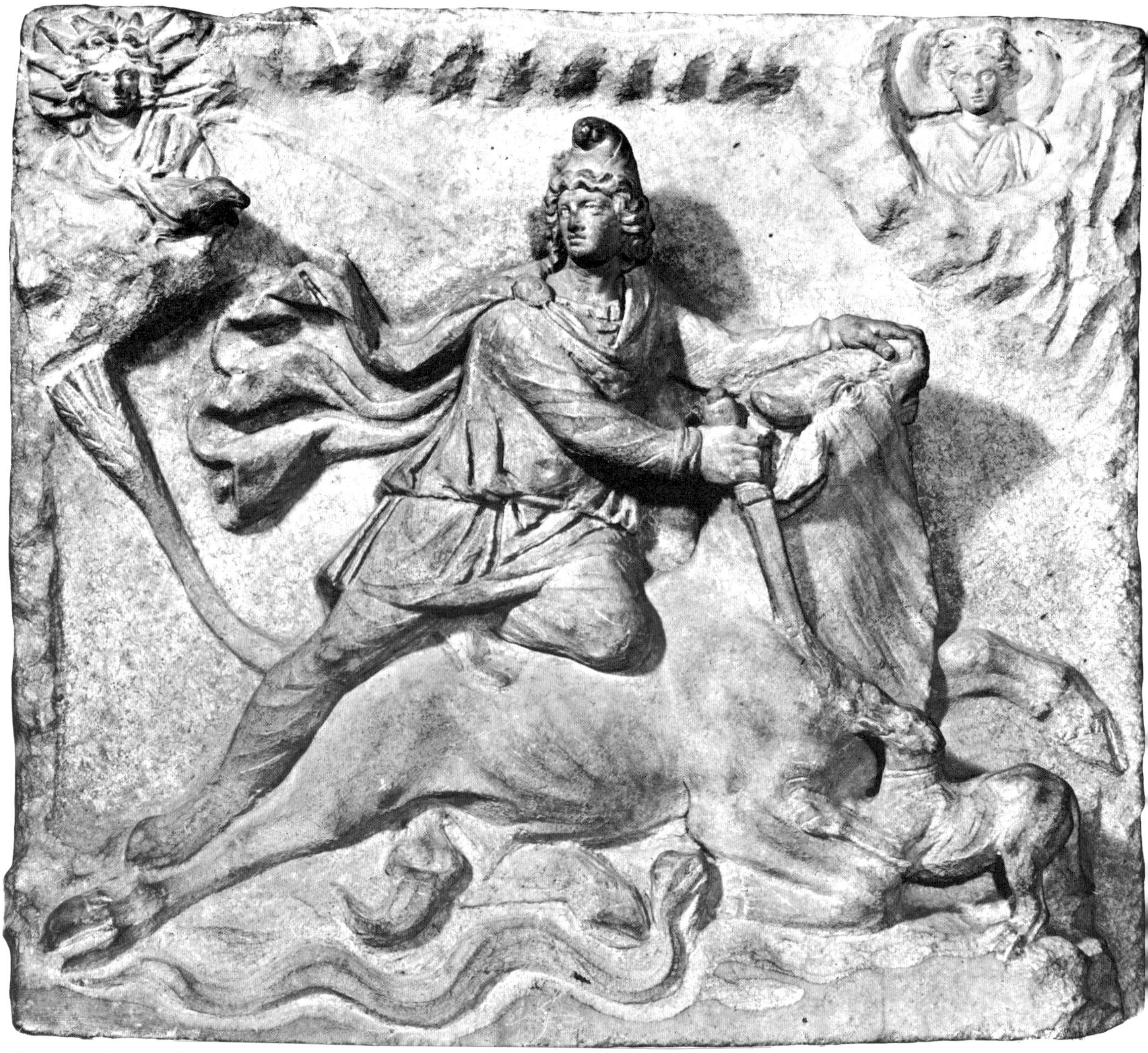

Mithras sacrificing the bull, with Sol and Luna. A god common to both Indian and Iranian mythology, though under somewhat different forms, Mithras was one of the great Persian gods. In pre-Zoroastrian times he was associated with Ahura Mazda as a god of light while under the Parthians his cult penetrated western Asia and was spread throughout Europe by the Roman armies. The immolation of a bull goes back to a belief in a cosmogonic rite. Mithraic altar. second century A.D.

Angra Mainyu – 'agonised or negative Thought' – became Ahriman. These two personages marked the two poles of existence. The first created life, the second death. The first consisted of light and truth, the second of darkness and falsehood. They could be defined by their antagonism: the god as anti-demon, the demon as anti-god. The real world was the result of their hand to hand struggle. All was conflict between these two principles.

This is the history of creation:

'Thus spoke Ahura Mazda to the holy Zarathustra (Zoroaster):

' "I have created a universe where none existed; if I had not made it the entire world would have gone towards the Airjana-Vaeja.

' "In opposition to this world, which is all life, Angra Mainyu created another which is all death, where there are only two months of summer and where winter is ten months long, months which so chill the earth that even the summer months are icy; and cold is the root of all evil.

' "Then I created Ghaon, the abode of Sughdra, the most delightful place on earth. It is sown with roses; there birds with ruby plumage are born.

' "Angra Mainyu then created the insects which are noxious to plants and animals.

' "Then I founded the holy and sublime city of Muru, and into it Angra Mainyu introduced lies and evil counsel.

' "Then I created Bashdi the enchanting, where surrounded by lush pastures a hundred thousand banners fly. Angra Mainyu sent wild beasts there and animals to devour the cattle that serve for man's use.

' "Afterwards I created Nissa, the city of prayer; and into it Angra Mainyu insinuated the doubt which gnaws at faith.

' "I created Haroju, the city of rich palaces. Angra Mainyu caused sloth to be born there and soon the city was poverty-stricken.

' "Thus each of the marvels I have given to men for their welfare has been counteracted by a baneful gift from Angra Mainyu. It is to him that the earth owes the evil instincts which infest it. It is he who established the criminal usage of burying or burning the dead, and all the misfortunes which ravage the race of mankind." '

Before becoming the spirit of evil Ahriman had, perhaps, been an underworld divinity. Indeed, among the devotees of Mithraism, whose temples were often grottoes or caverns, we find dedications: *Deo Arimanio.* In an early phase of the integration of this god with Mazdaism Ahura Mazda was supposed to have created two antithetical genii: Spenta Mainyu and Angra Mainyu, the beneficent spirit and the wicked spirit. This dualism was then subordinated to a deep-seated monotheism.

Even in the most dualistic form of the Iranian religion there is a dignity about the god which makes him more than the correlative of the demon: just as he must have existed alone in the golden age so would he exist alone in the future after exterminating his adversary.

The Powers of Good: The Amshaspends. Ormazd commanded six spirits who, like him, were 'Benign Immortals', Ameshas Spenta or Amshaspends. They were: Vohu-mano (Bahman), the 'Spirit of Good'; Asha-Vahishta (Arbidihist), 'Supreme Righteousness'; Khshathra-Vairya (Shahriver), 'Ideal Dominion'; Spenta-Aramaiti (Sipendarmith), 'Benign Piety'; Haurvatat (Khordadh), 'Perfection'; and Ameretat (Mourdad), 'Immortality'.

These 'powers' can be compared to the biblical archangels Gabriel, Michael and Raphael; though they are rather more closely related to Vedic-Brahmanic abstractions. Thus Asha-Vahishta is the perfection of Order (*asha* is *rita*, the original form of the *dharma* or the 'law', moral as well as cosmic). Khshathra-Vairya is the domination of the noble class which, in India, is the caste of the *kshatriyas*. Spenta-Aramaiti, daughter of Ormazd and the sky, whom Plutarch interpreted as Wisdom, is the beneficent Earth, *prithivi* of the Hindus; and the generous and spontaneous piety of which she is the incarnation recalls that which in India was named *bhakti* – or love composed of devotion, surrender and confidence. Haurvatat is fullness and achievement – the Indian *Paramita*, a term of health.

Ameretat is the letter, *amritatvam*, non-mortality thanks to the beverage of life, an ancient Aryan idea.

Each of these serene figures reigned over a particular order of reality, such as a part of the year or of the week, or a category of beings. Vohu-mano presided over useful animals; Asha-Vahishta governed fire; Khshathra-Vairya made the sun and the heavens move and ruled over metals; Aramaiti, Haurvatat and Ameretat commanded respectively the earth, the waters and plant life.

The Yazatas and the Fravashis. All nature was peopled by the Yazatas (Sanskrit *yajata*), genii to whom sacrifices were due. This class of divine beings was in a sense a duplication of the Amshaspends. The Amshaspends' chief protagonist was Zoroaster. The Yazatas belonged to a much more remote Iranian and even Aryan past. Nevertheless at a late period they are carefully listed and we are told that Ormazd was the first of the celestial Yazatas, while Zoroaster himself was the first of terrestrial Yazatas. Certain Yazatas corresponded to the heavenly bodies, to the elements, and to forces at the same time cosmic and moral – like the Amshaspends. Among the Yazatas primitive sacrificial fire played an important part as it did in Indian Brahmanism. Khwareno, glory or splendour (the *tejas* of India), had the radiant aspect of force and authority. In the triad Mithra-Sraosha-Rashnu the two last terms designated respectively Obedience and Justice. Verethraghna, who must not be confused with the Indian Vritrahan, was a genius of Victory; Indo-Greek or Indo-Scythian coins are fond of representing him as a kind of Nike.

Among good genii the Fravashis occupied a special position as guardian angels. Properly speaking the Fravashi was an important part of the human soul, created by Ormazd before a man's birth. During life it remained in the order of immaterial beings and it survived death.

The Powers of Evil: The Daevas. Angra Mainyu – Ahriman – was the prince of demons. It is striking that the demons of the *Zend-Avesta* are called by the same name as the gods of the Vedas – in Sanskrit *deva*, Persian *div*, Latin *divus*. This reversal of meaning may result from the fact that a specifically Iranian religious reform like that, for instance, of Zoroaster, altered the brilliant and serene cohort of the Aryan gods into dark and malignant genii, while in India they continued to be revered as celestial genii.

The diabolic nature of the Daevas consisted in their devotion to trickery and falsehood. Their vocation was to 'thwart' all efforts to achieve the good. Vohu-mano's opposite number was Ako-Mano, the 'Spirit of Evil' for whom Ahriman was immediately responsible. Indra had nothing in common with the august Vedic Indra except his warlike ardour, in this case devoted to the deception of men. On Sinvat, the bridge which souls must cross to reach the other world, Indra would lie in ambush to seize and throw them into the gulf below. During their lifetime he plunged people into moral uncertainty. In this he opposed the zeal of the moralising archangel Asha-Vahishta. Sauru – whose name is related to the Vedic terms *sars* or *sarva*, epithets of Rudra-Shiva – strove for the triumph of anarchy and tyranny over the regular exercise of royal authority which was the province of Khshathra-Vairya. Naonhai-

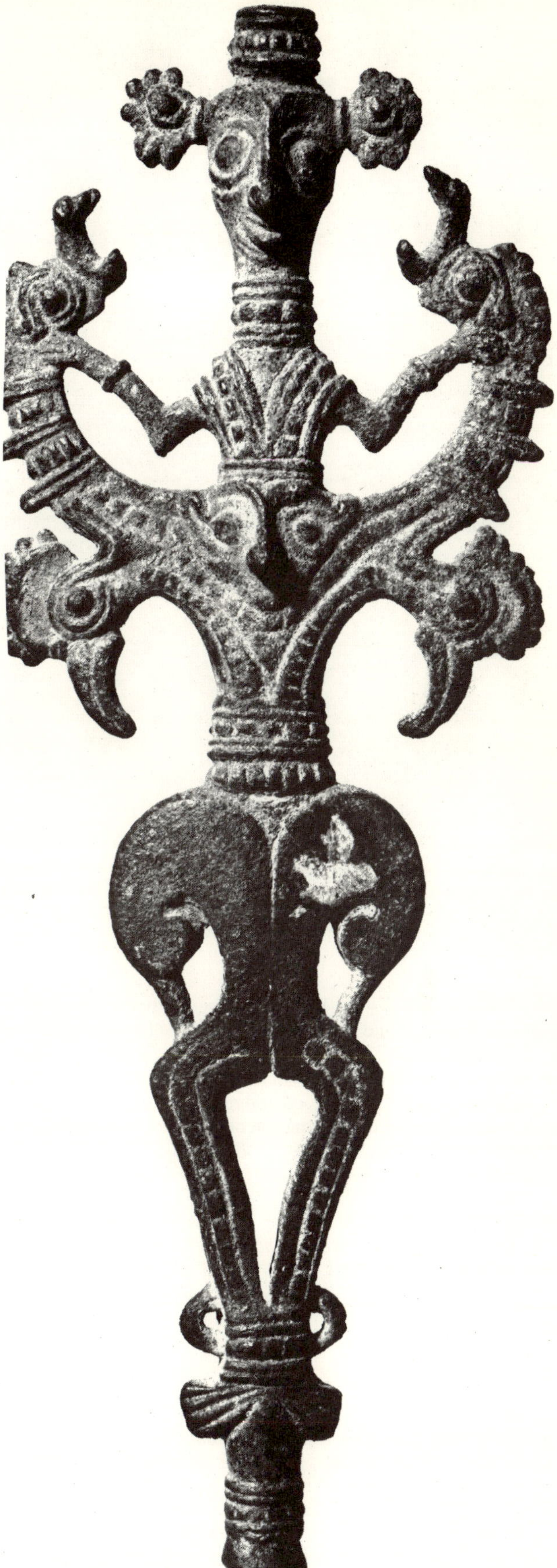

Bronze talisman or cultic standard from Luristan. The most intricate of the cast metalwork objects found in Luristan, over fifty of these talismans are known. Here a male anthropomorphic figure grasps the necks of two rearing monsters from whose backs grow the heads of two cocks or birds of prey while a further head sprouts from his waist. The figure has been tentatively identified by one authority as an early representation of the god Sraosha. *c.* 1,000 to 800 B.C.

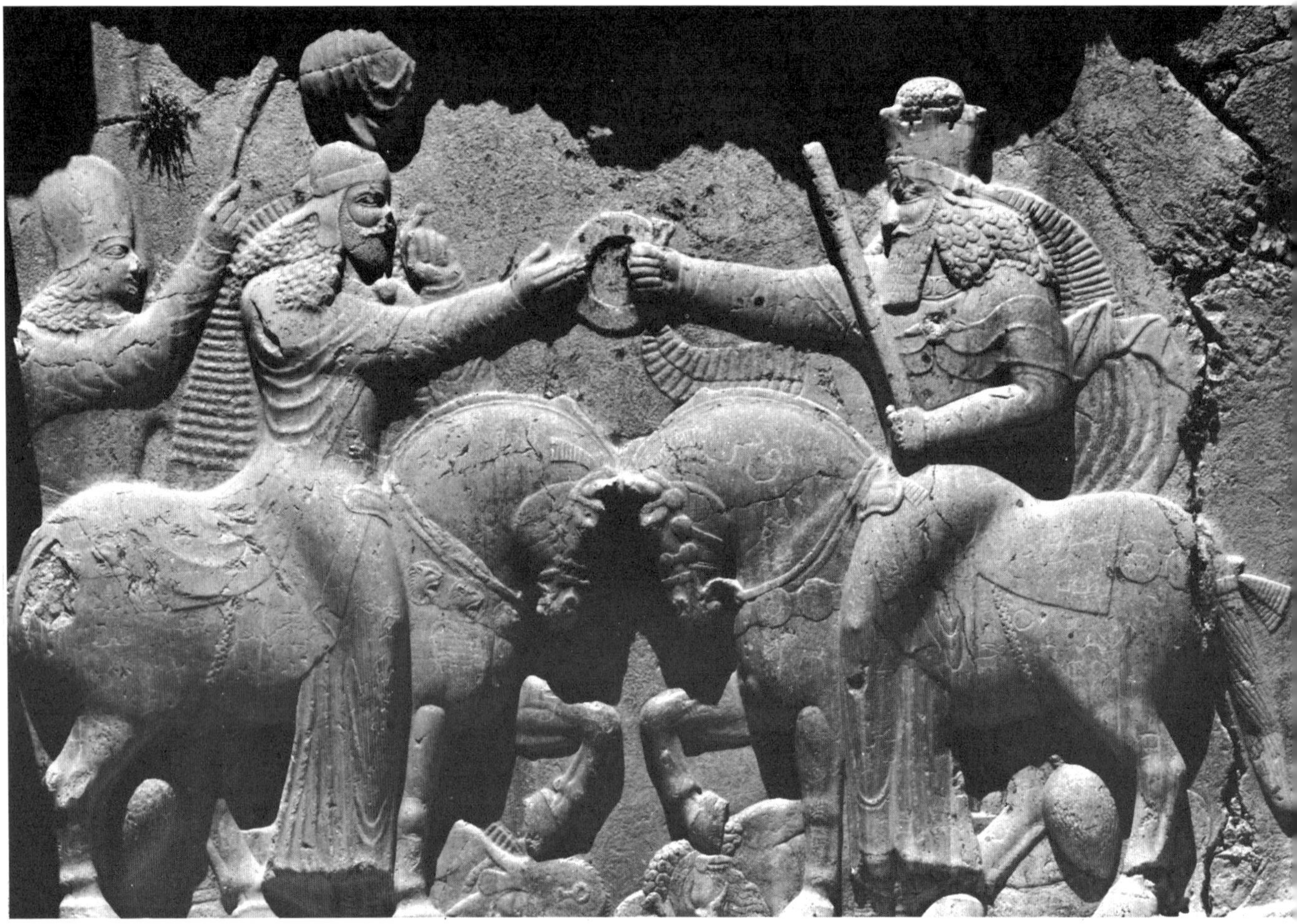

Equestrian investiture of Ardashir I by the god Ormazd. The worship of Ahura Mazda (or Ormazd, as his name became contracted) was taken over by the Sassanian kings in order to strengthen their claim to be the legitimate successors of the Achaemenian line. Here the first king of the Sassanian dynasty (on the left) is shown receiving his diadem from the god, whose horse tramples the evil spirit Ahriman. Ardashir's horse tramples the defeated Arsacid king. Relief on the cliff face at Naqsh-i-Rustem. Second quarter of the third century A.D.

thya (Naosihaithya) – the Vedic Nasatya (epithet of the Ashvins) – opposed Aramaiti and encouraged pride, rebellion and irreverence. Taurvi (Tauru) and Zairisha (Zairi) devoted themselves to degrading men and to their downfall. The antithesis of Haurvatat and Ameretat, they destroyed what was good and caused old age and decrepitude.

Aeshma, who was the incarnation of rage and devastation, formed a contrast with Sraosha. He was the Asmodeus (Aeshma daeva) of the *Book of Tobit*.

Drujs, Pairikas, Yatus. Many other demons sowed horror and crime. The Drujs, adversaries of the *asha,* were creatures of deceit, often female, always monstrous. The Pairikas (or Peri) disguised their malevolence under their charming appearance. They disturbed the normal action of the heavenly bodies and of the natural elements. The Yatus were sorcerers. The Kavis and the Karapans were priests of false religions.

Among the Drujs may be mentioned Nasu and Azidahaka. The former would assume the disguise of a fly and alight on corpses to hasten their corruption; it needed sharp eyes to get rid of him. The latter evolved into a serpent with three heads, six eyes and three pairs of fangs. Arab historians turned him into a mythical king of Babylon, Zohak, the constant enemy of Persia. An older tradition made him the adversary of Yima whom he had dethroned through jealousy. Thraetona (Feridun), the hero of the epic, overthrew the demon and chained him under Mount Demavand.

The vices to which women are subject were incorporated in the druj Jahi: a kiss which Ahriman once gave her introduced into the world the impurity of menstruation. Jahi furnished Milton with the prototype of Guilt.

Cosmogony. The creation of good principles by Ormazd and of bad principles by Ahriman, then the rivalry of these two powers, and finally the victory of Ormazd, is a cosmological myth which is strictly Zoroastrian and even more Sassanian. It partly covers a more ancient cosmogony of a ritualistic character, derived from the old Aryan background.

The twelve thousand years – the duration of this world – were divided into four periods, each lasting three millennia. Ormazd the un-created creator, at first proceeded with the immaterial elaboration of beings: he still limited himself to thinking of them. He thus foresaw the coming of Ahriman and Ahriman at once emerged from the darkness. Ormazd proposed peace between them but did not obtain it. He then declared war which should last for the nine remaining millennia and end in the triumph of the Light. The unconquerable weapon of victory was the sacred formula Ahuna Vairya, infallible like the Vedic hymns or the Hindu *mantras*. Zoroastrianism made this formula the evidence of Zarathustra's messianic mission – the affirmation that the prophet was the authentic Lord and Master who was to prepare the reign of Ormazd.

The second period of three thousand years was devoted to the actual creation of beings, either by God or by the Demon. The third period comprised the vicissitudes of the human race between the days of the first man until those of Zoroaster. The fourth was the period during which the victory of Zoroaster would become the final victory of Ormazd and the last judgment.

Myths of Primitive Humanity. Gayomart and the First Human Couple. The first man Gayomart, and the primitive bull, Gosh were the original creatures who produced all life. This human animal pair is evidence of the survival of archaic notions according to which everything resulted from the immolation of a victim by a primordial sacrificer. India, in its turn, preserved the memory of this belief in a cosmogonic rite. The bull of Mithraism was another residue of it. The death of Gosh and of Gayomart was the work of Ahriman.

The seed of Gayomart was buried for forty years in the earth and from it was born the first human couple: Mashya and Mashyoi. Ormazd said to them: 'You are human beings, masters of the world. In the perfection of thought I have created you the first of creatures. Think that which is good, say that which is good, do that which is good. Do not worship the Daevas.'

Their first thought was: 'That is God.' And they rejoiced one in the other, saying: 'Behold a human being.'

Their first act was to walk. Then they ate and said: 'It is Ormazd who made the waters, the earth, the tree, the ox, the stars, the moon, the sun and all other good things, both fruit and root.' Then a thought sent by the Demon occurred to them and they said: 'It is Angra Mainyu who created the water, the earth and so on... fruit and root.'

Thus they spoke, and the lie was to the taste of the demon and from it Angra Mainyu derived his first pleasure.

Initially pure, Mashya and Mashyoi thus became the victims of falsehood. Since the spirit of evil was more to blame than themselves the divine powers continued to protect them. In this way they learned how to make fire and use it, and how to provide for their needs. They gave birth to seven couples. From one of these, Siyamek and Siyameki, proceeded Fravak and Fravakain who were the ancestors of the fifteen races of mankind.

In these early days many things were revealed to man and civilisation was founded. The first king, Haoshyangha (Hoshang) and his successor Tahmouras, far from being oppressed by the Evil One, actually subjected his demons.

All this mythical history of primitive Persia lives again in the *Shah-Nameh* – or Book of the Kings – a sparkling poem of nearly sixty thousand verses which the Persian poet Firdusi composed in the tenth century. In it he made use of Avestaic traditions and Pahlavi literature. No better guide could be found for retracing the epic of Iran of which the following is a brief summary.

Husheng. The First King. Hoshang (Husheng) was the son of Siyamek. He began by avenging his father whom a Div (or Demon) had destroyed. Then, when he had assured the peace of his own kingdom, he set about civilising the world and spreading justice throughout the entire earth. First he discovered a mineral and, by his art, was able to separate the iron in it from the stone. He then invented the art of the blacksmith in order to fashion axes, saws and hoes. Afterwards he concerned himself with the distribution of water; he led it from the rivers and thus fertilised the fields. With the power which God had given him and with his own royal might, the wise Husheng domesticated animals which he used for the culti-

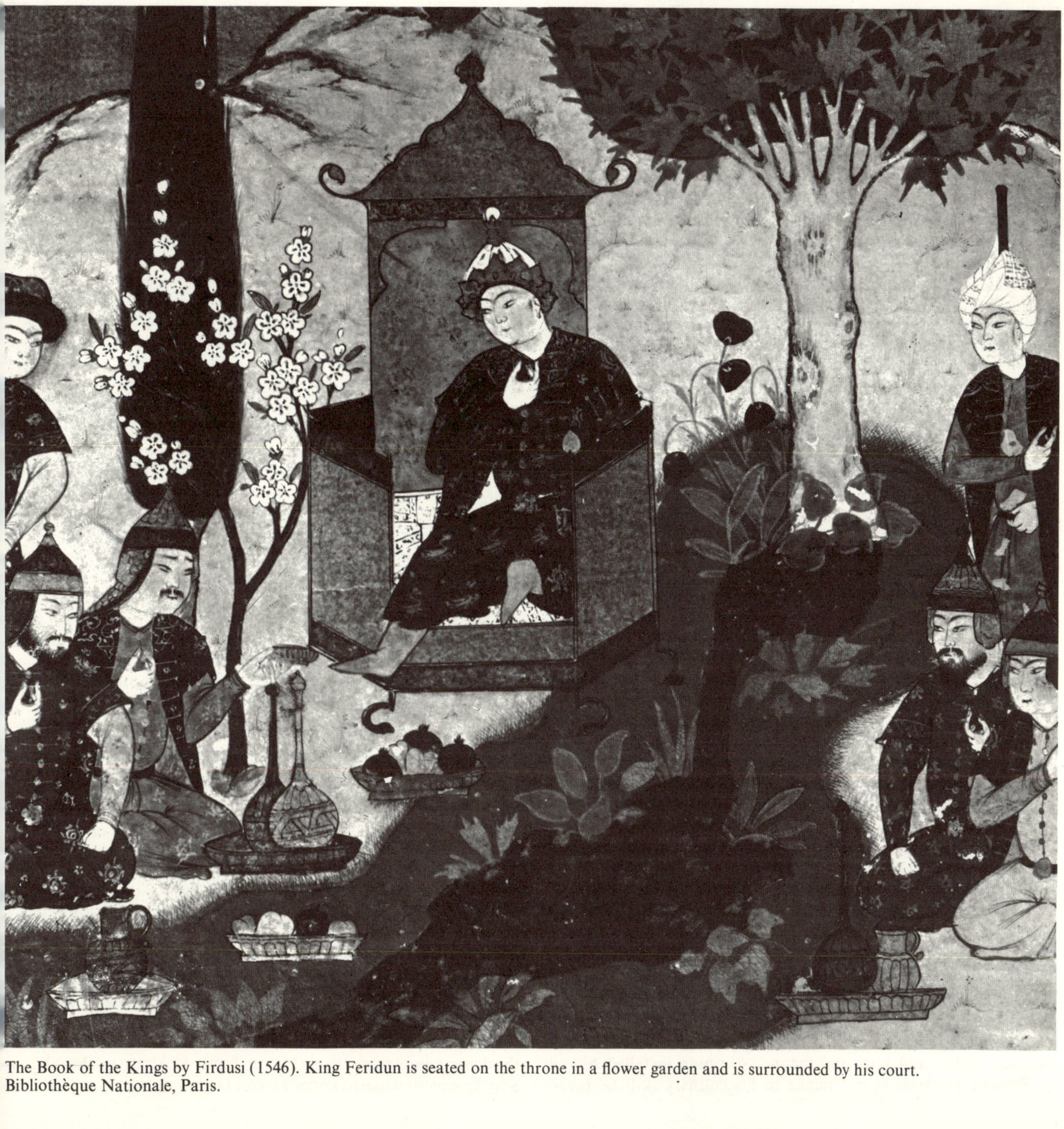

The Book of the Kings by Firdusi (1546). King Feridun is seated on the throne in a flower garden and is surrounded by his court. Bibliothèque Nationale, Paris.

vation of the ground. Wild animals he killed and with their skins he made clothing to cover men's bodies. 'He died, having in his lifetime achieved many works by the aid of spells and of thoughts without number.'

Tahmuras. The son of Husheng, Tahmuras, continued the civilising work of his father, teaching men to spin wool and weave carpets, to train cheetahs, gerfalcons and the royal hawk for the chase. 'He bound Ahriman by his spells and rode him like a swift steed. He saddled him and without respite made him carry him on a tour of the world.' But the wicked Divs took advantage of his absence to revolt. Tahmuras returned in haste to put down the rebellion. 'He was girded with the majesty of the master of the world. On his shoulder he bore a massive club. The courageous Divs and the enchanters all foregathered, forming an immense army of magicians. The black Div shouting aloud, led them, and their howling rose to the very heavens. The air darkened and the earth grew black and men's eyes were enveloped in shadows. Tahmuras, lord of the world, Tahmuras the Glorious, advanced with girded loins to do battle and wreak vengeance. On one side there was the noise and flame and smoke of the Divs; on the other the king's gallant men. Suddenly the king attacked the Divs. The combat was not long. He bound up two-thirds of them by magic and struck down the others with his heavy club. They were dragged away wounded and ignominiously tied together. They begged for mercy, saying: 'Do not kill us, and thou shalt learn from us a new art which will be useful to thee.' The illustrious king granted them their lives so that they might reveal their secret. When they had been delivered from their chains they begged his protection. They taught the king how to write and made him brilliant in learning.'

Jam or Yima (Jemshid). Jam or Yima, son of Tahmuras, is above all the prototype of the sovereign of the golden age. He lived in a sort of underground fortress, his *Var,* where he maintained the just laws and purity of the Aryan stock. In this he both resembles and differs from the Yama of India. Yama was the king of the dead and Yima, his Iranian equivalent, the ideal of the 'good shepherd'.

When, through the malevolence of the demon Mahrkusha, floods alternating with torrid summers threatened to devastate the earth and wipe out mankind and the animals, Ahura Mazda foresaw the tragedy and decided to save Yima, the just. He bade him build a hypogeum or subterranean dwelling where he should find shelter.

'Build a *var* as long as a horse can run, and of equal length and width. Into it carry representatives of every kind of beast, great and small, of men, dogs, birds, oxen and sheep.

'There thou shalt make water to flow. Thou shalt put birds in the trees along the water's edge, in verdure which is everlasting. There put specimens of all plants, the loveliest and most fragrant; and of all fruits, the most succulent. All these kinds of things and creatures shall remain and not perish as long as they are in the *var*.

'But put there no deformed creature, nor impotent, nor mad; neither wicked, nor deceitful, nor rancorous, nor jealous; nor a man with irregular teeth, nor a leper.

'In the upper part of the *var* thou shalt lay out nine avenues; in the middle, six; in the lower part, three.

'In the streets of the upper part thou shalt place one thousand couples, men and women; six hundred in the streets of the middle part; three hundred in the streets of the lower part.

'And over the *var* thou shalt open a window for the light.

'Yima wondered: "How shall I make this *var*?"

'Then Ahura Mazda said to him: "Thou shalt knead the earth with thy feet and thy hands as the potters do." '

This same Yima is found again in the *Shah-Nameh* under the name of Jemshid. To him, according to the poet, the manufacture of the first iron weapons was due, as well as the fabrication of linen and silk clothing, work in precious stones, the invention of perfume and the art of medicine. Unhappily Jemshid, intoxicated with power, committed the sin of pride and thus made himself vulnerable to the attacks of Zohak – the incarnation of the druj Azidahaka.

Zohak. He is a curious figure, this Zohak, the ambitious son of a desert king. Ahriman, the spirit of Evil, little by little succeeded in making him his creature. After having persuaded Zohak to kill his own father and seize the throne, Ahriman installed himself in Zohak's castle as chef. Thanks to his culinary skill he taught the king to eat the flesh of animals, an innovation which seemed startling and slightly sacrilegious to a vegetarian people. Zohak was delighted with these new dishes and offered to reward the demon. Ahriman asked for only one thing: 'That his gracious majesty permit me to kiss the top of his shoulders and there rest my eyes and face.' The request was granted and the demon-chief disappeared after having kissed the king.

But the king suddenly beheld a black snake spring from each of his shoulders. The snakes were cut away, but immediately grew again. All spells and remedies proved useless. Ahriman returned this time disguised as an illustrious doctor. He prescribed that the snakes should be fed each day with human brains.

Thenceforth Zohak was himself changed into a redoubtable demon. After he had vanquished Jemshid and had him sawn in two he reigned over the earth for a thousand years. 'The customs of decent men vanished, the desires of the wicked were accomplished. Virtue was despised, magic was held in honour, righteousness remained in hiding, vice flaunted itself openly.'

But one night in a dream Zohak saw himself vanquished and enchained by a young prince. The next day he summoned his Mobeds and asked them to interpret his dream. 'All were silent. Zirek Mobed who was wise and upright alone loosened his tongue before Zohak and said to him: "Empty thy head of wind, for none is born of his mother save to die. Wert thou a rampart of well-wrought iron the rotation of the heavens would break thee none-theless, and thou shouldst disappear. There will be someone to inherit thy throne and he will overthrow thy might. His name will be Feridun and for the earth he will be an august sky," ' In terror Zohak ordered the massacre of all children, hoping thus to destroy in his cradle him who it was intended should put an end to his reign.

Feridun. But no sooner had Feridun been born than his mother, the prudent Firanak, succeeded in saving his life. She confided him to the keeper of the garden where lived the miraculous cow Purmajeh, who suckled the infant hero. Afterwards she carried her son to Hindustan and put him under the care of a pious old mountaineer.

When he had grown up Feridun learned about Zohak's misdeeds from his mother, and swore to punish him. Now Zohak 'day and night continued to speak of Feridun; his tall stature was bent with fear, his heart suffered agony because of Feridun'. One day a man appeared at his palace, demanding justice. When the king asked him to name the person who had wronged him the man beat his head with his hands and said: 'I am Kaweh, the smith... It is thee whom I accuse in the bitterness of my soul... The brains of all my sons have been given to thy serpents to devour. I hold thee accountable for what thou hast done.'

Neither gifts nor words were able to appease the smith. Worse still, when he left the palace he stirred up the mob with his outcry. Finally he seized his smith's apron and tied it to the end of a lance to serve as a banner. He gathered together a group of partisans and led them towards Feridun's palace. Feridun received the smith and his banner as a sign of destiny, and decided to take up arms against Zohak.

Armed with a massive club Feridun set forth with his little army, his heart full of joy. As he marched an angel descended from heaven to teach him magic and to foretell the happiness of his future.

He crossed the Tigris by boldly spurring his horse into the river's swirling waters, and arrived at Zohak's palace. He entered it and no one dared to oppose him. The king was absent. The young hero smashed the talismans and set free the daughters of Jemshid – Shehrinaz and Arnewaz, the two lovely black-eyed girls whom Zohak had kept prisoners.

Meanwhile Zohak had been warned by a servant and was already on the way home, coming post-haste. He put on iron armour which rendered him unrecognisable and penetrated the palace. 'He saw the black-eyed Shehrinaz seated near Feridun, melting with tenderness and enchantment.' Maddened with rage and despair Zohak flung himself on Feridun, but Feridun was prepared for him. Just as Zohak drew his sword Feridun smote him with his club. An angel then intervened and commanded Feridun not to slay the demon, but instead to tie him up firmly and later to chain him in a rocky cavern situated under Mount Demavand.

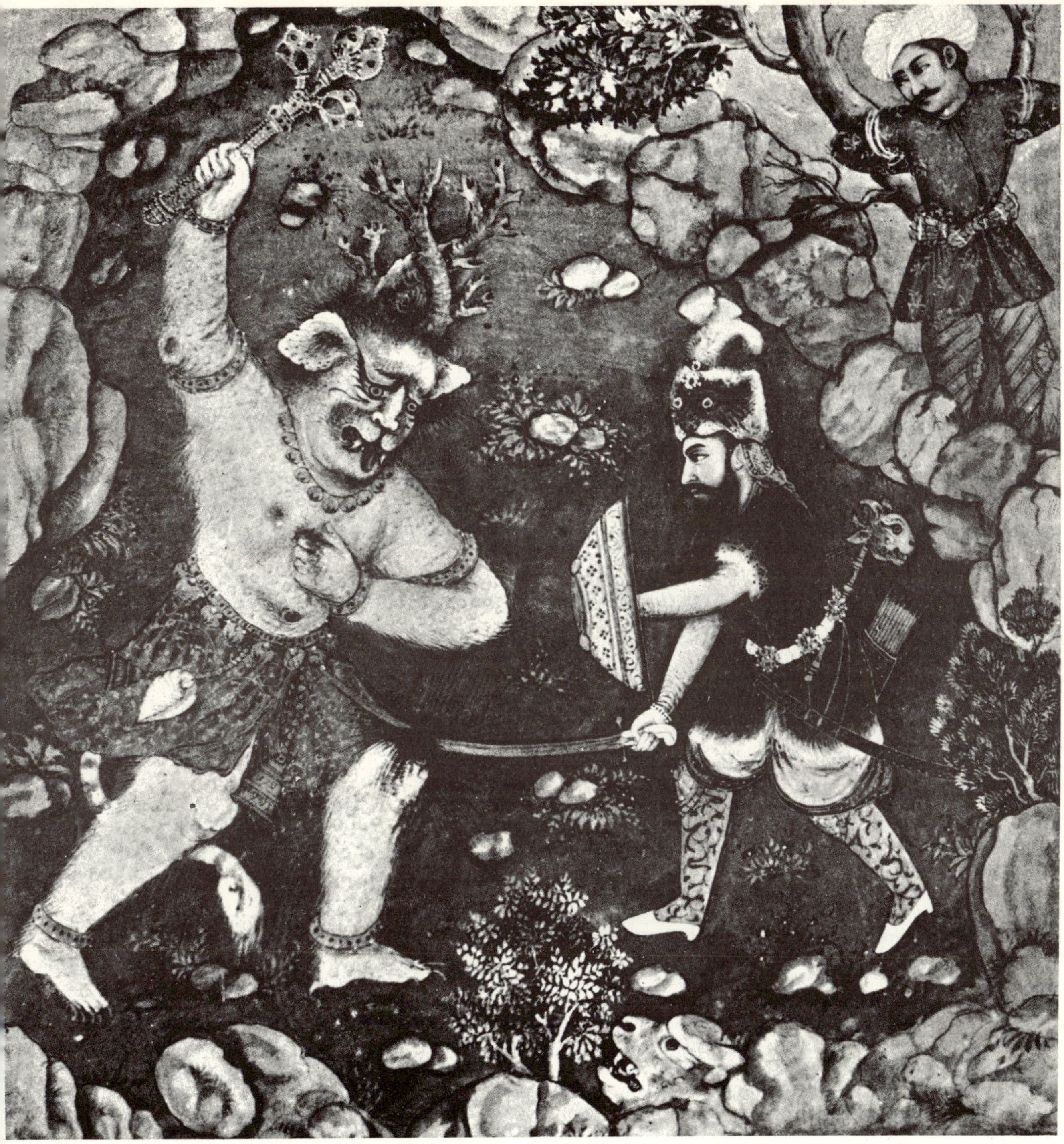

The Book of the Kings by Firdusi. Indo-Persian art, about 1620. Rustem battles with the White Demon in his cavern in order to free the king of Persia, Kai Kaus. Bibliothèque Nationale, Paris.

Feridun, having avenged Jemshid and his father, was at last able to mount the throne. 'The world remained in his power for five hundred years, during which not a day passed that he did not overthrow the foundations of unrighteousness. Wherever he beheld injustice, wherever he saw waste lands, he bound the hand of evil with the hand of good, as it befits a king to do!'

The Sons of Feridun: Minucher. When Feridun grew old he divided his vast kingdom between his three sons. To Selm, the eldest, fell the land of Roum and the West. To Tur he gave Turkestan and China. Irej, the youngest, inherited Iran. But Selm and Tur were discontented with their shares and decided to join forces and fight their young brother.

In vain the virtuous Irej, to whom this fratricidal struggle was repugnant, came alone and unarmed to his brothers, hoping to appease them by freely offering to give them all they wished for. Tur struck him on the head with his heavy golden chair; then, drawing a dagger, he covered Irej from head to foot with a torrent of blood, tearing the royal breast of his brother with the steel poniard. Finally he filled Irej's skull with musk and amber and sent it back to Feridun.

'Feridun kept watching the road. The army and the court early awaited the arrival of the young king. They were preparing to sally forth to meet him. Wine had been ordered, and singing and music...when black dust rose from the road. From the cloud of dust emerged a dromedary, mounted by a cavalier who was broken with sorrow. This bearer of sad news cried out with grief. To his breast he held a golden coffer. In the golden coffer was a silken cloth. In the silken cloth was placed the head of Irej...Feridun fell from his horse to the ground and all his warriors rent their garments; their cheeks were black and their eyes were white, for they had expected to be greeted by a very different sight...'

Heartbroken by the death of his beloved son Irej, old Feridun longed for revenge. An avenger finally appeared in the person of Minucher, the grandson of Irej. Attacked by Selm and Tur, who had again invaded Iran with their powerful army, Minucher defeated and put them to death. The battle was so furious and bloody that 'one might have said that the surface of the field was covered with tulips and that the feet of the war-elephants, sinking into the blood, appeared like so many pillars of coral'. His vengeance achieved, Feridun died, leaving the crown to Minucher.

Zal. For some time the young sovereign had had as a counsellor one of his lieutenants, the noble Sam, governor of Hindustan. Sam, shortly after returning to his province, became the father of a son, whose visage was fair as the sun but whose hair was white like that of an old man. Sam was ashamed of the strange appearance of the baby and had him exposed on a distant mountain. But a vulture, the noble Simurgh, was attracted by the cries of the infant and, taking him in its claws, bore him to its nest on the summit of Mount Elburz. The child grew and became a 'man who was like a tall cypress: his breast was like a hill of silver, his waist like a reed'. In the meantime Sam was stricken with remorse and, warned by a dream, began to seek for his son. He reached the distant mountain where he discovered Simurgh's rock. Simurgh consented to relinquish his adopted child and deposited him at Sam's feet. Sam blessed his innocent son and named him Zal.

The exploits of Zal, a hero full of wisdom and valour, are recounted at length in the *Shah-Nameh*. One of the most gracious episodes is that of his love for the beautiful Rudabeh.

One day while travelling through his father's domains Zal stopped at Kabul, where he stayed with Mihrab, one of Sam's vassals. There he was magnificently entertained. He learned moreover that Mihrab kept a daughter veiled whose visage was more beautiful than the sun. 'She is,' he was told, 'a silver cypress filled with colours and perfumes, a rose and a jasmine from head to foot. You would say that her features pour wine and that her hair is all of amber. Her body is moulded of rubies and jewels and the tresses of her hair are like a coat of mail made of musk.' The young prince immediately fell in love with the unknown beauty.

The maiden had also heard Zal praised for his strength and beauty and she too felt her heart filled with the fires of love. She confided in her slaves who, on the pretext of gathering roses, drew near Zal's camp and succeeded in speaking privately with him. Thus Zal obtained the promise of an interview with the princess.

Rudabeh secretly prepared a palace hung with Chinese brocades, filled with flowers, adorned with vases of gold and turquoise, scented with musk and amber and strewn with rubies and emeralds. There, on the terrace above the palace, she awaited Zal. As soon as she saw him she bade him welcome and as he sought some means of reaching her she loosened her long tresses and let them fall from the crenellated walls, calling down: 'O son of a gallant father, seize the ends of my black curls; for thee must I become as a noose.' Zal gazed at the moon-like beauty of Rudabeh's face and covered the musk-scented tresses with kisses so that she heard the sound of his lips. And he answered: 'May the sun never shine on the day when I lift a finger against a woman carried away with love!' From the hands of his slave he took a cord, made a running-knot and without further words tossed it in the air. The noose caught in the battlements and Zal climbed up at a bound. When he had mounted the high wall the lovely face of the fairy-like princess drew near to salute him. In her hand she took the hand of Zal and together they departed as though intoxicated. But the happiness of the young couple was threatened by a grave obstacle. The family of Mihrab, who was a direct descendant of Zohak, were hereditary enemies of the family of Minucher. The question was whether Zal would ever be able to obtain the consent of his father Sam and of his overlord, the mighty Minucher. He succeeded, however, after various trials, and because the astrologers who were consulted declared that 'this virtuous couple will have a son like unto a war-elephant, a stoutly girded son who will submit all men to the might of his sword and raise the king's throne above the clouds. Thanks to him evil days will fall upon Turan and prosperity will be spread throughout Iran.' And indeed this son was to be the glorious and invincible Rustem.

Rustem. The *Shah-Nameh* recounts how Zal's son Rustem (Rotastahm) installed the dynasty of the Kaianides on the throne and tells of the marvels he wrought not only against the Turanians beyond the Oxus but also against the demons. After the first two monarchs, Kai-Qobad and Kai-Kaus, Rustem secured the succession of the fortunate Kai-Khosrau. The following sovereign Lohresp, had a son during whose reign legend says Zoroaster lived. During the same legendary dynasty – which corresponds historically with the Achaemenians – was born Alexander, the reputed issue of the Persian king Darab and the daughter of Philip of Macedon.

The valour of Rustem symbolised the struggle between Iran and Turania, in other words between the peoples of the North and those of the East, ancestors of the Turks and the Mongols, who lived beyond the Oxus. Neither Rustem nor his father Zal appear in the *Zend-Avesta*. They belong, therefore, to a cycle of later legends with an Aryan basis. The cycle forms a military epic concentrated on a single hero whose exploits extend over several reigns.

The most celebrated of these exploits is the slaying of the White Demon in the mountains of Tabaristan. Another demon succeeded in surprising Rustem one day while he was asleep and throwing him into the sea. But the hero extricated himself from this peril as he had from all the others to which the malignity of the demons had exposed him. Only the treachery of the king himself, the king whom Rustem had served so well, was able to cause the hero's death. Jealous of Rustem's glory, the king had deep trenches dug in a game preserve; the bottom of the trenches bristled with spears, javelins and swords. Then the king said to Rustem: 'Should you care to hunt, I own a property where there are herds of wandering game. You must not fail to pay this charming spot a visit.' Rustem accepted the invitation. His horse Raksh scented the trap and refused to enter the treacherous preserve. But in vain; for Rustem stubbornly spurred him forward onto the fatal path. Together they plunged into one of the trenches and were cruelly lacerated. Rustem's wounds were fatal; but before he expired he at least had the satisfaction of killing the perfidious king with an arrow.

Eschatology. The Iranians, who held that the human soul was igneous or luminous, believed that the dead continued to exist. The idea, widespread among Indo-European peoples, of an underground abode of the dead gave them their conception of the *var* of Jam. Nevertheless the normal destiny of souls was the Light from which they came – hence a celestial abode. This integration with the Ahura, however, was not instantaneous. The Persians no doubt received from the Semites the notion of a last judgment together with related ideas: prophets and world salvation prepared by a Messiah.

As time ran out and the end approached the earth would become flatter, people would become more similar and, indeed, better. Ancient heroes, coming to life again, would exert themselves for the collective welfare. Thus Keresaspa, after his long lethargy, would exterminate Azidahaka (Zohak) whom previously Feridun had merely enchained. Many 'future helpers', many saviours, the Saoshyants, would suppress evil. Their moral and cosmic role was similar to that of the Buddha of the future, Maitreya, among the Indians. Such would be the direct, though distant, fruits of Zoroaster's apostolate: an ardent contribution to the final glory of Ormazd and the salvation of his creatures. According to the Armenian Eznik the final saviour should be a reincarnation of Gayomart, the first man.

The prototype of the Saoshyants was Zoroaster himself. The animating principle of his religious personality – that which the Iranians called his *daena* – would redouble its efficacy towards the end of time. The pre-eminent saviour, Astvatereta, who would be immaculately conceived by the virgin Vispataurvi, would promote the achievement of Mazda's work, not without the collaboration of minor saviours whose task would be to bring the reign of celestial Light to the different regions of the earth. Meanwhile the Amesha Spenta would make it shine forth in splendour in the world above. Each Virtue would triumph over its opposing Vice, and the very name of Angra Mainyu would in the end be forgotten. All creation would again become worthy of Ahura Mazda and bear witness to its creator.

A SUMMARY OF MOSLEM MYTHS

The Arabs before Islam. Before their conversion to Islam the Arabs, scattered through the vast peninsula between the Persian

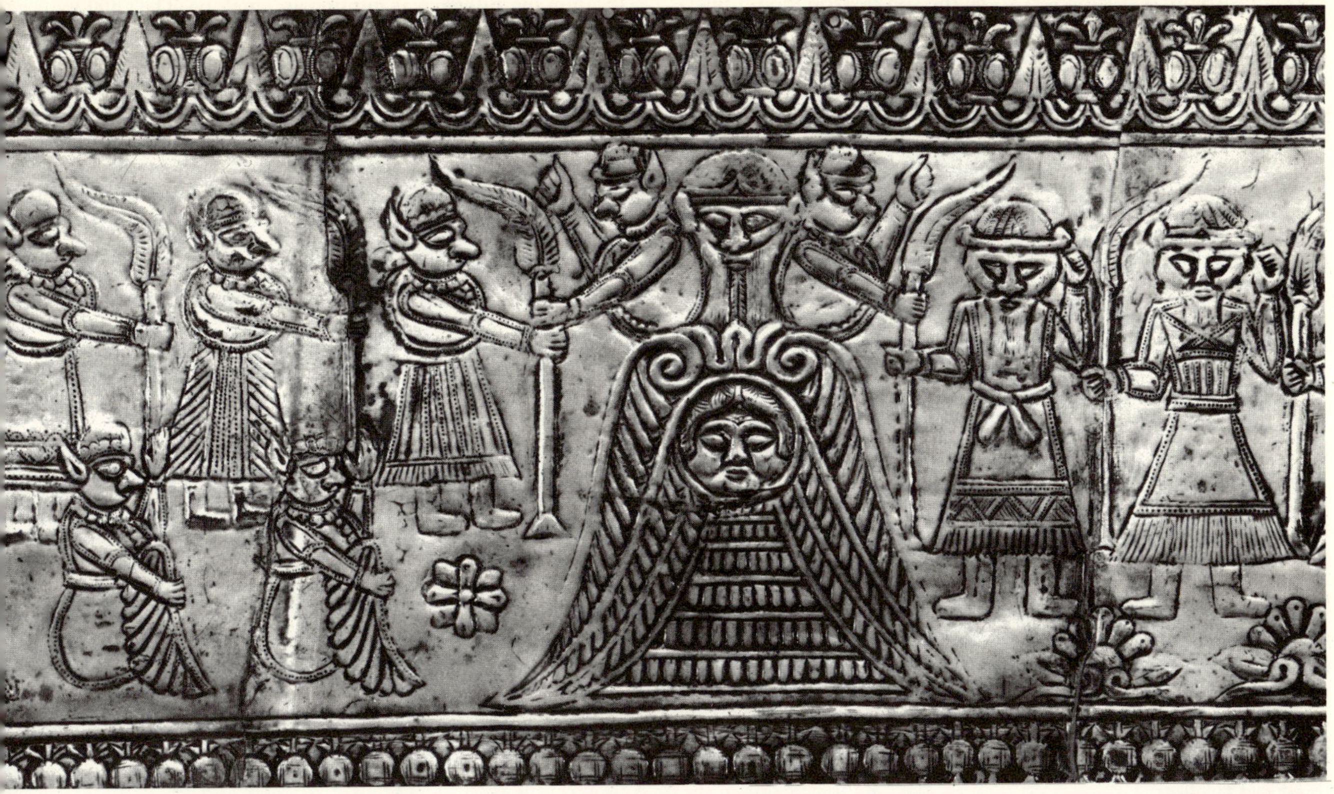

'he birth of Ahura Mazda and Ahriman. In the centre is the androgynous figure of Zurvan, the supreme god and personification of Time, while from is body emerge the twin forms of Ahura Mazda and Ahriman, the opposing principles of good and evil, born respectively of the value of his cts and his doubts concerning them. On either side are figures representing the three ages of man. Silver plaque from Luristan, eighth century B.C.

Gulf, the Indian Ocean and the Red Sea, practised a naturalistic and animistic religion, worshipping stones and trees. They peopled the universe with demons, benevolent and malevolent, the *jinns*, and with redoubtable genii, the *Efrit*, who delighted in assuming the most diverse forms in order to harm mankind. The cult of stones gave rise to idols which were usually no more than blocks of stone such as those of the goddesses Manat, venerated at Kodaid, and El Lat, whom Herodotus called Alilat, who was worshipped at Taif.

The gods were very numerous. Huart in his History of the Arabs enumerates nearly fifty of them. Among the Arabs of the South he distinguishes: Atthar (the Sun), a female divinity; Ankarih, Haubas, El-Makun, Khol and Sin (the moon-god borrowed from the Assyro-Babylonians). Among the Arabs of the North there were: Allat (the planet Venus); Ruda (the Evening Star); Itha, Raham and Chai-al-Kaum (the good and rewarding god who drinks no wine). The Koran mentions a few pagan divinities, among others the five idols who were erected by the descendants of Cain: Wadd, Sowa, Yaghut (he who helps, worshipped north of the Yemen in the form of a lion), Ya'uk (he who prevents or he who keeps) and Nasr, the vulture.

The goddess El-'Ozza was also held in high honour among the Koreishites. She was, it seems, offered human sacrifices. Finally there were Kozah, god of the storm and tempest, and Isaf and Naila who are still represented in Mecca by two standing stones.

The most venerated pagan sanctuary of the Arabs was the famous Kaaba at Mecca which held the black stone that was an object of general cult. Here pilgrims came from every part of Arabia. When the Abyssinian general Abraha, who had sworn to demolish the Kaaba, appeared before Mecca he was unable to enter the city because the elephant on which he was mounted knelt and stubbornly remained on its knees. Abraha's army had to beat a retreat pursued by birds who let fall from their beaks stones scarcely larger than lentils but sufficient nevertheless to pierce the fleeing soldiers through and through.

The Arabs also had their heroes whose exploits were recounted in the Moallakas, a kind of epic composition. The most celebrated was Antara el-Absi, son of Sheddad. He was both warrior and poet and lived towards the end of the sixth century. The *Story of Antar* which relates his valorous deeds and glorious end was among the most popular works of Arab literature.

Shiite Islam. There is scarcely any religion less propitious to the development of a mythology than Islam. Its dry and formal conception of the law excludes, at least in principle, not only individual phantasy but flights of popular imagination. In order to check the infinitely varied survivals of paganism – the multiplicity of gods, the worship of idols – and in order to maintain monotheism in its purity, the Moslems scorned anthropomorphic figures. Hence at the same time they confined their art to decoration inspired by geometry only; and to dogma they refused the licence of expressing itself in fables and symbols. The arid precision of the law was in their eyes the sole form of truth.

The civilisations of Aryan origin which were conquered by Islam – Persia and India – found this legalism repugnant and preserved their traditional myths as far as possible. In Persia the new religion converted – more or less profoundly – the whole population, and those who remained zealously faithful to Mazdaism had to expatriate themselves. These were the Parsees or the Ghebres who took refuge in Hindu territory. Nevertheless the national epic, in spite of its *Zend-Avesta* inspiration, retained its great prestige. And if the God of Mohammed was fanatically substituted for the Zoroastrian dualism there persisted in the souls of his Persian worshippers a rich and subtle mysticism which was unknown to the Arab conqueror.

Indeed the special quality of the Persian character turned Iran from orthodox Mohammedanism to the Shiite heresy. Shiites are those Moslems who revere Ali and maintain that Abu Bekr, Omar and Othman – the first three caliphs – committed an illegal crime by depriving Ali of the succession to the Prophet. Hence the veneration of the line which derived from Ali was to give rise to a new mythology, whose roots were Islamic but whose foliage was Iranian.

The twelve imams. Eleven descendants of Ali and his wife Fatima, Mohammed's daughter, constituted with Ali himself the twelve imams or 'directors'. They were semi-divine personages who were invested with moral functions. They ruled the twelve hours of the day and were worshipped in the order of their succession.

Ali, the 'approved' (Murteza), the 'Lion of God' (Haidar), purified the soul of sin. Fatima, too, was above all women 'pure' Hasan, their son, protected and on occasion avenged the faithful. His brother Hosein was a propitiator of divine mercy.

Zein el-Abidin was supposed to be the son of Hosein and Sherbanu, daughter of the last Sassanian king Yazdgard III. In this way began a development of Islam especially fitted to Persia with its mingling of religion and national tradition. The imam Zein el-Abidin indeed assumed a political character; he sheltered his devotees from tyranny and assured their favour with the sultans.

Mohammed el-Bagir was the patron of scholars; Jafer as-Sadiq, a master of piety; Musa al-Kazhim, a healer; Ali ar-Riza, a guide when one travelled; Mohammed at-Taqi dispensed not only the rewards of unselfishness but also those of riches; Alian-Naqi presided over justice, and also over charity. Abdallah Hasan watched over the decencies, formality and decorum of worldly as well as of religious behaviour He thus assured constant happiness. Mohammed al-Mahdi, who in infancy vanished underground, would announce the news of the imminent end of the world. Meanwhile he procured victory and saw that loans were repaid.

Art abstained from the impiety of representing the features of the imams. Their faces were veiled or their effigies symbolised by flames.

Influence of the Stars. In Moslem Persia astrology enjoyed great prestige, as it did throughout Islam and had done in ancient Chaldea. The Sun was the principle of heat as was the Moon of humidity. The planets represented dryness and cold. Jupiter and Venus exercised favourable influences; Saturn and Mars unfavourable. Mercury was ambiguous. He appeared as the patron of authors, while Mars was that of the blood-thirsty and Jupiter that of philosophers and men of religion. The Sun protected the powerful of this world, Saturn the cut-throats, and Venus the courtesans.

Genii and Demons. A union took place which reconciled Mazdaian demonology with the genii of the Koran. Among the latter may be mentioned the jinns, with their father Jann who was created before Adam. They were long faithful to the law of the Creator, but became corrupted by the sin of pride. Iblis, Satan, was born among them. His fault, too, was a lack of submission. The amalgamation of the two religions produced vague assimilations: Gayomart-Adam, the first man; Zoroaster-Ibrahim, the friend of God; Ahriman-Sheitan, the devil; and Ormazd-Allah, God.

The Hagiography of the Sufis. Mysticism occupied an outstanding place in Persian Islam as it did in the religions of neighbouring India. The Sufis of Persia, like the Hindu Yogis, sought absolute intuition in holiness and in gradual achievement of intelligence. Their vocation and their perfection were objects of legends.

Ibrahim ibn Edhem was hunting an antelope. The antelope – lik Saint Hubert's stag – came to him and said: 'Is it for this that tho wert brought into the world? Who has ordered thee to live in thi fashion?' The prince was touched with grace and decided to liv alone and in poverty.

According to another story the young prince saw bizarre creature on the roof of his palace who explained that they were looking fo camels. 'What!' he asked in bewilderment, 'Camels on roof-tops And they answered him: 'And yet thou seekest, on the thron to find God.'

Then there was Abdel-Kader Jilani who practised the super natural powers of yoga: levitation, the increase or decrease of hi stature. By means of hypnotism he would also transport a mediun through space or into the future. Other saints, anticipating wireless would trace magic circles and hear conversation which took plac at great distances.

The Phantasy of the Poets. The phantasy of the Persian poet displayed the wisdom of the mystics in a lighter vein.

In the twelfth century Attar described the destiny of souls as a flight of birds across the seven valleys of Seeking, Love, Knowledge Independence, Unity, Stupefaction and Annihilation The fina term symbolised the heart lost in the divine Ocean and thenceforth happy.

Jelal-ud-din Rumi (thirteenth century) in his *Mathnawi* write philosophy in the form of fables which recall those of La Fontaine For example, he explains the subjectivity of sense perceptions in thi manner: 'A master said to his pupil who was cross-eyed: "Go into the house and find a certain bottle." When the child saw two bottles he asked: "Which one shall I take?" "There are not two . . . Break one of them." The child obeyed and both disappeared.'

Biblical legends, transformed by a lively imagination and trans posed into symbols, provided many Persian myths. The story o Solomon and Absalom became, in the hands of Jami (fifteenth century) the following: a king decided to abstain from all connection with women. Nevertheless he succeeded in obtaining a son – Salaman. The king desired that this son should participate in the same purity. But Salaman was seduced by the charms of Absal the too ravishing nurse to whom he had been confided. The couple fled to the Isle of Voluptuousness. But the king, by the power of thought, put a thousand obstacles in the way of the two lovers who in despair threw themselves into the flames of a funeral pyre Only Absal was consumed. Suffering enlightened Salaman and having lost the desire and yearning for physical love, he became worthy of reigning.

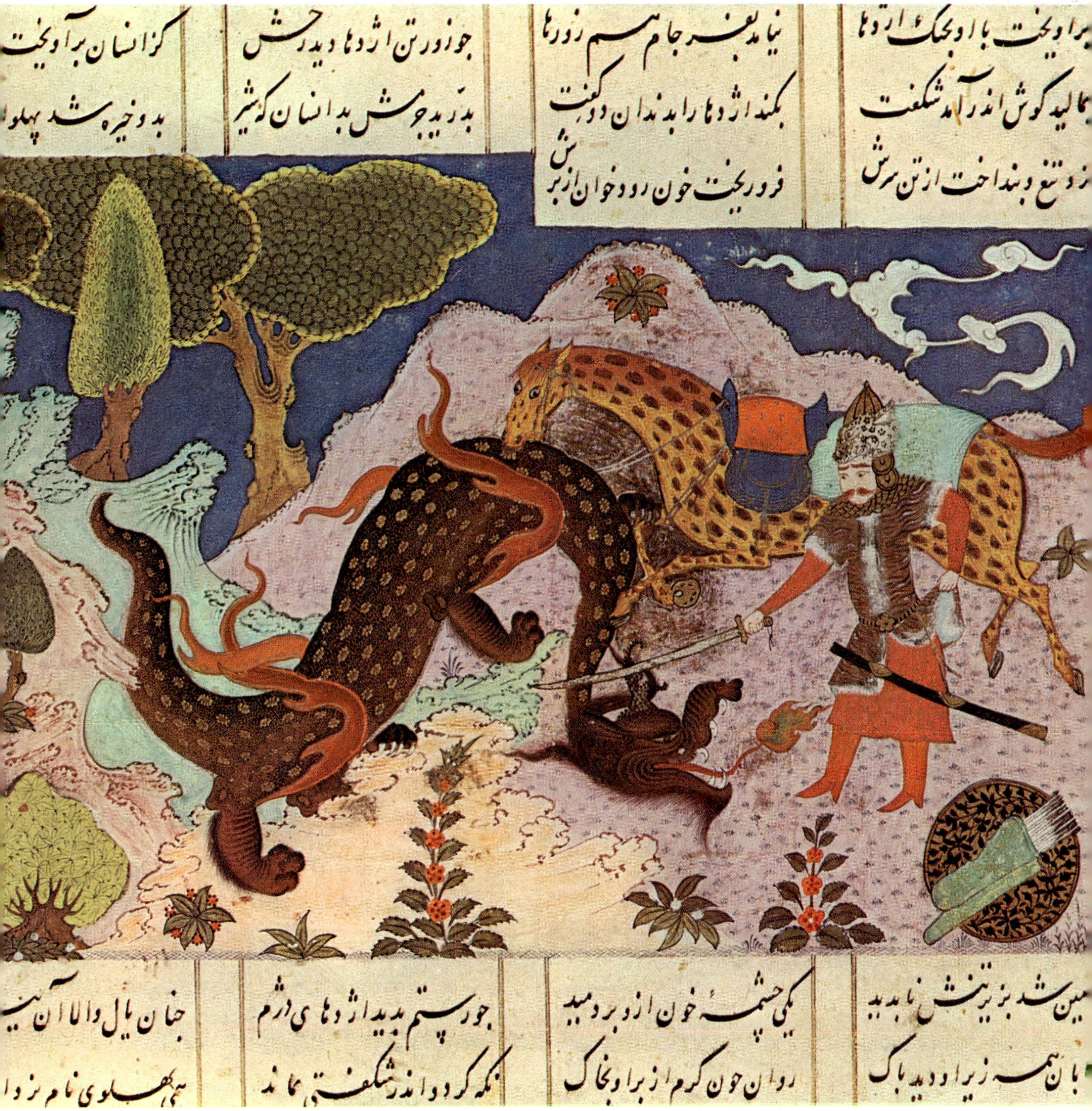

The Persian epic poem the *Shah-Nameh* (The Book of Kings) is one of the world's great sagas. Perhaps the most famous figure in the cycle is the hero Rustem, who symbolised the struggle of the Iranians or Aryans, with the savage peoples of the east. In this Persian miniature of 1486 he is seen killing a dragon which had attacked his horse.

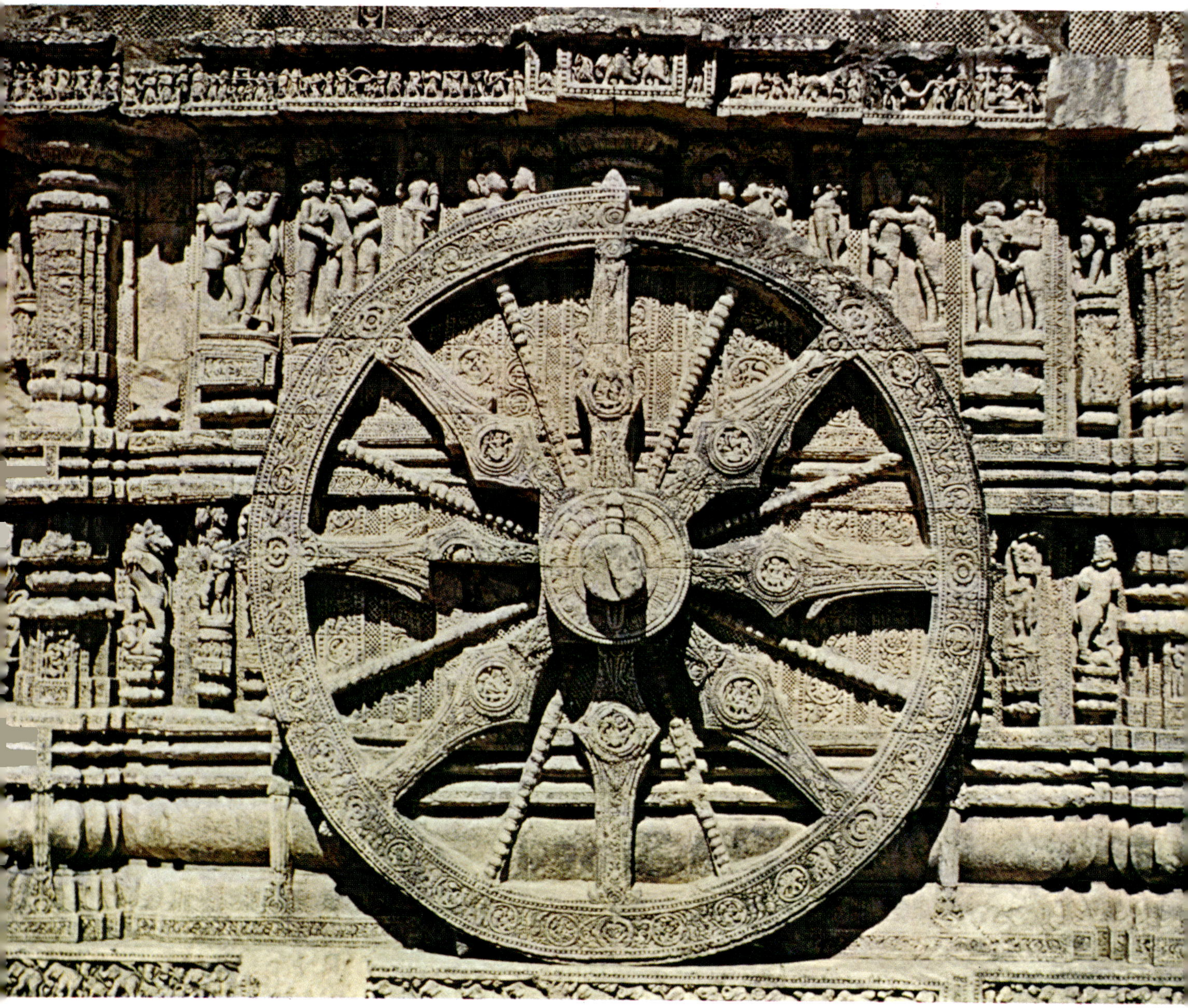

A remarkable expression of Hindu piety is the thirteenth-century sun temple of Vishnu-Surya at Konarak in Orissa. It is constructed in the shape of a giant solar chariot, borne on twelve great wheels each ten feet in diameter. The wheel is also the symbol of the view that life is lived in an endlessly recurring cycle, a basic Hindu belief.

INDIAN MYTHOLOGY

INTRODUCTION

Religious Complexity of Hindu Society. Indian mythology is an inextricable jungle of luxuriant growths. When you enter it you lose the light of day and all clear sense of direction. In a brief exposition one cannot aviod over-simplification. But at least one can point out how, in the most favourable circumstances, paths may be traced leading to a methodical exploration of this vast domain.

At every period the area including the two river basins – Indus and Ganges – and the plateau of the Deccan, contained a mixture of races devoid of unity but including every stage of civilisation, from the very primitive to the highly evolved. The Aryan invaders from the north-west settled at first in the Punjab (upper valley of the Indus and its tributaries) between 3000 and 1500 B.C., and must even then have come into contact with dark-skinned Dravidians of a rather advanced culture which may have been related to that of the Chaldeans (if we may judge from the excavations at Harappa), and with much 'wilder' tribes speaking Munda idioms, whose affinities were with the Negroids of Indo-China and Australia. A great peculiarity of India is that everything endures while everything changes, so that even to-day these three elements exist side by side, at once distinct and yet intermingled in an infinite number of amalgams, which moreover contain a certain number of Mongolian elements.

Thus, at the – theoretical – starting point of Indian mythology one must insist on the different factors, Munda, Dravidian and Aryan. But the first two have left no direct traces in very early times: they only appear through the medium of Brahmanic literature – the literature of the Aryans of India. The protohistoric expression of this literature exists in the *Vedas* and nowadays they are more and more recognised as possessing an 'Indian' and not merely 'Aryan' character. Moreover, the mixture of Aryan and non-Aryan myths which for a long time out of sheer prejudice was rated as 'late' and called 'Hinduism' dates from the earliest ages of 'Indianity', which includes the period of the *Vedas*.

Non-Aryan Cults. The aborigines, who spoke idioms related to the Munda, are to some extent involved with Totemism. The life of some vegetable or animal species was believed to be the life of the tribe and of the individuals who formed it. Sacrifice consisted in immolating a victim in order to absorb its vital principle – a custom sometimes implying cannibalism.

The Dravidians were less gross. They excluded blood sacrifices and the eating of raw meat, and were limited to the veneration of idols. The effigy of a divinity was sprinkled, perfumed, and hung with garlands. This pious and peaceful veneration remained in India under the name 'puja'. Still, if grossness did not appear in their rites, it was present in the divine forms which they revered. Even in our days, on the south-east slope of the Deccan, piety is shown to hideous she-ogres such as Kali and Durga, ferocious deities of Hinduism which show a Brahmanised separation. These female monsters symbolise the fecundity of Nature. The male element is also worshipped through the symbol of the phallus or *lingam*. The importance given to female forms of divinity indicates a social structure characterised by the matriarchy.

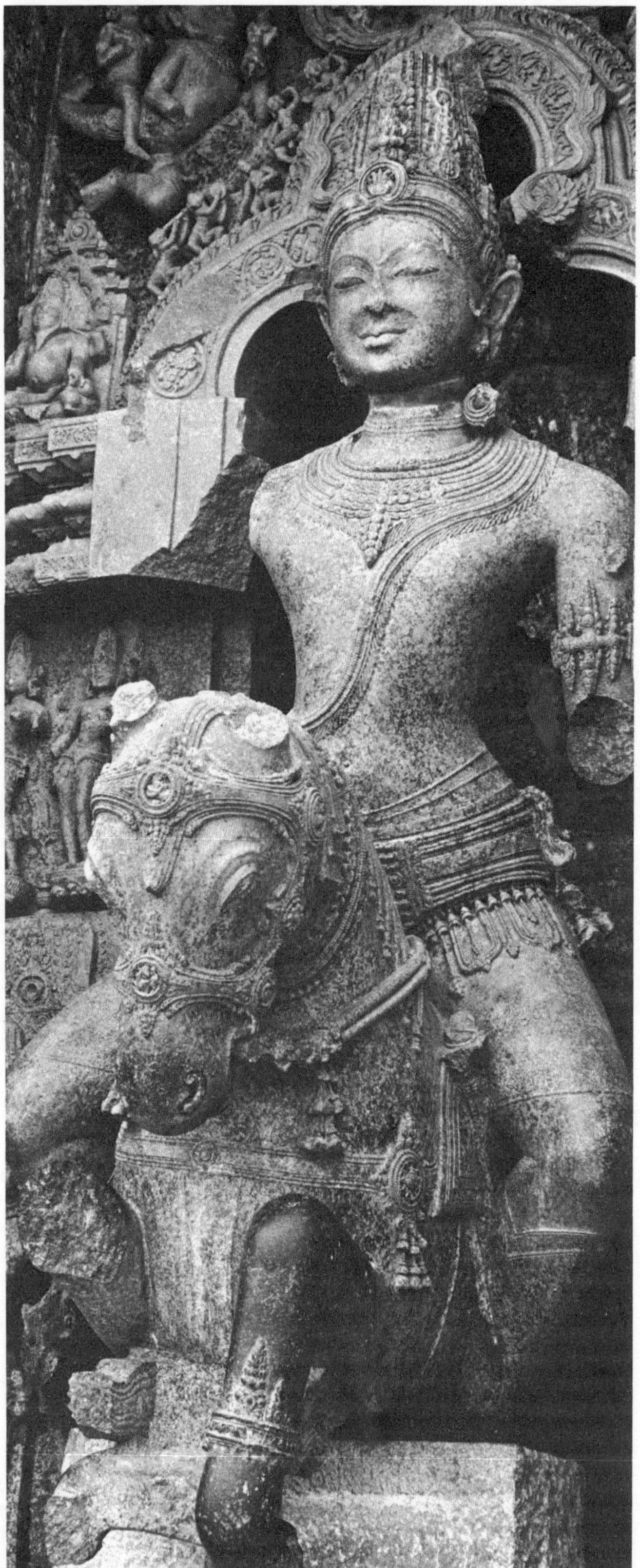

Vishnu in his manifestation as Surya the sun god, riding forth in majesty to bring light to mankind and to nourish and sustain him. According to the Brahma Purana, Surya revealed himself in twelve different forms of which Vishnu was the ninth. The horse was a constant symbol of the sun, the sun god's chariot being drawn by seven horses or mares. Sculpture from the sun temple at Konarak in Orissa, thirteenth century A.D.

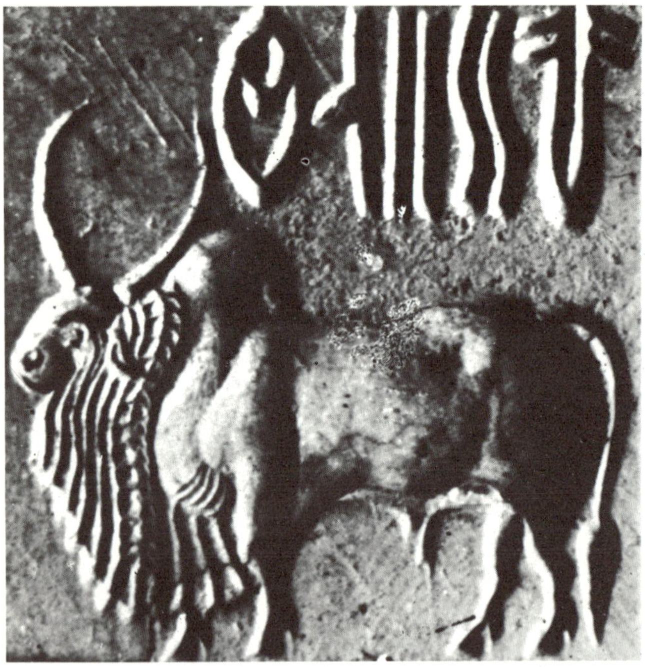

Steatite stamp-seal from Mohenjodaro – one of the two great cities of the pre-Aryan civilisation of the Indus valley. The frequent appearance of the bull in the art of the pre-Aryan period suggests that it was a sacred animal and it was often depicted in front of a censer. The pictographic characters have not yet been deciphered so that an important clue to the mystery of the Indus valley culture still remains to be found. Third millennium B.C.

The Aryan Tradition: the Vedo-Brahmanic Cult. From the beginning of its historical origins the Aryan element is marked by its family organisation. In everything is shown the wish to maintain the moral integrity of the Aryan clans in a conquered country. They long retained the aspect of victorious tribes settled among enemies; they were under military rule and consequently had the agnatic type of family. Living near one another in little republics, the germs of towns, or scattered in rural villages, the Aryan clans desired nothing so earnestly as the continuation and defence of their own traditions.

The result of this was that the social classes of the Aryans of Iran became the *castes* of the Aryans of India, with theoretically water-tight divisions. Religion, in theory a family affair, allowed only one priest – the father or the ancestor invested with authority; and it more and more assumed the aspect of a religion of caste. It remained a family affair, but was modified by different rites, according to whether the family belonged to the warrior nobility, the *Kshatriyas*; or to the priests, the *Brahmans*; or to the common people, the *Vaisyas*, who were entrusted with material affairs. This evolution in the direction of Caste shows the change of Indian Aryanism from the 'Vedic' stage to the 'Brahmanic' stage; although the Vedas were at least compiled if not conceived by a priesthood with a fundamentally Brahmanic spirit.

This forms the basis of religious notions. The Iranian *Asha* – the collection of the stable conditions of cosmic and social order – is changed to the *Dharma*, a social structure as well as an ontological reality, the right and duty of the Castes as well as fidelity to the Aryan ideal.

Each sect came to have its dharma, even those, such as the Jains and Buddhists, who rejected the Brahmanic tradition. There are as many varying mythologies as there are diversities contained within the Dharma.

THE BRAHMANIC DHARMA

Brahmanism is the inheritance of the Vedic tradition as the centre of the beliefs and cults proper to the Aryans of India. We find in it the conceptions proper to the warrior caste, those which especially affect the priestly caste, and popular beliefs. On top of all this came the more abstract mythology which was associated with the Brahmans themselves.

MYTHOLOGY OF THE WARRIOR CASTE

Long before the Brahmanic caste appeared in India, the ancestors of the Indo-Aryans, scattered over western Asia with no fixed abode, worshipped gods of a type befitting a conquering aristocracy. These gods are enumerated as the guarantors of a treaty whose memory has been preserved for us in the clay tablets of Bogaz-Keui, or Pteria, in Cappadocia. It is a treaty of peace, about 1400 B.C., between Mattinaza, king of the Mitanni, and Subbiluliuma, king of the Hittites. The witnesses cited are named Indra, Mitra, Varuna, and Nasatyas. The first three at least are represented as god-kings. They form a contrast to the cult-gods who were defined by the Brahmanic caste in the territory of India.

Indra. The Aryan, who set his yoke on the peoples of dark race, worshipped in Indra the grandiose projection of his own type. This god possesses on a large scale the defects and qualities of a Kshatriya, or at least of a primitive arya – he has their courage but also their intemperance. He cleaves demons asunder, as the Indo-European warriors overcame inferior races. This swashbuckler swills ambrosia, not to live but to get drunk. He is the only one of the Vedic gods who appears human in his characteristics and his morals, and to him are addressed by far the largest number (250) of hymns.

He is armed with arrows and rides in a chariot, like a noble. The myth transformed him into a cosmic force, and he wields a thunderbolt – the lightning – while his chariot becomes the sun. His victory over the dragon Vritra, the Enveloper or the Obstructor, ends with the liberation of the waters, like penned-up cows. To this end he splits mountains, and sends the torrents rushing towards the sea. His achievement determines the fecundity of Nature. By breaking the clouds he gives us back the sun and the dawn. As he supplies both light and water he appears not only as the god of war but as the principle of fertility.

We can estimate the importance of Indra's exploit only when we realise that in India the soil is exposed for months to a burning sun which makes it so hard that it can neither be dug nor sown. Therefore the god who brings the rain is very often invoked in the most flattering hymns. According to the poets of the Vedic epoch, the clouds brought by the sea-winds were enemies, greedy for the treasure hidden within them; they had to be conquered by a superior power before they would shower their wealth of water over the dry land.

Indra is the god of warriors, but also the god of Nature – a kind of Hercules with the aspect of Zeus. He reigns in the sky and triumphs in the storm, when he thunders and lets loose the rain. He is depicted with two arms, one of which holds a thunderbolt (vajra) and the other a bow; or with four arms, two of which hold lances similar to elephant goads. His steed, in fact, is the elephant Airavata, born from the sea of milk.

Indra, the prototype of the caste of nobles, has no legendary connection with gods of another origin. But an effort was made to link him closely with the god Agni. He was supposed to be Agni's twin brother, and therefore son of Heaven and of Earth. His wife – a mere reflection of himself – is Indrani, and his son Sitragupta.

Indra is Svargapati, the lord of heaven; Meghavahana, rider of the clouds; Vajri, the thunderer. He lives on mount Meru, the supposed centre of the earth, to the north of the Himalayas, and therefore between earth and heaven. The story of his battle with the demon shows us how the great Indra, Mahendra, came to deserve the title of powerful, Sakra; with this reservation, that popular inspiration degraded to the level of cunning an efficacy which from the very essence of the god should have been cosmic energy and the strength of a hero.

Indra and the Demon Vritra. Once upon a time there was a powerful Brahman by the name of Tvashtri who did not like Indra. To deprive Indra of his throne the Brahman created a son, and strengthened him with his own power. This son had three heads. With the first he read the Vedas; with the second he fed himself; and with the third he seemed to observe every inch of the horizon. He surpassed all men by the ardour of his asceticism and the pious humility of his heart. Indra became uneasy at the spectacle of the daily increase of a power which seemed destined to absorb the universe – and he decided to intervene. The most seductive girls of heaven were sent to tempt the young ascetic, but in vain. Indra

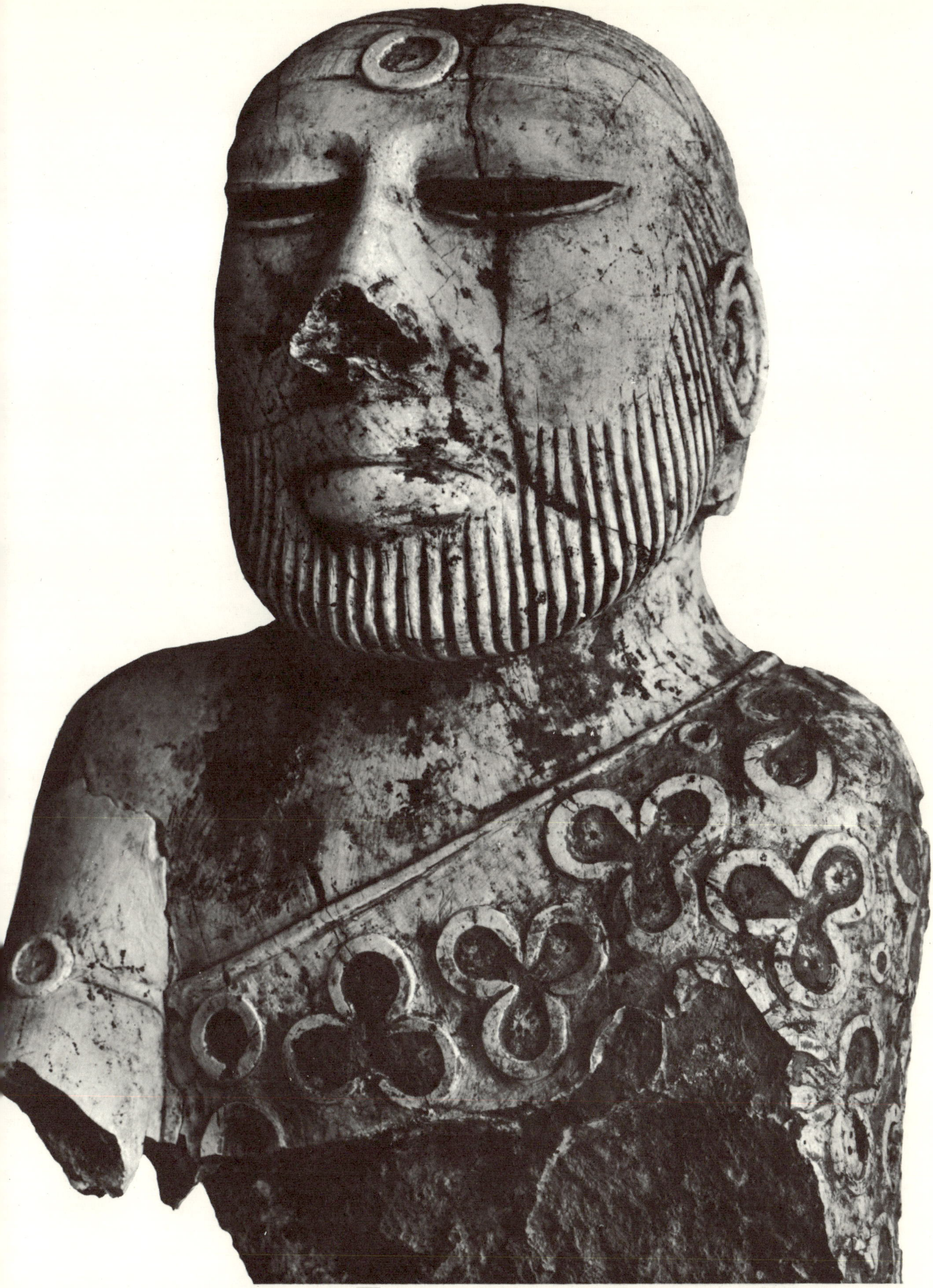

Steatite bust of a priest-king or deity from Mohenjodaro. The Indus valley civilisation was highly organised and there is evidence to suggest that it may have been ruled by priests or priest-kings like other civilisations of the same period. Scholars believe that much of its religion has survived in Hinduism – the darker side of the Siva cult, for example, being much older than the Aryan creeds which supposedly displaced it.

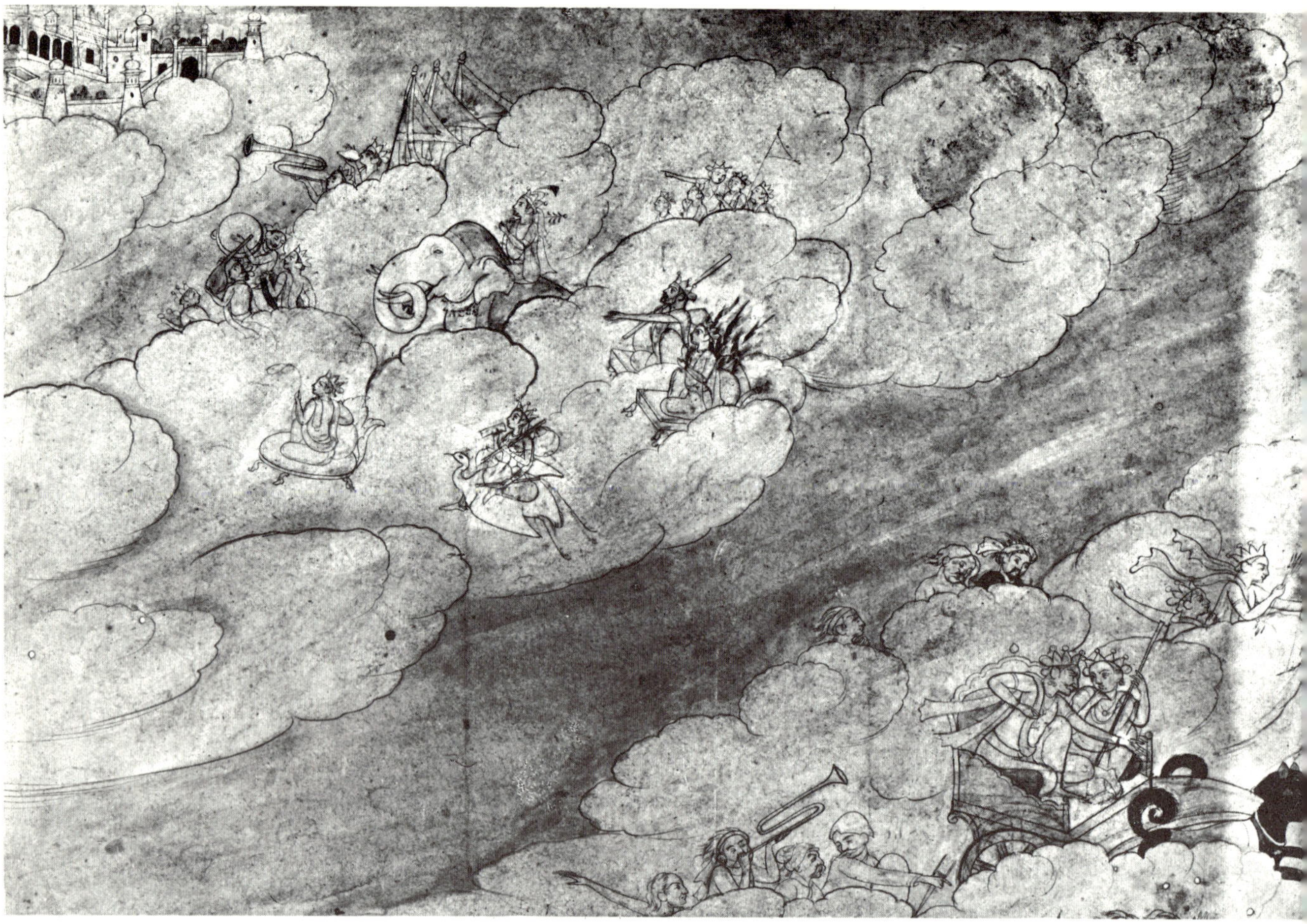

Indra and his queen Indrani enthroned in his movable heaven of Swarga among the clouds of Mount Meru. Beside him is his elephant Airavata while round about are the beatified figures of valorous warriors and groups of Apsaras and Gandharvas – heavenly nymphs and musicians. Originally the great god of the Aryan warrior caste, Indra was later relegated to the second rank but he remained the chief of the lesser gods. Rajput painting, nineteenth century A.D.

then decided that the youthful sage must die, and smote him with his thunderbolt. But even in death the body of the young Brahman radiated such glorious light over the world that Indra's fears were not calmed. He ordered a passing wood-cutter to cut off the dead man's three heads – and at that very instant great flights of doves and other birds burst forth.

To avenge his son, Tvashtri brought to life a demon which he named Vritra. This demon was so huge his head reached to the sky. He challenged Indra to fight. A horrible battle followed, and the demon was victorious. He seized the king of gods, cast him into his jaw, and swallowed him. The terrified gods did not know what to do. They had the inspiration to gag the demon, and as soon as he opened his mouth Indra contracted his body, jumped through the gaping jaws, and the battle started up again more furiously than ever. But the god was compelled to fly. In his humiliation he consulted the Rishi, and they all went together to get the advice of the god Vishnu who told them to make peace through the intervention of the Rishi, adding mysteriously that perhaps one day he would incarnate himself in a weapon which would slay the demon Vritra.

The Rishi succeeded in persuading Vritra to a reconciliation with his enemy, but with one condition. 'Give me your solemn promise,' he said, 'that Indra will never attack me with any weapon of wood, stone or iron, nor with anything dry, nor with anything wet. Promise too that he will never attack me by day nor by night.' The pact was agreed to.

However, Indra secretly meditated revenge. One evening he was on the sea-shore, and saw his enemy at no great distance; and suddenly he thought: 'The sun is setting on the horizon, darkness is coming on, but it is not yet night and it is not altogether day. If I could kill the demon now, between day and night, I should not have broken my promise.' While he mused he saw a vast column of foam rise from the sea, and Indra realised that it was neither dry nor wet nor stone nor iron nor wood. He seized the foam and hurled it at the demon who fell dead on the shore, for it was Vishnu who as he had promised had entered into this strange weapon, and nobody can resist him. The gods rejoiced and Nature with them; the sky was filled with light and a soft breeze began to blow; even the beasts of the field rejoiced. But Indra felt that he carried the burden of a great sin, for he had slain a Brahman.

Gods of Universal Power: Mitra and Varuna. Mitra and Varuna, made in India the sons of Aditi or Adityas, form a dyad. They are called kings (*Raja*), possessors of that power, *kshatram*, which forms the essence of the Kshatriya caste. They are endowed with universal power (samraj). Yet they scarcely possess human shape, which puts them in contrast to Indra. They have magical powers, *maya* and *asuras*, a term which comprehends not only the mysterious powers of certain devas (or gods) but the evil influence of demons.

Mitra and Varuna did not institute but maintain universal order, *rita*: that is their essential function. For this reason the former presides over friendship and ratifies contracts, while the latter looks after oaths. To carry out their functions as guardians and witnesses they must see, or shine, for in primitive minds these two ideas are interchangeable. And so one sees or shines during the day – Mitra or the Sun; the other at night – Varuna or the Moon. Their other characteristics are less significant and more arbitrary.

The Indian Mitra coincides with the Iranian Mithra, except that the former, unlike the latter, is not closely associated with a brother. But the Persians frequently linked his name with that of the great Ahura (asura) Mazda. From this standpoint Varuna should appear to us as an Indian transposition of the god preached by Zoroaster.

Nothing escapes him. He restrains with his bonds those who break rules. He rewards and punishes, taking into account intention and penitence. He directs the physical as well as the moral world. His decrees (vrata) regulate the motions of the heavens and the circulation of waters – two closely connected facts. Of course some ave exaggerated the apparent identity of Varuna with Uranus, s well as the supposedly marine character of Varuna. But the egulator of the seasons also controls the system of rains. This od presides over the sky, the air, and the waters. The wind is his reath, the stars are his eyes. He sees everything going on in the vorld, including every secret thought.

Shining with a 'sombre light' Varuna is especially linked with he moon, that reservoir of sacrificial liquid, Soma. He presides ver the care of this ambrosia throughout the alternating waxings nd wanings of the planet. Moreover, the moon is the abiding lace of the dead, and so Varuna shares with Yama, the first person vho died, the title of King of the Dead.

Varuna is represented as a white man riding on a sea monster, he *makara*, and holding a lasso – an allusion to his functions as udge. Hence his name of Pasi, as well as the epithets given him s the supremely wise, Prasetas, or as lord of the waters, Jalapati, adapati, Amburaja. It seems he fell in love with the nymph, Urvasi, t the same time as the Sun, Surya, and by her they had a son, Agastya, famous as an ascetic.

Lord of physical and moral order, Varuna is omnipresent. 'He ollows the track of the birds which fly in the sky like the wake of a ship' ploughing through the waves (*Rig-Veda*, I. 25); and knows he past and the future. He is a witness of every action, he is the 'third party' present at every gathering. No authority is equal to his.

Nasatyas or Asvins: Ribhus. There are almost as many opinions as experts in the interpretation of the last pair of gods mentioned as watching over the Mitanni. Their Vedic name most commonly used is 'the knights' or 'the horsemen', two golden or honey-coloured twins. They bring up the morning light of the sky, making a path through the clouds for the Dawn-goddess, Ushas. At the evening twilight they play a similar part, and perhaps they must be identified with the Morning and Evening star.

Their equivalence to the Greek Dioscuri cannot be called in question; they are Indo-European, and not solely Indian. They bear witness to that knightly ideal of the conquering aristocrats who introduced the horse to central and southern Asia.

Their name Nasatya, which can be interpreted from the root-form *nas*, meaning 'to save', seems to be an allusion to their mission of beneficence. They are the doctors of the gods, the friends of the sick and unfortunate. They heal the blind, and the lame, and give back their youth to the old. They are kindly disposed to love and marriage.

Their parents were the Sun and the cloud-goddess, Saranyu. As wife they have in common Surya, the daughter of Savitri, another aspect of solar light. Their whip scatters the dew. Their three-wheeled chariot was made by the triad of Rhibus, sons of the 'good archer', Sudhanvan. The name 'rhibu' implies genii skilled in constructing. They possess their own horses and prepare the equipment of the warrior gods, and they revolve chiefly round Indra.

A graceful legend attests the 'chivalrous' character of the Asvins. In spite of their beauty and their beneficence they found that entry to heaven was forbidden them by the gods, on account of their humble birth. And this is how the wealthy Syavana, who received eternal youth from them, persuaded Indra to allow them among the gods. This old Risi had a beautiful young wife, Sukanya. The twins watched her when she was bathing and said to her: 'O woman of delicious limbs, why did thy father bestow thee on such an old man, on the edge of the grave? Thou art radiant as summer lightning, we have seen none like thee even in heaven. Even without any ornament thou art an embellishment to the whole forest. How much more beautiful wouldst thou be in rich robes and splendid jewels! Abandon thine ancient husband and choose one of us, for youth does not endure.' She replied: 'I am devoted to my husband, Syavana.' They insisted: 'We will make thy husband young and beautiful, and then thou shalt choose which of us three thou wilt take as thy lord.' Sukanya repeated these words to her husband, who gave his consent. He bathed in the lake along with the Asvins, and all three emerged young and radiant. Sukanya, seeing all three alike, hesitated long in her choice, but when she finally recognised her husband she refused all except him. Syavana, delighted that he had kept his wife as well as receiving youth and beauty, persuaded Indra to allow the two horsemen to share the sacrifices made to the gods and to enjoy 'soma' with them.

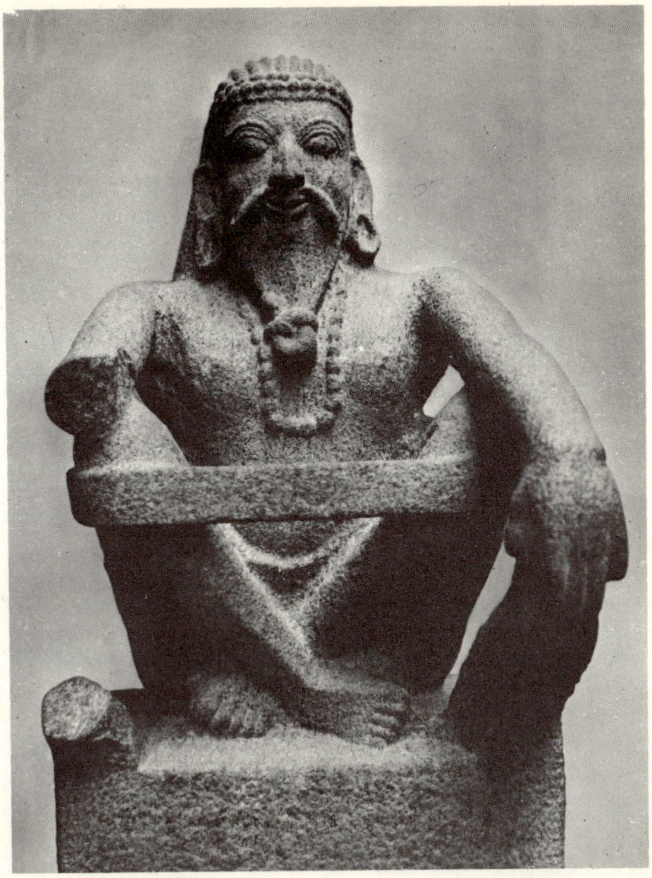

Agastya. The son of Varuna and the nymph Urvasi, Agastya was famous as an ascetic and was one of the great sages of Indian belief appearing in both canonical and epic stories as far back as Vedic times. Unrestricted to any particular period, he was, however, especially celebrated as the friend and protector of Rama whom he received in his hermitage on Mount Kunjara. His father was invoked as early as 1,400 B.C. Statue, eighth to ninth centuries A.D.

Myths of Royalty. With the historical times which succeeded the age of the Vedas we find following on the religion of Indra and the Adityas certain Kshatriyan rites which gave rise to myths of supreme power. The Brahmans were careful to take part in these rites, in order to lose no occasion of influencing the rival caste. Whether it was a matter of the frequent investitures or the rare consecration of a king, the ceremonies of the aristocracy were intended to endow the beneficiaries with the authority of the noble or of the king, and as every divinity tends to become the absolute god, so every petty king imagined himself a ruler without an equal. Hence the obsessive myth of the *cakravartin*, the controller of the universal Dharma, a sovereign on an equality with a demiurge. Here may be seen the most decisive influence of Persia on India, among so many fundamental and permanent affinities. The cakravartin unites the fascinating legitimacy of Varuna with the vigour of Indra.

The asvamedha or horse-sacrifice was the most solemn of these rites. The slaying of a sacred horse, the peculiarly Aryan animal and constant symbol of the Sun, marked the taking possession, by the exceptionally powerful sovereign who carried out the rite, of the four cardinal points – hence, of everything. A quasi-coupling of the animal with the queen founded in addition the fecundity of Nature. Nothing was spared to give splendour to a ceremony whereby henceforth a potentate became identified with the solar body, the heart of the universe. The Kshatriya thus became the centre of the world.

MYTHOLOGY OF THE PRIESTLY CASTE

Although its chief origins are derived from ancient Aryan practice, the mythology of the priestly caste corresponds to a later phase. In contrast to the simplicity of the religion of Indra, that of the Brahmans, the religion of Agni, allowed of endless developments and variations.

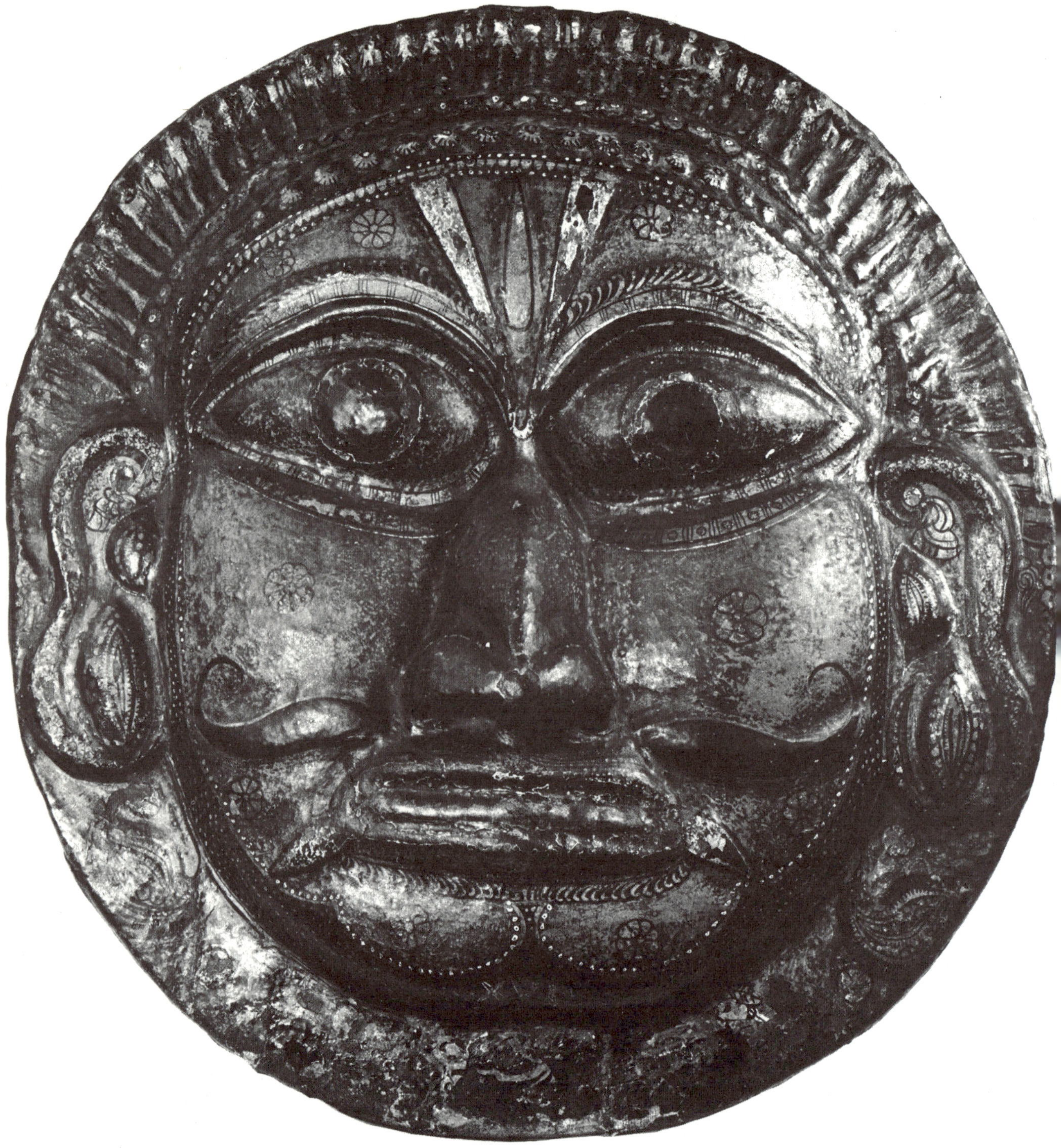

Surya, the sun god. One of the three great gods of the Vedic period, Surya was said to have a countenance so dazzling that his wife could no longer bear it and was forced to leave him. In order to enable her to return to her husband her father, the divine artificer Visvakarma, shaved off an eighth of the god's brilliance later using it to fashion the weapons of the gods. Wooden shield. Horniman Museum.

The Religion of Agni. Agni is a personification of fire, which had such immense prestige in the esteem of the Indo-Europeans, especially the Iranians. It started as the instrument of the cult, and became its object. The same flame wavers and crackles on the hearth, in the burning sunshine and in the flash of lightning. So Agni, like Indra, but in another sense, became the equivalent of the starry hearth-fire of the world and of the lightning which hurls down rain on the thirsty earth. They both, from this point of view, symbolise the relationship of Father Heaven and Mother Earth, which haunted Indo-European imagination.

The anthropomorphic transformation of Agni scarcely started, but his ritualistic descriptions occupy a privileged place in the Veda and the Brahmanas – the face smeared with butter, the wild hair, swift tongues, sharpened jaws, golden teeth, are all aspects of the flames on which the oblation is thrown; the diverse nature which is described both as eagle and bull; Agni is born from the rubbing together of two pieces of wood, the 'Aranis', and the poets marvel at the sight of a being so alive leaping from dry dead wood. His very growth is miraculous. Since his parents are incapable of providing for him, he devours them as soon as he is born, and then feeds on the oblations of clarified butter poured into his mouths of devouring flame. Agni also dwells in the waters and in the sky – under the form of lightning he tears asunder the cloud whose beneficent waters will fertilise the earth, and it is he who flames at the heart of the sun. He has many shapes, he plays the part of mediator – let us say mythically, of messenger – for the gods as well as for mankind. He despises nobody, since he is the guest of every hearth. He is the intimate protector of the home, he is the domestic priest, yet reconciles the various priestly functions. He watches with a thousand eyes over Man who feeds him and brings him offerings, protects him against his enemies and grants him immortality. In a funerary hymn Agni is requested to rewarm with his flames the immortal being which subsists in the dead man, and to lead him to the world of the Just. Agni carries a man through calamities as a ship carries him over the sea. The wealth of all worlds is under his power, and that is why he is invoked to obtain abundant food, prosperity, and all temporal goods generally. He is also invoked for the forgiveness of sins committed under the sway of passing folly.

He is called Agni, son of Heaven and of Earth, or the son of Brahma, or of Kasyapa and of Aditi, or of Angiras, king of the Manes. He is the husband of Svaha, and by her has three sons: Pavaka, Pavamana and Suci. Again, he is described as a red man with three legs, seven arms and black eyes and hair. He rides on a ram, and wears the Brahmanic cord with a garland of fruits. Flames spout from his mouth, and his body sends forth seven rays of light. His attributes are the axe, wood, the bellows (a fan), the torch, and the sacrificial spoon.

Agni made the sun, and filled the night with stars. The gods fear him and do him homage, for he knows the secrets of mortals.

According to the ritual directions, three different kinds of fire should be lighted – to the East, the ahavaniya or vaisvanara fire, for offerings to the gods; to the South, the dakshina (narasamsa) fire for the cult of the Manes; and to the West, the garhapatya fire for the cooking of food and for offerings. These hearths represent respectively the sky with the sun, the intermediate air (abode of the dead and domain of the winds), and the earth. The sacrificial rites symbolise the correspondences between these three worlds. Numerous myths express these fundamental correlations. We may note that of the *Bhrigus*, aerial gods of the storm who bring heaven and earth into communication; and the myth of *Matarisvan*, who receives and transmits the fire of heaven. The Bhrigus and the Matarisvan represent the wind, so closely connected with fire which is sometimes considered its cause and sometimes its effect.

According to a later tradition (Visnu Purana) Bhrigu was one of the first wise men, and ancestor of the family which bears his name; the word itself suggests fire, since it means 'born of flames'. Legend relates that one day Bhrigu cursed Agni. A woman named Puloma was betrothed to a demon, and Bhrigu seeing she was beautiful fell in love with her and, after marrying her according to the Vedic rites, secretly abducted her. But thanks to Agni's information the demon discovered the place where the young woman promised to him was hidden, and brought her back to his dwelling. Furious with Agni for helping the demon, Bhrigu cursed him, saying: 'Henceforth thou shalt eat of all things.' Agni demanded of Bhrigu the reason for this curse since he had only told the demon the truth. He pointed out that if a man is questioned and tells a lie he is cast into hell, along with seven generations of his ancestors and seven generations of his children. Moreover, the man who fails to give information is equally guilty. And Agni went on to say: 'I too can hurl curses but I respect the Brahmans and I control my anger. In truth I am the mouth of the gods and of the ancestors. When clarified butter is offered them, they receive it thanks to me, their mouth, so how can you tell me to eat all things?' Hearing these words, Bhrigu agreed to change his curse and said: 'As the sun purifies all Nature with his light and heat, so Agni shall purify everything which enters his flames.'

Soma. Another polymorphic deity. But this made him all the more efficient and venerable.

Soma (Haoma of the Avesta) is first and foremost a plant, an essential part of the ancient sacrificial offerings. It is also the juice of the plant, obtained by squeezing it between two mill-stones. Then it is golden nectar, the drink of the gods – a precious ambrosia which symbolises immortality and ensures victory over death to all who drink of it.

The myths show Soma in a multitude of different forms. Turn by turn he is a celestial bull, a bird, an embryo, a giant of the waters, the king of plants, the divine power which cures all evils, the dwelling place of Manes, and even the prince of poets! He is even the source of Inspiration and the principle of life. He rewards heroism and virtue. He is also the link between heaven and mankind. But very frequently (above all at a somewhat later epoch) Soma personifies the moon. Certain passages in the later Vedic hymns, or the Puranas, mark the transition between Soma considered as ambrosia and Soma as the moon. 'May the god Soma, he who is called the moon, liberate me.' Sometimes the two conceptions are confounded:

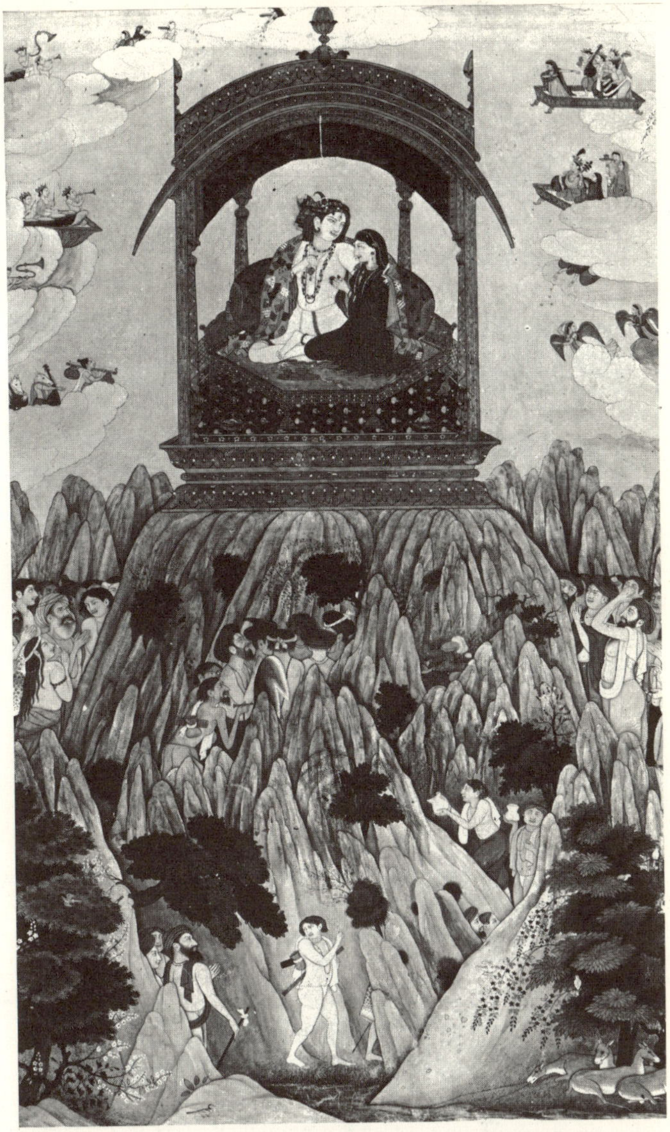

Siva and Parvati enthroned in their heaven on Mount Kailasa. Pilgrims climb the mountain with their offerings while gods and sages honour the divine couple. The daughter of Himavan, the god of the Himalayas, Parvati is the benign and gentle aspect of Siva's wife and is generally represented seated beside her husband discoursing on love or metaphysics. Though very beautiful she had first to win his love by practising great austerities. Kangra painting, eighteenth century A.D.

'Thanks to Soma the Adityas are powerful; thanks to Soma the earth is large; and Soma is placed in the midst of the stars. When the plant is crushed, he who drinks of it considers it as soma. But no one can drink what the priests consider as soma.'

Soma, the moon (the name in Sanskrit is masculine), was born from the churning of the sea. (This episode is related on page 379.) The twenty-seven lunar stations are his wives. They are the daughters of Daksha (also father-in-law of Siva and Kasyapa). The phenomenon of the periodical waning of the moon is sometimes explained by the fact that the gods, during its periods of regular rotation, drink in turn the soma it contains; but the waning is more usually attributed to a curse of Daksha. Daksha thought that Soma was too exclusively devoted to one of his daughters, Rohini, and condemned his son-in-law to die of consumption; but thanks to the urgent entreaties of his wives Soma's punishment was made periodical and not eternal. Another legend makes Soma spring from the eye of the wise man Atri, son of Brahma.

After the Rajasuya sacrifice celebrated at his coronation by a universal king with his subject princes, whereby his domination was sanctified, Soma looked upon his immense empire and was intoxicated with the glory which he had obtained. He became arrogant, and so licentious that he dared to carry off Tara, the wife of Brihaspati, the teacher of the gods. In vain Brihaspati tried to recover his wife, in vain Brahma ordered Soma to return Tara to

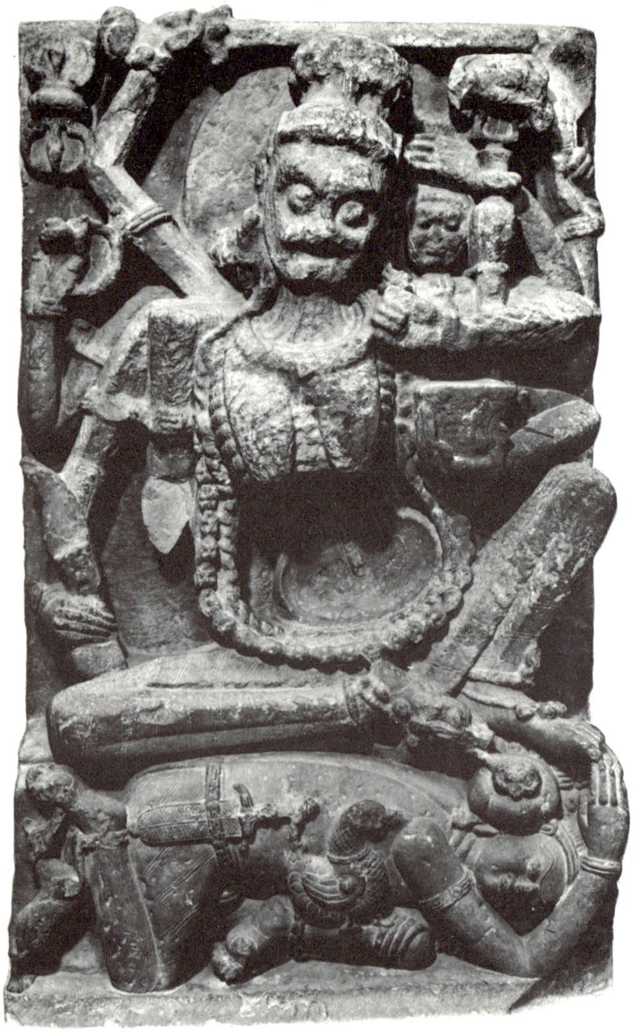

Kali Ma, the black mother. The fiercest and most bloodthirsty form assumed by Siva's consort, Kali is depicted naked to the hips wearing her ear-rings made of corpses, her necklace of snakes and her girdle of skulls. Above her head she brandishes a sword while in one of her left hands she grasps a giant's head. She is seated on the back of a crouching man – possibly her husband Siva.
Sculpture from Orissa, eleventh century A.D.

her husband. A great war broke out, with the gods on one side led by Tara, and on the other side Soma aided by the demons. Finally Tara appealed for protection to Brahma who compelled Soma to release his fair captive. But when she returned Brihaspati perceived that she was with child, and refused to receive her before her child was born. Miraculously obeying these injunctions the child was born at once. He was so radiant with power and beauty that both Soma and Brihaspati claimed him as their son. They questioned Tara, but her confusion prevented her from answering. The child became indignant and was about to utter a curse. But Brahma again intervened, quieted the child, and said to Tara: 'Tell me, my child, is he the son of Brihaspati or of Soma?' 'Of Soma', she confessed with a blush. As soon as she had spoken the Lord of constellations with radiant countenance embraced his son, saying: 'That is well, my son; indeed, you are intelligent.' And that is why he was called Buddha. Soma's son is considered as the founder of the lunar dynasties. He must not be confused with the Buddha who is claimed by the Buddhists. They are two quite different persons.

And now come other gods of priestly origin, so many personified aspects of ritual efficacy.

Savitar (Savitri). This god is the principle of movement which causes the sun to shine, the waters and the winds to circulate. Whoever acts has a share in him – Indra, Varuna, Mitra, and especially Surya, the Sun. As the universal motive power he is the equal of Prajapati, Puchan and Tvashtar. It is obvious how useful such an intermediary would be in the magical work of sacrifice.

Savitar has golden eyes, golden hands, and tongues of gold. He rides in a chariot drawn by glittering steeds with white hoofs. His golden arms are extended over all heaven in movements of benediction, infusing life into all creatures. He is the King of heaven, the other gods follow him, and he bestows immortality upon them. He is prayed to for the remission of sins, and to lead souls to the dwelling of the just. To him is devoted the *Gavatri*, the most sacred text of the Vedas, according to the Hindus. Every true Brahman should chant it when he rises, and this formula is supposed to exercise its magical powers on behalf of the reciter.

Surya. Like Savitar he stands for the Sun and is often identified with him, but he is a divinity of rather a different character, especially in the Puranas. He is described as a dark red man, with three eyes and four arms. Two of his hands hold water-lilies, the third blesses, and with the fourth he encourages his worshippers. Sometimes he is seated on a red lotus, and rays of glory spread from his body. In the Vishnu Purana (Book III, Chapter II), Surya marries Sanjna, the daughter of Visvakarma. After bearing him three children, she was so exhausted by the perpetual dazzling lavished by her husband that she had to leave him, and before going she arranged for Shaya (the Shade) to take her place. After several years Surya noticed the change, and went off to look for Sanjna. After various adventures he brought her home, but to prevent any further flights his father-in-law took away an eighth of Surya's splendour. Visvakarma, a skilled worker, made good use of this fragment of shining energy by using it to forge the disk of Vishnu, the trident of Siva, the lance of Karttikeya the god of war, and the weapons of Kuvera the god and guardian of wealth.

A passage in the Brahma Purana alludes to Surya's twelve names, each of which was followed by special epithets, as if they referred to twelve different solar divinities:

'The first form of the sun is Indra, lord of the gods and destroyer of their enemies; the second is Dhata, creator of all things; the third is Parjanya, who dwells in the clouds and with his rays sends down water on the earth; the fourth is Tvashta, who lives in all corporal forms; the fifth is Puchan, who provides food for all living things; the sixth is Aryama who brings sacrifices to fruition; the seventh derives his name from alms-giving and rejoices all beggars by his gifts; the eighth is named Vivasvan and causes good digestion; the ninth is Vishnu who constantly manifests himself to destroy the enemies of the gods; the tenth is Ansuman who keeps all vital organs in good health; the eleventh is Varuna who dwells in the heart of the waters and gives life to the universe; and the twelfth is Mitra who lives in the orb of the moon for the welfare of the three worlds. Such are the twelve splendours of the Sun, the supreme Spirit, who by their means plunges into the universe and irradiates even the secret souls of men.'

Ushas. This goddess, who symbolises the dawn, has been sung especially by the Vedic poets, and the hymns addressed to her are among the most beautiful in the Vedas.

She is the daughter of Heaven and the sister of Night. She is related to Varuna. Sometimes the Sun is spoken of as her husband, or Fire as her lover. In some hymns Ushas is praised as mother of the Sun. The Asvins are her friends. At one time Indra was thought of as her creator, but at another time he is hostile to her, and destroys her chariot with a thunderbolt.

Ushas travels in a shining chariot drawn by cows or reddish horses. The poets liken her sometimes to a charming girl dressed by her mother's care, and sometimes to a dancing-girl covered with jewels. Or she is a lovely girl coming out of her bath, or a wife dressed in magnificent clothes to meet her husband.

Ever-smiling, confident in the irresistible power of her charms, she moves forward half-opening her veils. She drives away darkness, and reveals treasures hidden in its folds. She gives light to the world even to the most distant horizon. She is the life and the health of all things. It is thanks to her that the birds can take flight in the morning.

Like the young mistress of a house, she awakens all creatures and orders them to their different work. She performs a service to the gods by waking those who intend to worship them and to light the fires of sacrifice. She is besought only to waken the good and the generous, and to let the wicked sleep.

She is young, she is born anew every morning, and yet old, since she is immortal. While generation after generation passes away, the dawn exists for ever.

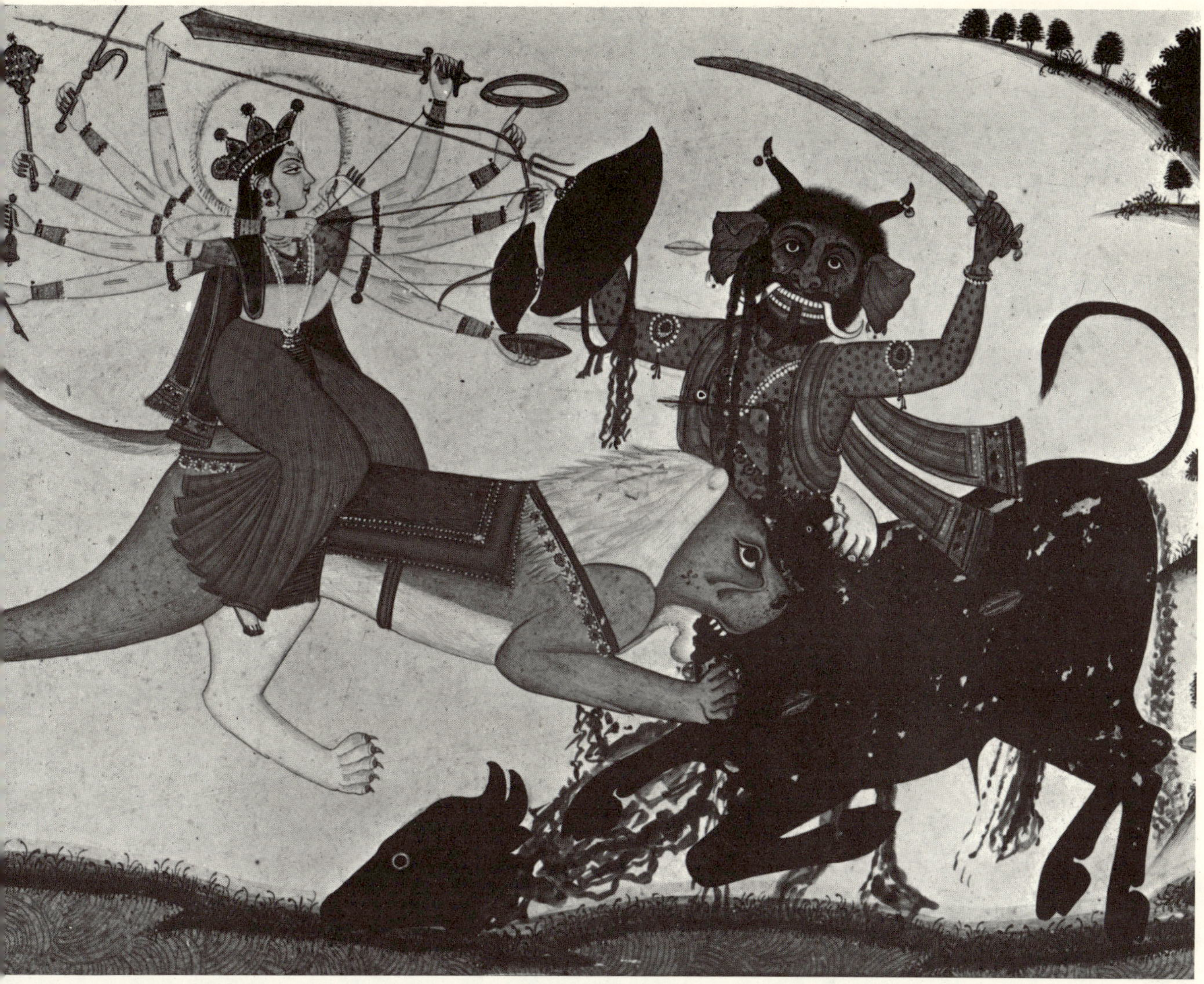

Durga slaying the demon Mahesasura. Durga, 'the inaccessible', was another of the fierce forms adopted by Siva's wife. Unlike Kali she was young and beautiful and was born fully grown as a warrior goddess whose purpose was to destroy demons, each of her ten arms being provided with weapons borrowed from the gods. Here, seated on her tiger, she attacks the demon Mahesasura who was threatening to dethrone the gods. Kangra painting, eighteenth century A.D.

Puchan. He brings all things, moving and immobile, into relationship with one another. For example, he carries out marriage. He protects, and he liberates. He provides food, and he fattens cattle. He must obviously be the reflection of some ancient fecundity rite. He often travels, he knows the roads, he is the guide and patron of travellers. He also leads the spirits of the dead into the other world. A hymn in the *Rig-Veda* invokes him as follows:

'Lead us, O Puchan, on our way. Son of the liberator, save us from agony; do thou walk before us. Drive away the evil and ravening wolf which seeks for us. Keep our road free from robbers, and set your foot on the burning weapons of the wretched exploiter, whoever he may be. O wise and miracle-powered Puchan, grant us your help as you gave it to our forefathers. O god through whom are all benedictions, your attribute is a gold lance – let us win riches easily. Make smooth our path when we travel. Give us strength. Lead us into rich pastures. May adversity never come our way... Feed and encourage us, and fill our bellies.'

And in another hymn:

'O Puchan, may we meet with a wise man who will guide us at once, saying: "Behold your way."'

'May Puchan take care of our cows and protect our horses. May he give us food. Come to us, O shining god, O liberator, may we meet together.'

Prajapati. Prajapati, the master of created beings, and Visvakarma, the universal agent, embody potency in a less concrete form, and in the Brahmanas are almost identical. They became independent only through a progress in abstraction, but Visvakarma had once been an epithet applied to Indra and the Sun; while Prajapati had been applied to Savitar and Soma. Visvakarma ordered all things and sees everything; he made the foundations and the distinctions of everything; Prajapati is a father and the protector of those who beget. Gods and asuras are his children. A loftier abstraction makes him the absolute, Brahma, and even the indefinable absolute, whose sole fitting name is 'Who?' (Ka).

Brihaspati. The final form is Bramanaspati, the master of magical power involved in ritual formula – he is the priesthood itself. This god is called the chaplain, the brahman, the brahmanic priest. In many places he is confused with Agni, and a special correlation links him with the fire of the South, the fire of the Manes, probably because of the importance attached by Hindus to funeral rites.

In Brahmanic literature, properly so called, which is later than the Vedic hymns, especially in the Brahmanas and Upanishads, the 'master of the Formula' and 'the master of created things' acquired a cosmological value. With these two entities we leave the pantheon and mythology, and touch the beginnings of metaphysics. Prajapati's origin is not a god but Thought (Taittiriya Brah. II, 2, 9, 10) or the Brahman (Brihadaranyaka Up., V, 5, 1); his demiurgic activity consists in begetting gods (*ibid.*) or creatures. And since they 'remained vaguely united he entered into them through form. That is why they say: "Prajapati is form." Then he entered into them by their name. And that is why they say: "Prajapati is the name."' (Tait. Br. II, 2, 7, 1).

The following divinities take us back to the Vedas.

Aditi. She is the mother of the Adityas, Mitra and Varuna. Literally Aditi means 'free from bonds'. No doubt this refers to the boundless

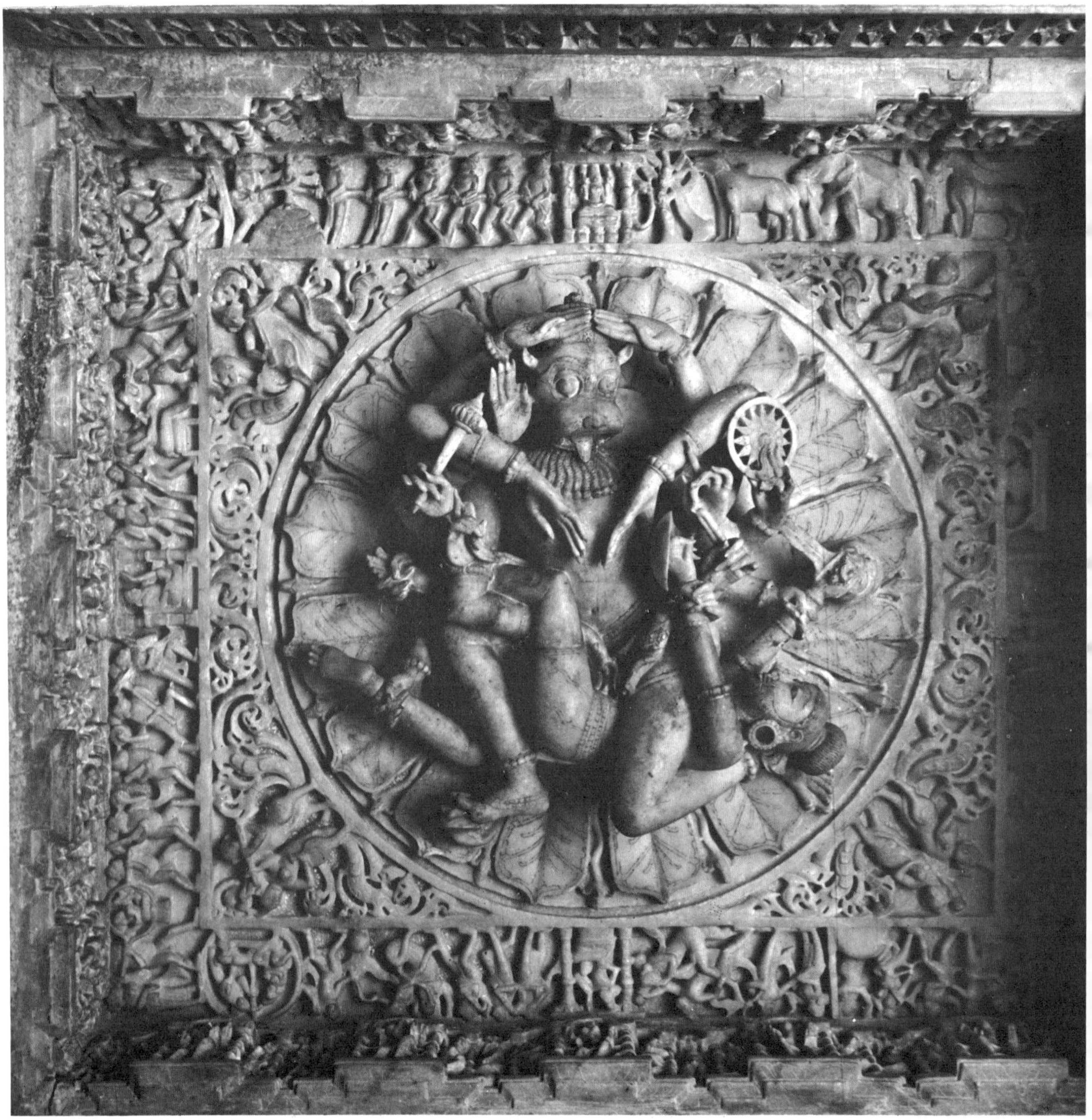

Vishnu seizing Hiranyakasipu. The god has assumed the form of a lion-headed man in order to slay the demon-king who has exiled the gods from heaven and attempted to murder his own son, a faithful devotee of the god. Hiranyakasipu was the first of three incarnations of the demon Ravana who could only obtain his redemption by dying at Vishnu's hands. Carved stone ceiling panel from the Vimlashan temple, Mount Abu. Eleventh century A. D.

sky, which is the abode of her 'children' sun and moon, night and day. The historian is tempted to rank this mother as later than her children, for they became Indian, while she is no older than 'Indianity'.

'Aditi is the sky, the air ... all gods, the five nations (Aryan). Aditi is the past and the future.

'The august mother of the supporters of justice (Mitra and Varuna), the wife of Order, we call you to our aid, O powerful, ever young, far-spreading, kind shelterer, good leader, Aditi!

'The solid earth and the sinless heavens, kind shelterer and good leader, Aditi, we call upon you. The divine ship with strong rowers which never sinks, may we meet with it, and free from sin attain salvation!'

Tvashtar. The special characteristic of Tvashtar is a hand at work. This 'worker' forged the thunderbolt of Indra as well as that cup reserved for ambrosia, the moon. He is called the universal exciter in all forms (savita visvarupa) and so he becomes the equivalent of Savitar, and therefore of solar nature.

The other gods are Nature gods and need no analysis or specia explanation: Vata or Vayu, the Wind; Parjanya, the Rain; Apa the Waters; Prithivi, the Earth.

POPULAR MYTHOLOGY: THE DEMONS

The Indian conception of demons is special to them, and moreove has many different aspects.

To start with, the line separating demons from gods is not ver clear. Generally 'Devas' are translated as 'gods' and 'Asuras' a 'demons', but in point of fact both are essentially beings gifted wit a remarkable and mysterious power which is manifested simultaneously by moral and physical attributes. For instance, Varun who enjoys a remarkable moral prestige is ranked an 'asura' whil Indra, unquestionably less refined, is a 'deva'. Surya, the sun, i called 'the asura-chaplain of the Devas'.

In the later Artharva Veda the word 'asura' is applied only t demons, and henceforth that is the generally received meaning. In Iran on the contrary the same term is used to mean the divinity, Ahura. Henceforth the Devas and the Asuras are often seen at war with one another.

According to the Satapatha Brahmana, Prajapati is their common ancestor. But the Devas rejected falsehood and chose the truth, while the Asuras rejected truth and chose falsehood. As they spoke only truth, the gods appeared to be weak; but in the end they became strong and attained prosperity. The Asuras at first by their lies won riches, but in the end found destruction. Another legend says that the Asuras when making sacrifice put the offerings in their own mouths, whereas the gods offer them to one another.

In spite of their rivalry with the Asuras, the Devas were glad to accept the help of their enemies for the churning of the sea, and at this task the demons showed quite as much skill and energy as the gods. (See page 379.)

Generally speaking, it is clear that the popular deities, only slightly Aryan and usually not Aryan at all, were described by the Aryans as demoniacal. Some of them have remained demons until our own times. Others were incorporated sooner or later into the Brahmanic pantheon, almost always retaining certain peculiarities which show their origin. For instance, the terrible forms of the cult of Siva in his aspect as destroyer, the fact that the demons are among his sectaries, and that he is sometimes called 'lord of demons' (Bhutapati) seem to point to a non-Aryan origin of his deity. The legend of his marriage with the daughter of Daksha is further confirmation of this hypothesis.

Daksha, one of the Prajapatis or lords of creation, out of vanity became violently hostile to Siva. Daksha's daughter, Sati, a real incarnation of feminine devotion and piety, had secretly given her heart to the cult of the condemned god. When the time came for her betrothal her father ordered a Svayamara (the ceremony where a king's daughter chose her husband from the assembled suitors) and purposely omitted to invite Siva. When Sati came forward, holding in her hand the garland of flowers which she was to cast round the neck of her chosen husband, she uttered a supreme invocation to the god she loved. 'If it is true that I am called Sati,' she exclaimed, throwing her flowers in the air. 'O Siva, take my garland!' And immediately Siva appeared, with her garland on his shoulders.

Yet later on this union was considered a mis-alliance. When Daksha went to war with his son-in-law, he called him 'the god with the monkey's eyes who married my daughter with her gazelle's eyes'. 'It was against my will', he says further, 'that I gave my daughter to this sullied personage, the abolisher of rites and destroyer of boundaries... He frequents horrible cemeteries, accompanied by crowds of spirits and ghosts, looking like a madman, naked, with dishevelled hair, wearing a garland of skulls and human bones... a lunatic beloved by lunatics, lord of the demons whose nature is wholly obscure. Alas! at the urging of Brahma I gave my virtuous daughter to this lord of furies, this evil heart.'

Often the demons have only a passing life. Sometimes created by the gods for some particular circumstance – for instance, to conquer the Asuras themselves – these evil beings afterwards disappear for ever as mysteriously as they were born.

Again, the gods and goddesses sometimes assume terrible shapes to fight with the demons. For instance, we shall see in the legend of Hiranyakasipu how Vishnu devours his victim in the form of a cruel monster with a lion's head.

But the most typical example of these metamporphoses is certainly that of Siva's wife.

Under the name of Parvati she is presented as a very beautiful young woman, seated beside her divine husband, discoursing with him sometimes of love and sometimes of lofty metaphysics.

In the shape of Uma she practises the harshest asceticism on the peaks of the Himalayas in order to attract Siva's attention and so be received into his favour.

But under the name of Durga, and in response to an appeal from the gods, she undertakes to destroy a demon who had dethroned them all. The battle is terrible. The demon changes into a buffalo, an elephant, and a giant with a thousand arms. But Durga is invincible. Mounted on a lion she overcomes the monster, and despatches him by thrusting her lance into his heart. Durga is represented with a serene and beautiful face, but she has ten arms, each with a weapon. One of her hands holds the lance which pierces the heart of the conquered demon. Her right foot is on the lion, and her left on the demon's neck.

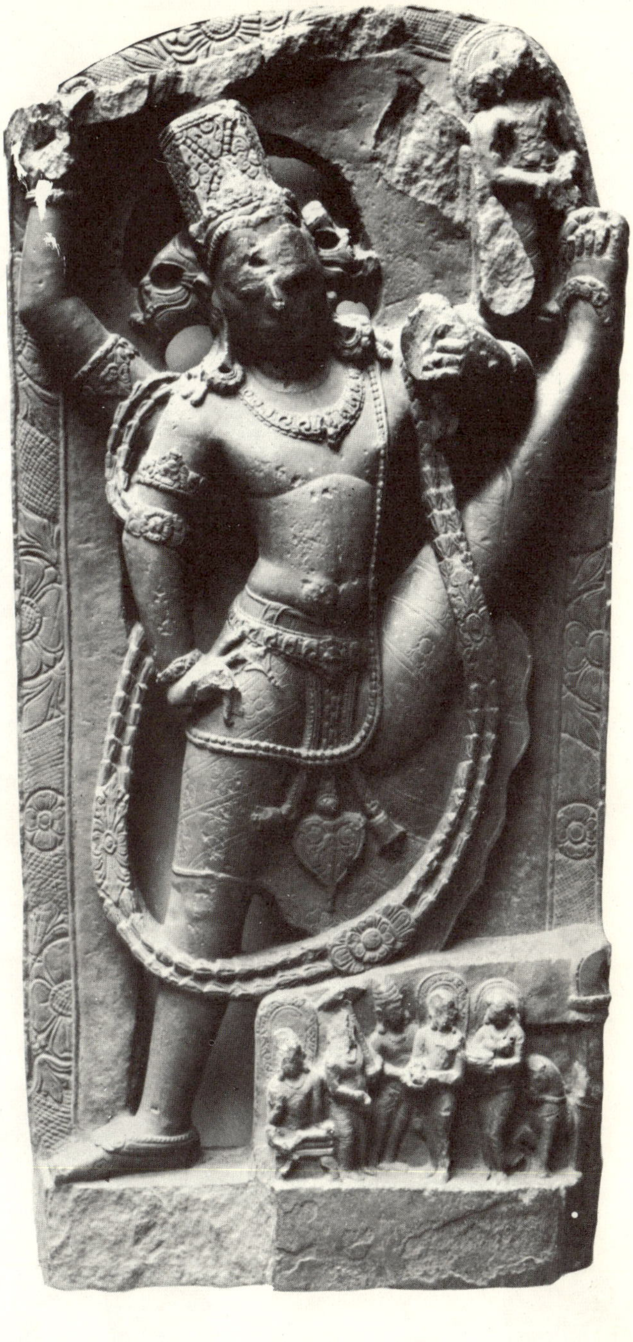

Vishnu traversing the universe. In order to win back heaven and earth from Bali, the grandson of Hiranyakasipu's devout son, Prahlada, Vishnu had agreed to be incarnated as a dwarf Brahman.
On the demon agreeing to his request for as much land as he could pace out in three steps he traversed the universe in two strides and cast Bali into the underworld on the third. Pala carving, tenth century A.D.

Siva's wife assumed as many as ten terrifying shapes to destroy the demons.

One of the most horrible and the most venerated was that of Kali, often called Kali Ma (the black mother). In this incarnation the goddess fought with Raktavija, chief of the army of demons. Seeing that gradually all his soldiers were being killed, Raktavija attacked the goddess himself. She smote him with her formidable weapons, but every drop of blood which fell from his body gave birth to a thousand giants as powerful as he. Kali was only able to overcome her adversary by drinking all his blood. Having conquered the giant she began to dance with joy so wildly that the whole earth quaked. At the request of the gods her husband begged her to stop, but in her sacred madness she did not even see him, cast him down among the dead and trod on his body. When at last she realised her mistake she was covered with shame. Kali is represented as a woman with a very dark complexion, with long

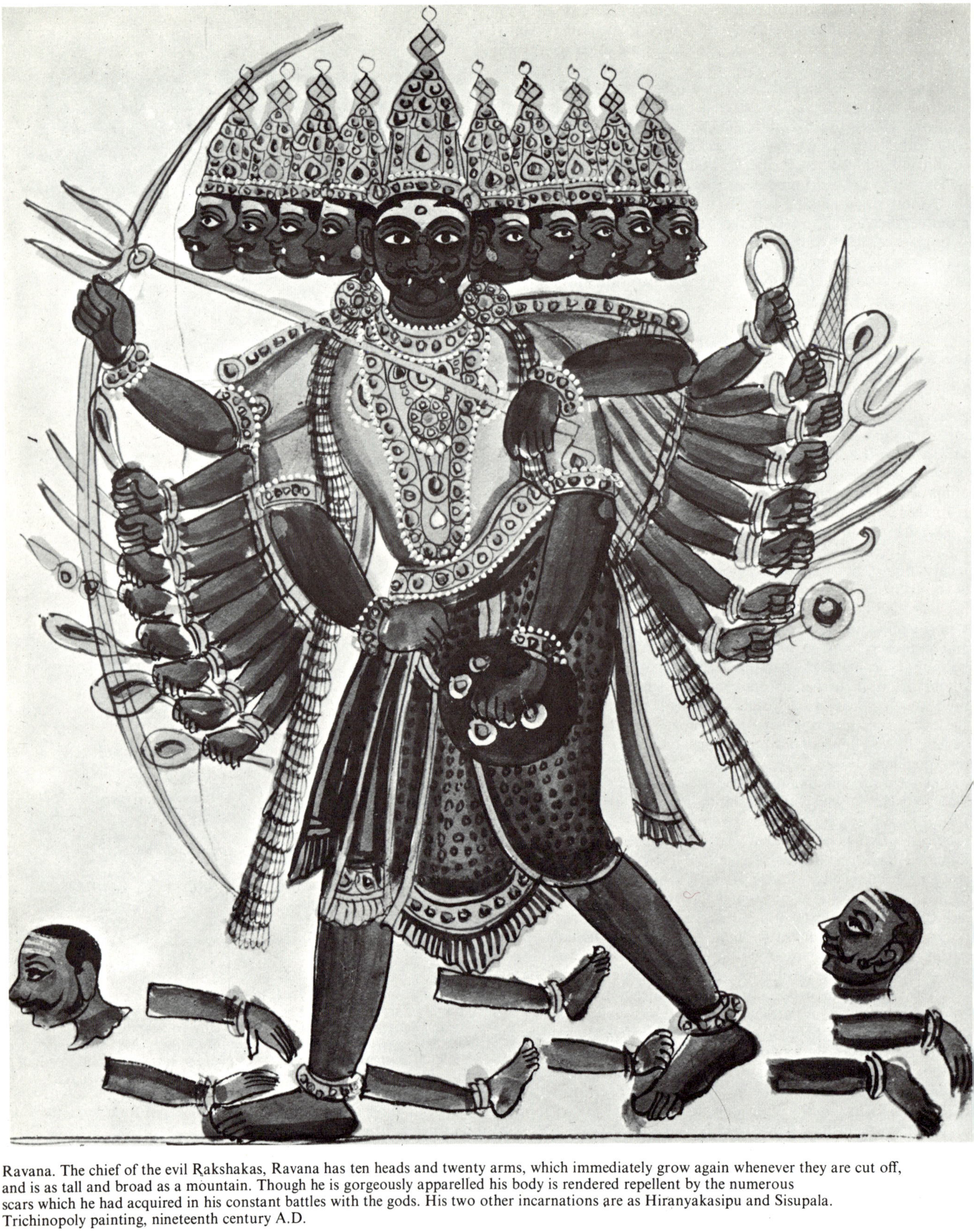

Ravana. The chief of the evil Rakshakas, Ravana has ten heads and twenty arms, which immediately grow again whenever they are cut off, and is as tall and broad as a mountain. Though he is gorgeously apparelled his body is rendered repellent by the numerous scars which he had acquired in his constant battles with the gods. His two other incarnations are as Hiranyakasipu and Sisupala. Trichinopoly painting, nineteenth century A.D.

loose hair, and four arms. One of her hands holds a sword; the second holds the severed head of the giant; and with the other two hands she encourages her worshippers. Her ear-rings are two corpses and she wears a necklace of human skulls. Her only garment is a girdle made up of two rows of hands. Her tongue hangs out, her eyes are red, as if she were drunk, her face and bosom are polluted with blood. The goddess is generally shown standing, with one foot on the leg and the other on the chest of Siva.

The Tattiriya Samhita puts evil beings into three categories – the Asuras are opposed to the gods, the Rakshasas to men, and the Pisakas to the dead. But these categories are much less clearly defined in practice than in theory.

The Asuras. The Asuras are a kind of very powerful Titans, skilled magicians and implacable enemies of the Devas. As will be observed in the legends which follow, they are sometimes superior to the gods and – this is a curious detail – their power has often been conferred on them by the gods themselves, who thus turn out to be the artisans of their own defeat.

The story of Jalandhara is characteristic of the various battles which were waged continually between the Devas and the Asuras.

One day Indra and the other gods paid a visit to Siva on mount Kailasi, and amused him with songs and dances. Siva was delighted by the music, and begged his visitors to ask a boon. Indra, in a defiant way, wished to become a warrior as powerful as Siva himself. The wish was granted, and the gods departed. Siva then began to wonder what use Indra would make of his new power; and as he meditated a shape of anger, black as darkness itself, rose before him and said: 'Give me your form, and tell me what I can do for you.' Siva told him to enter the river Ganga (the Ganges) and to wed her to the Ocean.

A son was born from this union – the earth quaked and wept, the three worlds echoed with claps of thunder. Brahma perceived the extraordinary strength of this miraculous child, gave him the name of Jalandhara and the gift of conquering the gods and possessing the three worlds.

Jalandhara's youth was filled with miracles – he soared over the oceans on the wings of the winds, and played with the lions he had tamed. Later his father gave him a splendid kingdom, and he wedded Vrinda, the daughter of a heavenly nymph, also renowned in legend.

Soon after his marriage he declared war on the gods under the pretext of regaining the wonders born from the churning of the sea of milk, which had been taken for himself by Indra.

The battle began, and on each side thousands of warriors were slain. The gods regained life and health thanks to magic plants gathered in the mountains. Jalandhara had received from Brahma himself the power of resurrecting the dead. Indra in his turn was attacked by Jalandhara, but Vishnu went to the rescue. The Asuras fought so valiantly that their arrows darkened the sky, but Vishnu drove them before him like dead leaves.

Jalandhara then flooded the mountains where the gods found the magic plants which restore life. Vishnu himself attacked Jalandhara, but this time the demon succeeded in overthrowing him, and only spared his life at the entreaty of the goddess, Lakshmi. Jalandhara, having conquered the Devas, drove them from heaven, and reposed in peace.

However, the gods refused to accept their fate, deprived as they were of their heavenly abodes, of sacrifices, and of ambrosia. They consulted Brahma, who led them to Siva. Seated on his throne, and accompanied by myriads of devoted followers, all of them naked, all deformed, with tangled curly hair, Siva advised the gods to pool their powers and to forge a weapon capable of annihilating their common foe. The gods, burning with anger, cast forth masses of flame, to which Siva added the burning rays of his third eye. Vishnu brought the fire of his rage, and also besought Siva to cause the demon to perish. Siva then approached the huge burning mass, set his heel on it, and began to revolve with dizzy speed. Thus a glistening disk was forged. Its rays singed the beard of Brahma, who peered at it too closely, and the gods, were blinded by it. But Siva hid the weapon under his arm, and the battle began again.

But now the war was complicated by a love affair – Jalandhara wanted to abduct Siva's wife, Parvati. She escaped him by changing into a lotus, and her ladies of honour were changed into bees and flew about her. On the other hand Vishnu was more cunning, and having assumed the form of Jalandhara succeeded in seducing his wife. But Vrinda discovered the trick and died of grief, laying curses on the seducer. Jalandhara was wild with rage when he heard of his wife's lamentable end. He gave up Parvati, returned to the battlefield, resurrected his dead heroes, and launched a final assault. Siva and Jalandhara defied each other to single combat. After a fierce struggle Siva brought forth the disk, and cut off the head of his adversary. But he had the power to make it constantly spring up again. Would Siva in his turn be beaten? No, for he called on the goddesses, wives of the gods. Transmuted into she-ogres they drank the Asura's blood, and thus Siva succeeded in mastering him and in regaining for the gods their possessions and their kingdom.

The Rakshasas. The Rakshasas often have a half-divine nature, but whereas the gods often display generosity, kindness, mastery and truth, the Rakshasas display the most deplorable passions – gluttony, lust, violence, perjury – at any rate in their relations with gods and men. Among themselves they show filial and conjugal affection, good faith and devotion. They are great Magicians, and have power to assume any shape they wish. The city of the Rakshasas is wonderfully beautiful, having been built by the architect of the gods, Visvakarma himself. They practise all the arts, and by austerity and penance sometimes obtain great favours of the gods.

In general the Rakshasas are not by nature evil beings, but creatures destined by inescapable fate (Dharma) to play a hostile or malevolent part in the life of such and such a person in such and such a situation. In some cases this part is the natural consequence of a former life, whose fruit thus comes to maturity.

An example is given us by the three incarnations of the demon Ravana. One day a being of high rank in the heaven of Vishnu committed a grave error. He had to return to earth to expiate it. He was given the choice between three incarnations as the enemy, or seven incarnations as the friend of Vishnu. He chose the former alternative as it was the quicker way to be free. In consequence certain incarnations of Vishnu have no other reason than the need for him to be on earth at the same time as his temporary enemy, and to slay him in order to procure his redemption.

Ravana's First Incarnation: Hiranyakasipu. Hiranyakasipu was a very powerful demon-king. Thanks to the power he had received from Brahma himself he succeeded in dethroning Indra and exiling the gods from heaven. He proclaimed himself king of the universe, and forbade worship of anyone but himself.

However, his son Prahlada consecrated himself to Vishnu, who had initiated him into the secrets of his heart. Hiranyakasipu, irritated by the sight of his son devoting himself to the cult of a mortal enemy, inflicted on the young man a series of cruel tortures in order to turn him from his vocation. But his fervour simply increased, and he began to preach the religion of Vishnu to men and demons.

Hiranyakasipu ordered the death of this unmanageable missionary. But the sword, poison, fire, wild elephants, and magic incantations failed to harm him, for Prahlada was protected by his god.

Hiranyakasipu once more called his son to him. Prahlada with immense gentleness tried again to convince his father of Vishnu's greatness and omnipresence, but the demon angrily exclaimed: 'If Vishnu is everywhere, how does it happen that my eyes don't see him?' He kicked one of the pillars in his audience chamber, saying: 'Is he here, for instance?' 'Even when invisible he is present in all things,' said Prahlada softly. Whereupon Hiranyakasipu uttered a blasphemy and kicked the pillar, which fell on the floor. Immediately Vishnu emerged from the pillar in the shape of a lion-headed man (in his incarnation as Narasimha), seized on the demon, and tore him to shreds.

Prahlada succeeded his father, and reigned with justice and wisdom. His grandson was the demon Bali, who also was a rival of the gods, but was as virtuous as he was powerful.

Bali reigned over heaven and earth. Only Vishnu could conquer so powerful a king. The gods besought him to be re-incarnated, so that he could regain the kingdom which belonged to them. And Vishnu agreed to be born again in the shape of a dwarf Brahman.

While Bali was offering up a sacrifice on the bank of the river sacred to the Narmada, the dwarf came to visit him. Bali knew his duty. He touched his forehead with the precious water which had cooled the Brahman's feet, bade him be welcome, and offered to grant whatever he desired. The dwarf replied modestly: 'I ask only a little piece of land, three steps, which I shall carefully pace out. I desire no more. A wise man does not ask for more than is necessary to him.' Although surprised by so humble a request, the king granted the gift.

Then Vishnu suddenly re-assumed his divine stature, and in two steps traversed the whole universe. He still had a third step to take. He turned to Bali and said: 'Asura, you promised me three steps of land. In two steps I have traversed the world – where shall I make the third? Every man who fails to give a Brahman what he has promised is doomed to fall. You have deceived me, and deserve to sink into the regions of hell.' 'I do not fear hell so much as a bad reputation,' answered Bali, and he presented his head for the god's third step, and was cast down into the depths of the underworld for ever.

Another legend has Bali slain by the hand of Indra during the battle waged between Indra and the demons led by Jalandhara. Bali fell, and a flood of jewels came from his mouth. Indra drew

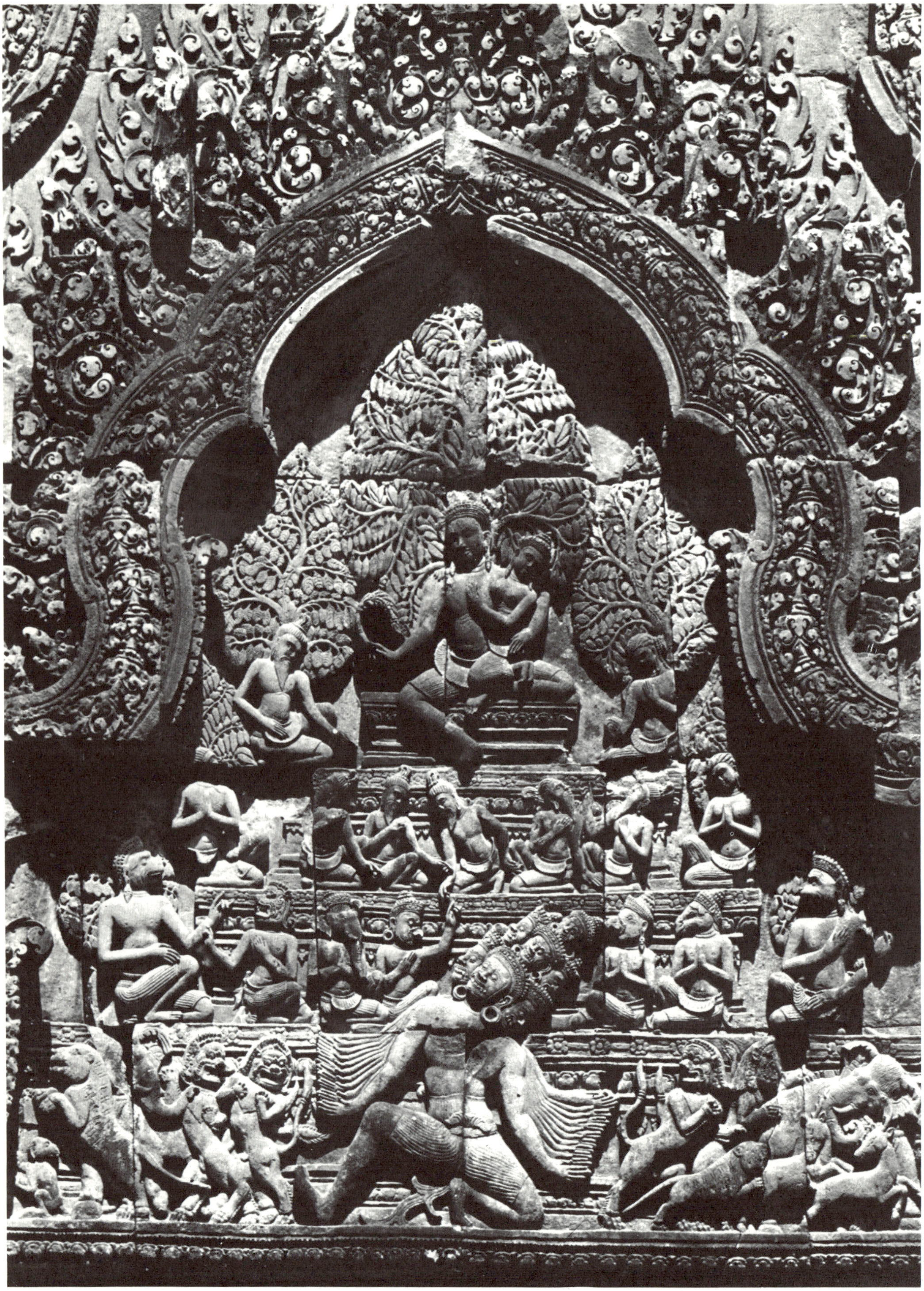

Ravana trying to shake Mount Kailasa, the abode of Siva and Parvati. The gigantic Rakshasa with his ten heads and twenty arms is shown below while the divine couple are seated on the summit of the mountain beneath a grove of trees. Ravana had tried to uproot the mountain and bring them down but Siva is holding him captive by the merest pressure of his big toe. Carved stone lintel, tenth century A.D. Banteai Srei, Angkor.

fear in surprise, and tore his body to pieces with a thunderbolt. Bali was so pure in his conduct that the various parts of his body gave birth to the germs of precious stones. Diamonds came from his bones, sapphires from his eyes, rubies from his blood, emeralds from his marrow, crystal from his flesh, and pearls from his teeth.

Second Incarnation: Ravana. The demon Ravana is the implacable enemy of Rama (an incarnation of Vishnu) and the abductor of Sita. His story will be given in great detail in the Ramayana account (see page 381). We shall merely note here that on the eve of the decisive battle in which he was slain Ravana had a short moment of lucidity in which he admitted the divinity of Rama. He then exclaimed: 'I must die by his hand. That is why I abducted the daughter of Janaka (Sita). Neither passion nor anger urged me to retain her. I want to die to attain the heaven of Vishnu.'

Alongside the story of Ravana, we hear of two brothers.

One of them, Kumbhakarna, is a sort of giant-ogre. As soon as he was born he stretched out his arms and grasped everything within his reach to allay his hunger. Later he seized five hundred Apsaras (heavenly nymphs) and abducted the wives of a hundred Rishis, not to mention cows and Brahmans.

To calm the fears aroused by this demon, Brahma wanted to confer on him the gift of eternal sleep; but Kumbhakarna asked to be allowed to wake up every six months and eat to repletion. In this bi-annual meal he is said to have devoured six thousand cows, ten thousand sheep, ten thousand goats, four hundred buffaloes, while drinking four thousand bowls of strong liquor in the skull of a wild boar. And he complained of his brother for not giving him more!

Ravana's other brother, Vibhishana, refused to join the war against Rama and urged his brother to give Sita back to her husband. But Ravana drove him away with curses. Rising into the air with four of his friends, Vibhishana passed over the sea and offered his services to Rama. They were accepted, and Rama undertook in exchange to place Vibhishana on the throne of Lanka (Ceylon) after the defeat of Ravana.

Third Incarnation: Sisupala. Sisupala was the son of a king, but he had three eyes and four arms. His father and mother were terrified by this omen, and were getting ready to abandon him when a voice rang through the air: 'Fear not! Cherish the child. His time is not yet come. He that will slay him by force of arms on the day of destiny is already born. Until then he will be the favourite of fortune and renown.' The queen his mother was somewhat comforted by these words, and said: 'Who is he who shall kill my son?' And the voice replied: 'You shall know him by this sign – when the child is on his knees his third eye will disappear and you will see his extra arms fall off.'

The king and queen then set out on their travels, and visited all the monarchs of the neighbouring lands. At each place they asked their host to take the child on his knees, but nothing of his appearance was changed. They returned home disappointed. Some time afterwards the young prince Krishna (another incarnation of Vishnu) paid them a visit accompanied by his elder brother. The two lads began to play with the child, and as soon as Krishna had taken him on his knees the baby's third eye withered away and his extra arms vanished. The queen then knew the future slayer of her son. Falling on her knees, she exclaimed: 'O my lord, grant me a boon.' 'Speak,' said the young god. 'Promise me that if my son should offend you, you will forgive him.' 'Certainly. Even if he offends me a hundred times, I will forgive him.'

However, the fate predicted had to befall. Many years later the king Yudhishthira celebrated a great sacrifice in honour of his cornonation. Kings and heroes were invited to his festivities. Krishna was present, and the royal family had decided to offer him their homage first of all. But one of the guests makes a protest. Sisupala bitterly reproaches the hosts, saying: 'You insult all the kings present by giving precedence to someone who has no right to it, either from his connections, his age, his lineage or for any other reason.' Sisupala argues his case so cleverly that some of the guests are ready to take his part. Would they prevent the consummation of the sacrifice, which would be a certain token of misfortune for the whole kingdom?

King Yudhishthira did everything he could to conciliate Sisupala, but he refused to be cajoled. Yudhishthira then turned to his old grandfather Brahma for his advice, and he answered smiling: 'The lord Krishna himself will decide the dispute. What can a dog do against a lion? This king seems like a lion so long as the real lion is not awake. Let us wait.' Sisupala was furious at being likened to a dog and insulted the venerable old man, who maintained his serenity, and prevented the others from intervening on his behalf to avenge him. He lifted his hand to command silence, and then told his guests the story of Sisupala and the predictions made long ago to his parents.

Sisupala's mad rage knew no bounds. He drew his sword and threatened the old man while again insulting him. The old man still remained calm and, turning his gaze towards Krishna, said with diginity: 'I fear nothing, for we have with us the lord we all

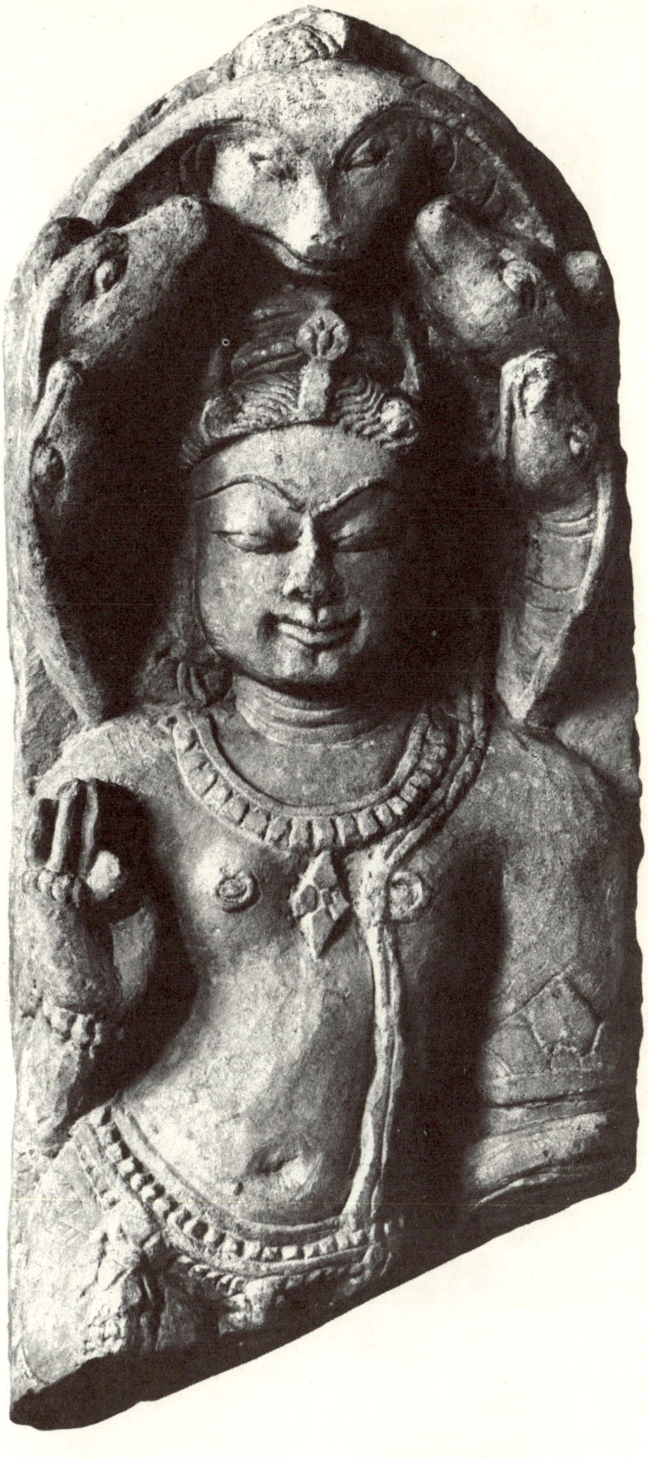

A Naga. The Nagas are a fabulous race of snakes who live in great splendour in the underworld kingdom of Patala and are renowned for their trickery and evil-doing. A few, however, are friendly with the gods and statues of divinised Nagas are still worshipped in the south of India. Here a Naga is portrayed in human form, while five cobras spread their hoods about his head. Sandstone, tenth century A.D.

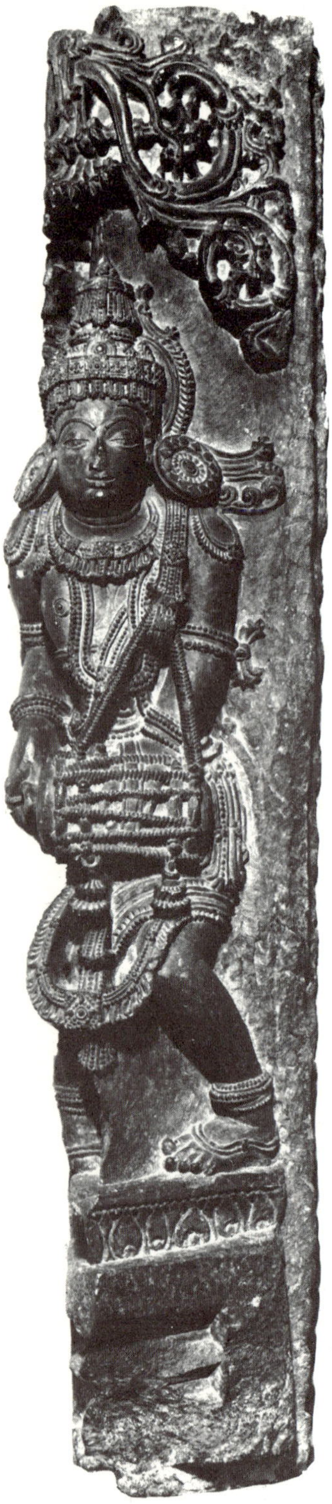

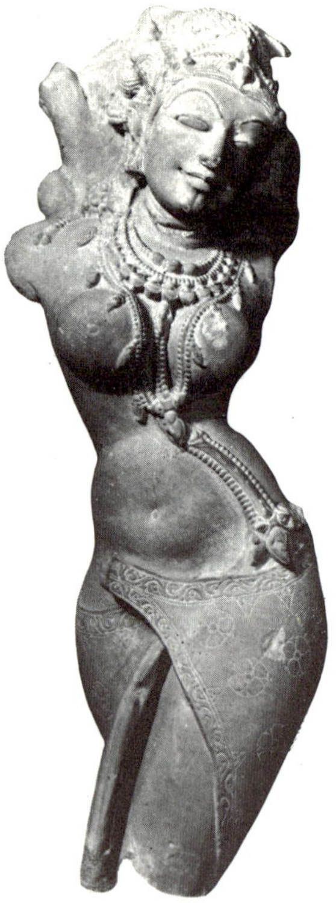

A Vrikshaka or tree-nymph. Like the water nymphs, or Apsaras, who haunted rivers and holy pools and later became the heavenly singers and dancers of Indra's heaven, she displays the voluptuous forms of an idealised type of feminine beauty. The pantheism of earlier ages still persists throughout India and many local deities may receive more fervent devotion than the more universally recognised gods. Statue in the post-Gupta style, ninth century A.D.

A Gandharva with a drum. The heavenly musicians of Indra's celestial abode of Swarga on the summit of Mount Meru, the Gandharvas perform at the banquets of the gods and are the licentious mates of the beautiful Apsaras. Originally the familiar spirits of the Indo-Europeans, they play a a part in the fecundity of nature and are the jealous guardians of the Soma. Hoysala potstone carving from Halebid in Mysore, thirteenth century A.D.

worship. Let anyone who wants a quick death contend with him – the dark-coloured god who bears in his hands the disk and the mace – and when he dies he will enter the god's body.'

All eyes were turned towards Krishna who looked mildly on the angry king. But when Sisupala repeated his threats and insults, the god said simply: 'The cup of your misdeeds is now full.' At that very moment the divine weapon, the flaming disk, rose behind Krishna, sped through the air and fell on the helmet of Sisupala, whom it cleft asunder from head to feet. Then the sinner's soul broke out like a mass of fire which moved forward to bow before Krishna, and was absorbed in his feet. Thus, as the elder had predicted, he was mingled with the god at his death.

Thus ended Sisupala who had sinned unto one hundred and one times and yet was pardoned, for even the god's enemies attain salvation by thinking of him continually.

The Pisakas are almost always vampires. The Bhutas and Pretas are sometimes ghosts, sometimes goblins. They are rather vague spirits who haunt in bands the cemeteries and other places of evil omen.

The Nagas. The Nagas are a fabulous race of snakes. They are powerful and dangerous, and usually appear in the form of ordinary snakes, but sometimes as fabulous snakes and, in some circumstances, in human form. There are snake-kings, such as that Takshaka whose glittering capital is the glory of the underworld kingdom.

Certain royal families or dynasties reckoned Nagas among their ancestors.

Statues of divinised Nagas are still commonly worshipped in the South of India. Needless to say a symbolical and highly metaphysical sense is now attached to the cult. The statues are always placed under a tree. On a private property custom even demands that an uncultivated space shall be left round the god-snakes for the jungle to grow freely. The popular belief is that if the snakes have their own domain reserved to them they are more likely to spare human beings.

In Mythology the Nagas and their wives, the Naginis, often play a fatal part, and their favourite methods are surprise and trickery. But there are exceptions. In epochs of cosmic rest Vishnu sleeps under the protection of the great snake, Sesha, who forms his bed while his seven raised heads give the god shade.

Reptiles in general are supposed to be gifted with amazing powers and the fact that they are amphibious seems to have greatly struck the imagination of the Indians.

Here briefly summarised are two legends from the Mahabharata where we come on Takshaka, king of the Nagas.

Parikchit. King Parikchit was passionately fond of hunting. One day when he was exhausted with fatigue and thirst after a long pursuit of a wounded gazelle, it happened that he unintentionally offended a hermit of the highest virtue who was observing a vow of silence in the heart of the forest. The wise man's son was indignant at this insult to his father, and placed his curse on the king, saying 'Within a week the snake Takshaka will burn you with his poison and you will die.'

When the king heard this fatal news he built a palace on top of a column which stood in the middle of a lake, and decided to shut himself up there. But Takshaka succeeded in overcoming the vigilance of the guards by a ruse. He changed some snakes into wandering monks and sent them to the king bearing offerings of water, the sacred plant and fruits. The king received them, accepted their gifts and dismissed them.

Then the king said to his ministers and friends: 'Let your excellencies eat with me the delicious fruits brought by these ascetics.' Among the open fruits there appeared a strange insect shining like red copper, with glittering eyes. The king picked up the insect and said: 'The sun is about to set, and I have now no fear of death. Let the hermit's speech be accomplished, let this insect bite me.' And he put it on his neck. Then the snake Takshaka, for he it was, wrapped the king in his coils and uttered a great roar.

Seeing the king caught in the snake's coils the counsellors burst into tears and suffered the keenest grief. They then fled from the monster's roaring, and even as they ran they saw the marvellous reptile rise into the air. Takshaka, king of the snakes, red as a lotus, traced across the forehead of heaven a line as straight as that which parts the hair on the head of a bride. The king fell dead as if struck by lightning, and the palace was wrapped in fire.

Afterwards they carried out for Parikchit all the ceremonies relating to the next world. Then the chaplain, the ministers, and all the assembled subjects acclaimed the new king, his son Janamejaya, who was still a child.

Utanka and the Ear-rings. A young Brahman student, Utanka, was told to take to his tutor's wife a pair of ear-rings, which had been given her by the queen. This queen (who was the wife of king Janamejaya, son of the king Parikchit who figures in the preceding tale) warned the young man that the king of snakes, Takshaka, had long coveted these jewels.

The Brahman set out, and on the way noticed a naked beggar who sometimes approached and sometimes disappeared from sight. Soon after, Utanka stopped to perform his ablutions, and laid the ear-rings on the ground. The beggar glided up swiftly towards the jewels, grasped them and fled. When his ablutions were

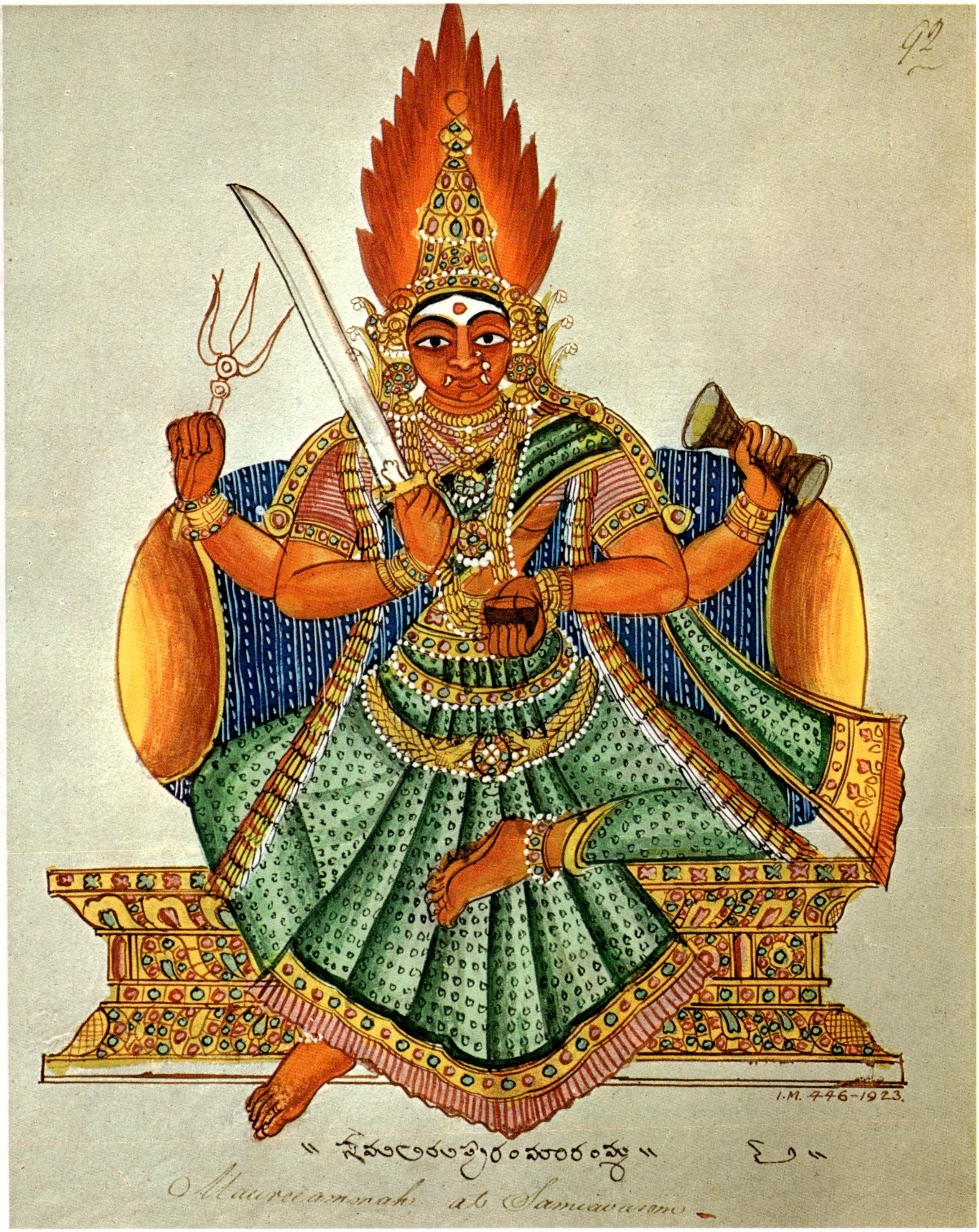

Durga Pratyangira. One of the many terrifying forms assumed by Siva's wife, the goddess is seated on a jewelled padnasana holding her husband's trident, sword and drum and a bowl for blood. Her name, in this south Indian representation, has Tantric associations while her form as Kali is seen in the long teeth and the tongues of fire. Kali (the black), in Vedic times, was the name of the fire god's black terrifying flame. Trichinopoly painting, nineteenth century A.D.

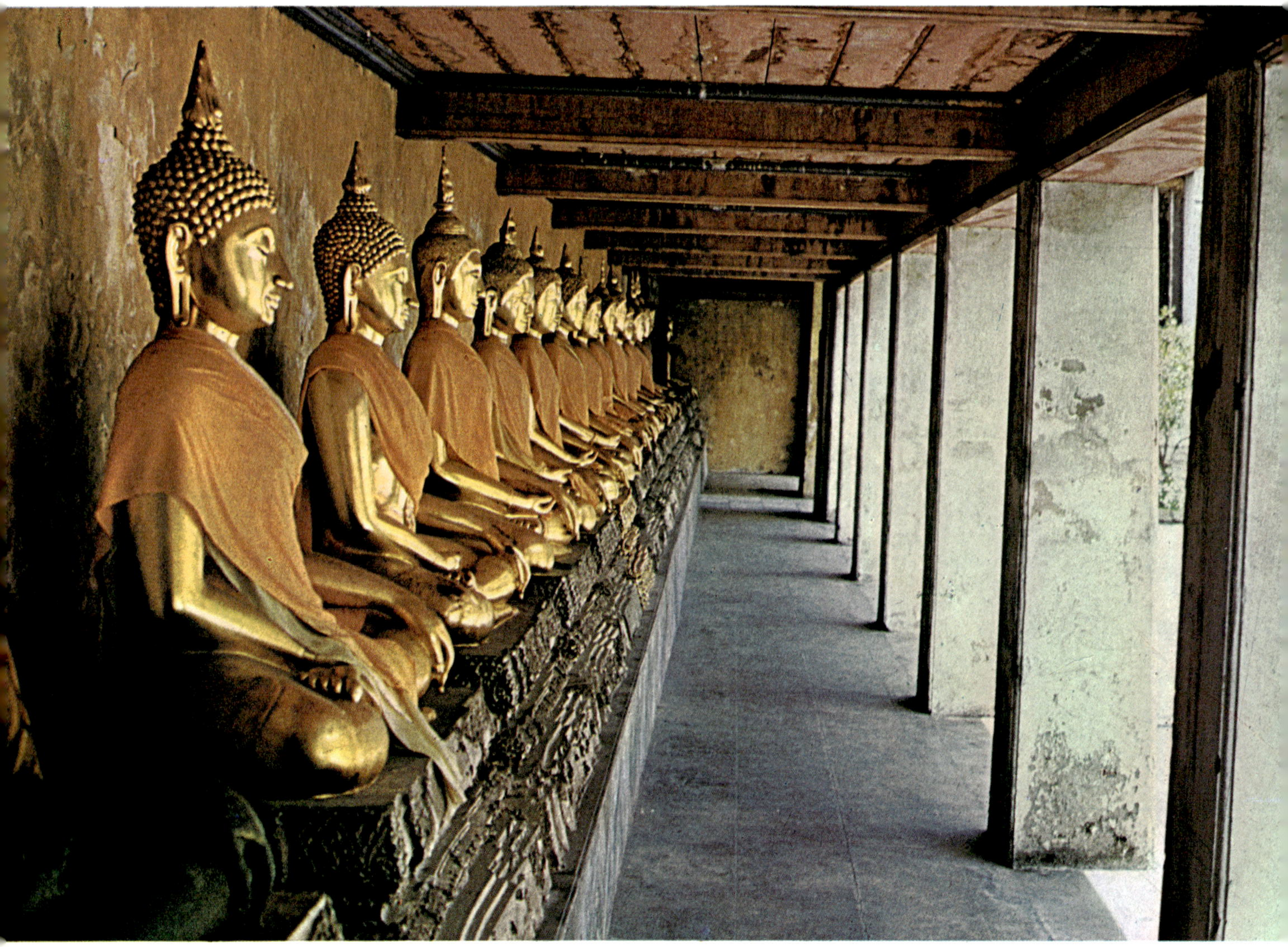

Buddhism spread rapidly through Asia, becoming a stronger influence outside India than in the land of its beginnings, and resulting in temples and images of a magnificence in contradiction to the benign simplicity of the religion's founder. This succession of gilded images, each one carefully clad in saffron robes, is in one of the inner courts of the great Wat Po temple in Bangkok.

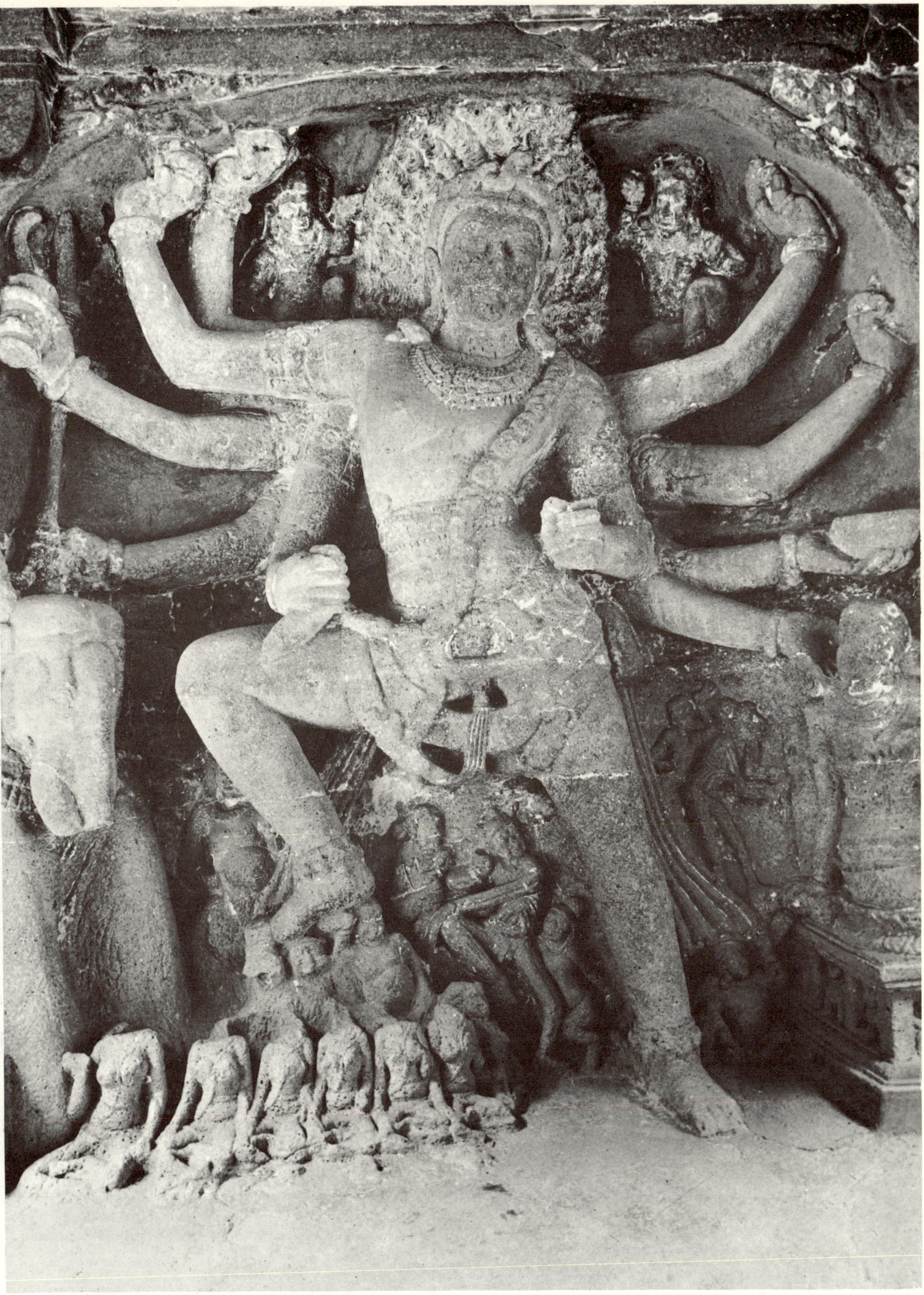

Rudra, the Vedic god of storms. A curious mixture of terrible and beneficent qualities, Rudra was both the prince of demons and the formidable archer whose arrows dispatched men and beasts to the other world and the divine physician and lord of cattle who also brought the healing rain. Many of his attributes were later given to Siva, particularly in his form as destroyer. Sculpture from the Ellora cave temple, eighth century A.D.

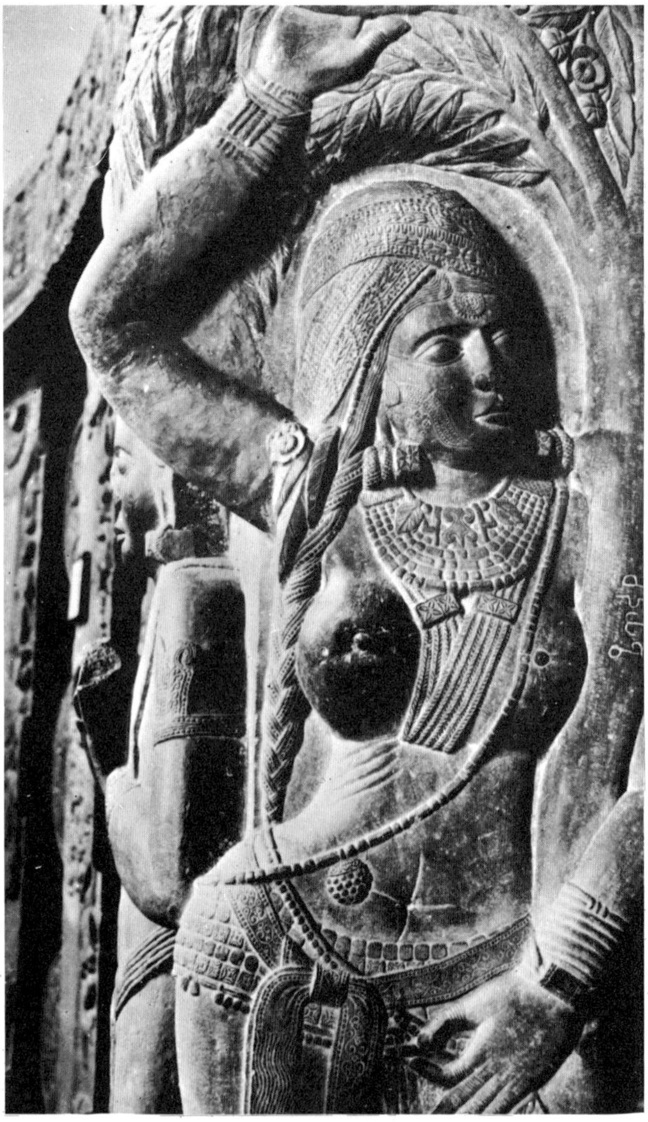

A Yakshi, or female Yaksha. Born of Night like their bloodthirsty brothers the Rakshasas, the Yakshas are the attendant spirits of Ravana's half-brother, Kubera, the god of wealth. They live in the Himalayas and are the guardians of hidden treasure. Though sometimes pictured in grotesque form, they are not usually enemies of mankind and are sometimes seen as graceful, otherworld figures like this. Balustrade carving from Bharut. Indian Museum, Calcutta.

finished Utanka discovered the theft, and eagerly pursued the thief. But at the moment when Utanka got his hands on him the robber abandoned his borrowed shape, became a snake again, and glided into a cleft which opened into the earth. Having thus returned to the world of snakes, the cunning Takshaka took refuge in his palace.

Utanka then remembered the queen's words. But how was he to get at Takshaka? He began to search the hole with the end of his staff, but without success. Indra saw he was overwhelmed with grief and sent his thunderbolt, saying: 'Go, and bring aid to this Brahman!' The thunder descended, entered the cleft by following the staff, and burst open the hole. Utanka followed in its tracks.

Having entered the limitless world of snakes, he found it was full of admirable establishments for games, both large and small, and crowded with hundreds of porticoes, turrets, palaces and temples, of different types of architecture. He then chanted a hymn in praise of the Nagas, but although the snakes were smothered with praise they did not return the jewels.

Thereupon Utanka entered into meditation. A marvellous symbolical vision of nights and days, of the year and the seasons, unrolled before his eyes; and then he saw Indra himself mounted on a horse. He praised the god in a sacred chant, and Indra, well-pleased, offered his help. Utanka asked: 'Put the snakes into my power.' 'Breathe on the crupper of my horse,' replied Indra. Utanka obeyed, and the steed suddenly caused an outburst of huge flames accompanied by smoke. The world of snakes was buried in the smoke; and terrified by the glow of the fire Takshaka hastily emerged from his palace and returned the ear-rings to the young Brahman.

Indra then lent Utanka his miraculous steed which brought the young man to his tutor in a second. He arrived just in time to hand the jewels at the time appointed to his tutor's wife as she had asked.

Rudra and the Maruts. The Indological school of Uppsala, K.F. Johansson and his followers E. Arbman and J. Charpentier, have lately found numerous traces of popular religion in the Vedas. The cult of Rudra plays a central part in it. This prince of demons (Bhudapati) is a savage figure, and god of the dead, in as much as he and his crew feed on the departed, like the followers of Odin in Nordic mythology. He is an earth god, but on the evidence of a single passage in the Rig-Veda which gives him the vajra (thunderbolt) scholars have been in too great a hurry to interpret him as a god of the hurricane or the storm. Rudra does not share in the sacrifice of Soma which extends to all Devas – he belongs to another category.

He is a formidable archer, whose shafts despatch men and beasts to the next world. The accuracy of his aim is praised by begging him to shoot at other places and not at the house of the suppliant. Once they are hit by him men and animals die of sickness. So this savage god is invoked as a doctor and a veterinary surgeon, on whom every cure depends. He dwells in the mountains, and thus his rule extends to heaven and the air as well as to earth.

The gods are as afraid of him as mortals are. One day when Prajapati committed incest with his own daughter Ushas who to escape him had changed into a gazelle, Rudra saw it as a mortal sin. In terror Prajapati called out: 'Don't shoot at me – I'll make you Lord of all animals!' Henceforth Rudra is named Pasupati, Lord of animals. But he shot all the same, and then wept to think that his shaft had struck the demiurge himself.

The Maruts are the sons of Rudra and Prisni (goddess of the dark season) and, as Hillebrandt has pointed out, seem to have been dead souls before they became the genii of wind and storm. In the most ancient texts they are 'Rudras', copies of the god of the dead, but when Rudra became a heavenly being they dropped the name and became gods of the atmosphere.

They are depicted as hustling the clouds, shaking mountains and wrecking forests. These energetic Rudras only become more gentle in order to please Rodasi, Rudra's wife, who likes to accompany them in her chariot.

Origins of Siva and Vishnu. This archaic popular god Rudra is the source of the god Siva who becomes of the first importance after the Vedic age – like Vishnu – in the religion of the masses. As we have seen, Siva also bore the title of prince of demons, Bhudapati. His name means 'the favourable' or 'the benevolent' and was meant to propitiate a dangerous deity who breathes pestilence and death. The god is essentially destructive but was endowed with benevolence by the piety of his worshippers who dreaded his dangerous manifestations. But his malevolent vocation brought round him all the atrocious and horrible deities revered by the Dravidians. Once presented as the wives of Siva these ogresses were consecrated by Hinduism – Uma, Durga and Parvati are three aspects of the same goddess. The name Tryambaka applied to Rudra already means the god accompanied by the three mother-goddesses, amba, ambika.

The cult of Vishnu has some frail links with Vedic mythology. He there appears as a solar god who traverses the three worlds in three steps. They are heaven, air, and earth, and he prefers to live in heaven. He is associated with Indra as conqueror of the dark Vritra, and there is no reason for surprise at this since Indra is the god of the warrior aristocracy and the sun was an emblem of royalty. Here we come again on the Maruts, the acolytes of Vishnu. We note that in his multiple forms this god, quite unlike Siva, was the object of pious devotion and tenderly affectionate worship.

Gandharvas Apsaras. The Gandharvas, the familiar spirits of the Indo-Europeans, belong to folk-lore. They are men-horses which the rites bring into masquerades like Carnival, which shows them in their generative function. The part they play in the fecundity of Nature is conjoined with that attributed to them by abstract reflection – according to which that part of the soul which moves

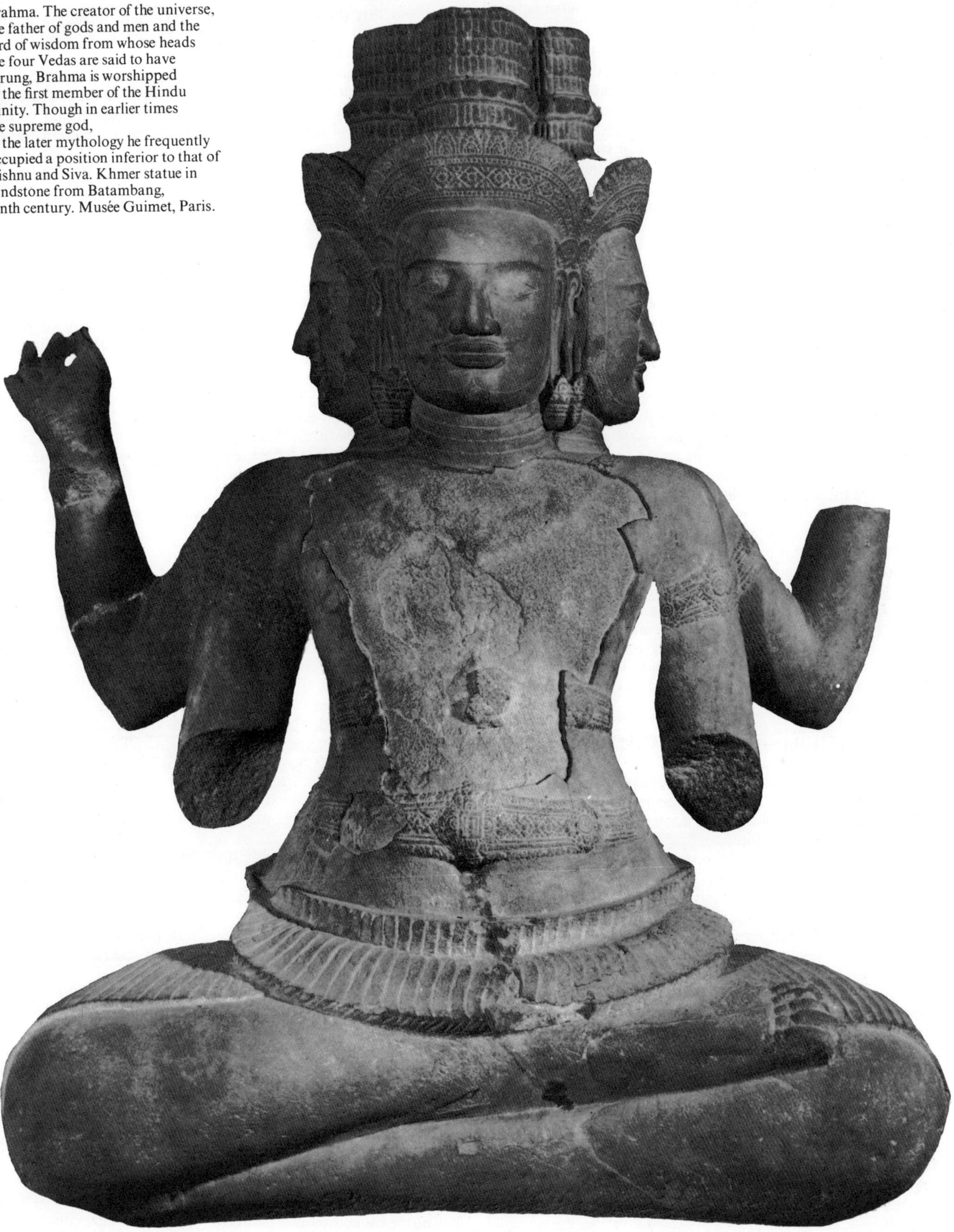

rahma. The creator of the universe, he father of gods and men and the ord of wisdom from whose heads he four Vedas are said to have prung, Brahma is worshipped s the first member of the Hindu rinity. Though in earlier times he supreme god, n the later mythology he frequently ccupied a position inferior to that of ishnu and Siva. Khmer statue in andstone from Batambang, enth century. Musée Guimet, Paris.

on from life to life is called 'gandharva'. The Gandharvas play heavenly music and jealously look after the Soma. They are the licentious mates of the Apsaras, nymphs who were first aquatic and then rustic, and in the first period of Brahmanism were supposed to dwell in figtrees and banana-plants.

The Vedic Apsara, Urvasi, gave rise to a legend which suggests the story of Psyche.

One day king Pururavas was hunting in the Himalayas and heard calls for help. Two Apsaras, playing among the flowers in a wood, were being carried off by demons. He was fortunate enough to be able to rescue them. Pururavas besought one of them, Urvasi, to respond to his love, and she consented on condition that she never saw her husband undressed. They lived together a long time and Urvasi hoped she was with child. However, the Gandharvas, who are the customary friends and companions of the Apsaras, regretted her absence and thought of a stratagem. Urvasi had two little lambs she always kept near her, and tied to her bed at night. Pururavas was laid beside her one night and the Gandharvas stole one of the lambs. 'Ah!' exclaimed Urvasi, 'they have taken my lamb as if there was not a man and a hero lying beside me!' Shortly afterwards they stole the second lamb, and she made exactly the same lament.

Pururavas thought: 'While I am here shall it be said there is no hero?' And without troubling to dress he leaped up to pursue the thieves. Then the Gandharvas filled the sky with flashes of lightning, and Urvasi saw her husband as clearly as in daylight. And she disappeared.

In despair the king sought throughout the land to find his beloved. At last he came to a lake where a flock of swans were swimming. They were Apsaras, and Urvasi was among them. Urvasi revealed herself, and Pururavas besought her to return with him and to grant him at least a moment's conversation. But Urvasi replied: 'What have I to say to you? I left you like the first dawn. Return home, Pururavas. I am like the wind, and hard to capture. You broke the pact which bound us. Return to your home, for it is hard to conquer me.' But seeing Pururavas' despair the Apsara at last allowed herself to be softened. 'Come back on the last day of the year,' she said. 'Then you can spend the night with me, and your son will have been born.' Pururavas returned on the last night of the year. The Gandharvas took him into a golden palace, and sent Urvasi to him. She said: 'In the morning the Gandharvas will grant you a boon. What will you choose?' 'Choose for me,' said Pururavas. 'Then say to them, "I want to become one of you."'

Next morning he made this wish. 'But,' said the Gandharvas, 'nowhere on earth does there burn the sacred fire which can make a man like unto us.' They gave him a dish containing fire, saying: 'You will make the sacrifices with this fire, and thus you will become a Gandharva like us.' Pururavas took the fire and returned home, bringing his son with him. But having left the fire for a moment he found it had disappeared. At the place where Pururavas had left the fire rose the tree Asvattha, and where he had left the dish containing the fire stood the tree Sami. He asked the advice of the Gandharvas. 'First cut the wood of the Sami tree, and then make a slim wand with the wood of the tree Asvattha. By turning one against the other you will make fire, the same fire you received from us.' In this way Pururavas learned how to make fire, and having cast his offerings into it, he became a Gandharva, and dwelt with Urvasi ever after.

ABSTRACT MYTHOLOGY OF THE BRAHMANAS

The abstractions of the latest collections of hymns opened the way for priestly scholasticism. The Vedas mentioned Visvakarma as the universal agent, Prajapati as the master of living things, Brihaspati as the master of the formula, Sraddha as faith. Brahmanas and Upanishads were to equate Prajapati and Brihaspati either with religious forces like the brahman, or with metaphysical notions like the atman, or with ancient mythological figures like the Purusha.

Brahman, a neuter term, is much older than the masculine name of the god Brahma and designates the essence of the Brahman caste, just as Kshatram designates the essence of the Kshatriya caste. Every existence, all knowledge depend on the brahman, as the keystone of the whole social order is the Brahman caste.

Brahman is also the sacred syllable Om, the eternal soul which penetrates the whole universe and is its cause.

Brahma and Sarasvati. Brahma, a masculine term, is the first person of the Hindu Trinity. He is essentially a creative god, the father of gods and men.

'This (world) was darkness, unknowable, without form, beyond reason and perception, as if utterly asleep.

'Then the august and self-existent Being, he who never unfolded, having unfolded this (universe) under the form of the great elements and others, having shown his energy, appeared to scatter the shades of darkness.

'This (Being) whom only the spirit can perceive, subtle, without distinct parts, eternal, including in himself all creatures, incomprehensible, appeared spontaneously.

'Wishing to draw different creatures from his body, he first by thought produced the waters and deposited his seed in them.

'This (seed) became a golden egg as brilliant as the sun, in which he himself was born (under the form of) Brahma, the first father of all worlds.

'The waters are called Naras, they are the daughters of Nara; and since they were his first dwelling-place (ayana) he took the name Narayana.

'From this (first) cause, indistinct, eternal, including in its being and not-being, came the Male, known in the world by th name of Brahma.

'In this egg the blessed one remained a whole year, then of him self, by the effort of his thought only, he divided the egg into two

'From the two halves he made heaven and earth, and betwee them the air and the eight cardinal points and the eternal abod of the waters.

'From himself he drew the Spirit, including in itself being an not-being, and from the Spirit he drew the feeling of self which conscious of personality and is master.

'And also the great (principle) the Soul, and all objects whic possess the three qualities, and successively the five organs of th senses which perceive material things.' (*Laws of Manu,* chap. I, v. 5

The god Brahma is depicted with four faces (caturanana), dresse in a white garment, riding on a swan, sometimes a peacock, or els seated on a lotus growing from Vishnu's navel. He holds varyin objects in his four hands – the four Vedas, the disk, the alms disl or the sacrificial spoon.

Sarasvati, his wife, is the goddess of music, wisdom, and know ledge, the mother of the Vedas. It was she who invented the de vanagari alphabet, Sanskrit. She is depicted as a beautiful youn woman with four arms. With one of her right hands she holds ou a flower to her husband, for she is always beside him; with the othe she holds a book of palm leaves, showing her love of learning. On of her left hands holds a garland and the other a little drum. A other times she is seated on a lotus, with only two arms and playin on the *vina.* Her name contains an allusion to a river, which ha led to the inference that originally she was a goddess of the waters

A legend explains Brahma's four faces, the birth of Sarasvati and the creation of the world.

Brahma first formed a woman from his own immaculate sub stance, and she was known as Satarupa, Sarasvati, Savitri, Gayatr or Brahmani. When he saw this lovely girl emerge from his own body Brahma fell in love with her. Satarupa moved to his right to avoid his gaze, but a head immediately sprang up from the god And when Satarupa turned to the left and then behind him, two new heads emerged. She darted towards heaven, and a fifth head was formed. Brahma then said to his daughter, 'Let us beget all kind of living things, men, Suras, Asuras.' Hearing these words Satarupa returned to earth, Brahma wedded her and they retired to a secre place where they remained together for a hundred (divine) years At that time Manu was born – he is also named Svayambhuva and Viraj.

Brahma's fifth head was eventually burned up by the fire of Siva' third eye.

Atman, the self, oneself (reflexive pronoun), designates what is manifested in the fact of consciousness as being the thinking prin ciple. The word derives from an Indo-European root meaning 'to breathe' – in India as in Europe 'spirit' takes its name from breathing.

Purusha, the Male, in the same texts and before that in the tenth book of Hymns is another name for the absolute Spirit. Here the continuity of the myth in the philosophy appears still more obvious What was to become the Spirit was first of all cosmic Man, whose different limbs formed each part of the world, and whose personality is at once the sacrificer and the victim, the sacrifice (yajna) being considered as reality itself.

Priests and Mythical Heroes. Several groups of mythical figures were conceived both as collective beings and as being summarised in a type-character, the centre of a cycle of legends. The social nature of these beings comes out clearly. Every Indian tradition in the first historical epochs is a matter of *kula,* of lineage, either family descent or religious association, or better still both together. These are the races of Rishis who preserved and transmitted the Vedic revelation, supposedly 'seen' by them, though in reality slowly elaborated by the poets, the influential ancestors of the Brahman caste.

The Atharvans (Iranian athravans) in ancient Aryan antiquity were priests of fire. Atharvan (in the singular) is a prototype of the priest, who produced Agni, fire by friction, and instituted the system of sacrifices. He lives with the gods in heaven. His son Dadhyanc also lights Agni. His affinity with Soma gave rise to some obscure myths, which are the expression of his sacerdotal essence.

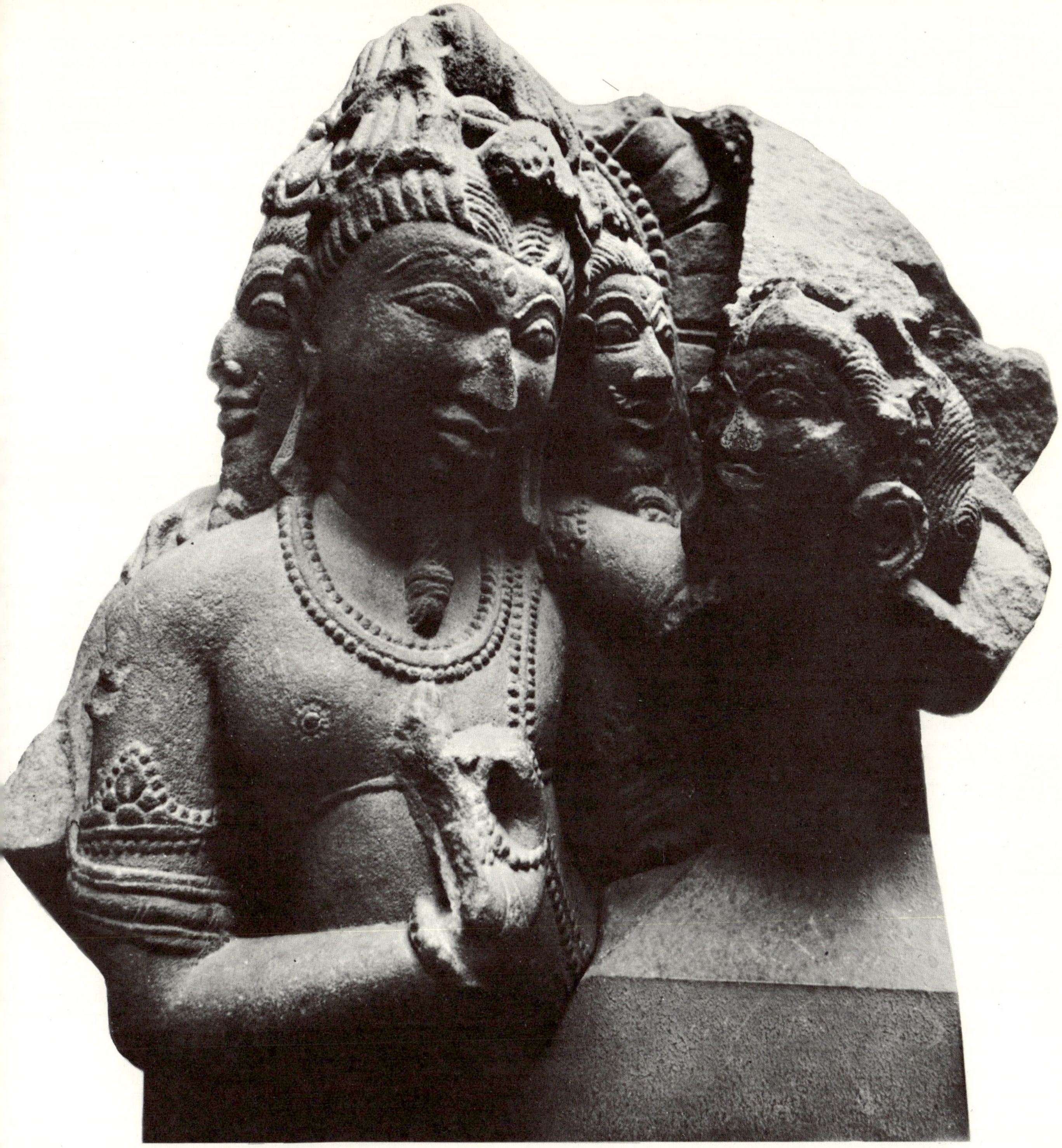

Brahma and Sarasvati. Originally a river goddess, Sarasvati was later made the consort of Brahma and is worshipped as the goddess of learning and the creative arts. According to one legend, she was born from the god's own body and it was in order to look upon her as she shyly fled his amorous gaze that Brahma grew five heads, one of which was later destroyed by Siva. Sculpture from Rajputana, tenth century A.D.

The Angiras are Rishis, sons of the gods, and are supposed to descend from a first Angira. They played the part of fathers to humanity. They too discovered Agni in wood, and presided over sacrifice, which earned them immortality as well as the friendship of Indra.

While the Angiris, true 'angeloi', performed – like angels – the function of intermediaries between gods and men, there are other beings which are theoretically entirely human, the Manus. We are told that Agni dwells with them, and the reason is that Manu, the first of the race, was also the founder of sacrifices. Manu was not only the first to offer sacrifices, he was the first man, the ancestor of humanity. He derived from Vivasvat, the rising Sun, like Yama, the first of the dead. Manu reigns over the living, Yama over the Manes. A part similar to that of Noah is attributed to Manu, who during a deluge was saved by a miraculous fish which later on came to be considered as an avatar of Vishnu. It seems very likely that the Semitic fable was the origin of this cycle of legends. In later times when sacrifice did not include the whole of human activity, Manu was credited with the part of legislator, and his name was attached to the most famous code of Brahman law.

Yama, judge of men and king of the invisible world, was born from Vivasvat, the Sun, and from Saranya, the daughter of Tvashtar. He was born before his mother grew weary of the glitter of her shining husband. He and his twin sister, Yami, made up the original couple from whom humanity is derived. Max Müller thought they meant Day and Night, which explains why they are inseparable and yet can never unite. Yami begged Yama to be her husband but the brother repelled her advances, saying that those who preach virtue should give the example of practising it.

As he was the first of all beings to die, Yama is the guide to everyone who adventures into the next world. He reigns there below, and inhabits a secret sanctuary of heaven bathed in supernatural light. In his kingdom, friend is restored to friend, the wife to the husband, children to their parents, and all live happy, protected from the ills of earthly existence. In this, the third, stage of heaven the Manes or Fathers (pitri) as well as the gods who come there, drink a Soma which delivers them from a second death. Two savage dogs guard the entrance.

We can now understand the epithets applied to Yama – Vaivasvata, son of Vivasvat; Kala, the weather; Dharmaraja, king of virtue; Pitripati, lord of the Fathers; Sraddhadeva, god of funeral ceremonies; Antaka, he who ends life; Kritanta, with the same meaning; Samana, the leveller; Samavurti, the impartial judge; Dandadhara, carrier of the stick, the punisher.

It is hard to touch Yama when at the appointed hour he comes to earth to seek his victim. Yet the sweet and beautiful Savitri, wife of Satyavat, by dint of a stubborn conjugal tenderness persuaded the god of death to spare her husband. As Yama carried off Satyavat's soul, Savitri followed his steps until at last the god was touched by such fidelity and promised to grant her wishes provided she would not ask him to bring her husband back to life. 'Then give me,' she said, 'a hundred strong sons born of Satyavat to carry on our stock.' Bound by his promise Yama had to bring the dead man to life.

Matarisvan: Bhrigus. Those mythical wise men, the earliest human beings, have transmitted to the most distant posterity the most precious of all knowledge – the technique of sacrificing in fire. The man who captured the thunderbolt in heaven, and gave to mortals the secret of the fiery element was Matarisvan.

We must also mention the Bhrigus, the 'shining ones', the name of a race destined to kindle and maintain Agni in human cults. The first bearer of this name designates one of the ten patriarchs instituted by Manu. A legend shows what authority these primitive men, in their capacity as possessors of the sacrificial knowledge, could exert over the most illustrious of the immortals. Certain wise men could not decide which of the three gods, Brahma, Vishnu and Siva, was most deserving of the Brahmans' worship; and Bhrigu was deputed to test the character of these gods. In approaching Brahma he intentionally omitted one of the signs which are due to him – the god gave Bhrigu a reprimand, but accepted his apologies and forgave him. Bhrigu then entered the dwelling of Siva and behaved in the same way. He would have been consumed to ashes by the angry god if he had not soothed him down with soft and humble words. Then he went to Vishnu who was lying down asleep, and woke him up with a kick in the chest. Far from getting into a rage the god asked if he had hurt himself and gently massaged his foot. 'Here is the greatest of the gods,' said Bhrigu. 'He surpasses the others by the most powerful weapons, kindness and generosity.'

COSMOGONY

The Vedas look upon the worlds – heaven, air, earth – sometimes as being constructed like a work of art, and sometimes as having derived from an organic development. Book X of the Hymns bridges the transition between the Vedic myths and the philosophical speculations of the Brahmans.

Before being and not-being there was a dark and watery chaos. Then a germ of life gifted with unity came to life by developing a sort of spontaneous heat, the 'tapas', which was at one and the same time heating, sweat and ascetic fervour. This principle felt and afterwards manifested the need to beget. (X, 129.).

In another explanation there was a primordial giant, a cosmic man, Purusha (the Male). The different parts of the world are his limbs, and in his unity this individual includes the first sacrificer and the first victim. (X, 90). In later metaphysics the term 'purusha' came to mean the spiritual principle.

In the work of creation there intervenes, with different meanings according to different traditions, the golden egg, the 'hiranyagarbha'. Produced by the primordial waters or brought into the world by Prajapati, this embryo gave birth to the supreme god, for instance the Brahman (*Satapatha Brahmana,* VI, 1, 1, 10). 'In this egg were the continents, the oceans, the mountains, the planets and the divisions of the universe, the gods, the demons and humanity. They say Brahma was born, which is a familiar way of saying that he manifested himself.' (*Vishnu-purana.*) At the end of a thousand years the egg opened, and Brahma who emerged from it meditated and started the work of creation. Seeing that the earth was submerged under the waters he assumed the aspect of a wild boar dived, and lifted it up on his tusks. At this period the old Vedic divinities were relegated to an inferior rank, even Varuna and Indra who, once the essential elements of the world had been created, had contributed to the establishment of its dimensions. Brahmanism thus preserves the ancient Vedic belief, according to which the gods maintain, without instituting, the fundamental order of things.

ESCHATOLOGY

According to the Rig-Veda, the dead are either buried or cremated. Cremation rapidly spread and was considered the normal way of attaining a definite dwelling place in the next world, in the sun or in the stars.

Later on all kinds of distinctions occurred. Only the spiritual principle, *asu* or *manas,* went to the sun, carried there by Agni. According to the *Satapatha Brahmana* there are two paths for the just – to the Fathers (pitri) and to the sun, while for the evil another leads to hell, naraka. In the Vedas the kingdom of Yama was a paradise for the good, but in the Puranas it is also a place of expiation for the wicked. According to the Upanishads we must distinguish between the journey to Brahma, the reward of perfect knowledge, which attains an abiding place from which there is no return, and the journey to heaven where after enjoying the reward deserved the soul returns to be reborn here below.

Thus we find a distinction which takes on the greatest importance in the faith of the Buddhists – on the one hand transmigration (samsara) without end, the normal condition of existence, and on the other hand the possibility of getting free for ever from this transmigration, that is to reach nirvana, for those who have completely understood the structure of things.

Heaven is a place where we possess the same goods as on earth, but without risking the troubles of earthly existence. One is provided with a glorious body. The idea of hell which may be discerned however in the *Athervabeda* became general at a later date. It has not a widely Indo-European character like the idea of a dwelling of the blessed in heavenly light.

THE HERETICAL DHARMAS

JAINISM

We call Jainism and Buddhism 'heretical' because these two religions, which began to spread through the area between the Himalayas and the Ganges in the 7th and 6th centuries before our era, threw off the Vedic tradition. They were far less concerned with giving mankind power over Nature than in freeing it from what they considered the basis of existence, the law of transmigration (samsara). Thus they are doctrines of salvation. Their propaganda does not lay claim to revelation or to some early authority. It limits itself to showing how a great man of wisdom found the path of deliverance for himself and for others, although he was wholly human. Consequently, at any rate at first, they contain no dogma, and no rites, but simply a law and an example.

Their mythology includes no theology, and is limited to a biography and moral exhortation. But the miraculous very soon crept into these alleged biographies, and the Churches by many popular legends multiplied their subjects almost to infinity. On the other hand, the moral mission very soon became involved in metaphysics, which in turn gave rise to unforeseen gods and myths. For these reasons, although theoretically all mythology is absent from these doctrines, there was an immense efflorescence of legends sprouting from the stem of both these heresies, especially from the Buddhist stem.

The Tirthamkaras. The assumption of Jainism, as of Buddhism, is the proposition that a man at grips with the normal conditions of existence is carried away by a sort of current, in which he will most likely succumb, and where he will inevitably be the victim of suffering and want. This strange conception, which their propaganda soon imposed on all India, including that of the Brahmans, derives from the fact that these heresies look upon existence as the result of action – every being is what he has made himself, and will become what he deserves to become according to the kind and quality of his actions. Death cannot annihilate the individual existence, because after it, retribution for things done – whether in the shape of reward or punishment – must be endured. This retribution involves fresh actions which in turn require new destinies, and so ad infinitum. Heavens and hells merely designate relative and temporary conditions. It would be madness to hope to reach salvation through the gods.

This law of transmigration of souls which brought even orthodox eschatology into confusion, seemed an endless servitude and pain to Indian consciences, which felt crushed by it. Henceforth every species of religious ingenuity and metaphysics strove to discover a means whereby the individual might escape this seemingly inevitable slavery. To escape from ignorance and want – that is the attainment of nirvana.

Every man who has 'found a ford' across the swirling, catastrophic current of the samsara is called Tirthamkara.

Such was the Jina, the initiator of Jainism, and such the Buddha, initiator of Buddhism. Both traversed the current by a clear intuition of the conditions of human misery reached after practising a stern asceticism.

To what extent the biography of a sage may be transformed by legend and thereby incorporated into mythology may be learned from M. A. Guérinot's *La Réligion Djaina*, 1926.

Humanity goes through alternating phases of progress and regression, and had reached an epoch when human suffering was continually on the increase. The Jina or Mahavira (Great Man) decided to leave his heavenly abode to save humanity. 'He took the form of an embryo in the womb of Devananda, wife of the Brahman Rishabhadatta who lived at Kundapura. That night as Devananda was in bed and half asleep she saw in her dreams fourteen apparitions of favourable omen – an elephant, a bull, a lion, the goddess Sri, a garland, the moon, the sun, a standard, a valuable vase, a lake of lotuses, the ocean, a heavenly dwelling, a heap of jewels, and finally a flame. Rishabhadatta was delighted. He perceived that a son would be born to him who would become skilled in the learning of the Brahmans.

'Now, Sakra, the king of the gods in heaven...thought it would be preferable to transfer the embryo of Mahavira from Devananda's womb to that of Trisala, the wife of the kshatriya Siddhartha...He called to him the leader of the heavenly infantry, Harinagamesi (the Man-with-the-antelope's-head) and ordered him to carry out this transposition...When Harinagamesi had completed his mission he left Trisala resting on a magnificent bed in an ornate dwelling filled with flowers and perfumes. In her turn she dreamed of fourteen unparalleled manifestations...

'From that moment Siddhartha found good fortune was his friend. He increased his possession of gold, silver, land and corn. His army increased in numbers and in power, and his glory shone in every direction. He decided that when his son was born he should be given then name of Vardhamana, he-who-grows, he-who-develops.'

(We now come to the birth of Mahavira.) '...That night the gods and goddesses came down from heaven to show their joy. The Demons rained flowers, fruits, gold and silver, pearls, diamonds, nectar, and sandal-wood on Siddhartha's palace...

'For thirty years (the Mahavira) lived a worldly life. He married Yasoda by whom he had a daughter, Riyadarsana. Then his parents, who followed the doctrines of Parsva, decided to leave this world. They lay down on a pile of grass and let themselves die of starvation. Vardhamana was now free from the vow he had made in his mother's womb, and decided to live after the fashion of wandering monks. He asked the permission of his brother and of the various authorities of the kingdom. Then he gave his wealth to the poor, and being thus freed from every bond became an ascetic.

'...The gods came down from heaven, approached...and did him homage...A procession was formed, made up of men, gods and demons, all shouting: "Victory! Victory!" The sky was as lovely as a lake covered with open lotus-flowers, while earth and air echoed with melodious instruments...'

Vardhamana spent twelve years in ascetic practices. Then once upon a time 'he sat down near an ancient temple under the tree Sala (teak), and remained motionless for two and a half days, fasting, and plunged in the deepest meditation. When he arose on the third day, enlightenment was complete. Vardhamana now possessed supreme and absolute knowledge; he was *kevalin*, omniscient...the perfect wise man, one of the blessed, an *arhat*; in short a *Jina*, a hero who had overcome evil and misery.

'...The gods were present (thirty years later, after he had spent that time in preaching) when he entered *nirvana* and became liberated, *mukta*, perfect, *siddha*.'

To sum up – we have a miraculous person vowed from all eternity to the salvation of the world, more than a god, since like men all the gods are mere supernumeraries compared with him, a discoverer, and a preacher of universal deliverance, the founder of a community. The Jain Church, made up of laymen led by monks and nuns, followed the master in propagating the Law. The real story was more modest, but with a religious genius of this type legend may be truer than historical reality.

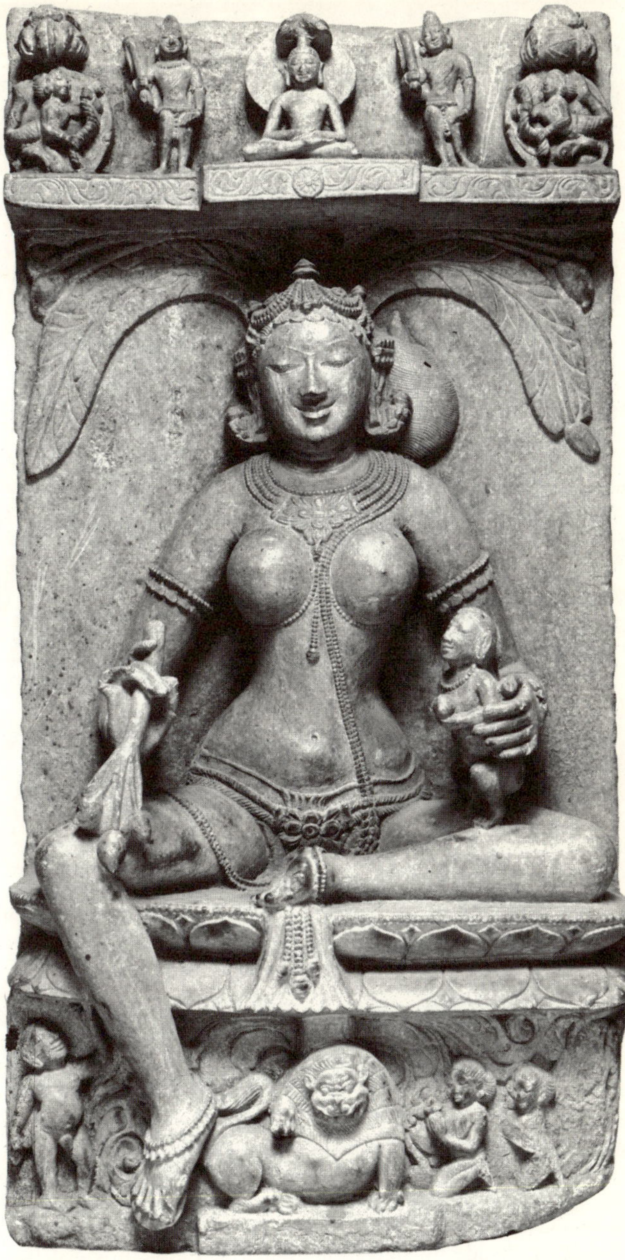

Jain mother goddess. This carving from the Jain temple at Orissa shows Parvati in her form as Ambika, or generatrix. Though the Jain religion was a revolt against the polytheism of Hinduism, many of the Hindu gods soon regained a foothold, though frequently under different names. Their role, however, was inferior to that of the Tirthamkaras and in order to attain Deliverance they themselves had first to become human-beings. Steatite, eleventh century A.D.

Other Tirthamkaras. The transposing of a human biography into terms of dogmatic myth is not solely a matter of adding the supernatural to the personality of the religious founder. It appears in the

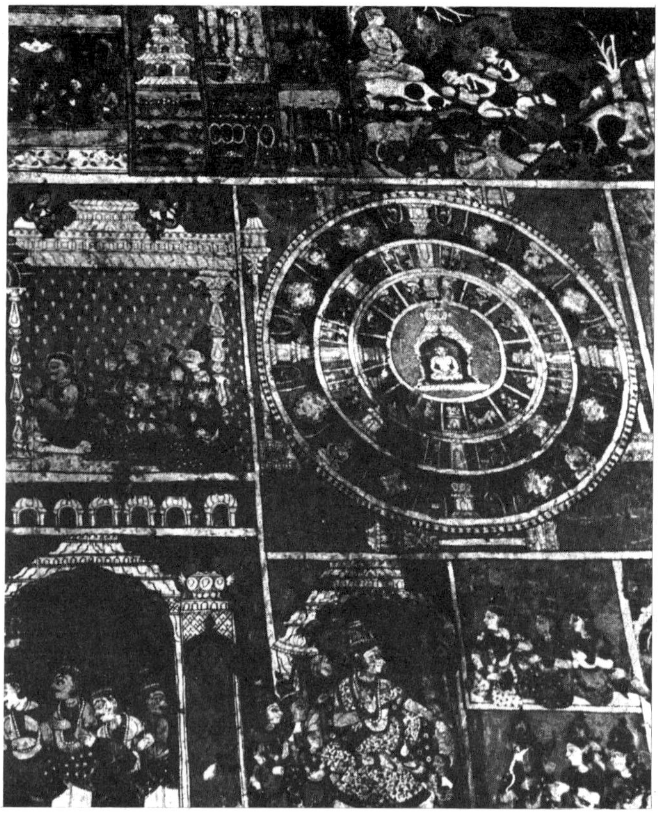

Jain wheel of life. For the Jains, as for the Buddhists, death does not put an end to an individual existence and the soul is constantly reborn on a higher or lower plane according to its merits in its previous life. To obtain release from this ceaseless cycle is the goal of their religion those who succeed being known as Tirthamkaras. Fresco in the nineteenth-century monastery at Sravanabelgola, Mysore.

endless multiplication of his personality into abstract types which mythology strives to make concrete. There are ten regions of the universe, in each of which arise twenty-four Tirthamkaras in each of the three ages, past, present and future. Thus we obtain seven hundred and twenty saviours of the world, of whom seven hundred and nineteen are pale reflections of the Jina.

In this way a stylised convention was formed from the real situation, wherein the Jina was preceded by the sect of the Nirgranthas, whose master was Parsva, practisers of austerity to the point of advocating suicide by starvation; but which also provided for a series of patriarchs who kept alive the tradition of the founder in the community. In the book by Guérinot already quoted will be found the description of twenty-four Tirthamkaras in that part of the world where India is situated, during the present epoch. Each one is defined by certain characteristics – such-and-such proportions of the body, such a colour, such-and-such symbols; such-and-such acolyte in human form, a yaksha or a yakshini; such-and-such a posture, of special significance from the position of the hands and legs, etc. To each one a special cult is appropriated.

BUDDHISM

Everything we have just described in Jainism is to be found under other aspects in Buddhism, which is indeed Jainism's younger brother. Theoretically the sect should have limited its activity to moral reform, the institution of a law or dharma, which in humble believers would lead to faith, and in saints to nirvana. But as a matter of fact, popular superstition and fable immediately imposed on it an exuberant mythology which completely altered the simplicity of the dogma. Just as in Europe Christianity followed the pagan cults which were transformed into hagiographies, so a whole popular religion soaked into the myths of Buddhism – for instance, the traditional agricultural rites at each season of the year. Such was the myth of Gavampati, the god of drought and wind, who was immolated to bring rain, of which traces may still be found in most Buddhist festivals. (See J. Przyluski, *Le Concile de Rajagriha*, 1926 – 1928).

LEGEND OF BUDDHA

H. Oldenberg has compiled from Pali writings a 'reasonable' – we will not say too 'historical' – biography of the sage of the Sakyas (Sakyamuni) who was to become the Buddha, the Enlightened. On the other hand, E. Senart has composed an entirely legendary biography on the same subject, derived from Sanskrit documents. In the latter the institutor of Buddhism, far from dwindling to a sage of human essence, turns out to be an aspect of the solar god, Vishnu, who came down on earth to save our species. In point of fact all the classic episodes of his life are more or less touched with the miraculous.

Buddha lived between about 563 and 483 B.C. in the north-east of India.

The future Buddha or Bodhisattva had already passed through thousands of existences to prepare himself for his final transmigration. Before coming down to earth for the last time he visited the heaven of the Tushitas (abode of the blessed) and preached the Law to the gods. But one day he perceived that his hour had come and was incarnated in the family of a king of the Sakyas, Suddhodhana, who reigned in Kapilavastu, on the borders of Nepal.

Birth and Childhood of Buddha. His conception was miraculous. Queen Maya, whose name literally means 'Illusions', warned by a presentiment, saw in a dream the Bodhisattva enter her womb in the shape of a lovely little elephant as white as snow. At this moment the whole universe showed its joy by miracles – musical instruments played without being touched, rivers stopped flowing to contemplate the Bodhisattva, trees and plants were covered with flowers and the lakes with lotuses. Next day Queen Maya's dream was interpreted by sixty-four Brahmans, who predicted the birth of a son destined to become either a universal emperor or a Buddha.

When the time of his birth drew near the queen retired to the garden of Lumbini and there, standing and holding on to a branch of the tree Sala with her right hand, she gave birth to the Bodhisattva who came forth from her right side without causing her the least pain. The child was received by Brahma and the other gods, but he began at once to walk, and a lotus appeared as soon as his foot touched the earth. He took seven steps in the direction of the seven cardinal points, and thus took possession of the world. On the very same day were born Yasodhara Devi who was to be his wife, the horse Kantaka which he was to ride when he deserted his palace to seek supreme knowledge, his squire Chandaka, his friend and favourite disciple Ananda, and the Bo-tree beneath which he came to know Enlightenment.

Five days after his birth the young prince received the name Siddhartha. On the seventh day Queen Maya died of joy, and was re-born among the gods, leaving her sister Mahaprajapati to take her place beside the young prince. The complete devotion of this adoptive mother has become legendary. A saintly old man from the Himalayas, the wealthy Asita, predicted the child's destiny and observed in him the eighty signs which are the pledges of a high religious vocation. When the child was taken by his parents to the temple, the statues of the gods bowed down before him.

When the young prince was twelve years old the king called a council of Brahmans. They revealed to him that the prince would devote himself to asceticism if he beheld the spectacle of old age, sickness and death, and if he afterwards met a hermit. The king preferred that his son should be a universal sovereign rather than a hermit. The sumptuous palaces with their vast and beautiful gardens in which the young man was destined to live were therefore surrounded with a triple wall well-guarded. Mention of the words 'death' and 'grief' was forbidden.

Buddha's Marriage. A little later it occurred to the Rajah that the surest way to bind the prince to his kingdom was marriage. With a view to discovering a princess who would awaken his son's love the king collected magnificent jewels, and announced that on a given day Siddhartha would distribute them among the neighbouring princesses. When all the presents had been given out there arrived the last girl, Yasodhara, daughter of Mahanama, one of the ministers. She asked the prince if he had nothing for her, and he, having met her glance, took the valuable ring from his finger and gave it to her. The exchange of glances and the remarkable gift did not escape

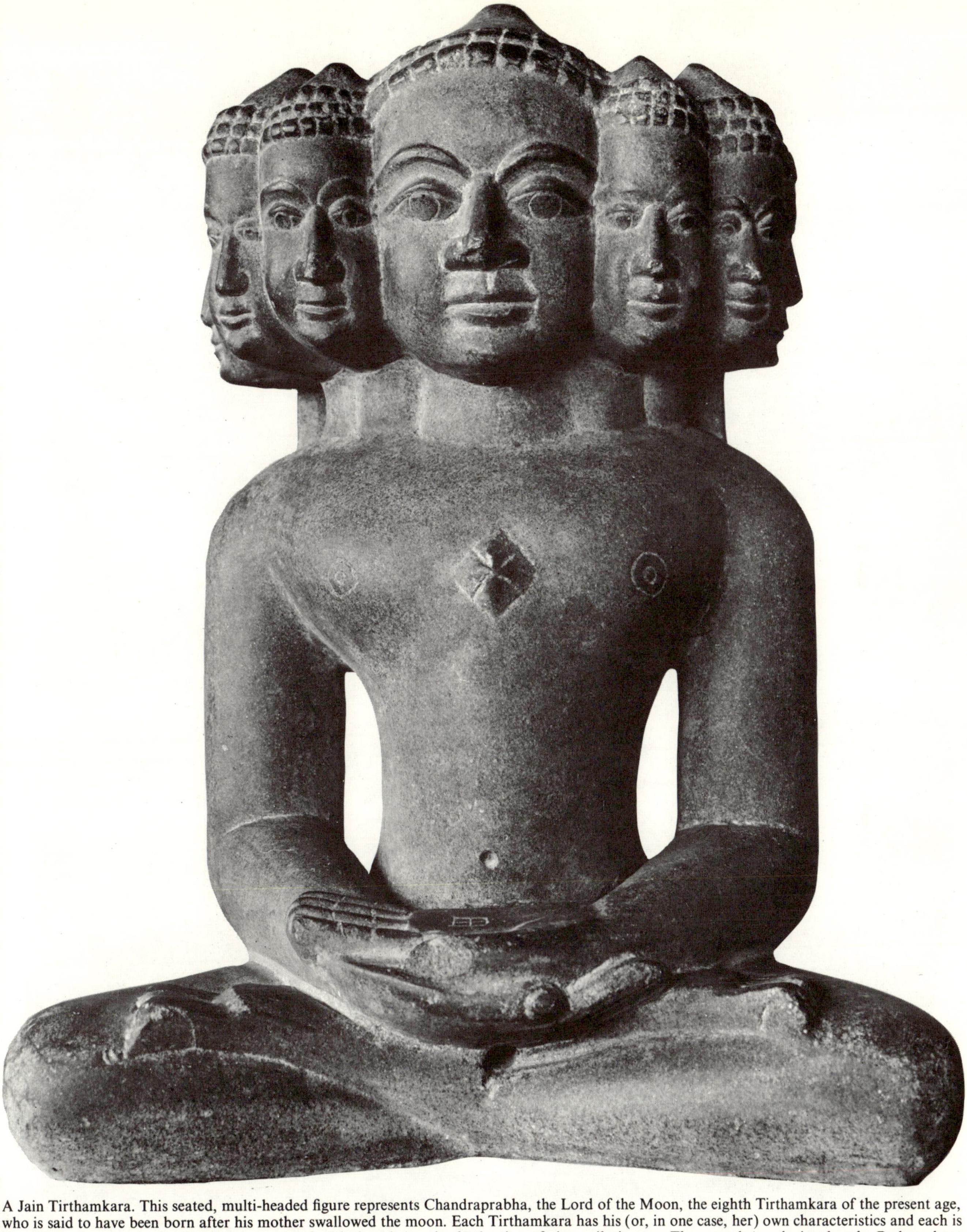

A Jain Tirthamkara. This seated, multi-headed figure represents Chandraprabha, the Lord of the Moon, the eighth Tirthamkara of the present age, who is said to have been born after his mother swallowed the moon. Each Tirthamkara has his (or, in one case, her) own characteristics and each is the object of a special cult, the places associated with them being the destination of pious pilgrimages. They are always depicted nude. Red sandstone.

the king's attention, and he asked for the girl in marriage.

However, the tradition of Sakyas compelled their princesses to take as husband only a true Kshatriya who could demonstrate his skill in all the accomplishments of his caste. Yasodhara's father had his doubts about Siddhartha, who had been brought up in the ease of court life. So a tournament was organised, and the prince came out first in all the competitions of riding, fencing and wrestling. Moreover, he was the only one who could string and shoot with the sacred bow of enormous size bequeathed by his ancestors. Princess Yasodhara was therefore married to him.

The Vocation and the Great Departure. But very soon his divine vocation awoke in him. The music of the different instruments which sounded in his ears, the graceful movements of the girls dancing for the delight of his eyes, ceased to move his senses, and on the contrary showed him the vanity and instability of human life. 'The life of the creature passes like the mountain torrent and like the flash of lightning.'

One day the prince called his equerry – he wanted to visit the town. The king ordered it to be swept and decorated and that every ugly or depressing sight should be hidden from his son. But these

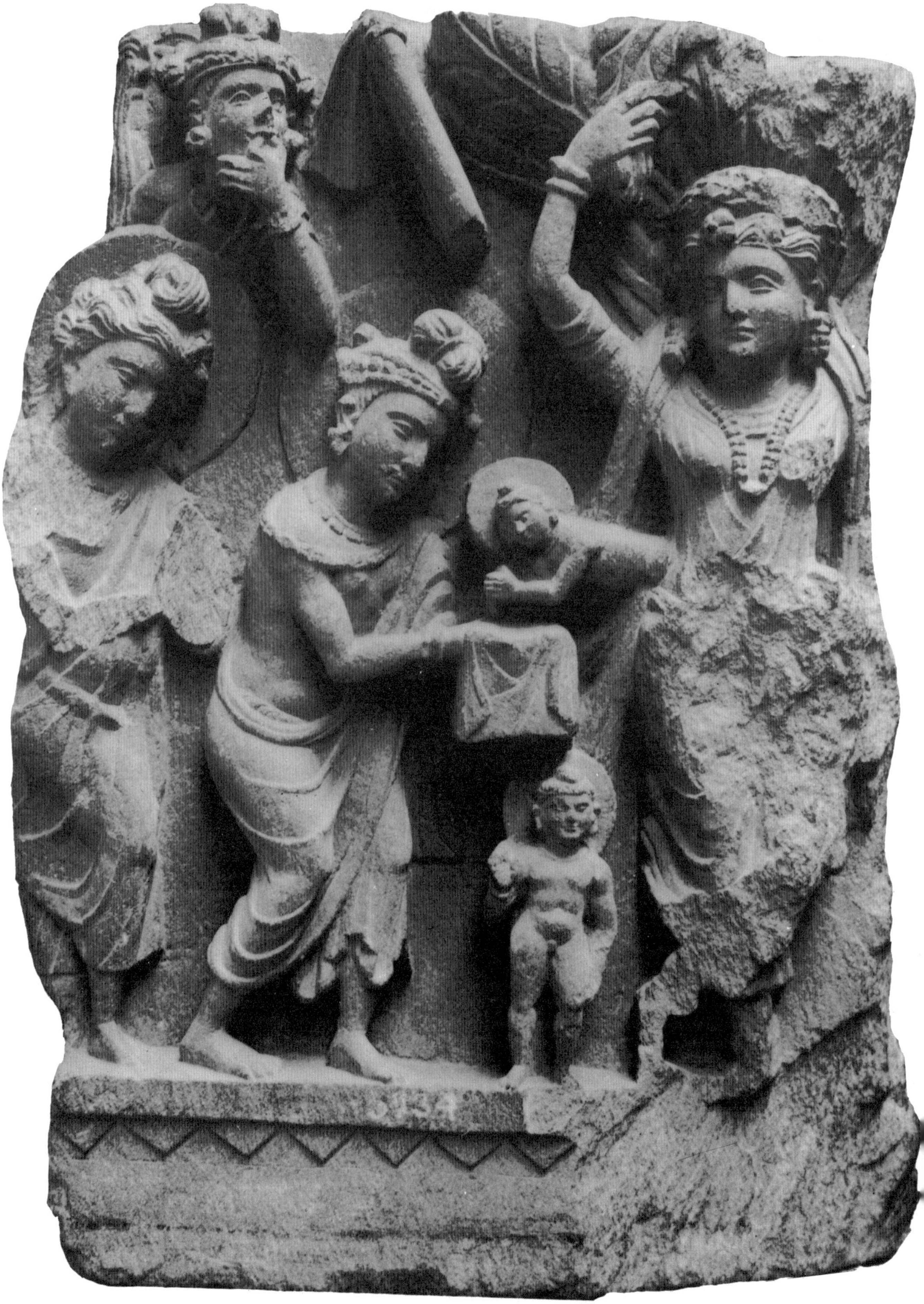

The birth of Buddha. After remaining childless until her forty-fifth year, Queen Maya has withdrawn to the garden of Lumbini to give birth to the son who will change the thoughts of mankind. Siddhartha is born from her side undefiled and full of awareness and instantly takes possession of the world. Queen Maya is reputed to have died seven days later but was converted by her son shortly after death.
Gandhara style relief, third century A.D.

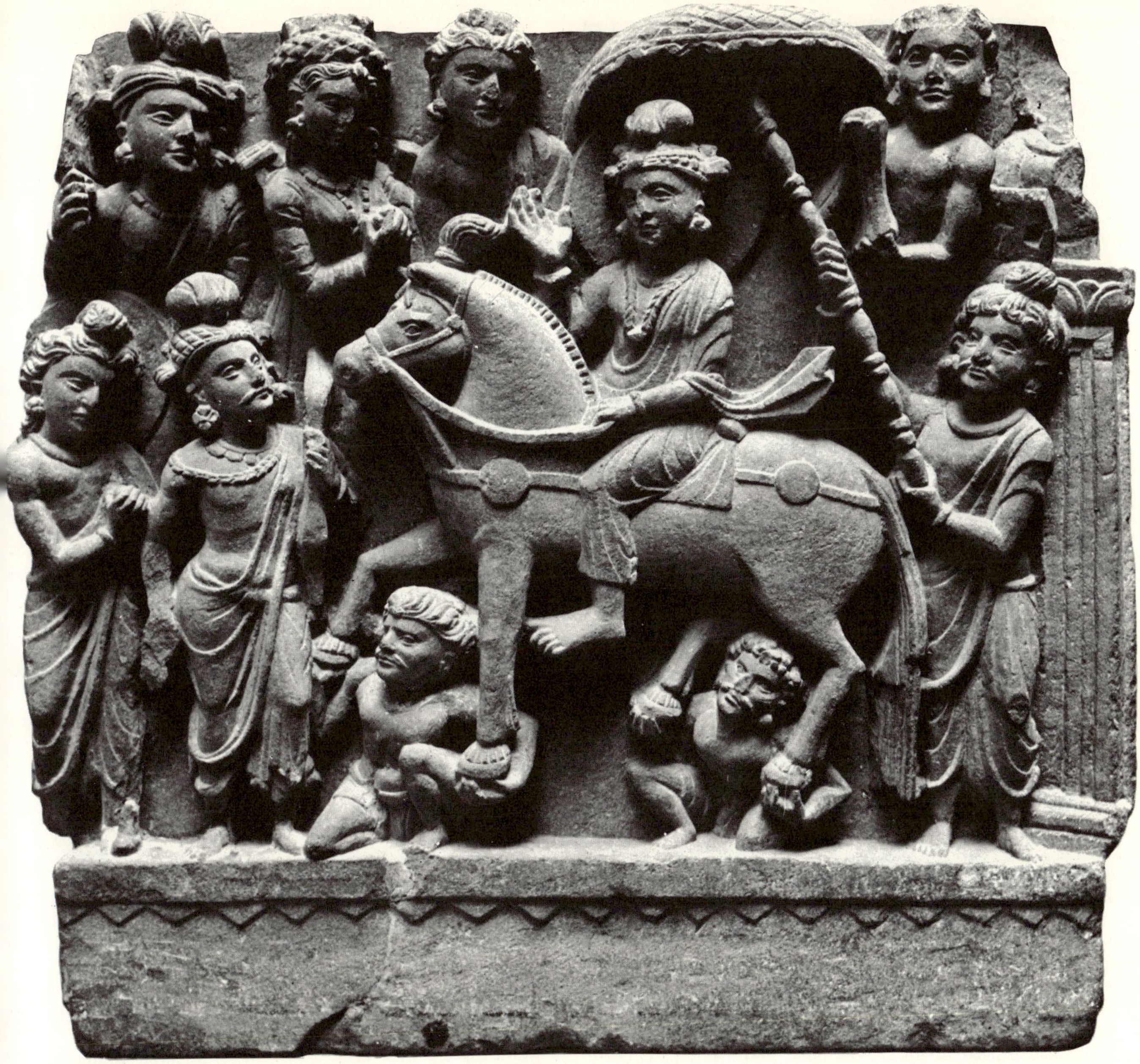

Siddhartha's departure. When he was twelve years old a council of Brahmans revealed that Siddhartha would devote himself to asceticism if ever he saw old age, sickness, death and a hermit. Now, despite his father's precautions, the prophecy has been fulfilled and the future Buddha steals away from the palace while the gods support his horse's hooves so that no sound shall awaken the sleeping guards. Gandhara style relief, third century A.D.

precautions were useless. As he rode through the streets the prince beheld a trembling, wrinkled old man, breathless with age, and bowed on his staff. With astonishment the young man learned that decrepitude is the inevitable fate of those who 'live out their lives'. When he got back to the palace he asked if there is any way of avoiding old age.

Similarly, another day he came on someone with an incurable disease, and then a funeral procession, and thus came to know of suffering and death.

Finally heaven threw in his way a begging ascetic, who told him that he had abandoned the world to pass beyond joy and suffering and attain peace of heart.

These experiences and his meditations on them suggested to Siddhartha that he should abandon his present life and become an ascetic. He spoke of it to his father – 'O king, all things in this world are changing and transitory. Let me go forth alone, a begging monk.'

The father was overwhelmed with grief at the thought of losing the son in whom lay all the hopes of his line. The guards round the walls were doubled, and there were continual amusements and pleasures devised in the palaces and gardens to prevent the young prince from thinking any more of leaving.

At this time Yasodhara gave birth to the little Rahula. But even this did not hinder Bodhisattva from his mission.

His decision became final when one sleepless night he beheld the spectacle of the harem – wan faces, bodies wilted in the involuntary relaxation of sleep and unconsciousness, an artless abandonment in the midst of disorder. 'Some dribbled, spattered with saliva; others ground their teeth; some snored and talked in their sleep. Some had their mouths wide open... It was like a foretaste of the horrors of the grave.'

His mind was made up. But before leaving, Siddhartha wanted to look for the last time on his beautiful wife, Yasodhara. She was asleep, holding their new-born child in her arms. He wanted to kiss his son but was afraid he might waken the mother, so left them both, and lifting the curtain heavy with jewels went out into the fresh night with its countless stars, and mounted his beautiful horse Kantaka, accompanied by his equerry Chandaka.

The gods in complicity sent sleep on the guards and lifted the horse's hoofs so that the noise of his shoes should waken nobody. At the gates of the town Siddhartha gave his horse to Chandaka and took farewell of these two friends urging them to console his father – and in mute farewell the horse licked his feet.

With one sweep of his sword the prince cut off his hair, and threw it upwards where it was gathered by the gods. A little later, meeting a hunter, he exchanged his own splendid garments for the man's rags, and thus transformed made his way to a hermitage where the Brahmans received him as a disciple.

Henceforth there was no more Siddhartha. He became the monk

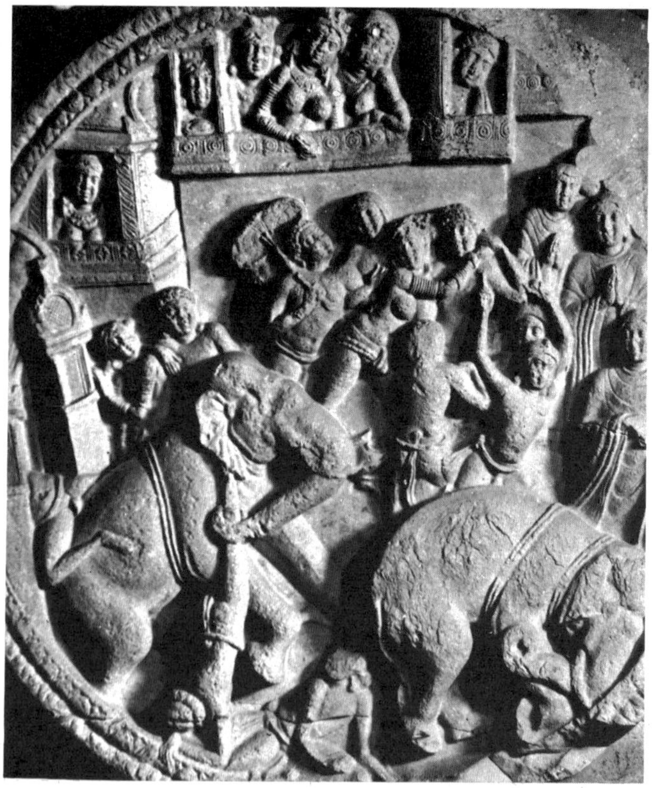

The drunken elephant, after spreading panic through the town, bows himself at the feet of Buddha. Amaravati, India.

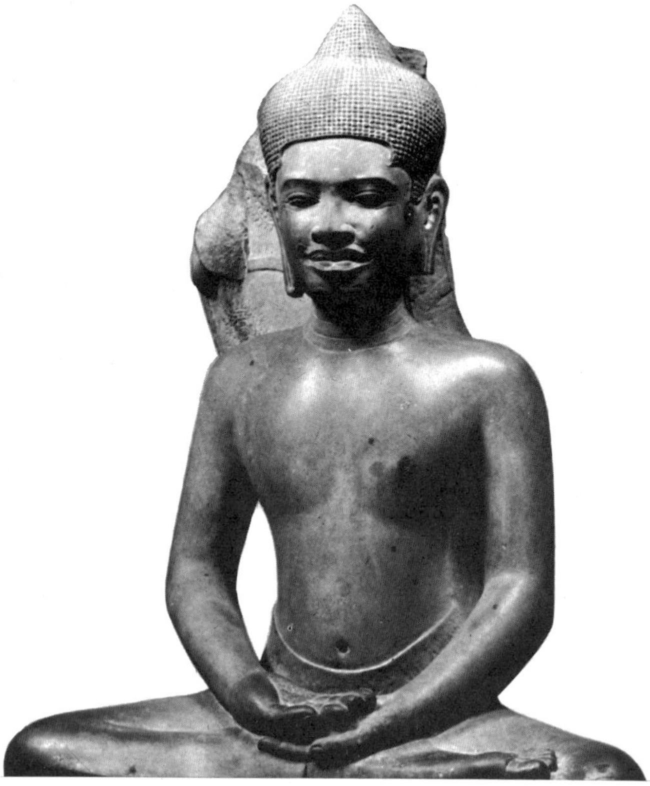

Buddha seated on Musilinda. After attaining Enlightenment beneath the sacred fig-tree at Bodhi-Gaya, Buddha spent a further period near the tree in meditation. In the fifth week a violent storm arose and in order to protect him from the soaking ground and teeming rain, the Naga kind, Musilinda, coiled himself beneath the sage and spread his hood (now missing) above his head. Sandstone from Bayon, Cambodia. Eleventh century A.D.

Gautama or, as he is still called, Sakyamuni, the ascetic of the Sakyas. He sought for wisdom as a disciple of the Yogis, living turn by turn in several hermitages, and especially with Arada Kalapa; but their doctrines did not teach him what he was seeking. He continued to wander, and at last stopped at Uruvilva on the bank of a very fine river. There he remained six years, practising dreadful austerities which reduced his body almost to nothing.

But he realised that excessive macerations destroy a man's strength and instead of freeing the mind make it impotent. He had to get beyond asceticism, as he had got beyond worldly life.

And the exhausted Bodhisattva, thin as a skeleton, accepted the bowl of rice offered him by a village girl, Sujata, who was moved to compassion by the ascetic's weakness. Then he bathed in the river. The five disciples who had shared his austerities abandoned him, much perturbed by his behaviour.

The Enlightenment. Siddhartha then started for Bodhi-Gaya and the tree of Wisdom. As he passed through the forest such light emanated from his body that the kingfishers and other birds were attracted and flew in circles about him. The peacocks joined other animals of the forest to escort him. A Naga king and his wife came out of their underground dwelling to worship him. The devas hung standards from the trees to show him his way.

And now the Bodhisattva reached the sacred fig-tree. It was the decisive hour of his career. He set a bundle of new-mown hay and sat down, uttering this vow:

'Here, on this seat, may my body dry up, may my skin and flesh waste away if I raise my body from this seat until I have attained the knowledge it is hard to attain during numerous kalpas!'

And the earth quaked six times.

Mara, the Buddhist demon, was warned of what was happening which would be the ruin of his power, and decided to interfere. He sent his three delicious daughters to tempt the Bodhisattva and divert him from his intentions. The girls sang and danced before his eyes. They were skilled in all the seductions of desire and pleasure, but the Bodhisattva remained as unmoved in his heart as in his countenance, as calm as a lotus on the smooth waters of a lake, as unmoved as the roots of the mountains.

Mara's daughters retired defeated. Then the demon tried an attack, with an army of devils, horrible creatures, some with a thousand mouths, others pot-bellied and deformed, drinking blood or devouring snakes, uttering inhuman cries, spreading darkness, armed with spears, bows and maces. They surrounded the tree of Wisdom, threatening the Bodhisattva, but found themselves paralysed with their arms bound to their sides.

Mara himself then made the supreme attempt. Riding on the clouds he hurled his terrible disk. But this weapon which could cut a mountain in two was impotent against the Bodhisattva. It was changed into a garland of flowers and hung suspended above his head.

Before sunset Mara was beaten. And the motionless Bodhisattva remained in meditation under the sacred tree. Night came, and with it the dawn of the Enlightenment he sought rose slowly on his heart. First he knew the exact conditions of all living beings, and then the causes of their rebirth. Throughout the world and in all ages he beheld beings live, die, and transmigrate. He remembered his own previous existences, and grasped the inevitable links of causes and effects. As he meditated on human suffering he was enlightened as to its genesis and the means which allow it to be destroyed.

When daylight appeared the Bodhisattva had attained perfect Enlightenment (bodhi) and had become a Buddha. The rays of light from his shining body reached the confines of space.

For seven days Buddha remained in meditation, and then stayed near the tree for another four weeks. In the fifth week a terrible storm arose, but the Naga king, Musilinda, made a seat for him from the coils of his body and a canopy with his open hood, and so sheltered him from the storm and the flood.

Henceforward two paths were open to Buddha. He could at once enter nirvana; or, renouncing for the time being his own deliverance, he could remain on earth to spread the good word. Mara urged him to leave the world, and Buddha himself realised that the doctrine is profound while men are not at all given to wisdom. Should he proclaim the Law to those who cannot understand it? For an instant

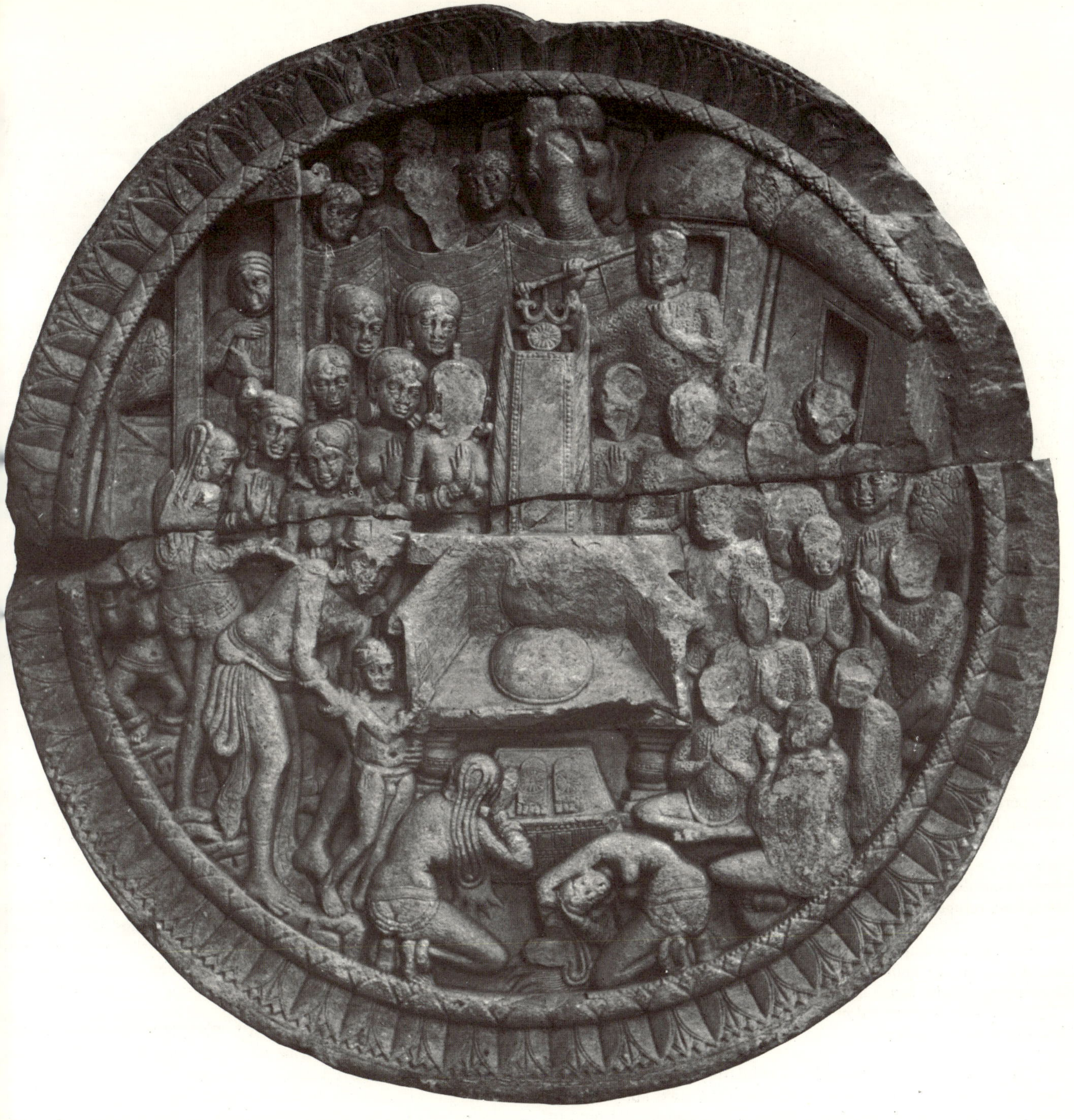

The presentation to Buddha of his son Rahula. Even the birth of his son, Rahula, to his beautiful young wife, Yasodhara, could not prevent Buddha from leaving the palace and following his vocation, but he later returned to the palace and converted his entire family, including Rahula, who became a monk. Buddha himself is not depicted, merely his footprints and his empty throne. Stone medallion from Amaravati, third century A.D.

he hesitated. But the gods united to implore him. Brahma in person came to beg him to preach his Law, and Buddha yielded to his wishes.

The Preaching. To whom was he first to address his preaching? His thoughts turned to the five disciples who had abandoned him. He went to Benares, and found them again. Seeing him coming from afar they agreed together: 'Here comes that Sramana Gautama, the dissolute, the glutton, spoiled by luxury... We have nothing in common with him. We must not go to meet him with respect, nor stand up... We must give him no carpet, no prepared drink, nowhere to set his feet.' But Buddha understood their thoughts, and turned on them the strength of his love. As a leaf is swept away by a torrent, so the hermits were conquered by his omnipotent goodness, and rose up to do homage to him whose first disciples they became.

So the first preaching took place at Benares, in the Gazelles' Park. According to the texts, the Buddha in his first sermon 'set in motion the wheel of the Law' (Dharmasakrapravartana). The Master's first message indicated at the outset the tone of primitive Buddhist doctrine – lucidity, moderation, charity.

'There are two extremes, O monks, which must be avoided. One is a life of pleasure, which is base and ignoble, contrary to the spirit, unworthy, vain. The other is a life of self-maceration, which is dreary, unworthy, vain. The Perfect, O monks, kept aloof from these two extremes and discovered the middle path which leads to rest, to knowledge, to enlightenment, and nirvana . . . Here, O monks, is the truth about pain. Birth, old age, sickness, death, separation from what we love, are pain. The origin of pain is the thirst for pleasure, the thirst for existence, the thirst for change. And here is the truth about the suppression of pain – the extinction of that thirst through the annihilation of desire.'

And again: 'I am come to fill the ignorant with knowledge. Almsgiving, knowledge, and virtue are goods which cannot be wasted. To do a little good is better than to accomplish difficult works...

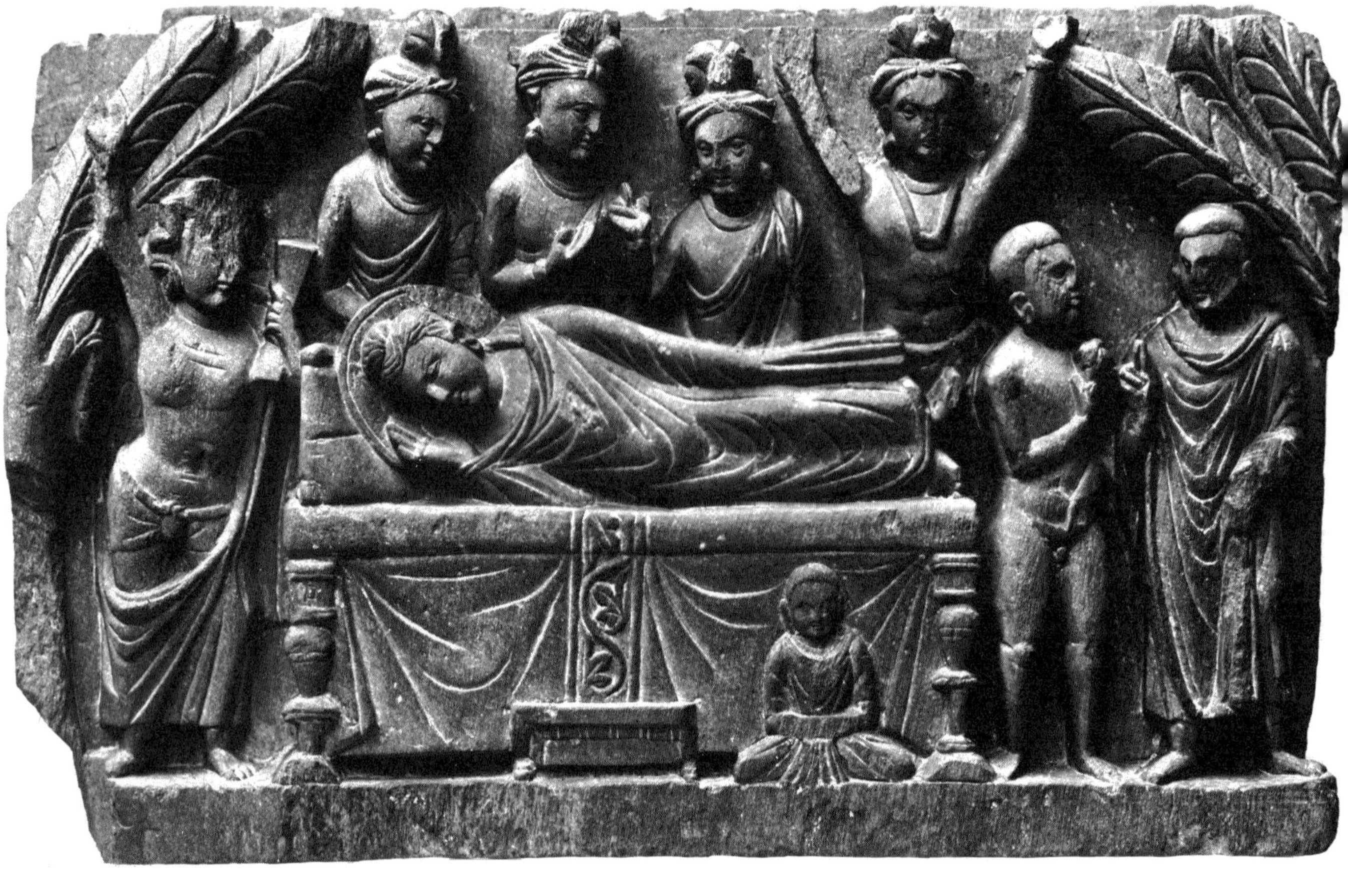

The passing of Buddha. The sage lies on the couch prepared for him by his disciple Ananda beneath a grove of miraculously flowering sal trees at Kusinagra while round about him are gathered his disciples and the Brahmans, kings and nobles summoned from the neighbouring countries to be at his side. After addressing his disciples Buddha entered into meditation and after a short period passed into nirvana. Gandhara relief, third century A.D.

The perfect man is nothing if he does not diffuse benefits on creatures, if he does not console the lonely... My doctrine is a doctrine of mercy... The way of salvation is open to all... Destroy your passions as an elephant throws down a hut built of reeds, but know that a man deceives himself if he thinks he can escape his passions by taking refuge in hermitages. The only remedy for evil is healthy reality.'

Thus began a wandering mission which lasted forty-four years. Buddha went up and down the land, followed by his disciples, converting all who heard him. Many episodes of this long ministration have been popularised in art or in legends. We mention here a few of the principal ones.

THE ANGRY ELEPHANT. Devadatta, Buddha's cousin, became his enemy. He made a royal elephant drunk, and turned it free in the streets at the moment when Buddha was going round to give alms. Smitten with terror the inhabitants fled, while the animal trampled on carriages and passers-by, and overthrew houses. Buddha's disciples implored him to leave, but he calmly kept on his way. But when a little girl carelessly crossing the road was almost killed by the raging elephant, Buddha spoke to it: 'Spare that innocent child – you were sent to attack me.' As soon as the elephant perceived Buddha, its rage was soothed as if by magic, and it came to kneel at the feet of the Blessed.

THE GREAT MIRACLE OF SRAVASTI. King Prasenajit organised a contest between Buddha and the members of a heretical sect he wished to convert. Numerous miracles were performed by Sakyamuni during this battle of miraculous powers. Two remained especially famous. The first is known as the miracle of water and fire. 'Bhagavat (the Blessed) plunged into meditation so profound that as soon as his spirit entered into it, he disappeared from the place where he was seated and shot into the air towards the West, where he appeared in the four postures of decency – that is to say, he walked, he stood up, he sat down, he lay down. He then rose to the region of light, and no sooner had he reached it than different lights spread from his body – blue, yellow, red and white lights, and others with the loveliest tints of crystal. He performed other miracles. Flames spread from the lower part of his body, while from the upper part fell a rain of cold water. He repeated in the South what he had done in the West and again in the four points of space.'

In the second episode Buddha is seen seated on a large golden lotus with a diamond stem formed by the Naga kings, with Brahma to his right and Indra to his left. Through the prestige of his omnipotence Buddha filled the whole sky with a countless number of similar lotuses, and in each of them was a Buddha similar to himself.

CONVERSION OF BUDDHA'S FAMILY. Buddha successively converted to his doctrine his father king Suddhodhana, his son Rahula, his cousin Ananda (who became his favourite disciple), his wife, and his adoptive mother, the good Mahaprajapati. Buddha ascended into heaven where he was greeted by his mother and the gods, who asked him to teach them the Law. At the end of three months this mission was ended, and the Blessed one returned to the earth by a ladder of gold and silver, with rungs of coral, ruby and emerald. And the gods escorted him.

The conversion of Nanda, Buddha's half-brother, was more difficult, and introduces a very human note, both poignant and comic. The young man had just married the prettiest girl in the district. The Blessed one came to the door. Nanda filled his bowl with alms, but Buddha refused to take it and go away. Nanda followed him, holding out the bowl, but received not a word or a gesture in reply. They came to the hermitage, and the mysterious, smiling Buddha caused his brother's head to be shaved, and forced him to put off his sumptuous clothes and dress in a monk's gown.

Poor Nanda submitted, but he was continually haunted by the charming memory of his young wife. One day he tried to run away, but mysterious powers prevented his escape. Sakyamuni took him on to a hill, where they saw a blind old monkey. 'Is your wife as beautiful as that monkey?' said Buddha to Nanda. Nanda's indignation was not soothed down until the Blessed carried him to the heaven of the thirty-three gods and into a magnificent palace inhabited by divine nymphs of incomparable beauty. Obviously his wife was a mere monkey compared with them. The nymphs revealed to him that after his death he was destined to become their lord and master.

On their return to the monastery Nanda became the most zealous of disciples, in the hope of being re-born in the heaven of the thirty-three gods. But a little later Buddha took him to hell, and showed him a vat of boiling water in which he would fall after his heavenly existence, in order to expiate his sensual desires. These successive visions led Nanda to meditate the doctrine, and he became a saint.

THE CHILD'S OFFERING. A little child wanted to make Buddha an offering, but had nothing in the world. So he collected the dust, and joining his two open hands childishly offered it to the Blessed. He was touched by this gesture of faith, and smilingly accepted the gift. Later on this innocent child was re-born in the form of the great Indian emperor, Asoka.

THE MONKEY'S OFFERING. A monkey offered Buddha a bowl of honey. Delighted to see his gift accepted, the monkey cut a caper, fell, and was killed. He was immediately re-born as the son of a Brahman.

Buddha's Death. At the age of eighty Buddha felt he had grown old. He visited all the communities he had founded, set them in order, and prepared for his end. He died at Kusinagara after eating an indigestible meal with one of his disciples, who was a smith. He died peacefully beside the river Hiranyavati, in a grove where Ananda had prepared his bed. The trees about him were covered with flowers. The Gandharvas played heavenly music. The disciples surrounded the dying man, and some wept despite their Master's exhortations.

'O disciples, everything created must perish. A man must separate from everything he has loved. Say not, we no longer have a Master ...When I am gone the doctrine I have preached will be your Master. Watch and pray without respite.'

After speaking these words, Buddha entered into meditation and then into ecstasy, and finally passed into nirvana. His body was burned on a funeral pyre which lighted itself, and was extinguished at the right moment by a miraculous rain. Relics of the Blessed one were preserved in the 'Stupas' which soon after were raised in India.

This biography which alongside the miraculous contains traits of high morality, not only flowered on the surface with repeated types of the Buddha in divergent forms, but also as it were in depth – Sakyamuni having deserved to become Buddha because of all his former lives, which formed part of his personality.

The Jatakas. Jatakas is the name given the stories relating to the lives of the Bodhisattva before the life in which he received the Bodhi, Enlightenment. Innumerable folklore stories have been incorporated in this literature. Many of the fables already current in India took on a Buddhist appearance. Moreover the Jatakas have a dogmatic value, since they show at work in reality that causal connection, which according to Buddhist philosophy forms the structure of things – every event in the present is to be explained by facts going farther and farther back into the past. This is the justification of the law of Kharma, by virtue of which every being, and the Bodhisattva in particular, becomes what he makes himself. Metaphysical dogma and popular belief thus coincide in the very idea of the Jataka.

Here, for instance, is the tale of The Devotion of the King-Monkey (Mahakapi-Jataka). In those days the Bodhisattva was a king-monkey. One day when he was disporting himself in an orchard of

Avalokitesvara. One of the five Dhyani-Bodhisattvas, Avalokitesvara is associated with the Dhyani-Buddha, Amitabha, and personifies Buddha's compassionate wish to remain on earth in order to share his knowledge. Although his normal abode is the paradise of Amitabha he prefers to bring help to the suffering and damned and instruct the unconverted. His serene and compassionate face is represented on the four sides of the tower of the eleventh century. Bayon temple in Cambodia.

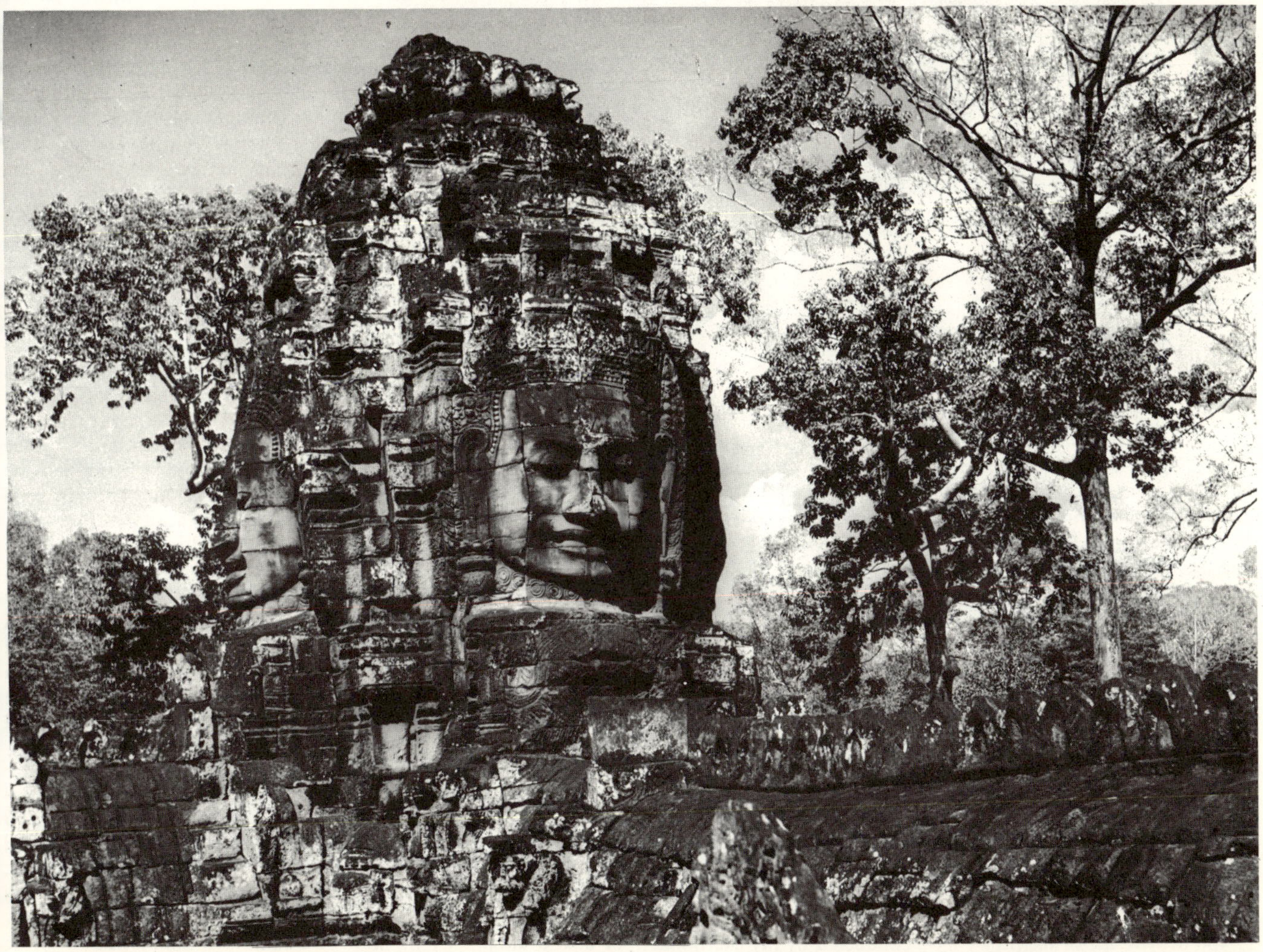

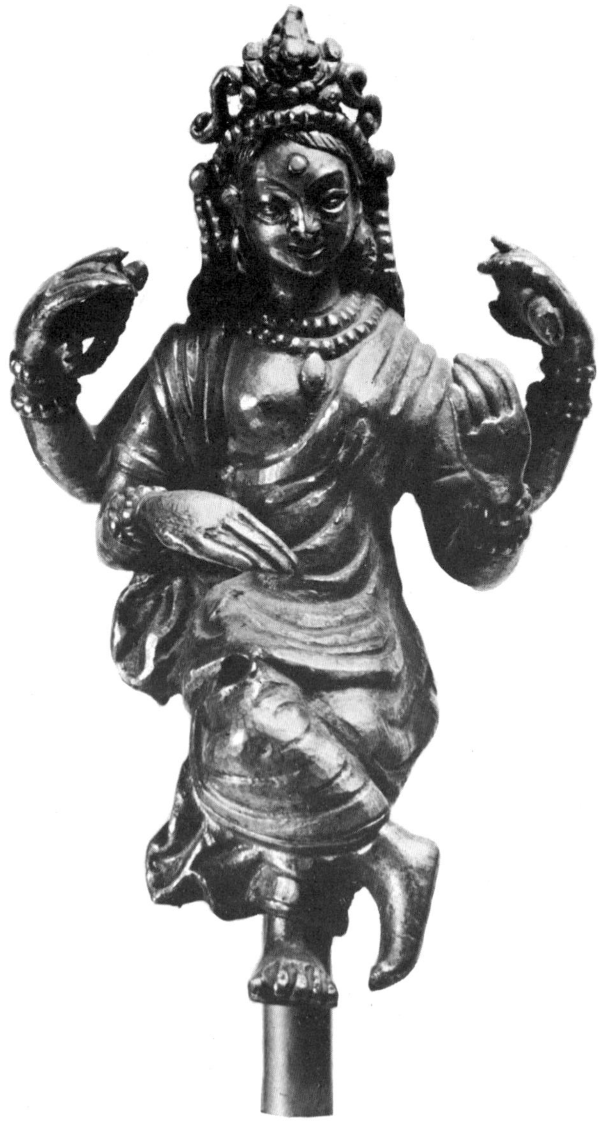

Tara. Like the gods of Hinduism, the Buddhas too have their saktis who take the form of goddesses and furnish mankind with knowledge or compassion. The most revered of these is Tara, the sakti of Avalokitesvara, who was born from his tears and in some countries shares his cult. Like Siva's wife she has a double character and can be both threatening and gentle.
Nepalese bronze, eighteenth century A.D.

mangoes along with eighty thousand of his subjects, the archers were ordered to surround the monkeys and to kill them. The poor creatures could only escape by crossing the Ganges. The king-monkey fastened to his waist a bamboo rope and tied the other end to the branch of a tree. He then crossed the river with one huge jump, but the rope was too short, and he could reach the bank only by clinging to a tree. On the living bridge thus formed the eighty thousand monkeys crossed and saved their lives. But Devadatta, Buddha's future cousin, was among the fugitives. Already the betrayer, he pretended to stumble, fell heavily on the back of the king-monkey and broke it as he passed. The heroic monkey was succoured by the king of Benares and made an edifying death, not without bestowing on his host some salutary advice for the government of his kingdom.

One of the principal Buddhist virtues is endless compassion for all creatures. We find an example in the story of the king, the dove and the falcon (Sibi-Jataka).

To test the integrity and charity of the king of the Sibis, Indra assumed the form of a falcon pursuing a dove, which itself is also a form of the metamorphosed god. The harried dove took refuge in the king's bosom. 'Fear nothing, beautiful bird, whose eyes are like the flowers of the asoka tree,' said the king. 'I save all living things which come to me for protection, even though I should lose my kingdom and my life itself.'

But now the falcon spoke: 'This dove is my food. By what right do you deprive me of the prey I have conquered by my exertions? I am devoured by hunger. You have no right to intervene in the differences of the birds of the air. If you mean to protect the dove think of me and how I shall die of hunger. If you refuse to yield me this bird you are cherishing, give me an equal weight of the flesh of your own body.'

'You are right,' said the king of the Sibis. 'Bring the scales.' He then cut off some of the flesh of his thigh and threw it into the scale having put the dove on the other one. The queens, the ministers and the attendants began to utter lamentations which rose up from the palace as the muttering of thunder from piled-up masses of cloud. The earth itself quaked at this act of integrity.

But the king continued to cut the flesh from his legs, his arms and his breast. The scale was piled up in vain, for the dove grew heavier and heavier. So much so that the king, now reduced to a skeleton decided he must give all himself, and entered the scale.

Then the gods appeared, and heavenly music was heard. A shower of ambrosia drenched the king's body, and completely healed him Flowers fell from heaven, the Gandharvas and Apsaras danced and sang. Indra resumed his divine form, and announced to the king of the Sibis that he would be re-incarnated in the body of the next Buddha.

Multiplication of Buddhas. The most ancient Buddhism or Little Vehicle admits that since the Sakyamuni had shown the path to salvation, other sages might in their turn attain bodhi and nirvana and thus become Buddhas. It particularly noticed the future Buddha, Maitreya.

Making use of the opportunity to multiply the number of Saviours, the Great Vehicle, which came into existence about the beginning of the Christian era and dominated Indian philosophy during the first seven centuries of that era, created the notion of transcendent persons, positive Buddhist divinities, although they were still called Bodhisattvas or Buddhas.

While the sage of the Sakyas represented the ideal of a slightly Brahman clan in the middle Ganges valley, the cults of the Great Vehicle came into existence on the borders of Iran in lands where there had been interpenetration of Hellenic, Persian and Indian influences.

The Graeco-Syrian gnosis, the Iranian religion of light, and Vishnu-ite sectarianism played their part in it, and perhaps also to some extent the faith of the Semites and Manichaeism. We must not forget that most of the biographies of the Sakyamuni were composed under the influence of the Great Vehicle, and that they owe to it the metaphysics which abounds in them.

The Artistic Representation of the Buddha Sakyamuni. A tangible proof of Western influence is shown by the artistic representation of the Buddha. Native art had always refrained from depicting the Blessed one's features, and he was symbolised by an empty throne or a solar wheel. When it was decided to give him plastic form, a Greek type was chosen. The Western sculptors dwelling in Bactriana represented him as Apollo. A. Foucher has demonstrated the continual evolution by imperceptible and gradual degrees from the most Hellenic Buddha to the most Japanese.

The Indian elements of this iconography were imposed by the Master's biography. The Buddha must be a monk, the Bodhisattva a prince. Here and there the same royal and divine type (the gods were kings in heaven, the kings gods on earth) appeared, but when the Buddha was to be represented the type was divested of lay ensigns of power and of worldly wealth. Both have a lens-shaped mark between the eyebrows, urna, which symbolised a tuft of luminous and radiant hair, but the Buddha has a protuberance of the skull, ushnisha, which incorporates with his anatomy the shape of a turban bound round a knot of hair. The attitudes of the body, asanas, express the kind and quality of his meditation; the position of the hands, mudras, complete this expression or indicate the action accomplished.

From Dipankara to Maitreya the Manushi-Buddhas. The most ancient precursor of Sakyamuni whose name has been preserved to us is Dipankara. During a former existence our Buddha presented him with flowers, and in return received from him an announcement, of his own mission. The legend of the distant predecessor reconciles as best it can the two etymologies of the name – *dvipa* an island, or *dipa* a lamp – by the idea of a luminous manifestation in the

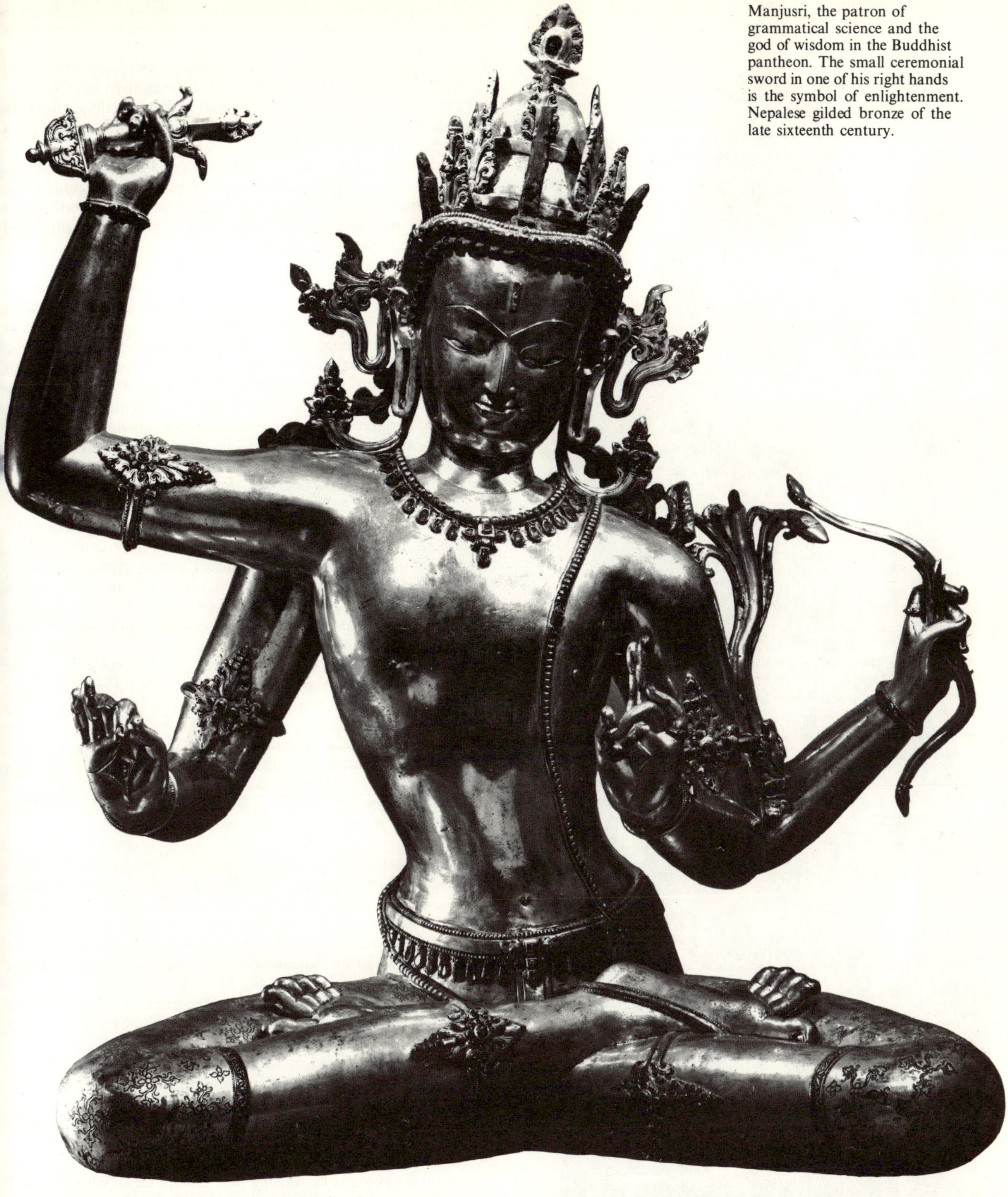

Manjusri, the patron of grammatical science and the god of wisdom in the Buddhist pantheon. The small ceremonial sword in one of his right hands is the symbol of enlightenment. Nepalese gilded bronze of the late sixteenth century.

midst of the waters, a divinity protecting sailors, especially in the 'Southern Isles'.

The epoch of the world to which we belong received six Blessed ones before the sage of the Sakyas – Vipasyin, Sikhin, Visvabhu, Krakuchanda, Kanakamuni, Ksyapa. An eighth is expected, Maitreya, who is still in the stage of a Bodhisattva. This pseudo-historical succession of Masters, who are given a role in the evolution of humanity, forms the series of 'human' Buddhas, Manushi.

The Dhyani-Buddhas. On the other hand the Buddhas of Meditation, Dhyani, are metaphysical essences, and yet iconography has much more frequently represented them in the creation of that section of Buddhism, the Great Vehicle, which conquered Tibet as well as the Far East. There are five of them:

Vairocana, whose colour is white, whose attribute is the disk, and his steed a dragon. He must derive from some solar hero. He became extremely popular with the Japanese Shingon sect.

Ratnasambhava is yellow, wears a jewel, and rides a lion. He reigns over the South.

Amitabha, Infinite Light, or Amitayus, Infinite Duration, is red, holds a lotus, and is escorted by a peacock. He reigns over the West, where he presides over a marvellous paradise, Sukhavati. All who believe in him will be re-born before final deliverance.

Amoghasiddhi is green, carries a double thunder-bolt, and is borne up by an eagle. His region is the North.

Akshobhya is blue, provided with a thunder-bolt and rides on an elephant. He watches over the East.

The Dhyani-Bodhisattvas: Avalokitesvara. From the meditation of the Dhyani-Buddhas emanate the Dhyani-Bodhisattvas: Saman-

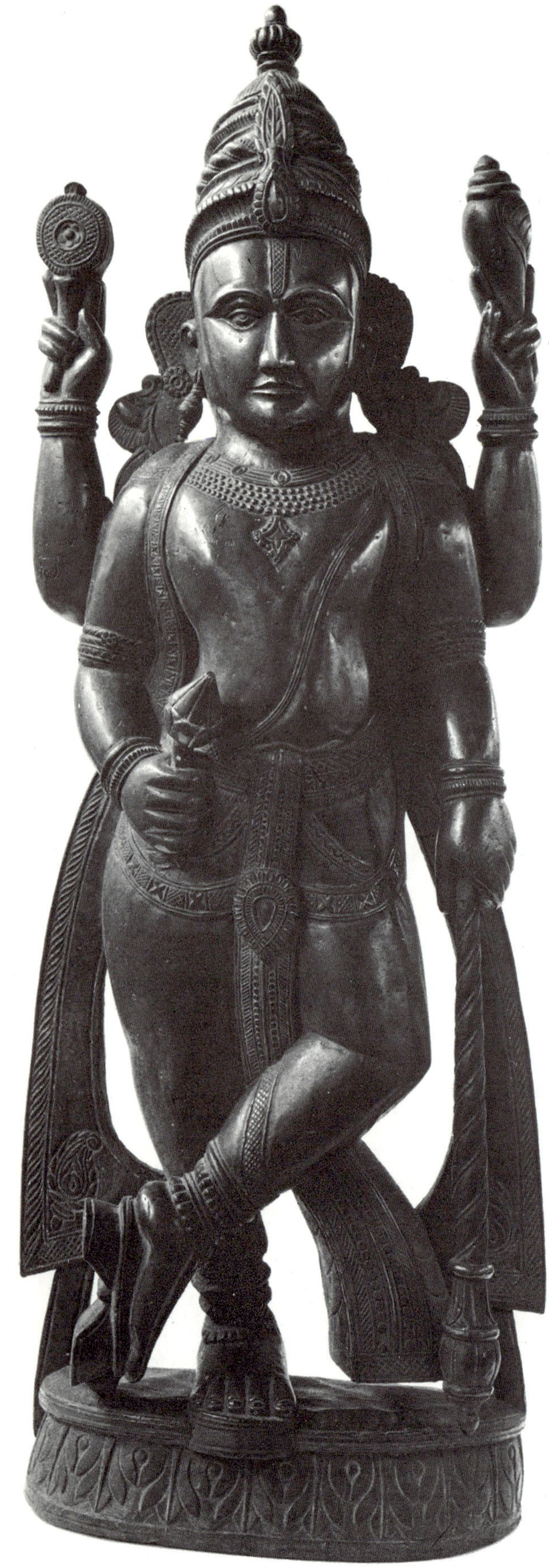

Vishnu. The second member of the Hindu triad, Vishnu is one of the most popular Hindu deities, his worship being of a particularly joyful character. Though his role is essentially that of preserver and restorer, his worshippers frequently claim for him the positions of supreme god and creator in addition. In his four hands he grasps his discus, his conchshell, a lotus-flower and his club. Elaborately carved wooden figure. Horniman Museum.

tabhadra, Vajrapani, Ratnapani, Avalokitesvara, Visvapani. Samantabhadra, one of the most constant intimates of Sakyamuni in the Mahayana texts, has the bearing of a god of action and symbolises happiness. He is green and rides an elephant. His cult is especially developed at Wo-meichen (Setzu-Zan) and in Nepal.

Vajrapani, wielder of the thunder-bolt, appears in the Gandharva sculptures sometimes as a Zeus, sometimes an Eros, even as a Hercules, a Pan or a Dionysus.

The representations show us the history of Vajrapani. He was first a yaksha, a faithful companion, a replica of Sakyamuni, and then becomes important in the Great Vehicle as a 'Bodhisattva of benign aspect or furious bearing', the ideal of the faithful and terror of the impious. (Foucher.)

Avalokitesvara, the Lord gifted with complete Enlightenment, remained in this world for the salvation of creatures, and is at the head of the Merciful. Under the name of Padmapani he holds a pink lotus, and to show that he derives from Amitabha he bears an effigy of him bound up with his hair. No person in suffering appeals to him in vain. As he has plenty of work in this world of misery a 'thousand' arms are not too many for him. The *Karandavy uha* describes his charitable wanderings, whether he takes cooling drinks to the damned in hell, or converts the she-ogres (Rakshasi) of Ceylon, or preaches the Law to beings incarnated as insects or worms in the region of Benares. So although his normal residence is the paradise of Amitabha, his chosen dwelling is the world of suffering which he prefers to the peace of nirvana.

China has transformed this Bodhisattva in a very curious way. To honour his capacity for love the Chinese have endowed him with the feminine aspect of the goddess Kuanyin (Kwannon) who, as she carries a child in her arms, has such a strange resemblance to the Virgin Mary and her divine son. In contrast to this very concrete image, India imagined this compassionate saviour as a cosmic being with innumerable forms:

'From his eyes were derived the sun and the moon, from his forehead Mahesvara, from his shoulders Brahma and other gods, from his heart Narayana, from his thighs Sarasvati, from his mouth the winds, from his feet the earth, from his belly Varuna... He is a lamp to the blind, a sunshade to those consumed by the heat of the sun, a stream for the thirsty; he takes away all fear from those who dread a disaster, he is a doctor to the sick, a father and mother to the unhappy (*Karandavyuha*, 14 and 18).' Mother! That was the shape in which he conquered the Far East.

Other Bodhisattvas – Manjusri, Maitreya, Kshitigarbha. Legend attributes a Chinese origin to the Bodhisattva Manjusri or Manjughsha. At least in the time of I-tsing the Hindus considered him as living in China, and he was especially venerated in the monastery of Ou-tai-Chan (Changsa). His name is only a translation of the Sanskrit Pancasika or Pancasirsha, the mountain with five peaks, certainly Indian, where a certain Kumarabhua, whose surname was Manjusri, attained to sanctity. According to Sylvain Levi, Manju is the Cutch translation of Kumara. The *Svayambhuprana* makes this Bodhisattva the patron of grammatical science and wisdom. He is portrayed as yellow, seated on a blue lion with a red maw, in the posture of teaching, a blue lotus in his hand – often with a sword, the sword of knowledge, or a book.

Maitreya, the Buddha of the future, still dwells in the heaven of Tushita whence the Sakyamuni of old descended. One of the latter's disciples, Kasyapa, having attained nirvana, dwells on the slope of mount Kukkutapada waiting for the moment when he will present the future Buddha with the robe of precedence most carefully preserved. Maitreya, who is represented as the colour of gold, is related at least by his name to Mitra, the solar god of the Iranians. Texts in Eastern Iranian studied by Ernest Leumann demonstrate the importance of the messianism of Maitreya in the southern part of Chinese Turkestan. Perhaps some historical character must be recognised as the origin of the cult of this bodhisattva – at least, such is the opinion of J. Takasuku and H. Ui, two Japanese Buddhologists who attribute some famous works of Yogasara inspiration to a certain Maitreya.

Kshitigarbha, very little honoured in India, but with effigies widely spread throughout central Asia, plays the part of an eschatological god. He regulates and surveys the six paths (gati) which are taken by souls after they have been judged – destinies of men, asuras, demons, of gods, animals, and the starving damned.

The paintings of Yueyen-Kwang show ten kings of hell gravitating about him. Here is reflected the mythical cosmography of Buddhism, which also appears by the admission of the four guards of the cardinal points, the Lokapalas, locked in their armour. This judgment, these judicial or police gods, are utterly in contradiction with the primitive Buddhist conception of Kharma, according to which every action in itself implied the just and necessary retribution, without any divine intervention. The development of the myth has carried us as far away from real Buddhism as from India proper.

The overwhelming monotony of these figures is not unintentional. The infinite number of these effigies, mythically different but metaphysically equivalent, was meant to reassure the faith of the humble, by showing how numerous the elect were. On the other hand it reveals to him who can understand, the essential truth of the Great Vehicle – that as the Law does not differ from nirvana, and as all is emptiness, Buddha is reduced to an empty form. If any life, denounced of course as illusory, circulates through these abstractions, it was provided by popular devotion to the extent that it treats the Buddhas as gods.

Buddhistic Hinduism. The popular cults forced their way even into the cold and lofty dogma of the Great Vehicle – there was a Buddhistic Hinduism as there had been a Brahmanic Hinduism.

Hideous, grimacing, grotesque figures point to an inspiration entirely different from the serenity of the saints. Yamantaka, the companion of Manjusri, wore a necklace of skulls, like Siva. He possesses several terrifying faces, and waves a number of arms. Trailokyavijaya has four heads and four threatening arms, and tramples on Siva's head. These two monsters demonstrate that a certain type of Buddhism tried to exceed the horror even of the Siva myths.

Alongside terror we have the ridiculous – the god of wealth, Jambhala, outrageously fat, and holding a lemon and a mangosteen, an amusing parody of the Brahman god Kuvera.

An unmistakable sign of Hinduism is the reappearance with scarcely any change of the old Dravidian she-ogres. Like Vishnu and Siva, the Buddhas had their saktis, who furnished mortals with knowledge, prajna, or compassion, karuna, while their quasi-husbands showed the path of salvation, upaya.

Tara, the most revered, shared in the cult devoted to Avalokitesvara, at least in Tibetan Tantrism. She was born from his tears. When she is red, yellow, blue, she threatens; when white or green, she is gentle and loving – a double character present in Siva's wife.

This sort of Bodhisattva of a feminine nature is among the Vidyadevis or Matrikadevis, goddesses of knowledge, or mother-goddesses, among whom may be noted:

Bhrikuti Tara, a special form of the preceding;

Kurukulla, represented as reddish, seated in a cavern, has four arms, of which the upper two threaten, and the lower two soothe;

Cunda – concerning whom the Tibetan Taranatha relates a fairy tale: 'Lucky for him was it that the son of the tree nymph and the Kshatriya chose her as patron, for with her help he slew the wicked queen whose bed every night was a grave for a new king of Bengal.' She has four or sixteen arms. 'Her kindly air contrasts with her threatening attributes. Thunder-bolt, disk, mace, sword, bow, arrow, axe, trident, etc. – nothing is absent from her arsenal; but for the worshipper who knows how to look, her first pair of hands is in the position of teaching, another in that of charity, while others hold the rosary, the golden lotus, and the flask of ambrosia; so that this strange divinity is as propitious to the good as she is terrible to the wicked' (Foucher, *Iconographie bouddhique du II siècle*, 144, 146);

Marici, the ray of dawn, a Buddhist Ushas, with a frontal eye, is sometimes terrible with her three grimacing faces and ten threatening arms.

Among the saktis of the Manushi-Buddhas is Sarasvati, the wife of Manjusri and goddess of teaching.

On the summit of this feminine pantheon reigns Prajna, Knowledge, corresponding to the supreme masculine abstraction, Adibuddha, original and fundamental essence of all Buddhas.

As the antithesis to this serenity let us mention Hariti, the mother suckling five hundred demons. She is associated with Pancika, a genius of opulence – her wealth is her fecundity, probably a relic of ancient agricultural rites.

This invasion of Buddhism by Tantrist mythology, attested by Tibetan Lamaism, illuminates a big historical problem with a very crude light. Let us not be surprised that Buddhism has disappeared from India, with the exception of Ceylon and Nepal – like the orthodoxy of Vedic tradition it has been absorbed by the sectarian religions.

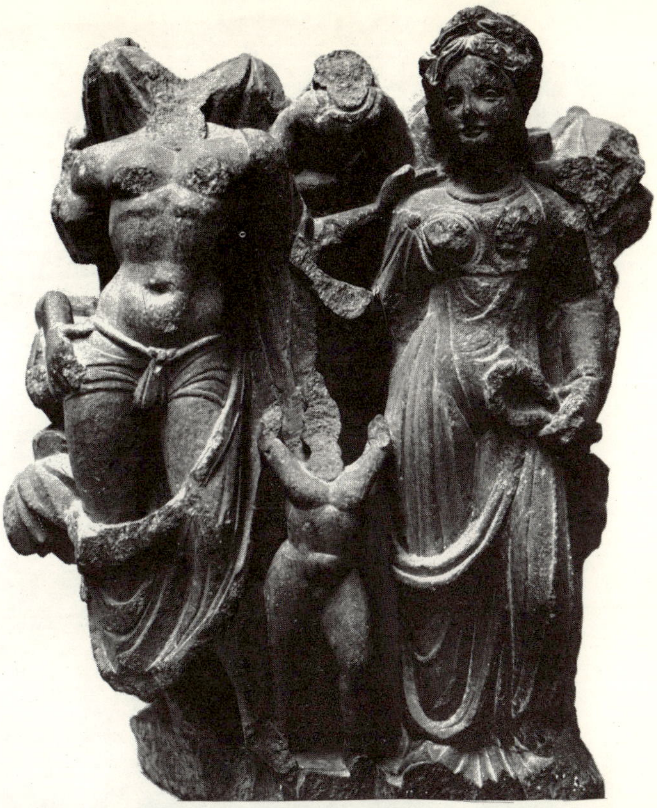

Pancika and Hariti. Buddhist philosophy proved too lofty and remote for the ordinary mind and the popular cults gradually forced their way even into the Great Vehicle itself, their frequently grotesque and hideous deities forming a marked contrast to the serenity of the saints. Two such popular deities – who were associated together – were Pancika, a genius of opulence, and Hariti, the mother suckling five hundred demons. Gandhara style relief, third century A.D.

MYTHOLOGY OF HINDUISM

We apply the word 'Hindu' to the population resulting from the mixture or propinquity of the different races of India; and the name 'Hinduism' is given to the social, religious, and mythological mixture produced by the interpenetration of the most divergent rites, beliefs and superstition. This syncretism occurred under the aegis of Brahmanism, because the Brahmans remained the most educated caste, destined to maintain the inheritance of Vedic tradition. But the history of Hinduism is that of the concessions which orthodoxy was forced to make to new or foreign beliefs and practices, since orthodoxy could only survive by giving its blessing to what it was unable to withstand.

RELIGION OF VISHNU

The Vishnu of Hinduism adds a large number of fantastic developments to the comparatively little personified Vishnu of the Vedic age, the principle of light 'penetrating', *vich*, the whole universe, which he crossed with three steps. The later epochs represented this god as dark blue, dressed in yellow, riding an eagle, Garuda, while his four arms carried a mace, a sea-shell, a disk and a lotus. The Vaikuntha heaven over which he reigns is made of gold and its palaces of precious stones. The crystal waters of the Ganges fall on the head of Druva and then on the seven Rishis, and so make their way to the sea. Vishnu is seated on white lotus flowers, having on his right his wife, the brilliant and perfumed Lakshmi, born from the churning of the sea and sprinkled with the Ganges by elephants with golden ewers, thus associating the ideal of love and beauty with the prestige of the supreme god. Here are some of the names or epithets of this first principle: Svayambhu who exists of himself, Ananta the infinite, Yajnesvara

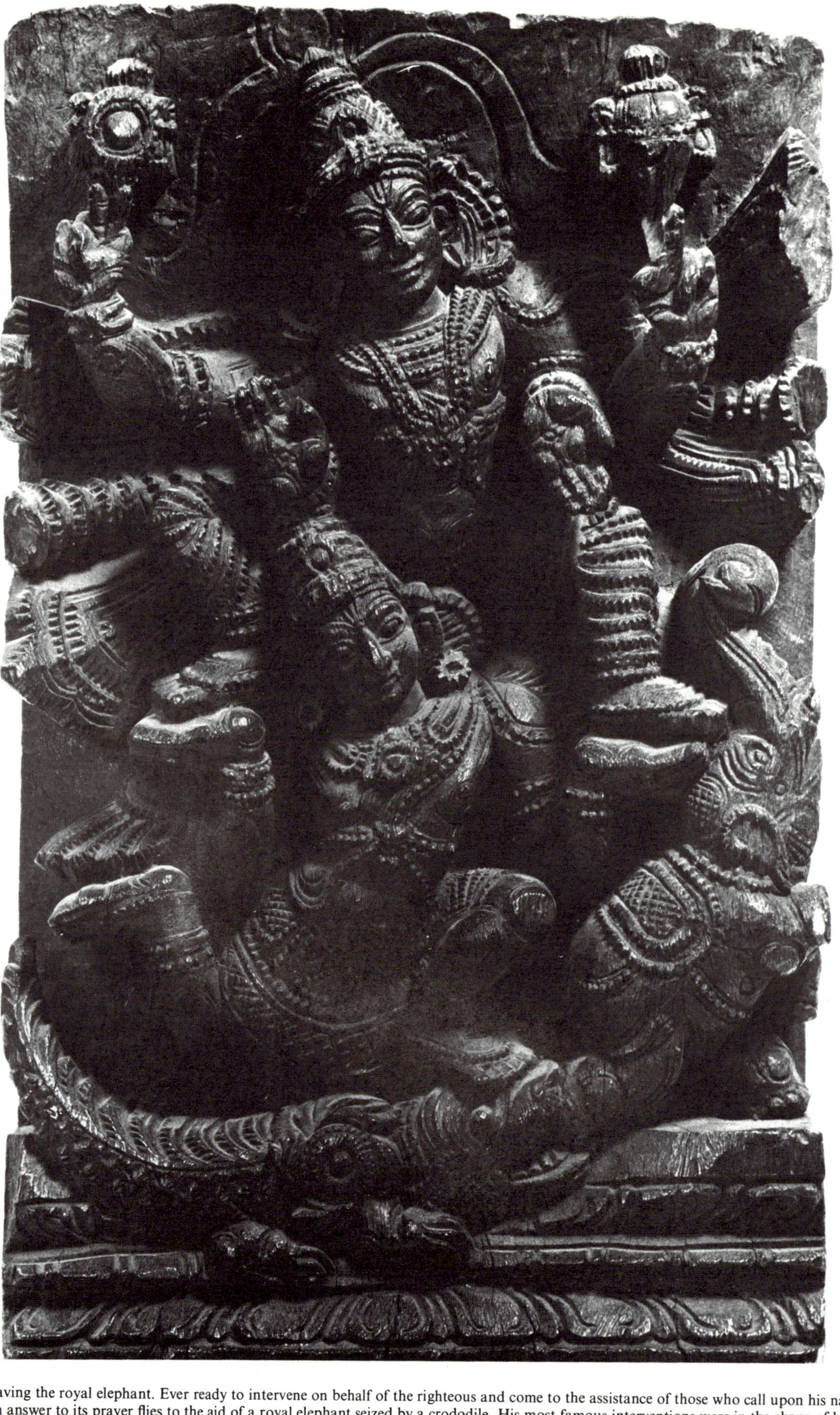

Vishnu saving the royal elephant. Ever ready to intervene on behalf of the righteous and come to the assistance of those who call upon his name, Vishnu in answer to its prayer flies to the aid of a royal elephant seized by a crododile. His most famous interventions were in the shape of his various human or supernatural incarnations or 'avatars'. Carved teakwood panel from a south Indian processional car, nineteenth century A.D.

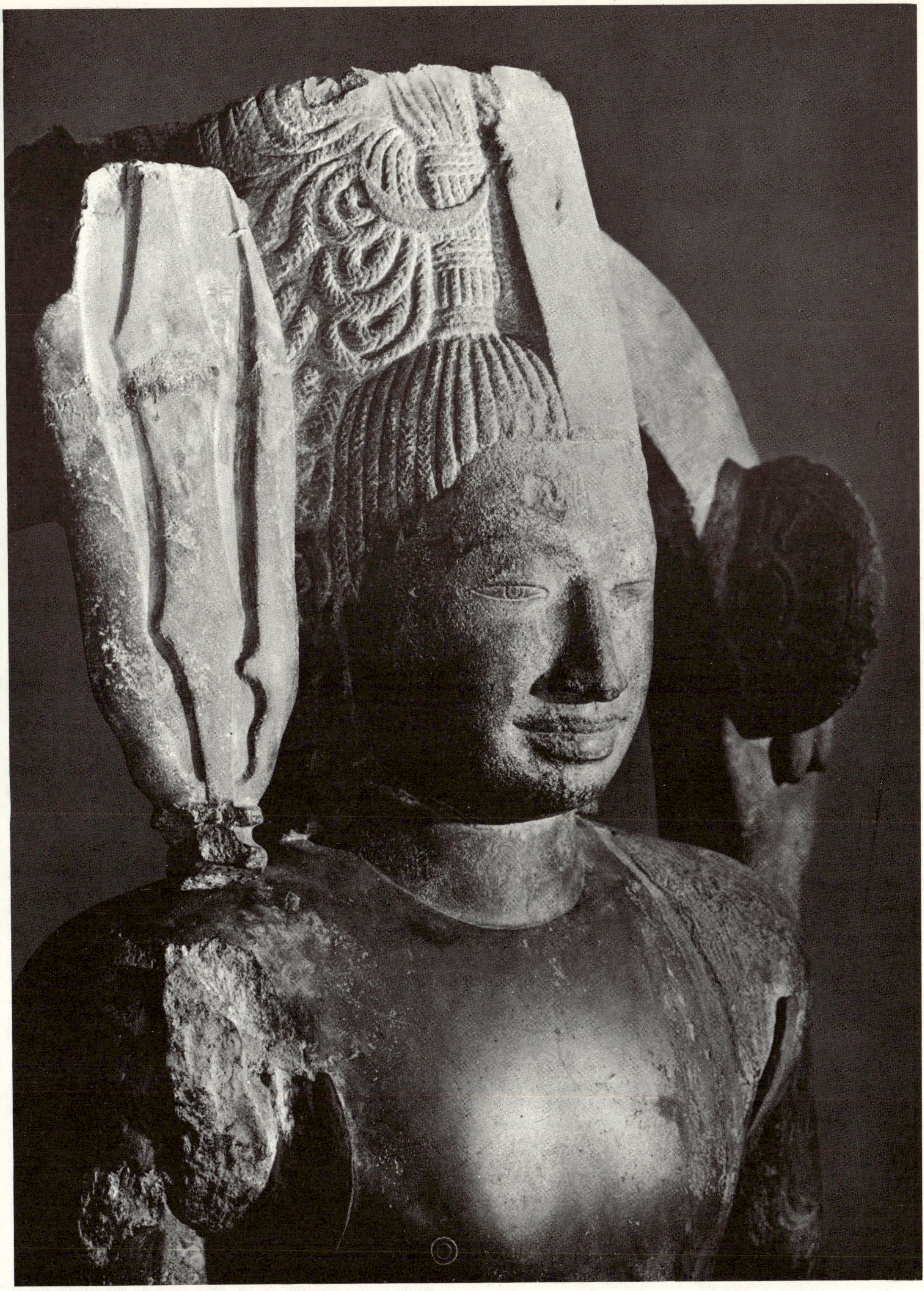

Hari-Hara. Both Vishnu's and Siva's followers claimed that their own god reigned supreme and an attempt was consequently made to combine the two into a composite deity, called Hari-Hara, who would be acceptable to both. This detail of a Khmer statue of the god shows him with Siva's features, surmounted by his ascetic's hair-knot, on the left and with Vishnu's features, surmounted by his cylindrical head-dress, on the right, Sandstone, sixth century, from Prei Krabas.

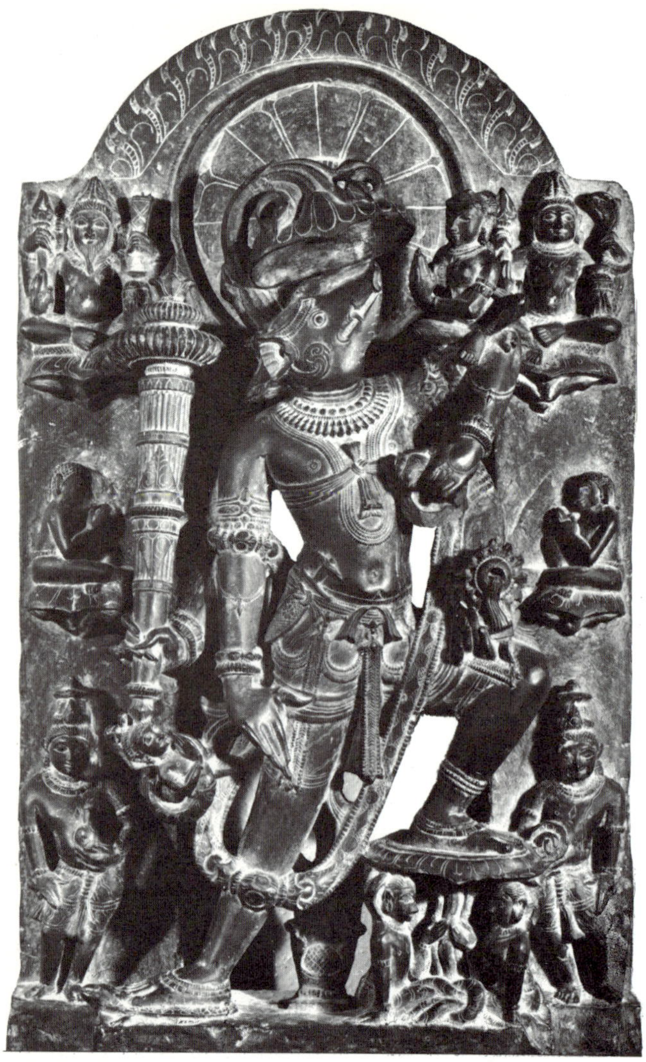

Varahavatara, Vishnu's boar avatar. Vishnu's avatar as a wild boar was also taken from an older legend concerning Brahma and tells how Vishnu took the form of a gigantic wild boar forty miles wide and four thousand miles tall to dive to the bottom of the ocean and recover the earth which had been taken prisoner by a demon. He is shown bearing the goddess of Earth on his left arm. Chauham style bronze, twelfth century A.D.

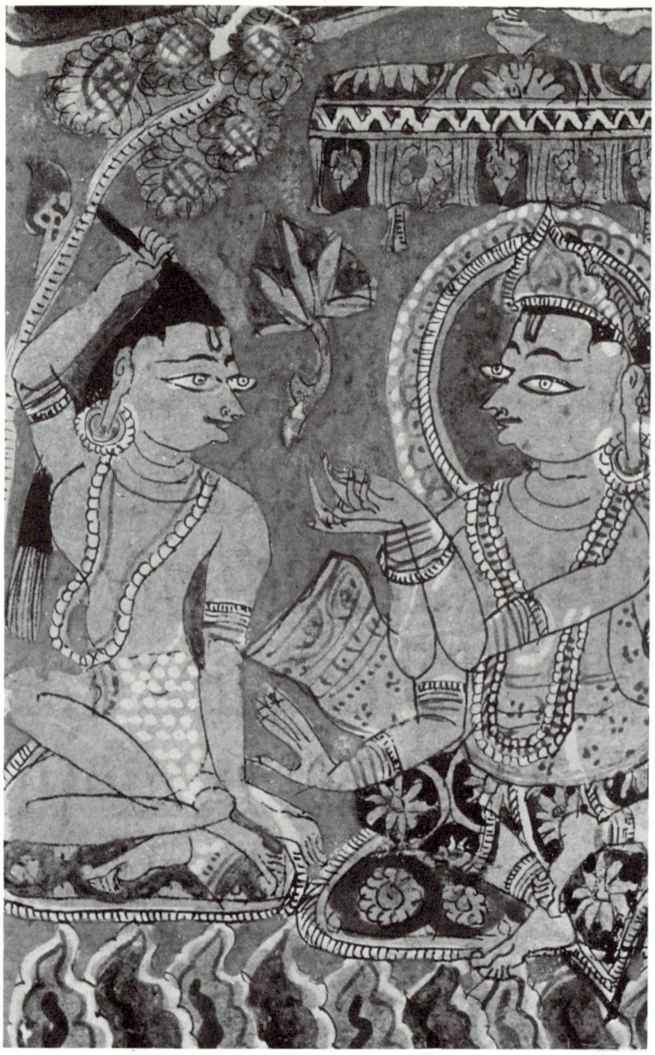

The consecration of Mahavira. Both Jainism and Buddhism threw off the Vedic tradition and their mythology was instead concentrated chiefly around the figure of a great human-being who through asceticism and meditation had managed to attain nirvana. Here the great teacher of Jainism receives his consecration at the hands of Sakra, the king of the gods, after attaining enlightenment beneath the Sala tree. Miniature from the *Kalpasutra*, Gujerat, fifteenth century A.D.

the lord of sacrifice, Hari the abducter who carries off souls to save them, Janarddana who captivates peoples' adoration, Mukunda the liberator, Madhava made of honey, Kesava the hairy whose hairs were the solar rays; Narauana, the source and refuge of beings. The variety of these forms is explicable historically by the fusion of different gods and demi-gods into a single figure under the action of a particular sentiment, a king of piety quite unknown to primitive Brahmanism, and called by the Hindus *Bhakti* made up of confidence, love, and the gift of self to the divinity.

The Avatars of Vishnu. In the intervals of successive creations, Vishnu sleeps on the cosmic waters, lying on the snake Sesha whose seven heads spread like a fan make a canopy for him. This slumber is not death but a state in which the god's virtuality slowly ripens to unfold again in another universe. These alternations of rest and activity, although each of them lasts for thousands of millions of centuries, are as regular and certain as an organic rhythm – India thinks of them as the god's in-breathing and out-breathing. To each cycle of creation there corresponds an 'avatar', literally 'a descent', of the god Vishnu. These avatars theoretically number ten, but the wealth of popular imagination has greatly increased the number. The lion avatar, Narasimha, has appeared in the story of Hiranyakasipu, and Vamana the dwarf in that of Bali.

Avatar of the Fish, Matsya. This implies ancient traditions to do with a flood. One day when the wise Manu was making his ablutions he found in the hollow of his hand a tiny little fish, which begged him to allow it to live. So he put it in a jar, but next day it was so much bigger that he had to carry it to a lake. Soon the lake was too small. 'Throw me into the sea,' said the fish, 'and I shall be more comfortable.' Then he warned Manu of a coming deluge. He sent him a large ship, with orders to load it with two of every living species and the seeds of every plant, and then to go on board himself.

Manu had only just carried out these orders when the ocean submerged everything, and nothing was to be seen but Vishnu in the form of a huge one-horned fish with golden scales. Manu moored his ship to the horn of the fish, using the large snake Vasuki as a rope. Thus mankind, the animals and the plants were saved from destruction.

Avatar of the Wild Boar, Varahavatara. When the earth was submerged by the deluge it was captured by demons. Vishnu in the form of a wild boar dashed across heaven and dived into the waters, where he tracked down the earth by his sense of smell. He killed the demon who held it prisoner, and came up to the surface of the water, bringing with him the earth which he lifted from the abyss on his tusks. The sculptors represented the Varahavatara in the form of a giant with the head of a wild boar, holding in his arms the goddess of Earth.

Avatar of the Turtle. This is connected with the episode of 'the churning of the sea', one of the most popular legends of Indian mythology.

Long ago Indra, king of the gods, was cursed by a great rishi named Durvasas. Thereafter Indra and the three worlds began to lose their first vigour. Vishnu appeared smiling and said: 'I will

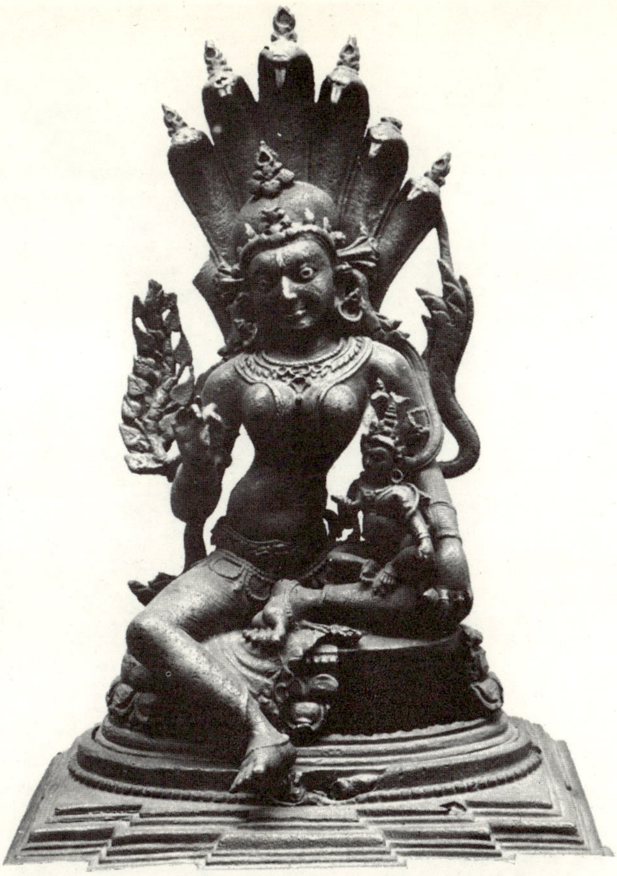

Manasa, the serpent goddess. Manasa (or Manasa-devi) is the sister of the great serpent king Sesha, or Ananta, upon whom Vishnu sleeps floating upon the cosmic waters, in the intervals of successive creations. Manasa is much worshipped in Bengal where she is invoked against the ever-present danger from poisonous snakes. Her cult is believed to be much older than this Hindu manifestation of it.
Chauham style slate carving, twelfth century A.D.

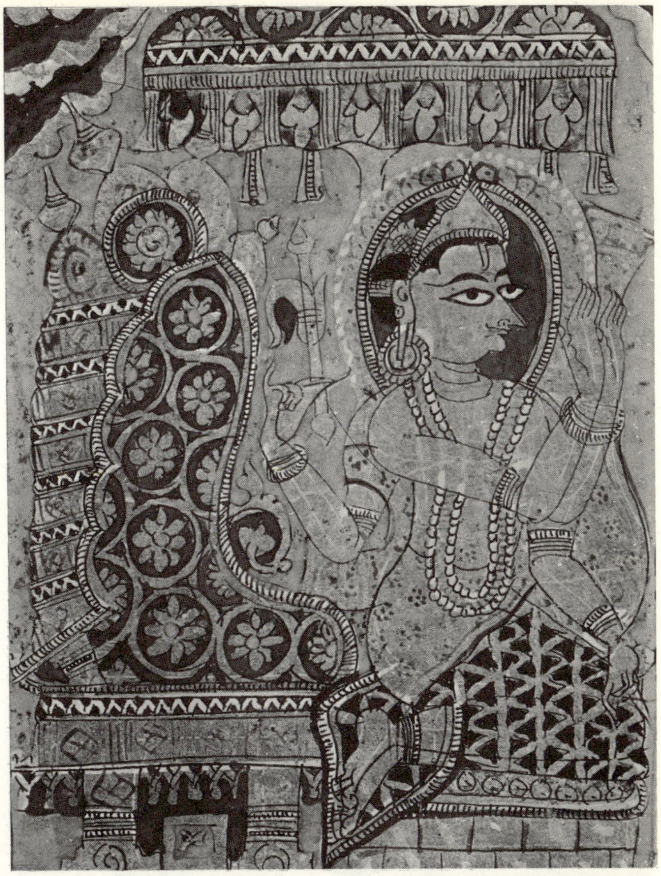

Sakra paying homage to the unborn Mahavira. The historical Mahavira probably lived in the seventh century B.C. but miraculous details soon accumulated around the events of his life and this is particularly noticeable in the account of his birth. According to legend he first took the form of an embryo in the womb of a Brahman's wife but Sakra later transferred him to that of Trisala, the wife of a kshatriya.
Gujerat miniature, fifteenth century A.D.

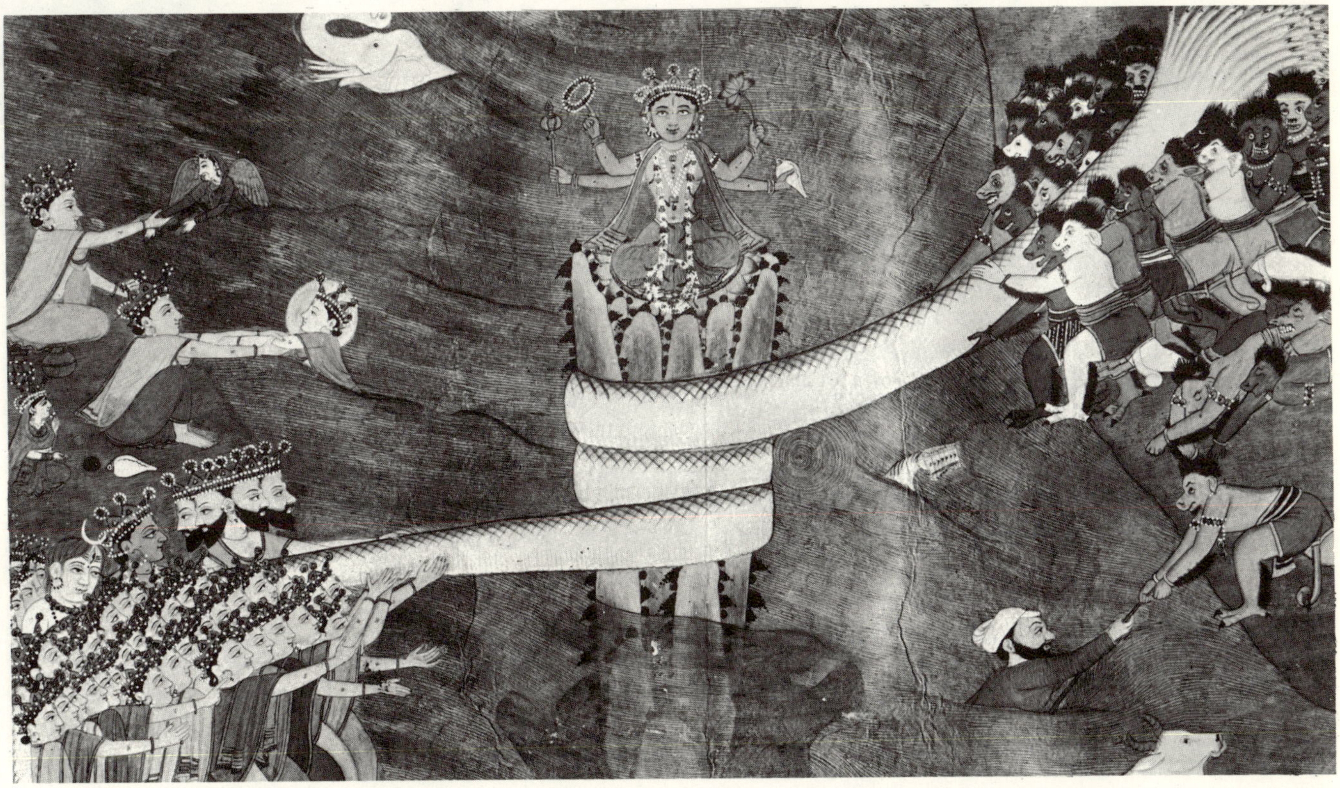

The churning of the sea of milk. The gods and demons are alternately hauling on the great snake Vasuki in order to produce the liquid of immortality, the gods (on the left) grasping its tail and the demons (on the right) its neck. Vishnu appears in his turtle avatar acting as a pivot for Mount Mandara while he is also seen seated on the summit of the mountain and assisting the gods.
Kangra painting, eighteenth century A.D.

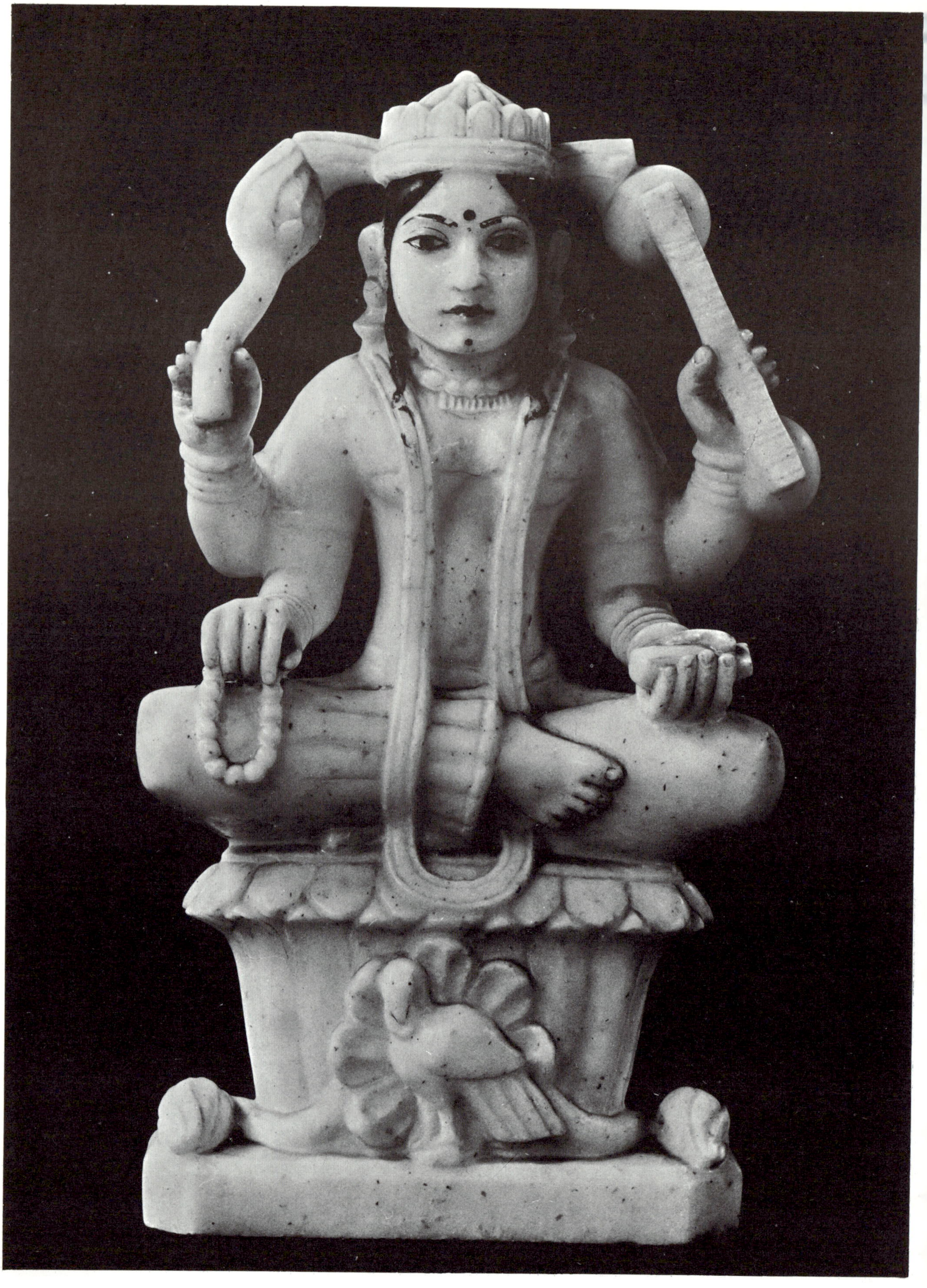

Lakshmi seated on a lotus. The wife of Vishnu and the epitome of feminine beauty, Lakshmi, or Sri, as she is sometimes called, is generally said to have been born radiant and fully grown at the churning of the sea of milk as one of the 'fourteen precious things'. The goddess of fortune and prosperity, she holds her traditional symbol, a lotus, in one of her four hands.
Painted marble figure. Horniman Museum.

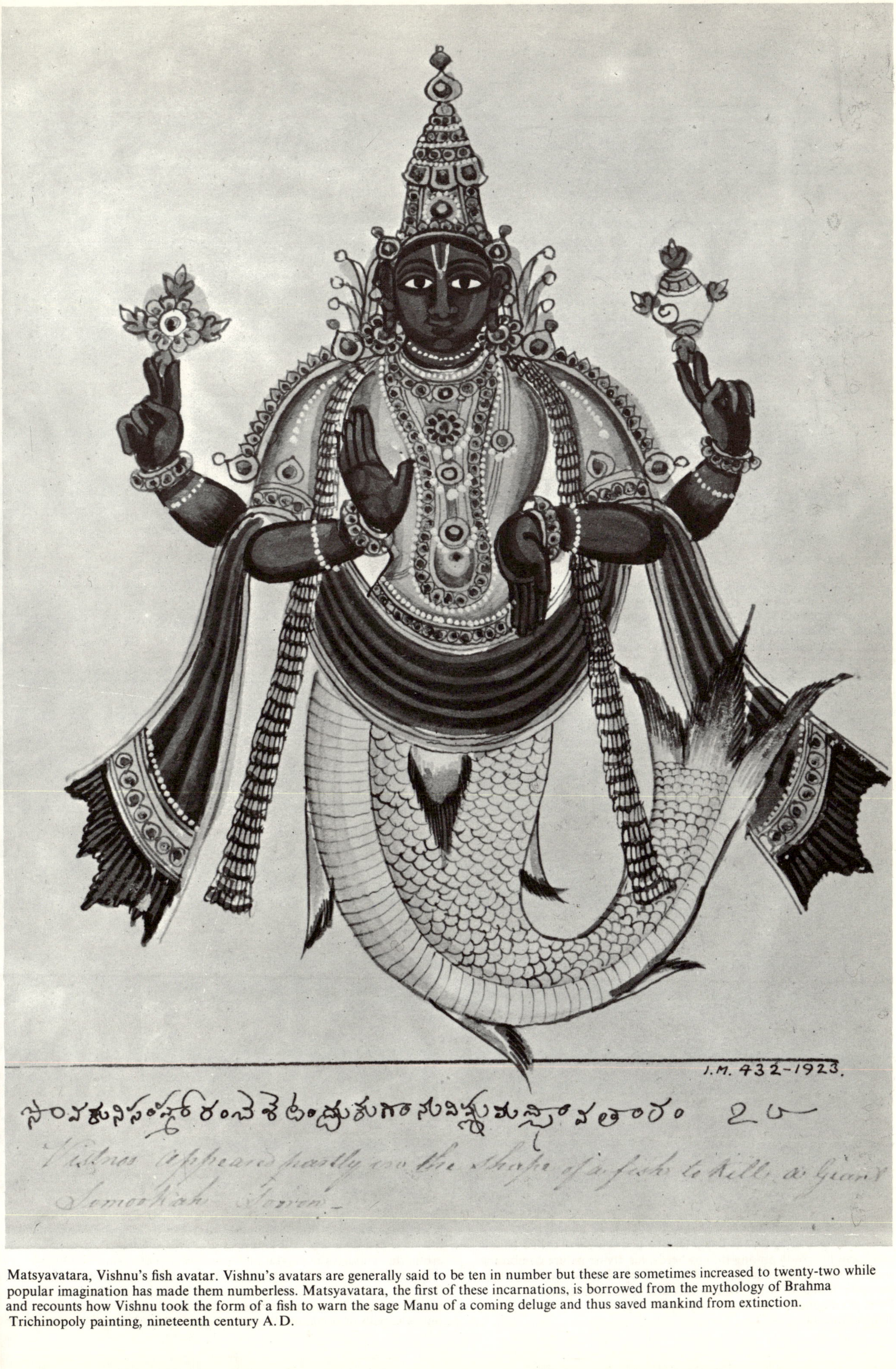

Matsyavatara, Vishnu's fish avatar. Vishnu's avatars are generally said to be ten in number but these are sometimes increased to twenty-two while popular imagination has made them numberless. Matsyavatara, the first of these incarnations, is borrowed from the mythology of Brahma and recounts how Vishnu took the form of a fish to warn the sage Manu of a coming deluge and thus saved mankind from extinction. Trichinopoly painting, nineteenth century A.D.

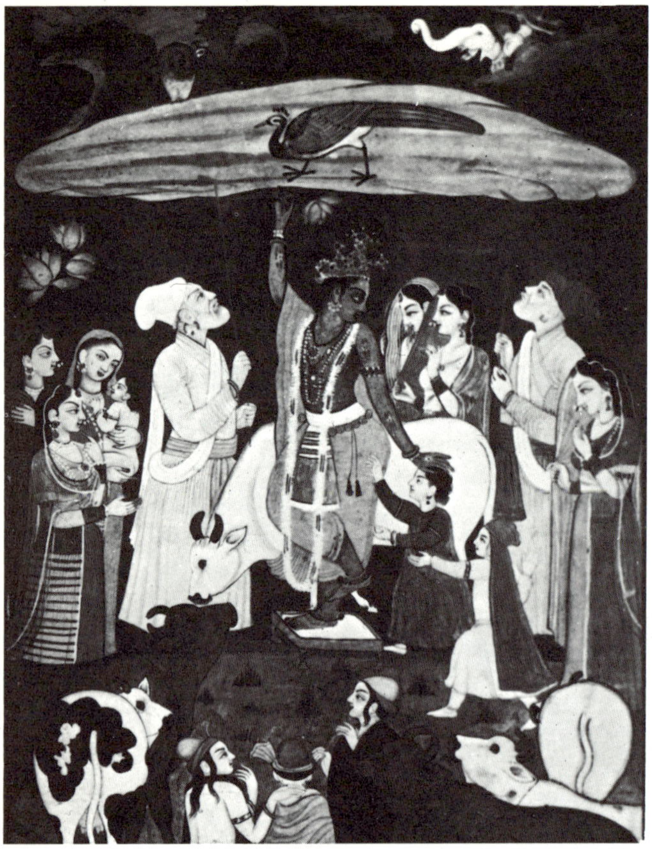

Krishna supporting Mount Govardhana. The best-loved and most human of Vishnu's incarnations, Krishna has playfully urged the herdsmen of Braj to worship Mount Govardhana instead of Indra and now he supports the mountain on his finger to shelter them and their animals from the deluge sent by the wrathful god who can be seen seated on his elephant among the storm-clouds. After seven days and nights Indra conceded defeat. Pahari painting, nineteenth century A.D.

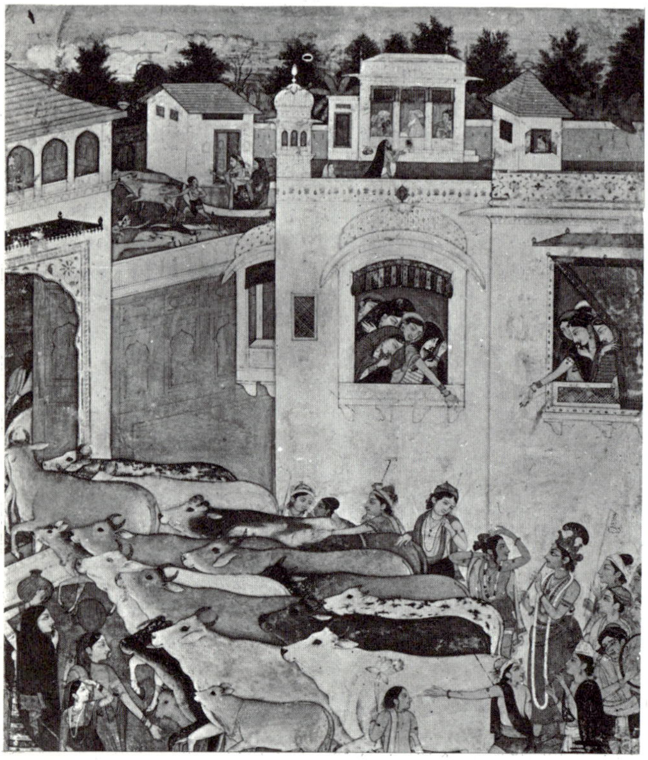

The hour of cowdust. In order to save his life, Krishna had been exchanged as a baby for the daughter of a poor cowherd called Nanda and spent his youth among the cowherds, his divine nature combining with the expression of joy in life. Here at the end of the day he brings the cattle home while the women cast him amorous glances. He is playing upon the flute. Kangra painting, late eighteenth century A.D.

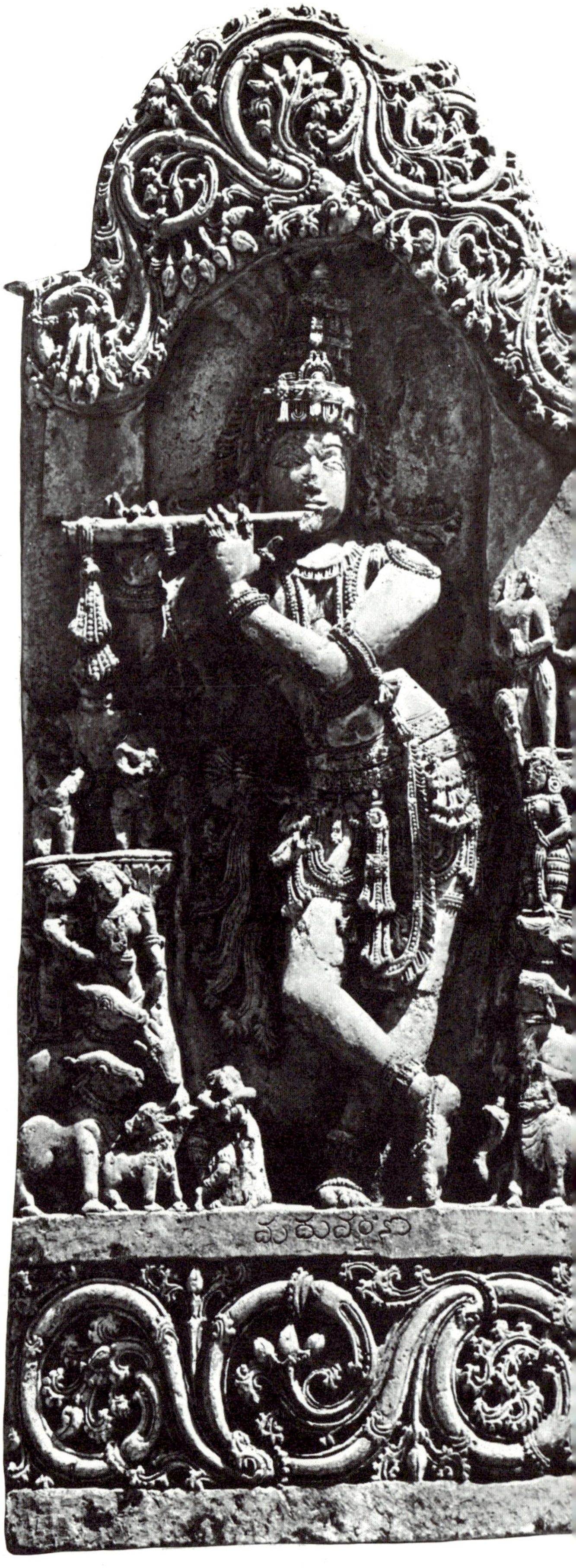

Krishna playing the flute – the irresistible call to love which has made his name synonymous with amorous pleasure and light-hearted eroticism. Though the playful and amorous aspects of his childhood and youth most seized the popular imagination, the call of Krishna's flute also signifies on a deeper level the irresistible call of the Infinite which would lead men and women from their homes and families onto the path of salvation. Stone carving. Belur, thirteenth century A.D.

give you back your power. This is what you must do. Take mount Mandara as a stick and the snake Vasuki as a rope and churn the sea of milk, and you will see it produces the liquid of immortality and other wonderful presents. But you must have the help of the demons. Make an alliance with them and tell them that you will share with them the fruits of your common labour. I shall myself take care that they don't get their share of ambrosia.'

So the gods made an alliance with the Asuras, and having taken mount Mandara as the stick and the snake Vasuki as the rope, they began their work. By its violent motions the mountain did great damage to the inhabitants of the ocean, and the heat created by its rotation destroyed the animals and birds living on its slopes. In fact the whole mountain would have been destroyed if Indra had not sent heavy rains down from heaven, to quench the flames and comfort the inhabitants. But owing to its weight and rapid motion the mountain bored into the earth and threatened to break through it. Vishnu, again invoked, assumed the form of a gigantic turtle, got beneath the mountain, and became its pivot. The churning went on faster than ever. So great is the power of Vishnu, and so numerous the forms that he is able to assume, that even while he supported the mountain he was also present, though invisible, among the gods and demons hauling at the rope. His energy also sustained Vasuki, king of the snakes, while everyone saw him seated in glory on the peak of Mandara.

The Snake suffered from this painful labour. While the gods pulled him by the tail and the demons by the head, torrents of venom escaped from his jaws and poured down on earth in a vast river which threatened to destroy gods, demons, men and animals. In their distress they called upon Siva, and Vishnu joined in their entreaties. Siva heard them and drank the poison to save the world from destruction, but it burnt his throat, and his neck still bears a blue mark which gave him the name of 'Nilakantha', blue throat.

At last the persevering efforts of gods and demons received their reward. First of all their eyes beheld Surabhi, the marvellous cow, mother and nurse of all living things. Then came Varuni goddess of wine, Parijata the tree of paradise, the delight of the nymphs of heaven, scenting the whole earth with the perfume of its flowers, and then all the Apsaras with their grace and enchanting beauty.

Then appeared the Moon which Siva grasped to wear on his forehead, and Lakshimi, the goddess of fortune, Vishnu's joy, seated radiant on a wide-open lotus. The heavenly musicians and the great sages began to sing her praises. The sacred rivers asked her to bathe in their waters. The sea of milk gave her a crown of immortal flowers. The great sacred elephants who support the world poured on her the holy water of the Ganges from golden ewers. As she was Vishnu's wife she sat on his knees, and refused to look at the demons who coveted the goddess of prosperity.

Among other products of the sea of milk must be mentioned Dhanvantari, doctor of the gods, and inventor of the Ayur-Vedic system of medicine; a miraculous horse, a sort of Pegasus; and a marvellous jewel which Vishnu placed on his breast.

The doctor of the gods was the last to appear, holding in his hand the cup which contained the liquid of immortality. The furious and impatient Asuras snatched it from him and fled. But Vishnu assumed the form of a most lovely woman, fascinated them by the illusion, and while the demons were arguing with each other, he took the ambrosia and brought it back to the gods. When they had drunk of it they regained their vigour and drove away the Asuras.

Krishna. Krishna is the most charming and human of Vishnu's incarnations.

He was born at Mathura, between Delhi and Agra. His mother

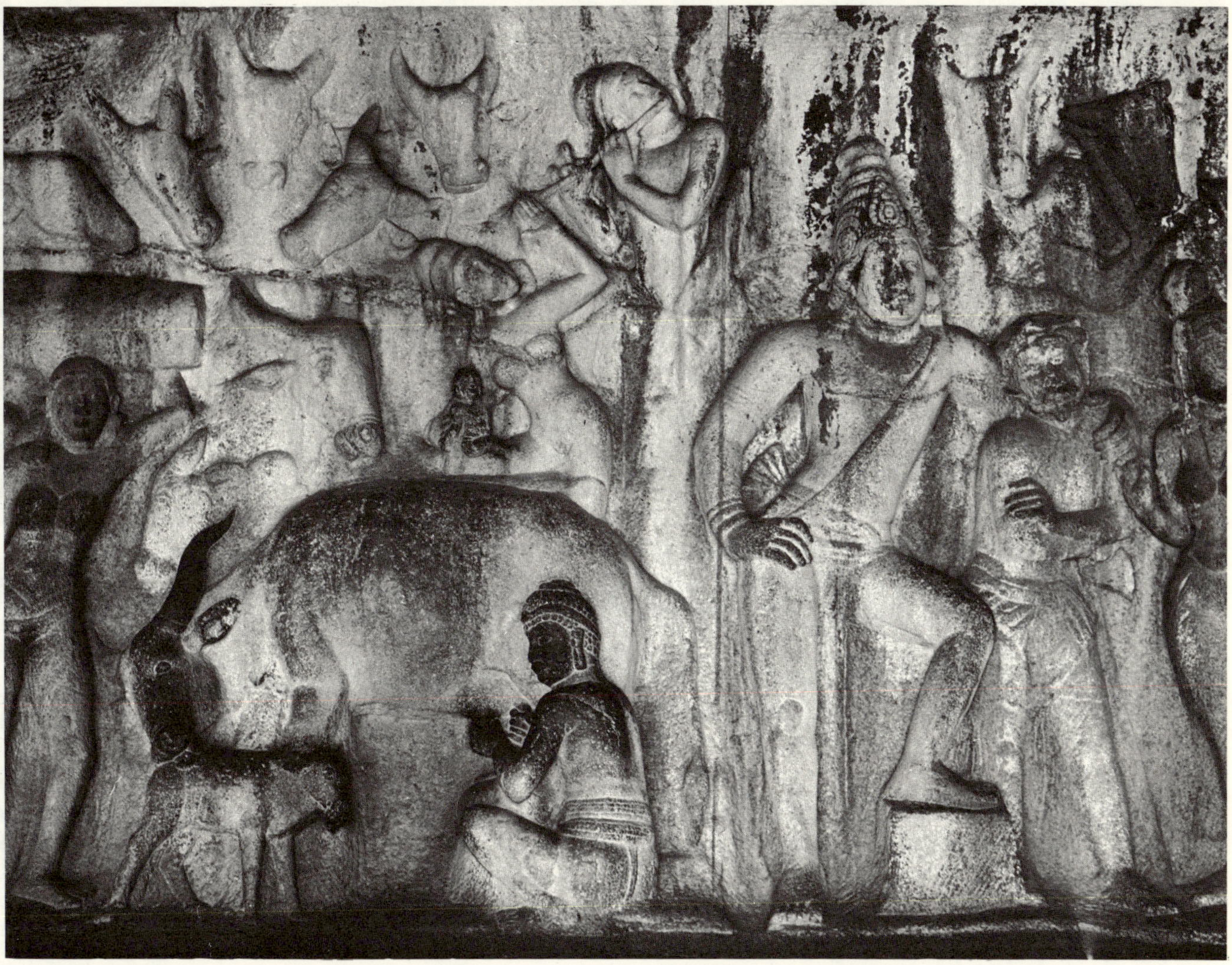

Krishna as a cowherd. His companions accepted his divinity as easily as he accepted the labours which were a part of his mortal form. To the Hindu there is nothing inconsistent in the portrayal of a manifestation of Vishnu milking a cow–his divine nature stressed by the tiara he wears, a feature of many representations of Vishnu himself. Relief from the 'Five Pandava Cave' in the temple complex at Mahabalipuram. Seventeenth century.

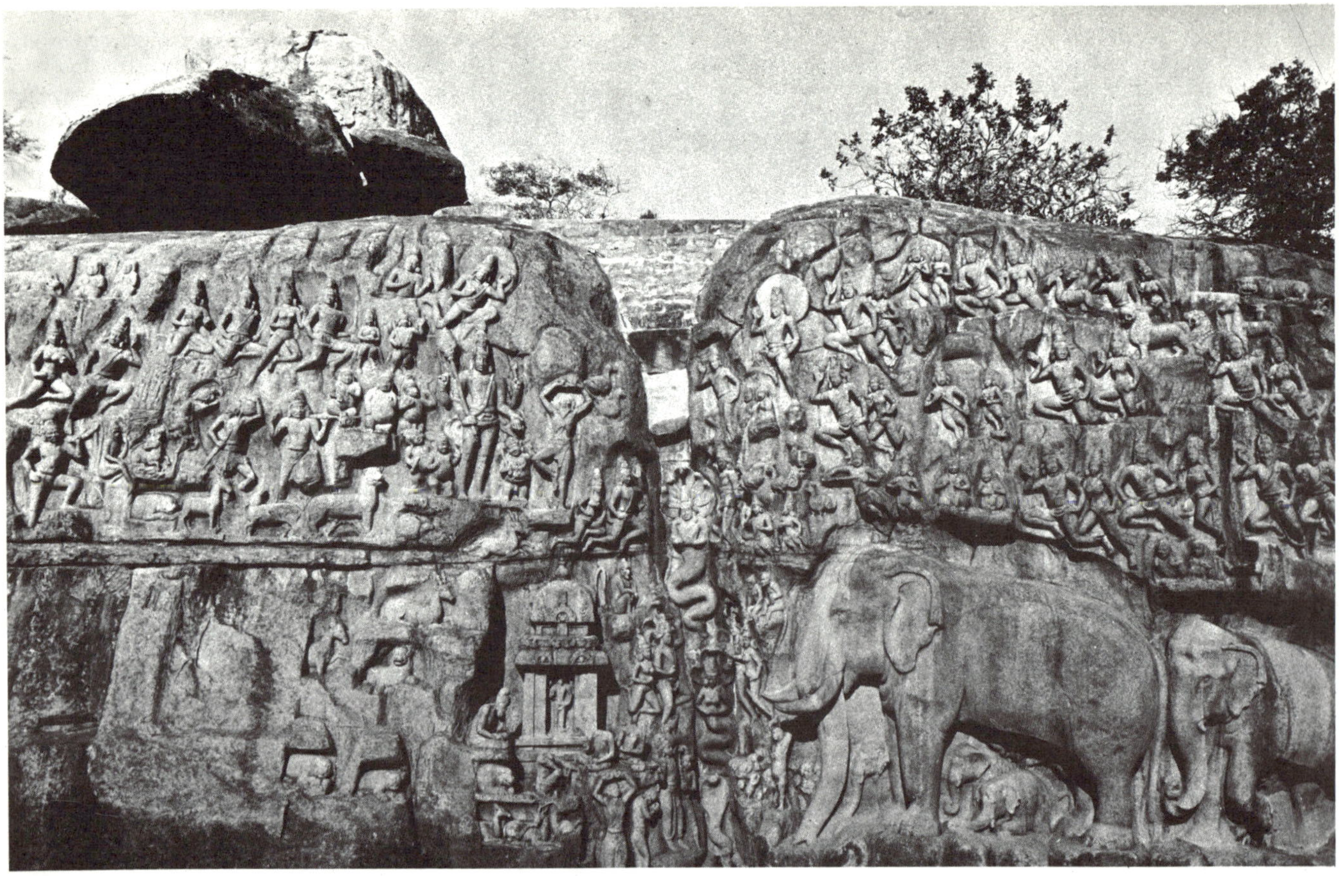

The penance of Arjuna. In his later life Krishna played an important part in the war between the five sons of Pandu and their cousins, the Kurus, and even became the charioteer of Arjuna, the third Pandu prince. Arjuna is shown on the upper left-hand portion of this great bas-relief at Mahabalipuram performing austerities in order to gain strength for the conflict while Siva stands beside him to enquire after his desires. Seventh century A.D.

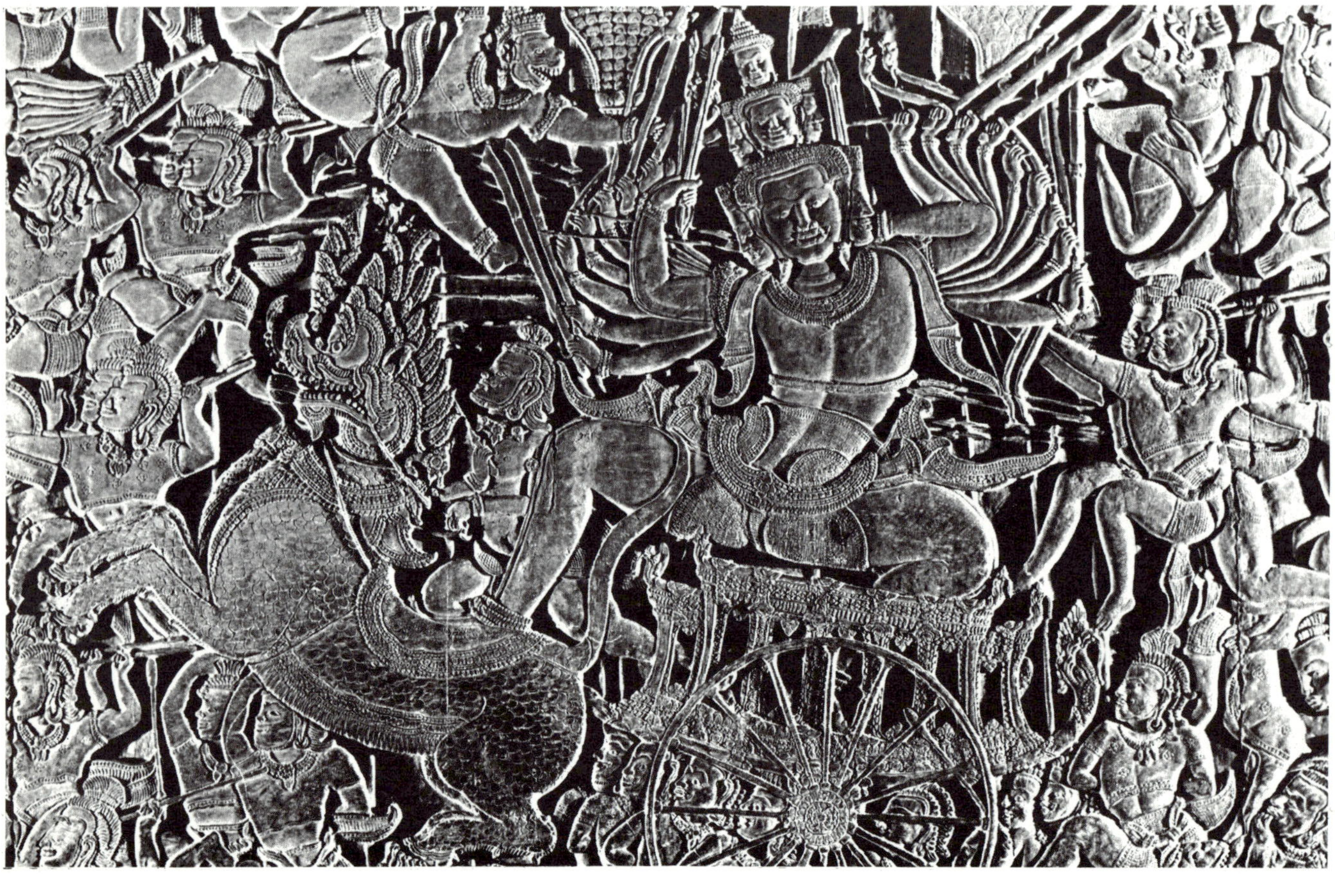

The battle of Lanka. In the centre Ravana, the king of the Rakshasas, is shown riding forth in his aerial chariot for the final confrontation with Rama, while Hanuman, the monkey general, attacks him from above. Ravana had carried off Rama's wife Sita to his island kingdom of Lanka but Rama finally killed him and recovered his wife. Rama was Vishnu's seventh avatar while Sita was a reincarnation of Lakshmi. Relief from Angkor Wat, twelfth century.

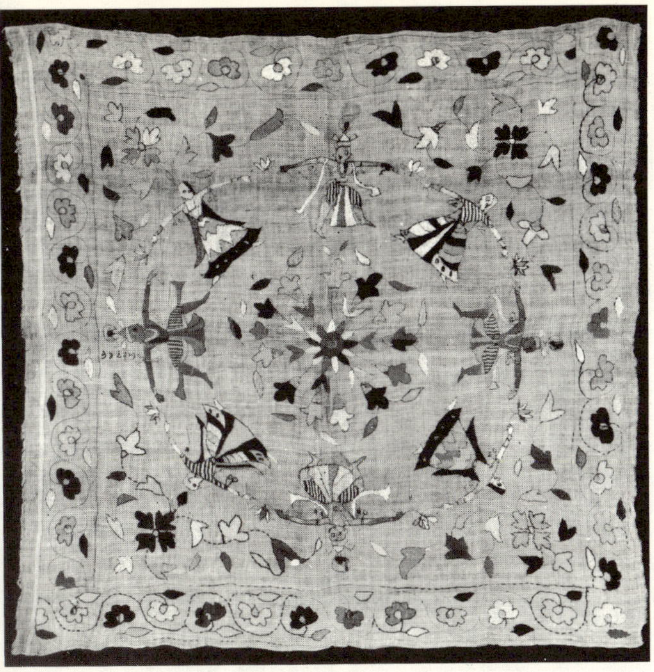

Krishna dancing with the cowgirls. One of Krishna's favourite pastimes before his marriage was dancing with the cowgirls of Braj. This nineteenth century embroidered handkerchief shows the famous episode from the *Gita-Govinda*, the Hindu 'Song of Songs', when after summoning them out of their homes one autumn evening to the sound of his flute he multiplied himself so that he could dance with each of the girls together.

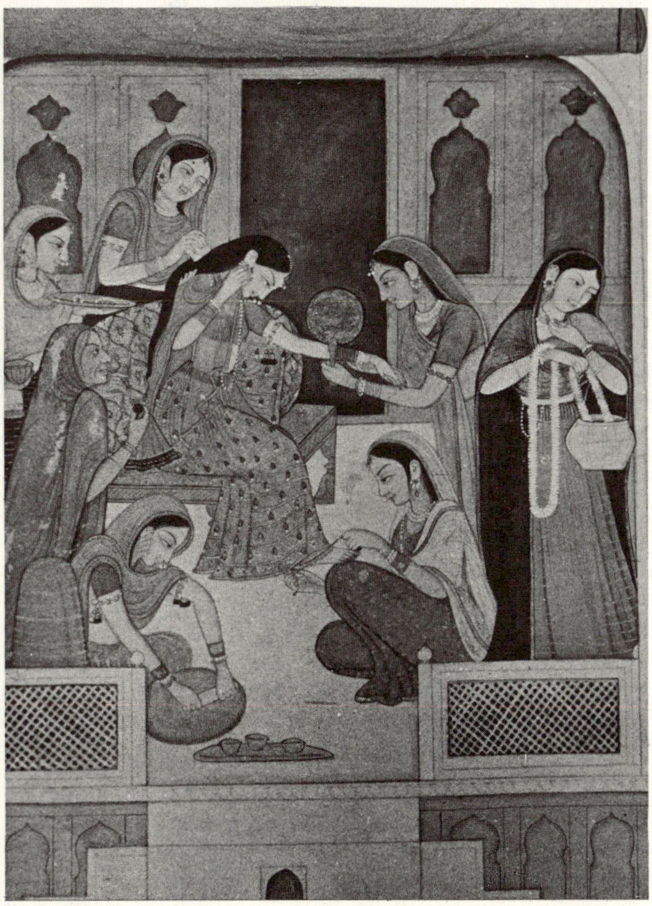

Rukmini being prepared for her marriage. Already in love with Krishna, the beautiful daughter of King Bhismaka is being prepared by her ladies for her marriage against her will to Sisupala, Krishna's evil cousin. In answer to her appeal, Krishna appeared at the last moment and carried her off to become his own wife. Rukmini was an incarnation of Lakshmi just as Krishna was an incarnation of Vishnu. Garwhal painting, eighteenth century A.D.

was Devaki, a sister of king Kamsa, who killed all her children as soon as they were born, since it had been predicted that he would be assassinated by one of them. Krishna owed his life to a ruse of his parents, who exchanged him for the daughter of a poor cowherd, in order to hide him from his uncle's anger. Krishna therefore spent his youth among keepers of herds, in the company of his brother Balarama.

Soon after his birth Krishna was already full of vigour, and sometimes of malice, and started his series of mighty deeds. He overthrew a cart, pulled up two trees together by the roots, fought successfully with a big water snake, and helped his brother Balarama to destroy a dangerous demon.

He played tricks on Indra himself. Once when the herdsmen were preparing to pay homage to the dispenser of rains, he advised them rather to honour the mountain which fed their herds, and the cattle who gave them milk. Krishna in this way appropriated to himself the cult devoted to Indra, for he appeared on the top of the mountain, saying: 'I am the mountain!' and took the first fruits of the offerings to himself. Indra was furious, and poured down cataracts of rain to drown the herdsmen and their cattle, but Krishna lifted the mountain and held it in the air with one finger, and thus protected his friends from the storm for seven days and nights. Indra was amazed, and came down from heaven with his wife Indrani, and they both begged his friendship for their son Arjuna.

In time Krishna became an adolescent. One day some shepherdesses went bathing in the Yamuna, and hearing their bursts of laughter he came up softly and stole their clothes, hiding with them in a neighbouring tree. When the shepherdesses came out of the water and could not find their clothes on the bank they did not know where to turn, and their trouble was increased when they noticed Krishna in the tree looking and laughing at them. Going back into the water they begged him to have pity on them, but he would not return their clothes except on the condition that they came to look for them one by one, with their hands folded in the attitude of prayer.

This incident is merely an introduction to many others like it. The herdsmen's wives and daughters, forgetting their customary reserve and modesty, left their work and their houses to follow Krishna into the forest, as soon as they heard the sound of his flute. The Bhagavata sometimes gently scolded them, but he also told them that through him they would obtain salvation. However Krishna is approached he gives liberation. Some knew and sought him as a son, some as a friend, some as a lover, or even as an enemy, but all received his blessing and deliverance.

The shepherdesses in love with Krishna became so numerous that they could not all hold his hand when he danced with them, so he multiplied himself into many forms, and each girl had the illusion that she was holding Krishna's hand in hers.

The erotic mysticism of the Hindu 'Song of Songs', the *Gita-Govinda*, was the delight of innumerable souls:

'Krishna enchanted the women by the pleasures he lavished on them. The contact of his limbs, soft and dark as a garland of lotus flowers, created amorous delight in them, while the women of the heifer-park kissed him as much as they desired...

'May those learned spirits who seek ecstasy in Vishnu derive from the song of Govinda the essence of love!'

When he was adult Krishna left the herdsmen and returned to Mathura. He killed Kamsa and a certain number of other evil-doers.

And then the Mahabharata allots him an important part in the famous war launched by the five sons of Pandu against their hundred cousins, the Kurus. Krishna was the friend and adviser of the Pandavas, and even became Arjuna's divine charioteer.

Arjuna hesitated to take part in the war, deploring the useless slaughter. Why kill one's friends and relations? Krishna, however, reminds him that he belongs to the caste of the warriors. He cannot go to heaven if he displays such cowardice. Besides they only kill and are killed in appearance. In reality the soul is eternal. All those on the battlefield have always existed and will never cease to exist.

These remarks induce Arjuna to ask Krishna a number of questions, and their dialogue forms the splendid philosophical poem, the *Bhagavad-Gita*.

After many hard fights the war ends with the total destruction of both armies. There are four survivors of the Kurus, and seven of the Pandavas including the god Krishna.

Soon after, Krishna himself accidentally dies, although he had

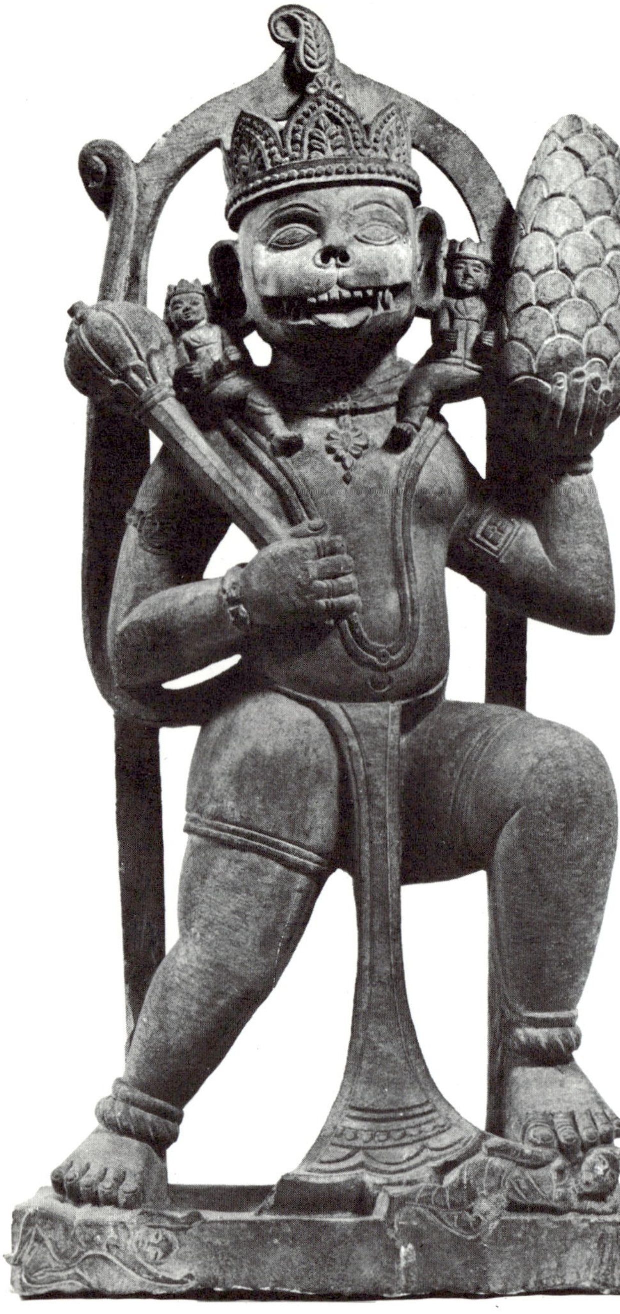

with Ravana and the Rakshasas, Hanuman was rewarded for his selfless courage and loyalty with immortality. As tall as a mountain and possessed of enormous strength and agility, it was he who discovered Sita in her hiding-place at Lanka after clearing the sea at a single bound. He was also renowned for his learning. Soapstone carving from Jaipur.

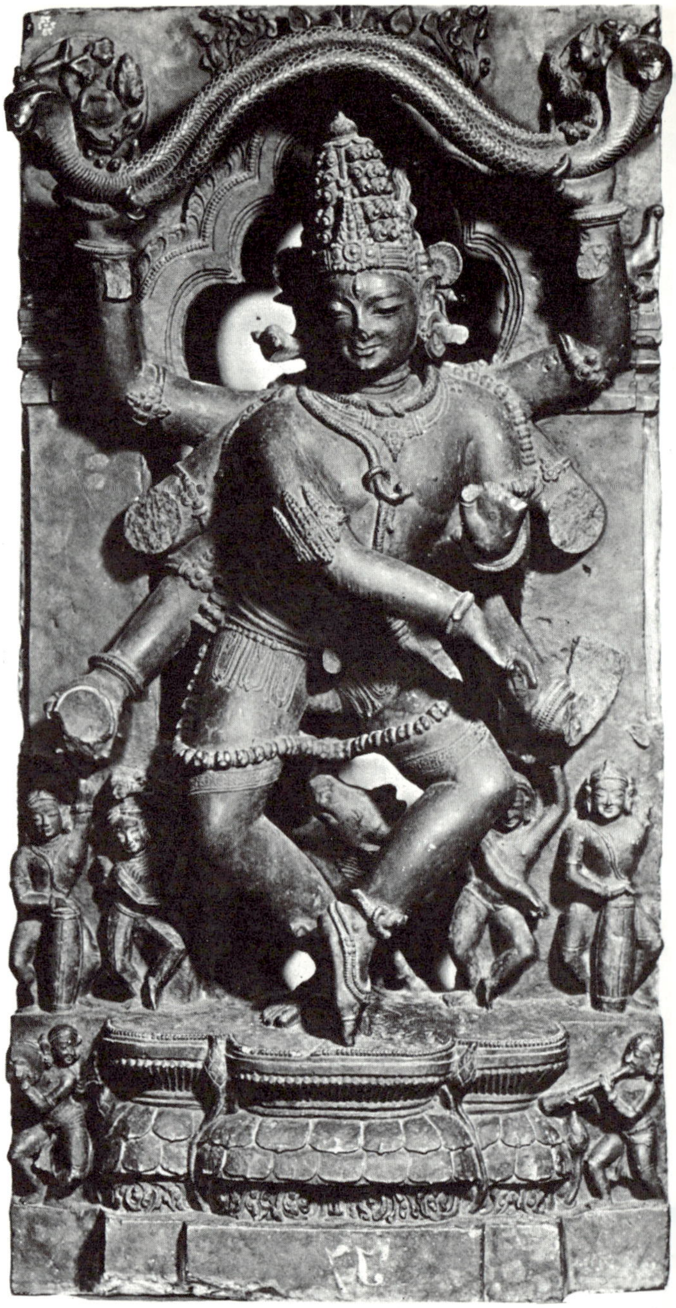

Siva dancing. The third member of the Hindu triad, Siva is shown holding two cobras above his head as he dances. Round his neck two further snakes are twined while he also wears a garland of skulls. There are many legends of Siva's dancing, an activity which symbolises the five cosmic functions of creation, conservation, destruction, incarnation and liberation. Stone carving, thirteenth century A.D.

foreseen his fate. Seated in the forest, in meditation, with his legs crossed, he exposed the soles of his feet. And the wise Durvasas had once cursed him in a moment of anger, saying that he would die from a wound in his foot. A hunter at a distance mistook Krishna for a deer he was following, and let fly a shaft which hit him in his one vulnerable place, the god's left heel. The hunter came up and was in despair at his mistake, but Krishna told him to fear nothing and not to grieve. These words of consolation were the last he spoke on this earth. Then, all radiant, he rose up into heaven, and the gods greeted him. Shadow then fell upon the earth.

Rama. 'The hero created by Valmiki', says Sylvain Levi, 'still remains for contemporary India the most perfect model of humanity. Rama's peaceable courage, always at the service of virtue, his passionate devotion to duty, his fine delicate sensibility, his filial piety, his conjugal tenderness, the communion of his spirit with all Nature, are traits of eternal beauty which time can neither destroy nor weaken.' (From Abbé Roussel's translation of the *Ramayana*.)

Rama was the son of king Dasaratha of Ayodhya, but was forced to renounce the throne and to go into exile by the intrigues of his step-mother. When he is leaving he advises his wife, the beautiful Sita, to stay in the palace. The life of the forest would be too rough and dangerous for her:

'You hear the dreadful roaring of lions mingled with the rushing of cataracts. There is not enough water, you walk along very difficult paths tangled with lianas and undergrowth, you sleep on beds of dead leaves, or on the bare earth, night after night, when you are worn out with fatigue. You have to be satisfied with fallen fruits, and sometimes to fast to the verge of extinction. Snakes with winding coils, like the streams in which they hide, boldly traverse the paths. It is the realm of wind, darkness, hunger, and the great terrors.'

But Sita insisted. She knew she had the right, for a wife's first duty is to share her husband's lot.

'Whether it is in asceticism, a hermitage, or in heaven, I want to be with you.

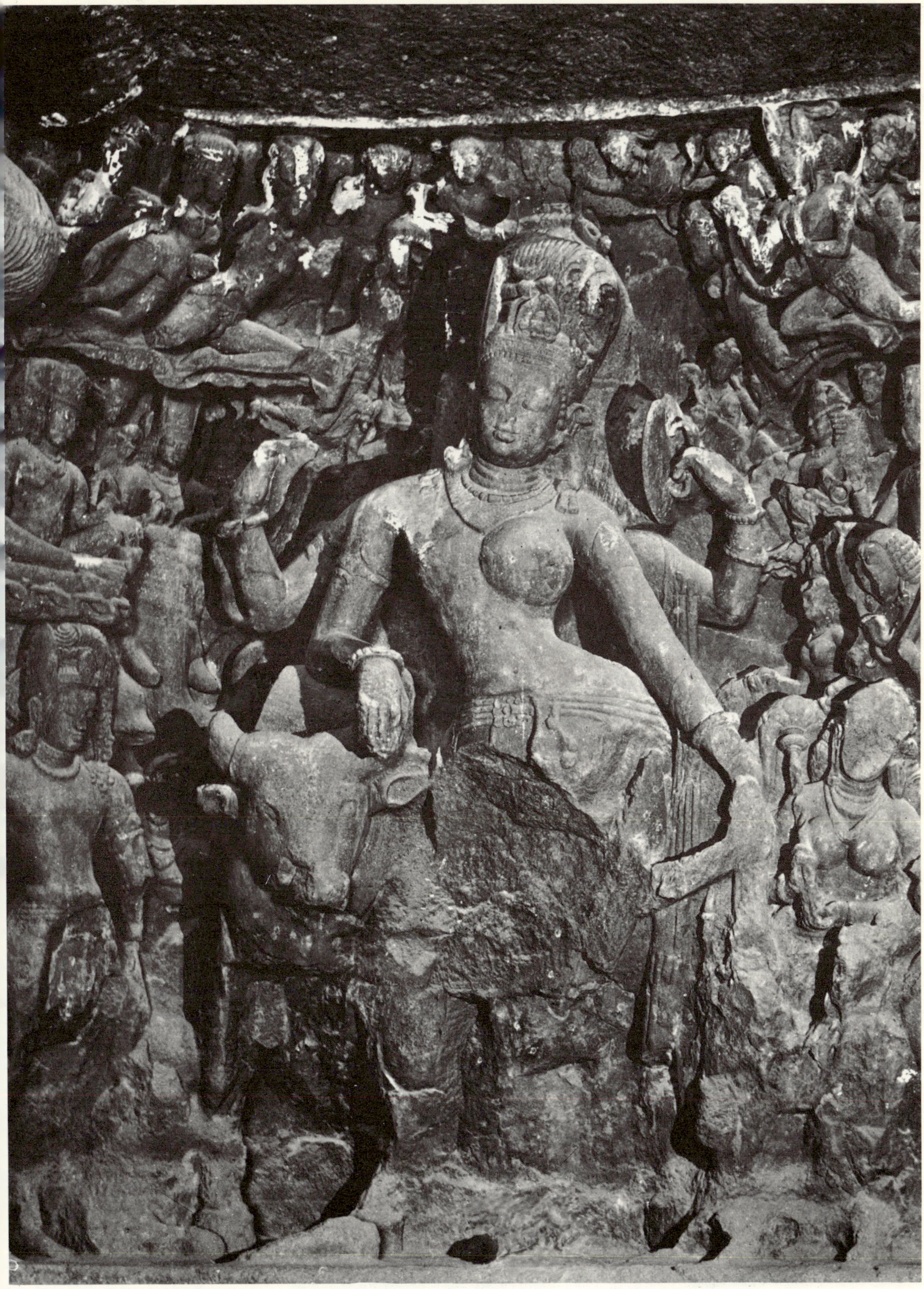

Ardhanarisvara. This curious composite figure, half-man and half-woman, represents Siva and his 'Sakti', or female nature, combined into one image which nevertheless represents the god alone, his essential nature being seen in the reconciliation of opposites. The figure is shown riding the bull Nandi, its seductive, one-breasted torso being surmounted by the high-domed head which represents the lingam. There are several stories accounting for this hermaphrodite form of the god. Sculpture from the Ellora Caves, seventh century A.D.

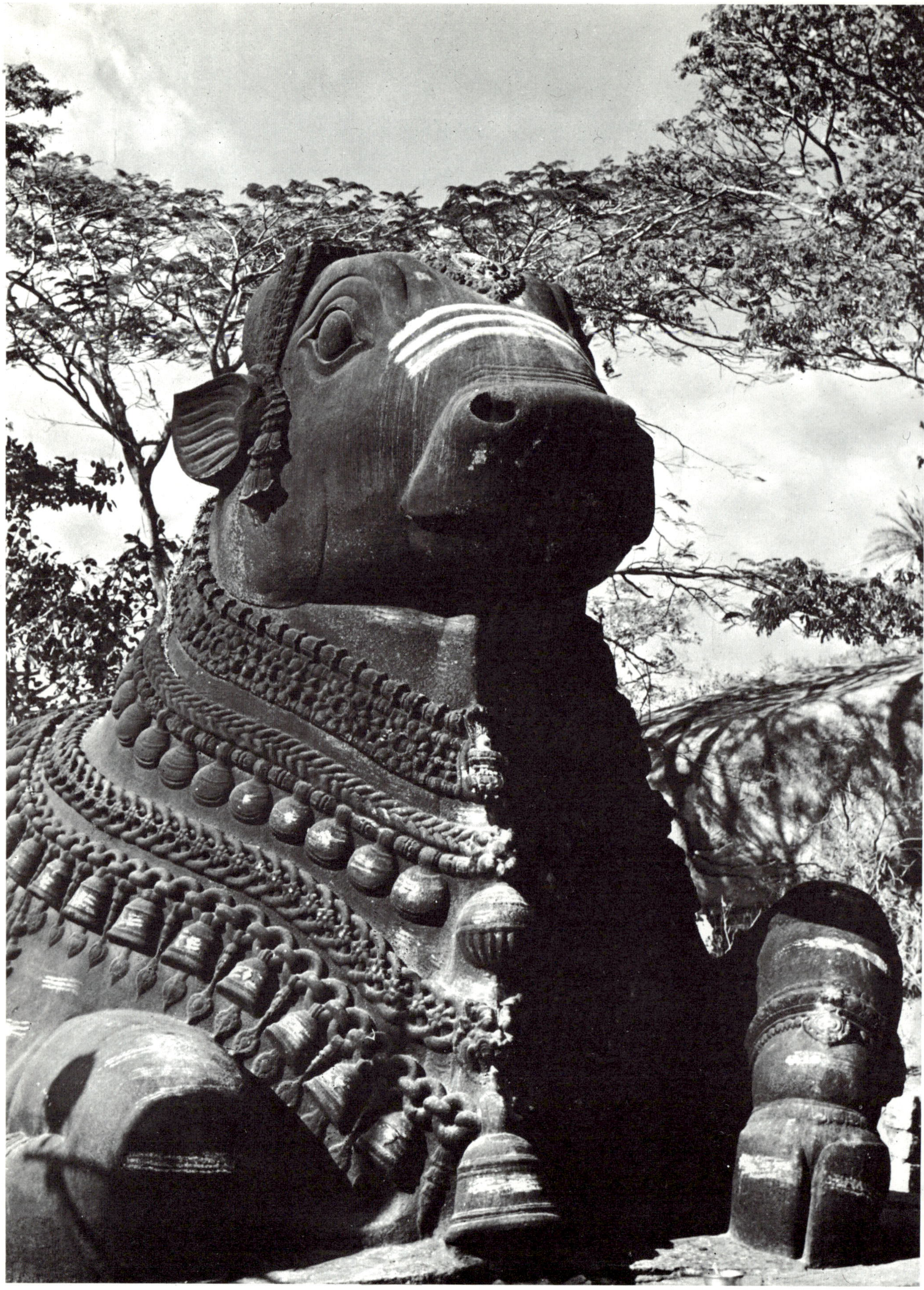

Nandi, the bull mount of Siva. The son of Kasyapa and Surahbi, the marvellous cow produced at the churning of the sea of milk, Nandi was Siva's chamberlain, mount, principal attendant and the provider of the music for his 'Tandava' dance as Siva Nataraja. He was also the guardian of all quadrupeds. He is generally portrayed of a milky white colour and his image is always conspicuous before the temples of Siva. Colossal stone carving from Mysore.

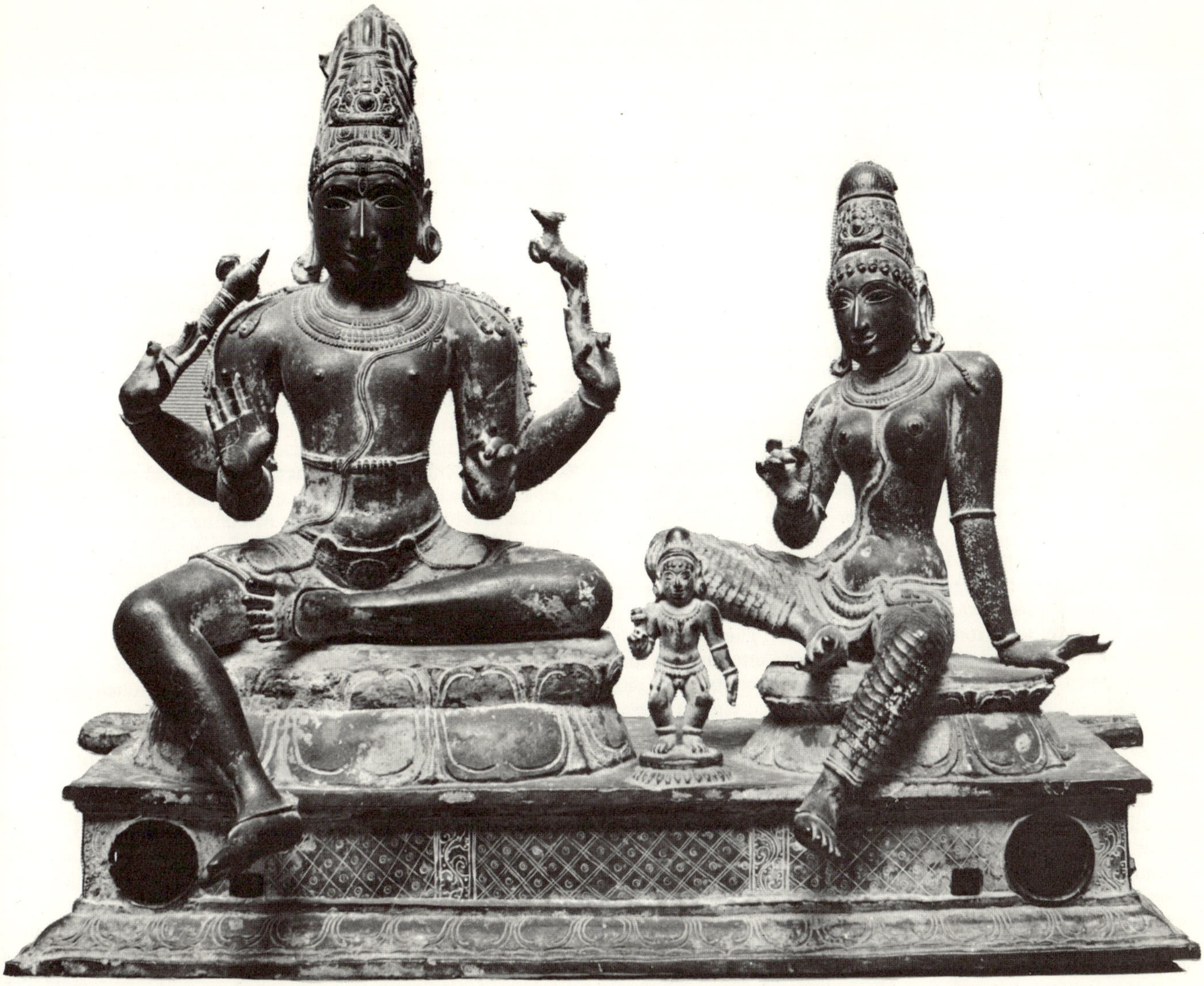

Siva and Parvati with their son Karttikeya. Numerous legends surround the birth of Karttikeya. According to one of these he was the son of Siva and Parvati, their union having been brought about by the gods for this purpose when danger threatened them. He later became the warrior god of the Hindus and is generally represented with six heads and twelve arms. He is also known as Skanda. Chola style bronze, sixteenth century A.D.

'I can never be tired walking after you. The reeds, the grass, the thorny bushes on the way will seem to me in your company as soft to the touch as a lawn or the skin of an antelope.

'The dust thrown up by the wind to cover me will seem, dear husband, rich sandal-wood powder.

'With you it is heaven, away from you hell. So it is. Be certain of it, O Rama, and be perfectly happy with me.'

Rama let himself be moved, and Sita followed him into exile along with his brother Lakshmana.

But Ravana, the king of the Rakshasas, desires Sita. He succeeds in drawing Rama away in pursuit of a magical gazelle, and carries off Sita by force in his aerial chariot. He keeps her a captive among his women in the kingdom of Lanka (Ceylon).

Rama, wild with despair and grief, looks madly for his wife, and vows to annihilate her abductor. An eagle among his friends indicates the trail, and a whole nation of monkeys put themselves at his service. Hanuman, one of the monkeys, is agile enough to clear the wall by an immense leap, and brings the hero back news of Sita whom he has cheered. Rama is sure of winning, but how can he take his army over the sea? He decides to ask the help of Ocean.

So, having formed a bed of the plant Kusa, Rama lay down on it, face to the East, and lifted his clasped hands to the sea, saying: 'The Ocean will yield, or I shall die.' Rama then remained there silent for three days with his spirit concentrated on the Ocean, but it made no answer. Then the hero became angry. He stood up, grasped his bow, tried to dry up the sea. He shot terrible arrows which pierced the waves, stirred up powerful storms and frightened the snakes and dolphins of the sea – and the gods shouted from heaven: 'Alas!' and 'Enough!'

But Ocean did not appear. Then having threatened him Rama fitted to his bow-string an arrow tipped with a charm given by Brahma, and shot. Darkness fell on heaven and earth, all creatures were seized with terror, the mountains trembled, and the depths of the sea were violently troubled. Then Ocean himself emerged from the waters, as the sun rises over mount Meru. Wearing a crown and spangled with glittering gems he was followed by the great rivers, the Ganga, the Sindhu, and others. He came to Rama with clasped hands, saying:

'O Rama, you know that each element possesses its own qualities. Mine are to be without bottom and difficult to cross. Neither love nor fear can give me the power to stay the eternal movement of the waters. But you can cross me, thanks to a bridge which I promise to uphold firmly. Secure the help of Nala, the son of Visvakarma (the smith of the gods). He is full of energy and as skilful as his father.' Having spoken, Ocean returned beneath his waves.

Thereupon, obeying Nala's orders, all the monkeys collected trees and rocks, carried them from the forest to the shore, and placed them on the sea. Some carried beams, some measured them, others rolled along enormous boulders. The rocks as they leaped into the sea made a noise like thunder. And at the end of five days a wide strong bridge was built. From a distance it looked on Ocean's head like the parting which divides the hair on a woman's head.

Rama and Lakshmana then started to cross the bridge with the army of monkeys. Other monkeys came swimming, and still others bounded through the air. The noise of this army overbore that of the waves and of Ocean.

Rama with his army soon reached the walls of Lanka, and a terrible battle began. It was at the expense of prodigies of valour that the hero's troops gradually overcame Ravana's.

After purification, and singing the hymn to the Sun, Rama in person had to fight, for Ravana came to attack him. They were like two fiery lions. One by one Rama with his arrows cut down the monster's ten heads, but fresh ones always sprang up. He then took a weapon which Agastya had given him – its wings were moved by the wind, its point was made of sunlight and fire, and it was as heavy as the mountains Meru and Mandara. After blessing this shaft with Vedic 'mantras' (sacred formulas) Rama fitted it to his bow and shot it. The shaft flew straight to its aim, pierced Ravana's chest and then, covered with blood, returned humbly to the hero's quiver.

Thus died the king of the Rakshasas. The gods rained down flowers on Rama's chariot, and sang hymns of praise, for the purpose which had caused Vishnu to assume human form was now attained.

Rama at first refused to receive the liberated Sita, for he wished to prove to everyone that in spite of her sojourn with Ravana his wife had remained unsullied. In despair at this repudiation Sita longed only for death, and had a funeral pyre built. She mounted it, and approaching the fire with clasped hands exclaimed: 'As my heart was never taken from Rama, so you, O Fire, the universal witness, will never take from me your protection!' Then she bravely entered the flames. While all the onlookers were uttering cries and lamentations, the fire was seen to rise up holding on its knees Sita who looked radiant as the morning sun. They cried out that it was a miracle, and Rama opened his arms to the Irreproachable, saying: 'I knew Sita's virtue, but I wished it to be justified before all the people. Without this test they would have said that Dasarath's son has yielded to desire and despises the traditional laws. But now all will know that she is truly mine, as the rays of the sun belong to their source.'

Rama then asked Indra to resurrect all his companions who had fallen on the battlefield, and then returned to Ayodhya, where he took in hand the government of the kingdom.

To close this series of Vishnu's avatars, let us mention Kalkin who, like Maitreya the future Buddha, has not yet appeared. The Kalki-Purana tells us what to expect from his beneficent intervention when his hour arrives. He will close the iron age, and annihilate the wicked. He will appear in the form of a giant with a horse's head. When his work is finished he will be re-absorbed in Vishnu until creation starts again, this time with a development opposite to the degeneration we now witness.

The elasticity of the 'avatar' system may be judged by the fact that Buddha himself was considered to be a form of Vishnu. Obviously it is an artificial interpretation, and yet contains a profound truth, since – as Senart has definitely proved – Sakyamuni belongs to the same solar myth which is implicit in all Vishnu's incarnations.

RELIGION OF SIVA

Vishnu is characterised by a tender devotion, and the religion of Siva is founded rather on asceticism. The god Siva is not a Bhagavat, but an Isvara, a Lord and Master. Although he wears the Brahman cord, he is the head of people without status like vampires and demons, as he is the head of those who have repudiated society, the ascetics. He is referred to by the same epithet as one of the Jain sects, 'digambara', naked 'clothed with space'. His chest is sometimes decked with a necklace of skulls. The question of his origin and his relations with the god Rudra have already been discussed (page 356).

Hindu art represents Siva in many very different forms. In his anthropomorphic aspect he usually has four arms – the two upper hands hold a drum and a doe, and the two others respectively make the gestures of giving and of reassuring. His forehead is sometimes marked by three horizontal stripes, and in the centre is a third eye. The god is dressed in a tiger-skin, with a snake for throat ornament, another for the sacred cord, while still others are coiled round his arms as bracelets. His hair is either tangled or braided and often stands erect with the high knot of the ascetic, decorated with a crescent moon and a trident. Sometimes amid the god's hair one can see the fifth head of Brahma or the goddess Ganga (Ganges). These different attributes correspond to episodes in his legend. He rides on the bull Nandi. Siva's personality swarms with contrasts. He destroys like time itself, and is also merciful. He is indifferent to pleasures, yet everywhere worshipped as the principle of generation under the symbol of the lingam (phallus). His whole activity points to the conviction, common to both Hinduism and Buddhism, that the same principle must be at the origin of good and of evil, of wretchedness and of salvation.

The philosophy of Sivaism is destructive of illusions, but leads neither to inaction nor to pessimism. On the contrary, its wisdom allows it to enter harmoniously into the great 'game', lila, of life, to take part in it by dancing with all one's heart and all one's joy.

Siva indeed is often represented under the form of Nataraja, the king of dancing. The halo fringed with fire which surrounds him then symbolises the whole cosmos.

A legend tells us that the god paid a visit to ten thousand Rishis who were heretics, in order to teach them the truth. But the Rishis received him with curses. As these had no effect they called up a terrible tiger which rushed at Siva to devour him. The smiling god took the skin off the tiger with the nail of his little finger, and hung it round himself like a shawl. Then the Rishis brought forth a horrible snake, and Siva hung it round his neck like a garland. Then appeared a demon dwarf, entirely black, armed with a mace. Siva set foot on his back and began to dance. Wearied by their efforts the hermits gazed at him in silence, captivated by the rapidity and dazzling splendour of the marvellous rhythm. Suddenly the heretics saw the heavens opened and the gods assembled to watch the dancer, and threw themselves at Siva's feet to worship him.

There are many other legends of Siva's dancing. The god destroys and creates in the dance 'Tandava', by which at the end of a cosmic period the world of appearances disappears but actually is re-integrated in the absolute. Siva has the genial intoxication and mystic fervour of Dionysus, with whom the Indo-Greeks confused him.

Siva's dance symbolises divine activity as the source of movement in the universe, particularly under the aspect of the cosmic functions of creation – conservation, destruction, incarnation and liberation. Its object is to rid men of illusion. When the god dances in cremation places, which are impure and full of fearful monsters, he is terrifying, the destroyer, and doubtless represents some pre-Aryan demon. It is also a way of showing that the demons are drawn into the dance of this universal god, and that in this way their evil powers are neutralised.

The place of cremation also symbolises the disciple's heart, where the self and its deeds are consumed, where everything has to disappear except the divine Dancer himself with whom the soul at last is identified. The supreme and perfect rhythm of this dynamic and triumphant joy is better expressed by dancing than by words. 'Ho whom no sign can describe is made known to us by his mystic dance,' says a poet of Southern India, a disciple of Siva.

Sivaism provides us with a magnificent cosmic synthesis where life and death continually give birth to one another, but where both are constantly dominated by a clear serene vision.

Siva Episodes. Siva's life abounds in instances of devotion and in earlier pages we saw how he swallowed the poison which threatened to destroy the world during the churning of the sea (page 367).

When the gods consented to the descent of Ganga (the Ganges), the heavenly river, the weight of this mass of water would have engulfed the earth, if the god with the trident had not offered himself to lessen the shock. Falling into his tangled hair, the heavenly Ganga wandered about the god's head for several years without finding an outlet. Finally Siva had to divide her into seven streams so that she could descend on earth without causing a catastrophe.

As they fell the waters made a noise like thunder, while fish and turtles fell with them. The Devas, the Rishis, the Gandharvas and the Yakshas, seated on their elephants or their horses or their chariots were amazed at the sight. All creatures rejoiced. The shining of the Devas and their jewels lighted up the whole sky like a hundred suns, the turtles and fish crossing it looked like flashes

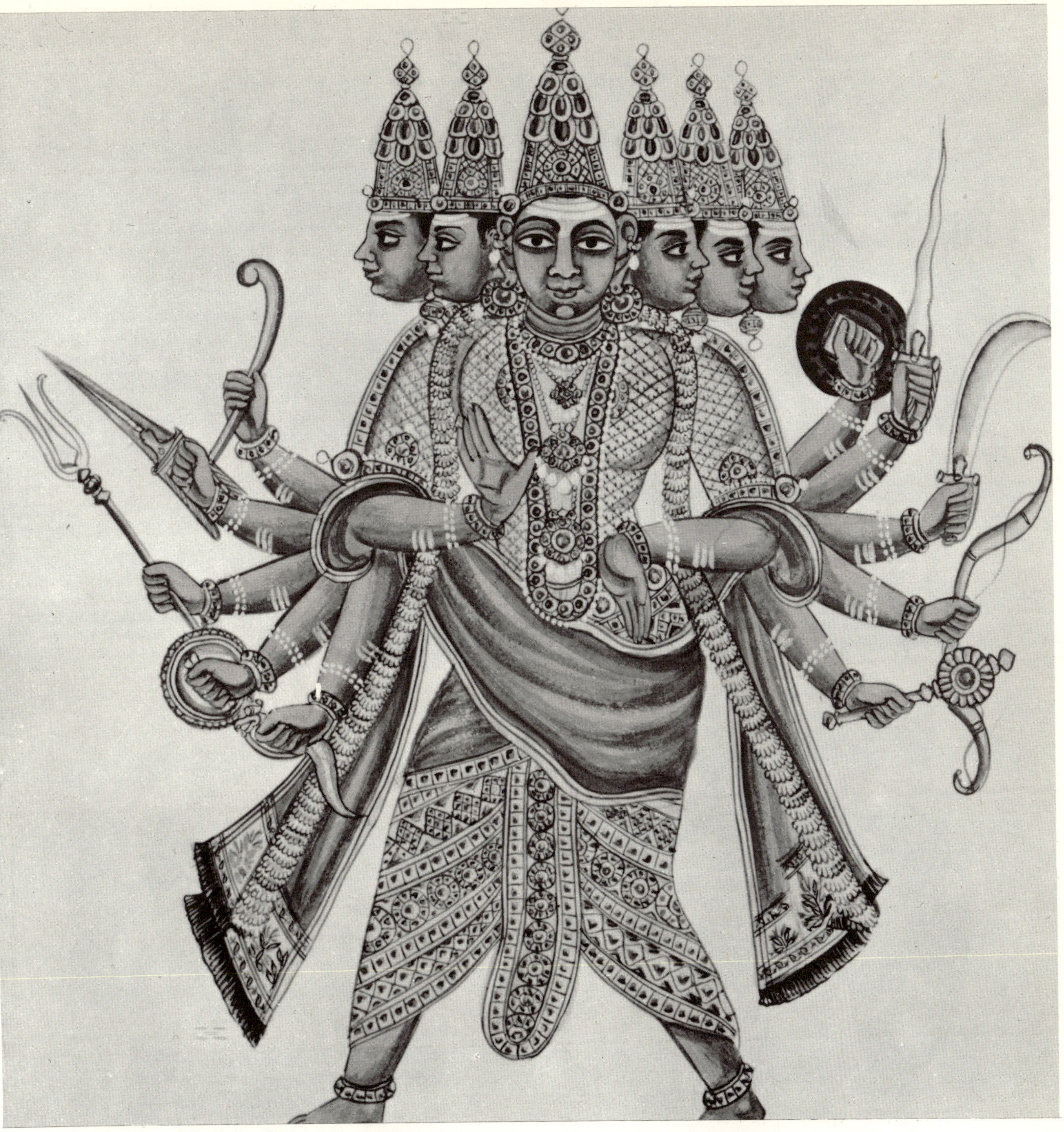

Karttikeya. The Hindu god of war is particularly popular in southern India and he is here shown in his south Indian form where he is known as Subrahmanya. Interested only in military exploits, he is generally said to dislike women though some accounts give him a wife. One account of his origins says that he acquired his six heads and twelve arms when Pãrvati squeezed what were originally six children too closely in her arms. Trichinopoly painting, nineteenth century A.D.

of lightning, and the pale foam flakes flew away like white birds. The waters poured on inexhaustibly, from heaven on to Siva's head and from Siva's head on to the earth; and there they split up into brooks and streams, climbing mountains and falling back into the valleys.

Parvati. The feminine divinity which personifies the 'power' (Sakti) of Siva is Parvati, daughter of the Himalayas, also named Uma, the gracious, and Bhairavi, the terrible, Ambika the generatrix, Sati the good wife, Gauri the brilliant, Kali the black, Durga the inaccessible. We have already had glimpses of this goddess's terrible aspects in dealing with her battles against demons.

According to the legend the appearance of Siva's third eye was caused by a frolic of his wife's. While he was meditating on the mountain, Uma imitating her husband observed a similar discipline, but one day she stole up mischievously behind her husband and covered his eyes with her lovely hands. Immediately the light of the world went out, the sun grew pallid and every creature trembled with fear. And then suddenly the darkness was dispelled, for a flaming eye had opened on Siva's forehead, a third eye like the sun, from which sprang flames which kindled all the Himalayas. The daughter of the mountain, grief-stricken and supplicating, displayed so much pain that with a kindly thought the god restored the mountains in all their splendour with their exuberant animals and plants.

Parvati often wearied of her husband's perpetual asceticism. In vain she waited patiently beside him in adoration; plunged in his meditations he did not even notice her presence.

To tear Siva away from his contemplations the gods one spring day sent him Love (Kamadeva) and his wife, Pleasure. Choosing the moment when Parvati was approaching her husband to worship him, Love drew his bow, but at the very moment when he was about to loose the shaft Siva saw him. and with a burning flash of his third eye consumed Love, who thereafter bore the name of Ananga, deprived of his limbs. While Pleasure mourned over him who, as

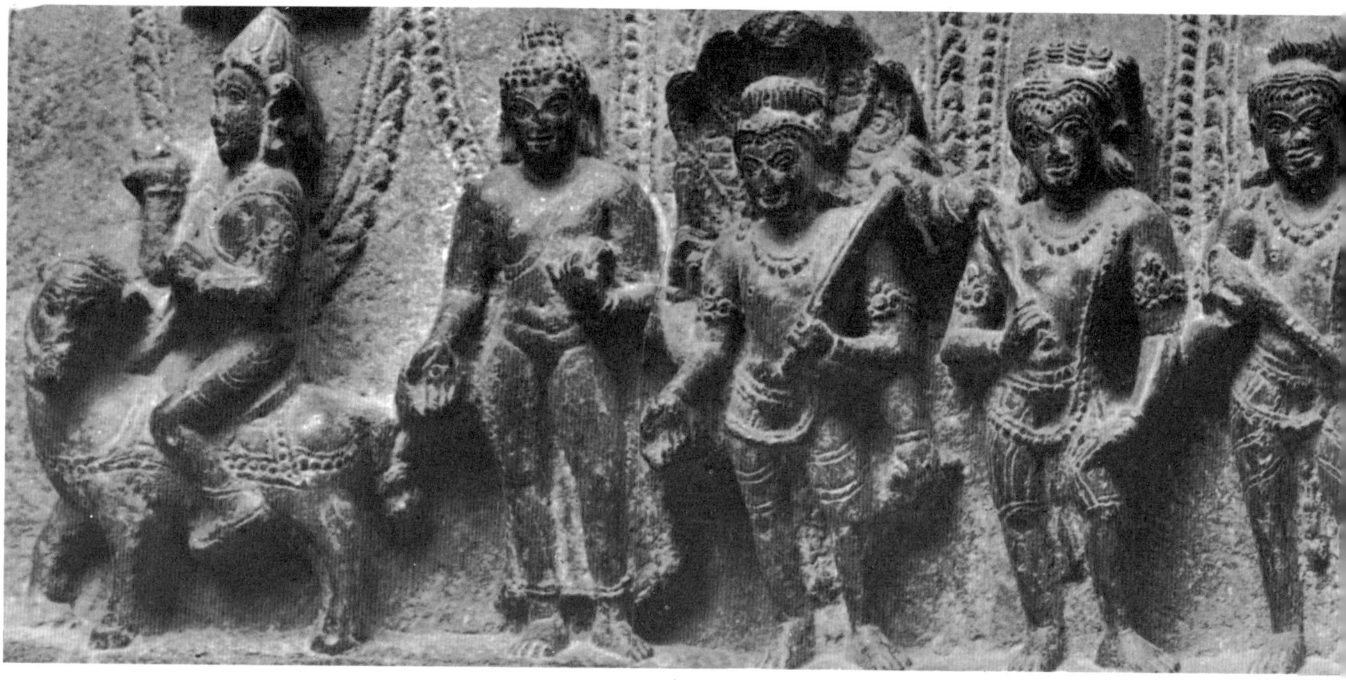

The ten avatars of Vishnu. (From right to left) Matsya, the fish; Kurma, the Turtle; Varaha, the Wild Boar; Narasimha, the Man-lion; Vamana, the Dwarf; Rama (with his bow); Parasurama, or Rama-with-the-Axe (the sixth avatar created to break the power of the warrior caste); and Balarama, Krishna's fair-skinned brother. The ninth avatar shown here is Buddha (declared by the Brahmans to be merely an avatar of Vishnu in an attempt to lessen the influence of his teaching) while finally comes Kalkin who will eventually destroy the present age of degeneration. Krishna, the most famous avatar of Vishnu is not shown here, having been accorded the statues of a separate divinity, and is replaced by his brother Balarama. Relief panel from Bihar, tenth century A.D.

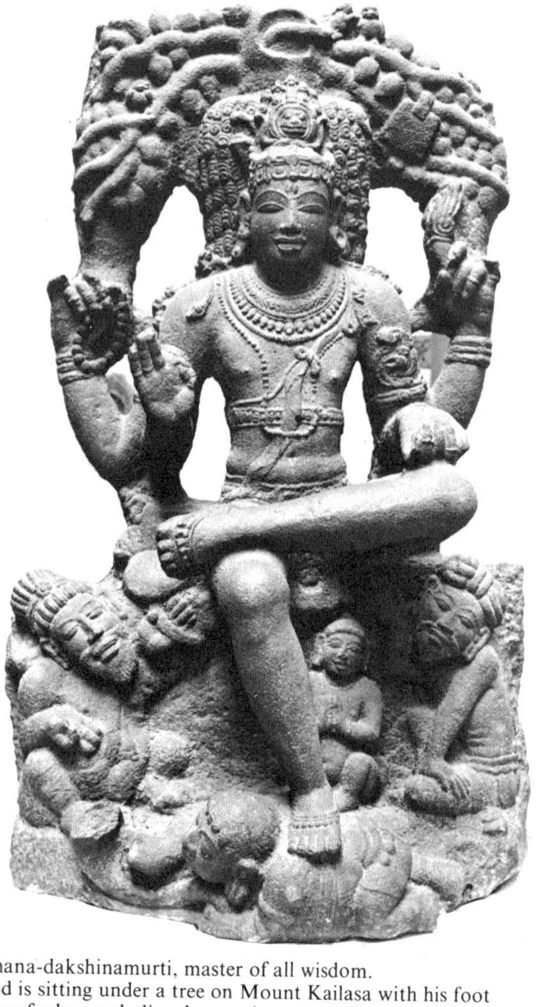

Siva Jnana-dakshinamurti, master of all wisdom.
The god is sitting under a tree on Mount Kailasa with his foot on a dwarf who symbolises human ignorance. Renowned for his wisdom, Siva on one occasion reduced the god of love to ashes for daring to inspire him with amorous thoughts while he was engaged in meditation and on another turned Parvati into a fisherwoman for being inattentive to his teaching. Basalt carving, fifteenth century.

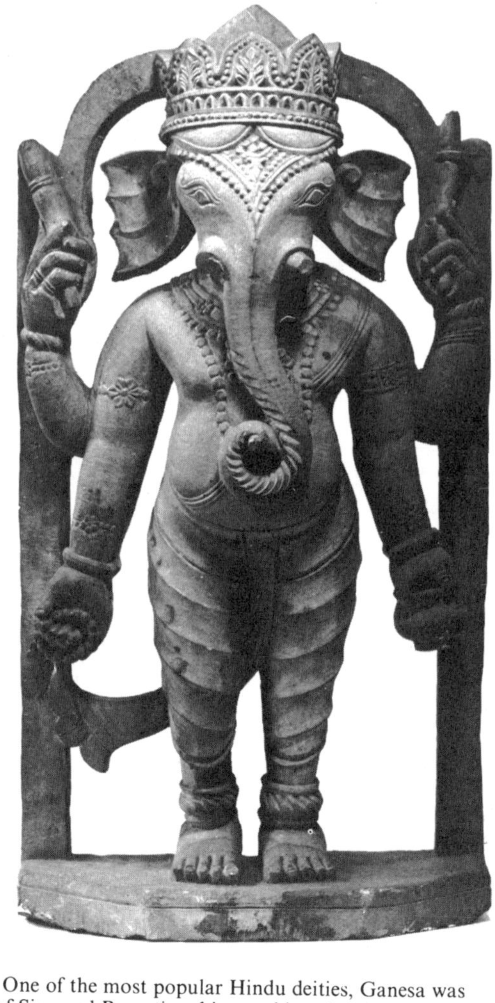

Ganesa. One of the most popular Hindu deities, Ganesa was the son of Siva and Parvati and is worshipped as the god of wisdom, good luck, prudence and the remover of obstacles.
In one account the four-armed god received his elephant's head after Siva had struck off his original one in a fury when he was attempting to guard his mother's privacy in her bath and refused his father admittance. Soapstone carving.

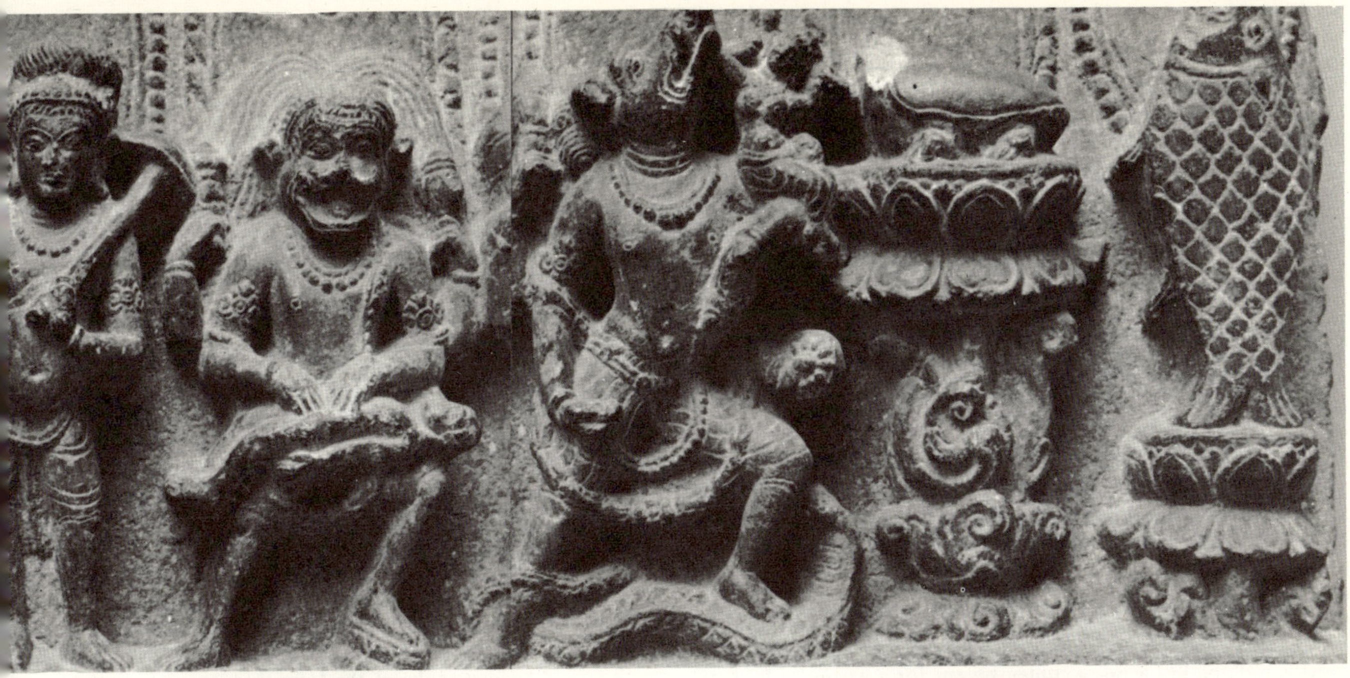

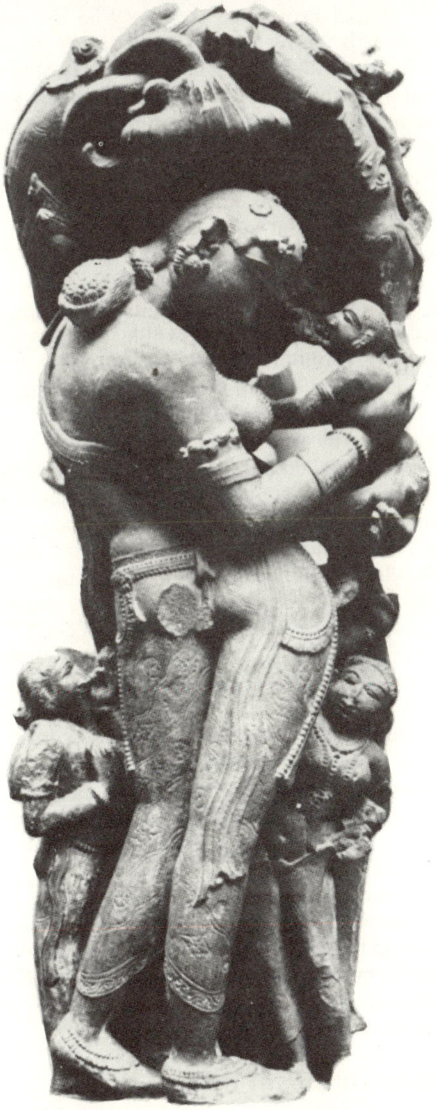

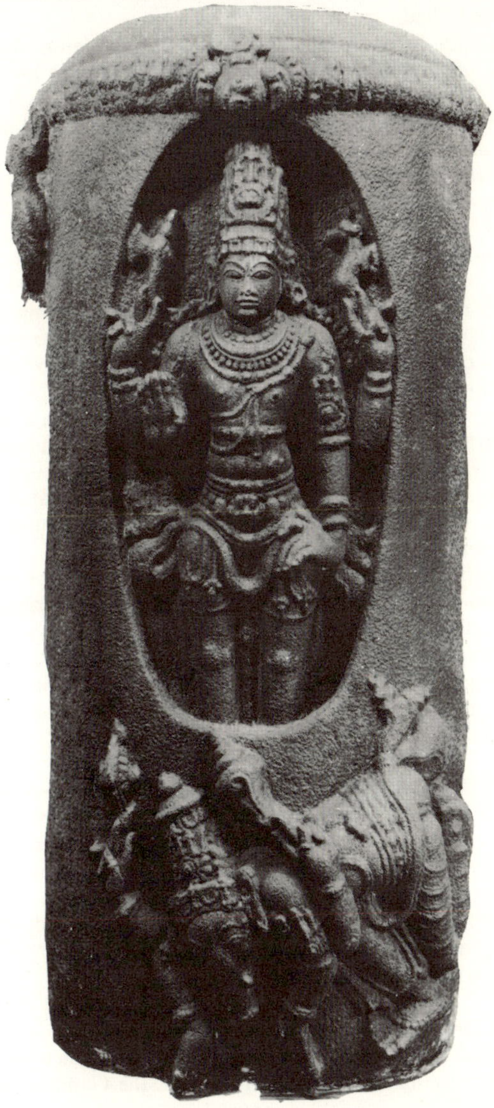

Karttikeya received by the Ganges. According to other accounts Karttikeya was the son not of Parvati but of Ganga, the goddess who personifies the sacred River Ganges. Ganga received six seeds of Agni, the fire god, when they were entrusted to her waters by Swaha, the daughter of a sage. Swaha visited Agni in a different guise for six nights, and from this union was born the warrior god. He rose from the Ganges with six heads, twelve arms and twelve legs. Statue from Khajuraho, eleventh century A.D.

Siva Lingodbhava. Though Siva's role in the Hindu triad is essentially that of destroyer, in Hindu belief destruction itself implies further reproduction and Siva is consequently regarded in addition as the great reproductive power. In this character of restorer he is worshipped in the form of the phallus, or lingam, within which he is portrayed standing, with Vishnu in the form of a wild boar at his feet. Basalt carving, thirteenth century A.D.

she believed, was for ever lost, a voice spoke to her saying: 'Your husband will return. When Siva weds Parvati he will give back Love's body to his soul.'

Parvati, weary of the god's indifference, had entered upon the life of a hermit. One day she was visited by a young Brahman who praised her for her faithful devotion, but tried to persuade her to return to the world. As she became angry the young man revealed that he was Siva himself. He promised her his love, but Parvati asked that first he should return the body of Kamadeva to his wife Pleasure. Siva agreed, and having taken Parvati to mount Kailasa at last consented to yield to her desire. Their embrace made the whole world tremble.

THE DESCENDANTS OF SIVA AND PARVATI

Ganesa. Ganesa is one of the most popular Hindu divinities. He was made by Parvati from the dew of her body mingled with dust, and acts as guardian to the goddess's gate. One day in an excess of zeal he tried to prevent Siva from entering, and for this he had his head cut off. But the indulgent Siva ordered that he should be brought the head of the first animal which happened to come along. Chance brought an elephant, and the resurrected son of Parvati received a new appearance.

Small and stocky with a fat stomach he has four arms, and carries in his hands an elephant-goad, a rosary, and an alms-bowl. His steed is nothing but a rat, a contemptuous form bestowed by him on a demon he had vanquished.

Ganesa's fat belly is the sign of his insatiable gluttony. They relate that one day after gorging himself with offerings he decided to take a ride to stir up his digestion. Mounted on his rat he was ambling along in the moonlight when a huge snake barred his way. The rat was frightened and leaped to one side, and Ganesa rebounded from earth so violently that he burst his belly!

To compel the snake to repair the damage he had caused, Ganesa took hold of him and rolled him round his damaged stomach. Recovering from the emotions of his accident the god was preparing to continue on his way when suddenly he heard great shouts of laughter ringing across the sky. It was the moon jeering at him! In a rage Ganesa broke off one his tusks and threw it in the mocker's face with a curse which periodically deprived the moon of his light, and lasts to this day.

Another version says that Ganesa tore out his tusk in a burst of enthusiasm to write down the Mahabharata from the dictation of the wise Vyasa. And in fact, despite the grotesque features of his legend, the elephant-headed god is the patron of literature. This should not surprise us, for Ganesa partakes of the natures of the two most intelligent beings, man and the elephant.

However he is above all a popular deity. Gentle, calm, propitious, he loves men and is loved by them. His good sense and friendliness are equally famous. He bestows riches, and assures the success of every undertaking. Nothing should be begun, not even the worship of another god, without first honouring Ganesa. He is particularly revered by the shop-keeping class. Even today if a bank fails the statues of Ganesa in the offices are turned round.

Karttikeya or Skanda. He is a war-god and was created by Siva at the request of the other gods to rid them of a demon. Siva directed the fire of his third eye on a lake, and instantly there emerged six children, who were suckled by the wives of Rishis. But one day when Parvati was cuddling them she squeezed so hard that they formed a single body. However, the six heads remained, and are figured in most statues of Karttikeya. This war god rides on a peacock, and carries a cock as his standard.

Kubera or Kuvera. He is a god of wealth, and also Siva's son. He hides, like his treasures, in the depths of the earth, listening to the music of artistic and horse-riding genii, like the Gandharvas and Kinnaras.

The Trimurti. Ingenious attempts were made to identify the two great sectarian gods, Vishnu and Siva, in the name of the idea that terror and love must have the same principle and the same end. For its part the Brahman caste altered its prototype of the absolute, brahman (neuter), a ritual formula, into a personal god, Brahma, masculine, who could be the equivalent of either Vishnu or Siva, and consequently bring them together. The representation of this Trimurti, triple aspect, is rather rare in sculpture.

Hinduism moreover has given birth to other composite deities. Hari-Hara is partly Vishnu and partly Siva, and is represented as divided into two halves by a vertical line, the right side bearing the attributes of Siva – the ascetic's hair-knot, the trident, the tiger-skin – and on the left Vishnu's tiara, disk and draped garment.

A curious figure is Ardhanarisvara (the god one half woman) considered however as solely an aspect of Siva – one half the statue represents the god, and the other half his 'Sakti', the manifestation of his energy in the feminine mode.

Far too often the Trimurti is used to suggest that India possessed a sort of Trinity with three equal figures. There is really only a rather artificial syncretism. Brahma, who personifies an abstraction, plays a very humble religious part in comparison with Vishnu and Siva, who for more than two thousand years have ruled the souls of Indians. However, the orthodoxy which was a possession of the priestly caste was preserved, thanks to the wholesale annexation of the sectarian cults. Once the Trimurti was formed, it received an adequate interpretation in each sect. Here is how Sivaism accepted it – the story is told by Brahma to the gods Rishis:

'In the night of Brahma when all beings were confounded in the same silent immobility, I observed the great Narayana, the soul of the universe with a thousand omniscient eyes, at once being and not-being, brooding over the waters without form, supported by the thousand-headed snake of the Infinite. Blinded by the shining I touched the eternal being and asked: "Who are you? Speak." Then lifting towards me his eyes like still sleepy lotus flowers he stood up, smiled, and said: "Welcome, my child, splendid Lord!" I was offended and replied: "How can you, a sinless god, treat me as a master treats a pupil, and call me child, I who am the cause of creation and of destruction, the creator of a thousand universes, the source of all that exists?" Vishnu replied: "Do you not know that I am Narayana, creator, preserver and destroyer of worlds, the eternal male, immortal source and centre of the universe? Even you were born from my imperishable body."

'And we argued together sharply over the sea without form, when to our eyes there appeared a glorious shining lingam, a pillar flaming with the light of a hundred fires able to destroy the universe, without beginning, without middle, without end, incomparable, indescribable. The great Vishnu was disturbed by these thousands of flames as I was, and said: "We must seek the source of this fire. I will descend, and you will ascend with all your strength." Then he took the form of a wild boar, like a mountain of blue collyrium, with sharp tusks, a long snout, a deep grunt, short strong feet, vigorous, irresistible. He descended for a thousand years but could not reach the base of the lingam. Meanwhile I had changed into a swan, entirely white, with burning eyes, wide wings, and my flight was as swift as the wind and thought itself. For a thousand years I flew up trying to reach the top of the pillar, but I could not reach it. When I returned I found the Vishnu had already returned weary.

'Then Siva appeared before us, and tamed by his magic we bowed before him. On all sides rose up his Om, eternal and clear. Vishnu said to him: "Our discussion has been fortunate, O god of gods, since you have appeared to put an end to it." And Siva replied: "In truth you are the creator, the preserver and the destroyer of worlds. My child, maintain both inertia and movement in the world. For I, the supreme indivisible Lord am three – Brahma, Vishnu and Siva; I create, I maintain, I destroy."'

The very variety of these combinations, their almost interchangeable character, show that in the end the gods are reducible to one another, according to the point of view adopted by the worshipper.

Under the swarming polytheism which animates Hindu mythology is hidden a profound doctrine of unity. 'God is One', says the Rig-Veda, 'but the sages, vipra, give him many names.'

EXPANSION OF HINDU MYTHOLOGY

While the mythology of the Little Vehicle conquered Indo-China, and that of the Great Vehicle Tibet, China, Japan, and the Indonesian archipelago, the mythology of Hinduism was exported to Cambodia and Java. Angkor-Wat, for instance, bears magnificent witness to it. There would scarcely exist an Indian statuary, either in the metropolis or the colonies, if mythology had not made the towering flight which we have tried to sketch the main lines.

CHINESE MYTHOLOGY

INTRODUCTION

Constitutive elements of Chinese mythology. It is well known that in China three different religions co-exist – Buddhism, Taoism and Confucianism, the two first of which have their own temples and priests: the Bonzes and Tao-shih, while the last has temples without priests. Chinese mythology has been formed from a mixture of elements belonging to these three religions, but these elements were not taken over intact. They suffered changes, sometimes rather profound changes, especially through the influence of plays and novels.

From early times and in the first years even of the Chinese Republic the official religion remained Confucianism. Every year the Emperor, followed by his courtiers, in spring and autumn made sacrifices to Heaven, the Sun, the Moon, the Soil, the god of War, Confucius, and the Ancestors, in each of their respective temples. Apart from that there was no special religious cult, except perhaps of Confucius himself. Some of these divinities were retained by the people in their mythology, but entirely changed their personality.

The same thing happened with the two other religions. Thus, certain Buddhist divinities may often be found under other names in mythology, while Taoism, to which Chinese mythology owes the greatest debt, was completely overturned and changed even to the personality of Lao-tzu, who is called its founder. In reality Lao-tzu was nearly a contemporary of Confucius (he is said to have lived in the sixth century B.C.) and like him was a philosopher. But popular legends endowed him with immortality and the power of conquering demons, claiming that he was the incarnation of the Celestial Master of the First Origin, one of the members of the Taoist supreme triad. After having spread his teaching and bestowed on his disciple, Yin Hsi, the Tao-te Ching or 'Book of the First Principle and its Virtue' he mounted a green ox and disappeared towards the West. He was never seen again.

The true founder of existing Taoism, which we shall call popular Taoism, was Chang Tao-ling who lived in the second century of our era and was deified in the eighth century. He received various revelations and, it seems, succeeded in preparing the drug of immortality. He fought with eight King-demons and conquered them thanks to his magic powers and his talismans; and finally after numerous exploits he ascended into heaven with his wife and two disciples, but not until he had passed on his various secret powers to his son.

Chang Tao-ling had bestowed on himself the title of Celestial-Master (T'ien-shih). His title passed from generation to generation of his descendants, and the writer recollects that at the beginning of the Republic the Celestial-Master of the epoch, a boy of about twelve, came to Peking to seek an audience of the president of the Republic, Yuan Shih-k'ai, who received him with great ceremony and confirmed him in his title.

Most of the divinities of Chinese mythology are of Taoist origin, and it should be added that many of them were made popular by two novels – *Travels in the West,* and *Romance of the Investiture of the Gods,* both dating from the Ming epoch, about the fifteenth century.

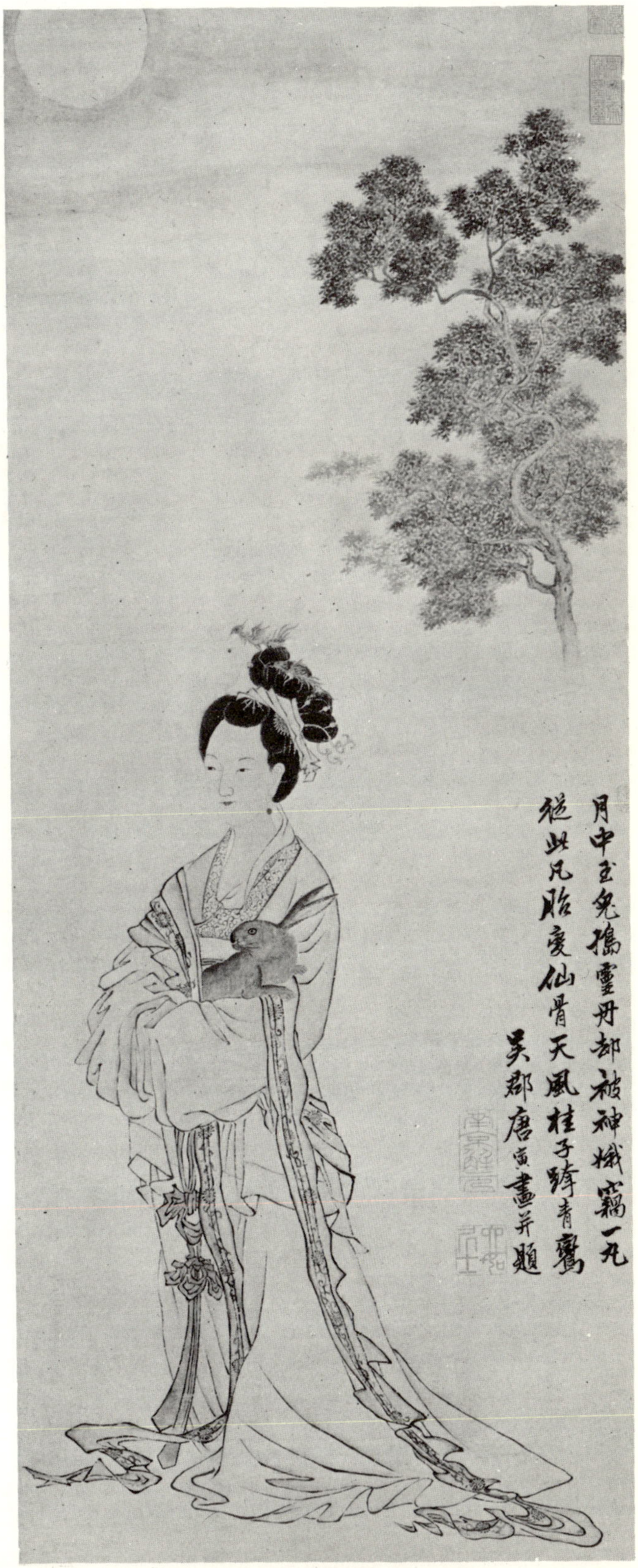

Ch'ang-o, the goddess of the Moon, The wife of I, the Excellent Archer, Ch'ang-o took up her abode in the Moon in order to escape her husband's wrath after she had swallowed the drug of immortality which had been given to him by the gods. The couple were later reconciled, however, and I would vist her in her lunar palace.
The goddess was always portrayed as a very beautiful young woman. Painting by T'ang Yin, Ming dynasty.

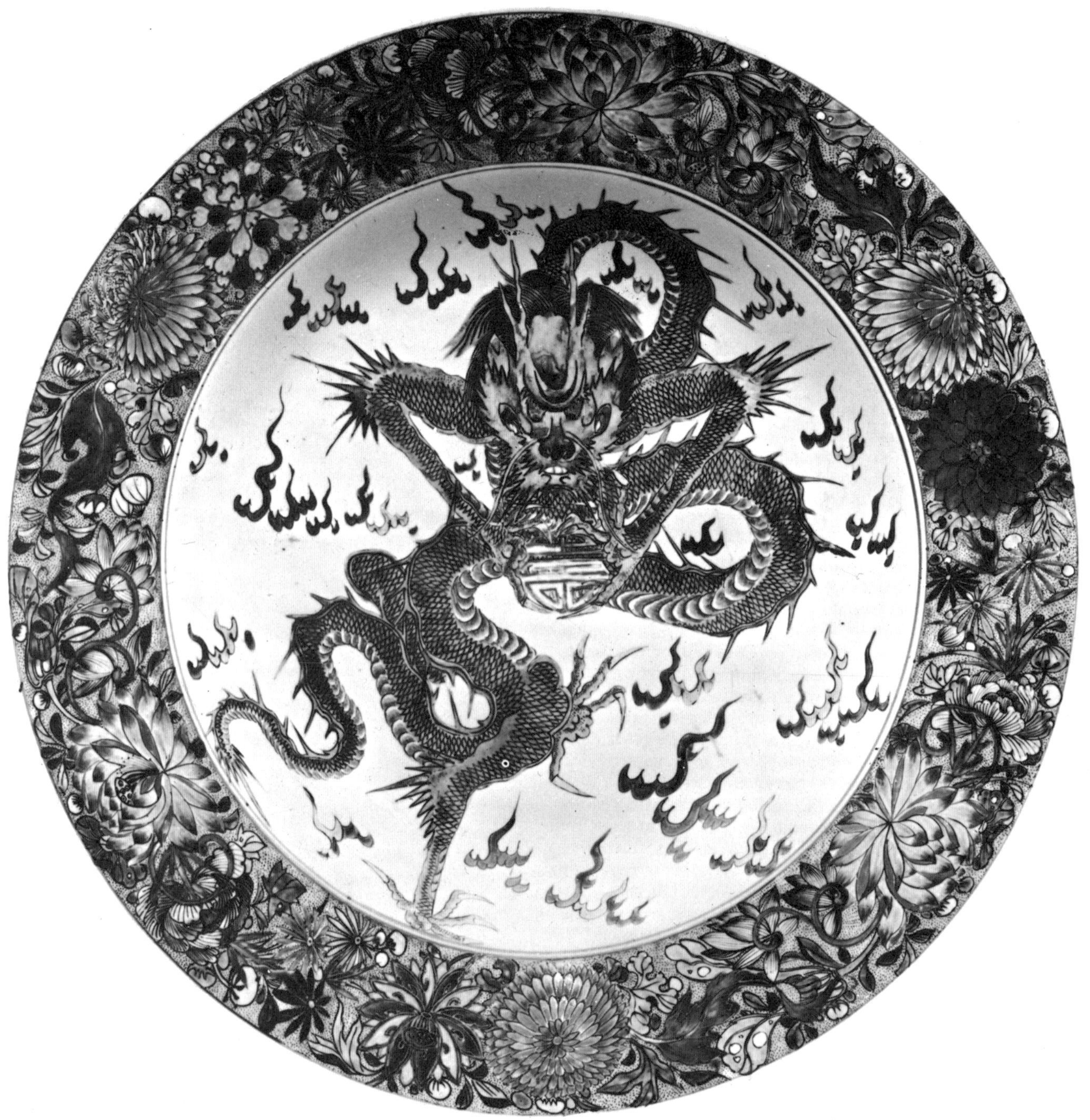

Porcelain dish decorated with a dragon holding a jewel in the form of a *shou* (longevity) character. The dragon is the symbol of the fertilising rain, the four Dragon-Kings who rule the four seas being responsible to the August Personage of Jade for distributing certain amounts of rain to given regions. The Dragon-Kings are approached both in times of drought and in times of excessive rain – in this case to avert floods. K'ang Hsi period.

Characteristics of the Chinese Pantheon. Perhaps the most curious fact about the Chinese Pantheon is that it is arranged in imitation of earthly organisation. It appears as a vast government administration, or, still more precisely, as a series of government departments, each one with its Minister and its personnel. The different gods are positive bureaucrats with a strict hierarchy of rank and with clearly defined powers. They keep registers, make reports, issue directives, with a regard for formalities and a superabundance of papers which the most pedantic administration on earth might well envy.

Every month they furnish a detailed report to their immediate superiors, and they every year give an account of their administration to the sovereign god, the August Personage of Jade, who then distributes his praise and his censure. The gods, according to circumstances, are then promoted or lowered in rank, and they may even be dismissed.

This is one of the most original characteristics of all Chinese mythology, for the gods are not immutable. Only function persists – the functionary changes. New gods take the place of the old. And these changes do not only occur in time, but in space. By that we must understand that in different regions the same powers are in many instances allotted to quite a varying number of different personages.

The explanation is that most Chinese gods are not in origin divine, but human; they are men who have been deified after their death.

These different facts explain the large number of divinities which inhabit Chinese mythology. It would be too long and too tedious to look over all of them in these pages and we shall deal only with the most important or most popular gods, referring those interested to Father Doré's *Recherches sur les Superstitions en Chine,* and to the chapter devoted to Chinese mythology by H. Maspero in the *Mythologie asiatique illustrée*. I make a point of stressing how much the present study owes to that work.

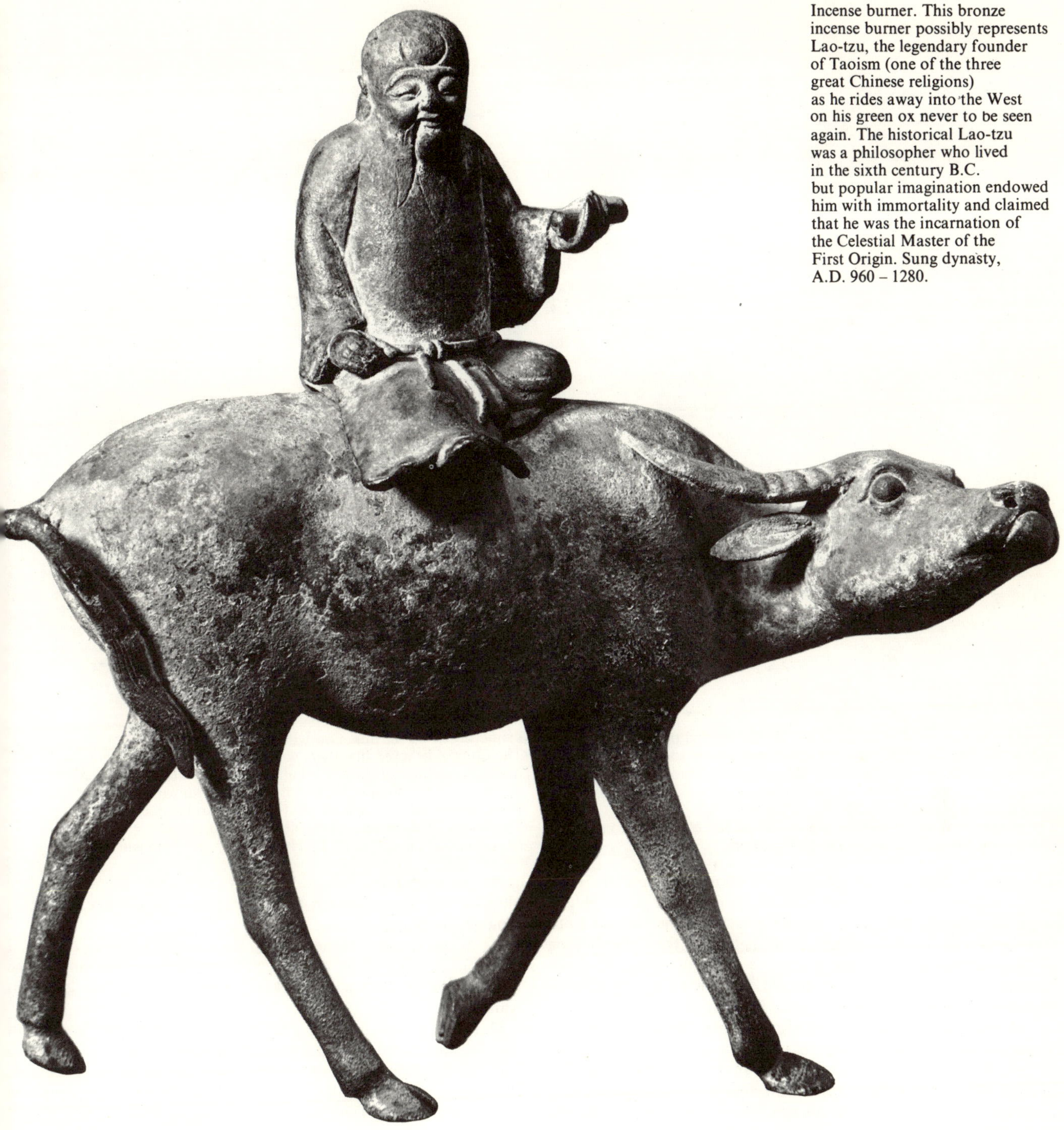

Incense burner. This bronze incense burner possibly represents Lao-tzu, the legendary founder of Taoism (one of the three great Chinese religions) as he rides away into the West on his green ox never to be seen again. The historical Lao-tzu was a philosopher who lived in the sixth century B.C. but popular imagination endowed him with immortality and claimed that he was the incarnation of the Celestial Master of the First Origin. Sung dynasty, A.D. 960 – 1280.

HEAVEN AND ITS GODS

Heaven is the dwelling of sidereal divinities, but they do not live together. Each god has his own palace, and moreover Heaven is divided into different levels, some say nine and others thirty-three. The gods with the highest seniority in office are the most important and live on the top level.

The August Personage of Jade. On the topmost level surrounded with his Court lives the August Personage of Jade (Yu-ti) also known as the August Supreme Emperor of Jade (Yu-huang-shang-ti) or again and most usually Father-Heaven (Lao-tien-yeh). They say he was one of the first gods who existed and that he created human beings – such at least is the tradition in Northern China. They add that Father-Heaven made human beings by modelling them in clay, and when his task was ended he put his statuettes to dry in the sun. At this moment a heavy shower of rain fell and Father-Heaven hastened to put his statuettes in shelter. But some of them were damaged by the rain, and they constitute the sick living on earth, while the healthy whose limbs are whole and complete are the statuettes which were not damaged.

Although recognised as the greatest of the gods, the August Personage of Jade is only the second person of the supreme triad, which includes the Heavenly Master of the First Origin, who preceded the August Personage of Jade, and the Heavenly Master of the Dawn of Jade of the Golden Door, who one day will succeed him.

The August Personage of Jade lives in a palace exactly similar to that of the Emperor who reigns over human beings. The doorway of this palace is guarded by Wang, a transcendental bureaucrat, who is armed with a stick and clad in armour and does duty as door-keeper. There the August Personage of Jade grants many audiences, for his Court is exactly like that of the human Emperor – he has his Ministers and his officers, represented by secondary

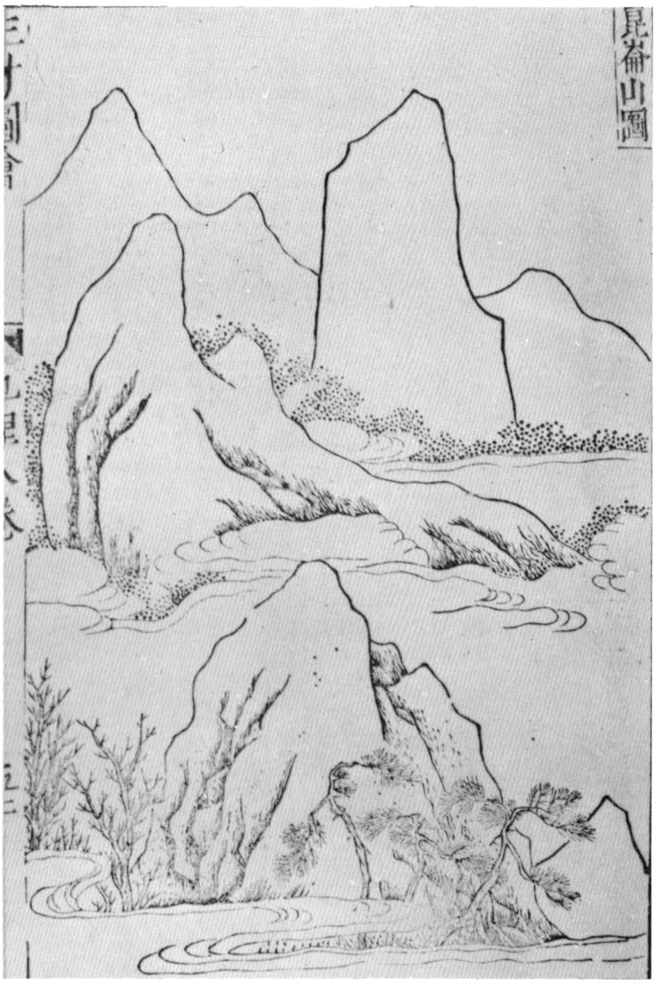

K'un-lun mountain. The abode of the Immortals and the blessed and meritorious dead, K'un-lun is ruled over by the Lady-Queen of the West, the Queen-Mother Wang, the wife of the Lord-King of the East. Her palace of jade is situated on the summit of the mountain while in its gardens grows the Peach tree of Immortality. The mountain is surrounded by water – some say of a vermilion colour. Illustration from *San-ts'ai t'u-hui*, 1607 edition.

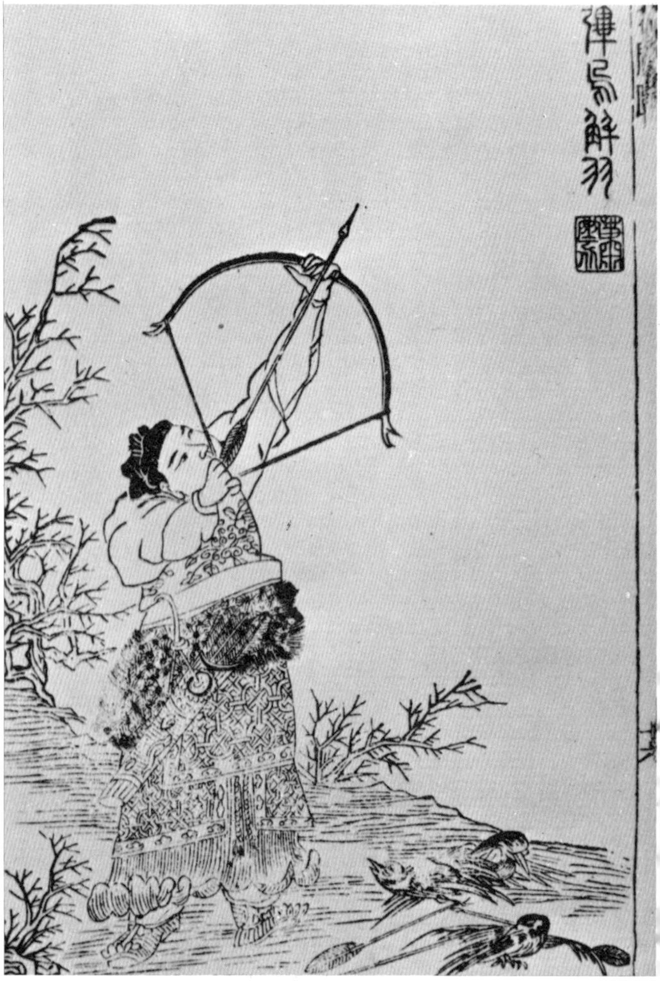

I shooting down the nine suns with his magic bow. The Chinese believed that there were originally ten suns – one for each hour of the day – but that one day all ten appeared in the sky together threatening to burn up the earth with their heat. Here I, the Excellent Archer, destroys the surplus ones. The bodies of three sun-ravens lie at his feet already. Illustration from *Li-sao t'u* by Hsiao Ch'ih-mu, 1645 edition.

gods, and he has an army of heavenly soldiers to fight the rebel Spirits when necessary. He has a family – a wife, sisters, daughters, nephews. Among the last-named we must note the Second Lord (Erh-lang) who drives away evil spirits, helped by the Celestial Dog (T'ien-kou). He is a god said to know seventy-two ways of transforming himself. He is much respected, and has numerous temples dedicated to him.

The wife of the August Personage of Jade, the Queen Mother Wang (Wang-mu niang-niang), is no doubt a popular corruption of the elderly character, the Lady-Queen of the West, who is spoken of in the Romance of the Emperor Mu (found in a tomb and dating from the fourth century). The ancient legends represent her as wife of the Lord-King of the East, dwelling on the K'un-lun mountains, which is the abode of the Immortals; the popular legends present her as the wife of the August Personage of Jade, living on the highest level of Heaven with her attendants. However, in spite of this transformation, she keeps her ancient attributes. She presides over the banquets of immortality which she gives to the gods, banquets mainly furnished with the peaches of immortality, P'an-t'ao, which ripen once every three thousand years on the peach-trees of the imperial orchard – which is why in China the peach is the symbol of longevity.

The August Personage of Jade is always represented wearing the high ceremonial costume, Chinese style, of the Emperor (note that the gods are always represented in Chinese and never in Manchu costume), with embroidered dragons on his robe. He wears on his head the headdress of the Emperors, formed by a flat board from which hang, in front and behind, thirteen pendants of coloured pearls on red strings, and his crossed hands hold the Imperial book of etiquette. He is seated on a throne, sometimes with secondary gods, his attendants, beside him, but more often alone. And like all gods who are supposed to have reached middle age, he wears long whiskers and a tuft of beard.

As to the Queen Mother Wang, she is usually represented as a beautiful young woman also in ceremonial dress, sometimes alone but sometimes with a peacock or surrounded by her ladies in waiting.

During the monarchy the Emperor every year made two solemn sacrifices to the August Personage of Jade, one in the winter solstice and one in spring. They were both celebrated in the huge Temple of Heaven situated in the south suburb of Peking. The Emperor was carried to the Temple in a monumental chair, accompanied by an imposing procession of princes, dignitaries, soldiers, and imposing procession of princes, dignitaries, soldiers, and dancers. He went up the three stages of the altar of Heaven, an enormous mound encircled with marble balustrades, bowed to the ground before the fire lighted in the god's honour, and made his offerings, which consisted of rolls of silk, disks of jade, various meats and many other libations.

NATURE DIVINITIES AND SIDEREAL GODS

Sun and Moon. We have already noted that the Sun and Moon were the objects of an official cult, but the people's worship was quite different. For them the Sun is a god who originally lived in the form of a cock but by following the Path obtained a human face. In the ordinary way he was only offered one sacrifice at the beginning of the year and another on his birthday, and that was all. There were very few Temples dedicated to him. The same is true of the Moon, except that it received more sacrifices. The festival of the Moon is one of the three great annual Chinese feasts, and takes place on the fifteenth day of the eighth month, at the full moon of the autumn equinox. It is especially a festival for women and children, who buy little figures representing either a white rabbit or a helmeted soldier dressed in his armour with a face like a hare, and make them a sacrifice consisting chiefly of fruit. They offer a sacrifice directly to the Moon when it has risen a little above the house-tops. In some families the sacrifice is made before a large paper panel with a representation of the Moon's palace with its inhabitant the Hare who makes the drug of immortality. The sacrifice consists of fruit, sweet cakes which are specially made and sold for the occasion, and a sprig of red amaranth. Men never take part in this ceremony, for in the popular mind the hare is the symbol of inverts – nobody knows why – and is considered their patron.

The Moon is also inhabited by a personage who is considered the Moon goddess, Ch'ang-o or Heng-o. She is the wife of I, the Excellent Archer, a mythological personage who brought down nine suns with his arrows, one day when the ten suns of primitive times took it into their heads to rise together and threatened to shrivel up the world. The gods had given him the drug of immortality and one day he returned home to find that she had drunk it. He was so angry she fled to the Moon, her husband in hot pursuit. She asked protection of the Hare, who fought with I and made him give up his intention of punishing his wife, who henceforth has lived in the Moon. She is represented as a very beautiful young woman, and her name is often mentioned in novels and poems for it is said currently of a pretty woman that she is as 'beautiful, as if Ch'ang-o had come down from the Moon'.

Rain, Thunder, Wind. Although Taoist religion includes a whole Ministry of Thunder made up of several divinities, the people recognise only one Thunder god called My Lord Thunder, Lei-kung. He is represented as a man of repulsive ugliness, with a body blue all over, furnished with wings and claws. He wears nothing but a loin-cloth, with one or more drums hanging at his side, and his hands hold a mallet and a chisel. There is general agreement that the chisel is used to strike the guilty whom the Thunder is ordered to punish, but there is less agreement about the uses of the mallet. Some say it is used to strike the drums to produce the rolls of thunder, but others think it is used to drive in the chisel.

By orders of Heaven, the Thunder punishes human beings guilty of some great crime which has remained undetected or which human laws do not touch (usually some act which has directly or indirectly caused somebody's death); it also punishes evil spirits who by practising Tao doctrine have succeeded in gaining personality and make use of it to harm mankind, etc. However, he is not always able to achieve this by himself, and he sometimes needs human help.

One day a hunter in pursuit of game had ventured far into a thick forest and was surprised by a violent storm. Flashes of lightning and thunder were continuous, and seemed to hover over a tree which lifted its tall branches not far from where the hunter stood. Looking up he saw a child holding in its hands a flag roughly made from a piece of cloth tied to a bit of wood. When the Thunder approached the child waved its flag, and the Thunder immediately retreated. It is well known that Thunder, like all the gods, dislikes unclean things and especially the blood of black dogs, and the hunter at once realised that the child was an evil spirit pursued by the Thunder and that his flag was made of some unclean material. By way of helping on the divine work, he loaded his gun and shot down the flag. The Thunder at once struck the tree, but the hunter who was too close to it was also touched and fainted away. When he recovered he found a little roll of paper on his body containing the words: 'Life prolonged for twelve years for helping on the work of Heaven', while at the foot of the shattered tree he found the corpse of a huge lizard, the real form of the child with the flag.

Thunder has no Temple of his own – at least, it is very rare to meet with one. Moreover the most worshipped gods are those who can give something, such as happiness, wealth, children, etc., so it is not surprising that nobody comes to ask anything from a god who can give nothing but a death entailing infamy; and yet there are some people who apply to him. Usually they are persons who have to complain of somebody else, and not being able to revenge themselves entrust their vengeance to the god, begging him to strike their enemies dead.

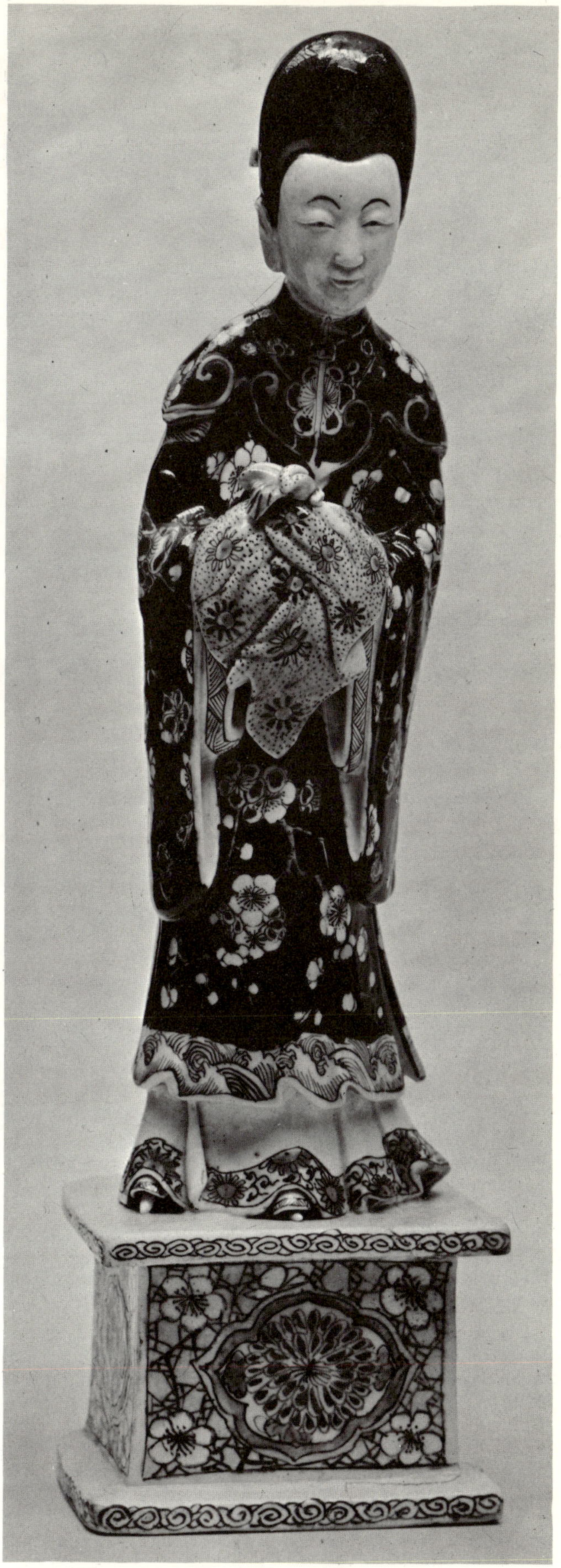

The Lady-Queen of the West, Hsi Wang Mu.
In ancient legends the wife of the Lord-King of the East, Hsi Wang Mu, ruled over the abode of the Immortals on K'un-lun. Popular legends made her the wife of the August Personage of Jade and placed her dwelling on the highest level of Heaven but she retained her attributes and continued to furnish the peaches of Immortality for the banquets of the gods. Porcelain figure.

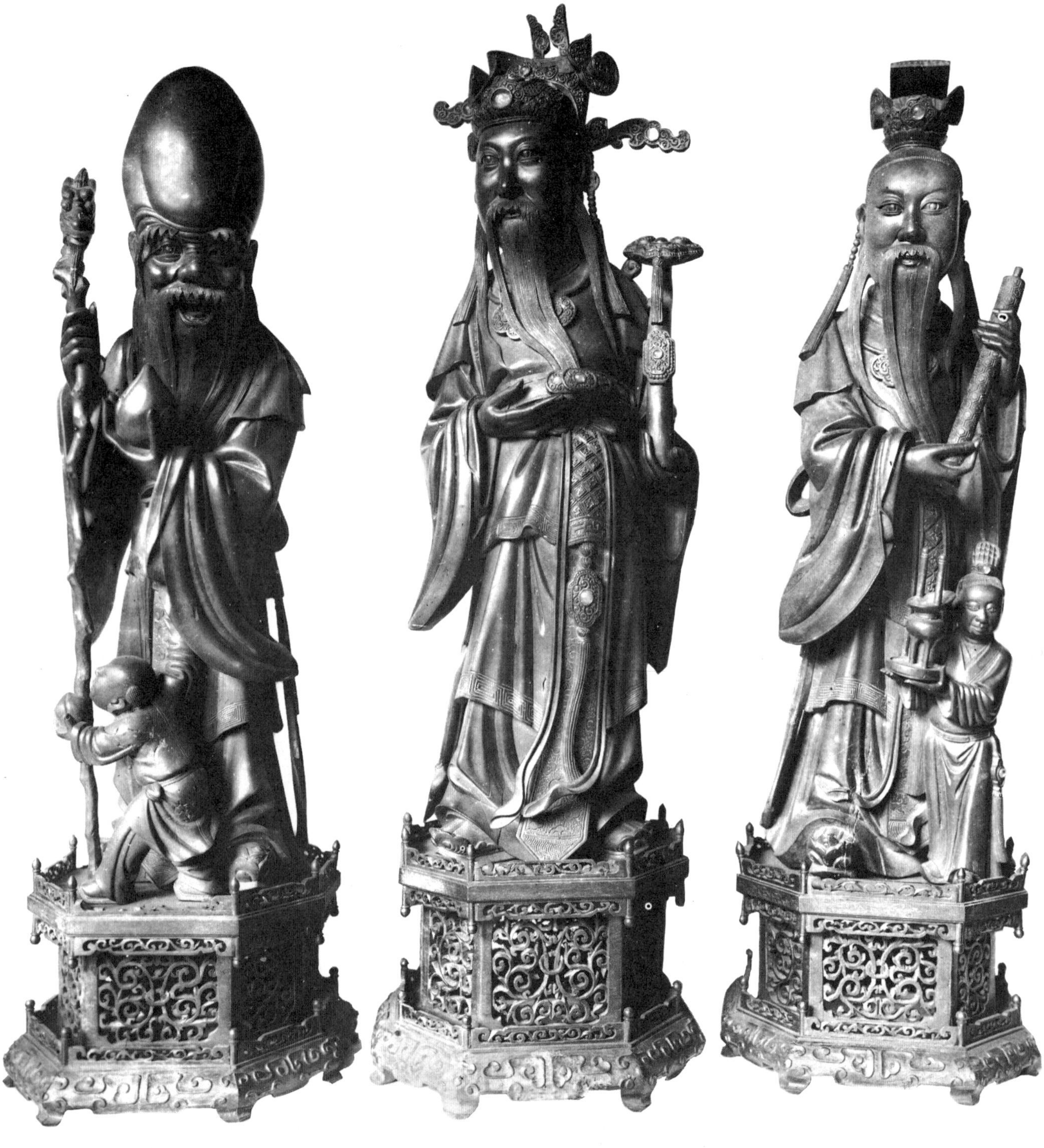

The gods of happiness. From left to right: Shou-hsing, the God of Long Life; Fu-hsing, the God of Happiness; Lu-hsing, the god of Salaries. Wood statuettes, eighteenth century. Musée Guimet, Paris.

During storms, Thunder, who can only make a noise, is helped by several other divinities. The flashes of lightning are produced by Mother-Lightning (Tien Mu) with the help of the mirrors she holds in her hands; the rain is produced by the Master of Rain (Yu-tzu) who with his sword sprinkles water from the pot he holds; the clouds are piled up by the Little Boy of the Clouds (Yun-t'ung); and the wind comes out of a kind of goatskin bottle carried by the Earl of Wind (Feng-po). Later on this last god was replaced by a goddess, an old woman named Mrs Wind (Feng-p'o-p'o). She may sometimes be seen moving among the clouds, riding on a tiger.

The Dragon-Kings: Lung-Wang. However, for the people these divinities are subordinate to the Dragon-Kings who depend directly on the August Personage of Jade, from whom they receive the order to distribute a certain amount of rain to a given region. There are four Dragon-Kings of importance, each of whom rules one of the four seas of which the earth is the centre, and they are mostly known to the people as four brothers under the names they have in *Travels in the West*, which differ from those given them by the Taoists. They are Ao Kuang, Ao Jun, Ao Shun and Ao Ch'in. Each lives in a palace called the Crystal Palace, and has his Ministers, his army consisting of fish, crabs and crayfish, and watchmen who see to the policing of the sea-bottom. These four Dragon-Kings are not much worshipped, although they have quite a lot of temples, because the local Dragon-Kings are much more respected. Indeed, every watercourse and every well has its Dragon-King. In northern China beside every well there is a tiny temple with the statue of its god, represented as a mandarin in ceremonial costume, and on the first and fifteenth of each month the owner of the well makes it a rudimentary sacrifice of three joss-sticks.

The Dragon-Kings bring rain, and so are resorted to in droughts. The ceremonies vary with the locality. In the big towns a procession is often organised, with the effigy of a dragon in cloth which serves specially for this event. The effigy is taken through the main streets of the town, preceded by a band and persons dancing. In the villages they don't do this. During bad droughts the village people go and ask for rain from the Dragon-Kings in the most important temple and offer an ample sacrifice. If at the end of a few days their prayers are not answered, the god's statue is taken out of the temple and left beside the road, for they rightly suppose that this treatment will cause suffering to a god who lives in the depths of waters, and that he will hasten to ask the August Personage of Jade for permission to send rain. On the other hand if after the sacrifice or the exposure of the stature it happens that enough rain falls to save the crops, the rejoicing is universal. A new sacrifice is made by the whole village, and important places may honour the god by giving a theatrical performance which lasts three days. Sometimes a number of neighbouring villages will club together to do the thing more handsomely. Naturally, if it rains too much or there is a threat of floods, the Dragon-Kings are again approached, but this time with a view to stopping the rain.

The God of Literature, Wen Ch'ang, and the God of Examinations, K'uei-hsing. The god of Examinations is the god of the four stars which form the waggon of Charles's Wain. He is a follower of the god of Literature, Wen Ch'ang. Only after he had lived through seventeen successive lives, filled with prodigious events, was Wen Ch'ang invested by the August Personage of Jade with the functions of Grand Emperor of Literature. He is usually represented sitting down, dressed as a mandarin, and holding a sceptre. Although his cult goes back to a very ancient epoch, Wen Ch'ang is less popular than his assistant, K'uei-hsing. Before the 1912 revolution, when the Imperial examinations took place regularly, there was a tablet or image of K'uei-hsing in every literary family. In some wealthy families it was not uncommon to see a little kiosk especially devoted to his cult, for he presides over examinations and chooses the person who is to come out top.

Like the god of Thunder, the god of Examinations is one of the ugliest in existence. He is usually represented making a grimace, standing on the head of a turtle Ao (which many people think is a fish) in an attitude resembling that of the genius of the Bastille, bending forward, with his left leg raised behind as if he is running. In his left hand he holds a bushel-basket and in his right a paintbrush. When the list of candidates is placed before the August Personage of Jade he indicates the name of the first successful candidate. He uses his brush to put a mark under the name of the lucky candidate, and uses his bushel to measure the talents of them all. They say also that the bushel is the distinctive sign of the god, since in China Charles's Wain or the Great Bear is called The Northern Bushel. There are two explanations of the turtle's head which he tramples under his foot. Some say that during his life on earth he came out first in the examination for his doctorate, but that when the reigning Emperor saw how ugly he was he refused to ratify the choice of the examiners. In his despair he tried to drown himself, but when he threw himself into the water, the turtle Ao received him on its head and took him back to land. The other explanation is less miraculous. The stairways of the imperial palace are all divided down the centre by a paved space on which is carved the head of the turtle Ao emerging from the water. When the Emperor gave an audience to the scholars who had passed their doctorate examinations the first was naturally placed just above this piece of carving. Hence it happened that each candidate received the wish 'may you alone stand on the head of Ao', and that is why the god of examinations was represented in this posture, as an omen of good luck.

Another of Wen Ch'ang's assistants is 'Red Jacket' who protects candidates who are not very well prepared. Thanks to him some of them sometimes succeed; but in spite of his goodwill, it is better to work hard and thus obtain the favour of K'uei-hsing or Wen Ch'ang, who never fail a deserving candidate.

A young student who had worked conscientiously returned home after the examination, dissatisfied with his essay. Fearing failure, he invoked Wen Ch'ang and begged him to intervene. While he was asleep the god appeared to him. The student saw him throwing a number of essays into a stove, and among them the candidate recognised his own. The god crumbled them to pieces and then took them out entirely altered. Wen Ch'ang handed the young man the corrected essay, and he learnt it by heart. When he awoke the candidate heard that during the night a fire had destroyed the building where the essays had been stored, so that the examinations had to be repeated. He did the work again, taking care to make use of the god's advice, and of course passed.

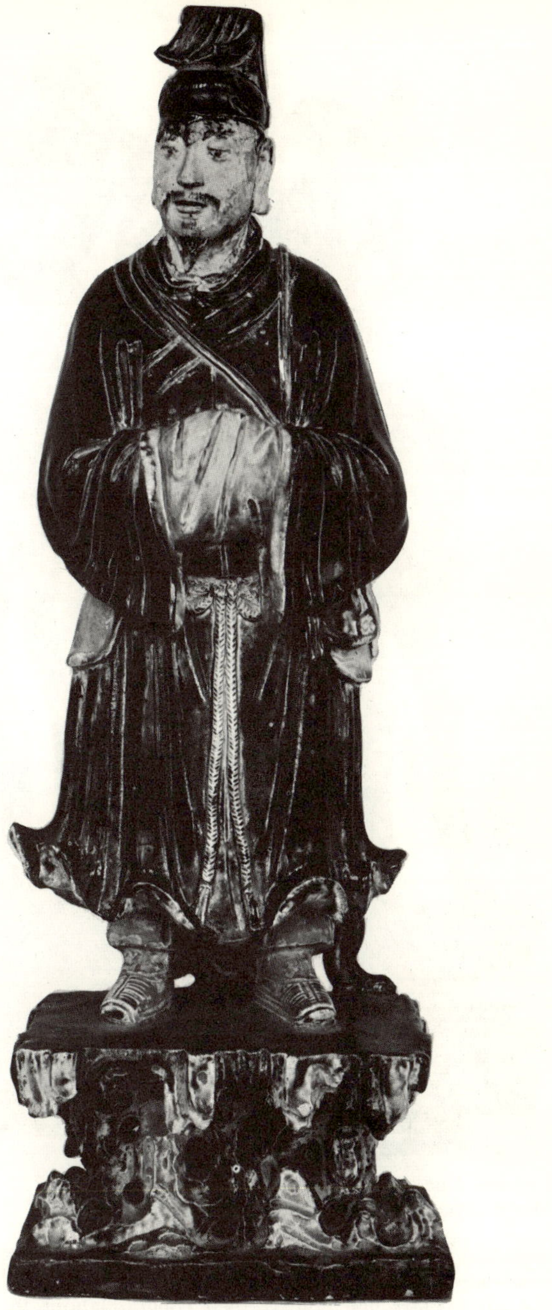

Lu Tung-pin. The last of the Eight Immortals – a group of legendary personages who attained immortality through the practice of Taoist doctrines and were privileged to be present at the banquets of the Lady Wang – Lu Tung-pin has the greatest number of legends attached to him. He is said to have assisted in the conversion of two of the others while the story of his own conversion furnished the plot of a play. Glazed pottery figure, Ming dynasty.

Gods of Happiness. The first of these gods is the god of Long Life, Shou-hsing. He is the star Canopus in the ship Argo. He is one of the easiest gods to recognise, for he has the face of an old man with pure white beard and eyebrows, and is especially noteworthy for an enormous bald head. He is usually represented standing, leaning on a large rough stick, with the peach of Immortality in one hand. He is often accompanied by a stork or a turtle, animals which were supposed to live to a great age, and thus became symbols of longevity. In China, as is well known, old age is considered a great blessing. So, although there is no regular worship of this god, who indeed has no temples, he is very much honoured. When there is a birthday celebration for an aged person (someone at least fifty) the image of the god, usually embroidered in silk, is hung up in a place of honour. Food and fruit are placed in front of it

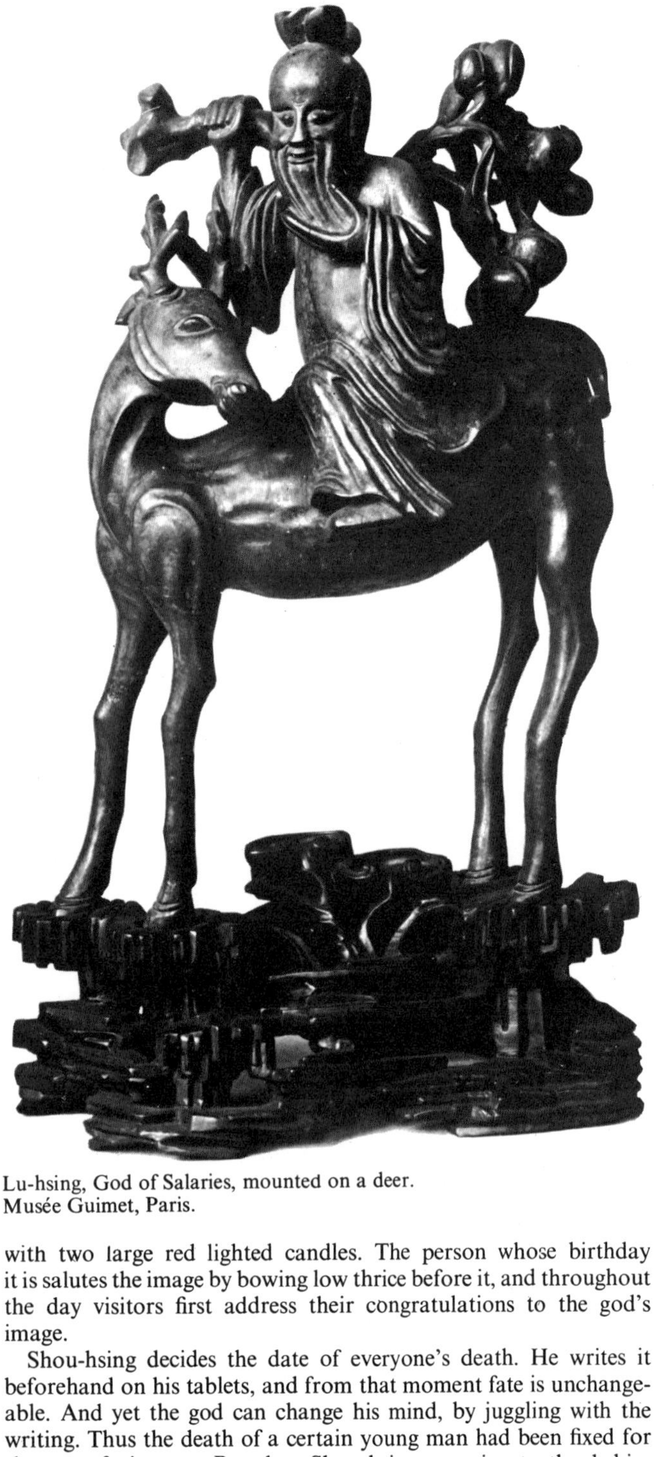

Lu-hsing, God of Salaries, mounted on a deer.
Musée Guimet, Paris.

with two large red lighted candles. The person whose birthday it is salutes the image by bowing low thrice before it, and throughout the day visitors first address their congratulations to the god's image.

Shou-hsing decides the date of everyone's death. He writes it beforehand on his tablets, and from that moment fate is unchangeable. And yet the god can change his mind, by juggling with the writing. Thus the death of a certain young man had been fixed for the age of nineteen. But then Shou-hsing, wanting to thank him for the gift of a jar of wine he had offered, just reversed the numbers one and nine, so that instead of 19 years he had 91 – which is what the change makes in Chinese.

The god of Long Life is one of a triad, which also includes the god of Happiness, Fu-hsing, and the god of Salaries, Lu-hsing. Both are historical persons divinised after their death. It seems that the god of Happiness in his life-time was a mandarin who lived at Tao-chou in the sixth century, though others see in him a general who saved the T'ang dynasty in the eighth century. The god of Salaries, or god of Functionaries, was a person who served the founder of the Han dynasty, in the third century before our era. Space is lacking to describe these divinities in more detail. We must limit ourselves to saying that these three gods often represented together either in human form – the gods of Happiness and of Salaries dressed in the robes of a mandarin – or in the form of symbols – bats for Happiness (in Chinese the word for bat is pronounced 'Fu', like happiness), a deer, called Lu, for the god of Salaries, and a stork or a peach or sometimes a pine for the god of Long Life.

The Heavenly Spinster, Chih-nii. Although she is a divinity and a daughter of the August Personage of Jade, so they say, there is no worship of the Heavenly Spinster, the goddess of the star Alpha in the Lyre. But she is the heroine of a pretty popular legend, and her name is often mentioned in Chinese folklore.

The goddess was continually spinning robes for the August Personage of Jade, robes of brocade and clouds which have no seams. To reward her for this work her father, taking pity on her loneliness, married her to the Heavenly Cow-herd (the Beta and Gamma stars in Aquila) but after her marriage the Spinster was so much absorbed in her love that she neglected her work. The August Personage of Jade lost his temper, and separated the couple by putting one of them to the right and the other to the left of the Heavenly River (the Milky Way) with permission to see each other once a year.

That, so to speak, is the goddess's official history. The people took it up and enlivened it, and this is what they relate.

The Cow-herd was a mere mortal, a little simple minded, whose father had bequeathed him a little bit of land and an ox to plough it. When he had reached a marriageable age his ox (who was a genius in disguise) said to him: 'Master, if you want a pretty wife without having to spend anything, go on a certain day to the river, and you will see all the girls bathing. Their clothes will be on the bank. Pick up a bundle and come back quickly. Hide them somewhere, and I promise you shall have a pretty wife.' The Cow-herd did as the ox suggested, and when he got home threw the clothes down an old well behind the house, and waited. Very soon their owner came along to ask for them. It was the Heavenly Spinster who for amusement had come down to earth with a few friends and had wanted to bathe, but now could not return to Heaven without her clothes. The Cow-herd therefore detained and married her. After several years he had a son by her and then a daughter, and one day his wife said to him: 'Now that we have been married so long and have children, tell me where you hid my heavenly clothes.' The unsuspicious Cow-herd showed her the hiding place. The Spinster hastened to take them out, dressed in them, and and returned to Heaven. The Cow-herd was in despair, especially as the children cried aloud for their mother; so he went and asked the advice of his ox. And the ox said: 'Master, put each of your children in a basket, and tie them to the ends of a pole which you can balance on your shoulders. Then take hold of my tail, shut your eyes, and I will take you to Heaven to rejoin your wife.' And this was done. When they got to Heaven, the Cow-herd requested an audience of the August Personage of Jade and demanded his wife. The August Personage of Jade sent for the Spinster, and having discovered that the facts alleged by the Cow-herd were true, he made him immortal, and appointed him to be god of a star to the west of the River, while the Spinster was to the East, with permission to meet once every seven days. But the couple misunderstood him, and thought they could meet only once a year on the seventh day of the seventh month, and that is what they have done ever since. As they cannot cross the River without a bridge, on that day all the magpies fly up to Heaven with the twig of a tree and make a foot-bridge for them to be able to meet.

This legend is spread all over China, and many poetic works refer to it. Moreover in northern China they say that on the seventh day of the seventh month it is bound to rain, at least in the morning (it falls by the way in the middle of the rainy season) because the Cow-herd and the Spinster weep for joy at seeing each other again, and their tears fall down on the earth.

GODS WHO TAKE CARE OF MANKIND

The Great Emperor of the Eastern Peak, T'ai-yueh-ta-ti or Tung-yueh-ta-ti. Although the August Personage of Jade is interested in everything that goes on in heaven and earth, he can't look after it all himself. So he detailed a god to look after mankind – he is the Great Emperor of the Eastern Peak, the god of the mountain T'ai-shan, in Shantung. This divinity is directly responsible to the August Personage of Jade, and has a large staff under his orders, for he presides over the life of men from their birth to their death, arranging their fate and determining their fortunes, honours, posterity, etc. Even the animals come under his jurisdiction. So he is widely worshipped. There is always a crowd in all his sanctuaries, and his temple in Peking, Tung-yueh-miao, was one of the richest. It is also one of the largest, for there are represented in it over eighty offices dependent on the god – offices of birth, of death, offices for the determination of social position, of wealth, of the number of children. There are also offices which keep registers of good and bad actions, and those for the retribution of these actions, etc. The personnel of the offices is recruited from the souls of the dead. In his temple the Emperor of the Eastern Peak is represented sitting down, wearing the costume of an Emperor, in a shape similar to that of the August Personage of Jade. Indeed, it would be very difficult to distinguish one from the other, if they were taken out of their surroundings. He is too important a god for his statue or picture to appear in family households. His devotees go to the temple to pay him their respects, and they go there when they have any request to make to the god.

The Emperor of the Eastern Peak has a daughter, the Princess of streaked Clouds, Pi-hsia-yuan-chun, also known as the Holy-Mother, Sheng-mu. She protects women and children, and usually presides over births. According to tradition, her husband is either the son of the western sea, or Mao Ying, who anciently attained immortality. The goddess, greatly venerated throughout China, is usually represented sitting, and with a headdress of three birds with outstretched wings. Her assistants are the Lady of Good Sight, who preserves children from eye maladies, and the Lady whose function it is to bring children.

The Princess of streaked Clouds has a Buddhist double in the person of the goddess Kuan-yin, who has in addition the surname of Sung-tzu niang-niang, the Lady who brings children. Draped in a large white veil, she sits on a lotus flower, and holds a child in her arms. Kuan-yin, goddess of fecundity, is equally expert in treating all sicknesses. So she is very popular, and her image is to be found in nearly every home. Every year long lines of pilgrims visit her Temple of Miao Feng Shan (the Mountain of the Wondrous Peak), situated about forty miles from Peking. Sick persons of all kinds come to implore the goddess to heal them, among the smoke of joss-sticks, the popping of crackers, and the creaking of rattles, which are supposed to win the favour of Kuan-yin.

Gods of Walls and Ditches, Ch'eng-huang and Gods of the Locality, T'u-ti. Every administrative area, town, or large village, has a god who protects it and takes care of the inhabitants, called the God of Walls and Ditches; and these gods are appointed by the August Personage of Jade. They are invariably divinised human beings, either heroes or mandarins of integrity, generally speaking persons who in their lifetime served and protected the people. After their death they are not reincarnated but are nominated as Ch'eng-huang of such and such a place, so that they can continue to protect the people. Chinese folklore contains a great many legends about these gods. The main outline changes very little. The inhabitants of a place are warned in a dream that on a certain date a person named Ch'eng-huang of the town will come to occupy his post; and on the date specified the noise of a procession and band is heard in the streets – the new god has arrived. Next day the inhabitants hasten to offer him a big arrival sacrifice. Very often, if the god is someone well known, they recast the statue in the temple consecrated to him and give it this person's head. Some legends say that when there is a vacancy for the post of god of Walls and Ditches, the gods arrange a competition for the candidates who are chosen from among living scholars. Such is the story of 'The Examination for God of Walls and Ditches' contained in the famous collection, *Tales of the Studio of Joy*.

In the popular mind the Ch'eng-huang plays the part of protector and governor to the place of which he is the god. His rank varies in accordance with the importance of the place he governs. Sometimes he corresponds only to a sub-prefect among human beings, sometimes to a prefect, while the Ch'eng-huang of Peking was the equal of the governor of the town. Human magistrates were far from disdaining them, and during the Empire sub-prefects were known to have asked their advice and help when a crime had been committed on their territory. With this in view they fasted for at least a day, offered a sacrifice to the god, and then slept that night in the temple. In their dreams the god pointed out the guilty party, usually by means of Sybilline poems. Needless to say, this custom has long since disappeared.

In the times before the Republic the festival of Ch'eng-huang took place in the spring of every year. The god's statue was carried round the town with great pomp, and this was called 'My Lord

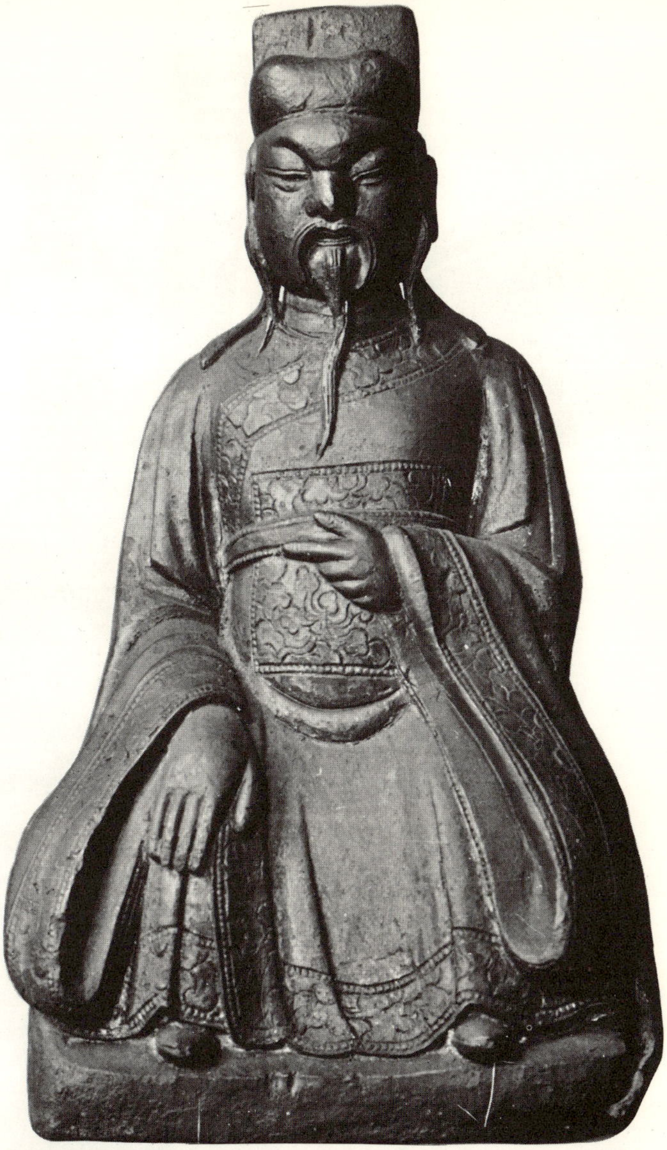

The God of Walls and Ditches (Ch'eng-huang).
Musée Guimet, Paris.

Ch'eng-huang's tour of inspection'. At the head of the procession went the God of the Place, represented either by his statue or by a notable in disguise. Following in his tracks they purified the streets with vinegar, and then came Ch'eng-huang's assistants, among them Mr White and Mr Black, who watch over the town, one by day and one by night; and Ox-Head and Horse-Face, who carry out the god's orders. Around these divinities marched groups of demons with hideous masks and penitents in the red robes of those to be tortured, amid a great waving of banners and a deafening noise of gongs. Finally came the statue of Ch'eng-huang carried in a rich palanquin and religiously escorted by the city dignitaries. As may be guessed, this ceremony occasioned great popular rejoicings.

The gods of Walls and Ditches only exist in administrative areas, in towns surrounded by walls (whence the name). This is not the case with the gods of Place (T'u-ti), who are less important gods but more popular. Each town, whether fortified or not, and every village, has one. There is a Place god for every street, every temple; every public building has one, and so it is with every dwelling. According to the legends they are sometimes famous persons who have been appointed to this work after their death, but as a rule they are anonymous. They are represented in the form of an old man with white beard, in ordinary clothes, carrying a long knotty stick, while his wife – who is always shown with him – is represented as a kindly old woman. Naturally the personality of the gods varies with the kind of place they look after. In the towns the Place god is a citizen, but in the country a peasant.

The Place god has very modest functions. He acts as a sort of

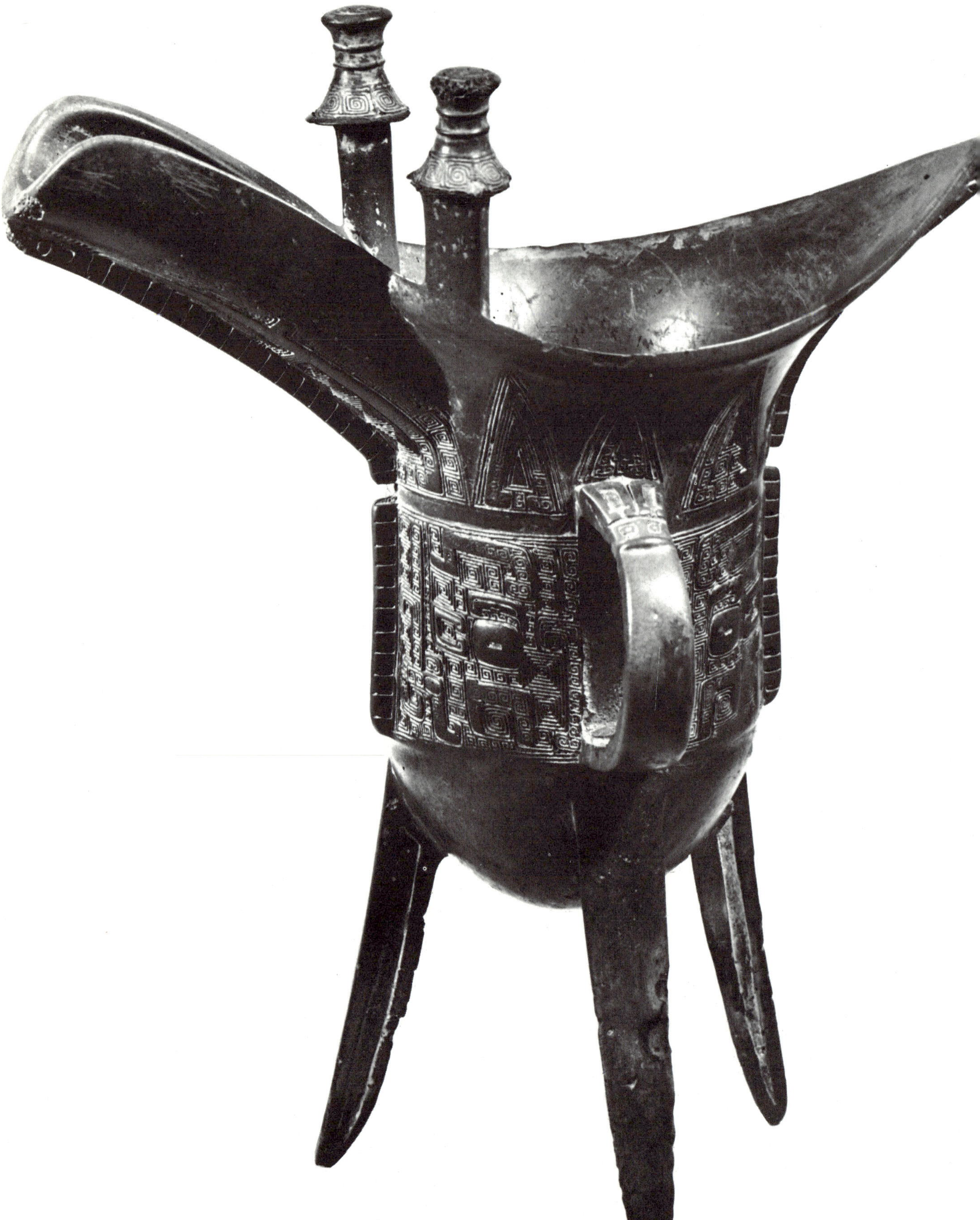

Bronze ritual vessel of the type *chueh*. Many such ritual vessels were buried in royal and other tombs from the time of the Shang dynasty, the *chueh* being used for pouring libations of wine to the spirits – the handles on the spout probably being designed to be gripped by tongs when the liquid was heated over a fire. Libations continued to be made to the gods until quite recent times. Shang dynasty, *c.* 1500 – 1027 B.C.

Kuan-yin, the goddess of mercy and compassion, was one of the best loved of all Chinese deities and representations of her featured in every home. She was sometimes portrayed as the Gentle Mother, carrying a child in her arms. Red amber statuette, Wellcome Historical Museum.

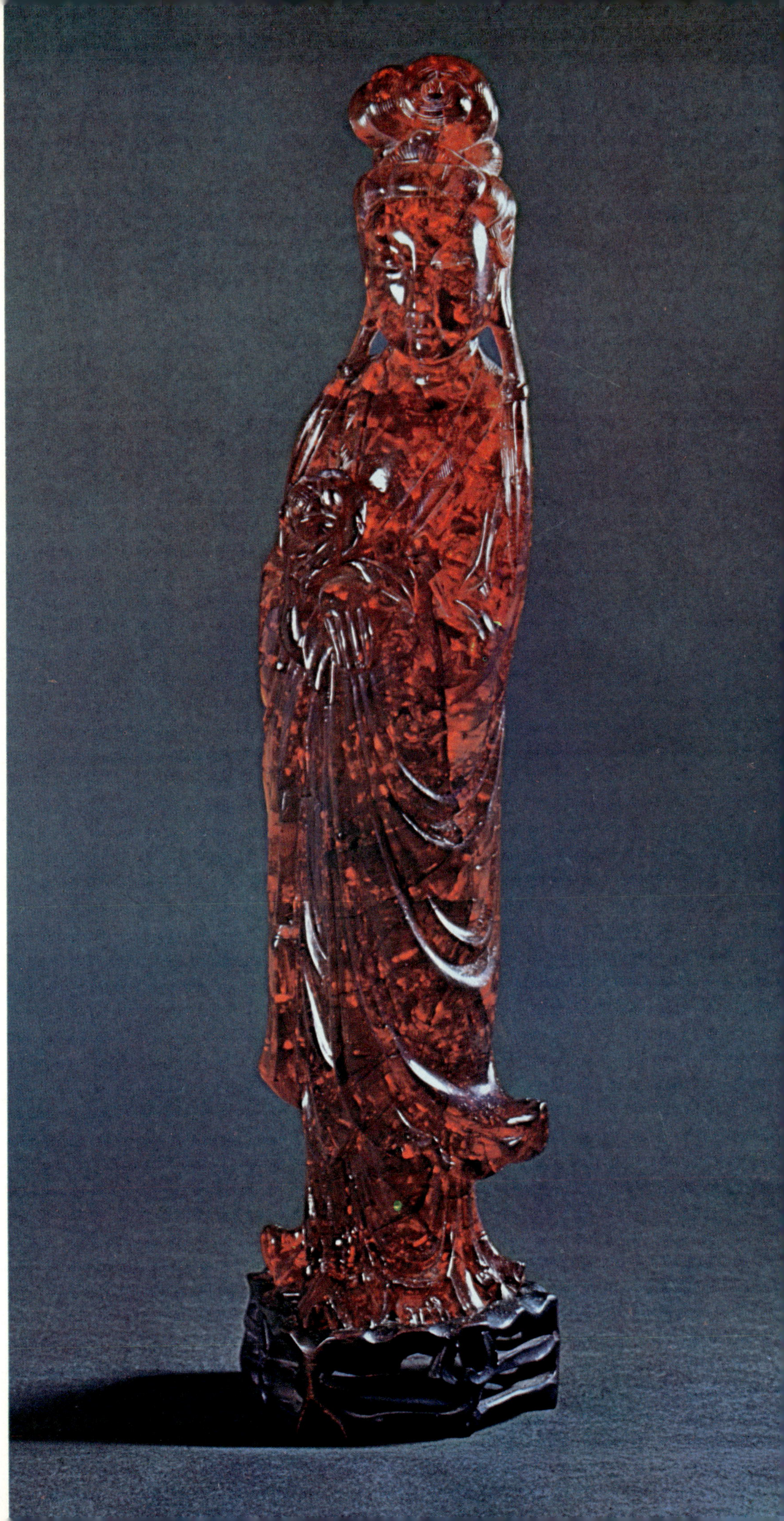

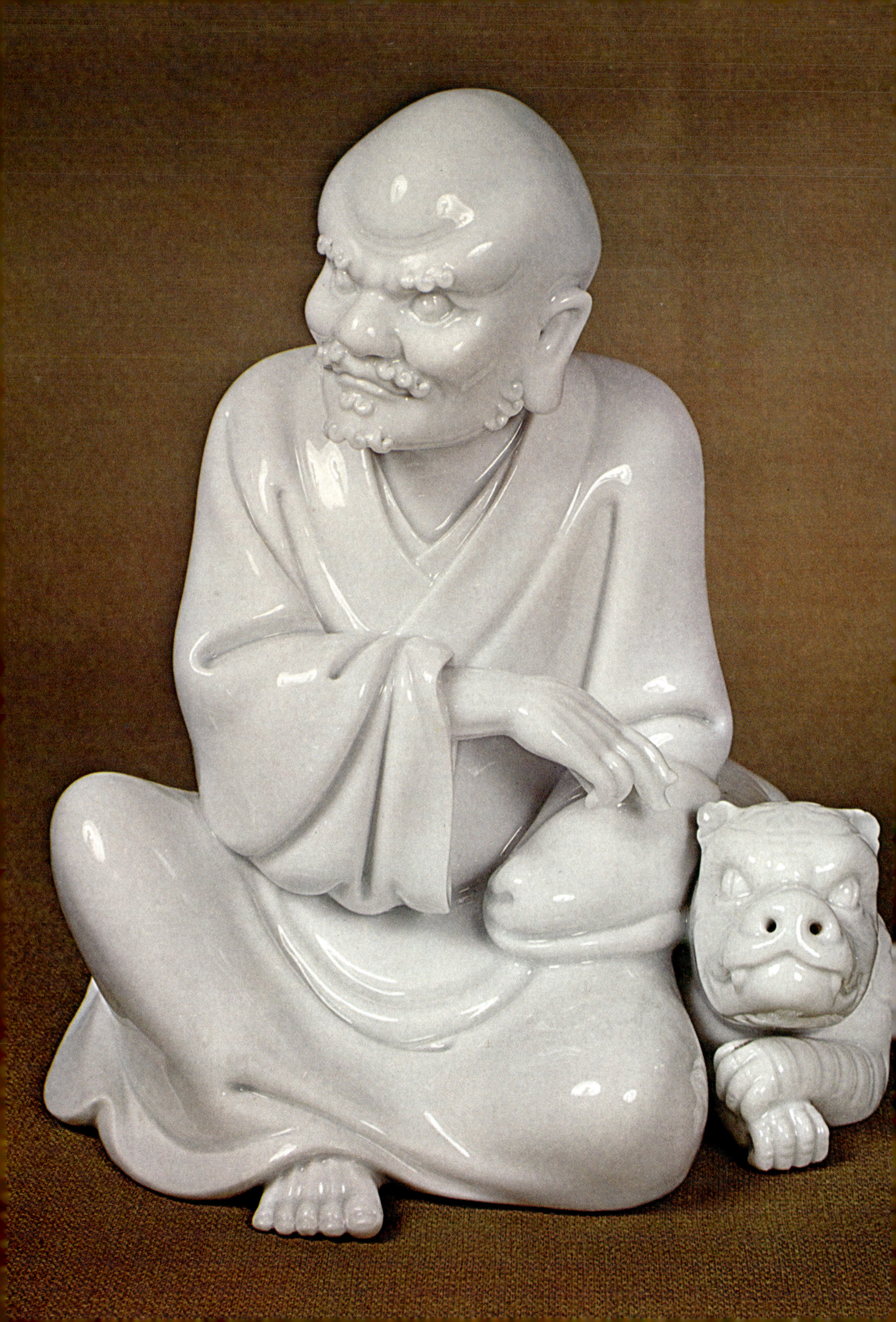

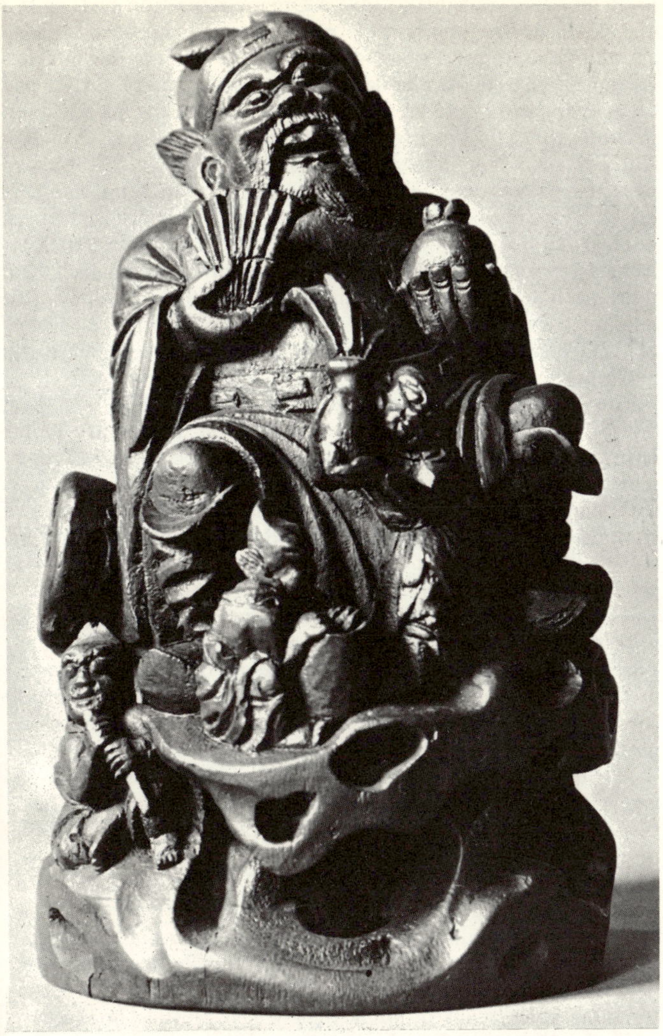

The God of Wealth. (Ts'ai-shen).

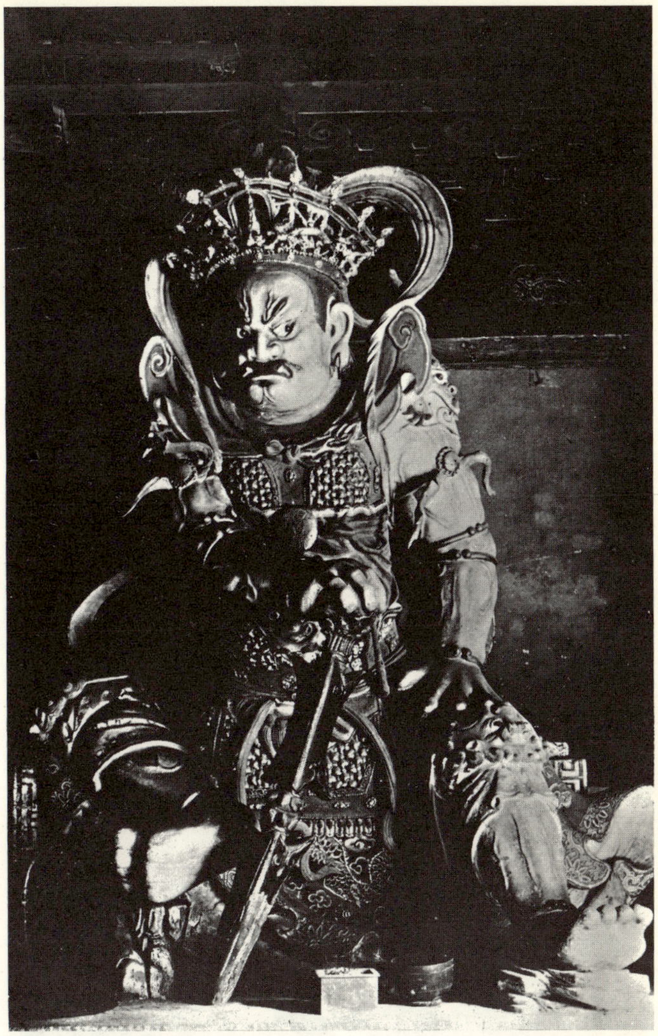

The sniffing general, Heng-chiang.

policeman to his territory, and in the country he has to scare off robbers and animals which raid the poultry yard, etc; but in recompense his cult is very wide-spread, and every family has a statue of him before which three joss-sticks are burned every morning and evening.

The Hearth god, Tsao-wang. The Hearth god is obviously domestic. He witnesses the acts and even words of every member of the family with which he lives, and keeps a record of them. Every year, on the twenty-third day of the twelfth month, he ascends into heaven to make his report to the August Personage of Jade, who on the basis of this report allots the family happiness or misfortune during the coming year.

The Hearth god is not represented by a statue but by a picture on paper – it will be seen why, later on. This image, coarsely printed and coloured, is placed in a sort of little wooden temple just over the hearth, or in some other part of the kitchen. It is essential that the image should face south. In the picture the god's wife, Tsao-wang nai-nai, is beside him, for she aids him in his duties by also keeping a record of the women's sayings and doings.

Apart from the three joss-sticks every morning, the family makes only two sacrifices a year to this god. The first takes place on the twenty-fourth day of the twelfth month when he has gone up to heaven to make his report to the August Personage of Jade. Among other offerings this sacrifice includes sweets which are specially made for the purpose and only sold at this time, as well as straw for the god's horse. After the sacrifice his picture is taken down from its niche and burned over a little fire of pine twigs to the noise of fire-crackers, but before starting the fire they are careful to put a bit of a sweet on his mouth so that he will 'speak sweet words' to the August Personage of Jade about the family he has just left. The Hearth god returns from Heaven on the first day of the new year. Another sacrifice is then offered up, always with firecrackers, and they hang up his picture in the kitchen, in the place it will occupy throughout the year.

There is an explanation of the fire-crackers set off during these sacrifices. They are special fire-crackers which bang off high in the air, and they say that this is to help the god up during his ascension, while on his return the fire-crackers show the god which house he must re-enter. Then, there is another custom, which is not to light a fire in the kitchen while the Hearth god is absent in Heaven, but this is observed less and less. During the god's absence, you can do anything you like, for the god is not there to record bad actions. But then it is also a time when the house, lacking its protector, is liable to all kinds of woes and calamities.

Door gods, Men-shen. On the outer doors of Chinese houses, which have two leaves, you often see represented two armed soldiers, stuck or painted on each of the leaves. One of them has a red or black face, and the other a white face – they are the Door gods. Originally these duties were entrusted to two mythical beings, Shen-t'u and Yu-lu, who in ancient mythology were supposed to prevent the spirits of the dead from escaping out of hell to disturb the peace of the living. The Ghosts' Door was placed between the branches of an enormous peach-tree planted on the top of a mountain. As soon as a malevolent soul appeared the two guards seized on him and threw him as food to the tigers. The figures of Shen-t'u and Yu-lu were later reproduced on the doors of houses to keep away evil spirits.

Later on, these two divinities were replaced by historical personages who had been promoted to the rank of gods – Yu-ch'ih Ching-te, and Ch'in Shu-pao. They had both been generals of the Emperor T'ai-tsung of the T'ang dynasty, and lived at the beginning of the seventh century. The explanation of why they were chosen as Door gods is to be fund in the *Travels in the West*. In the sixth chapter of that novel we are told that the Emperor T'ai-tsung, in spite of

A figure from Te-hua, Fukien, depicting a Lo-han with a tiger seated beside him in a peaceful attitude. The original disciples of Buddha were called Lo-hans by the Chinese, who received the doctrines in the first century A.D. However, the Chinese modified the teachings to such a degree that a different form was created. Late seventeenth century porcelain. Victoria and Albert Museum.

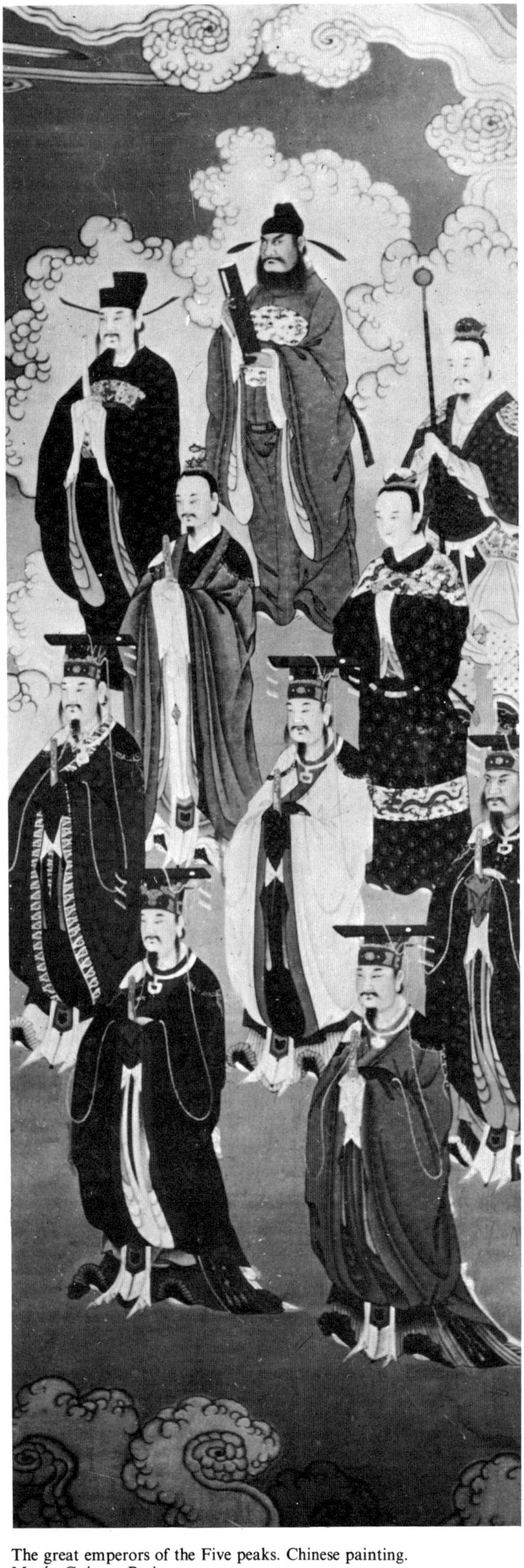

The great emperors of the Five peaks. Chinese painting. Musée Guimet, Paris.

his promise, was unable to save a Dragon-King who had made a mistake in distributing rain and was condemned to have his head cut off by the August Personage of Jade. The spirit of this Dragon-King held that the Emperor was responsible for his death, and every night came and created a disturbance at the palace door. In consequence the Emperor fell sick, and his two generals, Yu-ch'ih Ching-te and Ch'in Shupao, suggested that they should keep guard over the palace door. The spirit of the Dragon-King was thus driven away, but he went off and created a disturbance at the back door, a door with only one leaf, and was driven away by T'ai-tsung's Minister, Wei Cheng. The Emperor therefore had these three personages painted on all doors, and the tradition lasted until our own time, although it is rather uncommon to see a painting of Wei Cheng, but then doors with one leaf are not very numerous in China.

The Door gods are painted directly on to the doors of great houses, whereas humbler houses and those in the country simply have their printed and coloured images stuck on. They are represented in military dress, holding in one hand a long-handled mace, with a bow and arrows slung at their side. They keep away evil spirits and prevent them from entering the house they are guarding, and there are quantities of legends about their good services. In spite of which absolutely nothing is done in their worship.

And then it must be noted that in recent times they lost a great deal of their religious character. Except among the people, usually extremely superstitious, they had come to be considered rather as themes for decoration than as divinities, and they are on the way to disappearing completely. None are to be seen, for instance, on the doors of houses in Peking.

In Buddhist Temples, the Door gods are not Ch'in Shu-pao and Yu-ch'ih Ching-te, but are represented by different persons – the Sniffing General and the Puffing General (Heng-Ha-erh-Chiang) or else by the Heavenly Kings (T'ien Wang), the four brothers Mo-li. They are all represented by colossal grimacing figures placed in the first building of the temples. At first there were only the two generals, Sniffer and Puffer, one of whom has his mouth shut while the other has his mouth open. They are so called because during their lifetime it appears that one of them had the power of emitting from his nostrils jets of white light which mortals breathed in, while the other puffed fatal gases out of his mouth. Little by little in the course of ages these two personages have been replaced by the Celestial Kings.

When you enter a Buddhist temple you come into the inner hall, a kind of vestibule divided by a courtyard from the great hall, and there you see four enormous statues ranged along the walls. They represent soldiers with grimacing countenances, respectively holding a sword, an umbrella, a guitar and a striped marten – sometimes replaced by a snake. They are the Celestial Kings, guardians of the four directions.

Originally these personages were Buddhist divinities, named Vaisravana, Dhrtarastra, Virudhaka and Virupaksa. In course of time their personality changed under the influence of the novel, *Royal Investiture*. They are now considered to be the four brothers Mo-li, who were once generals famous for their deeds. The attributes they hold in their hands are simply the talismans by means of which they conquered their enemies during their mortal life. When the first flourished his sword he raised terrific whirlwinds which swept everything before them. The second merely had to open his umbrella and the sun was obscured, plunging the earth into deepest darkness while it poured with rain. The third controlled the direction of the winds by playing on his guitar. And the last annihilated his enemies by loosing his striped marten, who ate them up.

Like the Celestial Kings, the Sniffing and Puffing Generals were also once Buddhist divinities.

In these same outer halls may also be seen the statue of a young soldier, clad in shining armour and holding a knotty stick in his hands. This is Wei-t'o, chief of the thirty-two heavenly generals, and also assigned to guard doors.

POPULAR GODS

The God of Wealth, Ts'ai-shen. This god has certainly had more success than any of them. Not only do the people never fail to offer up a sacrifice to him on his birthday, but even persons who claim to be unbelievers and pay no sort of cult to other gods, salute his god with great respect on the appointed day.

The God of Wealth's anniversary is on the fifth day of the first month. On New Year's Day in Peking, the day on which all the gods descend on earth to make a tour of general inspection, the children run about the streets at night, shouting: 'We come to bring you the God of Wealth!' Each person hastens to buy one, and when other sellers appear the answer is: 'We already have one,' for it would not be in good taste to say: 'We don't want any more.' After it is purchased the image is placed beside that of other gods (the Star gods, the Hearth gods, etc.) and then they wait for the fifth day of the following month. On this day they sacrifice to the god a cock and a living carp specially reserved for this occasion, and then the image is burned on a fire of pine twigs accompanied by many fire-crackers, while the master of the house and all who live in it, without distinction of age or sex, come in succession to bow before the little fire.

The Taoists made the god of Wealth the head of a Ministry of Wealth with offices and a string of subordinates, such as the Celestial and Venerable Discoverer of Treasures, the Celestial and Venerable Bringer of Treasures, the Immortal of commercial profits, etc. But the people like to simplify, and usually they take one of these gods – in Peking the best known is the god of Wealth who increases Happiness, Tseng-fu-ts'ai-shen. The novel, the *Investiture of the Gods*, identified him with the wise man, Pi Kan, who lived towards the end of the Yin dynasty, and was put to death by order of the Emperor who wanted to find out if it is true, as people say, that the heart of a wise man is pierced with seven openings. Elsewhere general Chao of the dark Terrace is revered as the god of Wealth.

The Agent of Heaven, T'ien-Kuan, is another god who bestows happiness, and is one of a triad made up in addition to the Agent of the Earth, Ti-Kuan, who grants remission of sins and the Agent of Water, Shui-kuan, who averts evil. As M. Maspero has rightly pointed out, these three gods are the personification of the ancient Taoist ritual which insisted on a confession of sins written in triplicate, of which one was burned for Heaven, one buried for Earth, and the third sunk for Water. These three gods received twice a month an offering of cakes in the form of tortoises and chain-links, but the only one at all well known in our time is the Agent of Heaven, and that mainly thanks to the theatre, for it is the custom to begin every theatrical performance with a pantomime called 'the Agent of Heaven brings happiness', T'ien-kuan-ssu-fu. He appears in the form of a mandarin wearing ceremonial costume, with a smiling mask fringed with whiskers and a beard-tuft, does a sort of dance on the stage, carries rolled-up wishes for happiness which he unrolls as he presents them to the spectators. It is to be noted that this is one of the very rare occasions when a mask is used on the Chinese stage. The pantomime is also called 'the dance of the Agent who confers promotion', T'iao-chia-kuan; and formerly in public theatres, and still to this day in private performances given for some family rejoicing (birthday, birth of a child, etc.), the play is stopped and this pantomime is repeated as a sign of welcome to each distinguished guest as he arrives.

The Emperor Kuan, Kuan-ti. The worship of this god does not date from very far back. He receives two sorts of cult, one from official religion and the other from the people. For scholars Kuan-ti is god of War, in opposition to Confucius, the god of Literature, and as such he receives two sacrifices, in the spring and autumn of each year. This tradition was maintained even by the Republic, at least until the time of the nationalist government of Nanking; and the successive presidents as well as the last dictator, Chang-Tso-lin, officially offered sacrifices to him with great pomp. For the crowd Kuan-ti is a Taoist god, governor and protector of the people, mainly playing the part of judge. So the people appeal to him every time they have something to complain of, whether it is spirits (demons, illness, etc.) or human beings (unfriendly bureaucrats, brigands, cheats, etc.) and Kuan-ti sends his equerry Shou-ts'ang to punish them, or makes an appeal to the Thunder god or some other god to do it.

Kuan-ti is also famous for predicting the future. In most of the temples consecrated to him the necessary equipment may be found, consisting of eighty-one or sixty-four numbered slips, placed in a holder made from a hollow bamboo with a plug at one end. The suppliant wishing to know the future – the result of a relative's

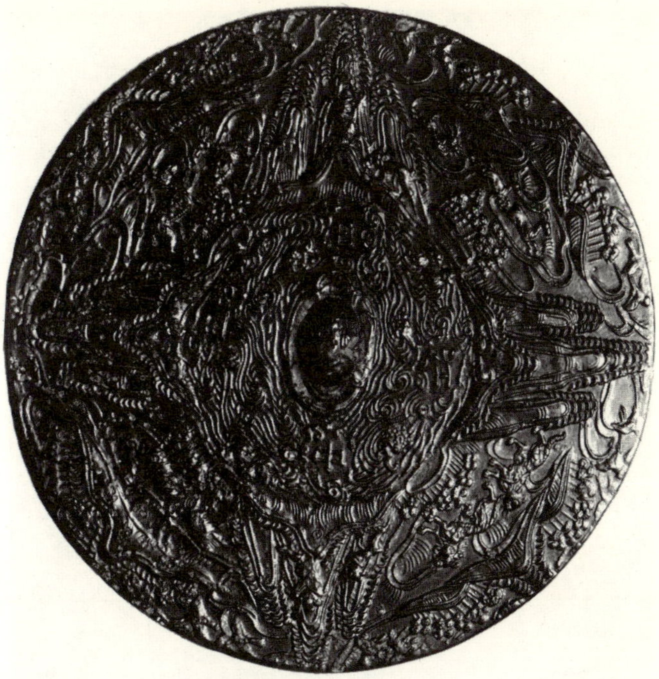

Cosmic mirror. The four cardinal directions are marked by the four cardinal mountains. According to the most popular Chinese creation myth the cardinal mountains were formed from the body of P'an-ku, the first man on earth. His head became the cardinal mountain of the East, his arms the mountains of the South and North and his feet the mountain of the West while some say that his belly became a further mountain – that of the centre. Bronze, T'ang dynasty (A.D. 618-906).

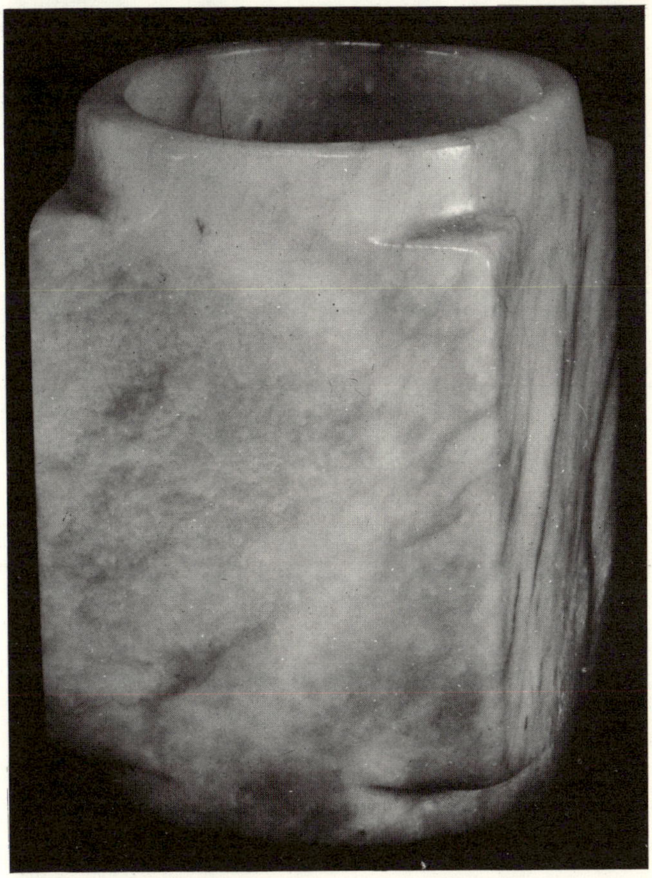

Jade *t'sung*. The *t'sung*, with its square, immovable shape, was a symbol of the earth for the Chinese while another ritual object, the perforated disk-shaped *pi*, was a symbol of heaven which was believed to be round and revolve above the flat surface of the earth. The belief that the earth was square was a very old one – its length and breadth according to one legend being 233,575 steps. Period of the Warring States, or early Han dynasty (206 B.C. – A.D. 220).

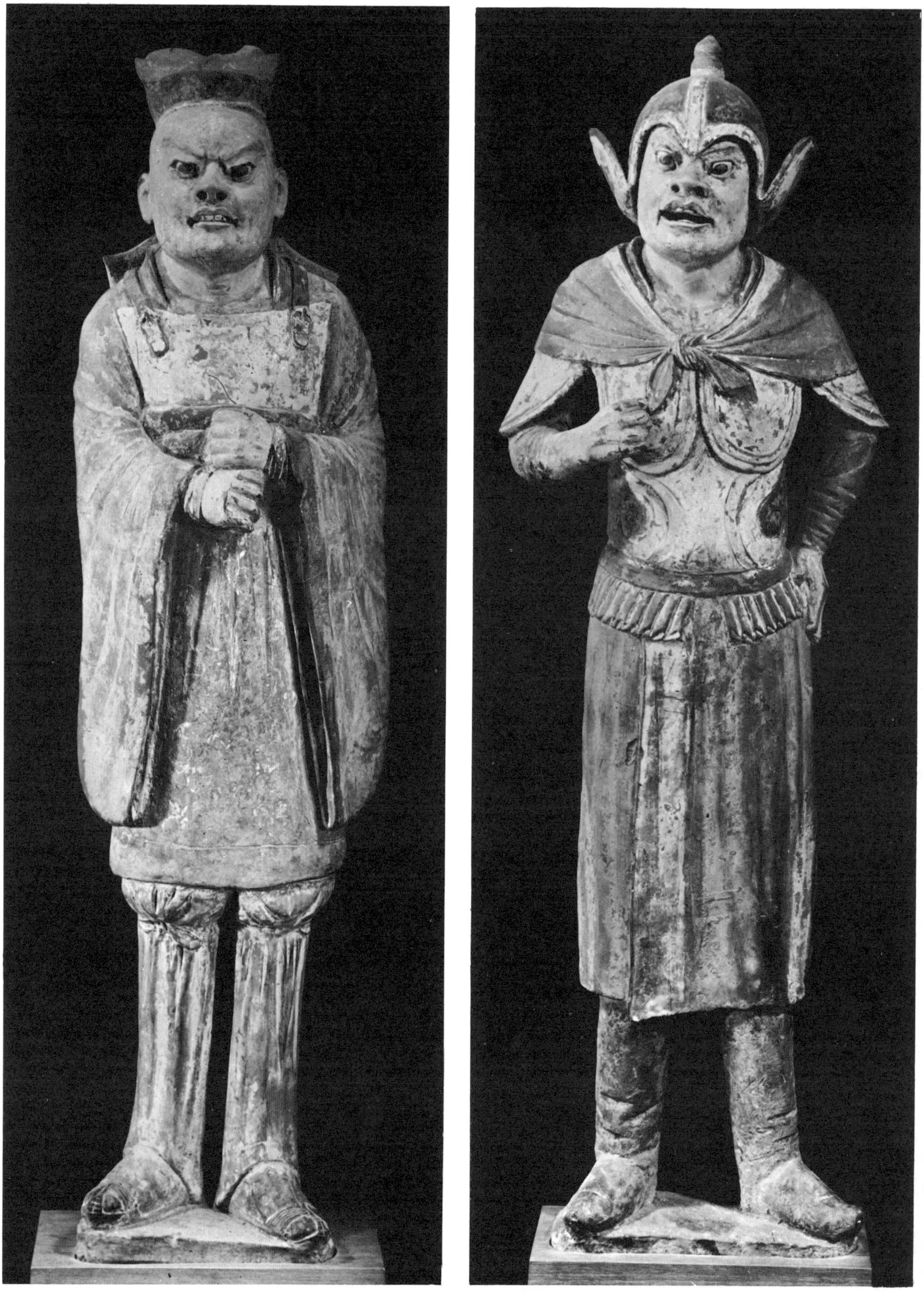

Pair of tomb attendants. Funerary figures were buried with the dead from early times either as replacements for the humans originally sacrificed on such occasions or as supernatural guardians. A pair of guardians very popular in everyday life were the Men-shen, or Door gods, whose images were painted or stuck on the doors of houses from the greatest to the lowliest in order to keep away evil spirits. Earthenware figures from Northern Wei, China.

illness, success of a journey, a marriage, a birth, or anything else, bows down before the god's statue, and then taking the holder in his hand shakes it until one of the slips falls out. There is also a register where against each number of the slips stands the prediction, usually written in rude poetry of the Sybilline style, and this register is consulted under the number of the fallen slip to find out the god's opinion. In some temples the predictions are printed on separate sheets of paper, and the priest in charge hands the suppliant the sheet corresponding to his number. Needless to say all this involves the payment of a small sum of money, euphemistically called Hsiang-huo-ch'ien, 'money to keep the incense burning'.

Kuan-ti was a general of the Han country in the epoch of the Three Kingdoms, renowned for his integrity and fidelity, and his real name was Kuan Yu. He died in 220, having been taken prisoner and beheaded by the rival country of Wu. He became famous mainly through the *Romance of the Three Kingdoms*, which relates his wonderful adventures, and through the plays derived from the novel. He is always presented as he is described there – dressed in green with a face as red as a jujube fruit. Almost invariably he is accompanied by his equerry, Shou-ts'ang, and his son Kuan P'ing, who stand beside him, and very often in the Temples the statue of his horse is to be seen too.

Another exorcist of demons and evil spirits is the Supreme Lord of the Dark Heaven (Hsuan-t'ien Shang-ti) who is also the Regent of Water. He appeared once to the Emperor Hui-tsung in the aspect of a man of colossal height, with loose hair, dressed in a black robe and a golden breast-plate. His naked feet rested on a turtle encircled by a snake. He is still represented with these features o-day.

The Eight Immortals, Pa-hsien. The eight Immortals are not, strictly speaking, gods. They are legendary personages who became immortal through the practice of Taoist doctrine, and who have the right to be present at the banquets given by the Lady Wang, wife of the August Personage of Jade.

These eight characters have nothing in common, and it is hard to say how the Taoists came to make them into an almost inseparable group. Their name does not appear in folklore until the Yuan dynasty, also called the Mongol dynasty, about the 13th or 14th century, and it was spread, we believe, thanks to the stage. The eight Immortals often accompany the effigy of the god of Long Life. They are:

Han Chung-li, usually represented as a man of ripe age with a slight corporation and a careless air. His name is supposed to have been Chung-li and he was believed to have lived in the time of the Han dynasty. His present name is made up of these different elements.

Chang-kuo Lao, an old man, known only by his miraculous donkey which could travel several dozens of thousands of leagues in a day, and when at rest could be folded up like a piece of paper.

Lan Ts'ai-ho, a street-singer, who, dressed in rags, with one foot bare and the other shod, goes round the streets singing. One day he was carried up to heaven by a stork.

T'ieh-kuai Li (Li with the Iron Crutch) was an ascetic instructed by Lao-tzu and another immortal, Master Wang-kiu. One day when he should have gone to Lao-tzu, only his soul went, after he had warned his disciple to watch over his body for seven days, and then to burn it if he did not return. On the sixth day the disciple's mother fell ill, and in his haste to go to her the disciple burnt his master's body. When Li's soul returned there was no longer a body for it to dwell in, so it entered the body of a beggar who had died of hunger. The God is represented as a beggar carrying a large calabash on his back and leaning on an iron crutch.

Han Hsiang-tzu was initiated into the doctrine by Lu Tung-pin who is mentioned below. *Ts'ao Kuo-chiu* converted by *Han Chung-li* and *Lu Tung-pin, Ho Hsien-ku* the Immortal Damsel Ho, who went to heaven in full daylight, are represented respectively as a young man in rich clothes with the little headdress of young lords, a man in the costume of a mandarin, and a girl wearing a lotus flower on her shoulder.

The last of the eight Immortals, Lu Tung-pin has the greatest number of legends attached to him. They say he likes to walk about among men looking like some ordinary person, and takes the opportunity to punish the wicked and reward the good. Among legends about him the best-known is that of his conversion,

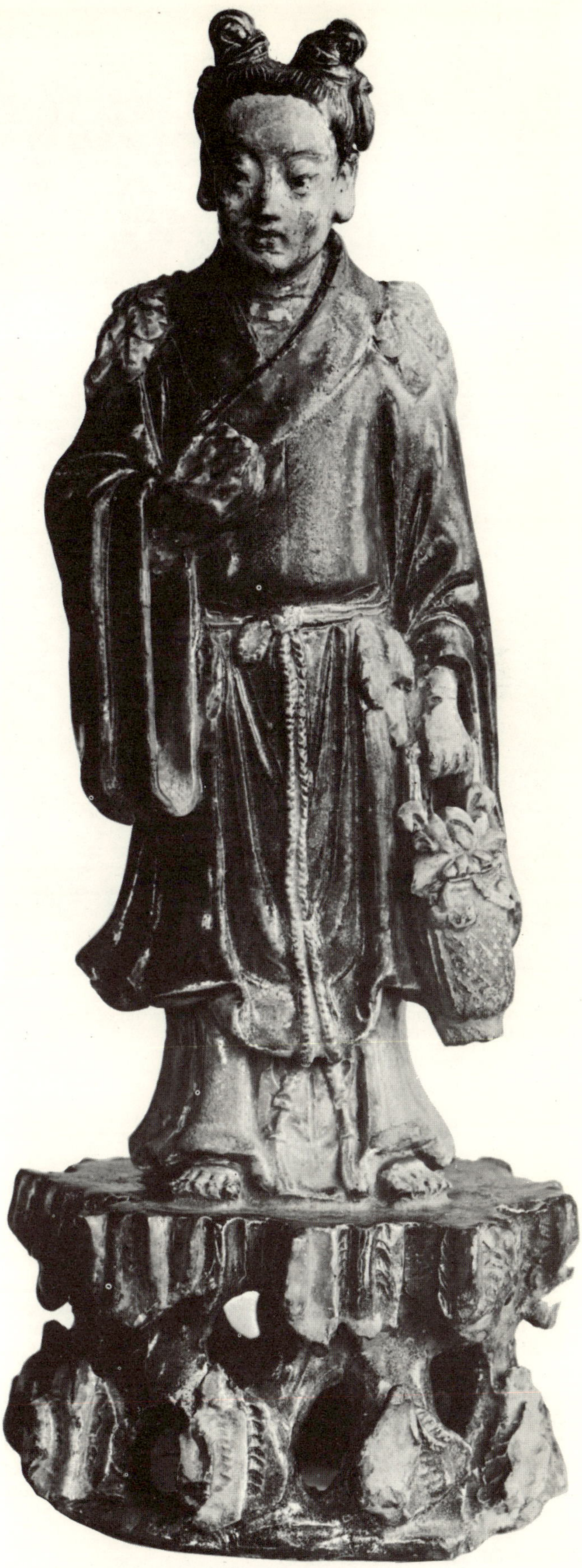

Lan Ts'ai-ho. Another of the Eight Immortals – the group of characters inseparably linked by the Taoists though in fact with little or nothing in common – Lan Ts'ai-ho was a street singer who, clad in rags and with only one foot shod, went through the streets singing of the delusive pleasures of life. He was later carried up to heaven. Figure in earthenware covered with dark blue and turquoise glazes, Ming dynasty. Victoria and Albert Museum.

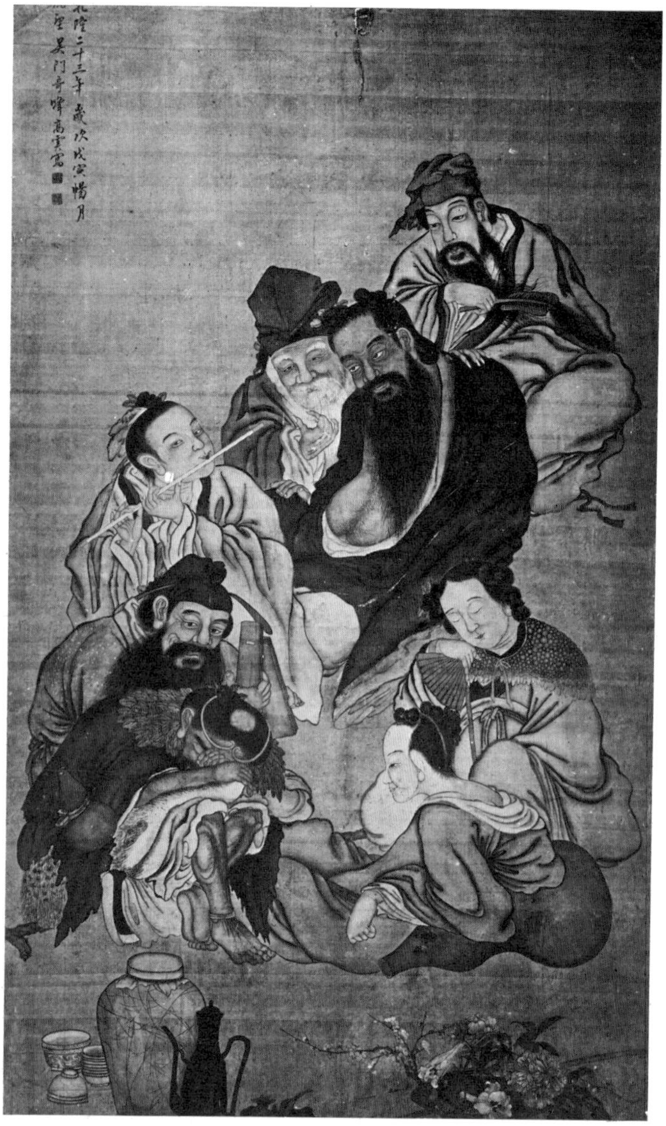

Pa-hsien (eight immortals). Painting by Kao-Yun, sixteenth century. Musée Guimet, Paris.

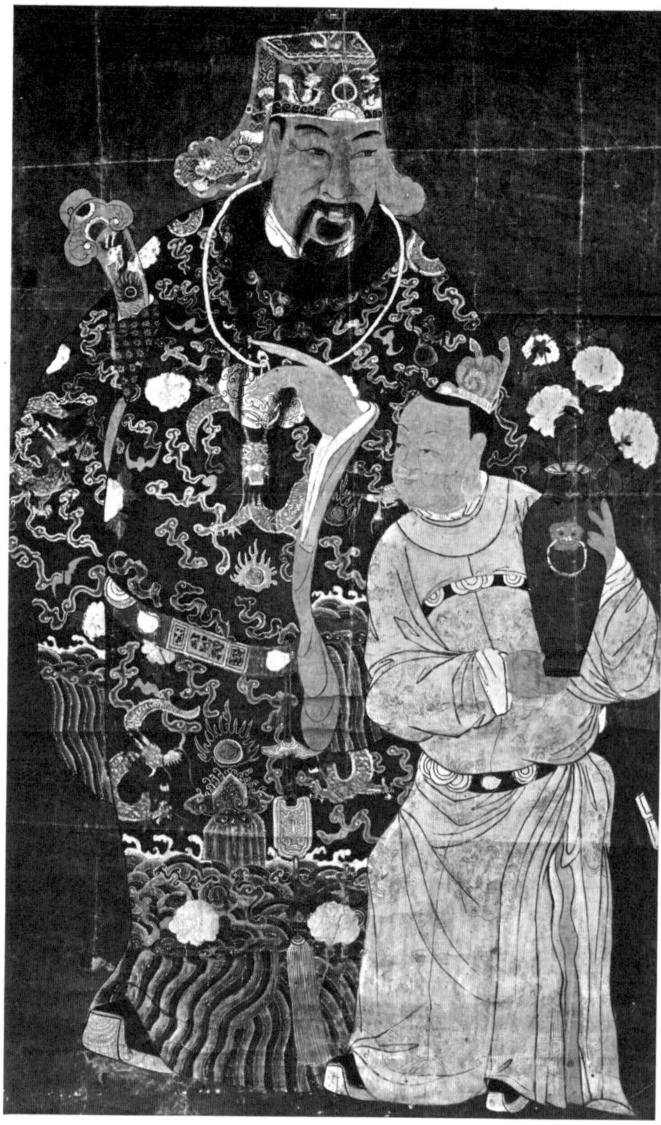

Ts'ai-shen, the god of wealth and good fortune, with a devotee. The most popular and universally worshipped of all the gods, Ts'ai-shen is offered sacrifices even by those who claim to be unbelievers. Water-colour on rice paper.

Huang-liangmeng, meaning the Dream of the Yellow Sorghum, which also furnished the plot for a play. When he was still only a student Lu Tung-pin stopped at an inn and met an Immortal in disguise with whom he talked for a moment. Then he went to sleep and saw the whole of his future life in a dream. At first he had numerous successes and was loaded with honours, but in the end he endured the worst misfortunes and perished miserably, killed by a brigand. When he awoke Lu Tung-pin decided to renounce the world.

Another equally well-known legend tells how he converted the girl-singer, White Peony, after three successive attempts in each of which he came to her in a different form. This Immortal is represented in the dress of a man of letters, carrying a fly-chaser and a sword, the Flying Sword, used by him to kill the Yellow Dragon which he carries on his back.

GODS OF THE PROFESSIONS

In addition to the gods we have been studying which are the objects of general worship, the Chinese pantheon also included a large number of divinities peculiar to each social class and to each profession. They are innumerable, and it is impossible to mention them all. Following M. Maspero, let us limit ourselves to mentioning a few.

Divinities of artisans. Artisans usually choose as their patrons those who are supposed to have been inventors in the different industries. Thus, general Sun Pin, who lived in the fourth century B.C., had his toes cut off, and to hide this deformity hid his feet in sheaths of leather, and thereby became the god of cobblers. Ts'ai Lun, who is supposed to have invented paper in the first century of our era is the god of stationers. A similar honour fell to I-ti who was the first maker of wine, to general Meng T'ien who invented the paint-brush, and to Ts'ang Chieh, who invented writing and is therefore adopted by the public tale-tellers.

Others are chosen because they distinguished themselves in their profession, or simply because they practised it. Thus Fan K'uei, who practised the humble occupation of a dog-skinner before he became the right arm of the founder of the Han dynasty, was adopted as their patron by the butchers. The carpenters have a cult for Lu Pan who, so they say, made a marvellous falcon which was able to fly. The thieves chose Sung Chiang, a famous brigand of the twelfth century. Even the prostitutes took it into their heads to look for a patron. And in some parts of China they found one in the person of P'an Chin-lien, a dissipated widow whose father-in-law murdered her in order to end her disorderly behaviour.

And then very often artisans content themselves with an anonymous deity, such as the god of the Shuttle for weavers, and the god of Garden Trees for gardeners.

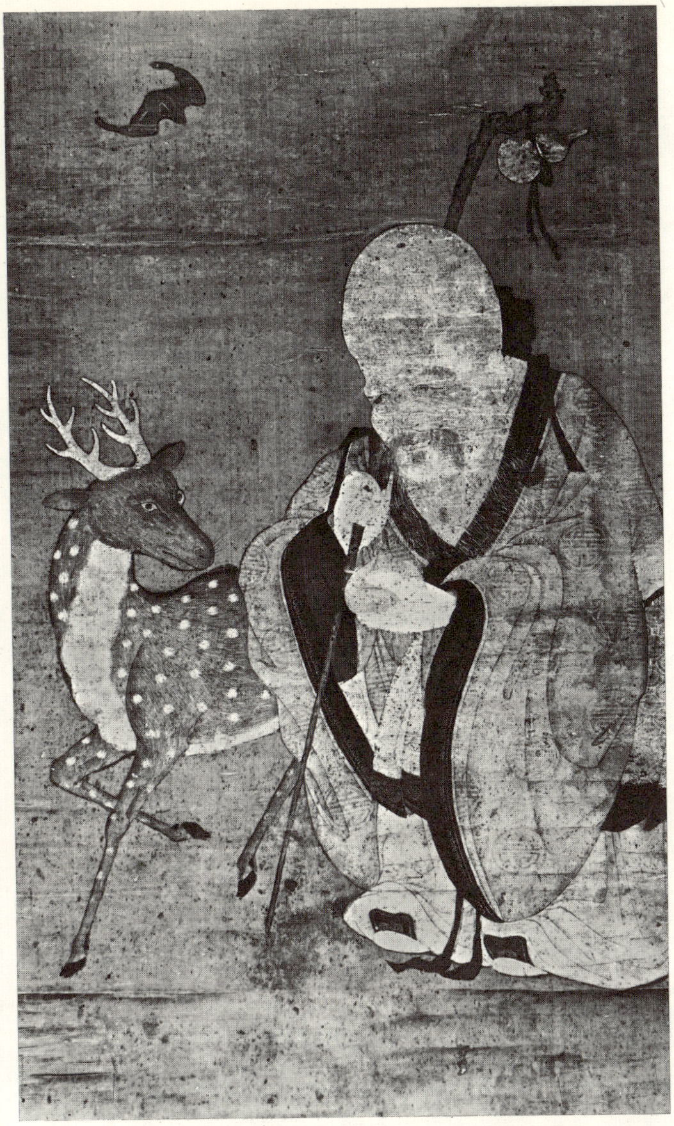

Shou-hsing, the God of Long Life. The bald-headed god is shown holding the Peach of immortality in his left hand and accompanied by a stag and a bat. One of a triad of gods which also includes Fu-hsing, the God of Happiness, and Lu-hsing, the God of Salaries, Shou-hsing is greatly revered although he has no temples or regular worship. It is he who decides the date of everybody's death. Screen painting.

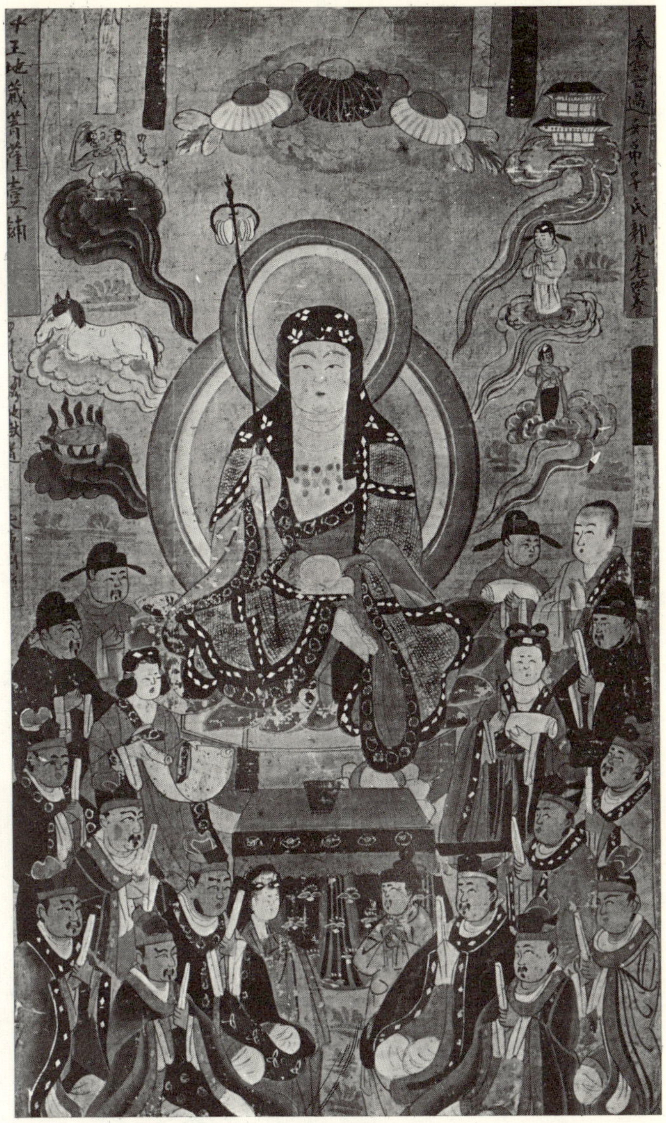

Ti-tsang (Ksitigarbha), the Merciful. Painting found at Tun-huang. Musée Guimet, Paris.

Sea gods. Like the rest of the universe, the sea is subject to the supreme authority of the August Personage of Jade, but the Chinese did not make it a divinity, any more than the other elements of Nature. However, they do recognise tutelary gods who protect navigators. The most popular as well as the highest in dignity is the Empress of Heaven, T'ien Hou, who must not be confused with the Queen-Mother Wang, wife of the August Personage of Jade.

Before she was promoted to her immortal destiny T'ien Hou was a girl in the island of Mei-chou which was famous for its piety. She had four brothers, all sailors, who sailed on different ships. One day when they were absent at sea the girl fainted and remained a long time unconscious. It was thought she was dead. With the aid of powerful stimulants she was brought back to life, but as soon as she emerged from her lethargy she complained that she had been awakened too soon. A little later three of her brothers returned, and related that they had been attacked by a violent storm during their voyage, and had been saved by their sister who appeared to them during the tempest and saved them from the danger. Only the fourth brother never came home – the girl had been revived before she had time to go to his aid.

After her death, which occurred very soon after this miracle, the girl of Mei-chou frequently showed the value of her intervention, either by helping sailors in peril or by helping to capture pirates or even by ending dangerous droughts. For which reason her cult continued to spread. She was first promoted to the title of Princess of Supernatural Favour, then in the sixteenth century was raised to the dignity of Queen, and in the eighteenth century received her definite title of Empress of Heaven.

She is represented as a woman sometimes seated on a lotus and sometimes on a throne. She wears the Imperial head dress, and holds either a sceptre or a tablet.

Country gods. According to the rites of Confucius, the Chinese recognise a god of the Soil, with whom they associate a god of Ploughing and a god of Harvests. They are impersonal deities, and have no mythic character. Formerly they were solemnly invoked at different periods of the year. The sacrifice which the Emperor offered up to the god of the Soil in spring and autumn was marked by the same pomp as that devoted to the god of Heaven. During the festival of the god of Ploughing the Emperor himself set his hand to the plough, and drew the first furrow.

Side by side with these official gods, the peasants venerate other deities of a more popular kind. Prince Millet, Hou Chi, the old god of cereals, has been supplanted by the Celestial Prince Liu, appointed to the functions of superintendent of the Five Cereals. The god Hu-shen is invoked as a protection against hail, since as he wishes he can send or withhold the disaster. Against locusts

Rhinoceros horn cup on a large, elaborately carved wooden stand. The cup itself is lavishly ornamented with pierced and relief decoration showing human and animal figures and foliage while the stand is carved to represent rocks and trees. Rhinoceros horns were believed to possess aphrodisiac and medicinal properties, and these cups were used to detect the presence of poison – any liquid dangerous to the drinker would froth, it was believed, when poured into a rhinoceros horn cup. The belief dates back to the T'ang dynasty, when the cups were also used to heal poisoned wounds. Originally they were quite plain but the example shown here dates from the early nineteenth century and is Cantonese work. Wellcome Medical Museum.

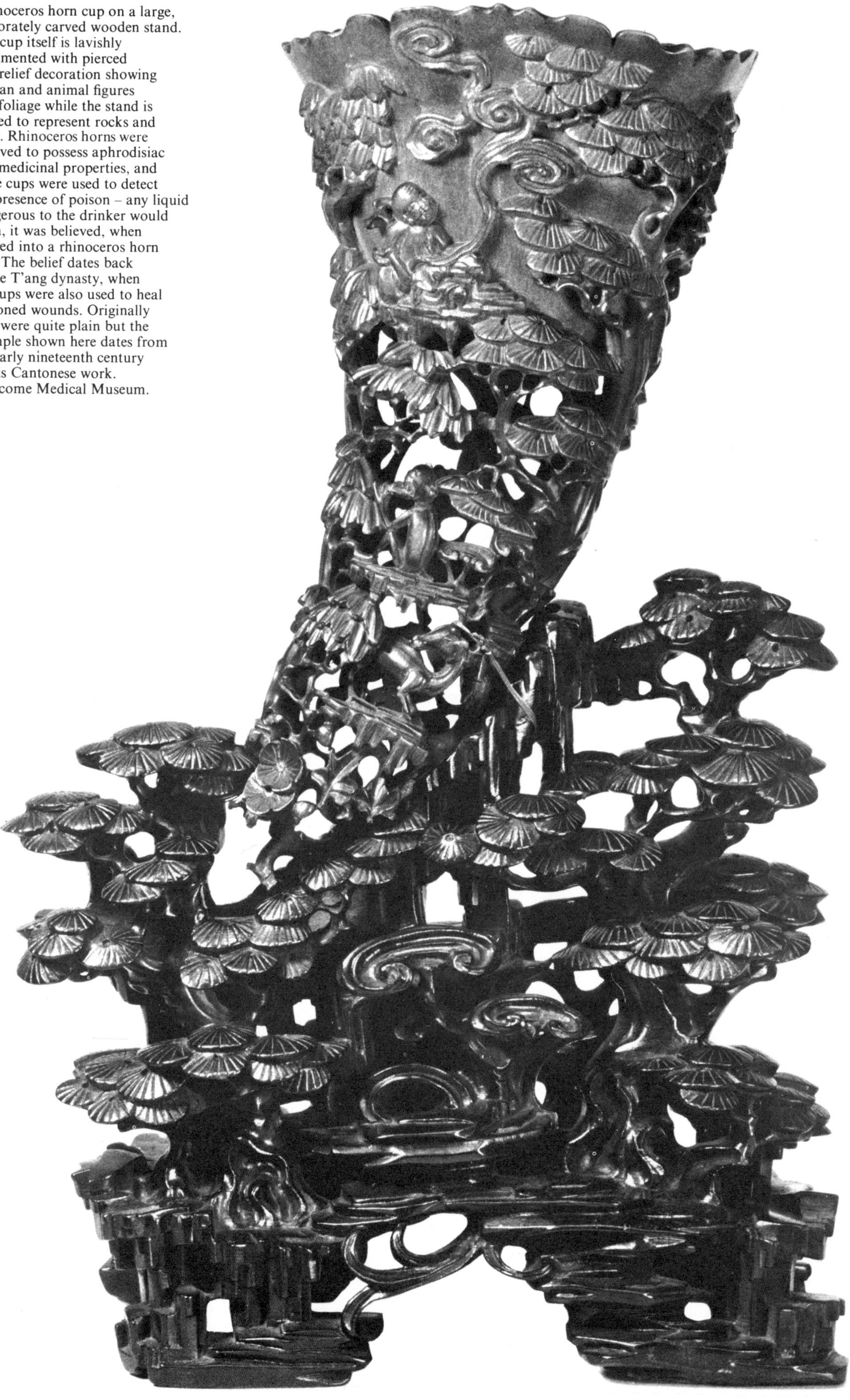

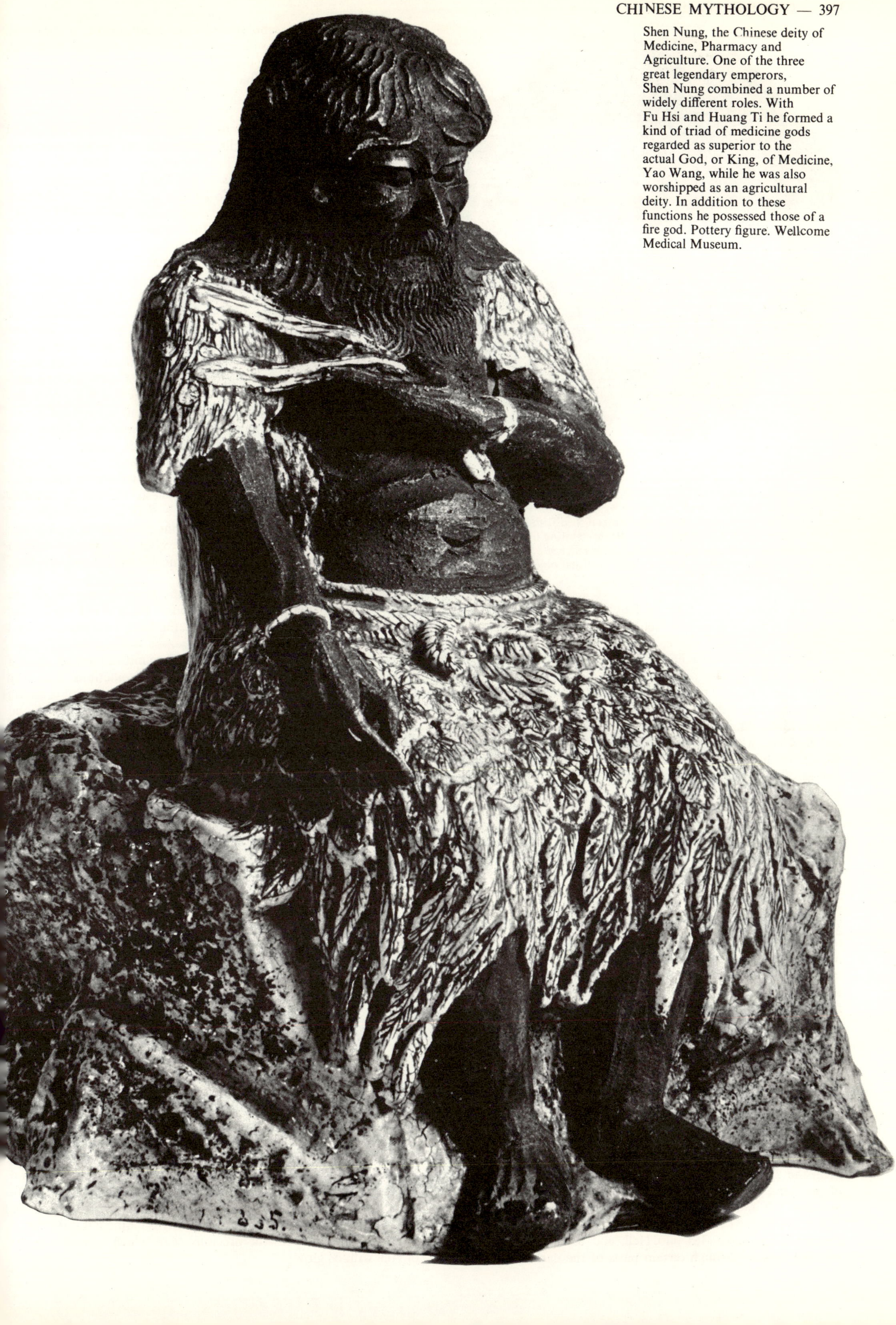

Shen Nung, the Chinese deity of Medicine, Pharmacy and Agriculture. One of the three great legendary emperors, Shen Nung combined a number of widely different roles. With Fu Hsi and Huang Ti he formed a kind of triad of medicine gods regarded as superior to the actual God, or King, of Medicine, Yao Wang, while he was also worshipped as an agricultural deity. In addition to these functions he possessed those of a fire god. Pottery figure. Wellcome Medical Museum.

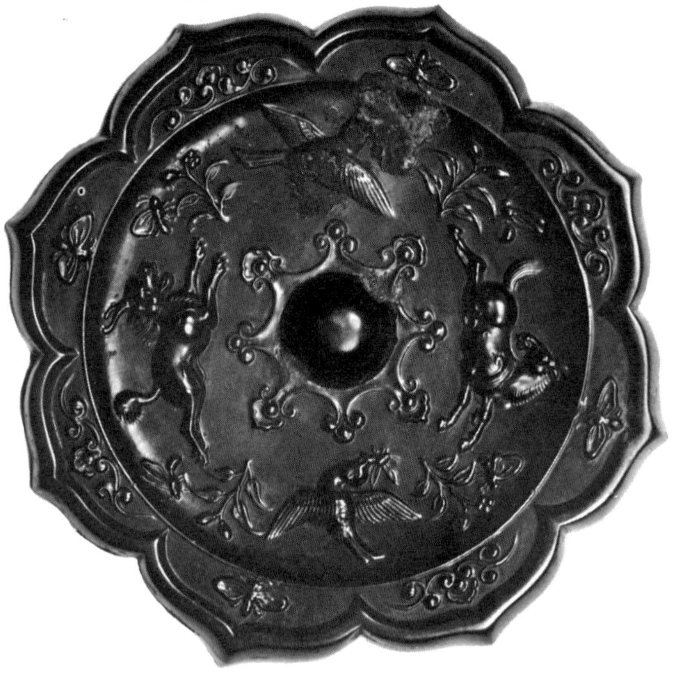

Bronze marriage mirror. The decoration on this bronze mirror is symbolical of the married couple, the horse and horned lion (respectively signifying speed and strength) standing for the man and the flowers for the woman. It is further embellished with birds and bees and formalized decorative motifs. Bronze casting first appeared in China during the Shang dynasty and rapidly reached a high artistic level. It was particularly employed for ornamental ritual objects. T'ang dynasty (618-906 A.D.).

they call on the Great General Pa-cha, who is represented as a man with a bird's beak and feet, while his hands are tipped with claws and he wears a petticoat. Cattle are under the protection of the god of Cattle-breeding, aided by the King-of-Oxen and the Transcendent Pig. During their lifetime they were both dangerous giants. The King-of-Oxen, who terrified his enemies by his enormous horns and buffalo ears, was yet tamed by the lady Nu-kua, who threaded a miraculous rope through his nose. Equally ferocious and hideous, with his black face, the Transcendent Pig had the impudence to swallow Erh-lang, the nephew of the August Personage of Jade himself, but he regretted it, for Erh-lang slew him. The breeding of silk-worms is under the protection of Lady Horse-head about whom there is a curious legend. Her father was kidnapped by pirates, which grieved her so much she refused to eat. Seeing the girl was in a decline, her mother vowed to marry her to the man who would bring back her husband. She spoke the vow aloud, and it was heard by the horse who was in love with his young mistress. The horse thereupon went off to look for the missing man, found him at last, and brought him home on his back. When he demanded his reward, the father flew into a violent rage, slew the poor animal, skinned him and put the skin to dry in the sun. A few days later as the girl passed it the skin leaped at her and carried her off. But the August Personage of Jade was on the watch. He changed the girl into a silk-worm and soon after took her up to Heaven. Since then the Lady Horse-head ranks among the Sovereign god's concubines.

HELL

Like all Chinese mythology, Hell is due to a mixture of Taoism and Buddhism, with a special preponderance given to the peculiarities of the Buddhist Hell.

The notion of Hell as it exists to-day among the people was, we believe, mainly disseminated by certain passages in novels, among them the *Travels in the West,* and the *Life of Yueh Fei*, a general of the Sung epoch, who was assassinated by order of the prime minister, Ch'in Kuei. In the first of these books, the Emperor T'ai-tsung of the T'ang dynasty was wrongly accused of killing the Dragon-King, descended into Hell, and before returning to life on earth passed through certain parts of the dark empire. In the other book a young scholar addresses a complaint to the gods, accusing them of lacking justice because of the death of Yueh Fei. He was summoned before the King of Hell, who showed him round his dominions to prove that there the wicked are punished and the good rewarded.

The Yama-Kings, Yen-wang. According to the most wide-spread version there are eighteen Hells, distributed among ten law-courts to which they are attached. These courts are presided over by the Shih-tien Yen-wang, the Kings of the Ten Law-Courts (the word Yen comes from Yama, the Indo-Iranian god of Death), while each Hell is reserved for the tortures which punish well-defined crimes.

The first of the Yama-Kings is the supreme master of the world of Hell as well as head of the first Law-Court. He is directly under the August Personage of Jade and the Great Emperor of the Southern Peak. He is popularly known as Yen-wang-yeh (the Lord Yama-King) although in reality the real Yama-King was dismissed by the August Personage of Jade for being too charitable and merciful, and was sent down to head the Fifth Law-Court. The first Yama-King receives the souls of the dead, investigates their actions during their past life, and if necessary sends them to other Kings to be punished. As to the nine others, eight of them are commissioned to punish criminal souls – thus the second King punishes dishonest male and female intermediaries and ignorant doctors, the third punishes bad mandarins, forgers, and back-biters, the fourth punishes misers, coiners, dishonest tradesmen and blasphemers, the fifth punishes murderers, unbelievers and the lustful, the sixth punishes sacrilege, the seventh is reserved for those who violated graves and sold or ate human flesh, the eighth punishes those who were lacking in filial piety, the ninth punishes arson and has for an annexe the Town of those Dying in Accidents, and finally the tenth King is entrusted with the Wheel of Transmigration, and takes care that the soul about to be reincarnated fits properly into the body assigned.

Another version says that each of the kings in turn judges the souls which go before each Law-Court, while the King of the Wheel of Transmigration decides on the form in which the soul just judged shall be re-born.

Naturally the tortures used in Hell are many and varied, so that each crime has its appropriate punishment, sometimes in a very logical way. Thus, blasphemers have their tongues torn out; misers and lying mandarins are compelled to swallow melted gold and silver, while still more guilty souls are flung on to mountains bristling with swords or plunged into boiling oil, or bound to a large red-hot hollow iron beam, or ground in mills or sawed in halves or cut into little pieces, etc.

The Kings of Hell have crowds of satellites to carry out their orders. These satellites are represented as stripped to the waist, with two lumps on their foreheads (which lumps are really meant for horns) and armed with a mace bearing iron spikes or with a trident. The Yama-Kings are represented in the dress of the Emperors, just like the August Personage of Jade and the Emperor of the Eastern Peak. On the images in books of piety they can only be distinguished by the inscription under each of them.

The Bodhisattva Ksitigarbha: Ti-tsang Wang-p'u-sa. In this Hell which is peopled by implacable ministers of justice, is there room for mercy? Yes, for the various regions of hell are continually visited by a compassionate and merciful deity, the Bodhisattva Ksitigarbha (in Chinese, Ti-tsang Wang-p'u-sa) whose occupation is to save the souls which come to him. In his human life Ti-tsang was a young Brahman who made a vow to save all souls engulfed in sin. To this end he devoted his successive existences, which were innumerable, and acquired such merit by his spirit of self-sacrifice that in the end Buddha entrusted to him the masses of gods and men 'so that he would not allow them for one day or one night to fall into evil birth'. In China this god is always invoked when somebody dies, so that he can come to the help of the dead person. His name Ti-tsang is a translation of the Sanskrit Ksitigarbha. The images of him show him as a bonze, sometimes with a shaved head like the Hindu bonzes, and sometimes wearing a ceremonial wreath such as is worn by Chinese bonzes. He holds in his right hand the metal wand hung with musical rings such as Chinese monks carry, and his left hand holds the precious pearl which lights the paths of Hell with its glow.

Life of the dead in Hell. When the registers of Death and Life kept by the Yama-King show that a man has reached the end of his earthly existence, the Yama-King sends two of his satellites to seize the man's soul and bring it before the infernal Law Courts. These satellites are named Ox-Head and Horse-Face, Niu-t'ou and Ma-mien, and they are represented with the head of the animal whose name they bear. They make their way to the man's house and take him off. And here comes out the value of the Door gods, for it is their duty to see that the warrant of arrest is authentic, and not until that is done will they allow Ox-Head and Horse-Face to enter.

They also say that these two satellites are not sent by the Yama-King but by the god of Walls and Ditches, who keeps a register of all the inhabitants in his area. And then again they say, for all the mythology of Hell is rather confused, that the persons charged to bring in the dead are the two Without-Duration, Wu-ch'ang, one of whom is white and the other black, who are called 'the Messengers who seize souls', Kou-hun-shih-che. Their statues are sometimes to be seen in the temples, and these two personages are represented wearing a long black or white robe which reaches to their feet, a tall pointed hat, a rope round their necks, and their tongues hanging out.

But whoever comes for them the souls (which retain their appearance for some time after leaving their robe of flesh) are taken first before the god of Walls and Ditches who puts them through a first series of questions and holds them for forty-nine days, either at liberty, or punishing them with the pillory or beating, according to what the dead person did in his lifetime. Sometimes it happens that owing to a similarity of name or some other error, the wrong soul is brought along; in which case the god allows it to return to earth and to re-enter the body in which it lived. This is perhaps the reason why the Chinese keep the bodies of the dead for several days before they are buried – at least seven, with a maximum of forty-nine.

After forty-nine days the god of Walls and Ditches hands over the soul to the Yama-King. He acts as judge, by consulting the

Kuan-ti, the God of War. One of the most popular Chinese gods, though he was not deified until the sixteenth century. Kuan-ti received two kinds of worship – the official, in his numerous temples throughout the country, and the popular, in which he was invoked as a protector against spirits and unfriendly human beings. He was also famous as a foreteller of the future. Fukien ware porcelain figure, Ming dynasty (A.D. 1368-1644).

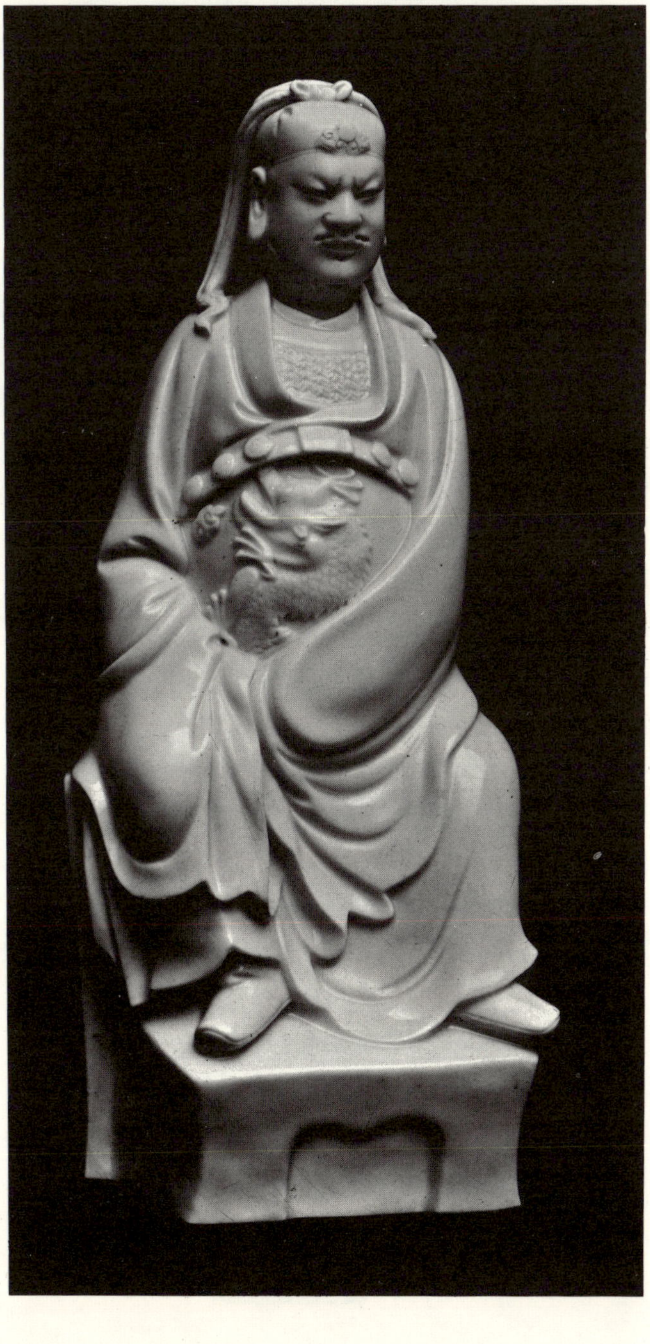

Han Hsiang-tzu, 'patron saint' of musicians, depicted playing the flute. One of the Eight Taoist Immortals, he is said to have been an historical figure – the grand-nephew of Han Yu (A.D. 764-824), the great statesman, writer and philosopher of the T'ang dynasty. He was also associated with magic and alchemy. Stoneware roof tile with coloured lead-glazes, Ming period. Seligman Collection.

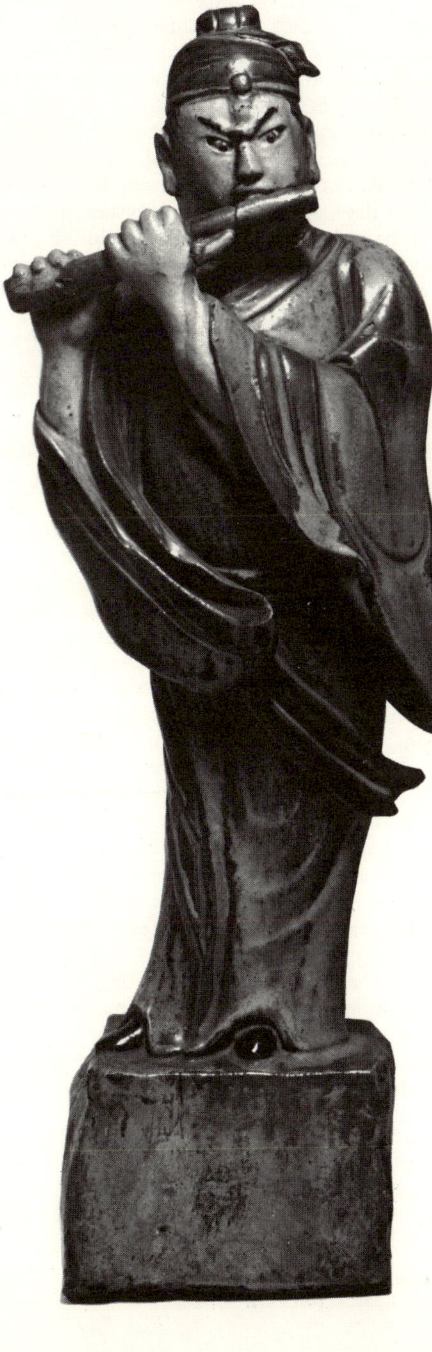

register which records all the good or evil actions of this soul, and if necessary sends it before whichever of the Yama-Kings is appointed to punish the crime of which the soul is guilty. As to those souls which have done good deeds, such as those of good sons, of good subjects, believers, and charitable persons etc., they either go to Buddha in the Land of Extreme Felicity in the West, or to the Mountain K'un-lun, the dwelling-place of the Immortals, or else they go straight to the tenth Yama-King to be re-born to another existence.

But let us return to the souls of sinners. They go before each of the Yama-Kings in turn, who punishes them for the crime under his jurisdiction. The people believe that persons who have committed very great crimes find that their souls must endure all the tortures of hell without distinction. Such, they say, was the case with the Minister Ch'in Kuei, already mentioned, and doubtless in this way the people work off the hatred they feel for some especially detested personage. After each torture the soul returns to its original form to undergo another. Thus, if it has been cut into little pieces, the pieces all join up again; and if it has been thrown in a cauldron of boiling oil, it becomes living as soon as it is taken out. When the soul has suffered all the punishments due for its sins, it finally goes before the tenth Yama-King who decides in what form, human or animal, it shall be re-born. The Buddhists believe there are six ways of re-birth – three of them are good, birth as a god, as a human being, or as an asura (a kind of demon); and three are bad, birth in hell, birth as a starving demon, birth as an animal. But people believe that birth as a human being is not necessarily a reward, for a man's soul may be condemned to re-birth in the body of a woman (in ancient times women were considered less honourable than men) or in the body of an invalid or a beggar, etc., while at other times a soul may be re-born an animal without having sinned. There are numerous tales on this theme. One of them relates that a man who had borrowed money from someone, died before he could pay his debt. After his death he asked permission of the Yama-King to be re-born as a colt in his creditor's family. Soon after his birth his master sold him for exactly the sum which was owing. The colt died soon after he was sold, and the soul which occupied it returned again to the Law-Courts of Hell to be judged. Another tale, which resembles the 'Dream of the Yellow Sorghum' mentioned in connection with the Immortal Lu Tung-pin, relates that a scholar who had just passed the Imperial examinations was walking in a Temple, and went into the room of a bonze to rest. There he fell asleep, and dreamed that he became a high dignitary and grew rich through telling lies. He then dreamed that he died, and was condemned to drink a quantity of molten gold equivalent to that which he had got unjustly. After this he dreamed that he was re-born in a family of beggars as a girl, and as she grew up was sold to be a scholar's concubine. He did not awake until he had dreamed that he had died a second time. Realising the vanity of this world's honours he retired to the mountain to seek the Path.

Souls re-incarnated in an animal do not thereby lose their human feelings. Whether born in the form of a cock or a pig, the soul will feel with human sensibilities all the suffering the animal feels when its throat is cut, and will even suffer from every slice of the knife which cuts it up. But it cannot express its anguish in human language, of which it has lost the use thanks to the Broth of Oblivion, Mi-hun-t'ang. This broth is compounded by the Lady Meng, who lives in a house built just inside the exit from Hell. All souls which pass her door on their way to the Wheel of Transmigration have to drink it willy-nilly. Under its influence the souls forget their former life, their existence in Hell and even their speech. There are legends relating to miraculous births – a child is able to speak as soon as born because the soul inhabiting its body had been successful in escaping the vigilance of the guardians of Hell, and had avoided drinking the Broth of Oblivion.

If after drinking this broth a soul is to be re-born in the form of an animal, the satellites of the Law Courts throw on his shoulders

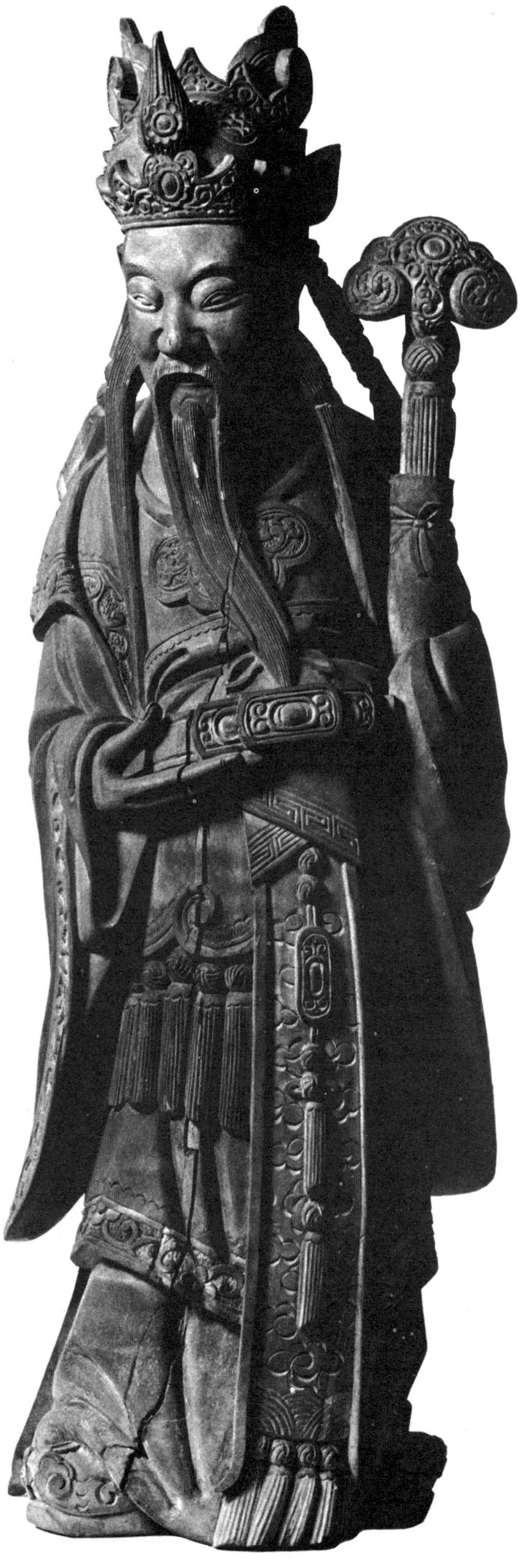

Wen Ch'ang, the God of Literature. Generally represented as a seated mandarin holding a sceptre in his left hand, Wen Ch'ang is said to have lived through seventeen successive lives before being invested by the August Personage of Jade with the functions of Grand Emperor of Literature. Like his follower K'uei-hsing, the God of Examinations, he was a benevolent god and never failed a deserving candidate. Carved wooden figure. Horniman Museum.

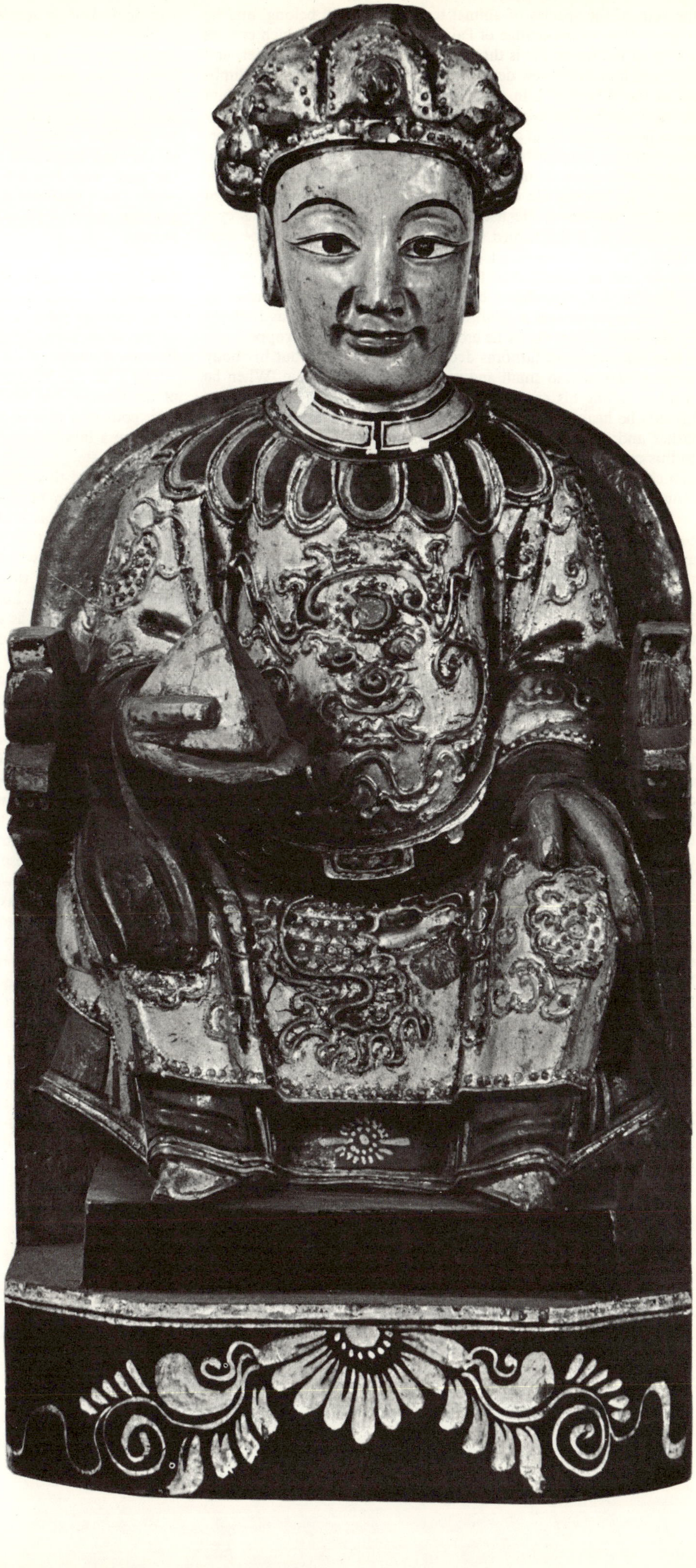

T'ien Hou, the Empress of Heaven. In addition to the gods who were generally worshipped, the Chinese pantheon also included a large number of divinities peculiar to each profession. T'ien Hou, a girl from the island of Mei-chou, became the favourite guardian of sailors after miraculously saving the lives of three of her brothers in a storm and her image was consequently placed in junks and sailing boats. Painted wooden figure. Horniman Museum.

the skin of the species of animal to which he will belong, and he is then taken to the Bridge of Pain, K'u-ch'u-ch'iao, which crosses a river of red water. He is thrown off the bridge into the water, and it carries him to his new destiny. They say also that the soul climbs on to the Wheel of Life and Death, which as it turns sends him down to earth. The tale just mentioned says: 'After walking a few paces he saw on a stand a beam of iron several feet in circumference, supporting a great wheel whose dimensions were an unknown number of leagues. Flames of five colours sprang from it, and their glow lit up heaven. He was struck by demons who compelled him to get on the wheel. He had scarcely jumped on it with his eyes shut when the wheel turned under his feet and he felt as if he were falling; he felt coolness all over his body, and opening his eyes he saw that he already had the body of a baby.

Another tale, translated by Father Wieger, mentions another case: 'Everything was a confusion to him. His body was buffeted by the wind. Suddenly as he crossed a red bridge he dropped into a lake ten thousand fathoms deep. He felt no pain, but his body became narrow and small and was no longer the same. When he stopped falling his eyes were closed and would not open, and in his ears he heard what seemed to be the sound of the voices of his father and mother. He seemed to be the plaything of a dream.' In this case, as in the tale before, the soul is being born in the body of a child; but of course the impression is quite different and much more unpleasant if it is the body of an animal.

Some details of Hell. Hell is a world on its own, with its own towns and country-side. The chief town is Feng-tu, which is entered by the souls of the dead through a big gate called the Gate of Demons, Kuei-men-kuan. The town contains the palaces of the Yama-Kings, the Law Courts, the places set aside for torture as well as the dwellings of the functionaries, the infernal satellites, and the souls waiting to be re-born. On the side opposite the Gate of Demons the town abuts on a river called the River Ḥow Nai-ho, crossed by three bridges. One bridge is in gold for the gods, one in silver for the souls of virtuous men, and the last for undeserving or criminal souls. This bridge is several leagues long, but has only three spans, and no rails. Criminal souls of certain categories, such as those who during their life-time profaned clothes of a purple colour, or women who lived dissipated lives, on trying to cross the bridge inevitably fall into the water rushing beneath. They then are preyed upon by bronze snakes and iron dogs who bite them and tear them to pieces.

The souls of the dead are not only responsible for their actions in the life they have just left, but also for those of their life before that, if for some reason they have not received punishment for them. Since these souls cannot remember their actions, owing to the Broth of Oblivion which they all drink on passing through Hell, they are when necessary placed in front of a huge mirror, the Mirror of the Wicked, Nieh-ching-t'ai, set up in the Court of the first Yama-King. In this mirror the souls see themselves with the appearance they had in their former life, and so perceive the crime they committed. The Yama-King bases the judgment he gives on this appearance.

Not far from the town of Feng-tu is the town of Those who Died in Accidents, Wang-ssu-ch'eng. It is under the ninth Yama-King. Everyone is sent there who dies before the date set down in the Registers of Life and Death, no matter whether they committed suicide or died by accident. The souls of these dead are condemned to live here like starving demons, with no hope of being re-born unless they can find someone to replace them. Thus the soul of a hanged man must bring the soul of another hanged man, and so with a drowned man. To allow them to find a replacement, these souls after three years in Hell are allowed to return freely to earth, to the place where they left their mortal bodies, and there they do all they can to arrange that men passing near the place shall die in the same way. For this reason the Chinese carefully avoid places where there has been a murder, a suicide, or an accident causing a human death, for fear of being made use of by the soul of the dead person.

The Chinese Paradise. As we have seen, when the souls of the just are not sent back immediately to a new life by the tenth Yama-King, they go either to the K'un-lun Mountain, the dwelling place of the Immortals, or to the Amitabha Buddha in the Land of Extreme Felicity in the West.

The K'un-lun Mountain has a close resemblance to the Olympus of the Greeks, but while the latter situated the dwelling place of their gods in a mountain of their own country, the Chinese placed theirs on a fabulous mountain far away from their land and at the earth's centre.

The ruler of this region is no other than the Lady Queen of the West, the Queen-Mother Wang, wife of the August Personage of Jade. The palace is built on the top of the mountain, it has nine storeys and is built entirely of jade. Around the palace are magnificent gardens in which grows the Peach-tree of Immortality. The Immortals live there, in an endless series of amusements and banquets. The only human beings allowed there are those permitted by the gods, as a reward for their virtues, to eat the marvellous fruit of the Peach-tree of Immortality during their earthly life.

The other just men admitted to the felicities of eternal life go to the Land of Extreme Felicity in the West. This land, which lies in the fathest west portion of the universe is separated from us by an infinity of worlds like our own. It is a place of all delights, closed in on all sides and embellished by seven rows of terraces with seven rows of trees whose branches are formed of precious stones sounding musically when the wind stirs them. There may be found lakes flowering with lotuses, with a floor of gold sand and banks paved with seven precious stones. Birds with many-coloured plumage and divine voices praise in their songs the five Virtues and the excellent Doctrines. Showers of blossom fall on the ground. In this Eden the righteous pass a life which is piously ordered: 'Every morning at dawn they go to offer flowers to all the Buddhas of other worlds, and they return to their world for meals.' Everything they hear – the song of the birds, the music of the wind in the trees of precious stones – makes them think of Buddha, the Law, and the Community. Their perilous transmigrations are over.

Happy are they, who in their life-time fervently called upon Amitabha. At the hour of their death their hearts will not be troubled, for Buddha himself will appear to them. He will receive their souls and place them in the lotuses of the lakes, in which they will remain enclosed until the day comes when, being cleansed from all impurities, they will escape from the opening flower and will go to mingle with the just who inhabit the Land of Extreme Felicity in the West.

JAPANESE MYTHOLOGY

INTRODUCTION

Sources of Japanese Mythology. When the ancestors of the Japanese, coming probably from Korea, settled in Japan, they met and made war upon the Ainus whom they drove into the north, while in the southern islands, especially Kyushu, they came upon various tribes whom they subdued and assimilated. They lived in tribes, each one of which had a chief, who, as we shall see later, was often a woman—a characteristic which struck the Chinese when they came into contact with the Japanese, probably about the beginning of our era. Besides China, Japan was also in touch with Korea, and these ancient relations with the Asiatic continent had their influence on the minds of the Japanese people. They also left distinct traces in their mythological tales. The southern tribes, living their sea-faring life, also had a share in building up Japanese mythology, and so had the local traditions peculiar to each of the different regions.

Oral traditions. The interlacing of local myths with foreign legend constitutes the mythology as it has been transmitted to us in the texts, and this is what makes the study such a delicate one. The difficulty is increased by the fact that the mythological tales were closely connected with the origins of the Japanese royal family, and therefore native scholars must not criticise or explain them in too rationalist a way. These myths were preserved by oral tradition, thanks to the Katari-be, a corporation of 'reciters' whose function was to recite these ancient legends during the great Shinto festivals. Japanese scholars believe that this corporation of reciters was closely linked with the priests and priestesses who, during the religious service, related ancient legends about the gods, the tribe or the district.

'The Katari-be seem to have sung their songs at the banquets of the Imperial Court or of the great families, and no doubt the poems described the origin of the gods and the ancestors.' (p. 5, N. Matsumoto, *Essai sur la Mythologie Japonaise*, Paris, 1928). In the beginning of the eighth century these tales were used to compile the old histories of Japan, and will be discussed later on. As we have seen, relations between Japan and China and Korea existed at the beginning of our era, as the facts of archaeology testify. We also know that Chinese learning and its form of writing were officially established in the year 405, when the learned Korean Wani arrived.

Buddhism was introduced around 522 and after various vicissitudes became the official religion. The Emperor Yomei (585—587) was the first sovereign to accept this foreign religion. In 592 the Empress Suiko came to the throne, and the regent Prince Shotoku was a devout Buddhist. Foreign customs influenced Japanese life so much that during a Shinto ceremony the descendants of the Koreans uttered the words in Chinese. It is natural to assume that the scholars who had to compose the history of Japan and the scribes who had to write it in Chinese must, under the influence of their Chinese education, have modified and embellished the ancient traditions in accordance with Chinese ideas.

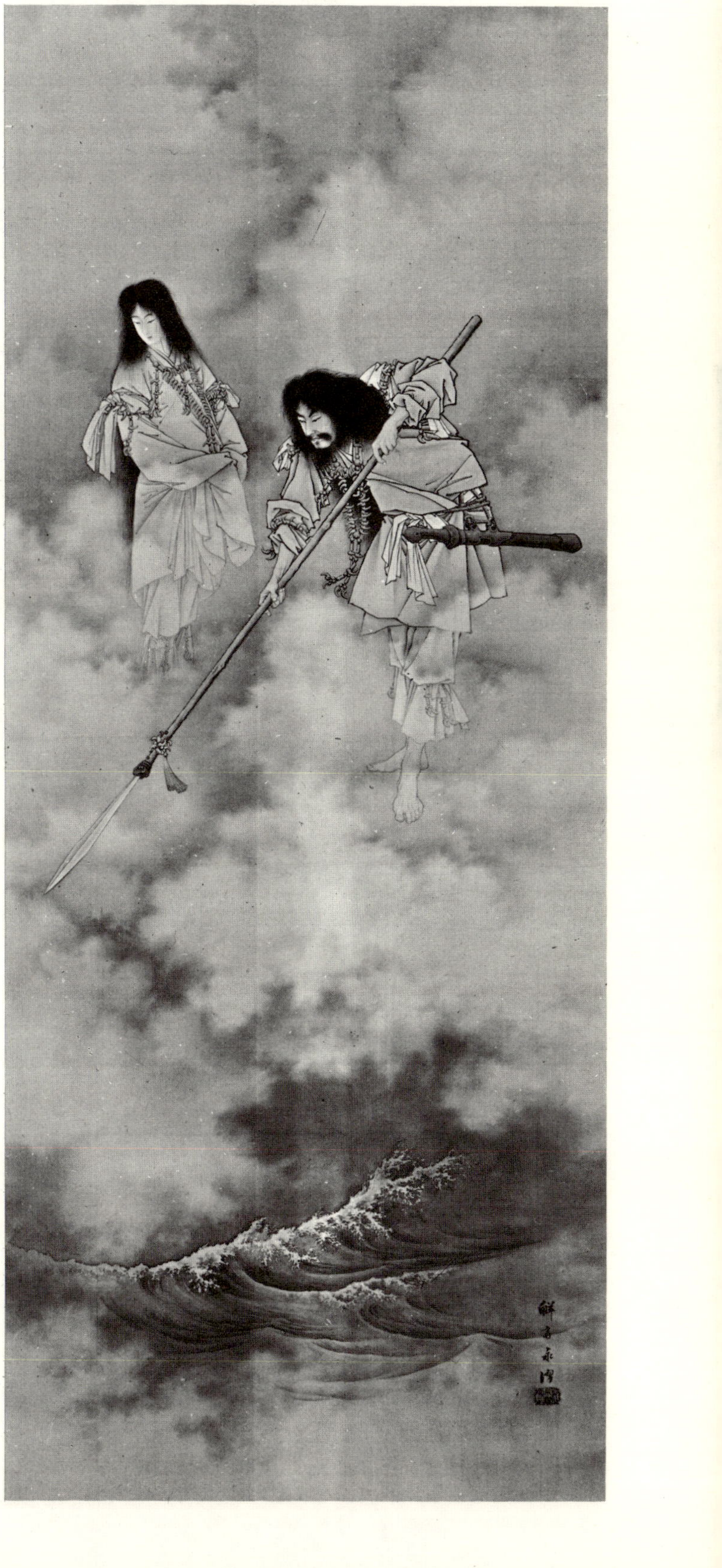

Izanagi and his sister Izanami creating the island of Onokoro. The last couple of the seven generations of gods who appeared when heaven and earth began, Izanagi and Izanami received the order to consolidate and fertilize the moving earth. Here Izanagi stirs the waters of the sea with his celestial lance to produce the island of Onokoro. The brother and sister then descended to it and engendered the islands of Japan and numerous deities. Silk painting, nineteenth century A.D.

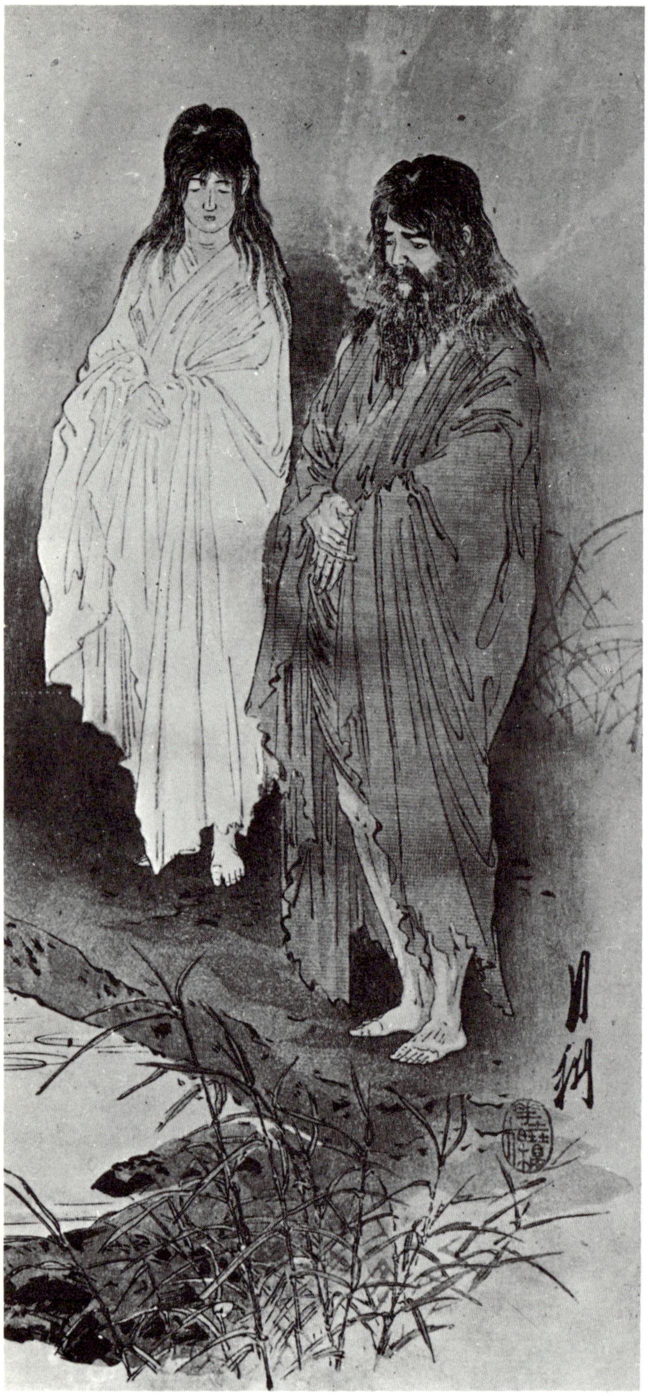

Izanami and Izanagi, standing on 'the Floating Bridge of Heaven', watch the wagtail as it approaches them.

Written sources. What are these written sources? First of all we have the *Kojiki*, the book of ancient things or of ancient words. The Emperor Temmu (672—686) realised that the ancient families in their contentions were changing the old traditions in order to provide more support for their rights and privileges. These alterations threatened to harm the reigning family. So in 681 he set up a Committee to put the old traditions into writing, but his death stopped the work. He had also given orders to Hieda-no-Are, one of his attendant ladies who had a very good memory, to learn all the old legends by heart. In 711 the Empress Gemmyo (707—715) ordered O no Yasumaro to collect the stories of Hieda-no-Are, to make a selection, and to set down the ancient traditions in the form of a book. In 712 the work was completed and presented to the Empress under the title of *Kojiki*. It is curious to find that O no Yasumaro was uncertain how to write the book. He would not write it entirely in Chinese for fear of distorting the character of the tales. But the Japanese syllabary was not then in existence, so like a good Japanese he made a compromise, sometimes writing in Chinese, sometimes using Chinese characters as the phonetic equivalents of Japanese syllables – which caused difficulties in reading the text. It must not be forgotten that the *Kojiki* was composed partly to settle the Imperial genealogy definitively and to place it above all controversy; and partly to do the same for the Shinto legends, source of the ritual and foundation of the state. In short, 'it was not so much a matter of writing a history as of establishing an orthodoxy.' (Cl. Maitre, *La Littérature historique du Japon des origines aux Ashikaga*, p. 53, B.E. F.E.O. October — December 1903.)

In 714 the same Empress also ordered a national history. Five years later, during the reign of the Emperor Gensho (715—726) Prince Toneri and O no Yasumaro compiled in Chinese the annals of Japan, *Nihon shoki,* (also called Nihongi) and presented them to the Emperor in 720. The first part of these annals, entitled *Jindaiki*, 'records of the age of the gods', deals with mythological legends and gives the different versions which existed at that time.

In 807 Imibe no Hironari wrote and presented to the throne the *Kogoshui*, 'gleanings of ancient words', to protest against the injuries caused by the Nakatomi family to the Imibe family in the protocol of religious services. Hironari relates several myths to show that the ancient traditions were well kept up in his family which therefore take precedence over the Nakatomi family. These myths are the same as those in the *Nihon shoki* and the *Kojiki*.

Tales and mythological information are also contained in the liturgical prayers, *norito,* included in 927 in the eighth volume of Ceremonial, *Engishiki,* which gives a great deal of information about Shinto matters. Following the Chinese custom, the Japanese government in 713 ordered the local authorities to draw up descriptions of their areas. These books were called *Fudoki,* but by far the greater number of these monographs have disappeared, and there remain only five *Fudoki* and fragments of others. They are a valuable source since they give local traditions which are a help to understanding the ancient myths. Mythological tales are also to be found in the *Manyoshu,* the first great anthology of Japanese poetry, compiled in the eighth century. In the *Shojiroku,* written in 814, and containing genealogies of the old nobility, there are traces of ancient traditions also.

To these written sources must be added the studies in Japanese folklore which during the past thirty years have been carried on with great energy. The numerous publications dealing with local traditions have enabled us to understand the old stories a little better. The studies of folklore in the Ryukyu islands have done much towards our understanding of the part played by women in the ancient traditions (N. Matsumoto '*L'état actuel des études de folklore au Japon*' p. 228, No 10. *Japon et Extrême Orient*, Paris, 1924). These folklore studies are especially interesting for the primitive religion of Japan, for in the course of history official Shinto has been influenced by foreign ideas, and has undergone certain modifications in consequence.

THE GREAT LEGENDS

The Kami. The Japanese deified the forces of Nature because they felt they were more powerful than themselves, and venerated them under the name *Kami.* High mountains, tall and ancient trees, rivers, were Kami and so, too, were great men. The word Kami means 'beings more highly placed', those who are venerated, and does not have the meaning of our word, god. The Japanese Kami are often characterised by the epithet chihaya-buru, which may be translated 'powerful'. The gods of Japanese mythology have bodies like those of human beings, and are endowed with all human qualities and defects. The myths speak perfectly frankly of certain exploits of the gods, which English translators prefer to give in Latin. Traditions tell us that the gods possessed two souls, one gentle, nigi-mi-tama, and one violent, ara-mi-tama. The Kami reacted according to the activity of one or the other. At times this soul can leave the body and manifest itself in an object. But the Kami of Japan are not omniscient. Those who live in Heaven do not know what is going on down in the world, and have to send messengers to find out. And they make use of divination to predict the future. The different gods can do good or do evil, but there are no essentially wicked Kami among them. True, when the god Izanagi (of whom we shall speak again) returns from Hell to earth

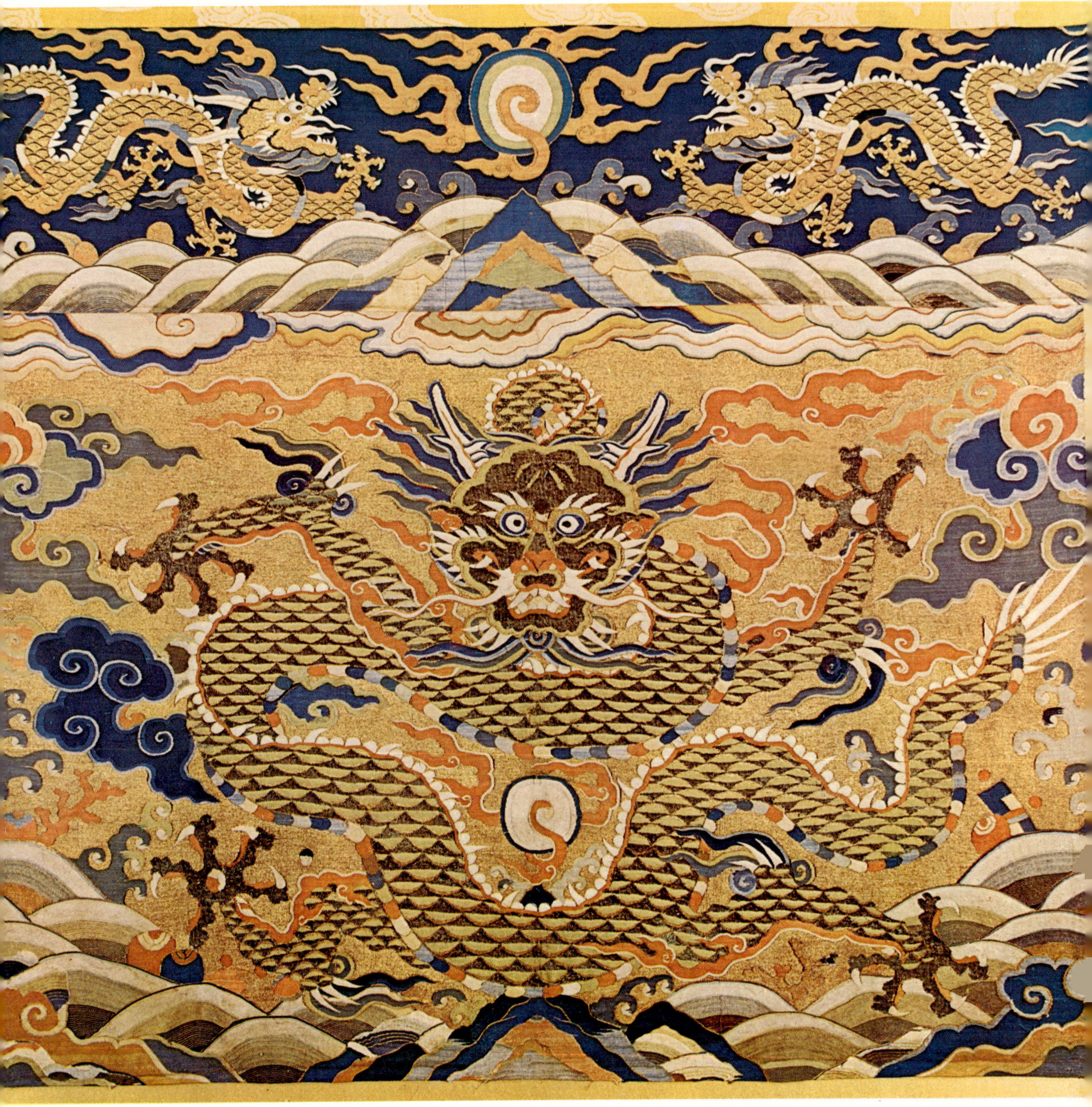

The dragon is an ancient symbol in China, representing both earth and water and above all the fertilising power of rain. A dragon horse is also said to have risen from the Yellow River and shown to Fu Hsi, the legendary first Emperor of China, a mystic chart inscribed on its back from which the written language of China evolved. The imperial dragon, insignia of the emperors, was always depicted with five toes. Ming Dynasty.

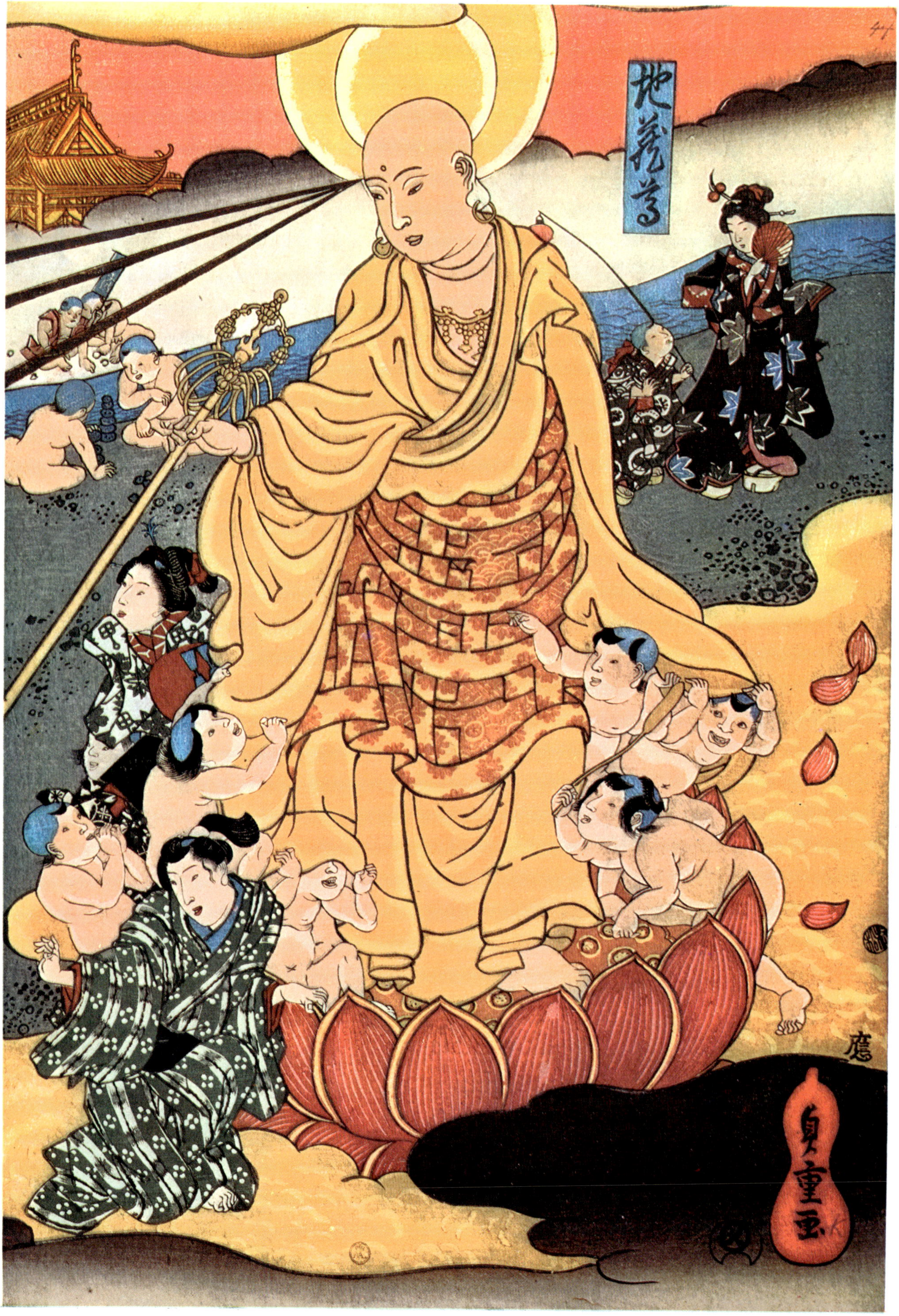

Hotei Osho, one of the Seven Gods of Happiness, is usually pictured as a jolly, plump priest surrounded by children. Though a popular embodiment of the bodhisattva Miroku (Maitreya in Indian Buddhism), the idea of the group of seven popular deities owes nothing to Buddhist teaching or tradition. It is a purely local and comparatively late concept. Coloured woodcut of the nineteenth century. Victoria and Albert Museum.

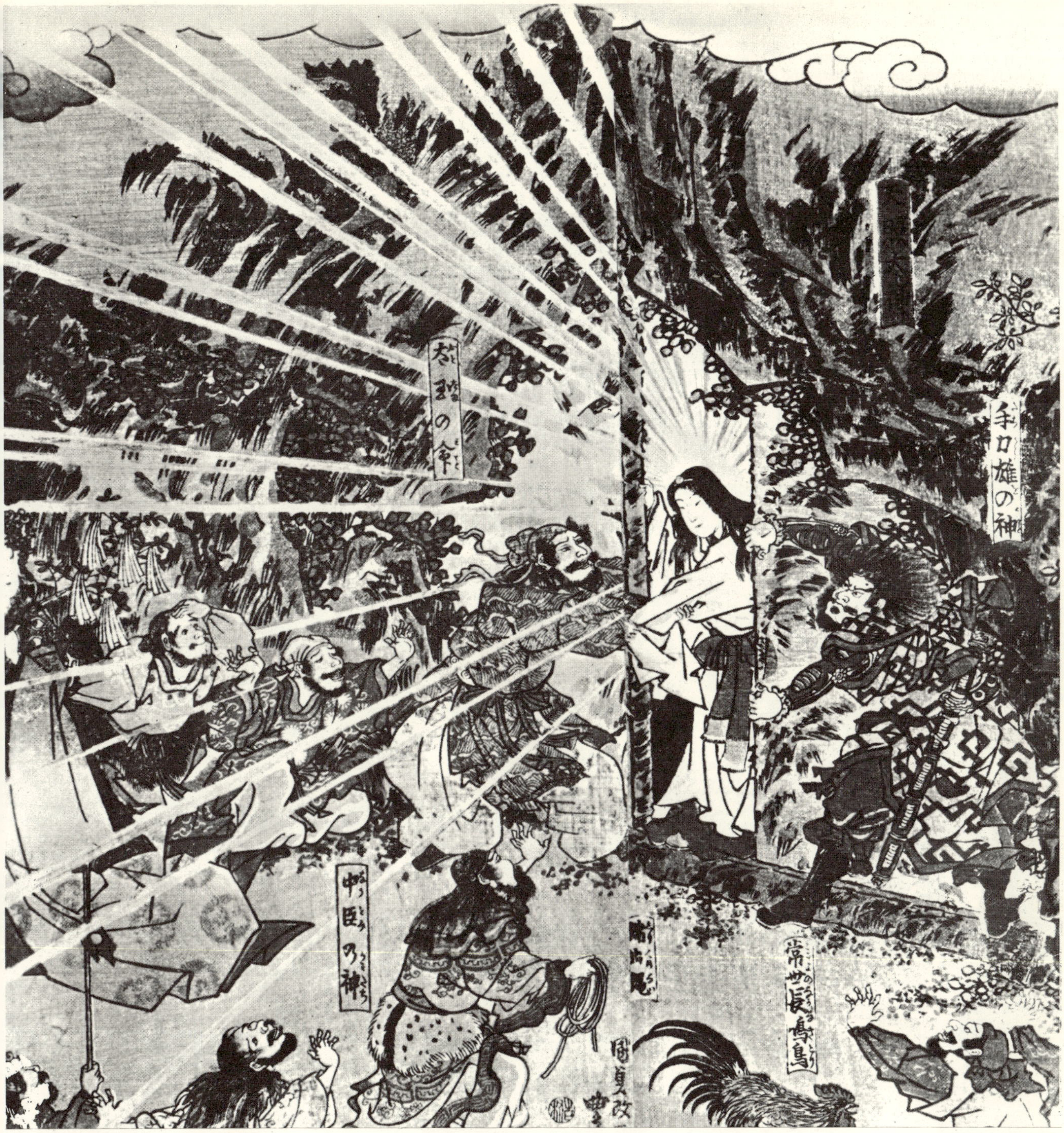

Amaterasu, attracted by the laughter of the gods, emerges from her cave. Kunisada Toyokuni II.

and washes off its impurities, the infernal mud gives birth to Yaso-Maga-Tsu-Bi, the god of multiple calamities; but then there appears Kamu-Nahobi, the god who puts things right again. All wicked things live in Hell, which is under the earth and these demons particularly represent the sicknesses and epidemics and calamities which afflict the inhabitants of Japan. But they are far less powerful than the Kami, who by the power of magic can conquer them or prevent them from coming out from under the earth.

Heaven, Earth, Hell. Japanese mythology divides the Kami into gods of Heaven, Ama-Tsu-Kami, and gods of Earth, Kuni-Tsu-Kami, the latter of which are more numerous and live in the islands of Japan. Still, some divinities rise up from earth to heaven, and on the other hand others come down to settle on earth. Heaven, which the Japanese describe by the word Ama, is not a far-off and inaccessible place. Its landscape is the same as Japan's, and it is crossed by the heavenly river, Ama no Gawa, which like Japanese rivers has a very wide bed covered with pebbles.

Formerly earth was linked with heaven by a sort of bridge, Ama no Hashidate, which allowed the gods to go to and fro. According to the *Tango-fudoki*, one day when the gods were all asleep this bridge or stairway collapsed into the sea. This formed the prolonged isthmus situated to the west of Kyoto in the sub-prefecture of Yosa, which is well known as one of the three most beautiful places in Japan.

Under the earth lies the kingdom of the dead, which is called 'land of darkness', Yomi-tsu-kuni, or 'land of roots', Ne no Kuni, and also 'the deep land', Soko no Kuni. There are two ways of entering Hell. There is a sloping and very winding road which begins in Izumo province and leads under ground; and the other is situated on the sea shore. It is a bottomless abyss which engulfs all the waters of the sea, and here on the day of grand purification all sins and all impurities are swept down with the waters. Palaces and cottages are built in this subterranean kingdom, the homes of male and female demons—the females are called shiko-me, ugly women, or hisa-me, frowning women. This kingdom of the dead is seldom mentioned in myths, but it is named notably when after the death of his wife Izanagi, the god Izanami goes down under the

Ofuda representing the goddess Amaterasu. (An ofuda consists of a sheet of paper folded round a stick of wood and represents the deity with whose name it is inscribed.) Amaterasu, the sun goddess, is said to have been born from Izanagi's left eye and is worshipped both as a heavenly body and spiritual deity and also as the ancestor of the Imperial family. This ofuda comes from her shrine at Ise, her cult centre since the first century A.D.

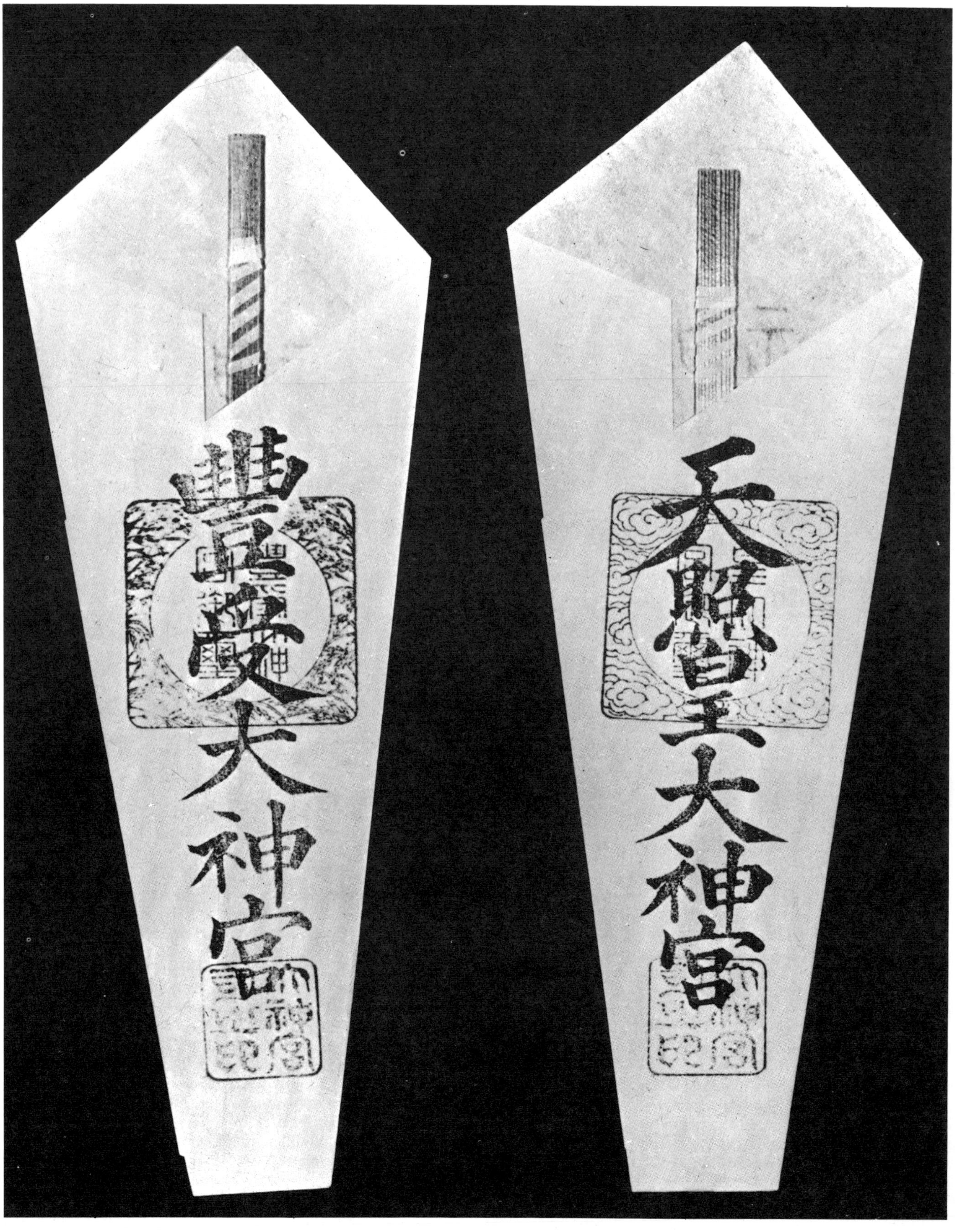

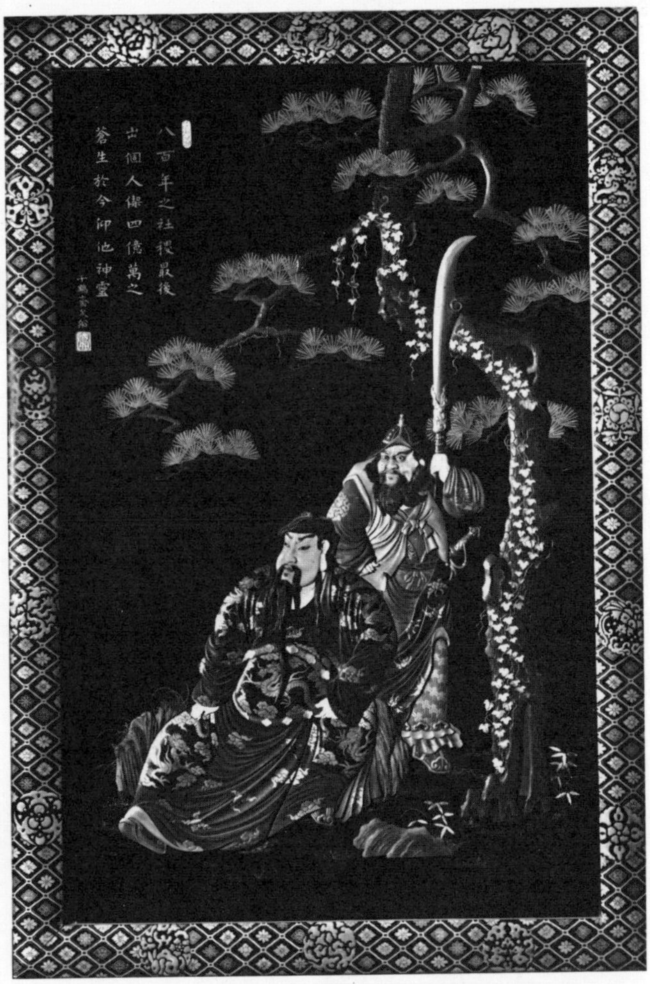

Ojin, or Hachiman, the Shinto god of war. The pantheon of Shinto gods was always increasing and, in addition to the mythological gods, historical personages also came in time to be considered as Kami. Among these were the Emperors Chuai and Ojin and the Empress Jingo all of whom were deified for their military exploits. At one time Buddhist elements were introduced into Ojin's cult but he later reverted to being a purely Shinto deity. Nineteenth century A.D.

earth to try to bring her back. Hell is also mentioned in a myth of Izumo province, where it is told how the god O-Kuni-Nushi went down there to consult Susanoo.

Japanese mythological traditions have not handed down to us the ancient beliefs about death. 'Probably', says Professor Florenz (*Lehrbuch der Religionsgeschichte, begründet von Chantepie de la Saussaye,* Verlag von J. C. B. Mohr, 4th new edition, Vol I, article *Die Japaner*, p. 267), 'the Shintoists felt a horror for everything which concerned death and corpses.' The idea of rewards and punishments after death came into Japan with Buddhist beliefs, but there is no mention of the topic in the old Shinto texts.

Origin of the gods and of the world. Japanese mythology tells us that 'at the time when heaven and earth began, three divinities were formed in the plain of high heaven'. They were born of themselves, and then hid. 'Later, when the earth was young and like floating oil, moving like a jelly-fish, from something which sprang up like the shoot of a reed there were born two divinities, and they too hid.' After that came seven generations of gods, and the last couple were called Izanagi and Izanami.

It is very probable that these beginnings of Japanese mythology, which show the influence of Chinese ideas, were set down by the compilers to act as an introduction to national traditions.

Izanagi and Izanami. Izanagi and Izanami received the order to consolidate and fertilise the moving earth. Standing on the 'floating bridge of heaven' they stirred up the waters of the sea with a lance which the gods had given them. When the water began to coagulate they withdrew the lance, and the drop which fell from its point formed the island of Onokoro, a word which means 'naturally coagulated'. The two deities then came down on this island, and created a column and a home.

Having looked well at one another Izanagi and Izanami decided to come together in order to beget countries.

They then walked round the column, Izanagi going round from the left and Izanami from the right. When they met the goddess Izanami exclaimed: 'What a pleasure to meet such a handsome young man!' But the god Izanagi was displeased with this exclamation, for the first words should have been spoken by him since he was the man. From this primordial union there was born 'a leech-child' whom his parents were unwilling to own. So they put him on a raft of reeds and set him adrift. Then the island of Awa was born, but they also refused to recognise it as their child.

They went off and consulted the gods, who explained to them that these unfortunate births were the result of Izanami's mistake in speaking first to her future husband and that they must walk round the column again and carry out the rite correctly. This the god Izanagi and the goddess Izanami did, and so gave birth to the many islands which constitute Japan as well as numerous gods—the god of Wind, of Trees, of Mountains etc. The last-born was the god of Fire, whose birth burned the goddess Izanami and caused her dreadful suffering. From her vomit, her urine, and her excrement other gods were born; and then she died. Izanagi lamented, and his tears gave birth to the goddess, Moaning-river. Furious with the baby who had caused the goddess's death, Izanagi picked up his sword and cut off the child's head. Drops of his blood, trickling down the blade, fell on the ground, and gave birth to eight different gods; and eight other deities symbolising different mountains came from various parts of the body.

Izanagi's descent into Hell. Izanagi was inconsolable for his wife's death, and went down to Hell and his wife came to meet him, but refused to return with him because she had already tasted the food of Hell. She suggested that she should go and discuss the question with the god of Hell, and begged her husband not to look inside the house. But the god became impatient and took the risk of following her. He broke off the 'made tooth' of his comb, that is, one of the two at the end of a comb, lighted it for a torch, and went into the palace. He found Izanami's body decomposing and full of worms, and watched over by eight Thunders. He fled in horror. Izanami called after him, 'You have humiliated me!' and set the ugly-girls-of-hell at him. Izanagi defended himself with various magical methods. So the goddess then sent eight Thunder gods and the soldiers of Hell. When he reached the end of the slope to Hell, Izanagi picked three peaches and threw them at the soldiers of Hell, who fled, and then blocked the entrance to Hell with a huge boulder. Izanami had pursued him, and found herself on the other side of the boulder. The two gods swore they would divorce, and so parted. The god Izanagi felt sullied by this contact with the world of the dead, and went off to the island of Tsukiji where he purified himself at the mouth of the little river Tachibana in Hyuga province. He threw away his stick, and from this stick was born the God-set-up-at-cross-roads. Then he took off his clothes and threw them away, each one of them producing a deity. He then dived into the river, and the impurities he had brought back from Hell gave birth to two gods of different ills. To cure these ills Izanagi gave birth to two gods who set the ills right, and to the 'sacred goddess'. Izanagi then dived into the sea, and from this bath are derived all the various sea gods. He washed his left eye, and so gave birth to the great goddess Amaterasu, goddess of the Sun; he then washed his right eye and brought into the world the goddess of the Moon, Tsukiyomi. Then he washed his nose, and gave birth to the god Susanoo. Izanagi ordered his elder daughter Amaterasu to rule the plain of Heaven, giving her his necklace of jewels. To the god of the Moon he entrusted the kingdom of night, and to the god Susanoo the plain of the seas. The goddess of the Sun and the god of the Moon obeyed the order of their father Izanagi, and took possession of Heaven and of the kingdom of night. Susanoo alone did not leave, and stayed where he was, weeping and groaning. Izanagi asked him the reason for these laments, and Susanoo said he wanted to go to the kingdom of his dead mother. The god Izanagi grew angry and drove him away, and Susanoo then said he wanted to say farewell to his elder sister before going down to the world underground.

Scholars who make a study of mythology have found certain

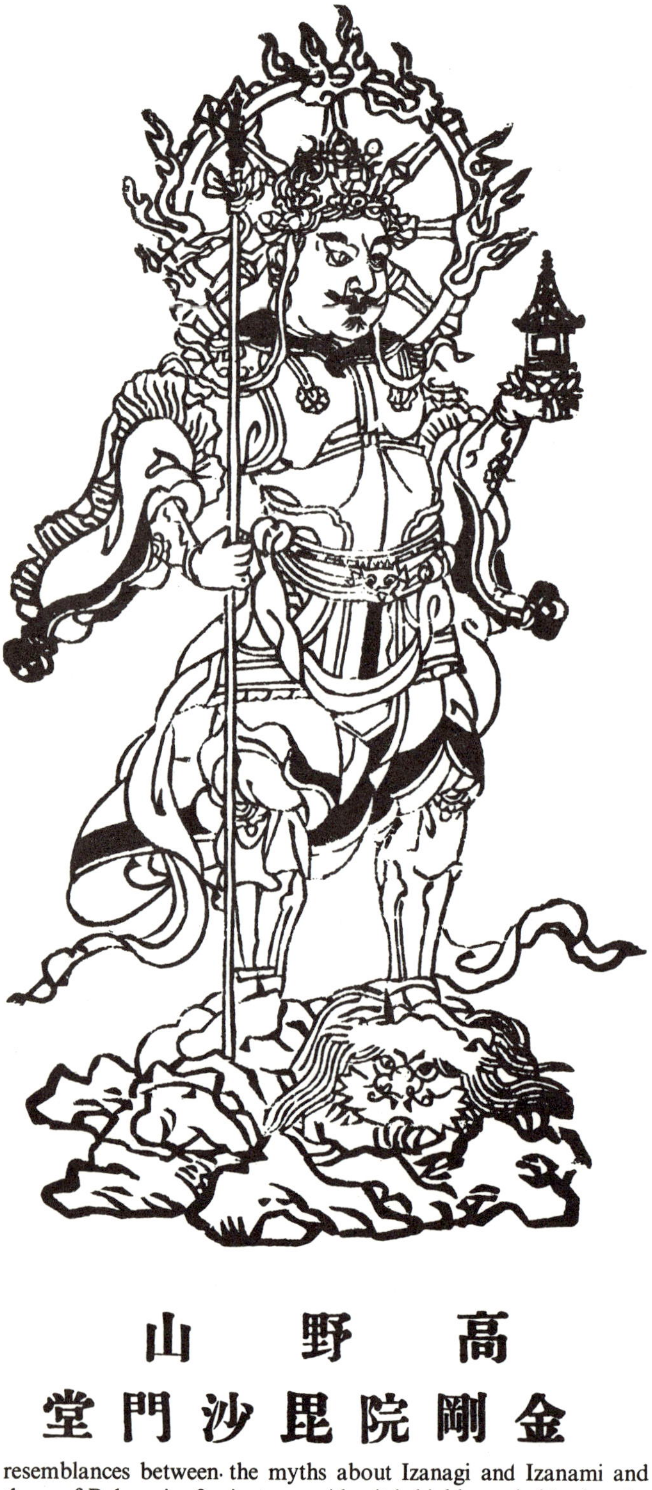

Bishamon trampling on a demon. Originally the heavenly guardian of the North, Bishamon (or Bishamonten) was later invoked as the protector of the law and of human life against illness and demons and as a god of war. As dispenser of wealth he was also included among the seven gods of happiness. He is portrayed as a soldier holding a lance and a reliquary in the shape of a pagoda. Woodcut from the Kongo-in shrine, Mount Koya.

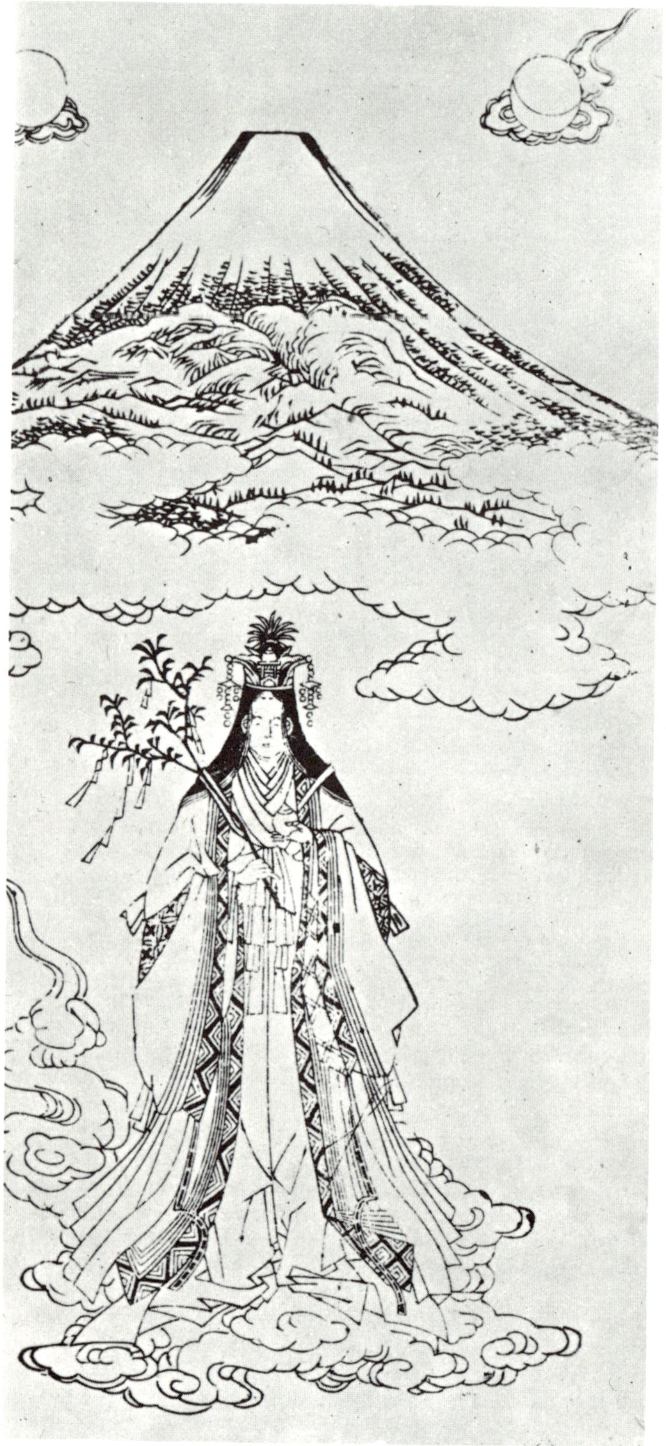

Sengen-Sama, the divinity of Fujiyama.

resemblances between the myths about Izanagi and Izanami and those of Polynesia, for instance. Also it is highly probable that the Chinese legend of Pan-Ku, whose left eye became the sun and his right eye the moon, was grafted on to an ancient tradition by the authors of the *Kojiki* and the *Nihon shoki.* As Mr N. Matsumoto has very rightly pointed out in his *Essai sur la Mythologie Japonaise*, the whole collection of these ancient traditions indicates that Susanoo represents the gods of Izumo province, and Amaterasu those of Yamato. The two tribes of these regions were enemies. The Imperial family, as we shall see later on, had the Sun goddess as an ancestor, and by recording the ancient traditions hoped to establish the supremacy of Yamato, which at the time when these texts were put down was already a historical fact. By a comparison of ancient texts and from the study of folklore, not only of Japan proper but of the Ryukyu islands, we observe that although Amaterasu was the Sun goddess she also has the character of a priestess, which is very understandable seeing that in ancient Japan 'the notions of god and priest were confounded', and consequently the lives of priests and priestesses influenced the building up of the myths. We shall see in myths to follow that Amaterasu, though Sun goddess, wove the gods' clothes, and we know that the Shinto priestesses were employed in weaving garments before the great ceremonies. The myths which tell us of the struggle between Amaterasu and her brother Susanoo probably are a reflection of the rivalry between a brother and his priestess-queen sister. On this rivalry we have the testimony of the Chinese historians who, in the annals of the Wei dynasty (220—264), relate that after the death of the priestess-queen Himeko of the kingdom of Yamato, a younger brother who had helped her was put on the throne, and that this succession led to civil wars. Peace was not restored until the eldest daughter of the dead queen ascended the throne.

Susanoo and Amaterasu. Let us return to the mythological stories of the *Kojiki* and *Nihon shoki.* Susanoo went up to Heaven to see his elder sister, but he made such a noise, shaking the mountains and rivers and making the earth quake, that the goddess thought it as well to take precautions in meeting him. So she slung a quiver on her back, and placed before her a bow whose string she vibrated. When she asked him why he had come, he said he had no evil intent, and had come simply to say good-bye to her before going to the distant land where his mother was.

The Sun goddess asked her brother for proofs of his goodwill. Susanoo proposed that each of them should create children—his would be boys and that would prove the sincerity of his intentions. Amaterasu took her brother's sword, broke it in three pieces and, after having chewed them, blew a light mist from her mouth which gave birth to three goddesses. Susanoo asked his sister for the five strings of jewels she was wearing and, after cracking them between his teeth, blew a light mist from his mouth and gave birth to five masculine deities. Amaterasu declared they were her children because they had been created from jewels which belonged to her.

It is interesting to note that in the historic epoch the eight children of Amaterasu and Susanoo were venerated as the eight 'princes' and considered as ancestors. The eldest male was the ancestor of the Emperors, and the others of the great families.

Susanoo was so pleased with his success that he lost all self-control. In the impetuosity of his victory he destroyed the rice-fields prepared by Amaterasu, filled in the irrigation ditches, and deposited excrement in the Temples built for the festival of First-fruits. The Sun goddess made excuses for her brother's misdeeds, but he continued them. One day when the goddess Amaterasu was weaving the gods' clothes in the sacred house Susanoo made a hole in the roof of the house, and threw down a piebald horse which he had already flayed. This terrible and unexpected apparition caused such a disturbance that one of the weaving women pricked herself with the shuttle and fell dead. The goddess Amaterasu was terrified and hid in a rocky cave of Heaven, blocking the entrance with a boulder. The world was plunged into darkness.

Some scholars have interpreted this disappearance of the sun as an allusion to an eclipse, but we are in agreement with Mr N. Matsumoto in his interpretation of the myth as the beginning of winter, since that event takes place after the festival of First-fruits.

Amaterasu's return. The darkness which covered the world greatly aided the wicked gods in their doings, and caused consternation among the good gods. The eight hundred myriads of gods all assembled in the dry bed of a river, to decide on what measures should be taken to bring back the Sun goddess. They approached the god 'Hoard-thoughts', and in accordance with his advice they collected cocks whose crow precedes the dawn. They gave orders for the making of a mirror and strings of jewels, which they hung on the branches of the Sakaki tree *(Cleyera japonica)* which they also decorated with cloth streamers. They uttered the ritual words. The goddess Ama no Uzume decked herself out with different plants, gathered some bamboo leaves, and then mounted a tub turned upside down which was placed outside the entrance to the cave. She then began to dance, drumming with her feet on the sounding tub. Carried away by divine ecstasy she took off all her clothes, and the eight hundred myriads of gods all roared with laughter. The Sun goddess hearing the crowing of the cocks, then the noise of Ama no Uzume dancing, and then the burst of laughter from the gods, was puzzled and asked the reason for all these noises. Ama no Uzume replied that the gods were rejoicing because they now had a better goddess than Amaterasu. Urged by her curiosity the Sun goddess looked out and saw the mirror which they had set up, and, much interested by its reflection, she came a little way out of the cave. The god of Force who had hidden himself close by seized her hand and forced her to come out completely. Then a rope was stretched in front of the cave to prevent Amaterasu from going back into it, and once more the world was lit up by the rays of the Sun goddess. The gods decided to punish Susanoo and forced him to pay a heavy fine. Then they cut off his beard and moustache, tore off the nails from his fingers and toes, and kicked him out of heaven.

We have already stressed the particular character of the Sun goddess's retreat after the festival of First-fruits. The obscene dance of the goddess Ama no Uzume is another sign that these traditions have an agricultural significance, for 'in primitive religion obscenity has always an agricultural significance, looking to the fertility of the fields', and the gods' laughter means that the life which had seemed extinct is about to be re-born. (P. L. Couchoud, *Le mythe de la danseuse obscène*. Mercure de France, 15 August 1929.)

Susanoo's exploits. When the god Susanoo was driven out of heaven, he came down to Izumo province. We have already said that the myths connected with this god come from that region. It must be also noted that Susanoo was not an essentially evil god. His character was such that it displayed itself in wicked deeds when he was controlled by his wicked soul, Ara-mi-tama, and in good deeds when his peaceful soul, Nigi-mi-tama, was in the ascendant. He was a fertility god, closely linked with agricultural beliefs. At one and the same time he is a god of Thunder, Storm and Rain. For this reason he is associated with snakes, for in ancient Japan the snake was considered as the god of Thunder. Mr N. Matsumoto points out that the main descendants of the god Susanoo are related either to water, thunder or the snake. The following pages from the *Nihon shoki* and the *Kojiki* relate myths about the god Susanoo.

When he came down to Izumo he met an old man and an old woman who were crying beside a girl. Susanoo asked the reason for these tears. The old man told him that he had had eight daughters and that every year a snake with eight heads from the Koshi district had come and devoured one of his daughters. Seven already had been eaten, and now the snake was coming to devour the last. Susanoo told them he was the brother of Amaterasu, and asked them to give him the girl. The old parents gladly agreed. Susanoo changed the girl into a comb which he stuck in his hair. Then he had eight bowls prepared and filled them with rice wine. When the terrible snake appeared it was attracted by the scent of the wine, and each head made for one of the bowls. The snake got drunk and went to sleep. Susanoo drew his sword, and cut the monster to pieces. In the middle of the snake's tail he found a wonderful sword which he presented to his sister the Sun goddess. In later stories this sword is given the name Kusanagi, and was transmitted to our own times as one of the three emblems of Imperial power. It is kept in the Temple of Atsuta, near the town of Nagoya.

Once he had got rid of the Snake, Susanoo built himself a palace at Suga, and lived there with his new wife. From this union was born the god O-Kuni-Nushi, who afterwards became Lord of Izumo.

Adventure of O-Kuni-Nushi. According to ancient traditions, O-Kuni-Nushi was a god of medicine connected with sorcery. The invention of therapeutic methods was attributed to him. The legend of the white hare of Inaba tells us that a skinned hare appealed to the eighty gods, brothers of O-Kuni-Nushi, and they advised it to bathe in the sea and then dry itself in the wind. The poor animal suffered dreadfully. It then met O-Kuni-Nushi, who felt sorry for its sufferings, and told it to wash in fresh water and then to roll in the pollen of sedges spread on the ground. The hare was completely cured, and when returning thanks declared that the princess Yakami would go to O-Kuni-Nushi, and not to his brothers. O-Kuni-Nushi's brothers were very angry at this, and by various subterfuges they managed to kill him, but he was resurrected through the intercession of his mother with the goddess Kami-Musubi. O-Kuni-Nushi once more became a strong young man. To save him from the rage of his brothers, his mother sent him to the underworld, to the god Susanoo. There he met Suseri-Hime, the god's daughter. She fell in love with him, and they were united. Susanoo received him, but put him to sleep in a room full of snakes. O-Kuni-Nushi was saved by a scarf which had been given him by Suseri-Hime. The next night he was sent to sleep in a room full of centipedes and wasps, but Suseri-Hime had given another scarf which protected him from the centipedes and wasps, and O-Kuni-Nushi came through that test unscathed. Then Susanoo shot a hissing arrow into the middle of a vast meadow and sent

Inari, the Rice God, with two foxes.
Musée Guimet, Paris.

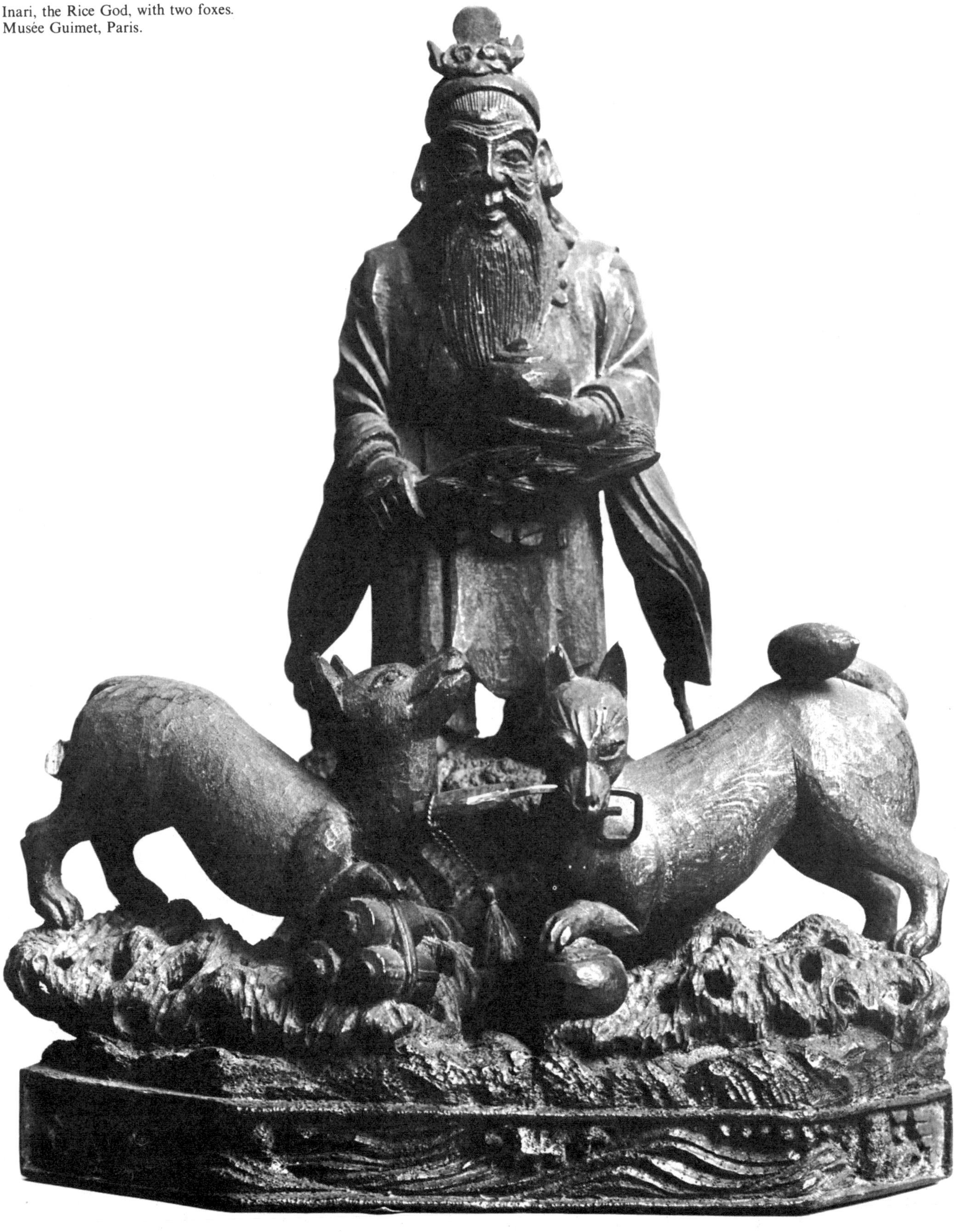

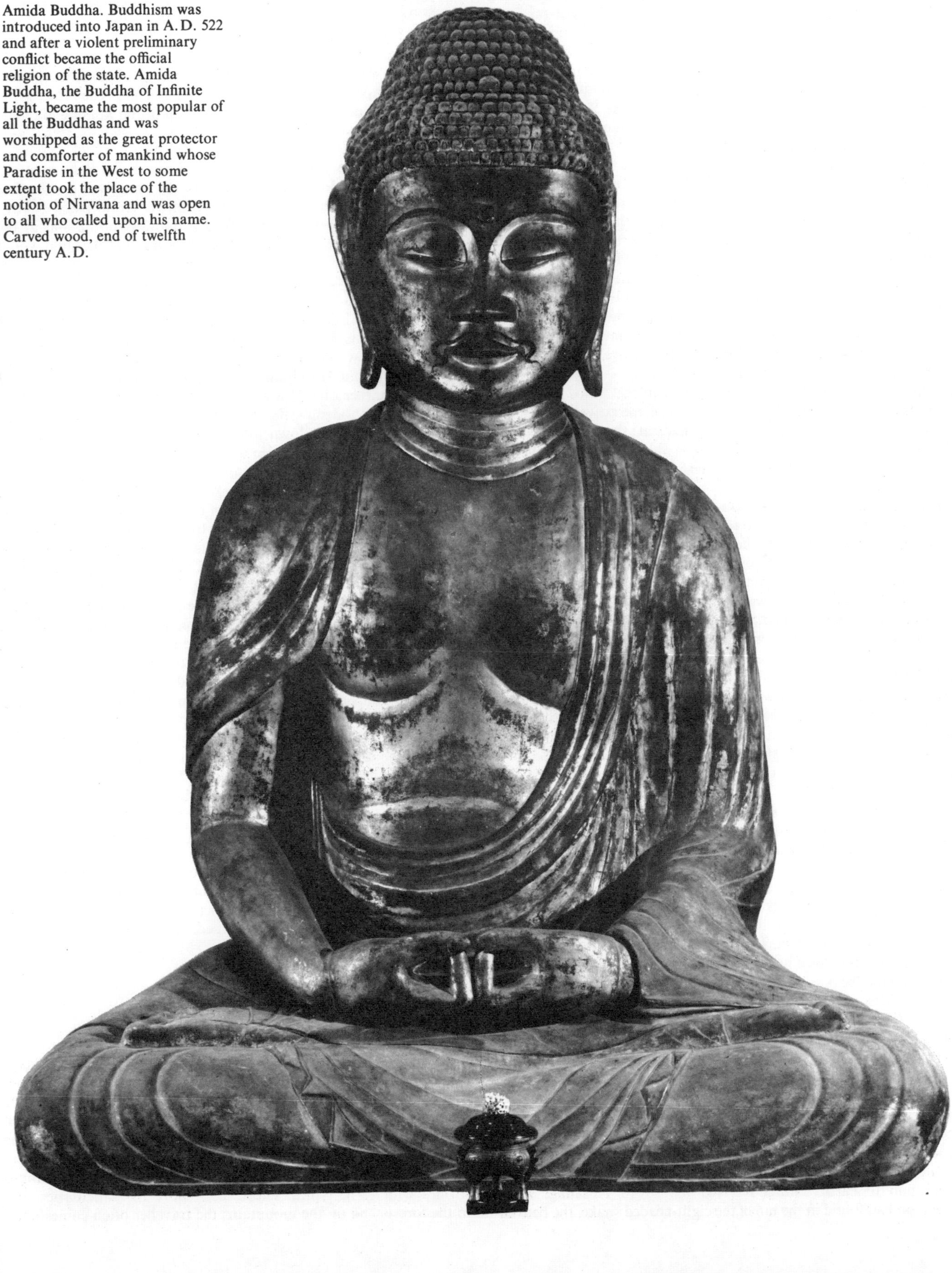

Amida Buddha. Buddhism was introduced into Japan in A.D. 522 and after a violent preliminary conflict became the official religion of the state. Amida Buddha, the Buddha of Infinite Light, became the most popular of all the Buddhas and was worshipped as the great protector and comforter of mankind whose Paradise in the West to some extent took the place of the notion of Nirvana and was open to all who called upon his name. Carved wood, end of twelfth century A.D.

O-Kuni-Nushi to look for it. When O-Kuni-Nushi was in the middle of the meadow Susanoo set fire to the grass, but O-Kuni-Nushi was saved by a mouse which showed him an underground room in which to shelter, and brought him the arrow. The god Susanoo then felt some confidence in him and, after asking-O-Kuni-Nushi to wash his hair, went to sleep. O-Kuni-Nushi took advantage of Susanoo's sleep to tie the god's hair to the rafters of the house, then put his wife Suseri-Hime on his back and fled, taking also the great god's sword, bow, arrows, and his harp, Koto. But the Koto brushed against a tree and awoke Susanoo, who started up and so pulled down the house. While Susanoo was freeing his hair O-Kuni-Nushi made good use of the time and had got far away when the god started in pursuit. On the slope of Hell Susanoo saw the abductor of his daughter in the distance, and advised him to fight his brothers with the sword and bow and shafts he had taken. In this way, he asserted, O-Kuni-Nushi would conquer them and reign over the world. He then asked him to make Suseri-Hime his chief wife, and to build his palace at the foot of mount Uka.

The myths about O-Kuni-Nushi then speak of a god who arrived in a drifting boat. This was Sukuna-Bikona, the son of the goddess Kami-Musubi, who was well received by O-Kuni-Nushi, and together they fortified the region. One day the god Sukuna-Bikona went to cape Kumanu, and disappeared in the direction of the region of Tokyo. O-Kuni-Nushi was in consternation when he found he was alone, and said to himself: 'Now I am quite alone to keep order in this land. Is there nobody to help me?' At that moment the sea was lit up with a divine light, and a god said: 'How could you rule this country if I were not at your side?' O-Kuni-Nushi asked the god who he was. 'I am your protecting deity, and I wish to be worshipped on mount Mimoro, where I live.' O-Kuni-Nushi worshipped this god, whose name is Omiwa.

The first part of official history related in the *Nihon shoki* ends with these legends of O-Kuni-Nushi. The narrative then comes back to the Sun goddess and her grandson, the ancestor of the Emperors of Japan. The events told in this second part all took place on earth or in the kingdom of the Sea god.

Amaterasu and Ninigi. Amaterasu decided to send her son Ame-no-Oshido-Mimi down to earth to reign over it as sovereign. But before leaving, the god looked at the earth from the floating bridge of Heaven, saw it was full of disturbances, and refused to go. The eight hundred myriads of gods were then ordered to meet, and the god-who-hoards-thoughts was told to work out a plan. After consultation the gods decided to send down the god Ame-no-Hohi to find out what was happening in the 'middle country of the land of reeds'. Three years passed without any news from him, so the gods sent down his son, with the same result. At last they chose Ame-no-Wakahiko, renowned for his courage, and gave him a divine bow and divine arrows. When he got down to earth the young god married O-Kuni-Nushi's daughter, Shitateru-Hime, and began to reign over the land. Eight years passed without any news of him reaching the gods. So the gods sent down to earth a pheasant to ask Ame-no-Wakahiko what he had been doing all this time. The pheasant settled on a tree opposite the door of the god's house, and one of the women said it was a bird of evil omen. So Ame-no-Wakahiko shot a divine arrow which pierced the bird, made a hole in heaven, and fell at the feet of Amaterasu and Taka-Mi-Musubi. Seeing the blood-stained arrow and recognising it as one he had given to Ame-no-Wakahiko, the god cursed it and flung it back. The arrow, hurled across the heavens, struck Ame-no-Wakahiko in the heart and killed him. The widow lamented and wept so bitterly that the gods of heaven heard her, and Ame-no-Wakahiko's parents came down to be present at his funeral. Ame-no-Wakahiko's funeral rites are described in great detail and are of much interest since this is the oldest document we possess about Shinto rites. The gods then sent to Izumo two gods who informed O-Kuni-Nushi that the Sun goddess had sent them to subjugate the land. O-Kuni-Nushi consulted his two sons. The elder accepted Amaterasu's suzerainty. The younger tried to resist, but was conquered by the power of the heavenly envoys and fled, promising however that he would not undertake anything against the Sun goddess. The gods returned to heaven to announce Izumo's submission. Meanwhile Amaterasu had a grandson, the god Ninigi, and decided to send him to earth. Ninigi received the sword Kusanagi which Susanoo had found in the tail of the eight-headed snake, the heavenly jewels, and the mirror which had caused Amaterasu to leave the cave, and as companions several deities, among them the goddess Ama-no-Uzume. When giving Ninigi the mirror, his grandmother Amaterasu said: 'Adore this mirror as our souls, adore it as you adore us.' The jewels, the sword Kusanagi and the mirror became the three emblems of the Imperial power.

The god Ninigi and his suite descended on mount Takachiho in the province of Hyuga, and built a palace on cape Kasasa. Japanese and Western scholars have had much discussion about this passage in the Japanese texts. Why should the grandson of the Sun goddess arrive at the island of Kyushu instead of at Izumo? Mr N. Matsumoto (*op. cit.* p. 104) quotes the opinion of a Japanese scholar, Professor K. Shiratori, who thinks the choice of the place may be explained by 'the political object of the compilers of these myths, who wanted to bring the hostile tribes of the island of Kyushu under the Imperial power'. That is perfectly comprehensible, given the state of mind in which the compilation of the *Kojiki* and *Nihon shoki* was undertaken.

Ninigi's sons. The god Ninigi married Kono-Hana-Sakuya-Hime, daughter of the Mountain god, but as she conceived on the first night he doubted her fidelity. The princess Kono-Hana-Sakuya was angry at this attitude. She built a doorless house and at the moment of birth set fire to the house, swearing that the child would perish if it were not Ninigi's. She brought forth three sons: Hoderi, Hosuseri and Hikohohodemi. Afterwards the texts speak of only two brothers. Hosuseri specialised in fishing, while Hikohohodemi became a clever hunter. One day the brothers tried to change over their occupations, but perceived that the results were bad. Hosuseri returned the bow and arrows to his younger brother, and asked for his fish-hook, but Hikohohodemi had lost the real fish-hook and gave him another one. Hosuseri refused to take it, as well as other hooks Hikohohodemi offered him. Hikohohodemi was grieved at the loss, and went down into the depths of the Ocean to visit the palace of the Sea god. He attracted the attention of the god's daughter, who presented him, and became his wife. He told his story to the Sea god, and the hook was found in the mouth of a red fish. Although life in the palace of the Sea god was very pleasant, Hikohohodemi persisted in wishing to return home. The sea god gave him two jewels, one which makes the tide rise, and another which makes it fall. His wife promised to rejoin him after a certain time. When Hikohohodemi got back he returned the fishhook to his brother, but as he continued to be a nuisance Hikohohodemi made use of the jewel which brings the high tide. The elder brother, finding himself covered with the sea, begged his pardon and promised to serve him. Hikohohodemi then threw into the sea the jewel which causes the low tide, and set his elder brother free.

The Sea god's daughter kept her word and rejoined Hikohohodemi. She told him she was about to have a child, but added that he must not be present at the birth nor try to watch her. Urged by curiosity Hikohohodemi looked between the walls of the hut, and saw his wife take the form of a dragon. She left the child with her husband and returned to her father the Sea god, but sent her sister to look after the child. This sister became the child's wife, and one of their sons, who received the names of Toyo-Mike-Nu and Kamu-Yamato-Iware-Hiko, is famous in history under his posthumous name of Jimmu-Tenno—he was the founder of the Imperial line of Japan. From this time the history of Japan officially began, but for a long time it was sown with ancient legends—the rivalry between Yamato and Izumo continued, and the wives of several Emperors were princesses of Izumo.

THE GODS

Ancient Japanese texts often speak of 'the eight hundred myriads of gods', a scarcely exaggerated number when you remember that every region, every town, every village and the most humble inhabitant possessed a local Kami and his attendants. In addition, as we have seen, every object whose shape or size differed from the normal—such as rocks, old trees etc.—was venerated as a Kami. Even in modern Japan we see not only the great Temples and Shinto shrines with torii, typical entrances, before the sanctuaries, but in the forests and on the mountains the traveller often comes upon small sanctuaries, hokora, dedicated to a local Kami or to a large rock or a very old tree.

The Sun goddess, Amaterasu. With so many deities, the established mythology is dominated by the Sun goddess, Amaterasu, who is worshipped not only as a heavenly body but as a spiritual divinity and the ancestor of the Imperial family. The Japanese people also venerate the sun which brings warmth and the harvest; and salute it in the morning by clapping hands. Amaterasu's chief shrine is at Ise. At first the goddess was worshipped in the Imperial palace itself. But, with the evolution of the Imperial power this proximity threatened difficulties, for the influence of the priestesses exercised through oracles deprived the Emperor of complete liberty. The Emperor Sujin (97—30 B.C.) decided to build a special sanctuary for the solar emblems, and appointed his own daughter to their worship. A little later the Emperor Suinin (29 B.C. to A.D. 70) handed over the cult of the goddess to his daughter Yamato-Hime. Looking for a suitable site she came to Ise province, and there, in accordance with an oracle of Amaterasu she built the sanctuary. Since that remote date the Shrine of Amaterasu has always been at Ise, where it is periodically restored but always by exactly copying the ancient shrine; and thanks to this, the style of the ancient architecture has remained until our own times.

This shrine houses the sacred mirror which is the Shintai of the deity, that is to say the object into which the goddess's spirit enters to be present at the ceremonies and to listen to the prayers addressed to her. It is the octagonal mirror which was made to bring Amaterasu out of the cave in which she was hiding. In the grounds attached to the Shrine at Ise are a large number of cocks which are considered as birds sacred to the sun because they salute the dawn. In ancient times a crow with several feet, Yata-Garasu, was also venerated as the messenger of Amaterasu. Very probably this belief was of foreign origin. The kite and the heavenly arrows are also considered to be emblems of the sun by the Shintoists.

Takami-Musubi. Although the Sun goddess occupied the first place in the official mythology she was not considered as an omnipotent deity. Thus, when Amaterasu called an assembly of the gods to appoint messengers to Izumo, the god Takami-Musubi was named with her; and legend also mentions him as being beside the goddess when Ninigi was sent down to earth. The Sun goddess does not act on her own will and pleasure, but asks advice of the other deities. She reigns over the high heavenly plain, but has to obtain her information about the earth from intermediaries. The seas and the world underground are not subject to her. We have already seen that the legends about the Sun contain traces of the lives of Shinto priestesses and their occupations. Amaterasu herself officiated in heaven, and carried out the ceremony of the new harvest, while she also wove divine garments. Up till our own times, in April and September, the festivals of divine garments were celebrated in the great Ise Shrine. Before dawn the pilgrims make their way to the sea-shore of Futami at Ise where two rocks, one large and one small, stand out of the sea, and are called 'the Wedded Rocks', Myoto-Ga-Seki. There is a place on this beach where the sun may be seen rising between these two rocks. The pilgrims adore the rising Sun by clapping their hands and piously saluting.

Wakahiru-Me. Amaterasu is far from being the only deity. The ancient texts mention others. Wakahiru-Me, Amaterasu's younger sister, according to the *Nihon shoki,* was weaving divine garments with her when Susanoo threw down the flayed horse into the room where they were sitting, and thus she is probably also a solar deity. Motoori Norinaga (1730—1801), the learned commentator of the *Kojiki,* interprets the name Waka, young, hiru, sun, and me, a woman, as meaning that this young sister of Amaterasu was a personification of the rising or morning sun.

Hiruko. According to a variant reading quoted in the *Nihon shoki,* the god Hiruko was born after the sun and moon, and his name is interpreted as 'the childleech'. Professor Florenz (*op. cit.* p. 286) considers this etymological explanation defective, and thinks that Hiruko was most probably a male solar deity thrown into the background by the cult of Amaterasu, the protecting divinity of the conquering Yamato tribe. In other texts we come upon a god whose name may be abridged to Nigihaya-hi, meaning 'swift-and-gentle-sun', that is the early morning sun. By a comparison of the texts we can determine that this solar god was the brother of Ninigi, the grandson of Amaterasu.

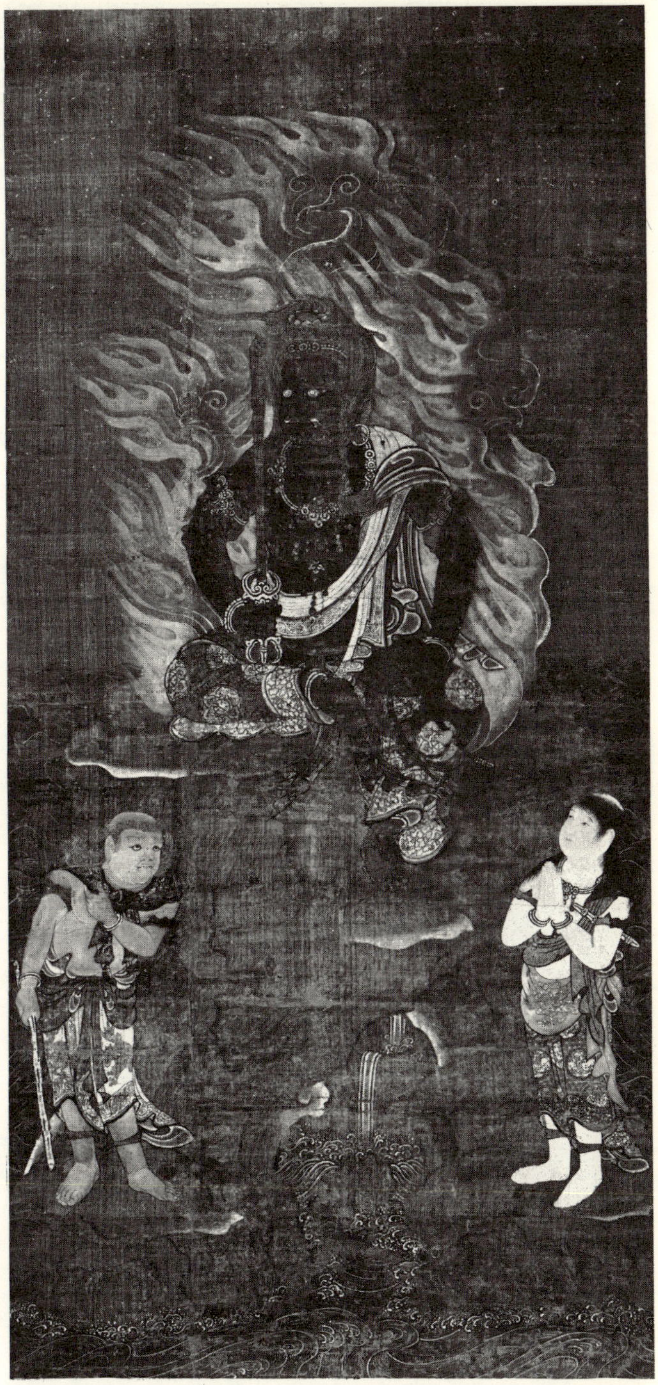

Fudo-Myoo attended by two doji. The most important of the five great Myoos, or terrible manifestations of the five great Buddhas whose wishes they carry out, Fudo-Myoo corresponds to the supreme Buddha, Dainichi Nyorai He is portrayed seated on a rock surrounded by a halo of flames, holding his sword in his right hand and the rope with which he binds those who oppose the Buddha in his left. Painting on silk, fourteenth century A.D.

The numerous compilations of the ancient texts were an attempt to build up a mythological whole from the ancient traditions and names of gods which had been preserved; and in so doing have greatly confused the origins of Japanese beliefs. Professor G. Kato, in his book on Shinto (*Annales du Musee Guimet*, vol. L, p. 135, 1931), quotes a typical case where four divinities have been arbitrarily amalgamated into one. It must also be remembered that the compilers of the *Nihon shoki* and *Kojiki* in building up an orthodoxy coolly dethroned or debased many divinities and tended to simplify greatly the original complicated structure according to their own personal beliefs and preferences.

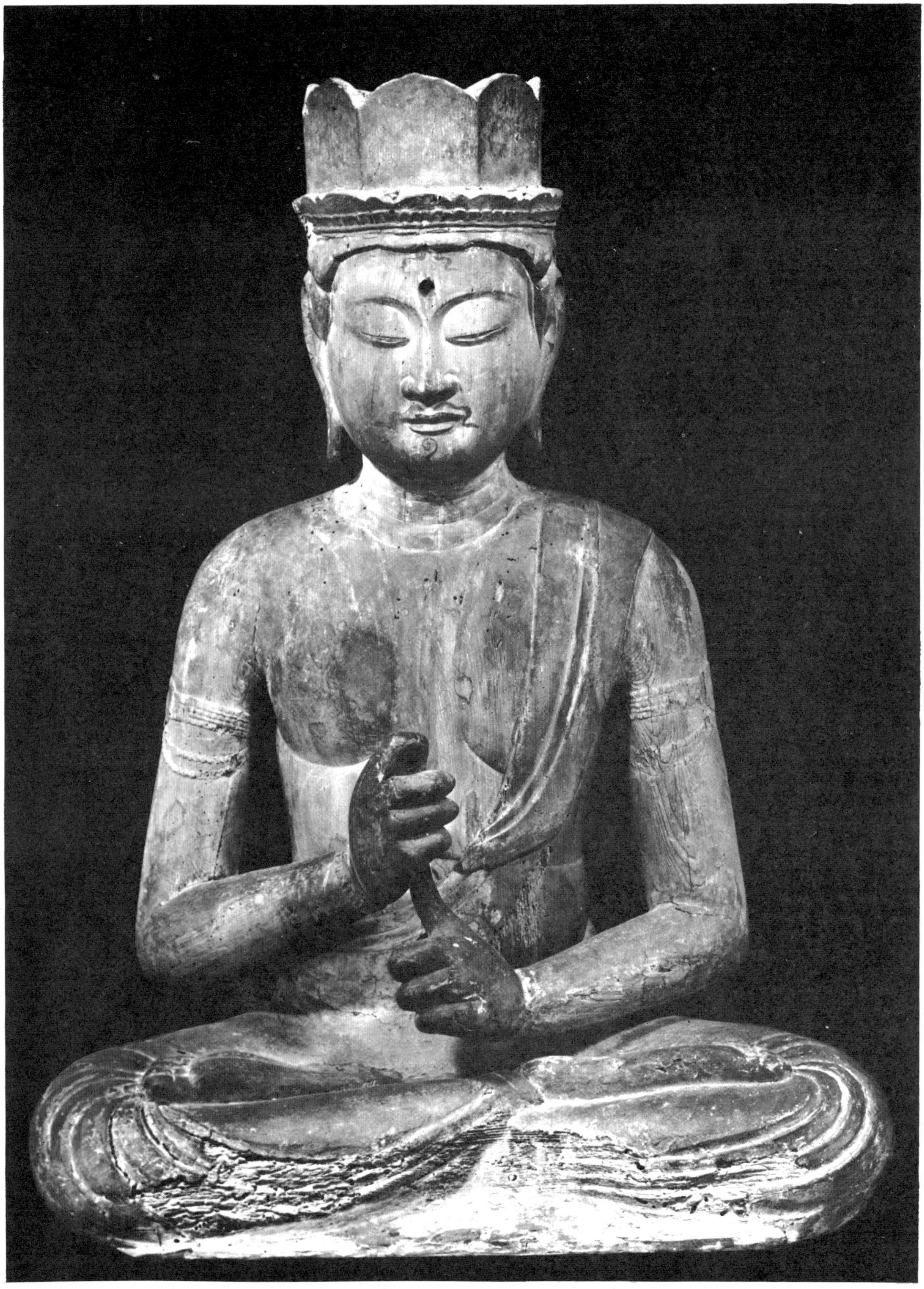

Dainichi Nyorai. The Buddha Maha-Vairocana was introduced into Japan at the beginning of the ninth century together with a large number of other Buddhist divinities and, under the name of Dainichi Nyorai, became the supreme deity of the esoteric Tendai, Shingon and Kegon sects. This early statue portrays the 'Great Illuminator' bejewelled and seated, making the gesture known as the 'fist of recognition' and wearing a diadem after the fashion of a bodhisattva. Wood, ninth century A.D.

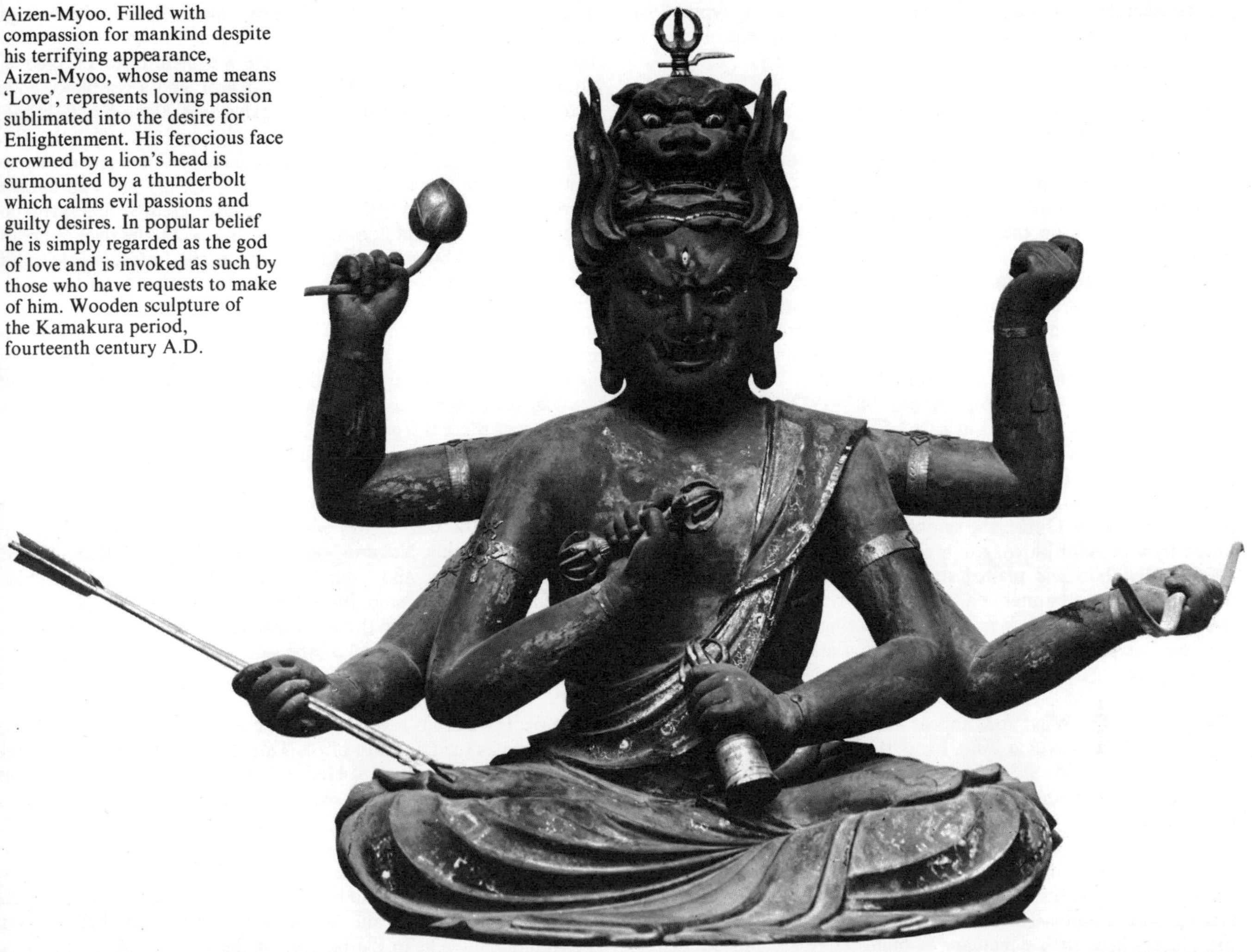

Aizen-Myoo. Filled with compassion for mankind despite his terrifying appearance, Aizen-Myoo, whose name means 'Love', represents loving passion sublimated into the desire for Enlightenment. His ferocious face crowned by a lion's head is surmounted by a thunderbolt which calms evil passions and guilty desires. In popular belief he is simply regarded as the god of love and is invoked as such by those who have requests to make of him. Wooden sculpture of the Kamakura period, fourteenth century A.D.

Tsuki-Yomi, god of the Moon. The cult of the moon has been greatly modified in the course of ages. The ancient texts inform us that Izanagi gave birth to the moon by washing his right eye. His Japanese name, Tsuki, moon, and Yomi, counter, that is to say, 'counter-of-the-months,' links him with the primitive calendar (N. Matsumoto, *op. cit.* p. 16, note 1). In Japan the lunar divinity is masculine, and in the ancient poems of the Manyoshu anthology his name is followed by the word Otoko, man, to stress his masculine character. This god has a shrine at Ise as well as at Kadono, and in both these sanctuaries is a mirror in which the god may manifest himself. It is curious to note that the Chinese picture of the hare in the moon preparing the drug of immortality has passed into the iconography of modern Japanese with certain modifications. The Japanese represent the white disk of the moon with a rabbit or a hare pounding rice in a mortar. This symbol is based on a pun. In Japanese, Mochi-zuki means to pound rice for cakes, and Mochi-zuki also means the full moon. Although the ideograms with which the two words are written are entirely different, the identity of the consonants was enough to produce the image.

The stars. As to the stars Mr G. Kato says: 'They never had a prominent place in early Shinto beliefs, although they included the god of evil, Amatsu-Mikaboshi, "the-august-star-of-heaven", in other terms Ama-no-Kagaseo, "the-brilliant-male".' Later on, due to the influence of Chinese and Buddhist beliefs, the Japanese god of stars was identified with the Pole Star, Myo-ken (in Sanskrit, Sudarsana), and finally with Ama-no-Minakanushi-no-kami, the-Divine-Lord-of-the-middle-heavens, the supreme heavenly deity (G. Kato, *op. cit.* p. 23—24). The legend of the annual meeting of the star of the Cowherd and the star of the Spinning Maiden over the Milky Way was brought to Japan during the reign of the Empress Koken (749—759) and utilised to found the festival of Tanabata, celebrated on the seventh evening of the seventh moon—whence the name Tanabata, which means seventh evening. (M.G. Cesselin, les 'Sekku' ou quèlques fêtes populaires, IV. *Tanabata no Sekku,* p. 194, No 10, April 1906. *Mélanges japonais,* Tokyo.)

Storm and thunder deities. It is curious to note that in later belief the god Susanoo was linked with the lunar cult, whereas in the myths generally he is rather the Storm or Thunder god and seems closely associated with agricultural rites. Mr N. Matsumoto (*op. cit.* p. 37 and following) has devoted to him a most interesting study, where he points out that the relationship between the ceremonies of expulsion and purification led, in the Middle Ages, to the god Susanoo being considered as the god of plague, and confused with a god of foreign origin, Gozu-Tenno, the Ox-headed-heavenly-King. The ancient texts also speak of the Thunder deities at the death of Izanami, whose body was guarded by eight Thunders who afterwards went in pursuit of Izanagi. But these thunders do not so much represent heavenly thunder, as the underground thunders which are so common in a volcanic country like Japan. The god Take-Mika-zuchi, who was sent by the other gods to subjugate Izumo province, is also considered a god of Thunder, who pursued the son of O-Kuni-Nushi to lake Suwa and conquered him. Aji-suki-takahikone, another son of the same god, is also a Thunder god. At his birth he cried and screamed, and they calmed him by carrying him to the top and then to the bottom of a ladder. 'In the Japanese mind the ladder is used to get to heaven, so this episode seems to allude to one of the characteristics of the Thunder, which is to come and go between heaven and earth. He was also placed in a boat which sailed between the eighty islands. The boat was the means by which the Thunder god connected heaven and earth (N. Matsumoto, *op. cit.* p. 57—58). Kami-Nari, the god of Rolling-Thunder, is greatly venerated, and many sanctuaries are devoted to him. Trees split by lightning, Kantoki no ki, are considered as sacred, and it is forbidden to cut them down. In the Annals of Japan for the year 618 of our era may be read the story of the official, Kawabe-no-Omi, who was ordered by the Emperor to cut down trees for the construction of ships. Among the trees was one which had been hit by lightning. The official made offerings to it and then gave orders for it to be cut down, but scarcely had the wood-cutters approached the tree when a terrible storm, with rain and thunder, broke over the forest. A sword plays the part of Shintai in the shrines which are consecrated to Kami-Nari, and is probably a symbol of lightning. The most venerated of the sanctuaries of Kami-Nari is situated at Kashima.

Rain gods. Rain also had its special gods, such as the god Taka-Okami who lives on mountains, and Kura-Okami who dwells in valleys and can cause snow as well as rain. Fujiwara-no-Kisaki, a concubine of the Emperor Temmu, says in effect in her poems that she has offered prayers to the god Kura-Okami so that he will send down snow-flakes on the Imperial palace *(Manyoshu,* volume II, poem 19).

In the description of Izumo province, it is stated that to the west of mount Kaminabi the wife of the god Aji-Suki-Taka-Hikone gave birth to the god Taki-Tsu-Hiko (Prince-cataract), and advised him to build a temple there. The god is a rock, and if prayers are said to it during a drought it sends rain.

The ceremonial of the Engi period (901—922) enumerates the ninety-five shrines to which in case of drought the Emperor sent messengers to ask the gods for rain.

But Japanese farmers have forgotten the old gods, and when there is a drought they get up a procession preceded by a Shintoist priest carrying the Gohei, the symbol of divinity. The priest is followed by a peasant blowing in a conch, and then comes a dragon made of bamboo and plaited straw. The procession is closed by peasants carrying banners on which are written prayers to bring rain. The peasants follow in a crowd, beating drums and making a noise. The procession makes its way to a lake or a river, where the image of the dragon is dipped in the water.

Gods of wind. The Wind gods appear at the beginning of the mythological narrative of *Nihon shoki.* From the breath of the god Izanagi came the Wind god, Shina-Tsu-Hiko, and to blow away the mist which covered the land the same god created the goddess, Shina-to-Be. This god and goddess are also mentioned in an incantation, Norito, in which it is said that the Wind god fills the void between heaven and earth, and bears up the earth. Besides these two chief deities, there is another couple of Wind gods—the god Tatsuta-Hiko and the goddess Tatsuta-Hime. They are named from Tatsuta, the place where their sanctuary is built. They are prayed to for good harvests. Fishermen and sailors were among their fervent worshippers, and wore their amulets to protect themselves against storms.

In one of the variants of the *Nihon shoki* it is said that the body of Ame-no-Wakahiko was brought down to earth from the plain of heaven by the Whirlwind god, who is named Haya-ji or Haya-Tsu-muji-no-Kami. Ryobu-Shinto (that is to say, the Japanese form of Buddhism which considered that all the gods of the Japanese pantheon were merely local manifestations of Buddhist divinities) has pictorially represented the Wind god in a terrible shape, carrying on his back a great bag from which he released the wind. The Thunder god was depicted among drums.

Earthquake gods. Among the scourges of Nature, earthquakes could not fail to impress the Japanese, but we find no mention of an Earthquake god. Not until the year 599 of our era, after an earthquake which no doubt was particularly violent, was there instituted a cult of the Earthquake god, Nai-no-Kami; and rather more than a century later several sanctuaries were dedicated to this formidable deity.

Mountain gods. In a volcanic country like Japan it was natural that the mountains should become gods. The extinct volcano Fujiyama is the most revered, and the sanctuary of the goddess Sengen-Sama is built on its peak. During the summer numbers of pilgrims climb the sacred mountain to worship the rising sun. At one time women were forbidden to go to the top, because they were then considered impure, but this restriction no longer exists. In addition to mount Fuji there are many other sacred mountains with shrines dedicated to different gods. In Shinano province there are Ontake-San and mount Nantai near lake Chuzenji; and in southern Japan, in Higo province, there is mount Aso, etc. In Japanese mythology we find the name of a deity O-Yama-Tsu-Mi, chief god and lord of mountains. He was born when Izanagi cut the Fire god into five pieces. The second god was Naka-Yama-Tsu-Mi, that is, the god of mountain slopes. The third was Ha-Yama-Tsu-Mi, the god of the lower mountain slopes; the fourth, Masaka-Yama-Tsu-Mi, the god of the steep slope; and the fifth Shigi-Yama-Tsu-Mi, the god of the mountain foot. In the *Kojiki* there are mentioned the god of mountain slopes, Saka-no-Mi-Wo-no-Kami, and a couple of gods of mountain minerals, Kana-Yama-Hiko and Kana-Yama-Hime

River gods. Rivers also had their gods called by the generic name Kawa-no-Kami (Kawa, river; Kami, god; no, of) and well-known rivers each had in addition their own god, greatly venerated on account of the frequent floods. In the year A.D. 22, the river Yamato was in flood and burst its banks; in a dream the Emperor saw a god who told him that the River god demanded a sacrifice of two men. A man was sacrificed and the banks repaired, while the second victim escaped by a subterfuge. The considerable number of persons drowned in Japanese rivers gave birth to the dwarf Kappa, who by his magic power draws people down into the water. The only way to avoid his clutch is to bow low to him, then he bows and pours all the water there is from a hole in his skull. Deprived of this water the Kappa can do no harm. There is also a god of river-mouths, called Minato-no-Kami.

Springs and wells also have their gods. The god of wells is named Mii-no-Kami, he who causes water to flow from the earth. In the *Kojiki* we read that Yakami, one of the wives of O-Kuni-Nushi, gave birth to a son, and from fear of the chief wife hid the child in the fork of a tree, whence his other name: Ki-no-Mata-No-Kami. When a new well is begun there is a special ceremony of purification, and when the well is finished a little salt is thrown in as purification offering.

Sea gods. The sea has several gods. The greatest is O-Wata-Tsu-Mi, also known as the Old Man of the Tide, Shio-Zuchi. When Izanagi washed off the impurities of Hell in the waters of the sea, he made several gods—the god of the sea bottom, god of the middle waters, and god of the surface. In the Engi epoch (901—922) the ceremonial mentions a shrine of the Sea god in Harima province, and the shrine of another Sea god in Chikuzen province. Fish and all sea creatures are ruled by the Sea god, and his messenger is the sea-monster which the ancient texts call Wani. We have already noted that the god Hikohohodemi went to the bottom of the sea to look for his brother's fish-hook, and lived in the palace of the Sea god who gave him the two jewels of the tides. At the time of the spread of Ryobu-Shinto, the Sea god had a sanctuary at Sumiyoshi, but became amalgamated with the Hindu god Varuna and thus developed into the very popular god, Suitengu, a great protector of sailors, with sanctuaries in almost all the big towns. On top of this mingling of personalities was engrafted the child Emperor, Antoku, who with his nurse died at sea during the battle of Dan-No-Ura. Thus grew up the belief that the god Suitengu, being a child himself, protects and comforts sick children.

The Fire god. The Fire god caused his mother's death when coming into the world and was killed by his father—on this occasion the god was called Kagu-Zuchi. In incantations he is always evoked under his other name of Ho-Masubi, the causer of fire, and in Ryobu-Shinto he becomes the god of mount Atago near Kyoto. He is supposed to be a protection against fire, so he is visited by many pilgrims who bring back amulets bearing the figure of a wild boar. The Fire god was greatly feared by the Japanese, for during the season of high winds their wooden houses were easily destroyed by fires. Twice a year the priests carried out at the Imperial palace a ritual intended to placate fire, and also to drive away all risk of burning from the Sovereign's dwelling. During this complicated ceremony some of the priests lighted fires by different methods in the four corners of the palace. Others read an incantation which related the myth of the god's birth, and enumerated the four ways to control him—with the help of the water-goddess, the gourd, river weed, and the clay-goddess, in accordance with the instructions given by Izanami. After that the priests read a list of the offerings which must be given to the Fire god to persuade him to spare His Majesty's palace.

The ritual customs of the shines demanded a pure fire which the priests made either by the friction of pieces of Hinoki wood (this is the Kiri-Bi fire) or by striking a hard stone with steel, which gives Uchi-bi fire. The priests of Shinto use it in their houses, and the Emperor's food is prepared over it. On New Year's Day at

Kyoto the faithful make their way to the Temple of Gion, and there receive from the priest's hands the pure fire, which they take home carefully to light the fire of their own hearths, and thus receive protection throughout the year. The matron overseers strike pure fire above the heads of geishas and courtesans to give them magical protection when they go out to clients.

Gods of the Road. The ancient texts mention several Road gods. Chimata-No-Kami is the god of crossroads and is mentioned in one of the norito. We must also note the god of innumerable roads, Yachimata-hiko, with whom goes a goddess of innumerable roads, Yachimato-hime; the god-of-the-place-not-to-be-visited, Kunado; and also the-god-of-the-place-not-to-be-violated, Funado. These gods are named also Sae-no-Kami, gods-who-ward-off (misfortunes), or the-ancestors-of-roads, Dosojin. They protect mankind against the wicked gods of Hell. It is to be noted that they have no sanctuaries, but twice a year ceremonies were celebrated in their honour at the entrance to a town or at a cross-roads, offerings were made them, and the ritual texts were read. To protect themselves against misfortunes and diseases which might be brought them by foreigners, the ancient Japanese celebrated ceremonies to the honour of the Sae-no-Kami two days before the arrival of an embassy. These protector gods are phallic gods, and their Shintai is a stick. When they are represented in human form, in stone or wood, their sex is always clearly indicated. Some Japanese scholars think the Road gods and the phallic gods were originally distinct, and only later were blended. However that may be, these gods were very popular in ancient Shinto, and as lords of procreation they were considered to be powerful protectors. In the Kogoshui we read that a phallus was set up in the middle of a field to protect the rice from locusts. In ancient times large stone phalluses were often placed at cross-roads, but the Buddhist priests opposed this belief, and replaced the ancient phallic emblems by wooden images of Mikado-Daimyojin (G. Kato, *op. cit.* p. 177). Then the Imperial government gave orders to take down the emblems of the cult and to remove them to unfrequented places. But the cult persists in popular belief, and there are still shrines where the god is venerated. The emblems are often to be found in the small domestic altars in courtesans' houses. Near forked trees in the mountains, little chapels containing a phallus are often found. Mr G. Kato has devoted a study of Japanese forms of phallic cult. *(A Study of the development of Religious Ideas among the Japanese People as illustrated by Japanese Phallicism.* Transactions of the Asiatic Society of Japan, vol I, suppl. 1924).

Rustic gods. We have already said that the ancient Japanese conceived that all aspects and phenomena of Nature were manifestations of different divinities. For this reason the *Kojiki* mentions among the gods derived from Izanagi and Izanami, the Princess-of-Grass, Kaya-Nu-hime, who is the goddess of fields and meadows, and is named Nu-Zuchi. Other texts mention gods of the tree trunks, Kuku-no-chi, and a god-who-protects-leaves, Hamori. In addition to the generalised divinities, each species of tree has a special god—oaks, for instance, are protected by Kashiwa-no-Kami. Large and beautiful trees are venerated, and often hung with a rope of plaited straw from which hang little pieces of paper called Shime-nawa, telling the passer-by of the tree's divine quality. In a hollow of the tree or in front of it there is made a tiny chapel where the faithful leave offerings. The tree Sakaki *(Cleyera japonica)* is particularly venerated, because it was the tree chosen by the gods on which to hang the mirror during the ceremony carried out to tempt the Sun goddess from her cave. In all Shinto shrines there are plantations of sakaki, and branches of the tree are laid before the altars. The big Japanese cedar called the tree of fire, Hinoki, is also considered as sacred, and is therefore planted round sanctuaries. Mr G. Kato (*op. cit.*, p. 21) says: 'It seems to me that, from Saka Shibutsu's *Daijingu Sankeiki* or *Journal of Pilgrimages to the Ise Shrines,* we may infer that so late as the fourteenth century there existed at Ise a Nature-cult which took the form of tree-worship. A cherry-tree called Sakura no miya was worshipped within the precincts of the great Shrine at Ise.'

Gods of Stones and Rocks. Stones and Rocks are also objects of veneration in Shinto. There existed an important god of rock, Oiwa Daimyojin, while in the Izushi Shrine stones are worshipped. We must not forget the stone which, according to the legend, the Empress Jingo (170—269 A.D.) carried on her belly in order to delay the birth of her child, because she was in command of a military expedition against Korea. This stone is now venerated, and is supposed to help women in childbirth. In Hizen province, a sanctuary is dedicated to a similar stone and bears the name Shrine-of-the-stone-helping-childbirth, Chinkai-Seki-no-Yashiro. Clay or earth, as matter, has a goddess called Hani-Yasu-no-Kami.

The goddess of Food. In the ancient texts the goddess of food is given different names—Uke-Mochi-No-Kami, she-who-possesses (Mochi), food (uke); Waka-Uke-Nome, the-young-woman-with-food; and Toyo-Uke-Bime, the princess-of-rich-food, etc. In the *Nihon shoki* we learn that Amaterasu sent her brother Tsuki-Yomi, the Food goddess. She invited him to a meal, and produced rice and other dishes from her mouth to set out several tables. Tsuki-Yomi was annoyed by such a meal, and killed the goddess Uke-Mochi. Amaterasu was angry at this murder, and separated from her brother. Uke-Mochi-No-Kami is worshipped in the Geku Shrine, which after that of the Sun goddess, is the most important of the Ise sanctuaries.

The Rice god. Inari, the Rice god, is closely related to the Food goddess, but his cult is far more extended and he has shrines with many red Torii, perhaps in greater number than any sanctuaries in Japan. In popular belief the god Inari is represented as a bearded old man sitting on a sack of rice, flanked by two foxes, who are his messengers. The people confuse Inari with his messengers, and worship the fox as the god of Rice. He is now considered as the god of Prosperity in all his forms, and is especially worshipped by tradesmen. In old Japan he was known as the patron of the smiths who forged swords.

Hearth gods. The hearth is protected by several deities. There are gods of the entrance and a couple of Kitchen gods named Oki-Tsu-Hiko and Oki-Tsu-Hime. There is a special god for the Imperial kitchen. The Emperor Keiko (A.D. 71—188) wished to reward the culinary talents of a deceased Imperial Prince, so dedicated a shrine to him, and promoted him to the rank of tutelary divinity of the Imperial kitchen (G. Kato, *op. cit.* p. 62). The god of the kitchen range, Kamado-no-Kami, is a greatly venerated deity in all houses. In old Japan special festivals were dedicated to the god of Pots, and all artisans who used pots in their occupation took part in them. During the ceremony of good wishes for the Palace, known as Otono-no-hogai, the procession visited the bathroom and the closets, where offerings were made of a few grains of rice and a few drops of rice-wine. The god of Closets was respected and feared because, according to the Japanese, evil gods always settle in unclean places, and from there afterwards send dangerous diseases.

Deified heroes. The pantheon of Shinto gods was always increasing. In addition to the mythological gods, historical personages were and are considered as Kami, but this is not a very ancient tendency. In the ninth century there is a mention of prayers addressed to a deceased Emperor to obtain rain or avoid a misfortune. Towards the beginning of the tenth century we find a written order to make offerings to the deceased sovereign as if he were a Kami. Among the deified sovereigns we must put to one side those to whom shrines were erected in order to calm their anger, or the desire for vengeance, which they might have felt from the suffering of their lifetime. Such was the Emperor Junnin (750 — 764) who was banished to Awaji island and then assassinated; such too Sutoku (1124—1141) who died in exile in Sanuki; Go-Toba (1184—1198), Tsuchi-Mikado (1199—1210) and Juntoku (1211—1221) who were exiled to different places after the defeat of their troops by the army of the military Government of Kama Kura; the Emperor Go-Daigo (1319 — 1338) who also tried to free himself from the control of the military Government of Kama Kura. He was banished to the island of Chiburi, succeeded in escaping and in re-assuming power, but had finally to abdicate after several years of hard struggle. And then there was the child Emperor Antoku, already mentioned, who died in 1185 in the naval battle of Danno-ura.

The sovereigns Chuai and Ojin, as well as the Empress Jingo, were deified for their military exploits. The last-named is venerated in the Shrine of Sumiyoshi for her expedition to Korea, which

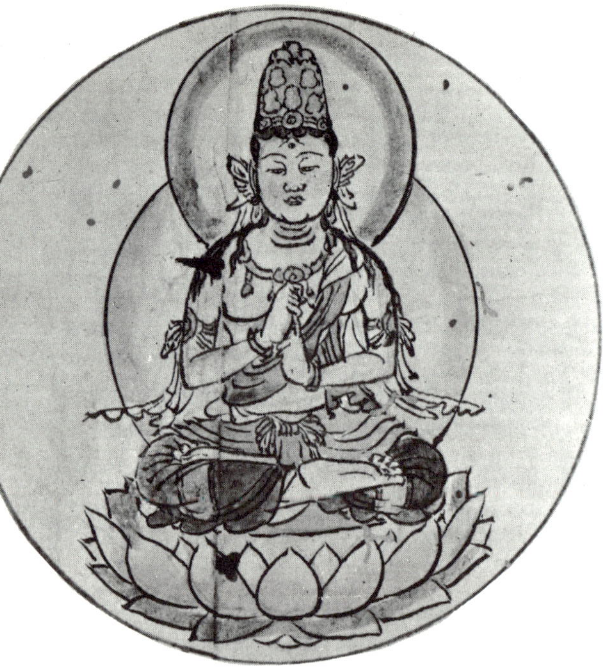

Ashuku Nyorai seated on a lotus. Ashuku Nyorai (the Buddha Aksobhya) is found in sacred paintings, or Mandalas, either alone or grouped with three other Buddhas around the figure of Dainichi Nyorai, the five Buddhas symbolising the five orients, five colours, five elements and five forms of knowledge. He is frequently identified with Yakushi Nyorai, the Divine Healer who stops epidemics and overcomes all diseases. Brush drawing, Kamakura period (thirteenth to fourteenth centuries A.D.).

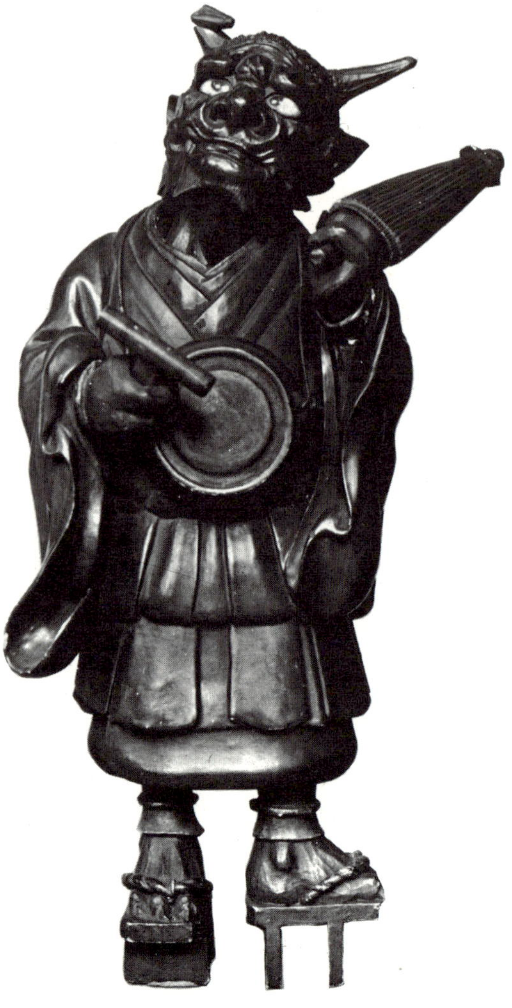

Oni, disguised as a begging monk converted to Buddhism. Musée Guimet, Paris.

probably occurred about the fourth century of our era. The Emperor Chuai fought the rebel tribes of Kyushu island, and died just before the expedition to Korea.

The Emperor Ojin, son of Chuai and Jingo, had a shrine at Usa, built in 712 by the Empress Gemmyo (708—714), and he became the god of War under the popular name of Hachiman. In the ninth century the Emperor Seiwa (died 876) built another shrine to him at Iwashimizu. The Ryobu-Shinto doctrines introduced Buddhist elements into his cult, and added on to his name a Buddhist epithet, Hachiman Daibosatsu. After the Imperial restoration of 1868 he once more became a purely Shinto deity. His shrines are still numerous, and always thronged with the pigeons who are his messengers. The Imperial government deified the legendary founder of the dynasty, the Emperor Jimmu, as well as the great reforming Emperor Kammu (719—781) and put up shrines to them. The Emperor Meiji, who died in 1912, and his wife, have been deified and have a sanctuary.

Statesmen also have become gods, and shrines have been built to them. The Minister Fujiwara Kamatari (614—669) has a shrine and receives offerings. Sugawara Michizane (845—903) is a Minister who died in exile. After his death his spirit brought misfortune to those who had calumniated him to the Emperor, and a small shrine was erected to him in 907, and a larger one in 947. He is considered as the protector of scholars, and the god of Calligraphy. He is called Tenjin, and his shrines are numerous.

The great military dictator Oda Nobunaga (1534—1582) is venerated in a Shinto shrine, and so is his successor Toyotomi Hideyoshi (1530—1598), Ieyasu (1524—1616), founder of the house of Tokugawa, which governed Japan for nearly three centuries, has sanctuaries where he is worshipped under the name of Tosho-Dai-gongen. Other examples might be quoted.

There were even persons to whom shrines were erected in their lifetime, and who were venerated as Kami before their death. Mr G. Kato has paid special attention to this question, and has devoted to it a volume of over four hundred pages, *Hompo Seishi no Kenkyu,* with an appendix in English: *Shinto worship of living human gods in the religious history of Japan,* 1932, Tokyo, as well as several articles in the *Transactions of the Meiji Japan Society*. He mentions the case of Honda Tadakazu (vol. XL, 1933), and that of Matsudaira Sadanobu (1758—1829) chief Minister of the Tokugawa and man of letters (vol. XXXIII, 1930). We will limit ourselves to these two examples.

BUDDHISM IN JAPAN

INTRODUCTION

Japanese Buddhist sects. It is probable that about the fourth century of our era certain elements of Buddhism (following the doctrines of the Mahayana, the Great Vehicle) entered Japan from China by way of Korea. However, it has been agreed to accept the year 522 as the official date of the introduction of Buddhism into Japan, since in that year the Korean kingdom of Paikche sent the Emperor of Japan a gilded bronze statue of Buddha and some volumes of Buddhist Sutras. The Emperor was not converted, but he allowed the great Soga family to adopt the new religion. After violent conflicts between the Buddhists and the old nationalist families, the new religion was proclaimed the religion of the state by the Prince Regent Shotoku in 592.

During the whole of the seventh and eighth centuries, in the course of the period called 'Nara' from the name of the temporary capital, Buddhism developed rapidly in Japan. There were then six main sects, the chief of which are the Sanron sect, the doctrine of the three books, founded by a Korean monk in 625; the Hosso sect, of Indian origin, introduced to Japan in 653; the Kegon sect introduced in 736 and based on the Avatamsaka sutra. The number of Buddhist divinities then introduced into Japan was still limited.

Towards the end of the eighth century the Buddhist clergy became a formidable power. To escape it the Emperor Kammu (783—805) decided to transfer the capital from Nara to Heian-kyo or Kyoto (794). It was the beginning of a new period, during which important religious reforms were carried out. Towards the year 804 the monks Dengyo Daishi and then Kobo Daishi came back from China, and taught the Tendai and Shingon doctrines. These were in opposition to the ancient Nara sects, not only from their mystical and secret aspect and from the pomp of their ceremonies, but also from their new doctrine of salvation made accessible to all human beings. Moreover, these new sects introduced a very large number of Buddhist divinities into Japan. Among these divinities the Dhyani Buddha, Vairocana, was the centre of a spiritual world which was represented by the aid of a drawing or Mandala. The world of ideas (Kongokai) must be distinguished from the world of forms (Taizokai). In each of these Mandalas the centre of the composition is occupied by Vairocana.

To the monk Dobo Daishi is also attributed the creation of Ryobu-Shinto or Shinto with two faces, whose doctrines unite the gods of Shinto with Buddhist divinities by identifying the one with the other. Thus Amaterasu, the Sun goddess, became a temporal manifestation of Vairocana.

In the twelfth century new Buddhist sects were introduced into Japan, notably the Jodo-Shu (Pure Land sect) which profoundly altered the preceding doctrines. Salvation for human beings is a Paradise which to some extent takes the place of the notion of Nirvana. It is governed by Amida Buddha. Corresponding to the existence of a Paradise there was a Hell, Jigoku, situated underground.

In the thirteenth century the monk Shinran Shonin reformed the sect, which then became 'the True Pure Land sect', Jodo-Shinshu. For the believers in this doctrine there was only one Buddha, Amida. His image only is allowed in Shinshu Temples. At the same period the monk Nichiren founded a sect based on the Sutra of the Lotus of Good Law, Saddharma pundarika sutra.

Limited by the space at our disposal and also by the impossibility of reviewing all the innumerable figures of the Buddhist pantheon, we shall limit ourselves to the most important, especially stressing the iconographic features which distinguish one from another.

BUDDHAS AND BODHISATTVAS

Amida. He is the most famous of the Dhyani Buddhas. He is especially favoured by the Shinshu and Jodo-Shu sects. He is the great protector of mankind, he comforts all who call upon his name, his Paradise in the West is open to all human beings. Standing with uncovered head in Indian dress he calls heaven and earth to witness that he will not enter Nirvana until he has saved all mankind. Many images represent him enthroned in the centre of the Sukhavati Paradise, or appearing behind the mountains, Yamagoshi no Amida, or coloured red and with his legs crossed, Kuharishiki no Amida. The esoteric sects recognise three Amidas—Muryoju (Amitayus), Muryoko (Amitabha) and Kanroo (Amrita).

Ashuku Nyorai. The cult of this Buddha does not exist in Japan. Yet his form will be found in Mandalas, either alone or joined with a group of divinities. He sits with crossed legs on a lotus. He has no head-dress. His outstretched right hand has the fingers pointing to earth, and his left first is clenched.

Dainichi Nyorai. Dainichi Nyorai, Maha-Vairocana tathagata, is the essential divinity of the Tendai, Shingon, and Kegon esoteric sects, and is the central figure of the Taizokai and Kongokai Mandalas.

Fugen Bosatsu. Fugen Bosatsu, Samantabhadra, is one of the most important Bodhisattvas. He represents wisdom, intelligence, understanding. He sits at the end of the Path of the extinction of errors. Thanks to his deep intuition and to his infinite kindness he understands the motives of all human actions. The uniformity of his compassion corresponds to the constancy of his contemplation. He is able to prolong human life. He is often depicted seated on a lotus supported by one or more white elephants. He may have two or twenty arms.

Hosho Nyorai. Hosho Nyorai, Ratnasambhava. He is the thrid Tathagata of the Kongokai Mandala. He looks after all treasures.

Kannon Bosatsu (Avalokitesvara, Kuan-yin). The cult of this Bodhisattva is one of the most venerated in Japan. It was practised from the first introduction of Buddhism, and the Horyuji monastery still preserves a beautiful bronze statue of Kannon dating from 651.

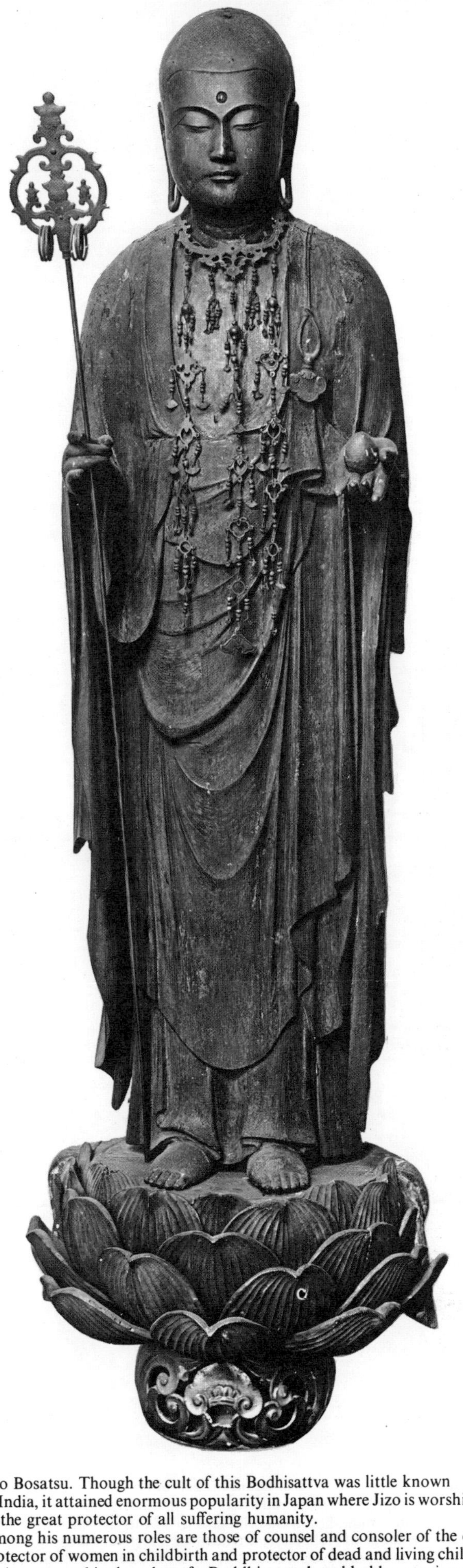

Jizo Bosatsu. Though the cult of this Bodhisattva was little known in India, it attained enormous popularity in Japan where Jizo is worshipped as the great protector of all suffering humanity.
Among his numerous roles are those of counsel and consoler of the dead, protector of women in childbirth and protector of dead and living children. He is portrayed in the robes of a Buddhist monk and holds a crozier and precious pearl. Wooden sculpture, thirteenth century A.D.

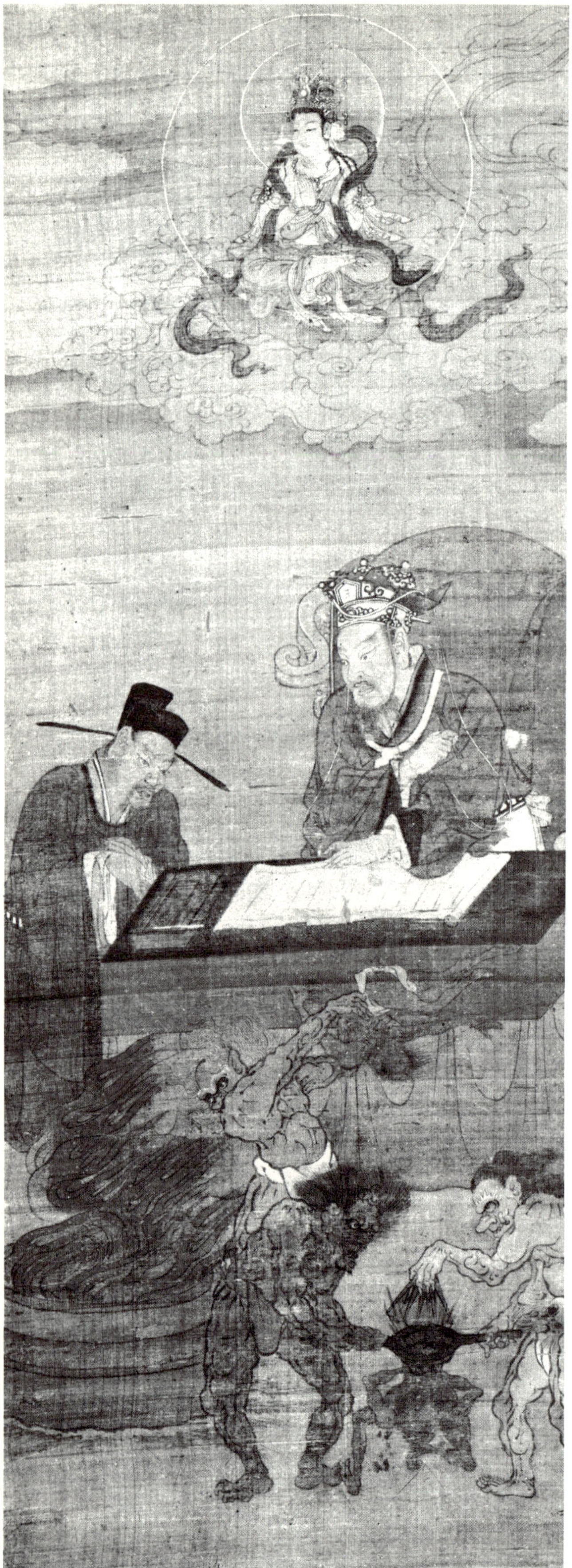

Emma-hoo enthroned in Hell. Incorporated into the Buddhist pantheon at an early stage as the deity entrusted with the enforcement of the law of retribution, Emma-hoo was both the ruler of the infernal world and the supreme judge of Hell. Here, attended by a secretary and a group of demons, he is portrayed seated at his desk dressed in the robes of a Chinese judge. Above him is his sister. Painting on silk, Kamakura period (thirteenth to fourteenth centuries A.D.).

His mercy is infinite, he comes to the help of all men. All Buddhist sects without exception worship him, and have put up innumerable sanctuaries to him. On the top of his head there is always placed a little image of Amida, recalling that Kannon Bosatsu is one of the two companions (disciple or manifestation, according to whether the sect is exoteric or esoteric) of this Buddha. There are seven forms of Kannon which are said to be the most widespread in Japan:

Senju Kannon (Kannon with the thousand arms or Sahasrabhuja sahasranetra) is figured in the centre of a vast halo formed out of a thousand hands, and in the palm of each is a human eye which symbolises his ever-vigilant compassion. Forty arms are attached to his body, and each holds an attribute or makes a mudra. Sometimes the centre head of this divinity is surmounted by twenty seven heads.

Nyo-i-rin Kannon (Cintamaricakra) usually has six arms, and each of the hands protects one of the six conditions. One holds a cintamani, the symbol of the satisfaction of vows; one a rosary, one a lotus or a wheel, the two others support his chin and rest on the lotus where the divinity is seated.

Ju-ichimen Kannon (Ekadasamukha) has eleven heads which the different sects group according to different combinations. 'Following the instructions of the Sutras, three faces—those in the centre and those in front—should have the expression of a Bodhisattva; the three faces to the left, an angry expression; and the three faces to the right should have the expression of a Bodhisattva but the canine teeth should project from the mouth. The face situated behind the head of the Bodhisattva laughs. The face at the top is either that of a Buddha or of a Nyorai and each of these heads carries the image of Amida on its diadem.'

Sho Kannon (Avalokitesvara). The All-Merciful comes to the aid of those who implore him. The Taizokai Mandala, which groups deities in the order of their power and the intentions they incarnate, places him to the right of Dainichi.

Bato Kannon (Hayagriva, the horse-headed Kannon). He is a manifestation of Amida. He has no crown. A horse's head placed on his hair recalls the charger of Cakravartiraja, which galloped tirelessly to the four points of the compass. He symbolises the Bodhisattva's universal activity in assisting the unfortunate and fighting demons. He protects the souls which destiny brings to the state of animals. His terrible face has a third eye and fangs. He sits on a lotus, and his hands form a mudra at the height of his breast.

Jundei Kannon (Sunde) uses his infinite virtues for the salvation of mankind. He has three eyes and eighteen arms. He is less often represented than the other forms of Kannon.

Fuku-kensaku Kannon (Amoghapasa) is a divinity of the Taizokai, World of Forms.

Miroku Bosatsu (Maitreya). The future Buddha. He dwells in the Tushita heaven and will come down on earth five thousand six hundred and seventy million years after the entry of Buddha into Nirvana. He revealed to Asanga the secret doctrines of the Mahayana, which explains his popularity among the esoteric sects. Ancient sculpture represents him sitting down, with his left foot on the ground, his right foot on his left knee, his right elbow on his right knee, and his left hand on his right ankle. His head is slightly bent, his right hand supports his chin, and there is a little Stupa on his crown. But sometimes he is to be met with having his legs crossed or standing on a lotus.

Among the ten names of Buddha is the name Nyorai, (Tathagata). This term corresponds with one of the forms under which Buddha manifests himself for the salvation of mankind.

Myoo. A great Myoo corresponds to each of the five great Buddhas. Dainichi (Mahavairocana), Ashuku (Akshobhya), Hosho (Ratnasambhava), Mida (Amithabha) and Fuku (Amonghavajra). These are terrible manifestations of the Buddhas, and are those who carry out their wishes.

A painting on the inside of the door of a Nara period shrine dedicated to Monju Bosatsu, the Japanese form of the Buddhist god of wisdom and compassion. The painting depicts one of the Lokapala (guardians of heaven), Jikoku Ten, who watches over the region of the east.

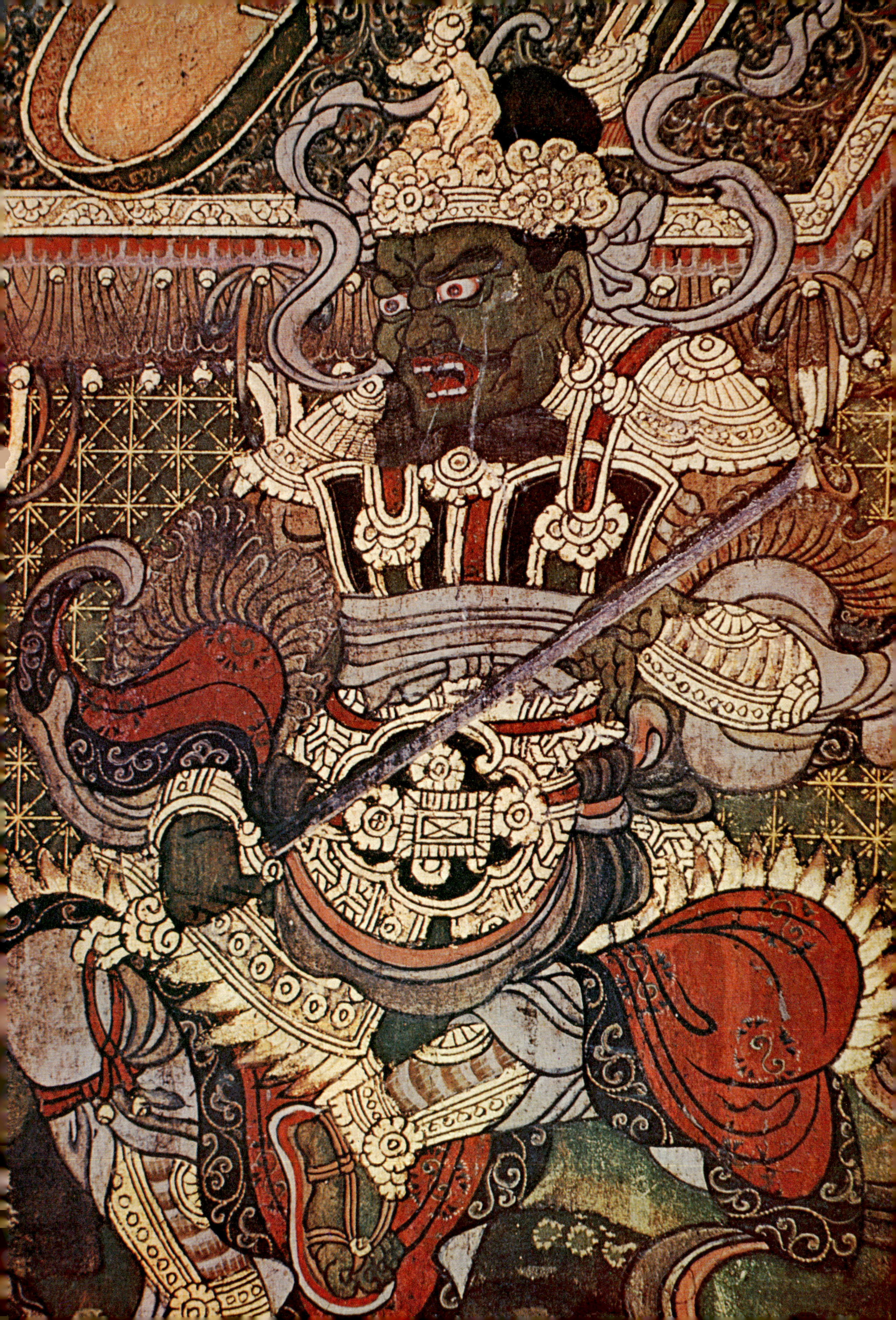

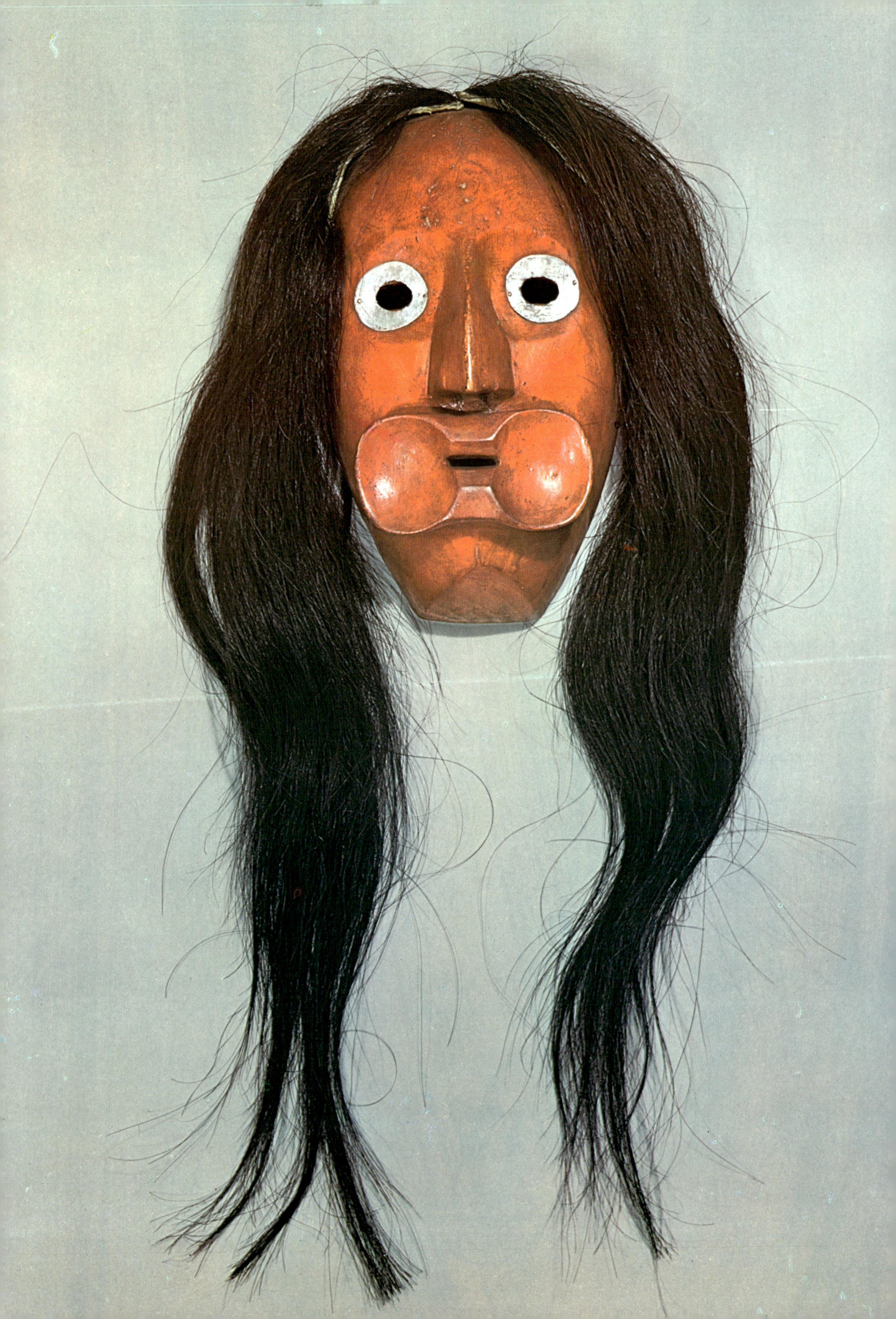

Dai-itoku-Myoo (Yamantaka) is the terrible manifestation of Amida, and lives in the region of the West. More powerful than the dragon, he does battle with evils and poisons. He is surrounded with flames and sits on a white ox or a rock. He has six heads with terrible faces, and also six arms and six legs. He conquered Emma-hoo, the king of Hell, whence his second name, Goemmason.

Fudo-Myoo (Arya acalanatha). The most important of the five great Myoo, one of the manifestations of Dainichi nyorai (Vairocana). He is surrounded by flames, the symbols of his virtues. His ferocious face is half hidden by his long hair. With his sword, which is the symbol of wisdom and mercy, he battles with the three poisons —avarice, anger and folly. He binds with his rope those who oppose the Buddha.

Gozanze-Myoo. He is the terrible manifestation of Ashuku, and lives in the region of the East. Each of his four faces bears a ferocious expression and has a third eye in the forehead. His eight hands hold different attributes. His left foot treads on Jizaiten (Mahesvara). His right foot presses the hand of Umahi (Uma), Jizaiten's wife.

Gundari-Myoo is the terrible manifestation of Hosho. He is represented standing on a lotus. His terrible face has three eyes, and fangs protrude from his mouth. A human skull is placed on his hair, and his red body has eight arms. Snakes are coiled round his wrists and ankles. This divinity is also called Nampo Gundari Yasha, because he lives to the south of mount Sumeru, and also Kanro (Amrita), because he gives heavenly nectar to poor human beings.

Kongo-yasha-Myoo (Vajrayaksha) is the terrible manifestation of Fuku. He protects the region of the North. He is surrounded by flames, poses on two lotus flowers, and lifts his left leg. He may have three heads and six arms, or one head and four arms. The front face has five eyes.

Kujaku-Myoo does not belong to the series of five Great Myoo. His looks are not terrible, and he is represented with the features of a Bodhisattva. He is always seated on a peacock. The esoteric sects consider him a manifestation of Sakyamuni. He gives proprotection against calamities, and is particularly resorted to for rain during periods of droughts.

Aizen-Myoo is a divinity who, under his terrible appearance, is full of compassion for mankind. His ferocious face with three eyes is topped by a lion's head with a bristling mane surmounted by a Vajra (thunder-bolt) which calms evil passions and guilty desires. He has six arms holding different attributes. In the secret Shingon sect Aizen-Myoo is in the centre of a Mandala.

Jizo Bosatsu (Kshitigarbha). The cult of this Bodhisattva, very little spread in India, had much popularity in central Asia, China, and especially Japan from the twelfth century. He is the great protector of all suffering humanity. Many sanctuaries are dedicated to him. His image has inspired sculptors and painters with masterpieces, and yet may be seen roughly carved alongside the roads of Japan. His considerable power is exercised in very different cases, whence the large number of different aspects in which he appears. There are six Jizo protectors of the six Paths or good and bad conditions which souls must undergo after judgment: that of Hell, that of the starving Demons, that of the world of animals, that of the demon Asuras, that of Men, that of the Devas. There are many tales displaying his infinite kindness—he saves the life of the warrior Toshihira, he averts fires, facilitates childbirth etc. One of the main devotions offered to him is as the pitying protector of children.

In the seventeenth century his power was increased and with it his popularity—he is able to redeem sinful souls from Hell and to bring them to Paradise. His most usual appearance is that of a Buddhist monk, seated or standing, holding a crozier (Khakkhara) in his right hand, and a precious pearl in the left. There is often a halo round his head.

The Jizo of the victorious army (Shogun Jizo) was associated with the divinity of mount Atago when Ryobu-Shinto was formed. In this particular form he has the appearance of a Chinese soldier on horseback, holding the crozier in one hand and the pearl in the other.

Kozuko Bosatsu. He lives in the koju world. The many images of him preserved in the Temples show him seated with crossed legs on a lotus supported by a lion.

Monju Bosatsu (Manjusri) was extremely popular in the ninth century and personifies intelligence, compassion, and contemplation. He is often associated with Fugen Bosatsu in the Shaka Nyorai trinity. This Bodhisattva is always accompanied by a lion. He is generally seated, holds in his hands the sword of intelligence which cuts the darkness of ignorance, and a book.

Yakushi Nyorai. Yakushi Nyorai (Bhaishajyaguru) is a divinity very popular in Japan from the eighth century, sometimes identified with Ashuku Nyorai or with Dainichi Nyorai. He is the divine healer who stops epidemics, whose knowledge can overcome every disease. He is usually represented under the aspect of a Buddha holding in his hand a little flask containing medicines. Sometimes he is accompanied by two other deities, the Bodhisattvas, Gakko, image of the Moon, and Nikko, image of the Sun.

HELL AND DEMONS

Emma-hoo (Yama-raja). Hell, Jigoku, is underground. It is made up of eight regions of fire and eight of ice. There are also subsidiary hells. The ruler of this infernal world is Emma-hoo (Yama-raja) who is also the supreme judge of Hell. Under his orders are eighteen generals and eighty thousand men. He is represented in the dress of a Chinese judge wearing a cap inscribed with the name Emma. The expression of his face is ferocious.

Emma-hoo only judges men, and leaves the task of deciding the fate of women to his sister. The sinner is taken before this formidable judge, who sits between the decapitated heads of Miru-me and Kagu-hana, from whom nothing can be hidden. All his past sins are reflected into the sinner's eyes by a huge mirror. His sins are weighed, and then Emma-hoo gives judgment. The sinner must stay in such-and-such a region of Hell according to the extent of his sins, unless his soul is saved by the prayers of the living. In this case a Bodhisattva rescues him from torture, and the sinner is reborn either on earth or in a Paradise.

Oni (devil-demons). The idea of ill-omened forces was introduced into Japan relatively late. Indian ideas and the Chinese doctrines of Yang and Yin were altered there and ended up in the creation of demons, Oni, and the birth of a new iconography. The Oni of Hell are distinguished from the Oni on earth. The former have red or green bodies, with the heads of oxen or horses. Their occupation consists in hunting for the sinner and taking him in a chariot of fire to Emma-hoo, god of Hell. The gaki demons are eternally tormented by thirst or hunger, and their bellies are enormous. The latter are maleficent demons who can assume the shape of a living being or of an inanimate object. There are invisible demons, but their presence may be detected because they sing, whistle, or talk. In the ninth century it was believed that very virtuous people only might sometimes witness their processions, invisible to all other mortals. They have the power to seize on a dead man's soul, and to appear to his relatives in his form.

We must also mention the Oni who are responsible for diseases and epidemics (they are dressed in red) and the Oni who are women changed into demons under the stress of jealousy or violent grief. Although they are maleficent spirits, the Oni in general are not very dangerous, and they may even be converted to Buddhism.

SUBSIDIARY DEITIES

Nio. The name of Nio is given to the two protectors of Buddhism who correspond to Vajrapani. Fukaotsu and Soko are placed on either side of the entry to Shrines.

Ida-ten, the Chinese Wei-t'o. Although of subsidiary importance this deity became very popular in China and still more in Japan from the seventh century onward. He guards the law, and watches over the discipline of monasteries and the good conduct of the monks. Ida-ten (General Wei) appeared in a dream to the Chinese monk Tao Hsuan (596 — 667). 'He is the first of the thirty-four generals of the four devaraja, placed directly under the orders of Him of the

A 'false face' mask of painted wood with human hair. These masks were worn by the Iroquois tribes of the east during rituals which celebrated the spirits of nature and drove away harmful ones. The occasions were primarily religious but there was a great deal of horseplay and some of the masks had a distinctly humorous aspect. British Museum.

South, Virudhaka, the protector of Buddhism and especially of monks and monasteries in the three regions of the South, the East, and the West gifted with absolute purity and free from all passion.'

In Japan the familiar expression 'running like Ida-ten', which means to run very fast, is derived from the following legend. When Buddha was dead but before they had closed the gold coffin, a demon named Sokushikki stole one of the sacred teeth and made off with it. The disciples, thunderstruck with surprise, were unable to stop him, and with one leap he went forty thousand yojana. Ida-ten alone pursued him, and regained the precious relic. In statues he is represented as a young man in the dress of a Chinese general, with his two hands resting on a weapon or holding it across his arms.

Buddha's disciples. Among the sixteen Rakan (Arhat) or disciples of Buddha we shall mention only Binzuru, the first among them. He aids human beings, and soothes the sick. However, entrance to Nirvana was refused him by Buddha because in his youth he broke the vow of chastity. He dwelt on mount Marishi. He is represented usually as an extremely old man with pure white hair and thick eyebrows.

Atago-Gongen. Atago-Gongen was a deity of Ryobu-Shinto who emigrated from the sanctuary of mount Atago at the beginning of the Meiji epoch, when the government expelled the Buddhist divinities from the Shinto sanctuaries. There he was confused with a deity of Thunder and Fire. In the eighth century the bronze Keishun built on top of mount Atago a Buddhist shrine consecrated to the Jizo of the victorious army. The iconography of Atago-Gongen was influenced by this proximity. The deity took on the appearance of a Chinese cavalry soldier carrying the emblems of Jizo, the precious pearl and the crozier. Today the mount Atago sanctuary is a Shinto shrine where a Fire god is worshipped.

Nijuhachi Bushu is the general name for the twenty-eight deities symbolising the constellations. They are sometimes considered as servants of Kannon.

Marishi-ten. Marici-deva is an all-powerful deva. He precedes the Sun. He is invisible, but the Japanese represent him in the costume of a Chinese lady, to indicate his Continental origin. He protects soldiers, and averts the danger of fires.

Shitenno. The Shitenno are four kings, heavenly guards, Lokapala. They are five hundred years old and live in the slopes of mount Sumeru, on the top of which dwells Taishaku-ten, whose vassals they are. They wear a ferocious expression, are dressed as Chinese soldiers, and trample on demons. They may be distinguished by their attributes. Jikoku (Dhritarashtra) protects the region of the East, he holds a sword and a little ossuary. Zocho (Virudhaka) protects the region of the South, he fights evil and does good, and holds a sword and shield. Komoku (Virupaksha) protects the region of the West, he holds a paint-brush or a spear in his hand, while the other hand is on his hip or holds the sheath of his sword. Tamon (Vaisramana) or Bishamon holds a sceptre and a little ossuary shaped like a pagoda. He protects the region of the North.

Kishimojin (Hariti) is a female divinity dwelling in China. At first she was a demon-woman who devoured children, but, after her conversion by Buddha, became their protector and also of women in childbirth. Mothers implore her to heal their sick children. The Shingon sect who brought her into Japan have kept her original name, Kariteimo. Many shrines were consecrated to her by the Nichiren sect. She is represented either standing with a baby to her breast and holding the flower of happiness, or sitting down in the Western fashion, surrounded with children.

Kompira (Kuvera) is a popular deity in Japan, the protector of sailors and bringer of prosperity. A large shrine is consecrated to him in the village of Kotohira on Shikoku island. The numerous pilgrims there receive a little slab of wood as an amulet, with the Chinese character for 'gold' engraved in a circle. The sailors of the Inland Sea had a special devotion to him in the Tokugawa period. To calm a storm the sailor cut his hair and threw it into the sea while uttering the name of the deity. He appears in the shape of a fat man sitting down cross-legged. In one hand he holds a purse.

Shichi Fukujin. The seven gods of happiness have different origins.

Ebisu and Daikoku are probably Shinto Kami. These gods wear Japanese clothes, and the lobes of their ears are swollen. Ebisu, the patron of work, holds a line in his hands and a big fish on a string. Daikoku, god of prosperity, holds the hammer of wealth and a big sack on his back, while he stands on two sacks of rice.

Benzaiten and Bishamonten are of Hindu origin. The first is the deity of love. She rides a dragon and plays the biwa, and her messenger is the snake. The second is the god of happiness and war. He is represented as a soldier holding a little pagoda and a lance.

The three other gods are of Chinese origin. Fukurokuju is the god of wisdom and long life, with a very high skull. He is accompanied by a stork. Jurojin, god of happiness and long life, leans on a long staff and is accompanied by a stag. Hotei Osho is a Buddhist priest with a fat stomach and a bald head, while the lobes of his ears are swollen. He holds a hand-screen and a large sack. He has been popularised in Europe under the name of Pusa.

MYTHOLOGY OF THE TWO AMERICAS

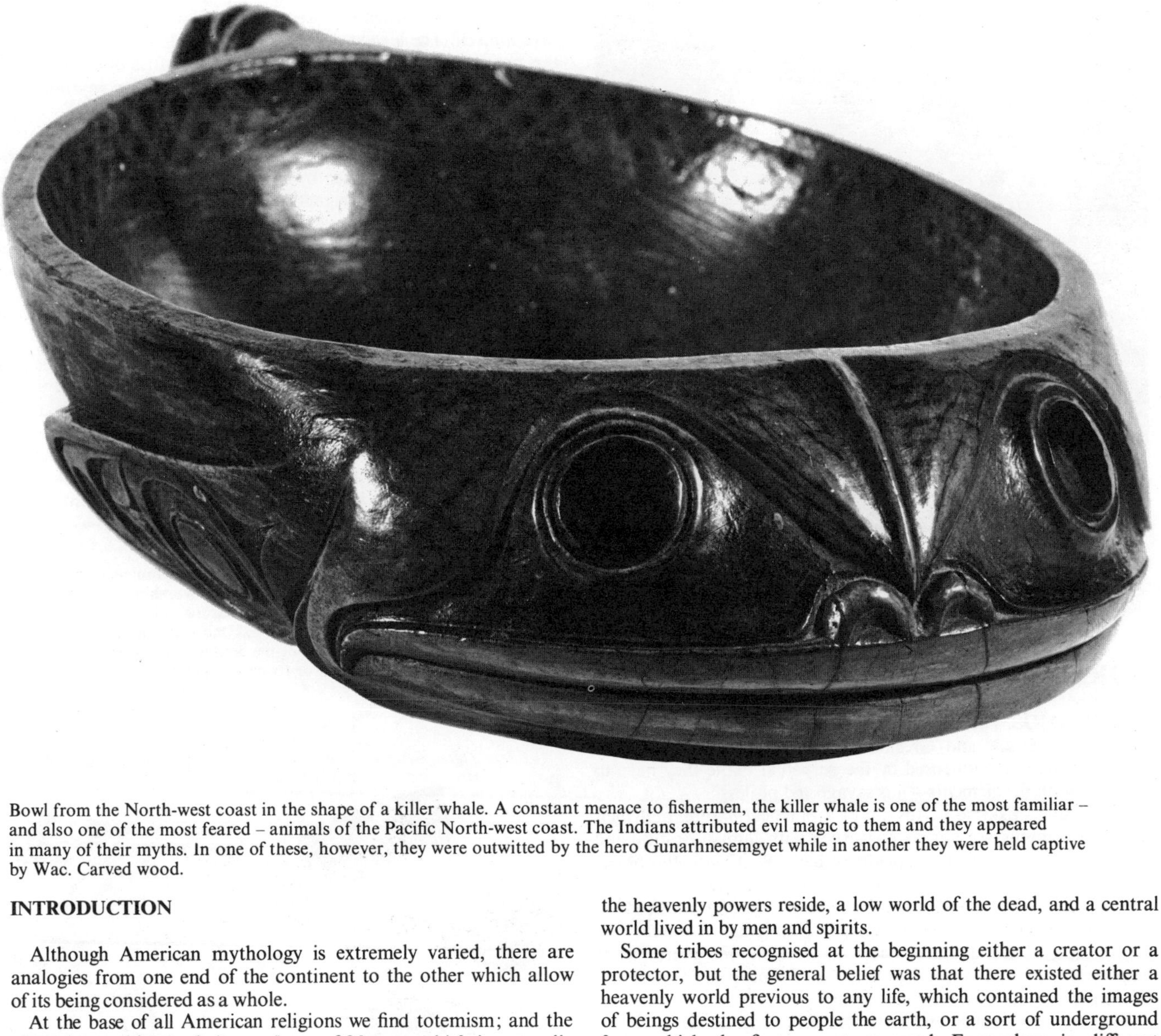

Bowl from the North-west coast in the shape of a killer whale. A constant menace to fishermen, the killer whale is one of the most familiar – and also one of the most feared – animals of the Pacific North-west coast. The Indians attributed evil magic to them and they appeared in many of their myths. In one of these, however, they were outwitted by the hero Gunarhnesemgyet while in another they were held captive by Wac. Carved wood.

INTRODUCTION

Although American mythology is extremely varied, there are analogies from one end of the continent to the other which allow of its being considered as a whole.

At the base of all American religions we find totemism; and the totem is an object, a being, a force of Nature, which is generally looked on as the ancestor of a group or clan or an individual, who take its name and identify themselves with it.

In exchange for the totem's help and protection all its representatives owe it a certain amount of deference and worship, rather as if it were an ancestor. But to make the totem favourable they have to multiply its effigies, make offerings and show it respect; in exchange for which they acquire rights over the totem which helps and protects them. In some of the more advanced civilisations, other and more evolved cults were attached to these primitive beliefs. Totemism itself became more complicated. The great gods appeared, and then was seen the rise of pantheons as full as those of Aztecs and Mayas, or in Peru the very complex cult of the Sun with all its hierarchy. The worship of divinities became general among the American peoples, and so too did the ideas about the formation of the universe. They believed in an upper world where the heavenly powers reside, a low world of the dead, and a central world lived in by men and spirits.

Some tribes recognised at the beginning either a creator or a protector, but the general belief was that there existed either a heavenly world previous to any life, which contained the images of beings destined to people the earth, or a sort of underground from which the first parents emerged. Everywhere in different forms may be found the heroes destined to create an organisation and laws, conquerors of the monsters which terrorised the earth, as well as the myth of the world's destruction by flood or fire, or the legend of the theft of fire. These explanatory myths and the heroic and divine legends were the expression among the American Indian populations of a more or less conscious, but sometimes very intense, religious emotion. An examination of them shows the evolution of human thought in its search for God.

In a limited study it is impossible to give a complete account of the mythology of the American peoples, but we shall try to give a clear if limited picture which will show the main outlines of the most important legends. The reader will find many reminiscences of classical or biblical mythologies. It is thought that these legends may have a common origin either in the great phenomena of Nature, or the cataclysms which in the past terrified primitive humanity.

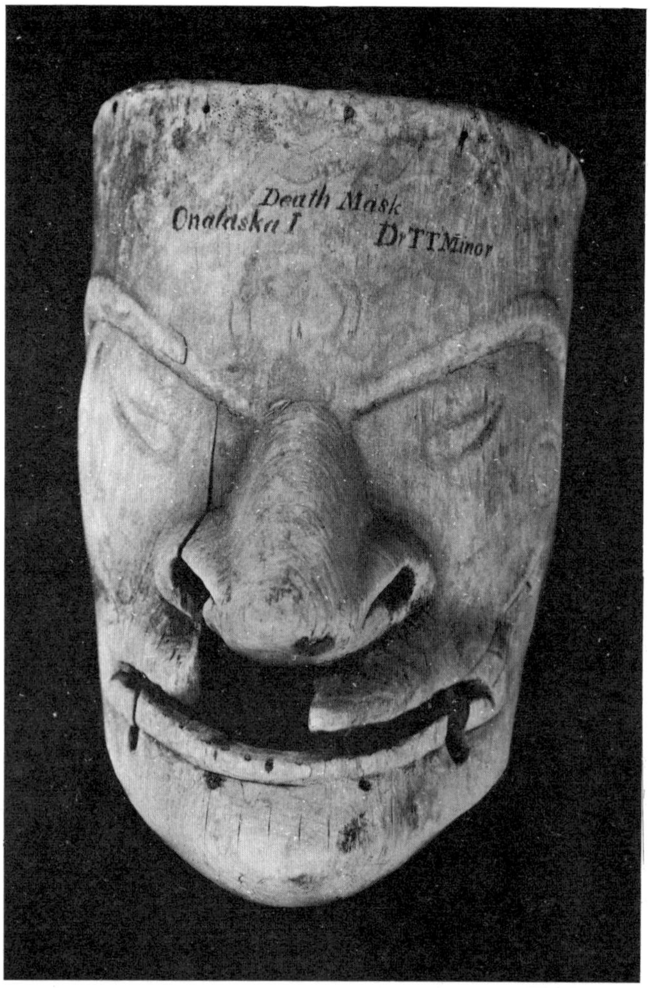

Funerary mask from the Aleutian Islands. The Eskimos believe in two realms of the dead while spectres and ghosts are also said to haunt the world.

NORTH AMERICA

THE ESKIMOS. The Eskimos occupy the area bounded by Hudson Bay, Bering Straits and Greenland.

Their religion is influenced by the perpetual battle they have to maintain with the elements—it is savage and pitiless.

In the main, Eskimo myths are of a practical nature, and their speculative myths are always concerned with human destiny and with the influence which actions may have on it, with the object of conciliating the gods and other supernatural powers.

For Eskimos the world is under the dominion of a multitude of invisible forces or 'Innua'. Everything in Nature has its Innua—the air, the sea, stones, animals. These may become the guardians or helpers of men, and then take the name of 'Torngak'. This, it will be seen, is an individual form of totemism.

The Innua of stones and bears are especially powerful. If the spirit of a bear becomes a man's Torngak, the man may be eaten by a bear and then brought back to life. He then becomes an Angakok or sorcerer.

Angakoks can make good or bad weather as they choose, can effect cures, see things hidden, and discover crimes by their second sight. Thus they form a kind of magistrature.

Angakoks have the Torngaks as their familiar spirits, and the name is derived from Torngasoak, the most powerful of spirits who command in his name. The Eskimos call him the Good Being, but are not agreed on the shape he assumes. Some say he has no shape, some say he looks like a bear, others represent him as a tall man with only one arm, and still others make him as small as a finger. He is immortal, but may be slain by the god Crepitus.

Torngarsak is not the creator of all things but has in him the characteristics of divinity, and in spite of his limited power the Eskimos call him the Great Spirit. At the same time they have spirits of fire, water, mountains and winds; and dog-faced demons. The souls of abortions become hideous spectres, and even ghosts are familiar to these people. A child whose mother was dead saw her spirit in broad daylight and heard her say: 'Don't be afraid, I'm your mother, and I love you.' For even in that land of ice Love is stronger than Death.

The goddess Sedna holds a very important place in the mythology and popular traditions of the Eskimos. She is thought of as the divinity of the sea and sea animals, but her power only extends to the material body of the beings in her submarine kingdom. She is hostile to the human race. Sedna is more feared by the Eskimos than any other deity, and they do their best to secure her favour by propitiatory sacrifices. The Eskimos think of her as being of gigantic size, and she has only one eye, the other having been torn out by her father when he threw her out of a boat, as some say, to save himself. The legend of Sedna contains elements showing that this personage, comparable with certain divinities of the Kalevala and the Edda, may be a theme common to many mythologies.

Here are the main lines of the legend:

'Sedna was a pretty Eskimo girl, the only child of a widowed father with whom she lived beside the sea. When Sedna reached marriageable age she was courted by a large number of young men from her own tribe and by foreigners from distant lands; but Sedna refused to marry, and took pleasure in rebuffing and hurting all her suitors. One day, however, there arrived from a distant land a young and handsome hunter dressed in splendid furs. He carried an ivory spear. His kayak approached the shore, but instead of landing he let his canoe rock among the waves and called to the girl in her hut, imploring her with a seductive song:

' "Follow me," he said, "into the land of birds, where there is never any hunger. You shall rest in my tent on warm bear skins, your lamp shall be always filled with oil, and your pot with meat. . ."

'Sedna, framed in the doorway of the cabin, rejected the stranger's alluring proposals. Although won by his first glance, she remained timid and confused. Was it not her duty to refuse? The stranger then began to implore her. He drew for Sedna an enchanting picture of his country, describing the ivory necklaces he would give

Amulet belt. This Netsilik Eskimo belt hung with amulets of bird skulls, teeth and talons is possibly connected with the worship of Koodjanuk, a spirit of the first rank, who has the appearance of a gigantic bird and heals the sick. Another bird famous in Eskimo mythology is Sedna's phantom lover. In Alaska the role of the demiurge is ascribed to a Crow Father who is said to have formed vegetation, animals and men out of clay.

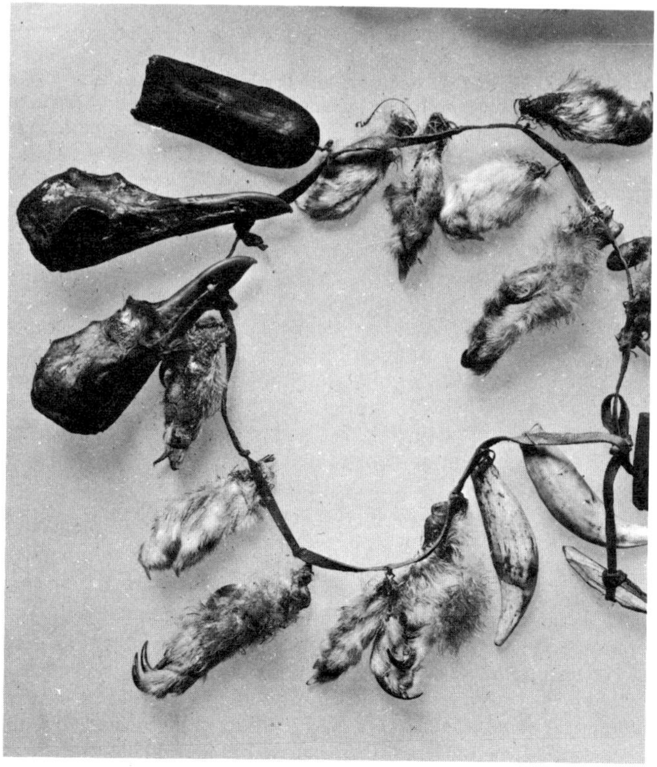

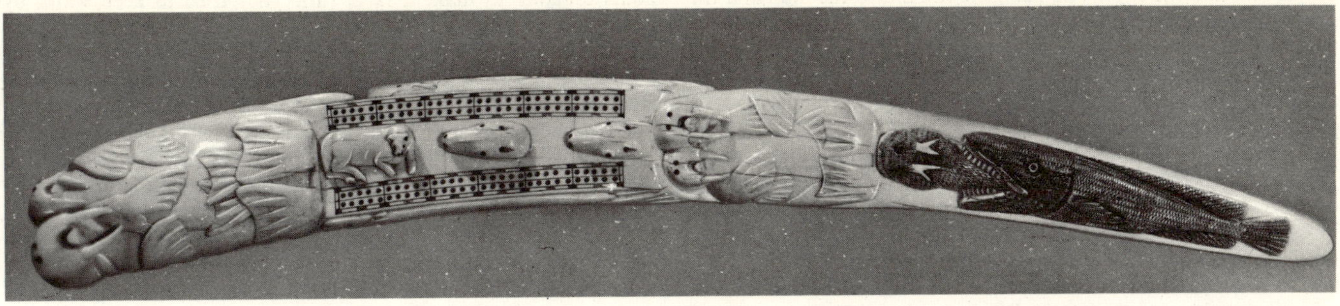

Ivory tusk carved with marine animals. For the Eskimos marine animals and the sea are under the dominion of the goddess Sedna who holds a very important place in their mythology and popular traditions and whose favour must be sought by propitiatory sacrifices. According to legend seals, ojuk, walruses and whales were born from her fingers and knuckles which were chopped off by her father when he threw her from his boat in order to appease the offended sea.

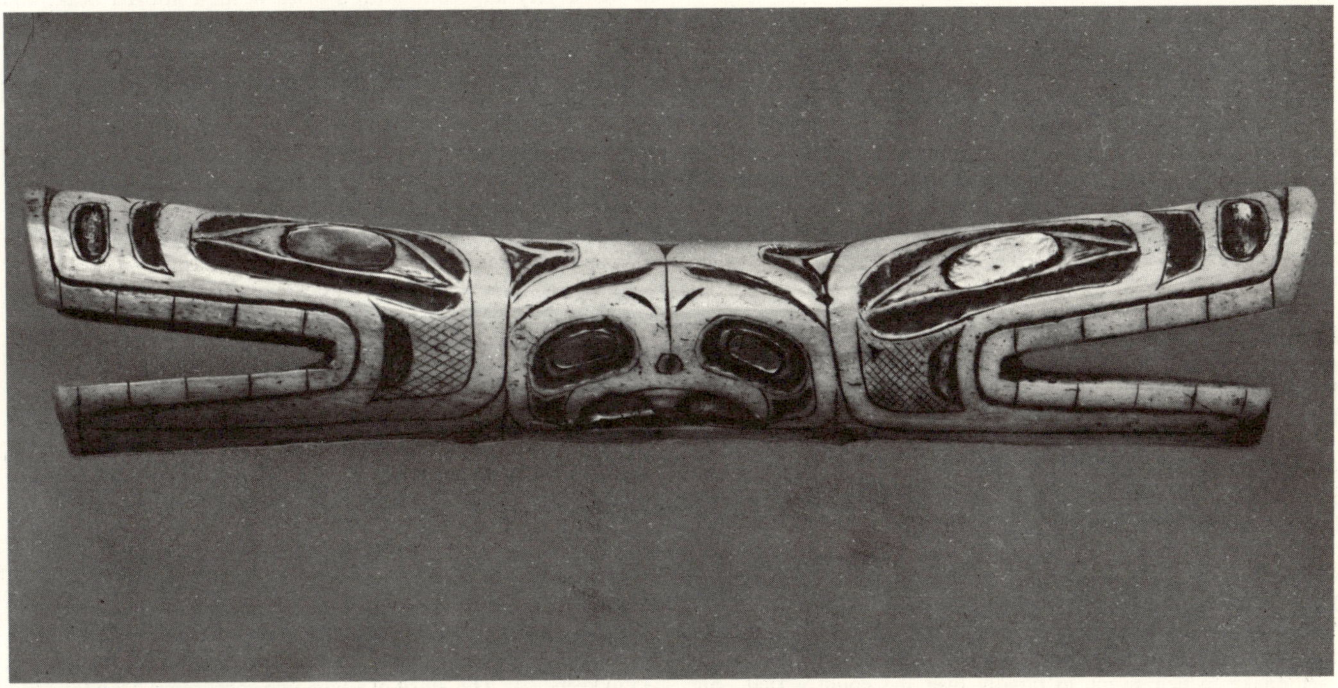

Eskimo shaman's charm. Eskimo shamans, or Angakoks, are believed to have the power to visit the 'other world' at will – either that below the sea in order to force Sedna to release seals in time of famine or that in the sky. They are also credited with the power to make good or bad weather, effect cures and discover crimes by second sight. They are frequently aided by the Torngaks. Ivory inlaid with mother of pearl.

her...and Sedna felt herself yielding, and little by little allowed herself to be drawn down to the sea. The stranger made her enter his boat, and started away. Thus it was that Sedna fled, and her father never again saw her on the shore where their home stood.

'Sedna's lover was not a man. He was only the phantom of a bird. Sometimes he took on the shape of a fulmar petrel, sometimes of a diving bird. He was a Bird-spirit with the power to assume human form and had fallen in love with the girl, and did not let her know his real nature.

'When Sedna knew the truth, her despair was immense, and her husband vainly tried to overcome the girl's repugnance. She could not grow accustomed to her seducer, and spent her days in grief and tears...

'Sedna's father, Angusta, was inconsolable for the loss of his daughter. One day he set out for the distant shore to which his child had been taken. When he arrived the Bird-spirit was away. Seeing his daughter plunged in grief, he took Sedna in his arms, carried her to the boat, and they set sail for their native land.

'When the fulmar returned he looked for his wife, but mysterious cries carried by the wind told him that Sedna had fled with her father, with lamentations and cries of anger. The bird reassumed his phantom form, entered his kayak, and set out in pursuit of the fugitive. Soon he came in sight of the boat which carried Sedna and her father, but when he saw the phantom he hid his daughter under some furs.

'The canoeist rapidly overhauled the boat, and demanded his wife: "Let me see Sedna, I beg you, let me see her." But the angry father refused to listen and continued on his way.

'Wild with despair, the Kokksaut—which is the name the Eskimos give to strange creatures—fell back. He had failed. Then was heard the beat of a furious wing—the phantom had changed back into a bird. Spreading his wings, the bird soared over the fugitives, uttering the strange cry of the loon, and then disappeared into the darkness. Suddenly a terrible storm, the dark storm of the Arctic ocean, swept across the sea. Sedna's father was smitten with horror, and fear of the man-bird gripped his heart. The horror at having offended the powers of heaven and earth gave him the strength to make a dreadful sacrifice. The waves clamoured for Sedna, and he must listen to their demand! Leaning forward, he seized his daughter and, with a horrible thrust, hurled her from the boat — hideous sacrifice, which was intended to appease the offended sea!

'Sedna's pale face appeared above the waves, while her hands desperately seized the side of the boat. The father, wild with terror, seized a great ivory axe and cut off the fingers clutching the boat. The girl sank into the water, while her chopped-off fingers were transformed into seals. Three times she strove to escape death, but she was lost, she was the prey of the ocean and nothing could save her. Thrice her father mutilated her wounded hands. The second knuckles gave birth to the ojuk (the deep-sea seals), the thrid became walruses, and from the remainder whales were born. When the sacrifice was completed, the sea grew calm, and the boat soon reached the shore. The father entered his tent, and fell into a deep sleep, exhausted as he was by suffering and grief. Sedna's dog was tied to the tent-pole, the *tupik*. During the night there was an exceptionally high tide which covered the shore, swallowing up the tent and the two living beings in it. And so the man and the dog were re-united with Sedna in the depths of the ocean. Since then they have reigned over an area called Adliden. It is the place where souls after their death are imprisoned to expiate the sins committed by the living. According to the gravity of the sin this punishment is temporary or eternal.'

Such is the legend of Sedna.

Sometimes when the Eskimos fail to catch any seals the Angakoks dive down to the bottom of the sea to compel Sedna to set them loose. According to ancient Greenland legend, the Angakok who wants to reach her must first pass through the kingdom of the dead, and then an abyss where there turns ceaselessly a wheel of ice and a boiling cauldron full of seals. When the Angakok has managed to escape the huge dog guarding the entry, he has to cross a second abyss on a bridge as slender as a knife edge.

Such, according to the Eskimos, are the dangers of a journey to the land of spirits.

The Eskimos see, moving around these higher spirits, an infinite number of lower spirits and monsters, some friendly to mankind, while others hunt them down implacably:

One day an Angakok went very far out to sea in pursuit of a seal. Suddenly he saw that he was surrounded by strange kayaks—they were fire spirits who had come to capture him. But there was an eddy among them, and the Angakok saw they were being pursued by a kayak whose prow opened and shut like a huge mouth, devouring everything which came its way. The fire spirits disappeared as quickly as they had arrived. The Angakok had been saved by his protecting spirit.

The Eskimos think that there is a lower world in the sky. The lower world is sometimes like the human world but with a paler sun and sky, and is sometimes formed of four caves placed one below the other, the first three being low and uncomfortable, while the lowest is spacious and pleasant.

The upper world beyond the dome of the sky turns around the summit of a mountain. As on earth there are hills and valleys, and it is the abode of the Innuas, heavenly bodies who were once men but were taken up into heaven and changed into stars.

The road which leads to the upper world is also full of danger. On the way to the moon somebody tries to make the travellers laugh, and if he succeeds, tears out their entrails.

Among the Eskimos are legends relating to the flood. In Alaska there existed the tradition of a terrible flood accompanied by an earthquake, which swept so rapidly over the country that only a few people managed to escape in their canoes, or took refuge on the tops of the highest mountains, consumed with terror.

The Eskimos of the Arctic ocean say that a flood swept over the earth, and that some people saved themselves by lashing their boats together to make a large raft. They tried to keep warm by lying close together as they were shivering in an icy wind. At last a sorcerer named Anodijum, which means 'Owl's son', threw his bow into the sea, saying: 'Enough, wind. Be still.' He then threw in his ear-rings and the waters grew less.

Here are some of the Eskimo divinities:

Agloolik: He lives under the ice, and is the tutelary spirit of the seal caves. He helps hunters to find game. He is considered a good spirit.

Aipalookvik: An evil spirit. He has a passion for destruction, and tries to bite and destroy boatmen. He lives in the sea.

Aulanerk: Lives in the sea. He is naked, and struggles, thus causing the waves. He is a source of joy to Eskimos.

Nootaikok: He is the spirit of icebergs. A benevolent spirit living in the sea. When invoked he procures seals.

Koodjanuk: Spirit of the first rank. At the creation of the world he was a very large bird with a black head, a hooked beak, and a white body. He is a benevolent spirit able to give satisfaction when invoked. He heals the sick.

Oluksak: Divinity of lakes. He lives on their banks. The Angakoks receive their inspiration through him as intermediary.

Tekkeitserktok: He is the god of the earth and of the district. All deer belong to him. This god's power is greater then that of all the other deities. He is offered numerous sacrifices every year before the hunting season.

Tootega: Looks like a little woman. This spirit has the ability to walk on water. It lives on an island in a stone house.

Akselloak: This is the spirit of rocking stones. Considered a good spirit.

Aumanil: Lives on land, and guides whales.

Eeyeekalduk: Lives on land, and looks like a little man. It is dangerous to look into his eyes. His face is black. He lives in a stone. This benevolent spirit tries to heal the sick.

Keelut: An earth spirit, looking like a hairless dog. Evil.

Kingmingoarkulluk: Lives on land, looks like a tiny Eskimo. When you see him he always sings joyously. Good.

Noesarnak: Lives on land. Looks like a woman with spindly legs. Is dressed in deer-skins, and carries a deer-skin mask. He must be treated very gingerly.

Ooyarrauyamitok: This deity has no special abode. Sometimes on earth, sometimes in heaven. If he is respected and invoked he gives the Eskimos meat, or at least the means of obtaining it.

Pukkeenegak: This spirit of a feminine appearance has a tattooed face. It wears very large boots and very pretty clothes. It is considered a benevolent deity, since it procures food and materials for making clothes, and gives children to the Eskimo women.

Sedna: Goddess of marine animals.

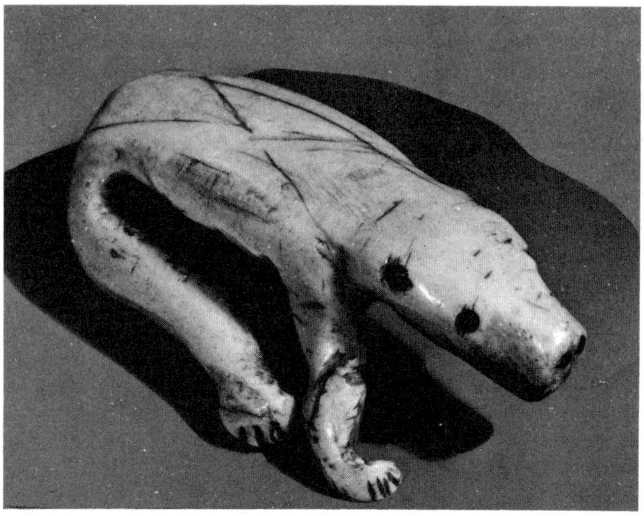

Polar bear charm. The Eskimo's life is a constant struggle against adverse forces – the vagaries of the weather, the shortage of food animals and the ever-present danger of death from exposure or at the jaws of wild animals – and these preoccupations are reflected in their myths and religious beliefs, many of their deities being concerned with hunting and the sea. This ivory figure is probably connected with sympathetic magic and was intended to bring luck in the hunt.

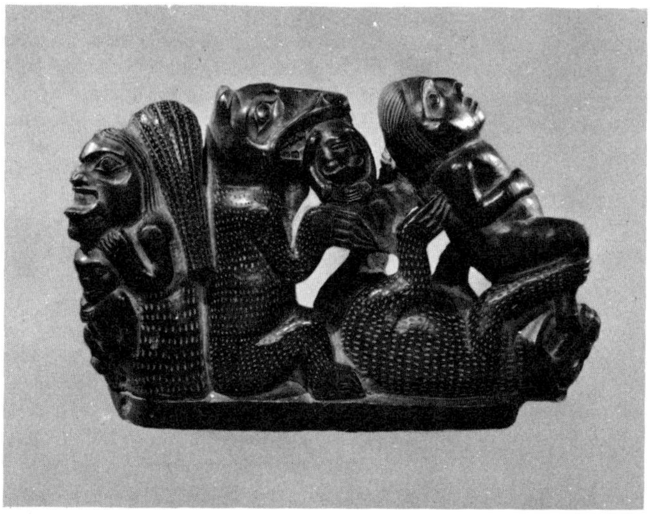

Haida Indian mythological carving in state. The Bear people myths of the Haida Indians of the Pacific North-west coast form one of the most complete reflections of age-old beliefs and have inspired some of the finest Indian art. The bears were not always, however, as hostile as this carving would suggest. The central figure in the legends is an Indian princess called Rhpisunt who was carried off by the Bear people and subsequently honoured by them.

Ataksak: Lives in heaven. Looks like a sphere. He is a personification of joy. He has several very brilliant cords on his clothes. When he dies his body also shines in the same way. He comes to the Eskimos by way of the Angakoks. He is considered to be a benevolent spirit.

INDIANS OF THE FOREST

The Algonquins. When the Whites began to colonise North America vast forests covered the regions which extend from the frozen steppes of Labrador and the shores of Hudson Bay down to the alluvial lands of the Gulf of Mexico. They were inhabited by many native tribes connected with the great Algonquin and Iroquois families, large warlike and hunting tribes.

The myths of these great tribes are peopled with ideal figures of civilising heroes, looked on half as the earliest men, and half as demiurges and creators. These beings are skilled in all the arts of magic, and have the power to change themselves into animals.

The Indians believe that everything in Nature — beings, plants, stones, etc.—is inhabited by a mysterious power, which spreads out and influences other beings. The Iroquois call it 'Orenda' and the Algonquins 'Manitou', and mean by it all magical powers or 'medicines' from the lowest to the highest. Men must get control of the small powers, and on the other hand do everything possible to gain the favour of the powerful Manitous, who are intelligent spirits.

According to the Algonquins of the North, the most powerful of all the Manitous is the Kitcki Manitou, the Great Spirit, who is the father of life and was never created. He is the fountain-head of all good things. And it is in his honour that the Indians 'smoke the pipe of peace'.

The Delawares relate how the Great Spirit instituted this rite:

'The tribes of the North collected in council had decided to exterminate the Delaware people when, suddenly, a bird of glittering white appeared among them, and hung with open wings above the head of the great chief's only daughter. She heard an inner voice saying to her: "Bring all the warriors together and tell them the Great Spirit's heart is sad and hidden in a dark cloud, because they seek to drink the blood of his first-born, the Lenni-Lennapi, the oldest of the tribes. To appease the anger of the Master of Life and to bring joy back to his heart, let all the warriors wash their hands in the blood of a fawn and then, bearing presents and their pipes let them all go together to their elders, let them distribute the presents, and smoke with them the great pipe of peace and fraternity which will unite them for ever." '

The Great Spirit who dwells in heaven is above all other powers. He is the master of light and is manifest in the sun. He is the breath of life, and penetrates everywhere in the shape of the winds. According to an Algonquin myth there exists another very important spirit, Michabo or the Great Hare, father of the race, born in an island called Michilimakinak.

The Great Hare made the earth, and is the inventor of fishing nets. He created water, fish, and a great deer. It was he who drove away the cannibal Manitous.

Michabo's house is situated at the place where the sun rises, and he seems to be a personification of the Dawn. The souls of good Indians live there, and feed on juicy fruits. Michabo also has the power of changing himself into a thousand different animals.

Cosmogony legends. Like almost all Indians, the Algonquin tribes believe in the Thunder Bird, a powerful spirit whose eyes flash lightning, while the beating of his wings is the rolling of thunder. He it is who prevents the earth from drying up and vegetation from dying. He is escorted by minor spirits who are represented in the form of birds resembling falcons or eagles.

Above the clouds which are the dwelling-place of winds and

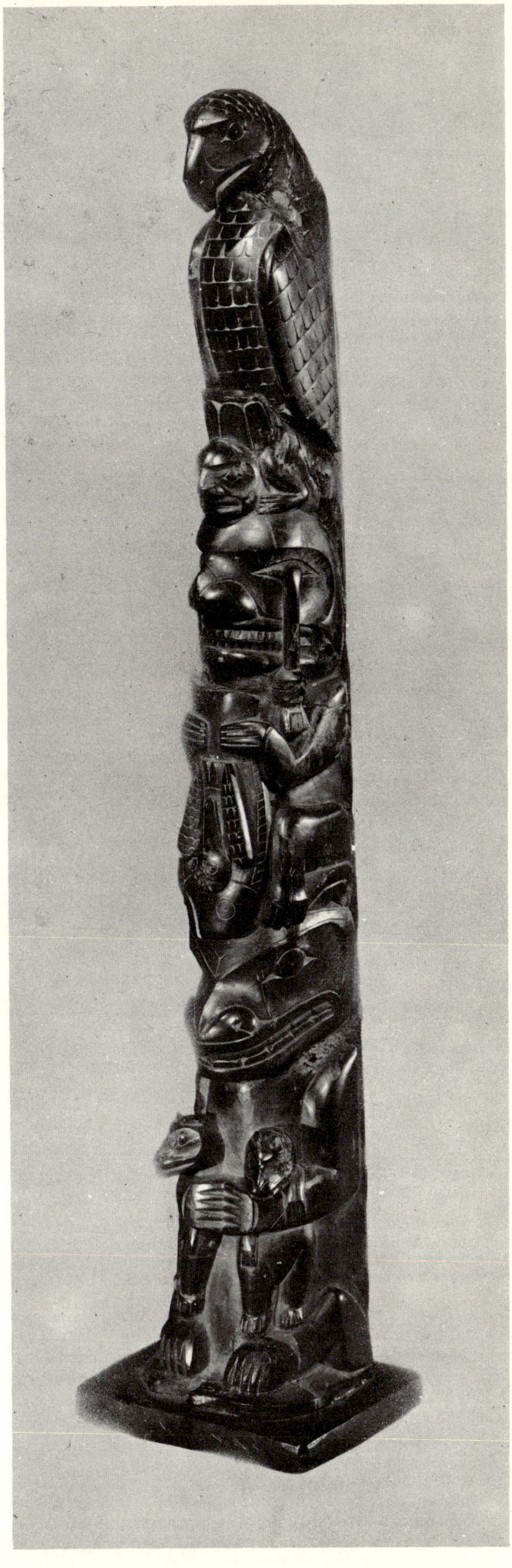

House totem from the Pacific North West.
The eagle at the top probably represents the Thunder Bird, an enormous supernatural creature with an eagle's head, the beating of whose wings produces the rolling of the thunder and whose eyes flash forth lightning. Though awe-inspiring it is not malignant for it is the Thunder Bird who prevents the earth from drying up and vegetation from dying. A belief in its existence was common to almost all the Indian tribes.

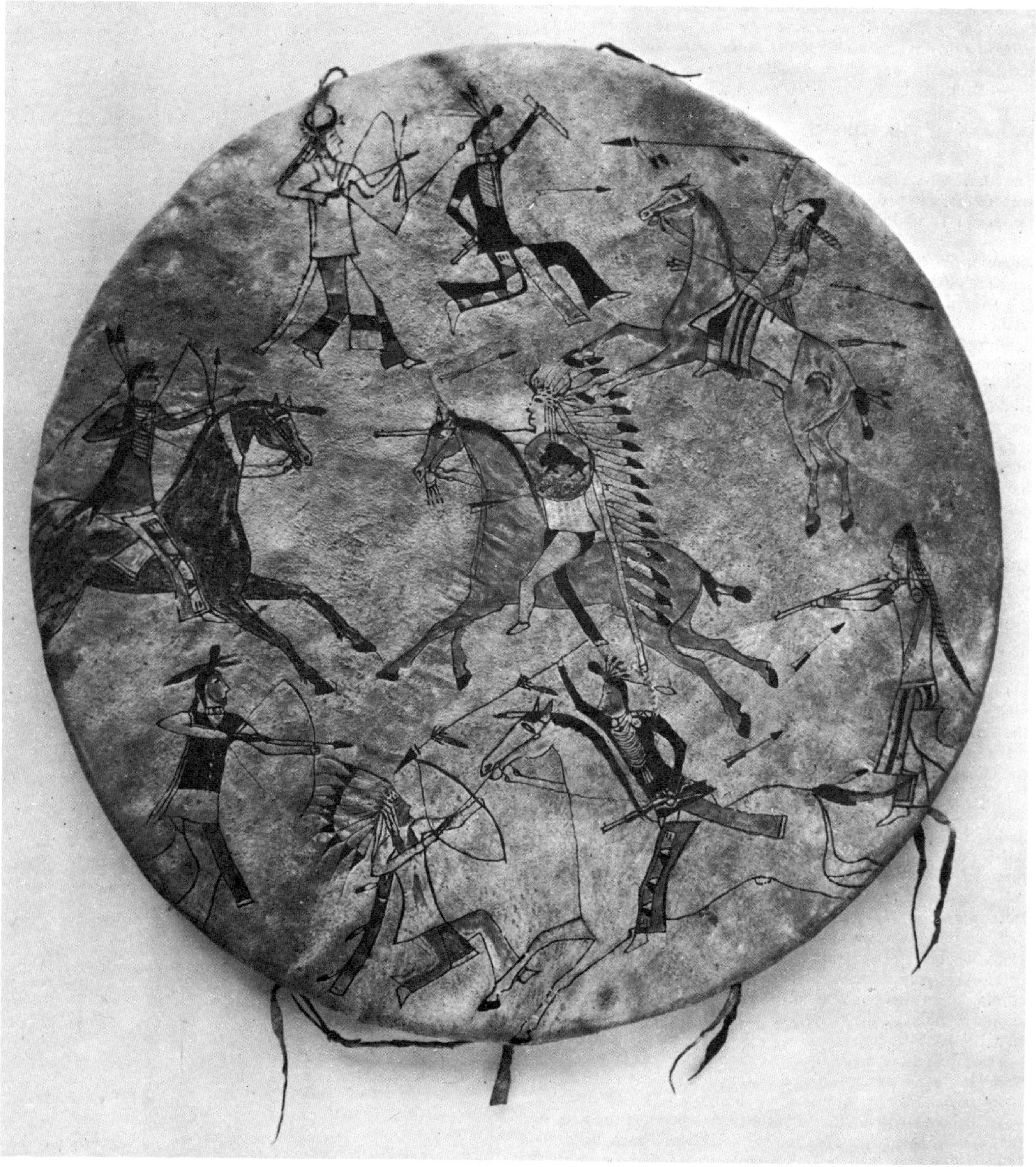

Sioux dance shield. In the centre is a mounted chieftain in his feathered head-dress while round about him other Indians are shown fighting with bows and arrows, spears and guns either on horseback or on foot. Though horses were unknown until introduction by the Spanish in the seventeenth century, they were quickly incorporated into Indian mythology and in a legend found among the Sioux tribes of Montana their invention is attributed to the tribal culture-hero, Coyote.

thunder, there is the abode of sun and moon, usually represented as a man and a woman, who are sometimes husband and wife but more often brother and sister. One Algonquin tribe relates that the sun armed with bow and arrows went hunting, but was away so long that his sister was alarmed, set out to look for him, and travelled for twenty days before she found him. Since then the moon has always made journeys of twenty days across the sky.

Above sun and moon live the stars.

Beneath the clouds is the Earth-Mother from whom is derived the Water of Life, who at her bosom feeds plants, animals and men. The Algonquins call her Nokomis, the Grandmother.

The birds act as intermediaries between human beings and the upper powers, while snakes and aquatic creatures communicate with the lower powers. Usually the world is divided into different levels—four for the upper world, four for the lower. At each of the four cardinal points lives one of four friendly spirits. The one to the North brings ice and snow which permit the hunting of wild animals; the South brings fruits, maize and tobacco; the West gives rain, and the East light and sun.

A legend of the Montagnais, belonging to the Algonquin family, relates how Michabo or the Great Hare re-established the world after the flood:

'One day Michabo went hunting, and the wolves he used as hunting-dogs plunged into a lake and did not return. Michabo

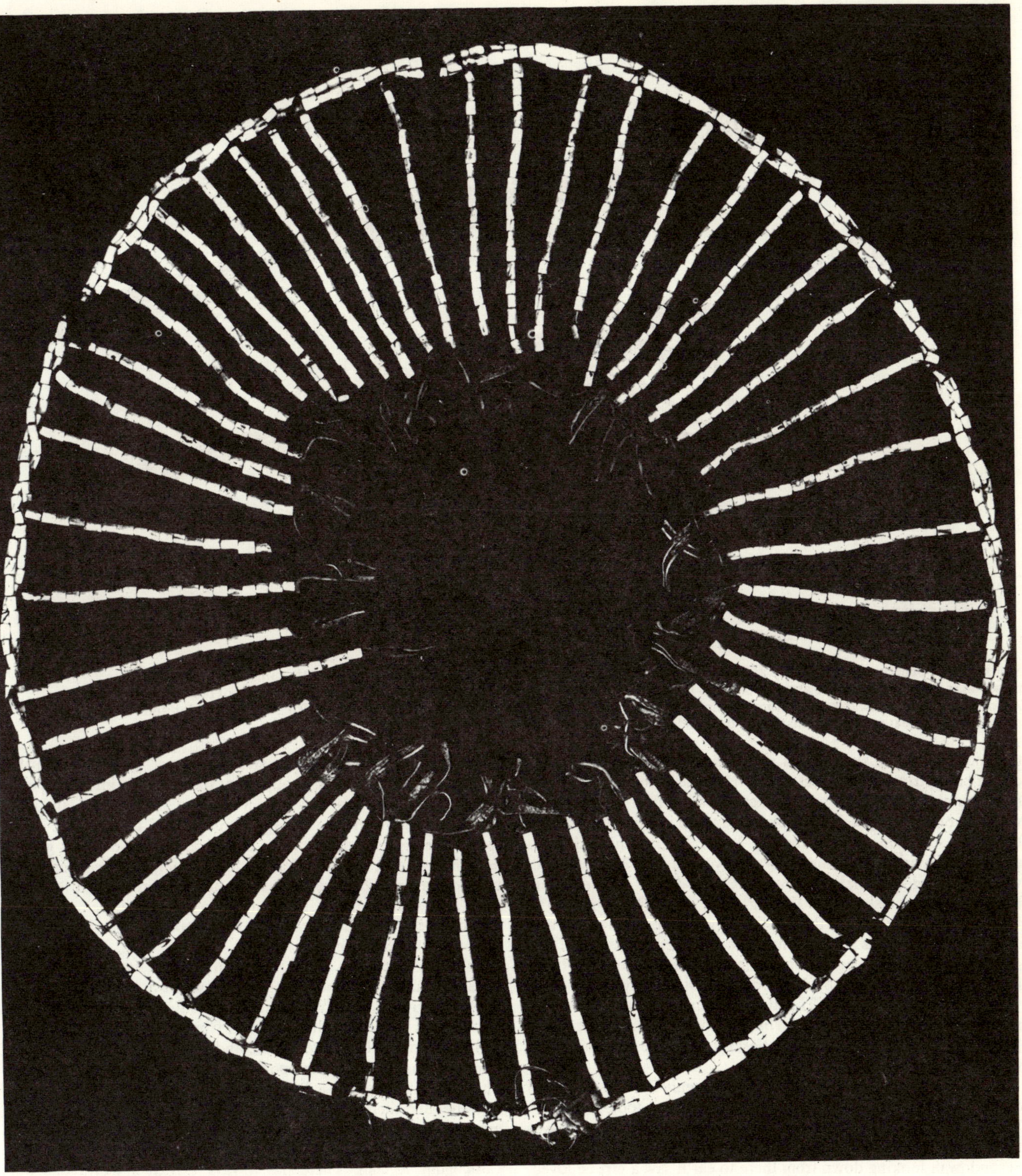

Wampum circle with fifty pendant strings made for the Confederacy of the Five Nations, the first step made by the North American Indians towards a settled nationhood. (The coming of the white man effectively destroyed it). A mnemonic, or memory-aiding device, it was in the care of important tribal dignitaries who used to keep records of tribal history. The foundation of many of the tribes and the creation of their social institutions were ascribed by the Indians to mythical animals.

looked for them everywhere, and at last a bird told him that the wolves were lost in the midst of the lake. When he wanted to go in and look for them, the water overflowed and covered the whole earth.

Michabo told the raven to bring him a lump of clay to re-make the world, but the raven could not find any. Michabo then sent an otter, which dived but brought nothing back. At last he sent out a musk rat which returned with some soil which Michabo used to re-make the earth. He fired arrows into tree-trunks, and they changed into branches. He took vengeance on those who had kept his wolves in the lake, and then married a musk-mouse by whom he had children to re-people the earth.'

Iroquois and Hurons. The most important among the chief gods of the Iroquois are Thunder, Wind and Echo. Stone giants play the part of 'Titans'. Among the oldest deities the Iroquois include their own ancestors and certain animals which assumed human form, and whose names were later used for the clans.

The giants are powerful magicians, very good hunters who are ignorant of the bow and arrows, and use stones as missiles. They have unbelievable strength, and when they fight, their weapons are trees of the biggest size which they uproot with the greatest ease. They are dreaded, for it seems they are given to cannibalism. One of the most important is Ga-oh, the giant who commands the winds. Side by side with this giant is Hino the Thunder spirit. He is

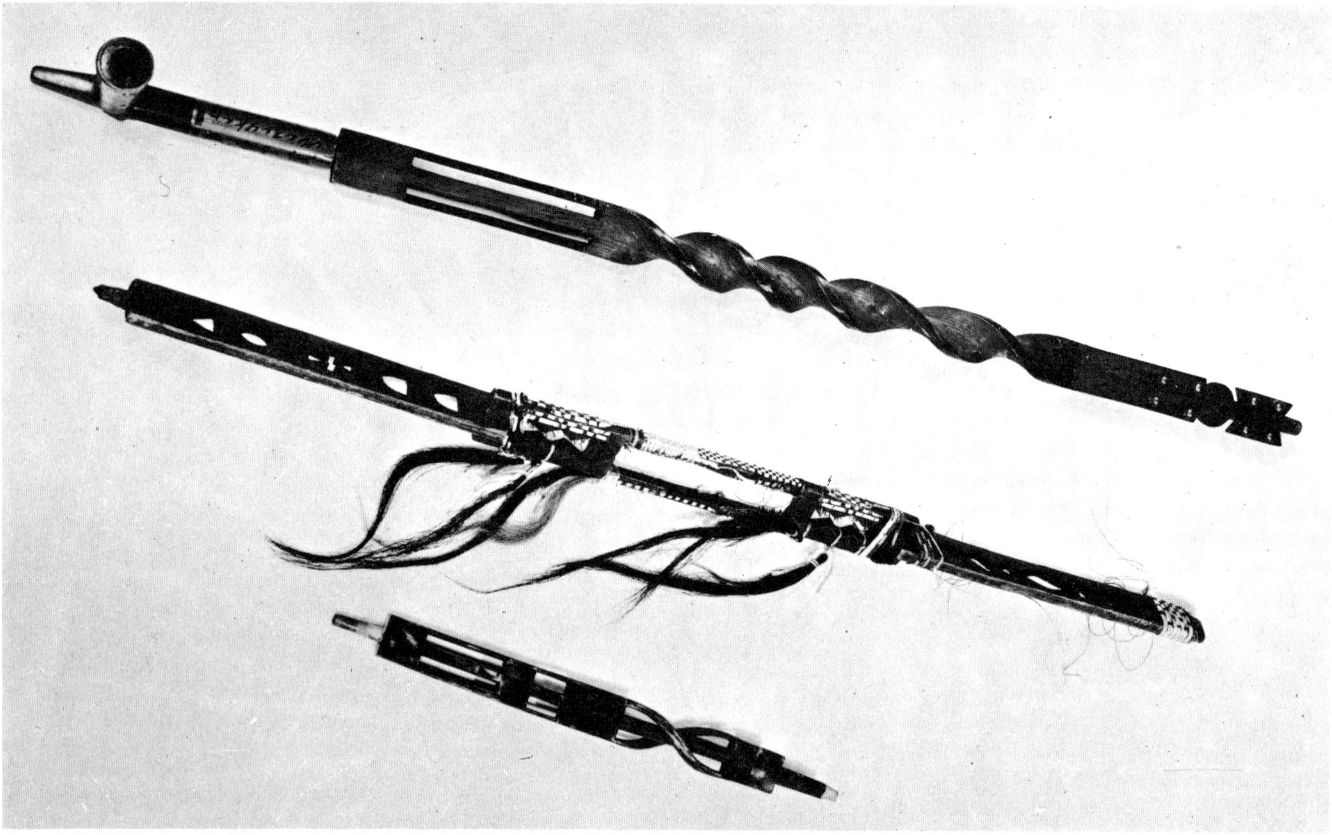

Sioux pipes. Tobacco was smoked by all the Indians of the Plains as a ceremonial or ritual activity. Rightly called 'pipes of peace' these Sioux pipes were smoked at tribal councils (which could last for several days), the tobacco producing a feeling of peace and well-being. According to the Delawares the custom of smoking peace pipes was originally instituted by the Great Spirit , or Kitcki Manitou, to avert their threatened extermination at the hands of the Northern tribes.

the guardian of the sky. Armed with a powerful bow and arrows of fire he destroys all harmful things. His wife is the Rainbow. He has a number of helpers, among them a boy named Gunnodoyak who was once a mortal. Hino took him up into his kingdom, armed him, and sent him to fight the Big Water Snake which devours mankind. Gunnodoyak himself was devoured but Hino and his warriors killed the Snake, recovered Gunnodoyak and took him back to heaven. Oshadagea, the Big Eagle of the Dew, is also in Hino's service. He lives in the Western sky and bears a lake of dew in the hollow of his back. When the destructive spirits of fire shrivel up all earthly vegetation, Oshadagea flies up and the beneficent moisture falls drop by drop from his outspread wings.

Above the clouds where Thunder lives, are the Sun and Moon, and above them are the stars. The Indians tell each other many legends of the stars. One of the prettiest is told by the Iroquois about the Morning star.

Sesondowah, the hunter, saw that the Heavenly Elk had wandered down to earth. In the heat of the chase his pursuit took him up to heaven, in the region above the Sun's dwelling, and there he was taken prisoner by Dawn who made him the watchman at her door. Sesondowah looking down from there to earth saw a girl he loved. When spring came he assumed the form of a blue bird and flew down to her. In summer he became a black bird, and in autumn a huge falcon which carried her off to heaven. Furious at this escapade Dawn chained him to her door, and changed the girl into a star which she tied on her forehead, so that he is consumed with longing to reach her and can never succeed. The star is called Gendenwitha, the Morning Star.

That is how the Iroquois conceive of the upper powers.

The most important of the lower powers is the Earth which the Iroquois call Eithinoha, Our Mother. They say that her daughter Onatha, Spirit of Wheat, went out one day to look for the Refreshing Dew and was carried off by the Spirit of Evil who imprisoned her in the darkness under the earth.

There she remained until the day when the sun found her and brought her back to the fields she had deserted. Since then Onatha has never again dared to go looking for dew.

On earth and under the earth dwell multitudes of strange and more or less invisible and mysterious beings in a certain order.

First come the dwarfs, grouped by the Iroquois into three categories: the Gahongas, living in water and rocks; the Gandayaks whose duty is to make vegetation fruitful and to take care of the fish in the rivers; and then the Ohdowas who live under ground and there are in charge of all kinds of monsters and venomous beasts. Under water live beings in human form dressed in snakeskins and wearing horns. Sometimes the beauty of their daughters attracts men, who disappear into the depths of the water and are for ever lost to their kin.

Other monsters live either in the forest or in underground dwellings. For instance among the Iroquois we have the Big Heads and the Stone Giants. The former are represented in the form of enormous heads covered with thick hair, from which project two paws with sharp nails. Their eyes flame, and their mouths are wide open. They fly among storms, supported by the profusion of their hair. They say that one day a Big Head followed an Indian girl to her wigwam, and there saw her eat chestnuts roasted on the fire; whereupon he seized and swallowed the burning brands, and killed himself.

Cosmogony legends. There has always existed a world like ours above the dome of the sky, and there the warriors, like those on earth, went hunting and at night slept in long huts.

The Iroquois and Huron myth describing creation, begins with this heavenly world in which pain was unknown.

'A little girl, Ataentsic, was born there soon after her father's death. It must be noted that this was the first death among the dwellers in heaven. His body was placed on a bed of state, and the child formed the habit of going to it and speaking to her father.

'When she grew up he told her to make a journey across the lands of the "Chief who owns the earth" whom she was to marry. The girl set out, crossed a river on the trunk of a maple, and, after escaping various dangers, came to the chief's hut pitched beside the "big tree of heaven". There after passing various tests she became the chief's wife. When he saw she was with child he became ferociously and unjustly jealous of the Fire Dragon. Ataentsic gave birth to a daughter, Breath of Wind. Representatives of all things and beings of creation then visited the chief and held council. Northern Lights guessed that Ataentsic's husband was jealous, and advised him to uproot the "tree of life", which he did at once, forming an abyss into which he cast his wife and child. Thus Ataentsic fell from the sky and as she passed through the air noticed a kind of blue light. She looked and thought she saw that she was falling towards a big lake, but saw no earth anywhere.

'Meanwhile the water creatures living in the lake noticed this body falling from the skies, and deicded to look for eath at the bottom of the lake.

'The otter and the turtle failed in their object, and only the musk rat succeeded in placing the earth he had brought up on the turtle's back. At that moment the shell grew enormously and became the solid earth. Ataentsic, borne up by the wings of birds, set foot on this soil.

'Her daughters, Breath of Wind, grew up, and one night received the visit of the Master of Winds, giving birth to twins, Ioskeha and Tawiscara. The twins hated each other, and fought before they were born, causing their mother's death. From her body Ataentsic made the sun and moon, but did not set them in the sky. Tawiscara persuaded his grandmother that Ioskeha alone had caused their mother's death. So she cast him out.

'He fled to his father, the Master of Winds, who gave him a bow and arrows and maize, thereby making him master animal and vegetable food. Ioskeha then created the various species of animals. He then overcame the dwarf Hadui who causes all diseases, and wrenched from him the secret of medicine and the ritual use of tobacco. He stole the sun and moon from Ataentsic and Tawiscara, and let them take their course in the sky. Then Ioskeha created mankind. Tawiscara tried to imitate him, but only succeeded in producing monsters, and in the end was sent into exile by his brother.'

In this myth Ioskeha appears as the great hero of creation, while his brother Tawiscara is the incarnation of all evil powers. They correspond to Osiris and Set. This legend also exists among the Algonquins, except that the names of the twin brothers are different.

The legend of the 'fished-up-earth', of which fragments are found in the myth of Ioskeha is frequently associated with that of the deluge.

The flood legends of the Iroquois and Hurons are analogous to those of the Algonquins. In a sentence—the Iroquois, Huron and Algonquin myths agree on looking for the origin of life in a higher world placed above the clouds. The Hurons recognise their ancestor in Ataentsic, who was cast out of heaven.

INDIANS OF THE PLAINS

Very different in appearance and life are the great plains of North America, which extend from the frozen regions of the Mackenzie river to the north of Mexico and the west of the Mississippi.

When the Whites reached them, these vast prairies gave pasture for innumerable herds of caribou in the north and bison in the south. There was abundance of game of all kinds, and the scattered Indian tribes lived comfortably on the products of the chase and of agriculture. Their horizon was boundless, with no thick forest or deep valleys to divert their gaze. According to the season and the area the Indian saw on all sides either the intense green of grass or the dazzling white of snow. Everywhere around him the sky seemed to touch the earth and to make a huge canopy covering a flat, circular earth. This apparent simplification of Nature on a grand scale appears in the mythology of the tribes of the plains. The world is governed by an all-powerful and invisible being, who takes precedence of all the other great gods. According to the tribe this supreme Being is called the Great Spirit, or the Master of Life, or our Father the Sky, or the Great Mystery.

The Sioux Indians call him Wakonda and the Pawnees Tirawa, or the Arch of Heaven. As a rule the Indians do not represent him in a definite form, but by symbols—dawn, for instance, suggesting the light white clouds floating very high in the sky. Wakonda is the source of all life and power; while the great gods whom the Indians revere are merely intermediaries between the distant, unknown Great Spirit and mankind. The gods are nearly always: The Sun, the Earth, the Moon, the Morning Star, Wind, Fire, Thunder, for the prairie Indians. For the agricultural tribes corn must be added. Among the Pawness, the Sun, 'Shakuru', is the greatest and most powerful. A very important ritual is observed

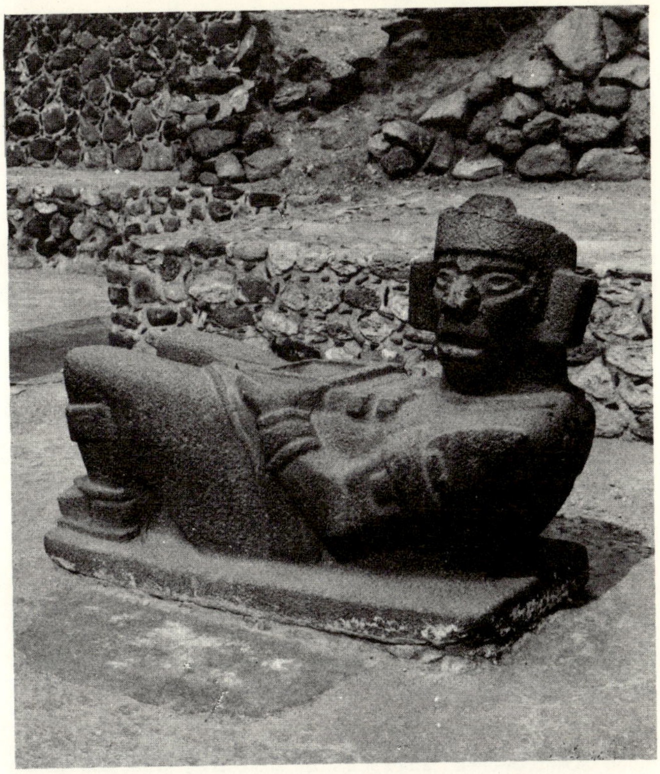

A chac-mool from the Toltec capital of Tula. These strange reclining figures holding shallow dishes in their laps and with averted, staring faces were placed at temple entrances and depicted attendants of the rain god Tlaloc (or the Mayan Chaac), their lumpy shape suggesting floating rain clouds. From Tula they spread to Aztec and Maya centres. The dishes in their laps have been variously interpreted as receptacles for offerings, rain or the hearts of sacrificial victims.

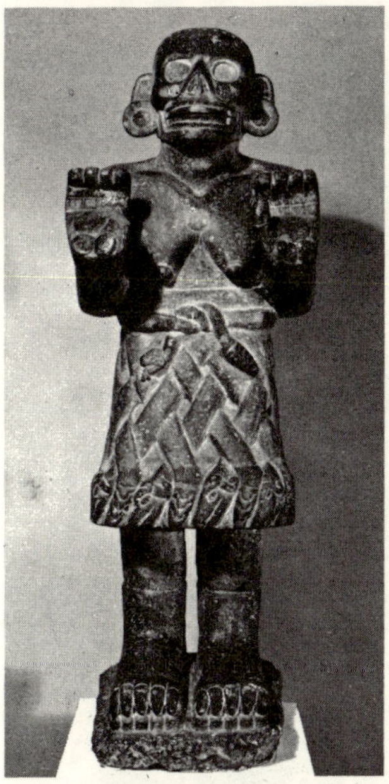

The goddess Coatlicue. An ancient earth and mother goddess, Coatlicue was adopted by the Aztecs and made the mother of Huitzilopochtli, the great war and storm god. According to myth she conceived him after already bearing a daughter and four hundred sons when a crown of feathers fell from heaven onto her breast. This awe-inspiring representation shows her with a death's-head and the serpent-woven skirt from which she took her name. Aztec statue in basalt, fifteenth century A.D.

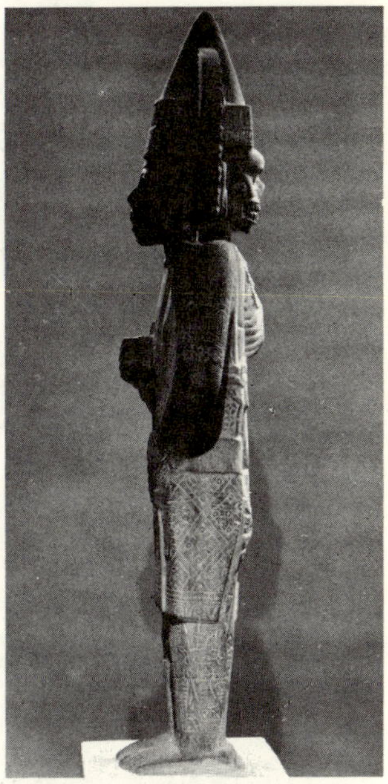

Quetzalcoatl. The great god and culture hero of old Mexico, the Plumed Serpent was the most powerful figure in the mythology of Mexico and Central America. This Huastec statue shows the young god in full life as the bright star Venus on the front left, while the back portrays the waning of power as day follows night and Venus is supplanted by the sun. The god wears his conical ocelot-skin cap and is dressed in elaborately decorated clothes, his customary attire.

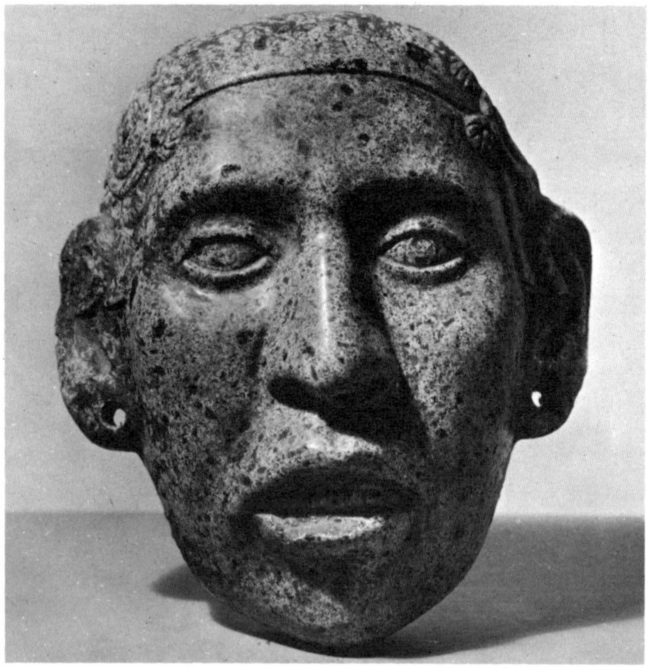

Mask of Tezcatlipoca. The arch enemy of Quetzalcoatl, Tezcatlipoca was one of the great gods of the Aztec pantheon and personified the summer sun which ripens the harvest but also brings drought and sterility. Blood sacrifices were a feature of his cult and every year the handsomest of the prisoners had his heart torn from his living body as an offering to the god. This stone mask is believed to come from the Xochimilco region of Mexico and is dated A.D. 1507.
Dumbarton Oaks, Washington.

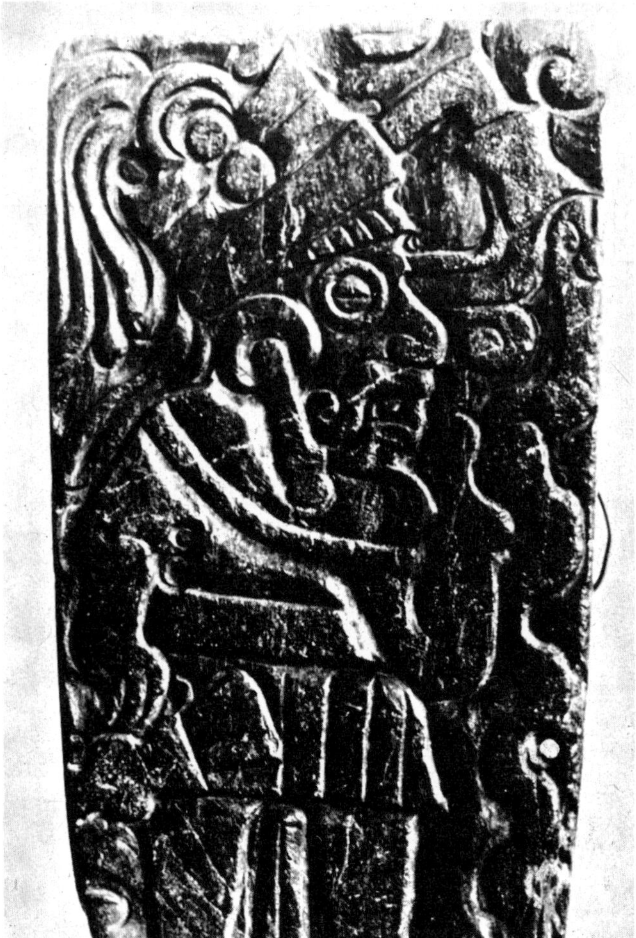

Tlaloc, the rain god of pre-colombian Mexico, carved in relief on a slab of serpentine. This very ancient deity is always recognisable even in stylistic representations, always being shown with completely circular eyes.

in his honour, and the 'dance of the Sun' is the greatest ceremony of the year among the tribes of the plains. It usually lasts a week, and consists of processions, symbolical dances and voluntary self-mutilations by warriors carrying out vows. It is also the great festival when the deeds of the young warriors are praised, and tribal affairs discussed.

Our Mother Earth is the start and finish of all life. She is the provider of all food. Ceremonies are also held in her honour, representing the marriage of Earth and Heaven, and the birth of life.

After the Sun the most important of the heavenly powers is the Morning Star. The Indians represent it as a young man painted in red (the colour of life), shod with moccasins, and wrapped in a large robe. On his head he wears a downy eagle's feather stained red, the image of the breath of life. To him the Great Spirit entrusted the Gift of Life which he is commanded to spread over the earth.

Formerly the Skidi Pawnees had the custom of sacrificing a virgin in his honour. The victim's body was cut into pieces, and buried in the fields to make them fertile.

The Black Feet relate a legend of the Morning Star's son:

'Once upon a time Morning Star noticed on earth Soatsaki, an Indian girl of great beauty, sleeping near her *tipi* (camp), and fell in love with her. He married her, and took her up to heaven, to the dwelling of his father and mother, the Sun and the Moon. There Soatsaki had a son, Little Star. The Moon, her Mother-in-Law, gave Soatsaki a pick as a present, and warned her not to use it to dig up the turnip which grew near the dwelling of the Spider Man. But curiosity got the better of the young woman, who tore up the forbidden turnip and found that she could see the Earth through the hole she had made. Seeing the *tipis* of her tribe she fell violently home-sick, and her heart grew deathly sad. To punish her disobedience the Sun, her father-in-law, decided to turn her out of heaven with her son, and lowered them to earth wrapped in an elk skin. But when the poor Indian girl found herself separated from her husband she soon died, leaving her son alone and poor.

'The child had a scar on his face and was nicknamed "Poia", Scar-face. When he grew up Poia fell in love with the chief's daughter, who rebuffed him because of his scar. In despair he made up his mind to seek his grandfather, the Sun, who would take away the scar, and so started out towards the West. When he reached the Pacific coast he halted, and passed three days in fasting and prayer, and on the morning of the fourth day a luminous trail unrolled before him across the ocean. Poia stepped boldly on to the miraculous path and reached the Sun's dwelling place. When he reached the sky he saw his father Morning Star battling with seven monstrous birds. Rushing to the rescue, he slew them all. In reward for this deed, the Sun took away the scar, and then after teaching him the ritual of the Sun dance, made him a gift of raven's feathers, a proof of his kinship with the Sun, and another of a flute which would win him the heart of his beloved. Poia returned to earth by another path called the Wolf Trail or the Milky Way, taught the Black Feet the Sun dance and having married the chief's daughter, took her up to heaven.'

The chief constellations have a place in Indian mythology, and each has a legend which varies from tribe to tribe. Thus the Great Bear is either an ermine or a coffin followed by mourning relatives, or seven brothers pursued by a monstrous bear, or seven young men reduced by poverty to changing themselves into stars and going up to heaven by unrolling a spider's web.

Alongside these heavenly powers the Indians of the plains revere the powers of Earth, Water, Fire and Air, and the different tribes represent them in different ways. Thus, the Sioux imagine that the water spirits are divided into two categories, those of the streams and those of the waters below ground. The former look like men, but the latter like women, though some believe that they form a hideous many-headed monster supporting the earth.

Thunder is the most important among the air spirits. In those vast plains where thunderstorms assume terrific proportions, the imagination of the natives naturally tried to explain these phenomena of Nature.

To them, thunder is the voice of the Great Spirit speaking in the clouds. They believe that thunder comes in the shape of a huge bird (the thunder-bird) accompanied by a swarm of smaller birds, the beating of whose wings causes the distant rolling which is heard rumbling among the clouds after each clap of thunder.

One of the Caddoan tribes, the Pawnees of Nebraska, tell a

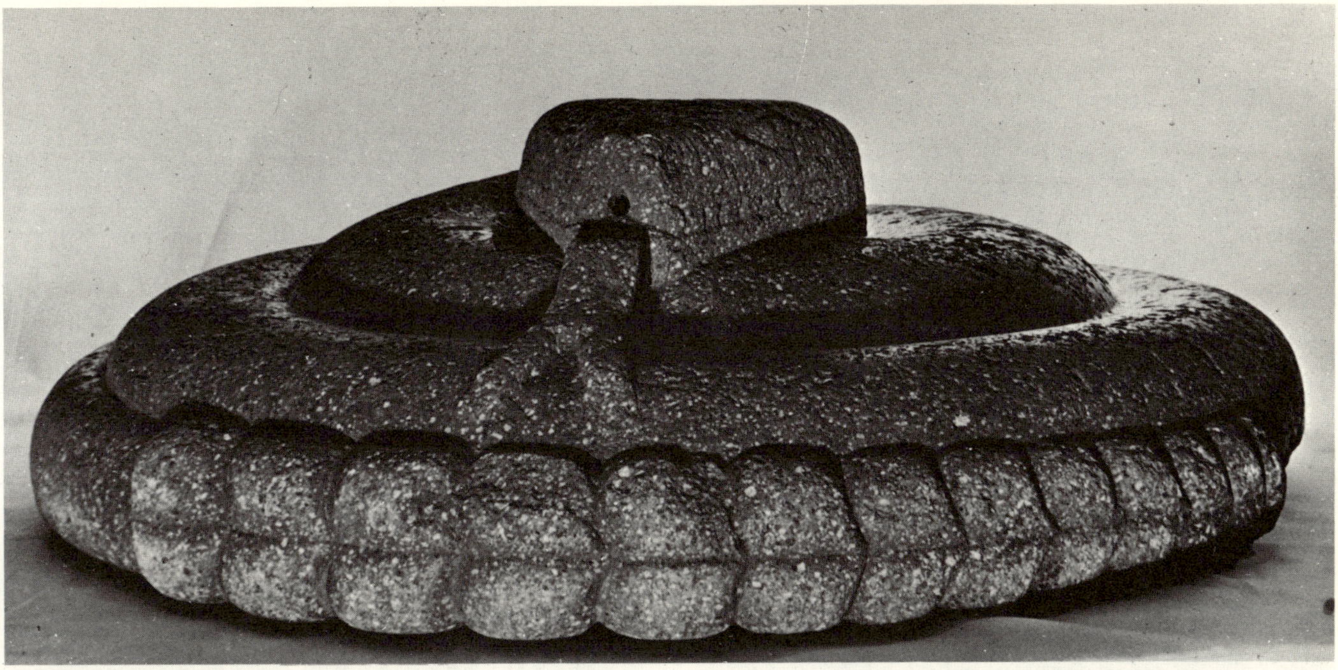

An Aztec carving showing a rattlesnake coiled with its head in the centre and its rattles wrapped around it on the outside. The thirteen rattles were probably the reason why the Aztecs, alone among Mexican peoples, carved ritual images of this snake. The number thirteen was particularly important in their methods of divination, the Divine Calendar, or 'Book of Destiny' (*tonalamatl*), which ruled their lives being divided into periods of thirteen days. Rhyolite porphyry, A.D. 1200 to 1521. Dumbarton Oaks, Washington.

cosmogony legend which explains the creation of the world as follows:

'In the beginning, Tirawa, the great chief and Atira his wife dwelt in heaven. All the other gods were seated about them. And Tirawa said to them: "I shall give each of you a task to carry out in heaven and a portion of my power, for I mean to create men in my image. They will all be under your protection, and you will take care of them." Thus, Shakuru the Sun was placed in the east to give light and heat; and Pah the moon in the west to give light by night. He said to Bright Star, the evening star: "You will stay in the west and you shall be called the mother of all things, for all beings shall be created by you." And to the Big Star, the morning star: "You shall stay in the east and be a warrior. Take care that none stays behind when you urge the people to the west." In the north he placed the Pole Star, and made it the first of heaven. In the south he placed the Star of Spirits or the Star of Death. Then he placed four other stars, one in the north-east, one in the north-west, one in the south-east and one in the south-west, and said to them: "Your task will be to support the sky."

'After he had done all this Tirawa said to the evening star: "I will send you clouds, winds, lightning and thunder, and when you receive them you will set them near the Heavenly Garden. There they will become human beings, I shall clothe them in buffalo robes and they shall be shod with moccasins." Immediately afterwards the clouds assembled, the winds began to blow, lightning and thunder entered the clouds. When the sky was entirely darkened, Tirawa dropped a pebble on the thick clouds which opened and revealed an immense expanse of water. Tirawa then armed the gods of the four stars of the quarters of heaven with maces and bade them smite the water, and the waters were separated and the earth appeared. On a fresh order from Tirawa the four gods began to sing songs in praise of the creation of the earth, and their voices brought together the gods of the elements, of clouds and winds, of lightning and thunder, and so caused a terrific thunderstorm to break, which by its violence split the earth into mountains and valleys. Then the four gods again began to sing in praise of forests and prairies, where-upon another storm broke which left the earth green and covered with trees and vegetation. They sang a third time, and the rivers and streams began to flow rapidly. At the fourth song, seeds of all kinds germinated and enriched the earth.

'Tirawa ordered the sun and moon to unite, to people this Earthly Paradise, and a son was born to them. The morning and evening

Quetzalcoatl in his manifestation as the wind god, when he is known as Ehecatl. This Aztec basalt statue shows him wearing the wind 'mask' which always identified him surmounted by his own distinctive conical cap. According to an early myth of the Nahua peoples who inhabited the high plateau before the arrival of the Aztecs, it was he who brought love into the world by bestirring the maiden Mayahuel. He represents spirit freed from any association with the world of matter.

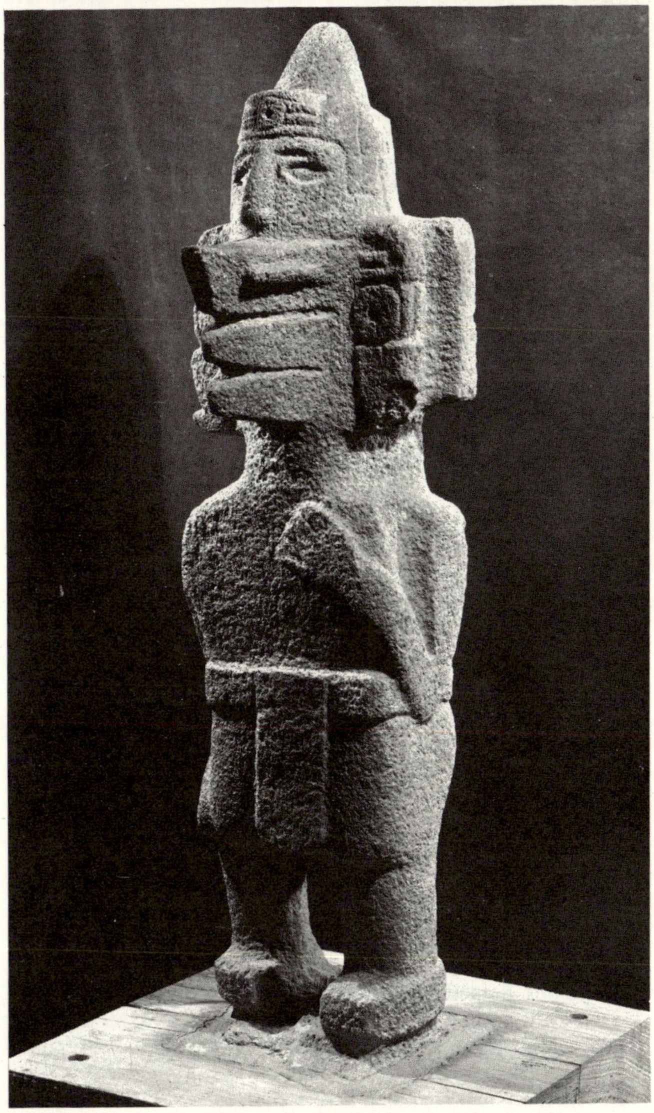

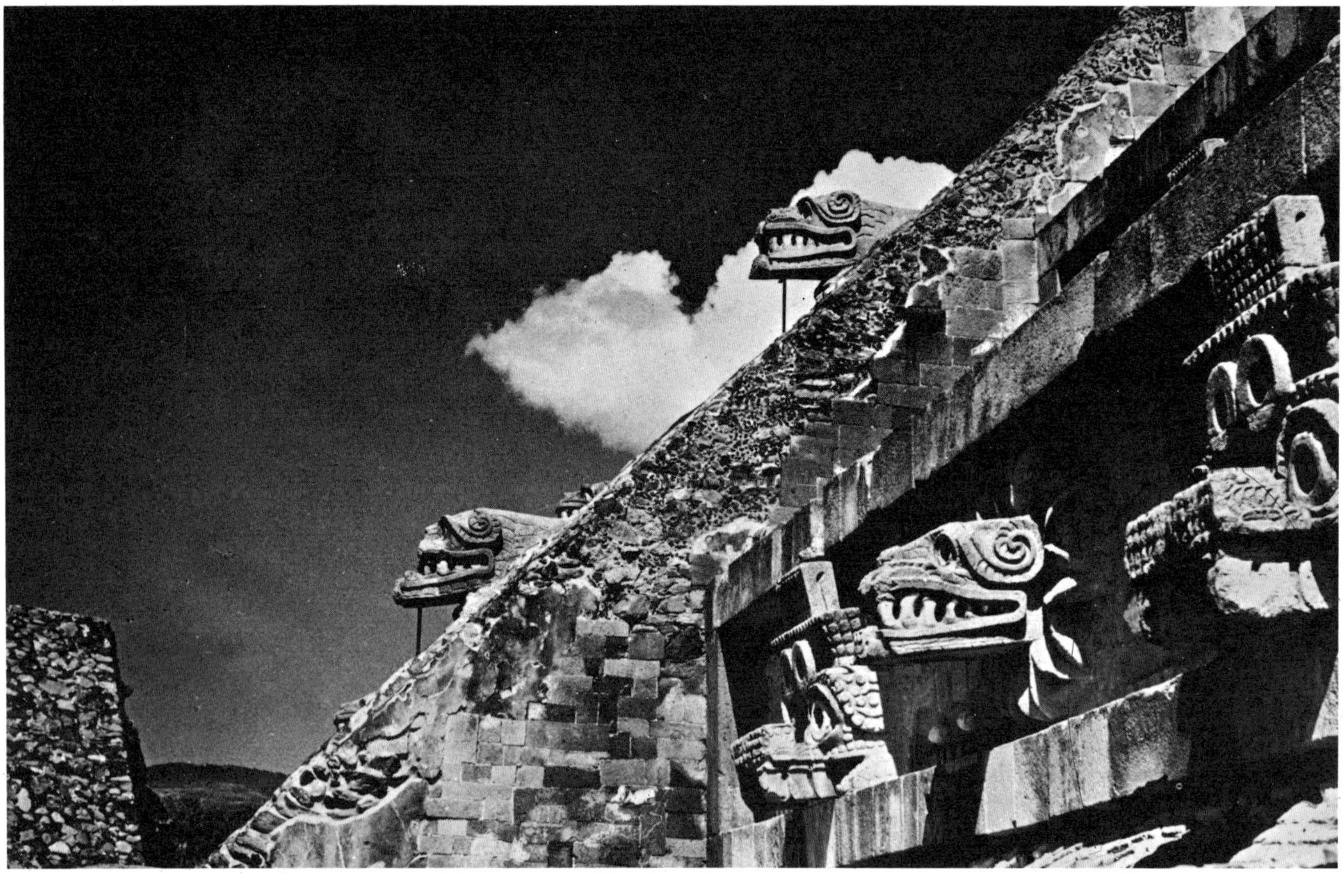

Detail of the side of the pyramid temple at Teotihuacan, which was dedicated to both Quetzalcoatl, the Plumed Serpent, and Tlaloc the rain god. The masks of the gods alternate: the serpent head with the goggle eyes of the rain god. Teotihuacan was the great religious centre of the Toltecs, an area three and a half miles long and two miles wide being devoted to the gods. This particular temple dates from the eighth century A.D.

stars also united, and they had a daughter. The two children were placed on earth and when they had grown up Tirawa sent gods to teach them the secrets of Nature. The woman was given seeds, and moisture to make them grow, a hut and a hearth. She learned the arts of fire and of speech. The man received male clothes and the weapons of a warrior. He learned the science of war-paint, and the names of the animals, the art of shooting with bow and arrows, of smoking and of fire stones.

'The Bright Star appeared to the young man, and taught him the ritual of sacrifice. Other men were created by the stars, and he became their chief and taught them what he had learned. A circular camp was built and laid out in the same order as the stars are fixed in heaven, in memory of the way in which the world had been created.'

The Pawnees also explain the origin of death: 'Before creating men Tirawa sent Lightning to explore the earth. Bright Star who has command of the elements gave him the sack of storms, in which he had enclosed the constellations which Morning Star drives before her. When he had travelled over the earth, Lightning laid down his sack and took out the stars, which he hung in the sky.

But one of the stars (called Coyote-Cheater because the coyote howls at it thinking it is the Morning Star which it precedes) was jealous of Bright Star's power, and sent a wolf to steal the sack of storms. The wolf succeeded, and let out all the beings shut up in the sack, but they were angry at not finding their master Lightning, and threw themselves upon the wolf and killed him. Since then death has never left the earth, and will never leave it until the day when all things vanish and the South Star, the star of death, will reign over the earth. Then the moon will redden and the sun go out. Men will be changed into little stars and will fly in heaven along the Milky Way, which is the path the dead take to go to heaven.'

Animal stories have a very considerable part in the legends of the Redskins. Sometimes they are spirits which put on an animal's skin, and they are always beings gifted with supernatural power. They teach men what rites should be performed, and give them remedies for sicknesses etc. Among the Pawness the coyote has been especially regarded as a heroic character in various legends.

The Hopi or Moqui Indians of Arizona give a different version in their myths of the creation of mankind. According to the Moqui, two deities, both named Huruing Wuhti, after filling the world with animals decided to create men and women. They took clay and moulded it and sang an incantation together, and soon the man and woman came to life.

THE PERICUS

The Pericu Indians of California paid no homage to created things. They had no festivals, no prayers, no vows. In heaven they recognised an all-powerful master named Niparaya, creator of heaven and earth, who gives food to all creatures. He is invisible, and has not a body like human beings.

Niparaya has a wife called Amayicoyondi and although he has no relations with her, having no body, nevertheless he had three sons by her. One is called Quaayayp, that is, Man. Amayicoyondi gave birth to the second on a red mountain. His name was Acaragui. Quaayayp took up his residence with the Indians of the south, in order to teach them. He was very powerful, and had a great number of servants who came down on earth with him. At last the Indians murdered him in violent enmity. He is dead even unto this day, but corruption cannot touch him, so that his blood flows continually. He does not speak, but an owl speaks to him.

In one myth the Pericus say that heaven is more populous than earth, and that at one time there was great strife between the inhabitants. Among them was Wac or Tupuran who was very powerful. He revolted against Niparaya, but was completely defeated and deprived of his power, driven out of heaven, and shut up with his followers in an underground cave, with the task of looking after whales and seeing they did not escape.

Thus there were two parties among the Californian Indians, those who followed Niparaya and were sensible and good, and those who preferred to follow Wac-Tupuran and were addicted to magic.

The Pericus thought that the stars were pieces of burning metal, that the moon was created by Cucumunic, and the stars by Purutabui.

The Guacure Indians among the tribes of the Loretto nation

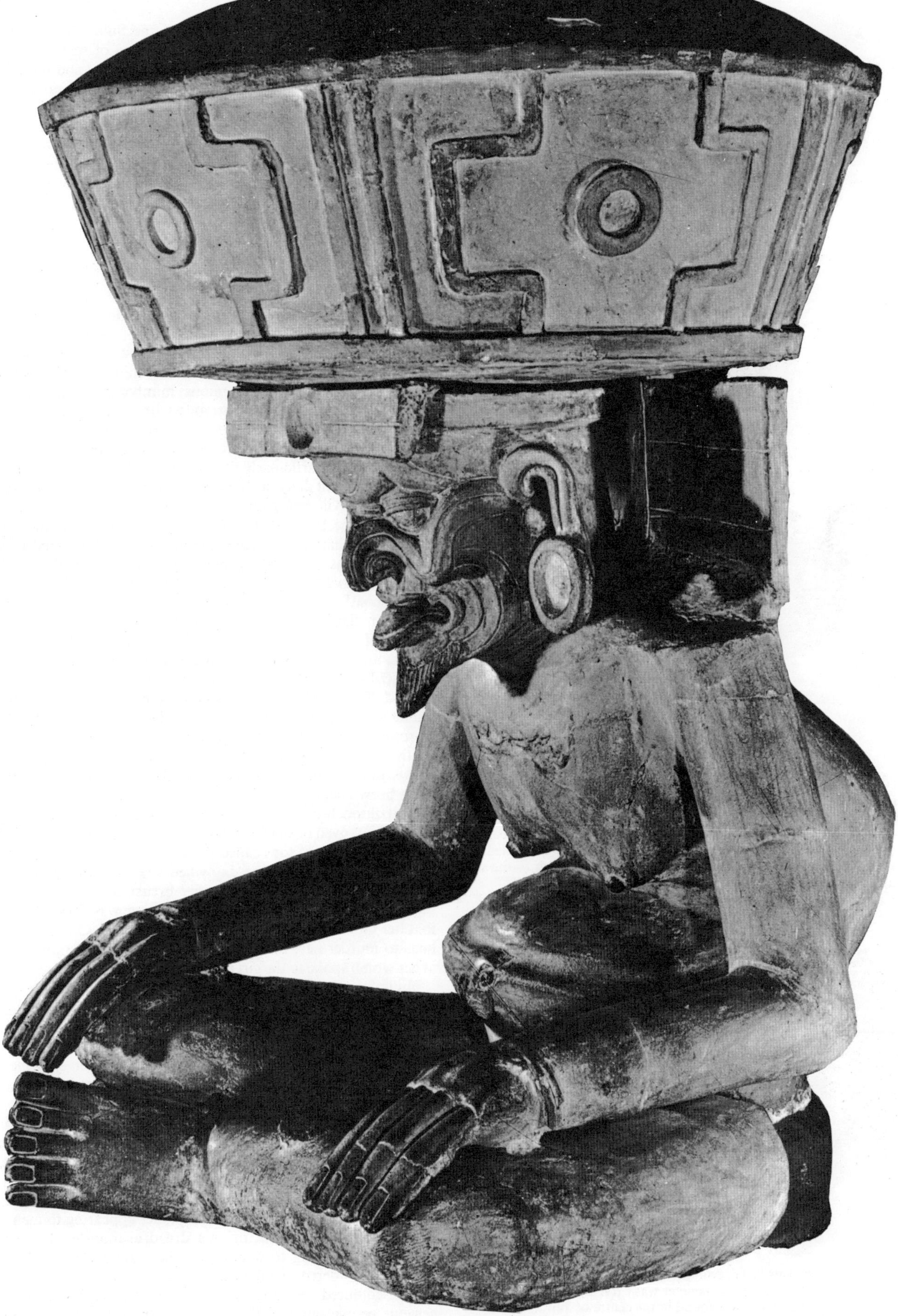

Xiuhtecuhtli, the fire god, as Huehueteotl, 'the old god at the centre'. One of the oldest deities of ancient America, this clay figure from the Veracruz culture shows him seated with a brazier on his head. Xiuhtecuhtli was lord of the present 'Sun', or era, his ceremonies being particularly important at the end of every fifty-two-year cycle when all fires were put out and a fresh one was kindled on a prisoner's breast in order to keep time moving.

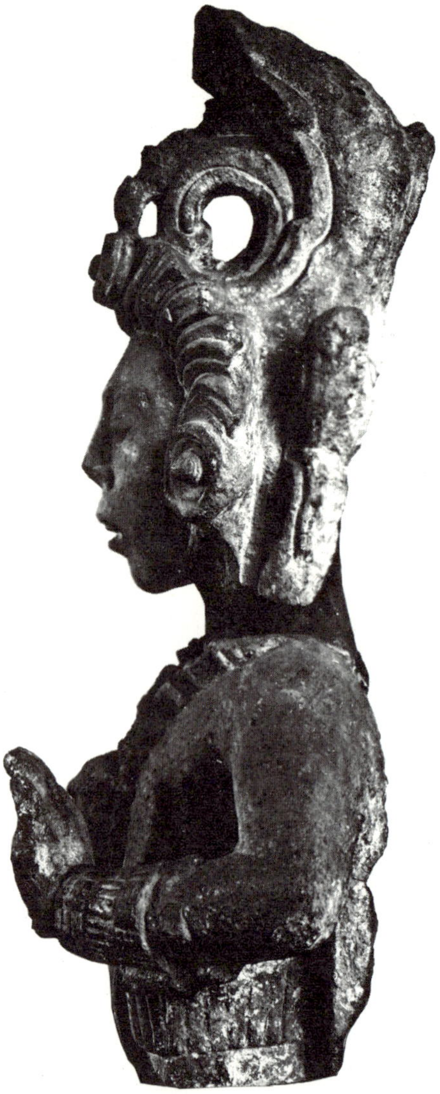

Yum Caax, the Maya god of maize. The counterpart of the Aztec Cinteotl, Yum Caax was associated with life, prosperity and fruitfulness, never with death. This sensitive portrait from Copan in Honduras reflects his benevolent character and the Maya's passionate attachment to the soil. The god is shown with the elongated, flattened forehead cultivated by the Maya aristocracy which was obtained by tying boards to the skull in childhood – the resultant shape symbolising an ear of maize.

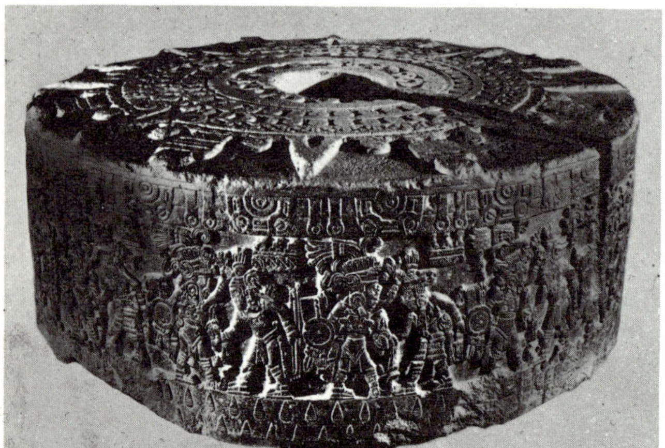

The stone of Tizoc. This large, cylindrical, drum-shaped stone two and a half feet high and eight feet in diameter was carved during the reign of the Aztec ruler Tizoc and was found in the centre of Tenochtitlan. A *techatl*, or sacrificial stone, it has a depression in the centre to hold the hearts of the victims while the bas-reliefs round the sides show future victims being captured and led off by the hair during a holy war.
Trachite, 1481 to 1486.

believed that the northern part of the sky was inhabited by spirits, whose chief was Gumongo. They it was who sent men plague and diseases.

Among other beliefs they think of the Sun, Moon and Stars, Evening and Morning, as having the forms of men and women, disappearing every evening in the western ocean, and re-appearing every morning in the east after having swum across the ocean during the night.

The Luiseno of Lower California say that a flood covered the highest mountains and destroyed most of mankind. Only a few were saved because they took refuge on the heights of Bonsald which alone were spared by the waters, when all the rest of the land was flooded. The survivors remained there until the flood ended.

MEXICO

Clan totemism no longer existed in Mexico at the time of the conquest. There remained only a sort of individual totemism, whereby, following on a significant dream, a man felt he was living in close sympathy with an animal or a thing. At that period the mythology included an enormous number of deities who were continually increasing. In accordance with the custom of conquering pagans, the Aztecs felt they ought to revere the gods of the conquered. Thus new cults grew up. Several of their great gods had such an origin, particularly Quetzalcoatl who was of Toltec origin, Tlaloc an ancient deity of the Otomi, Camaxtli formerly a god of the Chichimees, Xilonen, goddess of maize, deity of the Huastecs, etc.

As with the Indians of North America, the Mexican pantheon has the peculiarity of placing the gods in the 'quarters' of space. The north was the dwelling place of Tezcatlipoca, the south that of Huitzilopochtli, the east that of Tonatiuh, and the west that of Quetzalcoatl.

Certain figures of great gods stand out from the innumerable crowd of deities, Huitzilopochtli, Tezcatlipoca, Quetzalcoatl, Tlaloc, and his wife Chalchiuhtlicue, and Tzinteotl.

Huitzilopochtli (humming-bird of the South, or He of the South), the god of war, was worshipped in the temple of Tenochtitlan where numerous human sacrifices were made to him. He was also the storm-god. His attributes were humming-bird's feathers fastened to his left leg, a snake of fire, and a stick curved in the shape of a snake. In the manuscripts his face is shown crossed with blue lines and a brown band.

Huitzilopochtli was the son of the pious Coatlicue (She whose garment is woven of snakes) who was already the mother of a daughter and a number of sons called the Centzon-Huitznahuas (the Four hundred southerners). One day when she was praying a crown of feathers fell from heaven on to her breast, and soon after it was seen that she was with child. Her daughter was furious, believing that her mother was dishonoured, and urged the Centzon-Huitznahuas to murder her; but Huitzilopochtli whom the mother carried in her womb spoke to the girl and calmed her.

Huitzilopochtli was born fully armed in a sort of blue armour, like Athena springing from the head of Zeus, with humming-bird feathers decorating his head and left leg, and a blue javelin in his left hand—a sign of skill. His whole body was painted blue. He hurled himself on his sister and killed her, and then slew the Centzon-Huitznahuas and all who had plotted against his mother. He was the protector and guide of the Aztecs on their journeys.

Tezcatlipoca (Smoking Mirror) was the Sun god. He personified the summer sun, which ripens the harvest but also brings drought and sterility. He was linked with the Moon as the god of evening. Different names were given him, according to how he was invoked at festivals, some of which were sacred to him as god of music and dancing. He was invisible and impalpable, appearing to men sometimes as a flying shadow, or as a dreadful monster, but often as a jaguar. According to one legend the Aztecs thought that Tezcatlipoca wandered at night in the shape of a 'giant', wrapped in an ash-coloured veil and carrying his head in his hand. When nervous people saw him they died, but the brave man seized him, saying he would not let him go until sunrise. The 'giant' begged to be released, and then cursed. If the man succeeded in holding the monster until daylight, he changed his tone and offered wealth and invincible power if he was set free before dawn. The victorious

The solar stone at Macchu Picchu. The Incas believed they were descendants of Inti, the sun, and they were very skilled in astronomic observation. These stones – another exists at Ollontaytambo – served both ritual and astronomic requirements.

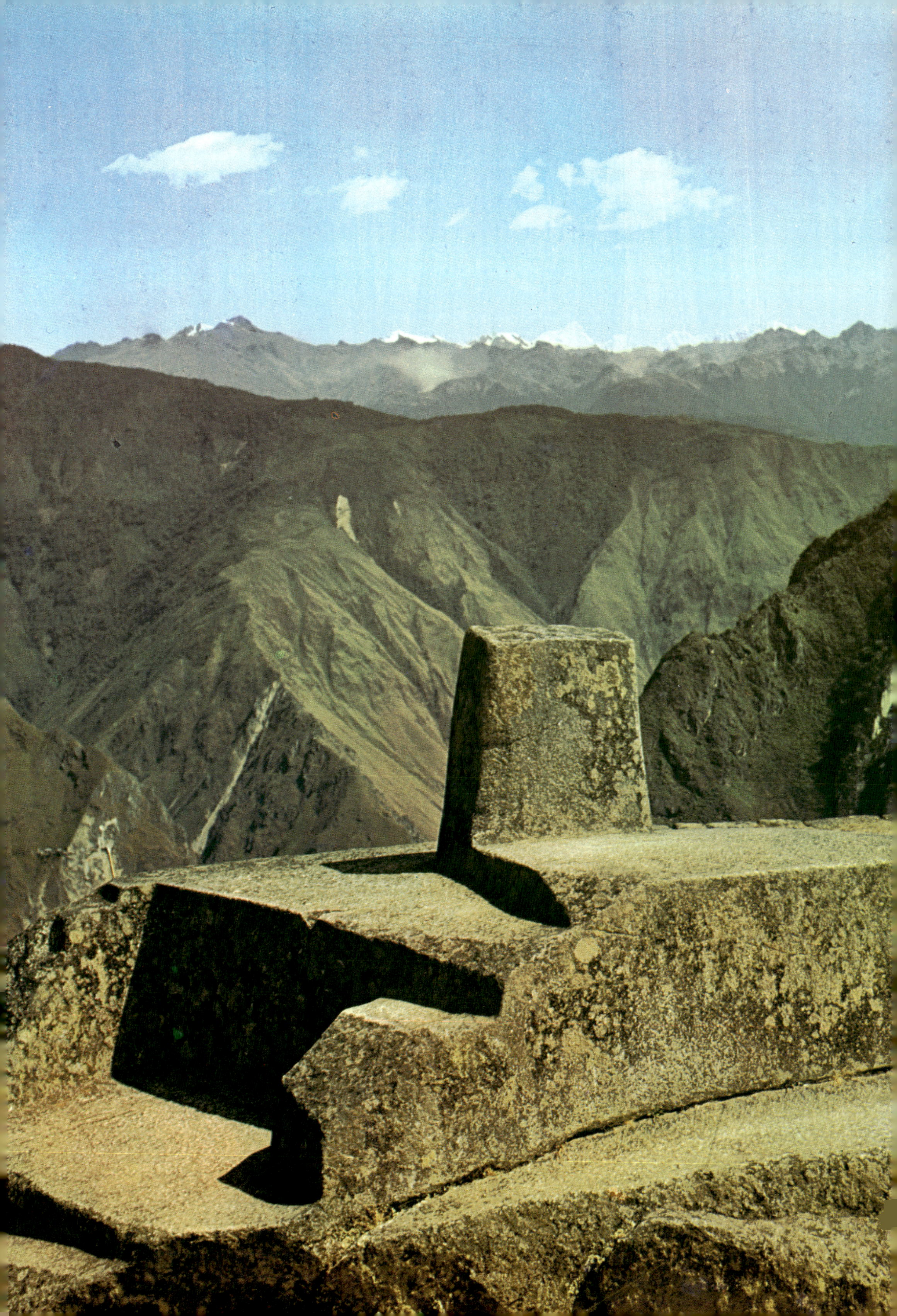

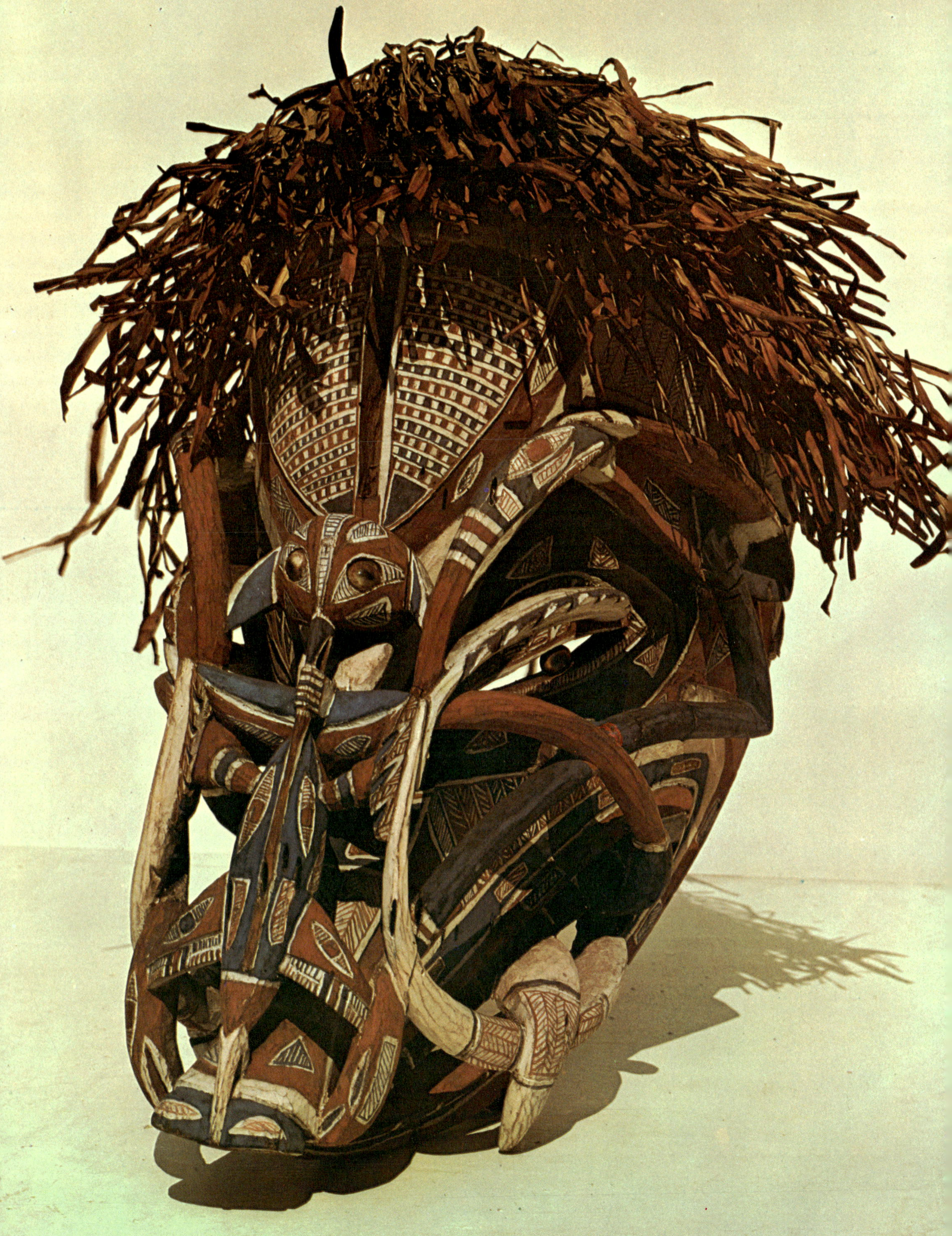

man received four thorns as a pledge of victory from the conquered. The brave man tore out his heart, and took it home; but when he unwrapped the cloth in which he had folded it he found nothing but white feathers or a thorn or ashes or an old rag. The Aztecs feared him more than any other god, and offered him blood sacrifices. Every year the handsomest among the prisoners was chosen to personify him. He was taught to sing and play the flute, to wear flowers and to smoke elegantly. He was richly garbed, and eight pages were assigned to wait on him. For a whole year he was heaped with honours and pleasure. Twenty days before the date fixed for his sacrifice, he received four girls as his wives, personifications of four goddesses. Then began a series of festivals and dances. After which when the fatal day had arrived the young god was taken with great pomp out of the town and sacrificed on the last terrace of the temple. With one cut of his obsidian knife the priest opened his breast and tore out the palpitating heart which he offered to the Sun. In Mexican mythology Tezcatlipoca was the great enemy of Quetzalcoatl, and the myth seems to indicate some great racial conflict.

In all his treacherous plottings Tezcatlipoca thought only of destroying the people of Tulla, that is to say, the Toltecs, whose most important god was Quetzalcoatl up till the time when after. the fall of the Toltecs he became one of the chief Aztec divinities.

One day the people of Tulla saw three sorcerers enter their town, one of whom in the form of a handsome young man was Tezcatlipoca. He succeeded in seducing the nieces of Quetzalcoatl, the daughter of the king Uemac, which enabled him to spread vice and disregard for the law throughout Tulla.

During an important festival he danced and sang a magic song. He was soon imitated by a multitude of people, but he led them on to a bridge which collapsed under their weight, and a large number of them were hurled into the river where they were changed into stones. Soon after he appeared to the Toltecs and showed them a puppet magically dancing on his hand. In their wonder they crowded round to see better, and many of them were suffocated. He then told them that they ought to stone him because of the harm he had done them. They obeyed, and killed him, but the sorcerer's body gave off such a dreadful strench that numbers of Toltecs died. At last after many casualties the Toltecs succeeded in dragging him out of the town. Tezcatlipoca is represented with a bear's face and brilliant eyes. His face was striped with yellow and black, his body was painted black, and he had bells on his ankles. He was the cause of disorder and war. He spread wealth. The Aztecs thought he had the power to destroy the world if he wished. Like most of the other gods, he rose from the dead and came back from heaven to earth.

Quetzalcoatl, the Snake-bird, god of wind, master of life, creator and civiliser, patron of every art and inventor of metallurgy, was originally a deity of Chololan, but was driven out by the intrigues of Tezcatlipoca and decided to return to the old land of Tlapallan after the fall of the Tulla. He burned his houses, built of silver and shells, buried his treasure, and set sail on the Eastern sea preceded by his attendants who had been changed into bright-hued birds, after promising his people he would return to them. Ever since then sentries were stationed on the East coast to watch for the god's return. When they saw the Spaniards wearing their bright breastplates, standing on ships which came from the East, they thought it was the return of Quetzalcoatl and sent to tell their emperor Montezuma. He sent presents to the new arrivals, including the snake mask incrusted with turquoises and the feather cloak, emblems of the god. Traditionally Quetzalcoatl is represented as a white-haired old man with a long beared dressed in a full robe. His face and whole body are painted black. He wears a mask with a pointed snout coloured red.

Tlaloc (pulp of the earth) was the god of mountains, rain, and springs. He belonged at first to the Otomi. Like the foregoing he is painted black, but wears a garland of white feathers topped with a green plume. Among his attributes occurs the mask of the two-headed snake.

Tlaloc lived on the mountain tops, and his dwelling Tlalocan was abundantly provided with food. There lived the goddesses of cereals, and especially of maize.

Tlaloc owned four pitchers of water which he used for watering the earth. The water of the first was good, and helped the growth of maize and fruits; that of the second produced spiders' webs

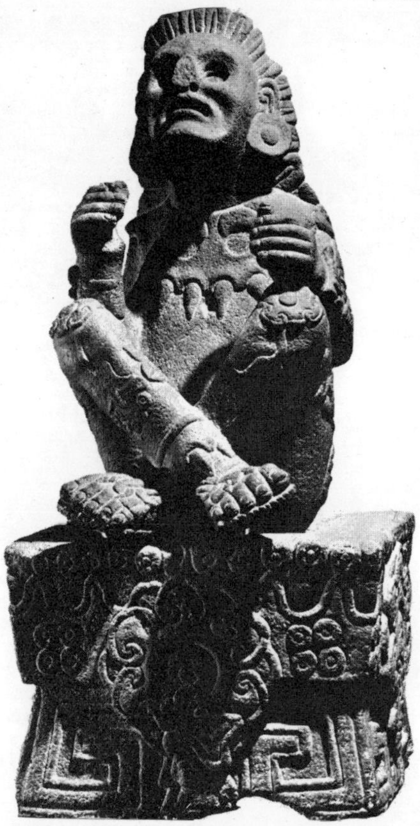

Xochipilli, the 'Prince of Flowers'. The male twin of Xochiquetzal, Xochipilli shared her joyous character and was the god of beauty, love, happiness and youth and also of music, dancing and gambling. He also presided over the seventh hour of the day.
Despite the happy nature of his functions he was always depicted with the head of a corpse. In later representations the two flower gods were particularly associated with Quetzalcoatl-Huitzilopochtli in whose temple their festival was celebrated.

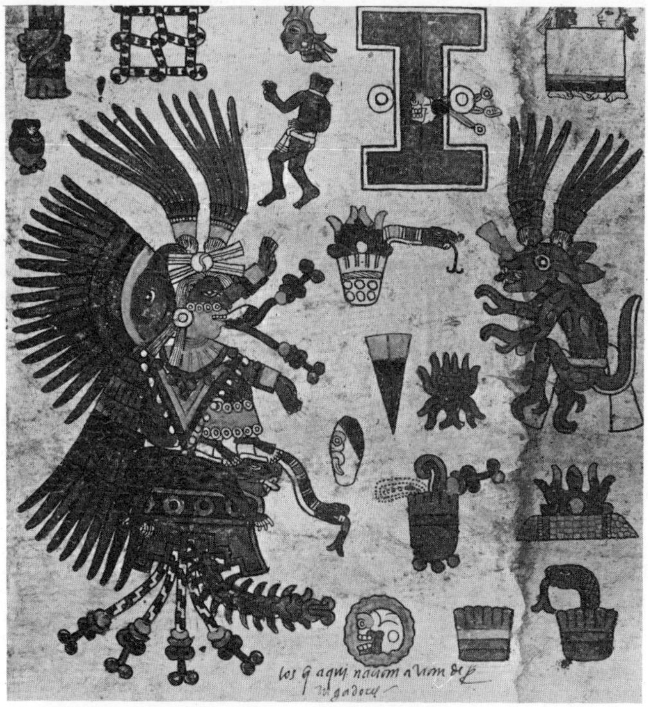

Xochiquetzal, the goddess of flowers and love. This detail from the *Codex Borbonicus*, a Mexican religious calendar of the sixteenth century, shows the goddess seated on a throne covered with an ocelet skin, and with a scroll indicating that she is speaking or singing issuing from her mouth. Lovely and gay, she lived on a mountain top surrounded by musicians and dancers but was stolen from her true husband, the rain god Tlaloc, by Tezcatlipoca. She is believed to have presided over the twentieth day of the Aztec calendar.

A head from one of the intricate and brilliantly decorated malanggans of New Ireland. The boar is a much prized creature in Melanesia but not often represented since the living animal is ever-present. The lower tusks are extended by the extraction of the upper incisors.
The lower ones then grow into circles – at the cost of much distress to the animal – and these are coveted as ornaments as tokens of prestige.

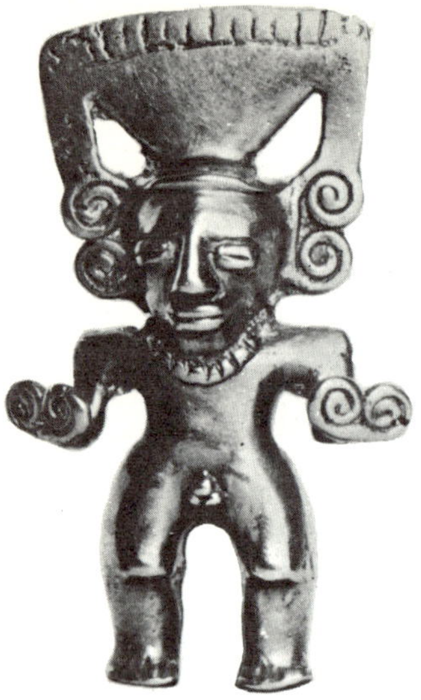

The 'Quetzalcoatl' found at Nicoya, Costa Rica. The execution of this work implies a Mexican influence in this area.

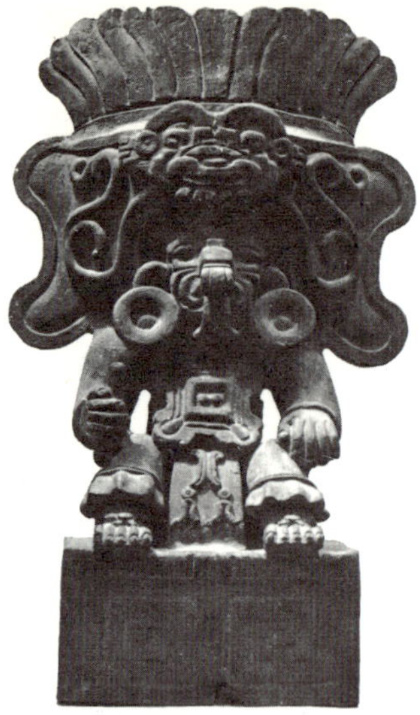

Cocijo, the Zapotec god of rain. One of the most frequently portrayed of the Zapotec gods, this funerary urn from Monte Alban shows him seated with his hands on his knees and his tongue protruding wearing an elaborate head-dress and enormous ear-plugs. Tlaloc, the Aztec rain god enjoyed a similar popularity and was also one of the chief gods of the pantheon. Though benign, his cult was marred by the sacrifice of innumerable children.

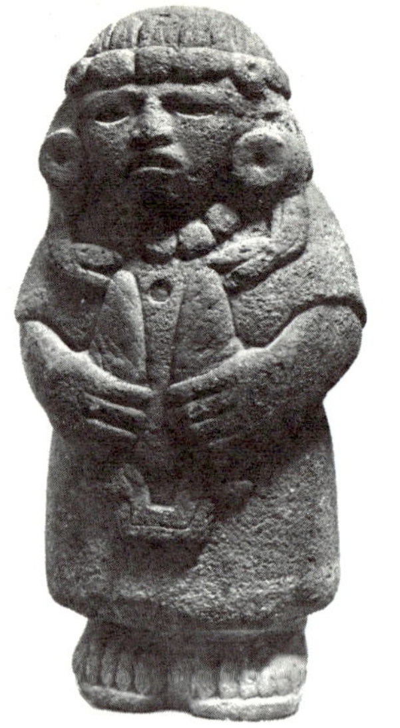

Xilonen, the Aztec goddess of the young corn. The female counterpart of Cinteotl, Xilonen was originally a deity of the Huastecs who was taken over by the conquering Aztecs. Her popularity, like that of all the ancient earth and fertility gods was greatest among the *macehuali*, or lower classes, especially those outside the towns. The Aztecs believed that maize was discovered by Quetzalcoatl who stole it for mankind from the ants. Statue in grey volcanic stone.

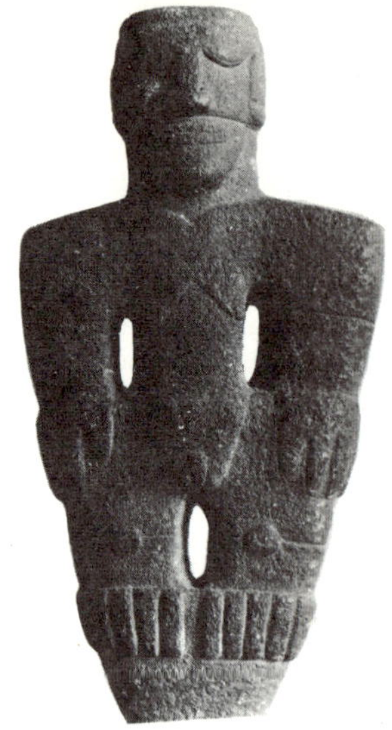

Stone idol, Costa Rica. Marquess of Peralta's Collection.

and caused blight among the cereals; that of the third turned to frost, and that of the fourth destroyed all fruits.

The cult of Tlaloc was the most horrible of all. Numerous children and babies at the breast were sacrificed to him. For the festival in his honour the priests started out to look for a large number of babies which they bought from their mothers... After killing them, they cooked and ate them... If the children cried and shed plenty of tears the spectators rejoiced, saying that rain was coming.

Chalchiuhtlicue, goddess of running water, springs and streams, was the wife or sister of Tlaloc. She was invoked for the protection of new-born children, marriages, and chaste loves.

An agricultural nation, the Aztecs possessed many deities of the earth's products, chief of whom was Tzinteotl, goddess of origins, who presided over procreation.

They had also a god of fire, of lust, of traders: Yacatecuhtli god of traders; Xiuhtecutli god of fire; Tlazolteotl goddess of guilty loves, of pleasure and filth. She is the Mexican Venus, about whom we find this legend:

'A certain Jappan wished to become a favourite of the gods, so he left his family and all his possessions to live a hermit's life in the desert. He discovered a very high rock on which he lived day and night, spending his time at his devotions. The gods wished to test his virtue, and commanded the demon Yaotl (the enemy) to spy on him, and try to punish him if he yielded. Yeotl sent him the most beautiful women who vainly urged him to come down. The goddess Tlazolteotl was annoyed by this, and appeared to Jappan who was deeply moved by her great beauty.

' "Brother Jappan", she said, "I am Tlazolteotl. I am amazed by your virtue and touched by your sufferings, and I went to console you. How can I reach you and talk to you more easily?" The hermit did not see the goddess's ruse, came down from his rock and helped her to climb it. And Jappan's virtue succumbed. Yaotl arrived at once, and in spite of his entreaties cut off his head. The gods changed him into a scorpion, and from shame he hid under the stone which had been the scene of his defeat.

'His wife, Tlahuitzin (the burning), was still alive. Yaotl went to look for her, brought her to the stone where the scorpion was, told her everything, and finally cut off her head. From her came another species of scorpion (fire-coloured). She joined her husband under the stone, and they had little scorpions of different colours. The gods thought that Yaotl had exceeded his instruction, so they punished him by changing him into a grasshopper.'

According to the Aztecs the 'nine heavens' are inhabited by: Tonatiuh, the sun; Meztli, the moon; Tlahuizcal-pantecuhtli, who was lord of the red glow of dawn, and also a great lover of sacrifices.

Among the very numerous other Mexican gods must be noted: Xochipili and Xochiquetzal, gods of the two sexes, of flowers, singing and dancing; Cihuatcoatl, goddess invoked at childbirth, who is sometimes friendly, sometimes hostile; Chicomecoatl, goddess of rural plenty, the Mexican Ceres; Xolotl, god of ball-play and protector of twins.

Among ill-defined deities are the Tepictoton, dwarfs who were the protectors of mountains and to whom children were sacrificed; the Yohual-tecuhtin, lords of the night to the number of ten, who determined the fates of men and one by one in turn ruled over their days.

According to a Mexican myth called 'Story of the four suns', the fifth of which is that which now gives us light, the gods created four successive worlds. Torrential rains followed and drowned all mankind except for a few who were changed into fish, under the first sun named Chalchiuhtonatiuh (sun of precious stones). Under the second sun Tletonatiuh (sun of fire) the men of that creation were destroyed by a rain of fire, and changed into chickens, dogs, etc. The third sun is called Yohualtonatiuh (sun of darkness). The men of this third creation fed on pitch and resin, and were either swallowed up by an earthquake or devoured by animals. The sun which shone on the fourth generation was Ehecatonatiuh (sun of wind or air). During this epoch men lived on fruits and were changed into monkeys.

The underworld was ruled by the infernal deities: Mictlantecuhtli and his wife Mictanchihuatl, who govern the 'nine underground rivers' and the souls of the dead.

The Aztecs, like nearly all peoples, had a tradition of a flood and of a confusion of languages. They say that humanity was wiped out by a flood, but one man Coxcoxtli and one woman Xochiquetzal escaped in a boat, and reached a mountain called Colhuacan. They had many children, who were dumb until the time when a dove on top of a tree made them the gift of languages; but these differed so much that the children could not understand each other.

CENTRAL AMERICA

Yucatan. The most interesting among the peoples of Central America are the Mayas of Yucatan and their southern neighbours the Quiche Mayas, nations of Toltec origin driven towards the isthmus by Aztec invasions. At the head of the mythological pantheon of the Yucatan Mayas is the god Hunab Ku (the one god), also called Kinebahan (mouth and eyes of the sun), whose wife was Ixazaluoh (water), the creator of weaving.

As was the case in Mexico, the Sun had a son, Itzamna, a civilising hero, inventor of drawing and letters, sometimes represented in the form of a red hand, to which the sick prayed. He brought back the dead to life, and for that reason there was a great cult of him in his town, Itzamal. Alms and presents were given to him. Many pilgrimages were made to him every year, during which squirrels were sacrificed to him and tissues offered up. In return Itzamna looked after the fertility of the fields and the abundance of water supply.

In their very extensive mythology must be mentioned the Bacabs, four wind gods, the pillars of heaven; Echua, the god of travellers; Yuncemil, the lord of death; Acat, the god of life, who shaped children in their mothers' wombs; Backlum-Chaam, the Maya Priapus, and Chin, god of vice.

The people of Yucatan also worshipped the god Cukulcan (bird-snake), of whom they told this legend:

'Once upon a time Cukulcan came from the west with nineteen companions, two of whom were gods of fish, two others gods of agriculture, and a god of thunder... They stayed ten years in Yucatan. Cukulcan made wise laws, and then set sail and disappeared in the direction of the rising sun...'

The people of Yucatan believed in a god of creation, benefactor of the world, Nohochacyum (the grandfather) among the Lacandons, and Nohochacyumchac among the modern Mayas. Among the former he was the son of two flowers. Nohochacyum was perpetually at war with an evil deity Hapikern, the enemy of mankind, and he had three brothers: Yantho who was associated with Xamani-qinqu, spirit of the north; Usukun a god ill-disposed to men, whose assistant is Kisin the earthquake; and Uyitzin, a benevolent god.

Beside these supreme gods was Akna (the mother) goddess of birth, whose husband was Akanchob.

Guatemala. In Guatemala, as in Honduras, we again come upon the cult of the sun and moon, whose gods Hun-Ahpu-Vuch and Hun-Ahpu-Mtye (grandfather and grandmother) are represented in human form but with the face of the sacred animal, the tapir. The son Gucumatz (the feathered snake) is the civilising and agricultural god, changing himself at will into different animals, and living in heaven and hell.

However, there exists another more powerful god, Hurakan, known also in the West Indies, and worshipped even by Gucumatz. He presides over the whirlwind and the rumblings of the thunderstorm. He gave the Quiche Mayas fire by rubbing his sandals together. His surname is Tohil, a name also given to Quetzalcoatl.

The basic idea of the Quiche myths is that of the sun, which dies and is born again, and also of the creation of mankind. Here is the Guatemala legend in which we find a curious cosmogony.

'In the beginning everything was under water, above which hovered Hurakan and Gucumatz, the givers of life. They said: "Earth!" and immediately the earth was created. The mountains rose out of the water, to the great joy of Gucumatz who congratulated Hurakan. (Here we note the superiority of the latter over Gucumatz.) The earth was covered with vegetation, and the creators peopled it with animals with the command to do them homage. But as the animals could not speak, they roared, howled or whistled, but could not make themselves understood. To punish them the gods decided they should be killed and eaten.

'They then made clay men who were unable to move their heads or speak or understand. They decided to make wooden men, but they lacked intelligence and feelings, and had no knowledge of their creators. The gods destroyed them. But some survived, and made little wooden monkeys.

'After consulting together Hurakan and Gucumatz decided to make four men of yellow and white maize. But as they were too

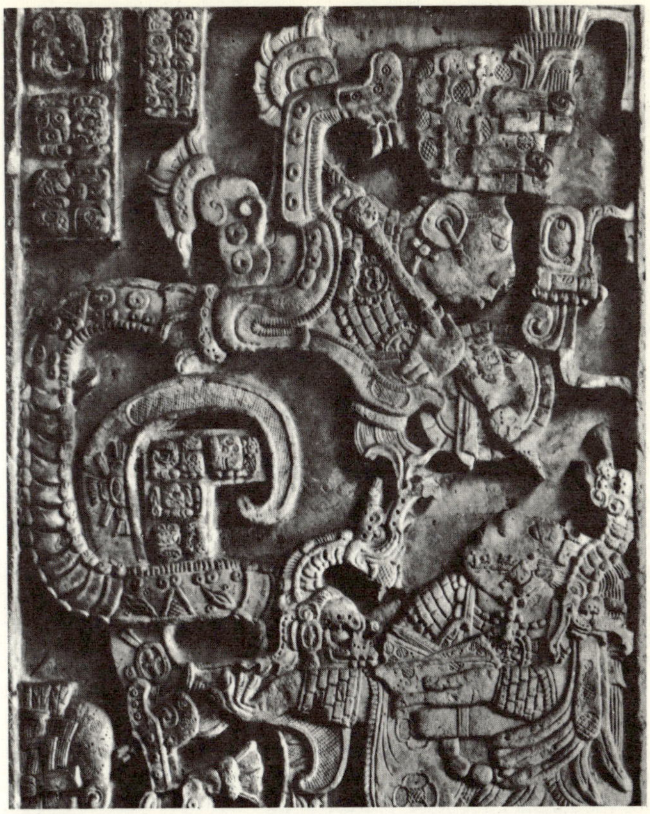

Priest and worshipper. This stone lintel from the Maya ceremonial centre of Menche (Yaxchilan) in Guatemala shows a worshipper kneeling before a priest who stands on the right wearing an elaborate plumed head-dress. The plumed head-dress probably indicates that he is a priest of Cukulcan (plumed serpent), the great god of the Mayas, who was later merged with the Aztec Quetzalcoatl with whom he shared many similarities. His priests traditionally stood at the head of the Maya priestly hierarchy.

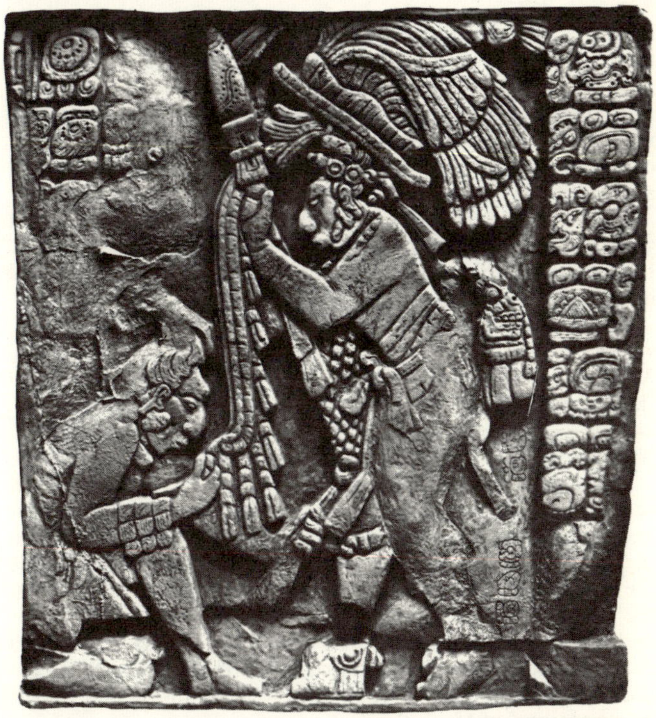

Serpent deity with a worshipper. Another of the elaborately carved lintels from the Maya ceremonial centre of Menche, this panel comes from House 'G' and shows a worshipper holding an offering in his left hand kneeling before a serpent deity. The inscription at the top shows the calendar round date 5 Imix 4 Mac which probably occurred in the year A.D. 681. Like the Aztecs the Mayas had an extraordinary preoccupation with time and their complex calendar system ruled their lives.

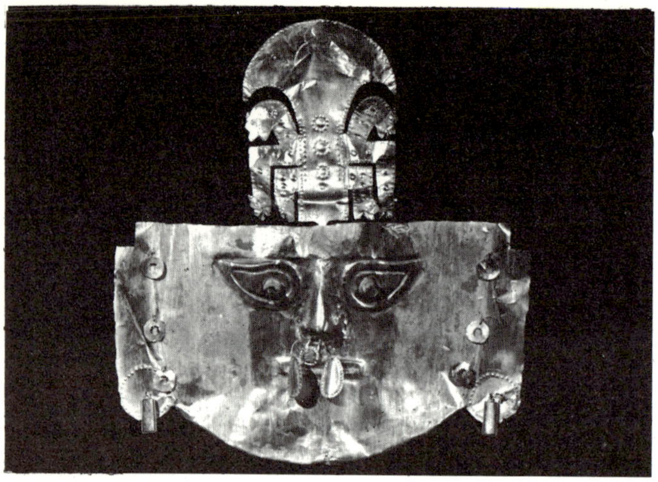

Gold funerary mask. Peruvian goldwork astounded the Conquistadors by its beauty and almost unbelievable profusion. This gold funerary mask from the pre-Inca Chimu culture gives some idea of the splendours that were lost in the Spanish melting pots. The Incas themselves believed that gold was formed from the sweat of the sun and its use was reserved exclusively for the Lord Inca, privileged nobles and religious purposes. Gold with emeralds and turquoise.
Twelfth to thirteenth centuries A.D.

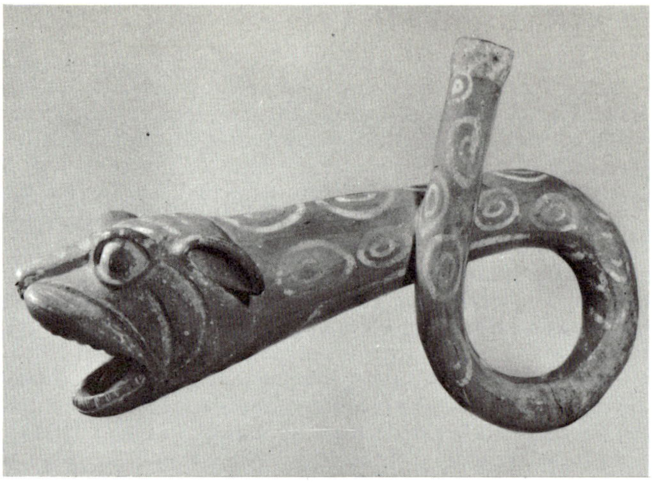

Jaguar-headed Mochica trumpet. A feline god was introduced into South America by the early Chavín culture at a time when animal totemism was still being practised and the jaguar and puma cults remained a feature of the Andean civilizations for a further thousand years. This looped pottery trumpet from the coastal Mochica empire was probably used in religious ceremonies. String instruments were unknown in pre-Hispanic America, music being provided solely by percussion and wind instruments.

perfect, the gods shortened their sight. During their sleep they created four women. And these were the ancestors of the Quiche tribe. However, they complained that they could not see clearly, for the sun had not yet appeared, so they went off to Tullan where they learned about their gods. It was very cold there, and they received fire from Tohil (Hurakan). But the sun did not appear, and the earth remained damp and cold. Speech was divided, and the ancestors no longer understood each other. They then left Tullan guided by Tohil and came to the Quiche country. There at last the sun appeared, followed by the moon and the stars. In their delight animals and men sang a hymn, and offered the gods blood from their ears and shoulders. Later they thought it better to shed the blood of victims.'

Honduras. In Honduras, where sun and moon also were worshipped, there is a rather strange legend of the 'White Woman':

'A white woman of matchless beauty came down from heaven to the town of Cealcoquin. There she built a palace ornamented with strange figures of men and animals, and placed a stone in the chief temple with mysterious figures on three of its sides. It was a talisman which she used to conquer all her enemies.

'Although she remained a virgin, she gave birth to three sons; and when she grew old she divided her kingdom with them. Then she had her bed carried to the highest part of the palace, and disappeared into the sky in the form of a beautiful bird...'

This legend has a great resemblance to a myth of the moon, whose three sons might well be the three visible phases of the moon. Moreover, in Honduras we find myths which are very similar to those of Mexico.

Nicaragua. The inhabitants of Nicaragua all had the same religion.

The gods of the Niquirans (one of the tribes in Nicaragua) lived in heaven and were immortal. The two chief deities were Tamagostad and the goddess Zipaltonal, creators of the earth and everything in it. They lived in the east. With them were Ecalchot, the wind god; the little Ciaga, a water god, who shared in the creation; Quiateot, the rain god; Misca, god of traders; Chiquinau, god of the air and the nine winds; and Vizetot, god of famine. After death, souls departed according to their deserts either to heaven with Tamagostad and Zipaltonal, or under the ground with Mictanteot (the Mictlantecuhtli of Mexico).

Among the underground gods is Masaya, the goddess of volcanoes, to whom sacrifices were made after earthquakes by throwing human victims into a crater. She is represented as a termagant with a black skin, thin hair and sagging breasts but she was consulted for her oracles which were highly esteemed.

There is every reason to think that Mexican influences were important in developing the early religious customs of this country.

Haiti. Totemism seems not to have existed among the Tainos of Haiti. All we find are some Zemis or idols, which are representations of individual protecting spirits, similar to the Mexican nahuals. These idols, considered as gods, were invoked for the conquest of enemies or the ripening of the harvest.

These supernatural beings revealed themselves to the Indian after a fast of six or seven days.

The Tainos had a god in heaven named Joca-huva, son of the goddess Atabei (these deities were not represented in images), and then Guabancex, the goddess of storms, winds and water, whose idol was made of stone; by her side was her messenger Guantauva, and Coatrischie, a deity who collects water among the mountains and lets it rush down on the lowlands to damage them.

Beside these gods the people of Haiti thought the world was peopled with souls of the dead or *opita*, who were gathered together in an island named Coaibai and went out only at night. Anyone who met an *opita* and tried to fight it was bound to die.

The myths of the Tainos of Haiti relate the creation of the world and the origin of the female sex, after a flood in which all the women were drowned and all the men changed into trees.

SOUTH AMERICA

THE CHIBCHAS OF CUNDINAMARCA. The inhabitants of central Colombia worshipped especially a great solar god, Bochica, creator of civilisation and all the arts. In a myth he is described as fighting with a demon named Chibchacum who after being defeated was forced as a punishment to support the earth on his shoulder. When Chibchacum changes his burden to the other shoulder there are earthquakes.

The myth of Bochica contains the story of a great flood:

'Long ago the people of the Cundinamarca plateau at Bogota lived as pure savages, without laws, agriculture or religion. One day there appeared an old man with a long thick beard, by name Bochica who belonged to a race different from that of the Chibchas. He taught the savages how to build huts and how to live together in society.

'His wife who was very beautiful and named Chia appeared after him, but she was wicked and enjoyed thwarting her husband's efforts at civilising. As she could not overcome Bochica's power she managed by her magical means that the river Funzha should rise, overflow and cover the whole plain. Many of the Indians died, and only a few managed to escape to the summits of the neighbouring mountains. Bochica was very angry, and exiled Chia from earth to the sky, where she became the moon given the task of lighting the nights. He then cleft the mountains which closed the valleys of the Magdalena from Cauca to Tequendama, so that the water might flow out. The Indians who had escaped the flood then returned to the Bogota Valley, where they built towns. Lake Guatavita still remains to prove this local deluge.

'Bochica gave them laws, taught them to cultivate the land, instituted the worship of the sun with periodical festivals, sacrifices, and pilgrimages. He then divided the power among two chiefs, and retired to heaven after passing two thousand years on earth as an ascetic.

'Everything we know about the mythology of the Chibchas is to be found in the basic theme of the civilising hero Bochica. In this mythology there is also mention of Nencatacoa, the god of weavers; of Chaquen, the guardian god of boundaries; of Bachue, goddess of water, protectress of vegetation and harvest; of Cuchavira, master of the air and the rainbow who healed the sick and protected women in childbirth; of a god of drunkenness who was not greatly venerated; and of Fomagata or Thomagata, a deity of terrifying appearance, the storm god, represented by his worshippers under the form of a fire spirit passing through the air and tyrannising over men, whom he sometimes liked to change into animals. Bochica had to make use of all his power to rid the land of this evil being. Thereafter Fomagata was reduced to impotence, but retained his right to appear in the Guesa procession, in the ritual dances, and in the assembly of the gods.

'He is represented with one eye, four ears, and a long tail. The Guesa (wanderer or vagabond) was a boy dedicated to sacrifice in honour of Bochica. He had to be taken from a village now called San Juan de los Llanos. It is from there, so they say, that Bochica first came.

'Up till the age of ten then, Guesa was brought up in the temple of the Sun at Sagamozo, never going out except to walk in the paths Bochica had used. During all his walks the Guesa received the highest honours and the most attentive care. At the age of fifteen he was taken to a column dedicated to the Sun, followed by masked priests of whom some represented Bochica and others his wife Chia, and still others the frog Ata. When they reached their destination the victim was bound to the column, and shot to death with arrows. Then they tore out his heart to offer to Bochica, and collected his blood in sacred vases.

'Here we again find the feature, so well-marked in Mexico and Central America, of the victim being associated with the deity he represents. The method of putting to death recalls the Mexican custom, but here the tearing out of the heart occurred after the Guesa's death. In a cosmogony myth we hear of the god Chiminiquagua (guardian of the sun), who opened the house in which the heavenly body was shut up. Huge black birds came forth, spreading sun-rays over the whole world.'

According to the Chibchas the human race was born from a woman who appeared on the shores of lake Iguaque holding a child in her arms. Later they were both changed into snakes, and disappeared into the lake, for which reason the Chibchas made offerings to it. A myth of Cundinamarca says that the souls of the dead were carried into the 'next world' on a canoe, made of spiders' webs, which took them to the centre of the earth by following the course of a great underground river. Hence the great respect for spiders.

ECUADOR. During the pre-Columbian period the coast of Ecuador was inhabited by civilised people, called the Caranques. They worshipped the sea, fish, tigers, lions, snakes and numerous richly decorated idols.

From this we can see that the Caranques were acquainted with totems. One of the two temples they owned was dedicated to Umina, the god of medicine, represented by a large emerald, which received divine honours and was visited by pilgrims. The pilgrims made offerings to the high priest of gold, silver, or precious stones. The other temple belonged to the Sun, and was associated with a splendid worship, celebrated during the festival of the winter solstice. Offerings and sacrifices were made to the Sun. The victims were usually animals, but the Caranques also sacrificed children, women, and prisoners of war. The priests examined the entrails of the animal victims, and so predicted the future. In their funeral rites they buried with the deceased the most beautiful and best beloved of his wives, as well as jewels and food.

The Canarians, an Indian tribe of Ecuador, relate the story of a flood from which two brothers escaped by going to the top of

Gold figure of a llama. The llama was the Incas' most common sacrificial victim – white or albino specimens being sacrificed for the health of the Inca while black ones were employed in an attempt to procure rain. They were also used in fertility and coming-of-age rites. Over twenty life-size figures of llamas with their young, all in pure gold, stood in the fields of the Coricancha in Cuzco, the most sacred of all the Inca shrines.

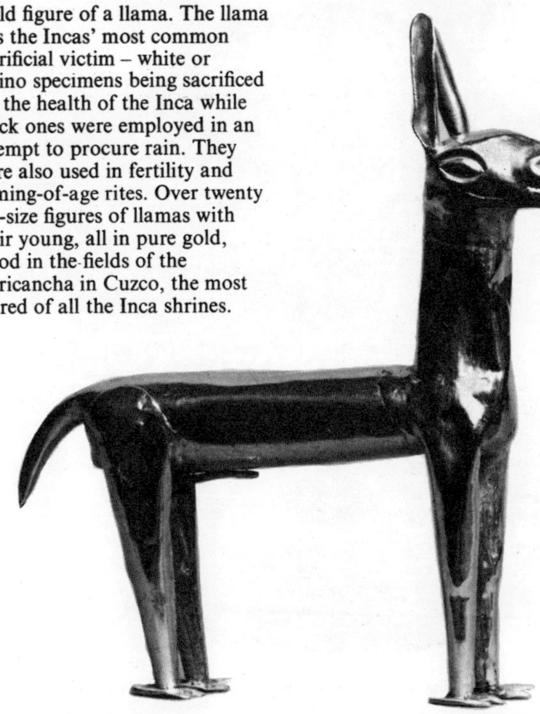

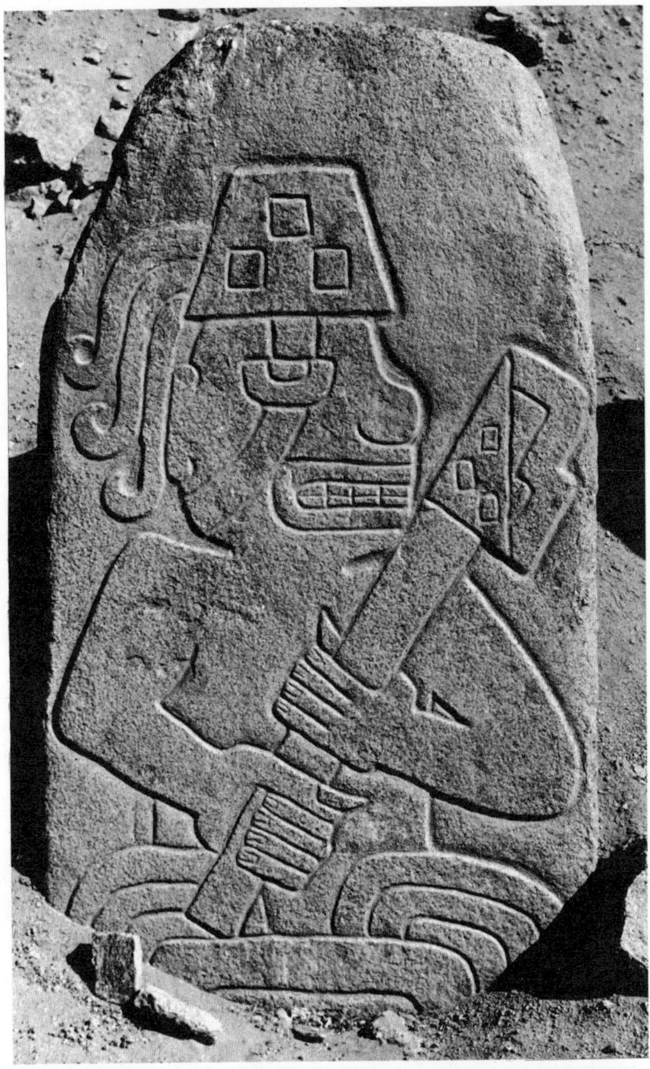

Carved stele from Cerro Sechin. One of a row of carved stones leading up to a temple in the early Peruvian religious centre of Cerro Sechin, this stele depicts a warrior grasping a club. Though the centre was connected with the Chavín culture there is no evidence of feline cults though there is of head-hunting. After the Inca conquest the gods of such local cultures were absorbed into the Inca pantheon and replaced by the cult of the Sun.

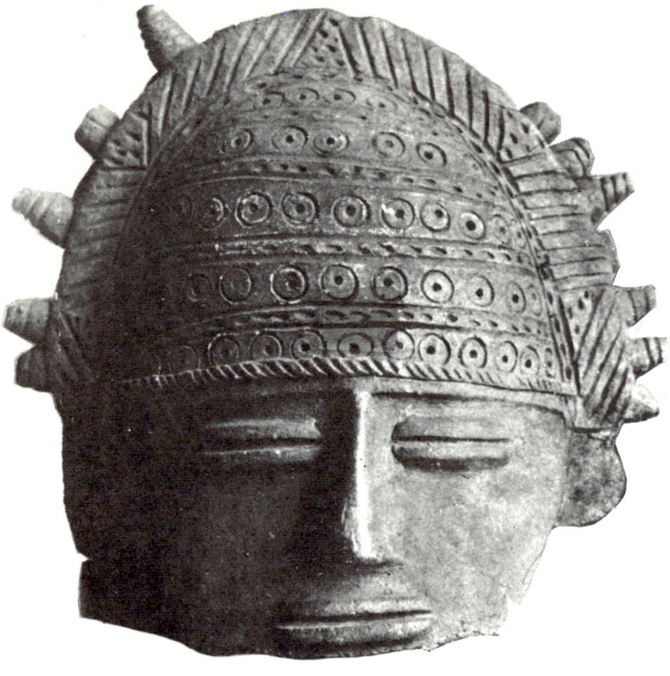

Part of an idol of the Chibchas, probably a water divinity. Colombia.

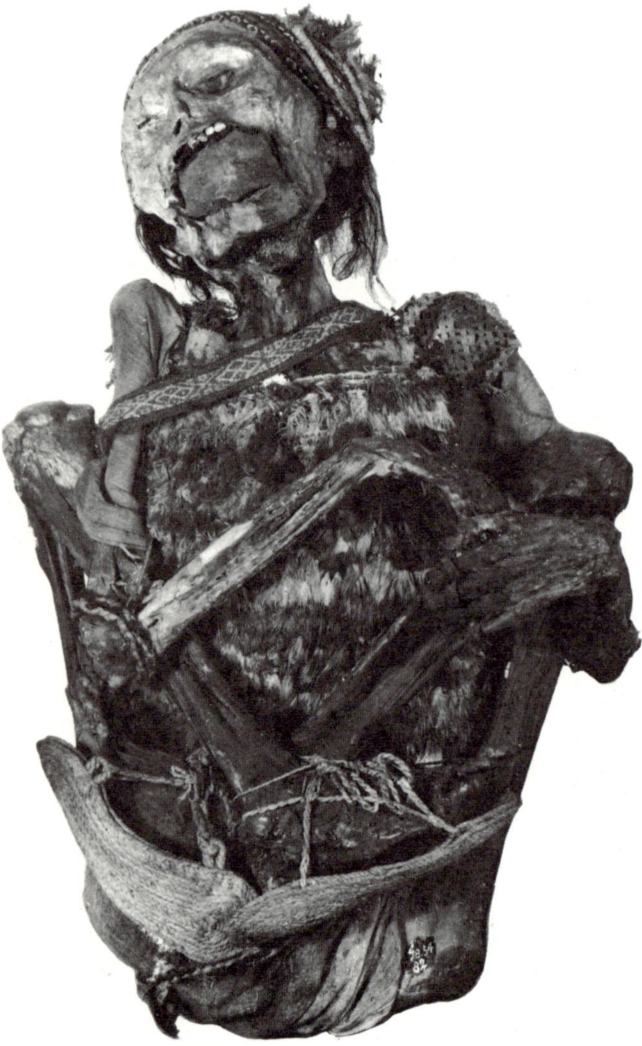

Female mummy bundle. The Incas venerated the dead who were regarded as *huacas*, a Quechua word meaning 'shrine', the mummies of previous emperors in particular being especially honoured and accorded the sort of worship only reserved for the great gods.
Burial was normally in this flexed position, the actual process of mummification generally being the result of natural dessication due to the dryness of the air. This richly dressed female mummy comes from the central coast of Peru.

a high mountain called Huaca-ynan. As the water rose the mountain grew higher, so that the two brothers escaped the disaster. When the waters retired, the provisions of the two brothers were all consumed, so they went down to the valley, and built a little house where they eked out existence on plants and roots. One day, when exhausted and almost dying of hunger, they returned home after a long excursion in search of food, and found that food and chicha were there, although they did not know who could have brought them. This happened ten days running. They agreed to try to find out who was so kind to them. The elder brother concealed himself, and soon there entered two macaws dressed as Canarians. As soon as the birds came in they began to prepare the food they had brought with them. When the man saw they were good-looking and had the faces of women, he came out of his hiding-place, but when the birds saw him they were angry and flew away without leaving anything to eat. The younger brother had been out looking for food, and when he returned he found nothing ready as had happened on other days. He asked his brother the reason, and both felt very cross. Next day the younger brother decided to hide himself, and wait for the birds. After three days the macaws came back, and started to prepare food. The two brothers waited until the two birds had finished cooking, and then closed the door. The two birds were very angry at being caught, and while the two brothers were catching the smaller, the other flew away. The two brothers married the smaller macaw, and had by her six boys and girls, from whom the Canarians are descended. Ever since then the Indians consider the Huaca-ynan mountain as sacred. They venerate macaws, and prize their feathers, which they use to deck themselves out for festivals.

THE INCAS

Before the Spanish conquest Peru included modern Peru, the republic of Ecuador to the north, part of Bolivia to the south-east, and part of Chile to the south.

Before they came under the civilising influence of the Incas, the ancient Peruvians accepted totemism. They worshipped animals, plants and stones, and took their names. Several Quiches (ancient Peruvians) believed they were descended from animals which they worshipped, such as the condor, the snake, and the jaguar, or from rivers and lakes. These protecting spirits were given the name of Huaca, by which they meant mysterious powers.

Along the coasts of Peru the chief totem was the sea, and its inhabitants were sub-totems.

Where the Incas established themselves totemism gave way to the cult of the Sun. The Peruvian name for the sun was Inti or Apu-Punchau (the head of day). They thought he had a human form, and his face was represented by a disk of gold surrounded with rays and flames. The Incas believed they were descended from Inti, and only they were allowed to utter his name.

Among divinities Mama Quilla, the moon, came immediately after the Sun, her brother and her husband. Her image was a silver disk with human features. She was the protecting goddess of married women. Many temples were dedicated to these chief deities, the most famous of which was the Coricancha of Cuzco.

The other deities grouped about the pair Sun-Moon and looked upon as their attendants were greatly venerated. Among them were Cuycha the rainbow, and Catequil the thunder and lightning god, represented carrying a sling and a mace. Children were sacrificed to him. Twins were looked upon as his children. Chasca (the long-haired star) was the planet Venus, and was thought to be a man acting as page to the Sun. Among the Incas this planet was the protectress of princesses and girls, the creatress and protectress of flowers. The other planets and stars were maids in waiting to the Moon. Other constellations were worshipped. The most revered were the Pleiads who protected cereals. Comets were a sign of the gods' wrath. In addition to these starry deities, they worshipped Pachamama (mother earth) and fire, Nina.

However, the Incas did not suppress all the cults older than that of the Sun and Moon. They retained two great gods whom they annexed to their pantheon – Viracocha (the foam or fat of the lake) and Pachacamac (he who animates the earth).

Pachacamac, who was outside the cycle of Inca gods, was considered the supreme god by the maritime population of Peru. His legend spread out from the valley of the Lurin, to the south of Lima, where he had his sanctuary, and makes him the rival of Viracocha. He renewed the world by changing the men created by Viracocha and teaching them the different arts and occupations. He must have been the god of fire, and so the Incas made him a son of the Sun, the master of giants. His worship required human victims. He uttered mysterious oracles. He was invisible, and it was forbidden to represent him in any form whatever. At Cuzco there was current a myth of the mountaineers of Pacari-Tambo (house of the morning):

'Once upon a time four pairs of brothers and sisters emerged from the caves of Pacari-Tambo. The eldest climbed up the mountain and threw a stone to each of the four cardinal points, saying that it was a token that he had assumed possession of the whole land. This angered the other three, the youngest of whom was the cleverest. He made up his mind to get rid of his brothers and reign alone. He persuaded the eldest to go into a cave, and shut him in with a huge rock. Then he got his second brother to come up the mountain with him under the pretext of looking for the eldest brother. But when they reached the top he threw the second brother into the void, and by magic changed him into a stone statue. The third brother fled in terror. So the youngest built Cuzco and had himself worshipped as son of the Sun under the name of Pirrhua-Manco or Manco-Capac. The first god was probably Pachacamac, god of underground fire; the second seems to have been a personification of the worship of stones; and the third Viracocha, the god who vanished.'

On the other hand the Incas taught that the Sun had three sons – Choun (one of the surnames of Viracocha), Pachacamac, and Manco-Capac.

Viracocha was originally also outside the cycle of the Inca gods, but was annexed to the 'cult of the Sun.' According to legend he lived in lake Titicaca, and represented its fertilising and procreative powers. He is the god of rain, and of the liquid element generally.

'Before the Sun appeared the earth was already peopled,' says the original myth of Viracocha. 'When he emerged from the depths of the lake he made the sun, the moon, the stars, and set them on their regular courses. Then he made several statues, which he brought to life, and commanded them to come out of the caves in which they had been carved. He then went to Cuzco and appointed Allcavica as king over the people in the town. The Incas descended from this Allcavica. Then Viracocha went away and disappeared into the water.'

Viracocha has neither flesh nor bones, and yet he runs very swiftly; he brings down the mountains and lifts up the valleys. He is represented with a beard, which is a symbol of water gods. His sister-wife was Mama-Cocha (rain and water). Beside these deities there existed special gods and powers of an animal nature, in which the Indians recognised mysterious power. Snakes were greatly revered, such as Urcaguary the god of underground treasures who is represented in the form of a large snake, with the head of a deer and little gold chains decorating his tail. The condor was thought to be the messenger of the gods. One of the peculiarities of the Inca religion is that they had 'Virgins of the Sun' or Aclla, who were real vestal virgins, maintaining the sacred fire under the control of matrons called Mama-Cuna who educated them and directed their work. The 'Virgins of the Sun' were chosen at the age of eight and shut up in cloisters, which they could not leave for six or seven years, and then only to marry chiefs of high rank.

Every Aclla convicted of relations with a man was buried alive, unless she could prove that she was with child, in which case it was supposed to be due to the Sun.

Human sacrifices occurred every year at the festivals celebrated in honour of the gods Inti, Pachacamac and Viracocha. Two or three children and large numbers of animals were massacred at these festivals. According to the myths, the earth was called Pacha, and above the earth were ranged four heavens inhabited by gods. The great god lived in the highest heaven.

The Incas thought that Inti, the sun, after crossing the sky, plunged into the western sea, which he partly dried up. He returned by swimming under the earth, and reappeared next morning rejuvenated by his bath.

Eclipses of the sun were held to indicate Inti's anger. The Peruvian

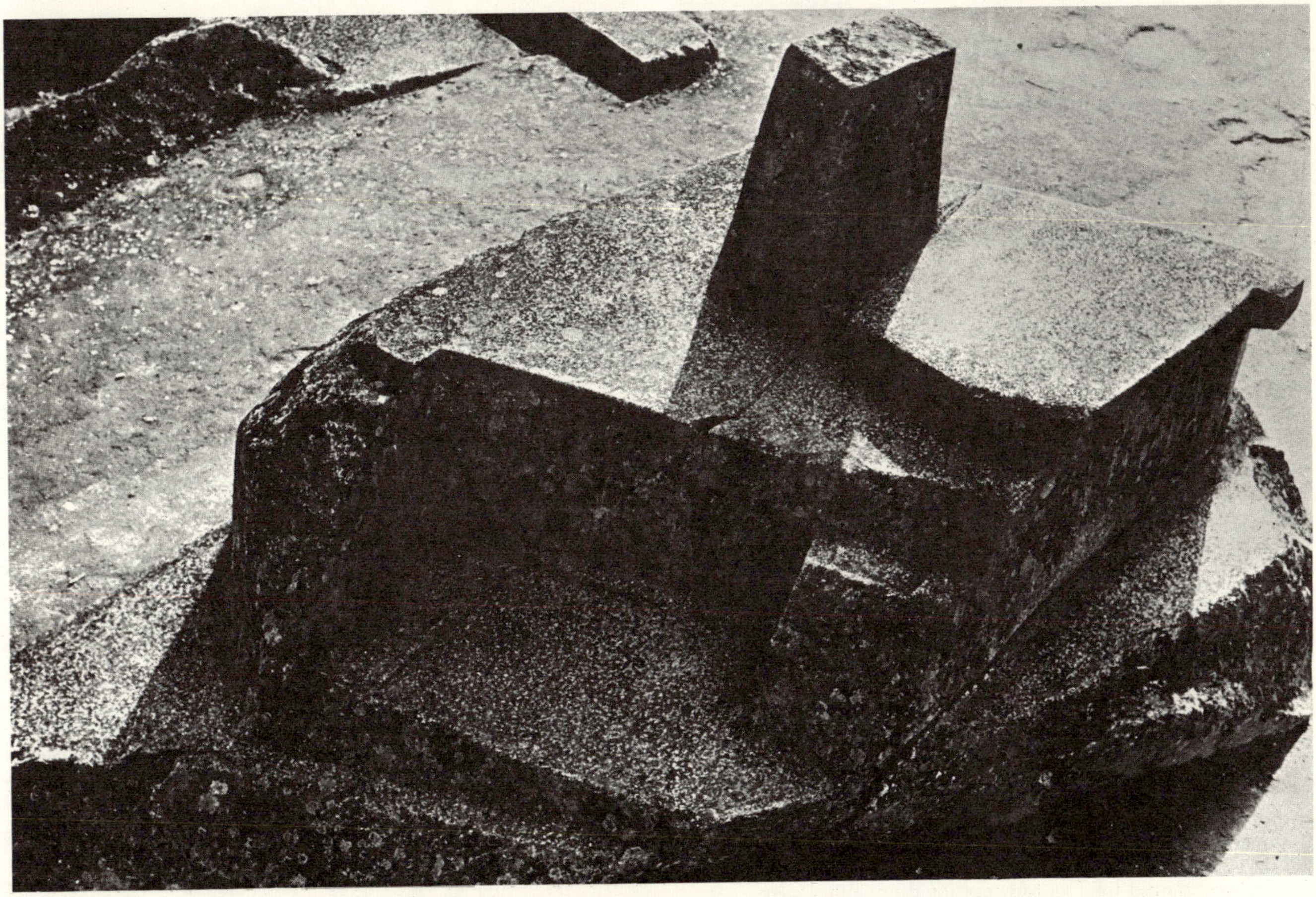

**The Intihuatana at Machu Picchu. Carved out of the solid rock, the Intihuatana (or 'Hitching Place of the Sun') was so constructed that the shadow from the central upright fell on different faces of the stone to mark different phases of the solar year.
The cult of the Sun pervaded Inca life and there were thousands of temples to the Sun throughout the empire.
It was believed that the Inca himself was directly descended from the sun-god, Inti.**

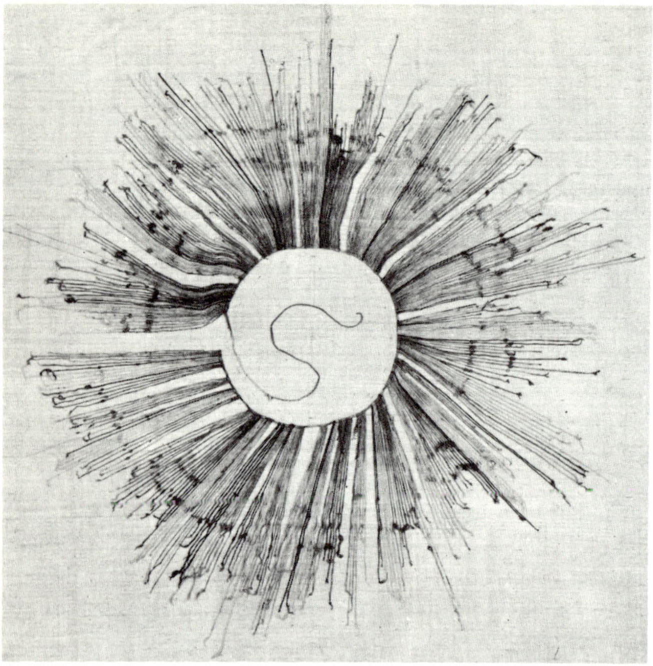

Quipu. The Incas have left no written records, the nearest approach they appear to have made to writing being in the form of the quipu, or knot-string record, a mnemonic device for recording statisics, and possibly also historical events by means of knotted strings of different lengths and colours. The destruction of the quipu 'archives' by the crusading padres in the seventeenth century and the grandual dying out of the quipu-camayocs, who alone could interpret them, has forever closed to us this aspect of Inca life and tradition.

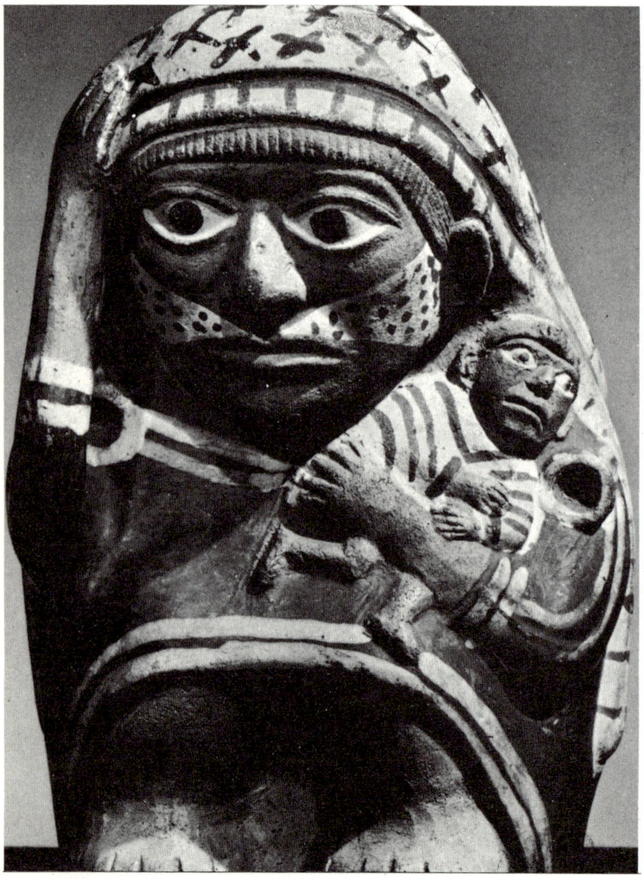

Mother and child. Like much early Peruvian pottery this vase from the Moche Valley near Trujillo gives us valuable insight into the customs and habits of daily life. Among the Incas, children were trained from an early age for the role they were to play in life. Girls, unlike boys, however, had a chance to better their social position and any who showed particular beauty or talent were selected as 'Chosen Women' to serve in the temples of the Sun.

myths of creation, of the origin of mankind, and of the flood, seem to have been local, as was the case in Mexico.

In a province of Peru to the east of Lima, the Indians say that once upon a time the world came near to total destruction. One day an Indian wanted to tie a llama in a good pasture, but the animal resisted, and in its way gave signs of grief. His owner said: 'Idiot! Why do you lament and refuse to browse? Are you not in a place with good grass?' 'Madman!' said the llama, 'learn that there is plenty of reason for my grief, for within five days the sea will rise and cover the whole earth!' The astonished Indian asked if there was no way of escaping. The llama told him to collect provisions for five days, and then to follow it to the top of the high mountain called Villca-Coto. So the man collected provisions, and led the llama on a leash. When they reached the top of the mountain they saw that all kinds of birds and animals had already taken refuge there. The sea began to rise, and covered all the plains and mountains except the top of Villca-Coto; and even there the waves dashed up so high that the animals were forced to crowd into a narrow area. The fox's tail dipped into the water, and that is why it has a black tip. Five days later the water ebbed, and the sea returned to its bed. But all human beings except one were drowned, and from him are descended all the nations on earth.

Another legend of the Peruvian Indians deals with the reappearance of men after the flood: 'In a place about sixty leagues from Cuzco the creator made a man of every nation, and painted the costume which each of the nations was to wear. He gave hair to those who were to have long hair, and clipped the hair of those who were to have short hair. To each he gave the speech he was to was to talk, suitable songs, and the seeds and food he was to grow. Then he gave life and soul to these men and women, and sent them underground. In this way each nation went to the region it was to occupy.'

Among the Incas there was a god of death, Supai, who lived inside the earth. Supai, the god of this dark world, is no more malevolent than Hades or Pluto, but he is a dreary and greedy god, always longing to increase the number of his subjects, so he must be placated, even at the cost of painful sacrifices. Thus, every year a hundred children were sacrificed to him.

THE ARAUCANIANS OF CHILE

The religious opinions of the Araucanians assumed a material form. The Araucanians do not appear to have got beyond fetishism, and give a corporeal form to all their divinities. They did not claim that all inanimate objects are inhabited by spirits, but think that spirits may live in them for a time. The Araucanians were acquainted with totemism, and practised the cult of ancestors. They did not recognise the existence of a superior being. They have no temples, no idols, no established religion.

The Araucanians imagined their chief gods to be evil spirits who had to be placated by propitiatory and expiatory sacrifices. The most powerful of the upper gods was Pillan, the god of thunder, who was also the provider of fire. He caused earthquakes, volcanic eruptions and lightning. The Indians represented him as a corporeal deity having several forms at once.

The chiefs and warriors killed during a war were absorbed into Pillan. The former became volcanoes, the latter clouds. Out of this belief arose a myth: 'During a storm the Indians looked at the sky to see in which direction the clouds were moving. They supposed that the clouds represented the battles between their peoples and the Spaniards. If the clouds moved to the south the Araucanians broke out into lamentations. If they went north, the Indians rejoiced at the defeat of their enemies.'

Pillan had at his disposal evil spirits called Huecuvus, who were able to change themselves into any shape they wished for the purpose of doing evil. The Araucanians attributed to them every disease, especially those they could not understand, and all physical phenomena occurring at a period when they should not, such as rain during the harvest, the blights which affected their plantations, etc. Among all the other servants of Pillan were the Cherruve, spirits represented in the form of snakes with human heads. These were the cause of comets and shooting stars, which Araucanians thought were omens of dreadful calamities to those of their villages towards which they fell.

Another deity was the god of winds, Meuler (whirlwind, water-

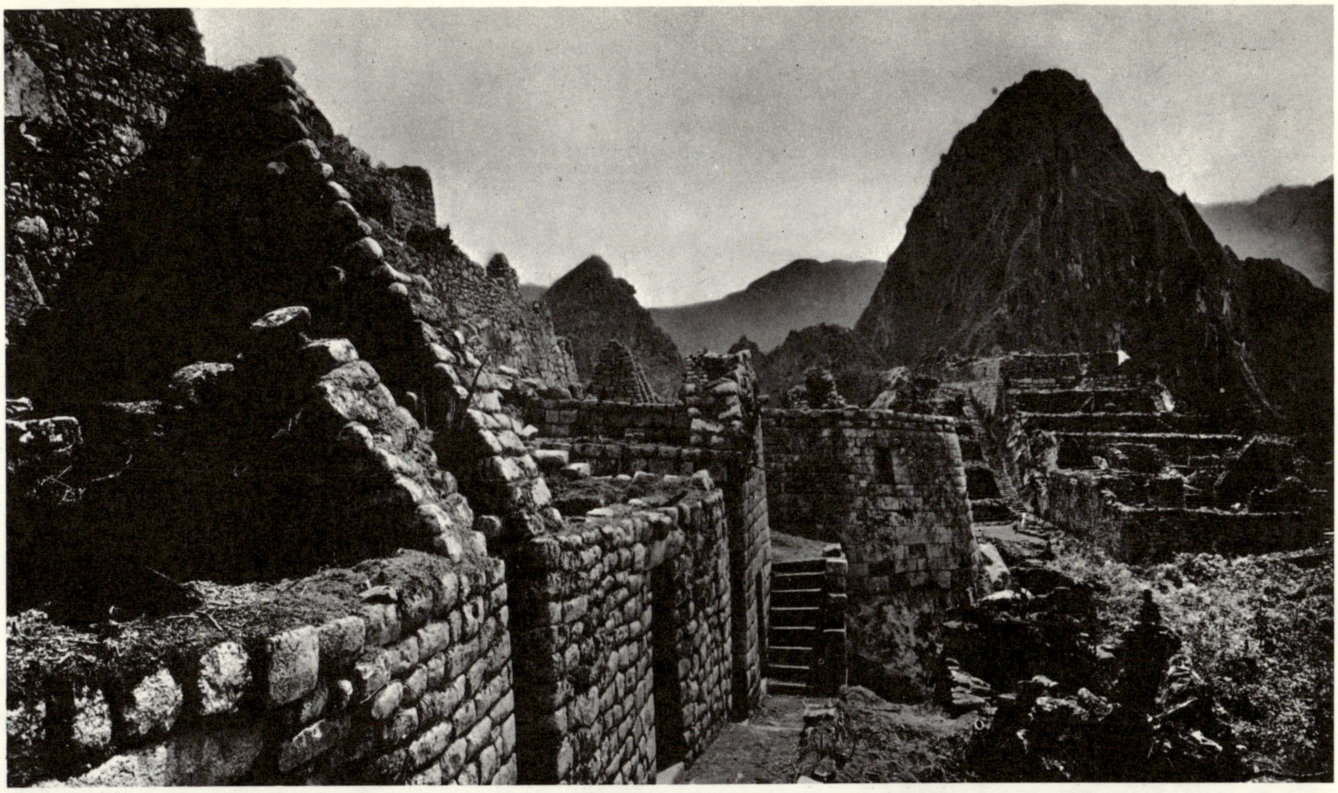

View of Machu Picchu. The most spectacular of all Inca sites, Machu Picchu hangs some 1,500 feet above the gorge of the Urubamba and was one of a series of fortress-sanctuaries protecting Cuzco. This view shows a street in the royal quarter with characteristic Inca masonry. It has been suggested that the choice of such an extraordinary site was made for religious reasons in the belief that the mountain was the place, some sixty leagues from Cuzco, where mankind found refuge and escaped destruction during the Flood.

spout, typhoon). He was represented as a lizard disappearing under ground when the typhoon burst.

The only beneficent deity among the Araucanians was 'Auchimalgen', the moon, the sun's wife. She protected the Indians against disasters, and drove away evil spirits by the fear she created in them. A red moon was the sign of the death of some great person. If one remembers how the Araucanians were connected with the Incas, it is very curious to note that they had no cult of the sun.

Ngurvilu, the god of water, rivers, and lakes, assumes the form of a wild cat, whose tail ends in a formidable claw. If any accident happens to an Indian in a boat or swimming, this deity is blamed for it.

Huaillepenyi, god of fog, appeared in the form of a ewe with a calf's head and the tail of a seal. He lived on the banks of rivers and lakes or on the sea-shore. When a deformed child was born, his deformity was attributed to the influence of this spirit.

Among secondary deities and inferior evil spirits is Chonchonyi. He is represented in the form of a human head whose very long ears served as wings to carry him where there were sick persons. When they are alone the spirit gets into their home, grapples with the sick person, kills him, and sucks his blood.

Colo-colo (basilisk) was born from a cock's egg, and causes fever and death, by drawing off the victim's saliva.

Pihuechenyi is a vampire which sucks the blood of Indians at night in the forest, and is represented as a winged snake.

Hell did not exist for the Araucanians. They merely believed that after death they assumed a corporeal but invisible form, and departed to another world which evil spirits could not enter. The Araucanians had no priestly caste, but there were fortune-tellers and sorcerers who possessed great influence among them. There is a tradition among the Araucanians of Chile that there was once a flood which very few Indians escaped. The survivors rook refuge on a high mountain called Thegtheg (the thundering or the glittering) which had three peaks and the ability to float on water. The flood was the result of a volcanic eruption accompanied by a violent earthquake; and whenever there is an earthquake the natives rush to the high mountains. They are afraid that after the earthquake the sea may again drown the world. On these occasions each person takes plenty of provisions, and in addition a wooden bowl to protect the head in case the Thegtheg should be carried up to the sun by the waters of the flood which was threatened.

THE GUARANI TUPIANS OR TUPINAMBAS OF BRAZIL

The Tupi mythology includes a series of civilising and creator heroes. The first of these heroes was Monan (ancient, old) who was the creator of mankind, and then destroyed the world with flood and fire; after whom came Maire-Monan (the transformer) who is often confused with his predecessor. He had the power of changing men and animals into other forms in order to punish them for their sins. He taught the Tupinambas the arts of governing and of cultivating the earth. A myth relates that he aroused the anger of men by his metamorphoses, so that they decided to kill him. For that end they arranged a festival during which Maire-Monan had to jump over three blazing bonfires.

He jumped the first but fainted above the second and was burned up. His bursting produced thunder, while the flames became lightning. Then he was carried up to heaven, where he became a star.

There was another hero, Maira-ata, who was thought to be a great wizard able to predict the future with the help of spirits. He holds a very important place in Brazilian mythology because he was the father of the mythical twins Ariconte and Tamendonare who caused the flood. They were mortal enemies these brothers, but were not by the same father. In a Tupinamba myth one was supposed to be the son of Maira-ata and the other of a mere mortal called Sarigoys. The mother of the twins, abandoned by Maira-ata, set out to look for him, guided by his child whom she carried in her womb. One day she came to the home of Sarigoys who offered his hospitality, and afterwards gave her another child. The mother went on her way until she came to a village where she fell a victim to the cruelty of the Indians, who cut her to pieces and ate her. The twins were rescued by a woman who brought them up. When they were men they decided they must avenge their mother, and with this in view they persuaded the murderers to accompany them to an island, under pretence of gathering fruit. While the Indians were on the island the brothers caused a storm which submerged them, after which they were changed into tigers. Having satisfied their wish for vengeance the twins then went to look for their father, whom they found in a village where he had become a wizard. He was very happy to see them, but before recognising them as his sons he put them through certain tests.

The first was shooting with bow and arrows, but the twins'

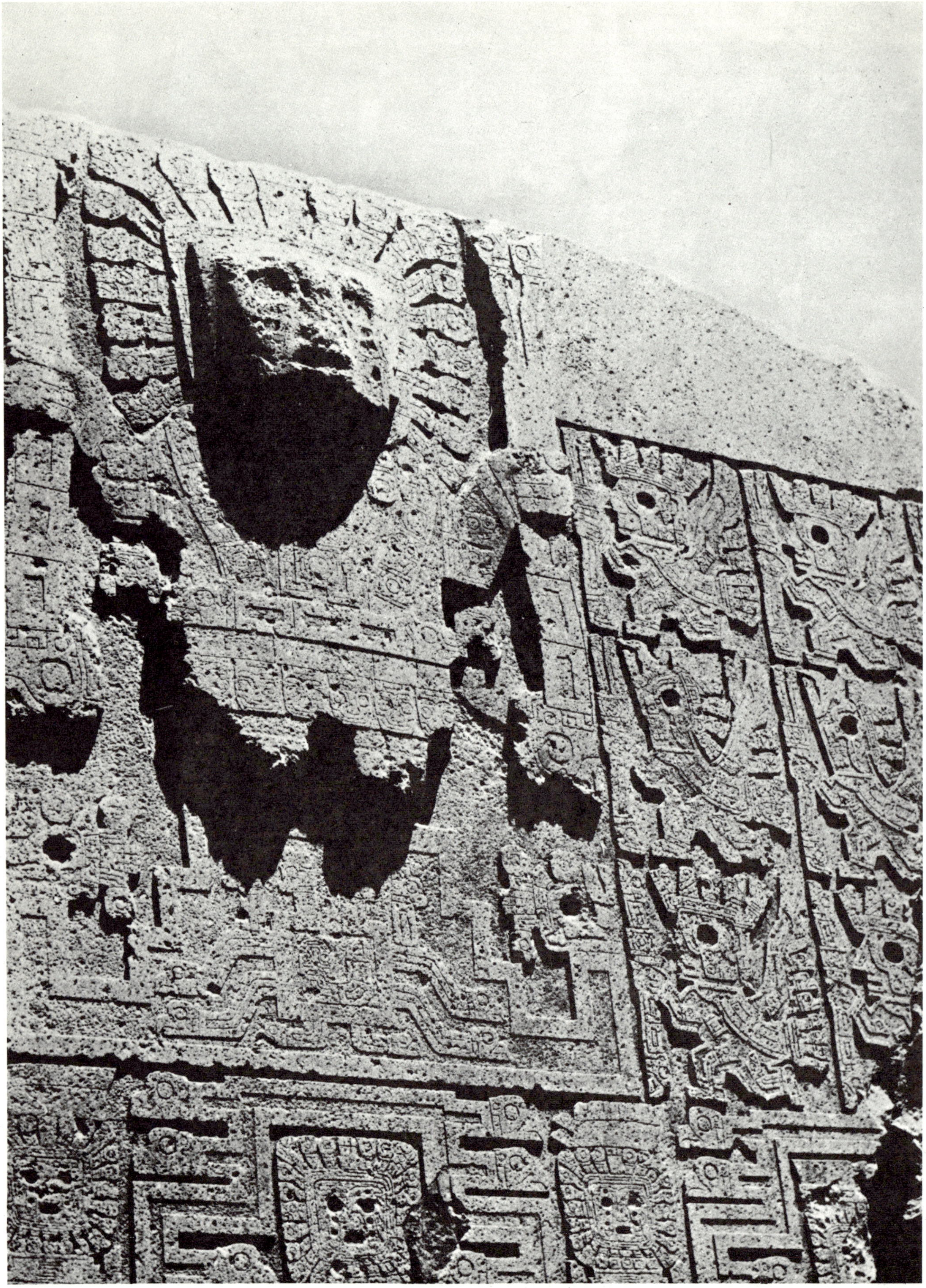

Detail of the Puerto del Sol (Sun door) at Tiahuanaco. Carved out of a single block of lava, the doorway shows a weeping god flanked by three rows of attendants. It has never been established who were the founders of the great city whose ruins lie on the Bolivian plateau near Lake Titicaca. There is much evidence of Sun worship and it is possible that the Incas destroyed it and dispersed the population, appropriating some ideas much as the Aztecs did in Mexico. *c.* 700 A.D.

arrows did not reach their targets but remained up in the air.

The second test was to pass three times through the stone Itha-Irapi, whose two halves dashed rapidly together. The son of Sarigoys went first, but was crushed. His brother picked up the fragments of his body and restored it to its former shape. They both were then able to pass through.

But Maira-ata was not satisfied with these tests, and insisted on a third. He told the twin brothers to go and steal the bait used by Agnen to catch the fish Alain which is the food of the dead. Once more the son of Sarigoys tried first to pass the test, and was torn to pieces by Agnen, but brought back to life by his brother. They tried again, and this time managed to steal the bait which they brought to Maira-ata, who then recognised them as his sons.

Among the Tupinambas there was another very important power, considered by the Indians as the demon of thunder and lightning, under the name Tupan. He was a kind of demon who received no worship and no prayers. He is represented as a short thick-set man with wavy hair. He was the youngest son of the civilising hero Nanderevusu and his wife Nandecy, for whom Tupan had a great affection. It is by order of his mother that Tupan leaves his home in the west to visit her in the east. Each journey causes a storm, and the noise of thunder comes from the hollow seat he uses as a boat to cross the sky. Two attendant birds take their place in his canoe, and are considered by the Indians as heralds of storms, which only stop when Tupan has reached his mother.

The Tupinambas thought they were surrounded by multitudes of spirits and genii. Among them was the Yurupari (demon) of the Tupians in the north, who haunts empty houses and places where the dead are buried. By the word Yurupari the Indians also meant the whole collections of demons or spirits of the wilds, whose malice made them dangerous.

Among the Tupians of the Amazon, Yurupari is a spirit of the forest, a kind of ogre, or god, according to the tribe.

Another greatly dreaded genius of the Tupinambas' mythology was named Agnen, mentioned above in the myth of the twin brothers, with whom he often did battle, and whose victim he was, but not until he had devoured one of them.

These evil genii were present at the start of creation. Although different from men, they are also mortal.

The most famous among the demons was Kurupira. He was a gnome of the forests and the protector of game, but ill disposed towards human beings. He is represented as a little man walking with his feet turned back. The Indians made offerings to this genius to appease his anger.

In the list of names of demons must be mentioned Macachera, the spirit of roads, considered by the Potiguara Indians as a messenger bringing good news, but by the Tupinambas as an enemy of human health. The Igpupiara were the genii of rivers who lived under water and killed the Indians. And there were the Baetata (will-o'th'-wisps).

Among the spirits benevolent to men were the Apoiaueue who made the rain fall when it was needed, and faithfully reported to God what happened on earth. The Tupinambas believed that after death the soul, *An*, goes to paradise, whose entrance is more or less accessible according to the soul's merits. This paradise is named the 'Land without Evil', and it is the home of the Ancestor, the civilising hero Maira. According to the myth of 'Land without Evil', Maira lives in the middle of a vast plain covered with flowers, and near his house is a large village whose inhabitants live in happiness. When they grow old, they don't die but become young again. There is no need to cultivate the fields, for crops grow there naturally. According to some, the 'Land without Evil' lies to the east, but according to others, to the west. At the time when they were discovered, the Indians of Brazil in the region of Rio de Janeiro had a legend of the world flood, as follows:

'A certain great wizard named Sommay, also known as Maira-ata, had two sons, named Tamendonare and Ariconte (the two twin brothers). The first-named had a wife, and was a good husband and father, but his brother Ariconte was just the opposite. He thought of nothing but fighting, and his one object was to engage the neighbouring peoples in contests, and to thwart his brother's justice and kindness. One day Ariconte came back from a fight, and showed his brother the bleeding arm of an enemy's body, and taunted him with these haughty words: "Get out of here, you coward! I'll take your wife and children, for you are not strong

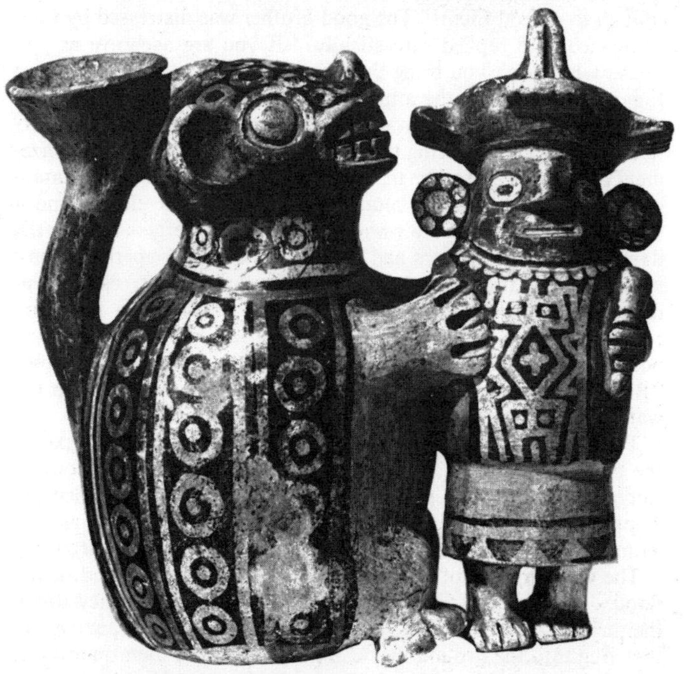

Feline grasping a man. Another example of the hold that felines had on the imagination of the early South American Indians, this little pottery vessel comes from Callejon de Huaylas in the northern Andes. These vessels, produced by specialist craftsmen, were used in burials and were filled with food and drink for the use of the dead person in the next world. Inca warriors were buried with their weapons while women were provided with their work-boxes and looms. Recuay culture.

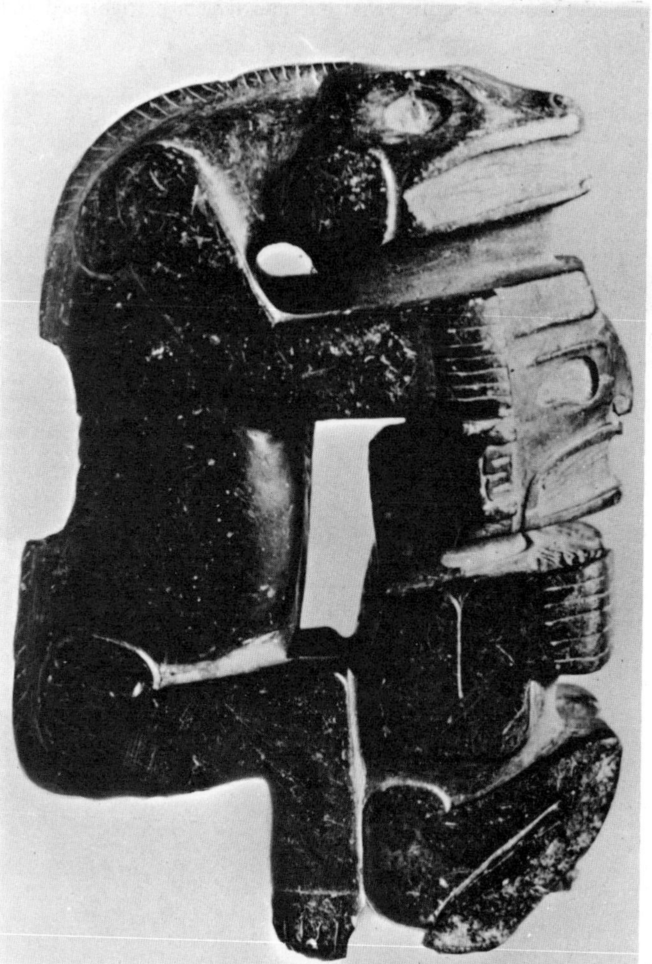

Idol, Muyrakytan. Brazil, Lower Amazon.

enough to defend them!" The good brother was distressed by such arrogance, and replied sarcastically: "If you are as brave as you boast, why didn't you bring the whole body of your enemy?" In a rage Ariconte threw the arm at his brother's door, and instantly the whole village was taken up into heaven, while the two brothers remained on earth. Seeing this, Tamendonare, either from amazement or anger, stamped on the earth so violently that a vast fountain gushed up higher than the mountains, as high as the clouds, and it went on flowing until the whole earth was submerged. Seeing the danger, the two brothers and their wives climbed up the highest mountain, and tried to save themselves by clinging to trees. Tamendonare and his wife climbed a tree called *pindora*, and the other brother with his wife climbed the tree *geniper*. While they were poised there Ariconte picked a fruit and gave it to his wife, saying: "Break it and drop a piece." By the sound of its meeting with the water they knew it was still high, and so waited.'

The Indians thought that all mankind died in this flood except the twin brothers and their wives, and that from the two couples came two different peoples, the Tonnasseares otherwise called the Tupinambas, and the Tonnaitz-Hoyanas also known as the Tominus, tribes which like the two brothers never stop quarrelling.

The Caryan tribe of Amazon Indians also have a legend of the flood: 'One day the Caryans were hunting wild pigs. They drove the animals into their dens, and killed each pig as it appeared. As they dug into the ground they came on a squirrel, then on a tapir, and then on a white squirrel. Then they found a human foot. In their terror they went for a powerful sorcerer called Anatina, who managed to dig up the man, calling out: "I'm Anatina! Bring me tobacco!" The Caryans did not understand him, and brought him flowers and fruits, which the sorcerer refused, pointing to a man who was smoking. The Caryans then understood, and brought him tobacco. He smoked until he fell down senseless on the ground. They took him to their village, and there he awoke and began to sing and dance. But his behaviour and language frightened the Caryans and they ran away. Anatina was greatly annoyed, and ran after them carrying a lot of calabashes full of water. He shouted to the Caryans to stop, but they did not, and in his wrath he broke one of the calabashes against the ground. The water at once began to rise, but the Caryans continued to run. Then he broke a second calabash, and another and another, and the water rose so high that the land was flooded, and only the mountains at the mouth of the Tapirapis rose above the flood. The Caryans took refuge on the two peaks of this mountain. Anatina then called to the fish, and asked them to throw the men into the sea. Several tried, but could not succeed. At last the *bicudo* (a fish with a long jaw looking like a beak) managed to climb the opposite slope of the mountain, and taking the Caryans in the rear, hurled them into the water. A big lagoon marks the place where they fell. Only a few Indians remained on the peaks, and only came down when the flood was over.'

Such is the mass of the chief legends in American mythology, and the reader will have noticed the similarities so easy to detect between this mythology and classical mythology, as well as with the chief traditions of the Hebrews.

Does this mean that Humanity was once upon a time reduced to a little group of individuals who later spread over the earth, bringing with them their legends which they altered through the centuries in accordance with new climates and new habits? Or, as seems more probable, are all these legends a confused account of great events on a planetary scale which were beheld in terror simultaneously by the men scattered everywhere over the world?

Looking over these cults and beliefs, we might make further instructive and curious comparisons. It would be the same for the Arts which grew up round them. The pyramids are one example. Another would be the ornaments to monuments, where we find details common to the Greeks, the Egyptians and the Hindus.

Our observations must be limited to these superficial suggestions, but study of them would be productive, and permit a deeper knowledge of the past of Humanity, still so vague to us.

OCEANIC MYTHOLOGY

THE PANTHEON OF OCEANIA

Complexity of the pantheon of Oceania. If, as is usually the case, mythology is taken to mean the genealogy, history and powers of gods, demi-gods and heroes, whose lives are imagined to resemble those of human beings, in short the pantheon of any given people, then it is very hard to give a brief general view of this pantheon for Oceania. It is quite possible to extract from travellers' books a long list of divinities, for instance in Polynesia Tangaroa, Tane, Rongo, Tu, and a host of other deities, some of whom turn up in a more or less large number of islands or archipelagos, either with the same name in variants of dialect, such as Tangaroa, Kanaloa, Taaroa, or with more or less synonymous names, or with approximate or even identical attributes. Thus, the chief Polynesian god, Tangaroa, is found in Micronesia under the more abstract name of Tabu-eriki (the sacred chief), in the anonymous thunder god of Ponape, the invisible god of the Ratak islands, the blind god of Bigar. The Polynesian god Rongo or Lono occurs in the Carolines, not only with the related names of Rongala (Fais island) and Mo-rogrog, but also with common features, notably those of being driven from heaven, to name one example, and for another of bringing fire to mankind.

But numerous differences are mingled with these resemblances. Sometimes, in the different islands of an archipelago, in the different districts of an island, even in a single tribe according to different individuals, the same god is endowed with different attributes, or unites in himself the attributes which elsewhere belong to different gods. Thus the Ngendei of the Fiji islands is the supporter of the world, so that when he moves he causes earthquakes; but at the same time he is the divinity of good harvests or of sterility, the revealer of fire, and king of the land of the dead like the Polynesian Mahiuki, the creator of the gods, the world and mankind, like the Polynesian Tangaroa, and, in addition, of cultivated crops which he showed mankind how to grow; he is also the author of a flood, a part attributed to different gods in Polynesia: Tawhaki, god of clouds and thunder in New Zealand; Tangaroa, Ru, god of the east wind, and Ruahatu a sea god in Tahiti; Hina, the Moon, in Hawaii. It also happens that in different regions different forms are attributed to the same god, or that when the god is represented in human form the sex is different.

On the other hand different gods in different populations receive the same attributes. Thus, the creation of the world is usually attributed to Tangaroa in Polynesia, but to Laulaati in Lifu island (Loyalty islands), to two deities, Tamakaia and Maui-Tikitiki (the latter of Polynesian origin), in Efate (New Hebrides), to Nobu in Eromanga (New Hebrides), to a prophet called by different names such as the unique, the old man, the man rejuvenated, or to his son Konori, in Geelvink Bay (New Guinea), and sometimes to Ngendei, sometimes to Ove in the Fiji islands. Again in the Fiji the origin of mankind is either attributed to Ngendei, who, according to some myths brought men forth by hatching out an egg similar to the world-egg of the Polynesian Tangaroa, or to several goddesses, particularly to Tuli, the daughter of Tangaroa, looked upon as the creatress of the world in the Samoan islands.

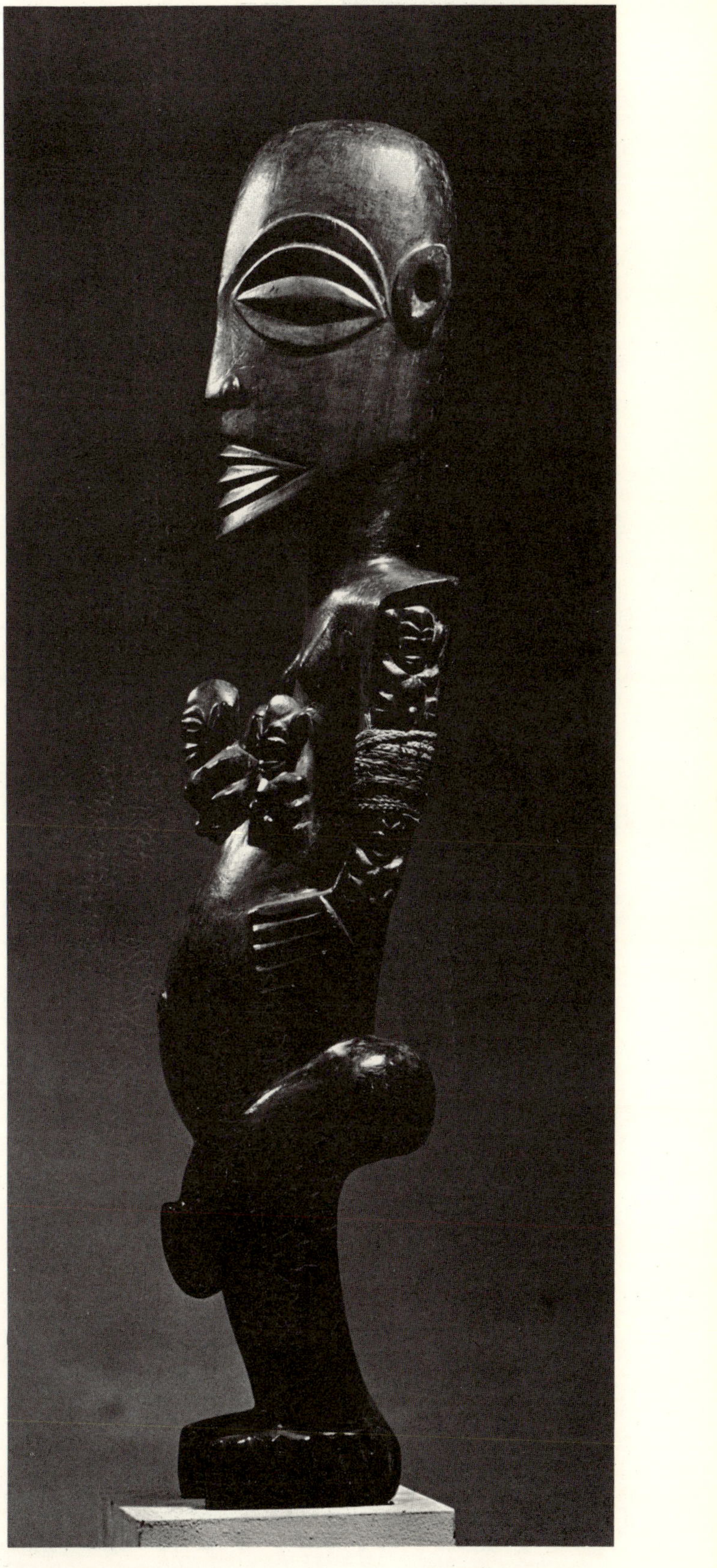

The god Rongo with his three sons. (Only two can be seen here; another is on the other side of his chest). One of these sons became the ancestor of the Ngariki tribe of the Mangaian Islands. Another possible interpretation of this figure is that it represents the demiurge Tangaroa in the act of creating gods and men. Tangaroa combines the attributes of both sexes, and even appears in other parts of the Pacific under the guise of a turtle or sea-serpent. Ironwood carving, Rarotonga, Cook Islands.

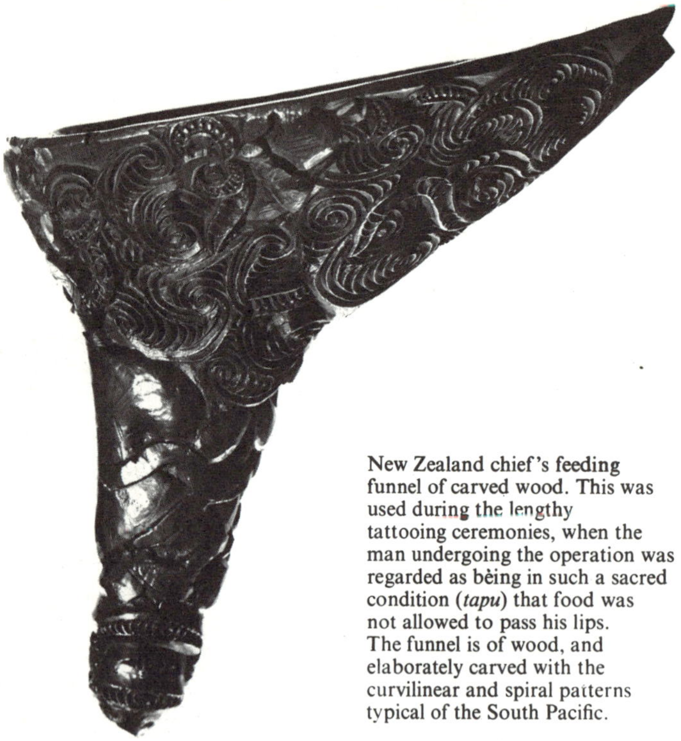

New Zealand chief's feeding funnel of carved wood. This was used during the lengthy tattooing ceremonies, when the man undergoing the operation was regarded as bèing in such a sacred condition (*tapu*) that food was not allowed to pass his lips. The funnel is of wood, and elaborately carved with the curvilinear and spiral patterns typical of the South Pacific.

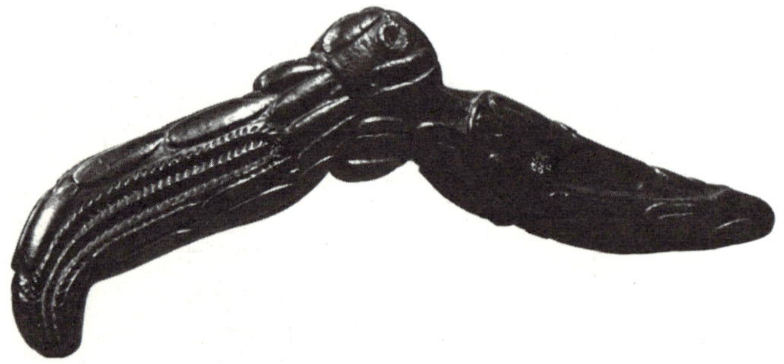

The bird-man of Easter Island. Birds occupied a prominent place in Easter Island legend and were under the protection of the local god Makemake, himself half human, half bird. The man who found the first sea-swallow's egg of the season (or, later, the chief whose servant first found the egg) became 'bird-man' for that year, and enjoyed ceremonial prestige. The egg was filled with *tapa* and used as a fertility charm. Woodcarving, Easter Island.

To introduce some order into this confusion, the best way, in our opinion, is to leave the names of the gods to one side, as well as their individuality as constituted by a collection of variable characteristics in the beliefs of different populations, often indeed within the same population, and to arrange them according to characteristics isolated by abstraction. Divinities, giving that word the very wide meaning of supernatural beings who always were or have become different from mankind, may be separated from one another by their nature or essence, which may be considered from the three standpoints of visible appearance, of attributes or functions, and of origin.

Physical appearance of divinities. Although as supernatural powers the divinities are of an essentially spiritual nature, this immaterial essence, as is the case with the human soul, is accompanied by appearances perceptible to the senses, and especially by visual form. Sometimes the divinities are thought of as possessing this form in themselves, so to speak, although human beings never see it; sometimes they may appear under this form in certain circumstances or to certain particularly favoured individuals; and sometimes, having no material form of themselves they borrow that of material beings or objects, in which they dwell or are incarnated in a more or less enduring way. It seems they can change not only by entering material beings of different forms; but also by changing their own forms; as is the case notably in the rather numerous legends of the 'Beauty and the Beast' type, to be met with in Indonesia, Melanesia, and Polynesia. These forms, not only the borrowed ones but those which are intrinsic, are very varied. There are anthropomorphic divinities, male or female, like most of the great gods of Polynesia or the protecting spirits of Dorei (New Guinea). Others are animals of all kinds and sizes: sharks, chiefly for the different sea gods (Tahiti, Fiji), sea-snakes, spider-crabs, crocodiles, snakes, eels (New Zealand), lizards (an incarnation of Tangaroa in Samoa), mice, frogs, flies, butterflies, grasshoppers, birds, especially the tropic-bird (above all the avian manifestations of Tahiti, and Tangaroa throughout Polynesia). The protecting spirit of the New Zealand prince Tinirau and his descendants was a divinity in the shape of a whale. In New Caledonia, Kabo Mandalat, the female demon who causes elephantiasis, is a gigantic hermit crab, with legs as big as coconut trees, living in the shell of an enormous *Delium-melanostoma*. In the Fiji islands there are some divinities which live in stones, but some, such as Ngendei's mother, are thought of as having really been stones. Divinities can also appear as meteors (thus in Torres Strait shooting stars were evil spirits, children of the stars, and in Fiji a comet is the child of Ngendei), and as sparks and sorts of vapour, a form often taken by souls of the dead at night.

Other divinities have the forms of fantastic beings. In New Zealand some are a sort of monster. The Ngendei of Fiji is half snake and half rock. Rati-mbati-ndua, the god of hell in various parts of Fiji, is a man with only one tooth (which is the meaning of his name) with which he devours the dead, while instead of arms he has wings with which he can fly through space like a burning meteor. Other divinities had wooden hands, eight eyes (a symbol of wisdom or clairvoyance), eight hands (symbol of dexterity), two bodies, twenty-four stomachs. Others again were hairy men of wood (New Zealand), ogres or other kinds of giant (Torres Strait, Fiji, Tahiti, Samoa, Tonga, Cook islands), or on the contrary were dwarfs, or men with white skin (such as the Pura of New Britain and Ruk island, the souls in the Banks islands, the earliest ancestors in New Zealand) recognised by the islanders in the first European travellers.

Attributes of divinities. Divinities may also be classified according to their attributes or functions, in other words according to that part of Nature in which they are interested and over which they preside. The idea of a providence regulating the whole universe, even when limited by the narrow horizon which for primitive people forms the limits of the world, if not wholly absent seems at least very little spread in Oceania, except perhaps in the esoteric doctrines of some colleges of priests, in New Zealand for instance. In general each divinity has a limited scope, rules over only a part of Nature, where it habitually lives. There are superintending divinities, which are also sometimes creative, of the sky, the sun, the moon, the stars (for instance, the Morning star in Dorei), the clouds, the winds, the rain, the sea, the earth, men, animals, and plants. Alongside these divinities of the great divisions of Nature, who might be called the great gods, exists a host of secondary divinities, attached to a limited area, an island, a part of the soil, a mountain, a volcano, a valley, a ravine, a watercourse, or a spring. Sometimes every tree and every stone has its particular divinity, which might equally well be called a spirit.

But whether their domain is large or small, some of these divinities play only a theoretical part, they serve merely to explain the existence and the properties of such and such a part of Nature, or such and such a known fact of actual experience. We shall come upon them again when dealing with mythology properly so called. Others have an incomparably more important interest for human beings since their influence is not exerted solely over Nature, but whether through its intermediary or directly on the destiny of mankind may be either profitable or harmful to them.

They subdivide themselves according to the extent of the human group in whose life they play a part, or, with whom, so to speak, they are concerned. Some are interested only in one person, others in a family, or a tribe, others again in a situation, an occupation, or a profession. Thus there are special divinities for war (Tu throughout the whole of Polynesia) and peace, for the fertility of the soil or the success of the plantations, for different industries or crafts (the building of houses and especially of roofs or of canoes, the weaving of nets, fishing, sailing), for healing, for household chores, for women and women's work (Hina the Moon, in Polynesia), for the physiology special to their sex (thus, in Hawaii Kapo was the divinity and at the same time the instrument of fertility and abortion), for marriage, for the arts (singing, dancing, dramatic art, tattooning), for games (among others, cock-fighting and surf riding). There were even divinities for thieves and for the different vices, even to love affairs of inverts. This division of labour among the divinities, if one may so put it, reached its maximum in Tahiti. For the sea alone there were thirteen divinities, each with special functions, and the pantheon included three hundred and sixty divinities with well-defined spheres.

Origin of divinities. From the point of view of their origin the divinities may be divided into two great categories, those who were never human beings, although they may have their form, and who make up the gods properly so called, and those who lived in a more or less distant past not only in the form but in the condition of men, whom we call spirits of the dead. The gods in their turn are eternal or, more precisely, original beings, *causa sui* as the metaphysicians say, who have always existed, and have no parents; or they may be the descendants of such. The earliest human beings were either begotten or created, fashioned by a god of one kind or the other. Among the ancestral spirits we may distinguish between those of ordinary dead persons who have no divine function except among their own descendants whose sole ancestors they are, and those of the dead who are especially famous for the deeds they did in their lifetime or for the benefits which humanity owes them; and these are the heroes, the type of whom may be found in the Polynesian Maui. Among his great deeds the most famous are that he brought up certain islands from the depths of the sea by fishing for them, that he compelled the sun to move more slowly, that he brought down fire to earth, and then, according to a tradition known only in New Zealand, that he attempted – unsuccessfully and at the cost of his own life – to make men immortal by penetrating the body of the great lady of darkness, Hine-nui-te-po.

Spirits of the dead. The spirits or ghosts correspond only partly with our current ideas about the souls of the dead. During life the body is linked with a different substance, which is a sort of double which is distinct in substance and is sometimes (New Caledonia), identified with its reflection. The soul detaches itself from the body momentarily during sleep, but completely at death, except in exceptional cases of resurrection. This separation of soul and body which results in the death of the body, does not cause the death of the soul, which continues to exist for all men, or according to the belief of some populations, exists only as a privilege for people of high rank. Moreover this survival is not necessarily permanent, and after a more or less lengthy series of partial deaths which, so to speak, are provisional survivals, may terminate in total annihilation (New Zealand). However this may be, the soul parted from the corpse retains an independent existence, imagined on the lines of that of the living and linked with a different but analogous body.

This survival of the soul may remain in the neighbourhood of its earthly dwelling and especially its burial-place, or in another world, sometimes alternately (New Caledonia), but generally and in a manner which is hard for us to conceive, simultaneously.

Souls reach the next world only after a long journey, which is made up of two parts, one on the earth, and the other from the earth to the next world. During this journey the soul retains the possibility of recovering earthly life. Without knowing it, the soul had a choice between two lines of conduct generally at the end of the journey on earth, for instance to stand on one or other of two neighbouring rocks, on one or other of the branches or roots of a tree; but sometimes on arriving in the next world, for example by eating or not eating the food placed before it. One of these lines of conduct made return to life impossible. From the time of leaving the body up till the time when it not only reached but was received into the next world, the soul was exposed to all sorts of dangers – evil powers, which are divinities properly so called, demons, or souls of other dead persons, tried in various ways to capture, kill or eat it.

The ideas about the position of the next world are very varied. Most often it is placed in the west, but sometimes it is situated on earth, sometimes under the earth or the sea (hell in the etymological sense), and sometimes above it, that is in the sky. To some extent it is not impossible to bring these different views into unity. The west is the point where the sun passes from the sky under the earth or under the sea, and thus is in a way the place of intersection of the heavenly and earthly worlds. Moreover, in islands of small area the horizon, which is identified with the utmost limit of the earth, is on the sea. The general idea seems to be simply that the soul leaves the precincts of the living for another world, whose difference from the earthly world is specified in a loose way. The tribes of New Caledonia who situate the infernal world in the north-east, consider that point as the utmost limit of the earth. Other reasons contributed to fixing the direction in which souls dwell. Thus, in Polynesia generally, by going west the souls were moving towards the land where the ancestors had lived, which seems to correspond to a historical reality.

The ideas about the number of resting places of souls are as different as those about their situation. Although the belief was not general, where it existed, for instance in the north of New Guinea, people admitted that every being or object had a soul just like men, and that these different souls went to an afterworld, either one common to all, or one reserved for special types of beings. For instance, in Tahiti there was an afterworld of pigs, in Rewa (Fiji islands) there was an afterworld of coconuts governed by a special

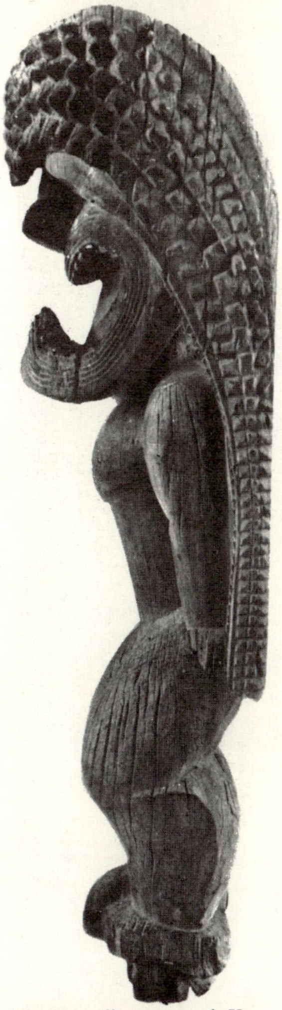

The Hawaiian war-god, Ku. Images like this, about four feet high, formerly stood in the precincts of Hawaiian temples. The pose of the body is typical of Polynesian sculpture – the legs slightly bent, the arms hanging down, the headdress merging with the head. Woodcarving, from Oahu, Hawaii.

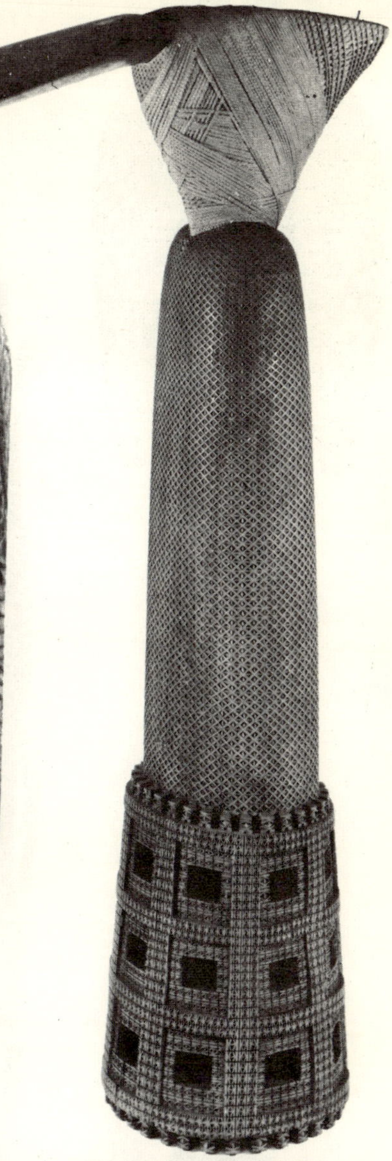

Chief's adze, symbol of the god Tane. Tane was a nature-god, son of Rangi (the Sky) and Papa (the Earth). He was particularly associated with forests, with trees and with wood, and was regarded with special veneration by anyone who worked in wood, such as house-builders and makers of canoes. The stone blade is bound to its wooden handle by tightly knotted threads. Mangaia, Cook Islands.

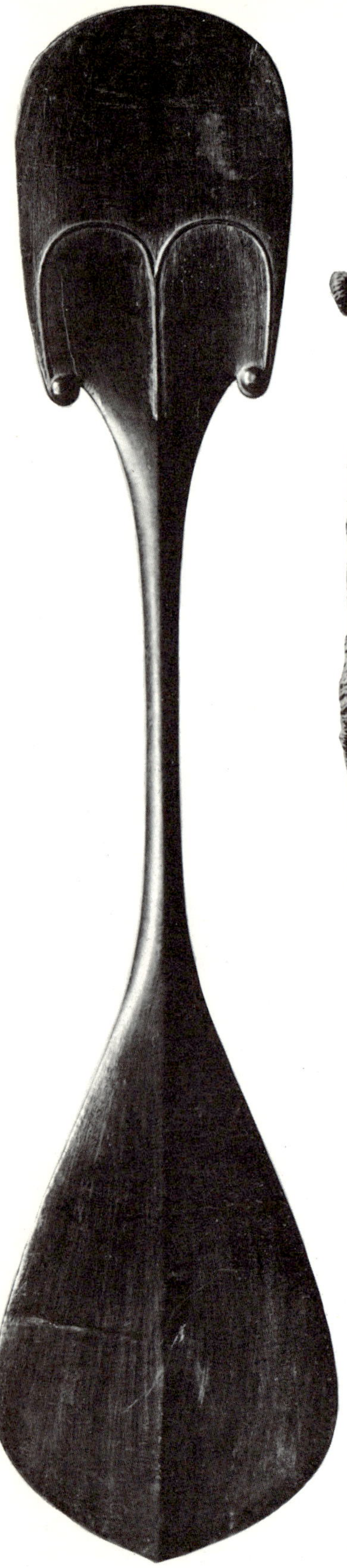

Ceremonial paddle.
This paddle *(rapa)* is made in the forms of a stylized man, and played various parts in cult rituals. When the sweet potato crop was in danger, either from pests or lack of rain, these paddles helped to ward off evil spirits.

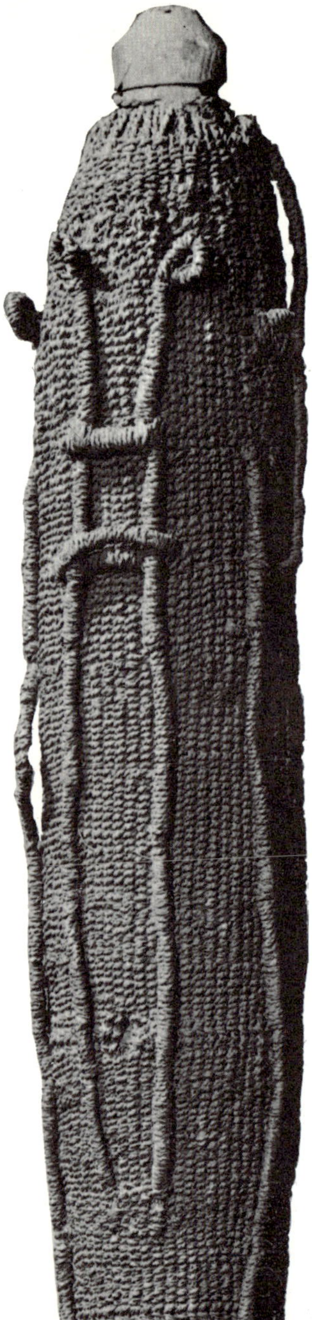

The war god Oro. Oro was worshipped all over Polynesia, but in Tahiti not represented by a carved human figure. Instead he was a bundle tied up with cords over a wooden core: limbs and facial features can, however, be recognized. Pleaded sinnet cloth on wood, Tahiti.

divinity to which they departed from all parts of the archipelago as soon as they had been eaten. Human souls had sometimes one, sometimes a number of afterworlds. Thus, not to mention the various heavenly worlds open to certain privileged souls, there were four infernal worlds in the Marquesas and ten in New Zealand.

Each of these afterworlds was ruled by a divinity who sometimes had no other function, while his name sometimes expressed both the afterworld he governed and the state of the souls in it, and sometimes had other occupations besides that of ruler of the dead. For instance, the divinity usually considered throughout Polynesia as the head of the afterworld was Miru, but in Hawaii she shared that function with Hakea; in the Fiji islands it was either Lothia (Lakemba), who turns up at Lifu (Loyalty islands) under the name of Locha, or it was Rati-mbati-ndua, the Lord with one tooth, or else the supreme god Ngendei. In New Zealand it was either Ngahue or Tawhaki who was also the thunder god, or it was the Great Lady of the shadows, Hine-nui-te-po, who sometimes ruled all the other worlds, sometimes only the four upper levels where the state of the souls was less agreeable, while the next three levels were ruled by Rohe, and the last three by the goddess Miru. At Tahiti the head of the afterworld reserved for the Areoi was Urutaetae; Hiro was at one and the same time head of the Areoi afterworld and of the afterworld of those who did not belong to the fraternity; in addition the god Oro presided over both afterworlds, and the divine bird Lota over that reserved for common people.

The different residences allotted to souls usually differed only in their conditions and, broadly, in the happiness of all those dwelling there; while according to other beliefs these variations were combined in a single residence; thus, at Raratonga there was a difference between the residence of the happy souls and that of the unhappy. This difference in conditions, which often amounted solely to a difference of food supply, had nothing in common with our idea of retribution after death; as a rule moral considerations had nothing to do with the matter. The state of each individual after his death depended on what he had possessed in his lifetime, on his power, his wealth, and the rites or sacrifices carried out for him by those who survived him – in a word, in one form or another, on his *mana*. For some tribes of New Caledonia his condition depended solely on his seniority as a soul arriving in the land of the dead.

The posthumous life of souls was in general merely a repetition of life on earth in another world. Generally speaking, it did not include any tortures or special privations; and sometimes it even seems as if in the next world all the souls without distinction enjoy the conditions reserved on earth for the privileged, with abundance and every kind of pleasure. In spite of the wide diversity of beliefs, they seem in agreement in recognising that whatever pleasures life after death may have in itself, so to speak, still it is not worth life on this earth, and dying is a great misfortune.

As a rule those souls which have reached the next world are not visible to ordinary mortals, but only to men gifted with a special clairvoyance. Those souls which for one reason or another have not reached the land of the dead, or who return from it, may be perceived by anybody, usually at night but sometimes by day. Sometimes they retain the physical appearance of the living in the form of a ghost, and sometimes they appear in the form of sparks or different animals.

As the souls of the dead should normally go to the other world, those who remained on earth were either miserable or vindictive; and if they managed to acquire superior powers they became evil spirits, greatly dreaded demons. Besides, even those souls which reached the other world regretted their life on earth. Even if the survivors had carried out all the funeral rites due and necessary to them, they still envied the living. The dead then were terrifying even to those whom they had loved in their lifetime. And yet it is unquestionably the fact that at the same time the ancestral spirits were looked on as tutelary powers, protecting spirits, from whom might be expected advice, help, protection, and favours of all kinds, quite as many, if not more, than might be expected from the more or less indifferent divinities, properly so called.

It is very hard to discover any rational explanation of this contradiction which must be the result of sentimental considerations, or, as they say, of affective logic. However, it is a plausible hypothesis that the ancestral spirits could not be looked on as endlessly hostile powers, since their actions had not prevented the family and tribal

Mask of basketwork from New Britain, worn in ancestor cult ceremonies, which are widespread in Melanesia.

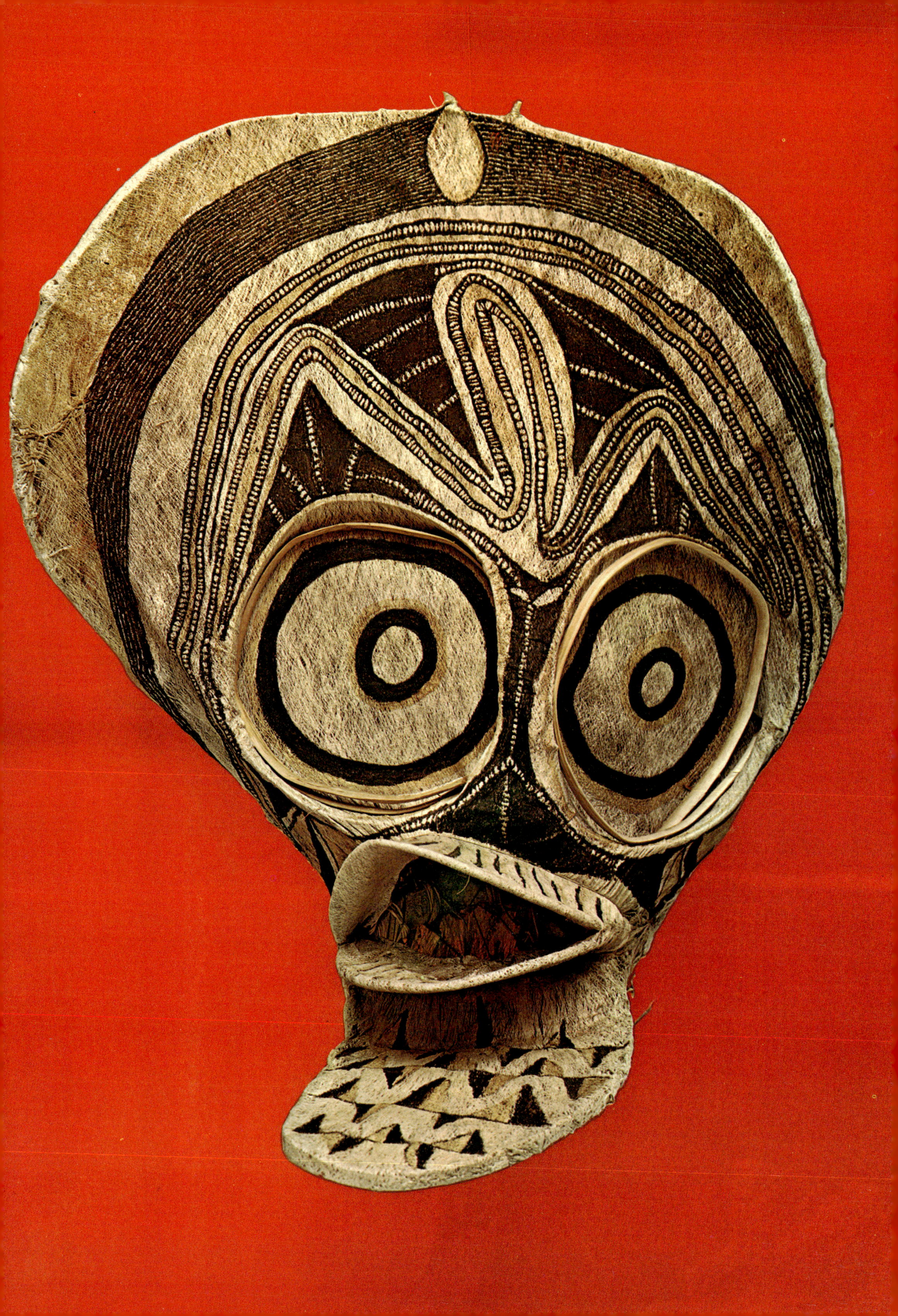

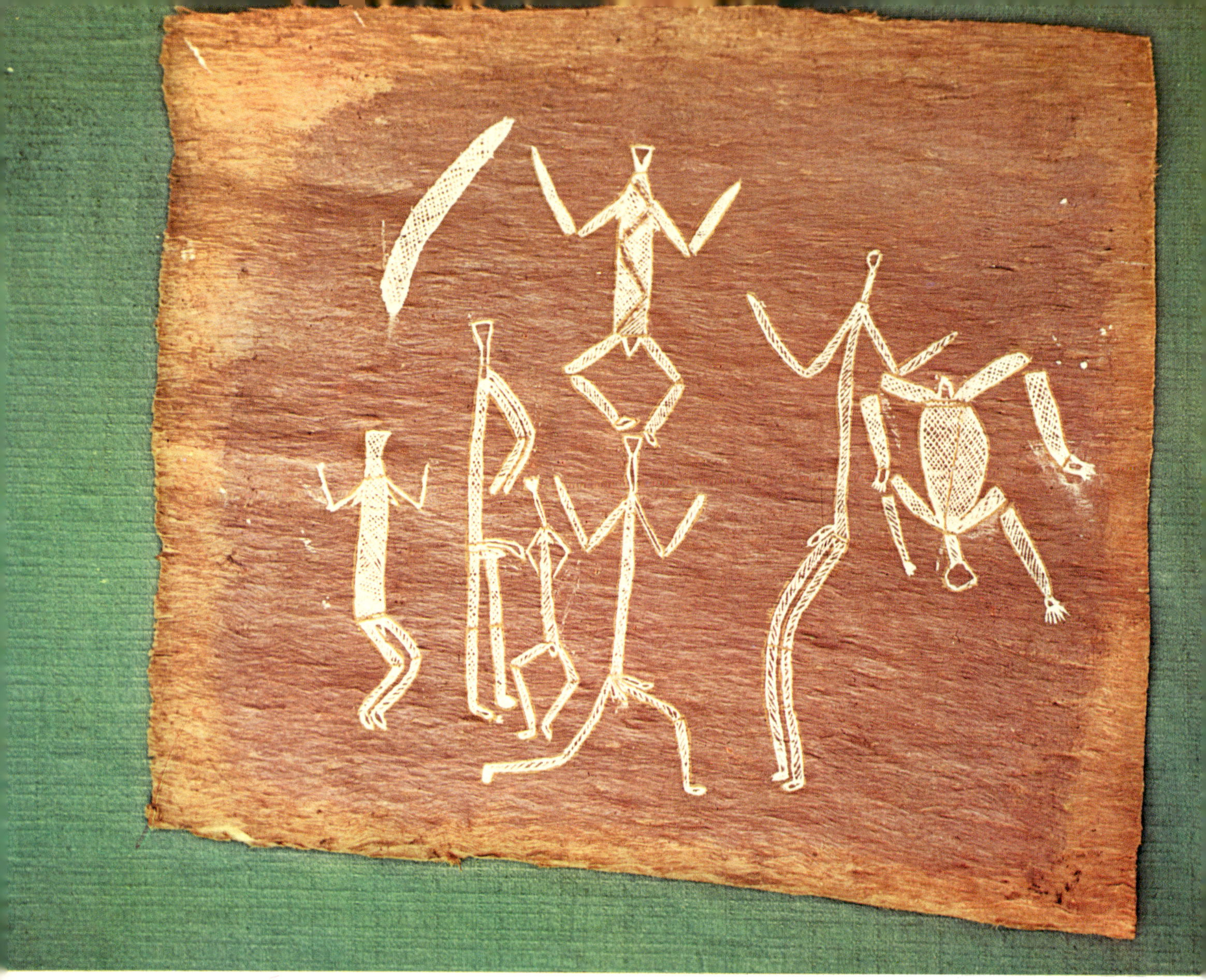

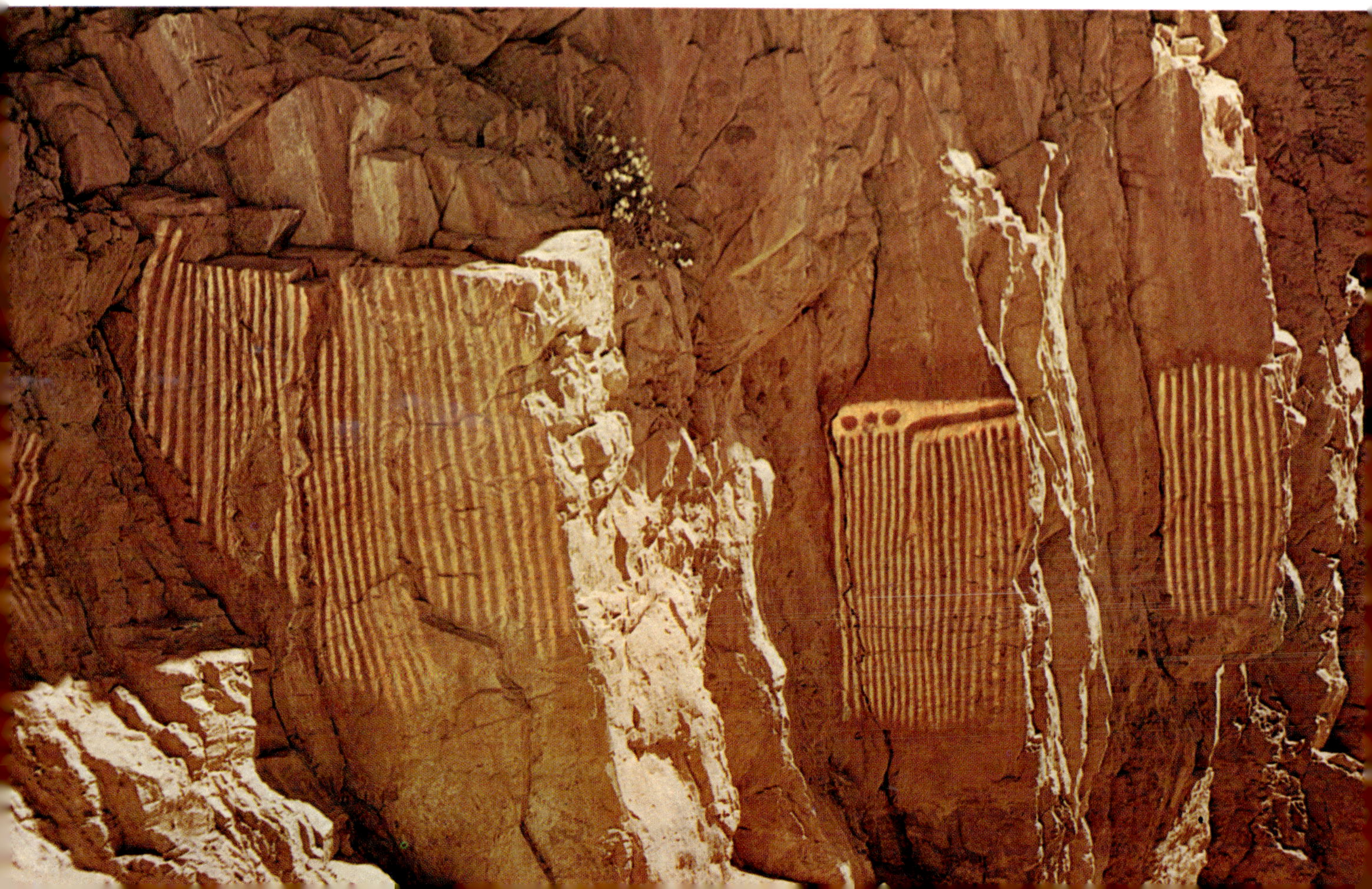

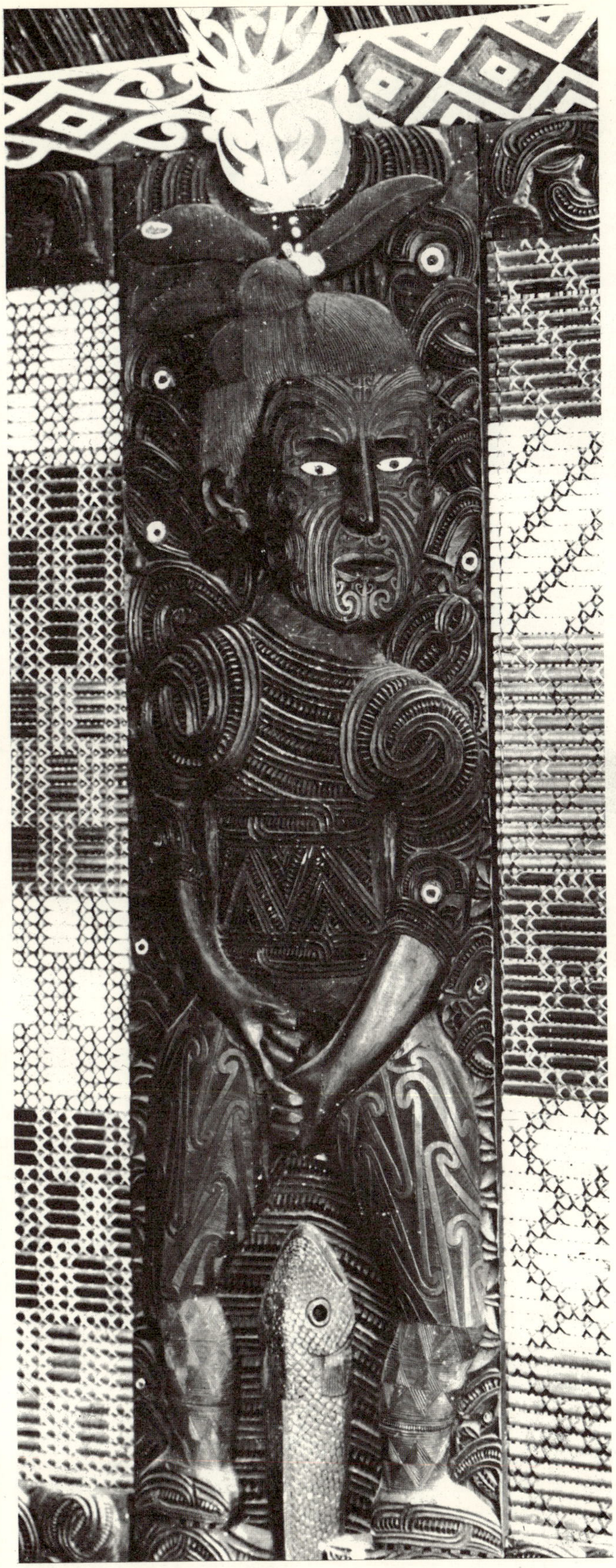

The god Maui pulling up the land. Maui plays in Polynesian mythology, a role not unlike that of Prometheus in Greek. He is credited with having pulled up the land from the ocean for men to live on, with championing them against the gods, and with stealing fire for them from the keeper of the underworld. This figure shows him pulling up North Island, New Zealand, symbolized by a fish. The eyes are shells. Woodcarving from a house at Whakewerawera, Rotorua, New Zealand.

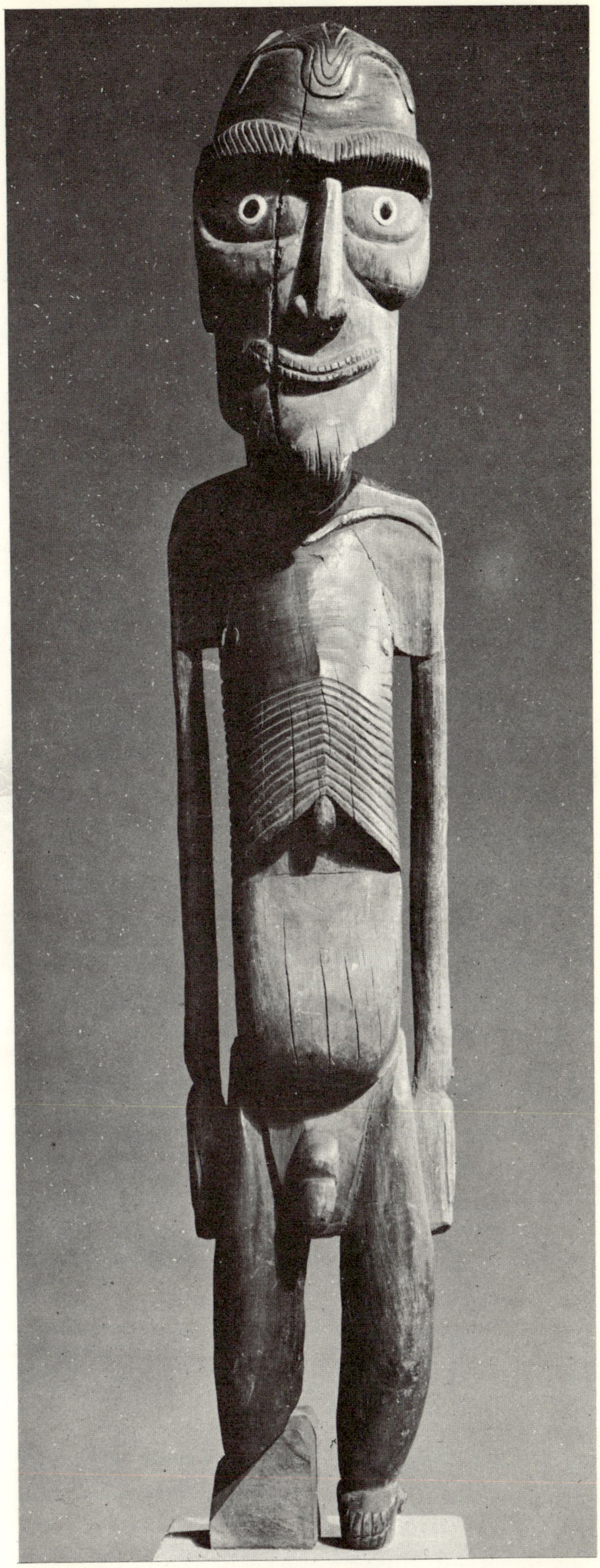

Ancestor figure from Easter Island. There is much disagreement among anthropologists concerning the appearance of emasculation in these figures. Some explain it as a stylistic feature merely (wood was extremely scarce and the sculptor had to make the most of small pieces); others deduce deficiency diseases; others food shortage; others again identify the figures as decaying corpses. They also seem to have a goitre on the neck. The eyes are inset with obsidian.

(*top*) In the rocks of the western Arnhem Land live the Mini spirits, who only emerge to dance when there is no wind, as they are so thin their bones would snap. Bark painting from Goulburn Island. (*bottom*) A witchetty grub totemic site of the Arunda aborigines in the Macdonnell Ranges of Australia. The paintings mark the place where the women of the Dreamtime (the mythical past) watched the performance of a sacred ceremony by the men of the tribe. In the Dreamtime women shared the knowledge of the tribal rites.

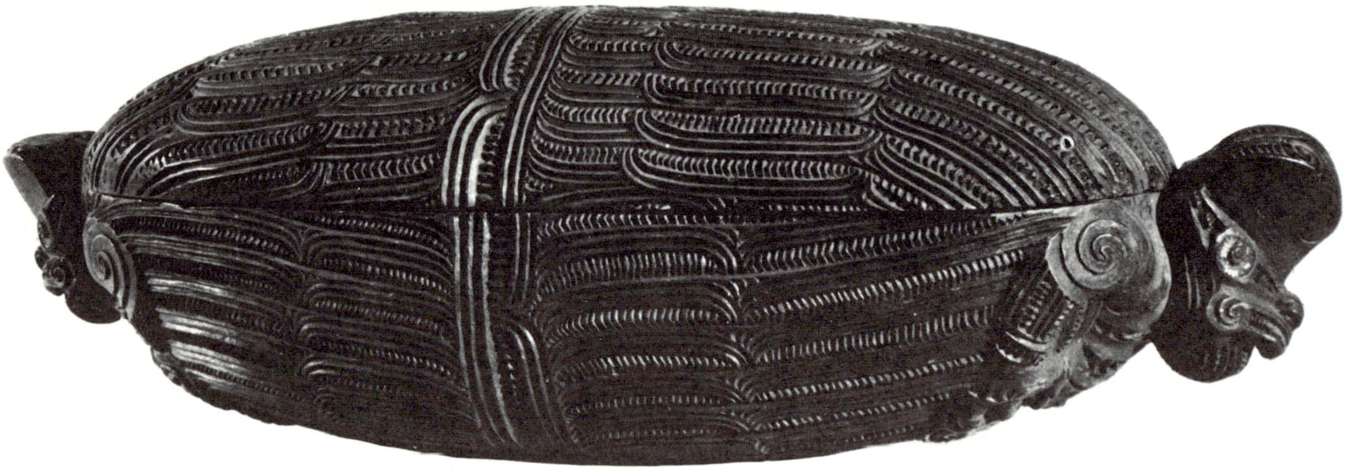

A Maori feather-box. Beautiful feathers were highly prized by the Maori and were widely used in cult ceremonial costume. This box in which they were kept is carved with feather-like patterns on the sides and has grotesque heads at each end. It is forty-two centimetres long and has a matching lid. Carved wood, New Zealand.

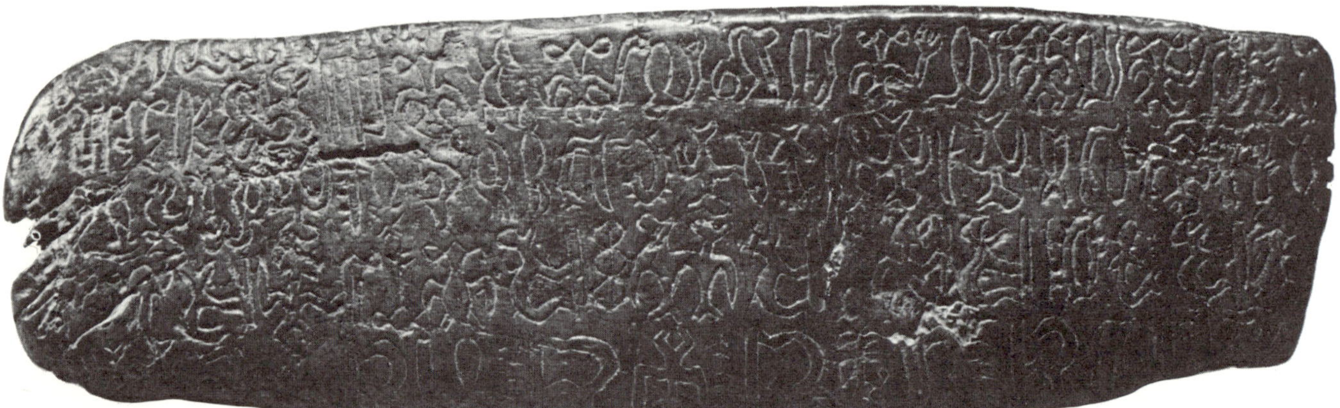

Inscribed tablet from Easter Island. This is one of the very few written documents of Oceanian mythology and is still undeciphered, though there are hopes of solving the riddle. It was made and used by the Rongorongo, men who combined the functions of bards and priests, and through whom the sacred stories were transmitted. The characters seem to be ideograms relating to ritual and history.

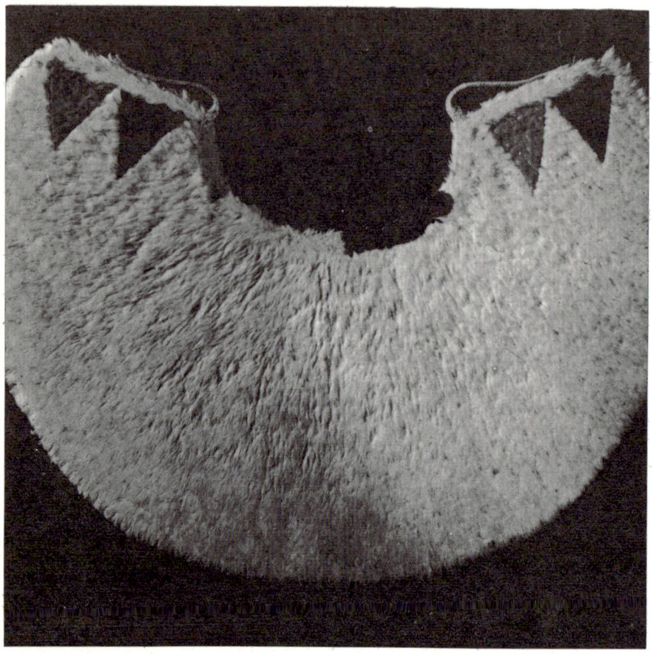

A nobleman's feather cape. In Hawaii the making of feather garments and decoration reached a peak of quality. A precise symbolism governed the use of the colours employed. This cape is yellow with red and black triangles. Red was a colour associated with divinity, as well as being a sign of noble rank.

life from continuing and even prospering, and so eventually they must have got rid of the malevolent feelings natural to them at the time when they had just been deprived of life. Perhaps as they became used to their life after death, they began to lose their memory and regret for their former state on earth and their envy of the survivors, and came to think only of their common stock. And as a matter of fact the protectors were not as a rule those recently dead, but the more or less far-off ancestors.

Confusion of the pantheon of Oceania. If the classification here presented of divinities or supernatural powers satisfies the tendencies of the logical mind, we must hasten to add that the beliefs of Oceania, like those of most primitive or savage peoples, show hardly any regard for accuracy and precision. The Graeco-Roman pantheon is scarcely known to us except through literary works and works of art, which present them in a finished form which these works themselves helped them to assume from times of antiquity, but the pantheon of Oceania comes to us as folklore, in the turmoil of life. In every community of the South Seas the original traditions have been supplanted or combined with or continue to exist side by side with beliefs which have either been brought in from abroad or invented by individual natives. Consequently the different gods who have names of their own have borrowed from one another some of their outstanding features as well as a part or the whole of their legendary history, and in addition at different times and places they have been placed in different categories, and the categories themselves have been more or less mixed up.

From a host of examples we may take, in the Marianas, Pountan, the night breeze, looked upon as a man of great inventiveness who for a long time lived in empty space before the existence of heaven

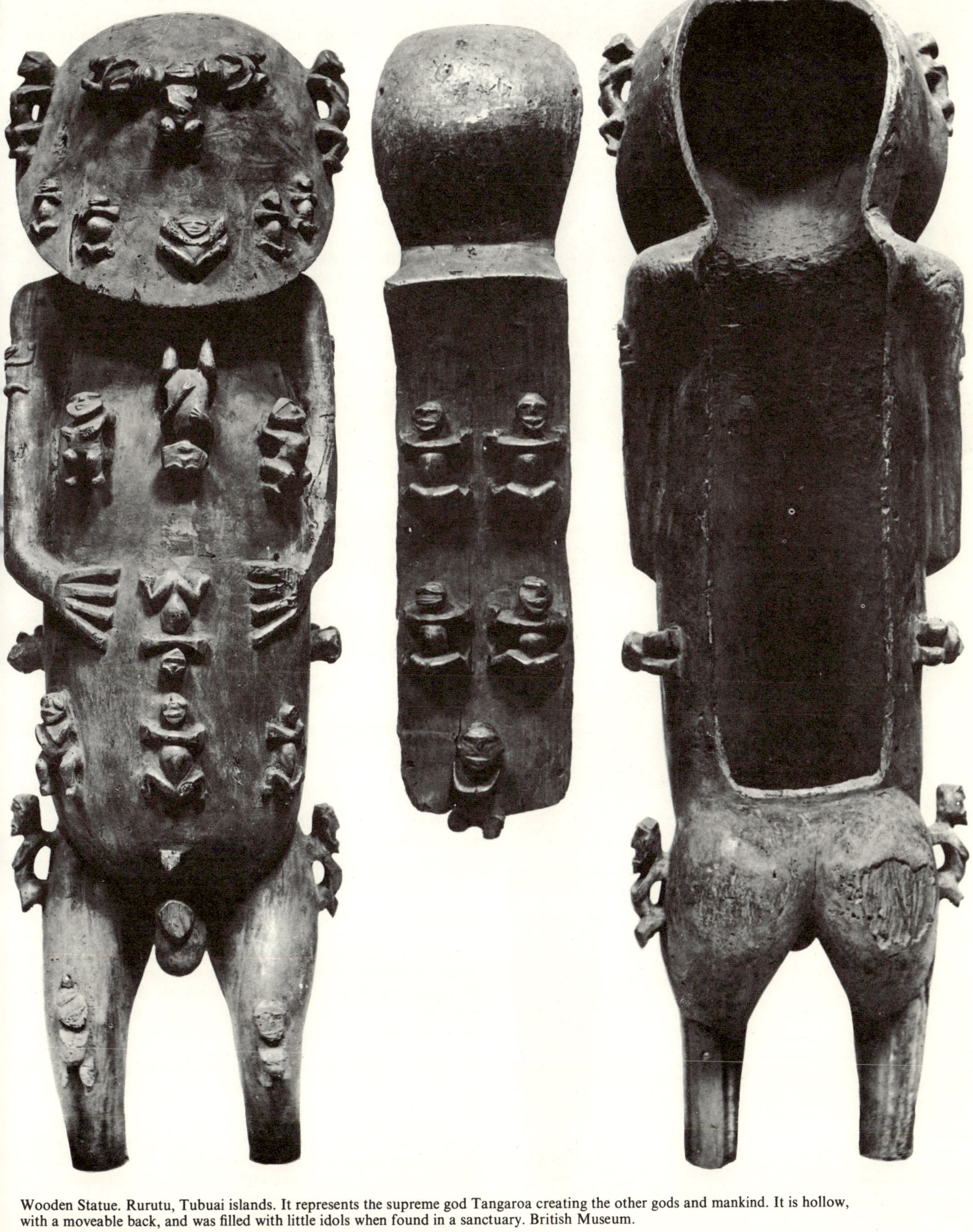

Wooden Statue. Rurutu, Tubuai islands. It represents the supreme god Tangaroa creating the other gods and mankind. It is hollow, with a moveable back, and was filled with little idols when found in a sanctuary. British Museum.

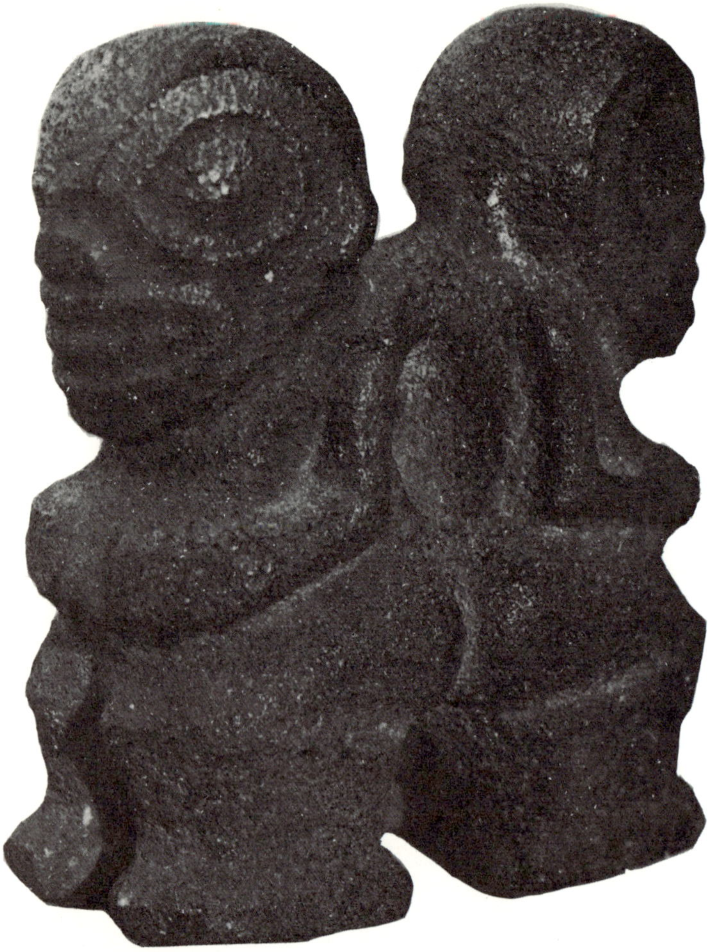

Double votive figures, *tiki*. These were used as weights for fishing nets, but identical figures recur in many other contexts – on canoes, war-clubs, stilts, fans and crowns. Tiki was a mortal man in Polynesian legend but became divine in Maori mythology. The big round eyes are characteristic of Marquesan art. Stone, Marquesas Islands.

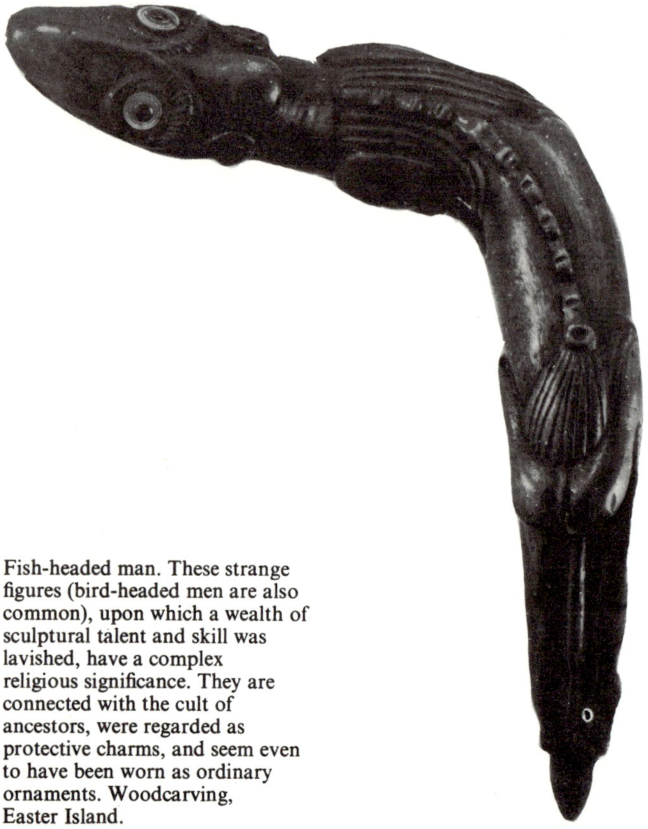

Fish-headed man. These strange figures (bird-headed men are also common), upon which a wealth of sculptural talent and skill was lavished, have a complex religious significance. They are connected with the cult of ancestors, were regarded as protective charms, and seem even to have been worn as ordinary ornaments. Woodcarving, Easter Island.

and earth – so at one and the same time he is a god and a hero. The two principal divinities of the New Hebrides, Tangaroa and Quat, are alternately or sometimes simultaneously looked upon as gods, demi-gods, heroes or mere spirits. In Ruk island and in New Britain, Nabaeo was at one time looked upon as a good spirit, but later became mainly evil. Pura, who began as a god, probably of the sky, came down to the rank of a simple hero; and the Marsaba of Ruk island who seems to have been originally god of the underworld is now only an evil spirit or vulgar demon. In New Zealand Tangaroa is not the supreme god, but one among other great gods, who shared in the creation but was not the sole creator. In Polynesia many of the great gods, and according to some Tahiti legends even Tangaroa, have been looked on as merely defied men.

In Tahiti, the oramatua, whose name means the ancestors, are no longer distinguished from other spirits. While in Tahiti and different parts of Polynesia, the atua, the gods, were distinguished by their name from the varua, the spirits, in Tanna (New Hebrides) spirits and gods are known by the same name, aremha, for the gods have dropped out of use or are thought of only as spirits. It is the same in New Guinea and in Balade (New Caledonia) though, on the other hand, in Ndeni (Santa Cruz islands) the ancestors have been raised to the rank of gods.

Throughout Polynesia the word tiki means both the protecting spirits and their idols, especially the little figures in green stone which the Maoris of New Zealand wore round their necks. But the function of protecting spirits is sometimes attributed to the gods properly so called, sometimes to Tangaroa or one of his children, or again to such and such a god to whom humanity owes the things most necessary to existence, such as light and food (vegetables and fish), or again to the souls of the ancestors, or to the first man who at one and the same time was a man and the descendant or creation of a god, or finally to some especially notable hero such as Maui, associated with the sun owing to certain details in his story.

Similarly the many sacred statues of Melanesia, especially the korwar of western New Guinea are not properly speaking idols, since the worship offered these images is actually not addressed to them but to the supernatural powers dwelling in them, and according to the definite statements of the natives they represent protecting spirits which are essentially the souls of ancestors. In many cases these spirits have been raised to the rank of deities, or on the contrary they are old gods who have fallen in rank, as may be seen from the animal form of their representations, or, when they are anthropomorphic, from their large mouths or long teeth for eating souls. In Micronesia, particularly the Marianas, the cult of ancestors has replaced that of the gods.

THE GREAT MYTHS OF OCEANIA

An examination of the pantheon, in our opinion, does not, properly speaking, constitute mythology, which according to etymology is the study of myths. A myth is not just any sort of legend, not even a legend in which superhuman personages take part, but an explanatory legend, meant to give the cause or origin of such and such a fact of actual experience. While legends are the primitive form of novels and history, myths are the original and living form of philosophy.

While studying the mythology of Oceania we shall not enquire whether the myths to be found in such and such an area, island or archipelago are native creations or importations. We shall limit ourselves to demonstrating, with reference to each of the main categories of empirical realities, the main types of mythical explanation invented in Oceania, quoting only the clearest examples. We shall have more than once to disentangle the various themes combined in a complex legend, and, which is more regrettable; shall be forced to pass over many a picturesque detail in silence. We resign ourselves to this, desirous above all to work scientifically and not in a literary way, less concerned with local colour than with the universal and constant aspiration of humanity to achieve the illusion of understanding.

What we must point out among the various peoples of Oceania is not the mere absence of myths concerning such and such a reality, which might be due to lack of information in us, but the deliberate refusal to give it a mythical explanation, because this thing has always existed, never had a beginning.

Thus among the mountain tribes in the north of Luzon, in

Minahassa, in the Palau islands and Western Carolines, all over Melanesia, in certain tales of New Zealand and the Chatham islands, the upper or heavenly world and the terrestrial world are thought to have existed for ever. It is the same in Australia, where the native populations of the north and east seem in addition to have believed generally that there have always been men, and that from the very beginning the animals always had their present characteristics. Similarly, in many legends we shall turn up, the earth is supposed to come out of the sea or to have been formed from materials brought from the sky to the sea, but the sea is thought of as having always existed.

Cosmogony myths. If in so many cases the mythical explanation takes for granted heaven and earth and sea as originally existing, beyond which it is not necessary to go, in others the myth sets out to explain their existence. These myths of the origin of the universe as a whole, or cosmonogy myths in the strict sense, may be divided into two main types. The first is creationist, and familiar to us from the mythology of the Judaeo-Christian religions. It was thought to exist among the tribes of south-east Australia, but the assertion of the earliest observers (most of them missionaries) that these peoples believed everything had been created in the beginning by a deity, seems to be a false generalisation; and it is probable that the natives used this explanation only to account for certain peculiarities of the land, such as mountains, rocks and rivers. In the central Carolines, there was in the beginning a goddess, Lukelong, who created the heavens and then the earth. In the Gilbert Islands heaven and earth were made by Naruau and his daughter Kobine. According to a legend of the Society Islands the heavenly god Taatoa embraced a rock, foundation of all things, and so produced the earth and the sea. A very detailed myth comes from the island of Nauru. In the beginning there was nothing but the sea, and above soared the Old-Spider. One day the Old-Spider found a giant clam, took it up, and tried to find if this object had any opening, but could find none. She tapped on it, and as it sounded hollow, she decided it was empty. By repeating a charm, she opened the two shells and slipped inside. She could see nothing, because the sun and moon did not then exist; and then, she could not stand up because there was not enough room in the shellfish. Constantly hunting about she at last found a snail. To endow it with power she placed it under her arm, lay down and slept for three days. Then she let it free, and still hunting about she found another snail bigger than the first one, and treated it in the same way. Then she said to the first snail: 'Can you open this room a little, so that we can sit down?' The snail said it could, and opened the shell a little. Old-Spider then took the snail, placed it in the west of the shell, and made it into the moon. Then there was a little light, which allowed Old-Spider to see a big worm. At her request he opened the shell a little wider, and from the body of the worm flowed a salted sweat which collected in the lower half-shell and became the sea. Then he raised the upper half-shell very high, and it became the sky. Rigi, the worm, exhausted by this great effort, then died. Old-Spider then made the sun from the second snail, and placed it beside the lower half-shell, which became the earth.

Belief in a creator god is to be met with in the Society Islands and in the doctrines of the New Zealand priests. In north-west Borneo two birds flew above the primeval sea, dived into it, and brought up two kinds of egg, from which they made heaven and earth.

In the second category of these cosmogony myths the gods are far from being the creators of the universe, and are only one of its elements with the same origin as all the others, that is to say a sort of Nothing which is the germ of all things. The rudimentary form of this conception occurs in Nias. In the beginning there was a thick fog, which condensed and became a being without speech or movement or head or arms or legs. This being in turn gave birth to another, which died, but a tree sprouted from its heart. Gods and men emerged from its buds. Similarly in the Society Islands, during the primeval darkness Ta'aroa existed in an egg, from which he afterwards emerged. The same theme, more fully developed, is found in various parts of Polynesia. In the beginning was Po, a void without light, heat, sound, form and movement. From this sort of chaos, or more precisely from this undifferentiated substance imperceptible by the senses, there gradually evolved movement

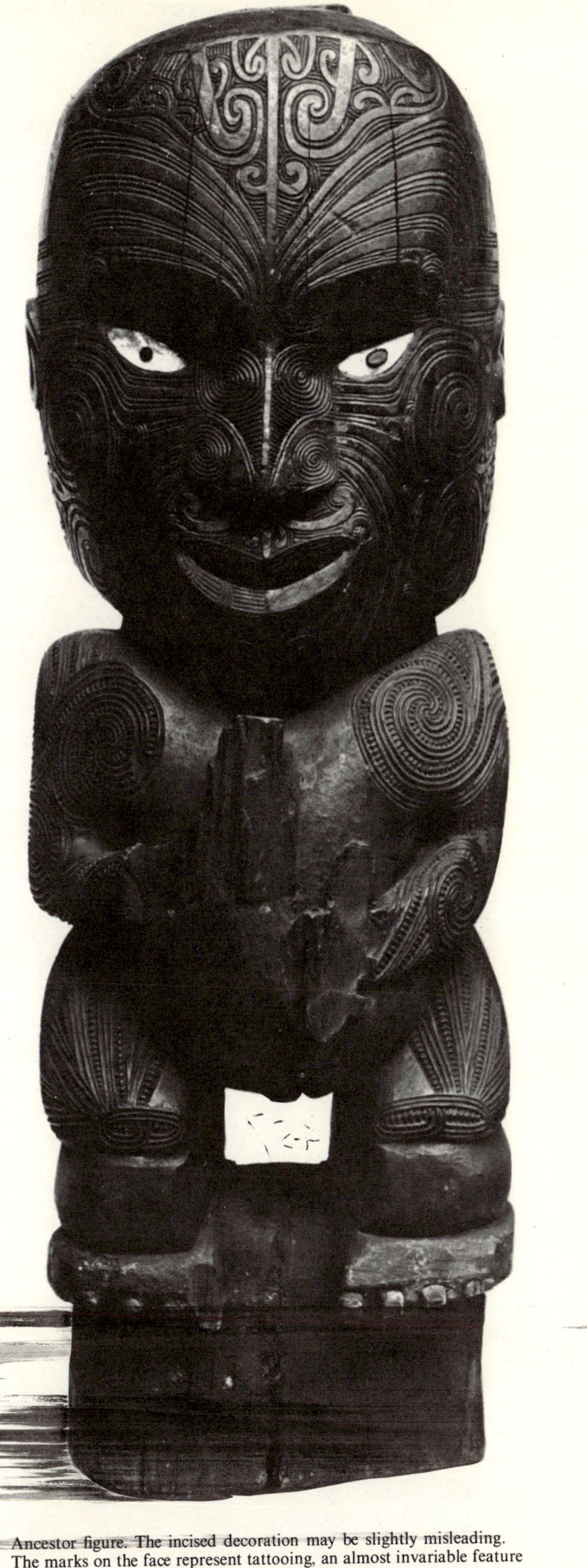

Ancestor figure. The incised decoration may be slightly misleading. The marks on the face represent tattooing, an almost invariable feature of cult-rituals in New Zealand, but those on the body merely serve to show the joints of the limbs. Ancestor worship is widespread throughout Polynesia. Wood-carving, New Zealand.

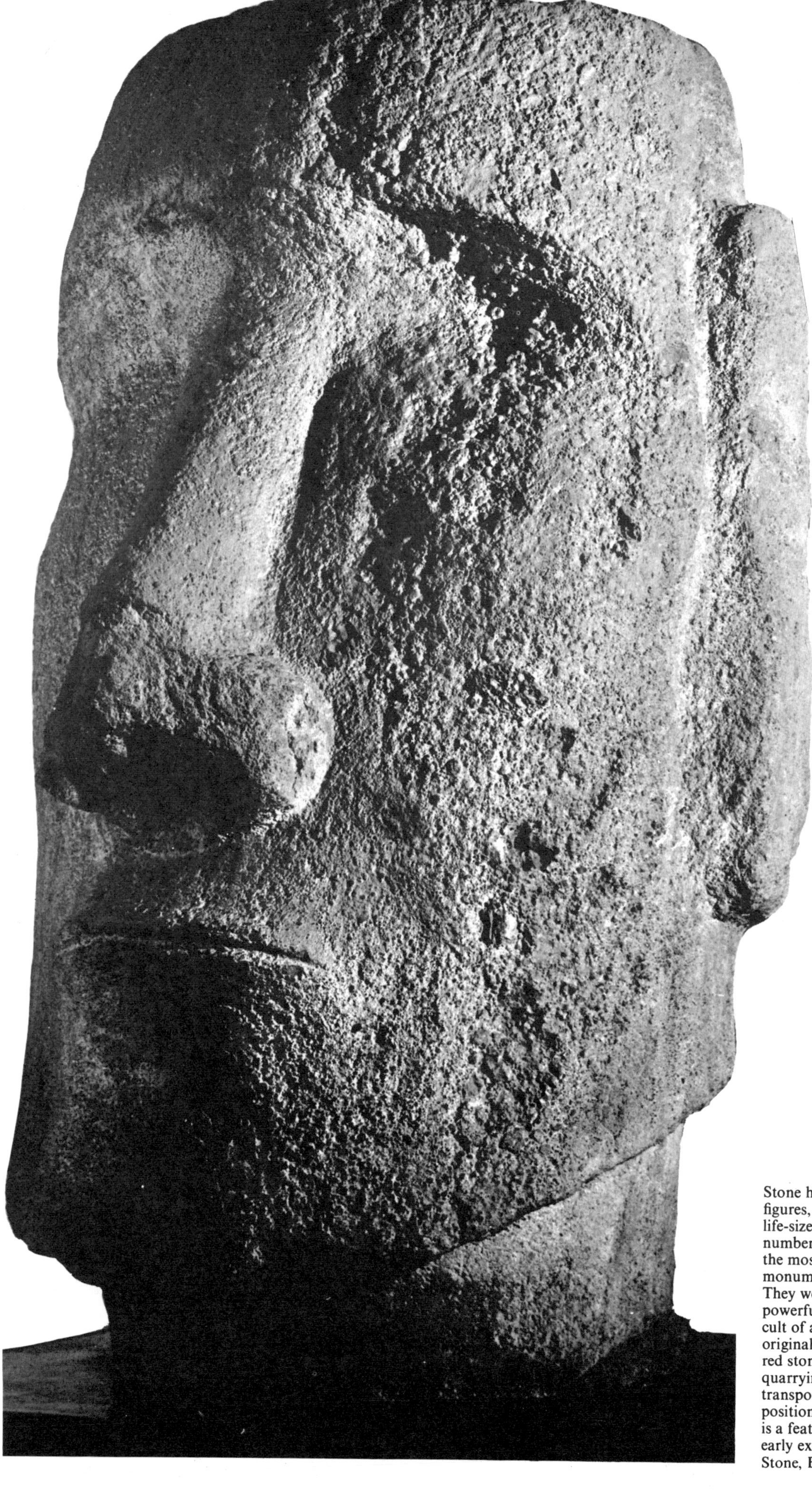

Stone head. These Easter Island figures, which are much over life-size and of which large numbers still survive, are perhaps the most astonishing religious monuments anywhere in Oceania. They were erected in rows by powerful families as part of the cult of ancestor-worship, and originally wore big 'top-knots' of red stone. The achievement of quarrying them from the rock bed, transporting them to their position and raising them upright is a feat of engineering which early explorers could hardly credit. Stone, Easter Island.

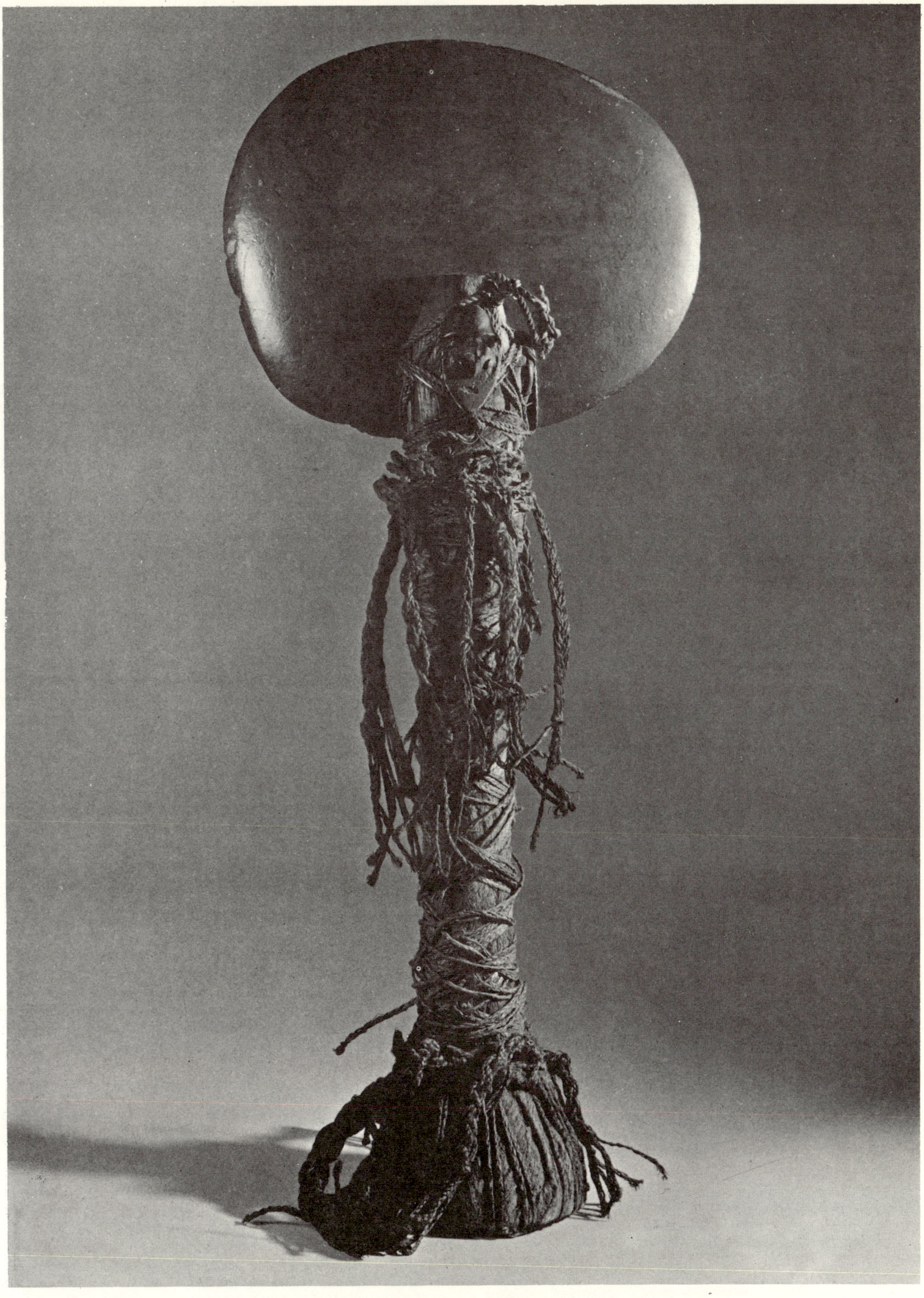

Ceremonial axe. Melanesian belief ascribed divine powers to these *tokis,* parade axes of jadeite or serpentine, quarried on Uen Island. The polished circular blade is lashed to a wooden handle which itself rests on half a coconut shell. This is then wrapped in *tapa* cloth and secured with red thongs. The whole is symbolic of the human body, made explicit here by a tiny head. It was used by the chief during rain-making ceremonies. Jadeite, wood, coconut and fibre, New Caledonia. Horniman Museum.

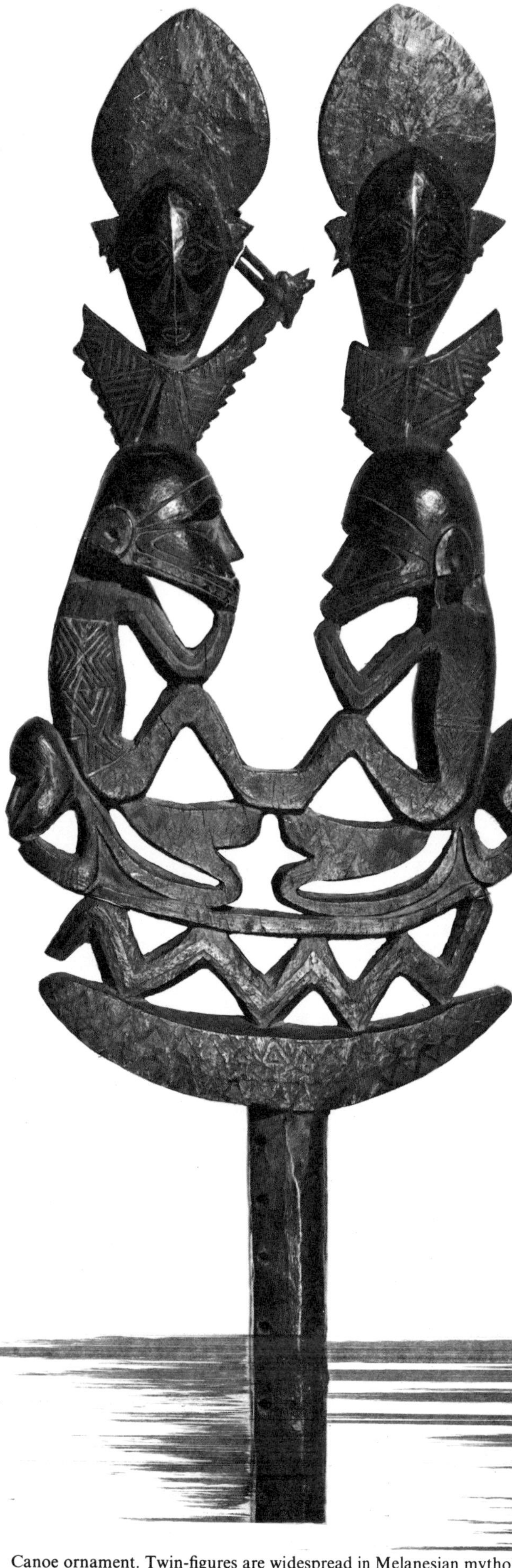

Canoe ornament. Twin-figures are widespread in Melanesian mythology and art. Here the double motif is repeated at each stage–crouching figures with others sitting on their backs, and two masks at the top. The masks, however, are not identical, but are given contrasted features. Woodcarving, Solomon Islands.

and sound, a waxing light, heat and damp, matter and form, and finally father Heaven and mother Earth, parents of the gods, men, and Nature. This conception is at one and the same time evolutionist, since it looks on the universe as the result of progressive development, and genealogical, inasmuch as each phase of the development is personified in a being descended from the one before. Let us take a comparatively simple example from the Ngaitahu of the southern island of New Zealand. Po begat Light, who begat Day-light, who begat enduring Light, who begat Without-possession, who begat Unpleasant, who begat Wobbly, who begat No-parents, who begat Damp, who married Huge Light and begat Raki (the sky). Similarly in the Marquesas Islands, the primeval void started a swelling, a whirling, a vague growth, a boiling, a swallowing; there came out an infinite number of supports or posts, the big and the little, the long and the short, the hooked and the curved, and above all there emerged the solid Foundation, space and light and innumerable rocks.

The cosmogony of Hawaii has a variation of the evolutionary theme, according to which the shadowy void from which all things emerged was simply the wreck of a preceding world. A similar idea is found in Samoa. The origin of the universe was a genealogical series of rocks, first of all the rocks on high and the land rocks (meaning, in short, heaven and earth) from which there emerged an octopus whose children were fire and water. A violent struggle occurred between their descendants in which victory went to water – the world was destroyed by flood, and later re-created by Tangaloa.

Perhaps it is not altogether useless to point out plainly that in concrete reality these various cosmogony myths are not so sharply opposed as they are in the abstract types in which we have classified them. They are sometimes combinations of those types, whose boundaries moreover cannot have been as clear in the minds of the natives as they are in ours.

For instance, according to a legend of the Marquesas, Atea (Light), derived by evolution and not by creation from Ta'aroa (Darkness), created heaven and earth, and moreover gave birth to a host of deities as children of marriage with Atanua (Dawn). Owing to the lack of additional definitions it is often impossible to discover whether the production of some constituent of the universe by its creator, who is usually more or less anthropomorphic, is an emanation, a creation by means of inert matter, or a procreation through union with a divinity of the opposite sex.

The Sea. The sea is an element of their environment which is especially important to islanders. For this reason perhaps in many parts of Indonesia, in Micronesia, on the northern borders of Melanesia, in western and central Polynesia, the existence of the sea is accepted as a primeval fact for which no explanation is sought. In the beginning there was a vast sea over which sailed a god (Society Islands, Marquesas), or a god soared above it (Samoa) or it was covered by skies inhabited by one or several deities (Society Islands, Tonga).

Still, there are in existence myths which attempt to explain the origin of the sea. One type makes it derive from a divine origin – it was the result of Ta'aroa's sweat in his efforts at creation (Nauru, western and central Polynesia), it came from the breakage of the ink sac in the primeval octopus (Samoa), it came from the amniotic fluid of a miscarriage of Atanua, daughter of the heavenly god, Atea (Marquesas).

According to another version, the sea came later than the earth, and at first it was only a little bit of salt water which somebody kept shut up and hidden. Others tried to get it from him, but when they lifted the lid the water flowed out and caused a flood (Baining in New Britain, Samoa). This is one of the forms of the flood legend, but we need not trouble with the others, which are not strictly speaking myths, but simply accounts of more or less historical events.

The Sky. The existence of the sky is usually taken as a primordial fact, just as with the sea. But in the Ralik group of the Marshall islands we find the following legend. When the deity Loa had created the world, the plants and the animals, a sea-gull flew up and formed the dome of the sky as a spider weaves its web.

If myths about the origin of the sky are very rare, there exists on the contrary a host of them to explain one of its most obvious

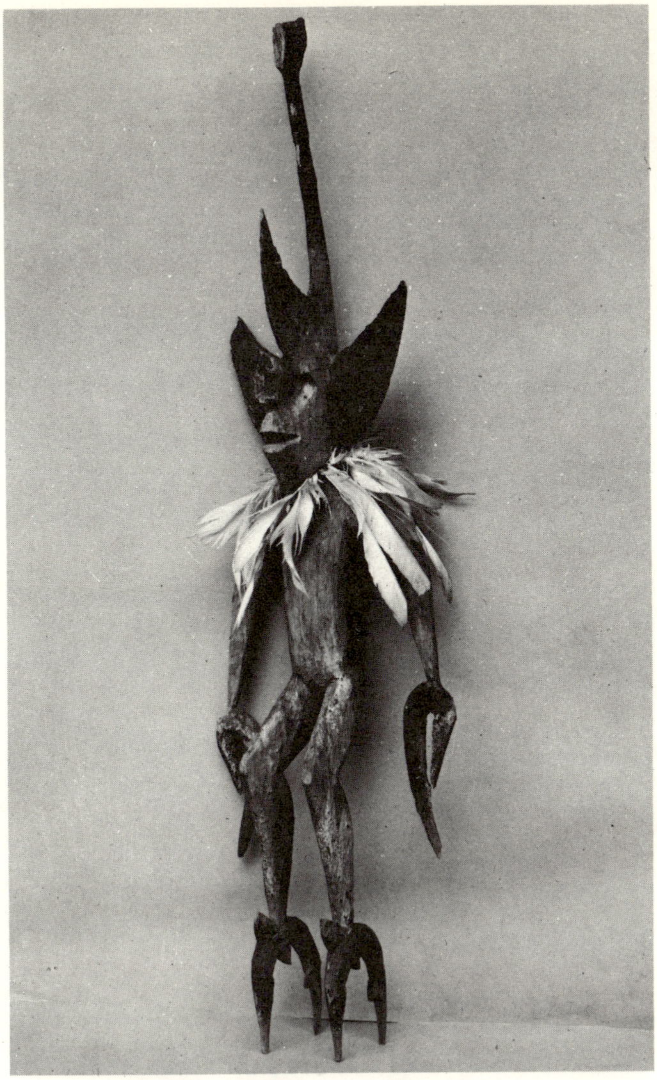

A sea-spirit. The sea enters Polynesian and Melanesian mythology at every point and the sea-spirit or *adaro* appears in many legends and cult practices under one guise or another. This figure, which had a propitiatory significance, wears a collar of feathers. Woodcarving, Solomon Islands.

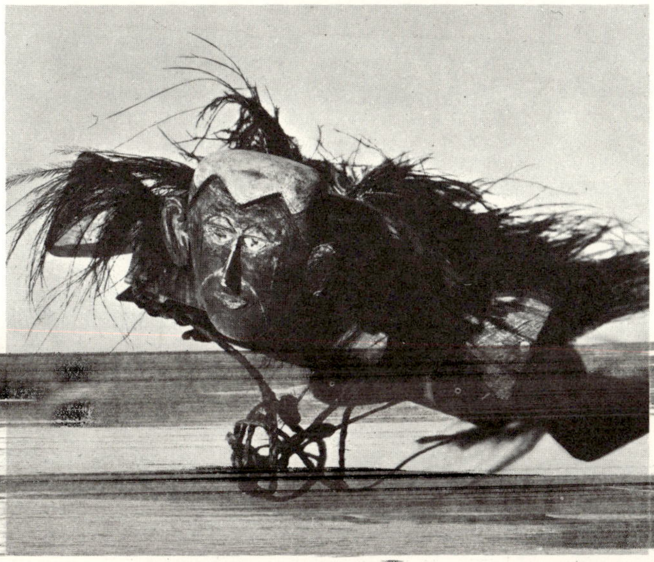

The malignant spirit Dogai. Dogai's special aptitude was to frustrate human enterprises, to make crops fail, to keep fish away from the nets, etc. Like other Melanesian deities, Dogai is a male god in some cultures, female in others, but retains the same character. To placate him, his image was fixed to the prows of canoes at certain times of the year, and masks representing him were worn at seasonal feasts. Wood and feathers, Torres Straits.

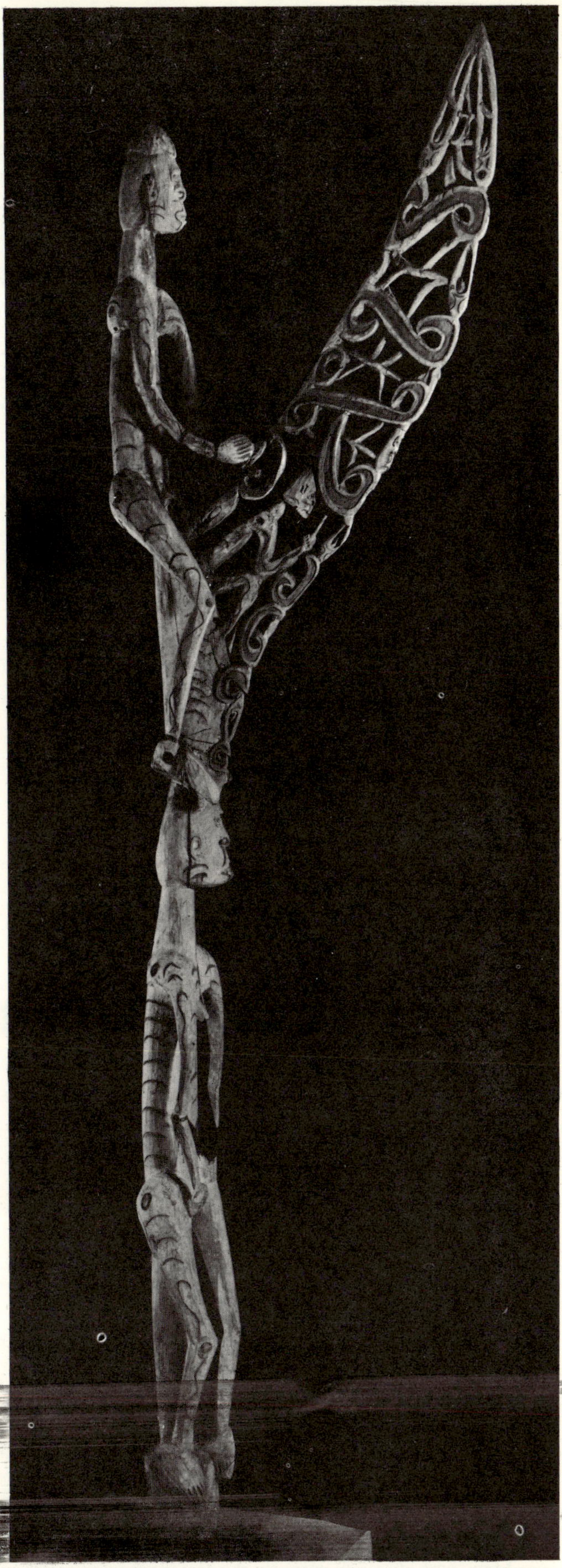

Top of a carved bis pole. The two men are ancestors killed in head-hunting raids, and the fretted projection between them probably represents the beak of the hornbill. This bird was one of the links between the world of the living and the world of the dead, which lay far away across the water. The lower part of these funerary poles were hollowed out like a canoe standing on end. Carved mangrove wood, Asmat District, S. W. New Guinea.

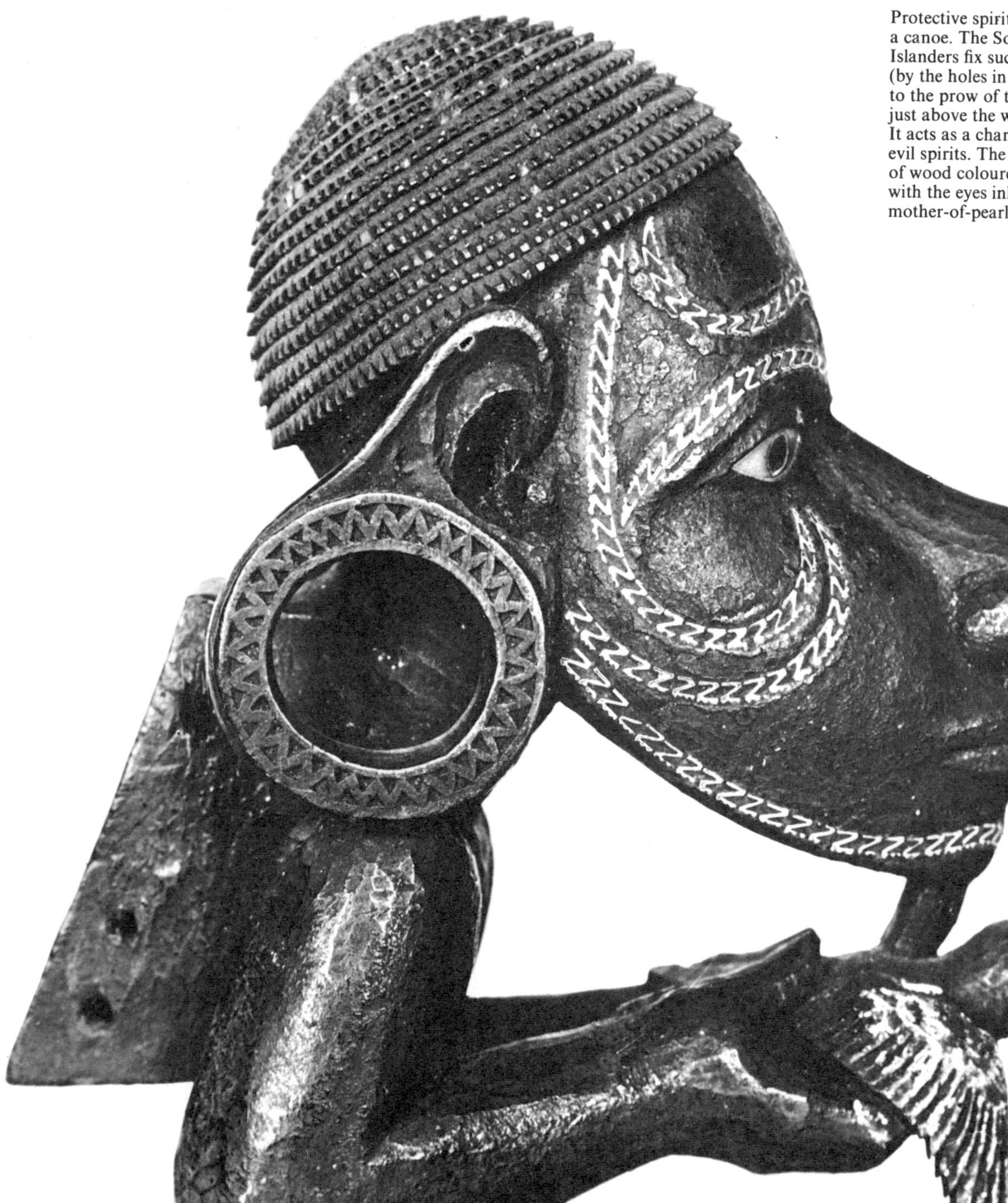

Protective spirit for a canoe. The Solomon Islanders fix such figures (by the holes in the back) to the prow of the canoe just above the water-line. It acts as a charm against evil spirits. The image is of wood coloured black with the eyes inlaid with mother-of-pearl.

physical properties, namely, its distance from the earth, or in other words the fact that it stays in the air without support. According to these beliefs, the sky was originally close to the earth (central Celebes, east Indonesia), so close that it stood on the leaves of certain plants, which owed their flattened shape to its weight (various archipelagoes in Polynesia), and only later was it lifted to its present position. In the legends of the Philippines, of various parts of Indonesia and Micronesia, of Efate (New Hebrides), the sky withdrew. In various archipelagoes of central Polynesia, in Samoa, in Hawaii, the lifting up of the sky is attributed to the hero Maui, who offered to carry out this feat if a woman gave him a drink of water from her gourd. Legends of central Polynesia, and especially of Samoa, show a transition towards another idea, according to which the separation of heaven and earth is a cosmic event, the act of such and such a god or several gods. This belief, far more widespread than the former, occurs over a large area.

The personification of sky and earth, which is to be found throughout eastern Indonesia, is particularly developed in New Zealand, where it gives the myth a most poetical form. Rangi, the Sky, in love with Papa, the Earth, who was beneath him, came down to her in the time of primeval darkness and immobility. Their close embrace crushed the host of gods to whom they had given birth, and all the beings placed between them; nothing could ripen or bear fruit. To escape this awkward situation, the gods determined to separate the Sky from the Earth. In one version the Sky himself urges his children to break their union. Once the separation was achieved, light spread over the terrestrial world.

Sun and Moon. Among various groups of Indonesia, and in the Society Islands and Hawaii, we find the mere assertion, with no details, that the Sun and Moon were created. Elsewhere they are looked upon as the children of a deity or of the first men or as formed from some of their parts. Thus, according to the Kavan of central Borneo, the Moon at least is one of the descendants of the armless

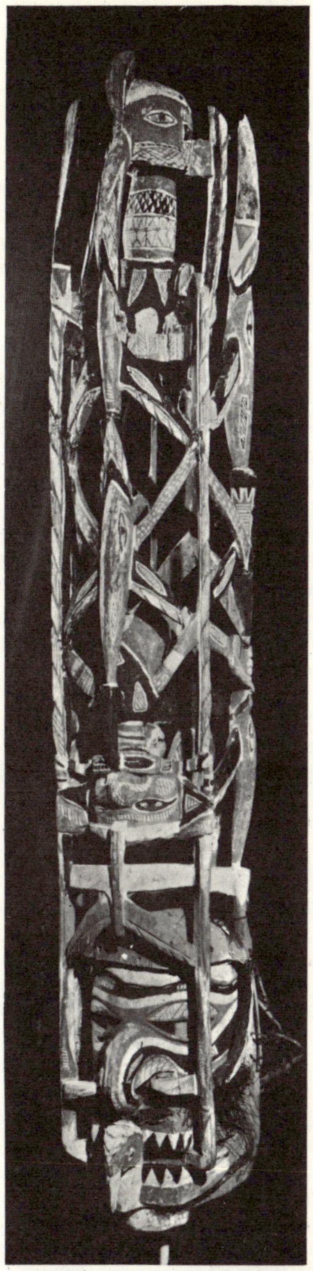

Cult objects of Malanggan ceremonies. A Malanggan is a group of carved wooden objects grouped on a decorated platform in honour of a dead man. The people of New Ireland prepare for these ceremonies months in advance, and the festival itself lasts for several weeks. The carvings are made by (or occasionally on behalf of) the dead man's clan. They show an amazing fertility of invention in both form and colour. Carved wood, fibre and shells, New Ireland.

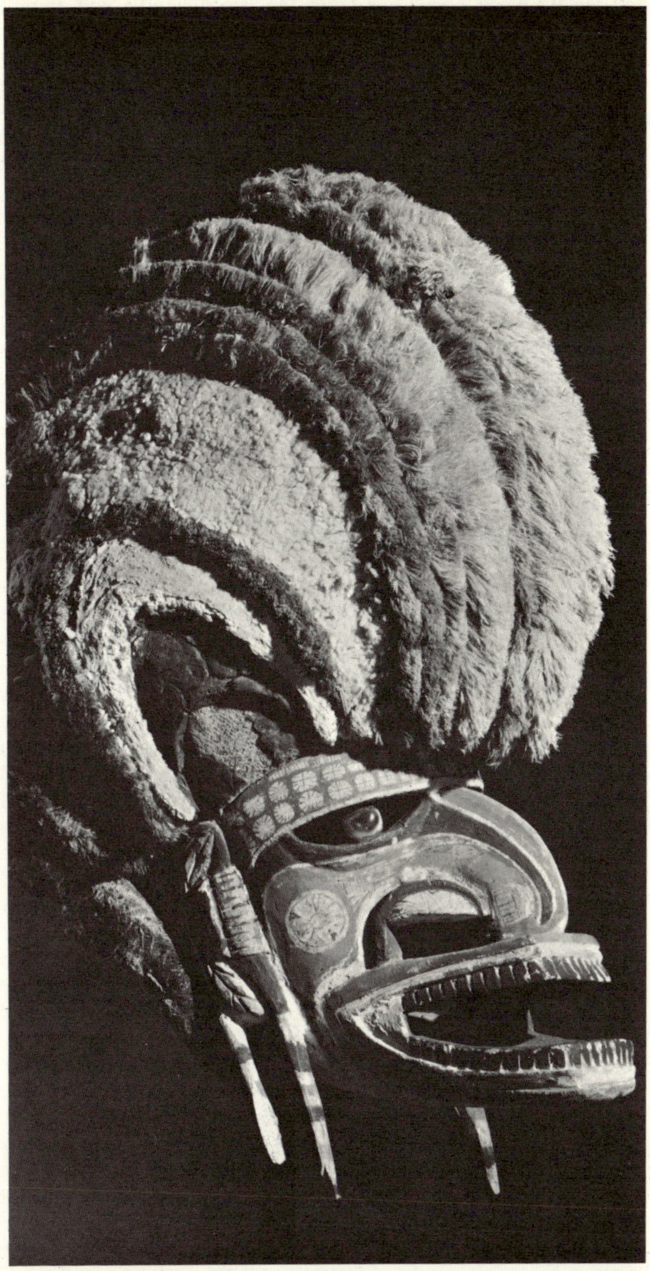

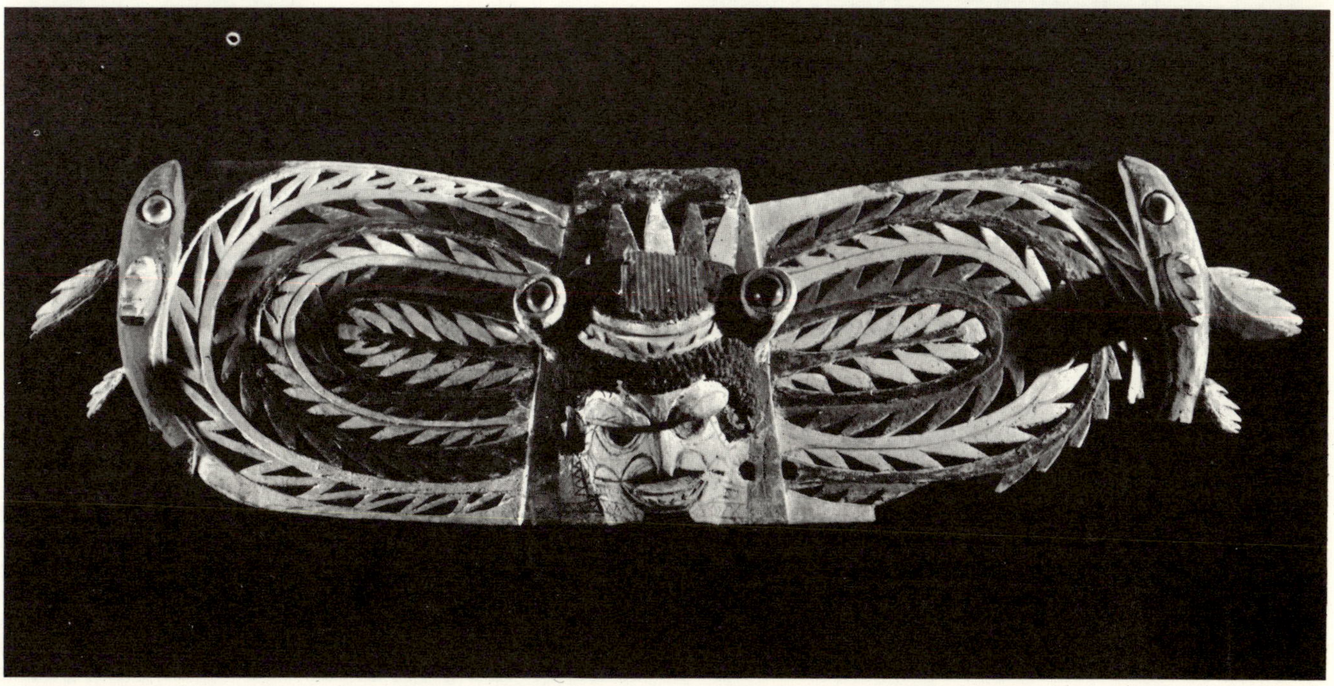

and legless being who came from the sword handle and spindle which fell from heaven. In the Gilbert Islands, the Sun and Moon, like the sea, are the children of the first man and the first woman, created by Na Reau. Although when he left them he had forbidden them to have children, they had three. Informed of their disobedience by his great messenger, the eel, Na Reau picked up his great club and went to the island where he had left them. In terror they threw themselves at his feet, begging him not to kill them. 'Our children', they said, 'are very useful to us. The Sun enables us to see clearly, and, when he is resting, the Moon takes his place; and the sea feeds us with its fish.' Convinced by this plea Na Reau departed without harming them. In Minahassa (Celebes) Sun, Moon and stars were formed from the body of a heavenly girl. In Nias, Sun and Moon were formed from the eyes of the armless and legless being, from whose heart sprang the tree with the buds which were the origin of men and gods. In Mangaia (Cook Islands) they are Vatea's eyes. In the Society Islands, in Samoa, and in New Zealand they are usually thought of as the children of Heaven who were later placed in the sky as eyes. In Queensland, the Sun (a woman) was made by the Moon, with two legs like men, but with a great number of arms which may be seen stretching out like rays when the Sun rises or sets.

Other myths doubtless inspired by the rising of the Sun and Moon looked upon them as beings who had passed from the earth to the sky. They may be classified into two types, according to whether these beings are things or men. In the Palau Islands the two primitive deities made the Sun and Moon by cutting two stones with an adze and then throwing them into the sky. In the Admiralty Islands, the two first inhabitants of the earth, after planting trees and creating edible plants, made two mushrooms and threw them into the sky – the one thrown by the man became the Moon, and the other thrown by the woman became the Sun. In Woodlark Island the only person at first to possess fire was an old woman. In vain her son scolded her for not wanting to share it. So he stole it from her, and gave it to the remainder of mankind. In her rage the old woman took the fire she had left, divided it into two parts and threw them into the sky – the larger became the Sun, the smaller the Moon. According to certain tribes in south-east Australia the Sun came from an emu's egg thrown into the sky. For instance, among the Euahlayi, at a time when there was no Sun but only the Moon and the stars, a man quarrelled with his friend the emu, ran to its nest, took one of its large eggs and threw it in the sky as hard as he could, and there it broke against a pile of wood kindling which at once caught fire. This greatly astonished the inhabitants of the earth, accustomed to semi-darkness, and almost blinded them. Such is the origin of the Sun. According to the Arunta of central Australia the Moon in the mythical period was the property of a man of the Opossum totem. Another man stole it. The man was unable to catch the thief and shouted to the Moon to get into the sky, which it did.

At Aneityum (New Hebrides) the Sun and Moon are considered as husband and wife. They first lived on the earth, somewhere in the east, but later the Sun climbed into the sky, telling the Moon to follow him, and she obeyed him. According to the Arunta and the tribes related to them, the Sun is a woman who emerged from the ground, like many of the primitive ancestral totems, and later went up into the sky carrying a torch. According to the Warramunga of northern Australia the Moon emerged from the ground in the form of a man (male). One day he met a woman, called to her, and they sat down to talk. A fire caused by the carelessness of two hawks surrounded them, and the woman was seriously burned. The Moon then cut one of his veins and poured blood on the woman, who was thus restored to life. They then both went up into the sky. According to shore-dwellers in Princess Charlotte's Bay (Queensland), two brothers were one day looking for honey, and one of them having put his arm into a hole in a tree, found he could not get it out. His brother came to his aid, but everyone else he asked, except the Moon, refused. The Moon (who was a man) climbed the tree, put his head into the hollow and sneezed violently, so that the sudden pressure of air enabled the prisoner to withdraw his arm. To avenge himself on those who had refused to help him, the man set light to the bush to burn them; but first of all he looked after the Moon's safety by moving him to different places, and at last into the sky, so that he could escape the fire.

Myths dealing with the alternation of day and night may be attached to Sun myths. They are divided into two classes, according to whether the myth explains the origin of the night, day having existed since the beginning, or, inversely, if it explains the origin of day, night having alone existed at first. The first type is characteristic of Melanesia, and may be found alongside the other in Australia.

In the Banks Islands, after Qat had formed men, pigs, trees and rocks, the daylight was endless. His brothers told him it was very disagreeable. So Qat took a pig, and went to buy the night-time from Night, who lived in another country. Night blackened his eyebrows, taught him how to sleep and how to make the dawn. Qat returned to his brothers, bringing with him a rooster and other birds to announce the dawn. He told his brothers to make beds of coconut leaves. Then for the first time they saw the Sun descending in the west, and they shouted to Qat that the Sun was going out. 'It will soon have gone entirely,' he said, and if you see a change on the face of the world, that will be the night.' Then he brought up night, and they said: 'What's this coming from the sea and covering the sky?' 'It's night,' he replied. 'Sit down on either side of your house, and when you feel something in your eyes, lie down and stay quiet.' It was quite dark, and their eyes began to blink. 'Qat, Qat! What is it? Are we dying?' 'Shut your eyes,' he said, 'that's right. Now sleep.' When night had lasted long enough, the rooster began to crow and the birds to twitter. Qat picked up a piece of red obsidian and cut the night, and the light which had been covered by darkness shone out again, and Qat's brothers woke up. According to the Sulka of New Britain, a man named Emakong brought night as well as fire back from his journey in the underworld of the snake-men. They gave him a parcel containing the night, the crickets which announce night, and the birds which announce the dawn. A simpler legend of certain tribes in Victoria states that in the beginning the Sun never set, but as human beings were weary of perpetual day (that is of not being able to sleep) the creating deity at last ordered the Sun to set.

Alongside these myths of the origin of night, Australia also furnishes the opposite myths of the origin of day. According to the tribes of the south-east, when the emu's egg thrown into the sky had given birth to the Sun by setting fire to a pile of kindling wood the heavenly deity, seeing the advantages of this fire for the world, decided to make it burn every day, and thus it has always been ever since. Every night he and his servants get together a pile of wood to make the daylight next morning. According to the Aruntas and their kindred in central Australia, the woman who climbed into the sky and became the Sun, comes down to earth every morning, and climbs back into the sky at night. In some areas they say that there are several suns which take turns to go up into the sky. According to the Narrinyeri of South Australia, the Sun is a woman who goes every night to visit the land of the dead. When she returns to earth, men ask her to remain with them, but she can stay only a moment, since she must be ready for her journey next day. In return for the favours she granted to such and such a man, she received as a gift a red kangaroo skin, and that is why when she arrives in the morning she is dressed in red. In this last myth we may detect the regret that the day is not long enough for all the daily tasks. The same feeling is expressed in the legends of New Zealand and Hawaii about the deeds of the hero Maui, who succeeded in delaying the Sun's motion

Some myths while explaining the origin of the Moon also account for the fact that its light is paler than the Sun's. According to a legend from Papua, a man digging a deep hole one day came on a small bright object. He picked it up, but the object began to grow bigger, and then slipping out of his hands rose up in the sky and became the Moon. The light of the Moon would have been brighter if it had stayed in the ground until it was born naturally, but as it was taken up prematurely, the light it gives is weak. In the Cook Islands, Vatea and Tonga-iti (or in one version, Tangaroa) were arguing about the origin of Papa's first child, each of them claiming to be the father. To pacify them, the child was cut into two pieces, and each received one of them. Vatea took the upper half which was his, and threw it into the sky, where it became the Sun. Tonga-iti at first kept on earth the lower part which had been allotted to him, but later, in imitation of Vatea he threw it also into the sky, and it became the Moon. But as it had lost its blood and had begun to decay, it shone with a paler light. In the Marquesas, the fact that the Moon is not so bright as the Sun is explained in different places by two opposite adjectives: black (dark) and white (pale). In the first case the blackness was caused because the deity who created the

Moon could not restrain his longing to eat porpoise, the skin of which is black. In the second case, the whiteness came from the fact that its mother Hanua when pregnant longed to eat coconut, the pulp of which is white.

The spots on the moon have also given rise to mythical explanations. In the Trust Territory of New Guinea the Moon at first was hidden by an old woman in a pitcher. Some boys noticed it and creeping up stealthily opened the pitcher. The Moon came out and rose into the sky, and the spots are the marks of the boys' hands as they tried to hold it back. In the Cook Islands the Moon (there thought of as male) fell in love with a pretty daughter of the blind Kui, came down to earth and eloped with her. To this day in the Moon you can see the girl with her heaps of leaves for the oven and her tongs to settle the embers. She is always at work making tapa (bark cloth) which may be seen in the Moon, as well as the stones to hold down the tapa when she spreads it out to bleach. According to a New Zealand story, Rona one night went out by moonlight to get water from a stream, but when she got there the Moon disappeared behind a cloud so that Rona stumbled over stones and roots. In her annoyance she insulted the Moon which was so annoyed that it came down to earth, seized Rona and carried her off with her water gourd, her basket and the tree to which she clung. You can see them all in the Moon to this day.

The phases of the Moon are explained in another Maori myth. Rona, who in this case is male, went to the Moon (also male) in pursuit of his wife. He and the Moon spend their lives eating each other, and that is why the Moon diminishes. Then they both regain strength and vigour by bathing in the live waters of Tane – after which they begin their struggle again. According to an Arunta myth, in the beginning a man of the Opossum totem died and was buried, but some time later came back to earth in the form of a child. On reaching adult age he died a second time and went up to heaven, where he became the Moon; since then the Moon dies and is reborn periodically. According to the Wongibon of New South Wales, the Moon is an old man who before going up to heaven hurt his back by falling off a rock, so that he walks bowed down. That is why the Moon has a bowed back each month when it appears.

Stars. In the Maori account of the separation of Heaven and Earth, Tane, after separating his parents, busied himself with clothing and adorning them. Seeing that his father, Heaven, was naked, Tane began by painting him red. But that was not enough, so he took the stars from the Mat of terror and from the Mat of sacred support. He set these stars in the sky during the daytime and they did not make much of a show, but at night the sky became splendid. In the Marquesas, large stars are the children of the Sun and Moon, and have multiplied among themselves like ants. According to the Mandayas of Mindanao the Sun and the Moon were married, had several children, and lived together happily for a long time. But at length they quarrelled, and the Moon deserted her husband. After the separation of their parents, the children died. The Moon gathered up their bodies, cut them into little pieces, and threw them into space. Those she threw into the air stayed in the sky and became stars. In Torres Straits the constellation of the Eagle is an ogress, and the constellation of the Dolphin a man who killed her.

In the districts of the north-west of Victoria, alpha and beta of the Centaur are two heroes, the Brambrambult brothers, who went to heaven after achieving various deeds. Their mother Dok became alpha of the Cross. According to the Narrinyeri of Encounter Bay (South Australia), Nepelle's two wives deserted him for Wyungare. To escape the vengeance of the indignant husband, they all three went up to heaven and became stars which may be seen to-day. The Euahlay of New South Wales have a similar legend. In Easter Island a husband tried to prevent his wife from bathing with another man, and she fled to heaven where she became a star. Her husband followed her, holding one of their children in each hand, and the three became Orion's Belt. But the wife would not accept them, and stayed in another part of the sky.

Atmospheric phenomena. In New Zealand various atmospheric phenomena are looked upon as manifestations of the grief felt by Heaven and Earth at their separation. In one version this explanation is presented in the form of the farewells uttered by the pair at the moment of leaving one another. Raki (Heaven) says to Papa (Earth): 'Papa, stay here. This is what will be a sign of my love for

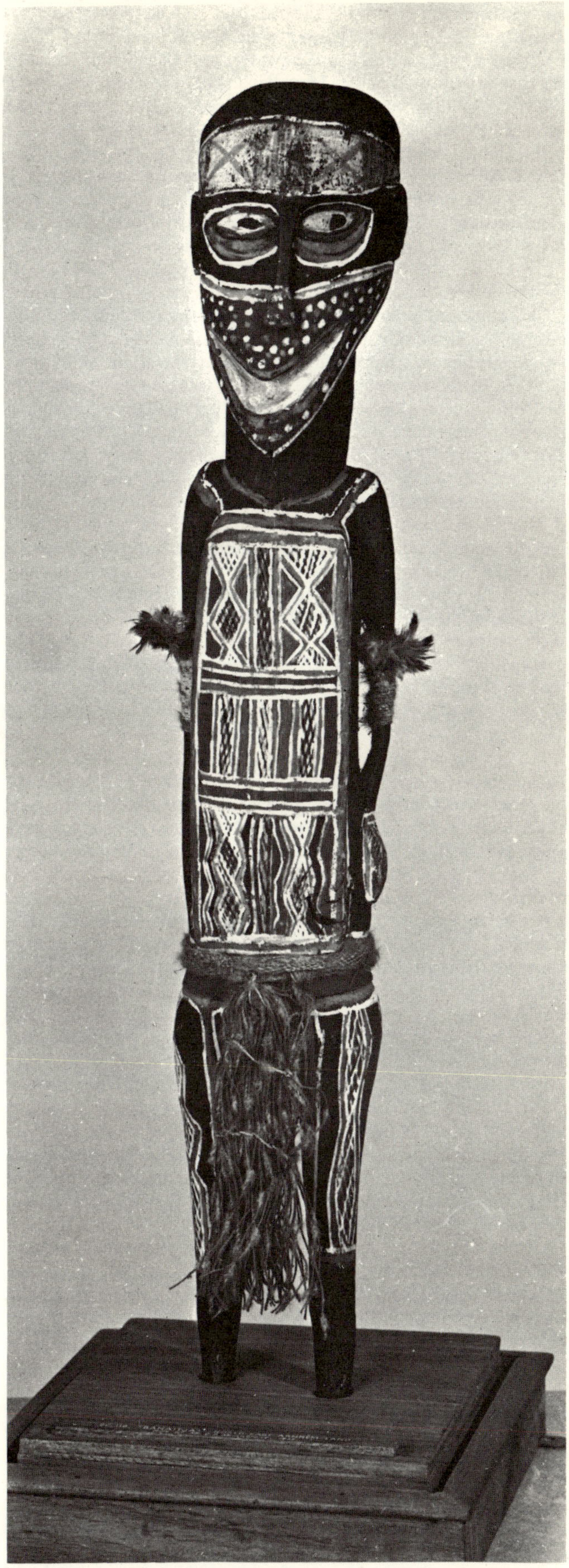

The Djanggawul brother. With his two sisters, says the myth, he arrived in Northern Australia from the sea, taught the aborigines to dig waterholes and cultivate crops, and gave them the basic beliefs of their religion. He is represented here with tattoo marks similar to those worn by the tribesmen themselves.
The artist's name is Mauwalan. Carved and painted wood, fibre and feathers, Yirrkalla, Arnhem Land, Australia.

you. In the eighth month I shall shed tears on you.' And these tears of Heaven weeping on the earth are the dew. Raki also said: 'Dear wife, stay where you are. In the winter time I shall sigh for you.' and that is the origin of ice. Then Papa spoke these farewell words to Raki: 'Go, dear husband, and in summer I shall lament for you, and the sighs of her loving heart rising up to heaven are the mists. In the Cook Islands, thunder is attributed to the daughter of Kui carried off by the Moon. In her new home she is always engaged in making tapa, which she holds down with stones when she spreads it out to bleach. From time to time she takes off the stones, and throws them away; the resulting noise is thunder.

The Earth. Most of the legends dealing with the origin of the earth make it come out of the sea, but they have variants which contradict one another. Generally speaking the production of the earth includes two succeeding moments – first the production of the solid earth and then of the vegetable world; but since these two productions have the same creator we may consider them together. Sometimes the earth simply came out of the sea (New Zealand), or from a rock which existed in the sea (Minahassa); or, again, a deity, sometimes a snake (Admiralty Islands) floating on the sea creates the earth there (Ralik group of the Marshall Islands). According to a legend of Nauru, the earth was separated from the sea by a butterfly, Rigi. Sometimes the earth is formed from matter thrown down or sent down from heaven by a deity: a rock (Kayan of Borneo, Samoa), the chips of the heavenly Carpenter (Tonga), sand either scattered on the sea (Yap in the Carolines, Dairi and Karo Battak of Sumatra) or on the head of a snake swimming in the sea (Toba Batak, south-east Borneo). Owing to constant identification of gods dwelling in heaven with birds, the god who throws a rock into the sea is sometimes replaced by a bird who drops an egg (Hawaii).

The Kayan of Borneo have special stories about the origin of the vegetable world. According to one of them, the surface of the rock thrown on to the original sea eventually collected mud which bred worms. Digging down into the rock they made sand which eventually covered the world of rock. According to another story, a lichen fell from heaven and stayed on the rock. Then came a worm whose excrements formed the first earth.

A very widespread myth considers that the islands in which it is accepted, and sometimes the neighbouring islands, were fished out of the sea. As a rule the fishing up is attributed to a deity (Gilbert Islands, New Hebrides, Futuna, Union Islands, some Polynesian archipelagoes). According to a legend of Samoa, Tangaloa caused this archipelago to be fished up by two of his servants as a refuge for two men who were the only survivors of the flood. The coastal tribes of the Gazelle peninsula (New Britain) attribute this feat to two brothers, who are at one and the same time the first men and civilising heroes. A similar legend may be found in the southern New Hebrides. In Hawaii, in Tonga, in New Zealand, the fishing up of the earth is one of the achievements of the hero Maui. The archipelagoes are explained either because the different islands were pulled up at different times (Aniwa, New Hebrides; Marquesas), or because an earth fished up whole broke into several pieces at the moment when it emerged (Hawaii).

Certain peculiarities of the land also were explained by myths, especially the unevenness of the ground. According to the Kayan of Borneo the valleys were hollowed out by a crab which fell from heaven and tore up the earth with its pincers. In the north-west of Borneo, when the two birds made heaven and earth from the two eggs they took out of the sea, the dimensions of the earth were larger than those of the sky. To adjust this, they crushed in the earth, and this caused the foldings which made mountains and valleys. In New Zealand, when the isle had been drawn up like a fish by Maui with the help of his brothers, they contrary to Maui's instructions began to cut up the fish. The valleys are the cuts made by their knives.

In Hawaii a certain fountain is the swimming pool which the son of a former chief made for his sister in the cave where they took refuge to escape from the persecutions of their step-mother. There are tribes in Victoria who explain their lakes in the same way as we have found the sea explained – the water which its owner kept shut up burst out as soon as there was an attempt to steal it.

In various Battak tribes of Sumatra, earthquakes are linked with cosmogony myths. Under various forms, all more or less determined, the idea is that the creation of the world was a disadvantage for a being already in existence, who reacted with a violent agitation which destroyed the earth. The creator took the necessary steps to prevent another destruction, but the agitation continues, and that is the cause of earthquakes.

Living beings. The mythical explanations of the origin of living beings seem to be rarer in the case of animals than of plants. In New Zealand plants and trees are looked upon as ornaments placed on the Earth either by her husband the Sky or by her son Tane, after the separation of the couple. According to some accounts, Tane first planted the trees with their roots in the air, but he found that this did not look well, and therefore planted the roots in the ground in the way they have always grown since. This curious detail must be compared with a theme which is to be found in Borneo and Yap (Carolines), for instance, of a big tree which hangs from the sky with its branches downward, and so provides men with a means of communication between earth and heaven.

In general, plant life is more or less explicitly credited with the utilitarian task of making the world habitable by giving shade or fruits. Sometimes the earliest dwellers on earth, who are usually of divine origin, are the creators of vegetation (Admiralty Islands, west Carolines) or go to another land to find their seeds (Minahassa), sometimes a deity creates them (Ralik group of the Marshall Islands, Marquesas), or sends or brings from heaven either the full-grown plants (central Carolines, Samoa), or their seeds (south-east Borneo, Tonga). According to the Kayan of central Borneo, there fell from the Sun the wooden handle of a sword, which took root and became a tall tree, and from the Moon a vine which grew up the tree. In the Marquesas a considerable number of trees were originally in the underworld. For instance the mei, the breadfruit tree. Pukuha Kaha went down into hell and returned to heaven after he had fastened a hook in the mei, and by gradually pulling he succeeded in bringing it up. The first mei was planted by Opimea in Atikota Bay. Another god, Tamaa, was the guardian of the coconut tree in hell. Mataia gave his daughter to Tamaa who came to live in Taihoe Bay and there planted the tree.

As to animals – in New Zealand we find the story of an old man and an old woman, who came from an egg which a bird dropped on the primeval sea, and got into a canoe with a boy who brought a dog and a girl who brought a pig, and so came to New Zealand. According to notion widely spread in Indonesia (Borneo, Philippines), the different species of animals are derived from the pieces of a being who varies and is cut up for different reasons in different areas. The Kayan of Borneo thought they were derived from the leaves and branches of a miraculous tree which in the beginning fell from heaven to earth. Some myths attribute to animals an origin like that of vegetation. For instance in the Ralik group of the Marshall Islands the deity Loa with the magic of the word created first the solid earth, then the world of vegetation, then the plants and then the birds. In Hawaii by gradual evolution all living forms, of vegetation as well as of animals, came from a shadowy chaos. First came the zoophytes and the corals, followed by worms and molluscs, parallel with the algae followed by reeds. When the mud caused by the decomposition of earlier living things raised the earth above the sea, there appeared plants with leaves, insects and birds. Then the sea produced the highest types, such as jellyfish, and whales, which monstrous creatures crawled on earth. Later appeared the food plants; in the fifth period, the pig; and in the sixth, mice on earth and porpoises in the sea. Then after a seventh period which saw the development of a series of abstract psychological qualities which were later embodied in mankind, there appeared women, men, and some of the great gods. Samoa also shows a conception of an evolutionary succession of vegetative life, but it is less clear.

The object of other myths is to explain, not the origin of living things as a whole, but the special characteristics of such and such a species. They are rather rare in the case of vegetation. Here is one about yams from Omba (New Hebrides). A wild yam insulted a kite, which seized it, flew up with it, and then let it drop. Another kite picked it up and dropped it again. The yam broke into two pieces which the kites shared. That is why some yams are good and some bad.

Myths concerning animals are uncommon in Indonesia and Polynesia, more usual in Melanesia, and are abundant in Australia,

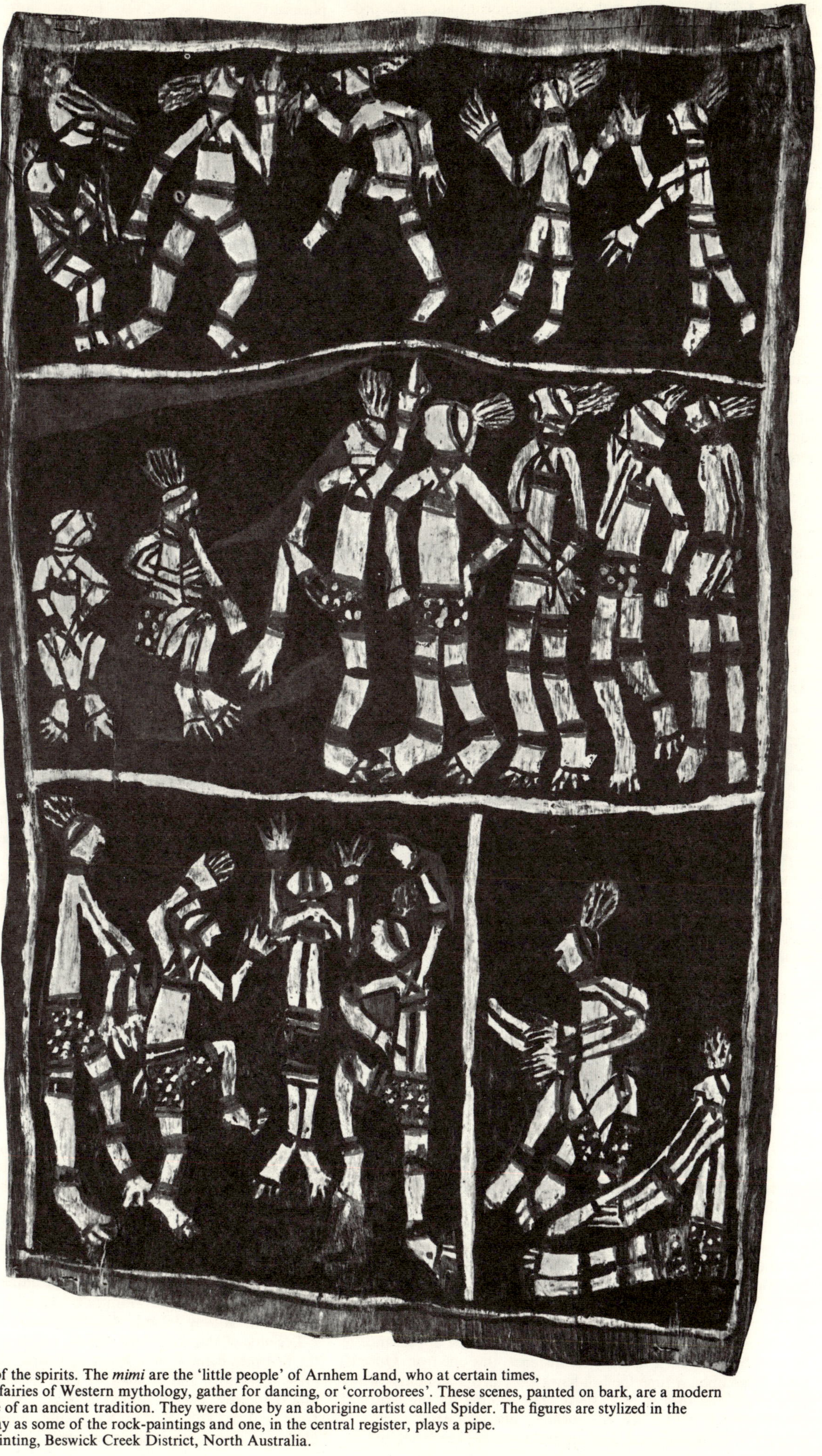

Dance of the spirits. The *mimi* are the 'little people' of Arnhem Land, who at certain times, like the fairies of Western mythology, gather for dancing, or 'corroborees'. These scenes, painted on bark, are a modern example of an ancient tradition. They were done by an aborigine artist called Spider. The figures are stylized in the same way as some of the rock-paintings and one, in the central register, plays a pipe.
Bark painting, Beswick Creek District, North Australia.

particularly in the east and south. Here are some instances. According to a tribe in Victoria, black swans are men who took refuge on a mountain during a flood, and turned into black swans at the moment when the water reached their feet. According to another tribe on the east coast of Australia, the pelican which was then entirely black, wanted to fight some men against whom he had vowed vengeance. To put himself on a war footing he began by painting himself white with pipe-clay. When he was half painted another pelican came along and, not recognising this parti-coloured creature, killed it. Since that time pelicans are half-black and half-white. In a legend of Papua the turtle was caught eating the bananas and sugar-canes belonging to Binama, the rhinoceros-bird, was brought to the bird's house and tied to a stake, ready to be killed and eaten. The birds went off hunting to complete the preparations for the feast, and the turtle was left alone with Binama's children, whom he persuaded to untie him so that they could all play together. He decked himself with Binama's jewellery and put a large wooden bowl on his back, which amused the children: When the turtle heard the others coming back, he fled and hid in the sea. They ran after him, throwing stones which smashed the jewels, but did the turtle no harm and did not break the bowl. Ever since then the turtle carries Binama's bowl on its back. According to a tribe in South Australia, the turtle originally had venomous fangs which were not essential for its safety since it could take refuge in water; but the snake had no fangs, and so no means of defence. The turtle gave its fangs to the snake, and received a snake's head in exchange. The red markings on the plumage of birds are attributed to fire. The red on top of the water-rail's head is due to the fact that Maui rubbed its head with a burning brand to punish it for having deceived him as to the way fire is produced (Hawaii). The red feathers in a wren's tail are because when he found fire in heaven he wanted to keep it to himself and hid it under his tail (Queensland). The Wongibons of New South Wales have a legend of the same kind about the black cockatoo and the sparrow hawk.

The calls of certain birds have also been given mythical explanations. According to some tribes in south-east Australia when the heavenly deity had arranged for the daily return of light, he decided first of all that the evening star should be the announcer of the imminent sunrise. But he saw this would not be enough, for people who were asleep would not see the star, and therefore he gave orders to a bird at every dawn when the evening star grew faint, to give a call like a laugh (the gourgourgahgah or kukuburra) which would awaken the world and announce that the sun was about to shine. An Australian legend explains the call and the thin red feet of the curlew. The curlew was originally a hawk. He was sent by the women of his tribe to hunt emus, but finding none he brought back as pretended results of his hunting pieces of meat cut from his own feet. His deception was discovered, and he became a curlew. Ever since then the curlew has had thin red feet and spends the night calling: 'Bou-you-gwai-gwai', which means 'O my poor red feet!'

A frequent type of myth explains at one and the same time the characteristics of two animals, those of the first being the result of a trick played on it by the second, and those of the second coming from the vengeance of the first. Such are the stories of the dog and the wallaby in the Gazelle peninsula (New Britain), of the kangaroo and the wombat (Victoria) the rat and the rail (Banks Islands), the emu and the bustard (New South Wales). Here, for instance, is a legend of the Euahlayis of New South Wales. Once upon a time the crow was white. One day the crane caught a lot of fish, and the crow asked for some, but the crane kept saying: 'Wait until they're cooked.' While the crane's back was turned he tried to steal some, but the crane saw him and threw a fish into his eyes. Blinded by this the crow fell on to the burnt grass rolling over in agony, and when he got up his eyes were white and his whole body black, as they are now. The crow waited his time to be avenged. One day the crane was asleep with its mouth open, and the crow stuck a fish-bone in the root of its tongue. When it woke up the crane tried to spit out the fish-bone but failed, and ever since then it can say nothing but 'gah-rah-gah'.

Other stories of the same kind deal not with the appearance of animals but with their habits – for instance, this one from Queensland. Once upon a time the fish-hawk poisoned a stretch of water with roots, and then went to sleep while waiting for the poisoned fish to come to the surface. Meanwhile a pheasant came along and seeing the fish killed them with spears. In return the hawk hid the pheasant's spears at the very top of a lofty tree. Eventually the pheasant discovered them, but being too lazy to climb so far up, he caused a flood which swept the fish-hawk out to sea. Ever since then the fish-hawk lives on coasts, and the pheasant keeps looking for his spears on the tops of the highest trees.

Mankind. Although the myths concerning the origins of mankind are extremely varied in their details, they can be reduced to a limited number of essential themes. The problem is to explain the presence on earth of living beings of human form and different sexes, who beget children in the normal way. Generally speaking, the myths only attempt to explain the origin of the groups in which they circulate, either ignoring or taking no interest in the rest of mankind. However, the Igorots of the Philippines, the natives of the Gilbert Islands, some tribes of the Northern Territory in Australia have an explanation of the origin of other human beings beside themselves. In some exceptional cases, mankind is thought to have derived from several couples (Baining of New Britain, Banks Islands), but the vast majority of legends derive them from a single original couple. Sometimes the myth merely explains the origin of one of the two individuals of the couple, either the male or the female, merely adding in some cases that one met the other (Battak of Sumatra, Minahassa, western Carolines, New Hebrides, Marquesas, Cook Islands, various tribes of Northern Australia), but usually it explains, and in the same way, the origin of both individuals, of the couple.

The first of these explanations is that of creation or manufacture from pre-existing matter by a deity. Sometimes they are satisfied by saying that the first men were created (Palau Islands, south-east Australia), but more often they give precise details of the method of creation and first of all of the matter employed.

The first men were made from grass according to the Ata of Mindanao, with two rushes according to the Igorot of Luzon, with the dirt on skin elsewhere in the Philippines, with excrement in Borneo, and also among the tribes at the northern and southern extremities of Australia. They were carved from stones (Toradjas of Celebes) or from the trunk of a tree (Admiralty and Banks Islands). According to different tribes of Borneo the creating gods made several successive attempts with different materials. But by far the most frequent explanation is that men were modelled from clay (Dairi Battak of Sumatra, Halmahera, Minahassa, Bagobos of Mindanao, New Hebrides, New Zealand, Society Islands, Marquesas, and Australian tribes near Melbourne).

After forming human beings, the god gives them life in various ways. Sometimes it is by incantation (Dairi Battak of Sumatra, Admiralty Islands), sometimes the god breathes in the vital principle, considered to be either his own breath (New Hebrides, Hawaii, New Zealand, Australian tribes in the neighbourhood of Melbourne) or the wind (Nias), or a fluid or liquid the god goes to heaven to find (south-east Borneo, Halmahera). In Minahassa when the god wanted to give life to his creatures he blew powdered ginger into their ears and over their heads; according to the Bogobo of Mindanao he spat on them; at Sumba and according to the Bilan of Mindanao he whipped them. These explanations were doubtless suggested by human methods of trying to revive a person who has fainted. Another method, which might be called psychological revulsion, is laughter. According to the Narrinyeri of Encounter Bay (South Australia) the creator of the first men formed them from excrement and then tickled them to make them laugh and to give them life. In the Banks Islands, the god danced and played on a drum before his still inanimate creations. Although in other cases, for instance among the Australia tribes in the neighbourhood of Melbourne, the god's dance is only an expression of his satisfaction with his work, it may here have the object of causing laughter, unless indeed it is a magical process, like incantation.

A curious variant on the creation theme is that where a male deity creates only a woman, and by his union with her becomes the ancestor of mankind (Admiralty Islands, Bougainville in the Solomons, Society Islands, New Zealand).

Legends of this kind form the transition to another type, where the first men came from a heavenly couple (Indonesia, Marquesas, Hawaii, Tahiti), and in some of these myths it is expressly stated that the ancestors of mankind were gods who came down to earth from heaven (Toba Battak, Kei Islands, Simbang in New Guinea, Hawaii, Kaitish, Northern Australia).

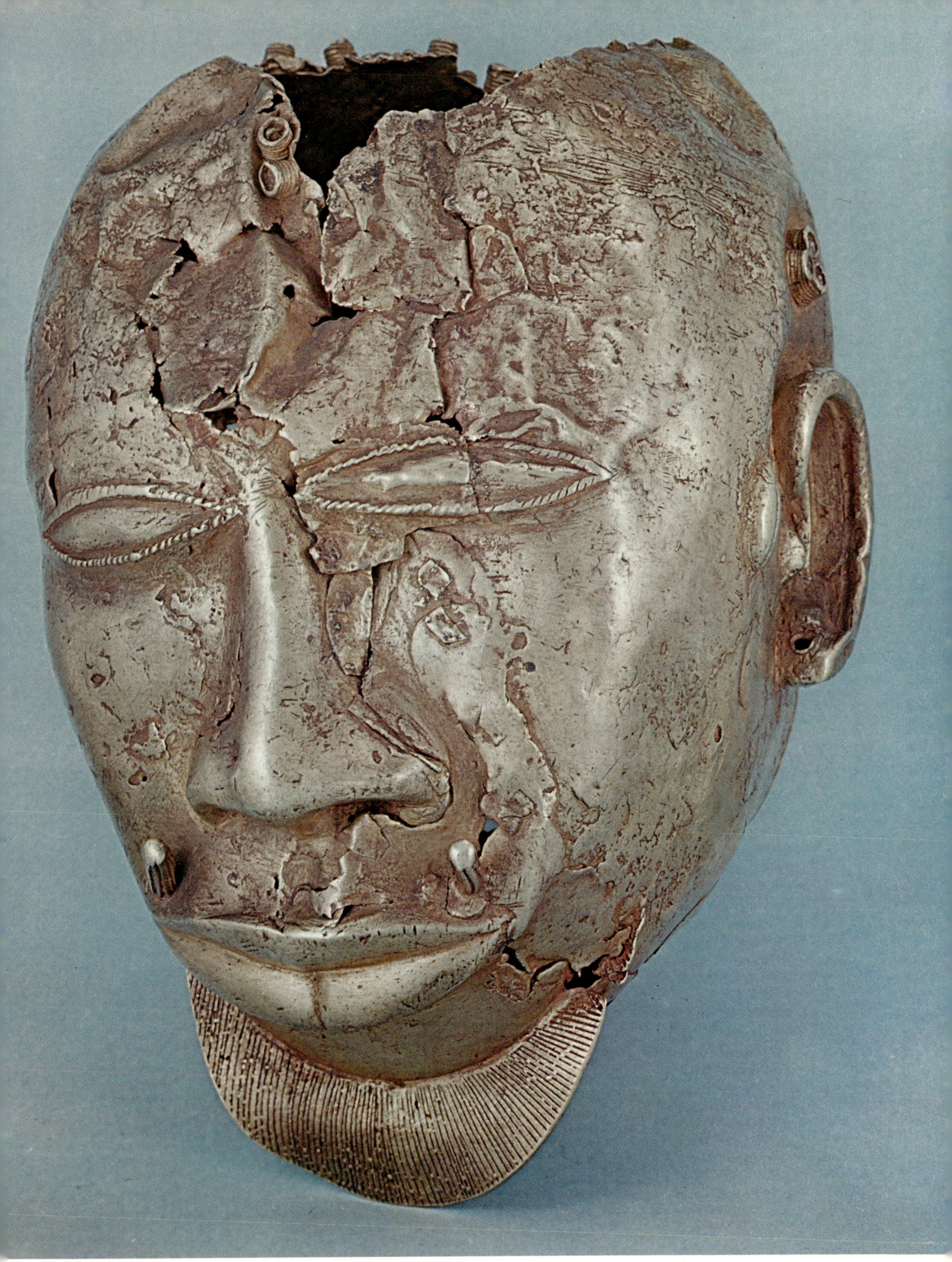

The god-like status of the Ashanti rulers was a direct expression of the power they wielded – as leaders of a strict military organisation the prestige and welfare of the nation stemmed directly from their gifts. The king was regarded as the representative of the sun itself and gold, symbolising this dynamic force, was his monopoly. This mask of pure gold is all that remains of past glory, the rest having been plundered, or recast for its material value. From the treasure of King Kofi Kakari.

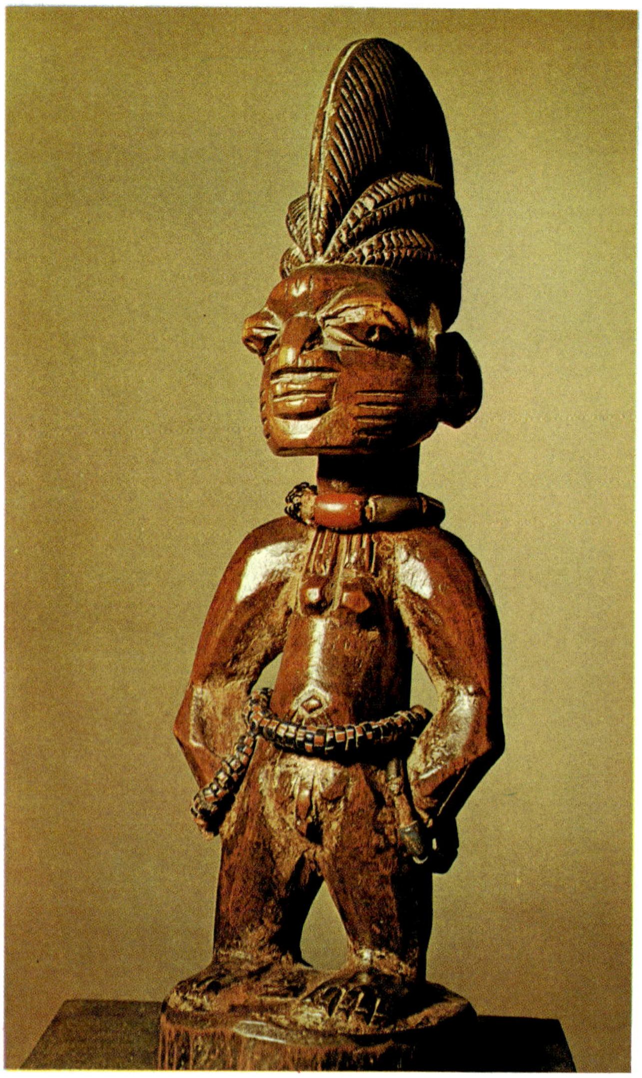

A votive figure of the Yoruba, representing a twin. These beautifully carved statuettes with their characteristic crested headdresses were made when a twin child died, and cherished so that the welfare of the surviving child was safe-guarded. Half of the soul was believed to exist in each twin and these figures provided a home for the soul of the child that died.

A Senufo 'fire-spitter', a mask worn by the Ghon cult of these people of the northern part of the Ivory Coast. It is worn during cleansing ceremonies to drive away witches and devourers of souls, when the uninitiated people of the village are confined to their huts. The mask is sometimes three feet long and sparks are produced from the mouth by means of burning tinder. The wearer, followed by a priest, is chosen for his ability to perform prodigious leaps; he flourishes a whip while horns are sounded to imitate the bellowing of a bull. Beautifully wrought in carved and polished wood, these masks take the form of familiar animals such as bulls, antelopes, or like the one in the picture, a mixture: the muzzle is that of a warthog and the horns of an antelope, while a chameleon climbs on to the human-looking head.

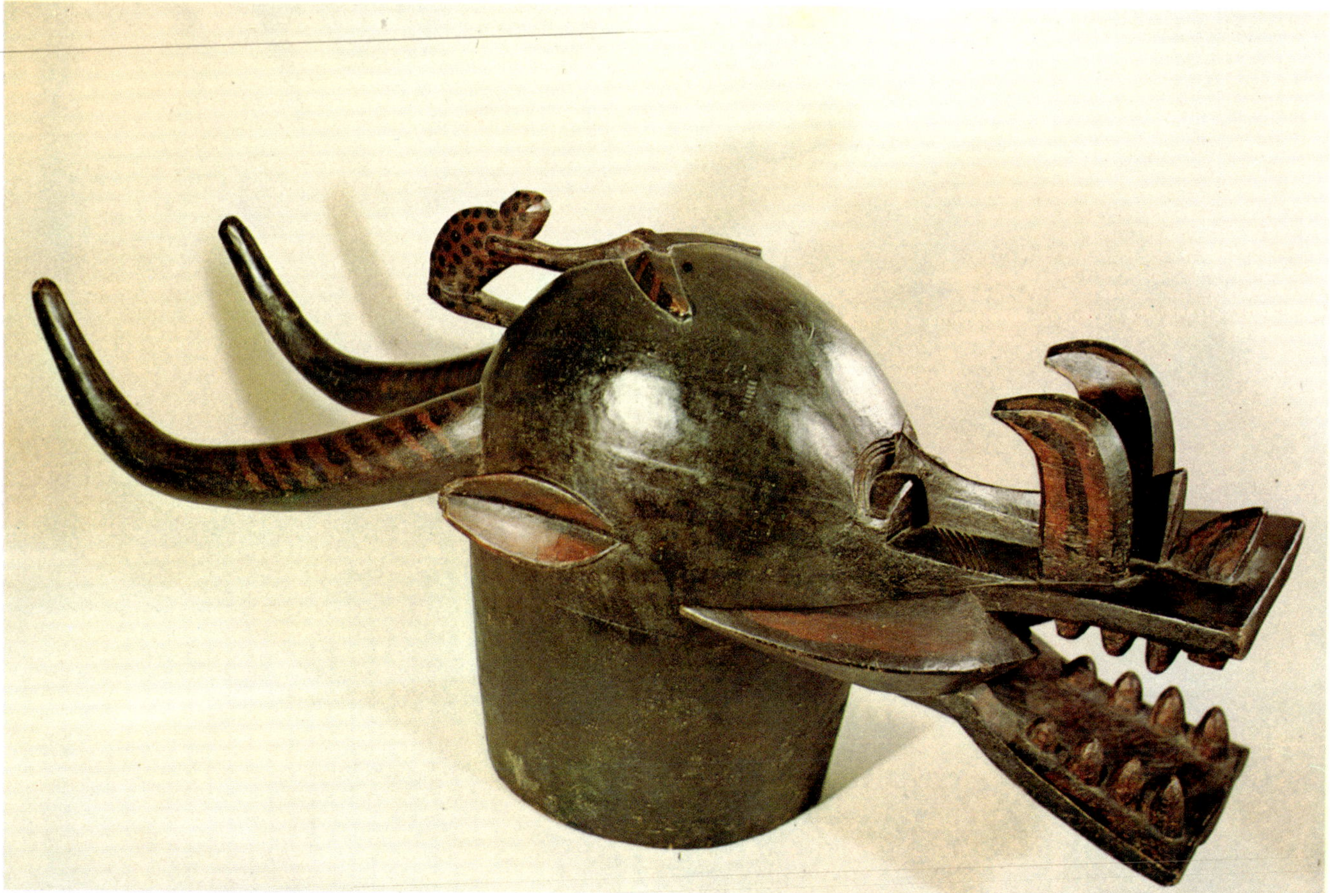

In some cases a goddess who comes down to earth becomes pregnant in some unusual way (Nomoi and elsewhere in the central Carolines, Mortlock), or children come out of her eyes and one of her arms (Nomoi). This birth of the first men by a sort of budding makes one of the transitions to the type of myth in which they are derived from trees, particularly widespread in Indonesia, and which may be also found in New Britain, in the Solomon Islands, at Niue, and in an Australian tribe of Victoria. According to the Kayan of Borneo, the first men were born from the union of a tree which came from heaven and a vine which embraced it.

Various legends derive the first men from birds' eggs (Mandaya in Mindanao, Admiralty Islands, Torres Straits, Fiji, Easter Island) or from turtles (Admiralty Island). The myths of the Admiralty Islands furnish a curious anticipation of the modern theory of mutations – a turtle or a dove laid at the same time several eggs, some of which produced animals of the same species, and the others produced men. Elsewhere the first men were produced not from eggs, properly so called, laid by living things, but from objects shaped like eggs, in earth (South-east Borneo) or from foam shaped like an egg by the waves which broke against a rock (Minahassa). In Formosa they came from a rock.

The first men were derived from a clot of blood, according to a belief especially widespread in Melanesia, and also to be found in Mindanao, the Marshall Islands, Samoa, and the Chatham Islands.

The first men are believed to have come out of the ground, in the Watubela and the Kei Islands of eastern Indonesia, and among the Elema of Papua. According to various Australian tribes, the ancestral totems of the different clans emerged from the ground sometimes in animal and sometimes in human form. In Samoa and Tonga, the first men came from a decaying worm, whose origin is itself variously explained. Elsewhere we find the belief that men did not originally have human form. According to a legend of the Society Islands, at first they were like balls on which arms and legs developed later. Similarly, according to various Australian tribes, the Arunta for example, and in Tasmania, the first men were 'inapertwa', beings of a rounded shape with only the rudiments of limbs, lacking mouths, eyes and ears, afterwards formed into normal men by deities or supernatural beings.

Various myths explain the difference of the sexes by a different origin for men and women. In the creationist myths they were formed by different deities or from different material. Thus, in the Palau Islands, the first man was created by the god, and the first woman by the goddess who formed the primeval couple. According to a legend of the Banks Islands, the first man was moulded in clay, and the first woman woven in basket-work; and among some of the Queensland tribes man was made from stone and woman from box-wood. A tribe in Victoria believe that the two first men were made out of clay by the god Pundgel, and the two first women were subsequently discovered at the bottom of a lake by his brother (or son) Pillyan.

In some of the Melanesian legends which deal with the origin of mankind, not as a creation but as a begetting or a metamorphosis, men and women were derived from different sources. For instance, among the Elemas of Papua the first man was born of the soil, and the first woman from a tree. According to the Baining of New Britain, the sun and the moon were at first the only beings in existence, and their children were stones and birds. The stones became men, and the birds became women, who inter-married and begat the first Baining. According to a legend of the Gazelle peninsula, the deity created the first two men, one of whom in his turn made the first two women from two coconuts.

There is also a mythical explanation of certain anthropological peculiarities. For instance, the Bilan of Mindanao explain in their way the depression of the nose just above the nostrils. The first deity who manufactured men made the nose with the nostrils turning upwards, and insisted on keeping it that way, although another god pointed out that in this way the race of men would be suffocated by the rain beating into their noses. So, when the first deity had his back turned, the other grasped the nose and turned it round into its present position – the hollows to be seen on either side are the marks of his fingers.

Other legends attempt to account for differences of race. In New Britain the difference between the dark-skinned Papuans and the lighter-skinned Melanesians is explained by the difference in colour of the coconuts which became the two first women. Among the

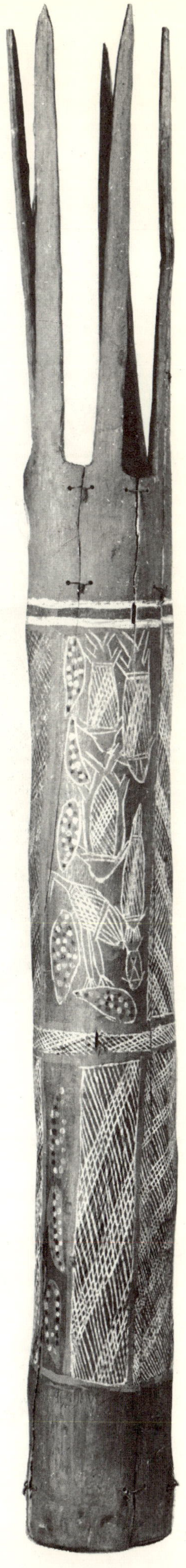

Log coffin. The log has been hollowed out, cut into sections and roughly shaped. It is only about four feet long and was made to hold the deceased's bones, some of which were inserted in circular holes. The five prongs at the top represent the fangs of a mythical monster. On the body, in a cross-hatching technique, are shown an assortment of strange animal, fish and bird forms. This may have come from Tjamuramara, a dreaming place of the Kartji group of the Wulaki District, Cape Stewart, Incised wood, Milingimbi Island, Australia.

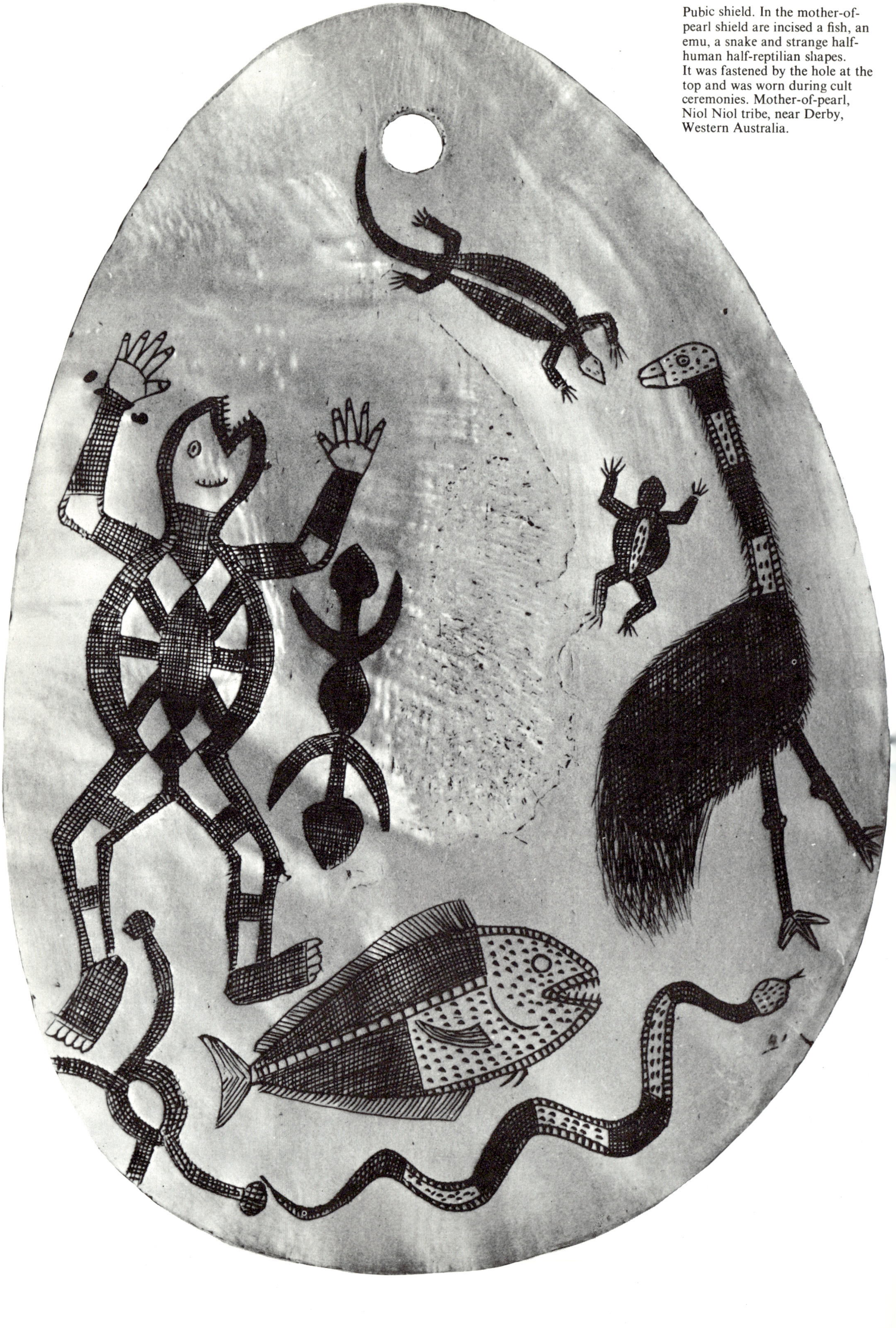

Pubic shield. In the mother-of-pearl shield are incised a fish, an emu, a snake and strange half-human half-reptilian shapes. It was fastened by the hole at the top and was worn during cult ceremonies. Mother-of-pearl, Niol Niol tribe, near Derby, Western Australia.

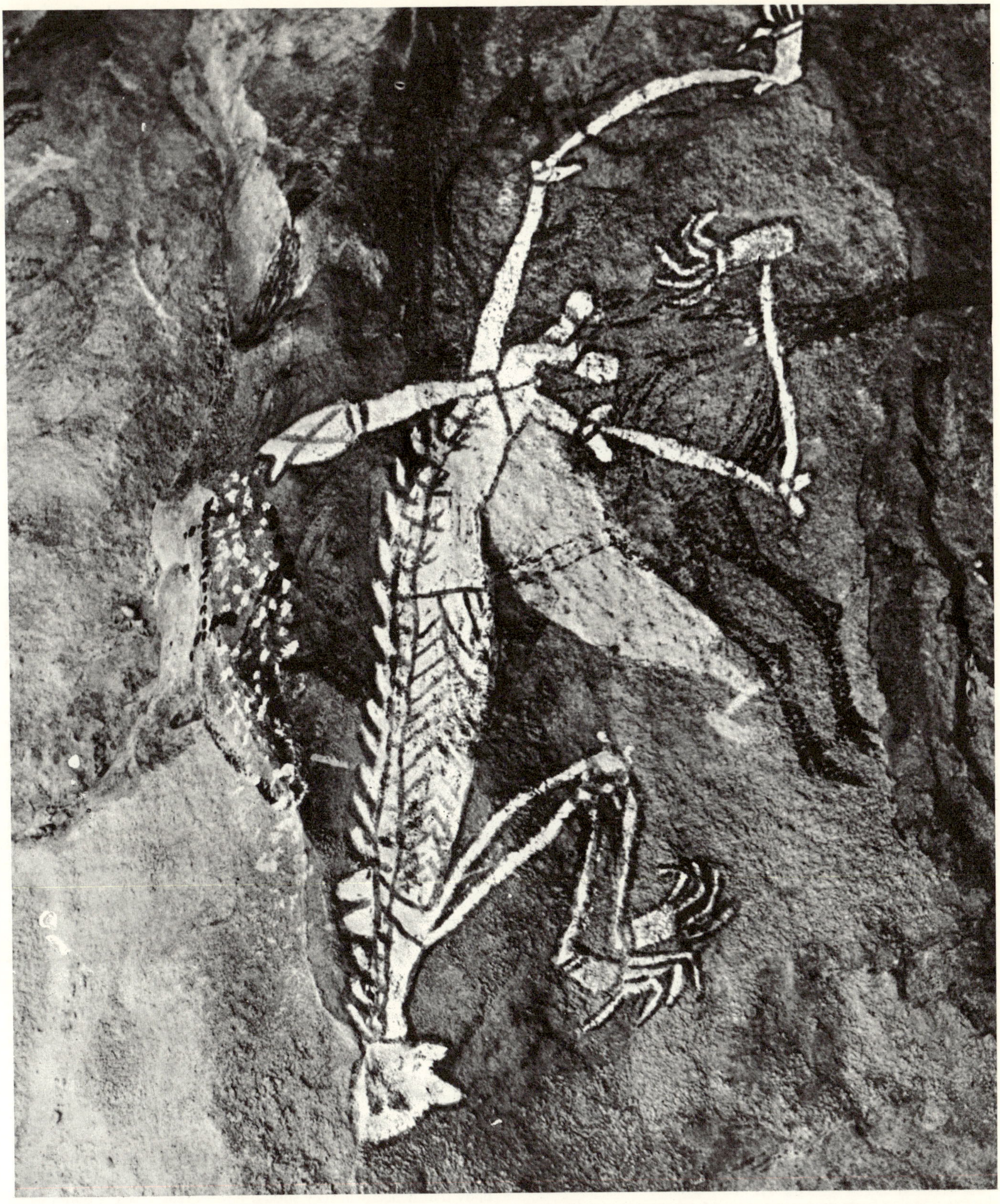

Fertility figure. Northern Australia is among the few places where rock paintings were executed and have survived. They are mostly connected with hunting and fertility magic, though parallels with love-charms have also been drawn. Artistically there are influences from Indonesia and New Guinea. There is no attempt to show modelling, the figures being merely sketched in outline. Paintings identical in style are also found on bark. Rock painting, from a cave in the Wellington Range, Arnhem Land, Australia.

Australian tribes in the neighbourhood of Melbourne the differences between the race with straight hair and the race with curly hair goes back to the first two men, to each of whom the creator gave one of these two kinds of hair.

Death. According to a belief spread through several areas of Oceania, mankind in the beginning was not mortal, or at least was not destined to be so, and only became mortal later. Man in his primitive condition is likened either to objects which do not die, such as stones (Baining of New Britain, Palau Islands), or trees and plants which spring up again after they are cut down (south-east Borneo, Palau Islands), or to beings whose death is only temporary and is followed by resurrection, like the moon which is reborn with each new moon (western Carolines, Arunta), crabs, and especially snakes which are reborn after changing their skins (Baining, Banks Islands, New Hebrides). As resurrection consists in the dead man rising from the grave, purely temporary death is compared to the property of the husk which rises to the surface when thrown into the water, while stones stay at the bottom (Australian tribes in New South Wales). To explain the origin of death, they say in the New Hebrides that in the beginning men changed their skins like snakes. They became mortal either because they failed to change their skins, or because when they had thrown off the old skin it was injured or destroyed by children at play. In Tana 'the old woman' became mortal because she washed herself, not in the river, but in the sea. In one type of fairly widespread legend, two divine or at any rate supernatural beings argue as to whether men should be mortal or not, and the second opinion is accepted (Carolines, Ambrym, New Zealand, Tahiti). In a variant from the western Carolines the sentence of an evil spirit which makes death inevitable happens only after a period during which men went to sleep and awoke with the moon. According to another version, the deity who created men went or sent somebody to find the vital principle, breath or liquid which would ensure men immortality as well as life; but in the meantime human beings were brought to life by another god or power, and so received only a precarious life (south-east Borneo, Toradja of Celebes). In the Banks Islands one deity created the first men, and then another tried to create some, but failed, and that is why men are mortal. In other myths the reason for death is failure, either by stupidity or negligence, to observe a precaution which would have resulted in the resurrection (western Carolines, New Britain, Banks Islands). Among the Dusun of North Borneo and the Baining of New Britain, men are mortal because they would not listen to the deity who showed the way to be immortal. According to the Arunta, death occurs because the people who were present when a dead man returned to life fled in terror, although he urged them not to do so. In the Admiralty Islands and in New South Wales, death is the punishment for a lack of graciousness, or of ingratitude. A legend of New Zealand makes the hero Maui try to bring mankind immortality by going down into the underworld, personified by some as 'the great Lady of night'; but he failed and lost his own life in the attempt.

Fire. The myths of various regions, and especially of New Guinea and Australia, allude specifically to a primitive state of mankind when fire was unknown, and when food was simply warmed in the sun's rays. The simplest if not the most practical way of getting fire is to obtain it from someone who already has it. In some myths the owner of fire from whom it is borrowed by mankind, produces it or contains it in his body (Nauru, New Guinea, Torres Straits). It is a deity in New Zealand, the Chatham Islands and Marquesas; a snake in the Admiralty Islands and in Queensland; a euro, a sort of kangaroo, among the Arunta.

The possessor of fire, the area in which he lives, and the person who obtains it, all vary greatly. A tribe in Victoria believe it was brought down from heaven by a man, a Queensland story says by a wren. It came from the lower world (New Britain, New Guinea, various archipelagoes in Polynesia), and was brought up by Maui (New Zealand). Among the Sulka of New Britain a man called Emakong brought it from the land of the snake-men who lived at the bottom of a river, into which the man had dived to look for a precious stone he had dropped. Elsewhere fire was brought from another part of the world, usually by an animal after various unsuccessful attempts (Igorot of the Philippines, Admiralty Islands, New Guinea, Torres Strait). In other myths the possessor of fire was a neighbour who kept it jealously; it was an old woman (Woodlark Island, Massim district, Papua), two women named Kangaroo-Rat and Bronze-winged Pigeon (New South Wales), the Bandicoot (Australian tribes, probably in Victoria). Sometimes the fire is stolen from its possessor by a trick, sometimes by force, sometimes by both together, as it was stolen by Maui from the water-rails in the Hawaii legend. Sometimes it is frankly given by its owner – a snake in the Admiralty Islands, snake-men in New Britain. In a New Zealand story the infernal deity of fire several times gives it to Maui in a friendly way, and only gets angry at repeated demands.

Borrowed fire must be most carefully preserved. In various legends people who had obtained it in that way allowed it to go out (central Celebes, Queensland, tribe in the neighourhood of Melbourne.

Social facts. There are some myths which relate to social customs or institutions, first of all to the Melanesian institution of dividing a tribe into two exogamous classes. At Omba (New Hebrides), each of the two classes originated with one of two daughters of the first woman who quarrelled – and here we meet descent traced through the female, which is one of the characteristics of this ethnological type. A legend of the Gazelle peninsula attributes this social division to a difference of race. One of the two first men asked the other to give him two light-coloured coconuts to make into two women. He gave one light and one dark, and each became a woman of corresponding colour. Then the first brother said to the other: 'If all mankind had had a light skin, it would have been immortal; but owing to your folly one group will descend from the light woman, and another group from the dark woman. Men with light skin must marry dark women, and men with dark skin light women.'

In Vao (New Hebrides) the custom of having separate fires for the men and the women is explained as follows. The first man and the first woman came out of a fruit which split in two when it fell from a tree on to a raised root. A bamboo rubbed by the wind against a dry branch produced fire, which the man kept going with brushwood. The woman, noticing the fire, looked over the root and asked what it was. The man said it was fire, and gave her some. Since then men and women have always had separate fires.

In Polynesia the practice of tattooing, which in all probability was anciently a magical charm, was revealed to men by the gods who invented it. The contrasts of light and shadow to be seen in the sky, the clouds, and the moon, must have been interpreted as tattooings of the corresponding deities. In New Zealand, the modern spiral tattooing which replaced the old tattooing imitated from basket-work, was brought back by Mata-ora after his journey to the underworld to look for his wife, Niwa-Reka.

In Australia many of the myths about the ancestors of mankind are especially concerned to explain how they came to teach certain customs and ceremonies to the peoples they met on their travels. A legend of Victoria gives the explanation of a taboo. The totemic 'bear' became an orphan while he was still young. The people in whose keeping he had been left took no care of him and often when they went hunting left him in the camp without even water to drink. One day they forgot to hang their water bottles out of his reach, and for once he was able to drink his fill. To avenge himself for previous ill treatment, he took all the water bottles and hung them on a tree. Then collecting the water of the streams he put it into other bottles which he hung on a tree, then climbed to its top, and made it grow until it was very tall. When the others returned, tired out, and thirsty from the hunt all day, they looked for their water bottles and could not find them. When they went to the river, it had run dry. Finally they noticed the little bear with all the water-bottles on top of the tree, and asked him if he had any water. 'Oh yes', he said, 'but you shan't have any, because you left me thirsty so often.' Several times they tried to climb the tree to take the water by force, but when they got a little way up the bear dropped water on them, which made them lose hold, so that they fell and were killed. In the end two sons of Pundjel came to their help. Unlike those who went before they climbed up in a spiral, so that when the bear threw down water it missed them. At last they succeeded in reaching the top, and the bear seeing that he was going to be captured, began to shout. Paying no attention to him, they beat him until all his bones were broken, and then threw him down. But instead of dying he changed into a real bear, and climbed up another tree. Then Pundjel's two sons came down and cut down the tree where the water bottles had been placed, and all the water in them went back to the rivers, which ever since have always contained water for people to use. Then Pundjel's two sons told everybody that henceforth they should never break a bear's bones when they killed one, and never flay him before they cooked him. So that is why unto this day the bear still lives in trees and still calls out when a man climbs a tree where he is. And he stays near water so that he can take it out of the streams if ever the order about not breaking his bones is transgressed.

CONCLUSION

This summary of the chief myths of Oceania shows that the problem of the origins of various types of beings or facts is stated in the same way as in the philosophies of which civilised societies are so proud. On the one hand as on the other, the hope is to understand origins by imagining them on the lines of this or that phenomenon observed in ordinary experience.

MYTHOLOGY OF BLACK AFRICA

INTRODUCTION

In Black Africa religion has nowhere reached a definitive form. Everywhere we find the worship of the forces of Nature personified – sun, moon, sky, mountains, rivers. But the undisciplined native imagination prevented the religion of Nature from expanding into poetic myths like those of India or Greece. The Negroes are quite ready to accept a supreme god who, as some of them think, created the first man and the first woman, while others think he created all things visible and invisible.

The religion of Nature is more highly developed in north-east Africa than fetishism, and as you go south fetishism gradually passess into idolatry.

Among the African sorcery is very powerful. Every medical treament has all the characteristics of exorcism, since magic remains secret while religion is open to all. Amulets and gri-gris are the usual manifestations of magic among the Africans. The object of those talismans is to protect their owner against disease, wounds, thieves and murderers, or to increase his wealth – in brief, to procure him everything profitable.

The African native thinks that the world and everything in it must be obedient to sorcerers, magicians who have the power of commanding the elements. This belief is bound up with another – the continuing existence of the soul after death. Magicians are able to call on souls to aid their powers. The souls of the dead often transmigrate into the bodies of animals, or may even be reincarnated in plants, when the natives think themselves bound to such by a close link of kinship. Thus the Zulus refrain from killing certain species of snakes which they think are the spirits of their relatives.

Africans attribute a spirit to every animate and inanimate object, and these spirits are the emanations of deities. Moreover, they are distinct from another, for there are spirits of natural phenomena and spirits of the ancestors.

Each family performs a regular cult to its ancestors. They represent demi-gods or the legendary heroes to whom they attribute magnificent exploits. Their lives end up by becoming legends.

Owing to the different kinds of ethnic groups occupying African territory and also to the low level at which the religious conceptions of the different peoples have usually become stabilised, it is impossible to undertake a regular exposition of African mythology. We shall have to limit ourselves to gleaning a few traditions or legends of a mythical nature among the various groups, without blinking the fact that such a method is inevitably incomplete and imperfect.

SOUTH-EASTERN GROUP

Madagascar. The Negroes of Madagascar believe in a supreme god, about whom are the *razanes,* the souls of the ancestors, and also in an evil spirit whom they call *angatch*.

For the Malagasy the souls of their ancestors are the intermediaries between the deities and human beings. The natives have a profound cult for them and make sacrifices to them. Among Malagasy spirits we must note those of fishing, hunting, agriculture, and war. The souls of chiefs transmigrate into the bodies of crocodiles, and those of the people into lynxes. There are idols in which the natives believe as they do in amulets. The Malagasy credit *Rabefihaza* with the origins of hunting, fishing with rod and line, and the invention of all snares.

A legend of south-west Madagascar deals with the origins of death and rain among the Malagasy, and at the same time explains the appearance of mankind on earth.

'Once upon a time *Ndriananahary* (God) sent down to earth

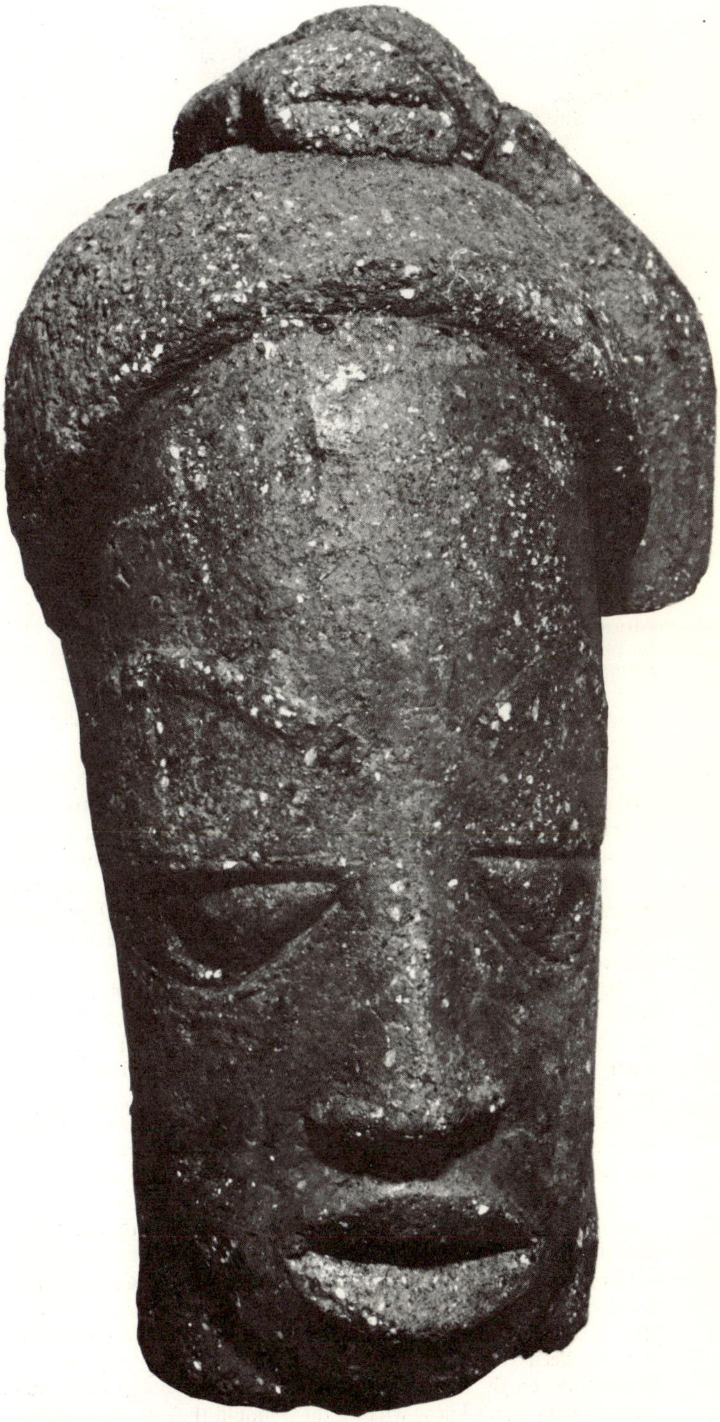

Nok head from Northern Nigeria. This serene, elongated head with its veiled, contemplative gaze and sensitively modelled nose and mouth was discovered in 1963 and is one of a number of remarkable terracotta heads found at Nok in northern Nigeria which are believed to be over two thousand years old. The strong naturalism suggests that they were portrait sculptures of kings or chiefs. African kings were not only regarded as divine but also as immortal, being reborn in their successors.

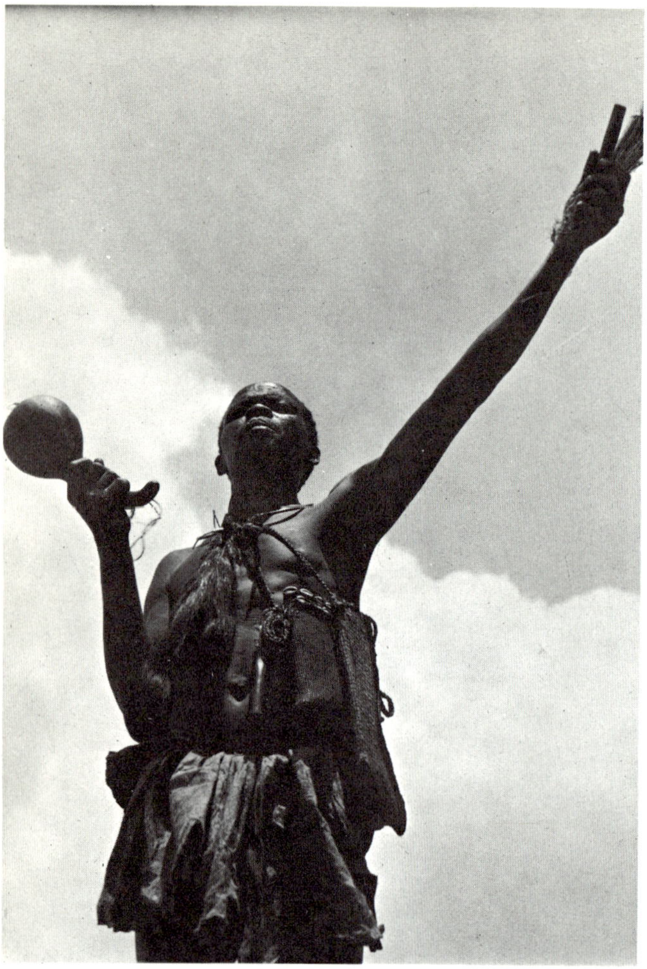

African rainmaker. Mythology and sorcery are still very much a part of the present in Africa today, many tribes believing that the world and everything in it must be obedient to sorcerers and magicians who have the power of commanding the elements. This man from the Congo region is a rainmaker and holds a gourd containing magical seeds in his right hand. Such men are also observers of nature and of the signs of the times.

his son Ataokoloinona (Water-a-Strange-Thing) to look into everything and advise on the possibility of creating living beings. At his father's order Ataokoloinona left the sky, and came down to the globe of the world. But, they say, it was so insufferably hot on earth that Ataokoloinona could not live there, and plunged into the depths of the ground to find a little coolness. He never appeared again.

'Ndriananahary waited a long time for his son to return. Extremely uneasy at not seeing him return at the time agreed, he sent servants to look for Ataokoloinona. They were men, who came down to earth, and each of them went a different way to try to find the missing person. But all their searching was fruitless.

'Ndriananahary's servants were wretched, for the earth was almost uninhabitable, it was so dry and hot, so arid and bare, and for lack of rain not one plant could grow on this barren soil.

'Seeing the uselessness of their efforts, men from time to time sent one of their number to inform Ndriananahary of the failure of their search, and to ask for fresh instructions.

'Numbers of them were thus despatched to the Creator, but unluckily not one returned to earth. They are the Dead. To this day messengers are still sent to Heaven since Ataokoloinona has not yet been found, and no reply from Ndriananahary has yet reached the earth, where the first men settled down and have multiplied. They don't know what to do – should they go on looking? Should they give up? Alas, not one of the messengers has returned to give up information on this point. And yet we still keep sending them, and the unsuccessful search continues.

'For this reason it is said that the dead never return to earth. To reward mankind for their persistence in looking for his son, Ndriananahary sent rain to cool the earth and to allow his servants to cultivate the plants they need for food.

'Such is the origin of fruitful rain.'

Another legend from the south of Madagascar shows how a man's fate comes from God:

Once upon a time, they say, there lived four men who could not agree, and each of them exerted himself in his own way.

One always carried an assegai, and went in pursuit of every living thing he saw, killing those he could catch, eating them or leaving them – that was his affair.

Another set snares for birds and animals. He killed some of those he caught so as to read omens in their entrails, and he kept the others to use at night as hunting gods – that was his affair.

On the other hand, another of these four men was attracted by any shining object, mica, iron, silver, fruit, anything of the sort, and when he saw it took up his abode there for the rest of the day – that was his affair.

And the fourth always carried a piece of iron to cultivate the earth.

Such were the circumstances of these four men.

As they could never agree, after some time they decided to make their way to God for him to arrange their fates and enable them to agree. So they set out, and they came to God, and it so happened that it was Friday, and God was pounding his rice. They told him their errand, and God said: 'Yes, but today I'm pounding rice and haven't time.' Then he gave a handful to each of them saying: 'Take this and keep it carefully, and on Monday I'll come to see you.' They said good-bye and went away, each with his rice in his hand. Then they made for the desert, separated, and each man went to his dwelling.

Soon after they had separated the man with the assegai saw a wild dog and went after it, and in the pursuit he forgot about the rice and dropped it. One of the others happened to come to the edge of a ravine cut out by a torrent. Seeing the glitter of something white, he put down his rice and started to climb down, but it happened that his liamba brushed away the rice from the edge of the ravine, and the torrent carried it away so that he lost it.

The bird-trapper went out at night, having heard the screech of an owl, and he went after it after putting down his rice outside his hut. On his way back he decided to put the rice into his salaka, but the rice had already been blown away by the wind and he could not find it. The fourth man came to a marshy place and began to dig; putting his rice into his lamba, he left it on a large clod of earth. When he had finished digging the wind overturned the lamba and with surprise he saw his rice scattered. He picked it up grain by grain and recovered about a quarter of it, so that at one and the same time he was pleased and sad, for if he had regained some of it the greater part was lost – for he considered as lost the rice which fell on the moist earth.

On Monday God arrived, called the four men together, and asked what had happened to the rice he had given them, and each told his tale. God replied: 'Do you see that you can't change the fate which God has given you? The fighting man is a fighting man, and that is the race of warriors. The sorcerer is a sorcerer, and that is the race of sorcerers. The trader is a trader, and that is the race of traders. And you, worker of the earth, you will be the race of workers of the earth, and of you I make the principle (i.e. the source) of the food of all the others. God follows men in the evil they do to lead them to the good. You used to disagree because of your different circumstances, for which you could see no reason. Henceforth, this is how you will arrange your behaviour.' Thus spoke God. And thereafter each of the men had his lot, which he loved.

Mozambique. The Negroes of Mozambique believe in the power of fetishes and amulets. But they recognise some deities, among them *Tilo* who, they think, is the god of the sky as well as a deity of thunder and rain. They also believe in survival after death, if we may judge by their funeral rites, especially the offering of food at graves, and again by the custom which used to be observed by the Uanyamuezis, that when a chief died three living slaves were buried in his grave to keep him company in the next world.

Many of these natives worship the sun and moon. A cosmogony myth of the Zambezi explains the spots on the moon: 'Formerly the moon was very pale and did not shine, and was jealous of the sun with its glittering feathers of light. She took advantage of a moment when the sun was looking at the other side of the earth, and stole some of his feathers of fire to adorn herself. But the sun found it out,

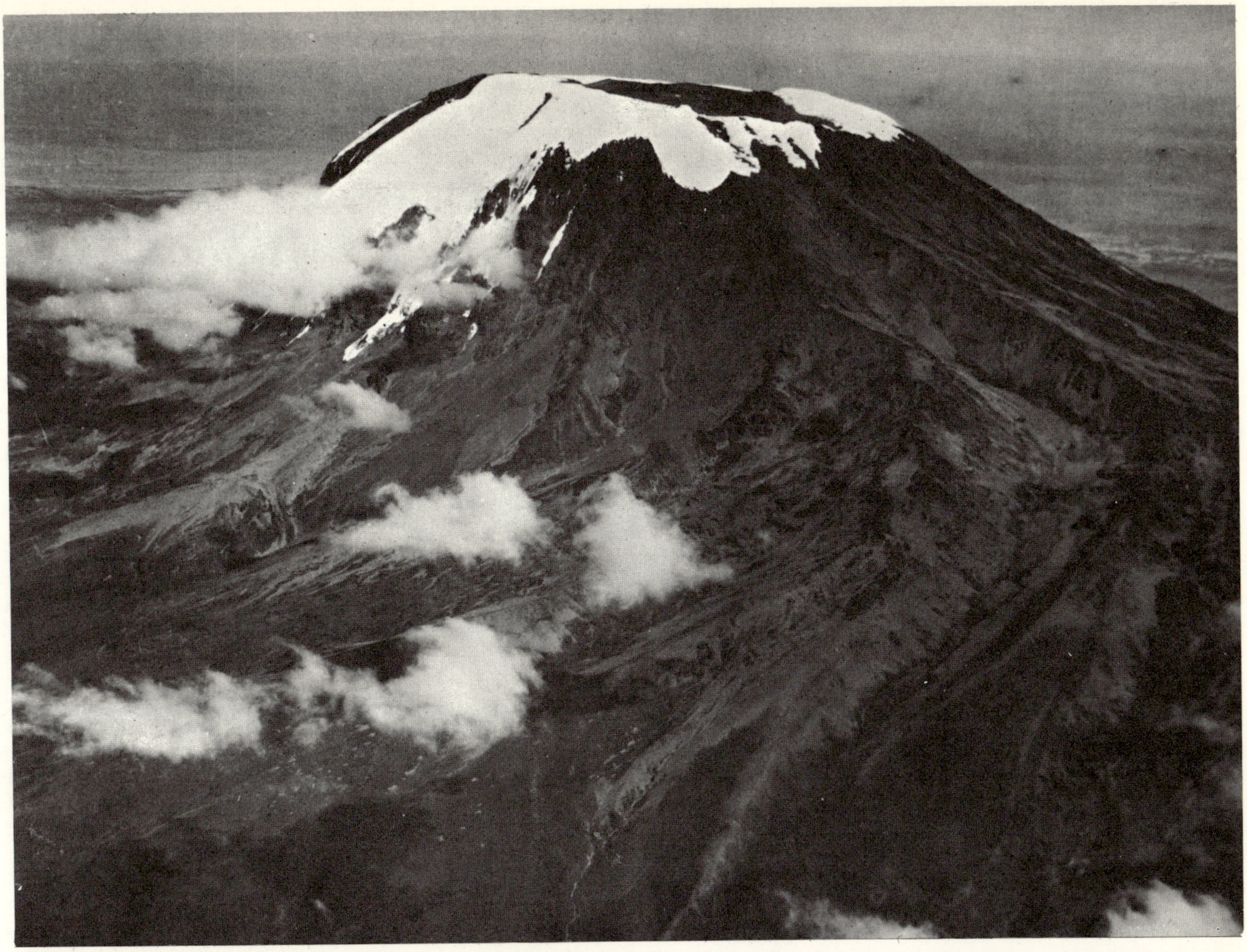

Mount Kilimanjaro. Snow-capped and wreathed in clouds, Mount Kilimanjaro is Africa's highest mountain and is located in the Northern Province of the former Tanganyika, now Tanzania. With Mount Kenya and Mount Cameroon it is one of the sacred mountains to which the African people of the region attribute their beginnings. In the Congo, also, mountains are considered sacred when a dead soul is believed to have taken up its dwelling there, its presence being the cause of mountain vertigo.

and in his anger splashed the moon with mud which remains stuck to it for all eternity. Ever since then the moon is bent on vengeance. Every ten years she surprises the sun when he is off guard, and cunningly spatters him with mud in his turn. Then the sun shows large spots and for some hours cannot shine, so that the whole earth is sad, and men and animals are greatly afraid, for they love the sun.' This myth indicates how the natives noticed eclipses and the various natural phenomena which result.

In the same Zambezi region there are traces of a myth which suggests that of the Greek giants attacking heaven. In this case men tried to kill the sun, *Nyambe*, by climbing up to it, but their temerity was severely punished.

The Macouas and the Banayis believe in a supreme being whom they call *Muluku*, and place in opposition an evil genius called *Minepa*. They have a myth of the creation of the first man and woman:

'In the beginning Muluku made two holes in the earth, and from one came a man, from the other a woman. God gave them land to cultivate, a pick, an axe, a pot, a plate and millet. He told them to cultivate the ground, to sow it with millet, to build a dwelling, and to cook their food in it. Instead of carrying out Muluku's advice, they ate the millet raw, broke the plates, put dirt in the pot, and then went and hid in the woods. Seeing that he had been disobeyed God called up the monkey and the she-monkey, and gave them the same tools and advice. They worked, cooked, and ate the millet. And God was well pleased. So he cut off the tails of the monkey and the she-monkey, and fastened them to the man and woman, saying to the monkeys: "Be men!" and to the humans: "Be monkeys!"'

In the northern part of south-east Africa, the Masai form an ethnic group which some ethnologists believe is related to the Semites. Like the Hebrews of old, the Masai call themselves God's chosen people, and their religious beliefs differ considerably from those of the neighbouring peoples. They worship a single god, *'Ng ai*, the creator of the universe. This word 'creator' applies to the inhabited world, for the Masai, like all the other Africans, believe the earth has always existed. 'In the beginning,' they say, 'there was only one man on earth, named Kintu. The daughter of Heaven saw him and fell in love with him, and persuaded her father to let him be her husband. Kintu was invited to Heaven, and thanks to the magic powers of the daughter of Heaven, succeeded in passing the tests the great god imposed on him, and then returned to earth with his divine wife, whose dowry included the domestic animals and useful plants. They would have been perfectly happy, but for a blunder on the part of Kintu. In taking leave of the newly wedded couple the great god had warned them not to retrace their steps. He feared on their behalf the anger of one his sons, Death, who had not been told of the marriage, and consequently had been absent.

'On the way, Kintu noticed that he had forgotten the corn for his chickens, and in spite of his wife's entreaties he went back to Heaven, where the god of Death was at that moment. He followed the man's steps, took his place near his dwelling, and killed all the children of Kintu and the daughter of Heaven. In vain they entreated the great god, who in the end, however, sent one of his sons to expel Death. But he was more nimble than his adversary, escaped all his devices, and established himself as henceforth the lord of the earth.'

Another tradition which circulates among the Masai, gives a different account of the origin of death. The great god wished to protect the race of men, and advised Le-eyo, his favourite, to say when a child died: 'Man dies and returns; the moon dies and does not return.' Soon after a child died, but as it was not one of his own, Le-eyo did not trouble to utter the formula. He did not remember it until misfortune struck him in the person of one of his own sons. But the great god told him when it was too late, and ever since then men have been subject to the law of Death.

Among the Masai the spirit of evil is represented by the demon *'Nenaunir*, who is also the god of the storm. The rainbow is also an evil power. One day he took it into his head to swallow the world. Luckily the Masai warriors attacked him with their arrows, and forced him to restore his prey.

Beside every Masai, 'Ng ai places a guardian angel who defends him against all dangers, and at the hour of death carries off his soul to the next world. The Masai believe in a future life, with rewards and punishments according to one's deserts. The wicked are doomed to wander for ever in an arid desert, while the virtuous enjoy eternal peace in vast meadows giving pasture to innumerable herds. However, it sometimes happens that the souls of the dead are reincarnated in certain snakes, which in consequence must not be killed.

SOUTHERN GROUP

The Bushmen, who appear to be related to the Hottentots, hold mythological and religious beliefs which are closely linked with their dances. Still, their use of amulets shows that they have a notion of supernatural forces and spirits. Among the Bushmen magic is founded on the belief that the world is peopled with invisible beings which can be seen only by the sorcerers. Among magical practices we will mention the method used by the Bushmen to cause rain. They light large fires which give off a black cloud whose colour resembles that of the rain-bearing clouds. The mythology of the Bushmen is marked by the part played in it by animals, who are supposed to be able to speak. Thus, the lion could speak by putting his tail in his mouth. In a neighbouring tribe of Bushmen who live in Hereroland, there exists a creation myth. It includes a sort of Yggdrasil tree, the tree from which men were born, and it is called 'Omumbo-rombonga'. Cattle also came from it. The Bushman deity is *Cagn*, creator of all things. The natives do not know where he lives, but the antelopes do. He has a wife: 'Coti'. Savages do not know how they came into the world, such things being known only to the initiated. (As with the Greeks, the Bushmen had secret societies for the conservation of beliefs and myths.) Cagn had two sons, 'Cogaz' and 'Gewi'. The three of them were great chiefs. Coti gave birth to a fawn, and since she insisted on knowing the character of her offspring and what its future would be, she made use of various sorceries. This myth relates to the origin of antelopes and their wildness. Cagn's relatives arrived and hunted the first eland too soon, which explains its timorous nature. One of Cagn's daughters married the snakes who were also men; they became subjects.

According to the Bushmen, Cagn's strength lay in one of his teeth. This suggests Samson, whose strength lay in his hair. Birds were his messengers, and told him all that was going on about him. Cagn could change his sandals into dogs, and set them on his enemies. The monkeys who had been men made fun of him, and he exiled them with curses to distant places.

He had the power to assume the form of an animal, such as the antelope. One day the thorns which once had been men attacked Cagn and killed him, and then the ants ate him. Not long afterwards his bones joined up again, and he returned to life.

Among the Bushmen of the western provinces, Cagn bears the name 'I Kaggen', a name which is identified with that of the praying mantis. I Kaggen's wife is 'Hyrax' (*Hyrax capensis*) and their adopted daughter is the porcupine, daughter of 'II Khwaihemm' (eat-all). She swallowed the whole world of beings and then vomited up her victims alive. I Kaggen had a similar fate.

The Bushmen pray to the sun, the moon and the stars. The moon belongs to the praying mantis, who made it out of an old shoe!

The natives also pray to the chameleon, which has the power to bring rain.

In the southern group, the Hottentots or Khoi-Khoi, a pastoral people, are on a higher level than their neighbours the Bushmen. The Hottentots had a cult of large stones, calling at the same time on a supernatural personage named Heitsi-Eibib. Like their Bushmen neighbours the Hottentots worshipped the praying mantis. The religion of the Hottentots seems to have consisted solely in magic and the cult devoted to souls of the dead by songs and dances. Heitsi-Eibib is more like a hero or a dead sorcerer, willing to aid the living. He had the power which is common to all sorcerers of being able to assume the form of any animal he wished. According to one myth he was born of a cow, and according to another of a virgin who ate a certain herb.

He did not create the animals, but he gave them their characteristics with his curses.

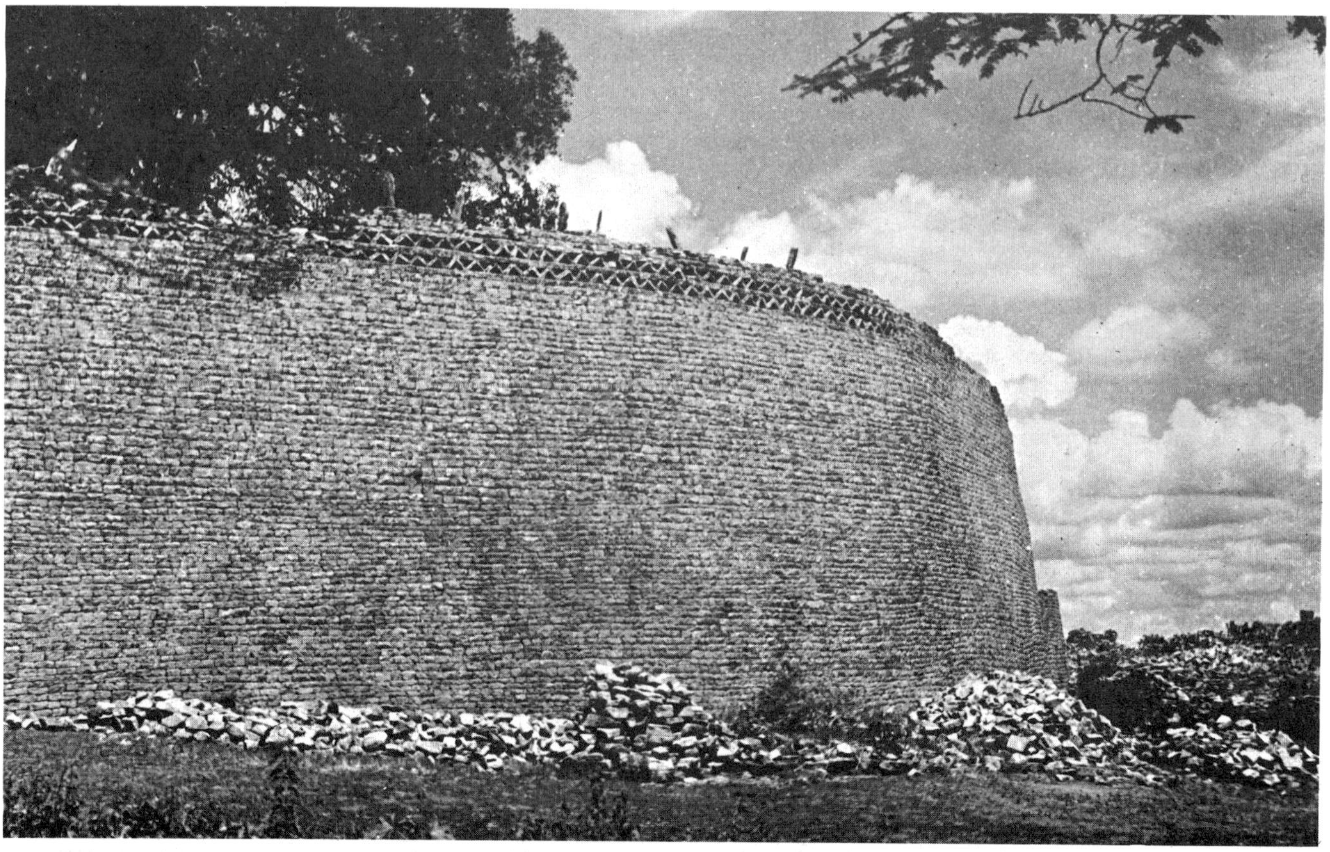

Outer wall of the 'Temple' at Zimbabwe, Southern Rhodesia. A ceremonial centre for probably close on a thousand years and, in later years, the capital of a vast empire, Zimbabwe's most sacred spot was located on the Acropolis where prayers were offered to Mwari through the intermediary of the dead Mambos (or kings) until the sacking of the city in the eighteen thirties. The reigning Mambo was concealed from public view by these massive walls – in reality those of his palace enclosure.

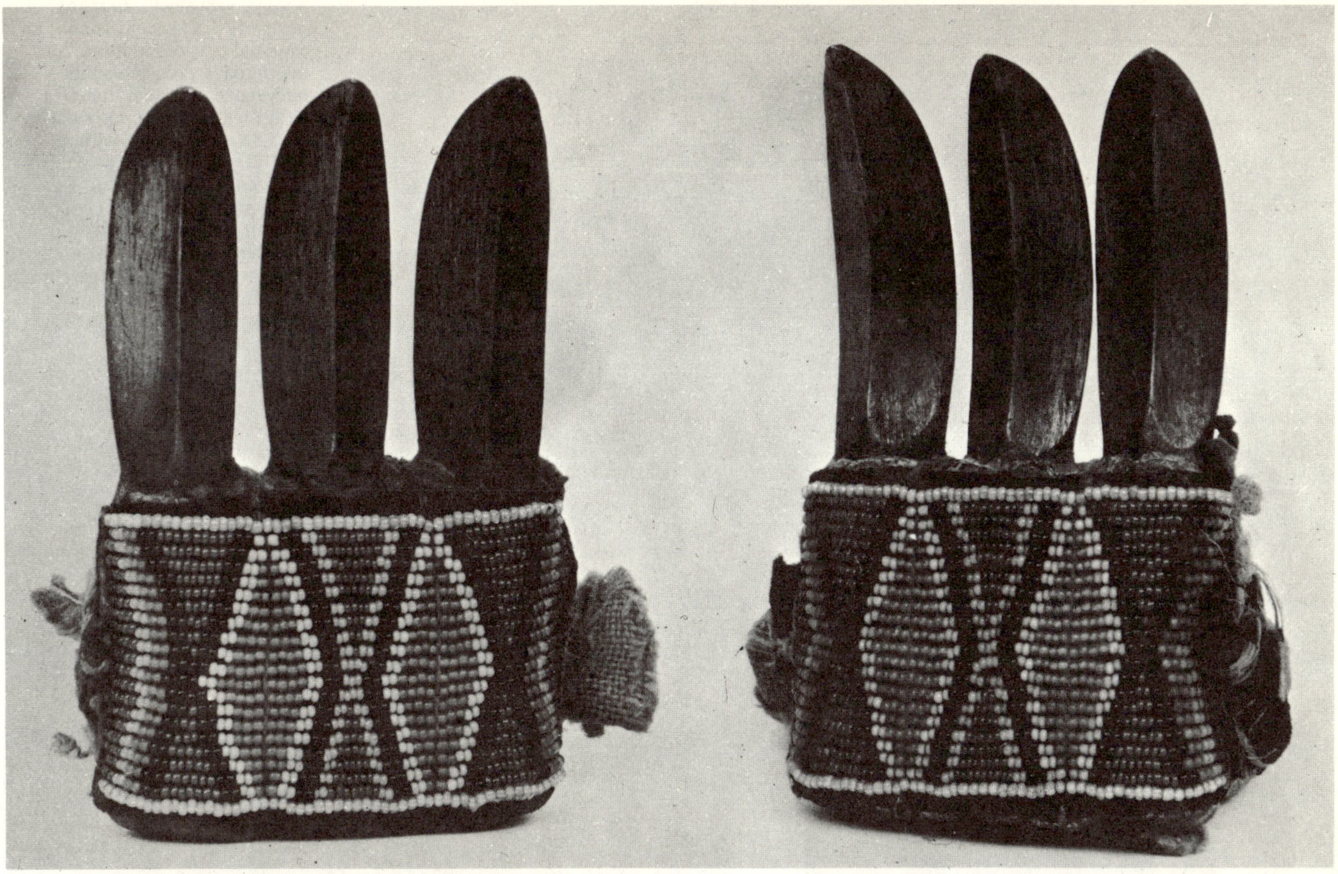

Crocodile-teeth ornaments, or charms, from Madagascar. A belief in the continued existence of the soul after death and in its transmigration into the bodies of various animals is common to many African peoples, the Negroes of Madagascar believing that such *razanes*, or ancestral souls, act as intermediaries between the gods and human beings. The most revered of these *razanes* are those of chiefs, which are believed to inhabit the bodies of crocodiles. Silver with coloured beadwork.

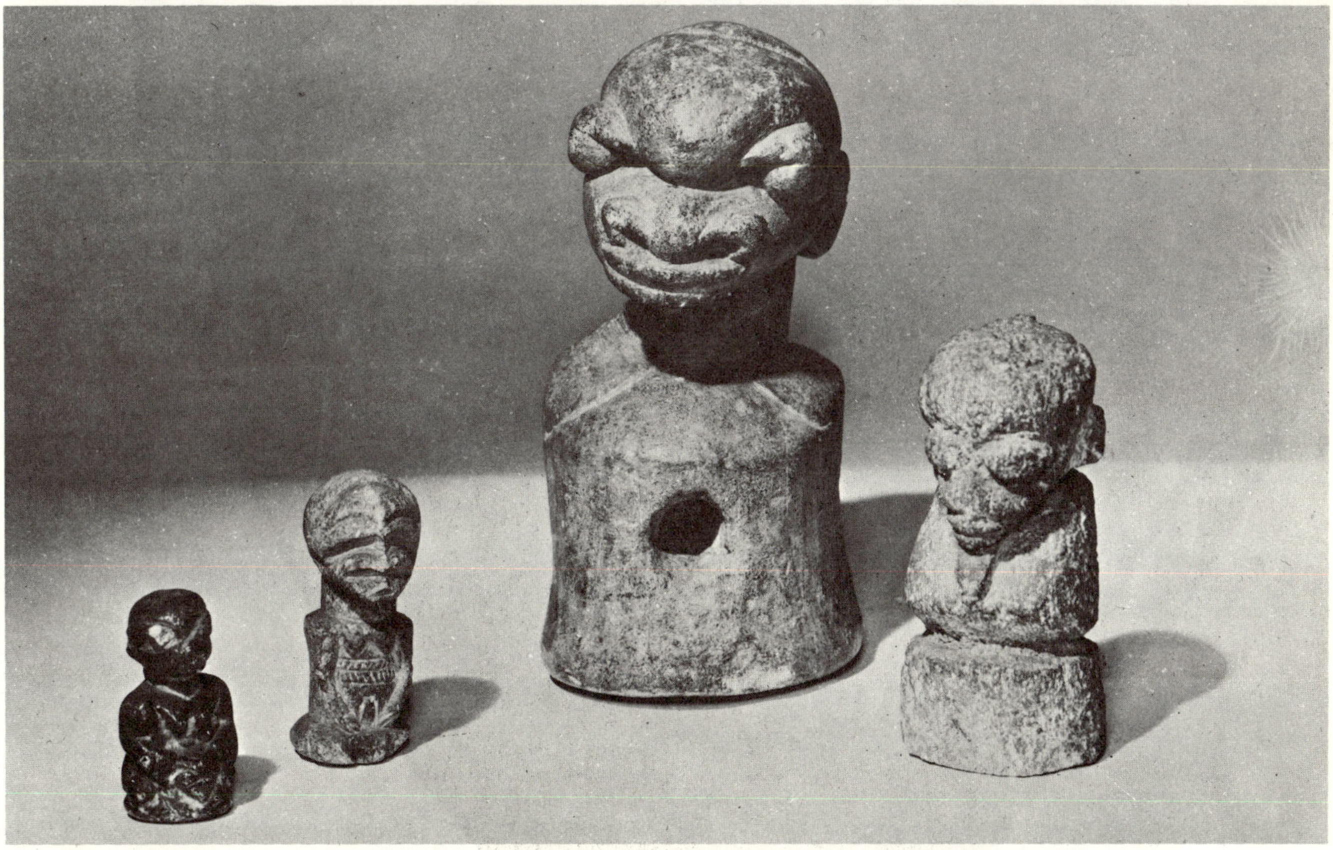

Four 'rice gods' from Sierra Leone. These four highly stylised steatite and soapstone figures from Sierra Leone are of great antiquity and may represent ancestors, though the common description of them as 'rice gods' would suggest that they portray an agricultural deity. The large figure in the centre, despite its protruding eyes, displays considerable naturalism, and may be a shrine. According to a Madagascan myth, rice was originally a celestial food but was brought down to earth by the daughter of the supreme god.

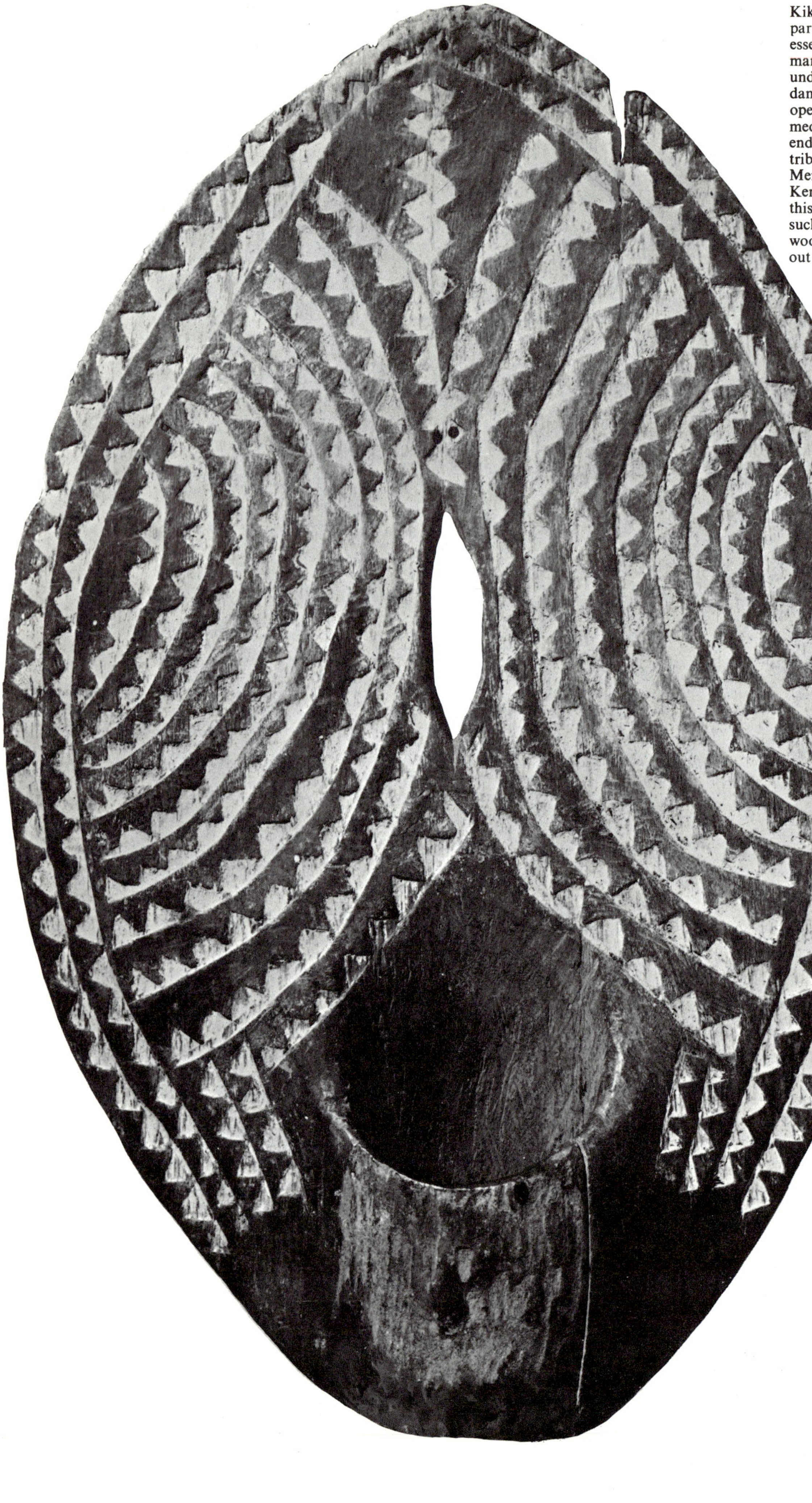

Kikuyu arm shield. In many parts of Africa cicumcision is an essential part of initiation into manhood, a process readily undergone in spite of the dangers attendant upon such an operation performed without medical refinement. The pain endured is both an offering to tribal gods and a test of courage. Men of the Kikuyu tribe of Kenya wear arm shields similar to this one on their right arms during such initiation rites. Carved wood with incised design picked out in colour.

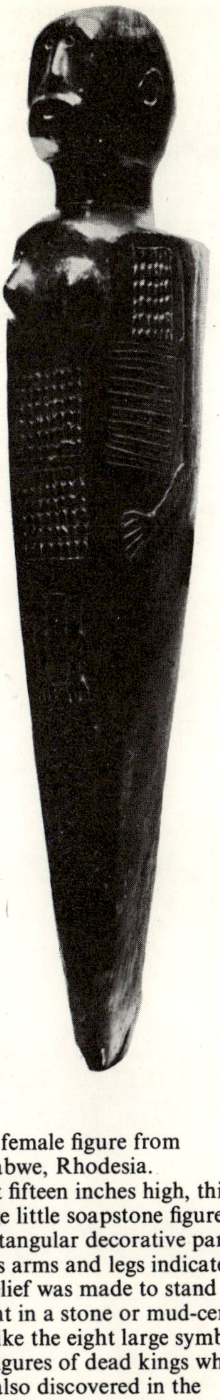

Small female figure from Zimbabwe, Rhodesia. About fifteen inches high, this strange little soapstone figure with its rectangular decorative panels and its arms and legs indicated in low relief was made to stand upright in a stone or mud-cement base like the eight large symbolic bird-figures of dead kings which were also discovered in the ruins of the city. Its purpose remains a mystery. The small size, however, would suggest a votive figure.

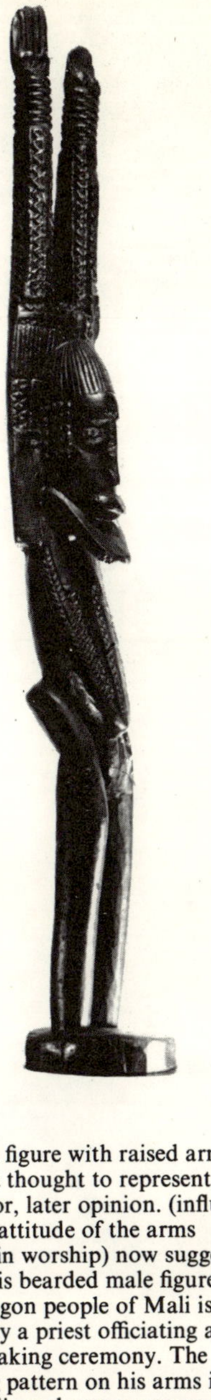

Dogon figure with raised arms. At first thought to represent an ancestor, later opinion. (influenced by the attitude of the arms raised in worship) now suggests that this bearded male figure from the Dogon people of Mali is possibly a priest officiating at a rain-making ceremony. The zig-zag pattern on his arms is symbolic and appears on many Dogon ritual objects. It represents the path followed by the creator during the formation of the world. Carved wood.

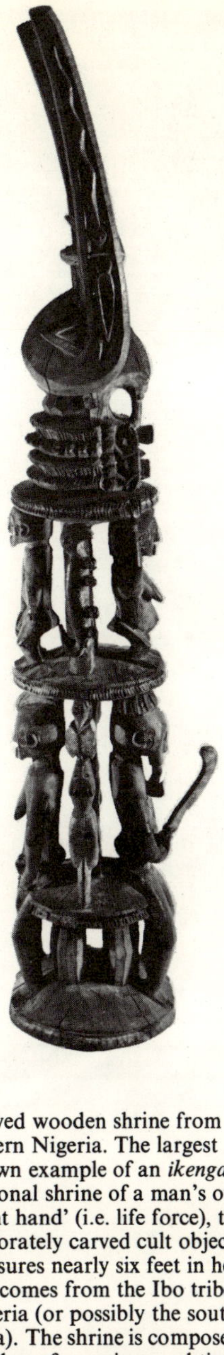

Carved wooden shrine from eastern Nigeria. The largest known example of an *ikenga*, or personal shrine of a man's own 'right hand' (i.e. life force), this elaborately carved cult object measures nearly six feet in height and comes from the Ibo tribe of Nigeria (or possibly the southern Igala). The shrine is composed of a number of superimposed tiers of diminishing width supported by human and animal figures and terminates in two curved 'wings' adorned with snakes.

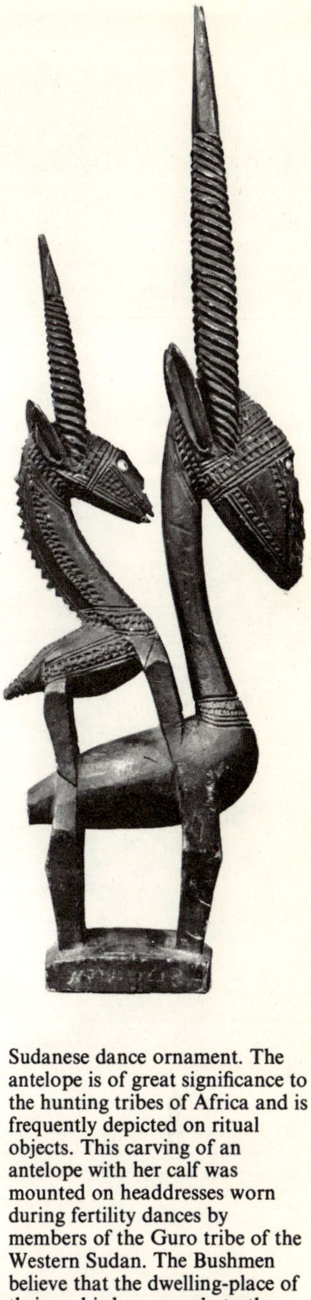

Sudanese dance ornament. The antelope is of great significance to the hunting tribes of Africa and is frequently depicted on ritual objects. This carving of an antelope with her calf was mounted on headdresses worn during fertility dances by members of the Guro tribe of the Western Sudan. The Bushmen believe that the dwelling-place of their god is known only to the antelopes and that he has the power to assume their shape. Carved wood with inlaid eyes.

They say that once the lion lived in trees like the birds, and it was owing to Heitsi-Eibib's curse that he came down and stayed on the ground. Heitsi-Eibib also cursed the hare, which escaped by running.

Among the Hottentots, Heitsi-Eibib's personality occurs again in the cult rendered him under the name of 'Tsui-Goab'. His enemy is a spirit by the name of 'Gaunab' who created the rainbow. The natives worship a pile of stones under which they think he is buried.

In addition to these legendary personages we must note the water spirits, a sort of red men with white hair; while the moon and the constellations are also worshipped.

Unlike the Hottentots, the Zulus are not very religious, but they do, like them, believe in the supernatural powers which are the prerogative of sorcerers.

According to one myth of the origin of the world, men emerged from a bed of reeds called 'uthlanga'. The first man was Unkulunkulu (the Very Old) who taught men their knowledge of the arts, the laws of marriage etc.

The Zulus have a myth about death, where Unkulunkulu plays the part of the supreme being.

One day Unkulunkulu said to the chameleon: 'Go, and say "Men shall not die!"' The chameleon started off, but he went very slowly, and stopped to eat the fruit of a mulberry. Others say he climbed a tree to warm himself in the sun, and went fast asleep. Meanwhile Unkulunkulu changed his mind, and sent a lizard after the chameleon telling him to deliver to men a message very different from the first one. The lizard set out, passed the lazy chameleon, and reached men first. He gave them the god's message, saying: 'Men shall die!' Then he returned to Unkulunkulu.

Soon after he had gone the chameleon arrived among men with his message of immortality. But men replied that the lizard had already been with them, bringing an exactly opposite message. 'We can't believe you,' they said. 'The lizard said, "Men shall die!"' And ever since no man has escaped death.

This legend may be found among other Bantu tribes, such as the Bechuana, the Basuto and the Baronga. But the natives have no worship of Unkulunkulu. Among them live the *iniangas*, magicians who have the power of making rain.

The iniangas also have the gift of being able to discover thieves and spell-binders. The sorcerers communicate with the spirits by whistling. The rain-makers are known by the name of 'sky shep-

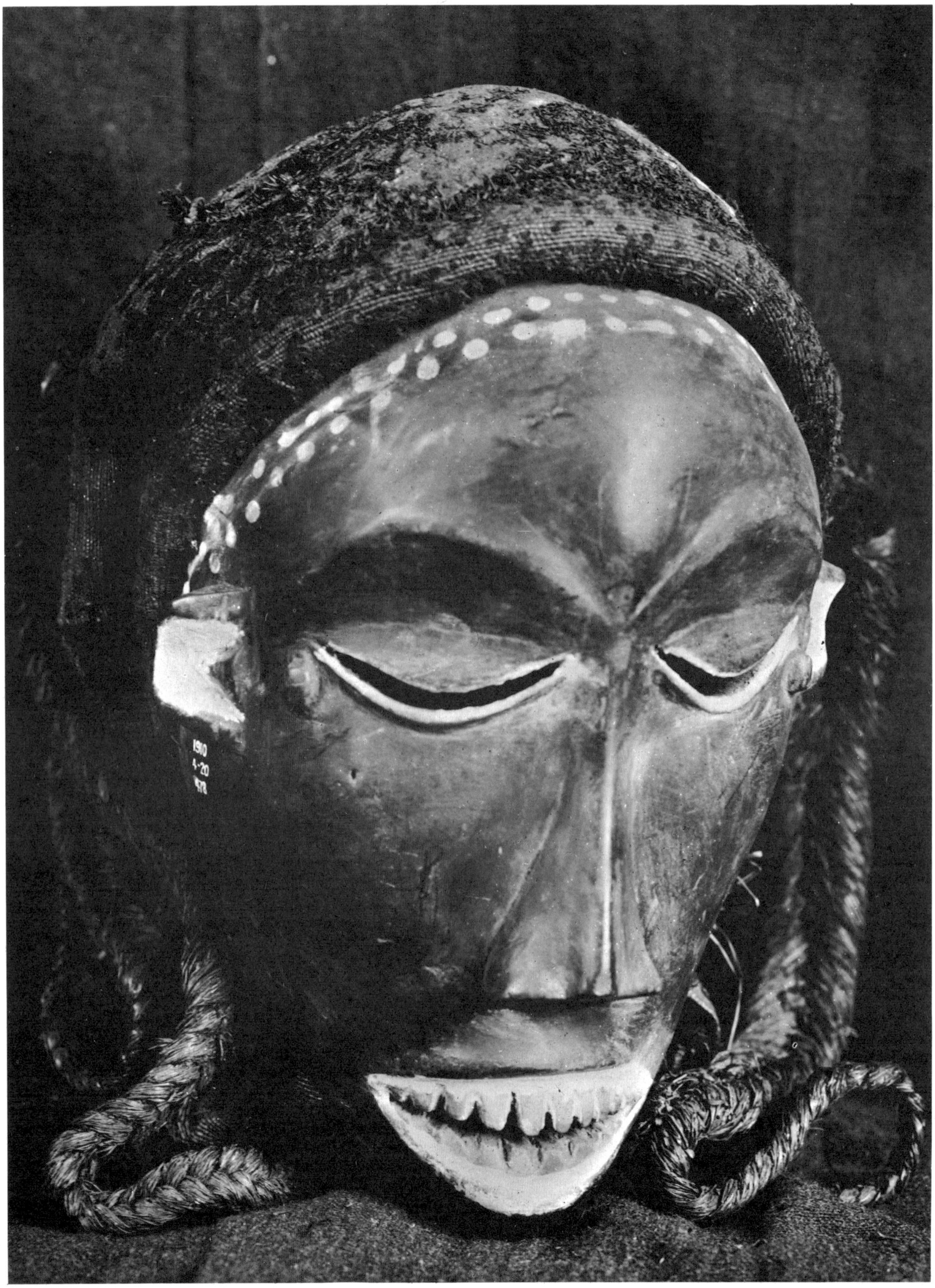

Bapende initiation mask. For the African peoples masks and representations of masks are powerful objects in themselves.
This initiation mask comes from the Bapende people of the Congo and was worn at the ceremonies which mark the passing of boys into manhood when adult religious lore and secrets are revealed to them and they become responsible members of the community. Though allegedly discovered by a woman, the use of masks with the Bapende is exclusively reserved for men. Carved and painted wood with cloth and fibre.

herds'. They look after the clouds as of the cows of a herd, and prevent them from bursting over the land worked by the tribe.

The Zulus think that clouds and lightning are just like living creatures.

THE CONGO GROUP

The people of Angola are idolaters. They believe that their fetishes – *muquixis*, little roughly carved statuettes of wood – can protect them from evil spells and make them happy. In addition to this belief, the natives of Angola think that the sorcerers can cause the death of one among them. The crow of a cock or the barking of a dog in the night are both the signs of a death. The people of Angola believe in a supreme being named Zambi, who lives in the sky. He is considered as the supreme judge after death. A myth of Lower Congo about the deluge says that long ago the sun met the moon and threw mud at it, which made it less bright. When this meeting happened there was a flood, and men then put their milk sticks behind their backs and were changed into monkeys.

The present race of men is a recent creation. Some natives say that during this flood men were changed into monkeys and women into lizards. In another myth the flood is supposed to have been caused during the formation of lake Dilolo, when a whole village perished with its inhabitants and domestic animals.

In the Congo group, the Fan or Pahouin profess a belief in the immortality of man in his bodily appearance. According to them, a man does not die, he is killed either by supernatural powers or by an accident. And the accident is usually attributed to an evil spirit or to an evil spell cast on the victim. When such cases happen the sorcerers take out the viscera from the corpse to find out whether the deceased was poisoned or whether someone 'ate his soul'. According to the Fan belief, the man or woman who ate the soul of the dead person will in turn fall ill and confess his crime.

Among the Fan the oldest traditions make mention of a single god, Nzame, whose name may be found very little altered among most of the Bantus.

This god is a vague being, he is invisible, and no image can be made of him.

According to a Pahouin myth, God formerly lived in the centre of Africa with his three sons, the White, the Black and the gorilla. He was very rich, with numerous wives and children. Men lived happily near God. But after the disobedience of the Negroes and the gorillas, God retired to the West coast, taking with him his white son and all his wealth. The gorilla went off to the recesses of the forest, and the Negroes were left to poverty and ignorance. So they are irresistibly attracted to the West which holds God, his white son, and his wealth. Apart from this conception of God, the real religion of the Pahouin is an animistic religion, the religion of spirits.

Spirits are ranged in two categories – the good and the bad. The worship of the Fan goes mainly to the latter, for all misfortunes come from them, and they must be placated by sacrifices of animals or by invocations to fetishes.

Spirits wander in space, leading a life with no other interests than terrifying the living, doing them harm, and taking vengeance on the beings who caused their death. They kill the living, and eat their hearts.

After death the soul does not approach God. Either it is reincarnated in the body of a crocodile or a snake, etc., or it dwells among trees, rocks, rapids, the tops of hills or mountains, which then become sacred. Mountain vertigo is explained by the presence of a spirit. The Pahouin think that souls are ruled by a very ugly, very wicked king, who can condemn a spirit to the supreme punishment of a second death. His name is Ngworekara. According to a native, spirits have very long hair scattered on their skulls, their eyes are asymmetrical, their gaze shame-faced, their ears are full of dirt and drooping, they have long noses, their mouths are like elephants' trunks, and they eat stinking ants, *nitotol.* Dances are arranged to frighten away the spirits. The Pahouin have idols which they paint red; most of them are female, but they attach less importance to them than to fetishes. As with most black tribes, fetishism has a very important place in Fan beliefs. The Bieri plays the biggest part among these fetishes. He is invoked in hunting and in war. Before praying to him, the native feeds him.

Here is the Pahouin explanation of the creation of man: 'God created man with clay, first in the shape of a lizard which he put

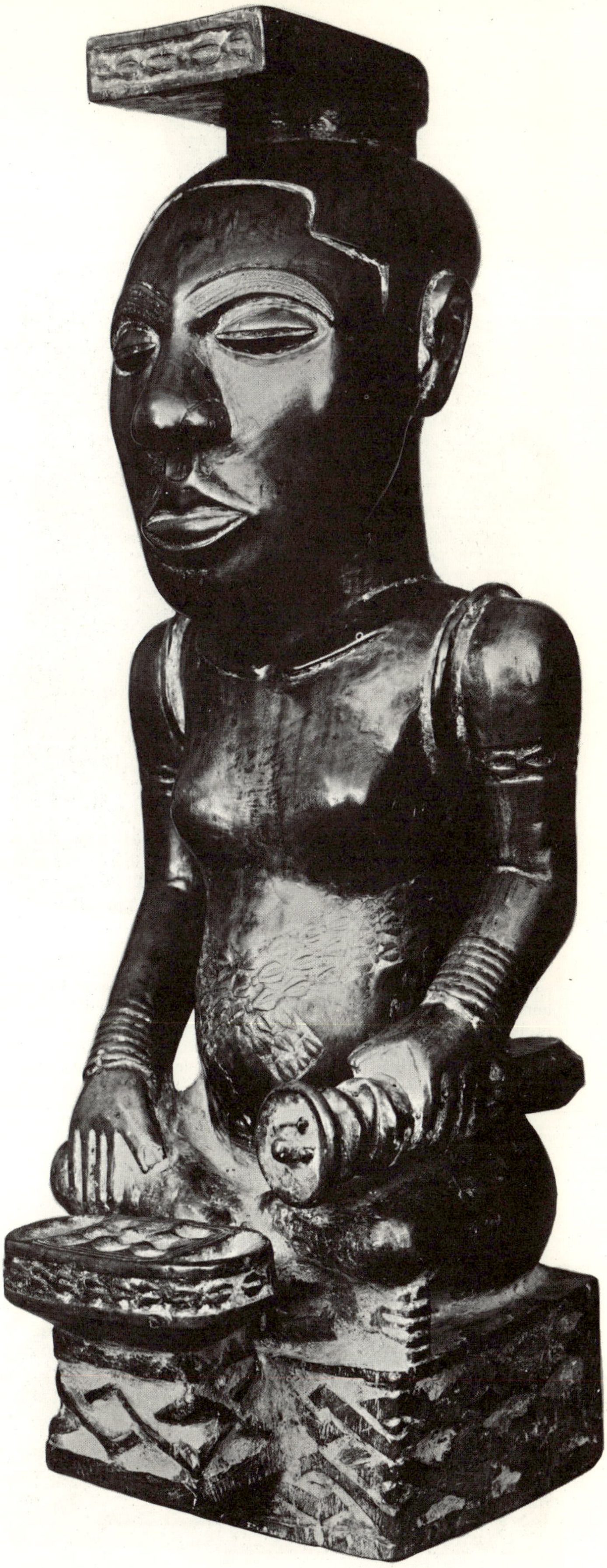

King Shamba Bolongongo. King Shamba of the Bushongo people of the Congo lived in the seventeenth century but was distinguished enough to become a legend in Africa. Famous for his wisdom and the benefits he brought his people, he is portrayed seated impassively before his mankala board in this Bakuba figure from Kasai province in the Congo. The game of mankala was introduced by the king to divert his subjects from the evils of gambling.

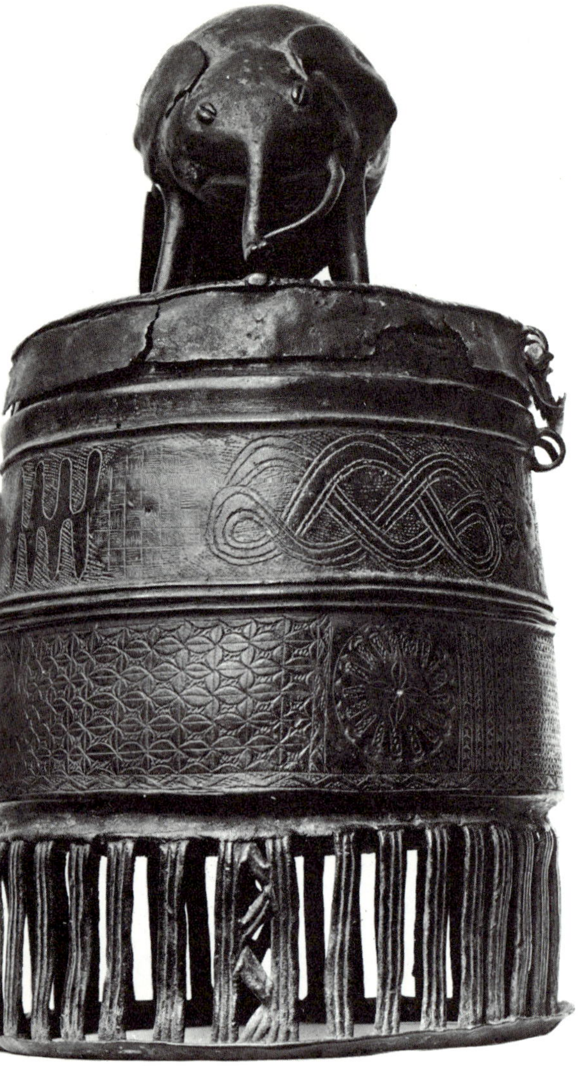

Ashanti Kuduo box. Kuduo boxes were ceremonial vessels employed at funeral rites, when they were filled with offerings and when honours were paid to the ancestors of the tribe. They remained the property of one man only and were buried with him when he died. This example is surmounted by the figure of an elephant and is decorated with incised and pierced ornament. The Ashanti people of Ghana have one of the most highly developed mythologies in Africa. Brass.

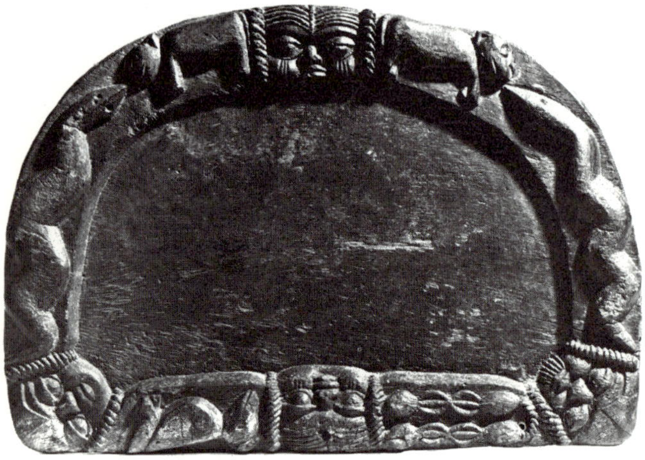

Yoruba divining board. Divination, and the origin of divination, play an important part in Yoruba mythology – the usual method employed by this people being to cast nuts (either on boards, the ground or from hand to hand) and then interpret the position of their fall – a method whose discovery is ascribed either to Ifa, the son of the supreme god, or to his messenger, Eschu. Carved wood with raised border showing familiar animals and the faces of deities.

in a pond and left there for seven days, after which he ordered him out. A man came out of the pond instead of a lizard.' The Yaunde of the Cameroons say that *Zamba* (God) created the earth and then came down to it, and had four sons: N'Kokon the learned, Otukut the idiot, Ngi the gorilla and Wo the chimpanzee. Zamba taught the Yaunde how to avoid troubles, and allotted duties to each one.

Among the Ubangui there is also belief in fetishes. If the native returns unsuccessful from hunting, he thinks his bad luck is due to an evil spell cast on him.

Diseases and death are never attributed to natural causes, they are the work of an evil spirit's vengeance. The fetish-doctors have considerable influence and practise as specialists. A native going out to hunt goes first of all to the fetish-doctor of hunting, who gives a fetish or a charm. There are fetish-doctors for whirlwinds, for alligators, for panthers, and for pregnant women.

Among the Kakar, a tribe of the Likuala region, there exists the 'man-panther' fetish-doctor. He is especially consulted to detect the committer of a crime or misdemeanour.

The Bomitaba, neighbours of the Kakar, also believe in spirits and in the immortality of the soul. When a native dies his *Mokadi* (spirit) wanders beside the family river where the spirits of his ancestors and relatives are already established. The Mokadi has power over men, to punish the living who caused his death. The fetish-doctors are also specialists among the Bomitaba, as they are with the other natives. There is even a fetish-doctor who receives communications from the dead in his dreams.

The Bomitaba have a cosmogony myth about the moon and its creation:

'Once upon a time there were two suns, the one we have and the moon. It was very tiresome for mankind, which being constantly in heat and light could not rest comfortably. One day one of the suns suggested to the other that they should bathe, and pretended to jump in a river; the other threw itself in and was quenched. Since that time there is only one sun, and though the moon lights men it no longer warms them.'

Among the Upotos of the Congo there is a myth relating why the immortality intended for men was given to the moon. One day *Libanza* (God) summoned before him the inhabitants of the moon and of the earth. The first immediately answered the call, and Libanza said to the moon: 'As a reward for coming at my summons, you shall not die, except for two days each month, and then only to rest, after which you will re-appear brighter than ever.' When the earth's inhabitants arrived much later, Libanza was angry and said to them: 'You did not come at my summons, and to punish you, you shall die one day, and never live again except to come to me!'

The Bambala of the Congo have a myth which says that men wanted to know what the moon is. They set a long pole in the ground, and a man climbed up it holding a second pole which he tied to the first. A third pole was added to the second, and so on. When this 'tower of Babel' had reached a considerable height, it collapsed, bringing down with it the whole population working at its construction who thus perished, victims of their curiosity.

A legend about the origin of death is to be found among the Negroes on the shores of lake Kivu.

After creating the first human beings, God told them they would never die. And so it was. In time men became very numerous, and Death tried to pick a quarrel with them, but God was on the watch and Death went under ground. One day God was not there, and Death seized a victim. A grave was dug, and she was buried in it. Some days later the earth on the grave began to rise as if the dead person was returning to life. The dead person was an old woman, who had left several children and daughters-in-law. She was about to rise from the dead, when one of her daughters-in-law noticed it. She ran off for boiling water which she poured on her mother-in-law's grave. Then, making a pestle she kept beating the ground saying: 'Die! What is dead should stay dead!'

Next day, the earth began to rise again, and she went on hitting it, saying: 'What is dead should stay dead!' And the mother-in-law who was returning to life, then died. And then God returned to the earth, and found that one woman was absent. He was told that she was dead. Seeing that Death had caused it, he said to the survivors: 'Stay here and remain in your dwellings, for I am going to pursue Death so that it makes no more victims.' They obeyed, and God went to look for Death. One day he discovered it, but it tried to escape and fled away at top speed. Just then an old woman came out of her hut to hide in the bush. She came face to face with Death who said: 'Hide me, and I'll reward you.' The old woman, who was not very bright, lifted to her armpits the skin which clothed her, Death slipped beneath and entered her belly.

At that moment God arrived, saw the old woman, and asked her if she had not seen Death go by. Before she had time to utter a word God threw himself on her saying: 'What use is she since she can have no more children? The best thing is to kill her, take Death out, and then kill it.' God had barely finished killing the old woman, when a young woman came out of her hut and surprised God cutting the old woman's throat. Death instantly fled from the old woman's body and hid in the young woman's. Seeing this God said: 'Well! Since they keep thwarting my efforts, let them take the consequences and die!'

In the Congo group are the Mundangs who lived beside the river 'Mayo-Kebbi'. They recognise three gods: *Massim Biambe* the creator, the omnipotent immaterial God; *Phebele*, the male god; and *Mebeli*, the female god.

Phebele and Mebeli had a child, Man, to whom Massim-Biambe gave a soul (*tchi*), breathing, and the breath of life. The Mundang thinks that animals have souls just as men have. Every time a living thing dies, its soul goes down a deep hole. Then the soul enters the body of a woman or of a female animal to create another being; but men's souls can only create men, and animals' souls beings of the same species.

God's ministers are the fetishes. Among them is one so constructed that a man can slip into it and make it move. This would suggest that the Mundangs have a demon.

The Bushongo, who live in Belgian Congo, to the east of Kisi and Loango, worship a god *Bumba*, who, so they say, created the universe by vomiting forth the sun, moon, stars and eight species of animals from which the others are derived. According to the traditions of this same people, heaven and earth at first lived united like husband and wife; but one day heaven went off in displeasure, and from that moment dates the separation of heavenly and terrestrial elements.

THE NILOTIC GROUP

Fetishism seems to dominate in this group as it does in the foregoing groups. The natives believe in metempsychosis and have a respectful cult of snakes. Among the Shilluk of the White Nile we find a creation legend, in which they explain the different colours of the human race by the choice of colours of the clay from which they were formed.

Juok was the god who created all men on earth. In the land of the Whites he found white earth or sand, and made it into men of the same colour. Then he came to Egypt where he made brown men from the Nile mud, and then to the Shilluk and created the Black from black earth. Then Juok said: 'I shall make man, but he must run and walk, so I shall give him two long legs like those of flamingoes.' That done, he said: 'Man must be able to cultivate millet, so I shall give him two arms – one to use the hoe and the other to pull up weeds.' Then he said: 'I shall give man two eyes to see with.' And so he did. Then he said: 'I shall give him a mouth to eat his millet.' And then he gave him a tongue and ears so that he could shout, dance, sing, speak, and listen to noises and speeches. Thus man was made perfect.

In Uganda the Nandi have a story which attributes death to a dog's bad temper. The dog had been told to bring men the news of their immortality, but thought he was not received with all the respect due to a divine messenger. So by way of revenge he changed the tale and condemned men to death, saying: 'All men will die like the moon, but you will not be re-born like the moon unless you give me food and drink.' Men laughed him to scorn and gave him drink on a stool. The dog was furious at not being looked upon as a man, and said: 'All men shall die – only the moon shall be re-born.'

The following tale belongs to the same part of Uganda. The Sun and the Moon one day agreed to kill all their children. The Sun carried out his part, but the Moon changed its mind and spared its descendants. So the Sun has no children, but those of the Moon are innumerable – the stars.

The Gallas have this myth about the origin of death. One day God sent a bird to men to tell them: 'You shall be immortal, and when you are old and feeble, all you have to do to be young again is to strip off your skins.' To show that the message was authentic God gave the bird a crest as a sign of its divine message. The bird set out, but on the way came upon a snake which was feeding on carrion. The bird looked longingly at the carrion, and said to the snake: 'Give me a little of that meat, and I'll tell you God's message.' 'It's of no interest to me,' said the snake, and went on eating. But the crested bird urged it to listen so much that the snake gave way. The bird then said: 'When men grow old they will die, but when you are old you'll change your skin and regain your youth.'

To punish the bird for having so treacherously altered his message, God afflicted him with a disease so painful that he utters his lamentations, perched on the top of a tree.

SUDAN AND VOLTA GROUPS

In the Sudan group most the Mandinga have become Mohammedans, but still retain their old animistic beliefs. Like the Senufo, they believe in a certain number of evil spirits, to which they must make sacrifices. They also believe in amulets and gri-gris. The same beliefs may be found among the Negroes of the Volta group, the Mossi, the Gurusi and the Bobo.

The Negroes of this group pay great attention to the cult of the dead. Among the Senufo, when an old person dies, his death is attributed to the will of the 'Master of all spirits,' while among the neighbouring tribes it is supposed to have been caused by malevolent supernatural powers. Among the Mossi the earth is thought to be a great moralist and avenging deity who is angered by crime. Thus, among the Bobo, a murderer had to make expiatory sacrifices to the earth which had been angered at seeing human blood shed. The sacrifices were carried out by a priest whose title was 'Chief of the Earth'.

The Gurmantshi of the Volta group are almost all fetishists, like most of the Mossi, Takamba and Bariba, who are their neighbours.

There is much superstition among them and a gross abuse of fetishism. Everything unexplained or inexplicable is referred to the idea of God. The native communicates with God through spirits as intermediaries, some of which have vast power which extends over the entire land. They have familiar spirits who protect the family's fields, and whose favour is obtained by making offerings. Each clan possesses its own *gri-gri*, the *Suanu* (Maneater) which the natives put above their doors to prevent the evil spirits from entering the house. The 'Man-eater' is the spirit of a man who died suddenly. Before undertaking anything of importance, the Gurmantshi consult the spirits through the sorcerers who are able to predict the future.

South of the Niger, the Menkiera offer sacrifices to rocks and stones which are the dwelling places of spirits, who exert their activity either for good or ill.

GUINEA AND SENEGAMBIA GROUPS

Among the Agni of Indene and Sanwi, religion derives fundamentally from animism and appears as a polytheism which has assimilated Mohammedan influence, and, since the end of the 15th century, Christian influences. The result of these influences was to modify the attributes as well as the powers of the chief deities. Such is the case with *Nyamia*, the supreme god, placed by the Blacks above all other gods since they came under Mohammedan influence.

Originally in fact Nyamia was in no way superior to *Asia*, the goddess of the earth, nor to *Asia-Bussu*, god of the bush, nor to *Pan*, son of the earth and of cultivation, but was equal to these important deities.

He represented the god of the sky, or the spirit of the sky, of the atmosphere, that is, the god of storms, rain, clouds, lightning etc.

Alongside these deities of the first rank were *Evua*, the sun, who received sacrifices and a worship similar to that given by the Blacks of the Volta group, the Mossi, the Gurusi, etc., and *Kaka-Guia*, a bull-headed god whose duty is to bring the souls of the dead to the supreme god, Nyamia. He in turn communicates with the living through spirits attached to such and such a place, which protect such and such a village.

These spirits are represented by different objects or fetishes possessing their protective power.

In exchange for the fetish's protection, its possessor or its representative is supposed to carry out the rites and ceremonies more or

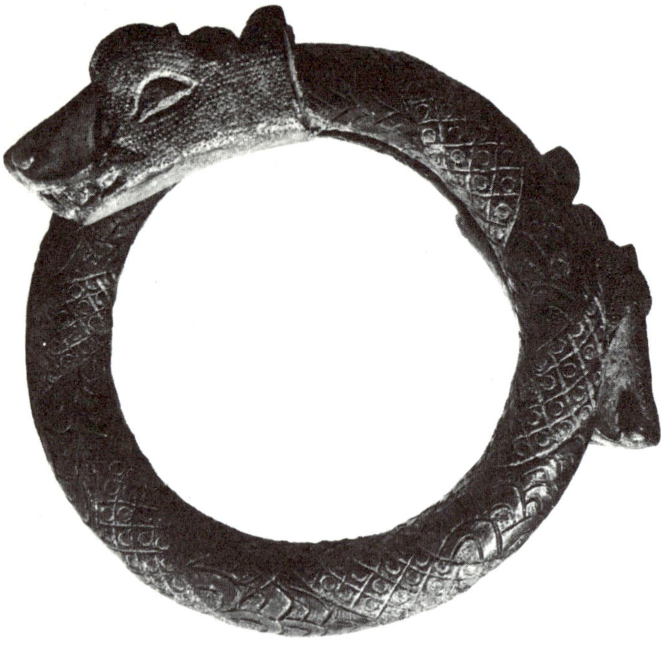

Snake bracelet from Dahomey. The snake depicted in a circle symbolised life, continuity and eternity to the many tribes of West Africa and in this respect was often shown in African art with its tail in its mouth. This bronze bracelet from Dahomey is probably intended to portray the celestial Rainbow Snake, Dan Ayido Hwedo, who encircles the world to integrate and unify its various parts. Snakes in various guises play an important part in African mythology.

less reserved for the spirit invoked.

Thus, Guruhi, a terrible god, exacts sacrifices on his altars from his believers, has the power to poison people and to torture those suspected of sorcery, and he gives his followers a greater power than that of the great chiefs themselves.

He is represented as a stool supporting an iron ball which is supposed to have fallen from heaven.

This god must not be looked upon by women, children or the uninitiated, under pain of the most severe punishment. In addition to these spirits, there are a certain number of deities derived from the tribes adjoining the Agni which have been incorporated into their belief.

First, we have Famien, who comes from Kitabo, and is represented as a rock-cave. Like Guruhi he exacts sacrifices from his believers. In exchange he takes care of the sick, drives away evil sorcerers, makes women fertile, etc. He has no particular dwelling, but stays with his owner, who thus becomes his fetish-doctor. The person who becomes the owner of Famien receives as a fetish a bag containing two knives, one of which is Famien, while the other is meant to make sacrifices to the gods, as well as two *kolas*, the deity's favourite fruit.

Another spirit called *Nampa* is made material by means of three balls made of roots and pounded leaves. He also is forbidden to women, children and the uninitiated.

Sunguin, like the preceding, is a foreigner. His materialisation includes a vase of black clay, a ball also in clay, and a roughly carved doll.

Sakarabru, the most important of these deities, is also alien to the Agni. Once upon a time he was the very powerful god of the village of Yacasse. In the hut reserved for fetishes at the entrance to the village, the walls are decorated with paintings of coiled snakes and alligators. A collection of wreaths, dried seeds, eggshells and bones is enclosed within. That is the den of Sakarabru, the demon of darkness. He is represented as a ball made of grains of maize. Like other spirits, he administers justice and is a healer. Moreover, he appears during the changes of season and renewals of the moon. At such times an actor impersonates the god, and dances a wild round. Sakarabru is a just god, but also a terrible and bloodthirsty one and much feared.

In the religion of the Agni we come on the cult of water, of streams, rivers, brooks, rivulets etc., a cult which originally required human sacrifices. In addition to these cults we must mention those relating to caves, rocks, hills and trees, as well as to certain sacred animals,

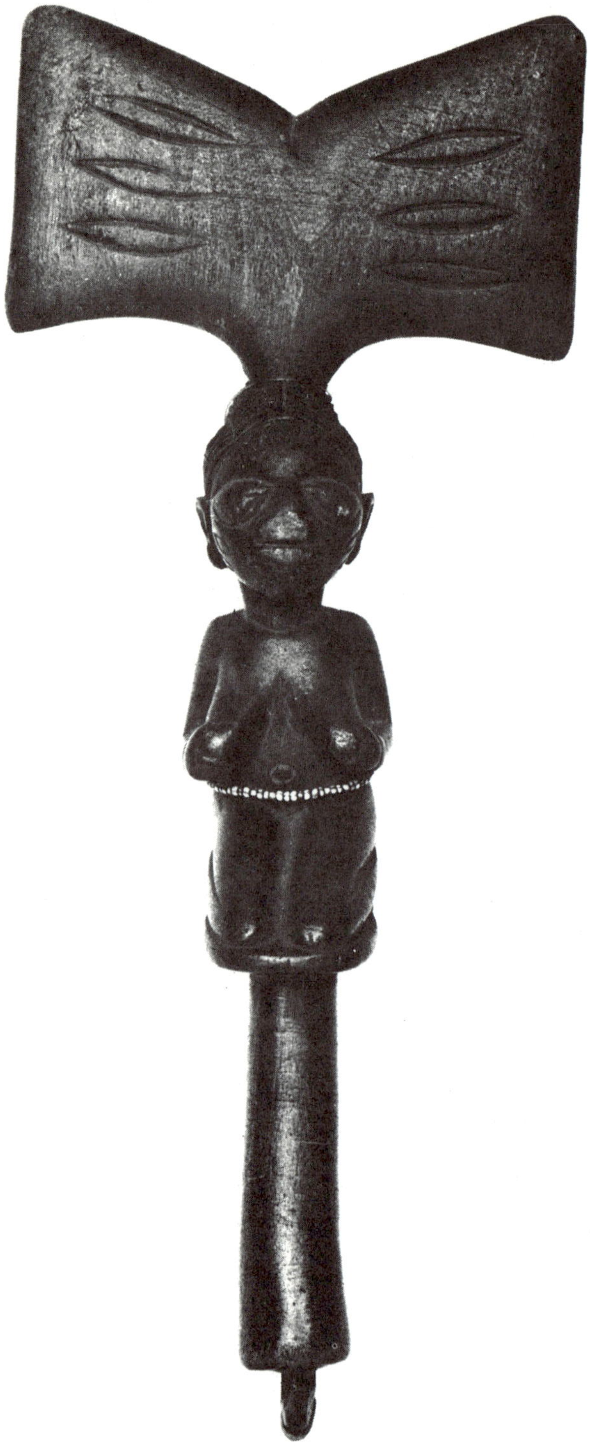

Double-headed ceremonial axe of the Shango cult. Shango is the storm god of the Yoruba people and is one of the sixteen great gods of their pantheon. Famed for his love of war and his knowledge of magic, he is also worshipped as a clan ancestor. This double axe-blade represents his magic thunder-bolt while the kneeling figure, bearing on her face the marks of the clan to which she belongs, represents one of his followers.

such as the leopard, the elephant, the snake, etc. The cult of the dead is particularly devoted to the double (*eoume*) of the deceased, which must be appeased. Like the other peoples of West Africa, the Agnis believe in the survival of a spiritual principle after death. The person who dies in a conspicuous way is afterwards re-incarnated in the womb of another woman of his tribe.

The dead are represented by little clay statuettes.

Before going on to the next group, we must mention an Ashanti legend which seems to show that the supreme god, *Nyamia*, had originally only a limited power, since this legend demonstrates that he could do nothing to change the social condition of anyone, because it is fixed by fate.

'A servant of the king of the Kumasi had a plantation which he visited every day. All the way there and during his work he complained of his lot and his poverty. One day he was lamenting as usual when he saw a large copper basin on a chain come down from heaven containing a white child with big ears. He recognised a *Nyamia ama*, a son of heaven, who said to him: "My father Nyamia sent me to look for you."

'The heavenly child made the man sit down beside him and the people of heaven hauled them up. The journey lasted a long time. At last they reached a door, which opened for the son of heaven. The man found himself in a large village, filled with a great many people who were talking, and in the midst of this space an old man dressed in a fine lion-cloth was seated on a throne of gold. He beckoned to the king of the Kumasi's servant to come forward, and said to him: "You are always complaining that I have made you one of the unfortunate. It isn't my fault. This village is occupied by the families of all men on earth – choose the dwelling you would like to stay in."

'God gave him a guide, and the man explored the village which was very large. He saw splendid houses occupied by people who did no work and had many servants. He saw wretched huts where the poor carried on the same occupations as poor human beings. In one of the houses he saw his parents and said to the guide: "There's my house." They returned to Nyamia, who said: "Look at your courtyard, you can see you have nothing, and you know that the child of poor parents can never become rich. If he gains some wealth, the money slips through his fingers. However, I am giving you a present. Here are two sacks, a large and a small, one of which is for you and the other for your master. You will not open yours until you have delivered my present to the king of the Kumasi."

'The child came for the man and took him back to earth. On the way the servant thought to himself: "Nobody knows that God has given me two sacks. I'll hide the big one and give my master the little one.

'When he got back to the plantation, the son of heaven left the man and went back to his father. The man then dug a hole and hid the big sack in it. He went to Kumasi where the king greeted him with joy, for he had thought the man was lost. The servant told his story, and handed over the little sack. The master opened it, and found it full of gold dust. In great joy the man who had been to heaven said to himself: "I'm rich." He ran to his field, dug up the big sack, and found it full of stones.

'Thus was verified the word of God – the poor man can never become rich.'

The religion of the people of Dahomey includes a fetishist cult. *Mahou* or *Mao* is the superior being, the good spirit. The *Rainbow Snake*, servant of Thunder, is also considered as a beneficent spirit. *Thunder*, who dwells in the clouds, is a dreaded spirit, whom the natives try to placate with offerings made by fetish-doctors.

The sea is a power surrounded by a large family – the splashing of the water, sirens, the python.

Alongside these spirits there are personal spirits who are particularly venerated. Such for the people of Dahomey are *Legba* and *Fa*.

Similar ideas may be found among the Baramba. With them the Wokolo is a little devil who must be avoided if you don't want to receive his treacherous arrows. Wokolo likes trees and the banks of streams. The Baramba have a special cult for trees, sacrifice domestic animals to them and smear the blood of the victims on the trunks, while praying to the spirit dwelling there.

The tribes speaking the Ewe language, who live in Togo, think that to this day God still makes human beings out of clay. When he wants to make a good man he uses good clay, and for a wicked man he uses bad clay. In the beginning God made a man and set him on earth, and then a woman. The two looked at each other, and burst out laughing. After which they wandered over the earth.

The same natives of Togo have a myth about death.

One day men sent a dog to God to ask that they might be reborn after death. The dog went off to carry his message. On the way he felt hungry, and went into a house where a man was boiling magical herbs. Meanwhile the frog had started off to tell God that men preferred not to live again. Nobody had told him to take this message. The dog who was watching the soup on the boil saw the frog go past, but thought: 'When I've had something to eat I can soon catch him up.' However, the frog arrived first and gave its message to God, and then along came the dog who explained his mission. God was extremely embarrassed and said to the dog: 'Really, I can't understand these two messages, but as the frog got here first, I shall grant its request.' And that is why men die, and never return to life.

In the Senegambia group, the 'Serers', who divide the Uolofs of the north from those of the south, are a very superstitious and fetish-ridden people. They believe in metempsychosis and are afraid of sorcerers, who are supposed to cause death. The Serers are primitive men, and have a superstitious belief for every natural force. They believe in one god, *Rock-Sene*, who shows his anger by thunder and lightning, and his kindness by rain and good harvests.

The Serers worship the spirits of the ancestors and the family spirits which they think live in baobabs or near burial places. The natives give offerings to them since after God they are the masters of good and evil. They have a cosmogony legend of the sun and moon. 'One day, the Sun's mother and the Moon's mother were bathing naked in a little waterfall. The Sun turned his back so as not to see his mother naked, but the Moon looked very keenly at her mother. After the bath the Sun was called by his mother who said: "My son, you have always respected me, may God bless you! You did not look at me in the waterfall; and as you turned your eyes away from me I pray God that he will allow no living being to look steadily at you." The Moon was called in turn by her mother, who said: "Daughter, you did not respect me in the waterfall, and you stared at me as if I were some bright object, so I want everyone to be able to look at you without ever tiring his eyes." '

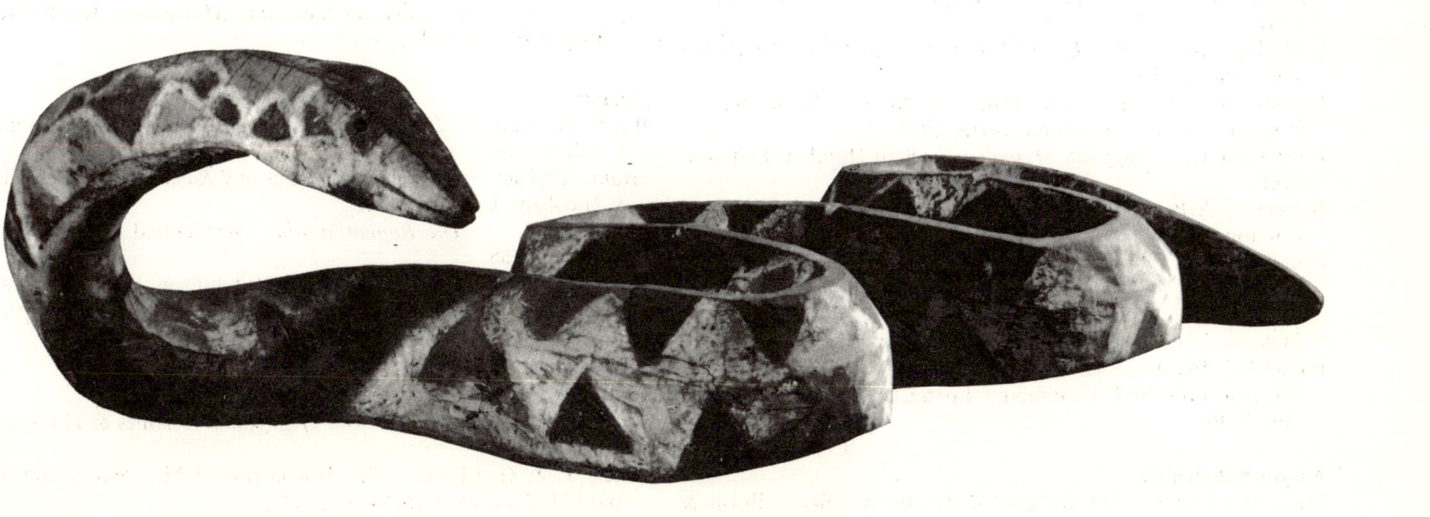

FURTHER READING LIST

General

Everyman Dictionary of Non-Classical Mythology. J.M. Dent, London and E.P. Dutton, New York. 1952.

Frazer, Sir James. *The Golden Bough.* 1 vol. ed. Macmillan, London and St. Martin's Press, New York. 1922.

Graves, Robert. *The White Goddess.* Faber & Faber, London. 1948.

MacCulloch, John A. and Gray, Louis H. *The Mythology of All Races.* 13 vols. Cooper Square Pubs. Inc., New York. 1922.

Smith, G.C. *Man and his Gods.* Jonathan Cape, London, 1953.

Standard Dictionary of Folklore, Mythology and Legend. 2 vols. Mayflower Pubs. Co., London and Funk & Wagnalls, New York. 1951.

Prehistoric

Howells, W.W. *The Heathens.* Victor Gollancz, London. 1959.

James, E.O. *Prehistoric Religions.* Thames & Hudson, London. 1957.

The Origin of Religions. Unicorn Press, London. 1937.

The Origins of Sacrifice. John Murray, London. 1933.

The Cult of the Mother Goddess. Thames & Hudson, London. 1959.

Maringer, J. *The Gods of Prehistoric Man.* Weidenfeld & Nicolson, London. 1960.

Egyptian

Cerny, J. *Ancient Egyptian Religions.* Hutchinson, London. 1952.

Desroches-Noblecourt, C. *Tutankhamen.* Penguin Books, Harmondsworth. 1965.

Gardiner, Sir Alan H. *Egypt of the Pharaohs.* Oxford Univ. Press. 1961.

Griffiths, John Gwyn. *The Conflict of Horus and Seth.* Liverpool Univ. Press. 1960.

Herodotus. *The Histories.* trans. by Aubrey de Selincourt. Penguin Classics, Harmondsworth. 1954.

Ions, Veronica. *Egyptian Mythology.* Paul Hamlyn, Feltham. 1968.

Mercier, S.A.B. *The Religions of Ancient Egypt.* Luzac & Co., London. 1949.

Murray, M.A. *Ancient Egyptian Legends.* John Murray, London. 1913.

The Splendour that was Egypt. Sidgwick & Jackson, London. 1949.

Plutarch. *Isis and Osiris.* Vol. V in Plutarch's *Moralia* (14 vols). Ed. and trans. by F.C. Babbit. Loeb Classical Library, London. 1936.

Assyro-Babylonian

Drioton, Etienne. *The Religion of the Ancient East.* Burns & Oates, London. 1959.

Gurney, O.R. *The Hittites.* Penguin Books, Harmondsworth. 1953.

Hooke, Samuel H. *Babylonian and Assyrian Religion.* Hutchinson, London. 1953.

James, E.O. *Myth and Ritual in the Ancient Near East.* Thames & Hudson, London. 1958.

Kramer, S.N. *History begins at Sumer.* Thames & Hudson, London. 1958.

Parrot, André. *Sumer.* Thames & Hudson, London. 1960.

Sanders, N.K. (trans.) *The Epic of Gilganesh.* Penguin Classics, Harmondsworth. 1960.

Phoenician

Driver, G.R. *Canaanite Myths and Legends.* T. & T. Clark, Edinburgh. 1956.

Gray, John. *The Canaanites.* Thames & Hudson, London. 1964.

Harden, D.E. *The Phoenicians.* Thames & Hudson, London. 1962.

Pritchard, J.B. *Ancient Near Eastern Texts relating to the Old Testament.* Oxford Univ. Press and Princeton Univ. Press. 1955.

Greek

Cook, A.B. *Zeus.* Cambridge Univ. Press. 1940.

Cottrell, Leonard. *The Bull of Minos.* Evans Bros., London. 1954.

Graves, Robert. *The Greek Myths.* 2 Vols. Penguin Books, Harmondsworth. 1948.

Harvey, Sir Paul. *Oxford Classical Dictionary.* Oxford Univ. Press. 1948.

Kerényi, C. *The Heroes of the Greeks.* Thames & Hudson, London. 1959.

Mylonas, G. *Eleusis and the Eleusinian Mysteries.* Routledge & Kegan Paul, London. 1962.

Roman

Bloch, Raymond. *The Origins of Rome.* Thames & Hudson, London. 1960.

Grant, Michael. *Myths of the Greeks and Romans.* Weidenfeld & Nicolson, London. 1962.

The Roman World. Weidenfeld & Nicolson, London. 1960.

Rose, H.J. *Ancient Roman Religion.* Hutchinson, London. 1949.

Warner, Rex. *Men and Gods.* Penguin Books, Harmondsworth. 1952.

Celtic

Branston, Brian. *The Lost Gods of England.* Thames & Hudson, London. 1958.

Jones, T. & G. (Trans.) *The Mabinogion.* J.M. Dent, London and E.P. Dutton, New York. 1963.

Ross, Anne. *Pagan Celtic Britain.* Routledge & Kegan Paul,

London and Columbia Univ. Press, New York. 1967.
Sjoestedt, Marie Louise. *Gods and Heroes of the Celts.* Methuen, London. 1967.
Yeats, W.B. *Mythologies.* Macmillan, London. 1959.

Teutonic
Branston, Brian. *Gods of the North.* Thames & Hudson, London. 1955.
Ellis, Davidson, H.R. *Gods and Myths of Northern Europe.* Penguin Books, Harmondsworth. 1964.
Jones, G. *Eirik the Red, and other Icelandic Sagas.* Oxford Univ. Press. 1961.
Oxenstierna, E.G. *The Norsemen.* Weidenfeld & Nicolson, London. 1965.
Vries, J.de. *Heroic Song and Heroic Legend.* Oxford Univ. Press. 1964.

Slavonic
Chadwick, N.K. *Russian Heroic Poetry.* Cambridge Univ. Press. 1932.
Downing, C. *Russian Tales and Legends.* Oxford Univ. Press. 1956.
Talbot Rice, T. *The Scythians.* Thames & Hudson, London. 1957.

Finni-Ugric
Kirby, W.F. (Trans.) *The Kalevala.* 2 vols. J.M. Dent, London and E.P. Dutton, New York. 1962.
Vorren, O. & Manker, E. *Lapp Life and Customs.* Oxford Univ. Press. 1962.

Ancient Persian
Ghirshman, Roman. *Persia, from the Origins to Alexander the Great.* Thames & Hudson, London. 1964.
Iran. The Parthians and Sassanians. Thames & Hudson, London. 1962.
Henning, W.B. *Zoroaster.* Oxford Univ. Press. 1951.
Vermaseren, M.J. *Mithras, the secret god.* Methuen, London. 1963.
Zaehner, R.C. *The Rise and Fall of Zoroastrianism.* Weidenfeld & Nicolson, London. 1961.

Indian
Archer, W.G. *The Loves of Krishna.* Allen & Unwin, London. 1957.
Basham, A.L. *The Wonder that was India.* Sidgwick & Jackson, London. 1954.
Dowson, J. *Classical Dictionary of Hindu Mythology.* Kegan Paul, London. 1961.
Humphreys, C. *Buddhism.* Penguin Books. Harmondsworth. 1951.
Ions, Veronica. *Indian Mythology.* Paul Hamlyn, Feltham. 1967.
Jaini, J. *Outlines of Jainism.* Cambridge Univ. Press. 1940.
Riencourt, Amaury de. *The Soul of India.* Jonathan Cape, London. 1961.
Stevenson, S. *The Heart of Jainism.* Oxford Univ. Press. 1915.
Weber, Max. *The Religion of India.* Allen & Unwin, London. 1958.
Zaehner, R.C. *Hinduism.* Oxford Univ. Press. 1962.

Chinese
Harvey, E.D. *The Mind of China.* Yale Univ. Press. 1933.
Reincourt, Amaury de. *The Soul of China.* Jonathan Cape, London. 1959.
Watson, W. *China.* Thames & Hudson, London. 1961.
Werner, E.T.C. *Myths and Legends of China.* Harrap, London. 1922.

Japanese
Anesaki, Mahasaru. *History of Japanese Religion.* Kegan Paul, London. 1930.
Aston, W.G. *Nihongi: Chronicles of Japan.* Allen & Unwin, London & Oxford Univ. Press, New York. 1956.
Kidder, J.E. *Japan.* Thames & Hudson, London. 1959.
Watts, Alan W. *The Way of Zen.* Thames & Hudson, London. 1957.

The Two Americas
Burland, Cottie. *The Gods of Mexico.* Eyre & Spottiswoode, London. 1967.
North American Indian Mythology. Paul Hamlyn, Feltham. 1965.
Bushnell, G.M.S. *The Ancient Peoples of the Andes.* Penguin Books, Harmondsworth. 1949.
Macmillan, C. *Glooskap's Country.* Oxford Univ. Press. 1956.
Martin, Paul Sidney. *Indians Before Columbus.* Chicago Univ. Press. 1947.
Mason, J.A. *The Ancient Civilisations of Peru.* Penguin Books, Harmondsworth. 1957.
Morley, S.G. *The Ancient Maya.* Oxford Univ. Press. 1946.
Nicholson, Irene. *Firefly in the Night.* Faber & Faber, London. 1959.
Mexican and Central American Mythology. Paul Hamlyn, Feltham. 1967.
Peterson, Fréderick. *Ancient Mexico.* Allen & Unwin, London. 1959.
Vaillant, G.C. *The Aztecs of Mexico.* Penguin Books, Harmondsworth. 1952.
Von Hagen, Victor W. *The Ancient Sun Kingdoms.* Thames & Hudson, London. 1962.
The Desert Kingdoms of Peru. Weidenfeld & Nicolson, London. 1965.

Oceanic
Beckwith, M. *Hawaiian Mythology.* Yale Univ. Press. 1940.
Berndt, R.M. *Djanggawul.* Routledge & Kegan Paul, London. 1952.
Kunapipi. F.W. Cheshire, Melbourne. 1951.
The World of the First Australians. Angus & Robertson, Sydney. 1965.
Grimble, Sir Arthur. *A Pattern of Islands.* John Murray, London. 1952.
Grey, Sir George. *Polynesian Mythology.* Whitcombe & Tombs, London and Christchurch. 1965.
Heyerdahl, Thor. *Aku-Aku.* Allen & Unwin, London. 1958.
McConnel, Ursula. *Myths of the Munkan.* Cambridge Univ. Press. 1957.
Métraux, A. *Easter Island.* Andre Deutsch, London. 1957.
Poignant, Roslyn. *Oceanic Mythology.* Paul Hamlyn, Feltham. 1968.
Suggs, R. C. *Island Civilisations of Polynesia.* Mentor Books, London. 1960.

African
Cardinall, A.W. *Tales Told in Togoland.* Oxford Univ. Press. 1931.
Fugi, A. *Fourteen Hundred Cowries.* Oxford Univ. Press. 1962.
Idowu, E.B. *Olodumare. God in Yoruba belief.* Longmans, London. 1962.
Itayemi, P. and Gurrey, P. *Folk Tales and Fables.* Penguin Africa Series, Harmondsworth, 1953.
Parrinder, E.G. *African Mythology.* Paul Hamlyn, Feltham. 1968.
West African Religions. Epworth Press, London. 1949.
Rattray, R.S. *Religion and Art in Ashanti.* Oxford Univ. Press. 1927.
Smith, E.W. and Parrinder, E.G. *African Ideas of God.* Edinburgh House Press, London. 1967.

ACKNOWLEDGMENTS

Black and white illustrations

2 British Museum. 3 Musée de l'Homme. 4 Paul Popper (top), Achille Weider (centre). 5 Paul Popper (top, bottom). 6 Yan. 7 Roger Viollet (bottom), Musée de l'Homme (top left), Foto Lala Aufsberg (top right). 9 British Museum. 11 John Freeman. 12 Larousse (top), Press Association (bottom). 13 Camera Press (left), Bulloz (right). 14 Giraudon (top), Forman Bros (bottom). 15 Forman Bros. 16 Giraudon. 17 Mansell Collection (top), Press Association (bottom). 18 British Museum (top, bottom). 19 Forman Bros. 20 Camera Press Ltd. 21 Giraudon. 22 British Museum (left), Forman Bros. (centre). 23 Mansell Collection. 24 Roger Viollet (top, bottom). 25 Roger Viollet (left), Mansell Collection (right). 26 Roger Viollet. 27 Forman Bros. (left), Giraudon (right). 28 Alinari. 30 Press Association (left), Bildarchive Foto Marburg (right). 31 Giraudon. 32 Forman Bros. (left, right). 33 Giraudon. 34 Mansell Collection. 35 Roger Viollet (top left), Mansell Collection (right). 36 Roger Viollet (top), Forman Bros. (bottom). 39 Bulloz. 40 British Museum (top left), Mansell Collection (bottom). 41 Forman Bros. (top, bottom). 42 Mansell Collection (top, centre). 43 Forman Bros. (left, right). 44 Mansell Collection (left), Forman Bros. (right). 45 Fitzwilliam Museum, Cambridge (top left), Roger Viollet (right). 46 British Museum. 47 Roger Viollet, 48 Forman Bros. 49 British Museum. 50 Archives Photographiques. 51 British Museum (top), Larousse (bottom left). 52 Directorate General of Antiquities, Baghdad, Iran. 53 British Museum (centre left, top centre), Giraudon (top left), Hirmer (top right). 54 Giraudon (top and centre), Musées Nationaux (bottom). 55 Roger Viollet (top), British Museum (bottom). 56 Mansell Collection. 57 Archives Photographiques. 58 Mansell Collection (top left, centre left). 59 Archives Photographiques. 60 Archives Photographiques (top), Mansell Collection (bottom). 61 Mansell Collection (top left), Giraudon (top centre), British Museum (top right). 62 British Museum. 63 Musées Nationaux. 64 Paul Popper. 65 Mansell Collection. 67 Archives Photographiques. 68 Paul Popper. 69 Archives Photographiques. 70 Mansell Collection (top, bottom). 71 University Museum, Philadelphia. 73 Giraudon. 74 Archives Photographiques (top left), Musselmany & Kurmly (bottom). 75 Giraudon. 76 Schaeffer. 77 National Museum of Lebanon (top), Antonello Perissinotto (bottom). 78 Antonello Perissinotto. 79 Camera Press Ltd. 80 Camera Press Ltd. 81–2 Antonello Perissinotto. 84 Paul Popper (top), Josephine Powell (bottom). 85 Alinari. 86 Archives Photographiques (left), Josephine Powell (bottom). 87 Giraudon (top) Josephine Powell (bottom). 88 British Museum (top left), Deutschen Archaeologisches Institut (top right), Paul Popper (bottom). 89 Bulloz (top left), Giraudon (top centre), Istanbul Archaeological Museum (top right). 90 Paul Popper. 91 Antiker Kleinkunst, Munish. 92 Brogi (bottom). 94 Boissonas. 95 Mansell Collection. 96 Boissonas. 99 Roger Viollet (bottom), Mansell Collection (top). 100 Bennett Associates Ltd. 101 Classical Studies Library. 102 Mansell Collection (top left), Deutsches Archaeologisches Institut, Rome. 103 Paul Popper. 104 Bulloz. 105 Giraudon. 107 Boissonas. 110 Mansell Collection. 111 Paul Popper (top), Mansell Collection (bottom). 112 Alinari. 113 Bennett Associates. 114 Dr Franz Stoedtner. 115, 116 Mansell Collection. 119 British Museum. 120, 122 Mansell Collection. 123 Alinari. 125 Berlin Staatliche Museen. 126 Alinari. 127 British Museum. 129 Boissonas. 130 Giraudon. 134 Mansell Collection. 137, 138–40 Alinari. 142 Giraudon. 148 Alinari. 151 Boissonas. 153 Brogi. 154 Anderson. 155, 156 Mansell Collection. 157 Paul Popper. 158 British Museum. 159 Mansell Collection. 160 Anderson. 162 Alinari. 164 Giraudon. 166 British Museum. 167 Paul Hamlyn Library. 168 Giraudon. 169 British Museum (top, bottom). 170 Mansell Collection (left), University of Philadelphia Museum. 171 British Museum. 172, 173, 174 Giraudon. 175 Alinari. 176 Ashmolean Museum. 177 Mansell Collection. 178 Laboritario Fotografico della Soprintendenza Alle Antichita della Campania, Naples. 179 Berlin Staatliche Museen. 180 Larousse (top), Mansell Collection (bottom). 181–3 Mansell Collection. 184 British Museum (top), Brogi (bottom). 185 Alinari (top), Victoria and Albert Museum (bottom right). 186–9 Alinari. 190 Ashmolean Museum (left), Mansell Collection (right). 192, 194 Alinari. 195 Laboratorio Fotografico della Soprintendenza alle Antichita della Campania Naples. 196 Kunsthistorisches Museum, Vienna. 197 Alinari. 199 F. Bruckmann. 200 Mansell Collection (top left), Larousse (top right, centre right, lower right). 201 Giraudon. 202, 203 Archives Photographiques. 204 Roger Viollet. 204 Alinari. 206 Alinari – Giraudon (left), Mansell Collection (right). 207 Paul Popper. 208 Larousse (top left, bottom left), Mansell Collection (right). 209 Soprintendenza alle Antichita dell' Etruria Meridionale – Rome (left), Mansell Collection (right). 210 Anderson. 211–3 Alinari. 214 Mansell Collection. 215 Anderson-Giraudon. 216 Alinari (left), British Museum (right). 217 Boissonnas (left), Mansell Collection (right). 218 British Museum (left), Mansell Collection (right). 219 Alinari (top, bottom). 220 Wim Swaan (top), Aquilea Museum (bottom). 221 Fitzwilliam Museum (top), Paul Popper (bottom). 222 Museum of Antiquities, the University, Newcastle. 223 Landesmuseum Stuttgart. 224 Larousse (top), Belzeaux-Zodiaque (bottom). 225 Giraudon (top), Ashmolean Museum (bottom). 226 Archives Photographiques. 227 Giraudon. 228 Rhein. Landesmuseum, Bonn (left), Landesmuseum Trier (right). 229 Giraudon. 230 Irish Tourist Photo (left), Larousse (right). 231 Larousse. 232–3 Musée d'Archeologie Borely. 234–5 Giraudon. 235 St Germain en-Laye Museum. 236 Musée d'Archeologie Borely. 237 Musée des Beaux Arts de Beaune (top), County Borough of Newport Museum and Art Gallery (bottom). 238 Guildhall Museum (left), Belzeaux-Zodiaque (right). 239 Photo Belzeaux (left), Wurtt. Landesmuseum Stuttgart (right). 241 National Museum of Ireland. 242–3 Yan. 243 National Museum of Ireland. 244–5 Universitetets Oldsaksamling, Oslo. 246 ATA Stockholm. 247 British

Museum. 248 Danish National Museum. 249 British Museum. 250 National Museum of Iceland (left), British Museum (right). 251 British Museum. 252 Bergen Museum, Norway. 253 Danish National Museum (left), Claes Clacsson (right). 256 British Museum (bottom). 257 British Museum (top). 258 Deutsche Fotothek, Dresden (top right). 259 British Museum (top left, centre left), ATA Stockholm (bottom left). 260 Courtesy of Norwegian Embassy. 261 British Museum (right), Universitetets Oldsaksamling, Oslo (left). 262 Universitetets Oldsaksamling, Oslo (top). 263 Universitetets Oldsaksamling, Oslo (top left, top right). 264 Nordisk Presse Foto, Copenhagen (left), ATA, Stockholm (right). 265 ATA, Stockholm (left). 267 Larousse. 269 Swedish Tourist Traffic Association. 271 Axel Poignant. 276 Universitetets Oldsaksamling, Oslo. 278 Larousse. 281 Giraudon. 282–5 Larousse. 286 Giraudon. 288–9 Larousse. 291–2 Giraudon (top and bottom). 293 Larousse. 295 Michael Holford. 297 Giraudon (top and bottom). 299 Lehtikuva. 300 Stall Museum für Völkerkunde. 301 National Museum of Finland. 302 John Massey Stewart. 303 Valerie Stalder. 304–5 Ateneum Art Gallery, Finland. 306–7 Valerie Stalder. 309 Paul Hamlyn Library. 310–1 Antonello Perissinotto. 312 Larousse. 313 British Museum (top), Giraudon (bottom). 315–6 Giraudon. 317 Cincinatti Art Museum. 318 Antonello Perissinotto. 319, 321 Larousse. 323 Giraudon. 325 J. Powell. 326 Archaeological Survey of India. 327 Larousse. 328 Museum of Fine Arts, Boston. 329 Boudot-Lamotte Photo. 330 Horniman Museum. 331 Museum of Fine Arts, Boston. 332 British Museum. 333 Victoria and Albert Museum. 334 Rapho. 335 Boudot-Lamotte Photo. 336 Victoria and Albert Museum. 338 Josephine Powell. 339 40 Victoria and Albert Museum. 341 Arpad Elfer. 342 Indian Museum, Calcutta. 343 Giraudon. 345 Boudot-Lamotte Photo. 347 Victoria and Albert Museum. 348 R. Lakshmi. 349 Victoria and Albert Museum. 350–1 Boudot-Lamotte Photo. 352 Archaeological Survey of India (left), Leonard Von Matt (right). 353 Boudot-Lamotte Photo. 354 British Museum. 355 High Commission of India. 356 J. Bordas. 357 Cleveland Museum of Art. 359 Boudot-Lamotte Photo. 360 Michael Holford. 361 Leonard Von Matt. 362 Victoria and Albert Museum (left), British Museum (right). 363 Indian Museum, Calcutta (top left), Freer Gallery of Art, Washington (top right), Brompton Studio (bottom). 364 Michael Holford. 365 Victoria and Albert Museum. 366 Hindu University, Benares (top left), Museum of Fine Arts, Boston (bottom left), Arpad Elfer (right). 367 Josephine Powell. 368 Paul Almasy (top), Yves Coffin (bottom). 369 Giraudon (top), Hindu University, Benares (bottom). 370 Horniman (left), Michael Holford (right). 371 J. Allan Cash. 372 Arpad Elfer. 373 Boudot-Lamotte Photo. 375 Victoria and Albert Museum. 376 Boudot-Lamotte Photo (bottom left), Larousse (bottom right). 377 Boudot-Lamotte Photo (bottom left), Musée Guimet (bottom right). 379 National Palace Museum, Taiwan. 380 Larousse. 381 Worcester Art Museum. 382 University, Hong Kong. 383 Metropolitan Museum of Art, N.Y. 384 Larousse. 385 University, Hong Kong. 386–7 Larousse. 388 Freer Gallery of Art, Washington D.C. 389–90 Larousse. 391–2 Seattle Art Museum. 393 Victoria and Albert Museum. 394 Giraudon (left), Bildarchiv Foto (right). 395 Bildarchiv Foto (left), Larousse (right). 396–7 Wellcome Medical Museum. 398 Seattle Art Museum. 399 Seattle Art Museum (left), Courtesy of the Arts Council of Great Britain (right). 400–1 Horniman Museum. 403 Museum of Fine Arts, Boston. 404–6 Larousse. 407 State Museum Moscow. 408–10 Larousse. 411 William Rockhill Nelson Gallery of Art, Kansas City. 413 Museum of Fine Arts, Boston. 414 Seattle Art Museum. 415 Museum of Fine Arts, Boston. 418 M. Sakamoto (top), Larousse (bottom). 419 Giraudon. 420 M. Sakamoto. 423 James H. Hooper Collection. 424 Smithsonian Institution (top), National Museum, Copenhagen (bottom). 425 Cincinnati Art Museum (top), British Museum (bottom). 426 James H. Hooper Collection (left), British Museum (right). 427 McCord Museum, McGill University. 428 Museum of American Indian, Heye Foundation, N.Y. 429–30 National Museum of Canada. 431 Paul Almasy (top), Giraudon (bottom left), Brooklyn Museum (bottom right). 432 Dumbarton Oaks, Washington (top), Larousse (bottom). 433 Dumbarton Oaks, Washington (top), Philadelphia Museum of Art, (bottom). 434 J. March-Penney. 435 National Museum of Anthropology, Mexico. 436 British Museum (top), National Museum of Anthropology, Mexico. 437 National Museum of Anthropology (top), Larousse (bottom). 438 Larousse (far left), J. March-Penney (left), Dr Kurt Stavenhagen (right), Larousse (far right). 439 British Museum. 440 Giraudon. 441 British Museum (top), Mike Andrews (bottom). 442 Larousse (top), Musée de l'Homme (bottom). 443 Mike Andrews. 444–5 Musée de l'homme. 446 Les Films du Chateau. 447 Musée de l'homme (top), Larousse (bottom). 449 Axel Poignant. 450 British Museum (top), Axel Poignant (bottom). 451 British Museum (left), John Webb (right). 452 Museum of Primitive Art, N.Y. 453 Dominion Museum, N.Z. (left), Brooklyn Museum (right). 454 Museum für Völkerkunde, Vienna (top), Axel Poignant (centre), American Museum of Natural History (bottom). 455 Larousse. 456 Dominion Museum, N.Z. (top), British Museum (bottom). 457 British Museum. 458 Musée de l'Homme. 459 Horniman Museum. 460 Cambridge Museum of Archaeology and Ethnology. 461 British Museum (top left), Cambridge Museum of Archaeology and Ethnology (bottom left), University Museum, Pennsylvania (right). 462 Museum für Völkerkunde, Basel. 463 Museum für Völkerkunde, Vienna (top left, bottom), Brooklyn Museum (top right). 465 National Gallery of S. Australia. 467 Kerry Dundas. 469 Smithsonian Institution. 470 Horniman Museum. 471 Axel Poignant. 473 Art Centrum. 474 Paul Popper. 475 Central Office of Information. 476 Paul Popper. 477 British Museum (top), Cambridge University of Archaeology and Ethnology (bottom). 478 Cambridge University of Archaeology and Ethnology. 479 British Museum (left), Art Centrum (left centre), Courtesy of the Arts Council of Great Britain (right centre), British Museum (right). 480–1 British Museum. 482 University Museum, Philadelphia (top), British Museum (bottom). 484 Musée de l'Homme (left), British Museum (right).

Colour Plates

Yves Coffin (facing page) 420. G. Donkin-Ure Smith Pty. 453 top. Werner Forman 277. Giraudon 53, 196, 276. Paul Hamlyn Library Frontis (recto), 52, 324, 340, 388, 389, 405, 421. Paul Hamlyn Library-Mansell Collection Frontis. Ann Hill 213. Hans Hinz 452. Kenneth Lowther 341. Naprojzi, Budapest 437. PAF International 212. Antonello Perissinotto 293. Axel Poignant 469. Paul Popper 4, 20, 453 bottom. Seattle Art Museum 404. Wim Swaan 5, 325. Wallace Collection 468. Roger Wood 21, 197, 292. Z. F. A. Dusseldorf 436.

INDEX

Main references are in bold type; references to captions are in italic

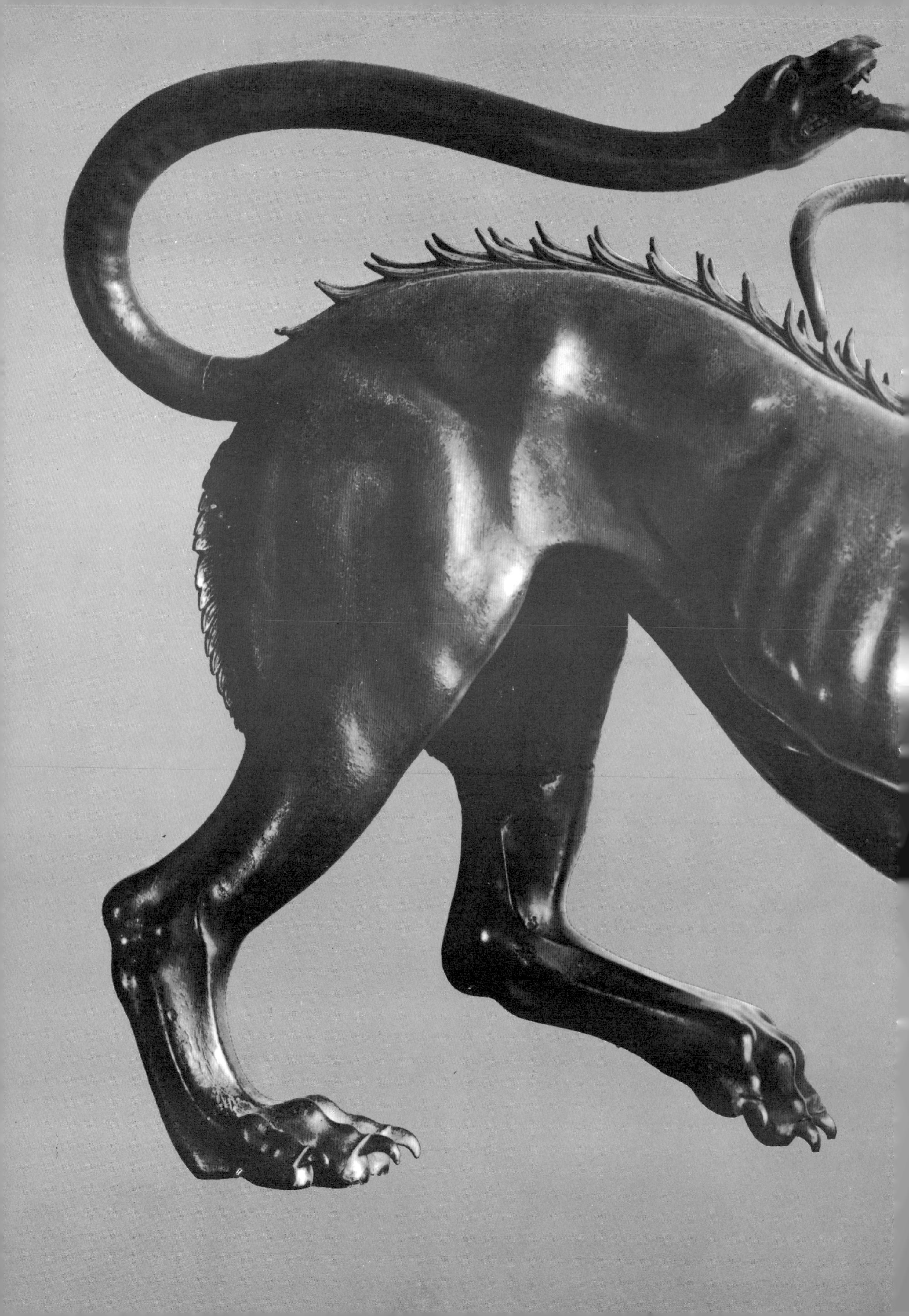